Associations USA

A Directory of Contact Information for
National Associations, Foundations, and Other Nonprofit
Organizations in the United States and Canada

1st Edition

Containing Mailing Addresses, Telephone Numbers, Web Site Addresses,
Fax Numbers, and Toll-Free Telephone Numbers for National Associations,
Private Foundations, and Other Nonprofit Organizations, Including
Non-Governmental Organizations, Political Action Committees,
Think Tanks, and Information Clearinghouses

615 Griswold Street • Detroit, Michigan 48226

Editorial Staff

Darren L. Smith, *Managing Editor*
Patricia H. Cook, *Production Editor*
Penny J. Hoffman, *Contributing Editor*

Renee Bulanda, Margaret M. Geist, Stephanie Kethman, Dawn D. Matthews,
and Cherry L. Stockdale, *Editorial Assistants*

Alicia Elkiss, *Administrative Associate/Verification Assistant*

Debbie Cerny, Jacqueline Elkiss, Jennie Hummel, Dena Kelly, Elizabeth K. Kelly,
Rhonda J. Oxman, and Sue Lynch, *Verification Assistants*

★ ★ ★ ★ ★

Omnigraphics, Inc.

Matthew P. Barbour, *Senior Vice President*
Kay Gill, *Vice President—Directories*
Kevin Hayes, *Operations Manager*
Leif Gruenberg, *Development Manager*
David P. Bianco, *Marketing Director*

Peter E. Ruffner, *Publisher*
Frederick G. Ruffner, Jr., *Chairman*

★ ★ ★ ★ ★

ISBN 0-7808-0732-4

Printed in the United States of America

Omnigraphics, Inc.
615 Griswold Street • Detroit, MI 48226
Phone Orders: 800-234-1340 • Fax Orders: 800-875-1340
Mail Orders: P.O. Box 625 • Holmes, PA 19043
www.omnigraphics.com

Table of Contents

About This Directory

Associations USA (AUSA) provides detailed contact information for nearly 14,200 national associations, private foundations, and other nonprofit organizations. Listings in the directory typically include the organization's name, address, and telephone number, and most include web site addresses. Fax and national toll-free numbers are also included as available.

Information contained in *AUSA* is obtained through original research carried out by editors with significant experience in the compilation of reference directories. The data compiled is then independently verified, primarily through direct telephone contact with the associations and other organizations listed.

While the principal focus of *Associations USA* is on U.S. organizations, a number of important Canadian organizations are listed in the directory as well.

What's Included in the Directory?

Associations USA lists:

- national, nonprofit membership associations, including those having individual members as well as those with corporate or institutional members;
- national, nonprofit, nonmembership organizations, such as NGOs (nongovernmental organizations), political action committees, public policy institutes (i.e., think tanks), information clearinghouses, and other nonprofit groups.
- foundations, including private, philanthropic foundations as well as educational and research foundations established by associations

Although *AUSA* focuses almost exclusively on national organizations, a special Appendix at the back of the directory provides listings for state and local area chambers of commerce in the U.S. as well as Canadian chambers of commerce. These organizations are excellent sources of information about a variety of matters in their respective areas.

What's *Not* Included

Types of listings that are specifically excluded from *Associations USA* are:

- For-profit organizations
- Defunct or otherwise inactive organizations
- Divisions, committees, special interest areas, and other subunits of national associations, except for subunits that operate autonomously and/or have contact data that is different from that of the parent group
- State, regional, or local branches or chapters of national organizations, except for certain state or regional groups that operate autonomously and may be of national interest
- Government departments or agencies

Listings Cover a Wide Range of Interests

AUSA listings include:

- Academic & Scholarly Societies
- Accreditation Organizations
- Agricultural Organizations
- Animals & Animal Welfare Groups
- Arts & Artists Organizations
- Charitable Organizations
- Children & Family Advocacy Groups
- Civic & Political Organizations
- Civil & Human Rights Organizations
- Computer User Groups
- Consumer Interest Associations
- Educational Associations
- Environmental Organizations
- Fraternities & Sororities
- Health & Health-Related Organizations
- Historical Societies
- Hobby & Affinity Groups
- Humanitarian Organizations

- Labor Unions
- Military & Veterans Organizations
- Nongovernmental Organizations (NGOs)
- Philanthropic Foundations
- Political Action Committees (PACs)
- Professional Associations
- Public Policy Institutes (Think Tanks)
- Religious Missions & Organizations
- Sports Organizations
- Trade & Business Associations
- Travel & Recreation Associations
- Women's Groups

Content of Individual Entries

Listings in *Associations USA* typically include the organization's name, address, and telephone number. More than 12,000 listings (about 85%) include fax numbers, and more than 13,000 listings (92%) provide a web site address. Where available, national toll-free numbers are included as well.

In some cases the editors of *AUSA* have determined that the most reliable contact information available for certain organizations is the web site. These usually are organizations that may not have a national office, and the designated contact person may change with some frequency, making it difficult to track the organization. However, many of these groups have now established web sites that provide detailed information about the organization and allow interested persons to apply for membership online, find conference and event schedules, and identify other useful information. Consequently, a limited number of listings in this directory (about 2-3% of the total) provide only the name and web site address.

Arrangement of Listings

Listings in the directory are presented in alphabetical order, by name of the organization and by principal subject keywords within the name. If the name contains no subject keywords or otherwise gives no indication of the group's interests, a keyword is assigned by the editors. Assigned keywords are presented in parentheses, followed by the organization's name and contact data. All keywords, whether assigned or otherwise, are interfiled alphabetically among the names. The overall arrangement of *Associations USA* makes it easy to find an organization by its name or its general area of interest without having to refer to a separate index.

If an organization's official name is an acronym or initialism (e.g., AARP), it is listed both by the acronym *and* according to the name its initials represent. Similarly, organizations that are well known by more than one name are listed by both names.

Organizations named for a person are alphabetized both by first and by last name (e.g., Frank Lloyd Wright Foundation and Wright Frank Lloyd Foundation).

Alphabetizing in *Associations USA* is word-by-word rather than letter-by-letter. Apostrophes, hyphens, slashes, conjunctions, and prepositions are ignored for sorting purposes, as are the parentheses that enclose assigned keywords. Punctuation is not used in this directory. If an association's name begins with the word 'The,' that word is dropped from the name for sorting purposes. If the association's name ends with 'Inc,' that is ignored in alphabetical sorting as well.

Appendix to Chambers of Commerce

Chambers of commerce are often excellent sources of information about other organizations, and the Appendix that follows the main body of listings in *Associations USA* lists three categories of chambers:

- state chambers of commerce in the United States;
- local chambers of commerce in U.S. communities or areas with a population of at least 25,000; and
- Canadian chambers of commerce.

Information provided for each chamber is the same as that given for listings in the main body of the book—name, address, phone number, and, as available, web address, fax number, and/or toll-free number.

Index to Acronyms

Most associations regularly use acronyms or initialisms as substitutes for the organization's full name, so it is not uncommon for a person to be familiar with an organization's acronym but not be sure of the group's actual name. The Acronyms Index at the back of this directory enables users to identify an organization when only its acronym is known. Each acronym listed in the index is accompanied by the organization's full name and the page number on which contact data for that organization is located.

In recent years a number of organizations have discontinued using their full names altogether, making their acronym the official name. In these situations, the acronym is presented in the index as both acronym *and* as the organization's name. For example, AARP has discontinued using the name American Association for Retired Persons and now refers to itself simply as AARP, so its index citation shows AARP as the acronym *and* as the name of the organization. (As an aid to those who might be more familiar with an organization's former, spelled-out name, that version is included among the listings in the main body of the book.)

Editor's Comments

The editors are grateful to the representatives of associations and organizations listed here for their willing cooperation in confirming and clarifying the information in this directory. We also welcome and appreciate all suggestions for additions, corrections, changes, and improvements for future editions of *Associations USA*. Contact:

Editor — Associations USA
Omnigraphics, Inc
2301 W. Sample Rd., Bldg. 3, Suite 7A
Pompano Beach, FL 33073
Phone: 954-979-8005
Fax: 954-972-0405

Associations USA

Associations USA

3HO Foundation — www.3ho.org
Rt 2 Box 4   Espanola NM 87532
Ph: 505-753-4988 ▪ Fx: 505-753-1999 ▪ TF: 888-346-2420

4-H Council, National — www.fourhcouncil.edu
7100 Connecticut Ave   Chevy Chase MD 20815
Ph: 301-961-2800 ▪ Fx: 301-961-2848

9to5 National Association of Working Women — www.9to5.org
152 W Wisconsin Ave Suite 408   Milwaukee WI 53203
Ph: 414-274-0925 ▪ Fx: 414-272-2870 ▪ TF: 800-522-0925

10th Regiment of Foot - American Contingent, His Majesty's — www.redcoat.org
61 Ivan St   Lexington MA 02420
Ph: 781-862-2586

20/20 Vision — www.2020vision.org
1828 Jefferson Pl NW   Washington DC 20036
Ph: 202-833-2020 ▪ Fx: 202-833-5307 ▪ TF: 800-669-1782

20-30 US & Canada Inc, Active — www.active20-30.com
915 L St Suite 1000   Sacramento CA 95814
Ph: 916-447-3217 ▪ Fx: 916-442-0382

52 Plus Joker — www.52plusjoker.org
670 Carlton Dr   Elgin IL 60120
Ph: 847-697-5819

60 Plus Association Inc — www.60plus.org
1600 Wilson Blvd Suite 960   Arlington VA 22209
Ph: 703-807-2070 ▪ Fx: 703-807-2073

92nd Street Young Men's & Young Women's Hebrew Association — www.92y.org
1395 Lexington Ave   New York NY 10128
Ph: 212-415-5765

100 Black Men of America Inc — www.100blackmen.org
141 Auburn Ave   Atlanta GA 30303
Ph: 404-688-5100 ▪ Fx: 404-688-1028 ▪ TF: 800-598-3411

100 Black Women, National Coalition of — www.ncbw.org
38 W 32nd St Suite 1610   New York NY 10001
Ph: 212-947-2196 ▪ Fx: 212-947-2477

401(k) Council of America, Profit Sharing/ — www.psca.org
10 S Riverside Plaza Suite 1610   Chicago IL 60606
Ph: 312-441-8550 ▪ Fx: 312-441-8559

1394 Trade Association — www.1394ta.org
1111 S Main St   Grapevine TX 76051
Ph: 817-410-5750 ▪ Fx: 817-410-5757

1812, General Society of the War of — www.societyofthewarof1812.org
1219 Charmuth Rd   Lutherville MD 21093
Ph: 410-825-3015

1812, National Society US Daughters of — www.iaw.on.ca/~jsek/usd1812.htm
1461 Rhode Island Ave NW   Washington DC 20005
Ph: 202-745-1812

2030 Center — www.2030.org
1025 Connecticut Ave NW Suite 205   Washington DC 20036
Ph: 202-822-6526 ▪ Fx: 202-955-5606 ▪ TF: 877-203-0674

A Alfred Taubman Center for State & Local Government — www.ksg.harvard.edu/taubmancenter
Harvard Univ John F Kennedy School of Government 79 JFK St   Cambridge MA 02138
Ph: 617-495-2199

A Better Chance — www.abetterchance.org
240 W 35th St 9th Fl   New York NY 10001
Ph: 646-346-1310 ▪ Fx: 646-346-1311 ▪ TF: 800-543-7181

A Cappella Society of America, Contemporary — www.casa.org
1850 Union St Suite 1449   San Francisco CA 94123
Ph: 415-563-5224 ▪ Fx: 415-563-5523

A Christian Ministry in the National Parks — www.acmnp.com
10 Justins Way   Freeport ME 04032
Ph: 207-865-6436 ▪ Fx: 207-865-6852 ▪ TF: 800-786-3450

A Course in Miracles, Foundation for — www.facim.org
41397 Buecking Dr   Temecula CA 92590
Ph: 909-296-6261 ▪ Fx: 909-296-9117

A Philip Randolph Institute — www.apri.org
1444 'I' St NW Suite 300   Washington DC 20005
Ph: 202-289-2774 ▪ Fx: 202-289-5289

a Wish with Wings Inc — www.awishwithwings.org
917 W Sanford St   Arlington TX 76012
Ph: 817-469-9474 ▪ Fx: 817-275-6005

AAA Foundation for Traffic Safety — www.aaafoundation.org
607 14th St NW Suite 201   Washington DC 20005
Ph: 202-638-5944 ▪ Fx: 202-638-5943

AACE International - Association for the Advancement of Cost Engineering — www.aacei.org
209 Prairie Ave Suite 100   Morgantown WV 26501
Ph: 304-296-8444 ▪ Fx: 304-291-5728 ▪ TF: 800-858-2678

AACSB International - Association to Advance Collegiate Schools of Business — www.aacsb.edu
600 Emerson Rd Suite 300   Saint Louis MO 63141
Ph: 314-872-8481 ▪ Fx: 314-872-8495

AAFRC Trust for Philanthropy — www.aafrc.org/philanthropy/
10293 N Meridian St Suite 175   Indianapolis IN 46290
Ph: 317-816-1613 ▪ Fx: 317-816-1633 ▪ TF: 800-462-2372

AAHP-HIAA — www.aahp.org
1129 20th St NW Suite 600   Washington DC 20036
Ph: 202-778-3200 ▪ Fx: 202-331-7487 ▪ TF: 877-291-2247

AARP — www.aarp.org
601 'E' St NW   Washington DC 20049
Ph: 202-434-2277 ▪ Fx: 202-434-2588 ▪ TF: 800-424-3410

AARP Grandparent Information Center — www.aarp.org/grandparents
601 'E' St NW   Washington DC 20049
Ph: 202-434-2296

AARP Public Policy Institute — www.aarp.org/ppi
601 'E' St NW   Washington DC 20049
Ph: 202-434-2277 ▪ Fx: 202-434-2588 ▪ TF: 800-424-3410

AAUW Educational Foundation — www.aauw.org/ef
c/o American Assn of University Women 1111 16th St NW   Washington DC 20036
Ph: 202-785-7602

Abandoned Infants Assistance Resource Center, National — aia.berkeley.edu
UC Berkeley Family Welfare Research Group 1950 Addison St Suite 104   Berkeley CA 94704
Ph: 510-643-8390 ▪ Fx: 510-643-7019

ABC Quilts — www.abcquilts.org
569 First New Hampshire Tpke Suite 3   Northwood NH 03261
Ph: 603-942-9211

Abdominal Surgeons, American Society of — www.abdominalsurg.org
675 Main St   Melrose MA 02176
Ph: 781-665-6102 ▪ Fx: 781-665-4127

Abduction, Jimmy Ryce Center for Victims of Predatory — www.jimmyryce.org
5050 Collins Ave Suite 1036   Miami Beach FL 33140
Ph: 305-864-1344 ▪ Fx: 305-864-4161 ▪ TF: 800-546-7923

Ability Center, National — www.nac1985.org
PO Box 682799   Park City UT 84068
Ph: 435-649-3991 ▪ Fx: 435-658-3992

Abortion Federation, National — www.prochoice.org
1755 Massachusetts Ave NW Suite 600   Washington DC 20036
Ph: 202-667-5881 ▪ Fx: 202-667-5890 ▪ TF: 800-772-9100

Abortion Funds, National Network of — www.nnaf.org
c/o CLPP Hampshire College   Amherst MA 01002
Ph: 413-559-5645 ▪ Fx: 413-559-6045

(Abortion) Human Life Foundation Inc — www.humanlifereview.com
215 Lexington Ave 4th Fl   New York NY 10016
Ph: 212-685-5210 ▪ Fx: 212-725-9793

Abortion Providers, National Coalition of — www.ncap.com
908 King St Suite 400W   Alexandria VA 22314
Ph: 703-684-0055 ▪ Fx: 703-684-5051

About-Face — www.about-face.org
PO Box 77665   San Francisco CA 94107
Ph: 415-436-0212

Abraham Lincoln Association — www.alincolnassoc.com
1 Old State Capitol Plaza   Springfield IL 62701
Ph: 217-782-2118 ▪ Fx: 217-785-7937

Abraham Lincoln Brigade, Veterans of the — www.alba-valb.org
799 Broadway Rm 227   New York NY 10003
Ph: 212-674-5552

Abraham Lincoln Museum, Friends of the
Lincoln Memorial Univ Box 2006   Harrogate TN 37752
Ph: 423-869-6235 ▪ Fx: 423-869-6350

Abraham Lincoln National Cemetery Support Committee
28 Kansas St   Frankfort IL 60423
Ph: 815-469-2176 ▪ Fx: 815-469-0295

Abrasive Engineering Society — www.abrasiveengineering.com
144 Moore Rd   Butler PA 16001
Ph: 724-282-6210

Abrasives Manufacturers' Association, Unified — www.uama.org
30200 Detroit Rd   Cleveland OH 44145
Ph: 440-899-0010 ▪ Fx: 440-892-1404

Abstract Artists, American
470 West End Ave Unit 9D   New York NY 10024
Ph: 212-874-0747

Abstracting & Information Services, National Federation of — www.nfais.org
1518 Walnut St Suite 307   Philadelphia PA 19102
Ph: 215-893-1561 ▪ Fx: 215-893-1564

Abundant Wildlife Society of North America — www.aws.vcn.com
PO Box 2   Beresford SD 57004
Ph: 605-751-0979

Abuse America, Prevent Child — www.preventchildabuse.org
200 S Michigan Ave 17th Fl   Chicago IL 60604
Ph: 312-663-3520 ▪ Fx: 312-939-8962 ▪ TF: 800-244-5373

Abuse of Children, American Professional Society on the — www.apsac.org
940 NE 13th St CHO 3B3406   Oklahoma City OK 73104
Ph: 405-271-8202 ▪ Fx: 405-271-2931

Abuse Defense & Resource Center, National Child — www.falseallegation.org
PO Box 638   Holland OH 43528
Ph: 419-865-0513 ▪ Fx: 419-865-0526

Abuse & Family Violence, National Council on Child www.nccafv.org
1025 Connecticut Ave NW Suite 1012   Washington DC 20036
Ph: 202-429-6695

Abuse & Incest National Network, Rape www.rainn.org
635-B Pennsylvania Ave SE   Washington DC 20003
Ph: 202-544-1034 ▪ Fax: 202-544-3556 ▪ TF: 800-656-4673

Abuse, National Center on Elder www.elderabusecenter.org
1225 'I' St NW Suite 725   Washington DC 20005
Ph: 202-898-2586 ▪ Fax: 202-898-2583

Abuse, National Committee for the Prevention of Elder www.preventelderabuse.org
1612 K St NW Suite 400   Washington DC 20006
Ph: 202-682-4140 ▪ Fax: 202-682-3984

Abuse & Routine Mutilation of Males, National Organization to www.noharmm.org
Halt the PO Box 460795   San Francisco CA 94146
Ph: 415-826-9351

Abuse, Survivors of Clergy - The Linkup www.thelinkup.org
291 N Hubbards Ln Suite B26   Louisville KY 40207
Ph: 502-290-4055 ▪ Fax: 502-290-4056

Abused by Priests, Survivors Network of Those www.snapnetwork.org
PO Box 6416   Chicago IL 60680
Ph: 312-409-2720

Abusers, Association for the Treatment of Sexual www.atsa.com
4900 SW Griffith Dr Suite 274   Beaverton OR 97005
Ph: 503-643-1023 ▪ Fax: 503-643-5084

ACA International - Association of Credit & Collection www.acainternational.org
Professionals PO Box 390106   Minneapolis MN 55439
Ph: 952-926-6547 ▪ Fax: 952-926-1624

Acacia International Fraternity www.acacia.org
8777 Purdue Rd Suite 130   Indianapolis IN 46268
Ph: 317-872-8210 ▪ Fax: 317-872-8213 ▪ TF: 888-345-1904

Acacia North American User Group www.anaug.org
401 N Michigan Ave   Chicago IL 60611
Ph: 312-644-6610 ▪ Fax: 312-644-6363

Academia, Accuracy in www.academia.org
4455 Connecticut Ave NW Suite 330   Washington DC 20008
Ph: 202-364-3085 ▪ Fax: 202-364-4098 ▪ TF: 800-787-0429

Academic Advising Association, National www.nacada.ksu.edu
Kansas State Univ 2323 Anderson Ave Suite 225   Manhattan
KS 66502
Ph: 785-532-5717 ▪ Fax: 785-532-7732

Academic Advisors for Athletics, National Association of www.nfoura.org
14606 Woodlake Terr   Louisville KY 40245
Ph: 502-253-9530 ▪ Fax: 502-253-9533

Academic Authors Association, Text & www.taaonline.net
PO Box 76477   Saint Petersburg FL 33734
Ph: 727-821-7277 ▪ Fax: 727-821-7271

Academic Chairmen of Plastic Surgery, Association of www.aacplasticsurgery.org
4900 B South 31st St   Arlington VA 22206
Ph: 703-820-7400 ▪ Fax: 703-931-4520

Academic Deans, American Conference of www.acad-edu.org
1818 R St NW   Washington DC 20009
Ph: 202-884-7419 ▪ Fax: 202-478-5005

Academic Emergency Medicine, Society for www.saem.org
901 N Washington Ave   Lansing MI 48906
Ph: 517-485-5484 ▪ Fax: 517-485-0801

Academic Exchange Service, German www.daad.org
871 United Nations Plaza   New York NY 10017
Ph: 212-758-3223 ▪ Fax: 212-755-5780

Academic Health Centers, Association of www.ahcnet.org
1400 16th St NW Suite 720   Washington DC 20036
Ph: 202-265-9600 ▪ Fax: 202-265-7514

(Academic) Honor Society of Phi Kappa Phi www.phikappaphi.org
LSU Baton Rouge PO Box 16000   Baton Rouge LA 70893
Ph: 225-388-4917 ▪ Fax: 225-388-4900 ▪ TF: 800-804-9880

Academic Language Therapy Association www.altaread.org
13140 Coit Rd Suite 320 LB 120   Dallas TX 75240
Ph: 972-233-9107 ▪ Fax: 972-490-4219

Academic Orthopaedic Society www.a-o-s.org
6300 N River Rd Suite 505   Rosemont IL 60018
Ph: 847-318-7330 ▪ Fax: 847-318-7339

(Academic) Phi Beta Kappa Society www.pbk.org
1606 New Hampshire Ave NW   Washington DC 20009
Ph: 202-265-3808 ▪ Fax: 202-986-1601

Academic & Professional Programs for the Americas, LASPAU: www.laspau.harvard.edu
25 Mount Auburn St   Cambridge MA 02138
Ph: 617-495-5255 ▪ Fax: 617-495-8990

Academic Psychiatry, Administrators in www.adminpsych.org
Univ of Michigan Dept of Psychiatry UH9C 9151   Ann Arbor MI
48109
Ph: 734-936-4860 ▪ Fax: 734-936-9983

Academic Radiology Departments, Society of Chairmen of www.scardonline.org
820 Jorie Blvd   Oak Brook IL 60523
Ph: 630-368-3731 ▪ Fax: 630-571-7837

Academic Rights, Coalition for Student & www.co-star.org
PO Box 491   Solebury PA 18963
Ph: 215-862-9096 ▪ Fax: 215-862-9097

Academic Standards & Traditions, Foundation for
545 Madison Ave 4th Fl   New York NY 10022
Ph: 212-486-1711

Academic Surgery, Association for www.aasurg.org
11300 W Olympic Blvd Suite 600   Los Angeles CA 90064
Ph: 310-437-0555 ▪ Fax: 310-437-0585

Academies of Engineering & Technological Sciences Inc, www.caets.org
International Council of 500 5th St NW   Washington DC
20001
Ph: 703-527-5782 ▪ Fax: 703-526-0570

Academy of Accounting Historians accounting.rutgers.edu/raw/aah
Univ of Alabama Culverhouse School of Accountancy Box
870220   Tuscaloosa AL 34587
Ph: 205-348-9784 ▪ Fax: 205-348-8453

Academy of Ambulatory Foot & Ankle Surgery www.academy-afs.org
1601 Walnut St Suite 1005   Philadelphia PA 19102
Ph: 215-569-3303 ▪ Fax: 215-569-3310 ▪ TF: 800-433-4892

Academy of American Poets www.poets.org
588 Broadway Suite 604   New York NY 10012
Ph: 212-274-0343 ▪ Fax: 212-274-9427

Academy of Aphasia www.academyofaphasia.org
PO Box 26532   Minneapolis MN 55426
Ph: 952-920-0966 ▪ Fax: 952-920-6098

Academy of Applied Science www.aas-world.org
24 Warren St   Concord NH 03301
Ph: 603-228-4530 ▪ Fax: 603-228-4730

Academy of Breastfeeding Medicine www.bfmed.org
191 Clarksville Rd   Princeton Junction NJ 08550
Ph: 609-799-6327 ▪ Fax: 609-799-7032 ▪ TF: 877-836-9947

Academy of Certified Archivists www.certifiedarchivists.org
48 Howard St   Albany NY 12207
Ph: 518-463-8644 ▪ Fax: 518-463-8656

Academy of Clinical Laboratory Physicians & Scientists depts.washington.edu/lmaclps
Univ of Chicago Dept of Pathology MC 0006 5841 S Maryland
Ave   Chicago IL 60637
Ph: 773-702-1878 ▪ Fax: 773-702-9082

Academy of Country Music www.acmcountry.com
4100 W Alameda Ave Suite 208   Burbank CA 91505
Ph: 818-842-8400 ▪ Fax: 818-842-8535

Academy of Criminal Justice Sciences www.acjs.org
7319 Hanover Pkwy Suite C   Greenbelt MD 20770
Ph: 301-446-6300 ▪ Fax: 301-446-2819 ▪ TF: 800-757-2257

Academy of Dental Materials Inc www.academydentalmaterials.org
PO Box 432   Morgantown WV 26507
Ph: 304-292-7343 ▪ Fax: 304-292-7099

Academy of Dental Sleep Medicine www.dentalsleepmed.org
1 Westbrook Corporate Ctr Suite 920   Westchester IL 60154
Ph: 708-273-9335 ▪ Fax: 708-492-0943

Academy of Dentistry International www.adint.org
3813 Gordon Creek Dr   Hicksville OH 43526
Ph: 419-542-0101 ▪ Fax: 419-542-6883

Academy of Dentistry for Persons with Disabilities scdonline.org/ADPD_Index.htm
211 E Chicago Ave Suite 740   Chicago IL 60611
Ph: 312-440-2660 ▪ Fax: 312-440-2824

Academy of Dispensing Audiologists www.audiologist.org
1 Windsor Cove Suite 305   Columbia SC 29223
Ph: 803-252-5646 ▪ Fax: 803-765-0860 ▪ TF: 800-445-8629

Academy for Eating Disorders www.aedweb.org
6728 Old McLean Village Dr   McLean VA 22101
Ph: 703-556-9222 ▪ Fax: 703-556-8729

Academy for Educational Development www.aed.org
1825 Connecticut Ave NW   Washington DC 20009
Ph: 202-884-8000 ▪ Fax: 202-884-8400

Academy of Forensic & Industrial Chiropractic Consultants aficc.tripod.com
18331 Gridely Rd Suite C   Cerritos CA 90703
Ph: 562-860-3662 ▪ Fax: 562-860-4377

Academy of General Dentistry www.agd.org
211 E Chicago Ave Suite 900   Chicago IL 60611
Ph: 312-440-4300 ▪ Fax: 312-440-0559 ▪ TF: 888-243-3368

Academy Health Sciences www.bemycoach.com
2578 Broadway Suite 112   New York NY 10025
Ph: 212-932-2381

Academy of Homiletics www.wlu.ca/~wwwsem/ah
Lincoln Christian Seminary 100 Campus View Dr   Lincoln IL
62656
Ph: 217-732-3168 ▪ Fax: 217-732-1821

Academy of International Business aib.msu.edu
Michigan State Univ Eli Broad College of Business 7 Eppley
Ctr   East Lansing MI 48824
Ph: 517-432-1452 ▪ Fax: 517-432-1009

Academy for International Health Studies www.aihs.com
37 Aspen Dr   South Glastonbury CT 06037
Ph: 860-430-1388 ▪ Fax: 860-430-1420

Academy of Laser Dentistry www.laserdentistry.org
PO Box 8667   Coral Springs FL 33075
Ph: 954-346-3776 ▪ Fax: 954-757-2598

Academy of Managed Care Pharmacy www.amcp.org
100 N Pitt St Suite 400   Alexandria VA 22314
Ph: 703-683-8416 ▪ Fax: 703-683-8417 ▪ TF: 800-827-2627

Academy of Managed Care Providers www.academymcp.org
1945 Palo Verde Ave Suite 202   Long Beach CA 90815
Ph: 562-682-3559 ▪ Fax: 562-799-3355 ▪ TF: 800-297-2627

Academy of Management www.aomonline.org
PO Box 3020   Briarcliff Manor NY 10510
Ph: 914-923-2607 ▪ Fax: 914-923-2615

Academy of Medical-Surgical Nurses www.medsurgnurse.org
PO Box 56   Pitman NJ 08071
Ph: 856-256-2323 ▪ Fax: 856-589-7463

Academy of Model Aeronautics www.modelaircraft.org
5161 E Memorial Dr   Muncie IN 47302
Ph: 765-287-1256 ▪ Fax: 765-289-4248 ▪ TF: 800-435-9262

Academy of Motion Picture Arts & Sciences www.oscars.org
8949 Wilshire Blvd   Beverly Hills CA 90211
Ph: 310-247-3000 ▪ Fax: 310-859-9619

Academy of Natural Sciences www.acnatsci.org
1900 Benjamin Franklin Pkwy   Philadelphia PA 19103
Ph: 215-299-1000 ▪ Fax: 215-299-1028

Academy of Organizational & Occupational Psychiatry www.aoop.org
717 Princess St   Alexandria VA 22314
Ph: 877-789-2667 ▪ Fax: 877-789-6050

Academy of Osseointegration www.osseo.org
85 W Algonquin Rd Suite 550   Arlington Heights IL 60005
Ph: 847-439-1919 ▪ Fax: 847-439-1569 ▪ TF: 800-656-7736

Academy of Parish Clergy
1851 King James Pkwy Suite 322   Westlake OH 44145
Ph: 440-835-0931
www.apclergy.org

Academy of Pharmacy Practice & Management
American Pharmacists Assn 2215 Constitution Ave
NW   Washington DC 20037
Ph: 202-628-4410 ▪ Fx: 202-783-2351
www.aphanet.org/APPMIntro.html

Academy of Political Science
475 Riverside Dr Suite 1274   New York NY 10115
Ph: 212-870-2500 ▪ Fx: 212-870-2202
www.epn.org/psq/psaops.html

Academy of Prosthodontics
6177 Orchard Lake Rd Suite 120   West Bloomfield MI 48322
Ph: 248-855-6655 ▪ Fx: 248-855-0803
www.academyprosthodontics.org

Academy of Psychosomatic Medicine
5824 N Magnolia Ave   Chicago IL 60660
Ph: 773-784-2025 ▪ Fx: 773-784-1304
www.apm.org

Academy of Radiology Research
1029 Vermont Ave NW Suite 505   Washington DC 20005
Ph: 202-347-5872 ▪ Fx: 202-347-5876
www.acadrad.org

Academy of Rehabilitative Audiology
PO Box 26532   Minneapolis MN 55426
Ph: 952-920-0484 ▪ Fx: 952-920-6098
www.audrehab.org

Academy of Religion & Psychical Research
PO Box 614   Bloomfield CT 06002
Ph: 860-242-4593
www.lightlink.com/arpr

Academy of Science Fiction Fantasy & Horror Films
334 W 54th St   Los Angeles CA 90037
Ph: 323-752-5811
www.saturnawards.org

Academy of Scientific Hypnotherapy
PO Box 12041   San Diego CA 92112
Ph: 619-427-6225 ▪ Fx: 619-427-5650

Academy of Security Educators & Trainers
PO Box 802   Berryville VA 22611
Ph: 540-554-2540 ▪ Fx: 540-554-2558
www.personalprotection.com/aset

Academy for State & Local Government
444 N Capitol St NW Suite 345   Washington DC 20001
Ph: 202-434-4850 ▪ Fx: 202-434-4851

Academy of Students of Pharmacy
American Pharmacists Assn 2215 Constitution Ave
NW   Washington DC 20037
Ph: 202-628-4410 ▪ Fx: 202-783-2351
www.aphanet.org/students/studentsnew.htm

Academy of Surgical Research
7500 Flying Cloud Rd Suite 900   Eden Prairie MN 55344
Ph: 952-253-6240 ▪ Fx: 952-835-4774
www.surgicalresearch.org

Academy of Television Arts & Sciences
5220 Lankershim Blvd   North Hollywood CA 91601
Ph: 818-754-2800 ▪ Fx: 818-761-2827
www.emmys.tv

Academy of Veterinary Allergy & Clinical Immunology
330 Waukegan Rd   Glenview IL 60025
Ph: 847-729-5200 ▪ Fx: 847-729-5214
www.avaci.org

Academy of Veterinary Homeopathy
PO Box 9280   Wilmington DE 19809
Ph: 866-652-1590
www.theavh.org

AcademyHealth
1801 K St NW Suite 701-L   Washington DC 20006
Ph: 202-292-6700 ▪ Fx: 202-292-6800
www.academyhealth.org

Access to Africa
115 W 30th St Suite 1205   New York NY 10001
Ph: 212-629-8001 ▪ Fx: 212-629-8033
www.itdp.org

Access Fund
PO Box 17010   Boulder CO 80308
Ph: 303-545-6772 ▪ Fx: 303-545-6774
www.accessfund.org

Access, Health Coalition on Liability &
PO Box 19008   Washington DC 20036
Ph: 202-293-4255 ▪ Fx: 202-296-7689
www.hcla.org

Access Point
PO Box 6359   Los Osos CA 93412
Ph: 805-534-1101 ▪ Fx: 805-534-1718 ▪ TF: 800-549-1749
www.accesspt.com

Access Professionals, American Society of
1444 'I' St NW Suite 700   Washington DC 20005
Ph: 202-216-9623 ▪ Fx: 202-216-9646
www.accesspro.org

Access Project
30 Winter St Suite 930   Boston MA 02108
Ph: 617-654-9911 ▪ Fx: 617-654-9922
www.accessproject.org

Access Research Network
PO Box 38069   Colorado Springs CO 80937
Ph: 719-633-1772 ▪ TF: 888-259-7102
www.arn.org

Access Systems Manufacturers Association, Door &
1300 Sumner Ave   Cleveland OH 44115
Ph: 216-241-7333 ▪ Fx: 216-241-0105
www.dasma.com

Accessibility Equipment Manufacturers Association
PO Box 380   Metamora IL 61548
Ph: 800-514-1100 ▪ Fx: 309-923-7964
www.aema.com

Accessible Apartment Clearinghouse, National
201 N Union St Suite 200   Alexandria VA 22314
Ph: 703-518-6141 ▪ Fx: 703-518-6191 ▪ TF: 800-421-1221
www.forrent.com/naac

Accessories Council
390 5th Ave Suite 710   New York NY 10018
Ph: 212-947-1135 ▪ Fx: 212-947-9258
www.accessoriescouncil.org

Accident Boards & Commissions, International Association of
Industrial   5610 Medical Cir Suite 14   Madison WI 53711
Ph: 608-663-6355 ▪ Fx: 608-663-1546
www.iaiabc.org

Accident Reconstruction Specialists Inc, National Association of
Professional   PO Box 65   Brandywine MD 20613
Ph: 301-843-0048
www.napars.org

ACCION International
56 Roland St Suite 300   Boston MA 02129
Ph: 617-625-7080 ▪ Fx: 617-625-7020
www.accion.org

ACCION USA
56 Roland St Suite 300   Boston MA 02129
Ph: 617-625-7080 ▪ Fx: 617-625-7020
www.accionusa.org

Accompanists & Coaches, National Association of
395 Riverside Dr Apt 13A   New York NY 10025
Ph: 212-316-6164 ▪ Fx: 212-663-1900

Accordion Musicological Society, American
334 S Broadway   Pitman NJ 08071
Ph: 856-854-6628

Accordionists Association, American
580 Kearny Ave   Kearny NJ 07032
Ph: 201-991-2233 ▪ Fx: 201-991-1944
www.ameraccord.com

Account Management Association, Strategic
150 N Wacker Dr Suite 2222   Chicago IL 60606
Ph: 312-251-3131 ▪ Fx: 312-251-3132
www.strategicaccounts.org

Accountancy, National Association of State Boards of
150 4th Ave N Suite 700   Nashville TN 37219
Ph: 615-880-4200 ▪ Fx: 615-880-4290 ▪ TF: 800-272-3926
www.nasba.org

Accountancy & Taxation, Accreditation Council for
1010 N Fairfax St   Alexandria VA 22314
Ph: 703-549-2228 ▪ Fx: 703-549-2984 ▪ TF: 888-289-7763
www.acatcredentials.org

Accountants, American Association of Attorney-Certified Public
24196 Alicia Pkwy Suite K   Mission Viejo CA 92691
Ph: 949-768-0336 ▪ TF: 888-288-9272
www.attorney-cpa.com

Accountants, American Institute of Certified Public
1211 Ave of the Americas   New York NY 10036
Ph: 212-596-6200 ▪ Fx: 212-596-6213 ▪ TF: 888-777-7077
www.aicpa.org

Accountants, American Society of Women
8405 Greensboro Dr Suite 800   McLean VA 22102
Ph: 703-506-3265 ▪ Fx: 703-506-3266
www.aswa.org

Accountants, American Woman's Society of Certified Public
136 S Keowee St   Dayton OH 45402
Ph: 937-222-1872 ▪ Fx: 937-222-5794 ▪ TF: 800-297-2721
www.awscpa.org

Accountants, Association of Government
2208 Mt Vernon Ave   Alexandria VA 22301
Ph: 703-684-6931 ▪ Fx: 703-548-9367 ▪ TF: 800-242-7211
www.agacgfm.org

Accountants, Association of Practicing Certified Public
Rockville MD 20850
Ph: 301-340-3340 ▪ Fx: 301-340-3343
www.ap-cpa.com

Accountants for Cooperatives, National Society of
6320 Augusta Dr Suite 800   Springfield VA 22150
Ph: 703-569-3088 ▪ Fx: 703-569-0235
www.nsacoop.org

Accountants Global Network
2851 S Parker Rd Suite 850   Aurora CO 80014
Ph: 303-743-7880 ▪ Fx: 303-743-7660 ▪ TF: 800-782-2272
www.agn.org

Accountants Inc, Institute of Management
10 Paragon Dr   Montvale NJ 07645
Ph: 201-573-9000 ▪ Fx: 201-573-8185 ▪ TF: 800-638-4427
www.imanet.org

Accountants International, Affiliated Conference of Practicing
30 Massachusetts Ave   North Andover MA 01845
Ph: 978-689-9420 ▪ Fx: 978-689-9404
www.acpaintl.org

Accountants, International Federation of
535 5th Ave 14th Fl   New York NY 10017
Ph: 212-286-9344 ▪ Fx: 212-286-9570
www.ifac.org

Accountants, National Association of Black
7249-A Hanover Pkwy   Greenbelt MD 20770
Ph: 301-474-6222 ▪ Fx: 301-474-3114
www.nabainc.org

Accountants, National Association of Forensic
2455 E Sunrise Blvd Suite 1201   Fort Lauderdale FL 33304
Ph: 954-535-5556 ▪ Fx: 954-537-4942 ▪ TF: 800-523-3680
www.nafanet.com

Accountants, National Society of
1010 N Fairfax St   Alexandria VA 22314
Ph: 703-549-6400 ▪ Fx: 703-549-2984 ▪ TF: 800-966-6679
www.nsacct.org

Accountants for the Public Interest
1420 N Charles St Suite 519   Baltimore MD 21201
Ph: 410-837-6533 ▪ Fx: 410-837-6532
www.geocities.com/api_woods/api/apihome.html

Accountants Societies, Council of Petroleum
PO Box 1190   Denison TX 75021
Ph: 903-463-5463 ▪ Fx: 903-463-5473
www.copas.org

Accountants Society of North America, Forensic
8712 W Dodge Rd Suite 200   Omaha NE 68114
Ph: 402-397-9433 ▪ Fx: 402-397-8649
www.fasna.org

Accountants in the US, Association of Chartered
341 Lafayette St Suite 4246   New York NY 10012
Ph: 212-334-2078 ▪ Fx: 212-431-5786
www.acaus.com

Accounting Administration, Association for
136 S Keowee St   Dayton OH 45402
Ph: 937-222-0030 ▪ Fx: 937-222-5794
www.cpaadmin.org

(Accounting) AGN International-North America
2851 S Parker Rd Suite 850   Aurora CO 80014
Ph: 303-743-7880 ▪ Fx: 303-743-7660 ▪ TF: 800-782-2272
www.agn.org

Accounting Association, American
5717 Bessie Dr   Sarasota FL 34233
Ph: 941-921-7747 ▪ Fx: 941-923-4093
aaahq.org

Accounting, Association of Latino Professionals in Finance &
510 W 6th St Suite 400   Los Angeles CA 90014
Ph: 213-243-0004 ▪ Fx: 213-243-0006
www.alpfa.org

(Accounting) BKR International
19 Fulton St Suite 306   New York NY 10038
Ph: 212-964-2115 ▪ Fx: 212-964-2133 ▪ TF: 800-257-4685
www.bkr.com

Accounting Education, Foundation for
530 5th Ave 5th Fl   New York NY 10036
Ph: 212-719-8300 ▪ Fx: 212-719-3365 ▪ TF: 800-537-3635

Accounting, Educational Foundation for Women in
PO Box 1925   Southeastern PA 19399
Ph: 610-407-9229 ▪ Fx: 610-644-3713
www.efwa.org

Accounting & Finance Council, National
American Trucking Assns 2200 Mill Rd   Alexandria VA 22314
Ph: 703-838-1915 ▪ Fx: 703-836-0751
truckline.com/cc/councils/nafc

Accounting Firms, International Group of
2250 Satellite Blvd Suite 115   Duluth GA 30097
Ph: 678-417-7730 ▪ Fx: 678-417-6977
www.igaf.org

Accounting Firms, National Associated Certified Public www.nacpaf.com
136 S Keowee St   Dayton OH 45402
Ph: 937-222-1024 ▪ Fx: 937-222-5794

Accounting Foundation, Financial www.fasb.org/facts
401 Merritt 7 PO Box 5116   Norwalk CT 06856
Ph: 203-847-0700 ▪ Fx: 203-849-9714

Accounting Historians, Academy of accounting.rutgers.edu/raw/aah
Univ of Alabama Culverhouse School of Accountancy Box
870220   Tuscaloosa AL 34587
Ph: 205-348-9784 ▪ Fx: 205-348-8453

(Accounting) IA International www.iai.org
9200 S Dadeland Blvd Suite 510   Miami FL 33156
Ph: 305-670-0580 ▪ Fx: 305-670-3818

Accounting Marketing, Association for www.accountingmarketing.org
14 W 3rd St Suite 200   Kansas City MO 64105
Ph: 816-221-1296 ▪ Fx: 816-472-7765

(Accounting) PKF North American Network www.pkfnan.org
3700 Crestwood Pkwy Suite 350   Duluth GA 30096
Ph: 770-279-4560 ▪ Fx: 770-279-4566

Accounting Standards Board, Financial www.fasb.org
401 Merritt 7 PO Box 5116   Norwalk CT 06856
Ph: 203-847-0700 ▪ Fx: 203-849-9714

Accounting & Systems Association, Insurance www.iasa.org
4705 University Dr Suite 280 PO Box 51340   Durham NC
27717
Ph: 919-489-0991 ▪ Fx: 919-489-1994

Accounts Payable Professionals, International www.iappnet.org
PO Box 590373   Orlando FL 32859
Ph: 407-351-322 ▪ Fx: 407-345-8361

ACCRA www.accra.org
PO Box 407   Arlington VA 22210
Ph: 703-522-4980 ▪ Fx: 703-522-4985

Accreditation of Allied Health Education Programs, Commission on www.caahep.org
35 E Wacker Dr Suite 1970   Chicago IL 60601
Ph: 312-553-9355 ▪ Fx: 312-553-9616

Accreditation of Ambulatory Surgery Facilities Inc, American Association for www.aaaasf.org
5101 Washington St Suite 2F PO Box
9500   Gurnee IL 60031
Ph: 888-545-5222 ▪ Fx: 847-775-1985

Accreditation, American Association for Laboratory www.a2la.org
5301 Buckeystown Pike Suite 350   Frederick MD 21704
Ph: 301-644-3248 ▪ Fx: 301-662-2974

Accreditation Association for Ambulatory Health Care www.aaahc.org
3201 Old Glenview Rd Suite 300   Wilmette IL 60091
Ph: 847-853-6060 ▪ Fx: 847-853-9028

Accreditation Board for Engineering & Technology Inc www.abet.org
111 Market Pl Suite 1050   Baltimore MD 21202
Ph: 410-347-7700 ▪ Fx: 410-625-2238

Accreditation Commission, Continuing Care www.ccaconline.org
2519 Connecticut Ave NW   Washington DC 20008
Ph: 202-783-7286 ▪ Fx: 202-220-0022

Accreditation, Commission on Office Laboratory www.cola.org
9881 Broken Land Pkwy Suite 200   Columbia MD 21046
Ph: 410-381-6581 ▪ Fx: 410-381-8611 ▪ TF: 800-981-9883

Accreditation, Commission on Opticianry www.coaccreditation.com
PO Box 3073   Merrifield VA 22116
Ph: 703-766-1600 ▪ Fx: 703-766-2834

Accreditation, Council on www.coanet.org
120 Wall St 11th Fl   New York NY 10005
Ph: 212-797-3000 ▪ Fx: 212-797-1428 ▪ TF: 866-262-8088

Accreditation Council for Accountancy & Taxation www.acatcredentials.org
1010 N Fairfax St   Alexandria VA 22314
Ph: 703-549-2228 ▪ Fx: 703-549-2984 ▪ TF: 888-289-7763

Accreditation Council Inc, Certified Claims Professional
PO Box 441110   Fort Washington MD 20749
Ph: 301-292-1988 ▪ Fx: 301-292-1787

Accreditation Council for Graduate Medical Education www.acgme.org
515 N State St Suite 2000   Chicago IL 60610
Ph: 312-755-5000 ▪ Fx: 312-755-7498

Accreditation, Council for Higher Education www.chea.org
1 Dupont Cir NW Suite 510   Washington DC 20036
Ph: 202-955-6126 ▪ Fx: 202-955-6129

Accreditation for Educational Programs for the EMS Professions, Committee on www.coaemsp.org
1248 Hardwood Rd   Bedford TX 76021
Ph: 817-283-9403 ▪ Fx: 817-354-8519

Accreditation HealthCare Commission, American www.urac.org
1220 L St NW Suite 400   Washington DC 20005
Ph: 202-216-9010 ▪ Fx: 202-216-9006

Accreditation of Healthcare Organizations, Joint Commission on www.jcaho.org
1 Renaissance Blvd   Oakbrook Terrace IL 60181
Ph: 630-792-5000 ▪ Fx: 630-792-5005

Accreditation of Laboratory Animal Care International, Association for Assessment & www.aaalac.org
11300 Rockville Pike Suite 1211   Rockville
MD 20852
Ph: 301-231-5353 ▪ Fx: 301-231-8282 ▪ TF: 800-926-0066

Accreditation for Law Enforcement Agencies, Commission on www.calea.org
10306 Eaton Pl Suite 320   Fairfax VA 22030
Ph: 703-352-4225 ▪ Fx: 703-591-2206 ▪ TF: 800-368-3757

(Accreditation) North Central Association Higher Learning Commission www.ncacihe.org
30 N La Salle St Suite 2400   Chicago IL 60602
Ph: 312-263-0456 ▪ Fx: 312-263-7462 ▪ TF: 800-621-7440

Accreditation in Occupational Hearing Conservation, Council for www.caohc.org
611 E Wells St   Milwaukee WI 53202
Ph: 414-276-5338 ▪ Fx: 414-276-2146

Accreditation Program Inc, Community Health www.chapinc.org
39 Broadway Suite 710   New York NY 10006
Ph: 212-480-8828 ▪ Fx: 212-480-8833 ▪ TF: 800-656-9656

Accreditation of Rehabilitation Facilities, Commission on www.carf.org
4891 E Grant Rd   Tucson AZ 85712
Ph: 520-325-1044 ▪ Fx: 520-318-1129

Accreditation Review Commission on Education for the Physician Assistant Inc www.arc-pa.org
1000 N Oak Ave   Marshfield WI 54449
Ph: 715-389-3785 ▪ Fx: 715-387-5163

Accreditation & School Improvement, North Central Association Commission on www.ncacasi.org
Arizona State Univ PO Box 873011   Tempe
AZ 85287
Ph: 480-965-8700 ▪ TF: 800-525-9517

Accreditation of Teacher Education, National Council for www.ncate.org
2010 Massachusetts Ave NW Suite 500   Washington DC 20036
Ph: 202-466-7496 ▪ Fx: 202-296-6620

Accreditation of Vascular Laboratories, Intersocietal Commission for the www.icavl.org
8840 Stanford Blvd Suite 4900   Columbia MD 21045
Ph: 410-872-0100 ▪ Fx: 410-872-0030

Accredited Marine Surveyors, Society of www.marinesurvey.org
4605 Cardina Blvd   Jacksonville FL 32210
Ph: 904-384-1494 ▪ Fx: 904-388-3958

Accredited Pet Cemetery Society www.accreditedpetcemeterysociety.org
3426 Brush Rd   Richfield OH 44286
Ph: 330-659-4270 ▪ Fx: 330-659-4254

Accredited Review Appraisers Council Inc arac.lincoln-grad.org
c/o Lincoln Graduate Ctr 303 W Cypress St   San Antonio TX
78212
Ph: 210-225-2897 ▪ Fx: 210-225-8450 ▪ TF: 800-531-5333

Accredited Schools, Northwest Association of www2.boisestate.edu/NASC
1910 University Dr   Boise ID 83725
Ph: 208-426-5727 ▪ Fx: 208-334-3228

Accrediting Agency for Clinical Laboratory Sciences, National www.naacls.org
8410 W Bryn Mawr Ave Suite 670   Chicago IL 60631
Ph: 773-714-8880 ▪ Fx: 773-714-8886

Accrediting Association of Bible Colleges www.gospelcom.net/aabc
5575 S Semoran Blvd Suite 26   Orlando FL 32822
Ph: 407-207-0808 ▪ Fx: 407-207-0840

Accrediting Association, International Christian www.oru.edu/oruef/icaa
7777 S Lewis Ave   Tulsa OK 74171
Ph: 918-495-6163 ▪ Fx: 918-495-6175

Accrediting Associations, Council of Arts www.arts-accredit.org
11250 Roger Bacon Dr Suite 21   Reston VA 20190
Ph: 703-437-0700 ▪ Fx: 703-437-6312

Accrediting Associations, National Federation of Nonpublic School State www.nfnssaa.org
6300 Father Tribou St   Little Rock AR 72205
Ph: 501-664-0340 ▪ Fx: 501-664-9075

Accrediting Board, Computing Sciences www.abet.org/cac1.html
Accreditation Board for Engineering & Technology Inc 111
Market Pl Suite 1050   Baltimore MD 21202
Ph: 410-347-7700 ▪ Fx: 410-625-2238

Accrediting Board, National Architectural www.naab.org
1735 New York Ave NW   Washington DC 20006
Ph: 202-783-2007 ▪ Fx: 202-783-2822

Accrediting Bureau of Health Education Schools www.abhes.org
7777 Leesburg Pike Suite 314 N   Falls Church VA 22043
Ph: 703-917-9503 ▪ Fx: 703-917-4109

Accrediting Commission of Career Schools & Colleges of Technology www.accsct.org
2101 Wilson Blvd Suite 302   Arlington VA 22201
Ph: 703-247-4212 ▪ Fx: 703-247-4533

Accrediting Commission for Community & Precollegiate Arts Schools www.arts-accredit.org
11250 Roger Bacon Dr Suite 21   Reston VA
20190
Ph: 703-437-0700 ▪ Fx: 703-437-6312

Accrediting Commission of Cosmetology Arts & Sciences, National www.naccas.org
4401 Ford Ave Suite 1300   Alexandria VA 22302
Ph: 703-600-7600 ▪ Fx: 703-379-2200

Accrediting Commission Inc, National League for Nursing www.nlnac.org
61 Broadway 33rd Fl   New York NY 10006
Ph: 212-363-5555 ▪ Fx: 212-812-0390 ▪ TF: 800-669-1656

Accrediting Council for Continuing Education & Training www.accet.org
1722 'N' St NW   Washington DC 20036
Ph: 202-955-1113 ▪ Fx: 202-955-1118

Accrediting Council on Education in Journalism & Mass Communications www.ukans.edu/~acejmc
Univ of Kansas School of Journalism
Stauffer-Flint Hall   Lawrence KS 66045
Ph: 785-864-3973 ▪ Fx: 785-864-5225

Accrediting Council for Independent Colleges & Schools www.acics.org
750 1st St NE Suite 980   Washington DC 20002
Ph: 202-336-6780 ▪ Fx: 202-842-2593

Accreditors, Association of Specialized & Professional www.aspa-usa.org
1020 W Byron St Suite 8G   Chicago IL 60613
Ph: 773-525-2160 ▪ Fx: 773-525-2162

(Accupressure) G-Jo Institute www.g-jo.com
PO Box 1460   Columbus NC 28722
Ph: 828-863-4660

Accuracy in Academia www.academia.org
4455 Connecticut Ave NW Suite 330   Washington DC 20008
Ph: 202-364-3085 ▪ Fx: 202-364-4098 ▪ TF: 800-787-0429

Accuracy in Media Inc www.aim.org
4455 Connecticut Ave NW Suite 330   Washington DC 20008
Ph: 202-364-4401 ▪ Fx: 202-364-4098 ▪ TF: 800-787-4567

ACDI/VOCA www.acdivoca.org
50 F St NW Suite 1075   Washington DC 20001
Ph: 202-638-4661 ▪ Fx: 202-626-8726 ▪ TF: 800-929-8622

Achilles Track Club www.achillestrackclub.org
42 W 38th St 4th Fl   New York NY 10018
Ph: 212-354-0300 ▪ Fx: 212-354-3978

Achromatopsia Network www.achromat.org
PO Box 214   Berkeley CA 94701
Ph: 510-540-4700 ▪ Fx: 510-540-4767

Acid Maltase Deficiency Association www.amda-pompe.org
PO Box 700248   San Antonio TX 78270
Ph: 210-494-6144 ▪ Fx: 210-497-3810

Acidemia Association, Organic www.oaanews.org
13210 35th Ave N   Plymouth MN 55441
Ph: 763-559-1797 ▪ Fx: 763-694-0017

Ackerman Institute for the Family   www.ackerman.org
149 E 78th St   New York NY 10021
Ph: 212-879-4900 ≋ Fx: 212-744-0206

ACORD   www.acord.org
PO Box 1529   Pearl River NY 10965
Ph: 845-620-1700 ≋ Fx: 845-620-3600 ≋ TF: 800-444-3341

Acoustic Neuroma Association   anausa.org
600 Peachtree Pkwy Suite 108   Cumming GA 30041
Ph: 770-205-8211 ≋ Fx: 770-205-0239

Acoustical Consultants, National Council of   www.ncac.com
66 Morris Ave Suite 1A   Springfield NJ 07081
Ph: 973-564-5859 ≋ Fx: 973-564-7480

Acoustical Society of America   asa.aip.org
2 Huntington Quadrangle Suite 1NO1   Melville NY 11747
Ph: 516-576-2360 ≋ Fx: 516-576-2377

Acoustical Society, Catgut   www.catgutacoustical.org
55 Park St   Montclair NJ 07042
Ph: 973-744-0371 ≋ Fx: 973-744-0375

ACRES Land Trust   www.acres-land-trust.org
2000 N Wells St   Fort Wayne IN 46808
Ph: 260-422-1004

Acrylic Council Inc   www.fabriclink.com/acryliccouncil
1285 Ave of the Americas 35th Fl   New York NY 10019
Ph: 212-554-4040 ≋ Fx: 212-554-4042

Acrylic Monomer Manufacturers Inc, Basic   www.bamm.net
941 Rhonda Pl SE   Leesburg VA 20175
Ph: 703-669-5688 ≋ Fx: 703-669-5689

Acrylic Painters Society, National Oil &   www.noaps.org
PO Box 676   Osage Beach MO 65049
Ph: 417-533-7550

(Acrylonitrile) AN Group Inc   www.angroup.org
1250 Connecticutt St NW Suite 700   Washington DC 20036
Ph: 202-419-1500 ≋ Fx: 202-659-8037

ACT Inc   www.deafblindadvocates.org
911 Regina Dr   Baltimore MD 21227
Ph: 410-247-5045 ≋ Fx: 410-381-6838

ACT UP   www.actupny.org
332 Bleecker St Suite G5   New York NY 10014
Ph: 212-966-4873

Acting Coaches & Teachers, Organization of Professional
3968 Eureka Dr   Studio City CA 91604
Ph: 323-877-4988

Action Against Hunger   www.aah-usa.org
247 W 37th St Suite 1201   New York NY 10018
Ph: 212-967-7800 ≋ Fx: 212-967-5480 ≋ TF: 877-777-1420

Action Center, International   www.iacenter.org
39 W 14th St Suite 206   New York NY 10011
Ph: 212-633-6646 ≋ Fx: 212-633-2889

ACTION for Child Protection   www.actionchildprotection.org
2101 Sardis Rd N Suite 204   Charlotte NC 28227
Ph: 704-845-2121 ≋ Fx: 704-845-8577

Action Committee for Rural Electrification
4301 Wilson Blvd   Arlington VA 22203
Ph: 703-907-5500 ≋ Fx: 703-907-6826

Action on Smoking & Health   www.ash.org
2013 H St NW   Washington DC 20006
Ph: 202-659-4310 ≋ Fx: 202-833-3921

Action Without Borders   www.idealist.org
79 5th Ave Suite 6614   New York NY 10003
Ph: 212-843-3973 ≋ Fx: 212-564-3377

Active 20-30 US & Canada Inc   www.active20-30.com
915 L St Suite 1000   Sacramento CA 95814
Ph: 916-447-3217 ≋ Fx: 916-442-0382

Active Lifestyles & Fitness, American Association for   www.aahperd.org/aaalf
1900 Association Dr   Reston VA 20191
Ph: 703-476-3430 ≋ Fx: 703-476-9527 ≋ TF: 800-213-7193

(Activism) Gray Panthers   www.graypanthers.org
733 15th St NW Suite 437   Washington DC 20005
Ph: 202-737-6637 ≋ Fx: 202-737-1160 ≋ TF: 800-280-5362

Activists, National Coalition of Education   www.nceaonline.org
1420 Walnut St Suite 720   Philadelphia PA 19102
Ph: 215-735-2418

Activists for Protective Animal Legislation
PO Box 11743   Costa Mesa CA 92627
Ph: 714-540-0583 ≋ Fx: 714-540-0365

Activity Professionals, National Certification Council for   www.nccap.org
PO Box 62589   Virginia Beach VA 23466
Ph: 757-552-0653 ≋ Fx: 757-552-0491

Acton Institute for the Study of Religion & Liberty   www.acton.org
161 Ottawa NW Suite 301   Grand Rapids MI 49503
Ph: 616-454-3080 ≋ Fx: 616-454-9454

Actors & Artistes of America, Associated
165 W 46th St   New York NY 10036
Ph: 212-869-0358 ≋ Fx: 212-869-1746

Actors' Equity Association   www.actorsequity.org
165 W 46th St   New York NY 10036
Ph: 212-869-8530 ≋ Fx: 212-719-9815

Actors' Fund of America   www.actorsfund.org
729 7th Ave 10th Fl   New York NY 10019
Ph: 212-221-7300 ≋ Fx: 212-764-0238

Actors' Guild of America Inc, Episcopal   www.actorsguild.org
1 E 29th St   New York NY 10016
Ph: 212-685-2927 ≋ Fx: 212-685-8793

Actors, Guild of Italian American   www.nygiaa.org
31 E 32nd St 12th Fl   New York NY 10016
Ph: 212-420-6590

Actors Guild, Screen   www.sag.org
5757 Wilshire Blvd   Los Angeles CA 90036
Ph: 323-954-1600 ≋ Fx: 323-549-6656

Actors, Hispanic Organization of Latin   www.hellohola.org
107 Suffolk St Suite 302   New York NY 10002
Ph: 212-253-1015 ≋ Fx: 212-253-9651

Actors Studio   www.actors-studio.com
432 W 44th St   New York NY 10036
Ph: 212-757-0870

Actuarial Society, Casualty   www.casact.org
1100 N Glebe Rd Suite 600   Arlington VA 22201
Ph: 703-276-3100 ≋ Fx: 703-276-3108

Actuaries, American Academy of   www.actuary.org
1100 17th St NW 7th Fl   Washington DC 20036
Ph: 202-223-8196 ≋ Fx: 202-872-1948

Actuaries, American Society of Pension   www.aspa.org
4245 N Fairfax Dr Suite 750   Arlington VA 22203
Ph: 703-516-9300 ≋ Fx: 703-516-9308

Actuaries, Conference of Consulting   www.ccactuaries.org
1110 W Lake Cook Rd Suite 235   Buffalo Grove IL 60089
Ph: 847-419-9090 ≋ Fx: 847-419-9091

Actuaries, Society of   www.soa.org
475 N Martingale Rd Suite 800   Schaumburg IL 60173
Ph: 847-706-3500 ≋ Fx: 847-706-3599

Acupuncture, American Academy of Medical   www.medicalacupuncture.org
4929 Wilshire Blvd Suite 428   Los Angeles CA 90010
Ph: 323-937-5514 ≋ Fx: 323-937-0959

Acupuncture Association, American
4262 Kissena Blvd   Flushing NY 11355
Ph: 718-886-4431 ≋ Fx: 718-463-0808

Acupuncture Detoxification Association, National   www.acudetox.com
PO Box 1927   Vancouver WA 98668
Ph: 360-254-0186 ≋ Fx: 360-260-8620 ≋ TF: 888-765-6232

Acupuncture & Oriental Medicine Alliance   www.aomalliance.org
6405 43rd Avenue Ct NW Suite B   Gig Harbor WA 98335
Ph: 253-851-6896 ≋ Fx: 253-851-6883

Acupuncture & Oriental Medicine, Council of Colleges of   www.ccaom.org
7501 Greenway Ctr Dr Suite 820   Greenbelt MD 20770
Ph: 301-313-0868 ≋ Fx: 301-313-0869

Acupuncture Society, International Veterinary   www.ivas.org
PO Box 271395   Fort Collins CO 80527
Ph: 970-266-0666 ≋ Fx: 970-266-0777

ACUTA - Association for Communications Technology Professionals in Higher Education   www.acuta.org
152 W Zandale Dr Suite 200   Lexington KY 40503
Ph: 859-278-3338 ≋ Fx: 859-278-3268

Acute Long Term Hospital Association   www.altha.org
1055 N Fairfax Suite 201   Alexandria VA 22314
Ph: 703-299-5571 ≋ Fx: 703-299-5574

Ad Council   www.adcouncil.org
261 Madison Ave 11th Fl   New York NY 10016
Ph: 212-922-1500 ≋ Fx: 212-922-1676

ADAPT   www.adapt.org
201 S Cherokee St   Denver CO 80223
Ph: 303-733-9324 ≋ Fx: 303-733-6211

Adaptive Sports Association   www.asadurango.org
PO Box 1884   Durango CO 81302
Ph: 970-259-0374 ≋ Fx: 970-259-2175

ADARA   www.adara.org
PO Box 480   Myersville MD 21773
Ph: 301-293-8969 ≋ Fx: 301-293-9698

Addiction Medicine, American Osteopathic Academy for
142 E Ontario St   Chicago IL 60611
Ph: 312-202-8163 ≋ Fx: 312-202-8463

Addiction Medicine, American Society of   www.asam.org
4601 N Park Ave Upper Arcade Suite 101   Chevy Chase MD 20815
Ph: 301-656-3920 ≋ Fx: 301-656-3815

Addiction Professionals, NAADAC - Association for   www.naadac.org
901 N Washington St Suite 600   Alexandria VA 22314
Ph: 703-741-7686 ≋ Fx: 800-377-1136 ≋ TF: 800-548-0497

Addiction Professionals, National Association of Lesbian/Gay   www.nalgap.org
901 N Washington St Suite 600   Alexandria VA 22314
Ph: 703-465-0539 ≋ Fx: 703-741-6989

Addiction Psychiatry, American Academy of   www.aaap.org
7301 Mission Rd Suite 252   Prairie Village KS 66208
Ph: 913-262-6161 ≋ Fx: 913-262-4311

(Addiction) Rational Recovery   www.rational.org
PO Box 800   Lotus CA 95651
Ph: 530-621-2667 ≋ Fx: 530-622-4296 ≋ TF: 800-303-2873

(Addiction Recovery) Nar-Anon World Service Office   www.naranon.com
22527 Crenshaw Blvd Suite 200B   Torance CA 90505
Ph: 310-547-5800

(Addiction Recovery) Triangle Club   www.triangleclub.org
2030 P St NW   Washington DC 20036
Ph: 202-659-8641

Addiction Treatment Providers, National Association of   www.naatp.org
313 West Liberty Suite 129   Lancaster PA 17603
Ph: 717-392-8480 ≋ Fx: 717-392-8481

Addictions, International Nurses Society on   www.intnsa.org
PO Box 10752   Raleigh NC 27605
Ph: 919-821-1292 ≋ Fx: 919-833-5743

Addictions & Offender Counselors, International Association of   www.counseling.org
5999 Stevenson Ave   Alexandria VA 22304
Ph: 800-347-6647 ≋ Fx: 800-473-2329

Addictions & Offender Counselors, International Association of
c/o American Counseling Assn 5999 Stevenson Ave   Alexandria VA 22304
Ph: 703-823-9800 ≋ Fx: 703-823-0252 ≋ TF: 800-347-6647

Addictive Disorders, American Academy of Health Care Providers in the   www.americanacademy.org
314 W Superior St Suite 702   Duluth MN 55802
Ph: 218-727-3940 ≋ Fx: 218-722-0346

Addicts Anonymous, Sex   www.saa-recovery.org
PO Box 70949   Houston TX 77270
Ph: 713-869-4902 ▪ Fx: 713-869-4176 ▪ TF: 800-477-8191

ADEAR Center   www.alzheimers.org
PO Box 8250   Silver Spring MD 20907
Ph: 301-495-3311 ▪ Fx: 301-495-3334 ▪ TF: 800-438-4380

ADED - Association for Driver Rehabilitation Specialists   www.driver-ed.org
711 S Vienna St   Ruston LA 71270
Ph: 318-257-5055 ▪ Fx: 318-255-4175 ▪ TF: 800-290-2344

Adhesion Society Inc   www.adhesionsociety.org
2 Davidson Hall-0212   Blacksburg VA 24061
Ph: 540-231-7257 ▪ Fx: 540-231-3971

Adhesive & Sealant Council Inc   www.ascouncil.org
7979 Old Georgetown Rd Suite 500   Bethesda MD 20814
Ph: 301-986-9700 ▪ Fx: 301-986-9795

Adirondack Council   www.adirondackcouncil.org
103 Hand Ave Suite 3   Elizabethtown NY 12932
Ph: 518-873-2240 ▪ Fx: 518-873-6675 ▪ TF: 877-873-2240

Adirondack Forty-Sixers   www.adk46r.org
PO Box 180   Cadyville NY 12918
Ph: 518-293-6401

Adirondack Historical Association
Adirondack Museum PO Box 99   Blue Mountain Lake NY
12812
Ph: 518-352-7311 ▪ Fx: 518-352-7653

Adirondack Mountain Club   www.adk.org
814 Goggins Rd   Lake George NY 12845
Ph: 518-668-4447 ▪ Fx: 518-668-3746 ▪ TF: 800-395-8080

Adirondack Trail Improvement Society
PO Box 565   Keene Valley NY 12943
Ph: 518-576-9157 ▪ Fx: 518-576-9949

Adjusters, National Association of Catastrophe   www.nacatadj.org
PO Box 821864   North Richland Hills TX 76180
Ph: 817-498-3466 ▪ Fx: 817-498-0480

Adjusters, Organized Flying   www.ofainc.com
1501 Bluff Dr   Round Rock TX 78681
Ph: 512-255-2740 ▪ Fx: 512-246-1066

Adjutants General Association of the US   www.agaus.org
1 Massachusetts Ave NW   Washington DC 20001
Ph: 202-789-0031 ▪ Fx: 202-682-9358

Adlerian Psychology, North American Society of   www.alfredadler.org
50 Northeast Dr   Hershey PA 17033
Ph: 717-579-8795 ▪ Fx: 717-533-8616

Administration, American Academy of Dental Practice   www.aadpa.org
1063 Whippoorwill Ln   Palatine IL 60067
Ph: 847-934-4404 ▪ Fx: 847-934-4410

Administration, National Association of Schools of Public Affairs &   www.naspaa.org
1120 G St NW Suite 730   Washington DC 20005
Ph: 202-628-8965 ▪ Fx: 202-626-4978

Administration Professionals, Association of College   www.acap.org
PO Box 1389   Staunton VA 24402
Ph: 540-885-1873 ▪ Fx: 540-885-6133

Administration, University Council for Educational   www.ucea.org
Univ of Missouri-Columbia 205 Hill Hall   Columbia MO 65211
Ph: 573-884-8300 ▪ Fx: 573-884-8302

Administrative Assistants, National Association of Executive Secretaries &   900 S Washington St Suite G-13   Falls Church   www.naesaa.com
VA 22046
Ph: 703-237-8616 ▪ Fx: 703-533-1153

Administrative Law Judges Conference, Federal   www.faljc.org
2000 Pennsylvania Ave NW Suite 260   Washington DC 20006
Ph: 202-675-3065 ▪ Fx: 202-219-3289

Administrative Management, American Association of Healthcare   www.aaham.org
11240 Waples Mill Rd Suite 200   Fairfax VA 22030
Ph: 703-281-4043 ▪ Fx: 703-359-7562

Administrative Professionals, International Association of   www.iaap-hq.org
10502 NW Ambassador Dr   Kansas City MO 64153
Ph: 816-891-6600 ▪ Fx: 816-891-9118

Administrators in Academic Psychiatry   www.adminpsych.org
Univ of Michigan Dept of Psychiatry UH9C 9151   Ann Arbor MI
48109
Ph: 734-936-4860 ▪ Fx: 734-936-9983

Administrators, American Academy of Medical   www.aameda.org
701 Lee St Suite 600   Des Plaines IL 60016
Ph: 847-759-8601 ▪ Fx: 847-759-8602

Administrators, American Association of School   www.aasa.org
801 N Quincy St Suite 700   Arlington VA 22203
Ph: 703-528-0700 ▪ Fx: 703-841-1543 ▪ TF: 800-771-1162

Administrators, American College of   www.aameda.org/Specialtygroups/cardiology.html
Cardiovascular   701 Lee St Suite 600   Des Plaines IL 60016
Ph: 847-759-8601 ▪ Fx: 847-759-8602

Administrators, American College of Managed Care   www.aameda.org
701 Lee St Suite 600   Des Plaines IL 60016
Ph: 847-759-8601 ▪ Fx: 847-759-8602

Administrators, American Federation of School   www.admin.org
1729 21st St NW   Washington DC 20009
Ph: 202-986-4209 ▪ Fx: 202-986-4211 ▪ TF: 800-354-2372

Administrators, Association of State Correctional   www.asca.net
213 Court St 6th Fl   Middletown CT 06457
Ph: 860-704-6410 ▪ Fx: 860-704-6420

Administrators, International Association of Museum Facility   www.iamfa.org
c/o High Museum of Art 1280 Peachtree Rd NE   Atlanta GA
30309
Ph: 404-733-4407 ▪ Fx: 404-733-4502

Administrators, National Association of County   www.countyadministrators.org
777 N Capitol St NE Suite 500   Washington DC 20002
Ph: 301-469-7460

Administrators of Schools & Programs for the Deaf, Conference of Educational   PO Box 1778   Saint Augustine FL 32085   www.ceasd.org
Ph: 904-810-5200 ▪ Fx: 904-810-5525

Administrators of Special Education, Council of   www.casecec.org
Fort Valley State Univ 1005 State University Dr   Fort Valley GA
31030
Ph: 478-825-7667 ▪ Fx: 478-825-7811

Administrators of Vocational Rehabilitation, Council of State   www.rehabnetwork.org
4733 Bethesda Ave Suite 330   Bethesda MD 20814
Ph: 301-654-8414 ▪ Fx: 301-654-5542

Admission Test Board, Secondary School   www.ssat.org
CN 5339   Princeton NJ 08543
Ph: 609-683-4440 ▪ Fx: 800-442-7728

Admissions Officers, American Association of Collegiate Registrars &   www.aacrao.org
1 Dupont Cir NW Suite 520   Washington DC 20036
Ph: 202-293-9161 ▪ Fx: 202-872-8857

Admissions Officers, National Association of College Deans Registrars &   Albany State Univ 504 College Dr   Albany GA   www.vsu.edu/nacdrao
31705
Ph: 229-430-4638 ▪ Fx: 229-430-2953

Admissions Professionals, National Association of Graduate   www.nagap.org
Iowa State Univ 10 Pearson Hall   Ames IA 50011
Ph: 515-294-2682 ▪ Fx: 515-294-3003

Adolescence, Society for Research on   www.s-r-a.org
3131 S State St Suite 302   Ann Arbor MI 48108
Ph: 734-998-6567 ▪ Fx: 734-998-9586

Adolescent Bipolar Foundation, Child &   www.bpkids.org
1187 Wilmette Ave PMB 331   Wilmette IL 60091
Ph: 847-256-8525 ▪ Fx: 847-920-9498

Adolescent Medicine, Society for   www.adolescenthealth.org
1916 NW Copper Oaks Cir   Blue Springs MO 64015
Ph: 816-224-8010 ▪ Fx: 816-224-8009

Adolescent Pregnancy Parenting & Prevention Inc, National Organization on   2401 Pennsylvania Ave NW Suite   www.noappp.org
350   Washington DC 20037
Ph: 202-293-8370 ▪ Fx: 202-293-8805 ▪ TF: 888-766-2777

Adolescent Psychiatry & Allied Professions, International Association for Child &   www.iacapap.org

Adolescent Psychiatry, American Academy of Child &   www.aacap.org
3615 Wisconsin Ave NW   Washington DC 20016
Ph: 202-966-7300 ▪ Fx: 202-966-2891 ▪ TF: 800-333-7636

Adolescent Psychiatry, American Society for   www.adolpsych.org
PO Box 570218   Dallas TX 75357
Ph: 972-686-6166 ▪ Fx: 972-613-5532

Adolescent Psychiatry, International Society for   www.isap-web.org
223 Sunset Blvd   Bronx NY 10473
Ph: 718-892-4868

Adolescent Psychiatry, Society of Professors of Child &
3615 Wisconsin Ave NW   Washington DC 20016
Ph: 202-966-7300 ▪ Fx: 202-966-2891

Adolph Coors Foundation   www.acoorsfdn.org
4100 E Mississippi Ave Suite 1850   Denver CO 80246
Ph: 303-388-1636 ▪ Fx: 303-388-1684

Adopt America Network   www.adoptamericanetwork.org
1025 N Reynolds Rd   Toledo OH 43615
Ph: 419-534-3350 ▪ Fx: 419-534-2995

Adopt a Husky Inc   www.adoptahusky.com
PO Box 275   Salem WI 53168
Ph: 262-909-2244 ▪ Fx: 262-878-1890

Adopt a Special Kid   www.adoptaspecialkid.org
7700 Edgewater Dr Suite 320   Oakland CA 94621
Ph: 510-553-1748 ▪ Fx: 510-553-1747 ▪ TF: 888-680-7349

Adoptable Children, North American Council on   www.nacac.org
970 Raymond Ave Suite 106   Saint Paul MN 55114
Ph: 651-644-3036 ▪ Fx: 651-644-9848

Adoptees & Natural Parents Organization
949 Lacon Dr   Newport News VA 23608
Ph: 757-874-9091

Adopting Children Everywhere, Families   www.faceadoptioninfo.org
PO Box 28058   Baltimore MD 21239
Ph: 410-488-2656

(Adoption) ALMA Society   www.almasociety.org
PO Box 85   Denville NJ 07834
Ph: 973-586-1358

Adoption ARC Inc   www.adoptionarc.com
4701 Pine St J-7   Philadelphia PA 19143
Ph: 215-748-1441 ▪ Fx: 215-842-9881 ▪ TF: 800-884-4004

Adoption Center, Greyhound   www.greyhounddog.org
PO Box 2433   La Mesa CA 91943
Ph: 619-443-0940 ▪ Fx: 619-443-0130 ▪ TF: 877-478-8364

Adoption Center, National   www.adopt.org
1500 Walnut St Suite 701   Philadelphia PA 19102
Ph: 215-735-9988 ▪ Fx: 215-735-9410

(Adoption) Children Awaiting Parents Inc   www.capbook.org
595 Blossom Rd Suite 306   Rochester NY 14610
Ph: 585-232-5110 ▪ Fx: 585-232-2634 ▪ TF: 888-835-8802

Adoption Congress, American   www.americanadoptioncongress.org
PO Box 42730   Washington DC 20015
Ph: 202-483-3399

Adoption, Council For Equal Rights in   www.adoptioncrossroads.org
444 E 76th St   New York NY 10021
Ph: 212-988-0110 ▪ Fx: 212-988-0291

Adoption Crossroads   www.adoptioncrossroads.org
444 E 76th St   New York NY 10021
Ph: 212-988-0110 ▪ Fx: 212-988-0291

Adoption, Dave Thomas Foundation for   www.davethomasfoundationforadoption.org
4288 W Dublin Granville Rd   Dublin OH 43017
Ph: 614-764-8454 ▪ Fx: 614-766-3871 ▪ TF: 800-275-3832

Adoption, Families for Private   www.ffpa.org
PO Box 6375   Washington DC 20015
Ph: 202-722-0338

Adoption Information Clearinghouse, National   naic.acf.hhs.gov
330 C St SW   Washington DC 20447
Ph: 703-352-3488 ▪ Fx: 703-385-3206 ▪ TF: 888-251-0075
Adoption Information, Institute for   www.adoptioninformationinstitute.org
PO Box 4405   Bennington VT 05201
Ph: 802-442-7135
Adoption Information Services   www.adoptioninfosvcs.com
558 Dovie Pl   Lawrenceville GA 30045
Ph: 770-339-7236
Adoption Institute, Evan B Donaldson   www.adoptioninstitute.org
120 Wall St 20th Fl   New York NY 10005
Ph: 212-269-5080 ▪ Fx: 212-269-1962
Adoption, National Council for   www.adoptioncouncil.org
225 N Washington St   Alexandria VA 22314
Ph: 703-299-6633 ▪ Fx: 703-299-6004
Adoption Network, Jewish Children's   www.users.qwest.net/~jcan
PO Box 147016   Denver CO 80214
Ph: 303-573-8113 ▪ Fx: 303-893-1447
Adoption Program, National Greyhound   www.ngap.org
4701 Bath St   Philadelphia PA 19137
Ph: 215-331-7918 ▪ Fx: 215-331-1947 ▪ TF: 800-348-2517
Adoption Search Information Services, Organized
PO Box 53-0761   Miami Shores FL 33153
Ph: 305-947-8788
Adoptive Families of America   www.adoptivefamilies.com
42 W 38th St Suite 901   New York NY 10018
Ph: 646-366-0830 ▪ Fx: 646-366-0842 ▪ TF: 800-372-3300
Adrenal Diseases Foundation, National   www.medhelp.org/nadf
505 Northern Blvd   Great Neck NY 11021
Ph: 516-487-4992
ADSC: International Association of Foundation Drilling   www.adsc-iafd.com
9696 Skillman St Suite 280 PO Box 550339   Dallas TX 75355
Ph: 214-343-2091 ▪ Fx: 214-343-2384
Adult Children of Alcoholics World Service Organization Inc   www.adultchildren.org
PO Box 3216   Torrance CA 90510
Ph: 310-534-1815
Adult Congenital Cardiac Disease, International Society for   www.isaccd.org
1500 Sunday Dr Suite 102   Raleigh NC 27607
Ph: 919-861-5578 ▪ Fx: 919-787-4916
Adult & Continuing Education, American Association for   www.aaace.org
4380 Forbes Blvd   Lanham MD 20706
Ph: 301-918-1913 ▪ Fx: 301-918-1846
Adult Day Services Association, National   www.nadsa.org
8201 Greensboro Dr Suite 300   McLean VA 22102
Ph: 703-610-9000 ▪ Fx: 703-610-9005 ▪ TF: 800-424-9046
Adult Development Network, Career Planning &   www.careernetwork.org
PO Box 1484   Pacifica CA 94044
Ph: 650-359-6911 ▪ Fx: 650-359-3089
Adult Education Professional Development Consortium, National   www.naepdc.org/
444 N Capitol St NW Suite 422   Washington DC 20001
Ph: 202-624-5250 ▪ Fx: 202-624-1497
Adult & Experiential Learning, Council for   www.cael.org
55 E Monroe St Suite 1930   Chicago IL 60603
Ph: 312-499-2600 ▪ Fx: 312-499-2601
Adult Immunization, National Coalition for   www.nfid.org/ncai
4733 Bethesda Ave Suite 750   Bethesda MD 20814
Ph: 301-656-0003 ▪ Fx: 301-907-0878
Adults With Special Learning Needs, National Association for   www.naasln.org
c/o Correctional Education Assn 4380 Forbes Blvd   Lanham MD 20706
Ph: 800-496-9222
AdvaMed   www.advamed.org
1200 G St NW Suite 400   Washington DC 20005
Ph: 202-783-8700 ▪ Fx: 202-783-8750
Advanced Medical Technology Association   www.advamed.org
1200 G St NW Suite 400   Washington DC 20005
Ph: 202-783-8700 ▪ Fx: 202-783-8750
Advanced Network & Services Inc   www.advanced.org
200 Business Park Dr   Armonk NY 10504
Ph: 914-765-1100 ▪ Fx: 914-273-1809
Advanced Television Systems Committee   www.atsc.org
1750 K St NW Suite 1200   Washington DC 20006
Ph: 202-872-9160 ▪ Fx: 202-872-9161
Advanced Transit Association   www.advancedtransit.org
Adventist Community Services   www.adventist.communityservices.org
12501 Old Columbia Pike   Silver Spring MD 20904
Ph: 301-680-6438 ▪ Fx: 301-680-6125 ▪ TF: 877-227-2702
Adventist Development & Relief Agency International   www.adra.org
12501 Old Columbia Pike   Silver Spring MD 20904
Ph: 301-680-6380 ▪ Fx: 301-680-6370 ▪ TF: 800-424-2372
Adventist World Aviation   www.flyawa.org
PO Box 251   Berrien Springs MI 49103
Ph: 269-473-0135 ▪ Fx: 269-471-4049
Adventure Cycling Association   www.adventurecycling.org
150 E Pine St PO Box 8308   Missoula MT 59802
Ph: 406-721-1776 ▪ Fx: 406-721-8754 ▪ TF: 800-755-2453
Adventure Travel Trade Association   www.adventuretravelbusiness.com
332 1/2 W Sackett St   Salida CO 81201
Ph: 719-530-0171 ▪ Fx: 719-530-0172
Adventures in Movement for the Handicapped   www.aimforthehandicapped.org
945 Danbury Rd   Dayton OH 45420
Ph: 937-294-4611 ▪ Fx: 937-294-3783 ▪ TF: 800-332-8210
Advertisers Inc, Association of National   www.ana.net
708 3rd Ave   New York NY 10017
Ph: 212-697-5950 ▪ Fx: 212-661-8428
Advertising Agencies, American Association of   www.aaaa.org
405 Lexington Ave 18th Fl   New York NY 10174
Ph: 212-682-2500 ▪ Fx: 212-682-8391

Advertising Agencies, Association of Hispanic   www.ahaa.org
8201 Greensboro Dr Suite 300   McLean VA 22102
Ph: 703-610-9014 ▪ Fx: 703-610-9005
Advertising Allowances Inc, National Association for Promotional &   www.napaa.org
13771 N Fountain Hills Blvd Suite 114   Fountain Hills AZ 85268
Ph: 480-837-9704 ▪ Fx: 602-296-0277
Advertising, American Academy of   www.americanacademyofadvertising.org
Advertising Association of America, Outdoor   www.oaaa.org
1850 M St NW Suite 1040   Washington DC 20036
Ph: 202-833-5566 ▪ Fx: 202-833-1522
Advertising Association, International   www.iaaglobal.org
521 5th Ave Suite 1807   New York NY 10175
Ph: 212-557-1133 ▪ Fx: 212-983-0455
Advertising Bureau, Cabletelevision   www.cabletvadbureau.com
830 3rd Ave 2nd Fl   New York NY 10022
Ph: 212-508-1200 ▪ Fx: 212-832-3268
Advertising Bureau, Interactive   www.iab.net
200 Park Ave S Suite 501   New York NY 10003
Ph: 212-949-9033
Advertising Bureau, Radio   www.rab.com
261 Madison Ave 23rd Fl   New York NY 10016
Ph: 212-681-7200 ▪ Fx: 212-681-7223 ▪ TF: 800-252-7234
(Advertising) Clio Awards Inc   www.clioawards.com
220 5th Ave Suite 1500   New York NY 10001
Ph: 212-683-4300 ▪ Fx: 212-683-4796 ▪ TF: 800-946-2546
Advertising Club The   www.theadvertisingclub.org
235 Park Ave S 6th Fl   New York NY 10003
Ph: 212-533-8080 ▪ Fx: 212-533-1929
Advertising Council Inc   www.adcouncil.org
261 Madison Ave 11th Fl   New York NY 10016
Ph: 212-922-1500 ▪ Fx: 212-922-1676
Advertising Dealers Association, Inflatable   www.inflatableads.com
136 S Keowee St   Dayton OH 45402
Ph: 937-222-1024 ▪ Fx: 937-222-5794
Advertising Div, Council of Better Business Bureaus Inc National   www.nadreview.org
70 W 36th St 13th Fl   New York NY 10018
Ph: 212-705-0114
Advertising Federation, American   www.aaf.org
1101 Vermont Ave NW Suite 500   Washington DC 20005
Ph: 202-898-0089 ▪ Fx: 202-898-0159 ▪ TF: 800-999-2231
Advertising Global Network, Marketing &   www.magnetglobal.org
464 Walnut St Suite 2-D   Pittsburgh PA 15238
Ph: 412-828-4031 ▪ Fx: 412-828-4057
Advertising International, Point-of-Purchase   www.popai.com
1660 L St NW 10th Fl   Washington DC 20036
Ph: 202-530-3000 ▪ Fx: 202-530-3030
Advertising & Marketing Association, Retail   www.rama-nrf.org
325 7th St NW Suite 1100   Washington DC 20004
Ph: 202-661-3052 ▪ Fx: 202-661-3049
Advertising & Marketing International Network   www.aminworldwide.com
12323 Nantucket   Wichita KS 67235
Ph: 316-722-2535 ▪ Fx: 316-722-8353
Advertising Media Credit Executives Association   www.amcea.org
8840 Columbia 100 Pkwy   Columbia MD 21045
Ph: 410-992-7609 ▪ Fx: 410-740-5574
Advertising, National Association Breweriana   www.nababrew.org
Advertising Photographers of America   www.apanational.org
PO Box 361309   Los Angeles CA 90036
Ph: 800-272-6264
Advertising for Publications Association, Digital Distribution of   www.ddap.org
PO Box 175   Marblehead MA 01945
Ph: 781-639-7785 ▪ Fx: 781-639-7786
Advertising Research Foundation   www.arfsite.org
641 Lexington Ave 11th Fl   New York NY 10022
Ph: 212-751-5656 ▪ Fx: 212-319-5265
Advertising Review Unit, Council of Better Business Bureaus Inc Children's   www.caru.org
70 W 36th St 13th Fl   New York NY 10018
Ph: 866-334-6272
Advertising, Television Bureau of   www.tvb.org
3 E 54th St 10th Fl   New York NY 10022
Ph: 212-486-1111 ▪ Fx: 212-935-5631
Advising Association, National Academic   www.nacada.ksu.edu
Kansas State Univ 2323 Anderson Ave Suite 225   Manhattan KS 66502
Ph: 785-532-5717 ▪ Fx: 785-532-7732
Advisors, Association of Insolvency & Restructuring   www.airacira.org
221 Stewart Ave Suite 207   Medford OR 97501
Ph: 541-858-1665 ▪ Fx: 541-858-9187
Advisors for Athletics, National Association of Academic   www.nfoura.org
14606 Woodlake Terr   Louisville KY 40245
Ph: 502-253-9530 ▪ Fx: 502-253-9533
Advisors for the Health Professions, National Association of   www.naahp.org
PO Box 1518   Champaign IL 61824
Ph: 217-355-0063 ▪ Fx: 217-355-1287
Advisors, National Association of Student Activity
1904 Association Dr   Reston VA 20191
Ph: 703-860-0200 ▪ Fx: 703-476-5432
(Advocacy) Capital Research Center   www.capitalresearch.org
1513 16th St NW   Washington DC 20036
Ph: 202-483-6900 ▪ Fx: 202-483-6902 ▪ TF: 800-459-3950
Advocacy Center, National Children's   www.nationalcac.org
210 Pratt Ave   Huntsville AL 35801
Ph: 256-533-5437 ▪ Fx: 256-534-6883
Advocacy Coalition, National Youth   www.nyacyouth.org
1638 R St NW Suite 300   Washington DC 20009
Ph: 202-319-7596 ▪ Fx: 202-319-7365 ▪ TF: 800-541-6922
Advocacy Institute   www.advocacy.org
1629 K St NW Suite 200   Washington DC 20006
Ph: 202-777-7575 ▪ Fx: 202-777-7577

Advocacy Project   www.advocacynet.org
1326 14th St NW   Washington DC 20005
Ph: 202-332-3900

Advocacy Systems, National Association of   www.protectionandadvocacy.com
Protection &   900 2nd St NE Suite 211   Washington DC
20002
Ph: 202-408-9514 ▪ Fx: 202-408-9520

Advocate Association, National Court Appointed Special   www.nationalcasa.org
100 W Harrison St North Tower Suite 500   Seattle WA 98119
Ph: 206-270-0072 ▪ Fx: 206-270-0078 ▪ TF: 800-628-3233

Advocates for Communication Technology for Deaf-Blind   www.deafblindadvocates.org
People Inc   911 Regina Dr   Baltimore MD 21227
Ph: 410-247-5045 ▪ Fx: 410-381-6838

Advocates for Highway & Auto Safety   www.saferoads.org
750 1st St NE Suite 901   Washington DC 20002
Ph: 202-408-1711 ▪ Fx: 202-408-1699

Advocates for Self-Government   www.self-gov.org
213 S Erwin St   Cartersville GA 30120
Ph: 770-386-8372 ▪ Fx: 770-386-8373

Advocates for Students, National Coalition of   www.ncasboston.org
100 Boylston St Suite 808   Boston MA 02116
Ph: 617-357-8507 ▪ Fx: 617-357-9549

Advocates for Women in Science Engineering & Mathematics   www.awsem.org
20000 NW Walker Rd   Beaverton OR 97006
Ph: 503-748-1504 ▪ Fx: 503-748-1470

Advocates for Youth   www.advocatesforyouth.org
1025 Vermont Ave NW Suite 200   Washington DC 20005
Ph: 202-347-5700 ▪ Fx: 202-347-2263

AeA: Advancing the Business of Technology   www.aeanet.org
5201 Great America Pkwy Suite 520   Santa Clara CA 95054
Ph: 408-987-4200 ▪ Fx: 408-970-8565 ▪ TF: 800-284-4232

Aerated Concrete Products Association, Autoclaved   www.aacpa.org
7638 Nashville St   Ringgold GA 30736
Ph: 706-965-4587

Aerial Firefighting Industry Association   www.afia.com
PO Box 523068   Springfield VA 22152
Ph: 703-644-6454 ▪ Fx: 703-644-4001

Aerobatic Club, International   www.iac.org
PO Box 3086   Oshkosh WI 54903
Ph: 920-426-4800 ▪ Fx: 920-426-6865

Aerobatics Model Pilots Association, Precision   www.control-line.org
158 Flying Cloud Isle   Foster City CA 94404
Ph: 650-345-0130 ▪ Fx: 650-578-8454

Aerobics Federation, US Competitive   www.sportaerobics-nac.com
Association of National Aerobic Championships Worldwide 8033
Sunset Blvd Suite 920   Los Angeles CA 90046
Ph: 323-850-3777 ▪ Fx: 323-850-7795

Aerobics & Fitness Association of America   www.afaa.com
15250 Ventura Blvd Suite 200   Sherman Oaks CA 91403
Ph: 818-905-0040 ▪ Fx: 818-990-5468 ▪ TF: 877-968-7263

Aeronautic Association, National   www.naa-usa.org
1815 N Fort Myer Dr Suite 500   Arlington VA 22209
Ph: 703-527-0226 ▪ Fx: 703-527-0229 ▪ TF: 800-644-9777

Aeronautical Repair Station Association   www.arsa.org
121 N Henry St   Alexandria VA 22314
Ph: 703-739-9543 ▪ Fx: 703-739-9488

Aeronautics, Academy of Model   www.modelaircraft.org
5161 E Memorial Dr   Muncie IN 47302
Ph: 765-287-1256 ▪ Fx: 765-289-4248 ▪ TF: 800-435-9262

Aeronautics & Astronautics, American Institute of   www.aiaa.org
1801 Alexander Bell Dr Suite 500   Reston VA 20191
Ph: 703-264-7500 ▪ Fx: 703-264-7657 ▪ TF: 800-639-2422

Aeroplanes Inc, World War I   www.aviation-history.com/ww1aero.htm
15 Crescent Rd   Poughkeepsie NY 12601
Ph: 845-473-3679 ▪ Fx: 845-452-7332

Aerosol Research, American Association for   www.aaar.org
17000 Commerce Pkwy Suite C   Mount Laurel NJ 08054
Ph: 856-439-9080 ▪ Fx: 856-439-0525

Aerospace & Agricultural Implement Workers of America, International   www.uaw.org
Union United Automobile   8000 E Jefferson Ave   Detroit MI
48214
Ph: 313-926-5000 ▪ Fx: 313-823-6016

Aerospace Education Foundation   www.aef.org
1501 Lee Hwy   Arlington VA 22209
Ph: 703-247-5839 ▪ Fx: 703-247-5853 ▪ TF: 800-291-8480

Aerospace & Electronics Systems Society, IEEE   www.ewh.ieee.org/soc/aes
IEEE Operations Ctr 445 Hoes Ln   Piscataway NJ 08854
Ph: 732-981-0060 ▪ Fx: 732-981-1721

(Aerospace Engineering) Sigma Gamma Tau   www.engr.twsu.edu/ae/sgt/sgthome.html
Wichita State Univ Dept of Aerospace Engineering   Wichita KS
67260
Ph: 316-978-6327 ▪ Fx: 316-978-3307

Aerospace Industries Association of America   www.aia-aerospace.org
1000 Wilson Blvd Suite 1700   Arlington VA 22209
Ph: 703-358-1000 ▪ Fx: 703-358-1011

Aerospace Industries Association, International Coordinating   www.aia-aerospace.org
Council of   1250 'I' St NW Suite 1200   Washington DC 20005
Ph: 202-371-8400 ▪ Fx: 202-371-8471

Aerospace Medical Association   www.asma.org
320 S Henry St   Alexandria VA 22314
Ph: 703-739-2240 ▪ Fx: 703-739-9652

Aerospace, Women in   www.womeninaerospace.org
PO Box 16721   Alexandria VA 22302
Ph: 202-547-9451

Aerospace Workers, International Association of Machinists &   www.iamaw.org
9000 Machinists Pl   Upper Marlboro MD 20772
Ph: 301-967-4500 ▪ Fx: 301-967-4588

Aesthetic Plastic Surgery, American Society for   www.surgery.org
11081 Winners Cir   Los Alamitos CA 90720
Ph: 562-799-2356 ▪ Fx: 562-799-1098 ▪ TF: 800-364-2147

Aesthetic Realism Foundation   www.aestheticrealism.org
141 Greene St   New York NY 10012
Ph: 212-777-4490 ▪ Fx: 212-777-4426

Aesthetic Surgery, International Confederation for Plastic   www.ipras.org
Reconstructive &   4 Executive Park Dr   Albany NY 12203
Ph: 518-438-1434 ▪ Fx: 518-489-1205

Aesthetics, American Society for   www.aesthetics-online.org
Marquette Univ 707 N 11th St Rm 322 PO Box
1881   Milwaukee WI 53201
Ph: 414-288-7831 ▪ Fx: 414-228-5415

Aesthetics, American Society for Dental   www.asdatoday.com
635 Madison Ave 13th Fl   New York NY 10022
Ph: 212-751-3263 ▪ Fx: 212-755-3263 ▪ TF: 800-454-2732

Aesthetics' International Association   www.dermascope.com/association.html
PO Box 468   Kaufman TX 75142
Ph: 972-203-8530 ▪ Fx: 972-226-2339 ▪ TF: 877-968-7539

AFCOM   www.afcom.com
742 E Chapman Ave   Orange CA 92866
Ph: 714-997-7966 ▪ Fx: 714-997-9743

Affective Disorders Association, Depression & Related   www.drada.org
2330 W Joppa Rd Suite 100   Lutherville MD 21093
Ph: 410-583-2919

Affiliated Conference of Practicing Accountants International   www.acpaintl.org
30 Massachusetts Ave   North Andover MA 01845
Ph: 978-689-9420 ▪ Fx: 978-689-9404

Affiliated Inventors Foundation   www.affiliatedinventors.com
1405 Potter Dr Suite 107   Colorado Springs CO 80909
Ph: 719-380-1234 ▪ Fx: 800-380-3862 ▪ TF: 800-525-5885

Affiliated Warehouse Companies Inc   www.awco.com
54 Village Ct PO Box 295   Hazlet NJ 07730
Ph: 732-739-2323 ▪ Fx: 732-739-4154

Affirmative Action, American Association for   www.affirmativeaction.org
12100 Sunset Hills Rd Suite 130   Reston VA 20190
Ph: 800-252-8952 ▪ Fx: 703-435-4390

Affirmative Action, Filipinos for   www.filipinos4action.org
310 8th St Suite 306   Oakland CA 94607
Ph: 510-465-9876 ▪ Fx: 510-465-7548

Affordable Housing Lenders, National Association of   www.taxcreditcoalition.org
1300 Connecticut Ave NW Suite 905   Washington DC 20036
Ph: 202-293-9850 ▪ Fx: 202-293-9852

Affordable Housing Management Association, National   www.nahma.org
526 W King St Suite 511   Alexandria VA 22314
Ph: 703-683-8630 ▪ Fx: 703-683-8634

Affordable Housing Tax Credit Coalition   www.taxcreditcoalition.org
401 9th St NW Suite 900   Washington DC 20004
Ph: 202-585-8739 ▪ Fx: 202-585-8080

Afghan Community in America
PO Box 311   Flushing NY 11352
Ph: 516-756-9198 ▪ Fx: 516-756-9236

AFIA - Alfalfa Processors Council   www.aapausa.org
8810 Craig Dr   Overland Park KS 66212
Ph: 913-648-6800 ▪ Fx: 913-648-2648

AFL-CIO, Building & Construction Trades Dept   www.buildingtrades.org
815 16th St NW Suite 600   Washington DC 20006
Ph: 202-347-1461

AFL-CIO Committee on Political Education
815 16th St NW   Washington DC 20006
Ph: 202-637-5000 ▪ Fx: 202-637-5058

AFL-CIO Working for America Institute   www.workingforamerica.org
815 16th NW   Washington DC 20006
Ph: 202-974-8100 ▪ Fx: 202-974-8101 ▪ TF: 800-842-4734

AFMA   www.afma.com
10850 Wilshire Blvd 9th Fl   Los Angeles CA 90024
Ph: 310-446-1000 ▪ Fx: 310-446-1600

Africa, Access to   www.itdp.org
115 W 30th St Suite 1205   New York NY 10001
Ph: 212-629-8001 ▪ Fx: 212-629-8033

Africa Action   www.africaaction.org
110 Maryland Ave NE Suite 508   Washington DC 20002
Ph: 202-546-7961 ▪ Fx: 202-546-1545

Africa-America Institute   www.aaionline.org
380 Lexington Ave 42nd Fl   New York NY 10168
Ph: 212-949-5666 ▪ Fx: 212-682-6174 ▪ TF: 800-745-3899

Africa Faith & Justice Network   afjn.cua.edu
3035 4th St NE   Washington DC 20017
Ph: 202-832-3412 ▪ Fx: 202-832-9051

Africa, Global Alliance for   www.globalallianceafrica.org
122 S DesPlaines St   Chicago IL 60661
Ph: 312-382-0607 ▪ Fx: 312-906-9930

Africa, Global Coalition for   www.gca-cma.org
1919 Pennsylvania Ave NW Suite 550   Washington DC 20006
Ph: 202-458-4338 ▪ Fx: 202-522-3259

Africa Inland Mission International   www.aim-us.org
PO Box 178   Pearl River NY 10965
Ph: 845-735-4014 ▪ Fx: 845-735-1814 ▪ TF: 800-254-0010

Africa, Operation Crossroads   oca.igc.org
PO Box 5570   New York NY 10027
Ph: 212-289-1949 ▪ Fx: 212-289-2526

Africa, Society of Missionaries of   www.missionariesofafrica.org/policies.php
1624 21st St NW   Washington DC 20009
Ph: 202-232-5154 ▪ Fx: 202-332-8640

Africa Travel Association   www.africa-ata.org
347 5th Ave Suite 610   New York NY 10016
Ph: 212-447-1926 ▪ Fx: 212-725-8253

Africa, Washington Office on   www.woaafrica.org
212 E Capitol St NE   Washington DC 20003
Ph: 202-547-7503 ▪ Fx: 202-547-7505

(African American) Alpha Kappa Alpha Sorority Inc   www.aka1908.com
5656 S Stony Island Ave   Chicago IL 60637
Ph: 773-684-1282 ▪ Fx: 773-288-8251

(African American) Alpha Phi Alpha Fraternity Inc   www.alphaphialpha.net
2313 Saint Paul St   Baltimore MD 21218
Ph: 410-554-0040 ▪ Fx: 410-554-0054

African American Breast Cancer Alliance   www.geocities.com/aabcainc
PO Box 8981   Minneapolis MN 55408
Ph: 612-825-3675

(African-American Children) Jack & Jill of America Inc   www.jack-and-jill.org
1930 17th St NW   Washington DC 20009
Ph: 202-667-7010 ▪ Fx: 202-667-6133

(African American) Delta Sigma Theta Sorority Inc   www.deltasigmatheta.org
1707 New Hampshire Ave NW   Washington DC 20009
Ph: 202-986-2400 ▪ Fx: 202-986-2513

(African-American Education) A Better Chance   www.abetterchance.org
240 W 35th St 9th Fl   New York NY 10001
Ph: 646-346-1310 ▪ Fx: 646-346-1311 ▪ TF: 800-543-7181

(African American) Iota Phi Theta Fraternity Inc   www.iotaphitheta.org
3001 Hewitt Ave Suite 390   Silver Spring MD 20906
Ph: 888-835-5109

(African American) Kappa Alpha Psi Fraternity Inc   www.kappaalphapsi.com
2322-24 N Broad St   Philadelphia PA 19132
Ph: 215-228-7184 ▪ Fx: 215-228-7181

African American Life & History, Association for the Study of   www.asalh.org
Howard Univ CB Powell Bldg 525 Bryant St Suite
C142   Washington DC 20059
Ph: 202-865-0053 ▪ Fx: 202-265-7920

African American Men, National Trust for the Development of
6811 Kenilworth Ave Suite 501   Riverdale MD 20737
Ph: 301-887-0100 ▪ Fx: 301-887-0405

African American Museums, Association of   www.blackmuseums.org

African-American Music, National Association for the Study & Performance of   www.naspaam.org

African-American Music Society
PO Box 2522   Springfield MA 01101
Ph: 413-734-2555 ▪ Fx: 413-731-9587

(African American) National Sales Network   www.salesnetwork.org
1075 Easton Ave Suite 11 PMB 316   Somerset NJ 08873
Ph: 732-246-5236

(African American) National Urban League Inc   www.nul.org
120 Wall St 8th Fl   New York NY 10005
Ph: 212-558-5300 ▪ Fx: 212-344-5332

(African American) Omega Psi Phi Fraternity Inc   www.oppf.org
3951 Snapfinger Pkwy   Decatur GA 30035
Ph: 404-284-5533 ▪ Fx: 404-284-0333

(African American) Phi Beta Sigma Fraternity Inc   www.pbs1914.org
145 Kennedy St NW   Washington DC 20011
Ph: 202-726-5434 ▪ Fx: 202-882-1681

(African American) Sigma Gamma Rho Sorority Inc   www.sgrho1922.org
8800 S Stony Island   Chicago IL 60617
Ph: 773-873-9000 ▪ Fx: 773-731-9642

African American Speakers Association, National   www.4naasa.org
3033 Western Ave   Park Forest IL 60466
Ph: 708-747-2219 ▪ TF: 877-866-2272

African-American Sportswriters & Broadcasters, National Association of
308A Deer Park Ave   Dix Hills NY 11746
Ph: 631-462-3933

African-American Studies & Affiliates, National Association of   www.naaas.org
PO Box 325   Biddeford ME 04005
Ph: 207-839-8004 ▪ Fx: 207-839-3776

(African-American) Transafrica Forum   www.transafricaforum.org
1426 21st NW 2nd Fl   Washington DC 20036
Ph: 202-223-1960 ▪ Fx: 202-223-1966

African-American Women Business Owners, Association of
3363 Alden Pl NE   Washington DC 20019
Ph: 202-399-3645

African-American Women's Clergy Association
214 P St NW   Washington DC 20001
Ph: 202-518-8488 ▪ Fx: 202-518-1273

African Americans in Human Resources, National Association of   www.naaahr.org

African Arts & Cultures, Homowo   www.homowo.org
4839 NE ML King Blvd Suite 209   Portland OR 97211
Ph: 503-288-3025 ▪ Fx: 503-331-6688

African Civilizations, Association for the Study of Classical   www.ascac.org
2274 W 20th St   Los Angeles CA 90018
Ph: 323-730-1155 ▪ Fx: 323-731-4998

African Development Institute   www.africainstitute.com
PO Box 1644   New York NY 10185
Ph: 888-619-7535 ▪ Fx: 201-461-3871

African Family Film Foundation   www.africanfamily.org
PO Box 630   Santa Cruz CA 95061
Ph: 831-426-3133

African Grapevine Inc   www.africangrapevine.com
PO Box 56140   Atlanta GA 30343
Ph: 404-233-8463 ▪ Fx: 770-482-7076 ▪ TF: 800-984-8463

African Heritage Center for African Dance & Music
4018 Minnesota Ave NE   Washington DC 20019
Ph: 202-399-5252

African Medical & Research Foundation   www.amref.org
19 W 44th St Suite 710   New York NY 10036
Ph: 212-768-2440 ▪ Fx: 212-768-4230

African Methodist Episcopal Church, Service & Development Agency of the   www.amecnet.org/sada/sada.htm
1134 11th St NW Suite 214   Washington DC 20001
Ph: 202-371-8722 ▪ Fx: 202-371-0981

African Missions, Society of   www.smafathers.org
23 Bliss Ave   Tenafly NJ 07670
Ph: 201-567-0450

African Parrot Society   www.wingscc.com/aps
PO Box 204   Clarinda IA 51632
Ph: 712-542-4190

African Scientific Institute   www.asi-org.net
PO Box 12153   Oakland CA 94604
Ph: 510-653-7027 ▪ Fx: 510-547-0387

African Studies Association   www.africanstudies.org
Rutgers Univ Douglass Campus 132 George St   New Brunswick
NJ 08901
Ph: 732-932-8173 ▪ Fx: 732-932-3394

African Studies, Institute of Near Eastern &   www.ineas.org
PO Box 425125   Cambridge MA 02142
Ph: 617-864-6327

African University Foundation   www.aufoundation.org/
545 Edgemere Dr   Indianapolis IN 46260
Ph: 317-259-8368 ▪ Fx: 317-259-4269

African Violet Society of America   www.avsa.org
2375 North St   Beaumont TX 77702
Ph: 409-839-4725 ▪ Fx: 409-839-4329 ▪ TF: 800-770-2872

African Wildlife Foundation   www.awf.org
1400 16th St NW Suite 120   Washington DC 20036
Ph: 202-939-3333 ▪ Fx: 202-939-3332 ▪ TF: 888-494-5354

Africanist Anthropology, Association for   www.ibiblio.org/afaa
c/o American Anthropological Assn 2200 Wilson Blvd Suite
600   Arlington VA 22201
Ph: 703-528-1902 ▪ Fx: 703-528-3546

Africare Inc   www.africare.org
440 R St NW   Washington DC 20001
Ph: 202-462-3614 ▪ Fx: 202-387-1034

Afro-American Artists, National Center of   www.ncaaa.org
300 Walnut Ave   Boston MA 02119
Ph: 617-442-8614 ▪ Fx: 617-445-5525

Afro-American Historical & Genealogical Society   www.aahgs.org
PO Box 73067   Washington DC 20056
Ph: 202-234-5350 ▪ Fx: 202-829-9280

AFS International Inc   www.afs.org
71 W 23rd St 17th Fl   New York NY 10010
Ph: 212-807-8686 ▪ Fx: 212-807-1001

AFSM International   www.afsmi.org
1342 Colonial Blvd Suite 25   Fort Myers FL 33907
Ph: 239-275-7887 ▪ Fx: 239-275-0794 ▪ TF: 800-333-9786

AFT Healthcare   www.aft.org/healthcare
American Federation of Teachers 555 New Jersey Ave
NW   Washington DC 20001
Ph: 202-879-4491 ▪ Fx: 202-393-5672

Aftermarket Association, Outdoor Power Equipment   www.opeaa.org
1726 M St NW Suite 1101   Washington DC 20036
Ph: 202-775-8605 ▪ Fx: 202-833-1577

Aftermarket Industry Association, Automotive   www.aftermarket.org
4600 East-West Hwy Suite 300   Bethesda MD 20814
Ph: 301-654-6664 ▪ Fx: 301-654-3299

Aftermarket Suppliers Association, Automotive   www.aftermarketsuppliers.org
10 Laboratory Dr PO Box 13966   Research Triangle Park NC
27709
Ph: 919-549-4800 ▪ Fx: 919-549-4824

Aga Khan Foundation USA   www.akdn.org/agency/akf.html
1825 K St NW Suite 901   Washington DC 20006
Ph: 202-293-2537 ▪ Fx: 202-785-1752

Aged, Jewish Association for Services for the   www.jasa.org
132 W 31st St 15th Fl   New York NY 10001
Ph: 212-273-5227

Aged Inc, National Caucus & Center on Black   www.ncba-aged.org
1220 L St NW Suite 800   Washington DC 20005
Ph: 202-637-8400 ▪ Fx: 202-347-0895

Agency for Instructional Technology   www.ait.net
1800 N Stonelake Dr Box A   Bloomington IN 47402
Ph: 812-339-2203 ▪ Fx: 812-333-4218 ▪ TF: 800-457-4509

Agents Alliance, American   www.agentsalliance.com
1768 Arrow Hwy Suite 105   LaVerne CA 91750
Ph: 909-392-0836 ▪ Fx: 909-392-0892 ▪ TF: 866-280-3222

Agents, American Association of Managing General   www.aamga.org
150 S Warner Rd Suite 156   King of Prussia PA 19406
Ph: 610-225-1999 ▪ Fx: 610-225-1996

Agents Association, Federal Bureau of Investigation   www.fbiaa.org
PO Box 250   New Rochelle NY 10801
Ph: 914-235-7580 ▪ Fx: 914-235-8235

Agents Inc, Association of Former OSI Special   www.afosisa-ncc.org
PO Box 52315   Springfield VA 22152
Ph: 703-978-6198

Agents of the FBI Inc, Society of Former Special   www.socxfbi.org
PO Box 1027   Quantico VA 22134
Ph: 703-640-6469 ▪ Fx: 703-640-6537

Agents & Managers, Association of Theatrical Press
165 W 46th St Suite 700   New York NY 10036
Ph: 212-719-3666 ▪ Fx: 212-302-1585 ▪ TF: 800-858-3667

Aggression, International Society for Research on   www.israsociety.com

Aggressive AIDS Prevention Inc   www.aggressive.org
PO Box 26227   San Francisco CA 94126
Ph: 415-255-6022 ▪ Fx: 415-267-6980

Aging, ABA Commission on Law &   www.abanet.org/aging
740 15th St NW 8th Fl   Washington DC 20005
Ph: 202-662-8690 ▪ Fx: 202-662-8698

Aging, American Association of Homes & Services for the   www2.aahsa.org
2519 Connecticut Ave NW   Washington DC 20008
Ph: 202-783-2242 ▪ Fx: 202-783-2255 ▪ TF: 800-508-9442

Aging, American Society on   www.asaging.org
833 Market St Suite 511   San Francisco CA 94103
Ph: 415-974-9600 ▪ Fx: 415-974-0300 ▪ TF: 800-537-9728

Aging Association, American   www.americanaging.org
110 Chesley Dr   Media PA 19063
Ph: 610-627-2626 ▪ Fx: 610-565-9747

Aging, Christian Foundation for Children &   www.cfcausa.org
1 Elmwood Ave   Kansas City KS 66103
Ph: 913-384-6500 ▪ Fx: 913-384-2211 ▪ TF: 800-875-6564

Aging, National Asian Pacific Center on   www.napca.org/
PO Box 21668   Seattle WA 98101
Ph: 206-624-1221 ▪ Fx: 206-624-1023

Aging, National Association of Area Agencies on   www.n4a.org
927 15th St NW 6th Fl   Washington DC 20005
Ph: 202-296-8130 ▪ Fx: 202-296-8134

Aging, National Association of State Units on   www.nasua.org
1201 15th St NW Sutie 350   Washington DC 20005
Ph: 202-898-2578 ▪ Fx: 202-898-2583

Aging, National Center on Women &   heller.brandeis.edu/national/ind.html
Brandeis University Heller Graduate School MS 035   Waltham MA 02454
Ph: 781-736-3866 ▪ Fx: 781-736-3865 ▪ TF: 800-929-1995

Aging, National Council on the   www.ncoa.org
300 D St SW Suite 801   Washington DC 20024
Ph: 202-479-1200 ▪ Fx: 202-479-0735 ▪ TF: 800-424-9046

Aging, National Hispanic Council on   www.nhcoa.org
2713 Ontario Rd NW   Washington DC 20009
Ph: 202-265-1288 ▪ Fx: 202-745-2522

Aging, National Indian Council on   www.nicoa.org
10501 Montgomery Blvd NE Suite 210   Albuquerque NM 87111
Ph: 505-292-2001 ▪ Fx: 505-292-1922

Aging, National Interfaith Coalition on   www.ncoa.org
300 D St SW   Washington DC 20024
Ph: 202-479-1200 ▪ Fx: 202-479-0735 ▪ TF: 800-424-9046

Aging, National Policy & Resource Center on Nutrition &   www.fiu.edu/~nutreldr
Florida International Univ University Park OE200   Miami FL 33199
Ph: 305-348-1517 ▪ Fx: 305-348-1518

Aging, National Resource Center on   www.med.und.nodak.edu/depts/rural//nrcnaa
Native American   PO Box 9037   Grand Forks ND 58202
Ph: 701-777-3437 ▪ Fx: 701-777-2389 ▪ TF: 800-896-7628

Aging Parents, Children of   www.caps4caregivers.org
1609 Woodbourne Rd Suite 302A   Levittown PA 19057
Ph: 215-945-6900 ▪ Fx: 215-945-8720 ▪ TF: 800-227-7294

Aging Programs, National Association of County   www.naco.org
440 1st St NW 8th Fl   Washington DC 20001
Ph: 202-942-4235 ▪ Fx: 202-393-2630

Aging & Public Policy, Pepper Institute on   www.pepperinstitute.org
Florida State Univ 207 Pepper Ctr 636 W Call St   Tallahassee FL 32306
Ph: 850-644-2831 ▪ Fx: 850-644-2304

Aging Research, Alliance for   www.agingresearch.org
2021 K St NW Suite 305   Washington DC 20006
Ph: 202-293-2856 ▪ Fx: 202-785-8574

Aging Research, American Federation for   www.afar.org
70 W 40th St 11th Fl   New York NY 10018
Ph: 212-703-9977 ▪ Fx: 212-997-0330 ▪ TF: 888-582-2327

Aging Research, American Foundation for   www.agingresearchfoundation.org
North Carolina State Univ Biochemistry Dept 128 Polk Hall   Raleigh NC 27695
Ph: 919-515-5679 ▪ Fx: 919-515-2047

Aging Services, Association of Jewish   www.ajas.org
316 Pennsylvania Ave SE Suite 402   Washington DC 20003
Ph: 202-543-7500 ▪ Fx: 202-543-4090

Aging Services Programs, National Association of Nutrition &   www.nanasp.org
1612 K St NW Suite 400   Washington DC 20006
Ph: 202-682-6899 ▪ Fx: 202-223-2099

Aging Society, National Academy on an   agingsociety.org
1030 15th St NW Suite 250   Washington DC 20005
Ph: 202-842-1275 ▪ Fx: 202-842-1150

Aging & Sports, International Association of   www.rit.edu/~pjr0120/csa/iapaas/main.html
Physical Activity   706 Madison Ave   Albany NY 12208
Ph: 518-465-6927 ▪ Fx: 518-462-1339

(Aging) SPRY Foundation   www.spry.org
10 G St NE Suite 600   Washington DC 20002
Ph: 202-216-0401 ▪ Fx: 202-216-0779

Aglow International   www.aglow.org
152 3rd Ave S Suite 103 PO Box 1749   Edmonds WA 98020
Ph: 425-775-7282 ▪ Fx: 425-778-9615 ▪ TF: 800-755-2456

AGN International-North America   www.agn.org
2851 S Parker Rd Suite 850   Aurora CO 80014
Ph: 303-743-7880 ▪ Fx: 303-743-7660 ▪ TF: 800-782-2272

Agni Yoga Society Inc   www.agniyoga.org
319 W 107th St   New York NY 10025
Ph: 212-864-7752 ▪ Fx: 212-864-7704

Agoraphobics in Motion   www.aim-hq.org
1719 Crooks Rd   Royal Oak MI 48067
Ph: 248-547-0400

Agri-Energy Roundtable   www.agribusinesscouncil.org/aer.htm
1312 18th St NW   Washington DC 20036
Ph: 202-887-0528 ▪ Fx: 202-887-9178

Agri-Marketing Association, National   www.nama.org
11020 King St Suite 205   Overland Park KS 66210
Ph: 913-491-6500 ▪ Fx: 913-491-6502 ▪ TF: 800-530-5646

Agribusiness Council   www.agribusinesscouncil.org
1312 18th St NW Suite 300   Washington DC 20036
Ph: 202-296-4563 ▪ Fx: 202-887-9178

Agribusiness League, United   www.ual.org
54 Corporate Pk   Irvine CA 92606
Ph: 949-975-1424 ▪ Fx: 949-975-1671 ▪ TF: 800-223-4590

Agricultural Agents, National Association of County   www.nacaa.com
252 N Park St   Decatur IL 62523
Ph: 217-876-1220 ▪ Fx: 217-877-5382

Agricultural Appraisers, American Society of   www.amagappraisers.com
1126 Eastland Dr N   Suite 100 PO Box 186   Twin Falls ID 83303
Ph: 208-733-2323 ▪ Fx: 208-733-2326 ▪ TF: 800-488-7570

Agricultural Aviation Association, National   www.agaviation.org
1005 'E' St SE   Washington DC 20003
Ph: 202-546-5722 ▪ Fx: 202-546-5726

Agricultural Aviation Foundation, International   www.agpilot.com
PO Box 1607   Mount Vernon WA 98273
Ph: 360-724-3881 ▪ TF: 888-490-8206

Agricultural Communicators of Tomorrow, National   nact.okstate.edu

Agricultural Consultants, American Society of   www.agconsultants.org
950 S Cherry St Suite 508   Denver CO 80246
Ph: 303-759-5091 ▪ Fx: 303-758-0190

Agricultural Economics Association, American   www.aaea.org
415 S Duff Ave Suite C   Ames IA 50010
Ph: 515-233-3202 ▪ Fx: 515-233-3101

Agricultural Editors' Association, American   www.ageditors.com
Box 156   New Prague MN 56071
Ph: 952-758-6502 ▪ Fx: 952-758-5813

Agricultural Education, National Council for   www.teamaged.org/councilindex.cfm
1410 King St Suite 400   Alexandria VA 22314
Ph: 703-838-5881 ▪ Fx: 703-838-5888 ▪ TF: 800-772-0939

Agricultural Educators, National Association of   www.naae.org
Univ of Kentucky 300 Garrigus Bldg   Lexington KY 40546
Ph: 859-257-2224 ▪ Fx: 859-323-3919 ▪ TF: 800-509-0204

Agricultural Employers, National Council of   www.ncaeonline.org
1112 16th St NW Suite 920   Washington DC 20036
Ph: 202-728-0300 ▪ Fx: 202-728-0303

Agricultural Engineers, American Society of   www.asae.org
2950 Niles Rd   Saint Joseph MI 49085
Ph: 269-429-0300 ▪ Fx: 269-429-3852 ▪ TF: 800-695-2723

Agricultural Film Manufacturers Association, Construction &   www.cafma.org
104 S Michigan Ave Suite 1500   Chicago IL 60603
Ph: 312-201-0101 ▪ Fx: 312-201-0214

Agricultural & Food Transporters Conference   www.truckline.com/cc/conferences/atc
2200 Mill Rd   Alexandria VA 22314
Ph: 703-838-7999 ▪ Fx: 703-519-1866

Agricultural History Society   www.majbill.vt.edu/history/aley/AHSIndex2.htm
Univ of Arkansas Little Rock Dept of History 2801 S University Ave   Little Rock AR 72204
Ph: 501-569-8782 ▪ Fx: 501-569-3059

Agricultural Implement Workers of America, International Union United   www.uaw.org
Automobile Aerospace &   8000 E Jefferson Ave   Detroit MI 48214
Ph: 313-926-5000 ▪ Fx: 313-823-6016

Agricultural & Industrial Manufacturers' Representatives   www.aimrareps.org
Association   7500 Flying Cloud Rd Suite 900   Eden Prairie MN 55344
Ph: 952-253-6230 ▪ Fx: 952-835-4774

Agricultural Law Association, American   www.aglaw-assn.org
415 S Duff Ave Suite C   Ames IA 50010
Ph: 515-956-4255 ▪ Fx: 515-233-3101

Agricultural Life & Labor Research Fund Inc, National Council on   www.ncall.org
20 E Division St PO Box 1092   Dover DE 19903
Ph: 302-678-9400 ▪ Fx: 302-678-9058

Agricultural Missions Inc
475 Riverside Dr Rm 850   New York NY 10015
Ph: 212-870-2554 ▪ Fx: 212-870-2959

Agricultural Policy Research Institute, Food &   www.fapri.iastate.edu
Iowa State University 578 Heady Hall   Ames IA 50011
Ph: 515-294-7519 ▪ Fx: 515-294-6336

Agricultural Relations Council   www.agriwashington.org
1150 18th St NW Suite 275   Washington DC 20036
Ph: 202-785-6710 ▪ Fx: 202-331-4212

Agricultural Research, Consultative Group on International   www.cgiar.org
1818 H St NW   Washington DC 20433
Ph: 202-473-8951 ▪ Fx: 202-473-8110

Agricultural Retailers Association   www.aradc.org
1156 15th St NW Suite 302   Washington DC 20005
Ph: 202-457-0825 ▪ Fx: 202-457-0864

Agricultural Retailers Association PAC
1156 15th St NW Suite 302   Washington DC 20005
Ph: 202-457-0825 ▪ Fx: 202-457-0864

Agricultural Science & Technology, Council for   www.cast-science.org
4420 W Lincoln Way   Ames IA 50014
Ph: 515-292-2125 ▪ Fx: 515-292-4512

Agricultural Student Organization, National Postsecondary   www.nationalpas.org
6060 FFA Dr PO Box 68960   Indianapolis IN 46268
Ph: 317-802-4220 ▪ Fx: 317-802-5220

Agricultural Trade Association, Western US   www.wusata.org
2500 Main St Suite 110   Vancouver WA 98660
Ph: 360-693-3373 ▪ Fx: 360-693-3464

(Agriculture) Alpha Gamma Rho   www.agrs.org
10101 N Ambassador Dr   Kansas City MO 64153
Ph: 816-891-9200 ▪ Fx: 816-891-9401

(Agriculture) Alpha Tau Alpha   bioinfo.clemson.edu/ataonline

Agriculture, American Farm Bureau Foundation for   www.agfoundation.org
225 Touhy Ave   Park Ridge IL 60068
Ph: 847-685-8764 ▪ Fx: 847-685-8969

Agriculture Council of America   www.agday.org
11020 King St Suite 205   Overland Park KS 66210
Ph: 913-491-1895 ▪ Fx: 913-491-6502 ▪ TF: 888-982-4329

Agriculture Council, National Urban   www.nuac.org
1015 18th St NW Suite 600   Washington DC 20036
Ph: 202-429-4344 ▪ Fx: 202-429-4342

(Agriculture) CropLife America   www.croplifeamerica.org
1156 15th St NW Suite 400   Washington DC 20005
Ph: 202-296-1585 ▪ Fx: 202-463-0474

(Agriculture) Fraternity of Alpha Zeta — www.alphazeta.org
1000 Executive Pkwy Suite 200 PO Box 410260 Saint Louis MO 63141
Ph: 314-576-7730 ▪ Fx: 314-576-7989

(Agriculture) Gamma Sigma Delta — www.gammasigmadelta.org

(Agriculture) Land Institute — www.landinstitute.org
2440 E Water Well Rd Salina KS 67401
Ph: 785-823-5376 ▪ Fx: 785-823-8728

Agriculture Movement, American — www.aaminc.org
PO Box 399 Sunray TX 79086
Ph: 806-733-2203 ▪ Fx: 806-733-2965

Agriculture, National Association of State Departments of — www.nasda.org
1156 15th St NW Suite 1020 Washington DC 20005
Ph: 202-296-9680 ▪ Fx: 202-296-9686

Agriculture, National Institute for Animal — www.animalagriculture.org
1910 Lyda Ave Bowling Green KY 42104
Ph: 270-782-9798 ▪ Fx: 270-782-0188

Agriculture Research Center, Hawaii — www2.hawaii.edu/~jzhu/harc.html
99-193 Aiea Heights Dr Suite 300 Aiea HI 96701
Ph: 808-487-5561 ▪ Fx: 808-486-5020

Agriculture & Rural Development, Association for International — aiard.org
Mississippi State Univ Dept of Agricultural Economics Box 5187 Mississippi State MS 39762
Ph: 662-325-0549 ▪ Fx: 662-325-8777

(Agriculture) Samuel Roberts Noble Foundation — www.noble.org
PO Box 2180 Ardmore OK 73402
Ph: 580-223-5810 ▪ Fx: 580-224-6217

Agriculture & the Self-Employed, Communicating for — www.selfemployedcountry.org
112 E Lincoln Ave Fergus Falls MN 56537
Ph: 218-739-3241 ▪ Fx: 218-739-3832 ▪ TF: 800-432-3276

Agriculture & Trade Policy, Institute for — www.iatp.org
2105 1st Ave S Minneapolis MN 55404
Ph: 612-870-0453 ▪ Fx: 612-870-4846

Agronomy, American Society of — www.agronomy.org
677 S Segoe Rd Madison WI 53711
Ph: 608-273-8080 ▪ Fx: 608-273-2021

Ahmanson Foundation
9215 Wilshire Blvd Beverly Hills CA 90210
Ph: 310-278-0770

AHS International — www.vtol.org
217 N Washington St Alexandria VA 22314
Ph: 703-684-6777 ▪ Fx: 703-739-9279

Aid to Artisans Inc — www.aidtoartisans.org
331 Wethersfield Ave Hartford CT 06114
Ph: 860-947-3344 ▪ Fx: 860-947-3350

Aid Association, Army & Air Force Mutual — www.aafmaa.com
102 Sheridan Ave Bldg 468 Fort Myer VA 22211
Ph: 703-526-1621 ▪ Fx: 703-522-1336 ▪ TF: 866-422-3622

Aid & Development Inc, Mercy-USA for — www.mercyusa.org
44450 Pinetree Dr Suite 201 Plymouth MI 48170
Ph: 734-454-0011 ▪ Fx: 734-454-0303 ▪ TF: 800-556-3729

Aid Inc, International — www.gospelcom.net/ia
17011 W Hickory St Spring Lake MI 49456
Ph: 616-846-7490 ▪ Fx: 616-846-3842 ▪ TF: 800-968-7490

Aid Society of USA, Russian Orthodox Catholic Mutual — www.rocmas.org
10 Downs Dr Wilkes-Barre PA 18705
Ph: 570-822-8591 ▪ Fx: 570-821-7060 ▪ TF: 877-476-2627

(AIDS) ACT UP — www.actupny.org
332 Bleecker St Suite G5 New York NY 10014
Ph: 212-966-4873

AIDS Action — www.aidsaction.org
1906 Sunderland Pl NW Washington DC 20036
Ph: 202-530-8030 ▪ Fx: 202-530-8031

AIDS Action Council — www.aidsaction.org
1906 Sunderland Pl NW Washington DC 20036
Ph: 202-530-8030 ▪ Fx: 202-530-8031

AIDS Care, Association of Nurses in — www.anacnet.org
3538 Ridgewood Rd Akron OH 44333
Ph: 330-670-0101 ▪ Fx: 330-670-0109 ▪ TF: 800-260-6780

AIDS Care, International Association of Physicians in — www.iapac.org
33 N LaSalle St Suite 1700 Chicago IL 60602
Ph: 312-795-4930 ▪ Fx: 312-795-4938

AIDS Coalition, National Episcopal — www.neac.org
520 Clinton Ave Brooklyn NY 11238
Ph: 718-857-9445 ▪ Fx: 718-638-3039 ▪ TF: 800-588-6628

AIDS Coalition to Unleash Power — www.actupny.org
332 Bleecker St Suite G5 New York NY 10014
Ph: 212-966-4873

AIDS Council, National Minority — www.nmac.org
1931 13th St NW Washington DC 20009
Ph: 202-483-6622 ▪ Fx: 202-483-1135

AIDS Directors, National Alliance of State & Territorial — www.nastad.org
444 N Capitol St NW Suite 339 Washington DC 20001
Ph: 202-434-8090 ▪ Fx: 202-434-8092

AIDS Foundation, Elizabeth Glaser Pediatric — www.pedaids.org
2950 31st St Suite 125 Santa Monica CA 90405
Ph: 310-314-1459 ▪ Fx: 310-314-1469 ▪ TF: 888-499-4673

AIDS Foundation, Elton John — www.ejaf.org
PO Box 17139 Beverly Hills CA 90209
Ph: 310-535-1775

AIDS Fund, Children's — www.childrensaidsfund.org
PO Box 16433 Washington DC 20041
Ph: 866-829-1560 ▪ Fx: 800-557-8529

AIDS Memorial Quilt, NAMES Project Foundation/ — www.aidsquilt.org
101 Krog St Atlanta GA 30307
Ph: 404-688-5500 ▪ Fx: 404-688-5552

AIDS, National Association of People with — www.napwa.org
1413 K St NW 7th Fl Washington DC 20005
Ph: 202-898-0414 ▪ Fx: 202-898-0435

AIDS Network, National Catholic — www.ncan.org
1400 W Devon Ave Suite 502 Chicago IL 60660
Ph: 773-508-7080 ▪ Fx: 773-508-7083

AIDS Prevention Inc, Aggressive — www.aggressive.org
PO Box 26227 San Francisco CA 94126
Ph: 415-255-6022 ▪ Fx: 415-267-6980

AIDS Prevention, American Institute for Teen
PO Box 395 Oberlin OH 44074
Ph: 440-774-5411 ▪ Fx: 440-233-6455

AIDS Prevention Center, National Native American — www.nnaapc.org
436 14th St Suite 1020 Oakland CA 94610
Ph: 510-444-2051 ▪ Fx: 510-444-1593 ▪ TF: 800-283-6880

AIDS Research, American Foundation for — www.amfar.org
120 Wall St 13th Fl New York NY 10005
Ph: 212-806-1600 ▪ Fx: 212-806-1601 ▪ TF: 800-392-6327

AIDS Resource Foundation for Children — www.aidsresource.org
Saint Clare's Home for Children 182 Roseville Ave Newark NJ 07107
Ph: 973-483-4250 ▪ Fx: 973-483-1998

(AIDS) Treatment Action Group — www.aidsinfonyc.org/tag
611 Broadway Suite 612 New York NY 10012
Ph: 212-253-7922 ▪ Fx: 212-253-7923

AIDS Treatment Data Network — www.atdn.org
611 Broadway Suite 613 New York NY 10012
Ph: 212-260-8868 ▪ Fx: 212-260-8869 ▪ TF: 800-734-7104

AIDS Vaccine Initiative, International — www.iavi.org
110 Williams St 27th Fl New York NY 10038
Ph: 212-847-1111 ▪ Fx: 212-847-1112

AIDSinfo — www.aidsinfo.nih.gov
PO Box 6303 Rockville MD 20849
Ph: 301-519-0459 ▪ Fx: 301-519-6616 ▪ TF: 800-448-0440

AIIM International - Enterprise Content Management Association — www.aiim.org
1100 Wayne Ave Suite 1100 Silver Spring MD 20910
Ph: 301-587-8202 ▪ Fx: 301-587-2711 ▪ TF: 800-477-2446

Aikido Association USA, Japan — tomiki.org
5752 S Kingston Way Englewood CO 80111
Ph: 303-740-7424 ▪ Fx: 303-337-1631

Aikido Federation, US — www.usaikifed.com
98 State St Northampton MA 01060
Ph: 413-586-7122

AIM Inc - Association for Automatic Identification & Mobility — www.aimglobal.org
125 Warrendale-Bayne Rd Warrendale PA 15086
Ph: 724-934-4470 ▪ Fx: 724-934-4495 ▪ TF: 800-338-0206

Air Balance Council, Associated — www.aabchq.com
1518 K St NW Washington DC 20005
Ph: 202-737-0202 ▪ Fx: 202-638-4833

Air Brake Association
2009 Oriole Trail LB Long Beach IN 46360
Ph: 219-874-3129 ▪ Fx: 219-874-3121

Air Cargo Association, International — www.tiaca.org
5600 NW 36th St Suite 620 Miami FL 33159
Ph: 786-265-7011 ▪ Fx: 786-265-7012

Air Carrier Association, National — www.naca.cc
1000 Wilson Blvd Suite 1700 Arlington VA 22209
Ph: 703-358-8060 ▪ Fx: 703-358-8070

Air Commando Association — www.aircommando.net
PO Box 7 Mary Esther FL 32569
Ph: 850-581-0099 ▪ Fx: 850-581-8988

AIR Commercial Real Estate Association — www.airea.com
700 S Flower St Suite 600 Los Angeles CA 90017
Ph: 213-687-8777 ▪ Fx: 213-687-8616

Air Companies, Institute of Clean — icac.com
1660 L St NW Suite 1100 Washington DC 20036
Ph: 202-457-0911 ▪ Fx: 202-331-1388

Air Conditioning Contractors of America — www.acca.org
2800 E Shirlington Rd Suite 300 Arlington VA 22206
Ph: 703-575-4477 ▪ Fx: 703-575-4449

Air Conditioning Contractors of America PAC
2800 Shirlington Rd Suite 300 Arlington VA 22206
Ph: 703-575-4477 ▪ Fx: 703-575-4449

Air Conditioning Contractors' National Association, Sheet Metal & — www.smacna.org
4201 Lafayette Center Dr Chantilly VA 20151
Ph: 703-803-2980 ▪ Fx: 703-803-3732

Air-Conditioning Engineers Inc, American Society of Heating Refrigerating & — www.ashrae.org
1791 Tullie Cir NE Atlanta GA 30329
Ph: 404-636-8400 ▪ Fx: 404-321-5478 ▪ TF: 800-527-4723

Air-Conditioning & Refrigeration Institute — www.ari.org
4100 N Fairfax Dr Suite 200 Arlington VA 22203
Ph: 703-524-8800 ▪ Fx: 703-528-3816

Air Conditioning Society Worldwide, Mobile — www.macsw.org
225 S Broad St Lansdale PA 19446
Ph: 215-631-7020 ▪ Fx: 215-631-7017

AIR Conference — www.aircon.org
1300 19th St NW Suite 750 Washington DC 20036
Ph: 202-861-7550 ▪ Fx: 202-861-7557

Air Courier Conference of America — www.aircour.org
2900 Linden Ln Suite 120 Silver Spring MD 20910
Ph: 301-962-7000 ▪ Fx: 301-495-8870

Air Diffusion Council — www.flexibleduct.org
1000 E Woodfield Rd Suite 102 Schaumburg IL 60173
Ph: 847-706-6750 ▪ Fx: 847-706-6751

Air Distribution Institute
4415 W Harrison St Suite 322 Hillside IL 60162
Ph: 708-449-2933 ▪ Fx: 708-449-0837

Air Duct Cleaners Association, National — www.nadca.com
1518 K St Suite 503 Washington DC 20005
Ph: 202-737-2926 ▪ Fx: 202-347-8847

Air Filtration Association, National — www.nafahq.org
PO Box 68639 Suite 503 Virginia Beach VA 23471
Ph: 757-313-7400 ▪ Fx: 757-497-1895

Air Force Aid Society Inc   www.afas.org
45 Nealy Ave Suite 100   Langley VA 23665
Ph: 757-764-3990 ▪ Fx: 757-764-6752

Air Force Association   www.afa.org
1501 Lee Hwy   Arlington VA 22209
Ph: 703-247-5800 ▪ Fx: 703-247-5853 ▪ TF: 800-727-3337

Air Force, Commemorative   www.commemorativeairforce.org
PO Box 62000   Midland TX 79711
Ph: 432-563-1000 ▪ Fx: 432-563-8046

Air Force Flight Surgeons, Society of US   www.sousaffs.org
PO Box 35387   Brooks AFB TX 78235
Ph: 210-536-2845 ▪ Fx: 210-536-1779

Air Force Historical Foundation   www.afhistoricalfoundation.com
1535 Command Dr Suite A-122   Andrews Air Force Base MD 20762
Ph: 301-736-1959 ▪ Fx: 301-981-3574

Air Force Missileers, Association of   www.afmissileers.org
PO Box 5693   Breckenridge CO 80424
Ph: 970-453-0500

Air Force Mutual Aid Association, Army &   www.aafmaa.com
102 Sheridan Ave Bldg 468   Fort Myer VA 22211
Ph: 703-526-1621 ▪ Fx: 703-522-1336 ▪ TF: 866-422-3622

Air Force Sergeants Association   www.afsahq.org
5211 Auth Rd   Suitland MD 20746
Ph: 301-899-3500 ▪ Fx: 301-899-8136 ▪ TF: 800-638-0594

Air & Gas Institute Inc, Compressed   www.cagi.org
1300 Sumner Ave   Cleveland OH 44115
Ph: 216-241-7333 ▪ Fx: 216-241-0105

Air Line Pilots Association   www.alpa.org
535 Herndon Pkwy   Herndon VA 20170
Ph: 703-689-2270 ▪ Fx: 703-689-4177

Air Line Pilots Association PAC   www.alpa.org
1625 Massachusetts Ave NW   Washington DC 20036
Ph: 202-797-4033 ▪ Fx: 202-797-4030

Air Medical Physician Association   www.ampa.org
383 F St   Salt Lake City UT 84103
Ph: 801-408-3699 ▪ Fx: 801-408-1668

Air Medical Services, Association of   www.aams.org
526 King St Suite 415   Alexandria VA 22314
Ph: 703-836-8732 ▪ Fx: 703-836-8920

Air Movement & Control Association International Inc   www.amca.org
30 W University Dr   Arlington Heights IL 60004
Ph: 847-394-0150 ▪ Fx: 847-253-0088

Air Pollution Control Officials, Association of Local   www.cleanairworld.org
444 N Capitol St NW Suite 307   Washington DC 20001
Ph: 202-624-7864 ▪ Fx: 202-624-7863

Air Pollution Program Administrators, State & Territorial   www.cleanairworld.org
444 N Capitol St NW Suite 307   Washington DC 20001
Ph: 202-624-7864 ▪ Fx: 202-624-7863

Air Safety Investigators, International Society of   www.isasi.org
107 E Holly Ave Suite 11   Sterling VA 20164
Ph: 703-430-9668 ▪ Fx: 703-430-4970

Air Serv International   www.airserv.org
6583 Merchant Pl Suite 100   Warrenton VA 20187
Ph: 540-428-2323 ▪ Fx: 540-428-2326

Air Shows, International Council of   www.airshows.org
751 Miller Dr SE Suite F-4   Leesburg VA 20175
Ph: 703-779-8510 ▪ Fx: 703-779-8511

Air & Stream Improvement Inc, National Council for   www.ncasi.org
PO Box 13318   Research Triangle Park NC 27709
Ph: 919-941-6400 ▪ Fx: 919-941-6401

Air & Surface Transport Nurses Association   www.astna.org
9101 E Kenyon Ave Suite 3000   Denver CO 80237
Ph: 800-897-6362 ▪ Fx: 303-770-1812

Air Traffic Control Association   www.atca.org
2300 Clarendon Blvd Suite 711   Arlington VA 22201
Ph: 703-522-5717 ▪ Fx: 703-527-7251

Air Traffic Controllers Association, National   www.natca.org
1325 Massachusetts Ave NW   Washington DC 20005
Ph: 202-628-5451 ▪ Fx: 202-628-5767 ▪ TF: 800-266-0895

Air Traffic Specialists, National Association of   www.naats.org
11303 Amherst Ave Suite 4   Wheaton MD 20902
Ph: 301-933-6228 ▪ Fx: 301-933-3902

Air Transport Association of America   www.air-transport.org
1301 Pennsylvania Ave NW Suite 1100   Washington DC 20004
Ph: 202-626-4000 ▪ Fx: 202-626-4181

Air Transport Association, International   www.iata.org
800 Pl Victoria PO Box 113   Montreal QC H4Z1M1
Ph: 514-874-0202 ▪ Fx: 514-874-9632

(Air Transport) Wings of Hope Inc   www.wings-of-hope.org
Spirit of St Louis Airport 18590 Edison Ave   Chesterfield MO 63005
Ph: 636-537-1302 ▪ Fx: 636-537-3139 ▪ TF: 800-448-9487

Air Transportation Association, National   www.nata-online.org
4226 King St   Alexandria VA 22302
Ph: 703-845-9000 ▪ Fx: 703-845-8176 ▪ TF: 800-808-6282

Air & Waste Management Association   www.awma.org
420 Fort Duquesne Blvd 1 Gateway Ctr 3rd Fl   Pittsburgh PA 15222
Ph: 412-232-3444 ▪ Fx: 412-232-3450 ▪ TF: 800-270-3444

Air Weather Association   www.airweaassn.org
1697 Capri Way   Charlottesville VA 22911
Ph: 434-296-2832 ▪ Fx: 434-296-9966

Airborne Association, American   www.americanairborneassn.org
10301 McKinstry Mill Rd   New Windsor MD 21776
Ph: 410-775-7733 ▪ Fx: 410-775-7760 ▪ TF: 888-567-2927

Airborne Law Enforcement Association   www.alea.org
PO Box 3683   Tulsa OK 74101
Ph: 918-599-0705 ▪ Fx: 918-583-2353

Airconditioning & Refrigeration Distributors International, Heating   www.hardinet.org
1389 Dublin Rd   Columbus OH 43215
Ph: 614-488-1835 ▪ Fx: 614-488-0482 ▪ TF: 888-253-2128

Aircraft Association, Experimental   www.eaa.org
3000 Poberezny Rd   Oshkosh WI 54902
Ph: 920-426-4800 ▪ Fx: 920-426-4828

Aircraft Builders Council   www.aircraftbuilders.com
4248 Park Glen Rd   Minneapolis MN 55416
Ph: 952-928-4662 ▪ Fx: 952-929-1318

Aircraft Electronics Association   www.aea.net
4217 S Hocker Dr   Independence MO 64055
Ph: 816-373-6565 ▪ Fx: 816-478-3100

Aircraft Finance Association, National   www.nafa-us.org
PO Box 85   Poolesville MD 20837
Ph: 301-349-2070 ▪ Fx: 301-972-7727

Aircraft Locknut Manufacturers Association   www.almanet.org
994 Old Eagle School Rd Suite 1019   Wayne PA 19087
Ph: 610-971-4850 ▪ Fx: 610-971-4859

Aircraft Mechanics Fraternal Association   www.amfa2000.org
PO Box 51955   Indianapolis IN 46251
Ph: 317-244-4413 ▪ Fx: 317-244-4418

Aircraft Owner & Pilot Associations, International Council of   www.iaopa.org
421 Aviation Way   Frederick MD 21701
Ph: 301-695-2000 ▪ Fx: 301-695-2375

Aircraft Owners & Pilots Association   www.aopa.org
421 Aviation Way   Frederick MD 21701
Ph: 301-695-2000 ▪ Fx: 301-695-2375 ▪ TF: 800-872-2672

Aircraft Owners & Pilots Association PAC
601 Pennsylvania Ave NW South Bldg Suite 875   Washington DC 20004
Ph: 202-737-7950 ▪ Fx: 202-737-7951 ▪ TF: 800-872-2672

Aircraft Resale Association, National   www.nara-dealers.com/
4226 King St   Alexandria VA 22302
Ph: 703-671-8273 ▪ Fx: 703-671-5848

Aircraft Trading, International Society of Transport   www.istat.org
5517 Talon Ct   Fairfax VA 22032
Ph: 703-978-8156 ▪ Fx: 703-503-5964

Airforwarders Association   www.airforwarders.org
1600 Duke St Suite 400   Alexandria VA 22314
Ph: 703-519-9846 ▪ Fx: 703-519-1716

Airlift Service, American Veterans Medical
931 Flanders Rd PO Box 1065   La Canada Flintridge CA 91011
Ph: 818-952-6212

Airlift/Tanker Association   www.atalink.org
9312 Convento Terr   Fairfax VA 22031
Ph: 703-385-2802 ▪ Fx: 703-385-2803

Airline Association, Cargo
1220 19th St NW Suite 400   Washington DC 20036
Ph: 202-293-1030 ▪ Fx: 202-293-4377

Airline Association, Regional   www.raa.org
2025 M St NW Suite 800   Washington DC 20036
Ph: 202-367-1100 ▪ Fx: 202-367-2100

Airline Entertainment Association, World   www.waea.org
8201 Greensboro Dr Suite 300   McLean VA 22102
Ph: 703-610-9021 ▪ Fx: 703-610-9005

Airline Industrial Relations Conference   www.aircon.org
1300 19th St NW Suite 750   Washington DC 20036
Ph: 202-861-7550 ▪ Fx: 202-861-7557

Airline Passengers Association, International   www.iapa.com
PO Box 700188   Dallas TX 75370
Ph: 972-404-9980 ▪ Fx: 972-233-5348 ▪ TF: 800-821-4272

Airline Personnel, Fellowship of Christian   www.fcap.org
136 Providence Rd   Fayetteville GA 30215
Ph: 770-461-9320 ▪ Fx: 770-461-2720

Airline Pilots Association, Retired   www.rapa.org
PO Box 293443   Sacramento CA 95829
Ph: 650-368-0200

Airline Pilots, Organization of Black   www.obap.org
8630 Fenton St Suite 126   Silver Spring MD 20910
Ph: 800-538-6227

Airline Suppliers Association   www.airlinesuppliers.com
1707 H St NW Suite 701   Washington DC 20006
Ph: 202-730-0270 ▪ Fx: 202-730-0274

Airlines Electronic Engineering Committee   www.arinc.com/aeec
2551 Riva Rd   Annapolis MD 21401
Ph: 410-266-4000 ▪ TF: 800-266-4180

Airlines Reporting Corp   www.arccorp.com
4100 N Fairfax Dr Suite 600   Arlington VA 22203
Ph: 703-816-8000 ▪ Fx: 703-816-8104

Airlines Travel Agent Network, International   www.iatan.org
300 Garden City Plaza Suite 342   Garden City NY 11530
Ph: 516-663-6000 ▪ Fx: 516-747-4462 ▪ TF: 800-294-2826

Airmen Memorial Foundation   www.amf.org
5211 Auth Rd   Suitland MD 20746
Ph: 301-899-3500 ▪ Fx: 301-899-8136 ▪ TF: 800-638-0594

Airplane Association, Antique   www.aaa-apm.org/aaa
22001 Bluegrass Rd   Ottumwa IA 52501
Ph: 641-938-2773 ▪ Fx: 641-938-2093

Airport Consultants Council   www.acconline.org
908 King St Suite 100   Alexandria VA 22314
Ph: 703-683-5900 ▪ Fx: 703-683-2564

Airport Duty Free Stores, International Association of   www.iaadfs.org
2025 M St NW Suite 800   Washington DC 20036
Ph: 202-367-1184 ▪ Fx: 202-429-5154

Airport Executives, American Association of   www.airportnet.org
601 Madison St Suite 400   Alexandria VA 22314
Ph: 703-824-0500 ▪ Fx: 703-820-1395

Airport Ground Transportation Association   www.agtaweb.org
UMSL Ctr for Transportation Studies 154 University Ctr 8001 Natural Bridge Rd   Saint Louis MO 63121
Ph: 314-516-7271 ▪ Fx: 314-516-7272

Airports Council International of North America
1775 K St NW Suite 500   Washington DC 20006
Ph: 202-293-8500 ▪ Fx: 202-331-1362
www.aci-na.org

Airship Association, Naval
2 Maryhill Dr   Saint Louis MO 63124
Ph: 314-991-3901 ▪ Fx: 314-991-9621
www.naval-airships.org/

Airways Systems Specialists, Professional
1150 17th St NW Suite 702   Washington DC 20036
Ph: 202-293-7277 ▪ Fx: 202-293-7727
www.passnational.org

Akhal-Teke Association of America
21314 129th Ave SE   Snohomish WA 98296
Ph: 425-485-4970 ▪ Fx: 360-668-4302
www.akhal-teke.org

Al-Anon Family Group Headquarters Inc
1600 Corporate Landing Pkwy   Virginia Beach VA 23454
Ph: 757-563-1600 ▪ Fx: 757-563-1655 ▪ TF: 888-425-2666
www.al-anon.org

Aladdin Knights of the Mystic Light
3935 Kelley Rd   Kevil KY 42053
Ph: 270-488-2116 ▪ Fx: 270-488-2055
www.aladdinknights.org

Alagille Syndrome Alliance
10630 SW Garden Park Pl   Tigard OR 97223
Ph: 503-639-6217
www.alagille.org

Alan Guttmacher Institute
120 Wall St 21st Fl   New York NY 10005
Ph: 212-248-1111 ▪ Fx: 212-248-1951
www.agi-usa.org

Alarm Association of America, National
PO Box 3409   Dayton OH 45401
Ph: 800-283-6285 ▪ Fx: 513-461-4759
www.naaa.org

Alarm Association Inc, Automatic Fire
PO Box 951807   Lake Mary FL 32795
Ph: 407-322-6288 ▪ Fx: 407-322-7488
www.afaa.org

Alarm Association, Central Station
440 Maple Ave E Suite 201   Vienna VA 22180
Ph: 703-242-4670 ▪ Fx: 703-242-4675
www.csaaul.org

Alarm Association, National Burglar & Fire
8300 Colesville Rd Suite 750   Silver Spring MD 20910
Ph: 301-585-1855 ▪ Fx: 301-585-1866
www.alarm.org

Alarm Distributors, National Independent Fire
1001 Office Park Rd Suite 105   West Des Moines IA 50625
Ph: 515-440-6057 ▪ Fx: 515-440-6055
www.nifad.org

Alaska Coalition
122 C St NW Suite 240   Washington DC 20001
Ph: 202-628-1843 ▪ Fx: 202-544-5197
www.alaskacoalition.org

Alaska Wilderness League
122 C St NW Suite 240   Washington DC 20002
Ph: 202-544-5205 ▪ Fx: 202-544-5197
www.alaskawild.org

Alaska Wildlife Alliance
PO Box 202022   Anchorage AK 99520
Ph: 907-277-0897 ▪ Fx: 907-277-7423
www.akwildlife.org

Alaska-Yukon Pioneers
2725 E Fir St Unit 71   Mount Vernon WA 98273
Ph: 360-428-1912 ▪ Fx: 360-428-4200

(Alaskan Tribes) Maniilaq Association
PO Box 256   Kotzebue AK 99752
Ph: 800-478-3312
www.maniilaq.org

Alateen
1600 Corporate Landing Pkwy   Virginia Beach VA 23454
Ph: 757-563-1600 ▪ Fx: 757-563-1655 ▪ TF: 888-425-2666
www.alateen.org

Alban Institute
7315 Wisconsin Ave Suite 1250 W   Bethesda MD 20814
Ph: 301-718-4407 ▪ Fx: 301-718-1958 ▪ TF: 800-486-1318
www.alban.org

Albert Einstein Institution
427 Newbury St   Boston MA 02115
Ph: 617-247-4882 ▪ Fx: 617-247-4035
www.aeinstein.org

Albert Schweitzer Fellowship
330 Brookline Ave   Boston MA 02215
Ph: 617-667-5111 ▪ Fx: 617-667-7989
www.schweitzerfellowship.org

Albertson JA & Kathryn Foundation
PO Box 70002   Boise ID 83707
Ph: 208-424-2600 ▪ Fx: 208-424-2626
www.jkaf.org

Albinism & Hypopigmentation, National Organization for
PO Box 959   East Hampstead NH 03826
Ph: 603-887-2310 ▪ Fx: 603-887-6049 ▪ TF: 800-473-2310
www.albinism.org

Alcohol Beverage Control Association, National
4216 King St W   Alexandria VA 22302
Ph: 703-578-4200 ▪ Fx: 703-820-3551
www.nabca.org

Alcohol Beverage Industries, World Association of
www.waabi.org

Alcohol & Drug Abuse Directors, National Association of State
808 17th St NW Suite 410   Washington DC 20006
Ph: 202-293-0090 ▪ Fx: 202-293-1250
www.nasadad.org

Alcohol & Drug Problems Association of North America
307 N Main St   Saint Charles MO 63301
Ph: 314-589-6702 ▪ Fx: 314-940-2358
www.adpana.com

Alcohol Drugs & Disability, National Association on
2165 Bunker Hill Dr   San Mateo CA 94402
Ph: 650-578-8047 ▪ Fx: 650-286-9205
www.naadd.org

Alcohol & Other Substance Abuse Issues, Inter-Association Task Force on   PO Box 430430   Denver CO 80250
Ph: 303-871-0901 ▪ Fx: 303-871-0907
www.iatf.org

Alcohol Policies, International Center for
1519 New Hampshire Ave NW   Washington DC 20036
Ph: 202-986-1159 ▪ Fx: 202-986-2080
www.icap.org

Alcohol Problems, American Council on
2376 Lakeside Dr   Birmingham AL 35244
Ph: 205-989-8177

Alcohol Research Information Service
430 Lathrop St   Lansing MI 48912
Ph: 517-485-9900 ▪ Fx: 517-485-1928

Alcohol Testing Industry Association, Drug &
1600 Duke St Suite 400   Alexandria VA 22314
Ph: 703-548-0901 ▪ Fx: 703-519-1716 ▪ TF: 800-355-1257
www.datia.org

Alcoholics Anonymous
475 Riverside Dr 11th Fl PO Box 459   New York NY 10163
Ph: 212-870-3400 ▪ Fx: 212-870-3003
www.aa.org

Alcoholics Chemically Dependent Persons & Significant Others, Jewish   850 7th Ave Suite 1201   New York NY 10019
Ph: 212-397-4197 ▪ Fx: 212-399-3525
www.jacsweb.org

Alcoholics Victorious
1045 Swift St   Kansas City MO 64116
Ph: 816-471-8020 ▪ Fx: 816-471-3718
av.iugm.org

Alcoholics World Service Organization Inc, Adult Children of
PO Box 3216   Torrance CA 90510
Ph: 310-534-1815
www.adultchildren.org

Alcoholism & Drug Dependence, National Council on
20 Exchange Pl Suite 2902   New York NY 10005
Ph: 212-269-7797 ▪ Fx: 212-269-7510 ▪ TF: 800-622-2255
www.ncadd.org

Alcoholism & Drug Dependency, International Commission for the Prevention of   12501 Old Columbia Pike   Silver Spring MD 20904
Ph: 301-680-6719 ▪ Fx: 301-680-6707

Alcoholism & Drug Dependency, National Committee for the Prevention of   12501 Old Columbia Pike   Silver Spring MD 20904
Ph: 301-680-6733 ▪ Fx: 301-680-6707

Alcoholism, International Society for Biomedical Research on
PO Box 202332   Denver CO 80220
Ph: 303-355-6420 ▪ Fx: 303-355-1207
www.isbra.com

Alcoholism Programs of North America Inc, Association of Halfway House   860 N Center St   Mesa AZ 85201
Ph: 480-610-8300 ▪ Fx: 480-964-2004 ▪ TF: 800-861-0599
www.ahhap.org

Alcoholism & Related Drug Problems Inc, National Catholic Council on   PO Box 248   Lafayette IN 47902
Ph: 765-420-0129 ▪ Fx: 765-420-0189
www.nccatoday.org

Alcoholism, Research Society on
7801 N Lamar Blvd Suite D-89   Austin TX 78752
Ph: 512-454-0022 ▪ Fx: 512-454-0812
www.rsoa.org

Alcor Life Extension Foundation
7895 E Acoma Dr Suite 110   Scottsdale AZ 85260
Ph: 480-905-1906 ▪ Fx: 480-922-9027 ▪ TF: 877-462-5267
www.alcor.org

Alcott Louisa May Memorial Association
PO Box 343   Concord MA 01742
Ph: 978-369-4118 ▪ Fx: 978-369-1367
www.louisamayalcott.org

ALEPH: Alliance for Jewish Renewal
7000 Lincoln Dr Suite B2   Philadelphia PA 19119
Ph: 215-247-9700 ▪ Fx: 215-247-9703
www.aleph.org

Alexander Graham Bell Association for the Deaf & Hard of Hearing
3417 Volta Pl NW   Washington DC 20007
Ph: 202-337-5220 ▪ Fx: 202-337-8314
www.agbell.org

Alexander Technique Inc, American Center for the
39 W 14th St Rm 507   New York NY 10011
Ph: 212-633-2229
www.acatnyc.org

Alexander Technique, American Society for the
PO Box 60008   Florence MA 01062
Ph: 413-584-2359 ▪ Fx: 413-584-3097 ▪ TF: 800-473-0620
www.alexandertech.com

Alfa Romeo Owners Club
10 Raskin Rd   Morristown NJ 07960
Ph: 973-285-9338 ▪ Fx: 973-285-9343
www.aroc-usa.org

Alfalfa Alliance, National
100 N Fruitland St Suite B   Kennewick WA 99336
Ph: 509-585-5460 ▪ Fx: 509-585-2671
www.alfalfa.org

Alfalfa Processors Council, AFIA -
8810 Craig Dr   Overland Park KS 66212
Ph: 913-648-6800 ▪ Fx: 913-648-2648
www.aapausa.org

Alfred P Sloan Foundation
630 5th Ave Suite 2550   New York NY 10111
Ph: 212-649-1649 ▪ Fx: 212-757-5117
www.sloan.org

Alger Horatio Association of Distinguished Americans
99 Canal Center Plaza   Alexandria VA 22314
Ph: 703-684-9444 ▪ Fx: 703-684-9445
www.horatioalger.com

Alhambra, Order of
4200 Leeds Ave   Baltimore MD 21229
Ph: 410-242-0660 ▪ Fx: 410-536-5729
www.orderalhambra.org

Alimentary Tract, Society for Surgery of the
900 Cummings Ctr Suite 221-U   Beverly MA 01915
Ph: 978-927-8330 ▪ Fx: 978-524-8890
www.ssat.com

Aliyah Center, Israel
633 3rd Ave 21st Fl   New York NY 10017
Ph: 212-339-6063 ▪ Fx: 212-318-6145
www.aliyah.org

Alkylphenols & Ethoxylates Research Council
1250 Connecticut Ave NW Suite 700   Washington DC 20036
Ph: 202-637-9071 ▪ Fx: 202-637-9178 ▪ TF: 866-273-7262
www.aperc.org

All-America Rose Selections
111 E Wacker Dr 18th Fl   Chicago IL 60601
Ph: 312-372-7090
www.rose.org

All-American Collegiate Golf Foundation
555 Madison Ave 12th Fl   New York NY 10022
Ph: 212-751-5170 ▪ Fx: 212-755-3762

All Indian Pueblo Council
PO Box 400   Albuquerque NM 87103
Ph: 505-881-1992 ▪ Fx: 505-883-7682
www.aipcinc.com

All Service Postal Chess Club
1805 S Van Buren St   Amarillo TX 79102
Ph: 806-374-5991
chessaspc.com

All Star Dairy Association Inc
PO Box 911050   Lexington KY 40591
Ph: 859-255-3644 ▪ Fx: 859-255-3647 ▪ TF: 800-930-3644
www.allstardairy.com

All-Terrain Vehicle Safety Institute
2 Jenner St Suite 150   Irvine CA 92618
Ph: 949-727-3727 ▪ Fx: 949-786-3323 ▪ TF: 800-887-2887
www.atvsafety.org

Allante Appreciation Group
PO Box 342   Florala AL 36442
Ph: 800-664-5224
www.allante.us

Allegheny Institute for Public Policy　　www.alleghenyinstitute.org
305 Mt Lebanon Blvd Suite 208　Pittsburgh PA 15234
Ph: 412-440-0079　▪ Fx: 412-440-0085

Allen Foundation for the Arts　　www.pgafoundations.com/arts.asp
505 5th Ave S Suite 900　Seattle WA 98104
Ph: 206-342-2000　▪ Fx: 206-342-3000

Allen Foundation for Music　　www.pgafoundations.com/music.asp
505 5th Ave S Suite 900　Seattle WA 98104
Ph: 206-342-2000　▪ Fx: 206-342-3000

Allen Paul G Charitable Foundation　　www.pgafoundations.com
505 5th Ave S Suite 900　Seattle WA 98104
Ph: 206-342-2000　▪ Fx: 206-342-3000

Allen Paul G Forest Protection Foundation　www.pgafoundations.com/forest.asp
505 5th Ave S Suite 900　Seattle WA 98104
Ph: 206-342-2000　▪ Fx: 206-342-3000

Allen Paul G Foundation for Medical Research　www.pgafoundations.com/med.asp
505 5th Ave S Suite 900　Seattle WA 98104
Ph: 206-342-2000　▪ Fx: 206-342-3000

Allen Paul G Virtual Education Foundation　www.pgafoundations.com/edu.asp
505 5th Ave S Suite 900　Seattle WA 98104
Ph: 206-342-2000　▪ Fx: 206-342-3000

Allergists, American Association of Certified
85 W Algonquin Rd Suite 550　Arlington Heights IL 60005
Ph: 847-427-8111　▪ Fx: 847-427-1294

Allergy, American Academy of Otolaryngic　　www.aaoaf.org
1900 M St NW Suite 680　Washington DC 20036
Ph: 202-955-5010　▪ Fx: 202-955-5016

Allergy & Anaphylaxis Network, Food　　www.foodallergy.org
10400 Eaton Pl Suite 107　Fairfax VA 22030
Ph: 703-691-3179　▪ Fx: 703-691-2713　▪ TF: 800-929-4040

Allergy Asthma & Immunology, American Academy of　www.aaaai.org
611 E Wells St 4th Fl　Milwaukee WI 53202
Ph: 414-272-6071　▪ Fx: 414-272-6070　▪ TF: 800-822-2762

Allergy Asthma & Immunology, American College of　allergy.mcg.edu
85 W Algonquin Rd Suite 550　Arlington Heights IL 60005
Ph: 847-427-1200　▪ Fx: 847-427-1294　▪ TF: 800-842-7777

Allergy Asthma & Immunology, Joint Council of　www.jcaai.org
50 N Brockway St Suite 3-3　Palatine IL 60067
Ph: 847-934-1918　▪ Fx: 847-934-1820

Allergy Bureau, National　　www.aaaai.org/nab
611 E Wells St 4th Fl　Milwaukee WI 53202
Ph: 414-272-6071　▪ Fx: 414-272-6070

Allergy & Clinical Immunology, Academy of Veterinary　www.avaci.org
330 Waukegan Rd　Glenview IL 60025
Ph: 847-729-5200　▪ Fx: 847-729-5214

Allergy Foundation of America, Asthma &　　www.aafa.org
1233 20th St NW Suite 402　Washington DC 20036
Ph: 202-466-7643　▪ Fx: 202-466-8940　▪ TF: 800-727-8462

Allergy & Immunology, American Board of　　www.abai.org
510 Walnut Suite 1701　Philadelphia PA 19106
Ph: 215-592-9466　▪ Fx: 215-592-9411

Allergy & Immunology, American Osteopathic College of
7025 E McDowell Rd Suite 1-B　Scottsdale AZ 85257
Ph: 480-585-1580　▪ Fx: 480-585-1581

Allergy Organization, World　　www.worldallergy.org
611 E Wells St　Milwaukee WI 53202
Ph: 414-276-1791　▪ Fx: 414-276-3349

Allergy Research Foundation, Practical　　www.drapp.com
PO Box 60　Buffalo NY 14223
Ph: 716-875-5578　▪ Fx: 716-875-5399

Alley Cat Allies　　www.alleycat.org
1801 Belmont Rd NW Suite 201　Washington DC 20009
Ph: 202-667-3630　▪ Fx: 202-667-3640

Alliance Against Fraud in Telemarketing & Electronic　www.fraud.org/aaft/aaftinfo.htm
Commerce　1701 K St NW Suite 1200　Washington DC 20006
Ph: 202-835-3323　▪ Fx: 202-835-0747

Alliance for Aging Research　　www.agingresearch.org
2021 K St NW Suite 305　Washington DC 20006
Ph: 202-293-2856　▪ Fx: 202-785-8574

Alliance for Animals　　www.afa.arlington.ma.us
232 Silver St　Boston MA 02127
Ph: 617-268-7800　▪ Fx: 617-269-0455

Alliance of Artists Communities　　www.artistcommunities.org
225 S Main St　Providence RI 02903
Ph: 401-351-4320　▪ Fx: 401-351-4507

Alliance for the Arts　　www.allianceforarts.org
330 W 42nd St Suite 1701　New York NY 10036
Ph: 212-947-6340　▪ Fx: 212-947-6416

Alliance of Automobile Manufacturers　　www.autoalliance.org
1401 'I' St NW Suite 900　Washington DC 20005
Ph: 202-326-5500　▪ Fx: 202-326-5598

Alliance of Cardiovascular Professionals　　www.acp-online.org
4356 Bonney Rd Suite 103　Virginia Beach VA 23452
Ph: 757-497-1225　▪ Fx: 757-497-3481

Alliance for Children & Families Inc　　www.alliance1.org
11700 W Lake Park Dr　Milwaukee WI 53224
Ph: 414-359-1040　▪ Fx: 414-359-1074

Alliance of Claims Assistance Professionals　　claims.org
873 Brentwood Dr　West Chicago IL 60185
Ph: 630-588-1260　▪ Fx: 630-690-0377　▪ TF: 877-275-8765

Alliance for Communities in Action
PO Box 30154　Bethesda MD 20824
Ph: 301-229-7707　▪ Fx: 301-229-0457

Alliance of Community Health Plans　　www.achp.org
2000 M St NW Suite 201　Washington DC 20036
Ph: 202-785-2247　▪ Fx: 202-785-4060

Alliance for Community Media　　www.alliancecm.org
666 11th St NW Suite 740　Washington DC 20001
Ph: 202-393-2650　▪ Fx: 202-393-2653

Alliance for Consumer Rights
132 Nassau St 2nd Fl　New York NY 10038
Ph: 212-349-9204　▪ Fx: 212-608-2310

Alliance for Continuing Medical Education　　www.acme-assn.org
1025 Montgomery Hwy Suite 105　Birmingham AL 35216
Ph: 205-824-1355　▪ Fx: 205-824-1357

Alliance Defense Fund　　www.alliancedefensefund.org
15333 N Pima Rd Suite 165　Scottsdale AZ 85260
Ph: 800-835-5233　▪ Fx: 480-444-0025

Alliance for Democracy　　www.thealliancefordemocracy.org
760 Main St PO Box 540115　Waltham MA 02451
Ph: 781-894-1179　▪ Fx: 781-894-0279

Alliance for Excellent Education　　www.all4ed.org
1101 Vermont Ave NW Suite 411　Washington DC 20005
Ph: 202-842-4888　▪ Fx: 202-842-1613

Alliance for Fire & Smoke Containment & Control　www.afscc.org
25 N Broadway　Tarrytown NY 10591
Ph: 914-332-0040　▪ Fx: 914-332-1541

Alliance of Foam Packaging Recyclers　　www.epspackaging.org
1298 Cronson Blvd Suite 201　Crofton MD 21114
Ph: 410-451-8340　▪ Fx: 410-451-8343　▪ TF: 800-944-8448

Alliance Francaise, French Institute　　www.fiaf.org
22 E 60th St　New York NY 10022
Ph: 212-355-6100　▪ Fx: 212-935-4119

Alliance of Guardian Angels　　www.guardianangels.org
982 E 89th St　Brooklyn NY 11236
Ph: 212-397-7822

Alliance for Healthy Homes　　www.afhh.org
227 Massachusetts Ave NE Suite 200　Washington DC 20002
Ph: 202-543-1147　▪ Fx: 202-543-4466

Alliance for Higher Education　　www.allianceedu.org
2602 Rutford Ave　Richardson TX 75080
Ph: 972-883-4920　▪ Fx: 972-713-8209

Alliance of Information & Referral Systems　　www.airs.org
PO Box 31668　Seattle WA 98103
Ph: 206-632-2477　▪ Fx: 206-632-0855

Alliance for International Educational & Cultural Exchange　www.alliance-exchange.org
1776 Massachusetts Ave NW Suite 620　Washington DC 20036
Ph: 202-293-6141　▪ Fx: 202-293-6144

Alliance for Justice　　www.afj.org
11 Dupont Cir NW 2nd Fl　Washington DC 20036
Ph: 202-822-6070　▪ Fx: 202-822-6068

Alliance for Life Ministries　　www.alliance4lifemin.org
PO Box 5468　Madison WI 53705
Ph: 608-833-7363

Alliance for Lupus Research　　www.lupusresearch.org
28 W 44th St Suite 1217　New York NY 10036
Ph: 212-218-2840　▪ Fx: 212-218-2848

Alliance of Minority Women for Business & Political Development
8604 2nd Ave Suite 125　Silver Spring MD 20910
Ph: 301-585-8051　▪ Fx: 301-681-3681

Alliance of Motion Picture & Television Producers　www.amptp.org
15503 Ventura Blvd　Encino CA 91436
Ph: 818-995-3600　▪ Fx: 818-382-1793

Alliance for National Renewal　　www.ncl.org
National Civic League 1319 F ST NW Suite 204　Washington
DC 20004
Ph: 202-783-2961　▪ Fx: 202-347-2161

Alliance for the New Humanity　　www.anhglobal.org

Alliance of Nonprofit Mailers　　www.nonprofitmailers.org
1211 Connecticut Ave NW Suite 620　Washington DC 20036
Ph: 202-462-5132

Alliance for Nonprofit Management　　www.allianceonline.org
1899 L St NW 6th Fl　Washington DC 20036
Ph: 202-955-8406

Alliance for Nuclear Accountability　　www.ananuclear.org
1914 N 34th St Suite 407　Seattle WA 98103
Ph: 206-547-3175　▪ Fx: 206-547-7158

Alliance of Poles of America　　www.allianceofpoles.com
6966 Broadway　Cleveland OH 44105
Ph: 216-883-3131

Alliance for the Polyurethanes Industry　　www.polyurethane.org
1300 Wilson Blvd　Arlington VA 22209
Ph: 703-741-5656　▪ Fx: 703-741-5655

Alliance for Public Technology　　apt.org
919 18th St NW Suite 900　Washington DC 20006
Ph: 202-263-2970　▪ Fx: 202-263-2960

Alliance for Rail Competition　　www.railcompetition.org
499 S Capitol St SW Suite 608　Washington DC 20036
Ph: 202-216-9270　▪ Fx: 202-216-9662

Alliance for Responsible Atmospheric Policy　　www.arap.org
2111 Wilson Blvd Suite 850　Arlington VA 22201
Ph: 703-243-0344　▪ Fx: 703-243-2874

Alliance for Retired Americans　　www.retiredamericans.org
888 16th St NW Suite 520　Washington DC 20006
Ph: 202-974-8222　▪ Fx: 202-974-8256　▪ TF: 888-373-6497

Alliance to Save Energy　　www.ase.org
1200 18th St NW Suite 900　Washington DC 20036
Ph: 202-857-0666　▪ Fx: 202-331-9588

Alliance of Small Island States　　www.sidsnet.org/aosis
800 2nd Ave 4th Fl　New York NY 10017
Ph: 212-599-6196　▪ Fx: 212-599-0797

Alliance for Sustainability　　www.afs.nonprofitoffice.com
Univ of Minnesota Hillel Center 1521 University Ave
SE　Minneapolis MN 55414
Ph: 612-331-1099　▪ Fx: 612-379-1527

Alliance for a Tax Free America
PO Box 476　Leonia NJ 07605
Ph: 201-947-7449　▪ Fx: 201-947-1503

Alliance for Telecommunications Industry Solutions   www.atis.org
1200 G St NW Suite 500   Washington DC 20005
Ph: 202-628-6380 ▪ Fax: 202-393-5453

Alliance of Transylvanian Saxons   www.atsaxons.com
5393 Pearl Rd   Cleveland OH 44129
Ph: 440-842-8442

Alliance for Work-Life Progress   www.awlp.org
14040 N Northsight Blvd   Scottsdale AZ 85260
Ph: 800-874-9383 ▪ Fax: 480-603-0791

Allied Artists of America   www.alliedartistsofamerica.org
15 Gramercy Park S   New York NY 10003
Ph: 212-582-6411

Allied Finance Adjusters Conference Inc   www.alliedfinanceadjusters.com
PO Box 20708   Chicago IL 60620
Ph: 800-621-3016

Allied Pilots Association   www.alliedpilots.org
14600 Trinity Blvd Suite 500   Fort Worth TX 76155
Ph: 817-302-2250 ▪ Fax: 817-302-2119 ▪ TF: 800-323-1470

Allied Social Science Associations   www.vanderbilt.edu/AEA
2014 Broadway Suite 305   Nashville TN 37203
Ph: 615-322-3509 ▪ Fax: 615-343-2986

Allied Stone Industries   www.alliedstone.com
PO Box 5133   Kansas City KS 66119
Ph: 913-371-7757 ▪ Fax: 913-371-7764

ALMA - International Loudspeaker Association   www.almainternational.org
191 Clarksville Rd   Princeton Junction NJ 08550
Ph: 609-799-8440 ▪ Fax: 609-799-7032

ALMA Society   www.almasociety.org
PO Box 85   Denville NJ 07834
Ph: 973-586-1358

Almond Board of California   www.almondboard.com
1150 9th St Suite 1500   Modesto CA 95354
Ph: 209-549-8262 ▪ Fax: 209-549-8267

Aloe Science Council, International   www.iasc.org
415 E Airport Fwy Suite 260   Irving TX 75062
Ph: 972-258-8772 ▪ Fax: 972-258-8777

Aloha International   www.alohainternational.org
4504 Kukui St Suite 11   Kapaa HI 96746
Ph: 808-823-8381

Alopecia Areata Foundation, National   www.naaf.org
PO Box 150760   San Rafael CA 94915
Ph: 415-456-4644 ▪ Fax: 415-472-5343

Alpaca Breeders & Owners Association   www.alpacainfo.com
17000 Commerce Pkwy Suite C   Mount Laurel NJ 08054
Ph: 856-439-1076 ▪ Fax: 856-439-0525 ▪ TF: 800-213-9522

Alpaca Breeders of the Rockies   www.alpacabreeders.org
47705 E County Rd 34   Bennett CO 80102
Ph: 303-644-4110

Alpenlite Travel Club   www.alpenlite.com/html/alpen_club_about.html
PO Box 1726   Clackamas OR 97015
Ph: 503-698-4461 ▪ Fax: 503-698-5521

Alpha-66   www.alpha66.org
1714 W Flagler St   Miami FL 33135
Ph: 305-541-5433 ▪ Fax: 305-541-2252

Alpha Beta Gamma International Business Honor Society   www.abg.org
75 Grasslands Rd   Valhalla NY 10595
Ph: 914-785-6877 ▪ Fax: 914-785-6481

Alpha Chi National College Honor Scholarship Society   www.harding.edu/alphachi
Harding University PO Box 12249   Searcy AR 72149
Ph: 501-279-4443 ▪ Fax: 501-279-4589 ▪ TF: 800-477-4225

Alpha Chi Omega   www.alphachiomega.org
5939 Castle Creek Pkwy N   Indianapolis IN 46250
Ph: 317-579-5050 ▪ Fax: 317-579-5051

Alpha Chi Rho Fraternity Inc   alphachirho.org
109 Oxford Way   Neptune NJ 07753
Ph: 732-869-1895 ▪ Fax: 732-988-5357

Alpha Chi Sigma   www.alphachisigma.org
2141 N Franklin Rd   Indianapolis IN 46219
Ph: 317-357-5944 ▪ Fax: 317-351-9702

Alpha Delta Kappa   www.alphadeltakappa.org
1615 W 92nd St   Kansas City MO 64114
Ph: 816-363-5525 ▪ Fax: 816-363-4010 ▪ TF: 800-247-2311

Alpha Delta Phi International Fraternity   www.alphadeltaphi.org
6126 Lincoln Ave   Morton Grove IL 60053
Ph: 847-965-1832 ▪ Fax: 847-965-1871

Alpha Delta Pi   www.alphadeltapi.org
1386 Ponce de Leon Ave NE   Atlanta GA 30306
Ph: 404-378-3164 ▪ Fax: 404-373-0084

Alpha Epsilon Delta   www.jmu.edu/orgs/nationalaed
James Madison University 701 Carrier Dr MSC
   4307   Harrisonburg VA 22807
Ph: 540-568-2594 ▪ Fax: 540-568-2595

Alpha Epsilon Phi Sorority   www.aephi.org
111 Prospect St 2nd Fl   Stamford CT 06901
Ph: 203-358-8744 ▪ Fax: 203-357-7975

Alpha Epsilon Pi Fraternity Inc   www.aepi.org
8815 Wesleyan Rd   Indianapolis IN 46268
Ph: 317-876-1913 ▪ Fax: 317-876-1057 ▪ TF: 800-223-2374

Alpha Gamma Delta   www.alphagammadelta.org
8701 Founders Rd   Indianapolis IN 46268
Ph: 317-872-2655 ▪ Fax: 317-875-5824

Alpha Gamma Rho   www.agrs.org
10101 N Ambassador Dr   Kansas City MO 64153
Ph: 816-891-9200 ▪ Fax: 816-891-9401

Alpha Kappa Alpha Sorority Inc   www.aka1908.com
5656 S Stony Island Ave   Chicago IL 60637
Ph: 773-684-1282 ▪ Fax: 773-288-8251

Alpha Kappa Delta International   www.alpha-kappa-delta.org
PO Box U-1147   Mobile AL 36688
Ph: 251-461-1700 ▪ Fax: 251-460-7925

Alpha Kappa Lambda, Fraternity of   www.akl.org
4735 Statesmen Dr Suite F   Indianapolis IN 46250
Ph: 317-585-4911 ▪ Fax: 317-585-4907

Alpha Kappa Psi   www.akpsi.com
9595 Angola Ct   Indianapolis IN 46268
Ph: 317-872-1553 ▪ Fax: 317-872-1567

Alpha Lambda Delta, National   www.mercer.edu/ald
PO Box 4403   Macon GA 31208
Ph: 478-744-9595 ▪ Fax: 478-744-9924

Alpha Mu Gamma   citywww.lacc.cc.ca.us/activities/honor/amg/homepage.html
855 N Vermont Ave   Los Angeles CA 90029
Ph: 323-644-9752

Alpha Omega Alpha Honor Medical Society   www.alphaomegaalpha.org
525 Middlefield Rd Suite 130   Menlo Park CA 94025
Ph: 650-329-0291 ▪ Fax: 650-329-1618

Alpha Omega International Dental Fraternity   www.ao.org
500 Commonwealth Dr   Warrendale PA 15086
Ph: 724-778-3419 ▪ Fax: 724-772-8349 ▪ TF: 800-677-8468

Alpha Omicron Pi Fraternity   www.alphaomicronpi.org
5390 Virginia Way   Brentwood TN 37027
Ph: 615-370-0920 ▪ Fax: 615-371-9736

Alpha One Foundation   www.alphaone.org
2937 SW 27th Ave Suite 302   Miami FL 33133
Ph: 305-567-9888 ▪ Fax: 305-567-1317 ▪ TF: 888-825-7421

Alpha Phi Alpha Fraternity Inc   www.alphaphialpha.net
2313 Saint Paul St   Baltimore MD 21218
Ph: 410-554-0040 ▪ Fax: 410-554-0054

Alpha Phi Delta Fraternity Inc   www.apd.org
916 62nd St   Brooklyn NY 11219
Ph: 718-745-9551 ▪ Fax: 718-745-9592

Alpha Phi International Fraternity   www.alphaphi.org
1930 Sherman Ave   Evanston IL 60201
Ph: 847-475-0663 ▪ Fax: 847-475-6820

Alpha Phi Omega   www.apo.org
14901 E 42nd St   Independence MO 64055
Ph: 816-373-8667 ▪ Fax: 816-373-5975

Alpha Pi Mu   www.alphapimu.eas.pdx.edu
PO Box 773   Portland OR 97207
Ph: 503-297-3604 ▪ Fax: 503-297-3694

Alpha Psi Omega   www.alphapsiomega.org
Wabash College Theater Dept   Crawfordsville IN 47933
Ph: 765-361-6394 ▪ Fax: 765-361-6341

Alpha Sigma Alpha   www.alphasigmaalpha.org
9550 Zionsville Rd Suite 160   Indianapolis IN 46268
Ph: 317-871-2920 ▪ Fax: 317-871-2924

Alpha Sigma Kappa   www.tc.umn.edu/~ask
1009 University Ave SE   Minneapolis MN 55414
Ph: 612-378-4759

Alpha Sigma Nu   www.marquette.edu/dept/ASN
Marquette Univ 707 Bldg Rm 330 PO Box 1881   Milwaukee WI
   53201
Ph: 414-288-7542 ▪ Fax: 414-288-3259

Alpha Sigma Phi National Fraternity   www.alphasigmaphi.org
710 Adams St   Carmel IN 46032
Ph: 317-843-1911 ▪ Fax: 317-843-2966 ▪ TF: 800-800-1845

Alpha Sigma Tau Sorority   www.alphasigmatau.org
1929 Canyon Rd   Birmingham AL 35216
Ph: 205-978-2179 ▪ Fax: 205-978-2182

Alpha Tau Alpha   bioinfo.clemson.edu/ataonline

Alpha Tau Omega Fraternity   www.ato.org
1 N Pennsylvania St 12th Fl   Indianapolis IN 46204
Ph: 317-684-1865 ▪ Fax: 317-684-1862

Alpha Xi Delta Women's Fraternity   www.alphaxidelta.org
8702 Founders Rd   Indianapolis IN 46268
Ph: 317-872-3500 ▪ Fax: 317-872-2947

Alpha Zeta, Fraternity of   www.alphazeta.org
1000 Executive Pkwy Suite 200 PO Box 410260   Saint Louis
   MO 63141
Ph: 314-576-7730 ▪ Fax: 314-576-7989

Alpha Zeta Omega Pharmaceutical Fraternity   www.azo.org/
4422 Porpoise Dr   Tampa FL 33617
Ph: 813-988-5338

Alpine Club, American   www.americanalpineclub.org
710 10th St Suite 100   Golden CO 80401
Ph: 303-384-0110 ▪ Fax: 303-384-0111

Alpines International   www.alpinesinternationalclub.com
485 McKinney Rd   Walla Walla WA 99362
Ph: 509-525-4606 ▪ Fax: 509-526-0673

ALS Association   www.alsa.org
27001 Agoura Rd Suite 150   Calabasas Hills CA 91301
Ph: 818-880-9007 ▪ Fax: 818-880-9006 ▪ TF: 800-782-4747

Alternate Postal Systems Inc, Association of   www.aapsinc.org
1725 Oaks Way   Oklahoma City OK 73131
Ph: 405-478-0161

Alternative Break Connection Inc, Break Away: The   www.alternativebreaks.org
2121 W Pensacola St Suite E-543   Tallahassee FL 32304
Ph: 850-644-0986 ▪ Fax: 850-644-3345

Alternative Community Schools, National Coalition of   www.ncacs.org
1289 Jewett   Ann Arbor MI 48104
Ph: 734-668-9171 ▪ TF: 888-771-9171

Alternative Energy Resources Organization   www.aeromt.org
432 N Last Chance Gulch   Helena MT 59601
Ph: 406-443-7272 ▪ Fax: 406-442-9120

Alternative Fuel Vehicle Network
11621 San Antonio Dr NE   Albuquerque NM 87122
Ph: 505-856-8585 ▪ Fax: 505-856-5904

Alternative Futures, Institute for   www.altfutures.com
100 N Pitt St Suite 235   Alexandria VA 22314
Ph: 703-684-5880 ▪ Fax: 703-684-0640

Alternative Medicines, National Association of www.rentamark.com/naam
PO Box 35189   Chicago IL 60707
Ph: 708-453-0080 ▪ Fx: 708-453-0083

Alternative Newsweeklies, Association of aan.org
1020 16th St NW 4th Fl   Washington DC 20036
Ph: 202-822-1955 ▪ Fx: 202-822-0929

Alternative Policies, Development Group for www.developmentgap.org
927 15th St NW 4th Fl   Washington DC 20005
Ph: 202-898-1566 ▪ Fx: 202-898-1612

Alternative Press Center www.altpress.org
PO Box 33109   Baltimore MD 21218
Ph: 410-243-2471 ▪ Fx: 410-235-5325

Alternative Schools, National Association for Legal Support of
PO Box 2823   Santa Fe NM 87504
Ph: 505-471-6928

(Alternative Technologies) Aprovecho Research Center www.aprovecho.net
80574 Hazelton Rd   Cottage Grove OR 97424
Ph: 503-942-8198

Alternative Therapists, American Society of www.asat.org
PO Box 703   Rockport MA 01966
Ph: 978-281-4400 ▪ Fx: 978-282-1144

Altrusa International Inc www.altrusa.com
332 S Michigan Ave Suite 1123   Chicago IL 60604
Ph: 312-427-4410 ▪ Fx: 312-427-8521

Aluminum Anodizers Council www.anodizing.org
1000 N Rand Rd Suite 214   Wauconda IL 60084
Ph: 847-526-2010 ▪ Fx: 847-526-3993

Aluminum Association www.aluminum.org
900 19th St NW Suite 300   Washington DC 20006
Ph: 202-862-5100 ▪ Fx: 202-862-5164

Aluminum Extruders Council aec.org
1000 N Rand Rd Suite 214   Wauconda IL 60084
Ph: 847-526-2010 ▪ Fx: 847-526-3993

Aluminum Foil Container Manufacturers Association www.afcma.org
10 Vecilla Ln   Hot Springs Village AR 71909
Ph: 501-922-7425 ▪ Fx: 501-922-0383

Alumni, American Council of Trustees & www.goacta.org
1726 M St NW Suite 800   Washington DC 20036
Ph: 202-467-6787 ▪ Fx: 202-467-6784 ▪ TF: 888-258-6648

Alzheimer's Association www.alz.org
225 N Michigan Ave Suite 1700   Chicago IL 60601
Ph: 312-335-8700 ▪ Fx: 312-335-1110 ▪ TF: 800-272-3900

Alzheimer's Disease Education & Referral Center www.alzheimers.org
PO Box 8250   Silver Spring MD 20907
Ph: 301-495-3311 ▪ Fx: 301-495-3334 ▪ TF: 800-438-4380

Amalgamated Transit Union www.atu.org
5025 Wisconsin Ave NW 3rd Fl   Washington DC 20016
Ph: 202-537-1645 ▪ Fx: 202-244-7824

Amateur Athletic Union of the US www.aausports.org
PO Box 22409   Lake Buena Vista FL 32830
Ph: 407-934-7200 ▪ Fx: 407-934-7242 ▪ TF: 800-228-4872

Amateur Ballroom Dancers Association, US www.usabda.org
PO Box 128   New Freedom PA 17349
Ph: 717-235-6656 ▪ Fx: 717-235-4183 ▪ TF: 800-447-9047

Amateur Baseball Congress, American www.aabc.us
118-119 Redfield Plaza   Marshall MI 49068
Ph: 269-781-2002 ▪ Fx: 269-781-2060

Amateur Baseball Federation, National www.nabf.com
PO Box 705   Bowie MD 20718
Ph: 301-262-5005

Amateur Chamber Music Players www.acmp.net
1123 Broadway Rm 304   New York NY 10010
Ph: 212-645-7424 ▪ Fx: 212-741-2678

Amateur Field Trial Clubs of America www.aftca.org
1300 Tripp Rd   Somerville TN 38068
Ph: 901-465-1556 ▪ Fx: 901-465-0427

Amateur Jump Rope Federation, US www.usajrf.org

Amateur Karate Federation, American www.aakf.org
1930 Wilshire Blvd Suite 1208   Los Angeles CA 90057
Ph: 213-483-8262 ▪ Fx: 213-483-4060

Amateur Press Association, American members.aol.com/aapa96
535 Kickerillo Dr   Houston TX 77079
Ph: 281-497-8493

Amateur Satellite Corp, Radio www.amsat.org
850 Sligo Ave Suite 600   Silver Spring MD 20910
Ph: 301-589-6062 ▪ Fx: 301-608-3410

Amateur Softball Association of America Inc www.softball.org
2801 NE 50th St   Oklahoma City OK 73111
Ph: 405-424-5266 ▪ Fx: 405-424-3855 ▪ TF: 800-654-8337

Amateur Trapshooting Association www.shootata.com
601 W National Rd   Vandalia OH 45377
Ph: 937-898-4638 ▪ Fx: 937-898-5472

Amazon Alliance www.amazonalliance.org
1367 Connecticut Ave NW Suite 400   Washington DC 20036
Ph: 202-785-3334 ▪ Fx: 202-785-3335

Ambassadors Foundation, Friendship www.faf.org
110 Mamaroneck Ave Suites 7 & 8   White Plains NY 10601
Ph: 914-328-8589 ▪ Fx: 914-328-8578 ▪ TF: 800-526-2908

AMBUCS Inc, National www.ambucs.com
3315 N Main St   High Point NC 27265
Ph: 336-869-2166 ▪ Fx: 336-887-8451

Ambulance Association, American www.the-aaa.org
8201 Greensboro Dr Suite 300   McLean VA 22102
Ph: 703-610-9018 ▪ Fx: 703-610-9005 ▪ TF: 800-523-4447

Ambulatory Behavioral Healthcare, Association for www.aabh.org
2301 Mt Vernon Ave Suite 100   Alexandria VA 22301
Ph: 703-836-2274 ▪ Fx: 703-836-0083

Ambulatory Care, American Academy of www.ambulatorymedicine.org
2813 S Hiawassee Rd Suite 206   Orlando FL 32835
Ph: 407-521-5789 ▪ Fx: 407-521-5790

Ambulatory Care, North American Association for www.nafac.com
18870 Rutledge Rd   Minneapolis MN 55391
Ph: 952-476-0015 ▪ Fx: 952-456-0646

Ambulatory Care Nursing, American Academy of www.aaacn.org
E Holly Ave Box 56   Pitman NJ 08071
Ph: 856-256-2350 ▪ Fx: 856-589-7463 ▪ TF: 800-262-6877

Ambulatory Foot & Ankle Surgery, Academy of www.academy-afs.org
1601 Walnut St Suite 1005   Philadelphia PA 19102
Ph: 215-569-3303 ▪ Fx: 215-569-3310 ▪ TF: 800-433-4892

Ambulatory Health Care, Accreditation Association for www.aaahc.org
3201 Old Glenview Rd Suite 300   Wilmette IL 60091
Ph: 847-853-6060 ▪ Fx: 847-853-9028

Ambulatory Pediatric Association www.ambpeds.org
6728 Old McLean Village Dr   McLean VA 22101
Ph: 703-556-9222 ▪ Fx: 703-556-8729

Ambulatory Surgery Association, Federated www.fasa.org
700 N Fairfax St Suite 306   Alexandria VA 22314
Ph: 703-836-8808 ▪ Fx: 703-549-0976

Ambulatory Surgery Centers, American Association of www.aaasc.org
PO Box 5271   Johnson City TN 37602
Ph: 423-915-1001 ▪ Fx: 423-282-9712 ▪ TF: 800-237-3768

Ambulatory Surgery Facilities Inc, American Association for www.aaaasf.org
Accreditation of 5101 Washington St Suite 2F PO Box
9500   Gurnee IL 60031
Ph: 888-545-5222 ▪ Fx: 847-775-1985

AMC Pacer Club clubs.hemmings.com/amcpacer
2628 Queenston Rd   Cleveland Heights OH 44118
Ph: 216-371-0226

AMC Rambler Club clubs.hemmings.com
2645 Ashton Rd   Cleveland Heights OH 44118
Ph: 216-371-5946

AMC World Clubs www.amcwc.com
7963 Depew St   Arvada CO 80003
Ph: 303-428-8760

AmCham Cuba www.amchamcuba.org
10454 Parthenon Ct   Bethesda MD 20817
Ph: 301-365-1745 ▪ Fx: 301-365-1829

(AME Church) Service & Development Agency Inc www.amecnet.org/sada/sada.htm
1134 11th St NW Suite 214   Washington DC 20001
Ph: 202-371-8722 ▪ Fx: 202-371-0981

America the Beautiful Fund www.america-the-beautiful.org
1730 K St NW Suite 1002   Washington DC 20006
Ph: 202-638-1649 ▪ Fx: 202-204-0028 ▪ TF: 800-522-3557

America-Israel Chamber of Commerce & Industry Inc www.israeltrade.org
120 W 45th St 18th Fl   New York NY 10036
Ph: 212-819-0430 ▪ Fx: 212-819-0431

America-Israel Council for Israeli-Palestinian Peace otherisrael.home.igc.org
224 Lake Dr   Kensington CA 94708
Ph: 510-526-8449

America Israel Friendship League www.aifl.org
134 E 39th St   New York NY 10016
Ph: 212-213-8630 ▪ Fx: 212-683-3475

America-Mideast Educational & Training Services www.amideast.org
1730 M St NW Suite 1100   Washington DC 20036
Ph: 202-776-9600 ▪ Fx: 202-776-7000

America Outdoors www.americaoutdoors.org
PO Box 10847   Knoxville TN 37939
Ph: 865-558-3595 ▪ Fx: 865-558-3598

(America Physical Therapy Association) PTPAC
1111 N Fairfax St   Alexandria VA 22314
Ph: 703-684-2782 ▪ Fx: 703-684-7343

America Scores www.americascores.org
1327 14th St NW Suite 100   Washington DC 20005
Ph: 202-234-4112 ▪ Fx: 202-234-4119

American Abstract Artists
470 West End Ave Unit 9D   New York NY 10024
Ph: 212-874-0747

American Academy of Actuaries www.actuary.org
1100 17th St NW 7th Fl   Washington DC 20036
Ph: 202-223-8196 ▪ Fx: 202-872-1948

American Academy of Addiction Psychiatry www.aaap.org
7301 Mission Rd Suite 252   Prairie Village KS 66208
Ph: 913-262-6161 ▪ Fx: 913-262-4311

American Academy of Advertising www.americanacademyofadvertising.org

American Academy of Allergy Asthma & Immunology www.aaaai.org
611 E Wells St 4th Fl   Milwaukee WI 53202
Ph: 414-272-6071 ▪ Fx: 414-272-6070 ▪ TF: 800-822-2762

American Academy of Ambulatory Care www.ambulatorymedicine.org
2813 S Hiawassee Rd Suite 206   Orlando FL 32835
Ph: 407-521-5789 ▪ Fx: 407-521-5790

American Academy of Ambulatory Care Nursing www.aaacn.org
E Holly Ave Box 56   Pitman NJ 08071
Ph: 856-256-2350 ▪ Fx: 856-589-7463 ▪ TF: 800-262-6877

American Academy of Anesthesiologist Assistants www.anesthetist.org
PO Box 13978   Tallahassee FL 32317
Ph: 850-656-8848 ▪ Fx: 850-656-3038

American Academy of Anti-Aging Medicine www.worldhealth.net
2415 N Greenview Ave   Chicago IL 60614
Ph: 773-528-4333 ▪ Fx: 773-528-5390

American Academy of Appellate Lawyers www.appellateacademy.org
15245 Shady Grove Rd Suite 130   Rockville MD 20850
Ph: 301-258-9210 ▪ Fx: 301-990-9771

American Academy of Arts & Letters
633 W 155th St   New York NY 10032
Ph: 212-368-5900 ▪ Fx: 212-491-4615

American Academy of Arts & Sciences www.amacad.org
136 Irving St   Cambridge MA 02138
Ph: 617-576-5000 ▪ Fx: 617-576-5050

American Academy of Audiology www.audiology.org
11730 Plaza America Dr Suite 300   Reston VA 22190
Ph: 703-790-8466 ▪ Fx: 703-790-8631 ▪ TF: 800-222-2336

American Academy for Cerebral Palsy & Developmental Medicine aacpdm.org
6300 N River Rd Suite 727   Rosemont IL 60018
Ph: 847-698-1635 ▪ Fx: 847-823-0536

American Academy of Child & Adolescent Psychiatry www.aacap.org
3615 Wisconsin Ave NW   Washington DC 20016
Ph: 202-966-7300 ▪ Fx: 202-966-2891 ▪ TF: 800-333-7636

American Academy of Clinical Neurophysiology www.aacnonline.com
104 13th St   Hudson WI 54016
Ph: 715-381-3440 ▪ Fx: 715-381-3442

American Academy of Clinical Psychiatrists www.aacp.com
PO Box 458   Glastonbury CT 06033
Ph: 860-633-5045 ▪ Fx: 860-633-6023

American Academy of Clinical Toxicology www.clintox.org
777 E Park Dr PO Box 8820   Harrisburg PA 17105
Ph: 717-558-7847 ▪ Fx: 717-558-7841

American Academy of Cosmetic Dentistry www.aacd.com
5401 World Dairy Dr   Madison WI 53718
Ph: 608-222-8583 ▪ Fx: 608-222-9540 ▪ TF: 800-543-9220

American Academy of Cosmetic Surgery www.cosmeticsurgery.org
737 N Michigan Ave Suite 820   Chicago IL 60611
Ph: 312-981-6760 ▪ Fx: 312-981-6787

American Academy of Craniofacial Pain www.aacfp.org
516 W Pipeline Rd   Hurst TX 76053
Ph: 817-282-1501 ▪ Fx: 817-282-8012 ▪ TF: 800-322-8651

American Academy of Dental Group Practice www.aadgp.org
2525 E Arizona Biltmore Cir Suite 127   Phoenix AZ 85016
Ph: 602-381-1185 ▪ Fx: 602-381-1093

American Academy of Dental Practice Administration www.aadpa.org
1063 Whippoorwill Ln   Palatine IL 60067
Ph: 847-934-4404 ▪ Fx: 847-934-4410

American Academy of Dermatology www.aad.org
930 E Woodfield Rd PO Box 4014   Schaumburg IL 60168
Ph: 847-330-0230 ▪ Fx: 847-330-0050

American Academy of Diplomacy www.academyofdiplomacy.org
1800 K St NW Suite 1014   Washington DC 20006
Ph: 202-331-3721 ▪ Fx: 202-833-4555

American Academy of Disability Evaluating Physicians www.aadep.org
150 N Wacker Dr Suite 1420   Chicago IL 60606
Ph: 312-658-1171 ▪ Fx: 312-658-1175 ▪ TF: 800-456-6095

American Academy of Emergency Medicine www.aaem.org
611 E Wells St   Milwaukee WI 53202
Ph: 800-884-2236 ▪ Fx: 414-276-3349

American Academy of Environmental Engineers www.enviro-engrs.org
130 Holiday Ct Suite 100   Annapolis MD 21401
Ph: 410-266-3311 ▪ Fx: 410-266-7653

American Academy of Environmental Medicine www.aaem.com
7701 E Kellogg Dr Suite 625   Wichita KS 67207
Ph: 316-684-5500 ▪ Fx: 316-684-5709

American Academy of Equine Art www.aaea.net
4089 Iron Works Pkwy   Lexington KY 40511
Ph: 859-281-6031 ▪ Fx: 859-281-6043

American Academy of Estate Planning Attorneys www.aaepa.com/
4365 Executive Dr Suite 850   San Diego CA 92121
Ph: 800-846-1555 ▪ Fx: 858-535-8241

American Academy of Esthetic Dentistry www.estheticacademy.org
401 N Michigan Ave   Chicago IL 60611
Ph: 312-321-5121 ▪ Fx: 312-673-6952

American Academy of Facial Plastic & Reconstructive Surgery   310 S Henry St   Alexandria VA 22314 www.facial-plastic-surgery.org
Ph: 703-299-9291 ▪ Fx: 703-299-8898 ▪ TF: 800-332-3223

American Academy of Family Physicians www.aafp.org
11400 Tomahawk Creek Pkwy   Leawood KS 66211
Ph: 913-906-6000 ▪ Fx: 913-906-6075 ▪ TF: 800-274-2237

American Academy of FertilityCare Professionals www.aafcp.org
11700 Studt Ave Suite C   Saint Louis MO 63141
Ph: 314-991-0327 ▪ Fx: 314-692-8097

American Academy of Fixed Prosthodontics
PO Box 1409   Bodega Bay CA 94923
Ph: 707-875-3040 ▪ Fx: 707-875-2927 ▪ TF: 800-880-5184

American Academy of Forensic Sciences www.aafs.org
410 N 21st St Suite 203 PO Box 669   Colorado Springs CO 80904
Ph: 719-636-1100 ▪ Fx: 719-636-1993

American Academy of Gnathologic Orthopedics www.aago.com
2651 Oak Grove Rd   Walnut Creek CA 94598
Ph: 925-939-5024 ▪ Fx: 925-676-7678 ▪ TF: 800-510-2246

American Academy of Gold Foil Operators www.goldfoil.org
1 Woods End Rd   Etna NH 03750
Ph: 603-643-2899

American Academy of Health Care Providers in the Addictive Disorders   314 W Superior St Suite 702   Duluth MN 55802 www.americanacademy.org
Ph: 218-727-3940 ▪ Fx: 218-722-0346

American Academy of Health Physics www.hps1.org/aahp
1313 Dolley Madison Blvd Suite 402   McLean VA 22101
Ph: 703-790-1745 ▪ Fx: 703-790-2672

American Academy of the History of Dentistry
Oregon Health Sciences Univ School of Dentistry 611 SW Campus Dr   Portland OR 97239
Ph: 503-494-4316

American Academy of Home Care Physicians www.aahcp.org
PO Box 1037   Edgewood MD 21040
Ph: 410-676-7966 ▪ Fx: 410-676-7980

American Academy of Hospice & Palliative Medicine www.aahpm.org
4700 W Lake Ave   Glenview IL 60025
Ph: 847-375-4712 ▪ Fx: 877-734-8671

American Academy of Implant Dentistry www.aaid-implant.org
211 E Chicago Ave Suite 750   Chicago IL 60611
Ph: 312-335-1550 ▪ Fx: 312-335-9090 ▪ TF: 877-335-2243

American Academy of Implant Prosthodontics
709 Haddonfield-Berlin Rd   Voorhees NJ 08043
Ph: 856-782-3990 ▪ Fx: 856-782-3775

American Academy of Insurance Medicine www.aaimedicine.org
174 Colonade Rd   Ottawa ON K2E7J5
Ph: 613-226-9601 ▪ Fx: 613-721-3581

American Academy of Kinesiology & Physical Education www.aakpe.org
c/o Human Kinetics Publishers Inc PO Box 5076   Champaign IL 61820
Ph: 217-351-5076 ▪ Fx: 217-351-2674 ▪ TF: 800-747-4457

American Academy for Liberal Education www.aale.org
1710 Rhode Island Ave NW 4th Fl   Washington DC 20036
Ph: 202-452-8611 ▪ Fx: 202-452-8620

American Academy of Matrimonial Lawyers www.aaml.org
150 N Michigan Ave Suite 2040   Chicago IL 60601
Ph: 312-263-6477 ▪ Fx: 312-263-7682

American Academy of Maxillofacial Prosthetics www.maxillofacialprosth.org
Univ of Florida College of Dentistry Dept of Prosthodontics Box 100435   Gainesville FL 32610
Ph: 352-846-2684 ▪ Fx: 352-846-2683

American Academy of Medical Acupuncture www.medicalacupuncture.org
4929 Wilshire Blvd Suite 428   Los Angeles CA 90010
Ph: 323-937-5514 ▪ Fx: 323-937-0959

American Academy of Medical Administrators www.aameda.org
701 Lee St Suite 600   Des Plaines IL 60016
Ph: 847-759-8601 ▪ Fx: 847-759-8602

American Academy of Medical Hypnoanalysts www.aamh.com
1022 Depot Hill Rd   Broomfield CO 80020
Ph: 888-454-9766 ▪ Fx: 303-465-1260

American Academy of Medical Management
6855 Jimmy Carter Blvd Suite 2100   Norcross GA 30071
Ph: 770-734-9904 ▪ Fx: 770-734-9709

American Academy of Ministry www.ministry.org
PO Box 681868   Franklin TN 37068
Ph: 615-599-9889 ▪ Fx: 615-599-8985 ▪ TF: 800-288-9673

American Academy of Neurological & Orthopaedic Surgeons www.aanos.org
2300 S Rancho Dr Suite 202   Las Vegas NV 89102
Ph: 702-388-7390 ▪ Fx: 702-388-7395

American Academy of Neurology www.aan.com
1080 Montreal Ave   Saint Paul MN 55116
Ph: 651-695-2717 ▪ Fx: 651-695-2791 ▪ TF: 800-879-1960

American Academy of Nurse Practitioners www.aanp.org
PO Box 10729   Glendale AZ 85318
Ph: 623-376-9467 ▪ Fx: 623-376-0369

American Academy of Nursing www.nursingworld.org/aan
600 Maryland Ave SW Suite 100 W   Washington DC 20024
Ph: 202-651-7238 ▪ Fx: 202-554-2641

American Academy of Nutrition www.nutritioneducation.com
1204-D Kenesaw Ave   Knoxville TN 37919
Ph: 865-524-8079 ▪ Fx: 865-524-8339 ▪ TF: 800-290-4226

American Academy of Ophthalmology www.aao.org
655 Beach St   San Francisco CA 94120
Ph: 415-561-8500 ▪ Fx: 415-561-8533 ▪ TF: 800-222-3937

American Academy of Ophthalmology PAC
1101 Vermont Ave NW Suite 700   Washington DC 20005
Ph: 202-737-6662 ▪ Fx: 202-737-7061

American Academy of Optometry www.aaopt.org
6110 Executive Blvd Suite 506   Rockville MD 20852
Ph: 301-984-1441 ▪ Fx: 301-984-4737

American Academy of Oral & Maxillofacial Pathology aaomp.org
710 E Ogden Ave Suite 600   Naperville IL 60563
Ph: 888-552-2667 ▪ Fx: 630-369-2488

American Academy of Oral & Maxillofacial Radiology www.aaomr.org
PO Box 1010   Evans GA 30809
Ph: 706-721-2607

American Academy of Oral Medicine www.aaom.org
2910 Lightfoot Dr   Baltimore MD 21209
Ph: 410-602-8585

American Academy of Orofacial Pain www.aaop.org
19 Mantua Rd   Mount Royal NJ 08061
Ph: 856-423-3629 ▪ Fx: 856-423-3420

American Academy of Orthopaedic Surgeons www.aaos.org
6300 N River Rd   Rosemont IL 60018
Ph: 847-823-7186 ▪ Fx: 847-823-8125

American Academy of Orthotists & Prosthetists www.oandp.org
526 King St Suite 201   Alexandria VA 22314
Ph: 703-836-0788 ▪ Fx: 703-836-0737

American Academy of Osteopathy www.academyofosteopathy.org
3500 DePauw Blvd Suite 1080   Indianapolis IN 46268
Ph: 317-879-1881 ▪ Fx: 317-879-0563

American Academy of Otolaryngic Allergy www.aaoaf.org
1900 M St NW Suite 680   Washington DC 20036
Ph: 202-955-5010 ▪ Fx: 202-955-5016

American Academy of Otolaryngology-Head & Neck Surgery www.entnet.org
1 Prince St   Alexandria VA 22314
Ph: 703-836-4444 ▪ Fx: 703-683-5100

American Academy of Pain Management www.aapainmanage.org
13947 Mono Way Suite A   Sonora CA 95370
Ph: 209-533-9744 ▪ Fx: 209-533-9750

American Academy of Pain Medicine www.painmed.org
4700 W Lake Ave   Glenview IL 60025
Ph: 847-375-4731 ▪ Fx: 847-375-6331 ▪ TF: 877-734-8750

American Academy of Pediatric Dentistry www.aapd.org
211 E Chicago Ave Suite 700   Chicago IL 60611
Ph: 312-337-2169 ▪ Fx: 312-337-6329

American Academy of Pediatrics www.aap.org
141 Northwest Point Blvd   Elk Grove Village IL 60007
Ph: 847-434-4000 ▪ Fx: 847-434-8000 ▪ TF: 800-433-9016

American Academy of Periodontology www.perio.org
737 N Michigan Ave Suite 800 Chicago IL 60611
Ph: 312-787-5518 ▪ Fx: 312-787-3670 ▪ TF: 800-282-4867

American Academy of Pharmaceutical Physicians aapp.org
1031 Pemberton Hill Rd Suite 101 Apex NC 27502
Ph: 919-355-1000 ▪ Fx: 919-355-1010

American Academy of Physical Medicine & Rehabilitation www.aapmr.org
1 IBM Plaza Suite 2500 Chicago IL 60611
Ph: 312-464-9700 ▪ Fx: 312-464-0227

American Academy of Physician Assistants www.aapa.org
950 N Washington St Alexandria VA 22314
Ph: 703-836-2272 ▪ Fx: 703-684-1924

American Academy of Physician Assistants PAC www.aapa.org/gandp/pac
950 N Washington St Alexandria VA 22314
Ph: 703-836-2272 ▪ Fx: 703-684-1924

American Academy on Physician & Patient www.physicianpatient.org
1000 Executive Pkwy Suite 220 Saint Louis MO 63141
Ph: 314-576-5333 ▪ Fx: 314-576-7989

American Academy of Podiatric Practice Management www.aappm.com
707 Turnpike St North Andover MA 01845
Ph: 978-686-6185 ▪ Fx: 978-685-9410

American Academy of Podiatric Sports Medicine www.aapsm.org
PO Box 723 Rockville MD 20848
Ph: 301-845-9887 ▪ Fx: 301-845-9888 ▪ TF: 800-438-3338

American Academy of Political & Social Science www.aapss.org
3814 Walnut St Philadelphia PA 19104
Ph: 215-746-6500 ▪ Fx: 215-898-1202

American Academy of Professional Coders www.aapc.com
309 W 700 South Salt Lake City UT 84101
Ph: 801-236-2200 ▪ Fx: 801-236-2258 ▪ TF: 800-626-2633

American Academy of Psychiatry & the Law www.aapl.org
1 Regency Dr PO Box 30 Bloomfield CT 06002
Ph: 860-242-5450 ▪ Fx: 860-286-0787 ▪ TF: 800-331-1389

American Academy of Psychotherapists www.coe.iup.edu/aap
PO Box 10589 Oakland CA 94610
Ph: 510-268-1786 ▪ Fx: 510-268-1787

American Academy of Religion www.aarweb.org
825 Houston Mill Rd Suite 300 Atlanta GA 30329
Ph: 404-727-3049 ▪ Fx: 404-727-7959

American Academy of Research Historians of Medieval Spain www.uca.edu/aarhms

American Academy of Restorative Dentistry www.restorativeacademy.com
985 Fuller Rd Colorado Springs CO 80920
Ph: 719-633-1060 ▪ Fx: 719-953-7926

American Academy of Safety Education www.veteransofsafety.org
Central Missouri State Univ Humphreys Bldg Warrensburg MO 64093
Ph: 660-543-4281 ▪ Fx: 660-543-4482

American Academy of Sanitarians Inc www.sanitarians.org
720 S Colorado Blvd Suite 960-S Denver CO 80246
Ph: 678-584-4912

American Academy of Sleep Medicine www.aasmnet.org
1 Westbrook Corporate Ctr Suite 920 Westchester IL 60154
Ph: 708-492-0930 ▪ Fx: 708-492-0943

American Academy of Somnology
PO Box 27077 Las Vegas NV 89126
Ph: 702-222-6463 ▪ Fx: 702-384-3264

American Academy of Sports Physicians
17445 Oak Creek Ct Encino CA 91316
Ph: 818-501-4433 ▪ Fx: 818-501-8855

American Academy of State Certified Appraisers
1438 W Main St Ephrata PA 17522
Ph: 717-721-3500 ▪ Fx: 717-721-3515 ▪ TF: 800-640-7601

American Academy of Tropical Medicine
PO Box 24224 Detroit MI 48224
Ph: 313-882-0641 ▪ Fx: 313-882-5110

American Academy of Veterinary & Comparative Toxicology
Murray State Univ Breathitt Veterinary Ctr 715 North Dr PO Box 2000 Hopkinsville KY 42240
Ph: 270-886-3959 ▪ Fx: 270-886-4295

American Academy of Veterinary Pharmacology & Therapeutics www.aavpt.org
621 W Hill St Champaign IL 61820
Ph: 217-359-0661 ▪ Fx: 217-244-1652

American Academy of Wound Management www.aawm.org
1255 23rd St NW Suite 200 Washington DC 20037
Ph: 202-521-0368 ▪ Fx: 202-833-3636

American Accordion Musicological Society
334 S Broadway Pitman NJ 08071
Ph: 856-854-6628

American Accordionists Association www.ameraccord.com
580 Kearny Ave Kearny NJ 07032
Ph: 201-991-2233 ▪ Fx: 201-991-1944

American Accounting Association aaahq.org
5717 Bessie Dr Sarasota FL 34233
Ph: 941-921-7747 ▪ Fx: 941-923-4093

American Accreditation HealthCare Commission Inc www.urac.org
1220 L St NW Suite 400 Washington DC 20005
Ph: 202-216-9010 ▪ Fx: 202-216-9006

American Action Fund for Blind Children & Adults www.actionfund.org
1800 Johnson St Baltimore MD 21230
Ph: 410-659-9314 ▪ Fx: 410-685-5653

American Acupuncture Association
4262 Kissena Blvd Flushing NY 11355
Ph: 718-886-4431 ▪ Fx: 718-463-0808

American Adoption Congress www.americanadoptioncongress.org
PO Box 42730 Washington DC 20015
Ph: 202-483-3399

American Advertising Federation www.aaf.org
1101 Vermont Ave NW Suite 500 Washington DC 20005
Ph: 202-898-0089 ▪ Fx: 202-898-0159 ▪ TF: 800-999-2231

American Agents Alliance www.agentsalliance.com
1768 Arrow Hwy Suite 105 LaVerne CA 91750
Ph: 909-392-0836 ▪ Fx: 909-392-0892 ▪ TF: 866-280-3222

American Aging Association www.americanaging.org
110 Chesley Dr Media PA 19063
Ph: 610-627-2626 ▪ Fx: 610-565-9747

American Agricultural Economics Association www.aaea.org
415 S Duff Ave Suite C Ames IA 50010
Ph: 515-233-3202 ▪ Fx: 515-233-3101

American Agricultural Editors' Association www.ageditors.com
Box 156 New Prague MN 56071
Ph: 952-758-6502 ▪ Fx: 952-758-5813

American Agricultural Law Association www.aglaw-assn.org
415 S Duff Ave Suite C Ames IA 50010
Ph: 515-956-4255 ▪ Fx: 515-233-3101

American Agriculture Movement www.aaminc.org
PO Box 399 Sunray TX 79086
Ph: 806-733-2203 ▪ Fx: 806-733-2965

American Aid Society of German Descendants www.geocities.com/aidsociety/americanaidsociety.html
6540 N Milwaukee Ave Chicago IL 60631
Ph: 773-763-9554

American Airborne Association www.americanairborneassn.com
10301 McKinstry Mill Rd New Windsor MD 21776
Ph: 410-775-7733 ▪ Fx: 410-775-7760 ▪ TF: 888-567-2927

American Airlines PAC
1101 17th St NW Suite 600 Washington DC 20036
Ph: 202-496-5666 ▪ Fx: 202-496-5660

American Alliance for Health Physical Education Recreation & Dance www.aahperd.org
1900 Association Dr Reston VA 20191
Ph: 703-476-3400 ▪ Fx: 703-476-9527 ▪ TF: 800-213-7193

American Alliance for Theatre & Education www.aate.com
7475 Wisconsin Ave Suite 300A Bethesda MD 20814
Ph: 301-951-7977

American Alpine Club www.americanalpineclub.org
710 10th St Suite 100 Golden CO 80401
Ph: 303-384-0110 ▪ Fx: 303-384-0111

American Amateur Baseball Congress www.aabc.us
118-119 Redfield Plaza Marshall MI 49068
Ph: 269-781-2002 ▪ Fx: 269-781-2060

American Amateur Karate Federation www.aakf.org
1930 Wilshire Blvd Suite 1208 Los Angeles CA 90057
Ph: 213-483-8262 ▪ Fx: 213-483-4060

American Amateur Press Association members.aol.com/aapa96
535 Kickerillo Dr Houston TX 77079
Ph: 281-497-8493

American Ambulance Association www.the-aaa.org
8201 Greensboro Dr Suite 300 McLean VA 22102
Ph: 703-610-9018 ▪ Fx: 703-610-9005 ▪ TF: 800-523-4447

American Amputee Foundation www.americanamputee.com
PO Box 250218 Hillcrest Stn Little Rock AR 72225
Ph: 501-666-2523 ▪ Fx: 501-666-8367

American Amusement Machine Association www.coin-op.org
450 E Higgins Rd Suite 201 Elk Grove Village IL 60007
Ph: 847-290-9088 ▪ Fx: 847-290-9121

American Anaplastology Association www.anaplastology.org
PO Box 27440 Seattle WA 98125
Ph: 206-268-0311

American Angora Goat Breeders Association
PO Box 195 Rocksprings TX 78880
Ph: 830-683-4483

American Angus Association www.angus.org
3201 Frederick Ave Saint Joseph MO 64506
Ph: 816-383-5100 ▪ Fx: 816-233-9703 ▪ TF: 800-821-5478

American Animal Hospital Association www.aahanet.org
PO Box 150899 Denver CO 80215
Ph: 303-986-2800 ▪ Fx: 303-986-1700 ▪ TF: 800-252-2242

American Anthropological Association www.aaanet.org
2200 Wilson Blvd Suite 600 Arlington VA 22201
Ph: 703-528-1902 ▪ Fx: 703-528-3546

American Anti-Slavery Group Inc www.iabolish.com
198 Tremont St Suite 421 Boston MA 02116
Ph: 617-426-8161 ▪ Fx: 617-507-8257 ▪ TF: 800-884-0719

American Anti-Vivisection Society www.aavs.org
801 Old York Rd Suite 204 Jenkintown PA 19046
Ph: 215-887-0816 ▪ Fx: 215-887-2088 ▪ TF: 800-723-2287

American Antiquarian Society www.americanantiquarian.org
185 Salisbury St Worcester MA 01609
Ph: 508-755-5221 ▪ Fx: 508-753-3311

American Apitherapy Society www.apitherapy.org
1209 Post Rd Scarsdale NY 10583
Ph: 914-725-7944 ▪ Fx: 914-723-0920

American Apparel & Footwear Association www.appareландfootwear.com
1601 N Kent St Suite 1200 Arlington VA 22209
Ph: 703-524-1864 ▪ Fx: 703-522-6741 ▪ TF: 800-520-2262

American Apparel & Footwear Association PAC
1601 N Kent St Suite 1200 Arlington VA 22209
Ph: 703-524-1864 ▪ Fx: 703-522-6741

American Apparel Producers' Network www.aapnetwork.net
PO Box 720693 Atlanta GA 30358
Ph: 404-843-3171

American-Arab Anti Discrimination Committee www.adc.org
4201 Connecticut Ave NW Suite 300 Washington DC 20008
Ph: 202-244-2990 ▪ Fx: 202-244-3196

American Arbitration Association Inc www.adr.org
1633 Broadway 10th Fl New York NY 10019
Ph: 212-484-4181 ▪ Fx: 212-246-7274 ▪ TF: 800-778-7879

American Archaeology, Society for www.saa.org
900 2nd St NE Suite 12 Washington DC 20002
Ph: 202-789-8200 ▪ Fx: 202-789-0284

American Archeology, Center for
PO Box 366   Kampsville IL 62053
Ph: 618-653-4316 ▪ Fx: 618-653-4232
www.caa-archeology.org

American Architectural Foundation
1799 New York Ave NW   Washington DC 20006
Ph: 202-626-7318 ▪ Fx: 202-626-7420
www.archfoundation.org

American Architectural Manufacturers Association
1827 Walden Office Sq Suite 550   Schaumburg IL 60173
Ph: 847-303-5664 ▪ Fx: 847-303-5774
www.aamanet.org

American Art Pottery Association
17736 Hwy 442   Independence LA 70443
Ph: 985-878-8640
www.amartpot.org

American Art, Smithsonian Archives of
750 9th St NW Suite 2200   Washington DC 20560
Ph: 202-275-2156 ▪ Fx: 202-275-1955
artarchives.si.edu

American Art Therapy Association
1202 Allanson Rd   Mundelein IL 60060
Ph: 847-949-6064 ▪ Fx: 847-566-4580 ▪ TF: 888-290-0878
www.arttherapy.org

American Artists Professional League
47 5th Ave   New York NY 10003
Ph: 212-645-1345

American Arts Alliance
1156 15th St NW Suite 820   Washington DC 20005
Ph: 202-387-8300 ▪ Fx: 202-833-2686
www.americanartsalliance.org

American Assembly
475 Riverside Dr Suite 456   New York NY 10115
Ph: 212-870-3500 ▪ Fx: 212-870-3555
www.columbia.edu/cu/amassembly

American Assembly for Men in Nursing
c/o NY State Nurses Assn 11 Cornell Rd   Latham NY 12110
Ph: 518-782-9400 ▪ Fx: 518-782-9530
www.aamn.org

American Associates Ben-Gurion University of the Negev
1430 Broadway 8th Fl   New York NY 10018
Ph: 212-687-7721 ▪ Fx: 212-302-6443 ▪ TF: 800-962-2248
www.aabgu.org

American Association for Accreditation of Ambulatory Surgery Facilities Inc   5101 Washington St Suite 2F PO Box 9500   Gurnee IL 60031
Ph: 888-545-5222 ▪ Fx: 847-775-1985
www.aaaasf.org

American Association for Active Lifestyles & Fitness
1900 Association Dr   Reston VA 20191
Ph: 703-476-3430 ▪ Fx: 703-476-9527 ▪ TF: 800-213-7193
www.aahperd.org/aaalf

American Association for Adult & Continuing Education
4380 Forbes Blvd   Lanham MD 20706
Ph: 301-918-1913 ▪ Fx: 301-918-1846
www.aaace.org

American Association for the Advancement of Science
1200 New York Ave NW   Washington DC 20005
Ph: 202-326-6400 ▪ Fx: 202-682-0816 ▪ TF: 800-731-4939
www.aaas.org

American Association for the Advancement of Slavic Studies   Harvard Univ 8 Story St 3rd Fl Box 14   Cambridge MA 02138
Ph: 617-495-0677 ▪ Fx: 617-495-0680
www.fas.harvard.edu/~aaass

American Association of Advertising Agencies
405 Lexington Ave 18th Fl   New York NY 10174
Ph: 212-682-2500 ▪ Fx: 212-682-8391
www.aaaa.org

American Association for Aerosol Research
17000 Commerce Pkwy Suite C   Mount Laurel NJ 08054
Ph: 856-439-9080 ▪ Fx: 856-439-0525
www.aaar.org

American Association for Affirmative Action
12100 Sunset Hills Rd Suite 130   Reston VA 20190
Ph: 800-252-8952 ▪ Fx: 703-435-4390
www.affirmativeaction.org

American Association of Airport Executives
601 Madison St Suite 400   Alexandria VA 22314
Ph: 703-824-0500 ▪ Fx: 703-820-1395
www.airportnet.org

American Association of Ambulatory Surgery Centers
PO Box 5271   Johnson City TN 37602
Ph: 423-915-1001 ▪ Fx: 423-282-9712 ▪ TF: 800-237-3768
www.aaasc.org

American Association of Anatomists
9650 Rockville Pike Suite 2408   Bethesda MD 20814
Ph: 301-634-7910 ▪ Fx: 301-634-7965
www.anatomy.org

American Association for Applied Linguistics
PO Box 361806   Birmingham AL 35236
Ph: 205-824-7700 ▪ Fx: 205-823-2760 ▪ TF: 866-821-7700
www.aaal.org

American Association for Artificial Intelligence
445 Burgess Dr Suite 100   Menlo Park CA 94025
Ph: 650-328-3123 ▪ Fx: 650-321-4457
www.aaai.org

American Association of Attorney-Certified Public Accountants
24196 Alicia Pkwy Suite K   Mission Viejo CA 92691
Ph: 949-768-0336 ▪ TF: 888-288-9272
www.attorney-cpa.com

American Association of Automatic Door Manufacturers
1300 Sumner Ave   Cleveland OH 44115
Ph: 216-241-7333 ▪ Fx: 216-241-0105
www.aaadm.com

American Association of Avian Pathologists
953 College Station Rd   Athens GA 30602
Ph: 706-542-5645 ▪ Fx: 706-542-0249
www.aaap.info

American Association of Bank Directors
4701 Sangamore Rd Suite P-15   Bethesda MD 20816
Ph: 301-263-9841 ▪ Fx: 301-229-2443
www.aabd.org

American Association of Bioanalysts
917 Locust St Suite 1100   Saint Louis MO 63101
Ph: 314-241-1445 ▪ Fx: 314-241-1449
www.aab.org

American Association of Blacks in Energy
927 15th St NW Suite 200   Washington DC 20005
Ph: 202-371-9530 ▪ Fx: 202-371-9218 ▪ TF: 800-466-0204
www.aabe.org

American Association of Blood Banks
8101 Glenbrook Rd   Bethesda MD 20814
Ph: 301-907-6977 ▪ Fx: 301-907-6895
www.aabb.org

American Association of Botanical Gardens & Arboreta
100 W 10th St Suite 614   Wilmington DE 19801
Ph: 302-655-7100 ▪ Fx: 302-655-8100
www.aabga.org

American Association of Bovine Practitioners
PO Box 1755   Rome GA 30162
Ph: 706-232-2220 ▪ Fx: 706-232-2232 ▪ TF: 800-269-2227
www.aabp.org

American Association for Budget & Program Analysis
PO Box 1157   Falls Church VA 22041
Ph: 703-941-4300 ▪ Fx: 703-941-1535
www.aabpa.org

American Association of Business Valuation Specialists
PO Box 13089   Tallahassee FL 32317
Ph: 850-878-3134 ▪ Fx: 850-878-1291
www.aabvs.com

American Association for Cancer Research
615 Chestnut St 17th Fl   Philadelphia PA 19106
Ph: 215-440-9300 ▪ Fx: 215-440-9313
www.aacr.org

American Association of Candy Technologists
175 Rock Rd   Glen Rock NJ 07452
Ph: 201-652-2655 ▪ Fx: 201-652-3419
www.aactcandy.org

American Association of Cardiovascular & Pulmonary Rehabilitation
401 N Michigan Ave Suite 2200   Chicago IL 60611
Ph: 312-321-5146 ▪ Fx: 312-527-6635
www.aacvpr.org

American Association for Career Education
2900 Amby Pl   Hermosa Beach CA 90254
Ph: 310-376-7378 ▪ Fx: 310-376-2926

American Association of Cereal Chemists Inc
3340 Pilot Knob Rd   Saint Paul MN 55121
Ph: 651-454-7250 ▪ Fx: 651-454-0766
www.aaccnet.org

American Association of Certified Allergists
85 W Algonquin Rd Suite 550   Arlington Heights IL 60005
Ph: 847-427-8111 ▪ Fx: 847-427-1294

American Association of Children's Residential Centers
2020 Pennsylvania Ave NW Suite 745   Washington DC 20006
Ph: 877-332-2272 ▪ Fx: 877-362-2272
www.aacrc-dc.org

American Association for Chinese Studies
City College-CUNY NAC R4/116   New York NY 10031
Ph: 212-650-6206
www.ccny.cuny.edu/aacs

American Association of Christian Schools
PO Box 1097   Independence MO 64051
Ph: 816-252-9900 ▪ Fx: 816-252-6700
www.aacs.org

American Association for Chronic Fatigue Syndrome
27 N Wacker Dr Suite 416   Chicago IL 60606
Ph: 847-258-7248 ▪ Fx: 847-748-8288
www.aacfs.org

American Association of Classified School Employees
7140 SW Childs Rd   Lake Oswego OR 97035
Ph: 503-620-5663 ▪ Fx: 503-684-4597
www.aacse.org

American Association for Clinical Chemistry Inc
2101 L St NW Suite 202   Washington DC 20037
Ph: 202-857-0717 ▪ Fx: 202-887-5093 ▪ TF: 800-892-1400
www.aacc.org

American Association of Clinical Endocrinologists
1000 Riverside Ave Suite 205   Jacksonville FL 32204
Ph: 904-353-7878 ▪ Fx: 904-353-8185
www.aace.com

American Association of Clinical Urologists Inc
1111 N Plaza Dr Suite 550   Schaumburg IL 60173
Ph: 847-517-1050 ▪ Fx: 847-517-7229
www.aacuweb.org

American Association of Code Enforcement
5310 E Main St Suite 104   Columbus OH 43213
Ph: 614-552-2633 ▪ Fx: 614-868-1177
www.aace1.com

American Association of Colleges of Nursing
1 Dupont Cir NW Suite 530   Washington DC 20036
Ph: 202-463-6930 ▪ Fx: 202-785-8320
www.aacn.nche.edu

American Association of Colleges of Osteopathic Medicine
5550 Friendship Blvd Suite 310   Chevy Chase MD 20815
Ph: 301-968-4100 ▪ Fx: 301-968-4101
www.aacom.org

American Association of Colleges of Pharmacy
1426 Prince St   Alexandria VA 22314
Ph: 703-739-2330 ▪ Fx: 703-836-8982
www.aacp.org

American Association of Colleges of Podiatric Medicine
1350 Piccard Dr Suite 322   Rockville MD 20850
Ph: 301-990-7400 ▪ Fx: 301-990-2807 ▪ TF: 800-922-9266
www.aacpm.org

American Association of Colleges for Teacher Education
1307 New York Ave NW Suite 300   Washington DC 20005
Ph: 202-293-2450 ▪ Fx: 202-457-8095
www.aacte.org

American Association of Collegiate Registrars & Admissions Officers
1 Dupont Cir NW Suite 520   Washington DC 20036
Ph: 202-293-9161 ▪ Fx: 202-872-8857
www.aacrao.org

American Association of Community Colleges
1 Dupont Cir NW Suite 410   Washington DC 20036
Ph: 202-728-0200 ▪ Fx: 202-833-2467
www.aacc.nche.edu

American Association of Community Psychiatrists
PO Box 570218   Dallas TX 75228
Ph: 972-613-0985 ▪ Fx: 972-613-5532
www.wpic.pitt.edu/aacp/

American Association of Community Theatre
8402 BriarWood Cir   Lago Vista TX 78645
Ph: 512-267-0711 ▪ Fx: 512-267-0712 ▪ TF: 866-687-2228
www.aact.org

American Association for Continuity of Care
PO Box 532   Dunedin FL 34697
Ph: 727-738-9653 ▪ Fx: 727-738-8099 ▪ TF: 800-816-1575
www.continuityofcare.com

American Association for Correctional Psychology
897 Oak Park Blvd Suite 124   Pismo Beach CA 93449
Ph: 805-489-0665
www.eaacp.org

American Association of Cosmetology Schools
15825 N 71st St Suite 100   Scottsdale AZ 85254
Ph: 480-281-0431 ▪ Fx: 480-905-0993 ▪ TF: 800-831-1086
www.beautyschools.org/index2.html

American Association of Credit Union Leagues
601 Pennsylvania Ave NW South Bldg Suite 600   Washington DC 20004
Ph: 202-638-5777 ▪ Fx: 202-638-7729
www.cuna.org/league

American Association of Critical-Care Nurses
101 Columbia   Aliso Viejo CA 92656
Ph: 949-362-2000 ▪ Fx: 949-362-2020 ▪ TF: 800-809-2273
www.aacn.org

American Association of Crop Insurers
1 Massachusetts Ave NW Suite 800   Washington DC 20001
Ph: 202-789-4100 ▪ Fx: 202-408-7763
users.erols.com/aaci

American Association of Crop Insurers PAC
1 Massachusetts Ave NW Suite 800   Washington DC 20001
Ph: 202-789-4100 ▪ Fx: 202-408-7763

American Association for Crystal Growth   www.crystalgrowth.org
25 4th St   Somerville NJ 08876
Ph: 908-575-0649 ▪ Fx: 908-575-0794

American Association of Daily Money Managers   www.aadmm.com
PO Box 8857   Gaithersburg MD 20898
Ph: 301-593-5462 ▪ Fx: 301-668-5760

American Association of Dental Editors   www.dentaleditors.org
750 N Lincoln Memorial Dr Suite 422   Milwaukee WI 53202
Ph: 414-272-2759 ▪ Fx: 414-272-2754

American Association of Dental Examiners   www.aadexam.org
211 E Chicago Ave Suite 760   Chicago IL 60611
Ph: 312-440-7464 ▪ Fx: 312-440-3525

American Association for Dental Research   www.iadr.com
1619 Duke St   Alexandria VA 22314
Ph: 703-548-0066 ▪ Fx: 703-548-1883

American Association of Diabetes Educators   www.aadenet.org
100 W Monroe St Suite 400   Chicago IL 60603
Ph: 312-424-2426 ▪ Fx: 312-424-2427 ▪ TF: 800-338-3633

American Association of Directors of Psychiatric Residency Training   www.aadprt.org
Univ of Connecticut Health Ctr Dept of Psychiatry 263
   Farmington Ave LG066   Farmington CT 06030
Ph: 860-679-8112 ▪ Fx: 860-679-1246

American Association of Drugless Practitioners   www.aadp.net
708 Madelaine Dr   Gilmer TX 75644
Ph: 903-843-6401 ▪ TF: 888-764-2237

American Association of Early Childhood Educators
3612 Bent Branch Ct   Falls Church VA 22041
Ph: 703-941-4329

American Association of Electrodiagnostic Medicine   www.aaem.net
421 1st Ave SW Suite 300E   Rochester MN 55902
Ph: 507-288-0100 ▪ Fx: 507-288-1225

American Association of Electronic Voice Phenomena   aaevp.com
PO Box 13111   Reno NV 89507
Ph: 775-329-5980

American Association for Employment in Education   www.aaee.org
3040 Riverside Dr Suite 125   Columbus OH 43221
Ph: 614-485-1111 ▪ Fx: 614-485-9609

American Association of Endodontists   www.aae.org
211 E Chicago Ave Suite 1100   Chicago IL 60611
Ph: 312-266-7255 ▪ Fx: 312-266-9867 ▪ TF: 800-872-3636

American Association of Engineering Societies   www.aaes.org
1828 L St NW Suite 906   Washington DC 20036
Ph: 202-296-2237 ▪ Fx: 202-296-1151 ▪ TF: 888-400-2237

American Association of Equine Practitioners   www.aaep.org
4075 Iron Works Pkwy   Lexington KY 40511
Ph: 859-233-0147 ▪ Fx: 859-233-1968 ▪ TF: 800-443-0177

American Association of Exporters & Importers   www.aaei.org
1200 G St NW Suite 800   Washington DC 20005
Ph: 202-661-2181 ▪ Fx: 202-661-2185

American Association of Eye & Ear Hospitals   www.aaeeh.org
1100 Wilson Blvd Suite 1200   Arlington VA 22209
Ph: 703-243-8848 ▪ Fx: 703-243-8664

American Association of Family & Consumer Sciences   www.aafcs.org
1555 King St Suite 400   Alexandria VA 22314
Ph: 703-706-4600 ▪ Fx: 703-706-4663 ▪ TF: 800-424-8080

American Association of Feline Practitioners   www.aafponline.org
618 Church St Suite 220   Nashville TN 37219
Ph: 615-259-7788 ▪ Fx: 615-254-7047 ▪ TF: 800-204-3514

American Association of Franchisees & Dealers   www.aafd.org
PO Box 81887   San Diego CA 92138
Ph: 619-209-3775 ▪ Fx: 619-209-3777 ▪ TF: 800-733-9858

American Association for Functional Orthodontics   www.aafo.org
106 S Kent St   Winchester VA 22601
Ph: 540-662-2200 ▪ Fx: 540-665-8910 ▪ TF: 800-441-3850

American Association of Fund-Raising Counsel   www.aafrc.org
10293 N Meridian St Suite 175   Indianapolis IN 46290
Ph: 317-816-1613 ▪ Fx: 317-816-1633 ▪ TF: 800-462-2372

American Association for Geodetic Surveying   www.acsm.net/aags
6 Montgomery Village Ave Suite 403   Gaithersburg MD 20879
Ph: 240-632-9716 ▪ Fx: 240-632-1321

American Association for Geriatric Psychiatry   www.aagpgpa.org
7910 Woodmont Ave Suite 1050   Bethesda MD 20814
Ph: 301-654-7850 ▪ Fx: 301-654-4137

American Association for Gifted Children   www.aagc.org
Duke University PO Box 90270   Durham NC 27708
Ph: 919-783-6152

American Association of Gynecological Laparoscopists   www.aagl.com
13021 E Florence Ave   Santa Fe Springs CA 90670
Ph: 562-946-8774 ▪ Fx: 562-946-0073 ▪ TF: 800-554-2245

American Association for Hand Surgery   www.handsurgery.org
20 N Michigan Ave Suite 700   Chicago IL 60602
Ph: 312-236-3307 ▪ Fx: 312-782-0553

American Association of Handwriting Analysts   www.handwriting.org/aaha
W8871 Gossfield Ln   Beaver Dam WI 53916
Ph: 920-887-2642 ▪ Fx: 920-887-3101

American Association for Health Education   www.aahperd.org/aahe
1900 Association Dr   Reston VA 20191
Ph: 703-476-3437 ▪ Fx: 703-476-6638 ▪ TF: 800-213-7193

American Association for Health Freedom   www.healthfreedom.net
9912 Georgetown Pike Suite D-2 PO Box 458   Great Falls VA
   22066
Ph: 703-759-0662 ▪ Fx: 703-759-6711 ▪ TF: 800-230-2762

American Association of Healthcare Administrative Management   www.aaham.org
11240 Waples Mill Rd Suite 200   Fairfax VA 22030
Ph: 703-281-4043 ▪ Fx: 703-359-7562

American Association of Healthcare Consultants   www.aahc.net
5 Revere Dr Suite 200   Northbrook IL 60062
Ph: 847-205-2718 ▪ Fx: 847-350-2241 ▪ TF: 888-350-2242

American Association for Higher Education   www.aahe.org
1 Dupont Cir NW Suite 360   Washington DC 20036
Ph: 202-293-6440 ▪ Fx: 202-293-0073

American Association of Hip & Knee Surgeons
704 N Florence Dr   Park Ridge IL 60068
Ph: 847-698-1200 ▪ Fx: 847-825-9294

American Association for the History of Medicine   www.histmed.org
East Carolina Univ School of Medicine Dept of Medical
   Humanities   Greenville NC 27858
Ph: 252-816-2797 ▪ Fx: 252-816-2319

American Association for the History of Nursing   www.aahn.org
PO Box 175   Lanoka Harbor NJ 08734
Ph: 609-693-7250 ▪ Fx: 609-693-1037

American Association for Homecare   www.aahomecare.org
625 Slaters Ln Suite 200   Alexandria VA 22314
Ph: 703-836-6263 ▪ Fx: 703-836-6730

American Association of Homes & Services for the Aging   www2.aahsa.org
2519 Connecticut Ave NW   Washington DC 20008
Ph: 202-783-2242 ▪ Fx: 202-783-2255 ▪ TF: 800-508-9442

American Association of Hospital Dentists   scdonline.org/AAHD_Index.htm
211 E Chicago Ave Suite 740   Chicago IL 60611
Ph: 312-440-2660 ▪ Fx: 312-440-2824

American Association of Housing Educators
Illinois State Univ Dept of Family & Consumer Sciences CB
   5060   Normal IL 61790
Ph: 309-438-5802 ▪ Fx: 309-438-5307

American Association of Immunologists   www.aai.org
9650 Rockville Pike   Bethesda MD 20814
Ph: 301-634-7178 ▪ Fx: 301-571-1816

American Association for the Improvement of Boxing   www.aaib.org
86 Fletcher Ave   Mount Vernon NY 10552
Ph: 914-664-4571 ▪ Fx: 914-664-3164

American Association of Independent News Distributors   www.aaind.org
900 Fox Valley Dr Suite 204   Longwood FL 32779
Ph: 407-774-9794 ▪ Fx: 407-774-6751

American Association of Individual Investors   www.aaii.com
625 N Michigan Ave   Chicago IL 60611
Ph: 312-280-0170 ▪ Fx: 312-280-9883 ▪ TF: 800-428-2244

American Association of Industrial Management   www.aaimnmta.com
293 Bridge St Stearns Bldg Suite 206   Springfield MA 01103
Ph: 413-737-8766 ▪ Fx: 413-737-9724 ▪ TF: 888-698-1968

American Association of Industrial Veterinarians
PO Box 488   Oskaloosa KS 66066
Ph: 785-863-2389 ▪ Fx: 785-863-3141

American Association of Insurance Management Consultants   www.aaimco.com
3925 Fenn Rd   Medina OH 44256
Ph: 330-725-8946 ▪ Fx: 330-723-6270

American Association of Insurance Services   www.aais.org
1745 S Naperville Rd   Wheaton IL 60187
Ph: 630-681-8347 ▪ Fx: 630-681-8356 ▪ TF: 800-564-2247

American Association of Integrated Healthcare Delivery Systems Inc   www.aaihds.org
4435 Waterfront Dr Suite 101   Glen Allen VA 23060
Ph: 804-747-5823 ▪ Fx: 804-747-5316

American Association for Klinefelter Syndrome Information & Support   www.aaksis.org
2945 W Farwell Ave   Chicago IL 60645
Ph: 773-761-5298

American Association for Laboratory Accreditation   www.a2la.org
5301 Buckeystown Pike Suite 350   Frederick MD 21704
Ph: 301-644-3248 ▪ Fx: 301-662-2974

American Association for Laboratory Animal Science   www.aalas.org
9190 Crestwyn Hills Dr   Memphis TN 38125
Ph: 901-754-8620 ▪ Fx: 901-753-0046

American Association of Law Libraries   www.aallnet.org
53 W Jackson Blvd Suite 940   Chicago IL 60604
Ph: 312-939-4764 ▪ Fx: 312-431-1097

American Association of Legal Nurse Consultants   www.aalnc.org
401 N Michigan Ave   Chicago IL 60611
Ph: 312-321-5177 ▪ Fx: 312-673-6655 ▪ TF: 877-402-2562

American Association for Leisure & Recreation   www.aahperd.org/aalr
1900 Association Dr   Reston VA 20191
Ph: 703-476-3400 ▪ Fx: 703-476-9527 ▪ TF: 800-213-7193

American Association of Limited Partners
4224 Montgomery Ave Suite 102   Bethesda MD 20814
Ph: 301-652-5066 ▪ Fx: 301-913-9146

American Association of Managed Care Nurses   www.aamcn.org
4435 Waterfront Dr Suite 101   Glen Allen VA 23060
Ph: 804-747-9698 ▪ Fx: 804-747-5316

American Association of Managing General Agents   www.aamga.org
150 S Warner Rd Suite 101   King of Prussia PA 19406
Ph: 610-225-1999 ▪ Fx: 610-225-1996

American Association for Marriage & Family Therapy   www.aamft.org
112 S Alfred St   Alexandria VA 22314
Ph: 703-838-9808 ▪ Fx: 703-838-9805

American Association of Meat Processors   www.aamp.com
PO Box 269   Elizabethtown PA 17022
Ph: 717-367-1168 ▪ Fx: 717-367-9096

American Association of Medical Assistants   www.aama-ntl.org
20 N Wacker Dr Suite 1575   Chicago IL 60606
Ph: 312-899-1500 ▪ Fx: 312-899-1259 ▪ TF: 800-228-2262

American Association of Medical Milk Commissions Inc
1824 N Hillhurst Ave   Los Angeles CA 90027
Ph: 323-664-1977 ▪ Fx: 323-664-0870

American Association of Medical Review Officers   www.aamro.com
PO Box 12873   Research Triangle Park NC 27709
Ph: 919-489-5407 ▪ Fx: 919-490-1010 ▪ TF: 800-489-1839

American Association of Medical Society Executives   www.aamse.org
611 E Wells St   Milwaukee WI 53202
Ph: 414-221-9275 ▪ Fx: 414-276-3349

American Association for Medical Transcription   www.aamt.org
100 Sycamore Ave   Modesto CA 95354
Ph: 209-527-9620 ▪ Fx: 209-527-9633 ▪ TF: 800-982-2182

American Association of Mental Health Professionals in Corrections
PO Box 160208   Sacramento CA 95816
Ph: 916-323-8305 ▪ Fx: 916-649-1070

American Association on Mental Retardation   www.aamr.org
444 N Capitol St NW Suite 846   Washington DC 20001
Ph: 202-387-1968 ▪ Fx: 202-387-2193 ▪ TF: 800-424-3688

American Association of Motor Vehicle Administrators   www.aamva.org
4301 Wilson Blvd Suite 400   Arlington VA 22203
Ph: 703-522-4200 ▪ Fx: 703-522-1553 ▪ TF: 800-515-8881

American Association for Museum Volunteers   www.aamv.org
1575 'I' St NW Suite 400   Washington DC 20005
Ph: 202-289-1818 ▪ Fx: 202-289-6578

American Association of Museums   www.aam-us.org
1575 'I' St NW Suite 400   Washington DC 20005
Ph: 202-289-1818 ▪ Fx: 202-289-6578

American Association of Naturopathic Physicians   www.naturopathic.org
3201 New Mexico Ave NW Suite 350   Washington DC 20016
Ph: 202-895-1392 ▪ Fx: 202-274-1992 ▪ TF: 866-538-2267

American Association of Neurological Surgeons   www.aans.org
5550 Meadowbrook Dr   Rolling Meadows IL 60068
Ph: 847-378-0500 ▪ Fx: 847-378-0600 ▪ TF: 888-566-2267

American Association of Neuropathologists   www.aanp-jnen.com
2095 Adelbert Rd   Cleveland OH 44106
Ph: 216-368-2488 ▪ Fx: 216-368-8964

American Association of Neuroscience Nurses   www.aann.org
4700 W Lake Ave   Glenview IL 60025
Ph: 847-375-4733 ▪ Fx: 877-734-8677 ▪ TF: 888-557-2266

American Association for Nude Recreation   www.aanr.com
1703 N Main St Suite E   Kissimmee FL 34744
Ph: 407-933-2064

American Association of Nurse Anesthetists   www.aana.com
222 S Prospect Ave   Park Ridge IL 60068
Ph: 847-692-7050 ▪ Fx: 847-692-6968

American Association of Nurse Anesthetists PAC
412 1st St SE Suite 12   Washington DC 20003
Ph: 202-484-8400 ▪ Fx: 202-484-8408

American Association of Nurse Attorneys   www.taana.org
7794 Grow Dr   Pensacola FL 32514
Ph: 850-474-3646 ▪ Fx: 850-484-8762 ▪ TF: 877-538-2262

American Association of Nutritional Consultants   www.aanc.net
400 Oak Hill Dr   Winona Lake IN 46590
Ph: 574-269-6165 ▪ Fx: 574-269-4060 ▪ TF: 888-828-2262

American Association of Occupational Health Nurses   www.aaohn.org
2920 Brandywine Rd Suite 100   Atlanta GA 30341
Ph: 770-455-7757 ▪ Fx: 770-455-7271 ▪ TF: 888-646-4631

American Association of Office Nurses   www.aaon.org
109 Kinderkamack Rd   Montvale NJ 07645
Ph: 201-391-2600 ▪ Fx: 201-573-8543 ▪ TF: 800-457-7504

American Association of Oral & Maxillofacial Surgeons   www.aaoms.org
9700 W Bryn Mawr Ave   Rosemont IL 60018
Ph: 847-678-6200 ▪ Fx: 847-678-6286 ▪ TF: 800-822-6637

American Association of Oriental Medicine   www.aaom.org
5530 Wisconsin Ave Suite 1210   Chevy Chase MD 20815
Ph: 301-941-1064 ▪ Fx: 301-986-9313 ▪ TF: 888-500-7999

American Association of Orthodontists   www.aaomembers.org
401 N Lindbergh Blvd   Saint Louis MO 63141
Ph: 314-993-1700 ▪ Fx: 314-997-1745 ▪ TF: 800-424-2841

American Association of Orthodontists PAC
401 N Lindbergh Blvd   Saint Louis MO 63141
Ph: 314-993-1700 ▪ Fx: 314-997-1745 ▪ TF: 800-424-2841

American Association of Orthopaedic Medicine   www.aaomed.org
PO Box 4997   Buena Vista CO 81211
Ph: 719-475-0032 ▪ Fx: 719-395-5615 ▪ TF: 800-922-2063

American Association of Owners & Breeders of Peruvian   www.aaobpph.org
Paso Horses   PO Box 476   Wilton CA 95693
Ph: 916-687-6232 ▪ Fx: 916-687-6691

American Association for Paralegal Educators   www.aafpe.org
407 Wekiva Springs Rd Suite 241   Longwood FL 32779
Ph: 407-834-6688 ▪ Fx: 407-834-4747

American Association of Pastoral Counselors   www.aapc.org
9504-A Lee Hwy   Fairfax VA 22031
Ph: 703-385-6967 ▪ Fx: 703-352-7725

American Association of Pathologists' Assistants   www.pathologistsassistants.org
1711 W County Rd B   Roseville MN 55113
Ph: 651-697-9264 ▪ Fx: 651-635-0307 ▪ TF: 800-532-2272

American Association for Pediatric Ophthalmology & Strabismus   www.aapos.org
PO Box 193832   San Francisco CA 94119
Ph: 415-561-8505 ▪ Fx: 415-561-8531

American Association of People with Disabilities   www.aapd-dc.org
1629 K St NW Suite 503   Washington DC 20006
Ph: 202-457-0046 ▪ Fx: 202-457-0473 ▪ TF: 800-840-8844

American Association of Petroleum Geologists   www.aapg.org
1444 S Boulder Ave   Tulsa OK 74119
Ph: 918-584-2555 ▪ Fx: 918-560-2694 ▪ TF: 800-364-2274

American Association of Pharmaceutical Scientists   www.aaps.org
2107 Wilson Blvd Suite 700   Arlington VA 22201
Ph: 703-243-2800 ▪ Fx: 703-243-9650

American Association of Physical Anthropologists   www.physanth.org
Univ of California Dept of Anthropology   Santa Barbara CA 93101
Ph: 805-685-8424

American Association of Physician Specialists Inc   www.aapsga.org
2296 Henderson Mill Rd Suite 206   Atlanta GA 30345
Ph: 770-939-8555 ▪ Fx: 770-939-8559 ▪ TF: 800-447-9397

American Association of Physicists in Medicine   www.aapm.org
1 Physics Ellipse   College Park MD 20740
Ph: 301-209-3350 ▪ Fx: 301-209-0862

American Association of Physics Teachers   www.aapt.org
1 Physics Ellipse   College Park MD 20740
Ph: 301-209-3300 ▪ Fx: 301-209-0845

American Association of Plastic Surgeons   www.aaps1921.org
4900B S 31st St   Arlington VA 22206
Ph: 703-820-7400 ▪ Fx: 703-931-4520

American Association of Podiatric Physicians & Surgeons
1328 Southern Ave SE Suite 200   Washington DC 20032
Ph: 202-562-2777 ▪ Fx: 202-562-5351

American Association of Poison Control Centers   www.aapcc.org
3201 New Mexico Ave Suite 330   Washington DC 20016
Ph: 202-362-7217 ▪ TF: 800-222-1222

American Association of Police Polygraphists   www.wordnet.net/aapp/
18160 Cottonwood Rd Suite 253   Sunriver OR 97707
Ph: 541-598-7332 ▪ Fx: 541-593-1021 ▪ TF: 888-743-5479

American Association of Political Consultants   www.theaapc.org
600 Pennsylvania Ave SE Suite 330   Washington DC 20003
Ph: 202-544-9815 ▪ Fx: 202-544-9816

American Association of Port Authorities   www.aapa-ports.org
1010 Duke St   Alexandria VA 22314
Ph: 703-684-5700 ▪ Fx: 703-684-6321

American Association of Preferred Provider Organizations   www.aappo.org
PO Box 429   Jeffersonville IN 47131
Ph: 812-246-4376 ▪ Fx: 812-246-4630

American Association of Premium Incentive Travel Suppliers &   www.traveltran.com
Agents   PO Box 35189   Chicago IL 60707
Ph: 708-453-0080 ▪ Fx: 708-453-0083

American Association of Private Railroad Car Owners Inc   www.aaprco.com
630-B Constitution Ave NE   Washington DC 20002
Ph: 202-547-5696 ▪ Fx: 202-547-5623

American Association of Professional Landmen   www.landman.org
4100 Fossil Creek Blvd   Fort Worth TX 76137
Ph: 817-847-7700 ▪ Fx: 817-847-7704 ▪ TF: 888-566-2275

American Association for Public Opinion Research   www.aapor.org
PO Box 14263   Lenexa KS 66285
Ph: 913-310-0118 ▪ Fx: 913-599-5340

American Association of Radon Scientists & Technologists   www.aarst.org
2502 S 5th Ave   Lebanon PA 17042
Ph: 717-949-3198 ▪ Fx: 717-949-3192 ▪ TF: 866-772-2778

American Association of Railroad Superintendents   www.supt.org
PO Box 456   Tinley Park IL 60477
Ph: 708-342-0210 ▪ Fx: 708-342-0257

American Association for Respiratory Care   www.aarc.org
11030 Ables Ln   Dallas TX 75229
Ph: 972-243-2272 ▪ Fx: 972-484-2720

American Association of Retired Persons   www.aarp.org
601 'E' St NW   Washington DC 20049
Ph: 202-434-2277 ▪ Fx: 202-434-2588 ▪ TF: 800-424-3410

American Association of Retirement Communities   www.the-aarc.org
700 Pelham Rd N   Jacksonville AL 36265
Ph: 256-782-5700 ▪ Fx: 256-782-5179

American Association of School Administrators   www.aasa.org
801 N Quincy St Suite 700   Arlington VA 22203
Ph: 703-528-0700 ▪ Fx: 703-841-1543 ▪ TF: 800-771-1162

American Association of School Librarians   www.ala.org/aasl
50 E Huron St   Chicago IL 60611
Ph: 312-280-4386 ▪ Fx: 312-664-7459 ▪ TF: 800-545-2433

American Association of Small Ruminant Practitioners   www.aasrp.org
1910 Lyda Ave Suite 200   Bowling Green KY 42104
Ph: 270-793-0781 ▪ Fx: 270-782-0188

American Association of Snowboard Instructors   www.aasi.org
133 S Van Gordon St Suite 101   Lakewood CO 80228
Ph: 303-987-9390 ▪ Fx: 800-222-4754

American Association of Spinal Cord Injury Psychologists &   www.aascipsw.org
Social Workers   75-20 Astoria Blvd   Jackson Heights NY 11370
Ph: 718-803-3782 ▪ Fx: 718-803-0414

American Association of State Climatologists   www.ncdc.noaa.gov/oa/climate/aasc.html

American Association of State Colleges & Universities   www.aascu.org
1307 New York Ave NW 5th Fl   Washington DC 20005
Ph: 202-293-7070 ▪ Fx: 202-296-5819

American Association of State Counseling Boards   www.aascb.org
3 Terrace Way Suite A   Greensboro NC 27403
Ph: 336-547-0914 ▪ Fx: 336-547-0017

American Association of State Highway & Transportation Officials   www.aashto.org
444 N Capitol St NW Suite 249   Washington DC 20001
Ph: 202-624-5800 ▪ Fx: 202-624-5806

American Association for State & Local History   www.aaslh.org
1717 Church St   Nashville TN 37203
Ph: 615-320-3203 ▪ Fx: 615-327-9013

American Association of Stratigraphic Palynologists Inc   www.palynology.org
600 N Dairy Ashford PO Box 2197   Houston TX 77252
Ph: 281-293-3189 ▪ Fx: 281-293-3833

American Association for the Study of Liver Diseases   www.aasld.org
1729 King St Suite 200   Alexandria VA 22314
Ph: 703-299-9766 ▪ Fx: 703-299-9622

American Association of Suicidology   www.suicidology.org
4201 Connecticut Ave NW Suite 408   Washington DC 20008
Ph: 202-237-2280 ▪ Fx: 202-237-2282

American Association of Sunday & Feature Editors   www.aasfe.org
Univ of Maryland Merrill College of Journalism 1117 Journalism Bldg   College Park MD 20742
Ph: 301-314-2631 ▪ Fx: 301-314-9166

American Association for the Surgery of Trauma   www.aast.org
Presbyterian Hospital Dept of Surgery 200 Lothrop St MS-F1264   Pittsburgh PA 15213
Ph: 412-647-0635 ▪ Fx: 412-647-1448

American Association of Surgical Physician Assistants   www.aaspa.com
PO Box 867   Bernardsville NJ 07924
Ph: 732-560-8378 ▪ Fx: 732-805-9582 ▪ TF: 888-882-2772

American Association of Swine Veterinarians   www.aasv.org
902 1st Ave   Perry IA 50220
Ph: 515-465-5255 ▪ Fx: 515-465-3832

American Association of Teachers of Arabic — www.wm.edu/aata
College of William & Mary PO Box 8795   Williamsburg VA 23187
Ph: 757-221-3145 ▪ Fx: 757-221-3637

American Association of Teachers of Esperanto
5140 San Lorenzo Dr   Santa Barbara CA 93111
Ph: 805-967-5241

American Association of Teachers of French — www.frenchteachers.org
Southern Illinois Univ MC 4510   Carbondale IL 62901
Ph: 618-453-5731 ▪ Fx: 618-453-5733

American Association of Teachers of German — www.aatg.org
112 Haddontowne Ct Suite 104   Cherry Hill NJ 08034
Ph: 856-795-5553 ▪ Fx: 856-795-9398

American Association of Teachers of Italian — www.italianstudies.org/aati
Univ of Wisconsin Dept of French & Italian 618 Van Hise Hall 1220 Linden Dr   Madison WI 53706
Ph: 608-262-3941 ▪ Fx: 608-265-3892

American Association of Teachers of Korean — www.fsu.edu/~aatk
Florida State Univ Dept of Modern Languages & Linguistics   Tallahassee FL 32306
Ph: 850-644-3728 ▪ Fx: 850-644-0524

American Association of Teachers of Slavic & East European Languages — www.aatseel.org
PO Box 7039   Berkeley CA 94707
Ph: 510-526-6614

American Association of Teachers of Spanish & Portuguese — www.aatsp.org
423 Exton Commons   Exton PA 19341
Ph: 610-363-7005 ▪ Fx: 610-363-7116

American Association of Teachers of Turkic Languages — www.princeton.edu/~ehgilson/aatt.html
Princeton Univ Near Eastern Studies 110 Jones Hall   Princeton NJ 08544
Ph: 609-258-1435 ▪ Fx: 609-258-1242

American Association of Textile Chemists & Colorists — www.aatcc.org
1 Davis Dr PO Box 12215   Research Triangle Park NC 27709
Ph: 919-549-8141 ▪ Fx: 919-549-8933

American Association for Thoracic Surgery — www.aats.org
900 Cummings Ctr Suite 221-U   Beverly MA 01915
Ph: 978-927-8330 ▪ Fx: 978-524-8890

American Association of Tissue Banks — www.aatb.org
1350 Beverly Rd Suite 220-A   McLean VA 22101
Ph: 703-827-9582 ▪ Fx: 703-356-2198

American Association of University Professors — www.aaup.org
1012 14th St NW Suite 500   Washington DC 20005
Ph: 202-737-5900 ▪ Fx: 202-737-5526 ▪ TF: 800-424-2973

American Association of University Women — www.aauw.org
1111 16th St NW   Washington DC 20036
Ph: 202-785-7700 ▪ Fx: 202-872-1425 ▪ TF: 800-326-2289

American Association of Variable Star Observers — www.aavso.org
25 Birch St   Cambridge MA 02138
Ph: 617-354-0484 ▪ Fx: 617-354-0665 ▪ TF: 800-223-0138

American Association of Veterinary Clinicians — www.craiggroup.com/aavc.htm
37 W Broad St Suite 480   Columbus OH 43215
Ph: 614-358-0417 ▪ Fx: 614-241-2215

American Association of Veterinary Immunologists — www.cvm.missouri.edu/aavi

American Association of Veterinary Parasitologists — www.aavp.org
2001 W Main St MS GL52 PO Box 708   Greenfield IN 46140
Ph: 317-277-4439 ▪ Fx: 317-651-4532

American Association of Veterinary State Boards — www.aavsb.org
4106 Central St   Kansas City MO 64111
Ph: 816-931-1504 ▪ Fx: 816-931-1604 ▪ TF: 877-698-8482

American Association for Vocational Instructional Materials — www.aavim.com
220 Smithonia Rd   Winterville GA 30683
Ph: 706-742-5355 ▪ Fx: 706-742-7005 ▪ TF: 800-228-4689

American Association of Women — www.amwomen.org
337 Washington Blvd Suite 1   Marina del Ray CA 90292
Ph: 310-822-4449 ▪ Fx: 310-822-4577 ▪ TF: 800-867-7777

American Association for Women in Community Colleges — www.pc.maricopa.edu/aawcc
1202 W Thomas Rd   Phoenix AZ 85013
Ph: 602-285-7449 ▪ Fx: 602-285-7832

American Association of Women Dentists — www.womendentists.org
330 S Wells Suite 1110   Chicago IL 60606
Ph: 312-913-9327 ▪ Fx: 312-461-0238 ▪ TF: 800-920-2293

American Association for Women Podiatrists Inc — www.aawpinc.com
PO Box 593   Pleasanton CA 94566
Ph: 925-785-8285 ▪ Fx: 925-426-5617

American Association for Women Radiologists — www.aawr.org
4550 Post Oak Pl Suite 342   Houston TX 77027
Ph: 713-623-8335 ▪ Fx: 713-960-0488

American Association of Woodturners — woodturner.org
3499 Lexington Ave N Suite 103   Shoreview MN 55126
Ph: 651-484-9094 ▪ Fx: 651-484-1724

American Association of Working People — www.aawp.org
4435 Waterfront Dr Suite 101   Glen Allen VA 23058
Ph: 804-527-1905 ▪ Fx: 804-747-5316 ▪ TF: 800-722-0376

American Association of Zoo Keepers — www.aazk.org
3601 SW 29th St Suite 133   Topeka KS 66614
Ph: 785-273-9149 ▪ Fx: 785-273-1980 ▪ TF: 800-242-4519

American Association of Zoo Veterinarians — www.aazv.org
6 N Pennell Rd   Media PA 19063
Ph: 610-892-4812 ▪ Fx: 610-892-4813

American Association for Zoological Nomenclature — www.iczn.org/aazn.htm
c/o Smithsonian Institution Dept of Zoology MRC 159   Washington DC 20013
Ph: 202-633-9786 ▪ Fx: 202-357-2986

American Astronautical Society — www.astronautical.org
6352 Rolling Mill Pl Suite 102   Springfield VA 22152
Ph: 703-866-0020 ▪ Fx: 703-866-3526

American Astronomical Society — www.aas.org
2000 Florida Ave NW Suite 400   Washington DC 20009
Ph: 202-328-2010 ▪ Fx: 202-234-2560

American Atheists — www.atheists.org
PO Box 5733   Parsippany NJ 07054
Ph: 908-276-7300 ▪ Fx: 908-276-7402

American Auditory Society — www.amauditorysoc.org
352 Sundial Ridge Cir   Dammeron Valley UT 84783
Ph: 435-574-0062 ▪ Fx: 435-574-0063

American Australian Association — www.americanaustralian.org
599 Lexington Ave 18th Fl   New York NY 10022
Ph: 212-338-6860 ▪ Fx: 212-338-6864

American-Austrian Society — www.geocities.com/americanaustriansociety
6630-D Eli Whitney Dr   Columbia MD 21046
Ph: 443-362-6422

American Auto Racing Writers & Broadcasters Association Inc — www.aarwba.org
922 N Pass Ave   Burbank CA 91505
Ph: 818-842-7005 ▪ Fx: 818-842-7020

American Autoimmune Related Disease Association — www.aarda.org
22100 Gratiot Ave   East Detroit MI 48021
Ph: 586-776-3900 ▪ Fx: 586-776-3903

American Automatic Control Council — www.a2c2.org
Wright State Univ Dept of Electrical Engineering 3640 Col Glenn Hwy   Dayton OH 45435
Ph: 937-775-5062 ▪ Fx: 937-775-3936

American Automobile Association — www.aaa.com
1000 AAA Dr Box 28   Heathrow FL 32746
Ph: 407-444-4240 ▪ Fx: 407-444-4247

American Automotive Leasing Association — www.aalafleet.com
675 N Washington St Suite 410   Alexandria VA 22314
Ph: 703-548-0777 ▪ Fx: 703-236-1949

American Bail Coalition — www.americanbailcoalition.com
1725 DeSales St NW Suite 800   Washington DC 20036
Ph: 202-659-6547 ▪ Fx: 202-296-8702 ▪ TF: 800-375-8390

American Bakers Association — www.americanbakers.org
1350 'I' St NW Suite 1290   Washington DC 20005
Ph: 202-789-0300 ▪ Fx: 202-898-1164

American Bakers Association PAC
1350 'I' St NW Suite 1290   Washington DC 20005
Ph: 202-789-0300 ▪ Fx: 202-898-1164

American Ballet Competition — www.dancecelebration.org
2000 Hamilton St Suite C200   Philadelphia PA 19130
Ph: 215-636-9000 ▪ Fx: 215-564-4206 ▪ TF: 880-052-3096

American Bamboo Society — www.americanbamboo.org

American Bandmasters Association — www.americanbandmasters.org
2221 Morgan Dr   Norman OK 73069
Ph: 405-321-3373 ▪ Fx: 405-321-4117

American Banjo Fraternity — www.abfbanjo.org
636 Pelis Rd   Newark NY 14513
Ph: 315-331-6717

American Bankers Association — www.aba.com
1120 Connecticut Ave NW   Washington DC 20036
Ph: 202-663-5000 ▪ Fx: 202-828-5045 ▪ TF: 800-226-5377

American Bankers Association PAC
1120 Connecticut Ave NW   Washington DC 20036
Ph: 202-663-5113 ▪ Fx: 202-663-7544

American Bankruptcy Institute — www.abiworld.org
44 Canal Center Plaza Suite 404   Alexandria VA 22314
Ph: 703-739-0800 ▪ Fx: 703-739-1060

American Bantam Association — www.the-coop.org/aba
PO Box 127   Augusta NJ 07822
Ph: 201-383-6944

American Baptist Association — www.abaptist.org
4605 N State Line   Texarkana TX 75503
Ph: 903-792-2783 ▪ Fx: 903-792-8128 ▪ TF: 800-264-2482

American Baptist Churches USA — www.abc-usa.org
PO Box 851   Valley Forge PA 19482
Ph: 610-768-2000 ▪ Fx: 610-768-2275 ▪ TF: 800-222-3872

American Baptist Historical Society — www.abc-usa.org/abhs
PO Box 851   Valley Forge PA 19482
Ph: 610-768-2269 ▪ Fx: 610-768-2266

American Baptist Homes & Hospitals Association — www.nationalministries.org/mission/abhha
PO Box 851   Valley Forge PA 19482
Ph: 800-222-3872 ▪ Fx: 610-768-2453

American Baptist International Ministries — www.internationalministries.org
PO Box 851   Valley Forge PA 19482
Ph: 610-768-2000 ▪ Fx: 610-768-2088 ▪ TF: 800-222-3872

American Baptist Women in Ministry — www.abwim.org
PO Box 851   Valley Forge PA 19482
Ph: 610-768-2000 ▪ Fx: 610-768-2275 ▪ TF: 800-222-3872

American Baptist Women's Ministries — www.abwministries.org
PO Box 851   Valley Forge PA 19482
Ph: 610-768-2000 ▪ Fx: 610-768-2275 ▪ TF: 800-222-3872

American Bar Association — www.abanet.org
750 N Lake Shore Dr   Chicago IL 60611
Ph: 312-988-5000 ▪ Fx: 312-988-6281 ▪ TF: 800-285-2221

American Bar Association Center for Professional Responsibility — www.abanet.org/cpr
541 N Fairbanks Ct 14th Fl   Chicago IL 60611
Ph: 312-988-5522 ▪ Fx: 312-988-5491

American Bar Foundation — www.abf-sociolegal.org
750 N Lake Shore Dr   Chicago IL 60611
Ph: 312-988-6500 ▪ Fx: 312-988-6579

American Bar Foundation, Fellows of the — fellows.abfn.org
750 N Lake Shore Dr   Chicago IL 60611
Ph: 312-988-6500 ▪ Fx: 312-988-6611

American Barefoot Club — barefoot.org
1251 Holy Cow Rd   Polk City FL 33868
Ph: 941-324-4141

American Bartenders' Association — www.americanbartenders.org
PO Box D   Plant City FL 33566
Ph: 800-935-3232 ▪ Fx: 813-752-2768

American Baseball Coaches Association www.abca.org
108 S University Ave Suite 3   Mount Pleasant MI 48858
Ph: 989-775-3300 ▪ Fx: 989-775-3600

American Baseball Foundation www.americanbaseball.org
1313 13th St S   Birmingham AL 35205
Ph: 205-558-4235 ▪ Fx: 205-918-0800

American Bashkir Curly Registry www.abcregistry.org
PO Box 151029   Ely NV 89315
Ph: 775-289-4999 ▪ Fx: 775-289-8579

American Bearing Manufacturers Association www.abma-dc.org
2025 M St NW Suite 800   Washington DC 20036
Ph: 202-367-1155 ▪ Fx: 202-367-2155

American Beauty Association www.abbies.org
15825 N 71st St   Scottsdale AZ 85254
Ph: 800-468-2274

American Beefalo World Registry www.abwr.org
2225 Old Stage Rd   Dillon MT 59725
Ph: 406-683-6564

American Beekeeping Federation www.abfnet.org
PO Box 1337   Jesup GA 31598
Ph: 912-427-4233 ▪ Fx: 912-427-8447

American Beethoven Society www2.sjsu.edu/depts/beethoven/abs/absociety.html
Ira F Brilliant Center for Beethoven Studies San Jose State Univ
1 Washington Sq   San Jose CA 95192
Ph: 408-808-2058 ▪ Fx: 408-808-2060

American Begonia Society www.begonias.org
157 Monument Rd   Rio Dell CA 95562
Ph: 707-764-5407

American Behcet's Disease Association www.behcets.com
PO Box 19952   Amarillo TX 79114
Ph: 800-723-4238

American Belgian Blue Breeders Association www.belgianblue.org
PO Box 154   Hedrick IA 52563
Ph: 641-656-2332 ▪ Fx: 641-653-2332

American Belgian Malinois Club www.breedclub.org/ABMC.htm
21710 Cove Point Farm Rd   Tilghman MD 21671
Ph: 410-886-2232

American Benedictine Academy www.osb.org/aba
Assumption Abbey 418 3rd Ave W   Richardton ND 58652
Ph: 701-974-3315 ▪ Fx: 701-974-3317

American Benefits Council www.appwp.org
1212 New York Ave NW Suite 1250   Washington DC 20005
Ph: 202-289-6700 ▪ Fx: 202-289-4582

American Berkshire Association www.americanberkshire.com
PO Box 2436   West Lafayette IN 47996
Ph: 765-497-3618 ▪ Fx: 765-497-2959

American Beverage Institute www.abionline.org
1775 Pennsylvania Ave NW Suite 1200   Washington DC 20006
Ph: 202-463-7110

American Beverage Licensees www.ablusa.org
5101 River Rd Suite 108   Bethesda MD 20816
Ph: 301-656-1494 ▪ Fx: 301-656-7539 ▪ TF: 800-311-8999

American Bible Society www.americanbible.org
1865 Broadway   New York NY 10023
Ph: 212-408-1200 ▪ Fx: 212-408-1512 ▪ TF: 800-322-4253

American Bicycle Association www.ababmx.com
1645 W Sunrise Blvd   Gilbert AZ 85233
Ph: 480-961-1903 ▪ Fx: 480-961-1842 ▪ TF: 800-886-1269

American Biological Safety Association www.absa.org
1202 Allanson Rd   Mundelein IL 60060
Ph: 847-949-1517 ▪ Fx: 847-566-4580

American Bird Conservancy www.abcbirds.org
4249 Loudoun Ave PO Box 249   The Plains VA 20198
Ph: 540-253-5780 ▪ Fx: 540-253-5782 ▪ TF: 888-247-3624

American Birding Association www.americanbirding.org
PO Box 6599   Colorado Springs CO 80934
Ph: 719-578-9703 ▪ Fx: 719-578-1480

American Bladesmith Society www.americanbladesmith.com
PO Box 1481   Cypress TX 77410
Ph: 281-225-9159 ▪ Fx: 281-225-9163

American Blind Lawyers Association
c/o American Council of the Blind 1155 15th St NW Suite
1004   Washington DC 20005
Ph: 202-467-5081 ▪ Fx: 202-467-5085 ▪ TF: 800-424-8666

American Blonde D'Aquitaine Association www.blondecattle.org
PO Box 470661   Tulsa OK 74147
Ph: 918-610-0842

American Board of Allergy & Immunology www.abai.org
510 Walnut Suite 1701   Philadelphia PA 19106
Ph: 215-592-9466 ▪ Fx: 215-592-9411

American Board of Anesthesiology www.abanes.org
4101 Lake Boone Trail Suite 510   Raleigh NC 27607
Ph: 919-881-2570 ▪ Fx: 919-881-2575

American Board of Bioanalysis www.abbcert.org
917 Locust St Suite 1100   Saint Louis MO 63101
Ph: 314-241-1445 ▪ Fx: 314-241-1449

American Board of Certification www.abcworld.org
44 Canal Center Plaza Suite 404   Alexandria VA 22314
Ph: 703-739-1023 ▪ Fx: 703-739-1060

American Board of Clinical Pharmacology Inc www.abcp.net
PO Box 40278   San Antonio TX 78229
Ph: 210-567-8505 ▪ Fx: 210-567-8500

American Board of Colon & Rectal Surgery www.abcrs.org
20600 Eureka Rd Suite 600   Taylor MI 48180
Ph: 734-282-9400 ▪ Fx: 734-282-9402

American Board of Criminalistics criminalistics.com
PO Box 1123   Wausau WI 54402
Ph: 715-845-3684 ▪ Fx: 715-845-4156

American Board of Dental Public Health www.aaphd.org
892 Overbrook Pl   West Palm Beach FL 33413
Ph: 561-686-2760 ▪ Fx: 561-686-4168

American Board of Dermatology www.abderm.org
Henry Ford Health System 1 Ford Pl   Detroit MI 48202
Ph: 313-874-1088 ▪ Fx: 313-872-3221

American Board of Emergency Medicine www.abem.org
3000 Coolidge Rd   East Lansing MI 48823
Ph: 517-332-4800 ▪ Fx: 517-332-2234

American Board of Endodontics www.aae.org/ABE1.html
211 E Chicago Ave Suite 1100   Chicago IL 60611
Ph: 312-266-7255 ▪ TF: 800-872-3636

American Board of Environmental www.americanboardofenvironmentalmedicine.org
Medicine   65 Wehrle Dr   Buffalo NY 14225
Ph: 716-833-2213 ▪ Fx: 716-833-2244

American Board of Examiners in Pastoral Counseling
13014 N Dale Mabry Hwy Suite 363   Tampa FL 33618
Ph: 813-926-5446

American Board of Examiners of Psychodrama Sociometry &
Group Psychotherapy   PO Box 15572   Washington DC 20003
Ph: 202-483-0514

American Board of Family Practice www.abfp.org
2228 Young Dr   Lexington KY 40505
Ph: 859-269-5626 ▪ Fx: 859-335-7501 ▪ TF: 888-995-5700

American Board of Forensic Anthropology www.csuchico.edu/anth/ABFA
c/o Lucas County Coroner's Office 2595 Arlington Ave   Toledo
OH 43614
Ph: 419-213-3908

American Board of Forensic Psychology Inc www.abfp.com
2815 Eastlake Ave E Suite 220   Seattle WA 98102
Ph: 206-320-0044 ▪ Fx: 206-320-7733

American Board of Funeral Service Education www.abfse.org
38 Florida Ave   Portland ME 04103
Ph: 207-878-6530 ▪ Fx: 207-797-7686

American Board of Genetic Counseling www.abgc.net
9650 Rockville Pike   Bethesda MD 20814
Ph: 301-571-1825 ▪ Fx: 301-634-7320

American Board of Independent Medical Examiners www.abime.org
111 Lions Dr Suite 217   Barrington IL 60010
Ph: 847-277-7902 ▪ Fx: 847-277-7912 ▪ TF: 800-234-3490

American Board of Industrial Hygiene www.abih.org
6015 W St Joseph Hwy Suite 102   Lansing MI 48917
Ph: 517-321-2638 ▪ Fx: 517-321-4624

American Board of Managed Care Nursing www.abmcn.org
4435 Waterfront Dr Suite 101   Glen Allen VA 23060
Ph: 804-527-1905 ▪ Fx: 804-747-5316

American Board of Medical Specialties www.abms.org
1007 Church St Suite 404   Evanston IL 60201
Ph: 847-491-9091 ▪ Fx: 847-328-3596

American Board of Nursing Specialties www.nursingcertification.org
610 Thornhill Ln   Aurora OH 44202
Ph: 330-995-9172 ▪ Fx: 330-995-9743

American Board of Nutrition www.uab.edu/nusc/abn.htm
Univ of Alabama Birmingham Dept of Nutrition Sciences 1675
University Blvd WEBB 232   Birmingham AL 35194
Ph: 205-975-5564 ▪ Fx: 205-934-7049

American Board of Obstetrics & Gynecology www.abog.org
2915 Vine St   Dallas TX 75204
Ph: 214-871-1619 ▪ Fx: 214-871-1943

American Board of Opticianry www.abo.org
6506 Loisdale Rd Suite 209   Springfield VA 22150
Ph: 703-719-5800 ▪ Fx: 703-719-9144 ▪ TF: 800-296-1379

American Board of Oral & Maxillofacial Surgery www.aboms.org
625 N Michigan Ave Suite 1820   Chicago IL 60611
Ph: 312-642-0070 ▪ Fx: 312-642-8584

American Board of Orthodontics www.americanboardortho.com
401 N Lindbergh Blvd Suite 308   Saint Louis MO 63141
Ph: 314-432-6130 ▪ Fx: 314-432-8170

American Board of Orthopaedic Surgery www.abos.org
400 Silver Cedar Ct   Chapel Hill NC 27514
Ph: 919-929-7103 ▪ Fx: 919-942-8988

American Board of Otolaryngology www.aboto.org
3050 Post Oak Blvd Suite 1700   Houston TX 77056
Ph: 713-850-0399 ▪ Fx: 713-850-1104

American Board of Pathology www.abpath.org
PO Box 25915   Tampa FL 33622
Ph: 813-286-2444 ▪ Fx: 813-289-5279

American Board of Pediatric Dentistry www.abpd.org
325 E Washington St Suite 101   Iowa City IA 52240
Ph: 319-341-9499

American Board of Pediatrics www.abp.org
111 Silver Cedar Ct   Chapel Hill NC 27514
Ph: 919-929-0461 ▪ Fx: 919-929-9255

American Board of Periodontology www.perio.org/amboard/amboard.html
737 N Michigan Ave Suite 800   Chicago IL 60611
Ph: 312-787-5518 ▪ Fx: 312-787-3670

American Board of Physical Medicine & Rehabilitation www.abpmr.org
3015 Allegro Park Ln SW   Rochester MN 55902
Ph: 507-282-1776 ▪ Fx: 507-282-9242

American Board of Plastic Surgery Inc www.abplsurg.org
1635 Market St 7 Penn Ctr Suite 400   Philadelphia PA 19103
Ph: 215-587-9322 ▪ Fx: 215-587-9622

American Board of Podiatric Orthopedics & Primary Podiatric www.abpoppm.org
Medicine   22910 Crenshaw Blvd Suite B   Torrance CA 90505
Ph: 310-891-0100 ▪ Fx: 310-891-0500

American Board of Preventive Medicine www.abprevmed.org
330 S Wells St Suite 1018   Chicago IL 60606
Ph: 312-939-2276 ▪ Fx: 312-939-2218

American Board of Professional Liability Attorneys www.abpla.org
5712 244th St   Douglaston NY 11362
Ph: 718-631-1400 ▪ Fx: 718-631-1456

American Board of Professional Psychology www.abpp.org
300 Drayton St 3rd Fl   Savannah GA 31401
Ph: 800-255-7792 ▪ Fx: 912-644-5655

American Board of Quality Assurance & Utilization Review   www.abqaurp.org
   Physicians   2120 Range Rd   Clearwater FL 33765
   Ph: 727-298-8777 ▪ Fx: 727-449-0555 ▪ TF: 800-998-6030

American Board of Rabbis - VAAD Harabonim of America   www.angelfire.com/ny2/abor
292 5th Ave 4th Fl   New York NY 10001
Ph: 212-714-3598

American Board of Radiology   www.theabr.org
5441 E Williams Blvd Suite 200   Tucson AZ 85711
Ph: 520-790-2900 ▪ Fx: 520-790-3200

American Board of Registration of Electroencephalographic &   www.abret.org
   Evoked Potential Technologists   1904 Croyden
     Dr   Springfield IL 62703
Ph: 217-553-3758 ▪ Fx: 217-585-6663

American Board of Sexology   www.sexologist.org
2431 Aloma Ave Suite 277   Winter Park FL 32792
Ph: 407-645-1641

American Board of Surgery   www.absurgery.org
1617 John F Kennedy Blvd Suite 860   Philadelphia PA 19103
Ph: 215-568-4000 ▪ Fx: 215-563-5718

American Board of Thoracic Surgery   www.abts.org
1560 Sherman Ave Suite 803   Evanston IL 60201
Ph: 847-475-1520 ▪ Fx: 847-475-6240

American Board of Toxicology   www.abtox.org
PO Box 30054   Raleigh NC 27612
Ph: 919-841-5022 ▪ Fx: 919-841-5042

American Board of Trial Advocates   www.abota.org
2001 Bryan St Suite 3000   Dallas TX 75201
Ph: 214-871-7523 ▪ Fx: 214-871-6025 ▪ TF: 800-932-2682

American Board of Urology   www.abu.org
2216 Ivy Rd Suite 210   Charlottesville VA 22903
Ph: 434-979-0059 ▪ Fx: 434-979-2066

American Board of Veterinary Practitioners Inc   www.abvp.com
618 Church St Suite 220   Nashville TN 37219
Ph: 615-254-3687 ▪ Fx: 615-254-7047

American Boarding Kennels Association   abka.org
1702 E Pikes Peak Ave   Colorado Springs CO 80909
Ph: 719-667-1600 ▪ Fx: 719-667-0116

American Boat & Yacht Council Inc   www.abycinc.org
3069 Solomon's Island Rd   Edgewater MD 21037
Ph: 410-956-1050 ▪ Fx: 410-956-2737

American Boiler Manufacturers Association   www.abma.com
4001 N 9th St Suite 226   Arlington VA 22203
Ph: 703-522-7350 ▪ Fx: 703-522-2665

American Bonanza Society   www.bonanza.org
1922 Midfield Rd PO Box 12888   Wichita KS 67277
Ph: 316-945-1700 ▪ Fx: 316-945-1710

American Bone Marrow Donor Registry   www.charityadvantage.com/abmdr
PO Box 8841   Mandeville LA 70470
Ph: 985-626-1749 ▪ Fx: 985-626-7414 ▪ TF: 800-745-2452

American Bonsai Society   www.absbonsai.org

American Book Producers Association   www.abpaonline.org
160 5th Ave   New York NY 10010
Ph: 212-645-2368 ▪ Fx: 212-242-6799 ▪ TF: 800-209-4575

American Booksellers Association   www.bookweb.org
828 S Broadway   Tarrytown NY 10591
Ph: 914-591-2665 ▪ Fx: 914-591-2720 ▪ TF: 800-637-0037

American Booksellers Foundation for Free Expression   www.abffe.com
139 Fulton St Suite 302   New York NY 10038
Ph: 212-587-4025 ▪ Fx: 212-587-2436

American Border Leicester Association   www.ablasheep.org
PO Box 947   Canby OR 97013
Ph: 503-266-7156

American Botanical Council   www.herbalgram.org
6200 Manor Rd   Austin TX 78723
Ph: 512-926-4900 ▪ Fx: 512-926-2345 ▪ TF: 800-373-7105

American Bowling Congress   www.bowl.com/bowl/abc
5301 S 76th St   Greendale WI 53129
Ph: 414-421-6400 ▪ Fx: 414-421-3014 ▪ TF: 800-514-2695

American Boxer Club   americanboxerclub.org

American Brahman Breeders Association   www.brahman.org
3003 South Loop W Suite 140   Houston TX 77054
Ph: 713-349-0854 ▪ Fx: 713-349-9795

American Brain Tumor Association   www.abta.org
2720 River Rd   Des Plaines IL 60018
Ph: 847-827-9910 ▪ Fx: 847-827-9918 ▪ TF: 800-886-2282

American Bridge Association   www.americanbridge.com
2828 Lakewood Ave SW   Atlanta GA 30315
Ph: 404-768-5517 ▪ Fx: 404-767-1871

American Bridge Teachers' Association   www.abtahome.com
14840 Crystal Cove Ct Suite 503   Fort Myers FL 33919
Ph: 239-437-4106

American British White Park Association   whitecattle.org
PO Box 249   Wheelock TX 77882
Ph: 979-828-2339 ▪ Fx: 979-208-9002

American Brittany Club   clubs.akc.org/brit
10370 Fleming Rd   Carterville IL 62918
Ph: 618-985-2336 ▪ Fx: 618-985-5103

American Broncho-Esophagological Association   www.abea.net
Univ of Utah Div of Otolaryngology 50 N Medical Dr
     3C120   Salt Lake City UT 84132
Ph: 801-581-7514 ▪ Fx: 801-585-5744

American Brush Manufacturers Association   www.abma.org
2111 W Plum St Suite 274   Aurora IL 60506
Ph: 630-631-5217 ▪ Fx: 630-897-9140

American Bryological & Lichenological Society   www.unomaha.edu/~abls/
Univ of Nevada Dept of Biological Sciences 4505 Maryland
     Pkwy Box 454004   Las Vegas NV 89154
Ph: 702-895-3119 ▪ Fx: 702-895-3956

American Buckskin Registry Association Inc   www.americanbuckskin.org
1141 Hartnell Ave PO Box 3850   Redding CA 96049
Ph: 530-223-1420

American Buddhist Association
4524 N Richmond St   Chicago IL 60625
Ph: 773-583-5794

American Buddhist Study Center   www.americanbuddhist.com
331 Riverside Dr   New York NY 10025
Ph: 212-864-7424

American Bureau of Metal Statistics   www.abms.com
PO Box 805   Chatham NJ 07928
Ph: 973-701-2299 ▪ Fx: 973-701-2152

American Bureau of Shipping   www.eagle.org
16855 Northchase Dr   Houston TX 77060
Ph: 281-877-6000 ▪ Fx: 281-877-6001

American Burn Association   www.ameriburn.org
625 N Michigan Ave Suite 1530   Chicago IL 60611
Ph: 312-642-9260 ▪ Fx: 312-642-9130 ▪ TF: 800-548-2876

American Bus Association   www.buses.org
1100 New York Ave NW Suite 575   Washington DC 20005
Ph: 202-842-1645 ▪ Fx: 202-842-0850 ▪ TF: 800-283-2877

(American Bus Association) BUSPAC
700 13th St NW Suite 575   Washington DC 20005
Ph: 202-842-1645 ▪ Fx: 202-842-0850 ▪ TF: 800-283-2877

American Business Conference   www.americanbusinessconference.org
1828 L St NW Suite 908   Washington DC 20003
Ph: 202-822-9300 ▪ Fx: 202-467-4070

American Business Media   www.americanbusinessmedia.com
675 3rd Ave Suite 415   New York NY 10017
Ph: 212-661-6360 ▪ Fx: 212-370-0736

American Business Women's Association   www.abwahq.org
9100 Ward Pkwy   Kansas City MO 64114
Ph: 816-361-6621 ▪ Fx: 816-361-4991 ▪ TF: 800-228-0007

American Businesspersons Association   www.aba-assn.com
350 Fairway Dr Suite 200   Deerfield Beach FL 33441
Ph: 954-571-1877 ▪ Fx: 954-571-8582 ▪ TF: 800-221-2168

American Butter Institute   www.butterinstitute.org
2101 Wilson Blvd Suite 400   Arlington VA 22201
Ph: 703-243-6111 ▪ Fx: 703-841-9328

American Cadet Alliance   www.marinecadets.org
PO Box 144   Sea Girt NJ 08750
Ph: 732-840-4500 ▪ Fx: 732-458-1075

American Camping Association   www.acacamps.org
5000 SR-67 N   Martinsville IN 46151
Ph: 765-342-8456 ▪ Fx: 765-349-6357 ▪ TF: 800-428-2267

American-Canadian Genealogical Society   www.acgs.org
PO Box 6478   Manchester NH 03108
Ph: 603-622-1554 ▪ Fx: 603-624-8843

American Cancer Society   www.cancer.org
1599 Clifton Rd NE   Atlanta GA 30329
Ph: 404-320-3333 ▪ Fx: 404-329-7985 ▪ TF: 800-227-2345

American Canoe Association   www.acanet.org
7432 Alban Station Blvd Suite B-232   Springfield VA 22150
Ph: 703-451-0141

American Carbon Society   www.americancarbonsociety.org

American Cargo War Risk Reinsurance Exchange   www.amich.org/acwHome.htm
30 Broad St 7th Fl   New York NY 10004
Ph: 212-405-2835 ▪ Fx: 212-240-0654

American Cash Flow Association   acfa-cashflow.org
PO Box 2668   Orlando FL 32802
Ph: 407-206-6523 ▪ Fx: 407-206-6507 ▪ TF: 800-253-1294

American Casting Association   www.americancastingassoc.org
1773 Lance End Ln   Fenton MO 63026
Ph: 636-225-9443 ▪ Fx: 636-225-7238

American Catahoula Association   www.catahoulas.org
PO Box 248   Abita Springs LA 70420
Ph: 985-892-6773

American Catholic Historical Society   www.amchs.org

American Cause The   www.theamericancause.org
8500 Leesburg Pike Suite 206   Vienna VA 22182
Ph: 703-356-4966 ▪ Fx: 703-356-4996

American Cave Conservation Association   www.cavern.org
119 E Main St PO Box 409   Horse Cave KY 42749
Ph: 270-786-1466 ▪ Fx: 270-786-1467

American Celiac Society/Dietary Support Coalition
PO Box 23455   New Orleans LA 70183
Ph: 504-737-3293 ▪ Fx: 504-737-3283

American Center for the Alexander Technique Inc   www.acatnyc.org
39 W 14th St Rm 507   New York NY 10011
Ph: 212-633-2229

American Center for Law & Justice   www.aclj.org
PO Box 64429   Virginia Beach VA 23467
Ph: 757-226-2489 ▪ Fx: 757-226-2836 ▪ TF: 800-296-4529

American Ceramic Society   www.acers.org
PO Box 6136   Westerville OH 43086
Ph: 614-890-4700 ▪ Fx: 614-899-6109

American Cetacean Society   www.acsonline.org
PO Box 1391   San Pedro CA 90733
Ph: 310-548-6279 ▪ Fx: 310-548-6950

American Chain Association   www.americanchainassn.com
6724 Lone Oak Blvd   Naples FL 34109
Ph: 941-514-3441 ▪ Fx: 941-514-3470

American Chamber of Commerce of Cuba in the US Inc   www.amchamcuba.org
10454 Parthenon Ct   Bethesda MD 20817
Ph: 301-365-1745 ▪ Fx: 301-365-1829

American Chamber of Commerce Executives   www.acce.org
4875 Eisenhower Ave Suite 250   Alexandria VA 22304
Ph: 703-998-0072 ▪ Fx: 703-212-9512 ▪ TF: 800-394-2223

American Cheese Society　www.cheesesociety.org
304 W Liberty St Suite 201　Louisville KY 40202
Ph: 502-583-3783 ▪ Fx: 502-589-3602

American Chemical Society　www.acs.org
1155 16th St NW　Washington DC 20036
Ph: 202-872-4600 ▪ Fx: 202-872-4615 ▪ TF: 800-227-5558

American Chemical Society Rubber Div　www.rubber.org
250 S Forge St 4th Fl　Akron OH 44309
Ph: 330-972-7814 ▪ Fx: 330-972-5269

American Chemistry Council　www.americanchemistry.com
1300 Wilson Blvd　Arlington VA 22209
Ph: 703-741-5000 ▪ Fx: 703-741-6000

American Chesterton Society　www.chesterton.org/
4117 Pebblebrook Cir　Minneapolis MN 55437
Ph: 952-831-3096 ▪ Fx: 952-831-0387

American Chestnut Foundation　www.acf.org
469 Main St Suite 1 PO Box 4044　Bennington VT 05201
Ph: 802-447-0110

American Cheviot Sheep Society　members.aol.com/culhamef/bcheviots/cheviot.htm
Rt 1 Box 120　New Richland MN 56072
Ph: 507-465-8474

American Chianina Association　www.chicattle.org
1708 N Prairie View Rd PO Box 890　Platte City MO 64079
Ph: 816-431-2808 ▪ Fx: 816-431-5381

American Children of SCORE　scoremusicensemble.org
8031 Great Run Ln PO Box 3423　Warrenton VA 20188
Ph: 540-428-2313 ▪ Fx: 540-428-2314

American Chiropractic Association　www.amerchiro.org
1701 Clarendon Blvd　Arlington VA 22209
Ph: 703-276-8800 ▪ Fx: 703-243-2593 ▪ TF: 800-986-4636

American Chiropractic Association Council on Sports Injuries &　www.acasc.org
Physical Fitness　PO Box 400 380 Wright Rd　Norwalk IA
52011
Ph: 515-981-9340 ▪ Fx: 515-981-9427 ▪ TF: 800-261-1495

American Chiropractic Association PAC
1701 Clarendon Blvd　Arlington VA 22209
Ph: 703-276-8800 ▪ Fx: 703-243-2593 ▪ TF: 800-986-4636

American Chiropractic College of Radiology　www.accr.org
PO Box 3053　La Habra CA 90632
Ph: 562-947-8755

American Chiropractic Registry of Radiologic Technologists
2330 Gull Rd　Kalamazoo MI 49048
Ph: 269-343-6666 ▪ Fx: 269-343-7236

American Choral Directors Association　www.acdaonline.org
502 SW 38th St PO Box 6310　Lawton OK 73506
Ph: 580-355-8161 ▪ Fx: 580-248-1465

American Christian Education, Foundation for　www.face.net
PO Box 9588　Chesapeake VA 23321
Ph: 757-488-6601 ▪ Fx: 757-488-5593 ▪ TF: 800-352-3223

American Chronic Pain Association　www.theacpa.org
PO Box 850　Rocklin CA 95677
Ph: 916-632-0922 ▪ Fx: 916-632-3208 ▪ TF: 800-533-3231

American Cinema Editors　www.ace-filmeditors.org
100 Universal City Plaza Bldg 2282 Rm 234　Universal City CA
91608
Ph: 818-777-2900 ▪ Fx: 818-733-5023

American Civil Defense Association　www.tacda.org
118 S Court St PO Box 1057　Starke FL 32091
Ph: 904-964-5397 ▪ Fx: 904-964-9641 ▪ TF: 800-425-5397

American Civil Liberties Union　www.aclu.org
125 Broad St 18th Fl　New York NY 10004
Ph: 212-549-2500 ▪ Fx: 212-549-2580 ▪ TF: 800-775-1158

American Civil Rights Institute　www.acri.org
PO Box 188350　Sacramento CA 95818
Ph: 916-444-2278 ▪ Fx: 916-444-2279

American Civil War Association
PO Box 30826　Alexandria VA 22310
Ph: 703-960-2053

American Classical League　www.aclclassics.org
Miami University　Oxford OH 45056
Ph: 513-529-7741 ▪ Fx: 513-529-7742

American Cleft Palate-Craniofacial Association　www.cleftpalate-craniofacial.org
104 S Estes Dr Suite 204　Chapel Hill NC 27514
Ph: 919-933-9044 ▪ Fx: 919-933-9604 ▪ TF: 800-242-5338

American Clinical & Climatological Association　www.accassoc.org
231 Albert Sabin Way ML 557　Cincinnati OH 45267
Ph: 513-558-4231 ▪ Fx: 513-558-0852

American Clinical Laboratory Association
1250 H St NW Suite 880　Washington DC 20005
Ph: 202-637-9466 ▪ Fx: 202-637-2050

American Clinical Neurophysiology Society　www.acns.org
PO Box 30　Bloomfield CT 06002
Ph: 860-243-3977 ▪ Fx: 860-286-0787

American Coal Ash Association　www.acaa-usa.org
15200 E Girard Ave Suite 3050　Aurora CO 80014
Ph: 720-870-7897 ▪ Fx: 720-870-7889

American Coalition for Fathers & Children　www.acfc.org
22365 El Toro Rd Suite 335　Lake Forest CA 92630
Ph: 800-978-3237 ▪ Fx: 949-859-1514

American Coaster Enthusiasts　www.aceonline.org
7700 Shawnee Mission Pkwy Suite 201　Overland Park KS
66202
Ph: 913-262-4512 ▪ Fx: 913-262-4513

American Cockatiel Society　www.acstiels.com
9527 60th Ln N　Pinellas Park FL 33782
Ph: 727-541-4724

American Cocoa Research Institute　www.chocolateandcocoa.org/acri/staff.htm
8320 Old Courthouse Rd Suite 300　Vienna VA 22182
Ph: 703-790-5011 ▪ Fx: 703-790-5752

American Coke & Coal Chemicals Institute　www.accci.org
1255 23rd St NW　Washington DC 20037
Ph: 202-452-1140 ▪ Fx: 202-833-3636

American College for Advancement in Medicine　www.acam.org
23121 Verdugo Dr Suite 204　Laguna Hills CA 92653
Ph: 949-583-7666 ▪ Fx: 949-455-9679 ▪ TF: 800-532-3688

American College of Allergy Asthma & Immunology　allergy.mcg.edu
85 W Algonquin Rd Suite 550　Arlington Heights IL 60005
Ph: 847-427-1200 ▪ Fx: 847-427-1294 ▪ TF: 800-842-7777

American College of Angiology　www.collegeofangiology.org
295 Northern Blvd Suite 104　Great Neck NY 11021
Ph: 516-466-4055 ▪ Fx: 516-466-4099

American College of Apothecaries　www.acainfo.org
2830 Summer Oaks Dr　Bartlett TN 38134
Ph: 901-383-8119 ▪ Fx: 901-383-8882

American College of Bankruptcy　www.amercol.org/
11350 Random Hills Rd Suite 800　Fairfax VA 22030
Ph: 703-934-6154 ▪ Fx: 703-802-0207

American College of Cardiology　www.acc.org
9111 Old Georgetown Rd　Bethesda MD 20814
Ph: 301-897-5400 ▪ Fx: 301-897-9745 ▪ TF: 800-253-4636

American College of Cardiovascular　www.aameda.org/Specialtygroups/cardiology.html
Administrators　701 Lee St Suite 600　Des Plaines IL 60016
Ph: 847-759-8601 ▪ Fx: 847-759-8602

American College of Chest Physicians　www.chestnet.org
3300 Dundee Rd　Northbrook IL 60062
Ph: 847-498-1400 ▪ Fx: 847-498-5460 ▪ TF: 800-343-2227

American College of Chiropractic Consultants　www.accc-chiro.com
2741 Ridge Rd　Lansing IL 60438
Ph: 708-895-3141 ▪ Fx: 708-895-2268

American College of Chiropractic Orthopedists　www.accoweb.org
1030 Broadway Suite 101　El Centro CA 92243
Ph: 760-370-9106 ▪ Fx: 760-352-3966

American College of Clinical Engineering　www.accenet.org
5200 Butler Pike　Plymouth Meeting PA 19462
Ph: 610-825-6067

American College of Clinical Pharmacology　www.accp1.org
3 Ellinwood Ct　New Hartford NY 13413
Ph: 315-768-6117 ▪ Fx: 315-768-6119

American College of Clinical Pharmacy　www.accp.com
3101 Broadway Suite 650　Kansas City MO 64111
Ph: 816-531-2177 ▪ Fx: 816-531-4990

American College of Community Midwives　www.collegeofmidwives.org
3889 Middlefield Rd　Palo Alto CA 94303
Ph: 650-328-8491

American College Counseling Association　www.collegecounseling.org
c/o American Counseling Assn 5999 Stevenson Ave　Alexandria
VA 22304
Ph: 703-823-9800 ▪ Fx: 703-823-0252 ▪ TF: 800-347-6647

American College of Counselors　www.angelfire.com/il/AmericanCollege
1124 1/2 S 5th St　Springfield IL 62703
Ph: 217-726-6220

American College Dance Festival Association　www.fsu.edu/~acdfa
1570 E Jefferson St　Rockville MD 20852
Ph: 301-770-4443 ▪ Fx: 301-468-5841

American College of Dentists　www.facd.org
839 Quince Orchard Blvd Suite J　Gaithersburg MD 20878
Ph: 301-977-3223 ▪ Fx: 301-977-3330 ▪ TF: 888-223-1920

American College of Emergency Physicians　www.acep.org
PO Box 619911　Dallas TX 75261
Ph: 972-550-0911 ▪ Fx: 972-580-2816 ▪ TF: 800-798-1822

American College of Epidemiology　www.acepidemiology.org
1500 Sunday Dr Suite 102　Raleigh NC 27607
Ph: 919-861-5573 ▪ Fx: 919-861-4916

American College of Eye Surgeons　www.aces-abes.org
2665 Oak Ridge Ct Suite A　Fort Myers FL 33901
Ph: 239-275-8881 ▪ Fx: 239-275-9969 ▪ TF: 888-335-0077

American College of Foot & Ankle Orthopedics & Medicine　www.acfaom.org
3525 Ellicott Mills Dr Suite N　Ellicott City MD 21043
Ph: 800-265-8263 ▪ Fx: 410-418-4805

American College of Foot & Ankle Pediatrics
6477 Auburn Dr　Virginia Beach VA 23464
Ph: 757-523-0414 ▪ Fx: 757-523-2047

American College of Foot & Ankle Surgeons　www.acfas.org
515 Busse Hwy　Park Ridge IL 60068
Ph: 847-292-2237 ▪ Fx: 847-292-2022 ▪ TF: 800-421-2237

American College of Forensic Examiners　www.acfei.com
2750 E Sunshine St　Springfield MO 65804
Ph: 417-881-3818 ▪ Fx: 417-881-4702

American College of Forensic Psychiatry　www.forensicpsychiatry.cc
PO Box 5870　Balboa Island CA 92662
Ph: 949-673-7773 ▪ Fx: 949-673-7710

American College of Gastroenterology　www.acg.gi.org
4900B S 31st St　Arlington VA 22206
Ph: 703-820-7400 ▪ Fx: 703-931-4520

American College Health Association　www.acha.org
PO Box 28937　Baltimore MD 21240
Ph: 410-859-1500 ▪ Fx: 410-859-1510

American College of Health Care Administrators　www.achca.org
300 N Lee St Suite 301　Alexandria VA 22314
Ph: 703-739-7900 ▪ Fx: 703-793-7901 ▪ TF: 888-882-2422

American College of Healthcare Architects　www.healtharchitects.org
8310 Nieman Rd PO Box 14548　Lenexa KS 66285
Ph: 913-492-4307 ▪ Fx: 913-599-5340

American College of Healthcare Executives　www.ache.org
1 N Franklin St Suite 1700　Chicago IL 60606
Ph: 312-424-2800 ▪ Fx: 312-424-0023

American College of International Physicians　www.acip.org
9323 Old Mount Vernon Rd　Alexandria VA 22309
Ph: 703-221-1500

American College of Laboratory Animal Medicine — www.aclam.org
Univ of Houston Houston TX 77204
Ph: 713-743-9191 ▪ Fx: 713-743-9200

American College of Legal Medicine — www.aclm.org
1111 N Plaza Dr Suite 550 Schaumburg IL 60173
Ph: 847-969-0283 ▪ Fx: 847-517-7229

American College of Managed Care Administrators — www.aameda.org
701 Lee St Suite 600 Des Plaines IL 60016
Ph: 847-759-8601 ▪ Fx: 847-759-8602

American College of Managed Care Medicine — www.acmcm.org
4435 Waterfront Dr Suite 101 Glen Allen VA 23060
Ph: 804-527-1906 ▪ Fx: 804-747-5316

American College of Medical Genetics — www.acmg.net
9650 Rockville Pike Bethesda MD 20814
Ph: 301-530-7127 ▪ Fx: 301-634-7275

American College of Medical Physics — www.acmp.org
12100 Sunset Hills Rd Suite 130 Reston VA 20190
Ph: 703-481-5001 ▪ Fx: 703-435-4390

American College of Medical Practice Executives — www.mgma.com/acmpe
104 Inverness Terr E Englewood CO 80112
Ph: 303-799-1111 ▪ Fx: 303-643-4427 ▪ TF: 888-608-5601

American College of Medical Quality — www.acmq.org
4334 Montgomery Ave 2nd Fl Bethesda MD 20814
Ph: 301-913-9149 ▪ Fx: 301-913-9142 ▪ TF: 800-924-2149

American College of Medical Toxicology — www.acmt.net
11240 Waples Mill Rd Suite 200 Fairfax VA 22030
Ph: 703-934-1223 ▪ Fx: 703-359-7562

American College of Mental Health Administration — www.acmha.org
324 Freeport Rd Pittsburgh PA 15238
Ph: 412-820-0670 ▪ Fx: 412-820-0669

American College of Mohs Micrographic Surgery & Cutaneous Oncology — www.mohscollege.org
611 E Wells St Milwaukee WI 53202
Ph: 414-347-1103 ▪ Fx: 414-272-6070 ▪ TF: 800-500-7224

American College of Mortgage Attorneys — www.acmaatty.org
15245 Shady Grove Rd Suite 130 Rockville MD 20850
Ph: 301-990-9075 ▪ Fx: 301-990-9771

American College of Musicians — www.pianoguild.com
808 Rio Grande St Austin TX 78701
Ph: 512-478-5775 ▪ Fx: 512-478-5843

American College of Neuropsychopharmacology — www.acnp.org
2014 Broadway Suite 320 Nashville TN 37203
Ph: 615-322-2075 ▪ Fx: 615-343-0662

American College of Nuclear Medicine — www.acnucmed.org
PO Box 175 Landisville PA 17538
Ph: 717-898-5008 ▪ Fx: 717-898-2555

American College of Nuclear Physicians — www.acnponline.org
1850 Samuel Morse Dr Reston VA 20190
Ph: 703-326-1190 ▪ Fx: 703-708-9015

American College of Nurse-Midwives — www.midwife.org
818 Connecticut Ave NW Suite 900 Washington DC 20006
Ph: 202-728-9860 ▪ Fx: 202-728-9897

American College of Nurse Practitioners — www.nurse.org/acnp/
1111 19th St NW Suite 404 Washington DC 20036
Ph: 202-659-2190 ▪ Fx: 202-659-2191

American College of Nutrition — www.am-coll-nutr.org
300 S Duncan Ave Suite 225 Clearwater FL 33755
Ph: 727-446-6086 ▪ Fx: 727-446-6202

American College of Obstetricians & Gynecologists — www.acog.com
409 12th St SW PO Box 96920 Washington DC 20090
Ph: 202-638-5577 ▪ Fx: 202-863-4284

American College of Occupational & Environmental Medicine — www.acoem.org
1114 N Arlington Heights Rd Arlington Heights IL 60004
Ph: 847-818-1800 ▪ Fx: 847-818-9266

American College of Oral & Maxillofacial Surgeons — www.acoms.org
1100 NW Loop 410 Suite 420 San Antonio TX 78213
Ph: 210-344-5674 ▪ Fx: 210-344-9754 ▪ TF: 800-522-6676

American College of Orgonomy — www.orgonomy.org
PO Box 490 Princeton NJ 08542
Ph: 732-821-1144 ▪ Fx: 732-821-0174

American College of Osteopathic Emergency Physicians — www.acoep.org
142 E Ontario St Suite 1250 Chicago IL 60611
Ph: 312-587-3709 ▪ Fx: 312-587-9951 ▪ TF: 800-521-3709

American College of Osteopathic Family Physicians — www.acofp.org
330 E Algonquin Rd Suite 1 Arlington Heights IL 60005
Ph: 847-228-6090 ▪ Fx: 847-228-9755 ▪ TF: 800-323-0794

American College of Osteopathic Internists — www.acoi.org
3 Bethesda Metro Ctr Suite 508 Bethesda MD 20814
Ph: 301-656-8877 ▪ Fx: 301-656-7133 ▪ TF: 800-327-5183

American College of Osteopathic Obstetricians & Gynecologists — www.acoog.com
900 Auburn Rd Pontiac MI 48342
Ph: 248-332-6360 ▪ Fx: 248-332-4607 ▪ TF: 800-875-6360

American College of Osteopathic Pediatricians — www.acopeds.org
142 E Ontario St Chicago IL 60611
Ph: 312-202-8174 ▪ Fx: 312-202-8224 ▪ TF: 877-231-2267

American College of Osteopathic Sclerotherapeutic Pain Management Inc — www.acopms.com
303 S Ingram Ct Middletown DE 19709
Ph: 302-376-8080 ▪ Fx: 302-376-8081 ▪ TF: 800-471-6114

American College of Osteopathic Surgeons — www.facos.org
123 N Henry St Alexandria VA 22314
Ph: 703-684-0416 ▪ Fx: 703-684-3280

American College Personnel Association — www.acpa.nche.edu
1 Dupont Cir NW Suite 300 Washington DC 20036
Ph: 202-835-2272 ▪ Fx: 202-296-3286

American College of Physician Executives — www.acpe.org
4890 W Kennedy Blvd Suite 200 Tampa FL 33609
Ph: 813-287-2000 ▪ Fx: 813-287-8993 ▪ TF: 800-562-8088

American College of Physicians — www.acponline.org
190 N Independence Mall W Philadelphia PA 19106
Ph: 215-351-2400 ▪ Fx: 215-351-2594 ▪ TF: 800-523-1546

American College of Preventive Medicine — www.acpm.org
1307 New York Ave NW Suite 200 Washington DC 20005
Ph: 202-466-2044 ▪ Fx: 202-466-2662

American College of Prosthodontists — www.prosthodontics.org
211 E Chicago Ave Suite 1000 Chicago IL 60611
Ph: 312-573-1260 ▪ Fx: 312-573-1257 ▪ TF: 800-378-1260

American College of Psychiatrists — www.acpsych.org
732 Addison St Suite C Berkeley CA 94710
Ph: 510-704-8020 ▪ Fx: 510-704-0113

American College of Psychoanalysts
434 Fox Run Ln Hampshire IL 60140
Ph: 847-683-7517 ▪ Fx: 847-683-3130

American College of Radiation Oncology — www.acro.org
4350 East-West Hwy Suite 401 Bethesda MD 20814
Ph: 301-718-6515 ▪ Fx: 301-656-0989

American College of Radiology — www.acr.org
1891 Preston White Dr Reston VA 20191
Ph: 703-648-8900 ▪ Fx: 703-295-6772 ▪ TF: 800-227-5463

American College of Real Estate Lawyers — www.acrel.org
11300 Rockville Pike Suite 903 Rockville MD 20852
Ph: 301-816-9811 ▪ Fx: 301-816-9786

American College of Rheumatology — www.rheumatology.org
1800 Century Pl Suite 250 Atlanta GA 30345
Ph: 404-633-3777 ▪ Fx: 404-633-1870

American College of Sports Medicine — www.acsm.org
401 W Michigan St Indianapolis IN 46206
Ph: 317-637-9200 ▪ Fx: 317-634-7817

American College of Surgeons — www.facs.org
633 N Saint Clair St Chicago IL 60611
Ph: 312-202-5000 ▪ Fx: 312-202-5001 ▪ TF: 800-621-4111

American College of Tax Counsel
1156 15th St NW Suite 900 Washington DC 20005
Ph: 202-637-3243 ▪ Fx: 202-393-0336

American College of Theriogenologists — www.theriogenology.org
PO Box 3065 Montgomery AL 36109
Ph: 334-395-4666 ▪ Fx: 334-395-3399

American College of Toxicology — actox.org
9650 Rockville Pike Bethesda MD 20814
Ph: 301-634-7840 ▪ Fx: 301-634-7852

American College of Trial Lawyers — www.actl.com
19900 MacArthur Blvd Suite 610 Irvine CA 92612
Ph: 949-752-1801 ▪ Fx: 949-752-1674

American College of Trust & Estate Counsel — www.actec.org
3415 S Sepulveda Blvd Suite 330 Los Angeles CA 90034
Ph: 310-398-1888 ▪ Fx: 310-572-7280

American College of Veterinary Dermatology — www.acvd.org
5610 Kearny Mesa Rd Suite B San Diego CA 92111
Ph: 858-560-9393 ▪ Fx: 858-560-0206

American College of Veterinary Internal Medicine — www.acvim.org
1997 Wadsworth Blvd Suite A Lakewood CO 80214
Ph: 303-231-9933 ▪ Fx: 303-231-0880 ▪ TF: 800-245-9081

American College of Veterinary Ophthalmologists — www.acvo.com
PO Box 1311 Meridian ID 83680
Ph: 208-466-7624 ▪ Fx: 208-466-7693

American College of Veterinary Pathologists — www.acvp.org
7600 Terrace Ave Suite 203 Middleton WI 53562
Ph: 608-833-8725 ▪ Fx: 608-831-5122

American College of Veterinary Radiology — www.acvr.ucdavis.edu
777 E Park Dr PO Box 8820 Harrisburg PA 17105
Ph: 717-558-7865 ▪ Fx: 717-558-7841

American College of Veterinary Surgeons — www.acvs.org
4401 East-West Hwy Suite 205 Bethesda MD 20814
Ph: 301-913-9550 ▪ Fx: 301-913-2034

American Collegians for Life — www.aclife.org
PO Box 1112 Washington DC 20013
Ph: 202-737-1007 ▪ Fx: 202-347-3245

American Collegiate Hockey Association — www.achahockey.org
PO Box 1013 Kent OH 44240
Ph: 330-221-4411

American Collegiate Retailing Association — www.acraretail.org

American Color Print Society — www.americancolorprintsociety.org

American Committee to Advance the Study of Petroglyphs & Pictographs PO Box 158 Shepherdstown WV 25443
Ph: 304-876-3208

American Committee on Italian Migration — www.acimimmigra.org
25 Carmine St New York NY 10014
Ph: 212-247-7373 ▪ Fx: 212-265-5793

American Committee for KEEP Inc — www.keep.or.jp/indexe.html
825 Green Bay Rd Suite 122 Wilmette IL 60091
Ph: 847-853-2500 ▪ Fx: 847-853-8901 ▪ TF: 800-368-5337

American Committee for Rescue & Resettlement of Iraqi Jews
1125 Park Ave New York NY 10029
Ph: 212-427-1246 ▪ Fx: 212-360-7009

American Committee for the Weizmann Institute of Science — www.weizmann-usa.org
130 E 59th St New York NY 10022
Ph: 212-895-7900 ▪ Fx: 212-895-7999

American Commodity Distribution Association — www.commodityfoods.org
11358 Barley Field Way Marriottsville MD 21104
Ph: 410-442-4612 ▪ Fx: 410-442-4613

American Communism, Historians of — www.historians.org/affiliates/hisn_am_communism.htm

American Comparative Literature Association — www.acla.org
Univ of Texas at Austin Program in Comparative Literature 1
University Stn B5003 Austin TX 78712
Ph: 512-471-8020

American Composers Alliance — www.composers.com
73 Spring St Rm 505 New York NY 10012
Ph: 212-362-8900 ▪ Fx: 212-925-6798

American Composers Forum
332 Minnesota St Suite E145   Saint Paul MN 55101
Ph: 651-228-1407 ▪ Fx: 651-291-7978
www.composersforum.org

American Composites Manufacturers Association
1010 Glebe Rd Suite 450   Arlington VA 22201
Ph: 703-525-0511 ▪ Fx: 703-525-0743
www.acmanet.org

American Computer Science League
PO Box 521   West Warwick RI 02893
Ph: 401-822-4312
www.acsl.org

American Computer Scientists Association Inc
6 Commerce Dr Suite 2000   Cranford NJ 07016
Ph: 908-272-0016 ▪ Fx: 908-272-6297
www.acsa2000.net

American Concrete Institute International
38800 Country Club Dr PO Box 9094   Farmington Hills MI 48331
Ph: 248-848-3700 ▪ Fx: 248-848-3701
www.aci-int.org

American Concrete Pavement Association
5420 Old Orchard Rd Suite A-100   Skokie IL 60077
Ph: 847-966-2272 ▪ Fx: 847-966-9970
www.pavement.com

American Concrete Pipe Association
222 W Las Colinas Blvd Suite 641   Irving TX 75039
Ph: 972-506-7216 ▪ Fx: 972-506-7682
www.concrete-pipe.org

American Concrete Pressure Pipe Association
11800 Sunrise Valley Dr Suite 309   Reston VA 20191
Ph: 703-391-9135 ▪ Fx: 703-391-9136
www.acppa.org

American Concrete Pumping Association
676 Enterprise Dr   Lewis Center OH 43035
Ph: 614-431-5618 ▪ Fx: 614-431-6944
www.concretepumpers.com

American Conference of Academic Deans
1818 R St NW   Washington DC 20009
Ph: 202-884-7419 ▪ Fx: 202-478-5005
www.acad-edu.org

American Conference of Cantors
1360 Center Dr Suite 110   Atlanta GA 30338
Ph: 770-390-0006 ▪ Fx: 770-390-0020 ▪ TF: 886-711-0006
www.accantors.org

American Conference of Governmental Industrial Hygienists
1330 Kemper Meadows Dr   Cincinnati OH 45240
Ph: 513-742-2020 ▪ Fx: 513-742-3355
www.acgih.org

American Conference for Irish Studies
www.acisweb.com

American Congregational Association
14 Beacon St   Boston MA 02108
Ph: 617-523-0604 ▪ Fx: 617-523-0491

American Congress of Community Supports & Employment Services
1875 'I' St NW 11th Fl   Washington DC 20006
Ph: 202-466-3355 ▪ Fx: 202-466-7571
www.accses.org

American Congress of Rehabilitation Medicine
6801 Lake Plaza Dr Suite B-205   Indianapolis IN 46220
Ph: 317-915-2250 ▪ Fx: 317-915-2245
www.acrm.org

American Congress on Surveying & Mapping
6 Montgomery Village Ave Suite 403   Gaithersburg MD 20879
Ph: 240-632-9716 ▪ Fx: 240-632-1321
www.acsm.net

American Conifer Society
PO Box 3422   Crofton MD 21114
Ph: 410-721-6611 ▪ Fx: 410-721-9636
www.conifersociety.org

American Connemara Pony Society
2360 Hunting Ridge Rd   Winchester VA 22603
Ph: 540-662-5953 ▪ Fx: 540-722-2277
www.acps.org

American Conservation Association
30 Rockefeller Plaza 56th Fl   New York NY 10112
Ph: 212-649-5822 ▪ Fx: 212-649-5921

American Conservative Union
1007 Cameron St   Alexandria VA 22314
Ph: 703-836-8602 ▪ Fx: 703-836-8606 ▪ TF: 800-228-7345
www.conservative.org

American Consumers Association
2633 Flossmoor Rd   Flossmoor IL 60422
Ph: 708-957-2900 ▪ Fx: 708-957-4155

American Contract Bridge League
2990 Airways Blvd   Memphis TN 38116
Ph: 901-332-5586 ▪ Fx: 901-398-7754 ▪ TF: 800-264-2743
www.acbl.org

American Coptic Association
PO Box 55   Saddle River NJ 07458
Ph: 201-451-0972 ▪ Fx: 201-451-3399
www.amcoptic.com

American Cormo Sheep Association
Rt 59 Box 25   Broadus MT 59317
Ph: 406-427-5449
www.cormosheep.com

American Corn Growers Association
PO Box 18157   Washington DC 20036
Ph: 202-835-0330 ▪ Fx: 202-463-0862
www.acga.org

American Correctional Association
4380 Forbes Blvd   Lanham MD 20706
Ph: 301-918-1800 ▪ Fx: 301-918-1900 ▪ TF: 800-222-5646
www.aca.org

American Correctional Chaplains Association
PO Box 661   Waupun WI 53963
Ph: 920-324-6298 ▪ Fx: 920-324-6254
www.correctionalchaplains.org

American Correctional Food Service Association
4248 Park Glen Rd   Minneapolis MN 55416
Ph: 952-928-4648 ▪ Fx: 952-929-1318
www.acfsa.org

American Correctional Health Services Association
250 Gatsby Pl   Alpharetta GA 30022
Ph: 877-918-1842 ▪ Fx: 770-650-5789
www.corrections.com/ACHSA

American Corriedale Association Inc
PO Box 391   Clay City IL 62824
Ph: 618-676-1046 ▪ Fx: 618-676-1133
www.americancorriedale.com

American Cotswold Record Association
PO Box 59   Plympton MA 02367
Ph: 781-585-2026

American Cotton Shippers Association
88 Union Ave Suite 1204   Memphis TN 38103
Ph: 901-525-2272 ▪ Fx: 901-527-6527
www.acsa-cotton.org

American Council on Alcohol Problems
2376 Lakeside Dr   Birmingham AL 35244
Ph: 205-989-8177

American Council of the Blind
1155 15th St NW Suite 1004   Washington DC 20005
Ph: 202-467-5081 ▪ Fx: 202-467-5085 ▪ TF: 800-424-8666
www.acb.org

American Council of Blind Lions
1155 15th St NW Suite 1004   Washington DC 20005
Ph: 202-467-5081 ▪ TF: 800-424-8666
www.acb.org/affiliates

American Council for Capital Formation
1750 K St NW Suite 400   Washington DC 20006
Ph: 202-293-5811 ▪ Fx: 202-785-8165
www.accf.org

American Council of Christian Churches
PO Box 5455   Bethlehem PA 18015
Ph: 610-865-3009 ▪ Fx: 610-865-3033
www.amcouncilcc.org

American Council for Construction Education
1300 Hudson Ln Suite 3   Monroe LA 71201
Ph: 318-323-2816 ▪ Fx: 318-323-2413
acce-hq.org

American Council on Consumer Interests
415 S Duff Ave Suite C   Ames IA 50010
Ph: 515-956-4666 ▪ Fx: 515-233-3101
consumerinterests.org

American Council for Drug Education
c/o Phoenix House 164 W 74th St   New York NY 10023
Ph: 212-595-5810 ▪ Fx: 212-721-7384 ▪ TF: 800-378-4435
www.acde.org

American Council on Education
1 Dupont Cir NW Suite 800   Washington DC 20036
Ph: 202-939-9300 ▪ Fx: 202-833-4760
www.acenet.edu

American Council for an Energy-Efficient Economy
1001 Connecticut Ave NW Suite 801   Washington DC 20036
Ph: 202-429-8873 ▪ Fx: 202-429-2248
www.aceee.org

American Council of Engineering Companies
1015 15th St NW 8th Fl   Washington DC 20005
Ph: 202-347-7474 ▪ Fx: 202-898-0068
www.acec.org

American Council on Exercise
4851 Paramount Dr   San Diego CA 92123
Ph: 858-279-8227 ▪ Fx: 858-279-8064 ▪ TF: 800-825-3636
www.acefitness.org

American Council on Germany
14 E 60th St Suite 606   New York NY 10022
Ph: 212-826-3636 ▪ Fx: 212-758-3445
www.acgusa.org

American Council for Headache Education
19 Mantua Rd   Mount Royal NJ 08061
Ph: 856-423-0258 ▪ Fx: 856-423-0082 ▪ TF: 800-255-2243
www.achenet.org

American Council of Hypnotist Examiners
700 S Central Ave   Glendale CA 91204
Ph: 818-242-1159 ▪ Fx: 818-247-9379 ▪ TF: 800-894-9766
www.sonic.net/hypno/ache.html

American Council of Independent Laboratories
1629 K St NW Suite 400   Washington DC 20006
Ph: 202-887-5872 ▪ Fx: 202-887-0021
www.acil.org

American Council on International Personnel
515 Madison Ave 6th Fl   New York NY 10022
Ph: 212-688-2437 ▪ Fx: 212-593-4697
www.acip.com

American Council for International Studies
343 Congress St Suite 3100   Boston MA 02210
Ph: 617-236-2051 ▪ Fx: 617-236-4703
www.acis.com

American Council for Judaism
PO Box 9009   Alexandria VA 22304
Ph: 703-836-2546
www.acjna.org

American Council of Learned Societies
633 3rd Ave   New York NY 10017
Ph: 212-697-1505 ▪ Fx: 212-949-8058
www.acls.org

American Council of Life Insurers
101 Constitution Ave NW Suite 700 W   Washington DC 20001
Ph: 202-624-2000 ▪ Fx: 202-624-2319
www.acli.com

American Council on Pharmaceutical Education
20 N Clark St Suite 2500   Chicago IL 60602
Ph: 312-664-3575 ▪ Fx: 312-664-4652
www.acpe-accredit.org

American Council for Polish Culture
35 Fernridge Rd   West Hartford CT 06107
Ph: 860-521-7621
www.polishcultureacpc.org

American Council on Rural Special Education
Utah State Univ 2865 Old Main Hill   Logan UT 84322
Ph: 435-797-3911
extension.usu.edu/acres

American Council on Science & Health
1995 Broadway 2nd Fl   New York NY 10023
Ph: 212-362-7044 ▪ Fx: 212-362-4919
www.acsh.org

American Council of Snowmobile Associations
271 Woodland Pass Suite 216   East Lansing MI 48823
Ph: 517-351-4362 ▪ Fx: 517-351-1363
www.snowmobileacsa.org

American Council of Spotted Asses
PO Box 121   New Melle MO 63365
Ph: 636-828-5430 ▪ Fx: 636-828-5431
www.spottedass.com

American Council on the Teaching of Foreign Languages
6 Executive Plaza   Yonkers NY 10701
Ph: 914-963-8830 ▪ Fx: 914-963-1275
www.actfl.org

American Council for Technology
11350 Random Hills Rd Suite 120   Fairfax VA 22030
Ph: 703-218-1955 ▪ Fx: 703-218-1960
www.actgov.org

American Council for Trade in Services
1030 15th St NW   Washington DC 20005
Ph: 202-842-1030 ▪ Fx: 202-842-1225
www.acts-talks.com

American Council of Trustees & Alumni
1726 M St NW Suite 800   Washington DC 20036
Ph: 202-467-6787 ▪ Fx: 202-467-6784 ▪ TF: 888-258-6648
www.goacta.org

American Council of Vedic Astrology
PO Box 2149   Sedona AZ 86339
Ph: 928-282-6595 ▪ Fx: 928-282-6097 ▪ TF: 800-900-6595
www.vedicastrology.org/

American Council for Voluntary International Action
1717 Massachusetts Ave NW Suite 701   Washington DC 20036
Ph: 202-667-8227 ▪ Fx: 202-667-8236
www.interaction.org

American Council of Young Political Leaders   www.acypl.org
1612 K St NW Suite 300   Washington DC 20006
Ph: 202-857-0999 ▪ Fx: 202-857-0027

American Councils for International Education   www.americancouncils.org
1776 Massachusetts Ave NW Suite 700   Washington DC 20036
Ph: 202-833-7522 ▪ Fx: 202-833-7523

American Counseling Association   www.counseling.org
5999 Stevenson Ave   Alexandria VA 22304
Ph: 703-823-9800 ▪ Fx: 703-823-0252 ▪ TF: 800-347-6647

American Countertrade Association   www.countertrade.org
818 Connecticut Ave NW 12th Fl   Washington DC 20006
Ph: 202-887-9011 ▪ Fx: 202-872-8324

American Cowboy Culture Association   www.cowboy.org
4124 62nd Dr   Lubbock TX 79413
Ph: 806-795-2455 ▪ Fx: 806-795-4749

American Craft Council   www.craftcouncil.org
72 Spring St   New York NY 10012
Ph: 212-274-0630 ▪ Fx: 212-274-0650 ▪ TF: 800-724-0859

American Cranberry Growers Association
PO Box 423   Tabernacle NJ 08088
Ph: 609-726-1330

American CranioSacral Therapy Association   www.acsta.com
11211 Prosperity Farms Rd Suite D-325   Palm Beach Gardens
FL 33410
Ph: 561-622-4334 ▪ Fx: 561-622-4771 ▪ TF: 800-233-5880

American Cream Draft Horse Association   www.americancreamdraft.org
193 Crossover Rd   Bennington VT 05201
Ph: 802-447-7612 ▪ Fx: 802-447-0711

American Creativity Association   www.amcreativityassoc.org
PO Box 5856   Philadelphia PA 19128
Ph: 888-837-1409

American Credit Union Mortgage Association   www.acuma.org
3419 Via Lido PMB 135   Newport Beach CA 92663
Ph: 949-645-5288 ▪ Fx: 949-645-5297

American Criminal Justice Association   www.acjalae.org
PO Box 601047   Sacramento CA 95860
Ph: 916-484-6553 ▪ Fx: 916-488-2227

American Cross Country Skiers   www.xcskiworld.com
PO Box 604   Bend OR 97709
Ph: 541-317-0217

American Cryonics Society Inc   www.americancryonics.org
PO Box 1509   Cupertino CA 95015
Ph: 650-254-2001 ▪ Fx: 650-254-0128 ▪ TF: 800-523-2001

American Crystallographic Association   www.hwi.buffalo.edu/aca
PO Box 96 Ellicott Stn   Buffalo NY 14205
Ph: 716-856-9600 ▪ Fx: 716-852-4846

American Culinary Federation Inc   www.acfchefs.org
10 San Bartola Dr   Saint Augustine FL 32086
Ph: 904-824-4468 ▪ Fx: 904-825-4758 ▪ TF: 800-624-9458

American Culinary Federation Chef & Child Foundation   www.acfchefs.org/ccf/ccf.html
10 San Bartola Dr   Saint Augustine FL 32086
Ph: 904-824-4468 ▪ Fx: 904-825-4758 ▪ TF: 800-624-9458

American Cultural Exchange   www.cultural.org
200 W Mercer St Suite 504   Seattle WA 98119
Ph: 206-217-9644 ▪ Fx: 206-217-9643

American Cultural Resources Association   www.acra-crm.org
6150 E Ponce de Leon Ave   Stone Mountain GA 30083
Ph: 770-498-5159 ▪ Fx: 770-498-3809

(American Culture) Free Congress Foundation   www.freecongress.org
717 2nd St NE   Washington DC 20002
Ph: 202-546-3000 ▪ Fx: 202-543-5605

American Cultures, Association of   www.taac.com
2554 W 16th St Suite 419   Yuma AZ 85364
Ph: 928-783-1757

American Cultures, Institute for the Study of   www.isacnet.org
233 12th St Suite 500 PO Box 2707   Columbus GA 31902
Ph: 706-243-6218 ▪ Fx: 706-322-7747

American Custom Gunmakers Guild   www.acgg.org
22 Vista View Dr   Cody WY 82414
Ph: 307-587-4297

American Daffodil Society   www.daffodilusa.org
4126 Winfield Rd   Columbus OH 43220
Ph: 614-451-4747 ▪ Fx: 614-451-2177

American Dairy Goat Association   www.adga.org
209 W Main St PO Box 865   Spindale NC 28160
Ph: 828-286-3801 ▪ Fx: 828-287-0476

American Dairy Products Institute   www.americandairyproducts.com
116 N York St Suite 200   Elmhurst IL 60126
Ph: 630-530-8700 ▪ Fx: 630-530-8707

American Dairy Science Association   www.adsa.org
1111 N Dunlap Ave   Savoy IL 61874
Ph: 217-356-3182 ▪ Fx: 217-398-4119

American Dance Guild   www.americandanceguild.org
PO Box 2006 Lenox Hill Stn   New York NY 10021
Ph: 212-932-2789

American Dance Therapy Association   www.adta.org
10632 Little Patuxent Pkwy Suite 108   Columbia MD 21044
Ph: 410-997-4040 ▪ Fx: 410-997-4048

American Darts Organization Inc   www.adodarts.com
230 N Crescent Way Suite K   Anaheim CA 92801
Ph: 714-254-0212 ▪ Fx: 714-254-0214

American Debate Association   www2.bc.edu/~katsulas

American Delaine & Merino Record Association   www.admra.org
59419 Walters Rd   Jacobsburg OH 43933
Ph: 740-686-2172

American Dental Assistants Association   www.dentalassistant.org
35 E Wacker Dr Suite 1730   Chicago IL 60601
Ph: 312-541-1550 ▪ Fx: 312-541-1496

American Dental Association   www.ada.org
211 E Chicago Ave   Chicago IL 60611
Ph: 312-440-2500 ▪ Fx: 312-440-2800

American Dental Education Association   www.adea.org
1625 Massachusetts Ave NW Suite 600   Washington DC 20036
Ph: 202-667-9433 ▪ Fx: 202-667-0642 ▪ TF: 800-353-2237

American Dental Hygienists' Association   www.adha.org
444 N Michigan Ave Suite 3400   Chicago IL 60611
Ph: 312-440-8900 ▪ Fx: 312-467-1806 ▪ TF: 800-243-2342

American Dental PAC
1111 14th St NW Suite 1100   Washington DC 20005
Ph: 202-898-2424 ▪ Fx: 202-898-2437

American Dental Society of Anesthesiology   www.adsa.org
211 E Chicago Ave Suite 780   Chicago IL 60611
Ph: 312-664-8270 ▪ Fx: 312-642-9713 ▪ TF: 800-722-7788

American Dental Trade Association   www.adta.com
4222 King St W   Alexandria VA 22302
Ph: 703-379-7755 ▪ Fx: 703-931-9429

American Design Drafting Association   www.adda.org
105 E Main St   Newbern TN 38059
Ph: 731-627-0802 ▪ Fx: 731-627-9321

American Dexter Cattle Association   www.dextercattle.org
404 High St   Prairie Home MO 65068
Ph: 660-841-9502

American Diabetes Association   www.diabetes.org
1701 N Beauregard St   Alexandria VA 22311
Ph: 703-549-1500 ▪ Fx: 703-836-2464 ▪ TF: 800-232-3472

American Dialect Society   www.americandialect.org
c/o Duke University Press Box 90660   Durham NC 27708
Ph: 919-687-3602 ▪ Fx: 919-688-2615 ▪ TF: 888-387-5765

American Dietetic Association   www.eatright.org
120 S Riverside Plaza Suite 2000   Chicago IL 60606
Ph: 312-899-0040 ▪ Fx: 312-899-4758 ▪ TF: 800-877-1600

American Disability Association   www.adanet.org
2201 6th Ave S   Birmingham AL 35233
Ph: 205-328-9090 ▪ Fx: 205-251-7417

American Disc Jockey Association   www.adja.org
2000 Corporate Dr Suite 408   Ladera Ranch CA 92694
Ph: 888-723-5776

American Ditchley Foundation
666 5th Ave 37th Fl   New York NY 10103
Ph: 212-541-3791 ▪ Fx: 212-541-3751

American Dog Breeder's Association   www.adba.cc
PO Box 1771   Salt Lake City UT 84110
Ph: 801-936-7513 ▪ Fx: 801-936-4229

American Dog Owners Association Inc   www.adoa.org
1654 Columbia Tpke   Castleton on Hudson NY 12033
Ph: 518-477-8469 ▪ Fx: 518-477-4034

American Dog Trainers Network   www.inch.com/~dogs
161 W 4th St   New York NY 10014
Ph: 212-727-7257

American Domestic Violence Crisis Line   www.awoscentral.com
3300 NW 185th Ave Suite 133   Portland OR 97229
Ph: 503-846-8748 ▪ Fx: 503-907-6554 ▪ TF: 866-879-6636

American Donkey & Mule Society   www.lovelongears.com
PO Box 1210   Lewisville TX 75067
Ph: 972-219-0781 ▪ Fx: 972-420-9980

American Double Dutch League   www.usaddl.org
4220 Eads St NE   Washington DC 20019
Ph: 800-982-2335

American Driver & Traffic Safety Education Association   www.adtsea.iup.edu
Indiana Univ of Pennsylvania Highway Safety Ctr R&P
Bldg   Indiana PA 15705
Ph: 724-357-4051 ▪ Fx: 724-357-7595 ▪ TF: 800-896-7703

American Driving Society Inc   www.americandrivingsociety.org
2324 Clark Rd   Lapeer MI 48446
Ph: 810-664-8666 ▪ Fx: 810-664-2405

American Druze Society   www.druze.com
PO Box 9276   Glendale CA 91226
Ph: 323-255-5237 ▪ Fx: 323-255-9155

American Economic Association   www.vanderbilt.edu/AEA
2014 Broadway Suite 305   Nashville TN 37203
Ph: 615-322-2595 ▪ Fx: 615-343-7590

American Edged Products Manufacturers Association   www.aepma.org
21165 Whitfield Pl Suite 105   Potomac Falls VA 20165
Ph: 703-433-9281 ▪ Fx: 703-433-0369

American Editorial Cartoonists, Association of   info.detnews.com/aaec
1121 Stoneferry Ln   Raleigh NC 27606
Ph: 919-859-5516 ▪ Fx: 919-859-3172

American Educational Research Association   www.aera.net
1230 17th St NW   Washington DC 20036
Ph: 202-223-9485 ▪ Fx: 202-775-1824

American Educational Trust   www.middleeastbooks.com
PO Box 53062   Washington DC 20009
Ph: 202-939-6050 ▪ TF: 800-368-5788

American Educators, Association of   www.aaeteachers.org
25201 Paseo de Alicia Suite 104   Laguna Hills CA 92653
Ph: 949-595-7979 ▪ Fx: 949-595-7970 ▪ TF: 800-704-7799

American Egg Board   www.aeb.org
1460 Renaissance Dr Suite 301   Park Ridge IL 60068
Ph: 847-296-7043 ▪ Fx: 847-296-7007

American Egyptian Cooperation Foundation   www.americanegyptiancoop.org
330 E 39th St Suite 32L   New York NY 10016
Ph: 212-867-2323 ▪ Fx: 212-697-0465

American Electrology Association   www.electrology.com
PO Box 687   Bodega Bay CA 94923
Ph: 707-875-9135

American Electroplaters & Surface Finishers Society Inc   www.aesf.org
12644 Research Pkwy   Orlando FL 32826
Ph: 407-281-6441 ▪ Fx: 407-281-6446

American Embryo Transfer Association   www.aeta.org
1111 N Dunlap Ave   Savoy IL 61847
Ph: 217-398-2217 ▪ Fx: 217-398-4119

American Endodontic Society   www.aesoc.com
1321 N Harbor Blvd Suite 201   Fullerton CA 92835
Ph: 714-870-5590 ▪ Fx: 714-526-2818

American Endurance Ride Conference   www.aerc.org
11960 Heritage Oak Pl Suite 9   Auburn CA 95603
Ph: 530-823-2260 ▪ Fx: 530-823-7805

American Engineering Association   www.aea.org
PO Box 820473   Fort Worth TX 76182
Ph: 972-264-6428

American Enterprise Institute for Public Policy Research   www.aei.org
1150 17th St NW Suite 1100   Washington DC 20036
Ph: 202-862-5800 ▪ Fx: 202-862-7177 ▪ TF: 800-862-5801

American Epilepsy Society   www.aesnet.org
342 N Main St   West Hartford CT 06117
Ph: 860-586-7505 ▪ Fx: 860-586-7550

American Equilibration Society   www.occlusion-tmj.org
8726 N Ferris Ave   Morton Grove IL 60053
Ph: 847-965-2888 ▪ Fx: 847-965-4888

American Equine Association
PO Box 658   Newfoundland NJ 07435
Ph: 973-948-7005 ▪ Fx: 973-697-1538

American Ethical Union   www.aeu.org
2 W 64th St   New York NY 10023
Ph: 212-873-6500 ▪ Fx: 212-362-0850

American Ethnological Society   www.aaanet.org/aes
c/o American Anthropological Assn 2200 Wilson Blvd Suite
    600   Arlington VA 22201
Ph: 703-528-1902 ▪ Fx: 703-528-3546

American-European Greyhound Alliance   www.ameurogreyhoundalliance.org/start.html
167 Saddle Hill Rd   Hopkinton MA 01748
Ph: 508-435-5969

American Evaluation Association   www.eval.org
16 Sconticut Neck Rd Suite 290   Fairhaven MA 02719
Ph: 508-748-3326 ▪ TF: 888-232-2275

American Ex-Prisoners of War   www.axpow.org
3201 E Pioneer Pkwy Suite 40   Arlington TX 76010
Ph: 817-649-2979 ▪ Fx: 817-649-0109

American Experiment, Center of the   www.amexp.org
1024 Plymouth Bldg 12 S 6th St   Minneapolis MN 55402
Ph: 612-338-3605 ▪ Fx: 612-338-3621

American Facsimile Association   2world.com/staging/afaxa
2200 Ben Franklin Pkwy Suite E105A   Philadelphia PA 19130
Ph: 215-981-0292 ▪ Fx: 215-981-0295

American Family Association   www.afa.net
PO Drawer 2440   Tupelo MS 38803
Ph: 662-844-5036 ▪ Fx: 662-842-7798

American Family Life PAC
1932 Wynnton Rd   Columbus GA 31999
Ph: 706-323-3431 ▪ Fx: 706-660-7278 ▪ TF: 800-992-3522

American Family Therapy Academy Inc   www.afta.org
1608 20th St NW 4th Fl   Washington DC 20009
Ph: 202-333-3690 ▪ Fx: 202-333-3692

American Fancy Rat & Mouse Association   www.afrma.org
9230 64th St   Riverside CA 92509
Ph: 626-966-0350

American Farm Bureau Federation   www.fb.com
225 W Touhy Ave   Park Ridge IL 60068
Ph: 847-685-8600 ▪ Fx: 847-685-8896

American Farm Bureau Foundation for Agriculture   www.agfoundation.org
225 Touhy Ave   Park Ridge IL 60068
Ph: 847-685-8764 ▪ Fx: 847-685-8969

American Farmland Trust   www.farmland.org
1200 18th St NW Suite 800   Washington DC 20036
Ph: 202-331-7300 ▪ Fx: 202-659-8339 ▪ TF: 800-431-1499

American Farrier's Association   www.americanfarriers.org
4509 Iron Works Pkwy Suite 1   Lexington KY 40511
Ph: 859-233-7411 ▪ Fx: 859-231-7862

American Federation for Aging Research   www.afar.org
70 W 40th St 11th Fl   New York NY 10018
Ph: 212-703-9977 ▪ Fx: 212-997-0330 ▪ TF: 888-582-2327

American Federation of Arts   www.afaweb.org
41 E 65th St   New York NY 10021
Ph: 212-988-7700 ▪ Fx: 212-861-2487 ▪ TF: 800-232-0270

American Federation of Astrologers   www.astrologers.com
6535 S Rural Rd   Tempe AZ 85283
Ph: 480-838-1751 ▪ Fx: 480-838-8293 ▪ TF: 888-301-7630

American Federation of Government Employees   www.afge.org
80 F St NW   Washington DC 20001
Ph: 202-737-8700 ▪ Fx: 202-639-6441

American Federation of Jews from Central Europe
570 7th Ave   New York NY 10018
Ph: 212-921-3871 ▪ Fx: 212-575-1918

American Federation of Labor & Congress of Industrial Organizations   www.aflcio.org
815 16th St NW   Washington DC 20006
Ph: 202-637-5000 ▪ Fx: 202-637-5058

American Federation for Medical Research   www.afmr.org
900 Cummings Ctr Suite 221-U   Beverly MA 01915
Ph: 978-927-8330 ▪ Fx: 978-524-8890

American Federation of Mineralogical Societies   www.amfed.org/
2706 Lascassas Pike   Murfreesboro TN 37130
Ph: 615-893-8270

American Federation of Motorcyclists   www.afmracing.com
6167 Jarvis Ave Suite 333   Newark CA 94560
Ph: 510-796-7005

American Federation of Musicians of the US & Canada   www.afm.org
1501 Broadway Suite 600   New York NY 10036
Ph: 212-869-1330 ▪ Fx: 212-764-6134 ▪ TF: 800-762-3444

American Federation of New Zealand Rabbit Breeders   www.geocities.com/newzealandrba
PO Box 171   Honeoye NY 14471
Ph: 585-229-5760

American Federation of Police & Concerned Citizens   www.aphf.org/afp_cc.html
6350 Horizon Dr   Titusville FL 32780
Ph: 321-264-0911 ▪ Fx: 321-264-0033

American Federation of School Administrators   www.admin.org
1729 21st St NW   Washington DC 20009
Ph: 202-986-4209 ▪ Fx: 202-986-4211 ▪ TF: 800-354-2372

American Federation of State County & Municipal Employees   www.afscme.org
1625 L St NW   Washington DC 20036
Ph: 202-452-4800 ▪ Fx: 202-429-1293

American Federation of Teachers   www.aft.org
555 New Jersey Ave NW   Washington DC 20001
Ph: 202-879-4400 ▪ Fx: 202-879-4556 ▪ TF: 800-238-1133

American Federation of Teachers Committee on Political Education
555 New Jersey Ave NW   Washington DC 20001
Ph: 202-879-4400 ▪ Fx: 202-879-4556 ▪ TF: 800-238-1133

American Federation of Television & Radio Artists   www.aftra.com
260 Madison Ave 7th Fl   New York NY 10016
Ph: 212-532-0800 ▪ Fx: 212-532-2242

American Feed Industry Association   www.afia.org
1501 Wilson Blvd Suite 1100   Arlington VA 22209
Ph: 703-524-0810 ▪ Fx: 703-524-1921

American Fence Association   www.americanfenceassociation.com
800 Roosevelt Rd Bldg C-20   Glen Ellyn IL 60137
Ph: 630-942-6598 ▪ Fx: 630-790-3095 ▪ TF: 800-822-4342

American Fern Society   www.amerfernsoc.org
Missouri Botanical Garden PO Box 229   Saint Louis MO 63166
Ph: 314-577-5100

American Ferret Association Inc   www.ferret.org
626-C Admiral Dr PMB 255   Annapolis MD 21401
Ph: 888-337-7381 ▪ Fx: 516-908-5215

American Festival of Microtonal Music Inc   www.afmm.org
318 E 70th St Suite 5FW   New York NY 10021
Ph: 212-517-3550 ▪ Fx: 212-517-5495

American Fiber Manufacturers Association Inc   www.afma.org
1530 Wilson Blvd Suite 690   Arlington VA 22209
Ph: 703-875-0432 ▪ Fx: 703-875-0907

American Fiberboard Association   www.fiberboard.org
1210 W Northwest Hwy   Palatine IL 60067
Ph: 847-934-8394 ▪ Fx: 847-934-8803

American Fibromyalgia Syndrome Association   www.afsafund.org
6380 E Tanque Verde Suite D   Tucson AZ 85715
Ph: 520-733-1570

American Film Institute   www.afi.com
2021 N Western Ave   Los Angeles CA 90027
Ph: 323-856-7600 ▪ Fx: 323-467-4578

American Filtration & Separations Society   www.afssociety.org
Univ of Houston Dept of Chemical Engineering 4800 Calhoun
    Rd   Houston TX 77204
Ph: 713-743-3671 ▪ Fx: 713-743-3679

American Finance Association   www.afajof.org
UC Berkeley Haas School of Business 545 Student Services
    Bldg   Berkeley CA 94729
Ph: 510-642-2397

American Financial Services Association   www.americanfinsvcs.com
919 18th St NW Suite 300   Washington DC 20006
Ph: 202-296-5544 ▪ Fx: 202-223-0321

American Financial Services Association Education Foundation   www.afsaef.org
919 18th St NW Suite 300   Washington DC 20006
Ph: 202-296-5544 ▪ Fx: 202-223-0321

American Financial Services Association PAC
919 18th St NW Suite 300   Washington DC 20006
Ph: 202-296-5544 ▪ Fx: 202-223-0321

American Fire Sprinkler Association Inc   www.firesprinkler.org
9696 Skillman St Suite 300   Dallas TX 75243
Ph: 214-349-5965 ▪ Fx: 214-343-8898

American First Day Cover Society   www.afdcs.org
PO Box 65960   Tucson AZ 85728
Ph: 520-321-0880 ▪ Fx: 520-321-0879

American Fisheries Society   www.fisheries.org
5410 Grosvenor Ln Suite 110   Bethesda MD 20814
Ph: 301-897-8616 ▪ Fx: 301-897-8096

American Flock Association   www.flocking.org
6 Beacon St Suite 1125   Boston MA 02108
Ph: 617-303-6288 ▪ Fx: 617-542-2199

American Floorcovering Alliance Inc
210 W Cuyler St   Dalton GA 30720
Ph: 706-278-4101 ▪ Fx: 706-278-5323 ▪ TF: 800-288-4101

American Floral Industry Association   www.afia.net
PO Box 420244   Dallas TX 75342
Ph: 214-742-2747 ▪ Fx: 214-742-2648

American Fly Fishing Trade Association   www.affta.com
PO Box 164   Kelso WA 98626
Ph: 360-636-0708 ▪ Fx: 360-636-3971

American Folklore Society   www.afsnet.org
Ohio State Univ Mershon Ctr 1501 Neil Ave   Columbus OH
    43201
Ph: 614-292-3375 ▪ Fx: 614-292-2407

American Football Coaches Association   www.afca.com
100 Legends Ln   Waco TX 76706
Ph: 254-754-9900 ▪ Fx: 254-754-7373

American Forage & Grassland Council   www.afgc.org
PO Box 94   Georgetown TX 78627
Ph: 512-868-2899 ▪ Fx: 512-931-1166 ▪ TF: 800-944-2342

American Foreign Relations, Society for Historians of   www.shafr.org

American Foreign Service Association   www.afsa.org
2101 'E' St NW   Washington DC 20037
Ph: 202-338-4045 ▪ Fx: 202-338-6820 ▪ TF: 800-704-2372

American Foreign Service Protective Association   www.afspa.org
1716 'N' St NW   Washington DC 20036
Ph: 202-833-4910   Fx: 202-833-4918

American Foreign Service Worldwide, Association of   www.aafsw.org
5125 McArthur Blvd NW Suite 36   Washington DC 20016
Ph: 202-362-6514   Fx: 202-362-6589

American Forensic Association   www.americanforensics.org
PO Box 256   River Falls WI 54022
Ph: 715-425-3198   Fx: 715-425-9533   TF: 800-228-5424

American Forest Foundation   www.affoundation.org
1111 19th St NW Suite 780   Washington DC 20036
Ph: 202-463-2462   Fx: 202-463-2461   TF: 888-889-4466

American Forest & Paper Association   www.afandpa.org
1111 19th St NW Suite 800   Washington DC 20036
Ph: 202-463-2700   Fx: 202-463-2785   TF: 800-878-8878

American Forest Resource Council   www.afrc.ws
1500 SW 1st Ave Suite 300   Portland OR 97201
Ph: 503-222-9505   Fx: 503-222-3255

American Forests   www.americanforests.org
734 15th St NW Suite 800 PO Box 2000   Washington DC 20013
Ph: 202-955-4500   Fx: 202-955-4588

American Forum for Global Education   www.globaled.org
120 Wall St Suite 2600   New York NY 10005
Ph: 212-624-1300   Fx: 212-624-1412   TF: 800-813-5056

American Foundation for Aging Research   www.agingresearchfoundation.org
North Carolina State Univ Biochemistry Dept 128 Polk Hall   Raleigh NC 27695
Ph: 919-515-5679   Fx: 919-515-2047

American Foundation for AIDS Research   www.amfar.org
120 Wall St 13th Fl   New York NY 10005
Ph: 212-806-1600   Fx: 212-806-1601   TF: 800-392-6327

American Foundation for the Blind   www.afb.org
11 Penn Plaza Suite 300   New York NY 10001
Ph: 212-502-7600   Fx: 212-502-7777   TF: 800-232-5463

American Foundation for Pharmaceutical Education
1 Church St Suite 202   Rockville MD 20850
Ph: 301-738-2160   Fx: 301-738-2161

American Foundation for Suicide Prevention   www.afsp.org
120 Wall St 22nd Fl   New York NY 10005
Ph: 212-363-3500   Fx: 212-363-6237   TF: 888-333-2377

American Foundation for Urologic Disease   www.afud.org
1000 Corporate Blvd Suite 110   Lithicum MD 21090
Ph: 410-689-3990   Fx: 410-689-3998   TF: 800-242-2383

American Foundry Society   www.afsinc.org
505 State St   Des Plaines IL 60016
Ph: 847-824-0181   Fx: 847-824-7848   TF: 800-537-4237

American Fox Terrier Club   www.aftc.org/
PO Box 1448   Edison NJ 08818
Ph: 732-777-0032   Fx: 732-777-0977

American Fracture Association   www.afa4docs.org
c/o Med Pro Orthopaedics 418 N 19th St   Phoenix AZ 85006
Ph: 602-254-9646

American Franchisee Association   www.franchisee.org
53 W Jackson Blvd Suite 205   Chicago IL 60604
Ph: 312-431-0545   Fx: 312-431-1132

American Fraternal Union   www.afu-life.com
111 4th Ave S PO Box 59   Ely MN 55731
Ph: 218-365-3143   Fx: 218-365-3181

American Freedom Center   www.homestead.com/americanfreedom
2002-A Guadalupe St Suite 284   Austin TX 78705
Ph: 512-453-7989   Fx: 512-453-7990

American Friends of Beth-Hatefutsoth
633 3rd Ave 21st Fl   New York NY 10017
Ph: 212-339-6034   Fx: 212-318-6176

American Friends of the Hakluyt Society   www.hakluyt.com/hak-soc-amer-top.htm
John Carter Brown Library PO Box 1894   Providence RI 02912
Ph: 401-863-2725   Fx: 401-863-3477

American Friends of the Hebrew University   www.afhu.org
11 E 69th St   New York NY 10021
Ph: 212-472-9800   Fx: 212-744-2324   TF: 800-567-2348

American Friends of the Israel Museum   www.imj.org.il
500 5th Ave Suite 2540   New York NY 10110
Ph: 212-997-5611   Fx: 212-997-5536

American Friends of Lafayette   www.friendsoflafayette.org
Lafayette College 316 Markle Hall   Easton PA 18042
Ph: 610-330-5200   Fx: 610-330-5700

American Friends of Neot-Kedumim   www.neot-kedumim.org.il
813 Rt 3   Halcott Center NY 12430
Ph: 845-254-5031   Fx: 845-254-9836

American Friends of the Paris Opera & Ballet
972 5th Ave   New York NY 10021
Ph: 212-439-1426   Fx: 212-439-1455

American Friends of Romania
4600 Connecticut Ave NW Unit 723   Washington DC 20008
Ph: 202-966-1922

American Friends of Saint David's Cathedral   www.afsdc.org
1001 Wilson Blvd Suite 405   Arlington VA 22209
Ph: 703-528-8192   Fx: 703-528-6186

American Friends Service Committee   www.afsc.org
1501 Cherry St   Philadelphia PA 19102
Ph: 215-241-7000   Fx: 215-241-7275

American Friends of the Shakespeare Birthplace Trust
625 Slaters Ln Suite 103   Alexandria VA 22314
Ph: 703-684-7703   Fx: 703-684-7594

American Friends of the Vatican Library   www.affi.com
581 E 14 Mile Rd   Clawson MI 48017
Ph: 248-588-1222

American Frozen Food Institute   www.affi.com
2000 Corporate Ridge Suite 1000   McLean VA 22102
Ph: 703-821-0770   Fx: 703-821-1350

American Frozen Food Institute PAC
2000 Corporate Ridge Suite 1000   McLean VA 22102
Ph: 703-821-0770   Fx: 703-821-1350

American Fuchsia Society   www.americanfuchsiasociety.org
243 Pinehaven Way   Pacifica CA 94044
Ph: 650-359-1227

American Furniture Manufacturers Association   www.afma4u.org
PO Box HP-7   High Point NC 27261
Ph: 336-884-5000   Fx: 336-884-5303

American Furniture Manufacturers Association PAC
1120 Connecticut Ave NW Suite 1080   Washington DC 20036
Ph: 202-466-7362   Fx: 202-429-4915

American Galloway Breeders' Association   www.galloway-world.org
310 W Spruce St   Missoula MT 59802
Ph: 406-728-5719   Fx: 406-721-6300

American Galvanizers Association   www.galvanizeit.org
6881 S Holly Cir Suite 108   Centennial CO 80112
Ph: 720-554-0900   Fx: 720-554-0909   TF: 800-468-7732

American Gaming Association   www.americangaming.org
555 13th St NW Suite 1010 E   Washington DC 20004
Ph: 202-637-6500   Fx: 202-637-6507

American Gas Association   www.aga.org
400 N Capitol St NW   Washington DC 20001
Ph: 202-824-7000   Fx: 202-824-7115

(American Gas Association) GASPAC
400 N Capitol St NW   Washington DC 20001
Ph: 202-824-7000   Fx: 202-824-7115

American Gastroenterological Association   www.gastro.org
4930 Del Ray Ave   Bethesda MD 20814
Ph: 301-654-2055   Fx: 301-654-5920

American Gathering of Jewish Holocaust Survivors
122 W 30th St Suite 205   New York NY 10001
Ph: 212-239-4230   Fx: 212-279-2926

American Gear Manufacturers Association   www.agma.org
500 Montgomery St Suite 350   Alexandria VA 22314
Ph: 703-684-0211   Fx: 703-684-0242

American Gelbvieh Association   www.gelbvieh.org
10900 Dover St   Westminster CO 80021
Ph: 303-465-2333   Fx: 303-465-2339

American Gem Society   www.ags.org
8881 W Sahara Ave   Las Vegas NV 89117
Ph: 702-255-6500   Fx: 702-255-7420

American Gem Trade Association   www.agta.org
PO Box 420643   Dallas TX 75342
Ph: 214-742-4367   Fx: 214-742-7334   TF: 800-972-1162

American Genetic Association   www.theaga.org
PO Box 257   Buckeystown MD 21717
Ph: 301-695-9292

American Geographical Society   www.amergeog.org
120 Wall St Suite 100   New York NY 10005
Ph: 212-422-5456   Fx: 212-422-5480

American Geological Institute   www.agiweb.org
4220 King St   Alexandria VA 22302
Ph: 703-379-2480   Fx: 703-379-7563

American Geophysical Union   www.agu.org
2000 Florida Ave NW   Washington DC 20009
Ph: 202-462-6900   Fx: 202-328-0566   TF: 800-966-2481

American Geriatrics Society   www.americangeriatrics.org
350 5th Ave Empire State Bldg Suite 801   New York NY 10018
Ph: 212-308-1414   Fx: 212-832-8646

American Glovebox Society   www.gloveboxsociety.org
PO Box 9099   Santa Rosa CA 95405
Ph: 800-530-1022   Fx: 707-578-4406

American Goat Society   www.americangoatsociety.com
PO Box 330   Broad Run VA 20137
Ph: 540-349-4709

American Gold Star Mothers Inc   www.goldstarmoms.com
2128 Leroy Pl NW   Washington DC 20008
Ph: 202-265-0991   Fx: 202-265-6963

American Golf Players Association   www.agpa.com
PO Box 33039   Phoenix AZ 85067
Ph: 602-279-4653   Fx: 602-241-9450   TF: 888-790-2472

American Grandprix Association   www.stadiumjumping.com/aga
1301 6th Ave W Suite 406   Bradenton FL 34205
Ph: 941-744-5465   Fx: 941-744-0874   TF: 800-237-8924

American Greyhound Track Operators Association   www.agtoa.com
Melbourne Greyhound Park 1100 N Wickham Rd   Melbourne FL 32935
Ph: 321-259-1143   Fx: 321-259-3437

American Ground Water Trust   www.agwt.org
16 Centre St   Concord NH 03301
Ph: 603-228-5444   Fx: 603-228-6557   TF: 800-423-7748

American Group Psychotherapy Association   www.agpa.org
25 E 21st St 6th Fl   New York NY 10010
Ph: 212-477-2677   Fx: 212-979-6627   TF: 877-668-2472

American Guernsey Association   www.usguernsey.com
7614 Slate Ridge Blvd PO Box 666   Reynoldsburg OH 43068
Ph: 614-864-2409   Fx: 614-864-5614

American Guild of English Handbell Ringers Inc   www.agehr.org
1055 E Centerville Stn Rd   Centerville OH 45459
Ph: 937-438-0085   Fx: 937-438-0434   TF: 800-878-5459

American Guild for Infant Survival
301 Eastwood Cir Suite 200   Virginia Beach VA 23454
Ph: 757-463-3845

American Guild of Music   www.americanguild.org
PO Box 599   Warren MI 48090
Ph: 248-336-9388

American Guild of Musical Artists   www.musicalartists.org
1430 Broadway 14th Fl   New York NY 10018
Ph: 212-265-3687   Fx: 212-262-9088   TF: 800-543-2462

American Guild of Organists www.agohq.org
475 Riverside Dr Suite 1260 New York NY 10115
Ph: 212-870-2310 ▪ Fx: 212-870-2163 ▪ TF: 800-246-5115

American Guild of Variety Artists
363 7th Ave 17th Fl New York NY 10001
Ph: 212-675-1003 ▪ Fx: 212-633-0097

American Hackney Horse Society www.hackneysociety.com
4059 Iron Works Pkwy Suite 3 Lexington KY 40511
Ph: 859-255-8694 ▪ Fx: 859-255-0177

American Haflinger Registry www.haflingerhorse.com
2746 State Rt 44 Rootstown OH 44272
Ph: 330-325-8116 ▪ Fx: 330-325-8178

American Hair Loss Council www.ahlc.org
125 7th St Suite 625 Pittsburgh PA 15222
Ph: 412-765-3666 ▪ Fx: 412-765-3669

American Hampshire Sheep Association www.countrylovin.com/ahsa/
15603 173rd Ave Milo IA 50166
Ph: 641-942-6402 ▪ Fx: 641-942-6502

American Handel Society www.americanhandelsociety.org
Univ of Maryland School of Music College Park MD 20742
Ph: 301-581-9602

American Handwriting Analysis Foundation iwhome.com/handwriting/applictn.htm
PO Box 6201 San Jose CA 95150
Ph: 408-377-6775 ▪ TF: 800-826-7774

American Hanoverian Society www.hanoverian.org
4067 Iron Works Pike Suite 1 Lexington KY 40511
Ph: 859-255-4141 ▪ Fx: 859-255-8467

American Hardware Manufacturers Association www.ahma.org
801 N Plaza Dr Schaumburg IL 60173
Ph: 847-605-1025 ▪ Fx: 847-605-1030

American Hardwood Export Council www.ahec.org
1111 19th St NW Suite 800 Washington DC 20036
Ph: 202-463-2720 ▪ Fx: 202-463-2787

American Harlequin Rabbit Club
1299 Josie Ln Conover NC 28613
Ph: 828-466-2274

American Harp Society Inc www.harpsociety.org
PO Box 38334 Los Angeles CA 90038
Ph: 323-825-4760 ▪ Fx: 323-469-3050

American Hatpin Society www.collectoronline.com/AHS/
20 Montecillo Dr Rolling Hills Estates CA 90274
Ph: 310-326-2196

American Headache Society ahsnet.org
19 Mantua Rd Mount Royal NJ 08061
Ph: 856-423-0043 ▪ Fx: 856-423-0082

American Health & Beauty Aids Institute www.proudlady.org
401 N Michigan Ave Suite 2200 Chicago IL 60611
Ph: 312-644-6610 ▪ Fx: 312-321-5194

American Health Care Association www.ahca.org
1201 L St NW Washington DC 20005
Ph: 202-842-4444 ▪ Fx: 202-842-3860 ▪ TF: 800-321-0343

American Health Care Association PAC
1201 L St NW Washington DC 20005
Ph: 202-842-4444 ▪ Fx: 202-842-3860 ▪ TF: 800-321-0343

American Health Information Management Association www.ahima.org
233 N Michigan Ave Suite 2150 Chicago IL 60601
Ph: 312-233-1100 ▪ Fx: 312-233-1090 ▪ TF: 800-335-5535

American Health Lawyers Association www.healthlawyers.org
1025 Connecticut Ave NW Suite 600 Washington DC 20036
Ph: 202-833-1100 ▪ Fx: 202-833-1105

American Health Planning Association www.ahpanet.org
7245 Arlington Blvd Suite 300 Falls Church VA 22042
Ph: 703-573-3103 ▪ Fx: 703-573-1276

American Health Quality Association www.ahqa.org
1140 Connecticut Ave NW Washington DC 20036
Ph: 202-331-5790 ▪ Fx: 202-331-9334

American Healthcare Radiology Administrators www.ahraonline.org
490-B Boston Post Rd Suite 101 Sudbury MA 01776
Ph: 978-443-7591 ▪ Fx: 978-443-8046 ▪ TF: 800-334-2472

American Hearing Impaired Hockey Association www.ahiha.org
1143 W Lake St Chicago IL 60607
Ph: 312-226-5880 ▪ Fx: 312-829-2098

American Hearing Research Foundation www.american-hearing.org
8 S Michigan Ave Suite 814 Chicago IL 60603
Ph: 312-726-9670 ▪ Fx: 312-726-9695

American Heart Association www.americanheart.org
7272 Greenville Ave Dallas TX 75231
Ph: 214-373-6300 ▪ Fx: 214-706-1191 ▪ TF: 800-242-8721

American Heartworm Society www.heartwormsociety.org
PO Box 667 Batavia IL 60510
Ph: 630-844-9676 ▪ Fx: 630-208-8398

American Hebrew Congregations, Union of www.uahcweb.org
633 3rd Ave New York NY 10017
Ph: 212-650-4000 ▪ Fx: 212-650-4159

American Helicopter Society International www.vtol.org
217 N Washington St Alexandria VA 22314
Ph: 703-684-6777 ▪ Fx: 703-739-9279

American Hellenic Educational Progressive Association www.ahepa.org
1909 Q St NW Suite 500 Washington DC 20009
Ph: 202-232-6300 ▪ Fx: 202-232-2140

American Hepato-Pancreato-Biliary Association www.ahpba.org
11300 W Olympic Blvd Suite 600 Los Angeles CA 90064
Ph: 310-437-0557 ▪ Fx: 310-437-0585

American Herb Association www.ahaherb.com/
PO Box 1673 Nevada City CA 95959
Ph: 916-265-9552

American Herbal Products Association www.ahpa.org
8484 Georgia Ave Suite 370 Silver Spring MD 20910
Ph: 301-588-1171 ▪ Fx: 301-588-1174

American Herbalists Guild www.americanherbalistsguild.com
1931 Gaddis Rd Canton GA 30115
Ph: 770-751-6021 ▪ Fx: 770-751-7472

American Hereford Association www.hereford.org
1501 Wyandotte St Kansas City MO 64108
Ph: 816-842-3757 ▪ Fx: 816-842-6931

American Hernia Society www.americanherniasociety.org
PO Box 536544 Orlando FL 32853
Ph: 407-898-1695 ▪ Fx: 407-894-2312

American Highland Cattle Association www.highlandcattle.org
4701 Marion St 200 Livestock Exchange Bldg Denver CO 80216
Ph: 303-292-9102 ▪ Fx: 303-292-9171

American Highway Users Alliance www.highways.org
1 Thomas Cir NW 10th Fl Washington DC 20005
Ph: 202-857-1200 ▪ Fx: 202-857-1220

American Hiking Society www.americanhiking.org
1422 Fenwick Ln Silver Spring MD 20910
Ph: 301-565-6704 ▪ Fx: 301-565-6714 ▪ TF: 800-972-8608

American Himalayan Rabbit Association ahra.homestead.com

American Historians, Organization of www.indiana.edu/~oah
112 N Bryan Ave Bloomington IN 47408
Ph: 812-855-7311 ▪ Fx: 812-855-0696

American Historic Racing Motorcycle Association www.ahrma.org
PO Box 1725 Goodlettsville TN 37070
Ph: 615-851-3674 ▪ Fx: 615-851-3678

American Historical Association www.historians.org
400 A St SE Washington DC 20003
Ph: 202-544-2422 ▪ Fx: 202-544-8307

American Historical Print Collectors Society www.ahpcs.org
PO Box 201 Fairfield CT 06824
Ph: 203-255-1627

American Historical Society of Germans from Russia www.ahsgr.org
631 D St Lincoln NE 68502
Ph: 402-474-3363 ▪ Fx: 402-474-7229

American History & Culture, Omohundro Institute of Early www.wm.edu/oieahc
PO Box 8781 Williamsburg VA 23187
Ph: 757-221-1110 ▪ Fx: 757-221-1047

American Hobbit Association
PO Box 51 Mason OH 45040
Ph: 513-398-4742

American Hockey Coaches Association www.ahcahockey.com
7 Concord St Gloucester MA 01930
Ph: 781-245-4177 ▪ Fx: 781-245-2492

American Holistic Health Association ahha.org
PO Box 17400 Anaheim CA 92817
Ph: 714-779-6152

American Holistic Medical Association www.holisticmedicine.org
12101 Menaul Blvd NE Suite C Albuquerque NM 87112
Ph: 505-292-7788 ▪ Fx: 505-293-7582

American Holistic Nurses' Association ahna.org
PO Box 2130 Flagstaff AZ 86003
Ph: 928-526-2196 ▪ Fx: 928-526-2752 ▪ TF: 800-278-2462

American Holistic Veterinary Medical Association www.ahvma.org
2218 Old Emmorton Rd Bel Air MD 21015
Ph: 410-569-0795 ▪ Fx: 410-569-2346

American Holsteiner Horse Association www.holsteiner.com
222 E Main St Suite 1 Georgetown KY 40324
Ph: 502-863-4239 ▪ Fx: 502-868-0722

American Home Life International www.amhomelife.org
1725 Oregon Pike Lancaster PA 17601
Ph: 717-560-2840 ▪ Fx: 717-560-2845

American Homebrewers Association www.beertown.org
736 Pearl St Boulder CO 80302
Ph: 303-447-0816 ▪ Fx: 303-447-2825 ▪ TF: 888-822-6273

American Homeowners Association www.ahahome.com
1100 Summer St 1st Fl Stamford CT 06905
Ph: 203-323-7715 ▪ Fx: 203-323-4558 ▪ TF: 800-470-2242

American Homeowners Foundation www.americanhomeowners.org
6776 Little Falls Rd Arlington VA 22213
Ph: 703-536-7776 ▪ Fx: 703-536-7079 ▪ TF: 800-489-7079

American Homeowners' Resource Center www.ahrc.com
PO Box 97 San Juan Capistrano CA 92693
Ph: 949-366-2125

American Horse Council www.horsecouncil.org
1616 H St NW 7th Fl Washington DC 20006
Ph: 202-296-4031 ▪ Fx: 202-296-1970

American Horse Protection Association www.americanhorseprotection.org
1000 29th St NW Suite T100 Washington DC 20007
Ph: 202-965-0500 ▪ Fx: 202-965-9621

American Horse Publications www.americanhorsepubs.org
49 Spinnaker Cir South Daytona FL 32119
Ph: 904-760-7743 ▪ Fx: 904-760-7728

American Horticultural Society www.ahs.org
7931 E Boulevard Dr Alexandria VA 22308
Ph: 703-768-5700 ▪ Fx: 703-768-8700 ▪ TF: 800-777-7931

American Horticultural Therapy Association www.ahta.org
909 York St Denver CO 80206
Ph: 303-370-8087 ▪ Fx: 303-331-5776 ▪ TF: 800-634-1603

American Hospital Association www.aha.org
1 N Franklin St Chicago IL 60606
Ph: 312-422-3000 ▪ Fx: 312-422-4796 ▪ TF: 800-424-4301

American Hospital Association PAC
325 7th St NW Suite 700 Washington DC 20004
Ph: 202-638-1100 ▪ Fx: 202-626-2345

American Hospitals, Federation of www.fahs.com
801 Pennsylvania Ave NW Suite 245 Washington DC 20004
Ph: 202-624-1500 ▪ Fx: 202-737-6462

American Hosta Society   www.hosta.org
9448 Mayfield Rd   Chesterland OH 44026
Ph: 440-729-9838 ▪ Fx: 440-729-2836

American Hot Rod Association   www.spokaneracewaypark.com/drags
111 N Hayford Rd   Spokane WA 99224
Ph: 509-244-2372 ▪ Fx: 509-244-2472

American Hotel & Lodging Association   www.ahla.com
1201 New York Ave NW Suite 600   Washington DC 20005
Ph: 202-289-3100 ▪ Fx: 202-289-3186

American Humane Association   www.americanhumane.org
63 Inverness Dr E   Englewood CO 80112
Ph: 303-792-9900 ▪ Fx: 303-792-5333 ▪ TF: 800-227-4645

American Humane Education Society
350 S Huntington Ave   Boston MA 02130
Ph: 617-522-7400 ▪ Fx: 617-522-4885

American Humanics   www.humanics.org
4601 Madison Ave   Kansas City MO 64112
Ph: 816-561-6415 ▪ Fx: 816-531-3527 ▪ TF: 800-343-6466

American Humanist Association   www.americanhumanist.org
1777 T St NW   Washington DC 20009
Ph: 202-238-9088 ▪ Fx: 202-238-9003 ▪ TF: 866-486-2647

American Hungarian Educators' Association   magyar.org/ahea

American Hungarian Foundation   www.ahfoundation.org
300 Somerset St PO Box 1084   New Brunswick NJ 08903
Ph: 732-846-5777 ▪ Fx: 732-249-7033

American Hungarian Library & Historical Society   www.hungarianhouse.org
213 E 82nd St   New York NY 10028
Ph: 212-249-9360

American Hydrogen Association   www.clean-air.org
1739 W 7th Ave   Mesa AZ 85202
Ph: 480-827-7915 ▪ Fx: 480-967-6601

American Hyperlexia Association   www.hyperlexia.org
195 W Spangler Suite B   Elmhurst IL 60126
Ph: 630-415-2212 ▪ Fx: 630-530-5908

American Hypnosis Association
18607 Ventura Blvd Suite 310   Tarzana CA 91356
Ph: 818-758-2730 ▪ Fx: 818-344-2262 ▪ TF: 800-990-0426

American Immigration Law Foundation   www.ailf.org
918 F St NW 6th Fl   Washington DC 20004
Ph: 202-742-5600 ▪ Fx: 202-742-5619

American Immigration Lawyers Association   www.aila.org
918 F St NW   Washington DC 20004
Ph: 202-216-2400 ▪ Fx: 202-783-7853

American Import Shippers Association   www.aisaship.com
662 Main St   New Rochelle NY 10801
Ph: 914-633-3770 ▪ Fx: 914-633-4041

American Independent Business Alliance   www.amiba.net
1510 5th St   Boulder CO 80302
Ph: 303-402-1575

American Indian Affairs, Association on   www.indian-affairs.org
PO Box 268   Sisseton SD 57262
Ph: 605-698-3998 ▪ Fx: 605-698-3316

American Indian Arts Council
725 Preston Forest Shopping Ctr Suite B   Dallas TX 75230
Ph: 214-891-9640 ▪ Fx: 214-891-0221

American Indian Arts, Institute for the Study of Traditional
PO Box 66124   Portland OR 97290
Ph: 503-233-8131

American Indian Cattlemen's Association, National
1541 Foster Rd   Toppenish WA 98948
Ph: 509-854-1329

American Indian College Fund   www.collegefund.org
8333 Greenwood Blvd   Denver CO 80221
Ph: 303-426-8900 ▪ Fx: 303-426-1200 ▪ TF: 800-776-3863

American Indian Council of Architects & Engineers   www.aicae.org

American Indian Court Judges Association, National   www.naicja.org
3618 Reder St   Rapid City SD 57702
Ph: 605-342-4804 ▪ Fx: 605-719-9357

American Indian Culture Research Center   www.bluecloud.org/dakota.html
Blue Cloud Abbey Box 98   Marvin SD 57251
Ph: 605-398-9200 ▪ Fx: 605-398-9201

American Indian Enterprise Development, National Center for   www.ncaied.org
953 E Juanita Ave   Mesa AZ 85204
Ph: 480-545-1298 ▪ Fx: 480-545-4208

American Indian Graduate Center   www.aigc.com
4520 Montgomery Blvd NE Suite 1-B   Albuquerque NM 87109
Ph: 505-881-4584 ▪ Fx: 505-884-0427 ▪ TF: 800-628-1920

American Indian Heritage Foundation   www.indians.org
PO Box 6330 6051 F Arlington Blvd   Falls Church VA 22040
Ph: 703-237-7500 ▪ Fx: 703-532-1921

American Indian Higher Education Consortium   www.aihec.org
121 Oronoco St   Alexandria VA 22314
Ph: 703-838-0400 ▪ Fx: 703-838-0388

American Indian Horse Registry   www.indianhorse.com
Rancho San Francisco 9028 State Park Rd   Lockhart TX 78644
Ph: 512-398-6642

American Indian Housing Council, National   naihc.indian.com
900 2nd St NE Suite 305   Washington DC 20002
Ph: 202-789-1754 ▪ Fx: 202-789-1758 ▪ TF: 800-284-9165

American Indian Institute   www.ou.edu/aii
Univ of Oklahoma College of Continuing Education 555
   Constitution Ave Suite 237   Norman OK 73072
Ph: 405-325-4127 ▪ Fx: 405-325-7757

American Indian Lore Association
960 Walhonding Ave   Logan OH 43138
Ph: 740-385-7136

American Indian Movement   www.aimovement.org
2717 Mission St Rm 303   San Francisco CA 94110
Ph: 415-552-1992

American Indian Physicians, Association of   www.aaip.com
1225 Sovereign Row Suite 103   Oklahoma City OK 73108
Ph: 405-946-7072 ▪ Fx: 405-946-7651

American Indian Research & Development Center
2233 W Lindsey Suite 118   Norman OK 73069
Ph: 405-364-0656 ▪ Fx: 405-364-5464

American Indian Ritual Object Repatriation Foundation   www.repatriationfoundation.org
463 E 57th St   New York NY 10022
Ph: 212-980-9441 ▪ Fx: 212-421-2746

American Indian Science & Engineering Society   www.aises.org
PO Box 9828   Albuquerque NM 87119
Ph: 505-765-1052 ▪ Fx: 505-765-5608

American Indian Youth, Running Strong for   www.indianyouth.org
8815 Telegraph Rd   Lorton VA 22079
Ph: 703-550-2123 ▪ Fx: 703-550-2473

American Indians, National Congress of   www.ncai.org
1301 Connecticut Ave NW Suite 200   Washington DC 20036
Ph: 202-466-7767 ▪ Fx: 202-466-7797

American-Indonesian Chamber of Commerce   www.aiccusa.org
317 Madison Ave Suite 520   New York NY 10017
Ph: 212-687-4505 ▪ Fx: 212-687-5844

American Industrial Hygiene Association   www.aiha.org
2700 Prosperity Ave Suite 250   Fairfax VA 22031
Ph: 703-849-8888 ▪ Fx: 703-207-3561

American Innerspring Manufacturers   www.aiminfo.org
1918 North Pkwy   Memphis TN 38112
Ph: 901-274-9030 ▪ Fx: 901-725-0510 ▪ TF: 800-882-5634

American Inns of Court   www.innsofcourt.org
1229 King St 2nd Fl   Alexandria VA 22314
Ph: 703-684-3590 ▪ Fx: 703-684-3607

American Institute of Aeronautics & Astronautics   www.aiaa.org
1801 Alexander Bell Dr Suite 500   Reston VA 20191
Ph: 703-264-7500 ▪ Fx: 703-264-7657 ▪ TF: 800-639-2422

American Institute of Architects   www.aiaonline.com
1735 New York Ave NW   Washington DC 20006
Ph: 202-626-7300 ▪ Fx: 202-626-7426 ▪ TF: 800-365-2724

American Institute of Architecture Students Inc   www.aiasnatl.com
1735 New York Ave NW   Washington DC 20006
Ph: 202-626-7472 ▪ Fx: 202-626-7414

American Institute of Bangladesh Studies   www.aibs.net
Pennsylvania State Univ 111 Sowers St Suite 501   State
   College PA 16801
Ph: 814-865-0436 ▪ Fx: 814-865-8299

American Institute of Biological Sciences   www.aibs.org
1444 'I' St NW Suite 200   Washington DC 20005
Ph: 202-628-1500 ▪ Fx: 202-628-1509 ▪ TF: 800-992-2427

American Institute of Biomedical Climatology   www.aibc.cc
1050 Eagle Rd   Newtown PA 18940
Ph: 215-968-4483

American Institute of Building Design   www.aibd.org
2505 Main St Suite 209B   Stratford CT 06961
Ph: 203-227-3640 ▪ Fx: 203-378-3568 ▪ TF: 800-366-2423

American Institute of Certified Planners   www.planning.org/aicp
1776 Massachusetts Ave NW Suite 400   Washington DC 20036
Ph: 202-872-0611 ▪ Fx: 202-872-0643

American Institute of Certified Public Accountants   www.aicpa.org
1211 Ave of the Americas   New York NY 10036
Ph: 212-596-6200 ▪ Fx: 212-596-6213 ▪ TF: 888-777-7077

American Institute of Chemical Engineers   www.aiche.org
3 Park Ave   New York NY 10016
Ph: 212-591-7338 ▪ Fx: 212-591-8897 ▪ TF: 800-242-4363

American Institute of Chemists   www.theaic.org
315 Chestnut St   Philadelphia PA 19106
Ph: 215-873-8224 ▪ Fx: 215-925-1954

American Institute of Commemorative Art   www.monuments-aica.com
11003 Fellswood Ct   Louisville KY 40243
Ph: 502-254-1375

American Institute for Conservation of Historic & Artistic Works   aic.stanford.edu
1717 K St NW Suite 200   Washington DC 20006
Ph: 202-452-9545 ▪ Fx: 202-452-9328

American Institute of Constructors   aicnet.org
466 94th Ave N   Saint Petersburg FL 33702
Ph: 727-578-0317 ▪ Fx: 727-578-9982

American Institute for Contemporary German Studies   www.aicgs.org
1400 16th St NW Suite 420   Washington DC 20036
Ph: 202-332-9312 ▪ Fx: 202-265-9531

American Institute for CPCU & Insurance Institute of America   www.aicpcu.org
720 Providence Rd PO Box 3016   Malvern PA 19355
Ph: 610-644-2100 ▪ Fx: 610-640-9576 ▪ TF: 800-644-2101

American Institute for Economic Research   www.aier.org
PO Box 1000   Great Barrington MA 01230
Ph: 413-528-1216 ▪ Fx: 413-528-0103

American Institute of Engineers   www.members-aie.org
4630 Appian Way Suite 206   El Sobrante CA 94803
Ph: 510-758-6240

American Institute of Fishery Research Biologists   www.iattc.org/aifrb/
Southwest Fisheries Science Ctr PO Box 271   La Jolla CA
   92038
Ph: 858-546-7177 ▪ Fx: 858-546-5653

American Institute of Floral Designers   www.aifd.org
720 Light St   Baltimore MD 21230
Ph: 410-752-3318 ▪ Fx: 410-752-8295

American Institute for Foreign Study   www.aifs.org
9 W Broad St   Stamford CT 06902
Ph: 203-399-5000 ▪ Fx: 203-399-5590 ▪ TF: 800-727-2437

American Institute for Foreign Study Foundation   www.aifs.com/aifsfoundation
9 W Broad St   Stamford CT 06902
Ph: 203-399-5414 ▪ Fx: 203-399-5593 ▪ TF: 800-322-4678

American Institute of Graphic Arts   www.aiga.org
164 5th Ave   New York NY 10010
Ph: 212-807-1990 ▪ Fx: 212-807-1799 ▪ TF: 800-548-1634

American Institute of the History of Pharmacy   www.aihp.org
777 Highland Ave   Madison WI 53705
Ph: 608-262-5378

American Institute of Homeopathy   www.homeopathyusa.org
801 N Fairfax St Suite 306   Alexandria VA 22314
Ph: 888-445-9988 ▪ Fx: 703-548-7792

American Institute of Hydrology   www.aihydro.org
2499 Rice St Suite 135   Saint Paul MN 55113
Ph: 651-484-8169 ▪ Fx: 651-484-8357

American Institute of Indian Studies   www.indiastudies.org
1130 E 59th St Foster Hall   Chicago IL 60637
Ph: 773-702-8638 ▪ Fx: 773-702-6636

American Institute of Inspectors   www.inspection.org
1421 Esplanade Ave Suite 7   Klamath Falls OR 97601
Ph: 541-273-6440 ▪ Fx: 541-273-1780 ▪ TF: 800-877-4770

American Institute for International Steel   www.aiis.org
1325 G St NW Suite 980   Washington DC 20005
Ph: 202-628-3878 ▪ Fx: 202-737-3134

American Institute of Life Threatening Illness & Loss   www.lifethreat.org/
Columbia-Presbyterian Medical Ctr 630 W 168th St   New York
    NY 10032
Ph: 718-601-4453 ▪ Fx: 718-549-7219

American Institute for Maghrib Studies   www.la.utexas.edu/research/mena/aims
Univ of Arizona Center for Middle Eastern Studies PO Box
    210080   Tucson AZ 85721
Ph: 520-626-6498

American Institute of Marine Underwriters   www.aimu.org
14 Wall St 8th Fl   New York NY 10005
Ph: 212-233-0550 ▪ Fx: 212-227-5102

American Institute of Massage Therapy Inc   www.aimtinc.com
1570 Brookhollow Dr Suite 200   Santa Ana CA 92705
Ph: 714-432-7879 ▪ Fx: 714-210-3199

American Institute for Medical & Biological Engineering   www.aimbe.org
1901 Pennsylvania Ave NW Suite 401   Washington DC 20006
Ph: 202-496-9660 ▪ Fx: 202-466-8489

American Institute of Mining Metallurgical & Petroleum Engineers   www.aimehq.org
8307 Shaffer Pkwy PO Box 270728   Littleton CO 80127
Ph: 303-948-4255 ▪ Fx: 303-948-4260

American Institute of Musical Studies   www.aimsgraz.org
6621 Snider Plaza   Dallas TX 75205
Ph: 214-363-2683 ▪ Fx: 214-363-6474

American Institute of Oral Biology   www.aiob.org
PO Box 7184   Loma Linda CA 92354
Ph: 909-558-4671 ▪ Fx: 909-558-0285

American Institute of Organbuilders   www.pipeorgan.org
PO Box 130982   Houston TX 77219
Ph: 713-529-2212

American Institute of Parliamentarians   www.parliamentaryprocedure.org
PO Box 2173   Wilmington DE 19899
Ph: 302-762-1811 ▪ Fx: 302-762-2170 ▪ TF: 888-664-0428

American Institute of Philanthropy   www.charitywatch.org
3450 N Lake Shore Dr Suite 2802E   Chicago IL 60657
Ph: 773-529-2300 ▪ Fx: 773-529-0024

American Institute of Physics   www.aip.org
1 Physics Ellipse   College Park MD 20740
Ph: 301-209-3100 ▪ Fx: 301-209-0843

American Institute of Polish Culture   www.ampolinstitute.org
1440 79th St Cswy Suite 117   Miami FL 33141
Ph: 305-864-2349 ▪ Fx: 305-865-5150

American Institute of Professional Bookkeepers   www.aipb.com
6001 Montrose Rd Suite 500   Rockville MD 20852
Ph: 301-770-7300 ▪ Fx: 800-541-0066 ▪ TF: 800-622-0121

American Institute of Professional Geologists   www.aipg.org
8703 Yates Dr Suite 200   Westminster CO 80031
Ph: 303-412-6205 ▪ Fx: 303-253-9220

American Institute for Public Service   www.jeffersonawards.org
100 W 10th St Suite 215   Wilmington DE 19801
Ph: 302-622-9101 ▪ Fx: 302-622-9108

American Institute for Shippers' Associations   www.shippers.org
PO Box 33457   Washington DC 20033
Ph: 202-628-0933 ▪ Fx: 202-296-7374

American Institute of Steel Construction   www.aisc.org
1 E Wacker Dr Suite 3100   Chicago IL 60601
Ph: 312-670-2400 ▪ Fx: 312-670-5403

American Institute of Stress   www.stress.org
124 Park Ave   Yonkers NY 10703
Ph: 914-963-1200 ▪ Fx: 914-965-6267

American Institute for Teen AIDS Prevention
PO Box 395   Oberlin OH 44074
Ph: 440-774-5411 ▪ Fx: 440-233-6455

American Institute of Timber Construction   www.aitc-glulam.org
7012 S Revere Pkwy Suite 140   Englewood CO 80112
Ph: 303-792-9559 ▪ Fx: 303-792-0669

American Institute of Ultrasound in Medicine   www.aium.org
14750 Sweitzer Ln Suite 100   Laurel MD 20707
Ph: 301-498-4100 ▪ Fx: 301-498-4450 ▪ TF: 800-638-5352

American Institute for Verdi Studies   www.nyu.edu/projects/verdi
New York Univ Music Dept 24 Waverly Pl Rm 268   New York
    NY 10003
Ph: 212-998-2587 ▪ Fx: 212-995-4147

American Institute of Wine & Food   www.aiwf.com
304 W Liberty St Suite 201   Louisville KY 40202
Ph: 800-274-2493 ▪ Fx: 502-589-3602

American Insurance Association   www.aiadc.org
1130 Connecticut Ave NW Suite 1000   Washington DC 20036
Ph: 202-828-7100 ▪ Fx: 202-293-1219

American Insurance PAC
1130 Connecticut Ave NW Suite 1000   Washington DC 20036
Ph: 202-828-7100 ▪ Fx: 202-293-1219

American Intellectual Property Law Association   www.aipla.org
2001 Jefferson Davis Hwy Suite 203   Arlington VA 22202
Ph: 703-415-0780 ▪ Fx: 703-415-0786

American Intellectual Property Law Association PAC
2001 Jefferson Davis Hwy Suite 203   Arlington VA 22202
Ph: 703-415-0780 ▪ Fx: 703-415-0786

American Intercultural Student Exchange   www.aise.com
7720 Herschel Ave   La Jolla CA 92037
Ph: 858-459-9761 ▪ Fx: 858-459-5301

American International Automobile Dealers Association   www.aiada.org
211 N Union St Suite 300   Alexandria VA 22314
Ph: 703-519-7800 ▪ Fx: 703-519-7810 ▪ TF: 800-462-4232

American-International Charolais Association   www.charolaisusa.com
PO Box 20247   Kansas City MO 64195
Ph: 816-464-5977 ▪ Fx: 816-464-5759

American International Health Alliance   www.aiha.com
1212 New York Ave NW Suite 750   Washington DC 20005
Ph: 202-789-1136 ▪ Fx: 202-789-1277

American International Marchigiana Society   www.marchigiana.org
PO Box 198   Walton KS 67151
Ph: 316-837-3303 ▪ Fx: 316-283-8379

American Irish Historical Society   www.aihs.org
991 5th Ave   New York NY 10028
Ph: 212-288-2263 ▪ Fx: 212-628-7927

American Iron Ore Association   www.aioa.org
302 W Superior St   Duluth MN 55802
Ph: 218-722-7724 ▪ Fx: 218-720-6707

American Iron & Steel Institute   www.steel.org
1140 Connecticut Ave NW Suite 705   Washington DC 20036
Ph: 202-452-7100 ▪ Fx: 202-463-6573

American Iron & Steel Institute PAC
1140 Connecticut Ave NW Suite 705   Washington DC 20036
Ph: 202-452-7100 ▪ Fx: 202-463-6573

American Israel Public Affairs Committee   www.aipac.org
440 1st St NW Suite 600   Washington DC 20001
Ph: 202-639-5200 ▪ Fx: 202-347-4918

American Italian Historical Association   www.mobilito.com/aiha
169 Country Club Rd   Chicago Heights IL 60411
Ph: 708-756-7168

American Ivy Society Inc   www.ivy.org

American Jail Association   www.corrections.com/aja
1135 Professional Ct   Hagerstown MD 21740
Ph: 301-790-3930

American Jersey Cattle Association   www.usjersey.com
6486 E Main St   Reynoldsburg OH 43068
Ph: 614-861-3636 ▪ Fx: 614-861-8040

American Jewish Archives   huc.edu/aja
3101 Clifton Ave   Cincinnati OH 45220
Ph: 513-221-1875 ▪ Fx: 513-221-7812

American Jewish Committee   www.ajc.org
165 E 56th St   New York NY 10022
Ph: 212-751-4000 ▪ Fx: 212-319-0975

American Jewish Congress   www.ajcongress.org
15 E 84th St   New York NY 10028
Ph: 212-879-4500 ▪ Fx: 212-249-3672

American Jewish Historical Society   www.ajhs.org
15 W 16th St   New York NY 10011
Ph: 212-294-6160 ▪ Fx: 212-294-6161

American Jewish Joint Distribution Committee   www.jdc.org
711 3rd Ave 10th Fl   New York NY 10017
Ph: 212-687-6200 ▪ Fx: 212-370-5467

American Jewish League for Israel   www.americanjewishleague.org
130 E 59th St   New York NY 10022
Ph: 212-371-1583 ▪ Fx: 212-371-3265

American Jewish Press Association   www.ajpa.org
1828 L St NW Suite 1000   Washington DC 20036
Ph: 202-785-2282 ▪ Fx: 202-785-2307

American Jewish Society for Service   www.ajss.org
15 E 26th St Rm 1029   New York NY 10010
Ph: 212-683-6178 ▪ Fx: 212-481-4174

American Jewish World Service   www.jws.org
45 W 36th St 10th Fl   New York NY 10018
Ph: 212-736-2597 ▪ Fx: 212-736-3463 ▪ TF: 800-889-7146

American Journalism Historians Association   www.berry.edu/ajha
Oklahoma Baptist Univ 500 W University St Box
    61201   Shawnee OK 74804
Ph: 405-878-2221

American Judges Association   aja.ncsc.dni.us
300 Newport Ave   Williamsburg VA 23185
Ph: 757-259-1841 ▪ Fx: 757-259-1520 ▪ TF: 800-616-6165

American Judicature Society   www.ajs.org
Drake Univ Opperman Ctr 2700 University Ave   Des Moines IA
    50311
Ph: 515-271-2281 ▪ Fx: 515-279-3090

American Judo & Jujitsu Federation   www.ajjf.org

American Junior Brahman Association   www.brahman.org/ajba.html
3003 South Loop W Suite 140   Houston TX 77054
Ph: 713-349-0854 ▪ Fx: 713-349-9795

American Junior Chianina Association   www.chicattle.org/ajca.html
PO Box 890   Platte City MO 64079
Ph: 816-431-2808 ▪ Fx: 816-431-5381

American Junior Golf Association   www.ajga.org
1980 Sports Club Dr   Braselton GA 30517
Ph: 770-868-4200 ▪ Fx: 770-868-4211 ▪ TF: 877-373-2542

American Junior Paint Horse Association   www.ajpha.com
PO Box 961023   Fort Worth TX 76161
Ph: 817-834-2746 ▪ Fx: 817-834-3152

American Junior Rodeo Association   home1.gte.net/ajra
4501 Armstrong St   San Angelo TX 76903
Ph: 915-658-8009

American Junior Shorthorn Association
8288 Hascall St   Omaha NE 68124
Ph: 402-393-7200 ▪ Fx: 402-393-7203
www.beefshorthornusa.com

American Junior Simmental Association
1 Simmental Way   Bozeman MT 59715
Ph: 406-587-4531
www.simmental.org/ajsainfo.html

American Juvenile Arthritis Organization
1330 W Peachtree St   Atlanta GA 30309
Ph: 404-965-7514 ▪ Fx: 404-872-0457
www.arthritis.org/communities

American Karakul Sheep Registry
11500 Hwy 5   Boonville MO 65233
Ph: 660-838-6340 ▪ Fx: 660-838-6322
www.karakulsheep.com

American Kennel Club
260 Madison Ave   New York NY 10016
Ph: 212-696-8200 ▪ Fx: 212-696-8299
www.akc.org

American Kenpo Karate International
PO Box 768   Evanston WY 82931
Ph: 307-789-4124
www.akki.com

American Kidney Fund
6110 Executive Blvd Suite 1010   Rockville MD 20852
Ph: 301-881-3052 ▪ Fx: 301-881-0898 ▪ TF: 800-638-8299
www.akfinc.org

American Killifish Association
280 Cold Springs Dr   Manchester PA 17345
Ph: 610-566-2098
www.aka.org

American Kitefliers Association
PO Box 1614   Walla Walla WA 99362
Ph: 509-529-9171 ▪ TF: 800-252-2550
www.aka.kite.org

American Knife & Tool Institute
22 Vista View   Cody WY 82414
Ph: 307-587-8296
www.akti.org

American Kodaly Educators, Organization of
1612 29th Ave S   Moorhead MN 56560
Ph: 218-227-6253 ▪ Fx: 218-277-6254
www.oake.org

American Kurdish Information Network
2600 Connecticut Ave NW Suite 1   Washington DC 20008
Ph: 202-483-6444 ▪ Fx: 202-483-6476
www.kurdistan.org

American Labor Education Center
2000 P St NW Suite 300   Washington DC 20036
Ph: 202-828-5170 ▪ Fx: 202-785-3862

American Ladder Institute
401 N Michigan Ave   Chicago IL 60611
Ph: 312-644-6610 ▪ Fx: 312-527-6705
www.americanladderinstitute.org

American Lamb Council
9875 Maroon Cir Suite 360   Centennial CO 80112
Ph: 303-771-3500 ▪ Fx: 303-771-8200
www.sheepusa.org

American Land Rights Association
30218 NE 82nd Ave PO Box 400   Battle Ground WA 98604
Ph: 360-687-3087 ▪ Fx: 360-687-2973
www.landrights.org

American Land Title Association
1828 L St NW Suite 705   Washington DC 20036
Ph: 202-296-3671 ▪ Fx: 202-223-5843 ▪ TF: 800-787-2582
www.alta.org

American Lands Alliance
726 7th St SE   Washington DC 20002
Ph: 202-547-9400 ▪ Fx: 202-547-9213
www.americanlands.org

American Langshan Club
18077 S Hwy 88   Claremore OK 74017
Ph: 918-341-2238

American Laryngological Association
www.alahns.org

American Laryngological Rhinological & Otological Society Inc
555 N 30th St   Omaha NE 68131
Ph: 402-346-5500 ▪ Fx: 402-346-5300
www.triological.org

American Latvian Association in the US
400 Hurley Ave   Rockville MD 20850
Ph: 301-340-1914 ▪ Fx: 301-340-8732
www.alausa.org

American Law Institute
4025 Chestnut St   Philadelphia PA 19104
Ph: 215-243-1600 ▪ Fx: 215-243-1664 ▪ TF: 800-253-6397
www.ali.org

American Law Institute - American Bar Association
4025 Chestnut St   Philadelphia PA 19104
Ph: 215-243-1600 ▪ Fx: 215-243-1664 ▪ TF: 800-253-6397
www.ali-aba.org

American Lawyers Auxiliary
541 N Fairbanks 15th Fl   Chicago IL 60611
Ph: 312-988-5522 ▪ TF: 800-285-2221
www.abanet.org/publiced/ala/

American Leadership Forum
PO Box 20089   Stanford CA 94309
Ph: 650-723-6127 ▪ Fx: 650-723-6131
www.alfnational.org

American League of Financial Institutions
900 19th St NW Suite 400   Washington DC 20006
Ph: 202-857-6176 ▪ Fx: 202-296-8716
www.alfi.org

American League of Lobbyists
PO Box 30005   Alexandria VA 22310
Ph: 703-960-3011 ▪ Fx: 703-960-4070
www.alldc.org

American Leather Chemists Association
1314 50th St Suite 103   Lubbock TX 79412
Ph: 806-744-1798 ▪ Fx: 806-744-1785
www.leatherchemists.org

American Lebanese Engineering Society
PO Box 690785   Orlando FL 32869
Ph: 407-422-6761 ▪ Fx: 407-422-9664

American Lebanese Syrian Associated Charities
501 St Jude Pl   Memphis TN 38105
Ph: 901-578-2000 ▪ Fx: 901-578-2805 ▪ TF: 800-822-6344
www.stjude.org

American Legion
700 N Pennsylvania St   Indianapolis IN 46204
Ph: 317-630-1200 ▪ Fx: 317-630-1223 ▪ TF: 800-433-3318
www.legion.org

American Legion Auxiliary
777 N Meridian St 3rd Fl   Indianapolis IN 46204
Ph: 317-955-3845 ▪ Fx: 317-955-3884
www.legion-aux.org

American Legion Baseball
PO Box 1055   Indianapolis IN 46206
Ph: 317-630-1213 ▪ Fx: 317-630-1369

American Legion Press Association, National
www.nalpa.legion.org

American Legion, Sons of the
PO Box 1055   Indianapolis IN 46206
Ph: 317-630-1200 ▪ Fx: 317-630-1413
www.sal.legion.org

American Legislative Exchange Council
1129 20th St NW Suite 500   Washington DC 20036
Ph: 202-466-3800 ▪ Fx: 202-466-3801
www.alec.org

American Leprosy Missions
1 ALM Way   Greenville SC 29601
Ph: 864-271-7040 ▪ Fx: 864-271-7062 ▪ TF: 800-543-3135
www.leprosy.org

American Library Association
50 E Huron St   Chicago IL 60611
Ph: 312-944-6780 ▪ Fx: 312-944-2641 ▪ TF: 800-545-2433
www.ala.org

American Licensed Practical Nurses Association
1090 Vermont Ave NW Suite 800   Washington DC 20005
Ph: 202-682-9000 ▪ Fx: 202-682-0168

American Life League
PO Box 1350   Stafford VA 22555
Ph: 540-659-4171 ▪ Fx: 540-659-2586 ▪ TF: 888-546-2580
www.all.org

American Lighting Association
2050 Stemmons Fwy Suite 10046   Dallas TX 75207
Ph: 214-698-9898 ▪ Fx: 214-698-9899 ▪ TF: 800-605-4448
www.americanlightingassoc.

American Liszt Society
Hog Mountain Rd   Fleishmanns NY 12430
Ph: 845-586-4457
www.americanlisztsociety.org

American Literacy Council
148 W 117th St   New York NY 10026
Ph: 212-663-4200 ▪ TF: 800-781-9985
www.americanliteracy.com

American Literary Translators Association
Univ of Texas at Dallas PO Box 830688 MC35   Richardson TX 75083
Ph: 972-883-2093 ▪ Fx: 972-883-6303
www.literarytranslators.org

American Lithotripsy Society
305 2nd Ave Suite 200   Waltham MA 02451
Ph: 781-895-9098 ▪ Fx: 781-895-9088
www.lithotripsy.org

American Littoral Society
Sandy Hook Bldg 18   Highlands NJ 07732
Ph: 732-291-0055 ▪ Fx: 732-872-8041
www.littoralsociety.org

American Livebearer Association
5 Zerbe St   Cressona PA 17929
Ph: 570-385-0573 ▪ Fx: 570-385-2781
www.livebearers.org

American Liver Foundation
75 Maiden Ln Suite 603   New York NY 10038
Ph: 212-668-1000 ▪ Fx: 212-483-8179 ▪ TF: 800-465-4837
www.liverfoundation.org

American Livestock Breeds Conservancy
PO Box 477   Pittsboro NC 27312
Ph: 919-542-5704 ▪ Fx: 919-545-0022
www.albc-usa.org

American Logistics Association
1133 15th St NW Suite 640   Washington DC 20005
Ph: 202-466-2520 ▪ Fx: 202-296-4419
www.ala-national.org

American Luggage Dealers Association
1114 State St   Santa Barbara CA 93101
Ph: 805-966-6909 ▪ Fx: 805-966-5710
www.luggagedealers.com

American Lumber Standard Committee Inc
PO Box 210   Germantown MD 20875
Ph: 301-972-1700 ▪ Fx: 301-540-8004
www.alsc.org

American Lung Association
61 Broadway 6th Fl   New York NY 10006
Ph: 212-315-8700 ▪ Fx: 212-315-8872 ▪ TF: 800-586-4872
www.lungusa.org

American Lutheran Publicity Bureau
PO Box 327   Delhi NY 13753
Ph: 607-746-7511
www.alpb.org

American Lyme Disease Foundation Inc
293 Rt 100   Somers NY 10589
Ph: 914-277-6970 ▪ Fx: 914-277-6974 ▪ TF: 800-876-5963
www.aldf.com

American Machine Tool Distributors' Association
1445 Research Blvd Suite 450   Rockville MD 20850
Ph: 301-738-1200 ▪ Fx: 301-738-9499 ▪ TF: 800-878-2683
www.amtda.org

American Maine-Anjou Association
204 Marshall Rd PO Box 1100   Platte City MO 64079
Ph: 816-431-9950 ▪ Fx: 816-431-9951
www.maine-anjou.org

American Malting Barley Association
740 N Plankinton Ave Suite 830   Milwaukee WI 53203
Ph: 414-272-4640
www.ambainc.org

American Managed Behavioral Healthcare Association
1101 Pennsylvania Ave NW 6th Fl   Washington DC 20004
Ph: 202-756-7726 ▪ Fx: 202-756-7308
www.ambha.org

American Management Association
1601 Broadway   New York NY 10019
Ph: 212-586-8100 ▪ Fx: 212-903-8168 ▪ TF: 800-262-6969
www.amanet.org

American Manufacturing Trade Action Coalition
910 16th St NW Suite 410   Washington DC 20006
Ph: 202-452-0866 ▪ Fx: 202-452-0739
www.amtacdc.org

American Marine Insurance Clearing House
30 Broad St 7th Fl   New York NY 10004
Ph: 212-405-2835 ▪ Fx: 212-344-1664
www.amich.org

American Maritain Association
3921 Glenview Dr   South Bend IN 46628
Ph: 574-271-1187 ▪ Fx: 574-271-1292
www.jacquesmaritain.org

American Maritime Congress
1300 'I' St NW Suite 250-W   Washington DC 20005
Ph: 202-842-4900 ▪ Fx: 202-842-3492
www.us-flag.org

American Maritime Officers Service
490 L'Enfant Plaza E SW Suite 7204   Washington DC 20024
Ph: 202-479-1133 ▪ Fx: 202-479-1136

American Marketing Association
311 S Wacker Dr Suite 5800   Chicago IL 60606
Ph: 312-542-9000 ▪ Fx: 312-542-9001 ▪ TF: 800-262-1150
www.marketingpower.com

American Massage Therapy Association www.amtamassage.org
820 Davis St Suite 100 Evanston IL 60201
Ph: 847-864-0123 ▪ Fx: 847-864-1178

American Master Mariners, Council of www.mastermariner.org
2700 Broening Hwy Dunmar Bldg Suite 115 Baltimore MD
21222
Ph: 410-285-7800

American Mathematical Association of Two-Year Colleges www.amatyc.org
Southwest Tennessee Community College 5983 Macon
Cove Memphis TN 38134
Ph: 901-333-4643 ▪ Fx: 901-383-4651

American Mathematical Society www.ams.org
PO Box 6248 Providence RI 02940
Ph: 401-455-4000 ▪ Fx: 401-331-3842 ▪ TF: 800-321-4267

American Measuring Tool Manufacturers Association www.amtma.com
1300 Sumner Ave Cleveland OH 44115
Ph: 216-241-7333 ▪ Fx: 216-241-0105

American Meat Institute www.meatami.com
1700 N Moore St Suite 1600 Arlington VA 22209
Ph: 703-841-2400 ▪ Fx: 703-527-0938

American Meat Institute PAC
1700 N Moore St Suite 1600 Arlington VA 22209
Ph: 703-841-2400 ▪ Fx: 703-527-0938

American Meat Science Association www.meatscience.org
1111 N Dunlap Ave Savoy IL 61874
Ph: 217-356-3182 ▪ Fx: 217-398-4119

American Medical Association www.ama-assn.org
515 N State St Chicago IL 60610
Ph: 312-464-5000 ▪ Fx: 312-464-4184 ▪ TF: 800-621-8335

American Medical Association www.ama-assn.org/ama/pub/category/3119.html
Foundation 515 N State St Chicago IL 60610
Ph: 312-464-4543 ▪ Fx: 312-464-5973

American Medical Association PAC
1101 Vermont Ave NW 12th Fl Washington DC 20005
Ph: 202-789-7400 ▪ Fx: 202-789-7485

American Medical Directors Association www.amda.com
10480 Little Patuxent Pkwy Suite 760 Columbia MD 21044
Ph: 410-740-9743 ▪ Fx: 410-740-4572 ▪ TF: 800-876-2632

American Medical Equestrian Association www.ameaonline.org
PO Box 130848 Birmingham AL 35213
Ph: 866-441-2632

American Medical Group Association www.amga.org
1422 Duke St Alexandria VA 22314
Ph: 703-838-0033 ▪ Fx: 703-548-1890

American Medical Informatics Association www.amia.org
4915 Saint Elmo Ave Suite 401 Bethesda MD 20814
Ph: 301-657-1291 ▪ Fx: 301-657-1296

American Medical Publishers Association www.ampaonline.org
14 Fort Hill Rd Huntington NY 11743
Ph: 631-423-0075

American Medical Rehabilitation Providers Association www.amrpa.org
1710 'N' St NW Washington DC 20036
Ph: 202-223-1920 ▪ Fx: 202-223-1925 ▪ TF: 888-346-4624

American Medical Society for Sports Medicine www.amssm.org
11639 Earnshaw St Overland Park KS 66210
Ph: 913-327-1415 ▪ Fx: 913-327-1491

American Medical Student Association www.amsa.org
1902 Association Dr Reston VA 20191
Ph: 703-620-6600 ▪ Fx: 703-620-5873 ▪ TF: 800-767-2266

American Medical Technologists www.amt1.com
710 Higgins Rd Park Ridge IL 60068
Ph: 847-823-5169 ▪ Fx: 847-823-0458 ▪ TF: 800-275-1268

American Medical Tennis Association www.mdtennis.org
1803 Cobbleston Dr Provo UT 84604
Ph: 800-326-2682 ▪ Fx: 801-374-0135

American Medical Women's Association www.amwa-doc.org
801 N Fairfax St Suite 400 Alexandria VA 22314
Ph: 703-838-0500 ▪ Fx: 703-549-3864

American Medical Writers Association www.amwa.org
40 W Gude Dr Suite 101 Rockville MD 20850
Ph: 301-294-5303 ▪ Fx: 301-294-9006

American Menopause Foundation Inc www.americanmenopause.org
350 5th Ave Suite 2822 New York NY 10118
Ph: 212-714-2398 ▪ Fx: 212-714-1252

American Men's Studies Association www.mensstudies.org
382 W Coyote Ln SE Albuquerque NM 87123
Ph: 505-323-2386 ▪ Fx: 505-323-3634

American Mensa Ltd www.us.mensa.org
1229 Corporate Dr W Arlington TX 76006
Ph: 817-607-0060 ▪ Fx: 817-649-5232 ▪ TF: 800-666-3672

American Mental Health Counselors Association www.amhca.org
801 N Fairfax St Suite 304 Alexandria VA 22314
Ph: 703-548-6002 ▪ Fx: 703-548-4775 ▪ TF: 800-326-2642

American Merchant Marine Library Association www.uss-ammla.com
20 Exchange Pl Suite 2901 New York NY 10005
Ph: 212-269-0711 ▪ Fx: 212-432-5492

American Metal Detecting Association www.amdaonline.net

American Metalcasting Consortium amc.aticorp.org
5300 International Blvd Charleston SC 29418
Ph: 843-760-3219 ▪ Fx: 843-767-3354

American Meteorological Society www.ametsoc.org
45 Beacon St Boston MA 02108
Ph: 617-227-2425 ▪ Fx: 617-742-8718

American Microscopical Society www.amicros.org
Bryn Mawr College Dept of Biology 101 N Merion Ave Bryn
Mawr PA 19010
Ph: 610-526-5094 ▪ Fx: 610-526-5086

American Military Medical Impression www.ww2medicine.org
PO Box 2026 Columbia MD 21045
Ph: 410-381-4293

American Military Uniform Collectors, Association of www.naples.net/clubs/aamuc
PO Box 1876 Elyria OH 44036
Ph: 440-365-5321

American Milking Devon Association www.milkingdevons.org
135 Old Bay Rd New Durham NH 03855
Ph: 603-859-6611

American Milking Shorthorn Junior Society www.milkingshorthorn.com/juniors.html
800 Pleasant St Beloit WI 53511
Ph: 608-365-3332 ▪ Fx: 608-365-6644

American Milking Shorthorn Society www.milkingshorthorn.com
800 Pleasant St Beloit WI 53511
Ph: 608-365-3332

American Miniature Horse Association www.swcp.com/amha
5601 S I-35 W Alvarado TX 76009
Ph: 817-783-5600 ▪ Fx: 817-783-6403

American Miniature Jersey Cattle Registry
PO Box 942 Rochester WA 98579
Ph: 360-273-7789

American Missionary Fellowship www.americanmissionary.org
672 Conestoga Rd PO Box 370 Villanova PA 19085
Ph: 610-527-4439 ▪ Fx: 610-527-4720

American Mobile Telecommunications Association www.amtausa.org
200 N Glebe Rd Suite 1000 Arlington VA 22203
Ph: 202-835-7819 ▪ Fx: 202-331-9062

American Mold Builders Association www.amba.org
701 E Irving Park Rd Suite 207 Roselle IL 60172
Ph: 630-980-7667 ▪ Fx: 630-980-9714

American Montessori Society www.amshq.org
281 Park Ave S 6th Fl New York NY 10010
Ph: 212-358-1250 ▪ Fx: 212-358-1256

American Monument Association www.imsa-online.com/ammonas.htm
30 Eden Alley Suite 301 Columbus OH 43215
Ph: 614-461-5852 ▪ Fx: 614-461-1497

American Morgan Horse Association www.morganhorse.com
PO Box 519 Shelburne VT 05482
Ph: 802-985-8430

American Mosquito Control Association www.mosquito.org
PO Box 234 Eatontown NJ 07727
Ph: 732-544-4645 ▪ Fx: 732-542-3267

American Mothers Inc www.americanmothers.org
15 Dupont Cir NW Washington DC 20036
Ph: 202-234-7375 ▪ Fx: 202-234-7390 ▪ TF: 877-242-4264

American Motility Society motilitysociety.org
45685 Harmony Ln Belleville MI 48111
Ph: 734-699-1130 ▪ Fx: 734-699-1136

American Motorcycle Heritage Foundation
Motorcycle Hall of Fame Museum 13515 Yarmouth
Dr Pickerington OH 43147
Ph: 614-856-2222 ▪ Fx: 614-856-2221

American Motorcyclist Association www.ama-cycle.org
13515 Yarmouth Dr Pickerington OH 43147
Ph: 614-856-1900 ▪ Fx: 614-856-1920 ▪ TF: 800-262-5646

American Motorcyclist Association PAC
13515 Yarmouth Dr Pickerington OH 43147
Ph: 614-856-1900 ▪ Fx: 614-856-1920

American Motors Drivers & Racers Association, National www.namdra.org
PO Box 987 Twin Lakes WI 53181
Ph: 262-396-9552

American Motors Owners Association www.amonational.com
1615 Purvis Ave Janesville WI 53545
Ph: 608-752-8247

American Motorsport International
7963 Depew St Arvada CO 80003
Ph: 303-428-8760 ▪ Fx: 303-428-1070

American Moving & Storage Association www.amconf.org
1611 Duke St Alexandria VA 22314
Ph: 703-683-7410 ▪ Fx: 703-683-7527

American Moving & Storage Association PAC
1611 Duke St Alexandria VA 22314
Ph: 703-683-7410 ▪ Fx: 703-683-7527

American Mule Association
264 Clovis Ave Clovis CA 93612
Ph: 559-324-6583

American Murray Grey Association www.murraygreybeefcattle.com
PO Box 224 New Bethlehem PA 16242
Ph: 814-275-2515 ▪ Fx: 814-275-2506

American Mushroom Institute www.americanmushroom.org
1 Massachusetts Ave NW Suite 800 Washington DC 20001
Ph: 202-842-4344 ▪ Fx: 202-408-7763

American Music Center www.amc.net
30 W 26th St Suite 1001 New York NY 10010
Ph: 212-366-5260 ▪ Fx: 212-366-5265

American Music Conference www.amc-music.org
5790 Armada Dr Carlsbad CA 92008
Ph: 760-431-9124 ▪ Fx: 760-438-7237

American Music Festival Association
PO Box 2987 Anaheim CA 92814
Ph: 562-948-2281 ▪ Fx: 562-948-4575

American Music, Institute for Studies in depthome.brooklyn.cuny.edu/isam
Brooklyn College of CUNY 2900 Bedford Ave Brooklyn NY
11210
Ph: 718-951-5655 ▪ Fx: 718-951-4858

American Music Scholarship Association www.amsa-wpc.org
441 Vine St Suite 1030 Cincinnati OH 45202
Ph: 513-421-5342 ▪ Fx: 513-421-2672

American Music, Society for www.american-music.org
Univ of Pittsburgh Stephen Foster Memorial 405 Bellefield
Hall Pittsburgh PA 15260
Ph: 412-624-3031 ▪ Fx: 412-624-7447

American Music Therapy Association　　www.musictherapy.org
8455 Colesville Rd Suite 1000　Silver Spring MD 20910
Ph: 301-589-3300 ▪ Fx: 301-589-5175

American Musical Instrument Society　　www.amis.org/
389 Main St Siote 202　Malden MA 02148
Ph: 781-397-8870

American Musicians Union
8 Tobin Ct　Dumont NJ 07628
Ph: 201-384-5378

American Musicological Society　　www.sas.upenn.edu/music/ams/
201 S 34th St　Philadelphia PA 19104
Ph: 215-898-8698 ▪ Fx: 215-573-2106

American Mustang & Burro Association Inc　　www.bardalisa.com
PO Box 788　Lincoln CA 95648
Ph: 530-633-9271 ▪ TF: 800-874-8453

American Name Society　　www.wtsn.binghamton.edu/ANS

American Naprapathic Association　　www.naprapathy.org
164 Division St Suite 202　Elgin IL 60120
Ph: 847-214-8642 ▪ Fx: 847-214-8645

American National CattleWomen Inc　　www.ancw.org
PO Box 3881　Englewood CO 80155
Ph: 303-694-0313 ▪ Fx: 303-694-2390

American National Standards Institute　　www.ansi.org
25 W 43rd St 4th Fl　New York NY 10036
Ph: 212-642-4900 ▪ Fx: 212-398-0023

American Nationalist Union　　www.anu.org

American Nature Study Society　　www.nature-study.org
Pocono Environmental Education Ctr RR 2 Box
1010　Dingmans Ferry PA 18328
Ph: 570-828-9692 ▪ Fx: 570-828-9695

American Naturopathic Medical Association　　www.anma.com
PO Box 96273　Las Vegas NV 89193
Ph: 702-897-7053 ▪ Fx: 702-897-7140

American Near East Refugee Aid　　www.anera.org
1522 K St NW Suite 202　Washington DC 20005
Ph: 202-347-2558 ▪ Fx: 202-682-1637

American Needlepoint Guild　　www.needlepoint.org
PO Box 1027　Cordova TN 38088
Ph: 901-755-3728 ▪ Fx: 901-755-3803

American Nephrology Nurses' Association　　anna.inurse.com
E Holly Ave Box 56　Pitman NJ 08071
Ph: 856-256-2320 ▪ Fx: 856-589-7463 ▪ TF: 888-600-2662

American Network of Community Options & Resources　　www.ancor.org
1101 King St Suite 380　Alexandria VA 22314
Ph: 703-535-7850 ▪ Fx: 703-535-7860

American Neurological Association　　www.aneuroa.org
5841 Cedar Lake Rd Suite 204　Minneapolis MN 55416
Ph: 952-545-6204 ▪ Fx: 952-545-6073

American Neuropsychiatric Association　　www.neuropsychiatry.com/ANPA/
700 Ackerman Rd Suite 550　Columbus OH 43202
Ph: 614-447-2077 ▪ Fx: 614-263-4366

American News Women's Club　　www.anwc.org
1607 22nd St NW　Washington DC 20008
Ph: 202-332-6770 ▪ Fx: 202-265-6092

American North Country Cheviot Sheep Association
8708 S County Rd 500 W　Reelsville IN 46171
Ph: 765-672-8205 ▪ Fx: 765-672-4275

American Nuclear Insurers　　www.amnucins.com
29 S Main St Suite 300-S　West Hartford CT 06107
Ph: 860-561-3433 ▪ Fx: 860-561-4655 ▪ TF: 888-561-3433

American Nuclear Society　　www.ans.org
555 N Kensington Ave　La Grange Park IL 60526
Ph: 708-352-6611 ▪ Fx: 708-352-0499 ▪ TF: 800-323-3044

American Numismatic Association　　www.money.org
818 N Cascade Ave　Colorado Springs CO 80903
Ph: 719-632-2646 ▪ Fx: 719-634-4085 ▪ TF: 800-367-9723

American Nursery & Landscape Association　　www.anla.org
1000 Vermont Ave NW Suite 300　Washington DC 20005
Ph: 202-789-2900 ▪ Fx: 202-789-1893

American Nurses Association　　www.ana.org
600 Maryland Ave SW Suite 100-W　Washington DC 20024
Ph: 202-651-7000 ▪ Fx: 202-651-7001 ▪ TF: 800-274-4262

American Nurses Association PAC　　www.nursingworld.org
600 Maryland Ave SW Suite 100W　Washington DC 20024
Ph: 202-554-4444 ▪ Fx: 202-651-7001

American Obesity Association　　www.obesity.org
1250 24th St NW Suite 300　Washington DC 20037
Ph: 202-776-7711 ▪ Fx: 202-776-7712 ▪ TF: 800-986-2373

American Occupational Therapy Association Inc　　www.aota.org
4720 Montgomery Ln PO Box 31220　Bethesda MD 20824
Ph: 301-652-2682 ▪ Fx: 301-652-7711

American Oil Chemists Society　　www.aocs.org
2211 W Bradley Ave　Champaign IL 61821
Ph: 217-359-2344 ▪ Fx: 217-351-8091 ▪ TF: 800-336-2627

American Optometric Association　　www.aoanet.org
243 N Lindbergh Blvd　Saint Louis MO 63141
Ph: 314-991-4100 ▪ Fx: 314-991-4101

American Optometric Student Association　　www.theaosa.org
243 N Lindbergh Blvd　Saint Louis MO 63141
Ph: 314-991-4100 ▪ Fx: 314-991-4101

American Orchid Society　　www.orchidweb.com
16700 AOS Ln　Delray Beach FL 33446
Ph: 561-404-2000 ▪ Fx: 561-404-2100

American Orff-Schulwerk Association　　www.aosa.org
PO Box 391080　Cleveland OH 44139
Ph: 440-543-5366 ▪ Fx: 440-543-2687

American Organ Transplant Association　　www.a-o-t-a.org
PO Box 41766　Houston TX 77244
Ph: 281-493-2047 ▪ Fx: 281-493-2099

American Organization for Bodywork Therapies of Asia　　www.aobta.org
1010 Haddonfield-Berlin Rd Suite 408　Voorhees NJ 08043
Ph: 856-782-1616 ▪ Fx: 856-782-1653

American Organization of Nurse Executives　　www.aone.org
1 N Franklin St 32nd Fl　Chicago IL 60606
Ph: 312-422-2800 ▪ Fx: 312-422-4503

American Oriental Society　　www.umich.edu/~aos
Univ of Michigan Hatcher Graduate Library　Ann Arbor MI
48109
Ph: 734-647-4760

American Ornithologists' Union　　www.aou.org
1313 Dolley Madison Blvd Suite 402　McLean VA 22101
Ph: 703-790-1745 ▪ Fx: 703-790-2672

American ORT　　www.aort.org
817 Broadway 10th Fl　New York NY 10003
Ph: 212-353-5800 ▪ Fx: 212-353-5888 ▪ TF: 800-364-9678

American Orthopaedic Association　　www.aoassn.org
6300 N River Rd Suite 505　Rosemont IL 60018
Ph: 847-318-7330 ▪ Fx: 847-318-7339

American Orthopaedic Foot & Ankle Society　　www.aofas.org
2517 Eastlake Ave E Suite 200　Seattle WA 98102
Ph: 206-223-1120 ▪ Fx: 206-223-1178 ▪ TF: 800-235-4855

American Orthopaedic Society for Sports Medicine　　www.sportsmed.org
6300 N River Rd Suite 500　Rosemont IL 60018
Ph: 847-292-4900 ▪ Fx: 847-292-4905 ▪ TF: 877-321-3500

American Orthopsychiatric Association　　www.amerortho.org
2001 N Beauregard St 12th Fl　Alexandria VA 22311
Ph: 703-797-2584 ▪ Fx: 703-684-5968

American Orthotic & Prosthetic Association　　www.aopanet.org
330 John Carlyle St Suite 200　Alexandria VA 22314
Ph: 571-431-0876 ▪ Fx: 571-431-0899

American Osteopathic Academy for Addiction Medicine
142 E Ontario St　Chicago IL 60611
Ph: 312-202-8163 ▪ Fx: 312-202-8463

American Osteopathic Academy of Orthopedics　　www.aoao.org
PO Box 291690　Davie FL 33329
Ph: 954-262-1700 ▪ Fx: 954-262-1748 ▪ TF: 800-741-2626

American Osteopathic Academy of Sports Medicine　　www.aoasm.org
7600 Terrace Ave Suite 203　Middleton WI 53562
Ph: 608-831-4400 ▪ Fx: 608-831-5185

American Osteopathic Association　　www.aoa-net.org
142 E Ontario St　Chicago IL 60611
Ph: 312-202-8000 ▪ Fx: 312-202-8200 ▪ TF: 800-621-1773

American Osteopathic Board of Emergency Medicine　　www.aobem.org
142 E Ontario St 8th Fl　Chicago IL 60611
Ph: 312-335-1065 ▪ Fx: 312-335-5489

American Osteopathic Board of Family Physicians　　www.aobfp.org
330 E Algonquin Rd Suite 6　Arlington Heights IL 60005
Ph: 847-640-8477

American Osteopathic Board of Pediatrics　　www.aobp.org
142 E Ontario St 6th Fl　Chicago IL 60611
Ph: 312-202-8267

American Osteopathic College of Allergy & Immunology
7025 E McDowell Rd Suite 1-B　Scottsdale AZ 85257
Ph: 480-585-1580 ▪ Fx: 480-585-1581

American Osteopathic College of Dermatology　　www.aocd.org
1501 E Illinois St PO Box 7525　Kirksville MO 63501
Ph: 660-665-2184 ▪ Fx: 660-627-2623 ▪ TF: 800-449-2623

**American Osteopathic College of Occupational & Preventive
Medicine**　PO Box 2606　Leesburg VA 20177　　www.aocopm.org
Ph: 800-558-8686 ▪ Fx: 703-443-0567

American Osteopathic College of Ophthalmology　　www.aocoohns.org/aoco.htm
405 W Grand Ave　Dayton OH 45405
Ph: 937-222-8820 ▪ Fx: 937-222-8840 ▪ TF: 800-455-9404

American Osteopathic College of Otolaryngology -　　www.aocoohns.org/aocohns.htm
Head & Neck Surgery　405 W Grand Ave　Dayton OH 45405
Ph: 937-222-8820 ▪ Fx: 937-222-8840 ▪ TF: 800-455-9404

American Osteopathic College of Pathologists Inc　　www.aocp-net.org
142 E Ontario St　Chicago IL 60611
Ph: 312-202-8197 ▪ Fx: 312-202-8224

American Osteopathic College of Physical Medicine & Rehabilitation　　www.aocpmr.org
314 S Knight Ave　Park Ridge IL 60068
Ph: 847-825-2515 ▪ Fx: 847-825-2509

American Osteopathic College of Radiology　　www.aocr.org
119 E 2nd St　Milan MO 63556
Ph: 660-265-4011 ▪ Fx: 660-265-3494 ▪ TF: 800-258-2627

American Osteopathic College of Rheumatology
193 Monroe Ave　Edison NJ 08820
Ph: 732-494-6688 ▪ Fx: 732-494-6689

American Ostrich Association　　www.ostriches.org
PO Box 163　Ranger TX 76470
Ph: 254-647-1645

American Otological Society　　otology-neurotology.org/AOS/AOS-home.html
2720 Tartan Way　Springfield IL 62707
Ph: 217-483-6966

American Outreach Association　　www.americanoutreach.org
PO Box 25042　Colorado Springs CO 80936
Ph: 719-592-1134

American Overseas Research Centers, Council of　　www.caorc.org
Smithsonian Institution　PO Box 37012 NHB Rm CE-123 MRC
178　Washington DC 20013
Ph: 202-842-8636 ▪ Fx: 202-786-2430

American Oxford Sheep Association
1960 E 2100 N Rd　Stonington IL 62567
Ph: 217-325-3515

American Pain Society　　www.ampainsoc.org
4700 W Lake Ave　Glenview IL 60025
Ph: 847-375-4715 ▪ Fx: 847-375-4777

American Paint Horse Association　　www.apha.com
PO Box 961023　Fort Worth TX 76161
Ph: 817-834-2742 ▪ Fx: 817-834-3152

American Pancreatic Association
UCLA School of Medicine 10833 LeConte Ave CHS72-259   Los
   Angeles CA 90095
Ph: 310-825-4976 ▪ Fx: 310-206-2472

American Paraplegia Society   www.apssci.org
75-20 Astoria Blvd   Jackson Heights NY 11370
Ph: 718-803-3782 ▪ Fx: 718-803-0414

American Park & Recreation Society
c/o National Recreation & Park Assn 22377 Belmont Ridge
   Rd   Ashburn VA 20148
Ph: 703-858-4741 ▪ Fx: 703-858-0794

American Parkinson Disease Association   www.apdaparkinson.com
1250 Hyland Blvd Suite 4B   Staten Island NY 10305
Ph: 718-981-8001 ▪ Fx: 718-981-4399 ▪ TF: 800-223-2732

American Part-Blooded Horse Registry   www.apbhorseregistry.com
4120 SE River Dr   Portland OR 97267
Ph: 503-654-6204

American Paso Fino Horse Association
PO Box 2363   Pittsburgh PA 15230
Ph: 724-437-5170 ▪ Fx: 724-438-4471

American Pathology Foundation   www.americanpathologyfoundation.org
1202 Allanson Rd   Mundelein IL 60060
Ph: 847-949-6055 ▪ Fx: 847-566-4580 ▪ TF: 877-993-9935

American Payroll Association   www.americanpayroll.org
30 E 33rd St 5th Fl   New York NY 10016
Ph: 212-686-2030 ▪ Fx: 212-686-4080

American Peanut Council   www.peanutsusa.com
1500 King St Suite 301   Alexandria VA 22314
Ph: 703-838-9500 ▪ Fx: 703-838-9508

American Peanut Research & Education   www.agr.okstate.edu/apres/welcome.htm
Society Inc   Oklahoma State Univ 376 Agriculture
   Hall   Stillwater OK 74078
Ph: 405-372-3052 ▪ Fx: 405-744-0354

American Peanut Shellers Association   www.peanut-shellers.org
PO Box 70157   Albany GA 31708
Ph: 229-888-2508 ▪ Fx: 229-888-5150

American Pediatric Society   www.aps-spr.org
3400 Research Forest Dr Suite B7   The Woodlands TX 77381
Ph: 281-419-0052 ▪ Fx: 281-419-0082

American Pediatric Surgical Association   www.eapsa.org
60 Revere Dr Suite 500   Northbrook IL 60062
Ph: 847-480-9576 ▪ Fx: 847-480-9282

American Pen Women Inc, National League of   www.americanpenwomen.org
1300 17th St NW   Washington DC 20036
Ph: 202-785-1997 ▪ Fx: 202-452-6868

American Pencil Collectors Society   www.pencilcollector.org

American Penstemon Society
1569 S Holland Ct   Lakewood CO 80232
Ph: 303-986-8096

American Peptide Society Inc   www.ampepsoc.org
2033 San Elijo Ave Suite 421   Cardiff by the Sea CA 92007
Ph: 858-455-4752

American Pesticide Control Officials, Association of   aapco.ceris.purdue.edu
PO Box 1249   Hardwick VT 05843
Ph: 802-472-6956 ▪ Fx: 802-472-6957

American Pet Boarding Association
22096 N Pet Ln   Prairie View IL 60069
Ph: 847-634-9444 ▪ Fx: 847-634-9460

American Pet Products Manufacturers Association Inc   www.appma.org
255 Glenville Rd   Greenwich CT 06831
Ph: 203-532-0000 ▪ Fx: 203-532-0551

American Petroleum Institute   api-ec.api.org
1220 L St NW   Washington DC 20005
Ph: 202-682-8000 ▪ Fx: 202-682-8029

American Pewter Guild
c/o Fischer Pewter 11940 Old Buckingham Rd   Midlothian VA
   23113
Ph: 804-379-3282 ▪ Fx: 804-897-1593

American Pharmacists Association   www.aphanet.org
2215 Constitution Ave NW   Washington DC 20037
Ph: 202-628-4410 ▪ Fx: 202-783-2351

American Pharmacists Association PAC   www.aphanet.org/govt/govaffair.html
2215 Constitution Ave NW   Washington DC 20037
Ph: 202-628-4410 ▪ Fx: 202-783-2351 ▪ TF: 800-237-2742

American Pheasant & Waterfowl Society   www3.upatsix.com/apws
W2270 US Hwy 10   Granton WI 54436
Ph: 715-238-7291 ▪ Fx: 715-238-7623

American Philatelic Research Library   www.stamps.org/TheLibrary/lib_AbouttheAPRL.htm
PO Box 8000   State College PA 16803
Ph: 814-237-3803 ▪ Fx: 814-237-6128

American Philatelic Society   www.stamps.org
100 Oakwood Ave PO Box 8000   State College PA 16803
Ph: 814-237-3803 ▪ Fx: 814-237-6128

American Philological Association   www.apaclassics.org
Univ of Pennsylvania 292 Logan Hall   249 S 36th
   St   Philadelphia PA 19104
Ph: 215-898-4975 ▪ Fx: 215-573-7874

American Philosophical Association   www.apa.udel.edu/apa
Univ of Delaware 31 Amstel Ave   Newark DE 19716
Ph: 302-831-1112 ▪ Fx: 302-831-8690

American Philosophical Society   www.amphilsoc.org
104 S 5th St   Philadelphia PA 19106
Ph: 215-440-3400 ▪ Fx: 215-440-3436

American Philosophy, Society for the Advancement of   www.american-philosophy.org
Southern Illinois Univ Dept of Philosophy MC 4505   Carbondale
   IL 62901
Ph: 618-536-6641

American Photographic Artisans Guild   apag.net

American Photographic Historical Society   www.superexpo.com/APHS.htm
1150 Ave of the Americas   New York NY 10036
Ph: 212-575-0483

American Physical Society   www.aps.org
1 Physics Ellipse   College Park MD 20740
Ph: 301-209-3200 ▪ Fx: 301-209-0865

American Physical Therapy Association   www.apta.org
1111 N Fairfax St   Alexandria VA 22314
Ph: 703-684-2782 ▪ Fx: 703-684-7343 ▪ TF: 800-999-2782

American Physicians, Association of   www.aap-online.org
Harvard Univ Dept of Medicine Channing Lab 181 Longwood
   Ave   Boston MA 02115
Ph: 617-277-0551 ▪ Fx: 617-731-1541

American Physicians Fellowship for Medicine in Israel   www.apfmed.org
2001 Beacon St Suite 210   Boston MA 02135
Ph: 617-232-5382 ▪ Fx: 617-739-2616

American Physicians & Surgeons Inc, Association of   www.aapsonline.org
1601 N Tucson Blvd Suite 9   Tucson AZ 85716
Ph: 520-327-4885 ▪ Fx: 520-325-4230 ▪ TF: 800-635-1196

American Physiological Society   www.the-aps.org
9650 Rockville Pike   Bethesda MD 20814
Ph: 301-634-7164 ▪ Fx: 301-634-7241

American Phytopathological Society   www.apsnet.org
3340 Pilot Knob Rd   Saint Paul MN 55121
Ph: 651-454-7250 ▪ Fx: 651-454-0766

American PIE   www.americanpie.org
316 Oak St PO Box 676   Northfield MN 55057
Ph: 507-645-5616 ▪ Fx: 507-645-5724 ▪ TF: 800-320-2743

American Pie Council   www.piecouncil.org
PO Box 368   Lake Forest IL 60045
Ph: 847-374-0170 ▪ Fx: 847-371-0199

American Pilots Association
499 S Capitol St SW Suite 409   Washington DC 20003
Ph: 202-484-0700 ▪ Fx: 202-484-9320

American Pinzgauer Association   www.pinzgauers.org
PO Box 147   Bethany MO 64424
Ph: 660-425-8617 ▪ Fx: 660-425-8374 ▪ TF: 800-914-9883

American Pipe Fittings Association Inc   www.apfa.com
201 Park Washington Ct   Falls Church VA 22046
Ph: 703-538-1786 ▪ Fx: 703-538-5603

American Planning Association   www.planning.org
1776 Massachusetts Ave NW   Washington DC 20036
Ph: 202-872-0611 ▪ Fx: 202-872-0643

American Plant Food Control Officials, Association of   www.aapfco.org
Univ of Kentucky 103 Regulatory Services Bldg   Lexington KY
   40546
Ph: 859-257-2668 ▪ Fx: 859-257-9478

American Plastics Council   www.americanplasticscouncil.org
1300 Wilson Blvd   Arlington VA 22209
Ph: 703-253-0700 ▪ Fx: 703-253-0710

American Platform Tennis Association   www.platformtennis.org
PO Box 43336   Upper Montclair NJ 07043
Ph: 973-744-1190 ▪ Fx: 973-783-4407 ▪ TF: 888-744-9490

American Podiatric Medical Association   www.apma.org
9312 Old Georgetown Rd   Bethesda MD 20814
Ph: 301-571-9200 ▪ Fx: 301-634-2752 ▪ TF: 800-275-2762

American Podiatric Medical Students' Association   www.apmsa.org
9312 Old Georgetown Rd   Bethesda MD 20814
Ph: 301-493-9667 ▪ Fx: 301-530-2752

American Podiatric Medical Writers Association
104-20 Queens Blvd Suite 17B   Forest Hills NY 11375
Ph: 718-897-9700 ▪ Fx: 718-896-5747

American Polar Society   www.oaedks.net/amerpolr.html

American Polarity Therapy Association   www.polaritytherapy.org
PO Box 19858   Boulder CO 80308
Ph: 303-545-2080 ▪ Fx: 303-545-2161 ▪ TF: 800-359-5620

American Political Science Association   www.apsanet.org
1527 New Hampshire Ave NW   Washington DC 20036
Ph: 202-483-2512 ▪ Fx: 202-483-2657

American Polygraph Association   www.polygraph.org
PO Box 8037   Chattanooga TN 37414
Ph: 423-892-3992 ▪ Fx: 423-894-5435 ▪ TF: 800-272-8037

American Polypay Sheep Association   www.countrylovin.com/polypay/
15603 173rd Ave   Milo IA 50166
Ph: 641-942-6402 ▪ Fx: 641-942-6502

American Pomological Society   hortweb.cas.psu.edu/aps/
103 Tyson Bldg   University Park PA 16802
Ph: 814-863-6163 ▪ Fx: 814-863-6139

American Poolplayers Association   www.poolplayers.com
1000 Lake St Louis Blvd Suite 325   Lake Saint Louis MO
   63367
Ph: 636-625-8611 ▪ Fx: 636-625-2975 ▪ TF: 800-372-2536

American Postal Chess Tournaments   www.correspondencechess.com/apct
PO Box 305   Western Springs IL 60558
Ph: 630-663-0688 ▪ Fx: 630-663-0689

American Postal Workers Union   www.apwu.org
1300 L St NW   Washington DC 20005
Ph: 202-842-4200 ▪ Fx: 202-842-8500

American Postal Workers Union   www.apwu.org/departments/legis/legisframe.htm
Committee on Political Action   1300 L St NW   Washington
   DC 20005
Ph: 202-842-4200

American Poultry Association   www.ampltya.com
133 Millville St   Mendon MA 01756
Ph: 508-473-8769

American Poultry International Inc
5420 I-55 N Suite B   Jackson MS 39211
Ph: 601-956-1715 ▪ Fx: 601-956-1755

American Power Boat Association   apba-racing.com
17640 Nine Mile Rd   Eastpointe MI 48021
Ph: 586-773-9700 ▪ Fx: 586-773-6490

American Practical Nurses Association
1090 Vermont Ave NW Suite 800   Washington DC 20005
Ph: 202-682-9000 ▪ Fx: 202-682-9298

American Prepaid Legal Services Institute   www.aplsi.org
541 N Fairbanks Ct   Chicago IL 60611
Ph: 312-988-5751 ▪ Fx: 312-988-5710

American Press Institute   www.americanpressinstitute.org
11690 Sunrise Valley Dr   Reston VA 20191
Ph: 703-620-3611 ▪ Fx: 703-620-5814

American Printing History Association   www.printinghistory.org

American Printing House for the Blind   www.aph.org
1839 Frankfort Ave PO Box 6085   Louisville KY 40206
Ph: 502-895-2405 ▪ Fx: 502-899-2274 ▪ TF: 800-223-1839

American Private Education, Council for   www.capenet.org
13017 Wisteria Dr PMB 457   Germantown MD 20874
Ph: 301-916-8460 ▪ Fx: 301-916-8485

American Probation & Parole Association   www.appa-net.org
2760 Research Park Dr   Lexington KY 40511
Ph: 859-244-8203 ▪ Fx: 859-244-8001

American Productivity & Quality Center   www.apqc.org
123 Post Oak Ln 3rd Fl   Houston TX 77024
Ph: 713-681-4020 ▪ Fx: 713-681-8578 ▪ TF: 800-776-9676

American Professional Practice Association   www.appa-assn.com
350 Fairway Dr Suite 200   Deerfield Beach FL 33441
Ph: 954-571-1877 ▪ Fx: 954-571-8582 ▪ TF: 800-221-2168

American Professional Society on the Abuse of Children www.apsac.org
940 NE 13th St CHO 3B3406   Oklahoma City OK 73104
Ph: 405-271-8202 ▪ Fx: 405-271-2931

American Prosecutors Research Institute   www.ndaa-apri.org/apri/
99 Canal Center Plaza Suite 510   Alexandria VA 22314
Ph: 703-549-9222 ▪ Fx: 703-836-3195

American Prostate Society   www.ameripros.org
7188 Ridge Rd PO Box 870   Hanover MD 21076
Ph: 410-859-3735 ▪ Fx: 410-850-0818 ▪ TF: 800-308-1106

American Prosthodontic Society   www.prostho.org
426 Hudson St   Hackensack NJ 07601
Ph: 201-440-7699 ▪ Fx: 201-440-7963 ▪ TF: 877-499-3500

American Psychiatric Association   www.psych.org
1000 Wilson Blvd Suite 1825   Arlington VA 22209
Ph: 703-907-7300 ▪ Fx: 703-907-1085 ▪ TF: 888-357-7924

American Psychiatric Nurses Association   www.apna.org
1555 Wilson Blvd Suite 515   Arlington VA 22209
Ph: 703-243-2443 ▪ Fx: 703-243-3390

American Psychoanalytic Association   www.apsa.org
309 E 49th St   New York NY 10017
Ph: 212-752-0450 ▪ Fx: 212-593-0571

American Psychological Association   www.apa.org
750 1st St NE   Washington DC 20002
Ph: 202-336-5500 ▪ Fx: 202-336-5502 ▪ TF: 800-374-2721

American Psychological Society   www.psychologicalscience.org
1010 Vermont Ave NW Suite 1100   Washington DC 20005
Ph: 202-783-2077 ▪ Fx: 202-783-2083

American Psychosomatic Society   www.psychosomatic.org
6728 Old McLean Village Dr   McLean VA 22101
Ph: 703-556-9222 ▪ Fx: 703-556-8729

American Psychotherapy Association   www.americanpsychotherapy.com
2750 E Sunshine St   Springfield MO 65804
Ph: 417-823-0173 ▪ Fx: 417-823-9959 ▪ TF: 800-205-9165

American Public Communications Council Inc   www.apcc.net
10302 Eaton Pl Suite 340   Fairfax VA 22030
Ph: 703-385-5300 ▪ Fx: 703-385-5301 ▪ TF: 800-868-2722

American Public Gas Association   www.apga.org
11094D Lee Hwy Suite 102   Fairfax VA 22030
Ph: 703-352-3890 ▪ Fx: 703-352-1271 ▪ TF: 800-927-4204

American Public Health Association   www.apha.org
800 'I' St NW   Washington DC 20001
Ph: 202-777-2742 ▪ Fx: 202-777-2534

American Public Human Services Association   www.aphsa.org
810 1st St NE Suite 500   Washington DC 20002
Ph: 202-682-0100 ▪ Fx: 202-289-6555

American Public Information on the Environment   www.americanpie.org
316 Oak St PO Box 676   Northfield MN 55057
Ph: 507-645-5616 ▪ Fx: 507-645-5724 ▪ TF: 800-320-2743

American Public Power Association   www.appanet.org
2301 M St NW   Washington DC 20037
Ph: 202-467-2900 ▪ Fx: 202-467-2910

American Public Transportation Association   www.apta.com
1666 K St NW   Washington DC 20006
Ph: 202-496-4800 ▪ Fx: 202-496-4321

American Public Works Association   www.apwa.net
2345 Grand Blvd Suite 500   Kansas City MO 64108
Ph: 816-472-6100 ▪ Fx: 816-472-1610

American Purchasing Society   www.american-purchasing.com
8 E Galena Blvd Suite 203   Aurora IL 60506
Ph: 630-859-0250 ▪ Fx: 630-859-0270

American Pyrotechnics Association   www.americanpyro.com
PO Box 30438   Bethesda MD 20824
Ph: 301-907-8181 ▪ Fx: 301-907-9148

American Quarter Horse Association   www.aqha.org
PO Box 200   Amarillo TX 79168
Ph: 806-376-4811 ▪ Fx: 806-349-6404 ▪ TF: 800-414-7433

American Quarter Horse Youth Association   www.aqha.com/youth
1600 Quarter Horse Dr PO Box 200   Amarillo TX 79168
Ph: 806-376-4811 ▪ Fx: 806-349-6409

American Quarter Pony Association   www.aqpa.com
PO Box 30   New Sharon IA 50207
Ph: 641-675-3669 ▪ Fx: 641-675-3969

American Quaternary Association   www4.nau.edu/amqua
Univ of Arkansas Dept of Geosciences   Fayetteville AR 72701
Ph: 501-575-3354 ▪ Fx: 501-575-3846

American Quilt Study Group   www.h-net.org/~aqsg/
PO Box 4737   Lincoln NE 68504
Ph: 402-472-5361 ▪ Fx: 402-472-5428

American Quilter's Society   www.aqsquilt.com
PO Box 3290   Paducah KY 42003
Ph: 270-898-7903 ▪ Fx: 270-898-1173

American Rabbit Breeders Association   www.arba.net
PO Box 426   Bloomington IL 61702
Ph: 309-664-7500 ▪ Fx: 309-664-0941

American Racing Pigeon Union   www.pigeon.org
PO Box 18465   Oklahoma City OK 73154
Ph: 405-848-5801 ▪ Fx: 405-848-5888 ▪ TF: 800-755-2778

American Radio Association   home.earthlink.net/~araplans
360 W 31st St 3rd Fl   New York NY 10001
Ph: 212-594-3600 ▪ Fx: 212-594-7422

American Radio Relay League   www.arrl.org
225 Main St   Newington CT 06111
Ph: 860-594-0200 ▪ Fx: 860-594-0259

American Radiological Nurses Association   www.arna.net
7794 Grow Dr   Pensacola FL 32514
Ph: 850-474-7292 ▪ Fx: 850-484-8762 ▪ TF: 866-486-2762

American Radium Society   www.americanradiumsociety.org
150485 S Cicero Ave   Oak Forest IL 60452
Ph: 708-687-1034 ▪ Fx: 708-687-1072

American Railway Development Association   www.amraildev.org
PO Box 44369   Eden Prairie MN 55344
Ph: 952-828-9750 ▪ Fx: 952-828-9751

American Railway Engineering & Maintenance-of-Way Association   www.arema.org
8201 Corporate Dr Suite 1125   Landover MD 20785
Ph: 301-459-3200 ▪ Fx: 301-459-8077

American Rambouillet Sheep Breeders' Association   www.rambouilletsheep.org
1610 S State Rd 3261   Levelland TX 79336
Ph: 806-894-3081 ▪ Fx: 806-894-5531 ▪ TF: 877-929-4414

American Rare Breed Association   www.arba.org
PO Box 757   Blooming Prairie MN 55917
Ph: 507-583-7718

American Real Estate & Urban Economics Association www.areuea.org
PO Box 1148   Portage MI 49081
Ph: 866-273-8321 ▪ Fx: 313-731-0174

American Recorder Society   ourworld.compuserve.com/homepages/recorder/
PO Box 631   Littleton CO 80160
Ph: 303-347-1120 ▪ Fx: 303-347-1181

American Recovery Association   www.repo.org
PO Box 231565   New Orleans LA 70183
Ph: 504-738-6404 ▪ Fx: 504-738-7910

American Recreation Coalition   www.funoutdoors.com
1225 New York Ave NW Suite 450   Washington DC 20005
Ph: 202-682-9530 ▪ Fx: 202-682-9529

American Recreational Golf Association   www.rentamark.com/arga
PO Box 35215   Chicago IL 60707
Ph: 708-453-0080 ▪ Fx: 708-453-0083

American Red Cross   www.redcross.org
2025 'E' St NW   Washington DC 20006
Ph: 202-303-4498 ▪ Fx: 202-639-3711 ▪ TF: 800-842-2200

American Red Cross International Services   www.redcross.org/services/intl
1730 'E' St NW   Washington DC 20006
Ph: 202-942-2506 ▪ Fx: 202-728-6404

American Red Cross Overseas Association
200 S Lebanon Rd   Loveland OH 45140
Ph: 513-683-1377

American Red Magen David for Israel   www.armdi.org
888 7th Ave Suite 403   New York NY 10106
Ph: 212-757-1627 ▪ Fx: 212-757-4662 ▪ TF: 866-632-2763

American Red Poll Association   www.redpollusa.org
PO Box 147   Bethany MO 64424
Ph: 660-425-7318 ▪ Fx: 660-425-8374

American Refugee Committee   www.archq.org
430 Oak Grove St Suite 204   Minneapolis MN 55403
Ph: 612-872-7060 ▪ Fx: 612-607-6499

American Registry of Diagnostic Medical Sonographers www.ardms.org
51 Monroe St Plaza East 1   Rockville MD 20850
Ph: 301-738-8401 ▪ Fx: 301-738-0312 ▪ TF: 800-541-9754

American Registry for Internet Numbers   www.arin.net
3635 Concorde Pkwy Suite 200   Chantilly VA 20151
Ph: 703-227-9840 ▪ Fx: 703-227-0676

American Registry of Medical Assistants
69 Southwick Rd   Westfield MA 01085
Ph: 413-562-7336 ▪ Fx: 413-562-9021 ▪ TF: 800-527-2762

American Registry of Professional Animal Scientists www.arpas.org
1111 N Dunlap Ave   Savoy IL 61874
Ph: 217-356-5390 ▪ Fx: 217-398-4119

American Registry of Radiologic Technologists   www.arrt.org
1255 Northland Dr   Saint Paul MN 55120
Ph: 651-687-0048 ▪ Fx: 651-687-0349

American Rehabilitation Counseling Association   www.nchrtm.okstate.edu/arca
c/o American Counseling Assn 5999 Stevenson Ave   Alexandria
    VA 22304
Ph: 703-823-9800 ▪ Fx: 703-823-0252 ▪ TF: 800-545-2223

American Rental Association   www.ararental.org
1900 19th St   Moline IL 61265
Ph: 309-764-2475 ▪ Fx: 309-764-1533 ▪ TF: 800-334-2177

American Rescue Dog Association   www.ardainc.org
PO Box 151   Chester NY 10918
Ph: 845-469-4173 ▪ Fx: 845-774-1054

American Rescue Team International   www.amerrescue.org
PO Box 534   Albuquerque NM 87103
Ph: 505-281-7977

American Rescue Workers Inc
643 Elmira St   Williamsport PA 17701
Ph: 570-323-8401 ▪ Fx: 570-323-0980
www.arwus.com

American Resort Development Association
1201 15th St NW Suite 400   Washington DC 20005
Ph: 202-371-6700 ▪ Fx: 202-289-8544
www.arda.org

American Resort Development Association PAC
1201 15th St NW Suite 400   Washington DC 20005
Ph: 202-371-6700 ▪ Fx: 202-289-8544

American Reusable Textile Association
PO Box 1053   Mulberry FL 33860
Ph: 863-660-5350
www.arta1.com

American Revenue Association
PO Box 728   Leesport PA 19533
Ph: 610-926-6200
www.revenuer.org

American Revolution, National Center for the
435 Devon Park Dr Bldg 800   Wayne PA 19087
Ph: 610-975-4939 ▪ Fx: 610-917-3188
www.valleyforgemuseum.org

American Revolution, National Society of the Children of the
1776 D St NW   Washington DC 20006
Ph: 202-638-3153 ▪ Fx: 202-737-3162
www.nscar.org

American Revolution, National Society Daughters of the
1776 D St NW   Washington DC 20006
Ph: 202-628-1776 ▪ Fx: 202-879-3252
www.dar.org

American Revolution, National Society of the Sons of the
1000 S 4th St   Louisville KY 40203
Ph: 502-589-1776 ▪ Fx: 502-589-1671
www.sar.org

American Revolution Round Table
6 Grovedale Rd   Niantic CT 06357
Ph: 860-739-6859 ▪ Fx: 860-786-8230
eve.kean.edu/~leew/arrt

(American Revolution) Society of the
Cincinnati   2118 Massachusetts Ave NW   Washington DC 20008
Ph: 202-785-2040 ▪ Fx: 202-785-0729
members.tripod.com/~Historic_Trust/cincinna.htm

American Rhinologic Society
3400 Bainbridge Ave 3rd Fl   Bronx NY 10467
Ph: 718-920-2991 ▪ Fx: 718-652-5194
www.american-rhinologic.org

American Rhodes Scholars, Association of
2717 Lincoln St   Evanston IL 60201
Ph: 847-869-5950 ▪ Fx: 847-869-6993
www.americanrhodes.org

American Rhododendron Society
11 Pinecrest Dr   Fortuna CA 95540
Ph: 707-725-3043 ▪ Fx: 707-725-1217
www.rhododendron.org

American Rights Coalition
7510 Lee Hwy   Chattanooga TN 37421
Ph: 423-893-7801 ▪ Fx: 423-893-7511 ▪ TF: 800-634-2224
www.tenlaws.com

American Risk & Insurance Association
716 Providence Rd PO Box 3028   Malvern PA 19355
Ph: 610-640-1997 ▪ Fx: 610-725-1007
www.aria.org

American River Touring Association Inc
20400 Casa Loma Rd   Groveland CA 95321
Ph: 209-962-7873 ▪ TF: 800-323-2782
www.arta.org

American Rivers
1025 Vermont Ave NW Suite 720   Washington DC 20005
Ph: 202-347-7550 ▪ Fx: 202-347-9240 ▪ TF: 800-296-6900
www.amrivers.org

American Road & Transportation Builders Association
1010 Massachusetts Ave NW   Washington DC 20001
Ph: 202-289-4434 ▪ Fx: 202-289-4435
www.artba-hq.org

American Rock Art Research Association
PO Box 210026   Tucson AZ 85721
Ph: 888-668-0052
www.arara.org

American Rock Mechanics Association
600 Woodland Terr   Alexandria VA 22302
Ph: 703-683-1808 ▪ Fx: 703-683-1815
www.armarocks.org

American Roentgen Ray Society
44211 Slatestone Ct   Leesburg VA 20176
Ph: 703-729-3353 ▪ Fx: 703-729-4839 ▪ TF: 800-438-2777
www.arrs.org

American Romagnola Association
3815 Touzalin Ave Suite 104   Lincoln NE 68507
Ph: 402-466-3334 ▪ Fx: 402-466-3338
www.americanromagnola.com

American Romanian Orthodox Youth
Romanian Orthodox Episcopate of America 2535 Grey Tower Rd   Jackson MI 49201
Ph: 517-522-4800
www.aroy.org

American Romney Breeders' Association
744 Riverbanks Rd   Grants Pass OR 97527
Ph: 541-476-6428
www.americanromney.org

American Rose Society
8877 Jefferson Paige Rd PO Box 30   Shreveport LA 71119
Ph: 318-938-5402 ▪ Fx: 318-938-5405 ▪ TF: 800-637-6534
www.ars.org

American Rosie the Riveter Association
2561 Rocky Ridge Rd   Birmingham AL 35243
Ph: 205-822-4106
www.rosietheriveter.net

American Royal Association
1701 American Royal Ct   Kansas City MO 64102
Ph: 816-221-9800 ▪ Fx: 816-221-8189 ▪ TF: 800-821-5857
www.americanroyal.com

American Running Association
4405 East-West Hwy Suite 405   Bethesda MD 20814
Ph: 301-913-9517 ▪ Fx: 301-913-9520 ▪ TF: 800-776-2732
www.americanrunning.org

American-Russian Chamber of Commerce & Industry
1101 Pennsylvania Ave NW 6th Fl   Washington DC 20004
Ph: 202-756-4943 ▪ Fx: 202-362-4634
www.arcci.org

American Saddlebred Horse Association
4093 Iron Works Pkwy   Lexington KY 40511
Ph: 859-259-2742 ▪ Fx: 859-259-1628
www.saddlebred.com

American Safe Deposit Association
98 W Madison St   Franklin IN 46131
Ph: 317-738-4432 ▪ Fx: 317-738-5267
www.tasda.com

American Sail Training Association
PO Box 1459   Newport RI 02840
Ph: 401-846-1775 ▪ Fx: 401-849-5400
tallships.sailtraining.org

American Saint Boniface Society
PO Box 1352   Bronx NY 10466
Ph: 718-994-0989 ▪ Fx: 718-994-6119

American Salers Association
19590 E Main St Suite 202   Parker CO 80138
Ph: 303-770-9292 ▪ Fx: 303-770-9302
www.salersusa.org

American Salers Junior Association
7383 Alton Way Suite 103   Englewood CO 80112
Ph: 303-770-9292 ▪ Fx: 303-770-9302
www.salersusa.org

American Salvage Pool Association
PO Box 6749   Glendale AZ 85312
Ph: 602-547-0052 ▪ Fx: 602-547-0246
www.aspa.com

American Satin Rabbit Breeders' Association
1895 Wilson Ave   Wilton IA 52778
Ph: 563-785-6365
www.asrba.com

American Savings Education Council
2121 K St NW Suite 600   Washington DC 20037
Ph: 202-659-0670 ▪ Fx: 202-775-6360
www.asec.org

American-Scandinavian Foundation
58 Park Ave   New York NY 10016
Ph: 212-879-9779 ▪ Fx: 212-249-3444
www.amscan.org

American/Schleswig-Holstein Heritage Society
PO Box 506   Walcott IA 52773
Ph: 563-284-4184
www.ashhs.org

American Scholastic Associates International
29256 Old US 20 W   Elkhart IN 46514
Ph: 574-389-0237 ▪ Fx: 574-522-3831 ▪ TF: 866-301-5515
www.asainternational.com

American School Band Directors' Association
PO Box 696   Guttenberg IA 52052
Ph: 319-252-2500
www.asbda.com

American School Counselor Association
1101 King St Suite 625   Alexandria VA 22314
Ph: 703-683-2722 ▪ Fx: 703-683-1619 ▪ TF: 800-306-4722
www.schoolcounselor.org

American School Food Service Association
700 S Washington St Suite 300   Alexandria VA 22314
Ph: 703-739-3900 ▪ Fx: 703-739-3915 ▪ TF: 800-877-8822
www.asfsa.org

American School Health Association
7263 State Rt 43   Kent OH 44240
Ph: 330-678-1601 ▪ Fx: 330-678-4526 ▪ TF: 800-445-2742
www.ashaweb.org

American Schools Association
PO Box 14260   Chicago IL 60614
Ph: 773-782-0046 ▪ Fx: 773-782-0113 ▪ TF: 800-230-2263
www.asaceu.com

American Schools of Oriental Research
656 Beacon St 5th Fl   Boston MA 02215
Ph: 617-353-6570 ▪ Fx: 617-353-6575
www.asor.org

American Schools in South America, Association of
14750 NW 77th Ct Suite 210   Miami Lakes FL 33016
Ph: 305-821-0345 ▪ Fx: 305-821-4244
www.aassa.com

American Scientific Glassblowers Society
PO Box 778   Madison NC 27025
Ph: 336-427-2406 ▪ Fx: 336-427-2496
www.asgs-glass.org

American Scottish Foundation
575 Madison Ave Suite 1006   New York NY 10022
Ph: 212-605-0338 ▪ Fx: 212-605-0222
www.americanscottishfoundation.com

American Scripture Gift Mission
PO Box 410280   Melbourne FL 32941
Ph: 321-255-7774 ▪ Fx: 321-255-8986 ▪ TF: 877-873-2746
www.gospelcom.net/asgm/

American Seafood Distributors Association
1901 N Fort Myer Dr Suite 700   Arlington VA 22209
Ph: 703-524-8880 ▪ Fx: 703-524-4619
www.freetradeinseafood.org

American Security Council Foundation
201A N Main St   Culpeper VA 22701
Ph: 540-547-1776 ▪ Fx: 540-547-9737
www.ascfusa.org/asc_home.htm

American Seed Research Foundation
225 Reinekers Ln Suite 650   Alexandria VA 22314
Ph: 703-837-8140 ▪ Fx: 703-837-9365
www.amseed.org/asrf

American Seed Trade Association
225 Reinekers Ln Suite 650   Alexandria VA 22314
Ph: 703-837-8140 ▪ Fx: 703-837-9365 ▪ TF: 888-890-7333
www.amseed.com

American Segmental Bridge Institute
9201 N 25th Ave Suite 150B   Phoenix AZ 85021
Ph: 602-997-9964 ▪ Fx: 602-997-9965
www.asbi-assoc.org

American Self-Help Group Clearinghouse
Saint Claires Health Services 100 E Hanover Ave Suite 202   Cedar Knolls NJ 07927
Ph: 973-326-8853 ▪ Fx: 973-326-9467
www.mentalhelp.net/selfhelp

American Self Protection Association Inc
825 Greengate Oval St   Sagamore Hills OH 44067
Ph: 330-467-1750
www.americanselfprotection.org

American Seminar Leaders Association
2405 E Washington Blvd   Pasadena CA 91104
Ph: 626-791-1211 ▪ Fx: 626-798-0701 ▪ TF: 800-735-0511
www.asla.com

American Senior Citizens Association
PO Box 41   Fayetteville NC 28302
Ph: 910-323-3641 ▪ Fx: 910-323-4343 ▪ TF: 800-323-6525
www.ncseniorcitizens.com

American Senior Fitness Association
PO Box 2575   New Smyrna Beach FL 32170
Ph: 386-423-6634 ▪ Fx: 386-427-0613 ▪ TF: 800-243-1478
www.seniorfitness.net

American Seniors Housing Association
5100 Wisconsin Ave NW Suite 307   Washington DC 20016
Ph: 202-237-0900 ▪ Fx: 202-237-1616
www.seniorshousing.org

American Sephardi Federation
15 W 16th St   New York NY 10011
Ph: 212-294-8350 ▪ Fx: 212-294-8348
www.asfonline.org

American Sewing Guild
9660 Hillcroft Suite 516   Houston TX 77096
Ph: 713-729-3000 ▪ Fx: 713-721-9230 ▪ TF: 877-422-6739
www.asg.org

American Sheep Industry Association
9785 Maroon Cir Suite 360   Centennial CO 80112
Ph: 303-771-3500 ▪ Fx: 303-771-8200
www.sheepusa.org

American Shetland Pony Club   www.shetlandminiature.com
81-B E Queenwood Rd   Morton IL 61550
Ph: 309-263-4044 ▪ Fx: 309-263-5113

American Shetland Sheepdog Association   www.assa.org
7274 S Chase Way   Littleton CO 80128
Ph: 303-979-8998

American Shipbuilding Association   www.americanshipbuilding.com
600 Pennsylvania Ave SE Suite 305   Washington DC 20003
Ph: 202-544-8170 ▪ Fx: 202-544-8252

American Shire Horse Association   www.shirehorse.org/
1211 Hill Harrell Rd   Effingham SC 29541
Ph: 843-629-0072

American Shore & Beach Preservation Association   www.asbpa.org
1724 Indian Way   Oakland CA 94611
Ph: 510-339-2818 ▪ Fx: 510-339-6710

American Shorin Kempo Karate Association   www.americanblackbeltacademy.com
1587 York St   Colorado Springs CO 80918
Ph: 719-598-0398 ▪ Fx: 719-268-2733

American Short Line & Regional Railroad Association   www.aslrra.org
50 F St NW Suite 7020   Washington DC 20005
Ph: 202-628-4500 ▪ Fx: 202-628-6430

American Shorthorn Association   www.beefshorthornusa.com
8288 Hascall St   Omaha NE 68124
Ph: 402-393-7200 ▪ Fx: 402-393-7203

American Shortwave Listeners Club
16182 Ballad Ln   Huntington Beach CA 92649
Ph: 714-846-1685

American Shotcrete Association   www.shotcrete.org
38800 Country Club Dr   Farmington Hills MI 48331
Ph: 248-848-3780 ▪ Fx: 248-848-3740

American Shoulder & Elbow Surgeons   www.ases-assn.org
6300 N River Rd Suite 727   Rosemont IL 60018
Ph: 847-698-1629 ▪ Fx: 847-823-0536

American Shrimp Processors Association
PO Box 50774   New Orleans LA 70150
Ph: 504-368-1571 ▪ Fx: 504-368-1573

American Shropshire Registry Association   www.shropshires.org
PO Box 635   Harvard IL 60033
Ph: 815-943-2034 ▪ Fx: 815-945-2034

American Sickle Cell Anemia Association   www.ascaa.org
10300 Carnegie Ave   Cleveland OH 44106
Ph: 216-229-8600 ▪ Fx: 216-229-4500

American SIDS Institute   www.sids.org
2480 Windy Hill Rd Suite 380   Marietta GA 30067
Ph: 770-612-1030 ▪ Fx: 770-612-8277 ▪ TF: 800-232-7437

American Sighthound Field Association   www.asfa.org

American Sightseeing International   www.americansightseeing.org
490 Post St Suite 1701   San Francisco CA 94102
Ph: 415-332-7916 ▪ Fx: 415-332-7980

American Simmental Association   www.simmental.org
1 Simmental Way   Bozeman MT 59718
Ph: 406-587-4531 ▪ Fx: 406-587-9301

American Single Shot Rifle Association   www.assra.com
PO Box 362   Delphos OH 45833
Ph: 419-692-3866 ▪ Fx: 419-695-3756

American Skin Association   www.skinassn.org
346 Park Ave S 4th Fl   New York NY 10010
Ph: 212-889-4858 ▪ Fx: 212-889-4959 ▪ TF: 800-499-7546

American Sleep Apnea Association   www.sleepapnea.org
1424 K St NW Suite 302   Washington DC 20005
Ph: 202-293-3650 ▪ Fx: 202-293-3656

American Slow Sand Association
PO Box 330   Ilion NY 13357
Ph: 315-895-7711 ▪ Fx: 315-895-7196

American Small Businesses Association   www.asbaonline.org
206 E College St Suite 201B   Grapevine TX 76051
Ph: 817-488-8770 ▪ Fx: 817-251-8578

American Social Health Association   www.ashastd.org
PO Box 13827   Research Triangle Park NC 27709
Ph: 919-361-8400 ▪ Fx: 919-361-8425 ▪ TF: 800-277-8922

American Society of Abdominal Surgeons   www.abdominalsurg.org
675 Main St   Melrose MA 02176
Ph: 781-665-6102 ▪ Fx: 781-665-4127

American Society of Access Professionals   www.accesspro.org
1444 'I' St NW Suite 700   Washington DC 20005
Ph: 202-216-9623 ▪ Fx: 202-216-9646

American Society of Addiction Medicine   www.asam.org
4601 N Park Ave Upper Arcade Suite 101   Chevy Chase MD 20815
Ph: 301-656-3920 ▪ Fx: 301-656-3815

American Society for Adolescent Psychiatry   www.adolpsych.org
PO Box 570218   Dallas TX 75357
Ph: 972-686-6166 ▪ Fx: 972-613-5532

American Society for the Advancement of Anesthesia & Sedation in Dentistry   www.sedation4dentists.com
6 E Union Ave   Bound Brook NJ 08805
Ph: 732-469-9050 ▪ Fx: 732-271-1985

American Society for Aesthetic Plastic Surgery   www.surgery.org
11081 Winners Cir   Los Alamitos CA 90720
Ph: 562-799-2356 ▪ Fx: 562-799-1098 ▪ TF: 800-364-2147

American Society for Aesthetics   www.aesthetics-online.org
Marquette Univ 707 N 11th St Rm 322 PO Box 1881   Milwaukee WI 53201
Ph: 414-288-7831 ▪ Fx: 414-228-5415

American Society on Aging   www.asaging.org
833 Market St Suite 511   San Francisco CA 94103
Ph: 415-974-9600 ▪ Fx: 415-974-0300 ▪ TF: 800-537-9728

American Society of Agricultural Appraisers   www.amagappraisers.com
1126 Eastland Dr N Suite 100 PO Box 186   Twin Falls ID 83303
Ph: 208-733-2323 ▪ Fx: 208-733-2326 ▪ TF: 800-488-7570

American Society of Agricultural Consultants   www.agconsultants.org
950 S Cherry St Suite 508   Denver CO 80246
Ph: 303-759-5091 ▪ Fx: 303-758-0190

American Society of Agricultural Engineers   www.asae.org
2950 Niles Rd   Saint Joseph MI 49085
Ph: 269-429-0300 ▪ Fx: 269-429-3852 ▪ TF: 800-695-2723

American Society of Agronomy   www.agronomy.org
677 S Segoe Rd   Madison WI 53711
Ph: 608-273-8080 ▪ Fx: 608-273-2021

American Society for the Alexander Technique   www.alexandertech.com
PO Box 60008   Florence MA 01062
Ph: 413-584-2359 ▪ Fx: 413-584-3097 ▪ TF: 800-473-0620

American Society of Alternative Therapists   www.asat.org
PO Box 703   Rockport MA 01966
Ph: 978-281-4400 ▪ Fx: 978-282-1144

American Society of Andrology   www.andrologysociety.com
1111 N Plaza Dr Suite 550   Schaumburg IL 60173
Ph: 847-619-4909 ▪ Fx: 847-517-7229

American Society of Anesthesia Technologists & Technicians   www.asat.org
5800 Foxridge Dr Suite 115   Mission KS 66202
Ph: 913-262-2249 ▪ Fx: 913-262-0174

American Society of Anesthesiologists   www.asahq.org
520 N Northwest Hwy   Park Ridge IL 60068
Ph: 847-825-5586 ▪ Fx: 847-825-1692

American Society of Anesthesiologists PAC
1101 Vermont Ave NW Suite 606   Washington DC 20005
Ph: 202-289-2222 ▪ Fx: 202-371-0384

American Society of Animal Science   www.asas.org
1111 N Dunlap Ave   Savoy IL 61874
Ph: 217-356-9050 ▪ Fx: 217-398-4119

American Society for Apheresis   www.apheresis.org
3900 E Timrod St   Tucson AZ 85711
Ph: 520-327-8584 ▪ Fx: 520-322-6778

American Society of Appraisers   www.appraisers.org
555 Herndon Pkwy Suite 125   Herndon VA 20170
Ph: 703-478-2228 ▪ Fx: 703-742-8471 ▪ TF: 800-272-8258

American Society for Artificial Internal Organs   www.asaio.com
PO Box C   Boca Raton FL 33429
Ph: 561-391-8589 ▪ Fx: 561-368-9153

American Society of Artists
PO Box 1326   Palatine IL 60078
Ph: 312-751-2500

American Society of Association Executives   www.asaenet.org
1575 'I' St NW   Washington DC 20005
Ph: 202-626-2723 ▪ Fx: 202-371-8825 ▪ TF: 888-950-2723

American Society for Automation in Pharmacy   www.asapnet.org
492 Norristown Rd Suite 160   Blue Bell PA 19422
Ph: 610-825-7783 ▪ Fx: 610-825-7641

American Society of Baking   www.asbe.org
27 E Napa St Suite G   Sonoma CA 95476
Ph: 707-935-0103 ▪ Fx: 707-935-0174 ▪ TF: 866-920-9885

American Society of Bariatric Physicians   www.asbp.org
5453 E Evans Pl   Denver CO 80222
Ph: 303-770-2526 ▪ Fx: 303-779-4834

American Society for Bariatric Surgery   www.asbs.org
7328 W University Ave Suite F   Gainesville FL 32607
Ph: 352-331-4900 ▪ Fx: 352-331-4975

American Society for Biochemistry & Molecular Biology   www.asbmb.org
9650 Rockville Pike   Bethesda MD 20814
Ph: 301-634-7145 ▪ Fx: 301-634-7126

American Society for Bioethics & Humanities   www.asbh.org
4700 W Lake Ave   Glenview IL 60025
Ph: 847-375-4745 ▪ Fx: 877-734-9385

American Society of Biomechanics   www.asb-biomech.org
Willamette Univ Sparks Ctr 5 900 State St   Salem OR 97301
Ph: 503-370-6423

American Society for Blood & Marrow Transplantation   www.asbmt.org
85 W Algonquin Rd Suite 550   Arlington Heights IL 60005
Ph: 847-427-0224 ▪ Fx: 847-427-9656

American Society of Body Engineers   www.asbe.net
2122 15 Mile Rd   Sterling Heights MI 48310
Ph: 586-268-8360 ▪ Fx: 586-268-2187

American Society for Bone & Mineral Research   www.asbmr.org
2025 M St NW Suite 800   Washington DC 20036
Ph: 202-367-1161 ▪ Fx: 202-367-2161

American Society of Bookplate Collectors & Designers   www.bookplate.org
PO Box 380340   Cambridge MA 02238
Ph: 781-393-9970 ▪ Fx: 781-393-9972

American Society of Botanical Artists   huntbot.andrew.cmu.edu/ASBA/asbotartists.html
47 5th Ave   New York NY 10003
Ph: 212-691-9080 ▪ Fx: 212-691-9130 ▪ TF: 866-691-9080

American Society for Breast Disease   www.asbd.org
PO Box 140186   Dallas TX 75214
Ph: 214-368-6836 ▪ Fx: 214-368-5719

American Society of Brewing Chemists   www.asbcnet.org
3340 Pilot Knob Rd   Saint Paul MN 55121
Ph: 651-454-7250 ▪ Fx: 651-454-0766

American Society of Business Publication Editors   www.asbpe.org
710 E Ogden Ave Suite 600   Naperville IL 60563
Ph: 630-579-3288 ▪ Fx: 630-369-2488

American Society of Cataract & Refractive Surgery   www.ascrs.org
4000 Legato Rd Suite 850   Fairfax VA 22033
Ph: 703-591-2220 ▪ Fx: 703-591-0614 ▪ TF: 800-451-1339

American Society for Cell Biology   www.ascb.org
8120 Woodmont Ave Suite 750   Bethesda MD 20814
Ph: 301-347-9300 ▪ Fx: 301-347-9310

American Society of Certified Engineering Technicians   www.ascet.org
PO Box 1348   Flowery Branch GA 30542
Ph: 770-967-9173 ▪ Fx: 770-967-8049

American Society for Church Growth   www.ascg.org
135 N Oakland Ave   Pasadena CA 91182
Ph: 626-584-5293 ▪ Fx: 626-584-5313 ▪ TF: 800-999-9578

American Society of Church History   www.churchhistory.org
PO Box 8517   Red Bank NJ 07701
Ph: 732-345-1787 ▪ Fx: 732-345-1788

American Society of Cinematographers   www.theasc.com
1782 N Orange Dr   Hollywood CA 90028
Ph: 323-876-5080 ▪ Fx: 323-876-4973 ▪ TF: 800-448-0145

American Society of Civil Engineers   www.asce.org
1801 Alexander Bell Dr   Reston VA 20191
Ph: 703-295-6000 ▪ Fx: 703-295-6333 ▪ TF: 800-548-2723

American Society of Clinical Hypnosis   www.asch.net
140 N Bloomingdale Rd   Bloomingdale IL 60108
Ph: 630-980-4740 ▪ Fx: 630-351-8490

American Society for Clinical Investigation   www.asci-jci.org
35 Research Dr Suite 300   Ann Arbor MI 48103
Ph: 734-222-6050 ▪ Fx: 734-222-6058

American Society for Clinical Laboratory Science   www.ascls.org
6701 Democracy Blvd Suite 300   Bethesda MD 20817
Ph: 301-657-2768 ▪ Fx: 301-657-2909

American Society for Clinical Nutrition   www.ascn.org
9650 Rockville Pike   Bethesda MD 20814
Ph: 301-634-7110 ▪ Fx: 301-571-1863

American Society of Clinical Oncology   www.asco.org
1900 Duke St Suite 200   Alexandria VA 22314
Ph: 703-299-0150 ▪ Fx: 703-299-1044 ▪ TF: 888-282-2552

American Society for Clinical Pathology   www.ascp.org
2100 W Harrison St   Chicago IL 60612
Ph: 312-738-1336 ▪ Fx: 312-738-1619 ▪ TF: 800-621-4142

American Society for Clinical Pharmacology & Therapeutics   www.ascpt.org
528 N Washington St   Alexandria VA 22314
Ph: 703-836-6981 ▪ Fx: 703-836-5223

American Society of Clinical Psychopharmacology Inc www.ascpp.org
PO Box 2257   New York NY 10116
Ph: 212-696-1088 ▪ Fx: 212-696-0563

American Society of Colon & Rectal Surgeons   www.fascrs.org
85 W Algonquin Rd Suite 550   Arlington Heights IL 60005
Ph: 847-290-9184 ▪ Fx: 847-290-9203

American Society for Colposcopy & Cervical Pathology   www.asccp.org
20 W Washington St Suite 1   Hagerstown MD 21740
Ph: 301-733-3640 ▪ Fx: 301-733-5775 ▪ TF: 800-787-7227

American Society of Composers Authors & Publishers   www.ascap.com
1 Lincoln Plaza   New York NY 10023
Ph: 212-621-6000 ▪ Fx: 212-724-9064 ▪ TF: 800-952-7227

American Society of Consultant Pharmacists   www.ascp.com
1321 Duke St   Alexandria VA 22314
Ph: 703-739-1300 ▪ Fx: 703-739-1321 ▪ TF: 800-355-2727

American Society of Consulting Arborists   www.asca-consultants.org
15245 Shady Grove Rd Suite 130   Rockville MD 20850
Ph: 301-947-0483 ▪ Fx: 301-990-9771

American Society of Contemporary Medicine Surgery & Ophthalmology
820 N Orleans St Suite 208   Chicago IL 60610
Ph: 312-440-0699 ▪ Fx: 312-440-0580 ▪ TF: 800-621-4002

American Society of Corporate Secretaries   ascs.org
521 5th Ave   New York NY 10175
Ph: 212-681-2000 ▪ Fx: 212-681-2005

American Society of Crime Laboratory Directors   www.ascld.org
PO Box 2710   Largo FL 33779
Ph: 727-549-6067 ▪ Fx: 727-549-6070

American Society of Criminology   www.asc41.com
1314 Kinnear Rd Suite 212   Columbus OH 43212
Ph: 614-292-9207 ▪ Fx: 614-292-6767

American Society of Cytopathology   www.cytopathology.org
400 W 9th St Suite 201   Wilmington DE 19801
Ph: 302-429-8802 ▪ Fx: 302-429-8807

American Society for Cytotechnology   www.asct.com
1500 Sunday Dr Suite 102   Raleigh NC 27607
Ph: 919-787-5181 ▪ Fx: 919-787-4916 ▪ TF: 800-948-3947

American Society of Danish Engineers
PO Box 606   Larchmont NY 10538
Ph: 914-834-0287 ▪ Fx: 914-834-0513

American Society for Deaf Children   www.deafchildren.org
PO Box 3355   Gettysburg PA 17325
Ph: 717-334-7922 ▪ Fx: 717-334-8808 ▪ TF: 800-942-2732

American Society for the Defense of Tradition Family & Property   www.tfp.org
PO Box 341   Hanover PA 17331
Ph: 717-225-7147 ▪ Fx: 717-225-7382

American Society of Dental Aesthetics   www.asdatoday.com
635 Madison Ave 13th Fl   New York NY 10022
Ph: 212-751-3263 ▪ Fx: 212-755-3263 ▪ TF: 800-454-2732

American Society for Dermatologic Surgery   www.asds-net.org
5550 Meadowbrook Dr Suite 120   Rolling Meadows IL 60008
Ph: 847-956-0900 ▪ Fx: 847-956-0999

American Society of Dermatological Retailers
320 Superior Ave Suite 395   Newport Beach CA 92663
Ph: 949-646-9098 ▪ Fx: 949-646-7298 ▪ TF: 800-469-3739

American Society of Dermatology   www.asd.org
2721 Capital Ave   Sacramento CA 95816
Ph: 916-446-5054 ▪ Fx: 916-446-0500

American Society of Dermatopathology   www.asdp.org
60 Revere Dr Suite 500   Northbrook IL 60062
Ph: 847-400-5820 ▪ Fx: 847-480-9282

American Society of Directors of Volunteer Services www.asdvs.org
1 N Franklin St 27th Fl   Chicago IL 60606
Ph: 312-422-3939 ▪ Fx: 312-422-4575

American Society of Dowsers   www.dowsers.org
PO Box 24   Danville VT 05828
Ph: 802-684-3417 ▪ Fx: 802-684-2565 ▪ TF: 800-711-9530

American Society of Echocardiography   asecho.org
1500 Sunday Dr Suite 102   Raleigh NC 27607
Ph: 919-861-5574 ▪ Fx: 919-787-4916

American Society for Eighteenth-Century Studies   asecs.press.jhu.edu
Wake Forest Univ PO Box 7867   Winston-Salem NC 27109
Ph: 336-727-4694 ▪ Fx: 336-727-4697

American Society of Electroneurodiagnostic Technologists Inc   www.aset.org
428 W 42nd St Suite B   Kansas City MO 64111
Ph: 816-931-1120 ▪ Fx: 816-931-1145

American Society of Emergency Radiology   www.erad.org
4550 Post Oak Pl Suite 342   Houston TX 77027
Ph: 713-965-0566 ▪ Fx: 713-960-0488

American Society for Engineering Education   www.asee.org
1818 'N' St NW Suite 600   Washington DC 20036
Ph: 202-331-3500 ▪ Fx: 202-265-8504

American Society for Engineering Management   www.engineering-management.org
PO Box 820   Rolla MO 65402
Ph: 573-341-2101 ▪ Fx: 573-364-3500

American Society for Enology & Viticulture   www.asev.org
PO Box 1855   Davis CA 95617
Ph: 530-753-3142 ▪ Fx: 530-753-3318

American Society for Environmental   www.h-net.org/~environ/ASEH/welcome_IE4.html
History   119 Pine St Suite 207   Seattle WA 98101
Ph: 206-343-0226 ▪ Fx: 206-343-0249

American Society of Equine Appraisers   www.equineappraiser.com
1126 Eastland Dr N Suite 100 PO Box 186   Twin Falls ID 93303
Ph: 208-733-2323 ▪ Fx: 208-733-2326 ▪ TF: 800-704-7020

American Society for Ethnohistory   ethnohistory.org
c/o Duke University Press Box 906660   Durham NC 27708
Ph: 919-687-3602 ▪ TF: 888-387-5687

American Society for Experimental NeuroTherapeutics   www.asent.org
611 E Wells St   Milwaukee WI 53202
Ph: 414-273-8290 ▪ Fx: 414-276-2146

American Society of Extra-Corporeal Technology   www.amsect.org
503 Carlisle Dr Suite 125   Herndon VA 20170
Ph: 703-435-8556 ▪ Fx: 703-435-0056

American Society of Farm Equipment   www.amagappraisers.com/farmeqip.htm
Appraisers   1126 Eastland Dr N Suite 100 PO Box 186   Twin
Falls ID 83303
Ph: 208-733-2323 ▪ Fx: 208-733-2326 ▪ TF: 800-488-7570

American Society of Farm Managers & Rural Appraisers   www.asfmra.org
950 S Cherry St Suite 508   Denver CO 80246
Ph: 303-758-3513 ▪ Fx: 303-758-0190

American Society of Forensic Geologists   www.forensicgeology.org
8401 Summerspring Ln   Raleigh NC 27615
Ph: 919-618-0810

American Society of Forensic Odontology   www.asfo.org
11 Tiffany Pl   Saratoga Springs NY 12866
Ph: 518-584-2342 ▪ Fx: 518-584-9706

American Society of the French Legion of Honor
22 E 60th St Rm 53   New York NY 10022
Ph: 212-751-8537 ▪ Fx: 212-755-7061

American Society of Furniture Designers   www.asfd.com
144 Woodland Dr   New London NC 28127
Ph: 910-576-1273 ▪ Fx: 910-573-1573

American Society of Gas Engineers   www.asge-national.org
2805 Barranca Pkwy   Irvine CA 92606
Ph: 949-733-4304 ▪ Fx: 949-733-4320

American Society for Gastrointestinal Endoscopy   www.asge.org
1520 Kensington Rd Suite 202   Oak Brook IL 60523
Ph: 630-573-0600 ▪ Fx: 630-573-0691

American Society of Gene Therapy   www.asgt.org
611 E Wells St   Milwaukee WI 53202
Ph: 414-278-1341 ▪ Fx: 414-276-3349

American Society of General Surgeons   www.theasgs.org
4200 Commercial Way   Glenview IL 60025
Ph: 847-391-9770 ▪ Fx: 847-391-9711 ▪ TF: 800-998-8322

American Society for Geriatric Dentistry   www.scdonline.org/ASGD_Index.htm
c/o Special Care Dentistry 211 E Chicago Ave Suite
740   Chicago IL 60611
Ph: 312-440-2660 ▪ Fx: 312-440-2824

American Society of Golf Course Architects   www.asgca.org
111 E Wacker Dr 18th Fl   Chicago IL 60601
Ph: 312-372-7090 ▪ Fx: 312-372-6160

American Society of Group Psychotherapy & Psychodrama   www.asgpp.org
301 N Harrison St Suite 508   Princeton NJ 08540
Ph: 609-452-1339 ▪ Fx: 609-936-1659

American Society of Hair Restoration Surgery   www.cosmeticsurgery.org
737 N Michigan Ave Suite 820   Chicago IL 60611
Ph: 312-981-6760 ▪ Fx: 312-981-6787

American Society of Hand Therapists   www.asht.org
401 N Michigan Ave Suite 2200   Chicago IL 60611
Ph: 312-321-6866 ▪ Fx: 312-673-6670

American Society of Handicapped Physicians
3424 S Culpepper Ct   Springfield MO 65804
Ph: 417-881-1570 ▪ Fx: 417-887-9830

American Society of Head & Neck Radiology   www.ashnr.org
2210 Midwest Rd Suite 207   Oak Brook IL 60523
Ph: 630-574-0220 ▪ Fx: 630-574-0661

American Society of Health-System Pharmacists   www.ashp.org
7272 Wisconsin Ave   Bethesda MD 20814
Ph: 301-657-3000 ▪ Fx: 301-664-8877

American Society for Healthcare Central Service Professionals   www.ashcsp.org
1 N Franklin St Suite 280   Chicago IL 60606
Ph: 312-422-3750 ▪ Fx: 312-422-4577

American Society for Healthcare Engineering   www.ashe.org
1 N Franklin St 28th Fl   Chicago IL 60606
Ph: 312-422-3800 ▪ Fx: 312-422-4571

American Society for Healthcare Environmental Services   www.ashes.org
1 N Franklin St Suite 2800   Chicago IL 60606
Ph: 312-422-3860 ▪ Fx: 312-422-4577

American Society for Healthcare Food Service Administrators   www.ashfsa.org
304 W Liberty St Suite 201   Louisville KY 40202
Ph: 800-620-6422

American Society for Healthcare Human Resources Administration   www.ashhra.org
1 N Franklin PO Box 75315   Chicago IL 60675
Ph: 312-422-3725 ▪ Fx: 312-422-4577

American Society for Healthcare Risk Management   www.ashrm.org
1 N Franklin St   Chicago IL 60606
Ph: 312-422-3980 ▪ Fx: 312-422-4580

American Society of Heating Refrigerating & Air-Conditioning Engineers Inc   1791 Tullie Cir NE   Atlanta GA 30329   www.ashrae.org
Ph: 404-636-8400 ▪ Fx: 404-321-5478 ▪ TF: 800-527-4723

American Society of Hematology   www.hematology.org
1900 M St NW Suite 200   Washington DC 20036
Ph: 202-776-0544 ▪ Fx: 202-776-0545

American Society of Highway Engineers   www.highwayengineers.org
113 Heritage Hills Rd   Uniontown PA 15401
Ph: 724-929-2760 ▪ Fx: 724-929-2234

American Society for Histocompatability & Immunogenetics   www.ashi-hla.org
17000 Commerce Pkwy Suite C   Mount Laurel NJ 08054
Ph: 856-638-0428 ▪ Fx: 856-439-0525

American Society of Home Inspectors   www.ashi.com
932 Lee St Suite 101   Des Plaines IL 60016
Ph: 847-759-2820 ▪ Fx: 847-759-1620 ▪ TF: 800-743-2744

American Society for Horticultural Science   www.ashs.org
113 South West St Suite 200   Alexandria VA 22314
Ph: 703-836-4606 ▪ Fx: 703-836-2024

American Society of Human Genetics   www.ashg.org/genetics/ashg
9650 Rockville Pike   Bethesda MD 20814
Ph: 301-571-1825 ▪ Fx: 301-634-7079

American Society of Hypertension   www.ash-us.org
148 Madison Ave 5th Fl   New York NY 10016
Ph: 212-696-9099 ▪ Fx: 212-696-0711

American Society of Ichthyologists & Herpetologists   www.asih.org
Florida International Univ Biology Dept 11200 SW 8th
St   Miami FL 33199
Ph: 305-919-5651 ▪ Fx: 305-919-5964

American Society of Indexers   www.asindexing.org
10200 W 44th Ave Suite 304   Wheat Ridge CO 80033
Ph: 303-463-2887 ▪ Fx: 303-422-8894

American Society for Information Science & Technology   www.asis.org
1320 Fenwick Ln Suite 510   Silver Spring MD 20910
Ph: 301-495-0900 ▪ Fx: 301-495-0810

American Society of Interior Designers   www.asid.org
608 Massachusetts Ave NE   Washington DC 20002
Ph: 202-546-3480 ▪ Fx: 202-546-3240

American Society of International Law   www.asil.org
2223 Massachusetts Ave NW   Washington DC 20008
Ph: 202-939-6000 ▪ Fx: 202-797-7133

American Society of Interventional & Therapeutic Neuroradiology   www.asitn.org
2210 Midwest Rd Suite 207   Oak Brook IL 60523
Ph: 630-574-0220 ▪ Fx: 630-574-0661

American Society of Inventors   www.americaninventor.org
PO Box 58426   Philadelphia PA 19102
Ph: 215-546-6601 ▪ Fx: 215-843-4234

American Society for Investigative Pathology   (no url)
9650 Rockville Pike   Bethesda MD 20814
Ph: 301-530-7130 ▪ Fx: 301-571-1879

American Society of Irrigation Consultants   www.asic.org
111 E Wacker Dr 18th Fl   Chicago IL 60601
Ph: 312-372-7090 ▪ Fx: 312-372-6160

American Society of Journalists & Authors   www.asja.org
1501 Broadway Suite 302   New York NY 10036
Ph: 212-997-0947 ▪ Fx: 212-768-7414

American Society of Laboratory Animal Practitioners   www.aslap.org
11300 Rockville Pike   Rockville MD 20852
Ph: 301-231-6349 ▪ Fx: 301-231-6071

American Society of Landscape Architects   www.asla.org
636 'I' St NW   Washington DC 20001
Ph: 202-898-2444 ▪ Fx: 202-898-1185 ▪ TF: 800-787-2752

American Society for Laser Medicine & Surgery   www.aslms.org
2404 Stewart Ave   Wausau WI 54401
Ph: 715-845-9283 ▪ Fx: 715-848-2493

American Society for Law Enforcement Training   www.aslet.org
121 N Court St   Frederick MD 21701
Ph: 301-668-9466 ▪ Fx: 301-668-9482

American Society of Law Medicine & Ethics   www.aslme.org
765 Commonwealth Ave 16th Fl   Boston MA 02215
Ph: 617-262-4990 ▪ Fx: 617-437-7596

American Society for Legal History   www.acls.org/asleghis.htm
Univ of Notre Dame PO Box R   Notre Dame IN 46556
Ph: 219-631-6984

American Society of Limnology & Oceanography   aslo.org
5400 Bosque Blvd Suite 680   Waco TX 76710
Ph: 254-399-9635 ▪ Fx: 254-776-3767 ▪ TF: 800-929-2756

American Society of Lipo-Suction Surgery   www.cosmeticsurgery.org
737 N Michigan Ave Suite 820   Chicago IL 60611
Ph: 312-981-6760 ▪ Fx: 312-981-6787

American Society of Magazine Editors   www.magazine.org/Editorial
810 7th Ave   New York NY 10022
Ph: 212-872-3737 ▪ Fx: 212-906-0128

American Society of Mammalogists   www.mammalsociety.org
810 E 10th St   Lawrence KS 66044
Ph: 785-843-1235 ▪ Fx: 785-843-1274 ▪ TF: 800-627-0629

American Society of Marine Artists   www.americansocietyofmarineartists.com
PO Box 369   Ambler PA 19002
Ph: 215-283-0888 ▪ Fx: 215-646-1581

American Society for Mass Spectrometry   www.asms.org
2019 Galisteo St Bldg 1   Santa Fe NM 87505
Ph: 505-989-4517 ▪ Fx: 505-989-1073

American Society of Master Dental Technologists   www.asmdt.com
PO Box 640248   Oakland Gardens NY 11364
Ph: 718-347-1239 ▪ Fx: 718-347-3113

American Society of Maxillofacial Surgeons   www.maxface.org
444 E Algonquin Rd   Arlington Heights IL 60005
Ph: 847-228-3338

American Society of Mechanical Engineers   www.asme.org
3 Park Ave   New York NY 10016
Ph: 212-591-7722 ▪ Fx: 212-591-7739 ▪ TF: 800-843-2763

American Society of Media Photographers   www.asmp.org
150 N 2nd St   Philadelphia PA 19106
Ph: 215-451-2767 ▪ Fx: 215-451-0880

American Society for Microbiology   www.asm.org
1752 'N' St NW   Washington DC 20036
Ph: 202-737-3600

American Society of Military Comptrollers   www.asmconline.org
2034 Eisenhower Ave Suite 145   Alexandria VA 22314
Ph: 703-549-0360 ▪ Fx: 703-549-3181 ▪ TF: 800-462-5637

American Society of Mining & Reclamation   ces.ca.uky.edu/asmr
3134 Montavesta Rd   Lexington KY 40502
Ph: 859-335-6529

American Society of Missiology   www.asmweb.org
64 Mercer St CN 821   Princeton NJ 08542
Ph: 609-497-3639 ▪ Fx: 609-430-0316

American Society of Music Arrangers & Composers   www.asmac.org
PO Box 17840   Encino CA 91416
Ph: 818-994-4661 ▪ Fx: 818-994-6181

American Society of Naturalists   www.amnat.org
Univ of Chicago Press PO Box 37005   Chicago IL 60637
Ph: 773-753-3347 ▪ Fx: 773-753-0811

American Society of Naval Engineers   www.navalengineers.org
1452 Duke St   Alexandria VA 22314
Ph: 703-836-6727 ▪ Fx: 703-836-7491

American Society of Nephrology   www.asn-online.com
1725 'I' St NW Suite 510   Washington DC 20006
Ph: 202-659-0599 ▪ Fx: 202-659-0709

American Society for Neurochemistry   www.ASNeurochem.org
9037 Ron Den Ln   Windermere FL 34786
Ph: 407-876-0750

American Society of Neuroimaging   www.asnweb.org
5841 Cedar Lake Rd Suite 204   Minneapolis MN 55416
Ph: 952-545-6291 ▪ Fx: 952-545-6073

American Society of Neuroradiology   www.asnr.org
2210 Midwest Rd Suite 207   Oak Brook IL 60523
Ph: 630-574-0220 ▪ Fx: 630-574-0661

American Society of Neurorehabilitation   www.asnr.com
5841 Cedar Lake Rd Suite 204   Minneapolis MN 55416
Ph: 952-545-6324 ▪ Fx: 952-545-6073

American Society of Newspaper Editors   www.asne.org
11690-B Sunrise Valley Dr   Reston VA 20191
Ph: 703-453-1122 ▪ Fx: 703-453-1133

American Society for Nondestructive Testing Inc   www.asnt.org
1711 Arlingate Ln   Columbus OH 43228
Ph: 614-274-6003 ▪ Fx: 614-274-6899 ▪ TF: 800-222-2768

American Society of Notaries   www.notaries.com
PO Box 940489   Maitland FL 32314
Ph: 800-422-1555 ▪ Fx: 800-224-6368

American Society of Nuclear Cardiology   www.asnc.org
9111 Old Georgetown Rd   Bethesda MD 20814
Ph: 301-493-2360 ▪ Fx: 301-493-2376

American Society for Nutritional Sciences   www.nutrition.org
9650 Rockville Pike   Bethesda MD 20814
Ph: 301-530-7050 ▪ Fx: 301-571-1892

American Society of Ophthalmic Administrators   www.asoa.org
4000 Legato Rd Suite 850   Fairfax VA 22033
Ph: 703-591-2222 ▪ Fx: 703-591-0614 ▪ TF: 800-451-1339

American Society of Ophthalmic Plastic & Reconstructive Surgery   www.asoprs.org
1133 W Morse Blvd Suite 201   Winter Park FL 32789
Ph: 407-647-8839 ▪ Fx: 407-629-2502

American Society of Ophthalmic Registered Nurses   www.asorn.org
PO Box 193030   San Francisco CA 94109
Ph: 415-561-8513 ▪ Fx: 415-561-8531

American Society of Orthopaedic Physician's Assistants   www.asopa.org
6300 N River Rd Suite 727   Rosemont IL 60018
Ph: 847-823-7186 ▪ Fx: 847-823-0536 ▪ TF: 800-998-6022

American Society of Pain Management Nurses   www.aspmn.org
7794 Grow Dr   Pensacola FL 32514
Ph: 850-473-0233 ▪ Fx: 850-484-8762 ▪ TF: 888-342-7766

American Society of Papyrologists   www.papyrology.org

American Society of Parasitologists   asp.unl.edu

American Society for Parenteral & Enteral Nutrition   www.clinnutr.org
8630 Fenton St Suite 412   Silver Spring MD 20910
Ph: 301-587-6315 ▪ Fx: 301-587-2365 ▪ TF: 800-727-4567

American Society of Pediatric Hematology/Oncology   www.aspho.org
4700 W Lake Ave   Glenview IL 60025
Ph: 847-375-4716 ▪ Fx: 877-734-9557

American Society of Pediatric Nephrology   www.aspneph.com
JW Riley Hospital for Children 702 Barnhill Dr Wells Research
Ctr Rm 2600-A   Indianapolis IN 46202
Ph: 317-278-0854 ▪ Fx: 317-278-3599

American Society of Pediatric Neuroradiology   www.asnr.org/aspnr
2210 Midwest Rd Suite 207   Oak Brook IL 60523
Ph: 630-574-0220 ▪ Fx: 630-574-0661

American Society for Pediatric Neurosurgery   www.aspn.org
James Whitcomb Riley Hospital For Children 1 Children's Sq
Suite 1730   Indianapolis IN 46202
Ph: 317-274-8852 ▪ Fx: 317-274-8895

American Society of Pension Actuaries
www.aspa.org
4245 N Fairfax Dr Suite 750   Arlington VA 22203
Ph: 703-516-9300 ▪ Fx: 703-516-9308

American Society of Perfumers
www.perfumers.org
PO Box 1551   West Caldwell NJ 07007
Ph: 201-991-0040 ▪ Fx: 201-991-0073

American Society of PeriAnesthesia Nurses
www.aspan.org
10 Melrose Ave Suite 110   Cherry Hill NJ 08003
Ph: 856-616-9600 ▪ Fx: 856-616-9601 ▪ TF: 877-737-9696

American Society of Pharmacognosy
www.phcog.org
PO Box 28665   Scottsdale AZ 85255
Ph: 623-202-3500 ▪ Fx: 623-572-3510

American Society for Pharmacology & Experimental Therapeutics
www.aspet.org
9650 Rockville Pike   Bethesda MD 20814
Ph: 301-634-7060 ▪ Fx: 301-634-7061

American Society for Photobiology
www.photobiology.org
PO Box 1897   Lawrence KS 66044
Ph: 785-843-1235 ▪ Fx: 785-843-1287

American Society for Photogrammetry & Remote Sensing
www.asprs.org
5410 Grosvenor Ln Suite 210   Bethesda MD 20814
Ph: 301-493-0290 ▪ Fx: 301-493-0208

American Society of Photographers
PO Box 316   Willimantic CT 06226
Ph: 860-423-1402 ▪ Fx: 860-423-9402 ▪ TF: 800-638-9609

American Society of Picture Professionals
www.aspp.com
409 S Washington St   Alexandria VA 22314
Ph: 703-229-0219 ▪ Fx: 703-299-0219

American Society of Plant Biologists
www.aspb.org
15501 Monona Dr   Rockville MD 20855
Ph: 301-251-0560 ▪ Fx: 301-279-2996

American Society of Plant Taxonomists
www.sysbot.org
Univ of Wyoming Dept of Botany 3165 1000 E University
Ave   Laramie WY 82071
Ph: 307-766-2556 ▪ Fx: 307-766-2851

American Society of Plastic Surgeons
www.plasticsurgery.org
444 E Algonquin Rd   Arlington Heights IL 60005
Ph: 847-228-9900 ▪ Fx: 847-228-9131 ▪ TF: 888-475-2784

American Society of Plastic Surgical Nurses
www.aspsn.org
3220 Pointe Pkwy Suite 500   Atlanta GA 30092
Ph: 678-291-0011 ▪ Fx: 678-291-9731

American Society for Plasticulture
www.plasticulture.org
526 Brittany Dr   State College PA 16803
Ph: 814-238-7045 ▪ Fx: 814-238-7051

American Society of Plumbing Engineers
www.aspe.org
8614 W Catalpa Ave Suite 1007   Chicago IL 60656
Ph: 773-693-2773

American Society of Podiatric Medical Assistants
www.aspma.org
2124 S Austin Blvd   Cicero IL 60804
Ph: 708-863-6303 ▪ Fx: 708-863-5375 ▪ TF: 888-882-7762

American Society of Podiatric Medicine
1111 Lane Concourse Dr Suite 111   Bay Harbor FL 33152
Ph: 305-866-9608 ▪ Fx: 305-866-1750

American Society of Polar Philatelists
www.polarphilatelists.org
PO Box 39   Exton PA 19341
Ph: 610-321-0740 ▪ Fx: 610-321-0219

American Society of Portrait Artists
www.asopa.com
PO Box 230216   Montgomery AL 36106
Ph: 334-270-9020 ▪ Fx: 334-270-0150 ▪ TF: 800-622-7672

American Society for Precision Engineering
www.aspe.net
PO Box 10826   Raleigh NC 27605
Ph: 919-839-8444 ▪ Fx: 919-839-8039

American Society for the Prevention of Cruelty to Animals
www.aspca.org
424 E 92nd St   New York NY 10128
Ph: 212-876-7700 ▪ Fx: 212-876-0014

American Society of Preventive Oncology
www.aspo.org
610 Walnut St Suite 256   Madison WI 53726
Ph: 608-263-9515 ▪ Fx: 608-263-4497

American Society of Primatologists
www.asp.org
Loyola Univ Psychology Dept   New Orleans LA 70118
Ph: 504-865-3255 ▪ Fx: 504-865-3970

American Society of Professional Estimators
www.aspenational.com
11141 Georgia Ave Suite 412   Wheaton MD 20902
Ph: 301-929-8848 ▪ Fx: 301-929-0231 ▪ TF: 800-378-4628

American Society for the Protection of Nature in Israel
www.aspni.org
28 Arrandale Ave   Great Neck NY 11024
Ph: 212-398-6750 ▪ Fx: 212-398-1665 ▪ TF: 800-411-0966

American Society for Psychical Research
www.aspr.org
5 W 73rd St   New York NY 10023
Ph: 212-799-5050 ▪ Fx: 212-496-2497

American Society of Psychopathology of Expression
74 Lawton St   Brookline MA 02446
Ph: 617-738-9821 ▪ Fx: 617-975-0411

American Society for Public Administration
www.aspanet.org
1120 G St NW Suite 700   Washington DC 20005
Ph: 202-393-7878 ▪ Fx: 202-638-4952

American Society for Quality
www.asq.org
600 N Plankinton Ave   Milwaukee WI 53201
Ph: 414-272-8575 ▪ Fx: 414-272-1734 ▪ TF: 800-248-1946

American Society of Questioned Document Examiners
www.asqde.org
PO Box 382684   Germantown TN 38183
Ph: 901-759-0729 ▪ Fx: 901-737-2643

American Society of Radiologic Technologists
www.asrt.org
15000 Central Ave SE   Albuquerque NM 87123
Ph: 505-298-4500 ▪ Fx: 505-298-5063 ▪ TF: 800-444-2778

American Society for Reconstructive Microsurgery
www.microsurg.org
20 N Michigan Ave Suite 700   Chicago IL 60602
Ph: 312-456-9579 ▪ Fx: 312-782-0553

American Society of Regional Anesthesia & Pain Medicine
www.asra.com
PO Box 11086   Richmond VA 23230
Ph: 804-282-0010 ▪ Fx: 804-282-0090

American Society for Reproductive Medicine
www.asrm.org
1209 Montgomery Hwy   Birmingham AL 35216
Ph: 205-978-5000 ▪ Fx: 205-978-5005

American Society of Retired Dentists
1 W Camino Real Blvd Suite 207   Boca Raton FL 33432
Ph: 561-395-2773 ▪ TF: 800-495-2773

American Society of Safety Engineers
www.asse.org
1800 E Oakton St   Des Plaines IL 60018
Ph: 847-699-2929 ▪ Fx: 847-768-3434

American Society of Sanitary Engineering
www.asse-plumbing.org
901 Canterbury Rd Suite A   Westlake OH 44145
Ph: 440-835-3040 ▪ Fx: 440-835-3488

American Society of Spine Radiology
www.theassr.org
2210 Midwest Rd Suite 207   Oak Brook IL 60523
Ph: 630-574-0220 ▪ Fx: 630-574-0661

American Society for Stereotactic & Functional Neurosurgery
Presbyterian Hospital   200 Lothrop St Suite B-400   Pittsburgh
PA 15213
Ph: 412-647-6782 ▪ Fx: 412-647-5559

American Society for Surgery of the Hand
www.assh.org
6300 N River Rd Suite 600   Rosemont IL 60018
Ph: 847-384-8300 ▪ Fx: 847-384-1435 ▪ TF: 888-576-2774

American Society of Swedish Engineers
www.asse-usa.org
780 3rd Ave   King of Prussia PA 19406
Ph: 610-265-4352 ▪ Fx: 610-265-4608

American Society of Theatre Consultants
www.theatreconsultants.org
12226 Mentz Hill Rd   Saint Louis MO 63128
Ph: 314-843-9218 ▪ Fx: 314-843-4955

American Society for Theatre Research
Brown Univ Dept of Theatre PO Box 1897   Providence RI
02912
Ph: 401-863-3289 ▪ Fx: 401-863-7529

American Society for Therapeutic Radiology & Oncology
www.astro.org
12500 Fair Lakes Cir Suite 375   Fairfax VA 22033
Ph: 703-502-1550 ▪ Fx: 703-502-7852 ▪ TF: 800-962-7876

American Society for Training & Development
www.astd.org
1640 King St Box 1443   Alexandria VA 22313
Ph: 703-683-8100 ▪ Fx: 703-683-1523 ▪ TF: 800-628-2783

American Society of Transplant Surgeons
www.asts.org
1020 N Fairfax St Suite 200   Alexandria VA 22314
Ph: 703-684-5990 ▪ Fx: 703-684-6303 ▪ TF: 888-990-2787

American Society of Transplantation
www.a-s-t.org
17000 Commerce Pkwy Suite C   Mount Laurel NJ 08054
Ph: 856-439-9986 ▪ Fx: 856-439-9982

American Society of Transportation & Logistics
www.astl.org
1700 N Moore St Suite 1900   Arlington VA 22209
Ph: 703-524-5011 ▪ Fx: 703-524-5017

American Society of Travel Agents
www.astanet.com
1101 King St Suite 200   Alexandria VA 22314
Ph: 703-739-2782 ▪ Fx: 703-684-8319 ▪ TF: 800-440-2782

American Society of Travel Agents PAC
1101 King St Suite 200   Alexandria VA 22314
Ph: 703-739-2782 ▪ Fx: 703-684-8319 ▪ TF: 800-275-2782

American Society of Trial Consultants
www.astcweb.org
1941 Greenspring Dr   Timonium MD 21093
Ph: 410-560-7949 ▪ Fx: 410-560-2563

American Society of Tropical Medicine & Hygiene
www.astmh.org
60 Revere Dr Suite 500   Northbrook IL 60062
Ph: 847-480-9592 ▪ Fx: 847-480-9282

American Society for Value Inquiry
Bergen Community College Humanities Dept 400 Paramus
Rd   Paramus NJ 07652
Ph: 201-447-9282 ▪ Fx: 201-612-8225

American Society for Virology
www.mcw.edu/asv

American Society of Women Accountants
www.aswa.org
8405 Greensboro Dr Suite 800   McLean VA 22102
Ph: 703-506-3265 ▪ Fx: 703-506-3266

American Sociological Association
www.asanet.org
1307 New York Ave NW Suite 700   Washington DC 20005
Ph: 202-383-9005 ▪ Fx: 202-638-0882

American Sokol
www.american-sokol.org
122 W 22nd St   Oak Brook IL 60523
Ph: 630-368-0771 ▪ Fx: 630-368-0758

American Solar Energy Society
www.ases.org
2400 Central Ave Suite A   Boulder CO 80301
Ph: 303-443-3130 ▪ Fx: 303-443-3212

American Southdown Breeders' Association
www.southdownsheep.org
HCR 13 Box 220   Fredonia TX 76842
Ph: 915-429-6226 ▪ Fx: 915-429-6225

American Soybean Association
www.amsoy.org
12125 Woodcrest Executive Dr Suite 100   Saint Louis MO
63141
Ph: 314-576-1770 ▪ Fx: 314-576-2786 ▪ TF: 800-688-7692

American Spaniel Club
www.asc-cockerspaniel.org
30 Cardinal Loop   Crossville TN 38555
Ph: 931-456-6690 ▪ Fx: 931-707-8504

American Specialty Toy Retailing Association
www.astratoy.org
4700 W Lake Ave   Glenview IL 60025
Ph: 847-375-4727 ▪ Fx: 888-840-2650

American Speech-Language-Hearing Association
www.asha.org
10801 Rockville Pike   Rockville MD 20852
Ph: 301-897-5700 ▪ Fx: 301-571-0457 ▪ TF: 800-498-2071

American Speech-Language-Hearing Association PAC
10801 Rockville Pike   Rockville MD 20852
Ph: 301-897-5700 ▪ Fx: 301-571-0457 ▪ TF: 800-638-8255

American Spice Trade Association
www.astaspice.org
2025 M St NW Suite 800   Washington DC 20036
Ph: 202-367-1127 ▪ Fx: 202-367-2127

American Spinal Injury Association www.asia-spinalinjury.org
345 E Superior St Suite 1436   Chicago IL 60611
Ph: 312-238-1242 ▪ Fx: 312-238-0869

American Spoon Collectors www.campanian.org/americanspoon.html
PO Box 243   Rhinecliff NY 12574
Ph: 845-876-0303 ▪ Fx: 845-876-2037

American Sport Touring Rider's Association
PO Box 672015   Marietta GA 30006
Ph: 770-222-0380

American Sportfishing Association www.asafishing.org
225 Reinekers Ln Suite 420   Alexandria VA 22314
Ph: 703-519-9691 ▪ Fx: 703-519-1872

American Sportfishing Association PAC www.asafishing.org
225 Reinekers Ln Suite 420   Alexandria VA 22314
Ph: 703-519-9691 ▪ Fx: 703-519-1872

American Sports Institute www.amersports.org
PO Box 1837   Mill Valley CA 94942
Ph: 415-383-5750 ▪ Fx: 415-383-5785

American Sportscasters Association www.americansportscasters.com
225 Broadway Suite 2030   New York NY 10007
Ph: 212-227-8080 ▪ Fx: 212-571-0556

American Staffing Association www.staffingtoday.net
277 S Washington St Suite 200   Alexandria VA 22314
Ph: 703-253-2020 ▪ Fx: 703-253-2053

American Stamp Dealers Association Inc www.asdaonline.com
3 School St Suite 205   Glen Cove NY 11542
Ph: 516-759-7000 ▪ Fx: 516-759-7014

American States, Organization of www.oas.org
1889 F St NW   Washington DC 20006
Ph: 202-458-3000 ▪ Fx: 202-458-3967

American Statistical Association www.amstat.org
1429 Duke St   Alexandria VA 22314
Ph: 703-684-1221 ▪ Fx: 703-684-2037 ▪ TF: 888-231-3473

American String Teachers Association www.astaweb.com
4153 Chain Bridge Rd   Fairfax VA 22030
Ph: 703-279-2113 ▪ Fx: 703-279-2114

American Student Association of Community Colleges www.asacc.org
2250 N University Pkwy Suite 4865   Provo UT 84604
Ph: 801-863-8620 ▪ Fx: 801-764-7229

American Student Dental Association www.asdanet.org
211 E Chicago Ave Suite 1160   Chicago IL 60611
Ph: 312-440-2795 ▪ Fx: 312-440-2820 ▪ TF: 800-621-8099

American Studies Association www.georgetown.edu/crossroads/asainfo.html
1120 19th St NW Suite 301   Washington DC 20036
Ph: 202-467-4783 ▪ Fx: 202-467-4786

American Studies, Fund for www.dcinternships.org
1706 New Hampshire Ave NW   Washington DC 20009
Ph: 800-741-6964 ▪ Fx: 202-318-0441

American Subcontractors Association Inc www.asaonline.com
1004 Duke St   Alexandria VA 22314
Ph: 703-684-3450 ▪ Fx: 703-836-3482

American Sugar Alliance www.sugaralliance.org
2111 Wilson Blvd Suite 600   Arlington VA 22201
Ph: 703-351-5055 ▪ Fx: 703-351-6698

American Sugar Cane League www.amscl.org
PO Box 938   Thibodaux LA 70302
Ph: 985-448-3707 ▪ Fx: 985-448-3722

American Sugar Cane League PAC
PO Box 938   Thibodaux LA 70302
Ph: 985-448-3707 ▪ Fx: 985-448-3722

American Sugarbeet Growers Association members.aol.com/asga
1156 15th St NW Suite 1101   Washington DC 20005
Ph: 202-833-2398 ▪ Fx: 202-833-2962

American Supplier Institute www.amsup.com
38701 Seven Mile Rd Suite 355   Livonia MI 48152
Ph: 734-464-1395 ▪ Fx: 734-464-1399 ▪ TF: 800-462-4500

American Supply Association www.asa.net
222 Merchandise Mart Plaza Suite 1400   Chicago IL 60654
Ph: 312-464-0090 ▪ Fx: 312-464-0091

American Supply Association PAC
222 Merchandise Mart Plaza Suite 1400   Chicago IL 60654
Ph: 312-464-0090 ▪ Fx: 312-464-0091

American Surgical Association www.americansurgical.info
900 Cummings Ctr Suite 221-U   Beverly MA 01915
Ph: 978-927-8330 ▪ Fx: 978-524-8890

American Surgical Hospital Association www.surgicalhospital.org
PO Box 23220   San Diego CA 92193
Ph: 858-490-8085 ▪ Fx: 858-490-9016 ▪ TF: 800-237-3768

American Swimming Coaches Association www.swimmingcoach.org
2101 N Andrews Ave Suite 107   Fort Lauderdale FL 33311
Ph: 954-563-4930 ▪ Fx: 954-563-9813 ▪ TF: 800-356-2722

American Swiss Foundation www.americanswiss.org
232 E 66th St   New York NY 10021
Ph: 212-754-0130 ▪ Fx: 212-754-4512

American Symphony Orchestra League www.symphony.org
33 W 60th St 5th Fl   New York NY 10023
Ph: 212-262-5161 ▪ Fx: 212-262-5198

American Tarentaise Association www.usa-tarentaise.com
PO Box 34705   Kansas City MO 64116
Ph: 816-421-1993 ▪ Fx: 816-421-1991

American Tax Token Society
12 Pheasant Dr   Asheville NC 28803
Ph: 828-684-1808

American Taxation Association www.atasection.org
c/o American Accounting Assn 5717 Bessie Dr   Sarasota FL
34233
Ph: 941-921-7747 ▪ Fx: 941-923-4093

American Technical Education Association www.ateaonline.org
North Dakota State College of Science 800 N 6th St   Wahpeton
ND 58076
Ph: 701-671-2240 ▪ Fx: 701-671-2260

American Telemedicine Association www.americantelemed.org
910 17th St NW Suite 314   Washington DC 20006
Ph: 202-223-3333 ▪ Fx: 202-223-2787

American Teleservices Association www.ataconnect.org
3815 River Crossing Pkwy Suite 20   Indianapolis IN 46240
Ph: 317-816-9336 ▪ Fx: 317-218-0323

American Tennis Association www.atanational.com
4640 Forbes Blvd Suite 200   Lanham MD 20706
Ph: 301-306-3193

American Textbook Council www.historytextbooks.org
475 Riverside Dr Rm 448   New York NY 10115
Ph: 212-870-2760 ▪ Fx: 212-870-3454

American Textile Industry Committee for Good www.atmi.org/About/ctte-atcigg.asp
Government 1130 Connecticut Ave NW Suite
1200   Washington DC 20036
Ph: 202-862-0500 ▪ Fx: 202-862-0570

American Textile Machinery Association www.atmanet.org
201 Park Washington Ct   Falls Church VA 22046
Ph: 703-538-1789 ▪ Fx: 703-241-5603

American Textile Manufacturers Institute www.atmi.org
1130 Connecticut Ave NW Suite 1200   Washington DC 20036
Ph: 202-862-0500 ▪ Fx: 202-862-0570

American Theatre Arts for Youth www.atafy.org
1429 Walnut St   Philadelphia PA 19102
Ph: 215-563-3501 ▪ Fx: 215-563-1588 ▪ TF: 800-523-4540

American Theatre Critics Association www.americantheatrecritics.org
c/o THEatre SERVICE PO Box 15282   Evansville IN 47716
Ph: 812-474-0549 ▪ Fx: 812-476-4168

American Theatre Organ Society Inc atos.org

American Theological Library Association www.atla.com
250 S Wacker Dr Suite 1600   Chicago IL 60606
Ph: 312-454-5100 ▪ Fx: 312-454-5505 ▪ TF: 888-665-2852

American Therapeutic Recreation Association www.atra-tr.org
1414 Prince St Suite 204   Alexandria VA 22314
Ph: 703-683-9420 ▪ Fx: 703-683-9431

American Thoracic Society www.thoracic.org
61 Broadway 4th Fl   New York NY 10006
Ph: 212-315-8600 ▪ Fx: 212-315-6498

American Thyroid Association www.thyroid.org
6066 Leesburg Pike Suite 650   Falls Church VA 22041
Ph: 703-998-8890 ▪ Fx: 703-998-8893

American Tinnitus Association www.ata.org
PO Box 5   Portland OR 97207
Ph: 503-248-9985 ▪ Fx: 503-248-0024 ▪ TF: 800-634-8978

American Topical Association www.americantopicalassn.org
PO Box 57   Arlington TX 76004
Ph: 817-274-1181 ▪ Fx: 817-274-1184

American Tort Reform Association www.atra.org
1101 Connecticut Ave NW Suite 400   Washington DC 20036
Ph: 202-682-1163 ▪ Fx: 202-682-1022

American Tract Society www.atstracts.org
1624 N 1st St   Garland TX 75046
Ph: 972-276-9408 ▪ Fx: 972-272-9642 ▪ TF: 800-548-7228

American Trade, Emergency Committee for www.ecattrade.com
1211 Connecticut Ave NW Suite 801   Washington DC 20036
Ph: 202-659-5147 ▪ Fx: 202-659-1347

American Traffic Safety Services Association www.atssa.com
15 Riverside Pkwy Suite 100   Fredericksburg VA 22406
Ph: 540-368-1701 ▪ Fx: 540-368-1717 ▪ TF: 800-272-8772

American Trails www.americantrails.org
PO Box 491797   Redding CA 96049
Ph: 530-547-2060 ▪ Fx: 530-547-2035

American Train Dispatchers Association atdd.homestead.com/atddpg1.html
1370 Ontario St Suite 1040   Cleveland OH 44113
Ph: 216-241-2770 ▪ Fx: 216-241-6286

American Trakehner Association www.americantrakehner.com
1514 W Church St   Newark OH 43055
Ph: 740-344-1111 ▪ Fx: 740-344-3225

American Transit Service Council www.transitatsc.org
1090 Vermont Ave NW Suite 1225   Washington DC 20005
Ph: 202-842-2818 ▪ Fx: 202-789-4328

American Translators Association www.atanet.org
225 Reinekers Ln Suite 590   Alexandria VA 22314
Ph: 703-683-6100 ▪ Fx: 703-683-6122

American Transplant Association www.americantransplant.org
980 N Michigan Ave Suite 1400   Chicago IL 60611
Ph: 800-494-4527

American Trauma Society www.amtrauma.org
8903 Presidential Pkwy Suite 512   Upper Marlboro MD 20772
Ph: 301-420-4189 ▪ Fx: 301-420-0617 ▪ TF: 800-556-7890

American Truck Dealers www.nada.org
8400 Westpark Dr   McLean VA 22102
Ph: 703-821-7230 ▪ Fx: 703-749-4700 ▪ TF: 800-252-6232

American Truck Historical Society www.aths.org
PO Box 901611   Kansas City MO 64190
Ph: 816-891-9900 ▪ Fx: 816-891-9903

(American Trucking Association) Truck PAC
430 1st St SE   Washington DC 20003
Ph: 202-544-6245 ▪ Fx: 202-675-6568

American Trucking Associations www.trucking.org
2200 Mill Rd   Alexandria VA 22314
Ph: 703-838-1700 ▪ Fx: 703-684-5751 ▪ TF: 800-282-5463

American Turkish Society www.americanturkishsociety.org
305 E 47th St 8th Fl   New York NY 10017
Ph: 212-583-7614 ▪ Fx: 212-583-7615

American Typecasting Fellowship
PO Box 263   Terra Alta WV 26764
Ph: 304-789-2455

American Underground Construction Association — www.auaonline.org
3001 Hennepin Ave S Suite D202   Minneapolis MN 55408
Ph: 612-825-8933 ▪ Fx: 612-825-8944

American Union of Men — groups.yahoo.com/group/aum
PO Box 80131   Santa Barbara CA 93117
Ph: 805-968-8068

American Urogynecologic Society — www.augs.org
2025 M St NW Suite 800   Washington DC 20036
Ph: 202-367-1167 ▪ Fx: 202-367-2167

American Urological Association — www.auanet.org
1000 Corporate Blvd   Linthicum MD 21090
Ph: 410-689-3700 ▪ Fx: 410-689-3800 ▪ TF: 866-746-4282

American-Uzbekistan Chamber of Commerce — www.erols.com/aucc
1800 Massachusetts Ave NW Suite 600   Washington DC 20036
Ph: 202-828-4317 ▪ Fx: 202-659-7010

American Values, Institute for — www.americanvalues.org
1841 Broadway Suite 211   New York NY 10023
Ph: 212-246-3942 ▪ Fx: 212-541-6665

American Vaulting Association — www.americanvaulting.org
642 Alford Pl NW   Bainbridge Island WA 98110
Ph: 206-780-9353 ▪ Fx: 206-780-9355

American Vegan Society — www.americanvegan.org
56 Dinshah Ln PO Box 369   Malaga NJ 08328
Ph: 856-694-2887 ▪ Fx: 856-694-2288

American Venous Forum — www.venous-info.com
900 Cummings Ctr Suite 221-U   Beverly MA 01915
Ph: 978-526-8330 ▪ Fx: 978-526-4018

American Veterans that Enlisted Underage — www.avteu.org
100 Village Ln   Philadelphia PA 19154
Ph: 215-632-2332 ▪ Fx: 215-637-9566 ▪ TF: 800-595-1006

American Veterans of Israel
136 E 39th St   New York NY 10016
Ph: 631-499-4327

American Veterans Medical Airlift Service
931 Flanders Rd PO Box 1065   La Canada Flintridge CA 91011
Ph: 818-952-6212

American Veterinary Dental Society — www.avds-online.org
618 Church St Suite 220   Nashville TN 37219
Ph: 800-332-2837 ▪ Fx: 615-254-7047

American Veterinary Distributors Association — www.avda.net
2105 Laurel Bush Rd Suite 200   Bel Air MD 21015
Ph: 443-640-1040 ▪ Fx: 443-640-1031

American Veterinary Exhibitors Association
712 N Broadway   Menominee WI 54751
Ph: 715-231-6312 ▪ Fx: 715-232-9936

American Veterinary Medical Association — www.avma.org
1931 N Meacham Rd Suite 100   Schaumburg IL 60173
Ph: 847-925-8070 ▪ Fx: 847-925-1329

American Veterinary Medical Association PAC
1101 Vermont Ave NW   Washington DC 20005
Ph: 202-789-0007 ▪ Fx: 202-842-4360

American Veterinary Medical Colleges, Association of — www.aavmc.org
1101 Vermont Ave NW Suite 710   Washington DC 20005
Ph: 202-371-9195 ▪ Fx: 202-842-0773

American Vineyard Foundation — www.avf.org
PO Box 5779   Napa CA 94581
Ph: 707-252-6911

American Vintners Association — www.americanwineries.org
1200 G St NW Suite 360   Washington DC 20005
Ph: 202-783-2756 ▪ Fx: 202-347-6341 ▪ TF: 800-879-4537

American Viola Society — www.americanviolasociety.org
13140 Coit Rd Suite 320 LB 120   Dallas TX 75240
Ph: 972-233-9107 ▪ Fx: 972-490-4219

American Vocational Education Research Association — tiger.coe.missouri.edu/~pavtat/AVERA

American Volkssport Association — www.ava.org
1001 Pat Booker Rd Suite 101   Universal City TX 78148
Ph: 210-659-2112 ▪ Fx: 210-659-1212 ▪ TF: 800-830-9255

American Volleyball Coaches Association — www.avca.org
1227 Lake Plaza Dr Suite B   Colorado Springs CO 80906
Ph: 719-576-7777 ▪ Fx: 719-576-7778

American Voyager Association — www.csonline.net/cybersite/american.htm
PO Box 253   Cypress IL 62923
Ph: 618-657-2664

American Waldensian Society — www.waldensian.org
102 Vultee St   Allentown PA 18103
Ph: 866-825-3373 ▪ Fx: 610-797-9723

American Walking Pony Association
PO Box 5282   Macon GA 31208
Ph: 478-743-2321 ▪ Fx: 478-742-6021

American Walnut Manufacturers Association — www.walnutassociation.org
PO Box 5046   Zionsville IN 46077
Ph: 317-873-8780

American Warmblood Registry — www.americanwarmblood.com
PO Box 211735   Royal Palm Beach FL 33421
Ph: 561-333-5848

American Warmblood Society — www.americanwarmblood.org
2 Buffalo Run   Center Ridge AR 72027
Ph: 501-893-2777 ▪ Fx: 501-893-2779

American Warmblood & Sport Horse Guild
PO Box 5512   Grants Pass OR 97527
Ph: 541-855-8942

American Watch Association
1201 Pennsylvania Ave NW PO Box 464   Washington DC 20044
Ph: 703-759-3377

American Watchmakers-Clockmakers Institute — www.awi-net.org
701 Enterprise Dr   Harrison OH 45030
Ph: 513-367-9800 ▪ Fx: 513-367-1414 ▪ TF: 866-367-2924

American Water Buffalo Association — www.americanwaterbuffalo.org
PO Box 13533   Gainesville FL 32604
Ph: 352-392-2643 ▪ Fx: 352-846-0816

American Water Resources Association — www.awra.org
4 W Federal St PO Box 1626   Middleburg VA 20118
Ph: 540-687-8390 ▪ Fx: 540-687-9395

American Water Ski Educational Foundation — www.waterskihalloffame.com
1251 Holy Cow Rd   Polk City FL 33868
Ph: 863-324-4341 ▪ Fx: 863-325-8259

American Water Works Association — www.awwa.org
6666 W Quincy Ave   Denver CO 80235
Ph: 303-794-7711 ▪ Fx: 303-347-0804 ▪ TF: 800-926-7337

American Watercraft Association — www.awahq.org
PO Box 1993   Ashburn VA 20147
Ph: 800-913-2921

American Waterways Operators — www.americanwaterways.com
801 N Quincy St Suite 200   Arlington VA 22203
Ph: 703-841-9300 ▪ Fx: 703-841-0389

American Way, People for the — www.pfaw.org
2000 M St NW Suite 400   Washington DC 20036
Ph: 202-467-4999 ▪ Fx: 202-293-2672 ▪ TF: 800-326-7329

American Welara Pony Society — www.WelaraRegistry.com/
PO Box 401   Yucca Valley CA 92286
Ph: 760-364-2048

American Welding Society — www.aws.org
550 NW Le Jeune Rd   Miami FL 33126
Ph: 305-443-9353 ▪ Fx: 305-443-7559 ▪ TF: 800-443-9353

American Wheelchair Bowling Association — www.awba.org
2912 Country Woods Ln   Palm Harbor FL 34683
Ph: 727-734-0023

American White Horse & American Creme Horse Registry — www.whitehorseranchnebraska.com/registry.htm
90000 Edwards Rd   Naper NE 68755
Ph: 402-832-5560

American Whitewater — www.americanwhitewater.org
1424 Fenwick Ln   Silver Spring MD 20910
Ph: 301-589-9453 ▪ Fx: 301-565-6714 ▪ TF: 866-262-8429

American Wholesale Booksellers Association — www.awba.com
702 S Michigan St   South Bend IN 46601
Ph: 574-288-4141

American Wholesale Marketers Association Inc — www.awmanet.org
2750 Prosperity Ave Suite 550   Fairfax VA 22031
Ph: 703-208-3358 ▪ Fx: 703-573-5738 ▪ TF: 800-482-2962

American Wildlands — www.wildlands.org
40 E Main St Suite 2   Bozeman MT 59715
Ph: 406-586-8175 ▪ Fx: 406-586-8242

American Wind Energy Association — www.awea.org
122 C St NW Suite 380   Washington DC 20001
Ph: 202-383-2500 ▪ Fx: 202-383-2505

American Wine Alliance for Research & Education — www.alcohol-aware.com
PO Box 765   Washington DC 20004
Ph: 800-700-4050

American Wine Society — www.americanwinesociety.com
3006 Latta Rd   Rochester NY 14612
Ph: 585-225-7613

American Wire Cloth Institute — www.wireclothinstitute.org
25 N Broadway   Tarrytown NY 10591
Ph: 914-332-0040 ▪ Fx: 914-332-1541

American Wire Producers Association — www.awpa.org
801 N Fairfax St Suite 211   Alexandria VA 22314
Ph: 703-299-4434 ▪ Fx: 703-299-9233

American Woman's Economic Development Corp — www.awed.org
216 E 45th St 10th Fl   New York NY 10017
Ph: 917-368-6100

American Woman's Society of Certified Public Accountants — www.awscpa.org
136 S Keowee St   Dayton OH 45402
Ph: 937-222-1872 ▪ Fx: 937-222-5794 ▪ TF: 800-297-2721

American Women in Radio & Television — www.awrt.org
8405 Greensboro Dr Suite 800   McLean VA 22102
Ph: 703-506-3290 ▪ Fx: 703-506-3266

American Wood-Preservers' Association — www.awpa.com
PO Box 388   Selma AL 36702
Ph: 334-874-9800 ▪ Fx: 334-874-9008

American Wood Preservers Institute — www.preservedwood.com
12100 Sunset Hills Rd Suite 130   Reston VA 20190
Ph: 703-204-0500 ▪ Fx: 703-204-4610 ▪ TF: 800-356-2974

American Yarn Spinners Association — www.aysa.org
PO Box 99   Gastonia NC 28053
Ph: 704-824-3522 ▪ Fx: 704-824-0630

American Yoga Association — www.americanyogaassociation.org
PO Box 19986   Sarasota FL 34276
Ph: 941-927-4977 ▪ Fx: 941-921-9844

American Youth Foundation — www.ayf.com
2331 Hampton Ave   Saint Louis MO 63139
Ph: 314-646-6000 ▪ Fx: 314-772-7542

American Youth Horse Council — www.ayhc.com
577 N Boyero Ave   Pueblo West CO 81007
Ph: 719-547-7677 ▪ TF: 800-879-2942

American Youth Hostels, Hostelling International - — www.hiusa.org
8401 Colesville Rd Suite 600   Silver Spring MD 20910
Ph: 301-495-1240 ▪ Fx: 301-495-6697

American Youth Soccer Organization — soccer.org
12501 S Isis Ave   Hawthorne CA 90250
Ph: 310-643-6455 ▪ Fx: 310-643-5310 ▪ TF: 800-872-2976

American Youth Work Center — www.youthtoday.org
1200 17th St NW 4th Fl   Washington DC 20036
Ph: 202-785-0764 ▪ Fx: 202-728-0657

American Zinc Association — www.zinc.org
2025 M St NW Suite 800   Washington DC 20036
Ph: 202-367-1151 ▪ Fx: 202-367-2232

American Zionist Movement www.azm.org
633 3rd Ave 21st Fl   New York NY 10017
Ph: 212-318-6100 ■ Fx: 212-935-3578

American Zionist Youth Foundation
633 3rd Ave 21st Fl   New York NY 10017
Ph: 212-318-6123 ■ TF: 800-274-7723

American Zoo & Aquarium Association www.aza.org
8403 Colesville Rd Suite 710   Silver Spring MD 20910
Ph: 301-562-0777 ■ Fx: 301-562-0888

Americans for the Arts www.artsusa.org
1000 Vermont Ave NW 6th Fl   Washington DC 20005
Ph: 202-371-2830 ■ Fx: 202-371-0424

Americans, Association of Retired www.ara-usa.org
6505 E 82nd St Suite 130   Indianapolis IN 46250
Ph: 800-806-6160 ■ Fx: 317-915-2510

Americans for Better Care of the Dying www.abcd-caring.org
4200 Wisconsin Ave NW Suite 418   Washington DC 20016
Ph: 202-895-2660 ■ Fx: 202-966-5410

Americans for Computer Privacy www.computerprivacy.org
1275 Pennsylvania Ave NW 10th Fl   Washington DC 20004
Ph: 202-393-5222 ■ Fx: 202-467-0810

Americans for Decency www.americansfordecency.com
3431 W Thunderbird Rd   Phoenix AZ 85053
Ph: 602-993-4353 ■ Fx: 602-993-4308

Americans for Democratic Action www.adaction.org
1625 K St NW Suite 210   Washington DC 20006
Ph: 202-785-5980 ■ Fx: 202-785-5969 ■ TF: 800-787-2734

Americans for Effective Law Enforcement www.aele.org
841 W Touhy Ave   Park Ridge IL 60068
Ph: 847-685-0700 ■ Fx: 847-685-9700

Americans for the Enforcement of Attorney Ethics rentamark.com/aeae
PO Box 35189   Chicago IL 60707
Ph: 773-283-3880

Americans for the Enforcement of Intellectual Property Rights rentamark.com/aeipr
PO Box 35189   Chicago IL 60707
Ph: 773-283-3880 ■ Fx: 708-453-0083

Americans for Fair Taxation www.fairtax.org
PO Box 27487   Houston TX 77227
Ph: 713-963-9023 ■ Fx: 713-963-8403 ■ TF: 800-324-7829

Americans for Gun Safety www.americansforgunsafety.com
2000 L St NW Suite 702   Washington DC 20036
Ph: 202-775-0300 ■ Fx: 202-775-0430

Americans for Immigration Control www.immigrationcontrol.com
PO Box 738   Monterey VA 24465
Ph: 540-468-2023 ■ Fx: 540-468-2026

Americans for Indian Opportunity www.aio.org
681 Juniper Hill Rd   Santa Ana Pueblo NM 87004
Ph: 505-867-0278 ■ Fx: 505-867-0441

Americans for Middle www.cafearabica.com/organizations/org12/orgameu1.html
East Understanding   475 Riverside Dr Suite 245   New York
NY 10115
Ph: 212-870-2053 ■ Fx: 212-870-2050

Americans for Nonsmokers' Rights www.no-smoke.org
2530 San Pablo Ave Suite J   Berkeley CA 94702
Ph: 510-841-3032 ■ Fx: 510-841-3071

Americans for Our Heritage & Recreation www.ahrinfo.org
1615 M St NW   Washington DC 20036
Ph: 202-429-2606 ■ Fx: 202-429-2621

Americans for Peace Now www.peacenow.org
1101 14th St NW 6th Fl   Washington DC 20005
Ph: 202-728-1893 ■ Fx: 202-728-1895

Americans for Religious Liberty www.arlinc.org
PO Box 6656   Silver Spring MD 20916
Ph: 301-260-2988 ■ Fx: 301-260-2989

Americans for Responsible Recreation www.arra-access.com

Americans for a Safe Israel www.afsi.org
1623 3rd Ave Suite 205   New York NY 10128
Ph: 212-828-2424 ■ Fx: 212-828-1717

Americans for Tax Reform www.atr.org
1920 L St NW Suite 200   Washington DC 20036
Ph: 202-785-0266 ■ Fx: 202-785-0261

Americans United for Life www.unitedforlife.org
310 S Peoria St Suite 300   Chicago IL 60607
Ph: 312-492-7234 ■ Fx: 312-492-7235 ■ TF: 800-626-6149

Americans United for Separation of Church & State www.au.org
518 C St NE   Washington DC 20002
Ph: 202-466-3234 ■ Fx: 202-466-2587 ■ TF: 800-875-3707

AmeriCares Foundation www.americares.org
161 Cherry St   New Canaan CT 06840
Ph: 203-966-5195 ■ Fx: 203-966-6028 ■ TF: 800-486-4357

America's Athletes with Disabilities www.americasathletes.org
8630 Fenton St Suite 920   Silver Spring MD 20910
Ph: 301-589-9042 ■ Fx: 301-589-9052 ■ TF: 800-238-7632

America's Blood Centers www.americasblood.org
725 15th St NW Suite 700   Washington DC 20005
Ph: 202-393-5725 ■ Fx: 202-393-1282 ■ TF: 888-872-5663

America's Charities www.charities.org
14150 Newbrook Dr Suite 110   Chantilly VA 20151
Ph: 703-222-3861 ■ Fx: 703-222-3867 ■ TF: 800-458-9505

America's Community Bankers www.acbankers.org
900 19th St NW Suite 400   Washington DC 20006
Ph: 202-857-3100 ■ Fx: 202-296-8716

Americas, Council of the www.counciloftheamericas.org
680 Park Ave   New York NY 10021
Ph: 212-628-3200 ■ Fx: 212-517-6247 ■ TF: 800-733-2342

America's Development Foundation www.adfusa.org
101 N Union St Suite 200   Alexandria VA 22314
Ph: 703-836-2717 ■ Fx: 703-836-3379

America's Future, Campaign for www.ourfuture.org
1025 Connecticut Ave NW Suite 205   Washington DC 20036
Ph: 202-955-5665 ■ Fx: 202-955-5606

America's Military Past, Council on www.campjamp.org
PO Box 1151   Fort Myer VA 22211
Ph: 703-912-6124 ■ Fx: 703-912-5666 ■ TF: 800-398-4693

Americas, Partners of the www.partners.net
1424 K St NW Suite 700   Washington DC 20005
Ph: 202-628-3300 ■ Fx: 202-628-3306

America's Promise - The Alliance for Youth www.americaspromise.org
909 N Washington St Suite 400   Alexandria VA 22314
Ph: 703-684-4500 ■ Fx: 703-535-3900 ■ TF: 800-365-0153

America's Second Harvest www.secondharvest.org
35 E Wacker Dr Suite 2000   Chicago IL 60601
Ph: 312-263-2303 ■ Fx: 312-263-5626 ■ TF: 800-771-2303

Americas Society www.americas-society.org
680 Park Ave   New York NY 10021
Ph: 212-249-8950 ■ Fx: 212-249-1880

Amerifax Cattle Association
PO Box 149   Hastings NE 68902
Ph: 402-463-5289 ■ Fx: 402-463-6652

Amerind Foundation Inc www.amerind.org
2100 N Amerind Rd PO Box 400   Dragoon AZ 85609
Ph: 520-586-3666 ■ Fx: 520-586-4679

AMF International www.amfi.org
PO Box 5470   Lansing IL 60438
Ph: 708-418-0020 ■ Fx: 708-418-0132

AMG International
6815 Shallowford Rd   Chattanooga TN 37421
Ph: 423-894-6060 ■ Fx: 423-894-6863 ■ TF: 800-241-7206

AMIDEAST www.amideast.org
1730 M St NW Suite 1100   Washington DC 20036
Ph: 202-776-9600 ■ Fx: 202-776-7000

Amigos de las Americas www.amigoslink.org
5618 Star Ln   Houston TX 77057
Ph: 713-782-5290 ■ Fx: 713-782-9267 ■ TF: 800-231-7796

Amish Religious Freedom, National Committee for www.holycrosslivonia.org/amish
30650 6 Mile Rd   Livonia MI 48152
Ph: 734-427-1414 ■ Fx: 734-427-1419

AMIT www.amitchildren.org
817 Broadway   New York NY 10003
Ph: 212-477-4720 ■ Fx: 212-353-2312 ■ TF: 800-989-2648

Amizade Ltd www.amizade.org
920 William Pitt Union   Pittsburgh PA 15260
Ph: 888-973-4443 ■ Fx: 412-648-1492

Ammonia Refrigeration, International Institute of www.iiar.org
1110 N Glebe Rd Suite 250   Arlington VA 22201
Ph: 703-312-4200 ■ Fx: 703-312-0065

Amnesty International USA www.amnestyusa.org
322 8th Ave   New York NY 10001
Ph: 212-807-8400 ■ Fx: 212-627-1451 ■ TF: 800-266-3789

Amon G Carter Foundation www.agcf.org
PO Box 1036   Fort Worth TX 76101
Ph: 817-332-2783 ■ Fx: 817-332-2787

AMORC, Rosicrucian Order www.rosicrucian.org
1342 Naglee Ave   San Jose CA 95191
Ph: 408-947-3600 ■ Fx: 408-947-3677

Amorphous Silica & Silicates Industry Association, Synthetic
1 PPG Pl   Pittsburgh PA 15272
Ph: 412-434-2801 ■ Fx: 412-434-3193

Amphibians & Reptiles, Society for the Study of www.ssarherps.org
PO Box 253   Marceline MO 64658
Ph: 660-256-3252

Amputation Foundation, National www.nationalamputation.org
40 Church St   Malverne NY 11565
Ph: 516-887-3600 ■ Fx: 516-887-3667

Amputee Coalition of America www.amputee-coalition.org
900 E Hill Ave Suite 285   Knoxville TN 37915
Ph: 865-524-8772 ■ Fx: 865-525-7917 ■ TF: 888-267-5669

Amputee Foundation, American www.americanamputee.org
PO Box 250218 Hillcrest Stn   Little Rock AR 72225
Ph: 501-666-2523 ■ Fx: 501-666-8367

Amputee Golf Association, National www.nagagolf.org
11 Walnut Hill Rd   Amherst NH 03031
Ph: 800-633-6242

Amusement Business Association, Outdoor www.oaba.org
1035 S Semoran Blvd Suite 1045A   Winter Park FL 32792
Ph: 407-681-9444 ■ Fx: 407-681-9445 ■ TF: 800-517-6222

Amusement Industry Manufacturers & Suppliers International www.aimsintl.org
1250 SE Port St Lucie Blvd Suite C   Port Saint Lucie FL 34952
Ph: 772-398-6701 ■ Fx: 772-398-6702

Amusement Machine Association, American www.coin-op.org
450 E Higgins Rd Suite 201   Elk Grove Village IL 60007
Ph: 847-290-9088 ■ Fx: 847-290-9121

Amusement & Music Operators Association www.amoa.com
1145 N Arlington Heights Rd Suite 300   Itasca IL 60143
Ph: 630-250-1430 ■ Fx: 630-250-3533 ■ TF: 800-937-2662

Amusement Parks & Attractions, International Association of www.iaapa.org
1448 Duke St   Alexandria VA 22314
Ph: 703-836-4800 ■ Fx: 703-836-9678

Amusement Photographers International, Antique & www.oldtimephotos.org
37 W Broad St Suite 480   Columbus OH 43215
Ph: 614-358-2828 ■ Fx: 614-241-2215

Amusement Ride Safety Officials, National Association of www.naarso.com
PO Box 638   Brandon FL 33509
Ph: 813-661-2779 ■ Fx: 813-685-5117 ■ TF: 800-669-9053

AMVETS www.amvets.org
4647 Forbes Blvd   Lanham MD 20706
Ph: 301-459-9600 ■ Fx: 301-459-7924 ■ TF: 877-726-8387

AN Group Inc — www.angroup.org
1250 Connecticutt St NW Suite 700   Washington DC 20036
Ph: 202-419-1500 ▪ Fx: 202-659-8037

Anachronism, Society for Creative — www.sca.org
PO Box 360789   Milpitas CA 95036
Ph: 408-263-9305 ▪ Fx: 408-263-0641

Anaerobe Society of the Americas — www.anaerobe.org
PO Box 452058   Los Angeles CA 90045
Ph: 310-216-9265 ▪ Fx: 310-216-9274

Analysts, Society of Quantitative — www.sqa-us.org
151 Herricks Rd Suite 1   Garden City Park NY 11040
Ph: 516-739-2510 ▪ Fx: 516-739-3803 ▪ TF: 800-284-6228

Analytical Chemistry & Spectroscopy Societies, Federation of — www.facss.org
PO Box 24379   Sante Fe NM 87502
Ph: 505-820-1648 ▪ Fx: 505-989-1073

Analytical Cytology, International Society for — www.isac-net.org
60 Revere Dr Suite 500   Northbrook IL 60062
Ph: 847-205-4722 ▪ Fx: 847-480-9282

Analytical Feminism, Society for — www.ukans.edu/~acudd/safhomepage.htm
Univ of Kentucky Dept of Philosophy Suite 1415   Lexington KY 40506
Ph: 859-257-1861

Analytical Laboratory Managers Association — www.labmanagers.org
2019 Galisteo St Bldg I   Santa Fe NM 87505
Ph: 505-989-4683 ▪ Fx: 505-989-1073

Analytical & Life Science Systems Association — www.alssa.org
225 Reinekers Ln Suite 625   Alexandria VA 22314
Ph: 703-836-1360 ▪ Fx: 703-836-6644

Ananda Marga New York Sector — www.anandamarga.org
97-38 42nd Ave Suite 1F   Corona NY 11368
Ph: 718-898-1603 ▪ Fx: 718-898-1604

Anaphylaxis Network, Food Allergy & — www.foodallergy.org
10400 Eaton Pl Suite 107   Fairfax VA 22030
Ph: 703-691-3179 ▪ Fx: 703-691-2713 ▪ TF: 800-929-4040

Anaplastology Association, American — www.anaplastology.org
PO Box 27440   Seattle WA 98125
Ph: 206-268-0311

Anatomists, American Association of — www.anatomy.org
9650 Rockville Pike Suite 2408   Bethesda MD 20814
Ph: 301-634-7910 ▪ Fx: 301-634-7965

Anatomy & Physiology Society, Human — www.hapsweb.org
8000 Bonhomme Ave Suite 412   Saint Louis MO 63105
Ph: 800-448-4277 ▪ Fx: 314-863-6457

Ancestral Research Association, Familia
PO Box 10359   Westminster CA 92685
Ph: 714-687-0390

Anchor Manufacturers Association, Concrete — www.concreteanchors.org
1603 Boone's Lick Rd   Saint Charles MO 63301
Ph: 636-925-2212 ▪ Fx: 636-946-3336

Ancient Egyptian Arabic Order Nobles Mystic Shrine — www.aeaonms.org
2239 Democrat Rd   Memphis TN 38132
Ph: 901-395-0150 ▪ Fx: 901-395-0115

Ancient Egyptian Order of Sciots — www.sciots.org
PO Box 501801   San Diego CA 92150
Ph: 858-755-0931

Ancient Forest International — www.ancientforests.org
PO Box 1850   Redway CA 95560
Ph: 707-923-4475

Ancient Greek Philosophy, Society for — sagp.binghamton.edu
Binghamton Univ Dept of Philosophy   Binghamton NY 13902
Ph: 607-777-2886 ▪ Fx: 607-777-2734

Ancient Historians, Association of — www.trentu.ca/ahc/aah
City College of New York Dept of Foreign Languages & Literatures NAC 5-223   New York NY 10031
Ph: 212-650-6731 ▪ Fx: 718-796-4392

Ancient & Honorable Artillery Company of Massachusetts — www.ahacsite.org
Armory Faneuil Hall   Boston MA 02109
Ph: 617-227-1638 ▪ Fx: 617-227-7221

Ancient & Illustrious Order Knights of Malta
2632 Skylark Dr   Wilmington DE 19808
Ph: 302-996-0800

Ancient Mystic Order of Bagmen of Baghdad Imperial Guild
6620 Cliffside Cir   Amarillo TX 79124
Ph: 806-373-8246

Andrew W Mellon Foundation — www.mellon.org
140 E 62nd St   New York NY 10021
Ph: 212-838-8400 ▪ Fx: 212-888-4172

Andrology, American Society of — www.andrologysociety.com
1111 N Plaza Dr Suite 550   Schaumburg IL 60173
Ph: 847-619-4909 ▪ Fx: 847-517-7229

Anemia & MDS International Foundation Inc, Aplastic — www.aamds.org
PO Box 613   Annapolis MD 21404
Ph: 410-867-0242 ▪ Fx: 410-867-0240 ▪ TF: 800-747-2820

Anemia Research Fund Inc, Fanconi — www.fanconi.org
1801 Willamette St Suite 200   Eugene OR 97401
Ph: 541-687-4658 ▪ Fx: 541-687-0548

Anesthesia & Critical Care Society, International Trauma — www.itaccs.com
PO Box 4826   Baltimore MD 21211
Ph: 410-235-7697 ▪ Fx: 410-235-8084

Anesthesia & Pain Medicine, American Society of Regional — www.asra.com
PO Box 11086   Richmond VA 23230
Ph: 804-282-0010 ▪ Fx: 804-282-0090

Anesthesia & Perinatology, Society for Obstetric — www.soap.org
2 Summit Park Dr Suite 140   Cleveland OH 44131
Ph: 216-447-7863 ▪ Fx: 216-642-1127

Anesthesia Research Society, International — www.iars.org
2 Summit Pk Dr Suite 140   Cleveland OH 44131
Ph: 216-642-1124 ▪ Fx: 216-642-1127

Anesthesia & Sedation in Dentistry, American Society for the Advancement of — www.sedation4dentists.com
6 E Union Ave   Bound Brook NJ 08805
Ph: 732-469-9050 ▪ Fx: 732-271-1985

Anesthesia, Society for Education in — www.seahq.org
520 N Northwest Hwy   Park Ridge IL 60068
Ph: 847-825-5586 ▪ Fx: 847-825-5658

Anesthesia Society, Navy — www.geocities.com/Vienna/2209/nas.html
Naval Medical Ctr Dept of Anesthesiology   San Diego CA 92134
Ph: 619-532-8943 ▪ Fx: 619-532-8945

Anesthesia, Society for Pediatric — www.pedsanesthesia.org
PO Box 11086   Richmond VA 23230
Ph: 804-282-9780 ▪ Fx: 804-282-0090

Anesthesia Technologists & Technicians, American Society of — www.asat.org
5800 Foxridge Dr Suite 115   Mission KS 66202
Ph: 913-262-2249 ▪ Fx: 913-262-0174

Anesthesiologist Assistants, American Academy of — www.anesthetist.org
PO Box 13978   Tallahassee FL 32317
Ph: 850-656-8848 ▪ Fx: 850-656-3038

Anesthesiologists, American Society of — www.asahq.org
520 N Northwest Hwy   Park Ridge IL 60068
Ph: 847-825-5586 ▪ Fx: 847-825-1692

Anesthesiologists, Association of University — www.auahq.org
520 Northwest Hwy   Park Ridge IL 60068
Ph: 847-825-5586

Anesthesiologists, Society of Cardiovascular — www.scahq.org
2209 Dickens Rd   Richmond VA 23230
Ph: 804-282-0084 ▪ Fx: 804-282-0090

Anesthesiology, American Board of — www.abanes.org
4101 Lake Boone Trail Suite 510   Raleigh NC 27607
Ph: 919-881-2570 ▪ Fx: 919-881-2575

Anesthesiology, American Dental Society of — www.adsa.org
211 E Chicago Ave Suite 780   Chicago IL 60611
Ph: 312-664-8270 ▪ Fx: 312-642-9713 ▪ TF: 800-722-7788

Anesthetists, American Association of Nurse — www.aana.com
222 S Prospect Ave   Park Ridge IL 60068
Ph: 847-692-7050 ▪ Fx: 847-692-6968

Anesthetists, International Federation of Nurse — www.ifna.info
222 S Prospect Ave   Park Ridge IL 60068
Ph: 847-692-7050 ▪ Fx: 847-692-6968

Angela Thirkell Society — www.angelathirkell.org
PO Box 7109   San Diego CA 92167
Ph: 619-222-8143 ▪ Fx: 619-255-3612

ANGELCARE — www.angelcare.org
PO Box 600370   San Diego CA 92160
Ph: 619-593-1222 ▪ Fx: 619-593-0222 ▪ TF: 888-264-5227

Angiography & Interventions, Society for Cardiac — www.scai.org
9111 Old Georgetown Rd   Bethesda MD 20814
Ph: 301-581-3450 ▪ Fx: 301-581-3408 ▪ TF: 800-992-7224

Angiology, American College of — www.collegeofangiology.org
295 Northern Blvd Suite 104   Great Neck NY 11021
Ph: 516-466-4055 ▪ Fx: 516-466-4099

Anglican Fellowship of Prayer — www.afp.org
3801 Appleton Way   Orlando FL 32806
Ph: 407-438-3166 ▪ Fx: 407-856-1578 ▪ TF: 800-711-6399

Anglican Musicians, Association of — www.anglicanmusicians.org
28 Ashton Rd   Fort Mitchell KY 41017
Ph: 859-344-9308

Anglican Society — www.anglicansociety.org
General Theological Seminary New York 175 9th Ave   New York NY 10011
Ph: 212-243-5150 ▪ Fx: 212-727-3907

Angola Chamber of Commerce, US- — www.us-angola.org
1100 Connecticut Ave NW Suite 1000   Washington DC 20036
Ph: 202-223-0540 ▪ Fx: 202-223-0551

Angora Goat Breeders Association, American
PO Box 195   Rocksprings TX 78880
Ph: 830-683-4483

Angus Association of America, Red — www.redangus.org
4201 N I-35   Denton TX 76207
Ph: 940-387-3502 ▪ Fx: 940-383-4036

Angus Association, American — www.angus.org
3201 Frederick Ave   Saint Joseph MO 64506
Ph: 816-383-5100 ▪ Fx: 816-233-9703 ▪ TF: 800-821-5478

Angus Association, National Junior — www.njaa.info
3201 Frederick Ave   Saint Joseph MO 64506
Ph: 816-383-5100 ▪ Fx: 816-233-9703

Animal Agriculture Alliance — www.animalagalliance.org
PO Box 9522   Arlington VA 22209
Ph: 703-562-5160 ▪ Fx: 703-524-1921

Animal Agriculture, National Institute for — www.animalagriculture.org
1910 Lyda Ave   Bowling Green KY 42104
Ph: 270-782-9798 ▪ Fx: 270-782-0188

Animal Alliance of Canada — www.animalalliance.ca
221 Broadview Ave Suite 101   Toronto ON M4M2G3
Ph: 416-462-9541 ▪ Fx: 416-462-9647

Animal Artists Inc, Society of — www.societyofanimalartists.com
47 5th Ave   New York NY 10003
Ph: 212-741-2880 ▪ Fx: 212-471-2262

Animal Behavior Society — www.animalbehavior.org
Indiana Univ 2611 E 10th St Suite 170   Bloomington IN 47408
Ph: 812-856-5541 ▪ Fx: 812-856-5542

Animal Breeders, National Association of — www.naab-css.org
PO Box 1033   Columbia MO 65205
Ph: 573-445-4406 ▪ Fx: 573-446-2279

Animal Care International, Association for Assessment & Accreditation of Laboratory — www.aaalac.org
11300 Rockville Pike Suite 1211   Rockville MD 20852
Ph: 301-231-5353 ▪ Fx: 301-231-8282 ▪ TF: 800-926-0066

Animal Concern Trust, Food   www.fact.cc
PO Box 14599   Chicago IL 60614
Ph: 773-525-4952 ▪ Fx: 773-525-5226

Animal Control Association, National   www.nacanet.org
132 S Cherry St   Olathe KS 66061
Ph: 913-768-1319 ▪ Fx: 913-768-1378

Animal Damage Control Association, National   nadca.unl.edu
PO Box 2180   Ardmore OK 73402
Ph: 580-223-5810

Animal Foundation, Morris   www.morrisanimalfoundation.org
45 Inverness Dr E   Englewood CO 80112
Ph: 303-790-2345 ▪ Fx: 303-790-4066 ▪ TF: 800-243-2345

Animal Health Association, US   www.usaha.org
PO Box K 227   Richmond VA 23229
Ph: 804-285-3210 ▪ Fx: 804-285-3367

Animal Health Institute   www.ahi.org
1325 G St NW Suite 700   Washington DC 20005
Ph: 202-637-2440 ▪ Fx: 202-393-1667

Animal Health Institute PAC
1325 G St NW Suite 700   Washington DC 20005
Ph: 202-637-2440 ▪ Fx: 202-393-1667

Animal Hospital Association, American   www.aahanet.org
PO Box 150899   Denver CO 80215
Ph: 303-986-2800 ▪ Fx: 303-986-1700 ▪ TF: 800-252-2242

Animal Humane Society, Hooved   www.hahs.org
10804 McConnell Rd PO Box 400   Woodstock IL 60098
Ph: 815-337-5563 ▪ Fx: 815-337-5569

Animal Interest Alliance, National   www.naiaonline.org
PO Box 66579   Portland OR 97290
Ph: 503-761-1139 ▪ Fx: 503-761-1289

Animal League, Doris Day   www.ddal.org
227 Massachusetts Ave NE Suite 100   Washington DC 20002
Ph: 202-546-1761 ▪ Fx: 202-546-2193

Animal Legal Defense Fund   www.aldf.org
127 4th St   Petaluma CA 94952
Ph: 707-769-7771 ▪ Fx: 707-769-0785

Animal Legislation, Activists for Protective
PO Box 11743   Costa Mesa CA 92627
Ph: 714-540-0583 ▪ Fx: 714-540-0365

Animal License Collectors, International Society of
928 SR 2206   Clinton KY 42031
Ph: 270-653-6060 ▪ Fx: 270-653-3030

Animal Medicine, American College of Laboratory   www.aclam.org
Univ of Houston   Houston TX 77204
Ph: 713-743-9191 ▪ Fx: 713-743-9200

Animal Medicine, International Association for Aquatic   iaaam.org

Animal Nations, United   www.uan.org
PO Box 188890   Sacramento CA 95818
Ph: 916-429-2457 ▪ Fx: 916-429-2456

Animal Orphanage, Wild   www.wildanimalorphanage.org
9626 Leslie Rd PO Box 690422   San Antonio TX 78269
Ph: 210-688-9038 ▪ Fx: 210-688-9514

Animal Poison Control Center, ASPCA   www.apcc.aspca.org
1717 S Philo Rd Suite 36   Urbana IL 61802
Ph: 217-337-5030 ▪ Fx: 217-337-0599 ▪ TF: 888-426-4435

Animal Practitioners, American Society of Laboratory   www.aslap.org
11300 Rockville Pike   Rockville MD 20852
Ph: 301-231-6349 ▪ Fx: 301-231-6071

Animal Protection Institute   www.api4animals.org
1122 'S' St   Sacramento CA 95814
Ph: 916-447-3085 ▪ Fx: 916-447-3070 ▪ TF: 800-348-7387

Animal Protective Legislation, Society for   www.saplonline.org
PO Box 3719   Washington DC 20027
Ph: 703-836-4300 ▪ Fx: 703-836-0400

Animal Reform Movement, Farm   www.farmusa.org
PO Box 30654   Bethesda MD 20824
Ph: 301-530-1737 ▪ Fx: 301-530-5747 ▪ TF: 800-632-8688

(Animal Reproduction) American College of Theriogenologists   www.theriogenology.org
PO Box 3065   Montgomery AL 36109
Ph: 334-395-4666 ▪ Fx: 334-395-3399

(Animal Reproduction) Society for Theriogenology   www.therio.org
PO Box 3007   Montgomery AL 36109
Ph: 334-395-4666 ▪ Fx: 334-270-3399

Animal Rights, Association of Veterinarians for   avar.org
PO Box 208   Davis CA 95617
Ph: 530-759-8106 ▪ Fx: 530-759-8116

Animal Rights Coalition   www.animalrightscoalition.com
PO Box 8750   Minneapolis MN 55408
Ph: 612-822-6161 ▪ Fx: 612-866-6604

Animal Rights, Feminists for   www.farinc.org
PO Box 41355   Tucson AZ 85717
Ph: 520-825-6852

Animal Rights International   www.ari-online.org
PO Box 767   Rye NY 10580
Ph: 914-934-0896 ▪ Fx: 914-934-0126

Animal Rights, International Society for   www.isaronline.org
965 Griffin Pond Rd   Clarks Summit PA 18411
Ph: 570-586-2200 ▪ Fx: 570-586-9580 ▪ TF: 800-543-4727

Animal Rights, Jews for   www.micahbooks.com/JAR.html
255 Humphrey St   Marblehead MA 01945
Ph: 617-631-7601

Animal Rights Mobilization   www.animalrightsmobilization.org
PO Box 805859   Chicago IL 60680
Ph: 773-381-1181 ▪ Fx: 773-381-1182

Animal Rights Network Inc   www.animalsandsociety.org
3500 Boston St Suite 325   Baltimore MD 21224
Ph: 410-675-4566 ▪ Fx: 410-675-0066

Animal Science, American Association for Laboratory   www.aalas.org
9190 Crestwyn Hills Dr   Memphis TN 38125
Ph: 901-754-8620 ▪ Fx: 901-753-0046

Animal Science, American Society of   www.asas.org
1111 N Dunlap Ave   Savoy IL 61874
Ph: 217-356-9050 ▪ Fx: 217-398-4119

Animal Science Societies, Federation of   www.fass.org
1111 N Dunlap Ave   Savoy IL 61874
Ph: 217-356-3182 ▪ Fx: 217-398-4119

Animal Scientists, American Registry of Professional   www.arpas.org
1111 N Dunlap Ave   Savoy IL 61874
Ph: 217-356-5390 ▪ Fx: 217-398-4119

Animal Suffering & Exploitation, Citizens to End   www.ceaseboston.org
PO Box 440456   Somerville MA 02144
Ph: 617-628-9030

Animal Testing, Johns Hopkins Center for Alternatives to   altweb.jhsph.edu
111 Market Pl Suite 840   Baltimore MD 21202
Ph: 410-223-1612 ▪ Fx: 410-223-1603

Animal Transportation Association   www.aata-animaltransport.org
1111 East Loop N   Houston TX 77029
Ph: 713-532-2177 ▪ Fx: 713-532-2166

Animal Transportation Association International Inc, Independent Pet &   www.ipata.com
745 Winding Trail   Holly Lake Ranch TX 75755
Ph: 903-769-2267 ▪ Fx: 903-769-2867

Animal Welfare Institute   www.awionline.org
PO Box 3650 Georgetown Stn   Washington DC 20007
Ph: 202-337-2332 ▪ Fx: 202-338-9478

Animal Welfare, International Fund for   www.ifaw.org
411 Main St PO Box 193   Yarmouth Port MA 02675
Ph: 508-744-2000 ▪ Fx: 508-744-2009 ▪ TF: 800-932-4329

Animal Welfare, Scientists Center for   www.scaw.com
7833 Walker Dr Suite 410   Greenbelt MD 20770
Ph: 301-345-3500 ▪ Fx: 301-345-3503

Animal Welfare Society, Performing   www.pawsweb.org
PO Box 849   Galt CA 95632
Ph: 209-745-2606 ▪ Fx: 209-745-1809

Animals, Alliance for   www.afa.arlington.ma.us
232 Silver St   Boston MA 02127
Ph: 617-268-7800 ▪ Fx: 617-269-0455

Animals, American Society for the Prevention of Cruelty to   www.aspca.org
424 E 92nd St   New York NY 10128
Ph: 212-876-7700 ▪ Fx: 212-876-0014

(Animals) Association of Sanctuaries   www.taosanctuaries.org
1013 Lesa Ln   Garland TX 75042
Ph: 972-485-5647 ▪ Fx: 972-487-9843

Animals, In Defense of   www.idausa.org
131 Camino Alto Suite E   Mill Valley CA 94941
Ph: 415-388-9641 ▪ Fx: 415-388-0388

(Animals) Delta Society   www.deltasociety.org
580 Naches Ave SW   Renton WA 98055
Ph: 425-226-7357 ▪ Fx: 425-235-1076

Animals in Entertainment, Coalition to Protect
PO Box 2448   Riverside CA 92516
Ph: 909-776-4040 ▪ Fx: 909-784-4262

Animals Foundation, Culture &   www.cultureandanimals.org
3509 Eden Croft Dr   Raleigh NC 27612
Ph: 919-782-3739 ▪ Fx: 919-782-6464

Animals Inc, Friends of   www.friendsofanimals.org
777 Post Rd Suite 205   Darien CT 06820
Ph: 203-656-1522 ▪ Fx: 203-656-0267 ▪ TF: 800-321-7387

Animals Inc, Fund for   www.fund.org
200 W 57th St Suite 705   New York NY 10019
Ph: 212-246-2096 ▪ Fx: 212-246-2633

Animals in Israel, Concern for Helping   www.chai-online.org
PO Box 3341   Alexandria VA 22302
Ph: 703-658-9650 ▪ Fx: 703-941-6132

Animals, Last Chance for   www.lcanimal.org
8033 Sunset Blvd Suite 835   Los Angeles CA 90046
Ph: 310-271-6096 ▪ Fx: 310-271-1890

Animals-Love, People-   www.peopleanimalslove.com
3201 New Mexico Ave NW Suite 350   Washington DC 20016
Ph: 202-895-1395 ▪ Fx: 202-274-1995

Animals & Nature, Interfaith Council for the Protection of
3691 Tuxedo Rd NW   Atlanta GA 30305
Ph: 404-814-1371

Animals, Orthopedic Foundation for   www.offa.org
2300 E Nifong Blvd   Columbia MO 65201
Ph: 573-442-0418 ▪ Fx: 573-875-5073

Animals, People for the Ethical Treatment of   www.peta-online.org
501 Front St   Norfolk VA 23510
Ph: 757-622-7382 ▪ Fx: 757-628-0782 ▪ TF: 800-483-4366

Animals, Psychologists for the Ethical Treatment of   www.psyeta.org
PO Box 1297   Washington Grove MD 20880
Ph: 301-963-4751

Animals & Public Policy, Tufts Center for   www.tufts.edu/vet/cfa
Tufts Univ School of Veterinary Medicine 200 Westboro Rd   North Grafton MA 01536
Ph: 508-839-7920 ▪ Fx: 508-839-2953

Animals Society, Voice for   www.v4a.org
PO Box 68119 162 Bonnie Doon Mall   Edmonton AB T6C4N6
Ph: 780-490-0905 ▪ Fx: 780-922-5287

Animals Voice Online   www.animalsvoice.com
1354 East Ave Suite 252   Chico CA 95926
Ph: 530-343-2498 ▪ TF: 800-828-6423

Animals, World Society for the Protection of   www.wspa.org.uk
34 Deloss St   Framingham MA 01702
Ph: 508-879-8350 ▪ Fx: 508-620-0786 ▪ TF: 800-883-9772

Animated Film Society, International   www.asifa-hollywood.org
721 S Victory Blvd   Burbank CA 91502
Ph: 818-842-8330 ▪ Fx: 818-842-5645

Animation, Women in   www.womeninanimation.org

Ankle Orthopedics & Medicine, American College of Foot &   www.acfaom.org
3525 Ellicott Mills Dr Suite N   Ellicott City MD 21043
Ph: 800-265-8263 ▪ Fx: 410-418-4805

Ankle Pediatrics, American College of Foot &
6477 Auburn Dr   Virginia Beach VA 23464
Ph: 757-523-0414 ▪ Fx: 757-523-2047

Ankle Society, American Orthopaedic Foot &   www.aofas.org
2517 Eastlake Ave E Suite 200   Seattle WA 98102
Ph: 206-223-1120 ▪ Fx: 206-223-1178 ▪ TF: 800-235-4855

Ankle Surgeons, American College of Foot &   www.acfas.org
515 Busse Hwy   Park Ridge IL 60068
Ph: 847-292-2237 ▪ Fx: 847-292-2022 ▪ TF: 800-421-2237

Ankole-Watusi International Registry   www.awir.org
22484 W 239th St   Spring Hill KS 66083
Ph: 913-592-4050

Anne Frank Center USA   www.annefrank.com
38 Crosby St Suite 5R   New York NY 10013
Ph: 212-431-7993 ▪ Fx: 212-431-8375

Annenberg Foundation   www.whannenberg.org
150 N Radnor-Chester Rd Suite 200   Radnor PA 19087
Ph: 610-341-9066 ▪ Fx: 610-964-8688

Annie E Casey Foundation   www.aecf.org
701 Saint Paul St   Baltimore MD 21202
Ph: 410-547-6600 ▪ Fx: 410-547-6624 ▪ TF: 800-222-1099

Annuities, National Association for Variable   www.navanet.org
11710 Plaza America Dr Suite 100   Reston VA 20190
Ph: 703-707-8830 ▪ Fx: 703-707-8831

Annuity Insurers, Committee of   www.annuity-insurers.org
c/o Davis & Harman LLP 1455 Pennsylvania Ave NW Suite
1200   Washington DC 20004
Ph: 202-347-2230 ▪ Fx: 202-393-3310

Anodizers Council, Aluminum   www.anodizing.org
1000 N Rand Rd Suite 214   Wauconda IL 60084
Ph: 847-526-2010 ▪ Fx: 847-526-3993

Anodizing Association, International Hard   www.ihanodizing.com
PO Box 579   Moorestown NJ 08057
Ph: 856-234-0330 ▪ Fx: 856-727-9504

Anorexia Nervosa & Associated Disorders, National Association of   www.anad.org
PO Box 7   Highland Park IL 60035
Ph: 847-831-3438 ▪ Fx: 847-433-4632

Antarctic & Southern Ocean Coalition   www.asoc.org
1630 Connecticut Ave Fl 3   Washington DC 20009
Ph: 202-234-2480 ▪ Fx: 202-387-4823

Antenna Measurement Techniques Association   www.amta.org

Antennas & Propagation Society, IEEE   www.ieeeaps.org
IEEE Operations Ctr 445 Hoes Ln   Piscataway NJ 08854
Ph: 732-981-0060 ▪ Fx: 732-981-1721

Anthology Film Archives   www.anthologyfilmarchives.org
32 2nd Ave   New York NY 10003
Ph: 212-505-5181 ▪ Fx: 212-477-2714

Anthropological Association, American   www.aaanet.org
2200 Wilson Blvd Suite 600   Arlington VA 22201
Ph: 703-528-1902 ▪ Fx: 703-528-3546

Anthropological Society, Kroeber   sscl.berkeley.edu/~kas
UC Berkeley Dept of Anthropology 232 Kroeber Hall   Berkeley
CA 94720
Ph: 510-642-3391 ▪ Fx: 510-643-8557

Anthropologists, American Association of Physical   www.physanth.org
Univ of California Dept of Anthropology   Santa Barbara CA
93101
Ph: 805-685-8424

Anthropologists, Association of Black   www.aaanet.org/aba
c/o American Anthropological Assn 2200 Wilson Blvd Suite
600   Arlington VA 22201
Ph: 703-528-1902 ▪ Fx: 703-528-3546

Anthropologists, Association of Latina & Latino   sbsi.csumb.edu/ALLA
c/o American Anthropological Assn 2200 Wilson Blvd Suite
600   Arlington VA 22201
Ph: 703-528-1902 ▪ Fx: 703-528-3546

Anthropologists, Association of Senior   www.aaanet.org/asa
c/o American Anthropological Assn 2200 Wilson Blvd Suite
600   Arlington VA 22201
Ph: 703-528-1902 ▪ Fx: 703-528-3546

Anthropologists, National Association of Student   www.aaanet.org/nasa
c/o American Anthropological Assn 2200 Wilson Blvd Suite
600   Arlington VA 22201
Ph: 703-528-1902 ▪ Fx: 703-528-3546

Anthropologists, Society of Lesbian & Gay   www.solga.org
c/o American Anthropological Assn 2200 Wilson Blvd Suite
600   Arlington VA 22201
Ph: 703-528-1902 ▪ Fx: 703-528-3546

Anthropology, American Board of Forensic   www.csuchico.edu/anth/ABFA
c/o Lucas County Coroner's Office 2595 Arlington Ave   Toledo
OH 43614
Ph: 419-213-3908

Anthropology, Association for Africanist   www.ibiblio.org/afaa
c/o American Anthropological Assn 2200 Wilson Blvd Suite
600   Arlington VA 22201
Ph: 703-528-1902 ▪ Fx: 703-528-3546

Anthropology, Association for Feminist   sscl.berkeley.edu/~afaweb
c/o American Anthropological Assn 2200 Wilson Blvd Suite
600   Arlington VA 22201
Ph: 703-528-1902 ▪ Fx: 703-528-3546

Anthropology, Association for Political & Legal   www.aaanet.org/apla
c/o American Anthropological Assn 2200 Wilson Blvd Suite
600   Arlington VA 22201
Ph: 703-528-1902 ▪ Fx: 703-528-3546

Anthropology in Community Colleges, Society for   ccanthro.bizland.com
c/o American Anthropological Assn 2200 Wilson Blvd Suite
600   Arlington VA 22201
Ph: 703-528-1902 ▪ Fx: 703-528-3545

Anthropology of Consciousness, Society for the   www.sacaaa.org
c/o American Anthropological Assn 2200 Wilson Blvd Suite
600   Arlington VA 22201
Ph: 703-528-1902 ▪ Fx: 703-528-3546

Anthropology, Council for Museum   www.nmnh.si.edu/cma
c/o American Anthropological Assn 2200 Wilson Blvd Suite
600   Arlington VA 22201
Ph: 703-528-1902 ▪ Fx: 703-528-3546

Anthropology, Council on Nutritional   www.aaanet.org/cna
c/o American Anthropological Assn 2200 Wilson Blvd Suite
600   Arlington VA 22201
Ph: 703-528-1902 ▪ Fx: 703-528-3546

Anthropology & Education, Council on   www.aaanet.org/cae
c/o American Anthropological Assn 2200 Wilson Blvd Suite
600   Arlington VA 22201
Ph: 703-528-1902 ▪ Fx: 703-528-3546

Anthropology of Europe, Society for the   www.h-net.org/~sae/sae
c/o American Anthropological Assn 2200 Wilson Blvd Suite
600   Arlington VA 22201
Ph: 703-528-1902 ▪ Fx: 703-528-3546

(Anthropology) Lambda Alpha   www.lambdaalpha.com
Ball State Univ Dept of Anthropology   Muncie IN 47306
Ph: 765-285-1575

Anthropology, National Association for the Practice of   www.practicinganthropology.org
c/o American Anthropological Assn 2200 Wilson Blvd Suite
600   Arlington VA 22201
Ph: 703-528-1902 ▪ Fx: 703-528-3546

Anthropology of North America, Society for the   faculty.kutztown.edu/ehrensal/sana2.html
c/o American Anthropological Assn 2200 Wilson Blvd Suite
600   Arlington VA 22201
Ph: 703-528-1902 ▪ Fx: 703-528-3546

Anthropology of Religion, Society for the   www.uwgb.edu/sar
c/o American Anthropological Assn 2200 Wilson Blvd Suite
600   Arlington VA 22201
Ph: 703-528-1902 ▪ Fx: 703-528-3546

Anthropology, Society for Applied   www.sfaa.net
PO Box 2436   Oklahoma City OK 73101
Ph: 405-843-5113 ▪ Fx: 405-843-8553

Anthropology, Society for Cultural   www.aaanet.org/sca
c/o American Anthropological Assn 2200 Wilson Blvd Suite
600   Arlington VA 22201
Ph: 703-528-1902 ▪ Fx: 703-528-3546

Anthropology, Society for Humanistic   www.smcm.edu/sha
c/o American Anthropological Assn 2200 Wilson Blvd Suite
600   Arlington VA 22201
Ph: 703-528-1902 ▪ Fx: 703-528-3546

Anthropology, Society for Latin American   www.aaanet.org/slaa/Slaa1.htm
c/o American Anthropological Assn 2200 Wilson Blvd Suite
600   Arlington VA 22201
Ph: 703-528-1902 ▪ Fx: 703-528-3546

Anthropology, Society for Linguistic   www.aaanet.org/sla
c/o American Anthropological Assn 2200 Wilson Blvd Suite
600   Arlington VA 22201
Ph: 703-528-1902 ▪ Fx: 703-528-3546

Anthropology, Society for Medical   www.medanthro.net
c/o American Anthropological Assn 2200 Wilson Blvd Suite
600   Arlington VA 22201
Ph: 703-528-1902 ▪ Fx: 703-528-3546

Anthropology, Society for Psychological   www.aaanet.org/SPA
c/o American Anthropological Assn 2200 Wilson Blvd Suite
600   Arlington VA 22201
Ph: 703-528-1902 ▪ Fx: 703-528-3546

Anthropology, Society for Urban National & Transnational/Global   www.sunta.org
c/o American Anthropological Assn 2200 Wilson Blvd Suite
600   Arlington VA 22201
Ph: 703-528-1902 ▪ Fx: 703-528-3546

Anthropology, Society for Visual   www.societyforvisualanthropology.org
c/o American Anthropological Assn 2200 Wilson Blvd Suite
600   Arlington VA 22201
Ph: 703-528-1902 ▪ Fx: 703-528-3546

Anthropology of Work, Society for the   www.aaanet.org/saw
c/o American Anthropological Assn 2200 Wilson Blvd Suite
600   Arlington VA 22201
Ph: 703-528-1902 ▪ Fx: 703-528-3546

Anthroposophical Medicine, Physicians Association for   www.paam.net
1923 Geddes Ave   Ann Arbor MI 48104
Ph: 734-930-9462 ▪ Fx: 734-662-1727

Anthroposophical Society in America   www.anthroposophy.org
1923 Geddes Ave   Ann Arbor MI 48104
Ph: 734-662-9355 ▪ Fx: 734-662-1727

Anti-Aging Medicine, American Academy of   www.worldhealth.net
2415 N Greenview Ave   Chicago IL 60614
Ph: 773-528-4333 ▪ Fx: 773-528-5390

Anti-Asian Violence, Committee Against   www.caaav.org
2473 Valentine Ave   Bronx NY 10458
Ph: 718-220-7391 ▪ Fx: 718-220-7398

Anti-Communism Crusade, Christian   www.schwarzreport.org
PO Box 129   Manitou Springs CO 80829
Ph: 719-685-9043 ▪ Fx: 719-685-9330

Anti-Counterfeiting Coalition, International   www.iacc.org
1725 K St NW Suite 1101   Washington DC 20006
Ph: 202-223-6667 ▪ Fx: 202-223-6668

Anti-Cruelty Society   www.anticruelty.org
510 N LaSalle St   Chicago IL 60610
Ph: 312-644-8338 ▪ Fx: 312-644-3878

Anti-Defamation League
823 United Nations Plaza   New York NY 10017
Ph: 212-885-7700 ▪ Fx: 212-697-0091
www.adl.org

Anti Discrimination Committee, American-Arab
4201 Connecticut Ave NW Suite 300   Washington DC 20008
Ph: 202-244-2990 ▪ Fx: 202-244-3196
www.adc.org

Anti-Drug Coalitions of America, Community
901 N Pitt St Suite 300   Alexandria VA 22314
Ph: 703-706-0560 ▪ Fx: 703-706-0565 ▪ TF: 800-542-2322
www.cadca.org

Anti-Fraud Association, National Health Care
1255 23rd St NW Suite 200   Washington DC 20037
Ph: 202-659-5955 ▪ Fx: 202-785-6764
www.nhcaa.org

Anti-Vivisection Society, American
801 Old York Rd Suite 204   Jenkintown PA 19046
Ph: 215-887-0816 ▪ Fx: 215-887-2088 ▪ TF: 800-723-2287
www.aavs.org

Anti-Vivisection Society, National
53 W Jackson Blvd Suite 1552   Chicago IL 60604
Ph: 312-427-6065 ▪ Fx: 312-427-6524 ▪ TF: 800-888-6287
www.navs.org

Antiochian Orthodox Christian Archdiocese of North America
358 Mountain Rd   Englewood NJ 07631
Ph: 201-871-1355 ▪ Fx: 201-871-7954
www.antiochian.org

Antiquarian Booksellers Association of America
20 W 44th St 4th Fl   New York NY 10036
Ph: 212-944-8291 ▪ Fx: 212-944-8293
www.abaa.org

Antiquarian Booksellers, International League of
400 Summit Ave   Saint Paul MN 55102
Ph: 651-290-0700 ▪ Fx: 651-290-0646
www.ilab-lila.com

Antiquarian Society, American
185 Salisbury St   Worcester MA 01609
Ph: 508-755-5221 ▪ Fx: 508-753-3311
www.americanantiquarian.org

Antique Airplane Association
22001 Bluegrass Rd   Ottumwa IA 52501
Ph: 641-938-2773 ▪ Fx: 641-938-2093
www.aaa-apm.org/aaa

Antique & Amusement Photographers International
37 W Broad St Suite 480   Columbus OH 43215
Ph: 614-358-2828 ▪ Fx: 614-241-2215
www.oldtimephotos.org

Antique & Art Dealers Association of America, National
220 E 57th St   New York NY 10022
Ph: 212-826-9707 ▪ Fx: 212-832-9493
naadaa.org

Antique Automobile Club of America
501 W Governor Rd PO Box 417   Hershey PA 17033
Ph: 717-534-1910 ▪ Fx: 717-534-9101
www.aaca.org

Antique Boat Club, Chris Craft
217 S Adams St   Tallahassee FL 32301
Ph: 850-224-2628 ▪ Fx: 850-224-1033
www.chris-craft.org

Antique & Classic Boat Society
422 James St   Clayton NY 13624
Ph: 315-686-2628 ▪ Fx: 315-686-2680
www.acbs.org

Antique & Collectible Show Promoters Association
PO Box 4389   Davidson NC 28036
Ph: 704-895-9088 ▪ Fx: 704-895-0230 ▪ TF: 800-287-7127
www.antiqueandcollectible.com

Antique Dealers League of America, Art &
1040 Madison Ave   New York NY 10021
Ph: 212-879-7558 ▪ Fx: 212-772-7197
www.artantiquedealersleague.com

Antique Engine Tractor & Toy Association
5731 Paradise Rd   Slatington PA 18080
Ph: 610-767-4768

Antique Fan Collectors Association
PO Box 5473   Sarasota FL 34277
Ph: 941-955-8232 ▪ Fx: 941-952-1491
www.fancollectors.org

Antique Malls, National Association of
PO Box 4389   Davidson NC 28036
Ph: 704-895-9088 ▪ Fx: 704-895-0230 ▪ TF: 800-287-7127
www.antiqueandcollectible.com

Antique Modelers, Society of
203 N Brockfield Dr   Sun City Center FL 33573
Ph: 813-634-7749
www.antiquemodeler.org

Antique Oldsmobile Club Inc, National
www.antiqueolds.org

Antique Phonograph Collectors Club
502 E 17th St   Brooklyn NY 11226
Ph: 718-941-6835 ▪ Fx: 718-941-1408

Antique Scale Collectors, International Society of
3616 Noakes St   Los Angeles CA 90023
Ph: 323-263-6878 ▪ Fx: 323-263-3147
www.isasc.org

Antique Telephone Collectors Association
PO Box 1252   McPherson KS 67460
Ph: 620-245-9555
www.atcaonline.com

Antique Truck Club of America
PO Box 9639   Apollo PA 15613
Ph: 724-727-9768
www.atca-inc.net/

Antique Wireless Association
PO Box E   Breesport NY 14816
Ph: 607-739-5443 ▪ Fx: 607-796-6230
www.antiquewireless.org

Antiques & Collectibles Dealer Association
PO Box 4389   Davidson NC 280396
Ph: 704-895-9088 ▪ Fx: 704-895-0230
www.antiqueandcollectible.com

Antiquities, Association for the Preservation of Virginia
204 W Franklin St   Richmond VA 23220
Ph: 804-648-1889
www.apva.org

Antiquities Research Association, New England
www.neara.org

Antiquities, Society for the Preservation of New England
141 Cambridge St   Boston MA 02114
Ph: 617-227-3956 ▪ Fx: 617-227-9204
www.spnea.org

Antiviral Research, International Society for
www.georgetown.edu/research/arc/ISAR

Anxiety Center, National
9 Brookside Rd   Maplewood NJ 07040
Ph: 973-763-6392 ▪ Fx: 973-763-4287
www.anxietycenter.com

(Anxiety Disorder) Agoraphobics in Motion
1719 Crooks Rd   Royal Oak MI 48067
Ph: 248-547-0400
www.aim-hq.org

Anxiety Disorders Association of America
8730 Georgia Ave Suite 600   Silver Spring MD 20910
Ph: 240-485-1001 ▪ Fx: 240-485-1035
www.adaa.org

(Anxiety Disorders) Freedom From Fear
308 Seaview Ave   Staten Island NY 10305
Ph: 718-351-1717 ▪ Fx: 718-667-8893 ▪ TF: 888-442-2022
www.freedomfromfear.org

AOAC International
481 N Frederick Ave Suite 500   Gaithersburg MD 20877
Ph: 301-924-7077 ▪ Fx: 301-924-7089 ▪ TF: 800-379-2622
www.aoac.org

AORN Inc
2170 S Parker Rd Suite 300   Denver CO 80231
Ph: 303-755-6300 ▪ Fx: 303-750-3212 ▪ TF: 800-755-2676
www.aorn.org

APA - Engineered Wood Association
7011 S 19th   Tacoma WA 98466
Ph: 253-565-6600 ▪ Fx: 253-565-7265
www.apawood.org

Apartment Association, National
201 N Union St Suite 200   Alexandria VA 22314
Ph: 703-518-6141 ▪ Fx: 703-518-6191 ▪ TF: 800-842-4054
www.naahq.org

Apartment Clearinghouse, National Accessible
201 N Union St Suite 200   Alexandria VA 22314
Ph: 703-518-6141 ▪ Fx: 703-518-6191 ▪ TF: 800-421-1221
www.forrent.com/naac

APCO International
351 N Williamson Blvd   Daytona Beach FL 32114
Ph: 386-322-2500 ▪ Fx: 386-322-2501 ▪ TF: 888-272-6911
www.apcointl.org

APhA Foundation
2215 Constitution Ave NW   Washington DC 20037
Ph: 202-429-7565 ▪ Fx: 202-429-6300
www.aphafoundation.org

Aphasia, Academy of
PO Box 26532   Minneapolis MN 55426
Ph: 952-920-0966 ▪ Fx: 952-920-6098
www.academyofaphasia.org

Aphasia Association, National
29 John St Suite 1103   New York NY 10038
Ph: 212-267-2814 ▪ Fx: 212-267-2812 ▪ TF: 800-922-4622
www.aphasia.org

Apheresis, American Society for
3900 E Timrod St   Tucson AZ 85711
Ph: 520-327-8584 ▪ Fx: 520-322-6778
www.apheresis.org

Apiary Inspectors of America
Minnesota Dept of Agriculture 90 W Plato Blvd   Saint Paul MN 55107
Ph: 651-297-2200 ▪ TF: 800-967-2474
www.mda.state.mn.us/apiary/aiahome.htm

APICS - Educational Society for Resource Management
5301 Shawnee Rd   Alexandria VA 22312
Ph: 703-354-8851 ▪ Fx: 703-354-8106 ▪ TF: 800-444-2742
www.apics.org

Apicultural Society of North America, Eastern
PO Box 300   Essex NY 12936
Ph: 518-963-7593
www.easternapiculture.org

Apitherapy Society, American
1209 Post Rd   Scarsdale NY 10583
Ph: 914-725-7944 ▪ Fx: 914-723-0920
www.apitherapy.org

Aplastic Anemia & MDS International Foundation Inc
PO Box 613   Annapolis MD 21404
Ph: 410-867-0242 ▪ Fx: 410-867-0240 ▪ TF: 800-747-2820
www.aamds.org

APMI International
105 College Rd E   Princeton NJ 08540
Ph: 609-452-7700 ▪ Fx: 609-987-8523
www.mpif.org

Apnea Association, American Sleep
1424 K St NW Suite 302   Washington DC 20005
Ph: 202-293-3650 ▪ Fx: 202-293-3656
www.sleepapnea.org

Apostle, Society of Saint Peter
366 5th Ave   New York NY 10001
Ph: 212-563-8700 ▪ Fx: 212-563-8725 ▪ TF: 800-431-2222
www.worldmissions-catholicchurch.org

Apostleship of the Sea in the US
3211 4th St NE   Washington DC 20017
Ph: 202-541-3226 ▪ Fx: 202-541-3351
www.aos-usa.org

Apostolate, Center for Applied Research in the
Georgetown Univ 2300 Wisconsin Ave NW Suite 400   Washington DC 20057
Ph: 202-687-8080 ▪ Fx: 202-687-8083
cara.georgetown.edu

Apostolate of the Chronically Sick & Disabled, CUSA - An
176 W 8th St   Bayonne NJ 07002
Ph: 201-437-0412
www.cusan.org

Apostolate for Family Consecration
Catholic Familyland 3375 County Rd Suite 36   Bloomingdale OH 43910
Ph: 740-765-5500 ▪ Fx: 740-765-5561 ▪ TF: 888-367-6279
www.familyland.org

Apostolate for Inclusion Ministry, National
PO Box 218   Riverdale MD 20738
Ph: 301-699-9500 ▪ TF: 800-736-1280
www.nafim.org

Apostolic Center, Father Judge
1292 Long Hill Rd   Stirling NJ 07980
Ph: 908-647-7112 ▪ Fx: 908-626-0350
www.fjac.org

Apostolic Development, Saint Vincent Pallotti Center for
415 Michigan Ave NE   Washington DC 20017
Ph: 202-529-3330 ▪ Fx: 202-529-0911 ▪ TF: 877-865-5465
www.pallotticenter.org

Apothecaries, American College of
2830 Summer Oaks Dr   Bartlett TN 38134
Ph: 901-383-8119 ▪ Fx: 901-383-8882
www.acainfo.org

APPA: Association of Higher Education Facilities Officers
1643 Prince St   Alexandria VA 22314
Ph: 703-684-1446 ▪ Fx: 703-549-2772
www.appa.org

Appalachia, Catholic Committee of
PO Box 662   Webster Springs WV 26288
Ph: 304-847-7215
www.cathcomappalachia.org

(Appalachia) Jesse Stuart Foundation Inc
1645 Winchester Ave PO Box 669   Ashland KY 41105
Ph: 606-326-1667 ▪ Fx: 606-325-2519
www.jsfbooks.com

Appalachian Bear Center
PO Box 364   Townsend TN 37882
Ph: 865-448-0143 ▪ Fx: 865-448-0141
www.appbears.org

Appalachian Consortium   people.uvawise.edu/appalcon
Appalachian State Univ Center for Appalachian Studies PO Box
   32018   Boone NC 28608
Ph: 828-262-2064 ▪ Fx: 828-262-6564 ▪ TF: 888-557-8163

Appalachian Hardwood Manufacturers Inc   www.appalachianwood.org
PO Box 427   High Point NC 27261
Ph: 336-885-8315 ▪ Fx: 336-886-8865

Appalachian Mountain Club   www.outdoors.org
5 Joy St   Boston MA 02108
Ph: 617-523-0636 ▪ Fx: 617-523-0722 ▪ TF: 800-262-4455

Appalachian Project, Christian   www.christianity.com/cap
322 Crab Orchard St   Lancaster KY 40446
Ph: 859-792-3051 ▪ Fx: 859-792-6560

Appalachian Studies Association   www.appalachianstudies.org
Marshall Univ 400 Hal Greer Blvd   Huntington WV 25755
Ph: 304-696-2904

Appalachian Trail Conference   www.appalachiantrail.org
799 Washington St   Harpers Ferry WV 25425
Ph: 304-535-6331 ▪ Fx: 304-535-2667

Appaloosa Horse Club   www.appaloosa.com
2720 W Pullman Rd   Moscow ID 83843
Ph: 208-882-5578 ▪ Fx: 208-882-8150

Appaloosa Sport Horse Association   www.appaloosasport.com
3380 Saxonburg Blvd   Glenshaw PA 15116
Ph: 412-767-4616

Apparel Association, International Textile &   www.itaa.org
PO Box 1360   Monument CO 80132
Ph: 719-488-3716

Apparel Association, Leather   www.leatherassociation.com
19 W 21st St Suite 403   New York NY 10010
Ph: 212-924-8895 ▪ Fx: 212-727-1218

Apparel Association, Professional   www.proapparel.com
994 Old Eagle School Rd Suite 1019   Wayne PA 19087
Ph: 610-971-4850 ▪ Fx: 610-971-4859 ▪ TF: 800-722-7712

Apparel Contractors Association, Ladies
147 W 36th St 15th Fl   New York NY 10001
Ph: 212-564-6161 ▪ Fx: 212-564-6166

Apparel & Footwear Association, American   www.apparelandfootwear.org
1601 N Kent St Suite 1200   Arlington VA 22209
Ph: 703-524-1864 ▪ Fx: 703-522-6741 ▪ TF: 800-520-2262

Apparel & Footwear Association PAC, American
1601 N Kent St Suite 1200   Arlington VA 22209
Ph: 703-524-1864 ▪ Fx: 703-522-6741

Apparel Manufacturers, Industrial Association of Juvenile
1430 Broadway Suite 1603   New York NY 10018
Ph: 212-244-2953 ▪ Fx: 212-221-3540

Apparel Manufacturers Suppliers, Southeastern   www.seams.org
4921-C Broad River Rd   Columbia SC 29212
Ph: 803-772-5861 ▪ Fx: 803-731-7709

Apparel Producers' Network, American   www.aapnetwork.net
PO Box 720693   Atlanta GA 30358
Ph: 404-843-3171

Apparel Production, Worldwide Responsible   www.wrapapparel.org
200 N Glebe Rd Suite 1016   Arlington VA 22203
Ph: 703-243-0970 ▪ Fx: 703-243-8247

Apparel Square Club, Intimate   thehugaward.org
326 Field Rd   Clinton Corners NY 12514
Ph: 845-758-5752 ▪ Fx: 845-758-2546

Apparel, US Association of Importers of Textiles &   www.usaita.com
13 E 16th St 6th Fl   New York NY 10003
Ph: 212-463-0089 ▪ Fx: 212-463-0583

Appeal of Conscience Foundation   www.appealofconscience.org
119 W 57th St Suite 820   New York NY 10019
Ph: 212-535-5800 ▪ Fx: 212-628-2513

Appellate Court Clerks, National Conference of   ncacc.ncsconline.org
300 Newport Ave   Williamsburg VA 23185
Ph: 757-259-1841 ▪ Fx: 757-259-1520

Appellate Lawyers, American Academy of   www.appellateacademy.org
15245 Shady Grove Rd Suite 130   Rockville MD 20850
Ph: 301-258-9210 ▪ Fx: 301-990-9771

Apple Association, US   www.usapple.org
8233 Old Courthouse Rd Suite 200   Vienna VA 22182
Ph: 703-442-8850 ▪ Fx: 703-790-0845 ▪ TF: 800-781-4443

Apple Processors Association   www.agriwashington.org/apa.html
1629 K St NW Suite 1100   Washington DC 20006
Ph: 202-785-6715 ▪ Fx: 202-331-4212

Apple Products Research & Education Council   www.appleproducts.org
5775 Peachtree-Dunwoody Rd Bldg G Suite 500   Atlanta GA
   30342
Ph: 404-252-3663 ▪ Fx: 404-252-0774

Appliance Manufacturers Association, Gas   www.gamanet.org
2107 Wilson Blvd Suite 600   Arlington VA 22201
Ph: 703-525-7060 ▪ Fx: 703-525-6790

Appliance Manufacturers, Association of Home   www.aham.org
1111 19th St NW Suite 402   Washington DC 20036
Ph: 202-872-5955 ▪ Fx: 202-872-9354

Appliance Parts Suppliers Association, National   www.napsaweb.org
PO Box 87067   Vancouver WA 98687
Ph: 360-834-3805 ▪ Fx: 360-834-3507

Appliance Service Association, National   www.nasa1.org
PO Box 2514   Kokomo IN 46904
Ph: 765-453-1820 ▪ Fx: 765-453-1895

Applications Group Inc, Open   www.openapplications.org
1950 Spectrum Cir Suite 400   Marietta GA 30067
Ph: 770-980-3418

Applications Standards Group, United   www.uasg.org
PO Box 1435   Des Moines IA 50305
Ph: 515-289-4467 ▪ Fx: 515-289-4468

Applicators Association, Interstate Professional
PO Box 1377   Milton WA 98354
Ph: 253-922-9437

Applied Computational Electromagnetics Society   aces.ee.olemiss.edu

Applied Ekistics, Educational Center for
1900 DeKalb Ave NE   Atlanta GA 30307
Ph: 404-378-2219 ▪ Fx: 404-378-8946

Applied Research Ethics National Association   www.primr.org/arena.html
132 Boylston St 4th Fl   Boston MA 02116
Ph: 617-423-4112 ▪ Fx: 617-423-1185

Applied Science, Academy of   www.aas-world.org
24 Warren St   Concord NH 03301
Ph: 603-228-4530 ▪ Fx: 603-228-4730

Applied Systems Client Network   www.ascnet.org
801 Douglas Ave Suite 205   Altamonte Springs FL 32714
Ph: 407-869-0404 ▪ Fx: 407-869-0418

Applied Technology Council   www.atcouncil.org
201 Redwood Shores Pkwy Suite 240   Redwood City CA 94065
Ph: 650-595-1542 ▪ Fx: 650-593-2320

Applied Voice Input/Output Society   www.avios.com
PO Box 20817   San Jose CA 95160
Ph: 408-323-1783 ▪ Fx: 408-323-1782

Appraisal Association, Professional Women's
1224 N Nokomis NE   Alexandria MN 56308
Ph: 320-763-7626 ▪ Fx: 320-763-9290

Appraisal Institute   www.appraisalinstitute.org
550 W Van Buren St Suite 1000   Chicago IL 60607
Ph: 312-335-4100 ▪ Fx: 312-335-4400

Appraiser Specialists, National Society of   pcb.lincoln-grad.org
303 W Cypress St PO Box 12617   San Antonio TX 78212
Ph: 210-271-0781 ▪ Fx: 210-225-8450 ▪ TF: 800-531-5333

Appraisers, American Academy of State Certified
1438 W Main St   Ephrata PA 17522
Ph: 717-721-3500 ▪ Fx: 717-721-3515 ▪ TF: 800-640-7601

Appraisers, American Society of   www.appraisers.org
555 Herndon Pkwy Suite 125   Herndon VA 20170
Ph: 703-478-2228 ▪ Fx: 703-742-8471 ▪ TF: 800-272-8258

Appraisers, American Society of Agricultural   www.amagappraisers.com
1126 Eastland Dr N   Suite 100 PO Box 186   Twin Falls ID
   83303
Ph: 208-733-2323 ▪ Fx: 208-733-2326 ▪ TF: 800-488-7570

Appraisers, American Society of Equine   www.equineappraiser.com
1126 Eastland Dr N Suite 100 PO Box 186   Twin Falls ID
   93303
Ph: 208-733-2323 ▪ Fx: 208-733-2326 ▪ TF: 800-704-7020

Appraisers, American Society of Farm Equipment   www.amagappraisers.com/farmeqip.htm
1126 Eastland Dr N Suite 100 PO Box 186   Twin Falls ID
   83303
Ph: 208-733-2323 ▪ Fx: 208-733-2326 ▪ TF: 800-488-7570

Appraisers, American Society of Farm Managers & Rural   www.asfmra.org
950 S Cherry St Suite 508   Denver CO 80246
Ph: 303-758-3513 ▪ Fx: 303-758-0190

Appraisers Association of America   www.appraisersassoc.org
386 Park Ave S Suite 2000   New York NY 10016
Ph: 212-889-5404 ▪ Fx: 212-889-5503

Appraisers Association, Independent Automotive Damage   www.iada.org
PO Box 12291   Columbus GA 31917
Ph: 800-369-4232 ▪ Fx: 888-423-2669

Appraisers, Association of Machinery & Equipment   www.amea.org
315 S Patrick St   Alexandria VA 22314
Ph: 703-836-7900 ▪ Fx: 703-836-9303 ▪ TF: 800-537-8629

Appraisers Council, Accredited Review   arac.lincoln-grad.org
c/o Lincoln Graduate Ctr 303 W Cypress St   San Antonio TX
   78212
Ph: 210-225-2897 ▪ Fx: 210-225-8450 ▪ TF: 800-531-5333

Appraisers, Institute of Business   www.go-iba.org
PO Box 17410   Plantation FL 33318
Ph: 954-584-1144 ▪ Fx: 954-584-1184 ▪ TF: 800-299-4130

Appraisers Institute, National Residential   www.nraiappraisers.com
2001 Cooper Foster Pk Rd   Amherst OH 44001
Ph: 440-282-7925 ▪ Fx: 440-282-8027

Appraisers, International Society of   www.isa-appraisers.org
1131 SW 7th St Suite 105   Renton WA 98055
Ph: 206-241-0359 ▪ Fx: 206-241-0436 ▪ TF: 888-472-5762

Appraisers, International Society of Livestock   www.amagappraisers.com/livestok.htm
1126 Eastland Dr N Suite 100 PO Box 186   Twin Falls ID
   83303
Ph: 208-733-2323 ▪ Fx: 208-733-2326 ▪ TF: 800-488-7570

Appraisers & Mortgage Underwriters, National Association   www.iami.org/nara.html
of Review   1224 N Nokomis NE   Alexandria MN 56308
Ph: 320-763-6870 ▪ Fx: 320-763-9290

Appraisers, National Association of Independent Fee   www.naifa.com
7501 Murdoch St   Saint Louis MO 63119
Ph: 314-781-6688 ▪ Fx: 314-781-2872

Appraisers, National Association of Jewelry
PO Box 6558   Annapolis MD 21401
Ph: 410-897-0889

Appraisers, National Association of Master   www.masterappraisers.org
303 W Cypress St   San Antonio TX 78212
Ph: 210-271-0781 ▪ Fx: 210-225-8450 ▪ TF: 800-229-6262

Appraisers, National Association of Real Estate   www.iami.org/narea
1224 N Nokomis NE   Alexandria MN 56308
Ph: 320-763-7626 ▪ Fx: 320-763-9290

Apprentices of the Plumbing Pipe Fitting Sprinkler Fitting Industry of   www.ua.org
the US & Canada, United Association of Journeymen &   901
   Massachusetts Ave NW   Washington DC 20001
Ph: 202-628-5823 ▪ Fx: 202-628-5024

Appropriate Technology in Health, Program for   www.path.org
1455 NW Leary St   Seattle WA 98107
Ph: 206-285-3500 ▪ Fx: 206-285-6619

Appropriate Technology, Institute for   www.i4at.org
89 Schoolhouse Rd PO Box 90   Summertown TN 38483
Ph: 931-964-4324 ▪ Fx: 931-964-2200

Appropriate Technology, National Center for www.ncat.org
PO Box 3838   Butte MT 59702
Ph: 406-494-4572 ▪ Fx: 406-494-2905 ▪ TF: 800-275-6228

Aprovecho Research Center www.aprovecho.net
80574 Hazelton Rd   Cottage Grove OR 97424
Ph: 503-942-8198

Aquacultural Engineering Society www.aesweb.org
c/o Freshwater Institute PO Box 1889   Shepherdstown WV
25443
Ph: 304-876-2815 ▪ Fx: 304-870-2208

Aquaculture Society, World www.was.org
Louisiana State Univ 143 JM Parker Coliseum   Baton Rouge LA
70803
Ph: 225-578-3137 ▪ Fx: 225-578-3493

Aquaculture Suppliers Association, US www.aquaculturesuppliers.com
PO Box 901303   Homestead FL 33090
Ph: 305-248-4205 ▪ Fx: 305-248-1756

Aquarium Association, American Zoo & www.aza.org
8403 Colesville Rd Suite 710   Silver Spring MD 20910
Ph: 301-562-0777 ▪ Fx: 301-562-0888

Aquatic Animal Medicine, International Association for iaaam.org

Aquatic Babies Congress, World www.waterbabies.org
776 21st Ave N   Saint Petersburg FL 33704
Ph: 727-896-7625 ▪ Fx: 727-896-0019

Aquatic Exercise Association aeawave.com
3439 Technology Dr Suite 6   Nokomis FL 34275
Ph: 941-486-8600 ▪ Fx: 941-486-8820 ▪ TF: 888-232-9283

Aquatic & Marine Science Libraries & Information Centers, www.iamslic.org
International Association of   Harbor Branch Oceanographic
Institution 5600 US 1 N   Fort Pierce FL 34946
Ph: 561-465-2400 ▪ Fx: 561-465-2446

Aquatic Network Inc, Women's www.womensaquatic.net
PO Box 4993   Washington DC 20008
Ph: 202-208-4646 ▪ Fx: 202-667-6916

Aquatic Plant Management Society Inc www.apms.org
PO Box 821265   Vicksburg MS 39182
Ph: 601-634-2656

Aquatic Research Interactive Inc www.arii.org
1100 W Columbus Dr   East Chicago IN 46312
Ph: 219-391-4138 ▪ Fx: 219-391-4168

Aquatics Bodywork Association, Worldwide aspen.forest.net/waba
PO Box 889   Middletown CA 95461
Ph: 707-987-3801 ▪ Fx: 707-987-9638

Arab American Institute www.aaiusa.org
1600 K St NW Suite 601   Washington DC 20006
Ph: 202-429-9210 ▪ Fx: 202-429-9214

Arab American Medical Association, National www.naama.com
801 S Adams Rd Suite 208   Birmingham MI 48009
Ph: 248-646-3661 ▪ Fx: 248-646-0617

Arab-American Press Guild
13313 Debell St   Arleta CA 91331
Ph: 818-896-5860

Arab Anti Discrimination Committee, American- www.adc.org
4201 Connecticut Ave NW Suite 300   Washington DC 20008
Ph: 202-244-2990 ▪ Fx: 202-244-3196

Arab Relations, National Council on US- www.ncusar.org
1140 Connecticut Ave NW Suite 1210   Washington DC 20036
Ph: 202-293-0801 ▪ Fx: 202-293-0903

Arab World & Islamic Resources www.awaironline.org
PO Box 174   Abiquiu NM 87510
Ph: 505-685-4533

Arabian Horse Association www.arabianhorses.org
10805 E Bethany Dr   Aurora CO 80014
Ph: 303-696-4500 ▪ Fx: 303-696-4599

Arabian Horse Owners Foundation www.arabianhorseowners.org
4101 N Bear Canyon Rd PO Box 30924   Tucson AZ 85749
Ph: 520-760-0682 ▪ Fx: 520-749-2572 ▪ TF: 800-892-0682

Arabian Horse Registry of America
12000 Zuni St   Westminster CO 80234
Ph: 303-450-4748 ▪ Fx: 303-450-2841

Arabian Jockey Club www.arabianracing.org
10805 E Bethany Dr   Aurora CO 80014
Ph: 303-696-4500 ▪ Fx: 303-696-4599

Arabian Society, North American Shagya- www.shagya.net
9797 S Rangeline Rd   Clinton IN 47842
Ph: 765-665-3851

Arabic, American Association of Teachers of www.wm.edu/aata
College of William & Mary PO Box 8795   Williamsburg VA
23187
Ph: 757-221-3145 ▪ Fx: 757-221-3637

Arabic Order Nobles Mystic Shrine, Ancient Egyptian www.aeaonms.org
2239 Democrat Rd   Memphis TN 38132
Ph: 901-395-0150 ▪ Fx: 901-395-0115

Arabic Sciences in America, Institute of Islamic & www.iiasa.org
8500 Hilltop Rd   Fairfax VA 22031
Ph: 703-641-4890 ▪ Fx: 703-641-4899

Araucanian Royalist Society, North American www.geocities.com/tourtoirac

Arba Sicula www.arbasicula.org
St Johns Univ Modern Foreign Languages Dept 8000 Utopia
Pkwy   Jamaica NY 11439
Ph: 718-990-5203 ▪ Fx: 718-990-5954

Arbeter Ring, Workmen's Circle/ www.circle.org
45 E 33rd St   New York NY 10016
Ph: 212-889-6800 ▪ Fx: 212-532-7518 ▪ TF: 800-922-2558

Arbitration Association Inc, American www.adr.org
1633 Broadway 10th Fl   New York NY 10019
Ph: 212-484-4181 ▪ Fx: 212-246-7274 ▪ TF: 800-778-7879

Arbitrators, National Academy of www.naarb.org
1 N Main St Suite 412   Cortland NY 13045
Ph: 607-756-8363 ▪ Fx: 607-756-8365

Arbor Day Foundation, National www.arborday.org
211 N 12th St   Lincoln NE 68508
Ph: 402-474-5655 ▪ Fx: 402-474-0820 ▪ TF: 888-448-7337

Arboreta, American Association of Botanical Gardens & www.aabga.org
100 W 10th St Suite 614   Wilmington DE 19801
Ph: 302-655-7100 ▪ Fx: 302-655-8100

Arboretum, Friends of the National www.fona.org
3501 New York Ave NE   Washington DC 20002
Ph: 202-544-8733 ▪ Fx: 202-544-5398

Arboriculture, International Society of www.isa-arbor.com
1400 W Anthony Dr PO Box 3129   Champaign IL 61826
Ph: 217-355-9411 ▪ Fx: 217-355-9516 ▪ TF: 888-472-8733

Arborist Association, National www.treecareindustry.org
3 Perimeter Rd Unit 1   Manchester NH 03103
Ph: 603-314-5380 ▪ Fx: 603-314-5386 ▪ TF: 800-733-2622

Arborists, American Society of Consulting www.asca-consultants.org
15245 Shady Grove Rd Suite 130   Rockville MD 20850
Ph: 301-947-0483 ▪ Fx: 301-990-9771

Arborists, Society of Municipal www.urban-forestry.com
PO Box 641   Watkinsville GA 30677
Ph: 706-769-7412 ▪ Fx: 706-769-7307

ARC Inc, Adoption www.adoptionarc.com
4701 Pine St Suite J-7   Philadelphia PA 19143
Ph: 215-748-1441 ▪ Fx: 215-842-9881 ▪ TF: 800-884-4004

Arc of the US The www.thearc.org
1010 Wayne Ave Suite 650   Silver Spring MD 20910
Ph: 301-565-3842 ▪ Fx: 301-565-3843 ▪ TF: 800-433-5255

Arcadian Federation of America, Pan www.panarcadian.org
880 N York Rd   Elmhurst IL 60126
Ph: 630-833-1900 ▪ Fx: 630-833-1956

Archaeological Conservancy www.americanarchaeology.com/aaabout.html
5301 Central Ave NE Suite 1218   Albuquerque NM 87108
Ph: 505-266-1540 ▪ Fx: 505-266-0311

Archaeological Institute of America www.archaeological.org
656 Beacon St 4th Fl   Boston MA 02215
Ph: 617-353-9361 ▪ Fx: 617-353-6550

Archaeological Society, Near East www.neasweb.org
Horn Archaeological Museum Andrews Univ   Berrien Springs
MI 49104
Ph: 269-471-3273 ▪ Fx: 269-471-3619

Archaeologists, National Association of State www.uiowa.edu/~osa/nasa

Archaeologists, Register of Professional www.rpanet.org
5024-R Campbell Blvd   Baltimore MD 21236
Ph: 410-933-3486 ▪ Fx: 410-931-8111

Archaeology, Institute of Nautical ina.tamu.edu
PO Drawer HG   College Station TX 77841
Ph: 979-845-6694 ▪ Fx: 979-847-9260

Archaeology, Society for American www.saa.org
900 2nd St NE Suite 12   Washington DC 20002
Ph: 202-789-8200 ▪ Fx: 202-789-0284

Archaeology, Society for Historical www.sha.org
19 Mantua Rd   Mount Royal NJ 08061
Ph: 856-224-0995 ▪ Fx: 856-423-3420

Archconfraternity of Christian Mothers www.capuchin.com/christia.htm
220 37th St   Pittsburgh PA 15201
Ph: 412-683-2400 ▪ Fx: 412-683-7155

Archeology, Center for American www.caa-archeology.org
PO Box 366   Kampsville IL 62053
Ph: 618-653-4316 ▪ Fx: 618-653-4232

Archeology, Society for Commercial www.sca-roadside.org
Bowling Green State Univ Dept of Popular Culture   Bowling
Green OH 43403
Ph: 419-372-2136

Archeology, Society for Industrial www.sia-web.org
Michigan Technological Univ Dept of Social Sciences 1400
Townsend Dr   Houghton MI 49931
Ph: 906-487-1889 ▪ Fx: 906-487-2468

Archery Association, National Field www.nfaa-archery.org
31407 Outer I-10   Redlands CA 92373
Ph: 909-794-2133 ▪ Fx: 909-794-8512 ▪ TF: 800-811-2331

Archery Range & Retailers Organization www.archeryretailers.com
156 N Main St Suite D   Oregon WI 53575
Ph: 608-835-9060 ▪ Fx: 608-835-9360

Archery Trade Association www.archerytrade.org
860 E 4500 South Suite 310   Salt Lake City UT 84107
Ph: 801-261-2380 ▪ Fx: 801-261-2389 ▪ TF: 866-266-2776

Archery, USA www.usarchery.org
1 Olympic Plaza   Colorado Springs CO 80909
Ph: 719-866-4576 ▪ Fx: 719-632-4733

Archibald Bush Foundation www.bushfoundation.org
332 Minnesota St Suite E-900   Saint Paul MN 55101
Ph: 651-227-0891 ▪ Fx: 651-297-6485

ArchiPAC
1735 New York Ave NW   Washington DC 20006
Ph: 202-626-7300 ▪ Fx: 202-626-7426

Architects, American College of Healthcare www.healtharchitects.org
8310 Nieman Rd PO Box 14548   Lenexa KS 66285
Ph: 913-492-4307 ▪ Fx: 913-599-5340

Architects, American Institute of www.aiaonline.com
1735 New York Ave NW   Washington DC 20006
Ph: 202-626-7300 ▪ Fx: 202-626-7426 ▪ TF: 800-365-2724

Architects, American Society of Golf Course www.asgca.org
111 E Wacker Dr 18th Fl   Chicago IL 60601
Ph: 312-372-7090 ▪ Fx: 312-372-6160

Architects, American Society of Landscape www.asla.org
636 'I' St NW   Washington DC 20001
Ph: 202-898-2444 ▪ Fx: 202-898-1185 ▪ TF: 800-787-2752

Architects & Engineers, American Indian Council of   www.aicae.org

Architects Engineers & Scientists Inc, Society of Turkish   www.m-l-m.org
821 United Nations Plaza 2nd Fl   New York NY 10017
Ph: 212-682-7688 ▪ Fx: 212-687-3026

Architects & Marine Engineers, Society of Naval   www.sname.org
601 Pavonia Ave 4th Fl   Jersey City NJ 07306
Ph: 201-798-4800 ▪ Fx: 201-798-4975

Architects, National Organization of Minority   www.noma.net
Howard Univ School of Architecture & Design 2366 6th St NW
Rm 100   Washington DC 20059
Ph: 202-686-2780

Architects, Society of American Registered   www.sara-national.org

Architectural Accrediting Board, National   www.naab.org
1735 New York Ave NW   Washington DC 20006
Ph: 202-783-2007 ▪ Fx: 202-783-2822

Architectural Engineering Institute   www.aeinstitute.org
1801 Alexander Bell Dr 1st Fl   Reston VA 20191
Ph: 703-295-6027 ▪ Fx: 703-295-6361

Architectural Foundation, American   www.archfoundation.org
1799 New York Ave NW   Washington DC 20006
Ph: 202-626-7318 ▪ Fx: 202-626-7420

Architectural Heritage Foundation   www.ahfboston.com
Old City Hall 45 School St   Boston MA 02108
Ph: 617-523-8678 ▪ Fx: 617-523-3782

Architectural Historians, Society of   www.sah.org
1365 N Astor St   Chicago IL 60610
Ph: 312-573-1365 ▪ Fx: 312-573-1141

Architectural Manufacturers Association, American   www.aamanet.org
1827 Walden Office Sq Suite 550   Schaumburg IL 60173
Ph: 847-303-5664 ▪ Fx: 847-303-5774

Architectural Metal Manufacturers, National Association of   www.naamm.org
8 S Michigan Ave Suite 1000   Chicago IL 60603
Ph: 312-332-0405 ▪ Fx: 312-332-0706

Architectural Precast Association   www.archprecast.org
6710 Winkler Rd Suite 8   Fort Myers FL 33919
Ph: 239-454-6989 ▪ Fx: 239-454-6787

Architectural Registration Boards, Council of Landscape   www.clarb.org
144 Church St NW Suite 201   Vienna VA 22180
Ph: 703-319-8380 ▪ Fx: 703-319-8290

Architectural Registration Boards, National Council of   www.ncarb.org
1801 K St NW Suite 1100   Washington DC 20006
Ph: 202-783-6500 ▪ Fx: 202-783-0290

Architectural Research Centers Consortium Inc   www.arccweb.org

Architectural Woodwork Institute   www.awinet.org
1952 Isaac Newton Sq W   Reston VA 20190
Ph: 703-733-0600 ▪ Fx: 703-733-0584

Architecture, Association of Collegiate Schools of   www.acsa-arch.org
1735 New York Ave NW 3rd Fl   Washington DC 20006
Ph: 202-785-2324 ▪ Fx: 202-628-0448

Architecture, Landscape   www.laprofession.org
818 18th St NW Suite 810   Washington DC 20006
Ph: 202-331-7070 ▪ Fx: 202-331-7079

Architecture, Friends of Cast Iron
235 E 87th St Room 6C   New York NY 10128
Ph: 212-369-6004

Architecture Students Inc, American Institute of   www.aiasnatl.org
1735 New York Ave NW   Washington DC 20006
Ph: 202-626-7472 ▪ Fx: 202-626-7414

Architecture, Van Alen Institute: Projects in Public   www.vanalen.org
30 W 22nd St   New York NY 10010
Ph: 212-924-7000 ▪ Fx: 212-366-5836

Archives of American Art, Smithsonian   artarchives.si.edu
750 9th St NW Suite 2200   Washington DC 20560
Ph: 202-275-2156 ▪ Fx: 202-275-1955

Archives & History of the United Methodist Church, General   www.gcah.org
Commission on   36 Madison Ave PO Box 127   Madison NJ
07940
Ph: 973-408-3189 ▪ Fx: 973-408-3909

Archives & Records Administrators, National Association of   www.nagara.org
Government   48 Howard St   Albany NY 12207
Ph: 518-463-8644 ▪ Fx: 518-463-8656

Archivists, Academy of Certified   www.certifiedarchivists.org
48 Howard St   Albany NY 12207
Ph: 518-463-8644 ▪ Fx: 518-463-8656

Archivists, Association of Moving Image   www.amianet.org
1313 N Vine St   Hollywood CA 90028
Ph: 323-463-1500 ▪ Fx: 323-463-1506

Archivists & Librarians in the History of the Health Sciences   www.alhhs.org
Virginia Commonwealth Univ Tompkins-McCaw Library Box
980582   Richmond VA 23298
Ph: 804-828-9898 ▪ Fx: 804-828-6089

Archivists, Society of American   www.archivists.org
527 S Wells St 5th Fl   Chicago IL 60607
Ph: 312-922-0140 ▪ Fx: 312-347-1452

Area Agencies on Aging, National Association of   www.n4a.org
927 15th St NW 6th Fl   Washington DC 20005
Ph: 202-296-8130 ▪ Fx: 202-296-8134

Area Business Publications, Association of   www.bizpubs.org
4929 Wilshire Blvd Suite 428   Los Angeles CA 90010
Ph: 323-937-5514 ▪ Fx: 323-937-0959

Argentine-American Chamber of Commerce Inc   www.argentinechamber.org
630 5th Ave 25th Fl   New York NY 10111
Ph: 212-698-2238 ▪ Fx: 212-698-2239

Arica Institute Inc   www.arica.org
PO Box 645   Kent CT 06757
Ph: 860-927-1006 ▪ Fx: 860-927-1007

Arison Foundation
3655 NW 87th Ave   Miami FL 33178
Ph: 305-599-2600 ▪ Fx: 305-406-4700

Arizona Cactus & Succulent Research   www.arizonacactus.com
8 S Cactus Ln   Bisbee AZ 85603
Ph: 520-432-7040 ▪ Fx: 520-432-7001

Ark-La-Tex Genealogical Association   www.rootsweb.com/~laaltga
PO Box 4463   Shreveport LA 71134
Ph: 318-746-4598

Arm Wrestling Association, New York   www.nycarms.com
PO Box 670952   Flushing NY 11367
Ph: 718-544-4592 ▪ Fx: 718-261-8111 ▪ TF: 877-692-2767

ARMA International   www.arma.org
13725 W 109th St Suite 101   Lenexa KS 66215
Ph: 913-341-3808 ▪ Fx: 913-341-3742 ▪ TF: 800-422-2762

Armadillo, International Order of the
PO Box 60305   Jacksonville FL 32236
Ph: 904-384-8594 ▪ Fx: 904-387-1806

Armed Forces Benefit Association   www.afba.com
909 N Washington St   Alexandria VA 22314
Ph: 703-549-4455 ▪ Fx: 703-706-5961 ▪ TF: 800-776-2322

Armed Forces Communications & Electronics Association   www.afcea.org
4400 Fair Lakes Ct   Fairfax VA 22033
Ph: 703-631-6100 ▪ Fx: 703-631-4693 ▪ TF: 800-336-4583

Armed Forces Hostess Association   www.army.mil/afha
The Pentagon Rm 1D110 6604 Army Pentagon   Washington
DC 20310
Ph: 703-697-3180 ▪ Fx: 703-693-9510

Armed Forces, National Conference on Ministry to the   www.ncmaf.org
4141 N Henderson Rd Suite 13   Arlington VA 22203
Ph: 703-276-7905 ▪ Fx: 703-276-7906

Armed Forces Optometric Society   www.afos2020.org
411 Sweetgrass Ct   Great Falls MT 59405
Ph: 406-452-5688 ▪ Fx: 406-452-5740

Armed Forces, Society of Medical Consultants to the   www.smcaf.org

Armed Services Mutual Benefit Association   www.asmba.com
PO Box 160384   Nashville TN 37216
Ph: 615-851-0800 ▪ Fx: 615-851-9484 ▪ TF: 800-251-8434

Armenian Assembly of America   www.aaainc.org
122 C St NW Suite 350   Washington DC 20001
Ph: 202-393-3434 ▪ Fx: 202-638-4904

Armenian Bar Association   www.armenianbar.org/
PO Box 29111   Los Angeles CA 90029
Ph: 323-666-6288

Armenian Church of America   www.armenianchurch.org
630 2nd Ave   New York NY 10016
Ph: 212-686-0710 ▪ Fx: 212-686-0245

Armenian Educational Foundation   www.aefweb.org
600 W Broadway Suite 130   Glendale CA 91204
Ph: 818-242-4154 ▪ Fx: 818-242-4913

Armenian Engineers & Scientists of America   www.aesa.org
417 W Arden Ave Suite 112C   Glendale CA 91203
Ph: 818-547-3372

Armenian Film Foundation   www.armenianfilmfoundation.com
2219 E Thousand Oaks Blvd Suite 292   Thousand Oaks CA
91362
Ph: 805-495-0717 ▪ Fx: 805-379-0667

Armenian General Benevolent Union   www.agbu.org
55 E 59th St 7th Fl   New York NY 10022
Ph: 212-319-6383 ▪ Fx: 212-319-6507

(Armenian) Hairenik Association Inc   www.hairenik.com
80 Bigelow Ave   Watertown MA 02472
Ph: 617-926-3974 ▪ Fx: 617-926-1750

Armenian Information Professionals, Association of
139 Cedar St   Cliffside Park NJ 07010
Ph: 201-941-2266 ▪ Fx: 201-941-5110

Armenian Missionary Association of America   www.amaa.org
31 W Century Rd   Paramus NJ 07652
Ph: 201-265-2607 ▪ Fx: 201-265-6015

Armenian National Committee of America   www.anca.org
888 17th St NW Suite 904   Washington DC 20006
Ph: 202-775-1918 ▪ Fx: 202-775-5648

Armenian National Education Committee
138 E 39th St   New York NY 10016
Ph: 212-689-7231 ▪ Fx: 212-689-7168

Armenian Numismatic Society
8511 Beverly Park Pl   Pico Rivera CA 90660
Ph: 562-695-0380

Armenian Relief Society Eastern US   www.arseastus.com
80 Bigelow Ave   Watertown MA 02472
Ph: 617-926-3801 ▪ Fx: 617-924-7238

Armenian Revolutionary Federation   www.arf.am/English/
80 Bigelow Ave   Watertown MA 02472
Ph: 617-926-3685 ▪ Fx: 617-926-5525

Armenian Students Association   www.asainc.org
333 Atlantic Ave   Warwick RI 02888
Ph: 401-461-6114 ▪ Fx: 401-461-6112

Armenian Studies & Research, National   www.commercemarketplace.com/home/naasr
Association for   395 Concord Ave   Belmont MA 02478
Ph: 617-489-1610 ▪ Fx: 617-484-1759

Armenian Studies Inc, Society of   armenianstudies.csufresno.edu/sas
California State Univ - Fresno 5245 N Backer Ave PB 4   Fresno
CA 93740
Ph: 559-278-4930 ▪ Fx: 559-278-2129

Armenian Women's Welfare Association Inc   www.awwa-inc.org
PO Box 191   Belmont MA 02478
Ph: 617-522-2600 ▪ Fx: 617-524-7024

Armenian Youth Federation   www.ayf.org
80 Bigelow Ave   Watertown MA 02472
Ph: 617-923-1933

Armor & Arms Club
40 Edgemont Rd   Montclair NJ 07042
Ph: 973-744-8838 ▪ Fx: 973-746-4814

Armored Car Association, National
1730 M St NW   Washington DC 20036
Ph: 202-296-3522 ▪ Fx: 202-296-7713

Armored Car Operators Association, Independent   www.iacoa.com
102 E Ave J   Lancaster CA 93535
Ph: 661-726-9864 ▪ Fx: 661-949-7877

Armored Transportation Institute
PO Box 333   Baltimore MD 21203
Ph: 410-229-1929 ▪ Fx: 410-229-1930 ▪ TF: 800-888-2129

Armorial Ancestry, Order of Americans of
PO Box 453   Abingdon MD 21009
Ph: 410-515-1824

Arms Club, Armor &
40 Edgemont Rd   Montclair NJ 07042
Ph: 973-744-8838 ▪ Fx: 973-746-4814

Arms Collectors & Makers Society Ltd, Miniature   www.miniaturearms.com
2502 Fresno Ln   Plainfield IL 60544
Ph: 815-254-8692 ▪ TF: 800-847-6788

Arms Control Association   www.armscontrol.org
1726 M St NW Suite 201   Washington DC 20036
Ph: 202-463-8270 ▪ Fx: 202-463-8273

Arms Reduction, Economists Allied for   www.ecaar.org
39 E Central Ave Suite 1   Pearl River NY 10965
Ph: 845-620-1542 ▪ Fx: 845-620-1866

Army & Air Force Mutual Aid Association   www.aafmaa.com
102 Sheridan Ave Bldg 468   Fort Myer VA 22211
Ph: 703-526-1621 ▪ Fx: 703-522-1336 ▪ TF: 866-422-3622

Army, Association of the US   www.ausa.org
2425 Wilson Blvd   Arlington VA 22201
Ph: 703-841-4300 ▪ Fx: 703-525-9039 ▪ TF: 800-336-4570

Army Aviation Association of America   www.quad-a.org
755 Main St Suite 4D   Monroe CT 06468
Ph: 203-268-2450 ▪ Fx: 203-268-5870

Army Corps Veterans' Association, Women's   www.armywomen.org

Army Distaff Foundation   www.armydistaff.org
6200 Oregon Ave NW   Washington DC 20015
Ph: 202-541-0105 ▪ Fx: 202-364-2856 ▪ TF: 800-541-4255

Army Emergency Relief   www.aerhq.org
200 Stovall St   Alexandria VA 22332
Ph: 703-328-0000 ▪ Fx: 703-325-7183

Army Historical Foundation   www.armyhistoryfnd.org
2425 Wilson Blvd   Arlington VA 22201
Ph: 703-522-7901 ▪ Fx: 703-522-7929 ▪ TF: 800-506-2672

(Army Intelligence) CID Agents Association   www.onin.com/cidaa
1896 Carlisle Rd   Traverse City MI 49686
Ph: 231-932-2388

Army & Navy Union USA   www.armynavy.net
2002 Tallmadge Ave   Kent OH 44240
Ph: 330-343-9015

Army Physician Assistants, Society of   www.sapa.org
6762 Candlewood Dr   Fort Myers FL 33919
Ph: 941-482-2162

Army Warrant Officers Association, US   www.penfed.org/usawoa
462 Herndon Pkwy Suite 207   Herndon VA 20170
Ph: 703-742-7727 ▪ Fx: 703-742-7728 ▪ TF: 800-587-2862

Aroid Society Inc, International   www.aroid.org

Aromatherapy & Herb Association, International   www.aromaherbshow.com
3541 W Acapulco Ln   Phoenix AZ 85053
Ph: 602-938-4439

Aromatherapy, National Association for Holistic   www.naha.org
4509 Interlake Ave N Suite 233   Seattle WA 98103
Ph: 206-547-2164 ▪ Fx: 206-547-2680 ▪ TF: 888-275-6242

Arrangers & Composers, American Society of Music   www.asmac.org
PO Box 17840   Encino CA 91416
Ph: 818-994-4661 ▪ Fx: 818-994-6181

ARRL Foundation Inc   www.arrl.org/arrlf
225 Main St   Newington CT 06111
Ph: 860-594-0230

Arrow, Order of the   www.oa-bsa.org
1325 W Walnut Hill Ln PO Box 152079   Irving TX 75015
Ph: 972-580-2438 ▪ Fx: 972-580-2399

Arrythmia Death Syndromes Foundation, Sudden   www.sads.org
508 E South Temple Suite 20   Salt Lake City UT 84102
Ph: 801-531-0937 ▪ Fx: 801-531-0945 ▪ TF: 800-786-7723

Arson Investigators, International Association of   www.fire-investigators.org
12770 Boenker Rd   Bridgeton MO 63044
Ph: 314-739-4224 ▪ Fx: 314-739-4219

Art, American Academy of Equine   www.aaea.net
4089 Iron Works Pkwy   Lexington KY 40511
Ph: 859-281-6031 ▪ Fx: 859-281-6043

Art, American Institute of Commemorative   www.monuments-aica.com
11003 Fellswood Ct   Louisville KY 40243
Ph: 502-254-1375

Art & Antique Dealers League of America   www.artantiquedealersleague.com
1040 Madison Ave   New York NY 10021
Ph: 212-879-7558 ▪ Fx: 212-772-7197

(Art) Arthur Szyk Society   www.szyk.org
1200 Edgehill Dr   Burlingame CA 94010
Ph: 650-343-9588 ▪ Fx: 650-579-6014

Art Association, College   www.collegeart.org
275 7th Ave   New York NY 10001
Ph: 212-691-1051 ▪ Fx: 212-627-2381

Art & Creative Materials Institute Inc   www.acminet.org
PO Box 479   Hanson MA 02341
Ph: 781-293-4100 ▪ Fx: 781-294-0808

Art & Dealers Association of America   www.artdealers.org
575 Madison Ave   New York NY 10022
Ph: 212-940-8590 ▪ Fx: 212-940-6484

Art Dealers Association of America, National Antique &   naadaa.org
220 E 57th St   New York NY 10022
Ph: 212-826-9707 ▪ Fx: 212-832-9493

Art Dealers Association of Canada   www.ad-ac.ca
55 St Clair Ave W Suite 255   Toronto ON M4V2Y7
Ph: 416-934-1583 ▪ Fx: 416-967-6320

Art Dealers, Association of International   www.artline.com/associations/ipa/ipa.html
Photography   1609 Connecticut Ave NW Suite
200   Washington DC 20009
Ph: 202-986-0105 ▪ Fx: 202-986-0448

Art Dealers Association, Private   www.pada.net
PO Box 872   New York NY 10021
Ph: 212-572-0772 ▪ Fx: 212-572-8398

Art & Design, Association of Independent Colleges of   www.aicad.org
3957 2nd St   San Francisco CA 94114
Ph: 415-642-8595 ▪ Fx: 415-642-8590

Art & Design, National Association of Schools of   nasad.arts-accredit.org
11250 Roger Bacon Dr Suite 21   Reston VA 20190
Ph: 703-437-0700 ▪ Fx: 703-437-6312

Art Directors Club   www.adcglobal.org
106 W 29th St   New York NY 10001
Ph: 212-643-1440 ▪ Fx: 212-643-4266

Art Directors Guild   www.artdirectors.org
11969 Ventura Blvd Suite 200   Studio City CA 91604
Ph: 818-762-9995 ▪ Fx: 818-762-9997

Art Dreco Institute   www.artdreco.com
30 Paloma Ave   San Francisco CA 94127
Ph: 415-333-8372 ▪ Fx: 415-239-6222

Art Editors, Association of   www.artedit.org
3912 Natchez Ave S   Saint Louis Park MN 55416
Ph: 952-922-1374

Art Education Association, National   www.naea-reston.org
1916 Association Dr   Reston VA 20191
Ph: 703-860-8000 ▪ Fx: 703-860-2960

Art Education, Council for   www.acminet.org/cfae.htm
PO Box 479   Hanson MA 02341
Ph: 781-293-4100 ▪ Fx: 781-294-0808

Art Foundation, Children's   www.stonesoup.com
PO Box 83   Santa Cruz CA 95063
Ph: 831-426-5557 ▪ Fx: 831-426-1161 ▪ TF: 800-447-4569

Art Foundation, Filipinas Americas Science &
1209 Park Ave   New York NY 10128
Ph: 212-427-6930 ▪ Fx: 212-427-6931

Art Foundation, Leslie-Lohman Gay   www.leslielohman.com
127-B Prince St   New York NY 10012
Ph: 212-673-7007 ▪ Fx: 212-260-0363

Art Fund, Public   www.publicartfund.org
1 E 53rd St 11th Fl   New York NY 10022
Ph: 212-980-4575 ▪ Fx: 212-980-3610

Art Glass Association   www.artglassassociation.com
PO Box 2537   Zanesville OH 43702
Ph: 740-454-1194 ▪ TF: 866-301-2421

Art Glass Collectors of America Inc, Fenton   fagcainc.wirefire.com
PO Box 384   Williamstown WV 26187
Ph: 304-375-6196 ▪ Fx: 304-375-4679

Art History, Association for Textual   www.uml.edu/Dept/History/ArtHistory/ATSAH
Scholarship in   112 Charles St Beacon Hill   Boston MA 02114
Ph: 617-367-1679 ▪ Fx: 617-557-2962

Art, International Center of Medieval   www.medievalart.org
The Cloisters Fort Tryon Pk   New York NY 10040
Ph: 212-928-1146 ▪ Fx: 212-928-9946

Art, International Council of the Museum of Modern
11 W 53rd St   New York NY 10019
Ph: 212-708-9470 ▪ Fx: 212-708-9740

Art International, Friends of Fiber
PO Box 468   Western Springs IL 60558
Ph: 708-246-9466

Art Libraries Society of North America   www.arlisna.org
329 March Rd Suite 232 Box 11   Kanata ON K2K2E1
Ph: 800-817-0621 ▪ Fx: 613-599-7027

Art Materials Trade Association, National   www.namta.org
15806 Brookway Dr Suite 300   Huntersville NC 28078
Ph: 704-892-6244 ▪ Fx: 704-892-6247

Art Museum Directors, Association of   www.aamd.org
41 E 65th St   New York NY 10021
Ph: 212-249-4423 ▪ Fx: 212-535-5039

Art Music Composers, Christian Fellowship of   www.cfamc.org
Houghton College Greatbatch School of Music   Houghton NY
14744
Ph: 585-567-9424

Art Pottery Association, American   www.amartpot.org
17736 Hwy 442   Independence LA 70443
Ph: 985-878-8640

Art Publishers Association   apa.pmai.org
3000 Picture Pl   Jackson MI 49201
Ph: 517-788-8100 ▪ Fx: 517-788-8371

Art Research Association, American Rock   www.arara.org
PO Box 210026   Tucson AZ 85721
Ph: 888-668-0052

Art Research, International Foundation for   www.ifar.org
500 5th Ave Suite 1234   New York NY 10110
Ph: 212-391-6234 ▪ Fx: 212-391-8794

Art Resources in Collaboration Inc   www.eyeondance.org/about
123 W 18th St 7th Fl   New York NY 10011
Ph: 212-206-6492

(Art) Salmagundi Club   www.salmagundi.org
47 5th Ave   New York NY 10003
Ph: 212-255-7740 ▪ Fx: 212-229-0172

Art & Science Foundation, Photographic
2100 NE 52nd St   Oklahoma City OK 73111
Ph: 405-424-4055 ▪ Fx: 405-424-4058

Art & Science, World Academy of   www.worldacademy.org/
301 19th Ave S   Minneapolis MN 55455
Ph: 612-624-5592 ▪ Fx: 612-625-3513

Art Services International   www.artservicesintl.org
1319 Powhatan St   Alexandria VA 22314
Ph: 703-548-4554 ▪ Fx: 703-548-3305

Art, Smithsonian Archives of American   artarchives.si.edu
750 9th St NW Suite 2200   Washington DC 20560
Ph: 202-275-2156 ▪ Fx: 202-275-1955

Art Therapy Association, American   www.arttherapy.org
1202 Allanson Rd   Mundelein IL 60060
Ph: 847-949-6064 ▪ Fx: 847-566-4580 ▪ TF: 888-290-0878

Art Therapy Credentials Board   www.atcb.org
3 Terrace Way Suite B   Greensboro NC 27403
Ph: 877-213-2822 ▪ Fx: 336-547-0017

Art, US Society for Education Through   www.public.asu.edu/~ifmls/usseafolder/ussea.html
Ohio State Univ 1739 N High St 4th Fl   Columbus OH 43210
Ph: 614-247-7612

Art, Women's Caucus for   www.nationalwca.com
PO Box 1498   New York NY 10013
Ph: 212-634-0007

Arthritis Foundation   www.arthritis.org
1330 W Peachtree St Suite 100   Atlanta GA 30309
Ph: 404-872-7100 ▪ Fx: 404-872-0457 ▪ TF: 800-283-7800

Arthritis Organization, American Juvenile   www.arthritis.org/communities
1330 W Peachtree St   Atlanta GA 30309
Ph: 404-965-7514 ▪ Fx: 404-872-0457

Arthritis Trust of America   www.arthritistrust.org
7376 Walker Rd   Fairview TN 37062
Ph: 615-799-1002

Arthroscopy Association of North America   www.aana.org
6300 N River Rd Suite 104   Rosemont IL 60018
Ph: 847-292-2262 ▪ Fx: 847-292-2268

Arthroscopy Knee Surgery & Orthopaedic Sports Medicine, International Society of   www.isakos.com
2678 Bishop Dr Suite 250   San Ramon CA 94583
Ph: 925-807-1197 ▪ Fx: 925-807-1199

Arthur DeMoss Foundation
777 S Flagler Dr Suite 1600   West Palm Beach FL 33401
Ph: 561-804-9000 ▪ Fx: 561-804-9025

Arthur Szyk Society   www.szyk.org
1200 Edgehill Dr   Burlingame CA 94010
Ph: 650-343-9588 ▪ Fx: 650-579-6014

Arthur Vining Davis Foundations   www.jvm.com/davis
225 Water St Suite 1510   Jacksonville FL 32202
Ph: 904-359-0670 ▪ Fx: 904-359-0675

Artificial Intelligence, American Association for   www.aaai.org
445 Burgess Dr Suite 100   Menlo Park CA 94025
Ph: 650-328-3123 ▪ Fx: 650-321-4457

Artificial Internal Organs, American Society for   www.asaio.com
PO Box C   Boca Raton FL 33429
Ph: 561-391-8589 ▪ Fx: 561-368-9153

Artillery Company of Massachusetts, Ancient & Honorable   www.ahacsite.org
Armory Faneuil Hall   Boston MA 02109
Ph: 617-227-1638 ▪ Fx: 617-227-7221

Artisans Inc, Aid to   www.aidtoartisans.org
331 Wethersfield Ave   Hartford CT 06114
Ph: 860-947-3344 ▪ Fx: 860-947-3350

Artisans Guild, American Photographic   apag.net

Artisans, International Guild of Miniature   www.igma.org
PO Box 629   Freedom CA 95019
Ph: 831-724-7974 ▪ Fx: 831-724-8605 ▪ TF: 800-711-4462

Artisans Order of Mutual Protection   www.artisansaomp.org
8100 Roosevelt Blvd   Philadelphia PA 19152
Ph: 215-708-1000 ▪ Fx: 215-708-1779

Artist-Blacksmith's Association of North America Inc   www.abana.org
PO Box 816   Farmington GA 30638
Ph: 706-310-1030 ▪ Fx: 706-769-7147

Artistas Latino Americanos, Grupo de
21 W 112th St Unit 9J   New York NY 10026
Ph: 212-369-3401 ▪ Fx: 212-480-9734

Artistes of America, Associated Actors &
165 W 46th St   New York NY 10036
Ph: 212-869-0358 ▪ Fx: 212-869-1746

Artistic Works, American Institute for Conservation of Historic &   aic.stanford.edu
1717 K St NW Suite 200   Washington DC 20006
Ph: 202-452-9545 ▪ Fx: 202-452-9328

Artists of America, Allied   www.alliedartistsofamerica.org
15 Gramercy Park S   New York NY 10003
Ph: 212-582-6411

Artists, American Abstract
470 West End Ave Unit 9D   New York NY 10024
Ph: 212-874-0747

Artists, American Guild of Musical   www.musicalartists.org
1430 Broadway 14th Fl   New York NY 10018
Ph: 212-265-3687 ▪ Fx: 212-262-9088 ▪ TF: 800-543-2462

Artists, American Guild of Variety
363 7th Ave 17th Fl   New York NY 10001
Ph: 212-675-1003 ▪ Fx: 212-633-0097

Artists, American Society of
PO Box 1326   Palatine IL 60078
Ph: 312-751-2500

Artists, American Society of Botanical   huntbot.andrew.cmu.edu/ASBA/asbotartists.html
47 5th Ave   New York NY 10003
Ph: 212-691-9080 ▪ Fx: 212-691-9130 ▪ TF: 866-691-9080

Artists, American Society of Marine   www.americansocietyofmarineartists.com
PO Box 369   Ambler PA 19002
Ph: 215-283-0888 ▪ Fx: 215-646-1581

Artists, American Society of Portrait   www.asopa.com
PO Box 230216   Montgomery AL 36106
Ph: 334-270-9020 ▪ Fx: 334-270-0150 ▪ TF: 800-622-7672

Artists, Association of Science Fiction & Fantasy   www.asfa-art.org

Artists Communities, Alliance of   www.artistcommunities.org
225 S Main St   Providence RI 02903
Ph: 401-351-4320 ▪ Fx: 401-351-4507

Artists Council of America, Original Doll   www.odaca.org
2917 SW Fairview Blvd   Portland OR 97201
Ph: 503-222-5809

Artists' Fellowship Inc   www.artistsfellowship.com/home.html
47 5th Ave   New York NY 10003
Ph: 646-230-9833

Artists & Galleries Association, Visual
350 5th Ave Suite 2820   New York NY 10118
Ph: 212-736-6666 ▪ Fx: 212-736-6767

Artists Guild Inc, Graphic   www.gag.org
90 John St Suite 403   New York NY 10038
Ph: 212-791-3400 ▪ Fx: 212-791-0333

Artists Guild, Original Paper Doll   www.opdag.com
PO Box 14   Kingfield ME 04947
Ph: 207-265-2500

Artists Inc, International Black Writers &   members.tripod.com/~IBWA
PO Box 43576   Los Angeles CA 90043
Ph: 323-964-3721

Artists, International Society of Copier
759 President St Suite 2H   Brooklyn NY 11215
Ph: 718-638-3264

Artists for Israel International   www.afii.org
PO Box 2056   New York NY 10163
Ph: 212-245-4188

Artists, National Association of Women   www.nawanet.org
80 5th Ave Suite 1405   New York NY 10011
Ph: 212-675-1616

Artists, National Center of Afro-American   www.ncaaa.org
300 Walnut Ave   Boston MA 02119
Ph: 617-442-8614 ▪ Fx: 617-445-5525

Artists, National Institute of American Doll   www.niada.org

Artists, National Society of   www.nsartists.org
PO Box 150   Santa Fe TX 77510
Ph: 409-425-3381

Artists, Network of Alternatives for Publishers Retailers &   www.napra.com
PO Box 9   Eastsound WA 98245
Ph: 360-376-2702 ▪ Fx: 360-376-2704 ▪ TF: 800-367-1907

Artists Network, International
PO Box 182   Bowdoinham ME 04008
Ph: 207-666-8453

Artists Professional League, American
47 5th Ave   New York NY 10003
Ph: 212-645-1345

Artists, Society of American Graphic   www.clt.astate.edu/elind/sagamain.htm
32 Union Sq Rm 214   New York NY 10003
Ph: 212-260-5706

Artists Inc, Society of Animal   www.societyofanimalartists.com
47 5th Ave   New York NY 10003
Ph: 212-741-2880 ▪ Fx: 212-471-2262

Artists Space   www.artistsspace.org
38 Greene St 3rd Fl   New York NY 10013
Ph: 212-226-3970 ▪ Fx: 212-966-1434

Artists, United Scenic   www.usa829.org
29 W 38th St 15th Fl   New York NY 10018
Ph: 212-581-0300 ▪ Fx: 212-977-2011 ▪ TF: 877-728-5635

Artists Using Science & Technology, YLEM: www.ylem.org
PO Box 2590   Alameda CA 94501
Ph: 650-856-9593

(Artists) Westbeth Corp   www.westbeth.org
463 West St   New York NY 10014
Ph: 212-691-1500 ▪ Fx: 212-691-1502

Artists & Writers Association, Renaissance   rawa.ru.org
c/o Ananda Marga New York Sectorial Office 97-38 42nd Ave   Corona NY 11368
Ph: 718-898-1603

Artists & Writers Network, Small Publishers   www.spawn.org
323 E Matilija St Suite 110   Ojai CA 93023
Ph: 818-886-4281 ▪ Fx: 818-886-3120

Artists, Young Concert   www.yca.org/
250 W 57th St Suite 1222   New York NY 10019
Ph: 212-307-6655 ▪ Fx: 212-581-8894

Arts Accrediting Associations, Council of   www.arts-accredit.org
11250 Roger Bacon Dr Suite 21   Reston VA 20190
Ph: 703-437-0700 ▪ Fx: 703-437-6312

Arts Administrators, National Council of
Univ of Kentucky College of Fine Arts   Lexington KY 40506
Ph: 606-257-1707

Arts Agencies, National Assembly of State   www.nasaa-arts.org
1029 Vermont Ave NW 2nd Fl   Washington DC 20005
Ph: 202-347-6352 ▪ Fx: 202-737-0526

Arts, Allen Foundation for the   www.pgafoundations.com/arts.asp
505 5th Ave S Suite 900   Seattle WA 98104
Ph: 206-342-2000 ▪ Fx: 206-342-3000

Arts, Alliance for the   www.allianceforarts.org
330 W 42nd St Suite 1701   New York NY 10036
Ph: 212-947-6340 ▪ Fx: 212-947-6416

Arts Alliance, American   www.americanartsalliance.org
1156 15th St NW Suite 820   Washington DC 20005
Ph: 202-387-8300 ▪ Fx: 202-833-2686

Arts Alliance, Asian American   www.aaartsalliance.org
74 Varick St Suite 302   New York NY 10013
Ph: 212-941-9208 ▪ Fx: 212-941-7978

Arts, American Federation of   www.afaweb.org
41 E 65th St   New York NY 10021
Ph: 212-988-7700 ▪ Fx: 212-861-2487 ▪ TF: 800-232-0270

Arts, American Institute of Graphic   www.aiga.org
164 5th Ave   New York NY 10010
Ph: 212-807-1990 ▪ Fx: 212-807-1799 ▪ TF: 800-548-1634

Arts, Americans for the   www.artsusa.org
1000 Vermont Ave NW 6th Fl   Washington DC 20005
Ph: 202-371-2830 ▪ Fx: 202-371-0424

ARTS Anonymous   www.artsanonymous.org
PO Box 230175   New York NY 10023
Ph: 212-873-7075

Arts, Association of Hispanic   www.latinoarts.org
155 Ave of the Americas 14th Fl   New York NY 10013
Ph: 212-727-7227 ▪ Fx: 212-427-0549

Arts, Bilingual Foundation of the   www.bfatheatre.org
421 N Ave 19   Los Angeles CA 90031
Ph: 323-225-4044 ▪ Fx: 323-225-1250

Arts Inc, Business Committee for the   www.bcainc.org
29-27 Queens Plaza N 4th Fl   Long Island City NY 11101
Ph: 718-482-9900 ▪ Fx: 718-482-9911

Arts & Business Council Inc   www.artsandbusiness.org
520 8th Ave Suite 319   New York NY 10018
Ph: 212-279-5910 ▪ Fx: 212-279-5915

Arts Centre, Asian American   www.artspiral.org
26 Bowery   New York NY 10013
Ph: 212-233-2154 ▪ Fx: 212-766-1287

Arts Council, American Indian
725 Preston Forest Shopping Ctr Suite B   Dallas TX 75230
Ph: 214-891-9640 ▪ Fx: 214-891-0221

Arts Council, Chinese American   www.mercurial.net/gallery456
456 Broadway 3rd Fl   New York NY 10013
Ph: 212-431-9740 ▪ Fx: 212-431-9789

Arts & Crafts Association, Indian   www.iaca.com
4010 Carlisle Blvd NE Suite C   Albuquerque NM 87107
Ph: 505-265-9149 ▪ Fx: 505-265-8251

Arts Crafts & Theatre Safety   www.caseweb.com/ACTS
181 Thompson St Suite 23   New York NY 10012
Ph: 212-777-0062 ▪ Fx: 212-673-4403

Arts & Cultural Environments, SPACES - Saving & Preserving
1804 N Van Ness Blvd   Los Angeles CA 90028
Ph: 323-463-1629

Arts & Culture, Center for   www.culturalpolicy.org
819 7th St NW Suite 505   Washington DC 20001
Ph: 202-783-5277 ▪ Fx: 202-783-4498

Arts Education Association, International Graphic   www.igaea.org
1899 Preston White Dr   Reston VA 20191
Ph: 703-758-0595

Arts Education Network, Kennedy Center   www.kennedy-center.org/education/kcaaen
Alliance for   John F Kennedy Ctr for the Performing Arts 2700
F St NW   Washington DC 20566
Ph: 202-416-8845 ▪ Fx: 202-416-8802 ▪ TF: 800-444-1324

Arts Employers of America, Graphic
100 Daingerfield Rd   Alexandria VA 22314
Ph: 703-519-8100 ▪ Fx: 703-548-3227

Arts Exchange, Center for US-China   www.columbia.edu/cu/china
423 W 118th St Suite 1E   New York NY 10027
Ph: 212-280-4648 ▪ Fx: 212-662-6346

Arts, Fellowship of United Methodists in Music & Worship   www.fummwa.org
PO Box 24787   Nashville TN 37202
Ph: 615-749-6875 ▪ Fx: 615-749-6874 ▪ TF: 800-952-8977

Arts Foundation, International Society for the Performing   www.ispa.org
17 Purdy Ave PO Box 909   Rye NY 10580
Ph: 914-921-1550 ▪ Fx: 914-921-1593

Arts Foundation, National   www.nafgallery.com
444 Oakton St   Skokie IL 60077
Ph: 847-674-7990 ▪ Fx: 847-675-8116

Arts, Global Alliance for Intelligent   www.global-alliance.com
PO Box 403   Northampton MA 01061
Ph: 413-584-3022

Arts Industry, Research & Engineering Council of the Graphic   www.recouncil.org
PO Box 1086   White Stone VA 22578
Ph: 804-436-9922 ▪ Fx: 804-436-9511

Arts, Institute for the Study of Traditional American Indian
PO Box 66124   Portland OR 97290
Ph: 503-233-8131

Arts, International Association for the Fantastic in the   wiz.cath.vt.edu/iafa

Arts & Knowledge of the Church, SPEAK Inc - Society for   www.speakinc.org
Promoting & Encouraging   805 County Rd 102   Eureka
Springs AR 72632
Ph: 479-253-9701 ▪ Fx: 479-253-1277

Arts & Letters, American Academy of
633 W 155th St   New York NY 10032
Ph: 212-368-5900 ▪ Fx: 212-491-4615

Arts & Letters, National Society of   www.arts-nsal.org
4227 46th St NW   Washington DC 20016
Ph: 202-363-5443

Arts, National Council on Education for the Ceramic   www.nceca.net
77 Erie Village Sq Suite 280   Erie CO 80516
Ph: 303-828-2811 ▪ Fx: 303-828-0911 ▪ TF: 866-266-2322

Arts, National Council for the Traditional   www.NCTA.net
1320 Fenwick Ln Suite 200   Silver Spring MD 20910
Ph: 301-565-0654 ▪ Fx: 301-565-0472

Arts, National Foundation for Advancement in the   www.nfaa.org
800 Brickell Ave Suite 500   Miami FL 33131
Ph: 305-377-1140 ▪ Fx: 305-377-1149 ▪ TF: 800-970-2787

Arts, National Guild of Community Schools of the   www.nationalguild.org
520 8th Ave Suite 302   New York NY 10018
Ph: 212-268-3337 ▪ Fx: 212-268-3995

Arts, National Hispanic Foundation for the   www.hispanicarts.org
1010 Wisconsin Ave NW Suite 210   Washington DC 20007
Ph: 202-293-8330 ▪ Fx: 202-965-5252

Arts, National Park Academy of the   www.artsfortheparks.com
PO Box 608   Jackson Hole WY 83001
Ph: 307-733-2787 ▪ Fx: 307-739-1199 ▪ TF: 800-553-2787

Arts, Paul VI Institute for the
619 10th St NW   Washington DC 20001
Ph: 202-347-1450 ▪ Fx: 202-347-1401

(Arts) Phi Beta Fraternity   www.phibeta.com
2110 Manor Green Dr   Madison WI 53711
Ph: 608-288-0561

Arts Presenters, Association of Performing   www.artspresenters.org
1112 16th St NW Suite 400   Washington DC 20036
Ph: 202-833-2787 ▪ Fx: 202-833-1543

Arts Preservation, Society for Folk   www.societyforfolkarts.com
69 Timberhill Ln   South Fallsburg NY 12779
Ph: 845-436-7314

Arts in Progress!, Cultural   www.capsart.org
1 S Delaware Ave   Yardley PA 19067
Ph: 215-369-0677

Arts Religion & Contemporary Culture, Society for the   www.sarcc.org
15811 Kutztown Rd Box 15   Maxatawny PA 19538
Ph: 610-683-7581

Arts Schools, Accrediting Commission for Community &   www.arts-accredit.org
Precollegiate   11250 Roger Bacon Dr Suite 21   Reston VA
20190
Ph: 703-437-0700 ▪ Fx: 703-437-6312

Arts Schools, International Network of Performing &   www.artsschoolsnetwork.org
Visual   173 Ridge View Dr   Berkeley Springs WV 25411
Ph: 304-258-1799 ▪ Fx: 304-258-0839

Arts & Sciences of America Inc, Polish Institute of   www.piasa.org
208 E 30th St   New York NY 10016
Ph: 212-686-4164 ▪ Fx: 212-545-1130

Arts & Sciences, American Academy of   www.amacad.org
136 Irving St   Cambridge MA 02138
Ph: 617-576-5000 ▪ Fx: 617-576-5050

Arts & Sciences, Council of Colleges of   www.ccas.net
PO Box 873108   Tempe AZ 85287
Ph: 480-727-6064 ▪ Fx: 480-727-6078

Arts Sciences & Technology, Leonardo -   mitpress2.mit.edu/e-journals/Leonardo
International Society for the   425 Market St 2nd Fl   San
Francisco CA 94105
Ph: 415-405-3335 ▪ Fx: 415-405-7758

Arts & Sciences in the US, Ukrainian Academy of
206 W 100th St   New York NY 10025
Ph: 212-222-1866 ▪ Fx: 212-864-3977

Arts Society, Percussive   www.pas.org
701 NW Ferris Ave   Lawton OK 73507
Ph: 580-353-1455 ▪ Fx: 580-353-1456

Arts Studio Collectors Association, Ceramic   www.cascollectors.com
PO Box 46   Madison WI 53701
Ph: 608-845-9286 ▪ Fx: 608-241-8770

Arts Suppliers Association, North American Graphic   www.nagasa.org
1604 New Hampshire Ave NW   Washington DC 20009
Ph: 202-328-8441 ▪ Fx: 202-328-8513

Arts Technical Foundation, Graphic   www.gain.net
200 Deer Run Rd   Sewickley PA 15143
Ph: 412-741-6860 ▪ Fx: 412-741-2311 ▪ TF: 800-910-4283

Arts Training, Association for Graphic   www.agatweb.org

Arts Trust, Decorative   www.decorativeartstrust.org
106 Bainbridge   Philadelphia PA 19147
Ph: 215-627-2859 ▪ Fx: 215-925-1144

(Arts) Willow Mixed Media Inc   www.hudsonvalley.com/willow
25 11th Ave   Glenford NY 12433
Ph: 845-657-2914

ArtTable   www.arttable.org
270 Lafayette St Suite 608   New York NY 10012
Ph: 212-343-1735 ▪ Fx: 212-343-1430

ArtWatch International Inc   www.artwatchinternational.org
Columbia Univ 931 Schermerhorn   New York NY 10027
Ph: 212-854-4569 ▪ Fx: 212-854-7329

(Arumanian) Society Farsarotul   www.farsarotul.org
466 Silver Ln PO Box 753   Trumbull CT 06611
Ph: 203-375-0600 ▪ Fx: 203-375-5003

ARZA/World Union North America   arza.org
633 3rd Ave   New York NY 10017
Ph: 212-650-4280 ▪ Fx: 212-650-4289

Asbestos Information Association/North America
1235 Jefferson Davis Hwy PMB 114   Arlington VA 22202
Ph: 703-560-2980 ▪ Fx: 703-560-2981

Asbestos Workers, International Association of Heat &   www.insulators.org
Frost Insulators &   9602 ML King Jr Hwy   Lanham MD
20706
Ph: 301-731-9101 ▪ Fx: 301-731-5058

ASCENT Alliance, CompTel/   www.comptel.org
1900 M St NW Suite 800   Washington DC 20036
Ph: 202-296-6650 ▪ Fx: 202-296-7585

ASEAN Business Council, US-   www.us-asean.org
1101 17th St NW Suite 411   Washington DC 20036
Ph: 202-289-1911 ▪ Fx: 202-289-0519

Asepsis Procedures, Organization for Safety &   www.osap.org
PO Box 6297   Annapolis MD 21401
Ph: 410-571-0003 ▪ Fx: 410-571-0028 ▪ TF: 800-298-6727

ASFE   www.asfe.org
8811 Colesville Rd Suite G106   Silver Spring MD 20910
Ph: 301-565-2733 ▪ Fx: 301-589-2017

Ashoka USA/Canada   www.ashoka.org/us-canada
1700 N Moore St Suite 2000   Arlington VA 22209
Ph: 703-527-8300 ▪ Fx: 703-527-8383

Asia America MultiTechnology Association www.aamasv.com
3300 Zanker Rd MD SJ2F8   San Jose CA 95134
Ph: 408-955-4505 ▪ Fx: 408-955-4516

Asia Foundation www.asiafoundation.org
465 California St 14th Fl   San Francisco CA 94104
Ph: 415-982-4640 ▪ Fx: 415-392-8863

Asia, Independent Scholars of www.hypersphere.com/isa
2321 Russell St Unit 3C   Berkeley CA 94705
Ph: 510-849-3791

Asia Institute, US- www.usasiainstitute.org
232 E Capitol St NE   Washington DC 20003
Ph: 202-544-3181 ▪ Fx: 202-543-1748

Asia Missionary Society, Voice of China & www.vocamissionarysociety.org
183 E Glenarm St PO Box 150   Pasadena CA 91102
Ph: 626-441-0640 ▪ Fx: 626-441-8124

(Asia-Pacific) East-West Center www.eastwestcenter.org
1601 East-West Rd   Honolulu HI 96848
Ph: 808-944-7111 ▪ Fx: 808-944-7376

Asia Society www.asiasociety.org
725 Park Ave   New York NY 10021
Ph: 212-288-6400 ▪ Fx: 212-517-8315

Asia, United Board for Christian Higher Education in www.unitedboard.org
475 Riverside Dr Suite 1221   New York NY 10115
Ph: 212-870-2610 ▪ Fx: 212-870-2322

(Asia) VIA www.viaprograms.org
PO Box 20266   Stanford CA 94309
Ph: 650-723-3228 ▪ Fx: 650-725-1805

Asian American Arts Alliance www.aaartsalliance.org
74 Varick St Suite 302   New York NY 10013
Ph: 212-941-9208 ▪ Fx: 212-941-7978

Asian American Arts Centre www.artspiral.org
26 Bowery   New York NY 10013
Ph: 212-233-2154 ▪ Fx: 212-766-1287

Asian American Chamber of Commerce, US Pan www.uspaacc.com
1329 18th St NW   Washington DC 20036
Ph: 202-296-5221 ▪ Fx: 202-296-5225

Asian American Curriculum Project Inc www.AsianAmericanBooks.com
83 W 37th Ave   San Mateo CA 94403
Ph: 650-357-1088 ▪ Fx: 650-357-6908 ▪ TF: 800-874-2242

Asian American Hotel Owners Association www.aahoa.com
66 Lenox Pointe NE   Atlanta GA 30324
Ph: 404-816-5759 ▪ Fx: 404-816-6260

Asian American Journalists Association www.aaja.org
1182 Market St Suite 320   San Francisco CA 94102
Ph: 415-346-2051 ▪ Fx: 415-346-6343

Asian American Legal Defense & Education Fund www.aaldef.org
99 Hudson St 12th Fl   New York NY 10013
Ph: 212-966-5932 ▪ Fx: 212-966-4303

Asian American Professionals, National Association of www.naaap.org

Asian American Studies, Association for www.aaastudies.org
Cornell Univ Asian American Studies Program 420 Rockefeller
   Hall   Ithaca NY 14853
Ph: 607-255-3320 ▪ Fx: 607-254-4996

Asian American Telecommunications Association, National www.naatanet.org
145 9th St Suite 350   San Francisco CA 94103
Ph: 415-863-0814 ▪ Fx: 415-863-7428

Asian CineVision Inc www.asiancinevision.org
133 W 19th St Suite 300   New York NY 10011
Ph: 212-989-1422 ▪ Fx: 212-727-3584

Asian History, Conference on www.historians.org/affiliates
Indiana Univ East Asian Studies Ctr   Bloomington IN 47405
Ph: 812-855-3765 ▪ Fx: 812-855-7762

Asian Music, Society for www.skidmore.edu/academics/asianmusic
Cornell Univ Dept of Music Lincoln Hall   Ithaca NY 14853
Ph: 607-255-5049 ▪ Fx: 607-254-2877

Asian Pacific American Bar Association, National www.napaba.org
733 15th St NW Suite 315   Washington DC 20005
Ph: 202-367-0796 ▪ Fx: 202-393-0995

Asian Pacific American Community Development, www.nationalcapacd.org
National Coalition for   1001 Connecticut Ave NW Suite
   730   Washington DC 20036
Ph: 202-223-2442 ▪ Fx: 202-223-4144

Asian Pacific American Families Against Substance Abuse, National www.napafasa.org
340 E Second St Suite 409   Los Angeles CA 90012
Ph: 213-625-5795 ▪ Fx: 213-625-5796

Asian Pacific American Institute for Congressional Studies www.apaics.org
1001 Connecticut Ave NW Suite 835   Washington DC 20036
Ph: 202-286-9200 ▪ Fx: 202-296-9236

Asian Pacific American Labor Alliance www.apalanet.org
815 16th St NW   Washington DC 20006
Ph: 202-974-8051 ▪ Fx: 202-974-8056

Asian Pacific American Law Student Association, National www.napalsa.org

Asian Pacific American Legal Consortium, National www.napalc.org
1140 Connecticut Ave NW Suite 1200   Washington DC 20036
Ph: 202-296-2300 ▪ Fx: 202-296-2318

Asian Pacific American Women's Forum, National www.napawf.org
1112 16th St NW Suite 110   Washington DC 20036
Ph: 202-293-2688 ▪ Fx: 202-463-2119

Asian Pacific Center on Aging, National www.napca.org/
PO Box 21668   Seattle WA 98101
Ph: 206-624-1221 ▪ Fx: 206-624-1023

Asian/Pacific Community Health Organizations, Association of www.aapcho.org
429 23rd St   Oakland CA 94612
Ph: 510-272-9536 ▪ Fx: 510-272-0817

Asian & Pacific Islander American Health Forum www.apiahf.org
450 Sutter St Suite 600   San Francisco CA 94108
Ph: 415-954-9988 ▪ Fx: 415-954-9999

Asian Studies, Association for www.aasianst.org
1021 E Huron St   Ann Arbor MI 48104
Ph: 734-665-2490 ▪ Fx: 734-665-3801

Asian Studies, International Association of www.caaav.org
PO Box 325   Biddeford ME 04005
Ph: 207-839-8004 ▪ Fx: 207-839-3776

Asian Violence, Committee Against Anti- www.caaav.org
2473 Valentine Ave   Bronx NY 10458
Ph: 718-220-7391 ▪ Fx: 718-220-7398

Asian Women in Business www.awib.org
358 5th Ave Suite 504   New York NY 10001
Ph: 212-868-1368 ▪ Fx: 212-868-1373

Asian Women's Health Organization, National www.nawho.org
250 Montgomery St Suite 900   San Francisco CA 94104
Ph: 415-989-9747 ▪ Fx: 415-989-9758

ASIFA - Hollywood www.asifa-hollywood.org
721 S Victory Blvd   Burbank CA 91502
Ph: 818-842-8330 ▪ Fx: 818-842-5645

ASIS International www.asisonline.org
1625 Prince St   Alexandria VA 22314
Ph: 703-519-6200 ▪ Fx: 703-519-6299

ASM International www.asm-intl.org
9639 Kinsman Rd   Materials Park OH 44073
Ph: 440-338-5151 ▪ Fx: 440-338-4634 ▪ TF: 800-336-5152

ASME Auxiliary Inc www.asme.org/auxiliary
3 Park Ave 23rd Fl   New York NY 10016
Ph: 212-591-7733 ▪ Fx: 212-591-7739 ▪ TF: 800-843-2763

ASME International www.asme.org
3 Park Ave   New York NY 10016
Ph: 212-591-7722 ▪ Fx: 212-591-7739 ▪ TF: 800-843-2763

Asociacion de Ingenieros Cubanos www.a-i-c.org
PO Box 557575   Miami FL 33255
Ph: 305-597-9858

ASPCA Animal Poison Control Center www.apcc.aspca.org
1717 S Philo Rd Suite 36   Urbana IL 61802
Ph: 217-337-5030 ▪ Fx: 217-337-0599 ▪ TF: 888-426-4435

ASPECT Foundation www.aspectfoundation.org
350 Sansome St Suite 740   San Francisco CA 94104
Ph: 415-228-8050 ▪ Fx: 415-228-8051 ▪ TF: 800-879-6884

Aspen Institute www.aspeninstitute.org
1 DuPont Cir NW Suite 700   Washington DC 20036
Ph: 202-736-5800 ▪ Fx: 202-467-0790

Asphalt Emulsion Manufacturers Association www.aema.org
3 Church Cir PMB 250   Annapolis MD 21401
Ph: 410-267-0023 ▪ Fx: 410-267-7546

Asphalt Institute www.asphaltinstitute.org
PO Box 14052   Lexington KY 40512
Ph: 859-288-4960 ▪ Fx: 859-288-4999

Asphalt Pavement Association, National www.hotmix.org
5100 Forbes Blvd   Lanham MD 20706
Ph: 301-731-4748 ▪ Fx: 301-731-4621 ▪ TF: 888-468-6499

Asphalt Paving Technologists, Association of www.asphalttechnology.org
4711 Clark Ave Suite G   White Bear Lake MN 55110
Ph: 651-293-9188 ▪ Fx: 651-293-9193

Asphalt Recycling & Reclaiming Association www.arra.org
3 Church Cir PMB 250   Annapolis MD 21401
Ph: 410-267-0023 ▪ Fx: 410-267-7546

Asphalt Roofing Manufacturers Association www.asphaltroofing.org
1156 15th St NW Suite 900   Washington DC 20005
Ph: 202-207-0917 ▪ Fx: 202-223-9741

ASPIRA Association Inc www.aspira.org
1444 'I' St NW Suite 800   Washington DC 20005
Ph: 202-835-3600 ▪ Fx: 202-835-3613

Aspirin Foundation of America www.aspirin.org
1555 Connecticut Ave NW Suite 200   Washington DC 20036
Ph: 800-432-3247 ▪ Fx: 202-737-8406

Assault League, Life After
1336 W Lindbergh St   Appleton WI 54914
Ph: 920-739-4489 ▪ Fx: 920-739-1990

Assault Prevention, National Center for www.ncap.org
606 Delsea Dr   Sewell NJ 08080
Ph: 856-582-7000 ▪ Fx: 856-582-3588 ▪ TF: 800-582-4206

Assemblies of God www.ag.org
1445 N Boonville Ave   Springfield MO 65802
Ph: 417-862-2781 ▪ Fx: 417-862-5554 ▪ TF: 800-641-4310

Assembly Managers, International Association of iaam.org
635 Fritz Dr   Coppell TX 75019
Ph: 972-906-7441 ▪ Fx: 972-906-7418 ▪ TF: 800-965-4582

Assembly of Turkish American Associations www.ataa.org
1526 18th St NW   Washington DC 20036
Ph: 202-483-9090 ▪ Fx: 202-483-9092

Assessing Officers, International Association of www.iaao.org
130 E Randolph St Suite 850   Chicago IL 60601
Ph: 312-819-6100 ▪ Fx: 312-819-6149

Assigned Names & Numbers, Internet Corp for www.icann.org
4676 Admiralty Way Suite 330   Marina del Rey CA 90292
Ph: 310-823-9358 ▪ Fx: 310-823-8649

Assigned Numbers Authority, Internet www.iana.org
USC ISI 4676 Admiralty Way Suite 330   Marina del Rey CA
   90292
Ph: 310-823-9358 ▪ Fx: 310-823-8649

Assist International www.assistintl.org
PO Box 66396   Scotts Valley CA 95067
Ph: 831-438-4582 ▪ Fx: 831-439-9602

Assistance Dogs of America Inc www.adai.org
8806 State Rt 64   Swanton OH 43558
Ph: 419-825-3622 ▪ Fx: 419-825-3710

Assistance League, National www.nal.org
PO Box 6637   Burbank CA 91510
Ph: 818-846-3777 ▪ Fx: 818-846-3535

Assistants, American Association of Pathologists' www.pathologistsassistants.org
1711 W County Rd B   Roseville MN 55113
Ph: 651-697-9264 ▪ Fx: 651-635-0307 ▪ TF: 800-532-2272

Assistants, Association of Celebrity Personal www.celebrityassistants.org
914 Westwood Blvd PMB 507   Los Angeles CA 90024
Ph: 310-322-7755

Assisted Living Federation of America www.alfa.org
11200 Waples Mill Rd Suite 150   Fairfax VA 22030
Ph: 703-691-8100 ▪ Fx: 703-691-8106

Assistive Technology Industry Association www.atia.org
401 N Michigan Ave   Chicago IL 60611
Ph: 312-321-5172 ▪ Fx: 312-673-6659 ▪ TF: 877-687-2842

Associate Missionaries of the Assumption
914 Main St Suite 5   Worcester MA 01610
Ph: 508-767-1356 ▪ Fx: 508-791-2936

Associate Reformed Presbyterian Church World Witness worldwitness.org
1 Cleveland St Suite 220   Greenville SC 29601
Ph: 864-233-5226 ▪ Fx: 864-233-5326

Associated Actors & Artistes of America
165 W 46th St   New York NY 10036
Ph: 212-869-0358 ▪ Fx: 212-869-1746

Associated Air Balance Council www.aabchq.com
1518 K St NW   Washington DC 20005
Ph: 202-737-0202 ▪ Fx: 202-638-4833

Associated Bodywork & Massage Professionals www.abmp.com
1271 Sugarbush Dr   Evergreen CO 80439
Ph: 303-674-8478 ▪ Fx: 303-674-0859 ▪ TF: 800-458-2267

Associated Builders & Contractors Inc www.abc.org
4250 N Fairfax Dr 9th Fl   Arlington VA 22203
Ph: 703-812-2000 ▪ Fx: 703-812-8203

Associated Builders & Contractors PAC
4250 N Fairfax Dr 9th Fl   Arlington VA 22203
Ph: 703-812-2000 ▪ Fx: 703-812-8203

Associated Church Press www.theacp.org
1410 Vernon St   Stoughton WI 53589
Ph: 608-877-0011 ▪ Fx: 608-877-0062

Associated Colleges of the Midwest www.acm.edu
205 W Wacker Dr Suite 1300   Chicago IL 60606
Ph: 312-263-5000 ▪ Fx: 312-263-5879

Associated Collegiate Press studentpress.journ.umn.edu
2221 University Ave SE Suite 121   Minneapolis MN 55414
Ph: 612-625-8335 ▪ Fx: 612-626-0720

Associated Construction Distributors International www.acdi.net
1605 SE Delaware Ave Suite B   Ankeny IA 50021
Ph: 515-964-1335 ▪ Fx: 515-964-7668

Associated Cooperage Industries of America www.acia.net
2100 Gardiner Ln Suite 100-E   Louisville KY 40205
Ph: 502-459-6113 ▪ Fx: 502-459-6114

Associated Equipment Distributors www.aednet.org
615 W 22nd St   Oak Brook IL 60523
Ph: 630-574-0650 ▪ Fx: 630-574-0132 ▪ TF: 800-388-0650

Associated General Contractors of America www.agc.org
333 John Carlyle St Suite 200   Alexandria VA 22314
Ph: 703-548-3118 ▪ Fx: 703-548-3119 ▪ TF: 800-242-1766

Associated General Contractors PAC www.agc.org/legislative_info
333 John Carlyle St Suite 200   Alexandria VA 22314
Ph: 703-548-3118 ▪ Fx: 703-548-3119 ▪ TF: 800-242-1766

Associated Humane Societies www.petfinder.org
124 Evergreen Ave   Newark NJ 07114
Ph: 973-824-7080 ▪ Fx: 973-824-2720

Associated Koi Clubs of America www.akca.org
258 Sherwood St   Costa Mesa CA 92627
Ph: 949-548-3690

Associated Landscape Contractors of America www.alca.org
150 Elden St Suite 270   Herndon VA 20170
Ph: 703-736-9666 ▪ Fx: 703-736-9668 ▪ TF: 800-395-2522

Associated Locksmiths of America aloa.org
3003 Live Oak St   Dallas TX 75204
Ph: 214-827-1701 ▪ Fx: 214-827-1810 ▪ TF: 800-532-2562

Associated Luxury Hotels www.alhi.com
1000 Connecticut Ave NW Suite 603   Washington DC 20036
Ph: 202-887-7020 ▪ Fx: 202-887-0085

Associated Owners & Developers www.constructionchannel.net/aod
PO Box 4163   McLean VA 22103
Ph: 703-734-2397 ▪ Fx: 703-734-2908 ▪ TF: 888-999-2536

Associated Parishes for Liturgy & Mission www.associatedparishes.org
PO Box 27141   Baltimore MD 21230
Ph: 410-752-0877

Associated Pipe Organ Builders of America www.apoba.com
PO Box 155   Chicago Ridge IL 60415
Ph: 800-473-5270

Associated Press Managing Editors www.apme.com
50 Rockefeller Plaza   New York NY 10020
Ph: 212-621-1838

Associated Professional Sleep Societies www.apss.org
1 Westbrook Corporate Ctr Suite 920   Westchester IL 60154
Ph: 708-492-0930 ▪ Fx: 708-492-0943

Associated Risk Managers International www.armnet.com
2 Pierce Pl   Itasca IL 60143
Ph: 630-285-4186 ▪ Fx: 630-285-3590

Associated Services for the Blind www.asb.org
919 Walnut St   Philadelphia PA 19107
Ph: 215-627-0600 ▪ Fx: 215-922-0692

Associated Specialty Contractors Inc www.assoc-spec-con.org
3 Bethesda Metro Ctr Suite 1100   Bethesda MD 20814
Ph: 301-657-3110 ▪ Fx: 301-215-4500

Associated Universities Inc www.aui.edu
1400 16th St NW Suite 730   Washington DC 20036
Ph: 202-462-1676 ▪ Fx: 202-232-7161

Associated Wire Rope Fabricators www.awrf.org
PO Box 20126   Lehigh Valley PA 18002
Ph: 610-974-9974 ▪ Fx: 610-691-6833

Associates for Biblical Research www.christiananswers.net/abr/abrhome.html
PO Box 144   Akron PA 17501
Ph: 800-430-0008

Association of Academic Chairmen of Plastic Surgery www.aacplasticsurgery.org
4900 B South 31st St   Arlington VA 22206
Ph: 703-820-7400 ▪ Fx: 703-931-4520

Association of Academic Health Centers www.ahcnet.org
1400 16th St NW Suite 720   Washington DC 20036
Ph: 202-265-9600 ▪ Fx: 202-265-7514

Association of Academic Health Sciences Libraries www.aahsl.org
2150 N 107th St Suite 205   Seattle WA 98133
Ph: 206-367-8704 ▪ Fx: 206-367-8777

Association for Academic Surgery www.aasurg.org
11300 W Olympic Blvd Suite 600   Los Angeles CA 90064
Ph: 310-437-0555 ▪ Fx: 310-437-0585

Association for Accounting Administration www.cpaadmin.org
136 S Keowee St   Dayton OH 45402
Ph: 937-222-0030 ▪ Fx: 937-222-5794

Association for Accounting Marketing www.accountingmarketing.org
14 W 3rd St Suite 200   Kansas City MO 64105
Ph: 816-221-1296 ▪ Fx: 816-472-7765

Association for Adult Development & Aging www.aadaweb.org
c/o American Counseling Assn 5999 Stevenson Ave   Alexandria
   VA 22304
Ph: 703-823-9800 ▪ Fx: 703-823-0252 ▪ TF: 800-347-6647

Association for Advanced Life Underwriting www.aalu.org
2901 Telestar Ct   Falls Church VA 22042
Ph: 703-641-9400 ▪ Fx: 703-641-9885 ▪ TF: 888-275-0092

Association of Advanced Rabbinical & Talmudic Schools
11 Broadway   New York NY 10004
Ph: 212-363-1991 ▪ Fx: 212-533-5335

Association for Advanced Training in the Behavioral Sciences www.aatbs.com
5126 Ralston St   Ventura CA 93003
Ph: 805-676-3030 ▪ Fx: 805-676-3033 ▪ TF: 800-472-1931

Association for the Advancement of Applied Sport Psychology www.aaasponline.org
801 Main St Suite 010   Louisville CO 80027
Ph: 303-494-5931

Association for the Advancement of Automotive Medicine www.carcrash.org
PO Box 4176   Barrington IL 60011
Ph: 847-844-3880 ▪ Fx: 847-844-3884

Association for the Advancement of Baltic Studies Inc www.balticstudies-aabs.lanet.lv
14743 Braemar Way   Darnestown MD 20878
Ph: 301-977-8491 ▪ Fx: 301-977-8492

Association for Advancement of Behavior Therapy www.aabt.org
305 7th Ave 16th Fl   New York NY 10001
Ph: 212-647-1890 ▪ Fx: 212-647-1865 ▪ TF: 800-685-2228

Association for the Advancement of the Blind & Retarded www.aabr.org
1508 College Pt Blvd   College Point NY 11356
Ph: 718-321-3800 ▪ Fx: 718-321-8688

Association for the Advancement of Computing in Education www.aace.org
PO Box 3728   Norfolk VA 23514
Ph: 757-623-7588 ▪ Fx: 703-997-8760

Association for the Advancement of Creative www.aacmchicago.org/aacmgoals.html
Musicians   PO Box 5757   Chicago IL 60680
Ph: 312-752-2212 ▪ Fx: 312-752-2226

Association for the Advancement of International Education www.aaie.org
San Diego State Univ College of Extended Studies 5250
   Campanile Dr Rm 2525   San Diego CA 92182
Ph: 619-594-2877 ▪ Fx: 619-594-8566

Association for the Advancement of Medical Instrumentation www.aami.org
1110 N Glebe Rd Suite 220   Arlington VA 22201
Ph: 703-525-4890 ▪ Fx: 703-276-0793 ▪ TF: 800-332-2264

Association for the Advancement of Psychology www.aapnet.org
PO Box 38129   Colorado Springs CO 80937
Ph: 800-869-6595 ▪ Fx: 719-520-0375

Association for the Advancement of Psychotherapy www.ajp.org
1300 Morris Park Ave Berfer Bldg Rm 406   Bronx NY 10461
Ph: 718-430-3503 ▪ Fx: 718-430-8907

Association for the Advancement of Wound Care www.aawcone.com
83 General Warren Blvd Suite 100   Malvern PA 19355
Ph: 610-560-0500 ▪ Fx: 610-560-0502 ▪ TF: 866-229-2999

Association of African American Museums www.blackmuseums.org

Association of African-American Women Business Owners
3363 Alden Pl NE   Washington DC 20019
Ph: 202-399-3645

Association for Africanist Anthropology www.ibiblio.org/afaa
c/o American Anthropological Assn 2200 Wilson Blvd Suite
   600   Arlington VA 22201
Ph: 703-528-1902 ▪ Fx: 703-528-3546

Association of Air Force Missileers www.afmissileers.org
PO Box 5693   Breckenridge CO 80424
Ph: 970-453-0500

Association of Air Medical Services www.aams.org
526 King St Suite 415   Alexandria VA 22314
Ph: 703-836-8732 ▪ Fx: 703-836-8920

Association of Alternate Postal Systems Inc www.aapsinc.org
1725 Oaks Way   Oklahoma City OK 73131
Ph: 405-478-0161

Association of Alternative Newsweeklies aan.org
1020 16th St NW 4th Fl   Washington DC 20036
Ph: 202-822-1955 ▪ Fx: 202-822-0929

Association for Ambulatory Behavioral Healthcare www.aabh.org
2301 Mt Vernon Ave Suite 100   Alexandria VA 22301
Ph: 703-836-2274 ▪ Fx: 703-836-0083

Association of American Chambers of Commerce in Latin America www.aaccla.org
1615 H St NW 3rd Fl   Washington DC 20062
Ph: 202-463-5485 ▪ Fx: 202-463-3126

Association of American Colleges & Universities www.aacu-edu.org
1818 R St NW   Washington DC 20009
Ph: 202-387-3760 ▪ Fx: 202-265-9532

Association of American Cultures   www.taac.com
2554 W 16th St Suite 419   Yuma AZ 85364
Ph: 928-783-1757

Association of American Editorial Cartoonists   info.detnews.com/aaec
1121 Stoneferry Ln   Raleigh NC 27606
Ph: 919-859-5516 ▪ Fx: 919-859-3172

Association of American Educators   www.aaeteachers.org
25201 Paseo de Alicia Suite 104   Laguna Hills CA 92653
Ph: 949-595-7979 ▪ Fx: 949-595-7970 ▪ TF: 800-704-7799

Association of American Foreign Service Worldwide   www.aafsw.org
5125 McArthur Blvd NW Suite 36   Washington DC 20016
Ph: 202-362-6514 ▪ Fx: 202-362-6589

Association of American Geographers   www.aag.org
1710 16th St NW   Washington DC 20009
Ph: 202-234-1450 ▪ Fx: 202-234-2744

Association on American Indian Affairs   www.indian-affairs.org
PO Box 268   Sisseton SD 57262
Ph: 605-698-3998 ▪ Fx: 605-698-3316

Association of American Indian Physicians   www.aaip.com
1225 Sovereign Row Suite 103   Oklahoma City OK 73108
Ph: 405-946-7072 ▪ Fx: 405-946-7651

Association of American Law Schools   www.aals.org
1201 Connecticut Ave NW Suite 800   Washington DC 20036
Ph: 202-296-8851 ▪ Fx: 202-296-8869

Association of American Medical Colleges   www.aamc.org
2450 'N' St NW   Washington DC 20037
Ph: 202-828-0400 ▪ Fx: 202-828-1125

Association of American Military Uniform Collectors   www.naples.net/clubs/aamuc
PO Box 1876   Elyria OH 44036
Ph: 440-365-5321

Association of American Pesticide Control Officials   aapco.ceris.purdue.edu
PO Box 1249   Hardwick VT 05843
Ph: 802-472-6956 ▪ Fx: 802-472-6957

Association of American Physicians   www.aap-online.org
Harvard Univ Dept of Medicine Channing Lab 181 Longwood
   Ave   Boston MA 02115
Ph: 617-277-0551 ▪ Fx: 617-731-1541

Association of American Physicians & Surgeons Inc   www.aapsonline.org
1601 N Tucson Blvd Suite 9   Tucson AZ 85716
Ph: 520-327-4885 ▪ Fx: 520-325-4230 ▪ TF: 800-635-1196

Association of American Plant Food Control Officials   www.aapfco.org
Univ of Kentucky 103 Regulatory Services Bldg   Lexington KY
   40546
Ph: 859-257-2668 ▪ Fx: 859-257-9478

Association of American Publishers Inc   www.publishers.org
71 5th Ave   New York NY 10003
Ph: 212-255-0200 ▪ Fx: 212-255-7007

Association of American Railroads   www.aar.org
50 F St NW   Washington DC 20001
Ph: 202-639-2100 ▪ Fx: 202-639-2466 ▪ TF: 800-544-7245

Association of American Rhodes Scholars   www.americanrhodes.org
2717 Lincoln St   Evanston IL 60201
Ph: 847-869-5950 ▪ Fx: 847-869-6993

Association of American Schools in South America   www.aassa.com
14750 NW 77th Ct Suite 210   Miami Lakes FL 33016
Ph: 305-821-0345 ▪ Fx: 305-821-4244

Association of American Universities   www.aau.edu
1200 New York Ave NW Suite 550   Washington DC 20005
Ph: 202-408-7500 ▪ Fx: 202-408-8184

Association of American University Presses   www.aaupnet.org
71 W 23rd St Suite 901   New York NY 10010
Ph: 212-989-1010 ▪ Fx: 212-989-0275

Association of American Veterinary Medical Colleges   www.aavmc.org
1101 Vermont Ave NW Suite 710   Washington DC 20005
Ph: 202-371-9195 ▪ Fx: 202-842-0773

Association of Ancient Historians   www.trentu.ca/ahc/aah
City College of New York Dept of Foreign Languages &
   Literatures NAC 5-223   New York NY 10031
Ph: 212-650-6731 ▪ Fx: 718-796-4392

Association of Anglican Musicians   www.anglicanmusicians.org
28 Ashton Rd   Fort Mitchell KY 41017
Ph: 859-344-9308

Association for Applied Psychophysiology & Biofeedback   www.aapb.org
10200 W 44th Ave Suite 304   Wheat Ridge CO 80033
Ph: 303-422-8436 ▪ Fx: 303-422-8894 ▪ TF: 800-477-8892

Association for Applied & Therapeutic Humor   www.aath.org
1951 W Camelback Rd Suite 445   Phoenix AZ 85015
Ph: 602-995-1454 ▪ Fx: 602-995-1449

Association of Area Business Publications   www.bizpubs.org
4929 Wilshire Blvd Suite 428   Los Angeles CA 90010
Ph: 323-937-5514 ▪ Fx: 323-937-0959

Association of Armenian Information Professionals
139 Cedar St   Cliffside Park NJ 07010
Ph: 201-941-2266 ▪ Fx: 201-941-5110

Association of Art Editors   www.artedit.org
3912 Natchez Ave S   Saint Louis Park MN 55416
Ph: 952-922-1374

Association of Art Museum Directors   www.aamd.org
41 E 65th St   New York NY 10021
Ph: 212-249-4423 ▪ Fx: 212-535-5039

Association for Asian American Studies   www.aaastudies.org
Cornell Univ Asian American Studies Program 420 Rockefeller
   Hall   Ithaca NY 14853
Ph: 607-255-3320 ▪ Fx: 607-254-4996

Association of Asian/Pacific Community Health Organizations   www.aapcho.org
429 23rd St   Oakland CA 94612
Ph: 510-272-9536 ▪ Fx: 510-272-0817

Association for Asian Studies   www.aasianst.org
1021 E Huron St   Ann Arbor MI 48104
Ph: 734-665-2490 ▪ Fx: 734-665-3801

Association of Asphalt Paving Technologists   www.asphalttechnology.org
4711 Clark Ave Suite G   White Bear Lake MN 55110
Ph: 651-293-9188 ▪ Fx: 651-293-9193

Association for Assessment & Accreditation of Laboratory Animal   www.aaalac.org
Care International   11300 Rockville Pike Suite
   1211   Rockville MD 20852
Ph: 301-231-5353 ▪ Fx: 301-231-8282 ▪ TF: 800-926-0066

Association for Assessment in Counseling & Education   aac.ncat.edu
c/o American Counseling Assn 5999 Stevenson Ave   Alexandria
   VA 22304
Ph: 703-823-9800 ▪ Fx: 703-823-0252 ▪ TF: 800-347-6647

Association for Astrological Networking Inc   www.afan.org
8306 Wilshire Blvd PMB 537   Beverly Hills CA 90211
Ph: 800-578-2326

Association for Astrological Psychology   www.aaperry.com
360 Quietwood Dr   San Rafael CA 94903
Ph: 415-479-5812

Association of Attorney-Mediators   www.attorney-mediators.org
PO Box 741955   Dallas TX 75374
Ph: 972-669-8101 ▪ Fx: 972-669-8180 ▪ TF: 800-280-1368

Association of Automotive Aftermarket Distributors
5050 Poplar Ave Suite 2020   Memphis TN 38157
Ph: 901-682-9090 ▪ Fx: 901-682-9098 ▪ TF: 800-727-8112

Association of Avian Veterinarians   www.aav.org
PO Box 811720   Boca Raton FL 33481
Ph: 561-393-8901 ▪ Fx: 561-393-8902

Association of Baptists for Scouting   www.bsa.net/abs
PO Box 152079   Irving TX 75015
Ph: 254-799-4696

Association of Baptists for World Evangelism   www.abwe.org
PO Box 8585   Harrisburg PA 17105
Ph: 717-774-7000 ▪ Fx: 717-774-1919

Association of Battery Recyclers
PO Box 290286   Tampa FL 33687
Ph: 813-626-6151 ▪ Fx: 813-622-8388

Association for Behavior Analysis   www.abainternational.org
1219 S Park St   Kalamazoo MI 49001
Ph: 269-492-9310 ▪ Fx: 269-492-9316

Association for the Behavioral Sciences & Medical Education   www.absame.org
1460 N Center Rd   Burton MI 48509
Ph: 810-715-4365 ▪ Fx: 810-715-4371

Association for Biology Laboratory Education   www.zoo.toronto.edu/able
Univ of California Irvine Dept of Ecology & Evolutionary
   Biology   Irvine CA 92697
Ph: 949-824-5573 ▪ Fx: 949-824-2181

Association of Biomolecular Resource Facilities   www.abrf.org
2019 Galisteo St Bldg 1   Santa Fe NM 87505
Ph: 505-983-8102 ▪ Fx: 505-989-1073

Association of Bituminous Contractors
815 Connecticut Ave NW Suite 620   Washington DC 20006
Ph: 202-785-4440 ▪ Fx: 202-331-8049

Association of Black Anthropologists   www.aaanet.org/aba
c/o American Anthropological Assn 2200 Wilson Blvd Suite
   600   Arlington VA 22201
Ph: 703-528-1902 ▪ Fx: 703-528-3546

Association of Black Cardiologists   www.abcardio.org
6849 Peachtree Dunwoody Rd NE Bldg 2   Atlanta GA 30328
Ph: 678-302-4222 ▪ Fx: 678-302-4223

Association of Black Psychologists   www.abpsi.org
PO Box 55999   Washington DC 20040
Ph: 202-722-0808 ▪ Fx: 202-722-5941

Association of Black Sociologists   www.blacksociologists.org
4200 Wisconsin Ave NW PMB 106-257   Washington DC 20016
Ph: 202-365-1759

Association of Boarding Schools   www.schools.com
4455 Connecticut Ave NW Suite A-200   Washington DC 20008
Ph: 202-966-8705 ▪ Fx: 202-966-8708 ▪ TF: 800-541-5908

Association of Boards of Certification   www.abccert.org
208 E 5th St   Ames IA 50010
Ph: 515-232-3623 ▪ Fx: 515-232-3778

Association of Bone & Joint Surgeons   www.abjs.org
6300 N River Rd Suite 727   Rosemont IL 60018
Ph: 847-698-1636 ▪ Fx: 847-823-4921

Association of Booksellers for Children   www.abfc.com
3900 Sumac Cir   Middleton WI 53562
Ph: 608-836-6050 ▪ Fx: 608-836-1438

Association for Borderlands Studies   www.absborderlands.org
Univ of San Diego 5998 Alcala Pk   San Diego CA 92110
Ph: 619-260-4090 ▪ Fx: 619-260-4161

Association of Brethren Caregivers   www.brethren.org/abc
1451 Dundee Ave   Elgin IL 60120
Ph: 847-742-5100 ▪ Fx: 847-742-5160 ▪ TF: 800-323-8039

Association of Brewers   www.beertown.org
736 Pearl St   Boulder CO 80302
Ph: 303-447-0816 ▪ Fx: 303-447-2825 ▪ TF: 888-822-6273

Association of Bridal Consultants   www.bridalassn.com
200 Chestnutland Rd   New Milford CT 06776
Ph: 860-355-0464 ▪ Fx: 860-354-1404

Association for Bridge Construction & Design   www.abcdpittsburgh.org
PO Box 23264   Pittsburgh PA 15222
Ph: 412-281-9900 ▪ Fx: 412-281-2056

Association for Business Communication   www.businesscommunication.org
Baruch College 1 Bernard Baruch Way Box B8-240   New York
   NY 10010
Ph: 646-312-3727 ▪ Fx: 646-349-5297

Association for Calligraphic Arts   www.calligraphicarts.org
1223 Woodward Ave   South Bend IN 46616
Ph: 574-287-2189 ▪ Fx: 574-233-6229

Association of Camp Nurses   www.campnurse.org
8630 Thorsonveien Rd NE   Bemidji MN 56601
Ph: 218-586-2633 ▪ Fx: 218-586-3661

Association for Canadian Studies in the US   www.acsus.org
1317 F St NW Suite 920   Washington DC 20004
Ph: 202-393-2580 ▪ Fx: 202-393-2582

Association Canado-Americaine   www.aca-assurance.com
52 Concord St PO Box 989   Manchester NH 03105
Ph: 603-625-8577 ▪ Fx: 603-625-1214 ▪ TF: 800-222-8577

Association for Car & Truck Rental Independents & Franchisees   www.actif.org
4248 Park Glen Rd   Minneapolis MN 55416
Ph: 952-928-4645 ▪ Fx: 952-929-1318 ▪ TF: 888-200-2795

Association of Career Management Consulting Firms International   www.aocfi.org
204 'E' St NE   Washington DC 20002
Ph: 202-547-6344 ▪ Fx: 202-547-6348

Association of Career Professionals International   www.acpinternational.org
204 'E' St NE   Washington DC 20002
Ph: 202-547-6377 ▪ Fx: 202-547-6348

Association for Career & Technical Education   www.acteonline.org
1410 King St   Alexandria VA 22314
Ph: 703-683-3111 ▪ Fx: 703-683-7424 ▪ TF: 800-826-9972

Association of Celebrity Personal Assistants   www.celebrityassistants.org
914 Westwood Blvd PMB 507   Los Angeles CA 90024
Ph: 310-322-7755

Association of Certified Fraud Examiners   www.cfenet.com
716 West Ave   Austin TX 78701
Ph: 512-478-9070 ▪ Fx: 512-478-9297 ▪ TF: 800-245-3321

Association of Certified Professional Wedding Consultants   www.acpwc.com
7791 Prestwick Cir   San Jose CA 95135
Ph: 408-528-9000 ▪ Fx: 408-528-9333

Association of Certified Wedding Consultants   www.weddingconsulting.com
PO Box 261163   Plano TX 75026
Ph: 972-596-7450 ▪ Fx: 972-985-4442 ▪ TF: 800-520-2292

Association of Chartered Accountants in the US   www.acaus.com
341 Lafayette St Suite 4246   New York NY 10012
Ph: 212-334-2078 ▪ Fx: 212-431-5786

Association for Chemoreception Sciences   www.achems.org
744 Duparc Cir   Tallahassee FL 32312
Ph: 850-531-0854

Association for Childhood Education International   www.udel.edu/bateman/acei
17904 Georgia Ave Suite 215   Olney MD 20832
Ph: 301-570-2111 ▪ Fx: 301-570-2212 ▪ TF: 800-423-3563

Association for Children with Down Syndrome Inc   www.acds.org
4 Fern Pl   Plainview NY 11803
Ph: 516-933-4700 ▪ Fx: 516-933-9524

Association for Children for Enforcement of Support   www.childsupport-aces.org
PO Box 7842   Fredericksburg VA 22404
Ph: 800-738-2237 ▪ Fx: 800-739-2237

Association of Children's Museums   www.childrensmuseums.org
1300 L St NW Suite 975   Washington DC 20005
Ph: 202-898-1080 ▪ Fx: 202-898-1086

Association of Children's Prosthetic-Orthotic Clinics   www.acpoc.org
6300 N River Rd Suite 727   Rosemont IL 60018
Ph: 847-698-1637 ▪ Fx: 847-823-0536

Association of Chiropractic Colleges   www.chirocolleges.org
4424 Montgomery Ave Suite 102   Bethesda MD 20814
Ph: 301-652-5066 ▪ Fx: 301-913-9146

Association of Christian Coin Dealers & Collectors
PO Box 236   Wymore NE 68466
Ph: 402-645-3341 ▪ Fx: 402-645-3342

Association of Christian Librarians   www.acl.org
PO Box 4   Cedarville OH 45314
Ph: 937-766-2255 ▪ Fx: 937-766-2337

Association of Christian Schools International   www.acsi.org
731 Chapel Hills Dr   Colorado Springs CO 80920
Ph: 719-528-6906 ▪ Fx: 719-531-0631 ▪ TF: 800-367-0798

Association of Christian Therapists   www.actheals.org
6728 Old McLean Village Dr   McLean VA 22101
Ph: 703-556-9222 ▪ Fx: 703-556-8729

Association of Cinema & Video Laboratories Inc   www.acvl.org

Association of Civilian Technicians   www.actnat.com
12620 Lake Ridge Dr   Woodbridge VA 22192
Ph: 703-494-4845 ▪ Fx: 703-494-0961

Association for Clinical Pastoral Education   www.acpe.edu
1549 Clairmont Rd Suite 103   Decatur GA 30033
Ph: 404-320-1472 ▪ Fx: 404-320-0849

Association of Clinical Research Professionals   www.acrpnet.org
500 Montgomery St Suite 800   Alexandria VA 22314
Ph: 703-254-8100 ▪ Fx: 703-254-8101

Association of Clinical Scientists   www.clinicalscience.org
PO Box 1287   Middlebury VT 05753
Ph: 802-462-2507 ▪ Fx: 802-462-2673

Association for Coffee Mill Enthusiasts   www.millmania.com

Association of Collecting Clubs   www.collectors.org/ACC
18222 Flower Hill Way Suite 299   Gaithersburg MD 20879
Ph: 301-926-8663 ▪ Fx: 301-926-7648

Association of College Administration Professionals   www.acap.org
PO Box 1389   Staunton VA 24402
Ph: 540-885-1873 ▪ Fx: 540-885-6133

Association of College Honor Societies   www.achsnatl.org
4990 Northwind Dr Suite 140   East Lansing MI 48823
Ph: 517-351-8335 ▪ Fx: 517-351-8336

Association of College & Research Libraries   www.ala.org/acrl.html
50 E Huron St   Chicago IL 60611
Ph: 312-280-2519 ▪ Fx: 312-280-2520 ▪ TF: 800-545-2433

Association of College Unions International   www.acui.org
120 W 7th St 1 City Ctr Suite 200   Bloomington IN 47404
Ph: 812-855-8550 ▪ Fx: 812-855-0162

Association of College & University Auditors   www.acua.org
342 N Main St   West Hartford CT 06117
Ph: 860-586-7561 ▪ Fx: 860-586-7550

Association of College & University Housing Officers International   www.acuho.ohio-state.edu
941 Chatham Ln Suite 318   Columbus OH 43221
Ph: 614-292-0099 ▪ Fx: 614-292-3205

Association of College & University Museums & Galleries   www.acumg.org
Ursinus College 601 E Main St   Collegeville PA 19426
Ph: 610-409-3500 ▪ Fx: 610-409-3664

Association for College & University Religious Affairs   www.upenn.edu/chaplain/acura
Northwestern Univ Chaplain 1870 Sheridan Rd   Evanston IL 60208
Ph: 847-491-7256 ▪ Fx: 847-491-7353

Association of Collegiate Business Schools & Programs   www.acbsp.org
7007 College Blvd Suite 420   Overland Park KS 66211
Ph: 913-339-9356 ▪ Fx: 913-339-6226

Association of Collegiate Conference & Events Directors-International   acced-i.colostate.edu
Colorado State Univ 8037 Campus Delivery   Fort Collins CO 80523
Ph: 970-491-5151 ▪ Fx: 970-491-0667 ▪ TF: 877-502-2233

Association of Collegiate Schools of Architecture   www.acsa-arch.org
1735 New York Ave NW 3rd Fl   Washington DC 20006
Ph: 202-785-2324 ▪ Fx: 202-628-0448

Association of Collegiate Schools of Planning   www.acsp.org
6311 Mallard Trace   Tallahassee FL 32312
Ph: 850-385-2054 ▪ Fx: 850-385-2084

Association of Commercial Finance Attorneys   www.afca.cc
25 Hooks Ln Suite 302   Baltimore MD 21208
Ph: 410-486-2600 ▪ Fx: 410-486-8438

Association for Communication Excellence   www.aceweb.org
Univ of Florida Mowry Rd Bldg 116 PO Box 110811   Gainesville FL 32611
Ph: 352-392-9588 ▪ Fx: 352-392-7902

Association of Community Cancer Centers   www.accc-cancer.org
11600 Nebel St Suite 201   Rockville MD 20852
Ph: 301-984-9496 ▪ Fx: 301-770-1949

Association for Community College Trustees   www.acct.org
1233 20th St NW Suite 605   Washington DC 20036
Ph: 202-775-4667 ▪ Fx: 202-223-1297

Association for Community Health Nursing Educators   www.uncc.edu/achne
11 Cornell Rd   Latham NY 12110
Ph: 518-782-9400 ▪ Fx: 518-782-9530

Association for Community Organization & Social Administration   www.acosa.org
20560 Bensley Ave   Lynwood IL 60411
Ph: 708-757-4187 ▪ Fx: 708-757-4234

Association of Community Organizations for Reform Now   www.acorn.org
739 8th St SE   Washington DC 20003
Ph: 202-547-2500 ▪ Fx: 202-547-2483 ▪ TF: 877-552-2676

Association of Community Tribal Schools
616 4th Ave W   Sisseton SD 57262
Ph: 605-698-3953 ▪ Fx: 605-698-7686

Association for Commuter Transportation   www.actweb.org
PO Box 15542   Washington DC 20003
Ph: 202-393-3497 ▪ Fx: 202-546-2196

Association for Comparative Economic Studies   www.wdi.bus.umich.edu/aces
Arizona State Univ Dept of Economics PO Box 873806   Tempe AZ 85287
Ph: 480-965-6524 ▪ Fx: 480-965-0748

Association for Competitive Technology   www.actonline.org
1413 K St NW 12th Fl   Washington DC 20005
Ph: 202-331-2130 ▪ Fx: 202-331-2139

Association for Comprehensive Energy Psychology   www.energypsych.org
PO Box 910244   San Diego CA 92191
Ph: 858-748-5963 ▪ Fx: 858-270-0370

Association for Computational Linguistics   www.aclweb.org
3 Landmark Ctr   East Stroudsburg PA 18301
Ph: 570-476-8006 ▪ Fx: 570-476-0860

Association of Computer Support Specialists   www.acss.org

Association for Computing Machinery   www.acm.org
1515 Broadway 17th Fl   New York NY 10036
Ph: 212-869-7440 ▪ Fx: 212-944-1318 ▪ TF: 800-342-6626

Association of Concert Bands   www.acbands.org
6613 Cheryl Ann Dr   Independence OH 44131
Ph: 216-524-1897 ▪ TF: 800-726-8720

Association for Conflict Resolution   www.acrnet.org
1015 18th St NW Suite 1150   Washington DC 20036
Ph: 202-464-9700 ▪ Fx: 202-464-9720

Association of Conservation Engineers   mdc.mo.gov/engineering/ace
WY State Parks & Historical Sites Div 122 W 25th St 1st Fl E   Cheyenne WY 82002
Ph: 307-777-6325 ▪ Fx: 307-777-6472

Association for Consortium Leadership   www.acl.odu.edu
1417 43rd St   Norfolk VA 23529
Ph: 757-683-3183 ▪ Fx: 757-683-4515

Association of Construction Inspectors   www.iami.org/aci
1224 N Nokomis NE   Alexandria MN 56308
Ph: 320-763-6350 ▪ Fx: 320-763-9290

Association of Consulting Chemists & Chemical Engineers   www.chemconsult.org
PO Box 297   Sparta NJ 07871
Ph: 973-729-6671 ▪ Fx: 973-729-7088

Association of Consulting Foresters of America   www.acf-foresters.com
732 N Washington St Suite 4A   Alexandria VA 22314
Ph: 703-548-0990 ▪ Fx: 703-548-6395 ▪ TF: 888-540-8733

Association for Consumer Research   acrweb.org
PO Box 2310   Valdosta GA 31604
Ph: 229-244-2380 ▪ Fx: 229-244-7881

Association of Contingency Planners International   www.acp-international.com
7044 S 13th St   Oak Creek WI 53154
Ph: 414-768-8000 ▪ Fx: 414-768-8001

Association for Continuing Higher Education   www.acheinc.org
2001 Mabelene Rd   Charleston SC 29406
Ph: 843-574-6658 ▪ Fx: 843-574-6470 ▪ TF: 800-807-2243

Association for Continuing Legal Education www.aclea.org
PO Box 4646   Austin TX 78765
Ph: 512-453-4340 ▪ Fx: 512-451-2911

Association for Convention Marketing Executives www.acmenet.org
204 'E' St NE   Washington DC 20002
Ph: 202-547-6340 ▪ Fx: 202-547-6348

Association of Cooperative Educators www.wisc.edu/uwcc/ace/ace.html
PO Box 64047   Saint Paul MN 55164
Ph: 651-451-5481 ▪ Fx: 651-451-5073

Association of Corporate Counsel www.acca.com
1025 Connecticut Ave NW Suite 200   Washington DC 20036
Ph: 202-293-4103 ▪ Fx: 202-293-4701

Association for Corporate Growth www.acg.org
1926 Waukegan Rd Suite 1   Glenview IL 60025
Ph: 847-657-6730 ▪ Fx: 847-657-6819 ▪ TF: 800-699-1331

Association of Corporate Travel Executives www.acte.org
515 King St Suite 340   Alexandria VA 22314
Ph: 703-683-5322 ▪ Fx: 703-683-2720 ▪ TF: 800-228-3669

Association for Correctional Research & Information www.happenings.com/lbennett
Management   2717 Cottage Way Suite 15   Sacramento CA
95825
Ph: 916-487-9334 ▪ Fx: 916-487-9929

Association for Counselor Education & Supervision www.acesonline.net
c/o American Counseling Assn 5999 Stevenson Ave   Alexandria
VA 22304
Ph: 703-823-9800 ▪ Fx: 703-823-0252 ▪ TF: 800-347-6647

Association for Counselors & Educators in Government
c/o American Counseling Assn 5999 Stevenson Ave   Alexandria
VA 22304
Ph: 703-823-9800 ▪ Fx: 703-823-0252

Association for Couples in Marriage Enrichment www.bettermarriages.org
PO Box 10596   Winston-Salem NC 27108
Ph: 336-724-1526 ▪ Fx: 336-721-4746 ▪ TF: 800-634-8325

Association of Coupon Professionals www.couponpros.org
200 E Howard St Suite 280   Des Plaines IL 60018
Ph: 847-297-7773

Association of Crafts & Creative Industries www.accicrafts.org
1100-H Brandywine Blvd PO Box 3388   Zanesville OH 43702
Ph: 740-452-4541 ▪ Fx: 740-452-2552

Association of Credit Union Internal Auditors www.acuia.org
PO Box 1926   Columbus OH 43216
Ph: 614-221-9702 ▪ Fx: 614-221-2335 ▪ TF: 866-254-8128

Association of Cuban Engineers www.a-i-c.org
PO Box 557575   Miami FL 33255
Ph: 305-597-9858

Association of Cultural Economics International www.acei.neu.edu
Northeastern Univ Dept of Economics 301 Lake Hall   Boston
MA 02115
Ph: 617-373-2839 ▪ Fx: 617-373-3640

Association for Death Education & Counseling www.adec.org
342 N Main St   West Hartford CT 06117
Ph: 860-586-7503 ▪ Fx: 860-586-7550

Association of Defensive Spray Manufacturers www.pepperspray.org
917 Locust St Suite 1100   Saint Louis MO 63101
Ph: 314-241-1445 ▪ Fx: 314-241-1449

Association of Departments of English www.ade.org
26 Broadway 3rd Fl   New York NY 10004
Ph: 646-576-5130 ▪ Fx: 646-834-4045

Association of Departments of Foreign Languages www.adfl.org
26 Broadway 3rd Fl   New York NY 10004
Ph: 646-576-5140 ▪ Fx: 646-493-0030

Association of Desk & Derrick Clubs www.addc.org
5153 E 51st St Suite 107   Tulsa OK 74135
Ph: 918-622-1749 ▪ Fx: 918-622-1675

Association of Destination Management Executives www.adme.org
3401 Quebec St Suite 4050   Denver CO 80207
Ph: 303-394-3905 ▪ Fx: 303-394-3450

Association for the Development of Human Potential
PO Box 3543   Spokane WA 99220
Ph: 509-838-6652 ▪ TF: 800-251-9273

Association for the Development of Religious Information Systems
PO Box 210735   Nashville TN 37221
Ph: 615-429-8744

Association of Diesel Specialists www.diesel.org
10 Laboratory Dr PO Box 13966   Research Triangle Park NC
27709
Ph: 919-549-4800 ▪ Fx: 919-549-4824

Association for Direct Instruction www.adihome.org
PO Box 10252   Eugene OR 97440
Ph: 541-485-1293 ▪ Fx: 541-683-7543

Association of Direct Response Fundraising Counsel www.adrfco.org
1612 K St NW Suite 510   Washington DC 20006
Ph: 202-293-9640 ▪ Fx: 202-887-9699

Association of Directory Marketing www.admworks.org
1187 Thorn Run Rd Suite 630   Moon Township PA 15108
Ph: 412-269-0663 ▪ Fx: 412-269-0655

Association of Directory Publishers www.adp.org
116 Cass St   Traverse City MI 49684
Ph: 800-267-9002 ▪ Fx: 231-486-2182

Association of Diving Contractors International www.adc-usa.org
5206 FM 1960 W Suite 202   Houston TX 77069
Ph: 281-893-8388 ▪ Fx: 281-893-5118

Association for Documentary Editing etext.virginia.edu/ade
Princeton Univ   Princeton NJ 08544
Ph: 609-258-5687 ▪ Fx: 609-258-1630

Association for Dressings & Sauces www.dressings-sauces.org
5775 Peachtree-Dunwoody Rd Bldg G Suite 500   Atlanta GA
30342
Ph: 404-252-3663 ▪ Fx: 404-252-0774

Association of Earth Science Editors www.aese.org

Association of Edison Illuminating Companies www.aeic.org
600 N 18th St PO Box 2641   Birmingham AL 35291
Ph: 205-257-2530 ▪ Fx: 205-257-2540

Association for Education in Journalism & Mass Communication www.aejmc.org/
234 Outlet Pointe Blvd Suite A   Columbia SC 29210
Ph: 803-798-0271 ▪ Fx: 803-772-3509

Association of Education Practitioners & Providers www.aepp.org/links/links.html
104 W Main St Suite 101 PO Box 348   Watertown WI 53094
Ph: 920-206-1474 ▪ Fx: 920-206-1475 ▪ TF: 800-252-3280

Association of Education & Rehabilitation of the Blind & www.aerbvi.org
Visually Impaired   1703 N Beauregard St Suite
440   Alexandria VA 22311
Ph: 703-671-4500 ▪ Fx: 703-671-6391

Association for the Education of Teachers of Science aets.chem.pitt.edu
East Carolina Univ College of Education Austin
324-A   Greenville NC 27858
Ph: 252-328-6736 ▪ Fx: 252-328-6218

Association for Educational Communications & Technology www.aect.org
1800 N Stonelake Dr Suite 2   Bloomington IN 47408
Ph: 812-335-7675 ▪ Fx: 812-335-7678 ▪ TF: 877-677-2328

Association of Educational Publishers www.edpress.org
510 Heron Dr Suite 309   Logan Township NJ 08085
Ph: 856-241-7772 ▪ Fx: 856-241-0709

Association of Educational Therapists www.aetonline.org
1804 W Burbank Blvd   Burbank CA 91506
Ph: 818-843-1183 ▪ Fx: 818-843-7423

Association of Educators in Radiological Sciences www.aers.org
PO Box 90204   Albuquerque NM 87199
Ph: 505-823-4740

Association for Efficient Environmental Energy Systems www.aeees.org
PO Box 598   Davis CA 95617
Ph: 530-750-0135 ▪ Fx: 530-750-0137

Association of Eminent Domain Professionals www.aedp.org
PO Box 6721   West Palm Beach FL 33405
Ph: 561-655-4144 ▪ Fx: 561-659-1824

Association of Energy Engineers www.aeecenter.org
4025 Pleasantdale Rd Suite 420   Atlanta GA 30340
Ph: 770-447-5083 ▪ Fx: 770-446-3969

Association of Energy Service Companies www.aesc.net
10200 Richmond Ave Suite 253   Houston TX 77042
Ph: 713-781-0758 ▪ Fx: 713-781-7542 ▪ TF: 800-692-0771

Association of Energy Services Professionals International www.aesp.org
17610 128th Trail N   Jupiter FL 33478
Ph: 561-575-2334 ▪ Fx: 561-575-4688

Association of Engineering Geologists www.aegweb.org
PO Box 460518   Denver CO 80246
Ph: 303-757-2926 ▪ Fx: 303-757-2969

Association for Engineering Graphics & Imaging Systems
800 Enterprise Dr Suite 202   Oak Brook IL 60523
Ph: 630-574-8200 ▪ Fx: 630-571-4731

Association for Enterprise Integration www.afei.org
2111 Wilson Blvd Suite 400   Arlington VA 22201
Ph: 703-247-9474 ▪ Fx: 703-522-3192

Association for Enterprise Opportunity www.microenterpriseworks.org/
1601 N Kent St Suite 1101   Arlington VA 22209
Ph: 703-841-7760 ▪ Fx: 703-841-7748

Association of Environmental Engineering & Science Professors www.aeesp.org

Association for Environmental Health & Sciences www.aehs.com
150 S Fearing St   Amherst MA 01002
Ph: 413-549-5170 ▪ Fx: 413-549-0059

Association of Environmental & Resource Economists www.aere.org/
1616 P St NW Rm 400   Washington DC 20036
Ph: 202-328-5077 ▪ Fx: 202-939-3460

Association of Episcopal Colleges www.cuac.org/aec
815 2nd Ave Suite 315   New York NY 10017
Ph: 212-716-6148 ▪ Fx: 212-986-5039

Association of Equipment Management Professionals www.equipment.org
410 20th St Suite 102   Glenwood Springs CO 81601
Ph: 970-384-0510 ▪ Fx: 970-384-0512

Association of Equipment Manufacturers www.aem.org
111 E Wisconsin Ave Suite 1000   Milwaukee WI 53202
Ph: 414-272-0943 ▪ Fx: 414-272-1170

Association of Executive Search Consultants www.aesc.org
12 E 41st St 17th Fl   New York NY 10017
Ph: 212-398-9556 ▪ Fx: 212-398-9560

Association Executives, American Society of www.asaenet.org
1575 'I' St NW   Washington DC 20005
Ph: 202-626-2723 ▪ Fx: 202-371-8825 ▪ TF: 888-950-2723

Association for Experiential Education www.aee.org
2305 Canyon Blvd Suite 100   Boulder CO 80302
Ph: 303-440-8844 ▪ Fx: 303-440-9581

Association for Facilities Engineering www.afe.org
8180 Corporate Park Dr Suite 305   Cincinnati OH 45242
Ph: 513-489-2473 ▪ Fx: 513-247-7422

Association of Family & Conciliation Courts www.afccnet.org
6515 Grand Teton Plaza Suite 210   Madison WI 53719
Ph: 608-664-3750 ▪ Fx: 608-664-3751

Association of Family Practice Residency Directors www.afprd.org
c/o Allen Press 11400 Tomahawk Creek Pkwy Suite
670   Leawood KS 66211
Ph: 913-906-6000 ▪ Fx: 913-906-6105 ▪ TF: 800-274-2237

Association of Farmworker Opportunity Programs www.afop.org
4350 N Fairfax Dr Suite 410   Arlington VA 22203
Ph: 703-528-4141 ▪ Fx: 703-528-4145

Association of Federal Communications Consulting Engineers www.afcce.org

Association for Federal Information Resources Management www.affirm.org
PO Box 2851   Washington DC 20013
Ph: 202-208-2780

Association for Feminist Anthropology　　　sscl.berkeley.edu/~afaweb
c/o American Anthropological Assn 2200 Wilson Blvd Suite
600　Arlington VA 22201
Ph: 703-528-1902 ▪ Fx: 703-528-3546

Association of Field Ornithologists　　　www.afonet.org
PO Box 1897　Lawrence KS 66044
Ph: 785-843-1221 ▪ Fx: 785-843-1274

Association of Film Commissioners International　　www.afci.org
314 N Main St Suite 307　Helena MT 59601
Ph: 406-495-8040 ▪ Fx: 406-495-8039

Association of Finance & Insurance Professionals　　www.afip.com
PO Box 212003　Bedford TX 76095
Ph: 817-428-2434 ▪ Fx: 817-581-4609

Association for Financial Counseling & Planning Education　www.afcpe.org
2112 Arlington Ave Suite H　Upper Arlington OH 43221
Ph: 614-485-9650 ▪ Fx: 614-485-9621

Association of Financial Guaranty Insurers　　www.afgi.org
c/o TowersGroup 15 W 39th St 14th Fl　New York NY 10018
Ph: 212-354-5020 ▪ Fx: 212-391-6920

Association for Financial Professionals　　www.afponline.org
7315 Wisconsin Ave Suite 600-W　Bethesda MD 20814
Ph: 301-907-2862 ▪ Fx: 301-907-2864

Association for Financial Technology　　www.fitech.org
5828 Zarley St Suite C　New Albany OH 43054
Ph: 614-895-1208 ▪ Fx: 614-895-3466

Association of Firearm & Tool Mark Examiners　　www.afte.org

Association of Flight Attendants　　www.afanet.org
1275 K St NW Suite 500　Washington DC 20005
Ph: 202-712-9799 ▪ Fx: 202-712-9798 ▪ TF: 800-424-2401

Association of Food & Drug Officials　　www.afdo.org
2550 Kingston Rd Suite 311　York PA 17402
Ph: 717-757-2888 ▪ Fx: 717-755-8089

Association of Food Industries Inc　　www.afius.org
3301 Rt 66 Bldg C Suite 205　Neptune NJ 08005
Ph: 732-922-3008 ▪ Fx: 732-922-3590

Association of Foreign Investors in Real Estate　　www.afire.org
1300 Pennsylvania Ave NW　Washington DC 20004
Ph: 202-312-1400 ▪ Fx: 202-312-1401

Association of Former Intelligence Officers　　www.afio.com
6723 Whittier Ave Suite 303A　McLean VA 22101
Ph: 703-790-0320 ▪ Fx: 703-790-0264

Association of Former OSI Special Agents Inc　　www.afosisa-ncc.org
PO Box 52315　Springfield VA 22152
Ph: 703-978-6198

Association of Fraternity Advisors　　www.fraternityadvisors.org
9640 N Augusta Dr Suite 433　Carmel IN 46032
Ph: 317-876-1632 ▪ Fx: 317-876-3981

Association of Free Community Papers　　www.afcp.org
1634 Miner St PO Box 1989　Idaho Springs CO 80452
Ph: 877-203-2327

Association of Freestanding Radiation Oncology Centers　www.afroc.org
1875 'I' St NW 12th Fl　Washington DC 20006
Ph: 888-334-4542 ▪ Fx: 202-466-5938

Association of Fulfillment Services　　www.associationfulfillment.com
3030 Malmo Dr　Arlington Heights IL 60005
Ph: 847-364-1222 ▪ Fx: 847-364-1268

Association of Full Gospel Women Clergy　　afgwc.org
PO Box 2628　Landover MD 20784
Ph: 301-879-6958

Association of Fund-Raising Distributors & Suppliers　　www.afrds.org
5775 Peachtree-Dunwoody Rd Bldg G Suite 500　Atlanta GA
30342
Ph: 404-252-3663 ▪ Fx: 404-252-0774

Association of Fundraising Professionals　　www.afpnet.org
1101 King St Suite 700　Alexandria VA 22314
Ph: 703-684-0410 ▪ Fx: 703-684-0404 ▪ TF: 800-666-3863

Association for Gay Lesbian & Bisexual Issues in Counseling　www.aglbic.org
c/o American Counseling Assn 5999 Stevenson Ave　Alexandria
VA 22304
Ph: 703-823-9800 ▪ Fx: 703-823-0252 ▪ TF: 800-347-6647

Association of Gay & Lesbian Psychiatrists　　www.aglp.org
4514 Chester Ave　Philadelphia PA 19143
Ph: 215-222-2800 ▪ Fx: 215-222-3881

Association for Gender Equity Leadership in Education　www.agele.org
317 S Division St PMB 54　Ann Arbor MI 48104
Ph: 734-449-5066

Association for General & Liberal Studies　　www.bsu.edu/web/agls
Ball State Univ English Dept RB 2109　Muncie IN 47306
Ph: 765-285-8406

Association of Genetic Technologists　　www.agt-info.org
PO Box 15945-288　Lenexa KS 66285
Ph: 913-541-0497 ▪ Fx: 913-599-5340

Association for Gerontology in Higher Education　　www.aghe.org
1030 15th St NW Suite 240　Washington DC 20005
Ph: 202-289-9806 ▪ Fx: 202-289-9824

Association for Gifted & Talented Students
PO Box 16037　Baton Rouge LA 70896
Ph: 504-388-2469 ▪ Fx: 504-388-1375 ▪ TF: 800-626-8811

Association of Girl Scout Executive Staff
222 S Riverside Plaza Suite 2120　Chicago IL 60606
Ph: 312-416-2500 ▪ Fx: 312-416-2932

Association of Golf Merchandisers　　www.agmgolf.org
PO Box 7247　Phoenix AZ 85011
Ph: 602-604-8250 ▪ Fx: 602-604-8251

Association of Gospel Rescue Missions　　www.agrm.org
1045 Swift St　Kansas City MO 64116
Ph: 816-471-8020 ▪ Fx: 816-471-3718 ▪ TF: 800-624-5156

Association of Governing Boards of Universities & Colleges　www.agb.org
1 Dupont Cir NW Suite 400　Washington DC 20036
Ph: 202-296-8400 ▪ Fx: 202-223-7053 ▪ TF: 800-356-6317

Association of Government Accountants　　www.agacgfm.org
2208 Mt Vernon Ave　Alexandria VA 22301
Ph: 703-684-6931 ▪ Fx: 703-548-9367 ▪ TF: 800-242-7211

Association for Governmental Leasing & Finance　　www.aglf.org
1255 23rd St NW Suite 200　Washington DC 20037
Ph: 202-742-2453 ▪ Fx: 202-833-3636

Association of Grace Brethren Ministers　　www.fgbc.org
1909 Neal Dr　Wooster OH 44691
Ph: 330-345-7826 ▪ Fx: 330-345-3348

Association of Graduate Liberal Studies Programs　www.udel.edu/aglsp
Univ of Delaware 219 McDowell Hall　Newark DE 19716
Ph: 302-831-4218 ▪ Fx: 302-831-4461

Association for Graphic Arts Training　　www.agatweb.org

Association of Graphic Communications　　www.agcomm.org
330 7th Ave 9th Fl　New York NY 10001
Ph: 212-279-2100 ▪ Fx: 212-279-5381

Association for Gravestone Studies　　www.gravestonestudies.org
278 Main St Suite 207　Greenfield MA 01301
Ph: 413-772-0836

Association of Halfway House Alcoholism Programs of North　www.ahhap.org
America Inc　860 N Center St　Mesa AZ 85201
Ph: 480-610-8300 ▪ Fx: 480-964-2004 ▪ TF: 800-861-0599

Association of Health Facility Survey Agencies　　www.ahfsa.org

Association of Health Insurance Advisors　　www.ahia.net
2901 Telestar Ct　Falls Church VA 22042
Ph: 703-770-8200 ▪ Fx: 703-770-8201

Association of Healthcare Internal Auditors　　www.ahia.org
PO Box 449　Onsted MI 49265
Ph: 517-467-7729 ▪ Fx: 517-467-6104 ▪ TF: 888-275-2442

Association for Healthcare Philanthropy　　www.ahp.org
313 Park Ave Suite 400　Falls Church VA 22046
Ph: 703-532-6243 ▪ Fx: 703-532-7170

Association of Hebrew Catholics　　www.hebrewcatholic.org
PO Box 980280　Ypsilanti MI 48198
Ph: 734-480-4242 ▪ Fx: 734-480-8990

Association Henri Capitant　　host.law.lsu.edu/ahclouisiana
Louisiana State Univ Paul M Hebert Law Ctr　Baton Rouge LA
70803
Ph: 225-578-1126 ▪ Fx: 225-578-3677

Association for High Technology Distribution　　www.ahtd.org
1900 Arch St　Philadelphia PA 19103
Ph: 215-564-3484 ▪ Fx: 215-963-9784

Association on Higher Education & Disability　　www.ahead.org
PO Box 540666　Waltham MA 02454
Ph: 781-788-0003 ▪ Fx: 781-788-0033

Association of Hispanic Advertising Agencies　　www.ahaa.org
8201 Greensboro Dr Suite 300　McLean VA 22102
Ph: 703-610-9014 ▪ Fx: 703-610-9005

Association of Hispanic Arts Inc　　www.latinoarts.org
155 Ave of the Americas 14th Fl　New York NY 10013
Ph: 212-727-7227 ▪ Fx: 212-427-0549

Association for the History of Chiropractic　　www.chiroweb.com/ahc
1000 Brady St　Davenport IA 52803
Ph: 563-884-5855 ▪ Fx: 563-884-5616

Association of Home Appliance Manufacturers　　www.aham.org
1111 19th St NW Suite 402　Washington DC 20036
Ph: 202-872-5955 ▪ Fx: 202-872-9354

Association of Home Appliance Manufacturers PAC
1111 19th St NW Suite 402　Washington DC 20036
Ph: 202-872-5955 ▪ Fx: 202-872-9354

Association of Home Office Underwriters　　www.alu-web.org/ahou
2300 Windy Ridge Pkwy Suite 600　Atlanta GA 30339
Ph: 770-984-3715 ▪ Fx: 770-984-6418

Association for Hospital Medical Education　　www.ahme.org
419 Beulah Rd　Pittsburgh PA 15235
Ph: 412-244-9302 ▪ Fx: 412-243-4693 ▪ TF: 866-617-4780

Association for Humanistic Psychology　　ahpweb.org
1516 Oak St Suite 320A　Alameda CA 94501
Ph: 510-769-6495 ▪ Fx: 510-769-6433

Association of Humanistic Rabbis　　www.iishj.org
28611 W 12 Mile Rd　Farmington Hills MI 48334
Ph: 248-476-9532 ▪ Fx: 248-476-8509

Association for Humanistic Sociology　　www.humanistsoc.org

Association of Image Consultants International　　www.aici.org
2695 Villa Creek Dr Suite 260　Dallas TX 75234
Ph: 972-755-1503 ▪ Fx: 972-755-2561 ▪ TF: 800-383-8831

Association of Independent Colleges of Art & Design　www.aicad.org
3957 2nd St　San Francisco CA 94114
Ph: 415-642-8595 ▪ Fx: 415-642-8590

Association of Independent Commercial Producers　　www.aicp.com
3 W 18th St 5th Fl　New York NY 10010
Ph: 212-929-3000 ▪ Fx: 212-929-3359

Association of Independent Corrugated Converters　www.aiccbox.org
113 S West St PO Box 25708　Alexandria VA 22313
Ph: 703-836-2422 ▪ Fx: 703-836-2795 ▪ TF: 877-836-2422

Association of Independent Information Professionals　　www.aiip.org
8550 United Plaza Blvd Suite 1001　Baton Rouge LA 70809
Ph: 225-408-4400 ▪ Fx: 225-922-4611 ▪ TF: 888-544-2447

Association of Independent Mailing Equipment Dealers　www.aimedweb.org
949 Winding Brook Ln　Walnut CA 91789
Ph: 909-444-9680 ▪ Fx: 909-594-9743 ▪ TF: 888-750-6245

Association of Independent Manufacturers'/Representatives Inc　www.aimr.net
PO Box 3467　Laguna Hills CA 92654
Ph: 949-859-2884 ▪ Fx: 949-855-2973 ▪ TF: 866-729-0975

Association for Independent Music　　www.afim.net
PO Box 16754　Rocky River OH 44116
Ph: 440-333-2208 ▪ Fx: 440-333-2280

Association of Independent Music Publishers www.aimp.org
PO Box 69473   Los Angeles CA 90069
Ph: 818-771-7301

Association of Independent Research Institutes www.airi.org
DAI Management Inc PO Box 844   Westminster MD 21158
Ph: 410-751-8900 ▪ Fx: 410-751-2662

Association of Independent Trust Companies www.aitco.net
710 E Ogden Ave Suite 600   Naperville IL 60563
Ph: 630-579-3290 ▪ Fx: 630-369-2488

Association of Independent Video & Filmmakers www.aivf.org
304 Hudson St 6th Fl   New York NY 10013
Ph: 212-807-1400 ▪ Fx: 212-463-8519

Association for India's Development www.aidindia.org
PO Box F   College Park MD 20741
Ph: 301-209-0508 ▪ Fx: 301-513-0565

Association of Industrial Metallizers Coaters & Laminators aimcal.org
2166 Gold Hill Rd   Fort Mill SC 29708
Ph: 803-802-7820 ▪ Fx: 803-802-7821

Association of Industrial Real Estate Brokers www.aireb.org
710 E Ogden Ave Suite 600   Naperville IL 60563
Ph: 630-579-3254 ▪ Fx: 630-369-2488

Association for Informal Logic & Critical Thinking ailact.mcmaster.ca

Association for Information & Dissemination Centers www.asidic.org
PO Box 3212   Maple Glen PA 19002
Ph: 215-654-9129

Association for Information Media & Equipment www.aime.org
PO Box 9844   Cedar Rapids IA 52409
Ph: 319-654-0608 ▪ Fx: 319-654-0609

Association for Information Systems www.aisnet.org
PO Box 2712   Atlanta GA 30301
Ph: 404-651-0348 ▪ Fx: 404-651-4938

Association of Information Technology Professionals www.aitp.org
401 N Michigan Ave Suite 2200   Chicago IL 60611
Ph: 312-245-1070 ▪ Fx: 312-527-6636 ▪ TF: 800-224-9371

Association of Ingersoll-Rand Distributors www.aird.org
1300 Sumner Ave   Cleveland OH 44115
Ph: 216-241-7333 ▪ Fx: 216-241-0105

Association of Insolvency & Restructuring Advisors www.airacira.org
221 Stewart Ave Suite 207   Medford OR 97501
Ph: 541-858-1665 ▪ Fx: 541-858-9187

Association for Institutional Research www.airweb.org
Florida State Univ 222 Stone Bldg   Tallahassee FL 32306
Ph: 850-644-4470 ▪ Fx: 850-644-8824

Association of Insurance Compliance Professionals www.aicp.net
12110 Sunset Hills Rd Suite 130   Reston VA 20190
Ph: 703-234-4074 ▪ Fx: 703-435-4390

Association for Integrative Medicine www.integrativemedicine.org
Box 1   Mont Clare PA 19453
Ph: 610-933-8145 ▪ Fx: 610-983-9162

Association for Integrative Studies www.units.muohio.edu/aisorg
Miami Univ School of Interdisciplinary Studies   Oxford OH
45056
Ph: 513-529-2213

Association for Interactive Marketing www.interactivehq.org
1430 Broadway 8th Fl   New York NY 10018
Ph: 212-790-1404 ▪ Fx: 212-391-9233 ▪ TF: 888-337-0008

Association of Internal Management Consultants Inc www.aimc.org
86 Clarendon Ave   Rutland VT 05777
Ph: 802-438-2882 ▪ Fx: 802-438-9859

Association for International Agriculture & Rural Development aiard.org
Mississippi State Univ Dept of Agricultural Economics Box
5187   Mississippi State MS 39762
Ph: 662-325-0549 ▪ Fx: 662-325-8777

Association of International Automobile Manufacturers www.aiam.org
1001 19th St N Suite 1200   Arlington VA 22209
Ph: 703-525-7788 ▪ Fx: 703-525-8817

Association of International Education Administrators wings.buffalo.edu/intled/aiea
Univ at Buffalo Office of International Education 411 Capen Hall
Box 601604   Buffalo NY 14260
Ph: 716-645-2368 ▪ Fx: 716-645-2528

Association of International Health Researchers
2665 Pleasant Valley Rd   Mobile AL 36606
Ph: 251-473-3946

Association of International Photography Art www.artline.com/associations/ipa/ipa.html
Dealers 1609 Connecticut Ave NW Suite 200   Washington DC
20009
Ph: 202-986-0105 ▪ Fx: 202-986-0448

Association for International Practical Training www.aipt.org
10400 Little Patuxent Pkwy Suite 250   Columbia MD 21044
Ph: 410-997-2200 ▪ Fx: 410-992-3924

Association for Investment Management & Research www.aimr.org
560 Ray C Hunt Dr PO Box 3668   Charlottesville VA 22903
Ph: 434-951-5499 ▪ Fx: 434-951-5262 ▪ TF: 800-247-8132

Association of Investment Management Sales Executives www.aimse.com
1320 19th St NW Suite 300   Washington DC 20036
Ph: 202-296-3560 ▪ Fx: 202-371-8977 ▪ TF: 800-343-5659

Association of Iron & Steel Engineers www.aise.org
3 Gateway Ctr Suite 1900   Pittsburgh PA 15222
Ph: 412-281-6323 ▪ Fx: 412-281-4657 ▪ TF: 800-966-6323

Association of Islamic Charitable Projects www.aicp.org
4431 Walnut St   Philadelphia PA 19104
Ph: 215-387-8888 ▪ Fx: 215-387-3815

Association of Jesuit Colleges & Universities www.ajcunet.edu
1 Dupont Cir NW Suite 405   Washington DC 20036
Ph: 202-862-9893 ▪ Fx: 202-862-8523

Association of Jewish Aging Services www.ajas.org
316 Pennsylvania Ave SE Suite 402   Washington DC 20003
Ph: 202-543-7500 ▪ Fx: 202-543-4090

Association of Jewish Center Professionals www.ajcp.org
15 E 26th St 10th Fl   New York NY 10010
Ph: 212-532-4949 ▪ Fx: 212-481-4174

Association of Jewish Family & Children's Agencies www.ajfca.org
557 Cranbury Rd Suite 2   East Brunswick NJ 08816
Ph: 732-432-7120 ▪ Fx: 732-432-7127 ▪ TF: 800-634-7346

Association of Jewish Libraries www.jewishlibraries.org
15 E 26th St Rm 1034   New York NY 10010
Ph: 212-725-5359

Association of Jewish Sponsored Camps www.jewishcamps.org
130 E 59th St   New York NY 10022
Ph: 212-751-0477 ▪ Fx: 212-755-9183

Association for Jewish Studies www.brandeis.edu/ajs
Center for Jewish History 15 W 16th St   New York NY 10011
Ph: 917-606-8249 ▪ Fx: 917-606-8282

Association of Junior Leagues International Inc www.ajli.org
132 W 31st St 11th Fl   New York NY 10001
Ph: 212-683-1515 ▪ Fx: 212-481-7196 ▪ TF: 800-955-3248

Association of Labor Relations Agencies www.alra.org

Association of Latina & Latino Anthropologists sbsi.csumb.edu/ALLA
c/o American Anthropological Assn 2200 Wilson Blvd Suite
600   Arlington VA 22201
Ph: 703-528-1902 ▪ Fx: 703-528-3546

Association of Latino Professionals in Finance & Accounting www.alpfa.org
510 W 6th St Suite 400   Los Angeles CA 90014
Ph: 213-243-0004 ▪ Fx: 213-243-0006

Association of Legal Administrators www.alanet.org
175 E Hawthorn Pkwy Suite 325   Vernon Hills IL 60061
Ph: 847-816-1212 ▪ Fx: 847-816-1213

Association for Library Collections & Technical Services www.ala.org/alcts
50 E Huron St   Chicago IL 60611
Ph: 312-280-5038 ▪ Fx: 312-280-5033 ▪ TF: 800-545-2433

Association for Library & Information Science Education www.alise.org
1009 Commerce Pk Suite 150   Oak Ridge TN 37839
Ph: 865-425-0155 ▪ Fx: 865-481-0390

Association for Library Service to Children www.ala.org/alsc
50 E Huron St   Chicago IL 60611
Ph: 312-280-2163 ▪ Fx: 312-944-7671 ▪ TF: 800-545-2433

Association for Library Trustees & Advocates www.ala.org/alta
50 E Huron St   Chicago IL 60611
Ph: 312-280-2161 ▪ Fx: 312-280-3256 ▪ TF: 800-545-2433

Association for Literary Scholars & Critics www.bu.edu/literary
Boston Univ 650 Beacon St Suite 510   Boston MA 02215
Ph: 617-358-1990 ▪ Fx: 617-358-1995

Association for Living History Farm & Agricultural Museums www.alhfam.org
8774 Rt 45 NW   North Bloomfield OH 44450
Ph: 440-685-4410

Association of Local Air Pollution Control Officials www.cleanairworld.org
444 N Capitol St NW Suite 307   Washington DC 20001
Ph: 202-624-7864 ▪ Fx: 202-624-7863

Association for Local Telecommunications Services www.alts.org
888 17th St NW 12th Fl   Washington DC 20006
Ph: 202-969-2587 ▪ Fx: 202-969-2581

Association of Machinery & Equipment Appraisers www.amea.org
315 S Patrick St   Alexandria VA 22314
Ph: 703-836-7900 ▪ Fx: 703-836-9303 ▪ TF: 800-537-8629

Association for Macular Diseases Inc www.macula.org/association/about.html
210 E 64th St 8th Fl   New York NY 10021
Ph: 212-605-3719 ▪ Fx: 212-628-0695

Association of Major City/County Building Officials
505 Huntmar Park Dr Suite 210   Herndon VA 20170
Ph: 703-481-2038 ▪ Fx: 703-481-3596

Association of Managed Care Dentists www.amcd.org
1223 Wilshire Blvd Suite 483   Santa Monica CA 90403
Ph: 310-453-3439 ▪ Fx: 310-453-7895 ▪ TF: 800-864-6848

Association of Management www.aom-iaom.org
920 S Battlefield Blvd Suite 100   Chesapeake VA 23322
Ph: 757-482-2273 ▪ Fx: 757-482-0325

Association Management Companies, International Association of www.iaamc.org
414 Plaza Dr Suite 209   Westmont IL 60559
Ph: 630-655-1669 ▪ Fx: 630-655-0391

Association of Management Consulting Firms www.amcf.org
380 Lexington Ave Suite 1700   New York NY 10168
Ph: 212-551-7887 ▪ Fx: 212-551-7934

Association for Management Information in Financial Services www.amifs.org
3895 Fairfax Ct   Atlanta GA 30339
Ph: 770-444-3557 ▪ Fx: 770-444-9084

Association of Manpower Franchise Owners
1123 N Water St   Milwaukee WI 53202
Ph: 414-276-2651 ▪ Fx: 414-276-7704

Association for Manufacturing Excellence www.trainingforum.com/ASN/AME
380 W Palatine Rd Suite 7   Wheeling IL 60090
Ph: 847-520-3282 ▪ Fx: 847-520-0163

Association for Manufacturing Technology www.amtonline.org
7901 Westpark Dr   McLean VA 22102
Ph: 703-893-2900 ▪ Fx: 703-893-1151 ▪ TF: 800-524-0475

Association of Marine Technicians www.am-tech.org
455 Knollwood Terr   Roswell GA 30075
Ph: 770-587-2432 ▪ Fx: 770-993-8982 ▪ TF: 800-467-0982

Association of Maternal & Child Health Programs www.amchp.org
1220 19th St NW Suite 801   Washington DC 20036
Ph: 202-775-0436 ▪ Fx: 202-775-0061

Association for Maximum Service Television www.mstv.org
PO Box 9897   Washington DC 20016
Ph: 202-966-1956 ▪ Fx: 202-966-9617

Association for Media-Based Continuing Education for Engineers Inc www.amcee.org
PO Box 210158   Tucson AZ 85721
Ph: 800-338-9344 ▪ Fx: 520-626-3708

Association of Medical Diagnostics Manufacturers
555 13th St NW Suite 7W-404   Washington DC 20004
Ph: 202-637-6837 ▪ Fx: 202-637-5910
www.amdm.org

Association of Medical Education & Research in Substance Abuse
125 Whipple St Suite 300   Providence RI 02908
Ph: 401-349-0000 ▪ Fx: 877-418-8769
www.amersa.org

Association of Medical Illustrators
5475 Mark Dabling Blvd Suite 108   Colorado Springs CO 80918
Ph: 719-598-8622 ▪ Fx: 719-599-3075
www.ami.org

Association of Medical School Pediatric Department Chairs
111 Silver Cedar Ct   Chapel Hill NC 27514
Ph: 919-942-1993 ▪ Fx: 919-929-9255

Association of Meeting Professionals
2025 M St NW Suite 800   Washington DC 20036
Ph: 202-973-8686 ▪ Fx: 202-973-8722
www.ampsweb.org

Association of Metropolitan Sewerage Agencies
1816 Jefferson Pl NW   Washington DC 20036
Ph: 202-833-2672 ▪ Fx: 202-833-4657
www.amsa-cleanwater.org

Association of Metropolitan Water Agencies
1717 K St NW Suite 801   Washington DC 20036
Ph: 202-331-2820 ▪ Fx: 202-785-1845
www.amwa.net

Association for Mexican Cave Studies
PO Box 7037   Austin TX 78713
Ph: 512-842-5709
www.amcs.org

Association of Midwest Fish & Wildlife Agencies
c/o Nebraska Game & Parks Commission 2200 N 33rd St   PO Box 30370   Lincoln NE 68503
Ph: 402-471-5539 ▪ Fx: 402-471-5528

Association of Military Banks of America
7417 Jenna Rd   Springfield VA 22153
Ph: 703-569-5163 ▪ Fx: 703-455-2110

Association of Military Colleges & Schools of the US
9429 Garden Ct   Potomac MD 20854
Ph: 301-765-0695 ▪ Fx: 301-983-0583
www.amcsus.org

Association of Military Surgeons of the US
9320 Old Georgetown Rd   Bethesda MD 20814
Ph: 301-897-8800 ▪ Fx: 301-530-5446 ▪ TF: 800-761-9320
www.amsus.org

Association of Millwork Distributors
10047 Robert Trent Jones Pkwy   New Port Richey FL 34655
Ph: 727-372-3665 ▪ Fx: 727-372-2879
www.nsdja.com

Association of Minority Health Professions Schools
507 Capitol Ct NE Suite 200   Washington DC 20002
Ph: 202-544-7499 ▪ Fx: 202-546-7105

Association of the Miraculous Medal
1811 W St Joseph St   Perryville MO 63775
Ph: 573-547-2508 ▪ Fx: 573-547-1389 ▪ TF: 800-264-6279
www.amm.org

Association for Molecular Pathology
9650 Rockville Pike   Bethesda MD 20814
Ph: 301-634-7939 ▪ Fx: 301-634-7990
www.ampweb.org

Association Montessori Internationale-USA
410 Alexander St   Rochester NY 14607
Ph: 716-461-5920 ▪ Fx: 716-461-0075 ▪ TF: 800-872-2643
www.montessori-ami.org

Association of Moving Image Archivists
1313 N Vine St   Hollywood CA 90028
Ph: 323-463-1500 ▪ Fx: 323-463-1506
www.amianet.org

Association for Multicultural Counseling & Development
c/o American Counseling Assn 5999 Stevenson Ave   Alexandria VA 22304
Ph: 703-823-9800 ▪ Fx: 703-823-0252

Association of MultiEthnic Americans Inc
PO Box 341304   Los Angeles CA 90034
Ph: 877-954-2632
www.ameasite.org/

Association of Muslim Scientists & Engineers
PO Box 38   Plainfield IN 46168
Ph: 517-947-6338
www.amse.net

Association of Muslim Social Scientists
PO Box 669   Herndon VA 20172
Ph: 703-471-1133 ▪ Fx: 703-471-3922
www.amss.net

Association of National Advertisers Inc
708 3rd Ave   New York NY 10017
Ph: 212-697-5950 ▪ Fx: 212-661-8428
www.ana.net

Association of Natural Medicine Pharmacists
PO Box 150727   San Rafael CA 94915
Ph: 415-479-1512 ▪ Fx: 415-472-2559
www.anmp.org

Association of Natural Resource Enforcement Trainers
402 W Washington St IGCS Rm W255D   Indianapolis IN 46204
Ph: 317-232-4014 ▪ Fx: 317-232-8035
www.anret.org

Association of Naval Aviation
2550 Huntington Ave Suite 201   Alexandria VA 22303
Ph: 703-960-2490 ▪ Fx: 703-960-4490
www.anahq.org

Association of North American Missions
PO Box 8667   Longview TX 75607
Ph: 903-234-2075
www.anamissions.org

Association of North American Radio Clubs Inc
www.anarc.org

Association of Northwest Steelheaders
PO Box 22065   Milwaukie OR 97269
Ph: 503-653-4176 ▪ Fx: 503-653-8769
www.nwsteelheaders.org

Association of Nurses in AIDS Care
3538 Ridgewood Rd   Akron OH 44333
Ph: 330-670-0101 ▪ Fx: 330-670-0109 ▪ TF: 800-260-6780
www.anacnet.org

Association of Occupational & Environmental Clinics
1010 Vermont Ave NW Suite 513   Washington DC 20005
Ph: 202-347-4976 ▪ Fx: 202-347-4950 ▪ TF: 888-347-2632
www.aoec.org

Association of Occupational Health Professionals
109 VIP Dr   Wexford PA 15090
Ph: 800-362-4347 ▪ Fx: 724-935-1560
www.aohp.org

Association of Official Racing Chemists
PO Box 8400 Stn T   Ottawa ON K1G3H8
Ph: 613-731-7137 ▪ Fx: 613-731-7984

Association of Official Seed Analysts
1763 E University Ave Suite A PMB 411   Las Cruces NM 88001
Ph: 505-522-1437
www.aosaseed.com

Association of Official Seed Certifying Agencies
55 SW 5th Ave Suite 150   Meridian ID 83642
Ph: 208-884-2493 ▪ Fx: 208-884-4201
www.aosca.org

Association of Ohio Longrifle Collectors
23003 State Rt 339   Beverly OH 45715
Ph: 740-984-4896

Association of Oil Pipe Lines
1101 Vermont Ave NW Suite 604   Washington DC 20005
Ph: 202-408-7970 ▪ Fx: 202-408-7983
www.aopl.org

Association of Old Crows
1000 N Payne St   Alexandria VA 22314
Ph: 703-549-1600 ▪ Fx: 703-549-2589 ▪ TF: 888-653-2769
www.crows.org

Association of Oldetime Barbell & Strongmen
33-30 150th St   Flushing NY 11354
Ph: 718-661-3195

Association of Oncology Social Work
1211 Locust St   Philadelphia PA 19107
Ph: 215-599-6093 ▪ Fx: 215-545-8107
www.aosw.org

Association of Orthodox Jewish Scientists
25 W 45th St Suite 1405   New York NY 10036
Ph: 212-840-1166 ▪ Fx: 212-840-1514
www.aojs.org

Association of Orthodox Jewish Teachers
1577 Coney Island Dr   Brooklyn NY 11230
Ph: 718-258-3585 ▪ Fx: 718-258-3586

Association of Osteopathic Directors & Medical Educators
142 E Ontario St   Chicago IL 60611
Ph: 312-202-8211 ▪ Fx: 312-202-8224
www.aodme.org

Association of Osteopathic State Executive Directors
2007 Apalachee Pkwy   Tallahassee FL 32301
Ph: 850-878-7364 ▪ Fx: 850-942-7538

Association of Otolaryngology Administrators
1805 Ardmore Blvd   Pittsburgh PA 15221
Ph: 412-243-5156 ▪ Fx: 412-243-5160
www.oto-online.org

Association for Outdoor Recreation & Education
2705 Robin St   Bloomington IL 61704
Ph: 309-829-9189
www.aore.org

Association of Pakistani Physicians of North America
6414 S Cass Ave   Westmont IL 60559
Ph: 630-968-8585 ▪ Fx: 630-968-8677
www.appna.org

Association of Paroling Authorities International
1941 Jefferson Davis Hwy CCM4 2nd Fl Rm 222   Arlington VA 22202
Ph: 703-607-1504 ▪ Fx: 703-607-2047
www.apaintl.org

Association of Partners for Public Lands
2401 Blueridge Ave Suite 303   Wheaton MD 20902
Ph: 301-946-9475 ▪ Fx: 301-946-9478
www.appl.org

Association of Pathology Chairs
9650 Rockville Pike   Bethesda MD 20814
Ph: 301-634-7880 ▪ Fx: 301-634-7990
www.apcprods.org

Association of Pediatric Oncology Nurses
4700 W Lake Ave   Glenview IL 60025
Ph: 847-375-4724 ▪ Fx: 877-734-8755
www.apon.org

Association of Pediatric Program Directors
6728 Old McLean Village Dr   McLean VA 22101
Ph: 703-556-9222 ▪ Fx: 703-556-8729
www.appd.org

Association of Performing Arts Presenters
1112 16th St NW Suite 400   Washington DC 20036
Ph: 202-833-2787 ▪ Fx: 202-833-1543
www.artspresenters.org

Association of Personal Computer User Groups
3150 Payne Ave Suite 12   Cleveland OH 44114
Ph: 301-423-1618
www.apcug.org

Association of Personal Historians
www.personalhistorians.org

Association of Pet Dog Trainers
PO Box 1781   Hobbs NM 88241
Ph: 800-738-3647
www.apdt.com

Association of Physician Assistant Programs
950 N Washington St   Alexandria VA 22314
Ph: 703-548-5538 ▪ Fx: 703-684-1924
www.apap.org

Association of Physician Assistants in Cardiovascular Surgery
PO Box 4834   Englewood CO 80155
Ph: 303-221-5651 ▪ Fx: 303-771-2550 ▪ TF: 877-221-5651
www.apacvs.org

Association of Physician Assistants in Obstetrics & Gynecology
PO Box 1109   Madison WI 53701
Ph: 800-545-0636

Association for Play Therapy
2050 N Winery Ave Suite 101   Fresno CA 93703
Ph: 559-252-2278 ▪ Fx: 559-252-2297
www.a4pt.org

Association for Political & Legal Anthropology
c/o American Anthropological Assn 2200 Wilson Blvd Suite 600   Arlington VA 22201
Ph: 703-528-1902 ▪ Fx: 703-528-3546
www.aaanet.org/apla

Association of Polysomnographic Technologists
1 Westbrook Corporate Ctr Suite 920   Westchester IL 60154
Ph: 708-492-0796 ▪ Fx: 708-273-9344
www.aptweb.org

Association for Population/Family Planning Libraries & Information Centers International
c/o Family Health International Library   PO Box 13950   Research Triangle Park NC 27709
Ph: 919-405-1433 ▪ Fx: 919-544-7261
www.aplici.org

Association for Postal Commerce
1901 N Fort Myer Dr Suite 401   Arlington VA 22209
Ph: 703-524-0096 ▪ Fx: 703-524-1871
www.postcom.org

Association of Postgraduate Physician Assistant Programs
PO Box 2128ABC   Philippi WV 26416
Ph: 304-457-6356 ▪ Fx: 304-457-6308
www.appap.org

Association for Practical & Professional Ethics   php.ucs.indiana.edu/~appe/home.html
618 E 3rd St   Bloomington IN 47405
Ph: 812-855-6450 ▪ Fx: 812-855-3315

Association of Practicing Certified Public Accountants   www.ap-cpa.org
Rockville MD 20850
Ph: 301-340-3340 ▪ Fx: 301-340-3343

Association of Presbyterian Colleges & Universities   www.apcu.net
100 Witherspoon St   Louisville KY 40202
Ph: 502-569-5364 ▪ Fx: 502-569-8766 ▪ TF: 888-728-7228

Association for the Preservation of Cape Cod   www.apcc.org
PO Box 398   Barnstable MA 02630
Ph: 508-362-4226 ▪ Fx: 508-362-4227 ▪ TF: 877-955-4142

Association for Preservation Technology International   apti.org
4513 Lincoln Ave Suite 213   Lisle IL 60532
Ph: 630-968-6400 ▪ Fx: 888-723-4242

Association for the Preservation of Virginia Antiquities   www.apva.org
204 W Franklin St   Richmond VA 23220
Ph: 804-648-1889

Association Presidents, Council of State   www.csap.org
800 Perry Hwy Suite 3   Pittsburgh PA 15229
Ph: 412-366-1177 ▪ Fx: 412-366-8804

Association of Private Enterprise Education   www.apee.org
Univ of Tennessee at Chattanooga 313 Fletcher Hall 615
McCallie Ave   Chattanooga TN 37403
Ph: 423-755-4118 ▪ Fx: 423-755-5218

Association of Productivity Specialists   www.a-p-s.org
New York NY 10175
Ph: 212-286-0943

Association of Professional Ball Players of America   www.apbpa.org
1820 W Orangewood Ave Suite 206   Orange CA 92868
Ph: 714-935-9993 ▪ Fx: 714-935-0431

Association of Professional Chaplains   www.professionalchaplains.org
1701 E Woodfield Rd Suite 760   Schaumburg IL 60173
Ph: 847-240-1014 ▪ Fx: 847-240-1015

Association of Professional Color Imagers   apci.pmai.org
3000 Picture Pl   Jackson MI 49201
Ph: 517-788-8100 ▪ Fx: 517-788-8371

Association of Professional Communication Consultants   www.consultingsuccess.org
3924 S Troost Ave   Tulsa OK 74105
Ph: 918-743-4793

Association of Professional Consultants   www.consultapc.org
PO Box 51193   Irvine CA 92619
Ph: 800-745-5050 ▪ Fx: 800-977-3272

Association of Professional Design Firms   www.apdf.org
601 108th Ave NE 19th Fl   Bellevue WA 98004
Ph: 425-943-3825 ▪ Fx: 425-943-3878

Association of Professional Directors of YMCAs in the US   www.apdymca.org
12 Broad St Suite 2-1   Westerly RI 02891
Ph: 401-604-0034 ▪ Fx: 401-604-0036

Association of Professional Energy Managers   www.apem.org
3916 W Oak St Suite D   Burbank CA 91505
Ph: 818-972-2159 ▪ Fx: 818-972-2863

Association of Professional Flight Attendants   www.apfa.org
1004 W Euless Blvd   Euless TX 76040
Ph: 817-540-0108 ▪ Fx: 817-540-2077 ▪ TF: 800-395-2732

Association of Professional Insurance Women   www.apiw.org
551 5th Ave Suite 1625   New York NY 10176
Ph: 212-867-0228 ▪ Fx: 212-867-2544

Association of Professional Investment Consultants   www.apic-ssb.com
1101 17th St NW Suite 703   Washington DC 20036
Ph: 202-464-4155 ▪ Fx: 202-464-4157

Association of Professional Landscape Designers   www.apld.org
1924 N 2nd St   Harrisburg PA 17102
Ph: 717-238-9780 ▪ Fx: 717-238-9985

Association of Professional Material Handling Consultants   www.mhia.org/apmhc
8720 Red Oak Blvd Suite 201   Charlotte NC 28217
Ph: 704-676-1184 ▪ Fx: 704-676-1199

Association of Professional Piercers   www.safepiercing.org
5446 Peachtree Industrial Blvd PMB 286   Chamblee GA 30341
Ph: 888-888-1277

Association of Professional Researchers for Advancement   www.aprahome.org
40 Shuman Blvd Suite 325   Naperville IL 60563
Ph: 630-717-8160 ▪ Fx: 630-717-8354

Association of Professional Schools of International Affairs   www.apsia.org
2101 Van Munching Hall   College Park MD 20742
Ph: 301-405-7553 ▪ Fx: 301-405-4675

Association for Professionals in Infection Control & Epidemiology Inc   www.apic.org
1275 K St NW Suite 1000   Washington DC 20005
Ph: 202-789-1890 ▪ Fx: 202-789-1899 ▪ TF: 888-278-2742

Association of Professors of Cardiology   www.cardiologyprofessors.org
9111 Old Georgetown Rd   Bethesda MD 20814
Ph: 301-493-2330 ▪ Fx: 301-897-9745

Association of Professors of Gynecology & Obstetrics   www.apgo.org
2130 Priest Bridge Dr Suite 7   Crofton MD 21114
Ph: 410-451-9560 ▪ Fx: 410-451-9568

Association of Professors of Medicine   www.im.org/apm
2501 M St NW Suite 550   Washington DC 20037
Ph: 202-861-7700 ▪ Fx: 202-861-9731

Association of Professors of Mission   www.asmweb.org/apm
1443 N Euclid Ave   Dayton OH 45406
Ph: 937-274-0821 ▪ Fx: 937-278-6237

Association of Professors & Researchers in Religious Education   www.mtso.edu/aprre
3081 Columbus Pike PO Box 80004   Delaware OH 43015
Ph: 740-362-3364 ▪ Fx: 740-362-5890

Association of Program Directors in Internal Medicine   www.im.org/APDIM
2501 M St NW Suite 550   Washington DC 20037
Ph: 202-887-9450 ▪ Fx: 202-887-9447 ▪ TF: 800-622-4558

Association of Program Directors in Radiology   www.apdr.org
820 Jorie Blvd   Oak Brook IL 60523
Ph: 630-368-3737 ▪ Fx: 630-571-7837

Association of Program Directors in Surgery   www.apds.org
4900-B S 31st St   Arlington VA 22206
Ph: 703-820-7400 ▪ Fx: 703-931-4520

Association on Programs for Female Officers
500 E 4th St   Chester PA 19013
Ph: 610-490-4340

Association of Progressive Rental Organizations   www.apro-rto.com
1504 Robin Hood Trail   Austin TX 78703
Ph: 512-794-0095 ▪ Fx: 512-794-0097 ▪ TF: 800-204-2776

Association of Proposal Management Professionals   www.apmp.org
PO Box 668   Dana Point CA 92629
Ph: 949-493-9398 ▪ Fx: 949-240-4844

Association for Psychoanalytic Medicine   www.theapm.org
4560 Delafield Ave   Riverdale NY 10471
Ph: 718-548-6088 ▪ Fx: 718-548-8302

Association for Psychological Type   www.aptcentral.org
4700 W Lake Ave   Glenview IL 60025
Ph: 847-375-4717 ▪ Fx: 877-734-9374

Association of Psychology Postdoctoral & Internship Centers   www.appic.org
10 G St NE Suite 750   Washington DC 20002
Ph: 202-589-0600 ▪ Fx: 202-589-0603

Association of Public Data Users   www.apdu.org
PO Box 12538   Arlington VA 22219
Ph: 703-807-2327 ▪ Fx: 703-528-2857

Association of Public Health Laboratories   www.aphl.org
2025 M St NW Suite 550   Washington DC 20036
Ph: 202-822-5227 ▪ Fx: 202-887-5098

Association for Public Policy Analysis & Management   www.appam.org
PO Box 18766   Washington DC 20036
Ph: 202-496-0130 ▪ Fx: 202-496-0134

Association of Public-Safety Communications Officials   www.apcointl.org
International Inc   351 N Williamson Blvd   Daytona Beach FL
32114
Ph: 386-322-2500 ▪ Fx: 386-322-2501 ▪ TF: 888-272-6911

Association of Public Television Stations   www.apts.org
666 11th St NW 11th Fl   Washington DC 20001
Ph: 202-654-4200 ▪ Fx: 202-654-4236

Association of Public Treasurers of the US & Canada   www.aptusc.org
1029 Vermont NW Suite 710   Washington DC 20005
Ph: 202-737-0660 ▪ Fx: 202-737-0662

Association Publications, Society of National   www.snaponline.org
8405 Greensboro Dr Suite 800   McLean VA 22102
Ph: 703-506-3285 ▪ Fx: 703-506-3266

Association for Puerto Rican-Hispanic Culture
83 Park Terr W   New York NY 10034
Ph: 212-942-2338

Association for Quality & Participation   www.aqp.org
PO Box 2005   Milwaukee WI 53201
Ph: 414-765-7219 ▪ Fx: 414-272-1247 ▪ TF: 800-733-3310

Association of Racing Commissioners International   www.arci.com
2343 Alexandria Dr Suite 200   Lexington KY 40504
Ph: 859-224-7070 ▪ Fx: 859-224-7071

Association of Railway Museums   www.railwaymuseums.org
PO Box 370   Tujunga CA 91043
Ph: 818-951-9151

Association of Real Estate License Law Officials   www.arello.org
PO Box 230159   Montgomery AL 36123
Ph: 334-260-2902 ▪ Fx: 334-260-2903

Association of Real Estate Women   www.arew.org
551 5th Ave Suite 3025   New York NY 10176
Ph: 212-599-6181 ▪ Fx: 212-687-4016

Association for Recorded Sound Collections   www.arsc-audio.org
PO Box 543   Annapolis MD 21404
Ph: 410-757-0488 ▪ Fx: 410-349-0175

Association of Regulatory Boards of Optometry   www.arbo.org
1750 S Brentwood Blvd Suite 503   Saint Louis MO 63144
Ph: 314-785-6000 ▪ Fx: 314-785-6002

Association of Rehabilitation Nurses   www.rehabnurse.org
4700 W Lake Ave   Glenview IL 60025
Ph: 847-375-4710 ▪ Fx: 877-734-9384

Association of Rehabilitation Programs in Computer Technology   www.arpct.org
503 S York St   Denver CO 80209
Ph: 303-733-2111 ▪ Fx: 303-733-2225

Association for Religion & Intellectual Life   www.aril.org
475 Riverside Dr Suite 1945   New York NY 10115
Ph: 212-870-2544 ▪ Fx: 212-870-2539

Association of Reporters of Judicial Decisions   arjd.washlaw.edu
5711 Nevada St   College Park MD 20740
Ph: 202-479-3194 ▪ Fx: 202-479-3240

Association of Reproductive Health Professionals   www.arhp.org
2401 Pennsylvania Ave NW Suite 350   Washington DC 20037
Ph: 202-466-3825 ▪ Fx: 202-466-3826

Association for Research of Childhood Cancer   www.arocc.org
PO Box 251   Buffalo NY 14225
Ph: 716-681-4433

Association of Research Directors
Alabama A&M Univ School of Agriculture &
Environmental   Normal AL 35762
Ph: 256-851-5781 ▪ Fx: 256-851-5906

Association for Research & Enlightenment   www.are-cayce.com
215 67th St   Virginia Beach VA 23451
Ph: 757-428-3588 ▪ Fx: 757-422-6921 ▪ TF: 800-333-4499

Association of Research Libraries   arl.cni.org
21 Dupont Cir NW Suite 800   Washington DC 20036
Ph: 202-296-2296 ▪ Fx: 202-872-0884

Association for Research in Nervous & Mental Disease   www.arnmd.org/arnmd

Association for Research in Otolaryngology   www.aro.org
19 Mantua Rd   Mount Royal NJ 08061
Ph: 856-423-0041 ▪ Fx: 856-423-3420

Association for Research in Vision & Ophthalmology
12300 Twinbrook Pkwy Suite 250   Rockville MD 20852
Ph: 240-221-2900 ▪ Fx: 240-221-0370
www.arvo.org

Association of Residents in Radiation Oncology
12500 Fair Lakes Cir Suite 375   Fairfax VA 22033
Ph: 703-502-1550 ▪ Fx: 703-502-7852 ▪ TF: 800-962-7876
www.arro.org

Association of Restorers
8 Medford Pl   New Hartford NY 13413
Ph: 315-733-1952
www.assoc-restorers.com

Association of Retail Marketing Services
244 Broad St   Red Bank NJ 07701
Ph: 732-842-5070 ▪ Fx: 732-219-1938
www.goarms.com

Association for Retail Technology Standards
325 7th St NW Suite 1100   Washington DC 20004
Ph: 202-626-8140
www.nrf-arts.org

Association of Retail Travel Agents
3161 Custer Dr Suite 8   Lexington KY 40517
Ph: 859-269-9739 ▪ Fx: 859-266-9396
www.artaonline.com

Association of Retired Americans
6505 E 82nd St Suite 130   Indianapolis IN 46250
Ph: 800-806-6160 ▪ Fx: 317-915-2510
www.ara-usa.org

Association of Rheumatology Health Professionals
1800 Century Pl Suite 250   Atlanta GA 30345
Ph: 404-633-3777 ▪ Fx: 404-633-1870
www.rheumatology.org/arhp

Association of Rotational Molders
2000 Spring Rd Suite 511   Oak Brook IL 60523
Ph: 630-571-0611 ▪ Fx: 630-571-0616
www.rotomolding.org

Association of Russian-American Scholars in the USA
PO Box 180035   Richmond Hill NY 11418
Ph: 518-785-6780

Association for Safe International Road Travel
11769 Gainsborough Rd   Potomac MD 20854
Ph: 301-983-5252 ▪ Fx: 301-983-3663
www.asirt.org

Association of Sanctuaries
1013 Lesa Ln   Garland TX 75042
Ph: 972-485-5647 ▪ Fx: 972-487-9843
www.taosanctuaries.org

Association of School Business Officials International
11401 N Shore Dr   Reston VA 20190
Ph: 703-478-0405 ▪ Fx: 703-478-0205
asbointl.org

Association of Schools of Allied Health Professions
1730 M St NW Suite 500   Washington DC 20036
Ph: 202-293-4848 ▪ Fx: 202-293-4852
www.asahp.org

Association of Schools & Colleges of Optometry
6110 Executive Blvd Suite 510   Rockville MD 20852
Ph: 301-231-5944 ▪ Fx: 301-770-1828
www.opted.org

Association of Schools of Journalism & Mass Communication
234 Outlet Pointe Blvd   Columbia SC 29210
Ph: 803-798-0271 ▪ Fx: 803-772-3509
www.aejmc.org

Association of Schools of Public Health
1101 15th St NW Suite 910   Washington DC 20005
Ph: 202-296-1099 ▪ Fx: 202-296-1252
www.asph.org

Association of Science Fiction & Fantasy Artists
www.asfa-art.org

Association of Science-Technology Centers Inc
1025 Vermont Ave NW Suite 500   Washington DC 20005
Ph: 202-783-7200 ▪ Fx: 202-783-7207
www.astc.org

Association of Scottish Games & Festivals
3000 Walnut Ave   Altoona PA 16601
Ph: 412-851-9900 ▪ Fx: 412-854-5963
www.asgf.org

Association of Senior Anthropologists
c/o American Anthropological Assn 2200 Wilson Blvd Suite
600   Arlington VA 22201
Ph: 703-528-1902 ▪ Fx: 703-528-3546
www.aaanet.org/asa

Association of Service & Computer Dealers International
131 NW 1st Ave Suite 206   Delray Beach FL 33444
Ph: 561-266-9016 ▪ Fx: 561-266-9017
www.ascdi.com

Association for Services Management International
1342 Colonial Blvd Suite 25   Fort Myers FL 33907
Ph: 239-275-7887 ▪ Fx: 239-275-0974 ▪ TF: 800-333-9786
www.afsmi.org

Association of Seventh-day Adventist Librarians
www.asdal.org

Association of Shareware Professionals
PO Box 1522   Martinsville IN 46151
Ph: 765-349-4740 ▪ Fx: 765-349-4744
www.asp-shareware.org

Association of Ship Brokers & Agents (USA) Inc
510 Sylvan Ave Suite 201   Englewood Cliffs NJ 07632
Ph: 201-569-2882 ▪ Fx: 201-569-9082
www.asba.org

Association of SIDS & Infant Mortality Programs
Stony Brook Univ School of Social Welfare   Stony Brook NY
11794
Ph: 631-444-3690 ▪ Fx: 631-444-6475
www.asip1.org

Association of Small Business Development Centers
8990 Burke Lake Rd   Burke VA 22015
Ph: 703-764-9850 ▪ Fx: 703-764-1234
www.asbdc-us.org

Association of Small Foundations
4905 Del Ray Ave Suite 308   Bethesda MD 20814
Ph: 301-907-3337 ▪ Fx: 301-907-0980 ▪ TF: 888-212-9922
smallfoundations.org

Association of Social Work Boards
400 South Ridge Pkwy Suite B   Culpeper VA 22701
Ph: 540-829-6880 ▪ Fx: 540-829-0142 ▪ TF: 800-225-6880
www.aswb.org

Association for the Sociology of Religion
3520 Wiltshire Dr   Holiday FL 34691
Ph: 727-844-5990 ▪ Fx: 727-844-7332
www.sociologyofreligion.com

Association of the Sons of Poland
333 Hackensack St   Carlstadt NJ 07072
Ph: 201-935-2807 ▪ Fx: 201-935-2752
www.sonsofpoland.com

Association of Southern Baptist Campus Ministers
PO Box 25118   Baton Rouge LA 70894
Ph: 225-343-0408 ▪ Fx: 225-343-0424

Association of Southern Baptist Colleges & Schools
PO Box 11655   Jackson TN 38308
Ph: 731-660-3497 ▪ Fx: 731-664-6459
www.baptistschools.org

Association of Space Explorers
1150 Gemini Ave   Houston TX 77058
Ph: 281-280-8172 ▪ Fx: 281-280-8173
www.space-explorers.org

Association of Specialists in Cleaning & Restoration
8229 Cloverleaf Dr Suite 460   Millersville MD 21108
Ph: 410-729-9900 ▪ Fx: 410-729-3603 ▪ TF: 800-272-7012
www.ascr.org

Association for Specialists in Group Work
Texas A&M Commerce Dept of Counseling 202 Education
N   Commerce TX 75429
Ph: 903-886-5630 ▪ Fx: 903-886-5780
www.asgw.org

Association of Specialized & Cooperative Library Agencies
50 E Huron St   Chicago IL 60611
Ph: 312-280-4395 ▪ Fx: 312-944-8085 ▪ TF: 800-545-2433
www.ala.org/ascla

Association of Specialized & Professional Accreditors
1020 W Byron St Suite 8G   Chicago IL 60613
Ph: 773-525-2160 ▪ Fx: 773-525-2162
www.aspa-usa.org

Association of Specialty Cut Flower Growers
PO Box 268   Oberlin OH 44074
Ph: 440-774-2887 ▪ Fx: 440-774-2435
www.ascfg.org

Association for Spiritual Ethical & Religious Values in Counseling
c/o American Counseling Assn 5999 Stevenson Ave   Alexandria
VA 22304
Ph: 703-823-9800 ▪ Fx: 703-823-0252 ▪ TF: 800-347-6647
www.aservic.org

Association of Staff Physician Recruiters
1711 W County Rd B Suite 300N   Roseville MN 55113
Ph: 651-635-0359 ▪ Fx: 651-635-0307 ▪ TF: 800-830-2777
www.aspr.org

Association of State Baptist Papers
c/o The Alabama Baptist Newspaper 3310 Independence
Dr   Birmingham AL 35209
Ph: 205-870-4720 ▪ Fx: 205-870-8957

Association of State Correctional Administrators
213 Court St 6th Fl   Middletown CT 06457
Ph: 860-704-6410 ▪ Fx: 860-704-6420
www.asca.net

Association of State Dam Safety Officials
450 Old Vine   Lexington KY 40507
Ph: 859-257-5140 ▪ Fx: 859-323-1958
www.damsafety.org

Association of State Democratic Chairs
430 S Capitol St SE   Washington DC 20003
Ph: 202-479-5121 ▪ Fx: 202-479-5123

Association of State Drinking Water Administrators
1025 Connecticut Ave NW Suite 903   Washington DC 20036
Ph: 202-293-7655 ▪ Fx: 202-293-7656
www.asdwa.org

Association of State Floodplain Managers
2809 Fish Hatchery Rd Suite 04   Madison WI 53713
Ph: 608-274-0123 ▪ Fx: 608-274-0696
www.floods.org

**Association of State & Interstate Water Pollution Control
Administrators**   750 1st St NE Suite 1010   Washington DC
20002
Ph: 202-898-0905 ▪ Fx: 202-898-0929
www.asiwpca.org

Association of State & Provincial Psychology Boards
PO Box 241245   Montgomery AL 36124
Ph: 334-832-4580 ▪ Fx: 334-269-6379 ▪ TF: 800-448-4069
www.asppb.org

**Association of State & Territorial Chronic Disease Program
Directors**   8201 Greensboro Dr Suite 300   McLean VA 22102
Ph: 703-610-9033 ▪ Fx: 703-610-9005
www.chronicdisease.org

Association of State & Territorial Dental Directors
322 Cannondale Rd   Jefferson City MO 65109
Ph: 573-636-0453 ▪ Fx: 573-636-0454
www.astdd.org

Association of State & Territorial Directors of Nursing
www.astdn.org

Association of State & Territorial Health Officials
1275 K St NW Suite 800   Washington DC 20005
Ph: 202-371-9090 ▪ Fx: 202-371-9797
www.astho.org

Association of State & Territorial Public Health Nutrition Directors
www.astphnd.org

Association of State & Territorial Solid Waste Management Officials
444 N Capitol St NW Suite 315   Washington DC 20001
Ph: 202-624-5828 ▪ Fx: 202-624-7875
www.astswmo.org

Association of State Wetland Managers
1434 Helderberg Trail PO Box 269   Berne NY 12023
Ph: 518-872-1804 ▪ Fx: 518-872-2171
www.aswm.org

Association of Steel Distributors
401 N Michigan Ave   Chicago IL 60611
Ph: 312-644-6610 ▪ Fx: 312-527-6705
www.steeldistributors.org

Association for the Study of African American Life & History
Howard Univ CB Powell Bldg 525 Bryant St Suite
C142   Washington DC 20059
Ph: 202-865-0053 ▪ Fx: 202-265-7920
www.asalh.org

Association for the Study of Classical African Civilizations
2274 W 20th St   Los Angeles CA 90018
Ph: 323-730-1155 ▪ Fx: 323-731-4998
www.ascac.org

Association for the Study of Dreams
PO Box 1592   Merced CA 95341
Ph: 209-724-0889 ▪ Fx: 209-724-9319
www.asdreams.org

Association for the Study of Higher Education
202 Hill Hall   Columbia MO 65211
Ph: 573-882-9645 ▪ Fx: 573-884-2197
www.ashe.missouri.edu

Association for the Study of Literature & Environment
Davidson College English Dept Box 7056   Davidson NC 28036
Ph: 704-894-2487
www.asle.umn.edu

Association for the Study of Nationalities
Columbia Univ 1216 IAB 420 W 118th St   New York NY 10027
Ph: 212-854-8487 ▪ Fx: 212-666-3481
www.nationalities.org

Association for the Study of Play
www.csuchico.edu/phed/tasp

Association for Supervision & Curriculum Development
1703 N Beauregard St   Alexandria VA 22311
Ph: 703-578-9600 ▪ Fx: 703-575-5400 ▪ TF: 800-933-2723
www.ascd.org

Association of Suppliers to the Paper Industry
201 Park Washington Ct   Falls Church VA 22046
Ph: 703-538-1787 ▪ Fx: 703-241-5603
www.aspinet.org

Association of Support Professionals
122 Barnard Ave   Watertown MA 02472
Ph: 617-924-3944   Fx: 617-924-7288
www.asponline.com

Association of Surfing Professionals
PO Box 309   Huntington Beach CA 92648
Ph: 714-848-8851   Fx: 714-848-8861
www.aspworldtour.com

Association for Surgical Education
SIU School of Medicine Dept of Surgery PO Box
19655   Springfield IL 62794
Ph: 217-545-3835
www.surgicaleducation.com

Association of Surgical Technologists
7108 S Alton Way Bldg C   Englewood CO 80112
Ph: 303-694-9130   Fx: 303-694-9169
www.ast.org

Association for Symbolic Logic
Vassar College PO Box 742   Poughkeepsie NY 12604
Ph: 845-437-7080   Fx: 845-437-7830
www.aslonline.org

Association of Talent Agents
9255 Sunset Blvd Suite 930   Los Angeles CA 90069
Ph: 310-274-0628   Fx: 310-274-5063
www.agentassociation.com

Association of Teachers of Japanese
Univ of Colorado-Boulder 279 UCB   Boulder CO 80309
Ph: 303-492-5487   Fx: 303-492-5856
www.colorado.edu/ealld/atj

Association for Technology in Music Instruction
atmi.music.org

Association for Teleservices International
12 Academy Ave   Atkinson NH 03811
Ph: 603-362-9489   Fx: 603-362-9486
www.atsi.org

Association of Test Publishers
1201 Pennsylvania Ave Suite 300   Washington DC 20004
Ph: 866-240-7909
www.testpublishers.org

**Association for Textual Scholarship in
Art History**   112 Charles St Beacon Hill   Boston MA 02114
Ph: 617-367-1679   Fx: 617-557-2962
www.uml.edu/Dept/History/ArtHistory/ATSAH

Association of Theatre Movement Educators
www.asu.edu/cfa/atme

Association of Theatrical Press Agents & Managers
165 W 46th St Suite 700   New York NY 10036
Ph: 212-719-3666   Fx: 212-302-1585   TF: 800-858-3667

Association of Theological Schools in the US & Canada
10 Summit Park Dr   Pittsburgh PA 15275
Ph: 412-788-6505   Fx: 412-788-6510
www.ats.edu

Association of Third World Studies Inc
Mississippi State Univ Dept of History   Mississippi State MS
39762
Ph: 662-325-4020
itc.gsw.edu/atws

Association for Transpersonal Psychology
PO Box 50187   Palo Alto CA 94303
Ph: 650-424-8764   Fx: 650-618-1851
www.atpweb.org

Association for Transportation Law Logistics & Policy
3 Church Cir PMB 250   Annapolis MD 21401
Ph: 410-267-0023   Fx: 410-267-7546
www.atllp.com

Association of Travel Marketing Executives
2005 Palmer Ave Suite 193   Larchmont NY 10538
Ph: 914-834-9110   Fx: 914-576-2831   TF: 800-525-3087
www.atme.org

Association for the Treatment of Sexual Abusers
4900 SW Griffith Dr Suite 274   Beaverton OR 97005
Ph: 503-643-1023   Fx: 503-643-5084
www.atsa.com

Association of Trial Lawyers of America
1050 31st St NW   Washington DC 20007
Ph: 202-965-3500   Fx: 202-625-7313   TF: 800-424-2725
www.atlanet.org

Association of Trial Lawyers PAC
1050 31st St NW   Washington DC 20007
Ph: 202-965-3500   Fx: 202-333-2861

Association for Tropical Biology & Conservation
US National Herbarium National Museum of Natural History
Botany MRC-166   Washington DC 20013
Ph: 202-357-2534   Fx: 202-786-2563
www.atbio.org

Association for Tropical Lepidoptera
PO Box 141210   Gainesville FL 32614
Ph: 352-392-5894   Fx: 352-373-3249
www.troplep.org

Association for Union Democracy
104 Montgomery St   Brooklyn NY 11225
Ph: 718-855-6650   Fx: 718-855-6799
www.uniondemocracy.org

Association of Unity Churches
401 SW Oldham Pkwy PO Box 610   Lee's Summit MO 64063
Ph: 816-524-7414   Fx: 816-525-4020
www.unity.org

Association of Universities for Research in Astronomy
1200 New York Ave NW Suite 350   Washington DC 20005
Ph: 202-483-2101   Fx: 202-483-2106
www.aura-astronomy.org

Association of University Anesthesiologists
520 Northwest Hwy   Park Ridge IL 60068
Ph: 847-825-5586
www.auahq.org

Association for University Business & Economic Research
Univ of Colorado Leeds School of Business UCB 419   Boulder
CO 80309
Ph: 303-492-3196   Fx: 303-492-3620
www.auber.org

Association of University Centers on Disabilities
8630 Fenton St Suite 410   Silver Spring MD 20910
Ph: 301-588-8252   Fx: 301-588-2842
www.aucd.org

Association of University Interior Designers
www.auid.org

Association of University Professors of Ophthalmology
PO Box 420369   San Francisco CA 94142
Ph: 415-561-8548   Fx: 415-561-8531

Association of University Programs in Health Administration
730 11th St NW 4th Fl   Washington DC 20001
Ph: 202-638-1448   Fx: 202-638-3429
www.aupha.org

Association of University Radiologists
820 Jorie Blvd   Oak Brook IL 60523
Ph: 630-368-3730   Fx: 630-571-7837
www.aur.org

Association of University Research Parks
12100 Sunset Hills Rd Suite 130   Reston VA 20190
Ph: 703-234-4088   Fx: 703-435-4390
www.aurrp.org

Association of University Technology Managers
60 Revere Dr Suite 500   Northbrook IL 60062
Ph: 847-559-0846   Fx: 847-480-9282
www.autm.net

Association for Unmanned Vehicle Systems International
3401 Columbia Pike Suite 400   Arlington VA 22204
Ph: 703-920-2720   Fx: 703-920-2889
www.auvsi.org

Association of the US Army
2425 Wilson Blvd   Arlington VA 22201
Ph: 703-841-4300   Fx: 703-525-9039   TF: 800-336-4570
www.ausa.org

Association of Vacuum Equipment Manufacturers International
71 Pinon Hill Pl NE   Albuquerque NM 87122
Ph: 505-856-6924   Fx: 505-856-6716
www.avem.org

Association of Vascular & Interventional Radiographers
10201 Lee Hwy Suite 500   Fairfax VA 22030
Ph: 703-691-2350   Fx: 703-691-8540
www.avir.org

Association of Veterinarians for Animal Rights
PO Box 208   Davis CA 95617
Ph: 530-759-8106   Fx: 530-759-8116
avar.org

Association of Volleyball Professionals
6080 Center Dr 6th Fl   Los Angeles CA 90045
Ph: 310-426-8000   Fx: 310-426-8010
www.avp.com

Association for Volunteer Administration
PO Box 32092   Richmond VA 23294
Ph: 804-672-3353   Fx: 804-672-3368
www.avaintl.org

Association of Waldorf Schools of North America
3911 Bannister Rd   Fair Oaks CA 95628
Ph: 916-961-0927   Fx: 916-961-0715
www.awsna.org

Association of the Wall & Ceiling Industries International
803 W Broad St Suite 600   Falls Church VA 22046
Ph: 703-534-8300   Fx: 703-534-8307
www.awci.org

Association of Water Technologies
8201 Greensboro Dr Suite 300   McLean VA 22102
Ph: 703-610-9012   Fx: 703-610-9005   TF: 800-858-6683
www.awt.org

Association for Wedding Professionals International
2730 Arden Way Suite 218   Sacramento CA 95825
Ph: 916-482-3010   Fx: 916-482-2025   TF: 800-242-4461
www.afwpi.com

Association of Western Pulp & Paper Workers
PO Box 4566   Portland OR 97208
Ph: 503-228-7486   Fx: 503-228-1346
www.awppw.org

Association of Winery Suppliers
21 Tamal Vista Blvd Suite 196   Corte Madera CA 94925
Ph: 415-927-2640   Fx: 415-927-0608

Association for Women in Aviation Maintenance
PO Box 1030   Edgewater FL 32132
Ph: 386-424-3580   Fx: 386-428-3514
www.awam.org

Association for Women in Communications
780 Ritchie Hwy River Reach Ctr Suite 280-S   Severna Park
MD 21146
Ph: 410-544-7442   Fx: 410-544-4640
www.womcom.org

Association for Women in Computing
41 Sutter St Suite 1006   San Francisco CA 94104
Ph: 415-905-4663
www.awc-hq.org

Association for Women Geoscientists
PO Box 30645   Lincoln NE 68505
Ph: 402-489-8122
www.awg.org

Association for Women Journalists
PO Box 2199   Fort Worth TX 76113
Ph: 817-685-3876
www.awjdfw.org/

Association for Women in Management
927 15th St NW Suite 1000   Washington DC 20005
Ph: 202-659-6364   Fx: 202-371-1467
www.womens.org

Association for Women in Mathematics
Univ of Maryland 4114 Computer & Space Science
Bldg   College Park MD 20742
Ph: 301-405-7892   Fx: 301-314-9363
www.awm-math.org

Association of Women in the Metal Industries
515 King St Suite 420   Alexandria VA 22314
Ph: 703-739-8335   Fx: 703-684-6048
www.awmi.com

Association for Women in Science Inc
1200 New York Ave NW Suite 650   Washington DC 20005
Ph: 202-326-8940   Fx: 202-326-8960   TF: 800-886-2947
www.awis.org

Association for Women in Sports Media
www.awsmonline.org

Association of Women Surgeons
414 Plaza Dr Suite 209   Westmont IL 60559
Ph: 630-655-0392   Fx: 630-655-0391
www.womensurgeons.org

Association of Women's Health Obstetric & Neonatal Nurses
2000 L St NW Suite 740   Washington DC 20036
Ph: 202-261-2400   Fx: 202-728-0575   TF: 800-673-8499
www.awhonn.org

Association for Women's Rights in Development
96 Spadina Ave Suite 401   Toronto ON M5V2J6
Ph: 416-594-3773   Fx: 416-594-0330
www.awid.org

Association of Woodworking & Furnishings Suppliers
5800 S Eastern Ave Suite 330   Los Angeles CA 90040
Ph: 323-838-9440   Fx: 323-838-9443   TF: 800-946-2837
www.awfssupplierfinder.org

Association for Work Process Improvement
185 Devonshire St Suite M102   Boston MA 02110
Ph: 617-426-1167   Fx: 617-521-8675   TF: 800-998-2974
www.tawpi.org

Association for World Travel Exchange
38 W 88th St   New York NY 10024
Ph: 212-787-7706   Fx: 212-580-9283
www.international-counselors.org

Association of Writers & Writing Programs
George Mason Univ 4400 University Dr Tallwood House MS
1E3   Fairfax VA 22030
Ph: 703-993-4301   Fx: 703-993-4302
awpwriter.org

Association of Yachting Professionals
PO Box 460248   Fort Lauderdale FL 33346
Ph: 954-522-0184   Fx: 954-462-6084

Associations, National Council of Nonprofit   www.ncna.org
1030 15th St NW Suite 870   Washington DC 20005
Ph: 202-962-0322 ▪ Fx: 202-962-0321

Associations, National Council of State Education
1201 16th St NW Suite 817   Washington DC 20036
Ph: 202-822-7745 ▪ Fx: 202-822-7113

Assumption, Associate Missionaries of the
914 Main St Suite 5   Worcester MA 01610
Ph: 508-767-1356 ▪ Fx: 508-791-2936

Assumption Guild   www.masscardsaa.com
PO Box 35190   Brighton MA 02135
Ph: 617-783-0495 ▪ Fx: 617-783-8030

Assyrian Academic Society   www.aas.net/jaas/
PO Box 3541   Skokie IL 60076
Ph: 773-461-6633

(Assyrian) Bet-Nahrain Inc   www.betnahrain.org
PO Box 4116   Modesto CA 95352
Ph: 209-538-4130 ▪ Fx: 209-538-2795

Astara   www.astara.org
792 W Arrow Hwy   Upland CA 91785
Ph: 909-981-4941 ▪ Fx: 909-920-9541

Asthma & Allergy Foundation of America   www.aafa.org
1233 20th St NW Suite 402   Washington DC 20036
Ph: 202-466-7643 ▪ Fx: 202-466-8940 ▪ TF: 800-727-8462

Asthma & Immunology, American Academy of Allergy   www.aaaai.org
611 E Wells St 4th Fl   Milwaukee WI 53202
Ph: 414-272-6071 ▪ Fx: 414-272-6070 ▪ TF: 800-822-2762

Asthma & Immunology, American College of Allergy   allergy.mcg.edu
85 W Algonquin Rd Suite 550   Arlington Heights IL 60005
Ph: 847-427-1200 ▪ Fx: 847-427-1294 ▪ TF: 800-842-7777

Asthma & Immunology, Joint Council of Allergy   www.jcaai.org
50 N Brockway St Suite 3-3   Palatine IL 60067
Ph: 847-934-1918 ▪ Fx: 847-934-1820

ASTM International   www.astm.org
100 Barr Harbor Dr PO Box C700   West Conshohocken PA 19428
Ph: 610-832-9500 ▪ Fx: 610-832-9555

Astrologers, American Federation of   www.astrologers.com
6535 S Rural Rd   Tempe AZ 85283
Ph: 480-838-1751 ▪ Fx: 480-838-8293 ▪ TF: 888-301-7630

Astrological Networking, Association for   www.afan.org
8306 Wilshire Blvd PMB 537   Beverly Hills CA 90211
Ph: 800-578-2326

Astrological Psychology, Association for   www.aaperry.com
360 Quietwood Dr   San Rafael CA 94903
Ph: 415-479-5812

Astrological Research, International Society for   www.isarastrology.com
PO Box 38613   Los Angeles CA 90038
Ph: 805-525-0461 ▪ Fx: 805-933-0301 ▪ TF: 800-982-1788

Astrology, American Council of Vedic   www.vedicastrology.org/
PO Box 2149   Sedona AZ 86339
Ph: 928-282-6595 ▪ Fx: 928-282-6097 ▪ TF: 800-900-6595

Astrology, Friends of   www.friendsofastrology.org
514 N Richmond Ave   Westmont IL 60559
Ph: 630-654-4742

Astronaut Council, Young   www.youngastronauts.com
5200 27th St NW   Washington DC 20015
Ph: 301-617-0923 ▪ Fx: 301-776-0858

Astronautical Society, American   www.astronautical.org
6352 Rolling Mill Pl Suite 102   Springfield VA 22152
Ph: 703-866-0020 ▪ Fx: 703-866-3526

Astronautics, American Institute of Aeronautics &   www.aiaa.org
1801 Alexander Bell Dr Suite 500   Reston VA 20191
Ph: 703-264-7500 ▪ Fx: 703-264-7657 ▪ TF: 800-639-2422

Astronomical League   www.astroleague.org/
11305 King St   Overland Park KS 66210
Ph: 913-469-0135

Astronomical Society, American   www.aas.org
2000 Florida Ave NW Suite 400   Washington DC 20009
Ph: 202-328-2010 ▪ Fx: 202-234-2560

Astronomical Society of the Pacific   www.astrosociety.org
390 Ashton Ave   San Francisco CA 94112
Ph: 415-337-1100 ▪ Fx: 415-337-5205

Astronomical Society, Von Braun   www.vbas.org
PO Box 1142   Huntsville AL 35807
Ph: 256-539-0316

Astronomy, Association of Universities for Research in   www.aura-astronomy.org
1200 New York Ave NW Suite 350   Washington DC 20005
Ph: 202-483-2101 ▪ Fx: 202-483-2106

At-Home Mothers, National Association of   www.athomemothers.com
406 E Buchanan Ave   Fairfield IA 52556
Ph: 515-472-3202 ▪ Fx: 515-469-3068

At-sea Processors Association   www.atsea.org
4039 21st Ave W Suite 400   Seattle WA 98199
Ph: 206-285-5139 ▪ Fx: 206-285-1841

Atheists, American   www.atheists.org
PO Box 5733   Parsippany NJ 07054
Ph: 908-276-7300 ▪ Fx: 908-276-7402

Athena, Maids of   www.ahepa.org/maids
1909 Q St NW Suite 500   Washington DC 20009
Ph: 202-232-6300 ▪ Fx: 202-232-2140

Atherosclerosis Imaging, Society of   www.sai.org
13140 Coit Rd Suite 320 LB 120   Dallas TX 75240
Ph: 972-233-9107 ▪ Fx: 972-490-4219

Atherosclerosis Society, International   www.athero.org
6550 Fannin St Suite 1211   Houston TX 77030
Ph: 713-797-0401 ▪ Fx: 713-796-8853

Athletes in Action   www.aia.com
651 Taylor Dr   Xenia OH 45385
Ph: 937-352-1000 ▪ Fx: 937-352-1101

Athletes with Disabilities, America's   www.americasathletes.org
8630 Fenton St Suite 920   Silver Spring MD 20910
Ph: 301-589-9042 ▪ Fx: 301-589-9052 ▪ TF: 800-238-7632

Athletes & Entertainers for Kids   www.aefk.org
3337 Colorado St   Long Beach CA 90814
Ph: 562-438-5905 ▪ Fx: 562-438-9175

Athletes, Fellowship of Christian   www.fca.org
8701 Leeds Rd   Kansas City MO 64129
Ph: 816-921-0909 ▪ Fx: 816-921-8755 ▪ TF: 800-289-0909

Athletes Outreach, Professional   www.pao.org
72 E Sunset Way PO Box 1044   Issaquah WA 98027
Ph: 425-392-6300 ▪ Fx: 425-392-7640

Athletes, US Association of Blind   www.usaba.org
33 N Institute St   Colorado Springs CO 80903
Ph: 719-630-0422 ▪ Fx: 719-630-0616

Athletic Administrators, National Association of Collegiate Women   www.nacwaa.org
4701 Wrightsville Ave Oak Park D-1   Wilmington NC 28403
Ph: 910-793-8244 ▪ Fx: 910-793-8246

Athletic Association of America, Dwarf   www.daaa.org
418 Willow Way   Lewisville TX 75077
Ph: 972-317-8299

Athletic Association, Central Intercollegiate   www.theciaa.com
303 Butler Farm Rd Suite 102   Hampton VA 23666
Ph: 757-865-0071 ▪ Fx: 757-865-8436

Athletic Association, National Christian College   www.thenccaa.com
302 W Washington St   Greenville SC 29601
Ph: 864-250-1199 ▪ Fx: 864-250-1141

Athletic Association, National Collegiate   www.ncaa.org
700 W Washington St PO Box 6222   Indianapolis IN 46206
Ph: 317-917-6222 ▪ Fx: 317-917-6888

Athletic Association, National Junior College   www.njcaa.org
PO Box 7305   Colorado Springs CO 80933
Ph: 719-590-9788 ▪ Fx: 719-590-7324

Athletic Association, University   www.uaa.rochester.edu
575 Mt Hope Ave   Rochester NY 14620
Ph: 716-273-5881 ▪ Fx: 716-275-8322

Athletic Business Management Association, College   nacda.ocsn.com/cabma/nacda-cabma.html
PO Box 16428   Cleveland OH 44116
Ph: 440-892-4000 ▪ Fx: 440-892-4007

Athletic Conference, Eastern College   www.ecac.com
1311 Craigville Beach Rd PO Box 3   Centerville MA 02632
Ph: 508-771-5060 ▪ Fx: 508-771-9481

Athletic Conference, Metro Atlantic   www.maacsports.com
712 Amboy Ave   Edison NJ 08837
Ph: 732-738-5455 ▪ Fx: 732-738-8366

Athletic Conference, Southwestern   www.swac.com
1527 5th Ave N   Birmingham AL 35204
Ph: 205-251-7573 ▪ Fx: 205-297-9820

Athletic Conference, Western   www.wacsports.com
9250 E Costilla Ave Suite300   Englewood CO 80112
Ph: 303-799-9221 ▪ Fx: 303-799-3888

Athletic Equipment, National Operating Committee on Standards for   www.nocsae.org
PO Box 12290   Overland Park KS 66282
Ph: 913-888-1340 ▪ Fx: 913-888-1065

Athletic Trainers Association, National   www.nata.org
2952 Stemmons Fwy Suite 200   Dallas TX 75247
Ph: 214-637-6282 ▪ Fx: 214-637-2206 ▪ TF: 800-879-6282

Athletic Union of the US, Amateur   www.aausports.org
PO Box 22409   Lake Buena Vista FL 32830
Ph: 407-934-7200 ▪ Fx: 407-934-7242 ▪ TF: 800-228-4872

Athletics, National Association of Academic Advisors for   www.nfoura.org
14606 Woodlake Terr   Louisville KY 40245
Ph: 502-253-9530 ▪ Fx: 502-253-9533

Athletics, National Association of Collegiate Directors of   nacda.ocsn.com
24651 Detroit Rd   Westlake OH 44145
Ph: 440-892-4000 ▪ Fx: 440-892-4007

Athletics, National Association of Intercollegiate   www.naia.org
23500 W 105th St   Olathe KS 66051
Ph: 913-791-0044 ▪ Fx: 913-791-9555

Atlantic Center for the Environment, Quebec-Labrador Foundation -   www.qlf.org
55 S Main St   Ipswich MA 01938
Ph: 978-356-0038 ▪ Fx: 978-356-7322

Atlantic Coast Collegiate Hockey League   www.acchockey.com
380 S State Rd 434   Altamonte Springs FL 32714
Ph: 407-296-5269

Atlantic Coast Conference   theacc.ocsn.com
PO Drawer ACC   Greensboro NC 27417
Ph: 336-854-8787 ▪ Fx: 336-854-7964

Atlantic Council of the United States   www.acus.org
910 17th St NW Suite 1000   Washington DC 20006
Ph: 202-463-7226 ▪ Fx: 202-463-7241

Atlantic Economic Society, International   www.iaes.org
4949 W Pine Blvd 2nd Fl   Saint Louis MO 63108
Ph: 314-454-0100 ▪ Fx: 314-454-9109

Atlantic Legal Foundation   www.atlanticlegal.org
205 E 42nd St 9th Fl   New York NY 10017
Ph: 212-573-1960 ▪ Fx: 212-573-1959

Atlantic Offshore Lobstermen's Association   www.offshorelobster.org
114 Adams Rd   Candia NH 03034
Ph: 603-483-3030 ▪ Fx: 603-483-4862

Atlantic Salmon Federation   www.asf.ca
PO Box 5200   Saint Andrews NB E5B3S8
Ph: 506-529-1033 ▪ Fx: 506-529-4438

Atlantic States Marine Fisheries Commission   www.asmfc.org
1444 'I' St NW 6th Fl   Washington DC 20005
Ph: 202-289-6400 ▪ Fx: 202-289-6051

Atlas Economic Research Foundation   www.atlasusa.org
4084 University Dr Suite 103   Fairfax VA 22030
Ph: 703-934-6969 ▪ Fx: 703-352-7530

ATM Forum
PO Box 22920   San Francisco CA 94122
Ph: 415-561-6275 ▪ Fx: 415-561-6120
www.atmforum.com

Atmospheric Policy, Alliance for Responsible
2111 Wilson Blvd Suite 850   Arlington VA 22201
Ph: 703-243-0344 ▪ Fx: 703-243-2874
www.arap.org

Atmospheric Research, University Corporation for
1850 Table Mesa Dr   Boulder CO 80305
Ph: 303-497-1000 ▪ Fx: 303-497-1654
www.ucar.edu

Atomic Bomb Survivors in the US, Committee of
1759 Sutter St   San Francisco CA 94115
Ph: 562-698-0855

Atomic Energy Liability Underwriters, Mutual
3158 River Rd Suite 103   Des Plaines IL 60018
Ph: 312-467-0003 ▪ Fx: 312-467-0774

ATP Tour Inc
201 ATP Tour Blvd   Ponte Vedra Beach FL 32082
Ph: 904-285-8000 ▪ Fx: 904-285-5966 ▪ TF: 800-527-4811
www.atptennis.com

Attention Deficit Disorder Association, National
1788 2nd St Suite 200   Highland Park IL 60035
Ph: 847-432-2332 ▪ Fx: 847-432-5874
www.add.org

Attention-Deficit/Hyperactivity Disorder, Children & Adults with
8181 Professional Pl Suite 201   Landover MD 20785
Ph: 301-306-7070 ▪ Fx: 301-306-7090 ▪ TF: 800-233-4050
www.chadd.org

Attention Deficit Information Network
58 Prince St   Needham MA 02492
Ph: 781-455-9895 ▪ Fx: 781-449-1232
www.addinfonetwork.com

Attorney-Certified Public Accountants, American Association of
24196 Alicia Pkwy Suite K   Mission Viejo CA 92691
Ph: 949-768-0336 ▪ TF: 888-288-9272
www.attorney-cpa.com

Attorney Ethics, Americans for the Enforcement of
PO Box 35189   Chicago IL 60707
Ph: 773-283-3880
rentamark.com/aeae

Attorney-Mediators, Association of
PO Box 741955   Dallas TX 75374
Ph: 972-669-8101 ▪ Fx: 972-669-8180 ▪ TF: 800-280-1368
www.attorney-mediators.org

Attorneys, American Academy of Estate Planning
4365 Executive Dr Suite 850   San Diego CA 92121
Ph: 800-846-1555 ▪ Fx: 858-535-8241
www.aaepa.com/

Attorneys, American Association of Nurse
7794 Grow Dr   Pensacola FL 32514
Ph: 850-474-3646 ▪ Fx: 850-484-8762 ▪ TF: 877-538-2262
www.taana.org

Attorneys, American Board of Professional Liability
5712 244th St   Douglaston NY 11362
Ph: 718-631-1400 ▪ Fx: 718-631-1456
www.abpla.org

Attorneys, American College of Mortgage
15245 Shady Grove Rd Suite 130   Rockville MD 20850
Ph: 301-990-9075 ▪ Fx: 301-990-9771
www.acmaatty.org

Attorneys, Association of Commercial Finance
25 Hooks Ln Suite 302   Baltimore MD 21208
Ph: 410-486-2600 ▪ Fx: 410-486-8438
www.afca.cc

Attorneys & Executives in Corporate Real Estate, International Association of   20106 S Sycamore Dr   Frankfort IL 60423
Ph: 815-464-6019 ▪ Fx: 815-464-8334
www.aecre.org

Attorneys General, National Association of
750 1st St NE Suite 1100   Washington DC 20002
Ph: 202-326-6000 ▪ Fx: 202-408-7014 ▪ TF: 888-245-6224
www.naag.org

Attorneys Group The
350 Fairway Dr Suite 200   Deerfield Beach FL 33441
Ph: 954-571-1877 ▪ Fx: 954-571-8582
www.tag-assn.com

Attorneys, National Academy of Elder Law
1604 N Country Club Rd   Tucson AZ 85716
Ph: 520-881-4005 ▪ Fx: 520-325-7925
www.naela.org

Attorneys, National Association of Assistant US
9001 Braddock Rd Suite 380   Springfield VA 22151
Ph: 703-426-4266 ▪ Fx: 800-528-3492 ▪ TF: 800-455-5661
www.naausa.org

Attorneys, National Association of College & University
1 Dupont Cir NW Suite 620   Washington DC 20036
Ph: 202-833-8390 ▪ Fx: 202-296-8379
www.nacua.org

Attorneys, National Association of County Civil
c/o National Assn of Counties 440 1st St NW   Washington DC 20001
Ph: 202-393-6226

Attorneys, National Association of Republican
PO Box 656513   Fresh Meadows NY 11365
Ph: 718-357-7075

Attorneys, National Association of Retail Collection
1620 'I' St NW Suite 165   Washington DC 20006
Ph: 202-861-0706 ▪ Fx: 202-463-8498 ▪ TF: 800-633-6069
www.narca.org

Attorneys Inc, National Network of Estate Planning
1 Valmont Plaza 4th Fl   Omaha NE 68154
Ph: 402-964-3700 ▪ Fx: 402-964-3800 ▪ TF: 888-837-4090
www.netplanning.com

Attorneys, USFN - America's Mortgage Banking
14471 Chambers Rd Suite 260   Tustin CA 92780
Ph: 714-838-7167 ▪ Fx: 714-573-2650 ▪ TF: 800-635-6128
www.usfn.org

Attractions, International Association of Amusement Parks &
1448 Duke St   Alexandria VA 22314
Ph: 703-836-4800 ▪ Fx: 703-836-9678
www.iaapa.org

Auction Association, National Auto
5320-D Spectrum Dr   Frederick MD 21703
Ph: 301-696-0400 ▪ Fx: 301-631-1359
www.naaa.com

Auction Warehouse Association, Burley
620 S Broadway St   Lexington KY 40508
Ph: 859-255-4504

Auctioneers Association, National
8880 Ballentine St   Overland Park KS 66214
Ph: 913-541-8084 ▪ Fx: 913-894-5281 ▪ TF: 888-541-8084
www.auctioneers.org

Audiences Inc, Young
115 E 92nd St   New York NY 10128
Ph: 212-831-8110 ▪ Fx: 212-289-1202
www.youngaudiences.org

Audio Engineering Society
60 E 42nd St Rm 2520   New York NY 10165
Ph: 212-661-8528 ▪ Fx: 212-682-0477 ▪ TF: 800-541-7299
www.aes.org

Audio Information Services, International Association of
www.iaais.org

Audio Publishers Association
8405 Greensboro Dr Suite 800   McLean VA 22102
Ph: 703-556-7172 ▪ Fx: 703-556-3236
www.audiopub.org

Audio Recording Services, Society of Professional
PO Box 770845   Memphis TN 38177
Ph: 901-747-3111 ▪ TF: 800-771-7727
www.spars.com

Audio Special Interest Group, Interactive
c/o MIDI Manufacturers Assn PO Box 3173   La Habra CA 90632
Ph: 714-736-9774 ▪ Fx: 714-736-9775
www.iasig.org

Audio Visual Communicators, International Association of
57 W Palo Verde Ave PO Box 250   Ocotillo CA 92259
Ph: 760-358-7000 ▪ Fx: 760-358-7569
www.iaavc.org

Audiologists, Academy of Dispensing
1 Windsor Cove Suite 305   Columbia SC 29223
Ph: 803-252-5646 ▪ Fx: 803-765-0860 ▪ TF: 800-445-8629
www.audiologist.org

Audiology, Academy of Rehabilitative
PO Box 26532   Minneapolis MN 55426
Ph: 952-920-0484 ▪ Fx: 952-920-6098
www.audrehab.org

Audiology, American Academy of
11730 Plaza America Dr Suite 300   Reston VA 22190
Ph: 703-790-8466 ▪ Fx: 703-790-8631 ▪ TF: 800-222-2336
www.audiology.org

Audiology Association, Educational
13153 N Del Mabry Hwy Suite 105   Tampa FL 33618
Ph: 813-968-2644 ▪ Fx: 813-968-3597 ▪ TF: 800-460-7322
www.edaud.org

Audiovideo Retailers Association, Professional
10 E 22nd St Suite 310   Lombard IL 60148
Ph: 630-268-1500 ▪ Fx: 630-953-8957
www.paralink.com

Audiovisual Catalogers, Online
Minnesota State Univ Memorial Library 3097 PO Box 8419   Mankato MN 56001
Ph: 507-389-5952
www.olacinc.org

Audit Bureau of Circulations
900 N Meacham Rd   Schaumburg IL 60173
Ph: 847-605-0909 ▪ Fx: 847-605-0483
www.accessabc.com

Audit Bureau for Media Measurement, Traffic
420 Lexington Ave Room 2520   New York NY 10170
Ph: 212-972-8075 ▪ Fx: 212-972-8928
www.tabonline.com

Audit & Control Association, Information Systems
3701 Algonquin Rd Suite 1010   Rolling Meadows IL 60008
Ph: 847-253-1545 ▪ Fx: 847-253-1443
www.isaca.org

Audit Network, Catholic Healthcare
231 S Bemiston Ave Suite 300   Saint Louis MO 63105
Ph: 314-802-2000 ▪ Fx: 314-802-2020
www.chanllc.com

(Auditing) BPA International
2 Corporate Dr Suite 900   Shelton CT 06484
Ph: 203-447-2800 ▪ Fx: 203-447-2900
www.bpai.com

Auditors, Association of College & University
342 N Main St   West Hartford CT 06117
Ph: 860-586-7561 ▪ Fx: 860-586-7550
www.acua.org

Auditors, Association of Credit Union Internal
PO Box 1926   Columbus OH 43216
Ph: 614-221-9702 ▪ Fx: 614-221-2335 ▪ TF: 866-254-8128
www.acuia.org

Auditors, Association of Healthcare Internal
PO Box 449   Onsted MI 49265
Ph: 517-467-7729 ▪ Fx: 517-467-6104 ▪ TF: 888-275-2442
www.ahia.org

Auditors Comptrollers & Treasurers, National Association of State
2401 Regency Rd Suite 302   Lexington KY 40503
Ph: 859-276-1147 ▪ Fx: 859-278-0507
www.nasact.org

Auditors, Institute of Internal
249 Maitland Ave   Altamonte Springs FL 32701
Ph: 407-937-1100 ▪ Fx: 407-937-1101
www.theiia.org

Auditors, National Association of Local Government
2401 Regency Rd Suite 302   Lexington KY 40503
Ph: 859-276-0686
www.nalga.org

Auditors, National Society of Insurance Premium
PO Box 1896   Columbus OH 43216
Ph: 614-221-9266 ▪ Fx: 614-221-2335 ▪ TF: 888-846-7472
www.nsipa.org

Auditory Society, American
352 Sundial Ridge Cir   Dammeron Valley UT 84783
Ph: 435-574-0062 ▪ Fx: 435-574-0063
www.amauditorysoc.org

Audubon Naturalist Society
8940 Jones Mill Rd   Chevy Chase MD 20815
Ph: 301-652-9188 ▪ Fx: 301-951-7179
www.audubonnaturalist.org

Audubon Society, National
700 Broadway   New York NY 10003
Ph: 212-979-3000 ▪ Fx: 212-979-3188
www.audubon.org

August Derleth Society
PO Box 481   Sauk City WI 53583
Ph: 608-643-3242 ▪ Fx: 608-643-5080
www.derleth.org

Augustana Historical Society
Augustana College 639 38th St   Rock Island IL 61201
Ph: 309-794-7166 ▪ Fx: 309-794-7443
www.augustana.edu/Historical

Auriton Solutions
1700 W Hwy 36 Suite 301   Roseville MN 55113
Ph: 651-631-8000 ▪ Fx: 651-697-7955 ▪ TF: 877-332-8700
www.auriton.org

Austen Jane Society of North America
106 Barlows Run   Williamsburg VA 23188
Ph: 800-836-3911
www.jasna.org

Australian Association, American
599 Lexington Ave 18th Fl   New York NY 10022
Ph: 212-338-6860 ▪ Fx: 212-338-6864
www.americanaustralian.org

Australian Cattle Dog Club of America
5041 Britton Ln   Jacksonville FL 32210
Ph: 904-771-5217 ▪ Fx: 904-908-9585
www.acdca.org

Australian Koala Foundation, Friends of the   www.savethekoala.com
c/o Nolan/Lehr Group Inc 224 W 29th St 15th Fl   New York NY 10001
Ph: 212-967-8200 ▪ Fx: 212-967-7292 ▪ TF: 800-695-6252

Australian New Zealand American Chambers of   www.austemb.org/chambers.htm
Commerce   c/o Embassy of Australia 1601 Massachusetts Ave NW   Washington DC 20036
Ph: 202-797-3028 ▪ Fx: 202-797-3457

Austrian Chamber of Commerce, US-   www.usatchamber.com
165 W 46th St   New York NY 10036
Ph: 212-819-0117 ▪ Fx: 212-819-0345

Austrian Society, American-   www.geocities.com/americanaustriansociety
6630-D Eli Whitney Dr   Columbia MD 21046
Ph: 443-362-6422

Austrian Studies, Center for   www.cas.umn.edu
Univ of Minnesota 267 19th Ave S 314 Social Science Bldg   Minneapolis MN 55455
Ph: 612-624-9811 ▪ Fx: 612-626-9004

Authors, American Society of Journalists &   www.asja.org
1501 Broadway Suite 302   New York NY 10036
Ph: 212-997-0947 ▪ Fx: 212-768-7414

Authors Association, Text & Academic   www.taaonline.net
PO Box 76477   Saint Petersburg FL 33734
Ph: 727-821-7277 ▪ Fx: 727-821-7271

Authors Guild   www.authorsguild.org
31 E 28th St 10th Fl   New York NY 10016
Ph: 212-563-5904 ▪ Fx: 212-564-5363

Authors League of America
31 E 28th St   New York NY 10016
Ph: 212-564-8350 ▪ Fx: 212-564-5363

Authors & Publishers, American Society of Composers   www.ascap.com
1 Lincoln Plaza   New York NY 10023
Ph: 212-621-6000 ▪ Fx: 212-724-9064 ▪ TF: 800-952-7227

Authorship Reading & Publishing, Society for the History of   www.sharpweb.org
PO Box 30   Wilmington NC 28402
Ph: 910-254-0308

Autism Network International   ani.autistics.org
PO Box 35448   Syracuse NY 13235
Ph: 315-476-2462 ▪ Fx: 315-425-1978

Autism Research Institute   autism.com/ari
4182 Adams Ave   San Diego CA 92116
Ph: 619-281-7165 ▪ Fx: 619-563-6840

Autism Research, National Alliance for   www.naar.org
99 Wall St Research Park   Princeton NJ 08540
Ph: 609-430-9160 ▪ Fx: 609-430-9163 ▪ TF: 888-777-6227

Autism Services Center   www.autismservicescenter.org
PO Box 507   Huntington WV 25710
Ph: 304-525-8014 ▪ Fx: 304-525-8026

Autism Society of America   www.autism-society.org
7910 Woodmont Ave Suite 300   Bethesda MD 20814
Ph: 301-657-0881 ▪ Fx: 301-657-0869 ▪ TF: 800-328-8476

Auto Association, Electric   www.eaaev.org
60 Alan Dr   Pleasant Hill CA 94523
Ph: 925-685-7580 ▪ TF: 800-537-2882

Auto Auction Association, National   www.naaa.com
5320-D Spectrum Dr   Frederick MD 21703
Ph: 301-696-0400 ▪ Fx: 301-631-1359

Auto Body Council, National   www.autobodycouncil.org
PO Box 4489   West Richland WA 99352
Ph: 509-545-3399 ▪ Fx: 509-545-4222 ▪ TF: 888-667-7443

Auto Club, US   www.usacracing.com
4910 W 16th St   Speedway IN 46224
Ph: 317-247-5151 ▪ Fx: 317-247-0123

Auto Collision Repair, I-CAR Inter-Industry Conference on   www.i-car.com
3701 Algonquin Rd Suite 400   Rolling Meadows IL 60008
Ph: 847-590-1191 ▪ Fx: 847-590-1215 ▪ TF: 800-422-7872

Auto Dealer Consultants Association, CPA   www.autodealercpas.com
1 Valmont Plaza 4th Fl   Omaha NE 68154
Ph: 402-964-3865 ▪ Fx: 402-964-3811 ▪ TF: 888-475-4476

Auto-Insurance Reform, Coalition for
7310 Stafford Rd   Alexandria VA 22307
Ph: 703-660-0799

Auto International Association   aiaglobal.org
4600 East-West Hwy Suite 300   Bethesda MD 20814
Ph: 301-654-6664 ▪ Fx: 301-654-3299

Auto Racing, National Association for Stock Car   www.nascar.com
1801 W International Speedway Blvd   Daytona Beach FL 32114
Ph: 386-253-0611 ▪ Fx: 386-947-6712

Auto Racing Writers & Broadcasters Association Inc, American   www.aarwba.org
922 N Pass Ave   Burbank CA 91505
Ph: 818-842-7005 ▪ Fx: 818-842-7020

Auto Safety, Advocates for Highway &   www.saferoads.org
750 1st St NE Suite 901   Washington DC 20002
Ph: 202-408-1711 ▪ Fx: 202-408-1699

Auto Safety, Center for   www.autosafety.org
1825 Connecticut Ave NW Suite 330   Washington DC 20009
Ph: 202-328-7700

Auto Theft Investigators, International Association of   www.iaati.org
PO Box 223   Clinton NY 13323
Ph: 315-853-1913 ▪ Fx: 315-793-0048

Autobody Craftsman Association   www.acanw.com
1124 Industry Dr   Tukwila WA 98188
Ph: 206-575-8893 ▪ Fx: 206-575-8894 ▪ TF: 800-526-3792

Autoclaved Aerated Concrete Products Association   www.aacpa.org
7638 Nashville St   Ringgold GA 30736
Ph: 706-965-4587

Autoimmune Related Disease Association, American   www.aarda.org
22100 Gratiot Ave   East Detroit MI 48021
Ph: 586-776-3900 ▪ Fx: 586-776-3903

Automated Builders Consortium   www.automatedbuildersconsortium.org
PO Box 865   Hershey PA 17033
Ph: 717-566-1525 ▪ Fx: 717-566-2114

Automated Building Association, Continental   www.caba.org
1200 Montreal Rd Bldg M-20   Ottawa ON K1A0R6
Ph: 613-990-7407 ▪ Fx: 613-991-9990 ▪ TF: 888-798-2222

Automated Imaging Association   www.machinevisiononline.org
900 Victors Way PO Box 3724   Ann Arbor MI 48106
Ph: 734-994-6088 ▪ Fx: 734-994-3338

Automatic Control Council, American   www.a2c2.org
Wright State Univ Dept of Electrical Engineering 3640 Col Glenn Hwy   Dayton OH 45435
Ph: 937-775-5062 ▪ Fx: 937-775-3936

Automatic Door Manufacturers, American Association of   www.aaadm.com
1300 Sumner Ave   Cleveland OH 44115
Ph: 216-241-7333 ▪ Fx: 216-241-0105

Automatic Fire Alarm Association Inc   www.afaa.org
PO Box 951807   Lake Mary FL 32795
Ph: 407-322-6288 ▪ Fx: 407-322-7488

Automatic Identification & Mobility, AIM Inc - Association for   www.aimglobal.org
125 Warrendale-Bayne Rd   Warrendale PA 15086
Ph: 724-934-4470 ▪ Fx: 724-934-4495 ▪ TF: 800-338-0206

Automatic Merchandising Association, National   www.vending.org
20 N Wacker Dr Suite 3500   Chicago IL 60606
Ph: 312-346-0370 ▪ Fx: 312-704-4140

Automatic Meter Reading Association   www.amra-intl.org
60 Revere Dr Suite 500   Northbrook IL 60062
Ph: 847-480-9628 ▪ Fx: 847-480-9282

Automatic Pistol Collectors Association, National   napca.net
PO Box 15738   Saint Louis MO 63163
Ph: 314-638-6505

Automatic Transmission Rebuilders Association   www.atra-gears.com
2400 Latigo Ave   Oxnard CA 93030
Ph: 805-604-2000 ▪ Fx: 805-604-2003

Automation Association, Measurement Control &   www.measure.org
PO Box 3698   Williamsburg VA 23187
Ph: 757-258-3100 ▪ Fx: 757-258-9066

Automation Consortium, Electronic Design   www.edac.org
111 W Saint John St Suite 220   San Jose CA 95113
Ph: 408-287-3322 ▪ Fx: 408-283-5283

Automation in Pharmacy, American Society for   www.asapnet.org
492 Norristown Rd Suite 160   Blue Bell PA 19422
Ph: 610-825-7783 ▪ Fx: 610-825-7641

Automation Society, IEEE Robotics &   www.ncsu.edu/IEEE-RAS
IEEE Operations Ctr 445 Hoes Ln   Piscataway NJ 08854
Ph: 732-981-0060 ▪ Fx: 732-981-1721

Automation Society, ISA - Instrumentation Systems &   www.isa.org
67 Alexander Dr   Research Triangle Park NC 27709
Ph: 919-549-8411 ▪ Fx: 919-549-8288

Automobile Aerospace & Agricultural Implement Workers of America, International Union United   www.uaw.org
8000 E Jefferson Ave   Detroit MI 48214
Ph: 313-926-5000 ▪ Fx: 313-823-6016

Automobile Association, American   www.aaa.com
1000 AAA Dr Box 28   Heathrow FL 32746
Ph: 407-444-4240 ▪ Fx: 407-444-4247

Automobile Association, Canadian   www.caa.ca
1145 Hunt Club Rd Suite 200   Ottawa ON K1V0Y3
Ph: 613-247-0117 ▪ Fx: 613-247-0118

Automobile Club of America, Antique   www.aaca.org
501 W Governor Rd PO Box 417   Hershey PA 17033
Ph: 717-534-1910 ▪ Fx: 717-534-9101

Automobile Dealers Association, American International   www.aiada.org
211 N Union St Suite 300   Alexandria VA 22314
Ph: 703-519-7800 ▪ Fx: 703-519-7810 ▪ TF: 800-462-4232

Automobile Dealers Association, National   www.nada.org
8400 Westpark Dr   McLean VA 22102
Ph: 703-821-7000 ▪ Fx: 703-821-7075 ▪ TF: 800-252-6232

Automobile Dealers Association, National Independent   www.niada.com
2521 Brown Blvd   Arlington TX 76006
Ph: 817-640-3838 ▪ Fx: 817-649-5866 ▪ TF: 800-682-3837

Automobile Dealers, National Association of Minority   www.namad.com/
8401 Corporate Dr Suite 404   Lanham MD 20785
Ph: 301-306-1614 ▪ Fx: 301-306-1493

Automobile Manufacturers, Alliance of   www.autoalliance.org
1401 'I' St NW Suite 900   Washington DC 20005
Ph: 202-326-5500 ▪ Fx: 202-326-5598

Automobile Manufacturers, Association of International   www.aiam.org
1001 19th St N Suite 1200   Arlington VA 22209
Ph: 703-525-7788 ▪ Fx: 703-525-8817

Automobile Manufacturers Association, Japan   www.japanauto.com
1050 17th St NW Suite 410   Washington DC 20036
Ph: 202-296-8537 ▪ Fx: 202-872-1212

Automotive Aftermarket Distributors, Association of   www.aftermarket.org
5050 Poplar Ave Suite 2020   Memphis TN 38157
Ph: 901-682-9090 ▪ Fx: 901-682-9098 ▪ TF: 800-727-8112

Automotive Aftermarket Industry Association   www.aftermarket.org
4600 East-West Hwy Suite 300   Bethesda MD 20814
Ph: 301-654-6664 ▪ Fx: 301-654-3299

Automotive Aftermarket Suppliers Association   www.aftermarketsuppliers.org
10 Laboratory Dr PO Box 13966   Research Triangle Park NC 27709
Ph: 919-549-4800 ▪ Fx: 919-549-4824

Automotive Analysts, Society of   www.cybersaa.org
3300 Washtenaw Ave Suite 220   Ann Arbor MI 48104
Ph: 734-677-3518 ▪ Fx: 734-677-2407

Automotive Body Parts Association   www.autobpa.org
2000 S Dairy Ashford Suite 420 PO Box 820689   Houston TX 77282
Ph: 281-531-0809 ▪ Fx: 281-531-9411 ▪ TF: 800-323-5832

Automotive Communications Council
4600 East-West Hwy Suite 300   Bethesda MD 20814
Ph: 240-333-1089 ▪ Fx: 301-654-3299
www.acc-online.org

Automotive Council, Overseas
10 Laboratory Dr PO Box 13966   Research Triangle Park NC
27709
Ph: 919-406-8810 ▪ Fx: 919-549-4824
www.oac-intl.org

Automotive Damage Appraisers Association, Independent
PO Box 12291   Columbus GA 31917
Ph: 800-369-4232 ▪ Fx: 888-423-2669
www.iada.org

Automotive Engine Rebuilders Association
330 Lexington Dr   Buffalo Grove IL 60089
Ph: 847-541-6550 ▪ Fx: 847-541-5808
www.aera.org

Automotive Engineers Inc, Society of
400 Commonwealth Dr   Warrendale PA 15096
Ph: 724-776-4841 ▪ Fx: 724-776-5760 ▪ TF: 877-606-7323
www.sae.org

Automotive Finance Association, National
217 St Charles Pl   Pittsburgh PA 15215
Ph: 412-781-5601 ▪ Fx: 412-781-5607
www.nafassociation.com

Automotive Fleet & Leasing Association
21061 S Western Ave   Torrance CA 90501
Ph: 310-533-2520 ▪ Fx: 310-533-2506
www.aflaonline.org

Automotive Historians, Society of
1102 Long Cove Rd   Gales Ferry CT 06335
Ph: 860-464-6466 ▪ Fx: 860-464-2614
www.autohistory.org

Automotive Industry Action Group
26200 Lahser Rd Suite 200   Southfield MI 48034
Ph: 248-358-3570 ▪ Fx: 248-358-3253
www.aiag.org

Automotive Leasing Association, American
675 N Washington St Suite 410   Alexandria VA 22314
Ph: 703-548-0777 ▪ Fx: 703-236-1949
www.aalafleet.com

Automotive Lift Institute
PO Box 33116   Indialantic FL 32903
Ph: 321-722-9993 ▪ Fx: 321-722-9931
www.autolift.org

Automotive Maintenance & Repair Association Inc
7101 Wisconsin Ave Suite 1200   Bethesda MD 20814
Ph: 301-634-4954
www.motorist.org

Automotive Medicine, Association for the Advancement of
PO Box 4176   Barrington IL 60011
Ph: 847-844-3880 ▪ Fx: 847-844-3884
www.carcrash.org

Automotive Occupant Restraints Council
1081 Dove Run Rd Suite 403   Lexington KY 40502
Ph: 859-269-4240 ▪ Fx: 859-269-4241
www.aorc.org

Automotive Oil Change Association
12810 Hillcrest Rd Suite 221   Dallas TX 75230
Ph: 972-458-9468 ▪ Fx: 972-458-9539 ▪ TF: 800-331-0329
www.aoca.org

Automotive Parts Rebuilders Association
14160 Newbrook Dr Suite 210   Chantilly VA 20151
Ph: 703-968-2772 ▪ Fx: 703-968-2878
www.apra.org

Automotive Public Relations Council
10 Laboratory Dr PO Box 13966   Research Triangle Park NC
27709
Ph: 919-549-4800 ▪ Fx: 919-549-4824
www.autopr.org

Automotive Radiator Service Association, National
PO Box 97   East Greenville PA 18041
Ph: 215-541-4500 ▪ Fx: 215-679-4977
www.narsa.org

Automotive Recyclers Association
3975 Fair Ridge Dr Suite 20N   Fairfax VA 22033
Ph: 703-385-1001 ▪ Fx: 703-385-1494
www.autorecyc.org

Automotive Refrigeration Products Institute
PO Box 9000   Fort Worth TX 76147
Ph: 817-732-4600 ▪ Fx: 817-732-9610

Automotive Service Association
1901 Airport Fwy   Bedford TX 76021
Ph: 817-283-6205 ▪ Fx: 817-685-0225 ▪ TF: 800-272-7467
www.asashop.org

Automotive Service Dealers Association, Gasoline &
9520 Seaview Ave   Brooklyn NY 11236
Ph: 718-241-1111 ▪ Fx: 718-763-6589

Automotive Service Excellence, National Institute for
101 Blue Seal Dr SE   Leesburg VA 20175
Ph: 703-669-6600 ▪ Fx: 703-713-0727 ▪ TF: 877-273-8324
www.asecert.org

Automotive Specialty Products Alliance
900 17th St NW Suite 300   Washington DC 20006
Ph: 202-833-7327 ▪ Fx: 202-872-8114
www.aspalliance.org

Automotive Teachers, North American Council of
11956 Bernardo Plaza Dr Dept 436   San Diego CA 92128
Ph: 858-487-8126 ▪ Fx: 858-487-3617
www.nacat.com

Automotive Technicians Education Foundation, National
101 Blue Seal Dr SE Suite 101   Leesburg VA 20175
Ph: 703-669-6650 ▪ Fx: 703-669-6125
www.natef.org

Automotive Trade Association Executives
8400 Westpark Dr   McLean VA 22102
Ph: 703-821-7072 ▪ Fx: 703-556-8581

Automotive Training Managers Council
101 Blue Seal Dr SE Suite 101   Leesburg VA 20175
Ph: 703-669-6670 ▪ Fx: 703-669-6126
www.atmc.org

Automotive Warehouse Distributors Association
4050 Pennsylvania Ave Suite 225   Kansas City MO 64111
Ph: 816-523-8693 ▪ Fx: 816-523-7293
www.awda.org

Auxiliary to Sons of Union Veterans of the Civil War
2449 Center Ave   Alliance OH 44601
Ph: 330-823-6919

Avian Pathologists, American Association of
953 College Station Rd   Athens GA 30602
Ph: 706-542-5645 ▪ Fx: 706-542-0249
www.aaap.info

Avian Trainers & Educators, International Association of
350 St Andrews Fairway   Memphis TN 38111
Ph: 901-685-9122 ▪ Fx: 901-685-7233
www.iaate.org

Avian Veterinarians, Association of
PO Box 811720   Boca Raton FL 33481
Ph: 561-393-8901 ▪ Fx: 561-393-8902
www.aav.org

Aviation, Adventist World
PO Box 251   Berrien Springs MI 49103
Ph: 269-473-0135 ▪ Fx: 269-471-4049
www.flyawa.org

Aviation Association of America, Army
755 Main St Suite 4D   Monroe CT 06468
Ph: 203-268-2450 ▪ Fx: 203-268-5870
www.quad-a.org

Aviation Association, Marine Corps
715 Broadway St PO Box 296   Quantico VA 22134
Ph: 703-630-1903 ▪ Fx: 703-630-2713 ▪ TF: 800-280-3001
www.flymcaa.org

Aviation Association, National Agricultural
1005 'E' St SE   Washington DC 20003
Ph: 202-546-5722 ▪ Fx: 202-546-5726
www.agaviation.org

Aviation Association, National Business
1200 18th St NW Suite 400   Washington DC 20036
Ph: 202-783-9000 ▪ Fx: 202-331-8364
www.nbaa.org

Aviation, Association of Naval
2550 Huntington Ave Suite 201   Alexandria VA 22303
Ph: 703-960-2490 ▪ Fx: 703-960-4490
www.anahq.org

Aviation Association, University
3410 Skyway Dr   Auburn AL 36830
Ph: 334-844-2434 ▪ Fx: 334-844-2432
uaa.auburn.edu

Aviation Crime Prevention Institute Inc
226 N Nova Rd   Ormond Beach FL 32174
Ph: 800-969-5473 ▪ Fx: 386-615-3378
www.acpi.org

Aviation Development Council
141-07 20th Ave Suite 404   Whitestone NY 11357
Ph: 718-746-0212

Aviation Distributors & Manufacturers Association
1900 Arch St   Philadelphia PA 19103
Ph: 215-564-3484 ▪ Fx: 215-963-9784
www.adma.org

Aviation Fellowship, Mission
1849 N Wabash Ave   Redlands CA 92374
Ph: 909-794-1151 ▪ Fx: 909-794-3016 ▪ TF: 800-359-7623
www.maf.org

Aviation Foundation, International Agricultural
PO Box 1607   Mount Vernon WA 98273
Ph: 360-724-3881 ▪ TF: 888-490-8206
www.agpilot.com

Aviation Insurance Association
14 W 3rd St Suite 200   Kansas City MO 64105
Ph: 816-221-8488 ▪ Fx: 816-472-2265
www.aiaweb.org

Aviation International, Women in
101 Corsair Dr Suite 101   Daytona Beach FL 32114
Ph: 386-226-7996 ▪ Fx: 386-226-7998
www.wai.org

(Aviation) LightHawk
PO Box 653   Lander WY 82520
Ph: 307-332-3242
www.lighthawk.org

Aviation Maintenance Association, Professional
717 Princess St   Alexandria VA 22314
Ph: 703-683-3171 ▪ Fx: 703-683-0018 ▪ TF: 866-865-7262
www.pama.org

Aviation Maintenance, Association for Women in
PO Box 1030   Edgewater FL 32132
Ph: 386-424-5780 ▪ Fx: 386-428-3534
www.awam.org

Aviation Manufacturers Association, General
1400 K St NW Suite 801   Washington DC 20005
Ph: 202-393-1500 ▪ Fx: 202-842-4063
www.gama.aero

Aviation Medical Association, Civil
PO Box 23864   Oklahoma City OK 73123
Ph: 405-840-0199 ▪ Fx: 405-848-1053
www.civilavmed.com

Aviation Officials, National Association of State
1010 Wayne Ave Suite 930   Silver Spring MD 20910
Ph: 301-588-0587 ▪ Fx: 301-585-1803
www.nasao.org

Aviation Organization, International Civil
999 University St   Montreal QC H3C5H7
Ph: 514-954-8219 ▪ Fx: 514-954-6077
www.icao.int

Aviation Preservation Society & Museum, Military
2260 International Pkwy   North Canton OH 44720
Ph: 330-896-6332
www.mapsairmuseum.org

Aviation Research & Education,
NASAO Center for   1010 Wayne Ave Suite 930   Silver Spring
MD 20910
Ph: 301-495-2848 ▪ Fx: 301-585-1803
www.nasao.org/center/Center_Home_Page.htm

Aviation Safety Institute
PO Box 690   Worthington OH 43085
Ph: 614-793-1679 ▪ Fx: 614-793-1708
www.aero-farm.com/asi/asi.htm

Aviation Technician Education Council
2090 Wexford Ct   Harrisburg PA 17112
Ph: 717-540-7121
www.atec-amt.org/

Aviation Women Association, International
PO Box 4491   New York NY 10163
Ph: 212-921-5100 ▪ Fx: 212-774-7415
www.iawa.org

Avion Travelcade Club
PO Box 624259   South Lake Tahoe CA 96154
Ph: 530-544-8285
www.avionclub.com

AVKO Dyslexia Research Foundation
3084 W Willard Rd   Clio MI 48420
Ph: 810-686-9283 ▪ Fx: 810-686-1101
www.spelling.org

Avocado Commission, California
38 Discovery Suite 150   Irvine CA 92618
Ph: 949-341-1955 ▪ Fx: 949-341-1970
www.avocado.org

AVS Science & Technology Society
120 Wall St 32nd Fl   New York NY 10005
Ph: 212-248-0200 ▪ Fx: 212-248-0245
www.avs.org

AVSC International Inc
440 9th Ave 3rd Fl   New York NY 10001
Ph: 212-561-8000 ▪ Fx: 212-561-8067 ▪ TF: 800-564-2872
www.engenderhealth.org

Awards & Recognition Association
4700 West Lake Ave   Glenview IL 60025
Ph: 847-375-4800 ▪ Fx: 877-734-9380 ▪ TF: 800-344-2148
www.ara.org

Awning Manufacturers Association, Professional
1801 County Rd 'B' W   Roseville MN 55113
Ph: 651-222-2508 ▪ Fx: 651-631-9334 ▪ TF: 800-225-4324
www.awninginfo.com

Ayn Rand Institute: The Center for the Advancement of Objectivism www.aynrand.org
2121 Alton Pkwy Suite 250   Irvine CA 92606
Ph: 949-222-6550 ▪ Fx: 949-222-6558

Ayrshire Breeders Association www.usayrshire.com
1224 Alton Darby Creek Rd Suite B   Columbus OH 43228
Ph: 614-335-0020 ▪ Fx: 614-335-0023

Azalea Society of America www.azaleas.org

B

B-24 Liberator Club, International www.bomberlegends.com/b24club.html
1672 Main St Suite E PMB 124   Ramona CA 92065
Ph: 760-788-3624 ▪ Fx: 760-789-8911

B-26 Marauder Historical Society b-26marauderarchive.org
PO Box 1786   Rockville MD 20849
Ph: 301-460-4488 ▪ Fx: 301-460-2075

Babbage Charles Institute www.cbi.umn.edu
Univ of Minnesota 211 Andersen Library 222 21st Ave
    S   Minneapolis MN 55455
Ph: 612-624-5050 ▪ Fx: 612-625-8054

Babe Ruth League Inc www.baberuthleague.org
1770 Brunswick Pike   Trenton NJ 08638
Ph: 609-695-1434 ▪ Fx: 609-695-2505

BACCHUS & GAMMA Peer Education Network bacchusgamma.org
2130 S University Blvd   Denver CO 80210
Ph: 303-871-0901 ▪ Fx: 303-871-0907

Back Country Horsemen of America www.backcountryhorse.com
PO Box 1367   Graham WA 98338
Ph: 360-832-2461 ▪ Fx: 360-832-2471 ▪ TF: 888-893-5161

Badminton, USA www.usabadminton.com
1 Olympic Plaza   Colorado Springs CO 80909
Ph: 719-578-4808 ▪ Fx: 719-578-4507

Baeck Leo Institute www.lbi.org
15 W 16th St   New York NY 10011
Ph: 212-744-6400 ▪ Fx: 212-988-1305

Bag Federation, Film & www.plasticbag.com
Society of the Plastics Industry Inc 1801 K St NW Suite
    600K   Washington DC 20006
Ph: 202-974-5215 ▪ Fx: 202-974-7675

Bagmen of Baghdad Imperial Guild, Ancient Mystic Order of
6620 Cliffside Cir   Amarillo TX 79124
Ph: 806-373-8246

Baha'is of the US, National Spiritual Assembly of the www.us.bahai.org
1233 Central St   Evanston IL 60201
Ph: 847-869-9039 ▪ TF: 800-999-9019

Bail Coalition, American www.americanbailcoalition.com
1725 DeSales St NW Suite 800   Washington DC 20036
Ph: 202-659-6547 ▪ Fx: 202-296-8702 ▪ TF: 800-375-8390

Baker Institute for Public Policy www.rice.edu/projects/baker
Rice University 6100 Main St Baker Hall Suite 120   Houston TX
    77005
Ph: 713-348-4683 ▪ Fx: 713-348-5993

Bakers of America Inc, Quality www.qba.com
70 Riverdale Ave   Greenwich CT 06831
Ph: 203-531-7100 ▪ Fx: 203-531-1406

Bakers Association, American www.americanbakers.org
1350 'I' St NW Suite 1290   Washington DC 20005
Ph: 202-789-0300 ▪ Fx: 202-898-1164

Bakers Association, Cookie & Snack
1128 Maple Dr NW   Cleveland TN 37312
Ph: 423-472-5856 ▪ Fx: 423-478-1273

Bakers Association, Independent www.independentbaker.org
1223 Potomac St NW PO Box 3731   Washington DC 20007
Ph: 202-333-8190 ▪ Fx: 202-337-3809

Bakers Association, Wholesale Variety
215 Eva St   Saint Paul MN 55107
Ph: 651-224-5761 ▪ Fx: 651-224-9047

Bakers Guild of America, Bread www.bbga.org
3203 Maryland Ave   North Versailles PA 15137
Ph: 412-823-2080 ▪ Fx: 412-823-2495

Bakery Association, International Dairy-Deli- www.iddanet.org
313 Price Pl Suite 202   Madison WI 53705
Ph: 608-238-7908 ▪ Fx: 608-238-6330

Bakery Association, RBA - Retailer's www.rbanet.com
14239 Park Center Dr   Laurel MD 20707
Ph: 301-725-2149 ▪ Fx: 301-725-2187 ▪ TF: 800-638-0924

Bakery Confectionery Tobacco Workers & Grain Millers www.bctgm.org
International Union   10401 Connecticut Ave   Kensington MD
    20895
Ph: 301-933-8600 ▪ Fx: 301-946-8452

Baking, American Society of www.asbe.org
27 E Napa St Suite G   Sonoma CA 95476
Ph: 707-935-0103 ▪ Fx: 707-935-0174 ▪ TF: 866-920-9885

Baking Association, Home www.homebaking.org
2931 SW Gainsboro Rd   Topeka KS 66614
Ph: 785-478-3283 ▪ Fx: 785-478-3024

Baking Industry Suppliers Association, BEMA - www.bema.org
825 Green Bay Rd Suite 120   Wilmette IL 60091
Ph: 847-920-1230 ▪ Fx: 847-920-1253

Balalaika & Domra Association of America www.bdaa.com
2801 Warner St   Madison WI 53713
Ph: 608-259-9440

Balance Pathology Resource Registry, NIDCD National Temporal www.tbregistry.org
Bone Hearing &   Massachusetts Eye & Ear Infirmary 243
    Charles St   Boston MA 02114
Ph: 617-573-3711 ▪ Fx: 617-573-3838 ▪ TF: 800-822-1327

Bald-Headed Men of America members.aol.com/BaldUSA/info.htm
102 Bald Dr   Morehead City NC 28557
Ph: 919-726-1855 ▪ Fx: 919-726-6061

Ball Players of America, Association of Professional www.apbpa.org
1820 W Orangewood Ave Suite 206   Orange CA 92868
Ph: 714-935-9993 ▪ Fx: 714-935-0431

Ballet, American Friends of the Paris Opera &
972 5th Ave   New York NY 10021
Ph: 212-439-1426 ▪ Fx: 212-439-1455

(Ballet) Cecchetti Council of America Inc www.cecchetti.org
23393 Meadows Ave   Flat Rock MI 48134
Ph: 734-379-6710 ▪ Fx: 734-379-3886

Ballet Competition, American www.dancecelebration.org
2000 Hamilton St Suite C200   Philadelphia PA 19130
Ph: 215-636-9000 ▪ Fx: 215-564-4206 ▪ TF: 880-052-3096

Ballet Theatre Foundation www.abt.org
American Ballet Theatre 890 Broadway 3rd Fl   New York NY
    10003
Ph: 212-477-3030 ▪ Fx: 212-254-5938

Balloon Federation of America www.bfa.net/
PO Box 400   Indianola IA 50125
Ph: 515-961-8809 ▪ Fx: 515-961-3537

Ballot Initiative Strategy Center www.ballot.org
1025 Connecticut Ave NW Suite 205   Washington DC 20036
Ph: 202-223-2373 ▪ Fx: 202-289-1530

Ballroom Dancers Association, US Amateur www.usabda.org
PO Box 128   New Freedom PA 17349
Ph: 717-235-6656 ▪ Fx: 717-235-4183 ▪ TF: 800-447-9047

Ballroom & Entertainment Association, National www.nbea.com
2799 Locust Rd   Decorah IA 52101
Ph: 563-382-3871

Baltic Studies Inc, Association for the Advancement of www.balticstudies-aabs.lanet.lv
14743 Braemar Way   Darnestown MD 20878
Ph: 301-977-8491 ▪ Fx: 301-977-8492

Bamboo Society, American www.americanbamboo.org

Banana Association, International www.eatmorebananas.com
1901 Pennsylvania Ave NW Suite 1100   Washington DC 20006
Ph: 202-303-3400 ▪ Fx: 202-303-3433

Band Association, National www.nationalbandassociation.org
PO Box 5032   Hattiesburg MS 39406
Ph: 601-297-8168 ▪ Fx: 601-266-6185

Band Association, National Catholic www.catholicbands.org
3334 N Normandy Ave   Chicago IL 60634
Ph: 773-282-9153

Band Association, North American Brass www.nabba.org

Band Directors' Association, American School www.asbda.com
PO Box 696   Guttenberg IA 52052
Ph: 319-252-2500

Band Directors International, Women www.eskimo.com/~moorhous

Band Directors National Association, College www.cbdna.org
Univ of Texas Box 8028   Austin TX 78713
Ph: 512-471-5883 ▪ Fx: 512-471-6589

Band Fraternity, Kappa Kappa Psi National Honorary www.kkytbs.org/kky
PO Box 849   Stillwater OK 74076
Ph: 405-372-2333 ▪ Fx: 405-372-2363 ▪ TF: 800-543-6505

Band Instrument Manufacturers, National Association of www.nabim.org
PO Box 5488   Long Island City NY 11105
Ph: 718-274-3210 ▪ Fx: 718-274-3214

Band Instrument Repair Technicians, National Association of www.napbirt.org
Professional   PO Box 51   Normal IL 61761
Ph: 309-452-4257 ▪ Fx: 309-452-4825

Band Sorority, Tau Beta Sigma National Honorary www.kkytbs.org/tbs
PO Box 849   Stillwater OK 74076
Ph: 405-372-2333 ▪ Fx: 405-372-2363 ▪ TF: 800-543-6505

Bandmasters Association, American www.americanbandmasters.org
2221 Morgan Dr   Norman OK 73069
Ph: 405-321-3373 ▪ Fx: 405-321-4117

Bands of America www.bands.org
39 W Jackson Pl   Indianapolis IN 46225
Ph: 317-636-2263 ▪ Fx: 317-524-6200 ▪ TF: 800-848-2263

Bands of America, Lesbian & Gay www.gaybands.org
PO Box 14874   San Francisco CA 94114
Ph: 415-554-0402 ▪ Fx: 415-621-4637

Bands, Association of Concert www.acbands.org
6613 Cheryl Ann Dr   Independence OH 44131
Ph: 216-524-1897 ▪ TF: 800-726-8720

Bangladesh Studies, American Institute of www.aibs.net
Pennsylvania State Univ 111 Sowers St Suite 501   State
    College PA 16801
Ph: 814-865-0436 ▪ Fx: 814-865-8299

Banjo Fraternity, American www.abfbanjo.org
636 Pelis Rd   Newark NY 14513
Ph: 315-331-6717

Bank Administration Institute www.bai.org
1 N Franklin St Suite 1000   Chicago IL 60606
Ph: 312-553-4600 ▪ Fx: 312-683-2321 ▪ TF: 800-224-9889

Bank Collectors of America, Mechanical www.mechanicalbanks.org
PO Box 13323   Pittsburgh PA 15242
Ph: 412-343-8733 ▪ Fx: 412-344-5273

Bank Collectors Club of America, Still www.stillbankclub.com

Bank Directors, American Association of www.aabd.org
4701 Sangamore Rd Suite P-15   Bethesda MD 20816
Ph: 301-263-9841 ▪ Fx: 301-229-2443

Bank Equipment & Systems Association, National Independent nibesa.com
5300 Sequoia Rd NW Suite 205   Albuquerque NM 87120
Ph: 505-839-7958 ▪ Fx: 505-839-0017 ▪ TF: 800-843-6082

Bank Information Center www.bicusa.org
733 15th St NW Suite 1126   Washington DC 20005
Ph: 202-737-7752 ▪ Fx: 202-737-1155

Bank Insurance & Securities Association www.bisanet.org
303 W Lancaster Ave Suite 2D   Wayne PA 19087
Ph: 610-989-9047 ▪ Fx: 610-989-9102

Bank Supervisors, Conference of State
1015 18th St NW 11th Fl Washington DC 20036
Ph: 202-296-2840 ▪ Fx: 202-296-1928 ▪ TF: 800-886-2727
www.csbs.org

Bankers, America's Community
900 19th St NW Suite 400 Washington DC 20006
Ph: 202-857-3100 ▪ Fx: 202-296-8716
www.acbankers.org

Bankers Association, American
1120 Connecticut Ave NW Washington DC 20036
Ph: 202-663-5000 ▪ Fx: 202-828-5045 ▪ TF: 800-226-5377
www.aba.com

Bankers Association, Consumer
1000 Wilson Blvd Suite 2500 Arlington VA 22209
Ph: 703-276-1750 ▪ Fx: 703-528-1290
www.cbanet.org

Bankers Association, Environmental
510 King St Suite 410 Alexandria VA 22314
Ph: 703-549-0977 ▪ Fx: 703-548-5945
www.envirobank.org

Bankers' Association for Finance & Trade
1120 Connecticut Ave NW Washington DC 20036
Ph: 202-663-7575 ▪ Fx: 202-663-5538
www.baft.org

Bankers Association, Hellenic American
PO Box 48 New York NY 10008
Ph: 212-421-1057
www.haba.org

Bankers Association, Mortgage
1919 Pennsylvania Ave NW Washington DC 20006
Ph: 202-557-2700 ▪ Fx: 202-721-0247 ▪ TF: 800-793-6222
www.mortgagebankers.org

Bankers Association, National
1513 P St NW Washington DC 20005
Ph: 202-588-5432 ▪ Fx: 202-588-5443
www.nationalbankers.org

Bankers Association, National Marine
200 E Randolph Dr Suite 5100 Chicago IL 60601
Ph: 312-946-6260
www.marinebankers.org

Bankers Association PAC, American
1120 Connecticut Ave NW Washington DC 20036
Ph: 202-663-5113 ▪ Fx: 202-663-7544

Bankers, Institute of International
299 Park Ave 17th Fl New York NY 10171
Ph: 212-421-1611 ▪ Fx: 212-421-1119
www.iib.org

Banking Advisory Network, Community
1 Valmont Plaza 4th Fl Omaha NE 68154
Ph: 402-964-3865 ▪ Fx: 402-964-3811 ▪ TF: 888-475-4476
www.bankingcpas.com

Banking Attorneys, USFN - America's Mortgage
14471 Chambers Rd Suite 260 Tustin CA 92780
Ph: 714-838-7167 ▪ Fx: 714-573-2650 ▪ TF: 800-635-6128
www.usfn.org

Banking, Women's World
8 W 40th St New York NY 10018
Ph: 212-768-8513 ▪ Fx: 212-768-8519
www.swwb.org

Bankruptcy, American College of
11350 Random Hills Rd Suite 800 Fairfax VA 22030
Ph: 703-934-6154 ▪ Fx: 703-802-0207
www.amercol.org/

Bankruptcy Institute, American
44 Canal Center Plaza Suite 404 Alexandria VA 22314
Ph: 703-739-0800 ▪ Fx: 703-739-1060
www.abiworld.org

Bankruptcy Judges, National Conference of
235 Secret Cove Dr Lexington SC 29072
Ph: 803-957-6225
www.ncbj.org

Bankruptcy Trustees, National Association of
1 Windsor Cove Suite 305 Columbia SC 29223
Ph: 803-252-5646 ▪ Fx: 803-765-0860
www.nabt.com

Banks of America, Association of Military
7417 Jenna Rd Springfield VA 22153
Ph: 703-569-5163 ▪ Fx: 703-455-2110

Banks, National Association of Equity Source
10451 Mill Run Cir Suite 400 Owings Mills MD 21117
Ph: 410-581-1373

Bankshot Operators, National Association of
785F Rockville Pike PMB 504 Rockville MD 20852
Ph: 301-309-0260 ▪ Fx: 301-309-0263 ▪ TF: 800-933-0140
www.nabo-assn.com

Banner Flag & Graphics Association
1801 County Rd 'B' W Roseville MN 55113
Ph: 651-222-2508 ▪ Fx: 651-631-9334 ▪ TF: 800-225-4324
www.bannerflag.com

Bantam Association, American
PO Box 127 Augusta NJ 07822
Ph: 201-383-6944
www.the-coop.org/aba

BAPS Care International Inc
195 Main St Suite 304 Metuchen NJ 08840
Ph: 732-744-9734 ▪ Fx: 732-744-0940 ▪ TF: 800-301-5594
www.baps-care.org

Baptist Association, American
4605 N State Line Texarkana TX 75503
Ph: 903-792-2783 ▪ Fx: 903-792-8128 ▪ TF: 800-264-2482
www.abaptist.org

Baptist Bible Fellowship International
PO Box 191 Springfield MO 65801
Ph: 417-862-5001 ▪ Fx: 417-865-0794
www.bbfi.org

Baptist Campus Ministers, Association of Southern
PO Box 25118 Baton Rouge LA 70894
Ph: 225-343-0408 ▪ Fx: 225-343-0424

Baptist Churches, General Association of Regular
1300 N Meacham Rd Schaumburg IL 60173
Ph: 847-843-1600 ▪ Fx: 847-843-3757 ▪ TF: 800-588-1600
www.garbc.org

Baptist Churches USA, American
PO Box 851 Valley Forge PA 19482
Ph: 610-768-2000 ▪ Fx: 610-768-2275 ▪ TF: 800-222-3872
www.abc-usa.org

Baptist Colleges & Schools, Association of Southern
PO Box 11655 Jackson TN 38308
Ph: 731-660-3497 ▪ Fx: 731-664-6459
www.baptistschools.org

Baptist Communicators Association
1715-K S Rutherford Blvd Suite 295 Murfreesboro TN 37130
Ph: 615-904-0152
www.baptistcommunicators.org

Baptist Convention of America Inc, National
1320 Pierre Ave Shreveport LA 71103
Ph: 318-221-3701 ▪ Fx: 318-222-7512
www.nbcamerica.net

Baptist Convention, Ethics & Religious Liberty Commission of the Southern 901 Commerce St Nashville TN 37203
Ph: 615-244-2495 ▪ Fx: 615-242-0065
www.erlc.com

Baptist Convention Inc, Progressive National
601 50th St NE Washington DC 20019
Ph: 202-396-0558 ▪ Fx: 202-398-4998 ▪ TF: 800-876-7622
www.pnbc.org

Baptist Convention, Southern
901 Commerce St Suite 750 Nashville TN 37203
Ph: 615-244-2355 ▪ Fx: 615-742-8919
www.sbc.net

Baptist Convention USA Inc, National
1700 Baptist World Ctr Dr Nashville TN 37207
Ph: 615-228-6292 ▪ Fx: 615-226-8757 ▪ TF: 866-531-3054
www.nationalbaptist.com

Baptist Disaster Relief, Southern
4200 North Point Pkwy Alpharetta GA 30022
Ph: 770-410-6442 ▪ Fx: 770-410-6014
www.namb.net/dr

Baptist Foundation, Southern
901 Commerce St Suite 600 Nashville TN 37203
Ph: 615-254-8823 ▪ Fx: 615-255-1832
www.sbfdn.org

Baptist General Conference
2002 S Arlington Heights Rd Arlington Heights IL 60005
Ph: 847-228-0200 ▪ Fx: 847-228-5376 ▪ TF: 800-323-4215
www.bgcworld.org

Baptist General Conference of the US & Canada, Seventh Day PO Box 1678 Janesville WI 53547
Ph: 608-752-5055 ▪ Fx: 608-752-7711
www.seventhdaybaptist.org

Baptist Historical Library & Archives, Southern
901 Commerce St Suite 400 Nashville TN 37203
Ph: 615-244-0344
www.sbhla.org

Baptist Historical Society, Seventh Day
PO Box 1678 Janesville WI 53547
Ph: 608-752-5055 ▪ Fx: 608-752-7711
home.inwave.com/sdbhist

Baptist Homes & Hospitals Association, American PO Box 851 Valley Forge PA 19482
Ph: 800-222-3872 ▪ Fx: 610-768-2453
www.nationalministries.org/mission/abhha

Baptist International Ministries, American
PO Box 851 Valley Forge PA 19482
Ph: 610-768-2000 ▪ Fx: 610-768-2088 ▪ TF: 800-222-3872
www.internationalministries.org

Baptist Mid-Missions
PO Box 308011 Cleveland OH 44130
Ph: 440-826-3930 ▪ Fx: 440-826-4457
www.bmm.org

Baptist Missionary Association of America
PO Box 30910 Little Rock AR 72206
Ph: 501-455-4977 ▪ Fx: 501-455-3636
www.bmaam.com

Baptist Missionary Society, Seventh Day
119 Main St Westerly RI 02891
Ph: 401-596-4326 ▪ Fx: 401-348-9494
sdbmissoc.home.mindspring.com

Baptist Missions, Continental
5900 Alpine NW Comstock Park MI 49321
Ph: 616-784-7190 ▪ Fx: 616-784-3330
www.cbmoffice.org

Baptist Papers, Association of State
c/o The Alabama Baptist Newspaper 3310 Independence
Dr Birmingham AL 35209
Ph: 205-870-4720 ▪ Fx: 205-870-8957

Baptist Peace Fellowship of North America
4800 Wedgewood Dr Charlotte NC 28210
Ph: 704-521-6051 ▪ Fx: 704-521-6053
www.bpfna.org

Baptist Professors of Religion, National Association of
Mercer University Macon GA 31207
Ph: 478-301-2758 ▪ Fx: 478-301-2384
www.cssr.org/soc_nabpr.htm

Baptist Women in Ministry, American
PO Box 851 Valley Forge PA 19482
Ph: 610-768-2000 ▪ Fx: 610-768-2275 ▪ TF: 800-222-3872
www.abwim.org

Baptist Women's Ministries, American
PO Box 851 Valley Forge PA 19482
Ph: 610-768-2000 ▪ Fx: 610-768-2275 ▪ TF: 800-222-3872
www.abwministries.org

Baptist World Alliance
405 N Washington St Falls Church VA 22046
Ph: 703-790-8980 ▪ Fx: 703-893-5160
www.bwanet.org

Baptist World Federation, Seventh Day
PO Box 1678 Janesville WI 53547
Ph: 608-752-5055 ▪ Fx: 608-752-7711
www.seventhdaybaptist.org

Baptists, General Association of General
100 Stinson Dr Poplar Bluff MO 63901
Ph: 573-785-7746 ▪ Fx: 573-785-0564
www.generalbaptist.com

Baptists International, Conservative
1501 W Mineral Ave Littleton CO 80120
Ph: 720-283-2000 ▪ Fx: 720-283-2111 ▪ TF: 800-487-4224
www.cbi.org

Baptists for Life
PO Box 3158 Grand Rapids MI 49501
Ph: 616-257-6800 ▪ Fx: 616-257-6805 ▪ TF: 800-968-6086
www.bfl.org

Baptists, National Association of Free Will
5233 Mt View Rd Antioch TN 37013
Ph: 615-731-6812 ▪ Fx: 615-731-0771 ▪ TF: 877-767-7659
www.nafwb.org

Baptists for Scouting, Association of
PO Box 152079 Irving TX 75015
Ph: 254-799-4696
www.bsa.net/abs

Baptists for World Evangelism, Association of
PO Box 8585 Harrisburg PA 17105
Ph: 717-774-7000 ▪ Fx: 717-774-1919
www.abwe.org

Bar Association, American
750 N Lake Shore Dr Chicago IL 60611
Ph: 312-988-5000 ▪ Fx: 312-988-6281 ▪ TF: 800-285-2221
www.abanet.org

Bar Association, Armenian
PO Box 29111 Los Angeles CA 90029
Ph: 323-666-6288
www.armenianbar.org/

Bar Association, Customs & International Trade
729 15th St NW Suite 800 Washington DC 20005
Ph: 202-783-6900 ▪ Fx: 202-783-6909
www.citba.org

Bar Association, Energy
2175 K St NW Suite 600 Washington DC 20037
Ph: 202-223-5625 ▪ Fx: 202-833-5596
www.eba-net.org

Bar Association, Federal   fedbar.org
2215 M St NW   Washington DC 20037
Ph: 202-785-1614 ▪ Fx: 202-785-1568

Bar Association, Federal Communications   www.fcba.org
1020 19th St NW Suite 325   Washington DC 20036
Ph: 202-293-4000 ▪ Fx: 202-293-4317

Bar Association, Hispanic National   www.hnba.com
815 Connecticut Ave NW Suite 500   Washington DC 20006
Ph: 202-223-4777 ▪ TF: 877-221-6569

Bar Association, Inter-American   www.iaba.org
1211 Connecticut Ave NW Suite 202   Washington DC 20036
Ph: 202-393-1217 ▪ Fx: 202-393-1241

Bar Association, Lawyer-Pilots   www.lpba.org/
PO Box 685   Poolesville MD 20837
Ph: 301-972-7700 ▪ Fx: 301-972-7727

Bar Association, National   www.nationalbar.org
1225 11th St NW   Washington DC 20001
Ph: 202-842-3900 ▪ Fx: 202-289-6170 ▪ TF: 800-621-2988

Bar Association, National Asian Pacific American   www.napaba.org
733 15th St NW Suite 315   Washington DC 20005
Ph: 202-367-0796 ▪ Fx: 202-393-0995

Bar Associations, National Conference of Women's   www.ncwba.org
PO Box 82366   Portland OR 97282
Ph: 503-775-4396 ▪ Fx: 503-657-3932

Bar Counsel, National Organization of   www.nobc.org
515 5th St NW Bldg A Rm 127   Washington DC 20001
Ph: 202-638-1501 ▪ Fx: 202-638-0862

Bar Examiners, National Conference of   www.ncbex.org
402 W Wilson St   Madison WI 53703
Ph: 608-280-8550 ▪ Fx: 608-280-8552

Bar Executives, National Association of   www.abanet.org/nabe
541 N Fairbanks Ct   Chicago IL 60611
Ph: 312-988-6008 ▪ Fx: 312-988-5492

Bar Foundation, American   www.abf-sociolegal.org
750 N Lake Shore Dr   Chicago IL 60611
Ph: 312-988-6500 ▪ Fx: 312-988-6579

Bar Foundation, Fellows of the American   fellows.abfn.org
750 N Lake Shore Dr   Chicago IL 60611
Ph: 312-988-6500 ▪ Fx: 312-988-6611

Bar Foundations, National Conference of   www.ncbf.org
541 N Fairbanks Ct Suite 1400   Chicago IL 60611
Ph: 312-988-5343 ▪ Fx: 312-988-5492

Bar Presidents, National Conference of   www.ncbp.org
541 N Fairbanks Ct Suite 1400   Chicago IL 60611
Ph: 312-988-5345 ▪ Fx: 312-988-5492

Bar-Related Title Insurers, National Association of   www.nabrti.com
2355 S Arlington Heights Rd Suite 230   Arlington Heights IL 60005
Ph: 847-545-0500 ▪ Fx: 847-545-0550

Barbara Bush Foundation for Family Literacy   www.barbarabushfoundation.com
1201 15th St SW Suite 420   Washington DC 20005
Ph: 202-955-6183 ▪ Fx: 202-955-5492

Barbecue Association, Hearth Patio &   www.hpba.org
1601 N Kent St Suite 1001   Arlington VA 22209
Ph: 703-522-0086 ▪ Fx: 703-522-0548

Barbecue Association, National   www.nbbqa.org
PO Box 9685   Kansas City MO 64134
Ph: 816-767-8311 ▪ Fx: 816-765-5860 ▪ TF: 888-909-2121

Barbell & Strongmen, Association of Oldetime
33-30 150th St   Flushing NY 11354
Ph: 718-661-3195

Barbeque Cookers Association, International   www.ibcabbq.org
PO Box 300556   Arlington TX 76007
Ph: 817-469-1579

Barber Shop Quartet Singing in America, Society for the Preservation & Encouragement of   www.spebsqsa.org
7930 Sheridan Rd   Kenosha WI 53143
Ph: 262-653-8440 ▪ Fx: 262-654-5552

Barber Supply Institute, Beauty &   www.bbsi.org/index2.html
15825 N 71st St Suite 100   Scottsdale AZ 85254
Ph: 480-281-0424 ▪ Fx: 480-905-0708 ▪ TF: 800-468-2274

Barefoot Club, American   barefoot.org
1251 Holy Cow Rd   Polk City FL 33868
Ph: 941-324-4341

Bariatric Physicians, American Society of   www.asbp.org
5453 E Evans Pl   Denver CO 80222
Ph: 303-770-2526 ▪ Fx: 303-779-4834

Bariatric Surgery, American Society for   www.asbs.org
7328 W University Ave Suite F   Gainesville FL 32607
Ph: 352-331-4900 ▪ Fx: 352-331-4975

Baronial Order of Magna Charta   www.magnacharta.com

Barr Foundation   www.oandp.com/barr
136 NE Olive Way   Boca Raton FL 33432
Ph: 561-394-6514 ▪ Fx: 561-391-7601

Barre Granite Association   www.barregranite.org
51 Church St PO Box 481   Barre VT 05641
Ph: 802-476-4131 ▪ Fx: 802-476-4765

Barrel Futurities of America Inc   www.barrelfuturitiesofamerica.com
4701 Parsons Rd   Springdale AR 72764
Ph: 501-756-3107 ▪ Fx: 501-756-9528

Barrel Horse Association, National   www.nbha.com
725 Broad St PO Box 1988   Augusta GA 30903
Ph: 706-722-7223 ▪ Fx: 706-722-9575

Bartenders' Association, American   www.americanbartenders.org
PO Box D   Plant City FL 33566
Ph: 800-935-3232 ▪ Fx: 813-752-2768

Barzona Cattle Breeders Association of America   www.mddc.com/havens

Baseball, American Legion
PO Box 1055   Indianapolis IN 46206
Ph: 317-630-1213 ▪ Fx: 317-630-1369

Baseball Association, National Beep   www.nbba.org
2231 W 1st Ave   Topeka KS 66606
Ph: 785-234-2156

(Baseball) Babe Ruth League Inc   www.baberuthleague.org
1770 Brunswick Pike   Trenton NJ 08638
Ph: 609-695-1434 ▪ Fx: 609-695-2505

Baseball Clubs, International League of Professional   www.ilbaseball.com
55 S High St Suite 202   Dublin OH 43017
Ph: 614-791-9300 ▪ Fx: 614-791-9009

Baseball Coaches Association, American   www.abca.org
108 S University Ave Suite 3   Mount Pleasant MI 48858
Ph: 989-775-3300 ▪ Fx: 989-775-3600

Baseball Congress, American Amateur   www.aabc.us
118-119 Redfield Plaza   Marshall MI 49068
Ph: 269-781-2002 ▪ Fx: 269-781-2060

Baseball Congress, National   www.nbcbaseball.com
PO Box 1420   Wichita KS 67201
Ph: 316-267-3372 ▪ Fx: 316-267-3382

Baseball Federation, National Amateur   www.nabf.com
PO Box 705   Bowie MD 20718
Ph: 301-262-5005

Baseball Foundation, American   www.americanbaseball.org
1313 13th St S   Birmingham AL 35205
Ph: 205-558-4235 ▪ Fx: 205-918-0800

Baseball Leagues, George Khoury Association of
5400 Meramec Bottom Rd   Saint Louis MO 63128
Ph: 314-849-8900 ▪ Fx: 314-849-8901

Baseball Leagues, National Association of Professional   www.minorleaguebaseball.com
201 Bayshore Dr SE   Saint Petersburg FL 33701
Ph: 727-822-6937 ▪ Fx: 727-821-5819

Baseball Inc, Little League   www.littleleague.org
PO Box 3485   Williamsport PA 17701
Ph: 570-326-1921 ▪ Fx: 570-326-1074

Baseball Players Association, Major League   bigleaguers.yahoo.com
12 E 49th St 24th Fl   New York NY 10017
Ph: 212-826-0808 ▪ Fx: 212-752-4378

Baseball Research, Society for American   www.sabr.org
812 Huron Rd E Suite 719   Cleveland OH 44115
Ph: 216-575-0500 ▪ Fx: 216-575-0502

Baseball/Softball Inc, PONY   www.pony.org
300 Clare Dr   Washington PA 15301
Ph: 724-225-1060 ▪ Fx: 724-225-9852

Baseball, USA   www.usabaseball.com
PO Box 1133   Durham NC 27702
Ph: 919-474-8721 ▪ Fx: 919-474-8822

Baseball Writers Association of America
78 Olive St   Lake Grove NY 11755
Ph: 631-981-7938 ▪ Fx: 631-585-4669

Basenji Club of America Inc   www.basenji.org
5102 Darnell   Houston TX 77096
Ph: 713-667-1266 ▪ Fx: 713-237-3782

Bashkir Curly Registry, American   www.abcregistry.org
PO Box 151029   Ely NV 89315
Ph: 775-289-4999 ▪ Fx: 775-289-8579

Basic Acrylic Monomer Manufacturers Inc   www.bamm.net
941 Rhonda Pl SE   Leesburg VA 20175
Ph: 703-669-5688 ▪ Fx: 703-669-5689

Basic Education, Council for   www.c-b-e.org
1319 F St NW Suite 900   Washington DC 20004
Ph: 202-347-4171 ▪ Fx: 202-347-5047

Basic Life Principles, Institute in   www.iblp.org
PO Box 1   Oak Brook IL 60522
Ph: 630-323-9800

Basketball Coaches Association, Women's   www.wbca.org
4646 Lawrenceville Hwy   Lilburn GA 30047
Ph: 770-279-8027 ▪ Fx: 770-279-8473

Basketball Coaches, National Association of   nabc.ocsn.com
9300 W 110th St Suite 640   Overland Park KS 66210
Ph: 913-469-1001 ▪ Fx: 913-469-1390

Basketball Officials, International Association of Approved   www.iaabo.org
12321 Middlebrook Rd Suite 290   Germantown MD 20875
Ph: 301-601-8013 ▪ Fx: 301-601-8018

Basketball Players Association, National   www.nbpa.com
2 Penn Plaza Suite 2430   New York NY 10121
Ph: 212-655-0880 ▪ Fx: 212-655-0881

Basketball Trainers Association, National
400 Colony Sq Suite 1750   Atlanta GA 30361
Ph: 404-875-4000 ▪ Fx: 404-892-8560

Basketball, USA   www.usabasketball.com
5465 Mark Dabling Blvd   Colorado Springs CO 80918
Ph: 719-590-4800 ▪ Fx: 719-590-4811

Basketball Writers Association, US   www.sportswriters.net/usbwa
1818 Chouteau Ave   Saint Louis MO 63103
Ph: 314-421-0339 ▪ Fx: 314-421-3505

Basque Studies in America, Society of   www.basque.ws
19 Colonial Gardens   Brooklyn NY 11209
Ph: 718-745-1141 ▪ Fx: 718-745-2503

Basset Hound Club of America Inc   www.basset-bhca.org
11 Barkalow Ave   Freehold NJ 07728
Ph: 732-577-9662

Bassists, International Society of   www.isbworldoffice.com
13140 Coit Rd Suite 320 LB 120   Dallas TX 75240
Ph: 972-233-9107 ▪ Fx: 972-490-4219

Bat Conservation International   www.batcon.org
PO Box 162603   Austin TX 78716
Ph: 512-327-9721 ▪ Fx: 512-327-9724 ▪ TF: 800-538-2287

Bath Association, National Kitchen &   www.nkba.org
687 Willow Grove St   Hackettstown NJ 07840
Ph: 908-852-0033 ▪ Fx: 908-852-1695 ▪ TF: 800-843-6522

Bath Enclosure Manufacturers Association
5709 SW 21st St   Topeka KS 66604
Ph: 785-273-0393
www.bathenclosures.org

Bathroom Designers, Society of Certified Kitchen &
687 Willow Grove St   Hackettstown NJ 07840
Ph: 908-852-0033 ▪ Fx: 908-852-1695 ▪ TF: 800-843-6522

Baton Twirling Association, National
PO Box 266   Janesville WI 53547
Ph: 608-754-2238 ▪ Fx: 608-754-1986

(Baton Twirling) US Twirling Association
44 Drexel Dr PO Box 390   Copiague NY 11726
Ph: 631-231-7434 ▪ Fx: 208-474-9067
www.ustwirling.com

Battered Women's Justice Project
2104 4th Ave S Suite B   Minneapolis MN 55404
Ph: 612-824-8768 ▪ Fx: 612-824-8965 ▪ TF: 800-903-0111
www.bwjp.org

Battery Association, Portable Rechargeable
1000 Parkwood Cir Suite 430   Atlanta GA 30339
Ph: 770-612-8826 ▪ Fx: 770-612-8841
www.prba.org

Battery Council International
401 N Michigan Ave   Chicago IL 60611
Ph: 312-644-6610 ▪ Fx: 312-321-6869
www.batterycouncil.org

Battery Manufacturers Association, Independent
401 N Michigan Ave 24th Fl   Chicago IL 60611
Ph: 312-245-1074 ▪ Fx: 312-527-6640 ▪ TF: 800-237-6126
www.thebatteryman.com

Battery Recyclers, Association of
PO Box 290286   Tampa FL 33687
Ph: 813-626-6151 ▪ Fx: 813-622-8388

Batting Institute, National Cotton
1918 N Parkway PO Box 820287   Memphis TN 38182
Ph: 901-274-9030 ▪ Fx: 901-725-0510
www.natbat.com

Battle of the Bulge, Veterans of the
PO Box 11129   Arlington VA 22210
Ph: 703-528-4058
www.tfl.net/bulge.html

Battle of Ormoc Bay Association
117 Tuscarora St   Harrisburg PA 17104
Ph: 717-238-0907
www.ormocbattle.com/veteran.htm

Battlefield Coalition, Save the
PO Box 110   Catharpin VA 20143
Ph: 703-754-4260

Battlefield Commissions, National Order of
4 Meadowlark Ln   Pinehurst NC 28374
Ph: 910-235-0007 ▪ Fx: 910-235-0579
www.battlefieldcommissions.org

Battleship Association, USS North Carolina
PO Box 480   Wilmington NC 28402
Ph: 910-251-5797 ▪ Fx: 910-251-5807
www.battleshippnc.com

Bau-Biologie & Ecology, International Institute for
1401 A Cleveland St   Clearwater FL 33755
Ph: 727-461-4371 ▪ Fx: 727-441-4373
www.bau-biologieusa.com

Bay of Pigs Veterans Association
1821 SW 9th St   Miami FL 33135
Ph: 305-649-4719 ▪ Fx: 305-649-9769

BBB OnLine
4200 Wilson Blvd Suite 800   Arlington VA 22203
Ph: 703-247-9370 ▪ Fx: 703-525-8277
www.bbbonline.org

BBB Wise Giving Alliance
4200 Wilson Blvd Suite 800   Arlington VA 22203
Ph: 703-276-0100 ▪ Fx: 703-525-8277
www.give.org

BDPA
6301 Ivy Ln Suite 700   Greenbelt MD 20770
Ph: 301-220-2180 ▪ Fx: 301-220-2185 ▪ TF: 800-727-2372
www.bdpa.org

Beach Education Advocates for Culture Health
Environment & Safety   PO Box 530702   Miami Shores FL
33153
Ph: 305-893-8838 ▪ Fx: 305-893-8823
www.beachesfoundation.org

Beach Preservation Association, American Shore &
1724 Indian Way   Oakland CA 94611
Ph: 510-339-2818 ▪ Fx: 510-339-6710
www.asbpa.org

Beaches Council, Clean
1225 New York Ave NW Suite 450   Washington DC 20006
Ph: 202-682-9507 ▪ Fx: 202-682-9506
www.cleanbeaches.org

Beachfront USA
www.bfusa.org

Beale Cipher & Treasure Association
8A Hobart Ave   Bayonne NJ 07002
Ph: 201-339-0442

Bear Center, Appalachian
PO Box 364   Townsend TN 37882
Ph: 865-448-0143 ▪ Fx: 865-448-0141
www.appbears.org

Bear Foundation, Great
802 E Front St PO Box 9383   Missoula MT 59807
Ph: 406-829-9378 ▪ Fx: 406-829-9371
www.greatbear.org

Bear Society, North American
4061 E Hartford Ave PO Box 55774   Phoenix AZ 85078
Ph: 602-971-2338 ▪ Fx: 602-971-2100
www.nonprofitnet.com/nabs

Beard James Foundation
167 W 12th St   New York NY 10011
Ph: 212-675-4984 ▪ Fx: 212-645-1438 ▪ TF: 800-362-3273
www.jamesbeard.org

Bearing Manufacturers Association, American
2025 M St NW Suite 800   Washington DC 20036
Ph: 202-367-1155 ▪ Fx: 202-367-2155
www.abma-dc.org

Bearing Specialists Association
800 Roosevelt Rd Bldg C Suite 20   Glen Ellyn IL 60137
Ph: 630-858-3838 ▪ Fx: 630-790-3095
www.bsahome.org

Bears of the World, Good
PO Box 13097   Toledo OH 43613
Ph: 419-531-5365
www.goodbearsoftheworld.org

Beauty Aids Institute, American Health &
401 N Michigan Ave Suite 2200   Chicago IL 60611
Ph: 312-644-6610 ▪ Fx: 312-321-5194
www.proudlady.org

Beauty Association, American
15825 N 71st St   Scottsdale AZ 85254
Ph: 800-468-2274
www.abbies.org

Beauty Association, World International Nail &
1221 N Lake View Ave   Anaheim CA 92807
Ph: 714-779-9883 ▪ Fx: 714-779-9971 ▪ TF: 800-624-5777

Beauty & Barber Supply Institute
15825 N 71st St Suite 100   Scottsdale AZ 85254
Ph: 480-281-0424 ▪ Fx: 480-905-0708 ▪ TF: 800-468-2274
www.bbsi.org/index2.html

Beauty Culturists' League Inc, National
25 Logan Cir NW   Washington DC 20005
Ph: 202-332-2695 ▪ Fx: 202-332-0940
www.nbcl.org

Becket Fund for Religious Liberty
1350 Connecticut Ave NW Suite 605   Washington DC 20036
Ph: 202-955-0095 ▪ Fx: 202-955-0090
www.becketfund.org

Bed & Breakfast Association, National
PO Box 332   Norwalk CT 06852
Ph: 203-847-6196 ▪ Fx: 203-847-0469
www.nbba.com

Beechcraft Society, World
500 SE Everett Mall Way Suite A7   Everett WA 98208
Ph: 425-267-9235
www.worldbeechcraft.com

Beef Association, National Cattlemen's
9110 E Nichols Ave Suite 300   Centennial CO 80112
Ph: 303-694-0305 ▪ Fx: 303-694-2851
www.beef.org

Beef Improvement Federation
www.beefimprovement.org

Beef Promotion & Research Board, Cattlemen's
9110 E Nichols Ave Suite 303   Centennial CO 80112
Ph: 303-220-9890 ▪ Fx: 303-220-9280
www.beefboard.org

Beefalo World Registry, American
2225 Old Stage Rd   Dillon MT 59725
Ph: 406-683-6564
www.abwr.org

Beefmaster Breeders United
6800 Park Ten Blvd Suite 290-W   San Antonio TX 78213
Ph: 210-732-3132 ▪ Fx: 210-732-7711
www.beefmasters.org

(Beekeeping) Apiary Inspectors of America
Minnesota Dept of Agriculture 90 W Plato Blvd   Saint Paul MN
55107
Ph: 651-297-2200 ▪ TF: 800-967-2474
www.mda.state.mn.us/apiary/aiahome.htm

Beekeeping Federation, American
PO Box 1337   Jesup GA 31598
Ph: 912-427-4233 ▪ Fx: 912-427-8447
www.abfnet.org

Beep Baseball Association, National
2231 W 1st Ave   Topeka KS 66606
Ph: 785-234-2156
www.nbba.org

Beer Can Collectors of America
747 Merus Ct   Fenton MO 63026
Ph: 636-343-6486
www.bcca.com

Beer Institute
122 C St NW Suite 750   Washington DC 20001
Ph: 202-737-2337 ▪ Fx: 202-737-7004 ▪ TF: 800-379-2739
www.beerinstitute.org

Beer Trade Association, Home Wine &
PO Box 1373   Valrico FL 33595
Ph: 813-685-4261 ▪ Fx: 813-681-5625
www.hwbta.org

Beer Wholesalers Association, National
1101 King St Suite 600   Alexandria VA 22314
Ph: 703-683-4300 ▪ Fx: 703-683-8965 ▪ TF: 800-300-6417
www.nbwa.org

Beet Sugar Association, US
1156 15th St NW Suite 1019   Washington DC 20005
Ph: 202-296-4820 ▪ Fx: 202-331-2065

Beet Sugar Development Foundation
800 Grant St Suite 300   Denver CO 80203
Ph: 303-832-4460 ▪ Fx: 303-832-4468
www.bsdf-assbt.org

Beethoven Society, American
Ira F Brilliant Center for Beethoven Studies San Jose State Univ
1 Washington Sq   San Jose CA 95192
Ph: 408-808-2058 ▪ Fx: 408-808-2060
www2.sjsu.edu/depts/beethoven/abs/absociety.html

(Beetles) Coleopterists Society
3294 Meadowview Rd   Sacramento CA 95832
Ph: 916-262-1160 ▪ Fx: 916-262-1190
www.coleopsoc.org

Before Columbus Foundation
655 13th St Suite 300   Oakland CA 94612
Ph: 510-268-9775

BEGINNINGS for Parents of Children Who Are Deaf or Hard of
Hearing Inc   PO Box 17646   Raleigh NC 27619
Ph: 919-850-2746 ▪ Fx: 919-850-2804 ▪ TF: 800-541-4327
www.ncbegin.org

Begonia Society, American
157 Monument Rd   Rio Dell CA 95562
Ph: 707-764-5407
www.begonias.org

Behavior Analysis, Association for
1219 S Park St   Kalamazoo MI 49001
Ph: 269-492-9310 ▪ Fx: 269-492-9316
www.abainternational.org

Behavior Analysis, Society for the Advancement of
1219 S Park St   Kalamazoo MI 49001
Ph: 269-492-9310 ▪ Fx: 269-492-9316
www.abainternational.org/saba

Behavior Genetics Association
Indiana Univ SE Dept of Psychology 4201 Grant Line Rd   New
Albany IN 47150
Ph: 812-941-2668 ▪ Fx: 812-941-2591
www.bga.org

Behavior, Institute for the Advancement of Human
4370 Alpine Rd Suite 209   Portola Valley CA 94028
Ph: 650-851-8411 ▪ Fx: 650-851-0406 ▪ TF: 800-258-8411
www.ibh.com

Behavior, Society for Quantitative Analyses of
234 Huron Ave   Cambridge MA 02139
Ph: 617-497-5270
sqab.psychology.org

Behavior Therapy, Association for Advancement of
305 7th Ave 16th Fl   New York NY 10001
Ph: 212-647-1890 ▪ Fx: 212-647-1865 ▪ TF: 800-685-2228
www.aabt.org

Behavioral & Applied Management, Institute of   www.ibam.com

Behavioral Health Directors, National Association of County   www.nacbhd.org
440 1st St NW   Washington DC 20001
Ph: 202-661-8816

Behavioral Health Nurses & Associates Inc, Consortium of   www.cbhna.org
1733 H St Suite 330 PMB 1214   Blaine WA 98230
Ph: 800-876-2236 ▪ Fx: 360-332-2280

Behavioral Healthcare, Association for Ambulatory   www.aabh.org
2301 Mt Vernon Ave Suite 100   Alexandria VA 22301
Ph: 703-836-2274 ▪ Fx: 703-836-0083

Behavioral Healthcare Association, American Managed   www.ambha.org
1101 Pennsylvania Ave NW 6th Fl   Washington DC 20004
Ph: 202-756-7726 ▪ Fx: 202-756-7308

Behavioral Healthcare, National Council for Community   www.nccbh.org
12300 Twinbrook Pkwy Suite 320   Rockville MD 20852
Ph: 301-984-6200 ▪ Fx: 301-881-7159

Behavioral Medicine, Society of   www.sbm.org
7600 Terrace Ave Suite 203   Middleton WI 53562
Ph: 608-827-7267 ▪ Fx: 608-831-5485

Behavioral Psychological & Cognitive Sciences,   www.thefederationonline.org
Federation of   750 1st NE Suite 5007   Washington DC 20002
Ph: 202-336-5920 ▪ Fx: 202-336-5953

(Behavioral Science) William Glasser Institute   www.wglasser.com
22024 Lassen St Suite 118   Chatsworth CA 91311
Ph: 818-700-8000 ▪ Fx: 818-700-0555 ▪ TF: 800-899-0688

Behavioral Sciences, Association for Advanced Training in the   www.aatbs.org
5126 Ralston St   Ventura CA 93003
Ph: 805-676-3030 ▪ Fx: 805-676-3033 ▪ TF: 800-472-1931

Behavioral Sciences & Medical Education, Association for the   www.absame.org
1460 N Center Rd   Burton MI 48509
Ph: 810-715-4365 ▪ Fx: 810-715-4371

Behavioral & Social Sciences, Cheiron: International   www.psych.yorku.ca/orgs/cheiron
Society for the History of

Behcet's Disease Association, American   www.behcets.com
PO Box 19952   Amarillo TX 79114
Ph: 800-723-4238

Beiderbecke Bix Memorial Society   www.bixsociety.org
PO Box 3688   Davenport IA 52808
Ph: 563-324-7170 ▪ Fx: 563-326-1732 ▪ TF: 888-249-5487

Belfer Center for Science & International Affairs   bcsia.ksg.harvard.edu
Harvard Univ John F Kennedy School of Government 79 JFK
St   Cambridge MA 02138
Ph: 617-495-1400

Belgian-American Chamber of Commerce in the US   www.belcham.org
245 Park Ave 24th Fl   New York NY 10167
Ph: 212-672-1632 ▪ Fx: 212-672-1644

Belgian American Educational Foundation   www.baef.be
195 Church St   New Haven CT 06510
Ph: 203-777-5765 ▪ Fx: 203-785-4951

Belgian Blue Breeders Association, American   www.belgianblue.org
PO Box 154   Hedrick IA 52563
Ph: 641-656-2332 ▪ Fx: 641-653-2332

Belgian Draft Horse Corp of America   www.belgiancorp.com
PO Box 335   Wabash IN 46992
Ph: 260-563-3205

Belgian Malinois Club, American   www.breedclub.org/ABMC.htm
21710 Cove Point Farm Rd   Tilghman MD 21671
Ph: 410-886-2232

Believe In Tomorrow National Children's Foundation   www.believeintomorrow.org
PO Box 21211   Baltimore MD 21228
Ph: 410-744-1032 ▪ Fx: 410-744-1984 ▪ TF: 800-933-5470

Bell Alexander Graham Association for the Deaf & Hard of Hearing   www.agbell.org
3417 Volta Pl NW   Washington DC 20007
Ph: 202-337-5220 ▪ Fx: 202-337-8314

Belleek Collector's International Society   www.belleek.ie
PO Box 1498   Great Falls VA 22066
Ph: 800-235-5335 ▪ Fx: 703-272-6271

Belt Association   www.idahogeology.org/Adjunct
c/o Idaho Geological Survey Univ of Idaho PO Box
443014   Moscow ID 83844
Ph: 208-885-7991 ▪ Fx: 208-885-5826

Belted Galloway Society   www.beltie.org
98 Eidson Rd   Staunton VA 24401
Ph: 540-885-9887 ▪ Fx: 540-885-9897

Belting Association, National Industrial   www.niba.org
N19 W24400 Riverwood Dr   Waukesha WI 53188
Ph: 262-523-9090 ▪ Fx: 262-523-9091 ▪ TF: 800-488-4845

BEMA - Baking Industry Suppliers Association   www.bema.org
825 Green Bay Rd Suite 120   Wilmette IL 60091
Ph: 847-920-1230 ▪ Fx: 847-920-1253

Ben-Gurion University of the Negev, American Associates   www.aabgu.org
1430 Broadway 8th Fl   New York NY 10018
Ph: 212-687-7721 ▪ Fx: 212-302-6443 ▪ TF: 800-962-2248

Bench Rest Shooters Association, National   nbrsa.benchrest.com
2835 Guilford Ln   Oklahoma City OK 73120
Ph: 405-842-9585 ▪ Fx: 405-842-9575

Benedictine Academy, American   www.osb.org/aba
Assumption Abbey 418 3rd Ave W   Richardton ND 58652
Ph: 701-974-3315 ▪ Fx: 701-974-3317

Benedictines for Peace   www.mountosb.org/bfp.html
Mount St Benedict Monastery 6101 E Lake Rd   Erie PA 16511
Ph: 814-899-0614 ▪ Fx: 814-898-4004

Benefit Administrators, Society of Professional   users.erols.com/spba
2 Wisconsin Cir Suite 670   Chevy Chase MD 20815
Ph: 301-718-7722 ▪ Fx: 301-718-9440

Benefit Association, Armed Forces   www.afba.org
909 N Washington St   Alexandria VA 22314
Ph: 703-549-4455 ▪ Fx: 703-706-5961 ▪ TF: 800-776-2322

Benefit Association, Armed Services Mutual   www.asmba.com
PO Box 160384   Nashville TN 37216
Ph: 615-851-0800 ▪ Fx: 615-851-9484 ▪ TF: 800-251-8434

Benefit Association, Military   www.militarybenefit.org
PO Box 221110   Chantilly VA 20153
Ph: 703-968-6200 ▪ Fx: 703-968-6423 ▪ TF: 800-336-0100

Benefit Fund of the USA, Workmen's   www.wbfusa.com
99 N Broadway   Hicksville NY 11801
Ph: 516-938-6060 ▪ Fx: 516-938-6882

Benefit Plans, International Foundation of Employee   www.ifebp.org
PO Box 69   Brookfield WI 53008
Ph: 262-786-6700 ▪ Fx: 262-786-8670 ▪ TF: 888-334-3327

Benefit Research Institute, Employee   www.ebri.org
2121 K St NW Suite 600   Washington DC 20037
Ph: 202-659-0670 ▪ Fx: 202-775-6312

Benefit Society, Slovene National   www.snpj.com
247 W Allegheny Rd   Imperial PA 15126
Ph: 724-695-1100 ▪ Fx: 724-695-1555 ▪ TF: 800-843-7675

Benefit Specialists, International Society of Certified Employee   www.iscebs.org
18700 W Bluemond Rd PO Box 209   Brookfield WI 53008
Ph: 262-786-8771 ▪ Fx: 262-786-8650

Benefits Council, American   www.appwp.org
1212 New York Ave NW Suite 1250   Washington DC 20005
Ph: 202-289-6700 ▪ Fx: 202-289-4582

Benefits, Council on Employee   www.ceb.org
4910 Moorland Ln   Bethesda MD 20814
Ph: 301-664-5940 ▪ Fx: 301-664-5944

Benefits Network Inc, Worldwide Employee   www.webnetwork.org
21165 Whitfield Pl   Potomac Falls VA 20165
Ph: 703-433-9696 ▪ Fx: 703-433-0369

Benevolent Association, National   www.nbacares.org
11780 Borman Dr   Saint Louis MO 63146
Ph: 314-993-9000 ▪ Fx: 314-993-9018

Benevolent & Protective Order of Elks of the USA   www.elks.org
2750 N Lakeview Ave   Chicago IL 60614
Ph: 773-755-4700 ▪ Fx: 773-755-4790

Benevolent Society Inc, International
PO Box 1276   Columbus GA 31902
Ph: 706-322-5671

Benjamin Franklin Education Foundation
6275 Hazeltine National Dr Suite 114   Orlando FL 32822
Ph: 407-240-8009 ▪ Fx: 407-240-8333

Benjamin Harrison Home Foundation, President   www.presidentbenjaminharrison.org
1230 N Delaware St   Indianapolis IN 46202
Ph: 317-631-1888 ▪ Fx: 317-632-5488

Benthological Society, North American   www.benthos.org
PO Box 1897   Lawrence KS 66044
Ph: 785-843-1235 ▪ Fx: 785-843-1274 ▪ TF: 800-627-0629

Benton Foundation   www.benton.org
1625 K St NW 11th Fl   Washington DC 20006
Ph: 202-638-5770 ▪ Fx: 202-638-5771

Berean Bible Society   www.bereanbiblesociety.org
PO Box 756   Germantown WI 53022
Ph: 262-255-4750 ▪ Fx: 262-255-4195

Berkeley Roundtable on the International Economy   brie.berkeley.edu/~briewww
Univ of California Berkeley 2234 Piedmont Ave   Berkeley CA
94720
Ph: 510-642-3067 ▪ Fx: 510-643-6617

Berkshire Association, American   www.americanberkshire.com
PO Box 2436   West Lafayette IN 47996
Ph: 765-497-3618 ▪ Fx: 765-497-2959

Best Buddies International   www.bestbuddies.org
100 SE 2nd St Suite 1990   Miami FL 33131
Ph: 305-374-2233 ▪ Fx: 305-374-5305

Bet-Nahrain Inc   www.betnahrain.org
PO Box 4116   Modesto CA 95352
Ph: 209-538-4130 ▪ Fx: 209-538-2795

Beta Alpha Psi   www.bap.org
1211 Ave of the Americas 6th Fl   New York NY 10036
Ph: 212-596-6090 ▪ Fx: 212-596-6288

Beta Beta Beta National Biological Honor Society   www.tri-beta.org
Univ of North Alabama Box 5079   Florence AL 35632
Ph: 256-765-6220 ▪ Fx: 256-765-6221

Beta Club, National   www.betaclub.org
151 Beta Club Way   Spartanburg SC 29306
Ph: 864-583-4553 ▪ Fx: 864-542-9300 ▪ TF: 800-845-8281

Beta Gamma Sigma Inc   www.betagammasigma.org
125 Weldon Pkwy   Maryland Heights MO 63043
Ph: 314-432-5650 ▪ Fx: 314-432-7083

Beta Phi Mu   www.beta-phi-mu.org
Florida State Univ School of Information Studies   Tallahassee
FL 32306
Ph: 850-644-3907 ▪ Fx: 850-644-9763

Beta Sigma Phi   www.betasigmaphi.org
1800 W 91st Pl   Kansas City MO 64114
Ph: 816-444-6800 ▪ Fx: 816-333-6206 ▪ TF: 800-821-3989

Beta Sigma Psi National Lutheran Fraternity   www.betasigmapsi.org
2408 Lebanon Ave   Belleville IL 62221
Ph: 618-235-0014 ▪ Fx: 618-235-0051

Beta Theta Pi   www.betathetapi.org
5134 Bonham Rd   Oxford OH 45056
Ph: 513-523-7591 ▪ Fx: 513-523-2381 ▪ TF: 800-800-2382

Beth-Hatefutsoth, American Friends of
633 3rd Ave 21st Fl   New York NY 10017
Ph: 212-339-6034 ▪ Fx: 212-318-6176

Bethany Christian Services International   www.bethany.org
901 Eastern Ave NE PO Box 294   Grand Rapids MI 49501
Ph: 616-224-7610 ▪ Fx: 616-224-7611

Bethany Fellowship Missions   www.bethfel.org
6820 Auto Club Rd Suite M   Minneapolis MN 55438
Ph: 952-829-2492 ▪ TF: 800-323-3417

Bethesda Lutheran Homes & Services Inc   www.blhs.org
600 Hoffman Dr   Watertown WI 53094
Ph: 920-261-3050 ▪ Fx: 920-261-8441 ▪ TF: 800-369-4636

Bethlehem Association   www.bethlehemassoc.org
PO Box 1111   Media PA 19063
Ph: 610-353-2010

Betsy-Tacy Society   www.betsy-tacysociety.org

Betta Congress, International   www.ibcbettas.org
923 Wadsworth St   Syracuse NY 13208
Ph: 315-454-4792

Better Business Bureaus Inc, Council of   www.bbb.org
4200 Wilson Blvd Suite 800   Arlington VA 22203
Ph: 703-276-0100 ▪ Fx: 703-525-8277

Better Government Association   bettergov.org
28 E Jackson Blvd Suite 1900   Chicago IL 60604
Ph: 312-427-8330 ▪ Fx: 312-427-8340

Better Hearing Institute   www.betterhearing.org
515 King St Suite 420   Alexandria VA 22314
Ph: 703-684-3391 ▪ Fx: 703-684-6048 ▪ TF: 888-432-7435

Better Sleep Council   www.bettersleep.org
501 Wythe St   Alexandria VA 22314
Ph: 703-683-8371 ▪ Fx: 703-683-4503

Better Vision Institute   www.visionsite.org
Vision Council of America 1700 Diagonal Rd Suite
500   Alexandria VA 22314
Ph: 703-548-4560 ▪ Fx: 703-548-4580 ▪ TF: 800-424-8422

Better World, Books for a   www.booksforabetterworld.org
PO Box 82307   Phoenix AZ 85071
Ph: 602-866-9281 ▪ Fx: 602-866-0035

Beverage Association, National United Merchants   www.numba.org
609 S Ann St   Homestead PA 15120
Ph: 412-636-3120 ▪ Fx: 412-636-3107

Beverage Dispensing Equipment Association, International   www.ibdea.org
4145 Amos Ave   Baltimore MD 21215
Ph: 410-764-0616 ▪ Fx: 410-764-6799

Beverage Industries, World Association of Alcohol   www.waabi.org

Beverage Institute, American   www.abionline.org
1775 Pennsylvania Ave NW Suite 1200   Washington DC 20006
Ph: 202-463-7110

Beverage Licensees, American   www.ablusa.org
5101 River Rd Suite 108   Bethesda MD 20816
Ph: 301-656-1494 ▪ Fx: 301-656-7539 ▪ TF: 800-311-8999

Beverage Packaging Association, International   www.ibpa.org
631 N Stephanie St Suite 564   Henderson NV 89014
Ph: 702-566-7103 ▪ Fx: 702-566-7166

Beverage Packaging Association, National
200 Dangerfield Rd   Alexandria VA 22314
Ph: 800-331-8816 ▪ Fx: 703-548-6563

Beverage Technologists, International Society of   www.bevtech.org
8110 S Suncoast Blvd   Homosassa FL 34446
Ph: 352-382-2008 ▪ Fx: 352-382-2018

Beyond Pesticides   www.beyondpesticides.org
701 'E' St SE Suite 200   Washington DC 20003
Ph: 202-543-5450 ▪ Fx: 202-543-4791

Biathlon Association, US   www.usbiathlon.org
29 Ethan Allen Ave   Colchester VT 05446
Ph: 802-654-7833 ▪ Fx: 802-654-7830 ▪ TF: 800-242-8456

Bible Association, National   www.nationalbible.org
1865 Broadway   New York NY 10023
Ph: 212-408-1390 ▪ Fx: 212-408-1448

Bible Center Inc, Christian Literature &   www.clbible.org
PO Box 7130   North Augusta SC 29861
Ph: 803-279-1981 ▪ Fx: 803-279-1270

Bible Centered Ministries International   www.bcmintl.org
309 Colonial Dr   Akron PA 17501
Ph: 717-859-6404 ▪ Fx: 717-859-6914 ▪ TF: 888-226-4685

Bible Collectors, International Society of   www.biblecollectors.org
2901 Pennsylvania Ave S   Saint Louis Park MN 55426
Ph: 952-929-3728

Bible Colleges, Accrediting Association of   www.gospelcom.net/aabc
5575 S Semoran Blvd Suite 26   Orlando FL 32822
Ph: 407-207-0808 ▪ Fx: 407-207-0840

Bible Curriculum In Public Schools, National Council on   www.bibleinschools.net
PO Box 9743   Greensboro NC 27429
Ph: 336-272-3799

Bible Fellowship International, Baptist   www.bbfi.org
PO Box 191   Springfield MO 65801
Ph: 417-862-5001 ▪ Fx: 417-865-0794

Bible Foundation, Braille   www.careministries.org/bbf.html
PO Box 948307   Maitland FL 32794
Ph: 407-834-3628 ▪ TF: 800-766-9080

Bible League   www.gospelcom.net/bibleleague
PO Box 28000   Chicago IL 60628
Ph: 708-367-8500 ▪ Fx: 708-367-8600 ▪ TF: 866-825-4636

Bible Prophecy Study Association   netministries.org/see/charmin/CM00407
339 E Laguna Dr   Tempe AZ 85282
Ph: 480-967-3066

Bible Sabbath Association   www.biblesabbath.org
HC 60 Box 8   Fairview OK 73737
Ph: 580-227-4494 ▪ Fx: 580-227-3200 ▪ TF: 888-687-5191

Bible Society, American   www.americanbible.org
1865 Broadway   New York NY 10023
Ph: 212-408-1200 ▪ Fx: 212-408-1512 ▪ TF: 800-322-4253

Bible Society, Berean   www.bereanbiblesociety.org
PO Box 756   Germantown WI 53022
Ph: 262-255-4750 ▪ Fx: 262-255-4195

Bible Society, International   www.gospelcom.net/ibs
1820 Jet Stream Dr   Colorado Springs CO 80921
Ph: 719-488-9200 ▪ Fx: 719-488-0810 ▪ TF: 800-524-1588

Bible Students Association, Dawn   www.dawnbible.com
199 Railroad Ave   East Rutherford NJ 07073
Ph: 201-438-6421 ▪ Fx: 201-531-8333 ▪ TF: 888-440-3296

Bible Studies, Neighborhood   www.neighborhoodbiblestudies.org
56 Main St   Dobbs Ferry NY 10522
Ph: 914-693-3273 ▪ Fx: 914-693-4345 ▪ TF: 800-369-0307

(Bible Study) Mailbox Club Inc   www.mailboxclub.org
404 Eager Rd   Valdosta GA 31602
Ph: 229-244-6812

Bible & Tract Society of New York Inc, Watchtower   www.watchtower.org
25 Columbia Heights   Brooklyn NY 11201
Ph: 718-560-5000

Bible Translators, Lutheran   www.gospelcom.net/lbt
303 N Lake St PO Box 2050   Aurora IL 60507
Ph: 630-897-0660 ▪ Fx: 630-897-3567 ▪ TF: 800-532-4253

Bible Translators, Wycliffe   www.wycliffe.org
PO Box 628200   Orlando FL 32862
Ph: 407-852-3600 ▪ Fx: 407-852-3601 ▪ TF: 800-992-5433

Bibles for the World   www.biblesfortheworld.org
PO Box 49759   Colorado Springs CO 80949
Ph: 719-630-7733 ▪ Fx: 719-630-1449 ▪ TF: 888-382-4253

Biblical Association of America, Catholic   studentorg.cua.edu/cbib
620 Michigan Ave NE 314   Caldwell Hall   Washington DC 20064
Ph: 202-319-5519 ▪ Fx: 202-319-4799

Biblical Literature, Society of   www.sbl-site.org
825 Houston Mill Rd Suite 350   Atlanta GA 30329
Ph: 404-727-3100 ▪ Fx: 404-727-3101

Biblical Research, Associates for   www.christiananswers.net/abr/abrhome.html
PO Box 144   Akron PA 17501
Ph: 800-430-0008

Biblical Research Institute, Interdisciplinary   www.ibri.org
PO Box 423 200 N Main St   Hatfield PA 19440
Ph: 215-368-5000 ▪ Fx: 215-368-7002

Biblical Witness Fellowship   www.biblicalwitness.org
PO Box 102   Candia NH 03034
Ph: 603-483-0597 ▪ Fx: 603-483-1035 ▪ TF: 800-494-9172

Bibliographical Society of America   www.bibsocamer.org
PO Box 1537 Lenox Hill Stn   New York NY 10021
Ph: 212-452-2710

Bicycle Association, American   www.ababmx.com
1645 W Sunrise Blvd   Gilbert AZ 85233
Ph: 480-961-1903 ▪ Fx: 480-961-1842 ▪ TF: 800-886-1269

Bicycle Dealers Association, National   nbda.com
777 W 19th St Suite O   Costa Mesa CA 92627
Ph: 949-722-6909 ▪ Fx: 949-722-1747

Bicycle Fund, International   www.ibike.org
4887 Columbia Dr S   Seattle WA 98108
Ph: 206-767-0848

Bicycle Helmet Safety Institute   www.helmets.org
4611 7th St S   Arlington VA 22204
Ph: 703-486-0100

Bicycle League, National   www.nbl.org
3958 Brown Park Dr Suite D   Hilliard OH 43026
Ph: 614-777-1625 ▪ Fx: 614-777-1680 ▪ TF: 800-866-2691

Bicycle Product Suppliers Association   bpsa.org
PO Box 187   Montgomeryville PA 18936
Ph: 215-393-3144 ▪ Fx: 215-893-4872

(Bicycles) Tandem Club of America   www.tandemclub.org
2220 Vanessa Dr   Birmingham AL 35242
Ph: 205-991-7766

Bicycling Association, International Mountain   www.imba.com
207 Canyon Blvd Suite 301 PO Box 7578   Boulder CO 80306
Ph: 303-545-9011 ▪ Fx: 303-545-9026 ▪ TF: 888-442-4622

Bicycling & Walking, National Center for   www.bikewalk.org
1506 21st St NW Suite 200   Washington DC 20036
Ph: 202-463-6622 ▪ Fx: 202-463-6625

Bicyclists, League of American   www.bikeleague.org
1612 K St NW Suite 800   Washington DC 20006
Ph: 202-822-1333 ▪ Fx: 202-822-1334

Bide-A-Wee Association   www.bideawee.org
410 E 38th St   New York NY 10016
Ph: 212-532-6395 ▪ Fx: 212-532-4210

Big Bend Natural History Association   www.nps.gov/bibe/BBNHA/bbnha.htm
PO Box 196   Big Bend National Park TX 79834
Ph: 432-477-2236 ▪ Fx: 432-477-2234

Big Brothers Big Sisters of America   www.bbbsa.org
230 N 13th St   Philadelphia PA 19107
Ph: 215-567-7000 ▪ Fx: 215-567-0394

Big Brothers, Catholic   www.cbbnyc.org
45 E 20th St 9th Fl   New York NY 10003
Ph: 212-477-2250 ▪ Fx: 212-477-2739

Big East Conference   www.bigeast.org
222 Richmond St Suite 110   Providence RI 02903
Ph: 401-272-9108 ▪ Fx: 401-274-5967

Big Little Book Club   www.biglittlebooks.com
PO Box 1242   Danville CA 94526
Ph: 925-837-2086

Big Picture Alliance   www.bigpicturealliance.org
1315 Walnut St Suite 1616   Philadelphia PA 19107
Ph: 215-735-5750 ▪ Fx: 215-735-9291

Big Ten Conference   www.bigten.org
1500 W Higgins Rd   Park Ridge IL 60068
Ph: 847-696-1010 ▪ Fx: 847-696-1150

Big West Conference   www.bigwest.org
2 Corporate Pk Suite 206   Irvine CA 92606
Ph: 949-261-2525 ▪ Fx: 949-261-2528

Bigfoot Information Center, Michigan/Canadian
152 W Sherman   Caro MI 48723
Ph: 989-673-2715

Bigfoot Studies, Center for
10926 Milano Ave   Norwalk CA 90650
Ph: 714-921-1014

Bike Association, International Police Mountain   www.ipmba.org
583 Fredrick Rd Suite 5B   Baltimore MD 21228
Ph: 410-744-2400 ▪ Fx: 410-744-5504 ▪ TF: 800-323-0037

Bike & Tea Society, Women's Mountain   www.wombats.org
PO Box 757   Fairfax CA 94978
Ph: 415-459-0980

Bikes Not Bombs   www.bikesnotbombs.org
59 Armory St Suite 103   Roxbury MA 02119
Ph: 617-442-0004 ▪ Fx: 617-445-2439

Biliary Association, American Hepato-Pancreato-   www.ahpba.org
11300 W Olympic Blvd Suite 600   Los Angeles CA 90064
Ph: 310-437-0557 ▪ Fx: 310-437-0585

Bilingual Education, National Association for   www.nabe.org
1030 15th St NW Suite 470   Washington DC 20005
Ph: 202-898-1829 ▪ Fx: 202-789-2866

Bilingual Foundation of the Arts   www.bfatheatre.org
421 N Ave 19   Los Angeles CA 90031
Ph: 323-225-4044 ▪ Fx: 323-225-1250

Bill & Melinda Gates Foundation   www.gatesfoundation.org
PO Box 23350   Seattle WA 98102
Ph: 206-709-3100 ▪ Fx: 206-709-3180 ▪ TF: 888-452-6352

Billfish Foundation   www.billfish.org
2161 E Commercial Blvd 2nd Fl   Fort Lauderdale FL 33308
Ph: 954-938-0150 ▪ Fx: 954-938-5311 ▪ TF: 800-438-8247

Billiard Association, US   www.uscarom.org
1800 Beach Dr Rm 1823   Gulfport MS 39507
Ph: 228-897-8290

Billiard Congress of America   www.bca-pool.com
4345 Beverly St Suite D   Colorado Springs CO 80918
Ph: 719-264-8300 ▪ Fx: 719-264-0900

Billiards Association, Women's Professional   www.wpba.com
6407 South Blvd   Charlotte NC 28217
Ph: 704-556-1128 ▪ Fx: 704-556-0699

Billing & Management Association, Healthcare   www.hbma.com
1540 S Coast Hwy Suite 203   Laguna Beach CA 92651
Ph: 877-640-4262 ▪ Fx: 949-376-3456

Billings Ovulation Method Association - USA   www.boma-usa.org
PO Box 16206   Saint Paul MN 55116
Ph: 651-699-8139 ▪ Fx: 651-699-8144

Billy Graham Evangelistic Association   www.billygraham.org
PO Box 779   Minneapolis MN 55440
Ph: 612-338-0500 ▪ Fx: 612-335-1289 ▪ TF: 877-247-2426

Binding Industries Association International   www.bindingindustries.org
100 Daingerfield Rd   Alexandria VA 22314
Ph: 703-519-8137 ▪ Fx: 703-548-3227

Binding Institute, Library   www.lbibinders.org
70 E Lake St Suite 300   Chicago IL 60601
Ph: 312-704-5020 ▪ Fx: 312-704-5025

Bio-Integral Resource Center   www.birc.org
PO Box 7414   Berkeley CA 94707
Ph: 510-524-2567 ▪ Fx: 510-524-1758

Bioanalysis, American Board of   www.abbcert.org
917 Locust St Suite 1100   Saint Louis MO 63101
Ph: 314-241-1445 ▪ Fx: 314-241-1449

Bioanalysts, American Association of   www.aab.org
917 Locust St Suite 1100   Saint Louis MO 63101
Ph: 314-241-1445 ▪ Fx: 314-241-1449

Biochemistry & Molecular Biology, American Society for   www.asbmb.org
9650 Rockville Pike   Bethesda MD 20814
Ph: 301-634-7145 ▪ Fx: 301-634-7126

BioCommunications Association   www.bca.org
220 Southwind Ln   Hillsborough NC 27278
Ph: 919-245-0906 ▪ Fx: 919-245-0909

Biodiesel Board, National   www.biodiesel.org
3337-A Emerald Ln PO Box 104898   Jefferson City MO 65110
Ph: 800-841-5849 ▪ Fx: 573-635-7913

Biodynamic Farming & Gardening Association Inc   www.biodynamics.com
25844 Butler Rd   Junction City OR 97448
Ph: 541-998-0105 ▪ Fx: 541-998-0106 ▪ TF: 888-561-7797

Bioelectromagnetics Society   www.bioelectromagnetics.org
2412 Cobblestone Way   Frederick MD 21702
Ph: 301-663-4252 ▪ Fx: 301-694-4948

Bioethics, Center for   bioethics.upenn.edu
Univ of Pennsylvania 3401 Market St Suite 320   Philadelphia
PA 19104
Ph: 215-898-7136 ▪ Fx: 215-573-3036

Bioethics, Center for Death Education &   www.uwlax.edu/sociology/cde&b
UW La Crosse Dept of Sociology/Archaeology 435 NH 1725
State St   La Crosse WI 54601
Ph: 608-785-6784 ▪ Fx: 608-785-8486

Bioethics Center, Midwest   www.midbio.org
1021-1025 Jefferson St   Kansas City MO 64105
Ph: 816-221-1100 ▪ Fx: 816-221-2002 ▪ TF: 800-344-3829

(Bioethics) Hastings Center   www.thehastingscenter.org
21 Malcolm Gordon Dr   Garrison NY 10524
Ph: 845-424-4040 ▪ Fx: 845-424-4545

Bioethics & Humanities, American Society for   www.asbh.org
4700 W Lake Ave   Glenview IL 60025
Ph: 847-375-4745 ▪ Fx: 877-734-9385

Bioethics, International Feminist Approaches to   www.msu.edu/~hlnelson/fab
California State Univ - Fresno 5340 N Campus Dr MS
SS78   Fresno CA 93740
Ph: 559-278-5721

Biofeedback, Association for Applied Psychophysiology &   www.aapb.org
10200 W 44th Ave Suite 304   Wheat Ridge CO 80033
Ph: 303-422-8436 ▪ Fx: 303-422-8894 ▪ TF: 800-477-8892

Biographical Society, New York Genealogical &   www.nygbs.org
122 E 58th St   New York NY 10022
Ph: 212-755-8532 ▪ Fx: 212-754-4218

Biological Engineering, American Institute for Medical &   www.aimbe.org
1901 Pennsylvania Ave NW Suite 401   Washington DC 20006
Ph: 202-496-9660 ▪ Fx: 202-466-8489

Biological Field Stations, Organization of   www.obfs.org
Santa Margarita Ecological Reserve 2648 N Stagecoach
Ln   Fallbrook CA 92028
Ph: 760-728-9306 ▪ Fx: 760-451-0769

Biological Honor Society, Beta Beta Beta National   www.tri-beta.org
Univ of North Alabama Box 5079   Florence AL 35632
Ph: 256-765-6220 ▪ Fx: 256-765-6221

Biological Psychiatry, Society of   www.sobp.org
4500 San Pablo Rd Mayo Clinic   Jacksonville FL 32224
Ph: 904-953-2842 ▪ Fx: 904-953-7117

Biological Rhythms, Society for Light Treatment &   www.websciences.org/sltbr
174 Cook St PO Box 591687   San Francisco CA 94159
Ph: 415-876-0716 ▪ Fx: 415-751-2758

Biological Safety Association, American   www.absa.org
1202 Allanson Rd   Mundelein IL 60060
Ph: 847-949-1517 ▪ Fx: 847-566-4580

Biological Sciences, American Institute of   www.aibs.org
1444 'I' St NW Suite 200   Washington DC 20005
Ph: 202-628-1500 ▪ Fx: 202-628-1509 ▪ TF: 800-992-2427

Biological Sciences Honor Society, Phi Sigma   www.phisigmasociety.org
Eastern Illinois Univ 2029 Life Science Bldg   Charleston IL
61920
Ph: 217-581-3126 ▪ Fx: 217-581-7141

Biologists, American Institute of Fishery Research   www.iattc.org/aifrb/
Southwest Fisheries Science Ctr PO Box 271   La Jolla CA
92038
Ph: 858-546-7177 ▪ Fx: 858-546-5653

Biologists, American Society of Plant   www.aspb.org
15501 Monona Dr   Rockville MD 20855
Ph: 301-251-0560 ▪ Fx: 301-279-2996

Biology, American Institute of Oral   www.aiob.org
PO Box 7184   Loma Linda CA 92354
Ph: 909-558-4671 ▪ Fx: 909-558-0285

Biology, American Society for Cell   www.ascb.org
8120 Woodmont Ave Suite 750   Bethesda MD 20814
Ph: 301-347-9300 ▪ Fx: 301-347-9310

Biology, Association for Tropical   www.atbio.org
US National Herbarium National Museum of Natural History
Botany MRC-166   Washington DC 20013
Ph: 202-357-2534 ▪ Fx: 202-786-2563

Biology, Federation of American Societies for Experimental   www.faseb.org
9650 Rockville Pike   Bethesda MD 20814
Ph: 301-530-7000 ▪ Fx: 301-530-7001 ▪ TF: 800-433-2732

Biology, International Federation for Cell   www.ifcbiol.org

Biology, International Society for the History Philosophy &   www.phil.vt.edu/ishpssb
Social Studies of   13423 Burma Rd SW   Vashon Island WA
98070
Ph: 206-567-5839

Biology, International Society for Plant Molecular   www.uga.edu/~ispmb
Univ of Georgia Dept of Biochemistry & Molecular
Biology   Athens GA 30602
Ph: 706-542-3239 ▪ Fx: 706-542-2090

Biology Laboratory Education, Association for   www.zoo.toronto.edu/able
Univ of California Irvine Dept of Ecology & Evolutionary
Biology   Irvine CA 92697
Ph: 949-824-5573 ▪ Fx: 949-824-2181

Biology & Medicine, Society for Experimental   www.sebm.org
197 W Spring Valley Ave   Maywood NJ 07607
Ph: 201-291-9080 ▪ Fx: 201-291-2988

Biology & Medicine, Society for Free Radical   www.sfrbm.org
2950 Buskirk Ave Suite 170   Walnut Creek CA 94597
Ph: 925-472-5904 ▪ Fx: 925-472-5901

Biology & Medicine, Society for Physical Regulation in   www.sprbm.org
2412 Cobblestone Way   Frederick MD 21702
Ph: 301-663-4556 ▪ Fx: 301-694-4948

Biology, Society for Conservation   www.conservationbiology.org
4245 N Fairfax Dr Suite 400   Arlington VA 22203
Ph: 703-276-2384 ▪ Fx: 703-995-4633

Biology, Society for Developmental   sdb.bio.purdue.edu
9650 Rockville Pike   Bethesda MD 20814
Ph: 301-571-0647 ▪ Fx: 301-571-5704

Biology, Society for In Vitro   www.sivb.org
9315 Largo Dr W Suite 255   Largo MD 20774
Ph: 301-324-5054 ▪ Fx: 301-324-5057

Biology, Society for Integrative & Comparative   www.sicb.org
1313 Dolley Madison Blvd Suite 402   McLean VA 22101
Ph: 703-790-1745 ▪ Fx: 703-790-2672 ▪ TF: 800-955-1236

Biology, Society for Leukocyte   www.leukocytebiology.org
9650 Rockville Pike   Bethesda MD 20814
Ph: 301-634-7810 ▪ Fx: 301-634-7813

Biology Teachers, National Association of   www.nabt.org
12030 Sunrise Valley Dr Suite 110   Reston VA 20191
Ph: 703-264-9696 ▪ Fx: 703-264-7778 ▪ TF: 800-406-0775

Biomass Energy Research Association   www.bera1.org
1116 'E' St SE   Washington DC 20003
Ph: 847-381-6200 ▪ Fx: 847-382-5595 ▪ TF: 800-247-1755

Biomaterials Foundation, Surfaces   www.surfaces.org
13355 10th Ave N Suite 108   Minneapolis MN 55441
Ph: 763-512-9103 ▪ Fx: 763-765-2329

Biomaterials, Society for   www.biomaterials.org
17000 Commerce Pkwy Suite C   Mount Laurel NJ 08054
Ph: 856-439-0826 ▪ Fx: 856-439-0525

Biomechanics, American Society of www.asb-biomech.org
Willamette Univ Sparks Ctr 5 900 State St   Salem OR 97301
Ph: 503-370-6423

Biomedical Climatology, American Institute of www.aibc.cc
1050 Eagle Rd   Newtown PA 18940
Ph: 215-968-4483

Biomedical Engineering Society www.bmes.org
8401 Corporate Dr Suite 225   Landover MD 20785
Ph: 301-459-1999 ▪ Fx: 301-459-2444

Biomedical Marketing Association www.bmaonline.org
10293 N Meridian St Suite 175   Indianapolis IN 46290
Ph: 317-816-1640 ▪ Fx: 317-816-1633

Biomedical Research on Alcoholism, International Society for www.isbra.com
PO Box 202332   Denver CO 80220
Ph: 303-355-6420 ▪ Fx: 303-355-1207

Biomedical Research, Foundation for www.fbresearch.org
818 Connecticut Ave NW Suite 200   Washington DC 20006
Ph: 202-457-0654 ▪ Fx: 202-457-0659

Biomedical Research, National Association for www.nabr.org
818 Connecticut Ave NW 2nd Fl   Washington DC 20006
Ph: 202-857-0540 ▪ Fx: 202-659-1902

Biometric Society, International www.tibs.org
1444 'I' St NW Suite 700   Washington DC 20005
Ph: 202-712-9049 ▪ Fx: 202-216-9646

Biomolecular Resource Facilities, Association of www.abrf.org
2019 Galisteo St Bldg 1   Santa Fe NM 87505
Ph: 505-983-8102 ▪ Fx: 505-989-1073

Biomolecular Screening, Society for www.sbsonline.org
36 Tamarack Ave Suite 348   Danbury CT 06811
Ph: 203-743-1336 ▪ Fx: 203-748-7557

Biophysical Society www.biophysics.org
9650 Rockville Pike   Bethesda MD 20814
Ph: 301-530-7114 ▪ Fx: 301-530-7133

Biosystematists, International Organization of Plant www.iopb.org

Biotech Medical Management Association www.bmma.org
10592 Perry Hwy Suite 300   Wexford PA 15090
Ph: 724-934-8440 ▪ Fx: 724-934-8449 ▪ TF: 888-990-2662

Biotech Trainers, Society of Pharmaceutical & www.spbt.org
4423 Pheasant Ridge Rd Suite 100   Roanoke VA 24014
Ph: 540-725-3859 ▪ Fx: 540-989-7482

Biotechnology Industry Organization www.bio.org
1225 'I' St NW Suite 400   Washington DC 20005
Ph: 202-962-9200 ▪ Fx: 202-962-9201

Bipolar Foundation, Child & Adolescent www.bpkids.org
1187 Wilmette Ave PMB 331   Wilmette IL 60091
Ph: 847-256-8525 ▪ Fx: 847-920-9498

Bipolar Support Alliance, Depression & www.dbsalliance.org
730 N Franklin St Suite 501   Chicago IL 60610
Ph: 312-642-0049 ▪ Fx: 312-642-7243 ▪ TF: 800-826-3632

Bird Banding Association, Eastern www.pronetisp.net/~bpbird

Bird Clubs of America www.birdclubsofamerica.org
PO Box 2005   Yorktown VA 23692
Ph: 757-898-5090

Bird Conservancy, American www.abcbirds.org
4249 Loudoun Ave PO Box 249   The Plains VA 20198
Ph: 540-253-5780 ▪ Fx: 540-253-5782 ▪ TF: 888-247-3624

Bird Rescue Research Center, International www.ibrrc.org
4369 Cordelia Rd   Fairfield CA 94534
Ph: 707-207-0380 ▪ Fx: 707-207-0395

Bird Sanctuary, World www.worldbirdsanctuary.org
125 Bald Eagle Ridge Rd   Valley Park MO 63088
Ph: 636-861-3225 ▪ Fx: 636-861-3240

Bird Studies Canada www.bsc-eoc.org
PO Box 160   Port Rowan ON N0E1M0
Ph: 519-586-3531 ▪ Fx: 519-586-3532 ▪ TF: 888-448-2473

Birding Association, American www.americanbirding.org
PO Box 6599   Colorado Springs CO 80934
Ph: 719-578-9703 ▪ Fx: 719-578-1480

(Birds of Prey) Hawk Mountain Sanctuary Association www.hawkmountain.org
1700 Hawk Mountain Rd   Kempton PA 19529
Ph: 610-756-6961 ▪ Fx: 610-756-4468

(Birds of Prey) Last Chance Forever www.lastchanceforever.org
PO Box 460993   San Antonio TX 78246
Ph: 210-499-4080 ▪ Fx: 210-499-4305

Birds of Prey Rehabilitation Foundation www.birds-of-prey.org
2290 S 104th St   Broomfield CO 80020
Ph: 303-460-0674

Birth, Center for Loss in Multiple www.climb-support.org
PO Box 91377   Anchorage AK 99509
Ph: 907-222-5321 ▪ Fx: 907-274-7029

(Birth Defect) Cornelia de Lange Syndrome Foundation Inc www.cdlsusa.org
302 W Main St Suite 100   Avon CT 06001
Ph: 860-676-8166 ▪ Fx: 860-676-8337 ▪ TF: 800-753-2357

Birth Defect Research for Children www.birthdefects.org
930 Woodcock Rd Suite 225   Orlando FL 32803
Ph: 407-895-0802 ▪ Fx: 407-895-0824

Birth Defects Foundation, March of Dimes www.modimes.org
1275 Mamaroneck Ave   White Plains NY 10605
Ph: 914-428-7100 ▪ Fx: 914-428-8203 ▪ TF: 888-663-4637

(Birth Defects) Pull-Thru Network www.pullthrough.org
2312 Savoy St   Hoover AL 35226
Ph: 205-978-2930

(Birth Defects) Teratology Society www.teratology.org
1821 Michael Faraday Dr Suite 300   Reston VA 20190
Ph: 703-438-3104 ▪ Fx: 703-438-3113

(Birthmark) Nevus Network www.nevusnetwork.org
PO Box 305   West Salem OH 44287
Ph: 419-853-4525

Birthparents, Concerned United www.cubirthparents.org
PO Box 230457   Encinitas CA 92023
Ph: 800-822-2777 ▪ Fx: 760-929-1879

Biscuit & Cracker Manufacturers Association www.thebcma.org
8484 Georgia Ave Suite 700   Silver Spring MD 20910
Ph: 301-608-1552 ▪ Fx: 301-608-1557

Bishop Hill Heritage Association www.bishophill.com
103 N Bishop Hill St PO Box 92   Bishop Hill IL 61419
Ph: 309-927-3345 ▪ Fx: 309-927-3010

Bishops in the Americas, Standing Conference of Canonical Orthodox www.scoba.us
8 E 79th St   New York NY 10021
Ph: 212-570-3500 ▪ Fx: 212-570-3569

Bison Association, National www.bisoncentral.com
4100 W 122nd Ave Suite 106   Westminster CO 80234
Ph: 303-292-2833 ▪ Fx: 303-292-2564

Bituminous Coal Operators Association
1500 K St NW   Washington DC 20005
Ph: 202-783-3195 ▪ Fx: 202-783-4862

Bituminous Contractors, Association of
815 Connecticut Ave NW Suite 620   Washington DC 20006
Ph: 202-785-4440 ▪ Fx: 202-331-8049

Bix Beiderbecke Memorial Society www.bixsociety.org
PO Box 3688   Davenport IA 52808
Ph: 563-324-7170 ▪ Fx: 563-326-1732 ▪ TF: 888-249-5487

BKR International www.bkr.com
19 Fulton St Suite 306   New York NY 10038
Ph: 212-964-2115 ▪ Fx: 212-964-2133 ▪ TF: 800-257-4685

Black Accountants, National Association of www.nabainc.org
7249-A Hanover Pkwy   Greenbelt MD 20770
Ph: 301-474-6222 ▪ Fx: 301-474-3114

Black Aged Inc, National Caucus & Center on www.ncba-aged.org
1220 L St NW Suite 800   Washington DC 20005
Ph: 202-637-8400 ▪ Fx: 202-347-0895

Black Airline Pilots, Organization of www.obap.org
8630 Fenton St Suite 126   Silver Spring MD 20910
Ph: 800-538-6227

Black America's Political Action Committee www.bampac.org
2029 P St NW Suite 202   Washington DC 20036
Ph: 202-785-9619 ▪ Fx: 202-785-9621 ▪ TF: 877-722-6722

Black Anthropologists, Association of www.aaanet.org/aba
c/o American Anthropological Assn 2200 Wilson Blvd Suite
600   Arlington VA 22201
Ph: 703-528-1902 ▪ Fx: 703-528-3546

Black Broadcasters Alliance www.thebba.org
3474 William Penn Hwy   Pittsburgh PA 15235
Ph: 412-829-9788 ▪ Fx: 412-829-0313

Black Cardiologists, Association of www.abcardio.org
6849 Peachtree Dunwoody Rd NE Bldg 2   Atlanta GA 30328
Ph: 678-302-4222 ▪ Fx: 678-302-4223

Black Catholic Congress, National www.nbccongress.org
320 Cathedral St   Baltimore MD 21201
Ph: 410-547-8496 ▪ Fx: 410-752-3958

Black Caucus Foundation Inc, Congressional www.cbcfinc.org
1720 Massachusetts Ave NW   Washington DC 20036
Ph: 202-263-2800 ▪ Fx: 202-775-0773 ▪ TF: 800-784-2577

Black Caucus of Local Elected Officials, National www.nbc-leo.org
1301 Pennsylvania Ave NW Suite 550   Washington DC 20004
Ph: 202-626-3000 ▪ Fx: 202-626-3043

Black Caucus of State Legislators, National www.nbcsl.com
444 N Capitol St NW Suite 622   Washington DC 20001
Ph: 202-624-5457 ▪ Fx: 202-508-3826

Black Chamber of Commerce, National www.nationalbcc.org
1350 Connecticut Ave NW Suite 825   Washington DC 20036
Ph: 202-466-6888 ▪ Fx: 202-466-4918

Black Chemists & Chemical Engineers, National Organization for www.nobcche.org
the Professional Advancement of   PO Box
77040   Washington DC 20013
Ph: 202-667-1699 ▪ Fx: 202-667-1705 ▪ TF: 800-776-1419

Black Child Development Institute, National www.nbcdi.org
1101 15th St NW Suite 900   Washington DC 20005
Ph: 202-833-2220 ▪ Fx: 202-833-8222

Black Churches, Congress of National
PO Box 65682   Washington DC 20035
Ph: 202-898-2422 ▪ Fx: 202-893-9300

Black Civic Participation Inc, National Coalition on www.bigvote.org
1025 Vermont Ave NW Suite 1010   Washington DC 20005
Ph: 202-659-4929 ▪ Fx: 202-659-5025

Black Coaches Association www.bcasports.org
201 S Capitol Ave Suite 495   Indianapolis IN 46225
Ph: 317-829-5600 ▪ Fx: 317-829-5601 ▪ TF: 877-789-1222

Black College Radio www.blackcollegeradio.com
PO Box 3191   Atlanta GA 30302
Ph: 404-523-6136 ▪ Fx: 404-523-5467

Black Community Crusade for Children www.childrensdefense.org/bccc
25 'E' St NW   Washington DC 20001
Ph: 202-628-8787 ▪ Fx: 202-662-3580

Black County Officials, National Association of
440 1st St NW Suite 410   Washington DC 20001
Ph: 202-347-6953 ▪ Fx: 202-393-6596

Black Culinarians Alliance www.blackculinarians.com
55 W 116th St Suite 234   New York NY 10026
Ph: 646-548-2949 ▪ Fx: 212-283-7157

Black Data Processing Associates www.bdpa.org
6301 Ivy Ln Suite 700   Greenbelt MD 20770
Ph: 301-220-2180 ▪ Fx: 301-220-2185 ▪ TF: 800-727-2372

Black Designers, Organization of www.core77.com/OBD
300 M St SW Suite N110   Washington DC 20024
Ph: 202-659-3918 ▪ Fx: 202-488-3838

Black Engineers, National Society of www.nsbe.org
1454 Duke St   Alexandria VA 22314
Ph: 703-549-2207 ▪ Fx: 703-683-5312

Black Engineers & Scientists, National Council of　　www.ncbes.org
1525 Aviation Blvd Suite C424　Redondo Beach CA 90278
Ph: 213-896-9779

Black Entertainment & Sports Lawyers Association　　www.besla.org
PO Box 441485　Fort Washington MD 20749
Ph: 301-248-1818 ▪ Fx: 301-248-0700

Black Family Life & Culture, Institute for the Advanced Study of　www.iasbflc.org
1484 9th St　Oakland CA 94607
Ph: 510-836-3245 ▪ Fx: 510-836-3248

Black Farmers & Agriculturalists Association　www.coax.net/people/lwf/bfaa.htm
PO Box 61　Tillery NC 27887
Ph: 252-826-2800 ▪ Fx: 252-826-3244

Black Filmmaker Foundation　　www.dvrepublic.com
670 Broadway Suite 300　New York NY 10012
Ph: 212-253-1690 ▪ Fx: 212-253-1689

Black Fund of America Inc, United　　www.ubfinc.org
2500 ML King Jr Ave SE PO Box 7051　Washington DC 20032
Ph: 202-783-9300 ▪ Fx: 202-347-2564

Black Human Resources Network　　www.bhrn.org
8855 Annapolis Rd Suite 301　Lanham MD 20706
Ph: 301-459-6200 ▪ Fx: 301-459-3134

Black Journalists, National Association of　　www.nabj.org
Univ of Maryland 8701-A Adelphi Rd　Adelphi MD 20783
Ph: 301-445-7100 ▪ Fx: 301-445-7101

Black Law Enforcement Executives, National Organization of　www.noblenatl.org
4609 Pinecrest Office Park Dr Suite F　Alexandria VA 22312
Ph: 703-658-1529 ▪ Fx: 703-658-9479

Black Law Students Association, National　　www.nblsa.org

Black Lawyers, National Conference of　　www.ncbl.org
PO Box 80043　Lansing MI 48908
Ph: 866-266-5091

Black Lung Association
PO Box 872　Crab Orchard WV 25827
Ph: 304-252-9654

Black Mayors, National Conference of　　www.blackmayors.org
1151 Cleveland Ave Suite D　East Point GA 30344
Ph: 404-765-6444 ▪ Fx: 404-765-6430

Black MBA Association, National　　www.nbmbaa.org
180 N Michigan Ave Suite 1400　Chicago IL 60601
Ph: 312-236-2622 ▪ Fx: 312-236-4131

Black McDonald's Operators Association, National　　www.nbmoa.org
PO Box 8204　Los Angeles CA 90008
Ph: 323-296-5495 ▪ Fx: 323-296-6134

Black Meeting Planners, National Coalition of　　www.ncbmp.com
8630 Fenton St Suite 126　Silver Spring MD 20910
Ph: 202-628-3952 ▪ Fx: 301-588-0011

Black Men of America Inc, 100　　www.100blackmen.org
141 Auburn Ave　Atlanta GA 30303
Ph: 404-688-5100 ▪ Fx: 404-688-1028 ▪ TF: 800-598-3411

Black Methodists for Church Renewal　　www.bmcr-umc.org
601 W Riverview Ave　Dayton OH 45406
Ph: 937-227-9460 ▪ Fx: 937-227-9463

Black Nurses Association, National
8630 Fenton St Suite 330　Silver Spring MD 20910
Ph: 301-589-3200 ▪ Fx: 301-589-3223

Black Owned Broadcasters, National Association of　　www.nabob.org
1155 Connecticut Ave NW 6th Fl　Washington DC 20036
Ph: 202-463-8970 ▪ Fx: 202-429-0657

Black Physicists, National Society of　　www.nsbp.org
6704 Lee Hwy Suite G　Arlington VA 22205
Ph: 703-536-4207 ▪ Fx: 703-536-4203

Black Police Association, National　　www.blackpolice.org
3251 Mt Pleasant St NW　Washington DC 20010
Ph: 202-986-2070 ▪ Fx: 202-986-0410

Black Political Scientists, National Conference of　www.poli.ncat.edu/ncobps
3695-F Cascade Rd SW Suite 212　Atlanta GA 30331
Ph: 404-880-8240

Black Professional Fire Fighters, International Association of　www.iabpff.org

Black Psychiatrists of America
24361 Greenfield Suite 300　Southfield MI 48075
Ph: 248-569-9344

Black Psychologists, Association of　　www.abpsi.org
PO Box 55999　Washington DC 20040
Ph: 202-722-0808 ▪ Fx: 202-722-5941

Black Public Administrators, National Forum for　　www.nfbpa.org
777 N Capitol St NE Suite 807　Washington DC 20002
Ph: 202-408-9300 ▪ Fx: 202-408-8558

Black Public Relations Society, National　　www.nbprs.org
6565 Sunset Blvd Suite 425　Hollywood CA 90028
Ph: 323-466-8221 ▪ Fx: 323-856-9510

Black Retail Action Group　　www.bragusa.org
PO Box 1192 Rockefeller Center Stn　New York NY 10185
Ph: 212-319-7751

Black Rock Coalition　　www.blackrockcoalition.org
PO Box 1054 Cooper Stn　New York NY 10276
Ph: 212-713-5097 ▪ Fx: 212-226-6707

Black School Educators, National Alliance of　　www.nabse.org
310 Pennsylvania Ave SE　Washington DC 20003
Ph: 202-608-6310 ▪ Fx: 202-608-6319 ▪ TF: 800-221-2654

Black Scientists Association, NIH　　bsa.od.nih.gov
PO Box 2262　Kensington MD 20891
Ph: 301-402-6425

Black Scuba Divers, National Association of　　www.nabsdivers.org

Black Sisters' Conference, National　　nbsc68.tripod.com
101 Q St NE　Washington DC 20002
Ph: 202-529-9250 ▪ Fx: 202-529-9370

Black Social Workers, National Association of　　www.nabsw.org
1220 11th St NW　Washington DC 20001
Ph: 202-589-1850 ▪ Fx: 202-589-1853

Black Sociologists, Association of　　www.blacksociologists.org
4200 Wisconsin Ave NW PMB 106-257　Washington DC 20016
Ph: 202-365-1759

Black State Troopers Coalition Inc, National　　www.nbstc.com
PO Box 70059　Nashville TN 37207
Ph: 877-996-2782

Black Storytellers, National Association of　　www.nabsnet.org
PO Box 67722　Baltimore MD 21215
Ph: 410-947-1117

Black Trade Unionists, Coalition of　　www.cbtu.org
PO Box 66268　Washington DC 20035
Ph: 202-429-1203 ▪ Fx: 202-429-1102

Black United Federation of Charities, National
1212 New York Ave NW Suite 550　Washington DC 20005
Ph: 202-289-7888 ▪ Fx: 202-289-5950

Black United Fund Inc, National　　www.nbuf.org
40 Clinton St 5th Fl　Newark NJ 07102
Ph: 973-643-5122 ▪ Fx: 973-648-8350 ▪ TF: 800-223-0866

Black Veterans for Social Justice Inc　　www.bvsj.org
665 Willoughby Ave　Brooklyn NY 11221
Ph: 718-852-6004 ▪ Fx: 718-852-4805

Black Women in Church & Society　　www.itc.edu/WSP/WSPBWCS.htm
700 ML King Jr Dr　Atlanta GA 30314
Ph: 404-527-5713 ▪ Fx: 404-527-5715

(Black Women) Iota Phi Lambda Sorority Inc　　www.iota1929.org
1462 W 113th Pl　Chicago IL 60643
Ph: 773-445-1315 ▪ TF: 800-982-4682

Black Women, National Coalition of 100　　www.ncbw.org
38 W 32nd St Suite 1610　New York NY 10001
Ph: 212-947-2196 ▪ Fx: 212-947-2477

Black Women Inc, National Congress of　　www.npcbw.org
8484 Georgia Ave Suite 420　Silver Spring MD 20910
Ph: 301-562-8000 ▪ Fx: 301-562-8303 ▪ TF: 877-274-1198

Black Women in Sisterhood for Action　　www.bisa-hq.org
PO Box 1592　Washington DC 20013
Ph: 202-543-6013 ▪ Fx: 202-543-5719

Black Women's Congress, International　　www.ibwc.info
555 Fenchurch St Suite 102　Norfolk VA 23510
Ph: 757-625-0500 ▪ Fx: 757-625-1905

Black Women's Health Imperative　　www.blackwomenshealth.org
600 Pennsylvania Ave SE Suite 310　Washington DC 20003
Ph: 202-548-4000 ▪ Fx: 202-543-9743

Black Women's Roundtable on Civic Participation　　www.bigvote.org/bwr.htm
1025 Vermont Ave NW Suite 1010　Washington DC 20005
Ph: 202-659-4929 ▪ Fx: 202-659-5025

Black World Foundation
PO Box 2869　Oakland CA 94618
Ph: 510-547-6633 ▪ Fx: 510-547-6679

Black Writers & Artists Inc, International　　members.tripod.com/~IBWA
PO Box 43576　Los Angeles CA 90043
Ph: 323-964-3721

Blacks in Criminal Justice, National Association of　www.nabcj.org
North Carolina Central Univ PO Box 19788　Durham NC 27707
Ph: 919-683-1801 ▪ Fx: 919-683-1903

Blacks in Energy, American Association of　　www.aabe.org
927 15th St NW Suite 200　Washington DC 20005
Ph: 202-371-9530 ▪ Fx: 202-371-9218 ▪ TF: 800-466-0204

Blacks in Government　　www.bignet.org
1820 11th St NW　Washington DC 20001
Ph: 202-667-3280 ▪ Fx: 202-667-3705

Blacks, Medical Education for South African　　www.mesab.org/
120 Albany St Suite 810　New Brunswick NJ 08901
Ph: 732-745-1292 ▪ Fx: 732-745-9794

Blacks for Reparations in America, National Coalition of　www.ncobra.com
PO Box 90604　Washington DC 20090
Ph: 202-291-8400 ▪ Fx: 202-291-4600

Blacksmith's Association of North America, Artist-　www.abana.org
PO Box 816　Farmington GA 30638
Ph: 706-310-1030 ▪ Fx: 706-769-7147

Blacksmiths Forgers & Helpers, International Brotherhood of　www.boilermakers.org
Boilermakers Iron Shipbuilders　753 State Ave Suite
　　570　Kansas City KS 66101
Ph: 913-371-2640 ▪ Fx: 913-281-8101

Blacksmiths & Weldors Association Inc, National　　blacksmithing.tripod.com
PO Box 123　Arnold NE 69120
Ph: 308-848-2913

Blade Collectors Inc, International
c/o Krause Publications 700 E State St　Iola WI 54990
Ph: 715-445-2214 ▪ Fx: 715-445-4087

Bladesmith Society, American　　www.americanbladesmith.com
PO Box 1481　Cypress TX 77410
Ph: 281-225-9159 ▪ Fx: 281-225-9163

Blazer Horse Association　　www.integrity.com/homes/lorenzo/bha.htm
820 N Can-Ada Rd　Star ID 83669
Ph: 208-286-7267

Blessings International　　www.blessing.org
PO Box 35292　Tulsa OK 74146
Ph: 918-250-8101 ▪ Fx: 918-250-1281 ▪ TF: 877-250-8101

Blind, American Council of the　　www.acb.org
1155 15th St NW Suite 1004　Washington DC 20005
Ph: 202-467-5081 ▪ Fx: 202-467-5085 ▪ TF: 800-424-8666

Blind, American Foundation for the　　www.afb.org
11 Penn Plaza Suite 300　New York NY 10001
Ph: 212-502-7600 ▪ Fx: 212-502-7777 ▪ TF: 800-232-5463

Blind, American Printing House for the　　www.aph.org
1839 Frankfort Ave PO Box 6085　Louisville KY 40206
Ph: 502-895-2405 ▪ Fx: 502-899-2274 ▪ TF: 800-223-1839

Blind, Associated Services for the　　www.asb.org
919 Walnut St　Philadelphia PA 19107
Ph: 215-627-0600 ▪ Fx: 215-922-0692

Blind Athletes, US Association of — www.usaba.org
33 N Institute St   Colorado Springs CO 80903
Ph: 719-630-0422 ▪ Fx: 719-630-0616

Blind, Canadian National Institute for the — www.cnib.ca
1929 Bayview Ave   Toronto ON M4G3E8
Ph: 416-480-7503

Blind Children & Adults, American Action Fund for — www.actionfund.org
1800 Johnson St   Baltimore MD 21230
Ph: 410-659-9314 ▪ Fx: 410-685-5653

Blind Children, National Organization of Parents of — www.nfb.org/nopbc/nopbc_what.htm
1800 Johnson St   Baltimore MD 21230
Ph: 410-659-9314

Blind, Christian Services for the — www.csbonline.org
1124 Fair Oaks PO Box 26   South Pasadena CA 91031
Ph: 626-799-3935 ▪ Fx: 626-403-9460

Blind & Dyslexic, Recording for the — www.rfbd.org
20 Roszel Rd   Princeton NJ 08540
Ph: 609-452-0606 ▪ Fx: 609-520-7990 ▪ TF: 800-221-4792

Blind Golfers' Association, US — www.blindgolf.com
3094 Shamrock St N   Tallahassee FL 32308
Ph: 850-893-4511

Blind, Gospel Association for the — www.careministries.org/gab.html
1450 SW 10th Ave Bldg B-2   Delray Beach FL 33444
Ph: 386-586-5885

Blind Inc, Guide Dog Foundation for the — www.guidedog.org
371 E Jericho Tkpe   Smithtown NY 11787
Ph: 631-265-2121 ▪ Fx: 631-361-5192 ▪ TF: 800-548-4337

Blind, Guide Dogs for the — www.guidedogs.com
PO Box 151200   San Rafael CA 94915
Ph: 415-499-4000 ▪ Fx: 415-499-4035 ▪ TF: 800-295-4050

Blind, Guiding Eyes for the — guidingeyes.org
611 Granite Springs Rd   Yorktown Heights NY 10598
Ph: 914-245-4024 ▪ Fx: 914-245-1609 ▪ TF: 800-942-0149

Blind & Handicapped, Skating Association for the — www.sabahinc.org
1200 East & West Rd   West Seneca NY 14224
Ph: 716-675-7222 ▪ Fx: 716-675-7223

Blind, Jewish Guild for the — www.jgb.org
15 W 65th St   New York NY 10023
Ph: 212-769-6200 ▪ Fx: 212-769-6266 ▪ TF: 800-284-4422

Blind Lawyers Association, American
c/o American Council of the Blind 1155 15th St NW Suite
1004   Washington DC 20005
Ph: 202-467-5081 ▪ Fx: 202-467-5085 ▪ TF: 800-424-8666

Blind, Leader Dogs for the — www.leaderdog.org
PO Box 5000   Rochester MI 48308
Ph: 248-651-9011 ▪ Fx: 248-651-5812 ▪ TF: 888-777-5332

Blind Lions, American Council of — www.acb.org/affiliates
1155 15th St NW Suite 1004   Washington DC 20005
Ph: 202-467-5081 ▪ TF: 800-424-8666

Blind Mission International, Christian — www.christianity.com/cbmi
450 E Park Ave   Greenville SC 29601
Ph: 864-239-0065 ▪ Fx: 864-239-0069 ▪ TF: 800-937-2264

Blind, National Council of State Agencies for the — www.ncsab.org
PO Box 25380   Washington DC 20027
Ph: 202-298-8468 ▪ Fx: 202-333-5881

Blind, National Federation of the — www.nfb.org
1800 Johnson St   Baltimore MD 21230
Ph: 410-659-9314 ▪ Fx: 410-685-5653

Blind, National Industries for the — www.nib.org
1901 N Beauregard St Suite 200   Alexandria VA 22311
Ph: 703-998-0770 ▪ Fx: 703-998-8268 ▪ TF: 800-433-2304

Blind People Inc, Advocates for Communication — www.deafblindadvocates.org
Technology for Deaf- 911 Regina Dr   Baltimore MD 21227
Ph: 410-247-5045 ▪ Fx: 410-381-6838

Blind & Retarded, Association for the Advancement of the — www.aabr.org
1508 College Pt Blvd   College Point NY 11356
Ph: 718-321-3800 ▪ Fx: 718-321-8688

Blind Students Inc, National Alliance of — www.blindstudents.org
1155 15th St NW Suite 1004   Washington DC 20005
Ph: 202-467-5081 ▪ Fx: 202-467-5085 ▪ TF: 800-424-8666

Blind & Visually Impaired, Association for Education & — www.aerbvi.org
Rehabilitation of the   1703 N Beauregard St Suite
440   Alexandria VA 22311
Ph: 703-671-4500 ▪ Fx: 703-671-6391

Blind Youths & Adults, Helen Keller National Center for Deaf- — hknc.org
141 Middle Neck Rd   Sands Point NY 11050
Ph: 516-944-8900 ▪ Fx: 516-944-7302

Blindness America, Prevent — www.preventblindness.org
500 E Remington Rd Suite 200   Schaumburg IL 60173
Ph: 847-843-2020 ▪ Fx: 847-843-8458 ▪ TF: 800-331-2020

Blindness, Foundation Fighting — www.blindness.org
11435 Cron Hill Dr   Owings Mills MD 21117
Ph: 410-568-0150 ▪ Fx: 410-363-2393 ▪ TF: 800-683-5555

(Blindness) Helen Keller Worldwide — www.hkworld.org
352 Park Ave S 12th Fl   New York NY 10010
Ph: 212-532-0544 ▪ Fx: 212-532-5860 ▪ TF: 877-535-5374

(Blindness) Keren-Or Inc — www.keren-or.org
350 7th Ave Suite 200   New York NY 10001
Ph: 212-279-4070 ▪ Fx: 212-279-4043

Blindness Inc, Research to Prevent — www.rpbusa.org
645 Madison Ave 21st Fl   New York NY 10022
Ph: 212-752-4333 ▪ Fx: 212-688-6231 ▪ TF: 800-621-0026

(Blindness) Ski for Light Inc — www.sfl.org
1455 W Lake St   Minneapolis MN 55408
Ph: 612-827-3232 ▪ Fx: 612-779-0211

Bloch RA Cancer Foundation — www.blochcancer.org
4400 Main St   Kansas City MO 64111
Ph: 816-932-8453 ▪ Fx: 816-931-7486 ▪ TF: 800-433-0464

Block & Bridle Club, National — www.blockandbridle.org
Colorado State Univ Dept of Dairy & Animal Science   University
Park PA 16802
Ph: 814-863-0734 ▪ Fx: 814-863-6042

Blonde D'Aquitaine Association, American — www.blondecattle.org
PO Box 470661   Tulsa OK 74147
Ph: 918-610-0842

Blood Banks, American Association of — www.aabb.org
8101 Glenbrook Rd   Bethesda MD 20814
Ph: 301-907-6977 ▪ Fx: 301-907-6895

Blood Centers, America's — www.americasblood.org
725 15th St NW Suite 700   Washington DC 20005
Ph: 202-393-5725 ▪ Fx: 202-393-1282 ▪ TF: 888-872-5663

Blood Donor Foundation, Cord — www.cordblooddonor.org
1200 Bayhill Dr Suite 301   San Bruno CA 94066
Ph: 650-635-1452 ▪ Fx: 650-635-1428

Blood Foundation, Children's — www.childrensbloodfoundation.org
333 E 38th Rm 830   New York NY 10016
Ph: 212-297-4336 ▪ Fx: 212-297-4340

Blood & Marrow Transplantation, American Society for — www.asbmt.org
85 W Algonquin Rd Suite 550   Arlington Heights IL 60005
Ph: 847-427-0224 ▪ Fx: 847-427-9656

Blood Purification, International Society of — www.isbp.org
Vanderbilt University Medical Ctr 1161 21st Ave S MCN
S-3301   Nashville TN 37232
Ph: 615-343-2220 ▪ Fx: 615-322-8653

Bloodhound Association, National Police
RR2 Box 1165   Milton PA 17847
Ph: 570-742-7310 ▪ Fx: 570-742-7319

Blouse Skirt & Undergarment Association, Greater — www.greaterblouse.org
225 W 34th St Suite 612   New York NY 10122
Ph: 212-563-5052 ▪ Fx: 212-563-5373

Blue Crab Industry Association, National — www.nfi.org
1901 N Fort Myer Dr Suite 700   Arlington VA 22209
Ph: 703-524-8883 ▪ Fx: 703-524-4619

Blue Cross & Blue Shield Association — www.bluecares.com
225 N Michigan Ave   Chicago IL 60601
Ph: 312-297-6000 ▪ Fx: 312-297-6609

Blue Goose International, Honorable Order of the — www.bluegoose.org
12940 Walnut Rd   Elm Grove WI 53122
Ph: 414-221-0341 ▪ Fx: 414-782-7608

Blue Knights International Law Enforcement Motorcycle Club Inc — www.blueknights.org
38 Alden St   Bangor ME 04401
Ph: 207-947-4600 ▪ Fx: 207-947-5814

Blueberry Association of North America, Wild — www.wildblueberries.com
59 Cottage St   Bar Harbor ME 04609
Ph: 207-288-2655 ▪ Fx: 207-288-2656 ▪ TF: 800-233-9453

Blueberry Council, North American — www.blueberry.org
4995 Golden Foothill Pkwy Suite 2   El Dorado Hills CA 95762
Ph: 916-933-9399 ▪ Fx: 916-933-9777

Bluebird Society, North American — www.nabluebirdsociety.org
PO Box 244   Wilmot OH 44689
Ph: 330-359-5511 ▪ Fx: 330-359-5455 ▪ TF: 888-235-1331

Bluegrass Music Association, International — www.ibma.org
2 Music Cir S Suite 100   Nashville TN 37203
Ph: 615-256-3222 ▪ Fx: 615-256-0450 ▪ TF: 888-438-4262

BlueRibbon Coalition — www.sharetrails.org
4555 Burley Dr   Pocatello ID 83202
Ph: 208-237-1008 ▪ Fx: 208-237-9424 ▪ TF: 800-258-3742

Blues Foundation — www.blues.org/
49 Union Ave   Memphis TN 38103
Ph: 901-527-2583 ▪ Fx: 901-529-4030 ▪ TF: 800-861-8795

Blues Music Association — www.bluesmusicassociation.org
PO Box 3122   Memphis TN 38173
Ph: 901-572-3843

Bluetick Breeders of America — www.bluetickbreedersofamerica.com
3205 Illinois Rt 78 S   Stockton IL 60815
Ph: 815-947-3090

BMW Motorcycle Owners of America — www.bmwmoa.org
PO Box 3982   Ballwin MO 63022
Ph: 636-394-7277 ▪ Fx: 636-537-9848

BMW Motorcycle Owners Ltd, Vintage — www.vintagebmw.org
PO Box 67   Exeter NH 03833
Ph: 603-772-9799

BMW Riders Association International — www.bmwra.org
PO Box 120430   West Melbourne FL 32912
Ph: 321-984-7800

BMW Vintage Club of America
PO Box S   San Rafael CA 94913
Ph: 415-897-0220 ▪ Fx: 415-898-0831

B'nai B'rith International — bnaibrith.org
2020 K St NW   Washington DC 20036
Ph: 202-857-6600 ▪ Fx: 202-857-6609 ▪ TF: 888-388-4224

B'nai B'rith Youth Organization — www.bbyo.org
2020 K St NW   Washington DC 20006
Ph: 202-857-6633 ▪ Fx: 202-857-6568

Bnai Zion Foundation Inc — www.bnaizion.org
136 E 39th St   New York NY 10016
Ph: 212-725-1211 ▪ Fx: 212-684-6327 ▪ TF: 800-564-6399

Bnei Akiva of the US & Canada — www.bneiakiva.org
7 Penn Plaza   New York NY 10010
Ph: 212-465-9536 ▪ Fx: 212-465-2155

Board Association, Structural — www.osbguide.com
25 Valleywood Dr Unit 27   Markham ON L3R5L9
Ph: 905-475-1100 ▪ Fx: 905-475-1101

Board of Certified Hazard Control Management — www.chcm-chsp.org
11900 Parklawn Dr Suite 451   Rockville MD 20852
Ph: 301-770-2540 ▪ Fx: 301-770-2183

Board of Certified Safety Professionals — www.bcsp.org
208 Burwash Ave   Savoy IL 61874
Ph: 217-359-9263 ▪ Fx: 217-359-0055

Board of Pharmaceutical Specialties   www.bpsweb.org
2215 Constitution Ave NW   Washington DC 20037
Ph: 202-429-7591 ▪ Fx: 202-429-6304

Boarding Schools, Association of   www.schools.com
4455 Connecticut Ave NW Suite A-200   Washington DC 20008
Ph: 202-966-8705 ▪ Fx: 202-966-8708 ▪ TF: 800-541-5908

BoardSource   www.boardsource.org
1828 L St NW Suite 900   Washington DC 20036
Ph: 202-452-6262 ▪ Fx: 202-452-6299 ▪ TF: 800-883-6262

Boat Association, American Power   apba-racing.com
17640 Nine Mile Rd   Eastpointe MI 48021
Ph: 586-773-9700 ▪ Fx: 586-773-6490

Boat Association, International Model Power   www.impba.com
2804 Woods Dr   Violet LA 70092
Ph: 504-276-4500

Boat Association, North American Model   www.namba.com
1815 Halley St   San Diego CA 92154
Ph: 619-424-6380 ▪ Fx: 619-424-8845

Boat Association, Pacific Dragon   www.pdbausa.org
PO Box 23693   Portland OR 97281
Ph: 503-639-2799 ▪ Fx: 503-670-1003

Boat Club, Chris Craft Antique   www.chris-craft.org
217 S Adams St   Tallahassee FL 32301
Ph: 850-224-2628 ▪ Fx: 850-224-1033

Boat Owners Alliance, National Party
181 Thames St   Groton CT 06340
Ph: 860-535-2066 ▪ Fx: 860-535-8389

Boat Owners Association of the US   www.boatus.com
880 S Pickett St   Alexandria VA 22304
Ph: 703-823-9550 ▪ Fx: 703-461-2847 ▪ TF: 800-937-9307

Boat Society, Antique & Classic   www.acbs.org
422 James St   Clayton NY 13624
Ph: 315-686-2628 ▪ Fx: 315-686-2680

Boat & Travel Club, Vagabundos del Mar   www.vagabundos.com
190 Main St   Rio Vista CA 94571
Ph: 707-374-5511 ▪ Fx: 707-374-6843 ▪ TF: 800-474-2252

Boat & Yacht Council Inc, American   www.abycinc.org
3069 Solomon's Island Rd   Edgewater MD 21037
Ph: 410-956-1050 ▪ Fx: 410-956-2737

Boaters Association, Christian   www.christianboater.org
PO Box 358   Canal Point FL 33438
Ph: 561-924-9522 ▪ Fx: 561-924-6097

Boating & Fishing Foundation, Recreational   www.rbff.org
601 N Fairfax St Suite 140   Alexandria VA 22314
Ph: 703-519-0013 ▪ Fx: 703-519-9565

Boating Law Administrators, National Association of State   www.nasbla.org
1500 Leestown Rd Suite 330   Lexington KY 40511
Ph: 859-225-9487 ▪ Fx: 859-231-6403

Boating Writers International   www.bwi.org
108 9th St   Wilmette IL 60091
Ph: 847-736-4142

(Boats) Catboat Association Inc   www.catboats.org
PO Box 72   Middleboro MA 02346
Ph: 508-947-5093 ▪ Fx: 508-947-2013

(Boats) Gar Wood Society   www.garwood.com
PO Box 6003   Syracuse NY 13217
Ph: 315-446-5654 ▪ Fx: 315-686-4104

(Boats) Houseboat Industry Association
200 E Randolph Dr Suite 5100   Chicago IL 60601
Ph: 312-946-6280 ▪ Fx: 312-946-0388 ▪ TF: 800-669-5462

(Boats) International Etchells Class Association Inc   www.etchells.org
PO Box 676   Jamestown RI 02835
Ph: 401-560-0022 ▪ Fx: 401-560-0013

(Boats) International Hobie Class Association   www.hobieclass.com
3334 Fulton   Victoria BC V9C2T9
Ph: 250-474-7580

(Boats) International Lightning Class Association   www.lightningclass.org
PO Box 10747   Murfreesboro TN 37129
Ph: 615-893-5274 ▪ Fx: 615-893-5205

(Boats) International Star Class Yacht Racing Association   www.starclass.org
1545 Waukegan Rd   Glenview IL 60025
Ph: 847-729-0630 ▪ Fx: 847-729-0718

(Boats) International Sunfish Class Association   www.sunfishclass.org
PO Box 300128   Waterford MI 48330
Ph: 248-673-2750

Boats Inc, PT   www.ptboats.org
PO Box 38070   Germantown TN 38183
Ph: 901-755-8440

(Boats) Traditional Small Craft Association   www.tsca.net
PO Box 350   Mystic CT 06355
Ph: 860-572-0711

(Boats) US Optimist Dinghy Association   www.usoda.org

Bobsled & Skeleton Federation, US   www.usbsf.com
421 Old Military Rd   Lake Placid NY 12946
Ph: 518-523-1842 ▪ Fx: 518-523-9491 ▪ TF: 800-262-7533

Bocce Association, World   www.worldbocce.org/USA
188 Industrial Dr Suite 17A   Elmhurst IL 60126
Ph: 630-834-8349 ▪ Fx: 630-832-2174 ▪ TF: 800-652-6623

Bocce Federation, US   www.bocce.com
44 Park Ln   Park Ridge IL 60068
Ph: 847-692-6223 ▪ Fx: 847-692-6221

Bockus International Society of Gastroenterology
300 Community Dr   Manhasset NY 11030
Ph: 516-562-4281 ▪ Fx: 516-562-2683

Bodies Ourselves, Our   www.ourbodiesourselves.org
34 Plympton St   Boston MA 02118
Ph: 617-451-3666 ▪ Fx: 617-451-3664

Body Engineers, American Society of   www.asbe.net
2122 15 Mile Rd   Sterling Heights MI 48310
Ph: 586-268-8360 ▪ Fx: 586-268-2187

Body Parts Association, Automotive   www.autobpa.com
2000 S Dairy Ashford Suite 420 PO Box 820689   Houston TX 77282
Ph: 281-531-0809 ▪ Fx: 281-531-9411 ▪ TF: 800-323-5832

Bodywork Association, Worldwide Aquatics   aspen.forest.net/waba
PO Box 889   Middletown CA 95461
Ph: 707-987-3801 ▪ Fx: 707-987-9638

Bodywork & Massage Professionals, Associated   www.abmp.com
1271 Sugarbush Dr   Evergreen CO 80439
Ph: 303-674-8478 ▪ Fx: 303-674-0859 ▪ TF: 800-458-2267

Bodywork Therapies of Asia, American Organization for   www.aobta.org
1010 Haddonfield-Berlin Rd Suite 408   Voorhees NJ 08043
Ph: 856-782-1616 ▪ Fx: 856-782-1653

Bohemia Ragtime Society   www.ragtimer.com
5059 Picket Dr   Colorado Springs CO 80918
Ph: 719-528-1547

Boiler Manufacturers Association, American   www.abma.com
4001 N 9th St Suite 226   Arlington VA 22203
Ph: 703-522-7350 ▪ Fx: 703-522-2665

Boiler Owners, Council of Industrial   www.cibo.org
6035 Burke Center Pkwy Suite 360   Burke VA 22015
Ph: 703-250-9042 ▪ Fx: 703-239-9042

Boiler & Pressure Vessel Inspectors, National Board of   www.nationalboard.org
1055 Crupper Ave   Columbus OH 43229
Ph: 614-888-8320 ▪ Fx: 614-847-1147

Boilermakers Iron Shipbuilders Blacksmiths Forgers & Helpers, International Brotherhood of   www.boilermakers.org
753 State Ave Suite 570   Kansas City KS 66101
Ph: 913-371-2640 ▪ Fx: 913-281-8101

Boise Peace Quilt Project   www.boisepeacequilt.org
PO Box 6469   Boise ID 83707
Ph: 208-343-3035 ▪ Fx: 208-323-0848

Bomb Survivors in the US, Committee of Atomic
1759 Sutter St   San Francisco CA 94115
Ph: 562-698-0855

BOMI Institute   www.bomi-edu.org
1521 Ritchie Hwy   Arnold MD 21012
Ph: 410-974-1410 ▪ Fx: 410-974-1935 ▪ TF: 800-235-2664

Bonanza Society, American   www.bonanza.org
1922 Midfield Rd PO Box 12888   Wichita KS 67277
Ph: 316-945-1700 ▪ Fx: 316-945-1710

Bond Lawyers, National Association of   www.nabl.org
250 S Wacker Dr Suite 1550   Chicago IL 60606
Ph: 312-648-9590 ▪ Fx: 312-648-9588

Bond Market Association   www.bondmarkets.com
360 Madison Ave   New York NY 10017
Ph: 646-637-9200 ▪ Fx: 646-637-9126

Bond Market Association PAC
1399 New York Ave NW 8th Fl   Washington DC 20005
Ph: 202-434-8400 ▪ Fx: 202-434-8456

Bond Producers, National Association of Surety   www.nasbp.org
5225 Wisconsin Ave NW Suite 600   Washington DC 20015
Ph: 202-686-3700 ▪ Fx: 202-686-3656

Bond & Share Society, International   www.scripophily.org
15 Dyatt Pl PO Box 430   Hackensack NJ 07602
Ph: 201-489-2440 ▪ Fx: 201-592-0282

Bone & Joint Surgeons, Association of   www.abjs.org
6300 N River Rd Suite 727   Rosemont IL 60018
Ph: 847-698-1636 ▪ Fx: 847-823-4921

Bone Marrow Donor Registry, American   www.charityadvantage.com/abmdr
PO Box 8841   Mandeville LA 70470
Ph: 985-626-1749 ▪ Fx: 985-626-7414 ▪ TF: 800-745-2452

Bone Marrow Foundation, Gift of Life   www.giftoflife.org
7700 Congress Ave   Boca Raton FL 33487
Ph: 561-988-0100 ▪ Fx: 561-988-0140 ▪ TF: 800-962-7769

Bone Marrow Transplant Registry, International   www.ibmtr.org
8701 Watertown Plank Rd PO Box 26509   Milwaukee WI 53226
Ph: 414-456-8325 ▪ Fx: 414-456-6530

Bone & Mineral Research, American Society for   www.asbmr.org
2025 M St NW Suite 800   Washington DC 20036
Ph: 202-367-1161 ▪ Fx: 202-367-2161

Bone & Mineral Society, International   www.ibmsonline.org
2025 M St NW Suite 800   Washington DC 20036
Ph: 202-367-1121 ▪ Fx: 202-367-2121

Bone & Related Disorders, Paget Foundation for Paget's Disease of   www.paget.org
120 Wall St Suite 1602   New York NY 10005
Ph: 212-509-5335 ▪ Fx: 212-509-8492 ▪ TF: 800-237-2438

Boniface Society, American Saint
PO Box 1352   Bronx NY 10466
Ph: 718-994-0989 ▪ Fx: 718-994-6119

Bonsai Clubs International   www.bonsai-bci.com
PO Box 8445   Metairie LA 70011
Ph: 504-832-8071 ▪ Fx: 504-834-2298

Bonsai Society, American   www.absbonsai.org

Book Arts, Center for   www.centerforbookarts.org
28 W 27th St 3rd Fl   New York NY 10001
Ph: 212-481-0295 ▪ Fx: 212-481-9853

Book Association of America, Periodical &   www.pbaa.net
481 8th Ave Suite 826   New York NY 10001
Ph: 212-563-6502 ▪ Fx: 212-563-4098

Book Bank, International   www.internationalbookbank.org
2201 Eagle St Unit D   Baltimore MD 21223
Ph: 410-362-0334 ▪ Fx: 410-362-0336 ▪ TF: 877-416-4265

Book, Center for the   www.loc.gov/loc/cfbook
Library of Congress 101 Independence Ave SE   Washington DC 20540
Ph: 202-707-5221 ▪ Fx: 202-707-0269

Book Center, National Yiddish
1021 West St   Amherst MA 01002
Ph: 413-256-4900 ▪ Fx: 413-256-4700
www.yiddishbookcenter.org

Book Club, Big Little
PO Box 1242   Danville CA 94526
Ph: 925-837-2086
www.biglittlebooks.com

Book Council, Children's
12 W 37th St 2nd Fl   New York NY 10018
Ph: 212-966-1990 ▪ Fx: 212-966-2073 ▪ TF: 800-999-2160
www.cbcbooks.org

Book Council, Jewish
15 E 26th St 10th Fl   New York NY 10010
Ph: 212-532-4949 ▪ Fx: 212-481-4174
www.jewishbookcouncil.org

Book Critics Circle, National
www.bookcritics.org

Book Exchange, US
2969 W 25th St   Cleveland OH 44113
Ph: 216-241-6960 ▪ Fx: 216-241-6966
www.usbe.com

Book & Film Carriers, National Magazine
100 Daingerfield Rd   Alexandria VA 22314
Ph: 703-837-1070 ▪ Fx: 703-837-1072
www.nmbfc.com

Book, First
1319 F St NW Suite 1000   Washington DC 20004
Ph: 202-393-1222 ▪ Fx: 202-628-1258 ▪ TF: 800-393-1222
www.firstbook.org

Book Industry Study Group Inc
19 W 21st St Suite 905   New York NY 10010
Ph: 646-336-7141 ▪ Fx: 646-336-6214
www.bisg.org

Book Manufacturers Institute Inc
65 William St Suite 300   Wellesley MA 02481
Ph: 781-239-0103 ▪ Fx: 781-239-0106
www.bmibook.org

Book Producers Association, American
160 5th Ave   New York NY 10010
Ph: 212-645-2368 ▪ Fx: 212-242-6799 ▪ TF: 800-209-4575
www.abpaonline.org

Book Project, International
1440 Delaware Ave   Lexington KY 40505
Ph: 859-254-6771 ▪ Fx: 859-253-2293 ▪ TF: 888-999-2665
www.intlbookproject.org

Book Publishers Association, Catholic
8404 Jamesport Dr   Rockford IL 61108
Ph: 815-332-3245
www.cbpa.org

Book Society, Miniature
620 Clinton Springs Ave   Cincinnati OH 45229
Ph: 513-556-1964
www.mbs.org

Book Workers, Guild of
521 5th Ave 17th Fl   New York NY 10175
Ph: 212-292-4444

Bookkeepers, American Institute of Professional
6001 Montrose Rd Suite 500   Rockville MD 20852
Ph: 301-770-7300 ▪ Fx: 800-541-0066 ▪ TF: 800-622-0121
www.aipb.com

Bookplate Collectors & Designers, American Society of
PO Box 380340   Cambridge MA 02238
Ph: 781-393-9970 ▪ Fx: 781-393-9972
www.bookplate.org

Books for Africa
253 E 4th St   Saint Paul MN 55101
Ph: 651-602-9844 ▪ Fx: 651-602-9848
www.booksforafrica.org

Books for a Better World
PO Box 82307   Phoenix AZ 85071
Ph: 602-866-9281 ▪ Fx: 602-866-0035
www.booksforabetterworld.org

Booksellers Association of America, Antiquarian
20 W 44th St 4th Fl   New York NY 10036
Ph: 212-944-8291 ▪ Fx: 212-944-8293
www.abaa.org

Booksellers Association, American
828 S Broadway   Tarrytown NY 10591
Ph: 914-591-2665 ▪ Fx: 914-591-2720 ▪ TF: 800-637-0037
www.bookweb.org

Booksellers Association, American Wholesale
702 S Michigan St   South Bend IN 46601
Ph: 574-288-4141
www.awba.com

Booksellers Association, Great Lakes
208 Franklin St PO Box 901   Grand Haven MI 49417
Ph: 616-847-2460 ▪ Fx: 616-842-0051 ▪ TF: 800-745-2460
www.books-glba.org

Booksellers for Children, Association of
3900 Sumac Cir   Middleton WI 53562
Ph: 608-836-6050 ▪ Fx: 608-836-1438
www.abfc.org

Booksellers Foundation for Free Expression, American
139 Fulton St Suite 302   New York NY 10038
Ph: 212-587-4025 ▪ Fx: 212-587-2436
www.abffe.org

Booksellers, International League of Antiquarian
400 Summit Ave   Saint Paul MN 55102
Ph: 651-290-0700 ▪ Fx: 651-290-0646
www.ilab-lila.com

Boomerang Association, US
www.usba.org

Boone & Crockett Club
250 Station Dr   Missoula MT 59801
Ph: 406-542-1888 ▪ Fx: 406-542-0784 ▪ TF: 888-840-4868
www.boone-crockett.org

Border Leicester Association, American
PO Box 947   Canby OR 97013
Ph: 503-266-7156
www.ablasheep.org

Border Patrol Council, National
www.nbpc.net

Borderland Sciences Research Foundation
PO Box 6250   Eureka CA 95502
Ph: 707-445-2247 ▪ Fx: 707-825-7779
www.borderlands.com

Borderlands Studies, Association for
Univ of San Diego 5998 Alcala Pk   San Diego CA 92110
Ph: 619-260-4090 ▪ Fx: 619-260-4161
www.absborderlands.org

Boston Theological Institute
Farwell Hall 210 Herrick Rd   Newton Centre MA 02459
Ph: 617-527-4880 ▪ Fx: 617-527-1073
www.bostontheological.org

Bostonian Society The
Old State House 206 Washington St   Boston MA 02109
Ph: 617-720-1713
www.bostonhistory.org

Botanical Artists, American Society of   huntbot.andrew.cmu.edu/ASBA/asbotartists.html
47 5th Ave   New York NY 10003
Ph: 212-691-9080 ▪ Fx: 212-691-9130 ▪ TF: 866-691-9080

Botanical Council, American
6200 Manor Rd   Austin TX 78723
Ph: 512-926-4900 ▪ Fx: 512-926-2345 ▪ TF: 800-373-7105
www.herbalgram.org

Botanical Gardens & Arboreta, American Association of
100 W 10th St Suite 614   Wilmington DE 19801
Ph: 302-655-7100 ▪ Fx: 302-655-8100
www.aabga.org

Botanical & Horticultural Libraries Inc, Council of   www2.ville.montreal.qc.ca/jardin/cbhl/cbhl.htm
Carnegie Mellon Univ Hunt Institute for Botanical
Documentation   Pittsburgh PA 15213
Ph: 412-268-7301 ▪ Fx: 412-268-5677

Botanical Medicine, North American College of
1116 Park Ave SW   Albuquerque NM 87102
Ph: 505-873-8107 ▪ Fx: 505-873-4530
www.nacbm.org

Botanical Society of America
1735 Neil Ave   Columbus OH 43210
Ph: 614-292-3519

Botany, Society for Economic
PO Box 1897   Lawrence KS 66044
Ph: 785-843-1235 ▪ Fx: 785-843-1274 ▪ TF: 800-627-0629
www.econbot.org

Bottle Club, Lilliputian
5626 Corning Ave   Los Angeles CA 90056
Ph: 323-294-3231

Bottled Water Association, International
1700 Diagonal Rd Suite 650   Alexandria VA 22314
Ph: 703-683-5213 ▪ Fx: 703-683-4074 ▪ TF: 800-928-3711
www.bottledwater.org

Bottler Association, Dr Pepper
PO Box 906   Rowlett TX 75030
Ph: 972-475-7397

Bovine Practitioners, American Association of
PO Box 1755   Rome GA 30162
Ph: 706-232-2220 ▪ Fx: 706-232-2232 ▪ TF: 800-269-2227
www.aabp.org

Bowhunter Education Foundation, National
101 1/2 N Front St   Townsend MT 59644
Ph: 406-266-3236 ▪ Fx: 406-266-3239
www.nbef.org

Bowhunters of America, Christian
2205 SR 571 W   Greenville OH 45331
Ph: 937-548-0623 ▪ TF: 877-912-5724
www.christianbowhunters.org

Bowhunters of America Inc, Physically Challenged
RD 1 Box 470   New Alexandria PA 15670
Ph: 724-668-7439
www.pcba-inc.org

Bowhunters Society, Professional
PO Box 246   Terrell NC 28682
Ph: 704-664-2534 ▪ Fx: 704-664-7471
www.bowsite.com/pbs

(Bowhunting) Pope & Young Club
273 Mill Creek Rd PO Box 548   Chatfield MN 55923
Ph: 507-867-4144
www.pope-young.org

Bowhunting Preservation Alliance
304 Brown St E PO Box 258   Comfrey MN 56019
Ph: 507-877-5300 ▪ Fx: 507-877-2149 ▪ TF: 866-266-2776
www.bowhuntingpreservation.org

Bowlers Association, Professional
719 2nd Ave Suite 701   Seattle WA 98104
Ph: 206-332-9688 ▪ Fx: 206-332-9722
www.pba.org

Bowlers to Veterans Link
PO Box 2289   Rockville MD 20847
Ph: 301-881-8333 ▪ Fx: 301-881-4042
www.bowlforveterans.org

Bowling Alliance, Young American
5301 S 76th St   Greendale WI 53129
Ph: 414-421-4700 ▪ Fx: 414-421-1301 ▪ TF: 800-514-2695
www.bowl.com/bowl/yaba

Bowling Association, American Wheelchair
2912 Country Woods Ln   Palm Harbor FL 34683
Ph: 727-734-0023
www.awba.org

Bowling Association, National
377 Park Ave S 7th Fl   New York NY 10016
Ph: 212-689-8308 ▪ Fx: 212-725-5063
www.tnbainc.org

Bowling Association, Professional Women's
7171 Cherryvale Blvd   Rockford IL 61112
Ph: 815-332-5756 ▪ Fx: 815-332-9636
pwba.com

Bowling Congress, American
5301 S 76th St   Greendale WI 53129
Ph: 414-421-6400 ▪ Fx: 414-421-3014 ▪ TF: 800-514-2695
www.bowl.com/bowl/abc

Bowling Congress, National Duckpin
4991 Fairview Ave   Linthicum Heights MD 21090
Ph: 410-636-2695 ▪ Fx: 410-636-3256
ndbc.org

Bowling Congress, Women's International
5301 S 76th St   Greendale WI 53129
Ph: 414-421-9000 ▪ Fx: 414-421-3014 ▪ TF: 800-514-2695
www.bowl.com/bowl/wibc

Bowling Federation, International
1631 Mesa Ave Suite A   Colorado Springs CO 80906
Ph: 719-636-2695 ▪ Fx: 719-636-3300
www.fiq.org

Bowling Instructors Association, US
PO Box 564   Palatine IL 60078
Ph: 847-359-0682 ▪ Fx: 847-550-0218

Bowling Lane Specialists, International Association of
5806 W 127th St   Alsip IL 60803
Ph: 708-371-8237 ▪ Fx: 708-371-8283
www.nairbowl.org

Bowling Pro Shop & Instructors Association, International
4337 N Golden State Blvd Suite 109   Fresno CA 93722
Ph: 559-275-9245 ▪ Fx: 559-275-9250 ▪ TF: 800-659-9444
www.ibpsia.org

Bowling Proprietors Association of America Inc
615 Six Flags Dr PO Box 5802   Arlington TX 76011
Ph: 817-649-5105 ▪ Fx: 817-633-2940
www.bpaa.com

Bowling, USA
5301 S 76th St   Greendale WI 53129
Ph: 800-514-2695
www.bowl.com/bowl/usa

Bowling USA, College
5301 S 76th St   Greendale WI 53129
Ph: 800-514-2695
www.bowl.com/bowl/cbusa

Bowling Writers Association of America www.bowlingwriters.com

Bowling Writers Association, National Women www.nwbw.freeservers.com
3001 21st St   Lubbock TX 79410
Ph: 806-795-3830

Bowling Writers, World
122 S Michigan Ave Suite 1506   Chicago IL 60603
Ph: 312-341-1110 ▪ Fx: 312-341-1480

Box Association, Fibre www.fibrebox.org
2850 Golf Rd Suite 412   Rolling Meadows IL 60008
Ph: 847-364-9600 ▪ Fx: 847-364-9639

Box Project Inc www.boxproject.org
PO Box 435   Plainville CT 06062
Ph: 860-747-8182 ▪ Fx: 860-793-8857 ▪ TF: 800-268-9928

Boxer Club, American americanboxerclub.org

Boxing, American Association for the Improvement of www.aaib.org
86 Fletcher Ave   Mount Vernon NY 10552
Ph: 914-664-4571 ▪ Fx: 914-664-3164

Boxing Federation, International www.ibf-usba-boxing.com
134 Evergreen Pl 9th Fl   East Orange NJ 07018
Ph: 973-414-0300 ▪ Fx: 973-414-0307

Boxing Federation, North American www.nabfnews.com

Boxing Inc, USA www.usaboxing.org
1 Olympic Plaza   Colorado Springs CO 80909
Ph: 719-866-4506 ▪ Fx: 719-632-3426

Boy Scouts of America www.scouting.org
PO Box 152079   Irving TX 75015
Ph: 972-580-2000 ▪ Fx: 972-580-2502

(Boy Scouts) Order of the Arrow www.oa-bsa.org
1325 W Walnut Hill Ln PO Box 152079   Irving TX 75015
Ph: 972-580-2438 ▪ Fx: 972-580-2399

Boys & Girls Clubs of America www.bgca.org
1230 W Peachtree St NW   Atlanta GA 30309
Ph: 404-487-5700 ▪ Fx: 404-487-5757 ▪ TF: 800-854-2582

Boys Ranch, Cal Farley's www.calfarleysboysranch.org
PO Box 1890   Amarillo TX 79174
Ph: 806-372-2341 ▪ Fx: 806-372-6638 ▪ TF: 800-687-3722

Boys' Schools Coalition, International www.boysschoolscoalition.org
7 Forehand Dr PO Box 117   Dennis MA 02638
Ph: 508-385-4563 ▪ Fx: 508-385-4273

Boys Town Jerusalem Foundation of America www.boystownjerusalem.com
12 W 31st St Suite 300   New York NY 10001
Ph: 212-244-2766 ▪ Fx: 212-244-2052 ▪ TF: 800-469-2697

Boys' Towns of Italy Inc www.boystown.it
250 E 63rd St Suite 204   New York NY 10021
Ph: 212-980-8770 ▪ Fx: 212-644-0766

BPA International www.bpai.com
2 Corporate Dr Suite 900   Shelton CT 06484
Ph: 203-447-2800 ▪ Fx: 203-447-2900

Brachial Plexus/Erb's Palsy Association Inc, National www.nbpepa.org
PO Box 23   Larsen WI 54947
Ph: 920-836-2151

Bradley Lynde & Harry Foundation Inc www.bradleyfdn.org
1241 N Franklin Pl   Milwaukee WI 53202
Ph: 414-291-9915 ▪ Fx: 414-291-9991

Brady Campaign to Prevent Gun Violence www.bradycampaign.org
1225 'I' St NW Suite 1100   Washington DC 20005
Ph: 202-898-0792 ▪ Fx: 202-371-9615

Brady Center to Prevent Gun Violence www.bradycenter.org
1225 'I' St NW Suite 1100   Washington DC 20005
Ph: 202-289-7319 ▪ Fx: 202-408-1851

Braford Breeders, United www.brafords.org
422 E Main St Suite 218   Nacogdoches TX 75961
Ph: 936-569-8200 ▪ Fx: 936-569-9556

Brahman Association, American Junior www.brahman.org/ajba.html
3003 South Loop W Suite 140   Houston TX 77054
Ph: 713-349-0854 ▪ Fx: 713-349-9795

Brahman Breeders Association, American www.brahman.org
3003 South Loop W Suite 140   Houston TX 77054
Ph: 713-349-0854 ▪ Fx: 713-349-9795

Braille Authority of North America www.brailleauthority.org
c/o Associated Services for the Blind 919 Walnut
St   Philadelphia PA 19107
Ph: 215-627-0600 ▪ Fx: 215-922-0692 ▪ TF: 800-223-1839

Braille Bible Foundation www.careministries.org/bbf.html
PO Box 948307   Maitland FL 32794
Ph: 407-834-3628 ▪ TF: 800-766-9080

Braille Institute of America Inc www.brailleinstitute.org
741 N Vermont Ave   Los Angeles CA 90029
Ph: 323-663-1111 ▪ Fx: 323-663-0867

Braille Institute of America, Jewish www.jbilibrary.org
110 E 30th St   New York NY 10016
Ph: 212-889-2525 ▪ Fx: 212-689-3692 ▪ TF: 800-433-1531

Braille Revival League
57 Grandview Ave   Watertown MA 02472
Ph: 617-926-9198 ▪ Fx: 617-923-0004 ▪ TF: 800-424-8666

Braille Workers, Lutheran www.lbwinc.org
13471 California St   Yucaipa CA 92399
Ph: 909-795-8977 ▪ Fx: 909-795-8970

Brain Injury Association of America www.biausa.org
8201 Greensboro Dr Suite 611   McLean VA 22102
Ph: 703-761-0750 ▪ Fx: 703-761-0755 ▪ TF: 800-444-6443

Brain Injury Resource Center www.headinjury.com
PO Box 84151   Seattle WA 98124
Ph: 206-621-8558 ▪ Fx: 206-329-4355

Brain Tumor Association, American www.abta.org
2720 River Rd   Des Plaines IL 60018
Ph: 847-827-9910 ▪ Fx: 847-827-9918 ▪ TF: 800-886-2282

Brain Tumor Society www.tbts.org
124 Watertown St Suite 3-H   Watertown MA 02472
Ph: 617-924-9997 ▪ Fx: 617-924-9998 ▪ TF: 800-770-8287

Brake Association, Air
2009 Oriole Trail LB   Long Beach IN 46360
Ph: 219-874-3129 ▪ Fx: 219-874-3121

Brake Manufacturers Council www.brakecouncil.org
PO Box 13966   Research Triangle Park NC 27709
Ph: 919-549-4800 ▪ Fx: 919-549-4824

Bramble Growers Association, North American www.nabga.com
13006 Mason Rd NE   Cumberland MD 21502
Ph: 301-724-4085 ▪ Fx: 301-724-3020

Brand Names Education Foundation www.bnef.org
1133 Ave of the Americas   New York NY 10036
Ph: 212-768-9885 ▪ Fx: 212-768-7796

Brangus Breeders Association, International www.int-brangus.org
5750 Epsilon PO Box 696020   San Antonio TX 78269
Ph: 210-696-4343 ▪ Fx: 210-696-8718

Brangus Breeders Association, International Junior www.int-brangus.org
5750 Epsilon PO Box 696020   San Antonio TX 78269
Ph: 210-696-4343 ▪ Fx: 210-696-8718

Brass Band Association, North American www.nabba.org

Brass & Bronze Ingot Industry
200 S Michigan Ave Suite 1100   Chicago IL 60604
Ph: 312-372-4000 ▪ Fx: 312-939-5617

Brass Fabricators Council Inc, Copper &
1050 17th St NW Suite 440   Washington DC 20036
Ph: 202-833-8575 ▪ Fx: 202-331-8267

Brass Servicenter Association, Copper & www.copper-brass.org
994 Old Eagle School Rd Suite 1019   Wayne PA 19087
Ph: 610-971-4850 ▪ Fx: 610-971-4859

Brass Society, Historic www.historicbrass.org
148 W 23rd St Unit 2A   New York NY 10011
Ph: 212-627-3820

Braunvieh Association of America www.braunvieh.org
3815 Touzalin Ave Suite 103   Lincoln NE 68507
Ph: 402-466-3292 ▪ Fx: 402-466-3293

Brazil Philatelic Association
462 W Walnut St   Long Beach NY 11561
Ph: 516-431-3412

Brazilian-American Chamber of Commerce Inc www.brazilcham.com
509 Madison Ave Suite 304   New York NY 10022
Ph: 212-751-4691 ▪ Fx: 212-751-7692

Brazilian-American Cultural Institute www.bacidc.org
4719 Wisconsin Ave NW   Washington DC 20016
Ph: 202-362-8334 ▪ Fx: 202-362-8337

Brazilian Studies Association www.brasaus.org
Latin American & Iberian Institute 1 Univ of New Mexico MSC02
1690   Albuquerque NM 87131
Ph: 505-277-2961 ▪ Fx: 505-277-5989

Bread Bakers Guild of America www.bbga.org
3203 Maryland Ave   North Versailles PA 15137
Ph: 412-823-2080 ▪ Fx: 412-823-2495

Bread & Roses www.breadandroses.org
233 Tarnalpais Dr Suite 100   Corte Madera CA 94925
Ph: 415-945-7120 ▪ Fx: 415-945-7128

Bread on the Waters www.breadonthewaters.com
91 Church Ln   Cloverdale CA 95425
Ph: 209-369-3202

Bread for the World www.bread.org
50 F St NW Suite 500   Washington DC 20001
Ph: 202-639-9400 ▪ Fx: 202-639-9401 ▪ TF: 800-822-7323

Break Away: The Alternative Break Connection Inc www.alternativebreaks.org
2121 W Pensacola St Suite E-543   Tallahassee FL 32304
Ph: 850-644-0986 ▪ Fx: 850-644-3345

Breakthrough Collaborative www.breakthroughcollaborative.org
40 1st St 5th Fl   San Francisco CA 94105
Ph: 415-442-0600 ▪ Fx: 415-442-0609

Breast Cancer Alliance, African American www.geocities.com/aabcainc
PO Box 8981   Minneapolis MN 55408
Ph: 612-825-3675

Breast Cancer Coalition, National www.stopbreastcancer.org
1707 L St NW Suite 1060   Washington DC 20036
Ph: 202-296-7477 ▪ Fx: 202-265-6854 ▪ TF: 800-622-2838

Breast Cancer Foundation, Susan G Komen www.komen.org
5005 LBJ Fwy Suite 250   Dallas TX 75244
Ph: 972-855-1600 ▪ Fx: 972-855-1605 ▪ TF: 800-462-9273

Breast Cancer, Mothers Supporting Daughters with www.mothersdaughters.org
21710 Bayshore Rd   Chestertown MD 21620
Ph: 410-778-1982 ▪ Fx: 410-778-1411

Breast Cancer Organization, Y-ME National www.y-me.org
212 W Van Buren St   Chicago IL 60607
Ph: 312-986-8338 ▪ Fx: 312-294-8597 ▪ TF: 800-221-2141

Breast Cancer Organizations, National Alliance of www.nabco.org
9 E 37th St 10th Fl   New York NY 10016
Ph: 212-889-0606 ▪ Fx: 212-689-1213 ▪ TF: 888-806-2226

Breast Disease, American Society of www.asbd.org
PO Box 140186   Dallas TX 75214
Ph: 214-368-6836 ▪ Fx: 214-368-5719

Breastfeeding Medicine, Academy of www.bfmed.org
191 Clarksville Rd   Princeton Junction NJ 08550
Ph: 609-799-6327 ▪ Fx: 609-799-7032 ▪ TF: 877-836-9947

Brecht Society, International german.lss.wisc.edu/brecht
Georgia Southern Univ Dept of Literature & Philosophy PO Box
8023   Statesboro GA 30460
Ph: 912-681-0155 ▪ Fx: 912-681-0653

Breeders Association of America, Racking Horse www.rackinghorse.com
67 Horse Ctr Rd   Decatur AL 35603
Ph: 256-353-7225 ▪ Fx: 256-353-7266

Breeders Association of America, Texas Longhorn   www.tlbaa.org
2315 N Main St Suite 402   Fort Worth TX 76106
Ph: 817-625-6241 ▪ Fx: 817-625-1388

Breeders Association, American Rabbit   www.arba.net
PO Box 426   Bloomington IL 61702
Ph: 309-664-7500 ▪ Fx: 309-664-0941

Breeders Association, International Brangus   www.int-brangus.org
5750 Epsilon PO Box 696020   San Antonio TX 78269
Ph: 210-696-4343 ▪ Fx: 210-696-8718

Breeders Association, National Saanen   nationalsaanenbreeders.com
PO Box 315   Santa Margarita CA 93453
Ph: 805-461-5547

Breeders Association, Thoroughbred Owners &   www.toba.org
PO Box 4367   Lexington KY 40544
Ph: 859-276-2291 ▪ Fx: 859-276-2462 ▪ TF: 888-606-8622

Breeders Association of the USA, Brown Swiss Cattle   www.brownswiss.com
800 Pleasant St   Beloit WI 53511
Ph: 608-365-4474 ▪ Fx: 608-365-5577

Breeders' & Exhibitors' Association, Tennessee Walking Horse   www.twhbea.com
PO Box 286   Lewisburg TN 37091
Ph: 931-359-1574 ▪ Fx: 931-359-2539 ▪ TF: 800-359-1574

Breeders International, Santa Gertrudis   www.santagertrudis.ws
PO Box 1257   Kingsville TX 78364
Ph: 361-592-9357 ▪ Fx: 361-592-8572

Breeders, National Association of Animal   www.naab-css.org
PO Box 1033   Columbia MO 65205
Ph: 573-445-4406 ▪ Fx: 573-446-2279

Breeders United, Beefmaster   www.beefmasters.org
6800 Park Ten Blvd Suite 290-W   San Antonio TX 78213
Ph: 210-732-3132 ▪ Fx: 210-732-7711

Breeding Specialist Group, Conservation   www.cbsg.org
12101 Johnny Cake Ridge Rd   Apple Valley MN 55124
Ph: 952-997-9800 ▪ Fx: 952-432-2757

Brennan Center for Justice   www.brennancenter.org
NYU School of Law 161 Ave of the Americas 12th Fl   New York NY 10013
Ph: 212-998-6730 ▪ Fx: 212-995-4550

Brethren Caregivers, Association of   www.brethren.org/abc
1451 Dundee Ave   Elgin IL 60120
Ph: 847-742-5100 ▪ Fx: 847-742-5160 ▪ TF: 800-323-8039

Brethren in Christ World Missions   www.bic-church.org/wm
431 Grantham Rd PO Box 390   Grantham PA 17027
Ph: 717-697-2634 ▪ Fx: 717-691-6053

Brethren, Church of the   www.brethren.org
1451 Dundee Ave   Elgin IL 60120
Ph: 847-742-5100 ▪ Fx: 847-742-6103 ▪ TF: 800-323-8039

Brethren Church Missionary Ministries   www.brethrenchurch.org
524 College Ave   Ashland OH 44805
Ph: 419-289-1708 ▪ Fx: 419-281-0450

Brethren Peace Fellowship
PO Box 455   New Windsor MD 21776
Ph: 410-848-5631

Bretton Woods Committee   www.brettonwoods.org
1990 M St NW Suite 450   Washington DC 20036
Ph: 202-331-1616 ▪ Fx: 202-785-9423

Breweriana Advertising, National Association   www.nababrew.org

Brewers, Association of   www.beertown.org
736 Pearl St   Boulder CO 80302
Ph: 303-447-0816 ▪ Fx: 303-447-2825 ▪ TF: 888-822-6273

Brewers' Association of America   www.brewersadvocate.com
501 Washington St Suite H   Durham NC 27701
Ph: 919-530-8140 ▪ Fx: 919-530-8160

Brewers Association of the Americas, Master   www.mbaa.com
3340 Pilot Knob Rd   Saint Paul MN 55121
Ph: 651-454-7250 ▪ Fx: 651-454-0766

Brewing Chemists, American Society of   www.asbcnet.org
3340 Pilot Knob Rd   Saint Paul MN 55121
Ph: 651-454-7250 ▪ Fx: 651-454-0766

Brick Collectors' Association, International
3265 Hood Ct   Wichita KS 67204
Ph: 316-831-9713

Brick Industry Association   www.brickinfo.org
11490 Commerce Pk Dr Suite 300   Reston VA 20191
Ph: 703-620-0010 ▪ Fx: 703-620-3928

Bricklayers & Allied Craftworkers, International Council of Employers of   www.icebac.org
1776 'I' St NW   Washington DC 20006
Ph: 202-783-3788 ▪ Fx: 202-393-0222 ▪ TF: 888-880-8222

Bricklayers & Allied Craftworkers, International Union of   www.bacweb.org
1776 'I' St NW Suite 500   Washington DC 20006
Ph: 202-783-3788 ▪ Fx: 202-393-0219 ▪ TF: 800-331-1077

Bridal Consultants, Association of   www.bridalassn.com
200 Chestnutland Rd   New Milford CT 06776
Ph: 860-355-0464 ▪ Fx: 860-354-1404

Bridge Association, American   www.americanbridge.com
2828 Lakewood Ave SW   Atlanta GA 30315
Ph: 404-768-5517 ▪ Fx: 404-767-1871

Bridge Construction & Design, Association for   www.abcdpittsburgh.org
PO Box 23264   Pittsburgh PA 15222
Ph: 412-281-9900 ▪ Fx: 412-281-2056

Bridge Grid Flooring Manufacturers Association   www.abcdpittsburgh.org/BGFMA.htm
201 Castle Dr   West Mifflin PA 15122
Ph: 412-469-3985

Bridge Institute, American Segmental   www.asbi-assoc.org
9201 N 25th Ave Suite 150B   Phoenix AZ 85021
Ph: 602-997-9964 ▪ Fx: 602-997-9965

Bridge League, American Contract   www.acbl.org
2990 Airways Blvd   Memphis TN 38116
Ph: 901-332-5586 ▪ Fx: 901-398-7754 ▪ TF: 800-264-2743

Bridge Structural Ornamental & Reinforcing Iron Workers, International Association of   www.ironworkers.org
1750 New York Ave NW Suite 400   Washington DC 20006
Ph: 202-383-4800 ▪ Fx: 202-638-4856 ▪ TF: 800-368-0105

Bridge Teachers' Association, American   www.abtahome.com
14840 Crystal Cove Ct Suite 503   Fort Myers FL 33919
Ph: 239-437-4106

Bridge Tunnel & Turnpike Association, International   www.ibtta.org
1146 19th St NW Suite 800   Washington DC 20036
Ph: 202-659-4620 ▪ Fx: 202-659-0500

Bridges, National Society for the Preservation of Covered   www.vermontbridges.com/nspcb1st.htm
44 Cleveland Ave   Worcester MA 01603
Ph: 508-756-4516

Bridle Club, National Block &   www.blockandbridle.org
Colorado State Univ Dept of Dairy & Animal Science   University Park PA 16802
Ph: 814-863-0734 ▪ Fx: 814-863-6042

Bright Belt Warehouse Association
PO Box 12004   Raleigh NC 27605
Ph: 919-828-8988

Bright Futures Farm   www.brightfuturesfarm.org
44793 Harrison Rd   Spartansburg PA 16434
Ph: 814-827-8270 ▪ Fx: 814-827-8278

Bright Hope International   www.brighthope.org
2060 Stonington Ave   Hoffman Estates IL 60195
Ph: 847-519-0012 ▪ Fx: 847-519-0024

Brith Sholom   www.brithsholom.com
6410 N Broad St   Philadelphia PA 19126
Ph: 215-878-5696 ▪ Fx: 215-878-5699

British-American Business Association   www.babawashington.org
PO Box 16482   Washington DC 20041
Ph: 202-293-0010 ▪ Fx: 202-296-3332

British-American Business Council   www.babc.org
52 Vanderbilt Ave 20th Fl   New York NY 10017
Ph: 212-661-4060 ▪ Fx: 212-661-4074

British American Educational Foundation   www.baef.org
PO Box 33   Larchmont NY 10538
Ph: 914-834-2064 ▪ Fx: 914-833-3718

British Genealogy & Family History, International Society for
PO Box 3115   Salt Lake City UT 84110
Ph: 801-272-2178

British Schools & Universities Club of New York   www.bsuc.org
24 E 39th St   New York NY 10016
Ph: 212-713-5713

British Schools & Universities Foundation   www.bsuf.org
575 Madison Ave Suite 1006   New York NY 10022
Ph: 212-662-5576

British Studies, North American Conference on   www.nacbs.org

British White Park Association, American   whitecattle.org
PO Box 249   Wheelock TX 77882
Ph: 979-828-2339 ▪ Fx: 979-208-9002

Brittany Club, American   clubs.akc.org/brit
10370 Fleming Rd   Carterville IL 62918
Ph: 618-985-2336 ▪ Fx: 618-985-5103

(Brittle Bone Disorder) Osteogenesis Imperfecta Foundation   www.oif.org
804 W Diamond Ave Suite 210   Gaithersburg MD 20878
Ph: 301-947-0083 ▪ Fx: 301-947-0456 ▪ TF: 800-981-2663

Broadcast Association for Community Affairs, National
13502 Whittier Blvd Suite H Box 341   Whittier CA 90605
Ph: 562-698-6280 ▪ Fx: 562-698-9912

Broadcast Cable Financial Management Association   www.bcfm.com
932 Lee St Suite 204   Des Plaines IL 60016
Ph: 847-296-0200 ▪ Fx: 847-296-7510

Broadcast Designers Association   www.bda.tv
2029 Century Pk E Suite 555   Los Angeles CA 90067
Ph: 310-712-0040 ▪ Fx: 310-712-0039

Broadcast Education Association   www.beaweb.org
1771 'N' St NW   Washington DC 20036
Ph: 202-429-5354 ▪ TF: 888-380-7222

Broadcast Employees & Technicians-Communications Workers of America, National Association of   www.nabetcwa.org
501 3rd St NW Suite 880   Washington DC 20001
Ph: 202-434-1254 ▪ Fx: 202-434-1426

Broadcast Engineers, Society of   www.sbe.org
9247 N Meridian St Suite 305   Indianapolis IN 46260
Ph: 317-846-9000 ▪ Fx: 317-846-9120

Broadcast Monitors, International Association of   www.iabm.com
PO Box 986   Irmo SC 29063
Ph: 800-236-1741 ▪ Fx: 888-732-9004

Broadcast Music Inc   www.bmi.com
320 W 57th St   New York NY 10019
Ph: 212-586-2000 ▪ Fx: 212-489-2368

Broadcast Technology Society, IEEE   www.ieee.org/organizations/society/bt
IEEE Operations Ctr 445 Hoes Ln   Piscataway NJ 08854
Ph: 732-981-0060 ▪ Fx: 732-981-1721

Broadcasters Alliance, Black   www.thebba.org
3474 William Penn Hwy   Pittsburgh PA 15235
Ph: 412-829-9788 ▪ Fx: 412-829-0313

Broadcasters Association Inc, American Auto Racing Writers &   www.aarwba.org
922 N Pass Ave   Burbank CA 91505
Ph: 818-842-7005 ▪ Fx: 818-842-7020

Broadcasters Inc, Country Radio   www.crb.org
819 18th Ave S   Nashville TN 37203
Ph: 615-327-4487 ▪ Fx: 615-329-4492

Broadcasters' Foundation   broadcastersfoundation.org
7 Lincoln Ave   Greenwich CT 06830
Ph: 203-862-8577 ▪ Fx: 203-629-5739

Broadcasters, National Association of   www.nab.org
1771 'N' St NW   Washington DC 20036
Ph: 202-429-5300 ▪ Fx: 202-429-5406

Broadcasters, National Association of African-American Sportswriters &
308A Deer Park Ave   Dix Hills NY 11746
Ph: 631-462-3933

Broadcasters, National Association of Black Owned   www.nabob.org
1155 Connecticut Ave NW 6th Fl   Washington DC 20036
Ph: 202-463-8970 ■ Fx: 202-429-0657

Broadcasters, National Association of Farm   www.nafb.com
700 Branch St Suite 8 PO Box 500   Platte City MO 64079
Ph: 816-431-4032 ■ Fx: 816-431-4087

Broadcasters, National Federation of Community   www.nfcb.org
970 Broadway Suite 1000   Oakland CA 94612
Ph: 510-451-8200 ■ Fx: 510-451-8208

Broadcasters, National Religious   www.nrb.org
9510 Technology Dr   Manassas VA 20110
Ph: 703-330-7000 ■ Fx: 703-330-7100

Broadcasting & Communications Association, Satellite   www.sbca.com
225 Reinekers Ln Suite 600   Alexandria VA 22314
Ph: 703-549-6990 ■ Fx: 703-549-7640 ■ TF: 800-541-5981

Broadcasting, Corporation for Public   www.cpb.org
401 9th St NW   Washington DC 20004
Ph: 202-879-9600 ■ Fx: 202-879-9700 ■ TF: 800-272-2190

Broadcasting Management Association, Public   www.pbma.org
PO Box 50008   Columbia SC 29250
Ph: 803-799-5517 ■ Fx: 803-771-4831

Broadcasting Service, Public   www.pbs.org
1320 Braddock Pl   Alexandria VA 22314
Ph: 703-739-5000 ■ Fx: 703-739-0775

Broadcasting System Inc, Intercollegiate   www.ibsradio.org
367 Windsor Hwy   New Windsor NY 12553
Ph: 845-565-0003 ■ Fx: 845-565-7446

Broker Management Council   www.bmcsales.com
PO Box 150229   Arlington TX 76015
Ph: 817-561-7272 ■ Fx: 817-561-7275

Brokerage Managers, Council of Real Estate   www.crb.com
430 N Michigan Ave Suite 300   Chicago IL 60611
Ph: 312-321-4400 ■ Fx: 312-329-8882 ■ TF: 800-621-8738

Brokers & Agents (USA) Inc, Association of   www.asba.org
510 Sylvan Ave Suite 201   Englewood Cliffs NJ 07632
Ph: 201-569-2882 ■ Fx: 201-569-9082

Brokers, National Association of Equipment Leasing   www.naelb.org
5024-R Campbell Blvd   Baltimore MD 21236
Ph: 410-931-8100 ■ Fx: 410-931-8111 ■ TF: 800-996-2352

Bromeliad Society International   www.bsi.org
PO Box 12981   Gainesville FL 32604
Ph: 352-372-6589 ■ Fx: 352-372-8823

Brominated Solvents Committee
1250 Connecticut Ave NE Suite 700   Washington DC 20036
Ph: 202-637-9040 ■ Fx: 202-637-9178

Broncho-Esophagological Association, American   www.abea.net
Univ of Utah Div of Otolaryngology 50 N Medical Dr
    3C120   Salt Lake City UT 84132
Ph: 801-581-7514 ■ Fx: 801-585-5744

Bronze Ingot Industry, Brass &
200 S Michigan Ave Suite 1100   Chicago IL 60604
Ph: 312-372-4000 ■ Fx: 312-939-5617

Brookings Institution   www.brook.edu
1775 Massachusetts Ave NW   Washington DC 20036
Ph: 202-797-6000 ■ Fx: 202-797-6004 ■ TF: 800-275-1447

Brotherhood of the Knights of the Vine   www.kov.org
2210 Northpoint Pkwy   Santa Rosa CA 95407
Ph: 707-579-3781 ■ Fx: 707-579-3996

Brotherhood of Locomotive Engineers & Trainmen   www.ble.org
1370 Ontario St Mezzanine Level   Cleveland OH 44113
Ph: 216-241-2630 ■ Fx: 216-241-6516

Brotherhood of Maintenance of Way Employees   www.bmwe.org
20300 Civic Ctr Dr Suite 320   Southfield MI 48076
Ph: 248-948-1010 ■ Fx: 248-948-7150

Brotherhood of Railroad Signalmen   www.brs.org
601 W Golf Rd Box U   Mount Prospect IL 60056
Ph: 847-439-3732 ■ Fx: 847-439-3743

Brotherhood of Saint Andrew   www.brotherhoodstandrew.org
PO Box 632   Ambridge PA 15003
Ph: 724-266-4810 ■ Fx: 724-266-5810

Brotherhood of Shoe & Allied Craftsmen
PO Box 390   East Bridgewater MA 02333
Ph: 508-378-9300 ■ Fx: 508-588-9735

Brother's Brother Foundation   www.brothersbrother.org
1200 Galveston Ave   Pittsburgh PA 15233
Ph: 412-321-3160 ■ Fx: 412-321-3325 ■ TF: 888-323-1916

Brown Foundation Inc   www.brownfoundation.org
PO Box 130646   Houston TX 77219
Ph: 713-523-6867 ■ Fx: 713-523-2917

Brown Swiss Cattle Breeders Association of the USA   www.brownswiss.com
800 Pleasant St   Beloit WI 53511
Ph: 608-365-4474 ■ Fx: 608-365-5577

Bruderhof Communities   www.bruderhof.org
PO Box 903   Rifton NY 12471
Ph: 845-658-8351 ■ Fx: 845-658-3144

Brush Manufacturers Association, American   www.abma.org
2111 W Plum St Suite 274   Aurora IL 60506
Ph: 630-631-5217 ■ Fx: 630-897-9140

Brush Inc, Pen &   www.penandbrush.org
16 E 10th St   New York NY 10003
Ph: 212-475-3669 ■ Fx: 212-475-6018

Bryological & Lichenological Society, American   www.unomaha.edu/~abls/
Univ of Nevada Dept of Biological Sciences 4505 Maryland
    Pkwy Box 454004   Las Vegas NV 89154
Ph: 702-895-3119 ■ Fx: 702-895-3956

Buchanan James Foundation for the Preservation   www.lanccounty.com/wheatland
    of Wheatland   1120 Marietta Ave   Lancaster PA 17603
Ph: 717-392-8721 ■ Fx: 717-295-8825

Buck Pearl S International   www.pearl-s-buck.org/psbi
520 Dublin Rd   Perkasie PA 18944
Ph: 215-249-0100 ■ Fx: 215-249-9657 ■ TF: 800-220-2825

Buckminster Fuller Institute   www.bfi.org
111 N Main St   Sebastopol CA 95472
Ph: 707-824-2242 ■ Fx: 707-824-2243 ■ TF: 800-967-6277

Buckskin Horse Association, International   www.ibha.net
PO Box 268   Shelby IN 46377
Ph: 219-552-1013

Buckskin Registry Association Inc, American   www.americanbuckskin.com
1141 Hartnell Ave PO Box 3850   Redding CA 96049
Ph: 530-223-1420

Buddhist Association, American
4524 N Richmond St   Chicago IL 60625
Ph: 773-583-5794

Buddhist Association, Burma-America
1708 Powder Mill Rd   Silver Spring MD 20903
Ph: 301-439-4035

Buddhist Association, Dharma Realm   www.drba.org
Sagely City of 10 Thousand Buddhas 2001 Talmage Rd PO Box
    217   Talmage CA 95481
Ph: 707-462-0939 ■ Fx: 707-462-0949

Buddhist Churches of America   www.buddhistchurchesofamerica.com
1710 Octavia St   San Francisco CA 94109
Ph: 415-776-5600 ■ Fx: 415-771-6293

Buddhist Peace Fellowship   www.bpf.org
PO Box 3470   Berkeley CA 94703
Ph: 510-655-6169 ■ Fx: 510-655-1369

Buddhist Society, Cambodian   www.cambodian-buddhist.org
13800 New Hampshire Ave   Silver Spring MD 20904
Ph: 301-622-6544

(Buddhist) Soka Gakkai International-USA   www.sgi-usa.org
606 Wilshire Blvd   Santa Monica CA 90401
Ph: 310-260-8900 ■ Fx: 310-260-8917 ■ TF: 800-626-1313

Buddhist Study Center, American   www.americanbuddhist.org
331 Riverside Dr   New York NY 10025
Ph: 212-864-7424

Budget, Committee for a Responsible Federal   www.crfb.org
1630 Connecticut Ave NW 7th Fl   Washington DC 20009
Ph: 202-986-6599 ■ Fx: 202-986-3696

Budget Officers, National Association of State   www.nasbo.org
444 N Capitol St NW Suite 642   Washington DC 20001
Ph: 202-624-5382 ■ Fx: 202-624-7745

Budget & Policy Priorities, Center on   www.cbpp.org
820 1st St NE Suite 510   Washington DC 20002
Ph: 202-408-1080 ■ Fx: 202-408-1056

Budget & Program Analysis, American Association for   www.aabpa.org
PO Box 1157   Falls Church VA 22041
Ph: 703-941-4300 ■ Fx: 703-941-1535

Buick Club of America   www.buickclub.org
PO Box 360775   Columbus OH 43236
Ph: 614-472-3939 ■ Fx: 614-472-3222

Build PAC
1201 15th St NW   Washington DC 20005
Ph: 202-822-0200 ■ Fx: 202-822-0559 ■ TF: 800-368-5242

Builders Association, American Road & Transportation   www.artba-hq.org
1010 Massachusetts Ave NW   Washington DC 20001
Ph: 202-289-4434 ■ Fx: 202-289-4435

Builders Association, National Frame   nfba.org
4840 W 15th St Suite 1000   Lawrence KS 66049
Ph: 785-843-2444 ■ Fx: 785-843-7555 ■ TF: 800-557-6957

Builder's Association of North America, Log Home   www.loghomebuilders.org
22203 State Rt 203   Monroe WA 98272
Ph: 360-794-4469

Builders Consortium, Automated   www.automatedbuildersconsortium.com
PO Box 865   Hershey PA 17033
Ph: 717-566-1525 ■ Fx: 717-566-2114

Builders & Contractors Inc, Associated   www.abc.org
4250 N Fairfax Dr 9th Fl   Arlington VA 22203
Ph: 703-812-2000 ■ Fx: 703-812-8203

Builders Council, Aircraft   www.aircraftbuilders.com
4248 Park Glen Rd   Minneapolis MN 55416
Ph: 952-928-4662 ■ Fx: 952-929-1318

Builders Exchange Executives, International   www.ibee.org
43636 Woodward Ave Suite 300   Bloomfield Hills MI 48302
Ph: 248-409-1504 ■ Fx: 248-409-1503

Builders' Hardware Manufacturers Association   www.buildershardware.com
355 Lexington Ave 17th Fl   New York NY 10017
Ph: 212-297-2122 ■ Fx: 212-370-9047

Builders Institute, Home   www.hbi.org
1201 15th St NW 6th Fl   Washington DC 20005
Ph: 202-371-0600 ■ Fx: 202-266-8999

Builders, National Association of Home   www.nahb.org
1201 15th St NW   Washington DC 20005
Ph: 202-266-8200 ■ TF: 800-368-5242

Building Association, Continental Automated   www.caba.org
1200 Montreal Rd Bldg M-20   Ottawa ON K1A0R6
Ph: 613-990-7407 ■ Fx: 613-991-9990 ■ TF: 888-798-2222

Building Association, Energy & Environmental   www.eeba.org
10740 Lyndale Ave S Suite 10W   Bloomington MN 55420
Ph: 952-881-1098 ■ Fx: 952-881-3048

Building Codes & Standards, National Conference of States on   www.ncsbcs.org
505 Huntmar Park Dr Suite 210   Herndon VA 20170
Ph: 703-437-0100 ■ Fx: 703-481-3596

Building & Construction Trades Dept AFL-CIO   www.buildingtrades.org
815 16th St NW Suite 600   Washington DC 20006
Ph: 202-347-1461

Building Contractors & Erectors Association, Metal   www.mbcea.org
28 Lowry Dr PO Box 117   West Milton OH 45383
Ph: 937-698-4127 ■ Fx: 937-698-6153 ■ TF: 800-866-6722

Building Council, US Green www.usgbc.org
1015 18th St NW Suite 805 Washington DC 20036
Ph: 202-828-7422 ▪ Fx: 202-828-5110

Building Design, American Institute of www.aibd.org
2505 Main St Suite 209B Stratford CT 06961
Ph: 203-227-3640 ▪ Fx: 203-378-3568 ▪ TF: 800-366-2423

Building Granite Quarries Association, National www.nbgqa.com
1220 L St NW Suite 100-167 Washington DC 20005
Ph: 800-557-2848

Building Industry Consulting Services International www.bicsi.org
8610 Hidden River Pkwy Tampa FL 33637
Ph: 813-979-1991 ▪ Fx: 813-971-4311 ▪ TF: 800-242-7405

Building Inspection Engineers, National Academy of www.nabie.org
PO Box 520 York Harbor ME 03911
Ph: 800-294-7729 ▪ Fx: 207-351-1915

Building Institute, Modular www.mbinet.org
413 Park St Charlottesville VA 22902
Ph: 804-296-3288 ▪ Fx: 804-296-3361 ▪ TF: 888-811-3288

Building Manufacturers Association, Metal www.mbma.com
1300 Sumner Ave Cleveland OH 44115
Ph: 216-241-7333 ▪ Fx: 216-241-0105

Building Material Dealers Association www.bmda.com
12540 SW Main St Suite 200 Tigard OR 97223
Ph: 503-624-0561 ▪ Fx: 503-620-1016 ▪ TF: 800-666-2632

Building Material Dealers Association, National Lumber & www.dealer.org
40 Ivy St SE Washington DC 20003
Ph: 202-547-2230 ▪ Fx: 202-547-7640 ▪ TF: 800-634-8645

Building Material Distribution Association, North American www.nbmda.org
401 N Michigan Ave Suite 2400 Chicago IL 60611
Ph: 312-644-6610 ▪ Fx: 312-321-6869 ▪ TF: 888-747-7862

Building Officials, Association of Major City/County
505 Huntmar Park Dr Suite 210 Herndon VA 20170
Ph: 703-481-2038 ▪ Fx: 703-481-3596

Building Owners & Managers Association International www.boma.org
1201 New York Ave NW Suite 300 Washington DC 20005
Ph: 202-408-2662 ▪ Fx: 202-371-0181 ▪ TF: 800-426-6292

Building Owners & Managers Institute www.bomi-edu.org
1521 Ritchie Hwy Arnold MD 21012
Ph: 410-974-1410 ▪ Fx: 410-974-1935 ▪ TF: 800-235-2664

Building Sciences, National Institute of www.nibs.org
1090 Vermont Ave NW Suite 700 Washington DC 20005
Ph: 202-289-7800 ▪ Fx: 202-289-1092

Building Service Contractors Association International www.bscai.org
10201 Lee Hwy Suite 225 Fairfax VA 22030
Ph: 703-359-7090 ▪ Fx: 703-352-0493 ▪ TF: 800-368-3414

Building Service Contractors, World Federation of www.wfbsc.org
10201 Lee Hwy Suite 225 Fairfax VA 22030
Ph: 703-359-7090 ▪ Fx: 703-352-0493

Building Stone Institute www.buildingstone.org
PO Box 507 Purdys NY 10578
Ph: 914-232-5725 ▪ Fx: 914-232-5259

Building Trades Employers Association
180 Linden Oaks Suite 110 Rochester NY 14625
Ph: 585-586-0710 ▪ Fx: 585-586-1580

Buildings Industry Council, Sustainable www.sbicouncil.org
1331 H St NW Suite 1000 Washington DC 20005
Ph: 202-628-7400 ▪ Fx: 202-393-5043

Buildings & Urban Habitat, Council on Tall www.ctbuh.org
Illinois Institute of Technology SR Crown Hall 3360 S State
St Chicago IL 60616
Ph: 312-909-0253

Bulb Society Inc, International www.bulbsociety.com

Bulk Container Association, Flexible Intermediate www.fibca.com
PO Box 26068 Macon GA 31221
Ph: 478-757-1006 ▪ Fx: 478-757-9444

Bulk Vendors Association, National www.nbva.org
191 N Wacker Dr Suite 1800 Chicago IL 60606
Ph: 312-521-2400 ▪ Fx: 312-521-2300

Bullet Association, Cast www.castbulletassoc.org
12857 S Rd Hoyt KS 66440
Ph: 785-986-6675

Bureau of Wholesale Sales Representatives www.bwsr.com
1100 Spring St NW Suite 700 Atlanta GA 30309
Ph: 404-870-7600 ▪ Fx: 404-870-7601 ▪ TF: 800-877-1808

Burgess Thornton W Society www.thorntonburgess.org
6 Discovery Hill Rd East Sandwich MA 02537
Ph: 508-888-6870 ▪ Fx: 508-888-1919

Burglar & Fire Alarm Association, National www.alarm.org
8300 Colesville Rd Suite 750 Silver Spring MD 20910
Ph: 301-585-1855 ▪ Fx: 301-585-1866

Burial Association, Hebrew Free
224 W 35th St Rm 300 New York NY 10001
Ph: 212-239-1662 ▪ Fx: 212-239-1981

Burial Vault Association, National Concrete ncbva.org
900 Fox Valley Dr Suite 204 Longwood FL 32779
Ph: 407-788-1996 ▪ Fx: 407-774-6751 ▪ TF: 800-538-1423

Burley Auction Warehouse Association
620 S Broadway St Lexington KY 40508
Ph: 859-255-4504

Burley Tobacco Growers Cooperative Association www.burleytobacco.com
620 S Broadway Lexington KY 40508
Ph: 859-252-3561 ▪ Fx: 859-231-9804

Burma-America Buddhist Association
1708 Powder Mill Rd Silver Spring MD 20903
Ph: 301-439-4035

Burma Coalition, Free www.freeburmacoalition.org
1101 Pennsylvania Ave SW Suite 204 Washington DC 20003
Ph: 202-547-5985 ▪ Fx: 202-547-6118

Burma-India Veterans Association, China-
PO Box 780676 Orlando FL 32878
Ph: 407-282-0346

Burmese Cat Fanciers, United
2395 NE 185th St North Miami Beach FL 33180
Ph: 305-931-0104

Burn Association, American www.ameriburn.org
625 N Michigan Ave Suite 1530 Chicago IL 60611
Ph: 312-642-9260 ▪ Fx: 312-642-9130 ▪ TF: 800-548-2876

Burn Survivors, Phoenix Society for www.phoenix-society.org
2153 Wealthy St SE Suite 215 East Grand Rapids MI 49506
Ph: 616-458-2773 ▪ Fx: 616-458-2831 ▪ TF: 800-888-2876

Burn Victim Foundation, National www.nbvf.org
PO Box 409 Basking Ridge NJ 07920
Ph: 908-953-9091 ▪ Fx: 908-953-9099

Burns United Support Group
PO Box 36416 Grosse Pointe MI 48236
Ph: 313-881-5577 ▪ Fx: 313-417-8702

Burro Association Inc, American Mustang & www.bardalisa.com
PO Box 788 Lincoln CA 95648
Ph: 530-633-9271 ▪ TF: 800-874-8453

Burro Program, National Wild Horse & wildhorseandburro.blm.gov
PO Box 3270 Sparks NV 89432
Ph: 775-475-2222 ▪ Fx: 775-861-6711 ▪ TF: 800-417-9647

Burros, International Society for the Protection of Mustangs & www.ispmb.org
PO Box 55 Lantry SD 57636
Ph: 605-964-6866 ▪ Fx: 605-365-6991

Burroughs Bibliophiles www.jeddak.com

Burroughs John Association Inc www.johnburroughs.org
15 W 77th St New York NY 10024
Ph: 212-769-5169

Bus Association, American www.buses.org
1100 New York Ave NW Suite 575 Washington DC 20005
Ph: 202-842-1645 ▪ Fx: 202-842-0850 ▪ TF: 800-283-2877

Bus Traffic Association, National www.bustraffic.org
700 13th St NE Suite 575 Washington DC 20005
Ph: 202-898-2700 ▪ Fx: 202-842-0850

Buses International Association www.busesintl.com
PO Box 9337 Spokane WA 99209
Ph: 509-328-2494 ▪ Fx: 509-325-5396

Bush Archibald Foundation www.bushfoundation.org
332 Minnesota St Suite E-900 Saint Paul MN 55101
Ph: 651-227-0891 ▪ Fx: 651-297-6485

Bush Barbara Foundation for Family Literacy www.barbarabushfoundation.com
1201 15th St SW Suite 420 Washington DC 20005
Ph: 202-955-6183 ▪ Fx: 202-955-5492

Business, AACSB International - Association to Advance www.aacsb.edu
Collegiate Schools of 600 Emerson Rd Suite 300 Saint
Louis MO 63141
Ph: 314-872-8481 ▪ Fx: 314-872-8495

Business, Academy of International aib.msu.edu
Michigan State Univ Eli Broad College of Business 7 Eppley
Ctr East Lansing MI 48824
Ph: 517-432-1452 ▪ Fx: 517-432-1009

Business Administration, National Association of Church www.nacba.net
100 N Central Expy Suite 914 Richardson TX 75080
Ph: 972-699-7555 ▪ Fx: 972-699-7617 ▪ TF: 800-898-8085

Business Alliance, American Independent www.amiba.net
1510 5th St Boulder CO 80302
Ph: 303-402-1575

Business Alliance for Commerce in Hemp www.chrisconrad.com
PO Box 1716 El Cerrito CA 94530
Ph: 510-215-8326

Business Alliance for International Economic Development www.fintrac.com/alliance
1615 L St NW Suite 520 Washington DC 20036
Ph: 202-429-8855 ▪ Fx: 202-429-8857

(Business) Alpha Kappa Psi www.akpsi.com
9595 Angola Ct Indianapolis IN 46268
Ph: 317-872-1553 ▪ Fx: 317-872-1567

Business Appraisers, Institute of www.go-iba.org
PO Box 17410 Plantation FL 33318
Ph: 954-584-1144 ▪ Fx: 954-584-1184 ▪ TF: 800-299-4130

Business, Asian Women in www.awib.org
358 5th Ave Suite 504 New York NY 10001
Ph: 212-868-1368 ▪ Fx: 212-868-1373

Business Associates, World
1000 Connecticut Ave NW Suite 202 Washington DC 20036
Ph: 202-466-5428 ▪ Fx: 202-452-8540

Business Association, British-American www.babawashington.org
PO Box 16482 Washington DC 20041
Ph: 202-293-0010 ▪ Fx: 202-296-3332

Business Association, Canada-US
600 Renaissance Ctr Suite 1100 Detroit MI 48243
Ph: 313-567-2208 ▪ Fx: 313-567-2164

Business Association, Latin www.lbausa.com
5400 E Olympic Blvd Suite 130 Los Angeles CA 90022
Ph: 323-721-4000 ▪ Fx: 323-722-5050 ▪ TF: 800-371-4522

Business Association, National www.nationalbusiness.org
5151 Beltline Rd Suite 1150 Dallas TX 75240
Ph: 972-458-0900 ▪ Fx: 972-960-9149 ▪ TF: 800-456-0440

Business Association, National Cooperative www.ncba.org
1401 New York Ave NW Suite 1100 Washington DC 20005
Ph: 202-638-6222 ▪ Fx: 202-638-1374

Business Association Inc, National Nurses in www.nnba.net
867 Levitt Pkwy Rockledge FL 32955
Ph: 321-633-4610 ▪ TF: 877-353-8888

Business Association, National Small www.nsba.biz
1156 15th St NW Suite 1100 Washington DC 20005
Ph: 202-393-8830 ▪ Fx: 202-872-8543 ▪ TF: 800-345-6728

Business Aviation Association, National   www.nbaa.org
1200 18th St NW Suite 400   Washington DC 20036
Ph: 202-783-9000 ▪ Fx: 202-331-8364

(Business) Beta Alpha Psi   www.bap.org
1211 Ave of the Americas 6th Fl   New York NY 10036
Ph: 212-596-6090 ▪ Fx: 212-596-6288

(Business) Beta Gamma Sigma Inc   www.betagammasigma.org
125 Weldon Pkwy   Maryland Heights MO 63043
Ph: 314-432-5650 ▪ Fx: 314-432-7083

Business Brokers Association, International   www.ibba.org
401 N Michigan Ave Suite 2200   Chicago IL 60611
Ph: 312-321-4097 ▪ Fx: 312-673-6599 ▪ TF: 888-686-4222

Business Center Association International, Office   www.officebusinesscenters.com
200 E Campus View Blvd Suite 200   Columbus OH 43235
Ph: 614-985-3633 ▪ Fx: 614-985-3601 ▪ TF: 800-237-4741

Business Coalition on Health, National   www.nbch.org
1015 18th St NW Suite 730   Washington DC 20036
Ph: 202-775-9300 ▪ Fx: 202-775-1569

(Business) CommerceNet   www.commerce.net
510 Logue Ave   Mountain View CA 94043
Ph: 650-962-2600 ▪ Fx: 650-962-2601 ▪ TF: 888-255-1900

Business Committee for the Arts Inc   www.bcainc.org
29-27 Queens Plaza N 4th Fl   Long Island City NY 11101
Ph: 718-482-9900 ▪ Fx: 718-482-9911

Business Communication, Association for   www.businesscommunication.org
Baruch College 1 Bernard Baruch Way Box B8-240   New York
NY 10010
Ph: 646-312-3727 ▪ Fx: 646-349-5297

Business Communications Alliance, Integrated   www.ibacweb.org
139 E Oakland Ave   Doylestown PA 18901
Ph: 215-489-1722 ▪ Fx: 215-489-1799

Business Communications Council, Health Industry   www.hibcc.org
2525 E Arizona Biltmore Cir Suite 127   Phoenix AZ 85016
Ph: 602-381-1091 ▪ Fx: 602-381-1093

Business Communicators, International Association of   www.iabc.com
1 Hallidie Plaza Suite 600   San Francisco CA 94102
Ph: 415-544-4700 ▪ Fx: 415-544-4747 ▪ TF: 800-766-4222

Business Conference, American   www.americanbusinessconference.org
1828 L St NW Suite 908   Washington DC 20003
Ph: 202-822-9300 ▪ Fx: 202-467-4070

Business Consultants, Institute of Certified Healthcare   www.ichbc.org
307 N Michigan Ave Suite 800   Chicago IL 60601
Ph: 312-360-0384 ▪ Fx: 312-360-0388 ▪ TF: 800-447-1684

Business Council   www.businesscouncil.com
PO Box 20147   Washington DC 20041
Ph: 202-298-7650 ▪ Fx: 202-785-0296

Business Council of America, Small   www.sbca.net
800 Delaware Ave 7th Fl   Wilmington DE 19899
Ph: 302-691-7222 ▪ Fx: 877-404-1329

Business Council Inc, Arts &   www.artsandbusiness.org
520 8th Ave Suite 319   New York NY 10018
Ph: 212-279-5910 ▪ Fx: 212-279-5915

Business Council, Canadian American   www.canambusco.org
1900 K St NW   Washington DC 20006
Ph: 202-496-7340 ▪ Fx: 202-496-7756

Business Council, Hungarian-US
c/o US Chamber of Commerce 1615 H St NW   Washington DC
20062
Ph: 202-463-5482 ▪ Fx: 202-463-3114

Business Council for International Understanding   www.bciu.org
1212 Ave of the Americas 10th Fl   New York NY 10036
Ph: 212-490-0460 ▪ Fx: 212-697-8526

Business Council, Lithuanian-US
c/o US Chamber of Commerce 1615 H St NW   Washington DC
20062
Ph: 202-463-5601 ▪ Fx: 202-463-3114

Business Council Ltd, Moroccan American   www.usa-morocco.org
1085 Commonwealth Ave Suite 194   Boston MA 02215
Ph: 617-319-3400 ▪ Fx: 508-230-9943

Business Council Inc, National Minority   www.nmbc.org
25 W 45th St Suite 301   New York NY 10036
Ph: 212-997-4753 ▪ Fx: 212-997-5102

Business Council, National Women's   www.nwbc.gov
409 3rd St SW Suite 210   Washington DC 20024
Ph: 202-205-3850 ▪ Fx: 202-205-6825

Business Council, Polish-US
c/o US Chamber of Commerce 1615 H St NW   Washington DC
20062
Ph: 202-463-5482 ▪ Fx: 202-463-3114

Business Council, Romanian-US
c/o US Chamber of Commerce 1615 H St NW   Washington DC
20062
Ph: 202-463-5482 ▪ Fx: 202-463-3114

Business Council for Southeastern Europe, US   www.usbizcouncil.org
PO Box 1521 Wall St Stn   New York NY 10268
Ph: 212-439-9025 ▪ Fx: 212-439-9105 ▪ TF: 800-203-8900

Business Council for Sustainable Energy   www.bcse.org
1200 18th St NW 9th Fl   Washington DC 20036
Ph: 202-785-0507 ▪ Fx: 202-785-0514

Business Council, US-ASEAN   www.us-asean.org
1101 17th St NW Suite 411   Washington DC 20036
Ph: 202-289-1911 ▪ Fx: 202-289-0519

Business Council, US-China   www.uschina.org
1818 N St NW Suite 200   Washington DC 20036
Ph: 202-429-0340 ▪ Fx: 202-775-2476

Business Council, US-Japan   www.usjbc.org
2000 L St NW Suite 515   Washington DC 20036
Ph: 202-728-0068 ▪ Fx: 202-728-0073

Business Council, US-Russia   www.usrbc.org
1701 Pennsylvania Ave NW Suite 520   Washington DC 20006
Ph: 202-739-9180 ▪ Fx: 202-659-5920

Business Council, US-Saudi Arabian   www.us-saudi-business.org
1401 New York Ave NW Suite 720   Washington DC 20005
Ph: 202-638-1212 ▪ Fx: 202-638-2894

Business Council, US-Taiwan   www.us-taiwan.org
1700 N Moore St Suite 703   Arlington VA 22209
Ph: 703-465-2930 ▪ Fx: 703-465-2937

Business Council, US-Thailand   www.ustbc.org
3050 K St NW Suite 205   Washington DC 20007
Ph: 202-337-5973 ▪ Fx: 202-337-0039

(Business) Delta Sigma Pi   www.dspnet.org
330 S Campus Ave Box 230   Oxford OH 45056
Ph: 513-523-1907 ▪ Fx: 513-523-7292

Business Development Centers, Association of Small   www.asbdc-us.org
8990 Burke Lake Rd   Burke VA 22015
Ph: 703-764-9850 ▪ Fx: 703-764-1234

Business & Economic Research, Association for University   www.auber.org
Univ of Colorado Leeds School of Business UCB 419   Boulder
CO 80309
Ph: 303-492-3196 ▪ Fx: 303-492-3620

Business Economics, National Association for   www.nabe.com
1233 20th St NW Suite 505   Washington DC 20036
Ph: 202-463-6223 ▪ Fx: 202-463-6239

(Business & Economics) Phi Chi Theta   www.phichitheta.org
5215 N O'Connor Blvd Suite 200   Irving TX 75039
Ph: 972-443-9889 ▪ Fx: 214-350-8011

Business Economists, Conference of
28790 Chagrin Blvd Suite 350   Cleveland OH 44122
Ph: 216-464-2137 ▪ Fx: 216-464-0397

Business Editors & Writers, Society of American   www.sabew.org
Missouri School of Journalism 134A Neff Annex   Columbia MO
65211
Ph: 573-882-7862 ▪ Fx: 573-884-1372

Business Education Association, National   www.nbea.org
1914 Association Dr   Reston VA 20191
Ph: 703-860-8300 ▪ Fx: 703-620-4483

(Business Education) Delta Pi Epsilon   www.dpe.org
PO Box 4340   Little Rock AR 72214
Ph: 501-219-1866 ▪ Fx: 501-219-1876

Business Education, International Assembly for Collegiate   www.iacbe.org
PO Box 25217   Overland Park KS 66225
Ph: 913-631-3009 ▪ Fx: 913-631-9154

Business Education, International Society for   www.siec-isbe.org
PO Box 20457   Carson City NV 89721
Ph: 775-882-1445 ▪ Fx: 775-882-1449

Business Espionage Controls & Countermeasures Association   www.becca-online.org
PO Box 55582   Shoreline WA 98155
Ph: 206-364-4672 ▪ Fx: 206-367-3316

Business Ethics, Society for   www.societyforbusinessethics.org
Loyola Univ of Chicago School of Business Administration 820
N Michigan Ave   Chicago IL 60611
Ph: 312-915-6994 ▪ Fx: 312-915-6988

Business Executives for National Security   www.bens.org
1717 Pennsylvania Ave NW Suite 350   Washington DC 20006
Ph: 202-296-2125 ▪ Fx: 202-296-2490 ▪ TF: 800-296-2125

Business Exporters Association, Small   www.sbea.org
1156 15th St NW Suite 1100   Washington DC 20005
Ph: 202-659-9320 ▪ Fx: 202-872-5843

Business, FCIB: Association of Executives in Finance
Credit & International   8840 Columbia 100 Pkwy   Columbia
MD 21045   www.fcibglobal.com
Ph: 410-423-1840 ▪ Fx: 410-423-1845 ▪ TF: 888-256-3242

Business Fellows, Society of International   www.sibf.org
191 Peachtree St NE Suite 3220   Atlanta GA 30303
Ph: 404-525-7423 ▪ Fx: 404-525-5331

Business Forms Management Association   www.bfma.org
319 SW Washington St Suite 710   Portland OR 97204
Ph: 503-227-3393 ▪ Fx: 503-274-7667

Business & Government, Center for   www.ksg.harvard.edu/cbg/
Harvard Univ John F Kennedy School of Government Weil Hall
79 JFK St   Cambridge MA 02138
Ph: 617-384-7329 ▪ Fx: 617-496-0063

Business, Graduate Women in   www.gwib.org

Business-Higher Education Forum   www.acenet.edu/programs/bhef
1 Dupont Cir NW Suite 800   Washington DC 20036
Ph: 202-939-9345 ▪ Fx: 202-833-4723

Business & Home Safety, Institute for   www.ibhs.org
4775 E Fowler Ave   Tampa FL 33617
Ph: 813-286-3400 ▪ Fx: 813-286-9960 ▪ TF: 866-675-4247

Business Honor Society, Alpha Beta Gamma International   www.abg.org
75 Grasslands Rd   Valhalla NY 10595
Ph: 914-785-6877 ▪ Fx: 914-785-6481

Business Incubation Association, National   www.nbia.org
20 E Circle Dr   Athens OH 45701
Ph: 740-593-4331 ▪ Fx: 740-593-1996

Business & Industrial Chaplaincy, National Institute of   www.nibic.com
1770 St James Pl Suite 550   Houston TX 77056
Ph: 713-266-2456 ▪ Fx: 713-266-0845

Business & Industry Council Educational Foundation, US   www.usbusiness.org
910 16th St NW Suite 300   Washington DC 20006
Ph: 202-728-1990 ▪ Fx: 202-728-1981

Business & Industry Council, US   www.usbusiness.org
910 16th St NW Suite 300   Washington DC 20006
Ph: 202-728-1980 ▪ Fx: 202-728-1981

Business Industry Political Action Committee   www.bipac.org
888 16th St NW Suite 305   Washington DC 20006
Ph: 202-833-1880 ▪ Fx: 202-833-2338

Business & Institutional Furniture Manufacturers Association   www.bifma.com
2680 Horizon Dr SE Suite A-1   Grand Rapids MI 49546
Ph: 616-285-3963 ▪ Fx: 616-285-3765

Business, International Council for Small www.icsb.org
George Washington Univ School of Business & Public
Management 2115 G St NW Suite 403   Washington DC
20052
Ph: 202-994-0704 ▪ Fx: 202-994-4930

Business International Trade Educators, North American Small www.nasbite.org
Wright State Univ 120 Rike Hall 3640 Colonel Glenn
Hwy   Dayton OH 45435
Ph: 937-775-3524 ▪ Fx: 937-775-3545

Business Leaders of America - Phi Beta Lambda Inc, Future www.fbla-pbl.org
1912 Association Dr   Reston VA 20191
Ph: 703-860-3334 ▪ Fx: 703-758-0749 ▪ TF: 800-325-2946

Business Leaders, National Association of www.nabl.com/
4132 Shoreline Dr Suite J   Earth City MO 63045
Ph: 314-344-1111 ▪ Fx: 314-928-9110

Business Legislative Council, Small www.sblc.org
1010 Massachusetts Ave NW Suite 400   Washington DC 20001
Ph: 202-639-8500 ▪ Fx: 202-296-5333

Business Management Association, Radiology www.rbma.org
8001 Irvine Center Dr Suite 1060   Irvine CA 92618
Ph: 949-340-5000 ▪ Fx: 949-340-5001 ▪ TF: 888-224-7262

Business Marketing Association www.marketing.org
400 N Michigan Ave 15th Fl   Chicago IL 60611
Ph: 312-409-4262 ▪ Fx: 312-409-4266 ▪ TF: 800-664-4262

Business Media, American www.americanbusinessmedia.com
675 3rd Ave Suite 415   New York NY 10017
Ph: 212-661-6360 ▪ Fx: 212-370-0736

Business Music Association, International www.ibma.net
PO Box 940   Franklin NC 28744
Ph: 828-369-2322

Business, National Federation of Independent www.nfib.com
1201 F St NW Suite 200   Washington DC 20004
Ph: 202-554-9000 ▪ Fx: 202-554-0496 ▪ TF: 800-552-6342

(Business) Newcomen Society of the US www.newcomen.org
211 Welsh Pool Rd Suite 240   Exton PA 19341
Ph: 610-363-6600 ▪ Fx: 610-363-0612

Business Officers' Association, National www.nboa.net
PO Box 4576   Boulder CO 80306
Ph: 720-564-0475 ▪ Fx: 720-564-4951

Business Officers, Community College www.ccbo.org
PO Box 5565   Charlottesville VA 22905
Ph: 434-293-2825 ▪ Fx: 434-245-8453

Business Officers, National Association of College & University www.nacubo.org
2501 M St NW Suite 400   Washington DC 20037
Ph: 202-861-2500 ▪ Fx: 202-861-2583

Business Officials International, Association of School asbointl.org
11401 N Shore Dr   Reston VA 20190
Ph: 703-478-0405 ▪ Fx: 703-478-0205

Business Organizations, National Association for
10451 Mill Run Cir Suite 400   Owings Mills MD 21117
Ph: 410-581-1373

Business Owners, Association of African-American Women
3363 Alden Pl NE   Washington DC 20019
Ph: 202-399-3645

Business Owners, National Association of Women www.nawbo.org
8405 Greensboro Dr Suite 800   McLean VA 22102
Ph: 703-506-3268 ▪ Fx: 703-506-3266 ▪ TF: 800-556-2926

(Business) Phi Theta Pi Fraternity www.phithetapi.org
2103 Cortez Rd   Jacksonville FL 32246
Ph: 888-608-9841 ▪ Fx: 904-641-9006

Business Political Action Committees, National Association of www.nabpac.org
1133 21st St NW Suite M-100   Washington DC 20036
Ph: 202-572-6279 ▪ Fx: 202-546-4243

Business Products Credit Association www.bpca.org
119 Hill Ave   Ballwin MO 63011
Ph: 636-394-7777 ▪ Fx: 636-394-7099

Business & Professional Women/USA www.bpwusa.org
1900 M St NW Suite 310   Washington DC 20036
Ph: 202-293-1100 ▪ Fx: 202-861-0298

Business & Professional Women's Clubs Inc, National Association of Negro www.nanbpwc.org
1806 New Hampshire Ave NW   Washington DC
20009
Ph: 202-483-4206 ▪ Fx: 202-462-7253

Business & Professional Women's Foundation www.bpwusa.org
1900 M St NW Suite 310   Washington DC 20036
Ph: 202-293-1100 ▪ Fx: 202-861-0298

Business Professionals of America www.bpa.org
5454 Cleveland Ave   Columbus OH 43231
Ph: 614-895-7277 ▪ Fx: 614-895-1165 ▪ TF: 800-334-2007

Business Professionals, Consumer Science www.consumerexpert.org
PO Box 2065   Lake Oswego OR 97035
Ph: 503-620-6690 ▪ Fx: 503-620-6898

Business Publication Editors, American Society of www.asbpe.org
710 E Ogden Ave Suite 600   Naperville IL 60563
Ph: 630-579-3288 ▪ Fx: 630-369-2488

Business Publications, Association of Area www.bizpubs.org
4929 Wilshire Blvd Suite 428   Los Angeles CA 90010
Ph: 323-937-5514 ▪ Fx: 323-937-0959

Business Research, Center for Women's www.nfwbo.org
1411 K St NW Suite 1350   Washington DC 20005
Ph: 202-638-3060 ▪ Fx: 202-638-3064

(Business Research) Institute for the Future www.iftf.org
2744 Sand Hill Rd   Menlo Park CA 94025
Ph: 650-854-6322 ▪ Fx: 650-854-7850

Business, Research Institute for Small & Emerging www.riseb.org
722 12th St NW   Washington DC 20005
Ph: 202-628-8382 ▪ Fx: 202-628-8392

Business Roundtable www.brtable.org
1615 L St NW Suite 1100   Washington DC 20036
Ph: 202-872-1260 ▪ Fx: 202-466-3509

Business Schools & Programs, Association of Collegiate www.acbsp.org
7007 College Blvd Suite 420   Overland Park KS 66211
Ph: 913-339-9356 ▪ Fx: 913-339-6226

(Business) SCORE Association www.score.org
409 3rd St SW 6th Fl   Washington DC 20024
Ph: 202-205-6762 ▪ Fx: 202-205-7636 ▪ TF: 800-634-0245

Business for Social Responsibility www.bsr.org
111 Sutter St 12th Fl   San Francisco CA 94104
Ph: 415-984-3200 ▪ Fx: 415-984-3201

Business Software Alliance www.bsa.org
1150 18th St Suite 700   Washington DC 20036
Ph: 202-872-5500 ▪ Fx: 202-872-5501 ▪ TF: 888-667-4722

Business Survival Committee, Small www.sbsc.org
1920 L St NW Suite 200   Washington DC 20036
Ph: 202-785-0238 ▪ Fx: 202-822-8118

Business Teacher Education, National Association for www.nbea.org
1914 Association Dr   Reston VA 20191
Ph: 703-860-8300 ▪ Fx: 703-620-4483

Business of Technology, AeA: Advancing the www.aeanet.org
5201 Great America Pkwy Suite 520   Santa Clara CA 95054
Ph: 408-987-4200 ▪ Fx: 408-970-8565 ▪ TF: 800-284-4232

Business Technology Association www.bta.org
12411 Wornall Rd   Kansas City MO 64145
Ph: 816-941-3100 ▪ Fx: 816-941-2829 ▪ TF: 800-316-9721

Business Today www.businesstoday.org
48 University Pl   Princeton NJ 08544
Ph: 609-258-1111 ▪ Fx: 609-258-1222

Business Travel Agents, National Association of
3699 Wilshire Blvd Suite 700   Los Angeles CA 90010
Ph: 213-382-3335

Business Travel Association, National www.nbta.org
110 N Royal St 4th Fl   Alexandria VA 22314
Ph: 703-684-0836 ▪ Fx: 703-684-0263

Business, US Council for International www.uscib.org
1212 Ave of the Americas 18th Fl   New York NY 10036
Ph: 212-354-4480 ▪ Fx: 212-944-0012

Business Valuation Specialists, American Association of www.aabvs.com
PO Box 13089   Tallahassee FL 32317
Ph: 850-878-3134 ▪ Fx: 850-878-1291

Business Volunteers Unlimited www.businessvolunteers.org
200 Public Sq   Cleveland OH 44113
Ph: 216-736-7711 ▪ Fx: 216-736-7710

Business Women's Association, American www.abwahq.org
9100 Ward Pkwy   Kansas City MO 64114
Ph: 816-361-6621 ▪ Fx: 816-361-4991 ▪ TF: 800-228-0007

Businesses Association, American Small www.asbaonline.org
206 E College St Suite 201B   Grapevine TX 76051
Ph: 817-488-8770 ▪ Fx: 817-251-8578

Businessmen to Christ, Connecting www.cbmc.com
6650 E Brainerd Rd Suite 100   Chattanooga TN 37421
Ph: 423-698-4444 ▪ Fx: 423-629-4434 ▪ TF: 800-575-2262

Businesspersons Association, American www.aba-assn.com
350 Fairway Dr Suite 200   Deerfield Beach FL 33441
Ph: 954-571-1877 ▪ Fx: 954-571-8582 ▪ TF: 800-221-2168

Businesspersons Association, Disabled www.disabledbusiness.com
SDSU Interwork Institute 3590 Camino del Rio N Suite
117   San Diego CA 92108
Ph: 619-594-8805 ▪ Fx: 619-594-4208

BUSPAC
700 13th St NW Suite 575   Washington DC 20005
Ph: 202-842-1645 ▪ Fx: 202-842-0850 ▪ TF: 800-283-2877

Butter Institute, American www.butterinstitute.org
2101 Wilson Blvd Suite 400   Arlington VA 22201
Ph: 703-243-6111 ▪ Fx: 703-841-9328

Butterfly Association, North American www.naba.org
4 Delaware Rd   Morristown NJ 07960
Ph: 973-285-0907 ▪ Fx: 973-285-0936

Butterfly Lovers International
210 Columbus Ave   San Francisco CA 94104
Ph: 415-864-1169

Buyer Agents, National Association of Exclusive www.naeba.org
191 Clarksville Rd   Princeton Junction NJ 08550
Ph: 609-799-4382 ▪ Fx: 609-799-7032

Buyer's Agent Council, Real Estate www.rebac.net
430 N Michigan Ave   Chicago IL 60611
Ph: 312-329-8656 ▪ Fx: 312-329-8632 ▪ TF: 800-648-6224

Buyers Association, International Entertainment www.ieba.org
PO Box 128376   Nashville TN 37212
Ph: 615-463-0161 ▪ Fx: 615-463-0163 ▪ TF: 888-999-4322

Buyers, National Association of Educational www.naeb.org
450 Wireless Blvd   Hauppauge NY 11788
Ph: 631-273-2600 ▪ Fx: 631-952-3660

Buying Points Association, National Peanut
PO Box 314   Tifton GA 31793
Ph: 229-386-1716 ▪ Fx: 229-386-8757

By Word of Mouth Storytelling Guild shorock.com/folk/bwom
PO Box 56   Frankford MO 63441
Ph: 573-784-2589 ▪ Fx: 573-784-2364

Byam Wally Caravan Club International www.wbcci.org
PO Box 612   Jackson Center OH 45334
Ph: 937-596-5211 ▪ Fx: 937-596-5542

Byelorussian-American Youth Organization
PO Box 1123   New Brunswick NJ 08903
Ph: 732-560-8610

C

Cabinet Manufacturers Association, Kitchen www.kcma.org
1899 Preston White Dr   Reston VA 20191
Ph: 703-264-1690 ▪ Fx: 703-620-6530

Cable Engineers Association, Insulated   www.icea.net
PO Box 1568 Carrollton GA 30112
Ph: 770-830-0369 ▪ Fx: 770-830-8501

Cable Financial Management Association, Broadcast   www.bcfm.com
932 Lee St Suite 204 Des Plaines IL 60016
Ph: 847-296-0200 ▪ Fx: 847-296-7510

Cable & Telecommunications Association for Marketing   www.ctam.com
201 N Union St Suite 440 Alexandria VA 22314
Ph: 703-549-4200 ▪ Fx: 703-684-1167

Cable & Telecommunications Association, National   www.ncta.com
1724 Massachusetts Ave NW Washington DC 20036
Ph: 202-775-3550 ▪ Fx: 202-775-1055

Cable Telecommunications Engineers, Society of   www.scte.org
140 Philips Rd Exton PA 19341
Ph: 610-363-6888 ▪ Fx: 610-363-5898 ▪ TF: 800-542-5040

Cable & Telecommunications Human Resources Association   www.cthra.com
1755 Park St Suite 260 Naperville IL 60563
Ph: 630-416-1166 ▪ Fx: 630-416-9798

Cable & Telecommunications, Women in   www.wict.org
14555 Avion Pkwy Suite 250 Chantilly VA 20151
Ph: 703-234-9810 ▪ Fx: 703-817-1595

Cable Television Cooperative Inc, National   www.cabletvco-op.org
11200 Corporate Ave Lenexa KS 66219
Ph: 913-599-5900 ▪ Fx: 913-599-5903

Cable Television Laboratories Inc   www.cablelabs.com
400 Centennial Pkwy Louisville CO 80027
Ph: 303-661-9100 ▪ Fx: 303-661-9199

Cable Television Public Affairs Association   www.ctpaa.org
PO Box 33697 Washington DC 20033
Ph: 202-775-1081 ▪ Fx: 202-955-1134 ▪ TF: 800-210-3396

CableLabs   www.cablelabs.com
400 Centennial Pkwy Louisville CO 80027
Ph: 303-661-9100 ▪ Fx: 303-661-9199

Cabletelevision Advertising Bureau   www.cabletvadbureau.com
830 3rd Ave 2nd Fl New York NY 10022
Ph: 212-508-1200 ▪ Fx: 212-832-3268

Cabrini Mission Corps   cabrini-missioncorps.org
610 King of Prussia Rd Radnor PA 19087
Ph: 610-971-0821 ▪ Fx: 610-971-0396

Cactus & Succulent Research, Arizona   www.arizonacactus.com
8 S Cactus Ln Bisbee AZ 85603
Ph: 520-432-7040 ▪ Fx: 520-432-7001

Cactus & Succulent Society of America   www.cssainc.org
6811 S 230th East Ave Broken Arrow OK 74014
Ph: 918-357-2401

Cadet Alliance, American   www.marinecadets.org
PO Box 144 Sea Girt NJ 08750
Ph: 732-840-4500 ▪ Fx: 732-458-1075

Cadet Corps, Naval Sea   www.seacadets.org
2300 Wilson Blvd Arlington VA 22201
Ph: 703-243-6910 ▪ Fx: 703-243-3985

Cadillac-Lasalle Club   www.cadillaclasalleclub.org
PO Box 360835 Columbus OH 43236
Ph: 614-478-4622 ▪ Fx: 614-472-3222

Cadmium Association, International   www.cadmium.org
PO Box 924 Great Falls VA 22066
Ph: 703-759-7400 ▪ Fx: 703-759-7003

Cafritz Morris & Gwendolyn Foundation   www.cafritzfoundation.org
1825 K St NW 14th Fl Washington DC 20006
Ph: 202-223-3100 ▪ Fx: 202-296-7567

Cal Farley's Boys Ranch   www.calfarleysboysranch.org
PO Box 1890 Amarillo TX 79174
Ph: 806-372-2341 ▪ Fx: 806-372-6638 ▪ TF: 800-687-3722

CAL/N-X-211 Collectors Society   www.isoc.net/astuder/calnx211

Calico Cat Registry International
PO Box 944 Morongo Valley CA 92256
Ph: 760-363-6511

California Association of Winegrape Growers   www.cawg.org
555 University Ave Suite 250 Sacramento CA 95825
Ph: 916-924-5370

California Avocado Commission   www.avocado.org
38 Discovery Suite 150 Irvine CA 92618
Ph: 949-341-1955 ▪ Fx: 949-341-1970

California Date Commission   www.datesaregreat.com
PO Box 1736 Indio CA 92202
Ph: 760-347-4510 ▪ Fx: 760-347-6374 ▪ TF: 800-223-8748

California Fig Advisory Board   www.californiafigs.com
7395 N Palm Bluffs Ave Suite 106 Fresno CA 93711
Ph: 559-440-5400 ▪ Fx: 559-438-5405

California Kiwifruit Commission   www.kiwifruit.org
9845 Horn Rd Suite 160 Sacramento CA 95827
Ph: 916-362-7490 ▪ Fx: 916-362-7993

California Pioneers, Society of   www.californiapioneers.org
300 4th St San Francisco CA 94107
Ph: 415-957-1849 ▪ Fx: 415-957-9858

California Pistachio Commission   www.pistachios.org
1318 E Shaw Ave Suite 420 Fresno CA 93710
Ph: 559-221-8294 ▪ Fx: 559-221-8044

California Redwood Association   www.calredwood.org
405 Enfrente Dr Suite 200 Novato CA 94949
Ph: 415-382-0662 ▪ Fx: 415-382-8531 ▪ TF: 888-225-7339

California Strawberry Commission   www.calstrawberry.com
PO Box 269 Watsonville CA 95077
Ph: 831-724-1301 ▪ Fx: 831-724-5973

California Table Grape Commission   www.tablegrape.com
392 W Fallbrook Ave Suite 101 Fresno CA 93711
Ph: 559-447-8350 ▪ Fx: 559-447-9180

Californian Rabbit Specialty Club, National   home.woh.rr.com/crsc
22162 S Hunter Rd Colton OR 97017
Ph: 503-824-2138

Call for Action   www.callforaction.org
5272 River Rd Suite 300 Bethesda MD 20816
Ph: 301-657-8260 ▪ Fx: 301-657-2914 ▪ TF: 800-647-1756

Call to Action USA   www.cta-usa.org
2135 W Roscoe St Chicago IL 60618
Ph: 773-404-0004 ▪ Fx: 773-404-1610

Call Center Industry Advisory Board   www.ciac-cert.org
330 Franklin Rd Suite 135A PMB 390 Brentwood TN 37027
Ph: 615-373-2376

Callerlab - International Association of Square Dance Callers   www.callerlab.org
467 Forrest Ave Suite 118 Cocoa FL 32922
Ph: 321-639-0039 ▪ Fx: 321-639-0851

Calligraphers Guild, Washington   www.calligraphersguild.org
PO Box 3688 Merrifield VA 22116
Ph: 301-897-8637

Calligraphic Arts, Association for   www.calligraphicarts.org
1223 Woodward Ave South Bend IN 46616
Ph: 574-287-2189 ▪ Fx: 574-233-6229

Calligraphy, Society for   www.societyforcalligraphy.org
PO Box 64174 Los Angeles CA 90064
Ph: 323-931-6146

Calorie Control Council   www.caloriecontrol.org
5775 Peachtree-Dunwoody Rd Bldg G Suite 500 Atlanta GA 30342
Ph: 404-252-3663 ▪ Fx: 404-252-0774

Calvin Coolidge Memorial Foundation   www.calvin-coolidge.org
PO Box 97 Plymouth VT 05056
Ph: 802-672-3389 ▪ Fx: 802-672-3369

CAM International   caminternational.gospelcom.net
8625 La Prada Dr Dallas TX 75228
Ph: 214-327-8206 ▪ Fx: 214-327-8201 ▪ TF: 800-366-2264

Camara de Comercio Latina de Estados Unidos   www.camacol.org
1417 W Flagler St Miami FL 33135
Ph: 305-642-3870 ▪ Fx: 305-642-0653

Camaro Club, Worldwide   www.worldwidecamaro.com
5140 S Washington Ave Titusville FL 32780
Ph: 321-269-9680 ▪ Fx: 321-383-2059 ▪ TF: 800-456-1957

Cambodian Buddhist Society   www.cambodian-buddhist.org
13800 New Hampshire Ave Silver Spring MD 20904
Ph: 301-622-6544

Cambridge In America   www.cantab.org
309 W 49th St 4th Fl New York NY 10019
Ph: 212-984-0960 ▪ Fx: 212-984-0970

Camel Hair Manufacturers Institute, Cashmere &   www.cashmere.org
6 Becaon St Suite 1125 Boston MA 02108
Ph: 617-542-7481 ▪ Fx: 617-542-2199

Camerawork, San Francisco   www.sfcamerawork.org
1246 Folsom St San Francisco CA 94103
Ph: 415-863-1001 ▪ Fx: 415-863-1015

Camille & Henry Dreyfus Foundation   www.dreyfus.org
555 Madison Ave New York NY 10022
Ph: 212-753-1760

Camp Association, National   www.summercamp.org
610 5th Ave PO Box 5371 New York NY 10185
Ph: 845-354-5504 ▪ Fx: 845-354-5501 ▪ TF: 800-966-2267

Camp Counselor Program, YMCA International   www.ymcaiccp.org
5 W 63rd St 2nd Fl New York NY 10023
Ph: 212-727-8800 ▪ Fx: 212-727-8814

Camp Fire Conservation Fund Inc
230 Camp Fire Rd Chappaqua NY 10514
Ph: 914-941-0199 ▪ Fx: 914-923-0977

Camp Fire USA   www.campfire.org
4601 Madison Ave Kansas City MO 64112
Ph: 816-756-1950 ▪ Fx: 816-756-0258

Camp Nurses, Association of   www.campnurse.org
8630 Thorsonveien Rd NE Bemidji MN 56601
Ph: 218-586-2633 ▪ Fx: 218-586-3661

Campaign for America's Future   www.ourfuture.org
1025 Connecticut Ave NW Suite 205 Washington DC 20036
Ph: 202-955-5665 ▪ Fx: 202-955-5606

(Campaign Finance Reform) Public Campaign   www.publiccampaign.org
1320 19th St NW Suite M-1 Washington DC 20036
Ph: 202-293-0222 ▪ Fx: 202-293-0202

Campaign Fund, Women's   www.wcfonline.org
734 15th St NW Suite 500 Washington DC 20005
Ph: 202-393-8164 ▪ Fx: 202-393-0649 ▪ TF: 800-446-8170

Campaign for Working Families   www.campaignforfamilies.org
2800 Shirlington Rd Suite 605 Arlington VA 22206
Ph: 703-671-8800 ▪ Fx: 703-671-8899

Campbell J Bulow Foundation
50 Hurt Plaza Suite 850 Atlanta GA 30303
Ph: 404-658-9066 ▪ Fx: 404-659-4802

Campbell Joseph Foundation   www.jcf.org
PO Box 36 San Anselmo CA 94979
Ph: 800-330-6984

Campers, International Brotherhood of Motorcycle   www.ibmc.org
PO Box 375 Helper UT 84526
Ph: 435-650-3290

Campers & RVers, Family   www.fcrv.org
4808 Transit Rd Bldg 2 Depew NY 14043
Ph: 716-668-6242 ▪ TF: 800-245-9755

Campgrounds, National Association of RV Parks &   www.arvc.org
113 Park Ave Falls Church VA 22046
Ph: 703-241-8801 ▪ Fx: 703-241-1004

Camping Association, American   www.acacamps.org
5000 SR-67 N Martinsville IN 46151
Ph: 765-342-8456 ▪ Fx: 765-349-6357 ▪ TF: 800-428-2267

Camping International/USA, Christian   cci.gospelcom.net/ccihome
PO Box 62189 Colorado Springs CO 80962
Ph: 719-260-9400 ▪ Fx: 719-260-6398

Camps, Association of Jewish Sponsored   www.jewishcamps.org
130 E 59th St   New York NY 10022
Ph: 212-751-0477 ▪ Fx: 212-755-9183

Campus Activities, National Association for   www.naca.org
13 Harbison Way   Columbia SC 29212
Ph: 803-732-6222 ▪ Fx: 803-749-1047 ▪ TF: 800-845-2338

Campus Children's Centers, National Coalition for   www.campuschildren.org
Univ of Northern Iowa 119 Schindler Education Ctr   Cedar Falls
IA 50614
Ph: 319-273-3113 ▪ Fx: 319-273-3109 ▪ TF: 800-813-8207

Campus Compact   www.compact.org
Brown Univ Box 1970   Providence RI 02912
Ph: 401-867-3950 ▪ Fx: 401-867-3925

Campus Crusade for Christ International   www.ccci.org
100 Lake Hart Dr   Orlando FL 32832
Ph: 407-826-2000 ▪ Fx: 407-826-2749 ▪ TF: 877-924-7478

Campus Law Enforcement Administrators, International Association of   www.iaclea.org
342 W Main St   West Hartford CT 06117
Ph: 860-586-7517 ▪ Fx: 860-586-7550

Campus Ministries USA, Chi Alpha   www.chialpha.com
3728 W Chestnut Expy   Springfield MO 65802
Ph: 417-862-2781 ▪ Fx: 417-865-9947

Campus Ministry Association, Catholic   www.ccmanet.org
1118 Pendleton St Suite 300   Cincinnati OH 45210
Ph: 513-842-0167 ▪ Fx: 513-842-0171 ▪ TF: 888-714-6631

Campus Ministry Association, National   www.campusministry.net
2 Ocean Dune Cir   Palm Coast FL 32137
Ph: 386-446-8066

Can Collectors, National Pop   www.one-mans-junk.com/npcc/npcc.htm

Can Manufacturers Institute Inc   www.cancentral.com
1625 Massachusetts Ave NW Suite 500   Washington DC 20036
Ph: 202-232-4677 ▪ Fx: 202-232-5756

Can & Tube Institute, Composite   www.cctiwdc.org
50 S Pickett St   Alexandria VA 22310
Ph: 703-823-7234 ▪ Fx: 703-823-7237

Canada Foundation, Heritage   www.heritagecanada.org
5 Blackburn Ave   Ottawa ON K1N8A2
Ph: 613-237-1066 ▪ Fx: 613-237-5987

Canada Labour Congress   www.clc-ctc.ca
2841 Riverside Dr   Ottawa ON K1V8X7
Ph: 613-521-3400 ▪ Fx: 613-521-4655

Canada-US Business Association
600 Renaissance Ctr Suite 1100   Detroit MI 48243
Ph: 313-567-2208 ▪ Fx: 313-567-2164

Canada's Research-Based Pharmaceutical Companies   www.canadapharma.org
55 Metcalfe St Suite 1220   Ottawa ON K1P6L5
Ph: 613-236-0455 ▪ Fx: 613-236-6756

Canadian Academy of Sport Medicine   www.casm-acms.org
1010 Polytek St Unit 14 Suite 100   Ottawa ON K1J9H9
Ph: 613-748-5851 ▪ Fx: 613-748-5792 ▪ TF: 877-585-2394

Canadian American Business Council   www.canambusco.org
1900 K St NW   Washington DC 20006
Ph: 202-496-7340 ▪ Fx: 202-496-7756

Canadian Association of Chemical Distributors   www.cacd.ca
627 Lyons Ln Suite 301   Oakville ON L6J5Z7
Ph: 905-844-9140 ▪ Fx: 905-844-5706

Canadian Association of Children's Librarians   www.cla.ca/divisions/capl/cacl.htm
328 Frank St   Ottawa ON K2P0X8
Ph: 613-232-9625 ▪ Fx: 613-563-9895

Canadian Association of College & University   www.cla.ca/divisions/cacul/cacul.htm
Libraries   328 Frank St   Ottawa ON K2P0X8
Ph: 613-232-9625 ▪ Fx: 613-563-9895

Canadian Association of Law Libraries   www.callacbd.ca
PO Box 1570   Kingston ON K7L5C8
Ph: 613-531-9338 ▪ Fx: 613-531-0626

Canadian Association of Pharmacy Technicians   www.capt.ca
PO Box 1271 Stn A   Toronto ON M4Y2V8
Ph: 416-410-1142

Canadian Association of Private Language Schools   www.capls.ca
12880 54A Ave   Surrey BC V3X3C9
Ph: 604-507-2577 ▪ Fx: 604-502-0373

Canadian Association of Public Libraries   www.cla.ca/divisions/capl/capl.htm
328 Frank St   Ottawa ON K2P0X8
Ph: 613-232-9625 ▪ Fx: 613-563-9895

Canadian Association of Retired Persons   www.50plus.com
1304-27 Queen St E   Toronto ON M5C2M6
Ph: 416-363-8748 ▪ Fx: 416-363-8747 ▪ TF: 800-363-9736

Canadian Association of Special Libraries &   www.cla.ca/caslis/index.htm
Information Services   328 Frank St   Ottawa ON K2P0X8
Ph: 613-232-9625 ▪ Fx: 613-563-9895

Canadian Automobile Association   www.caa.ca
1145 Hunt Club Rd Suite 200   Ottawa ON K1V0Y3
Ph: 613-247-0117 ▪ Fx: 613-247-0118

Canadian Bigfoot Information Center, Michigan/
152 W Sherman   Caro MI 48723
Ph: 989-673-2715

Canadian Council for International Cooperation   www.ccic.ca
1 Nicholas St Suite 300   Ottawa ON K1N7B7
Ph: 613-241-7007 ▪ Fx: 613-241-5302

Canadian Federation of Humane Societies   www.cfhs.ca
30 Concourse Gate Suite 102   Nepean ON K2E7V7
Ph: 613-224-8072 ▪ Fx: 613-723-0252 ▪ TF: 888-678-2347

Canadian Genealogical Society, American-   www.acgs.org
PO Box 6478   Manchester NH 03108
Ph: 603-622-1554 ▪ Fx: 603-624-8843

Canadian Health Libraries Association   www.chla-absc.ca
3324 Yonge St   Toronto ON M4N3R1
Ph: 416-485-0377 ▪ Fx: 416-485-6877

Canadian Kennel Club   www.ckc.ca
89 Skyway Ave Suite 100   Etobicoke ON M9W6R4
Ph: 416-675-5511 ▪ Fx: 416-675-6506 ▪ TF: 800-250-8040

Canadian Library Association   www.cla.ca
328 Frank St   Ottawa ON K2P0X8
Ph: 613-232-9625 ▪ Fx: 613-563-9895

Canadian Library Trustees Association   www.cla.ca/divisions/clta/clta.htm
328 Frank St   Ottawa ON K2P0X8
Ph: 613-232-9625 ▪ Fx: 613-563-9895

Canadian Marine Manufacturers Association   www.cmma.ca
243 North Service Rd W Suite 106   Oakville ON L6M3E5
Ph: 905-845-4999 ▪ Fx: 905-845-1701

Canadian Medical Association   www.cma.ca
1867 Alta Vista Dr   Ottawa ON K1G3Y6
Ph: 613-731-9331 ▪ Fx: 613-731-7314

Canadian National Institute for the Blind   www.cnib.ca
1929 Bayview Ave   Toronto ON M4G3E8
Ph: 416-480-7503

Canadian Nature Federation   www.cnf.ca
1 Nicholas St Suite 606   Ottawa ON K1N7B7
Ph: 613-562-3447 ▪ Fx: 613-562-3371 ▪ TF: 800-267-4088

Canadian Parks & Recreation Association   www.cpra.ca
2197 Riverside Dr Suite 404   Ottawa ON K1H7X3
Ph: 613-523-5315 ▪ Fx: 613-523-1182

Canadian Parks & Wilderness Society   www.cpaws.org
880 Wellington St Suite 506   Ottawa ON K1R6K7
Ph: 613-569-7226 ▪ Fx: 613-569-7098 ▪ TF: 800-333-9453

Canadian Peregrine Foundation   www.peregrine-foundation.ca
250 Merton St Suite 104   Toronto ON M4S1B1
Ph: 416-481-1233 ▪ Fx: 416-481-7158 ▪ TF: 888-709-3944

Canadian School Library Association   www.cla.ca/divisions/csla
328 Frank St   Ottawa ON K2P0X8
Ph: 613-232-9625 ▪ Fx: 613-563-9895

Canadian Studies in the US, Association for   www.acsus.org
1317 F St NW Suite 920   Washington DC 20004
Ph: 202-393-2580 ▪ Fx: 202-393-2582

Canadian Veterinary Medical Association   www.cvma-acmv.org
339 Booth St   Ottawa ON K1R7K1
Ph: 613-236-1162 ▪ Fx: 613-236-9681

Canadian Water Resources Association   www.cwra.org
400 Clyde Rd PO Box 1329   Cambridge ON N1R7G6
Ph: 519-622-4764 ▪ Fx: 519-621-4844

Canadian Wildlife Federation   www.cwf-fcf.org
350 Michael Cowpland Dr   Kanata ON K2M2W1
Ph: 613-599-9594 ▪ Fx: 613-599-4428 ▪ TF: 800-563-9453

Canadians, Council of   www.canadians.org
151 Slater St Suite 502   Ottawa ON K1P5H3
Ph: 613-233-2773 ▪ Fx: 613-233-6776 ▪ TF: 800-387-7177

Canal Society of New York State   www.canalsnys.org

CANARIE   www.canarie.ca
110 O'Connor St 4th Fl   Ottawa ON K1P1H1
Ph: 613-943-5454 ▪ Fx: 613-943-5443

Cancer, Association for Research of Childhood   www.arocc.org
PO Box 251   Buffalo NY 14225
Ph: 716-681-4433

Cancer Care Inc   www.cancercare.org
275 7th Ave 22nd Fl   New York NY 10001
Ph: 212-712-8080 ▪ Fx: 212-771-2845 ▪ TF: 800-813-4673

Cancer Centers, Association of Community   www.accc-cancer.org
11600 Nebel St Suite 201   Rockville MD 20852
Ph: 301-984-9496 ▪ Fx: 301-770-1949

Cancer Coalition, National Breast   www.stopbreastcancer.org
1707 L St NW Suite 1060   Washington DC 20036
Ph: 202-296-7477 ▪ Fx: 202-265-6854 ▪ TF: 800-622-2838

Cancer Coalition, National Ovarian   www.ovarian.org
500 NE Spanish River Blvd Suite 14   Boca Raton FL 33431
Ph: 561-393-0005 ▪ Fx: 561-393-7275 ▪ TF: 888-682-7426

Cancer Control Society   www.cancercontrolsociety.com
2043 N Berendo St   Los Angeles CA 90027
Ph: 323-663-7801 ▪ Fx: 323-663-7757

Cancer Foundation, Candlelighters Childhood   www.candlelighters.org
PO Box 498   Kensington MD 20895
Ph: 301-962-3520 ▪ Fx: 301-962-3521 ▪ TF: 800-366-2223

Cancer Foundation Inc, Carcinoid   www.carcinoid.org
333 Mamaroneck Ave Suite 492   White Plains NY 10605
Ph: 212-722-3132 ▪ Fx: 212-683-5919

Cancer Foundation, Gynecologic   www.wcn.org/gcf
230 W Monroe St Suite 2528   Chicago IL 60606
Ph: 312-578-1439 ▪ Fx: 312-578-9769

Cancer Foundation, Oral   www.oralcancerfoundation.org
3419 Via Lido Suite 205   Newport Beach CA 92663
Ph: 949-646-8000 ▪ Fx: 949-496-3331

Cancer Foundation, RA Bloch   www.blochcancer.org
4400 Main St   Kansas City MO 64111
Ph: 816-932-8453 ▪ Fx: 816-931-7486 ▪ TF: 800-433-0464

Cancer Foundation, Skin   www.skincancer.org
245 5th Ave Suite 1403   New York NY 10016
Ph: 212-725-5176 ▪ Fx: 212-725-5751 ▪ TF: 800-754-6490

Cancer Foundation, Susan G Komen Breast   www.komen.org
5005 LBJ Fwy Suite 250   Dallas TX 75244
Ph: 972-855-1600 ▪ Fx: 972-855-1605 ▪ TF: 800-462-9273

Cancer Information Service   cis.nci.nih.gov
National Cancer Institute 9000 Rockville Pike Bldg 31 Rm
10A16   Bethesda MD 20892
Ph: 301-496-4000 ▪ Fx: 301-496-8664 ▪ TF: 800-422-6237

(Cancer) Make Today Count
1235 E Cherokee St   Springfield MO 65804
Ph: 417-885-3324 ▪ Fx: 417-888-7426 ▪ TF: 800-432-2273

Cancer, Mothers Supporting Daughters with Breast
21710 Bayshore Rd   Chestertown MD 21620
Ph: 410-778-1982 ▪ Fx: 410-778-1411
www.mothersdaughters.org

Cancer National Alliance, Ovarian
910 17th St NW Suite 413   Washington DC 20006
Ph: 202-331-1332 ▪ Fx: 202-292-2292
www.ovariancancer.org

Cancer Network, Women's
230 W Monroe St Suite 2528   Chicago IL 60606
Ph: 312-578-1439 ▪ Fx: 312-578-9769
www.wcn.org

Cancer Organization, Y-ME National Breast
212 W Van Buren St   Chicago IL 60607
Ph: 312-986-8338 ▪ Fx: 312-294-8597 ▪ TF: 800-221-2141
www.y-me.org

Cancer Organizations, National Alliance of Breast
9 E 37th St 10th Fl   New York NY 10016
Ph: 212-889-0606 ▪ Fx: 212-689-1213 ▪ TF: 888-806-2226
www.nabco.org

Cancer, People Against
604 East St PO Box 10   Otho IA 50569
Ph: 515-972-4444 ▪ Fx: 515-972-4415
www.peopleagainstcancer.com

Cancer Prevention, Institute for
390 5th Ave   New York NY 10018
Ph: 212-953-1900 ▪ Fx: 212-687-2339
www.ifcp.us

Cancer Prevention Resource Center, National HPV & Cervical   PO Box 13827   Research Triangle Park NC 27709
Ph: 919-361-8400 ▪ Fx: 919-361-8425
www.ashastd.org/hpvccrc

Cancer Registrars Association, National
1340 Braddock Pl Suite 203   Alexandria VA 22314
Ph: 703-299-6640 ▪ Fx: 703-299-6620
www.ncra-usa.org

Cancer Registry, Gilda Radner Familial Ovarian
Roswell Park Cancer Institute Elm & Carlton Sts   Buffalo NY 14263
Ph: 716-845-4503 ▪ Fx: 716-845-8266 ▪ TF: 800-682-7426
www.ovariancancer.com

Cancer Research, American Association for
615 Chestnut St 17th Fl   Philadelphia PA 19106
Ph: 215-440-9300 ▪ Fx: 215-440-9313
www.aacr.org

Cancer Research Foundation of America
1600 Duke St Suite 110   Alexandria VA 22314
Ph: 703-836-4412 ▪ Fx: 703-836-4413 ▪ TF: 800-227-2732
www.crfa.org

Cancer Research, Native American
3022 S Nova Rd   Pine CO 80470
Ph: 303-838-9359 ▪ Fx: 303-838-7629
natamcancer.org

(Cancer) Sisters Network
8787 Woodway Dr Suite 4206   Houston TX 77063
Ph: 713-781-0255 ▪ Fx: 713-780-8998
sistersnetworkinc.org

Cancer Society, American
1599 Clifton Rd NE   Atlanta GA 30329
Ph: 404-320-3333 ▪ Fx: 404-329-7985 ▪ TF: 800-227-2345
www.cancer.org

Cancer Society, National Children's
1015 Locust St Suite 600   Saint Louis MO 63101
Ph: 314-241-1600 ▪ Fx: 314-241-6949 ▪ TF: 800-532-6459
www.children-cancer.org

Cancer Society, Veterinary
PO Box 1763   Spring Valley CA 91979
Ph: 619-474-8929 ▪ Fx: 619-474-8947
www.vetcancersociety.org

Cancer Survivorship, National Coalition for
1010 Wayne Ave Suite 770   Silver Spring MD 20910
Ph: 301-650-9127 ▪ Fx: 301-565-9670
www.canceradvocacy.org

Cancer Therapy, Foundation for Advancement in
PO Box 1242 Old Chelsea Stn   New York NY 10113
Ph: 212-741-2790
www.fact-ltd.org

Cancer Treatment, Patient Advocates for Advanced
1143 Parmelee NW   Grand Rapids MI 49504
Ph: 616-453-1477 ▪ Fx: 616-453-1846
www.paactusa.org

(Cancer) United Order True Sisters Inc
100 State St Suite 1020   Albany NY 12207
Ph: 518-436-1670 ▪ Fx: 518-436-1573
www.uots.org

Candle Association, National
1156 15th St Suite 900   Washington DC 20005
Ph: 202-393-2210 ▪ Fx: 202-393-0336
www.candles.org

Candlelighters Childhood Cancer Foundation
PO Box 498   Kensington MD 20895
Ph: 301-962-3520 ▪ Fx: 301-962-3521 ▪ TF: 800-366-2223
www.candlelighters.org

Candy Technologists, American Association of
175 Rock Rd   Glen Rock NJ 07452
Ph: 201-652-2655 ▪ Fx: 201-652-3419
www.aactcandy.org

Canid Survival & Research Center, Wild
PO Box 760   Eureka MO 63025
Ph: 636-938-5900 ▪ Fx: 636-938-6490
www.wolfsanctuary.org

Canine Association, US Police
PO Box 80   Springboro OH 45066
Ph: 800-531-1614
www.uspcak9.com

Canine Companions for Independence
2965 Dutton Ave   Santa Rosa CA 95407
Ph: 707-577-1700 ▪ Fx: 707-577-1711 ▪ TF: 800-572-2275
www.caninecompanions.org

Canine Defense Fund
1654 Columbia Tpke   Castleton on Hudson NY 12033
Ph: 518-477-8469 ▪ Fx: 518-477-4034
www.adoa.org/participate/cdf00.php

(Cannabis) Business Alliance for Commerce in Hemp
PO Box 1716   El Cerrito CA 94530
Ph: 510-215-8326
www.chrisconrad.com

Canners Association, National Meat
1700 N Moore St Suite 1600   Arlington VA 22209
Ph: 703-841-2400 ▪ Fx: 703-527-0938
www.meatami.com/content/AboutAMI/canners.htm

Canoe Association, American
7432 Alban Station Blvd Suite B-232   Springfield VA 22150
Ph: 703-451-0141
www.acanet.org

Canoe Association, US
606 Ross St   Middletown OH 45044
Ph: 513-422-3739
www.uscanoe.com

Canoe Heritage Association Ltd, Wooden
www.wcha.org

Canoe/Kayak, USA
230 S Tryon St Suite 220   Charlotte NC 28202
Ph: 704-348-4330 ▪ Fx: 704-348-4418
www.usacanoekayak.org

Canola Association, US
600 Penn Ave SE Suite 320   Washington DC 20003
Ph: 202-969-8113 ▪ Fx: 202-969-7036

Canon Law Society of America
Catholic Univ Caldwell Hall Rm 431   Washington DC 20064
Ph: 202-269-3491 ▪ Fx: 202-319-5719
www.clsa.org

Canon Law Society, North American
www.rbsocc.org/organizations.html

Canonical Orthodox Bishops in the Americas, Standing Conference of
8 E 79th St   New York NY 10021
Ph: 212-570-3500 ▪ Fx: 212-570-3569
www.scoba.us

Cantors, American Conference of
1360 Center Dr Suite 110   Atlanta GA 30338
Ph: 770-390-0006 ▪ Fx: 770-390-0020 ▪ TF: 886-711-0006
www.accantors.org

Cantors Assembly
Jewish Theological Seminary 3080 Broadway Suite 613   New York NY 10027
Ph: 212-678-8834 ▪ Fx: 212-662-8989
www.cantors.org

Canyonlands Field Institute
PO Box 68   Moab UT 84532
Ph: 435-259-7750 ▪ Fx: 435-259-2335 ▪ TF: 800-860-5262
www.canyonlandsfieldinst.org

Cape Cod, Association for the Preservation of
PO Box 398   Barnstable MA 02630
Ph: 508-362-4226 ▪ Fx: 508-362-4227 ▪ TF: 877-955-4142
www.apcc.org

Capital Association, National Community
620 Chestnut St Suite 572   Philadelphia PA 19106
Ph: 215-923-4754 ▪ Fx: 215-923-4755
www.communitycapital.org

Capital Formation, American Council for
1750 K St NW Suite 400   Washington DC 20006
Ph: 202-293-5811 ▪ Fx: 202-785-8165
www.accf.org

Capital Markets Credit Analysis Society Inc
151 Herricks Rd Suite 1   Garden City Park NY 11040
Ph: 516-739-2510 ▪ Fx: 516-739-3803 ▪ TF: 800-284-6228
www.cmcas.org

Capital Press Club
PO Box 19403   Washington DC 20036
Ph: 202-628-1122
www.cpcomm.org

Capital Research Center
1513 16th St NW   Washington DC 20036
Ph: 202-483-6900 ▪ Fx: 202-483-6902 ▪ TF: 800-459-3950
www.capitalresearch.org

Capitant, Association Henri
Louisiana State Univ Paul M Hebert Law Ctr   Baton Rouge LA 70803
Ph: 225-578-1126 ▪ Fx: 225-578-3677
host.law.lsu.edu/ahclouisiane

Capitol Hill Club
300 1st St SE   Washington DC 20003
Ph: 202-484-4590 ▪ Fx: 202-479-9110
www.capitolhillclub.com

Capitol Hill, National Republican Club of
300 1st St SE   Washington DC 20003
Ph: 202-484-4590 ▪ Fx: 202-479-9110
www.capitolhillclub.com

Capitol Hill Restoration Society
420 10th St NE PO Box 15264   Washington DC 20003
Ph: 202-543-0425
www.chrs.org

Capitol Historical Society, US
200 Maryland Ave NE   Washington DC 20002
Ph: 202-543-8919 ▪ Fx: 202-544-8244
www.uschs.org

CapitolWatch
PO Box 71   Great Falls VA 22066
Ph: 202-544-2600 ▪ Fx: 703-430-6378
www.capitolwatch.org

Captive Nations Committee, National
PO Box 1171   Washington DC 20013
Ph: 202-547-0018 ▪ Fx: 202-543-5502

Car Care Council
4600 East-West Hwy Suite 300   Bethesda MD 20814
Ph: 240-333-1088
www.carcare.org

Car Collectors Association, Toy
PO Box 1824   Bend OR 97709
Ph: 541-318-7176
www.toynutz.com/TCCA.html

Car & Truck Rental Independents & Franchisees, Association for
4248 Park Glen Rd   Minneapolis MN 55416
Ph: 952-928-4645 ▪ Fx: 952-929-1318 ▪ TF: 888-200-2795
www.actif.org

Caravan Club International, Wally Byam
PO Box 612   Jackson Center OH 45334
Ph: 937-596-5211 ▪ Fx: 937-596-5542
www.wbcci.org

Carbide Producers Association, Cemented
30200 Detroit Rd   Cleveland OH 44145
Ph: 440-899-0010 ▪ Fx: 440-892-1404
www.ccpa.org

Carbide & Tool Engineers, Society of
ASM International 9639 Kinsman Rd   Materials Park OH 44072
Ph: 440-338-5151 ▪ Fx: 440-338-4634
www.scte10.org

Carbon Monoxide Referral & Resources
508 Westgate Rd   Baltimore MD 21229
Ph: 410-362-6400 ▪ Fx: 410-362-6401
www.mcsrr.org

Carbon Society, American
www.americancarbonsociety.org

Carcinoid Cancer Foundation Inc
333 Mamaroneck Ave Suite 492   White Plains NY 10605
Ph: 212-722-3132 ▪ Fx: 212-683-5919
www.carcinoid.org

Card Manufacturers Association, International
PO Box 727   Princeton Junction NJ 08550
Ph: 609-799-4900 ▪ Fx: 609-799-7032
www.icma.com

Cardiac Angiography & Interventions, Society for
9111 Old Georgetown Rd   Bethesda MD 20814
Ph: 301-581-3450 ▪ Fx: 301-581-3408 ▪ TF: 800-992-7224
www.scai.org

Cardiac Disease, International Society for Adult Congenital
1500 Sunday Dr Suite 102   Raleigh NC 27607
Ph: 919-861-5578 ▪ Fx: 919-787-4916
www.isaccd.org

Cardiac Imaging, North American Society for www.nasci.org
PO Box 20085 Stanford CA 94309
Ph: 650-216-6621 ▪ Fx: 650-556-1678

Cardiac Surgery, International Society for Minimally Invasive www.ismics.org
900 Cummings Ctr Suite 221-U Beverly MA 01915
Ph: 978-927-8330 ▪ Fx: 978-524-8890

Cardigan Welsh Corgi Club of America www.cardigancorgis.com
7446 Park Pl Boulder CO 80301
Ph: 303-530-7107

Cardinal Mindszenty Foundation www.mindszenty.org
PO Box 11321 Saint Louis MO 63105
Ph: 314-727-6279 ▪ Fx: 314-727-5897

Cardiologists, Association of Black www.abcardio.org
6849 Peachtree Dunwoody Rd NE Bldg 2 Atlanta GA 30328
Ph: 678-302-4222 ▪ Fx: 678-302-4223

Cardiology, American College of www.acc.org
9111 Old Georgetown Rd Bethesda MD 20814
Ph: 301-897-5400 ▪ Fx: 301-897-9745 ▪ TF: 800-253-4636

Cardiology, American Society of Nuclear www.asnc.org
9111 Old Georgetown Rd Bethesda MD 20814
Ph: 301-493-2360 ▪ Fx: 301-493-2376

Cardiology, Association of Professors of www.cardiologyprofessors.org
9111 Old Georgetown Rd Bethesda MD 20814
Ph: 301-493-2330 ▪ Fx: 301-897-9745

Cardiology, Society of Geriatric www.sgcard.org
9111 Old Georgetown Rd Bethesda MD 20814
Ph: 301-581-3449 ▪ Fx: 301-581-3456

Cardiovascular Administrators, www.aameda.org/Specialtygroups/cardiology.html
American College of 701 Lee St Suite 600 Des Plaines IL
60016
Ph: 847-759-8601 ▪ Fx: 847-759-8602

Cardiovascular Anesthesiologists, Society of www.scahq.org
2209 Dickens Rd Richmond VA 23230
Ph: 804-282-0484 ▪ Fx: 804-282-0090

Cardiovascular Magnetic Resonance, Society for www.scmr.org
19 Mantua Rd Mount Royal NJ 08061
Ph: 856-423-8955 ▪ Fx: 856-423-3420

Cardiovascular Professionals, Alliance of www.acp-online.org
4356 Bonney Rd Suite 103 Virginia Beach VA 23452
Ph: 757-497-1225 ▪ Fx: 757-497-3481

Cardiovascular Professionals, Society of Invasive www.sicp.com
PO Box 61606 Virginia Beach VA 23466
Ph: 757-497-3694 ▪ Fx: 757-497-0010

Cardiovascular & Pulmonary Rehabilitation, American Association of www.aacvpr.org
401 N Michigan Ave Suite 2200 Chicago IL 60611
Ph: 312-321-5146 ▪ Fx: 312-527-6635

Cardiovascular Surgery, Association of Physician Assistants in www.apacvs.org
PO Box 4834 Englewood CO 80155
Ph: 303-221-5651 ▪ Fx: 303-771-2550 ▪ TF: 877-221-5651

Cardiovascular & Wellness Nutritionists, Sports www.scandpg.org
PO Box 60820 Colorado Springs CO 80960
Ph: 719-635-6005 ▪ Fx: 719-635-3587

Care Alliance, National School-Age www.nsaca.org
1137 Washington Ave Boston MA 02124
Ph: 617-298-5012 ▪ Fx: 617-298-5022

Care, American Association for Continuity of www.continuityofcare.com
PO Box 532 Dunedin FL 34697
Ph: 727-738-9653 ▪ Fx: 727-738-8099 ▪ TF: 800-816-1575

CARE USA www.care.org
151 Ellis St NE Atlanta GA 30303
Ph: 404-681-2552 ▪ Fx: 404-589-2630 ▪ TF: 800-422-7385

Career Assessment Professionals, Vocational Evaluation & www.vecap.org
PO Box 26273 Colorado Springs CO 80936
Ph: 719-638-4787 ▪ Fx: 719-638-6153

Career Coaches, Professional Association of Resume Writers & www.parw.com
1388 Brightwaters Blvd NE Saint Petersburg FL 33704
Ph: 727-821-2274 ▪ Fx: 727-894-1277 ▪ TF: 800-822-7279

Career College Association www.career.org
10 G St NE Suite 750 Washington DC 20002
Ph: 202-336-6700 ▪ Fx: 202-336-6828

Career & Community Leaders of America, Family www.fcclainc.org
1910 Association Dr Reston VA 20191
Ph: 703-476-4900 ▪ Fx: 703-860-2713 ▪ TF: 800-234-4425

Career Development Association, National www.ncda.org
10820 E 45th St Suite 210 Tulsa OK 74146
Ph: 918-663-7060 ▪ Fx: 918-663-7058 ▪ TF: 866-367-6232

Career Education, American Association for
2900 Amby Pl Hermosa Beach CA 90254
Ph: 310-376-7378 ▪ Fx: 310-376-2926

Career Management Consulting Firms International, Association of www.aocfi.org
204 'E' St NE Washington DC 20002
Ph: 202-547-6344 ▪ Fx: 202-547-6348

Career Planning & Adult Development Network www.careernetwork.org
PO Box 1484 Pacifica CA 94044
Ph: 650-359-6911 ▪ Fx: 650-359-3089

Career Professionals International, Association of www.acpinternational.org
204 'E' St NE Washington DC 20002
Ph: 202-547-6377 ▪ Fx: 202-547-6348

Career & Technical Education, Association for www.acteonline.org
1410 King St Alexandria VA 22314
Ph: 703-683-3111 ▪ Fx: 703-683-7424 ▪ TF: 800-826-9972

Career Transition for Dancers www.careertransition.org
165 W 64th St Suite 701 New York NY 10036
Ph: 212-764-0172 ▪ Fx: 212-764-0343

Caregiver Alliance, Family www.caregiver.org
690 Market St Suite 600 San Francisco CA 94104
Ph: 415-434-3388 ▪ Fx: 415-434-3508 ▪ TF: 800-445-8106

Caregivers, Association of Brethren www.brethren.org/abc
1451 Dundee Ave Elgin IL 60120
Ph: 847-742-5100 ▪ Fx: 847-742-5160 ▪ TF: 800-323-8039

Caregivers Association, National Family www.nfcacares.org
10400 Connecticut Ave Suite 500 Kensington MD 20895
Ph: 301-942-6430 ▪ Fx: 301-942-2302 ▪ TF: 800-896-3650

Caregiving Foundation, National www.caregivingfoundation.org
801 N Pitt St Suite 116 Alexandria VA 22314
Ph: 703-299-9300 ▪ Fx: 703-299-9304 ▪ TF: 800-930-1357

Caregiving, National Alliance for www.caregiving.org
4720 Montgomery Ln Suite 642 Bethesda MD 20814
Ph: 301-718-8444 ▪ Fx: 301-652-7711

Cargo Airline Association
1220 19th St NW Suite 400 Washington DC 20036
Ph: 202-293-1030 ▪ Fx: 202-293-4377

Cargo Bureau Inc, National www.natcargo.org
17 Battery Pl Suite 1232 New York NY 10004
Ph: 212-785-8300 ▪ Fx: 212-785-8333

Cargo Gear Bureau, International www.icgb.com
120 W 44th St Suite 401 New York NY 10036
Ph: 917-510-9938 ▪ Fx: 917-510-9974

Cargo Security Council, National www.cargosecurity.com
3 Church Cir Suite 292 Annapolis MD 21401
Ph: 410-956-0941 ▪ Fx: 410-956-0679 ▪ TF: 800-976-0403

Cargo War Risk Reinsurance Exchange, American www.amich.org/acwHome.htm
30 Broad St 7th Fl New York NY 10004
Ph: 212-405-2835 ▪ Fx: 212-240-0654

Caribbean American Chamber of Commerce & Industry
Brooklyn Navy Yard Bldg 5 63 Flushing Ave Brooklyn NY
11205
Ph: 718-834-4544 ▪ Fx: 718-834-9774

Caribbean-Central American Action www.claa.org
1818 'N' St NW Suite 500 Washington DC 20036
Ph: 202-466-7464 ▪ Fx: 202-822-0075

Caribbean Conservation Corp www.cccturtle.org
4424 NW 13th St Suite A-1 Gainesville FL 32609
Ph: 352-373-6441 ▪ Fx: 352-375-2449 ▪ TF: 800-678-7853

Caribbean Culture Center
408 W 58th St New York NY 10019
Ph: 212-307-7420 ▪ Fx: 212-315-1086

Caribbean, Ecumenical Program on Central America & the www.epica.org
1470 Irving St NW Washington DC 20010
Ph: 202-332-0292 ▪ Fx: 202-332-1184

Caribbean Studies, Institute of icsdc.org
1612 7th St NW Washington DC 20001
Ph: 202-829-1887 ▪ Fx: 202-829-1667

Caring, Community of www.communityofcaring.org
1325 G St NW Washington DC 20005
Ph: 202-393-1251 ▪ Fx: 202-715-1146

Caring Inc, Partnership for www.partnershipforcaring.org
1620 'I' St NW Suite 202 Washington DC 20006
Ph: 202-296-8071 ▪ Fx: 202-296-8352 ▪ TF: 800-989-9455

Carmelite Order of the Blessed Virgin Mary of Mount carmelnet.org/toc/toc.htm
Carmel, Lay 8501 Bailey Rd Darien IL 60561
Ph: 630-969-5050 ▪ Fx: 630-969-7519

Carnegie Corp of New York www.carnegie.org
437 Madison Ave 26th Fl New York NY 10022
Ph: 212-371-3200 ▪ Fx: 212-754-4073

Carnegie Council on Ethics & International Affairs www.carnegiecouncil.org
Merrill House 170 E 64th St New York NY 10021
Ph: 212-838-4120 ▪ Fx: 212-752-2432

Carnegie Endowment for International Peace www.ceip.org
1779 Massachusetts Ave NW Washington DC 20036
Ph: 202-483-7600 ▪ Fx: 202-483-1840

Carnegie Foundation for the Advancement of Teaching www.carnegiefoundation.org
555 Middlefield Rd Menlo Park CA 94025
Ph: 650-566-5100 ▪ Fx: 650-326-0278

Carnegie Hero Fund Commission www.carnegiehero.org
425 6th Ave Suite 1640 Pittsburgh PA 15219
Ph: 412-281-1302 ▪ Fx: 412-281-5751 ▪ TF: 800-447-8900

Carnival Glass Association, International www.woodsland.com/ICGA
PO Box 306 Mentone IN 46539
Ph: 574-353-7678

Carpenters' Company of the City & County www.ushistory.org/carpentershall/company
of Philadelphia 320 Chestnut St Philadelphia PA 19106
Ph: 215-925-0167 ▪ Fx: 215-925-3880

Carpenters & Joiners of America, United Brotherhood of www.carpenters.org
101 Constitution Ave NW Washington DC 20001
Ph: 202-546-6206 ▪ Fx: 202-543-5724

Carpenter's Legislative Improvement Committee
101 Constitution Ave NW 10th Fl Washington DC 20001
Ph: 202-546-6206 ▪ Fx: 202-547-8979

Carpet Cushion Council www.carpetcushion.org
PO Box 546 Riverside CT 06878
Ph: 203-637-1312 ▪ Fx: 203-698-1022

Carpet & Rug Institute www.carpet-rug.com
310 S Holiday Ave Dalton GA 30720
Ph: 706-278-3176 ▪ Fx: 706-278-8835 ▪ TF: 800-882-8846

Carr Center for Human Rights Policy www.ksg.harvard.edu/cchrp
Harvard Univ John F Kennedy School of Government 79 JFK
St Cambridge MA 02138
Ph: 617-495-5819 ▪ Fx: 617-495-4297

Carreras International Leukemia Foundation, Friends www.carrerasfoundation.org
of the Jose 1100 Fairview Ave N D5-100 PO Box
19024 Seattle WA 98109
Ph: 206-667-7108 ▪ Fx: 206-667-6498

Carriage Association of America www.caaonline.com
177 Pointers-Auburn Rd Salem NJ 08079
Ph: 856-935-1616 ▪ Fx: 856-935-9362 ▪ TF: 800-571-1616

Carriage Club of America, Horseless www.hcca.org
49637 Hwy 41 Oakhurst CA 93644
Ph: 559-658-8800 ▪ TF: 888-832-2374

Carriers Association, Express www.expresscarriers.com
PO Box 4307 Bethlehem PA 18018
Ph: 610-740-5857 ▪ Fx: 866-322-3299 ▪ TF: 866-322-7447

Carriers' Association, Lake www.lcaships.com
614 W Superior Ave Suite 915 Cleveland OH 44113
Ph: 216-621-1107 ▪ Fx: 216-241-8262

Carriers Association, Motor Freight www.mfca.org
499 S Capitol St SW Suite 502A Washington DC 20003
Ph: 202-554-3060 ▪ Fx: 202-554-3160

Carriers & Rigging Association, Specialized www.scranet.org
2750 Prosperity Ave Suite 620 Fairfax VA 22031
Ph: 703-698-0291 ▪ Fx: 703-698-0297

Carrying Capacity Network www.carryingcapacity.org
2000 P St NW Suite 310 Washington DC 20036
Ph: 202-296-4548 ▪ Fx: 202-296-4609

(Cars) Alfa Romeo Owners Club www.aroc-usa.org
10 Raskin Rd Morristown NJ 07960
Ph: 973-285-9338 ▪ Fx: 973-285-9343

(Cars) Allante Appreciation Group www.allante.us
PO Box 342 Florala AL 36442
Ph: 800-664-5224

(Cars) AMC World Clubs www.amcwc.com
7963 Depew St Arvada CO 80003
Ph: 303-428-8760

(Cars) American Motors Owners Association www.amonational.com
1615 Purvis Ave Janesville WI 53545
Ph: 608-752-8247

(Cars) Antique Automobile Club of America www.aaca.org
501 W Governor Rd PO Box 417 Hershey PA 17033
Ph: 717-534-1910 ▪ Fx: 717-534-9101

(Cars) BMW Vintage Club of America
PO Box S San Rafael CA 94913
Ph: 415-897-0220 ▪ Fx: 415-898-0831

(Cars) Buick Club of America www.buickclub.org
PO Box 360775 Columbus OH 43236
Ph: 614-472-3939 ▪ Fx: 614-472-3222

(Cars) Cadillac-LaSalle Club www.cadillaclasalleclub.org
PO Box 360835 Columbus OH 43236
Ph: 614-478-4622 ▪ Fx: 614-472-3222

(Cars) Checker Car Club of America www.checkercabs.org
10530 W Alabama Ave Sun City AZ 85351
Ph: 623-974-4987

(Cars) Citroen Car Club home.comcast.net/~citroenquarterly
PO Box 130030 Boston MA 02113
Ph: 617-742-6604

(Cars) Classic Car Club of America www.classiccarclub.org
1645 Des Plaines River Rd Suite 7A Des Plaines IL 60018
Ph: 847-390-0443 ▪ Fx: 847-390-7118

(Cars) Classic Chevy Club International www.classicchevy.com
5140 S Washington Ave Titusville FL 32780
Ph: 407-299-1957 ▪ Fx: 407-299-3341 ▪ TF: 800-456-1957

(Cars) Classic Thunderbird Club International www.ctci.org
1308 E 29th St Signal Hill CA 90806
Ph: 562-426-2709 ▪ Fx: 562-426-7023

(Cars) Corvair Society of America www.corvair.org
PO Box 607 Lemont IL 60439
Ph: 630-257-6530

(Cars) Crown Victoria Association clubs.hemmings.com/crownvictoria
PO Box 6 Bryan OH 43506
Ph: 419-636-2475 ▪ Fx: 419-636-8449

(Cars) Edsel Club www.edselworld.com
19296 Tuckaway Ct Fort Myers FL 33903
Ph: 941-731-8027

(Cars) Fairlane Club of America www.fairlaneclubofamerica.com
340 Clicktown Rd Church Hill TN 37642
Ph: 423-245-6678 ▪ Fx: 423-245-2456

(Cars) Falcon Club of America www.falconclub.com
PO Box 113 Jacksonville AR 72078
Ph: 501-982-9721

(Cars) Ferrari Club of America www.ferrariclubofamerica.org
PO Box 720597 Atlanta GA 30358
Ph: 800-328-0444 ▪ Fx: 770-936-9392

(Cars) Goodguys Rod & Custom Association www.good-guys.com
PO Box 424 Alamo CA 94507
Ph: 925-838-9876 ▪ Fx: 925-820-8241

(Cars) International Mercury Owners Association www.mercuryclub.com
6445 W Grand Ave Chicago IL 60707
Ph: 773-622-6445 ▪ Fx: 773-622-3602

(Cars) Jaguar Clubs of North America Inc www.jcna.com
1000 Glenbrook Rd Anchorage KY 40223
Ph: 888-258-2524

(Cars) Late Great Chevrolet Association www.lategreatchevy.com
2166 S Orange Blossom Trail Apopka FL 32703
Ph: 407-886-1619 ▪ Fx: 407-886-7571 ▪ TF: 800-683-1961

(Cars) Maserati Club www.themaseraticlub.com

(Cars) Mercedes-Benz Club of America www.mbca.org
1907 Lelaray St Colorado Springs CO 80909
Ph: 719-633-6427 ▪ Fx: 719-633-9283 ▪ TF: 800-637-2360

(Cars) Model A Ford Club of America Inc www.mafca.com
250 S Cypress St La Habra CA 90631
Ph: 562-697-2712 ▪ Fx: 562-690-7452

(Cars) Model A Restorers Club www.modelaford.org
24800 Michigan Ave Dearborn MI 48124
Ph: 313-278-1455

(Cars) Model T Ford Club of America www.mtfca.com
PO Box 126 Centerville IN 47330
Ph: 765-855-5248 ▪ Fx: 765-855-3428

(Cars) Nash Car Club of America www.nashcarclub.org
1N274 Prarie Glen Ellyn IL 60137
Ph: 630-469-5848

(Cars) National American Motors Drivers & Racers Association www.namdra.org
PO Box 987 Twin Lakes WI 53181
Ph: 262-396-9552

(Cars) National Antique Oldsmobile Club Inc www.antiqueolds.org

(Cars) National Corvette Restorers Society www.ncrs.org
6291 Day Rd Cincinnati OH 45252
Ph: 513-385-8526 ▪ Fx: 513-385-8554

(Cars) National Impala Association www.impala.blackhills.com
2928 4th Ave PO Box 968 Spearfish SD 57783
Ph: 605-642-5864 ▪ Fx: 605-642-5868

(Cars) National Nostalgic Nova www.nnnova.com
PO Box 2344 York PA 17405
Ph: 717-252-4192 ▪ Fx: 717-252-1666

(Cars) National Street Rod Association www.nsra-usa.com
4030 Park Ave Memphis TN 38111
Ph: 901-452-4030 ▪ Fx: 901-452-6772

(Cars) Packard Club www.packardclub.org
PO Box 360806 Columbus OH 43236
Ph: 614-478-4946 ▪ Fx: 614-472-3222 ▪ TF: 800-478-0012

(Cars) Plymouth Owners Club Inc www.plymouthbulletin.com
PO Box 416 Cavalier ND 58220
Ph: 701-549-3746 ▪ Fx: 701-549-3744

(Cars) Porsche Club of America www.pca.org
PO Box 5900 Springfield VA 22150
Ph: 703-451-9000 ▪ Fx: 703-451-0145

(Cars) Professional Car Society www.professionalcar.org
5405 Heritage Ln Kingsport TN 37664
Ph: 423-288-3454

(Cars) REO Club of America clubs.hemmings.com/frameset.cfm?club=reo
7971 Vernon Rd Cicero NY 13039
Ph: 315-458-4721

(Cars) Rolls-Royce Owners' Club www.rroc.org
191 Hempt Rd Mechanicsburg PA 17050
Ph: 717-697-4671 ▪ Fx: 717-697-7820

(Cars) Sports Car Club of America www.scca.com
PO Box 19400 Topeka KS 66619
Ph: 785-357-7222 ▪ Fx: 785-232-7228 ▪ TF: 800-770-2055

(Cars) Sportscar Vintage Racing Association www.svra.com
257 Dekalb Industrial Way Decatur GA 30030
Ph: 404-298-3323 ▪ Fx: 404-298-3325

(Cars) Studebaker Driver's Club Inc www.studebakerdriversclub.com
PO Box 1743 Maple Grove MN 55311
Ph: 763-420-7829 ▪ Fx: 763-420-7849

(Cars) United Street Machine Association Inc www.usmacarshows.com
430 N Batchewana St Clawson MI 48017
Ph: 248-280-0342

(Cars) Veteran Motor Car Club of America www.vmcca.org
4441 W Altadena Ave Glendale AZ 85304
Ph: 800-428-7327

(Cars) Vintage Chevrolet Club of America www.vcca.org
PO Box 5387 Orange CA 92863
Ph: 714-633-1310

(Cars) Vintage Thunderbird Club International www.vintagethunderbirdclub.org

(Cars) Worldwide Camaro Club www.worldwidecamaro.com
5140 S Washington Ave Titusville FL 32780
Ph: 321-269-9680 ▪ Fx: 321-383-2059 ▪ TF: 800-456-1957

Carson Rachel Council Inc members.aol.com/rccouncil/ourpage
PO Box 10779 Silver Spring MD 20914
Ph: 301-593-7507 ▪ Fx: 301-593-6251

Carson Rachel Homestead Association www.rachelcarsonhomestead.org
613 Marion Ave Box 46 Springdale PA 15144
Ph: 724-274-5459 ▪ Fx: 724-275-1259

Carter Amon G Foundation www.agcf.org
PO Box 1036 Fort Worth TX 76101
Ph: 817-332-2783 ▪ Fx: 817-332-2787

Carter Center www.cartercenter.org
1 Copenhill 453 Freedom Pkwy Atlanta GA 30307
Ph: 404-331-3900 ▪ Fx: 404-331-0283

Cartographic Information Society, North American www.nacis.org/
PO Box 399 Milwaukee WI 53201
Ph: 414-229-6282 ▪ Fx: 414-229-3624 ▪ TF: 800-558-8993

Cartography & Geographic Information Society www.acsm.net/cagis
6 Montgomery Village Ave Suite 403 Gaithersburg MD 20879
Ph: 240-632-9716 ▪ Fx: 240-632-1321

Cartoonists Association www.cartoonistsassociation.com
National Writers Union 113 University Pl 6th Fl New York NY 10003
Ph: 212-254-0279 ▪ Fx: 212-254-0673

Cartoonists, Association of American Editorial info.detnews.com/aaec
1121 Stoneferry Ln Raleigh NC 27606
Ph: 919-859-5516 ▪ Fx: 919-859-3172

Cartoonists Northwest www.cartoonists.net
PO Box 31122 Seattle WA 98103
Ph: 425-226-7623 ▪ Fx: 425-227-0511

Carver Roy J Charitable Trust www.carvertrust.org
202 Iowa Ave Muscatine IA 52761
Ph: 563-263-4010 ▪ Fx: 563-263-1547

Carvers Association, National Wood www.chipchats.org
7424 Miami Ave Cincinnati OH 45243
Ph: 513-561-9051

Carving Association, International Wildfowl iwfca.com

Carwash Association, International www.carwashes.com
401 N Michigan Ave Chicago IL 60611
Ph: 312-321-5199 ▪ Fx: 312-245-1085

Carwash Owners & Suppliers Association
1822 South St Racine WI 53404
Ph: 262-639-2320 ▪ Fx: 262-639-4393

Cascade Policy Institute www.cascadepolicy.org
813 SW Alder St Suite 450 Portland OR 97205
Ph: 503-242-0900 ▪ Fx: 503-242-3822

Case Collectors Club www.casesales.com/ccc
PO Box 4000 Bradford PA 16701
Ph: 814-368-4123 ▪ Fx: 814-368-1736 ▪ TF: 800-523-6350

Case Management, National Association of www.yournacm.addr.com

Case Management Society of America www.cmsa.org
8201 Cantrell Rd Suite 230 Little Rock AR 72227
Ph: 501-225-2229 ▪ Fx: 501-221-9068

Case Method Research & Application, World Association for www.wacra.org
23 Mackintosh Ave Needham MA 02492
Ph: 781-444-8982 ▪ Fx: 781-444-1548 ▪ TF: 800-523-6468

Casey Annie E Foundation www.aecf.org
701 Saint Paul St Baltimore MD 21202
Ph: 410-547-6600 ▪ Fx: 410-547-6624 ▪ TF: 800-222-1099

Cash Flow Association, American acfa-cashflow.org
PO Box 2668 Orlando FL 32802
Ph: 407-206-6523 ▪ Fx: 407-206-6507 ▪ TF: 800-253-1294

Cashmere & Camel Hair Manufacturers Institute www.cashmere.org
6 Becaon St Suite 1125 Boston MA 02108
Ph: 617-542-7481 ▪ Fx: 617-542-2199

Casing Association, International Natural Sausage www.insca.org
12339 Carroll Ave Rockville MD 20852
Ph: 301-231-9811 ▪ Fx: 301-231-4871

Casing Association, North American Natural www.nanca.org
666 11th St NW Washington DC 20001
Ph: 202-331-8234 ▪ Fx: 202-331-8191

Casino Chips & Gaming Tokens Collectors Club Inc www.ccgtcc.com
PO Box 368 Wellington OH 44090
Ph: 440-647-4335 ▪ TF: 877-422-4822

Casino & Theme Party Operators, National Association of www.casinoparties.com
18946 Des Moines Memorial Dr Bldg 5 SeaTac WA 98146
Ph: 206-241-4777 ▪ Fx: 206-241-6956 ▪ TF: 800-355-8299

Casket & Funeral Supply Association of America www.cfsaa.org
51 Sherwood Terr Suite D-1 Lake Bluff IL 60044
Ph: 847-295-6630 ▪ Fx: 847-295-6647

Cast Bullet Association www.castbulletassoc.org
12857 S Rd Hoyt KS 66440
Ph: 785-986-6675

Cast Iron Architecture, Friends of
235 E 87th St Room 6C New York NY 10128
Ph: 212-369-6004

Cast Iron Soil Pipe Institute www.cispi.org
5959 Shallowford Rd Suite 419 Chattanooga TN 37421
Ph: 423-892-0137 ▪ Fx: 423-892-0817

Cast Polymer Alliance, International www.icpa-hq.org
1010 N Glebe Rd Suite 450 Arlington VA 22201
Ph: 703-525-0320 ▪ Fx: 703-525-0743 ▪ TF: 800-414-4272

Cast Stone Institute www.caststone.org
10 W Kimball St Winder GA 30680
Ph: 770-868-5909 ▪ Fx: 770-868-5910

Caster & Wheel Manufacturers, Institute of www.mhia.org/psc
8720 Red Oak Blvd Suite 201 Charlotte NC 28217
Ph: 704-676-1190 ▪ Fx: 704-676-1199 ▪ TF: 800-345-1815

Casting Association, American www.americancastingassoc.org
1773 Lance End Ln Fenton MO 63026
Ph: 636-225-9443 ▪ Fx: 636-225-7238

Casting Industry Suppliers Association www.cisa.org
223 W Jackson Blvd Suite 800 Chicago IL 60606
Ph: 312-957-1701 ▪ Fx: 312-957-1702

Casting Institute, Investment www.investmentcasting.org
136 Summit Ave Montvale NJ 07645
Ph: 201-573-9770 ▪ Fx: 201-573-9771

Casting Project, Non-Traditional www.ntcp.org
1560 Broadway Suite 1600 New York NY 10036
Ph: 212-730-4750 ▪ Fx: 212-730-4820

Casting Research Institute, Iron www.ironcasting.org
2802 Fisher Rd Columbus OH 43204
Ph: 614-275-4201 ▪ Fx: 614-275-4203

Castor Oil Association, International www.icoa.org
656 Linwood Ave Ridgewood NJ 07450
Ph: 201-652-0889 ▪ Fx: 201-652-7383

Casual Furniture Retailers www.casualfurniture.org
710 E Ogden Ave Suite 600 Naperville IL 60563
Ph: 630-579-3262 ▪ Fx: 630-369-2488 ▪ TF: 800-956-2237

Casualty Actuarial Society www.casact.org
1100 N Glebe Rd Suite 600 Arlington VA 22201
Ph: 703-276-3100 ▪ Fx: 703-276-3108

Casualty Insurers of America, Property www.allianceai.org
2600 S River Rd Des Plaines IL 60018
Ph: 847-297-7800 ▪ Fx: 847-297-5064

Cat Collectors www.catcollectors.com
PO Box 150784 Nashville TN 37215
Ph: 615-297-7403 ▪ Fx: 615-383-7403

Cat Fanciers' Federation Inc www.cffinc.org
PO Box 661 Gratis OH 45330
Ph: 937-787-9009 ▪ Fx: 937-787-4290

Cat Friends, Feral www.feralcatfriends.org
8255 White Oak Rd Garner NC 27529
Ph: 919-662-5365

Cat Registry International, Calico
PO Box 944 Morongo Valley CA 92256
Ph: 760-363-6511

Cat Society, Library www.ironfrog.com/libcats/lcs.html
PO Box 274 Moorhead MN 56560
Ph: 218-236-7205

Catacomb Society, International www.catacombsociety.org
3 Lewis St PO Box 130439 Boston MA 02113
Ph: 617-742-1285 ▪ Fx: 617-742-1550

Catahoula Association, American www.catahoulas.org
PO Box 248 Abita Springs LA 70420
Ph: 985-892-6773

Catalog Council, Direct Marketing Association Inc www.the-dma.org/councils/catalog
1120 Ave of the Americas New York NY 10036
Ph: 212-768-7277 ▪ Fx: 212-302-6714

Catalog Managers Association, National www.ncmacat.org
4600 East-West Hwy Suite 300 Bethesda MD 20814
Ph: 301-654-6664 ▪ Fx: 301-654-3299

Catalogue Raisonne Scholars Association
15 Lawrence Hall Dr Suite 2 Williamstown MA 01267
Ph: 413-597-2335

Catalysis Society, North American www.nacatsoc.org
c/o DuPont Co PO Box 80262 Wilmington DE 19880
Ph: 302-695-2488 ▪ Fx: 302-695-8347

Catalysis Society, Organic Reactions www.orcs.org

Catalyst Inc www.catalystwomen.org
120 Wall St 5th Fl New York NY 10005
Ph: 212-514-7600 ▪ Fx: 212-514-8470

Cataract & Refractive Surgery, American Society of www.ascrs.org
4000 Legato Rd Suite 850 Fairfax VA 22033
Ph: 703-591-2220 ▪ Fx: 703-591-0614 ▪ TF: 800-451-1339

Catastrophe Adjusters, National Association of www.nacatadj.org
PO Box 821864 North Richland Hills TX 76180
Ph: 817-498-3466 ▪ Fx: 817-498-0480

Catboat Association Inc www.catboats.org
PO Box 72 Middleboro MA 02346
Ph: 508-947-5093 ▪ Fx: 508-947-2013

Catechetical Leadership, National Conference for www.nccl.org
3021 4th St NE Washington DC 20017
Ph: 202-636-3826 ▪ Fx: 202-832-2712

Catechumenate, North American Forum on the www.naforum.org
3033 4th St NE Washington DC 20017
Ph: 202-529-9493 ▪ Fx: 202-529-9497

Caterers Association, International www.icacater.org
1200 17th St NW Washington DC 20036
Ph: 888-604-5844

Caterers Association - International, Mobile Industrial www.mobilecaterers.com
304 W Liberty St Suite 201 Louisville KY 40202
Ph: 502-583-3783 ▪ Fx: 502-589-3602 ▪ TF: 800-620-6422

Catering Executives, National Association of www.nace.net
5565 Sterrett Pl Suite 328 Columbia MD 21044
Ph: 410-997-9055 ▪ Fx: 410-997-8834

Catfish Farmers of America
1100 Hwy 82 E Suite 202 Indianola MS 38751
Ph: 662-887-2699 ▪ Fx: 662-887-6857

Catfish Institute www.catfishinstitute.com
1100 Hwy 82 E PO Box 924 Indianola MS 38751
Ph: 662-887-2988 ▪ Fx: 662-247-2644

Catgut Acoustical Society www.catgutacoustical.org
55 Park St Montclair NJ 07042
Ph: 973-744-0371 ▪ Fx: 973-744-0375

Cathedral Association, National www.cathedral.org/cathedral
Washington National Cathedral 3101 Wisconsin Ave
NW Washington DC 20016
Ph: 202-537-6243 ▪ Fx: 202-364-6600 ▪ TF: 800-622-6304

Cather Willa Pioneer Memorial & Educational Foundation www.willacather.org
413 N Webster Red Cloud NE 68970
Ph: 402-746-2653 ▪ Fx: 402-746-2652

Catholic Academy for Communication Arts Professionals www.catholicacademy.org
901 Irving Ave Dayton OH 45409
Ph: 937-229-2303 ▪ Fx: 937-229-2300

Catholic Academy of Sciences in the USA
PO Box 9611 Washington DC 20016
Ph: 301-963-0459 ▪ Fx: 301-963-6049

Catholic Activities Inc, Foundations & Donors Interested in www.fadica.org
1350 Connecticut Ave NW Suite 303 Washington DC 20036
Ph: 202-223-3550 ▪ Fx: 202-296-9295

Catholic Activities, Raskob Foundation for www.rfca.org
PO Box 4019 Wilmington DE 19807
Ph: 302-655-4440

Catholic Aid Association www.catholicaid.com
3499 Lexington Ave N Saint Paul MN 55126
Ph: 651-490-0170 ▪ Fx: 651-490-0746 ▪ TF: 800-568-6670

Catholic AIDS Network, National www.ncan.org
1400 W Devon Ave Suite 502 Chicago IL 60660
Ph: 773-508-7080 ▪ Fx: 773-508-7083

Catholic Alliance, Lithuanian
71-73 S Washington St Wilkes-Barre PA 18701
Ph: 570-823-8876

Catholic Association of Foresters www.catholicforesters.com
347 Commonwealth Ave Boston MA 02115
Ph: 617-536-8221 ▪ Fx: 617-536-2819 ▪ TF: 800-282-2263

Catholic Band Association, National www.catholicbands.org
3334 N Normandy Ave Chicago IL 60634
Ph: 773-282-9153

Catholic Biblical Association of America studentorg.cua.edu/cbib
620 Michigan Ave NE 314 Caldwell Hall Washington DC
20064
Ph: 202-319-5519 ▪ Fx: 202-319-4799

Catholic Big Brothers www.cbbnyc.org
45 E 20th St 9th Fl New York NY 10003
Ph: 212-477-2250 ▪ Fx: 212-477-2739

Catholic Bishops, US Conference of www.usccb.org
3211 4th St NE Washington DC 20017
Ph: 202-541-3000 ▪ Fx: 202-541-3322

Catholic Book Publishers Association www.cbpa.org
8404 Jamesport Dr Rockford IL 61108
Ph: 815-332-3245

(Catholic) Call to Action USA
2135 W Roscoe St   Chicago IL 60618
Ph: 773-404-0004 ▪ Fx: 773-404-1610
www.cta-usa.org

Catholic Campaign for Human Development
3211 4th St NE   Washington DC 20017
Ph: 202-541-3210 ▪ Fx: 202-541-3329 ▪ TF: 800-946-4243
www.nccbuscc.org/chd

Catholic Campus Ministry Association
1118 Pendleton St Suite 300   Cincinnati OH 45210
Ph: 513-842-0167 ▪ Fx: 513-842-0171 ▪ TF: 888-714-6631
www.ccmanet.org

Catholic Cemetery Conference, National
710 N River Rd   Des Plaines IL 60016
Ph: 847-824-8131 ▪ Fx: 847-824-9608
www.ntriplec.org

Catholic Central Union of America
3835 Westminster Pl   Saint Louis MO 63108
Ph: 314-371-1653
www.socialjusticereview.org

Catholic Chaplains, National Association of
PO Box 070473   Milwaukee WI 53207
Ph: 414-483-4898 ▪ Fx: 414-483-6712
www.nacc.org

Catholic Charities USA
1731 King St Suite 200   Alexandria VA 22314
Ph: 703-549-1390 ▪ Fx: 703-549-1656
www.catholiccharitiesusa.org

Catholic Church Extension Society of the USA
150 S Wacker Dr 20th Fl   Chicago IL 60606
Ph: 312-236-7240 ▪ Fx: 312-236-5276 ▪ TF: 800-842-7804
www.catholic-extension.org

Catholic Clergy, National Organization for Continuing Education of Roman   1337 W Ohio St   Chicago IL 60622
Ph: 312-226-1890 ▪ Fx: 312-829-8915
www.nocercc.org

Catholic Committee of Appalachia
PO Box 662   Webster Springs WV 26288
Ph: 304-847-7215
www.cathcomappalachia.org

Catholic Committee on Scouting, National
PO Box 152079   Irving TX 75015
Ph: 972-580-2114 ▪ Fx: 972-580-7870
www.nccs-bsa.org

Catholic Conference Directors, National Association of State
1042 Burlington Ln   Frankfort KY 40601
Ph: 502-875-4345 ▪ Fx: 502-875-2841
www.nasccd.org

Catholic Congress, National Black
320 Cathedral St   Baltimore MD 21201
Ph: 410-547-8496 ▪ Fx: 410-752-3958
www.nbccongress.org

Catholic Council on Alcoholism & Related Drug Problems Inc, National   PO Box 248   Lafayette IN 47902
Ph: 765-420-0129 ▪ Fx: 765-420-0189
www.nccatoday.org

(Catholic) Crosier Missions
3510 Vivian Ave   Shoreview MN 55126
Ph: 651-486-7456 ▪ Fx: 651-287-1130 ▪ TF: 800-407-5875
www.crosier.org

Catholic Daughters of the Americas
10 W 71st St   New York NY 10023
Ph: 212-877-3041 ▪ Fx: 212-724-5923
www.catholicdaughters.org

Catholic Development Conference, National
80 Front St   Hempstead NY 11550
Ph: 516-481-6000 ▪ Fx: 516-489-9287 ▪ TF: 888-879-6232
www.ncdcusa.org

Catholic Education, National Association of Boards Commissions & Councils of   National Catholic Educational Assn 1077 30th St NW Suite 100   Washington DC 20007
Ph: 202-337-6232 ▪ Fx: 202-333-6706
www.ncea.org/departments/nabcccc

Catholic Educational Association, National
1077 30th St NW Suite 100   Washington DC 20007
Ph: 202-337-6232 ▪ Fx: 202-333-6706
www.ncea.org

Catholic Family Life Ministers, National Association of
300 College Park   Dayton OH 45469
Ph: 937-229-3324 ▪ Fx: 937-229-4902
www.nacflm.org

Catholic Federation, Italian
675 Hegenberger Rd Suite 230   Oakland CA 94621
Ph: 510-633-9058 ▪ Fx: 510-633-9758 ▪ TF: 888-423-1924
icf.org

Catholic Federation, Slovak
St John the Baptist Rectory 108 N Main St   Taylor PA 18517
Ph: 570-562-1341 ▪ Fx: 570-562-2807

(Catholic) Glenmary Home Missioners
PO Box 465618   Cincinnati OH 45246
Ph: 513-874-8900 ▪ Fx: 513-874-1690
www.glenmary.org

Catholic Golden Age
PO Box 249   Olyphant PA 18447
Ph: 570-586-1091 ▪ Fx: 570-586-7721 ▪ TF: 800-836-5699
www.catholicgoldenage.org

Catholic Health Association of the US
4455 Woodson Rd   Saint Louis MO 63134
Ph: 314-427-2500 ▪ Fx: 314-427-0029
www.chausa.org

Catholic Healthcare Audit Network
231 S Bemiston Ave Suite 300   Saint Louis MO 63105
Ph: 314-802-2000 ▪ Fx: 314-802-2000
www.chanllc.com

Catholic Historical Society, American
www.amchs.org

(Catholic) Holy Cross Family Ministries
518 Washington St   North Easton MA 02356
Ph: 508-238-4095 ▪ Fx: 508-238-3953 ▪ TF: 800-299-7729
www.familyrosary.org

(Catholic) Human Life International
4 Family Life Ln   Front Royal VA 22630
Ph: 540-635-7884 ▪ Fx: 540-636-7363 ▪ TF: 800-549-5433
www.hli.org

(Catholic) Kappa Gamma Pi
10215 Chardon Rd   Chardon OH 44024
Ph: 440-286-3764 ▪ Fx: 440-286-4379
www.kappagammapi.org

Catholic Knights
1100 W Wells St   Milwaukee WI 53233
Ph: 414-273-6266 ▪ Fx: 414-223-3201 ▪ TF: 800-927-2547
www.catholicknights.com

Catholic Knights of America
3525 Hampton Ave   Saint Louis MO 63139
Ph: 314-351-1029 ▪ Fx: 314-351-9937
www.ckoa.com

Catholic Kolping Society of America
PO Box 4907   Clifton NJ 07015
Ph: 973-478-8635 ▪ Fx: 973-478-8049 ▪ TF: 877-659-7237
www.kolping.org

Catholic Laymen, National Committee of
215 Lexington Ave 4th Fl   New York NY 10016
Ph: 212-685-6666 ▪ Fx: 212-725-9793

Catholic League for Religious & Civil Rights
450 7th Ave   New York NY 10123
Ph: 212-371-3191 ▪ Fx: 212-371-3394
www.catholicleague.org

Catholic Legal Immigration Network Inc
McCormick Pavilion 415 Michigan Ave NE   Washington DC 20017
Ph: 202-635-2556
www.cliniclegal.org

Catholic Lesbians Inc, Conference for
www.catholicwomenl2l.org

Catholic Library Association
100 North St Suite 224   Pittsfield MA 01201
Ph: 413-443-2252
www.cathla.org

Catholic Life Insurance
1635 NE Loop 410 Suite 300   San Antonio TX 78209
Ph: 210-828-9921 ▪ Fx: 210-828-4629 ▪ TF: 800-262-2548
www.catholiclifeinsurance.com

Catholic Medical Association
159 Washington St Suite 3   Boston MA 02135
Ph: 617-782-3356 ▪ Fx: 617-782-3362
www.cathmed.org

Catholic Medical Mission Board
10 W 17th St   New York NY 10011
Ph: 212-242-7757 ▪ Fx: 212-807-9161 ▪ TF: 800-678-5659
www.cmmb.org

Catholic Migration Commission, International
MRS/US Conference of Catholic Bishops 3211 4th St NE   Washington DC 20017
Ph: 202-541-3389 ▪ Fx: 202-722-8755
www.icmc.net

Catholic Mission Association, US
3029 4th St NE   Washington DC 20017
Ph: 202-832-3112 ▪ Fx: 202-832-3688
www.uscatholicmission.org

Catholic Music & Video Association, United
PO Box 230   Donnellson IA 52625
Ph: 319-835-9340 ▪ Fx: 319-835-9071 ▪ TF: 877-668-2682
www.ucmva.com

Catholic Mutual Aid Society of USA, Russian Orthodox
10 Downs Dr   Wilkes-Barre PA 18705
Ph: 570-822-8591 ▪ Fx: 570-821-7060 ▪ TF: 877-476-2627
www.rocmas.org

Catholic Near East Welfare Association
1011 1st Ave   New York NY 10022
Ph: 212-826-1480 ▪ Fx: 212-838-1344 ▪ TF: 800-442-6392
www.cnewa.org

Catholic Negro American Mission Board
2021 H St NW   Washington DC 20006
Ph: 202-331-8542 ▪ Fx: 202-331-8544

Catholic Network of Volunteer Service
6930 Carroll Ave Suite 506   Takoma Park MD 20912
Ph: 301-270-0900 ▪ Fx: 301-270-0901 ▪ TF: 800-543-5046
www.cnvs.org

Catholic Office for the Deaf, National
7202 Buchanan St   Hyattsville MD 20784
Ph: 301-577-1684 ▪ Fx: 301-577-1690
www.ncod.org

(Catholic) Opus Dei Foundation
524 North Ave Suite 203   New Rochelle NY 10801
Ph: 914-235-1201 ▪ Fx: 914-235-7805
www.opusdei.org

Catholic Order of Foresters
355 Shuman Blvd PO Box 3012   Naperville IL 60566
Ph: 630-983-4900 ▪ Fx: 630-983-4057 ▪ TF: 800-552-0145
www.catholicforester.com

Catholic Peace Fellowship
PO Box 41   Notre Dame IN 46556
Ph: 574-631-7666
www.catholicpeacefellowship.org

Catholic Pharmacists Guild of the US, National
1012 Surrey Hills Dr   Saint Louis MO 63117
Ph: 314-645-0085

Catholic Press Association
3555 Veterans Memorial Hwy Unit O   Ronkonkoma NY 11779
Ph: 631-471-4730 ▪ Fx: 631-471-4804
www.catholicpress.org

Catholic Press Society, Lithuanian
4545 W 63rd St   Chicago IL 60629
Ph: 773-585-9500 ▪ Fx: 773-585-8284

Catholic Relief Services
209 W Fayette St   Baltimore MD 21201
Ph: 410-625-2220 ▪ Fx: 410-685-1635 ▪ TF: 800-235-2772
www.catholicrelief.org

Catholic Rural Life Conference, National
4625 Beaver Ave   Des Moines IA 50310
Ph: 515-270-2634 ▪ Fx: 515-270-9447
www.ncrlc.com

Catholic Scholars, Fellowship of
916 S Wolcott St   Chicago IL 60612
Ph: 312-355-3336
www.catholicscholars.org

Catholic School Teachers, National Association of
1700 Sansom St Suite 903   Philadelphia PA 19103
Ph: 215-665-0993 ▪ Fx: 215-568-8270 ▪ TF: 800-996-2278
www.nacst.org

Catholic Slovak Ladies Association, First
24950 Chagrin Blvd   Beachwood OH 44122
Ph: 216-464-8015 ▪ Fx: 216-464-9260 ▪ TF: 800-464-4642
www.fcsla.org

Catholic Slovak Union of the US & Canada, First
6611 Rockside Rd   Independence OH 44131
Ph: 216-642-9406 ▪ Fx: 216-642-4310 ▪ TF: 800-533-6682
www.fcsu.com

Catholic Society of Foresters, National
320 S School St   Mount Prospect IL 60056
Ph: 800-344-0273
www.ncsf.org

Catholic Sokol, Slovak
205 Madison St PO Box 899   Passaic NJ 07055
Ph: 800-886-7656
www.slovakcatholicsokol.org

Catholic Stewardship Council, International
1275 K St NW Suite 980   Washington DC 20005
Ph: 202-289-1093 ▪ Fx: 202-682-9018
www.catholicstewardship.org

Catholic Theological Society of America
John Carroll Univ 20700 North Park Blvd   University Heights OH 44118
Ph: 216-397-1631 ▪ Fx: 216-397-1804
www.jcu.edu/ctsa

Catholic Union of America, Polish Roman
984 N Milwaukee Ave   Chicago IL 60622
Ph: 773-782-2600 ▪ Fx: 773-278-4595 ▪ TF: 800-772-8632
www.prcua.org

Catholic Union of the US, Croatian www.ccu-usa.org
1 E Old Ridge Rd PO Box 602 Hobart IN 46342
Ph: 219-942-1191 ▪ Fx: 219-942-8808

Catholic Union of the USA, Greek www.gcuusa.com
5400 Tuscarawas Rd Beaver PA 15009
Ph: 724-495-3400 ▪ Fx: 724-495-3421 ▪ TF: 800-722-4428

Catholic Union, Western www.wculife.com
510 Maine St Quincy IL 62301
Ph: 217-223-9721 ▪ Fx: 217-223-9726 ▪ TF: 800-223-4928

(Catholic) Wanderer Forum Foundation www.wandererforum.org
PO Box 542 Hudson WI 54016
Ph: 651-276-1429

Catholic War Veterans Auxiliary www.cwv.org/laux/laux.htm
441 N Lee St Alexandria VA 22314
Ph: 703-549-3622 ▪ Fx: 703-684-5196

Catholic War Veterans of the USA www.cwv.org
441 N Lee St Alexandria VA 22314
Ph: 703-549-3622 ▪ Fx: 703-684-5196

(Catholic) We Believe www.webelieve.cc
1899 Pinehurst Ave Saint Paul MN 55116
Ph: 651-698-1857 ▪ Fx: 651-699-8390

(Catholic) Women for Faith & Family www.wf-f.org
PO Box 3286 Saint Louis MO 63132
Ph: 314-863-8385 ▪ Fx: 314-863-5858

Catholic Women, National Council of www.nccw.org
200 N Glebe Rd Suite 703 Arlington VA 22203
Ph: 703-224-0990 ▪ Fx: 703-224-0991 ▪ TF: 800-506-9407

Catholic Worker Movement www.catholicworker.org
36 E 1st St New York NY 10003
Ph: 212-777-9617

Catholic Workman www.catholicworkman.org
1201 1st St NE PO Box 47 New Prague MN 56071
Ph: 952-758-2229 ▪ Fx: 952-758-6221 ▪ TF: 800-346-6231

Catholic Youth Ministry, National Federation for www.nfcym.org
415 Michigan Ave NE Suite 40 Washington DC 20017
Ph: 202-636-3825 ▪ Fx: 202-526-7544

Catholics in America, Providence Association of Ukrainian
817 N Franklin St Philadelphia PA 19123
Ph: 215-627-4984 ▪ Fx: 215-238-1933

Catholics, Association of Hebrew www.hebrewcatholic.org
PO Box 980280 Ypsilanti MI 48198
Ph: 734-480-4242 ▪ Fx: 734-480-8990

Catholics for a Free Choice www.catholicsforchoice.org
1436 U St NW Suite 301 Washington DC 20009
Ph: 202-986-6093 ▪ Fx: 202-332-7995

Catholics Inc, North American Conference of Separated & Divorced www.nacsdc.org
PO Box 360 Richland OR 97870
Ph: 541-893-6089

Catholics Speak Out www.quixote.org/cso
PO Box 5206 Hyattsville MD 20782
Ph: 301-699-0042 ▪ Fx: 301-864-2182

Catholics United for the Faith www.cuf.org
827 N 4th St Steubenville OH 43952
Ph: 740-283-2482 ▪ TF: 800-693-2484

Cato Institute www.cato.org
1000 Massachusetts Ave NW Washington DC 20001
Ph: 202-842-0200 ▪ Fx: 202-842-3490

(Cats) Alley Cat Allies www.alleycat.org
1801 Belmont Rd NW Suite 201 Washington DC 20009
Ph: 202-667-3630 ▪ Fx: 202-667-3640

(Cats) Calico Cat Registry International
PO Box 944 Morongo Valley CA 92256
Ph: 760-363-6511

(Cats) Cat Fanciers' Federation Inc www.cffinc.org
PO Box 661 Gratis OH 45330
Ph: 937-787-9009 ▪ Fx: 937-787-4290

(Cats) Feral Cat Friends www.feralcatfriends.org
8255 White Oak Rd Garner NC 27529
Ph: 919-662-5365

(Cats) International Cat Association www.tica.org
PO Box 2684 Harlingen TX 78551
Ph: 956-428-8046 ▪ Fx: 956-428-8047

(Cats) United Burmese Cat Fanciers
2395 NE 185th St North Miami Beach FL 33180
Ph: 305-931-0104

(Cats) United Silver Fanciers www.unitedsilverfanciers.com

(Cattle) American Angus Association www.angus.org
3201 Frederick Ave Saint Joseph MO 64506
Ph: 816-383-5100 ▪ Fx: 816-233-9703 ▪ TF: 800-821-5478

(Cattle) American Belgian Blue Breeders Association www.belgianblue.org
PO Box 154 Hedrick IA 52563
Ph: 641-656-2332 ▪ Fx: 641-653-2332

(Cattle) American Blonde D'Aquitaine Association www.blondecattle.org
PO Box 470661 Tulsa OK 74147
Ph: 918-610-0842

(Cattle) American Brahman Breeders Association www.brahman.org
3003 South Loop W Suite 140 Houston TX 77054
Ph: 713-349-0854 ▪ Fx: 713-349-9795

(Cattle) American British White Park Association whitecattle.org
PO Box 249 Wheelock TX 77882
Ph: 979-828-2339 ▪ Fx: 979-208-9002

(Cattle) American Chianina Association www.chicattle.org
1708 N Prairie View Rd PO Box 890 Platte City MO 64079
Ph: 816-431-2808 ▪ Fx: 816-431-5381

(Cattle) American Galloway Breeders' Association www.galloway-world.org
310 W Spruce St Missoula MT 59802
Ph: 406-728-5719 ▪ Fx: 406-721-6300

(Cattle) American Gelbvieh Association www.gelbvieh.org
10900 Dover St Westminster CO 80021
Ph: 303-465-2333 ▪ Fx: 303-465-2339

(Cattle) American Guernsey Association www.usguernsey.com
7614 Slate Ridge Blvd PO Box 666 Reynoldsburg OH 43068
Ph: 614-864-2409 ▪ Fx: 614-864-5614

(Cattle) American-International Charolais Association www.charolaisusa.com
PO Box 20247 Kansas City MO 64195
Ph: 816-464-5977 ▪ Fx: 816-464-5759

(Cattle) American International Marchigiana Society www.marchigiana.org
PO Box 198 Walton KS 67151
Ph: 316-837-3303 ▪ Fx: 316-283-8379

(Cattle) American Junior Brahman Association www.brahman.org/ajba.html
3003 South Loop W Suite 140 Houston TX 77054
Ph: 713-349-0854 ▪ Fx: 713-349-9795

(Cattle) American Junior Chianina Association www.chicattle.org/ajca.html
PO Box 890 Platte City MO 64079
Ph: 816-431-2808 ▪ Fx: 816-431-5381

(Cattle) American Junior Shorthorn Association www.beefshorthornusa.com
8288 Hascall St Omaha NE 68124
Ph: 402-393-7200 ▪ Fx: 402-393-7203

(Cattle) American Junior Simmental Association www.simmental.org/ajsainfo.html
1 Simmental Way Bozeman MT 59715
Ph: 406-587-4531

(Cattle) American Maine-Anjou Association www.maine-anjou.org
204 Marshall Rd PO Box 1100 Platte City MO 64079
Ph: 816-431-9950 ▪ Fx: 816-431-9951

(Cattle) American Milking Devon Association www.milkingdevons.org
135 Old Bay Rd New Durham NH 03855
Ph: 603-859-6611

(Cattle) American Milking Shorthorn Junior Society www.milkingshorthorn.com/juniors.html
800 Pleasant St Beloit WI 53511
Ph: 608-365-3332 ▪ Fx: 608-365-6644

(Cattle) American Milking Shorthorn Society www.milkingshorthorn.com
800 Pleasant St Beloit WI 53511
Ph: 608-365-3332

(Cattle) American Murray Grey Association www.murraygreybeefcattle.com
PO Box 224 New Bethlehem PA 16242
Ph: 814-275-2515 ▪ Fx: 814-275-2506

(Cattle) American Pinzgauer Association www.pinzgauers.org
PO Box 147 Bethany MO 64424
Ph: 660-425-8617 ▪ Fx: 660-425-8374 ▪ TF: 800-914-9883

(Cattle) American Red Poll Association www.redpollusa.com
PO Box 147 Bethany MO 64424
Ph: 660-425-7318 ▪ Fx: 660-425-8374

(Cattle) American Romagnola Association www.americanromagnola.com
3815 Touzalin Ave Suite 104 Lincoln NE 68507
Ph: 402-466-3334 ▪ Fx: 402-466-3338

(Cattle) American Salers Association www.salersusa.org
19590 E Main St Suite 202 Parker CO 80138
Ph: 303-770-9292 ▪ Fx: 303-770-9302

(Cattle) American Salers Junior Association www.salersusa.org
7383 Alton Way Suite 103 Englewood CO 80112
Ph: 303-770-9292 ▪ Fx: 303-770-9302

(Cattle) American Shorthorn Association www.beefshorthornusa.com
8288 Hascall St Omaha NE 68124
Ph: 402-393-7200 ▪ Fx: 402-393-7203

(Cattle) American Simmental Association www.simmental.org
1 Simmental Way Bozeman MT 59718
Ph: 406-587-4531 ▪ Fx: 406-587-9301

(Cattle) American Tarentaise Association www.usa-tarentaise.com
PO Box 34705 Kansas City MO 64116
Ph: 816-421-1993 ▪ Fx: 816-421-1991

(Cattle) Ankole-Watusi International Registry www.awir.org
22484 W 239th St Spring Hill KS 66083
Ph: 913-592-4050

Cattle Association, American Dexter www.dextercattle.org
404 High St Prairie Home MO 65068
Ph: 660-841-9502

Cattle Association, American Highland www.highlandcattle.org
4701 Marion St 200 Livestock Exchange Bldg Denver CO 80216
Ph: 303-292-9102 ▪ Fx: 303-292-9171

Cattle Association, American Jersey www.usjersey.com
6486 E Main St Reynoldsburg OH 43068
Ph: 614-861-3636 ▪ Fx: 614-861-8040

Cattle Association, Amerifax
PO Box 149 Hastings NE 68902
Ph: 402-463-5289 ▪ Fx: 402-463-6652

Cattle Association, Red & White Dairy www.redandwhitecattle.com
3085 S Valley Rd Crystal Spring PA 15536
Ph: 814-735-4221 ▪ Fx: 814-735-3473

(Cattle) Ayrshire Breeders Association www.usayrshire.com
1224 Alton Darby Creek Rd Suite B Columbus OH 43228
Ph: 614-335-0020 ▪ Fx: 614-335-0023

(Cattle) Belted Galloway Society www.beltie.org
98 Eidson Rd Staunton VA 24401
Ph: 540-885-9887 ▪ Fx: 540-885-9897

(Cattle) Braunvieh Association of America www.braunvieh.org
3815 Touzalin Ave Suite 103 Lincoln NE 68507
Ph: 402-466-3292 ▪ Fx: 402-466-3293

Cattle Breeders Association of America, Barzona www.mddc.com/havens

Cattle Breeders Association, Parthenais www.parthenaiscattle.org/
PO Box 550 Bells TX 75414
Ph: 903-965-4259 ▪ Fx: 903-965-5452 ▪ TF: 800-762-0164

Cattle Breeders Association of the USA, Brown Swiss www.brownswiss.com
800 Pleasant St Beloit WI 53511
Ph: 608-365-4474 ▪ Fx: 608-365-5577

Cattle Breeders Society & Registry, International Miniature www.minicattle.com
25204 156th Ave SE Covington WA 98042
Ph: 253-631-1911 ▪ Fx: 253-631-5774

Cattle Dog Club of America, Australian   www.acdca.org
5041 Britton Ln   Jacksonville FL 32210
Ph: 904-771-5217 ▪ Fx: 904-908-9585

(Cattle) International Brangus Breeders Association   www.int-brangus.org
5750 Epsilon PO Box 696020   San Antonio TX 78269
Ph: 210-696-4343 ▪ Fx: 210-696-8718

(Cattle) International Junior Brangus Breeders Association   www.int-brangus.org
5750 Epsilon PO Box 696020   San Antonio TX 78269
Ph: 210-696-4343 ▪ Fx: 210-696-8718

(Cattle) National Junior Angus Association   www.njaa.info
3201 Frederick Ave   Saint Joseph MO 64506
Ph: 816-383-5100 ▪ Fx: 816-233-9703

(Cattle) National Junior Hereford Association   www.hereford.org
PO Box 014059   Kansas City MO 64101
Ph: 816-842-3757 ▪ Fx: 816-842-6931

(Cattle) National Junior Santa Gertrudis   www.santagertrudis.ws/jrwelcome.html
Association   PO Box 1257   Kingsville TX 78364
Ph: 361-592-9357 ▪ Fx: 361-592-8572

(Cattle) North American Corriente Association   www.corrientecattle.org
PO Box 12359   North Kansas City MO 64116
Ph: 816-421-1992 ▪ Fx: 816-421-1991

(Cattle) North American Junior Limousin Association   www.nalf.org/programs/juniors.html
7383 S Alton Way Suite 100   Englewood CO 80112
Ph: 303-220-1693 ▪ Fx: 303-220-1884

(Cattle) North American Limousin Foundation   www.nalf.org
7383 S Alton Way Suite 100   Englewood CO 80112
Ph: 303-220-1693 ▪ Fx: 303-220-1884

(Cattle) North American Normande Association   www.normandeassociation.com
30698 Ottoman Ave   Elroy WI 53929
Ph: 866-685-8491

(Cattle) Piedmontese Association of the US   pauscattle.org
343 Barrett Rd   Elsberry MO 63343
Ph: 573-384-5685 ▪ Fx: 573-384-5567

(Cattle) Red Angus Association of America   www.redangus.org
4201 N I-35   Denton TX 76207
Ph: 940-387-3502 ▪ Fx: 940-383-4036

Cattle Registry, American Miniature Jersey
PO Box 942   Rochester WA 98579
Ph: 360-273-7789

(Cattle) Santa Gertrudis Breeders International   www.santagertrudis.ws
PO Box 1257   Kingsville TX 78364
Ph: 361-592-9357 ▪ Fx: 361-592-8572

(Cattle) Texas Longhorn Breeders Association of America   www.tlbaa.org
2315 N Main St Suite 402   Fort Worth TX 76106
Ph: 817-625-6241 ▪ Fx: 817-625-1388

(Cattle) United Braford Breeders   www.brafords.org
422 E Main St Suite 218   Nacogdoches TX 75961
Ph: 936-569-8200 ▪ Fx: 936-569-9556

Cattlemen's Association, National American Indian
1541 Foster Rd   Toppenish WA 98948
Ph: 509-854-1329

Cattlemen's Beef Association, National   www.beef.org
9110 E Nichols Ave Suite 300   Centennial CO 80112
Ph: 303-694-0305 ▪ Fx: 303-694-2851

Cattlemen's Beef Promotion & Research Board   www.beefboard.org
9110 E Nichols Ave Suite 303   Centennial CO 80112
Ph: 303-220-9890 ▪ Fx: 303-220-9280

CattleWomen Inc, American National   www.ancw.org
PO Box 3881   Englewood CO 80155
Ph: 303-694-0313 ▪ Fx: 303-694-2390

Caucus - Association of Technology Procurement Professionals   www.caucusnet.com
PO Drawer 2970   Winter Park FL 32790
Ph: 407-740-5600 ▪ Fx: 407-740-0368

Cavalier King Charles Spaniel Club USA   www.ckcsc.org
PO Box 330   Conway NH 03818
Ph: 603-447-5218 ▪ Fx: 603-447-5419

Cavalry Association, US   www.uscavalry.org
PO Box 2325   Fort Riley KS 66442
Ph: 785-784-5797

Cave Conservation Association, American   www.cavern.org
119 E Main St PO Box 409   Horse Cave KY 42749
Ph: 270-786-1466 ▪ Fx: 270-786-1467

Cave Diving, National Association for   www.safecavediving.com
PO Box 14492   Gainesville FL 32604
Ph: 352-331-7666 ▪ TF: 888-565-6223

Cave Research Foundation   www.cave-research.org
3473 Regalwoods Dr   Doraville GA 30340
Ph: 770-491-8587

Cave Studies, Association for Mexican   www.amcs.org
PO Box 7037   Austin TX 78713
Ph: 512-842-5709

Caves Association, National   www.cavern.com
PO Box 280   Park City KY 42160
Ph: 270-749-2228 ▪ Fx: 270-749-2428 ▪ TF: 866-552-2837

CBA International   www.cbaonline.org
PO Box 62000   Colorado Springs CO 80962
Ph: 719-265-9895 ▪ Fx: 719-272-3510 ▪ TF: 800-252-1950

CBInternational   www.cbi.org
1501 W Mineral Ave   Littleton CO 80120
Ph: 720-283-2000 ▪ Fx: 720-283-2111 ▪ TF: 800-487-4224

CCHS Family Network   www.cchsnetwork.org

CCIM Institute   www.ccim.org
430 N Michigan Ave Suite 800   Chicago IL 60611
Ph: 312-321-4460

CDS International Inc   www.cdsintl.org
871 United Nations Plaza 15th Fl   New York NY 10017
Ph: 212-497-3500 ▪ Fx: 212-497-3535

Cecchetti Council of America Inc   www.cecchetti.org
23393 Meadows Ave   Flat Rock MI 48134
Ph: 734-379-6710 ▪ Fx: 734-379-3886

CEDAM International   www.cedam.org
1 Fox Rd   Croton-on-Hudson NY 10520
Ph: 914-271-5365 ▪ Fx: 914-271-4723

Cedar Lumber Association, Western Red   www.wrcla.org
1501-700 W Pender St   Vancouver BC V6C1G8
Ph: 604-684-0266 ▪ Fx: 604-687-4930

Cedar Pole Association, Western Red   www.preservedwood.com/wrcpa/main.html
2405 61st Ave SE   Mercer Island WA 98040
Ph: 800-410-1917 ▪ Fx: 206-275-4755

Cedar Shake & Shingle Bureau   www.cedarbureau.org
PO Box 1178   Sumas WA 98295
Ph: 604-820-7700 ▪ Fx: 604-820-0266 ▪ TF: 800-843-3578

Cedars of Lebanon of North America, Tall   www.mastermason.com/tcl
2609 N Front St   Harrisburg PA 17110
Ph: 717-232-5991 ▪ Fx: 717-232-5997

CEF   www.innercite.com/~cef
2700 Zinfandel Dr   Rancho Cordova CA 95670
Ph: 916-853-1914 ▪ Fx: 916-853-1921

Ceiling Industries International, Association of the Wall &   www.awci.org
803 W Broad St Suite 600   Falls Church VA 22046
Ph: 703-534-8300 ▪ Fx: 703-534-8307

Ceilings & Interior Systems Construction Association   cisca.org
1500 Lincoln Hwy Suite 202   Saint Charles IL 60174
Ph: 630-584-1919 ▪ Fx: 630-584-2003

Celebrity Assistants, New York   www.nycelebrityassistants.org
459 Columbus Ave Suite 216   New York NY 10024
Ph: 212-803-5444

Celebrity Personal Assistants, Association of   www.celebrityassistants.org
914 Westwood Blvd PMB 507   Los Angeles CA 90024
Ph: 310-322-7755

Celiac Disease Foundation   www.celiac.org
13251 Ventura Blvd Suite 1   Studio City CA 91604
Ph: 818-990-2354 ▪ Fx: 818-990-2379

Celiac Disease Research, Friends of   www.friendsofceliac.com
8832 N Port Washington Rd Suite 204   Milwaukee WI 53217
Ph: 414-540-6679 ▪ Fx: 414-540-0587

Celiac Society/Dietary Support Coalition, American
PO Box 23455   New Orleans LA 70183
Ph: 504-737-3293 ▪ Fx: 504-737-3283

Celiac Sprue Association/USA Inc   www.csaceliacs.org
PO Box 31700   Omaha NE 68131
Ph: 402-558-0600 ▪ Fx: 402-558-1347

Cell Biology, American Society for   www.ascb.org
8120 Woodmont Ave Suite 750   Bethesda MD 20814
Ph: 301-347-9300 ▪ Fx: 301-347-9310

Cell Biology, International Federation for   www.ifcbiol.org

Cellular Telecommunications & Internet Association   www.wow-com.com
1400 16th St NW Suite 600   Washington DC 20036
Ph: 202-785-0081 ▪ Fx: 202-785-0721

Cellulose Insulation Manufacturers Association   www.cellulose.org
136 S Keowee St   Dayton OH 45402
Ph: 937-222-2462 ▪ Fx: 937-222-5794 ▪ TF: 888-881-2462

Celtic League American Branch   www.celticleague.org
PO Box 20153   New York NY 10017
Ph: 800-626-2358

Cement Association of Canada   www.cement.ca
1500-60 Queen St   Ottawa ON K1P5Y7
Ph: 613-236-9471 ▪ Fx: 613-563-4498

Cement Association, Portland   www.cement.org
5420 Old Orchard Rd   Skokie IL 60077
Ph: 847-966-6200 ▪ Fx: 847-966-9781

Cement Employers Association
122 Broad St 2nd Fl   Bethlehem PA 18018
Ph: 610-868-8060 ▪ Fx: 610-861-2884

Cement Kiln Recycling Coalition   www.ckrc.org
1730 K St NW Suite 710   Washington DC 20006
Ph: 202-466-6802 ▪ Fx: 202-466-5009

Cement Masons' International Association of the US & Canada,   www.opcmia.org
Operative Plasterers' &   14405 Laurel Pl Suite 300   Laurel
MD 20707
Ph: 301-470-4200 ▪ Fx: 301-470-2502

Cemented Carbide Producers Association   www.ccpa.org
30200 Detroit Rd   Cleveland OH 44145
Ph: 440-899-0010 ▪ Fx: 440-892-1404

Cemeteries, International Association of Pet   www.iaopc.org
5055 Rt 11 PO Box 163   Ellenburg Depot NY 12935
Ph: 518-594-3000 ▪ Fx: 518-594-8801

Cemetery Conference, National Catholic   www.ntriplec.org
710 N River Rd   Des Plaines IL 60016
Ph: 847-824-8131 ▪ Fx: 847-824-9608

Cemetery Consumer Service Council   www.icfa.org/ccsc.htm
PO Box 2028   Reston VA 20195
Ph: 703-391-8407 ▪ Fx: 703-391-8416

Cemetery & Funeral Association, International   www.icfa.org
1895 Preston White Dr Suite 220   Reston VA 20191
Ph: 703-391-8400 ▪ Fx: 703-391-8416 ▪ TF: 800-645-7700

Cemetery Support Committee, Abraham Lincoln National
28 Kansas St   Frankfort IL 60423
Ph: 815-469-2176 ▪ Fx: 815-469-0295

Censored, Project   www.projectcensored.org
1801 E Cotati Ave   Rohnert Park CA 94928
Ph: 707-664-2500 ▪ Fx: 707-664-2108

Censorship, National Coalition Against   www.ncac.org
275 7th Ave 9th Fl   New York NY 10001
Ph: 212-807-6222 ▪ Fx: 212-807-6245

Cent Collectors, Society of Lincoln   www.slcc.nasc.net
13515 Magnolia Blvd   Sherman Oaks CA 91423
Ph: 818-789-7805

Center for the Advancement of Human Rights www.cahr.fsu.edu
Florida State Univ MC 1602 426 W Jefferson St   Tallahassee FL
32301
Ph: 850-664-4500 ▪ Fx: 850-664-4633

Center for Advancement of Public Policy www.capponline.org
1735 'S' St NW   Washington DC 20009
Ph: 202-797-0606 ▪ Fx: 202-265-6245

Center for American Archeology www.caa-archeology.org
PO Box 366   Kampsville IL 62053
Ph: 618-653-4316 ▪ Fx: 618-653-4232

Center of the American Experiment www.amexp.org
1024 Plymouth Bldg 12 S 6th St   Minneapolis MN 55402
Ph: 612-338-3605 ▪ Fx: 612-338-3621

Center for Applications of Psychological Type www.capt.org
2815 NW 13th St Suite 401   Gainesville FL 32609
Ph: 352-375-0160 ▪ Fx: 352-378-0503 ▪ TF: 800-777-2278

Center for Applied Linguistics www.cal.org
4646 40th St NW   Washington DC 20016
Ph: 202-362-0700 ▪ Fx: 202-362-3740

Center for Applied Research in the Apostolate cara.georgetown.edu
Georgetown Univ 2300 Wisconsin Ave NW Suite
400   Washington DC 20057
Ph: 202-687-8080 ▪ Fx: 202-687-8083

Center for Arts & Culture www.culturalpolicy.org
819 7th St NW Suite 505   Washington DC 20001
Ph: 202-783-5277 ▪ Fx: 202-783-4498

Center for Austrian Studies www.cas.umn.edu
Univ of Minnesota 267 19th Ave S 314 Social Science
Bldg   Minneapolis MN 55455
Ph: 612-624-9811 ▪ Fx: 612-626-9004

Center for Auto Safety www.autosafety.org
1825 Connecticut Ave NW Suite 330   Washington DC 20009
Ph: 202-328-7700

Center for Bigfoot Studies
10926 Milano Ave   Norwalk CA 90650
Ph: 714-921-1014

Center for Bioethics bioethics.upenn.edu
Univ of Pennsylvania 3401 Market St Suite 320   Philadelphia
PA 19104
Ph: 215-898-7136 ▪ Fx: 215-573-3036

Center for the Book www.loc.gov/loc/cfbook
Library of Congress 101 Independence Ave SE   Washington DC
20540
Ph: 202-707-5221 ▪ Fx: 202-707-0269

Center for Book Arts www.centerforbookarts.org
28 W 27th St 3rd Fl   New York NY 10001
Ph: 212-481-0295 ▪ Fx: 212-481-9853

Center on Budget & Policy Priorities www.cbpp.org
820 1st St NE Suite 510   Washington DC 20002
Ph: 202-408-1080 ▪ Fx: 202-408-1056

Center for Business & Government www.ksg.harvard.edu/cbg/
Harvard Univ John F Kennedy School of Government Weil Hall
79 JFK St   Cambridge MA 02138
Ph: 617-384-7329 ▪ Fx: 617-496-0063

Center for Chemical Process Safety www.aiche.org/ccps/index.htm
3 Park Ave   New York NY 10016
Ph: 212-591-7319 ▪ Fx: 212-591-8895

Center for the Child Care Workforce www.ccw.org
555 New Jersey Ave NW   Washington DC 20001
Ph: 202-662-8005 ▪ Fx: 202-662-8006

Center for Christian-Jewish Understanding www.ccju.org
Sacred Heart Univ 5151 Park Ave   Fairfield CT 06432
Ph: 203-365-7592 ▪ Fx: 203-365-4815

Center for Citizen Initiatives www.ccisf.org
PO Box 29912   San Francisco CA 94129
Ph: 415-561-7777 ▪ Fx: 415-561-7778 ▪ TF: 888-729-7071

Center for Clean Air Policy www.ccap.org
750 1st St NE Suite 940   Washington DC 20002
Ph: 202-408-9260 ▪ Fx: 202-408-8896

Center for Cognitive Liberty & Ethics www.cognitiveliberty.org
PO Box 73481   Davis CA 95617
Ph: 530-750-7912 ▪ TF: 888-950-6463

Center for Commercial-Free Public Education
1714 Franklin St   Oakland CA 94612
Ph: 510-268-1100 ▪ Fx: 510-268-1277 ▪ TF: 800-867-5841

Center for Community Change www.communitychange.org
1000 Wisconsin Ave NW   Washington DC 20007
Ph: 202-342-0519 ▪ Fx: 202-333-5462

Center for Community Solutions www.ccssd.org
4508 Mission Bay Dr   San Diego CA 92109
Ph: 858-272-5777 ▪ Fx: 858-272-5361 ▪ TF: 888-272-2767

Center for Computer-Assisted Legal Instruction www.cali.org
1313 5th Ave SE   Minneapolis MN 55414
Ph: 612-625-3419 ▪ Fx: 612-379-3875

Center on Conscience & War www.nisbco.org
1830 Connecticut Ave NW   Washington DC 20009
Ph: 202-483-2220 ▪ Fx: 202-483-1246 ▪ TF: 800-379-2679

Center for Constructive Change www.constructivechange.org
801 Duke St   Alexandria VA 22314
Ph: 703-684-4735 ▪ Fx: 703-684-4738

Center for Contemporary Opera www.conopera.org
PO Box 258   New York NY 10044
Ph: 212-785-2757 ▪ Fx: 212-758-0389

Center for Critical Thinking www.criticalthinking.org
PO Box 220   Dillon Beach CA 94929
Ph: 707-878-9100 ▪ Fx: 707-878-9111 ▪ TF: 800-833-3645

Center for Cuban Studies www.cubaupdate.org
124 W 23rd St   New York NY 10011
Ph: 212-242-0559 ▪ Fx: 212-242-1937

Center for Dao-Confucianism www.wam.umd.edu/~tkang
1318 Randolph St NE   Washington DC 20017
Ph: 202-526-6818

Center for Death Education & Bioethics www.uwlax.edu/sociology/cde&b
UW La Crosse Dept of Sociology/Archaeology 435 NH 1725
State St   La Crosse WI 54601
Ph: 608-785-6784 ▪ Fx: 608-785-8486

Center for Defense Information www.cdi.org
1779 Massachusetts Ave NW Suite 615   Washington DC 20036
Ph: 202-332-0600 ▪ Fx: 202-462-4559

Center for Democracy www.centerfordemocracy.org
1101 15th St NW Suite 505   Washington DC 20005
Ph: 202-429-9141 ▪ Fx: 202-293-1768

Center for Democracy & Technology www.cdt.org
1634 'I' St NW 11th Fl   Washington DC 20006
Ph: 202-637-9800 ▪ Fx: 202-637-0968

Center For Democratic Renewal www.publiceye.org/cdr
PO Box 50469   Atlanta GA 30302
Ph: 404-221-0025 ▪ Fx: 404-221-0045

Center for Design Planning
2300 E Mallory St   Pensacola FL 32503
Ph: 850-432-8478

Center for Development of Human Services www.bsc-cdhs.org
1695 Elmwood Ave   Buffalo NY 14207
Ph: 716-876-7600 ▪ Fx: 716-876-2237

Center for Digital Democracy www.democraticmedia.org
1718 Connecticut Ave NW Suite 200   Washington DC 20009
Ph: 202-986-2220

Center for Dispute Settlement www.cdsusa.org
1666 Connecticut Ave NW Suite 500   Washington DC 20009
Ph: 202-265-9572 ▪ Fx: 202-332-3951

Center for Ecoliteracy www.ecoliteracy.org
2522 San Pablo Ave   Berkeley CA 94702
Ph: 510-845-4595 ▪ Fx: 510-845-1439

Center for Economic Options Inc www.centerforeconomicoptions.org
214 Capital St Suite 200   Charleston WV 25301
Ph: 304-345-1298 ▪ Fx: 304-342-0641

Center for Economic & Social Rights www.cesr.org
162 Montague St 2nd Fl   Brooklyn NY 11201
Ph: 718-237-9145 ▪ Fx: 718-237-9147

Center for Energy Efficiency & Renewable Technologies
1100 11th St Suite 311   Sacramento CA 95814
Ph: 916-442-7785 ▪ Fx: 916-447-2940 ▪ TF: 877-758-4462

Center for Environmental Information www.rochesterenvironment.org
55 Saint Paul St   Rochester NY 14604
Ph: 716-262-2870 ▪ Fx: 716-262-4156

Center for Environmental Study www.cesmi.org
528 Bridge St NW Suite 1C   Grand Rapids MI 49504
Ph: 616-988-2854 ▪ Fx: 616-988-2857

Center for Equal Opportunity www.ceousa.org
14 Pidgeon Hill Dr Suite 500   Sterling VA 20165
Ph: 703-421-5443 ▪ Fx: 703-421-6401

Center for the Evangelical United Brethren Heritage www.united.edu/eubcenter
1810 Harvard Blvd   Dayton OH 45406
Ph: 937-278-5817 ▪ Fx: 937-275-5701

Center for Exhibition Industry Research www.ceir.org
2301 S Lake Shore Dr Suite E 1002   Chicago IL 60616
Ph: 312-808-2347 ▪ Fx: 312-949-3472

Center for Family Support Inc www.cfsny.org
333 7th Ave 9th Fl   New York NY 10001
Ph: 212-629-7939 ▪ Fx: 212-239-2211

Center for First Amendment Studies www.csulb.edu/~crsmith/1amendment.html
CSU Long Beach   Long Beach CA 90840
Ph: 562-985-4313 ▪ Fx: 562-985-4259

Center for Health Care Strategies Inc www.chcs.org
PO Box 3469   Princeton NJ 08543
Ph: 609-895-8101 ▪ Fx: 609-895-9648

Center for Health Environment & Justice www.chej.org/
PO Box 6806   Falls Church VA 22040
Ph: 703-237-2249 ▪ Fx: 703-237-8389

Center on Human Policy soeweb.syr.edu/thechp
805 S Crouse Ave   Syracuse NY 13244
Ph: 315-443-3851 ▪ Fx: 315-443-4338 ▪ TF: 800-894-0826

Center for Immigration Studies www.cis.org
1522 K St NW Suite 820   Washington DC 20005
Ph: 202-466-8185 ▪ Fx: 202-466-8076

Center for Individual Rights www.cir-usa.org
1233 20th St NW Suite 300   Washington DC 20036
Ph: 202-833-8400 ▪ Fx: 202-833-8410

Center for Institutional & International Initiatives www.acenet.edu/programs/ciii.cfm
American Council on Education 1 Dupont Cir NW   8th
Fl   Washington DC 20036
Ph: 202-939-9427

Center for International Development at Harvard University www.cid.harvard.edu
Harvard Univ John F Kennedy School of Government 1 Eliot St
Bldg   79 JFK St   Cambridge MA 02138
Ph: 617-496-7294 ▪ Fx: 617-496-8753

Center for International Environmental Law www.ciel.org
1367 Connecticut Ave NW Suite 300   Washington DC 20036
Ph: 202-785-8700 ▪ Fx: 202-785-8701

Center for International Policy www.ciponline.org
1717 Massachusetts Ave NW Suite 801   Washington DC 20036
Ph: 202-232-3317 ▪ Fx: 202-232-3440

Center for International Private Enterprise www.cipe.org
1155 15th St NW Suite 700   Washington DC 20005
Ph: 202-721-9200 ▪ Fx: 202-721-9250

Center of International Studies www.wws.princeton.edu/~cis
Princeton University Bendheim Hall   Princeton NJ 08544
Ph: 609-258-4852 ▪ Fx: 609-258-3988

Center for Investigative Reporting   www.muckraker.org
131 Steuart St Suite 600   San Francisco CA 94105
Ph: 415-543-1200 ▪ Fx: 415-543-8311

Center for Jewish Genetic Diseases Inc   www.nfjgd.org
Mt Sinai Medical Center 5th Ave at 100 St   New York NY 10029
Ph: 212-659-6774

Center for Judicial Accountability Inc   www.judgewatch.org
PO Box 69 Gedney Stn   White Plains NY 10605
Ph: 914-421-1200 ▪ Fx: 914-428-4994

Center for Labor & Community Research   www.clcr.org
3411 W Diversey Ave Suite 10   Chicago IL 60647
Ph: 773-278-5418 ▪ Fx: 773-278-5918

Center for Law & Education   www.cleweb.org
1875 Connecticut Ave NW Suite 510   Washington DC 20009
Ph: 202-986-3000 ▪ Fx: 202-986-6648

Center for Law in the Public Interest   www.clipi.org
10951 W Pico Blvd 3rd Fl   Los Angeles CA 90064
Ph: 310-470-3000 ▪ Fx: 310-474-7083

Center for Law & Religious Freedom   www.clsnet.org
4208 Evergreen Ln Suite 222   Annandale VA 22003
Ph: 703-642-1070 ▪ Fx: 703-642-1075

Center for Law & Social Policy   www.clasp.org
1015 15th St NW Suite 400   Washington DC 20005
Ph: 202-906-8000 ▪ Fx: 202-842-2885

Center for Lesbian & Gay Studies   www.clags.org
City Univ of New York 365 5th Ave Rm 7115   New York NY 10016
Ph: 212-817-1955 ▪ Fx: 212-817-2985

Center for Libertarian Studies   www.libertarianstudies.org
851 Burlway Rd Suite 202   Burlingame CA 94010
Ph: 800-325-7257 ▪ Fx: 650-401-5530

Center for Lifelong Learning   www.acenet.edu/clll
1 Dupont Cir NW Suite 250   Washington DC 20036
Ph: 202-939-9475 ▪ Fx: 202-833-4760

Center for Loss in Multiple Birth   www.climb-support.org
PO Box 91377   Anchorage AK 99509
Ph: 907-222-5321 ▪ Fx: 907-274-7029

Center for Management Effectiveness   www.cmeinc.org
PO Box 1202   Pacific Palisades CA 90272
Ph: 310-459-6052 ▪ Fx: 310-459-9307 ▪ TF: 888-819-0200

Center for Mathematical Studies in Economics &   www.kellogg.nwu.edu/research/math
Management Sciences   Northwestern University 2001 Sheridan Rd Leverone Hall Rm 580   Evanston IL 60208
Ph: 847-491-3527 ▪ Fx: 847-491-2530

Center for Media Education   www.cme.org
2120 L St NW Suite 200   Washington DC 20037
Ph: 202-331-7833 ▪ Fx: 202-331-7841

Center for Media & Public Affairs   www.cmpa.com
2100 L St NW Suite 300   Washington DC 20037
Ph: 202-223-2942

Center for Medical Consumers   www.medicalconsumers.org
130 MacDougal St   New York NY 10012
Ph: 212-674-7105 ▪ Fx: 212-674-7100

Center for Medical Ethics & Mediation   www.cmem.org
PO Box 86110   San Diego CA 92138
Ph: 619-296-7268

Center for Migration Studies of New York Inc   www.cmsny.org
209 Flagg Pl   Staten Island NY 10304
Ph: 718-351-8800 ▪ Fx: 718-667-4598

Center on National Labor Policy
5211 Port Royal Rd Suite 103   North Springfield VA 22151
Ph: 703-321-9180 ▪ Fx: 703-321-9325

Center for National Policy   www.cnponline.org
1 Massachusetts Ave NW Suite 333   Washington DC 20001
Ph: 202-682-1800 ▪ Fx: 202-682-1818

Center for Neighborhood Technology   www.cnt.org
2125 W North Ave   Chicago IL 60647
Ph: 773-278-4800 ▪ Fx: 773-278-3840

Center for Nonproliferation Studies   www.cns.miis.edu
460 Pierce St   Monterey CA 93940
Ph: 831-647-4154 ▪ Fx: 831-546-3518

Center for Nonviolent Communication   cnvc.org
2428 Foothill Blvd Suite E   La Crescenta CA 91214
Ph: 818-957-9393 ▪ Fx: 818-957-1424 ▪ TF: 800-255-7696

Center for Nonviolent Social Change Inc, Martin Luther   www.thekingcenter.com
King Jr   449 Auburn Ave NE   Atlanta GA 30312
Ph: 404-524-1956 ▪ Fx: 404-526-8969

Center for Oceans Law & Policy   www.virginia.edu/colp
Univ of Virginia School of Law 580 Massie Rd   Charlottesville VA 22903
Ph: 804-924-7441 ▪ Fx: 804-924-7362

Center for Organ Recovery & Education   www.core.org
204 Sigma Dr   Pittsburgh PA 15238
Ph: 800-366-6777 ▪ Fx: 412-963-3563

Center for Patient Advocacy   www.patientadvocacy.org
1350 Beverly Rd Suite 108   McLean VA 22101
Ph: 703-748-0400 ▪ Fx: 703-748-0402 ▪ TF: 800-846-7444

Center for Plant Conservation   www.mobot.org/CPC
PO Box 299   Saint Louis MO 63166
Ph: 314-577-9450 ▪ Fx: 314-577-9465

Center for Policy Alternatives   www.cfpa.org
1875 Connecticut Ave NW Suite 710   Washington DC 20009
Ph: 202-387-6030 ▪ Fx: 202-387-8529 ▪ TF: 800-935-0699

Center for Policy Analysis on Palestine   www.palestinecenter.org
2425-35 Virginia Ave NW   Washington DC 20037
Ph: 202-338-1290 ▪ Fx: 202-338-7742

Center for Policy Research   www-cpr.maxwell.syr.edu
Syracuse University Eggers Hall Rm 426   Syracuse NY 13244
Ph: 315-443-3114 ▪ Fx: 315-443-1081

Center for Popular Economics   www.populareconomics.org
Box 785   Amherst MA 01004
Ph: 413-545-0743

Center for Process Studies   www.ctr4process.org
Claremont School of Theology 1325 N College Ave   Claremont CA 91711
Ph: 909-621-5330 ▪ Fx: 909-621-2760

Center for Professional Well-Being   www.cpwb.org
21 W Colony Pl Suite 150   Durham NC 27705
Ph: 919-489-9167 ▪ Fx: 919-419-0011

Center for Public Dialogue
10615 Brunswick Ave   Kensington MD 20895
Ph: 301-933-3535

Center for Public Integrity   www.publicintegrity.org
910 17th St NW 7th Fl   Washington DC 20006
Ph: 202-466-1300 ▪ Fx: 202-466-1101

Center for Public Justice   www.cpjustice.org
2444 Solomons Island Rd Suite 201   Annapolis MD 21401
Ph: 410-571-6300 ▪ Fx: 410-571-6365 ▪ TF: 866-275-8784

Center for Public Leadership   www.ksg.harvard.edu/leadership
Harvard Univ John F Kennedy School of Government 79 JFK St   Cambridge MA 02138
Ph: 617-496-8866 ▪ Fx: 617-496-3337

Center for Reproductive Law & Policy Inc   www.crlp.org
120 Wall St 14th Fl   New York NY 10005
Ph: 917-637-3600 ▪ Fx: 917-637-3666

Center for Research Libraries   wwwcrl.uchicago.edu
6050 S Kenwood Ave   Chicago IL 60637
Ph: 773-955-4545 ▪ Fx: 773-955-4339 ▪ TF: 800-621-6044

Center for Resource Management   www.crminc.com
2 Highland Rd S   Hampton NH 03842
Ph: 603-394-7040 ▪ Fx: 603-394-7483

Center for Respect of Life & Environment   www.crle.org
2100 L St NW   Washington DC 20037
Ph: 202-778-6133 ▪ Fx: 202-778-6138

Center for Responsive Politics   www.opensecrets.org
1101 14th St NW Suite 1030   Washington DC 20005
Ph: 202-857-0044 ▪ Fx: 202-857-7809

Center for Rural Affairs   www.cfra.org
PO Box 406   Walthill NE 68067
Ph: 402-846-5428 ▪ Fx: 402-846-5420

Center for Science in the Public Interest   www.cspinet.org
1875 Connecticut Ave NW Suite 300   Washington DC 20009
Ph: 202-332-9110 ▪ Fx: 202-265-4954

Center for Seafarers' Rights   www.seamenschurch.org
241 Water St   New York NY 10038
Ph: 212-349-9090 ▪ Fx: 212-349-8342

Center for Social Gerontology   www.tcsg.org
2307 Shelby Ave   Ann Arbor MI 48103
Ph: 734-665-1126 ▪ Fx: 734-665-2071

Center for Social & Legal Research   www.privacyexchange.org
2 University Plaza Suite 414   Hackensack NJ 07601
Ph: 201-996-1154 ▪ Fx: 201-996-1883

Center for Social Studies Education
901 Old Hickory Rd   Pittsburgh PA 15243
Ph: 412-341-1967 ▪ Fx: 412-341-6533

Center for Socialist History   csh.gn.apc.org/
PO Box 626   Alameda CA 94501
Ph: 510-601-6460

Center for Strategic & International Studies   www.csis.org
1800 K St NW Suite 400   Washington DC 20006
Ph: 202-887-0200 ▪ Fx: 202-775-3199

Center for the Study of the College Fraternity   www.indiana.edu/~cscf
Indiana Univ Franklin Hall 002   Bloomington IN 47405
Ph: 812-855-1228

Center for the Study of Democratic Societies   www.centersds.com
PO Box 475   Manhattan Beach CA 90267
Ph: 310-798-2737 ▪ Fx: 310-374-0440

Center for the Study of Human Rights   www.columbia.edu/cu/humanrights
420 W 118th St Suite 1187   New York NY 10027
Ph: 212-854-2479 ▪ Fx: 212-316-4578

Center for the Study of Political Graphics   www.politicalgraphics.org
8124 W 3rd St Suite 211   Los Angeles CA 90048
Ph: 323-653-4662 ▪ Fx: 323-653-6991

Center for the Study of the Presidency   www.thepresidency.org
1020 19th NW Suite 250   Washington DC 20036
Ph: 202-872-9800 ▪ Fx: 202-872-9811

Center for the Study of Religion &   puffin.creighton.edu/human/csrs/centerhome.html
Society   Creighton Univ   Omaha NE 68178
Ph: 402-280-2504

Center for Study of Responsive Law   www.csrl.org
PO Box 19367   Washington DC 20036
Ph: 202-387-8030 ▪ Fx: 202-234-5176

Center for the Study of Social Policy   www.cssp.org
1575 'I' St NW Suite 500   Washington DC 20005
Ph: 202-371-1565 ▪ Fx: 202-371-1472

Center for Sutton Movement Writing   www.dancewriting.org
PO Box 517   La Jolla CA 92038
Ph: 858-456-0098 ▪ Fx: 858-456-0020

Center for Third World Organizing   www.ctwo.org
1218 E 21st St   Oakland CA 94606
Ph: 510-533-7583 ▪ Fx: 510-533-0923

Center for UFO Studies, J Allen Hynek   www.cufos.org
2457 W Peterson Ave Suite 6   Chicago IL 60659
Ph: 773-271-3611

Center for US-China Arts Exchange   www.columbia.edu/cu/china
423 W 118th St Suite 1E   New York NY 10027
Ph: 212-280-4648 ▪ Fx: 212-662-6346

Center for Voting & Democracy   www.fairvote.org
6930 Carroll Ave Suite 610   Takoma Park MD 20912
Ph: 301-270-4616 ▪ Fx: 301-270-4133

Center for War Peace & the News Media   www.nyu.edu/cwpnm
New York Univ 418 Lafayette Suite 554   New York NY 10003
Ph: 212-998-7960 ▪ Fx: 212-995-4143

Center for War/Peace Studies   www.cwps.org
180 W 80th St Suite 211   New York NY 10024
Ph: 212-579-4206 ▪ Fx: 212-579-4362

Center for Waste Reduction Technologies   www.aiche.org/cwrt
3 Park Ave   New York NY 10016
Ph: 212-591-7462 ▪ Fx: 212-591-8895

Center for Whale Research   www.whaleresearch.com
PO Box 1577   Friday Harbor WA 98250
Ph: 360-378-5835 ▪ Fx: 360-378-5954

Center for Women Policy Studies   www.centerwomenpolicy.org
1211 Connecticut Ave NW Suite 312   Washington DC 20036
Ph: 202-872-1770 ▪ Fx: 202-296-8962

Center for Women's Business Research   www.nfwbo.org
1411 K St NW Suite 1350   Washington DC 20005
Ph: 202-638-3060 ▪ Fx: 202-638-3064

Center for World Indigenous Studies   www.cwis.org
1001 Cooper Point Rd SW Suite 140 PMB 214   Olympia WA
98502
Ph: 360-754-1990 ▪ Fx: 253-276-0084

Center for World Thanksgiving   www.thanksgiving.org
c/o Thanks-Giving Square PO Box 131770   Dallas TX 75313
Ph: 214-969-1977 ▪ Fx: 214-754-0152 ▪ TF: 888-305-1205

Central America & the Caribbean, Ecumenical Program on   www.epica.org
1470 Irving St NW   Washington DC 20010
Ph: 202-332-0292 ▪ Fx: 202-332-1184

Central American Action, Caribbean-   www.claa.org
1818 'N' St NW Suite 500   Washington DC 20036
Ph: 202-466-7464 ▪ Fx: 202-822-0075

Central American Resource Center   www.carecen-la.org
1459 Columbia Rd NW   Washington DC 20009
Ph: 202-328-9799

Central Association of the Miraculous Medal   www.cammonline.org
475 E Chelten Ave   Philadelphia PA 19144
Ph: 215-848-1010 ▪ Fx: 215-848-1014 ▪ TF: 800-523-3674

Central Collegiate Hockey Association   www.ccha.com
23995 Freeway Park Dr   Farmington Hills MI 48335
Ph: 248-888-0600 ▪ Fx: 248-888-0664

Central Conference of American Rabbis   www.ccarnet.org
355 Lexington Ave 18th Fl   New York NY 10017
Ph: 212-972-3636 ▪ Fx: 212-692-0819 ▪ TF: 800-935-2227

Central Intercollegiate Athletic Association   www.theciaa.com
303 Butler Farm Rd Suite 102   Hampton VA 23666
Ph: 757-865-0071 ▪ Fx: 757-865-8436

Central Organization for Jewish Outreach
770 Eastern Pkwy   Brooklyn NY 11213
Ph: 718-953-2353

Central Rabbinical Congress of the USA & Canada
85 Division Ave   Brooklyn NY 11211
Ph: 718-384-6765 ▪ Fx: 718-486-5574

Central States Collegiate Hockey League   www.cschl.com
2475 Archdale   West Bloomfield MI 48324
Ph: 248-366-7914 ▪ Fx: 248-366-7915

Central Station Alarm Association   www.csaaul.org
440 Maple Ave E Suite 201   Vienna VA 22180
Ph: 703-242-4670 ▪ Fx: 703-242-4675

Central Yiddish Culture Organization
25 E 21st St 3rd Fl   New York NY 10010
Ph: 212-505-8305 ▪ Fx: 212-505-8044

Centre for Development & Population Activities   www.cedpa.org
1400 16th St NW Suite 100   Washington DC 20036
Ph: 202-667-1142 ▪ Fx: 202-332-4496

Century Foundation   www.tcf.org
41 E 70th St   New York NY 10021
Ph: 212-535-4441 ▪ Fx: 212-535-7534

CEO Clubs   www.ceoclubs.org
295 Greenwich St Suite 514   New York NY 10007
Ph: 212-925-7911 ▪ Fx: 212-925-7463

(CEOs) Business Council   www.businesscouncil.com
PO Box 20147   Washington DC 20041
Ph: 202-298-7650 ▪ Fx: 202-785-0886

Ceramic Arts, National Council on Education for the   www.nceca.net
77 Erie Village Sq Suite 280   Erie CO 80516
Ph: 303-828-2811 ▪ Fx: 303-828-0911 ▪ TF: 866-266-2322

Ceramic Arts Studio Collectors Association   www.cascollectors.com
PO Box 46   Madison WI 53701
Ph: 608-845-9286 ▪ Fx: 608-241-8770

Ceramic Decorators, Society of Glass &   www.sgcd.org
47 N 4th St   Zanesville OH 43702
Ph: 740-588-9882 ▪ Fx: 740-588-0245

Ceramic Engineering Fraternity, Keramos National   www.ceramics.org/keramos
Professional   c/o Seagate Technology 389 Disc Dr MS
COL-MW1   Longmont CO 80503
Ph: 720-684-2034 ▪ Fx: 720-684-2677

Ceramic Engineers, National Institute of
PO Box 6136   Westerville OH 43086
Ph: 614-890-4700

Ceramic Fibers Coalition, Refractory   www.rcfc.net
1133 Connecticut Ave NW Suite 1200   Washington DC 20036
Ph: 202-775-2388 ▪ Fx: 202-833-8491

Ceramic Society, American   www.acers.org
PO Box 6136   Westerville OH 43086
Ph: 614-890-4700 ▪ Fx: 614-899-6109

Ceramic Tile Distributors Association   www.ctdahome.org
800 Roosevelt Rd Bldg C Suite 20   Glen Ellyn IL 60137
Ph: 630-545-9415 ▪ Fx: 630-790-3095 ▪ TF: 800-938-2832

Ceramic Tile Institute of America Inc   www.ctioa.org
12061 Jefferson Blvd   Culver City CA 90230
Ph: 310-574-7800 ▪ Fx: 310-821-4655

Ceramics Association, US Advanced   www.advancedceramics.org
1800 M St NW Suite 300   Washington DC 20036
Ph: 202-293-6253 ▪ Fx: 202-223-5537

Cereal Chemists Inc, American Association of   www.aaccnet.org
3340 Pilot Knob Rd   Saint Paul MN 55121
Ph: 651-454-7250 ▪ Fx: 651-454-0766

Cerebral Palsy Associations Inc, United   www.ucp.org
1660 L St NW Suite 700   Washington DC 20036
Ph: 202-776-0406 ▪ Fx: 202-776-0414 ▪ TF: 800-872-5827

Cerebral Palsy & Developmental Medicine, American Academy for   aacpdm.org
6300 N River Rd Suite 727   Rosemont IL 60018
Ph: 847-698-1635 ▪ Fx: 847-823-0536

(Cerebral Palsy) UCP National   www.ucp.org
1660 L St NW Suite 700   Washington DC 20036
Ph: 202-776-0406 ▪ Fx: 202-776-0414 ▪ TF: 800-872-5827

Ceremonial Association, Gallup Inter-Tribal Indian   www.gallupnm.org/ceremonial
226 W Coal Ave   Gallup NM 87301
Ph: 505-863-3896 ▪ Fx: 505-722-5158 ▪ TF: 888-685-2564

Certification, American Board of   www.abcworld.org
44 Canal Center Plaza Suite 404   Alexandria VA 22314
Ph: 703-739-1023 ▪ Fx: 703-739-1060

Certification, Association of Boards of   www.abccert.org
208 E 5th St   Ames IA 50010
Ph: 515-232-3623 ▪ Fx: 515-232-3778

Certification Board, Electronic Components   www.eccb.org

Certification Board for Nutrition Specialists   www.cert-nutrition.org
300 S Duncan Ave Suite 225   Clearwater FL 33755
Ph: 727-446-6086 ▪ Fx: 727-446-6202

Certification Board, Orthopaedic Nurses   www.orthonurse.org/certification/oncb.cfm
401 N Michigan Ave Suite 2200   Chicago IL 60611
Ph: 800-289-6266 ▪ Fx: 312-527-6658

Certification Board, Pharmacy Technician   www.ptcb.org
2215 Constitution Ave NW   Washington DC 20037
Ph: 202-429-7576 ▪ Fx: 202-429-7596

Certification Commission, National   pages.zdnet.com/washdc/certification
PO Box 15282   Chevy Chase MD 20825
Ph: 301-847-0102 ▪ Fx: 301-847-0103

Certification, Commission on Rehabilitation Counselor   www.crccertification.com
1835 Rohlwing Rd Suite E   Rolling Meadows IL 60008
Ph: 847-394-2104 ▪ Fx: 847-394-2172

Certification of Computing Professionals, Institute for   www.iccp.org
2350 E Devon Ave Suite 115   Des Plaines IL 60018
Ph: 847-299-4227 ▪ Fx: 847-299-4280 ▪ TF: 800-843-8227

Certification Corp, Solar Rating &   www.solar-rating.org
c/o Florida Solar Energy Ctr 1679 Clearlake Rd   Cocoa FL
32922
Ph: 321-638-1537 ▪ Fx: 321-638-1010

Certification Council for Activity Professionals, National   www.nccap.org
PO Box 62589   Virginia Beach VA 23466
Ph: 757-552-0653 ▪ Fx: 757-552-0491

Certification in Engineering Technologies, National Institute for   www.nicet.org
1420 King St   Alexandria VA 22314
Ph: 703-548-1518 ▪ Fx: 703-682-2756 ▪ TF: 888-476-4238

Certification in Geriatric Pharmacy, Commission for   www.ccgp.org
1321 Duke St   Alexandria VA 22314
Ph: 703-535-3038 ▪ Fx: 703-739-1500

Certification of Health Environmental & Safety Technologies,   www.cchest.org
Council on   208 Burwash Ave   Savoy IL 61874
Ph: 217-359-2686 ▪ Fx: 217-359-0055

Certification Institute, Human Resource   www.hrci.org
Society for Human Resource Management 1800 Duke
St   Alexandria VA 22314
Ph: 703-548-3440

Certification, Institute of Inspection Cleaning & Restoration   www.iicrc.org
2715 E Mill Plain Blvd   Vancouver WA 98661
Ph: 360-693-5675 ▪ Fx: 360-693-4858

Certification Inc, National Council for Therapeutic Recreation   www.nctrc.org
7 Elmwood Dr   New City NY 10956
Ph: 845-639-1439 ▪ Fx: 845-639-1471

Certification in Occupational Therapy Inc, National Board for   www.nbcot.org
800 S Frederick Ave Suite 200   Gaithersburg MD 20877
Ph: 301-990-7979 ▪ Fx: 301-869-8492

Certification of Work Adjustment & Vocational Evaluation   www.ccwaves.org
Specialists, Commission on   1835 Rohlwing Rd Suite
E   Rolling Meadows IL 60008
Ph: 847-342-1796 ▪ Fx: 847-394-2108

Certified Claims Professional Accreditation Council Inc
PO Box 441110   Fort Washington MD 20749
Ph: 301-292-1988 ▪ Fx: 301-292-1787

Certified Clinical Hypnotherapists, National Board of   www.natboard.com
1110 Fiddler Ln Suite L-1   Silver Spring MD 20910
Ph: 301-608-0123 ▪ Fx: 301-588-9535 ▪ TF: 800-449-8144

Certified Consultants, National Bureau of   www.national-bureau.com
1850 5th Ave   San Diego CA 92101
Ph: 619-239-7076 ▪ Fx: 619-296-3580 ▪ TF: 800-543-1114

Certified Contractors NetWork   www.contractors.net
134 Sibley Ave   Ardmore PA 19003
Ph: 610-642-9505 ▪ Fx: 610-642-5842

Certified Counselors Inc, National Board for   www.nbcc.org
3 Terrace Way Suite D   Greensboro NC 27403
Ph: 336-547-0607 ▪ Fx: 336-547-0017 ▪ TF: 800-398-5389

Certified Engineering Technicians, American Society of   www.ascet.org
PO Box 1348   Flowery Branch GA 30542
Ph: 770-967-9173 ▪ Fx: 770-967-8049

Certified Financial Planner Board of Standards Inc   www.cfp-board.org
1700 Broadway Suite 2100   Denver CO 80290
Ph: 303-830-7500 ▪ Fx: 303-860-7388 ▪ TF: 888-237-6275

Certified Hazard Control Management, Board of   www.chcm-chsp.org
11900 Parklawn Dr Suite 451   Rockville MD 20852
Ph: 301-770-2540 ▪ Fx: 301-770-2183

Certified Horsemanship Association   www.cha-ahse.org
5318 Old Bullard Rd   Tyler TX 75703
Ph: 903-509-2473 ▪ Fx: 903-509-2474 ▪ TF: 800-399-0138

Certified Milk Producers Association of America
8300 Pine Ave   Chino CA 91710
Ph: 909-399-3560 ▪ Fx: 909-399-3627

Certified Pipe Welding Bureau, National   www.mcaa.org/ncpwb
1385 Piccard Dr   Rockville MD 20850
Ph: 301-869-5800 ▪ Fx: 301-990-9690

Certified Planners, American Institute of   www.planning.org/aicp
1776 Massachusetts Ave NW Suite 400   Washington DC 20036
Ph: 202-872-0611 ▪ Fx: 202-872-0643

Certified Professional Insurance Agents Society   www.cpia.com
PO Box 35718   Richmond VA 23235
Ph: 804-674-6466 ▪ Fx: 804-276-1300 ▪ TF: 877-674-2472

Certified Professional Managers, Institute of   cob.jmu.edu/icpm
James Madison University MSC 5504   Harrisonburg VA 22807
Ph: 540-568-3247 ▪ Fx: 540-801-8650 ▪ TF: 800-568-4120

Certified Public Accountants, American Association of   www.attorney-cpa.com
Attorney- 24196 Alicia Pkwy Suite K   Mission Viejo CA 92691
Ph: 949-768-0336 ▪ TF: 888-288-9272

Certified Public Accountants, American Institute of   www.aicpa.org
1211 Ave of the Americas   New York NY 10036
Ph: 212-596-6200 ▪ Fx: 212-596-6213 ▪ TF: 888-777-7077

Certified Public Accountants, American Woman's Society of   www.awscpa.org
136 S Keowee St   Dayton OH 45402
Ph: 937-222-1872 ▪ Fx: 937-222-5794 ▪ TF: 800-297-2721

Certified Public Accountants, Association of Practicing   www.ap-cpa.org
Rockville MD 20850
Ph: 301-340-3340 ▪ Fx: 301-340-3343

Certified Public Accounting Firms, National Associated   www.nacpaf.com
136 S Keowee St   Dayton OH 45402
Ph: 937-222-1024 ▪ Fx: 937-222-5794

Certified Records Managers, Institute of   www.icrm.org
318 Oak St   Syracuse NY 13203
Ph: 315-234-1904 ▪ Fx: 315-474-1784 ▪ TF: 877-244-3128

Certified Safety Professionals, Board of   www.bcsp.org
208 Burwash Ave   Savoy IL 61874
Ph: 217-359-9263 ▪ Fx: 217-359-0055

Certifying Agencies, Association of Official Seed   www.aosca.org
55 SW 5th Ave Suite 150   Meridian ID 83642
Ph: 208-884-2493 ▪ Fx: 208-884-4201

Cervical Cancer Prevention Resource Center, National HPV &   www.ashastd.org/hpvccrc
PO Box 13827   Research Triangle Park NC 27709
Ph: 919-361-8400 ▪ Fx: 919-361-8425

Cervical Pathology, American Society for Colposcopy &   www.asccp.org
20 W Washington St Suite 1   Hagerstown MD 21740
Ph: 301-733-3640 ▪ Fx: 301-733-5775 ▪ TF: 800-787-7227

Cervical Spine Research Society   www.csrs.org
6300 N River Rd Suite 727   Rosemont IL 60018
Ph: 847-698-1628 ▪ Fx: 847-823-0536

Cesarean Awareness Network Inc, International   www.ican-online.org
1304 Kingsdale Ave   Redondo Beach CA 90278
Ph: 310-542-6400 ▪ Fx: 310-542-5368 ▪ TF: 800-686-4226

Cessna Pilots Association   www.cessna.org
3409 Corsair Cir PO Box 5817   Santa Maria CA 93456
Ph: 805-922-2580 ▪ Fx: 805-922-7249

Cetacean Society, American   www.acsonline.org
PO Box 1391   San Pedro CA 90733
Ph: 310-548-6279 ▪ Fx: 310-548-6950

Cetacean Society International   www.csiwhalesalive.org
PO Box 953   Georgetown CT 06829
Ph: 203-431-1606

CFIDS Association of America Inc   www.cfids.org
PO Box 220398   Charlotte NC 28222
Ph: 704-364-0466 ▪ Fx: 704-365-9755 ▪ TF: 800-442-3437

Chain Association, American   www.americanchainassn.org
6724 Lone Oak Blvd   Naples FL 34109
Ph: 941-514-3441 ▪ Fx: 941-514-3470

Chain Drug Marketing Association   www.chaindrug.com
43157 W Nine-Mile Rd PO Box 995   Novi MI 48376
Ph: 248-449-9300 ▪ Fx: 248-449-4634 ▪ TF: 800-935-2362

Chain Drug Stores, National Association of   www.nacds.org
413 N Lee St   Alexandria VA 22314
Ph: 703-549-3001 ▪ Fx: 703-836-4869 ▪ TF: 800-678-6223

Chain Link Fence Manufacturers Institute   www.chainlinkinfo.org
10015 Old Columbia Rd Suite B-215   Columbia MD 21046
Ph: 301-596-2583 ▪ Fx: 301-596-2594

Chain Restaurants, National Council of   www.nccr.net
325 7th St NW Suite 1100   Washington DC 20004
Ph: 202-626-8183 ▪ Fx: 202-626-8185

Chain Salon Association, International   www.icsa.cc
13331 Millbank Dr   Plainfield IL 60544
Ph: 815-254-7477 ▪ Fx: 815-609-3969 ▪ TF: 866-444-4272

Challenged Homeschoolers Associated Network, National   www.nathhan.com
PO Box 39   Porthill ID 83853
Ph: 208-267-6246

Challenger Center for Space Science Education   www.challenger.org
1250 N Pitt St   Alexandria VA 22314
Ph: 703-683-9740 ▪ Fx: 703-683-7546 ▪ TF: 800-987-8277

Chamber of Commerce, American-Uzbekistan   www.erols.com/aucc
1800 Massachusetts Ave NW Suite 600   Washington DC 20036
Ph: 202-828-4317 ▪ Fx: 202-659-7010

Chamber of Commerce Executives, American   www.acce.org
4875 Eisenhower Ave Suite 250   Alexandria VA 22304
Ph: 703-998-0072 ▪ Fx: 703-212-9512 ▪ TF: 800-394-2223

Chamber of Commerce & Industry, Caribbean American
Brooklyn Navy Yard Bldg 5 63 Flushing Ave   Brooklyn NY 11205
Ph: 718-834-4544 ▪ Fx: 718-834-9774

Chamber of Commerce, International   www.iccwbo.org
1212 Ave of the Americas   New York NY 10036
Ph: 212-354-4480 ▪ Fx: 212-575-0327

Chamber of Commerce, National Black   www.nationalbcc.org
1350 Connecticut Ave NW Suite 825   Washington DC 20036
Ph: 202-466-6888 ▪ Fx: 202-466-4918

Chamber of Commerce, Norwegian-American   www.nacc.no
800 3rd Ave 23rd Fl   New York NY 10022
Ph: 212-421-1655 ▪ Fx: 212-838-0374

Chamber of Commerce, Romanian-American   www.racc.ro
5530 Wisconsin Ave Suite 1110   Chevy Chase MD 20815
Ph: 301-656-9022 ▪ Fx: 301-656-9008

Chamber of Commerce in the US, Belgian-American   www.belcham.org
245 Park Ave 24th Fl   New York NY 10167
Ph: 212-672-1632 ▪ Fx: 212-672-1644

Chamber of Commerce, US Hispanic   www.ushcc.com
2175 K St NW Suite 100   Washington DC 20037
Ph: 202-842-1212 ▪ Fx: 202-842-3221 ▪ TF: 800-874-2286

Chamber of Commerce, US Junior   www.usjaycees.org
PO Box 7   Tulsa OK 74102
Ph: 918-584-2481 ▪ Fx: 918-584-4422 ▪ TF: 800-529-2337

Chamber of Commerce, US Pan Asian American   www.uspaacc.com
1329 18th St NW   Washington DC 20036
Ph: 202-296-5221 ▪ Fx: 202-296-5225

Chamber Foundation, National   www.uschamber.com/ncf
1615 H St NW   Washington DC 20062
Ph: 202-463-5500 ▪ Fx: 202-463-3129 ▪ TF: 800-638-6582

Chamber International, Junior   www.juniorchamber.org
16120 Chesterfield Pkwy W Suite 250   Chesterfield MO 63017
Ph: 636-449-3100 ▪ Fx: 636-449-3107 ▪ TF: 800-905-5499

Chamber Litigation Center, National   www.uschamber.com/nclc
c/o US Chamber of Commerce 1615 H St NW   Washington DC 20062
Ph: 202-659-6000

Chamber Music America   www.chamber-music.org
305 7th Ave 5th Fl   New York NY 10001
Ph: 212-242-2022 ▪ Fx: 212-242-7955

Chamber Music Players, Amateur   www.acmp.net
1123 Broadway Rm 304   New York NY 10010
Ph: 212-645-7424 ▪ Fx: 212-741-2678

Chamber of Shipping of America
1730 M St NW Suite 407   Washington DC 20036
Ph: 202-775-4399 ▪ Fx: 202-659-3795

Champagne D'Argent Rabbit Federation
1704 Heisel Ave   Pekin IL 61554
Ph: 309-347-1347

Champions for Life International   www.lifechampions.org
PO Box 761101   Dallas TX 75376
Ph: 972-298-1101 ▪ Fx: 972-298-1104

Championship Association of Mechanics   www.racecrews.org
8435 Georgetown Rd Suite 200   Indianapolis IN 46268
Ph: 317-802-0001 ▪ Fx: 317-802-0003

Champlin Foundations   fdncenter.org/grantmaker/champlin
300 Centerville Rd Suite 300S   Warwick RI 02886
Ph: 401-736-0370 ▪ Fx: 401-736-7248

Change, Center for Constructive   www.constructivechange.org
801 Duke St   Alexandria VA 22314
Ph: 703-684-4735 ▪ Fx: 703-684-4738

Change, Initiatives of   www.us.initiativesofchange.org
1156 15th St NW Suite 910   Washington DC 20005
Ph: 202-872-9077 ▪ Fx: 202-872-9137

Change Ringers, North American Guild of   www.nagcr.org
829 N 25th St   Philadelphia PA 19130
Ph: 215-765-8736 ▪ Fx: 215-276-5238

Change, Teaching for   www.teachingforchange.org
PO Box 73038   Washington DC 20056
Ph: 202-588-7204 ▪ Fx: 202-238-0109 ▪ TF: 800-763-9131

Chaos Theory in Psychology & Life Sciences,   www.societyforchaostheory.org
Society for Univ of Oregon Dept of Psychology CMB 1227   Eugene OR 97403
Ph: 541-346-1996 ▪ Fx: 541-346-4911

Chaplain Services Inc, Christian
PO Box 86307   Los Angeles CA 90086
Ph: 213-353-9435 ▪ Fx: 213-353-9436

Chaplaincy, National Institute of Business & Industrial   www.nibic.com
1770 St James Pl Suite 550   Houston TX 77056
Ph: 713-266-2456 ▪ Fx: 713-266-0845

Chaplains Association, American Correctional   www.correctionalchaplains.org
PO Box 661   Waupun WI 53963
Ph: 920-324-6298 ▪ Fx: 920-324-6254

Chaplains, Association of Professional   www.professionalchaplains.org
1701 E Woodfield Rd Suite 760   Schaumburg IL 60173
Ph: 847-240-1014 ▪ Fx: 847-240-1015

Chaplains Association of the USA, Military   www.mca-usa.org
PO Box 7056   Arlington VA 22207
Ph: 703-276-2189

Chaplains Council, JWB Jewish   www.jcca.org/JWB
15 E 26th St   New York NY 10010
Ph: 212-532-4949 ▪ Fx: 212-481-4174

Chaplains, Federation of Fire   www.ffcfirechaplains.org
185 County Rd Suite 1602   Clifton TX 76634
Ph: 254-622-8514

Chaplains, International Conference of Police   www.icpc4cops.org
PO Box 5590   Destin FL 32540
Ph: 850-654-9736 ▪ Fx: 850-654-9742

Chaplains, National Association of Catholic   www.nacc.org
PO Box 070473   Milwaukee WI 53207
Ph: 414-483-4898 ▪ Fx: 414-483-6712

Chapter 13 Trustees, National Association of   www.nactt.com
1 Windsor Cove Suite 305   Columbia SC 29205
Ph: 803-252-5646 ▪ Fx: 803-765-0860 ▪ TF: 800-445-8629

(Charitable) BAPS Care International Inc   www.baps-care.org
195 Main St Suite 304   Metuchen NJ 08840
Ph: 732-744-9734 ▪ Fx: 732-744-0940 ▪ TF: 800-301-5594

(Charitable) Brother's Brother Foundation   www.brothersbrother.org
1200 Galveston Ave   Pittsburgh PA 15233
Ph: 412-321-3160 ▪ Fx: 412-321-3325 ▪ TF: 888-323-1916

(Charitable) Children to Children   www.childrentochildren.org

(Charitable) Enersol Inc   www.enersol.org
55 Middlesex St Suite 221   Chelmsford MA 01863
Ph: 978-251-1828 ▪ Fx: 978-251-5291

Charitable Foundation, Paul G Allen   www.pgafoundations.com
505 5th Ave S Suite 900   Seattle WA 98104
Ph: 206-342-2000 ▪ Fx: 206-342-3000

(Charitable) Gifts In Kind International   www.giftsinkind.org
333 N Fairfax St Suite 100   Alexandria VA 22314
Ph: 703-836-2121 ▪ Fx: 703-549-1481

(Charitable) HOPE worldwide   www.hopeww.org
353 W Lancaster Ave Suite 200   Wayne PA 19087
Ph: 610-254-8800 ▪ Fx: 610-254-8989

(Charitable) Intimate Apparel Square Club   thehugaward.org
326 Field Rd   Clinton Corners NY 12514
Ph: 845-758-5752 ▪ Fx: 845-758-2546

(Charitable) Jack & Jill of America Foundation Inc   www.jackandjillfoundation.org
PO Box 468   Pickerington OH 43147
Ph: 614-864-7085 ▪ Fx: 614-864-7093

(Charitable) NewTithing Group   www.newtithing.org
1 Market Stewart Tower Suite 2105   San Francisco CA 94105
Ph: 415-274-2765 ▪ Fx: 415-274-2756

Charitable Projects, Association of Islamic   www.aicp.org
4431 Walnut St   Philadelphia PA 19104
Ph: 215-387-8888 ▪ Fx: 215-387-3815

(Charitable) Rotary Foundation   www.rotary.org/foundation
1560 Sherman Ave   Evanston IL 60201
Ph: 847-866-3000 ▪ Fx: 847-328-4101

Charitable Statistics, National Center for   nccsdataweb.urban.org
Urban Institute 2100 M St NW   Washington DC 20037
Ph: 202-833-7200 ▪ TF: 866-518-3874

Charitable Trust, MJ Murdock   www.murdock-trust.org
703 Broadway St Suite 710   Vancouver WA 98660
Ph: 360-694-8415 ▪ Fx: 360-694-1819

Charitable Trust, Roy J Carver   www.carvertrust.org
202 Iowa Ave   Muscatine IA 52761
Ph: 563-263-4010 ▪ Fx: 563-263-1547

Charitable Trusts, Pew   www.pewtrusts.org
2005 Market St 1 Commerce Sq Suite 1700   Philadelphia PA 19103
Ph: 215-575-9050 ▪ Fx: 215-575-4939 ▪ TF: 800-634-4850

(Charitable) United Way of America   national.unitedway.org
701 N Fairfax St   Alexandria VA 22314
Ph: 703-836-7100 ▪ Fx: 703-683-7840 ▪ TF: 800-892-2757

(Charitable) United Way International   www.uwint.org
701 N Fairfax St   Alexandria VA 22314
Ph: 703-519-0092 ▪ Fx: 703-519-0097

Charities Aid Foundation   www.cafonline.org
1800 Diagonal Rd Suite 150   Alexandria VA 22314
Ph: 703-549-8931 ▪ Fx: 703-549-8934

Charities of America, Conservation & Preservation   www.conservenow.org
21 Tamal Vista Blvd Suite 209   Corte Madera CA 94925
Ph: 800-626-6685

Charities of America, Independent   www.independentcharities.org
21 Tamal Vista Blvd Suite 209   Corte Madera CA 94925
Ph: 800-477-0733 ▪ Fx: 415-924-1379

Charities of America, Italian
8320 Queens Blvd   Elmhurst NY 11373
Ph: 718-478-3100 ▪ Fx: 718-478-2665

Charities of America, Women Children & Family Service   www.womenandchildren.org
21 Tamal Vista Blvd Suite 209   Corte Madera CA 94925
Ph: 800-626-6481 ▪ Fx: 415-924-1379

Charities, American Lebanese Syrian Associated   www.stjude.org
501 St Jude Pl   Memphis TN 38105
Ph: 901-578-2000 ▪ Fx: 901-578-2805 ▪ TF: 800-822-6344

Charities, America's   www.charities.org
14150 Newbrook Dr Suite 110   Chantilly VA 20151
Ph: 703-222-3861 ▪ Fx: 703-222-3867 ▪ TF: 800-458-9505

Charities, Community Health   www.healthcharities.org
200 N Glebe Rd Suite 801   Arlington VA 22203
Ph: 703-528-1007 ▪ Fx: 703-528-1365 ▪ TF: 800-654-0845

Charities, International Orthodox Christian   www.iocc.org
110 West Rd Suite 360   Baltimore MD 21204
Ph: 410-243-9820 ▪ Fx: 410-243-9824 ▪ TF: 877-803-4622

Charities, National Black United Federation of
1212 New York Ave NW Suite 550   Washington DC 20005
Ph: 202-289-7888 ▪ Fx: 202-289-5950

Charities, Ronald McDonald House   www.rmhc.org
1 Kroc Dr   Oak Brook IL 60523
Ph: 630-623-7048 ▪ Fx: 630-623-7488

Charities USA, Catholic   www.catholiccharitiesusa.org
1731 King St Suite 200   Alexandria VA 22314
Ph: 703-549-1390 ▪ Fx: 703-549-1656

Charity of the Incarnate Word, Sisters of   www.ccvisanantonio.org
4503 Broadway   San Antonio TX 78209
Ph: 210-828-2224 ▪ Fx: 210-828-9741

(Charity) NGA   www.nga-inc.org
820 Newtown Rd   Warminster PA 18974
Ph: 215-682-9183 ▪ Fx: 215-682-9185 ▪ TF: 866-295-9974

Charity, Variety International - The Children's   www.varietychildrenscharity.com
350 5th Ave Suite 1119   New York NY 10118
Ph: 212-695-3818 ▪ Fx: 212-695-3857

Charles A & Anne Morrow Lindbergh Foundation   www.lindberghfoundation.org
2150 3rd Ave N Suite 310   Anoka MN 55303
Ph: 763-576-1596 ▪ Fx: 763-576-1664

Charles Babbage Institute   www.cbi.umn.edu
Univ of Minnesota 211 Andersen Library 222 21st Ave S   Minneapolis MN 55455
Ph: 612-624-5050 ▪ Fx: 612-625-8054

Charles Darwin Foundation   www.galapagos.org
407 N Washington St Suite 105   Falls Church VA 22046
Ph: 703-538-6833 ▪ Fx: 703-538-6835

Charles Hayden Foundation   fdncenter.org/grantmaker/hayden
140 Broadway 51st Fl   New York NY 10005
Ph: 212-785-3677 ▪ Fx: 212-785-3689

Charles & Helen Schwab Foundation   www.schwabfoundation.org
1650 S Amphlett Blvd Suite 300   San Mateo CA 94402
Ph: 650-655-2412 ▪ Fx: 650-655-2411

Charles Ives Society Inc   www.charlesives.org
Indiana Univ School of Music   Bloomington IN 47405
Ph: 812-855-7097 ▪ Fx: 812-855-4936

Charles the Martyr, Society of King   www.skcm-usa.org
291 Bacon St   Waltham MA 02451
Ph: 781-899-3165

Charles Stewart Mott Foundation   www.mott.org
503 S Saginaw St Suite 1200   Flint MI 48502
Ph: 810-238-5651 ▪ Fx: 810-766-1753

Charolais Association, American-International   www.charolaisusa.com
PO Box 20247   Kansas City MO 64195
Ph: 816-464-5977 ▪ Fx: 816-464-5759

Chartered Accountants in the US, Association of   www.acaus.com
341 Lafayette St Suite 4246   New York NY 10012
Ph: 212-334-2078 ▪ Fx: 212-431-5786

Chatlos Foundation   www.chatlos.org
PO Box 915048   Longwood FL 32791
Ph: 407-862-5077

Chautauqua Society, Jewish   www.nftb.org/jcs.html
633 3rd Ave   New York NY 10017
Ph: 212-650-4100 ▪ Fx: 212-650-4189 ▪ TF: 800-765-6200

Check Payment Systems Association   www.cpsa-checks.org
2025 M St NW Suite 800   Washington DC 20036
Ph: 202-857-1144 ▪ Fx: 202-223-4579

Checker Car Club of America   www.checkercabs.org
10530 W Alabama Ave   Sun City AZ 85351
Ph: 623-974-4987

Cheese Importers Association of America
460 Park Ave 11th Fl   New York NY 10022
Ph: 212-753-7500 ▪ Fx: 212-688-2870

Cheese Institute, National
1250 H St NW Suite 900   Washington DC 20005
Ph: 202-737-4332 ▪ Fx: 202-331-7820

Cheese Makers Association, Wisconsin   www.wischeesemakersassn.org
8030 Excelsior Dr Suite 305   Madison WI 53717
Ph: 608-828-4550 ▪ Fx: 608-828-4551

Cheese Society, American   www.cheesesociety.org
304 W Liberty St Suite 201   Louisville KY 40202
Ph: 502-583-3783 ▪ Fx: 502-589-3602

Chef Association, US Personal   uspca.com
481 Rio Rancho Blvd NE   Rio Rancho NM 87124
Ph: 505-896-3522 ▪ Fx: 505-994-6399 ▪ TF: 800-995-2138

Chef & Child Foundation, American Culinary Federation   www.acfchefs.org/ccf/ccf.html
10 San Bartola Dr   Saint Augustine FL 32086
Ph: 904-824-4468 ▪ Fx: 904-825-4758 ▪ TF: 800-624-9458

Chefs Association, Research   www.culinology.com
5775 Peachtree-Dunwoody Rd Bldg G Suite 500   Atlanta GA 30342
Ph: 404-252-3663 ▪ Fx: 404-252-0774

Chefs de Cuisine Association of America
301 E 45th St Suite 2B   New York NY 10017
Ph: 212-599-2717

Chefs & Restaurateurs, Women   www.womenchefs.org
304 W Liberty St Suite 201   Louisville KY 40202
Ph: 502-581-0300 ▪ Fx: 502-589-3602 ▪ TF: 877-927-7787

Cheiron: International Society for the History of Behavioral & Social Sciences   www.psych.yorku.ca/orgs/cheiron

Chemical & Associated Technologies Association, Drug   www.dcat.org
1 Washington Blvd Suite 7   Robbinsville NJ 08691
Ph: 609-448-1000 ▪ Fx: 609-448-1944 ▪ TF: 800-640-3228

Chemical Coaters Association International   www.ccaiweb.com
PO Box 54316   Cincinnati OH 45254
Ph: 513-624-6767 ▪ Fx: 513-624-0601 ▪ TF: 800-926-2848

Chemical Contamination, Citizens for Alternatives to
8735 Maple Grove Rd   Lake MI 48632
Ph: 517-544-3318 ▪ Fx: 517-544-2828

Chemical Credit Association, National   www.ncca1.org
1100 Main St   Buffalo NY 14209
Ph: 716-878-2894 ▪ Fx: 716-878-2866

Chemical Distributors, Canadian Association of   www.cacd.ca
627 Lyons Ln Suite 301   Oakville ON L6J5Z7
Ph: 905-844-9140 ▪ Fx: 905-844-5706

Chemical Distributors, National Association of   www.nacd.com
1560 Wilson Blvd Suite 1200   Arlington VA 22209
Ph: 703-527-6223 ▪ Fx: 703-527-7747

Chemical Ecology, International Society of   www.chemecol.org
North Dakota State Univ Dept of Entomology   Fargo ND 58105
Ph: 701-231-6444 ▪ Fx: 701-231-8557

Chemical Education, Institute for   ice.chem.wisc.edu
Univ of Wisconsin-Madison Dept of Chemistry 1101 University Ave   Madison WI 53706
Ph: 608-262-3033 ▪ Fx: 608-265-8094 ▪ TF: 800-991-5534

Chemical Engineers, American Institute of   www.aiche.org
3 Park Ave   New York NY 10016
Ph: 212-591-7338 ▪ Fx: 212-591-8897 ▪ TF: 800-242-4363

Chemical Fabrics & Film Association   www.chemicalfabricsandfilm.com
1300 Sumner Ave   Cleveland OH 44115
Ph: 216-241-7333 ▪ Fx: 216-241-0105

Chemical Heritage Foundation   www.chemheritage.org
315 Chestnut St   Philadelphia PA 19106
Ph: 215-925-2222 ▪ Fx: 215-925-1954

Chemical Industry - American Section, Society of   www.soci.org/SCI
15 W 72nd St Suite 12N   New York NY 10023
Ph: 212-873-4449 ▪ Fx: 212-873-4446

Chemical Industry, Sales Association of the
66 Morris Ave Suite 2A   Springfield NJ 07081
Ph: 973-379-1100 ▪ Fx: 973-379-6507

Chemical Manufacturers Association, Synthetic Organic   www.socma.com
1850 M St NW Suite 700   Washington DC 20036
Ph: 202-721-4100 ▪ Fx: 202-296-8120

Chemical Process Industry Inc, Materials Technology Institute   www.mti-link.org
of the   1215 Fern Ridge Pkwy Suite 206   Saint Louis MO
63141
Ph: 314-576-7712 ▪ Fx: 314-576-6078

Chemical Process Safety, Center for   www.aiche.org/ccps/index.htm
3 Park Ave   New York NY 10016
Ph: 212-591-7319 ▪ Fx: 212-591-8895

Chemical Producers & Distributors Association   www.cpda.com
1430 Duke St   Alexandria VA 22314
Ph: 703-548-7700 ▪ Fx: 703-548-3149

Chemical Research Inc, Council for   www.ccrhq.org
1620 L St NW Suite 620   Washington DC 20036
Ph: 202-429-3971 ▪ Fx: 202-429-3976

Chemical Sciences in Development, International Organization for   www.iocd.org

Chemical Society, American   www.acs.org
1155 16th St NW   Washington DC 20036
Ph: 202-872-4600 ▪ Fx: 202-872-4615 ▪ TF: 800-227-5558

Chemical Sources Association   www.chemsources.org
500 Plaza Dr PO Box 3189   Secaucus NJ 07096
Ph: 201-392-8900 ▪ Fx: 201-348-3877

Chemical Studies, National Institute for   www.nicsinfo.org
2300 MacCorkle Ave SE   Charleston WV 25304
Ph: 304-346-6264 ▪ Fx: 304-346-6349

Chemical Workers Union Council, International   www.icwuc.org
1655 W Market St   Akron OH 44313
Ph: 330-867-2444 ▪ Fx: 330-867-0544

Chemically Dependent Persons & Significant Others, Jewish   www.jacsweb.org
Alcoholics   850 7th Ave Suite 1201   New York NY 10019
Ph: 212-397-4197 ▪ Fx: 212-399-3525

Chemically Hypersensitive, National Foundation for the   www.mcsrelief.com
4407 Swinson Rd   Rhodes MI 48652
Ph: 989-689-6369 ▪ Fx: 989-689-6877

Chemicals Association, Fire Retardant   www.fireretardants.com
1801 K St NW Suite 1000-L   Washington DC 20006
Ph: 202-530-4590 ▪ Fx: 202-530-4700

Chemicals Association, Pine   www.pinechemicals.org
3350 Riverwood Pkwy SE Suite 1900   Atlanta GA 30339
Ph: 770-984-5340 ▪ Fx: 770-984-5341

(Chemistry) Alpha Chi Sigma   www.alphachisigma.org
2141 N Franklin Rd   Indianapolis IN 46219
Ph: 317-357-5944 ▪ Fx: 317-351-9702

Chemistry Inc, American Association for Clinical   www.aacc.org
2101 L St NW Suite 202   Washington DC 20037
Ph: 202-857-0717 ▪ Fx: 202-887-5093 ▪ TF: 800-892-1400

Chemistry Council, American   www.americanchemistry.com
1300 Wilson Blvd   Arlington VA 22209
Ph: 703-741-5000 ▪ Fx: 703-741-6000

Chemistry Council, Chlorine   www.c3.org
1300 Wilson Blvd   Arlington VA 22209
Ph: 703-741-5000 ▪ Fx: 703-741-6000

Chemistry, International Union of Pure & Applied   www.iupac.org
PO Box 13757   Research Triangle Park NC 27709
Ph: 919-485-8700 ▪ Fx: 919-485-8706

(Chemistry) Phi Lambda Upsilon   www.cpac.washington.edu/~campbell/plu
Univ of Washington Chemistry Dept Box 351700   Seattle WA
98195
Ph: 506-616-6085

Chemistry, Society of Environmental Toxicology &   www.setac.org
1010 N 12th Ave   Pensacola FL 32501
Ph: 850-469-1500 ▪ Fx: 850-469-9778 ▪ TF: 888-899-2088

Chemistry & Spectroscopy Societies, Federation of Analytical   www.facss.org
PO Box 24379   Sante Fe NM 87502
Ph: 505-820-1648 ▪ Fx: 505-989-1073

Chemists Inc, American Association of Cereal   www.aaccnet.org
3340 Pilot Knob Rd   Saint Paul MN 55121
Ph: 651-454-7250 ▪ Fx: 651-454-0766

Chemists, American Institute of   www.theaic.org
315 Chestnut St   Philadelphia PA 19106
Ph: 215-873-8224 ▪ Fx: 215-925-1954

Chemists, American Society of Brewing   www.asbcnet.org
3340 Pilot Knob Rd   Saint Paul MN 55121
Ph: 651-454-7250 ▪ Fx: 651-454-0766

(Chemists) AOAC International   www.aoac.org
481 N Frederick Ave Suite 500   Gaithersburg MD 20877
Ph: 301-924-7077 ▪ Fx: 301-924-7089 ▪ TF: 800-379-2622

Chemists Association, American Leather   www.leatherchemists.org
1314 50th St Suite 103   Lubbock TX 79412
Ph: 806-744-1798 ▪ Fx: 806-744-1785

Chemists, Association of Official Racing
PO Box 8400 Stn T   Ottawa ON K1G3H8
Ph: 613-731-7137 ▪ Fx: 613-731-7984

Chemists & Chemical Engineers, Association of Consulting   www.chemconsult.org
PO Box 297   Sparta NJ 07871
Ph: 973-729-6671 ▪ Fx: 973-729-7088

Chemists & Chemical Engineers, National Organization for the   www.nobcche.org
Professional Advancement of Black   PO Box
77040   Washington DC 20013
Ph: 202-667-1699 ▪ Fx: 202-667-1705 ▪ TF: 800-776-1419

Chemists & Colorists, American Association of Textile   www.aatcc.org
1 Davis Dr PO Box 12215   Research Triangle Park NC 27709
Ph: 919-549-8141 ▪ Fx: 919-549-8933

Chemists, National Registry of Certified   www.nrcc6.org
927 S Walter Reed Dr Suite 11   Arlington VA 22204
Ph: 703-979-9001

Chemists, Society of Cosmetic   www.scconline.org
120 Wall St Suite 2400   New York NY 10005
Ph: 212-668-1500 ▪ Fx: 212-668-1504

Chemists, Society of Flavor   www.flavorchemist.org
86 Watertower Plaza Suite 343   Leominster MA 01453
Ph: 978-840-4596 ▪ Fx: 978-383-0580

Chemoreception Sciences, Association for   www.achems.org
744 Duparc Cir   Tallahassee FL 32312
Ph: 850-531-0854

Chemotherapy Foundation
183 Madison Ave Rm 403   New York NY 10016
Ph: 212-213-9292 ▪ Fx: 212-213-3831

ChemPAC
1913 'I' St NW   Washington DC 20006
Ph: 202-872-8110 ▪ Fx: 202-872-8114

Cherokee National Historical Society Inc   www.cherokeeheritage.org
PO Box 515   Tahlequah OK 74465
Ph: 918-456-6007 ▪ Fx: 918-456-6165 ▪ TF: 888-999-6007

Cherry Growers & Industries Foundation, National   www.usacherries.com
PO Box 30285   Lansing MI 48909
Ph: 517-669-4264 ▪ Fx: 517-669-3354

Cherry Marketing Institute   www.cherrymkt.org
PO Box 30285   Lansing MI 48909
Ph: 517-669-4264 ▪ Fx: 517-669-3354

Chesapeake & Ohio Historical Society   www.cohs.org
PO Box 79   Clifton Forge VA 24422
Ph: 540-862-2210 ▪ Fx: 540-863-9159 ▪ TF: 800-453-2647

Chess Club, All Service Postal   chessaspc.com
1805 S Van Buren St   Amarillo TX 79102
Ph: 806-374-5991

Chess Collectors International   www.chesscollectors.com
PO Box 166   Commack NY 11725
Ph: 631-543-7667 ▪ Fx: 631-543-7901

Chess Federation, US   www.uschess.org
3054 US Rt 9 W   New Windsor NY 12553
Ph: 845-562-8350 ▪ Fx: 845-561-2437 ▪ TF: 800-388-5464

Chess Journalists of America   www.correspondencechess.com/cja
22 Budd St   Morristown NJ 07960
Ph: 973-984-3832

Chess in the Schools   www.chessintheschools.org
520 8th Ave Fl 2   New York NY 10018
Ph: 212-643-0225 ▪ Fx: 212-564-3083

Chess Tournaments, American Postal   www.correspondencechess.com/apct
PO Box 305   Western Springs IL 60558
Ph: 630-663-0688 ▪ Fx: 630-663-0689

Chest Physicians, American College of   www.chestnet.org
3300 Dundee Rd   Northbrook IL 60062
Ph: 847-498-1400 ▪ Fx: 847-498-5460 ▪ TF: 800-343-2227

Chester White Swine Record Association   www.cpsswine.com/chester/chesterwhites.htm
PO Box 9758   Peoria IL 61612
Ph: 309-691-0151 ▪ Fx: 309-691-0168

Chesterton Society, American   www.chesterton.org/
4117 Pebblebrook Cir   Minneapolis MN 55437
Ph: 952-831-3096 ▪ Fx: 952-831-0387

Chestnut Foundation, American   www.acf.org
469 Main St Suite 1 PO Box 4044   Bennington VT 05201
Ph: 802-447-0110

Cheviot Sheep Association, American North Country
8708 S County Rd 500 W   Reelsville IN 46171
Ph: 765-672-8205 ▪ Fx: 765-672-4275

Cheviot Sheep Society, American   members.aol.com/culhamef/bcheviots/cheviot.htm
Rt 1 Box 120   New Richland MN 56072
Ph: 507-465-8474

Chevrolet Association, Late Great   www.lategreatchevy.com
2166 S Orange Blossom Trail   Apopka FL 32703
Ph: 407-886-1963 ▪ Fx: 407-886-7571 ▪ TF: 800-683-1961

Chevrolet Club of America, Vintage   www.vcca.org
PO Box 5387   Orange CA 92863
Ph: 714-633-1310

Chevy Club International, Classic   www.classicchevy.com
5140 S Washington Ave   Titusville FL 32780
Ph: 407-299-1957 ▪ Fx: 407-299-3341 ▪ TF: 800-456-1957

Chewing Gum Manufacturers, National Association of   www.nacgm.org
17000 Commerce Pkwy Suite C   Mount Laurel NJ 08054
Ph: 856-439-0500 ▪ Fx: 856-439-0525

Chi Alpha Campus Ministries USA   www.chialpha.com
3728 W Chestnut Expy   Springfield MO 65802
Ph: 417-862-2781 ▪ Fx: 417-865-9947

Chi Eta Phi Sorority Inc   www.chietaphi.com
3029 13th St NW   Washington DC 20009
Ph: 202-232-3858 ▪ Fx: 202-232-3460

Chi Omega Fraternity   www.chiomega.com
3395 Players Club Pkwy   Memphis TN 38125
Ph: 901-748-8600 ▪ Fx: 901-748-8686 ▪ TF: 800-488-4664

Chi Phi Fraternity   www.chiphi.org
850 Indian Trail Rd NW   Lilburn GA 30047
Ph: 404-231-1824 ▪ Fx: 404-237-5090

Chi Psi Fraternity www.chipsi.org
147 Maple Row Blvd Suite 200   Hendersonville TN 37075
Ph: 615-826-9966 Fx: 615-826-9986

Chi Sigma Iota www.csi-net.org
PO Box 35448   Greensboro NC 27425
Ph: 336-841-8180

Chi Upsilon Sigma National Latin Sorority Inc, Corazones www.justbecus.org
Unidos Siempre/   99 Park Ave Suite 278A   New York NY
10016
Ph: 212-969-0793 Fx: 212-867-7904

Chian Federation of America www.chianfed.org
44-01 Broadway   Astoria NY 11103
Ph: 718-204-2550 Fx: 718-278-6199

Chianina Association, American www.chicattle.org
1708 N Prairie View Rd PO Box 890   Platte City MO 64079
Ph: 816-431-2808 Fx: 816-431-5381

Chianina Association, American Junior www.chicattle.org/ajca.html
PO Box 890   Platte City MO 64079
Ph: 816-431-2808 Fx: 816-431-5381

Chicago Council on Foreign Relations www.ccfr.org
116 S Michigan Ave 10th Fl   Chicago IL 60603
Ph: 312-726-3860 Fx: 312-726-4491

Chicano Studies, National Association for Chicana & www.naccs.org

Chicanos & Native Americans in Science, Society for Advancement of www.sacnas.org
PO Box 8526   Santa Cruz CA 95061
Ph: 831-459-0170 Fx: 831-459-0194

Chicken Council, National www.eatchicken.com/about_sponsors
1015 15th St NW Suite 930   Washington DC 20005
Ph: 202-296-2622 Fx: 202-293-4005

Chief Administrators, National Association of State www.nasca.org
167 W Main St Suite 600   Lexington KY 40507
Ph: 859-231-1931 Fx: 859-514-9188

Chief Executives Organization
7920 Norfolk Ave Suite 400   Bethesda MD 20814
Ph: 301-656-9220 Fx: 301-656-9221 TF: 800-634-2655

(Chief Executives) TEC International Inc www.teconline.com
11452 El Camino Real Suite 400   San Diego CA 92130
Ph: 858-627-4050 Fx: 800-934-4540 TF: 800-274-2367

Chief Justices, Conference of ccj.ncsc.dni.us
300 Newport Ave   Williamsburg VA 23185
Ph: 757-259-1841 Fx: 757-259-1520

Chief Officers of State Library Agencies www.cosla.org
167 W Main St Suite 600   Lexington KY 40507
Ph: 859-514-9151 Fx: 859-514-9166

Chief Petty Officers' Association, National www.members.tripod.com/NCPOA/main.html
106 Waring Welfare Rd   Boerne TX 78006
Ph: 830-537-4899

Chief Petty Officers Association, US Coast Guard www.uscgcpoa.org
5520-G Hempstead Way   Springfield VA 22151
Ph: 703-941-0395 Fx: 703-941-0397

Chief Warrant & Warrant Officers Association www.cwoauscg.org
200 V St SW   Washington DC 20024
Ph: 202-544-7753 Fx: 202-484-0641

Chiefs of Police, International Association of www.theiacp.org
515 N Washington St   Alexandria VA 22314
Ph: 703-836-6767 Fx: 703-836-4543 TF: 800-843-4227

Chiefs of Police, National Association of www.aphf.org/nacop.html
6350 Horizon Dr   Titusville FL 32780
Ph: 321-264-0911 Fx: 321-264-0033

Chihuahuan Desert Research Institute www.cdri.org
PO Box 905   Fort Davis TX 79734
Ph: 915-364-2499 Fx: 915-364-2504

Child Abuse America, Prevent www.preventchildabuse.org
200 S Michigan Ave 17th Fl   Chicago IL 60604
Ph: 312-663-3520 Fx: 312-939-8962 TF: 800-244-5373

Child Abuse Defense & Resource Center, National www.falseallegation.org
PO Box 638   Holland OH 43528
Ph: 419-865-0513 Fx: 419-865-0526

Child Abuse & Family Violence, National Council on www.nccafv.org
1025 Connecticut Ave NW Suite 1012   Washington DC 20036
Ph: 202-429-6695

(Child Abuse) Jacob Wetterling Foundation www.jwf.org
2314 University Ave W Suite 14   Saint Paul MN 55114
Ph: 651-714-4673 Fx: 651-714-9098

Child Abuse, National Center for Prosecution of www.ndaa-apri.org
99 Canal Ctr Plaza Suite 510   Alexandria VA 22314
Ph: 703-739-0321 Fx: 703-549-6259

Child & Adolescent Bipolar Foundation www.bpkids.org
1187 Wilmette Ave PMB 331   Wilmette IL 60091
Ph: 847-256-8525 Fx: 847-920-9498

Child & Adolescent Psychiatry & Allied Professions, International www.iacapap.org
Association for

Child & Adolescent Psychiatry, American Academy of www.aacap.org
3615 Wisconsin Ave NW   Washington DC 20016
Ph: 202-966-7300 Fx: 202-966-2891 TF: 800-333-7636

Child & Adolescent Psychiatry, Society of Professors of
3615 Wisconsin Ave NW   Washington DC 20016
Ph: 202-966-7300 Fx: 202-966-2891

(Child Advocacy) Hear My Voice www.hearmyvoice.org
1100 N Main St Suite 201   Ann Arbor MI 48104
Ph: 734-747-9654 Fx: 734-747-9559 TF: 800-958-6423

Child Alert Foundation www.childalert.org
Rt 87 S   Box 357   Dushore PA 18614
Ph: 570-928-8422 Fx: 570-928-8110

Child Care Association, National www.nccanet.org
1016 Rosser St   Conyers GA 30012
Ph: 770-922-8198 Fx: 770-388-7772 TF: 800-543-7161

Child Care Executives, National Fellowship of www.nfcce.org/fset.htm
1101 Hartman St   McKeesport PA 15132
Ph: 412-673-1992 Fx: 412-673-1996

Child Care Inc, International www.gospelcom.net/icc
3620 N High St Suite 110   Columbus OH 43214
Ph: 614-447-9952 Fx: 614-447-1123 TF: 800-722-4453

Child Care, National Association for Family www.nafcc.org
5202 Pinemont Dr   Salt Lake City UT 84123
Ph: 801-269-9338 Fx: 801-268-9507 TF: 800-359-3817

Child Care, National Resource Center for Health & Safety in nrc.uchsc.edu
Univ of Colorado Health Sciences Ctr at Fitzsimons CMS F 541
PO Box 6508   Aurora CO 80045
Ph: 303-724-0665 Fx: 303-724-0960 TF: 800-598-5437

Child Care Professionals, National Association of www.naccp.org
7610 Hwy 71 W Suite E   Austin TX 78735
Ph: 512-301-5557 Fx: 512-301-5080 TF: 800-537-1118

Child Care Resource & Referral Agencies, National Association of www.naccrra.org
1319 F St NW Suite 500   Washington DC 20004
Ph: 202-393-5501 Fx: 202-393-1109 TF: 800-424-2246

Child Care Workforce, Center for the www.ccw.org
555 New Jersey Ave NW   Washington DC 20001
Ph: 202-662-8005 Fx: 202-662-8006

Child Daycare, National Association for Sick www.nascd.com
1716 5th Ave N   Birmingham AL 35203
Ph: 205-324-8447 Fx: 205-324-8050

Child Development, Foundation for www.ffcd.org
145 E 32nd St 14th Fl   New York NY 10016
Ph: 212-213-8337 Fx: 212-213-5897

Child Development Institute, National Black www.nbcdi.org
1101 15th St NW Suite 900   Washington DC 20005
Ph: 202-833-2220 Fx: 202-833-8222

Child Development, Society for Research in www.srcd.org
3131 S State St Suite 302   Ann Arbor MI 48108
Ph: 734-998-6578 Fx: 734-998-6569

Child Evangelism Fellowship Inc www.gospelcom.net/cef
PO Box 348   Warrenton MO 63383
Ph: 636-456-4321 TF: 800-748-7710

Child & Family Policy Center www.cfpciowa.org
218 6th Ave Suite 1021   Des Moines IA 50309
Ph: 515-280-9027 Fx: 515-244-8997

Child Find of America Inc www.childfindofamerica.org
PO Box 277   New Paltz NY 12561
Ph: 845-255-1848 Fx: 845-255-5706 TF: 800-426-5678

Child Find Canada www.childfind.ca
1-1808 Main St   Winnipeg MB R2V2A3
Ph: 204-339-5584 Fx: 204-339-5587 TF: 800-387-7962

Child Foundation, American Culinary Federation Chef & www.acfchefs.org/ccf/ccf.html
10 San Bartola Dr   Saint Augustine FL 32086
Ph: 904-824-4468 Fx: 904-825-4758 TF: 800-624-9458

Child Health Foundation www.childhealthfoundation.org
10630 Little Patuxent Pkwy Century Plaza Suite 126   Columbia
MD 21044
Ph: 301-596-4514 Fx: 410-992-5641

Child Health Programs, Association of Maternal & www.amchp.org
1220 19th St NW Suite 801   Washington DC 20036
Ph: 202-775-0436 Fx: 202-775-0061

Child Lures Prevention www.childlures.org
5166 Shelburne Rd   Shelburne VT 05482
Ph: 802-985-8458 Fx: 802-985-8418

Child Neurology Society www.childneurologysociety.org
1000 W County Rd   Saint Paul MN 55126
Ph: 651-486-9447 Fx: 651-486-9436

Child, Nurses for the Rights of the nurses.cirp.org
369 Montezuma Ave Suite 354   Santa Fe NM 87501
Ph: 505-989-7377

(Child Product Safety) Danny Foundation www.dannyfoundation.org
1415 Danville Blvd Suite 202   Alamo CA 94507
Ph: 925-833-2669 Fx: 925-314-8133 TF: 800-833-2669

Child Protection, ACTION for www.actionchildprotection.org
2101 Sardis Rd N Suite 204   Charlotte NC 28227
Ph: 704-845-2121 Fx: 704-845-8577

Child Quest International www.childquest.org
1625 The Alameda Suite 500   San Jose CA 95126
Ph: 408-287-4673 Fx: 408-287-4676 TF: 888-818-4673

Child Resource Institute, International www.icrichild.org
1581 Le Roy Ave   Berkeley CA 94708
Ph: 510-644-1000 Fx: 510-525-4106

Child Rights Inc, Committee for Mother &
6536 Colgate Ave   Los Angeles CA 90048
Ph: 323-634-0543 Fx: 323-936-7762

Child Safety Council, National
PO Box 1368   Jackson MI 49204
Ph: 517-764-6070 Fx: 517-764-3068 TF: 800-222-1464

(Child Safety) Hug-a-Tree & Survive www.tbt.com/hugatree
PO Box 712739   Santee CA 92072
Ph: 619-286-7536

(Child Sexual Abuse) Stop it Now! www.stopitnow.com
PO Box 495   Haydenville MA 01039
Ph: 413-268-3096 Fx: 413-268-3098 TF: 888-773-8368

(Child Support) Association for Children for Enforcement www.childsupport-aces.org
of Support   PO Box 7842   Fredericksburg VA 22404
Ph: 800-738-2237 Fx: 800-739-2237

Child Support Enforcement Association, National www.ncsea.org
444 N Capitol St NW Suite 414   Washington DC 20001
Ph: 202-624-8180 Fx: 202-624-8828

Child Trends www.childtrends.org
4301 Connecticut Ave NW Suite 100   Washington DC 20008
Ph: 202-362-5580 Fx: 202-362-5533

Child Welfare Administrators, National Association of Public
810 1st St NE Suite 500   Washington DC 20002
Ph: 202-682-0100 Fx: 202-289-6555

Child Welfare Association, National Indian www.nicwa.org
5100 SW Macadam Ave Suite 300   Portland OR 97239
Ph: 503-222-4044 Fx: 503-222-4007

Child Welfare Institute
3950 Shackleford Rd Suite 175   Duluth GA 30096
Ph: 770-935-8484 ▪ Fx: 770-935-0344
www.gocwi.org

Child Welfare League of America
440 1st St NW 3rd Fl   Washington DC 20001
Ph: 202-638-2952 ▪ Fx: 202-638-4004
www.cwla.org

Childbearing Centers, National Association of
3123 Gottschall Rd   Perkiomenville PA 18074
Ph: 215-234-8068 ▪ Fx: 215-234-8829
www.birthcenters.org

Childbirth Education Association, International
PO Box 20048   Minneapolis MN 55420
Ph: 952-854-8660 ▪ Fx: 952-854-8772 ▪ TF: 800-624-4934
www.icea.org

Childbirth, InterNational Association of Parents & Professionals for Safe Alternatives in   Rt 4 Box 646   Marble Hill MO 63764
Ph: 573-238-2010
www.napsac.org

(Childbirth) Lamaze International
2025 M St NW Suite 800   Washington DC 20036
Ph: 202-367-1128 ▪ Fx: 202-367-2128 ▪ TF: 800-368-4404
www.lamaze-childbirth.com

Childbirth Without Pain Education Association
20134 Snowden St   Detroit MI 48235
Ph: 313-341-3816 ▪ Fx: 313-345-9850

Childcare International
3350 Airport Dr   Bellingham WA 98226
Ph: 360-647-2283 ▪ Fx: 360-647-2392 ▪ TF: 800-553-2328
www.childcare-intl.org

Childhelp USA
15757 N 78th St   Scottsdale AZ 85260
Ph: 480-922-8212 ▪ Fx: 480-922-7061 ▪ TF: 800-422-4453
www.childhelpusa.org

Childhood Association, Holy
366 5th Ave   New York NY 10001
Ph: 212-563-8700 ▪ Fx: 212-563-8725
www.worldmissions-catholicchurch.org

Childhood Association, Southern Early
PO Box 55930   Little Rock AR 72215
Ph: 501-221-1648 ▪ Fx: 501-227-5297 ▪ TF: 800-305-7322
www.southernearlychildhood.org

Childhood Cancer, Association for Research of
PO Box 251   Buffalo NY 14225
Ph: 716-681-4433
www.arocc.org

Childhood Cancer Foundation, Candlelighters
PO Box 498   Kensington MD 20895
Ph: 301-962-3520 ▪ Fx: 301-962-3521 ▪ TF: 800-366-2223
www.candlelighters.org

Childhood Education International, Association for
17904 Georgia Ave Suite 215   Olney MD 20832
Ph: 301-570-2111 ▪ Fx: 301-570-2212 ▪ TF: 800-423-3563
www.udel.edu/bateman/acei

Childhood Education, Professional Association for
1290 Sutter St Suite 200   San Francisco CA 94109
Ph: 415-749-6851 ▪ Fx: 415-749-6861 ▪ TF: 800-924-2460
www.pacenet.org

Childhood Educators, American Association of Early
3612 Bent Branch Ct   Falls Church VA 22041
Ph: 703-941-4329

Childhood Lead Poisoning, Coalition to End
2714 Hudson St   Baltimore MD 21224
Ph: 410-534-6447 ▪ Fx: 410-534-6475 ▪ TF: 800-370-5323
www.leadsafe.org

Childhood Resources, Institute for
268 Bush St   San Francisco CA 94104
Ph: 415-864-1169 ▪ Fx: 510-540-0171 ▪ TF: 800-551-8697

Childhood Teacher Educators, National Association of Early
www.naecte.org

Childreach
155 Plan Way   Warwick RI 02886
Ph: 401-738-5600 ▪ Fx: 401-738-5608 ▪ TF: 800-556-7918
www.childreach.org

Children Inc
PO Box 5381   Richmond VA 23220
Ph: 804-359-4562 ▪ Fx: 804-353-7541 ▪ TF: 800-538-5381
www.children-inc.org

Children & Adults with Attention-Deficit/Hyperactivity Disorder
8181 Professional Pl Suite 201   Landover MD 20785
Ph: 301-306-7070 ▪ Fx: 301-306-7090 ▪ TF: 800-233-4050
www.chadd.org

Children & Aging, Christian Foundation for
1 Elmwood Ave   Kansas City KS 66103
Ph: 913-384-6500 ▪ Fx: 913-384-2211 ▪ TF: 800-875-6564
www.cfcausa.org

Children of Aging Parents
1609 Woodbourne Rd Suite 302A   Levittown PA 19057
Ph: 215-945-6900 ▪ Fx: 215-945-8720 ▪ TF: 800-227-7294
www.caps4caregivers.org

Children, AIDS Resource Foundation for
Saint Clare's Home for Children 182 Roseville Ave   Newark NJ 07107
Ph: 973-483-4250 ▪ Fx: 973-483-1998
www.aidsresource.org

Children, American Association for Gifted
Duke University PO Box 90270   Durham NC 27708
Ph: 919-783-6152
www.aagc.org

Children, American Coalition for Fathers &
22365 El Toro Rd Suite 335   Lake Forest CA 92630
Ph: 800-978-3237 ▪ Fx: 949-859-1514
www.acfc.org

Children, American Professional Society on the Abuse of
940 NE 13th St CHO 3B3406   Oklahoma City OK 73104
Ph: 405-271-8202 ▪ Fx: 405-271-2931
www.apsac.org

Children of the American Revolution, National Society of the
1776 D St NW   Washington DC 20006
Ph: 202-638-3153 ▪ Fx: 202-737-3162
www.nscar.org

(Children) With Arms Wide Open Foundation
525 E College Ave   Tallahassee FL 32301
Ph: 850-222-3882 ▪ Fx: 850-222-1461
www.witharmswideopen.org

Children, Association of Booksellers for
3900 Sumac Cir   Middleton WI 53562
Ph: 608-836-6050 ▪ Fx: 608-836-1438
www.abfc.com

Children, Association for Library Service to
50 E Huron St   Chicago IL 60611
Ph: 312-280-2163 ▪ Fx: 312-944-7671 ▪ TF: 800-545-2433
www.ala.org/alsc

Children Association Inc, North America Missing
136 Rt 420 Hwy   South Esk NB E1V4N8
Ph: 506-627-1209 ▪ Fx: 506-622-3515
www.namca.com

Children Awaiting Parents Inc
595 Blossom Rd Suite 306   Rochester NY 14610
Ph: 585-232-5110 ▪ Fx: 585-232-2634 ▪ TF: 888-835-8802
www.capbook.org

Children, Black Community Crusade for
25 'E' St NW   Washington DC 20001
Ph: 202-628-8787 ▪ Fx: 202-662-3580
www.childrensdefense.org/bccc

Children to Children
www.childrentochildren.org

Children, Commission on Missing & Exploited
616 Adams Ave   Memphis TN 38105
Ph: 901-405-8441 ▪ Fx: 901-575-8856
www.comec.org

Children, Committee for
801 1st Ave S Suite 100   Seattle WA 98134
Ph: 206-343-1223 ▪ Fx: 206-438-6765 ▪ TF: 800-634-4449
www.cfchildren.org

Children of the Confederacy
c/o United Daughters of the Confederacy 328 North
   Blvd   Richmond VA 23220
Ph: 804-355-1636 ▪ Fx: 804-353-1396
hqudc.org/CofC

Children, Council for Exceptional
1110 N Glebe Rd   Arlington VA 22201
Ph: 703-620-3660 ▪ Fx: 703-264-9494 ▪ TF: 888-232-7733
www.cec.sped.org

Children of Deaf Adults International Inc
PO Box 30715   Santa Barbara CA 93130
Ph: 805-682-0997
www.coda-international.org

(Children) Devil Pups Inc
2160 Lords Landing   Virginia Beach VA 23454
Ph: 757-496-8796 ▪ Fx: 757-496-8797
www.devilpups.com

Children with Disabilities, National Dissemination Center for
PO Box 1492   Washington DC 20013
Ph: 202-884-8200 ▪ Fx: 202-884-8441 ▪ TF: 800-695-0285
www.nichcy.org

Children with Down Syndrome Inc, Association for
4 Fern Pl   Plainview NY 11803
Ph: 516-933-4700 ▪ Fx: 516-933-9524
www.acds.org

(Children) Dream Factory Inc
1218 S 3rd St   Louisville KY 40203
Ph: 502-637-8700 ▪ Fx: 502-637-8744 ▪ TF: 800-456-7556
www.dreamfactoryinc.com

Children for Enforcement of Support, Association for
PO Box 7842   Fredericksburg VA 22404
Ph: 800-738-2237 ▪ Fx: 800-739-2237
www.childsupport-aces.org

Children & Families Inc, Alliance for
11700 W Lake Park Dr   Milwaukee WI 53224
Ph: 414-359-1040 ▪ Fx: 414-359-1074
www.alliance1.org

Children & Families, National Coalition for the Protection of
800 Compton Rd Suite 9224   Cincinnati OH 45231
Ph: 513-521-6227 ▪ Fx: 513-521-6337
www.eos.net/ncpcf

Children & Families, National Law Center for
3819 Plaza Dr   Fairfax VA 22030
Ph: 703-691-4626
www.nationallawcenter.org

Children & Family Service Charities of America, Women
21 Tamal Vista Blvd Suite 209   Corte Madera CA 94925
Ph: 800-626-6481 ▪ Fx: 415-924-1379
www.womenandchildren.org

(Children) Famous Fone Friends
9101 Sawyer St   Los Angeles CA 90035
Ph: 310-204-5683
www.nancycartwright.com/volunteer_fff.html

Children, Feed the
PO Box 36   Oklahoma City OK 73101
Ph: 405-942-0228 ▪ Fx: 405-945-4177 ▪ TF: 800-627-4556
www.feedthechildren.org

Children, Find the
3250 Ocean Park Blvd Suite 333   Santa Monica CA 90405
Ph: 310-314-3213 ▪ Fx: 310-314-3169 ▪ TF: 888-477-6721
www.findthechildren.com

Children Inc, French-American Aid for
575 Madison Ave Suite 2409   New York NY 10022
Ph: 212-486-9593 ▪ Fx: 212-486-9594
www.aidforchildren.org

Children, Futures for
9600 Tennyson St NE   Albuquerque NM 87122
Ph: 505-821-2828 ▪ Fx: 505-821-4141 ▪ TF: 800-545-6843
www.futuresforchildren.org

(Children) Give Kids the World Village
210 S Bass Rd   Kissimmee FL 34746
Ph: 407-396-1114 ▪ Fx: 407-396-1207 ▪ TF: 800-995-5437
www.gktw.org

Children, Healing the
PO Box 9065   Spokane WA 99209
Ph: 509-327-4281 ▪ Fx: 509-327-4284 ▪ TF: 877-432-5543
www.healingchildren.org

(Children) Hole in the Wall Gang Camps Inc
265 Church St   New Haven CT 06510
Ph: 203-562-1203 ▪ Fx: 203-562-1207
www.hitwgcamps.org

Children, INMED Partnerships for
45449 Severn Way Suite 161   Sterling VA 20166
Ph: 703-444-4477 ▪ Fx: 703-444-4471 ▪ TF: 800-521-1175
www.inmed.org

Children, Institute for the Advancement of Philosophy for   Montclair State Univ 14 Normal Ave   Upper Montclair NJ 07043
Ph: 973-655-4977
www.montclair.edu/pages/iapc

Children International
2000 E Red Bridge Rd   Kansas City MO 64131
Ph: 816-942-2000 ▪ Fx: 816-942-3714 ▪ TF: 800-888-3089
children.org

(Children) Kids Meeting Kids
380 Riverside Dr Box 8H   New York NY 10025
Ph: 212-662-2327 ▪ Fx: 212-222-1416
kidsmeetingkids.org

Children & the Law, ABA Center on
740 15th St NW 9th Fl   Washington DC 20005
Ph: 202-662-1720 ▪ Fx: 202-662-1755
www.abanet.org/child

Children of Lesbians & Gays Everywhere
3543 18th St Suite 1   San Francisco CA 94110
Ph: 415-861-5437 ▪ Fx: 415-255-8345
www.colage.org

Children, National Association of Counsel for
1825 Marion St Suite 340   Denver CO 80218
Ph: 888-828-6222
www.naccchildlaw.org

Children, National Association for the Education of Young
1509 16th St NW   Washington DC 20036
Ph: 202-232-8777 ▪ Fx: 202-328-1846 ▪ TF: 800-424-2460
www.naeyc.org

Children, National Association for Gifted www.nagc.org
1707 L St NW Suite 550   Washington DC 20036
Ph: 202-785-4268 ▪ Fx: 202-785-4248

Children, National Center for Missing & Exploited www.missingkids.com
699 Prince St   Alexandria VA 22314
Ph: 703-274-3900 ▪ Fx: 703-274-2095 ▪ TF: 800-843-5678

Children, National Congress for Fathers & www.ncfc.net
9454 Wilshire Blvd Suite 907   Beverly Hills CA 90212
Ph: 310-247-6051 ▪ TF: 800-733-3237

Children of the Night www.childrenofthenight.org
14530 Sylvan St   Van Nuys CA 91411
Ph: 818-908-4474 ▪ Fx: 818-908-1468 ▪ TF: 800-551-1300

Children, North American Council on Adoptable www.nacac.org
970 Raymond Ave Suite 106   Saint Paul MN 55114
Ph: 651-644-3036 ▪ Fx: 651-644-9848

Children Now www.childrennow.org
1212 Broadway 5th Fl   Oakland CA 94612
Ph: 510-763-2444 ▪ Fx: 510-763-1974

Children, Parents of Murdered www.pomc.com
100 E 8th St Suite B-41   Cincinnati OH 45202
Ph: 513-721-5683 ▪ Fx: 513-345-4489 ▪ TF: 888-818-7662

Children & Parents, World Association for www.wacap.org
315 S 2nd St   Renton WA 98055
Ph: 206-575-4550 ▪ Fx: 206-575-4148

(Children) Pearl S Buck International www.pearl-s-buck.org/psbi
520 Dublin Rd   Perkasie PA 18944
Ph: 215-249-0100 ▪ Fx: 215-249-9657 ▪ TF: 800-220-2825

Children in Poverty, National Center for cpmcnet.columbia.edu/dept/nccp
215 W 125th St 3rd Fl   New York NY 10027
Ph: 646-284-9600 ▪ Fx: 646-284-9623

Children, Project www.interwebinc.com/children/
PO Box 933   Greenwood Lake NY 10925
Ph: 845-477-3472 ▪ Fx: 845-477-2334

(Children) Rainbows www.rainbows.org
2100 Golf Rd Suite 370   Rolling Meadows IL 60008
Ph: 847-952-1770 ▪ Fx: 847-952-1774 ▪ TF: 800-266-3206

Children of Russia www.leahi.net/russia
4117 Kahala Ave   Honolulu HI 96816
Ph: 808-737-5248 ▪ Fx: 808-737-7806

Children, Save the www.savethechildren.org
54 Wilton Rd   Westport CT 06880
Ph: 203-221-4000 ▪ Fx: 203-227-5667 ▪ TF: 800-243-5075

Children of SCORE, American scoremusicensemble.org
8031 Great Run Ln PO Box 3423   Warrenton VA 20188
Ph: 540-428-2313 ▪ Fx: 540-428-2314

Children, SEE (Signing Exact English) Center for the www.seecenter.org
Advancement of Deaf   PO Box 1181   Los Alamitos CA 90720
Ph: 562-430-1467 ▪ Fx: 562-795-6614

Children Services, Jewish Board of Family & www.jbfcs.org
120 W 57th St   New York NY 10019
Ph: 212-582-9100 ▪ Fx: 212-956-5676 ▪ TF: 888-523-2769

Children, Society for Ear Nose & Throat Advances in www.sentac.org
3333 Burnet Ave   Cincinnati OH 45229
Ph: 513-636-2287

Children, Spaulding for www.spaulding.org
16250 Northland Dr Suite 120   Southfield MI 48075
Ph: 248-443-7080 ▪ Fx: 248-443-7099 ▪ TF: 877-767-5437

Children with Special Needs, Federation for www.fcsn.org
1135 Tremont St Suite 420   Boston MA 02120
Ph: 617-236-7210 ▪ Fx: 617-572-2094 ▪ TF: 800-331-0688

Children, Stand For www.stand.org
516 SE Morrison St Suite 206   Portland OR 97214
Ph: 503-235-2305 ▪ Fx: 503-963-9517 ▪ TF: 800-663-4032

(Children) Sunshine Foundation www.sunshinefoundation.org
1041 Mill Creek Dr   Feasterville PA 19053
Ph: 215-396-4770 ▪ Fx: 215-396-4774 ▪ TF: 800-767-1976

Children, Treasures for Little www.treasuresforlittlechildren.com
8201 Pleasant Ave S   Bloomington MN 55420
Ph: 952-888-1079

Children, Voices for America's www.voicesforamericaschildren.org
1522 K St NW Suite 600   Washington DC 20005
Ph: 202-289-0777 ▪ Fx: 202-289-0776

Children of War www.thechildrenofwar.org
PO Box 11321   Burke VA 22009
Ph: 703-923-0455

Children Who Are Deaf or Hard of Hearing Inc, BEGINNINGS www.ncbegin.org
for Parents of   PO Box 17646   Raleigh NC 27619
Ph: 919-850-2746 ▪ Fx: 919-850-2804 ▪ TF: 800-541-4327

Children, World Council for Gifted & Talented www.worldgifted.org
18401 Hiawatha St   Northridge CA 91326
Ph: 818-368-7501 ▪ Fx: 818-368-2163

Children, World Opportunities International/Help the www.helpthechildren.org
1415 Cahuenga Blvd   Hollywood CA 90028
Ph: 323-466-7187 ▪ Fx: 323-871-1546

Children, Yes I Can Foundation for Exceptional yesican.cec.sped.org
1110 N Glebe Rd Suite 300   Arlington VA 22201
Ph: 703-264-3660 ▪ Fx: 703-264-9494 ▪ TF: 800-224-6830

Children & Young People, International Association of Theatre www.assitej-usa.org
for   724 2nd Ave S   Nashville TN 37210
Ph: 615-254-5719 ▪ Fx: 615-254-3255

Children Youth & Families, Grantmakers for www.gcyf.org
1522 K St NW Suite 1100   Washington DC 20005
Ph: 202-962-3940 ▪ Fx: 202-393-4148

Children's Adoption Network, Jewish www.users.qwest.net/~jcan
PO Box 147016   Denver CO 80214
Ph: 303-573-8113 ▪ Fx: 303-893-1447

Children's Advertising Review Unit, Council of Better Business www.caru.org
Bureaus Inc   70 W 36th St 13th Fl   New York NY 10018
Ph: 866-334-6272

Children's Advocacy Center, National www.nationalcac.org
210 Pratt Ave   Huntsville AL 35801
Ph: 256-533-5437 ▪ Fx: 256-534-6883

Children's Agencies, Association of Jewish Family & www.ajfca.org
557 Cranbury Rd Suite 2   East Brunswick NJ 08816
Ph: 732-432-7120 ▪ Fx: 732-432-7127 ▪ TF: 800-634-7346

Children's AIDS Fund www.childrensaidsfund.org
PO Box 16433   Washington DC 20041
Ph: 866-829-1560 ▪ Fx: 800-557-8529

Children's Alliance, Vanished www.vca.org
991 W Hedding St Suite 101   San Jose CA 95126
Ph: 408-296-1113 ▪ Fx: 408-296-1117 ▪ TF: 800-826-4743

Children's Art Foundation www.stonesoup.com
PO Box 83   Santa Cruz CA 95063
Ph: 831-426-5557 ▪ Fx: 831-426-1161 ▪ TF: 800-447-4569

Children's Blood Foundation www.childrensbloodfoundation.org
333 E 38th Rm 830   New York NY 10016
Ph: 212-297-4336 ▪ Fx: 212-297-4340

Children's Book Council www.cbcbooks.org
12 W 37th St 2nd Fl   New York NY 10018
Ph: 212-966-1990 ▪ Fx: 212-966-2073 ▪ TF: 800-999-2160

Children's Book Writers & Illustrators, Society of www.scbwi.org
8271 Beverly Blvd   Los Angeles CA 90048
Ph: 323-782-1010 ▪ Fx: 323-782-1892

Children's Cancer Society, National www.children-cancer.org
1015 Locust Suite 600   Saint Louis MO 63101
Ph: 314-241-1600 ▪ Fx: 314-241-6949 ▪ TF: 800-532-6459

Children's Center, Kempe www.kempecenter.org
1825 Marion St   Denver CO 80218
Ph: 303-864-5300 ▪ Fx: 303-864-5179

Children's Centers, National Coalition for Campus www.campuschildren.org
Univ of Northern Iowa 119 Schindler Education Ctr   Cedar Falls
IA 50614
Ph: 319-273-3113 ▪ Fx: 319-273-3109 ▪ TF: 800-813-8207

Children's Charity, Variety International - The www.varietychildrenscharity.com
350 5th Ave Suite 1119   New York NY 10118
Ph: 212-695-3818 ▪ Fx: 212-695-3857

Children's Craniofacial Association www.ccakids.com
13140 Coit Rd Suite 307   Dallas TX 75240
Ph: 214-570-9099 ▪ Fx: 214-570-8811 ▪ TF: 800-535-3643

Children's Defense Fund www.childrensdefense.org
25 'E' St NW   Washington DC 20001
Ph: 202-628-8787 ▪ Fx: 202-662-3510 ▪ TF: 800-233-1200

Children's Express Foundation Inc
1101 14th St NW 3rd Fl   Washington DC 20005
Ph: 202-737-7377 ▪ Fx: 202-737-0193

Children's Eye Care Foundation, National www.mentalhealth.about.com
PO Box 795069   Dallas TX 75379
Ph: 972-407-0404 ▪ Fx: 972-407-0616

Children's Foundation www.childrensfoundation.net
725 15th St NW Suite 505   Washington DC 20005
Ph: 202-347-3300 ▪ Fx: 202-347-3382

Children's Foundation, Believe In Tomorrow National www.believeintomorrow.org
PO Box 21211   Baltimore MD 21228
Ph: 410-744-1032 ▪ Fx: 410-744-1984 ▪ TF: 800-933-5470

Children's Foundation, Starlight www.starlight.org
5900 Wilshire Blvd Suite 2530   Los Angeles CA 90036
Ph: 323-634-0080 ▪ Fx: 323-634-0090 ▪ TF: 800-274-7827

Children's Fund Inc, Christian www.christianchildrensfund.org
2821 Emerywood Pkwy   Richmond VA 23294
Ph: 804-756-2700 ▪ Fx: 804-756-2718 ▪ TF: 800-776-6767

Children's Fund, United Nations www.unicef.org
3 UN Plaza   New York NY 10017
Ph: 212-326-7000 ▪ Fx: 212-888-7465 ▪ TF: 800-553-1200

Children's Health Fund www.childrenshealthfund.org
317 E 64th St   New York NY 10021
Ph: 212-535-9400 ▪ Fx: 212-535-7488

Children's HeartLink www.childrensheartlink.org
5075 Arcadia Ave   Minneapolis MN 55436
Ph: 952-928-4860 ▪ Fx: 952-928-4859

Children's Hospice International www.chionline.org
901 N Pitt St Suite 230   Alexandria VA 22314
Ph: 703-684-0330 ▪ Fx: 703-684-0226 ▪ TF: 800-242-4453

(Children's Hospitals) Children's Miracle Network www.cmncan.ca
4220 Steeles Ave W Suite C18   Woodbridge ON L4L3S8
Ph: 905-265-9750 ▪ Fx: 905-265-9749

(Children's Hospitals) Children's Miracle Network www.cmn.org
4525 S 2300 East   Salt Lake City UT 84117
Ph: 801-278-8900 ▪ Fx: 801-277-8787

Children's Hospitals & Related Institutions, National www.childrenshospitals.net
Association of   401 Wythe St   Alexandria VA 22314
Ph: 703-684-1355 ▪ Fx: 703-684-1589

(Children's Hospitals) Shrine of North America www.shrinershq.org
2900 N Rocky Point Dr   Tampa FL 33607
Ph: 813-281-0300 ▪ Fx: 813-281-2519

Children's Leukemia Research Association www.childrensleukemia.org
585 Stewart Ave Suite 18   Garden City NY 11530
Ph: 516-222-1944 ▪ Fx: 516-222-0457

Children's Librarians, Canadian Association of www.cla.ca/divisions/capl/cacl.htm
328 Frank St   Ottawa ON K2P0X8
Ph: 613-232-9625 ▪ Fx: 613-563-9895

Children's Literacy Initiative www.cliontheweb.org
2314 Market St   Philadelphia PA 19103
Ph: 215-561-4676 ▪ Fx: 215-561-4677 ▪ TF: 888-408-3388

Children's Literature Association www.childlitassn.org
PO Box 138   Battle Creek MI 49016
Ph: 269-965-8180 ▪ Fx: 269-965-3568

Children's Medical Ministries www.childrenmed.org
PO Box 3382   Crofton MD 21114
Ph: 301-261-3211 ▪ Fx: 301-721-4647

Children's Mental Health, Federation of Families for
1101 King St Suite 420   Alexandria VA 22314
Ph: 703-684-7710 ■ Fx: 703-836-1040
www.ffcmh.org

Children's Miracle Network
4220 Steeles Ave W Suite C18   Woodbridge ON L4L3S8
Ph: 905-265-9750 ■ Fx: 905-265-9749
www.cmncan.ca

Children's Miracle Network
4525 S 2300 East   Salt Lake City UT 84117
Ph: 801-278-8900 ■ Fx: 801-277-8787
www.cmn.org

Children's Museums, Association of
1300 L St NW Suite 975   Washington DC 20005
Ph: 202-898-1080 ■ Fx: 202-898-1086
www.childrensmuseums.org

Children's Organ Transplant Association
2501 Cota Dr   Bloomington IN 47403
Ph: 812-336-8872 ■ Fx: 812-336-8885 ■ TF: 800-366-2682
www.cota.org

Children's Organization, Global
PO Box 67583   Los Angeles CA 90067
Ph: 310-581-2234 ■ Fx: 310-581-6155
www.globalchild.org

(Children's Products) Parents' Choice Foundation
201 W Padonia Rd Suite 303   Timonium MD 21093
Ph: 410-308-3858 ■ Fx: 410-308-3877
www.parents-choice.org

Children's Prosthetic-Orthotic Clinics, Association of
6300 N River Rd Suite 727   Rosemont IL 60018
Ph: 847-698-1637 ■ Fx: 847-823-0536
www.acpoc.org

Children's Residential Centers, American Association of
2020 Pennsylvania Ave NW Suite 745   Washington DC 20006
Ph: 877-332-2272 ■ Fx: 877-362-2272
www.aacrc-dc.org

Children's Rights
404 Park Ave S 11th Fl   New York NY 10016
Ph: 212-683-2210 ■ Fx: 212-683-4015
www.childrensrights.org

Children's Rights Council
6200 Editors Park Dr Suite 103   Hyattsville MD 20782
Ph: 301-559-3120 ■ Fx: 301-559-3124 ■ TF: 800-787-5437
www.gocrc.com

Children's Services, Holt International
1195 City View PO Box 2880   Eugene OR 97402
Ph: 541-687-2202 ■ Fx: 541-683-6175
www.holtinternational.org

Children's Surgical Aid International
37 St Paul's Pl   Hempstead NY 11550
Ph: 516-485-7909 ■ Fx: 516-481-5393
www.csaintl.org

Children's Survival Fund Inc
4211 Surfside Cir   Missouri City TX 77459
Ph: 281-403-3808 ■ TF: 800-426-9885
home.houston.rr.com/csf

Children's Villages-USA, SOS
1317 F St NW Suite 550   Washington DC 20004
Ph: 202-347-7920 ■ Fx: 202-347-7334 ■ TF: 800-886-5767
www.soschildrensvillages.org

Children's Welfare Society Inc, Russian
200 Park Ave S Suite 1617   New York NY 10003
Ph: 212-473-6263 ■ Fx: 212-473-6301 ■ TF: 888-732-7297
www.rcws.org

Children's Wish Foundation International
8615 Roswell Rd   Atlanta GA 30350
Ph: 770-393-9474 ■ Fx: 770-393-0683 ■ TF: 800-323-9474
www.childrenswish.org

Chile-US Chamber of Commerce
801 Brickell Ave Suite 900   Miami FL 33131
Ph: 305-789-6690 ■ Fx: 305-372-0189
www.chileus.org

Chimie Industrielle American Section, Societe de
PO Box 873 Grand Central Stn   New York NY 10163
Ph: 212-725-9539
www.societe.org

Chimney Safety Institute of America
2155 Commercial Dr   Plainfield IN 46168
Ph: 317-837-5362 ■ Fx: 317-837-5365 ■ TF: 800-536-0118
www.csia.org

Chimney Sweep Guild, National
2155 Commercial Dr   Plainfield IN 46168
Ph: 317-837-1500 ■ Fx: 317-837-5365
www.ncsg.org

China Arts Exchange, Center for US-
423 W 118th St Suite 1E   New York NY 10027
Ph: 212-280-4648 ■ Fx: 212-662-6346
www.columbia.edu/cu/china

China & Asia Missionary Society, Voice of
183 E Glenarm St PO Box 150   Pasadena CA 91102
Ph: 626-441-0640 ■ Fx: 626-441-8124
www.vocamissionarysociety.org

China Association, Yale-
442 Temple St PO Box 208223   New Haven CT 06520
Ph: 203-432-0881 ■ Fx: 203-432-7246
www.yalechina.org/

China-Burma-India Veterans Association
PO Box 780676   Orlando FL 32878
Ph: 407-282-0346

China Business Council, US-
1818 N St NW Suite 200   Washington DC 20036
Ph: 202-429-0340 ■ Fx: 202-775-2476
www.uschina.org

China Chamber of Commerce, USA-
55 W Monroe St Suite 630   Chicago IL 60603
Ph: 312-368-9030 ■ Fx: 312-368-9922
www.usccc.org

China Clay Producers Association
4885 Riverside Dr Suite 108   Macon GA 31210
Ph: 478-757-1211 ■ Fx: 478-757-1949
www.kaolin.com

China Fellowship Inc, Evangelize
437 S Garfield   Monterey Park CA 91754
Ph: 626-288-8828 ■ Fx: 626-288-6727
www.ecfusa.org

China, Friends of Free
PO Box 4134   Merrifield VA 22116
Ph: 703-573-8677 ■ Fx: 703-573-2134

China, Human Rights in
350 5th Ave Suite 3309   New York NY 10118
Ph: 212-239-4495 ■ Fx: 212-239-2561
www.hrichina.org

China Institute in America
125 E 65th St   New York NY 10021
Ph: 212-744-8181 ■ Fx: 212-628-4159
www.chinainstitute.org

China Painters, World Organization of
2641 NW 10th St   Oklahoma City OK 73107
Ph: 405-521-1234 ■ Fx: 405-521-1265
www.theshop.net/wocporg

China Peoples Friendship Association, US
1214 W Schwartz St   Carbondale IL 62901
Ph: 618-549-1555 ■ Fx: 618-549-9766
www.uscpfa.org

(China) Pickard Collectors Club
300 E Grove St   Bloomington IL 61701
Ph: 309-828-5533 ■ Fx: 309-829-2266

China Relations, National Committee on US-
71 W 23rd St Suite 1901   New York NY 10010
Ph: 212-645-9677 ■ Fx: 212-645-1695
www.ncuscr.org

(China) Tea Leaf Club International
PO Box 377   Belton MO 64012
Ph: 816-331-5546
www.tealeafclub.com

Chincoteague Pony Association, National
2595 Jensen Rd   Bellingham WA 98226
Ph: 360-671-8338 ■ Fx: 360-671-7603
www.pony-chincoteague.com

Chinese American Arts Council
456 Broadway 3rd Fl   New York NY 10013
Ph: 212-431-9740 ■ Fx: 212-431-9789
www.mercurial.net/gallery456

Chinese American Citizens Alliance
1044 Stockton St   San Francisco CA 94108
Ph: 415-434-2222
www.cacanational.org

Chinese American Civic Council
PO Box 166082   Chicago IL 60616
Ph: 312-225-0234

Chinese American Forum
PO Box 719   Saint Charles MO 63302
Ph: 636-561-8134 ■ Fx: 636-561-8031
www.cafmag.org

Chinese-American Librarians Association
PO Box 4992   Irvine CA 92616
Ph: 949-824-6832 ■ Fx: 949-857-1988
www.cala-web.org

(Chinese Americans) Committee of 100
677 5th Ave 3rd Fl   New York NY 10022
Ph: 212-371-6565 ■ Fx: 212-371-9009
www.committee100.org

Chinese Americans, Organization of
1001 Connecticut Ave NW Suite 601   Washington DC 20036
Ph: 202-223-5500 ■ Fx: 202-296-0540
www.ocanatl.org

Chinese Christian Mission
PO Box 750759   Petaluma CA 94975
Ph: 707-762-1314 ■ Fx: 707-762-1713
www.ccmusa.org

Chinese Consolidated Benevolent Association
62-64 Mott St   New York NY 10013
Ph: 212-226-6280 ■ Fx: 212-226-6764
ccbany.org

Chinese Culture Foundation of San Francisco
750 Kearny St 3rd Fl   San Francisco CA 94108
Ph: 415-986-1822 ■ Fx: 415-986-2825
www.c-c-c.org

Chinese Economists Society
733 15th St NW Suite 910   Washington DC 20005
Ph: 202-347-8588 ■ Fx: 202-347-8510
www.china-ces.org

Chinese Language Teachers Association
Univ of Hawaii Center for Chinese Studies 416 Moore
Hall   Honolulu HI 96822
Ph: 808-956-2692
clta.deall.ohio-state.edu

Chinese Music Society of North America
PO Box 5275   Woodridge IL 60517
Ph: 630-910-1551 ■ Fx: 630-910-1561
www.chinesemusic.net

Chinese Snuff Bottle Society Inc, International
2601 N Charles St   Baltimore MD 21218
Ph: 410-467-9400 ■ Fx: 410-243-3451
www.snuffbottle.org

Chinese Studies, American Association for
City College-CUNY NAC R4/116   New York NY 10031
Ph: 212-650-6206
www.ccny.cuny.edu/aacs

Ching Hai International Association, Supreme Master
PO Box 730247   San Jose CA 95173
Ph: 408-998-2342
www.chinghai.com

Chirofeed International
2627 Capital Mall Dr Suite B 3-A   Olympia WA 98502
Ph: 360-786-6322 ■ Fx: 360-786-5677

Chiropractic Association, American
1701 Clarendon Blvd   Arlington VA 22209
Ph: 703-276-8800 ■ Fx: 703-243-2593 ■ TF: 800-986-4636
www.amerchiro.org

**Chiropractic Association Council on Sports Injuries & Physical
Fitness, American**   PO Box 400 380 Wright Rd   Norwalk IA
52011
Ph: 515-981-9340 ■ Fx: 515-981-9427 ■ TF: 800-261-1495
www.acasc.org

Chiropractic, Association for the History of
1000 Brady St   Davenport IA 52803
Ph: 563-884-5855 ■ Fx: 563-884-5616
www.chiroweb.com/ahc

Chiropractic College of Radiology, American
PO Box 3053   La Habra CA 90632
Ph: 562-947-8755
www.accr.org

Chiropractic Colleges, Association of
4424 Montgomery Ave Suite 102   Bethesda MD 20814
Ph: 301-652-5066 ■ Fx: 301-913-9146
www.chirocolleges.org

Chiropractic Consultants, Academy of Forensic & Industrial
18331 Gridely Rd Suite C   Cerritos CA 90703
Ph: 562-860-3662 ■ Fx: 562-860-4377
aficc.tripod.com

Chiropractic Consultants, American College of
2741 Ridge Rd   Lansing IL 60438
Ph: 708-895-3141 ■ Fx: 708-895-2268
www.accc-chiro.com

Chiropractic Education, Council on
8049 N 85th Way   Scottsdale AZ 85258
Ph: 480-443-8877 ■ Fx: 480-483-7333
www.cce-usa.org

Chiropractic Education, Foundation for the Advancement of
PO Box 1052   Levittown PA 19058
Ph: 800-397-9722
www.f-a-c-e.com

Chiropractic Education & Research, Foundation for
PO Box 400   Norwalk IA 50211
Ph: 515-981-9888 ■ Fx: 515-981-9427 ■ TF: 800-622-6309
www.fcer.org

Chiropractic Examiners, National Board of
901 54th Ave   Greeley CO 80634
Ph: 970-356-9100
www.nbce.org

Chiropractic Licensing Boards, Federation of   www.fclb.org
901 54th Ave Suite 101   Greeley CO 80634
Ph: 970-356-3500 ▪ Fx: 970-356-3599

Chiropractic Orthopedists, American College of   www.accoweb.org
1030 Broadway Suite 101   El Centro CA 92243
Ph: 760-370-9106 ▪ Fx: 760-352-3966

Chiropractic Physiological Therapeutics & Rehabilitation, Council on   www.ccptr.org
312 Courtyard Dr   Hillsborough NJ 08844
Ph: 908-722-9075 ▪ Fx: 908-722-1144

Chiropractic Registry of Radiologic Technologists, American
2330 Gull Rd   Kalamazoo MI 49048
Ph: 269-343-6666 ▪ Fx: 269-343-7236

Chiropractors Association, Christian   www.christianchiropractors.org
PO Box 9715   Fort Collins CO 80525
Ph: 970-482-1404 ▪ Fx: 970-482-1538 ▪ TF: 800-999-1970

Chiropractors Association, International   www.chiropractic.org
1110 N Glebe Rd Suite 1000   Arlington VA 22201
Ph: 703-528-5000 ▪ Fx: 703-528-5023 ▪ TF: 800-423-4690

Chiropractors & Organizations, Federation of Straight   www.straightchiropractic.com
2276 Wassergass Rd   Hellertown PA 18055
Ph: 610-838-3030 ▪ Fx: 610-838-3031 ▪ TF: 800-521-9856

Chirurgiens, Order of Descendants of Colonial Physicians &
9317 Bent Tree Cir   Wichita KS 67226
Ph: 316-634-1930

Chlorinated Paraffins Industry Association   www.regnet.com/cpia
1250 Connecticut Ave NW Suite 700   Washington DC 20036
Ph: 202-637-9040 ▪ Fx: 202-637-9178

Chlorinators, National Association of Gas
21939 Camille Dr   Nuevo CA 92567
Ph: 949-364-1990 ▪ Fx: 949-364-2009

Chlorine Chemistry Council   www.c3.org
1300 Wilson Blvd   Arlington VA 22209
Ph: 703-741-5000 ▪ Fx: 703-741-6000

Chlorine Institute Inc   www.cl2.org
2001 L St NW Suite 506   Washington DC 20036
Ph: 202-775-2790 ▪ Fx: 202-223-7225

Chocolate Manufacturers Association
8320 Old Courthouse Rd Suite 300   Vienna VA 22182
Ph: 703-790-5011 ▪ Fx: 703-790-5752 ▪ TF: 800-433-1200

CHOICE   www.choice-phila.org
1233 Locust St Suite 301   Philadelphia PA 19107
Ph: 215-985-3355 ▪ Fx: 215-985-2838

Choice, Catholics for a Free   www.catholicsforchoice.org
1436 U St NW Suite 301   Washington DC 20009
Ph: 202-986-6093 ▪ Fx: 202-332-7995

Choice, Republicans for   www.republicansforchoice.com/
2760 Eisenhower Ave Suite 260   Alexandria VA 22314
Ph: 703-960-9882 ▪ Fx: 703-329-2411

Choice Inc, Victims of   www.victimsofchoice.com
PO Box 815   Naperville IL 60566
Ph: 630-378-1680 ▪ Fx: 630-759-5030 ▪ TF: 888-267-3998

Choir Association of the US, Latvian
7886 Anita Dr   Philadelphia PA 19111
Ph: 215-725-6953

Choir, National Christian   nationalchristianchoir.org
983-A Russell Ave   Gaithersburg MD 20879
Ph: 301-670-6331 ▪ Fx: 301-330-7299 ▪ TF: 800-599-4710

Choral Directors Association, American   www.acdaonline.org
502 SW 38th St PO Box 6310   Lawton OK 73506
Ph: 580-355-8161 ▪ Fx: 580-248-1465

Choral Music, International Federation for   ifcm.net
Univ of Illinois at Chicago Dept of Performing Arts 1040 W
Harrison St MC 255   Chicago IL 60607
Ph: 312-996-8744 ▪ Fx: 312-996-0954

Choreographers, Society of Stage Directors &   www.ssdc.org
1501 Broadway Suite 1701   New York NY 10036
Ph: 212-391-1070 ▪ Fx: 212-302-6195

Choristers Guild   www.choristersguild.org
2834 W Kingsley Rd   Garland TX 75041
Ph: 972-271-1521 ▪ Fx: 972-840-3113

Chorus America   www.chorusamerica.org
1156 15th St NW Suite 310   Washington DC 20005
Ph: 202-331-7577 ▪ Fx: 202-331-7599

Choruses, Gay & Lesbian Association of   www.galachoruses.org
PO Box 65084   Washington DC 20035
Ph: 202-467-5830 ▪ Fx: 202-467-5831

Choruses Inc, Intercollegiate Men's   www.cco.caltech.edu/~dgc/imc.html
Kansas State Univ 109 McCain Auditorium   Manhattan KS
66506
Ph: 785-532-3824 ▪ Fx: 785-532-5709

Chosin Few   home.hawaii.rr.com/chosin
238 Cornwall Cir   Chalfont PA 18914
Ph: 215-822-9093 ▪ Fx: 215-822-0163 ▪ TF: 888-999-7819

Chris Craft Antique Boat Club   www.chris-craft.org
217 S Adams St   Tallahassee FL 32301
Ph: 850-224-2628 ▪ Fx: 850-224-1033

Christ Child Society Inc, National   www.nationalchristchildsoc.org
5105 Wisconsin Ave NW Suite 304   Washington DC 20016
Ph: 202-363-9516 ▪ Fx: 202-966-2880 ▪ TF: 800-814-2149

Christ for the City International   www.cfci.org
PO Box 241827   Omaha NE 68124
Ph: 402-592-8332 ▪ TF: 888-526-7551

Christ, Community of   www.cofchrist.org
1001 W Walnut St   Independence MO 64050
Ph: 816-833-1000 ▪ Fx: 816-521-3085 ▪ TF: 800-825-2806

Christ, Connecting Businessmen to   www.cbmc.com
6650 E Brainerd Rd Suite 100   Chattanooga TN 37421
Ph: 423-698-4444 ▪ Fx: 423-629-4434 ▪ TF: 800-575-2262

Christ in India, Friends of   www.foci.org
Greenfield Hill Congregational Church 1045 Old Academy
Rd   Fairfield CT 06430
Ph: 203-259-5596

Christ International, Campus Crusade for   www.ccci.org
100 Lake Hart Dr   Orlando FL 32832
Ph: 407-826-2000 ▪ Fx: 407-826-2749 ▪ TF: 877-924-7478

Christ International, Fellowship of Companies for   www.myfcci.org
12201 Pangborn Ave   Downey CA 90241
Ph: 562-803-3400 ▪ Fx: 562-803-3344

Christ International, Peace Officers for   www.pofci.org
3000 W MacArthur Blvd Suite 426   Santa Ana CA 92704
Ph: 714-426-7632 ▪ Fx: 714-426-0792

Christ International, Transport for   www.transportforchrist.org
PO Box 303   Denver PA 17517
Ph: 717-859-4870 ▪ Fx: 717-859-4798

Christ for the Nations Inc   www.cfni.org
PO Box 769000   Dallas TX 75376
Ph: 214-376-1711 ▪ Fx: 214-302-6228 ▪ TF: 800-933-2364

Christ, Truckers for   www.truckersforchrist.org
PO Box 1311   Taylorsville NC 28681
Ph: 828-632-8842

Christ Truth Ministries   prisonministry.net/ctm
PO Box 610   Upland CA 91785
Ph: 909-981-2838 ▪ Fx: 909-981-2839

Christ/USA, Youth for   community.gospelcom.net/Brix/yfcusa/public
PO Box 228822   Denver CO 80222
Ph: 303-843-9000 ▪ Fx: 303-843-9002 ▪ TF: 800-735-3252

Christ, Women Nationally Active for   www.nafwb.org/wnac
5233 Mt View Rd PO Box 5002   Antioch TN 37011
Ph: 615-731-6812 ▪ Fx: 615-731-0771

Christar   www.christar.org
PO Box 14866   Reading PA 19612
Ph: 610-375-0300 ▪ Fx: 610-375-6862 ▪ TF: 800-755-7955

Christian Accrediting Association, International   www.oru.edu/oruef/icaa
7777 S Lewis Ave   Tulsa OK 74171
Ph: 918-495-6163 ▪ Fx: 918-495-6175

Christian Aid Mission   www.christianaid.org
PO Box 9037   Charlottesville VA 22906
Ph: 434-977-5650 ▪ TF: 800-977-5650

Christian Airline Personnel, Fellowship of   www.fcap.org
136 Providence Rd   Fayetteville GA 30215
Ph: 770-461-9320 ▪ Fx: 770-461-2720

(Christian) Alban Institute   www.alban.org
7315 Wisconsin Ave Suite 1250 W   Bethesda MD 20814
Ph: 301-718-4407 ▪ Fx: 301-718-1958 ▪ TF: 800-486-1318

(Christian) American Rescue Workers Inc   www.arwus.com
643 Elmira St   Williamsport PA 17701
Ph: 570-323-8401 ▪ Fx: 570-323-0980

Christian Anti-Communism Crusade   www.schwarzreport.org
PO Box 129   Manitou Springs CO 80829
Ph: 719-685-9043 ▪ Fx: 719-685-9330

Christian Appalachian Project   www.christianity.com/cap
322 Crab Orchard St   Lancaster KY 40446
Ph: 859-792-3051 ▪ Fx: 859-792-6560

Christian Archdiocese of North America, Antiochian Orthodox   www.antiochian.org
358 Mountain Rd   Englewood NJ 07631
Ph: 201-871-1355 ▪ Fx: 201-871-7954

Christian Association of the USA, Young Women's   www.ywca.org
1015 18th St NW Suite 1100   Washington DC 20036
Ph: 202-467-0801 ▪ Fx: 202-467-0802 ▪ TF: 800-992-2871

(Christian) Athletes in Action   www.aia.com
651 Taylor Dr   Xenia OH 45385
Ph: 937-352-1000 ▪ Fx: 937-352-1101

Christian Athletes, Fellowship of   www.fca.org
8701 Leeds Rd   Kansas City MO 64129
Ph: 816-921-0909 ▪ Fx: 816-921-8755 ▪ TF: 800-289-0909

Christian Benefit Association, Loyal   www.lcba.com
PO Box 13005   Erie PA 16514
Ph: 814-453-4331 ▪ Fx: 814-453-3211 ▪ TF: 800-234-5222

Christian Blind Mission International   www.christianity.com/cbmi
450 E Park Ave   Greenville SC 29601
Ph: 864-239-0065 ▪ Fx: 864-239-0069 ▪ TF: 800-937-2264

Christian Boaters Association   www.christianboater.org
PO Box 358   Canal Point FL 33438
Ph: 561-924-9522 ▪ Fx: 561-924-6097

Christian Booksellers Association   www.cbaonline.org
PO Box 62000   Colorado Springs CO 80962
Ph: 719-265-9895 ▪ Fx: 719-272-3510 ▪ TF: 800-252-1950

Christian Bowhunters of America   www.christianbowhunters.org
2205 SR 571 W   Greenville OH 45331
Ph: 937-548-0623 ▪ TF: 877-912-5724

(Christian) Bread on the Waters   www.breadonthewaters.com
91 Church Ln   Cloverdale CA 95425
Ph: 209-369-3202

(Christian) Bruderhof Communities   www.bruderhof.org
PO Box 903   Rifton NY 12471
Ph: 845-658-8351 ▪ Fx: 845-658-3144

Christian Camping International/USA   cci.gospelcom.net/ccihome
PO Box 62189   Colorado Springs CO 80962
Ph: 719-260-9400 ▪ Fx: 719-260-6398

(Christian) Champions for Life International   www.lifechampions.org
PO Box 761101   Dallas TX 75376
Ph: 972-298-1101 ▪ Fx: 972-298-1104

Christian Chaplain Services Inc
PO Box 86307   Los Angeles CA 90086
Ph: 213-353-9435 ▪ Fx: 213-353-9436

Christian Charities, International Orthodox   www.iocc.org
110 West Rd Suite 360   Baltimore MD 21204
Ph: 410-243-9820 ▪ Fx: 410-243-9824 ▪ TF: 877-803-4622

(Christian) Chi Alpha Campus Ministries USA   www.chialpha.com
3728 W Chestnut Expy   Springfield MO 65802
Ph: 417-862-2781 ▪ Fx: 417-865-9947

Christian Children's Fund Inc   www.christianchildrensfund.org
2821 Emerywood Pkwy   Richmond VA 23294
Ph: 804-756-2700 ▪ Fx: 804-756-2718 ▪ TF: 800-776-6767

Christian Chiropractors Association   www.christianchiropractors.org
PO Box 9715   Fort Collins CO 80525
Ph: 970-482-1404 ▪ Fx: 970-482-1538 ▪ TF: 800-999-1970

Christian Choir, National   nationalchristianchoir.org
983-A Russell Ave   Gaithersburg MD 20879
Ph: 301-670-6331 ▪ Fx: 301-330-7299 ▪ TF: 800-599-4710

(Christian) Church Army USA   www.churcharmyusa.org
210 W North Ave PO Box 1425   Pittsburgh PA 15212
Ph: 412-231-5442 ▪ Fx: 412-231-5481

Christian Church (Disciples of Christ)   www.disciples.org
PO Box 1986   Indianapolis IN 46206
Ph: 317-635-3100 ▪ Fx: 317-635-3700

Christian Churches, American Council of   www.amcouncilcc.org
PO Box 5455   Bethlehem PA 18015
Ph: 610-865-3009 ▪ Fx: 610-865-3033

Christian Churches, National Association of Congregational   www.naccc.org
8473 S Howell Ave   Oak Creek WI 53154
Ph: 414-764-1620 ▪ Fx: 414-764-0319 ▪ TF: 800-262-1620

Christian Coalition of America   www.cc.org
499 S Capitol St SW Suite 615   Washington DC 20003
Ph: 202-479-6900 ▪ Fx: 202-479-4260 ▪ TF: 888-440-2262

Christian Coin Dealers & Collectors, Association of
PO Box 236   Wymore NE 68466
Ph: 402-645-3341 ▪ Fx: 402-645-3342

Christian College Athletic Association, National   www.thenccaa.org
302 W Washington St   Greenville SC 29601
Ph: 864-250-1199 ▪ Fx: 864-250-1141

Christian College Consortium   www.ccconsortium.org
50 Stark Hwy S   Dunbarton NH 03046
Ph: 603-774-6623 ▪ Fx: 603-774-6628

Christian Colleges & Universities, Council for   www.cccu.org
321 8th St NE   Washington DC 20002
Ph: 202-546-8713 ▪ Fx: 202-546-8913

Christian Community Development Association   www.ccda.org
3817 W Ogden Ave   Chicago IL 60623
Ph: 773-762-0994 ▪ Fx: 773-762-5772

Christian Concern, International   www.persecution.org
2020 Pennsylvania Ave NW Suite 941   Washington DC 20006
Ph: 301-989-1708 ▪ Fx: 301-989-1709 ▪ TF: 800-422-5441

Christian Convention, North American   www.naccctheconnectingplace.org
110 Boggs Ln Suite 330   Cincinnati OH 45246
Ph: 513-772-9970 ▪ Fx: 513-772-9980

Christian Council on Persons With Disabilities   www.ccpd.org
1100 W 42nd St Suite 223   Indianapolis IN 46208
Ph: 317-923-2273

Christian Cycling Club USA, International   www.ironclad.org
PO Box 411757   Aurora CO 80044
Ph: 720-870-3707

Christian Disaster Response International   www.cdresponse.org
PO Box 3339   Winter Haven FL 33885
Ph: 863-551-9554 ▪ Fx: 863-551-1422 ▪ TF: 866-551-9554

(Christian) East-West Ministries International   www.eastwestministries.org
4450 Sojourn Dr Suite 100   Addison TX 75001
Ph: 214-265-8300 ▪ Fx: 214-265-8503

Christian Education, Foundation for American   www.face.net
PO Box 9588   Chesapeake VA 23321
Ph: 757-488-6601 ▪ Fx: 757-488-5593 ▪ TF: 800-352-3223

Christian Education, North American Professors of   www.napce.org
c/o Cook Communications Ministries 4050 Lee Vance
   View   Colorado Springs CO 80918
Ph: 719-536-0100

Christian Educators Association International   www.ceai.org
PO Box 41300   Pasadena CA 91114
Ph: 626-798-1124 ▪ Fx: 626-798-2346 ▪ TF: 888-798-1124

Christian Educators, Professional Association of   www.gospelcom.net/paceinc
PO Box 140284   Dallas TX 75214
Ph: 214-841-3566 ▪ Fx: 214-841-3773 ▪ TF: 800-829-9410

Christian Endeavor International   www.teamce.com
309 S Main St   Mount Vernon OH 43050
Ph: 740-397-2622 ▪ Fx: 740-397-0198 ▪ TF: 800-260-3234

Christian Endeavor Union, World's   www.christianendeavorworldwide.org
3575 Valley Rd PO Box 326   Liberty Corner NJ 07938
Ph: 908-604-9440 ▪ Fx: 908-604-6190

Christian Ethics, Society of   www.scethics.org
St Johns University PO Box 5633   Collegeville MN 56321
Ph: 320-363-3525 ▪ Fx: 320-363-3145

(Christian) Evangelical Association for the Promotion   www.tonycampolo.org/eape.shtml
   of Education 1300 Eagle Rd   Saint Davids PA 19087
Ph: 610-341-1722 ▪ Fx: 610-341-4372

(Christian) Faith at Work Inc   www.faithatwork.com
106 E Broad St Suite B   Falls Church VA 22046
Ph: 703-237-3426 ▪ Fx: 703-237-0157

Christian Family Life   www.christianfamilylife.org
5301 Harris Blvd   Charlotte NC 28269
Ph: 704-596-9630 ▪ Fx: 704-596-4522

Christian Family Movement   www.cfm.org
PO Box 925   Evansville IN 47706
Ph: 812-962-5508 ▪ Fx: 812-962-5509

Christian Family Renewal
PO Box 73   Clovis CA 93613
Ph: 559-347-9324

Christian Fellowship of Art Music Composers   www.cfamc.org
Houghton College Greatbatch School of Music   Houghton NY
   14744
Ph: 585-567-9424

Christian Fellowship, Nurses   www.intervarsity.org/ncf
PO Box 7895   Madison WI 53707
Ph: 608-274-9001

Christian Fellowship, Officers'   www.gospelcom.net/ocf
3784 S Inca St   Englewood CO 80110
Ph: 800-424-1984

Christian Fellowship, Unitarian Universalist   www.uua.org/uucf
PO Box 629   Lancaster MA 01523
Ph: 978-365-2427 ▪ Fx: 978-368-0194

Christian Fellowship/USA, InterVarsity   www.intervarsity.org
6400 Schroeder Rd   Madison WI 53711
Ph: 608-274-9001 ▪ Fx: 608-274-7882

Christian Firefighters International, Fellowship of   fellowshipofchristianfirefighters.com
PO Box 901   Fort Collins CO 80522
Ph: 970-407-0083 ▪ TF: 800-322-9848

(Christian) First Fruit Inc   www.firstfruit.org
14 Corporate Plaza   Newport Beach CA 92660
Ph: 949-720-3774 ▪ Fx: 949-760-5349

Christian Foundation for Children & Aging   www.cfcausa.org
1 Elmwood Ave   Kansas City KS 66103
Ph: 913-384-6500 ▪ Fx: 913-384-2211 ▪ TF: 800-875-6564

Christian Freedom International   www.christianfreedom.org
PO Box 535   Front Royal VA 22630
Ph: 540-636-8907 ▪ TF: 800-323-2273

(Christian) Genesis Institute   www.genesisinstitute.org
10220 N Nevada St Suite 280   Spokane WA 99218
Ph: 509-467-7913 ▪ Fx: 509-467-0344

(Christian) HBI Global Partners   hbi.gospelcom.net
PO Box 584   Forest VA 24551
Ph: 434-525-5847 ▪ TF: 877-424-4634

Christian Herald Association
132 Madison Ave   New York NY 10016
Ph: 212-684-2800 ▪ Fx: 212-684-3740

Christian Higher Education in Asia, United Board for   www.unitedboard.org
475 Riverside Dr Suite 1221   New York NY 10115
Ph: 212-870-2610 ▪ Fx: 212-870-2322

Christian Historical Society, Congregational   www.cchsonline.org
14 Beacon St   Boston MA 02108
Ph: 617-523-0470 ▪ Fx: 617-523-0491

(Christian) Holy Face Association   www.holyface.org
PO Box 1000 Stn A   Montreal QC H3C2W9
Ph: 514-747-0357 ▪ Fx: 514-747-9147

(Christian) IFCA International   www.ifca.org
PO Box 810   Grandville MI 49468
Ph: 616-531-1840 ▪ Fx: 616-531-1814 ▪ TF: 800-347-1840

(Christian) India Partners   www.indiapartners.org
PO Box 5470   Eugene OR 97405
Ph: 541-683-0696 ▪ Fx: 541-683-2773 ▪ TF: 888-870-9085

Christian Instrumentalists & Directors Association   www.cidaonline.com

(Christian) Interserve USA   www.interserve.org
PO Box 418 7000 Ludlow St   Upper Darby PA 19082
Ph: 610-352-0581 ▪ Fx: 610-352-4394 ▪ TF: 800-809-4440

(Christian) Japan ICU Foundation Inc   www.jicuf.org
475 Riverside Dr Suite 439   New York NY 10115
Ph: 212-870-3386 ▪ Fx: 212-870-2696

Christian-Jewish Understanding, Center for   www.ccju.org
Sacred Heart Univ 5151 Park Ave   Fairfield CT 06432
Ph: 203-365-7592 ▪ Fx: 203-365-4815

(Christian) Jimmy Swaggart Ministries   www.jsm.org
8919 World Ministry Blvd   Baton Rouge LA 70810
Ph: 225-768-8300 ▪ Fx: 225-769-2244 ▪ TF: 800-288-8350

Christian Labor Association of the USA
405 Centerstone Ct PO Box 65   Zeeland MI 49464
Ph: 616-772-9164 ▪ Fx: 616-772-9830

(Christian) Lasallian Volunteers   www.cbconf.org/cbc.nsf/pages/volunteers
4351 Garden City Dr Suite 200   Landover MD 20785
Ph: 301-459-9410 ▪ Fx: 301-459-8056

Christian Law Association   www.christianlaw.org
PO Box 4010   Seminole FL 33775
Ph: 727-399-8300 ▪ Fx: 727-398-3907

Christian Leadership Conference for Israel, National   www.nclci.org
43422 W Oaks Dr Suite 300   Novi MI 48377
Ph: 248-557-4540 ▪ Fx: 248-557-4527

Christian Leadership Conference, Southern   www.sclcnational.org
591-A Edgewood Ave SE   Atlanta GA 30312
Ph: 404-522-1420 ▪ Fx: 404-527-4333

Christian Legal Society   www.clsnet.org
4208 Evergreen Ln Suite 222   Annandale VA 22003
Ph: 703-642-1070 ▪ Fx: 703-642-1075

(Christian) Legatus   www.legatus.org
24 Frank Lloyd Wright Dr PO Box 511   Ann Arbor MI 48106
Ph: 734-930-3854 ▪ Fx: 734-668-2448

Christian Librarians, Association of   www.acl.org
PO Box 4   Cedarville OH 45314
Ph: 937-766-2255 ▪ Fx: 937-766-2337

(Christian) Life Action Ministries   www.lifeaction.org
PO Box 31   Buchanan MI 49107
Ph: 269-684-5905 ▪ Fx: 269-684-0923

Christian Life Community of the USA, National   www.clc-usa.org
3691 Lindell Blvd   Saint Louis MO 63108
Ph: 314-977-7370

Christian Literature & Bible Center Inc   www.clbible.org
PO Box 7130   North Augusta SC 29861
Ph: 803-279-1981 ▪ Fx: 803-279-1270

Christian Living, Peale Center for
66 E Main St   Pawling NY 12564
Ph: 845-855-5000 ▪ Fx: 845-855-1036 ▪ TF: 800-431-2344

(Christian) Logoi   www.logoi.org
14540 SW 136th St Suite 200   Miami FL 33186
Ph: 305-232-5880

Christian Magicians, Fellowship of   www.gospelcom.net/fcm

Christian Management Association   www.christianity.com/cma
PO Box 4090   San Clemente CA 92674
Ph: 949-487-0900 ▪ Fx: 949-487-0927

Christian Medical & Dental Associations   www.cmdahome.org
PO Box 7500   Bristol TN 37620
Ph: 423-844-1000 ▪ Fx: 423-844-1005

Christian Military Fellowship   www.cmfhq.org
PO Box 1207   Englewood CO 80150
Ph: 303-761-1959 ▪ Fx: 303-761-4577 ▪ TF: 800-798-7875

Christian Ministry in the National Parks, A   www.acmnp.com
10 Justins Way   Freeport ME 04032
Ph: 207-865-6436 ▪ Fx: 207-865-6852 ▪ TF: 800-786-3450

Christian Mission, Chinese   www.ccmusa.org
PO Box 750759   Petaluma CA 94975
Ph: 707-762-1314 ▪ Fx: 707-762-1713

Christian Mission for the Deaf   www.cmdeaf.org
PO Box 28005   Detroit MI 48228
Ph: 313-933-1424

(Christian) Mission: Moving Mountains   www.movingmountains.org
PO Box 1168   Burnsville MN 55337
Ph: 952-440-9100 ▪ Fx: 952-440-9104 ▪ TF: 800-545-7980

Christian & Missionary Alliance   www.cmalliance.org
PO Box 35000   Colorado Springs CO 80935
Ph: 719-599-5999 ▪ Fx: 719-593-8692

Christian Missionary Fellowship   www.cmfi.org
5525 E 82nd St PO Box 501020   Indianapolis IN 46250
Ph: 317-578-2700 ▪ Fx: 317-578-2827

Christian Missions in Many Lands   www.cmmlusa.org
PO Box 13   Spring Lake NJ 07762
Ph: 732-449-8880 ▪ Fx: 732-974-0888

(Christian) Moms in Touch International   www.momsintouch.com
PO Box 1120   Poway CA 92074
Ph: 800-949-6667 ▪ Fx: 858-486-5132

Christian Mothers, Archconfraternity of   www.capuchin.com/christia.htm
220 37th St   Pittsburgh PA 15201
Ph: 412-683-2400 ▪ Fx: 412-683-7155

Christian Motorcyclists Association   www.cmausa.org
PO Box 9   Hatfield AR 71945
Ph: 870-389-6196 ▪ Fx: 870-389-6199

Christian Motorsports Ministries   www.christianmotorsports.com
PO Box 129   Mansfield PA 16933
Ph: 570-549-2282 ▪ Fx: 570-549-3366

(Christian) Mustard Seed Foundation   www.msfdn.org
3330 N Washington Blvd Suite 100   Arlington VA 22201
Ph: 703-524-5620 ▪ Fx: 703-524-5643

(Christian Mystics) Rosicrucian Fellowship   www.rosicrucianfellowship.org
2222 Mission Ave PO Box 713   Oceanside CA 92049
Ph: 760-757-6600 ▪ Fx: 760-721-3806

(Christian) National Enthronement Center   communications.sscc.org/enthronement
PO Box 111   Fairhaven MA 02719
Ph: 508-999-2680 ▪ Fx: 508-993-8233

(Christian) Navigators   home.navigators.org/us
PO Box 6000   Colorado Springs CO 80934
Ph: 719-598-1212 ▪ Fx: 719-260-0479

(Christian) Nocturnal Adoration Society   www.sjbrcc.org/nas.html
Saint Jean Baptiste Catholic Church 184 E 76th St   New York
NY 10021
Ph: 212-288-5082 ▪ Fx: 212-717-8397

(Christian) NOEL   www.noelforlife.org
405 Frederick Ave   Sewickley PA 15143
Ph: 412-749-0455 ▪ Fx: 412-749-0422 ▪ TF: 800-707-6635

(Christian) OMS International   www.omsinternational.org
941 Fry Rd Box A   Greenwood IN 46142
Ph: 317-881-6751 ▪ Fx: 317-888-5275

(Christian) Oral Roberts University Educational Fellowship   www.oru.edu/oruef
7777 S Lewis Ave   Tulsa OK 74171
Ph: 918-495-6163 ▪ Fx: 918-495-6175

(Christian) Order of the Daughters of the King   www.dok-national.org
Margaret J Franklin Ctr 101 Weatherstone Dr Suite
870   Woodstock GA 30188
Ph: 770-517-8552 ▪ Fx: 770-517-8066

Christian Peace Officers USA, Fellowship of   www.fcpo.org
PO Box 3686   Chattanooga TN 37404
Ph: 423-622-1234 ▪ Fx: 423-622-9725

Christian Philosophers, Society of   www.siu.edu/~scp
Calvin College Dept of Philosophy 3201 Burton St SE   Grand
Rapids MI 49546
Ph: 616-526-6421

Christian Pilots Association   www.christianpilots.org
PO Box 90452   Los Angeles CA 90009
Ph: 562-208-2912

(Christian) Pioneer Clubs   www.pioneerclubs.org
PO Box 788   Wheaton IL 60189
Ph: 630-293-1600 ▪ Fx: 630-293-3053 ▪ TF: 800-694-2582

(Christian) Pro Sanctity Movement   www.prosanctity.org
205 S Pine Dr   Fullerton CA 92833
Ph: 714-956-1020 ▪ Fx: 714-525-8948

(Christian) Promise Keepers   www.promisekeepers.org
PO Box 103001   Denver CO 80250
Ph: 303-964-7600 ▪ Fx: 303-433-1036 ▪ TF: 800-888-7595

Christian Publishers Association, Evangelical   www.ecpa.org
1969 E Broadway Rd Suite 2   Tempe AZ 85282
Ph: 480-966-3998 ▪ Fx: 480-966-1944

(Christian) Reasons to Believe   www.reasons.org
PO Box 5978   Pasadena CA 91117
Ph: 626-335-1480 ▪ Fx: 626-852-0178 ▪ TF: 800-482-7836

Christian Record Services   www.christianrecord.org
4444 S 52nd St   Lincoln NE 68516
Ph: 402-488-0981 ▪ Fx: 402-488-7582

Christian Reformed Church in North America   www.crcna.org
2850 Kalamazoo Ave SE   Grand Rapids MI 49560
Ph: 616-224-0744 ▪ Fx: 616-224-5895 ▪ TF: 800-272-5125

Christian Reformed World Relief Committee   www.crwrc.org
2850 Kalamazoo Ave SE   Grand Rapids MI 49560
Ph: 616-224-0740 ▪ Fx: 616-224-0806 ▪ TF: 800-552-7972

Christian Released Time Ministries, Fellowship of   www.rtce.org
5722 Lime Ave   Long Beach CA 90805
Ph: 562-428-7733 ▪ Fx: 562-728-7633 ▪ TF: 800-360-7943

(Christian Relief) Global Action International   www.globalactionintl.org
PO Box 717   Carlsbad CA 92018
Ph: 760-438-3979 ▪ Fx: 760-602-0383

Christian Relief Services   www.christianrelief.org
8815 Telegraph Rd   Lorton VA 22079
Ph: 703-550-2472 ▪ Fx: 703-550-2473 ▪ TF: 800-337-3543

Christian Research Institute   www.equip.org
PO Box 7000   Rancho Santa Margarita CA 92688
Ph: 949-858-6100 ▪ Fx: 949-858-6111 ▪ TF: 800-700-6274

Christian Schools, American Association of   www.aacs.org
PO Box 1097   Independence MO 64051
Ph: 816-252-9900 ▪ Fx: 816-252-6700

Christian Schools International   www.gospelcom.net/csi
3350 E Paris Ave SE   Grand Rapids MI 49512
Ph: 616-957-1070 ▪ Fx: 616-957-5022 ▪ TF: 800-635-8288

Christian Schools International, Association of   www.acsi.org
731 Chapel Hills Dr   Colorado Springs CO 80920
Ph: 719-528-6906 ▪ Fx: 719-531-0631 ▪ TF: 800-367-0798

Christian Service Club
2110 Enterprise St SE   Grand Rapids MI 49508
Ph: 616-455-2490

Christian Services for the Blind   www.csbonline.org
1124 Fair Oaks PO Box 26   South Pasadena CA 91031
Ph: 626-799-3935 ▪ Fx: 626-403-9460

(Christian) Sinsinawa Dominicans   www.sinsinawa.org
585 County Rd Z   Sinsinawa WI 53824
Ph: 608-748-4411 ▪ Fx: 608-748-4491

(Christian) Society of the Little Flower   www.littleflower.org
1313 Frontage Rd   Darien IL 60561
Ph: 630-968-9400 ▪ Fx: 630-968-9542 ▪ TF: 800-621-2806

Christian Sociological Society   www.christiansociology.com

(Christian) Sojourners   www.sojo.net
2401 15th St NW   Washington DC 20009
Ph: 202-328-8842 ▪ Fx: 202-328-8757 ▪ TF: 800-714-7474

Christian Solidarity International   www.csi-int.ch
870 Hampshire Rd Suite T   Westlake Village CA 91361
Ph: 805-777-7107 ▪ TF: 888-676-5700

(Christian) STEER Inc   www.steerinc.com
PO Box 1236   Bismarck ND 58502
Ph: 701-258-4911 ▪ Fx: 701-258-7684

Christian Stewardship Association   www.stewardship.org
770 N Highschool Rd PO Box 531340   Indianapolis IN 46253
Ph: 317-244-4272 ▪ Fx: 317-244-4329

Christian Studies Association, International   www.jis3.org/abouticsa.htm
1065 Pine Bluff Dr   Pasadena CA 91107
Ph: 626-351-0419

Christian Tattoo Association   www.xtat.org
2815 Gull Rd   Kalamazoo MI 49048
Ph: 269-998-7738

Christian Technologists Association, International   www.gospelcom.net/icta
15455 Gleneagle Dr Suite 210   Colorado Springs CO 80921
Ph: 719-785-0120 ▪ Fx: 719-785-0117

Christian Therapists, Association of   www.actheals.org
6728 Old McLean Village Dr   McLean VA 22101
Ph: 703-556-9222 ▪ Fx: 703-556-8729

(Christian) Trans World Radio   www.gospelcom.net/twr
PO Box 8700   Cary NC 27512
Ph: 919-460-3700 ▪ Fx: 919-460-3702 ▪ TF: 800-456-7897

(Christian) Turning Point Ministries   www.turningpointministries.org
6101 Preservation Dr PO Box 22127   Chattanooga TN 37422
Ph: 423-899-4770 ▪ Fx: 423-899-4547 ▪ TF: 800-879-4770

(Christian) United World Mission Inc   www.uwm.org
9401-B Southern Pines Blvd   Charlotte NC 28273
Ph: 704-357-3355 ▪ Fx: 704-357-6389 ▪ TF: 800-825-5896

Christian Unity, Council on   www.disciples.org/ccu
130 E Washington St PO Box 1986   Indianapolis IN 46206
Ph: 317-713-2585 ▪ Fx: 317-713-2588

(Christian) Voice of the Martyrs   www.persecution.com
PO Box 443   Bartlesville OK 74005
Ph: 918-337-8015 ▪ Fx: 918-338-0189 ▪ TF: 800-747-0085

(Christian) Watchman Fellowship   www.watchman.org
3337 W Pioneer Pkwy PO Box 13340   Arlington TX 76094
Ph: 817-277-0023 ▪ Fx: 817-227-8089

(Christian) Way International The   www.theway.org
5555 Wierwille Rd PO Box 328   New Knoxville OH 45871
Ph: 419-753-2523 ▪ Fx: 419-753-2903

(Christian) Word of Life Fellowship Inc   www.wol.org
PO Box 600   Schroon Lake NY 12870
Ph: 518-494-6000 ▪ Fx: 518-494-6306 ▪ TF: 800-331-9673

(Christian) World Convention (Christian - Churches of   worldconv.home.comcast.net
Christ - Disciples of Christ) 4800 B Franklin Rd   Nashville
TN 37220
Ph: 615-331-1824 ▪ Fx: 615-331-1864

(Christian) Young Life   www.younglife.org
PO Box 520   Colorado Springs CO 80901
Ph: 719-381-1800 ▪ Fx: 719-381-1750

Christianity & Ecology, North American Coalition for   www.nacce.org
PO Box 40011   Saint Paul MN 55104
Ph: 612-698-0349

Christianity, Forum for Scriptural
308 E Main St PO Box 150   Wilmore KY 40390
Ph: 606-858-4661 ■ Fx: 606-858-4972 ■ TF: 800-487-7784

(Christianity) Gateways to Better Education   www.gtbe.org
PO Box 514   Lake Forest CA 92609
Ph: 949-586-5437 ■ Fx: 949-457-6361

Christians in America, Fellowship of Orthodox   www.orthodoxfellowship.org
10 Downs Dr   Wilkes-Barre PA 18705
Ph: 570-825-3158 ■ Fx: 570-825-0136

Christians in Government   www.christiansingovernment.org
PO Box 71654   Los Angeles CA 90071
Ph: 213-250-5016

Christians' Israel Public Action Campaign   www.cipaconline.org
PO Box 18173   Washington DC 20036
Ph: 202-234-3600 ■ Fx: 202-332-3221

Christians & Jews, International Fellowship of   www.ifcj.org
30 N LaSalle St Suite 2600   Chicago IL 60602
Ph: 312-641-7200 ■ Fx: 312-641-7201 ■ TF: 800-486-8844

Christians for Life, Orthodox   www.oclife.org
PO Box 805   Melville NY 11747
Ph: 631-271-4408

Christians for Peace in El Salvador   www.crispaz.org
122 Dewitt Dr   Boston MA 02120
Ph: 617-445-5115 ■ Fx: 617-249-0769

Christians in Social Work, North American Association of   www.nacsw.org
PO Box 121   Botsford CT 06404
Ph: 203-270-8780 ■ TF: 888-426-4712

Christians in the Visual Arts   www.civa.org
255 Grapevine Rd   Wenham MA 01984
Ph: 978-867-4124 ■ Fx: 978-867-4125

Christmas Tree Association, National   www.realchristmastrees.org
1000 Executive Pkwy Suite 220   Saint Louis MO 63141
Ph: 314-205-0944 ■ Fx: 314-576-7989

Christopher Columbus Philatelic Society
11258 Goodnight Ln Suite 105   Dallas TX 75229
Ph: 972-241-2326 ■ Fx: 972-243-4381

Christopher Reeve Paralysis Foundation   www.christopherreeve.org
500 Morris Ave   Springfield NJ 07081
Ph: 973-379-2690 ■ Fx: 973-912-9433 ■ TF: 800-225-0292

Christophers The   www.christophers.org
12 E 48th St   New York NY 10017
Ph: 212-759-4050 ■ Fx: 212-838-5073 ■ TF: 888-298-4050

Chromosome 18 Registry & Research Society   www.chromosome18.org
6302 Fox Head   San Antonio TX 78247
Ph: 210-657-4968

(Chromosome Disorders) Support Organization for Trisomy   www.trisomy.org
18/13 & Other Related Disorders   2982 S Union
St   Rochester NY 14624
Ph: 585-594-4621 ■ Fx: 585-594-1957 ■ TF: 800-716-7638

Chronic Care Consortium, National   www.nccconline.org
801 Pennsylvania Ave Suite 245   Washington DC 20004
Ph: 202-624-1516

Chronic Disease Program Directors, Association of   www.chronicdisease.org
State & Territorial   8201 Greensboro Dr Suite 300   McLean
VA 22102
Ph: 703-610-9033 ■ Fx: 703-610-9005

(Chronic Fatigue) CFIDS Association of America Inc   www.cfids.org
PO Box 220398   Charlotte NC 28222
Ph: 704-364-0466 ■ Fx: 704-365-9755 ■ TF: 800-442-3437

Chronic Fatigue Syndrome, American Association for   www.aacfs.org
27 N Wacker Dr Suite 416   Chicago IL 60606
Ph: 847-258-7248 ■ Fx: 847-748-8288

Chronic Granulomatous Disease Association   home.socal.rr.com/cgda
2616 Monterey Rd   San Marino CA 91108
Ph: 626-441-4118

Chronic Pain Association, American   www.theacpa.org
PO Box 850   Rocklin CA 95677
Ph: 916-632-0922 ■ Fx: 916-632-3208 ■ TF: 800-533-3231

Chronic Pain Outreach Association, National   www.chronicpain.org
PO Box 274   Millboro VA 24460
Ph: 540-862-9437 ■ Fx: 540-862-9485

Chrysanthemum Society, National   www.mums.org
10107 Homar Pond Dr   Fairfax Station VA 22039
Ph: 703-978-7981

Church Alliance, Evangelical   www.keynet.net/~eca/index.html
PO Box 9   Bradley IL 60915
Ph: 815-937-0720 ■ Fx: 815-937-0001

Church of America, Armenian   www.armenianchurch.org
630 2nd Ave   New York NY 10016
Ph: 212-686-0710 ■ Fx: 212-686-0245

Church in America, Reformed   www.rca.org
475 Riverside Dr 18th Fl   New York NY 10115
Ph: 212-870-3071 ■ Fx: 212-870-2499 ■ TF: 800-722-9977

Church Army USA   www.churcharmyusa.org
210 W North Ave PO Box 1425   Pittsburgh PA 15212
Ph: 412-231-5442 ■ Fx: 412-231-5481

Church of the Brethren   www.brethren.org
1451 Dundee Ave   Elgin IL 60120
Ph: 847-742-5100 ■ Fx: 847-742-6103 ■ TF: 800-323-8039

Church Business Administration, National Association of   www.nacba.net
100 N Central Expy Suite 914   Richardson TX 75080
Ph: 972-699-7555 ■ Fx: 972-699-7617 ■ TF: 800-898-8085

Church of Christ Justice & Witness Ministries, United   www.ucc.org/justice/index.html
700 Prospect Ave   Cleveland OH 44115
Ph: 216-736-3704 ■ Fx: 216-736-3703

Church of Christ Scientist   www.tfccs.com
175 Huntington Ave   Boston MA 02115
Ph: 617-450-2000 ■ Fx: 617-450-7575 ■ TF: 800-288-7090

Church of Christ, United   www.ucc.org
700 Prospect Ave   Cleveland OH 44115
Ph: 216-736-2100 ■ Fx: 216-736-2103

Church Food Service, National Association of   www.nacfs.org
PO Box 550413   Atlanta GA 30355
Ph: 404-261-1794 ■ Fx: 404-240-8276

Church of the Foursquare Gospel, International   www.foursquare.org
1910 W Sunset Blvd Suite 200   Los Angeles CA 90026
Ph: 213-989-4200 ■ Fx: 213-989-4590 ■ TF: 888-635-4234

Church of God in Christ Inc   www.cogic.org
938 Mason St   Memphis TN 38126
Ph: 901-947-9300 ■ Fx: 901-947-9359

Church of God Ministries   www.chog.org
1201 E 5th St PO Box 2420   Anderson IN 46018
Ph: 765-642-0256 ■ Fx: 765-642-5652 ■ TF: 800-848-2464

Church of God World Missions   www.cogwm.org
PO Box 8016   Cleveland TN 37320
Ph: 423-478-7190 ■ Fx: 423-478-7155 ■ TF: 800-345-7492

Church Goods Association, National   www.ncgaweb.com
800 Roosevelt Rd Bldg C Suite 20   Glen Ellyn IL 60137
Ph: 630-942-6599 ■ Fx: 630-790-3095

Church Growth, American Society for   www.ascg.org
135 N Oakland Ave   Pasadena CA 91182
Ph: 626-584-5293 ■ Fx: 626-584-5313 ■ TF: 800-999-9578

Church History, American Society of   www.churchhistory.org
PO Box 8517   Red Bank NJ 07701
Ph: 732-345-1787 ■ Fx: 732-345-1788

Church Institute, Seamen's   www.seamenschurch.org
241 Water St   New York NY 10038
Ph: 212-349-9090 ■ Fx: 212-349-8342

Church of Jesus Christ of Latter-Day Saints   www.lds.org
50 E North Temple St   Salt Lake City UT 84150
Ph: 801-240-1000 ■ Fx: 801-240-2033 ■ TF: 800-453-3860

Church Library Association, Evangelical   www.eclalibraries.org
PO Box 353   Glen Ellyn IL 60138
Ph: 630-681-7591 ■ Fx: 630-681-7592 ■ TF: 800-223-0001

Church Ministries, Wider   www.ucc.org/wcm
700 Prospect Ave NE 7th Fl   Cleveland OH 44115
Ph: 216-736-2320 ■ Fx: 216-736-3203

Church Inc, Missionary   www.mcusa.org
3811 Vanguard Dr PO Box 9127   Fort Wayne IN 46899
Ph: 219-747-2027 ■ Fx: 219-747-5331

Church Movement, Unity Fellowship
5148 W Jefferson Blvd   Los Angeles CA 90016
Ph: 323-938-8322 ■ Fx: 323-965-8322

Church Music Association of America   www.musicasacra.com
Christendom College 134 Christendom Dr   Front Royal VA
22630
Ph: 540-636-2900 ■ Fx: 540-636-1655

Church Music Publishers Association   www.cmpamusic.org
PO Box 158992   Nashville TN 37215
Ph: 615-791-0273 ■ Fx: 615-790-8847

Church of the Nazarene   www.nazarene.org
6401 The Paseo   Kansas City MO 64131
Ph: 816-333-7000

Church Pension Group   www.cpg.org
445 5th Ave   New York NY 10016
Ph: 212-592-1800 ■ Fx: 212-779-3370 ■ TF: 800-223-6602

Church Periodical Club   arc.episcopalchurch.org/cpc
815 2nd Ave   New York NY 10017
Ph: 800-334-7626 ■ Fx: 212-867-0395

Church Personnel Administrators, National Association of   www.nacpa.org
100 E 8th St   Cincinnati OH 45202
Ph: 513-421-3134 ■ Fx: 513-421-3085

(Church Planting) Mission to the World   www.mtw.org
1600 N Brown Rd   Lawrenceville GA 30043
Ph: 678-823-0004 ■ Fx: 678-823-0027

Church Press, Associated   www.theacp.org
1410 Vernon St   Stoughton WI 53589
Ph: 608-877-0011 ■ Fx: 608-877-0062

(Church Reform) Catholics Speak Out   www.quixote.org/cso
PO Box 5206   Hyattsville MD 20782
Ph: 301-699-0042 ■ Fx: 301-864-2182

Church Renewal, Black Methodists for   www.bmcr-umc.org
601 W Riverview Ave   Dayton OH 45406
Ph: 937-227-9460 ■ Fx: 937-227-9463

Church & School of Wicca   www.wicca.org
PO Box 297-IN   Hinton WV 25951
Ph: 304-466-2613 ■ Fx: 304-466-1353

Church, Seventh-day Adventist World   www.adventist.org
12501 Old Columbia Pike   Silver Spring MD 20904
Ph: 301-680-6000 ■ Fx: 301-680-6307

Church & Society, Black Women in   www.itc.edu/WSP/WSPBWCS.htm
700 ML King Jr Dr   Atlanta GA 30314
Ph: 404-527-5713 ■ Fx: 404-527-5715

Church, SPEAK Inc - Society for Promoting & Encouraging   www.speakinc.org
Arts & Knowledge of the   805 County Rd 102   Eureka
Springs AR 72632
Ph: 479-253-9701 ■ Fx: 479-253-1277

Church & State, Americans United for Separation of   www.au.org
518 C St NE   Washington DC 20002
Ph: 202-466-3234 ■ Fx: 202-466-2587 ■ TF: 800-875-3707

Church & Synagogue Library Association   www.worldaccessnet.com/~csla
PO Box 19357   Portland OR 97280
Ph: 503-244-6919 ■ Fx: 503-977-3734 ■ TF: 800-542-2752

Church Universal & Triumphant
PO Box 5000   Gardiner MT 59030
Ph: 800-245-5445 ■ Fx: 800-221-8307

Church Women United   www.churchwomen.org
475 Riverside Dr Rm1626   New York NY 10115
Ph: 212-870-2347 ■ Fx: 212-870-2338 ■ TF: 800-298-5551

Church World Service   www.churchworldservice.org
475 Riverside Dr 7th Fl   New York NY 10115
Ph: 212-870-2061 ■ TF: 800-456-1310

Church World Service Emergency Response Program www.cwserp.org
475 Riverside Dr 7th Fl   New York NY 10115
Ph: 212-870-3151 ▪ Fx: 212-870-2236

Churches of America, Buddhist www.buddhistchurchesofamerica.com
1710 Octavia St   San Francisco CA 94109
Ph: 415-776-5600 ▪ Fx: 415-771-6293

Churches, American Council of Christian www.amcouncilcc.org
PO Box 5455   Bethlehem PA 18015
Ph: 610-865-3009 ▪ Fx: 610-865-3033

Churches, Association of Unity www.unity.org
401 SW Oldham Pkwy PO Box 610   Lee's Summit MO 64063
Ph: 816-524-7414 ▪ Fx: 816-525-4020

Churches' Center for Theology & Public Policy www.cctpp.org
4500 Massachusetts Ave NW   Washington DC 20016
Ph: 202-885-8659 ▪ Fx: 202-885-8585 ▪ TF: 800-882-4987

Churches of Christ in the USA, National Council of the www.ncccusa.org
475 Riverside Dr 8th Fl   New York NY 10115
Ph: 212-870-2227 ▪ Fx: 212-870-2030

Churches, Congress of National Black
PO Box 65682   Washington DC 20035
Ph: 202-898-2422 ▪ Fx: 202-893-9300

Churches, International Council of Community iccc-world.org
21116 Washington Pkwy   Frankfort IL 60423
Ph: 815-464-5690 ▪ Fx: 815-464-5692

Churches, National Spiritualist Association of www.nsac.org
PO Box 217   Lily Dale NY 14752
Ph: 716-595-2000 ▪ Fx: 716-595-2020

Churches, Universal Fellowship of Metropolitan Community www.mcchurch.org
8704 Santa Monica Blvd 2nd Fl   West Hollywood CA 90069
Ph: 310-360-8640 ▪ Fx: 310-360-8680

Churches - US Office, World Council of www.wcc-coe.org
475 Riverside Dr Rm 1371   New York NY 10115
Ph: 212-870-3260 ▪ TF: 888-212-2920

Churchill Centre www.winstonchurchill.org
1150 17th St NW Suite 307   Washington DC 20036
Ph: 202-223-5511 ▪ Fx: 202-223-4944 ▪ TF: 888-972-1874

Churchill Winston Foundation of the US www.thechurchillscholarships.com
PO Box 1240   New York NY 10028
Ph: 212-879-3480

Churchmen, Fellowship of Concerned netministries.org/see/charmin/CM06091
4800 Dupont Ave S   Minneapolis MN 55409
Ph: 612-824-3933

Churchmen, National Guild of
PO Box 34548   San Diego CA 92163
Ph: 619-542-8660 ▪ Fx: 619-542-8585

Churro Sheep Association, Navajo- www.navajo-churrosheep.com
PO Box 94   Ojo Caliente NM 87549
Ph: 505-737-0488

CID Agents Association www.onin.com/cidaa
1896 Carlisle Rd   Traverse City MI 49686
Ph: 231-932-2388

CIES - Food Business Forum www.ciesnet.com
8455 Colesville Rd Suite 710   Silver Spring MD 20910
Ph: 301-563-3383 ▪ Fx: 301-563-3386

Cigar Association of America Inc
1707 H St NW Suite 800   Washington DC 20006
Ph: 202-223-8204 ▪ Fx: 202-833-0379

Cincinnati, Society of the members.tripod.com/~Historic_Trust/cincinna.htm
2118 Massachusetts Ave NW   Washington DC 20008
Ph: 202-785-2040 ▪ Fx: 202-785-0729

CINE www.cine.org
1112 16th St NW Suite 510   Washington DC 20036
Ph: 202-785-1136 ▪ Fx: 202-785-4114

Cinema Editors, American www.ace-filmeditors.org
100 Universal City Plaza Bldg 2282 Rm 234   Universal City CA 91608
Ph: 818-777-2900 ▪ Fx: 818-733-5023

Cinema & Media Studies, Society for www.cinemastudies.org
Univ of Texas Press PO Box 7819   Austin TX 78713
Ph: 512-471-4531

Cinema Society, Travel Adventure www.travelfilms.org
765 Beverly Park Pl   Jackson MI 49203
Ph: 877-279-7604

Cinema & Video Laboratories, Association of www.acvl.org

Cinematographers, American Society of www.theasc.com
1782 N Orange Dr   Hollywood CA 90028
Ph: 323-876-5080 ▪ Fx: 323-876-4973 ▪ TF: 800-448-0145

Cinephiles/Cinecon Inc, Society for www.cinecon.org
3405 Glendale Blvd Suite 251   Los Angeles CA 90039
Ph: 800-411-0455

CineVision Inc, Asian www.asiancinevision.org
133 W 19th St Suite 300   New York NY 10011
Ph: 212-989-1422 ▪ Fx: 212-727-3584

Cipher & Treasure Association, Beale
8A Hobart Ave   Bayonne NJ 07002
Ph: 201-339-0442

Circle K International www.circlek.org
3636 Woodview Trace   Indianapolis IN 46268
Ph: 317-875-8755 ▪ Fx: 317-879-0204 ▪ TF: 800-549-2647

Circle Sanctuary Network www.circlesanctuary.org
PO Box 219   Mount Horeb WI 53572
Ph: 608-924-2216 ▪ Fx: 608-924-5961

Circuits & Systems Society, IEEE www.ieee-cas.org
IEEE Operations Ctr 445 Hoes Ln   Piscataway NJ 08854
Ph: 732-981-0060 ▪ Fx: 732-981-1721

Circulations, Audit Bureau of www.accessabc.com
900 N Meacham Rd   Schaumburg IL 60173
Ph: 847-605-0909 ▪ Fx: 847-605-0483

Circum-Pacific Council for Energy & Mineral Resources www.circum-pacificcouncil.org
345 Middlefield Rd MS 973   Menlo Park CA 94025
Ph: 650-329-5430 ▪ Fx: 650-329-4936

Circumcision, Doctors Opposing faculty.washington.edu/gcd/DOC
2442 NW Market St Suite 42   Seattle WA 98107
Ph: 360-385-1882

Circumcision Information Resource Centers, National Organization of www.nocirc.org
PO Box 2512   San Anselmo CA 94979
Ph: 415-488-9883 ▪ Fx: 415-488-9660

(Circumcision) National Organization to Halt the Abuse & Routine Mutilation of Males www.noharmm.org   PO Box 460795   San Francisco CA 94146
Ph: 415-826-9351

(Circumcision) Nurses for the Rights of the Child nurses.cirp.org
369 Montezuma Ave Suite 354   Santa Fe NM 87501
Ph: 505-989-7377

(Circumnavigation) Joshua Slocum Society www.joshuaslocumsocietyintl.org
International   15 Codfish Hill Rd Ext   Bethel CT 06801
Ph: 203-790-6616 ▪ Fx: 203-790-6617

Circumpolar Conservation Union www.circumpolar.org
1612 K St NW Suite 401   Washington DC 20006
Ph: 202-675-8370

Circus Fans Association of America www.circusfans.org

Circus Project, National
56 Lion Ln   Westbury NY 11590
Ph: 516-334-2123 ▪ Fx: 516-334-2249

Cities International, Sister www.sister-cities.org
1301 Pennsylvania Ave NW Suite 850   Washington DC 20004
Ph: 202-347-8630 ▪ Fx: 202-393-6524

Cities, National League of www.nlc.org
1301 Pennsylvania Ave NW Suite 550   Washington DC 20004
Ph: 202-626-3000 ▪ Fx: 202-626-3043

(Citizen Diplomacy) Sister Cities International www.sister-cities.org
1301 Pennsylvania Ave NW Suite 850   Washington DC 20004
Ph: 202-347-8630 ▪ Fx: 202-393-6524

Citizen Initiatives, Center for www.ccisf.org
PO Box 29912   San Francisco CA 94129
Ph: 415-561-7777 ▪ Fx: 415-561-7778 ▪ TF: 888-729-7071

Citizen Participation, Civicus: World Alliance for www.civicus.org
1112 16th St NW   Washington DC 20036
Ph: 202-331-8518 ▪ Fx: 202-331-8774

Citizen Soldier www.citizen-soldier.org
267 5th St Suite 901   New York NY 10016
Ph: 212-679-2250 ▪ Fx: 212-679-2252

Citizens Against Government Waste www.cagw.org
1301 Connecticut Ave NW Suite 400   Washington DC 20036
Ph: 202-467-5300 ▪ Fx: 202-467-4253 ▪ TF: 800-232-6479

Citizens Alliance for VD Awareness
800 W Central Rd Suite 128   Mount Prospect IL 60056
Ph: 847-398-3378 ▪ Fx: 847-398-7309

Citizens for Alternatives to Chemical Contamination
8735 Maple Grove Rd   Lake MI 48632
Ph: 517-544-3318 ▪ Fx: 517-544-2828

Citizens for a Better Environment www.cbemw.org
152 W Wisconsin Ave Suite 510   Milwaukee WI 53203
Ph: 414-271-7280 ▪ Fx: 414-271-5904 ▪ TF: 866-256-5988

Citizens Coal Council www.citizenscoalcouncil.org
110 Maryland Ave NE Suite 408   Washington DC 20002
Ph: 202-544-6210 ▪ Fx: 202-544-7164

Citizens' Commission on Civil Rights www.cccr.org
2000 M St NW Suite 400   Washington DC 20036
Ph: 202-659-5565 ▪ Fx: 202-223-5302

Citizens for Community Values www.ccv.org
11175 Reading Rd Suite 103   Cincinnati OH 45241
Ph: 513-733-5775 ▪ Fx: 513-733-5794

Citizens Crime Commissions, National Association of www.crimecom.org/naccc
125 N Market Suite 115   Wichita KS 67202
Ph: 316-267-1235

Citizens Development Corps www.cdc.org
1726 M St NW Suite 1100   Washington DC 20036
Ph: 202-872-0933 ▪ Fx: 202-872-0923 ▪ TF: 800-394-1945

Citizens for Educational Freedom www.educational-freedom.org
9333 Clayton Rd   Saint Louis MO 63124
Ph: 314-997-6361 ▪ Fx: 314-997-6321

Citizens to End Animal Suffering & Exploitation www.ceaseboston.org
PO Box 440456   Somerville MA 02144
Ph: 617-628-9030

Citizens Flag Alliance www.cfa-inc.org
PO Box 7197   Indianapolis IN 46207
Ph: 317-630-1384 ▪ Fx: 317-630-1385

Citizens for Impartial Justice www.cijonline.org

Citizens for Law & Order Inc www.cloinc.org
PO Box 412   Carlsbad CA 92018
Ph: 760-631-2028

Citizens Network for Foreign Affairs www.cnfa.com
1111 19th St NW Suite 900   Washington DC 20036
Ph: 202-296-3920 ▪ Fx: 202-296-3948 ▪ TF: 888-872-2632

Citizens Network for Sustainable Development www.citnet.org
11426 Rockville Pike Suite 306   Rockville MD 20852
Ph: 301-770-6375 ▪ Fx: 301-770-6377

Citizens' Research Foundation
UC Berkeley Institute of Government Studies 104 Moses Hall   Berkeley CA 94720
Ph: 510-642-5158 ▪ Fx: 510-642-5537

Citizens for a Sound Economy www.cse.org
1900 M St NW 5th Fl   Washington DC 20036
Ph: 202-783-3870 ▪ Fx: 202-783-4687 ▪ TF: 888-564-6273

Citizens United for Rehabilitation of Errants www.curenational.org
PO Box 2310   Washington DC 20013
Ph: 202-789-2126

Citizens United Resisting Euthanasia
303 Truman St Berkeley Springs WV 25411
Ph: 304-258-5433 Fx: 304-258-5420

Citizenship, National Conference on   www.ncoc.net
1300 19th St NW Suite 800 Washington DC 20036
Ph: 202-778-0448

Citriculture, International Society of   www.lal.ufl.edu/ISC_Citrus_homepage.htm
UC Riverside Dept of Botany & Plant Sciences Riverside CA 92521
Ph: 909-787-4412 Fx: 909-787-4437

Citroen Car Club   home.comcast.net/~citroenquarterly
PO Box 130030 Boston MA 02113
Ph: 617-742-6604

Citrus Label Society   www.citruslabelsociety.com
131 Miramonte Dr Fullerton CA 92835
Ph: 714-871-2864 Fx: 714-871-0249

City Council, National Farm-   www.farmcity.org
225 Touhy Ave Park Ridge IL 60068
Ph: 847-685-8764 Fx: 847-685-8969

City/County Building Officials, Association of Major
505 Huntmar Park Dr Suite 210 Herndon VA 20170
Ph: 703-481-2038 Fx: 703-481-3596

City/County Management Association, International   www.icma.org
777 N Capitol St NE Suite 500 Washington DC 20002
Ph: 202-289-4262 Fx: 202-962-3500

City Health Officials, National Association of County &   www.naccho.org
1100 17th St 2nd Fl Washington DC 20036
Ph: 202-783-5550 Fx: 202-783-1583

City Human Services Officials, US Conference of
1620 'I' St NW Washington DC 20006
Ph: 202-293-7330 Fx: 202-293-2352

City International, Christ for the   www.cfci.org
PO Box 241802 Omaha NE 68124
Ph: 402-592-8332 TF: 888-526-7551

City & Regional Magazine Association   www.citymag.org
4929 Wilshire Blvd Suite 428 Los Angeles CA 90010
Ph: 323-937-5514 Fx: 323-937-0959

City Schools, Council of the Great   www.cgcs.org
1301 Pennsylvania Ave NW Suite 702 Washington DC 20004
Ph: 202-393-2427 Fx: 202-393-2400

CityKids Foundation   www.citykids.com
57 Leonard St New York NY 10013
Ph: 212-925-3320 Fx: 212-925-0128

Cityteam Ministries   www.cityteam.org
2304 Zanker Rd San Jose CA 95131
Ph: 408-232-5600 Fx: 408-428-9505 TF: 888-248-9832

(Civic) Cosmopolitan International   www.cosmopolitan.org
7341 W 80th St Overland Park KS 66204
Ph: 913-648-4330 Fx: 913-648-4630 TF: 800-648-4331

Civic Council, Chinese American
PO Box 166082 Chicago IL 60616
Ph: 312-225-0234

Civic League, National   www.ncl.org
1445 Market St Suite 300 Denver CO 80202
Ph: 303-571-4343 Fx: 303-571-4404

Civic Participation, Black Women's Roundtable on   www.bigvote.org/bwr.htm
1025 Vermont Ave NW Suite 1010 Washington DC 20005
Ph: 202-659-4929 Fx: 202-659-5025

Civic Participation Inc, National Coalition on Black   www.bigvote.org
1025 Vermont Ave NW Suite 1010 Washington DC 20005
Ph: 202-659-4929 Fx: 202-659-5025

Civicus: World Alliance for Citizen Participation   www.civicus.org
1112 16th St NW Washington DC 20036
Ph: 202-331-8518 Fx: 202-331-8774

Civil Affairs Association   www.civilaffairsassoc.org
10130 Hyla Brook Rd Columbia MD 21044
Ph: 410-992-7724 Fx: 410-740-5046

Civil Air Patrol   www.cap.gov
105 S Hansell St Bldg 714 Maxwell AFB AL 36112
Ph: 334-953-6047

Civil Attorneys, National Association of County
c/o National Assn of Counties 440 1st St NW Washington DC 20001
Ph: 202-393-6226

Civil Aviation Medical Association   www.civilavmed.com
PO Box 23864 Oklahoma City OK 73123
Ph: 405-840-0199 Fx: 405-848-1053

Civil Aviation Organization, International   www.icao.int
999 University St Montreal QC H3C5H7
Ph: 514-954-8219 Fx: 514-954-6077

Civil Defense Association, American   www.tacda.org
118 S Court St PO Box 1057 Starke FL 32091
Ph: 904-964-5397 Fx: 904-964-9641 TF: 800-425-5397

Civil Engineering Research Foundation   www.cerf.org
2131 K St NW Suite 700 Washington DC 20037
Ph: 202-785-6420 Fx: 202-833-2604

Civil Engineers, American Society of   www.asce.org
1801 Alexander Bell Dr Reston VA 20191
Ph: 703-295-6000 Fx: 703-295-6333 TF: 800-548-2723

Civil Justice, Lawyers for   www.lfcj.com
1140 Connecticut Ave NW Suite 503 Washington DC 20036
Ph: 202-429-0045 Fx: 202-429-6892

Civil Liberties Institute, Meiklejohn   www.sfsu.edu/~mclicfc
PO Box 673 Berkeley CA 94701
Ph: 510-848-0599 Fx: 510-848-6008

(Civil Liberties) Rutherford Institute   www.rutherford.org
PO Box 7482 Charlottesville VA 22906
Ph: 434-978-3888 Fx: 434-978-1789

Civil Liberties Union, American   www.aclu.org
125 Broad St 18th Fl New York NY 10004
Ph: 212-549-2500 Fx: 212-549-2580 TF: 800-775-1158

Civil Rights, Catholic League for Religious &   www.catholicleague.org
450 7th Ave New York NY 10123
Ph: 212-371-3191 Fx: 212-371-3394

Civil Rights, Citizens' Commission on   www.cccr.org
2000 M St NW Suite 400 Washington DC 20036
Ph: 202-659-5565 Fx: 202-223-5302

Civil Rights Institute, American   www.acri.org
PO Box 188350 Sacramento CA 95818
Ph: 916-444-2278 Fx: 916-444-2279

Civil Rights, Leadership Conference on   www.civilrights.org/lccr/index.html
1629 K St NW Suite 1000 Washington DC 20006
Ph: 202-466-3311 Fx: 202-466-3435

Civil Rights Organizations of America, Human &   www.hcr.org
21 Tamal Vista Blvd Suite 209 Corte Madera CA 94925
Ph: 415-924-1108 Fx: 415-924-1379 TF: 800-686-6347

(Civil Rights) Southern Regional Council   www.southerncouncil.org
133 Carnegie Way NW Suite 1030 Atlanta GA 30303
Ph: 404-522-8764 Fx: 404-522-8791

Civil Rights Under Law, Lawyers' Committee for   www.lawyerscommittee.org
1401 New York Ave NW Suite 400 Washington DC 20005
Ph: 202-662-8600 Fx: 202-783-0857

Civil Service Commission, International   icsc.un.org
2 United Nations Plaza 10th Fl New York NY 10017
Ph: 212-963-5465 Fx: 212-963-0159

Civil Service Employees, National Association of
6829 Park Ridge Blvd San Diego CA 92120
Ph: 619-466-3150

Civil War Association, American
PO Box 30826 Alexandria VA 22310
Ph: 703-960-2053

Civil War, Auxiliary to Sons of Union Veterans of the
2449 Center Ave Alliance OH 44601
Ph: 330-823-6919

(Civil War) North-South Skirmish Association Inc   www.n-ssa.org
PO Box 361 Bloomfield Hills MI 48303
Ph: 248-447-5909 Fx: 248-447-5944

Civil War Preservation Trust   www.civilwar.org
1331 H St NW Suite 1001 Washington DC 20005
Ph: 202-367-1861 Fx: 202-367-1865 TF: 888-606-1400

Civil War Society
33756 Black Mountain Rd Tollhouse CA 93667
Ph: 559-855-8636 Fx: 559-855-8639

Civilian Conservation Corps Alumni, National Association of   www.cccalumni.org
16 Hancock Ave PO Box 16429 Saint Louis MO 63125
Ph: 314-487-8666 Fx: 314-487-9488

Civilian Managers Association, Naval   www.ncmanational.org
PO Box 215 Portsmouth VA 23705
Ph: 757-396-3862 Fx: 757-396-3170

Civilizations, International Society for the Comparative Study of   www.iscsc.net

Civitan International   www.civitan.org
1 Civitan Pl PO Box 130744 Birmingham AL 35213
Ph: 205-591-8910 Fx: 205-592-6307 TF: 800-248-4826

Civitas   www.civitas.org
1327 W Washington Blvd Suite 3D Chicago IL 60607
Ph: 312-266-6700 Fx: 312-226-6733

Claim Association, International   www.claim.org
1225 23rd St NW Suite 200 Washington DC 20037
Ph: 202-452-0143 Fx: 202-833-3636

Claims Assistance Professionals, Alliance of   claims.org
873 Brentwood Dr West Chicago IL 60185
Ph: 630-588-1260 Fx: 630-690-0377 TF: 877-275-8765

Claims Council, National Truck & Heavy Equipment   www.nthecc.org

Claims Professional Accreditation Council Inc, Certified
PO Box 441110 Fort Washington MD 20749
Ph: 301-292-1988 Fx: 301-292-1787

CLAL - National Jewish Center for Learning & Leadership   www.clal.org
440 Park Ave S 4th Fl New York NY 10016
Ph: 212-779-3300 Fx: 212-779-1009

Claretians The   www.claretians.org
205 W Monroe St Chicago IL 60606
Ph: 312-236-7782 Fx: 312-236-7230

Clarinet Association, International   www.clarinet.org
PO Box 5039 Wheaton IL 60189
Ph: 630-665-3602 Fx: 630-665-3848

Clark Edna McConnell Foundation   www.emcf.org
250 Park Ave Suite 900 New York NY 10177
Ph: 212-551-9100 Fx: 212-986-4558

Classic Car Club of America   www.classiccarclub.org
1645 Des Plaines River Rd Suite 7A Des Plaines IL 60018
Ph: 847-390-0443 Fx: 847-390-7118

Classic Chevy Club International   www.classicchevy.com
5140 S Washington Ave Titusville FL 32780
Ph: 407-299-1957 Fx: 407-299-3341 TF: 800-456-1957

Classic Thunderbird Club International   www.ctci.org
1308 E 29th St Signal Hill CA 90806
Ph: 562-426-2709 Fx: 562-426-7023

Classical Caucus, Women's   home.gwu.edu/~camatteo/Womens_Classical_Caucus
Univ of Illinois at Urbana-Champaign Dept of the Classics 4080 Foreign Languages Bldg 707 S Mathews Ave Urbana IL 61801
Ph: 217-333-1008

Classical League, American   www.aclclassics.org
Miami University Oxford OH 45056
Ph: 513-529-7741 Fx: 513-529-7742

Classical League, National Junior   www.njcl.org
Miami Univ 422 Wells Mill Dr Oxford OH 45056
Ph: 513-529-7741 Fx: 513-529-7742

Classification Management Society, National   www.classmgmt.com
994 Old Eagle School Rd Suite 1019 Wayne PA 19087
Ph: 610-971-4856 Fx: 610-971-4859

Classification Society of North America www.pitt.edu/~csna/csna.html
Univ of Illinois at Chicago 601 S Morgan St IDS Dept MC
294   Chicago IL 60607
Ph: 312-996-2676 ▪ Fx: 312-413-0385

Classroom Publishers Association
5335 Wisconsin Ave NW Suite 920   Washington DC 20015
Ph: 202-965-2650 ▪ Fx: 202-244-5167

Claver, Junior Daughters of Peter www.knightsofpeterclaver.com
1825 Orleans Ave   New Orleans LA 70116
Ph: 504-821-4225 ▪ Fx: 504-821-4253

Claver, Junior Knights of Peter www.knightsofpeterclaver.com
1825 Orleans Ave   New Orleans LA 70116
Ph: 504-821-4225 ▪ Fx: 504-821-4253

Claver, Knights of Peter www.knightsofpeterclaver.com
1825 Orleans Ave   New Orleans LA 70116
Ph: 504-821-4225 ▪ Fx: 504-821-4253

Clay Henry Memorial Foundation www.henryclay.org
120 Sycamore Rd   Lexington KY 40502
Ph: 859-266-8581 ▪ Fx: 859-268-7266

Clay Minerals Society cms.lanl.gov
PO Box 460130   Aurora CO 80046
Ph: 303-680-9002 ▪ Fx: 303-680-9003

Clay Pipe Institute, National www.ncpi.org
PO Box 759   Lake Geneva WI 53147
Ph: 262-248-9094

Clay Producers Association, China www.kaolin.com
4885 Riverside Dr Suite 108   Macon GA 31210
Ph: 478-757-1211 ▪ Fx: 478-757-1949

Clay & Slate Institute, Expanded Shale www.escsi.org
2225 E Murray Holladay Rd Suite 102   Salt Lake City UT 84117
Ph: 801-272-7070 ▪ Fx: 801-272-3377

Clays Association, National Sporting www.mynsca.com
5931 Roft Rd   San Antonio TX 78253
Ph: 210-688-3371 ▪ Fx: 210-688-3014 ▪ TF: 800-877-5338

Clean Air Companies, Institute of icac.com
1660 L St NW Suite 1100   Washington DC 20036
Ph: 202-457-0911 ▪ Fx: 202-331-1388

Clean Air Policy, Center for www.ccap.org
750 1st St NE Suite 940   Washington DC 20002
Ph: 202-408-9260 ▪ Fx: 202-408-8896

Clean Beaches Council www.cleanbeaches.org
1225 New York Ave NW Suite 450   Washington DC 20006
Ph: 202-682-9507 ▪ Fx: 202-682-9506

Clean Fuels Development Coalition www.cleanfuelsdc.org
1925 N Lynn St Suite 725   Arlington VA 22209
Ph: 703-276-2332 ▪ Fx: 703-276-8447

Clean Harbors Cooperative
4601 Tremley Pt Rd   Linden NJ 07036
Ph: 908-862-7500 ▪ Fx: 908-862-7560

Clean Islands International Inc www.islands.org
8219 Elvaton Dr   Pasadena MD 21122
Ph: 410-647-2500 ▪ Fx: 410-647-4554 ▪ TF: 888-647-2501

Clean Water Action www.cleanwateraction.org
4455 Connecticut Ave NW Suite A-300   Washington DC 20008
Ph: 202-895-0420 ▪ Fx: 202-895-0438

Clean Water Fund www.cleanwaterfund.org
4455 Connecticut Ave NW Suite A300-16   Washington DC
20008
Ph: 202-895-0432 ▪ Fx: 202-895-0438

Cleaners Association, National www.nca-i.com
252 W 29th St 2nd Fl   New York NY 10001
Ph: 212-967-3002 ▪ Fx: 212-967-2240

Cleaners Association, National Air Duct www.nadca.com
1518 K St Suite 503   Washington DC 20005
Ph: 202-737-2926 ▪ Fx: 202-347-8847

Cleaning Association, International Window www.iwca.org
6418 Grovedale Dr Suite 101B   Alexandria VA 22310
Ph: 703-971-7771 ▪ Fx: 703-971-7772 ▪ TF: 800-875-4922

Cleaning Equipment Trade Association www.ceta.org
7691 Central Ave NE Suite 201   Fridley MN 55432
Ph: 763-786-9200 ▪ Fx: 763-786-7775 ▪ TF: 800-441-0111

Cleaning Management Institute www.cm-instituteonline.com
c/o National Trade Publications Inc 13 Century Hill Dr   Latham
NY 12110
Ph: 518-783-1281 ▪ Fx: 518-783-1386

Cleaning & Restoration, Association of Specialists in www.ascr.org
8229 Cloverleaf Dr Suite 460   Millersville MD 21108
Ph: 410-729-9900 ▪ Fx: 410-729-3603 ▪ TF: 800-272-7012

Cleaning Technicians, International Society of www.isct.org
109 Mill Stone Dr   Dothan AL 36305
Ph: 334-702-1984 ▪ Fx: 334-792-2999

Clearwater Inc, Hudson River Sloop www.clearwater.org
112 Market St   Poughkeepsie NY 12601
Ph: 845-454-7673

Cleft Palate-Craniofacial Association, American www.cleftpalate-craniofacial.org
104 S Estes Dr Suite 204   Chapel Hill NC 27514
Ph: 919-933-9044 ▪ Fx: 919-933-9604 ▪ TF: 800-242-5338

Cleft Palate Foundation www.cleftline.org
104 S Estes Dr Suite 204   Chapel Hill NC 27514
Ph: 919-933-9044 ▪ Fx: 919-933-9604 ▪ TF: 800-242-5338

Cleptomaniacs & Shoplifters Anonymous Inc www.shoplifersanonymous.com

Clergy Abuse, Survivors of - The Linkup www.thelinkup.org
291 N Hubbards Ln Suite B26   Louisville KY 40207
Ph: 502-290-4055 ▪ Fx: 502-290-4056

Clergy, Academy of Parish www.apclergy.org
1851 King James Pkwy Suite 322   Westlake OH 44145
Ph: 440-835-0931

Clergy Association, African-American Women's
214 P St NW   Washington DC 20001
Ph: 202-518-8488 ▪ Fx: 202-518-1273

Clergy, Association of Full Gospel Women afgwc.org
PO Box 2628   Landover MD 20784
Ph: 301-879-6958

Clergy International, Wesleyan/Holiness Women www.messiah.edu/whwc
Messiah College 1 College Ave   Grantham PA 17027
Ph: 717-691-6021

Clergy, National Organization for Continuing Education of Roman Catholic www.nocercc.org
1337 W Ohio St   Chicago IL 60622
Ph: 312-226-1890 ▪ Fx: 312-829-8915

Clerks, International Institute of Municipal www.iimc.com
8331 Utica Ave Suite 200   Rancho Cucamonga CA 91730
Ph: 909-944-4162 ▪ Fx: 909-944-8545 ▪ TF: 800-251-1639

Clerkship Directors in Internal Medicine www.im.org/cdim
2501 M St NW Suite 550   Washington DC 20037
Ph: 202-861-8600 ▪ Fx: 202-861-9731

Cleveland Bay Horse Society of North America www.clevelandbay.org
PO Box 483   Goshen NH 03752
Ph: 603-863-5193

Client Network, Applied Systems www.ascnet.org
801 Douglas Ave Suite 205   Altamonte Springs FL 32714
Ph: 407-869-0404 ▪ Fx: 407-869-0418

Climate Coalition, Global www.globalclimate.org
1275 K St NW   Washington DC 20005
Ph: 202-682-9161 ▪ Fx: 202-628-3622

Climate Institute www.climate.org
333 1/2 Pennsylvania Ave SE   Washington DC 20003
Ph: 202-547-0104 ▪ Fx: 202-547-0111

Climatological Association, American Clinical & www.accassoc.org
231 Albert Sabin Way ML 557   Cincinnati OH 45267
Ph: 513-558-4231 ▪ Fx: 513-558-0852

Climatologists, American Association of State www.ncdc.noaa.gov/oa/climate/aasc.html

Climatology, American Institute of Biomedical www.aibc.cc
1050 Eagle Rd   Newtown PA 18940
Ph: 215-968-4483

Clinical Associates, Organization of Regulatory & www.orcanw.org
PO Box 3490   Redmond WA 98052
Ph: 206-464-0825

Clinical Chemistry Inc, American Association for www.aacc.org
2101 L St NW Suite 202   Washington DC 20037
Ph: 202-857-0717 ▪ Fx: 202-887-5093 ▪ TF: 800-892-1400

Clinical & Climatological Association, American www.accassoc.org
231 Albert Sabin Way ML 557   Cincinnati OH 45267
Ph: 513-558-4231 ▪ Fx: 513-558-0852

Clinical Engineering, American College of www.accenet.org
5200 Butler Pike   Plymouth Meeting PA 19462
Ph: 610-825-6067

Clinical Immunology Society www.clinimmsoc.org
611 E Wells St   Milwaukee WI 53202
Ph: 414-224-8095 ▪ Fx: 414-272-6070

Clinical Investigation, American Society for www.asci-jci.org
35 Research Dr Suite 300   Ann Arbor MI 48103
Ph: 734-222-6050 ▪ Fx: 734-222-6058

Clinical Laboratory Management Association www.clma.org
989 Old Eagle School Rd Suite 815   Wayne PA 19087
Ph: 610-995-9580 ▪ Fx: 610-995-9568

Clinical Laboratory Science, American Society for www.ascls.org
6701 Democracy Blvd Suite 300   Bethesda MD 20817
Ph: 301-657-2768 ▪ Fx: 301-657-2909

Clinical Laboratory Sciences, National Accrediting Agency for www.naacls.org
8410 W Bryn Mawr Ave Suite 670   Chicago IL 60631
Ph: 773-714-8880 ▪ Fx: 773-714-8886

Clinical Ligand Assay Society www.clas.org
3139 S Wayne Rd   Wayne MI 48184
Ph: 734-722-6290 ▪ Fx: 734-722-7006

Clinical Magnetic Resonance Society www.cmrs.com
4550 Post Oak Pl Suite 342   Houston TX 77027
Ph: 713-623-8336 ▪ Fx: 713-960-0488 ▪ TF: 877-841-2522

Clinical Orthopaedic Society www.cosociety.org
PO Box 531823   Indianapolis IN 46253
Ph: 317-388-0329 ▪ Fx: 317-388-8984 ▪ TF: 800-843-9735

Clinical Scientists, Association of www.clinicalscience.org
PO Box 1287   Middlebury VT 05753
Ph: 802-462-2507 ▪ Fx: 802-462-2673

Clinical Social Work Federation www.cswf.org
PO Box 3740   Arlington VA 22203
Ph: 703-522-3866 ▪ Fx: 703-522-9441 ▪ TF: 800-270-9739

Clinical Trials, Society for www.sctweb.org
600 Wyndhurst Ave Suite 112   Baltimore MD 21210
Ph: 410-433-4722 ▪ Fx: 410-435-8631

Clinicians, American Association of Veterinary www.craiggroup.com/aavc.htm
37 W Broad St Suite 480   Columbus OH 43215
Ph: 614-358-0417 ▪ Fx: 614-241-2215

Clinics, Association of Children's Prosthetic-Orthotic www.acpoc.org
6300 N River Rd Suite 727   Rosemont IL 60018
Ph: 847-698-1637 ▪ Fx: 847-823-0536

Clinics, Association of Occupational & Environmental www.aoec.org
1010 Vermont Ave NW Suite 513   Washington DC 20005
Ph: 202-347-4976 ▪ Fx: 202-347-4950 ▪ TF: 888-347-2632

Clinton Presidential Center www.clintonpresidentialcenter.org
55 W 125th St   New York NY 10027
Ph: 212-348-8882 ▪ Fx: 212-348-9245

Clio Awards Inc www.clioawards.com
220 5th Ave Suite 1500   New York NY 10001
Ph: 212-683-4300 ▪ Fx: 212-683-4796 ▪ TF: 800-946-2546

Clock Association, Self Winding
1161 E Marcellus St   Long Beach CA 90807
Ph: 562-422-5158

Clock Collectors, National Association of Watch & www.nawcc.org
514 Poplar St   Columbia PA 17512
Ph: 717-684-8261 ▪ Fx: 717-684-0878

Clockmakers Institute, American Watchmakers-   www.awi-net.org
701 Enterprise Dr   Harrison OH 45030
Ph: 513-367-9800 ▪ Fx: 513-367-1414 ▪ TF: 866-367-2924

Cloisonne Collectors Club
PO Box 96   Rockport MA 01966
Ph: 978-546-6930

Close Up Foundation Inc   www.closeup.org
44 Canal Ctr Plaza   Alexandria VA 22314
Ph: 703-706-3300 ▪ Fx: 703-706-0000 ▪ TF: 800-256-7387

Closure Manufacturers Association   www.cmadc.org
1627 K St NW Suite 800   Washington DC 20006
Ph: 202-223-9050 ▪ Fx: 202-785-3603

Clothing Manufacturers Association of the USA
730 Broadway 10th Fl   New York NY 10003
Ph: 212-529-0823

Clowns of America International   www.coai.org
PO Box 6468   Lee's Summit MO 64064
Ph: 816-373-5696 ▪ TF: 888-522-5696

Club Association, National   www.natlclub.org
1201 15th St NW Suite 450   Washington DC 20005
Ph: 202-822-9822 ▪ Fx: 202-822-9808 ▪ TF: 800-625-6221

Club Managers Association of America   www.cmaa.org
1733 King St   Alexandria VA 22314
Ph: 703-739-9500 ▪ Fx: 703-739-0124

Clubmakers Society, Professional   www.proclubmakers.org
70 Persimmon Ridge Dr   Louisville KY 40245
Ph: 502-241-2816 ▪ Fx: 502-241-2817 ▪ TF: 800-548-6094

Clun Forest Association, North American   www.clunforestsheep.org
Bramble Hill 21777 Randall Dr   Houston MN 55943
Ph: 507-864-7585

CLUW Center for Education & Research   www.cluw.org/programs-edresearch.html
1925 K St NW Suite 402   Washington DC 20006
Ph: 202-223-8360 ▪ Fx: 202-776-0537

Clydesdale Breeders of the USA   www.clydesusa.com
17346 Kelley Rd   Pecatonica IL 61063
Ph: 815-247-8780 ▪ Fx: 815-247-8337

CMF International   www.cmfi.org
5525 E 82nd St PO Box 501020   Indianapolis IN 46250
Ph: 317-578-2700 ▪ Fx: 317-578-2827

Co-Anon Family Groups   www.co-anon.org
PO Box 12722   Tucson AZ 85732
Ph: 520-513-5028

(Co-Dependency) Co-Anon Family Groups   www.co-anon.org
PO Box 12722   Tucson AZ 85732
Ph: 520-513-5028

Co-Dependents Anonymous Inc   www.codependents.org
PO Box 33577   Phoenix AZ 85067
Ph: 602-277-7991

Co-op America   www.coopamerica.org
1612 K St NW Suite 600   Washington DC 20006
Ph: 202-872-5307 ▪ Fx: 202-331-8166 ▪ TF: 800-584-7336

Co-op PAC
50 F St NW Suite 900   Washington DC 20001
Ph: 202-626-8700 ▪ Fx: 202-626-8722

Coach Federation, International   www.coachfederation.org
1441 'I' St NW Suite 700   Washington DC 20005
Ph: 202-712-9039 ▪ Fx: 202-216-9646 ▪ TF: 888-423-3131

Coaches Association of America, College Swimming   www.cscaa.org
PO Box 63285   Colorado Springs CO 80962
Ph: 719-266-0064 ▪ Fx: 719-266-6844

Coaches Association of America, Golf   gcaa.collegiategolf.com
1225 W Main St Suite 110   Norman OK 73069
Ph: 405-329-4222 ▪ Fx: 405-573-7888 ▪ TF: 866-422-2669

Coaches Association of America, National Soccer   www.nscaa.com
6700 Squibb Rd Suite 215   Mission KS 66202
Ph: 913-362-1747 ▪ Fx: 913-362-3439 ▪ TF: 800-458-0678

Coaches Association, American Baseball   www.abca.org
108 S University Ave Suite 3   Mount Pleasant MI 48858
Ph: 989-775-3300 ▪ Fx: 989-775-3600

Coaches Association, American Football   www.afca.com
100 Legends Ln   Waco TX 76706
Ph: 254-754-9900 ▪ Fx: 254-754-7373

Coaches Association, American Hockey   www.ahcahockey.com
7 Concord St   Gloucester MA 01930
Ph: 781-245-4177 ▪ Fx: 781-245-2492

Coaches Association, American Swimming   www.swimmingcoach.org
2101 N Andrews Ave Suite 107   Fort Lauderdale FL 33311
Ph: 954-563-4930 ▪ Fx: 954-563-9813 ▪ TF: 800-356-2722

Coaches Association, American Volleyball   www.avca.org
1227 Lake Plaza Dr Suite B   Colorado Springs CO 80906
Ph: 719-576-7777 ▪ Fx: 719-576-7778

Coaches Association, Black   www.bcasports.org
201 S Capitol Ave Suite 495   Indianapolis IN 46225
Ph: 317-829-5600 ▪ Fx: 317-829-5601 ▪ TF: 877-789-1222

Coaches Association, Indoor Soccer   www.isca.net
9606 Aero Dr   San Diego CA 92123
Ph: 858-836-4422 ▪ Fx: 858-836-4421

Coaches Association, International Shooting
17446 SW Granada Dr   Beaverton OR 97007
Ph: 503-642-5873 ▪ Fx: 503-649-5182

Coaches Association, National Golf   www.ngca.com
180 N LaSalle St Suite 1822   Chicago IL 60601
Ph: 312-551-0814 ▪ Fx: 312-551-0815

Coaches Association, National Wrestling   www.nwcaadmin.bluestep.net/my/shared/home.jsp
PO Box 254   Manheim PA 17545
Ph: 717-653-8009 ▪ Fx: 717-653-8270

Coaches Association, National Youth Sports   www.nays.org
2050 Vista Pkwy   West Palm Beach FL 33411
Ph: 561-684-1141 ▪ Fx: 561-684-2546 ▪ TF: 800-729-2057

Coaches Association, NFHS   www.nfhs.org/nfca.htm
PO Box 690   Indianapolis IN 46206
Ph: 317-972-6900 ▪ Fx: 317-822-5700

Coaches Association, US Cross Country   www.usccca.org
Michigan State Univ Jenison Fieldhouse   East Lansing MI 48824
Ph: 517-355-1640 ▪ Fx: 517-432-3339

Coaches Association, US Fencing   www.usfca.org
PO Box 1966   Hoboken NJ 07030
Ph: 888-927-6687

Coaches Association, US Women's Track
7263 Heartcrest Ln   Centerville OH 45458
Ph: 937-434-0383

Coaches Association, Women's Basketball   www.wbca.org
4646 Lawrenceville Hwy   Lilburn GA 30047
Ph: 770-279-8027 ▪ Fx: 770-279-8473

Coaches, National Association of Accompanists &
395 Riverside Dr Apt 13A   New York NY 10025
Ph: 212-316-6164 ▪ Fx: 212-663-1900

Coaches, National Association of Basketball   nabc.ocsn.com
9300 W 110th St Suite 640   Overland Park KS 66210
Ph: 913-469-1001 ▪ Fx: 913-469-1390

Coaches & Teachers, Organization of Professional Acting
3968 Eureka Dr   Studio City CA 91604
Ph: 323-877-4988

Coal Ash Association, American   www.acaa-usa.org
15200 E Girard Ave Suite 3050   Aurora CO 80014
Ph: 720-870-7897 ▪ Fx: 720-870-7889

Coal Chemicals Institute, American Coke &   www.accci.org
1255 23rd St NW   Washington DC 20037
Ph: 202-452-1140 ▪ Fx: 202-833-3636

Coal Council, Citizens   www.citizenscoalcouncil.org
110 Maryland Ave NE Suite 408   Washington DC 20002
Ph: 202-544-6210 ▪ Fx: 202-544-7164

Coal Lessors, National Council of
300 Summers St Suite 1050   Charleston WV 25301
Ph: 304-346-0569 ▪ Fx: 304-346-6516

Coal Operators Association, Bituminous
1500 K St NW   Washington DC 20005
Ph: 202-783-3195 ▪ Fx: 202-783-4862

Coal Technology Association   www.coaltechnologies.com
601 Suffield Dr   Gaithersburg MD 20878
Ph: 301-294-6080 ▪ Fx: 301-294-7480

Coalition for the Advancement of Jewish Education   www.caje.org
261 W 35th St 12th Fl   New York NY 10001
Ph: 212-268-4210 ▪ Fx: 212-268-4214

Coalition for American Leadership Abroad   www.colead.org
2101 'E' St NW   Washington DC 20037
Ph: 202-944-5519 ▪ Fx: 202-338-6820

Coalition of Americans to Protect Sports
200 Castlewood Dr   North Palm Beach FL 33408
Ph: 561-842-4225 ▪ Fx: 561-863-8984

Coalition for Auto-Insurance Reform
7310 Stafford Rd   Alexandria VA 22307
Ph: 703-660-0799

Coalition of Black Trade Unionists   www.cbtu.org
PO Box 66268   Washington DC 20035
Ph: 202-429-1203 ▪ Fx: 202-429-1102

Coalition for the Defense of Human Rights   www.dhimmi.com
195 Jamestown Rd   Macomb IL 61455
Ph: 309-833-6039

Coalition for Education in the Life Sciences   www.wisc.edu/cbe/cels

Coalition to End Childhood Lead Poisoning   www.leadsafe.org
2714 Hudson St   Baltimore MD 21224
Ph: 410-534-6447 ▪ Fx: 410-534-6475 ▪ TF: 800-370-5323

Coalition for Environmentally Responsible Economies   www.ceres.org
99 Chauncy St 6th Fl   Boston MA 02111
Ph: 617-247-0700 ▪ Fx: 617-267-5400

Coalition of Essential Schools   www.essentialschools.org/
1814 Franklin St Suite 700   Oakland CA 94612
Ph: 510-433-1451 ▪ Fx: 510-433-1455

Coalition for Fair Lumber Imports   www.fairlumbercoalition.org
1775 Pennsylvania Ave NW Suite 600   Washington DC 20006
Ph: 202-862-4505 ▪ Fx: 202-862-1093

Coalition for Government Procurement   www.coalgovpro.org
1990 M St NW Suite 400   Washington DC 20036
Ph: 202-331-0975 ▪ Fx: 202-822-9788

Coalition of Higher Education Assistance Organizations   www.coheao.org
1101 Vermont Ave NW Suite 400   Washington DC 20005
Ph: 202-289-3910 ▪ Fx: 202-371-0197

Coalition on Human Needs   www.chn.org
1120 Connecticut Ave NW Suite 919   Washington DC 20036
Ph: 202-223-2532 ▪ Fx: 202-223-2538

Coalition for the International Criminal Court   www.iccnow.org
777 UN Plaza   New York NY 10017
Ph: 212-687-2176 ▪ Fx: 212-599-1332

Coalition for International Justice   www.cij.org
2001 'S' St NW Suite 740   Washington DC 20009
Ph: 202-483-9234 ▪ Fx: 202-483-9263

Coalition for Juvenile Justice   www.juvjustice.org/
1211 Connecticut Ave NW Suite 414   Washington DC 20036
Ph: 202-467-0864 ▪ Fx: 202-887-0738

Coalition of Labor Union Women   www.cluw.org
1925 K St NW Suite 402   Washington DC 20006
Ph: 202-223-8360 ▪ Fx: 202-776-0537

Coalition of Labor Union Women Center for   www.cluw.org/programs-edresearch.html
Education & Research   1925 K St NW Suite 402   Washington DC 20006
Ph: 202-223-8360 ▪ Fx: 202-776-0537

Coalition of National Health Education Organizations hsc.usf.edu/CFH/cnheo

Coalition for Networked Information www.cni.org
21 Dupont Cir NW Euram Bldg Suite 800   Washington DC 20036
Ph: 202-296-5098 ▪ Fx: 202-872-0884

Coalition to Protect Animals in Entertainment
PO Box 2448   Riverside CA 92516
Ph: 909-776-4040 ▪ Fx: 909-784-4262

Coalition of Publicly Traded Partnerships www.ptpcoalition.org
805 15th St NW Suite 500   Washington DC 20005
Ph: 202-371-9770 ▪ Fx: 202-371-6601

Coalition for Responsible Waste Incineration www.crwi.org
1752 'N' St NW Suite 800   Washington DC 20036
Ph: 202-452-1241 ▪ Fx: 202-887-8044

Coalition of Service Industries www.uscsi.org
1090 Vermont Ave NW Suite 420   Washington DC 20005
Ph: 202-289-7460 ▪ Fx: 202-775-1726

Coalition to Stop Gun Violence www.csgv.org
1023 15th St NW Suite 600   Washington DC 20005
Ph: 202-408-0061 ▪ Fx: 202-408-0062

Coalition for Student & Academic Rights www.co-star.org
PO Box 491   Solebury PA 18963
Ph: 215-862-9096 ▪ Fx: 215-862-9097

Coalition of Visionary Resources www.covr.org
1667 N Magnolia Ave   Tucson AZ 85712
Ph: 520-320-9338

COALPAC
101 Constitution Ave NW Suite 500E   Washington DC 20001
Ph: 202-463-2625 ▪ Fx: 202-463-6152

COAR Peace Mission
4395 Rocky River Dr   Cleveland OH 44135
Ph: 216-252-5572 ▪ Fx: 216-252-5573

Coast Alliance www.coastalliance.org
600 Pennsylvania Ave SE Suite 340   Washington DC 20003
Ph: 202-546-9554 ▪ Fx: 202-546-9609

Coast Defense Study Group Inc www.cdsg.org
1560 Somerville Rd   Bel Air MD 21015
Ph: 410-838-6509

Coast Guard Chief Petty Officers Association, US www.uscgcpoa.org
5520-G Hempstead Way   Springfield VA 22151
Ph: 703-941-0395 ▪ Fx: 703-941-0397

Coastal Conservation Association www.joincca.org
6919 Portwest Dr Suite 100   Houston TX 77024
Ph: 713-626-4234 ▪ Fx: 713-626-5852 ▪ TF: 800-201-3474

Coastal States Organization www.sso.org/cso
444 N Capitol St NW Hall of the States Suite 322   Washington DC 20001
Ph: 202-508-3860 ▪ Fx: 202-508-3843

Coaster Enthusiasts, American www.aceonline.org
7700 Shawnee Mission Pkwy Suite 201   Overland Park KS 66202
Ph: 913-262-4512 ▪ Fx: 913-262-4513

Coaters & Laminators, Association of Industrial Metallizers aimcal.org
2166 Gold Hill Rd   Fort Mill SC 29708
Ph: 803-802-7820 ▪ Fx: 803-802-7821

Coating Association, National Coil www.coilcoating.org
1300 Sumner Ave   Cleveland OH 44115
Ph: 216-241-7333 ▪ Fx: 216-241-0105

Coating Association, Surface Engineering
1300 Sumner Ave   Cleveland OH 44115
Ph: 216-241-7333 ▪ Fx: 216-241-0105

Coatings Association, National Paint & www.paint.org
1500 Rhode Island Ave NW   Washington DC 20005
Ph: 202-462-6272 ▪ Fx: 202-462-8549

Coatings Technology, Federation of Societies for www.coatingstech.org
492 Norristown Rd   Blue Bell PA 19422
Ph: 610-940-0777 ▪ Fx: 610-940-0292

Coblentz Society www.coblentz.org
1330 Zephyr Ct   Cumming GA 30041
Ph: 770-205-0248 ▪ TF: 877-477-4626

Cocaine Anonymous World Services Inc www.ca.org
3740 Overland Ave Suite C   Los Angeles CA 90034
Ph: 310-559-5833 ▪ Fx: 310-559-2554 ▪ TF: 800-347-8998

Cochlear Implant Association Inc www.cici.org

Cockatiel Society, American www.acstiels.com
9527 60th Ln N   Pinellas Park FL 33782
Ph: 727-541-4724

Cocker Spaniel Club of America Inc, English www.ecsca.org
PO Box 252   Hales Corners WI 53130
Ph: 414-529-9714

Cocoa Merchants' Association of America www.cocoamerchants.com
26 Broadway Suite 707   New York NY 10004
Ph: 212-363-7334 ▪ Fx: 212-363-7678

Cocoa Research Institute, American www.chocolateandcocoa.org/acri/staff.htm
8320 Old Courthouse Rd Suite 300   Vienna VA 22182
Ph: 703-790-5011 ▪ Fx: 703-790-5752

Code Council, International www.iccsafe.org
5203 Leesburg Pike Suite 600   Falls Church VA 22041
Ph: 703-931-4533 ▪ Fx: 703-379-1546

Code Council Inc, Uniform www.uc-council.org
1009 Lenox Dr Suite 202   Lawrenceville NJ 08648
Ph: 609-620-0200 ▪ Fx: 609-620-1200

Code Enforcement, American Association of www.aace1.com
5310 E Main St Suite 104   Columbus OH 43213
Ph: 614-552-2633 ▪ Fx: 614-868-1177

Code Management Association, Electronic Commerce www.eccma.org
2980 Linden St Suite E-2   Bethlehem PA 18017
Ph: 610-861-5990 ▪ Fx: 610-861-5992

Coders, American Academy of Professional www.aapc.com
309 W 700 South   Salt Lake City UT 84101
Ph: 801-236-2200 ▪ Fx: 801-236-2258 ▪ TF: 800-626-2633

Coexistence Initiative www.coexistence.net
477 Madison Ave 4th Fl   New York NY 10022
Ph: 212-303-9445 ▪ Fx: 212-980-4027

Coffee Association of America, Specialty www.scaa.org
330 Golden Shore Suite 50   Long Beach CA 90802
Ph: 562-624-4100 ▪ Fx: 562-624-4101

Coffee Association of USA Inc, National www.ncausa.org
15 Maiden Ln Suite 1405   New York NY 10038
Ph: 212-766-4007 ▪ Fx: 212-766-5815

Coffee Mill Enthusiasts, Association of www.millmania.com

Coffin-Lowry Syndrome Foundation www.clsf.info
3045 255th Ave SE   Sammamish WA 98075
Ph: 425-427-0939

Cognate Studies, International Organization for Septuagint & ccat.sas.upenn.edu/ioscs

Cognitive Liberty & Ethics, Center for www.cognitiveliberty.org
PO Box 73481   Davis CA 95617
Ph: 530-750-7912 ▪ TF: 888-950-6463

Cognitive Science Society Inc www.cognitivesciencesociety.org

Cognitive Sciences, Federation of Behavioral Psychological & www.thefederationonline.org
750 1st NE Suite 5007   Washington DC 20002
Ph: 202-336-5920 ▪ Fx: 202-336-5953

Coif, Order of the www.orderofthecoif.org
Univ of North Carolina Law Library CB 3385   Chapel Hill NC 27599
Ph: 919-962-1321 ▪ Fx: 919-962-1193

Coil Coating Association, National www.coilcoating.org
1300 Sumner Ave   Cleveland OH 44115
Ph: 216-241-7333 ▪ Fx: 216-241-0105

Coil Winding Association, Electrical Manufacturing & www.emcw.org
PO Box 278   Imperial Beach CA 91933
Ph: 619-435-3629 ▪ Fx: 619-435-3639 ▪ TF: 800-984-3629

Coin Coalition
601 13th St NW Suite 900 S   Washington DC 20005
Ph: 202-783-5594

Coin Dealers & Collectors, Association of Christian
PO Box 236   Wymore NE 68466
Ph: 402-645-3341 ▪ Fx: 402-645-3342

Coin Laundry Association www.coinlaundry.org
1315 Butterfield Rd Suite 212   Downers Grove IL 60515
Ph: 630-963-5547 ▪ Fx: 630-963-5864 ▪ TF: 800-570-5629

Coke & Coal Chemicals Institute, American www.accci.org
1255 23rd St NW   Washington DC 20037
Ph: 202-452-1140 ▪ Fx: 202-833-3636

Cold Finished Steel Bar Institute www.cfsbi.com
201 Park Washington Ct   Falls Church VA 22046
Ph: 703-538-3543 ▪ Fx: 703-241-5603

Cold Formed Parts & Machine Institute ww3.cfpmi.org
25 N Broadway   Tarrytown NY 10591
Ph: 914-332-0040 ▪ Fx: 914-332-1541

Cold Storage Construction, International Association for www.iacsc.org
1500 King St Suite 201   Alexandria VA 22314
Ph: 703-373-4300 ▪ Fx: 703-373-4301

Coleopterists Society www.coleopsoc.org
3294 Meadowview Rd   Sacramento CA 95832
Ph: 916-262-1160 ▪ Fx: 916-262-1190

Colitis Foundation of America, Crohn's & www.ccfa.org
386 Park Ave S 17th Fl   New York NY 10016
Ph: 212-685-3440 ▪ Fx: 212-779-4098 ▪ TF: 800-932-2423

Collaborative Family Healthcare Association www.cfhcc.org
PO Box 20838   Rochester NY 14602
Ph: 716-482-8210 ▪ Fx: 716-482-2901

Collectible Show Promoters Association, Antique & www.antiqueandcollectible.com
PO Box 4389   Davidson NC 28036
Ph: 704-895-9088 ▪ Fx: 704-895-0230 ▪ TF: 800-287-7127

Collectibles Dealer Association, Antiques & www.antiqueandcollectible.com
PO Box 4389   Davidson NC 280396
Ph: 704-895-9088 ▪ Fx: 704-895-0230

Collectibles & Giftmakers Guild www.collectiblesguild.org
77 W Washington St Suite 1716   Chicago IL 60602
Ph: 312-379-2935 ▪ Fx: 312-379-2939

(Collecting) 52 Plus Joker www.52plusjoker.org
670 Carlton Dr   Elgin IL 60120
Ph: 847-697-5819

Collecting Clubs, Association of www.collectors.org/ACC
18222 Flower Hill Way Suite 299   Gaithersburg MD 20879
Ph: 301-926-8663 ▪ Fx: 301-926-7648

Collection Attorneys, National Association of Retail www.narca.org
1620 'I' St NW Suite 165   Washington DC 20006
Ph: 202-861-0706 ▪ Fx: 202-463-8498 ▪ TF: 800-633-6069

Collection Professionals, ACA International - Association of Credit & www.acainternational.org
PO Box 390106   Minneapolis MN 55439
Ph: 952-926-6547 ▪ Fx: 952-926-1624

Collectors of America Inc, Heisey www.heiseymuseum.org/hca
National Heisey Glass Museum 169 W Church St   Newark OH 43055
Ph: 740-345-2932 ▪ Fx: 740-345-9638

Collectors Club www.collectorsclub.org
22 E 35th St   New York NY 10016
Ph: 212-683-0559 ▪ Fx: 212-481-1269

Collectors, International Association of Commercial www.commercialcollector.com
4040 W 70th St   Minneapolis MN 55435
Ph: 952-925-0760 ▪ Fx: 952-926-1624

Collectors, National Association of www.collectors.org/NAC
18222 Flower Hill Way Suite 299   Gaithersburg MD 20879
Ph: 301-926-8663 ▪ Fx: 301-926-7648

Collectors of Religion on Stamps
425 N Linwood Ave Suite 110   Appleton WI 54914
Ph: 920-734-2417 ▪ Fx: 920-734-6711

College Administration Professionals, Association of   www.acap.org
PO Box 1389   Staunton VA 24402
Ph: 540-885-1873 ▪ Fx: 540-885-6133

College Admission Counseling, National Association for   www.nacac.com
1631 Prince St   Alexandria VA 22314
Ph: 703-836-2222 ▪ Fx: 703-836-8015 ▪ TF: 800-822-6285

College of American Pathologists   www.cap.org
325 Waukegan Rd   Northfield IL 60093
Ph: 847-832-7000 ▪ Fx: 847-832-8000 ▪ TF: 800-323-4040

College of American Pathologists PAC
1350 'I' St NW Suite 590   Washington DC 20005
Ph: 202-354-7100 ▪ Fx: 202-354-7155

College Art Association   www.collegeart.org
275 7th Ave   New York NY 10001
Ph: 212-691-1051 ▪ Fx: 212-627-2381

College Association, Career   www.career.org
10 G St NE Suite 750   Washington DC 20002
Ph: 202-336-6700 ▪ Fx: 202-336-6828

College Athletic Association, National Christian   www.thenccaa.org
302 W Washington St   Greenville SC 29601
Ph: 864-250-1199 ▪ Fx: 864-250-1141

College Athletic Association, National Junior   www.njcaa.org
PO Box 7305   Colorado Springs CO 80933
Ph: 719-590-9788 ▪ Fx: 719-590-7324

College Athletic Business Management   nacda.ocsn.com/cabma/nacda-cabma.html
Association   PO Box 16428   Cleveland OH 44116
Ph: 440-892-4000 ▪ Fx: 440-892-4007

College Auxiliary Services, National Association of   www.nacas.org
7 Boars Head Ln   Charlottesville VA 22903
Ph: 434-245-8425 ▪ Fx: 434-245-8453

College Band Directors National Association   www.cbdna.org
Univ of Texas Box 8028   Austin TX 78713
Ph: 512-471-5883 ▪ Fx: 512-471-6589

College Board   www.collegeboard.com
45 Columbus Ave   New York NY 10023
Ph: 212-713-8000 ▪ Fx: 212-713-8184 ▪ TF: 800-927-4302

College Bowling USA   www.bowl.com/bowl/cbusa
5301 S 76th St   Greendale WI 53129
Ph: 800-514-2695

College Coalition, Women's   www.womenscolleges.org
125 Michigan Ave NE Suite 340   Washington DC 20017
Ph: 202-234-0443 ▪ Fx: 202-234-0445

College Composition & Communication, Conference on   www.ncte.org/groups/cccc
1111 W Kenyon Rd   Urbana IL 61801
Ph: 217-328-3870 ▪ Fx: 217-278-3763 ▪ TF: 800-369-6283

College Consortium for International Studies   www.ccisabroad.org
2000 P St NW Suite 503   Washington DC 20036
Ph: 202-223-0330 ▪ Fx: 202-223-0999 ▪ TF: 800-453-6956

College Counseling Association, American   www.collegecounseling.org
c/o American Counseling Assn 5999 Stevenson Ave   Alexandria
VA 22304
Ph: 703-823-9800 ▪ Fx: 703-823-0252 ▪ TF: 800-347-6647

College Dance Festival Association, American   www.fsu.edu/~acdfa
1570 E Jefferson St   Rockville MD 20852
Ph: 301-770-4443 ▪ Fx: 301-468-5841

College Deans Registrars & Admissions Officers,   www.vsu.edu/nacdrao
National Association of   Albany State Univ 504 College
Dr   Albany GA 31705
Ph: 229-430-4638 ▪ Fx: 229-430-2953

College Designers Association, University &   www.ucda.com
153 Front St   Smyrna TN 37167
Ph: 615-459-4559 ▪ Fx: 615-459-5229

College of Diplomates of the American Board of Orthodontics   www.cdabo.org
8005 W 110 St Suite 214   Overland Park KS 66210
Ph: 913-451-1443 ▪ Fx: 913-451-1453

College English Association   www.as.ysu.edu/~english/cea/ceaindex.htm

College Fraternity, Center for the Study of the   www.indiana.edu/~cscf
Indiana Univ Franklin Hall 002   Bloomington IN 47405
Ph: 812-855-1228

College Fraternity Editors Association   www.cfea.org
11020 NW Ambassador Dr Suite 30   Kansas City MO 64153
Ph: 816-891-9445 ▪ Fx: 816-891-0838

College Fund, American Indian   www.collegefund.org
8333 Greenwood Blvd   Denver CO 80221
Ph: 303-426-8900 ▪ Fx: 303-426-1200 ▪ TF: 800-776-3863

College Fund Inc, United Negro   www.uncf.org
8260 Willow Oaks Corporate Dr   Fairfax VA 22031
Ph: 703-205-3400 ▪ Fx: 703-205-3597 ▪ TF: 800-331-2244

College Gymnastics Association   tigger.uic.edu/~cjgym
52 Evelyn Rd   Needham MA 02494
Ph: 781-444-3893 ▪ Fx: 781-455-0782

College Health Association, American   www.acha.org
PO Box 28937   Baltimore MD 21240
Ph: 410-859-1500 ▪ Fx: 410-859-1510

College of Healthcare Information Management Executives   www.cio-chime.org
3300 Washtenaw Ave Suite 225   Ann Arbor MI 48104
Ph: 734-665-0000 ▪ Fx: 734-665-4922

College Hockey America   info.bemidjistate.edu/sports/cha
3163 Birchmont Dr NE   Bemidji MN 56601
Ph: 218-755-2767 ▪ Fx: 218-755-3898

College Honor Societies, Association of   www.achsnatl.org
4990 Northwind Dr Suite 140   East Lansing MI 48823
Ph: 517-351-8335 ▪ Fx: 517-351-8336

(College Honor Society) Mortar Board Inc   www.mortarboard.org
1200 Chambers Rd Suite 201   Columbus OH 43212
Ph: 614-488-4094 ▪ Fx: 614-488-4095 ▪ TF: 800-989-6266

College Language Association   www.clascholars.org

College, League for Innovation in the Community   www.league.org
4505 E Chandler Blvd Suite 250   Phoenix AZ 85048
Ph: 480-705-8200 ▪ Fx: 480-705-8201

College Media Advisers   www.collegemedia.org
Univ of Memphis Dept of Journalism   Memphis TN 38152
Ph: 901-678-2403 ▪ Fx: 901-678-4798

College Music Society   www.music.org
312 E Pine St   Missoula MT 59802
Ph: 406-721-9616 ▪ Fx: 406-721-9419

College of Optometrists in Vision Development   www.covd.org
243 N Lindbergh Blvd Suite 310   Saint Louis MO 63141
Ph: 314-991-4007 ▪ Fx: 314-991-1167 ▪ TF: 888-268-3770

College Parents of America   www.collegeparents.org
8300 Boone Blvd Suite 500   Vienna VA 22182
Ph: 703-761-6702 ▪ TF: 888-256-4627

College of Performance Management   www.cpm-pmi.org
101 S Whiting St Suite 320   Alexandria VA 22304
Ph: 703-370-7885 ▪ Fx: 703-370-1757

College Personnel Association, American   www.acpa.nche.edu
1 Dupont Cir NW Suite 300   Washington DC 20036
Ph: 202-835-2272 ▪ Fx: 202-296-3286

College Radio, Black   www.blackcollegeradio.com
PO Box 3191   Atlanta GA 30302
Ph: 404-523-6136 ▪ Fx: 404-523-5467

College Reading & Learning Association   www.crla.net
PO Box 6251   Auburn CA 95604
Ph: 530-823-1076 ▪ Fx: 530-823-6331

College Republican National Committee   www.crnc.org
600 Pennsylvania Ave SE Suite 215   Washington DC 20003
Ph: 202-608-1411 ▪ Fx: 202-608-1429 ▪ TF: 888-765-3564

College & Research Libraries, Association of   www.ala.org/acrl.html
50 E Huron St   Chicago IL 60611
Ph: 312-280-2519 ▪ Fx: 312-280-2520 ▪ TF: 800-545-2433

(College Sports) Atlantic Coast Conference   theacc.ocsn.com
PO Drawer ACC   Greensboro NC 27417
Ph: 336-854-8787 ▪ Fx: 336-854-7964

(College Sports) Big East Conference   www.bigeast.org
222 Richmond St Suite 110   Providence RI 02903
Ph: 401-272-9108 ▪ Fx: 401-274-5967

(College Sports) Big Ten Conference   www.bigten.org
1500 W Higgins Rd   Park Ridge IL 60068
Ph: 847-696-1010 ▪ Fx: 847-696-1150

(College Sports) Big West Conference   www.bigwest.org
2 Corporate Pk Suite 206   Irvine CA 92606
Ph: 949-261-2525 ▪ Fx: 949-261-2528

College Sports Information Directors of America   www.cosida.com
202 Tudor Rd   Ithaca NY 14850
Ph: 607-273-5891

(College Sports) Pacific 10 Conference   www.pac-10.org
800 S Broadway Suite 400   Walnut Creek CA 94596
Ph: 925-932-4411 ▪ Fx: 925-932-4601

(College Sports) Southeastern Conference   www.secsports.com
2201 Richard Arrington Blvd N   Birmingham AL 35203
Ph: 205-458-3000 ▪ Fx: 205-458-3031

(College Sports) Southern Conference   www.soconsports.com
905 E Main St   Spartanburg SC 29302
Ph: 864-591-5100

(College Sports) Southwestern Athletic Conference   www.swac.org
1527 5th Ave N   Birmingham AL 35204
Ph: 205-251-7573 ▪ Fx: 205-297-9820

(College Sports) Western Athletic Conference   www.wacsports.com
9250 E Costilla Ave Suite300   Englewood CO 80112
Ph: 303-799-9221 ▪ Fx: 303-799-3888

College Stores, National Association of   www.nacs.org
500 E Lorain St   Oberlin OH 44074
Ph: 440-775-7777 ▪ Fx: 440-775-4769 ▪ TF: 800-622-7498

College Swimming Coaches Association of America   www.cscaa.org
PO Box 63285   Colorado Springs CO 80962
Ph: 719-266-0064 ▪ Fx: 719-266-6844

College Trustees, Association of Community   www.acct.org
1233 20th St NW Suite 605   Washington DC 20036
Ph: 202-775-4667 ▪ Fx: 202-223-1297

College Unions International, Association of   www.acui.org
120 W 7th St 1 City Ctr Suite 200   Bloomington IN 47404
Ph: 812-855-8550 ▪ Fx: 812-855-0162

College & University Attorneys, National Association of   www.nacua.org
1 Dupont Cir NW Suite 620   Washington DC 20036
Ph: 202-833-8390 ▪ Fx: 202-296-8379

College & University Auditors, Association of   www.acua.org
342 N Main St   West Hartford CT 06117
Ph: 860-586-7561 ▪ Fx: 860-586-7550

College & University Business Officers, National Association of   www.nacubo.org
2501 M St NW Suite 400   Washington DC 20037
Ph: 202-861-2500 ▪ Fx: 202-861-2583

College & University Food Services, National Association of   www.nacufs.org
1405 S Harrison Rd Suite 305   East Lansing MI 48824
Ph: 517-332-2494 ▪ Fx: 517-332-8144

College & University Housing Officers International,   www.acuho.ohio-state.edu
Association of   941 Chatham Ln Suite 318   Columbus OH
43221
Ph: 614-292-0099 ▪ Fx: 614-292-3205

College & University Libraries, Canadian   www.cla.ca/divisions/cacul/cacul.htm
Association of   328 Frank St   Ottawa ON K2P0X8
Ph: 613-232-9625 ▪ Fx: 613-563-9895

College & University Media Centers, Consortium of   www.ccumc.org
Iowa State Univ Instructional Technology Ctr 1200
Communications Bldg   Ames IA 50011
Ph: 515-294-1811 ▪ Fx: 515-294-8089

College & University Museums & Galleries, Association of www.acumg.org
Ursinus College 601 E Main St   Collegeville PA 19426
Ph: 610-409-3500 ▪ Fx: 610-409-3664

College & University Planning, Society for www.scup.org
339 E Liberty St Suite 300   Ann Arbor MI 48104
Ph: 734-998-7832 ▪ Fx: 734-998-6532

College & University Professional Association for Human Resources www.cupahr.org
1233 20th St NW Suite 301   Washington DC 20036
Ph: 202-429-0311 ▪ Fx: 202-429-0149

College & University Religious Affairs, Association for www.upenn.edu/chaplain/acura
Northwestern Univ Chaplain 1870 Sheridan Rd   Evanston IL 60208
Ph: 847-491-7256 ▪ Fx: 847-491-7353

College-University Resource Institute Inc www.curi-inc.org
4953 'W' St NW   Washington DC 20007
Ph: 202-337-0889

Colleges, Accrediting Association of Bible www.gospelcom.net/aabc
5575 S Semoran Blvd Suite 26   Orlando FL 32822
Ph: 407-207-0808 ▪ Fx: 407-207-0840

Colleges, American Association of Community www.aacc.nche.edu
1 Dupont Cir NW Suite 410   Washington DC 20036
Ph: 202-728-0200 ▪ Fx: 202-833-2467

Colleges, American Association for Women in Community www.pc.maricopa.edu/aawcc
1202 W Thomas Rd   Phoenix AZ 85013
Ph: 602-285-7449 ▪ Fx: 602-285-7832

Colleges, American Mathematical Association of Two-Year www.amatyc.org
Southwest Tennessee Community College 5983 Macon Cove   Memphis TN 38134
Ph: 901-333-4643 ▪ Fx: 901-383-4651

Colleges of Art & Design, Association of Independent www.aicad.org
3957 2nd St   San Francisco CA 94114
Ph: 415-642-8595 ▪ Fx: 415-642-8590

Colleges of Arts & Sciences, Council of www.ccas.net
PO Box 873108   Tempe AZ 85287
Ph: 480-727-6064 ▪ Fx: 480-727-6078

Colleges, Association of American Medical www.aamc.org
2450 'N' St NW   Washington DC 20037
Ph: 202-828-0400 ▪ Fx: 202-828-1125

Colleges, Association of American Veterinary Medical www.aavmc.org
1101 Vermont Ave NW Suite 710   Washington DC 20005
Ph: 202-371-9195 ▪ Fx: 202-842-0773

Colleges, Association of Chiropractic www.chirocolleges.org
4424 Montgomery Ave Suite 102   Bethesda MD 20814
Ph: 301-652-5066 ▪ Fx: 301-913-9146

Colleges, Association of Episcopal www.cuac.org/aec
815 2nd Ave Suite 315   New York NY 10017
Ph: 212-716-6148 ▪ Fx: 212-986-5039

Colleges, Association of Governing Boards of Universities & www.agb.org
1 Dupont Cir NW Suite 400   Washington DC 20036
Ph: 202-296-8400 ▪ Fx: 202-223-7053 ▪ TF: 800-356-6317

Colleges Association, Great Lakes www.glca.org
535 W William St Suite 301   Ann Arbor MI 48103
Ph: 734-761-4833 ▪ Fx: 734-761-3939

Colleges, Council of Independent www.cic.edu
1 Dupont Cir NW Suite 320   Washington DC 20036
Ph: 202-466-7230 ▪ Fx: 202-466-7238

Colleges & Employers, National Association of www.naceweb.org
62 Highland Ave   Bethlehem PA 18017
Ph: 610-868-1421 ▪ Fx: 610-868-0208 ▪ TF: 800-544-5272

Colleges, Journalism Association of Community www.jacconline.org

Colleges of the Midwest, Associated www.acm.edu
205 W Wacker Dr Suite 1300   Chicago IL 60606
Ph: 312-263-5000 ▪ Fx: 312-263-5879

Colleges, National Association of Private Nontraditional Schools & www.napnsc.org
182 Thompson Rd   Grand Junction CO 81503
Ph: 970-243-5441 ▪ Fx: 970-242-4392

Colleges, National Council of State Directors of Community www.statedirectors.org
1 Dupont Cir NW Suite 410   Washington DC 20036
Ph: 202-728-0200 ▪ Fx: 202-833-2467

Colleges, New England Association of Schools & www.neasc.org
209 Burlington Rd   Bedford MA 01730
Ph: 781-271-0022 ▪ Fx: 781-271-0950

Colleges of Nursing, American Association of www.aacn.nche.edu
1 Dupont Cir NW Suite 530   Washington DC 20036
Ph: 202-463-6930 ▪ Fx: 202-785-8320

Colleges of Optometry, Association of Schools & www.opted.org
6110 Executive Blvd Suite 510   Rockville MD 20852
Ph: 301-231-5944 ▪ Fx: 301-770-1828

Colleges of Osteopathic Medicine, American Association of www.aacom.org
5550 Friendship Blvd Suite 310   Chevy Chase MD 20815
Ph: 301-968-4100 ▪ Fx: 301-968-4101

Colleges of Pharmacy, American Association of www.aacp.org
1426 Prince St   Alexandria VA 22314
Ph: 703-739-2330 ▪ Fx: 703-836-8982

Colleges of Podiatric Medicine, American Association of www.aacpm.org
1350 Piccard Dr Suite 322   Rockville MD 20850
Ph: 301-990-7400 ▪ Fx: 301-990-2807 ▪ TF: 800-922-9266

Colleges & Schools, Accrediting Council for Independent www.acics.org
750 1st St NE Suite 980   Washington DC 20002
Ph: 202-336-6780 ▪ Fx: 202-842-2593

Colleges & Schools, Association of Southern Baptist www.baptistschools.org
PO Box 11655   Jackson TN 38308
Ph: 731-660-3497 ▪ Fx: 731-664-6459

Colleges & Schools, Middle States Association of www.msache.org
3624 Market St   Philadelphia PA 19104
Ph: 215-662-5600 ▪ Fx: 215-662-5950 ▪ TF: 800-355-1258

Colleges & Schools, Southern Association of www.sacs.org
1866 Southern Ln   Decatur GA 30033
Ph: 404-679-4500 ▪ Fx: 404-679-4556 ▪ TF: 800-248-7701

Colleges & Schools of the US, Association of Military www.amcsus.org
9429 Garden Ct   Potomac MD 20854
Ph: 301-765-0695 ▪ Fx: 301-983-0583

Colleges, Society for Anthropology in Community ccanthro.bizland.com
c/o American Anthropological Assn 2200 Wilson Blvd Suite 600   Arlington VA 22201
Ph: 703-528-1902 ▪ Fx: 703-528-3545

Colleges for Teacher Education, American Association of www.aacte.org
1307 New York Ave NW Suite 300   Washington DC 20005
Ph: 202-293-2450 ▪ Fx: 202-457-8095

Colleges of Technology, Accrediting Commission of Career Schools & www.accsct.org
2101 Wilson Blvd Suite 302   Arlington VA 22201
Ph: 703-247-4212 ▪ Fx: 703-247-4533

Colleges & Universities, American Association of State www.aascu.org
1307 New York Ave NW 5th Fl   Washington DC 20005
Ph: 202-293-7070 ▪ Fx: 202-296-5819

Colleges & Universities, Association of American www.aacu-edu.org
1818 R St NW   Washington DC 20009
Ph: 202-387-3760 ▪ Fx: 202-265-9532

Colleges & Universities, Association of Jesuit www.ajcunet.edu
1 Dupont Cir NW Suite 405   Washington DC 20036
Ph: 202-862-9893 ▪ Fx: 202-862-8523

Colleges & Universities, Association of Presbyterian www.apcu.net
100 Witherspoon St   Louisville KY 40202
Ph: 502-569-5364 ▪ Fx: 502-569-8766 ▪ TF: 888-728-7228

Colleges & Universities, Council for Christian www.cccu.org
321 8th St NE   Washington DC 20002
Ph: 202-546-8713 ▪ Fx: 202-546-8913

Colleges & Universities, Hispanic Association of www.hacu.net
8415 Datapoint Dr Suite 400   San Antonio TX 78229
Ph: 210-692-3805 ▪ Fx: 210-692-0823 ▪ TF: 800-780-4228

Colleges & Universities, National Association of Independent www.naicu.edu
1025 Connecticut Ave NW Suite 700   Washington DC 20036
Ph: 202-785-8866 ▪ Fx: 202-835-0003

Colleges, Western Association of Schools & www.wascweb.org
985 Atlantic Ave Suite 100   Alameda CA 94501
Ph: 510-748-9001 ▪ Fx: 510-748-9797

Collegians for Life, American www.aclife.org
PO Box 1112   Washington DC 20013
Ph: 202-737-1007 ▪ Fx: 202-347-3245

Collegiate Athletic Association, National www.ncaa.org
700 W Washington St PO Box 6222   Indianapolis IN 46206
Ph: 317-917-6222 ▪ Fx: 317-917-6888

Collegiate Business Education, International Assembly for www.iacbe.org
PO Box 25217   Overland Park KS 66225
Ph: 913-631-3009 ▪ Fx: 913-631-9154

Collegiate Business Schools & Programs, Association of www.acbsp.org
7007 College Blvd Suite 420   Overland Park KS 66211
Ph: 913-339-9356 ▪ Fx: 913-339-6226

Collegiate Commissioners Association
2201 Richard Arlington Blvd N   Birmingham AL 35203
Ph: 205-458-3000

Collegiate Conference & Events Directors-International, Association of acced-i.colostate.edu
Colorado State Univ 8037 Campus Delivery   Fort Collins CO 80523
Ph: 970-491-5151 ▪ Fx: 970-491-0667 ▪ TF: 877-502-2233

Collegiate Directors of Athletics, National Association of nacda.ocsn.com
24651 Detroit Rd   Westlake OH 44145
Ph: 440-892-4000 ▪ Fx: 440-892-4007

Collegiate Golf Foundation, All-American
555 Madison Ave 12th Fl   New York NY 10022
Ph: 212-751-5170 ▪ Fx: 212-755-3762

Collegiate Hockey Association, American www.achahockey.org
PO Box 1013   Kent OH 44240
Ph: 330-221-4411

Collegiate Hockey Association, Central www.ccha.com
23995 Freeway Park Dr   Farmington Hills MI 48335
Ph: 248-888-0600 ▪ Fx: 248-888-0664

Collegiate Hockey Association, NorthEast www.necha.org
PO Box 58   Keene NH 03431
Ph: 603-363-4508

Collegiate Hockey Association, Western wcha.ocsn.com
2190 S High St   Denver CO 80208
Ph: 303-871-4223 ▪ Fx: 303-871-2600

(Collegiate Hockey) Hockey East Association www.hockeyeastonline.com
591 North Ave Suite 2   Wakefield MA 01880
Ph: 781-245-2122 ▪ Fx: 781-245-2492

Collegiate Hockey League, Atlantic Coast www.acchockey.com
380 S State Rd 434   Altamonte Springs FL 32714
Ph: 407-296-5269

Collegiate Hockey League, Central States www.cschl.com
2475 Archdale   West Bloomfield MI 48324
Ph: 248-366-7914 ▪ Fx: 248-366-7915

Collegiate Hockey League, Southwest www.schl.org
1533 Fairfield Ct   Lewisville TX 75077
Ph: 972-436-1560 ▪ Fx: 972-436-1560

Collegiate Hockey League, Tri-State www.tschl.com
Purdue University   West Lafayette IN 47907
Ph: 765-494-8931 ▪ Fx: 765-494-8956

Collegiate Licensing Association, International nacda.ocsn.com/icla/nacda-icla.html
24651 Detroit Rd   Westlake OH 44145
Ph: 440-892-4000 ▪ Fx: 440-892-4007

Collegiate Marketing Administrators, National Association of nacda.ocsn.com/nacma
PO Box 16428   Cleveland OH 44116
Ph: 440-892-4000 ▪ Fx: 440-892-4007

Collegiate Press, Associated studentpress.journ.umn.edu
2221 University Ave SE Suite 121   Minneapolis MN 55414
Ph: 612-625-8335 ▪ Fx: 612-626-0720

Collegiate Registrars & Admissions Officers, American Association of www.aacrao.org
1 Dupont Cir NW Suite 520   Washington DC 20036
Ph: 202-293-9161 ▪ Fx: 202-872-8857

Collegiate Roller Hockey Association, National   www.ncrha.org

Collegiate Schools of Architecture, Association of   www.acsa-arch.org
1735 New York Ave NW 3rd Fl   Washington DC 20006
Ph: 202-785-2324   Fx: 202-628-0448

**Collegiate Schools of Business, AACSB International -
Association to Advance**   600 Emerson Rd Suite 300   Saint
Louis MO 63141   www.aacsb.edu
Ph: 314-872-8481   Fx: 314-872-8495

Collegiate Schools of Planning, Association of   www.acsp.org
6311 Mallard Trace   Tallahassee FL 32312
Ph: 850-385-2054   Fx: 850-385-2084

(Collegiate Sports) Metro Atlantic Athletic Conference   www.maacsports.com
712 Amboy Ave   Edison NJ 08837
Ph: 732-738-5455   Fx: 732-738-8366

Collegiate Water Polo Association   www.collegiatewaterpolo.org
28 W Airy St   Norristown PA 19401
Ph: 610-277-6787   Fx: 610-277-7382

Collegiate Women Athletic Administrators, National Association of   www.nacwaa.org
4701 Wrightsville Ave Oak Park D-1   Wilmington NC 28403
Ph: 910-793-8244   Fx: 910-793-8246

Collegiate Wrestling Association, National   www.ncwa.net
11411 N Central Expy Suite 100W   Dallas TX 75243
Ph: 214-378-8700   Fx: 214-378-9900

Collegium Internationale Neuro-Psychopharmacologicum   www.cinp.org
2014 Broadway Suite 320   Nashville TN 37203
Ph: 615-343-2068   Fx: 615-343-2069

Collision Repair, I-CAR Inter-Industry Conference on Auto   www.i-car.com
3701 Algonquin Rd Suite 400   Rolling Meadows IL 60008
Ph: 847-590-1191   Fx: 847-590-1215   TF: 800-422-7872

Collision Repair Specialists, Society of   www.scrs.com
PO Box 4519   West Richland WA 99353
Ph: 509-943-8919   Fx: 509-943-8942   TF: 877-841-0660

Colombian-American Association   www.colombianamerican.org
30 Vesey St Suite 506   New York NY 10007
Ph: 212-233-7776   Fx: 212-233-7779

Colombian American Chamber of Commerce   www.colombiachamber.com
250 Catalonia Ave Suite 407   Coral Gables FL 33134
Ph: 305-446-2542   Fx: 305-448-5026

Colon Hydrotherapy, International Association for   www.i-act.org
PO Box 461285   San Antonio TX 78246
Ph: 210-366-2888   Fx: 210-366-2999

Colon & Rectal Surgeons, American Society of   www.fascrs.org
85 W Algonquin Rd Suite 550   Arlington Heights IL 60005
Ph: 847-290-9184   Fx: 847-290-9203

Colon & Rectal Surgery, American Board of   www.abcrs.org
20600 Eureka Rd Suite 600   Taylor MI 48180
Ph: 734-282-9400   Fx: 734-282-9402

Colonial Coverlet Guild of America
5617 Blackstone   La Grange IL 60525
Ph: 708-352-3812

Colonial Dames of America, National Society of the   www.nscda.org
2715 Q St NW   Washington DC 20007
Ph: 202-337-0972   Fx: 202-337-0348

Colonial Dames XVII Century, National Society   www.colonialdames17c.net
1300 New Hampshire Ave NW   Washington DC 20036
Ph: 202-293-1700   Fx: 202-466-6099

Colonial New England, National Society Sons of   www.nsscne.org

Colonial Physicians & Chirurgiens, Order of Descendants of
9317 Bent Tree Cir   Wichita KS 67226
Ph: 316-634-1930

Colonial Society of Massachusetts   www.colonialsociety.org
87 Mt Vernon St   Boston MA 02108
Ph: 617-227-2782

Colonial Tavern Keepers, Flagon & Trencher   nctimes.net/~churchyj/fandt_home.html
Society: Descendants of   7916 Quill Point Dr   Bowie MD
20720
Ph: 301-352-2919

Colonial Williamsburg Foundation   www.history.org
PO Box 1776   Williamsburg VA 23187
Ph: 757-229-1000   Fx: 757-220-7259

Color Association of the US   www.colorassociation.com
315 W 39th St Studio 507   New York NY 10018
Ph: 212-947-7774   Fx: 212-594-6987

Color Council, Inter-Society   www.iscc.org
11491 Sunset Hills Rd Suite 301   Reston VA 20190
Ph: 703-318-0263   Fx: 703-318-0514

Color Imagers, Association of Professional   apci.pmai.org
3000 Picture Pl   Jackson MI 49201
Ph: 517-788-8100   Fx: 517-788-8371

Color Manufacturers, International Association of   www.iacmcolor.org
1620 'I' St NW Suite 925   Washington DC 20006
Ph: 202-293-5800   Fx: 202-463-8998

Color Marketing Group   www.colormarketing.org
5904 Richmond Hwy Suite 408   Alexandria VA 22303
Ph: 703-329-8500   Fx: 703-329-0155

Color Pigments Manufacturers Association   www.cpma.com
PO Box 20839   Alexandria VA 22320
Ph: 703-684-4044   Fx: 703-684-1795

Color Print Society, American   www.americancolorprintsociety.org

Colorado Dude & Guest Ranch Association   www.coloradoranch.com
PO Box 2120   Granby CO 80446
Ph: 970-887-3128   Fx: 970-887-1229

Colorado Ranger Horse Association   www.coloradoranger.com
RD 1 Box 1290   Wampum PA 16157
Ph: 412-535-4841

Colored People, National Association for the Advancement of   www.naacp.org
4805 Mount Hope Dr   Baltimore MD 21215
Ph: 410-358-8900   Fx: 410-486-9255   TF: 877-622-2798

Colored Women's Clubs Inc, National Association of
1601 R St NW   Washington DC 20009
Ph: 202-667-4080   Fx: 202-667-4113

Colored Wool Growers Association, Natural   www.ncwga.org
429 W US 30   Valparaiso IN 46385
Ph: 219-759-9665

Colorists, American Association of Textile Chemists &   www.aatcc.org
1 Davis Dr PO Box 12215   Research Triangle Park NC 27709
Ph: 919-549-8141   Fx: 919-549-8933

Colposcopy & Cervical Pathology, American Society for   www.asccp.org
20 W Washington St Suite 1   Hagerstown MD 21740
Ph: 301-733-3640   Fx: 301-733-5775   TF: 800-787-7227

Columbia Scholastic Press Advisers Association   www.columbia.edu/cu/cspa/CSPAA.html
Columbia Univ MC 5711   New York NY 10027
Ph: 212-854-9400   Fx: 212-854-9401

Columbia Scholastic Press Association   www.columbia.edu/cu/cspa
Columbia University MC 5711   New York NY 10027
Ph: 212-854-9400   Fx: 212-854-9401

Columbia Sheep Breeders Association of America   www.columbiasheep.org
PO Box 272   Upper Sandusky OH 43351
Ph: 740-482-2608

Columbus Christopher Philatelic Society
11258 Goodnight Ln Suite 105   Dallas TX 75229
Ph: 972-241-2326   Fx: 972-243-4381

Columbus Foundation, Before
655 13th St Suite 300   Oakland CA 94612
Ph: 510-268-9775

Columbus, Knights of   www.kofc.org
1 Columbus Plaza   New Haven CT 06510
Ph: 203-752-4000   Fx: 203-773-3000

Columnists, National Society of Newspaper   www.columnists.com
1410 Stiener St Suite 709   San Francisco CA 94115
Ph: 415-563-5403

Combat Correspondents Association, US Marine Corps   www.usmccca.org
238 Cornwall Cir   Chalfont PA 18914
Ph: 215-822-6898   Fx: 215-822-0163   TF: 888-999-7819

Combustion Institute   www.combustioninstitute.org
5001 Baum Blvd Suite 635   Pittsburgh PA 15213
Ph: 412-687-1366   Fx: 412-687-0340

ComCARE Alliance   www.comcare.org
888 17th St NW 12th Fl   Washington DC 20006
Ph: 202-429-0574   Fx: 202-296-2962

Comics Magazine Association of America
355 Lexington Ave 17th Fl   New York NY 10017
Ph: 212-297-2122   Fx: 212-370-9047

Commemorative Air Force   www.commemorativeairforce.org
PO Box 62000   Midland TX 79711
Ph: 432-563-1000   Fx: 432-563-8046

Commemorative Art, American Institute of   www.monuments-aica.com
11003 Fellswood Ct   Louisville KY 40243
Ph: 502-254-1375

Commerce Association, Electronic   www.theeca.org
1432 Fenwick Ln Suite 200   Silver Spring MD 20910
Ph: 301-608-9600

CommerceNet   www.commerce.net
510 Logue Ave   Mountain View CA 94043
Ph: 650-962-2600   Fx: 650-962-2601   TF: 888-255-1900

Commercial Alert   www.commercialalert.org
4110 SE Hawthorne Blvd Suite 123   Portland OR 97214
Ph: 503-235-8012   Fx: 503-235-5073

Commercial Collectors, International Association of   www.commercialcollector.com
4040 W 70th St   Minneapolis MN 55435
Ph: 952-925-0760   Fx: 952-926-1624

Commercial Development & Marketing Association   www.cdmaonline.org
1900 Arch St   Philadelphia PA 19103
Ph: 215-564-3484   Fx: 215-963-9784

Commercial Finance Association   www.cfa.com
225 W 34th St Suite 1815   New York NY 10122
Ph: 212-594-3490   Fx: 212-564-6053

Commercial Finance Attorneys, Association of   www.afca.cc
25 Hooks Ln Suite 302   Baltimore MD 21208
Ph: 410-486-2600   Fx: 410-486-8438

Commercial Food Equipment Service Association   www.cfesa.com
2211 W Meadowview Rd Suite 20   Greensboro NC 27407
Ph: 336-346-4700   Fx: 336-346-4745

Commercial-Free Public Education, Center for
1714 Franklin St   Oakland CA 94612
Ph: 510-268-1100   Fx: 510-268-1277   TF: 800-867-5841

Commercial Law League of America   www.clla.org
150 N Michigan Ave Suite 600   Chicago IL 60601
Ph: 312-781-2000   Fx: 312-781-2010   TF: 800-978-2552

Commercial Mortgage Securities Association   www.cmbs.org
30 Broad St 28th Fl   New York NY 10004
Ph: 212-509-1844   Fx: 212-509-1895

Commercial Producers, Association of Independent   www.aicp.com
3 W 18th St 5th Fl   New York NY 10010
Ph: 212-929-3000   Fx: 212-929-3359

Commercial Real Estate Association, AIR   www.airea.com
700 S Flower St Suite 600   Los Angeles CA 90017
Ph: 213-687-8777   Fx: 213-687-8616

Commercial Recreation Association, Resort &   www.r-c-r-a.org
PO Box 2437   Aurora IL 60507
Ph: 630-892-2175   Fx: 630-801-4202

Commercial Travelers Association, Order of United   www.uct.org
632 N Park St PO Box 159019   Columbus OH 43215
Ph: 614-228-3276   Fx: 614-228-1898   TF: 800-848-0123

Commercial Vehicle Safety Alliance   www.cvsa.org
1101 17th St NW Suite 803   Washington DC 20036
Ph: 202-775-1623   Fx: 202-775-1624

Commercial Workers International Union, United Food & www.ufcw.org
1775 K St NW Washington DC 20006
Ph: 202-223-3111 ▪ Fx: 202-466-1562 ▪ TF: 800-551-4010

Commission on Accreditation of Allied Health Education Programs www.caahep.org
35 E Wacker Dr Suite 1970 Chicago IL 60601
Ph: 312-553-9355 ▪ Fx: 312-553-9616

Commission on Accreditation for Law Enforcement Agencies www.calea.org
10306 Eaton Pl Suite 320 Fairfax VA 22030
Ph: 703-352-4225 ▪ Fx: 703-591-2206 ▪ TF: 800-368-3757

Commission on Accreditation of Rehabilitation Facilities www.carf.org
4891 E Grant Rd Tucson AZ 85712
Ph: 520-325-1044 ▪ Fx: 520-318-1129

Commission for Certification in Geriatric Pharmacy www.ccgp.org
1321 Duke St Alexandria VA 22314
Ph: 703-535-3038 ▪ Fx: 703-739-1500

Commission on Certification of Work Adjustment & Vocational www.ccwaves.org
Evaluation Specialists 1835 Rohlwing Rd Suite E Rolling
Meadows IL 60008
Ph: 847-342-1796 ▪ Fx: 847-394-2108

Commission on Dietetic Registration www.cdrnet.org
120 S Riverside Plaza Suite 2000 Chicago IL 60606
Ph: 312-899-0040 ▪ Fx: 312-899-4772

Commission on Missing & Exploited Children www.comec.org
616 Adams Ave Memphis TN 38105
Ph: 901-405-8441 ▪ Fx: 901-575-8856

Commission on Office Laboratory Accreditation www.cola.org
9881 Broken Land Pkwy Suite 200 Columbia MD 21046
Ph: 410-381-6581 ▪ Fx: 410-381-8611 ▪ TF: 800-981-9883

Commission on Opticianry Accreditation www.coaccreditation.com
PO Box 3073 Merrifield VA 22116
Ph: 703-766-1600 ▪ Fx: 703-766-2834

Commission on Presidential Debates www.debates.org
1200 New Hampshire Ave NW PO Box 445 Washington DC
20036
Ph: 202-872-1020 ▪ Fx: 202-783-5923

Commission on Professionals in Science & Technology www.cpst.org
1200 New York Ave NW Suite 390 Washington DC 20005
Ph: 202-326-7080 ▪ Fx: 202-842-1603

Commission on Rehabilitation Counselor Certification www.crccertification.com
1835 Rohlwing Rd Suite E Rolling Meadows IL 60008
Ph: 847-394-2104 ▪ Fx: 847-394-2172

Commissioned Officers Association of the US Public Health www.coausphs.org
Service 8201 Corporate Dr Suite 560 Landover MD 20785
Ph: 301-731-9080 ▪ Fx: 301-731-9084

Commissioners Association, Collegiate
2201 Richard Arlington Blvd N Birmingham AL 35203
Ph: 205-458-3000

Committee of 100 www.committee100.org
677 5th Ave 3rd Fl New York NY 10022
Ph: 212-371-6565 ▪ Fx: 212-371-9009

Committee of 200 www.c200.org
625 N Michigan Ave Suite 500 Chicago IL 60611
Ph: 312-751-3477 ▪ Fx: 312-943-9401

Committee to Abolish Sport Hunting www.all-creatures.org/cash
PO Box 562 New Paltz NY 12561
Ph: 845-255-4227 ▪ Fx: 845-256-9113

Committee on Accreditation for Educational Programs for the www.coaemsp.org
EMS Professions 1248 Hardwood Rd Bedford TX 76021
Ph: 817-283-9403 ▪ Fx: 817-354-8519

Committee for Accuracy in Middle East Reporting in America www.camera.org
PO Box 35040 Boston MA 02135
Ph: 617-789-3672 ▪ Fx: 617-787-7853

Committee Against Anti-Asian Violence www.caaav.org
2473 Valentine Ave Bronx NY 10458
Ph: 718-220-7391 ▪ Fx: 718-220-7398

Committee of Annuity Insurers www.annuity-insurers.org
c/o Davis & Harman LLP 1455 Pennsylvania Ave NW Suite
1200 Washington DC 20004
Ph: 202-347-2230 ▪ Fx: 202-393-3310

Committee of Atomic Bomb Survivors in the US
1759 Sutter St San Francisco CA 94115
Ph: 562-698-0855

Committee for Children www.cfchildren.org
801 1st Ave S Suite 100 Seattle WA 98134
Ph: 206-343-1223 ▪ Fx: 206-438-6765 ▪ TF: 800-634-4449

Committee of Concerned Scientists www.libertynet.org/ccs
53-34 208th St Bayside NY 11364
Ph: 718-229-2813 ▪ Fx: 718-229-7540

Committee for a Democratic Majority
301 4th St NE Suite 202 Washington DC 20002
Ph: 202-544-4889 ▪ Fx: 202-546-2285

Committee for Economic Development www.ced.org
261 Madison Ave 25th Fl New York NY 10016
Ph: 212-688-2063 ▪ Fx: 212-758-9068

Committee for Education Funding www.cef.org
122 C St NW Suite 280 Washington DC 20001
Ph: 202-383-0083 ▪ Fx: 202-383-0097

Committee on Institutional Cooperation www.cic.uiuc.edu
302 E John St Suite 1705 Champaign IL 61820
Ph: 217-333-8475 ▪ Fx: 217-244-7127

Committee of Interns & Residents www.cirseiu.org
520 8th Ave Suite 1200 New York NY 10018
Ph: 212-356-8100 ▪ Fx: 212-356-8111

Committee on Lesbian & Gay History www.usc.edu/clgh
College of William & Mary PO Box 8795 Williamsburg VA
23187
Ph: 757-221-2453 ▪ Fx: 757-221-3737

Committee on Letter Carriers Political Education
100 Indiana Ave NW Washington DC 20001
Ph: 202-393-4695 ▪ Fx: 202-737-1540

Committee on the Middle East www.middleeast.org/archives/come.htm
PO Box 18367 Washington DC 20036
Ph: 202-362-5266 ▪ Fx: 202-362-6965

Committee on Missionary Evangelism www.comemissions.com
PO Box 88085 Grand Rapids MI 49518
Ph: 616-455-8228

Committee for Mother & Child Rights Inc
6536 Colgate Ave Los Angeles CA 90048
Ph: 323-634-0543 ▪ Fx: 323-936-7762

Committee for Nuclear Responsibility www.ratical.org/radiation/CNR
PO Box 421993 San Francisco CA 94142
Ph: 415-776-8299

Committee Opposed to Militarism & the Draft www.comdsd.org
PO Box 15195 San Diego CA 92175
Ph: 760-753-7518

Committee for Private Offshore Rescue & Towing www.c-port.org
1600 Duke St Suite 220 Alexandria VA 22314
Ph: 703-519-1713 ▪ Fx: 703-519-1716

Committee to Protect Journalists www.cpj.org
330 7th Ave 12th Fl New York NY 10001
Ph: 212-465-1004 ▪ Fx: 212-465-9568

Committee on Public Doublespeak
National Council of Teachers of English 1111 W
Kenyon Urbana IL 61801
Ph: 217-328-3870 ▪ Fx: 217-328-9645 ▪ TF: 800-369-6283

Committee on Research Materials on www.library.wisc.edu/guides/SEAasia/cormosea
Southeast Asia

Committee for a Responsible Federal Budget www.crfb.org
1630 Connecticut Ave NW 7th Fl Washington DC 20009
Ph: 202-986-6599 ▪ Fx: 202-986-3696

Committee for the Scientific Investigation of Claims of the Paranormal www.csicop.org
PO Box 703 Amherst NY 14226
Ph: 716-636-1425 ▪ Fx: 716-636-1733 ▪ TF: 800-634-1610

Committee in Solidarity with the People of El Salvador www.cispes.org
PO Box 8560 New York NY 10117
Ph: 212-465-8115 ▪ Fx: 212-465-8998

Committee for a Strong Economy
9300 Livingston Rd Fort Washington MD 20744
Ph: 301-248-6200 ▪ Fx: 301-248-7104 ▪ TF: 800-248-6862

Committee for the Study of the American Electorate www.gspm.org/csae
601 Pennsylvania Ave NW South Bldg Suite 900 Washington
DC 20004
Ph: 202-546-3221 ▪ Fx: 202-546-3571

Committee to Support the Revolution in Peru www.csrp.org
PO Box 1246 Berkeley CA 94701
Ph: 415-252-5786 ▪ Fx: 415-252-7414

Committee for a Unified Independent Party www.cuip.org
225 Broadway Suite 2010 New York NY 10007
Ph: 212-962-1811 ▪ Fx: 212-803-1899

Commodity Distribution Association, American www.commodityfoods.org
11358 Barley Field Way Marriottsville MD 21104
Ph: 410-442-4612 ▪ Fx: 410-442-4613

Common Cause www.commoncause.org
1250 Connecticut Ave NW Suite 600 Washington DC 20036
Ph: 202-833-1200 ▪ Fx: 202-659-3716 ▪ TF: 800-926-1064

Common Destiny Alliance www.education.umd.edu/CODA
Univ of Maryland College of Education 2110 Benjamin
Bldg College Park MD 20742
Ph: 301-405-0639 ▪ Fx: 301-405-3573

Common Dreams www.commondreams.org
PO Box 443 Portland ME 04112
Ph: 207-775-0488 ▪ Fx: 207-775-0489

Common Ground Alliance www.commongroundalliance.com
14500 Avion Pkwy Suite 300 Chantilly VA 20151
Ph: 703-818-3274

Common Property, International Association for the Study of www.iascp.org
PO Box 2355 Gary IN 46409
Ph: 219-980-1433 ▪ Fx: 219-980-2801

Common Sense About Kids & Guns www.kidsandguns.org
418 C St NE Washington DC 20002
Ph: 202-546-0200 ▪ Fx: 202-546-6250 ▪ TF: 877-955-5437

Commonwealth Fund www.cmwf.org
1 E 75th St New York NY 10021
Ph: 212-606-3800 ▪ Fx: 212-249-1276

Commonwealth Institute www.comw.org
PO Box 398105 Cambridge MA 02139
Ph: 617-547-4474 ▪ Fx: 617-868-1267

Communal Studies Association www.communalstudies.info
PO Box 122 Amana IA 52203
Ph: 319-622-6446

Communicating for Agriculture & the Self-Employed www.selfemployedcountry.org
112 E Lincoln Ave Fergus Falls MN 56537
Ph: 218-739-3241 ▪ Fx: 218-739-3832 ▪ TF: 800-432-3276

Communication Advancement, Council for Electronic Revenue www.cerca.org/
600 Cameron St Suite 309 Alexandria VA 22314
Ph: 703-340-1655

Communication Arts Professionals, Catholic Academy for www.catholicacademy.org
901 Irving Ave Dayton OH 45409
Ph: 937-229-2303 ▪ Fx: 937-229-2300

Communication, Association for Business www.businesscommunication.org
Baruch College 1 Bernard Baruch Way Box B8-240 New York
NY 10010
Ph: 646-312-3727 ▪ Fx: 646-349-5297

Communication Association, International www.icahdq.org
1730 Rhode Island Ave NW Suite 300 Washington DC 20036
Ph: 202-530-9855 ▪ Fx: 202-530-9851

Communication Association, National www.natcom.org
1765 'N' St NW Washington DC 20036
Ph: 202-464-4622 ▪ Fx: 202-464-4600

Communication, Center for Nonviolent　　cnvc.org
2428 Foothill Blvd Suite E　La Crescenta CA 91214
Ph: 818-957-9393 ▪ Fx: 818-957-1424 ▪ TF: 800-255-7696

(Communication) Civitas　　www.civitas.org
1327 W Washington Blvd Suite 3D　Chicago IL 60607
Ph: 312-266-6700 ▪ Fx: 312-226-6733

Communication, Conference on College Composition &　　www.ncte.org/groups/cccc
1111 W Kenyon Rd　Urbana IL 61801
Ph: 217-328-3870 ▪ Fx: 217-278-3763 ▪ TF: 800-369-6283

Communication Consultants, Association of Professional　　www.consultingsuccess.org
3924 S Troost Ave　Tulsa OK 74105
Ph: 918-743-4793

Communication Contractors Association, Power &　　www.pccaweb.org
103 Orinoco St Suite 200　Alexandria VA 22314
Ph: 703-212-7734 ▪ Fx: 703-548-3733 ▪ TF: 800-542-7222

Communication Excellence, Association for　　www.aceweb.org
Univ of Florida Mowry Rd Bldg 116 PO Box
110811　Gainesville FL 32611
Ph: 352-392-9588 ▪ Fx: 352-392-7902

Communication, Foundation for Student　　www.businesstoday.org
48 University Pl　Princeton NJ 08544
Ph: 609-258-1111 ▪ Fx: 609-258-1222

Communication Institute for Online Scholarship　　www.cios.org
PO Box 57　Rotterdam Junction NY 12150
Ph: 518-887-2443 ▪ Fx: 518-887-5186

Communication, International Council for Computer　　www.icccgovernors.org
PO Box 9745　Washington DC 20016
Ph: 703-836-7787

Communication, International Training in　　www.itcintl.com
2519 Woodland Dr　Anaheim CA 92801
Ph: 714-995-3660 ▪ Fx: 714-995-6974

Communication, Society for Technical　　www.stc.org
901 N Stuart St Suite 904　Arlington VA 22203
Ph: 703-522-4114 ▪ Fx: 703-522-2075

Communication Technology for Deaf-Blind People Inc,　www.deafblindadvocates.org
Advocates for　911 Regina Dr　Baltimore MD 21227
Ph: 410-247-5045 ▪ Fx: 410-381-6838

(Communication) Toastmasters International　　www.toastmasters.org
PO Box 9052　Mission Viejo CA 92690
Ph: 949-858-8255 ▪ Fx: 949-858-1207

Communications, Accrediting Council on Education in　www.ukans.edu/~acejmc
Journalism & Mass　Univ of Kansas School of Journalism
Stauffer-Flint Hall　Lawrence KS 66045
Ph: 785-864-3973 ▪ Fx: 785-864-5225

Communications Alliance, Integrated Business　　www.ibacweb.org
139 E Oakland Ave　Doylestown PA 18901
Ph: 215-489-1722 ▪ Fx: 215-489-1799

Communications Association, Forestry Conservation　　www.fcca.info
444 N Capitol St NW　Washington DC 20001
Ph: 202-624-8474 ▪ Fx: 202-624-5407

Communications, Association of Graphic　　www.agcomm.org
330 7th Ave 9th Fl　New York NY 10001
Ph: 212-279-2100 ▪ Fx: 212-279-5381

Communications Association, Health Sciences　　www.hesca.org
39 Wedgewood Dr Suite A　Jewett City CT 06351
Ph: 860-376-5915 ▪ Fx: 860-376-6621

Communications Association, Interactive Multimedia & Collaborative　　www.imcca.org
PO Box 756　Syosset NY 11771
Ph: 516-818-8184 ▪ Fx: 516-922-2170

Communications Association International, Media　　www.mca-i.org
401 N Michigan Ave　Chicago IL 60611
Ph: 312-321-5171 ▪ Fx: 312-673-6716

Communications Association, International Prepaid　　www.i-pca.org
904 Massachusetts Ave NE　Washington DC 20002
Ph: 202-544-4448 ▪ Fx: 202-547-7417 ▪ TF: 800-958-7824

Communications Association International, Wireless　　www.wcai.com
1333 H St NW Suite 700W　Washington DC 20005
Ph: 202-452-7823 ▪ Fx: 202-452-0041

Communications Association, Portable Computer &　　www.pcca.org
PO Box 680　Hood River OR 97031
Ph: 541-490-5140

Communications Association, Satellite Broadcasting &　　www.sbca.com
225 Reinekers Ln Suite 600　Alexandria VA 22314
Ph: 703-549-6990 ▪ Fx: 703-549-7640 ▪ TF: 800-541-5981

Communications, Association for Women in　　www.womcom.org
780 Ritchie Hwy River Reach Ctr Suite 280-S　Severna Park
MD 21146
Ph: 410-544-7442 ▪ Fx: 410-544-4640

Communications Bar Association, Federal　　www.fcba.org
1020 19th St NW Suite 325　Washington DC 20036
Ph: 202-293-4000 ▪ Fx: 202-293-4317

(Communications) ComCARE Alliance　　www.comcare.org
888 17th St NW 12th Fl　Washington DC 20006
Ph: 202-429-0574 ▪ Fx: 202-296-2962

Communications Consortium, International Packet　　www.packetcomm.org
2400 Camino Ramon Suite 275　San Ramon CA 94583
Ph: 925-275-6635 ▪ Fx: 925-275-6691

Communications Consulting Engineers, Association of Federal　　www.afcce.org

Communications Council Inc, American Public　　www.apcc.net
10302 Eaton Pl Suite 340　Fairfax VA 22030
Ph: 703-385-5300 ▪ Fx: 703-385-5301 ▪ TF: 800-868-2722

Communications Council, Automotive　　www.acc-online.org
4600 East-West Hwy Suite 300　Bethesda MD 20814
Ph: 240-333-1089 ▪ Fx: 301-654-3299

Communications Council, Land Mobile　　www.lmcc.org
1110 N Glebe Rd Suite 500　Arlington VA 22201
Ph: 202-331-7773 ▪ Fx: 202-331-9062

Communications & Electronics Association, Armed Forces　　www.afcea.org
4400 Fair Lakes Ct　Fairfax VA 22033
Ph: 703-631-6100 ▪ Fx: 703-631-4693 ▪ TF: 800-336-4583

Communications, Foundation for American　　www.facsnet.org
85 S Grand Ave　Pasadena CA 91105
Ph: 626-584-0010 ▪ Fx: 626-584-0627

Communications Fraud Control Association　　www.cfca.org
3030 N Central Ave Suite 707　Phoenix AZ 85012
Ph: 602-265-2322 ▪ Fx: 602-265-1015

Communications Industries Association, International　　www.infocomm.org
11242 Waples Mill Rd Suite 200　Fairfax VA 22030
Ph: 703-273-7200 ▪ Fx: 703-278-8082 ▪ TF: 800-659-7469

Communications Industry Association, Computer &　　www.ccianet.org
666 11th St NW Suite 600　Washington DC 20001
Ph: 202-783-0070 ▪ Fx: 202-783-0534

Communications, Institute for Global　　www.igc.org
PO Box 29904　San Francisco CA 94129
Ph: 415-561-6100 ▪ Fx: 415-561-6101

Communications International Inc, Population　　www.population.org
777 United Nations Plaza 5th Fl　New York NY 10017
Ph: 212-687-3366 ▪ Fx: 212-661-4188 ▪ TF: 877-724-7627

Communications International Union, Graphic　　www.gciu.org
1900 L St NW 9th Fl　Washington DC 20036
Ph: 202-462-1400 ▪ Fx: 202-721-0600

Communications International Union, Transportation　　www.tcunion.org
3 Research Pl　Rockville MD 20850
Ph: 301-948-4910 ▪ Fx: 301-948-1369

Communications Marketing Association　　www.commktga.com
PO Box 36275　Denver CO 02365
Ph: 303-988-3515 ▪ Fx: 303-988-3517

Communications Media Management Association　　www.cmma.net
PO Box 227　Wheaton IL 60189
Ph: 630-653-2772 ▪ Fx: 630-653-2882

Communications, National Association of Minorities in　　www.namic.com
600 Anton Blvd Suite 1100　Costa Mesa CA 92625
Ph: 714-371-4077 ▪ Fx: 714-371-2103

Communications, North American Center For Emergency　　www.nacec.org
PO Box 174　Aurora MN 55705
Ph: 218-229-2887

Communications Officials International Inc, Association of　www.apcointl.org
Public-Safety　351 N Williamson Blvd　Daytona Beach FL
32114
Ph: 386-322-2500 ▪ Fx: 386-322-2501 ▪ TF: 888-272-6911

(Communications) REACT International Inc　　www.reactintl.org
5210 Auth Rd Suite 403　Suitland MD 20746
Ph: 301-316-2900 ▪ Fx: 301-316-2903

Communications Resources, Professional Association for Investment　　www.paicr.org
1320 19th St NW Suite 300　Washington DC 20036
Ph: 202-371-9750 ▪ Fx: 202-371-8977 ▪ TF: 800-561-0751

Communications Society, IEEE　　www.comsoc.org
IEEE Operations Ctr 445 Hoes Ln　Piscataway NJ 08854
Ph: 732-981-0060 ▪ Fx: 732-981-1721

Communications Specialists, International Society of　　www.iscs.cc
201 Blue Sky Dr　Marietta GA 30068
Ph: 770-973-0662 ▪ Fx: 770-973-1410

Communications Supply Service Association　　www.cssa.net
5700 Murray St　Little Rock AR 72209
Ph: 501-562-7666 ▪ Fx: 501-562-7616 ▪ TF: 800-252-2772

Communications & Technology, Association for Educational　　www.aect.org
1800 N Stonelake Dr Suite 2　Bloomington IN 47408
Ph: 812-335-7675 ▪ Fx: 812-335-7678 ▪ TF: 877-677-2328

Communications Technology Professionals in Higher Education,　www.acuta.org
ACUTA - Association for　152 W Zandale Dr Suite
200　Lexington KY 40503
Ph: 859-278-3338 ▪ Fx: 859-278-3268

Communications Workers of America　　www.cwa-union.org
501 3rd St NW　Washington DC 20001
Ph: 202-434-1100 ▪ Fx: 202-434-1436

Communications Workers of America, National Association of　www.nabetcwa.org
Broadcast Employees & Technicians-　501 3rd St NW Suite
880　Washington DC 20001
Ph: 202-434-1254 ▪ Fx: 202-434-1426

Communications Workers of America Printing Publishing & Media
Workers Sector　501 3rd St NW Suite 950　Washington DC
20001
Ph: 202-434-1238 ▪ Fx: 202-434-1245

Communicators Association, Baptist　www.baptistcommunicators.org
1715-K S Rutherford Blvd Suite 295　Murfreesboro TN 37130
Ph: 615-904-0152

Communicators Association, Turf & Ornamental　　www.toca.org
120 W Main St PO Box 156　New Prague MN 56071
Ph: 952-758-6340 ▪ Fx: 952-758-5813

Communicators Council, Religion　www.religioncommunicators.org
475 Riverside Dr Rm 1948A　New York NY 10115
Ph: 212-870-2985 ▪ Fx: 212-870-3578

Communicators, International Association of Audio Visual　　www.iaavc.org
57 W Palo Verde Ave PO Box 250　Ocotillo CA 92259
Ph: 760-358-7000 ▪ Fx: 760-358-7569

Communicators, International Association of Business　　www.iabc.com
1 Hallidie Plaza Suite 600　San Francisco CA 94102
Ph: 415-544-4700 ▪ Fx: 415-544-4747 ▪ TF: 800-766-4222

Communicators International, Utility　　www.uci-online.com
5525 E Grandview Dr　Scottsdale AZ 85254
Ph: 602-971-1989 ▪ Fx: 602-971-2738

Communicators, National Association of Government　　www.nagc.com
10366 Democracy Ln Suite B　Fairfax VA 22030
Ph: 703-691-0377 ▪ Fx: 703-706-9583

Communicators of Tomorrow, National Agricultural　　nact.okstate.edu

Communism, Historians of American　www.historians.org/affiliates/hisn_am_communism.htm

Communist Party USA　　www.cpusa.org
235 W 23rd St 7th Fl　New York NY 10011
Ph: 212-989-4994 ▪ Fx: 212-229-1713

Communitarian Network   www.gwu.edu/~ccps
2130 H St NW Suite 703   Washington DC 20052
Ph: 202-994-7997 ▪ Fx: 202-994-1606 ▪ TF: 800-245-7460

Communities in Action, Alliance for
PO Box 30154   Bethesda MD 20824
Ph: 301-229-7707 ▪ Fx: 301-229-0457

Communities, Institute for Sustainable   www.iscvt.org
535 Stone Cutters Way   Montpelier VT 05602
Ph: 802-229-2900 ▪ Fx: 802-229-2919

(Communities) National Training & Information Center   www.ntic-us.org
810 N Milwaukee Ave   Chicago IL 60622
Ph: 312-243-3035 ▪ Fx: 312-243-7044

Communities, Partners for Livable   www.livable.com
1429 21st St NW   Washington DC 20036
Ph: 202-887-5990 ▪ Fx: 202-466-4845

Communities in Schools Inc   www.cisnet.org
277 S Washington St Suite 210   Alexandria VA 22314
Ph: 703-519-8999 ▪ Fx: 703-519-7537 ▪ TF: 800-247-4543

(Communities) Up With People   www.upwithpeople.org
1675 Broadway Suite 1460   Denver CO 80202
Ph: 303-460-7100 ▪ Fx: 303-225-4649 ▪ TF: 877-264-8856

Community Action Foundation, National   www.ncaf.org
810 1st St NE Suite 530   Washington DC 20002
Ph: 202-842-2092 ▪ Fx: 202-842-2095

Community Action on Latin America   www.sit.wisc.edu/~omsuarez/cala.html
731 State St   Madison WI 53703
Ph: 608-251-3241 ▪ Fx: 608-251-3267

Community Action Partnership   www.communityactionpartnership.com
1100 17th St NW Suite 500   Washington DC 20036
Ph: 202-265-7546 ▪ Fx: 202-265-8850

Community Affairs, National Broadcast Association for
13502 Whittier Blvd Suite H Box 341   Whittier CA 90605
Ph: 562-698-6280 ▪ Fx: 562-698-9912

Community Anti-Drug Coalitions of America   www.cadca.org
901 N Pitt St Suite 300   Alexandria VA 22314
Ph: 703-706-0560 ▪ Fx: 703-706-0565 ▪ TF: 800-542-2322

Community Assistance, Foundation for International   www.villagebanking.org
1101 14th St NW 11th Fl   Washington DC 20005
Ph: 202-682-1510 ▪ Fx: 202-682-3510

Community Assistance Program, Rural   www.rcap.org
1522 K St NW Suite 400   Washington DC 20005
Ph: 202-408-1273 ▪ Fx: 202-408-8165 ▪ TF: 888-321-7227

Community Associations Institute   www.caionline.org
225 Reinekers Ln Suite 300   Alexandria VA 22314
Ph: 703-548-8600 ▪ Fx: 703-684-1581

Community Bankers of America, Independent   www.icba.org
1 Thomas Cir NW Suite 400   Washington DC 20005
Ph: 202-659-8111 ▪ Fx: 202-659-9216 ▪ TF: 800-422-8439

Community Bankers, America's   www.acbankers.org
900 19th St NW Suite 400   Washington DC 20006
Ph: 202-857-3100 ▪ Fx: 202-296-8716

Community Banking Advisory Network   www.bankingcpas.com
1 Valmont Plaza 4th Fl   Omaha NE 68154
Ph: 402-964-3865 ▪ Fx: 402-964-3811 ▪ TF: 888-475-4476

Community-Based Long-Term Care, National Institute on   www.ncoa.org
c/o National Council on the Aging 300 D St SW Suite 801   Washington DC 20024
Ph: 202-479-1200 ▪ Fx: 202-479-0735

Community Behavioral Healthcare, National Council for   www.nccbh.org
12300 Twinbrook Pkwy Suite 320   Rockville MD 20852
Ph: 301-984-6200 ▪ Fx: 301-881-7159

Community Board, Native American   www.nativeshop.org
PO Box 572   Lake Andes SD 57356
Ph: 605-487-7072 ▪ Fx: 605-487-7964

Community Broadcasters, National Federation of   www.nfcb.org
970 Broadway Suite 1000   Oakland CA 94612
Ph: 510-451-8200 ▪ Fx: 510-451-8208

Community Cancer Centers, Association of   www.accc-cancer.org
11600 Nebel St Suite 201   Rockville MD 20852
Ph: 301-984-9496 ▪ Fx: 301-770-1949

Community Capital Association, National   www.communitycapital.org
620 Chestnut St Suite 572   Philadelphia PA 19106
Ph: 215-923-4754 ▪ Fx: 215-923-4755

Community of Caring   www.communityofcaring.org
1325 G St NW   Washington DC 20005
Ph: 202-393-1251 ▪ Fx: 202-715-1146

Community Centers Association of North America, Jewish   www.jcca.org
15 E 26th St 10th Fl   New York NY 10010
Ph: 212-532-4949 ▪ Fx: 212-481-4174

Community Change, Center for   www.communitychange.org
1000 Wisconsin Ave NW   Washington DC 20007
Ph: 202-342-0519 ▪ Fx: 202-333-5462

Community of Christ   www.cofchrist.org
1001 W Walnut St   Independence MO 64050
Ph: 816-833-1000 ▪ Fx: 816-521-3085 ▪ TF: 800-825-2806

Community Churches, International Council of   iccc-world.org
21116 Washington Pkwy   Frankfort IL 60423
Ph: 815-464-5690 ▪ Fx: 815-464-5692

Community Churches, Universal Fellowship of Metropolitan   www.mccchurch.org
8704 Santa Monica Blvd 2nd Fl   West Hollywood CA 90069
Ph: 310-360-8640 ▪ Fx: 310-360-8680

Community College Business Officers   www.ccbo.org
PO Box 5565   Charlottesville VA 22905
Ph: 434-293-2825 ▪ Fx: 434-245-8453

Community College Humanities Association   www.ccha-assoc.org
Essex County College 303 University Ave   Newark NJ 07102
Ph: 973-877-3577 ▪ Fx: 973-877-3578

Community College, League for Innovation in the   www.league.org
4505 E Chandler Blvd Suite 250   Phoenix AZ 85048
Ph: 480-705-8200 ▪ Fx: 480-705-8201

Community College Trustees, Association of   www.acct.org
1233 20th St NW Suite 605   Washington DC 20036
Ph: 202-775-4667 ▪ Fx: 202-223-1297

Community Colleges, American Association of   www.aacc.nche.edu
1 Dupont Cir NW Suite 410   Washington DC 20036
Ph: 202-728-0200 ▪ Fx: 202-833-2467

Community Colleges, American Association for Women in   www.pc.maricopa.edu/aawcc
1202 W Thomas Rd   Phoenix AZ 85013
Ph: 602-285-7449 ▪ Fx: 602-285-7832

Community Colleges, American Student Association of   www.asacc.org
2250 N University Pkwy Suite 4865   Provo UT 84604
Ph: 801-863-8020 ▪ Fx: 801-764-7229

Community Colleges for International Development   www.ccid.kirkwood.cc.ia.us
6301 Kirkwood Blvd SW   Cedar Rapids IA 52406
Ph: 319-398-5653 ▪ Fx: 319-398-1255

Community Colleges, Journalism Association of   www.jacconline.org

Community Colleges, National Council of State Directors of   www.statedirectors.org
1 Dupont Cir NW Suite 410   Washington DC 20036
Ph: 202-728-0200 ▪ Fx: 202-833-2467

Community Colleges, Society for Anthropology in   ccanthro.bizland.com
c/o American Anthropological Assn 2200 Wilson Blvd Suite 600   Arlington VA 22201
Ph: 703-528-1902 ▪ Fx: 703-528-3545

Community Corrections Association, International   www.iccaweb.org
PO Box 1987   La Crosse WI 54602
Ph: 608-785-0200 ▪ Fx: 608-784-5335

Community for Creative Non-Violence   users.erols.com/ccnv
425 2nd St NW   Washington DC 20001
Ph: 202-393-1909 ▪ Fx: 202-783-3254

Community Development Agencies, Council of State   www.coscda.org
1825 K St NW Suite 515   Washington DC 20006
Ph: 202-293-5820 ▪ Fx: 202-293-2820

Community Development Association, Christian   www.ccda.org
3817 W Ogden Ave   Chicago IL 60623
Ph: 773-762-0994 ▪ Fx: 773-762-5772

Community Development Association, National   www.ncdaonline.org
522 21st St NW Suite 120   Washington DC 20006
Ph: 202-293-7587 ▪ Fx: 202-887-5546

Community Development Council Inc, Ethiopian   www.ecdcinternational.org
1038 S Highland St   Arlington VA 22204
Ph: 703-685-0510 ▪ Fx: 703-685-0529

Community Development Credit Unions, National Federation of   www.natfed.org
120 Wall St 10th Fl   New York NY 10005
Ph: 212-809-1850 ▪ Fx: 212-809-3274 ▪ TF: 800-437-8711

(Community Development) Enterprise Foundation   www.enterprisefoundation.org
10227 Wincopin Cir Suite 500   Columbia MD 21044
Ph: 410-964-1230 ▪ Fx: 410-964-1918 ▪ TF: 800-624-4298

(Community Development) Los Ninos   www.losninosinternational.org
287 G St   Chula Vista CA 91910
Ph: 619-426-9110 ▪ Fx: 619-426-6664 ▪ TF: 866-567-6466

Community Development, National Coalition for Asian Pacific American   www.nationalcapacd.org
1001 Connecticut Ave NW Suite 730   Washington DC 20036
Ph: 202-223-2442 ▪ Fx: 202-223-4144

Community Development Society   comm-dev.org
17 S High St Suite 200   Columbus OH 43215
Ph: 614-221-1900 ▪ Fx: 614-221-1989

Community Development Venture Capital Alliance   www.cdvca.org
330 7th Ave 19th Fl   New York NY 10001
Ph: 212-594-6747 ▪ Fx: 212-594-6717

Community & Economic Development, National Association for County   www.nacced.org
2025 M St NW Suite 800   Washington DC 20036
Ph: 202-367-1149 ▪ Fx: 202-367-2149

Community Economic Development, National Congress for   www.ncced.org
1030 15th St NW Suite 325   Washington DC 20005
Ph: 202-289-9020 ▪ Fx: 202-289-7051 ▪ TF: 877-446-2233

Community Economics Inc, Institute for   www.iceclt.org
57 School St   Springfield MA 01105
Ph: 413-746-8660 ▪ Fx: 413-746-8862

Community Education Association, National   www.ncea.com
3929 Old Lee Hwy Suite 91-A   Fairfax VA 22030
Ph: 703-359-8973 ▪ Fx: 703-359-0972

Community Education, National Association for Family &   www.nafce.org
73 Cavalier Blvd Suite 106   Florence KY 41042
Ph: 877-712-4477 ▪ Fx: 859-525-6496

Community Education, National Center for   www.nccenet.org
1017 Avon St   Flint MI 48503
Ph: 810-238-0463 ▪ Fx: 810-238-9211 ▪ TF: 800-811-1105

Community Environmental Council   www.communityenvironmentalcouncil.org
930 Miramonte Dr   Santa Barbara CA 93109
Ph: 805-963-0583 ▪ Fx: 805-962-9080

Community Financial Services Association of America   www.cfsa.net
515 King St Suite 300   Alexandria VA 22314
Ph: 703-684-1029 ▪ Fx: 703-684-7912

Community Health Accreditation Program Inc   www.chapinc.org
39 Broadway Suite 710   New York NY 10006
Ph: 212-480-8828 ▪ Fx: 212-480-8833 ▪ TF: 800-656-9656

Community Health Centers, National Association of   www.nachc.com
7200 Wisconsin Ave Suite 210   Bethesda MD 20814
Ph: 301-347-0400 ▪ Fx: 301-347-0459

Community Health Charities   www.healthcharities.org
200 N Glebe Rd Suite 801   Arlington VA 22203
Ph: 703-528-1007 ▪ Fx: 703-528-1365 ▪ TF: 800-654-0845

Community Health Nursing Educators, Association of   www.uncc.edu/achne
11 Cornell Rd   Latham NY 12110
Ph: 518-782-9400 ▪ Fx: 518-782-9530

Community Health Organizations, Association of Asian/Pacific   www.aapcho.org
429 23rd St   Oakland CA 94612
Ph: 510-272-9536 ▪ Fx: 510-272-0817

(Community Improvement) National People's Action
810 N Milwaukee Ave   Chicago IL 60622
Ph: 312-243-3038 ▪ Fx: 312-243-7044
www.npa-us.org

Community & Justice, National Conference for
475 Park Ave S 19th Fl   New York NY 10016
Ph: 212-545-1300 ▪ Fx: 212-545-8053
www.nccj.org

Community Leaders of America, Family Career &
1910 Association Dr   Reston VA 20191
Ph: 703-476-4900 ▪ Fx: 703-860-2713 ▪ TF: 800-234-4425
www.fcclainc.org

Community Leadership Association
200 S Meridian St Suite 250   Indianapolis IN 46225
Ph: 317-637-7408 ▪ Fx: 317-637-7413
www.communityleadership.org

Community Learning & Information Network
1750 K St NW Suite 1200   Washington DC 20006
Ph: 202-857-2330 ▪ Fx: 202-857-0643
www.clin.org

Community Media, Alliance for
666 11th St NW Suite 740   Washington DC 20001
Ph: 202-393-2650 ▪ Fx: 202-393-2653
www.alliancecm.org

Community Mediation, National Association for
1527 New Hampshire Ave NW 4th Fl   Washington DC 20036
Ph: 202-667-9700 ▪ Fx: 202-667-8629
www.nafcm.org

Community Options & Resources, American Network of
1101 King St Suite 380   Alexandria VA 22314
Ph: 703-535-7850 ▪ Fx: 703-535-7860
www.ancor.org

Community Organization, Interreligious Foundation for
402 W 145th St   New York NY 10031
Ph: 212-926-5757 ▪ Fx: 212-926-5842
www.ifconews.org

Community Organization & Social Administration, Association for
20560 Bensley Ave   Lynwood IL 60411
Ph: 708-757-4187 ▪ Fx: 708-757-4234
www.acosa.org

Community Organizations for Reform Now, Association of
739 8th St SE   Washington DC 20003
Ph: 202-547-2500 ▪ Fx: 202-547-2483 ▪ TF: 877-552-2676
www.acorn.org

Community Papers, Association of Free
1634 Miner St PO Box 1989   Idaho Springs CO 80452
Ph: 877-203-2327
www.afcp.org

Community Pharmacists Association, National
205 Daingerfield Rd   Alexandria VA 22314
Ph: 703-683-8200 ▪ Fx: 703-683-3619 ▪ TF: 800-544-7447
www.ncpanet.org

Community Reinvestment Coalition, National
733 15th St NW Suite 540   Washington DC 20005
Ph: 202-628-8866 ▪ Fx: 202-628-9800
www.ncrc.org

Community for Religious Research & Education
St Francis Univ Dept of Religious Studies   Loretto PA 15940
Ph: 814-472-3396 ▪ Fx: 814-472-2776

Community Research, Center for Labor &
3411 W Diversey Ave Suite 10   Chicago IL 60647
Ph: 773-278-5418 ▪ Fx: 773-278-5918
www.clcr.org

Community Schools, National Coalition of Alternative
1289 Jewett   Ann Arbor MI 48104
Ph: 734-668-9171 ▪ TF: 888-771-9171
www.ncacs.org

Community Service Inc, Joint Action in
5225 Wisconsin Ave NW Suite 404   Washington DC 20015
Ph: 202-537-0996 ▪ Fx: 202-363-0239 ▪ TF: 800-522-7773
www.jacsinc.org

Community Service Inc, Women in
1900 N Beauregard St Suite 103   Alexandria VA 22311
Ph: 703-671-0500 ▪ Fx: 703-671-4489 ▪ TF: 800-442-9427
www.charityadvantage.com/wics

Community Services, Adventist
12501 Old Columbia Pike   Silver Spring MD 20904
Ph: 301-680-6438 ▪ Fx: 301-680-6125 ▪ TF: 877-227-2702
www.adventist.communityservices.org

Community Services Programs, National Association for State
400 N Capitol St NW   Washington DC 20001
Ph: 202-624-5866 ▪ Fx: 202-624-8472
www.nascsp.org

Community Solutions, Center for
4508 Mission Bay Dr   San Diego CA 92109
Ph: 858-272-5777 ▪ Fx: 858-272-5361 ▪ TF: 888-272-2767
www.ccssd.org

Community Supports & Employment Services, American Congress of
1875 'I' St NW 11th Fl   Washington DC 20006
Ph: 202-466-3355 ▪ Fx: 202-466-7571
www.accses.org

Community Theatre, American Association of
8402 BriarWood Cir   Lago Vista TX 78645
Ph: 512-267-0711 ▪ Fx: 512-267-0712 ▪ TF: 866-687-2228
www.aact.org

Community Transportation Association of America
1341 G St NW Suite 1000   Washington DC 20005
Ph: 202-628-1480 ▪ Fx: 202-737-9197 ▪ TF: 800-527-8279
www.ctaa.org

Community Tribal Schools, Association of
616 4th Ave W   Sisseton SD 57262
Ph: 605-698-3953 ▪ Fx: 605-698-7686

Community Values, Citizens for
11175 Reading Rd Suite 103   Cincinnati OH 45241
Ph: 513-733-5775 ▪ Fx: 513-733-5794
www.ccv.org

Commuter Programs, National Clearinghouse for
Univ of Maryland 1120 Stamp Student Union   College Park MD 20742
Ph: 301-314-5274 ▪ Fx: 301-314-9874
www.cacs.umd.edu/NCCP

Commuter Transportation, Association for
PO Box 15542   Washington DC 20003
Ph: 202-393-3497 ▪ Fx: 202-546-2196
www.actweb.org

Companies for Christ International, Fellowship of
12201 Pangborn Ave   Downey CA 90241
Ph: 562-803-3400 ▪ Fx: 562-803-3344
www.myfcci.org

Companies, Council of Growing
PO Box 10863   McLean VA 22102
Ph: 703-893-5343 ▪ Fx: 703-893-5222 ▪ TF: 800-929-3165

Companion Program, Senior
2900 Newton St NE   Washington DC 20018
Ph: 212-529-7700 ▪ Fx: 202-832-0127
www.seniorcorps.org/joining/scp

Company of Fifers & Drummers Inc
PO Box 277   Ivoryton CT 06442
Ph: 860-767-2237 ▪ Fx: 860-767-9765
companyoffifeanddrum.org

Comparative & International Education Society
www.cies.ws

Comparative Literature Association, American
Univ of Texas at Austin Program in Comparative Literature 1 University Stn B5003   Austin TX 78712
Ph: 512-471-8020
www.acla.org

Compassion in Dying Federation
6312 SW Capitol Hwy Suite 415   Portland OR 97239
Ph: 503-221-9556 ▪ Fx: 503-228-9160
www.compassionindying.org

Compassion International
PO Box 65000   Colorado Springs CO 80962
Ph: 719-487-7000 ▪ Fx: 719-481-5738 ▪ TF: 800-336-7539
www.compassion.com

Compassionate American Samaritans, Foundation of
PO Box 428760   Cincinnati OH 45242
Ph: 513-621-5300 ▪ Fx: 513-621-5307
www.focas-us.org

Compassionate Friends
PO Box 3696   Oak Brook IL 60522
Ph: 630-990-0010 ▪ Fx: 630-990-0246 ▪ TF: 877-969-0010
www.compassionatefriends.com

Compatible Technology International
Hamline Univ Box 109 1536 Hewitt Ave   Saint Paul MN 55104
Ph: 651-632-3912 ▪ Fx: 651-632-3913
www.compatibletechnology.org

Compensation, Employers Council on Flexible
927 15th St NW Suite 1000   Washington DC 20005
Ph: 202-659-4300 ▪ Fx: 202-371-1467
www.ecfc.org

Competency Assurance, National Organization for
2025 M St NW Suite 800   Washington DC 20036
Ph: 202-367-1165 ▪ Fx: 202-367-2165
www.noca.org

Competitive Intelligence Professionals, Society of
1700 Diagonal Rd Suite 600   Alexandria VA 22314
Ph: 703-739-0696 ▪ Fx: 703-739-2524
www.scip.org

Competitive Technology, Association for
1413 K St NW 12th Fl   Washington DC 20005
Ph: 202-331-2130 ▪ Fx: 202-331-2139
www.actonline.org

Competitiveness, Council on
1500 K St NW Suite 850   Washington DC 20005
Ph: 202-682-4292 ▪ Fx: 202-682-5150
www.compete.org

Compliance Professionals, Association of Insurance
12110 Sunset Hills Rd Suite 130   Reston VA 20190
Ph: 703-234-4074 ▪ Fx: 703-435-4390
www.aicp.net

Compliance Professionals Inc, National Society of
22 Kent Rd   Cornwall Bridge CT 06754
Ph: 860-672-0843 ▪ Fx: 860-672-3005
www.nscp.org

Components Packaging & Manufacturing Technology Society, IEEE
445 Hoes Ln PO Box 1331   Piscataway NJ 08855
Ph: 732-562-5529 ▪ Fx: 732-981-1769
www.cpmt.org

Composer, Meet the
75 9th Ave 3R Suite C   New York NY 10011
Ph: 212-645-6949 ▪ Fx: 212-645-9669
www.meetthecomposer.org

Composers Alliance, American
73 Spring St Rm 505   New York NY 10012
Ph: 212-362-8900 ▪ Fx: 212-925-6798
www.composers.com

Composers, American Society of Music Arrangers &
PO Box 17840   Encino CA 91416
Ph: 818-994-4661 ▪ Fx: 818-994-6181
www.asmac.org

Composers Authors & Publishers, American Society of
1 Lincoln Plaza   New York NY 10023
Ph: 212-621-6000 ▪ Fx: 212-724-9064 ▪ TF: 800-952-7227
www.ascap.com

Composers, Christian Fellowship of Art Music
Houghton College Greatbatch School of Music   Houghton NY 14744
Ph: 585-567-9424
www.cfamc.org

Composers Forum, American
332 Minnesota St Suite E145   Saint Paul MN 55101
Ph: 651-228-1407 ▪ Fx: 651-291-7978
www.composersforum.org

Composers' League, Southeastern
6812 Dina Leigh Ct   Springfield VA 22153
Ph: 540-463-8852
www.runet.edu/~scl-web/

Composers & Lyricists, Society of
400 S Beverly Dr Suite 214   Beverly Hills CA 90212
Ph: 310-281-2812 ▪ Fx: 310-284-4861
www.thescl.com

Composers USA, National Association of
PO Box 49256   Los Angeles CA 90049
Ph: 310-838-4465 ▪ Fx: 310-373-3244
www.music-usa.org/nacusa

Composite Can & Tube Institute
50 S Pickett St   Alexandria VA 22310
Ph: 703-823-7234 ▪ Fx: 703-823-7237
www.cctiwdc.org

Composite Panel Association
18922 Premiere Ct   Gaithersburg MD 20879
Ph: 301-670-0604 ▪ Fx: 301-840-1252
www.pbmdf.com

Composites Manufacturers Association, American
1010 Glebe Rd Suite 450   Arlington VA 22201
Ph: 703-525-0511 ▪ Fx: 703-525-0743
www.acmanet.org

Composition & Communication, Conference on College
1111 W Kenyon Rd   Urbana IL 61801
Ph: 217-328-3870 ▪ Fx: 217-278-3763 ▪ TF: 800-369-6283
www.ncte.org/groups/cccc

Composting Council
4250 Veterans Memorial Hwy Suite 275   Holbrook NY 11741
Ph: 631-737-4931 ▪ Fx: 631-737-4939
www.compostingcouncil.org

Compounding Pharmacists, International Academy of
PO Box 1365   Sugar Land TX 77487
Ph: 281-933-8400 ▪ Fx: 281-495-0602 ▪ TF: 800-927-4227
www.iacprx.org

Comprehensive Health Education Foundation
22419 Pacific Hwy S   Seattle WA 98198
Ph: 206-824-2907 ▪ Fx: 206-824-3072 ▪ TF: 800-323-2433
www.chef.org

Compressed Air & Gas Institute Inc
1300 Sumner Ave   Cleveland OH 44115
Ph: 216-241-7333 ▪ Fx: 216-241-0105
www.cagi.org

Compressed Gas Association
4221 Walney Rd 5th Fl   Chantilly VA 20151
Ph: 703-788-2700 ▪ Fx: 703-961-1831
www.cganet.com

Compressor Remanufacturers Association, International
PO Box 33092 Kansas City MO 64114
Ph: 816-333-7205 ▪ Fx: 816-822-8826

CompTel/ASCENT Alliance www.comptel.org
1900 M St NW Suite 800 Washington DC 20036
Ph: 202-296-6650 ▪ Fx: 202-296-7585

Comptrollers, American Society of Military www.asmconline.org
2034 Eisenhower Ave Suite 145 Alexandria VA 22314
Ph: 703-549-0360 ▪ Fx: 703-549-3181 ▪ TF: 800-462-5637

Comptrollers & Treasurers, National Association of State Auditors www.nasact.org
2401 Regency Rd Suite 302 Lexington KY 40503
Ph: 859-276-1147 ▪ Fx: 859-278-0507

Compulsive Eaters Anonymous - HOW www.ceahow.org
5500 E Atherton St Suite 227B Long Beach CA 90815
Ph: 562-342-9344 ▪ Fx: 562-342-9346

Compulsive Gambling of New Jersey Inc, Council on www.800gambler.org
3635 Quakerbridge Rd Suite 7 Hamilton NJ 08619
Ph: 609-588-5515 ▪ Fx: 609-588-5665 ▪ TF: 800-426-2537

Computational Electromagnetics Society, Applied aces.ee.olemiss.edu

Computational Linguistics, Association for www.aclweb.org
3 Landmark Ctr East Stroudsburg PA 18301
Ph: 570-476-8006 ▪ Fx: 570-476-0860

Computational Mechanics, US Association for www.usacm.org
Scientific Computation Research Ctr 7011 CIL Bldg Troy NY 12180
Ph: 518-276-3590 ▪ Fx: 518-276-4886

Computer Applications in Radiology, Society for www.scarnet.org
10105 Cottesmore Ct Great Falls VA 22066
Ph: 703-757-0054 ▪ Fx: 703-757-0454

Computer Assisted Language Instruction Consortium www.calico.org
601 University Dr 214 Centennial Hall San Marcos TX 78666
Ph: 512-245-2360 ▪ Fx: 512-245-8298

Computer-Assisted Legal Instruction, Center for www.cali.org
1313 5th Ave SE Minneapolis MN 55414
Ph: 612-625-3419 ▪ Fx: 612-944-1318

Computer Capacity Management, Institute for www.demandtech.com
1020 8th Ave S Suite 6 Naples FL 34102
Ph: 239-261-8945 ▪ Fx: 239-261-5456 ▪ TF: 800-531-6143

Computer Communication, International Council for www.icccgovernors.org
PO Box 9745 Washington DC 20016
Ph: 703-836-7787

Computer & Communications Association, Portable www.pcca.org
PO Box 680 Hood River OR 97031
Ph: 541-490-5140

Computer & Communications Industry Association www.ccianet.org
666 11th St NW Suite 600 Washington DC 20001
Ph: 202-783-0070 ▪ Fx: 202-783-0534

Computer Consultant Businesses, National Association of www.naccb.org
1800 Diagonal Rd Suite 520 Alexandria VA 22314
Ph: 703-838-2050 ▪ Fx: 703-838-3610

Computer Consultants Association, Independent www.icca.org
11131 S Towne Sq Suite F Saint Louis MO 63123
Ph: 314-892-1675 ▪ Fx: 314-487-1345 ▪ TF: 800-774-4222

Computer Dealers International, Association of Service & www.ascdi.com
131 NW 1st Ave Suite 206 Delray Beach FL 33444
Ph: 561-266-9016 ▪ Fx: 561-266-9017

Computer Engineering Department Heads Association, Electrical & www.ecedha.org
549 W Randolph St Suite 600 Chicago IL 60661
Ph: 312-559-3724 ▪ Fx: 312-559-3329

Computer Event Marketing Association www.cemaonline.com
10 River Rd Suite 203 Uxbridge MA 01569
Ph: 978-443-3330 ▪ Fx: 978-449-4715 ▪ TF: 866-702-2362

Computer Information Systems, International Association for www.iacis.org

Computer Integrated Textile Design Association www.citda.org/
405 Battleground Ave Suite 204 Greensboro NC 27401
Ph: 336-379-0603 ▪ Fx: 336-379-0851

Computer Law Association www.cla.org
3028 Javier Rd Suite 402 Fairfax VA 22031
Ph: 703-560-7747 ▪ Fx: 703-207-7028

Computer Library Center Inc, Online www.oclc.org
6565 Frantz Rd Dublin OH 43017
Ph: 614-764-6000 ▪ Fx: 614-764-6096 ▪ TF: 800-848-5878

Computer Measurement Group www.cmg.org
151 Fries Mill Rd Suite 104 Turnersville NJ 08012
Ph: 856-401-1700 ▪ Fx: 856-401-1708 ▪ TF: 800-436-7264

Computer Memory Card International Association, Personal www.pc-card.com
2635 N 1st St Suite 209 San Jose CA 95134
Ph: 408-433-2273 ▪ Fx: 408-433-9558

Computer Music Association, International www.computermusic.org

Computer Network, Museum www.mcn.edu
329 March Rd Suite 232 Box 11 Ottawa ON K2K2E1
Ph: 888-211-1477 ▪ Fx: 613-599-7027

(Computer Networks) Network Professional Association www.npanet.org
1405 Warner Ave Tustin CA 92780
Ph: 714-258-8381 ▪ Fx: 714-258-8391

Computer Privacy, Americans for www.computerprivacy.org
1275 Pennsylvania Ave NW 10th Fl Washington DC 20004
Ph: 202-393-5222 ▪ Fx: 202-467-0810

Computer Professionals for Social Responsibility www.cpsr.org
PO Box 717 Palo Alto CA 94302
Ph: 650-322-3778 ▪ Fx: 650-322-4748

Computer Science League, American www.acsl.org
PO Box 521 West Warwick RI 02893
Ph: 401-822-4312

Computer Scientists Association, American www.acsa2000.net
6 Commerce Dr Suite 2000 Cranford NJ 07016
Ph: 908-272-0016 ▪ Fx: 908-272-6297

Computer Security Institute www.gocsi.com
600 Harrison St San Francisco CA 94107
Ph: 415-947-6000 ▪ Fx: 415-905-2218

Computer Society, IEEE www.computer.org
IEEE Operations Ctr 445 Hoes Ln Piscataway NJ 08854
Ph: 732-981-0060 ▪ Fx: 732-981-1721

Computer Support Specialists, Association of www.acss.org

(Computer Systems) SCSI Trade Association www.scsita.org
Presidio of San Francisco PO Box 29920 San Francisco CA 94129
Ph: 415-561-6273 ▪ Fx: 415-561-6120

Computer Systems Security, International Association for www.iacss.com
6 Swarthmore Ln Dix Hills NY 11746
Ph: 631-499-1616 ▪ Fx: 631-462-9178

Computer Technology, Association of Rehabilitation Programs in www.arpct.org
503 S York St Denver CO 80209
Ph: 303-733-2111 ▪ Fx: 303-733-2225

Computer User Groups, Association of Personal www.apcug.org
3150 Payne Ave Suite 12 Cleveland OH 44114
Ph: 301-423-1618

Computers in Jewish Life, Institute for
7074 N Western Ave Chicago IL 60645
Ph: 773-262-9200 ▪ Fx: 773-262-9298

(Computers) Per Scholas www.perscholas.org
1231 Lafayette Ave Bronx NY 10474
Ph: 718-991-8400 ▪ Fx: 718-991-0362 ▪ TF: 800-877-4068

Computing, Association for Women in www.awc-hq.org
41 Sutter St Suite 1006 San Francisco CA 94104
Ph: 415-905-4663

Computing in Education, Association for the Advancement of www.aace.org
PO Box 3728 Norfolk VA 23514
Ph: 757-623-7588 ▪ Fx: 703-997-8760

Computing Machinery, Association for www.acm.org
1515 Broadway 17th Fl New York NY 10036
Ph: 212-944-1318 ▪ Fx: 800-342-6626

Computing Professionals, Institute for Certification of www.iccp.org
2350 E Devon Ave Suite 115 Des Plaines IL 60018
Ph: 847-299-4227 ▪ Fx: 847-299-4280 ▪ TF: 800-843-8227

Computing Research Association www.cra.org
1100 17th St NW Suite 507 Washington DC 20036
Ph: 202-234-2111 ▪ Fx: 202-667-1066

Computing Sciences Accrediting Board Inc www.abet.org/cac1.html
Accreditation Board for Engineering & Technology Inc 111 Market Pl Suite 1050 Baltimore MD 21202
Ph: 410-347-7700 ▪ Fx: 410-625-2238

(Computing Systems) USENIX Association www.usenix.org
2560 9th St Suite 215 Berkeley CA 94710
Ph: 510-528-8649 ▪ Fx: 510-548-5738

Computing Technology Industry Association www.comptia.org
1815 S Meyers Rd Suite 300 Oakbrook Terrace IL 60181
Ph: 630-268-1818 ▪ Fx: 630-268-1384

(Computing) Upsilon Pi Epsilon Association www.acm.org/upe
California State Univ Chico Dept of Computer Science Chico CA 95929
Ph: 530-898-6442 ▪ Fx: 530-898-5995

Concern America www.concernamerica.org
2015 N Broadway PO Box 1790 Santa Ana CA 92702
Ph: 714-953-8575 ▪ Fx: 714-953-1242 ▪ TF: 800-266-2376

Concern for Helping Animals in Israel www.chai-online.org
PO Box 3341 Alexandria VA 22302
Ph: 703-658-9650 ▪ Fx: 703-941-6132

Concern International, Project www.projectconcern.org
3550 Afton Rd San Diego CA 92123
Ph: 858-279-9690 ▪ Fx: 858-694-0294

Concern Worldwide US Inc www.concernusa.org
104 E 40th St Suite 903 New York NY 10016
Ph: 212-557-8000 ▪ Fx: 212-557-8004

Concerned Educators Against Forced Unionism www.nrtwc.org
8001 Braddock Rd Suite 500 Springfield VA 22160
Ph: 703-321-8519 ▪ Fx: 703-321-9319 ▪ TF: 800-326-3600

Concerned Scientists, Committee of www.libertynet.org/ccs
53-34 208th St Bayside NY 11364
Ph: 718-229-2813 ▪ Fx: 718-229-7540

Concerned United Birthparents www.cubirthparents.org
PO Box 230457 Encinitas CA 92023
Ph: 800-822-2777 ▪ Fx: 760-929-1879

Concerned Women for America www.cwfa.org
1015 15th St NW Suite 1100 Washington DC 20005
Ph: 202-488-7000 ▪ Fx: 202-488-0806

Concert Artists, Young www.yca.org/
250 W 57th St Suite 1222 New York NY 10019
Ph: 212-307-6655 ▪ Fx: 212-581-8894

Concert Bands, Association of www.acbands.org
6613 Cheryl Ann Dr Independence OH 44131
Ph: 216-524-1897 ▪ TF: 800-726-8720

Concessionaires, National Association of www.naconline.org
35 E Wacker Dr Suite 1816 Chicago IL 60601
Ph: 312-236-3858 ▪ Fx: 312-236-7809

Conciliation Courts, Association of Family & www.afccnet.org
6515 Grand Teton Plaza Suite 210 Madison WI 53719
Ph: 608-664-3750 ▪ Fx: 608-664-3751

Concord Coalition www.concordcoalition.org
1011 Arlington Blvd Suite 300 Arlington VA 22209
Ph: 703-894-6222 ▪ Fx: 703-894-6231 ▪ TF: 888-333-4248

Concord Grape Association www.concordgrape.org
5775 Peachtree-Dunwoody Rd Bldg G Suite 500 Atlanta GA 30342
Ph: 404-252-3663 ▪ Fx: 404-252-0774

Concordia Deaconess Conference
Concordia Univ 7400 Augusta St River Forest IL 60305
Ph: 708-209-3136 ▪ Fx: 708-209-3176

Concrete Anchor Manufacturers Association www.concreteanchors.org
1603 Boone's Lick Rd Saint Charles MO 63301
Ph: 636-925-2212 ▪ Fx: 636-946-3336

Concrete Association, National Precast www.precast.org
10333 N Meridian St Suite 272 Indianapolis IN 46290
Ph: 317-571-9500 ▪ Fx: 317-571-0041 ▪ TF: 800-366-7731

Concrete Association, National Ready Mixed www.nrmca.org
900 Spring St Silver Spring MD 20910
Ph: 301-587-1400 ▪ Fx: 301-585-4219

Concrete Association, Tilt-up www.tilt-up.org
113 1st St W PO Box 204 Mount Vernon IA 52314
Ph: 319-895-6911 ▪ Fx: 319-895-8830

Concrete Burial Vault Association, National ncbva.org
900 Fox Valley Dr Suite 204 Longwood FL 32779
Ph: 407-788-1996 ▪ Fx: 407-774-6751 ▪ TF: 800-538-1423

Concrete Form Association, Insulating www.forms.org
1730 Dewes St Suite 2 Glenview IL 60025
Ph: 847-657-9730 ▪ Fx: 847-657-9728 ▪ TF: 888-864-4232

Concrete Foundations Association of North America www.cfawalls.org
113 1st St W PO Box 204 Mount Vernon IA 52314
Ph: 319-895-6940 ▪ Fx: 319-895-8830 ▪ TF: 866-232-9255

Concrete Institute International, American www.aci-int.org
38800 Country Club Dr PO Box 9094 Farmington Hills MI
48331
Ph: 248-848-3700 ▪ Fx: 248-848-3701

Concrete Institute, Precast/Prestressed www.pci.org
209 W Jackson Blvd Suite 500 Chicago IL 60606
Ph: 312-786-0300 ▪ Fx: 312-786-0353

Concrete Masonry Association, National www.ncma.org
13750 Sunrise Valley Dr Herndon VA 20171
Ph: 703-713-1900 ▪ Fx: 703-713-1910

Concrete Pavement Association, American www.pavement.com
5420 Old Orchard Rd Suite A-100 Skokie IL 60077
Ph: 847-966-2272 ▪ Fx: 847-966-9970

Concrete Pavement Institute, Interlocking icpi.org
1444 'I' St NW Suite 700 Washington DC 20005
Ph: 202-712-9036 ▪ Fx: 202-408-0285 ▪ TF: 800-241-3652

Concrete Pipe Association, American www.concrete-pipe.org
222 W Las Colinas Blvd Suite 641 Irving TX 75039
Ph: 972-506-7216 ▪ Fx: 972-506-7682

Concrete Plant Manufacturers Bureau www.cpmb.org
900 Spring St Silver Spring MD 20910
Ph: 301-587-1400 ▪ Fx: 301-587-1605

Concrete Pressure Pipe Association, American www.acppa.org
11800 Sunrise Valley Dr Suite 309 Reston VA 20191
Ph: 703-391-9135 ▪ Fx: 703-391-9136

Concrete Producers Association, Ornamental www.ornamentalconcrete.org
502 Kay Ave SE Bemidji MN 56601
Ph: 218-751-1982 ▪ Fx: 218-751-2186

Concrete Products Association, Autoclaved Aerated www.aacpa.org
7638 Nashville St Ringgold GA 30736
Ph: 706-965-4587

Concrete Pumping Association, American www.concretepumpers.com
676 Enterprise Dr Lewis Center OH 43035
Ph: 614-431-5618 ▪ Fx: 614-431-6944

Concrete Reinforcing Steel Institute www.crsi.org
933 N Plum Grove Rd Schaumburg IL 60173
Ph: 847-517-1200 ▪ Fx: 847-517-1206

Concrete Repair Institute, International www.icri.org
3166 S River Rd Suite 132 Des Plaines IL 60018
Ph: 847-827-0830 ▪ Fx: 847-827-0832

Concrete Research Council, Reinforced
Texas A&M Univ Dept of Civil Engineering MS 3136 College
Station TX 77843
Ph: 979-845-1940 ▪ Fx: 979-845-6554

Concrete Sawing & Drilling Association www.csda.org
10901 D Roosevelt Blvd N Suite 100A Saint Petersburg FL
33716
Ph: 727-577-5004 ▪ Fx: 727-577-5012

Conditioning Association, National Strength & www.nsca-lift.org
PO Box 9908 Colorado Springs CO 80932
Ph: 719-632-6722 ▪ Fx: 719-632-6367 ▪ TF: 800-815-6826

Conductors Guild www.conductorsguild.org
5300 Glenside Dr Suite 2207 Richmond VA 23228
Ph: 804-553-1378 ▪ Fx: 804-553-1876

Confectioners Association of the US, National www.candyusa.org
8320 Old Courthouse Rd Suite 300 Vienna VA 22182
Ph: 703-790-5750 ▪ Fx: 703-790-5752 ▪ TF: 800-433-1200

Confectioners International, Retail www.retailconfectioners.org
1807 Glenview Rd Suite 204 Glenview IL 60025
Ph: 847-724-6120 ▪ Fx: 847-724-2719 ▪ TF: 800-545-5381

Confectionery Sales Association, National www.candyhalloffame.com
10225 Berea Rd Suite B Cleveland OH 44102
Ph: 216-631-8200 ▪ Fx: 216-631-8210

Confectionery Tobacco Workers & Grain Millers International www.bctgm.org
Union, Bakery 10401 Connecticut Ave Kensington MD 20895
Ph: 301-933-8600 ▪ Fx: 301-946-8452

Confederacy, Children of the hqudc.org/CofC
c/o United Daughters of the Confederacy 328 North
Blvd Richmond VA 23220
Ph: 804-355-1636 ▪ Fx: 804-353-1396

Confederacy, United Daughters of the www.hqudc.org
328 North Blvd Richmond VA 23220
Ph: 804-355-1636 ▪ Fx: 804-353-1396

Confederate Memorial Association www.confederate.org
PO Box 6010 Washington DC 20005
Ph: 202-483-5700

Confederate Memorial Literary Society www.moc.org
1201 E Clay St Richmond VA 23219
Ph: 804-649-1861 ▪ Fx: 804-644-7150

Confederate Veterans, Sons of www.scv.org
PO Box 59 Columbia TN 38402
Ph: 800-380-1896 ▪ Fx: 931-381-6712

Conference on Asian History www.historians.org/affiliates
Indiana Univ East Asian Studies Ctr Bloomington IN 47405
Ph: 812-855-3765 ▪ Fx: 812-855-7762

Conference Board Inc www.conference-board.org
845 3rd Ave New York NY 10022
Ph: 212-759-0900 ▪ Fx: 212-980-7014

Conference Board of the Mathematical Sciences www.cbmsweb.org
1529 18th St NW Washington DC 20036
Ph: 202-293-1170 ▪ Fx: 202-293-3412

Conference of Business Economists
28790 Chagrin Blvd Suite 350 Cleveland OH 44122
Ph: 216-464-2137 ▪ Fx: 216-464-0397

Conference for Catholic Lesbians Inc www.catholicwomenl2l.org

Conference Center Administrators, International Association of www.iacca.org
1685 S Colorado Blvd Unit S Denver CO 80222
Ph: 303-757-3303 ▪ Fx: 303-753-1455

Conference Centers, International Association of www.iacconline.org
243 N Lindbergh Blvd Saint Louis MO 63141
Ph: 314-993-8575 ▪ Fx: 314-993-8919

Conference of Chief Justices ccj.ncsc.dni.us
300 Newport Ave Williamsburg VA 23185
Ph: 757-259-1841 ▪ Fx: 757-259-1520

Conference on College Composition & Communication www.ncte.org/groups/cccc
1111 W Kenyon Rd Urbana IL 61801
Ph: 217-328-3870 ▪ Fx: 217-278-3763 ▪ TF: 800-369-6283

Conference of Consulting Actuaries www.ccactuaries.org
1110 W Lake Cook Rd Suite 235 Buffalo Grove IL 60089
Ph: 847-419-9090 ▪ Fx: 847-419-9091

Conference on Consumer Finance Law www.theccfl.com
Oklahoma City Univ School of Law 2501 N Blackwelder
Ave Oklahoma City OK 73106
Ph: 405-521-5363 ▪ Fx: 405-521-5089

Conference of Educational Administrators of Schools & Programs www.ceasd.org
for the Deaf PO Box 1778 Saint Augustine FL 32085
Ph: 904-810-5200 ▪ Fx: 904-810-5525

Conference & Events Directors-International, Association acced-i.colostate.edu
of Collegiate Colorado State Univ 8037 Campus
Delivery Fort Collins CO 80523
Ph: 970-491-5151 ▪ Fx: 970-491-0667 ▪ TF: 877-502-2233

Conference on Faith & History www.huntington.edu/cfh
Gordon College Dept of History Wrenham MA 01984
Ph: 978-867-4415

Conference of Historical Journals
Univ of Arkansas Dept of History Old Main 416 Fayetteville AR
72701
Ph: 501-575-5884

Conference on Jewish Material Claims Against Germany www.claimscon.org
15 E 26th St Rm 906 New York NY 10010
Ph: 646-536-9100 ▪ Fx: 212-679-2126

Conference of Major Superiors of Men www.cmsm.org
8808 Cameron St Silver Spring MD 20910
Ph: 301-588-4030 ▪ Fx: 301-587-4575

Conference Management Association Inc, Religious www.rcmaweb.org
1 RCA Dome Suite 120 Indianapolis IN 46225
Ph: 317-632-1888 ▪ Fx: 317-632-7909

Conference of Minority Public Administrators www.natcompa.org
1120 G St NW Suite 700 Washington DC 20005
Ph: 202-393-7878 ▪ Fx: 202-638-4952

Conference of Minority Transportation Officials www.comto.org
1725 DeSales St NW Suite 808 Washington DC 20036
Ph: 202-289-0567 ▪ Fx: 202-289-1214

Conference of Philosophical Societies
D'Youville College Div of Liberal Arts Buffalo NY 14201
Ph: 716-881-7786

Conference of Presidents of Major American www.conferenceofpresidents.org
Jewish Organizations 633 3rd Ave 21st Fl New York NY
10017
Ph: 212-318-6111 ▪ Fx: 212-644-4135

Conference of Prince Hall Grand Masters
PO Box 1588 Muskogee OK 74402
Ph: 918-683-3123 ▪ Fx: 918-687-4845

Conference of Radiation Control Program Directors www.crcpd.org
205 Capitol Ave Frankfort KY 40601
Ph: 502-227-4543 ▪ Fx: 502-227-7862

Conference on Safe Transportation of Hazardous Articles www.costha.com
7803 Hill House Ct Fairfax Station VA 22039
Ph: 703-451-4031 ▪ Fx: 703-451-4207

Conference of State Bank Supervisors www.csbs.org
1015 18th St NW 11th Fl Washington DC 20036
Ph: 202-296-2840 ▪ Fx: 202-296-1928 ▪ TF: 800-886-2727

Conference of State Court Administrators cosca.ncsc.dni.us
National Ctr for State Courts 300 Newport Ave PO Box
8798 Williamsburg VA 23187
Ph: 757-259-1841 ▪ Fx: 757-259-1520 ▪ TF: 800-877-1233

Confessing Synod Ministries www.confessingsynod.org
East Liberty Lutheran Church 5707 Penn Ave Pittsburgh PA
15206
Ph: 412-362-1712

Conflict Inc, Creative Response to www.ccrcglobal.org
521 N Broadway Box 271 Nyack NY 10960
Ph: 845-353-1796 ▪ Fx: 845-358-4924

Conflict Resolution, Association for www.acrnet.org
1015 18th St NW Suite 1150 Washington DC 20036
Ph: 202-464-9700 ▪ Fx: 202-464-9720

Conflict Resolution Center International www.conflictres.org
204 37th St   Pittsburgh PA 15201
Ph: 412-687-6210 ▪ Fx: 412-687-6232

Conflict Resolution, Institute for International Mediation & www.iimcr.org
1424 K St NW Suite 650   Washington DC 20005
Ph: 202-347-2042 ▪ Fx: 202-347-2440

Conflict Resolution, Institute for Mediation & www.mediate.com/imcr
384 E 149th St Suite 330   Bronx NY 10455
Ph: 718-585-1190 ▪ Fx: 718-585-1962

Conflict Resolution, National Conference on Peacemaking & www.apeacemaker.net
3070 Bristol Pike Bldg 1 Suite 116   Bensalem PA 19020
Ph: 215-245-6993 ▪ Fx: 215-245-6994 ▪ TF: 877-397-3223

Confraternity of Penitents www.penitents.org
520 Oliphant Ln   Middletown RI 02842
Ph: 401-849-5421

Confrerie de la Chaine des Rotisseurs www.chaineus.org
444 Park Ave S Suite 301   New York NY 10016
Ph: 212-683-3770 ▪ Fx: 212-683-3882

Confucianism, Center for Dao- www.wam.umd.edu/~tkang
1318 Randolph St NE   Washington DC 20017
Ph: 202-526-6818

Congenital Cardiac Disease, International Society for Adult www.isaccd.org
1500 Sunday Dr Suite 102   Raleigh NC 27607
Ph: 919-861-5578 ▪ Fx: 919-787-4916

(Congenital Central Hypoventilation Syndrome) CCHS www.cchsnetwork.org
Family Network

Congregation of the Blessed Sacrament www.blessedsacrament.com
5384 Wilson Mills Rd   Cleveland OH 44143
Ph: 440-449-2103 ▪ Fx: 440-449-3862

Congregation Shema Yisrael www.shema.com
28600 Lahser Rd PO Box 804   Southfield MI 48037
Ph: 248-593-5150

Congregation of Sisters of Saint Agnes www.csasisters.org/
330 County Rd K   Fond du Lac WI 54935
Ph: 920-923-2121 ▪ Fx: 920-823-3194

Congregational Association, American
14 Beacon St   Boston MA 02108
Ph: 617-523-0604 ▪ Fx: 617-523-0491

Congregational Christian Churches, National Association of www.naccc.org
8473 S Howell Ave   Oak Creek WI 53154
Ph: 414-764-1620 ▪ Fx: 414-764-0319 ▪ TF: 800-262-1620

Congregational Christian Historical Society www.cchsonline.org
14 Beacon St   Boston MA 02108
Ph: 617-523-0470 ▪ Fx: 617-523-0491

Congres du travail du Canada www.clc-ctc.ca
2841 Riverside Dr   Ottawa ON K1V8X7
Ph: 613-521-3400 ▪ Fx: 613-521-4655

Congress of Independent Unions
303 Ridge St   Alton IL 62002
Ph: 618-462-2447 ▪ Fx: 618-462-5579

Congress of Industrial Organizations, American Federation of Labor & www.aflcio.org
815 16th St NW   Washington DC 20006
Ph: 202-637-5000 ▪ Fx: 202-637-5058

Congress for Jewish Culture
25 E 21st St   New York NY 10010
Ph: 212-505-8040 ▪ Fx: 212-505-8044

Congress of National Black Churches
PO Box 65682   Washington DC 20035
Ph: 202-898-2422 ▪ Fx: 202-893-9300

Congress, National Committee for an Effective www.ncec.org
122 C St NW Suite 650   Washington DC 20001
Ph: 202-639-8300 ▪ Fx: 202-639-5038

Congress of Neurological Surgeons www.neurosurgeon.org
10 N Martingale Rd Suite 190   Schaumburg IL 60173
Ph: 847-240-2500 ▪ Fx: 847-240-0804 ▪ TF: 877-517-1267

Congress of Racial Equality www.core-online.org
817 Broadway 3rd Fl   New York NY 10003
Ph: 212-598-4000 ▪ Fx: 212-982-0184

Congress on Research in Dance www.cordance.org
SUNY College at Brockport Dept of Dance 350 New Campus
Dr   Brockport NY 14420
Ph: 716-395-2590 ▪ Fx: 716-395-5413

Congress of Russian-Americans www.russian-americans.org
2460 Sutter St   San Francisco CA 94115
Ph: 415-928-5841 ▪ Fx: 415-928-5831

Congress of Secular Jewish Organizations www.csjo.org
19657 Villa Dr N   Southfield MI 48076
Ph: 248-569-8127 ▪ Fx: 248-569-5222

Congress, US Association of Former Members of www.usafmc.org
233 Pennsylvania Ave SE Suite 200   Washington DC 20003
Ph: 202-543-8676 ▪ Fx: 202-543-7145

Congress Watch www.citizen.org/congress
215 Pennsylvania Ave SE 3rd Fl   Washington DC 20003
Ph: 202-546-4996 ▪ Fx: 202-547-7392 ▪ TF: 800-289-3787

Congressional Black Caucus Foundation Inc www.cbcfinc.org
1720 Massachusetts Ave NW   Washington DC 20036
Ph: 202-263-2800 ▪ Fx: 202-775-0773 ▪ TF: 800-784-2577

Congressional Club www.congressionalclub.org
2001 New Hampshire Ave NW   Washington DC 20009
Ph: 202-332-1155 ▪ Fx: 202-797-0698

Congressional Committee, National Republican nrcc.org
320 1st St SE   Washington DC 20003
Ph: 202-479-7000 ▪ Fx: 202-863-0693

Congressional Economic Leadership Institute www.celi.org
201 Massachusetts Ave NE Suite C-6   Washington DC 20002
Ph: 202-546-5007 ▪ Fx: 202-546-7037

Congressional Hispanic Caucus Institute www.chci.org
911 2nd St NE   Washington DC 20002
Ph: 202-543-1771 ▪ Fx: 202-546-2143 ▪ TF: 800-392-3532

Congressional Hunger Center www.hungercenter.org
229 1/2 Pennsylvania Ave SE   Washington DC 20003
Ph: 202-547-7022 ▪ Fx: 202-547-7575

Congressional Management Foundation www.cmfweb.org
513 Capitol Ct NE Suite 300   Washington DC 20002
Ph: 202-546-0100 ▪ Fx: 202-547-0936

Congressional Medal of Honor Society www.cmohs.org
40 Patriots Point Rd   Mount Pleasant SC 29464
Ph: 843-884-8862 ▪ Fx: 843-884-1471

Congressional Sportsmen's Foundation www.sportsmenslink.org
110 North Carolina Ave SE   Washington DC 20003
Ph: 202-543-6850 ▪ Fx: 202-543-6853

Congressional Studies, Asian Pacific American Institute for www.apaics.org
1001 Connecticut Ave NW Suite 835   Washington DC 20036
Ph: 202-286-9200 ▪ Fx: 202-296-9236

Conifer Society, American www.conifersociety.org
PO Box 3422   Crofton MD 21114
Ph: 410-721-6611 ▪ Fx: 410-721-9636

Connect For Kids www.connectforkids.org
1625 K St NW Suite 1100   Washington DC 20006
Ph: 202-638-5770 ▪ Fx: 202-638-5771 ▪ TF: 877-236-8666

Connected International Meeting Professionals Association www.cimpa.org
9200 Bayard Pl   Fairfax VA 22032
Ph: 703-978-6287 ▪ Fx: 703-978-5524

Connecting Businessmen to Christ www.cbmc.com
6650 E Brainerd Rd Suite 100   Chattanooga TN 37421
Ph: 423-698-4444 ▪ Fx: 423-629-4434 ▪ TF: 800-575-2262

Connector & Interconnection Technology, International Institute of www.iicit.org
PO Box 665   Hudson MA 01749
Ph: 978-568-0717 ▪ Fx: 978-568-0716 ▪ TF: 800-854-4248

Connemara Pony Society, American www.acps.org
2360 Hunting Ridge Rd   Winchester VA 22603
Ph: 540-662-5953 ▪ Fx: 540-722-2277

Conrad Joseph Society of America www.engl.unt.edu/~jgpeters/Conrad

Conrad N Hilton Foundation www.hiltonfoundation.org
100 W Liberty St Suite 840   Reno NV 89501
Ph: 775-323-4221 ▪ Fx: 775-323-4150

Conscience Foundation, Appeal of www.appealofconscience.org
119 W 57th St Suite 820   New York NY 10019
Ph: 212-535-5800 ▪ Fx: 212-628-2513

Conscience & War, Center on www.nisbco.org
1830 Connecticut Ave NW   Washington DC 20009
Ph: 202-483-2220 ▪ Fx: 202-483-1246 ▪ TF: 800-379-2679

Consciousness, Society for the Anthropology of www.sacaaa.org
c/o American Anthropological Assn 2200 Wilson Blvd Suite
600   Arlington VA 22201
Ph: 703-528-1902 ▪ Fx: 703-528-3546

Consecration, Apostolate for Family www.familyland.org
Catholic Familyland 3375 County Rd Suite 36   Bloomingdale
OH 43910
Ph: 740-765-5500 ▪ Fx: 740-765-5561 ▪ TF: 888-367-6279

Conservancy, Great Outdoors www.thegreatoutdoors.org
4311 Manatee Ave W Suite 210   Bradenton FL 34209
Ph: 941-708-3456 ▪ Fx: 941-708-3535

Conservation Alliance, Predator www.predatorconservation.org
PO Box 6733   Bozeman MT 59771
Ph: 406-587-3389 ▪ Fx: 406-587-3178

Conservation Association, American
30 Rockefeller Plaza 56th Fl   New York NY 10112
Ph: 212-649-5822 ▪ Fx: 212-649-5921

Conservation Association, Coastal www.joincca.org
6919 Portwest Dr Suite 100   Houston TX 77024
Ph: 713-626-4234 ▪ Fx: 713-626-5852 ▪ TF: 800-201-3474

Conservation Association, Purple Martin www.purplemartin.org
Edinboro Univ of Pennsylvania   Edinboro PA 16444
Ph: 814-734-4420 ▪ Fx: 814-734-5803

Conservation Association, Student www.thesca.org
PO Box 550   Charlestown NH 03603
Ph: 603-543-1700 ▪ Fx: 603-543-1828 ▪ TF: 888-722-9675

Conservation Association, Western Forestry & www.westernforestry.org
4033 SW Canyon Rd   Portland OR 97221
Ph: 503-226-4562 ▪ Fx: 503-226-2515

Conservation Biology, Society for www.conservationbiology.org
4245 N Fairfax Dr Suite 400   Arlington VA 22203
Ph: 703-276-2384 ▪ Fx: 703-995-4633

(Conservation) Boone & Crockett Club www.boone-crockett.org
250 Station Dr   Missoula MT 59801
Ph: 406-542-1888 ▪ Fx: 406-542-0784 ▪ TF: 888-840-4868

Conservation Breeding Specialist Group www.cbsg.org
12101 Johnny Cake Ridge Rd   Apple Valley MN 55124
Ph: 952-997-9800 ▪ Fx: 952-432-2757

Conservation Communications Association, Forestry www.fcca.info
444 N Capitol St NW   Washington DC 20001
Ph: 202-624-8474 ▪ Fx: 202-624-5407

Conservation Corps Alumni, National Association of Civilian www.cccalumni.org
16 Hancock Ave PO Box 16429   Saint Louis MO 63125
Ph: 314-487-8666 ▪ Fx: 314-487-9488

Conservation Corps, National Association of Service & www.nascc.org
666 11th St NW Suite 1000   Washington DC 20001
Ph: 202-737-6272 ▪ Fx: 202-737-6277 ▪ TF: 800-666-2722

Conservation Districts, National Association of www.nacdnet.org
509 Capitol Ct NE   Washington DC 20002
Ph: 202-547-6223 ▪ Fx: 202-547-6450

Conservation Engineers, Association of mdc.mo.gov/engineering/ace
WY State Parks & Historical Sites Div 122 W 25th St 1st Fl
E   Cheyenne WY 82002
Ph: 307-777-6325 ▪ Fx: 307-777-6472

Conservation Fund www.conservationfund.org
1800 N Kent St Suite 1120   Arlington VA 22209
Ph: 703-525-6300 ▪ Fx: 703-525-4610

Conservation of Historic & Artistic Works, American Institute for aic.stanford.edu
1717 K St NW Suite 200   Washington DC 20006
Ph: 202-452-9545 ▪ Fx: 202-452-9328

Conservation International www.conservation.org
1919 M St NW Suite 600   Washington DC 20036
Ph: 202-912-1000 ▪ Fx: 202-912-1030 ▪ TF: 800-529-5660

Conservation, International Institute for Energy www.iiec.org
10005 Leamoore Ln Suite 100   Vienna VA 22181
Ph: 703-281-7263 ▪ Fx: 703-968-6678

(Conservation) Izaak Walton League of America www.iwla.org
707 Conservation Ln   Gaithersburg MD 20878
Ph: 301-548-0150 ▪ Fx: 301-548-0146 ▪ TF: 800-453-5463

Conservation Leadership, Institute for www.icl.org
6930 Carroll Ave Suite 420   Takoma Park MD 20912
Ph: 301-270-2900 ▪ Fx: 301-270-0610

Conservation of Nature & Natural Resources, International Union for www.iucn.org
USA Multilateral Office 1630 Connecticut Ave NW 3rd
Fl   Washington DC 20009
Ph: 202-387-4826 ▪ Fx: 202-387-4823

(Conservation) Open Space Institute www.openspaceinstitute.org
1350 Broadway Suite 201   New York NY 10018
Ph: 212-629-3981 ▪ Fx: 212-244-3441

Conservation & Preservation Charities of America www.conservenow.org
21 Tamal Vista Blvd Suite 209   Corte Madera CA 94925
Ph: 800-626-6685

Conservation, Society Promoting Environmental www.spec.bc.ca
2150 Maple St   Vancouver BC V6J3T3
Ph: 604-736-7732 ▪ Fx: 604-736-7115

Conservation Society, Sea Shepherd www.seashepherd.org
PO Box 2616   Friday Harbor WA 98250
Ph: 360-370-5650 ▪ Fx: 360-370-5651

Conservation Society, Soil & Water www.swcs.org
945 SW Ankeny Rd   Ankeny IA 50021
Ph: 515-289-2216 ▪ Fx: 515-289-1227 ▪ TF: 800-843-7645

Conservation Society, Tongass www.ptialaska.net/~tongass
PO Box 23377   Ketchikan AK 99901
Ph: 907-225-5827

Conservation Treaty Support Fund www.conservationtreaty.org
3705 Cardiff Rd   Chevy Chase MD 20815
Ph: 301-654-3150 ▪ Fx: 301-652-6390

Conservation Union, Circumpolar www.circumpolar.org
1612 K St NW Suite 401   Washington DC 20006
Ph: 202-675-8870

Conservation Voters, League of www.lcv.org
1920 L St NW Suite 800   Washington DC 20036
Ph: 202-785-8683 ▪ Fx: 202-835-0491

Conservative Caucus www.conservativeusa.org
450 Maple Ave E Suite 306   Vienna VA 22180
Ph: 703-938-9626 ▪ Fx: 703-281-4108

Conservative Judaism in Israel, Masorti Foundation for www.masorti.org
475 Riverside Dr Suite 832   New York NY 10115
Ph: 212-870-2216 ▪ Fx: 212-870-2218 ▪ TF: 877-287-7414

Conservative Judaism, United Synagogue of www.uscj.org
155 5th Ave   New York NY 10010
Ph: 212-533-7800 ▪ Fx: 212-353-9439

Conservative Union, American www.conservative.org
1007 Cameron St   Alexandria VA 22314
Ph: 703-836-8602 ▪ Fx: 703-836-8606 ▪ TF: 800-228-7345

Conservatree www.conservatree.com
100 2nd Ave   San Francisco CA 94118
Ph: 415-721-4230 ▪ Fx: 415-883-6264

Consistent Life www.consistent-life.org
PO Box 792   Garner NC 27529
Ph: 919-779-8766 ▪ Fx: 919-779-1912

Consortium for Advanced Manufacturing - International www.cam-i.com
6737 Brentwood Stair Rd Suite 214   Fort Worth TX 76112
Ph: 817-496-4644 ▪ Fx: 817-496-4674

Consortium for the Advancement of Private Higher Education www.cic.edu/caphe
1 Dupont Cir NW Suite 320   Washington DC 20036
Ph: 202-466-7230 ▪ Fx: 202-466-7238

Consortium of Behavioral Health Nurses & Associates Inc www.cbhna.org
1733 H St Suite 330 PMB 1214   Blaine WA 98230
Ph: 800-876-2236 ▪ Fx: 360-332-2280

Consortium of College & University Media Centers www.ccumc.org
Iowa State Univ Instructional Technology Ctr 1200
Communications Bldg   Ames IA 50011
Ph: 515-294-1811 ▪ Fx: 515-294-8089

Consortium for Graduate Study in Management www.cgsm.org
200 S Hanley Rd Suite 1102   Saint Louis MO 63105
Ph: 314-877-5500 ▪ Fx: 314-877-5505 ▪ TF: 888-658-6814

Consortium of Humanities Centers & Institutes www.fas.harvard.edu/~chci
Harvard Univ Humanities Ctr 12 Quincy St   Cambridge MA
02138
Ph: 617-495-0738 ▪ Fx: 617-495-0730

Consortium Leadership, Association for www.acl.odu.edu
1417 43rd St   Norfolk VA 23529
Ph: 757-683-3183 ▪ Fx: 757-683-4515

Consortium for North American Higher Education Collaboration www.conahec.org
Univ of Arizona PO Box 210300   Tucson AZ 85721
Ph: 520-621-7761 ▪ Fx: 520-626-2675

Consortium of Physicians from Latin America www.cophyla.org
1850 E 17th St Suite 219   Santa Ana CA 92705
Ph: 714-836-1116 ▪ Fx: 714-245-1664

Consortium for School Networking www.cosn.org
1710 Rhode Island Ave NW Suite 900   Washington DC 20036
Ph: 202-861-2676 ▪ Fx: 202-861-0888 ▪ TF: 866-267-8747

Consortium of Social Science Associations www.cossa.org
1522 K St NW Suite 836   Washington DC 20005
Ph: 202-842-3525 ▪ Fx: 202-842-2788

Consortium for the Study of Intelligence www.intelligenceconsortium.org
1730 Rhode Island Ave NW Suite 500   Washington DC 20036
Ph: 202-429-0129 ▪ Fx: 202-659-5429

Constellation Foundation www.constellation.org
301 E Pratt St Pier 1   Baltimore MD 21202
Ph: 410-539-1797 ▪ Fx: 410-539-6238

Constitution & Parliament Association, World www.wcpa.biz

Constitution Society www.constitution.org
7793 Burnet Rd Unit 37   Austin TX 78757
Ph: 512-374-9585

Constitutional Rights Foundation www.crf-usa.org
601 S Kingsley Dr   Los Angeles CA 90005
Ph: 213-487-5590 ▪ Fx: 213-386-0459 ▪ TF: 800-488-4273

Construction & Agricultural Film Manufacturers Association www.cafma.org
104 S Michigan Ave Suite 1500   Chicago IL 60603
Ph: 312-201-0101 ▪ Fx: 312-201-0214

Construction Association, American Underground www.auaonline.org
3001 Hennepin Ave S Suite D202   Minneapolis MN 55408
Ph: 612-825-8933 ▪ Fx: 612-825-8944

Construction Association, Ceilings & Interior Systems cisca.org
1500 Lincoln Hwy Suite 202   Saint Charles IL 60174
Ph: 630-584-1919 ▪ Fx: 630-584-2003

Construction Association, Metal www.metalconstruction.org
4700 W Lake Ave   Glenview IL 60025
Ph: 847-375-4718 ▪ Fx: 877-665-2235

Construction & Design, Association for Bridge www.abcdpittsburgh.org
PO Box 23264   Pittsburgh PA 15222
Ph: 412-281-9900 ▪ Fx: 412-281-2056

Construction Distributors International, Associated www.acdi.net
1605 SE Delaware Ave Suite B   Ankeny IA 50021
Ph: 515-964-1335 ▪ Fx: 515-964-7668

Construction Education, American Council for acce-hq.org
1300 Hudson Ln Suite 3   Monroe LA 71201
Ph: 318-323-2816 ▪ Fx: 318-323-2413

Construction Education & Research, National Center for www.nccer.org
3600 NW 43rd St Bldg G PO Box 141104   Gainesville FL
32606
Ph: 352-334-0911 ▪ Fx: 352-334-0932

Construction Employers Council, Residential www.aboutrcec.org
2000 Spring Rd Suite 502   Oak Brook IL 60523
Ph: 630-990-3536 ▪ Fx: 630-990-3537

Construction Estimators Association of America, Professional www.pcea.org
PO Box 680336   Charlotte NC 28216
Ph: 704-987-9978 ▪ Fx: 704-987-9979 ▪ TF: 877-521-7232

Construction Financial Management Association www.cfma.org
29 Emmons Dr Suite F-50   Princeton NJ 08540
Ph: 609-452-8000 ▪ Fx: 609-452-0474

Construction Industry CPAs/Consultants Association www.cicpac.com
111 E Wacker Dr Suite 990   Chicago IL 60601
Ph: 800-869-0491 ▪ Fx: 312-729-9800

Construction Industry Employers Association www.conexbuff.com
625 Ensminger Rd   Tonawanda NY 14150
Ph: 716-875-3435 ▪ Fx: 716-875-4412

Construction Innovation Forum www.cif.org
43636 Woodward Ave Suite 300   Bloomfield Hills MI 48302
Ph: 248-409-1500 ▪ Fx: 248-409-1503

Construction Inspectors, Association of www.iami.org/aci
1224 N Nokomis NE   Alexandria MN 56308
Ph: 320-763-6350 ▪ Fx: 320-763-9290

Construction, International Association for Cold Storage www.iacsc.org
1500 King St Suite 201   Alexandria VA 22314
Ph: 703-373-4300 ▪ Fx: 703-373-4301

Construction & Maintenance Association, National Railroad www.nrcma.org
122 C St NW Suite 850   Washington DC 20001
Ph: 202-638-7790 ▪ Fx: 202-638-1045 ▪ TF: 800-883-1557

Construction Management Association of America cmaanet.org
7918 Jones Branch Dr Suite 540   McLean VA 22102
Ph: 703-356-2622 ▪ Fx: 703-356-6388

Construction Marketing Research Council cmrc.net
4625 S Wendler Dr Suite 111   Tempe AZ 85282
Ph: 602-431-0637 ▪ Fx: 602-431-1441

Construction, National Association of Women in www.nawic.org
327 S Adams St   Fort Worth TX 76104
Ph: 817-877-5551 ▪ Fx: 817-877-0324 ▪ TF: 800-552-3506

Construction Owners Association of America www.coaa.org
PO Box 56205   Atlanta GA 30343
Ph: 404-659-2485 ▪ Fx: 404-577-3551 ▪ TF: 800-994-2622

Construction Owners & Executives USA, Women www.wcoeusa.org
4410A Connecticut Ave NW   Washington DC 20008
Ph: 800-788-3548

Construction, Professional Women in www.pwcusa.org
315 E 56th St   New York NY 10022
Ph: 212-486-7745 ▪ Fx: 212-486-0228

Construction Specifications Institute www.csinet.org
99 Canal Ctr Plaza Suite 300   Alexandria VA 22314
Ph: 703-684-0300 ▪ Fx: 703-684-0465 ▪ TF: 800-689-2900

Construction Trades Dept AFL-CIO, Building & www.buildingtrades.org
815 16th St NW Suite 600   Washington DC 20006
Ph: 202-347-1461

Construction Writers Association www.constructionwriters.org
PO Box 5586   Buffalo Grove IL 60089
Ph: 847-398-7756 ▪ Fx: 847-590-5241

Constructive Change, Center for www.constructivechange.org
801 Duke St   Alexandria VA 22314
Ph: 703-684-4735 ▪ Fx: 703-684-4738

Constructors, American Institute of aicnet.org
466 94th Ave N   Saint Petersburg FL 33702
Ph: 727-578-0317 ▪ Fx: 727-578-9982

Constructors, NEA - Association of Union — www.nea-online.org
1501 Lee Hwy Suite 202   Arlington VA 22209
Ph: 703-524-3336 ▪ Fx: 703-524-3364

Consular Officers Retired, Diplomatic & — www.dacorbacon.org
1801 F St NW   Washington DC 20006
Ph: 202-682-0500 ▪ Fx: 202-842-3295 ▪ TF: 800-344-9127

Consultant Association, International Lactation — www.ilca.org
1500 Sunday Dr Suite 102   Raleigh NC 27607
Ph: 919-861-5577 ▪ Fx: 919-787-4916

Consultant Businesses, National Association of Computer — www.naccb.org
1800 Diagonal Rd Suite 520   Alexandria VA 22314
Ph: 703-838-2050 ▪ Fx: 703-838-3610

Consultant Pharmacists, American Society of — www.ascp.com
1321 Duke St   Alexandria VA 22314
Ph: 703-739-1300 ▪ Fx: 703-739-1321 ▪ TF: 800-355-2727

Consultants, American Association of Healthcare — www.aahc.net
5 Revere Dr Suite 200   Northbrook IL 60062
Ph: 847-205-2718 ▪ Fx: 847-350-2241 ▪ TF: 888-350-2242

Consultants, American Association of Insurance Management — www.aaimco.com
3925 Fenn Rd   Medina OH 44256
Ph: 330-725-8946 ▪ Fx: 330-723-6270

Consultants, American Association of Legal Nurse — www.aalnc.org
401 N Michigan Ave   Chicago IL 60611
Ph: 312-321-5177 ▪ Fx: 312-673-6655 ▪ TF: 877-402-2562

Consultants, American Association of Nutritional — www.aanc.net
400 Oak Hill Dr   Winona Lake IN 46590
Ph: 574-269-6165 ▪ Fx: 574-269-4060 ▪ TF: 888-828-2262

Consultants, American Association of Political — www.theaapc.org
600 Pennsylvania Ave SE Suite 330   Washington DC 20003
Ph: 202-544-9815 ▪ Fx: 202-544-9816

Consultants, American College of Chiropractic — www.accc-chiro.com
2741 Ridge Rd   Lansing IL 60438
Ph: 708-895-3141 ▪ Fx: 708-895-2268

Consultants, American Society of Agricultural — www.agconsultants.org
950 S Cherry St Suite 508   Denver CO 80246
Ph: 303-759-5091 ▪ Fx: 303-758-0190

Consultants, American Society of Irrigation — www.asic.org
111 E Wacker Dr 18th Fl   Chicago IL 60601
Ph: 312-372-7090 ▪ Fx: 312-372-6160

Consultants, American Society of Theatre — www.theatreconsultants.org
12226 Mentz Hill Rd   Saint Louis MO 63128
Ph: 314-843-9218 ▪ Fx: 314-843-4955

Consultants, American Society of Trial — www.astcweb.org
1941 Greenspring Dr   Timonium MD 21093
Ph: 410-560-7949 ▪ Fx: 410-560-2563

Consultants to the Armed Forces, Society of Medical — www.smcaf.org

Consultants, Association of Bridal — www.bridalassn.com
200 Chestnutland Rd   New Milford CT 06776
Ph: 860-355-0464 ▪ Fx: 860-354-1404

Consultants Association, Construction Industry CPAs/ — www.cicpac.com
111 E Wacker Dr Suite 990   Chicago IL 60601
Ph: 800-869-0491 ▪ Fx: 312-729-9800

Consultants Association, CPA Auto Dealer — www.autodealercpas.com
1 Valmont Plaza 4th Fl   Omaha NE 68154
Ph: 402-964-3865 ▪ Fx: 402-964-3811 ▪ TF: 888-475-4476

Consultants, Association of Executive Search — www.aesc.org
12 E 41st St 17th Fl   New York NY 10017
Ph: 212-398-9556 ▪ Fx: 212-398-9560

Consultants Association, Freight Transportation — www.transportpros.org
PO Box 53087   Albuquerque NM 87153
Ph: 505-299-0615

Consultants Association, Independent Computer — www.icca.org
11131 S Towne Sq Suite F   Saint Louis MO 63123
Ph: 314-892-1675 ▪ Fx: 314-487-1345 ▪ TF: 800-774-4222

Consultants Association, Independent Educational — www.educationalconsulting.org
3251 Old Lee Hwy Suite 510   Fairfax VA 22030
Ph: 703-591-4850 ▪ Fx: 703-591-4860 ▪ TF: 800-808-4322

Consultants Association of Internal Management — www.aimc.org
86 Clarendon Ave   Rutland VT 05777
Ph: 802-438-2882 ▪ Fx: 802-438-9859

Consultants Association, Investment Management — www.imca.org
9101 E Kenyon Ave Suite 3000   Denver CO 80237
Ph: 303-770-3377 ▪ Fx: 303-770-1812

Consultants, Association of Professional — www.consultapc.org
PO Box 51193   Irvine CA 92619
Ph: 800-745-5050 ▪ Fx: 800-977-3272

Consultants, Association of Professional Communication — www.consultingsuccess.org
3924 S Troost Ave   Tulsa OK 74105
Ph: 918-743-4793

Consultants, Association of Professional Investment — www.apic-ssb.com
1101 17th St NW Suite 703   Washington DC 20036
Ph: 202-464-4155 ▪ Fx: 202-464-4157

Consultants, Association of Professional Material Handling — www.mhia.org/apmhc
8720 Red Oak Blvd Suite 201   Charlotte NC 28217
Ph: 704-676-1184 ▪ Fx: 704-676-1199

Consultants Association, Professional & Technical — www.patca.org
543 Vista Mar Ave   Pacifica CA 94044
Ph: 408-971-5902 ▪ Fx: 650-359-3089 ▪ TF: 800-747-2822

Consultants Association Inc, Qualitative Research — www.qrca.org
PO Box 967   Camden TN 30320
Ph: 731-584-8080 ▪ Fx: 731-584-7882 ▪ TF: 888-674-7722

Consultants Council, Airport — www.acconline.org
908 King St Suite 100   Alexandria VA 22314
Ph: 703-683-5900 ▪ Fx: 703-683-2564

Consultants, Institute of Certified Healthcare Business — www.ichbc.org
307 N Michigan Ave Suite 800   Chicago IL 60601
Ph: 312-360-0384 ▪ Fx: 312-360-0388 ▪ TF: 800-447-1684

Consultants Institute, Roof — www.rci-online.org
1500 Sunday Dr Suite 204   Raleigh NC 27607
Ph: 919-859-0742 ▪ Fx: 919-859-1328 ▪ TF: 800-828-1902

Consultants, Institute of Tax — www.taxprofessionals.homestead.com/welcome.html
7500 212th St SW Suite 205   Edmonds WA 98026
Ph: 425-774-3521 ▪ Fx: 425-672-0461

Consultants International, Association of Image — www.aici.org
2695 Villa Creek Dr Suite 260   Dallas TX 75234
Ph: 972-755-1503 ▪ Fx: 972-755-2561 ▪ TF: 800-383-8831

Consultants, International Association of Professional Security — www.iapsc.org
525 SW 5th St Suite A   Des Moines IA 50309
Ph: 515-282-8192 ▪ Fx: 515-282-9117

Consultants, International Association of Registered Financial — www.iarfc.org
2507 N Verity Pkwy PO Box 42506   Middletown OH 45042
Ph: 513-424-6395 ▪ Fx: 513-424-5752 ▪ TF: 800-532-9060

Consultants, International Society of Hospitality — www.ishc.com
515 King St Suite 420   Alexandria VA 22314
Ph: 703-684-6681 ▪ Fx: 703-684-6048

Consultants, National Association of Healthcare — www.healthcon.org
1255 23rd St NW Suite 200   Washington DC 20037
Ph: 202-452-8282 ▪ Fx: 202-833-3636

Consultants, National Association of Independent Crop — www.naicc.org
349 E Nolley Dr   Collierville TN 38017
Ph: 901-861-0511 ▪ Fx: 901-861-0512

Consultants, National Association of Legal Search — www.nalsc.org
The Biltmore 817 W Peachtree St Suite 208   Atlanta GA 30308
Ph: 404-879-5080 ▪ Fx: 404-879-5075 ▪ TF: 866-394-9347

Consultants, National Bureau of Certified — www.national-bureau.com
1850 5th Ave   San Diego CA 92101
Ph: 619-239-7076 ▪ Fx: 619-296-3580 ▪ TF: 800-543-1114

Consultants, National Council of Acoustical — www.ncac.com
66 Morris Ave Suite 1A   Springfield NJ 07081
Ph: 973-564-5859 ▪ Fx: 973-564-7480

Consultants, National Society of Environmental — nsec.lincoln-grad.org
303 W Cypress St   San Antonio TX 78212
Ph: 210-271-0781 ▪ Fx: 210-225-8450 ▪ TF: 800-486-3676

Consultants Society International, Foodservice — www.fcsi.org
304 W Liberty St Suite 201   Louisville KY 40202
Ph: 502-583-3783 ▪ Fx: 502-589-3602

Consultants, Society of Medical-Dental Management — www.smdmc.org
125 Strafford Ave Suite 300   Wayne PA 19087
Ph: 800-826-2264 ▪ Fx: 610-687-7702

Consultants, Society of Telecommunications — www.stcconsultants.org
PO Box 416   Fall River Mills CA 96028
Ph: 530-336-7070 ▪ Fx: 530-336-7060 ▪ TF: 800-782-7670

Consultants USA Inc, Institute of Management — www.imcusa.org
2025 M St NW Suite 800   Washington DC 20036
Ph: 202-367-1134 ▪ Fx: 202-367-2134 ▪ TF: 800-221-2557

Consultative Group on International Agricultural Research — www.cgiar.org
1818 H St NW   Washington DC 20433
Ph: 202-473-8951 ▪ Fx: 202-473-8110

Consulting Actuaries, Conference of — www.ccactuaries.org
1110 W Lake Cook Rd Suite 235   Buffalo Grove IL 60089
Ph: 847-419-9090 ▪ Fx: 847-419-9091

Consulting Arborists, American Society of — www.asca-consultants.org
15245 Shady Grove Rd Suite 130   Rockville MD 20850
Ph: 301-947-0483 ▪ Fx: 301-990-9771

Consulting Chemists & Chemical Engineers, Association of — www.chemconsult.com
PO Box 297   Sparta NJ 07871
Ph: 973-729-6671 ▪ Fx: 973-729-7088

Consulting Engineers, Association of Federal Communications — www.afcce.org

Consulting Firms, Association of Management — www.amcf.org
380 Lexington Ave Suite 1700   New York NY 10168
Ph: 212-551-7887 ▪ Fx: 212-551-7934

Consulting Firms, International Association of Career — www.iaccf.com
1910 Cochran Rd Suite 740   Pittsburgh PA 15220
Ph: 800-565-2182

Consulting Firms International, Association of Career Management — www.aocfi.org
204 'E' St NE   Washington DC 20002
Ph: 202-547-6344 ▪ Fx: 202-547-6348

Consulting Foresters of America, Association of — www.acf-foresters.com
732 N Washington St Suite 4A   Alexandria VA 22314
Ph: 703-548-0990 ▪ Fx: 703-548-6395 ▪ TF: 888-540-8733

Consulting Services International, Building Industry — www.bicsi.org
8610 Hidden River Pkwy   Tampa FL 33637
Ph: 813-979-1991 ▪ Fx: 813-971-4311 ▪ TF: 800-242-7405

Consumer Advocacy, Society for Healthcare — www.shca-aha.org
1 Franklin St 31st Fl N   Chicago IL 60606
Ph: 312-422-3726 ▪ Fx: 312-422-4581

Consumer Advocates, National Association of — www.naca.net
1730 Rhode Island NW Suite 805   Washington DC 20036
Ph: 202-452-1989 ▪ Fx: 202-452-0099

Consumer Advocates, National Association of State Utility — www.nasuca.org
8300 Colesville Rd Suite 101   Silver Spring MD 20910
Ph: 301-589-6313 ▪ Fx: 301-589-6380

Consumer Affairs Exchange, Insurance — www.icae.org

Consumer Agency Administrators, National Association of — www.nacaanet.org
750 Old Hickory Blvd Bldg 2 Suite 150   Brentwood TN 37027
Ph: 615-371-6125

Consumer Alert — www.consumeralert.org
1001 Connecticut Ave NW Suite 1128   Washington DC 20036
Ph: 202-467-5809 ▪ Fx: 202-467-5814

Consumer Bankers Association — www.cbanet.org
1000 Wilson Blvd Suite 2500   Arlington VA 22209
Ph: 703-276-1750 ▪ Fx: 703-528-1290

Consumer Credit Administrators, National Association of — www.naccaonline.org
PO Box 20871   Columbus OH 43220
Ph: 614-326-1165 ▪ Fx: 614-326-1162

Consumer Credit Insurance Association — www.cciaonline.com
542 S Dearborn St Suite 400   Chicago IL 60605
Ph: 312-939-2242 ▪ Fx: 312-939-8287

Consumer Data Industry Association   www.cdiaonline.org
1090 Vermont Ave NW Suite 200   Washington DC 20005
Ph: 202-371-0910 ▪ Fx: 202-371-0134

(Consumer Education) Myvesta.org Inc   www.myvesta.org
6 Taft Ct Suite 200   Rockville MD 20850
Ph: 301-762-5270 ▪ TF: 800-698-3782

Consumer Electronics Association   www.ce.org
2500 Wilson Blvd   Arlington VA 22201
Ph: 703-907-7600 ▪ Fx: 703-907-7675

Consumer Electronics Society, IEEE   www.ewh.ieee.org/soc/ces
IEEE Operations Ctr 445 Hoes Ln   Piscataway NJ 08854
Ph: 732-981-0060 ▪ Fx: 732-981-1721

Consumer Energy Council of America   www.cecarf.org
2000 L St NW Suite 802   Washington DC 20036
Ph: 202-659-0404 ▪ Fx: 202-659-0407

Consumer Federation of America   www.consumerfed.org
1424 16th St NW Suite 604   Washington DC 20036
Ph: 202-387-6121

Consumer Federation of America Foundation   www.consumerfed.org/backpage/cfaf.html
1424 16th St NW Suite 604   Washington DC 20036
Ph: 202-387-6121 ▪ Fx: 202-265-7989

Consumer Finance Law, Conference on   www.theccfl.com
Oklahoma City Univ School of Law 2501 N Blackwelder
Ave   Oklahoma City OK 73106
Ph: 405-521-5363 ▪ Fx: 405-521-5089

Consumer Financial Education, Institute of   www.financial-education-icfe.org
PO Box 34070   San Diego CA 92163
Ph: 619-232-8811 ▪ Fx: 619-239-1401

Consumer Healthcare Products Association   www.chpa-info.org
1150 Connecticut Ave NW Suite 1200   Washington DC 20036
Ph: 202-429-9260 ▪ Fx: 202-223-6835

(Consumer Hotlines) Call for Action   www.callforaction.org
5272 River Rd Suite 300   Bethesda MD 20816
Ph: 301-657-8260 ▪ Fx: 301-657-2914 ▪ TF: 800-647-1756

(Consumer Interest) Private Citizen Inc   privatecitizen.com
PO Box 233   Naperville IL 60566
Ph: 630-393-2370 ▪ TF: 800-288-5865

Consumer Interests, American Council on   consumerinterests.org
415 S Duff Ave Suite C   Ames IA 50010
Ph: 515-956-4666 ▪ Fx: 515-233-3101

Consumer Law Center, National   www.consumerlaw.org
77 Summer St 10th Fl   Boston MA 02110
Ph: 617-542-8010 ▪ Fx: 617-542-8028

Consumer Mortgage Coalition
801 N Pennsylvania Ave NW Suite 625   Washington DC 20004
Ph: 202-544-3550 ▪ Fx: 202-543-1438

Consumer Project on Technology   www.cptech.org
PO Box 19367   Washington DC 20036
Ph: 202-387-8030 ▪ Fx: 202-234-5176

Consumer Protection Council Inc, Transportation   transportlaw.com/tcpc
120 Main St   Huntington NY 11743
Ph: 631-427-0100 ▪ Fx: 631-549-8962

Consumer Research, Association for   acrweb.org
PO Box 2310   Valdosta GA 31604
Ph: 229-244-2380 ▪ Fx: 229-244-7881

Consumer Rights, Alliance for
132 Nassau St 2nd Fl   New York NY 10038
Ph: 212-349-9204 ▪ Fx: 212-608-2310

Consumer Science Business Professionals   www.consumerexpert.org
PO Box 2065   Lake Oswego OR 97035
Ph: 503-620-6690 ▪ Fx: 503-620-6898

Consumer Sciences, American Association of Family &   www.aafcs.org
1555 King St Suite 400   Alexandria VA 22314
Ph: 703-706-4600 ▪ Fx: 703-706-4663 ▪ TF: 800-424-8080

Consumer Sciences Education Association, Family &   www.cwu.edu/~fandcs/fcsea
Central Washington Univ Dept of Family & Consumer Science
400 E 8th Ave   Ellensburg WA 98926
Ph: 509-963-2766 ▪ Fx: 509-963-2787

Consumer Sciences, National Extension Association of Family &   www.neafcs.org
PO Box 239   Great Falls VA 22066
Ph: 703-759-1040 ▪ Fx: 703-759-4801 ▪ TF: 800-808-9133

Consumer Shows, National Association of   www.publicshows.com
147 SE 102nd St   Portland OR 97216
Ph: 503-253-0832 ▪ Fx: 503-253-9172 ▪ TF: 800-728-6227

Consumer Specialty Products Association   www.cspa.org
900 17th St NW Suite 300   Washington DC 20006
Ph: 202-872-8110 ▪ Fx: 202-872-8114

Consumers Association, American
2633 Flossmoor Rd   Flossmoor IL 60422
Ph: 708-957-2900 ▪ Fx: 708-957-4155

Consumers, Center for Medical   www.medicalconsumers.org
130 MacDougal St   New York NY 10012
Ph: 212-674-7105 ▪ Fx: 212-674-7100

Consumers League, National   www.natlconsumersleague.org
1701 K St NW Suite 1200   Washington DC 20006
Ph: 202-835-3323 ▪ Fx: 202-835-0747 ▪ TF: 800-876-7060

Consumers' Research Council of America   www.consumersresearchcncl.org
2020 Pennsylvania Ave NW Suite 300A   Washington DC 20006
Ph: 202-835-9698 ▪ Fx: 202-835-9793

Consumers Resource Council, Electricity   www.elcon.org
1333 H St NW West Tower 8th Fl   Washington DC 20005
Ph: 202-682-1390 ▪ Fx: 202-289-6370

Consumers' Self-Help Clearinghouse, National Mental Health   www.mhselfhelp.org
1211 Chestnut St Suite 1207   Philadelphia PA 19107
Ph: 215-751-1810 ▪ Fx: 215-636-6312 ▪ TF: 800-553-4539

Consumers United for Rail Equity   www.railcure.org
1050 Thomas Jefferson St NW 7th Fl   Washington DC 20007
Ph: 202-298-1800 ▪ Fx: 202-338-2416

Consumers for World Trade   www.cwt.org
1001 Connecticut Ave NW Suite 1110   Washington DC 20006
Ph: 202-293-2944 ▪ Fx: 202-293-0495

Contact Lens Association of Ophthalmologists   www.clao.org
721 Papworth Ave Suite 205   Metairie LA 70005
Ph: 504-835-3937 ▪ Fx: 504-833-5884

Contact Lens Council   www.contactlenscouncil.org
8201 Corporate Dr Suite 850   Landover MD 20785
Ph: 301-459-2618 ▪ Fx: 301-459-1802 ▪ TF: 800-884-4252

Contact Lens Examiners, National   www.abo-ncle.org
6506 Loisdale Rd Suite 209   Springfield VA 22150
Ph: 703-719-5800 ▪ Fx: 703-719-9144 ▪ TF: 800-296-1379

Contact Lens Manufacturers Association   www.contactlenses.org
PO Box 368   Kensington MD 20895
Ph: 301-231-8544 ▪ Fx: 301-231-8545

Contact Lens Society of America   www.clsa.info
441 Carlisle Dr   Herndon VA 20170
Ph: 703-437-5100 ▪ Fx: 703-437-0727 ▪ TF: 800-296-9776

Container Association, Flexible Intermediate Bulk   www.fibca.com
PO Box 26068   Macon GA 31221
Ph: 478-757-1006 ▪ Fx: 478-757-9444

Container Association, National Wooden Pallet &   www.nwpca.com
329 S Patrick St   Alexandria VA 22314
Ph: 703-519-6104 ▪ Fx: 703-519-4720

Container Distributors, National Association of   www.nacd.net
1900 Arch St   Philadelphia PA 19103
Ph: 215-564-3484 ▪ Fx: 215-564-2175

Container Institute, Plastic Shipping   www.pscionline.org
1920 'N' St NW Suite 800   Washington DC 20036
Ph: 202-973-2709 ▪ Fx: 202-331-8330

Container Institute, Steel Shipping   www.steelcontainers.com
1101 14th St NW Suite 1020   Washington DC 20005
Ph: 202-408-1900 ▪ Fx: 202-408-1972

Container Lessors, Institute of International   www.iicl.org
555 Pleasantville Rd Suite 140S   Briarcliff Manor NY 10510
Ph: 914-747-9100 ▪ Fx: 914-747-4600

Container Manufacturers Association, Aluminum Foil   www.afcma.org
10 Vecilla Ln   Hot Springs Village AR 71909
Ph: 501-922-7425 ▪ Fx: 501-922-0383

Container Resources, National Association for PET   www.napcor.com
10800 Sikes Pl Suite 240   Charlotte NC 28277
Ph: 704-845-5070 ▪ Fx: 704-845-5276

Containerization & Intermodal Institute
195 Fairfield Ave Suite 4D   West Caldwell NJ 07006
Ph: 973-226-0160 ▪ Fx: 973-364-1212

Contemporary A Cappella Society of America   www.casa.org
1850 Union St Suite 1449   San Francisco CA 94123
Ph: 415-563-5224 ▪ Fx: 415-563-5523

Contemporary Culture, Society for the Arts Religion &   www.sarcc.org
15811 Kutztown Rd Box 15   Maxatawny PA 19538
Ph: 610-683-7581

Contemporary Opera, Center for   www.conopera.org
PO Box 258   New York NY 10044
Ph: 212-785-2757 ▪ Fx: 212-758-0389

Contemporary Studies, Institute for   www.icspress.com
310 Harrison St   Oakland CA 94611
Ph: 510-238-5010 ▪ Fx: 510-238-8440 ▪ TF: 800-326-0263

Content Rating Association, Internet   www.icra.org
1130 Connecticut Ave NW Suite 501   Washington DC 20036
Ph: 202-331-8651 ▪ Fx: 202-331-8652

Continence, National Association for   www.nafc.org
PO Box 1019   Charleston SC 29402
Ph: 843-377-0900 ▪ Fx: 843-377-0905 ▪ TF: 800-252-3337

Continence Nurses Society, Wound Ostomy &   www.wocn.org
4700 W Lake Ave   Glenview IL 60025
Ph: 888-224-9626 ▪ Fx: 866-615-8560

Continence, Simon Foundation for   www.simonfoundation.org
PO Box 815   Wilmette IL 60091
Ph: 847-864-3913 ▪ Fx: 847-864-9758 ▪ TF: 800-237-4666

Continental Automated Building Association   www.caba.org
1200 Montreal Rd Bldg M-20   Ottawa ON K1A0R6
Ph: 613-990-7407 ▪ Fx: 613-991-9990 ▪ TF: 888-798-2222

Continental Baptist Missions   www.cbmoffice.org
5900 Alpine NW   Comstock Park MI 49321
Ph: 616-784-7190 ▪ Fx: 616-784-3330

Continental Divide Trail Society   www.cdtsociety.org
3704 N Charles St Suite 601 B   Baltimore MD 21218
Ph: 410-235-9610 ▪ Fx: 410-243-1960

Continental Dorset Club   www.dorsets.homestead.com
PO Box 506   North Scituate RI 02857
Ph: 401-647-4676 ▪ Fx: 401-647-4679

Contingency Planners International, Association of   www.acp-international.com
7044 S 13th St   Oak Creek WI 53154
Ph: 414-768-8000 ▪ Fx: 414-768-8001

Continuing Care Accreditation Commission   www.ccaconline.org
2519 Connecticut Ave NW   Washington DC 20008
Ph: 202-783-7286 ▪ Fx: 202-220-0022

Continuing Education, American Association for Adult &   www.aaace.org
4380 Forbes Blvd   Lanham MD 20706
Ph: 301-918-1913 ▪ Fx: 301-918-1846

(Continuing Education) American Law Institute - American Bar Association   4025 Chestnut St   Philadelphia PA 19104   www.ali-aba.org
Ph: 215-243-1600 ▪ Fx: 215-243-1664 ▪ TF: 800-253-6397

Continuing Education Association, University   www.ucea.edu
1 Dupont Cir NW Suite 615   Washington DC 20036
Ph: 202-659-3130 ▪ Fx: 202-785-0374

Continuing Education & Training, Accrediting Council for   www.accet.org
1722 'N' St NW   Washington DC 20036
Ph: 202-955-1113 ▪ Fx: 202-955-1118

Continuing Education & Training, International Association for   www.iacet.org
1620 'I' St NW Suite 615   Washington DC 20006
Ph: 202-463-2905 ▪ Fx: 202-463-8497

Continuing Education & Training, National Council for www.nccet.org
PO Box 130623 Carlsbad CA 92013
Ph: 760-753-8375 ▪ Fx: 760-942-7296

Continuing Higher Education, Association for www.acheinc.org
2001 Mabelene Rd Charleston SC 29406
Ph: 843-574-6658 ▪ Fx: 843-574-6470 ▪ TF: 800-807-2243

Continuing Legal Education, Association for www.aclea.org
PO Box 4646 Austin TX 78765
Ph: 512-453-4340 ▪ Fx: 512-451-2911

Continuity of Care, American Association for www.continuityofcare.com
PO Box 532 Dunedin FL 34697
Ph: 727-738-9653 ▪ Fx: 727-738-8099 ▪ TF: 800-816-1575

Contract Bridge League, American www.acbl.org
2990 Airways Blvd Memphis TN 38116
Ph: 901-332-5586 ▪ Fx: 901-398-7754 ▪ TF: 800-264-2743

Contract Industry Council, Service www.go-scic.com
204 S Monroe St Tallahassee FL 32302
Ph: 850-681-1058 ▪ Fx: 850-681-6713

Contract Management Association, National www.ncmahq.org
8260 Greensboro Dr Suite 200 McLean VA 22102
Ph: 571-382-0082 ▪ Fx: 703-448-0939 ▪ TF: 800-344-8096

Contract Manufacturing & Packaging Association www.contractpackaging.org
519 N Highland Ave Jackson TN 38301
Ph: 731-422-7994 ▪ Fx: 731-427-2430

Contract Services Association of America www.csa-dc.org
1000 Wilson Blvd Suite 1800 Arlington VA 22209
Ph: 703-243-2020 ▪ Fx: 703-243-3601

Contractors of America, Associated General www.agc.org
333 John Carlyle St Suite 200 Alexandria VA 22314
Ph: 703-548-3118 ▪ Fx: 703-548-3119 ▪ TF: 800-242-1766

Contractors of America, Mechanical Service www.mcaa.org/msca
1385 Piccard Dr Rockville MD 20850
Ph: 301-869-5800 ▪ Fx: 301-990-9690

Contractors Inc, Associated Builders & www.abc.org
4250 N Fairfax Dr 9th Fl Arlington VA 22203
Ph: 703-812-2000 ▪ Fx: 703-812-8203

Contractors' Association, Engineering home.flash.net/~eca
8310 Florence Ave Downey CA 90240
Ph: 562-861-0929 ▪ Fx: 562-923-6179 ▪ TF: 800-293-2240

Contractors Association, North American
1702 W Market St Greensboro NC 27403
Ph: 336-370-4979 ▪ Fx: 336-370-4946

Contractors & Erectors Association, Metal Building www.mbcea.org
28 Lowry Dr PO Box 117 West Milton OH 45383
Ph: 937-698-4127 ▪ Fx: 937-698-6153 ▪ TF: 800-866-6722

Contractors, National Association of Minority www.namconline.org
666 11th St NW Suite 520 Washington DC 20001
Ph: 202-347-8259 ▪ Fx: 202-628-1876

Contractors NetWork, Certified www.contractors.net
134 Sibley Ave Ardmore PA 19003
Ph: 610-642-9505 ▪ Fx: 610-642-5842

Contribution Administrators Inc, National Association of www.nagdca.org
Government Defined 167 W Main St Suite 600 Lexington KY
40507
Ph: 859-514-9161 ▪ Fx: 859-514-9166

Control & Automation Association, Measurement www.measure.org
PO Box 3698 Williamsburg VA 23187
Ph: 757-258-3100 ▪ Fx: 757-258-9066

Control Systems Society, IEEE www.ieeecss.org
IEEE Operations Ctr 445 Hoes Ln Piscataway NJ 08854
Ph: 732-981-0060 ▪ Fx: 732-981-1721

Controlled Environment Testing Association www.cetainternational.org
1500 Sunday Dr Suite 102 Raleigh NC 27607
Ph: 919-787-5576 ▪ Fx: 919-787-4916

Controlled Release Society www.controlledrelease.org
13355 10th Ave N Suite 108 Minneapolis MN 55441
Ph: 763-512-0909 ▪ Fx: 763-765-2329

Controlled Substance Authorities, National Association of State www.nascsa.org
72 Brook St Quincy MA 02170
Ph: 617-472-0520 ▪ Fx: 617-472-0521

Controllers Association, National Tuberculosis
2951 Flowers Rd S Suite 102 Atlanta GA 30341
Ph: 770-455-0801 ▪ Fx: 770-455-4221 ▪ TF: 888-455-0801

Convenience Stores, National Association of www.nacsonline.com
1600 Duke St Alexandria VA 22314
Ph: 703-684-3600 ▪ Fx: 703-836-4564 ▪ TF: 800-966-6227

Convention of American Instructors of the Deaf www.caid.org/
PO Box 377 Bedford TX 76095
Ph: 817-354-8414

Convention & Exhibitors Association, Healthcare www.hcea.org
5775 Peachtree-Dunwoody Rd Bldg G Suite 500 Atlanta GA
30342
Ph: 404-252-3663 ▪ Fx: 404-252-0774

Convention Industry Council www.conventionindustry.org
8201 Greensboro Dr Suite 300 McLean VA 22102
Ph: 703-610-9030 ▪ Fx: 703-610-9005 ▪ TF: 800-725-8982

Convention Management Association, Professional www.pcma.org
2301 S Lake Shore Dr Suite 1001 Chicago IL 60616
Ph: 312-423-7262 ▪ Fx: 312-423-7222 ▪ TF: 877-827-7262

Convention Marketing Executives, Association for www.acmenet.org
204 'E' St NE Washington DC 20002
Ph: 202-547-6340 ▪ Fx: 202-547-6348

Convention & Visitor Bureaus, International Association of www.iacvb.org
2025 M St NW Suite 500 Washington DC 20036
Ph: 202-296-7888 ▪ Fx: 202-296-7889

Converters, Association of Independent Corrugated www.aiccbox.org
113 S West St PO Box 25708 Alexandria VA 22313
Ph: 703-836-2422 ▪ Fx: 703-836-2795 ▪ TF: 877-836-2422

Converting Equipment Manufacturers Association www.cema-converting.org
2166 Gold Hill Rd Fort Mill SC 29708
Ph: 803-802-7820 ▪ Fx: 803-802-7821

Converting Technologies, NPES: Association for Suppliers of www.npes.org
Printing Publishing & 1899 Preston White Dr Reston VA
20191
Ph: 703-264-7200 ▪ Fx: 703-620-0994

Conveyor Equipment Manufacturers Association www.cemanet.org
6724 Lone Oak Blvd Naples FL 34109
Ph: 941-514-3441 ▪ Fx: 941-514-3470

Cook Frederick A Society www.cookpolar.org

Cookers International, Solar solarcookers.org
1919 21st St Suite 101 Sacramento CA 95814
Ph: 916-455-4499 ▪ Fx: 916-455-4498

Cookie & Snack Bakers Association
1128 Maple Dr NW Cleveland TN 37312
Ph: 423-472-5856 ▪ Fx: 423-478-1273

Cooking Club of America www.cookingclub.com
12301 Whitewater Dr Minnetonka MN 55343
Ph: 888-850-2802

Cookware Manufacturers Association www.cookware.org
PO Box 531335 Mountain Brook AL 35253
Ph: 205-802-7600 ▪ Fx: 205-802-7610

Cooley's Anemia Foundation www.thalassemia.org
129-09 26th Ave Suite 203 Flushing NY 11354
Ph: 718-321-2873 ▪ Fx: 718-321-3340 ▪ TF: 800-522-7222

Coolidge Calvin Memorial Foundation www.calvin-coolidge.org
PO Box 97 Plymouth VT 05056
Ph: 802-672-3389 ▪ Fx: 802-672-3369

Cooling Institute, Evaporative www.evapcooling.org
New Mexico State Univ MSC 3ECI PO Box 30001 Las Cruces
NM 88003
Ph: 505-646-4104 ▪ Fx: 505-646-2960

Cooling Technology Institute www.cti.org
PO Box 73383 Houston TX 77273
Ph: 281-583-4087 ▪ Fx: 281-537-1721

Cooper Ornithological Society www.cooper.org
PO Box 1897 Lawrence KS 66044
Ph: 800-627-0629 ▪ Fx: 785-843-1274

Cooperage Industries of America, Associated www.acia.net
2100 Gardiner Ln Suite 100-E Louisville KY 40205
Ph: 502-459-6113 ▪ Fx: 502-459-6114

Cooperation, North American Students of www.umich.edu/~nasco
PO Box 7715 Ann Arbor MI 48107
Ph: 734-663-0889 ▪ Fx: 734-663-5072

Cooperative Business Association, National www.ncba.org
1401 New York Ave NW Suite 1100 Washington DC 20005
Ph: 202-638-6222 ▪ Fx: 202-638-1374

Cooperative Education, National Commission for www.co-op.edu
360 Huntington Ave 384 CP Boston MA 02115
Ph: 617-373-3770 ▪ Fx: 617-373-3463

Cooperative Educators, Association of www.wisc.edu/uwcc/ace/ace.html
PO Box 64047 Saint Paul MN 55164
Ph: 651-451-5481 ▪ Fx: 651-451-5073

Cooperative Housing Foundation Inc www.chfhq.org
8601 Georgia Ave Suite 800 Silver Spring MD 20910
Ph: 301-587-4700 ▪ Fx: 301-587-7315

Cooperatives/Land Assistance Fund, Federation www.federationsoutherncoop.com
of Southern 2769 Church St East Point GA 30344
Ph: 404-765-0991 ▪ Fx: 404-765-9178

Cooperatives, National Council of Farmer www.ncfc.org
50 F St NW Suite 900 Washington DC 20001
Ph: 202-626-8700 ▪ Fx: 202-626-8722

Cooperatives, National Society of Accountants for www.nsacoop.org
6320 Augusta Dr Suite 800 Springfield VA 22150
Ph: 703-569-3088 ▪ Fx: 703-569-0235

Coordinating Research Council Inc www.crcao.org
3650 Mansell Rd Suite 140 Alpharetta GA 30022
Ph: 678-795-0506 ▪ Fx: 678-795-0509

Coors Adolph Foundation www.acoorsfdn.org
4100 E Mississippi Ave Suite 1850 Denver CO 80246
Ph: 303-388-1636 ▪ Fx: 303-388-1684

Copier Artists, International Society of
759 President St Suite 2H Brooklyn NY 11215
Ph: 718-638-3264

Copier Dealers Association www.cdainfo.org
PO Box 627 Cockeysville MD 21030
Ph: 410-252-4800

Copper Association, International www.copperinfo.com
260 Madison Ave 16th Fl New York NY 10016
Ph: 212-251-7240 ▪ Fx: 212-251-7245

Copper & Brass Fabricators Council Inc
1050 17th St NW Suite 440 Washington DC 20036
Ph: 202-833-8575 ▪ Fx: 202-331-8267

Copper & Brass Servicenter Association Inc www.copper-brass.org
994 Old Eagle School Rd Suite 1019 Wayne PA 19087
Ph: 610-971-4850 ▪ Fx: 610-971-4859

Copper Development Association Inc www.copper.org
260 Madison Ave 16th Fl New York NY 10016
Ph: 212-251-7200 ▪ Fx: 212-251-7234 ▪ TF: 800-232-3282

Coptic Association, American www.amcoptic.com
PO Box 55 Saddle River NJ 07458
Ph: 201-451-0972 ▪ Fx: 201-451-3399

Coptic Orphans Support Association www.copticorphans.org
PO Box 2881 Merrifield VA 22116
Ph: 703-641-8910 ▪ Fx: 703-641-8787 ▪ TF: 800-499-2989

Copyright Clearance Center Inc www.copyright.com
222 Rosewood Dr Danvers MA 01923
Ph: 978-750-8400 ▪ Fx: 978-646-8600

Copyright Society of the USA www.csusa.org
352 7th Ave Suite 307 New York NY 10001
Ph: 212-354-6401 ▪ Fx: 212-354-2847

Copywriters Council of America   www.lgroup.addr.com/CCA.htm
7 Putter Ln PO Box 102   Middle Island NY 11953
Ph: 631-924-8555 ▪ Fx: 631-924-3890

Coral Reef Alliance, Global   www.globalcoral.org
37 Pleasant St   Cambridge MA 02139
Ph: 617-864-4226 ▪ Fx: 617-864-0433

Corazones Unidos Siempre/Chi Upsilon Sigma National Latin   www.justbecus.org
Sorority Inc   99 Park Ave Suite 278A   New York NY 10016
Ph: 212-969-0793 ▪ Fx: 212-867-7904

Cord Blood Donor Foundation   www.cordblooddonor.org
1200 Bayhill Dr Suite 301   San Bruno CA 94066
Ph: 650-635-1452 ▪ Fx: 650-635-1428

Cordage Institute   www.ropecord.com
994 Old Eagle School Rd Suite 1019   Wayne PA 19087
Ph: 610-971-4854 ▪ Fx: 610-971-4859

Cordell Hull Foundation for International Education   www.payson.tulane.edu/cordellhull
135 E 50th St Suite 3H   New York NY 10022
Ph: 212-759-3311

CoreNet Global Inc   www.corenetglobal.org
260 Peachtree St NW Suite 1500   Atlanta GA 30303
Ph: 404-589-3200 ▪ Fx: 404-589-3201 ▪ TF: 800-726-8111

Cormo Sheep Association, American   www.cormosheep.com
Rt 59 Box 25   Broadus MT 59317
Ph: 406-427-5449

Corn Growers Association, American   www.acga.org
PO Box 18157   Washington DC 20036
Ph: 202-835-0330 ▪ Fx: 202-463-0862

Corn Growers Association, National   www.ncga.com
632 Cepi Dr   Chesterfield MO 63005
Ph: 636-733-9004 ▪ Fx: 636-733-9005

Corn Refiners Association Inc   www.corn.org
1701 Pennsylvania Ave NW Suite 950   Washington DC 20006
Ph: 202-331-1634 ▪ Fx: 202-331-2054

Cornelia de Lange Syndrome Foundation Inc   www.cdlsusa.org
302 W Main St Suite 100   Avon CT 06001
Ph: 860-676-8166 ▪ Fx: 860-676-8337 ▪ TF: 800-753-2357

Cornish American Heritage Society   www.cousinjack.org

Coro Foundation   www.coro.org
1010 W 39th St   Kansas City MO 64111
Ph: 816-931-0751 ▪ Fx: 816-756-0924

Corporal Punishment & Alternatives,   www.temple.edu/education/ncscpa/ncscpa.html
National Center for the Study of   Temple Univ 253 Ritter
     Annex   Philadelphia PA 19122
Ph: 215-204-6091 ▪ Fx: 215-204-6013

Corporal Punishment in Schools, National Coalition   www.stophitting.com/disatschool
to Abolish   155 W Main St Suite 1603   Columbus OH 43215
Ph: 614-221-8829 ▪ Fx: 614-221-2110

(Corporate Accountability) Infact   www.infact.org
46 Plympton St   Boston MA 02118
Ph: 617-695-2525 ▪ Fx: 617-695-2626 ▪ TF: 800-688-8797

Corporate Angel Network Inc   www.corpangelnetwork.org
Westchester County Airport 1 Loop Rd   White Plains NY 10604
Ph: 914-328-1313 ▪ Fx: 914-328-3938

Corporate Council, National Hispanic   www.nhcc-hq.org
1530 Wilson Blvd Suite 110   Arlington VA 22209
Ph: 703-807-5137 ▪ Fx: 703-807-0567

Corporate Counsel, Association of   www.acca.com
1025 Connecticut Ave NW Suite 200   Washington DC 20036
Ph: 202-293-4103 ▪ Fx: 202-293-4701

Corporate Counsel Inc, Federation of Defense &   www.thefederation.org
11812-A N 56th St   Tampa FL 33617
Ph: 813-983-0022 ▪ Fx: 813-988-5837

Corporate Directors, National Association of   www.nacdonline.org
1828 L St NW Suite 801   Washington DC 20036
Ph: 202-775-0509 ▪ Fx: 202-775-4857

Corporate Facility Advisors   www.corfac.com
2000 N 15th St Suite 101   Arlington VA 22201
Ph: 703-528-3500 ▪ Fx: 703-528-0113

Corporate Growth, Association for   www.acg.org
1926 Waukegan Rd Suite 1   Glenview IL 60025
Ph: 847-657-6730 ▪ Fx: 847-657-6819 ▪ TF: 800-699-1331

Corporate Housing Providers Association   www.corporatehousingproviders.org
7150 Winton Dr Suite 300   Indianapolis IN 46268
Ph: 317-328-4631 ▪ Fx: 317-280-8527

Corporate Meeting Professionals, Society of   www.scmp.org
217 Ridgemont Ave   San Antonio TX 78209
Ph: 210-822-6522 ▪ Fx: 210-882-9838

Corporate & Professional Recruitment, International Association of   www.iacpr.org
20 N Wacker Dr Suite 2262   Chicago IL 60606
Ph: 312-630-9881 ▪ Fx: 312-630-9882

Corporate Real Estate, International Association of   www.aecre.org
Attorneys & Executives in   20106 S Sycamore Dr   Frankfort
     IL 60423
Ph: 815-464-6019 ▪ Fx: 815-464-8334

Corporate Real Estate Service Advisors   www.cresa.com
405 Lexington Ave 47th Fl   New York NY 10174
Ph: 212-758-3131 ▪ Fx: 212-980-1977

Corporate Responsibility, Hispanic Association on   www.hacr.org
1444 'I' St NW Suite 850   Washington DC 20005
Ph: 202-835-9672 ▪ Fx: 202-457-0455

Corporate Responsibility, Interfaith Center on   www.iccr.org
475 Riverside Dr Rm 550   New York NY 10115
Ph: 212-870-2295 ▪ Fx: 212-870-2023

Corporate Secretaries, American Society of   ascs.org
521 5th Ave   New York NY 10175
Ph: 212-681-2000 ▪ Fx: 212-681-2005

Corporate Theatre Fund, National   www.nctf.org
1 E 53rd St 3rd Fl   New York NY 10022
Ph: 212-750-6895 ▪ Fx: 212-750-6977

Corporate Travel Executives, Association of   www.acte.org
515 King St Suite 340   Alexandria VA 22314
Ph: 703-683-5322 ▪ Fx: 703-683-2720 ▪ TF: 800-228-3669

Corporate Treasurers, National Association of   www.nact.org
12100 Sunset Hills Rd Suite 130   Reston VA 20190
Ph: 703-437-4377 ▪ Fx: 703-435-4390

Corporation for Jefferson's Poplar Forest   www.poplarforest.org
PO Box 419   Forest VA 24551
Ph: 434-525-1806 ▪ Fx: 434-525-7252

Corporation for National Research Initiatives   www.cnri.reston.va.us
1895 Preston White Dr Suite 100   Reston VA 20191
Ph: 703-620-8990 ▪ Fx: 703-620-0913

Corporation for Public Broadcasting   www.cpb.org
401 9th St NW   Washington DC 20004
Ph: 202-879-9600 ▪ Fx: 202-879-9700 ▪ TF: 800-272-2190

Corporation for Research & Educational Networking   www.cren.net
1150 18th St NW Suite 1030   Washington DC 20036
Ph: 202-293-5909 ▪ Fx: 202-293-2853

Corpus - National Association for an Inclusive Priesthood   www.corpus.org
PO Box 104   High Bridge NJ 08829
Ph: 908-638-6877 ▪ Fx: 908-638-8220

Correction Officers, Federation of Police Security &   www.fopsco-afspa.org
71 E Cherry St   Rahway NJ 07065
Ph: 732-388-3323 ▪ Fx: 732-388-5620

Correctional Administrators, Association of State   www.asca.net
213 Court St 6th Fl   Middletown CT 06457
Ph: 860-704-6410 ▪ Fx: 860-704-6420

Correctional Association, American   www.aca.org
4380 Forbes Blvd   Lanham MD 20706
Ph: 301-918-1800 ▪ Fx: 301-918-1900 ▪ TF: 800-222-5646

Correctional Chaplains Association, American   www.correctionalchaplains.org
PO Box 661   Waupun WI 53963
Ph: 920-324-6298 ▪ Fx: 920-324-6254

Correctional Education Association   www.ceanational.com
4380 Forbes Blvd   Lanham MD 20706
Ph: 301-918-1915 ▪ Fx: 301-918-1846 ▪ TF: 800-783-1232

Correctional Food Service Association, American   www.acfsa.org
4248 Park Glen Rd   Minneapolis MN 55416
Ph: 952-928-4648 ▪ Fx: 952-929-1318

Correctional Health Care, National Commission on   www.ncchc.org
1300 W Belmont Ave   Chicago IL 60657
Ph: 773-880-1460 ▪ Fx: 773-880-2424

Correctional Health Services Association, American   www.corrections.com/ACHSA
250 Gatsby Pl   Alpharetta GA 30022
Ph: 877-918-1842 ▪ Fx: 770-650-5789

Correctional Industries Association   www.nationalcia.org
1202 N Charles St   Baltimore MD 21201
Ph: 410-230-3972 ▪ Fx: 410-230-3981

Correctional Psychology, American Association for   www.eaacp.org
897 Oak Park Blvd Suite 124   Pismo Beach CA 93449
Ph: 805-489-0665

Correctional Research & Information Management,   www.happenings.com/lbennett
Association for   2717 Cottage Way Suite 15   Sacramento CA
     95825
Ph: 916-487-9334 ▪ Fx: 916-487-9929

Correctional Training Personnel, International Association of   www.iactp.org
PO Box 11018   Albany NY 12211
Ph: 518-783-6939

Correctional Vendors Association
3000 K St NW Suite 500   Washington DC 20007
Ph: 202-672-5579 ▪ Fx: 202-672-5399

Corrections, American Association of Mental Health Professionals in
PO Box 160208   Sacramento CA 95816
Ph: 916-323-8305 ▪ Fx: 916-649-1070

Corrections Association, International Community   www.iccaweb.org
PO Box 1987   La Crosse WI 54602
Ph: 608-785-0200 ▪ Fx: 608-784-5335

Correspondents Association, Radio-Television
c/o Senate Radio-TV Gallery US Capitol Rm S-325   Washington
     DC 20510
Ph: 202-224-6421 ▪ Fx: 202-224-4882

Correspondents Association, US Marine Corps Combat   www.usmccca.org
238 Cornwall Cir   Chalfont PA 18914
Ph: 215-822-6898 ▪ Fx: 215-822-0163 ▪ TF: 888-999-7819

Corriedale Association Inc, American   www.americancorriedale.com
PO Box 391   Clay City IL 62824
Ph: 618-676-1046 ▪ Fx: 618-676-1133

Corriente Association, North American   www.corrientecattle.org
PO Box 12359   North Kansas City MO 64116
Ph: 816-421-1992 ▪ Fx: 816-421-1991

Corrosion Society, NACE International: www.nace.org
1440 S Creek Dr   Houston TX 77084
Ph: 281-228-6200 ▪ Fx: 281-228-6300

Corrugated Case Association, International   www.iccanet.org
2850 Golf Rd Suite 412   Rolling Meadows IL 60008
Ph: 847-364-9600 ▪ Fx: 847-364-9639

Corrugated Converters, Association of Independent   www.aiccbox.org
113 S West St PO Box 25708   Alexandria VA 22313
Ph: 703-836-2422 ▪ Fx: 703-836-2795 ▪ TF: 877-836-2422

Corrugated Packaging Foundation, International   icpf.corrugated.org
113 S West St PO Box 25708   Alexandria VA 22313
Ph: 703-836-2422 ▪ Fx: 703-836-2795

Corrugated Steel Pipe Association, National   www.ncspa.org
13140 Coit Rd Suite 320 LB 120   Dallas TX 75240
Ph: 972-850-9107 ▪ Fx: 972-490-4219

Corvair Society of America   www.corvair.org
PO Box 607   Lemont IL 60439
Ph: 630-257-6530

Corvette Restorers Society, National   www.ncrs.org
6291 Day Rd   Cincinnati OH 45252
Ph: 513-385-8526 ▪ Fx: 513-385-8554

COSA
PO Box 14537   Minneapolis MN 55414
www.cosa-recovery.org
Ph: 763-537-6904

Cosmetic Chemists, Society of
120 Wall St Suite 2400   New York NY 10005
www.scconline.org
Ph: 212-668-1500 ▪ Fx: 212-668-1504

Cosmetic Dentistry, American Academy of
5401 World Dairy Dr   Madison WI 53718
www.aacd.com
Ph: 608-222-8583 ▪ Fx: 608-222-9540 ▪ TF: 800-543-9220

Cosmetic Executive Women
21 E 40th St Suite 1700   New York NY 10016
www.cew.org
Ph: 212-685-5955 ▪ Fx: 212-685-3334

Cosmetic Industry Assoc, Foragers
135 E 55th St 8th Fl PH   New York NY 10022
www.cosmeticindex.com/ci/for
Ph: 212-759-1991 ▪ Fx: 212-755-4841

Cosmetic Ingredient Review
1101 17th St NW Suite 310   Washington DC 20036
www.cir-safety.org
Ph: 202-331-0651 ▪ Fx: 202-331-0088

Cosmetic Manufacturers & Distributors Inc, Independent
1220 W Northwest Hwy   Palatine IL 60067
www.icmad.org
Ph: 847-991-4499 ▪ Fx: 847-991-8161 ▪ TF: 800-334-2623

Cosmetic Professionals, Society of Permanent
69 N Broadway St   Des Plaines IL 60016
www.spcp.org
Ph: 847-635-1330 ▪ Fx: 847-635-1326

Cosmetic Surgery, American Academy of
737 N Michigan Ave Suite 820   Chicago IL 60611
www.cosmeticsurgery.org
Ph: 312-981-6760 ▪ Fx: 312-981-6787

Cosmetic Toiletry & Fragrance Association Inc
1101 17th St NW Suite 300   Washington DC 20036
www.ctfa.org
Ph: 202-331-1770 ▪ Fx: 202-331-1969

Cosmetic Toiletry & Fragrance Association PAC
1101 17th St NW Suite 300   Washington DC 20036
www.ctfa.org
Ph: 202-331-1770 ▪ Fx: 202-331-1969

Cosmetology Arts & Sciences, National Accrediting Commission of
4401 Ford Ave Suite 1300   Alexandria VA 22302
www.naccas.org
Ph: 703-600-7600 ▪ Fx: 703-379-2200

Cosmetology Association, National
401 N Michigan Ave Suite 2200   Chicago IL 60611
www.behindthechair.com/ncacares
Ph: 312-644-6610 ▪ Fx: 312-464-6118

Cosmetology Inc, National-Interstate Council of State Boards of
7622 Briarwood Cir   Little Rock AR 72205
www.nictesting.org
Ph: 501-227-8262 ▪ Fx: 501-227-8212

Cosmetology Schools, American Association of
15825 N 71st St Suite 100   Scottsdale AZ 85254
www.beautyschools.org/index2.html
Ph: 480-281-0431 ▪ Fx: 480-905-0993 ▪ TF: 800-831-1086

Cosmopolitan International
7341 W 80th St   Overland Park KS 66204
www.cosmopolitan.org
Ph: 913-648-4330 ▪ Fx: 913-648-4630 ▪ TF: 800-648-4331

Cost Engineering, AACE International - Association for the Advancement of   209 Prairie Ave Suite 100   Morgantown WV 26501
www.aacei.org
Ph: 304-296-8444 ▪ Fx: 304-291-5728 ▪ TF: 800-858-2678

Cost Engineering Council, International
www.icoste.org

Cost Estimating & Analysis, Society of
101 S Whiting St Suite 201   Alexandria VA 22304
www.sceaonline.net
Ph: 703-751-8069 ▪ Fx: 703-461-7328

Costume Designers Guild
4730 Woodman Ave Suite 430   Sherman Oaks CA 91423
www.costumedesignersguild.com
Ph: 818-905-1557 ▪ Fx: 818-905-1560

Costume Jewelry Club, Vintage Fashion &
PO Box 265   Glen Oaks NY 11004
www.lizjewel.com/vf
Ph: 718-939-3095 ▪ Fx: 718-939-7988

Costume Jewelry Salesman's Association
403 Charles St   Providence RI 02904
Ph: 401-272-3090 ▪ Fx: 401-274-5114 ▪ TF: 800-225-2452

Costume Society of America
55 Edgewater Dr PO Box 73   Earleville MD 21919
www.costumesocietyamerica.com
Ph: 410-275-1619 ▪ Fx: 410-275-8936 ▪ TF: 800-272-9447

Costumers Association, National
6914 Upper Trail Cir   Mesa AZ 85207
www.costumers.org
Ph: 800-622-1321 ▪ Fx: 480-654-6223

Cotswold Record Association, American
PO Box 59   Plympton MA 02367
Ph: 781-585-2026

Cottage Industry Miniaturists Trade Association Inc
PO Box 42849   Evergreen Park IL 60805
www.cimta.org/cimta.htm
Ph: 773-233-5522 ▪ Fx: 773-233-5506

Cotton Inc
6399 Weston Pkwy   Cary NC 27513
www.cottoninc.com
Ph: 919-678-2220 ▪ Fx: 919-678-2230 ▪ TF: 800-334-5868

Cotton Advisory Committee, International
1629 K St NW Suite 702   Washington DC 20006
www.icac.org
Ph: 202-463-6660 ▪ Fx: 202-463-6950

Cotton Association, Southern
88 Union Ave Suite 1204   Memphis TN 38103
www.southerncottonassociation.com
Ph: 901-525-2272 ▪ Fx: 901-527-8303

Cotton Batting Institute, National
1918 N Parkway PO Box 820287   Memphis TN 38182
www.natbat.com
Ph: 901-274-9030 ▪ Fx: 901-725-0510

Cotton Council of America, National
1918 North Pkwy   Memphis TN 38112
www.cotton.org
Ph: 901-274-9030 ▪ Fx: 901-725-0510 ▪ TF: 800-377-9030

Cotton Council International
1521 New Hampshire Ave NW   Washington DC 20036
www.cottonusa.org
Ph: 202-745-7805 ▪ Fx: 202-483-4040

Cotton Foundation
1918 North Pkwy   Memphis TN 38112
www.cotton.org/cf
Ph: 901-274-9030 ▪ Fx: 901-725-0510

Cotton Ginners' Association, National
PO Box 820285   Memphis TN 38182
Ph: 901-274-9030 ▪ Fx: 901-725-0510

Cotton Ginners Association, Southern
874 Cotton Gin Pl   Memphis TN 38106
www.southerncottonginners.org
Ph: 901-947-3104 ▪ Fx: 901-947-3103

Cotton Growers Inc, Plains
4517 W Loop 289   Lubbock TX 79414
www.plainscotton.org
Ph: 806-792-4904 ▪ Fx: 806-792-4906

Cotton Shippers Association, American
88 Union Ave Suite 1204   Memphis TN 38103
www.acsa-cotton.org
Ph: 901-525-2272 ▪ Fx: 901-527-6527

(Cotton) Supima
4141 E Broadway Rd   Phoenix AZ 85040
www.supima.com
Ph: 602-437-1364 ▪ Fx: 602-437-0143

Cotton Warehouse Association of America
499 S Capitol St NW Suite 600   Washington DC 20003
Ph: 202-554-1233 ▪ Fx: 202-554-1230

Cottonseed Products Association, National
104 Timber Creek Dr Suite 200   Cordova TN 38108
www.cottonseed.com
Ph: 901-682-0800 ▪ Fx: 901-682-2856

Council on Accreditation
120 Wall St 11th Fl   New York NY 10005
www.coanet.org
Ph: 212-797-3000 ▪ Fx: 212-797-1428 ▪ TF: 866-262-8088

Council for Accreditation in Occupational Hearing Conservation
611 E Wells St   Milwaukee WI 53202
www.caohc.org
Ph: 414-276-5338 ▪ Fx: 414-276-2146

Council of Administrators of Special Education
Fort Valley State Univ 1005 State University Dr   Fort Valley GA 31030
www.casecec.org
Ph: 478-825-7667 ▪ Fx: 478-825-7811

Council for Adult & Experiential Learning
55 E Monroe St Suite 1930   Chicago IL 60603
www.cael.org
Ph: 312-499-2600 ▪ Fx: 312-499-2601

Council for the Advancement of Standards in Higher Education
1 Dupont Cir NW Suite 300   Washington DC 20036
www.cas.edu
Ph: 202-862-1400 ▪ Fx: 202-296-3286

Council for Advancement & Support of Education
1307 New York Ave NW Suite 1000   Washington DC 20005
www.case.org
Ph: 202-328-5900 ▪ Fx: 202-387-4973 ▪ TF: 800-554-8536

Council for Affordable Health Insurance
112 S West St Suite 400   Alexandria VA 22314
www.cahi.org
Ph: 703-836-6200 ▪ Fx: 703-836-6550

Council for Affordable & Rural Housing
121 N Washington St Suite 301   Alexandria VA 22314
www.carh.org
Ph: 703-837-9001 ▪ Fx: 703-837-8467

Council for Agricultural Science & Technology
4420 W Lincoln Way   Ames IA 50014
www.cast-science.org
Ph: 515-292-2125 ▪ Fx: 515-292-4512

Council for Aid to Education
215 Lexington Ave 21st Fl   New York NY 10016
www.cae.org
Ph: 212-661-5800 ▪ Fx: 212-661-9766

Council of American Maritime Museums
c/o Maine Maritime Museum 243 Washington St   Bath ME 04530
www.councilofamericanmaritimemuseums.org
Ph: 207-443-1316 ▪ Fx: 207-443-1663

Council of American Master Mariners Inc
2700 Broening Hwy Dunmar Bldg Suite 115   Baltimore MD 21222
www.mastermariner.org
Ph: 410-285-7800

Council of American Overseas Research Centers
Smithsonian Institution   PO Box 37012 NHB Rm CE-123 MRC 178   Washington DC 20013
www.caorc.org
Ph: 202-842-8636 ▪ Fx: 202-786-2430

Council for American Private Education
13017 Wisteria Dr PMB 457   Germantown MD 20874
www.capenet.org
Ph: 301-916-8460 ▪ Fx: 301-916-8485

Council of American Survey Research Organizations
3 Upper Devon Rd   Port Jefferson NY 11777
www.casro.org
Ph: 631-928-6954 ▪ Fx: 631-928-6041

Council of the Americas
680 Park Ave   New York NY 10021
www.counciloftheamericas.org
Ph: 212-628-3200 ▪ Fx: 212-517-6247 ▪ TF: 800-733-2342

Council on America's Military Past USA Inc
PO Box 1151   Fort Myer VA 22211
www.campjamp.org
Ph: 703-912-6124 ▪ Fx: 703-912-5666 ▪ TF: 800-398-4693

Council on Anthropology & Education
c/o American Anthropological Assn 2200 Wilson Blvd Suite 600   Arlington VA 22201
www.aaanet.org/cae
Ph: 703-528-1902 ▪ Fx: 703-528-3546

Council for Art Education Inc
PO Box 479   Hanson MA 02341
www.acminet.org/cfae.htm
Ph: 781-293-4100 ▪ Fx: 781-294-0808

Council of Arts Accrediting Associations
11250 Roger Bacon Dr Suite 21   Reston VA 20190
www.arts-accredit.org
Ph: 703-437-0700 ▪ Fx: 703-437-6312

Council for Basic Education
1319 F St NW Suite 900   Washington DC 20004
www.c-b-e.org
Ph: 202-347-4171 ▪ Fx: 202-347-5047

Council of Better Business Bureaus Inc
4200 Wilson Blvd Suite 800   Arlington VA 22203
www.bbb.org
Ph: 703-276-0100 ▪ Fx: 703-525-8277

Council of Better Business Bureaus Inc Children's Advertising Review Unit   70 W 36th St 13th Fl   New York NY 10018
www.caru.org
Ph: 866-334-6272

Council of Better Business Bureaus Inc National Advertising Div
70 W 36th St 13th Fl   New York NY 10018
www.nadreview.org
Ph: 212-705-0114

Council of Better Business Bureaus Inc Wise Giving Alliance
4200 Wilson Blvd Suite 800   Arlington VA 22203
www.give.org
Ph: 703-276-0100 ▪ Fx: 703-525-8277

Council on Botanical & Horticultural   www2.ville.montreal.qc.ca/jardin/cbhl/cbhl.htm
Libraries Inc   Carnegie Mellon Univ Hunt Institute for Botanical
    Documentation   Pittsburgh PA 15213
    Ph: 412-268-7301 ■ Fx: 412-268-5677

Council of Canadians   www.canadians.org
    151 Slater St Suite 502   Ottawa ON K1P5H3
    Ph: 613-233-2773 ■ Fx: 613-233-6776 ■ TF: 800-387-7177

Council for Certification of Health Environmental & Safety   www.cchest.org
Technologies   208 Burwash Ave   Savoy IL 61874
    Ph: 217-359-2686 ■ Fx: 217-359-0055

Council for Chemical Research Inc   www.ccrhq.org
    1620 L St NW Suite 620   Washington DC 20036
    Ph: 202-429-3971 ■ Fx: 202-429-3976

Council of Chief State School Officers   www.ccsso.org
    1 Massachusetts Ave NW Suite 700   Washington DC 20001
    Ph: 202-408-5505 ■ Fx: 202-408-8072

Council on Chiropractic Education   www.cce-usa.org
    8049 N 85th Way   Scottsdale AZ 85258
    Ph: 480-443-8877 ■ Fx: 480-483-7333

Council on Chiropractic Physiological Therapeutics & Rehabilitation   www.ccptr.org
    312 Courtyard Dr   Hillsborough NJ 08844
    Ph: 908-722-9075 ■ Fx: 908-722-1144

Council for Christian Colleges & Universities   www.cccu.org
    321 8th St NE   Washington DC 20002
    Ph: 202-546-8713 ■ Fx: 202-546-8913

Council on Christian Unity   www.disciples.org/ccu
    130 E Washington St PO Box 1986   Indianapolis IN 46206
    Ph: 317-713-2585 ■ Fx: 317-713-2588

Council of Citizens With Low Vision   www.cclvi.org
    1155 15th St NW Suite 1004   Washington DC 20005
    Ph: 202-467-5081 ■ Fx: 202-467-5085 ■ TF: 800-424-8666

Council of Colleges of Acupuncture & Oriental Medicine   www.ccaom.org
    7501 Greenway Ctr Dr Suite 820   Greenbelt MD 20770
    Ph: 301-313-0868 ■ Fx: 301-313-0869

Council of Colleges of Arts & Sciences   www.ccas.net
    PO Box 873108   Tempe AZ 85287
    Ph: 480-727-6064 ■ Fx: 480-727-6078

Council on Competitiveness   www.compete.org
    1500 K St NW Suite 850   Washington DC 20005
    Ph: 202-682-4292 ■ Fx: 202-682-5150

Council on Compulsive Gambling of New Jersey Inc   www.800gambler.org
    3635 Quakerbridge Rd Suite 7   Hamilton NJ 08619
    Ph: 609-588-5515 ■ Fx: 609-588-5665 ■ TF: 800-426-2537

Council for Court Excellence   www.courtexcellence.org
    1717 K St NW Suite 510   Washington DC 20036
    Ph: 202-785-5917 ■ Fx: 202-785-5922

Council of Defense & Space Industry Associations   www.codsia.org
    1000 Wilson Blvd Suite 1800   Arlington VA 22209
    Ph: 703-243-2020 ■ Fx: 703-243-8539

Council of Development Finance Agencies   www.cdfa.net
    301 NW 63rd Ave Suite 500   Oklahoma City OK 73116
    Ph: 405-848-6059 ■ Fx: 405-842-3299

Council on Education of the Deaf   www.deafed.net
    Gallaudet Univ 800 Florida Ave NE FH 207   Washington DC
    20002
    Ph: 202-651-5525 ■ Fx: 202-651-5749

Council of Educational Facility Planners International   www.cefpi.com
    9180 E Desert Cove Dr Suite 104   Scottsdale AZ 85260
    Ph: 480-391-0840 ■ Fx: 480-391-0940

Council for Electronic Revenue Communication Advancement   www.cerca.org/
    600 Cameron St Suite 309   Alexandria VA 22314
    Ph: 703-340-1655

Council for Elementary Science International   unr.edu/homepage/crowther/cesi.html
    511 Marion Dr   Columbia MO 65203
    Ph: 573-874-1038

Council on Employee Benefits   www.ceb.org
    4910 Moorland Ln   Bethesda MD 20814
    Ph: 301-664-5940 ■ Fx: 301-664-5944

Council of Energy Resource Tribes   www.certredearth.com
    695 S Colorado Blvd Suite 10   Denver CO 80246
    Ph: 303-282-7576 ■ Fx: 303-282-7584

Council of Engineers & Scientists Organizations   www.cesounions.org/
    15205 52nd Ave S   Seattle WA 98188
    Ph: 206-433-0991

Council For Equal Rights in Adoption   www.adoptioncrossroads.org
    444 E 76th St   New York NY 10021
    Ph: 212-988-0110 ■ Fx: 212-988-0291

Council for Ethics in Economics   www.businessethics.org
    191 W Nationwide Blvd Suite 300B   Columbus OH 43215
    Ph: 614-221-8661 ■ Fx: 614-221-8707

Council for European Studies   www.europanet.org
    Columbia Univ 1203A International Affairs Bldg   MC 3310 420
    W 118th St   New York NY 10027
    Ph: 212-854-4172 ■ Fx: 212-854-8808

Council for Excellence in Government   www.excelgov.org
    1301 K St NW Suite 450 West   Washington DC 20005
    Ph: 202-728-0418 ■ Fx: 202-728-0422

Council for Exceptional Children   www.cec.sped.org
    1110 N Glebe Rd   Arlington VA 22201
    Ph: 703-620-3660 ■ Fx: 703-264-9494 ■ TF: 888-232-7733

Council of Families with Visual Impairment
    1155 15th St NW Suite 1004   Washington DC 20005
    Ph: 202-467-5081 ■ Fx: 202-467-5085 ■ TF: 800-424-8666

Council on Family Health   www.cfhinfo.org
    1155 Connecticut Ave Suite 1200-B   Washington DC 20036
    Ph: 202-331-7710 ■ Fx: 202-223-6835

Council of Fashion Designers of America   www.cfda.com
    1412 Broadway Suite 2006   New York NY 10018
    Ph: 212-302-1821 ■ Fx: 212-768-0515

Council of Fleet Specialists   www.cfshq.com
    315 Delaware St   Kansas City MO 64105
    Ph: 816-421-2600 ■ Fx: 816-421-7532

Council on Foreign Relations Inc   www.cfr.org
    Harold Pratt House 58 E 68th St   New York NY 10021
    Ph: 212-434-9400 ■ Fx: 212-434-9800

Council on Forest Engineering   www.cofe.org
    620 SW 4th St   Corvallis OR 97333
    Ph: 541-754-7558 ■ Fx: 541-754-7559

Council on Foundations   www.cof.org
    1828 L St NW Suite 300   Washington DC 20036
    Ph: 202-466-6512 ■ Fx: 202-785-3926

Council for Government Reform   www.govreform.org
    3124 N 10th St   Arlington VA 22201
    Ph: 703-243-7400 ■ Fx: 703-243-7403

Council on Governmental Ethics Laws   www.cogel.org
    PO Box 417   Locust Grove VA 22508
    Ph: 540-972-3662 ■ Fx: 540-972-3693

Council on Governmental Relations   www.cogr.edu
    1200 New York Ave NW Suite 320   Washington DC 20005
    Ph: 202-289-6655 ■ Fx: 202-289-6698

Council of Graduate Schools   www.cgsnet.org
    1 Dupont Cir NW Suite 430   Washington DC 20036
    Ph: 202-223-3791 ■ Fx: 202-331-7157

Council of the Great City Schools   www.cgcs.org
    1301 Pennsylvania Ave NW Suite 702   Washington DC 20004
    Ph: 202-393-2427 ■ Fx: 202-393-2400

Council of Growing Companies
    PO Box 10863   McLean VA 22102
    Ph: 703-893-5343 ■ Fx: 703-893-5222 ■ TF: 800-929-3165

Council on Hemispheric Affairs   www.coha.org
    1444 'I' St NW Suite 211   Washington DC 20005
    Ph: 202-216-9261 ■ Fx: 202-216-9193 ■ TF: 888-922-9261

Council for Higher Education Accreditation   www.chea.org
    1 Dupont Cir NW Suite 510   Washington DC 20036
    Ph: 202-955-6126 ■ Fx: 202-955-6129

Council of Hotel & Restaurant Trainers   www.chart.org
    PO Box 2835   Westfield NJ 07091
    Ph: 800-463-5918 ■ Fx: 800-427-5436

Council of Independent Colleges   www.cic.edu
    1 Dupont Cir NW Suite 320   Washington DC 20036
    Ph: 202-466-7230 ■ Fx: 202-466-7238

Council of Independent Restaurants of America   www.ciraonline.org
    304 W Liberty St Suite 201   Louisville KY 40202
    Ph: 502-583-3783 ■ Fx: 502-589-3602

Council for Indian Education   www.cie-mt.org
    1240 Burlington Ave   Billings MT 59102
    Ph: 406-652-7598 ■ Fx: 406-652-0536

Council of Industrial Boiler Owners   www.cibo.org
    6035 Burke Center Pkwy Suite 360   Burke VA 22015
    Ph: 703-250-9042 ■ Fx: 703-239-9042

Council of Infrastructure Financing Authorities   www.cifanet.org
    805 15th St NW Suite 500   Washington DC 20005
    Ph: 202-371-9694 ■ Fx: 202-371-6601

Council of Institutional Investors   www.cii.org
    1730 Rhode Island Ave NW Suite 512   Washington DC 20036
    Ph: 202-822-0800 ■ Fx: 202-822-0801

Council of Insurance Agents & Brokers   www.ciab.com
    701 Pennsylvania Ave NW Suite 750   Washington DC 20004
    Ph: 202-783-4400 ■ Fx: 202-783-4410

Council on International Educational Exchange   www.ciee.org
    3 Copley Pl 2nd Fl   Boston MA 02116
    Ph: 617-247-0350 ■ Fx: 617-247-2911 ■ TF: 888-268-6245

Council for International Exchange of Scholars   www.cies.org
    3007 Tilden St NW Suite 5L   Washington DC 20008
    Ph: 202-686-4000 ■ Fx: 202-362-3442

Council of International Investigators   www.cii2.org
    2150 N 107th St Suite 205   Seattle WA 98133
    Ph: 206-361-8869 ■ Fx: 206-367-8777 ■ TF: 888-759-8884

Council of International Programs USA   www.cipusa.org
    1700 E 13th St Suite 4ME   Cleveland OH 44114
    Ph: 216-566-1088 ■ Fx: 216-566-1490

Council for International Tax Education   www.fdta-cite.org
    PO Box 1012   White Plains NY 10602
    Ph: 914-328-5656 ■ Fx: 914-328-5757

Council of Ivy Group Presidents   www.ivyleaguesports.com
    228 Alexander St 1st Fl   Princeton NJ 08544
    Ph: 609-258-6426 ■ Fx: 609-258-1690

Council of Landscape Architectural Registration Boards   www.clarb.org
    144 Church St NW Suite 201   Vienna VA 22180
    Ph: 703-319-8380 ■ Fx: 703-319-8290

Council of Large Public Housing Authorities   www.clpha.org
    1250 'I' St NW Suite 901A   Washington DC 20005
    Ph: 202-638-1300 ■ Fx: 202-638-2364

Council on Law in Higher Education   www.clhe.org
    111 Coconut Key Ct   Palm Beach Gardens FL 33418
    Ph: 561-622-5765 ■ Fx: 561-624-9198

Council for Learning Disabilities   www.cldinternational.org
    PO Box 4014   Leesburg VA 20177
    Ph: 571-258-1010 ■ Fx: 571-258-1011

Council of Lebanese American Organizations   www.clao.com
    PO Box 181116   Cleveland OH 44118
    Ph: 216-932-9936

Council on Library & Information Resources   www.clir.org
    1775 Massachusetts Ave NW Suite 500   Washington DC 20036
    Ph: 202-939-4750 ■ Fx: 202-939-4765

Council on Library Media Technicians Inc   colt.ucr.edu
    Daniel Boone Regional Library 100 W Broadway   Columbia MO
    65203
    Ph: 573-443-3161 ■ Fx: 573-874-0862

Council on Licensure Enforcement & Regulation www.clearhq.org
403 Marquis Ave Suite 100   Lexington KY 40502
Ph: 859-269-1289 ▪ Fx: 859-231-1943

Council of Literary Magazines & Presses www.clmp.org
154 Christopher St Suite 3C   New York NY 10014
Ph: 212-741-9110 ▪ Fx: 212-741-9112

Council of Logistics Management www.clm1.org
2805 Butterfield Rd Suite 200   Oak Brook IL 60523
Ph: 630-574-0985 ▪ Fx: 630-574-0989

Council of Manufacturing Associations www.nam.org/ac
National Assn of Manufacturers 1331 Pennsylvania Ave
NW   Washington DC 20004
Ph: 202-637-3000 ▪ Fx: 202-637-3182

Council for Marketing & Opinion Research www.cmor.org
4147-U Crossgate Dr   Cincinnati OH 45236
Ph: 513-985-0001 ▪ Fx: 513-985-0119 ▪ TF: 800-887-2667

Council of Medical Specialty Societies www.cmss.org
51 Sherwood Terr Suite M   Lake Bluff IL 60044
Ph: 847-295-3456 ▪ Fx: 847-295-3759

Council for Museum Anthropology www.nmnh.si.edu/cma
c/o American Anthropological Assn 2200 Wilson Blvd Suite
600   Arlington VA 22201
Ph: 703-528-1902 ▪ Fx: 703-528-3546

Council for the National Interest www.cnionline.org
1250 4th St SW Suite WG-1   Washington DC 20024
Ph: 202-863-2951 ▪ Fx: 202-863-2952 ▪ TF: 800-296-6958

Council on National Literatures annehenrypaolucci.homestead.com/CNL1.html
68-02 Metropolitan Ave   Middle Village NY 11379
Ph: 718-821-3916

Council for Nutritional Anthropology www.aaanet.org/cna
c/o American Anthropological Assn 2200 Wilson Blvd Suite
600   Arlington VA 22201
Ph: 703-528-1902 ▪ Fx: 703-528-3546

Council on Occupational Education www.council.org
41 Perimeter Ctr East NE Suite 640   Atlanta GA 30346
Ph: 770-396-3898 ▪ Fx: 770-396-3790 ▪ TF: 800-917-2081

Council on Ocean Law
1600 H St NW 2nd Fl   Washington DC 20006
Ph: 202-347-3766

Council for Opportunity in Education www.trioprograms.org
1025 Vermont Ave NW Suite 900   Washington DC 20005
Ph: 202-347-7430 ▪ Fx: 202-347-0786

Council for a Parliament of the World's Religions www.cpwr.org
PO Box 1630   Chicago IL 60690
Ph: 312-629-2990 ▪ Fx: 312-629-2991

Council of Petroleum Accountants Societies www.copas.org
PO Box 1190   Denison TX 75021
Ph: 903-463-5463 ▪ Fx: 903-463-5473

Council of Professional Associations on Federal Statistics www.copafs.org
1429 Duke St Suite 402   Alexandria VA 22314
Ph: 703-836-0404 ▪ Fx: 703-684-3410

Council for Professional Recognition www.cdacouncil.org
2460 16th St NW   Washington DC 20009
Ph: 202-265-9090 ▪ Fx: 202-265-9161 ▪ TF: 800-424-4310

Council of Protocol Executives
101 W 12th St PH-H   New York NY 10011
Ph: 212-633-6934

Council of Public Relations Firms www.prfirms.org
27 Jefferson Plaza 2nd Fl   Princeton NJ 08540
Ph: 201-444-4457 ▪ Fx: 877-773-2937 ▪ TF: 877-773-4767

**Council on Quality & Leadership in Support for People
with Disabilities**   100 West Rd Suite 406   Towson MD 21204 www.thecouncil.org
Ph: 410-583-0060 ▪ Fx: 410-583-0063

Council of Real Estate Brokerage Managers www.crb.com
430 N Michigan Ave Suite 300   Chicago IL 60611
Ph: 312-321-4400 ▪ Fx: 312-329-8882 ▪ TF: 800-621-8738

Council for Research in Values & Philosophy www.crvp.org
PO Box 261 Cardinal Stn   Washington DC 20064
Ph: 202-319-6089

Council of Residential Specialists www.crs.com
430 N Michigan Ave Suite 300   Chicago IL 60611
Ph: 312-321-4400 ▪ Fx: 312-329-8882 ▪ TF: 800-462-8841

Council for Resource Development www.crdnet.org
1 Dupont Cir NW Suite 410   Washington DC 20036
Ph: 202-822-0750 ▪ Fx: 202-822-5014

Council for Responsible Genetics www.gene-watch.org
5 Upland Rd Suite 3   Cambridge MA 02140
Ph: 617-868-0870 ▪ Fx: 617-491-5344

Council for Responsible Nutrition www.crnusa.org
1875 'I' St NW Suite 400   Washington DC 20006
Ph: 202-872-1488 ▪ Fx: 202-872-9594

Council of Sailing Associations www.ussailing.org/csa
PO Box 1260   Portsmouth RI 02871
Ph: 401-683-0800 ▪ Fx: 401-683-0840

Council of Science Editors www.councilofscienceeditors.org
12100 Sunset Hills Rd Suite 130   Reston VA 20190
Ph: 703-437-4377 ▪ Fx: 703-435-4399

Council of Scientific Society Presidents cssp.us
1155 16th St NW   Washington DC 20036
Ph: 202-872-4452

Council of Scottish Clans & Associations Inc www.cosca.net
PO Box 2828   Moultrie GA 31776
Ph: 229-985-6540 ▪ Fx: 229-985-0936

Council for Secular Humanism www.secularhumanism.org
PO Box 664   Amherst NY 14226
Ph: 716-636-7571 ▪ Fx: 716-636-1733

Council on Size & Weight Discrimination www.cswd.org
PO Box 305   Mount Marion NY 12456
Ph: 845-679-1209 ▪ Fx: 845-679-1206

Council on Social Work Education www.cswe.org
1725 Duke St Suite 500   Alexandria VA 22314
Ph: 703-683-8080 ▪ Fx: 703-683-8099

Council of Societies for the Study of Religion www.cssr.org
Valparaiso Univ   Valparaiso IN 46383
Ph: 219-464-5515 ▪ Fx: 219-464-6714 ▪ TF: 888-422-2777

Council for Spiritual & Ethical Education www.csee.org
1465 Northside Dr Suite 220   Atlanta GA 30318
Ph: 404-355-4460 ▪ Fx: 404-355-4435 ▪ TF: 800-298-4599

Council on Standards for International Educational Travel www.csiet.org
212 S Henry St   Alexandria VA 22314
Ph: 703-739-9050 ▪ Fx: 703-739-9035

Council of State Administrators of Vocational Rehabilitation www.rehabnetwork.org
4733 Bethesda Ave Suite 330   Bethesda MD 20814
Ph: 301-654-8414 ▪ Fx: 301-654-5542

Council of State Association Presidents www.csap.org
800 Perry Hwy Suite 3   Pittsburgh PA 15229
Ph: 412-366-1177 ▪ Fx: 412-366-8804

Council of State Community Development Agencies www.coscda.org
1825 K St NW Suite 515   Washington DC 20006
Ph: 202-293-5820 ▪ Fx: 202-293-2820

Council of State Governments www.csg.org
2760 Research Park Dr PO Box 11910   Lexington KY 40578
Ph: 859-244-8000 ▪ Fx: 859-244-8001 ▪ TF: 800-800-1910

Council of State Science Supervisors csss.enc.org

Council on State Taxation www.statetax.org
122 C St NW Suite 330   Washington DC 20001
Ph: 202-484-5222 ▪ Fx: 202-484-5229

Council of State & Territorial Epidemiologists www.cste.org
2872 Woodcock Blvd Suite 303   Atlanta GA 30341
Ph: 770-458-3811 ▪ Fx: 770-458-8516

Council on Tall Buildings & Urban Habitat www.ctbuh.org
Illinois Institute of Technology SR Crown Hall 3360 S State
St   Chicago IL 60616
Ph: 312-909-0253

Council of Teachers of Southeast Asian Languages www.cotseal.org

Council on Technology Teacher Education teched.vt.edu/ctte
International Technology Education Assn 1914 Association
Dr   Reston VA 20191
Ph: 703-860-2100 ▪ Fx: 703-860-0353

Council for Textile Recycling www.smartasn.org
7910 Woodmont Ave Suite 1130   Bethesda MD 20814
Ph: 301-718-0671 ▪ Fx: 301-656-1079

Council on Undergraduate Research www.cur.org
734 15th St NW Suite 550   Washington DC 20005
Ph: 202-783-4810 ▪ Fx: 202-783-4811

Council on Union-Free Environment www.cueinc.com
825 W Bitters Rd Suite 103   San Antonio TX 78216
Ph: 866-409-4283 ▪ Fx: 210-545-4284

Council of Writers Organizations
12724 Sagamore Rd   Leawood KS 66209
Ph: 913-451-9023 ▪ Fx: 913-451-4866

Council of Writing Program Administrators www.wpacouncil.org

Counsel, American Association of Fund-Raising www.aafrc.org
10293 N Meridian St Suite 175   Indianapolis IN 46290
Ph: 317-816-1613 ▪ Fx: 317-816-1633 ▪ TF: 800-462-2372

Counsel, American College of Tax
1156 15th St NW Suite 900   Washington DC 20005
Ph: 202-637-3243 ▪ Fx: 202-393-0336

Counsel, American College of Trust & Estate www.actec.org
3415 S Sepulveda Blvd Suite 330   Los Angeles CA 90034
Ph: 310-398-1888 ▪ Fx: 310-572-7280

Counsel Association of America, Investment www.icaa.org
1050 17th St NW Suite 725   Washington DC 20036
Ph: 202-293-4222 ▪ Fx: 202-293-4223

Counsel, Association of Corporate www.acca.com
1025 Connecticut Ave NW Suite 200   Washington DC 20036
Ph: 202-293-4103 ▪ Fx: 202-293-4701

Counsel, Association of Direct Response Fundraising www.adrfco.org
1612 K St NW Suite 510   Washington DC 20006
Ph: 202-293-9640 ▪ Fx: 202-887-9699

Counsel for Children, National Association of www.naccchildlaw.org
1825 Marion St Suite 340   Denver CO 80218
Ph: 888-828-6222

Counsel Inc, Federation of Defense & Corporate www.thefederation.org
11812-A N 56th St   Tampa FL 33617
Ph: 813-983-0022 ▪ Fx: 813-988-5837

Counsel, National Association of Railroad Trial www.usnartc.org
881 Alma Real Dr Suite 218   Pacific Palisades CA 90272
Ph: 310-459-7659 ▪ Fx: 310-459-6603

(Counseling) Access Point www.accesspt.com
PO Box 6359   Los Osos CA 93412
Ph: 805-534-1101 ▪ Fx: 805-534-1718 ▪ TF: 800-549-1749

Counseling, American Board of Examiners in Pastoral
13014 N Dale Mabry Hwy Suite 363   Tampa FL 33618
Ph: 813-926-5446

Counseling, American Board of Genetic www.abgc.net
9650 Rockville Pike   Bethesda MD 20814
Ph: 301-571-1825 ▪ Fx: 301-634-7320

Counseling Association, American www.counseling.org
5999 Stevenson Ave   Alexandria VA 22304
Ph: 703-823-9800 ▪ Fx: 703-823-0252 ▪ TF: 800-347-6647

Counseling Association, American College www.collegecounseling.org
c/o American Counseling Assn 5999 Stevenson Ave   Alexandria
VA 22304
Ph: 703-823-9800 ▪ Fx: 703-823-0252 ▪ TF: 800-347-6647

Counseling Association, American Rehabilitation   www.nchrtm.okstate.edu/arca
c/o American Counseling Assn 5999 Stevenson Ave   Alexandria VA 22304
Ph: 703-823-9800 ▪ Fx: 703-823-0252 ▪ TF: 800-545-2223

Counseling, Association for Death Education &   www.adec.org
342 N Main St   West Hartford CT 06117
Ph: 860-586-7503 ▪ Fx: 860-586-7550

Counseling, Association for Gay Lesbian & Bisexual Issues in   www.aglbic.org
c/o American Counseling Assn 5999 Stevenson Ave   Alexandria VA 22304
Ph: 703-823-9800 ▪ Fx: 703-823-0252 ▪ TF: 800-347-6647

Counseling Association for Humanistic Education & Development
c/o American Counseling Assn 5999 Stevenson Ave   Alexandria VA 22304
Ph: 703-823-9800 ▪ Fx: 703-823-0252 ▪ TF: 800-347-6647

Counseling Association, National Employment   www.employmentcounseling.org
5999 Stevenson Ave   Alexandria VA 22304
Ph: 703-823-0252 ▪ Fx: 800-473-2329 ▪ TF: 800-347-6647

Counseling Association, National Rehabilitation   nrca-net.org
8807 Sudley Rd Suite 102   Manassas VA 20110
Ph: 703-361-2077 ▪ Fx: 703-361-2489

Counseling, Association for Spiritual Ethical & Religious Values in   www.aservic.org
c/o American Counseling Assn 5999 Stevenson Ave   Alexandria VA 22304
Ph: 703-823-9800 ▪ Fx: 703-823-0252 ▪ TF: 800-347-6647

Counseling Boards, American Association of State   www.aascb.org
3 Terrace Way Suite A   Greensboro NC 27403
Ph: 336-547-0914 ▪ Fx: 336-547-0017

Counseling & Development, Association for Multicultural
c/o American Counseling Assn 5999 Stevenson Ave   Alexandria VA 22304
Ph: 703-823-9800 ▪ Fx: 703-823-0252

Counseling & Education, Association for Assessment in   aac.ncat.edu
c/o American Counseling Assn 5999 Stevenson Ave   Alexandria VA 22304
Ph: 703-823-9800 ▪ Fx: 703-823-0252 ▪ TF: 800-347-6647

(Counseling) Love in Action   www.loveinaction.org
PO Box 171444   Memphis TN 38187
Ph: 901-751-8468 ▪ Fx: 901-751-1922

Counseling, National Association for College Admission   www.nacac.com
1631 Prince St   Alexandria VA 22314
Ph: 703-836-2222 ▪ Fx: 703-836-8015 ▪ TF: 800-822-6285

(Counseling) National Career Development Association   www.ncda.org
10820 E 45th St Suite 210   Tulsa OK 74146
Ph: 918-663-7060 ▪ Fx: 918-663-7058 ▪ TF: 866-367-6232

Counseling, National Foundation for Credit   www.nfcc.org
801 Roeder Rd Suite 900   Silver Spring MD 20910
Ph: 301-589-5600 ▪ Fx: 301-495-5623 ▪ TF: 800-388-2227

Counseling & Planning Education, Association for Financial   www.afcpe.org
2112 Arlington Ave Suite H   Upper Arlington OH 43221
Ph: 614-485-9650 ▪ Fx: 614-485-9621

Counseling Services, International Association of   www.iacsinc.org
101 S Whiting St Suite 211   Alexandria VA 22304
Ph: 703-823-9840 ▪ Fx: 703-823-9843

Counselor Association, American School   www.schoolcounselor.org
1101 King St Suite 625   Alexandria VA 22314
Ph: 703-683-2722 ▪ Fx: 703-683-1619 ▪ TF: 800-306-4722

Counselor Certification, Commission on Rehabilitation   www.crccertification.com
1835 Rohlwing Rd Suite E   Rolling Meadows IL 60008
Ph: 847-394-2104 ▪ Fx: 847-394-2172

Counselor Education & Supervision, Association for   www.acesonline.net
c/o American Counseling Assn 5999 Stevenson Ave   Alexandria VA 22304
Ph: 703-823-9800 ▪ Fx: 703-823-0252 ▪ TF: 800-347-6647

Counselors, American Association of Pastoral   www.aapc.org
9504-A Lee Hwy   Fairfax VA 22031
Ph: 703-385-6967 ▪ Fx: 703-352-7725

Counselors, American College of   www.angelfire.com/il/AmericanCollege
1124 1/2 S 5th St   Springfield IL 62703
Ph: 217-726-6220

Counselors Association, American Mental Health   www.amhca.org
801 N Fairfax St Suite 304   Alexandria VA 22314
Ph: 703-548-6002 ▪ Fx: 703-548-4775 ▪ TF: 800-326-2642

Counselors & Educators in Government, Association for
c/o American Counseling Assn 5999 Stevenson Ave   Alexandria VA 22304
Ph: 703-823-9800 ▪ Fx: 703-823-0252

Counselors, International Association of Addictions & Offender   www.counseling.org
5999 Stevenson Ave   Alexandria VA 22304
Ph: 800-347-6647 ▪ Fx: 800-473-2329

Counselors, International Association of Addictions & Offender
c/o American Counseling Assn 5999 Stevenson Ave   Alexandria VA 22304
Ph: 703-823-9800 ▪ Fx: 703-823-0252 ▪ TF: 800-347-6647

Counselors, International Association of Marriage & Family   www.iamfc.com
c/o American Counseling Assn 5999 Stevenson Ave   Alexandria VA 22304
Ph: 703-823-9800 ▪ Fx: 703-823-0252 ▪ TF: 800-545-2223

Counselors, National Association of   nac.lincoln-grad.org
c/o Lincoln Graduate Ctr 303 W Cypress St   San Antonio TX 78212
Ph: 210-271-0781 ▪ Fx: 210-225-8450

Counselors, National Association of Fraternal Insurance
PO Box 357   Sheboygan WI 53082
Ph: 920-458-1996 ▪ Fx: 920-457-4661

Counselors Inc, National Board for Certified   www.nbcc.org
3 Terrace Way Suite D   Greensboro NC 27403
Ph: 336-547-0607 ▪ Fx: 336-547-0017 ▪ TF: 800-398-5389

Counselors of Real Estate   www.cre.org
430 N Michigan Ave 2nd Fl   Chicago IL 60611
Ph: 312-329-8427 ▪ Fx: 312-329-8881

Counselors For Social Justice   www.counselorsforsocialjustice.org
c/o American Counseling Assn 5999 Stevenson Ave   Alexandria VA 22304
Ph: 703-823-9800 ▪ Fx: 703-823-0252 ▪ TF: 800-347-6647

Counselors & Therapists, International Association of   www.iact.org
10915 Bonita Beach Rd SE Suite 1101   Bonita Springs FL 34135
Ph: 941-498-9710 ▪ Fx: 941-498-1215

Counterfeiting Coalition, International Anti-   www.iacc.org
1725 K St NW Suite 1101   Washington DC 20006
Ph: 202-223-6667 ▪ Fx: 202-223-6668

Counterfeits Project, Spiritual   www.scp-inc.org
PO Box 4308   Berkeley CA 94704
Ph: 510-540-0300 ▪ Fx: 510-540-1107

Counterpart International Inc   www.counterpart.org
1200 18th St NW Suite 1100   Washington DC 20036
Ph: 202-296-9676 ▪ Fx: 202-296-9679

Countertrade Association, American   www.countertrade.org
818 Connecticut Ave NW 12th Fl   Washington DC 20006
Ph: 202-887-9011 ▪ Fx: 202-872-8324

Counties, National Association of   www.naco.org
440 1st St NW   Washington DC 20001
Ph: 202-393-6226 ▪ Fx: 202-393-2630

Country Dance & Song Society   www.cdss.org
132 Main St PO Box 338   Haydenville MA 01039
Ph: 413-268-7426 ▪ Fx: 413-268-7471

Country Music, Academy of   www.acmcountry.com
4100 W Alameda Ave Suite 208   Burbank CA 91505
Ph: 818-842-8400 ▪ Fx: 818-842-8535

Country Music Association   www.cmaworld.com
1 Music Cir S   Nashville TN 37203
Ph: 615-244-2840 ▪ Fx: 615-726-0314 ▪ TF: 800-998-4636

Country Music Association, National Traditional   www.oldtimemusic.bigstep.com/
PO Box 492   Anita IA 50020
Ph: 712-762-4363

Country Music Foundation Inc   www.ncma.org
222 5th Ave S   Nashville TN 37203
Ph: 615-416-2001 ▪ Fx: 615-255-2245

Country Music Showcase International   www.cmshowcase.org
PO Box 368   Carlisle IA 50047
Ph: 515-989-3748 ▪ Fx: 515-989-0235

Country Radio Broadcasters Inc   www.crb.org
819 18th Ave S   Nashville TN 37203
Ph: 615-327-4487 ▪ Fx: 615-329-4492

County Administrators, National Association of   www.countyadministrators.org
777 N Capitol St NE Suite 500   Washington DC 20002
Ph: 301-469-7460

County Aging Programs, National Association of   www.naco.org
440 1st St NW 8th Fl   Washington DC 20001
Ph: 202-942-4235 ▪ Fx: 202-393-2630

County Agricultural Agents, National Association of   www.nacaa.com
252 N Park St   Decatur IL 62523
Ph: 217-876-1220 ▪ Fx: 217-877-5382

County Association Executives, National Council of
440 1st St NW 8th Fl   Washington DC 20001
Ph: 202-942-4291 ▪ Fx: 202-942-4203

County Behavioral Health Directors, National Association of   www.nacbhd.org
440 1st St NW   Washington DC 20001
Ph: 202-661-8816

County Building Officials, Association of Major City/
505 Huntmar Park Dr Suite 210   Herndon VA 20170
Ph: 703-481-2038 ▪ Fx: 703-481-3596

County & City Health Officials, National Association of   www.naccho.org
1100 17th St 2nd Fl   Washington DC 20036
Ph: 202-783-5550 ▪ Fx: 202-783-1583

County Civil Attorneys, National Association of
c/o National Assn of Counties 440 1st St NW   Washington DC 20001
Ph: 202-393-6226

County Community & Economic Development, National Association for   www.nacced.org
2025 M St NW Suite 800   Washington DC 20036
Ph: 202-367-1149 ▪ Fx: 202-367-2149

County Engineers, National Association of   www.countyengineers.org
c/o National Assn of Counties 440 1st St NW   Washington DC 20001
Ph: 202-393-6226

County Executives of America   www.countyexecutives.org
1010 Massachusetts Ave NW Suite 100   Washington DC 20001
Ph: 202-289-4805 ▪ Fx: 202-289-4809 ▪ TF: 800-296-8438

County Information Technology Administrators, National Association of   c/o National Assn of Counties 440 1st St NW   Washington DC 20001
Ph: 202-393-6226

County Intergovernmental Relations Officials, National Association of   c/o National Assn of Counties 440 1st St NW   Washington DC 20001
Ph: 202-393-6226

County Management Association, International City/   www.icma.org
777 N Capitol St NE Suite 500   Washington DC 20002
Ph: 202-289-4262 ▪ Fx: 202-962-3500

County & Municipal Employees, American Federation of State   www.afscme.org
1625 L St NW   Washington DC 20036
Ph: 202-452-4800 ▪ Fx: 202-429-1293

County Officials, National Association of Black
440 1st St NW Suite 410   Washington DC 20001
Ph: 202-347-6953 ▪ Fx: 202-393-6596

County Park & Recreation Officials, National Association of   www.nacpro.org
c/o Harris County Public Infrastructure Dept 1001 Preston Ave 7th Fl   Houston TX 77002
Ph: 713-755-5583

County Planners, National Association of
c/o National Assn of Counties 440 1st St NW   Washington DC 20001
Ph: 202-393-6226

County Recorders Election Officials & Clerks, National Association of   www.nacrc.org
PO Box 3159   Durham NC 27715
Ph: 919-384-8446 ■ Fx: 919-383-0035

County Surveyors, National Association of   www.naco.org/nacs/index.html
c/o National Assn of Counties 440 1st St NW   Washington DC 20001
Ph: 202-393-6226 ■ Fx: 202-393-2630

County Treasurers & Finance Officers, National Association of   www.nactfo.org
c/o National Assn of Counties 440 1st St NW   Washington DC 20001
Ph: 202-393-6226

Couple to Couple League International   www.ccli.org
PO Box 111184   Cincinnati OH 45211
Ph: 513-471-2000 ■ Fx: 513-557-2449

Couples in Marriage Enrichment, Association for   www.bettermarriages.org
PO Box 10596   Winston-Salem NC 27108
Ph: 336-724-1526 ■ Fx: 336-721-4746 ■ TF: 800-634-8325

Coupon Professionals, Association of   www.couponpros.org
200 E Howard St Suite 280   Des Plaines IL 60018
Ph: 847-297-7773

Courage   couragerc.net
210 W 31st St   New York NY 10001
Ph: 212-268-1010 ■ Fx: 212-268-7150

Courier Association of the Americas, Messenger   www.mcaa.com
1156 15th St NW Suite 900   Washington DC 20005
Ph: 202-785-3298 ■ Fx: 202-223-9741

Court Administrators, Conference of State   cosca.ncsc.dni.us
National Ctr for State Courts 300 Newport Ave PO Box 8798   Williamsburg VA 23187
Ph: 757-259-1841 ■ Fx: 757-259-1520 ■ TF: 800-877-1233

Court Appointed Special Advocate Association, National   www.nationalcasa.org
100 W Harrison St North Tower Suite 500   Seattle WA 98119
Ph: 206-270-0072 ■ Fx: 206-270-0078 ■ TF: 800-628-3233

Court Clerks Association, Federal   www.fcca.ws

Court Clerks, National Conference of Appellate   ncacc.ncsconline.org
300 Newport Ave   Williamsburg VA 23185
Ph: 757-259-1841 ■ Fx: 757-259-1520

Court, Coalition for the International Criminal   www.iccnow.org
777 UN Plaza   New York NY 10017
Ph: 212-687-2176 ■ Fx: 212-599-1332

Court Excellence, Council for   www.courtexcellence.org
1717 K St NW Suite 510   Washington DC 20036
Ph: 202-785-5917 ■ Fx: 202-785-5922

Court Judges, National Conference of Specialized   www.abanet.org/jd/ncscj
541 N Fairbanks Ct MS 13.2   Chicago IL 60611
Ph: 312-988-5705 ■ Fx: 312-988-5709

Court Management, National Association for   www.nacmnet.org
National Ctr for State Courts 300 Newport Ave   Williamsburg VA 23185
Ph: 757-259-1841 ■ Fx: 757-259-1520

Court Reporters Association, National   www.ncraonline.org
8224 Old Courthouse Rd   Vienna VA 22182
Ph: 703-556-6272 ■ Fx: 703-556-6291 ■ TF: 800-272-6272

Court Reporters Association, US   www.uscra.org
PO Box 465   Chicago IL 60690
Ph: 800-628-2730

Courts, Association of Family & Conciliation   www.afccnet.org
6515 Grand Teton Plaza Suite 210   Madison WI 53719
Ph: 608-664-3750 ■ Fx: 608-664-3751

Courts, Fund for Modern   www.moderncourts.org
351 W 54th St   New York NY 10019
Ph: 212-541-6741 ■ Fx: 212-541-7301

Courts, National Center for State   www.ncsconline.org
300 Newport Ave   Williamsburg VA 23185
Ph: 757-253-2000 ■ Fx: 757-564-2022 ■ TF: 800-616-6164

Cousteau Society   www.cousteausociety.org
710 Settlers Landing Rd   Hampton VA 23669
Ph: 757-722-9300 ■ Fx: 757-722-8185 ■ TF: 800-441-4395

COVA/CVAG Inc   www.covacvag.org
PO Box 2136   West Paterson NJ 07424
Ph: 973-881-8838 ■ Fx: 973-279-3779

Covenant House   www.covenanthouse.org
346 W 17th St   New York NY 10011
Ph: 212-727-4000 ■ Fx: 212-727-6516 ■ TF: 800-999-9999

Cover Society, Western   www.westerncoversociety.org

Covered Bridges, National Society for the Preservation of   www.vermontbridges.com/nspcb1st.htm
44 Cleveland Ave   Worcester MA 01603
Ph: 508-756-4516

Coverlet Guild of America, Colonial
5617 Blackstone   La Grange IL 60525
Ph: 708-352-3812

Cowboy Culture Association, American   www.cowboy.org
4124 62nd Dr   Lubbock TX 79413
Ph: 806-795-2455 ■ Fx: 806-795-4749

Cowboys Association, Professional Rodeo   www.prorodeo.com
101 Pro Rodeo Dr   Colorado Springs CO 80919
Ph: 719-593-8840 ■ Fx: 719-548-4876

CPA Associates International Inc   www.cpaai.com
301 Rt 17 N 7th Fl   Rutherford NJ 07070
Ph: 201-804-8686 ■ Fx: 201-804-9222

CPA Auto Dealer Consultants Association   www.autodealercpas.com
1 Valmont Plaza 4th Fl   Omaha NE 68154
Ph: 402-964-3865 ■ Fx: 402-964-3811 ■ TF: 888-475-4476

CPA Health Care Advisors Association, National   www.hcaa.com
1 Valmont Plaza 4th Fl   Omaha NE 68154
Ph: 402-964-3865 ■ Fx: 402-964-3811 ■ TF: 888-475-4476

CPA Manufacturing Services Association   www.manufacturingcpas.com
1 Valmont Plaza 4th Fl   Omaha NE 68154
Ph: 402-964-3865 ■ Fx: 402-964-3811 ■ TF: 888-475-4476

CPA Practitioners, National Conference of   www.nccpap.org
50 Jericho Tpke Suite 106   Jericho NY 11753
Ph: 516-333-8282 ■ Fx: 516-333-4099 ■ TF: 888-488-5400

CPAmerica International   www.afai.com
11801 Research Dr   Alachua FL 32615
Ph: 386-418-4001 ■ Fx: 386-418-4002

CPAs/Consultants Association, Construction Industry   www.cicpac.com
111 E Wacker Dr Suite 990   Chicago IL 60601
Ph: 800-869-0491 ■ Fx: 312-729-9800

CPCU & Insurance Institute of America, American Institute for   www.aicpcu.org
720 Providence Rd PO Box 3016   Malvern PA 19355
Ph: 610-644-2100 ■ Fx: 610-640-9576 ■ TF: 800-644-2101

CPCU Society   www.cpcusociety.org
720 Providence Rd Kahler Hall PO Box 3009   Malvern PA 19355
Ph: 800-932-2728 ■ Fx: 610-251-2780

Crab Industry Association, National Blue   www.nfi.org
1901 N Fort Myer Dr Suite 700   Arlington VA 22209
Ph: 703-524-8883 ■ Fx: 703-524-4619

Cracker Manufacturers Association, Biscuit &   www.thebcma.org
8484 Georgia Ave Suite 700   Silver Spring MD 20910
Ph: 301-608-1552 ■ Fx: 301-608-1557

Craft Association, National   www.craftassoc.com
2012 Ridge Rd E Suite 120   Rochester NY 14622
Ph: 585-266-5472 ■ Fx: 585-785-3231 ■ TF: 800-715-9594

Craft Council, American   www.craftcouncil.org
72 Spring St   New York NY 10012
Ph: 212-274-0630 ■ Fx: 212-274-0650 ■ TF: 800-724-0859

Craft Designers, Society of   www.craftdesigners.org
PO Box 3388   Zanesville OH 43702
Ph: 740-452-4541 ■ Fx: 740-454-2552

Craft Retailers Association for Tomorrow   www.craftonline.org
1900 Arch St   Philadelphia PA 19103
Ph: 215-563-3484 ■ Fx: 215-564-2175

Craft Yarn Council of America   www.craftyarncouncil.com
PO Box 9   Gastonia NC 28053
Ph: 704-824-7838

Crafted with Pride in USA Council   www.craftedwithpride.org
PO Box 65326   Washington DC 20032
Ph: 202-775-0658 ■ Fx: 202-775-0311

Crafts Association, Indian Arts &   www.iaca.com
4010 Carlisle Blvd NE Suite C   Albuquerque NM 87107
Ph: 505-265-9149 ■ Fx: 505-265-8251

Crafts & Creative Industries, Association of   www.accicrafts.org
1100-H Brandywine Blvd PO Box 3388   Zanesville OH 43702
Ph: 740-452-4541 ■ Fx: 740-452-2552

Crafts & Theatre Safety, Arts   www.caseweb.com/ACTS
181 Thompson St Suite 23   New York NY 10012
Ph: 212-777-0062 ■ Fx: 212-673-4403

Craftsman Association, Autobody   www.acanw.com
1124 Industry Dr   Tukwila WA 98188
Ph: 206-575-8893 ■ Fx: 206-575-8894 ■ TF: 800-526-3792

Craftsmen Inc, Elder   www.eldercraftsmen.org
610 Lexington Ave   New York NY 10022
Ph: 212-319-8128 ■ Fx: 212-319-8141

Craftsmen, International Society of Folk Harpers &   www.folkharpsociety.org
4110 Brandemere Way   Houston TX 77066
Ph: 832-249-7885

Cranberry Growers Association, American
PO Box 423   Tabernacle NJ 08088
Ph: 609-726-1330

Cranberry Institute   www.cranberryinstitute.org/
3203-B Cranberry Hwy   East Wareham MA 02538
Ph: 508-759-6855 ■ Fx: 508-759-6294 ■ TF: 800-295-4132

Crane Foundation, International   www.savingcranes.org
PO Box 447   Baraboo WI 53913
Ph: 608-356-9462 ■ Fx: 608-356-9465

Crane Manufacturers Association of America   www.mhia.org/psc
8720 Red Oak Blvd Suite 201   Charlotte NC 28217
Ph: 704-676-1190 ■ Fx: 704-676-1199 ■ TF: 800-345-1815

Crane Working Group, North American   www.nacwg.org
341 W Olympic Pl   Seattle WA 98119
Ph: 206-286-8607

Cranial Academy   www.cranialacademy.com
8202 Clearvista Pkwy Suite 9D   Indianapolis IN 46256
Ph: 317-594-0411 ■ Fx: 317-594-9299

Cranio-Mandibular Orthopedics, International College of   tmj-iccmo.org
619 N 35th St Suite 307   Seattle WA 98103
Ph: 206-633-4355 ■ Fx: 206-633-4352 ■ TF: 800-446-1763

Craniofacial Association, American Cleft Palate-   www.cleftpalate-craniofacial.org
104 S Estes Dr Suite 204   Chapel Hill NC 27514
Ph: 919-933-9044 ■ Fx: 919-933-9604 ■ TF: 800-242-5338

Craniofacial Association, Children's   www.ccakids.com
13140 Coit Rd Suite 307   Dallas TX 75240
Ph: 214-570-9099 ■ Fx: 214-570-8811 ■ TF: 800-535-3643

Craniofacial Association, Faces: National   www.faces-cranio.org
PO Box 11082   Chattanooga TN 37401
Ph: 423-266-1632 ■ Fx: 423-267-3124 ■ TF: 800-332-2373

(Craniofacial) Forward Face   www.forwardface.org
317 E 34th St Suite 901A   New York NY 10016
Ph: 212-684-5860 ■ Fx: 212-684-5864

Craniofacial Pain, American Academy of   www.aacfp.org
516 W Pipeline Rd   Hurst TX 76053
Ph: 817-282-1501 ■ Fx: 817-282-8012 ■ TF: 800-322-8651

CranioSacral Therapy Association, American   www.acsta.org
11201 Prosperity Farms Rd Suite D-325   Palm Beach Gardens FL 33410
Ph: 561-622-4334 ■ Fx: 561-622-4771 ■ TF: 800-233-5880

Crazy Horse Memorial Foundation www.crazyhorse.org
Ave of the Chiefs   Crazy Horse SD 57730
Ph: 605-673-4681 ▪ Fx: 605-673-2185

Cream Draft Horse Association, American www.americancreamdraft.org
193 Crossover Rd   Bennington VT 05201
Ph: 802-447-7612 ▪ Fx: 802-447-0711

Creation Research, Institute for www.icr.org
10946 N Woodside Ave   Santee CA 92071
Ph: 619-448-0900 ▪ Fx: 619-448-3469

Creative Anachronism, Society for www.sca.org
PO Box 360789   Milpitas CA 95036
Ph: 408-263-9305 ▪ Fx: 408-263-0641

Creative Coalition www.thecreativecoalition.org
665 Broadway Suite 804   New York NY 10012
Ph: 212-614-2121 ▪ Fx: 212-614-2142

Creative Dance, International Association for www.dancecreative.org
103 Princeton Ave   Providence RI 02907
Ph: 401-521-0546

Creative Education Foundation Inc www.creativeeducationfoundation.org
289 Bay Rd   Hadley MA 01035
Ph: 413-559-6614 ▪ Fx: 413-559-6615 ▪ TF: 800-447-2774

Creative Grandparenting Inc www.creativegrandparenting.org
100 W 10th St Suite 1007   Wilmington DE 19801
Ph: 302-656-2122 ▪ Fx: 302-656-2123

Creative Materials Institute Inc, Art & www.acminet.org
PO Box 479   Hanson MA 02341
Ph: 781-293-4100 ▪ Fx: 781-294-0808

Creative Music Foundation Inc www.creativemusicstudio.org
PO Box 671   Woodstock NY 12498
Ph: 845-679-8847

Creative Musicians, Association for the www.aacmchicago.org/aacmgoals.html
Advancement of   PO Box 5757   Chicago IL 60680
Ph: 312-752-2212 ▪ Fx: 312-752-2226

Creative Musicians Coalition www.aimcmc.com
1024 W Wilcox Ave   Peoria IL 61604
Ph: 309-685-4843 ▪ Fx: 309-685-4878 ▪ TF: 800-882-4262

Creative Response to Conflict Inc www.ccrcglobal.org
521 N Broadway Box 271   Nyack NY 10960
Ph: 845-353-1796 ▪ Fx: 845-358-4924

Creativity Association, American www.amcreativityassoc.org
PO Box 5856   Philadelphia PA 19128
Ph: 888-837-1409

Credential Evaluation Services, National Association of www.naces.org
c/o International Education Research Foundation PO Box
3665   Culver City CA 90231
Ph: 310-258-9451 ▪ Fx: 310-342-7086

Credentialing Agency for Laboratory Personnel Inc, National www.nca-info.org
PO Box 15945-289   Lenexa KS 66285
Ph: 913-438-5110 ▪ Fx: 913-599-5340

Credentials Board, Art Therapy www.atcb.org
3 Terrace Way Suite B   Greensboro NC 27403
Ph: 877-213-2822 ▪ Fx: 336-547-0017

(Credit) ACCION International www.accion.org
56 Roland St Suite 300   Boston MA 02129
Ph: 617-625-7080 ▪ Fx: 617-625-7020

Credit Administrators, National Association of Consumer www.naccaonline.org
PO Box 20871   Columbus OH 43220
Ph: 614-326-1165 ▪ Fx: 614-326-1162

Credit Analysis Society Inc, Capital Markets www.cmcas.org
151 Herricks Rd Suite 1   Garden City Park NY 11040
Ph: 516-739-2510 ▪ Fx: 516-739-3803 ▪ TF: 800-284-6228

Credit Association, Business Products www.bpca.org
119 Hill Ave   Ballwin MO 63011
Ph: 636-394-7777 ▪ Fx: 636-394-7099

Credit Association, National Chemical www.ncca1.org
1100 Main St   Buffalo NY 14209
Ph: 716-878-2894 ▪ Fx: 716-878-2866

Credit & Collection Professionals, ACA International - www.acainternational.org
Association of   PO Box 390106   Minneapolis MN 55439
Ph: 952-926-6547 ▪ Fx: 952-926-1624

Credit Council, Farm www.fccouncil.com
50 F St NW Suite 900   Washington DC 20001
Ph: 202-626-8710 ▪ Fx: 202-626-8718

Credit Counseling, National Foundation for www.nfcc.org
801 Roeder Rd Suite 900   Silver Spring MD 20910
Ph: 301-589-5600 ▪ Fx: 301-495-5623 ▪ TF: 800-388-2227

Credit Executives Association, Advertising Media www.amcea.org
8840 Columbia 100 Pkwy   Columbia MD 21045
Ph: 410-992-7609 ▪ Fx: 410-740-5574

Credit Insurance Association, Consumer www.cciaonline.com
542 S Dearborn St Suite 400   Chicago IL 60605
Ph: 312-939-2242 ▪ Fx: 312-939-8007

Credit Insurance Association, Foreign www.fcia.com
40 Rector St 11th Fl   New York NY 10006
Ph: 212-885-1500 ▪ Fx: 212-885-1535

Credit & International Business, FCIB: Association of Executives www.fcibglobal.com
in Finance   8840 Columbia 100 Pkwy   Columbia MD 21045
Ph: 410-423-1840 ▪ Fx: 410-423-1845 ▪ TF: 888-256-3242

(Credit) Katalysis Partnership www.katalysis.org
1331 N Commerce St   Stockton CA 95202
Ph: 209-943-6165 ▪ Fx: 209-947-7046

Credit Management, National Association of www.nacm.org
8840 Columbia 100 Pkwy   Columbia MD 21045
Ph: 410-740-5560 ▪ Fx: 410-740-5574 ▪ TF: 800-955-8815

Credit Professionals International www.creditprofessionals.org
525B N Laclede Stn Rd   Saint Louis MO 63119
Ph: 314-961-0031 ▪ Fx: 314-961-0040

Credit Reporting Association, National www.ncrainc.org
125 E Lake St Suite 200   Bloomingdale IL 60108
Ph: 630-539-1525 ▪ Fx: 630-539-1526

Credit Research Foundation www.crfonline.org
8840 Columbia 100 Pkwy   Columbia MD 21045
Ph: 410-740-5499 ▪ Fx: 410-740-5574

Credit Union Association, Information Technologies www.itcua.org
PO Box 160   Del Mar CA 92014
Ph: 858-792-3883 ▪ Fx: 858-792-3884

Credit Union Chairmen, National Association of www.nacuc.org
PO Box 160   Del Mar CA 92014
Ph: 858-792-3883 ▪ Fx: 858-792-3884 ▪ TF: 888-987-4247

Credit Union Council, Defense www.dcuc.org
601 Pennsylvania Ave W Suite 600   Washington DC 20004
Ph: 202-638-3930 ▪ Fx: 202-638-3410 ▪ TF: 800-356-9655

Credit Union Council, Education www.ecuc.org
PO Box 7558   Spanish Fort AL 36577
Ph: 251-626-3399 ▪ Fx: 251-626-3565

Credit Union Executives Society www.cues.org
5510 Research Park Dr   Madison WI 53711
Ph: 608-271-2664 ▪ Fx: 608-271-2303 ▪ TF: 800-252-2664

Credit Union Internal Auditors, Association of www.acuia.org
PO Box 1926   Columbus OH 43216
Ph: 614-221-9702 ▪ Fx: 614-221-2335 ▪ TF: 866-254-8128

Credit Union Leagues, American Association of www.cuna.org/league
601 Pennsylvania Ave NW South Bldg   Suite 600   Washington
DC 20004
Ph: 202-638-5777 ▪ Fx: 202-638-7729

Credit Union Legislative Action Council of CUNA
601 Pennsylvania Ave NW South Bldg   Suite 600   Washington
DC 20004
Ph: 202-638-5777 ▪ Fx: 202-638-7734

Credit Union Management Association, National
4989 Rebel Trail NW   Atlanta GA 30327
Ph: 404-255-6828 ▪ Fx: 404-851-1752

Credit Union Mortgage Association, American www.acuma.org
3419 Via Lido PMB 135   Newport Beach CA 92663
Ph: 949-645-5288 ▪ Fx: 949-645-5297

Credit Union National Association www.cuna.org
5710 Mineral Point Rd   Madison WI 53705
Ph: 608-231-4000 ▪ Fx: 608-231-4858 ▪ TF: 800-356-9655

Credit Union Services Organizations, National Association of www.nacuso.org
3419 Via Lido PMB 135   Newport Beach CA 92663
Ph: 949-645-5296 ▪ Fx: 949-645-5297 ▪ TF: 888-462-2870

Credit Union Supervisors, National Association of State www.nascus.org
1655 N Fort Myer Dr Suite 300   Arlington VA 22209
Ph: 703-528-8351 ▪ Fx: 703-528-3248

Credit Union Supervisory & Auditing Committees, National www.nacusac.org
Association of   PO Box 160   Del Mar CA 92014
Ph: 858-792-3883 ▪ Fx: 858-792-3884 ▪ TF: 800-287-5949

Credit Unions, National Association of Federal www.nafcunet.org
3138 10th St N   Arlington VA 22201
Ph: 703-522-4770 ▪ Fx: 703-524-1082 ▪ TF: 800-336-4644

Credit Unions, National Council of Postal www.ncpcu.org
PO Box 160   Del Mar CA 92014
Ph: 858-792-3883 ▪ Fx: 858-792-3884

Credit Unions, National Federation of Community Development www.natfed.org
120 Wall St 10th Fl   New York NY 10005
Ph: 212-809-1850 ▪ Fx: 212-809-3274 ▪ TF: 800-437-8711

Credit Unions Inc, World Council of www.woccu.org
5710 Minerial Point Rd   Madison WI 53705
Ph: 608-231-7130 ▪ Fx: 608-238-8020 ▪ TF: 800-356-2644

Cremation Association of North America www.cremationassociation.org
401 N Michigan Ave Suite 2100   Chicago IL 60611
Ph: 312-644-6610 ▪ Fx: 312-245-6869

Creme Horse Registry, American White www.whitehorseranchnebraska.com/registry.htm
Horse & American   90000 Edwards Rd   Naper NE 68755
Ph: 402-832-5560

Creutzfeldt-Jakob Disease Foundation Inc www.cjdfoundation.org
PO Box 5312   Akron OH 44334
Ph: 330-665-5590 ▪ Fx: 330-668-2474 ▪ TF: 800-659-1991

CREW Network www.crewnetwork.org
1201 Wakarusa Dr Suite C3   Lawrence KS 66049
Ph: 785-832-1808 ▪ Fx: 785-832-1551

Crime Bureau, National Insurance www.nicb.org
10330 S Roberts Rd   Palos Hills IL 60465
Ph: 708-430-2430 ▪ Fx: 708-430-5025 ▪ TF: 800-447-6282

Crime Commissions, National Association of Citizens www.crimecom.org/naccc
125 N Market Suite 115   Wichita KS 67202
Ph: 316-267-1235

Crime & Delinquency, National Council on www.nccd-crc.org
1970 Broadway Suite 500   Oakland CA 94612
Ph: 510-208-0500 ▪ Fx: 510-208-0511

Crime, International Association for the Study of Organized www.iasoc.net
c/o National Institute of Justice 810 7th St NW   Washington
DC 20531
Ph: 202-616-1960 ▪ Fx: 202-307-6256

Crime Investigation Association International, High Technology www.htcia.org
1474 Freeman Dr   Amissville VA 20106
Ph: 540-937-5019 ▪ Fx: 540-937-7848

Crime Laboratory Directors, American Society of www.ascld.org
PO Box 2710   Largo FL 33779
Ph: 727-549-6067 ▪ Fx: 727-549-6070

Crime, National Center for Victims of www.ncvc.org
2000 M St NW Suite 480   Washington DC 20036
Ph: 202-467-8700 ▪ Fx: 202-467-8701 ▪ TF: 800-394-2255

Crime Prevention Council, National www.ncpc.org
1000 Connecticut Ave NW 13th Fl   Washington DC 20036
Ph: 202-466-6272 ▪ Fx: 202-296-1356

Crime Prevention Institute, Aviation www.acpi.org
226 N Nova Rd   Ormond Beach FL 32174
Ph: 800-969-5473 ▪ Fx: 386-615-3378

Crime Stoppers International   www.c-s-i.org
PO Box 614 Arlington TX 76004
Ph: 817-446-6253 ▪ TF: 800-245-0009

Crime Victim Compensation Boards, National Association of   www.nacvcb.org
PO Box 16003 Alexandria VA 22302
Ph: 703-313-9500

(Crime Victims) Klaas Kids Foundation   www.klaaskids.org
PO Box 925 Sausalito CA 94966
Ph: 415-331-6867 ▪ Fx: 415-331-5633

Crime Watch of America, Youth   www.ycwa.org
9200 S Dadeland Blvd Suite 417 Miami FL 33156
Ph: 305-670-2409 ▪ Fx: 305-670-3805

Crimes Investigators, International Association of Financial   www.iafci.org
873 Embarcadero Dr Suite 5 El Dorado Hills CA 95762
Ph: 916-939-5000 ▪ Fx: 916-939-0395

Criminal Court, Coalition for the International   www.iccnow.org
777 UN Plaza New York NY 10017
Ph: 212-687-2176 ▪ Fx: 212-599-1332

Criminal Defense Lawyers, National Association of   www.nacdl.org
1150 18th St NW Suite 950 Washington DC 20036
Ph: 202-872-8600 ▪ Fx: 202-872-8690

Criminal Justice Association, American   www.acjalae.org
PO Box 601047 Sacramento CA 95860
Ph: 916-484-6553 ▪ Fx: 916-488-2227

Criminal Justice Association, National   www.ncja.org
720 7th St NW 3rd Fl Washington DC 20001
Ph: 202-628-8550 ▪ Fx: 202-628-0080

Criminal Justice Legal Foundation   www.cjlf.org
PO Box 1199 Sacramento CA 95812
Ph: 916-446-0345 ▪ Fx: 916-446-1194

Criminal Justice, National Association of Blacks in   www.nabcj.org
North Carolina Central Univ PO Box 19788 Durham NC 27707
Ph: 919-683-1801 ▪ Fx: 919-683-1903

(Criminal Justice) National Center on Institutions & Alternatives   www.ncianet.org
7222 Ambassador Rd Baltimore MD 21244
Ph: 410-265-1490

(Criminal Justice) Osborne Association   www.osborneny.org
36-31 38th St Long Island City NY 11101
Ph: 718-707-2600 ▪ Fx: 718-707-3103

Criminal Justice Policy Foundation   www.cjpf.org
8730 Georgia Ave Suite 400 Silver Spring MD 20910
Ph: 301-589-6020 ▪ Fx: 301-589-5056

Criminal Justice Sciences, Academy of   www.acjs.org
7319 Hanover Pkwy Suite C Greenbelt MD 20770
Ph: 301-446-6300 ▪ Fx: 301-446-2819 ▪ TF: 800-757-2257

Criminal Justice Section, ABA   www.abanet.org/crimjust
740 15th St NW 10th Fl Washington DC 20005
Ph: 202-662-1500 ▪ Fx: 202-662-1501

Criminal Psychology, Society for Police &   cep.jmu.edu/spcp/
Southwest Texas State Univ Dept of Criminal Justice San Marcos TX 78666
Ph: 512-530-8211

Criminalistics, American Board of   criminalistics.com
PO Box 1123 Wausau WI 54402
Ph: 715-845-3684 ▪ Fx: 715-845-4156

Criminology, American Society of   www.asc41.com
1314 Kinnear Rd Suite 212 Columbus OH 43212
Ph: 614-292-9207 ▪ Fx: 614-292-6767

Crisis Line, American Domestic Violence   www.awoscentral.com
3300 NW 185th Ave Suite 133 Portland OR 97229
Ph: 503-846-8748 ▪ Fx: 503-907-6554 ▪ TF: 866-879-6636

CRISTA Ministries   www.crista.org
19303 Fremont Ave N Seattle WA 98133
Ph: 206-546-7200 ▪ Fx: 206-546-7484 ▪ TF: 800-442-4003

Cristina Foundation, National   www.cristina.org
500 W Putnam Ave Greenwich CT 06830
Ph: 203-863-9100 ▪ Fx: 203-863-9230

Critical Care Medicine, Society of   www.sccm.org
701 Lee St Suite 200 Des Plaines IL 60016
Ph: 847-827-6869 ▪ Fx: 847-827-6886

Critical-Care Nurses, American Association of   www.aacn.org
101 Columbia Aliso Viejo CA 92656
Ph: 949-362-2000 ▪ Fx: 949-362-2020 ▪ TF: 800-809-2273

Critical Care Society, International Trauma Anesthesia &   www.itaccs.org
PO Box 4826 Baltimore MD 21211
Ph: 410-235-7697 ▪ Fx: 410-235-8084

Critical Thinking, Association for Informal Logic &   ailact.mcmaster.ca

Critical Thinking, Center for   www.criticalthinking.org
PO Box 220 Dillon Beach CA 94929
Ph: 707-878-9100 ▪ Fx: 707-878-9111 ▪ TF: 800-833-3645

Critics Association, American Theatre   www.americantheatrecritics.org
c/o THEatre SERVICE PO Box 15282 Evansville IN 47716
Ph: 812-474-0549 ▪ Fx: 812-476-4168

Critics, Association of Literary Scholars &   www.bu.edu/literary
Boston Univ 650 Beacon St Suite 510 Boston MA 02215
Ph: 617-358-1990 ▪ Fx: 617-358-1995

Critics Association of North America, Music   www.mcana.org
722 Dulaney Valley Rd Suite 259 Baltimore MD 21204
Ph: 410-435-3881

Critics Circle, National Book   www.bookcritics.org

Critics Circle, Outer
101 W 57th St New York NY 10019
Ph: 212-765-8557 ▪ Fx: 212-765-7979

Croatian Catholic Union of the US   www.ccu-usa.org
1 E Old Ridge Rd PO Box 602 Hobart IN 46342
Ph: 219-942-1191 ▪ Fx: 219-942-8808

Croatian Fraternal Union of America   www.croatianfraternalunion.org
100 Delaney Dr Pittsburgh PA 15235
Ph: 412-351-3909 ▪ Fx: 412-823-1594

Croatian Fraternal Union of America Junior   www.croatianfraternalunion.org/jrfed.html
Cultural Federation 100 Delaney Dr Pittsburgh PA 15235
Ph: 412-351-3909 ▪ Fx: 412-823-1594

Croatian Philatelic Society   www.croatianstamps.com
PO Box 696 Fritch TX 79036
Ph: 806-857-0129

Crockett Club, Boone &   www.boone-crockett.org
250 Station Dr Missoula MT 59801
Ph: 406-542-1888 ▪ Fx: 406-542-0784 ▪ TF: 888-840-4868

Crohn's & Colitis Foundation of America   www.ccfa.org
386 Park Ave S 17th Fl New York NY 10016
Ph: 212-685-3440 ▪ Fx: 212-779-4098 ▪ TF: 800-932-2423

Crop Consultants, National Association of Independent   www.naicc.org
349 E Nolley Dr Collierville TN 38017
Ph: 901-861-0511 ▪ Fx: 901-861-0512

Crop Improvement Association, Organic   www.ocia.org
6400 Cornhusker Hwy Suite 125 Lincoln NE 68507
Ph: 402-477-2323 ▪ Fx: 402-477-4325

Crop Insurance Research Bureau   www.cropinsurance.org
9200 Indian Creek Pkwy Suite 220 Overland Park KS 66210
Ph: 913-338-0470 ▪ Fx: 913-661-1640

Crop Insurance Services, National   www.ag-risk.org
7201 W 129th St Suite 200 Overland Park KS 66213
Ph: 913-685-2767 ▪ Fx: 913-685-3080 ▪ TF: 800-951-6247

Crop Insurers, American Association of   users.erols.com/aaci
1 Massachusetts Ave NW Suite 800 Washington DC 20001
Ph: 202-789-4100 ▪ Fx: 202-408-7763

Crop Science Society of America   www.crops.org
677 S Segoe Rd Madison WI 53711
Ph: 608-273-8080 ▪ Fx: 608-273-2021

CropLife America   www.croplifeamerica.org
1156 15th St NW Suite 400 Washington DC 20005
Ph: 202-296-1585 ▪ Fx: 202-463-0474

Croquet Association, US   www.croquetamerica.com
700 Florida Mango Rd West Palm Beach FL 33406
Ph: 561-478-0760 ▪ Fx: 561-686-5507

Croquet Foundation of America   www.croquetamerica.com
700 Florida Mango Rd West Palm Beach FL 33406
Ph: 561-478-0760 ▪ Fx: 561-686-5507

Crosier Missions   www.crosier.org
3510 Vivian Ave Shoreview MN 55126
Ph: 651-486-7456 ▪ Fx: 651-287-1130 ▪ TF: 800-407-5875

Cross Country Coaches Association, US   www.usccca.org
Michigan State Univ Jenison Fieldhouse East Lansing MI 48824
Ph: 517-355-1640 ▪ Fx: 517-432-3339

Cross Country Ski Areas Association   www.xcski.org
259 Bolton Rd Winchester NH 03470
Ph: 603-239-4341 ▪ Fx: 603-239-6387 ▪ TF: 877-779-2754

Cross Country Skiers, American   www.xcskiworld.com
PO Box 604 Bend OR 97709
Ph: 541-317-0217

Cross-Cultural Dance Resources   www.ccdr.org
518 S Agassiz St Flagstaff AZ 86001
Ph: 520-774-8108

Cross-Cultural Research, Society for   www.sccr.org
Western Connecticut State Univ 233 N Quaker Ln West Hartford CT 06119
Ph: 203-837-8678

Cross-Cultural Shamanism Network
PO Box 270 Williams OR 97544
Ph: 541-846-1313 ▪ Fx: 541-846-1204

Crossbowmen of the US Inc, National   www.usarchery.org/divisions/crossbow/xbow.htm
3731 SW 144th Ave Miramar FL 33027
Ph: 954-704-0770 ▪ Fx: 954-704-9566

Crossing Contractors Association, Directional   www.dcca.org
13355 Noel Rd Suite 1940 Dallas TX 75240
Ph: 972-386-9545 ▪ Fx: 972-386-9547

Crowding the Rim   www.crowdingtherim.com
345 Middlefield Rd MS 973 Menlo Park CA 94025
Ph: 650-329-5430 ▪ Fx: 650-329-4936

Crown Victoria Association   clubs.hemmings.com/crownvictoria
PO Box 6 Bryan OH 43506
Ph: 419-636-2475 ▪ Fx: 419-636-8449

Cruise Liner Society, World Ocean &   www.oceancruisenews.com
PO Box 4850 Stamford CT 06907
Ph: 203-329-2787

Cruise Lines International Association   www.cruising.org
500 Fifth Ave Suite 1407 New York NY 10110
Ph: 212-921-0066 ▪ Fx: 212-921-0549

Cruise Lines, International Council of   www.iccl.org
2111 Wilson Blvd 8th Fl Arlington VA 22201
Ph: 703-522-8463 ▪ Fx: 703-522-3811 ▪ TF: 800-595-9338

Cruise Oriented Agencies, National Association of   www.nacoaonline.com
7600 Red Rd Suite 128 Miami FL 33143
Ph: 305-663-5626 ▪ Fx: 305-663-5625

Cruising Association, Seven Seas   www.ssca.org
1525 S Andrews Ave Suite 217 Fort Lauderdale FL 33316
Ph: 954-463-2431 ▪ Fx: 954-463-7183

Crusade for Christ International, Campus   www.ccci.org
100 Lake Hart Dr Orlando FL 32832
Ph: 407-826-2000 ▪ Fx: 407-826-2749 ▪ TF: 877-924-7478

Crustacean Society   www.vims.edu/tcs
PO Box 1897 Lawrence KS 66044
Ph: 785-843-1221 ▪ Fx: 785-843-1274

Cryogenic Society of America   www.cryogenicsociety.org
1033 South Blvd Suite 13 Oak Park IL 60302
Ph: 708-383-6220 ▪ Fx: 708-383-9337

(Cryonics) Alcor Life Extension Foundation   www.alcor.org
7895 E Acoma Dr Suite 110 Scottsdale AZ 85260
Ph: 480-905-1906 ▪ Fx: 480-922-9027 ▪ TF: 877-462-5267

Cryonics Society Inc, American   www.americancryonics.org
PO Box 1509   Cupertino CA 95015
Ph: 650-254-2001 ▪ Fx: 650-254-0128 ▪ TF: 800-523-2001
Cryosurgeons, Society of Urologic
1950 Old Tustin Ave   Santa Ana CA 92705
Ph: 714-550-9155 ▪ Fx: 714-550-9234
Cryptozoology, International Society of
PO Box 43070   Tucson AZ 85733
Ph: 520-884-8369
Crystal Growth, American Association for   www.crystalgrowth.org
25 4th St   Somerville NJ 08876
Ph: 908-575-0649 ▪ Fx: 908-575-0794
Crystallographic Association, American   www.hwi.buffalo.edu/aca
PO Box 96 Ellicott Stn   Buffalo NY 14205
Ph: 716-856-9600 ▪ Fx: 716-852-4846
CSA Fraternal Life   www.csafraternallife.org
122 W 22nd St   Oak Brook IL 60523
Ph: 630-472-0500 ▪ Fx: 630-472-1100 ▪ TF: 800-543-3272
(Cuba) Alpha-66   www.alpha66.org
1714 W Flagler St   Miami FL 33135
Ph: 305-541-5433 ▪ Fx: 305-541-2252
(Cuba) Venceremos Brigade   www.venceremosbrigade.org
PO Box 5202   Englewood NJ 07631
Ph: 212-560-4360
Cuban American National Council   www.cnc.org
1223 SW 4th St   Miami FL 33135
Ph: 305-642-3484 ▪ Fx: 305-642-9122
Cuban American National Foundation   www.canfnet.org
1312 SW 27th Ave Suite 301   Miami FL 33145
Ph: 305-642-2220 ▪ Fx: 305-592-7889
Cuban American Women of the USA, National Association of
308 38th St   Union City NJ 07087
Ph: 201-864-4879
Cuban Engineers, Association of   www.a-i-c.org
PO Box 557575   Miami FL 33255
Ph: 305-597-9858
Cuban Studies, Center for   www.cubaupdate.org
124 W 23rd St   New York NY 10011
Ph: 212-242-0559 ▪ Fx: 212-242-1937
Cuddle Inc, Project   www.projectcuddle.org
2973 Harbor Blvd Suite 326   Costa Mesa CA 92626
Ph: 714-432-9681 ▪ Fx: 714-433-6815 ▪ TF: 888-628-3353
Cued Speech Association, National   www.cuedspeech.org
23970 Hermitage Rd   Cleveland OH 44122
Ph: 216-292-6213 ▪ TF: 800-459-3529
Culinaire Philanthropique, Societe   www.societeculinaire.com
305 E 47th St Suite 11B   New York NY 10017
Ph: 212-308-0628 ▪ Fx: 212-308-0588
Culinarians Alliance, Black   www.blackculinarians.com
55 W 116th St Suite 234   New York NY 10026
Ph: 646-548-2949 ▪ Fx: 212-283-7157
Culinary Federation Inc, American   www.acfchefs.org
10 San Bartola Dr   Saint Augustine FL 32086
Ph: 904-824-4468 ▪ Fx: 904-825-4758 ▪ TF: 800-624-9458
Culinary Federation Chef & Child Foundation, American   www.acfchefs.org/ccf/ccf.html
10 San Bartola Dr   Saint Augustine FL 32086
Ph: 904-824-4468 ▪ Fx: 904-825-4758 ▪ TF: 800-624-9458
Culinary Professionals, International Association of   www.iacp.com
304 W Liberty St Suite 201   Louisville KY 40202
Ph: 502-581-9786 ▪ Fx: 502-589-3602
Cult Awareness Network   www.cultawarenessnetwork.org
1680 N Vine St Suite 415   Los Angeles CA 90028
Ph: 323-468-0567 ▪ Fx: 323-468-0568 ▪ TF: 800-556-3055
Cultural Affairs, Institute of   www.ica-usa.org
215 NE 40th St Suite C-2   Seattle WA 98105
Ph: 206-323-2100 ▪ Fx: 206-547-4057
Cultural Anthropology, Society for   www.aaanet.org/sca
c/o American Anthropological Assn 2200 Wilson Blvd Suite
600   Arlington VA 22201
Ph: 703-528-1902 ▪ Fx: 703-528-3546
Cultural Arts in Progress!   www.capsart.org
1 S Delaware Ave   Yardley PA 19067
Ph: 215-369-0677
Cultural Association, India American
1281 Cooper Lake Rd SE   Smyrna GA 30082
Ph: 770-436-3719
Cultural Association, Pacific Islanders'   www.pica-org.org
1016 Lincoln Blvd Suite 5   San Francisco CA 94131
Ph: 415-281-0221
Cultural Economics International, Association for   www.acei.neu.edu
Northeastern Univ Dept of Economics 301 Lake Hall   Boston
MA 02115
Ph: 617-373-2839 ▪ Fx: 617-373-3640
Cultural Environments, SPACES - Saving & Preserving Arts &
1804 N Van Ness Blvd   Los Angeles CA 90028
Ph: 323-463-1629
Cultural Exchange, Alliance for International Educational &   www.alliance-exchange.org
1776 Massachusetts Ave NW Suite 620   Washington DC 20036
Ph: 202-293-6141 ▪ Fx: 202-293-6144
(Cultural Exchange) US Servas Inc   www.usservas.org
11 John St Rm 505   New York NY 10038
Ph: 212-267-0252 ▪ Fx: 212-267-0292
Cultural Institute, Brazilian-American   www.bacidc.org
4719 Wisconsin Ave NW   Washington DC 20016
Ph: 202-362-8334 ▪ Fx: 202-362-8337
Cultural Integration Fellowship   www.culturalintegration.org
360 Cumberland St   San Francisco CA 94114
Ph: 415-626-2442
Cultural Preservation Council, Ethnic
6500 S Pulaski Rd   Chicago IL 60629
Ph: 773-582-5143 ▪ Fx: 773-582-5133

Cultural Resources Association, American   www.acra-crm.org
6150 E Ponce de Leon Ave   Stone Mountain GA 30083
Ph: 770-498-5159 ▪ Fx: 770-498-3809
Cultural Services & Educational Aid, Society for French American   www.facsea.org
972 5th Ave   New York NY 10021
Ph: 212-439-1439 ▪ Fx: 212-439-1455 ▪ TF: 800-937-3624
Cultural Survival Inc   www.cs.org
215 Prospect St   Cambridge MA 02139
Ph: 617-441-5400 ▪ Fx: 617-441-5417
Cultural Trade Association, Japanese-American
PO Box 4804   Panorama City CA 91412
Ph: 818-780-0815 ▪ Fx: 818-780-8501
Culture & Animals Foundation   www.cultureandanimals.org
3509 Eden Croft Dr   Raleigh NC 27612
Ph: 919-782-3739 ▪ Fx: 919-782-6464
Culture, Center for Arts &   www.culturalpolicy.org
819 7th St NW Suite 505   Washington DC 20001
Ph: 202-783-5277 ▪ Fx: 202-783-4498
Cultures, Institute for the Study of American   www.isacnet.org
233 12th St Suite 500 PO Box 2707   Columbus GA 31902
Ph: 706-243-6218 ▪ Fx: 706-322-7747
Curators International, Independent   www.ici-exhibitions.org
799 Broadway Suite 205   New York NY 10003
Ph: 212-254-8200 ▪ Fx: 212-477-4781
Curling Association, US   www.usacurl.org
PO Box 866   Stevens Point WI 54481
Ph: 715-344-1199 ▪ Fx: 715-344-2279 ▪ TF: 888-287-5377
Curling Association, US Women's   www.uswca.org
916 9th St S   Virginia MN 55792
Ph: 218-741-0253
Curriculum Development, Association for Supervision &   www.ascd.org
1703 N Beauregard St   Alexandria VA 22311
Ph: 703-578-9600 ▪ Fx: 703-575-5400 ▪ TF: 800-933-2723
Curriculum & Instruction, World Council for   www.alliant.edu/gsoe/wcci
Alliant International Univ Cross Cultural Studies Institute School
of Education 10455 Pomerado Rd   San Diego CA 92131
Ph: 858-635-4719 ▪ Fx: 858-635-4714
Curriculum Project Inc, Asian American   www.AsianAmericanBooks.com
83 W 37th Ave   San Mateo CA 94403
Ph: 650-357-1088 ▪ Fx: 650-357-6908 ▪ TF: 800-874-2242
Cursillo Movement, National   www.natl-cursillo.org
PO Box 210226   Dallas TX 75211
Ph: 214-339-6321 ▪ Fx: 214-339-6322
CUSA - An Apostolate of the Chronically Sick & Disabled   www.cusan.org
176 W 8th St   Bayonne NJ 07002
Ph: 201-437-0412
Cushing's Support & Research Foundation   www.csrf.net
65 E India Row Suite 22-B   Boston MA 02110
Ph: 617-723-3674
Cushion Council, Carpet   www.carpetcushion.org
PO Box 546   Riverside CT 06878
Ph: 203-637-1312 ▪ Fx: 203-698-1022
Cushman Club of America   cushmanclubofamerica.com
PO Box 661   Union Springs AL 36089
Ph: 334-738-3874
Cushman Foundation   cushforams.niu.edu
Smithsonian Institution Dept of Paleobiology
MRC-121   Washington DC 20560
Ph: 202-357-1390 ▪ Fx: 202-786-2832
Custer Battlefield Historical & Museum Association   www.cbhma.org
PO Box 902   Hardin MT 59034
Ph: 406-665-2060 ▪ Fx: 406-665-3133
Custody Association, Joint   www.jointcustody.org
10606 Wilkins Ave   Los Angeles CA 90024
Ph: 310-475-5352 ▪ Fx: 310-475-6541
Custom Electronic Design & Installation Association   www.cedia.net
7150 Winton Dr Suite 300   Indianapolis IN 46268
Ph: 317-328-4336 ▪ Fx: 317-280-8527 ▪ TF: 800-669-5329
Custom Roll Forming Institute   www.metalforming.com/division/crfid
Precision Metal Forming Assn 6363 Oak Tree Blvd   Cleveland
OH 44131
Ph: 216-901-8800 ▪ Fx: 216-901-9190
Custom Tailors & Designers Association of America   www.ctda.com
PO Box 53052   Washington DC 20009
Ph: 202-387-7220 ▪ Fx: 202-387-7713
Customer Service Association, International   www.icsa.com
401 N Michigan Ave   Chicago IL 60611
Ph: 312-321-6800 ▪ Fx: 312-245-1084 ▪ TF: 800-360-4272
(Customer Service) SOCAP International   www.socap.org
675 N Washington St Suite 200   Alexandria VA 22314
Ph: 703-519-3700 ▪ Fx: 703-549-4886
Customs Brokers & Forwarders Association of America Inc, National   www.ncbfaa.org
1200 18th St NW Suite 901   Washington DC 20036
Ph: 202-466-0222 ▪ Fx: 202-466-0226
Customs & International Trade Bar Association   www.citba.org
729 15th St NW Suite 800   Washington DC 20005
Ph: 202-783-6900 ▪ Fx: 202-783-6909
Cut Flower Growers, Association of Specialty   www.ascfg.org
PO Box 268   Oberlin OH 44074
Ph: 440-774-2887 ▪ Fx: 440-774-2435
Cutting Horse Association, National   www.nchacutting.com
260 Bailey Ave   Fort Worth TX 76107
Ph: 817-244-6188 ▪ Fx: 817-244-2015
Cutting Tool Institute, US   www.uscti.org
1300 Sumner Ave   Cleveland OH 44115
Ph: 216-241-7333 ▪ Fx: 216-241-0105
Cycad Society   www.cycad.org
1109 Grand Bois Rd   Breaux Bridge LA 70517
Ph: 337-845-4153

Cycling Association, Adventure   www.adventurecycling.org
150 E Pine St PO Box 8308   Missoula MT 59802
Ph: 406-721-1776 ▪ Fx: 406-721-8754 ▪ TF: 800-755-2453

Cycling Association Inc, Ultra Marathon   www.ultracycling.com
PO Box 18028   Boulder CO 80308
Ph: 303-545-9566 ▪ Fx: 303-545-9619

Cycling Association, US Deaf   home.earthlink.net/~skedsmo/usdca.htm

Cycling Club USA, International Christian   www.ironclad.org
PO Box 411757   Aurora CO 80044
Ph: 720-870-3707

Cycling Inc, USA   www.usacycling.org
1 Olympic Plaza   Colorado Springs CO 80909
Ph: 719-866-4581 ▪ Fx: 719-866-4628

(Cycling) Wheelmen   www.thewheelmen.org
14 Mulford Ln   Montclair NJ 07042
Ph: 973-509-2523 ▪ Fx: 973-509-2562

Cypress Manufacturers Association, Southern   www.cypressinfo.org
400 Penn Center Blvd Suite 530   Pittsburgh PA 15235
Ph: 412-829-0770 ▪ Fx: 412-829-0844 ▪ TF: 877-607-7262

Cystic Fibrosis Foundation   www.cff.org
6931 Arlington Rd Suite 200   Bethesda MD 20814
Ph: 301-951-4422 ▪ Fx: 301-951-6378 ▪ TF: 800-344-4823

**Cytochemistry, International Federation of Societies for
Histochemistry &**   Univ of Washington Dept of Biological   www.ifshc.org
     Structure PO Box 357420   Seattle WA 98195
Ph: 206-616-5894 ▪ Fx: 206-616-5842

Cytokine Society, International   www.weizmann.ac.il/cytokine
119 Davis Rd Suite 5A   Augusta GA 30907
Ph: 706-722-7511 ▪ Fx: 706-228-4678

Cytology, International Society for Analytical   www.isac-net.org
60 Revere Dr Suite 500   Northbrook IL 60062
Ph: 847-205-4722 ▪ Fx: 847-480-9282

Cytopathology, American Society of   www.cytopathology.org
400 W 9th St Suite 201   Wilmington DE 19801
Ph: 302-429-8802 ▪ Fx: 302-429-8807

Cytotechnology, American Society for   www.asct.com
1500 Sunday Dr Suite 102   Raleigh NC 27607
Ph: 919-787-5181 ▪ Fx: 919-787-4916 ▪ TF: 800-948-3947

Czech, International Association of Teachers of   www.language.brown.edu/NAATC/

Czechoslovak Genealogical Society International   www.cgsi.org
PO Box 16225   Saint Paul MN 55116
Ph: 952-922-1280

Czechoslovak Society of Arts & Sciences   www.svu2000.org
5529 Whitley Park Terr   Bethesda MD 20814
Ph: 301-564-9081 ▪ Fx: 301-564-9069

D

Dachshund Club of America Inc   www.dachshund-dca.org
1793 Berme Rd   Kerhonkson NY 12446
Ph: 845-626-4137

Dads & Daughters   www.dadsanddaughters.org
34 E Superior St Suite 200   Duluth MN 55802
Ph: 888-824-3237 ▪ Fx: 218-728-0314

Daedalians, Order of   www.daedalians.org
PO Box 249   Randolph AFB TX 78148
Ph: 210-945-2111 ▪ Fx: 210-945-2112

Daffodil Society, American   www.daffodilusa.org
4126 Winfield Rd   Columbus OH 43220
Ph: 614-451-4747 ▪ Fx: 614-451-2177

Daguerreian Society   www.daguerre.org
3045 W Liberty Ave Suite 9   Pittsburgh PA 15216
Ph: 412-343-5525 ▪ Fx: 412-563-5972

Dairies, Quality Chekd   www.qchekd.com
1733 Park St   Naperville IL 60563
Ph: 630-717-1110 ▪ Fx: 630-717-1126

Dairy Association Inc, All Star   www.allstardairy.com
PO Box 911050   Lexington KY 40591
Ph: 859-255-3644 ▪ Fx: 859-255-3647 ▪ TF: 800-930-3644

Dairy Cattle Association, Red & White   www.redandwhitecattle.com
3085 S Valley Rd   Crystal Spring PA 15536
Ph: 814-735-4221 ▪ Fx: 814-735-3473

Dairy Council, National   www.nationaldairycouncil.org
10255 W Higgins Rd Suite 900   Rosemont IL 60018
Ph: 847-803-2000 ▪ Fx: 847-803-2077

Dairy-Deli-Bakery Association, International   www.iddanet.org
313 Price Pl Suite 202   Madison WI 53705
Ph: 608-238-7908 ▪ Fx: 608-238-6330

Dairy Export Council, US   www.usdec.org
2101 Wilson Blvd Suite 400   Arlington VA 22201
Ph: 703-528-3049 ▪ Fx: 703-528-3705

Dairy Farmers PAC
10220 N Ambassador Dr Northpointe Tower   Kansas City MO
     64153
Ph: 816-801-6455 ▪ Fx: 816-801-6592

Dairy Federation, US National Committee to the International   www.usnac.org
PO Box 930398   Verona WI 53593
Ph: 608-848-6455 ▪ Fx: 608-848-7675

Dairy Foods Association, International   www.idfa.org
1250 H St NW Suite 900   Washington DC 20005
Ph: 202-737-4332 ▪ Fx: 202-331-7820

Dairy Goat Association, American   www.adga.org
209 W Main St PO Box 865   Spindale NC 28160
Ph: 828-286-3801 ▪ Fx: 828-287-0476

Dairy Herd Improvement Association Inc, National   www.dhia.org
3021 E Dublin Granville Rd Suite 102   Columbus OH 43231
Ph: 614-890-3630 ▪ Fx: 614-890-3667

Dairy Management Inc   www.dairyinfo.com
10255 W Higgins Rd Suite 900   Rosemont IL 60018
Ph: 847-803-2000 ▪ Fx: 847-803-2077

Dairy Products Association, Wisconsin
8383 Greenway Blvd   Middleton WI 53562
Ph: 608-836-3336 ▪ Fx: 608-836-3334

Dairy Products Institute, American   www.americandairyproducts.com
116 N York St Suite 200   Elmhurst IL 60126
Ph: 630-530-8700 ▪ Fx: 630-530-8707

Dairy Science Association, American   www.adsa.org
1111 N Dunlap Ave   Savoy IL 61874
Ph: 217-356-3182 ▪ Fx: 217-398-4119

Dairy Shrine, National   dairyshrine.org
1224 Alton Darby Creek Rd   Columbus OH 43228
Ph: 614-878-5333 ▪ Fx: 614-870-2622

Dalmatian Club of America   www.thedca.org
2316 McCrary Rd   Richmond TX 77469
Ph: 281-342-8407

Dam Safety Officials, Association of State   www.damsafety.org
450 Old Vine   Lexington KY 40507
Ph: 859-257-5140 ▪ Fx: 859-323-1958

DAMA - Data Management Association International   www.dama.org
PO Box 5786   Bellevue WA 98006
Ph: 425-562-2636 ▪ Fx: 425-562-0376

Damage Appraisers Association, Independent Automotive   www.iada.org
PO Box 12291   Columbus GA 31917
Ph: 800-369-4232 ▪ Fx: 888-423-2669

Damage Control Association, National Animal   nadca.unl.edu
PO Box 2180   Ardmore OK 73402
Ph: 580-223-5810

Damien Ministries   www.damienministries.org
PO Box 10202   Washington DC 20018
Ph: 202-526-3020 ▪ Fx: 202-526-9770

Dams, US Society on   www.ussdams.org
1616 17th St Suite 483   Denver CO 80202
Ph: 303-628-5430 ▪ Fx: 303-628-5431

Dance Alliance, International   www.idanews.com
1120 Broderick St   San Francisco CA 94115
Ph: 415-922-0560 ▪ Fx: 415-922-0588

**Dance, American Alliance for Health Physical Education
Recreation &**   1900 Association Dr   Reston VA 20191   www.aahperd.org
Ph: 703-476-3400 ▪ Fx: 703-476-9527 ▪ TF: 800-213-7193

(Dance) Art Resources in Collaboration Inc   www.eyeondance.org/about
123 W 18th St 7th Fl   New York NY 10011
Ph: 212-206-6492

Dance Association, National   www.aahperd.org/nda
1900 Association Dr   Reston VA 20191
Ph: 703-476-3421 ▪ Fx: 703-476-9527 ▪ TF: 800-213-7193

Dance, Congress on Research in   www.cordance.org
SUNY College at Brockport Dept of Dance 350 New Campus
     Dr   Brockport NY 14420
Ph: 716-395-2590 ▪ Fx: 716-395-5413

Dance Education Association, National   www.ndea.org
4948 St Elmo Ave Suite 301   Bethesda MD 20814
Ph: 301-657-2880 ▪ Fx: 301-657-2882

Dance Educators of America   www.deadance.com
PO Box 607   Pelham NY 10803
Ph: 914-636-3200 ▪ Fx: 914-636-5895 ▪ TF: 800-229-3868

Dance Festival Association, American College   www.fsu.edu/~acdfa
1570 E Jefferson St   Rockville MD 20852
Ph: 301-770-4443 ▪ Fx: 301-468-5841

Dance Films Association   www.dancefilmsassn.org
48 W 21st St Suite 907   New York NY 10010
Ph: 212-727-0764

Dance, Foundation for Pacific   home.att.net/~pacificdance
PO Box 621435   Littleton CO 80162
Ph: 303-933-2157

Dance Guild, American   www.americandanceguild.org
PO Box 2006 Lenox Hill Stn   New York NY 10021
Ph: 212-932-2789

Dance Guild, Sacred   www.sacreddanceguild.org
305 Townsend Ave   New Haven CT 06512
Ph: 203-469-4277

Dance History Scholars Inc, Society of   www.sdhs.org
3416 Primm Ln   Birmingham AL 35216
Ph: 205-978-1404 ▪ Fx: 205-823-2760

Dance Institute, National   www.nationaldance.org/
594 Broadway Rm 805   New York NY 10012
Ph: 212-226-0083 ▪ Fx: 212-226-0761 ▪ TF: 877-634-4255

Dance, International Association for Creative   www.dancecreative.org
103 Princeton Ave   Providence RI 02907
Ph: 401-521-0546

**Dance, International Council for Health Physical Education
Recreation Sport &**   1900 Association Dr   Reston VA 20191   www.ichpersd.org
Ph: 703-476-3462 ▪ Fx: 703-476-9527 ▪ TF: 800-213-7193

(Dance) Lloyd Shaw Foundation   www.lloydshaw.org
1620 Los Alamos SW   Albuquerque NM 87104
Ph: 505-247-3921

Dance Masters of America   dma-national.org
214-10 41st Ave   Bayside NY 11361
Ph: 718-225-4013 ▪ Fx: 718-225-4293 ▪ TF: 866-564-6362

Dance Merchants of America, United   www.udma.org
1609 Tabor Ct   Lafayette IN 47909
Ph: 765-471-0442 ▪ Fx: 765-477-5840 ▪ TF: 800-304-8362

Dance & Music, African Heritage Center for African
4018 Minnesota Ave NE   Washington DC 20019
Ph: 202-399-5252

Dance, National Association of Schools of   nasd.arts-accredit.org
11250 Roger Bacon Dr Suite 21   Reston VA 20190
Ph: 703-437-0700 ▪ Fx: 703-437-6312

Dance Notation Bureau   dancenotation.org/DNB
151 W 30th St Rm 202   New York NY 10001
Ph: 212-564-0985 ▪ Fx: 212-904-1426

Dance Resources, Cross-Cultural   www.ccdr.org
518 S Agassiz St   Flagstaff AZ 86001
Ph: 520-774-8108

Dance & Song Society, Country   www.cdss.org
132 Main St PO Box 338   Haydenville MA 01039
Ph: 413-268-7426 ▪ Fx: 413-268-7471

Dance Teachers Association, Professional   www.dancecaravan.com/PDTA/PDTA.html
PO Box 38   Waldwick NJ 07463
Ph: 201-652-7767 ▪ Fx: 201-652-2599 ▪ TF: 800-462-8679

Dance Teachers, International Association of Round   www.roundalab.org
355 N Orchard St Suite 200   Boise ID 83706
Ph: 208-377-1232 ▪ Fx: 208-377-1236 ▪ TF: 800-346-7522

Dance Theater Workshop   www.dtw.org
219 W 19th St   New York NY 10011
Ph: 212-691-6500 ▪ Fx: 212-633-1974

Dance Therapy Association, American   www.adta.org
10632 Little Patuxent Pkwy Suite 108   Columbia MD 21044
Ph: 410-997-4040 ▪ Fx: 410-997-4048

Dance/USA   www.danceusa.org
1156 15th St NW Suite 820   Washington DC 20005
Ph: 202-833-1717 ▪ Fx: 202-833-2686

Dancers Association, US Amateur Ballroom   www.usabda.org
PO Box 128   New Freedom PA 17349
Ph: 717-235-6656 ▪ Fx: 717-235-4183 ▪ TF: 800-447-9047

Dancers, Career Transition for   www.careertransition.org
165 W 64th St Suite 701   New York NY 10036
Ph: 212-764-0172 ▪ Fx: 212-764-0343

Dangerous Goods Advisory Council   www.dgac.org
1101 Vermont Ave NW Suite 301   Washington DC 20005
Ph: 202-289-4550 ▪ Fx: 202-289-4074 ▪ TF: 800-634-1598

Danish-American Chamber of Commerce   www.daccny.com
885 2nd Ave 18th Fl   New York NY 10017
Ph: 212-980-6240 ▪ Fx: 212-754-1904

Danish American Heritage Society   www.dana.edu/dahs
4105 Stone Brooke Rd   Ames IA 50010
Ph: 515-232-7479

Danish Engineers, American Society of
PO Box 606   Larchmont NY 10538
Ph: 914-834-0287 ▪ Fx: 914-834-0513

Danish Sisterhood of America   www.danishsisterhood.org
1000 Elysian Ave   Penngrove CA 94951
Ph: 707-794-8630 ▪ Fx: 707-794-8429

Danny Foundation   www.dannyfoundation.org
1415 Danville Blvd Suite 202   Alamo CA 94507
Ph: 925-833-2669 ▪ Fx: 925-314-8133 ▪ TF: 800-833-2669

Dante Society of America   www.dantesociety.org

Dao-Confucianism, Center for   www.wam.umd.edu/~tkang
1318 Randolph St NE   Washington DC 20017
Ph: 202-526-6818

D'Aquitaine Association, American Blonde   www.blondecattle.org
PO Box 470661   Tulsa OK 74147
Ph: 918-610-0842

DARE America   www.dare.com
PO Box 512090   Los Angeles CA 90051
Ph: 310-215-0575 ▪ Fx: 310-215-0180 ▪ TF: 800-223-3273

Dark-Fried Tobacco Growers Association, Eastern
1109 S Main St PO Box 517   Springfield TN 37172
Ph: 615-384-4543 ▪ Fx: 615-384-4545

Dark-Sky Association, International   www.darksky.org
3225 N 1st Ave   Tucson AZ 85719
Ph: 520-293-3198 ▪ Fx: 520-293-3192

Darling JN 'Ding' Foundation   www.ding-darling.org
785 Crandon Blvd Suite 1206   Key Biscayne FL 33149
Ph: 305-361-9788 ▪ Fx: 305-361-9789

Dart Association, National   www.ndadarts.com
5613 W 74th St   Indianapolis IN 46278
Ph: 317-387-1299 ▪ Fx: 317-387-0999 ▪ TF: 800-808-9884

Darts Organization Inc, American   www.adodarts.com
230 N Crescent Way Suite K   Anaheim CA 92801
Ph: 714-254-0212 ▪ Fx: 714-254-0214

Darwin Charles Foundation   www.galapagos.org
407 N Washington St Suite 105   Falls Church VA 22046
Ph: 703-538-6833 ▪ Fx: 703-538-6835

(Data Centers) AFCOM   www.afcom.com
742 E Chapman Ave   Orange CA 92866
Ph: 714-997-7966 ▪ Fx: 714-997-9743

Data Interchange Standards Association   www.disa.org
7600 Leesburg Pike Suite 430   Falls Church VA 22043
Ph: 703-970-4480 ▪ Fx: 703-970-4488

Data Interchange, Workgroup for Electronic   www.wedi.org
12020 Sunrise Valley Dr Suite 100   Reston VA 20191
Ph: 703-391-2716 ▪ Fx: 703-391-2759

Data Management Association International, DAMA -   www.dama.org
PO Box 5786   Bellevue WA 98006
Ph: 425-562-2636 ▪ Fx: 425-562-0376

Data Processing Associates, Black   www.bdpa.org
6301 Ivy Ln Suite 700   Greenbelt MD 20770
Ph: 301-220-2180 ▪ Fx: 301-220-2185 ▪ TF: 800-727-2372

Data Users, Association of Public   www.apdu.org
PO Box 12538   Arlington VA 22219
Ph: 703-807-2327 ▪ Fx: 703-528-2857

DataCenter   www.datacenter.org
1904 Franklin St Suite 900   Oakland CA 94612
Ph: 510-835-4692 ▪ Fx: 510-835-3017 ▪ TF: 800-735-3741

Date Commission, California   www.datesaregreat.com
PO Box 1736   Indio CA 92202
Ph: 760-347-4510 ▪ Fx: 760-347-6374 ▪ TF: 800-223-8748

Date Rape, National Clearinghouse on Marital &   www.ncmdr.org
2325 Oak St   Berkeley CA 94708
Ph: 510-524-1582

DateAble Inc   www.dateable.org
7830 Wisconsin Ave   Bethesda MD 20814
Ph: 301-656-8723 ▪ Fx: 301-657-4327

Daughters of the American Revolution, National Society   www.dar.org
1776 D St NW   Washington DC 20006
Ph: 202-628-1776 ▪ Fx: 202-879-3252

Daughters of Isabella   www.daughtersofisabella.org
PO Box 9585   New Haven CT 06535
Ph: 203-865-2570 ▪ Fx: 203-865-5586

Daughters of the King, Order of the   www.dok-national.org
Margaret J Franklin Ctr 101 Weatherstone Dr Suite
870   Woodstock GA 30188
Ph: 770-517-8552 ▪ Fx: 770-517-8066

Daughters of the Nile   www.daughtersofthenile.com
2001 Broadway PO Box 1322   Helena MT 59601
Ph: 406-443-4949

Daughters of Penelope   www.ahepa.org/dop
1909 Q St NW Suite 500   Washington DC 20009
Ph: 202-234-9741 ▪ Fx: 202-483-6983

Daughters of the Republic of Texas Inc   www.drtl.org/DRTInc
510 E Anderson Ln   Austin TX 78752
Ph: 512-339-1997 ▪ Fx: 512-339-1998

Daughters of Scotia   www.daughtersofscotia.org
7595 Carter Rd   Sagamore Hills OH 44067
Ph: 330-467-6387 ▪ Fx: 330-724-9307

Dave Thomas Foundation for Adoption   www.davethomasfoundationforadoption.org
4288 W Dublin Granville Rd   Dublin OH 43017
Ph: 614-764-8454 ▪ Fx: 614-766-3871 ▪ TF: 800-275-3832

David & Lucile Packard Foundation   www.packard.org
300 2nd St Suite 200   Los Altos CA 94022
Ph: 650-948-7658 ▪ Fx: 650-948-5793

Davis Arthur Vining Foundations   www.jvm.com/davis
225 Water St Suite 1510   Jacksonville FL 32202
Ph: 904-359-0670 ▪ Fx: 904-359-0675

Dawn Bible Students Association   www.dawnbible.com
199 Railroad Ave   East Rutherford NJ 07073
Ph: 201-438-6421 ▪ Fx: 201-531-8333 ▪ TF: 888-440-3296

Day of Prayer International Committee, World   www.worlddayofprayer.net
475 Riverside Dr Rm 560   New York NY 10115
Ph: 212-870-3049 ▪ Fx: 212-864-8648

Day School Association, Solomon Schechter
155 5th Ave   New York NY 10010
Ph: 212-533-7800 ▪ Fx: 212-353-9439

Day Services Association, National Adult   www.nadsa.org
8201 Greensboro Dr Suite 300   McLean VA 22102
Ph: 703-610-9000 ▪ Fx: 703-610-9005 ▪ TF: 800-424-9046

Daycare, National Association for Sick Child   www.nascd.com
1716 5th Ave N   Birmingham AL 35203
Ph: 205-324-8447 ▪ Fx: 205-324-8050

Deaconess Association, Lutheran   www.valpo.edu/lda
1304 La Porte Ave   Valparaiso IN 46383
Ph: 219-464-6925 ▪ Fx: 219-464-6928

Deaconess Conference, Concordia
Concordia Univ 7400 Augusta St   River Forest IL 60305
Ph: 708-209-3136 ▪ Fx: 708-209-3176

(Deaf) ADARA   www.adara.org
PO Box 480   Myersville MD 21773
Ph: 301-293-8969 ▪ Fx: 301-293-9698

Deaf Adults International Inc, Children of   www.coda-international.org
PO Box 30715   Santa Barbara CA 93130
Ph: 805-682-0997

Deaf-Blind People Inc, Advocates for Communication   www.deafblindadvocates.org
Technology for   911 Regina Dr   Baltimore MD 21227
Ph: 410-247-5045 ▪ Fx: 410-381-6838

Deaf-Blind Youths & Adults, Helen Keller National Center for   hknc.org
141 Middle Neck Rd   Sands Point NY 11050
Ph: 516-944-8900 ▪ Fx: 516-944-7302

Deaf Children, American Society for   www.deafchildren.org
PO Box 3355   Gettysburg PA 17325
Ph: 717-334-7922 ▪ Fx: 717-334-8808 ▪ TF: 800-942-2732

Deaf Children, SEE (Signing Exact English) Center for the   www.seecenter.org
Advancement of   PO Box 1181   Los Alamitos CA 90720
Ph: 562-430-1467 ▪ Fx: 562-795-6614

Deaf, Christian Mission for   www.cmdeaf.org
PO Box 28005   Detroit MI 48228
Ph: 313-933-1424

Deaf, Conference of Educational Administrators of Schools &   www.ceasd.org
Programs for the   PO Box 1778   Saint Augustine FL 32085
Ph: 904-810-5200 ▪ Fx: 904-810-5525

Deaf, Convention of American Instructors of the   www.caid.org/
PO Box 377   Bedford TX 76095
Ph: 817-354-8414

Deaf, Council on Education of the   www.deafed.net
Gallaudet Univ 800 Florida Ave NE FH 207   Washington DC
20002
Ph: 202-651-5525 ▪ Fx: 202-651-5749

Deaf Cycling Association, US   home.earthlink.net/~skedsmo/usdca.htm

Deaf, Dogs for the   www.dogsforthedeaf.org
10175 Wheeler Rd   Central Point OR 97502
Ph: 541-826-9220 ▪ Fx: 541-826-6696 ▪ TF: 800-990-2647

Deaf Education Center, National   clerccenter.gallaudet.edu
800 Florida Ave NE   Washington DC 20002
Ph: 202-651-5051 ▪ Fx: 202-651-5054

Deaf & Hard of Hearing, Alexander Graham Bell Association for the   www.agbell.org
3417 Volta Pl NW   Washington DC 20007
Ph: 202-337-5220 ▪ Fx: 202-337-8314

Deaf or Hard of Hearing Inc, BEGINNINGS for Parents of Children Who Are   PO Box 17646   Raleigh NC 27619
Ph: 919-850-2746 ▪ Fx: 919-850-2804 ▪ TF: 800-541-4327
www.ncbegin.org

Deaf, National Association of the
814 Thayer Ave Suite 250   Silver Spring MD 20910
Ph: 301-587-1788 ▪ Fx: 301-587-1791
www.nad.org

Deaf, National Catholic Office for the
7202 Buchanan St   Hyattsville MD 20784
Ph: 301-577-1684 ▪ Fx: 301-577-1690
www.ncod.org

Deaf, National Fraternal Society of the
1118 S 6th St   Springfield IL 62703
Ph: 217-789-7429 ▪ Fx: 217-289-7489
www.nfsd.com

Deaf, National Theatre of the
55 Van Dyke Ave Suite 312   Hartford CT 06106
Ph: 860-724-5179 ▪ Fx: 860-550-7974 ▪ TF: 800-300-5179
ntd.org

Deaf Inc, Registry of Interpreters for the
333 Commerce St   Alexandria VA 22314
Ph: 703-838-0030 ▪ Fx: 703-838-0454
www.rid.org

Deaf Sports Federation, USA
102 N Krohn Pl   Sioux Falls SD 57103
Ph: 605-367-5760 ▪ Fx: 605-367-5958
www.usadsf.org

Deaf Inc, Telecommunications for the
8630 Fenton St Suite 604   Silver Spring MD 20910
Ph: 301-589-3006 ▪ Fx: 301-589-3797
www.tdi-online.org

Deafness Research Foundation
1050 17th St NW Suite 701   Washington DC 20036
Ph: 202-289-5850 ▪ Fx: 202-289-1805
www.drf.org

Dealers Association, International Fine Print
15 Gramercy Park S Suite 7A   New York NY 10003
Ph: 212-674-6095 ▪ Fx: 212-674-6783
www.printdealter.com

Dealers Election Action Committee
8400 Westpark Dr 3rd Fl MS 3   McLean VA 22102
Ph: 703-821-7110 ▪ Fx: 703-442-3168 ▪ TF: 877-501-3322

Death with Dignity National Center
11 Dupont Cir NW Suite 202   Washington DC 20036
Ph: 202-969-1669 ▪ Fx: 202-969-1668
www.deathwithdignity.org

Death Education & Bioethics, Center for
UW La Crosse Dept of Sociology/Archaeology 435 NH 1725 State St   La Crosse WI 54601
Ph: 608-785-6784 ▪ Fx: 608-785-8486
www.uwlax.edu/sociology/cde&b

Death Education & Counseling, Association for
342 N Main St   West Hartford CT 06117
Ph: 860-586-7503 ▪ Fx: 860-586-7550
www.adec.org

Death, International Institute for the Study of
1000 Island Blvd Suite 512   Aventura FL 33160
Ph: 305-936-1408

Death Penalty Information Center
1320 18th St NW   Washington DC 20036
Ph: 202-293-6970 ▪ Fx: 202-822-4787
www.deathpenaltyinfo.org

Death Penalty, National Coalition to Abolish the
920 Pennsylvania Ave SE   Washington DC 20003
Ph: 202-543-9577 ▪ Fx: 202-543-7798 ▪ TF: 888-286-2237
www.ncadp.org

Death Resource Center, National SIDS/Infant
2070 Chain Bridge Rd Suite 450   Vienna VA 22182
Ph: 703-821-8955 ▪ Fx: 703-821-2098 ▪ TF: 866-866-7437
www.sidscenter.org

Death Syndromes Foundation, Sudden Arrythmia
508 E South Temple Suite 20   Salt Lake City UT 84102
Ph: 801-531-0937 ▪ Fx: 801-531-0945 ▪ TF: 800-786-7723
www.sads.org

DeBakey Michael E International Surgical Society
1 Baylor Plaza   Houston TX 77030
Ph: 713-798-4557 ▪ Fx: 713-796-9605
www.mediss.org

Debate Association, American
www2.bc.edu/~katsulas

Debate & Theatre Association, NFHS Speech
PO Box 690   Indianapolis IN 46206
Ph: 317-972-6900 ▪ Fx: 317-822-5700
www.nfhs.org/sdta.htm

Debates, Commission on Presidential
1200 New Hampshire Ave NW PO Box 445   Washington DC 20036
Ph: 202-872-1020 ▪ Fx: 202-783-5923
www.debates.org

Debs Eugene V Foundation
PO Box 843   Terre Haute IN 47808
Ph: 812-237-3443 ▪ Fx: 812-237-8072
eugenevdebs.com

Debtors Anonymous
PO Box 920888   Needham MA 02492
Ph: 781-453-2743
www.debtorsanonymous.org

DECA - Decathlon Association
Mount St Mary's College 16300 Old Emmitsburg Rd   Emmitsburg MD 21727
Ph: 301-447-6122 ▪ Fx: 301-447-6255
www.decathlonusa.org

Decalogue Society of Lawyers
39 S LaSalle St Suite 410   Chicago IL 60603
Ph: 312-263-6493 ▪ Fx: 312-263-6512

Decathlon Association, DECA -
Mount St Mary's College 16300 Old Emmitsburg Rd   Emmitsburg MD 21727
Ph: 301-447-6122 ▪ Fx: 301-447-6255
www.decathlonusa.org

Decency, Americans for
3431 W Thunderbird Rd   Phoenix AZ 85053
Ph: 602-993-4353 ▪ Fx: 602-993-4308
www.americansfordecency.com

(Decentralism) EF Schumacher Society
140 Jug End Rd   Great Barrington MA 01230
Ph: 413-528-1737 ▪ Fx: 413-528-4472
www.smallisbeautiful.org

Decision Sciences Institute
35 Broad St   Atlanta GA 30303
Ph: 404-651-4073 ▪ Fx: 404-651-2804
www.decisionsciences.org/

Declaration Foundation
721 R 2nd St NE   Washington DC 20002
Ph: 202-544-9555 ▪ Fx: 202-544-9724 ▪ TF: 888-458-5976
www.declaration.net

Decorating Contractors of America, Painting &
11960 Westline Industrial Dr Suite 201   Saint Louis MO 63146
Ph: 314-514-7322 ▪ Fx: 314-514-9417 ▪ TF: 800-332-7322
www.pdca.com

Decorating Retailers Association, Paint &
403 Axminister Dr   Fenton MO 63026
Ph: 636-326-2636 ▪ Fx: 636-326-1823 ▪ TF: 800-737-0107
www.pdra.org

Decorative Arts Trust
106 Bainbridge   Philadelphia PA 19147
Ph: 215-627-2859 ▪ Fx: 215-925-1144
www.decorativeartstrust.org

Decorative Fabric Distributors, National Association of
1 Windsor Cove Suite 305   Columbia SC 29223
Ph: 803-252-5646 ▪ Fx: 803-765-0860 ▪ TF: 800-445-8629
www.nadfd.com

Decorative Painters, Society of
393 N McLean Blvd   Wichita KS 67203
Ph: 316-269-9300 ▪ Fx: 316-269-9191
www.decorativepainters.org

Decorators, Society of Glass & Ceramic
47 N 4th St   Zanesville OH 43702
Ph: 740-588-9882 ▪ Fx: 740-588-0245
www.sgcd.org

Decoy Collectors Association, Midwest
6 E Scott St Suite 3   Chicago IL 60610
Ph: 312-337-7957 ▪ Fx: 312-337-9679
www.midwestdecoy.org

Dedicated Wooden Money Collectors
2084 N Brook Cir   York PA 17403
Ph: 717-845-4295

Deep Foundations Institute
120 Charlotte Pl 3rd Fl   Englewood Cliffs NJ 07632
Ph: 201-567-4232 ▪ Fx: 201-567-4436
www.dfi.org

Deer Farmers Association, North American
1720 W Wisconsin Ave   Appleton WI 54914
Ph: 920-734-0934 ▪ Fx: 920-734-0955
www.nadefa.org

Deerfield Inc, Historic
PO Box 321   Deerfield MA 01342
Ph: 413-774-5581 ▪ Fx: 413-775-7220
www.historic-deerfield.org

Defamation, Gay & Lesbian Alliance Against
248 W 35th St 8th Fl   New York NY 10001
Ph: 212-629-3322 ▪ Fx: 212-629-3225
www.glaad.org

Defender Investigator Association, National
2600 Dixwell Ave Suite 7   Hamden CT 06514
Ph: 203-281-6342 ▪ Fx: 203-248-8932
www.ndia.net

Defenders of Property Rights
1350 Connecticut Ave Suite 410   Washington DC 20036
Ph: 202-822-6770 ▪ Fx: 202-822-6774
www.yourpropertyrights.org

Defenders of Wildlife
1130 17th St NW   Washington DC 20006
Ph: 202-682-9400 ▪ Fx: 202-682-1331 ▪ TF: 800-989-8981
www.defenders.org

Defense Association, American Civil
118 S Court St PO Box 1057   Starke FL 32091
Ph: 904-964-5397 ▪ Fx: 904-964-9641 ▪ TF: 800-425-5397
www.tacda.org

Defense Association, Men's
17854 Lyons St   Forest Lake MN 55025
Ph: 651-464-7887 ▪ Fx: 651-464-7135
www.mensdefense.org

Defense Committee Inc, Leonard Peltier
PO Box 583   Lawrence KS 66044
Ph: 785-842-5774 ▪ Fx: 785-842-5796
www.leonardpeltier.org

Defense & Corporate Counsel Inc, Federation of
11812-A N 56th St   Tampa FL 33617
Ph: 813-983-0022 ▪ Fx: 813-988-5837
www.thefederation.org

Defense Council of America, Serbian National
5782 N Elston Ave   Chicago IL 60646
Ph: 773-775-7772 ▪ Fx: 773-775-7779
www.snd-us.com

Defense Council Foundation, National
1220 King St Suite 1   Alexandria VA 22314
Ph: 703-836-3443 ▪ Fx: 703-836-5402
www.ndcf.org

Defense Counsel, International Association of
1 N Franklin St Suite 1205   Chicago IL 60606
Ph: 312-368-1494 ▪ Fx: 312-368-1854
www.iadclaw.org

Defense Credit Union Council
601 Pennsylvania Ave W Suite 600   Washington DC 20004
Ph: 202-638-3930 ▪ Fx: 202-638-3410 ▪ TF: 800-356-9655
www.dcuc.org

Defense & Disarmament Studies, Institute for
675 Massachusetts Ave 8th Fl   Cambridge MA 02139
Ph: 617-354-4337 ▪ Fx: 617-354-1450
www.idds.org

Defense Equipment Exhibitors Association, International
6233 Nelway Dr   McLean VA 22101
Ph: 703-760-0762 ▪ Fx: 703-760-0764
www.ideea.org

Defense Fire Protection Association
PO Box 1310   Falls Church VA 22041
Ph: 703-521-3926 ▪ Fx: 703-521-0849
www.dfpa.org

Defense Foundation Inc, National Right to Work Legal
8001 Braddock Rd Suite 600   Springfield VA 22160
Ph: 703-321-8510 ▪ Fx: 703-321-9613 ▪ TF: 800-325-7892
www.nrtw.org

Defense Fund, Alliance
15333 N Pima Rd Suite 165   Scottsdale AZ 85260
Ph: 800-835-5233 ▪ Fx: 480-444-0025
www.alliancedefensefund.org

Defense Fund, Animal Legal
127 4th St   Petaluma CA 94952
Ph: 707-769-7771 ▪ Fx: 707-769-0785
www.aldf.org

Defense Fund, Children's
25 'E' St NW   Washington DC 20001
Ph: 202-628-8787 ▪ Fx: 202-662-3510 ▪ TF: 800-233-1200
www.childrensdefense.org

Defense Industrial Association, National
2111 Wilson Blvd Suite 400   Arlington VA 22201
Ph: 703-522-1820 ▪ Fx: 703-522-1885
www.ndia.org

Defense Information, Center for
1779 Massachusetts Ave NW Suite 615   Washington DC 20036
Ph: 202-332-0600 ▪ Fx: 202-462-4559
www.cdi.org

Defense Intel Alumni Association Inc
PO Box 86   McLean VA 22101
Ph: 202-231-3414
www.dialumni.org

Defense Lawyers, National Association of Criminal   www.nacdl.org
1150 18th St NW Suite 950   Washington DC 20036
Ph: 202-872-8600 ▪ Fx: 202-872-8690

Defense Organization, Jewish   www.jdo.org
PO Box 159 FDR Stn   New York NY 10150
Ph: 212-252-3383

Defense Research Institute   www.dri.org
150 N Michigan Ave Suite 300   Chicago IL 60601
Ph: 312-795-1101 ▪ Fx: 312-795-0747 ▪ TF: 800-667-8108

Defense Resource Center, Libel   www.ldrc.com
80 8th Ave Suite 200   New York NY 10011
Ph: 212-337-0200 ▪ Fx: 212-337-9893

Defense & Space Industry Association, Council of   www.codsia.org
1000 Wilson Blvd Suite 1800   Arlington VA 22209
Ph: 703-243-2020 ▪ Fx: 703-243-8539

Defense Study Group Inc, Coast   www.cdsg.org
1560 Somerville Rd   Bel Air MD 21015
Ph: 410-838-6509

Defense Transportation Association, National   www.ndtahq.com
50 S Pickett St Suite 220   Alexandria VA 22304
Ph: 703-751-5011 ▪ Fx: 703-823-8761

Defensive Spray Manufacturers, Association of   www.pepperspray.org
917 Locust St Suite 1100   Saint Louis MO 63101
Ph: 314-241-1445 ▪ Fx: 314-241-1449

Defined Contribution Council, National   www.ndcconline.org
9101 E Kenyon Ave Suite 3000   Denver CO 80237
Ph: 303-770-5353 ▪ Fx: 303-770-1812

Degree of Honor Protective Association   www.degreeofhonor.com
445 Minnesota St Suite 1600   Saint Paul MN 55101
Ph: 651-228-7600 ▪ Fx: 651-224-7446

Delaine & Merino Record Association, American   www.admra.org
59419 Walters Rd   Jacobsburg OH 43933
Ph: 740-686-2172

Delancey Street Foundation
600 Embarcadero   San Francisco CA 94107
Ph: 415-957-9800 ▪ Fx: 415-512-5141

Deli-Bakery Association, International Dairy-   www.iddanet.org
313 Price Pl Suite 202   Madison WI 53705
Ph: 608-238-7908 ▪ Fx: 608-238-6330

Delinquency, National Council on Crime &   www.nccd-crc.org
1970 Broadway Suite 500   Oakland CA 94612
Ph: 510-208-0500 ▪ Fx: 510-208-0511

Delivery Systems Inc, American Association of Integrated Healthcare   www.aaihds.org
4435 Waterfront Dr Suite 101   Glen Allen VA 23060
Ph: 804-747-5823 ▪ Fx: 804-747-5316

Delphi International Program   www.worldlearning.org/delphi
1015 18th St NW Suite 1000   Washington DC 20036
Ph: 202-898-0950 ▪ Fx: 202-842-0885

Delta Chi Fraternity Inc   www.deltachi.com
314 Church St PO Box 1817   Iowa City IA 52244
Ph: 319-337-4811 ▪ Fx: 319-337-5529

Delta Delta Delta Fraternity   www.tridelta.org
2331 Brookhollow Plaza Dr PO Box 5987   Arlington TX 76005
Ph: 817-633-8001 ▪ Fx: 817-652-0212

Delta Dental Plans Association   www.deltadental.com
1515 W 22nd St Suite 1200   Oak Brook IL 60523
Ph: 630-574-6001 ▪ Fx: 630-574-6999

Delta Epsilon Sigma   des.barry.edu
Barry Univ 11300 NE 2nd Ave   Miami FL 33161
Ph: 305-899-3020 ▪ Fx: 305-899-3026

Delta Gamma   www.deltagamma.org
3250 Riverside Dr PO Box 21397   Columbus OH 43221
Ph: 614-481-8169 ▪ Fx: 614-481-0133

Delta Kappa Epsilon Fraternity   www.dke.org
2238 47th St NW   Washington DC 20001
Ph: 800-560-3353 ▪ Fx: 202-478-0374

Delta Kappa Phi Fraternity Inc   www.delta-kappa-phi.org
9 Mt Hope St   Lowell MA 01854
Ph: 978-452-8388

Delta Nu Alpha Transportation Fraternity   www.deltanualpha.org
1451 Elm Hill Pike Suite 205   Nashville TN 37210
Ph: 615-360-6863 ▪ Fx: 615-360-1891

Delta Omega   www.deltaomega.org

Delta Omicron   www.delta-omicron.org

Delta Phi Epsilon International Sorority   www.dphie.org
16A Worthington Dr   Maryland Heights MO 63043
Ph: 314-275-2626 ▪ Fx: 314-275-2655

Delta Phi Epsilon Professional Foreign   www.deltaphiepsilon.net/National_Fraternity.html
Service Fraternity Inc   PO Box 25401   Washington DC 20027
Ph: 202-337-7116

Delta Phi Fraternity Inc   deltaphi.org
PO Box 81521   Athens GA 30608
Ph: 706-552-1444 ▪ Fx: 706-552-5444

Delta Pi Epsilon   www.dpe.org
PO Box 4340   Little Rock AR 72214
Ph: 501-219-1866 ▪ Fx: 501-219-1876

Delta Psi Kappa
PO Box 90264   Indianapolis IN 46290
Ph: 317-255-4379 ▪ Fx: 317-334-8721

Delta Sigma Delta   www.deltsig.com
296 15th Ave   Nekoosa WI 54457
Ph: 715-325-6320 ▪ Fx: 715-325-3057 ▪ TF: 800-335-8744

Delta Sigma Phi Fraternity   www.deltasig.org
1331 N Delaware St   Indianapolis IN 46202
Ph: 317-634-1899 ▪ Fx: 317-634-1410

Delta Sigma Pi   www.dspnet.org
330 S Campus Ave Box 230   Oxford OH 45056
Ph: 513-523-1907 ▪ Fx: 513-523-7292

Delta Sigma Theta Sorority Inc   www.deltasigmatheta.org
1707 New Hampshire Ave NW   Washington DC 20009
Ph: 202-986-2400 ▪ Fx: 202-986-2513

Delta Society   www.deltasociety.org
580 Naches Ave SW   Renton WA 98055
Ph: 425-226-7357 ▪ Fx: 425-235-1076

Delta Tau Delta Fraternity   www.delts.org
10000 Allisonville Rd   Fishers IN 46038
Ph: 317-284-0203 ▪ Fx: 317-284-0214

Delta Theta Phi   www.deltathetaphi.org
38640 Butternut Ridge Rd   Elyria OH 44035
Ph: 440-458-4381 ▪ Fx: 440-458-4380 ▪ TF: 800-783-2600

Delta Upsilon International Fraternity   www.deltau.org
8705 Founders Rd PO Box 68942   Indianapolis IN 46268
Ph: 317-875-8900 ▪ Fx: 317-876-1629

Delta Waterfowl Foundation   www.deltawaterfowl.org
1305 E Central Ave   Bismarck ND 58501
Ph: 701-222-8857 ▪ Fx: 701-223-4645 ▪ TF: 888-987-3695

Delta Zeta Sorority   www.deltazeta.org
202 E Church St   Oxford OH 45056
Ph: 513-523-7597 ▪ Fx: 513-523-1921

Deltiologists of America   www.deltiologists-america.com

Demeter Association Inc   www.demeter-usa.org
Britt Rd   Aurora NY 13026
Ph: 315-364-5617 ▪ Fx: 315-364-5224

Democracy, Alliance for   www.thealliancefordemocracy.org
760 Main St PO Box 540115   Waltham MA 02451
Ph: 781-894-1179 ▪ Fx: 781-894-0279

Democracy, Association for Union   www.uniondemocracy.org
104 Montgomery St   Brooklyn NY 11225
Ph: 718-855-6650 ▪ Fx: 718-855-6799

Democracy, Center for   www.centerfordemocracy.org
1101 15th St NW Suite 505   Washington DC 20005
Ph: 202-429-9141 ▪ Fx: 202-293-1768

Democracy & Development, Fund for   www.centerfordemocracy.org
1101 15th St NW Suite 205   Washington DC 20005
Ph: 202-296-5353 ▪ Fx: 202-296-5433

Democracy, Institute on Religion &   www.ird-renew.org
1110 Vermont Ave NW Suite 1180   Washington DC 20005
Ph: 202-969-8430 ▪ Fx: 202-969-8429

Democracy, National Endowment for   www.ned.org
1101 15th St NW Suite 700   Washington DC 20005
Ph: 202-293-9072 ▪ Fx: 202-223-6042

Democracy, National Initiative for   ni4d.us
1600 N Oak St Suite 1412   Arlington VA 22209
Ph: 703-516-4056 ▪ Fx: 703-516-4057

Democracy & Technology, Center for   www.cdt.org
1634 'I' St NW 11th Fl   Washington DC 20006
Ph: 202-637-9800 ▪ Fx: 202-637-0968

(Democracy) We The People   www.wtp.org
200 Harrison St   Oakland CA 94607
Ph: 510-836-3273 ▪ Fx: 510-836-3063

Democrat Network, New   www.newdem.org
777 N Capitol St NE Suite 410   Washington DC 20002
Ph: 202-544-9200 ▪ Fx: 202-547-2929

Democratic Action, Americans for   www.adaction.org
1625 K St NW Suite 210   Washington DC 20006
Ph: 202-785-5980 ▪ Fx: 202-785-5969 ▪ TF: 800-787-2734

Democratic Chairs, Association of State
430 S Capitol St SE   Washington DC 20003
Ph: 202-479-5121 ▪ Fx: 202-479-5123

Democratic Club, National   www.natdemclub.org
30 Ivy St SE   Washington DC 20003
Ph: 202-543-2035 ▪ Fx: 202-479-4273

Democratic Club, Woman's National   www.democraticwoman.org
1526 New Hampshire Ave NW   Washington DC 20036
Ph: 202-232-7363 ▪ Fx: 202-986-2791

Democratic Council, National Jewish   www.njdc.org
PO Box 75308   Washington DC 20013
Ph: 202-216-9060 ▪ Fx: 202-216-9061

Democratic Governors Association   www.democraticgovernors.org
499 S Capitol St SW Suite 422   Washington DC 20003
Ph: 202-772-5600 ▪ Fx: 202-772-5602

Democratic Majority, Committee for a
301 4th St NE Suite 202   Washington DC 20002
Ph: 202-544-4889 ▪ Fx: 202-546-2285

Democratic National Committee   www.democrats.org
430 S Capitol St SE   Washington DC 20003
Ph: 202-863-8000 ▪ Fx: 202-863-8081 ▪ TF: 800-934-8683

Democratic Renewal, Center For   www.publiceye.org/cdr
PO Box 50469   Atlanta GA 30302
Ph: 404-221-0025 ▪ Fx: 404-221-0045

Democratic Socialists of America   www.dsausa.org
180 Varick St 12th Fl   New York NY 10014
Ph: 212-727-8610 ▪ Fx: 212-727-8616

Democratic Societies, Center for the Study of   www.centersds.com
PO Box 475   Manhattan Beach CA 90267
Ph: 310-798-2737 ▪ Fx: 310-374-0440

Democratic Union, Teamsters for a   www.tdu.org
PO Box 10128   Detroit MI 48210
Ph: 313-842-2600 ▪ Fx: 313-842-0227

Democratic Women, National Federation of   www.nfdw.org
19432 Burlington Dr   Detroit MI 48203
Ph: 313-892-6199 ▪ Fx: 313-892-8424

Democrats of America, Young   www.yda.org
PO Box 77496   Washington DC 20013
Ph: 202-639-8585 ▪ Fx: 202-318-3221 ▪ TF: 877-639-8585

Democrats, National Stonewall   www.stonewalldemocrats.org
PO Box 9330   Washington DC 20005
Ph: 202-625-1382 ▪ Fx: 202-625-1383

DeMolay International   www.demolay.org
10200 N Ambassabor Dr   Kansas City MO 64153
Ph: 816-891-8333 ▪ Fx: 816-891-9062 ▪ TF: 800-336-6529

Demolition Contractors, National Association of   www.demolitionassociation.com
16 N Franklin St Suite 203   Doylestown PA 18901
Ph: 215-348-4949 ▪ Fx: 215-348-8422 ▪ TF: 800-541-2412

Demos: A Network for Ideas & Action   www.demos-usa.org
220 5th Ave 5th Fl   New York NY 10001
Ph: 212-633-1405 ▪ Fx: 212-633-2015

DeMoss Arthur Foundation
777 S Flagler Dr Suite 1600   West Palm Beach FL 33401
Ph: 561-804-9000 ▪ Fx: 561-804-9025

Densitometry, International Society for Clinical   www.iscd.org
342 N Main St   West Hartford CT 06117
Ph: 860-586-7563 ▪ Fx: 860-586-7550

Dental Aesthetics, American Society for   www.asdatoday.com
635 Madison Ave 13th Fl   New York NY 10022
Ph: 212-751-3263 ▪ Fx: 212-755-3263 ▪ TF: 800-454-2732

Dental Assistants Association, American   www.dentalassistant.org
35 E Wacker Dr Suite 1730   Chicago IL 60601
Ph: 312-541-1550 ▪ Fx: 312-541-1496

Dental Assistants Association, National   www.ndaonline.org
3517 16th St NW   Washington DC 20010
Ph: 202-588-1697 ▪ Fx: 202-588-1244

Dental Assisting National Board   www.danb.org
676 N St Clair St Suite 1880   Chicago IL 60611
Ph: 312-642-3368 ▪ Fx: 312-642-1475 ▪ TF: 800-367-3262

Dental Association, American   www.ada.org
211 E Chicago Ave   Chicago IL 60611
Ph: 312-440-2500 ▪ Fx: 312-440-2800

Dental Association, American Student   www.asdanet.org
211 E Chicago Ave Suite 1160   Chicago IL 60611
Ph: 312-440-2795 ▪ Fx: 312-440-2820 ▪ TF: 800-621-8099

Dental Association, Hispanic   www.hdassoc.org
188 W Randolph St Suite 415   Chicago IL 60601
Ph: 312-577-4013 ▪ Fx: 312-577-0052 ▪ TF: 800-852-7921

Dental Association, Holistic   www.holisticdental.org
PO Box 5007   Durango CO 81301
Ph: 970-259-1091

Dental Association, Indian   www.dentalhealthindia.com
146-02 89th Ave   Jamaica NY 11435
Ph: 718-523-8438

Dental Association, National   www.ndaonline.org
3517 16th St NW   Washington DC 20010
Ph: 202-588-1697 ▪ Fx: 202-588-1244

Dental Association, National Medical &   www.polishnmda.com
72-41 Grand Ave   Maspeth NY 11378
Ph: 718-478-3333

Dental Associations, Christian Medical &   www.cmdahome.com
PO Box 7500   Bristol TN 37620
Ph: 423-844-1000 ▪ Fx: 423-844-1005

Dental Directors, Association of State & Territorial   www.astdd.org
322 Cannondale Rd   Jefferson City MO 65109
Ph: 573-636-0453 ▪ Fx: 573-636-0454

Dental Editors, American Association of   www.dentaleditors.org
750 N Lincoln Memorial Dr Suite 422   Milwaukee WI 53202
Ph: 414-272-2759 ▪ Fx: 414-272-2754

Dental Education Association, American   www.adea.org
1625 Massachusetts Ave NW Suite 600   Washington DC 20036
Ph: 202-667-9433 ▪ Fx: 202-667-0642 ▪ TF: 800-353-2237

Dental Examiners, American Association of   www.aadexam.org
211 E Chicago Ave Suite 760   Chicago IL 60611
Ph: 312-440-7464 ▪ Fx: 312-440-3525

Dental Fraternity, Alpha Omega International   www.ao.org
500 Commonwealth Dr   Warrendale PA 15086
Ph: 724-778-3419 ▪ Fx: 724-772-8349 ▪ TF: 800-677-8468

Dental Fraternity, Psi Omega
1040 Savannah Hwy   Charleston SC 29407
Ph: 843-556-0573 ▪ Fx: 843-556-6311

Dental Fraternity, Xi Psi Phi   www.xipsiphi.org
1623 Washington Ave Suite 300   Alton IL 62002
Ph: 618-463-1889

Dental Group Management Association   www.dgma.org
2525 E Arizona Biltmore Cir Suite 127   Phoenix AZ 85016
Ph: 602-381-8980 ▪ Fx: 602-381-1093

Dental Group Practice, American Academy of   www.aadgp.org
2525 E Arizona Biltmore Cir Suite 127   Phoenix AZ 85016
Ph: 602-381-1185 ▪ Fx: 602-381-1093

Dental Hygienists' Association, American   www.adha.org
444 N Michigan Ave Suite 3400   Chicago IL 60611
Ph: 312-440-8900 ▪ Fx: 312-467-1806 ▪ TF: 800-243-2342

Dental Hygienists' Association, National   www.ndaonline.org
3517 16th St NW   Washington DC 20010
Ph: 202-588-1697 ▪ Fx: 202-588-1244

(Dental Hygienists) Sigma Phi Alpha   www.sigmaphialpha.org
Univ of Texas Health Science Ctr Dental Branch PO Box
20068   Houston TX 77225
Ph: 713-500-4085

Dental Laboratories, National Association of   www.nadl.org
1530 Metropolitan Blvd   Tallahassee FL 32308
Ph: 850-205-5626 ▪ Fx: 850-222-0053 ▪ TF: 800-950-1150

Dental Management Consultants, Society of Medical-   www.smdmc.org
125 Strafford Ave Suite 300   Wayne PA 19087
Ph: 800-826-2264 ▪ Fx: 610-687-7702

Dental Materials Inc, Academy of   www.academydentalmaterials.org
PO Box 432   Morgantown WV 26507
Ph: 304-292-7343 ▪ Fx: 304-292-7099

Dental PAC, American
1111 14th St NW Suite 1100   Washington DC 20005
Ph: 202-898-2424 ▪ Fx: 202-898-2437

Dental Plans Association, Delta   www.deltadental.com
1515 W 22nd St Suite 1200   Oak Brook IL 60523
Ph: 630-574-6001 ▪ Fx: 630-574-6999

Dental Plans, National Association of   www.nadp.org
8111 LBJ Fwy Suite 935   Dallas TX 75251
Ph: 972-458-6998 ▪ Fx: 972-458-2258

Dental Practice Administration, American Academy of   www.aadpa.org
1063 Whippoorwill Ln   Palatine IL 60067
Ph: 847-934-4404 ▪ Fx: 847-934-4410

Dental Public Health, American Board of   www.aaphd.org
892 Overbrook Pl   West Palm Beach FL 33413
Ph: 561-686-2760 ▪ Fx: 561-686-4168

Dental Research, American Association for   www.iadr.org
1619 Duke St   Alexandria VA 22314
Ph: 703-548-0066 ▪ Fx: 703-548-1883

Dental Research, International Association for   www.iadr.org
1619 Duke St   Alexandria VA 22314
Ph: 703-548-0066 ▪ Fx: 703-548-1883

Dental Sleep Medicine, Academy of   www.dentalsleepmed.org
1 Westbrook Corporate Ctr Suite 920   Westchester IL 60154
Ph: 708-273-9335 ▪ Fx: 708-492-0943

Dental Society, American Veterinary   www.avds-online.org
618 Church St Suite 220   Nashville TN 37219
Ph: 800-332-2837 ▪ Fx: 615-254-7047

Dental Society of Anesthesiology, American   www.adsa.org
211 E Chicago Ave Suite 780   Chicago IL 60611
Ph: 312-664-8270 ▪ Fx: 312-642-9713 ▪ TF: 800-722-7788

Dental Technologists, American Society of Master   www.asmdt.org
PO Box 640248   Oakland Gardens NY 11364
Ph: 718-347-1239 ▪ Fx: 718-347-3113

Dental Tennis Association, US   www.dentaltennis.org
2180 Briarcliff Dr   Idaho Falls ID 83404
Ph: 800-445-2524 ▪ Fx: 208-523-9004

Dental Trade Alliance   www.dmanews.org
123 S Broad St Suite 2030   Philadelphia PA 19109
Ph: 215-731-9975 ▪ Fx: 215-731-9984

Dental Trade Association, American   www.adta.com
4222 King St W   Alexandria VA 22302
Ph: 703-379-7755 ▪ Fx: 703-931-9429

Dentistry, Academy of General   www.agd.org
211 E Chicago Ave Suite 900   Chicago IL 60611
Ph: 312-440-4300 ▪ Fx: 312-440-0559 ▪ TF: 888-243-3368

Dentistry, Academy of Laser   www.laserdentistry.org
PO Box 8667   Coral Springs FL 33075
Ph: 954-346-3776 ▪ Fx: 954-757-2598

Dentistry, American Academy of Cosmetic   www.aacd.com
5401 World Dairy Dr   Madison WI 53718
Ph: 608-222-8583 ▪ Fx: 608-222-9540 ▪ TF: 800-543-9220

Dentistry, American Academy of Esthetic   www.estheticacademy.org
401 N Michigan Ave   Chicago IL 60611
Ph: 312-321-5121 ▪ Fx: 312-673-6952

Dentistry, American Academy of the History of
Oregon Health Sciences Univ School of Dentistry 611 SW
Campus Dr   Portland OR 97239
Ph: 503-494-4316

Dentistry, American Academy of Implant   www.aaid-implant.org
211 E Chicago Ave Suite 750   Chicago IL 60611
Ph: 312-335-1550 ▪ Fx: 312-335-9090 ▪ TF: 877-335-2243

Dentistry, American Academy of Pediatric   www.aapd.org
211 E Chicago Ave Suite 700   Chicago IL 60611
Ph: 312-337-2169 ▪ Fx: 312-337-6329

Dentistry, American Academy of Restorative   www.restorativeacademy.com
985 Fuller Rd   Colorado Springs CO 80920
Ph: 719-633-1060 ▪ Fx: 719-953-7926

Dentistry, American Board of Pediatric   www.abpd.org
325 E Washington St Suite 101   Iowa City IA 52240
Ph: 319-341-9499

Dentistry, American Society for the Advancement of   www.sedation4dentists.com
Anesthesia & Sedation in   6 E Union Ave   Bound Brook NJ
08805
Ph: 732-469-9050 ▪ Fx: 732-271-1985

Dentistry, American Society for Geriatric   www.scdonline.org/ASGD_Index.htm
c/o Special Care Dentistry 211 E Chicago Ave Suite
740   Chicago IL 60611
Ph: 312-440-2660 ▪ Fx: 312-440-2824

(Dentistry) Delta Sigma Delta   www.deltsig.org
296 15th Ave   Nekoosa WI 54457
Ph: 715-325-6320 ▪ Fx: 715-325-3057 ▪ TF: 800-335-8744

Dentistry for the Handicapped, National Foundation of   www.nfdh.org
1800 15th St Unit 100   Denver CO 80202
Ph: 303-534-5360 ▪ Fx: 303-534-5290 ▪ TF: 888-471-6334

Dentistry International, Academy of   www.adint.org
3813 Gordon Creek Dr   Hicksville OH 43526
Ph: 419-542-0101 ▪ Fx: 419-542-6883

Dentistry, International Academy for Sports   www.acadsportsdent.org
118 Faye St   Farmersville IL 62533
Ph: 217-227-3431 ▪ Fx: 217-227-3438 ▪ TF: 800-273-1788

(Dentistry) International Association for Disability & Oral Health   www.iadh.org
Ohio State Univ College of Dentistry 305 W 12th Ave PO Box
182357   Columbus OH 43218
Ph: 614-292-1232 ▪ Fx: 614-292-4522

Dentistry for Persons with Disabilities, Academy of   scdonline.org/ADPD_Index.htm
211 E Chicago Ave Suite 740   Chicago IL 60611
Ph: 312-440-2660 ▪ Fx: 312-440-2824

(Dentistry) Pierre Fauchard Academy   www.fauchard.org
PO Box 80330   Las Vegas NV 89180
Ph: 702-651-5013 ▪ Fx: 702-651-5537 ▪ TF: 800-232-0099

Dentistry, Special Care   scdonline.org
211 E Chicago Ave Suite 740   Chicago IL 60611
Ph: 312-440-2660 ▪ Fx: 312-440-2824

Dentists, American Association of Hospital   scdonline.org/AAHD_Index.htm
211 E Chicago Ave Suite 740   Chicago IL 60611
Ph: 312-440-2660 ▪ Fx: 312-440-2824

Dentists, American Association of Women   www.womendentists.org
330 S Wells Suite 1110   Chicago IL 60606
Ph: 312-913-9327 ▪ Fx: 312-461-0238 ▪ TF: 800-920-2293

Dentists, American College of   www.facd.org
839 Quince Orchard Blvd Suite J   Gaithersburg MD 20878
Ph: 301-977-3223 ▪ Fx: 301-977-3330 ▪ TF: 888-223-1920

Dentists, American Society of Retired
1 W Camino Real Blvd Suite 207   Boca Raton FL 33432
Ph: 561-395-2773 ▪ TF: 800-495-2773

Dentists, Association of Managed Care   www.amcd.org
1223 Wilshire Blvd Suite 483   Santa Monica CA 90403
Ph: 310-453-3439 ▪ Fx: 310-453-7895 ▪ TF: 800-864-6848

Dentists, International College of   www.icd.org
51 Monroe St Suite 1400   Rockville MD 20850
Ph: 301-251-8861 ▪ Fx: 301-738-9143

Dentists, National Association of Seventh-day   www.llu.edu/llu/dentistry/nasdad
Adventist   PO Box 101   Loma Linda CA 92354
Ph: 909-558-8187 ▪ Fx: 909-558-4607

Dentists, National Association of VA Physicians &   www.navapd.org
11 Canal Ctr Plaza Suite 110   Alexandria VA 22314
Ph: 703-548-0280 ▪ Fx: 703-683-7939

Dentists, Union of American Physicians &   www.uapd.com
1330 Broadway Suite 730   Oakland CA 94612
Ph: 510-839-0193 ▪ Fx: 510-763-8756

Denturist Association, National   www.nationaldenturist.com
PO Box 308   Towanda PA 18848
Ph: 570-265-0238 ▪ Fx: 570-265-0239 ▪ TF: 888-599-7958

Department Store Union, Retail Wholesale &   www.rwdsu.info
30 E 29th St   New York NY 10016
Ph: 212-684-5300 ▪ Fx: 212-779-2809

Depreciation Professionals, Society of   www.depr.org
8100-M4 Wyoming Blvd NE Suite 228   Albuquerque NM 87113
Ph: 505-792-4604 ▪ Fx: 505-922-1495

Depression After Delivery Inc   www.depressionafterdelivery.com
91 E Somerset St   Raritan NJ 08869
Ph: 908-575-9121 ▪ Fx: 908-541-9713 ▪ TF: 800-944-4773

Depression & Bipolar Support Alliance   www.dbsalliance.org
730 N Franklin St Suite 501   Chicago IL 60610
Ph: 312-642-0049 ▪ Fx: 312-642-7243 ▪ TF: 800-826-3632

Depression & Related Affective Disorders Association   www.drada.org
2330 W Joppa Rd Suite 100   Lutherville MD 21093
Ph: 410-583-2919

Depressive Illness Inc, National Foundation for   www.depression.org
PO Box 2257   New York NY 10116
Ph: 800-239-1265

Derby Rallies Inc, National   www.ndr.org
6644 Switzer St   Shawnee KS 66203
Ph: 913-962-0706

Derleth August Society   www.derleth.org
PO Box 481   Sauk City WI 53583
Ph: 608-643-3242 ▪ Fx: 608-643-5080

Dermatologic Association, Pacific   www.pacificderm.org
2950 Buskirk Ave Suite 170   Walnut Creek CA 94597
Ph: 925-472-5910 ▪ Fx: 925-472-5901

Dermatologic Surgery, American Society for   www.asds-net.org
5550 Meadowbrook Dr Suite 120   Rolling Meadows IL 60008
Ph: 847-956-0900 ▪ Fx: 847-956-0999

Dermatological Retailers, American Society of
320 Superior Ave Suite 395   Newport Beach CA 92663
Ph: 949-646-9098 ▪ Fx: 949-646-7298 ▪ TF: 800-469-3739

Dermatological Societies, International League of   www.ilds.org
PO Box 35069   Sarasota FL 34232
Ph: 941-346-1226 ▪ Fx: 941-927-1936

Dermatological Society, Noah Worcester   www.noahw.org
61 Donna Rd   Newton MA 02459
Ph: 617-641-9761 ▪ Fx: 617-527-4423

Dermatology, American Academy of   www.aad.org
930 E Woodfield Rd PO Box 4014   Schaumburg IL 60168
Ph: 847-330-0230 ▪ Fx: 847-330-0050

Dermatology, American Board of   www.abderm.org
Henry Ford Health System 1 Ford Pl   Detroit MI 48202
Ph: 313-874-1088 ▪ Fx: 313-872-3221

Dermatology, American College of Veterinary   www.acvd.org
5610 Kearny Mesa Rd Suite B   San Diego CA 92111
Ph: 858-560-9393 ▪ Fx: 858-560-0206

Dermatology, American Osteopathic College of   www.aocd.org
1501 E Illinois St PO Box 7525   Kirksville MO 63501
Ph: 660-665-2184 ▪ Fx: 660-627-2623 ▪ TF: 800-449-2623

Dermatology, American Society of   www.asd.org
2721 Capital Ave   Sacramento CA 95816
Ph: 916-446-5054 ▪ Fx: 916-446-0500

Dermatology, International Society of   www.intsocdermatol.org
847 S Randall Rd Suite 412   Elgin IL 60123
Ph: 847-429-9535 ▪ Fx: 847-429-9545

Dermatology Nurses Association   www.dnanurse.org
PO Box 56   Pitman NJ 08071
Ph: 856-256-2330 ▪ Fx: 856-589-7463 ▪ TF: 800-454-4362

Dermatology Society, History of   www.dermato.med.br/hds
1819 John F Kennedy Blvd Suite 465   Philadelphia PA 19103
Ph: 215-563-8333 ▪ Fx: 215-563-3044

Dermatology Inc, Society for Investigative   www.sidnet.org
820 W Superior Ave 7th Fl   Cleveland OH 44113
Ph: 216-579-9300 ▪ Fx: 216-579-9333

Dermatology, Society for Pediatric   www.pedsderm.net
5422 N Bernard St   Chicago IL 60625
Ph: 773-583-9780 ▪ Fx: 773-583-9765

Dermatopathology, American Society of   www.asdp.org
60 Revere Dr Suite 500   Northbrook IL 60062
Ph: 847-400-5820 ▪ Fx: 847-480-9282

Derrick Clubs, Association of Desk &   www.addc.org
5153 E 51st St Suite 107   Tulsa OK 74135
Ph: 918-622-1749 ▪ Fx: 918-622-1675

Desalination Association, International   www.idadesal.org
PO Box 387   Topsfield MA 01983
Ph: 978-887-0410 ▪ Fx: 978-887-0411

Descendants of Founders of New Jersey   www.njfounders.org
109 Christopher St   Montclair NJ 07042
Ph: 973-744-2926

D'Escoffier, Les Dames   www.ldei.org

Desert Fishes Council   www.desertfishes.org
PO Box 337   Bishop CA 93515
Ph: 760-872-8751

Desert Protective Council   www.dpcinc.org
PO Box 3635   San Diego CA 92163
Ph: 619-543-0757

Desert Research Institute, Chihuahuan   www.cdri.org
PO Box 905   Fort Davis TX 79734
Ph: 915-364-2499 ▪ Fx: 915-364-2504

Desert Tortoise Preserve Committee   www.tortoise-tracks.org
4067 Mission Inn Ave   Riverside CA 92501
Ph: 909-683-3872 ▪ Fx: 909-683-6949

Design, American Institute of Building   www.aibd.org
2505 Main St Suite 209B   Stratford CT 06961
Ph: 203-227-3640 ▪ Fx: 203-378-3568 ▪ TF: 800-366-2423

Design, Association for Bridge Construction &   www.abcdpittsburgh.org
PO Box 23264   Pittsburgh PA 15222
Ph: 412-281-9900 ▪ Fx: 412-281-2056

Design Association, Computer Integrated Textile   www.citda.org/
405 Battleground Ave Suite 204   Greensboro NC 27401
Ph: 336-379-0603 ▪ Fx: 336-379-0851

Design Association, International Furnishings &   www.ifda.com
191 Clarksville Rd   Princeton Junction NJ 08550
Ph: 609-799-3423 ▪ Fx: 609-799-7023

Design Association, International Interior   www.iida.org
13-122 Merchandise Mart   Chicago IL 60654
Ph: 312-467-1950 ▪ Fx: 312-467-0779 ▪ TF: 888-799-4432

Design Association, Surface   www.surfacedesign.org
PO Box 360   Sebastopol CA 95473
Ph: 707-829-3110 ▪ Fx: 707-829-3285

Design Automation Consortium, Electronic   www.edac.org
111 W Saint John St Suite 220   San Jose CA 95113
Ph: 408-287-3322 ▪ Fx: 408-283-5283

Design-Build Institute of America   www.dbia.org
1010 Massachusetts Ave NW 3rd Fl   Washington DC 20001
Ph: 202-682-0110 ▪ Fx: 202-682-5877 ▪ TF: 866-692-0110

Design Drafting Association, American   www.adda.org
105 E Main St   Newbern TN 38059
Ph: 731-627-0802 ▪ Fx: 731-627-9321

Design Firms, Association of Professional   www.apdf.org
601 108th Ave NE 19th Fl   Bellevue WA 98004
Ph: 425-943-3825 ▪ Fx: 425-943-3878

Design Management Institute   www.dmi.org
29 Temple Pl 2nd Fl   Boston MA 02111
Ph: 617-338-6380 ▪ Fx: 617-338-6570

Design, National Association of Schools of Art &   nasad.arts-accredit.org
11250 Roger Bacon Dr Suite 21   Reston VA 20190
Ph: 703-437-0700 ▪ Fx: 703-437-6312

Design Planning, Center for
2300 E Mallory St   Pensacola FL 32503
Ph: 850-432-8478

Design Professionals Association
415 Taft Ave   Glen Ellyn IL 60137
Ph: 630-858-9500 ▪ Fx: 630-344-1414

Design Qualification, National Council for Interior   www.ncidq.org
1200 18th St NW Suite 1001   Washington DC 20036
Ph: 202-721-0220 ▪ Fx: 202-721-0221

Design Research Association, Environmental   home.telepath.com/~edra
PO Box 7146   Edmond OK 73083
Ph: 405-330-4863 ▪ Fx: 405-330-4150

Design, Society for Environmental Graphic   www.segd.org
1000 Vermont Ave Suite 400   Washington DC 20005
Ph: 202-638-5555 ▪ Fx: 202-638-0891

Designers of America, Council of Fashion   www.cfda.com
1412 Broadway Suite 2006   New York NY 10018
Ph: 212-302-1821 ▪ Fx: 212-768-0515

Designers, American Society of Interior   www.asid.org
608 Massachusetts Ave NE   Washington DC 20002
Ph: 202-546-3480 ▪ Fx: 202-546-3240

Designers Association of America, Custom Tailors &   www.ctda.com
PO Box 53052   Washington DC 20009
Ph: 202-387-7220 ▪ Fx: 202-387-7713

Designers Association, Broadcast   www.bda.tv
2029 Century Pk E Suite 555   Los Angeles CA 90067
Ph: 310-712-0040 ▪ Fx: 310-712-0039

Designers, Association of Professional Landscape   www.apld.org
1924 N 2nd St   Harrisburg PA 17102
Ph: 717-238-9780 ▪ Fx: 717-238-9985

Designers Association, University & College   www.ucda.com
153 Front St   Smyrna TN 37167
Ph: 615-459-4559 ▪ Fx: 615-459-5229

Designers Guild, Costume   www.costumedesignersguild.com
4730 Woodman Ave Suite 430   Sherman Oaks CA 91423
Ph: 818-905-1557 ▪ Fx: 818-905-1560

Designers Guild, Professional Knitwear
W3090 County Rd Y   Lomira WI 53048
Ph: 920-583-4298

Designers, International Association of Lighting www.iald.org
200 World Trade Ctr Merchandise Mart Suite 9-104   Chicago IL 60654
Ph: 312-527-3677 ▪ Fx: 312-527-3680

Designers, Organization of Black www.core77.com/OBD
300 M St SW Suite N110   Washington DC 20024
Ph: 202-659-3918 ▪ Fx: 202-488-3838

Designers & Producers Association, Exhibit www.edpa.com
5775 Peachtree Dunwoody Rd Bldg G Suite 500   Atlanta GA 30342
Ph: 404-303-7310 ▪ Fx: 404-252-0774

Designers Society of America, Industrial www.idsa.org
45195 Business Ct Suite 250   Dulles VA 20166
Ph: 703-707-6000 ▪ Fx: 703-787-8501

Designers, Society of Certified Kitchen & Bathroom
687 Willow Grove St   Hackettstown NJ 07840
Ph: 908-852-0033 ▪ Fx: 908-852-1695 ▪ TF: 800-843-6522

Designers, Society of Craft www.craftdesigners.org
PO Box 3388   Zanesville OH 43702
Ph: 740-452-4541 ▪ Fx: 740-454-2552

Designers, Society of Piping Engineers & www.spedweb.org
1 Main St Suite 719   Houston TX 77002
Ph: 713-221-8089 ▪ Fx: 713-226-5230

Designers Inc, Society of Publication www.spd.org
60 E 42nd St Suite 721   New York NY 10165
Ph: 212-983-8585 ▪ Fx: 212-983-2308

Designs for Change www.designsforchange.org
29 E Madison St Suite 950   Chicago IL 60602
Ph: 312-236-7252 ▪ Fx: 312-236-7927

Desk & Derrick Clubs, Association of www.addc.org
5153 E 51st St Suite 107   Tulsa OK 74135
Ph: 918-622-1749 ▪ Fx: 918-622-1675

Destination Management Executives, Association of www.adme.org
3401 Quebec St Suite 4050   Denver CO 80207
Ph: 303-394-3905 ▪ Fx: 303-394-3450

Destructive Decisions, Students Against www.saddonline.com
255 Main St   Marlborough MA 01752
Ph: 508-481-3568 ▪ Fx: 508-481-5759 ▪ TF: 877-723-3462

Detergent Association, Soap & www.cleaning101.com
1500 K St NW Suite 300   Washington DC 20005
Ph: 202-347-2900 ▪ Fx: 202-347-4110

Detoxification Association, National Acupuncture www.acudetox.com
PO Box 1927   Vancouver WA 98668
Ph: 360-254-0186 ▪ Fx: 360-260-8620 ▪ TF: 888-765-6232

Developers, Associated Owners & www.constructionchannel.net/aod
PO Box 4163   McLean VA 22103
Ph: 703-734-2397 ▪ Fx: 703-734-2908 ▪ TF: 888-999-2536

Developing World, Our www.magiclink.net/~odw
13004 Paseo Presada   Saratoga CA 95070
Ph: 408-379-4431 ▪ Fx: 408-376-0755

Development Agencies, National Association of State www.nasda.com
12884 Harbor Dr   Woodbridge VA 22192
Ph: 703-490-6777 ▪ Fx: 703-492-4404

Development, American Society for Training & www.astd.org
1640 King St Box 1443   Alexandria VA 22313
Ph: 703-683-8100 ▪ Fx: 703-683-1523 ▪ TF: 800-628-2783

Development Association, National Community www.ncdaonline.org
522 21st St NW Suite 120   Washington DC 20006
Ph: 202-293-7587 ▪ Fx: 202-887-5546

Development Companies, National Association of www.nadco.org
6764 Old McLean Village Dr   McLean VA 22101
Ph: 703-748-2575 ▪ Fx: 703-748-2582

Development Corp, Operation Blessing International Relief & www.ob.org
977 Centerville Tpke   Virginia Beach VA 23463
Ph: 757-226-3401 ▪ Fx: 757-226-3411 ▪ TF: 800-730-2537

Development Corps, Citizens www.cdc.org
1726 M St NW Suite 1100   Washington DC 20036
Ph: 202-872-0933 ▪ Fx: 202-872-0923 ▪ TF: 800-394-1945

Development Council, National www.ndc-online.org
51 E 42nd St Suite 300   New York NY 10017
Ph: 212-682-1106 ▪ Fx: 212-573-6118

Development Council, Pacific Basin
711 Kapiolana Blvd Suite 1075   Honolulu HI 96813
Ph: 808-596-7229 ▪ Fx: 808-596-7249

Development Environment & Security, Pacific Institute for Studies in www.pacinst.org
654 13th St   Oakland CA 94612
Ph: 510-251-1600 ▪ Fx: 510-251-2203

Development Federation, World www.wdf.org
35 Technology Park Suite 150   Norcross GA 30092
Ph: 770-446-6996 ▪ Fx: 770-263-8825

Development Finance Agencies, Council of www.cdfa.net
301 NW 63rd Ave Suite 500   Oklahoma City OK 73116
Ph: 405-848-6059 ▪ Fx: 405-842-3299

Development Foundation, America's www.adfusa.org
101 N Union St Suite 200   Alexandria VA 22314
Ph: 703-836-2717 ▪ Fx: 703-836-3379

Development Foundation, Pan American www.padf.org
2600 16th St NW 4th Fl   Washington DC 20009
Ph: 202-458-3969 ▪ Fx: 202-458-6316

Development, Fund for Democracy &
1101 15th St NW Suite 205   Washington DC 20005
Ph: 202-296-5353 ▪ Fx: 202-296-5433

Development GAP www.developmentgap.org
927 15th St NW 4th Fl   Washington DC 20005
Ph: 202-898-1566 ▪ Fx: 202-898-1612

Development Group for Alternative Policies www.developmentgap.org
927 15th St NW 4th Fl   Washington DC 20005
Ph: 202-898-1566 ▪ Fx: 202-898-1612

Development at Harvard University, Center for International www.cid.harvard.edu
Harvard Univ John F Kennedy School of Government 1 Eliot St Bldg   79 JFK St   Cambridge MA 02138
Ph: 617-496-7294 ▪ Fx: 617-496-8753

(Development) HOPE International www.hopeinternational.net
PO Box 10001   Lancaster PA 17605
Ph: 877-982-4673 ▪ Fx: 717-464-9046

Development Institute, First Nations www.firstnations.org
11917 Main St   Fredericksburg VA 22408
Ph: 540-371-5615 ▪ Fx: 540-371-3505 ▪ TF: 800-682-5384

Development, Institute for Integral www.institutefortraining.com
PO Box 2172   Colorado Springs CO 80901
Ph: 719-634-7943 ▪ Fx: 719-630-7025 ▪ TF: 800-544-9562

Development, Inter-American Council for Integral www.cidi.oas.org
1889 F St NW Rm 220I   Washington DC 20006
Ph: 202-458-3783 ▪ Fx: 202-458-3526

Development, International Center for Law in
777 United Nations Plaza Suite 7E   New York NY 10017
Ph: 212-687-0036 ▪ Fx: 212-370-9844

Development Inc, Mercy-USA for Aid & www.mercyusa.org
44450 Pinetree Dr Suite 201   Plymouth MI 48170
Ph: 734-454-0011 ▪ Fx: 734-454-0303 ▪ TF: 800-556-3729

Development Organizations, National Association of www.nado.org
400 N Capitol St NW Suite 390   Washington DC 20001
Ph: 202-624-7806 ▪ Fx: 202-624-8813

(Development) Plenty International www.plenty.org
PO Box 394   Summertown TN 38483
Ph: 931-964-4864

Development Policy, Institute for Food & www.foodfirst.org
398 60th St   Oakland CA 94618
Ph: 510-654-4400 ▪ Fx: 510-654-4551

Development & Population Activities, Centre for www.cedpa.org
1400 16th St NW Suite 100   Washington DC 20036
Ph: 202-667-1142 ▪ Fx: 202-332-4496

Development & Relief Agency International, Adventist www.adra.org
12501 Old Columbia Pike   Silver Spring MD 20904
Ph: 301-680-6380 ▪ Fx: 301-680-6370 ▪ TF: 800-424-2372

(Development) Third World Conference Foundation www.twcfinternational.org
1525 E 53rd St Suite 435   Chicago IL 60615
Ph: 773-241-6688 ▪ Fx: 773-241-7898

Development - USA, Society for International www.sidint.org
1875 Connecticut Ave NW   Washington DC 20009
Ph: 202-884-8590 ▪ Fx: 202-884-8499

Development, Village Earth - Consortium for Sustainable Village-Based www.villageearth.org
PO Box 797   Fort Collins CO 80522
Ph: 970-491-5754 ▪ Fx: 970-491-2729 ▪ TF: 800-648-8043

Development, World Learning for International www.worldlearning.org
1015 15th St NW Suite 750   Washington DC 20005
Ph: 202-408-5420 ▪ Fx: 202-408-5397

Developmental Biology, Society for sdb.bio.purdue.edu
9650 Rockville Pike   Bethesda MD 20814
Ph: 301-571-0647 ▪ Fx: 301-571-5704

Developmental Disabilities Councils, National Association of www.naddc.org
1234 Massachusetts Ave NW Suite 103   Washington DC 20005
Ph: 202-347-1234 ▪ Fx: 202-347-4023

Developmental Disabilities, National Association of Councils on www.nacdd.org
1234 Massachusetts Ave NW Suite 103   Washington DC 20005
Ph: 202-347-1234 ▪ Fx: 202-347-4023

Developmental Disabilities Nurses Association www.ddna.org
1733 H St Suite 330 PMB 1214   Blaine WA 98230
Ph: 800-888-6733 ▪ Fx: 360-332-2280

Developmental Disabilities Services, National Association of State Directors of www.nasddds.org
113 Oronoco St   Alexandria VA 22314
Ph: 703-683-4202 ▪ Fx: 703-684-1395

Developmental Education, National Association for www.nade.net
2447 Tissin Ave Suite 207   Findlay OH 45840
Ph: 419-424-9360 ▪ Fx: 419-423-9078 ▪ TF: 877-881-9876

Developmental Medicine, American Academy for Cerebral Palsy & aacpdm.org
6300 N River Rd Suite 727   Rosemont IL 60018
Ph: 847-698-1635 ▪ Fx: 847-823-0536

Developmental Neuroscience, International Society for developmental-neuroscience.org

Devil Pups Inc www.devilpups.com
2160 Lords Landing   Virginia Beach VA 23454
Ph: 757-496-8796 ▪ Fx: 757-496-8797

Devon Association, American Milking www.milkingdevons.org
135 Old Bay Rd   New Durham NH 03855
Ph: 603-859-6611

Dewey John Society johndeweysociety.org

Dexter Cattle Association, American www.dextercattle.org
404 High St   Prairie Home MO 65068
Ph: 660-841-9502

DFK International/USA Inc www.dfkusa.com
1255 23rd St NW Suite 200   Washington DC 20037
Ph: 202-452-1588 ▪ Fx: 202-833-3636

DGA-PAC
7920 W Sunset Blvd   Los Angeles CA 90046
Ph: 310-289-2000 ▪ Fx: 310-289-2029

DH Lawrence Society of North America www.wsu.edu/~hydev/dhlsna.htm

Dharma Realm Buddhist Association www.drba.org
Sagely City of 10 Thousand Buddhas 2001 Talmage Rd PO Box 217   Talmage CA 95481
Ph: 707-462-0939 ▪ Fx: 707-462-0949

Diabetes Association, American www.diabetes.org
1701 N Beauregard St   Alexandria VA 22311
Ph: 703-549-1500 ▪ Fx: 703-836-2464 ▪ TF: 800-232-3472

Diabetes Educators, American Association of www.aadenet.org
100 W Monroe St Suite 400   Chicago IL 60603
Ph: 312-424-2426 ▪ Fx: 312-424-2427 ▪ TF: 800-338-3633

Diabetes Exercise & Sports Association
8001 Montcastle Dr   Nashville TN 37221
Ph: 800-898-4322
www.diabetes-exercise.org

Diabetes Research Foundation International, Juvenile
120 Wall St   New York NY 10005
Ph: 212-785-9500 ▪ Fx: 212-785-9595 ▪ TF: 800-533-2873
www.jdf.org

Diagnostic Medical Sonographers, American Registry of
51 Monroe St Plaza East 1   Rockville MD 20850
Ph: 301-738-8401 ▪ Fx: 301-738-0312 ▪ TF: 800-541-9754
www.ardms.org

Diagnostic Medical Sonography, Society of
2745 N Dallas Pkwy Suite 350   Plano TX 75093
Ph: 214-473-8057 ▪ Fx: 214-473-8563 ▪ TF: 800-229-9506
www.sdms.org

Diagnostics Manufacturers, Association of Medical
555 13th St NW Suite 7W-404   Washington DC 20004
Ph: 202-637-6837 ▪ Fx: 202-637-5910
www.amdm.org

Diakonia of the Americas & Caribbean
1304 LaPorte Ave   Valparaiso IN 46383
Ph: 219-464-6925 ▪ Fx: 219-464-6928
diakonia-world.org/dotac

Dialect Society, American
c/o Duke University Press Box 90660   Durham NC 27708
Ph: 919-687-3602 ▪ Fx: 919-688-2615 ▪ TF: 888-387-5765
www.americandialect.org

Dialogue, Center for Public
10615 Brunswick Ave   Kensington MD 20895
Ph: 301-933-3535

Dialogue on Diversity Inc
1730 K St NW Suite 304   Washington DC 20006
Ph: 703-631-0650 ▪ Fx: 703-631-0617
www.dialogueondiversity.org

Dialogue Foundation
PO Box 20210   Shaker Heights OH 44120
Ph: 216-491-1830
www.dialoguefoundation.com

Dialysis, International Society for Peritoneal
66 Martin St   Milton ON L9T2R2
Ph: 905-875-2456 ▪ Fx: 905-875-2864 ▪ TF: 888-834-1001
www.ispd.org

Dialysis & Transplantation, North American Society for
4010 Bentley Dr   Pearland TX 77584
Ph: 281-997-1944
www.nasdat.org

Diamond Association of America, Industrial
PO Box 29460   Columbus OH 43229
Ph: 614-797-2265 ▪ Fx: 614-797-2264
www.superabrasives.org

Diamond & Colorstone Association, Indian
56 W 45th St Suite 705   New York NY 10036
Ph: 212-921-4488 ▪ Fx: 212-768-7935

Diamond Council of America
3212 W End Ave Suite 202   Nashville TN 37203
Ph: 615-385-5301 ▪ Fx: 615-385-4955
www.diamondcouncil.org

Diamond Dealers Club
580 5th Ave   New York NY 10036
Ph: 212-869-9777 ▪ Fx: 212-869-5164

Diamond Manufacturers & Importers Association of America
PO Box 5297   New York NY 10185
Ph: 212-944-2066

Diamond Trade & Precious Stone Association of America
11 W 47th St   New York NY 10036
Ph: 212-790-3806 ▪ Fx: 212-869-5511

Dian Fossey Gorilla Fund International
800 Cherokee Ave SE   Atlanta GA 30315
Ph: 404-624-5881 ▪ Fx: 404-624-5999 ▪ TF: 800-851-0203
www.gorillafund.org

Diaper Services, National Association of
994 Old Eagle School Rd Suite 1019   Wayne PA 19087
Ph: 610-971-4850 ▪ Fx: 610-971-4859
www.diapernet.com

Dictionary Society of North America
Univ of Wisconsin-Madison 600 N Park St 6129 HC White
Hall   Madison WI 53706
Ph: 608-233-3051 ▪ Fx: 608-263-3817
polyglot.lss.wisc.edu/dsna

Die Casting Association, North American
9701 W Higgins Rd Suite 880   Rosemont IL 60018
Ph: 847-292-3600 ▪ Fx: 847-292-3620
www.diecasting.org

Die Stampers & Engravers Union of North America, International
Plate Printers   14 C St SW Rm 213-5a   Washington DC
20228
Ph: 202-874-2554

Diecasting Development Council
9701 W Higgins Rd Suite 855   Rosemont IL 60018
Ph: 847-292-3625 ▪ Fx: 847-292-3613
www.diecasting.org/ddc

Diecutting & Diemaking, International Association of
651 W Terra Cotta Ave Suite 132   Crystal Lake IL 60014
Ph: 815-455-7519 ▪ Fx: 815-455-7510 ▪ TF: 800-828-4233
www.iadd.org

Dielectrics & Electrical Insulation Society, IEEE
IEEE Operations Ctr 445 Hoes Ln   Piscataway NJ 08854
Ph: 732-981-0060 ▪ Fx: 732-981-1721
tdei.sju.edu/deis

Diesel Specialists, Association of
10 Laboratory Dr PO Box 13966   Research Triangle Park NC
27709
Ph: 919-549-4800 ▪ Fx: 919-549-4824
www.diesel.org

(Diet) Feingold Association of the US
127 E Main St Suite 106   Riverhead NY 11901
Ph: 631-369-9340 ▪ Fx: 631-369-2988 ▪ TF: 800-321-3287
www.feingold.org

Dietary Managers Association
406 Surrey Woods Dr   Saint Charles IL 60174
Ph: 630-587-6336 ▪ Fx: 630-587-6308
www.dmaonline.org

Dietary Support Coalition, American Celiac Society/
PO Box 23455   New Orleans LA 70183
Ph: 504-737-3293 ▪ Fx: 504-737-3283

Dietetic Association, American
120 S Riverside Plaza Suite 2000   Chicago IL 60606
Ph: 312-899-0040 ▪ Fx: 312-899-4758 ▪ TF: 800-877-1600
www.eatright.org

Dietetic Association, Seventh-day Adventist
6100 Leoni Rd   Grizzly Flats CA 95636
Ph: 530-626-3610 ▪ Fx: 530-626-8524
www.sdada.org

Dietetic Registration, Commission on
120 S Riverside Plaza Suite 2000   Chicago IL 60606
Ph: 312-899-0040 ▪ Fx: 312-899-4772
www.cdrnet.org

Digestive Disease National Coalition
507 Capitol Ct NE Suite 200   Washington DC 20002
Ph: 202-544-7497 ▪ Fx: 202-546-7105
www.ddnc.org

Digestive Health & Nutrition, Foundation for
4930 Del Ray Ave   Bethesda MD 20814
Ph: 301-222-4002 ▪ Fx: 301-222-4010
www.fdhn.org

Digital Arts & Sciences, International Academy of
3515 24th St   San Francisco CA 94110
Ph: 415-824-2268 ▪ Fx: 415-826-9111
www.iadas.net

Digital Democracy, Center for
1718 Connecticut Ave NW Suite 200   Washington DC 20009
Ph: 202-986-2220
www.democraticmedia.org

Digital Distribution of Advertising for Publications Association
PO Box 175   Marblehead MA 01945
Ph: 781-639-7785 ▪ Fx: 781-639-7786
www.ddap.org

Digital Enterprise Alliance, International
100 Daingerfield Rd   Alexandria VA 22314
Ph: 703-837-1070 ▪ Fx: 703-837-1072
www.idealliance.org

Digital Freedom Network
520 Broad St 3rd Fl   Newark NJ 07102
Ph: 973-438-3712 ▪ Fx: 973-438-1735
www.dfn.org

Digital Imaging Association, Heidelberg
1 Barney Rd Suite 232   Clifton Park NY 12065
Ph: 518-373-1225 ▪ Fx: 518-373-9205
www.hdia.org

Digital Imaging Association, International
PO Box 81261   Chamblee GA 30366
Ph: 770-452-8119 ▪ Fx: 770-234-9058
pwr.com/ldia

Digital Imaging Marketing Association
3000 Picture Pl   Jackson MI 49201
Ph: 517-788-8100 ▪ Fx: 517-788-8371
dima.pmai.org

(Digital Music) MIDI Manufacturers Association Inc
PO Box 3173   La Habra CA 90632
Ph: 714-736-9774 ▪ Fx: 714-736-9775
www.midi.org

Digital Printing & Imaging Association
10015 Main St   Fairfax VA 22031
Ph: 703-385-1339 ▪ Fx: 703-359-1336
www.dpia.org

'Ding' Darling Foundation, JN
785 Crandon Blvd Suite 1206   Key Biscayne FL 33149
Ph: 305-361-9788 ▪ Fx: 305-361-9789
www.ding-darling.org

Dinghy Association, US Optimist
www.usoda.org

Dinshah Health Society
PO Box 707   Malaga NJ 08328
Ph: 856-692-4686 ▪ Fx: 856-696-7890
www.dinshahhealth.org

Diocesan Ecumenical Officers, National Association of
8003 Mobud Dr   Houston TX 77036
Ph: 713-774-0097 ▪ Fx: 713-774-0320
www.nadeo.com

Diocesan Liturgical Commissions, Federation of
415 Michigan Ave NE Suite 70   Washington DC 20017
Ph: 202-635-6990 ▪ Fx: 202-529-2452
www.fdlc.org

Diocesan Vocation Directors, National Conference of
PO Box 1570   Little River SC 29566
Ph: 843-280-7191 ▪ Fx: 843-280-0681
www.ncdvd.org

Diplomacy, American Academy of
1800 K St NW Suite 1014   Washington DC 20006
Ph: 202-331-3721 ▪ Fx: 202-833-4555
www.academyofdiplomacy.org

Diplomatic & Consular Officers Retired
1801 F St NW   Washington DC 20006
Ph: 202-682-0500 ▪ Fx: 202-842-3295 ▪ TF: 800-344-9127
www.dacorbacon.org

(Diplomats) Hospitality & Information Service
1630 Crescent Pl NW   Washington DC 20009
Ph: 202-232-3002 ▪ Fx: 202-667-1475
www.this4diplomats.org

Direct Instruction, Association for
PO Box 10252   Eugene OR 97440
Ph: 541-485-1293 ▪ Fx: 541-683-7543
www.adihome.org

Direct Marketing Association Inc
1120 Ave of the Americas   New York NY 10036
Ph: 212-768-7277 ▪ Fx: 212-302-6714
www.the-dma.org

Direct Marketing Association Inc Catalog Council
1120 Ave of the Americas   New York NY 10036
Ph: 212-768-7277 ▪ Fx: 212-302-6714
www.the-dma.org/councils/catalog

Direct Marketing Association Inc Nonprofit
Federation   1111 19th St NW Suite 1180   Washington DC
20036
Ph: 202-628-4380 ▪ Fx: 202-628-4383
www.the-dma.org/nonprofitfederation

Direct Marketing Association, North American Farmers'
62 White Loaf Rd   Southampton MA 01073
Ph: 413-529-0386
www.nafdma.com

Direct Marketing Association Inc
Telephone Preference Service   PO Box 1559   Carmel NY
10512
Ph: 212-768-7277
www.dmaconsumers.org/offtelephonelist.html

Direct Marketing Educational Foundation
1120 Ave of the Americas   New York NY 10036
Ph: 212-768-7277 ▪ Fx: 212-302-6714
www.the-dma.org/dmef

Direct Marketing Fundraisers Association
224 7th St   Garden City NY 11530
Ph: 516-746-6700 ▪ Fx: 516-294-8141
www.dmfa.org

Direct Relief International
27 S La Patera Ln   Santa Barbara CA 93117
Ph: 805-964-4767 ▪ Fx: 805-681-4838 ▪ TF: 800-676-1638
www.directrelief.org

Direct Response Fundraising Counsel, Association of
1612 K St NW Suite 510   Washington DC 20006
Ph: 202-293-9640 ▪ Fx: 202-887-9699
www.adrfco.org

Direct Selling Association
1275 Pennsylvania Ave NW Suite 800   Washington DC 20004
Ph: 202-347-8866 ▪ Fx: 202-347-0055
www.dsa.org

Direct Selling Associations, World Federation of — www.wfdsa.org
1275 Pennsylvania Ave NW Suite 800   Washington DC 20004
Ph: 202-347-8866 ▪ Fx: 202-347-0055

Direct Selling Education Foundation — www.dsef.org
1275 Pennsylvania Ave NW Suite 800   Washington DC 20004
Ph: 202-347-8866 ▪ Fx: 202-347-8401

Direct Voice
1111 19th St NW   Washington DC 20036
Ph: 202-955-5030 ▪ Fx: 202-955-0085

Directed Energy Professional Society — www.deps.org
PO Box 9874   Albuquerque NM 87119
Ph: 505-998-4910 ▪ Fx: 505-242-2249

Directional Crossing Contractors Association — www.dcca.org
13355 Noel Rd Suite 1940   Dallas TX 75240
Ph: 972-386-9545 ▪ Fx: 972-386-9547

Directors Guild of America — www.dga.org
7920 W Sunset Blvd   Los Angeles CA 90046
Ph: 310-289-2000 ▪ Fx: 310-289-2029 ▪ TF: 800-421-4173

Directors Guild of Canada — www.dgc.ca
1 Eglinton Ave E Suite 604   Toronto ON M4P3A1
Ph: 416-482-6640 ▪ Fx: 416-482-6639 ▪ TF: 888-972-0098

(Directors Guild) DGA-PAC
7920 W Sunset Blvd   Los Angeles CA 90046
Ph: 310-289-2000 ▪ Fx: 310-289-2029

Directors of Health Promotion & Education — www.dhpe.org
1101 15th St NW Suite 601   Washington DC 20005
Ph: 202-659-2230 ▪ Fx: 202-659-2339

Directors of YMCAs in the US, Association of Professional — www.apdymca.org
12 Broad St Suite 2-1   Westerly RI 02891
Ph: 401-604-0034 ▪ Fx: 401-604-0036

Directory Marketing, Association of — www.admworks.org
1187 Thorn Run Rd Suite 630   Moon Township PA 15108
Ph: 412-269-0663 ▪ Fx: 412-269-0655

Directory Publishers, Association of — www.adp.org
116 Cass St   Traverse City MI 49684
Ph: 800-267-9002 ▪ Fx: 231-486-2182

Disabilities, Academy of Dentistry for Persons with — scdonline.org/ADPD_Index.htm
211 E Chicago Ave Suite 740   Chicago IL 60611
Ph: 312-440-2660 ▪ Fx: 312-440-2824

Disabilities, American Association of People with — www.aapd-dc.org
1629 K St NW Suite 503   Washington DC 20006
Ph: 202-457-0046 ▪ Fx: 202-457-0473 ▪ TF: 800-840-8844

Disabilities, America's Athletes with — www.americasathletes.org
8630 Fenton St Suite 920   Silver Spring MD 20910
Ph: 301-589-9042 ▪ Fx: 301-589-9052 ▪ TF: 800-238-7632

Disabilities Association of America, Learning — www.ldanatl.org
4156 Library Rd   Pittsburgh PA 15234
Ph: 412-341-1515 ▪ Fx: 412-344-0224 ▪ TF: 888-300-6710

Disabilities, Association of University Centers on — www.aucd.org
8630 Fenton St Suite 410   Silver Spring MD 20910
Ph: 301-588-8252 ▪ Fx: 301-588-2842

Disabilities, Christian Council on Persons With — www.ccpd.org
1100 W 42nd St Suite 223   Indianapolis IN 46208
Ph: 317-923-2273

Disabilities, Council for Learning — www.cldinternational.org
PO Box 4014   Leesburg VA 20177
Ph: 571-258-1010 ▪ Fx: 571-258-1011

Disabilities, Council on Quality & Leadership in Support for People with — www.thecouncil.org
100 West Rd Suite 406   Towson MD 21204
Ph: 410-583-0060 ▪ Fx: 410-583-0063

Disabilities Councils, National Association of Developmental — www.naddc.org
1234 Massachusetts Ave NW Suite 103   Washington DC 20005
Ph: 202-347-1234 ▪ Fx: 202-347-4023

Disabilities, Family Resource Center on — www.frcd.org
20 E Jackson Blvd Rm 300   Chicago IL 60604
Ph: 312-939-3513 ▪ Fx: 312-939-7297 ▪ TF: 800-952-4199

Disabilities, National Association of Councils on Developmental — www.nacdd.org
1234 Massachusetts Ave NW Suite 103   Washington DC 20005
Ph: 202-347-1234 ▪ Fx: 202-347-4023

Disabilities, National Center for Learning — www.ncld.org
381 Park Ave S Suite 1401   New York NY 10016
Ph: 212-545-7510 ▪ Fx: 212-545-9665 ▪ TF: 888-575-7373

Disabilities, National Coalition for Students with — www.ncsd.org
1413 K St NW 9th Fl   Washington DC 20005
Ph: 202-347-8772 ▪ Fx: 202-393-5886

Disabilities, National Dissemination Center for Children with — www.nichcy.org
PO Box 1492   Washington DC 20013
Ph: 202-884-8200 ▪ Fx: 202-884-8441 ▪ TF: 800-695-0285

Disabilities Network, YAI/National Institute for People with — www.yai.org
460 W 34th St   New York NY 10001
Ph: 212-273-6100 ▪ Fx: 212-563-4836

Disabilities Nurses Association, Developmental — www.ddna.org
1733 H St Suite 330 PMB 1214   Blaine WA 98230
Ph: 800-888-6733 ▪ Fx: 360-332-2280

Disabilities Services, National Association of State Directors of Developmental — www.nasddds.org
113 Oronoco St   Alexandria VA 22314
Ph: 703-683-4202 ▪ Fx: 703-684-1395

Disabilities, World Association of People with — www.wapd.org
4503 Sunnyview Dr Suite 1121 PO Box 14111   Oklahoma City OK 73135
Ph: 405-672-4440 ▪ Fx: 405-672-4441

Disability Association, American — www.adanet.org
2201 6th Ave S   Birmingham AL 35233
Ph: 205-328-9090 ▪ Fx: 205-251-7417

Disability, Association on Higher Education & — www.ahead.org
PO Box 540666   Waltham MA 02454
Ph: 781-788-0003 ▪ Fx: 781-788-0033

Disability Evaluating Physicians, American Academy of — www.aadep.org
150 N Wacker Dr Suite 1420   Chicago IL 60606
Ph: 312-658-1171 ▪ Fx: 312-658-1175 ▪ TF: 800-456-6095

Disability Evaluating Professionals, National Association of — www.nadep.com
PO Box 13801   Midlothian VA 23113
Ph: 804-378-7275

Disability Management Employer Coalition — www.dmec.org
6343 El Cajon Blvd Suite 110   San Diego CA 92115
Ph: 619-698-0431 ▪ Fx: 619-749-7872 ▪ TF: 800-789-3632

Disability, National Association on Alcohol Drugs & — www.naadd.org
2165 Bunker Hill Dr   San Mateo CA 94402
Ph: 650-578-8047 ▪ Fx: 650-286-9205

Disability, National Catholic Partnership on — www.ncpd.org
415 Michigan Ave NE Suite 240   Washington DC 20017
Ph: 202-529-2933 ▪ Fx: 202-529-4678

Disability, National Organization on — www.nod.org
910 16th St NW Suite 600   Washington DC 20006
Ph: 202-293-5960 ▪ Fx: 202-293-7999

Disability & Oral Health, International Association for — www.iadh.org
Ohio State Univ College of Dentistry 305 W 12th Ave PO Box 182357   Columbus OH 43218
Ph: 614-292-1232 ▪ Fx: 614-292-4522

Disability Resources Inc — www.disabilityresources.org
4 Glatter Ln   Centereach NY 11720
Ph: 631-585-0290

Disability Rights Advocates — www.dralegal.org
449 15th St Suite 303   Oakland CA 94612
Ph: 510-451-8644 ▪ Fx: 510-451-8511

Disability Rights Center Inc — www.drcnh.org
18 Low Ave PO Box 3660   Concord NH 03302
Ph: 603-228-0432 ▪ Fx: 603-255-2077 ▪ TF: 800-834-1721

Disability Rights Education & Defense Fund — www.dredf.org
2212 6th St   Berkeley CA 94710
Ph: 510-644-2555 ▪ Fx: 510-841-8645

Disability Services, National Center for — www.ncds.org
201 IU Willets Rd   Albertson NY 11507
Ph: 516-747-5400 ▪ Fx: 516-393-2668

Disability Sports Alliance, National — www.ndsaonline.org
25 W Independence Way   Kingston RI 02881
Ph: 401-792-7130 ▪ Fx: 401-792-7132

Disability Studies, Society for — www.uic.edu/orgs/sds
Univ of Chicago Dept of Disability & Human Development 1640 W Roosevelt Rd Suite 236   Chicago IL 60608
Ph: 312-996-4664 ▪ Fx: 312-996-7743

Disability, World Institute on — www.wid.org
510 16th St Suite 100   Oakland CA 94612
Ph: 510-763-4100 ▪ Fx: 510-763-4109

(Disabled) ADAPT — www.adapt.org
201 S Cherokee St   Denver CO 80223
Ph: 303-733-9324 ▪ Fx: 303-733-6211

Disabled & Alone/Life Services for the Handicapped — www.disabledandalone.org
352 Park Ave S 11th Fl   New York NY 10010
Ph: 212-532-6740 ▪ Fx: 212-532-3588 ▪ TF: 800-995-0066

Disabled American Veterans — www.dav.org
3725 Alexandria Pike   Cold Spring KY 41076
Ph: 859-441-7300 ▪ Fx: 859-441-1416 ▪ TF: 877-426-2838

Disabled American Veterans Auxiliary — www.dav.org/dava
3725 Alexandria Pike   Cold Spring KY 41076
Ph: 859-441-7300 ▪ Fx: 859-442-2095

(Disabled) Best Buddies International — www.bestbuddies.org
100 SE 2nd St Suite 1990   Miami FL 33131
Ph: 305-374-2233 ▪ Fx: 305-374-5305

Disabled Businesspersons Association — www.disabledbusiness.com
SDSU Interwork Institute 3590 Camino del Rio N Suite 117   San Diego CA 92108
Ph: 619-594-8805 ▪ Fx: 619-594-4208

Disabled Collectors' Correspondence Club — www.members.aol.com/disabledcc

Disabled, CUSA - An Apostolate of the Chronically Sick & — www.cusan.org
176 W 8th St   Bayonne NJ 07002
Ph: 201-437-0412

(Disabled) Easter Seals — www.easterseals.com
230 W Monroe St Suite 1800   Chicago IL 60606
Ph: 312-726-6200 ▪ Fx: 312-726-1494 ▪ TF: 800-221-6827

(Disabled) Extensions for Independence — www.mouthstick.net
555 Saturn Blvd Suite B368   San Diego CA 92154
Ph: 619-423-7709 ▪ TF: 866-632-7149

(Disabled) HEATH Resource Center — www.heath.gwu.edu
George Washington Univ 2121 K St NW Suite 220   Washington DC 20037
Ph: 202-973-0904 ▪ Fx: 202-973-0908 ▪ TF: 800-544-3284

(Disabled) Inspiration Ministries — www.inspirationministries.org
PO Box 948   Walworth WI 53184
Ph: 262-275-6131 ▪ Fx: 262-275-3355

Disabled, International Center for the — www.icdrehab.org
340 E 24th St   New York NY 10010
Ph: 212-585-6000 ▪ Fx: 212-585-6161

(Disabled) Just One Break Inc — www.justonebreak.com
120 Wall St   New York NY 10005
Ph: 212-785-7300 ▪ Fx: 212-785-4513

(Disabled) Lifespire — www.lifespire.org
345 Hudson St 3rd Fl   New York NY 10014
Ph: 212-741-0100 ▪ Fx: 212-463-9814

(Disabled) Mobility International USA — www.miusa.org
PO Box 10767   Eugene OR 97440
Ph: 541-343-1284 ▪ Fx: 541-343-6812

(Disabled) National Accessible Apartment Clearinghouse — www.forrent.com/naac
201 N Union St Suite 200   Alexandria VA 22314
Ph: 703-518-6141 ▪ Fx: 703-518-6191 ▪ TF: 800-421-1221

(Disabled) National Cristina Foundation — www.cristina.org
500 W Putnam Ave   Greenwich CT 06830
Ph: 203-863-9100 ▪ Fx: 203-863-9230

Disabled, National Legal Center for the Medically Dependent &
1 S 6th St   Terre Haute IN 47808
Ph: 812-232-2434 ▪ Fx: 812-235-3658

(Disabled) NISH   www.nish.org
8401 Old Courthouse Rd   Vienna VA 22182
Ph: 703-560-6800 ▪ Fx: 703-849-8916

Disabled Sports USA   www.dsusa.org
451 Hungerford Dr Suite 100   Rockville MD 20850
Ph: 301-217-0960 ▪ Fx: 301-217-0968

(Disabled) TASH   www.tash.org
29 W Susquehanna Ave Suite 210   Baltimore MD 21204
Ph: 410-828-8274 ▪ Fx: 410-828-6706

Disabled Veterans, Friends of Israel   fidv-bh.com
419 Park Ave S Suite 905   New York NY 10016
Ph: 212-689-3220 ▪ Fx: 212-689-3236 ▪ TF: 800-648-2125

(Disabled) VSA Arts   www.vsarts.org
1300 Connecticut Ave NW Suite 700   Washington DC 20036
Ph: 202-628-2800 ▪ Fx: 202-737-0725 ▪ TF: 800-933-8721

Disarmament Peace & Security, NGO Committee on   disarm.igc.org
777 United Nations Plaza Rm 3-B   New York NY 10017
Ph: 212-687-5340 ▪ Fx: 212-687-1643

Disarmament Studies, Institute for Defense &   www.idds.org
675 Massachusetts Ave 8th Fl   Cambridge MA 02139
Ph: 617-354-4337 ▪ Fx: 617-354-1450

Disaster Assistance, Presbyterian   www.pcusa.org/pda
100 Witherspoon St   Louisville KY 40202
Ph: 502-569-5839 ▪ Fx: 502-569-8039 ▪ TF: 888-728-7228

Disaster, National Voluntary Organizations Active in   www.nvoad.org
14253 Ballinger Terr   Burtonsville MD 20866
Ph: 301-890-2119

Disaster Preparedness, Doctors for   www.oism.org/ddp
1601 N Tucson Blvd Suite 9   Tucson AZ 85716
Ph: 520-325-2680 ▪ Fx: 520-325-4230

Disaster Preparedness & Emergency Response Association   www.disasters.org
International   PO Box 797   Longmont CO 80502
Ph: 303-809-4412

Disaster Recovery Association, International   www.idra.com
c/o BWT Assoc PO Box 4515   Shrewsbury MA 01545
Ph: 508-845-6000 ▪ Fx: 508-842-9003

(Disaster Recovery) DRI International   www.drii.org
201 Park Washington Ct   Falls Church VA 22046
Ph: 703-538-1792 ▪ Fx: 703-241-5603

Disaster Relief, Southern Baptist   www.namb.net/dr
4200 North Point Pkwy   Alpharetta GA 30022
Ph: 770-410-6442 ▪ Fx: 770-410-6014

Disaster Response International, Christian   www.cdresponse.org
PO Box 3339   Winter Haven FL 33885
Ph: 863-551-9554 ▪ Fx: 863-551-1422 ▪ TF: 866-551-9554

Disaster Response, Lutheran   www.ldr.org
8765 W Higgins Rd   Chicago IL 60631
Ph: 773-380-2822 ▪ Fx: 773-380-2493 ▪ TF: 800-638-3522

Disaster Search Dog Foundation, National   www.ndsdf.org
206 N Signal St Suite R   Ojai CA 93023
Ph: 805-646-1015 ▪ Fx: 805-640-1848

Disaster Service, Mennonite   mds.mennonite.net
1018 Main St   Akron PA 17501
Ph: 717-859-2210 ▪ Fx: 717-859-4910

Disc Jockey Association, American   www.adja.com
2000 Corporate Dr Suite 408   Ladera Ranch CA 92694
Ph: 888-723-5776

(Disciples of Christ), Christian Church   www.disciples.org
PO Box 1986   Indianapolis IN 46206
Ph: 317-635-3100 ▪ Fx: 317-635-3700

Disciples of Christ Historical Society   www.dishistsoc.org
1101 19th Ave S   Nashville TN 37212
Ph: 615-327-1444 ▪ Fx: 615-327-1445

Disciples Ecumenical Consultative Council
130 E Washington St PO Box 1986   Indianapolis IN 46206
Ph: 317-713-2585 ▪ Fx: 317-713-2588

Disciples Peace Fellowship   www.homelandministries.org/DPF
PO Box 1986   Indianapolis IN 46206
Ph: 317-713-2679 ▪ Fx: 317-635-4426 ▪ TF: 888-346-2631

Discoveries, Society for the History of   www.sochistdisc.org
5502 Laurel Ridge Dr   Alpharetta GA 30005
Ph: 770-772-6366

Discovery Institute   www.discovery.org
1511 3rd Ave Suite 808   Seattle WA 98101
Ph: 206-629-2041 ▪ Fx: 206-682-5320

Discrimination Committee, American-Arab Anti   www.adc.org
4201 Connecticut Ave NW Suite 300   Washington DC 20008
Ph: 202-244-2990 ▪ Fx: 202-244-3196

Discrimination, Council on Size & Weight   www.cswd.org
PO Box 305   Mount Marion NY 12456
Ph: 845-679-1209 ▪ Fx: 845-679-1206

Disease Association, American Behcet's   www.behcets.com
PO Box 19952   Amarillo TX 79114
Ph: 800-723-4238

Disease Foundation, Hereditary   www.hdfoundation.org
1303 Pico Blvd   Santa Monica CA 90405
Ph: 310-450-9913 ▪ Fx: 310-450-9532

Disease, International Society on Metabolic Eye
1125 Park Ave   New York NY 10128
Ph: 212-427-1246 ▪ Fx: 212-360-7009

Disease Management Association of America   www.dmaa.org
1129 20th St NW Suite 850   Washington DC 20036
Ph: 202-861-1490 ▪ Fx: 202-861-1477

Disease Program Directors, Association of State &   www.chronicdisease.org
Territorial Chronic   8201 Greensboro Dr Suite 300   McLean
VA 22102
Ph: 703-610-9033 ▪ Fx: 703-610-9005

(Diseases) Alpha One Foundation   www.alphaone.org
2937 SW 27th Ave Suite 302   Miami FL 33133
Ph: 305-567-9888 ▪ Fx: 305-567-1317 ▪ TF: 888-825-7421

Diseases Association, Iron Overload   www.ironoverload.org
433 Westwind Dr   North Palm Beach FL 33408
Ph: 561-840-8512 ▪ Fx: 561-842-9881

Diseases, International Society for Infectious   www.isid.org
181 Longwood Ave   Boston MA 02115
Ph: 617-277-0551 ▪ Fx: 617-731-1541

(Diseases) MHE Coalition   www.mhecoalition.com
8838 Holly Ln   Olmsted Falls OH 44138
Ph: 440-235-6325

(Diseases) National Fragile X Foundation   www.fragilex.org
PO Box 190488   San Francisco CA 94119
Ph: 925-938-9300 ▪ Fx: 925-938-9315 ▪ TF: 800-688-8765

(Diseases) VHL Family Alliance   www.vhl.org
171 Clinton Rd   Brookline MA 02445
Ph: 617-277-5667 ▪ Fx: 617-734-8233 ▪ TF: 800-767-4845

Disk Drive Equipment & Materials Association, International   www.idema.com
470 Lakeside Dr Suite A   Sunnyvale CA 94085
Ph: 408-991-9430 ▪ Fx: 408-991-9434

Disneyana Enthusiasts, World Chapter of
PO Box 22647   Lake Buena Vista FL 32830
Ph: 407-275-2756

Disorders, National Organization for Rare   www.rarediseases.org
55 Kenosia Ave PO Box 1968   Danbury CT 06813
Ph: 203-744-0100 ▪ Fx: 203-798-2291 ▪ TF: 800-999-6673

Disorders, Paget Foundation for Paget's Disease of Bone & Related   www.paget.org
120 Wall St Suite 1602   New York NY 10005
Ph: 212-509-5335 ▪ Fx: 212-509-8492 ▪ TF: 800-237-2438

Dispensing Equipment Association, International Beverage   www.ibdea.org
4145 Amos Ave   Baltimore MD 21215
Ph: 410-764-0616 ▪ Fx: 410-764-6799

Display Association, International Laser   www.laserist.org
3721 SE Henry St   Portland OR 97202
Ph: 503-407-0289

Display Distributors Association
1267 Mission St   San Francisco CA 94103
Ph: 415-861-4400 ▪ Fx: 415-861-4496 ▪ TF: 800-862-4400

Dispute Settlement, Center for   www.cdsusa.org
1666 Connecticut Ave NW Suite 500   Washington DC 20009
Ph: 202-265-9572 ▪ Fx: 202-332-3951

Dissociation, International Society for the Study of   www.issd.org
60 Revere Dr Suite 500   Northbrook IL 60062
Ph: 847-480-0899 ▪ Fx: 847-480-9282

Distaff Foundation, Army   www.armydistaff.org
6200 Oregon Ave NW   Washington DC 20015
Ph: 202-541-0105 ▪ Fx: 202-364-2856 ▪ TF: 800-541-4255

Distance Education & Training Council   www.detc.org
1601 18th St NW   Washington DC 20009
Ph: 202-234-5100 ▪ Fx: 202-332-1386

Distance Learning Association, US   www.usdla.org
8 Winter St   Boston MA 02108
Ph: 800-275-5162 ▪ Fx: 617-399-1771

Distilled Spirits Council of the US Inc   www.discus.org
1250 'I' St NW Suite 400   Washington DC 20005
Ph: 202-628-3544 ▪ Fx: 202-682-8888 ▪ TF: 888-862-7597

Distillers Grains Technology Council   www.distillersgrains.org
Lutz Hall Rm 435   Louisville KY 40292
Ph: 502-852-1575 ▪ Fx: 502-852-1577

Distillery Wine & Allied Workers Div UFCW International Union
219 Paterson Ave   Little Falls NJ 07424
Ph: 973-237-1241 ▪ Fx: 973-890-1956

Distribution Business Management Association   www.dcenter.com
2938 Columbia Ave Suite 1102   Lancaster PA 17603
Ph: 717-295-0033 ▪ Fx: 717-299-2154

Distribution Contractors Association   www.dca-online.org
101 W Renner Rd Suite 250   Richardson TX 75082
Ph: 972-680-0261 ▪ Fx: 972-680-0461

Distribution & LTL Carriers Association   www.dltlca.org
2200 Mill Rd Suite 600   Alexandria VA 22314
Ph: 703-838-1806 ▪ Fx: 703-684-8143

Distributive Education Clubs of America   www.deca.org
1908 Association Dr   Reston VA 20191
Ph: 703-860-5000 ▪ Fx: 703-860-4013

Distributors Association, Independent   www.idaparts.org
13370 Branch View Ln Suite 100   Dallas TX 75234
Ph: 972-241-1124 ▪ Fx: 972-484-3599

District Attorneys Association, National   www.ndaa.org
99 Canal Center Plaza Suite 510   Alexandria VA 22314
Ph: 703-549-9222 ▪ Fx: 703-836-3195

District Attorneys, National College of   www.law.sc.edu/ncda/
Univ of South Carolina Carolina Plaza 937 Assembly
St   Columbia SC 29208
Ph: 803-544-5005 ▪ Fx: 803-544-5301

Ditchley Foundation, American
666 5th Ave 37th Fl   New York NY 10103
Ph: 212-541-3791 ▪ Fx: 212-541-3751

Dive Rescue Specialists, International Association of   www.iadrs.org
201 N Link Ln   Fort Collins CO 80524
Ph: 970-482-1562 ▪ Fx: 970-482-0893 ▪ TF: 800-423-7791

Divers Alert Network   www.diversalertnetwork.org
Peter D Bennett Ctr 6 W Colony Pl   Durham NC 27705
Ph: 919-684-2948 ▪ Fx: 919-490-6630 ▪ TF: 800-446-2671

Divers, International Association of Nitrox & Technical   www.iantd.com
9628 NE 2nd Ave Suite D   Miami Shores FL 33138
Ph: 305-751-4873 ▪ Fx: 305-751-3958

Divers, National Association of Black Scuba — www.nabsdivers.org

(Diversity) Coexistence Initiative — www.coexistence.net
477 Madison Ave 4th Fl   New York NY 10022
Ph: 212-303-9445 ▪ Fx: 212-980-4027

Diversity Inc, Dialogue on — www.dialogueondiversity.org
1730 K St NW Suite 304   Washington DC 20006
Ph: 703-631-0650 ▪ Fx: 703-631-0617

Divine Science Federation International — www.divinesciencefederation.org
3617 Wyoming St   Saint Louis MO 63116
Ph: 314-664-4143 ▪ TF: 800-664-9680

Divine Science Ministers Association — www.divinescienceministersassociation.org
6565 Premier Dr   Nashville TN 37209
Ph: 615-354-1222

(Diving) CEDAM International — www.cedam.org
1 Fox Rd   Croton-on-Hudson NY 10520
Ph: 914-271-5365 ▪ Fx: 914-271-4723

Diving Contractors International, Association of — www.adc-usa.org
5206 FM 1960 W Suite 202   Houston TX 77069
Ph: 281-893-8388 ▪ Fx: 281-893-5118

Diving Equipment & Marketing Association — www.dema.org
3750 Convoy St Suite 310   San Diego CA 92111
Ph: 858-616-6408 ▪ Fx: 858-616-6495 ▪ TF: 800-862-3483

Diving, Institute of — www.diveweb.com/iod
17314 Panama City Beach Pkwy   Panama City Beach FL 32413
Ph: 850-235-4101

Diving Instructors International, Professional Association of — www.padi.com
30151 Tomas St   Rancho Santa Margarita CA 92688
Ph: 949-858-7234 ▪ Fx: 949-858-0106 ▪ TF: 800-729-7234

Diving, National Association for Cave — www.safecavediving.com
PO Box 14492   Gainesville FL 32604
Ph: 352-331-7666 ▪ TF: 888-565-6223

Diving Inc, US — www.usadiving.org
201 S Capitol Ave Suite 430   Indianapolis IN 46225
Ph: 317-237-5252 ▪ Fx: 317-237-5257

Divorced Catholics Inc, North American Conference of Separated & — www.nacsdc.org
PO Box 360   Richland OR 97870
Ph: 541-893-6089

Do Something — www.dosomething.org
423 W 55th St 8th Fl   New York NY 10019
Ph: 212-523-1175 ▪ Fx: 212-582-1307

Doctors of America, Flying — www.fdoamerica.org
1235 N Decatur Rd   Atlanta GA 30306
Ph: 404-815-7044 ▪ Fx: 404-892-6672

Doctors Association, Mission — www.missiondoctors.org
3424 Wilshire Blvd   Los Angeles CA 90010
Ph: 626-285-8868 ▪ Fx: 626-309-1716

Doctors for Disaster Preparedness — www.oism.org/ddp
1601 N Tucson Blvd Suite 9   Tucson AZ 85716
Ph: 520-325-2680 ▪ Fx: 520-325-4230

Doctors Opposing Circumcision — faculty.washington.edu/gcd/DOC
2442 NW Market St Suite 42   Seattle WA 98107
Ph: 360-385-1882

Doctors Without Borders USA Inc — www.doctorswithoutborders.org
6 E 39th St 8th Fl   New York NY 10016
Ph: 212-679-6800 ▪ Fx: 212-679-7016 ▪ TF: 888-392-0392

Doctors to the World — www.dttw.org
3654 S Oneida Way PO Box 37167   Denver CO 80237
Ph: 303-758-5405 ▪ Fx: 303-758-4124

Doctors of the World — www.doctorsoftheworld.org
375 W Broadway 4th Fl   New York NY 10012
Ph: 212-226-9890 ▪ Fx: 212-226-7026 ▪ TF: 800-817-4357

Document Examiners, National Association of — www.documentexaminers.org
3490 US Rt 1 Suite 3B   Princeton NJ 08540
Ph: 866-569-0833

Document Management Industries Association — www.dmia.org
433 E Monroe Ave   Alexandria VA 22301
Ph: 703-836-6232 ▪ Fx: 703-836-2241 ▪ TF: 800-336-4641

Document Systems Foundation, Electronic — www.edsf.org
24238 Hawthorne Blvd   Torrance CA 90505
Ph: 310-541-1481 ▪ Fx: 310-541-4803

(Document Technologies) Xplor International — www.xplor.org
24238 Hawthorne Blvd   Torrance CA 90505
Ph: 310-373-3633 ▪ Fx: 310-375-4240 ▪ TF: 800-669-7567

Documentary Association, International — www.documentary.org
1201 W 5th St Suite M320   Los Angeles CA 90017
Ph: 213-534-3600 ▪ Fx: 213-534-3610

Documentary Editing, Association for — etext.virginia.edu/ade
Princeton Univ   Princeton NJ 08544
Ph: 609-258-5687 ▪ Fx: 609-258-1630

Dodge Geraldine R Foundation — www.grdodge.org
163 Madison Ave   Morristown NJ 07962
Ph: 973-540-8442 ▪ Fx: 973-540-1211

Dog Association, American Rescue — www.ardainc.org
PO Box 151   Chester NY 10918
Ph: 845-469-4173 ▪ Fx: 845-774-1054

Dog Association, North American Police Work — www.napwda.com
4222 Manchester Ave   Perry OH 44081
Ph: 440-259-3169 ▪ Fx: 440-259-3170 ▪ TF: 888-422-6463

Dog Breeder's Association, American — www.adba.cc
PO Box 1771   Salt Lake City UT 84110
Ph: 801-936-7513 ▪ Fx: 801-936-4229

Dog Center, National Service — www.deltasociety.org/dsb000.htm
c/o Delta Society   580 Naches Ave SW Suite 101   Renton WA 98055
Ph: 425-226-7357 ▪ Fx: 425-235-1076

Dog Club of America, Australian Cattle — www.acdca.org
5041 Britton Ln   Jacksonville FL 32210
Ph: 904-771-5217 ▪ Fx: 904-908-9585

Dog Club of America, German Shepherd — www.gsdca.org
PO Box 429   Applegate CA 95703
Ph: 530-878-2826

Dog Foundation, Fidelco Guide — www.fidelco.org
PO Box 142   Bloomfield CT 06002
Ph: 860-243-5200 ▪ Fx: 860-243-7215

Dog Foundation, National Disaster Search — www.ndsdf.org
206 N Signal St Suite R   Ojai CA 93023
Ph: 805-646-1015 ▪ Fx: 805-640-1848

Dog Groomers Association of America Inc, National — www.nationaldoggroomers.com
PO Box 101   Clark PA 16113
Ph: 724-962-2711 ▪ Fx: 724-962-1919

Dog Inc, International Hearing — www.ihdi.org
5901 E 89th Ave   Henderson CO 80640
Ph: 303-287-3277 ▪ Fx: 303-287-3425

Dog Owners Association Inc, American — www.adoa.org
1654 Columbia Tpke   Castleton on Hudson NY 12033
Ph: 518-477-8469 ▪ Fx: 518-477-4034

Dog Racing Association, International Sled — www.isdra.org
22702 Rebel Rd   Merrifield MN 56465
Ph: 218-765-4297 ▪ Fx: 218-765-3246

Dog Registry, National — www.natldogregistry.com
PO Box 116   Woodstock NY 12498
Ph: 845-679-2355 ▪ TF: 800-637-3647

Dog Services, National Education for Assistance — www.neads.org
PO Box 213   West Boylston MA 01583
Ph: 978-422-9064 ▪ Fx: 978-422-3255

Dog Society, North American Sheep —
Rt 3 Box 107   McLeansboro IL 62859
Ph: 618-757-2238

Dog Trainers, Association of Pet — www.apdt.com
PO Box 1781   Hobbs NM 88241
Ph: 800-738-3647

Dog Trainers Network, American — www.inch.com/~dogs
161 W 4th St   New York NY 10014
Ph: 212-727-7257

Dog Users Inc, Guide — www.gdui.org
57 Grandview Ave   Watertown MA 02472
Ph: 617-926-9198 ▪ Fx: 617-923-0004 ▪ TF: 888-858-1008

Dog Writers Association of America Inc — www.dwaa.org
173 Union Rd   Coatesville PA 19320
Ph: 610-384-2436 ▪ Fx: 610-384-2471

(Dogs) Adopt a Husky Inc — www.adoptahusky.com
PO Box 275   Salem WI 53168
Ph: 262-909-2244 ▪ Fx: 262-878-1890

Dogs of America Inc, Assistance — www.adai.org
8806 State Rt 64   Swanton OH 43558
Ph: 419-825-3622 ▪ Fx: 419-825-3710

Dogs of America, Guide — www.guidedogsofamerica.org
13445 Glenoaks Blvd   Sylmar CA 91342
Ph: 818-362-5834 ▪ Fx: 818-362-6870 ▪ TF: 800-459-4843

(Dogs) American Belgian Malinois Club — www.breedclub.org/ABMC.htm
21710 Cove Point Farm Rd   Tilghman MD 21671
Ph: 410-886-2232

(Dogs) American Boxer Club — americanboxerclub.org

(Dogs) American Brittany Club — clubs.akc.org/brit
10370 Fleming Rd   Carterville IL 62918
Ph: 618-985-2336 ▪ Fx: 618-985-5103

(Dogs) American Catahoula Association — www.catahoulas.org
PO Box 248   Abita Springs LA 70420
Ph: 985-892-6773

(Dogs) American Fox Terrier Club — www.aftc.org/
PO Box 1448   Edison NJ 08818
Ph: 732-777-0032 ▪ Fx: 732-777-0977

(Dogs) American Rare Breed Association — www.arba.org
PO Box 757   Blooming Prairie MN 55917
Ph: 507-583-7718

(Dogs) American Shetland Sheepdog Association — www.assa.org
7274 S Chase Way   Littleton CO 80128
Ph: 303-979-8998

(Dogs) American Sighthound Field Association — www.asfa.org

(Dogs) American Spaniel Club — www.asc-cockerspaniel.org
30 Cardinal Loop   Crossville TN 38555
Ph: 931-456-6690 ▪ Fx: 931-707-8504

(Dogs) Basenji Club of America Inc — www.basenji.org
5102 Darnell   Houston TX 77096
Ph: 713-667-1266 ▪ Fx: 713-237-3782

(Dogs) Basset Hound Club of America Inc — www.basset-bhca.org
11 Barkalow Ave   Freehold NJ 07728
Ph: 732-577-9662

Dogs for the Blind, Leader — www.leaderdog.org
PO Box 5000   Rochester MI 48308
Ph: 248-651-9011 ▪ Fx: 248-651-5812 ▪ TF: 888-777-5332

(Dogs) Bluetick Breeders of America — www.bluetickbreedersofamerica.com
3205 Illinois Rt 78 S   Stockton IL 60815
Ph: 815-947-3090

(Dogs) Canadian Kennel Club — www.ckc.ca
89 Skyway Ave Suite 100   Etobicoke ON M9W6R4
Ph: 416-675-5511 ▪ Fx: 416-675-6506 ▪ TF: 800-250-8040

(Dogs) Cardigan Welsh Corgi Club of America — www.cardigancorgis.com
7446 Park Pl   Boulder CO 80301
Ph: 303-530-7107

(Dogs) Cavalier King Charles Spaniel Club USA — www.ckcsc.org
PO Box 330   Conway NH 03818
Ph: 603-447-5218 ▪ Fx: 603-447-5419

(Dogs) Dachshund Club of America Inc — www.dachshund-dca.org
1793 Berme Rd   Kerhonkson NY 12446
Ph: 845-626-4137

(Dogs) Dalmatian Club of America   www.thedca.org
2316 McCrary Rd   Richmond TX 77469
Ph: 281-342-8407

Dogs for the Deaf   www.dogsforthedeaf.org
10175 Wheeler Rd   Central Point OR 97502
Ph: 541-826-9220 ▪ Fx: 541-826-6696 ▪ TF: 800-990-2647

(Dogs) English Cocker Spaniel Club of America Inc   www.ecsca.org
PO Box 252   Hales Corners WI 53130
Ph: 414-529-9104

(Dogs) English Springer Rescue America Inc   www.springerrescue.org
2721 Walker Lee Rd   Los Alamitos CA 90720
Ph: 800-921-1047

(Dogs) Golden Retriever Club of America   www.grca.org

(Dogs) Greyhound Adoption Center   www.greyhoundog.org
PO Box 2433   La Mesa CA 91943
Ph: 619-443-0940 ▪ Fx: 619-443-0130 ▪ TF: 877-478-8364

(Dogs) Guiding Eyes for the Blind   guidingeyes.org
611 Granite Springs Rd   Yorktown Heights NY 10598
Ph: 914-245-4024 ▪ Fx: 914-245-1609 ▪ TF: 800-942-0149

(Dogs) Hunting Retriever Club Inc   www.hrc-ukc.com

Dogs International Inc, Therapy   www.tdi-dog.org
88 Bartley Rd   Flanders NJ 07836
Ph: 973-252-9800 ▪ Fx: 973-252-7171

(Dogs) Jack Russell Terrier Club of America   www.terrier.com
PO Box 4527   Lutherville MD 21094
Ph: 410-561-3655 ▪ Fx: 410-560-2563

(Dogs) Mastiff Club of America Inc   mastiff.org
PO Box 609   Fruitland Park FL 34731
Ph: 352-787-8549

(Dogs) National Greyhound Adoption Program   www.ngap.org
4701 Bath St   Philadelphia PA 19137
Ph: 215-331-7918 ▪ Fx: 215-331-1947 ▪ TF: 800-348-2517

(Dogs) National REGAP Network   www.regap.org
PO Box 4454   Cary IL 60013
Ph: 847-217-1836

(Dogs) National Retriever Club   www.working-retriever.com/nrc
4379 S Howell Ave Suite 17   Milwaukee WI 53207
Ph: 414-481-2760 ▪ Fx: 414-481-2743

(Dogs) National Shiba Club of America   www.shibas.org
4360 Deer Spring Rd   Middletown MD 21769
Ph: 301-371-7815

(Dogs) Norwegian Elkhound Association of America   www.neaa.net
21738 Hampton Ct   Kildeer IL 60047
Ph: 847-438-3670

(Dogs) Old English Sheepdog Club of   www.oldenglishsheepdogclubofamerica.org
America Inc   N 64 W 20708 Mill Rd Suite 1015   Menomonee
Falls WI 53501
Ph: 262-252-3936

(Dogs) Operation K9 Rescue Inc   www.operationk9rescue.com
PO Box 235207   Encinitas CA 92023
Ph: 760-497-7764

(Dogs) Otterhound Club of America   clubs.akc.org/ohca
2185 Seeman St SW   East Sparta OH 44626
Ph: 330-484-4845

(Dogs) Paws With a Cause   www.pawswithacause.org
4646 S Division St   Wayland MI 49348
Ph: 616-877-7297 ▪ Fx: 616-877-0248 ▪ TF: 800-253-7297

(Dogs) Pembroke Welsh Corgi Club of America   www.pembrokecorgi.org
PO Box 2141   Duxbury MA 02331
Ph: 781-934-0110 ▪ Fx: 781-934-6597

Dogs Inc, Pilot   www.pilotdogs.org
625 W Town St   Columbus OH 43215
Ph: 614-221-6367 ▪ Fx: 614-221-1577

(Dogs) Professional Handlers Association Inc   www.infodog.com/misc/pha/phamain.htm
17017 Norbrook Dr   Olney MD 20832
Ph: 301-924-0089

(Dogs) Seeing Eye   www.seeingeye.org
PO Box 375   Morristown NJ 07963
Ph: 973-539-4425 ▪ Fx: 973-539-0922

(Dogs) Silky Terrier Club of America   www.silky-terrier-club.com

(Dogs) Skye Terrier Club of America   clubs.akc.org/skye
11567 Sutters Mill Cir   Gold River CA 95670
Ph: 916-631-8716

(Dogs) Staffordshire Terrier Club of America   www.amstaff.org

Dogs on Stamps Study Unit   www.dossu.org
202A Newport Rd   Monroe Township NJ 08831
Ph: 609-655-7411

Dogs Inc, Support   www.supportdogs.org
9510 Page Ave   Saint Louis MO 63132
Ph: 314-423-1988 ▪ Fx: 314-423-5564

(Dogs) United Schutzhund Clubs of America   www.germanshepherddog.com
3810 Paule Ave   Saint Louis MO 63125
Ph: 314-638-9686 ▪ Fx: 314-683-0609

(Dogs) US Kerry Blue Terrier Club   www.uskbtc.com
2458 Eastridge Dr   Hamilton OH 45011
Ph: 513-863-5041

(Dogs) Westminster Kennel Club   www.westminsterkennelclub.org
149 Madison Ave Suite 803   New York NY 10016
Ph: 212-213-3165

Dole Institute of Politics   www.doleinstitute.org
704 W 12th St   Lawrence KS 66044
Ph: 785-749-3911 ▪ Fx: 785-749-3907

Doll Artists Council of America, Original   www.odaca.org
2917 SW Fairview Blvd   Portland OR 97201
Ph: 503-222-5809

Doll Artists Guild, Original Paper   www.opdag.com
PO Box 14   Kingfield ME 04947
Ph: 207-265-2500

Doll Artists, National Institute of American   www.niada.org

Doll Clubs Inc, United Federation of   www.ufdc.org
10900 N Pomona Ave   Kansas City MO 64153
Ph: 816-891-7040 ▪ Fx: 816-891-8360

Doll Makers Association, International   www.idmadolls.com
1204 Bakers Bridge Rd   Douglasville GA 30134
Ph: 770-949-1737

Doll Makers, International Foundation of   www.ifdm.org
PO Box 120187   Clermont FL 34712
Ph: 352-394-1404 ▪ Fx: 352-394-1270

Dollars for Scholars   www.scholarshipamerica.org/dfs
Scholarship America 1 Scholarship Way   Saint Peter MN 56082
Ph: 507-931-1682 ▪ Fx: 507-931-9168 ▪ TF: 800-537-4180

Dolphin Research Center   www.dolphins.org
58901 Overseas Hwy   Marathon FL 33050
Ph: 305-289-1121 ▪ Fx: 305-743-7627

Domestic Violence, ABA Commission on   www.abanet.org/domviol
740 15th St NW 9th Fl   Washington DC 20005
Ph: 202-662-1737 ▪ Fx: 202-662-1594

Domestic Violence Crisis Line, American   www.awoscentral.com
3300 NW 185th Ave Suite 133   Portland OR 97229
Ph: 503-846-8748 ▪ Fx: 503-907-6554 ▪ TF: 866-879-6636

(Domestic Violence) FaithTrust Institute   www.faithtrustinstitute.org
2400 N 45th St Suite 10   Seattle WA 98103
Ph: 206-634-1903 ▪ Fx: 206-634-0115

Domestic Violence Hotline, National   www.ndvh.org
PO Box 161810   Austin TX 78716
Ph: 800-799-7233

Domestic Violence, National Coalition Against   www.ncadv.org
1201 E Colfax Ave Suite 385   Denver CO 80218
Ph: 303-839-1852 ▪ Fx: 303-831-9251 ▪ TF: 800-799-7233

Domestic Violence, National Network to End   www.nnedv.org
660 Pennsylvania Ave SE Suite 303   Washington DC 20003
Ph: 202-543-5566 ▪ Fx: 202-543-5626

Domestic Violence, National Resource Center on   www.nrcdv.org
6400 Flank Dr Suite 1300   Harrisburg PA 17112
Ph: 717-545-6400 ▪ Fx: 717-545-9456 ▪ TF: 800-537-2238

Domra Association of America, Balalaika &   www.bdaa.com
2801 Warner St   Madison WI 53713
Ph: 608-259-9440

Donald W Reynolds Foundation   www.dwreynolds.org
1701 Village Ctr Cir   Las Vegas NV 89134
Ph: 702-804-6000 ▪ Fx: 702-804-6099

Donaldson Evan B Adoption Institute   www.adoptioninstitute.org
120 Wall St 20th Fl   New York NY 10005
Ph: 212-269-5080 ▪ Fx: 212-269-1962

Donkey Association, National Miniature
6450 Dewey Rd   Rome NY 13440
Ph: 315-336-0154 ▪ Fx: 315-339-4414

Donkey & Mule Society, American   www.lovelongears.com
PO Box 1210   Lewisville TX 75067
Ph: 972-219-0781 ▪ Fx: 972-420-9980

Donkey Registry, International Miniature   www.qis.net/~minidonk/imdr.htm
1338 Hughes Shop Rd   Westminster MD 21158
Ph: 410-875-0118 ▪ Fx: 410-857-9145

Donor Program, National Marrow   www.marrow.org
3001 Broadway St NE Suite 500   Minneapolis MN 55413
Ph: 612-627-5800 ▪ Fx: 612-627-8125 ▪ TF: 800-526-7809

Donor Registry, American Bone Marrow   www.charityadvantage.com/abmdr
PO Box 8841   Mandeville LA 70470
Ph: 985-626-1749 ▪ Fx: 985-626-7414 ▪ TF: 800-745-2452

Door & Access Systems Manufacturers Association International   www.dasma.com
1300 Sumner Ave   Cleveland OH 44115
Ph: 216-241-7333 ▪ Fx: 216-241-0105

Door Association, International   www.doors.org
PO Box 246   West Milton OH 45383
Ph: 800-355-4432 ▪ Fx: 937-698-6153

Door & Hardware Institute   www.dhi.org
14150 Newbrook Dr Suite 200   Chantilly VA 20151
Ph: 703-222-2010 ▪ Fx: 703-222-2410

Door Institute, Insulated Steel   www.isdi.org
30200 Detroit Rd   Cleveland OH 44145
Ph: 440-899-0010 ▪ Fx: 440-892-1404

Door Institute, Steel   www.steeldoor.org
30200 Detroit Rd   Cleveland OH 44145
Ph: 440-899-0010 ▪ Fx: 440-892-1404

Door Manufacturers, American Association of Automatic   www.aaadm.com
1300 Sumner Ave   Cleveland OH 44115
Ph: 216-241-7333 ▪ Fx: 216-241-0105

Door Manufacturers Association, Window &   www.wdma.com
1400 E Touhy Ave Suite 470   Des Plaines IL 60018
Ph: 847-299-5200 ▪ Fx: 847-299-1286 ▪ TF: 800-223-2301

Doris Day Animal League   www.ddal.org
227 Massachusetts Ave NE Suite 100   Washington DC 20002
Ph: 202-546-1761 ▪ Fx: 202-546-2193

Doris Duke Charitable Foundation   fdncenter.org/grantmaker/dorisduke
650 5th Ave 19th Fl   New York NY 10019
Ph: 212-974-7000 ▪ Fx: 212-974-7095

Dorset Club, Continental   www.dorsets.homestead.com
PO Box 506   North Scituate RI 02857
Ph: 401-647-4676 ▪ Fx: 401-647-4679

Double Dutch League, American   www.usaddl.com
4220 Eads St NE   Washington DC 20019
Ph: 800-982-2335

Double Reed Society, International   www.idrs.org
2423 Lawndale Rd   Finksburg MD 21048
Ph: 410-871-0658 ▪ Fx: 410-871-0659

Doublespeak, Committee on Public
National Council of Teachers of English 1111 W
Kenyon   Urbana IL 61801
Ph: 217-328-3870 ▪ Fx: 217-328-9645 ▪ TF: 800-369-6283

Dow Herbert H & Grace A Foundation   www.hhdowfoundation.org
1018 W Main St   Midland MI 48640
Ph: 989-631-3699 ▪ Fx: 989-631-0675 ▪ TF: 800-362-4849

Dow Jones Newspaper Fund Inc   djnewspaperfund.dowjones.com
4300 Rt 1 N PO Box 300   Princeton NJ 08543
Ph: 609-452-2820 ▪ Fx: 609-520-5804 ▪ TF: 800-639-7386

Down Syndrome Inc, Association for Children with   www.acds.org
4 Fern Pl   Plainview NY 11803
Ph: 516-933-4700 ▪ Fx: 516-933-9524

Down Syndrome Congress, National   www.ndsccenter.org
1370 Center Dr Suite 102   Atlanta GA 30338
Ph: 770-604-9500 ▪ Fx: 770-604-9898 ▪ TF: 800-232-6372

Down Syndrome, National Association for   www.nads.org
PO Box 4542   Oak Brook IL 60522
Ph: 630-325-9112 ▪ Fx: 630-325-8842

Down Syndrome Society, National   www.ndss.org
666 Broadway 8th Fl   New York NY 10012
Ph: 212-460-9330 ▪ Fx: 212-979-2873 ▪ TF: 800-221-4602

Downtown Association, International   ida-downtown.org
1250 H St NW 10th Fl   Washington DC 20005
Ph: 202-393-6801 ▪ Fx: 202-393-6869

Dowsers, American Society of   www.dowsers.org
PO Box 24   Danville VT 05828
Ph: 802-684-3417 ▪ Fx: 802-684-2565 ▪ TF: 800-711-9530

Dozenal Society of America   www.dozens.org

Dr Pepper Bottler Association
PO Box 906   Rowlett TX 75030
Ph: 972-475-7397

Draft, Committee Opposed to Militarism & the   www.comdsd.org
PO Box 15195   San Diego CA 92175
Ph: 760-753-7518

Draft Horse Association, American Cream   www.americancreamdraft.org
193 Crossover Rd   Bennington VT 05201
Ph: 802-447-7612 ▪ Fx: 802-447-0711

Draft Horse Corp of America, Belgian   www.belgiancorp.com
PO Box 335   Wabash IN 46992
Ph: 260-563-3205

Drafting Association, American Design   www.adda.org
105 E Main St   Newbern TN 38059
Ph: 731-627-0802 ▪ Fx: 731-627-9321

Drag Racers Association, United   www.udra.org
18823 High Point   Chagrin Falls OH 44023
Ph: 440-543-4272

Dragon Boat Association, Pacific   www.pdbausa.org
PO Box 23693   Portland OR 97281
Ph: 503-639-2799 ▪ Fx: 503-670-1003

Dragonfly Society of the Americas   www.afn.org/~iori/dsaintro.html

Drainage Institute, Plumbing &   www.pdionline.org
800 Turnpike St Suite 300   North Andover MA 01845
Ph: 978-557-0720 ▪ Fx: 978-557-0721 ▪ TF: 800-589-8956

Drama, Institute of Outdoor   www.unc.edu/depts/outdoor
Univ of North Carolina 1700 Airport Rd CB 3240   Chapel Hill
NC 27599
Ph: 919-962-1328 ▪ Fx: 919-962-4212

Drama Therapy, National Association for   www.nadt.org
15 Post Lake Ln   Pittsford NY 14534
Ph: 585-381-5618 ▪ Fx: 585-383-1474

Dramatists Guild of America Inc   www.dramaguild.com
1501 Broadway Suite 701   New York NY 10036
Ph: 212-398-9366 ▪ Fx: 212-944-0420

Dramatists, New   newdramatists.org
424 W 44th St   New York NY 10036
Ph: 212-757-6960 ▪ Fx: 212-265-4738

Dramaturgs of the Americas, Literary Managers &   www.lmda.org
Village Stn PO Box 728   New York NY 10014
Ph: 212-561-0315

Drawing Center   www.drawingcenter.org
35 Wooster St   New York NY 10013
Ph: 212-219-2166 ▪ Fx: 212-966-2976

Drawings Association Inc, Master   www.masterdrawings.org
29 E 36th St   New York NY 10016
Ph: 212-685-0008 ▪ Fx: 212-685-4740

Dream Factory Inc   www.dreamfactoryinc.com
1218 S 3rd St   Louisville KY 40203
Ph: 502-637-8700 ▪ Fx: 502-637-8744 ▪ TF: 800-456-7556

Dreams, Association for the Study of   www.asdreams.org
PO Box 1592   Merced CA 95341
Ph: 209-724-0889 ▪ Fx: 209-724-9319

Dredging Associations, World Organization of   www.westerndredging.org
PO Box 5797   Vancouver WA 98668
Ph: 360-750-0209 ▪ Fx: 360-750-1445

Dredging Contractors of America
643 S Washington St   Alexandria VA 22314
Ph: 703-518-8408 ▪ Fx: 703-578-8490

Dress for Success Worldwide   www.dressforsuccess.org
32 E 31st St 7th Fl   New York NY 10016
Ph: 212-532-1922 ▪ Fx: 212-684-9563

Dressage Federation, US   www.usdf.org
PO Box 6669   Lincoln NE 68506
Ph: 402-434-8550 ▪ Fx: 402-434-8570

Dressings & Sauces, Association for   www.dressings-sauces.org
5775 Peachtree-Dunwoody Rd Bldg G Suite 500   Atlanta GA
30342
Ph: 404-252-3663 ▪ Fx: 404-252-0774

Dreyfus Camille & Henry Foundation   www.dreyfus.org
555 Madison Ave   New York NY 10022
Ph: 212-753-1760

DRI International   www.drii.org
201 Park Washington Ct   Falls Church VA 22046
Ph: 703-538-1792 ▪ Fx: 703-241-5603

Drilling Association, Concrete Sawing &   www.csda.org
10901 Roosevelt Blvd N Suite 100A   Saint Petersburg FL
33716
Ph: 727-577-5004 ▪ Fx: 727-577-5012

Drilling Association, National   www.nda4u.com
10901D Roosevelt Blvd N Suite 100   Saint Petersburg FL
33716
Ph: 727-577-5006 ▪ Fx: 727-577-5012

Drilling Contractors, International Association of   www.iadc.org
PO Box 4287   Houston TX 77210
Ph: 713-292-1945 ▪ Fx: 713-292-1946

Drilling Engineering Association   www.dea.main.com

Drinking Water Administrators, Association of State   www.asdwa.org
1025 Connecticut Ave NW Suite 903   Washington DC 20036
Ph: 202-293-7655 ▪ Fx: 202-293-7656

Driver Employer Council of America   www.decausa.org
1225 'I' St NW Suite 1000   Washington DC 20005
Ph: 202-371-0100 ▪ Fx: 202-842-0011

Driver Rehabilitation Specialists, ADED - Association for   www.driver-ed.org
711 S Vienna St   Ruston LA 71270
Ph: 318-257-5055 ▪ Fx: 318-255-4175 ▪ TF: 800-290-2344

Driver & Traffic Safety Education Association, American   www.adtsea.iup.edu
Indiana Univ of Pennsylvania Highway Safety Ctr R&P
Bldg   Indiana PA 15705
Ph: 724-357-4051 ▪ Fx: 724-357-7595 ▪ TF: 800-896-7703

Drivers Association, Owner-Operator Independent   www.ooida.com
1 NW OOIDA Dr   Grain Valley MO 64029
Ph: 816-229-5791 ▪ TF: 800-444-5791

Drivers Association, Professional   www.stuntplayers.com/links
5235 Mission Oaks Blvd   Camarillo CA 93012
Ph: 818-774-3889 ▪ Fx: 805-491-0708

Drivers & Racers Association, National American Motors   www.namdra.org
PO Box 987   Twin Lakes WI 53181
Ph: 262-396-9552

Driving School Association of the Americas Inc   www.thedsaa.org
6031 W Center St   Milwaukee WI 53210
Ph: 800-270-3722 ▪ Fx: 414-328-1177

Driving Society Inc, American   www.americandrivingsociety.org
2324 Clark Rd   Lapeer MI 48446
Ph: 810-664-8666 ▪ Fx: 810-664-2405

Dropout Prevention Center, National   www.dropoutprevention.org
Clemson Univ 209 Martin St   Clemson SC 29631
Ph: 864-656-2599 ▪ Fx: 864-656-0136

(Drug Abuse) DARE America   www.dare.com
PO Box 512090   Los Angeles CA 90051
Ph: 310-215-0575 ▪ Fx: 310-215-0180 ▪ TF: 800-223-3273

Drug Abuse Directors, National Association of State Alcohol &   www.nasadad.org
808 17th St NW Suite 410   Washington DC 20006
Ph: 202-293-0090 ▪ Fx: 202-293-1250

Drug Abuse Problems Inc, National Association on   www.nadap.org
355 Lexington Ave 2nd Fl   New York NY 10017
Ph: 212-986-1170 ▪ Fx: 212-697-2939

Drug & Alcohol Testing Industry Association   www.datia.org
1600 Duke St Suite 400   Alexandria VA 22314
Ph: 703-548-0901 ▪ Fx: 703-519-1716 ▪ TF: 800-355-1257

Drug Awareness, Family Council on   www.fcda.org
PO Box 1716   El Cerrito CA 94530
Ph: 510-215-8326

Drug Chemical & Associated Technologies Association   www.dcat.org
1 Washington Blvd Suite 7   Robbinsville NJ 08691
Ph: 609-448-1900 ▪ Fx: 609-448-1944 ▪ TF: 800-640-3228

Drug Dependence, National Council on Alcoholism &   www.ncadd.org
20 Exchange Pl Suite 2902   New York NY 10005
Ph: 212-269-7797 ▪ Fx: 212-269-7510 ▪ TF: 800-622-2255

**Drug Dependency, International Commission for the Prevention of
Alcoholism &**   12501 Old Columbia Pike   Silver Spring MD
20904
Ph: 301-680-6719 ▪ Fx: 301-680-6707

**Drug Dependency, National Committee for the Prevention of
Alcoholism &**   12501 Old Columbia Pike   Silver Spring MD
20904
Ph: 301-680-6733 ▪ Fx: 301-680-6707

Drug Education, American Council for   www.acde.org
c/o Phoenix House 164 W 74th St   New York NY 10023
Ph: 212-595-5810 ▪ Fx: 212-721-7384 ▪ TF: 800-378-4435

Drug-Free America, Partnership for a   www.drugfreeamerica.org
405 Lexington Ave Suite 1601   New York NY 10174
Ph: 212-922-1560 ▪ Fx: 212-922-1570 ▪ TF: 888-575-3115

Drug-Free Workplace, Institute for a   www.drugfreeworkplace.org
1225 'I' St NW Suite 1000   Washington DC 20005
Ph: 202-842-7400 ▪ Fx: 202-842-0022

Drug Information Association   www.diahome.org
800 Enterprise Rd Suite 200   Horsham PA 19044
Ph: 215-442-6100 ▪ Fx: 215-442-6199

Drug Law Institute, Food &   www.fdli.org
1000 Vermont Ave NW Suite 200   Washington DC 20005
Ph: 202-371-1420 ▪ Fx: 202-371-0649 ▪ TF: 800-956-6293

Drug Manufacturers Association of Canada, Nonprescription   www.ndmac.ca
1111 Prince of Wales Dr Suite 406   Ottawa ON K2C3T2
Ph: 613-723-0777 ▪ Fx: 613-723-0779

Drug Marketing Association, Chain   www.chaindrug.com
43157 W Nine-Mile Rd PO Box 995   Novi MI 48376
Ph: 248-449-9300 ▪ Fx: 248-449-4634 ▪ TF: 800-935-2362

Drug Officials, Association of Food &   www.afdo.org
2550 Kingston Rd Suite 311   York PA 17402
Ph: 717-757-2888 ■ Fx: 717-755-8089
Drug Policy Alliance   www.drugpolicy.org
70 W 36th St 16 Fl   New York NY 10018
Ph: 212-613-8020 ■ Fx: 212-613-8021
(Drug Prevention) Teen Challenge International   www.teenchallenge.com
3728 W Chestnut Expy   Springfield MO 65802
Ph: 417-862-6969 ■ Fx: 417-862-8209 ■ TF: 800-814-5729
Drug Problems Association of North America, Alcohol &   www.adpana.com
307 N Main St   Saint Charles MO 63301
Ph: 314-589-6702 ■ Fx: 314-940-2358
Drug Problems Inc, National Catholic Council on Alcoholism &   www.nccatoday.org
Related   PO Box 248   Lafayette IN 47902
Ph: 765-420-0129 ■ Fx: 765-420-0189
Drug Programs, National Council for Prescription   www.ncpdp.org
9240 E Raintree Dr   Scottsdale AZ 85260
Ph: 480-477-1000 ■ Fx: 480-767-1042
Drug Stores, National Association of Chain   www.nacds.org
413 N Lee St   Alexandria VA 22314
Ph: 703-549-3001 ■ Fx: 703-836-4869 ■ TF: 800-678-6223
Drugless Practitioners, American Association of   www.aadp.net
708 Madelaine Dr   Gilmer TX 75644
Ph: 903-843-6401 ■ TF: 888-764-2237
Drugs & Disability, National Association on Alcohol   www.naadd.org
2165 Bunker Hill Dr   San Mateo CA 94402
Ph: 650-578-8047 ■ Fx: 650-286-9205
Drum Corps International   www.dci.org
470 S Irmen Dr   Addison IL 60101
Ph: 630-628-7888 ■ Fx: 630-628-7971 ■ TF: 800-495-7469
Drummers Inc, Company of Fifers &   companyoffifeanddrum.org
PO Box 277   Ivoryton CT 06442
Ph: 860-767-2237 ■ Fx: 860-767-9765
Drunk Driving, Mothers Against   www.madd.org
511 E John Carpenter Fwy Suite 700   Irving TX 75062
Ph: 214-744-6233 ■ Fx: 972-869-2207 ■ TF: 800-438-6233
Druze Society, American   www.druze.com
PO Box 9276   Glendale CA 91226
Ph: 323-255-5237 ■ Fx: 323-255-9155
Dry Bean Council, National
8233 Old Courthouse Rd Suite 210   Vienna VA 22182
Ph: 703-556-9305 ■ Fx: 703-556-9301
Dry Cleaning International Union, Laundry &
307 4th Ave Suite 405   Pittsburgh PA 15222
Ph: 412-471-4829 ■ Fx: 412-471-1840
Dry Pea & Lentil Council, International   www.pea-lentil.com
2780 W Pullman Rd   Moscow ID 83843
Ph: 208-882-3023 ■ Fx: 208-882-6406
Drycleaners Congress, International   www.idcnews.org
9016 Oak Branch Dr   Apex NC 27502
Ph: 919-363-5062 ■ Fx: 919-387-8326
DSL Forum   www.dslforum.org
39355 California St Suite 307   Fremont CA 94538
Ph: 510-608-5905 ■ Fx: 510-608-5917
Dually Diagnosed, National Association for the   www.thenadd.org
132 Fair St   Kingston NY 12401
Ph: 845-331-4336 ■ Fx: 845-331-4569 ■ TF: 800-331-5362
Duckpin Bowling Congress, National   ndbc.org
4991 Fairview Ave   Linthicum Heights MD 21090
Ph: 410-636-2695 ■ Fx: 410-636-3256
Ducks Unlimited Inc   www.ducks.org
1 Waterfowl Way   Memphis TN 38120
Ph: 901-758-3825 ■ Fx: 901-758-3850 ■ TF: 800-453-8257
Duct Cleaners Association, National Air   www.nadca.com
1518 K St Suite 503   Washington DC 20005
Ph: 202-737-2926 ■ Fx: 202-347-8847
Ductile Iron Pipe Research Association   www.dipra.org
245 Riverchase Pkwy E Suite 'O'   Birmingham AL 35244
Ph: 205-402-8700 ■ Fx: 205-402-8730
Ductile Iron Society   www.ductile.org
28938 Lorain Rd Suite 202   North Olmsted OH 44070
Ph: 440-734-8040 ■ Fx: 440-734-8182
Dude & Guest Ranch Association, Colorado   www.coloradoranch.com
PO Box 2120   Granby CO 80446
Ph: 970-887-3128 ■ Fx: 970-887-1229
Dude Ranchers' Association   www.duderanch.org
PO Box 2307   Cody WY 82414
Ph: 307-587-2339 ■ Fx: 307-587-2776
(DUI) RID-USA Inc   www.rid-usa.org
PO Box 520   Schenectady NY 12301
Ph: 518-372-0034 ■ Fx: 518-370-4917
Duke Doris Charitable Foundation   fdncenter.org/grantmaker/dorisduke
650 5th Ave 19th Fl   New York NY 10019
Ph: 212-974-7000 ■ Fx: 212-974-7095
Duke Endowment   www.dukeendowment.org
100 N Tryon St Suite 3500   Charlotte NC 28202
Ph: 704-376-0291 ■ Fx: 704-376-9336
DuPont Workers, International Brotherhood of   www.dupontworkers.com
PO Box 16333   Louisville KY 40256
Ph: 502-569-3232
Durum Growers Association, US   www.durumgrowers.com
4023 State St   Bismarck ND 58503
Ph: 701-222-2204 ■ Fx: 701-223-0018 ■ TF: 877-463-8786
Dutch Warmblood Studbook in North America   www.nawpn.org
PO Box 0   Sutherlin OR 97479
Ph: 541-459-3232 ■ Fx: 541-459-2967
Duty Free Stores, International Association of Airport   www.iaadfs.org
2025 M St NW Suite 800   Washington DC 20036
Ph: 202-367-1184 ■ Fx: 202-429-5154

Dwarf Athletic Association of America   www.daaa.org
418 Willow Way   Lewisville TX 75077
Ph: 972-317-8299
Dwarf Fruit Tree Association, International   www.idfta.org
14 S Main St   Middleburg PA 17842
Ph: 570-837-1551 ■ Fx: 570-837-0090
(Dwarfs) Little People of America   www.lpaonline.org
5289 NE Elam Young Pkwy Suite F-700   Hillsboro OR 97124
Ph: 503-846-1562 ■ Fx: 503-846-1590 ■ TF: 888-572-2001
(Dyes) ETAD North America   www.etad.com
1850 M St NW Suite 700   Washington DC 20036
Ph: 202-721-4154 ■ Fx: 202-296-8120
Dying, Americans for Better Care of the   www.abcd-caring.org
4200 Wisconsin Ave NW Suite 418   Washington DC 20016
Ph: 202-895-2660 ■ Fx: 202-966-5410
Dying Federation, Compassion in   www.compassionindying.org
6312 SW Capitol Hwy Suite 415   Portland OR 97239
Ph: 503-221-9556 ■ Fx: 503-228-9160
Dying Project, Living/   www.livingdying.org
PO Box 357   Fairfax CA 94978
Ph: 415-456-3915
Dynamic Youth Ministries   www.gospelcom.net/dym
1333 Alger SE PO Box 7259   Grand Rapids MI 49510
Ph: 616-241-5616 ■ Fx: 616-241-5558
Dyslexia Association, International   www.interdys.org
8600 LaSalle Rd Chester Bldg Suite 382   Baltimore MD 21286
Ph: 410-296-0232 ■ Fx: 410-321-5069 ■ TF: 800-222-3123
Dyslexia Research Foundation, AVKO   www.spelling.org
3084 W Willard Rd   Clio MI 48420
Ph: 810-686-9283 ■ Fx: 810-686-1101
Dyslexic, Recording for the Blind &   www.rfbd.org
20 Roszel Rd   Princeton NJ 08540
Ph: 609-452-0606 ■ Fx: 609-520-7990 ■ TF: 800-221-4792
Dystonia Medical Research Foundation   www.dystonia-foundation.org
1 E Wacker Dr Suite 2430   Chicago IL 60601
Ph: 312-755-0198 ■ Fx: 312-803-0138 ■ TF: 800-377-3978
Dystrophic Epidermolysis Bullosa Research Association of America   www.debra.org
5 W 36th St Suite 404   New York NY 10018
Ph: 212-868-1573 ■ Fx: 212-868-9296

E

Eagle Forum   www.eagleforum.org
PO Box 618   Alton IL 62002
Ph: 618-462-5415 ■ Fx: 618-462-8909
Eagle Scout Association, National   www.scouting.org/nesa
1325 W Walnut Hill Ln PO Box 152079   Irving TX 75015
Ph: 972-580-2000 ■ Fx: 972-580-2399
Eagles, Grand Aerie Fraternal Order of   www.foe.com
1623 Gateway Cir S   Grove City OH 43123
Ph: 614-883-2200 ■ Fx: 614-883-2201
Ear Hospitals, American Association of Eye &   www.aaeeh.org
1100 Wilson Blvd Suite 1200   Arlington VA 22209
Ph: 703-243-8848 ■ Fx: 703-243-8664
Ear Nose & Throat Advances in Children, Society for   www.sentac.org
3333 Burnet Ave   Cincinnati OH 45229
Ph: 513-636-2287
Early American Decoration, Historical Society of   www.hsead.org
Farmers Museum PO Box 30   Cooperstown NY 13326
Ph: 607-547-5667
Early American History & Culture, Omohundro Institute of   www.wm.edu/oieahc
PO Box 8781   Williamsbury VA 23187
Ph: 757-221-1110 ■ Fx: 757-221-1047
Early American Industries Association   www.eaiainfo.org
167 Bakerville Rd   South Dartmouth MA 02748
Ph: 508-993-9578
Early American Republic, Society for Historians of the   www.sla.purdue.edu/jer
Early Childhood Association, Southern   www.southernearlychildhood.org
PO Box 55930   Little Rock AR 72215
Ph: 501-221-1648 ■ Fx: 501-227-5297 ■ TF: 800-305-7322
Early Childhood Educators, American Association of
3612 Bent Branch Ct   Falls Church VA 22041
Ph: 703-941-4329
Early Childhood Teacher Educators, National Association of   www.naecte.org
Early Music America   www.earlymusic.org
11421 1/2 Bellflower Rd   Cleveland OH 44106
Ph: 216-229-1685 ■ Fx: 216-229-1688 ■ TF: 888-722-5288
Early Sites Research Society   www.diggit.org
PO Box 4175   Independence MO 64050
Ph: 816-254-4658
Early Typewriter Collectors Association   www.home.earthlink.net/~dcrehr/etc.html
PO Box 641824   Los Angeles CA 90064
Ph: 310-477-5229
EARS Inc, International Order of   www.cornislandstorytellingfestival.org
12019 Donohue Ave   Louisville KY 40243
Ph: 502-245-0643 ■ Fx: 502-254-7542
Earth Charter USA Campaign   www.earthcharterusa.org/
2100 L St NW   Washington DC 20037
Ph: 202-778-6133 ■ Fx: 202-778-6138
Earth Communications Office   www.earthcomm.org
12021 Wilshire Blvd Suite 557   Los Angeles CA 90025
Ph: 310-656-0577 ■ Fx: 310-656-1657
Earth Day Network   www.earthday.net
1616 P St NW Suite 200   Washington DC 20036
Ph: 202-518-0044 ■ Fx: 202-518-8794
Earth Day USA   www.earthday.net
811 1st Ave Suite 466   Seattle WA 98104
Ph: 206-876-2000 ■ Fx: 206-876-2015

Earth Education, Institute for   www.eartheducation.org
Cedar Cove   Greenville WV 24945
Ph: 304-832-6404 ▪ Fx: 304-832-6077

(Earth Engineering) ASFE   www.asfe.org
8811 Colesville Rd Suite G106   Silver Spring MD 20910
Ph: 301-565-2733 ▪ Fx: 301-589-2017

Earth, Friends of the   www.foe.org
1025 Vermont Ave NW Suite 300   Washington DC 20005
Ph: 202-783-7400 ▪ Fx: 202-783-0444 ▪ TF: 877-843-8687

Earth, International Society for a Complete   www.hollow-earth.org
PO Box 1952   Kapaa HI 96746
Ph: 808-245-3820

Earth Island Institute   www.earthisland.org
300 Broadway Suite 28   San Francisco CA 94133
Ph: 415-788-3666 ▪ Fx: 415-788-7324

Earth, Kids for Saving   www.kidsforsavingearth.org
PO Box 421118   Minneapolis MN 55442
Ph: 763-559-1234 ▪ Fx: 763-559-6980

Earth Network, Sacred   www.sacredearthnetwork.org
592 Main St   Amherst MA 01002
Ph: 413-253-6998 ▪ Fx: 413-253-1657

Earth Policy Institute   www.earth-policy.org
1350 Connecticut Ave NW Suite 403   Washington DC 20036
Ph: 202-496-9290 ▪ Fx: 202-496-9325

Earth Science Editors, Association of   www.aese.org

Earth Science Teachers Association, National   www.nestanet.org

(Earth Sciences) Sigma Gamma Epsilon   www.earth.uni.edu/SGE
Univ of Oklahoma 100 E Boyd Rm N-131   Norman OK 73019
Ph: 405-325-3031 ▪ Fx: 405-325-7069

Earth Sciences Society, History of   www.historyearthscience.org
PO Box 455   Poncha Springs CO 81242
Ph: 719-539-4113 ▪ Fx: 719-539-4542

Earth Scientists, Society of Independent Professional   www.sipes.org
4925 Greenville Ave Suite 1106   Dallas TX 75206
Ph: 214-363-1780 ▪ Fx: 214-363-8195

Earth Share   www.earthshare.org
7735 Old Georgetown Rd Suite 900   Bethesda MD 20814
Ph: 240-333-0300 ▪ TF: 800-875-3863

Earth Society Foundation   www.earthsocietyfoundation.org
399 E 72nd St PH-B   New York NY 10021
Ph: 212-988-1800 ▪ Fx: 212-988-0700 ▪ TF: 800-332-7843

EarthAction International   www.earthaction.org
30 Cottage St   Amherst MA 01002
Ph: 413-549-8118 ▪ Fx: 413-549-0544

Earthday Resources   www.earthdayresources.org
29 Temple Pl   Boston MA 02111
Ph: 877-327-8446

Earthjustice   www.earthjustice.org
426 17th St 6th Fl   Oakland CA 94612
Ph: 510-550-6700 ▪ Fx: 510-550-6740

Earthquake Engineering, National Information Service for   nisee.berkeley.edu
Univ of California Berkeley 1301 S 46th St RFS 453   Richmond
CA 94804
Ph: 510-231-9403 ▪ Fx: 510-231-9461

Earthquake Engineering Research Institute   www.eeri.org
499 14th St Suite 320   Oakland CA 94612
Ph: 510-451-0905 ▪ Fx: 510-451-5411

EarthRights International   www.earthrights.org
1612 K St NW Suite 401   Washington DC 20006
Ph: 202-466-5188 ▪ Fx: 202-466-5189

EarthSave International   www.earthsave.org
PO Box 96   New York NY 10108
Ph: 718-459-7503 ▪ Fx: 718-228-2491 ▪ TF: 800-362-3648

Earthstewards Network   www.earthstewards.org
PO Box 10697   Bainbridge Island WA 98110
Ph: 206-842-7986 ▪ Fx: 206-842-8918

Earthwatch Institute   www.earthwatch.org
3 Clock Tower Pl Suite 100   Maynard MA 01754
Ph: 978-461-0081 ▪ Fx: 978-461-2332 ▪ TF: 800-776-0188

East European Research, National Council for Eurasian &   www.nceeer.org
910 17th St NW Suite 300   Washington DC 20006
Ph: 202-822-6950 ▪ Fx: 202-822-6955

East Meets West Foundation   www.eastmeetswest.org
PO Box 29292   Oakland CA 94604
Ph: 510-763-7045 ▪ Fx: 510-763-6545

East-West Center   www.eastwestcenter.org
1601 East-West Rd   Honolulu HI 96848
Ph: 808-944-7111 ▪ Fx: 808-944-7376

East-West Ministries International   www.eastwestministries.org
4450 Sojourn Dr Suite 100   Addison TX 75001
Ph: 214-265-8300 ▪ Fx: 214-265-8503

Easter Seals   www.easterseals.com
230 W Monroe St Suite 1800   Chicago IL 60606
Ph: 312-726-6200 ▪ Fx: 312-726-1494 ▪ TF: 800-221-6827

Eastern Apicultural Society of North America   www.easternapiculture.org
PO Box 300   Essex NY 12936
Ph: 518-963-7593

Eastern Bird Banding Association   www.pronetisp.net/~bpbird

Eastern College Athletic Conference   www.ecac.com
1311 Craigville Beach Rd PO Box 3   Centerville MA 02632
Ph: 508-771-5060 ▪ Fx: 508-771-9481

Eastern Dark-Fried Tobacco Growers Association
1109 S Main St PO Box 517   Springfield TN 37172
Ph: 615-384-4543 ▪ Fx: 615-384-4545

Eastern Star, General Grand Chapter Order of the   www.easternstar.org/ggc/frame.html
1618 New Hampshire Ave NW   Washington DC 20009
Ph: 202-667-4737 ▪ Fx: 202-462-5162 ▪ TF: 800-648-1182

EastWest Institute   www.iews.org
700 Broadway 2nd Fl   New York NY 10003
Ph: 212-824-4100 ▪ Fx: 212-824-4149

Eaters Anonymous - HOW, Compulsive   www.ceahow.org
5500 E Atherton St Suite 227B   Long Beach CA 90815
Ph: 562-342-9344 ▪ Fx: 562-342-9346

Eating Disorders, Academy for   www.aedweb.org
6728 Old McLean Village Dr   McLean VA 22101
Ph: 703-556-9222 ▪ Fx: 703-556-8729

Eating Disorders Association, National   www.nationaleatingdisorders.org
603 Stewart St Suite 803   Seattle WA 98101
Ph: 206-382-3587 ▪ Fx: 206-829-8501 ▪ TF: 800-931-2237

Eating Disorders Professionals, International Association of   www.iaedp.com
PO Box 1295   Pekin IL 61555
Ph: 309-346-3341 ▪ Fx: 309-346-2874 ▪ TF: 800-800-8126

eBusiness Association   www.ebusinessassociation.org
PO Box 804   Adams Basin NY 14410
Ph: 716-234-1322 ▪ Fx: 716-377-8949

Eccles George S & Dolores Dore Foundation
79 S Main St 12th Fl   Salt Lake City UT 84111
Ph: 801-246-5355 ▪ Fx: 801-350-3510

Echocardiography, American Society of   asecho.org
1500 Sunday Dr Suite 102   Raleigh NC 27607
Ph: 919-861-5574 ▪ Fx: 919-787-4916

Ecoliteracy, Center for   www.ecoliteracy.org
2522 San Pablo Ave   Berkeley CA 94702
Ph: 510-845-4595 ▪ Fx: 510-845-1439

Ecologic Development Fund   www.ecologic.org
PO Box 383405   Cambridge MA 02238
Ph: 617-441-6300 ▪ Fx: 617-441-6307

Ecological Economics, International Society for   www.ecoeco.org
1313 Dolley Madison Blvd Suite 402   McLean VA 22101
Ph: 703-790-1745 ▪ Fx: 703-790-2672

Ecological Farming Association   www.eco-farm.org
406 Main St Suite 313   Watsonville CA 95076
Ph: 831-763-2111 ▪ Fx: 831-763-2112

Ecological Institute, Thorne   www.thorne-eco.org
PO Box 19107   Boulder CO 80308
Ph: 303-499-3647 ▪ Fx: 720-565-3873

Ecological Restoration International, Society for   www.ser.org
1955 W Grant Rd Suite 150   Tucson AZ 85745
Ph: 520-622-5485 ▪ Fx: 520-622-5491

Ecological Society of America   www.esa.org
1707 H St NW Suite 400   Washington DC 20006
Ph: 202-833-8773 ▪ Fx: 202-833-8775

Ecological & Toxicological Association of Dyes & Organic   www.etad.com
Pigments Manufacturers   1850 M St NW Suite
700   Washington DC 20036
Ph: 202-721-4154 ▪ Fx: 202-296-8120

Ecology Action League, Human   members.aol.com/HEALNatnl
PO Box 29629   Atlanta GA 30359
Ph: 404-248-1898 ▪ Fx: 404-248-0162

Ecology & Ethnology, International Council for Human   www.ichee.org
PO Box 7024   New York NY 10128
Ph: 212-410-6560

Ecology, Foundation for Deep   www.deepecology.org
Fort Cronkhite Bldg 1062   Sausalito CA 94965
Ph: 415-229-9339 ▪ Fx: 415-229-9340

Ecology, International Institute for Bau-Biologie &   www.bau-biologieusa.com
1401 A Cleveland St   Clearwater FL 33755
Ph: 727-461-4371 ▪ Fx: 727-441-4373

Ecology, International Society of Chemical   www.chemecol.org
North Dakota State Univ Dept of Entomology   Fargo ND 58105
Ph: 701-231-6444 ▪ Fx: 701-231-8557

(Ecology) For Mother Earth   www.motherearth.org
Old First Presbyterian Church 1101 Bryder Rd   Columbus OH
43205
Ph: 614-252-9255 ▪ Fx: 614-443-6125

Ecology, North American Coalition for Christianity &   www.nacce.org
PO Box 40011   Saint Paul MN 55104
Ph: 612-698-0349

Ecology, North American Coalition on Religion &
5 Thomas Cir NW   Washington DC 20005
Ph: 202-462-2591 ▪ Fx: 202-462-6534

Ecology, Society for Human   www.societyforhumanecology.org
College of the Atlantic 105 Eden St   Bar Harbor ME 04609
Ph: 207-288-5015 ▪ Fx: 207-288-3780

Ecology, Society for Vector   www.sove.org/
1966 Compton Ave   Corona CA 92881
Ph: 909-340-9792 ▪ Fx: 909-340-2515

Econometric Society   www.econometricsociety.org/es
Northwestern Univ Dept of Economics   Evanston IL 60208
Ph: 847-491-3615 ▪ Fx: 847-491-5427

Economic Agenda Project, Women's   www.weap.org
449 15th St 2nd Fl   Oakland CA 94612
Ph: 510-451-7379 ▪ Fx: 510-986-8628

Economic Analysis, Institute for   www.iea-macro-economics.org
262 Harvard St Suite 12   Cambridge MA 02139
Ph: 617-864-9933

Economic Association, American   www.vanderbilt.edu/AEA
2014 Broadway Suite 305   Nashville TN 37203
Ph: 615-322-2595 ▪ Fx: 615-343-7590

Economic Association International, Western   www.weainternational.org
7400 Center Ave Suite 109   Huntington Beach CA 92647
Ph: 714-898-3222 ▪ Fx: 714-891-6715

Economic Association, Southern   www.okstate.edu/economics/journal/south1.html
Oklahoma State Univ College of Business Admin   Stillwater OK
74078
Ph: 405-744-7645 ▪ Fx: 405-744-5180

Economic Botany, Society for   www.econbot.org
PO Box 1897   Lawrence KS 66044
Ph: 785-843-1235 ▪ Fx: 785-843-1274 ▪ TF: 800-627-0629

Economic Cooperation, Foundation for Russian-American   www.fraec.org
2601 4th Ave Suite 310   Seattle WA 98121
Ph: 206-443-1935 ▪ Fx: 206-443-0954

Economic Developers Association, National Rural   www.nreda.org
431 E Locust Suite 300   Des Moines IA 50309
Ph: 515-284-1421 ▪ Fx: 515-243-2049

(Economic Development) ACCRA   www.accra.org
PO Box 407   Arlington VA 22210
Ph: 703-522-4980 ▪ Fx: 703-522-4985

Economic Development Associates, Mennonite   www.meda.org
1821 Oregon Pike Suite 201   Lancaster PA 17601
Ph: 717-560-6546 ▪ Fx: 717-560-6549 ▪ TF: 800-665-7026

Economic Development, Business Alliance for International   www.fintrac.com/alliance
1615 L St NW Suite 520   Washington DC 20036
Ph: 202-429-8855 ▪ Fx: 202-429-8857

Economic Development, Committee for   www.ced.org
261 Madison Ave 25th Fl   New York NY 10016
Ph: 212-688-2063 ▪ Fx: 212-758-9068

Economic Development Corp, American Woman's   www.awed.org
216 E 45th St 10th Fl   New York NY 10017
Ph: 917-368-6100

Economic Development Council, International   www.iedconline.org
734 15th St NW Suite 900   Washington DC 20005
Ph: 202-223-7800 ▪ Fx: 202-223-4745

Economic Development & Law Center, National   www.nedlc.org
2201 Broadway Suite 815   Oakland CA 94612
Ph: 510-251-2600 ▪ Fx: 510-251-0600

Economic Development, National Association for County Community &   www.nacced.org
2025 M St NW Suite 800   Washington DC 20036
Ph: 202-367-1149 ▪ Fx: 202-367-2149

Economic Development, National Congress for Community   www.ncced.org
1030 15th St NW Suite 325   Washington DC 20005
Ph: 202-289-9020 ▪ Fx: 202-289-7051 ▪ TF: 877-446-2233

(Economic Development) Reach-Out International   www.reach-out-international.org
1968 Wooddale Ct   Baton Rouge LA 70806
Ph: 225-928-3123 ▪ Fx: 225-924-1512

Economic Education, Estonian American Fund for
4 Noyes Ct   Silver Spring MD 20910
Ph: 301-587-9115 ▪ Fx: 301-587-0730

Economic Education, Foundation for   www.fee.org
30 S Broadway   Irvington-on-Hudson NY 10533
Ph: 914-591-7230 ▪ Fx: 914-591-8910 ▪ TF: 800-960-4333

Economic Education, National Council on   www.ncee.net
1140 6th Ave 2nd Fl   New York NY 10036
Ph: 212-730-7007 ▪ Fx: 212-730-1793 ▪ TF: 800-338-1192

Economic Education, National Schools Committee for   www.nscee.org
30 S Broadway   Irvington-on-Hudson NY 10533
Ph: 914-591-7230 ▪ Fx: 914-591-8910

Economic Geologists, Society of   www.segweb.org
7811 Shaffer Pkwy   Littleton CO 80127
Ph: 720-981-7882 ▪ Fx: 720-981-7874

Economic Growth, International Center for   www.iceg.org
777 Campus Commons Rd Suite 200   Sacramento CA 95825
Ph: 916-563-7180 ▪ Fx: 916-929-0448

Economic History Association   eh.net/EHA
Univ of Kansas Department of Economics 213 Summerfield Hall   Lawrence KS 66045
Ph: 785-864-2847 ▪ Fx: 785-864-5270

Economic Justice Institute Inc   www.law.wisc.edu/eji
975 Bascom Mall   Madison WI 53706
Ph: 608-262-9143

Economic Leadership Institute, Congressional   www.celi.org
201 Massachusetts Ave NE Suite C-6   Washington DC 20002
Ph: 202-546-5007 ▪ Fx: 202-546-7037

Economic Options Inc, Center for   www.centerforeconomicoptions.org
214 Capital St Suite 200   Charleston WV 25301
Ph: 304-345-1298 ▪ Fx: 304-342-0641

Economic Policy Institute   www.epinet.org
1660 L St NW Suite 1200   Washington DC 20036
Ph: 202-775-8810 ▪ Fx: 202-775-0819

Economic Processing Zones Association, World   www.wepza.org
PO Box 986   Flagstaff AZ 86002
Ph: 928-779-0052 ▪ Fx: 928-774-8589

Economic Public Policy Studies, Phoenix Center for Advanced Legal &   www.phoenix-center.org
5335 Wisconsin Ave NW Suite 440   Washington DC 20015
Ph: 202-274-0235

Economic Research, American Institute for   www.aier.org
PO Box 1000   Great Barrington MA 01230
Ph: 413-528-1216 ▪ Fx: 413-528-0103

Economic Research, Association for University Business &   www.auber.org
Univ of Colorado Leeds School of Business UCB 419   Boulder CO 80309
Ph: 303-492-3196 ▪ Fx: 303-492-3620

Economic Research Foundation, Atlas   www.atlasusa.org
4084 University Dr Suite 103   Fairfax VA 22030
Ph: 703-934-6969 ▪ Fx: 703-352-7530

Economic Round Table, Women's   www.wert.org
1633 Broadway 37th Fl   New York NY 10019
Ph: 212-492-4439 ▪ Fx: 212-492-4436

Economic & Security Alternatives, National Center for   www.ncesa.org
2000 P St NW Suite 330   Washington DC 20036
Ph: 202-986-1373 ▪ Fx: 202-986-7938

Economic & Social Rights, Center for   www.cesr.org
162 Montague St 2nd Fl   Brooklyn NY 11201
Ph: 718-237-9145 ▪ Fx: 718-237-9147

Economic Society, International Atlantic   www.iaes.org
4949 W Pine Blvd 2nd Fl   Saint Louis MO 63108
Ph: 314-454-0100 ▪ Fx: 314-454-9109

Economic Strategy Institute   www.econstrat.org
1401 H St NW Suite 560   Washington DC 20005
Ph: 202-289-1288 ▪ Fx: 202-289-1319

Economic Studies, Association for Comparative   www.wdi.bus.umich.edu/aces
Arizona State Univ Dept of Economics PO Box 873806   Tempe AZ 85287
Ph: 480-965-6524 ▪ Fx: 480-965-0748

Economic Studies, Joint Center for Political &   www.jointcenter.org
1090 Vermont Ave NW Suite 1100   Washington DC 20005
Ph: 202-789-3500 ▪ Fx: 202-789-6390

Economic Theory, Society for the Advancement of
Univ of Illinois 330 Wohlerf Hall 1206 S 6th St   Champaign IL 61820
Ph: 217-333-0120 ▪ Fx: 217-244-6678

Economic Trends, Foundation on   www.biotechcentury.org
1660 L St NW Suite 216   Washington DC 20036
Ph: 202-466-2823 ▪ Fx: 202-429-9602

Economics Association, American Agricultural   www.aaea.org
415 S Duff Ave Suite C   Ames IA 50010
Ph: 515-233-3202 ▪ Fx: 515-233-3101

Economics Association, American Real Estate & Urban   www.areuea.org
PO Box 1148   Portage MI 49081
Ph: 866-273-8321 ▪ Fx: 313-731-0174

Economics, Center for Popular   www.populareconomics.org
Box 785   Amherst MA 01004
Ph: 413-545-0743

Economics, Council for Ethics in   www.businessethics.org
191 W Nationwide Blvd Suite 300B   Columbus OH 43215
Ph: 614-221-8661 ▪ Fx: 614-221-8707

Economics & the Environment, Foundation for Research on   www.free-eco.org
945 Technology Blvd Suite 101F   Bozeman MT 59718
Ph: 406-585-1776 ▪ Fx: 406-585-3000

Economics & Finance Association, North American   www.naefa.org
Ohio Univ Dept of Economics   Athens OH 45701
Ph: 740-593-2034 ▪ Fx: 740-593-0181

Economics, Foundation for Teaching   www.fte.org
260 Russell Blvd Suite B   Davis CA 95616
Ph: 530-757-4630 ▪ Fx: 530-757-4636

Economics Institute of Bard College, Levy   www.levy.org
Blithewood   Annandale-on-Hudson NY 12504
Ph: 845-758-7700 ▪ Fx: 845-758-1149

Economics Inc, Institute for Community   www.iceclt.org
57 School St   Springfield MA 01105
Ph: 413-746-8660 ▪ Fx: 413-746-8862

Economics, Institute for International   www.iie.com
1750 Massachusetts Ave NW   Washington DC 20036
Ph: 202-328-9000 ▪ Fx: 202-328-5432

Economics International, Association for Cultural   www.acei.neu.edu
Northeastern Univ Dept of Economics 301 Lake Hall   Boston MA 02115
Ph: 617-373-2839 ▪ Fx: 617-373-3640

Economics, International Association for Energy   www.iaee.org
28790 Chagrin Blvd Suite 350   Cleveland OH 44122
Ph: 216-464-5365 ▪ Fx: 216-464-2737

Economics, International Society for Ecological   www.ecoeco.org
1313 Dolley Madison Blvd Suite 402   McLean VA 22101
Ph: 703-790-1745 ▪ Fx: 703-790-2672

Economics, International Society of Statistical Science in
536 Oasis Dr   Santa Rosa CA 95407
Ph: 707-575-3529

Economics & Management Sciences, Center for Mathematical Studies in   www.kellogg.nwu.edu/research/math
Northwestern University 2001 Sheridan Rd Leverone Hall Rm 580   Evanston IL 60208
Ph: 847-491-3527 ▪ Fx: 847-491-2530

(Economics) Milken Institute   www.milkeninstitute.org
1250 4th St   Santa Monica CA 90401
Ph: 310-570-4600 ▪ Fx: 310-570-4601

Economics, National Association for Business   www.nabe.com
1233 20th St NW Suite 505   Washington DC 20036
Ph: 202-463-6223 ▪ Fx: 202-463-6239

Economics, National Association of Forensic   www.nafe.net
PO Box 30067   Kansas City MO 64112
Ph: 816-235-2833 ▪ Fx: 816-235-5263

(Economics) Proutist Universal North America   www.prout.org/ny
PO Box 56533   Washington DC 20040
Ph: 301-231-0110

Economics Society, History of   eh.net/HE/HisEcSoc

Economics, Union for Radical Political   www.urpe.org
37 Howe St   New Haven CT 06511
Ph: 203-777-4605

Economics, US Association for Energy   www.usaee.org
28790 Chagrin Blvd Suite 350   Cleveland OH 44122
Ph: 216-464-2785 ▪ Fx: 216-464-2768

Economies, Coalition for Environmentally Responsible   www.ceres.org
99 Chauncy St 6th Fl   Boston MA 02111
Ph: 617-247-0700 ▪ Fx: 617-267-5400

Economists Allied for Arms Reduction   www.ecaar.org
39 E Central Ave Suite 1   Pearl River NY 10965
Ph: 845-620-1542 ▪ Fx: 845-620-1866

Economists, Association of Environmental & Resource   www.aere.org/
1616 P St NW Rm 400   Washington DC 20036
Ph: 202-328-5077 ▪ Fx: 202-939-3460

Economists Club, National   www.national-economists.org
PO Box 19281   Washington DC 20036
Ph: 703-739-9404 ▪ Fx: 703-739-9405

Economists, Conference of Business
28790 Chagrin Blvd Suite 350   Cleveland OH 44122
Ph: 216-464-2137 ▪ Fx: 216-464-0397
Economists Society, Chinese   www.china-ces.org
733 15th St NW Suite 910   Washington DC 20005
Ph: 202-347-8588 ▪ Fx: 202-347-8510
Economy, American Council for an Energy-Efficient   www.aceee.org
1001 Connecticut Ave NW Suite 801   Washington DC 20036
Ph: 202-429-8873 ▪ Fx: 202-429-2248
Economy, Berkeley Roundtable on the International   brie.berkeley.edu/~briewww
Univ of California Berkeley 2234 Piedmont Ave   Berkeley CA 94720
Ph: 510-642-3067 ▪ Fx: 510-643-6617
Economy, Citizens for a Sound   www.cse.org
1900 M St NW 5th Fl   Washington DC 20036
Ph: 202-783-3870 ▪ Fx: 202-783-4687 ▪ TF: 888-564-6273
Economy, National Center on Education & the   www.ncee.org
555 13th St NW Suite 500 W   Washington DC 20004
Ph: 202-783-3668 ▪ Fx: 202-783-3672
Economy Research Center, Political   www.perc.org
2048 Analysis Dr Suite A   Bozeman MT 59718
Ph: 406-578-9591 ▪ Fx: 406-586-7555
Ecosystem Alliance, Northwest   www.ecosystem.org
1208 Bay St Suite 201   Bellingham WA 98225
Ph: 360-671-9950 ▪ Fx: 360-671-8429
Ecotourism Society, International   www.ecotourism.org
733 15th St NW Suite 1000   Washington DC 20005
Ph: 202-347-9203 ▪ Fx: 202-387-7915
ECRI   www.ecri.org
5200 Butler Pike   Plymouth Meeting PA 19462
Ph: 610-825-6000 ▪ Fx: 610-834-1275
Ecuadorian-American Association
30 Vesey St Suite 506   New York NY 10007
Ph: 212-233-7776 ▪ Fx: 212-233-7779
Ecuadorian-American Chamber of Commerce North America
4100 Westheimer Rd Suite 200   Houston TX 77027
Ph: 713-877-8534 ▪ Fx: 713-960-1052
Ecumenical Consultative Council, Disciples
130 E Washington St PO Box 1986   Indianapolis IN 46206
Ph: 317-713-2585 ▪ Fx: 317-713-2588
Ecumenical Council, Reformed
2050 Breton Rd SE Suite 102   Grand Rapids MI 49546
Ph: 616-949-2910
Ecumenical & Interreligious Staff, National Association of
PO Box 7093   Tacoma WA 98406
Ph: 253-759-0141 ▪ Fx: 253-759-9689
Ecumenical Officers, National Association of Diocesan   www.nadeo.com
8003 Mobud Dr   Houston TX 77036
Ph: 713-774-0097 ▪ Fx: 713-774-0320
Ecumenical Program on Central America & the Caribbean   www.epica.org
1470 Irving St NW   Washington DC 20010
Ph: 202-332-0292 ▪ Fx: 202-332-1184
Ecumenical Theological Seminary   www.etseminary.org
2930 Woodward Ave   Detroit MI 48201
Ph: 313-831-5200 ▪ Fx: 313-831-1353
Ecumenists, North American Academy of   www.naae.net
211 Easton Dr   Lakeland FL 33803
Ph: 863-682-8415
Eden Alternative   www.edenalt.com
742 Turnpike Rd   Sherburne NY 13460
Ph: 607-674-5232 ▪ Fx: 607-674-6723
Edgar Allan Poe Society of Baltimore   www.eapoe.org
(Edgar Cayce) Association for Research & Enlightenment   www.are-cayce.com
215 67th St   Virginia Beach VA 23451
Ph: 757-428-3588 ▪ Fx: 757-422-6921 ▪ TF: 800-333-4499
Edged Products Manufacturers Association, American   www.aepma.org
21165 Whitfield Pl Suite 105   Potomac Falls VA 20165
Ph: 703-433-9281 ▪ Fx: 703-433-0369
Edible Oils, Institute of Shortening &   www.iseo.org
1750 New York Ave NW Suite 120   Washington DC 20006
Ph: 202-783-7960 ▪ Fx: 202-393-1367
Edison Birthplace Association Inc   www.tomedison.org
Edison Birthplace Museum 9 Edison Dr PO Box 451   Milan OH 44846
Ph: 419-499-2135 ▪ Fx: 419-499-3241
Edison Electric Institute   www.eei.org
701 Pennsylvania Ave NW   Washington DC 20004
Ph: 202-508-5000 ▪ Fx: 202-508-5794 ▪ TF: 800-334-4688
Edison Illuminating Companies, Association of   www.aeic.org
600 N 18th St PO Box 2641   Birmingham AL 35291
Ph: 205-257-2530 ▪ Fx: 205-257-2540
Edison Welding Institute   www.ewi.org
1250 Arthur E Adams Dr   Columbus OH 43221
Ph: 614-688-5000 ▪ Fx: 614-688-5001
Edith Stein Guild
Church of Saint John the Baptist 210 W 31st St   New York NY 10001
Ph: 212-564-9070 ▪ Fx: 212-279-2823
Editing, Association for Documentary   etext.virginia.edu/ade
Princeton Univ   Princeton NJ 08544
Ph: 609-258-5687 ▪ Fx: 609-258-1630
Editorial Cartoonists, Association of American   info.detnews.com/aaec
1121 Stoneferry Ln   Raleigh NC 27606
Ph: 919-859-5516 ▪ Fx: 919-859-3172
Editorial Council, International Foodservice   www.ifec-is-us.com
PO Box 491   Hyde Park NY 12538
Ph: 845-229-6973 ▪ Fx: 845-229-6993
Editorial Freelancers Association   www.the-efa.org
71 W 23rd St Suite 1910   New York NY 10010
Ph: 212-929-5400 ▪ Fx: 212-929-5439 ▪ TF: 866-929-5400

Editorial Projects in Education Inc   www.edweek.org
6935 Arlington Rd Suite 100   Bethesda MD 20814
Ph: 301-280-3100 ▪ Fx: 301-280-3200
Editorial Writers, National Conference of   www.ncew.org
3899 N Front St   Harrisburg PA 17110
Ph: 717-703-3015 ▪ Fx: 717-703-3014
Editors, American Association of Dental   www.dentaleditors.org
750 N Lincoln Memorial Dr Suite 422   Milwaukee WI 53202
Ph: 414-272-2759 ▪ Fx: 414-272-2754
Editors, American Association of Sunday & Feature   www.aasfe.org
Univ of Maryland Merrill College of Journalism 1117 Journalism Bldg   College Park MD 20742
Ph: 301-314-2631 ▪ Fx: 301-314-9166
Editors, American Cinema   www.ace-filmeditors.org
100 Universal City Plaza Bldg 2282 Rm 234   Universal City CA 91608
Ph: 818-777-2900 ▪ Fx: 818-733-5023
Editors, American Society of Business Publication   www.asbpe.org
710 E Ogden Ave Suite 600   Naperville IL 60563
Ph: 630-579-3288 ▪ Fx: 630-369-2488
Editors, American Society of Magazine   www.magazine.org/Editorial
810 7th Ave   New York NY 10022
Ph: 212-872-3737 ▪ Fx: 212-906-0128
Editors, American Society of Newspaper   www.asne.org
11690-B Sunrise Valley Dr   Reston VA 20191
Ph: 703-453-1122 ▪ Fx: 703-453-1133
Editors, Associated Press Managing   www.apme.com
50 Rockefeller Plaza   New York NY 10020
Ph: 212-621-1838
Editors' Association, American Agricultural   www.ageditors.com
Box 156   New Prague MN 56071
Ph: 952-758-6502 ▪ Fx: 952-758-5813
Editors, Association of Art   www.artedit.org
3912 Natchez Ave S   Saint Louis Park MN 55416
Ph: 952-922-1374
Editors Association, College Fraternity   www.cfea.org
11020 NW Ambassador Dr Suite 30   Kansas City MO 64153
Ph: 816-891-9445 ▪ Fx: 816-891-0838
Editors, Association of Earth Science   www.aese.org
Editors, Council of Science   www.councilofscienceeditors.org
12100 Sunset Hills Rd Suite 130   Reston VA 20190
Ph: 703-437-4377 ▪ Fx: 703-435-4399
Editors, International Society of Weekly Newspaper   www.iswne.org
Missouri Southern State Univ 3950 E Newman Rd   Joplin MO 64801
Ph: 417-625-9736 ▪ Fx: 417-659-4445
Editors, Investigative Reporters &   www.ire.org
Missouri School of Journalism 138 Neff Annex   Columbia MO 65211
Ph: 573-882-2042 ▪ Fx: 573-882-5431
Editors, National Association of Real Estate   www.naree.org
1003 NW 6th Terr   Boca Raton FL 33486
Ph: 561-391-3599
Editors & Writers, Society of American Business   www.sabew.org
Missouri School of Journalism 134A Neff Annex   Columbia MO 65211
Ph: 573-882-7862 ▪ Fx: 573-884-1372
Edna Hibel Society   www.hibel.com/society.htm
PO Box 9721   Coral Springs FL 33075
Ph: 954-731-6699
Edna McConnell Clark Foundation   www.emcf.org
250 Park Ave Suite 900   New York NY 10177
Ph: 212-551-9100 ▪ Fx: 212-986-4558
Edsel Club   www.edselworld.com
19296 Tuckaway Ct   Fort Myers FL 33903
Ph: 941-731-8027
Education Accreditation, Council for Higher   www.chea.org
1 Dupont Cir NW Suite 510   Washington DC 20036
Ph: 202-955-6126 ▪ Fx: 202-955-6129
Education Activists, National Coalition of   www.nceaonline.org
1420 Walnut St Suite 720   Philadelphia PA 19102
Ph: 215-735-2418
Education Administrators, Association of International   wings.buffalo.edu/intled/aiea
Univ at Buffalo Office of International Education 411 Capen Hall Box 601604   Buffalo NY 14260
Ph: 716-645-2368 ▪ Fx: 716-645-2528
Education, Alliance for Excellent   www.all4ed.org
1101 Vermont Ave NW Suite 411   Washington DC 20005
Ph: 202-842-4888 ▪ Fx: 202-842-1613
Education, Alliance for Higher   www.allianceedu.org
2602 Rutford Ave   Richardson TX 75080
Ph: 972-883-4920 ▪ Fx: 972-713-8209
(Education) Alpha Delta Kappa   www.alphadeltakappa.org
1615 W 92nd St   Kansas City MO 64114
Ph: 816-363-5525 ▪ Fx: 816-363-4010 ▪ TF: 800-247-2311
Education, American Academy for Liberal   www.aale.org
1710 Rhode Island Ave NW 4th Fl   Washington DC 20036
Ph: 202-452-8611 ▪ Fx: 202-452-8620
Education, American Academy of Safety   www.veteransofsafety.org
Central Missouri State Univ Humphreys Bldg   Warrensburg MO 64093
Ph: 660-543-4281 ▪ Fx: 660-543-4482
Education, American Alliance for Theatre &   www.aate.com
7475 Wisconsin Ave Suite 300A   Bethesda MD 20814
Ph: 301-951-7977
Education, American Association for Adult & Continuing   www.aaace.org
4380 Forbes Blvd   Lanham MD 20706
Ph: 301-918-1913 ▪ Fx: 301-918-1846

Education, American Association of Colleges for Teacher   www.aacte.org
1307 New York Ave NW Suite 300   Washington DC 20005
Ph: 202-293-2450 ▪ Fx: 202-457-8095

Education, American Association for Employment in   www.aaee.org
3040 Riverside Dr Suite 125   Columbus OH 43221
Ph: 614-485-1111 ▪ Fx: 614-485-9609

Education, American Association for Higher   www.aahe.org
1 Dupont Cir NW Suite 360   Washington DC 20036
Ph: 202-293-6440 ▪ Fx: 202-293-0073

Education, American Council on   www.acenet.edu
1 Dupont Cir NW Suite 800   Washington DC 20036
Ph: 202-939-9300 ▪ Fx: 202-833-4760

Education, American Council on Rural Special   extension.usu.edu/acres
Utah State Univ 2865 Old Main Hill   Logan UT 84322
Ph: 435-797-3911

Education, American Councils for International   www.americancouncils.org
1776 Massachusetts Ave NW Suite 700   Washington DC 20036
Ph: 202-833-7522 ▪ Fx: 202-833-7523

Education, American Forum for Global   www.globaled.org
120 Wall St Suite 2600   New York NY 10005
Ph: 212-624-1300 ▪ Fx: 212-624-1412 ▪ TF: 800-813-5056

(Education) American ORT   www.aort.org
817 Broadway 10th Fl   New York NY 10003
Ph: 212-353-5800 ▪ Fx: 212-353-5888 ▪ TF: 800-364-9678

Education in Asia, United Board for Christian Higher   www.unitedboard.org
475 Riverside Dr Suite 1221   New York NY 10115
Ph: 212-870-2610 ▪ Fx: 212-870-2322

Education for Asian Pacifics, Leadership   www.leap.org
327 E 2nd St Suite 226   Los Angeles CA 90012
Ph: 213-485-1422 ▪ Fx: 213-485-0050

Education for Assistance Dog Services, National   www.neads.org
PO Box 213   West Boylston MA 01583
Ph: 978-422-9064 ▪ Fx: 978-422-3255

Education Assistance Organizations, Coalition of Higher   www.coheao.org
1101 Vermont Ave NW Suite 400   Washington DC 20005
Ph: 202-289-3910 ▪ Fx: 202-371-0197

Education Associates, Global   www.globaleduc.org
475 Riverside Dr Suite 1850   New York NY 10115
Ph: 212-870-3290 ▪ Fx: 212-870-2729

Education, Association for the Advancement of International   www.aaie.org
San Diego State Univ College of Extended Studies 5250
   Campanile Dr Rm 2525   San Diego CA 92182
Ph: 619-594-2877 ▪ Fx: 619-594-8566

Education Association, American Driver & Traffic Safety   www.adtsea.iup.edu
Indiana Univ of Pennsylvania Highway Safety Ctr R&P
   Bldg   Indiana PA 15705
Ph: 724-357-4051 ▪ Fx: 724-357-7595 ▪ TF: 800-896-7703

Education, Association for Assessment in Counseling &   aac.ncat.edu
c/o American Counseling Assn 5999 Stevenson Ave   Alexandria
   VA 22304
Ph: 703-823-9800 ▪ Fx: 703-823-0252 ▪ TF: 800-347-6647

Education, Association for the Behavioral Sciences & Medical   www.absame.org
1460 N Center Rd   Burton MI 48509
Ph: 810-715-4365 ▪ Fx: 810-715-4371

Education, Association for Biology Laboratory   www.zoo.toronto.edu/able
Univ of California Irvine Dept of Ecology & Evolutionary
   Biology   Irvine CA 92697
Ph: 949-824-5573 ▪ Fx: 949-824-2181

Education Association, Broadcast   www.beaweb.org
1771 'N' St NW   Washington DC 20036
Ph: 202-429-5354 ▪ TF: 888-380-7222

Education, Association for Career & Technical   www.acteonline.org
1410 King St   Alexandria VA 22314
Ph: 703-683-3111 ▪ Fx: 703-683-7424 ▪ TF: 800-826-9972

Education, Association for Continuing Higher   www.acheinc.org
2001 Mabelene Rd   Charleston SC 29406
Ph: 843-574-6658 ▪ Fx: 843-574-6470 ▪ TF: 800-807-2243

Education, Association for Continuing Legal   www.aclea.org
PO Box 4646   Austin TX 78765
Ph: 512-453-4340 ▪ Fx: 512-451-2911

Education, Association for Experiential   www.aee.org
2305 Canyon Blvd Suite 100   Boulder CO 80302
Ph: 303-440-8844 ▪ Fx: 303-440-9581

Education Association, Federal   www.feaonline.org
1101 15th St NW Suite 1002   Washington DC 20005
Ph: 202-822-7850 ▪ Fx: 202-822-7816

Education, Association for Financial Counseling & Planning   www.afcpe.org
2112 Arlington Ave Suite H   Upper Arlington OH 43221
Ph: 614-485-9650 ▪ Fx: 614-485-9621

Education, Association for Gender Equity Leadership in   www.agele.org
317 S Division St PMB 54   Ann Arbor MI 48104
Ph: 734-449-5066

Education, Association for Gerontology in Higher   www.aghe.org
1030 15th St NW Suite 240   Washington DC 20005
Ph: 202-289-9806 ▪ Fx: 202-289-9824

Education Association, International Graphic Arts   www.igaea.org
1899 Preston White Dr   Reston VA 20191
Ph: 703-758-0595

Education Association, Jesuit Secondary   www.jsea.org
1616 P St NW Suite 400   Washington DC 20036
Ph: 202-667-3888 ▪ Fx: 202-387-6305

Education Association, Journalism   www.jea.org
Kansas State Univ 103 Kedzie Hall   Manhattan KS 66506
Ph: 785-532-5532 ▪ Fx: 785-532-5563

Education Association, National   www.nea.org
1201 16th St NW   Washington DC 20036
Ph: 202-833-4000 ▪ Fx: 202-822-7974

Education Association, National Business   www.nbea.org
1914 Association Dr   Reston VA 20191
Ph: 703-860-8300 ▪ Fx: 703-620-4483

Education Association, National Community   www.ncea.com
3929 Old Lee Hwy Suite 91-A   Fairfax VA 22030
Ph: 703-359-8973 ▪ Fx: 703-359-0972

Education Association, National Indian   www.niea.org
700 N Fairfax St Suite 210   Alexandria VA 22314
Ph: 703-838-2870 ▪ Fx: 703-838-1620

Education Association, National Rural   www.nrea.net
Univ of Oklahoma 820 Van Vleet Oval Rm 227   Norman OK
   73109
Ph: 405-324-7959

Education Association, Association of Outdoor Recreation &   www.aore.org
2705 Robin St   Bloomington IL 61704
Ph: 309-829-9189

Education Association, Religious   www.religiouseducation.net
c/o Interdenomination Theological Ctr 700 ML King Jr Dr
   SW   Atlanta GA 30314
Ph: 404-527-7739 ▪ Fx: 404-527-0901

Education, Association for the Study of Higher   www.ashe.missouri.edu
202 Hill Hall   Columbia MO 65211
Ph: 573-882-9645 ▪ Fx: 573-884-2197

Education, Association for Surgical   www.surgicaleducation.com
SIU School of Medicine Dept of Surgery PO Box
   19655   Springfield IL 62794
Ph: 217-545-3835

Education Association, University Continuing   www.ucea.edu
1 Dupont Cir NW Suite 615   Washington DC 20036
Ph: 202-659-3130 ▪ Fx: 202-785-0374

Education Associations, National Council of State
1201 16th St NW Suite 817   Washington DC 20036
Ph: 202-822-7745 ▪ Fx: 202-822-7113

Education Associations, National Council of Urban   www.nea.org/ncuea
1201 16th St NW Suite 410   Washington DC 20036
Ph: 202-822-7376 ▪ Fx: 202-822-7624

Education, Center for Commercial-Free Public
1714 Franklin St   Oakland CA 94612
Ph: 510-268-1100 ▪ Fx: 510-268-1277 ▪ TF: 800-867-5841

Education, Center for Law &   www.cleweb.org
1875 Connecticut Ave NW Suite 510   Washington DC 20009
Ph: 202-986-3000 ▪ Fx: 202-986-6648

Education, Center for Social Studies
901 Old Hickory Rd   Pittsburgh PA 15243
Ph: 412-341-1967 ▪ Fx: 412-341-6533

Education Centers, National Association of Private Special   www.napsec.org
1522 K St NW Suite 1032   Washington DC 20005
Ph: 202-408-3338 ▪ Fx: 202-408-3340

Education for the Ceramic Arts, National Council on   www.nceca.net
77 Erie Village Sq Suite 280   Erie CO 80516
Ph: 303-828-2811 ▪ Fx: 303-828-0911 ▪ TF: 866-266-2322

Education & Certification, National Association of State Directors   www.nasdtec.org
of Teacher   39 Nathan Ellis Hwy PMB 134   Mashpee MA
   02649
Ph: 508-539-8844 ▪ Fx: 508-539-8868

Education Clubs of America, Distributive   www.deca.org
1908 Association Dr   Reston VA 20191
Ph: 703-860-5000 ▪ Fx: 703-860-4013

Education, Coalition for the Advancement of Jewish   www.caje.org
261 W 35th St 12th Fl   New York NY 10001
Ph: 212-268-4210 ▪ Fx: 212-268-4214

Education Collaboration, Consortium for North American Higher   www.conahec.org
Univ of Arizona PO Box 210300   Tucson AZ 85721
Ph: 520-621-7761 ▪ Fx: 520-626-2675

Education Commission of the States   www.ecs.org
700 Broadway Suite 1200   Denver CO 80203
Ph: 303-299-3600 ▪ Fx: 303-296-8332

Education Committee, Armenian National
138 E 39th St   New York NY 10016
Ph: 212-689-7231 ▪ Fx: 212-689-7168

Education Concerns for Hunger Organization   www.echonet.org
17391 Durrance Rd   Fort Myers FL 33917
Ph: 941-543-3246 ▪ Fx: 941-543-5317

Education, Consortium for the Advancement of Private Higher   www.cic.edu/caphe
1 Dupont Cir NW Suite 320   Washington DC 20036
Ph: 202-466-7230 ▪ Fx: 202-466-7238

Education Consortium, American Indian Higher   www.aihec.org
121 Oronoco St   Alexandria VA 22314
Ph: 703-838-0400 ▪ Fx: 703-838-0388

Education Consortium, National Association of State Directors   www.careertech.org
of Career Technical   444 N Capitol St NW Suite
   830   Washington DC 20001
Ph: 202-737-0303 ▪ Fx: 202-737-1106

Education Consortium for Urban Affairs, Higher   www.hecua.org
2233 University Ave W Suite 210   Saint Paul MN 55114
Ph: 651-646-8831 ▪ Fx: 651-659-9421 ▪ TF: 800-554-1089

Education Cooperation, National Association for Industry-   www2.pcom.net/naiec/
235 Hendricks Blvd   Buffalo NY 14226
Ph: 716-834-7047

Education, Cordell Hull Foundation for International   www.payson.tulane.edu/cordellhull
135 E 50th St Suite 3H   New York NY 10022
Ph: 212-759-3311

Education, Council of Administrators of Special   www.casecec.org
Fort Valley State Univ 1005 State University Dr   Fort Valley GA
   31030
Ph: 478-825-7667 ▪ Fx: 478-825-7811

Education, Council for the Advancement of Standards in Higher   www.cas.edu
1 Dupont Cir NW Suite 300   Washington DC 20036
Ph: 202-862-1400 ▪ Fx: 202-296-3286

Education, Council for Advancement & Support of   www.case.org
1307 New York Ave NW Suite 1000   Washington DC 20005
Ph: 202-328-5900 ▪ Fx: 202-387-4973 ▪ TF: 800-554-8536

Education, Council for Aid to www.cae.org
215 Lexington Ave 21st Fl   New York NY 10016
Ph: 212-661-5800 ▪ Fx: 212-661-9766

(Education), Council for American Private www.capenet.org
13017 Wisteria Dr PMB 457   Germantown MD 20874
Ph: 301-916-8460 ▪ Fx: 301-916-8485

Education, Council on Anthropology & www.aaanet.org/cae
c/o American Anthropological Assn 2200 Wilson Blvd Suite
600   Arlington VA 22201
Ph: 703-528-1902 ▪ Fx: 703-528-3546

Education, Council for Basic www.c-b-e.org
1319 F St NW Suite 900   Washington DC 20004
Ph: 202-347-4171 ▪ Fx: 202-347-5047

Education, Council for International Tax www.fdta-cite.org
PO Box 1012   White Plains NY 10602
Ph: 914-328-5656 ▪ Fx: 914-328-5757

Education, Council on Occupational www.council.org
41 Perimeter Ctr East NE Suite 640   Atlanta GA 30346
Ph: 770-396-3898 ▪ Fx: 770-396-3790 ▪ TF: 800-917-2081

Education, Council for Opportunity in www.trioprograms.org
1025 Vermont Ave NW Suite 900   Washington DC 20005
Ph: 202-347-7430 ▪ Fx: 202-347-0786

Education Credit Union Council www.ecuc.org
PO Box 7558   Spanish Fort AL 36577
Ph: 251-626-3399 ▪ Fx: 251-626-3565

Education of the Deaf, Council on www.deafed.net
Gallaudet Univ 800 Florida Ave NE FH 207   Washington DC
20002
Ph: 202-651-5525 ▪ Fx: 202-651-5749

Education Development Center Inc www.edc.org
55 Chapel St   Newton MA 02458
Ph: 617-969-7100 ▪ Fx: 617-969-3401

Education, Directors of Health Promotion & www.dhpe.org
1101 15th St NW Suite 601   Washington DC 20005
Ph: 202-659-2230 ▪ Fx: 202-659-2339

Education & Disability, Association on Higher www.ahead.org
PO Box 540666   Waltham MA 02454
Ph: 781-788-0003 ▪ Fx: 781-788-0033

Education & the Economy, National Center on www.ncee.org
555 13th St NW Suite 500 W   Washington DC 20004
Ph: 202-783-3668 ▪ Fx: 202-783-3672

Education, Editorial Projects in www.edweek.org
6935 Arlington Rd Suite 100   Bethesda MD 20814
Ph: 301-280-3100 ▪ Fx: 301-280-3200

Education, Evangelical Association for the www.tonycampolo.org/eape.shtml
Promotion of   1300 Eagle Rd   Saint Davids PA 19087
Ph: 610-341-1722 ▪ Fx: 610-341-4372

Education Excellence Partnership www.ed.gov/pubs/Strengthen/part7.html
1615 L St NW Suite 1100   Washington DC 20036
Ph: 202-872-1260 ▪ TF: 800-237-6278

Education Facilities Officers, APPA: Association of Higher www.appa.org
1643 Prince St   Alexandria VA 22314
Ph: 703-684-1446 ▪ Fx: 703-549-2772

Education Forum, Business-Higher www.acenet.edu/programs/bhef
1 Dupont Cir NW Suite 800   Washington DC 20036
Ph: 202-939-9345 ▪ Fx: 202-833-4723

Education, Foundation for the Advancement of Chiropractic www.f-a-c-e.com
PO Box 1052   Levittown PA 19058
Ph: 800-397-9722

Education, Foundation for the Advancement of Monetary www.fame.org
PO Box 625 FDR Stn   New York NY 10150
Ph: 212-818-1206 ▪ Fx: 212-754-6543

Education, Foundation for American Christian www.face.net
PO Box 9588   Chesapeake VA 23321
Ph: 757-488-6601 ▪ Fx: 757-488-5593 ▪ TF: 800-352-3223

Education Foundation, Benjamin Franklin
6275 Hazeltine National Dr Suite 114   Orlando FL 32822
Ph: 407-240-8009 ▪ Fx: 407-240-8333

Education Foundation Inc, Creative www.creativeeducationfoundation.org
289 Bay Rd   Hadley MA 01035
Ph: 413-559-6614 ▪ Fx: 413-559-6615 ▪ TF: 800-447-2774

Education Foundation & Entrepreneurs Workshop, www.inventorsworkshop.org
Inventors Workshop International   1029 Castillo St   Santa
Barbara CA 93101
Ph: 805-967-5722 ▪ Fx: 805-899-4927

Education, Foundation for Independent Higher www.fihe.org
1920 'N' St NW Suite 210   Washington DC 20036
Ph: 202-367-0333 ▪ Fx: 202-367-0334

Education Foundation, Latin American www.laef.org
924 W Colfax Ave Suite 103   Denver CO 80204
Ph: 303-446-0541 ▪ Fx: 303-446-0526

Education Foundation, Luso-American www.luso-american.org/laef
PO Box 2967   Dublin CA 94568
Ph: 925-828-3883

Education Foundation, Nellie Mae www.nmefdn.org
1250 Hancock St Suite 205N   Quincy MA 02169
Ph: 781-348-4200 ▪ Fx: 781-348-4299 ▪ TF: 877-635-5436

Education Foundation, Paul G Allen Virtual www.pgafoundations.com/edu.asp
505 5th Ave S Suite 900   Seattle WA 98104
Ph: 206-342-2000 ▪ Fx: 206-342-3000

Education, Friends Association for Higher www.earlham.edu/~fahe
1501 Cherry St   Philadelphia PA 19102
Ph: 215-241-7116 ▪ Fx: 215-241-7278

Education, Friends Council on www.friendscouncil.org
1507 Cherry St   Philadelphia PA 19102
Ph: 215-241-7245 ▪ Fx: 215-241-7299

Education Fund, WAND www.wand.org
691 Massachusetts Ave   Arlington MA 02476
Ph: 781-643-6740 ▪ Fx: 781-643-6744

Education Funding, Committee for www.cef.org
122 C St NW Suite 280   Washington DC 20001
Ph: 202-383-0083 ▪ Fx: 202-383-0097

(Education) I Have a Dream Foundation www.ihad.org
330 7th Ave 20th Fl   New York NY 10001
Ph: 212-293-5480 ▪ Fx: 212-293-5478

Education Information, National Center for www.ncei.com
1901 Pennsylvania Ave NW Suite 207   Washington DC 20006
Ph: 202-822-8280 ▪ Fx: 202-822-8284

Education, Institute for Independent www.ifie.org
PO Box 42428   Washington DC 20015
Ph: 202-362-9344 ▪ Fx: 202-362-0513

Education, Institute of International www.iie.org
809 UN Plaza   New York NY 10017
Ph: 212-883-8200 ▪ Fx: 212-984-5452

Education, Institute for Responsive www.responsiveeducation.org
Northeastern Univ 21 Lake Hall   Boston MA 02115
Ph: 617-373-2595 ▪ Fx: 617-373-8839

Education, International Assembly for Collegiate Business www.iacbe.org
PO Box 25217   Overland Park KS 66225
Ph: 913-631-3009 ▪ Fx: 913-631-9154

Education International, Association for Childhood www.udel.edu/bateman/acei
17904 Georgia Ave Suite 215   Olney MD 20832
Ph: 301-570-2111 ▪ Fx: 301-570-2212 ▪ TF: 800-423-3563

Education, International Association for the Study of Cooperation in www.iasce.net
PO Box 390   Readfield ME 04355
Ph: 207-685-3171 ▪ Fx: 207-685-4455

Education in Journalism & Mass Communication, Association for www.aejmc.org/
234 Outlet Pointe Blvd Suite A   Columbia SC 29210
Ph: 803-798-0271 ▪ Fx: 803-772-3509

Education in Journalism & Mass Communications, www.ukans.edu/~acejmc
Accrediting Council on   Univ of Kansas School of Journalism
Stauffer-Flint Hall   Lawrence KS 66045
Ph: 785-864-3973 ▪ Fx: 785-864-5225

(Education) Kappa Delta Pi www.kdp.org
3707 Woodview Trace   Indianapolis IN 46268
Ph: 317-871-4900 ▪ Fx: 317-704-2323 ▪ TF: 800-284-3167

Education Knowledge Industry Association, National www.nekia.org
1718 Connecticut Ave NW Suite 700   Washington DC 20009
Ph: 202-518-0847 ▪ Fx: 202-785-3849

Education Law Association www.educationlaw.org
300 College Pk MD 0528   Dayton OH 45469
Ph: 937-229-3589 ▪ Fx: 937-229-3845

Education Leadership Association, National Science www.nsela.org
PO Box 99381   Raleigh NC 27624
Ph: 919-848-1871 ▪ Fx: 919-848-0496

Education, Liaison Committee on Medical www.lcme.org
American Medical Assn 515 N State St   Chicago IL 60610
Ph: 312-464-4933 ▪ Fx: 312-464-5830

Education in the Life Sciences, Coalition for www.wisc.edu/cbe/cels

Education, Lifetime Institute for Family
9 Old Kings Hwy S 4th Fl   Darien CT 06820
Ph: 203-656-3600 ▪ Fx: 203-656-2221 ▪ TF: 800-832-0277

Education Loan Programs, National Council of Higher www.nchelp.org
1100 Connecticut Ave NW 12th Fl   Washington DC 20036
Ph: 202-822-2106 ▪ Fx: 202-822-2142

Education, Lumina Foundation for www.luminafoundation.org
30 S Meridian St Suite 700   Indianapolis IN 46204
Ph: 317-951-5704 ▪ Fx: 317-951-5063 ▪ TF: 800-834-5756

Education Management Systems, National Center for Higher www.nchems.org
PO Box 9752   Boulder CO 80301
Ph: 303-497-0301 ▪ Fx: 303-497-0338

Education, MENC: National Association for Music www.menc.org
1806 Robert Fulton Dr   Reston VA 20191
Ph: 703-860-4000 ▪ Fx: 703-860-1531 ▪ TF: 800-336-3768

Education for Minorities Network, Quality qemnetwork.qem.org
1818 'N' St NW Suite 350   Washington DC 20036
Ph: 202-659-1818 ▪ Fx: 202-659-5408

(Education) Montessori Foundation www.montessori.org
1001 Bern Creek Loop   Sarasota FL 34240
Ph: 941-379-6626 ▪ Fx: 941-379-6671

Education, National Academy of www.nae.nyu.edu
New York Univ School of Education 726 Broadway   Rm
509   New York NY 10003
Ph: 212-998-9035 ▪ Fx: 212-995-4435

Education, National Association for Bilingual www.nabe.org
1030 15th St NW Suite 470   Washington DC 20005
Ph: 202-898-1829 ▪ Fx: 202-789-2866

Education, National Association of Boards www.ncea.org/departments/nabccce
Commissions & Councils of Catholic   National Catholic
Educational Assn 1077 30th St NW Suite
100   Washington DC 20007
Ph: 202-337-6232 ▪ Fx: 202-333-6706

Education, National Association for Developmental www.nade.net
2447 Tissin Ave Suite 207   Findlay OH 45840
Ph: 419-424-9360 ▪ Fx: 419-423-9078 ▪ TF: 877-881-9876

Education, National Association for Equal Opportunity in Higher www.nafeo.org
8701 Georgia Ave Suite 200   Silver Spring MD 20910
Ph: 301-650-2440 ▪ Fx: 301-495-3306

Education, National Association for Family & Community www.nafce.org
73 Cavalier Blvd Suite 106   Florence KY 41042
Ph: 877-712-4477 ▪ Fx: 859-525-6496

Education, National Association for Humane & Environmental www.nahee.org
PO Box 362   East Haddam CT 06423
Ph: 860-434-8666 ▪ Fx: 860-434-9579

Education, National Association for Humanities www.nahe.org
Brigham Young Univ PO Box 26100   Provo UT 84602
Ph: 801-378-2212 ▪ Fx: 801-378-2284

Education, National Association of Partners In
901 N Pitt St Suite 320   Alexandria VA 22314
Ph: 703-836-4880 ▪ Fx: 703-836-6941
www.napehq.org

Education, National Association for Physical Education in Higher
Northern Illinois Univ Dept of Kinesiology & Physical Education
Anderson Hall   DeKalb IL 60015
Ph: 815-753-1894
www.napehe.org

(Education) National Association of Precollege Directors   45 Wintonbury Ave   Bloomfield CT 06002
Ph: 860-769-5283 ▪ Fx: 860-769-5287
www.jhuapl.edu/NAPD/aboutNAPD.htm

Education, National Association of State Boards of
277 S Washington St Suite 100   Alexandria VA 22314
Ph: 703-684-4000 ▪ Fx: 703-836-2313 ▪ TF: 800-368-5023
www.nasbe.org

Education, National Association of State Directors of Migrant
500 Mero St Rm 832   Frankfort KY 40601
Ph: 502-564-3791
www.nasdme.org

Education, National Association of State Directors of Special
1800 Diagonal Rd Suite 320   Alexandria VA 22314
Ph: 703-519-3800 ▪ Fx: 703-519-3808
www.nasdse.org

Education, National Association of Trade & Industrial
PO Box 1665   Leesburg VA 20177
Ph: 703-777-1740
www.skillsusa.org/NATIE

Education, National Association for Year-Round
PO Box 711386   San Diego CA 92171
Ph: 619-276-5298 ▪ Fx: 858-571-5754
www.nayre.org

Education, National Center for Community
1017 Avon St   Flint MI 48503
Ph: 810-238-0463 ▪ Fx: 810-238-9211 ▪ TF: 800-811-1105
www.nccenet.org

Education, National Coalition for Women & Girls in
c/o National Women's Law Ctr 11 Dupont Cir NW Suite
800   Washington DC 20036
Ph: 202-785-7730 ▪ Fx: 202-588-5185
www.ncwge.org

Education, National Commission for Cooperative
360 Huntington Ave 384 CP   Boston MA 02115
Ph: 617-373-3770 ▪ Fx: 617-373-3463
www.co-op.edu

Education, National Council for Agricultural
1410 King St Suite 400   Alexandria VA 22314
Ph: 703-838-5881 ▪ Fx: 703-838-5888 ▪ TF: 800-772-0939
www.teamaged.org/councilindex.cfm

Education, National Council for Geographic
Jacksonville State Univ 206A Martin Hall   Jacksonville AL
36265
Ph: 256-782-5293 ▪ Fx: 256-782-5336
www.ncge.org

Education, National Council for History
26915 Westwood Rd Suite B2   Westlake OH 44145
Ph: 440-835-1776 ▪ Fx: 440-835-1295
www.history.org/nche

Education, National Council on Measurement in
1230 17th St NW   Washington DC 20036
Ph: 202-223-9318 ▪ Fx: 202-775-1824
www.ncme.org

(Education) National Paideia Center
400 Silver Cedar Ct Suite 200   Chapel Hill NC 27514
Ph: 919-962-3128 ▪ Fx: 919-962-3139
www.paideia.org

Education, National Schools Committee for Economic
30 S Broadway   Irvington-on-Hudson NY 10533
Ph: 914-591-7230 ▪ Fx: 914-591-8910
www.nscee.org

Education, National Society for the Study of
Univ of Illinois College of Education 1040 W Harrison St M/C
147 Chicago IL 60607
Ph: 312-996-4529 ▪ Fx: 312-996-6400
www.uic.edu/educ/nsse

Education, NEA Foundation for the Improvement of
1201 16th St NW   Washington DC 20036
Ph: 202-822-7840 ▪ Fx: 202-822-7779
www.nfie.org

Education Network, BACCHUS & GAMMA Peer
2130 S University Blvd   Denver CO 80210
Ph: 303-871-0901 ▪ Fx: 303-871-0907
bacchusgamma.org

Education Network, Public
601 13th St NW Suite 900 N   Washington DC 20005
Ph: 202-628-7460 ▪ Fx: 202-628-1893
www.publiceducation.org

Education Network, Public Leadership
1001 Connecticut Ave NW Suite 900   Washington DC 20036
Ph: 202-872-1585 ▪ Fx: 202-872-0141
www.plen.org

Education, North American Professors of Christian
c/o Cook Communications Ministries 4050 Lee Vance
View   Colorado Springs CO 80918
Ph: 719-536-0100
www.napce.org

Education, Parents & Teachers Against Violence in
PO Box 1033   Alamo CA 94507
Ph: 925-831-1661 ▪ Fx: 925-838-8914
www.nospank.net

Education Partnership, National Science & Technology
2500 Wilson Blvd Suite 210   Arlington VA 22201
Ph: 703-907-7400 ▪ Fx: 703-907-7401
www.nationalstep.org

Education Partnership, Planning & Visual
3368A Oxford Ave   Saint Louis MO 63143
Ph: 314-645-0701
www.visualstore.com/pave

(Education) Phi Delta Kappa International
408 N Union St   Bloomington IN 47402
Ph: 812-339-1156 ▪ Fx: 812-339-0018 ▪ TF: 800-766-1156
www.pdkintl.org

Education for the Physician Assistant Inc, Accreditation Review Commission on   1000 N Oak Ave   Marshfield WI
54449
Ph: 715-389-3785 ▪ Fx: 715-387-5163
www.arc-pa.org

(Education) Pi Lambda Theta
PO Box 6626   Bloomington IN 47407
Ph: 800-487-3411 ▪ Fx: 812-339-3462
www.pilambda.org

Education Practitioners & Providers, Association of
104 W Main St Suite 101 PO Box 348   Watertown WI 53094
Ph: 920-206-1474 ▪ Fx: 920-206-1475 ▪ TF: 800-252-3280
www.aepp.org/links/links.html

Education, Professional Association for Childhood
1290 Sutter St Suite 200   San Francisco CA 94109
Ph: 415-749-6851 ▪ Fx: 415-749-6861 ▪ TF: 800-924-2460
www.pacenet.org

Education Program Administrators, National Association of Federal
830 Virginia Ave   Sheybogan WI 53081
Ph: 920-459-6718 ▪ Fx: 920-803-7761
www.nafepa.org

Education Programs, Commission on Accreditation of Allied Health
35 E Wacker Dr Suite 1970   Chicago IL 60601
Ph: 312-553-9355 ▪ Fx: 312-553-9616
www.caahep.org

Education in Radiologic Technology, Joint Review Committee on
20 N Wacker Dr Suite 900   Chicago IL 60606
Ph: 312-704-5300 ▪ Fx: 312-704-5304
www.jrcert.org

Education Research Association, American Vocational
tiger.coe.missouri.edu/~pavtat/AVERA

Education Research, Foundation for Interior Design
146 Monroe Ctr NW Suite 1318   Grand Rapids MI 49503
Ph: 616-458-0400 ▪ Fx: 616-458-0460
www.fider.org

Education Research Foundation, International
PO Box 3665   Culver City CA 90231
Ph: 310-258-9451 ▪ Fx: 310-342-7086
www.ierf.org

Education Research Institute, National Home
PO Box 13939   Salem OR 97309
Ph: 503-364-1490 ▪ Fx: 503-364-2827
www.nheri.org

Education & Research in Substance Abuse, Association of Medical
125 Whipple St Suite 300   Providence RI 02908
Ph: 401-349-0000 ▪ Fx: 877-418-8769
www.amersa.org

Education of Roman Catholic Clergy, National Organization for Continuing   1337 W Ohio St   Chicago IL 60622
Ph: 312-226-1890 ▪ Fx: 312-829-8915
www.nocercc.org

Education in the Sciences, Foundation for Advanced
1 Cloister Ct Suite 230   Bethesda MD 20814
Ph: 301-496-7976 ▪ Fx: 301-402-0174
www.faes.org

Education Service of North America, Jewish
111 8th Ave Suite 11-E   New York NY 10011
Ph: 212-284-6950 ▪ Fx: 212-284-6951
www.jesna.org

(Education) SkillsUSA-VICA Inc
PO Box 3000   Leesburg VA 20177
Ph: 703-777-8810 ▪ Fx: 703-777-8999 ▪ TF: 800-321-8422
www.skillsusa.org

Education, Society for the Advancement of Excellence in
1889 Springfield Rd Suite 225   Kelowna BC V1Y5V5
Ph: 250-717-1163 ▪ Fx: 250-717-1134
www.excellenceineducation.ca

Education Society, Comparative & International
www.cies.ws

Education Society, History of
Slippery Rock Univ 220 McKay Educational Bldg   Slippery Rock
PA 16057
Ph: 724-738-4557 ▪ Fx: 724-738-4548
www.sru.edu/depts/scc/hes/hes.htm

Education Society, IEEE
IEEE Operations Ctr 445 Hoes Ln   Piscataway NJ 08854
Ph: 732-981-0060 ▪ Fx: 732-981-1721
www.ewh.ieee.org/soc/es

Education Society, National Humane
PO Box 340   Charles Town WV 25414
Ph: 304-725-0506 ▪ Fx: 304-725-1523
www.nhes.org

Education Society, Philosophy of
Southern Illinois Univ College of Education   Carbondale IL
62901
Ph: 618-536-4434
cuip.net/pes

Education, Society for Values in Higher
Portland State Univ PO Box 751   Portland OR 97207
Ph: 503-725-2575 ▪ Fx: 503-725-2577
www.svhe.org

Education of Students, Institute for the International
33 N LaSalle St 15th Fl   Chicago IL 60602
Ph: 312-944-1750 ▪ Fx: 312-944-1448 ▪ TF: 800-995-2300
www.iesabroad.org

Education of Teachers of Science, Association for the
East Carolina Univ College of Education Austin
324-A   Greenville NC 27858
Ph: 252-328-6736 ▪ Fx: 252-328-6218
aets.chem.pitt.edu

(Education) Telluride Association
217 West Ave   Ithaca NY 14850
Ph: 607-273-5011 ▪ Fx: 607-272-2667
www.tellurideassociation.org

Education Through Art, US Society for   www.public.asu.edu/~ifmls/usseafolder/ussea.html
Ohio State Univ 1739 N High St 4th Fl   Columbus OH 43210
Ph: 614-247-7612

Education & Training, Accrediting Council for Continuing
1722 'N' St NW   Washington DC 20036
Ph: 202-955-1113 ▪ Fx: 202-955-1118
www.accet.org

Education & Training Council, Distance
1601 18th St NW   Washington DC 20009
Ph: 202-234-5100 ▪ Fx: 202-332-1386
www.detc.org

Education & Training, International Association for Continuing
1620 'I' St NW Suite 615   Washington DC 20006
Ph: 202-463-2905 ▪ Fx: 202-463-8497
www.iacet.org

Education & Training, National Council for Continuing
PO Box 130623   Carlsbad CA 92013
Ph: 760-753-8375 ▪ Fx: 760-942-7296
www.nccet.org

Education Training & Research, International Society for Intercultural   8835 SW Canyon Ln Suite 110   Portland OR
97225
Ph: 503-297-4622 ▪ Fx: 503-297-4695
www.sietarusa.org

Education Trust
1725 K St NW Suite 200   Washington DC 20006
Ph: 202-293-1217 ▪ Fx: 202-293-2605
www2.edtrust.org/edtrust

Education, United Ministries in Higher
7407 Steele Creek Rd   Charlotte NC 28217
Ph: 704-588-2182 ▪ Fx: 704-588-3652
www.umhe.org

Education & Welfare Association, Presbyterian Health
100 Witherspoon St Rm 3041   Louisville KY 40202
Ph: 502-569-5794 ▪ Fx: 502-569-8034 ▪ TF: 888-728-7228
www.pcusa.org/phewa

(Education) Women's American ORT
315 Park Ave S   New York NY 10010
Ph: 212-505-7700 ▪ Fx: 212-674-3057 ▪ TF: 800-519-2678
www.waort.org

(Education) Women's International Center
PO Box 880736   San Diego CA 92168
Ph: 619-295-6446 ▪ Fx: 619-296-1633
www.wic.org

Education Inc, World   www.worlded.org
44 Farnsworth St   Boston MA 02210
Ph: 617-482-9485 ▪ Fx: 617-482-0617

Education Writers Association   www.ewa.org
2122 P St NW Suite 201   Washington DC 20037
Ph: 202-452-8830 ▪ Fx: 202-452-9837

Education of Young Children, National Association for the   www.naeyc.org
1509 16th St NW   Washington DC 20036
Ph: 202-232-8777 ▪ Fx: 202-328-1846 ▪ TF: 800-424-2460

Educational Accountability, National Center for   www.nc4ea.org
4030-2 W Braker Ln   Austin TX 78759
Ph: 512-232-0770 ▪ Fx: 512-232-0777

Educational Activities, Institute for Development of   www.idea.org
259 Regency Ridge   Dayton OH 45459
Ph: 937-434-6969 ▪ Fx: 937-434-5203

Educational Administration, University Council for   www.ucea.org
Univ of Missouri-Columbia 205 Hill Hall   Columbia MO 65211
Ph: 573-884-8300 ▪ Fx: 573-884-8302

Educational Administrators of Schools & Programs for the Deaf, Conference of   PO Box 1778   Saint Augustine FL 32085   www.ceasd.org
Ph: 904-810-5200 ▪ Fx: 904-810-5525

Educational Aid, Society for French American Cultural Services &   www.facsea.org
972 5th Ave   New York NY 10021
Ph: 212-439-1439 ▪ Fx: 212-439-1455 ▪ TF: 800-937-3624

Educational Association, National Catholic   www.ncea.org
1077 30th St NW Suite 100   Washington DC 20007
Ph: 202-337-6232 ▪ Fx: 202-333-6706

Educational Association, National Young Farmer   www.nyfea.org
PO Box 20326   Montgomery AL 36120
Ph: 334-288-0097

Educational Audiology Association   www.edaud.org
13153 N Del Mabry Hwy Suite 105   Tampa FL 33618
Ph: 813-968-2644 ▪ Fx: 813-968-3597 ▪ TF: 800-460-7322

Educational Buyers, National Association of   www.naeb.org
450 Wireless Blvd   Hauppauge NY 11788
Ph: 631-273-2600 ▪ Fx: 631-952-3660

Educational Center for Applied Ekistics
1900 DeKalb Ave NE   Atlanta GA 30307
Ph: 404-378-2219 ▪ Fx: 404-378-8946

Educational Communications & Technology, Association for   www.aect.org
1800 N Stonelake Dr Suite 2   Bloomington IN 47408
Ph: 812-335-7675 ▪ Fx: 812-335-7678 ▪ TF: 877-677-2328

Educational Consultants Association, Independent   www.educationalconsulting.org
3251 Old Lee Hwy Suite 510   Fairfax VA 22030
Ph: 703-591-4850 ▪ Fx: 703-591-4860 ▪ TF: 800-808-4322

Educational & Cooperative Union of America, Farmers   www.nfu.org
11900 E Cornell Ave   Aurora CO 80014
Ph: 303-337-5500 ▪ Fx: 303-368-1390 ▪ TF: 800-347-1961

Educational & Cultural Exchange, Alliance for International   www.alliance-exchange.org
1776 Massachusetts Ave NW Suite 620   Washington DC 20036
Ph: 202-293-6141 ▪ Fx: 202-293-6144

Educational Development, Academy for   www.aed.org
1825 Connecticut Ave NW   Washington DC 20009
Ph: 202-884-8000 ▪ Fx: 202-884-8400

Educational Equity Concepts Inc   www.edequity.org
100 5th Ave   New York NY 10011
Ph: 212-243-1110 ▪ Fx: 212-627-0407

Educational Exchange, Council on International   www.ciee.org
3 Copley Pl 2nd Fl   Boston MA 02116
Ph: 617-247-0350 ▪ Fx: 617-247-2911 ▪ TF: 888-268-6245

(Educational Exchange) Delphi International Program   www.worldlearning.org/delphi
1015 18th St NW Suite 1000   Washington DC 20036
Ph: 202-898-0950 ▪ Fx: 202-842-0885

Educational Facility Planners International, Council of   www.cefpi.com
9180 E Desert Cove Dr Suite 104   Scottsdale AZ 85260
Ph: 480-391-0840 ▪ Fx: 480-391-0940

Educational Fellowship, Oral Roberts University   www.oru.edu/oruef
7777 S Lewis Ave   Tulsa OK 74171
Ph: 918-495-6163 ▪ Fx: 918-495-6175

Educational Foundation, AAUW   www.aauw.org/ef
c/o American Assn of University Women 1111 16th St
   NW   Washington DC 20036
Ph: 202-785-7602

Educational Foundation of America   www.efaw.org
35 Church Ln   Westport CT 06880
Ph: 203-226-6498 ▪ Fx: 203-227-0424

Educational Foundation, Armenian   www.aefweb.org
600 W Broadway Suite 130   Glendale CA 91204
Ph: 818-242-4154 ▪ Fx: 818-242-4913

Educational Foundation, Belgian American   www.baef.be
195 Church St   New Haven CT 06510
Ph: 203-777-5765 ▪ Fx: 203-785-4951

Educational Foundation, British American   www.baef.org
PO Box 33   Larchmont NY 10538
Ph: 914-834-2064 ▪ Fx: 914-833-3718

Educational Foundation Inc, Givat Haviva   www.givathaviva.org
114 W 26th Suite 1001   New York NY 10001
Ph: 212-989-9272 ▪ Fx: 212-989-9840

Educational Foundation, National Restaurant Association   www.nraef.org
175 W Jackson Blvd Suite 1500   Chicago IL 60604
Ph: 312-715-1010 ▪ TF: 800-765-2122

Educational Foundation for Nuclear Science   www.thebulletin.org/nuclear/efns.html
6042 S Kimbark Ave   Chicago IL 60637
Ph: 773-702-2555 ▪ Fx: 773-702-0725

Educational Foundation, Threefold   www.threefold.org
260 Hungry Hollow Rd   Chestnut Ridge NY 10977
Ph: 845-352-5020 ▪ Fx: 845-352-5071

Educational Foundation, US Business & Industry Council   www.usbusiness
910 16th St NW Suite 300   Washington DC 20006
Ph: 202-728-1990 ▪ Fx: 202-728-1981

Educational Foundation for Women in Accounting   www.efwa.org
PO Box 1925   Southeastern PA 19399
Ph: 610-407-9229 ▪ Fx: 610-644-3713

Educational Freedom, Citizens for   www.educational-freedom.org
9333 Clayton Rd   Saint Louis MO 63124
Ph: 314-997-6361 ▪ Fx: 314-997-6321

Educational Leadership, Institute for   www.iel.org
1001 Connecticut Ave NW Suite 310   Washington DC 20036
Ph: 202-822-8405 ▪ Fx: 202-872-4050

Educational Media, National Information Center for   www.nicem.com
PO Box 8640   Albuquerque NM 87198
Ph: 505-998-0800 ▪ Fx: 505-256-1080 ▪ TF: 800-926-8328

Educational Negotiators, North American Association of   www.naen.org
6678 County Rd 32   Norwich NY 13815
Ph: 305-588-2800

Educational Networking, Corporation for Research &   www.cren.net
1150 18th St NW Suite 1030   Washington DC 20036
Ph: 202-293-5909 ▪ Fx: 202-293-2853

Educational Office Professionals, National Association of   www.naeop.org
PO Box 12619   Wichita KS 67277
Ph: 316-942-4822 ▪ Fx: 316-942-7100

Educational Paperback Association   www.edupaperback.org
PO Box 1399   East Hampton NY 11937
Ph: 212-879-6850

Educational Publishers, Association of   www.edpress.org
510 Heron Dr Suite 309   Logan Township NJ 08085
Ph: 856-241-7772 ▪ Fx: 856-241-0709

Educational Records Bureau   www.erbtest.org
220 E 42nd St   New York NY 10017
Ph: 212-672-9800 ▪ Fx: 212-370-4096

Educational Research Analysts   www.textbookreviews.org
PO Box 7518   Longview TX 75607
Ph: 903-753-5993 ▪ Fx: 903-753-7788

Educational Research Association, American   www.aera.net
1230 17th St NW   Washington DC 20036
Ph: 202-223-9485 ▪ Fx: 202-775-1824

Educational Research Service   www.ers.org
2000 Clarendon Blvd   Arlington VA 22201
Ph: 703-243-2100 ▪ Fx: 703-243-1985 ▪ TF: 800-741-9308

Educational Theatre Association   www.etassoc.org
2343 Auburn Ave   Cincinnati OH 45219
Ph: 513-421-3900 ▪ Fx: 513-421-7077

Educational Therapists, Association of   www.aetonline.org
1804 W Burbank Blvd   Burbank CA 91506
Ph: 818-843-1183 ▪ Fx: 818-843-7423

Educational Trust, American   www.middleeastbooks.com
PO Box 53062   Washington DC 20009
Ph: 202-939-6050 ▪ TF: 800-368-5788

Educators Against Forced Unionism, Concerned   www.nrtwc.org
8001 Braddock Rd Suite 500   Springfield VA 22160
Ph: 703-321-8519 ▪ Fx: 703-321-9319 ▪ TF: 800-326-3600

Educators, American Association of Early Childhood
3612 Bent Branch Ct   Falls Church VA 22041
Ph: 703-941-4329

Educators, American Association of Housing
Illinois State Univ Dept of Family & Consumer Sciences CB
   5060   Normal IL 61790
Ph: 309-438-5802 ▪ Fx: 309-438-5307

Educators, American Association for Paralegal   www.aafpe.org
407 Wekiva Springs Rd Suite 241   Longwood FL 32779
Ph: 407-834-6688 ▪ Fx: 407-834-4747

Educators Assembly, Jewish   www.jewisheducators.org
300 Forest Dr   East Hills NY 11548
Ph: 516-484-9585 ▪ Fx: 516-484-9586

Educators, Association of American   www.aaeteachers.org
25201 Paseo de Alicia Suite 104   Laguna Hills CA 92653
Ph: 949-595-7979 ▪ Fx: 949-595-7970 ▪ TF: 800-704-7799

Educators' Association, American Hungarian   magyar.org/ahea

Educators, Association of Cooperative   www.wisc.edu/uwcc/ace/ace.html
PO Box 64047   Saint Paul MN 55164
Ph: 651-451-5481 ▪ Fx: 651-451-5073

Educators Association International, Christian   www.ceai.org
PO Box 41300   Pasadena CA 91114
Ph: 626-798-1124 ▪ Fx: 626-798-2346 ▪ TF: 888-798-1124

Educators, Association of Theatre Movement   www.asu.edu/cfa/atme

Educators in Government, Association for Counselors &
c/o American Counseling Assn 5999 Stevenson Ave   Alexandria
   VA 22304
Ph: 703-823-9800 ▪ Fx: 703-823-0252

Educators, International Society of Travel & Tourism   www.istte.org
23220 Edgewater   Saint Clair Shores MI 48082
Ph: 586-294-0208

(Educators) Kappa Kappa Iota   www.kappakappaiota.org
1875 E 15th St   Tulsa OK 74104
Ph: 918-744-0389 ▪ Fx: 918-744-0578 ▪ TF: 800-678-0389

Educators, NAFSA: Association of International   www.nafsa.org
1307 New York Ave NW 8th Fl   Washington DC 20005
Ph: 202-737-3699 ▪ Fx: 202-737-3657

Educators, National Alliance of Black School   www.nabse.org
310 Pennsylvania Ave SE   Washington DC 20003
Ph: 202-608-6310 ▪ Fx: 202-608-6319 ▪ TF: 800-221-2654

Educators, National Association of Agricultural   www.naae.org
Univ of Kentucky 300 Garrigus Bldg   Lexington KY 40546
Ph: 859-257-2224 ▪ Fx: 859-323-3919 ▪ TF: 800-509-0204

Educators, National Association of Maritime
124 N Van Ave   Houma LA 70363
Ph: 985-879-3866 ▪ Fx: 985-879-3911

Educators, National Association of Professional   www.teacherspet.com/napeindex.htm
900 17th St Suite 300   Washington DC 20006
Ph: 202-848-8969

Educators, National Seafood
PO Box 60006   Richmond Beach WA 98160
Ph: 206-546-6410 ▪ Fx: 206-546-6411

Educators, Nature & Environmental Writers - College & University   www.new-cue.org
Saint Thomas Aquinas College   Sparkill NY 10976
Ph: 845-398-4247 ▪ Fx: 845-398-4224

Educators, Organization of American Kodaly   www.oake.org
1612 29th Ave S   Moorhead MN 56560
Ph: 218-227-6253 ▪ Fx: 218-277-6254

Educators, Professional Association of Christian   www.gospelcom.net/paceinc
PO Box 140284   Dallas TX 75214
Ph: 214-841-3566 ▪ Fx: 214-841-3773 ▪ TF: 800-829-9410

Educators in Radiological Sciences, Association of   www.aers.org
PO Box 90204   Albuquerque NM 87199
Ph: 505-823-4740

Educators for Social Responsibility   www.esrnational.org
23 Garden St   Cambridge MA 02138
Ph: 617-492-1764 ▪ Fx: 617-864-5164 ▪ TF: 800-370-2515

Educators, Society of Park & Recreation   www.nrpa.org
c/o National Recreation & Park Assn 22377 Belmont Ridge
   Rd   Ashburn VA 20148
Ph: 703-858-0784 ▪ Fx: 703-858-0794

Educators & Trainers, Academy of Security   www.personalprotection.com/aset
PO Box 802   Berryville VA 22611
Ph: 540-554-2540 ▪ Fx: 540-554-2558

EDUCAUSE   www.educause.edu
1150 18th St NW Suite 1010   Washington DC 20036
Ph: 202-872-4200 ▪ Fx: 202-872-4318

EF Foundation for Foreign Study   www.effoundation.org
1 Education St   Cambridge MA 02141
Ph: 888-447-4273 ▪ Fx: 617-619-1401

EF Schumacher Society   www.smallisbeautiful.org
140 Jug End Rd   Great Barrington MA 01230
Ph: 413-528-1737 ▪ Fx: 413-528-4472

Efficient Environmental Energy Systems, Association for   www.aeees.org
PO Box 598   Davis CA 95617
Ph: 530-750-0135 ▪ Fx: 530-750-0137

Egg Association, US Poultry &   www.poultryegg.org
1530 Cooledge Rd   Tucker GA 30084
Ph: 770-493-9401 ▪ Fx: 770-493-9257

Egg Board, American   www.aeb.org
1460 Renaissance Dr Suite 301   Park Ridge IL 60068
Ph: 847-296-7043 ▪ Fx: 847-296-7007

Egg Clearinghouse Inc   www.eggs.org
PO Box 187   Dover NH 03821
Ph: 603-749-8137 ▪ Fx: 603-749-2707

Egg Export Council, USA Poultry &   www.usapeec.org
2300 W Park Place Blvd Suite 100   Stone Mountain GA 30087
Ph: 770-413-0006 ▪ Fx: 770-413-0007

Egg Producers, United   www.unitedegg.com
1720 Windward Concourse Suite 230   Alpharetta GA 30005
Ph: 770-360-9220 ▪ Fx: 770-360-7058

Egyptian Arabic Order Nobles Mystic Shrine, Ancient   www.aeaonms.org
2239 Democrat Rd   Memphis TN 38132
Ph: 901-395-0150 ▪ Fx: 901-395-0115

Egyptian Cooperation Foundation, American   www.americanegyptiancoop.org
330 E 39th St Suite 32L   New York NY 10016
Ph: 212-867-2323 ▪ Fx: 212-697-0465

Egyptian Order of Sciots, Ancient   www.sciots.org
PO Box 501801   San Diego CA 92150
Ph: 858-755-0931

Egyptians Relief Association   www.egyptiansrelief.org
6121 Winnepeg Dr   Burke VA 22015
Ph: 703-818-2573 ▪ Fx: 703-503-8816

EIFS Industry Members Association   www.eima.com
3000 Corporate Center Dr Suite 270   Morrow GA 30260
Ph: 770-968-7945 ▪ Fx: 770-968-5818 ▪ TF: 800-294-3462

Eighteenth-Century Scottish Studies Society   www.ecsss.org
New Jersey Institute of Technology   Newark NJ 07102
Ph: 973-596-3377 ▪ Fx: 973-642-4689

Eighteenth-Century Studies, American Society for   asecs.press.jhu.edu
Wake Forest Univ PO Box 7867   Winston-Salem NC 27109
Ph: 336-727-4694 ▪ Fx: 336-727-4697

Einstein Albert Institution   www.aeinstein.org
427 Newbury St   Boston MA 02115
Ph: 617-247-4882 ▪ Fx: 617-247-4035

Eire Philatelic Association   www.eirephilatelicassoc.org
PO Box 704   Bernardsville NJ 07924
Ph: 908-766-2728 ▪ Fx: 908-766-7783

Eisenhower Mamie Doud Birthplace Foundation   www.booneiowa.com
PO Box 55   Boone IA 50036
Ph: 515-432-1896 ▪ Fx: 515-432-3097

Ekistics, Educational Center for Applied
1900 DeKalb Ave NE   Atlanta GA 30307
Ph: 404-378-2219 ▪ Fx: 404-378-8946

El Salvador, Christians for Peace in   www.crispaz.org
122 Dewitt Dr   Boston MA 02120
Ph: 617-445-5115 ▪ Fx: 617-249-0769

El Salvador, Committee in Solidarity with the People of   www.cispes.org
PO Box 8560   New York NY 10117
Ph: 212-465-8115 ▪ Fx: 212-465-8998

(El Salvador) SHARE Foundation   www.share-elsalvador.org
598 Bosworth St Suite 1   San Francisco CA 94131
Ph: 415-239-2595 ▪ Fx: 415-239-0785

El Toro International Yacht Racing Association   www.eltoroyra.org
1014 Hopper Ave Suite 419   Santa Rosa CA 95403
Ph: 707-526-6621 ▪ Fx: 707-526-3838

EL Wiegand Foundation
165 W Liberty St Suite 200 Wiegand Ctr   Reno NV 89501
Ph: 775-333-0310 ▪ Fx: 775-333-0314

Elbow Surgeons, American Shoulder &   www.ases-assn.org
6300 N River Rd Suite 727   Rosemont IL 60018
Ph: 847-698-1629 ▪ Fx: 847-823-0536

Elder Abuse, National Center on   www.elderabusecenter.org
1225 'I' St NW Suite 725   Washington DC 20005
Ph: 202-898-2586 ▪ Fx: 202-898-2583

Elder Abuse, National Committee for the Prevention of   www.preventelderabuse.org
1612 K St NW Suite 400   Washington DC 20006
Ph: 202-682-4140 ▪ Fx: 202-682-3984

Elder Craftsmen Inc   www.eldercraftsmen.org
610 Lexington Ave   New York NY 10022
Ph: 212-319-8128 ▪ Fx: 212-319-8141

Elder Law Attorneys, National Academy of   www.naela.com
1604 N Country Club Rd   Tucson AZ 85716
Ph: 520-881-4005 ▪ Fx: 520-325-7925

Eldercare Locator   www.eldercare.gov
927 15th St NW 6th Fl   Washington DC 20005
Ph: 202-296-8130 ▪ Fx: 202-296-8134 ▪ TF: 800-677-1116

Elderhostel Inc   www.elderhostel.org
11 Ave de Lafayette   Boston MA 02111
Ph: 617-426-7788 ▪ Fx: 877-426-2166 ▪ TF: 877-426-8056

(Elderly Health Care) National PACE Association   www.natlpaceassn.org
801 N Fairfax St Suite 309   Alexandria VA 22314
Ph: 703-535-1565 ▪ Fx: 703-535-1566

Elderly, Legal Counsel for the
601 'E' St NW Bldg A 4th Fl   Washington DC 20049
Ph: 202-434-2170 ▪ Fx: 202-434-6464

Elderly, Little Brothers - Friends of the   www.littlebrothers.org
954 W Washington Blvd 5th Fl   Chicago IL 60607
Ph: 312-829-3055 ▪ Fx: 312-829-3077

Elderly, National Association for Hispanic
1452 W Temple St Suite 100   Los Angeles CA 90026
Ph: 213-202-5900 ▪ Fx: 213-202-5905

Elected Officials, National Black Caucus of Local   www.nbc-leo.org
1301 Pennsylvania Ave NW Suite 550   Washington DC 20004
Ph: 202-626-3000 ▪ Fx: 202-626-3043

Election Directors, National Association of State   www.nased.org
Council of State Governments 444 N Capitol St NW Suite
   401   Washington DC 20001
Ph: 202-624-5460 ▪ Fx: 202-624-5452

Election Officials & Clerks, National Association of County Recorders   www.nacrc.org
PO Box 3159   Durham NC 27715
Ph: 919-384-8446 ▪ Fx: 919-383-0035

(Election Reform) Citizens' Research Foundation
UC Berkeley Institute of Government Studies 104 Moses
   Hall   Berkeley CA 94720
Ph: 510-642-5158 ▪ Fx: 510-642-5537

Election Systems, International Foundation for   www.ifes.org
1101 15th NW Suite 300   Washington DC 20005
Ph: 202-828-8507 ▪ Fx: 202-466-8466

Electorate, Committee for the Study of the American   www.gspm.org/csae
601 Pennsylvania Ave NW South Bldg Suite 900   Washington
   DC 20004
Ph: 202-546-3221 ▪ Fx: 202-546-3571

Electric Auto Association   www.eaaev.org
60 Alan Dr   Pleasant Hill CA 94523
Ph: 925-685-7580 ▪ TF: 800-537-2882

Electric Cooperative Association, National Rural   www.nreca.org
4301 Wilson Blvd   Arlington VA 22203
Ph: 703-907-5500 ▪ Fx: 703-907-5528

Electric Drive Transportation Association   www.evaa.org
701 Pennsylvania Ave NW 3rd Fl   Washington DC 20004
Ph: 202-408-0774 ▪ Fx: 202-508-5924

Electric Institute, Edison   www.eei.org
701 Pennsylvania Ave NW   Washington DC 20004
Ph: 202-508-5000 ▪ Fx: 202-508-5794 ▪ TF: 800-334-4688

Electric Power Supply Association   www.epsa.org
1401 New York Ave 11th Fl   Washington DC 20005
Ph: 202-628-8200 ▪ Fx: 202-628-8260

Electric Power Supply Association PAC
1401 New York Ave NW 11th Fl   Washington DC 20005
Ph: 202-628-8200

Electric Railroaders' Association   www.electricrailroaders.org
PO Box 3323   New York NY 10163
Ph: 212-986-4482

Electric Reliability Council, North American   www.nerc.com
116-390 Village Blvd   Princeton NJ 08540
Ph: 609-452-8060 ▪ Fx: 609-452-9550

(Electric Utility) EUCG Inc   www.eucg.org
20165 N 67th Ave Suite 122   Glendale AZ 85308
Ph: 623-572-4140 ▪ Fx: 623-572-4141

Electrical Apparatus Recyclers League, Professional   www.pearl1.org
6257 Lakepoint Pl   Parker CO 80134
Ph: 303-840-1059 ▪ Fx: 720-851-6090

Electrical Apparatus Service Association   www.easa.com
1331 Baur Blvd   Saint Louis MO 63132
Ph: 314-993-2220 ▪ Fx: 314-993-1269

Electrical Association, Energy Telecommunications &   www.entelec.org
14015 Park Dr Suite 206   Tomball TX 77375
Ph: 281-357-8700 ▪ Fx: 281-357-8777 ▪ TF: 888-503-8700

Electrical Associations, International League of   www.ileaweb.org
2901 Metro Dr Suite 203   Bloomington MN 55425
Ph: 952-854-4405 ▪ Fx: 952-854-7076

Electrical & Computer Engineering Department Heads Association   www.ecedha.org
549 W Randolph St Suite 600   Chicago IL 60661
Ph: 312-559-3724 ▪ Fx: 312-559-3329

Electrical Contracting Foundation   www.electri21.org
3 Bethesda Metro Ctr Suite 1100   Bethesda MD 20814
Ph: 301-215-4538 ▪ Fx: 301-215-4500

Electrical Contractors Association, National — www.necanet.org
3 Bethesda Metro Ctr Suite 1100   Bethesda MD 20814
Ph: 301-657-3110 ▪ Fx: 301-215-4500

Electrical Contractors, Independent — www.ieci.org
4401 Ford Ave Suite 1100   Alexandria VA 22302
Ph: 703-549-7351 ▪ Fx: 703-549-7448 ▪ TF: 800-456-4324

Electrical Contractors PAC — www.necanet.org/government
3 Bethesda Metro Ctr Suite 1100   Bethesda MD 20814
Ph: 301-657-3110 ▪ Fx: 301-215-4500

Electrical Distributors Inc, National Association of — www.naed.org
1100 Corporate Sq Dr Suite 100   Saint Louis MO 63132
Ph: 314-991-9000 ▪ Fx: 314-991-3060 ▪ TF: 888-791-2512

Electrical & Electronics Engineers, Institute of — www.ieee.org
3 Park Ave 17th Fl   New York NY 10016
Ph: 212-419-7900 ▪ Fx: 212-752-4929 ▪ TF: 800-678-4333

Electrical Equipment Representatives Association — www.eera.org
PO Box 419264   Kansas City MO 64141
Ph: 816-561-5323 ▪ Fx: 816-561-1249

Electrical Generating Systems Association — www.egsa.org
1650 S Dixie Hwy Suite 500   Boca Raton FL 33432
Ph: 561-750-5575 ▪ Fx: 561-395-8557

Electrical Inspectors, International Association of — www.iaei.org
901 Waterfall Way Suite 602   Richardson TX 75080
Ph: 972-235-1455 ▪ Fx: 972-235-6858 ▪ TF: 800-786-4234

Electrical Insulation Conference — www.electricalinsulation.org
13707 Brook Hollow Ct   Fort Wayne IN 46814
Ph: 219-625-5987 ▪ Fx: 219-625-3693

Electrical Insulation Society, IEEE Dielectrics & — tdei.sju.edu/deis
IEEE Operations Ctr 445 Hoes Ln   Piscataway NJ 08854
Ph: 732-981-0060 ▪ Fx: 732-981-1721

Electrical Manufacturers Association, National — www.nema.org
1300 N 17th St Suite 1847   Rosslyn VA 22209
Ph: 703-841-3200 ▪ Fx: 703-841-5900

Electrical Manufacturers Representatives Association, National — www.nemra.org
660 White Plains Rd   Tarrytown NY 10591
Ph: 914-524-8650 ▪ Fx: 914-524-8655

Electrical Manufacturing & Coil Winding Association — www.emcw.org
PO Box 278   Imperial Beach CA 91933
Ph: 619-435-3629 ▪ Fx: 619-435-3639 ▪ TF: 800-984-3629

Electrical Radio & Machine Workers of America, United — www.ranknfile-ue.org
1 Gateway Ctr Suite 1400   Pittsburgh PA 15222
Ph: 412-471-8919 ▪ Fx: 412-471-8999

Electrical Testing Association, InterNational — www.netaworld.org
106 Stone St PO Box 687   Morrison CO 80465
Ph: 303-697-8441 ▪ Fx: 303-697-8431 ▪ TF: 888-300-6382

Electrical Workers, International Brotherhood of — www.ibew.org
1125 15th St NW   Washington DC 20005
Ph: 202-833-7000 ▪ Fx: 202-467-6316

Electrical Workers PAC, International Brotherhood of
1125 15th St NW   Washington DC 20005
Ph: 202-833-7000 ▪ Fx: 202-467-6316

Electricity Consumers Resource Council — www.elcon.org
1333 H St NW West Tower 8th Fl   Washington DC 20005
Ph: 202-682-1390 ▪ Fx: 202-289-6370

Electro-Optics Manufacturers' Association, Laser & — www.leoma.com
123 Kent Rd   Pacifica CA 94044
Ph: 650-738-1492 ▪ Fx: 650-738-1769

Electrochemical Society — www.electrochem.org
65 S Main St   Pennington NJ 08534
Ph: 609-737-1902 ▪ Fx: 609-737-2743

Electrocoat Association — www.electrocoat.org
PO Box 541083   Cincinnati OH 45244
Ph: 513-753-5501 ▪ Fx: 513-753-5557 ▪ TF: 800-579-8806

Electrodiagnostic Medicine, American Association of — www.aaem.net
421 1st Ave SW Suite 300E   Rochester MN 55902
Ph: 507-288-0100 ▪ Fx: 507-288-1225

Electroencephalographic & Evoked Potential Technologists, American Board of Registration of — www.abret.org
1904 Croyden Dr   Springfield IL 62703
Ph: 217-553-3758 ▪ Fx: 217-585-6663

Electrologists, International Guild of Professional — www.igpe.org
803 N Main St Suite 3A   High Point NC 27262
Ph: 336-841-6631 ▪ Fx: 336-841-5187 ▪ TF: 800-830-3247

Electrology Association, American — www.electrology.com
PO Box 687   Bodega Bay CA 94923
Ph: 707-875-9135

Electromagnetic Compatibility Society, IEEE — www.ewh.ieee.org/soc/emcs
IEEE Operations Ctr 445 Hoes Ln   Piscataway NJ 08854
Ph: 732-981-0060 ▪ Fx: 732-981-1721

Electromagnetics Society, Applied Computational — aces.ee.olemiss.edu

Electron Devices Society, IEEE — www.ieee.org/organizations/society/eds
IEEE Operations Ctr 445 Hoes Ln   Piscataway NJ 08854
Ph: 732-981-0060 ▪ Fx: 732-981-1721

Electroneurodiagnostic Technologists Inc, American Society of — www.aset.org
428 W 42nd St Suite B   Kansas City MO 64111
Ph: 816-931-1120 ▪ Fx: 816-931-1145

Electronic Article Surveillance Manufacturers Association, International — www.ieasma.org
1800 K St NW   Washington DC 20006
Ph: 202-466-4212 ▪ Fx: 202-466-7414

Electronic Commerce, Alliance Against Fraud in Telemarketing & — www.fraud.org/aaft/aaftinfo.htm
1701 K St NW Suite 1200   Washington DC 20006
Ph: 202-835-3323 ▪ Fx: 202-835-0747

Electronic Commerce Association — www.theeca.com
1432 Fenwick Ln Suite 200   Silver Spring MD 20910
Ph: 301-608-9600

Electronic Commerce Code Management Association — www.eccma.org
2980 Linden St Suite E-2   Bethlehem PA 18017
Ph: 610-861-5990 ▪ Fx: 610-861-5992

Electronic Components Certification Board Inc — www.eccb.org

Electronic Components Institute, Variable — www.veci-vrci.com
PO Box 1070   Vista CA 92085
Ph: 760-631-0178 ▪ Fx: 760-631-7827

Electronic Data Interchange, Workgroup for — www.wedi.org
12020 Sunrise Valley Dr Suite 100   Reston VA 20191
Ph: 703-391-2716 ▪ Fx: 703-391-2759

Electronic Design Automation Consortium — www.edac.org
111 W Saint John St Suite 220   San Jose CA 95113
Ph: 408-287-3322 ▪ Fx: 408-283-5283

Electronic Design & Installation Association, Custom — www.cedia.net
7150 Winton Dr Suite 300   Indianapolis IN 46268
Ph: 317-328-4336 ▪ Fx: 317-280-8527 ▪ TF: 800-669-5329

Electronic Device Failure Analysis Society — www.edfas.org
ASM International 9639 Kinsman Rd   Materials Park OH 44073
Ph: 440-338-5151 ▪ Fx: 440-338-4634

Electronic Distribution Network Association, Hotel — www.hedna.org
333 John Carlyle St Suite 600   Alexandria VA 22314
Ph: 703-837-6181 ▪ Fx: 703-548-5738

Electronic Distributors Association, National — www.nedassoc.org
1111 Alderman Dr Suite 400   Alpharetta GA 30005
Ph: 678-393-9990 ▪ Fx: 678-393-9998 ▪ TF: 800-347-6332

Electronic Document Systems Foundation — www.edsf.org
24238 Hawthorne Blvd   Torrance CA 90505
Ph: 310-541-1481 ▪ Fx: 310-541-4803

Electronic Electrical Salaried Machine & Furniture Workers, International Union of — www.iue-cwa.org
1275 K St NW Suite 600   Washington DC 20005
Ph: 202-513-6300 ▪ Fx: 202-513-6357

Electronic Engineering Committee, Airlines — www.arinc.com/aeec
2551 Riva Rd   Annapolis MD 21401
Ph: 410-266-4000 ▪ TF: 800-266-4180

Electronic Frontier Foundation Inc — www.eff.org
454 Shotwell St   San Francisco CA 94110
Ph: 415-436-9333 ▪ Fx: 415-436-9993

Electronic Funds Transfer Association — www.efta.org
950 Herndon Pkwy Suite 390   Herndon VA 20170
Ph: 703-435-9800 ▪ Fx: 703-435-7157

Electronic Industries Alliance — www.eia.org
2500 Wilson Blvd   Arlington VA 22201
Ph: 703-907-7500 ▪ Fx: 703-907-7501

Electronic Keyboard Manufacturers, International Association of — www.iaekm.org

Electronic Payments Association, NACHA - — www.nacha.org
13665 Dulles Technology Dr Suite 300   Herndon VA 20171
Ph: 703-561-1100 ▪ Fx: 703-787-0996 ▪ TF: 800-487-9180

Electronic Privacy Information Center — epic.org
1718 Connecticut Ave NW Suite 200   Washington DC 20009
Ph: 202-483-1140 ▪ Fx: 202-483-1248

Electronic Publishers Association, Newsletter & — www.newsletters.org
1501 Wilson Blvd Suite 509   Arlington VA 22209
Ph: 703-527-2333 ▪ Fx: 703-841-0629 ▪ TF: 800-356-9302

Electronic Retailing Association — www.retailing.org
2101 Wilson Blvd Suite 1002   Arlington VA 22201
Ph: 703-841-1751 ▪ Fx: 703-841-1860 ▪ TF: 800-987-6462

Electronic Revenue Communication Advancement, Council for — www.cerca.org/
600 Cameron St Suite 309   Alexandria VA 22314
Ph: 703-340-1655

Electronic Transactions Association — www.electran.org
1101 16th St NW Suite 402   Washington DC 20036
Ph: 202-828-2635 ▪ Fx: 202-828-2639 ▪ TF: 800-695-5509

Electronic Voice Phenomena, American Association of — aaevp.com
PO Box 13111   Reno NV 89507
Ph: 775-329-5980

(Electronic Warfare) Association of Old Crows — www.crows.org
1000 N Payne St   Alexandria VA 22314
Ph: 703-549-1600 ▪ Fx: 703-549-2589 ▪ TF: 888-653-2769

(Electronics) 1394 Trade Association — www.1394ta.org
1111 S Main St   Grapevine TX 76051
Ph: 817-410-5750 ▪ Fx: 817-410-5757

Electronics Association, Aircraft — www.aea.net
4217 S Hocker Dr   Independence MO 64055
Ph: 816-373-6565 ▪ Fx: 816-478-3100

Electronics Association, Armed Forces Communications & — www.afcea.org
4400 Fair Lakes Ct   Fairfax VA 22033
Ph: 703-631-6100 ▪ Fx: 703-631-4693 ▪ TF: 800-336-4583

Electronics Association, Consumer — www.ce.org
2500 Wilson Blvd   Arlington VA 22201
Ph: 703-907-7600 ▪ Fx: 703-907-7675

Electronics Association, National Marine — www.nmea.org
7 Riggs Ave   Severna Park MD 21146
Ph: 410-975-9425 ▪ Fx: 410-975-9450

Electronics Engineers, Institute of Electrical & — www.ieee.org
3 Park Ave 17th Fl   New York NY 10016
Ph: 212-419-7900 ▪ Fx: 212-752-4929 ▪ TF: 800-678-4333

Electronics Industries, IPC-Association Connecting — www.ipc.org
2215 Sanders Rd   Northbrook IL 60062
Ph: 847-509-9700 ▪ Fx: 847-509-9798

Electronics Manufacturers Initiative, National — www.nemi.org
2214 Rock Hill Rd Suite 110   Herndon VA 20170
Ph: 703-834-0330 ▪ Fx: 703-834-2735

Electronics Representatives Association — www.era.org
444 N Michigan Ave Suite 1960   Chicago IL 60611
Ph: 312-527-3050 ▪ Fx: 312-527-3783 ▪ TF: 800-776-7377

Electronics Service Dealers Association, National — www.nesda.com
3608 Pershing Ave   Fort Worth TX 76107
Ph: 817-921-9061 ▪ Fx: 817-921-3741

Electronics Society, IEEE Industrial — www.ewh.ieee.org/soc/ies
IEEE Operations Ctr 445 Hoes Ln   Piscataway NJ 08854
Ph: 732-981-0060 ▪ Fx: 732-981-1721

Electronics Standards Association, Video   www.vesa.org
920 Hillview Ct Suite 140   Milpitas CA 95035
Ph: 408-957-9270

Electronics Technicians Association International   www.eta-sda.com
5 Depot St   Greencastle IN 46135
Ph: 765-653-8262 ▪ Fx: 765-653-4287 ▪ TF: 800-288-3824

Electronics Technicians, International Society of Certified   www.iscet.org
3608 Pershing Ave   Fort Worth TX 76107
Ph: 817-921-9101 ▪ Fx: 817-921-3741 ▪ TF: 800-946-0201

Electrophoresis Society   www.aesociety.org
3338 Carlyle Terr   Lafayette CA 94549
Ph: 925-284-7186 ▪ Fx: 925-283-5621

Electroplaters & Surface Finishers Society Inc, American   www.aesf.org
12644 Research Pkwy   Orlando FL 32826
Ph: 407-281-6441 ▪ Fx: 407-281-6446

Electrostatic Discharge Association   www.esda.org
7900 Turin Rd Bldg 3   Rome NY 13440
Ph: 315-339-6937 ▪ Fx: 315-339-6793

Elementary School Principals, National Association of   www.naesp.org
1615 Duke St   Alexandria VA 22314
Ph: 703-684-3345 ▪ Fx: 703-548-6021 ▪ TF: 800-386-2377

Elementary Science International, Council for   unr.edu/homepage/crowther/cesi.html
511 Marion Dr   Columbia MO 65203
Ph: 573-874-1038

Elephant Research Foundation
106 E Hickory Grove   Bloomfield Hills MI 48304
Ph: 248-540-3947 ▪ Fx: 248-540-3948

Elevator Constructors, International Union of   www.iuec.org
7154 Columbia Gateway Dr   Columbia MD 21046
Ph: 410-953-6150 ▪ Fx: 410-953-6169

Elevator Contractors, National Association of   www.naec.org
1298 Wellbrook Cir NE Suite A   Conyers GA 30012
Ph: 770-760-9660 ▪ Fx: 770-760-9714

Elevator Escalator Safety Foundation   www.eesf.org
362 Pinehill Dr   Mobile AL 36606
Ph: 334-479-2199 ▪ TF: 888-743-3723

Elevator Industry Inc, National   www.neii.org
1677 County Rd 64 PO Box 838   Salem NY 12865
Ph: 518-854-3100 ▪ Fx: 518-854-3257

Elevator Safety Authorities International, National Association of   www.naesai.org
4541 N 12th St   Phoenix AZ 85014
Ph: 602-266-9701 ▪ Fx: 602-265-0093

Elizabeth Glaser Pediatric AIDS Foundation   www.pedaids.org
2950 31st St Suite 125   Santa Monica CA 90405
Ph: 310-314-1459 ▪ Fx: 310-314-1469 ▪ TF: 888-499-4673

Elk Breeders Association, North American   www.naelk.org
PO Box 1640   Platte City MO 64079
Ph: 816-431-3605 ▪ Fx: 816-431-2705

Elk Foundation, Rocky Mountain   www.rmef.org
PO Box 8249   Missoula MT 59807
Ph: 406-523-4500 ▪ Fx: 406-523-4550 ▪ TF: 800-225-5355

Elkhound Association of America, Norwegian   www.neaa.net
21738 Hampton Ct   Kildeer IL 60047
Ph: 847-438-3670

Elks of the USA, Benevolent & Protective Order of   www.elks.org
2750 N Lakeview Ave   Chicago IL 60614
Ph: 773-755-4700 ▪ Fx: 773-755-4790

Ellis Island Foundation, Statue of Liberty-   www.ellisisland.org
292 Madison Ave   New York NY 10017
Ph: 212-561-4500 ▪ Fx: 212-779-1990

Ellison Medical Foundation   www.ellisonfoundation.org
4710 Bethesda Ave Suite 204   Bethesda MD 20814
Ph: 301-657-1830 ▪ Fx: 301-657-1828

Elm Research Institute   www.libertyelm.com
11 Kit St   Keene NH 03431
Ph: 603-358-6198 ▪ Fx: 603-358-6305

Elton John AIDS Foundation   www.ejaf.org
PO Box 17139   Beverly Hills CA 90209
Ph: 310-535-1775

Elvish Linguistic Fellowship   www.elvish.org

Elwyn Inc   www.elwyn.org
111 Elwyn Rd   Elwyn PA 19063
Ph: 610-891-2000 ▪ Fx: 610-891-2458

Ely-Chatelaine, Free Territory of   www.worldfreeinternet.net/ftec
PO Box 7075   Laguna Niguel CA 92607
Ph: 949-581-5348

Emanuel Foundation for Hungarian Culture
97-45 Queens Blvd Suite 614   Rego Park NY 11374
Ph: 718-896-8300 ▪ Fx: 718-896-8323

Embalming Chemical Manufacturers Association   www.embalmers.com
1370 Honeyspot Rd Ext   Stratford CT 06615
Ph: 203-375-2984 ▪ Fx: 203-378-9160 ▪ TF: 800-243-6104

Embossing Association, Foil Stamping &   www.fsea.com
536 NW Tyler Ct Suite 204   Topeka KS 66608
Ph: 785-232-8776 ▪ Fx: 785-232-8747

Embroiderers Association, Pleaters Stitchers &
225 W 39th St   New York NY 10018
Ph: 212-398-5400 ▪ Fx: 212-398-3141

Embroiderers Guild of America   www.needlearts.com/ega
335 W Broadway Suite 100   Louisville KY 40202
Ph: 502-589-6956 ▪ Fx: 502-584-7900

Embroidery Council of America   www.embroiderycouncil.org
409 Henry St   Fairview NJ 07022
Ph: 201-943-7730

Embroidery Trade Association   www.embroiderytrade.org
12300 Ford Rd Suite 135   Dallas TX 75234
Ph: 972-906-6720 ▪ Fx: 972-755-2561 ▪ TF: 800-727-3014

Embryo Transfer Association, American   www.aeta.org
1111 N Dunlap Ave   Savoy IL 61847
Ph: 217-398-2217 ▪ Fx: 217-398-4119

Embryo Transfer Society, International   www.iets.org
1111 N Dunlap Ave   Savoy IL 61874
Ph: 217-356-3182 ▪ Fx: 217-398-4119

Emerald Isle Immigration Center of New York   www.eiic.org
59-26 Woodside Ave   Woodside NY 11377
Ph: 718-478-5502 ▪ Fx: 718-446-3727

(Emergency Care) ECRI   www.ecri.org
5200 Butler Pike   Plymouth Meeting PA 19462
Ph: 610-825-6000 ▪ Fx: 610-834-1275

Emergency Committee for American Trade   www.ecattrade.com
1211 Connecticut Ave NW Suite 801   Washington DC 20036
Ph: 202-659-5147 ▪ Fx: 202-659-1347

Emergency Communications, North American Center For   www.nacec.org
PO Box 174   Aurora MN 55705
Ph: 218-229-2887

Emergency Department Practice Management Association   www.edpma.org
8405 Greensboro Dr Suite 800   McLean VA 22102
Ph: 703-506-3292 ▪ Fx: 703-506-3266

Emergency Equipment Dealers Association, National   www.needa.org
8421 Frost Way   Annandale VA 22003
Ph: 703-280-4622 ▪ Fx: 703-280-0942

Emergency Management Association, National   www.nemaweb.org
PO Box 11910   Lexington KY 40578
Ph: 859-244-8000 ▪ Fx: 859-244-8239

Emergency Manufacturers & Services Association, Fire &   www.femsa.org
PO Box 147   Lynnfield MA 01940
Ph: 781-334-2771

Emergency Medical Services Training Coordinators, National Council of State   www.ncsemstc.org
201 Park Washington Ct   Falls Church VA 22046
Ph: 703-538-1794 ▪ Fx: 703-241-5603

Emergency Medical Technicians, National Association of   www.naemt.org
PO Box 1400   Clinton MS 39060
Ph: 800-346-2368

Emergency Medical Technicians, National Registry of   www.nremt.org
6610 Bush Blvd PO Box 29233   Columbus OH 43229
Ph: 614-888-4484 ▪ Fx: 614-888-8920

Emergency Medicine, American Academy of   www.aaem.org
611 E Wells St   Milwaukee WI 53202
Ph: 800-884-2236 ▪ Fx: 414-276-3349

Emergency Medicine, American Board of   www.abem.org
3000 Coolidge Rd   East Lansing MI 48823
Ph: 517-332-4800 ▪ Fx: 517-332-2234

Emergency Medicine, American Osteopathic Board of   www.aobem.org
142 E Ontario St 8th Fl   Chicago IL 60611
Ph: 312-335-1065 ▪ Fx: 312-335-5489

Emergency Medicine Physician Assistants, Society of   www.sempa.org
950 N Washington St   Alexandria VA 22314
Ph: 703-519-7334 ▪ Fx: 703-684-1924

Emergency Medicine Residents' Association   www.emra.org
1125 Executive Cir   Irving TX 75038
Ph: 972-550-0920 ▪ Fx: 972-580-2829 ▪ TF: 800-798-1822

Emergency Medicine, Society for Academic   www.saem.org
901 N Washington Ave   Lansing MI 48906
Ph: 517-485-5484 ▪ Fx: 517-485-0801

Emergency Number Association, National   www.nena9-1-1.org
4350 N Fairfax Dr Suite 750   Arlington VA 22203
Ph: 703-812-4600 ▪ Fx: 703-812-4675 ▪ TF: 800-332-3911

Emergency Nurses Association   www.ena.org
915 Lee St   Des Plaines IL 60016
Ph: 847-460-4000 ▪ Fx: 847-460-4001 ▪ TF: 800-900-9659

Emergency Physicians, American College of   www.acep.org
PO Box 619911   Dallas TX 75261
Ph: 972-550-0911 ▪ Fx: 972-580-2816 ▪ TF: 800-798-1822

Emergency Physicians, American College of Osteopathic   www.acoep.org
142 E Ontario St Suite 1250   Chicago IL 60611
Ph: 312-587-3709 ▪ Fx: 312-587-9951 ▪ TF: 800-521-3709

Emergency Radiology, American Society of   www.erad.org
4550 Post Oak Pl Suite 342   Houston TX 77027
Ph: 713-965-0566 ▪ Fx: 713-960-0488

Emergency Relief, Army   www.aerhq.org
200 Stovall St   Alexandria VA 22332
Ph: 703-328-0000 ▪ Fx: 703-325-7183

Emergency Relief, World   www.worldemergency.org
2270 Camino Vida Roble Suite D   Carlsbad CA 92009
Ph: 760-930-8001 ▪ Fx: 760-930-9085 ▪ TF: 888-484-2543

Emergency Response Association International, Disaster Preparedness &   www.disasters.org
PO Box 797   Longmont CO 80502
Ph: 303-809-4412

Emergency Response Program, Church World Service   www.cwserp.org
475 Riverside Dr 7th Fl   New York NY 10115
Ph: 212-870-3151 ▪ Fx: 212-870-2236

Emerging Business, Research Institute for Small &   www.riseb.org
722 12th St NW   Washington DC 20005
Ph: 202-628-8382 ▪ Fx: 202-628-8392

Emerging Markets Traders Association   www.emta.org
360 Madison Ave 18th Fl   New York NY 10017
Ph: 646-637-9100 ▪ Fx: 646-637-9128

Emerson Ralph Waldo Memorial Association
3 Post Office Sq 10th Fl   Boston MA 02109
Ph: 617-423-5705 ▪ Fx: 617-423-6656

EMILY's List   www.emilyslist.org
1120 Connecticut Ave NW Suite 1100   Washington DC 20036
Ph: 202-326-1400 ▪ Fx: 202-326-1415 ▪ TF: 800-683-6459

Eminent Domain Professionals, Association of   www.aedp.org
PO Box 6721   West Palm Beach FL 33405
Ph: 561-655-4144 ▪ Fx: 561-659-1824

Emission Controls Association, Manufacturers of   meca.org
1660 L St NW Suite 1100   Washington DC 20036
Ph: 202-296-4797 ▪ Fx: 202-331-1388

Emmaus Ministries www.streets.org
921 W Wilson Ave   Chicago IL 60640
Ph: 773-334-6063 ▪ Fx: 773-334-8638 ▪ TF: 800-378-4445

Emotions Anonymous International www.emotionsanonymous.org
2233 University Ave W Suite 402 PO Box 4245   Saint Paul MN 55104
Ph: 651-647-9712 ▪ Fx: 651-647-1593

Employee Assistance Professionals Association Inc www.eapassn.n
2101 Wilson Blvd Suite 500   Arlington VA 22201
Ph: 703-522-6272 ▪ Fx: 703-522-4585

Employee Assistance Society of North America www.easna.org
230 E Ohio St Suite 400   Chicago IL 60611
Ph: 312-644-0828 ▪ Fx: 312-644-8557

Employee Benefit Plans, International Foundation of www.ifebp.org
PO Box 69   Brookfield WI 53008
Ph: 262-786-6700 ▪ Fx: 262-786-8670 ▪ TF: 888-334-3327

Employee Benefit Research Institute www.ebri.org
2121 K St NW Suite 600   Washington DC 20037
Ph: 202-659-0670 ▪ Fx: 202-775-6312

Employee Benefit Specialists, International Society of Certified www.iscebs.org
18700 W Bluemond Rd PO Box 209   Brookfield WI 53008
Ph: 262-786-8771 ▪ Fx: 262-786-8650

Employee Benefits, Council on www.ceb.org
4910 Moorland Ln   Bethesda MD 20814
Ph: 301-664-5940 ▪ Fx: 301-664-5944

(Employee Benefits) ESOP Association www.esopassociation.org
1726 M St NW Suite 501   Washington DC 20036
Ph: 202-293-2971 ▪ Fx: 202-293-7568 ▪ TF: 866-366-3832

Employee Benefits Network Inc, Worldwide www.webnetwork.org
21165 Whitfield Pl   Potomac Falls VA 20165
Ph: 703-433-9696 ▪ Fx: 703-433-0369

Employee Involvement Association www.eianet.org
7925 E Lakeview   Mesa AZ 85208
Ph: 480-358-1791 ▪ Fx: 480-358-1866

Employee Ownership, National Center for www.nceo.org
1736 Franklin St 8th Fl   Oakland CA 94612
Ph: 510-208-1300 ▪ Fx: 510-272-9510

Employee Relocation Council www.erc.org
1717 Pennsylvania Ave NW Suite 800   Washington DC 20006
Ph: 202-857-0857 ▪ Fx: 202-467-4012 ▪ TF: 888-372-2255

Employee Retirement Systems, National Conference on Public www.ncpers.org
444 N Capitol St NW Suite 221   Washington DC 20001
Ph: 202-624-1456 ▪ Fx: 202-624-1439 ▪ TF: 877-202-5706

Employee Services Management Association www.esmassn.org
2211 York Rd Suite 207   Oak Brook IL 60523
Ph: 630-368-1280 ▪ Fx: 630-368-1286

Employees, American Association of Classified School www.aacse.org
7140 SW Childs Rd   Lake Oswego OR 97035
Ph: 503-620-5663 ▪ Fx: 503-684-4597

Employees Education & Assistance Fund, Federal www.feea.org
8441 W Bowles Ave Suite 200   Littleton CO 80123
Ph: 303-933-7580 ▪ Fx: 303-933-7587 ▪ TF: 800-323-4140

Employees, Independent Association of Publishers' www.iape1096.org
14 Washington Rd Suite 521   Princeton Junction NJ 08550
Ph: 609-799-1520 ▪ Fx: 609-716-0626 ▪ TF: 800-325-8273

Employees Organization, National Weather Service www.nwseo.org
601 Pennsylvania Ave Suite 900   Washington DC 20004
Ph: 703-293-9651 ▪ Fx: 703-293-9653

Employees of Public Agencies, Worldwide Assurance for www.waepa.org
7651 Leesburg Pike   Falls Church VA 22043
Ph: 703-790-8010 ▪ Fx: 703-790-4606 ▪ TF: 800-368-3484

Employees Roundtable, Public www.theroundtable.org
PO Box 75248   Washington DC 20013
Ph: 202-927-4926 ▪ Fx: 202-927-4920

Employer Coalition, Disability Management www.dmec.org
6343 El Cajon Blvd Suite 110   San Diego CA 92115
Ph: 619-698-0431 ▪ Fx: 619-749-7872 ▪ TF: 800-789-3632

Employer Labor Relations Association, National Public www.npelra.org
1617 Duke St   Alexandria VA 22314
Ph: 703-836-9626 ▪ Fx: 703-836-9628 ▪ TF: 800-296-2230

Employer Organizations, National Association of Professional www.napeo.org
901 N Pitt St Suite 150   Alexandria VA 22314
Ph: 703-836-0466 ▪ Fx: 703-836-0976

Employer Support of the Guard & Reserve, National Committee for www.esgr.org
1555 Wilson Blvd Suite 200   Arlington VA 22209
Ph: 703-696-1386 ▪ Fx: 703-696-1411 ▪ TF: 800-336-4590

Employers of America www.employerhelp.org
1431 4th St SW Box 305   Mason City IA 50401
Ph: 641-424-3187 ▪ TF: 800-728-3187

Employers Association www.employersassoc.com
3020 W Arrowood Rd   Charlotte NC 28273
Ph: 704-522-8011 ▪ Fx: 704-522-8105

Employers Association, Building Trades
180 Linden Oaks Suite 110   Rochester NY 14625
Ph: 585-586-0710 ▪ Fx: 585-586-1580

Employers Association, Construction Industry www.conexbuff.com
625 Ensminger Rd   Tonawanda NY 14150
Ph: 716-875-3435 ▪ Fx: 716-875-4412

Employers of Bricklayers & Allied Craftworkers, International Council of www.icebac.org
1776 'I' St NW   Washington DC 20006
Ph: 202-783-3788 ▪ Fx: 202-393-0222 ▪ TF: 888-880-8222

Employers Council on Flexible Compensation www.ecfc.org
927 15th St NW Suite 1000   Washington DC 20005
Ph: 202-659-4300 ▪ Fx: 202-371-1467

Employers, National Association of Colleges & www.naceweb.org
62 Highland Ave   Bethlehem PA 18017
Ph: 610-868-1421 ▪ Fx: 610-868-0208 ▪ TF: 800-544-5272

Employers, National Association of Waterfront
2011 Pennsylvania Ave NW Suite 301   Washington DC 20006
Ph: 202-296-2810 ▪ Fx: 202-331-7479

Employers, National Council of Agricultural www.ncaeonline.org
1112 16th St NW Suite 920   Washington DC 20036
Ph: 202-728-0300 ▪ Fx: 202-728-0303

Employment Advisory Council, Equal www.eeac.org
1015 15th St NW Suite 1200   Washington DC 20005
Ph: 202-789-8650 ▪ Fx: 202-789-2291

Employment Association, National Student nseastudemp.org
PO Box 23606   Eugene OR 97402
Ph: 541-484-6935

Employment Counseling Association, National www.employmentcounseling.org
5999 Stevenson Ave   Alexandria VA 22304
Ph: 703-823-0252 ▪ Fx: 800-473-2329 ▪ TF: 800-347-6647

Employment in Education, American Association for www.aaee.org
3040 Riverside Dr Suite 125   Columbus OH 43221
Ph: 614-485-1111 ▪ Fx: 614-485-9609

Employment Inc, Homeworkers Organized for More www.homecoop.net
PO Box 10   Orland ME 04472
Ph: 207-469-7961 ▪ Fx: 207-469-1023

Employment Law Project, National www.nelp.org
55 John St 7th Fl   New York NY 10038
Ph: 212-285-3025 ▪ Fx: 212-285-3044

Employment Lawyers Association, National www.nela.org
44 Montgomery St Suite 2080   San Francisco CA 94104
Ph: 415-296-7629 ▪ Fx: 415-677-9445

Employment Policies Institute www.epionline.org
1775 Pennsylvania Ave NW Suite 1200   Washington DC 20006
Ph: 202-463-7650 ▪ Fx: 202-463-7107

Employment Policy Foundation www.epf.org
1015 15th St NW Suite 1200   Washington DC 20005
Ph: 202-789-8685 ▪ Fx: 202-789-8684

Employment Security, International Association of Personnel in
International Assn of Workforce Professionals 1801 Louisville Rd   Frankfort KY 40601
Ph: 502-223-4459 ▪ Fx: 502-223-4127 ▪ TF: 888-898-9960

Employment Services, American Congress of Community Supports & www.accses.org
1875 'I' St NW 11th Fl   Washington DC 20006
Ph: 202-466-3355 ▪ Fx: 202-466-7571

Employment, Women Work! National Network for Women's www.womenwork.org
1625 K St NW Suite 300   Washington DC 20006
Ph: 202-467-6346 ▪ Fx: 202-467-5366 ▪ TF: 800-235-2732

Empower America www.empoweramerica.org
1775 Pennsylvania Ave NW 11th Fl   Washington DC 20006
Ph: 202-452-8200 ▪ Fx: 202-833-0388

Empowerment Training Project, Student www.trainings.org
119 Somerset St 2nd Fl   New Brunswick NJ 08901
Ph: 732-247-2197

EMS Directors, National Association of State www.nasemsd.org
201 Park Washington Ct   Falls Church VA 22046
Ph: 703-538-1799 ▪ Fx: 703-241-5603

EMS Educators, National Association of www.naemse.org
700 N Bell Ave Suite 260   Carnegie PA 15106
Ph: 412-429-9550 ▪ Fx: 412-429-9554

EMS Physicians, National Association of www.naemsp.org
PO Box 15945-281   Lenexa KS 66214
Ph: 913-492-5858 ▪ Fx: 913-599-5340 ▪ TF: 800-228-3677

EMS Pilots Association, National www.nemspa.org
526 King St Suite 415   Alexandria VA 22314
Ph: 703-836-8930 ▪ Fx: 703-836-8920

EMS Professions, Committee on Accreditation for Educational Programs for the www.coaemsp.org
1248 Hardwood Rd   Bedford TX 76021
Ph: 817-283-9403 ▪ Fx: 817-354-8519

Emunah of America www.emunah.org
7 Penn Plaza 7th Fl   New York NY 10001
Ph: 212-564-9045 ▪ Fx: 212-643-9731 ▪ TF: 800-368-6440

En Foco Inc www.enfoco.org
32 E Knightsbridge Rd   Bronx NY 10468
Ph: 718-584-7718

Enamel Institute, Porcelain www.porcelainenamel.com
PO Box 920220   Norcross GA 30010
Ph: 770-281-8980 ▪ Fx: 770-625-4923

Enclosure Association, National Patio
12625 Frederick St Suite 1-5 315   Moreno Valley CA 92553
Ph: 909-485-8881 ▪ Fx: 909-924-3078

Encompass www.encompassus.org
401 N Michigan Ave 22nd Fl   Chicago IL 60611
Ph: 312-321-5151 ▪ Fx: 312-673-4609 ▪ TF: 877-354-9887

End-of-Life Choices www.endoflifechoices.org
PO Box 101810   Denver CO 80250
Ph: 303-639-1202 ▪ Fx: 303-639-1224 ▪ TF: 800-247-7421

Endangered Species Act Reform Coalition, National www.nesarc.org
1050 Thomas Jefferson St 7th Fl   Washington DC 20007
Ph: 202-333-7481 ▪ Fx: 202-338-2416

Endangered Species Coalition www.stopextinction.org
1101 14th St NW Suite 1001   Washington DC 20005
Ph: 202-408-7707 ▪ Fx: 202-408-7820

Endocrine Fellows Foundation www.endocrinefellows.org
5959 W Century Blvd Suite 575   Los Angeles CA 90045
Ph: 310-216-1066 ▪ TF: 877-877-6515

Endocrine Society www.endo-society.org
4350 East-West Hwy Suite 500   Bethesda MD 20814
Ph: 301-941-0200 ▪ Fx: 301-941-0259

Endocrinologists, American Association of Clinical www.aace.com
1000 Riverside Ave Suite 205   Jacksonville FL 32204
Ph: 904-353-7878 ▪ Fx: 904-353-8185

Endocrinology & Infertility, Society for Reproductive www.socrei.org
1209 Montgomery Hwy   Birmingham AL 35216
Ph: 205-978-5000 ▪ Fx: 205-978-5005

Endocrinology, Women in www.women-in-endo.org
Brigham & Women's Hospital Endocrine Div 22 Longwood Ave   Boston MA 02115
Ph: 617-732-5768 ▪ Fx: 617-732-5764

Endodontic Society, American   www.aesoc.com
1321 N Harbor Blvd Suite 201 Fullerton CA 92835
Ph: 714-870-5590 ▪ Fx: 714-526-2818

Endodontics, American Board of   www.aae.org/ABE1.html
211 E Chicago Ave Suite 1100 Chicago IL 60611
Ph: 312-266-7255 ▪ Fx: 800-872-3636

Endodontists, American Association of   www.aae.org
211 E Chicago Ave Suite 1100 Chicago IL 60611
Ph: 312-266-7255 ▪ Fx: 312-266-9867 ▪ TF: 800-872-3636

Endometriosis Association   www.endometriosisassn.org
8585 N 76th Pl Milwaukee WI 53223
Ph: 414-355-2200 ▪ Fx: 414-355-6065 ▪ TF: 800-992-3636

Endoscopic Surgeons, Society of American Gastrointestinal   www.sages.org
11300 W Olympic Blvd Suite 600 Los Angeles CA 90064
Ph: 310-437-0544 ▪ Fx: 310-437-0585

Endoscopy, American Society for Gastrointestinal   www.asge.org
1520 Kensington Rd Suite 202 Oak Brook IL 60523
Ph: 630-573-0600 ▪ Fx: 630-573-0691

Endurance Ride Conference, American   www.aerc.org
11960 Heritage Oak Pl Suite 9 Auburn CA 95603
Ph: 530-823-2260 ▪ Fx: 530-823-7805

Energy, Alliance to Save   www.ase.org
1200 18th St NW Suite 900 Washington DC 20036
Ph: 202-857-0666 ▪ Fx: 202-331-9588

Energy, American Association of Blacks in   www.aabe.org
927 15th St NW Suite 200 Washington DC 20005
Ph: 202-371-9530 ▪ Fx: 202-371-9218 ▪ TF: 800-466-0204

Energy Assistance Directors' Association, National   www.neada.org
1615 M St NW Suite 800 Washington DC 20036
Ph: 202-237-5199 ▪ Fx: 202-237-7316

Energy Association, American Wind   www.awea.org
122 C St NW Suite 380 Washington DC 20001
Ph: 202-383-2500 ▪ Fx: 202-383-2505

Energy Association, Geothermal   www.geo-energy.org
209 Pennsylvania Ave SE Washington DC 20003
Ph: 202-454-5261 ▪ Fx: 202-454-5265

Energy Association, International District   www.districtenergy.org
125 Turnpike Rd Suite 4 Westborough MA 01581
Ph: 508-366-9339 ▪ Fx: 508-366-0019

Energy Association, US   www.usea.org
1300 Pennsylvania Ave NW Suite 550 Washington DC 20004
Ph: 202-312-1230 ▪ Fx: 202-682-1826

Energy Bar Association   www.eba-net.org
2175 K St NW Suite 600 Washington DC 20037
Ph: 202-223-5625 ▪ Fx: 202-833-5596

Energy, Business Council for Sustainable   www.bcse.org
1200 18th St NW 9th Fl Washington DC 20036
Ph: 202-785-0507 ▪ Fx: 202-785-0514

Energy Communities Alliance   www.energyca.org
1101 Connecticut Ave NW Suite 1000 Washington DC 20036
Ph: 202-828-2318 ▪ Fx: 202-828-2488

Energy Conservation, International Institute for   www.iiec.org
10005 Leamoore Ln Suite 100 Vienna VA 22181
Ph: 703-281-7263 ▪ Fx: 703-968-6678

Energy Council of America, Consumer   www.cecarf.org
2000 L St NW Suite 802 Washington DC 20036
Ph: 202-659-0404 ▪ Fx: 202-659-0407

Energy Council, Lignite   www.lignite.com
1016 E Owens Ave Suite 200 Bismarck ND 58502
Ph: 701-258-7117 ▪ Fx: 701-258-2755

Energy Council, National Food &   www.nfec.org
601 Business Loop 70W Suite 216D Columbia MO 65203
Ph: 573-875-7155 ▪ Fx: 573-449-5322

Energy Credit Association, International   www.ieca.net
8325 Lantern View Ln Saint John IN 46373
Ph: 219-365-7313 ▪ Fx: 219-365-0327

Energy Economics, International Association for   www.iaee.org
28790 Chagrin Blvd Suite 350 Cleveland OH 44122
Ph: 216-464-5365 ▪ Fx: 216-464-2737

Energy Economics, US Association for   www.usaee.org
28790 Chagrin Blvd Suite 350 Cleveland OH 44122
Ph: 216-464-2785 ▪ Fx: 216-464-2768

Energy Education, Foundation for Water &   www.fwee.org

Energy Efficiency & Renewable Energy   www.eere.energy.gov/consumerinfo
Clearinghouse US Dept of Energy PO Box 3048 Merrifield
VA 22116
Ph: 800-363-3732 ▪ Fx: 703-893-0400

Energy Efficiency & Renewable Technologies, Center for
1100 11th St Suite 311 Sacramento CA 95814
Ph: 916-442-7785 ▪ Fx: 916-447-2940 ▪ TF: 877-758-4462

Energy-Efficient Economy, American Council for an   www.aceee.org
1001 Connecticut Ave NW Suite 801 Washington DC 20036
Ph: 202-429-8873 ▪ Fx: 202-429-2248

Energy Engineers, Association of   www.aeecenter.org
4025 Pleasantdale Rd Suite 420 Atlanta GA 30340
Ph: 770-447-5083 ▪ Fx: 770-446-3969

Energy & the Environment, Women's Council on   www.wcee.org
PO Box 33211 Washington DC 20033
Ph: 703-351-7850

Energy & Environmental Building Association   www.eeba.org
10740 Lyndale Ave S Suite 10W Bloomington MN 55420
Ph: 952-881-1098 ▪ Fx: 952-881-3048

Energy Foundation, National   www.nef1.org
3676 California Ave Suite A117 Salt Lake City UT 84104
Ph: 801-908-5800 ▪ Fx: 801-908-5400

Energy Frontiers International   www.energyfrontiers.org
1110 N Glebe Rd Suite 610 Arlington VA 22201
Ph: 703-276-6655 ▪ Fx: 703-276-7662

Energy Information Service, Nuclear   www.neis.org
PO Box 1637 Evanston IL 60204
Ph: 847-869-7650 ▪ Fx: 847-869-7658

Energy, International Association for Hydrogen   www.iahe.org
PO Box 248266 Coral Gables FL 33124
Ph: 305-284-4666 ▪ Fx: 305-284-4792

Energy Management Institute, National   www.nemionline.org
601 N Fairfax St Suite 250 Alexandria VA 22314
Ph: 703-739-7100 ▪ Fx: 703-683-7615 ▪ TF: 800-458-6525

Energy Managers, Association of Professional   www.apem.org
3916 W Oak St Suite D Burbank CA 91505
Ph: 818-972-2159 ▪ Fx: 818-972-2863

Energy Medicine, International Society for the Study of Subtle Energies &   www.issseem.org
11005 Ralston Rd Suite 100D Arvada CO 80004
Ph: 303-425-4625 ▪ Fx: 303-425-4685

Energy & Mineral Law Foundation   www.emlf.org
Univ of Kentucky Mineral Law Ctr Rm 21 Law Bldg Lexington
KY 40507
Ph: 859-257-7140 ▪ Fx: 859-257-2884

Energy & Mineral Resources, Circum-Pacific Council for   www.circum-pacificcouncil.org
345 Middlefield Rd MS 973 Menlo Park CA 94025
Ph: 650-329-5430 ▪ Fx: 650-329-4936

Energy Officials, National Association of State   www.naseo.org
1414 Prince St Suite 200 Alexandria VA 22314
Ph: 703-299-8800 ▪ Fx: 703-299-6208

Energy Professional Society, Directed   www.deps.org
PO Box 9874 Albuquerque NM 87119
Ph: 505-998-4910 ▪ Fx: 505-242-2249

Energy Psychology, Association for Comprehensive   www.energypsych.org
PO Box 910244 San Diego CA 92191
Ph: 858-748-5963 ▪ Fx: 858-270-0370

Energy Research Association, Biomass   www.bera1.org
1116 'E' St SE Washington DC 20003
Ph: 847-381-6320 ▪ Fx: 847-382-5595 ▪ TF: 800-247-1755

Energy Research Institute
6850 Rattlesnake Hammock Rd Naples FL 34113
Ph: 813-793-1922 ▪ Fx: 813-793-1260

Energy Resource Tribes, Council of   www.certredearth.com
695 S Colorado Blvd Suite 10 Denver CO 80246
Ph: 303-282-7576 ▪ Fx: 303-282-7584

Energy Resources Organization, Alternative   www.aeromt.org
432 N Last Chance Gulch Helena MT 59601
Ph: 406-443-7272 ▪ Fx: 406-442-9120

Energy Roundtable, Agri-   www.agribusinesscouncil.org/aer.htm
1312 18th St NW Washington DC 20036
Ph: 202-887-0528 ▪ Fx: 202-887-9178

Energy Security Council   www.energysecuritycouncil.org
5555 San Felipe Rd Suite 101 Houston TX 77056
Ph: 713-296-1893 ▪ Fx: 713-296-1895

Energy Service Companies, Association of   www.aesc.net
10200 Richmond Ave Suite 253 Houston TX 77042
Ph: 713-781-0758 ▪ Fx: 713-781-7542 ▪ TF: 800-692-0771

Energy Service Companies, National Association of   www.naesco.org
1615 M St SW Suite 800 Washington DC 20036
Ph: 202-822-0950 ▪ Fx: 202-822-0955

Energy Services Association, National   www.nesanet.org
6430 FM 1960 W Suite 213 Houston TX 77069
Ph: 713-856-6525 ▪ Fx: 713-856-6199

Energy Services Professionals International, Association of   www.aesp.org
17610 128th Trail N Jupiter FL 33478
Ph: 561-575-2334 ▪ Fx: 561-575-4688

Energy Society, American Solar   www.ases.org
2400 Central Ave Suite A Boulder CO 80301
Ph: 303-443-3130 ▪ Fx: 303-443-3212

Energy Study Institute, Environmental &   www.eesi.org
122 C St NW Suite 722 Washington DC 20001
Ph: 202-628-6500 ▪ Fx: 202-737-5299

Energy Systems, Association for Efficient Environmental   www.aeees.org
PO Box 598 Davis CA 95617
Ph: 530-750-0135 ▪ Fx: 530-750-0137

Energy Telecommunications & Electrical Association   www.entelec.org
14015 Park Dr Suite 206 Tomball TX 77375
Ph: 281-357-8700 ▪ Fx: 281-357-8777 ▪ TF: 888-503-8700

Energy Traffic Association   www.energytraffic.org
3303 Main St Suite 207 Houston TX 77002
Ph: 713-827-1199 ▪ Fx: 713-464-0702

Enersol Inc   www.enersol.org
55 Middlesex St Suite 221 Chelmsford MA 01863
Ph: 978-251-1828 ▪ Fx: 978-251-5291

EngenderHealth   www.engenderhealth.org
440 9th Ave 3rd Fl New York NY 10001
Ph: 212-561-8000 ▪ Fx: 212-561-8067 ▪ TF: 800-564-2872

Engine Manufacturers Association   www.enginemanufacturers.org
2 N LaSalle St Suite 2200 Chicago IL 60602
Ph: 312-827-8700 ▪ Fx: 312-827-8737

Engine Parts Manufacturers Association, National
4012 E Harbor Rd Suite 141 Port Clinton OH 43452
Ph: 419-734-2501

Engine Rebuilders Association, Automotive   www.aera.org
330 Lexington Dr Buffalo Grove IL 60089
Ph: 847-541-6550 ▪ Fx: 847-541-5808

Engine Remanufacturers Association, Production   www.pera.org
14160 Newbrook Dr Suite 210 Chantilly VA 20151
Ph: 703-968-2772 ▪ Fx: 703-968-2878

Engine Service Association, Outdoor Power Equipment &   www.opeesa.com
210 Allen Dr Exton PA 19341
Ph: 610-363-3844 ▪ Fx: 610-363-3817

Engine Tractor & Toy Association, Antique
5731 Paradise Rd Slatington PA 18080
Ph: 610-767-4768

Engineered Wood Association, APA - www.apawood.org
7011 S 19th Tacoma WA 98466
Ph: 253-565-6600 ▪ Fx: 253-565-7265

Engineered Wood Research Foundation www.engineeredwood.org
PO Box 11700 Tacoma WA 98411
Ph: 253-565-6600 ▪ Fx: 253-565-7265

Engineering, American Institute for Medical & Biological www.aimbe.org
1901 Pennsylvania Ave NW Suite 401 Washington DC 20006
Ph: 202-496-9660 ▪ Fx: 202-466-8489

Engineering, American Society for Precision www.aspe.net
PO Box 10826 Raleigh NC 27605
Ph: 919-839-8444 ▪ Fx: 919-839-8039

Engineering Association, American www.aea.org
PO Box 820473 Fort Worth TX 76182
Ph: 972-264-6428

(Engineering) CEF www.innercite.com/~cef
2700 Zinfandel Dr Rancho Cordova CA 95670
Ph: 916-853-1914 ▪ Fx: 916-853-1921

Engineering Coating Association, Surface
1300 Sumner Ave Cleveland OH 44115
Ph: 216-241-7333 ▪ Fx: 216-241-0105

Engineering College Magazines Associated www.ecmaweb.org
Univ of Minnesota Institute of Technology 1701 University Ave
SE Minneapolis MN 55414
Ph: 612-626-7959

Engineering Companies, American Council of www.acec.org
1015 15th St NW 8th Fl Washington DC 20005
Ph: 202-347-7474 ▪ Fx: 202-898-0068

Engineering Consortium, International www.iec.org
549 W Randolph St Suite 600 Chicago IL 60661
Ph: 312-559-4100 ▪ Fx: 312-559-4111

Engineering Contractors' Association home.flash.net/~eca
8310 Florence Ave Downey CA 90240
Ph: 562-861-0929 ▪ Fx: 562-923-6179 ▪ TF: 800-293-2240

Engineering Department Heads Association, Electrical & Computer www.ecedha.org
549 W Randolph St Suite 600 Chicago IL 60661
Ph: 312-559-3724 ▪ Fx: 312-559-3329

Engineering Education, American Society for www.asee.org
1818 'N' St NW Suite 600 Washington DC 20036
Ph: 202-331-3500 ▪ Fx: 202-265-8504

(Engineering) Eta Kappa Nu Association www.hkn.org
PO Box 3535 Lisle IL 60532
Ph: 800-406-2590 ▪ Fx: 800-864-2051

Engineering Fraternity, Theta Tau Professional www.thetatau.org
815 Brazos St Suite 710 Austin TX 78701
Ph: 512-472-1904 ▪ Fx: 512-472-4820 ▪ TF: 800-264-1904

Engineering Geologists, Association of www.aegweb.org
PO Box 460518 Denver CO 80246
Ph: 303-757-2926 ▪ Fx: 303-757-2969

Engineering Geophysical Society, Environmental & www.eegs.org
1720 S Bellaire St Suite 110 Denver CO 80222
Ph: 303-531-7517 ▪ Fx: 303-820-3844

Engineering Graphics & Imaging Systems, Association for
800 Enterprise Dr Suite 202 Oak Brook IL 60523
Ph: 630-574-8200 ▪ Fx: 630-571-4731

Engineering Institute, Architectural www.aeinstitute.org
1801 Alexander Bell Dr 1st Fl Reston VA 20191
Ph: 703-295-6027 ▪ Fx: 703-295-6361

Engineering, Inter-American Association of Sanitary &
Environmental 601 Wythe St Alexandria VA 22314 www.aidis-usa.org
Ph: 703-684-2400

Engineering Management, American Society for www.engineering-management.org
PO Box 820 Rolla MO 65402
Ph: 573-341-2101 ▪ Fx: 573-364-3500

Engineering Management Society, IEEE www.ewh.ieee.org/soc/ems
IEEE Operations Ctr 445 Hoes Ln Piscataway NJ 08854
Ph: 732-981-0060 ▪ Fx: 732-981-1721

Engineering in Medicine & Biology Society, IEEE www.eng.unsw.edu.au/embs/index.html
IEEE Operations Ctr 445 Hoes Ln Piscataway NJ 08854
Ph: 732-981-0060 ▪ Fx: 732-981-1721

Engineering Ministries International www.emiusa.org
110 S Weber St Suite 104 Colorado Springs CO 80903
Ph: 719-633-2078 ▪ Fx: 719-633-2970

Engineering, National Academy of www.nae.edu
2101 Constitution Ave NW Washington DC 20418
Ph: 202-334-3200 ▪ Fx: 202-334-1563

Engineering, National Action Council for Minorities in www.nacme.org
440 Hamilton Ave Suite 302 White Planes NY 10601
Ph: 914-539-4010 ▪ Fx: 914-539-4032

Engineering Program Administrators, National Association of
Minority 1133 W Morse Blvd Suite 201 Winter Park FL www.namepa.org
32789
Ph: 407-647-8839 ▪ Fx: 407-629-2502

Engineering Programs & Advocates Network, Women in www.wepan.org
Purdue Univ 1284 CIVL Bldg Rm G167 West Lafayette IN
47907
Ph: 765-494-5387 ▪ Fx: 765-494-9152

Engineering & Science Professors, Association of Environmental www.aeesp.org

Engineering Science Inc, Society of www.sesinc.org
Texas A & M University 701 HR Bright Bldg 3141
TAMU College Station TX 77843
Ph: 979-845-1604

Engineering Societies, American Association of www.aaes.org
1828 L St NW Suite 906 Washington DC 20036
Ph: 202-296-2237 ▪ Fx: 202-296-1151 ▪ TF: 888-400-2237

Engineering Society, Abrasive www.abrasiveengineering.com
144 Moore Rd Butler PA 16001
Ph: 724-282-6210

Engineering, Society for the Advancement of Material & Process org.et.byu.edu/sampe
PO Box 2459 Covina CA 91722
Ph: 626-331-0616 ▪ Fx: 626-332-8929 ▪ TF: 800-562-7360

Engineering Society, American Indian Science & www.aises.org
PO Box 9828 Albuquerque NM 87119
Ph: 505-765-1052 ▪ Fx: 505-765-5608

Engineering Society, American Lebanese
PO Box 690785 Orlando FL 32869
Ph: 407-422-6761 ▪ Fx: 407-422-9664

Engineering Society, IEEE Product Safety ewh.ieee.org/soc/pses
IEEE Operations Ctr 445 Hoes Ln Piscataway NJ 08854
Ph: 732-981-0060 ▪ Fx: 732-981-1721

Engineering Society, Standards www.ses-standards.org
13340 SW 96th Ave Miami FL 33176
Ph: 305-971-4798 ▪ Fx: 305-971-4799

Engineering & Surveying, National Council of Examiners for www.ncees.org
280 Seneca Creek Rd Clemson SC 29633
Ph: 864-654-6824 ▪ Fx: 864-654-6033 ▪ TF: 800-250-3196

Engineering Task Force, Internet www.ietf.cnri.reston.va.us
1895 Preston White Dr Suite 100 Reston VA 20191
Ph: 703-620-8990 ▪ Fx: 703-620-0913

(Engineering) Tau Beta Pi Association www.tbp.org
PO Box 2697 Knoxville TN 37901
Ph: 865-546-4578 ▪ Fx: 865-546-4579 ▪ TF: 800-828-2382

Engineering Technical Society, Junior www.jets.org
1420 King St Suite 405 Alexandria VA 22314
Ph: 703-548-5387 ▪ Fx: 703-548-0769

Engineering Technicians, American Society of Certified www.ascet.com
PO Box 1348 Flowery Branch GA 30542
Ph: 770-967-9173 ▪ Fx: 770-967-8049

Engineering & Technological Sciences Inc, International Council of www.caets.org
Academies of 500 5th St NW Washington DC 20001
Ph: 703-527-5782 ▪ Fx: 703-526-0570

Engineering Technologies, National Institute for Certification in www.nicet.org
1420 King St Alexandria VA 22314
Ph: 703-548-1518 ▪ Fx: 703-682-2756 ▪ TF: 888-476-4238

Engineering & Technology Inc, Accreditation Board for www.abet.org
111 Market Pl Suite 1050 Baltimore MD 21202
Ph: 410-347-7700 ▪ Fx: 410-625-2238

(Engineering Technology) Tau Alpha Pi www.taualphapi.org

Engineering Workforce Commission www.ewc-online.org
American Assn of Engineering Societies 1828 L St NW Suite
906 Washington DC 20036
Ph: 202-296-2237 ▪ Fx: 202-296-1151 ▪ TF: 888-400-2237

Engineers, American Indian Council of Architects & www.aicae.org

Engineers, American Institute of www.members-aie.org
4630 Appian Way Suite 206 El Sobrante CA 94803
Ph: 510-758-6240

Engineers, American Society of Civil www.asce.org
1801 Alexander Bell Dr Reston VA 20191
Ph: 703-295-6000 ▪ Fx: 703-295-6333 ▪ TF: 800-548-2723

Engineers, American Society of Danish
PO Box 606 Larchmont NY 10538
Ph: 914-834-0287 ▪ Fx: 914-834-0513

Engineers, American Society of Highway www.highwayengineers.org
113 Heritage Hills Rd Uniontown PA 15401
Ph: 724-929-2760 ▪ Fx: 724-929-2234

Engineers, American Society of Mechanical www.asme.org
3 Park Ave New York NY 10016
Ph: 212-591-7722 ▪ Fx: 212-591-7739 ▪ TF: 800-843-2763

Engineers, American Society of Naval www.navalengineers.org
1452 Duke St Alexandria VA 22314
Ph: 703-836-6727 ▪ Fx: 703-836-7491

Engineers, American Society of Swedish www.asse-usa.org
780 3rd Ave King of Prussia PA 19406
Ph: 610-265-4352 ▪ Fx: 610-265-4608

Engineers, Association of Cuban www.a-i-c.org
PO Box 557575 Miami FL 33255
Ph: 305-597-9858

Engineers Association, Korean-American Scientists & www.ksea.org
1952 Gallows Rd Suite 300 Vienna VA 22182
Ph: 703-748-1221 ▪ Fx: 703-748-1331

Engineers, Association of Muslim Scientists & www.amse.net
PO Box 38 Plainfield IN 46168
Ph: 517-947-6338

Engineers Associations, National Council of Structural dwp.bigplanet.com/engineers
203 N Wabash Ave Suite 2010 Chicago IL 60601
Ph: 312-372-8035 ▪ Fx: 312-372-5673

Engineers & Designers, Society of Piping www.spedweb.org
1 Main St Suite 719 Houston TX 77002
Ph: 713-221-8089 ▪ Fx: 713-226-5230

Engineers, International Federation of Professional & Technical www.ifpte.org
8630 Fenton St Suite 400 Silver Spring MD 20910
Ph: 301-565-9016 ▪ Fx: 301-565-0018

Engineers, International Union of Operating www.iuoe.org
1125 17th St NW Washington DC 20036
Ph: 202-429-9100 ▪ Fx: 202-778-2616

Engineers, National Association of County www.countyengineers.org
c/o National Assn of Counties 440 1st St NW Washington DC
20001
Ph: 202-393-6226

Engineers, National Association of Power www.powerengineers.com
1 Springfield St Chicopee MA 01013
Ph: 413-592-6273 ▪ Fx: 413-592-1998

Engineers, National Organization for the Professional www.nobcche.org
Advancement of Black Chemists & Chemical PO Box
77040 Washington DC 20013
Ph: 202-667-1699 ▪ Fx: 202-667-1705 ▪ TF: 800-776-1419

Engineers, National Society of Black — www.nsbe.org
1454 Duke St   Alexandria VA 22314
Ph: 703-549-2207 ■ Fx: 703-683-5312

Engineers, National Society of Professional — www.nspe.org
1420 King St   Alexandria VA 22314
Ph: 703-684-2800 ■ Fx: 703-836-4875

Engineers in Private Practice, Professional — www.nspe.org/pepp
1420 King St   Alexandria VA 22314
Ph: 703-684-2804 ■ Fx: 703-836-4875

Engineers & Scientists of America, Armenian — www.aesa.org
417 W Arden Ave Suite 112C   Glendale CA 91203
Ph: 818-547-3372

Engineers & Scientists, National Council of Black — www.ncbes.org
1525 Aviation Blvd Suite C424   Redondo Beach CA 90278
Ph: 213-896-9779

Engineers & Scientists Organizations, Council of — www.cesounions.org/
15205 52nd Ave S   Seattle WA 98188
Ph: 206-433-0991

Engineers Society of America, Ukrainian — www.uesa.org

Engineers, Society of American Military — www.same.org
607 Prince St   Alexandria VA 22314
Ph: 703-549-3800 ■ Fx: 703-684-0231 ■ TF: 800-336-3097

Engineers, Society of Carbide & Tool — www.scte10.org
ASM International 9639 Kinsman Rd   Materials Park OH 44072
Ph: 440-338-5151 ■ Fx: 440-338-4634

Engineers, Society of Hispanic Professional — www.shpe.org
5400 E Olympic Blvd Suite 210   Los Angeles CA 90022
Ph: 323-725-3970 ■ Fx: 323-725-0316

Engineers, Society of Marine Port — www.smpe.org
PO Box 466   Avenel NJ 07001
Ph: 732-381-7673 ■ Fx: 732-381-2046

Engineers, Society of Motion Picture & Television — www.smpte.org
595 W Hartsdale Ave   White Plains NY 10607
Ph: 914-761-1100 ■ Fx: 914-761-3115

Engineers, Society of Petroleum Evaluation — www.spee.org
1001 McKinney St Suite 801   Houston TX 77002
Ph: 713-651-1639 ■ Fx: 713-951-9659

Engineers, Society of Reliability — www.sre.org

Engineers, Society of Women — www.societyofwomenengineers.org
230 E Ohio St Suite 400   Chicago IL 60611
Ph: 312-596-5223 ■ Fx: 312-596-5252

Engineers & Technicians Association, Refrigerating — www.reta.com
4700 W Lake Ave   Glenview IL 60025
Ph: 847-375-4738 ■ Fx: 877-218-8369

English Association, College — www.as.ysu.edu/~english/cea/ceaindex.htm

English, Association of Departments of — www.ade.org
26 Broadway 3rd Fl   New York NY 10004
Ph: 646-576-5130 ■ Fx: 646-834-4045

English Cocker Spaniel Club of America Inc — www.ecsca.org
PO Box 252   Hales Corners WI 53130
Ph: 414-529-9714

English First — www.englishfirst.org
8001 Forbes Pl Suite 102   Springfield VA 22151
Ph: 703-321-8818 ■ Fx: 703-321-7636

English Handbell Ringers Inc, American Guild of — www.agehr.org
1055 E Centerville Stn Rd   Centerville OH 45459
Ph: 937-438-0085 ■ Fx: 937-438-0434 ■ TF: 800-878-5459

English Language Acquisition & Language Instruction Educational Programs, National Clearinghouse for — www.ncela.gwu.edu
George Washington Univ 2121 K St NW Suite 260   Washington DC 20037
Ph: 202-467-0867 ■ Fx: 800-531-9347 ■ TF: 800-321-6223

English Language & Literature, Society for the Preservation of — www.spellorg.com
PO Box 321   Braselton GA 30517
Ph: 770-586-0184 ■ Fx: 770-868-0578

(English Language) Sigma Tau Delta — www.english.org
Northern Illinois Univ Dept of English   DeKalb IL 60115
Ph: 815-753-1612

English in the Liturgy, International Commission on
1522 K St NW Suite 1000   Washington DC 20005
Ph: 202-347-0800

English, National Council of Teachers of — www.ncte.org
1111 W Kenyon Rd   Urbana IL 61801
Ph: 217-328-3870 ■ Fx: 217-328-0977 ■ TF: 800-369-6283

English Sheepdog Club of America Inc, Old — www.oldenglishsheepdogclubofamerica.org
N 64 W 20708 Mill Rd Suite 1015   Menomonee Falls WI 53501
Ph: 262-252-3936

English-Speaking Union of the US — www.english-speakingunion.org
144 E 39th St   New York NY 10006
Ph: 212-818-1200 ■ Fx: 212-867-4177

English Springer Rescue America Inc — www.springerrescue.org
2721 Walker Lee Rd   Los Alamitos CA 90720
Ph: 800-921-1047

English Trade Association, Western- — www.wetaonline.org
451 E 58th Ave Suite 4323   Denver CO 80216
Ph: 303-295-2001 ■ Fx: 303-295-6108

ENGLISH Inc, US — www.us-english.org
1747 Pennsylvania Ave NW Suite 1050   Washington DC 20006
Ph: 202-833-0100 ■ Fx: 202-833-0108 ■ TF: 800-873-4547

Engraved Graphics Association, International — www.iega.org
305 Plus Park Blvd   Nashville TN 37217
Ph: 615-366-1094 ■ Fx: 615-366-4192 ■ TF: 800-821-3138

Engraved Stationery Manufacturers Association
305 Plus Park Blvd   Nashville TN 37217
Ph: 615-366-1094 ■ Fx: 615-366-4192

Engravers Association of the US, Machine Printers &
690 Warren Ave   Providence RI 02914
Ph: 401-438-5849

Engravers Union of North America, International Plate Printers Die Stampers &   14 C St SW Rm 213-5a   Washington DC 20228
Ph: 202-874-2554

Enlightenment, Association for Research & — www.are-cayce.com
215 67th St   Virginia Beach VA 23451
Ph: 757-428-3588 ■ Fx: 757-422-6921 ■ TF: 800-333-4499

(Enlightenment) Astara — www.astara.org
792 W Arrow Hwy   Upland CA 91785
Ph: 909-981-4941 ■ Fx: 909-920-9541

(Enlightenment) SOL Association for Research Inc — www.solarpress.com
PO Box 2276   North Canton OH 44720
Ph: 330-497-9645

Enlisted Association of the National Guard of the US — www.eangus.org
3133 Mt Vernon Ave   Alexandria VA 22305
Ph: 703-519-3846 ■ Fx: 703-519-3849 ■ TF: 800-234-3264

Enlisted Association, Retired — www.trea.org
13130 E Colfax Ave   Aurora CO 80011
Ph: 303-340-3939 ■ Fx: 303-340-4516

Enlisted Reserve Association, Naval — www.nera.org
6703 Farragut Ave   Falls Church VA 22042
Ph: 703-534-1329 ■ Fx: 703-534-3617 ■ TF: 800-776-9020

Eno Transportation Foundation — www.enotrans.com
1634 'I' St NW Suite 500   Washington DC 20006
Ph: 202-879-4700 ■ Fx: 202-879-4719

Enology & Viticulture, American Society for — www.asev.org
PO Box 1855   Davis CA 95617
Ph: 530-753-3142 ■ Fx: 530-753-3318

Enrolled Agents, National Association of — www.naea.org
200 Orchard Ridge Dr Suite 302   Gaithersburg MD 20878
Ph: 301-212-9608 ■ Fx: 301-990-1611 ■ TF: 800-424-4339

Enteral Nutrition, American Society for Parenteral & — www.clinnutr.org
8630 Fenton St Suite 412   Silver Spring MD 20910
Ph: 301-587-6315 ■ Fx: 301-587-2365 ■ TF: 800-727-4567

Enterprise Content Management Association, AIIM International - — www.aiim.org
1100 Wayne Ave Suite 1100   Silver Spring MD 20910
Ph: 301-587-8202 ■ Fx: 301-587-2711 ■ TF: 800-477-2446

Enterprise Development, Foundation for — www.fed.org
2020 K St NW Suite 400   Washington DC 20036
Ph: 202-530-8920 ■ Fx: 202-530-5702

Enterprise Development International — www.endpoverty.org
10395 Democracy Ln   Fairfax VA 22030
Ph: 703-277-3360 ■ Fx: 703-277-3348 ■ TF: 800-936-2253

Enterprise Development, National Center for American Indian — www.ncaied.org
953 E Juanita Ave   Mesa AZ 85204
Ph: 480-545-1298 ■ Fx: 480-545-4208

Enterprise Foundation — www.enterprisefoundation.org
10227 Wincopin Cir Suite 500   Columbia MD 21044
Ph: 410-964-1230 ■ Fx: 410-964-1918 ■ TF: 800-624-4298

Enterprise Integration, Association for — www.afei.org
2111 Wilson Blvd Suite 400   Arlington VA 22201
Ph: 703-247-9474 ■ Fx: 703-522-3192

Enterprise Opportunity, Association for — www.microenterpriseworks.org/
1601 N Kent St Suite 1101   Arlington VA 22209
Ph: 703-841-7760 ■ Fx: 703-841-7748

EnterpriseWorks Worldwide Inc — www.enterpriseworks.org
1828 L St NW Suite 1000   Washington DC 20036
Ph: 202-293-4600 ■ Fx: 202-293-4598

Entertainers for Kids, Athletes & — www.aefk.org
3337 Colorado St   Long Beach CA 90814
Ph: 562-438-5905 ■ Fx: 562-438-9175

Entertainment Association, National Ballroom & — www.nbea.com
2799 Locust Rd   Decorah IA 52101
Ph: 563-382-3871

Entertainment Association, World Airline — www.waea.org
8201 Greensboro Dr Suite 300   McLean VA 22102
Ph: 703-610-9021 ■ Fx: 703-610-9005

(Entertainment) Bread & Roses — www.breadandroses.org
233 Tarnalpais Dr Suite 100   Corte Madera CA 94925
Ph: 415-945-7120 ■ Fx: 415-945-7128

Entertainment Buyers Association, International — www.ieba.org
PO Box 128376   Nashville TN 37212
Ph: 615-463-0161 ■ Fx: 615-463-0163 ■ TF: 888-999-4322

(Entertainment) Friars Club — www.friarsclub.com
57 E 55th St   New York NY 10022
Ph: 212-751-7272 ■ Fx: 212-355-0217

Entertainment Industries Council Inc — eiconline.org
1760 Reston Pkwy Suite 415   Reston VA 20190
Ph: 703-481-1414 ■ Fx: 703-481-1418

Entertainment Industry Educators Association, Music & — www.meiea.org
6363 St Charles Ave PO Box 83   New Orleans LA 70118
Ph: 504-865-3975

Entertainment Industry Foundation — www.eifoundation.org
11132 Ventura Blvd Suite 401   Studio City CA 91604
Ph: 818-760-7722 ■ Fx: 818-760-7898

Entertainment Industry, International Association for the Leisure & — www.ialei.org
33 Henniker St   Hillsborough NH 03244
Ph: 603-464-6498 ■ Fx: 603-464-6497 ■ TF: 888-464-6498

Entertainment Merchants Association, Interactive — www.iema.org
64 Danbury Rd Suite 700   Wilton CT 06897
Ph: 203-761-6780 ■ Fx: 203-761-6184

Entertainment Services & Technology Association — www.esta.org
875 Sixth Ave Suite 1005   New York NY 10001
Ph: 212-244-1505 ■ Fx: 212-244-1502

Entertainment Software Association — www.theesa.com
1211 Connecticut Ave NW Suite 600   Washington DC 20036
Ph: 202-223-2400 ■ Fx: 202-223-2401

Entertainment & Sports Lawyers Association, Black — www.besla.org
PO Box 441485   Fort Washington MD 20749
Ph: 301-248-1818 ■ Fx: 301-248-0700

Enthronement Center, National   communications.sscc.org/enthronement
PO Box 111   Fairhaven MA 02719
Ph: 508-999-2680 ▪ Fx: 508-993-8233

Entomological Society of America   www.entsoc.org
10001 Derekwood Ln Suite 100   Lanham MD 20706
Ph: 301-731-4535 ▪ Fx: 301-731-4538

Entomologists Society, Young   www.members.aol.com/yesbugs/bugclub.html
6907 W Grand River Ave   Lansing MI 48906
Ph: 517-886-0630

Entrepreneurial Parents, National Association of   www.en-parent.com/NAEP.htm
PO Box 320722   Fairfield CT 06432
Ph: 203-371-6212

Entrepreneurs Organization, Young   www.yeo.org
1199 N Fairfax St Suite 200   Alexandria VA 22314
Ph: 703-519-6700 ▪ Fx: 703-519-1864

Entrepreneurs Workshop, Inventors Workshop   www.inventorsworkshop.org
International Education Foundation &   1029 Castillo
St   Santa Barbara CA 93101
Ph: 805-967-5722 ▪ Fx: 805-899-4927

Entrepreneurship Institute   www.tei.net
3592 Corporate Dr Suite 101   Columbus OH 43231
Ph: 614-895-1153 ▪ Fx: 614-895-1473

Envelope Manufacturers Association   www.envelope.org
300 N Washington St Suite 500   Alexandria VA 22314
Ph: 703-739-2200 ▪ Fx: 703-739-2209

Environic Foundation International   www.environicfoundation.org
3503 Hutch Pl   Chevy Chase MD 20815
Ph: 301-654-7160 ▪ Fx: 301-654-3710

(Environment) Access Fund   www.accessfund.org
PO Box 17010   Boulder CO 80308
Ph: 303-545-6772 ▪ Fx: 303-545-6774

Environment, American Public Information on the   www.americanpie.org
316 Oak St PO Box 676   Northfield MN 55057
Ph: 507-645-5616 ▪ Fx: 507-645-5724 ▪ TF: 800-320-2743

Environment Association, New   web.syr.edu/~hs38/neaindex.htm
270 Fenway Dr   Syracuse NY 13224
Ph: 315-446-8009

Environment, Association for the Study of Literature &   www.asle.umn.edu
Davidson College English Dept Box 7056   Davidson NC 28036
Ph: 704-894-2487

Environment Balance Inc, Population-   www.balance.org
2000 P St NW Suite 600   Washington DC 20036
Ph: 202-955-5700 ▪ Fx: 202-955-6161 ▪ TF: 800-866-6269

Environment, Center for Respect of Life &   www.crle.org
2100 L St NW   Washington DC 20037
Ph: 202-778-6133 ▪ Fx: 202-778-6138

Environment Center, World   www.wec.org
419 Park Ave S Suite 500   New York NY 10016
Ph: 212-683-4700 ▪ Fx: 212-683-5053

(Environment) Charles A & Anne Morrow   www.lindberghfoundation.org
Lindbergh Foundation   2150 3rd Ave N Suite 310   Anoka MN
55303
Ph: 763-576-1596 ▪ Fx: 763-576-1664

Environment, Citizens for a Better   www.cbemw.org
152 W Wisconsin Ave Suite 510   Milwaukee WI 53203
Ph: 414-271-7280 ▪ Fx: 414-271-5904 ▪ TF: 866-256-5988

(Environment) Coast Alliance   www.coastalliance.org
600 Pennsylvania Ave SE Suite 340   Washington DC 20003
Ph: 202-546-9554 ▪ Fx: 202-546-9609

(Environment) Cousteau Society   www.cousteausociety.org
710 Settlers Landing Rd   Hampton VA 23669
Ph: 757-722-9300 ▪ Fx: 757-722-8185 ▪ TF: 800-441-4395

(Environment) Earth Island Institute   www.earthisland.org
300 Broadway Suite 28   San Francisco CA 94133
Ph: 415-788-3666 ▪ Fx: 415-788-7324

(Environment) Earth Share   www.earthshare.org
7735 Old Georgetown Rd Suite 900   Bethesda MD 20814
Ph: 240-333-0300 ▪ TF: 800-875-3863

(Environment) Earthwatch Institute   www.earthwatch.org
3 Clock Tower Pl Suite 100   Maynard MA 01754
Ph: 978-461-0081 ▪ Fx: 978-461-2332 ▪ TF: 800-776-0188

Environment Federation, Water   www.wef.org
601 Wythe St   Alexandria VA 22314
Ph: 703-684-2400 ▪ Fx: 703-684-2492 ▪ TF: 800-666-0206

Environment, Foundation for Research on Economics & the   www.free-eco.org
945 Technology Blvd Suite 101F   Bozeman MT 59718
Ph: 406-585-1776 ▪ Fx: 406-585-3000

(Environment) Friends of the Earth Canada   www.foecanada.org
260 Saint Patrick St Suite 206   Ottawa ON K1N5K5
Ph: 613-241-0085 ▪ Fx: 613-241-7998 ▪ TF: 888-385-4444

(Environment) Green Seal   www.greenseal.org
1001 Connecticut Ave NW Suite 827   Washington DC 20036
Ph: 202-872-6400 ▪ Fx: 202-872-4324

(Environment) Greenpeace Canada   www.greenpeace.ca
250 Dundas St W Suite 605   Toronto ON M5T2Z5
Ph: 416-597-8408 ▪ Fx: 416-597-8422 ▪ TF: 800-320-7183

(Environment) Greenpeace USA   www.greenpeace.org
702 H St NW Suite 300   Washington DC 20001
Ph: 202-462-1177 ▪ Fx: 202-462-4507 ▪ TF: 800-326-0959

Environment, Institute for the Human
2572 Acacia Ave   Sonoma CA 95476
Ph: 707-935-9335 ▪ Fx: 707-935-9593

(Environment) Jesse Smith Noyes Foundation   www.noyes.org
6 E 39th St 12th Fl   New York NY 10016
Ph: 212-684-6577 ▪ Fx: 212-689-6549

Environment & Justice, Center for Health   www.chej.org/
PO Box 6806   Falls Church VA 22040
Ph: 703-237-2249 ▪ Fx: 703-237-8389

Environment, Kids for a Clean   www.kidsface.org
PO Box 158254   Nashville TN 37215
Ph: 615-331-7381 ▪ Fx: 615-333-9879 ▪ TF: 800-952-3223

(Environment) National Anxiety Center   www.anxietycenter.com
9 Brookside Rd   Maplewood NJ 07040
Ph: 973-763-6392 ▪ Fx: 973-763-4287

Environment, Quebec-Labrador Foundation - Atlantic Center for the   www.qlf.org
55 S Main St   Ipswich MA 01938
Ph: 978-356-0038 ▪ Fx: 978-356-7322

(Environment) Rare   www.rarecenter.org
1840 Wilson Blvd Suite 204   Arlington VA 22201
Ph: 703-522-5070 ▪ Fx: 703-522-5027

Environment, Responsible Industry for a Sound   www.pestfacts.org
1156 15th St NW Suite 400   Washington DC 20005
Ph: 202-872-3860 ▪ Fx: 202-463-0474

Environment & Safety, Beach Education Advocates for   www.beachesfoundation.org
Culture Health   PO Box 530702   Miami Shores FL 33153
Ph: 305-893-8838 ▪ Fx: 305-893-8823

Environment & Security, Pacific Institute for Studies in Development   www.pacinst.org
654 13th St   Oakland CA 94612
Ph: 510-251-1600 ▪ Fx: 510-251-2203

(Environment) Surfrider Foundation USA   www.surfrider.org
122 S El Camino Real Suite 67   San Clemente CA 92672
Ph: 949-492-8170 ▪ Fx: 949-492-8142 ▪ TF: 800-743-7873

(Environment) Thornton W Burgess Society   www.thorntonburgess.org
6 Discovery Hill Rd   East Sandwich MA 02537
Ph: 508-888-6870 ▪ Fx: 508-888-1919

(Environment) Windstar Foundation   www.wstar.org
PO Box 656   Snowmass CO 81654
Ph: 970-927-5435

Environment, Women's Council on Energy & the   www.wcee.org
PO Box 33211   Washington DC 20033
Ph: 703-351-7850

Environmental Action Coalition, Student   www.seac.org
PO Box 31909   Philadelphia PA 19104
Ph: 215-222-4711

Environmental Alliance for Senior Involvement   www.easi.org
PO Box 250   Catlett VA 20119
Ph: 540-788-3274 ▪ Fx: 540-788-9301

Environmental Assessment Association   www.iami.org/eaa.html
1224 N Nokomis NE   Alexandria MN 56308
Ph: 320-763-5190 ▪ Fx: 320-763-9290

Environmental Assistance Foundation, Legal   www.leaflaw.org
1114 Thomasville Rd Suite E   Tallahassee FL 32303
Ph: 850-681-2591 ▪ Fx: 850-224-1275

Environmental Balancing Bureau, National   www.nebb.org
8575 Grovemont Cir   Gaithersburg MD 20877
Ph: 301-977-3698 ▪ Fx: 301-977-9589

Environmental Bankers Association   www.envirobank.org
510 King St Suite 410   Alexandria VA 22314
Ph: 703-549-0977 ▪ Fx: 703-548-5945

Environmental Building Association, Energy &   www.eeba.org
10740 Lyndale Ave S Suite 10W   Bloomington MN 55420
Ph: 952-881-1098 ▪ Fx: 952-881-3048

Environmental Careers Organization   www.eco.org
179 South St   Boston MA 02111
Ph: 617-426-4375 ▪ Fx: 617-423-0998

Environmental Clinics, Association of Occupational &   www.aoec.org
1010 Vermont Ave NW Suite 513   Washington DC 20005
Ph: 202-347-4976 ▪ Fx: 202-347-4950 ▪ TF: 888-347-2632

Environmental Conservation, Society Promoting   www.spec.bc.ca
2150 Maple St   Vancouver BC V6J3T3
Ph: 604-736-7732 ▪ Fx: 604-736-7115

Environmental Consultants, National Society of   nsec.lincoln-grad.org
303 W Cypress St   San Antonio TX 78212
Ph: 210-271-0781 ▪ Fx: 210-225-8450 ▪ TF: 800-486-3676

Environmental Council, Community   www.communityenvironmentalcouncil.org
930 Miramonte Dr   Santa Barbara CA 93109
Ph: 805-963-0583 ▪ Fx: 805-962-9080

Environmental Council, National Tribal   www.ntec.org
2501 Rio Grande Blvd NW Suite A   Albuquerque NM 87104
Ph: 505-242-2175 ▪ Fx: 505-242-2654

Environmental Council of the States   www.sso.org/ecos
444 N Capitol St NW Suite 445   Washington DC 20001
Ph: 202-624-3660 ▪ Fx: 202-624-3666

Environmental Defense   www.environmentaldefense.org
257 Park Ave S 17th Fl   New York NY 10010
Ph: 212-505-2100 ▪ Fx: 212-505-2375 ▪ TF: 800-225-5333

Environmental Design Research Association   home.telepath.com/~edra
PO Box 7146   Edmond OK 73083
Ph: 405-330-4863 ▪ Fx: 405-330-4150

Environmental Education, National Association for Humane &   www.nahee.org
PO Box 362   East Haddam CT 06423
Ph: 860-434-8666 ▪ Fx: 860-434-9579

Environmental Education, North American Association for   www.naaee.org
1707 H St NW Suite 900   Washington DC 20006
Ph: 202-261-6481 ▪ Fx: 202-261-6464

Environmental Education & Training Foundation, National   www.neetf.org
1707 H St NW Suite 900   Washington DC 20006
Ph: 202-833-2933 ▪ Fx: 202-261-6464

Environmental & Energy Study Institute   www.eesi.org
122 C St NW Suite 722   Washington DC 20001
Ph: 202-628-6500 ▪ Fx: 202-737-5299

Environmental Energy Systems, Association for Efficient   www.aeees.org
PO Box 598   Davis CA 95617
Ph: 530-750-0135 ▪ Fx: 530-750-0137

Environmental & Engineering Geophysical Society   www.eegs.org
1720 S Bellaire St Suite 110   Denver CO 80222
Ph: 303-531-7517 ▪ Fx: 303-820-3844

Environmental Engineering, Inter-American Association of   www.aidis-usa.org
Sanitary &   601 Wythe St   Alexandria VA 22314
Ph: 703-684-2400

Environmental Engineering & Science Professors, Association of   www.aeesp.org

Environmental Engineers, American Academy of   www.enviro-engrs.org
130 Holiday Ct Suite 100   Annapolis MD 21401
Ph: 410-266-3311   Fx: 410-266-7653

Environmental Ethics, Forest Service Employees for   www.fseee.org
PO Box 11615   Eugene OR 97440
Ph: 541-484-2692   Fx: 541-484-3004

Environmental Geochemistry & Health, Society for   www.segh.net
4698 S Forrest Ave   Springfield MO 65810
Ph: 417-885-1166   Fx: 417-881-6920

Environmental Graphic Design, Society for   www.segd.org
1000 Vermont Ave Suite 400   Washington DC 20005
Ph: 202-638-5555   Fx: 202-638-0891

Environmental Health Administrators, National   depts.washington.edu/clehaweb
Conference of Local   Univ of Washington Dept of
   Environmental Health CB 357234   Seattle WA 98195
Ph: 206-616-2097   Fx: 206-616-8123

Environmental Health Association, National   www.neha.org
720 S Colorado Blvd Suite 970S   Denver CO 80246
Ph: 303-756-9090   Fx: 303-691-9490

Environmental Health & Safety Council of North America, Silicones   www.sehsc.com
11921 Freedom Dr Suite 550   Reston VA 20190
Ph: 703-904-4322   Fx: 703-925-5955

Environmental Health & Sciences, Association for   www.aehs.com
150 S Fearing St   Amherst MA 01002
Ph: 413-549-5170   Fx: 413-549-0579

Environmental Health, Society for Occupational &   www.soeh.org
6728 Old McLean Village Dr   McLean VA 22101
Ph: 703-556-9222   Fx: 703-556-8729

Environmental Health Strategies, National Center for   www.ncehs.org
1100 Rural Ave   Voorhees NJ 08043
Ph: 856-429-5358

Environmental History, American   www.h-net.org/~environ/ASEH/welcome_IE4.html
Society for   119 Pine St Suite 207   Seattle WA 98101
Ph: 206-343-0226   Fx: 206-343-0249

Environmental Industry Associations   www.envasns.org
4301 Connecticut Ave NW Suite 300   Washington DC 20008
Ph: 202-244-4700   Fx: 202-966-4818   TF: 800-927-5007

Environmental Information Association   www.eia-usa.org
4915 Auburn Ave Suite 204   Bethesda MD 20814
Ph: 301-961-4999   Fx: 301-961-3094

Environmental Information, Center for   www.rochesterenvironment.org
55 Saint Paul St   Rochester NY 14604
Ph: 716-262-2870   Fx: 716-262-4156

Environmental Journalists, Society of   www.sej.org
321 Old York Rd Suite 200   Jenkintown PA 19046
Ph: 215-884-8174   Fx: 215-884-8175

Environmental Law Alliance Worldwide   www.elaw.org
1877 Garden Ave   Eugene OR 97403
Ph: 541-687-8454   Fx: 541-687-0535

Environmental Law, Center for International   www.ciel.org
1367 Connecticut Ave NW Suite 300   Washington DC 20036
Ph: 202-785-8700   Fx: 202-785-8701

Environmental Law Institute   www.eli.org
1616 P St NW Suite 200   Washington DC 20036
Ph: 202-939-3800   Fx: 202-939-3868   TF: 800-433-5120

Environmental Law Societies, National Association of   www.naels.org

Environmental Management Association   www.emaweb.org
38575 Mallast St   Harrison Township MI 48045
Ph: 866-999-4362

Environmental Management, National Association for   www.naem.org
1612 K St NW Suite 1102   Washington DC 20006
Ph: 202-986-6616   Fx: 202-530-4408   TF: 800-391-6236

Environmental Medicine, American Academy of   www.aaem.com
7701 E Kellogg Dr Suite 625   Wichita KS 67207
Ph: 316-684-5500   Fx: 316-684-5709

Environmental Medicine, American   www.americanboardofenvironmentalmedicine.org
Board of   65 Wehrle Dr   Buffalo NY 14225
Ph: 716-833-2213   Fx: 716-833-2244

Environmental Medicine, American College of Occupational &   www.acoem.org
1114 N Arlington Heights Rd   Arlington Heights IL 60004
Ph: 847-818-1800   Fx: 847-818-9266

Environmental Mutagen Society   www.ems-us.org
1821 Michael Faraday Dr Suite 330   Reston VA 20190
Ph: 703-438-8220   Fx: 703-438-3113

Environmental Network, Indigenous   www.ienearth.org
PO Box 485   Bemidji MN 56601
Ph: 218-751-4967   Fx: 218-751-0561

Environmental Packaging Association, International Molded Pulp   www.impepa.org
1425 W Mequon Rd Suite A   Mequon WI 53092
Ph: 262-241-0522   Fx: 262-241-3766

Environmental Policy Project, Science &   www.sepp.org
1600 S Eads St Suite 712-S   Arlington VA 22202
Ph: 703-920-2744

(Environmental Policy) World Resources Institute   www.wri.org
10 G St NE Suite 800   Washington DC 20002
Ph: 202-729-7600   Fx: 202-729-7610

Environmental Practice, Institute of Professional   www.ipep.org
600 Forbes Ave 333 Fisher Hall   Pittsburgh PA 15282
Ph: 412-396-1703   Fx: 412-396-1704

Environmental Professionals, National Association of   www.naep.org
PO Box 2086   Bowie MD 20718
Ph: 301-860-1140   Fx: 301-860-1141   TF: 888-251-9902

Environmental Professionals, National Association of Local   www.nalgep.org/
Government   1333 New Hampshire Ave NW Suite
   1100   Washington DC 20036
Ph: 202-638-6254   Fx: 202-393-2866

Environmental Professionals, National Registry of   www.nrep.org
PO Box 2099   Glenview IL 60025
Ph: 847-724-6631   Fx: 847-724-4223

Environmental Protection Information Center   www.wildcalifornia.org
PO Box 397   Garberville CA 95542
Ph: 707-923-2931   Fx: 707-923-4210

Environmental & Resource Economists, Association of   www.aere.org/
1616 P St NW Rm 400   Washington DC 20036
Ph: 202-328-5077   Fx: 202-939-3460

Environmental Safety & Health Association, Semiconductor   seshaonline.org
1313 Dolley Madison Blvd Suite 402   McLean VA 22101
Ph: 703-790-1745   Fx: 703-790-2672

Environmental & Safety Technologies, Council on Certification   www.cchest.org
of Health   208 Burwash Ave   Savoy IL 61874
Ph: 217-359-2686   Fx: 217-359-0055

Environmental Sanity, Youth for   www.yesworld.org
420 Bronco Rd   Soquel CA 95073
Ph: 877-293-7226   Fx: 831-462-6970

Environmental Sciences & Technology, Institute of   www.iest.org
5005 Newport Dr Suite 506   Rolling Meadows IL 60008
Ph: 847-255-1561   Fx: 847-255-1699

Environmental Services, American Society for Healthcare   www.ashes.org
1 N Franklin St Suite 2800   Chicago IL 60606
Ph: 312-422-3860   Fx: 312-422-4577

Environmental Study, Center for   www.cesmi.org
528 Bridge St NW Suite 1C   Grand Rapids MI 49504
Ph: 616-988-2854   Fx: 616-988-2857

(Environmental Sustainability) Planet Drum Foundation   www.planetdrum.org
PO Box 31251   San Francisco CA 94131
Ph: 415-285-6556   Fx: 415-285-6563

Environmental Technologists, Federation of   www.fetinc.org
PO Box 624   Slinger WI 53086
Ph: 262-644-0070   Fx: 262-644-7106

Environmental Technology Council   www.etc.org
734 15th St NW Suite 720   Washington DC 20005
Ph: 202-783-0870   Fx: 202-737-2038

Environmental Toxicology & Chemistry, Society of   www.setac.org
1010 N 12th Ave   Pensacola FL 32501
Ph: 850-469-1500   Fx: 850-469-9778   TF: 888-899-2088

Environmental Training Association, National   www.ehs-training.org
5320 N 16th St Suite 114   Phoenix AZ 85016
Ph: 602-956-6099   Fx: 602-956-6399

Environmental Traveling Companions   www.etctrips.org
Fort Mason Ctr Landmark Bldg C   San Francisco CA 94123
Ph: 415-474-7662   Fx: 415-474-3919

Environmental Trust, National   www.net.org
1200 18th St NW 5th Fl   Washington DC 20036
Ph: 202-887-8800   Fx: 202-887-8877

Environmental Working Group   www.ewg.org
1436 U St NW Suite 100   Washington DC 20009
Ph: 202-667-6982   Fx: 202-232-2592

Environmental Writers - College & University Educators, Nature &   www.new-cue.org
Saint Thomas Aquinas College   Sparkill NY 10976
Ph: 845-398-4247   Fx: 845-398-4224

Environmentally Responsible Economies, Coalition for   www.ceres.org
99 Chauncy St 6th Fl   Boston MA 02111
Ph: 617-247-0700   Fx: 617-267-5400

Epidemiologic Research, Society for   www.epiresearch.org
PO Box 990   Clearfield UT 84098
Ph: 801-525-0231   Fx: 801-774-9211

Epidemiologists, Council of State & Territorial   www.cste.org
2872 Woodcock Blvd Suite 303   Atlanta GA 30341
Ph: 770-458-3811   Fx: 770-458-8516

Epidemiology of America, Society for Healthcare   www.shea-online.org
19 Mantua Rd   Mount Royal NJ 08061
Ph: 856-423-0087   Fx: 856-423-3420

Epidemiology, American College of   www.acepidemiology.org
1500 Sunday Dr Suite 102   Raleigh NC 27607
Ph: 919-861-5573   Fx: 919-861-4916

Epidemiology Inc, Association for Professionals in Infection Control &   www.apic.org
1275 K St NW Suite 1000   Washington DC 20005
Ph: 202-789-1890   Fx: 202-789-1899   TF: 888-278-2742

Epilepsy Foundation   www.epilepsyfoundation.org
4351 Garden City Dr   Landover MD 20785
Ph: 301-459-3700   Fx: 301-577-2684   TF: 800-332-1000

Epilepsy Society, American   www.aesnet.org
342 N Main St   West Hartford CT 06117
Ph: 860-586-7505   Fx: 860-586-7550

Epiphyllum Society of America   www.epiphyllum.org
PO Box 1395   Monrovia CA 91017
Ph: 310-670-8148

Episcopal Actors' Guild of America Inc   www.actorsguild.org
1 E 29th St   New York NY 10016
Ph: 212-685-2927   Fx: 212-685-8793

Episcopal AIDS Coalition, National   www.neac.org
520 Clinton Ave   Brooklyn NY 11238
Ph: 718-857-9445   Fx: 718-638-3039   TF: 800-588-6628

Episcopal Church, Historical Society of the   www.hsec-usa.org
PO Box 2247   Manchaca TX 78652
Ph: 512-282-3234   Fx: 512-280-3902   TF: 800-553-7745

Episcopal Church Missionary Community   www.episcopalian.org/ecmc
PO Box 278   Ambridge PA 15003
Ph: 724-266-2810   Fx: 724-266-6773

Episcopal Church USA   www.ecusa.anglican.org
815 2nd Ave   New York NY 10017
Ph: 212-716-6000   Fx: 212-867-0395   TF: 800-334-7626

Episcopal Colleges, Association of   www.cuac.org/aec
815 2nd Ave Suite 315   New York NY 10017
Ph: 212-716-6148   Fx: 212-986-5039

Episcopal Evangelical Education Society   members.aol.com/eeesociety/EEESPAGE.html
2300 9th St S Suite 301   Arlington VA 22204
Ph: 703-521-3264   Fx: 703-521-6758

(Episcopal) Faith Alive — www.faithalive.org
431 Richmond Pl NE   Albuquerque NM 87106
Ph: 505-255-3233 ▪ Fx: 505-255-2282

Episcopal Migration Ministries — demo.episcopalchurch.org/emm
815 2nd Ave   New York NY 10017
Ph: 212-716-6252 ▪ Fx: 212-972-0860 ▪ TF: 800-334-7626

Episcopal Relief & Development — www.er-d.org
815 2nd Ave   New York NY 10017
Ph: 212-867-8400 ▪ Fx: 212-983-6377 ▪ TF: 800-334-7626

Episcopal Schools, National Association of — www.episcopalschools.org
815 2nd Ave Suite 313   New York NY 10017
Ph: 212-716-6134 ▪ Fx: 212-286-9366 ▪ TF: 800-334-7626

EPS Molders Association — www.epsmolders.org
1298 Cronson Blvd Suite 201   Crofton MD 21114
Ph: 410-451-8341 ▪ Fx: 410-451-8343 ▪ TF: 800-607-3772

Epsilon Sigma Alpha International — www.esaintl.com
363 W Drake Rd   Fort Collins CO 80526
Ph: 970-223-2824 ▪ Fx: 970-223-4456

Epsilon Sigma Phi — espnational.org
PO Box 357340   Gainesville FL 32635
Ph: 352-378-6665 ▪ Fx: 352-375-0722

Equal Employment Advisory Council — www.eeac.org
1015 15th St NW Suite 1200   Washington DC 20005
Ph: 202-789-8650 ▪ Fx: 202-789-2291

Equal Justice Works — www.equaljusticeworks.org
2120 L St Suite 450   Washington DC 20037
Ph: 202-466-3686 ▪ Fx: 202-429-9766

Equal Opportunity, Center for — www.ceousa.org
14 Pidgeon Hill Dr Suite 500   Sterling VA 20165
Ph: 703-421-5443 ▪ Fx: 703-421-6401

Equal Opportunity in Higher Education, National Association for — www.nafeo.org
8701 Georgia Ave Suite 200   Silver Spring MD 20910
Ph: 301-650-2440 ▪ Fx: 301-495-3306

Equal Rights Advocates — www.equalrights.org
1663 Mission St Suite 250   San Francisco CA 94103
Ph: 415-621-0672 ▪ Fx: 415-621-6744

Equality Inc, Project — www.projectequality.org
7132 Main St   Kansas City MO 64114
Ph: 816-361-9222 ▪ Fx: 816-361-8997

Equestrian Association, American Medical — www.ameaonline.org
PO Box 130848   Birmingham AL 35213
Ph: 866-441-2632

Equestrian Association, Gladstone
PO Box 119   Gladstone NJ 07934
Ph: 908-234-0151 ▪ Fx: 908-234-0863

Equestrian Federation Inc, US — www.usef.org
4047 Iron Works Pkwy   Lexington KY 40511
Ph: 859-225-6900 ▪ Fx: 859-231-6662

(Equestrian Sports) US Eventing Association — www.eventingusa.com
525 Old Waterford Rd NW   Leesburg VA 20176
Ph: 703-779-0440 ▪ Fx: 703-779-0550

Equestrian Team, US — www.uset.org
PO Box 355   Gladstone NJ 07934
Ph: 908-234-1251 ▪ Fx: 908-234-9417

Equilibration Society, American — www.occlusion-tmj.org
8726 N Ferris Ave   Morton Grove IL 60053
Ph: 847-965-2888 ▪ Fx: 847-965-4888

Equine Advocates — www.equineadvocates.com
PO Box 700   Bedford NY 10506
Ph: 845-278-3095

Equine Appraisers, American Society of — www.equineappraiser.com
1126 Eastland Dr N Suite 100 PO Box 186   Twin Falls ID 93303
Ph: 208-733-2323 ▪ Fx: 208-733-2326 ▪ TF: 800-704-7020

Equine Art, American Academy of — www.aaea.net
4089 Iron Works Pkwy   Lexington KY 40511
Ph: 859-281-6031 ▪ Fx: 859-281-6043

Equine Association, American
PO Box 658   Newfoundland NJ 07435
Ph: 973-948-7005 ▪ Fx: 973-697-1538

Equine Practitioners, American Association of — www.aaep.org
4075 Iron Works Pkwy   Lexington KY 40511
Ph: 859-233-0147 ▪ Fx: 859-233-1968 ▪ TF: 800-443-0177

Equine Rescue League Inc — erl.freeyellow.com
PO Box 4366   Leesburg VA 20177
Ph: 703-771-1240

Equipment Appraisers, Association of Machinery & — www.amea.org
315 S Patrick St   Alexandria VA 22314
Ph: 703-836-7900 ▪ Fx: 703-836-9303 ▪ TF: 800-537-8629

Equipment Dealers Association, North American — www.naeda.com
1195 Smizer Mill Rd   Fenton MO 63026
Ph: 636-349-5000 ▪ Fx: 636-349-5443

Equipment Dealers, International Association of Used — www.iaued.org
214 Edgewood Dr Suite 100   Wilmington DE 19809
Ph: 302-765-3471

Equipment Distributors, Associated — www.aednet.org
615 W 22nd St   Oak Brook IL 60523
Ph: 630-574-0650 ▪ Fx: 630-574-0132 ▪ TF: 800-388-0650

Equipment Leasing Association of America — www.elaonline.org
4301 N Fairfax Dr Suite 550   Arlington VA 22203
Ph: 703-527-8655 ▪ Fx: 703-527-2649

Equipment Leasing Brokers, National Association of — www.naelb.org
5024-R Campbell Blvd   Baltimore MD 21236
Ph: 410-931-8100 ▪ Fx: 410-931-8111 ▪ TF: 800-996-2352

Equipment Leasing, United Association of — www.uael.org
78120 Calle Estado Suite 201   La Quinta CA 92253
Ph: 760-564-2227 ▪ Fx: 760-564-2206

Equipment Management Professionals, Association of — www.equipment.org
410 20th St Suite 102   Glenwood Springs CO 81601
Ph: 970-384-0510 ▪ Fx: 970-384-0512

Equipment Managers Council of America — www.emca.org
PO Box 794   South Amboy NJ 08879
Ph: 908-309-3905 ▪ Fx: 732-721-0754

Equipment Manufacturers, Association of — www.aem.org
111 E Wisconsin Ave Suite 1000   Milwaukee WI 53202
Ph: 414-272-0943 ▪ Fx: 414-272-1170

Equipment Manufacturers Association, Converting — www.cema-converting.org
2166 Gold Hill Rd   Fort Mill SC 29708
Ph: 803-802-7820 ▪ Fx: 803-802-7821

Equipment Manufacturers Association, Farm — www.farmequip.org
1000 Executive Pkwy Suite 100   Saint Louis MO 63141
Ph: 314-878-2304 ▪ Fx: 314-878-1742

Equipment Manufacturers Association, Motor & — www.mema.org
10 Laboratory Dr PO Box 13966   Research Triangle Park NC 27709
Ph: 919-549-4800 ▪ Fx: 919-549-4824 ▪ TF: 800-227-4655

Equipment Market Association, Specialty — www.sema.org
1575 S Valley Vista Dr   Diamond Bar CA 91765
Ph: 909-396-0289 ▪ Fx: 909-860-0184

Equipment Service Association — www.2esa.org
5264 Crystal Creek Dr   Pace FL 32571
Ph: 850-995-1996 ▪ Fx: 850-995-7099

Equipment & Tool Institute — www.etools.org
10 Laboratory Dr   Research Triangle Park NC 27709
Ph: 919-406-8844 ▪ Fx: 919-406-1306

Equitable Reserve Association — www.equitablereserve.com
116 S Commercial St PO Box 448   Neenah WI 54957
Ph: 920-722-1574 ▪ Fx: 920-722-5400 ▪ TF: 800-722-1574

Equity Source Banks, National Association of
10451 Mill Run Cir Suite 400   Owings Mills MD 21117
Ph: 410-581-1373

Equus, Project — www.projectequus.org
PO Box 18030   Boulder CO 80308
Ph: 720-565-2889

Erb's Palsy Association Inc, National Brachial Plexus/ — www.nbpepa.org
PO Box 23   Larsen WI 54947
Ph: 920-836-2151

Erectors Association, Metal Building Contractors & — www.mbcea.org
28 Lowry Dr PO Box 117   West Milton OH 45383
Ph: 937-698-4127 ▪ Fx: 937-698-6153 ▪ TF: 800-866-6722

Erectors Fabricators & Riggers, National Council of
10382 Main St Suite 200 PO Box 280   Fairfax VA 22030
Ph: 703-591-1870 ▪ Fx: 703-591-1895

Ergonomics Society, Human Factors & — hfes.org
PO Box 1369   Santa Monica CA 90406
Ph: 310-394-1811 ▪ Fx: 310-394-2410

Erickson Milton H Foundation Inc — www.erickson-foundation.org
3606 N 24th St   Phoenix AZ 85016
Ph: 602-956-6196 ▪ Fx: 602-956-0519

ERISA Industry Committee — www.eric.org
1400 L St NW Suite 350   Washington DC 20005
Ph: 202-789-1400 ▪ Fx: 202-789-1120

Erosion Control Association, International — www.ieca.org
3001 S Lincoln Ave Suite A   Steamboat Springs CO 80487
Ph: 970-879-3010 ▪ Fx: 970-879-8563 ▪ TF: 800-455-4322

Errants, Citizens United for Rehabilitation of — www.curenational.org
PO Box 2310   Washington DC 20013
Ph: 202-789-2126

Errors Freaks & Oddities Collector's Club — www.efoers.org
955 S Grove Blvd Suite 65   Kingsland GA 31548
Ph: 912-729-1573 ▪ Fx: 912-729-1585

Escalator Safety Foundation, Elevator — www.eesf.org
362 Pinehill Dr   Mobile AL 36606
Ph: 334-479-2199 ▪ TF: 888-743-3723

Escapees RV Club — www.escapees.com
100 Rainbow Dr   Livingston TX 77351
Ph: 936-327-8873 ▪ Fx: 936-327-4388 ▪ TF: 888-757-2582

ESM Association — www.esmassn.org
2211 York Rd Suite 207   Oak Brook IL 60523
Ph: 630-368-1280 ▪ Fx: 630-368-1286

ESOP Association — www.esopassociation.org
1726 M St NW Suite 501   Washington DC 20036
Ph: 202-293-2971 ▪ Fx: 202-293-7568 ▪ TF: 866-366-3832

ESOP Association PAC
1726 M St NW Suite 501   Washington DC 20036
Ph: 202-293-2971 ▪ Fx: 202-293-7568

Esophagological Association, American Broncho- — www.abea.net
Univ of Utah Div of Otolaryngology 50 N Medical Dr
   3C120   Salt Lake City UT 84132
Ph: 801-581-7514 ▪ Fx: 801-585-5744

Esperantic Studies Foundation — www.esperantic.org

Esperanto, American Association of Teachers of
5140 San Lorenzo Dr   Santa Barbara CA 93111
Ph: 805-967-5241

Esperanto League for North America — www.esperanto-usa.org
PO Box 1129   El Cerrito CA 94530
Ph: 510-653-0998 ▪ Fx: 510-653-1468 ▪ TF: 800-377-3726

Espionage Controls & Countermeasures Association, Business — www.becca-online.org
PO Box 55582   Shoreline WA 98155
Ph: 206-364-4672 ▪ Fx: 206-367-3316

Espionage Research Institute — www.espionbusiness.com
10903 Indian Head Hwy Suite 304   Fort Washington MD 20744
Ph: 301-292-6430 ▪ Fx: 301-292-4635

Essential Information Inc — www.essential.org
PO Box 19405   Washington DC 20036
Ph: 202-387-8030 ▪ Fx: 202-234-5176

Essential Schools, Coalition of — www.essentialschools.org/
1814 Franklin St Suite 700   Oakland CA 94612
Ph: 510-433-1451 ▪ Fx: 510-433-1455

Estate Counsel, American College of Trust & www.actec.org
3415 S Sepulveda Blvd Suite 330   Los Angeles CA 90034
Ph: 310-398-1888 ▪ Fx: 310-572-7280

Estate Planners & Councils, National Association of www.naepc.org
1120 Chester Ave Suite 470   Cleveland OH 44114
Ph: 866-226-2224 ▪ Fx: 216-696-2582

Estate Planning Attorneys, American Academy of www.aaepa.com/
4365 Executive Dr Suite 850   San Diego CA 92121
Ph: 800-846-1555 ▪ Fx: 858-535-8241

Estate Planning Attorneys Inc, National Network of www.netplanning.com
1 Valmont Plaza 4th Fl   Omaha NE 68154
Ph: 402-964-3700 ▪ Fx: 402-964-3800 ▪ TF: 888-837-4090

Estate Planning, National Association of Financial & www.nafep.com
525 E 4500 S Suite F-100   Salt Lake City UT 84107
Ph: 801-266-9900 ▪ Fx: 801-266-1019

Esthetic Dentistry, American Academy of www.estheticacademy.org
401 N Michigan Ave   Chicago IL 60611
Ph: 312-321-5121 ▪ Fx: 312-673-6952

Estimators, American Society of Professional www.aspenational.com
11141 Georgia Ave Suite 412   Wheaton MD 20902
Ph: 301-929-8848 ▪ Fx: 301-929-0231 ▪ TF: 800-378-4628

Estimators Association of America, Professional Construction www.pcea.org
PO Box 680336   Charlotte NC 28216
Ph: 704-987-9978 ▪ Fx: 704-987-9979 ▪ TF: 877-521-7232

Estonian American Fund for Economic Education
4 Noyes Ct   Silver Spring MD 20910
Ph: 301-587-9115 ▪ Fx: 301-587-0730

Estonian American National Council Inc www.estosite.org
243 E 34th St   New York NY 10016
Ph: 212-685-0776 ▪ Fx: 212-683-4418

Estonian Relief Committee Inc
243 E 34th St   New York NY 10016
Ph: 212-685-7467 ▪ Fx: 212-683-4418

Estuarine Research Federation www.erf.org
2018 Daffodil Rd PO Box 510   Port Republic MD 20676
Ph: 410-586-0997 ▪ Fx: 410-586-9226

Eta Kappa Nu Association www.hkn.org
PO Box 3535   Lisle IL 60532
Ph: 800-406-2590 ▪ Fx: 800-864-2051

Eta Sigma Gamma www.bsu.edu/web/esg
2000 University Ave   Muncie IN 47306
Ph: 765-285-2258 ▪ Fx: 765-285-3210 ▪ TF: 800-715-2559

ETAD North America www.etad.com
1850 M St NW Suite 700   Washington DC 20036
Ph: 202-721-4154 ▪ Fx: 202-296-8120

Etch A Sketch Club www.etch-a-sketch.com
Ohio Art Co 1 Toy St PO Box 111   Bryan OH 43506
Ph: 419-636-3141 ▪ Fx: 419-636-7614 ▪ TF: 800-641-6226

Etchells Class Association Inc, International www.etchells.org
PO Box 676   Jamestown RI 02835
Ph: 401-560-0022 ▪ Fx: 401-560-0013

Ethical Education, Council for Spiritual & www.csee.org
1465 Northside Dr Suite 220   Atlanta GA 30318
Ph: 404-355-4460 ▪ Fx: 404-355-4435 ▪ TF: 800-298-4599

Ethical & Religious Values in Counseling, Association for Spiritual www.aservic.org
c/o American Counseling Assn 5999 Stevenson Ave   Alexandria
VA 22304
Ph: 703-823-9800 ▪ Fx: 703-823-0252 ▪ TF: 800-347-6647

Ethical Research, International Foundation for www.ifer.org
53 W Jackson Blvd Suite 1552   Chicago IL 60604
Ph: 312-427-6025 ▪ Fx: 312-427-6524

Ethical Treatment of Animals, People for the www.peta-online.org
501 Front St   Norfolk VA 23510
Ph: 757-622-7382 ▪ Fx: 757-628-0782 ▪ TF: 800-483-4366

Ethical Treatment of Animals, Psychologists for the www.psyeta.org
PO Box 1297   Washington Grove MD 20880
Ph: 301-963-4751

Ethical Union, American www.aeu.org
2 W 64th St   New York NY 10023
Ph: 212-873-6500 ▪ Fx: 212-362-0850

Ethics, American Society of Law Medicine & www.aslme.org
765 Commonwealth Ave 16th Fl   Boston MA 02215
Ph: 617-262-4990 ▪ Fx: 617-437-7596

Ethics, Americans for the Enforcement of Attorney rentamark.com/aeae
PO Box 35189   Chicago IL 60707
Ph: 773-283-3880

Ethics, Association for Practical & Professional php.ucs.indiana.edu/~appe/home.html
618 E 3rd St   Bloomington IN 47405
Ph: 812-855-6450 ▪ Fx: 812-855-3315

Ethics, Center for Cognitive Liberty & www.cognitiveliberty.org
PO Box 73481   Davis CA 95617
Ph: 530-750-7912 ▪ TF: 888-950-6463

Ethics in Economics, Council for www.businessethics.org
191 W Nationwide Blvd Suite 300B   Columbus OH 43215
Ph: 614-221-8661 ▪ Fx: 614-221-8707

Ethics, Forest Service Employees for Environmental www.fseee.org
PO Box 11615   Eugene OR 97440
Ph: 541-484-2692 ▪ Fx: 541-484-3004

Ethics & International Affairs, Carnegie Council on www.carnegiecouncil.org
Merrill House 170 E 64th St   New York NY 10021
Ph: 212-838-4120 ▪ Fx: 212-752-2432

Ethics Laws, Council on Governmental www.cogel.org
PO Box 417   Locust Grove VA 22508
Ph: 540-972-3662 ▪ Fx: 540-972-3693

Ethics Inc, Leave No Trace Center for Outdoor www.lnt.org
PO Box 997   Boulder CO 80306
Ph: 303-442-8222 ▪ Fx: 303-442-8217 ▪ TF: 800-332-4100

Ethics & Mediation, Center for Medical www.cmem.org
PO Box 86110   San Diego CA 92138
Ph: 619-296-7268

Ethics National Association, Applied Research www.primr.org/arena.html
132 Boylston St 4th Fl   Boston MA 02116
Ph: 617-423-4112 ▪ Fx: 617-423-1185

Ethics Officer Association www.eoa.org
411 Waverley Oaks Rd Suite 324   Waltham MA 02452
Ph: 781-647-9333 ▪ Fx: 781-647-9399

Ethics & Public Policy Center www.eppc.org
1015 15th St NW Suite 900   Washington DC 20005
Ph: 202-682-1200 ▪ Fx: 202-408-0632

Ethics & Religious Liberty Commission of the Southern Baptist www.erlc.com
Convention   901 Commerce St   Nashville TN 37203
Ph: 615-244-2495 ▪ Fx: 615-242-0065

Ethics Resource Center www.ethics.org
1747 Pennsylvania Ave NW Suite 400   Washington DC 20006
Ph: 202-737-2258 ▪ Fx: 202-737-2227

Ethics & Ritual, Women's Alliance for Theology www.his.com/~mhunt
8035 13th St   Silver Spring MD 20910
Ph: 301-589-2509 ▪ Fx: 301-589-3150

Ethics, Society for Business www.societyforbusinessethics.org
Loyola Univ of Chicago School of Business Administration 820
N Michigan Ave   Chicago IL 60611
Ph: 312-915-6994 ▪ Fx: 312-915-6988

Ethics, Society of Christian www.scethics.org
St Johns University PO Box 5633   Collegeville MN 56321
Ph: 320-363-3525 ▪ Fx: 320-363-3145

Ethiopian Community Development Council Inc www.ecdcinternational.org
1038 S Highland St   Arlington VA 22204
Ph: 703-685-0510 ▪ Fx: 703-685-0529

Ethiopian Community Mutual Assistance Association
552 Massachusetts Ave Suite 201   Cambridge MA 02139
Ph: 617-492-4232 ▪ Fx: 617-492-7685

Ethiopian Jewry, North American Conference on www.nacoej.org
132 Nassau St Suite 412   New York NY 10038
Ph: 212-233-5200 ▪ Fx: 212-233-5243

Ethiopian Jewry, Struggle to Save www.studentstruggle.org
2472 Broadway Suite 316   New York NY 10025
Ph: 866-376-7735

Ethnic Affairs, National Center for Urban
PO Box 20 Cardinal Stn   Washington DC 20064
Ph: 202-319-5129 ▪ Fx: 202-319-6289

Ethnic Cultural Preservation Council
6500 S Pulaski Rd   Chicago IL 60629
Ph: 773-582-5143 ▪ Fx: 773-582-5133

Ethnic History Society, Immigration & www.iehs.org
American Univ 4400 Massachusetts NW   Washington DC
20016
Ph: 202-885-2410

Ethnic Studies, National Association for www.ethnicstudies.org
Arizona State Univ College of Arts & Sciences 4701 W
Thunderbird Rd MC 3051   Glendale AZ 85306
Ph: 602-543-4111 ▪ Fx: 602-965-3451

Ethnobiology, Society of www.ethnobiology.org
Univ of North Carolina Dept of Anthropology CB 3115 Alumni
Bldg   Chapel Hill NC 27599
Ph: 919-962-3841 ▪ Fx: 919-962-1613

Ethnohistory, American Society for ethnohistory.org
c/o Duke University Press Box 906660   Durham NC 27708
Ph: 919-687-3602 ▪ TF: 888-387-5687

Ethnological Society, American www.aaanet.org/aes
c/o American Anthropological Assn 2200 Wilson Blvd Suite
600   Arlington VA 22201
Ph: 703-528-1902 ▪ Fx: 703-528-3546

Ethnology, International Council for Human Ecology & www.ichee.org
PO Box 7024   New York NY 10128
Ph: 212-410-6560

Ethnomusicology, Society for www.ethnomusicology.org
Indiana University 1165 E 3rd St Morrison Hall
005   Bloomington IN 47405
Ph: 812-855-0389 ▪ Fx: 812-855-6673

Ethoxylates Research Council, Alkylphenols & www.aperc.org
1250 Connecticut Ave NW Suite 700   Washington DC 20036
Ph: 202-637-9071 ▪ Fx: 202-637-9178 ▪ TF: 866-273-7262

Ethylene Oxide Sterilization Association www.eosa.org
1815 H St NW Suite 500   Washington DC 20006
Ph: 202-296-6300 ▪ Fx: 202-775-5929

ETOUSA Veterans Association, SHAEF/ www.shaef.org
2301 Broadway   San Francisco CA 94115
Ph: 415-921-8322

ETR Associates www.etr.org
4 Carbonero Way   Scotts Valley CA 95066
Ph: 831-438-4060

Etruscan Foundation www.etruscanfoundation.org
c/o Grants Management Assoc 77 Summer St Suite
800   Boston MA 02110
Ph: 617-426-7080 ▪ Fx: 617-426-7087

EUCG Inc www.eucg.org
20165 N 67th Ave Suite 122   Glendale AZ 85308
Ph: 623-572-4140 ▪ Fx: 623-572-4141

Eugene O'Neill Society
PO Box 402   Danville CA 94526
Ph: 925-820-1818 ▪ Fx: 925-828-0265

Eugene O'Neill Theater Center www.oneilltheatercenter.org
305 Great Neck Rd   Waterford CT 06385
Ph: 860-443-5378 ▪ Fx: 860-443-9653

Eugene V Debs Foundation eugenevdebs.com
PO Box 843   Terre Haute IN 47808
Ph: 812-237-3443 ▪ Fx: 812-237-8072

Euphonium Association, International Tuba- www.tubaonline.org
2253 Downing St   Denver CO 80205
Ph: 303-832-4676 ▪ Fx: 303-832-0839

Eurasia, Initiative for Social Action & Renewal in   www.isar.org
1601 Connecticut Ave NW Suite 301   Washington DC 20009
Ph: 202-387-3034 ▪ Fx: 202-667-3291

Eurasia, NCSJ: Advocates on Behalf of Jews in Russia Ukraine   www.ncsj.org
the Baltic States &   2020 K St NW Suite 7800   Washington
DC 20036
Ph: 202-898-2500 ▪ Fx: 202-898-0822

Eurasian & East European Research, National Council for   www.nceeer.org
910 17th St NW Suite 300   Washington DC 20006
Ph: 202-822-6950 ▪ Fx: 202-822-6955

Europe, Society for the Anthropology of   www.h-net.org/~sae/sae
c/o American Anthropological Assn 2200 Wilson Blvd Suite
600   Arlington VA 22201
Ph: 703-528-1902 ▪ Fx: 703-528-3546

Europe, US Business Council for Southeastern   www.usbizcouncil.org
PO Box 1521 Wall St Stn   New York NY 10268
Ph: 212-439-9025 ▪ Fx: 212-439-9105 ▪ TF: 800-203-8900

European-American Business Council   www.eabc.org
910 17th St NW Suite 1106   Washington DC 20006
Ph: 202-728-0777 ▪ Fx: 202-728-2937

European/American Issues Forum   www.eaif.org
297 El Camino Real Suite 155   San Bruno CA 94066
Ph: 650-952-8489 ▪ Fx: 650-869-7215

European Greyhound Alliance, American-   www.ameurogreyhoundalliance.org/start.html
167 Saddle Hill Rd   Hopkinton MA 01748
Ph: 508-435-5969

European Studies, Council for   www.europanet.org
Columbia Univ 1203A International Affairs Bldg   MC 3310 420
W 118th St   New York NY 10027
Ph: 212-854-4172 ▪ Fx: 212-854-8808

European Travel Commission   www.visiteurope.com
1 Rockefeller Plaza Suite 214   New York NY 10020
Ph: 212-218-1200 ▪ Fx: 212-218-1205

Euthanasia & Assisted Suicide, International Task   www.internationaltaskforce.org
Force on   PO Box 760   Steubenville OH 43952
Ph: 740-282-3810 ▪ Fx: 740-282-0769 ▪ TF: 800-958-5678

Euthanasia, Citizens United Resisting
303 Truman St   Berkeley Springs WV 25411
Ph: 304-258-5433 ▪ Fx: 304-258-5420

Euthanasia Research & Guidance Organization   www.finalexit.org
24829 Norris Ln   Junction City OR 97448
Ph: 541-998-1873

Evaluating Professionals, National Association of Disability   www.nadep.com
PO Box 13801   Midlothian VA 23113
Ph: 804-378-7275

Evaluation Association, American   www.eval.org
16 Sconticut Neck Rd Suite 290   Fairhaven MA 02719
Ph: 508-748-3326 ▪ TF: 888-232-2275

Evan B Donaldson Adoption Institute   www.adoptioninstitute.org
120 Wall St 20th Fl   New York NY 10005
Ph: 212-269-5080 ▪ Fx: 212-269-1962

Evangelical Alliance, World   www.worldevangelical.org
PO Box 1839   Edmonds WA 98020
Ph: 425-778-5513 ▪ Fx: 425-640-3671

Evangelical Association for the Promotion of   www.tonycampolo.org/eape.shtml
Education   1300 Eagle Rd   Saint Davids PA 19087
Ph: 610-341-1722 ▪ Fx: 610-341-4372

Evangelical Christian Publishers Association   www.ecpa.org
1969 E Broadway Rd Suite 2   Tempe AZ 85282
Ph: 480-966-3998 ▪ Fx: 480-966-1944

Evangelical Church Alliance   www.keynet.net/~eca/index.html
PO Box 9   Bradley IL 60915
Ph: 815-937-0720 ▪ Fx: 815-937-0001

Evangelical Church Library Association   www.eclalibraries.org
PO Box 353   Glen Ellyn IL 60138
Ph: 630-681-7591 ▪ Fx: 630-681-7592 ▪ TF: 800-223-0001

Evangelical Council for Financial Accountability   www.ecfa.org
440 W Jubal Early Dr   Winchester VA 22601
Ph: 540-535-0103 ▪ Fx: 540-353-0533 ▪ TF: 800-323-9473

Evangelical Education Society, Episcopal   members.aol.com/eeesociety/EEESPAGE.html
2300 9th St S Suite 301   Arlington VA 22204
Ph: 703-521-3264 ▪ Fx: 703-521-6758

Evangelical Fellowship of Mission Agencies
4201 N Peachtree Rd Suite 300   Atlanta GA 30341
Ph: 770-457-6677 ▪ Fx: 770-457-0037

Evangelical Free Church Mission   www.efcm.org
901 E 78th St   Bloomington MN 55420
Ph: 952-854-1300 ▪ Fx: 952-853-8474 ▪ TF: 800-745-2202

Evangelical Friends International   www.evangelical-friends.org
5350 Broadmoor Cir NW   Canton OH 44709
Ph: 330-493-1660 ▪ Fx: 330-493-0852

Evangelical Lutheran Church in America   www.elca.org
8765 W Higgins Rd   Chicago IL 60631
Ph: 773-380-2700 ▪ Fx: 773-380-1465 ▪ TF: 800-638-3522

Evangelical Lutheran Synod, Wisconsin   www.wels.net
2929 N Mayfair Rd   Milwaukee WI 53222
Ph: 414-256-3888 ▪ Fx: 414-256-3899

Evangelical Missiological Society   www.missiology.org/EMS
PO Box 794   Wheaton IL 60189
Ph: 630-752-5533 ▪ Fx: 630-752-5916

Evangelical Philosophical Society   www.epsociety.org
Biola Univ McNally 66 13800 Biola Ave   La Mirada CA 90639
Ph: 562-906-4570 ▪ Fx: 562-906-4592

Evangelical Press Association   www.gospelcom.net/epa
PO Box 28129   Crystal MN 55428
Ph: 763-535-4793 ▪ Fx: 763-535-4794

Evangelical Theological Society   www.etsjets.org
200 Russell Woods Dr   Lynchburg VA 24502
Ph: 434-237-5309

Evangelical Training Association   www.etaworld.org
110 Bridge St   Wheaton IL 60189
Ph: 630-668-6400 ▪ Fx: 630-668-8437 ▪ TF: 800-369-8291

Evangelical United Brethren Heritage, Center for the   www.united.edu/eubcenter
1810 Harvard Blvd   Dayton OH 45406
Ph: 937-278-5817 ▪ Fx: 937-275-5701

Evangelicals Concerned Inc   www.ecinc.org
311 E 72nd St   New York NY 10021
Ph: 212-517-3171

Evangelicals, National Association of   www.nae.net
701 G St SW   Washington DC 20024
Ph: 202-789-1011 ▪ Fx: 202-842-0392

Evangelicals for Social Action   www.esa-online.org
10 E Lancaster Ave   Wynnewood PA 19096
Ph: 610-645-9390 ▪ Fx: 610-649-8090 ▪ TF: 800-650-6600

Evangelism, Association of Baptists for World   www.abwe.org
PO Box 8585   Harrisburg PA 17105
Ph: 717-774-7000 ▪ Fx: 717-774-1919

Evangelism, Committee on Missionary   www.comemissions.com
PO Box 88085   Grand Rapids MI 49518
Ph: 616-455-8228

Evangelism, Fellowship of Associates of Medical   www.fameworld.org
PO Box 33548   Indianapolis IN 46203
Ph: 317-358-2480 ▪ Fx: 317-358-2483

Evangelism Fellowship Inc, Child   www.gospelcom.net/cef
PO Box 348   Warrenton MO 63383
Ph: 636-456-4321 ▪ TF: 800-748-7710

Evangelism International, Literacy &   www.literacyevangelism.org
1800 S Jackson Ave   Tulsa OK 74107
Ph: 918-585-3826 ▪ Fx: 918-585-3224 ▪ TF: 800-266-7139

Evangelism & Missions Information Service   bgc.gospelcom.net/emis
500 College Ave   Wheaton IL 60187
Ph: 630-752-7158 ▪ Fx: 630-752-7155

(Evangelism) National Cursillo Movement   www.natl-cursillo.org
PO Box 210226   Dallas TX 75211
Ph: 214-339-6321 ▪ Fx: 214-339-6322

(Evangelism) Open Air Campaigners USA   www.oacusa.org
PO Box D   Nazareth PA 18064
Ph: 610-746-0508 ▪ Fx: 610-746-0509

Evangelistic Association, Billy Graham   www.billygraham.org
PO Box 779   Minneapolis MN 55440
Ph: 612-338-0500 ▪ Fx: 612-335-1289 ▪ TF: 877-247-2426

Evangelistic Association, Luis Palau   www.palau.org
PO Box 50   Portland OR 97207
Ph: 503-614-1500 ▪ Fx: 503-614-1599

Evangelistic Faith Missions   www.efm-missions.org
PO Box 609   Bedford IN 47421
Ph: 812-275-7531 ▪ Fx: 812-275-7532 ▪ TF: 877-864-7480

Evangelistic Fellowship, Presbyterian   www.pefministry.org
4211 Flat Shoals Pkwy   Decatur GA 30034
Ph: 404-244-0740 ▪ Fx: 404-244-0914 ▪ TF: 800-225-5733

Evangelize China Fellowship Inc   www.ecfusa.org
437 S Garfield   Monterey Park CA 91754
Ph: 626-288-8828 ▪ Fx: 626-288-6727

Evaporative Cooling Institute Inc   www.evapcooling.org
New Mexico State Univ MSC 3ECI   PO Box 30001   Las Cruces
NM 88003
Ph: 505-646-4104 ▪ Fx: 505-646-2960

Evelyn & Walter Haas Jr Fund   www.haasjr.org
1 Market St Suite 400   San Francisco CA 94105
Ph: 415-856-1400 ▪ Fx: 415-856-1500

Event Marketing Association, Computer   www.cemaonline.com
10 River Rd Suite 203   Uxbridge MA 01569
Ph: 978-443-3330 ▪ Fx: 978-449-4715 ▪ TF: 866-702-2362

Eventing Association, US   www.eventingusa.com
525 Old Waterford Rd NW   Leesburg VA 20176
Ph: 703-779-0440 ▪ Fx: 703-779-0550

Events Association, International Festivals &   www.ifea.com
2601 Eastover Terr   Boise ID 83706
Ph: 208-433-0950 ▪ Fx: 208-433-9812

Events Directors-International, Association of Collegiate   acced-i.colostate.edu
Conference &   Colorado State Univ 8037 Campus
Delivery   Fort Collins CO 80523
Ph: 970-491-5151 ▪ Fx: 970-491-0667 ▪ TF: 877-502-2233

Events Society, International Special   www.ises.com
401 N Michigan Ave   Chicago IL 60611
Ph: 312-312-6853 ▪ Fx: 312-673-6953 ▪ TF: 800-688-4737

Everglades, Friends of the   www.everglades.org
7800 Red Rd Suite 215K   South Miami FL 33143
Ph: 305-669-0858 ▪ Fx: 305-669-4108

Evergreen Freedom Foundation   www.effwa.org
PO Box 552   Olympia WA 98507
Ph: 360-956-3482 ▪ Fx: 360-352-1874

Evergreen International   www.evergreen-intl.org
PO Box 3   Salt Lake City UT 84110
Ph: 801-363-3837 ▪ Fx: 801-264-8641 ▪ TF: 800-391-1000

Every Child by Two   www.ecbt.org
666 11th St NW Suite 202   Washington DC 20001
Ph: 202-783-7034 ▪ Fx: 202-783-7042

Evidence Inc, International Association for Property &   www.iape.org
903 N San Fernando Blvd Suite 4   Burbank CA 91504
Ph: 818-846-2926 ▪ Fx: 818-846-4543 ▪ TF: 800-449-4273

Evidence Photographers International Council Inc   www.epic-photo.org
600 Main St   Honesdale PA 18431
Ph: 570-253-5450 ▪ Fx: 570-253-5011 ▪ TF: 800-356-3742

Evolution, Society for the Study of   lsul.la.asu.edu/evolution
810 E 10th St PO Box 1897   Lawrence KS 66044
Ph: 785-843-1235

Ewing Marion Kauffman Foundation   www.emkf.org
4801 Rockhill Rd   Kansas City MO 64110
Ph: 816-932-1000 ▪ Fx: 816-932-1100 ▪ TF: 800-489-4900

Ex-Gays, Parents & Friends of　　www.pfox.org
PO Box 561　Fort Belvoir VA 22060
Ph: 703-739-8220

Examination Board of Professional Home Inspectors　www.homeinspectionexam.org
932 Lee St Suite 202　Des Plaines IL 60016
Ph: 847-298-7750　Fx: 847-299-2505

Examiners, Association of Certified Fraud　www.cfenet.com
716 West Ave　Austin TX 78701
Ph: 512-478-9070　Fx: 512-478-9297　TF: 800-245-3321

Examiners, Association of Firearm & Tool Mark　www.afte.org

Examiners for Engineering & Surveying, National Council of　www.ncees.org
280 Seneca Creek Rd　Clemson SC 29633
Ph: 864-654-6824　Fx: 864-654-6033　TF: 800-250-3196

Examiners of Long Term Care Administrators, National Association of Boards of　www.nabweb.org
1444 'I' St NW Suite 700　Washington DC 20005
Ph: 202-712-9040　Fx: 202-216-9646

Examiners, National Association of Document　www.documentexaminers.org
3490 US Rt 1 Suite 3B　Princeton NJ 08540
Ph: 866-569-0833

Exceptional Children, Council for　www.cec.sped.org
1110 N Glebe Rd　Arlington VA 22201
Ph: 703-620-3660　Fx: 703-264-9494　TF: 888-232-7733

Exceptional Children, Yes I Can Foundation for　yesican.cec.sped.org
1110 N Glebe Rd Suite 300　Arlington VA 22201
Ph: 703-264-3660　Fx: 703-264-9494　TF: 800-224-6830

Exchange Club, National　www.nationalexchangeclub.com
3050 W Central Ave　Toledo OH 43606
Ph: 419-535-3232　Fx: 419-535-1989　TF: 800-924-2643

(Exchange Programs) InterExchange Inc　www.interexchange.org
161 6th Ave　New York NY 10013
Ph: 212-924-0446　Fx: 212-924-0575

(Exchange Programs) Meridian International Center　www.meridian.org
1630 Crescent Pl NW　Washington DC 20009
Ph: 202-667-6800　Fx: 202-667-1475

Exchange of Scholars, Council for International　www.cies.org
3007 Tilden St NW Suite 5L　Washington DC 20008
Ph: 202-686-4000　Fx: 202-362-3442

Exchange of Students Technology Experience, International Association for the　10400 Little Patuxent Pkwy Suite 250　Columbia MD 21044
Ph: 410-997-3069　Fx: 410-997-5186

Exchanger Manufacturers Association, Tubular　www.tema.org
25 N Broadway　Tarrytown NY 10591
Ph: 914-332-0040　Fx: 914-332-1541

Exchangors, National Council of　www.infoville.com/nce
PO Box 668　Morro Bay CA 93443
Ph: 800-324-1031　Fx: 866-332-3004

Excipients Council of the Americas, International Pharmaceutical　www.ipecamericas.org
1655 N Fort Myer Dr Suite 700　Arlington VA 22209
Ph: 703-875-2127　Fx: 703-525-5157

Executive Assistants, Health Care　www.hceaonline.com
1 N Franklin Ave 31st Fl N　Chicago IL 60606
Ph: 312-422-3851　Fx: 312-422-4575

Executive Housekeepers Association, International　www.ieha.org
1001 Eastwind Dr Suite 301　Westerville OH 43081
Ph: 614-895-7166　Fx: 614-895-1248　TF: 800-200-6342

Executive Leadership Council　www.elcinfo.com
1010 Wisconsin Ave NW Suite 520　Washington DC 20007
Ph: 202-298-8226　Fx: 202-298-8074

Executive Recruiters, National Association of　www.naer.org
1320 Tower Rd Suite 2262　Schaumburg IL 60173
Ph: 847-598-3680　Fx: 847-885-5681

Executive Search Consultants, Association of　www.aesc.org
12 E 41st St 17th Fl　New York NY 10017
Ph: 212-398-9556　Fx: 212-398-9560

Executive Search Roundtable Inc　www.esroundtable.org

Executive Secretaries & Administrative Assistants, National Association of　www.naesaa.com
900 S Washington St Suite G-13　Falls Church VA 22046
Ph: 703-237-8616　Fx: 703-533-1153

Executive Service Corps, International　www.iesc.org
901 15th St NW Suite 350　Washington DC 20005
Ph: 202-326-0280　Fx: 202-326-0280　TF: 800-243-4372

Executive Service Corps, National　www.nesc.org
120 Wall St 16th Fl　New York NY 10005
Ph: 212-269-1234　Fx: 212-269-0959

Executive Staff, Association of Girl Scout
222 S Riverside Plaza Suite 2120　Chicago IL 60606
Ph: 312-416-2500　Fx: 312-416-2932

Executive Women in Government　www.execwomeningov.org
PO Box 1046　Laurel MD 20725
Ph: 301-725-3500　Fx: 301-725-5323

Executive Women in Hospitality, Network of　www.newh.org
PO Box 322　Shawano WI 54166
Ph: 715-526-5267　Fx: 715-526-5979

Executive Women International　www.executivewomen.org
515 South 700 E Suite 2-A　Salt Lake City UT 84102
Ph: 801-355-2800　Fx: 801-355-2852

Executive Women's Golf Association　www.ewga.org
300 Ave of the Champions Suite 140　Palm Beach Gardens FL 33418
Ph: 561-691-0096　Fx: 561-691-0012　TF: 800-407-1477

Executives, American Society of Association　www.asaenet.org
1575 'I' St NW　Washington DC 20005
Ph: 202-626-2723　Fx: 202-371-8825　TF: 888-950-2723

Executives Association, Fraternity　www.fea-inc.org
8777 Purdue Rd Suite 130　Indianapolis IN 46268
Ph: 317-872-8210　Fx: 317-872-8213

Executives Association, Senior　www.seniorexecs.org
PO Box 44808　Washington DC 20026
Ph: 202-927-7000　Fx: 202-927-5192

Executives, Automotive Trade Association
8400 Westpark Dr　McLean VA 22102
Ph: 703-821-7072　Fx: 703-556-8581

Executives International, Financial　www.fei.org
200 Campus Dr PO Box 674　Florham Park NJ 07932
Ph: 973-765-1000　Fx: 973-765-1018

Executives, National Association for Female　www.nafe.org
260 Madison Ave 3rd Fl　New York NY 10016
Ph: 212-351-6400　TF: 800-927-6233

Exercise, American Council on　www.acefitness.org
4851 Paramount Dr　San Diego CA 92123
Ph: 858-279-8227　Fx: 858-279-8064　TF: 800-825-3636

Exercise Association, Aquatic　aeawave.com
3439 Technology Dr Suite 6　Nokomis FL 34275
Ph: 941-486-8600　Fx: 941-486-8820　TF: 888-232-9283

Exercise Safety Association　www.exercisesafety.com
PO Box 3340　Spring Hill FL 34611
Ph: 352-683-5246　Fx: 352-666-7862

Exercise & Sports Association, Diabetes　www.diabetes-exercise.org
8001 Montcastle Dr　Nashville TN 37221
Ph: 800-898-4322

Exhaust Cleaning Association, International Kitchen　www.ikeca.org
1518 K St NW Suite 503　Washington DC 20005
Ph: 202-393-5955　Fx: 202-638-4833

Exhibit Designers & Producers Association　www.edpa.com
5775 Peachtree Dunwoody Rd Bldg G Suite 500　Atlanta GA 30342
Ph: 404-303-7310　Fx: 404-252-0774

Exhibition Industry Research, Center for　www.ceir.org
2301 S Lake Shore Dr Suite E 1002　Chicago IL 60616
Ph: 312-808-2347　Fx: 312-949-3472

Exhibition Management, International Association for　www.iaem.org
PO Box 802425　Dallas TX 75380
Ph: 972-458-8002　Fx: 972-458-8119

Exhibitors Association, International Defense Equipment　www.ideea.com
6233 Nelway Dr　McLean VA 22101
Ph: 703-760-0762　Fx: 703-760-0764

Exhibitors' Association, Tennessee Walking Horse Breeders' &　www.twhbea.com
PO Box 286　Lewisburg TN 37091
Ph: 931-359-1574　Fx: 931-359-2539　TF: 800-359-1574

Exhibitors Association, Trade Show　www.tsea.org
2301 S Lake Shore Dr Suite 1005　Chicago IL 60616
Ph: 312-842-8732　Fx: 312-842-8744

Exiles, Society of the Descendants of the Schwenkfeldian　www.centralschwenkfelder.com/exile
105 Seminary St　Pennsburg PA 18073
Ph: 215-679-3103　Fx: 215-679-8175

Existential Philosophy, Society for Phenomenology &　www.spep.org
Seattle Univ Dept of Philosophy 900 Broadway　Seattle WA 98122
Ph: 206-296-5473　Fx: 206-296-5997

Exodus International North America　www.exodus-international.org
PO Box 540119　Orlando FL 32854
Ph: 407-599-6872　Fx: 407-599-0011　TF: 888-264-0877

Exotic Wildlife Association　www.exoticwildlifeassociation.com
HC 7　Box 24C　Ingram TX 78025
Ph: 830-367-7761　Fx: 830-895-4998

Expandable Polystyrene Resin Suppliers Council
1300 Wilson Blvd　Arlington VA 22209
Ph: 703-253-0649　Fx: 703-253-0651

Expanded Shale Clay & Slate Institute　www.escsi.org
2225 E Murray Holladay Rd Suite 102　Salt Lake City UT 84117
Ph: 801-272-7070　Fx: 801-272-3377

Expansion Joint Manufacturers Association Inc　www.ejma.org
25 N Broadway　Tarrytown NY 10591
Ph: 914-332-0040　Fx: 914-332-1541

Expansionist Party of the US　members.aol.com/XPUS
295 Smith St　Newark NJ 07106
Ph: 973-416-6151

Expediting Management Association　www.expedite.org

Experience Works Inc　www.experienceworks.org
2200 Clarendon Blvd Suite 1000　Arlington VA 22201
Ph: 703-522-7272　Fx: 703-522-0141　TF: 866-397-9757

Experiential Education, Association for　www.aee.org
2305 Canyon Blvd Suite 100　Boulder CO 80302
Ph: 303-440-8844　Fx: 303-440-9581

Experiential Education, National Society for　www.nsee.org
9001 Braddock Rd Suite 380　Springfield VA 22151
Ph: 703-426-4268　Fx: 703-426-8400　TF: 800-803-4170

Experiential Learning, Council for Adult &　www.cael.org
55 E Monroe St Suite 1930　Chicago IL 60603
Ph: 312-499-2600　Fx: 312-499-2601

Experiment, Center of the American　www.amexp.org
1024 Plymouth Bldg 12 S 6th St　Minneapolis MN 55402
Ph: 612-338-3605　Fx: 612-338-3621

Experimental Aircraft Association　www.eaa.org
3000 Poberezny Rd　Oshkosh WI 54902
Ph: 920-426-4800　Fx: 920-426-4828

Experimental Biology, Federation of American Societies for　www.faseb.org
9650 Rockville Pike　Bethesda MD 20814
Ph: 301-530-7000　Fx: 301-530-7001　TF: 800-433-2732

Experimental Biology & Medicine, Society for　www.sebm.org
197 W Spring Valley Ave　Maywood NJ 07607
Ph: 201-291-9080　Fx: 201-291-2988

Experimental Hematology, International Society for　www.iseh.org
2025 M St NW Suite 800　Washington DC 20036
Ph: 202-367-1183　Fx: 202-367-2183

Experimental Mechanics Inc, Society for   www.sem.org
7 School St   Bethel CT 06801
Ph: 203-790-6373 ▪ Fx: 203-790-4472

Experimental NeuroTherapeutics, American Society for   www.asent.org
611 E Wells St   Milwaukee WI 53202
Ph: 414-273-8290 ▪ Fx: 414-276-2146

Experimental Psychology, Society of Multivariate   www.smep.org
Univ of Oklahoma Psychology Dept   Norman OK 73019
Ph: 405-325-4511 ▪ Fx: 405-325-4737

Experimental Test Pilots, Society of   www.setp.org
PO Box 986   Lancaster CA 93584
Ph: 661-942-9574 ▪ Fx: 661-940-0398

Experimental Therapeutics, American Society for Pharmacology &   www.aspet.org
9650 Rockville Pike   Bethesda MD 20814
Ph: 301-634-7060 ▪ Fx: 301-634-7061

Exploited Children, National Center for Missing &   www.missingkids.com
699 Prince St   Alexandria VA 22314
Ph: 703-274-3900 ▪ Fx: 703-274-2095 ▪ TF: 800-843-5678

Exploration Geophysicists, Society of   www.seg.org
8801 S Yale Ave   Tulsa OK 74137
Ph: 918-493-3516 ▪ Fx: 918-497-5557

Exploration Inc, Society for Mining Metallurgy &   www.smenet.org
8307 Shaffer Pkwy   Littleton CO 80127
Ph: 303-973-9550 ▪ Fx: 303-973-3845 ▪ TF: 800-763-3132

Explorers Club   www.explorers.org
46 E 70th St   New York NY 10021
Ph: 212-628-8383 ▪ Fx: 212-288-4449

Explorers, South American   www.saexplorers.org
126 Indian Creek Rd   Ithaca NY 14850
Ph: 607-277-0488 ▪ Fx: 607-277-6122 ▪ TF: 800-274-0568

Explosives Engineers, International Society of   www.isee.org
30325 Bainbridge Rd   Cleveland OH 44139
Ph: 440-349-4400 ▪ Fx: 440-349-3788

Explosives, Institute of Makers of   www.ime.org
1120 19th St NW Suite 310   Washington DC 20036
Ph: 202-429-9280 ▪ Fx: 202-293-2420

Export Association, Phosphate Chemicals   www.phoschem.com
100 S Saunders Rd Suite 300   Lake Forest IL 60045
Ph: 847-739-1200

Export Companies, National Association of   www.nexco.org
PO Box 3949 Grand Central Stn   New York NY 10163
Ph: 877-291-4901 ▪ Fx: 646-349-9628

Export Council, American Hardwood   www.ahec.org
1111 19th St NW Suite 800   Washington DC 20036
Ph: 202-463-2720 ▪ Fx: 202-463-2787

Export Council, Softwood   www.softwood.org
520 SW 6th Ave Suite 810   Portland OR 97204
Ph: 503-248-0406 ▪ Fx: 503-248-0402

Export Council, USA Poultry & Egg   www.usapeec.org
2300 W Park Place Blvd Suite 100   Stone Mountain GA 30087
Ph: 770-413-0006 ▪ Fx: 770-413-0007

Export Federation Inc, US Meat   www.usmef.org
1050 17th St Suite 2200   Denver CO 80265
Ph: 303-623-6328 ▪ Fx: 303-623-0297

Export Grain Association, North American
1250 I St NW   Washington DC 20005
Ph: 202-682-4030 ▪ Fx: 202-682-4033

Export Institute USA   www.exportinstitute.com
6901 W 84th St Suite 157   Minneapolis MN 55438
Ph: 952-943-1505 ▪ TF: 800-943-3171

Exporters Association, Leaf Tobacco
3716 National Dr Suite 114   Raleigh NC 27612
Ph: 919-782-5151 ▪ Fx: 919-781-0915

Exporters Association, Small Business   www.sbea.org
1156 15th St NW Suite 1100   Washington DC 20005
Ph: 202-659-9320 ▪ Fx: 202-872-5843

Exporters & Importers, American Association of   www.aaei.org
1200 G St NW Suite 800   Washington DC 20005
Ph: 202-661-2181 ▪ Fx: 202-661-2185

Exporters, National Council of Music Importers &
PO Box 5488   Long Island City NY 11105
Ph: 718-274-3210 ▪ Fx: 718-274-3214

Exporters, Northwest Fruit
105 S 18th St Suite 227   Yakima WA 98901
Ph: 509-576-8004 ▪ Fx: 509-576-3646

Exposition Service Contractors Association   www.esca.org
22 Corporate Cir Suite 400   Henderson NV 89074
Ph: 702-319-9561 ▪ Fx: 702-450-7732 ▪ TF: 877-792-3722

Exposure Analysis, International Society of   www.iseaweb.org
c/o JSI Research & Training Institute 44 Farnsworth St   Boston MA 02210
Ph: 617-482-9485 ▪ Fx: 617-482-0617

Express Carriers Association   www.expresscarriers.com
PO Box 4307   Bethlehem PA 18018
Ph: 610-740-5857 ▪ Fx: 866-322-3299 ▪ TF: 866-322-7447

Expression, American Society of Psychopathology of
74 Lawton St   Brookline MA 02446
Ph: 617-738-9821 ▪ Fx: 617-975-0411

Extension Association of Family & Consumer Sciences, National   www.neafcs.org
PO Box 239   Great Falls VA 22066
Ph: 703-759-1040 ▪ Fx: 703-759-4801 ▪ TF: 800-808-9133

(Extension System) Epsilon Sigma Phi   espnational.org
PO Box 357340   Gainesville FL 32635
Ph: 352-378-6665 ▪ Fx: 352-375-0722

Extensions for Independence   www.mouthstick.net
555 Saturn Blvd Suite B368   San Diego CA 92154
Ph: 619-423-7709 ▪ TF: 866-632-7149

Extra-Corporeal Technology, American Society of   www.amsect.org
503 Carlisle Dr Suite 125   Herndon VA 20170
Ph: 703-435-8556 ▪ Fx: 703-435-0056

Extra Touch Florist Association   www.etfassociation.org
332 E Main St   Northville MI 48167
Ph: 248-692-0008 ▪ Fx: 248-380-1830 ▪ TF: 888-419-1515

Extract Manufacturers Association of the US, Flavor &   www.femaflavor.org
1620 'I' St NW Suite 925   Washington DC 20006
Ph: 202-293-5800 ▪ Fx: 202-463-8998

Extropy Institute   www.extropy.org
10709 Pointe View Dr   Austin TX 78738
Ph: 512-263-2749

Eye Bank Association of America   www.restoresight.org
1015 18th St NW Suite 1010   Washington DC 20036
Ph: 202-775-4999 ▪ Fx: 202-429-6036

Eye Care Foundation, National Children's   www.mentalhealth.about.com
PO Box 795069   Dallas TX 75379
Ph: 972-407-0404 ▪ Fx: 972-407-0616

Eye Disease, International Society on Metabolic
1125 Park Ave   New York NY 10128
Ph: 212-427-1246 ▪ Fx: 212-360-7009

Eye & Ear Hospitals, American Association of   www.aaeeh.org
1100 Wilson Blvd Suite 1200   Arlington VA 22209
Ph: 703-243-8848 ▪ Fx: 703-243-8664

Eye Expeditions International Inc, Surgical   www.seeintl.org
27 E de La Guerra St Suite C-2   Santa Barbara CA 93101
Ph: 805-963-3303 ▪ Fx: 805-965-3564 ▪ TF: 800-208-6733

Eye Foundation, International   www.iefusa.org
10801 Connecticut Ave   Kensington MD 20895
Ph: 240-290-0263 ▪ Fx: 240-290-0269

Eye Surgeons, American College of   www.aces-abes.org
2665 Oak Ridge Ct Suite A   Fort Myers FL 33901
Ph: 239-275-8881 ▪ Fx: 239-275-9969 ▪ TF: 888-335-0077

Eye Surgeons, Society of
10801 Connecticut Ave   Kensington MD 20814
Ph: 240-290-0263 ▪ Fx: 240-290-0269

Eyecare Inc, Society for Excellence in   www.excellenteyesurgery.com
2850 Countrybrook Dr Suite F16   Palm Harbor FL 34684
Ph: 630-699-1929 ▪ Fx: 727-786-6622

Eyes for the Needy, New
549 Millburn Ave PO Box 332   Short Hills NJ 07078
Ph: 973-376-4903 ▪ Fx: 973-376-3807

F

F-4 Phantom II Society   www.f4phantom.com
PO Box 8335   Van Nuys CA 91409
Ph: 818-781-9703 ▪ Fx: 818-781-9618

Fabric Distributors, National Association of Decorative   www.nadfd.com
1 Windsor Cove Suite 305   Columbia SC 29223
Ph: 803-252-5646 ▪ Fx: 803-765-0860 ▪ TF: 800-445-8629

Fabric Manufacturers, International Society of Industrial
1337 Garden Cir Dr   Newberry SC 29108
Ph: 803-276-2684

Fabricare Institute, International   www.ifi.org
12251 Tech Rd   Silver Spring MD 20904
Ph: 301-622-1900 ▪ Fx: 301-236-9320 ▪ TF: 800-638-2627

Fabricators Association, International Solid Surface   www.issfa.net
975 American Pacific Dr   Henderson NV 89014
Ph: 702-567-8150 ▪ Fx: 702-567-8145

Fabricators & Manufacturers Association International   www.fmametalfab.org
833 Featherstone Rd   Rockford IL 61107
Ph: 815-399-8700 ▪ Fx: 815-484-7700 ▪ TF: 800-432-2832

Fabricators & Riggers, National Council of Erectors
10382 Main St Suite 200 PO Box 280   Fairfax VA 22030
Ph: 703-591-1870 ▪ Fx: 703-591-1895

Fabrics Association International, Industrial   www.ifai.com
1801 County Rd 'B' W   Roseville MN 55113
Ph: 651-222-2508 ▪ Fx: 651-631-9334 ▪ TF: 800-225-4324

Fabrics & Film Association, Chemical   www.chemicalfabricsandfilm.com
1300 Sumner Ave   Cleveland OH 44115
Ph: 216-241-7333 ▪ Fx: 216-241-0105

Fabrics Industry, INDA: Association of the Nonwoven   www.inda.org
1300 Crescent Green Suite 100   Cary NC 27511
Ph: 919-233-1210 ▪ Fx: 919-233-1282

Fabrics Institute, US Industrial   www.ifai.com/membership/divisions
1801 County Rd 'B' W   Roseville MN 55113
Ph: 651-222-2508 ▪ Fx: 651-631-9334

Faces: National Craniofacial Association   www.faces-cranio.org
PO Box 11082   Chattanooga TN 37401
Ph: 423-266-1632 ▪ Fx: 423-267-3124 ▪ TF: 800-332-2373

(Facial Disfigurement) Let's Face It USA   www.faceit.org
PO Box 29972   Bellingham WA 98228
Ph: 360-676-7325

Facial Plastic & Reconstructive Surgery, American Academy of   www.facial-plastic-surgery.org
310 S Henry St   Alexandria VA 22314
Ph: 703-299-9291 ▪ Fx: 703-299-8898 ▪ TF: 800-332-3223

Facial Reconstruction, National Foundation for   www.nffr.org
317 E 34th St   New York NY 10016
Ph: 212-263-6656 ▪ Fx: 212-263-7534

(Facial Reconstruction) Operation Smile   www.operationsmile.org
6435 Tidewater Dr   Norfolk VA 23509
Ph: 757-321-7645 ▪ Fx: 757-321-7660 ▪ TF: 888-677-6453

Facilities Administrators, National Association of State   www.nasfa.net
2760 Research Park Dr PO Box 11910   Lexington KY 40578
Ph: 859-244-8181 ▪ Fx: 859-244-8001

Facilities Engineering, Association for   www.afe.org
8180 Corporate Park Dr Suite 305   Cincinnati OH 45242
Ph: 513-489-2473 ▪ Fx: 513-247-7422

Facilities Executives, International Society of   www.isfe.org
200 Corporate Pl 2B   Peabody MA 01960
Ph: 978-536-0108 ▪ Fx: 978-536-0199

Facilities Officers, APPA: Association of Higher Education
www.appa.org
1643 Prince St   Alexandria VA 22314
Ph: 703-684-1446 ▪ Fx: 703-549-2772

Facility Administrators, International Association of Museum
www.iamfa.org
c/o High Museum of Art 1280 Peachtree Rd NE   Atlanta GA
30309
Ph: 404-733-4407 ▪ Fx: 404-733-4502

Facility Management Association, International
www.ifma.org
1 E Greenway Plaza Suite 1100   Houston TX 77046
Ph: 713-623-4362 ▪ Fx: 713-623-6124

Facility Planners International, Council of Educational
www.cefpi.com
9180 E Desert Cove Dr Suite 104   Scottsdale AZ 85260
Ph: 480-391-0840 ▪ Fx: 480-391-0940

Facing History & Ourselves National Foundation Inc
www.facing.org
16 Hurd Rd   Brookline MA 02445
Ph: 617-232-1595 ▪ Fx: 617-232-0281

Facsimile Association, American
2world.com/staging/afaxa
2200 Ben Franklin Pkwy Suite E105A   Philadelphia PA 19130
Ph: 215-981-0292 ▪ Fx: 215-981-0295

Fair Collectors Society, World's
members.aol.com/Bbqprod/wfcs.html
PO Box 20806   Sarasota FL 34276
Ph: 941-923-2590

Fairlane Club of America
www.fairlaneclubofamerica.com
340 Clicktown Rd   Church Hill TN 37642
Ph: 423-245-6678 ▪ Fx: 423-245-2456

Fairness & Accuracy in Reporting
www.fair.org
112 W 27th St 6th Fl   New York NY 10001
Ph: 212-633-6700 ▪ Fx: 212-727-7668

Fairness Everywhere, National Organization Taunting Safety &
www.notsafe.org
PO Box 5743   Santa Barbara CA 93150
Ph: 805-966-0611

Fairs & Expositions, International Association of
www.iafenet.org
PO Box 985   Springfield MO 65801
Ph: 417-862-5771 ▪ Fx: 417-862-0156 ▪ TF: 800-516-0313

Faith Alive
www.faithalive.org
431 Richmond Pl NE   Albuquerque NM 87106
Ph: 505-255-3233 ▪ Fx: 505-255-2282

Faith & Family, Women for
www.wf-f.org
PO Box 3286   Saint Louis MO 63132
Ph: 314-863-8385 ▪ Fx: 314-863-5858

Faith & History, Conference on
www.huntington.edu/cfh
Gordon College Dept of History   Wrenham MA 01984
Ph: 978-867-4415

Faith & Justice Network, Africa
afjn.cua.edu
3035 4th St NE   Washington DC 20017
Ph: 202-832-3412 ▪ Fx: 202-832-9051

Faith Ministries, International Convention of
www.icfm.org
5500 Woodland Park Blvd   Arlington TX 76013
Ph: 817-451-9620 ▪ Fx: 817-451-9621

Faith North America, Forward in
www.forwardinfaith.com
2905 Lackland Rd   Fort Worth TX 76116
Ph: 817-735-1675 ▪ Fx: 817-735-1351 ▪ TF: 800-225-3661

Faith, Society for the Propagation of the
www.worldmissions-catholicchurch.org
365 5th Ave   New York NY 10001
Ph: 212-563-8700 ▪ Fx: 212-563-8725 ▪ TF: 800-431-2222

Faith & Technology, Servants in
www.sifat.org
2944 County Rd 113   Lineville AL 36266
Ph: 256-396-2017 ▪ Fx: 256-396-2501

Faith at Work Inc
www.faithatwork.com
106 E Broad St Suite B   Falls Church VA 22046
Ph: 703-237-3426 ▪ Fx: 703-237-0157

FaithTrust Institute
www.faithtrustinstitute.org
2400 N 45th St Suite 10   Seattle WA 98103
Ph: 206-634-1903 ▪ Fx: 206-634-0115

Falcon Club of America
www.falconclub.com
PO Box 113   Jacksonville AR 72078
Ph: 501-982-9721

False Claims Act Legal Center
www.taf.org
1220 19th St NW Suite 501   Washington DC 20036
Ph: 202-296-4826 ▪ Fx: 202-296-4838 ▪ TF: 800-873-2573

Familia Ancestral Research Association
PO Box 10359   Westminster CA 92685
Ph: 714-687-0390

Families in Action, National
www.nationalfamilies.org
2957 Clairmont Rd NE Suite 50   Atlanta GA 30329
Ph: 404-248-9676 ▪ Fx: 404-248-1312

Families Adopting Children Everywhere
www.faceadoptioninfo.org
PO Box 28058   Baltimore MD 21239
Ph: 410-488-2656

Families Against Mandatory Minimums
www.famm.org
1612 K St NW Suite 700   Washington DC 20006
Ph: 202-822-6700 ▪ Fx: 202-822-6704

Families Against Substance Abuse, National Asian Pacific
www.napafasa.org
American   340 E Second St Suite 409   Los Angeles CA 90012
Ph: 213-625-5795 ▪ Fx: 213-625-5796

Families Inc, Alliance for Children &
www.alliance1.org
11700 W Lake Park Dr   Milwaukee WI 53224
Ph: 414-359-1040 ▪ Fx: 414-359-1074

Families of American Prisoners & Missing in Southeast
www.pow-miafamilies.org
Asia, National League of   1005 N Glebe Rd Suite
170   Arlington VA 22201
Ph: 703-465-7432 ▪ Fx: 703-465-7433

Families Anonymous
www.familiesanonymous.org
PO Box 3475   Culver City CA 90231
Ph: 310-815-8010 ▪ Fx: 310-815-9682 ▪ TF: 800-736-9805

Families, Campaign for Working
www.campaignforfamilies.org
2800 Shirlington Rd Suite 605   Arlington VA 22206
Ph: 703-671-8800 ▪ Fx: 703-671-8899

Families & Friends of Lesbians & Gays, Parents
www.pflag.org
1726 M St NW Suite 400   Washington DC 20036
Ph: 202-467-8180 ▪ Fx: 202-467-8194

Families, Grantmakers for Children Youth &
www.gcyf.org
1522 K St NW Suite 1100   Washington DC 20005
Ph: 202-962-3940 ▪ Fx: 202-393-4148

Families, Labor Project for Working
www.laborproject.org
2521 Channing Way Suite 5555   Berkeley CA 94720
Ph: 510-643-7088 ▪ Fx: 510-642-6432

Families, National Coalition for the Protection of Children &
www.eos.net/ncpcf
800 Compton Rd Suite 9224   Cincinnati OH 45231
Ph: 513-521-6227 ▪ Fx: 513-521-6337

Families, National Law Center for Children &
www.nationallawcenter.org
3819 Plaza Dr   Fairfax VA 22030
Ph: 703-691-4626

Families, National Partnership for Women &
www.nationalpartnership.org
1875 Connecticut Ave NW Suite 650   Washington DC 20009
Ph: 202-986-2600 ▪ Fx: 202-986-2539

Families for Private Adoption
www.ffpa.org
PO Box 6375   Washington DC 20015
Ph: 202-722-0338

Families USA
www.familiesusa.org
1334 G St NW Suite 300   Washington DC 20005
Ph: 202-628-3030 ▪ Fx: 202-347-2417 ▪ TF: 800-593-5041

Families with Visual Impairment, Council of
1155 15th St NW Suite 1004   Washington DC 20005
Ph: 202-467-5081 ▪ Fx: 202-467-5085 ▪ TF: 800-424-8666

Families Worldwide
www.fww.org
5248 Pinemont Dr Suite C-190   Salt Lake City UT 84123
Ph: 801-268-6461 ▪ Fx: 801-268-6471

Family, Ackerman Institute for the
www.ackerman.org
149 E 78th St   New York NY 10021
Ph: 212-879-4900 ▪ Fx: 212-744-0206

Family of the Americas Foundation
www.familyplanning.net
PO Box 1170   Dunkirk MD 20754
Ph: 301-627-3346 ▪ Fx: 301-327-0847 ▪ TF: 800-443-3395

Family Association, American
www.afa.net
PO Drawer 2440   Tupelo MS 38803
Ph: 662-844-5036 ▪ Fx: 662-842-7798

Family Association, National
www.familyassociation.org

Family Association, National Military
www.nmfa.org
2500 N Van Dorn St Suite 102   Alexandria VA 22302
Ph: 703-931-6632 ▪ Fx: 703-931-4600

Family Association, Teaching
www.teaching-family.org
4356 Bonney Rd Suite 103   Virginia Beach VA 23452
Ph: 757-497-3023 ▪ Fx: 757-497-0010

Family-Based Treatment Association, Foster
www.ffta.org
294 Union St   Hackensack NJ 07601
Ph: 800-414-3382 ▪ Fx: 201-862-0331

Family Campers & RVers
www.fcrv.org
4808 Transit Rd Bldg 2   Depew NY 14043
Ph: 716-668-6242 ▪ TF: 800-245-9755

Family Career & Community Leaders of America
www.fcclainc.org
1910 Association Dr   Reston VA 20191
Ph: 703-476-4900 ▪ Fx: 703-860-2713 ▪ TF: 800-234-4425

Family Caregiver Alliance
www.caregiver.org
690 Market St Suite 600   San Francisco CA 94104
Ph: 415-434-3388 ▪ Fx: 415-434-3508 ▪ TF: 800-445-8106

Family Caregivers Association, National
www.nfcacares.org
10400 Connecticut Ave Suite 500   Kensington MD 20895
Ph: 301-942-6430 ▪ Fx: 301-942-2302 ▪ TF: 800-896-3650

Family Child Care, National Association for
www.nafcc.org
5202 Pinemont Dr   Salt Lake City UT 84123
Ph: 801-269-9338 ▪ Fx: 801-268-9507 ▪ TF: 800-359-3817

Family & Children Services, Jewish Board of
www.jbfcs.org
120 W 57th St   New York NY 10019
Ph: 212-582-9100 ▪ Fx: 212-956-5676 ▪ TF: 888-523-2769

Family & Children's Agencies, Association of Jewish
www.ajfca.org
557 Cranbury Rd Suite 2   East Brunswick NJ 08816
Ph: 732-432-7120 ▪ Fx: 732-432-7127 ▪ TF: 800-634-7346

Family & Community Education, National Association for
www.nafce.org
73 Cavalier Blvd Suite 106   Florence KY 41042
Ph: 877-712-4477 ▪ Fx: 859-525-6496

Family & Conciliation Courts, Association of
www.afccnet.org
6515 Grand Teton Plaza Suite 210   Madison WI 53719
Ph: 608-664-3750 ▪ Fx: 608-664-3751

Family Consecration, Apostolate for
www.familyland.org
Catholic Familyland 3375 County Rd Suite 36   Bloomingdale
OH 43910
Ph: 740-765-5500 ▪ Fx: 740-765-5561 ▪ TF: 888-367-6279

Family & Consumer Sciences, American Association of
www.aafcs.org
1555 King St Suite 400   Alexandria VA 22314
Ph: 703-706-4600 ▪ Fx: 703-706-4663 ▪ TF: 800-424-8080

Family & Consumer Sciences Education Association
www.cwu.edu/~fandcs/fcsea
Central Washington Univ Dept of Family & Consumer Science
400 E 8th Ave   Ellensburg WA 98926
Ph: 509-963-2766 ▪ Fx: 509-963-2787

Family & Consumer Sciences, National Extension Association of
www.neafcs.org
PO Box 239   Great Falls VA 22066
Ph: 703-759-1040 ▪ Fx: 703-759-4801 ▪ TF: 800-808-9133

Family Council on Drug Awareness
www.fcda.org
PO Box 1716   El Cerrito CA 94530
Ph: 510-215-8326

Family Counselors, International Association of Marriage &
www.iamfc.com
c/o American Counseling Assn 5999 Stevenson Ave   Alexandria
VA 22304
Ph: 703-823-9800 ▪ Fx: 703-823-0252 ▪ TF: 800-545-2223

Family Court Judges, National Council of Juvenile &
www.ncjfcj.org
Univ of Nevada PO Box 8970   Reno NV 89507
Ph: 775-784-6012 ▪ Fx: 775-784-6628

Family Education, Lifetime Institute for
9 Old Kings Hwy S 4th Fl   Darien CT 06820
Ph: 203-656-3600 ▪ Fx: 203-656-2221 ▪ TF: 800-832-0277

Family Farm Coalition, National   www.nffc.net
110 Maryland Ave NE Suite 307   Washington DC 20002
Ph: 202-543-5675   Fx: 202-543-0978   TF: 800-639-3276

Family Film Foundation, African   www.africanfamily.org
PO Box 630   Santa Cruz CA 95061
Ph: 831-426-3133

Family Firm Institute   www.ffi.org
200 Lincoln St Suite 201   Boston MA 02111
Ph: 617-482-3045   Fx: 617-482-3049

Family, Focus on the   www.family.org
8605 Explorer Dr   Colorado Springs CO 80995
Ph: 719-531-3400   Fx: 719-548-4670   TF: 800-232-6459

Family Health, Council on   www.cfhinfo.org
1155 Connecticut Ave Suite 1200-B   Washington DC 20036
Ph: 202-331-7373   Fx: 202-223-6835

Family Healthcare Association, Collaborative   www.cfhcc.org
PO Box 20838   Rochester NY 14602
Ph: 716-482-8210   Fx: 716-482-2901

Family History Forum, Irish   www.ifhf.org
PO Box 67   Plainview NY 11803
Ph: 516-616-3587

Family History, International Society for British Genealogy &
PO Box 3115   Salt Lake City UT 84110
Ph: 801-272-2178

Family & Home Network   www.familyandhome.org
9493-C Silver King Ct   Fairfax VA 22031
Ph: 703-866-4164   Fx: 703-352-1076   TF: 800-783-4666

Family Learning Association   www.kidscanlearn.com
3925 E Hagan St Suite 101   Bloomington IN 47401
Ph: 812-323-9862   Fx: 812-331-2776

Family Life, Christian   www.christianfamilylife.org
5301 Harris Blvd   Charlotte NC 28269
Ph: 704-596-9630   Fx: 704-596-4522

Family Life & Culture, Institute for the Advanced Study of Black   www.iasbflc.org
1484 9th St   Oakland CA 94607
Ph: 510-836-3245   Fx: 510-836-3248

Family Life Ministers, National Association of Catholic   www.nacflm.org
300 College Park   Dayton OH 45469
Ph: 937-229-3324   Fx: 937-229-4902

Family Life PAC, American
1932 Wynnton Rd   Columbus GA 31999
Ph: 706-323-3431   Fx: 706-660-7278   TF: 800-992-3522

Family Literacy, Barbara Bush Foundation for   www.barbarabushfoundation.com
1201 15th St SW Suite 420   Washington DC 20005
Ph: 202-955-6183   Fx: 202-955-5492

Family Literacy, National Center for   www.famlit.org
325 W Main St Suite 300   Louisville KY 40202
Ph: 502-584-1133   Fx: 502-584-0172   TF: 877-326-5481

Family Medicine, Society of Teachers of   www.stfm.org
11400 Tomahawk Creek Pkwy Suite 540   Leawood KS 66211
Ph: 913-906-6000   Fx: 913-906-6096

Family Motor Coach Association   www.fmca.com
8291 Clough Pike   Cincinnati OH 45244
Ph: 513-474-3622   Fx: 513-474-2332   TF: 800-543-3622

Family Movement, Christian   www.cfm.org
PO Box 925   Evansville IN 47706
Ph: 812-962-5508   Fx: 812-962-5509

Family Physicians, American Academy of   www.aafp.org
11400 Tomahawk Creek Pkwy   Leawood KS 66211
Ph: 913-906-6000   Fx: 913-906-6075   TF: 800-274-2237

Family Physicians, American College of Osteopathic   www.acofp.org
330 E Algonquin Rd Suite 1   Arlington Heights IL 60005
Ph: 847-228-6090   Fx: 847-228-9755   TF: 800-323-0794

Family Physicians, American Osteopathic Board of   www.aobfp.org
330 E Algonquin Rd Suite 6   Arlington Heights IL 60005
Ph: 847-640-8477

Family Physicians, Uniformed Services Academy of   www.usafp.org
2301 N Parham Rd Suite 4   Richmond VA 23229
Ph: 804-968-4436   Fx: 804-968-4418

Family Plan, Save a   www.safp.org
PO Box 3622   London ON N6A4L4
Ph: 519-672-1115   Fx: 519-672-6379

Family Planning Libraries & Information Centers International, Association for Population/   www.aplici.org
c/o Family Health International
Library PO Box 13950   Research Triangle Park NC 27709
Ph: 919-405-1433   Fx: 919-544-7261

(Family Planning) Pathfinder International   www.pathfind.org
9 Galen St Suite 217   Watertown MA 02472
Ph: 617-924-7200   Fx: 617-924-3833

Family Planning & Reproductive Health Association, National   www.nfprha.org
1627 K St NW 12th Fl   Washington DC 20006
Ph: 202-293-3114   Fx: 202-293-1990

Family Policy Center, Child &   www.cfpciowa.org
218 6th Ave Suite 1021   Des Moines IA 50309
Ph: 515-280-9027   Fx: 515-244-8997

Family Practice, American Board of   www.abfp.org
2228 Young Dr   Lexington KY 40505
Ph: 859-269-5626   Fx: 859-335-7501   TF: 888-995-5700

Family Practice Residency Directors, Association of   www.afprd.org
c/o Allen Press 11400 Tomahawk Creek Pkwy Suite
670   Leawood KS 66211
Ph: 913-906-6000   Fx: 913-906-6105   TF: 800-274-2237

Family Pride Coalition   www.familypride.org
PO Box 65327   Washington DC 20035
Ph: 202-331-5015   Fx: 202-331-0080

Family & Property, American Society for the Defense of Tradition   www.tfp.org
PO Box 341   Hanover PA 17331
Ph: 717-225-7147   Fx: 717-225-7382

Family Relations, National Council on   www.ncfr.com
3989 Central Ave NE Suite 550   Minneapolis MN 55421
Ph: 763-781-9331   Fx: 763-781-9348   TF: 888-781-9331

Family Renewal, Christian
PO Box 73   Clovis CA 93613
Ph: 559-347-9324

Family Research Council   www.frc.org
801 G St NW   Washington DC 20001
Ph: 202-393-2100   Fx: 202-393-2134   TF: 800-225-4008

Family Research Institute   familyresearchinst.org
PO Box 2640   Colorado Springs CO 80962
Ph: 303-681-3113   Fx: 303-681-3427

Family Resource Center on Disabilities   www.frcd.org
20 E Jackson Blvd Rm 300   Chicago IL 60604
Ph: 312-939-3513   Fx: 312-939-7297   TF: 800-952-4199

Family Service Charities of America, Women Children &   www.womenandchildren.org
21 Tamal Vista Blvd Suite 209   Corte Madera CA 94925
Ph: 800-626-6481   Fx: 415-924-1379

Family Support America   www.familysupportamerica.org
20 N Wacker Dr Suite 1100   Chicago IL 60606
Ph: 312-338-0900   Fx: 312-338-1522

Family Support Inc, Center for   www.cfsny.org
333 7th Ave 9th Fl   New York NY 10001
Ph: 212-629-7939   Fx: 212-239-2211

Family Therapy Academy Inc, American   www.afta.org
1608 20th St NW 4th Fl   Washington DC 20009
Ph: 202-333-3690   Fx: 202-333-3692

Family Therapy, American Association for Marriage &   www.aamft.org
112 S Alfred St   Alexandria VA 22314
Ph: 703-838-9808   Fx: 703-838-9805

Family Violence, National Council on Child Abuse &   www.nccafv.org
1025 Connecticut Ave NW Suite 1012   Washington DC 20036
Ph: 202-429-6695

Family Violence Prevention Fund   endabuse.org
383 Rhode Island St Suite 304   San Francisco CA 94103
Ph: 415-252-8900   Fx: 415-252-8991   TF: 888-792-2873

Family, Women for Faith &   www.wf-f.org
PO Box 3286   Saint Louis MO 63132
Ph: 314-863-8385   Fx: 314-863-5858

Famous Fone Friends   www.nancycartwright.com/volunteer_fff.html
9101 Sawyer St   Los Angeles CA 90035
Ph: 310-204-5683

Fan Collectors Association, Antique   www.fancollectors.org
PO Box 5473   Sarasota FL 34277
Ph: 941-955-8232   Fx: 941-952-1491

Fanconi Anemia Research Fund Inc   www.fanconi.org
1801 Willamette St Suite 200   Eugene OR 97401
Ph: 541-687-4658   Fx: 541-687-0548

Fantastic in the Arts, International Association for the   wiz.cath.vt.edu/iafa

Fantasy Artists, Association of Science Fiction &   www.asfa-art.org

Fantasy Gaming Society, International   www.ifgs.org
PO Box 3577   Boulder CO 80307
Ph: 303-443-1012

Fantasy & Horror Films, Academy of Science Fiction   www.saturnawards.org
334 W 54th St   Los Angeles CA 90037
Ph: 323-752-5811

Fantasy Writers of America Inc, Science Fiction &   www.sfwa.org
PO Box 877   Chestertown MD 21620
Ph: 410-778-3052

Farm & Agricultural Museums, Association for Living History   www.alhfam.org
8774 Rt 45 NW   North Bloomfield OH 44450
Ph: 440-685-4410

Farm Aid   www.farmaid.org
11 Ward St Suite 200   Somerville MA 02143
Ph: 617-354-2922   Fx: 617-354-6992   TF: 800-327-6243

Farm Animal Reform Movement   www.farmusa.org
PO Box 30654   Bethesda MD 20824
Ph: 301-530-1737   Fx: 301-530-5747   TF: 800-632-8688

Farm Broadcasters, National Association of   www.nafb.com
700 Branch St Suite 8 PO Box 500   Platte City MO 64079
Ph: 816-431-4032   Fx: 816-431-4087

Farm Bureau Federation, American   www.fb.com
225 W Touhy Ave   Park Ridge IL 60068
Ph: 847-685-8600   Fx: 847-685-8896

Farm Bureau Foundation for Agriculture, American   www.agfoundation.org
225 Touhy Ave   Park Ridge IL 60068
Ph: 847-685-8764   Fx: 847-685-8969

Farm-City Council, National   www.farmcity.org
225 Touhy Ave   Park Ridge IL 60068
Ph: 847-685-8764   Fx: 847-685-8969

Farm Coalition, National Family   www.nffc.net
110 Maryland Ave NE Suite 307   Washington DC 20002
Ph: 202-543-5675   Fx: 202-543-0978   TF: 800-639-3276

Farm Credit Council   www.fccouncil.com
50 F St NW Suite 900   Washington DC 20001
Ph: 202-626-8710   Fx: 202-626-8718

Farm Equipment Appraisers, American   www.amagappraisers.com/farmeqip.htm
Society of   1126 Eastland Dr N Suite 100 PO Box 186   Twin
Falls ID 83303
Ph: 208-733-2323   Fx: 208-733-2326   TF: 800-488-7570

Farm Equipment Manufacturers Association   www.farmequip.org
1000 Executive Pkwy Suite 100   Saint Louis MO 63141
Ph: 314-878-2304   Fx: 314-878-1742

Farm Equipment Wholesalers Association   www.fewa.org
Box 1347   Iowa City IA 52244
Ph: 319-354-5156   Fx: 319-354-5157

Farm Foundation   www.farmfoundation.org
1211 W 22nd St Suite 216   Oak Brook IL 60523
Ph: 630-571-9393   Fx: 630-571-9580

Farm Labor Organizing Committee AFL-CIO   floc.com
1221 Broadway St   Toledo OH 43609
Ph: 419-243-3456   Fx: 419-243-5655

Farm Managers & Rural Appraisers, American Society of www.asfmra.org
950 S Cherry St Suite 508   Denver CO 80246
Ph: 303-758-3513 ▪ Fx: 303-758-0190

Farm Safety 4 Just Kids www.fs4jk.org
PO Box 458   Earlham IA 50072
Ph: 515-758-2827 ▪ Fx: 515-758-2517 ▪ TF: 800-423-5437

Farm Safety, National Institute for www.ag.ohio-state.edu/~agsafety/NIFS/nifs.htm
Univ of Wisconsin 460 Henry Mall   Madison WI 53706
Ph: 608-265-0568 ▪ Fx: 608-262-1228

Farm Sanctuary www.farmsanctuary.org
PO Box 150   Watkins Glen NY 14891
Ph: 607-583-2225 ▪ Fx: 607-583-2041

Farm Show Council, North American www.ag.ohio-state.edu/~farmshow

Farm Worker Health Services Inc www.farmworkerhealth.org
1221 Massachusetts Ave NW Suite 5   Washington DC 20005
Ph: 202-347-7377 ▪ Fx: 202-347-6385

Farm Worker Ministry, National www.nfwm.org
438 N Skinker Blvd   Saint Louis MO 63130
Ph: 314-726-6470 ▪ Fx: 314-726-6427

Farm Workers, United www.ufw.org
PO Box 62   Keene CA 93531
Ph: 661-822-5571 ▪ Fx: 661-823-6177

Farmer Cooperatives, National Council of www.ncfc.org
50 F St NW Suite 900   Washington DC 20001
Ph: 202-626-8700 ▪ Fx: 202-626-8722

Farmer Educational Association, National Young www.nyfea.org
PO Box 20326   Montgomery AL 36120
Ph: 334-288-0097

Farmers & Agriculturalists Association, Black www.coax.net/people/lwf/bfaa.htm
PO Box 61   Tillery NC 27887
Ph: 252-826-2800 ▪ Fx: 252-826-3244

Farmers of America, Catfish
1100 Hwy 82 E Suite 202   Indianola MS 38751
Ph: 662-887-2699 ▪ Fx: 662-887-6857

Farmers' Direct Marketing Association, North American www.nafdma.com
62 White Loaf Rd   Southampton MA 01073
Ph: 413-529-0386

Farmers Educational & Cooperative Union of America www.nfu.org
11900 E Cornell Ave   Aurora CO 80014
Ph: 303-337-5500 ▪ Fx: 303-368-1390 ▪ TF: 800-347-1961

Farmers, Institute for the Advancement of Hawaiian www.opihi.com/sovereignty
86-649 Puuhulu Rd   Waianae HI 96792
Ph: 808-697-3045 ▪ Fx: 808-696-7774

Farmers, International Flying www.flyingfarmers.org
PO Box 9124   Wichita KS 67277
Ph: 316-943-4234 ▪ Fx: 800-266-5415

Farmers Organization, National www.nfo.org
528 Billy Sunday Rd Suite 100   Ames IA 50010
Ph: 515-292-2000 ▪ Fx: 515-292-7106 ▪ TF: 800-247-2110

FarmHouse Fraternity www.farmhouse.org
11020 NW Ambassador Dr Suite 330   Kansas City MO 64153
Ph: 816-891-9445 ▪ Fx: 816-891-0838

Farming Association, Ecological www.eco-farm.org
406 Main St Suite 313   Watsonville CA 95076
Ph: 831-763-2111 ▪ Fx: 831-763-2112

Farming Association, Humane www.hfa.org
PO Box 3577   San Rafael CA 94912
Ph: 415-771-2253 ▪ Fx: 415-485-0106

Farming & Gardening Association Inc, Biodynamic www.biodynamics.com
25844 Butler Rd   Junction City OR 97448
Ph: 541-998-0105 ▪ Fx: 541-998-0106 ▪ TF: 888-561-7797

Farmland Trust, American www.farmland.org
1200 18th St NW Suite 800   Washington DC 20036
Ph: 202-331-7300 ▪ Fx: 202-659-8339 ▪ TF: 800-431-1499

Farms International www.farmsinternational.com
PO Box 270   Knife River MN 55609
Ph: 218-834-2676

Farmworker Health, National Center for www.ncfh.org
1770 FM 967   Buda TX 78610
Ph: 512-312-2700 ▪ Fx: 512-312-2600

Farmworker Justice Fund www.fwjustice.org
1010 Vermont Ave NW Suite 915   Washington DC 20005
Ph: 202-783-2628 ▪ Fx: 202-783-2561

Farmworker Opportunity Programs, Association of www.afop.org
4350 N Fairfax Dr Suite 410   Arlington VA 22203
Ph: 703-528-4141 ▪ Fx: 703-528-4145

Farrier's Association, American www.americanfarriers.org
4509 Iron Works Pkwy Suite 1   Lexington KY 40511
Ph: 859-233-7411 ▪ Fx: 859-231-7862

Farsarotul, Society www.farsarotul.org
466 Silver Ln PO Box 753   Trumbull CT 06611
Ph: 203-375-0600 ▪ Fx: 203-375-5003

Fashion Accessories Association, National www.accessoryweb.com
350 5th Ave Suite 2030   New York NY 10118
Ph: 212-947-3424 ▪ Fx: 212-629-0361

Fashion Accessories Shippers Association Inc www.accessoryweb.com
350 5th Ave Suite 2030   New York NY 10118
Ph: 212-947-3424 ▪ Fx: 212-629-0361

Fashion & Costume Jewelry Club, Vintage www.lizjewel.com/vf
PO Box 265   Glen Oaks NY 11004
Ph: 718-939-3095 ▪ Fx: 718-939-7888

Fashion Designers of America, Council of www.cfda.com
1412 Broadway Suite 2006   New York NY 10018
Ph: 212-302-1821 ▪ Fx: 212-768-0515

Fashion Group International www.fgi.org
597 5th Ave 8th Fl   New York NY 10017
Ph: 212-593-1715 ▪ Fx: 212-593-1925

Fashion Products Association, Home
355 Lexington Ave 17th Fl   New York NY 10017
Ph: 212-297-2122 ▪ Fx: 212-370-9047

Fastener Distributors Association, National www.nfda-fastener.org
1717 E 9th St Suite 1185   Cleveland OH 44114
Ph: 216-579-1571 ▪ Fx: 216-579-1531

Fastener Industry Coalition
1717 E 9th St Suite 1185   Cleveland OH 44114
Ph: 216-579-1571 ▪ Fx: 216-579-1531

Fasteners Distributors Association, Specialty Tools & www.stafda.org
PO Box 44   Elm Grove WI 53122
Ph: 262-784-4774 ▪ Fx: 262-784-5059 ▪ TF: 800-352-2981

Fasteners Institute, Industrial www.industrial-fasteners.org
1717 E 9th St Suite 1105   Cleveland OH 44114
Ph: 216-241-1482 ▪ Fx: 216-241-5901

Fat Acceptance, National Association to Advance www.naafa.org
PO Box 188620   Sacramento CA 95818
Ph: 916-558-6880 ▪ Fx: 916-558-6881

Father Judge Apostolic Center www.fjac.org
1292 Long Hill Rd   Stirling NJ 07980
Ph: 908-647-7112 ▪ Fx: 908-626-0350

Fathering, National Center for www.fathers.com
PO Box 413888   Kansas City MO 64141
Ph: 913-384-4661 ▪ Fx: 913-384-4665 ▪ TF: 800-593-3237

Fathers & Children, American Coalition for www.acfc.org
22365 El Toro Rd Suite 335   Lake Forest CA 92630
Ph: 800-978-3237 ▪ Fx: 949-859-1514

Fathers & Children, National Congress for www.ncfc.net
9454 Wilshire Blvd Suite 907   Beverly Hills CA 90212
Ph: 310-247-6051 ▪ TF: 800-733-3237

Fathers Network www.fathersnetwork.org
16120 NE 8th St   Bellevue WA 98008
Ph: 425-747-4004 ▪ Fx: 425-747-1069

Fathers Resource Center, Men & www.fathers.org
807 Brazos St Suite 315   Austin TX 78701
Ph: 512-472-3237 ▪ Fx: 512-499-8056

Fats & Proteins Research Foundation Inc www.fprf.org
16551 Old Colonial Rd   Bloomington IL 61704
Ph: 309-829-7744 ▪ Fx: 309-829-5147

Fauchard Pierre Academy www.fauchard.org
PO Box 80330   Las Vegas NV 89180
Ph: 702-651-5013 ▪ Fx: 702-651-5537 ▪ TF: 800-232-0099

FBI Inc, Society of Former Special Agents of the www.socxfbi.org
PO Box 1027   Quantico VA 22134
Ph: 703-640-6469 ▪ Fx: 703-640-6537

FCIB: Association of Executives in Finance Credit & www.fcibglobal.com
International Business 8840 Columbia 100 Pkwy   Columbia
MD 21045
Ph: 410-423-1840 ▪ Fx: 410-423-1845 ▪ TF: 888-256-3242

Fear, Freedom From www.freedomfromfear.org
308 Seaview Ave   Staten Island NY 10305
Ph: 718-351-1717 ▪ Fx: 718-667-8893 ▪ TF: 888-442-2022

Feature Editors, American Association of Sunday & www.aasfe.org
Univ of Maryland Merrill College of Journalism 1117 Journalism
Bldg   College Park MD 20742
Ph: 301-314-2631 ▪ Fx: 301-314-9166

Feature Project, Independent www.ifp.org
104 W 29th St 12th Fl   New York NY 10001
Ph: 212-465-8200 ▪ Fx: 212-465-8525

Fed-Search www.fed-search.org

Federal Administrative Law Judges Conference www.faljc.org
2000 Pennsylvania Ave NW Suite 260   Washington DC 20006
Ph: 202-675-3065 ▪ Fx: 202-219-3289

Federal Bar Association fedbar.org
2215 M St NW   Washington DC 20037
Ph: 202-785-1614 ▪ Fx: 202-785-1568

Federal Budget, Committee for a Responsible www.crfb.org
1630 Connecticut Ave NW 7th Fl   Washington DC 20009
Ph: 202-986-6599 ▪ Fx: 202-986-3696

Federal Bureau of Investigation Agents Association www.fbiaa.org
PO Box 250   New Rochelle NY 10801
Ph: 914-235-7580 ▪ Fx: 914-235-8235

Federal Communications Bar Association www.fcba.org
1020 19th St NW Suite 325   Washington DC 20036
Ph: 202-293-4000 ▪ Fx: 202-293-4317

Federal Communications Consulting Engineers, Association of www.afcce.org

Federal Court Clerks Association www.fcca.ws

Federal Credit Unions, National Association of www.nafcunet.org
3138 10th St N   Arlington VA 22201
Ph: 703-522-4770 ▪ Fx: 703-524-1082 ▪ TF: 800-336-4644

Federal Education Association www.feaonline.org
1101 15th St NW Suite 1002   Washington DC 20005
Ph: 202-822-7850 ▪ Fx: 202-822-7816

Federal Education Program Administrators, National Association of www.nafepa.org
830 Virginia Ave   Sheybogan WI 53081
Ph: 920-459-6718 ▪ Fx: 920-803-7761

Federal Employees Education & Assistance Fund www.feea.org
8441 W Bowles Ave Suite 200   Littleton CO 80123
Ph: 303-933-7580 ▪ Fx: 303-933-7587 ▪ TF: 800-323-4140

Federal Employees, National Alliance of Postal & www.napfe.com
1628 11th St NW   Washington DC 20001
Ph: 202-939-6325 ▪ Fx: 202-939-6389

Federal Employees, National Association of Retired www.narfe.org
606 N Washington St   Alexandria VA 22314
Ph: 703-838-7760 ▪ Fx: 703-838-7785 ▪ TF: 800-627-3394

Federal Employees, National Federation of www.nffe.org
1016 16th St NW Suite 300   Washington DC 20036
Ph: 202-862-4400 ▪ Fx: 202-862-4432

Federal Executives, National Association of Hispanic www.nahfe.org
PO Box 469   Herndon VA 20172
Ph: 703-787-0291 ▪ Fx: 703-787-4675

Federal Extravagance, Seniors Against   www.s-a-f-e.org
413 Delaware Ave Wilmington DE 19803
Ph: 302-478-0676

Federal Government, Society for History in the   www.shfg.org
PO Box 14139 Ben Franklin Stn Washington DC 20044
Ph: 202-501-5350 ▪ Fx: 202-219-2176

Federal Information Resources Management, Association for   www.affirm.org
PO Box 2851 Washington DC 20013
Ph: 202-208-2780

Federal Judges Association   www.federaljudgesassoc.org
111 W Washington St Suite 1100 Chicago IL 60602
Ph: 312-641-1441 ▪ Fx: 312-641-1288

Federal Labor Relations Professionals, Society of
PO Box 25112 Arlington VA 22202
Ph: 703-685-4130 ▪ Fx: 703-685-1144

Federal Law Enforcement Officers Association   www.fleoa.org
PO Box 326 Lewisberry PA 17339
Ph: 717-938-2300 ▪ Fx: 717-932-2262

Federal Managers Association   www.fedmanagers.org
1641 Prince St Alexandria VA 22314
Ph: 703-683-8700 ▪ Fx: 703-683-8707

Federal Network for Sustainability   www.federalsustainability.org
1331 H St NW Suite 1000 Washington DC 20005
Ph: 202-628-6100 ▪ Fx: 202-393-5043

Federal Physicians Association   www.fedphy.org
9001 Braddock Rd Suite 380 Springfield VA 22151
Ph: 703-323-9888 ▪ Fx: 703-426-8400 ▪ TF: 800-403-3374

Federal Probation & Pretrial Officers Association   www.fppoa.org
350 S Main St Suite 160 Salt Lake City UT 84101
Ph: 801-524-6943

Federal Search Foundation   www.fed-search.org

Federal Statistics, Council of Professional Associations on   www.copafs.org
1429 Duke St Suite 402 Alexandria VA 22314
Ph: 703-836-0404 ▪ Fx: 703-684-3410

Federal Superannuates National Association   www.fsna.com
1052 St Laurent Blvd Ottawa ON K1K3B4
Ph: 613-745-2559 ▪ Fx: 613-745-5457

Federal Trial Judges, National Conference of   www.abanet.org/jd/ncftjweb.html
541 N Fairbanks Ct Chicago IL 60611
Ph: 312-988-5689 ▪ Fx: 312-988-5709

Federal Veterinarians, National Association of   users.erols.com/nafv
1101 Vermont Ave NW Suite 710 Washington DC 20005
Ph: 202-289-6334 ▪ Fx: 202-842-4360

Federalist Society for Law & Public Policy Studies   www.fed-soc.org
1015 18th St NW Suite 425 Washington DC 20036
Ph: 202-822-8138 ▪ Fx: 202-296-8061

Federally Employed Women Inc   www.few.org
PO Box 27687 Washington DC 20038
Ph: 202-898-0994

Federally Impacted Schools, National Association of   www.sso.org/nafis
444 N Capitol St NW Suite 419 Washington DC 20001
Ph: 202-624-5455 ▪ Fx: 202-624-5468

Federated Ambulatory Surgery Association   www.fasa.org
700 N Fairfax St Suite 306 Alexandria VA 22314
Ph: 703-836-8808 ▪ Fx: 703-549-0976

Federation of American Hospitals   www.fahs.com
801 Pennsylvania Ave NW Suite 245 Washington DC 20004
Ph: 202-624-1500 ▪ Fx: 202-737-6462

Federation for American Immigration Reform   www.fairus.org
1666 Connecticut Ave NW Suite 400 Washington DC 20009
Ph: 202-328-7004 ▪ Fx: 202-387-3447 ▪ TF: 877-627-3247

Federation of American Scientists   www.fas.org
1717 K St NW Suite 209 Washington DC 20036
Ph: 202-546-3300 ▪ Fx: 202-675-1010

Federation of American Societies for Experimental Biology   www.faseb.org
9650 Rockville Pike Bethesda MD 20814
Ph: 301-530-7000 ▪ Fx: 301-530-7001 ▪ TF: 800-433-2732

Federation of Analytical Chemistry & Spectroscopy Societies   www.facss.org
PO Box 24379 Sante Fe NM 87502
Ph: 505-820-1648 ▪ Fx: 505-989-1073

Federation of Animal Science Societies   www.fass.org
1111 N Dunlap Ave Savoy IL 61874
Ph: 217-356-3182 ▪ Fx: 217-398-4119

Federation of Associations of Regulatory Boards   www.farb.org
1603 Orrington Ave Suite 2080-F Evanston IL 60201
Ph: 847-328-7909 ▪ Fx: 847-864-0588

Federation of Behavioral Psychological & Cognitive Sciences   www.thefederationonline.org
750 1st NE Suite 5007 Washington DC 20002
Ph: 202-336-5920 ▪ Fx: 202-336-5953

Federation for Children with Special Needs   www.fcsn.org
1135 Tremont St Suite 420 Boston MA 02120
Ph: 617-236-7210 ▪ Fx: 617-572-2094 ▪ TF: 800-331-0688

Federation of Chiropractic Licensing Boards   www.fclb.org
901 54th Ave Suite 101 Greeley CO 80634
Ph: 970-356-3500 ▪ Fx: 970-356-3599

Federation of Defense & Corporate Counsel Inc   www.thefederation.org
11812-A N 56th St Tampa FL 33617
Ph: 813-983-0022 ▪ Fx: 813-988-5837

Federation of Diocesan Liturgical Commissions   www.fdlc.org
415 Michigan Ave NE Suite 70 Washington DC 20017
Ph: 202-635-6990 ▪ Fx: 202-529-2452

Federation of Environmental Technologists Inc   www.fetinc.org
PO Box 624 Slinger WI 53086
Ph: 262-644-0070 ▪ Fx: 262-644-7106

Federation of Families for Children's Mental Health   www.ffcmh.org
1101 King St Suite 420 Alexandria VA 22314
Ph: 703-684-7710 ▪ Fx: 703-836-1040

Federation of Fire Chaplains   www.ffcfirechaplains.org
185 County Rd Suite 1602 Clifton TX 76634
Ph: 254-622-8514

Federation of Fly Fishers   www.fedflyfishers.org
PO Box 1595 Bozeman MT 59771
Ph: 406-585-7592 ▪ Fx: 406-585-7596

Federation of Gay Games   www.gaygames.org
584 Castro St Suite 343 San Francisco CA 94114
Ph: 415-695-0222 ▪ Fx: 800-877-1373

Federation of International Trade Associations   www.fita.org
11800 Sunrise Valley Dr Suite 210 Reston VA 20191
Ph: 703-620-1588 ▪ Fx: 703-620-4922

Federation Internationale des Quilleurs   www.fiq.org
1631 Mesa Ave Suite A Colorado Springs CO 80906
Ph: 719-636-2695 ▪ Fx: 719-636-3300

Federation of Jewish Men's Clubs   fjmc.org
475 Riverside Dr Suite 832 New York NY 10115
Ph: 212-749-8100 ▪ Fx: 212-316-4271 ▪ TF: 800-288-3562

Federation of Masons of the World
1017 E 11th St Austin TX 78702
Ph: 512-477-5380 ▪ Fx: 512-477-5313

Federation of Materials Societies   www.materialsocieties.org
910 17th St NW Suite 800 Washington DC 20006
Ph: 202-296-9282 ▪ Fx: 202-833-3014

Federation of Modern Painters & Sculptors
234 W 21st St New York NY 10011
Ph: 212-255-4858

Federation of Podiatric Medical Boards   www.fpmb.org
PO Box 880187 Boca Raton FL 33474
Ph: 561-477-3060

Federation of Police Security & Correction Officers   www.fopsco-afspa.org
71 E Cherry St Rahway NJ 07065
Ph: 732-388-3323 ▪ Fx: 732-388-5620

Federation of Protestant Welfare Agencies   www.fpwa.org
281 Park Ave S New York NY 10010
Ph: 212-777-4800 ▪ Fx: 212-673-4085

Federation of Societies for Coatings Technology   www.coatingstech.org
492 Norristown Rd Blue Bell PA 19422
Ph: 610-940-0777 ▪ Fx: 610-940-0292

Federation of Southern Cooperatives/Land Assistance Fund   www.federationsoutherncoop.com
2769 Church St East Point GA 30344
Ph: 404-765-0991 ▪ Fx: 404-765-9178

Federation of State Boards of Physical Therapy   www.fsbpt.org
509 Wythe St Alexandria VA 22314
Ph: 703-299-3100 ▪ Fx: 703-299-3110 ▪ TF: 800-881-1430

Federation of State Humanities Councils   www.statehumanities.com
1600 Wilson Blvd Suite 902 Arlington VA 22209
Ph: 703-908-9700 ▪ Fx: 703-908-9706

Federation of State Medical Boards of the US Inc   www.fsmb.org
400 Fuller Wiser Rd Suite 300 Euless TX 76039
Ph: 817-868-4000 ▪ Fx: 817-868-4099 ▪ TF: 800-876-5396

Federation of Straight Chiropractors & Organizations   www.straightchiropractic.com
2276 Wassergass Rd Hellertown PA 18055
Ph: 610-838-3030 ▪ Fx: 610-838-3031 ▪ TF: 800-521-9856

Federation of Tax Administrators   www.taxadmin.org
444 N Capitol St NW Suite 348 Washington DC 20001
Ph: 202-624-5890 ▪ Fx: 202-624-7888

Federation of Turkish-American Associations Inc   www.ftaa.org
821 United Nations Plaza 2nd Fl New York NY 10017
Ph: 212-682-7688 ▪ Fx: 212-687-3026

Federation of Woman's Exchanges
19 Upper Price Rd Saint Louis MO 63132
Ph: 314-997-4364 ▪ Fx: 314-872-3505

FedPAC
801 Pennsylvania Ave NW Suite 245 Washington DC 20004
Ph: 202-624-1500 ▪ Fx: 202-737-6462

Feed Association, National Grain &   www.ngfa.org
1250 I St NW Suite 1003 Washington DC 20005
Ph: 202-289-0873 ▪ Fx: 202-289-5388

Feed Association, Pacific Northwest Grain &   www.pnwgfa.org
200 SW Market St Suite 348 Portland OR 97201
Ph: 503-227-0234 ▪ Fx: 503-227-0059

Feed the Children   www.feedthechildren.org
PO Box 36 Oklahoma City OK 73101
Ph: 405-942-0228 ▪ Fx: 405-945-4177 ▪ TF: 800-627-4556

Feed Industry Association, American   www.afia.org
1501 Wilson Blvd Suite 1100 Arlington VA 22209
Ph: 703-524-0810 ▪ Fx: 703-524-1921

Feingold Association of the US   www.feingold.org
127 E Main St Suite 106 Riverhead NY 11901
Ph: 631-369-9340 ▪ Fx: 631-369-2988 ▪ TF: 800-321-3287

Feldenkrais Educational Foundation of North America   www.feldenkrais.com
3611 SW Hood Ave Suite 100 Portland OR 97201
Ph: 503-221-6612 ▪ Fx: 503-221-6616 ▪ TF: 800-775-2118

Feline Practitioners, American Association of   www.aafponline.org
618 Church St Suite 220 Nashville TN 37219
Ph: 615-259-7788 ▪ Fx: 615-254-7047 ▪ TF: 800-204-3514

Fellows of the American Bar Foundation   fellows.abfn.org
750 N Lake Shore Dr Chicago IL 60611
Ph: 312-988-6500 ▪ Fx: 312-988-6611

Fellowship of Associates of Medical Evangelism   www.fameworld.org
PO Box 33548 Indianapolis IN 46203
Ph: 317-358-2480 ▪ Fx: 317-358-2483

Fellowship of Catholic Scholars   www.catholicscholars.org
916 S Wolcott St Chicago IL 60612
Ph: 312-355-3336

Fellowship of Christian Airline Personnel   www.fcap.org
136 Providence Rd Fayetteville GA 30215
Ph: 770-461-9320 ▪ Fx: 770-461-2720

Fellowship of Christian Athletes   www.fca.org
8701 Leeds Rd Kansas City MO 64129
Ph: 816-921-0909 ▪ Fx: 816-921-8755 ▪ TF: 800-289-0909

Fellowship of Christian Firefighters International fellowshipofchristianfirefighters.com
PO Box 901   Fort Collins CO 80522
Ph: 970-407-0083   ▪ TF: 800-322-9848

Fellowship of Christian Magicians www.gospelcom.net/fcm

Fellowship of Christian Peace Officers USA www.fcpo.org
PO Box 3686   Chattanooga TN 37404
Ph: 423-622-1234   ▪ Fx: 423-622-9725

Fellowship of Christian Released Time Ministries www.rtce.org
5722 Lime Ave   Long Beach CA 90805
Ph: 562-428-7733   ▪ Fx: 562-728-7633   ▪ TF: 800-360-7943

Fellowship of Companies for Christ International www.myfcci.org
12201 Pangborn Ave   Downey CA 90241
Ph: 562-803-3400   ▪ Fx: 562-803-3344

Fellowship of Concerned Churchmen netministries.org/see/charmin/CM06091
4800 Dupont Ave S   Minneapolis MN 55409
Ph: 612-824-3933

Fellowship Foundation, Woodrow Wilson National www.woodrow.org
5 Vaughn Dr CN 5281   Princeton NJ 08540
Ph: 609-452-7007   ▪ Fx: 609-452-0066

(Fellowship) Gyro International www.gyro-international.org
1019 Mentor Ave PO Box 489   Painesville OH 44077
Ph: 440-352-2501   ▪ Fx: 440-352-3882

Fellowship International Mission www.gospelcom.net/fim/
555 S 24th St   Allentown PA 18104
Ph: 610-435-9099   ▪ Fx: 610-435-1641   ▪ TF: 888-346-9099

Fellowship of Missions www.fellowshipofmissions.org
140 Jacqueline Dr   Berea OH 44017
Ph: 440-243-0156

Fellowship of Orthodox Christians in America www.orthodoxfellowship.org
10 Downs Dr   Wilkes-Barre PA 18705
Ph: 570-825-3158   ▪ Fx: 570-825-0136

Fellowship in Prayer www.sacredjourney.org
291 Witherspoon St   Princeton NJ 08540
Ph: 609-924-6863   ▪ Fx: 609-924-6910

Fellowship of Reconciliation www.forusa.org
PO Box 271   Nyack NY 10960
Ph: 845-358-4601   ▪ Fx: 845-358-4924

Fellowship of Saint James
PO Box 410788   Chicago IL 60641
Ph: 773-481-1090   ▪ Fx: 773-481-1095

Fellowship of Saint John the Divine www.antiochian.org/Fellowship
Antiochian Orthodox Christian Archdiocese 358 Mountain
   Rd   Englewood NJ 07631
Ph: 201-871-1355   ▪ Fx: 201-871-7954

Fellowship of United Methodists in Music & Worship Arts www.fummwa.org
PO Box 24787   Nashville TN 37202
Ph: 615-749-6875   ▪ Fx: 615-749-6874   ▪ TF: 800-952-8977

(Fellowships) John Simon Guggenheim Memorial Foundation www.gf.org
90 Park Ave 33rd Fl   New York NY 10016
Ph: 212-687-4470   ▪ Fx: 212-697-3248

Female Executives, National Association for www.nafe.com
260 Madison Ave 3rd Fl   New York NY 10016
Ph: 212-351-6400   ▪ TF: 800-927-6233

Female Health, World Foundation for Medical Studies in www.wffh.org
405 Main St Suite 8   Port Washington NY 11050
Ph: 516-944-8655   ▪ Fx: 516-944-8663

Female Officers, Association on Programs for
500 E 4th St   Chester PA 19013
Ph: 610-490-4340

Feminism, Society for Analytical www.ukans.edu/~acudd/safhomepage.htm
Univ of Kentucky Dept of Philosophy Suite 1415   Lexington KY
   40506
Ph: 859-257-1861

Feminist Anthropology, Association for sscl.berkeley.edu/~afaweb
c/o American Anthropological Assn 2200 Wilson Blvd Suite
   600   Arlington VA 22201
Ph: 703-528-1902   ▪ Fx: 703-528-3546

Feminist Approaches to Bioethics, International www.msu.edu/~hlnelson/fab
California State Univ - Fresno 5340 N Campus Dr MS
   SS78   Fresno CA 93740
Ph: 559-278-5721

Feminist Karate Union www.geocities.com/wellesley/5466
1426 S Jackson St 3rd Fl   Seattle WA 98107
Ph: 206-325-3878

Feminist Majority Foundation www.feminist.org
1600 Wilson Blvd Suite 801   Arlington VA 22209
Ph: 703-522-2214   ▪ Fx: 703-522-2219

Feminists for Animal Rights www.farinc.org
PO Box 41355   Tucson AZ 85717
Ph: 520-825-6852

Fence Association, American www.americanfenceassociation.com
800 Roosevelt Rd Bldg C-20   Glen Ellyn IL 60137
Ph: 630-942-6598   ▪ Fx: 630-790-3095   ▪ TF: 800-822-4342

Fence Manufacturers Institute, Chain Link www.chainlinkinfo.org
10015 Old Columbia Rd Suite B-215   Columbia MD 21046
Ph: 301-596-2583   ▪ Fx: 301-596-2594

Fencing Association, Intercollegiate ifa.ecac.org
PO Box 3   Centerville MA 02632
Ph: 508-771-5060   ▪ Fx: 508-771-9481

Fencing Association, US www.usfencing.org
1 Olympic Plaza   Colorado Springs CO 80909
Ph: 719-866-4511   ▪ Fx: 719-632-5737

Fencing Coaches Association, US www.usfca.org
PO Box 1966   Hoboken NJ 07030
Ph: 888-927-6687

Feng Shui Institute of America www.windwater.com
PO Box 488   Wabasso FL 32970
Ph: 561-589-9900   ▪ Fx: 561-589-1611

Fenton Art Glass Collectors of America Inc fagcainc.wirefire.com
PO Box 384   Williamstown WV 26187
Ph: 304-375-6196   ▪ Fx: 304-375-4679

Fenton Glass Society, National www.fentonglasssociety.org
PO Box 4008   Marietta OH 45750
Ph: 740-374-3345   ▪ Fx: 740-376-9708

Feral Cat Friends www.feralcatfriends.org
8255 White Oak Rd   Garner NC 27529
Ph: 919-662-5365

Fern Society, American www.amerfernsoc.org
Missouri Botanical Garden PO Box 229   Saint Louis MO 63166
Ph: 314-577-5100

Ferrari Club of America www.ferrariclubofamerica.org
PO Box 720597   Atlanta GA 30358
Ph: 800-328-0444   ▪ Fx: 770-936-9392

Ferret Association Inc, American www.ferret.org
626-C Admiral Dr PMB 255   Annapolis MD 21401
Ph: 888-337-7381   ▪ Fx: 516-908-5215

Ferret Fanciers Club
2916 Perrysville Ave   Pittsburgh PA 15214
Ph: 412-322-1161

Fertility Research Foundation www.frfbaby.com
877 Park Ave   New York NY 10021
Ph: 212-744-5500   ▪ Fx: 212-744-6536

FertilityCare Professionals, American Academy of www.aafcp.org
11700 Studt Ave Suite C   Saint Louis MO 63141
Ph: 314-991-0327   ▪ Fx: 314-692-8097

Fertilizer Development Center, International www.ifdc.org
PO Box 2040   Muscle Shoals AL 35662
Ph: 256-381-6600   ▪ Fx: 256-381-7408

Fertilizer Industry Round Table www.firt.org
1914 Baldwin Mill Rd   Forest Hill MD 21050
Ph: 410-557-8026

Fertilizer Institute www.tfi.org
820 1st St NE Suite 430   Washington DC 20002
Ph: 202-962-0490   ▪ Fx: 202-962-0575

Festival of Microtonal Music Inc, American www.afmm.org
318 E 70th St Suite 5FW   New York NY 10021
Ph: 212-517-3550   ▪ Fx: 212-517-5495

Festival Organizations, International Federation of www.morenofidof.org
4230 Stansbury Ave Suite 105   Sherman Oaks CA 91423
Ph: 818-789-7596   ▪ Fx: 818-784-9141

Festivals, Association of Scottish Games & www.asgf.org
3000 Walnut Ave   Altoona PA 16601
Ph: 412-851-9900   ▪ Fx: 412-854-5963

Festivals & Events Association, International www.ifea.com
2601 Eastover Terr   Boise ID 83706
Ph: 208-433-0950   ▪ Fx: 208-433-9812

Fetal Medicine, Society for Maternal www.smfm.org
409 12th St SW   Washington DC 20024
Ph: 202-863-2476   ▪ Fx: 202-554-1132

FFA Organization, National www.ffa.org
6060 FFA Dr   Indianapolis IN 46268
Ph: 317-802-6060   ▪ Fx: 317-802-6061   ▪ TF: 800-772-0939

FIABCI-USA www.fiabci-usa.com
2000 N 15th St Suite 101   Arlington VA 22201
Ph: 703-524-4279

Fiber Art International, Friends of
PO Box 468   Western Springs IL 60558
Ph: 708-246-9466

Fiber Association, Mid Atlantic www.mafafiber.org
PO Box 701   Scranton PA 18501
Ph: 570-961-2304   ▪ Fx: 570-961-5110

Fiber Economics Bureau Inc www.fibereconomics.com
1530 Wilson Blvd Suite 690   Arlington VA 22209
Ph: 703-875-0676   ▪ Fx: 703-875-0675

Fiber Manufacturers Association Inc, American www.afma.org
1530 Wilson Blvd Suite 690   Arlington VA 22209
Ph: 703-875-0432   ▪ Fx: 703-875-0907

Fiber Society fs.tx.ncsu.edu
North Carolina State Univ College of Textiles   Raleigh NC
   27695
Ph: 919-515-6555   ▪ Fx: 919-515-4556

Fiberboard Association, American www.fiberboard.org
1210 W Northwest Hwy   Palatine IL 60067
Ph: 847-934-8394   ▪ Fx: 847-934-8803

Fiberglass Tank & Pipe Institute www.fiberglasstankandpipe.com
11150 Wilcrest Dr Suite 101   Houston TX 77099
Ph: 281-568-4100   ▪ Fx: 281-568-4500

Fibre Box Association www.fibrebox.org
2850 Golf Rd Suite 412   Rolling Meadows IL 60008
Ph: 847-364-9600   ▪ Fx: 847-364-9639

Fibre Channel Industry Association www.fibrechannel.org
PO Box 29920   San Francisco CA 94129
Ph: 415-561-6270   ▪ Fx: 415-561-6120

Fibrodysplasia Ossificans Progressiva Association, International www.ifopa.org
PO Box 196217   Winter Springs FL 32719
Ph: 407-365-4194   ▪ Fx: 407-365-3213

Fibromyalgia Partnership Inc, National www.fmpartnership.org
140 Zinn Way PO Box 160   Linden VA 22642
Ph: 866-725-4404   ▪ Fx: 866-666-2727

Fibromyalgia Syndrome Association, American www.afsafund.org
6380 E Tanque Verde Suite D   Tucson AZ 85715
Ph: 520-733-1570

Fiddlers' Association, National Oldtime
309 State St   Weiser ID 83672
Ph: 800-437-1280   ▪ Fx: 208-414-0255

Fiddling Revival Ltd, Scottish www.scottishfiddling.org
1938 Rose Villa St   Pasadena CA 91107
Ph: 626-792-6323   ▪ Fx: 626-793-9401

Fidelco Guide Dog Foundation   www.fidelco.org
PO Box 142   Bloomfield CT 06002
Ph: 860-243-5200 ▪ Fx: 860-243-7215

Fiduciaries, National Council of Real Estate Investment   www.ncreif.org
2 Prudential Plaza 180 N Stetson Ave Suite 2515   Chicago IL 60601
Ph: 312-819-5890 ▪ Fx: 312-819-5891

Fiduciary & Risk Management Association   www.thefirma.org
PO Box 48297   Athens GA 30604
Ph: 706-354-0083 ▪ Fx: 706-353-3994

Field Hockey Association, US   www.usfieldhockey.com
1 Olympic Plaza   Colorado Springs CO 80909
Ph: 719-866-4567 ▪ Fx: 719-632-0979

Field Selling Association, National   www.nfsa.com
1900 Arch St   Philadelphia PA 19103
Ph: 215-564-1627 ▪ Fx: 215-564-2175

Field Stations, Organization of Biological   www.obfs.org
Santa Margarita Ecological Reserve 2648 N Stagecoach Ln   Fallbrook CA 92028
Ph: 760-728-9306 ▪ Fx: 760-451-0769

Field Trial Clubs of America, Amateur   www.aftca.org
1300 Tripp Rd   Somerville TN 38068
Ph: 901-465-1556 ▪ Fx: 901-465-0427

Fifers & Drummers Inc, Company of   companyoffifeanddrum.org
PO Box 277   Ivoryton CT 06442
Ph: 860-767-2237 ▪ Fx: 860-767-9765

Fifty-Plus Lifelong Fitness   www.50plus.org
2483 E Bayshore Rd Suite 202   Palo Alto CA 94303
Ph: 650-843-1750 ▪ Fx: 650-843-1758

Fig Advisory Board, California   www.californiafigs.com
7395 N Palm Bluffs Ave Suite 106   Fresno CA 93711
Ph: 559-440-5400 ▪ Fx: 559-438-5405

Fight Directors, Society of American   www.safd.org
350 W 51st St Suite 3A   New York NY 10019
Ph: 212-315-3956 ▪ TF: 800-659-6579

Figure Skating Association, US   www.usfsa.org
20 1st St   Colorado Springs CO 80906
Ph: 719-635-5200 ▪ Fx: 719-635-9548

Figures Collectors Club
11174 Hunts Corners Rd   Clarence NY 14031
Ph: 716-741-8399 ▪ Fx: 716-759-7462

Filipinas Americas Science & Art Foundation
1209 Park Ave   New York NY 10128
Ph: 212-427-6930 ▪ Fx: 212-427-6931

Filipino American Associations, National Federation of   www.naffaa.org
1444 'N' St NW   Washington DC 20005
Ph: 202-986-9330 ▪ Fx: 202-478-5109

Filipino American National Historical Society   www.fanhs-national.org
810 18th Ave Rm 100   Seattle WA 98122
Ph: 206-322-0203 ▪ Fx: 206-461-4879

Filipinos for Affirmative Action   www.filipinos4action.org
310 8th St Suite 306   Oakland CA 94607
Ph: 510-465-9876 ▪ Fx: 510-465-7548

Film Advisory Board Inc   www.filmadvisoryboard.org
7045 Hawthorn Ave Suite 305   Hollywood CA 90028
Ph: 323-461-6541 ▪ Fx: 323-469-8541

Film Archives, Anthology   www.anthologyfilmarchives.org
32 2nd Ave   New York NY 10003
Ph: 212-505-5181 ▪ Fx: 212-477-2714

Film Arts Foundation   www.filmarts.org
145 9th St Suite 101   San Francisco CA 94103
Ph: 415-552-8760 ▪ Fx: 415-552-0882

Film Association, Chemical Fabrics &   www.chemicalfabricsandfilm.com
1300 Sumner Ave   Cleveland OH 44115
Ph: 216-241-7333 ▪ Fx: 216-241-0105

Film Association, International Window   www.iwfa.com
PO Box 3871   Martinsville VA 24115
Ph: 276-666-4932

Film & Bag Federation   www.plasticbag.com
Society of the Plastics Industry Inc 1801 K St NW Suite 600K   Washington DC 20006
Ph: 202-974-5215 ▪ Fx: 202-974-7675

Film Carriers, National Magazine Book &   www.nmbfc.com
100 Daingerfield Rd   Alexandria VA 22314
Ph: 703-837-1070 ▪ Fx: 703-837-1072

Film Commissioners International, Association of   www.afci.org
314 N Main St Suite 307   Helena MT 59601
Ph: 406-495-8040 ▪ Fx: 406-495-8039

Film Festival, USA   www.usafilmfestival.com
6116 N Central Expy Suite 105   Dallas TX 75206
Ph: 214-821-6300 ▪ Fx: 214-821-6364

Film Foundation, African Family   www.africanfamily.org
PO Box 630   Santa Cruz CA 95061
Ph: 831-426-3133

Film Foundation, Armenian   www.armenianfilmfoundation.org
2219 E Thousand Oaks Blvd Suite 292   Thousand Oaks CA 91362
Ph: 805-495-0717 ▪ Fx: 805-379-0667

Film Institute, American   www.afi.com
2021 N Western Ave   Los Angeles CA 90027
Ph: 323-856-7600 ▪ Fx: 323-467-4578

Film Manufacturers Association, Construction & Agricultural   www.cafma.org
104 S Michigan Ave Suite 1500   Chicago IL 60603
Ph: 312-201-0101 ▪ Fx: 312-201-0214

Film Music Society   www.filmmusicsociety.org
15125 Ventura Blvd Suite 201   Sherman Oaks CA 91403
Ph: 818-789-6404 ▪ Fx: 818-789-6414

Film, National Center for Jewish   www.jewishfilm.org
Brandeis Univ Lown 102 MS 053   Waltham MA 02454
Ph: 781-899-7044 ▪ Fx: 781-736-2070

Film Seminars, International   www.flahertyseminar.org
6 E 39th St 12th Fl   New York NY 10016
Ph: 212-448-0457 ▪ Fx: 212-448-0458

Film Society, International Animated   www.asifa-hollywood.com
721 S Victory Blvd   Burbank CA 91502
Ph: 818-842-8330 ▪ Fx: 818-842-5645

Film/Video Arts   www.fva.com
462 Broadway Suite 520   New York NY 10013
Ph: 212-941-8787 ▪ Fx: 212-219-8924

Film & Video Foundation, University   www.ufva.com
Univ of Illinois Press 1325 S Oak St   Champaign IL 61820
Ph: 217-224-0626 ▪ Fx: 217-244-9910 ▪ TF: 866-244-0626

Film & Video Preservation, National Center for
c/o American Film Institute 2021 N Western Ave   Los Angeles CA 90027
Ph: 323-856-7708 ▪ Fx: 323-586-7616

Film & Video, Women in   www.wifv.org
1919 M St NW Suite 225   Washington DC 20036
Ph: 202-429-9438 ▪ Fx: 202-429-9440

Film, Women in   www.wif.org
8857 W Olympic Blvd Suite 201   Beverly Hills CA 90211
Ph: 310-657-5144 ▪ Fx: 310-657-5154

Filmmaker Foundation, Black   www.dvrepublic.com
670 Broadway Suite 300   New York NY 10012
Ph: 212-253-1690 ▪ Fx: 212-253-1689

Filmmakers, Association of Independent Video &   www.aivf.org
304 Hudson St 6th Fl   New York NY 10013
Ph: 212-807-1400 ▪ Fx: 212-463-8519

Films Association, Dance   www.dancefilmsassn.org
48 W 21st St Suite 907   New York NY 10010
Ph: 212-727-0764

Filter Manufacturers Council   www.filtercouncil.org
10 Laboratory Dr PO Box 13966   Research Triangle Park NC 27709
Ph: 919-549-4800 ▪ Fx: 919-549-4824

Filtration Association, National Air   www.nafahq.org
PO Box 68639 Suite 503   Virginia Beach VA 23471
Ph: 757-313-7400 ▪ Fx: 757-497-1895

Filtration & Separations Society, American   www.afssociety.org
Univ of Houston Dept of Chemical Engineering 4800 Calhoun Rd   Houston TX 77204
Ph: 713-743-3671 ▪ Fx: 713-743-3679

Finance & Accounting, Association of Latino Professionals in   www.alpfa.org
510 W 6th St Suite 400   Los Angeles CA 90014
Ph: 213-243-0004 ▪ Fx: 213-243-0006

Finance Adjusters Conference Inc, Allied   www.alliedfinanceadjusters.com
PO Box 20708   Chicago IL 60620
Ph: 800-621-3016

Finance Adjusters, National   www.nfa.org
1370 W North Ave   Baltimore MD 21217
Ph: 410-728-2400 ▪ Fx: 410-523-8336

Finance Advisors, National Association of Independent Public   www.naipfa.com
PO Box 304   Montgomery IL 60538
Ph: 800-624-7321

Finance Agencies, Council of Development   www.cdfa.net
301 NW 63rd Ave Suite 500   Oklahoma City OK 73116
Ph: 405-848-6059 ▪ Fx: 405-842-3299

Finance Agencies, National Association of Local Housing   www.nalhfa.org
2025 M St NW Suite 800   Washington DC 20036
Ph: 202-367-1197 ▪ Fx: 202-367-2197

Finance Association, American   www.afajof.org
UC Berkeley Haas School of Business 545 Student Services Bldg   Berkeley CA 94729
Ph: 510-642-2397

Finance Association, Commercial   www.cfa.com
225 W 34th St Suite 1815   New York NY 10122
Ph: 212-594-3490 ▪ Fx: 212-564-6053

Finance, Association for Governmental Leasing &   www.aglf.org
1255 23rd St NW Suite 200   Washington DC 20037
Ph: 202-742-2453 ▪ Fx: 202-833-3636

Finance Association, Insurance Premium
2890 Niagara Falls PO Box 726   Amherst NY 14226
Ph: 716-695-8757 ▪ Fx: 716-695-8758

Finance Association, National Aircraft   www.nafa-us.org
PO Box 85   Poolesville MD 20837
Ph: 301-349-2070 ▪ Fx: 301-972-7727

Finance Association, National Automotive   www.nafassociation.com
217 St Charles Pl   Pittsburgh PA 15215
Ph: 412-781-5601 ▪ Fx: 412-781-5607

Finance Association, North American Economics &   www.naefa.org
Ohio Univ Dept of Economics   Athens OH 45701
Ph: 740-593-2034 ▪ Fx: 740-593-0181

Finance Attorneys, Association of Commercial   www.afca.cc
25 Hooks Ln Suite 302   Baltimore MD 21208
Ph: 410-486-2600 ▪ Fx: 410-486-8438

Finance Council, National Accounting &   truckline.com/cc/councils/nafc
American Trucking Assns 2200 Mill Rd   Alexandria VA 22314
Ph: 703-838-1915 ▪ Fx: 703-836-0751

Finance Credit & International Business, FCIB: Association of Executives in   www.fcibglobal.com
8840 Columbia 100 Pkwy   Columbia MD 21045
Ph: 410-423-1840 ▪ Fx: 410-423-1845 ▪ TF: 888-256-3242

(Finance & Development) Bretton Woods Committee   www.brettonwoods.org
1990 M St NW Suite 450   Washington DC 20036
Ph: 202-331-1616 ▪ Fx: 202-785-9423

Finance, Institute of International   www.iif.com
2000 Pennsylvania Ave NW Suite 8500   Washington DC 20006
Ph: 202-857-3600 ▪ Fx: 202-775-1430

Finance & Insurance Professionals, Association of   www.afip.com
PO Box 212003   Bedford TX 76095
Ph: 817-428-2434 ▪ Fx: 817-581-4609

Finance Law, Conference on Consumer　　www.theccfl.com
Oklahoma City Univ School of Law 2501 N Blackwelder
Ave　Oklahoma City OK 73106
Ph: 405-521-5363 ▪ Fx: 405-521-5089

Finance Officers Association, Government　　www.gfoa.org
203 N LaSalle St Suite 2700　Chicago IL 60601
Ph: 312-977-9700 ▪ Fx: 312-977-4806

Finance Officers, National Association of County Treasurers &　www.nactfo.org
c/o National Assn of Counties 440 1st St NW　Washington DC
20001
Ph: 202-393-6226

Finance & Trade, Bankers' Association for　　www.baft.org
1120 Connecticut Ave NW　Washington DC 20036
Ph: 202-663-7575 ▪ Fx: 202-663-5538

Finance, Women in Housing &　　www.whfdc.org
717 Princess St　Alexandria VA 22314
Ph: 703-683-4742 ▪ Fx: 703-683-0018

Financial Accountability, Evangelical Council for　www.ecfa.org
440 W Jubal Early Dr　Winchester VA 22601
Ph: 540-535-0103 ▪ Fx: 540-353-0533 ▪ TF: 800-323-9473

Financial Accounting Foundation　　www.fasb.org/facts
401 Merritt 7 PO Box 5116　Norwalk CT 06856
Ph: 203-847-0700 ▪ Fx: 203-849-9714

Financial Accounting Standards Board　　www.fasb.org
401 Merritt 7 PO Box 5116　Norwalk CT 06856
Ph: 203-847-0700 ▪ Fx: 203-849-9714

Financial Advisors, National Association of Insurance &　www.naifa.org
2901 Telestar Ct　Falls Church VA 22042
Ph: 703-770-8100 ▪ TF: 877-866-2432

Financial Advisors, National Association of Personal　www.napfa.org
3250 N Arlington Suite 109　Arlington Heights IL 60004
Ph: 847-537-7722 ▪ Fx: 847-483-5415 ▪ TF: 800-366-2732

Financial Aid Administrators, National Association of Student　www.nasfaa.org
1129 20th St NW Suite 400　Washington DC 20036
Ph: 202-785-0453 ▪ Fx: 202-785-1487

Financial Consultants, International Association of Registered　www.iarfc.org
2507 N Venty Pkwy PO Box 42506　Middletown OH 45042
Ph: 513-424-6395 ▪ Fx: 513-424-5752 ▪ TF: 800-532-9060

(Financial Counseling) Auriton Solutions　　www.auriton.org
1700 W Hwy 36 Suite 301　Roseville MN 55113
Ph: 651-631-8000 ▪ Fx: 651-697-7955 ▪ TF: 877-332-8700

Financial Counseling & Planning Education, Association for　www.afcpe.org
2112 Arlington Ave Suite H　Upper Arlington OH 43221
Ph: 614-485-9650 ▪ Fx: 614-485-9621

Financial Crimes Investigators, International Association of　www.iafci.org
873 Embarcadero Dr Suite 5　El Dorado Hills CA 95762
Ph: 916-939-5000 ▪ Fx: 916-939-0395

Financial Education, Institute of Consumer　www.financial-education-icfe.org
PO Box 34070　San Diego CA 92163
Ph: 619-232-8811 ▪ Fx: 619-239-1401

Financial & Estate Planning, National Association of　www.nafep.com
525 E 4500 S Suite F-100　Salt Lake City UT 84107
Ph: 801-266-9900 ▪ Fx: 801-266-1019

Financial Examiners, Society of　　www.sofe.org
174 Grace Blvd　Altamonte Springs FL 32714
Ph: 407-682-4930 ▪ Fx: 407-682-3175 ▪ TF: 800-787-7633

Financial Executives International　　www.fei.org
200 Campus Dr PO Box 674　Florham Park NJ 07932
Ph: 973-765-1000 ▪ Fx: 973-765-1018

Financial Executives, International Newspaper　www.infe.org
21525 Ridgetop Cir Suite 200　Sterling VA 20166
Ph: 703-421-4060 ▪ Fx: 703-421-4068

Financial Guaranty Insurers, Association of　www.afgi.org
c/o TowersGroup 15 W 39th St 14th Fl　New York NY 10018
Ph: 212-354-5020 ▪ Fx: 212-391-6920

Financial Institutions, American League of　www.alfi.org
900 19th St NW Suite 400　Washington DC 20006
Ph: 202-857-6176 ▪ Fx: 202-296-8716

Financial Management Association, Broadcast Cable　www.bcfm.com
932 Lee St Suite 204　Des Plaines IL 60016
Ph: 847-296-0200 ▪ Fx: 847-296-7510

Financial Management Association, Construction　www.cfma.org
29 Emmons Dr Suite F-50　Princeton NJ 08540
Ph: 609-452-8000 ▪ Fx: 609-452-0474

Financial Management Association, Healthcare　www.hfma.org
2 Westbrook Corporate Ctr Suite 700　Westchester IL 60154
Ph: 708-531-9600 ▪ Fx: 708-531-0032 ▪ TF: 800-252-4362

Financial Management Association International　www.fma.org
USF College of Business Admin 4202 E Fowler Ave Suite
3331　Tampa FL 33620
Ph: 813-974-2084 ▪ Fx: 813-974-3318

Financial Management Association, IT　　www.itfma.com
PO Box 30188　Santa Barbara CA 93130
Ph: 805-687-7390 ▪ Fx: 805-687-7382

Financial Management, International Consortium on Governmental　www.icgfm.org/
444 N Capitol St Suite 234　Washington DC 20001
Ph: 202-624-8461 ▪ Fx: 202-624-5473

Financial Managers Society　　www.fmsinc.org
100 W Monroe St Suite 810　Chicago IL 60603
Ph: 312-578-1300 ▪ TF: 800-275-4367

Financial Markets Association　　www.securagroup.com
7799 Leesburg Pike Suite 800N　Falls Church VA 22043
Ph: 703-749-1579 ▪ Fx: 703-749-1688

Financial Planner Board of Standards Inc, Certified　www.cfp-board.org
1700 Broadway Suite 2100　Denver CO 80290
Ph: 303-830-7500 ▪ Fx: 303-860-7388 ▪ TF: 888-237-6275

Financial Planners Institute, Registered　　www.rfpi.com
2001 Cooper Foster Park Rd　Amherst OH 44001
Ph: 440-282-7176 ▪ Fx: 440-282-8027

Financial Planning Association　　www.fpanet.org
5775 Glenridge Dr NE Suite B300　Atlanta GA 30328
Ph: 404-845-0011 ▪ Fx: 404-845-3660 ▪ TF: 800-945-4237

Financial Professionals, Association for　　www.afponline.org
7315 Wisconsin Ave Suite 600-W　Bethesda MD 20814
Ph: 301-907-2862 ▪ Fx: 301-907-2864

Financial Service Centers of America Inc　　www.fisca.org
25 Main St 5th Fl　Hackensack NJ 07602
Ph: 201-487-0412 ▪ Fx: 201-487-3954

Financial Service Professionals, Society of　　www.financialpro.org
270 S Bryn Mawr Ave　Bryn Mawr PA 19010
Ph: 610-526-2500 ▪ Fx: 610-527-4010 ▪ TF: 800-392-6900

Financial Services Association of America, Community　www.cfsa.net
515 King St Suite 300　Alexandria VA 22314
Ph: 703-684-1029 ▪ Fx: 703-684-7912

Financial Services Association, American　www.americanfinsvcs.com
919 18th St NW Suite 300　Washington DC 20006
Ph: 202-296-5544 ▪ Fx: 202-223-0321

Financial Services Association Education Foundation, American　www.afsaef.org
919 18th St NW Suite 300　Washington DC 20006
Ph: 202-296-5544 ▪ Fx: 202-223-0321

Financial Services Association, International　　www.ifsa.org
9 Sylvan Way 1st Fl　Parsippany NJ 07054
Ph: 973-656-1900 ▪ Fx: 973-656-1915

Financial Services, Association for Management Information in　www.amifs.org
3895 Fairfax Ct　Atlanta GA 30339
Ph: 770-444-3557 ▪ Fx: 770-444-9084

Financial Services Coalition, Urban　　www.ufscnet.org
1300 L St NW Suite 825　Washington DC 20005
Ph: 202-289-8335 ▪ Fx: 202-842-0567

(Financial Services) GAMA International　　www.gamaweb.com
2901 Telestar Ct　Falls Church VA 22042
Ph: 703-770-8184 ▪ Fx: 703-770-8182 ▪ TF: 800-345-2687

(Financial Services) LOMA　　www.loma.org
2300 Windy Ridge Pkwy Suite 600　Atlanta GA 30339
Ph: 770-984-6432 ▪ Fx: 770-984-6420 ▪ TF: 800-275-5662

Financial Services Roundtable　　www.fsround.org
805 15th St Suite 600　Washington DC 20005
Ph: 202-289-4322 ▪ Fx: 202-289-1903

Financial Services Technology Consortium　www.fstc.org
44 Wall St 12th Fl　New York NY 10005
Ph: 212-461-7116 ▪ Fx: 646-349-3629

Financial Services Volunteer Corps　　www.fsvc.org
10 E 53rd St 24th Fl　New York NY 10022
Ph: 212-771-1400 ▪ Fx: 212-421-2162

Financial Services, Women in Insurance &　www.w-wifs.org
9101 LBJ Fwy Suite 450　Dallas TX 75243
Ph: 469-621-3525 ▪ TF: 800-753-3973

Financial Technology, Association for　　www.fitech.org
5828 Zarley St Suite C　New Albany OH 43054
Ph: 614-895-1208 ▪ Fx: 614-895-3466

Financial & Technology Professionals, Hospitality　www.hftp.org
11709 Boulder Ln Suite 110　Austin TX 78726
Ph: 512-249-5333 ▪ Fx: 512-249-1533 ▪ TF: 800-856-4242

Financial Women International　　www.fwi.org
200 N Glebe Rd Suite 820　Arlington VA 22203
Ph: 703-807-2007 ▪ Fx: 703-807-0111

Financial Writers' Association, New York　　www.nyfwa.org
PO Box 338　Ridgewood NJ 07451
Ph: 201-612-0100 ▪ Fx: 201-612-9915

Financiers, International Society of　　www.insofin.com
PO Box 398　Naples NC 28760
Ph: 828-698-7805 ▪ Fx: 828-698-7806

Financing Authorities, Council of Infrastructure　www.cifanet.org
805 15th St NW Suite 500　Washington DC 20005
Ph: 202-371-9694 ▪ Fx: 202-371-6601

Find the Children　　www.findthechildren.com
3250 Ocean Park Blvd Suite 333　Santa Monica CA 90405
Ph: 310-314-3213 ▪ Fx: 310-314-3169 ▪ TF: 888-477-6721

Fine Arts Deans, International Council of　　www.icfad.org
Pennsylvania State Univ 111 Arts Bldg　University Park PA
16802
Ph: 814-865-2593 ▪ Fx: 814-865-2018

Fine Print Dealers Association, International　www.printdealter.com
15 Gramercy Park S Suite 7A　New York NY 10003
Ph: 212-674-6095 ▪ Fx: 212-674-6783

Finishers, National Association of Metal　　www.namf.org
12644 Research Parkway Suite 105　Orlando FL 32826
Ph: 407-281-6445 ▪ Fx: 407-281-7345

Finishers Society Inc, American Electroplaters & Surface　www.aesf.org
12644 Research Pkwy　Orlando FL 32826
Ph: 407-281-6441 ▪ Fx: 407-281-6446

Finishing Contractors Association　www.finishingcontractors.org
8150 Leesburg Pike Suite 1210　Vienna VA 22182
Ph: 703-448-9001 ▪ Fx: 703-448-9002

Finishing Job Shops Association, Mass　　www.mfjsa.com
808 13th St　Moline IL 61244
Ph: 309-755-1101 ▪ Fx: 309-755-1121

Finishing Suppliers' Association, Metal　　www.mfsa.org
112 J Elden St　Herndon VA 20170
Ph: 703-709-5729 ▪ Fx: 703-709-1036

Finnish American Chamber of Commerce Inc　www.finlandtrade.com
866 United Nations Plaza　New York NY 10017
Ph: 212-821-0225 ▪ Fx: 212-750-4418

Finnish-American Historical Society of the West　www.finamhsw.com
PO Box 5522　Portland OR 97228
Ph: 503-654-0448

Finnsheep Breeders Association　　www.finnsheep.org
143 Gravel Ln　Lexington VA 24450
Ph: 540-463-4594

Fiqh Council of North America
750-A Miller Dr SE Leesburg VA 20175
Ph: 703-779-7477 ▪ Fx: 703-779-7999

Fire Alarm Association Inc, Automatic   www.afaa.org
PO Box 951807 Lake Mary FL 32795
Ph: 407-322-6288 ▪ Fx: 407-322-7488

Fire Alarm Association, National Burglar &   www.alarm.org
8300 Colesville Rd Suite 750 Silver Spring MD 20910
Ph: 301-585-1855 ▪ Fx: 301-585-1866

Fire Alarm Distributors, National Independent   www.nifad.org
1001 Office Park Rd Suite 105 West Des Moines IA 50625
Ph: 515-440-6057 ▪ Fx: 515-440-6055

Fire Apparatus Manufacturers Association   www.fama.org
PO Box 397 Lynnfield MA 01940
Ph: 781-334-2911

Fire Buff Associates Inc, International   www.ifba.org
955 Regina Dr Baltimore MD 21227
Ph: 410-242-8672 ▪ Fx: 410-242-4688

Fire Chaplains, Federation of   www.ffcfirechaplains.org
185 County Rd Suite 1602 Clifton TX 76634
Ph: 254-622-8514

Fire Chiefs, International Association of   www.iafc.org
4025 Fair Ridge Dr Suite 300 Fairfax VA 22033
Ph: 703-273-0911 ▪ Fx: 703-273-9363

Fire Council, National Volunteer   www.nvfc.org
1050 17th St NW Suite 490 Washington DC 20036
Ph: 202-887-5700 ▪ Fx: 202-887-5291 ▪ TF: 888-275-6832

Fire Department Safety Officers Association   www.fdsoa.org
30 Main St Suite 6 PO Box 149 Ashland MA 01721
Ph: 508-881-3114 ▪ Fx: 508-881-1128

Fire & Emergency Manufacturers & Services Association   www.femsa.org
PO Box 147 Lynnfield MA 01940
Ph: 781-334-2771

Fire Equipment Distributors, National Association of   www.nafed.org
104 S Michigan Ave Suite 300 Chicago IL 60603
Ph: 312-263-8100 ▪ Fx: 312-263-8111

Fire Equipment Manufacturers Association Inc   www.yourfirstdefense.com
1300 Sumner Ave Cleveland OH 44115
Ph: 216-241-7333 ▪ Fx: 216-241-0105

Fire Equipment Service Association, United
500 Telser Rd Lake Zurich IL 60047
Ph: 847-438-2343 ▪ Fx: 847-438-1869

Fire Fighters, International Association of   www.iaff.org
1750 New York Ave NW 3rd Fl Washington DC 20006
Ph: 202-737-8484 ▪ Fx: 202-737-8418

Fire Fighters, International Association of Black Professional   www.iabpff.org

Fire Foundation, National Historical
6101 E Van Buren St Phoenix AZ 85008
Ph: 602-275-3473 ▪ Fx: 602-275-0896

Fire, International Association of Wildland   www.iawfonline.org
4025 Fair Ridge Dr Fairfax VA 22033
Ph: 785-423-1818 ▪ Fx: 785-542-3511

Fire Investigators, National Association of   www.nafi.org
857 Tallevast Rd Sarasota FL 34243
Ph: 941-359-2800 ▪ Fx: 941-351-5849 ▪ TF: 877-506-6234

Fire Marshals Association, International   www.nfpa.org/MemberSections/IFMA/IFMA.asp
c/o NFPA International 1 Batterymarch Park Quincy MA 02169
Ph: 617-770-3000 ▪ Fx: 617-770-0700

Fire Marshals, National Association of State   www.firemarshals.org
PO Box 4127 Clifton Park NY 12065
Ph: 518-317-0018 ▪ Fx: 518-383-9647 ▪ TF: 877-996-2736

Fire Photographers Association, International   www.ifpaonline.com
143 40th St New Orleans LA 70124
Ph: 504-482-9616 ▪ Fx: 504-482-9636

Fire Professionals of America, International Union Security Police &   www.spfpa.org
25510 Kelly Rd Roseville MI 48066
Ph: 586-772-7250 ▪ Fx: 586-772-9644 ▪ TF: 800-228-7492

Fire Protection Association, Defense   www.dfpa.org
PO Box 1310 Falls Church VA 22041
Ph: 703-521-3926 ▪ Fx: 703-521-0849

Fire Protection Engineers, Society of   www.sfpe.org
7315 Wisconsin Ave Suite 1225W Bethesda MD 20814
Ph: 301-718-2910 ▪ Fx: 301-718-2242

Fire Retardant Chemicals Association   www.fireretardants.org
1801 K St NW Suite 1000-L Washington DC 20006
Ph: 202-530-4590 ▪ Fx: 202-530-4700

(Fire Safety Standards) NFPA International   www.nfpa.org
1 Batterymarch Pk Quincy MA 02169
Ph: 617-770-3000 ▪ Fx: 617-770-0700 ▪ TF: 800-344-3555

Fire Service Instructors, International Society of   www.isfsi.org
PO Box 2320 Stafford VA 22555
Ph: 540-657-2490 ▪ Fx: 540-657-0154 ▪ TF: 800-435-0005

Fire Service Training Association, International   www.ifsta.org
Fire Protection Publications Oklahoma State Univ 930 N
  Willis Stillwater OK 74078
Ph: 405-744-5723 ▪ Fx: 405-744-8204 ▪ TF: 800-654-4055

Fire Service, Women in the   www.wfsi.org
PO Box 5446 Madison WI 53705
Ph: 608-233-4768 ▪ Fx: 608-233-4879

Fire & Smoke Containment & Control, Alliance for   www.afscc.org
25 N Broadway Tarrytown NY 10591
Ph: 914-332-0040 ▪ Fx: 914-332-1541

Fire Sprinkler Association Inc, American   www.firesprinkler.org
9696 Skillman St Suite 300 Dallas TX 75243
Ph: 214-349-5965 ▪ Fx: 214-343-8898

Fire Sprinkler Association, National   www.nfsa.org
40 Jon Barrett Rd PO Box 1000 Patterson NY 12563
Ph: 845-878-4200 ▪ Fx: 845-878-4215

Fire Suppression Systems Association   www.fssa.net
5024-R Campbell Blvd Baltimore MD 21236
Ph: 410-931-8100 ▪ Fx: 410-931-8111

Firearm & Tool Mark Examiners, Association of   www.afte.org

Firearms Dealers, National Association of Federally Licensed
150 SE 12th St Suite 200 Fort Lauderdale FL 33316
Ph: 954-467-9994 ▪ Fx: 954-463-2501

Firearms Instructors, International Association of Law Enforcement   www.ialefi.com
25 Country Club Rd Suite 707 Gilford NH 03249
Ph: 603-524-8787 ▪ Fx: 603-524-8856

(Firearms) National Mossberg Collectors Association   www.mossbergcollectors.org
PO Box 487 Festus MO 63028
Ph: 636-937-6401

Firearms Research & Identification Association
PO Box 620 Wrightwood CA 92397
Ph: 760-249-6837 ▪ Fx: 760-249-1098

Firefighters International, Fellowship of Christian   fellowshipofchristianfirefighters.com
PO Box 901 Fort Collins CO 80522
Ph: 970-407-0083 ▪ TF: 800-322-9848

Firefighting Industry Association, Aerial   www.afia.com
PO Box 523068 Springfield VA 22152
Ph: 703-644-6454 ▪ Fx: 703-644-4001

Firemen & Oilers, National Conference of   www.ncfo.org
1023 15th St NW 10th Fl Washington DC 20005
Ph: 202-962-0981 ▪ Fx: 202-872-1222

Firemen's Insurance Association, Police &   www.pfia.net
101 E 116th St Carmel IN 46032
Ph: 317-581-1913 ▪ Fx: 317-571-5946 ▪ TF: 800-221-7342

FIREPAC   www.iaff.org
1750 New York Ave NW 3rd Fl Washington DC 20006
Ph: 202-737-8484 ▪ Fx: 202-737-8418

Firestop Contractors International Association   www.fcia.org
1257 Golf Cir Wheaton IL 60187
Ph: 630-690-0682 ▪ Fx: 630-690-2871

Firestop Council, International   www.firestop.org
25 N Broadway Tarrytown NY 10591
Ph: 914-332-0040 ▪ Fx: 914-332-1541

Fireworks Association, National   www.nationalfireworks.org
8224 NW Bradford Ct Kansas City MO 64151
Ph: 816-505-3589 ▪ Fx: 816-741-4058

Firm Institute, Family   www.ffi.org
200 Lincoln St Suite 201 Boston MA 02111
Ph: 617-482-3045 ▪ Fx: 617-482-3049

FIRST   www.usfirst.org
200 Bedford St Manchester NH 03101
Ph: 603-666-3906 ▪ Fx: 603-666-3907 ▪ TF: 800-871-8326

First Amendment Lawyers Association   www.fala.org
200 S Wacker Dr Suite 3100 Chicago IL 60606
Ph: 312-236-0606 ▪ Fx: 312-332-6008

First Amendment Project   www.thefirstamendment.org
1736 Franklin St 9th Fl Oakland CA 94612
Ph: 510-208-7744 ▪ Fx: 510-208-4562

First Book   www.firstbook.org
1319 F St NW Suite 1000 Washington DC 20004
Ph: 202-393-1222 ▪ Fx: 202-628-1258 ▪ TF: 800-393-1222

First Candle/SIDS Alliance   www.firstcandle.org
1314 Bedford Ave Suite 210 Baltimore MD 21208
Ph: 410-653-8226 ▪ Fx: 410-653-8709 ▪ TF: 800-221-7437

First Catholic Slovak Ladies Association   www.fcsla.com
24950 Chagrin Blvd Beachwood OH 44122
Ph: 216-464-8015 ▪ Fx: 216-464-9260 ▪ TF: 800-464-4642

First Catholic Slovak Union of the US & Canada   www.fcsu.com
6611 Rockside Rd Independence OH 44131
Ph: 216-642-9406 ▪ Fx: 216-642-4310 ▪ TF: 800-533-6682

First Flight Society   www.firstflight.org
PO Box 1903 Kitty Hawk NC 27949
Ph: 252-441-1903 ▪ Fx: 252-441-4349

First Fruit Inc   www.firstfruit.org
14 Corporate Plaza Newport Beach CA 92660
Ph: 949-720-3774 ▪ Fx: 949-760-5349

First Hungarian Literary Society   www.onkepzo.com
323 E 79th St New York NY 10021
Ph: 212-288-5002

First Nations Development Institute   www.firstnations.org
11917 Main St Fredericksburg VA 22408
Ph: 540-371-5615 ▪ Fx: 540-371-3505 ▪ TF: 800-682-5384

First Voice International   www.firstvoiceint.org
2400 'N' St NW Washington DC 20037
Ph: 202-861-2261 ▪ Fx: 202-861-6407

FISA   www.fisanet.org
1207 Sunset Dr Greensboro NC 27408
Ph: 336-274-6311 ▪ Fx: 336-691-1839

(Fiscal Responsibility) Concord Coalition   www.concordcoalition.org
1011 Arlington Blvd Suite 300 Arlington VA 22209
Ph: 703-894-6222 ▪ Fx: 703-894-6231 ▪ TF: 888-333-4248

(Fish) American Livebearer Association   www.livebearers.org
5 Zerbe St Cressona PA 17929
Ph: 570-385-0573 ▪ Fx: 570-385-2781

Fish Association, International Game   www.igfa.org
IGFA Fishing Hall of Fame & Museum 300 Gulf Stream
  Way Dania Beach FL 33004
Ph: 954-927-2628 ▪ Fx: 954-924-4299

Fish Farms Association, Florida Tropical   www.ftffa.org
PO Box 1519 Winter Haven FL 33882
Ph: 863-293-5710 ▪ Fx: 863-299-5154

(Fish) International Betta Congress   www.ibcbettas.org
923 Wadsworth St Syracuse NY 13208
Ph: 315-454-4792

Fish Meal & Oil Association, National
1901 N Fort Myer Dr Suite 700   Arlington VA 22209
Ph: 703-524-8884 ▪ Fx: 703-524-4619

Fish Society, Native   www.nativefishsociety.org
PO Box 19570   Portland OR 97280
Ph: 503-977-0287 ▪ Fx: 503-977-0026

Fish & Wildlife Agencies, Association of Midwest
c/o Nebraska Game & Parks Commission 2200 N 33rd St PO
Box 30370   Lincoln NE 68503
Ph: 402-471-5539 ▪ Fx: 402-471-5528

Fish & Wildlife Agencies, International Association of   www.iafwa.org
444 N Capitol St NW Suite 544   Washington DC 20001
Ph: 202-624-7890 ▪ Fx: 202-624-7891

Fish & Wildlife Agencies, Southeastern Association of   www.seafwa.org
8500 Freshwater Farms Rd   Tallahassee FL 32309
Ph: 850-893-1204 ▪ Fx: 850-893-6204

Fish & Wildlife Association, National Military   www.nmfwa.org
6300 Somerset Way   Cambria CA 93428
Ph: 805-238-8265

Fish & Wildlife Commission, Great Lakes Indian   www.glifwc.org
100 Maple St PO Box 9   Odanah WI 54861
Ph: 715-682-6619

Fish & Wildlife Foundation, National   www.nfwf.org
1120 Connecticut Ave NW Rm 900   Washington DC 20036
Ph: 202-857-0166 ▪ Fx: 202-857-0162

FishAmerica Foundation   www.fishamerica.org
225 Reinekers Ln Suite 420   Alexandria VA 22314
Ph: 703-519-9691 ▪ Fx: 703-519-1872

Fisheries Association, Middle Atlantic
7 Dey St Suite 801   New York NY 10007
Ph: 212-732-4340 ▪ Fx: 212-732-6644

Fisheries Association, Northwest   www.northwestfisheries.org
2208 SW Market St Suite 318   Seattle WA 98107
Ph: 206-789-6197 ▪ Fx: 206-789-8147

Fisheries Association Inc, Southeastern   www.southeasternfish.org
1118-B Thomasville Rd   Tallahassee FL 32303
Ph: 850-224-0612 ▪ Fx: 850-222-3663

Fisheries Commission, Atlantic States Marine   www.asmfc.org
1444 'I' St NW 6th Fl   Washington DC 20005
Ph: 202-289-6400 ▪ Fx: 202-289-6051

Fisheries Commission, Pacific States Marine   www.psmfc.org
205 SE Spokane St Suite 100   Portland OR 97027
Ph: 503-595-3100 ▪ Fx: 503-595-3232

Fisheries Development Association, New England   www.fishfacts.com
197 8th St Suite 600A   Charlestown MA 02129
Ph: 617-886-0793 ▪ Fx: 617-886-0173

Fisheries Economics & Trade, International Institute of   oregonstate.edu/dept/iifet
Oregon State Univ Dept of Agricultural & Resource
Economics   Corvallis OR 97331
Ph: 541-737-1416 ▪ Fx: 541-737-2563

Fisheries Institute Inc, National   www.nfi.org
1901 N Fort Myer Dr Suite 700   Arlington VA 22209
Ph: 703-524-8880 ▪ Fx: 703-524-4619

Fisheries Network, Women's   www.fis.com/wfn
2442 NW Market St Suite 243   Seattle WA 98107
Ph: 206-789-1987

Fisheries Society, American   www.fisheries.org
5410 Grosvenor Ln Suite 110   Bethesda MD 20814
Ph: 301-897-8616 ▪ Fx: 301-897-8096

Fisheries & Wildlife Programs, National   www.ag.iastate.edu/departments/aecl/naufwp
Association of University   Univ of Montana 310 Lewis Hall
Box 173460   Bozeman MT 59717
Ph: 406-994-2270 ▪ Fx: 406-994-3190

Fisherman Foundation, Future   www.futurefisherman.org
225 Reinekers Ln Suite 420   Alexandria VA 22314
Ph: 703-519-9691 ▪ Fx: 703-519-1872

Fishermen's Associations, Pacific Coast Federation of   www.pcffa.org
PO Box 29370   San Francisco CA 94159
Ph: 415-561-5080 ▪ Fx: 415-561-5464

Fishers, Federation of Fly   www.fedflyfishers.org
PO Box 1595   Bozeman MT 59771
Ph: 406-585-7592 ▪ Fx: 406-585-7596

Fishery Management Council, Pacific   www.pcouncil.org
7700 NE Ambassador Pl Suite 200   Portland OR 97220
Ph: 503-820-2280 ▪ Fx: 503-820-2299 ▪ TF: 866-806-7204

Fishery Research Biologists, American Institute of   www.iattc.org/aifrb/
Southwest Fisheries Science Ctr PO Box 271   La Jolla CA
92038
Ph: 858-546-7177 ▪ Fx: 858-546-5653

Fishes Association, North American Native   www.nanfa.org
1107 Argonne Dr   Baltimore MD 21218
Ph: 410-243-9050

Fishing Club, North American   www.fishingclub.com
12301 Whitewater Dr   Minnetonka MN 55343
Ph: 800-843-6232 ▪ Fx: 952-936-9755

Fishing Foundation, Recreational Boating &   www.rbff.org
601 N Fairfax St Suite 140   Alexandria VA 22314
Ph: 703-519-0013 ▪ Fx: 703-519-9565

Fitness, American Association for Active Lifestyles &   www.aahperd.org/aaalf
1900 Association Dr   Reston VA 20191
Ph: 703-476-3430 ▪ Fx: 703-476-9527 ▪ TF: 800-213-7193

Fitness, American Chiropractic Association Council on Sports   www.acasc.org
Injuries & Physical   PO Box 400 380 Wright Rd   Norwalk IA
52011
Ph: 515-981-9340 ▪ Fx: 515-981-9427 ▪ TF: 800-261-1495

Fitness Association of America, Aerobics &   www.afaa.org
15250 Ventura Blvd Suite 200   Sherman Oaks CA 91403
Ph: 818-905-0040 ▪ Fx: 818-990-5468 ▪ TF: 877-968-7263

Fitness Association, American Senior   www.seniorfitness.net
PO Box 2575   New Smyrna Beach FL 32170
Ph: 386-423-6634 ▪ Fx: 386-427-0613 ▪ TF: 800-243-1478

Fitness Association, International Physical   www.ipfa.org
415 W Court St   Flint MI 48503
Ph: 810-239-2166 ▪ Fx: 810-239-9390 ▪ TF: 877-520-4732

Fitness Association, US Water   www.uswfa.com
PO Box 3279   Boynton Beach FL 33424
Ph: 561-732-9908 ▪ Fx: 561-732-0950

Fitness, Fifty-Plus Lifelong   www.50plus.org
2483 E Bayshore Rd Suite 202   Palo Alto CA 94303
Ph: 650-843-1750 ▪ Fx: 650-843-1758

Fitness, National Association for Health &   www.physicalfitness.org
201 S Capitol Ave Suite 560   Indianapolis IN 46225
Ph: 317-237-5630 ▪ Fx: 317-237-5632

(Fitness Professionals) IDEA Inc   www.ideafit.com
6190 Cornerstone Ct E Suite 204   San Diego CA 92121
Ph: 858-535-8979 ▪ Fx: 858-535-8234 ▪ TF: 800-999-4332

Fittings Association, Plastic Pipe &   www.ppfahome.com
800 Roosevelt Rd Bldg C Suite 20   Glen Ellyn IL 60137
Ph: 630-858-6540 ▪ Fx: 630-790-3095

Fittings Industry Inc, Manufacturers Standardization Society   www.mss-hq.com
of the Valve &   127 Park St NE   Vienna VA 22180
Ph: 703-281-6613 ▪ Fx: 703-281-6671

Fixed Income Analysts Society Inc   www.fiasi.org
151 Herricks Rd Suite 1   Garden City Park NY 11040
Ph: 516-739-2510 ▪ Fx: 516-739-3803 ▪ TF: 800-284-6228

Fixture Manufacturers, National Association of Store   www.nasfm.org
3595 Sheridan St Suite 200   Hollywood FL 33021
Ph: 954-893-7300 ▪ Fx: 954-893-7500

Flag Alliance, Citizens   www.cfa-inc.org
PO Box 7197   Indianapolis IN 46207
Ph: 317-630-1384 ▪ Fx: 317-630-1385

Flag Dealers Association, National Independent   www.flaginfo.com
710 E Ogden Ave Suite 600   Naperville IL 60563
Ph: 630-579-3274 ▪ Fx: 630-369-2488 ▪ TF: 877-544-3524

Flag Foundation, National   www.americanflags.com
Flag Plaza 1275 Bedford Ave   Pittsburgh PA 15219
Ph: 412-261-1776 ▪ Fx: 412-261-9132 ▪ TF: 800-615-1776

Flag Foundation, US   www.americanflags.com
Flag Plaza 1275 Bedford Ave   Pittsburgh PA 15219
Ph: 412-261-1776 ▪ Fx: 412-261-9132 ▪ TF: 800-615-1776

Flag & Graphics Association, Banner   www.bannerflag.com
1801 County Rd 'B' W   Roseville MN 55113
Ph: 651-222-2508 ▪ Fx: 651-631-9334 ▪ TF: 800-225-4324

Flag Manufacturers Association of America
17000 Commerce Pkwy Suite C   Mount Laurel NJ 08054
Ph: 856-439-0500 ▪ Fx: 856-439-0525

Flag Research Center   flagspot.net/flags/vex-frc.html
PO Box 580   Winchester MA 01890
Ph: 781-729-9410 ▪ Fx: 781-721-4817

Flagon & Trencher Society: Descendants of   nctimes.net/~churchyj/fandt_home.html
Colonial Tavern Keepers   7916 Quill Point Dr   Bowie MD
20720
Ph: 301-352-2919

(Flags) North American Vexillological Association   www.nava.org

Flavor Chemists, Society of   www.flavorchemist.org
86 Watertower Plaza Suite 343   Leominster MA 01453
Ph: 978-840-4596 ▪ Fx: 978-383-0580

Flavor & Extract Manufacturers Association of the US   www.femaflavor.org
1620 'I' St NW Suite 925   Washington DC 20006
Ph: 202-293-5800 ▪ Fx: 202-463-8998

Flavor & Fragrance Commerce, Women in   www.wffc.org
3301 Rt 66 Bldg C Suite 205   Neptune NJ 07753
Ph: 732-922-0500 ▪ Fx: 732-922-0560

Flavors & Food-Ingredient Systems Inc, National Association of   www.naffs.org
3301 Rt 66 Bldg C Suite 205   Neptune NJ 07753
Ph: 732-922-3218 ▪ Fx: 732-922-3590

Fleet Administrators, National Association of   www.nafa.org
100 Wood Ave S Suite 310   Iselin NJ 08830
Ph: 732-494-8100 ▪ Fx: 732-494-6789

Fleet Administrators, National Conference of State   ncsfa.state.ut.us
PO Box 159   Litchfield Park AZ 85340
Ph: 623-772-9096 ▪ Fx: 623-772-9098

Fleet & Leasing Association, Automotive   www.aflaonline.org
21061 S Western Ave   Torrance CA 90501
Ph: 310-533-2520 ▪ Fx: 310-533-2506

Fleet Reserve Association   www.fra.org
125 N West St   Alexandria VA 22314
Ph: 703-683-1400 ▪ Fx: 703-549-6610 ▪ TF: 800-372-1924

Fleet Specialists, Council of   www.cfshq.com
315 Delaware St   Kansas City MO 64105
Ph: 816-421-2600 ▪ Fx: 816-421-7532

Fleischner Society   www.fleischner.org
c/o Intelligent Meeting Managers 4550 Post Oak Pl Suite
342   Houston TX 77027
Ph: 713-965-0566 ▪ Fx: 713-960-0488

Flemish Americans, Genealogical Society of   www.rootsweb.com/~gsfa
18740 13 Mile Rd   Roseville MI 48066
Ph: 586-776-9579

Flemish Giant Rabbit Breeders, National Federation of   www.nffgrb.org
2259 Barbara Dr   Camarillo CA 93012
Ph: 805-491-2029

Flexible Compensation, Employers Council on   www.ecfc.org
927 15th St NW Suite 1000   Washington DC 20005
Ph: 202-659-4300 ▪ Fx: 202-371-1467

Flexible Intermediate Bulk Container Association   www.fibca.com
PO Box 26068   Macon GA 31221
Ph: 478-757-1006 ▪ Fx: 478-757-9444

Flexible Packaging Association   www.flexpack.org
971 Corporate Blvd Suite 403   Linthicum MD 21090
Ph: 410-694-0800 ▪ Fx: 410-694-0900

Flexographic Prepress Platemakers Association — www.fppa.net
2105 Laurel Bush Rd Suite 200   Bel Air MD 21015
Ph: 443-640-1045 ▪ Fx: 443-640-1031

Flexographic Technical Association — www.flexography.org
900 Marconi Ave   Ronkonkoma NY 11779
Ph: 631-737-6020 ▪ Fx: 631-737-6813

Flight Attendants, Association of — www.afanet.org
1275 K St NW Suite 500   Washington DC 20005
Ph: 202-712-9799 ▪ Fx: 202-712-9798 ▪ TF: 800-424-2401

Flight Attendants, Association of Professional — www.apfa.org
1004 W Euless Blvd   Euless TX 76040
Ph: 817-540-0108 ▪ Fx: 817-540-2077 ▪ TF: 800-395-2732

Flight Instructors, National Association of — www.nafinet.org
EAA Aviation Ctr PO Box 3086   Oshkosh WI 54903
Ph: 920-426-6801 ▪ Fx: 920-426-4881

Flight Paramedics Association, National — www.flightparamedic.org
383 F St   Salt Lake City UT 84103
Ph: 800-381-6372

Flight Safety Foundation — www.flightsafety.org
601 Madison St Suite 300   Alexandria VA 22314
Ph: 703-739-6700 ▪ Fx: 703-739-6708

Flight Society, First — www.firstflight.org
PO Box 1903   Kitty Hawk NC 27949
Ph: 252-441-1903 ▪ Fx: 252-441-4349

Flight Surgeons, Society of US Air Force — www.sousaffs.org
PO Box 35387   Brooks AFB TX 78235
Ph: 210-536-2845 ▪ Fx: 210-536-1779

Flights for Kids, Miracle — www.miracleflights.org
2756 N Green Valley Pkwy Suite 115   Green Valley NV 89014
Ph: 702-261-0494 ▪ Fx: 702-261-0497 ▪ TF: 800-358-1711

Flock Association, American — www.flocking.org
6 Beacon St Suite 1125   Boston MA 02108
Ph: 617-303-6288 ▪ Fx: 617-542-2199

Floodplain Managers, Association of State — www.floods.org
2809 Fish Hatchery Rd Suite 04   Madison WI 53713
Ph: 608-274-0123 ▪ Fx: 608-274-0696

Floor Covering Association, World — www.wfca.org
2211 E Howell Ave   Anaheim CA 92806
Ph: 714-978-6440 ▪ Fx: 714-978-6066 ▪ TF: 800-624-6880

Floor Covering Distributors, National Association of — www.nafcd.org
401 N Michigan Ave Suite 2400   Chicago IL 60611
Ph: 312-321-6836 ▪ Fx: 312-673-6962

Floor Covering Installation Contractors Association — www.fcica.com
7439 Millwood Dr   West Bloomfield MI 48322
Ph: 248-661-5015 ▪ Fx: 248-661-5018

Floor Covering Institute, Resilient — www.rfci.com
401 E Jefferson St Suite 102   Rockville MD 20850
Ph: 301-340-8580 ▪ Fx: 301-340-7283

Floorcovering Alliance Inc, American
210 W Cuyler St   Dalton GA 30720
Ph: 706-278-4101 ▪ Fx: 706-278-5323 ▪ TF: 800-288-4101

Flooring Association, National Wood — www.woodfloors.org
111 Chesterfield Industrial Blvd   Chesterfield MO 63005
Ph: 636-519-9663 ▪ Fx: 636-519-9664 ▪ TF: 800-422-4556

Flooring Manufacturers Association, Maple — www.maplefloor.org
60 Revere Dr Suite 500   Northbrook IL 60062
Ph: 847-480-9138 ▪ Fx: 847-480-9282

Flooring Manufacturers Association, NOFMA: Wood — www.nofma.org
PO Box 3009   Memphis TN 38173
Ph: 901-526-5016 ▪ Fx: 901-526-7022

Flora Neotropica, Organization for — www.nybg.org/bsci/ofn
New York Botanical Garden   Bronx NY 10458
Ph: 718-817-8625 ▪ Fx: 718-817-8648

Floral Association, International Freeze-Dry — www.ifdfa.org
11407 N Main St Suite A   High Point NC 27263
Ph: 336-861-6737 ▪ TF: 888-554-9706

Floral Council, Fresh Produce & — www.fpfc.org
6301 Beach Blvd Suite 150   Buena Park CA 90621
Ph: 714-739-0177 ▪ Fx: 714-739-0226

Floral Designers, American Institute of — www.aifd.org
720 Light St   Baltimore MD 21230
Ph: 410-752-3318 ▪ Fx: 410-752-8295

Floral Industry Association, American — www.afia.net
PO Box 420244   Dallas TX 75342
Ph: 214-742-2747 ▪ Fx: 214-742-2648

Floresta USA — www.floresta.org
4903 Morena Blvd Suite 1215   San Diego CA 92117
Ph: 858-274-3718 ▪ Fx: 858-274-3728 ▪ TF: 800-633-5319

Florida Trail Association — www.florida-trail.org
5415 SW 13th St   Gainesville FL 32608
Ph: 352-378-8823 ▪ Fx: 352-378-4550 ▪ TF: 877-445-3352

Florida Tropical Fish Farms Association — www.ftffa.com
PO Box 1519   Winter Haven FL 33882
Ph: 863-293-5710 ▪ Fx: 863-299-5154

Florist Association, Extra Touch — www.etfassociation.org
332 E Main St   Northville MI 48167
Ph: 248-692-0008 ▪ Fx: 248-380-1830 ▪ TF: 888-419-1515

Florist & Florist Supplier Association, Wholesale — www.wffsa.org
147 Old Solomons Island Rd Suite 302   Annapolis MD 21401
Ph: 410-573-0400 ▪ Fx: 410-573-5001 ▪ TF: 888-289-3372

Florists, Society of American — www.safnow.org
1601 Duke St   Alexandria VA 22314
Ph: 703-836-8700 ▪ Fx: 703-836-8705 ▪ TF: 800-336-4743

Flotation Device Manufacturers Association, Personal — www.pfdma.org
200 E Randolph Dr Suite 510   Chicago IL 60601
Ph: 312-946-6280 ▪ Fx: 312-946-0388

Flour Distributors, National Association of
PO Box 165067   Little Rock AR 72216
Ph: 501-372-0636 ▪ Fx: 501-372-2468

Flower Essence Society — www.flowersociety.org
PO Box 459   Nevada City CA 95959
Ph: 530-265-9163 ▪ Fx: 530-265-0584 ▪ TF: 800-736-9222

Flower Growers Association, International Cut — www.rosesinc.org
PO Box 99   Haslett MI 48840
Ph: 517-655-3726 ▪ Fx: 517-655-3727 ▪ TF: 800-968-7673

Flower Growers, Association of Specialty Cut — www.ascfg.org
PO Box 268   Oberlin OH 44074
Ph: 440-774-2887 ▪ Fx: 440-774-2435

Flower, Society of the Little — www.littleflower.org
1313 Frontage Rd   Darien IL 60561
Ph: 630-968-9400 ▪ Fx: 630-968-9542 ▪ TF: 800-621-2806

Flower Society, New England Wild — www.newfs.org
180 Hemenway Rd   Framingham MA 01701
Ph: 617-877-7630 ▪ Fx: 617-877-3658

Fluid Controls Institute — www.fluidcontrolsinstitute.org
1300 Sumner Ave   Cleveland OH 44115
Ph: 216-241-7333 ▪ Fx: 216-241-0105

Fluid Power Association, National — www.nfpa.com
3333 N Mayfair Rd Suite 101   Milwaukee WI 53222
Ph: 414-778-3344 ▪ Fx: 414-778-3361

Fluid Power Distributors Association — www.fpda.org
PO Box 1420   Cherry Hill NJ 08034
Ph: 856-424-8998 ▪ Fx: 856-424-9248

Fluid Power Society — www.ifps.org
PO Box 1420   Cherry Hill NJ 08034
Ph: 856-489-8983 ▪ Fx: 856-424-9248 ▪ TF: 800-303-8520

Fluid Sealing Association — www.fluidsealing.com
994 Old Eagle School Rd Suite 1019   Wayne PA 19087
Ph: 610-971-4850 ▪ Fx: 610-971-4859

Fluorescent Mineral Society — www.uvminerals.org
PO Box 572694   Tarzana CA 91357
Ph: 818-343-6637

Fly Fishers, Federation of — www.fedflyfishers.org
PO Box 1595   Bozeman MT 59771
Ph: 406-585-7592 ▪ Fx: 406-585-7596

Fly Fishing Trade Association, American — www.affta.com
PO Box 164   Kelso WA 98626
Ph: 360-636-0708 ▪ Fx: 360-636-3971

Flying Adjusters, Organized — www.ofainc.com
1501 Bluff Dr   Round Rock TX 78681
Ph: 512-255-2740 ▪ Fx: 512-246-1066

(Flying Disc Sports) Ultimate Players Association — www.upa.org
714 Pearl St Side Suite   Boulder CO 80302
Ph: 303-447-3472 ▪ Fx: 303-447-3483 ▪ TF: 800-872-4384

Flying Doctors of America — www.fdoamerica.org
1235 N Decatur Rd   Atlanta GA 30306
Ph: 404-815-7044 ▪ Fx: 404-892-6672

(Flying Doctors of Mercy) LIGA International Inc — liga.blytheco.com
1464 N Fitzgerald Ave Hangar 2   Rialto CA 92376
Ph: 909-875-6300 ▪ Fx: 909-875-6900

Flying Farmers, International — www.flyingfarmers.org
PO Box 9124   Wichita KS 67277
Ph: 316-943-4234 ▪ Fx: 800-266-5415

Flying Physicians Association — www.fpadrs.org
PO Box 677427   Orlando FL 32867
Ph: 407-359-1423 ▪ Fx: 407-359-1167

Flying Veterinarians Association
101 Bingham Rd   Columbia MO 65203
Ph: 573-449-4497

Foam Packaging Recyclers, Alliance of — www.epspackaging.org
1298 Cronson Blvd Suite 201   Crofton MD 21114
Ph: 410-451-8340 ▪ Fx: 410-451-8343 ▪ TF: 800-944-8448

Focus on the Family — www.family.org
8605 Explorer Dr   Colorado Springs CO 80995
Ph: 719-531-3400 ▪ Fx: 719-548-4670 ▪ TF: 800-232-6459

Foil Container Manufacturers Association, Aluminum — www.afcma.org
10 Vecilla Ln   Hot Springs Village AR 71909
Ph: 501-922-7425 ▪ Fx: 501-922-0383

Foil Operators, American Academy of Gold — www.goldfoil.org
1 Woods End Rd   Etna NH 03750
Ph: 603-643-2899

Foil Stamping & Embossing Association — www.fsea.com
536 NW Tyler Ct Suite 204   Topeka KS 66608
Ph: 785-232-8776 ▪ Fx: 785-232-8747

Folk Alliance — www.folk.org
962 Wayne Ave Suite 902   Silver Spring MD 20910
Ph: 301-588-8185 ▪ Fx: 301-588-8186

Folk Art Federation of America, Italian — www.italian-american.com/ifafa

Folk Art Society of America — www.folkart.org
PO Box 17041   Richmond VA 23226
Ph: 804-285-4532 ▪ TF: 800-527-3655

Folk Arts Preservation, Society for — www.societyforfolkarts.com
69 Timberhill Ln   South Fallsburg NY 12779
Ph: 845-436-7314

Folk Harpers & Craftsmen, International Society of — www.folkharpsociety.org
4110 Brandemere Way   Houston TX 77066
Ph: 832-249-7885

Folk Music Association, World — www.wfma.net
PO Box 40553   Washington DC 20016
Ph: 202-362-2225 ▪ Fx: 202-244-1543 ▪ TF: 800-779-2226

Folklore Society, American — www.afsnet.org
Ohio State Univ Mershon Ctr 1501 Neil Ave   Columbus OH 43201
Ph: 614-292-3375 ▪ Fx: 614-292-2407

Folklore Society, Tennessee — www.middleenglish.org/tennfolk
Box 201   Murfreesboro TN 37132
Ph: 615-898-2573 ▪ Fx: 615-898-5098

Fone Friends, Famous   www.nancycartwright.com/volunteer_fff.html
9101 Sawyer St   Los Angeles CA 90035
Ph: 310-204-5683

Food Additives Council, International
5775 Peachtree-Dunwoody Rd Bldg G Suite 500   Atlanta GA 30342
Ph: 404-252-3663 ▪ Fx: 404-252-0774

Food & Agricultural Policy Research Institute   www.fapri.iastate.edu
Iowa State University 578 Heady Hall   Ames IA 50011
Ph: 515-294-7519 ▪ Fx: 515-294-6336

Food for All   www.foodforall.org
3246 Prospect St NW   Washington DC 20007
Ph: 202-965-6499 ▪ Fx: 202-965-5177 ▪ TF: 800-896-5101

Food Allergy & Anaphylaxis Network   www.foodallergy.org
10400 Eaton Pl Suite 107   Fairfax VA 22030
Ph: 703-691-3179 ▪ Fx: 703-691-2713 ▪ TF: 800-929-4040

Food & Allied Service Trades AFL-CIO   www.fastaflcio.org
1925 K St NW Suite 400   Washington DC 20006
Ph: 202-737-7200 ▪ Fx: 202-737-7208

Food, American Institute of Wine &   www.aiwf.com
304 W Liberty St Suite 201   Louisville KY 40202
Ph: 800-274-2493 ▪ Fx: 502-589-3602

Food Animal Concern Trust   www.fact.cc
PO Box 14599   Chicago IL 60614
Ph: 773-525-4952 ▪ Fx: 773-525-5226

Food Association, International Frozen
2000 Corporate Ridge Suite 1000   McLean VA 22102
Ph: 703-821-0770 ▪ Fx: 703-821-1350

Food Business Forum, CIES -   www.ciesnet.com
8455 Colesville Rd Suite 710   Silver Spring MD 20910
Ph: 301-563-3383 ▪ Fx: 301-563-3386

(Food Choices) EarthSave International   www.earthsave.org
PO Box 96   New York NY 10108
Ph: 718-459-7503 ▪ Fx: 718-228-2491 ▪ TF: 800-362-3648

Food & Commercial Workers International Union, United   www.ufcw.org
1775 K St NW   Washington DC 20006
Ph: 202-223-3111 ▪ Fx: 202-466-1562 ▪ TF: 800-551-4010

Food Day, US National Committee for World
2175 K St NW   Washington DC 20437
Ph: 202-653-2404 ▪ Fx: 202-653-5760

Food & Development Policy, Institute for   www.foodfirst.org
398 60th St   Oakland CA 94618
Ph: 510-654-4400 ▪ Fx: 510-654-4551

Food Distribution Research Society   fdrs.ag.utk.edu
Michigan State Univ 211C Agriculture Hall   East Lansing MI 48824
Ph: 517-353-7226 ▪ Fx: 517-432-1800

Food Distributors Association, National Poultry &   www.npfda.org
958 McEver Rd Ext Unit B-8   Gainesville GA 30504
Ph: 770-535-9901 ▪ Fx: 770-535-7385 ▪ TF: 877-845-1545

Food & Drug Law Institute   www.fdli.org
1000 Vermont Ave NW Suite 200   Washington DC 20005
Ph: 202-371-1420 ▪ Fx: 202-371-0649 ▪ TF: 800-956-6293

Food & Drug Officials, Association of   www.afdo.org
2550 Kingston Rd Suite 311   York PA 17402
Ph: 717-757-2888 ▪ Fx: 717-755-8089

Food & Energy Council, National   www.nfec.org
601 Business Loop 70W Suite 216D   Columbia MO 65203
Ph: 573-875-7155 ▪ Fx: 573-449-5322

Food Equipment Service Association, Commercial   www.cfesa.com
2211 W Meadowview Rd Suite 20   Greensboro NC 27407
Ph: 336-346-4700 ▪ Fx: 336-346-4745

Food First   www.foodfirst.org
398 60th St   Oakland CA 94618
Ph: 510-654-4400 ▪ Fx: 510-654-4551

Food for the Hungry Inc   www.fh.org
PO Box 12349   Scottsdale AZ 85267
Ph: 480-998-3100 ▪ Fx: 480-443-1420 ▪ TF: 800-248-6437

Food Industries Inc, Association of   www.afius.org
3301 Rt 66 Bldg C Suite 205   Neptune NJ 08005
Ph: 732-922-3008 ▪ Fx: 732-922-3590

Food Industry Association Executives   www.fiae.net
PO Box 2510   Flemington NJ 08822
Ph: 908-782-7833 ▪ Fx: 908-782-6907

Food Industry, Joint Labor Management Committee of the Retail
3720 Farragut Ave Suite 301   Kensington MD 20895
Ph: 301-942-5400 ▪ Fx: 301-942-5409

Food Industry Suppliers, International Association of   www.iafis.org
1451 Dolley Madison Blvd   McLean VA 22101
Ph: 703-761-2600 ▪ Fx: 703-761-4334

Food Information Council, International   www.ific.org
1100 Connecticut Ave NW Suite 430   Washington DC 20036
Ph: 202-296-6540 ▪ Fx: 202-296-6547

Food-Ingredient Systems Inc, National Association of Flavors &   www.naffs.org
3301 Rt 66 Bldg C Suite 205   Neptune NJ 07753
Ph: 732-922-3218 ▪ Fx: 732-922-3590

Food Institute   www.foodinstitute.org
1 Broadway   Elmwood Park NJ 07407
Ph: 201-791-5570 ▪ Fx: 201-791-5222

Food Institute, Italian Wine &   www.italianwineandfoodinstitute.com
60 E 42nd St Suite 1341 PO Box 789   New York NY 10150
Ph: 212-867-4111 ▪ Fx: 212-867-4114

Food Logistics Organization, World   www.wflo.org
1500 King St Suite 201   Alexandria VA 22314
Ph: 703-373-4300 ▪ Fx: 703-373-4301

Food Marketing Institute   www.fmi.org
655 15th St NW Suite 700   Washington DC 20005
Ph: 202-220-0600 ▪ Fx: 202-429-4519

Food Marketing Institute PAC
655 15th St NW   Washington DC 20005
Ph: 202-220-0600 ▪ Fx: 202-429-4519

Food & Packaging Systems Inc, Research & Development Associates for Military   www.militaryfood.org
16607 Blanco Rd Suite 1506   San Antonio TX 78232
Ph: 210-493-8024 ▪ Fx: 210-493-8036

Food Policy Research Institute, International   www.ifpri.org
2033 K St NW   Washington DC 20006
Ph: 202-862-5600 ▪ Fx: 202-467-4439

Food for the Poor Inc   www.foodforthepoor.com
550 SW 12th Ave Bldg 4   Deerfield Beach FL 33442
Ph: 954-427-2222 ▪ Fx: 954-570-7654 ▪ TF: 800-282-7667

Food Processing Machinery Association   www.fpmsa.org
200 Daingerfield Rd   Alexandria VA 22314
Ph: 703-684-1080 ▪ Fx: 703-548-6563 ▪ TF: 800-833-4337

Food Processors Association, National   www.nfpa-food.org
1350 'I' St NW Suite 300   Washington DC 20005
Ph: 202-639-5900 ▪ Fx: 202-639-5932 ▪ TF: 800-355-0983

Food Processors Association, National Suppliers to
PO Box 59149   Minneapolis MN 55459
Ph: 612-341-9600 ▪ Fx: 612-341-9648

Food Processors Institute   www.fpi-food.org
1350 'I' St NW   Washington DC 20005
Ph: 202-639-5945 ▪ Fx: 202-639-5932 ▪ TF: 800-355-0983

Food Programme, Friends of the World   www.friendsofwfp.org
1341 Connecticut Ave NW   Washington DC 20036
Ph: 202-530-1694

Food Protection, International Association for   www.foodprotection.org
6200 Aurora Ave Suite 200W   Des Moines IA 50322
Ph: 515-276-3344 ▪ Fx: 515-276-8655 ▪ TF: 800-369-6337

Food Research & Action Center   www.frac.org
1875 Connecticut Ave NW Suite 540   Washington DC 20009
Ph: 202-986-2200 ▪ Fx: 202-986-2525

Food Service Administrators, American Society for Healthcare   www.ashfsa.org
304 W Liberty St Suite 201   Louisville KY 40202
Ph: 800-620-6422

Food Service Association, American Correctional   www.acfsa.org
4248 Park Glen Rd   Minneapolis MN 55416
Ph: 952-928-4648 ▪ Fx: 952-929-1318

Food Service Association, American School   www.asfsa.org
700 S Washington St Suite 300   Alexandria VA 22314
Ph: 703-739-3900 ▪ Fx: 703-739-3915 ▪ TF: 800-877-8822

Food Service Association, International Inflight   www.ifsanet.com
5775 Peachtree-Dunwoody Rd Bldg G Suite 500   Atlanta GA 30342
Ph: 404-252-3663 ▪ Fx: 404-252-0774

Food Service Executives Association, International   www.ifsea.com
836 San Bruno Ave   Henderson NV 89015
Ph: 702-564-0997 ▪ Fx: 702-564-4836 ▪ TF: 888-234-3732

Food Service Management Institute, National   www.nfsmi.org
PO Drawer 188   University MS 38677
Ph: 662-915-7658 ▪ Fx: 662-915-5615 ▪ TF: 800-321-3054

Food Service Management, National Society for Healthcare   www.hfm.org
204 'E' St NE   Washington DC 20002
Ph: 202-546-7236 ▪ Fx: 202-547-6348

Food Service, National Association of Church   www.nacfs.org
PO Box 550413   Atlanta GA 30355
Ph: 404-261-1794 ▪ Fx: 404-240-8276

Food Services, National Association of College & University   www.nacufs.org
1405 S Harrison Rd Suite 305   East Lansing MI 48824
Ph: 517-332-2494 ▪ Fx: 517-332-8144

Food Shippers of America   www.foodshippersofamerica.org
6166 Booror Rd   Grove City OH 43123
Ph: 614-875-3955

Food & Stormwater Management Agencies, National Association of   www.nafsma.org
1299 Pennsylvania Ave NW 8th Fl W   Washington DC 20004
Ph: 202-218-4122 ▪ Fx: 202-478-1734

Food Technologists, Institute of   www.ift.org
525 W Van Buren St Suite 1000   Chicago IL 60607
Ph: 312-782-8424 ▪ Fx: 312-782-8348 ▪ TF: 800-438-3663

Food Trade Inc, National Association for the Specialty   www.specialtyfoodmarket.com
120 Wall St 27th Fl   New York NY 10005
Ph: 212-482-6440 ▪ Fx: 212-482-6459 ▪ TF: 800-627-3869

Food Transporters Conference, Agricultural &   www.truckline.com/cc/conferences/atc
2200 Mill Rd   Alexandria VA 22314
Ph: 703-838-7999 ▪ Fx: 703-519-1866

Food & Wine Institute, Greek
34-80 48th St   Long Island City NY 11101
Ph: 718-729-5277 ▪ Fx: 718-361-9725

Food Wine & Travel Writers Association, International   www.ifwtwa.org
PO Box 8249   Calabasas CA 91372
Ph: 818-999-9959 ▪ Fx: 818-347-7545

Foods Association, National Frozen & Refrigerated   www.nfraweb.org
4755 Linglestown Rd Suite 300   Harrisburg PA 17112
Ph: 717-657-8601 ▪ Fx: 717-657-9862

Foods Association, National Nutritional   www.nnfa.org
3931 MacArthur Blvd Suite 101   Newport Beach CA 92660
Ph: 949-622-6272 ▪ Fx: 949-622-6266 ▪ TF: 800-966-6632

Foods Association, Refrigerated   www.refrigeratedfoods.org
2971 Flowers Rd S Suite 266   Atlanta GA 30341
Ph: 770-452-0660 ▪ Fx: 770-455-3879 ▪ TF: 800-719-1309

Foodservice Consultants Society International   www.fcsi.org
304 W Liberty St Suite 201   Louisville KY 40202
Ph: 502-583-3783 ▪ Fx: 502-589-3602

Foodservice Distributors Association, International   www.ifdaonline.org
201 Park Washington Ct   Falls Church VA 22046
Ph: 703-532-9400 ▪ Fx: 703-538-4673

Foodservice Editorial Council, International   www.ifec-is-us.com
PO Box 491   Hyde Park NY 12538
Ph: 845-229-6973 ▪ Fx: 845-229-6993

Foodservice Equipment Distributors Association   www.feda.com
223 W Jackson Blvd Suite 620   Chicago IL 60606
Ph: 312-427-9605 ▪ Fx: 312-427-9607 ▪ TF: 800-677-9605

Foodservice Equipment Manufacturers, North American Association of www.nafem.org
161 N Clark Suite 2020   Chicago IL 60601
Ph: 312-821-0201 ▪ Fx: 312-821-0202

Foodservice Forum, Women's www.womensfoodserviceforum.com
1 General Mills Blvd MS W05D   Golden Valley MN 55426
Ph: 763-293-1150 ▪ Fx: 763-293-1114

Foodservice Group www.fsgroup.com
4149 Lakeshore Way   Marietta GA 30067
Ph: 770-977-1476 ▪ Fx: 770-973-6662

Foodservice & Hospitality Alliance, Multicultural www.mfha.net
65 Weybosset St Suite 50   Providence RI 02903
Ph: 401-751-8883 ▪ Fx: 401-751-8333

Foodservice Industry, Manufacturers' Agents Association for the www.mafsi.org
2814 Spring Rd Suite 211   Atlanta GA 30339
Ph: 770-433-9844 ▪ Fx: 770-433-2450

Foodservice Management, Society for www.sfm-online.org
304 W Liberty St Suite 201   Louisville KY 40202
Ph: 502-583-3783 ▪ Fx: 502-589-3602

Foodservice Manufacturers Association, International www.ifmaworld.com
180 N Stetson Ave 2 Prudential Plaza Suite 4400   Chicago IL
60601
Ph: 312-540-4400 ▪ Fx: 312-540-4401

Foodservice & Packaging Institute www.fpi.org
150 S Washington St Suite 204   Falls Church VA 22046
Ph: 703-538-2800 ▪ Fx: 703-538-2187

Foot & Ankle Orthopedics & Medicine, American College of www.acfaom.org
3525 Ellicott Mills Dr Suite N   Ellicott City MD 21043
Ph: 410-265-8263 ▪ Fx: 410-418-4805

Foot & Ankle Pediatrics, American College of
6477 Auburn Dr   Virginia Beach VA 23464
Ph: 757-523-0414 ▪ Fx: 757-523-2047

Foot & Ankle Society, American Orthopaedic www.aofas.org
2517 Eastlake Ave E Suite 200   Seattle WA 98102
Ph: 206-223-1120 ▪ Fx: 206-223-1178 ▪ TF: 800-235-4855

Foot & Ankle Surgeons, American College of www.acfas.org
515 Busse Hwy   Park Ridge IL 60068
Ph: 847-292-2237 ▪ Fx: 847-292-2022 ▪ TF: 800-421-2237

Foot & Ankle Surgery, Academy of Ambulatory www.academy-afs.org
1601 Walnut St Suite 1005   Philadelphia PA 19102
Ph: 215-569-3303 ▪ Fx: 215-569-3310 ▪ TF: 800-433-4892

Football Coaches Association, American www.afca.com
100 Legends Ln   Waco TX 76706
Ph: 254-754-9900 ▪ Fx: 254-754-7373

Football League Players Association, National www.nflpa.org
2021 L St NW Suite 600   Washington DC 20036
Ph: 202-463-2200 ▪ Fx: 202-857-0380 ▪ TF: 800-372-2000

Football League, US Flag & Touch www.usftl.com
7709 Ohio St   Mentor OH 44060
Ph: 440-974-8735 ▪ Fx: 440-974-8441

Football Researchers Association, Professional www.footballresearch.com/
12870 Rt 30   North Huntingdon PA 15642
Ph: 724-863-6345

Football Writers Association of America www.sportswriters.net/fwaa
c/o Dallas Morning News 18652 Vista Del Sol   Dallas TX 75287
Ph: 972-713-6198

Footprint Association, International www.footprinter.org
PO Box 2487   Walnut Creek CA 94595
Ph: 925-944-1763 ▪ Fx: 925-944-1771 ▪ TF: 888-944-1763

Footwear Association, American Apparel & www.apparelandfootwear.org
1601 N Kent St Suite 1200   Arlington VA 22209
Ph: 703-524-1864 ▪ Fx: 703-522-6741 ▪ TF: 800-520-2262

Footwear Association, Pedorthic www.pedorthics.org
7150 Columbia Gateway Dr Suite G   Columbia MD 21046
Ph: 410-381-7278 ▪ Fx: 410-381-1167 ▪ TF: 800-673-8447

Footwear Distributors & Retailers of America www.fdra.org
1319 F St NW Suite 700   Washington DC 20004
Ph: 202-737-5660 ▪ Fx: 202-638-2615

Footwear Distributors & Retailers of America PAC
1319 F St NW Suite 700   Washington DC 20004
Ph: 202-737-5660 ▪ Fx: 202-638-2615

Footwear Foundation, Two Ten www.twoten.org
1466 Main St   Waltham MA 02451
Ph: 781-736-1500 ▪ Fx: 781-736-1555 ▪ TF: 800-346-3210

For Mother Earth www.motherearth.org
Old First Presbyterian Church 1101 Bryder Rd   Columbus OH
43205
Ph: 614-252-9255 ▪ Fx: 614-443-6125

Forage & Grassland Council, American www.afgc.org
PO Box 94   Georgetown TX 78627
Ph: 512-868-2899 ▪ Fx: 512-931-1166 ▪ TF: 800-944-2342

Foragers Cosmetic Industry Associates www.cosmeticindex.com/ci/for
135 E 55th St 8th Fl PH   New York NY 10022
Ph: 212-759-1991 ▪ Fx: 212-755-4841

(Foraminiferal Research) Cushman Foundation cushforams.niu.edu
Smithsonian Institution Dept of Paleobiology
MRC-121   Washington DC 20560
Ph: 202-357-1390 ▪ Fx: 202-786-2832

Ford Club of America Inc, Model A www.mafca.com
250 S Cypress St   La Habra CA 90631
Ph: 562-697-2712 ▪ Fx: 562-690-7452

Ford Club of America, Model T www.mtfca.com
PO Box 126   Centerville IN 47330
Ph: 765-855-5248 ▪ Fx: 765-855-3428

Ford Dealers Alliance www.dealersalliance.org
401 Hackensack Ave   Hackensack NJ 07601
Ph: 201-342-4542 ▪ Fx: 201-342-3997

Ford Family Foundation www.tfff.org
1600 NW Stewart Pkwy   Roseburg OR 97470
Ph: 541-957-5574 ▪ Fx: 541-957-5720

Ford Foundation www.fordfound.org
320 E 43rd St   New York NY 10017
Ph: 212-573-5000 ▪ Fx: 212-351-3677

Ford Motor Minority Dealers Association www.fmmda.org
16000 W Nine-Mile Rd Suite 603   Southfield MI 48075
Ph: 248-557-2500 ▪ Fx: 248-557-2882 ▪ TF: 800-247-0293

Ford's Theatre Society www.fordstheatre.org
511 10th St NW   Washington DC 20004
Ph: 202-638-2941 ▪ Fx: 202-347-6269 ▪ TF: 800-899-2367

Fordson Tractor Club
250 Robinson Rd   Cave Junction OR 97523
Ph: 541-592-3203

Foreign Affairs, Citizens Network for www.cnfa.com
1111 19th St NW Suite 900   Washington DC 20036
Ph: 202-296-3920 ▪ Fx: 202-296-3948 ▪ TF: 888-872-2632

Foreign Credit Insurance Association www.fcia.com
40 Rector St 11th Fl   New York NY 10006
Ph: 212-885-1500 ▪ Fx: 212-885-1535

Foreign Investors in Real Estate, Association of www.afire.com
1300 Pennsylvania Ave NW   Washington DC 20004
Ph: 202-312-1400 ▪ Fx: 202-312-1401

(Foreign Language) Alpha citywww.lacc.cc.ca.us/activities/honor/amg/homepage.html
Mu Gamma   855 N Vermont Ave   Los Angeles CA 90029
Ph: 323-644-9752

(Foreign Language) Phi Sigma Iota www.phisigmaiota.org
Univ of South Florida World Language Education 4202 E Fowler
Ave   Tampa FL 33620
Ph: 813-974-2746 ▪ Fx: 813-974-6944 ▪ TF: 800-673-5599

Foreign Languages, American Council on the Teaching of www.actfl.org
6 Executive Plaza   Yonkers NY 10701
Ph: 914-963-8830 ▪ Fx: 914-963-1275

Foreign Languages, Association of Departments of www.adfl.org
26 Broadway 3rd Fl   New York NY 10004
Ph: 646-576-5140 ▪ Fx: 646-458-0030

Foreign Languages, Northeast Conference on the www.dickinson.edu/nectfl
Teaching of   Dickinson College PO Box 1773   Carlisle PA
17013
Ph: 717-245-1977 ▪ Fx: 717-245-1976

Foreign Mission Association of North America, www.ifmamissions.org
Interdenominational   PO Box 398   Wheaton IL 60189
Ph: 630-682-9270 ▪ Fx: 630-682-9278

Foreign Missions, Independent Board for Presbyterian www.ibpfm.org
246 W Walnut Ln   Philadelphia PA 19144
Ph: 215-438-0511 ▪ Fx: 215-438-0560

Foreign Policy Association www.fpa.org
470 Park Ave S 2nd Fl   New York NY 10016
Ph: 212-481-8100 ▪ Fx: 212-481-9275 ▪ TF: 800-628-5754

Foreign Policy Institute www.sais-jhu.edu
Johns Hopkins Univ Paul H Nitze School of Advanced
International Studies   Washington DC 20036
Ph: 202-663-5600

Foreign Policy Research Institute www.fpri.org
1528 Walnut St Suite 610   Philadelphia PA 19102
Ph: 215-732-3774 ▪ Fx: 215-732-4401

Foreign Press Association, Hollywood
646 N Robertson Blvd   West Hollywood CA 90069
Ph: 310-657-1731 ▪ Fx: 310-657-5576

Foreign Press Association of New York www.foreignpressnewyork.com
333 E 46th St Suite 1K   New York NY 10017
Ph: 212-370-1054 ▪ Fx: 212-370-1058

Foreign Relations, Chicago Council on www.ccfr.org
116 S Michigan Ave 10th Fl   Chicago IL 60603
Ph: 312-726-3860 ▪ Fx: 312-726-4491

Foreign Relations Inc, Council on www.cfr.org
Harold Pratt House 58 E 68th St   New York NY 10021
Ph: 212-434-9400 ▪ Fx: 212-434-9800

Foreign Relations, Society for Historians of American www.shafr.org

Foreign Service Association, American www.afsa.org
2101 'E' St NW   Washington DC 20037
Ph: 202-338-4045 ▪ Fx: 202-338-6820 ▪ TF: 800-704-2372

Foreign Service Fraternity Inc, Delta www.deltaphiepsilon.net/National_Fraternity.html
Phi Epsilon Professional   PO Box 25401   Washington DC
20027
Ph: 202-337-7116

Foreign Service Protective Association, American www.afspa.org
1716 'N' St NW   Washington DC 20036
Ph: 202-833-4910 ▪ Fx: 202-833-4918

Foreign Service Worldwide, Association of American www.aafsw.org
5125 McArthur Blvd NW Suite 36   Washington DC 20016
Ph: 202-362-6514 ▪ Fx: 202-362-6589

Foreign Student Service Council
1930 18th St NW Suite 21   Washington DC 20009
Ph: 202-232-4979 ▪ Fx: 202-667-9305

Foreign Study, American Institute for www.aifs.org
9 W Broad St   Stamford CT 06902
Ph: 203-399-5000 ▪ Fx: 203-399-5590 ▪ TF: 800-727-2437

Foreign Study, EF Foundation for www.effoundation.org
1 Education St   Cambridge MA 02141
Ph: 888-447-4273 ▪ Fx: 617-619-1401

Foreign Study Foundation, American Institute for www.aifs.com/aifsfoundation
9 W Broad St   Stamford CT 06902
Ph: 203-399-5414 ▪ Fx: 203-399-5593 ▪ TF: 800-322-4678

Foreign Trade Council, National www.nftc.org
1625 K St NW Suite 200   Washington DC 20006
Ph: 202-887-0278 ▪ Fx: 202-452-8160

Foreign-Trade Zones, National Association of www.naftz.org
1000 Connecticut Ave NW Suite 1001   Washington DC 20036
Ph: 202-331-1950 ▪ Fx: 202-331-1994

Foreign Wars of the US, Veterans of www.vfw.com
406 W 34th St   Kansas City MO 64111
Ph: 816-756-3390 ▪ Fx: 816-968-1149

Forensic Accountants, National Association of www.nafanet.com
2455 E Sunrise Blvd Suite 1201   Fort Lauderdale FL 33304
Ph: 954-535-5556 ▪ Fx: 954-537-4942 ▪ TF: 800-523-3680

Forensic Accountants Society of North America www.fasna.org
8712 W Dodge Rd Suite 200   Omaha NE 68114
Ph: 402-397-9433 ▪ Fx: 402-397-8649

Forensic Anthropology, American Board of www.csuchico.edu/anth/ABFA
c/o Lucas County Coroner's Office 2595 Arlington Ave   Toledo
OH 43614
Ph: 419-213-3908

Forensic Association, American www.americanforensics.org
PO Box 256   River Falls WI 54022
Ph: 715-425-3198 ▪ Fx: 715-425-9533 ▪ TF: 800-228-5424

Forensic Economics, National Association of www.nafe.net
PO Box 30067   Kansas City MO 64112
Ph: 816-235-2833 ▪ Fx: 816-235-5263

Forensic Examiners, American College of www.acfei.com
2750 E Sunshine St   Springfield MO 65804
Ph: 417-881-3818 ▪ Fx: 417-881-4702

Forensic Geologists, American Society of www.forensicgeology.org
8401 Summerspring Ln   Raleigh NC 27615
Ph: 919-618-0810

Forensic & Industrial Chiropractic Consultants, Academy of aficc.tripod.com
18331 Gridely Rd Suite C   Cerritos CA 90703
Ph: 562-860-3662 ▪ Fx: 562-860-4377

Forensic League, National www.nflonline.org
125 Watson St   Ripon WI 54971
Ph: 920-748-6206 ▪ Fx: 920-748-9478

Forensic Odontology, American Society of www.asfo.org
11 Tiffany Pl   Saratoga Springs NY 12866
Ph: 518-584-2342 ▪ Fx: 518-584-9706

Forensic Psychiatry, American College of www.forensicpsychiatry.cc
PO Box 5870   Balboa Island CA 92662
Ph: 949-673-7773 ▪ Fx: 949-673-7710

Forensic Psychology Inc, American Board of www.abfp.com
2815 Eastlake Ave E Suite 220   Seattle WA 98102
Ph: 206-320-0044 ▪ Fx: 206-320-7733

Forensic Sciences, American Academy of www.aafs.org
410 N 21st St Suite 203 PO Box 669   Colorado Springs CO
80904
Ph: 719-636-1100 ▪ Fx: 719-636-1993

Forensic Sciences Foundation Inc www.aafs.org
410 N 21st St PO Box 669   Colorado Springs CO 80901
Ph: 719-636-1100 ▪ Fx: 719-636-1993

Forensic Toxicologists, International Association of www.tiaft.org

Foresight Institute www.foresight.org
PO Box 61058   Palo Alto CA 94306
Ph: 650-917-1122 ▪ Fx: 650-917-1123

Forest Association, Intermountain www.ifia.com
3731 N Ramsey Rd Suite 110   Coeur d'Alene ID 83815
Ph: 208-667-4641 ▪ Fx: 208-664-0557

Forest Council, Native www.forestcouncil.org
PO Box 2190   Eugene OR 97402
Ph: 541-431-2600 ▪ Fx: 541-461-2156

Forest Engineering, Council on www.cofe.org
620 SW 4th St   Corvallis OR 97333
Ph: 541-754-7558 ▪ Fx: 541-754-7559

Forest Foundation, American www.affoundation.org
1111 19th St NW Suite 780   Washington DC 20036
Ph: 202-463-2462 ▪ Fx: 202-463-2461 ▪ TF: 888-889-4466

Forest Foundation, National www.natlforests.org/
2715 M St NW Suite 410   Washington DC 20007
Ph: 202-298-6740 ▪ Fx: 202-298-6758

Forest Foundation, Tropical www.tropicalforestfoundation.org
2121 Eisenhower Ave Suite 200   Alexandria VA 22314
Ph: 703-518-8834 ▪ Fx: 703-518-8974

Forest History Society www.lib.duke.edu/forest
701 Vickers Ave   Durham NC 27701
Ph: 919-682-9319 ▪ Fx: 919-682-2349

Forest Industries Telecommunications www.landmobile.com
871 Country Club Rd Suite A   Eugene OR 97401
Ph: 541-485-8441 ▪ Fx: 541-485-7556

Forest Institute, World www.worldforestry.org/wfi
4033 SW Canyon Rd   Portland OR 97221
Ph: 503-228-1367 ▪ Fx: 503-228-4608

Forest International, Ancient www.ancientforests.org
PO Box 1850   Redway CA 95560
Ph: 707-923-4475

Forest Landowners Association www.forestlandowners.com
PO Box 450209   Atlanta GA 31145
Ph: 404-325-2954 ▪ Fx: 404-325-2955 ▪ TF: 800-325-2954

Forest Network, Native www.nativeforest.org/
PO Box 8251   Missoula MT 59807
Ph: 406-542-7343 ▪ Fx: 406-542-7347

Forest & Paper Association, American www.afandpa.org
1111 19th St NW Suite 800   Washington DC 20036
Ph: 202-463-2700 ▪ Fx: 202-463-2785 ▪ TF: 800-878-8878

Forest Products Association, Southern www.sfpa.org
PO Box 641700   Kenner LA 70064
Ph: 504-443-4464 ▪ Fx: 504-443-6612

(Forest Products) Hoo-Hoo International www.hoo-hoo.org
PO Box 118   Gurdon AR 71743
Ph: 870-353-4997 ▪ Fx: 870-353-4151 ▪ TF: 800-979-9950

Forest Products Society www.forestprod.org
2801 Marshall Ct   Madison WI 53705
Ph: 608-231-1361 ▪ Fx: 608-231-2152 ▪ TF: 800-354-7164

Forest Protection Foundation, Paul G Allen www.pgafoundations.com/forest.asp
505 5th Ave S Suite 900   Seattle WA 98104
Ph: 206-342-2000 ▪ Fx: 206-342-3000

Forest Recreation Association, National www.nfra.org
PO Box 488   Woodlake CA 93286
Ph: 559-564-2365 ▪ Fx: 559-564-2048

Forest Resource Council, American www.afrc.ws
1500 SW 1st Ave Suite 300   Portland OR 97201
Ph: 503-222-9505 ▪ Fx: 503-222-3255

Forest Resources Association Inc www.forestresources.org
600 Jefferson Plaza Suite 350   Rockville MD 20852
Ph: 301-838-9385 ▪ Fx: 301-838-9481

Forest Service Employees for Environmental Ethics www.fseee.org
PO Box 11615   Eugene OR 97440
Ph: 541-484-2692 ▪ Fx: 541-484-3004

Forest Trust www.theforesttrust.org
PO Box 519   Santa Fe NM 87504
Ph: 505-983-8992 ▪ Fx: 505-986-0798

Foresters of America, Association of Consulting www.acf-foresters.com
732 N Washington St Suite 4A   Alexandria VA 22314
Ph: 703-548-0990 ▪ Fx: 703-548-6395 ▪ TF: 888-540-8733

Foresters, Catholic Association of www.catholicforesters.com
347 Commonwealth Ave   Boston MA 02115
Ph: 617-536-8221 ▪ Fx: 617-536-2819 ▪ TF: 800-282-2263

Foresters, Catholic Order of www.catholicforester.com
355 Shuman Blvd PO Box 3012   Naperville IL 60566
Ph: 630-983-4900 ▪ Fx: 630-983-4057 ▪ TF: 800-552-0145

Foresters, Independent Order of www.foresters.biz
789 Don Mills Rd   Toronto ON M3C1T9
Ph: 416-429-3000 ▪ Fx: 416-429-3896 ▪ TF: 800-828-1540

Foresters, International Society of Tropical www.istf-bethesda.org
5400 Grosvenor Ln   Bethesda MD 20814
Ph: 301-897-8720 ▪ Fx: 301-897-3690

Foresters, National Association of State www.stateforesters.org
444 N Capitol St NW Suite 540   Washington DC 20001
Ph: 202-624-5415 ▪ Fx: 202-624-5407

Foresters, National Catholic Society of www.ncsf.org
320 S School St   Mount Prospect IL 60056
Ph: 800-344-0273

Foresters, Society of American www.safnet.org
5400 Grosvenor Ln   Bethesda MD 20814
Ph: 301-897-8720 ▪ Fx: 301-897-3690

Forestry Center, World www.worldforestry.org
4033 SW Canyon Rd   Portland OR 97221
Ph: 503-228-1367 ▪ Fx: 503-228-4608

Forestry & Conservation Association, Western www.westernforestry.org
4033 SW Canyon Rd   Portland OR 97221
Ph: 503-226-4562 ▪ Fx: 503-226-2515

Forestry Conservation Communications Association www.fcca.info
444 N Capitol St NW   Washington DC 20001
Ph: 202-624-8474 ▪ Fx: 202-624-5407

Forests, American www.americanforests.org
734 15th St NW Suite 800 PO Box 2000   Washington DC
20013
Ph: 202-955-4500 ▪ Fx: 202-955-4588

Forests, National Council on Private www.ncpf.org
5400 Grosvenor Ln   Bethesda MD 20814
Ph: 301-897-8720 ▪ Fx: 301-897-3690

Forests, Save America's www.saveamericasforests.org
4 Library Ct SE   Washington DC 20003
Ph: 202-544-9219 ▪ Fx: 202-544-7462

Forfeiture Endangers American Rights Foundation www.fear.org
20 Sunnyside Suite A-419   Mill Valley CA 94941
Ph: 415-389-8551 ▪ TF: 888-332-7001

Forging Industry Association www.forging.org
25 W Prospect Ave Suite 300   Cleveland OH 44115
Ph: 216-781-6260 ▪ Fx: 216-781-0102

Forging Industry Educational & Research Foundation www.forgings.org
25 W Prospect Ave Suite 300   Cleveland OH 44115
Ph: 216-781-5040 ▪ Fx: 216-781-0102

Formalwear Association, International www.formalwear.org
401 N Michigan Ave   Chicago IL 60611
Ph: 312-644-6610 ▪ Fx: 312-321-4098

Former Intelligence Officers, Association of www.afio.com
6723 Whittier Ave Suite 303A   McLean VA 22101
Ph: 703-790-0320 ▪ Fx: 703-790-0264

Forming Institute Inc, Scaffolding Shoring & www.ssfi.org
1300 Sumner Ave   Cleveland OH 44115
Ph: 216-241-7333 ▪ Fx: 216-241-0105

Forms Management Association, Business www.bfma.org
319 SW Washington St Suite 710   Portland OR 97204
Ph: 503-227-3393 ▪ Fx: 503-274-7667

Forth Interest Group www.forth.org

Fortune Society www.fortunesociety.org
53 W 23rd St 8th Fl   New York NY 10010
Ph: 212-691-7554 ▪ Fx: 212-255-4948

Forty & Eight fortyandeight.org
777 N Meridian St Rm 204   Indianapolis IN 46204
Ph: 317-634-1804 ▪ Fx: 317-632-9365

Forum for Investor Advice www.investoradvice.org
7200 Wisconsin Ave Suite 709   Bethesda MD 20814
Ph: 301-656-7998 ▪ Fx: 301-656-5019

Forum for Scriptural Christianity www.forscrist.org
308 E Main St PO Box 150   Wilmore KY 40390
Ph: 606-858-4661 ▪ Fx: 606-858-4972 ▪ TF: 800-487-7784

Forward Face www.forwardface.org
317 E 34th St Suite 901A   New York NY 10016
Ph: 212-684-5860 ▪ Fx: 212-684-5864

Forward in Faith North America
2905 Lackland Rd   Fort Worth TX 76116
Ph: 817-735-1675 ▪ Fx: 817-735-1351 ▪ TF: 800-225-3661
www.forwardinfaith.com

Forwarders Association of America Inc, Household Goods
2320 Mill Rd Suite 102   Alexandria VA 22314
Ph: 703-684-3780 ▪ Fx: 703-684-3784
www.hhgfaa.org

Forwarders Association of America Inc, National Customs Brokers &
1200 18th St NW Suite 901   Washington DC 20036
Ph: 202-466-0222 ▪ Fx: 202-466-0226
www.ncbfaa.org

Fossey Dian Gorilla Fund International
800 Cherokee Ave SE   Atlanta GA 30315
Ph: 404-624-5881 ▪ Fx: 404-624-5999 ▪ TF: 800-851-0203
www.gorillafund.org

Foster Family-Based Treatment Association
294 Union St   Hackensack NJ 07601
Ph: 800-414-3382 ▪ Fx: 201-862-0331
www.ffta.org

Foster Grandparent Program
PO Box 70675   Washington DC 20024
Ph: 202-678-4215 ▪ Fx: 202-561-2414
www.seniorcorps.org/joining/fgp

Foster Grandparent Program Directors, National Association of
Foster Grandparent Program City Hall 4th Fl   Kansas City MO 64106
Ph: 816-513-3221 ▪ Fx: 816-513-3212
www.nafgpd.org

Foster Parent Association, National
7512 Stanich Ave Suite 6   Gig Harbor WA 98335
Ph: 253-853-4000 ▪ Fx: 253-853-4001 ▪ TF: 800-557-5238
www.nfpainc.org

Foundation for A Course in Miracles
41397 Buecking Dr   Temecula CA 92590
Ph: 909-296-6261 ▪ Fx: 909-296-9117
www.facim.org

Foundation for Academic Standards & Traditions
545 Madison Ave 4th Fl   New York NY 10022
Ph: 212-486-1711

Foundation for Accounting Education
530 5th Ave 5th Fl   New York NY 10036
Ph: 212-719-8300 ▪ Fx: 212-719-3365 ▪ TF: 800-537-3635

Foundation for Advanced Education in the Sciences
1 Cloister Ct Suite 230   Bethesda MD 20814
Ph: 301-496-7976 ▪ Fx: 301-402-0174
www.faes.org

Foundation for Advancement in Cancer Therapy
PO Box 1242 Old Chelsea Stn   New York NY 10113
Ph: 212-741-2790
www.fact-ltd.org

Foundation for the Advancement of Chiropractic Education
PO Box 1052   Levittown PA 19058
Ph: 800-397-9722
www.f-a-c-e.com

Foundation for the Advancement of Hispanic Americans
6004 Roxbury Ave   Springfield VA 22152
Ph: 703-866-1578 ▪ Fx: 703-354-2329

Foundation for the Advancement of Monetary Education
PO Box 625 FDR Stn   New York NY 10150
Ph: 212-818-1206 ▪ Fx: 212-754-6543
www.fame.org

Foundation for the Advancement of Sephardic Studies & Culture   34 W 15th St 3rd Fl   New York NY 10011
Ph: 212-960-5492 ▪ Fx: 212-960-0067
www.sephardicstudies.org

Foundation for Advances in Medicine & Science
PO Box 832   Mahwah NJ 07430
Ph: 201-818-1010 ▪ Fx: 201-818-0086 ▪ TF: 800-443-0263
www.scanning.org

Foundation of the American Board of Trial Advocates
2001 Bryan St Bryan Tower Suite 3000   Dallas TX 75201
Ph: 214-871-7523 ▪ Fx: 214-871-6025 ▪ TF: 800-932-2682
www.abota.org/foundation

Foundation for American Christian Education
PO Box 9588   Chesapeake VA 23321
Ph: 757-488-6601 ▪ Fx: 757-488-5593 ▪ TF: 800-352-3223
www.face.net

Foundation for American Communications
85 S Grand Ave   Pasadena CA 91105
Ph: 626-584-0010 ▪ Fx: 626-584-0627
www.facsnet.org

Foundation for Biomedical Research
818 Connecticut Ave NW Suite 200   Washington DC 20006
Ph: 202-457-0654 ▪ Fx: 202-457-0659
www.fbresearch.org

Foundation Center
79 5th Ave 2nd Fl   New York NY 10003
Ph: 212-620-4230 ▪ Fx: 212-807-3691 ▪ TF: 800-424-9836
fdncenter.org

Foundation for Child Development
145 E 32nd St 14th Fl   New York NY 10016
Ph: 212-213-8337 ▪ Fx: 212-213-5897
www.ffcd.org

Foundation for Chiropractic Education & Research
PO Box 400   Norwalk IA 50211
Ph: 515-981-9888 ▪ Fx: 515-981-9427 ▪ TF: 800-622-6309
www.fcer.org

Foundation of Compassionate American Samaritans
PO Box 428760   Cincinnati OH 45242
Ph: 513-621-5300 ▪ Fx: 513-621-5307
www.focas-us.org

Foundation for Deep Ecology
Fort Cronkhite Bldg 1062   Sausalito CA 94965
Ph: 415-229-9339 ▪ Fx: 415-229-9340
www.deepecology.org

Foundation for Digestive Health & Nutrition
4930 Del Ray Ave   Bethesda MD 20814
Ph: 301-222-4002 ▪ Fx: 301-222-4010
www.fdhn.org

Foundation Drilling, ADSC: International Association of
9696 Skillman St Suite 280 PO Box 550339   Dallas TX 75355
Ph: 214-343-2091 ▪ Fx: 214-343-2384
www.adsc-iafd.com

Foundation for Economic Education
30 S Broadway   Irvington-on-Hudson NY 10533
Ph: 914-591-7230 ▪ Fx: 914-591-8910 ▪ TF: 800-960-4333
www.fee.org

Foundation on Economic Trends
1660 L St NW Suite 216   Washington DC 20036
Ph: 202-466-2823 ▪ Fx: 202-429-9602
www.biotechcentury.org

Foundation for Enterprise Development
2020 K St NW Suite 400   Washington DC 20036
Ph: 202-530-8920 ▪ Fx: 202-530-5702
www.fed.org

Foundation Fighting Blindness
11435 Cron Hill Dr   Owings Mills MD 21117
Ph: 410-568-0150 ▪ Fx: 410-363-2393 ▪ TF: 800-683-5555
www.blindness.org

Foundation Francisco Marroquin
PO Box 2422   Stuart FL 34995
Ph: 772-286-6450 ▪ Fx: 772-280-0670
www.ffmnet.org

Foundation for Global Community
222 High St   Palo Alto CA 94301
Ph: 650-328-7756 ▪ Fx: 650-328-7785 ▪ TF: 800-707-7932
www.globalcommunity.org

Foundation for Independent Higher Education
1920 'N' St NW Suite 210   Washington DC 20036
Ph: 202-367-0333 ▪ Fx: 202-367-0334
www.fihe.org

Foundation for Interior Design Education Research
146 Monroe Ctr NW Suite 1318   Grand Rapids MI 49503
Ph: 616-458-0400 ▪ Fx: 616-458-0460
www.fider.org

Foundation for International Community Assistance
1101 14th St NW 11th Fl   Washington DC 20005
Ph: 202-682-1510 ▪ Fx: 202-682-3510
www.villagebanking.org

Foundation for International Cooperation
1237 S Western Ave   Park Ridge IL 60068
Ph: 847-518-0934 ▪ Fx: 847-518-8384 ▪ TF: 800-890-3543
www.ficcultureswap.org

Foundation for Middle East Peace
1761 'N' St NW   Washington DC 20036
Ph: 202-835-3650 ▪ Fx: 202-835-3651
www.fmep.org

Foundation for Moral Restoration
PO Box 1009   Ashburn VA 20146
Ph: 703-724-4141

Foundation for North American Wild Sheep
PO Box 146   Douglas WY 82633
Ph: 307-358-3693 ▪ Fx: 307-358-3262
www.fnaws.org

Foundation for Pacific Dance
PO Box 621435   Littleton CO 80162
Ph: 303-933-2157
home.att.net/~pacificdance

Foundation for Pavement Preservation
PO Box 23093   Lansing MI 48909
Ph: 517-381-0549
www.fp2.org

Foundation for PEACE
PO Box 98381   Raleigh NC 27624
Ph: 919-850-9696 ▪ Fx: 919-876-3621

Foundation for Physical Therapy
1111 Fairfax St   Alexandria VA 22314
Ph: 800-875-1378 ▪ Fx: 703-683-6743
www.apta.org/Foundation

Foundation for the Preservation of the Mahayana Tradition
PO Box 888   Taos NM 87571
Ph: 505-758-7766 ▪ Fx: 505-758-7765
www.fpmt.org

Foundation for Research on Economics & the Environment
945 Technology Blvd Suite 101F   Bozeman MT 59718
Ph: 406-585-1776 ▪ Fx: 406-585-3000
www.free-eco.org

Foundation for Russian-American Economic Cooperation
2601 4th Ave Suite 310   Seattle WA 98121
Ph: 206-443-1935 ▪ Fx: 206-443-0954
www.fraec.org

Foundation for Shamanic Studies
PO Box 1939   Mill Valley CA 94942
Ph: 415-380-8282
www.shamanism.org

Foundation for Student Communication Inc
48 University Pl   Princeton NJ 08544
Ph: 609-258-1111 ▪ Fx: 609-258-1222
www.businesstoday.org

Foundation for the Study of Independent Social Ideas
310 Riverside Dr Suite 1201   New York NY 10025
Ph: 212-316-3120 ▪ Fx: 212-316-3145

Foundation for Teaching Economics
260 Russell Blvd Suite B   Davis CA 95616
Ph: 530-757-4630 ▪ Fx: 530-757-4636
www.fte.org

Foundation for Water & Energy Education
www.fwee.org

Foundation for Women's Resources
1115 San Jacinto Blvd Suite 250   Austin TX 78701
Ph: 512-459-1167 ▪ Fx: 512-459-1408
www.womensresources.org

Foundations Association, Concrete
113 1st St W PO Box 204   Mount Vernon IA 52314
Ph: 319-895-6940 ▪ Fx: 319-895-8830 ▪ TF: 866-232-9255
www.cfawalls.org

Foundations, Association of Small
4905 Del Ray Ave Suite 308   Bethesda MD 20814
Ph: 301-907-3337 ▪ Fx: 301-907-0980 ▪ TF: 888-212-9922
smallfoundations.org

Foundations, Council on
1828 L St NW Suite 300   Washington DC 20036
Ph: 202-466-6512 ▪ Fx: 202-785-3926
www.cof.org

Foundations & Donors Interested in Catholic Activities Inc
1350 Connecticut Ave NW Suite 303   Washington DC 20036
Ph: 202-223-3550 ▪ Fx: 202-296-9295
www.fadica.org

Founders' Society of America, Steel
780 McArdle Dr Suite G   Crystal Lake IL 60014
Ph: 815-455-8240 ▪ Fx: 815-455-8241
www.sfsa.org

Founders Society, Non-Ferrous
1480 Renaissance Dr Suite 310   Park Ridge IL 60068
Ph: 847-299-0950 ▪ Fx: 847-299-3598
www.nffs.org

Foundry Society, American
505 State St   Des Plaines IL 60016
Ph: 847-824-0181 ▪ Fx: 847-824-7848 ▪ TF: 800-537-4237
www.afsinc.org

Foursquare Gospel, International Church of the
1910 W Sunset Blvd Suite 200   Los Angeles CA 90026
Ph: 213-989-4200 ▪ Fx: 213-989-4590 ▪ TF: 888-635-4234
www.foursquare.org

Fox Michael J Foundation for Parkinson's Research
PO Box 4777 Grand Central Stn   New York NY 10163
Ph: 800-708-7644
www.michaeljfox.org

Fox Terrier Club, American
PO Box 1448   Edison NJ 08818
Ph: 732-777-0032 ▪ Fx: 732-777-0977
www.aftc.org/

Fox Trotting Horse Breed Association Inc, Missouri
PO Box 1027   Ava MO 65608
Ph: 417-683-2468 ▪ Fx: 417-683-6144
www.mfthba.com

Foxhounds Association of America, Masters of
PO Box 363   Millwood VA 22646
Ph: 540-955-5680 ▪ Fx: 540-955-5682
www.mfha.com

Fracture Association, American
c/o Med Pro Orthopaedics 418 N 19th St   Phoenix AZ 85006
Ph: 602-254-9646
www.afa4docs.org

Fragile X Foundation, National
PO Box 190488   San Francisco CA 94119
Ph: 925-938-9300 ▪ Fx: 925-938-9315 ▪ TF: 800-688-8765
www.fragilex.org

Fragrance Association Inc, Cosmetic Toiletry &
1101 17th St NW Suite 300   Washington DC 20036
Ph: 202-331-1770 ▪ Fx: 202-331-1969
www.ctfa.org

Fragrance Commerce, Women in Flavor &
3301 Rt 66 Bldg C Suite 205   Neptune NJ 07753
Ph: 732-922-0500 ▪ Fx: 732-922-0560
www.wffc.org

Fragrance Foundation
145 E 32nd St   New York NY 10016
Ph: 212-725-2755 ▪ Fx: 212-779-9058
www.fragrance.org

Fragrance Materials Association of the US
1620 'I' St NW Suite 925   Washington DC 20006
Ph: 202-293-5800 ▪ Fx: 202-463-8998
www.fmafragrance.org

Frame Builders Association, National
4840 W 15th St Suite 1000   Lawrence KS 66049
Ph: 785-843-2444 ▪ Fx: 785-843-7555 ▪ TF: 800-557-6957
nfba.org

Frame Business Council, Timber
217 Main St   Hamilton MT 59840
Ph: 406-375-0713 ▪ Fx: 406-375-6401 ▪ TF: 888-560-9251
www.timberframe.org

Frame Study, International Institute for
www.iifs.org

Framers Association, Professional Picture
3000 Picture Pl   Jackson MI 49201
Ph: 517-788-8100 ▪ Fx: 517-788-8371
www.ppfa.com

Framers Guild, Timber
PO Box 60   Beckett MA 01223
Ph: 413-623-9926 ▪ Fx: 888-453-0879 ▪ TF: 888-453-0879
www.tfguild.org

Framing Manufacturers Association, Metal
401 N Michigan Ave   Chicago IL 60611
Ph: 312-644-6610 ▪ Fx: 312-321-4098
www.metalframingmfg.org

FRAN-PAC
1350 New York Ave NW Suite 900   Washington DC 20005
Ph: 202-628-8000 ▪ Fx: 202-628-0812 ▪ TF: 800-543-1038
www.franchise.org

Franchise Association, International
1350 New York Ave NW Suite 900   Washington DC 20005
Ph: 202-628-8000 ▪ Fx: 202-628-0812 ▪ TF: 800-543-1038
www.franchise.org

Franchisee Association, American
53 W Jackson Blvd Suite 205   Chicago IL 60604
Ph: 312-431-0545 ▪ Fx: 312-431-1132
www.franchisee.org

Franchisee Association, National
3901 Roswell NE Suite 312   Marietta GA 30062
Ph: 770-971-0808 ▪ Fx: 770-971-3799
www.nfabk.org

Franchisees, Association for Car & Truck Rental Independents &
4248 Park Glen Rd   Minneapolis MN 55416
Ph: 952-928-4645 ▪ Fx: 952-929-1318 ▪ TF: 888-200-2795
www.actif.org

Franchisees & Dealers, American Association of
PO Box 81887   San Diego CA 92138
Ph: 619-209-3775 ▪ Fx: 619-209-3777 ▪ TF: 800-733-9858
www.aafd.org

Franchising, Women in
53 W Jackson Blvd Suite 205   Chicago IL 60604
Ph: 312-431-1467 ▪ Fx: 312-431-1469 ▪ TF: 800-222-4943
www.womeninfranchising.com

Francisco Marroquin, Foundation
PO Box 2422   Stuart FL 34995
Ph: 772-286-6450 ▪ Fx: 772-280-0670
www.ffmnet.org

(Franco-American) Association Canado-Americaine
52 Concord St PO Box 989   Manchester NH 03105
Ph: 603-625-8577 ▪ Fx: 603-625-1214 ▪ TF: 800-222-8577
www.aca-assurance.com

Frank Lloyd Wright Foundation
Taliesin West PO Box 4430   Scottsdale AZ 85261
Ph: 480-860-2700 ▪ Fx: 480-391-4009
www.franklloydwright.org

Frank Lloyd Wright Foundation
Taliesin West PO Box 4430   Scottsdale AZ 85261
Ph: 480-860-2700 ▪ Fx: 480-391-4009
www.franklloydwright.org

Frank Lloyd Wright Preservation Trust
931 Chicago Ave   Oak Park IL 60302
Ph: 708-848-1976 ▪ Fx: 708-848-1248
www.wrightplus.org

Franklin Benjamin Education Foundation
6275 Hazeltine National Dr Suite 114   Orlando FL 32822
Ph: 407-240-8009 ▪ Fx: 407-240-8333

Franklin & Eleanor Roosevelt Institute
4079 Albany Post Rd   Hyde Park NY 12538
Ph: 212-259-1259
www.feri.org

Franklin Inc, Friends of
PO Box 40048   Philadelphia PA 19106
Ph: 215-236-0300 ▪ Fx: 215-440-3423
www.benfranklin2006.org

Franklin Furnace Archive Inc
45 John St Suite 611   New York NY 10038
Ph: 212-766-2606 ▪ Fx: 212-766-2740
www.franklinfurnace.org

(Fraternal) Benevolent & Protective Order of Elks of the USA
2750 N Lakeview Ave   Chicago IL 60614
Ph: 773-755-4700 ▪ Fx: 773-755-4790
www.elks.org

Fraternal Congress of America, National
1240 Iroquois Ave Suite 300   Naperville IL 60563
Ph: 630-355-6633 ▪ Fx: 630-355-0042
www.nfcanet.org

Fraternal Insurance Counselors, National Association of
PO Box 357   Sheboygan WI 53082
Ph: 920-458-1996 ▪ Fx: 920-457-4661

Fraternal Life, CSA
122 W 22nd St   Oak Brook IL 60523
Ph: 630-472-0500 ▪ Fx: 630-472-1100 ▪ TF: 800-543-3272
www.csafraternallife.org

(Fraternal) Moose International Inc
Rt 31   Mooseheart IL 60539
Ph: 630-859-2000 ▪ Fx: 630-859-6618
www.mooseintl.org

Fraternal Order of Eagles, Grand Aerie
1623 Gateway Cir S   Grove City OH 43123
Ph: 614-883-2200 ▪ Fx: 614-883-2201
www.foe.com

(Fraternal) Order of Knights of Pythias
59 Coddington St Suite 202   Quincy MA 02169
Ph: 617-472-8800 ▪ Fx: 617-376-0363
www.pythias.org

Fraternal Order of Police
1410 Donelson Pike Suite A-17   Nashville TN 37217
Ph: 615-399-0900 ▪ Fx: 615-399-0400 ▪ TF: 800-451-2711
www.grandlodgefop.org

(Fraternal) Supreme Council of the Royal Arcanum
61 Batterymarch St PO Box 392   Boston MA 02110
Ph: 617-426-4135 ▪ Fx: 617-426-2322 ▪ TF: 888-272-2686
www.royalarcanum.com

Fraternal Union, American
111 4th Ave S PO Box 59   Ely MN 55731
Ph: 218-365-3143 ▪ Fx: 218-365-3181
www.afu-life.com

Fraternity Advisors, Association of
9640 N Augusta Dr Suite 433   Carmel IN 46032
Ph: 317-876-1632 ▪ Fx: 317-876-3981
www.fraternityadvisors.org

Fraternity of Alpha Kappa Lambda
4735 Statesmen Dr Suite F   Indianapolis IN 46250
Ph: 317-585-4911 ▪ Fx: 317-585-4907
www.akl.org

Fraternity of Alpha Zeta
1000 Executive Pkwy Suite 200 PO Box 410260   Saint Louis
MO 63141
Ph: 314-576-7730 ▪ Fx: 314-576-7989
www.alphazeta.org

Fraternity Association Inc, Professional
345 N Charles St 3rd Fl   Baltimore MD 21201
Ph: 888-771-4732
www.profraternity.org

Fraternity, Center for the Study of the College
Indiana Univ Franklin Hall 002   Bloomington IN 47405
Ph: 812-855-1228
www.indiana.edu/~cscf

Fraternity Editors Association, College
11020 NW Ambassador Dr Suite 30   Kansas City MO 64153
Ph: 816-891-9445 ▪ Fx: 816-891-0838
www.cfea.org

Fraternity Executives Association
8777 Purdue Rd Suite 130   Indianapolis IN 46268
Ph: 317-872-8210 ▪ Fx: 317-872-8213
www.fea-inc.org

Fraud Agencies, International Association of Insurance
PO Box 10018   Kansas City MO 64171
Ph: 816-756-5285 ▪ Fx: 816-756-5287
www.iaifa.org

Fraud Control Association, Communications
3030 N Central Ave Suite 707   Phoenix AZ 85012
Ph: 602-265-2322 ▪ Fx: 602-265-1015
www.cfca.org

Fraud Education Fun, Taxpayers Against
1220 19th St NW Suite 501   Washington DC 20036
Ph: 202-296-4826 ▪ Fx: 202-296-4838 ▪ TF: 800-873-2573
www.taf.org

Fraud Examiners, Association of Certified
716 West Ave   Austin TX 78701
Ph: 512-478-9070 ▪ Fx: 512-478-9297 ▪ TF: 800-245-3321
www.cfenet.com

Fraud Information Center, National
1701 K St NW Suite 1200   Washington DC 20006
Ph: 202-835-3323 ▪ Fx: 202-835-0747 ▪ TF: 800-876-7060
www.fraud.org

Fraud in Telemarketing & Electronic Commerce, Alliance Against   1701 K St NW Suite 1200   Washington DC 20006
Ph: 202-835-3323 ▪ Fx: 202-835-0747
www.fraud.org/aaft/aaftinfo.htm

Fraud Watch, Internet
c/o National Fraud Information Ctr 1701 K St NW Suite 1200   Washington DC 20006
Ph: 202-835-3323 ▪ Fx: 202-835-0747 ▪ TF: 800-876-7060
www.fraud.org/internet/intinfo.htm

Freaks & Oddities Collector's Club, Errors
955 S Grove Blvd Suite 65   Kingsland GA 31548
Ph: 912-729-1573 ▪ Fx: 912-729-1585
www.efoers.org

Frederick A Cook Society
www.cookpolar.org

Free Burma Coalition
1101 Pennsylvania Ave SW Suite 204   Washington DC 20003
Ph: 202-547-5985 ▪ Fx: 202-547-6118
www.freeburmacoalition.org

Free China, Friends of
PO Box 4134   Merrifield VA 22116
Ph: 703-573-8677 ▪ Fx: 703-573-2134

Free Community Papers, Association of
1634 Miner St PO Box 1989   Idaho Springs CO 80452
Ph: 877-203-2327
www.afcp.org

Free Congress Foundation
717 2nd St NE   Washington DC 20002
Ph: 202-546-3000 ▪ Fx: 202-543-5605
www.freecongress.org

Free Enterprise, Students in
1959 E Kerr St   Springfield MO 65803
Ph: 417-831-9505 ▪ Fx: 417-831-6165 ▪ TF: 800-677-7433
www.sife.org

Free Expression, American Booksellers Foundation for
139 Fulton St Suite 302   New York NY 10038
Ph: 212-587-4025 ▪ Fx: 212-587-2436
www.abffe.com

Free Expression, Thomas Jefferson Center for the Protection of
400 Worrell Dr   Charlottesville VA 22911
Ph: 434-295-4784 ▪ Fx: 434-296-3621
www.tjcenter.org

Free Men, National Coalition of
PO Box 129   Manhasset NY 11030
Ph: 516-482-6378 ▪ TF: 888-223-1280
www.ncfm.org

Free Minds Inc
PO Box 3818   Manhattan Beach CA 90266
Ph: 310-545-7831 ▪ Fx: 310-545-0068
www.freeminds.org

Free Papers of America, Independent
107 Hemlock Dr   Rio Grande NJ 08242
Ph: 609-886-0141 ▪ Fx: 609-889-8835 ▪ TF: 800-441-4372
www.ifpa.com

Free Radical Biology & Medicine, Society for
2950 Buskirk Ave Suite 170   Walnut Creek CA 94597
Ph: 925-472-5904 ▪ Fx: 925-472-5901
www.sfrbm.org

Free Software Foundation
59 Temple Pl Suite 330   Boston MA 02111
Ph: 617-542-5942 ▪ Fx: 617-542-2652
www.gnu.org/fsf/fsf.html

Free Sons of Israel Inc
247-25 Jamaica Ave   Bellerose NY 11426
Ph: 718-347-1614
www.freesons.org

Free Territory of Ely-Chatelaine   www.worldfreeinternet.net/ftec
PO Box 7075   Laguna Niguel CA 92607
Ph: 949-581-5348

(Free Will Baptists) Master's Men   www.nafwb.org/mm
PO Box 5002   Antioch TN 37011
Ph: 615-760-6141 ▪ Fx: 615-731-0049 ▪ TF: 877-767-8039

Free Will Baptists, National Association of   www.nafwb.org
5233 Mt View Rd   Antioch TN 37013
Ph: 615-731-6812 ▪ Fx: 615-731-0771 ▪ TF: 877-767-7659

Freedom Alliance   www.freedomalliance.org
22570 Markey Ct   Dulles VA 20166
Ph: 703-444-7940 ▪ Fx: 703-444-9893

Freedom Center, American   www.homestead.com/americanfreedom
2002-A Guadalupe St Suite 284   Austin TX 78705
Ph: 512-453-7989 ▪ Fx: 512-453-7990

Freedom Federation, Individual
PO Box 392   Lathrup Village MI 48076
Ph: 517-738-7496

Freedom Forum   www.freedomforum.org
1101 Wilson Blvd   Arlington VA 22209
Ph: 703-528-0800 ▪ Fx: 703-284-3770

Freedom Foundation, Evergreen   www.effwa.org
PO Box 552   Olympia WA 98507
Ph: 360-956-3482 ▪ Fx: 360-352-1874

Freedom From Fear   www.freedomfromfear.org
308 Seaview Ave   Staten Island NY 10305
Ph: 718-351-1717 ▪ Fx: 718-667-8893 ▪ TF: 888-442-2022

Freedom, Frontiers of   www.ff.org
12011 Lee Jackson Memorial Hwy Suite 310   Fairfax VA 22033
Ph: 703-246-0110 ▪ Fx: 703-246-0129

Freedom House   www.freedomhouse.org
1319 18th St NW   Washington DC 20036
Ph: 202-296-5101 ▪ Fx: 202-296-5078

Freedom from Hunger   www.freefromhunger.org
1644 DaVinci Ct   Davis CA 95616
Ph: 530-758-6200 ▪ Fx: 530-758-6241

Freedom of Information Center   www.missouri.edu/~foiwww/
Univ of Missouri 133 Neff Annex   Columbia MO 65211
Ph: 573-882-4856 ▪ Fx: 573-884-6204

Freedom, Institute for Health   www.forhealthfreedom.org
1825 'I' St NW Suite 400   Washington DC 20006
Ph: 202-429-6610 ▪ Fx: 202-861-1973

Freedom, International Coalition for Religious   www.religiousfreedom.com
7777 Leesburg Pike Suite 404 N-A   Falls Church VA 22043
Ph: 703-790-1500 ▪ Fx: 703-790-5562

Freedom Network, Digital   www.dfn.org
520 Broad St 3rd Fl   Newark NJ 07102
Ph: 973-438-3712 ▪ Fx: 973-438-1735

Freedom Outreach, Personal   www.pfo.org
PO Box 26062   Saint Louis MO 63136
Ph: 314-921-9800

Freedom, Women's International League for Peace & - US Section   www.wilpf.org
1213 Race St   Philadelphia PA 19107
Ph: 215-563-7110 ▪ Fx: 215-563-5527

Freelancers Association, Editorial   www.the-efa.org
71 W 23rd St Suite 1910   New York NY 10010
Ph: 212-929-5400 ▪ Fx: 212-929-5439 ▪ TF: 866-929-5400

Freeman-Sheldon Parent Support Group   www.fspsg.org
509 E Northmont Way   Salt Lake City UT 84103
Ph: 801-364-7060

Freestanding Radiation Oncology Centers, Association of   www.afroc.org
1875 'I' St NW 12th Fl   Washington DC 20006
Ph: 888-334-4542 ▪ Fx: 202-466-5938

Freeze-Dry Floral Association, International   www.ifdfa.com
11407 N Main St Suite A   High Point NC 27263
Ph: 336-861-6737 ▪ TF: 888-554-9706

Freight Carriers Association, Motor   www.mfca.org
499 S Capitol St SW Suite 502A   Washington DC 20003
Ph: 202-554-3060 ▪ Fx: 202-554-3160

Freight Traffic Association, National Motor   www.nmfta.org
2200 Mill Rd   Alexandria VA 22314
Ph: 703-838-1810 ▪ Fx: 703-683-1094

Freight Transportation Association, National   www.nftahq.org
PO Box 1321   Exton PA 19341
Ph: 610-363-7747 ▪ Fx: 610-363-2971

Freight Transportation Consultants Association   www.transportpros.com
PO Box 53087   Albuquerque NM 87153
Ph: 505-299-0615

French-American Aid for Children Inc   www.aidforchildren.org
575 Madison Ave Suite 2409   New York NY 10022
Ph: 212-486-9593 ▪ Fx: 212-486-9594

French, American Association of Teachers of   www.frenchteachers.org
Southern Illinois Univ MC 4510   Carbondale IL 62901
Ph: 618-453-5731 ▪ Fx: 618-453-5733

French American Cultural Services & Educational Aid, Society for   www.facsea.org
972 5th Ave   New York NY 10021
Ph: 212-439-1439 ▪ Fx: 212-439-1455 ▪ TF: 800-937-3624

French-American Foundation   www.frenchamerican.org
28 W 44th St Suite 1420   New York NY 10036
Ph: 212-829-8800 ▪ Fx: 212-829-8810

French Institute Alliance Francaise   www.fiaf.org
22 E 60th St   New York NY 10022
Ph: 212-355-6100 ▪ Fx: 212-935-4119

French Legion of Honor, American Society of the
22 E 60th St Rm 53   New York NY 10022
Ph: 212-751-8537 ▪ Fx: 212-755-7061

Fresh-Cut Produce Association, International   www.fresh-cuts.org
1600 Duke St Suite 440   Alexandria VA 22314
Ph: 703-299-6282 ▪ Fx: 703-299-6288

Fresh Produce Association of the Americas   www.fpaota.org
30 N Huggins St PO Box 848   Nogales AZ 85628
Ph: 520-287-2707 ▪ Fx: 520-287-2948

Fresh Produce & Floral Council   www.fpfc.org
6301 Beach Blvd Suite 150   Buena Park CA 90621
Ph: 714-739-0177 ▪ Fx: 714-739-0226

Freshwater Society   www.freshwater.org
2500 Shadywood Rd   Excelsior MN 55331
Ph: 952-471-9773 ▪ Fx: 952-471-7685

Friars Club   www.friarsclub.com
57 E 55th St   New York NY 10022
Ph: 212-751-7272 ▪ Fx: 212-355-0217

Friction Materials Standards Institute   www.fmsi.org
588 Monroe Tpke   Monroe CT 06468
Ph: 203-452-1877 ▪ Fx: 203-452-7951

Friends of the Abraham Lincoln Museum
Lincoln Memorial Univ Box 2006   Harrogate TN 37752
Ph: 423-869-6235 ▪ Fx: 423-869-6350

Friends of Animals Inc   www.friendsofanimals.org
777 Post Rd Suite 205   Darien CT 06820
Ph: 203-656-1522 ▪ Fx: 203-656-0267 ▪ TF: 800-321-7387

Friends Association for Higher Education   www.earlham.edu/~fahe
1501 Cherry St   Philadelphia PA 19102
Ph: 215-241-7116 ▪ Fx: 215-241-7278

Friends of Astrology   www.friendsofastrology.org
514 N Richmond Ave   Westmont IL 60559
Ph: 630-654-4742

Friends of the Australian Koala Foundation   www.savethekoala.com
c/o Nolan/Lehr Group Inc 224 W 29th St 15th Fl   New York NY
   10001
Ph: 212-967-8200 ▪ Fx: 212-967-7292 ▪ TF: 800-695-6252

Friends of Cast Iron Architecture
235 E 87th St Room 6C   New York NY 10128
Ph: 212-369-6004

Friends of Celiac Disease Research   www.friendsofceliac.com
8832 N Port Washington Rd Suite 204   Milwaukee WI 53217
Ph: 414-540-6679 ▪ Fx: 414-540-0587

Friends of Christ in India   www.foci.org
Greenfield Hill Congregational Church 1045 Old Academy
   Rd   Fairfield CT 06430
Ph: 203-259-5596

Friends Committee on National Legislation   www.fcnl.org
245 2nd St NE   Washington DC 20002
Ph: 202-547-6000 ▪ Fx: 202-547-6019

Friends Council on Education   www.friendscouncil.org
1507 Cherry St   Philadelphia PA 19102
Ph: 215-241-7245 ▪ Fx: 215-241-7299

Friends of the Earth   www.foe.org
1025 Vermont Ave NW Suite 300   Washington DC 20005
Ph: 202-783-7400 ▪ Fx: 202-783-0444 ▪ TF: 877-843-8687

Friends of the Earth Canada   www.foecanada.org
260 Saint Patrick St Suite 206   Ottawa ON K1N5K5
Ph: 613-241-0085 ▪ Fx: 613-241-7998 ▪ TF: 888-385-4444

Friends of the Earth PAC   foepac.org
1025 Vermont Ave NW Suite 300   Washington DC 20005
Ph: 202-783-7400 ▪ Fx: 202-783-0444

Friends of the Everglades   www.everglades.org
7800 Red Rd Suite 215K   South Miami FL 33143
Ph: 305-669-0858 ▪ Fx: 305-669-4108

Friends of Fiber Art International
PO Box 468   Western Springs IL 60558
Ph: 708-246-9466

Friends of Franklin Inc   www.benfranklin2006.org
PO Box 40048   Philadelphia PA 19106
Ph: 215-236-0300 ▪ Fx: 215-440-3423

Friends of Free China
PO Box 4134   Merrifield VA 22116
Ph: 703-573-8677 ▪ Fx: 703-573-2134

Friends General Conference   www.fgcquaker.org
1216 Arch St Suite 2B   Philadelphia PA 19107
Ph: 215-561-1700 ▪ Fx: 215-561-0759 ▪ TF: 800-966-4556

Friends' Health Connection   www.friendshealthconnection.org
PO Box 114   New Brunswick NJ 08903
Ph: 732-418-1811 ▪ Fx: 732-249-9897 ▪ TF: 800-483-7436

Friends of Hibakusha
1765 Sutter St Suite 2   San Francisco CA 94115
Ph: 415-567-7599 ▪ Fx: 415-931-6158

Friends Historical Association   www.haverford.edu/library/fha/fha.html
Haverford College Library 370 Lancaster Ave   Haverford PA
   19041
Ph: 610-896-1161 ▪ Fx: 610-896-1102

Friends of India Society International   www.fisiusa.org
PO Box 73327   Houston TX 77273
Ph: 281-494-1909

Friends of the Israel Defense Forces   www.israelsoldiers.org
298 5th Ave 5th Fl   New York NY 10001
Ph: 212-244-3118 ▪ Fx: 212-244-3119

Friends of Israel Disabled Veterans   fidv-bh.com
419 Park Ave S Suite 905   New York NY 10016
Ph: 212-689-3220 ▪ Fx: 212-689-3236 ▪ TF: 800-648-2125

Friends of Israel Gospel Ministry Inc   foi.org
PO Box 908   Bellmawr NJ 08099
Ph: 856-853-5590 ▪ Fx: 856-853-9565 ▪ TF: 800-257-7843

Friends of the Jose Carreras International Leukemia   www.carrerasfoundation.org
Foundation   1100 Fairview Ave N D5-100 PO Box
   19024   Seattle WA 98109
Ph: 206-667-7108 ▪ Fx: 206-667-6498

Friends of Karen Inc   www.friendsofkaren.org
118 Titicus Rd   Purdys NY 10578
Ph: 914-277-4547 ▪ Fx: 914-277-4967 ▪ TF: 800-637-2774

Friends of the Kennedy Center www.kennedy-center.org/support/volunteers
Kennedy Ctr for the Performing Arts 2700 F St
NW Washington DC 20566
Ph: 202-416-4600 ▪ Fx: 202-416-8076 ▪ TF: 800-444-1324

Friends of Libraries USA www.folusa.com
1420 Walnut St Suite 450 Philadelphia PA 19102
Ph: 215-790-1674 ▪ Fx: 215-545-3821 ▪ TF: 800-936-5872

Friends of Lindenwald
1013 Old Post Rd PO Box 64 Kinderhook NY 12106
Ph: 518-758-9689 ▪ Fx: 518-758-6986

Friends of the London Library Inc, International
515 Madison Ave Suite 3702 New York NY 10022
Ph: 212-644-4858 ▪ Fx: 212-644-4859

Friends of Morocco morocco.home.att.net
PO Box 2579 Washington DC 20013
Ph: 703-660-9292

Friends of the National Arboretum www.fona.org
3501 New York Ave NE Washington DC 20002
Ph: 202-544-8733 ▪ Fx: 202-544-5398

Friends of the National Library of Medicine www.fnlm.org
1555 Connecticut Ave NW Suite 200 Washington DC 20036
Ph: 202-462-0992 ▪ Fx: 202-462-9043

Friends of the National Parks at Gettysburg www.friendsofgettysburg.org
304B York St PO Box 4622 Gettysburg PA 17325
Ph: 717-334-0772 ▪ Fx: 717-334-3118

Friends of the National Zoo www.fonz.org
National Zoological Pk Washington DC 20008
Ph: 202-673-4973 ▪ Fx: 202-673-4890

Friends of Nigeria Inc friendsofnigeria.org
1203 Cambria Ct Iowa City IA 52246
Ph: 319-351-3375

Friends of Old-Time Radio
PO Box 4321 Hamden CT 06514
Ph: 203-248-2887 ▪ Fx: 203-281-1322

Friends of Peace Pilgrim www.peacepilgrim.org/FoPP
7350 Dorado Canyon Rd Somerset CA 95684
Ph: 530-620-0333 ▪ Fx: 530-620-7085

Friends of the River www.friendsoftheriver
915 20th St Sacramento CA 95814
Ph: 916-442-3155 ▪ Fx: 916-442-3396

Friends of Rwanda Association
8391 Red Fox Way Elk Grove CA 95758
Ph: 916-683-3356 ▪ Fx: 916-688-7295

Friends of the Sea Lion Marine Mammal Center www.fslmmc.org
20612 Laguna Canyon Rd Laguna Beach CA 92651
Ph: 949-494-3050 ▪ Fx: 949-494-2802

Friends of the Sea Otter www.seaotters.org
2150 Garden Rd Suite A-3 Monterey CA 93940
Ph: 831-373-2747 ▪ Fx: 831-373-2749

Friends Service Committee, American www.afsc.org
1501 Cherry St Philadelphia PA 19102
Ph: 215-241-7000 ▪ Fx: 215-241-7275

Friends of the Shakers www.maineshakers.com/friends.html
707 Shaker Rd New Gloucester ME 04260
Ph: 207-926-4597

Friends of Terra Cotta Inc www.preserve.org/fotc
771 West End Ave Suite 10E New York NY 10025
Ph: 212-662-0768

Friends of the Third World www.friendsofthethirdworld.org
611 W Wayne St Fort Wayne IN 46802
Ph: 219-422-6821 ▪ Fx: 219-422-1650

Friends United Meeting www.fum.org
101 Quaker Hill Dr Richmond IN 47374
Ph: 765-962-7573 ▪ Fx: 765-966-1293

Friends of the World Food Programme www.friendsofwfp.org
1341 Connecticut Ave NW Washington DC 20036
Ph: 202-530-1694

Friendship Ambassadors Foundation www.faf.org
110 Mamaroneck Ave Suites 7 & 8 White Plains NY 10601
Ph: 914-328-8589 ▪ Fx: 914-328-8578 ▪ TF: 800-526-2908

Friendship Association, US China Peoples www.uscpfa.org
1214 W Schwartz St Carbondale IL 62901
Ph: 618-549-1555 ▪ Fx: 618-549-9766

Friendship Centres, National Association of www.nafc-aboriginal.com
275 MacLaren St Ottawa ON K2P0L9
Ph: 613-563-4844 ▪ Fx: 613-563-1819

Friendship Force International www.friendshipforce.org
34 Peachtree St Suite 900 Atlanta GA 30303
Ph: 404-522-9490 ▪ Fx: 404-688-6148

Friendship, US Council for International
745 Leader Bldg Cleveland OH 44114
Ph: 216-861-5542 ▪ Fx: 216-861-5064

Frontiers of Freedom www.ff.org
12011 Lee Jackson Memorial Hwy Suite 310 Fairfax VA 22033
Ph: 703-246-0110 ▪ Fx: 703-246-0129

Frozen Food Association, International
2000 Corporate Ridge Suite 1000 McLean VA 22102
Ph: 703-821-0770 ▪ Fx: 703-821-1350

Frozen Food Institute, American www.affi.com
2000 Corporate Ridge Suite 1000 McLean VA 22102
Ph: 703-821-0770 ▪ Fx: 703-821-1350

Frozen Pizza Institute, National www.affi.com/nfpi/nfpihomepage.htm
2000 Corporate Ridge Suite 1000 McLean VA 22102
Ph: 703-821-0770 ▪ Fx: 703-821-1350

Frozen & Refrigerated Foods Association, National www.nfraweb.org
4755 Linglestown Rd Suite 300 Harrisburg PA 17112
Ph: 717-657-8601 ▪ Fx: 717-657-9862

Fruit Explorers Inc, North American www.nafex.org
1716 Apples Rd Chapin IL 62628
Ph: 217-245-7589

Fruit Exporters, Northwest
105 S 18th St Suite 227 Yakima WA 98901
Ph: 509-576-8004 ▪ Fx: 509-576-3646

Fruit Tree Association, International Dwarf www.idfta.org
14 S Main St Middleburg PA 17842
Ph: 570-837-1551 ▪ Fx: 570-837-0090

Fruit & Vegetable Association, United Fresh www.uffva.org
1901 Pennsylvania Ave NW Suite 1100 Washington DC 20006
Ph: 202-303-3400 ▪ Fx: 202-303-3433

Fuchsia Society, American www.americanfuchsiasociety.org
243 Pinehaven Way Pacifica CA 94044
Ph: 650-359-1227

(Fuel) National Biodiesel Board www.biodiesel.org
3337-A Emerald Ln PO Box 104898 Jefferson City MO 65110
Ph: 800-841-5849 ▪ Fx: 573-635-7913

Fuels Association, Oxygenated www.ofa.net
1401 New York Ave NW Suite 520 Washington DC 20005
Ph: 202-393-6190 ▪ Fx: 202-393-6199

Fuels Association, Renewable www.ethanolrfa.org
1 Massachusetts Ave NW Suite 820 Washington DC 20001
Ph: 202-289-3835 ▪ Fx: 202-289-7519

Fuels Development Coalition, Clean www.cleanfuelsdc.org
1925 N Lynn St Suite 725 Arlington VA 22209
Ph: 703-276-2332 ▪ Fx: 703-276-8447

Fuels Institute, Pellet www.pelletheat.org
1601 N Kent St Suite 1001 Arlington VA 22209
Ph: 703-522-6778 ▪ Fx: 703-522-0548

Fulbright Association www.fulbright.org
666 11th St NW Suite 525 Washington DC 20001
Ph: 202-347-5543 ▪ Fx: 202-347-6540

Fulfillment Service Association, Mailing & www.mfsanet.org
1421 Prince St Suite 410 Alexandria VA 22314
Ph: 703-836-9200 ▪ Fx: 703-548-8204 ▪ TF: 800-333-6272

Fulfillment Services, Association of www.associationfulfillment.com
3030 Malmo Dr Arlington Heights IL 60005
Ph: 847-364-1222 ▪ Fx: 847-364-1268

Fuller Buckminster Institute www.bfi.org
111 N Main St Sebastopol CA 95472
Ph: 707-824-2242 ▪ Fx: 707-824-2243 ▪ TF: 800-967-6277

Fully Informed Jury Association www.fija.org
PO Box 5570 Helena MT 59604
Ph: 406-442-7800 ▪ Fx: 406-442-9332 ▪ TF: 800-835-5879

Function Point Users Group, International www.ifpug.org
191 Clarksville Rd Princeton Junction NJ 08550
Ph: 609-799-4900 ▪ Fx: 609-799-7032

Functional Orthodontics, American Association for www.aafo.org
106 S Kent St Winchester VA 22601
Ph: 540-662-2200 ▪ Fx: 540-665-8910 ▪ TF: 800-441-3850

Fund for American Studies www.dcinternships.org
1706 New Hampshire Ave NW Washington DC 20009
Ph: 800-741-6964 ▪ Fx: 202-318-0441

Fund for Animals Inc www.fund.org
200 W 57th St Suite 705 New York NY 10019
Ph: 212-246-2096 ▪ Fx: 212-246-2633

Fund for Assuring an Independent Retirement
100 Indiana Ave NW Suite 813 Washington DC 20001
Ph: 202-662-2833 ▪ Fx: 202-756-7400

Fund for Democracy & Development
1101 15th St NW Suite 205 Washington DC 20005
Ph: 202-296-5353 ▪ Fx: 202-296-5433

Fund for Modern Courts www.moderncourts.org
351 W 54th St New York NY 10019
Ph: 212-541-6741 ▪ Fx: 212-541-7301

Fund for an OPEN Society www.opensoc.org
1315 Walnut St Suite 1708 Philadelphia PA 19107
Ph: 215-546-0511 ▪ Fx: 215-546-0514

Fund for Peace www.fundforpeace.org
1701 K St NW 11th Fl Washington DC 20006
Ph: 202-223-7940 ▪ Fx: 202-223-7947

Fund for Podiatric Medical Education www.apma.org/fpme/fundmain.htm
9312 Old Georgetown Rd Bethesda MD 20814
Ph: 301-581-9200 ▪ Fx: 301-530-2752

Fund-Raising Counsel, American Association of www.aafrc.org
10293 N Meridian St Suite 175 Indianapolis IN 46290
Ph: 317-816-1613 ▪ Fx: 317-816-1633 ▪ TF: 800-462-2372

Fund-Raising Distributors & Suppliers, Association of www.afrds.org
5775 Peachtree-Dunwoody Rd Bldg G Suite 500 Atlanta GA
30342
Ph: 404-252-3663 ▪ Fx: 404-252-0774

Fund for UFO Research Inc fufor.com

Funding, Committee for Education www.cef.org
122 C St NW Suite 280 Washington DC 20001
Ph: 202-383-0083 ▪ Fx: 202-383-0097

Funding Network, Women's www.wfnet.org
1375 Sutter St Suite 406 San Francisco CA 94109
Ph: 415-441-0706 ▪ Fx: 415-441-0827

Fundraisers Association, Direct Marketing www.dmfa.org
224 7th St Garden City NY 11530
Ph: 516-746-6700 ▪ Fx: 516-294-8141

Fundraising Counsel, Association of Direct Response www.adrfco.org
1612 K St NW Suite 510 Washington DC 20006
Ph: 202-293-9640 ▪ Fx: 202-887-9699

Fundraising Professionals, Association of www.afpnet.org
1101 King St Suite 700 Alexandria VA 22314
Ph: 703-684-0410 ▪ Fx: 703-684-0540 ▪ TF: 800-666-3863

Fundraising Ticket Manufacturers, National Association of www.naftm.org
1885 University Ave W Suite 246 Saint Paul MN 55104
Ph: 651-644-4710

Funds Transfer Association, Electronic   www.efta.org
950 Herndon Pkwy Suite 390   Herndon VA 20170
Ph: 703-435-9800 ▪ Fx: 703-435-7157

Funeral Association, International Cemetery &   www.icfa.org
1895 Preston White Dr Suite 220   Reston VA 20191
Ph: 703-391-8400 ▪ Fx: 703-391-8416 ▪ TF: 800-645-7700

Funeral Consumers Alliance   www.funerals.org
33 Patchen Rd   South Burlington VT 05403
Ph: 802-865-8300 ▪ Fx: 802-865-2626 ▪ TF: 800-765-0107

Funeral Directors of America, Jewish   www.jfda.org
150 Lynnway Suite 506   Lynn MA 01902
Ph: 781-477-9300 ▪ Fx: 781-477-9393

Funeral Directors Association, National   www.nfda.org
13625 Bishop's Dr   Brookfield WI 53005
Ph: 262-789-1880 ▪ Fx: 262-789-6977 ▪ TF: 800-228-6332

Funeral Directors International, Preferred   www.pfdi.org
PO Box 335   Indian Rocks Beach FL 33785
Ph: 727-524-8100 ▪ Fx: 727-524-8200 ▪ TF: 888-655-1566

Funeral Directors & Morticians Association, National   www.nfdma.com
3951 Snapfinger Pkwy Suite 570   Decatur GA 30035
Ph: 404-286-6680 ▪ Fx: 404-286-6573 ▪ TF: 800-434-0958

(Funeral Homes) International Order of the Golden Rule   www.ogr.org
13523 Lakefront Dr   Bridgeton MO 63045
Ph: 314-209-7142 ▪ Fx: 314-209-1289 ▪ TF: 800-367-8030

Funeral Homes, Selected Independent   www.selectedfuneralhomes.org
500 Lake Cook Rd Suite 205   Deerfield IL 60015
Ph: 847-236-9401 ▪ Fx: 847-236-9968 ▪ TF: 800-323-4219

Funeral Service Consumer Assistance Program
PO Box 486   Elm Grove WI 53122
Ph: 800-662-7666

Funeral Service Education, American Board of   www.abfse.org
38 Florida Ave   Portland ME 04103
Ph: 207-878-6530 ▪ Fx: 207-797-7686

Funeral Service Examining Boards Inc, International Conference of   www.cfseb.org
1885 Shelby Ln   Fayetteville AR 72704
Ph: 479-442-7076 ▪ Fx: 479-442-7090

Funeral Supply Association of America, Casket &   www.cfsaa.org
51 Sherwood Terr Suite D-1   Lake Bluff IL 60044
Ph: 847-295-6630 ▪ Fx: 847-295-6647

Fur Commission USA   www.furcommission.com
826 Orange Ave PMB 506   Coronado CA 92118
Ph: 619-575-0139 ▪ Fx: 619-575-5578

Fur Information Council of America   www.fur.org
8424 A Santa Monica Blvd Suite 860   West Hollywood CA 90069
Ph: 323-848-7940 ▪ Fx: 323-848-2931

Furnishings Association, National Home   www.nhfa.org
PO Box 2396   High Point NC 27261
Ph: 336-886-6100 ▪ Fx: 336-801-6102 ▪ TF: 800-888-9590

Furnishings & Design Association, International   www.ifda.com
191 Clarksville Rd   Princeton Junction NJ 08550
Ph: 609-799-3423 ▪ Fx: 609-799-7023

Furnishings Marketing Authority, International Home   www.furnituremarket.org
PO Box 5243   High Point NC 27262
Ph: 336-869-1000 ▪ Fx: 336-869-6999

Furnishings Suppliers, Association of Woodworking &   www.awfssupplierfinder.org
5800 S Eastern Ave Suite 330   Los Angeles CA 90040
Ph: 323-838-9440 ▪ Fx: 323-838-9443 ▪ TF: 800-946-2837

Furniture Action Council, Upholstered   www.ufac.org
PO Box 2436   High Point NC 27261
Ph: 336-885-5065 ▪ Fx: 336-885-5072

Furniture Association, International Wholesale   www.iwfa.net
164 S Main St Suite 310 PO Box 2482   High Point NC 27261
Ph: 336-884-1566 ▪ Fx: 336-884-1350

Furniture Association, Scientific Equipment &   www.sefalabs.com
1205 Franklin Ave   Garden City NY 11530
Ph: 516-294-5424 ▪ Fx: 516-294-2758

Furniture Association, Unfinished   www.unfinishedfurniture.org
17000 Commerce Pkwy Suite C   Mount Laurel NJ 08054
Ph: 856-439-0500 ▪ Fx: 856-439-0525 ▪ TF: 800-487-8321

Furniture Dealers Association, Independent Office Products &   www.iopfda.org
301 N Fairfax St   Alexandria VA 22314
Ph: 703-549-9040 ▪ Fx: 703-683-7552

Furniture Designers, American Society of   www.asfd.com
144 Woodland Dr   New London NC 28127
Ph: 910-576-1273 ▪ Fx: 910-573-1573

Furniture Distribution Association, Office   www.theofda.org
6 Main St PO Box 326   Petersham MA 01366
Ph: 978-724-3267 ▪ Fx: 978-724-3507

Furniture Manufacturers Association, American   www.afma4u.org
PO Box HP-7   High Point NC 27261
Ph: 336-884-5000 ▪ Fx: 336-884-5303

Furniture Manufacturers Association, Business & Institutional   www.bifma.com
2680 Horizon Dr SE Suite A-1   Grand Rapids MI 49546
Ph: 616-285-3963 ▪ Fx: 616-285-3765

Furniture Manufacturers Association, Summer & Casual
PO Box HP-7   High Point NC 27261
Ph: 336-884-5000 ▪ Fx: 336-884-5303

Furniture Rental Association, International   www.ifra.org
9202 N Meridian St Suite 200   Indianapolis IN 46260
Ph: 317-571-5613 ▪ Fx: 317-571-5603

Furniture Retailers Association, National Independent Nursery   www.babyexpressstores.com
12302 Hart Ranch   San Antonio TX 78249
Ph: 210-699-1133 ▪ Fx: 210-699-3232

Furniture Retailers, Casual   www.casualfurniture.org
710 E Ogden Ave Suite 600   Naperville IL 60563
Ph: 630-579-3262 ▪ Fx: 630-369-2488 ▪ TF: 800-956-2237

Furniture & Transportation Logistics Council, International   www.iftlc.org
PO Box 889   Gardner MA 01440
Ph: 978-632-1913 ▪ Fx: 978-630-2917

Furniture Workers, International Union of Electronic Electrical Salaried Machine &   www.iue-cwa.org
1275 K St NW Suite 600   Washington DC 20005
Ph: 202-513-6300 ▪ Fx: 202-513-6357

Fusion Power Associates   www.fusionpower.org
2 Professional Dr Suite 249   Gaithersburg MD 20879
Ph: 301-258-0545 ▪ Fx: 301-975-9869

Futon Association International   www.futon.org
10705-7 Rocket Blvd   Orlando FL 32824
Ph: 407-447-1706 ▪ TF: 800-327-3262

Future Business Leaders of America - Phi Beta Lambda Inc   www.fbla-pbl.org
1912 Association Dr   Reston VA 20191
Ph: 703-860-3334 ▪ Fx: 703-758-0749 ▪ TF: 800-325-2946

Future, Campaign for America's   www.ourfuture.org
1025 Connecticut Ave NW Suite 205   Washington DC 20036
Ph: 202-955-5665 ▪ Fx: 202-955-5606

Future Fisherman Foundation   www.futurefisherman.org
225 Reinekers Ln Suite 420   Alexandria VA 22314
Ph: 703-519-9691 ▪ Fx: 703-519-1872

Future, Institute for the   www.iftf.org
2744 Sand Hill Rd   Menlo Park CA 94025
Ph: 650-854-6322 ▪ Fx: 650-854-7850

Future Problem Solving Program   www.fpsp.org
2028 Regency Rd   Lexington KY 40503
Ph: 859-276-4336 ▪ Fx: 859-276-4306 ▪ TF: 800-256-1499

Future Society, World   www.wfs.org
7910 Woodmont Ave Suite 450   Bethesda MD 20814
Ph: 301-656-8274 ▪ Fx: 301-951-0394 ▪ TF: 800-989-8274

Futures Association, National   www.nfa.futures.org
200 W Madison St   Chicago IL 60606
Ph: 312-781-1300 ▪ Fx: 312-781-1467 ▪ TF: 800-366-6321

Futures for Children   www.futuresforchildren.org
9600 Tennyson St NE   Albuquerque NM 87122
Ph: 505-821-2828 ▪ Fx: 505-821-4141 ▪ TF: 800-545-6843

Futures Foundation, Global   www.globalff.org
415 Jackson St 2nd Fl   San Francisco CA 94111
Ph: 415-364-3803 ▪ Fx: 415-693-9163

Futures Industry Association   www.fiafii.org
2001 Pennsylvania Ave NW Suite 600   Washington DC 20006
Ph: 202-466-5460 ▪ Fx: 202-296-3184

Fuzzy Information Processing Society, North American   morden.csee.usf.edu/Nafipsf

G

G-Jo Institute   www.g-jo.com
PO Box 1460   Columbus NC 28722
Ph: 828-863-4660

Gabriel Marcel Society   www.lemoyne.edu/gms
Loyola Univ Philosophy Dept 6363 St Charles Ave   New Orleans LA 70118
Ph: 504-865-3940 ▪ Fx: 504-865-3347

Gaia Institute   www.gaia-inst.org
440 City Island Ave   Bronx NY 10464
Ph: 718-885-1906

GALA Choruses Inc   www.galachoruses.org
PO Box 65084   Washington DC 20035
Ph: 202-467-5830 ▪ Fx: 202-467-5831

Galiceno Horse Breeders Association
PO Box 219   Godley TX 76044
Ph: 817-389-3547

Galleries, Association of College & University Museums &   www.acumg.org
Ursinus College 601 E Main St   Collegeville PA 19426
Ph: 610-409-3500 ▪ Fx: 610-409-3664

Galleries Association, Visual Artists &
350 5th Ave Suite 2820   New York NY 10118
Ph: 212-736-6666 ▪ Fx: 212-736-6767

Galloway Breeders' Association, American   www.galloway-world.org
310 W Spruce St   Missoula MT 59802
Ph: 406-728-5719 ▪ Fx: 406-721-6300

Gallup Inter-Tribal Indian Ceremonial Association   www.gallupnm.org/ceremonial
226 W Coal Ave   Gallup NM 87301
Ph: 505-863-3896 ▪ Fx: 505-722-5158 ▪ TF: 888-685-2564

Galvanizers Association, American   www.galvanizeit.org
6881 S Holly Cir Suite 108   Centennial CO 80112
Ph: 720-554-0900 ▪ Fx: 720-554-0909 ▪ TF: 800-468-7732

Gam-Anon International Service Office Inc   gam-anon.org
PO Box 157   Whitestone NY 11357
Ph: 718-352-1671 ▪ Fx: 718-746-2571

GAMA International   www.gamaweb.com
2901 Telestar Ct   Falls Church VA 22042
Ph: 703-770-8184 ▪ Fx: 703-770-8182 ▪ TF: 800-345-2687

Gamblers Anonymous   www.gamblersanonymous.org
PO Box 17173   Los Angeles CA 90017
Ph: 213-386-8789 ▪ Fx: 213-386-0030

(Gambling) Gam-Anon International Service Office Inc   gam-anon.org
PO Box 157   Whitestone NY 11357
Ph: 718-352-1671 ▪ Fx: 718-746-2571

Gambling Inc, National Council on Problem   www.ncpgambling.org
208 G St NE 1st Fl   Washington DC 20002
Ph: 202-547-9204 ▪ Fx: 202-547-9206 ▪ TF: 800-522-4700

Gambling of New Jersey Inc, Council on Compulsive   www.800gambler.org
3635 Quakerbridge Rd Suite 7   Hamilton NJ 08619
Ph: 609-588-5515 ▪ Fx: 609-588-5665 ▪ TF: 800-426-2537

Game Developers Association, International   www.igda.org
600 Harrison St   San Francisco CA 94107
Ph: 415-947-6235 ▪ Fx: 415-947-6090

Game Fish Association, International www.igfa.org
IGFA Fishing Hall of Fame & Museum 300 Gulf Stream
 Way Dania Beach FL 33004
Ph: 954-927-2628 ▪ Fx: 954-924-4299

Game Manufacturers Association www.gama.org
80 Garden Center Suite 116 Broomfield CO 80020
Ph: 303-635-2223 ▪ Fx: 303-469-2878

Gamebird Association, North American
1214 Brooks Ave Raleigh NC 27607
Ph: 919-782-6758

Games Association, National Senior www.nsga.com/
PO Box 82059 Baton Rouge LA 70884
Ph: 225-766-6800 ▪ Fx: 225-766-9115

Games, Federation of Gay www.gaygames.org
584 Castro St Suite 343 San Francisco CA 94114
Ph: 415-695-0222 ▪ Fx: 800-877-1373

Games & Festivals, Association of Scottish www.asgf.org
3000 Walnut Ave Altoona PA 16601
Ph: 412-851-9900 ▪ Fx: 412-854-5963

Games, National Congress of State www.stategames.org
290 Roberts St East Hartford CT 06108
Ph: 860-528-4588 ▪ Fx: 860-291-8032

Gaming Association, American www.americangaming.org
555 13th St NW Suite 1010 E Washington DC 20004
Ph: 202-637-6500 ▪ Fx: 202-637-6507

Gaming Association, National Indian www.indiangaming.org
224 2nd St SE Washington DC 20003
Ph: 202-546-7711 ▪ Fx: 202-546-1755 ▪ TF: 800-286-6442

Gaming Association, North American Simulation & www.nasaga.org
PO Box 78636 Indianapolis IN 46278
Ph: 317-387-1424 ▪ Fx: 317-387-1921 ▪ TF: 888-432-4263

Gaming Regulators Association, North American www.nagra.org
26 E Exchange St Suite 500 Saint Paul MN 55101
Ph: 651-203-7244 ▪ Fx: 651-290-2266

Gaming Society, International Fantasy www.ifgs.org
PO Box 3577 Boulder CO 80307
Ph: 303-443-1012

Gaming Society, Strategy www.gametableonline.com/StrategyGamingSociety.htm
87-6 Park Ave Worcester MA 01605
Ph: 508-831-5334

Gaming Standards Association www.gamingstandards.com
39355 California St Suite 307 Fremont CA 94538
Ph: 510-744-4007

Gaming States, National Council of Legislators from
139 Lancaster St Albany NY 12210
Ph: 518-449-4699 ▪ Fx: 518-432-5651

Gaming Tokens Collectors Club Inc, Casino Chips & www.ccgtcc.com
PO Box 368 Wellington OH 44090
Ph: 440-647-4335 ▪ TF: 877-422-4822

Gamma Beta Phi Society www.gammabetaphi.org
105 Michell Rd Suite 204 Oak Ridge TN 37830
Ph: 865-483-6212 ▪ Fx: 865-483-9801 ▪ TF: 800-628-9920

Gamma Iota Sigma www.gammaiotasigma.org
2586 Oakstone Dr Columbus OH 43231
Ph: 614-891-4242 ▪ Fx: 614-891-7698

Gamma Phi Beta International Sorority www.gammaphibeta.org
12737 E Euclid Dr Englewood CO 80111
Ph: 303-799-1874 ▪ Fx: 303-799-1876

Gamma Sigma Delta www.gammasigmadelta.org

Gamma Theta Upsilon www.gtuhonors.org
Univ of Wisconsin La Crosse Dept of Geography La Crosse WI
 54601
Ph: 608-785-8333 ▪ Fx: 608-785-8332

Gar Wood Society www.garwood.com
PO Box 6003 Syracuse NY 13217
Ph: 315-446-5654 ▪ Fx: 315-686-4104

Garden Club of America www.gcamerica.org
14 E 60th St 3rd Fl New York NY 10022
Ph: 212-753-8287

Garden Clubs Inc, National www.gardenclub.org
4401 Magnolia Ave Suite 1600 Saint Louis MO 63110
Ph: 314-776-7574 ▪ Fx: 314-776-5108 ▪ TF: 800-550-6007

Garden Dealers Association, Lawn & www.lgda.org
2411 E Skelly Dr Suite 105 Tulsa OK 74105
Ph: 800-752-5296 ▪ Fx: 918-749-1718

Garden Marketing & Distribution Association, Lawn & www.lgmda.org
1900 Arch St Philadelphia PA 19103
Ph: 215-564-3484 ▪ Fx: 215-564-2175

Garden Writers Association www.gwaa.org
10210 Leatherleaf Ct Manassas VA 20111
Ph: 703-257-1032 ▪ Fx: 703-257-0213

Gardeners of America tgoa-mgca.org
PO Box 241 Johnston IA 50131
Ph: 515-278-0295 ▪ Fx: 515-278-6245

Gardening Association Inc, Biodynamic Farming & www.biodynamics.com
25844 Butler Rd Junction City OR 97448
Ph: 541-998-0105 ▪ Fx: 541-998-0106 ▪ TF: 888-561-7797

Gardening Association, Mailorder www.mailordergardening.com
5836 Rockburn Woods Way Elkridge MD 21075
Ph: 410-540-9830 ▪ Fx: 410-540-9827

Gardening Association, National www.garden.org
1100 Dorset St South Burlington VT 05403
Ph: 802-863-5251 ▪ Fx: 802-864-6889 ▪ TF: 800-538-7476

Gardening Club, National Home www.gardeningclub.org
12301 Whitewater Dr Minnetonka MN 55343
Ph: 952-988-7404 ▪ TF: 800-324-8454

Gardening Society, International Water Lily & Water www.iwgs.org
6828 26th St W Bradenton FL 34207
Ph: 941-756-0880

Gardens & Arboreta, American Association of Botanical www.aabga.org
100 W 10th St Suite 614 Wilmington DE 19801
Ph: 302-655-7100 ▪ Fx: 302-655-8100

Garment Council, UFCW Textile &
4207 Lebanon Pike Suite 200 Hermitage TN 37076
Ph: 615-889-9221 ▪ Fx: 615-885-3102

Garment Industry Development Corp www.gidc.org
275 7th Ave 9th Fl New York NY 10001
Ph: 212-366-6160 ▪ Fx: 212-366-6162

Gas Appliance Manufacturers Association www.gamanet.org
2107 Wilson Blvd Suite 600 Arlington VA 22201
Ph: 703-525-7060 ▪ Fx: 703-525-6790

Gas Association of America, Interstate Natural www.ingaa.org
10 G St NE Suite 700 Washington DC 20002
Ph: 202-216-5900 ▪ Fx: 202-216-0870 ▪ TF: 888-854-6422

Gas Association, American www.aga.org
400 N Capitol St NW Washington DC 20001
Ph: 202-824-7000 ▪ Fx: 202-824-7115

Gas Association, American Public www.apga.org
11094D Lee Hwy Suite 102 Fairfax VA 22030
Ph: 703-352-3890 ▪ Fx: 703-352-1271 ▪ TF: 800-927-4204

Gas Association, Compressed www.cganet.com
4221 Walney Rd 5th Fl Chantilly VA 20151
Ph: 703-788-2700 ▪ Fx: 703-961-1831

Gas Association, National Propane www.npga.org
1150 17th St NW Suite 310 Washington DC 20036
Ph: 202-466-7200 ▪ Fx: 202-466-7205

Gas Association, US Oil &
901 F St NW Suite 601 Washington DC 20004
Ph: 202-638-4400 ▪ Fx: 202-638-5967

Gas Chlorinators, National Association of
21939 Camille Dr Nuevo CA 92567
Ph: 949-364-1990 ▪ Fx: 949-364-2009

Gas Compact Commission, Interstate Oil & www.iogcc.oklaosf.state.ok.us
PO Box 53127 Oklahoma City OK 73152
Ph: 405-525-3556 ▪ Fx: 405-525-3592 ▪ TF: 800-822-4015

Gas Engineers, American Society of www.asge-national.org
2805 Barranca Pkwy Irvine CA 92606
Ph: 949-733-4304 ▪ Fx: 949-733-4320

Gas Institute Inc, Compressed Air & www.cagi.org
1300 Sumner Ave Cleveland OH 44115
Ph: 216-241-7333 ▪ Fx: 216-241-0105

Gas Machinery Research Council www.gmrc.org
3030 LBJ Fwy Suite 1300 LB-60 Dallas TX 75234
Ph: 972-620-4024 ▪ Fx: 972-620-1613

Gas Processors Association www.gasprocessors.com
6526 E 60th St Tulsa OK 74145
Ph: 918-493-3872 ▪ Fx: 918-493-3875

Gas Processors Suppliers Association gpsa.gasprocessors.com
6526 E 60th St Tulsa OK 74145
Ph: 918-493-3872 ▪ Fx: 918-493-3875

Gas Supply Association, Natural www.ngsa.org
805 15th St NW Suite 510 Washington DC 20005
Ph: 202-326-9300 ▪ Fx: 202-326-9330

Gas Turbine Institute, International www.asme.org/igti
5775B Glenridge Dr Suite 370 Atlanta GA 30328
Ph: 404-847-0072 ▪ Fx: 404-847-0151

Gas Vehicle Coalition, Natural www.ngvc.org
400 N Capitol St NW Washington DC 20001
Ph: 202-824-7360 ▪ Fx: 202-824-7367

Gases & Welding Distributors Association www.gawda.org
1900 Arch St Philadelphia PA 19103
Ph: 215-564-3484 ▪ Fx: 215-963-9784

Gasification Technologies Council www.gasification.org
1110 N Glebe Rd Suite 610 Arlington VA 22201
Ph: 703-276-0110 ▪ Fx: 703-276-0141

Gasket Fabricators Association www.gasketfab.com
994 Old Eagle School Rd Suite 1019 Wayne PA 19087
Ph: 610-971-4850 ▪ Fx: 610-971-4859

Gasoline & Automotive Service Dealers Association
9520 Seaview Ave Brooklyn NY 11236
Ph: 718-241-1111 ▪ Fx: 718-763-6589

Gasoline Marketers of America, Society of Independent www.sigma.org
11911 Freedom Dr Suite 590 Reston VA 20190
Ph: 703-709-7000 ▪ Fx: 703-709-7007

GASPAC
400 N Capitol St NW Washington DC 20001
Ph: 202-824-7000 ▪ Fx: 202-824-7115

Gastroenterological Association, American www.gastro.org
4930 Del Ray Ave Bethesda MD 20814
Ph: 301-654-2055 ▪ Fx: 301-654-5920

Gastroenterology, American College of www.acg.gi.org
4900B S 31st St Arlington VA 22206
Ph: 703-820-7400 ▪ Fx: 703-931-4520

Gastroenterology, Bockus International Society of
300 Community Dr Manhasset NY 11030
Ph: 516-562-4281 ▪ Fx: 516-562-2683

Gastroenterology Hepatology & Nutrition, North American Society for Pediatric www.naspghan.org
PO Box 6 Flourtown PA 19031
Ph: 215-233-0808 ▪ Fx: 215-233-3918

Gastroenterology Nurses & Associates Inc, Society of www.sgna.org
401 N Michigan Ave Chicago IL 60611
Ph: 312-321-5165 ▪ Fx: 312-527-6658 ▪ TF: 800-245-7462

Gastrointestinal Disorders, International Foundation for Functional www.iffgd.org
PO Box 170864 Milwaukee WI 53217
Ph: 414-964-1799 ▪ Fx: 414-964-7176 ▪ TF: 888-964-2001

Gastrointestinal Endoscopic Surgeons, Society of American www.sages.org
11300 W Olympic Blvd Suite 600 Los Angeles CA 90064
Ph: 310-437-0544 ▪ Fx: 310-437-0585

Gastrointestinal Endoscopy, American Society for — www.asge.org
1520 Kensington Rd Suite 202   Oak Brook IL 60523
Ph: 630-573-0600 ▪ Fx: 630-573-0691

Gastrointestinal Radiologists, Society of — www.sgr.org
4550 Post Oak Pl Suite 342   Houston TX 77027
Ph: 713-965-0566 ▪ Fx: 713-960-0488

Gates Bill & Melinda Foundation — www.gatesfoundation.org
PO Box 23350   Seattle WA 98102
Ph: 206-709-3100 ▪ Fx: 206-709-3180 ▪ TF: 888-452-6352

Gates Family Foundation — www.gatesfamilyfoundation.org
3575 Cherry Creek North Dr Suite 100   Denver CO 80209
Ph: 303-722-1881 ▪ Fx: 303-316-3038

Gateways to Better Education — www.gtbe.org
PO Box 514   Lake Forest CA 92609
Ph: 949-586-5437 ▪ Fx: 949-457-6361

Gathering of Nations Ltd — www.gatheringofnations.com
3301 Coors Blvd NW Suite R300   Albuquerque NM 87120
Ph: 505-836-2810 ▪ Fx: 505-839-0475

Gaucher Foundation, National — www.gaucherdisease.org
5410 Edson Ln Suite 260   Rockville MD 20852
Ph: 301-816-1515 ▪ Fx: 301-816-1516 ▪ TF: 800-428-2437

Gay Addiction Professionals, National Association of Lesbian/ — www.nalgap.org
901 N Washington St Suite 600   Alexandria VA 22314
Ph: 703-465-0539 ▪ Fx: 703-741-6989

Gay Art Foundation, Leslie-Lohman — www.leslielohman.org
127-B Prince St   New York NY 10012
Ph: 212-673-7007 ▪ Fx: 212-260-0363

Gay Bands of America, Lesbian & — www.gaybands.org
PO Box 14874   San Francisco CA 94114
Ph: 415-554-0402 ▪ Fx: 415-621-4637

Gay Environment, Senior Action in a — www.sageusa.org
305 7th Ave 16th Fl   New York NY 10001
Ph: 212-741-2247 ▪ Fx: 212-366-1947

Gay Games, Federation of — www.gaygames.org
584 Castro St Suite 343   San Francisco CA 94114
Ph: 415-695-0222 ▪ Fx: 800-877-1373

Gay History, Committee on Lesbian & — www.usc.edu/clgh
College of William & Mary PO Box 8795   Williamsburg VA 23187
Ph: 757-221-2453 ▪ Fx: 757-221-3737

Gay Journalists Association, National Lesbian & — www.nlgja.org
1420 K St NW Suite 910   Washington DC 20005
Ph: 202-588-9888 ▪ Fx: 202-588-1818

Gay Law Association, National Lesbian & — www.nlgla.org
200 E Lexington St Suite 1511   Baltimore MD 21202
Ph: 508-892-8290 ▪ Fx: 410-244-0775

Gay & Lesbian Alliance Against Defamation — www.glaad.org
248 W 35th St 8th Fl   New York NY 10001
Ph: 212-629-3322 ▪ Fx: 212-629-3225

Gay & Lesbian Association of Choruses Inc — www.galachoruses.org
PO Box 65084   Washington DC 20035
Ph: 202-467-5830 ▪ Fx: 202-467-5831

Gay Lesbian & Bisexual Issues in Counseling, Association for — www.aglbic.org
c/o American Counseling Assn 5999 Stevenson Ave   Alexandria VA 22304
Ph: 703-823-9800 ▪ Fx: 703-823-0252 ▪ TF: 800-347-6647

Gay & Lesbian Human Rights Commission, International — www.iglhrc.org
1375 Sutter St Suite 222   San Francisco CA 94109
Ph: 415-561-0633 ▪ Fx: 415-561-0619

Gay & Lesbian National Hotline — www.glnh.org
2261 Market St PMB 296   San Francisco CA 94114
Ph: 415-355-0999 ▪ Fx: 415-552-5498 ▪ TF: 888-415-3022

Gay & Lesbian Psychiatrists, Association of — www.aglp.org
4514 Chester Ave   Philadelphia PA 19143
Ph: 215-222-2800 ▪ Fx: 215-222-3881

Gay & Lesbian Scientists & Technical Professionals, National Organization of — www.noglstp.org/
PO Box 91803   Pasadena CA 91109
Ph: 626-791-7689

Gay Lesbian & Straight Education Network — www.glsen.org/
121 W 27th St Suite 804   New York NY 10001
Ph: 212-727-0135 ▪ Fx: 212-727-0254

Gay & Lesbian Task Force, National — www.ngltf.org
1325 Massachusetts Ave NW Suite 600   Washington DC 20005
Ph: 202-393-5177 ▪ Fx: 202-393-2241

Gay & Lesbian Travel Association, International — www.iglta.org
4331 N Federal Hwy Suite 304   Fort Lauderdale FL 33308
Ph: 954-776-2626 ▪ Fx: 954-776-3303 ▪ TF: 800-448-8550

Gay & Lesbian Victory Fund — www.victoryfund.org
1705 DeSales St NW Suite 500   Washington DC 20036
Ph: 202-842-8679 ▪ Fx: 202-289-3863

Gay Men's Health Crisis — www.gmhc.org
119 W 24th St   New York NY 10011
Ph: 212-367-1000 ▪ Fx: 212-367-1220 ▪ TF: 800-243-7692

Gay Officers' Action League — www.goalny.org
PO Box 2038 Canal St Stn   New York NY 10013
Ph: 212-691-4625

Gay Rodeo Association, International — www.igra.com
900 E Colfax Ave   Denver CO 80218
Ph: 303-832-4472 ▪ Fx: 303-860-9105

Gay Square Dance Clubs, International Association of — www.iagsdc.org
PO Box 87507   San Diego CA 92138
Ph: 800-835-6462

Gay Studies, Center for Lesbian & — www.clags.org
City Univ of New York 365 5th Ave Rm 7115   New York NY 10016
Ph: 212-817-1955 ▪ Fx: 212-817-2985

Gays Everywhere, Children of Lesbians & — www.colage.org
3543 18th St Suite 1   San Francisco CA 94110
Ph: 415-861-5437 ▪ Fx: 415-255-8345

Gays & Lesbians, Pro-Life Alliance of — www.plagal.org
PO Box 33292   Washington DC 20033
Ph: 202-223-6697 ▪ Fx: 202-265-9737

Gays, Parents Families & Friends of Lesbians & — www.pflag.org
1726 M St NW Suite 400   Washington DC 20036
Ph: 202-467-8180 ▪ Fx: 202-467-8194

Gays, Parents & Friends of Ex- — www.pfox.org
PO Box 561   Fort Belvoir VA 22060
Ph: 703-739-8220

Gear Manufacturers Association, American — www.agma.org
500 Montgomery St Suite 350   Alexandria VA 22314
Ph: 703-684-0211 ▪ Fx: 703-684-0242

Geekcorps — www.geekcorps.org
1121 Mass MoCA Way   North Adams MA 01247
Ph: 413-664-0030 ▪ Fx: 413-664-0032

Gelbvieh Association, American — www.gelbvieh.org
10900 Dover St   Westminster CO 80021
Ph: 303-465-2333 ▪ Fx: 303-465-2339

Gem & Lapidary Dealers Association — www.glda.com
PO Box 2391   Tucson AZ 85702
Ph: 520-792-9431 ▪ Fx: 520-882-2836

Gem Society, American — www.ags.org
8881 W Sahara Ave   Las Vegas NV 89117
Ph: 702-255-6500 ▪ Fx: 702-255-7420

Gem Trade Association, American — www.agta.org
PO Box 420643   Dallas TX 75342
Ph: 214-742-4367 ▪ Fx: 214-742-7334 ▪ TF: 800-972-1162

Gemological Institute of America — www.gia.org
5345 Armada Dr   Carlsbad CA 92008
Ph: 760-603-4000 ▪ Fx: 760-603-4003 ▪ TF: 800-421-7250

Gen Art — www.genart.org
133 W 25th St 6th Fl E   New York NY 10001
Ph: 212-255-7300 ▪ Fx: 212-255-7400

Gender Education & Advocacy — www.gender.org
PO Box 33724   Decatur GA 30033
Ph: 404-299-1775

Gender Education, International Foundation for — www.ifge.org
PO Box 540229   Waltham MA 02454
Ph: 781-899-2212 ▪ Fx: 781-899-5703

Gender Equity Leadership in Education, Association for — www.agele.org
317 S Division St PMB 54   Ann Arbor MI 48104
Ph: 734-449-5066

Gene Resources, National Council on —
1738 Thousand Oaks Blvd   Berkeley CA 94707
Ph: 510-524-8973 ▪ Fx: 510-526-3092

Gene Stratton-Porter Memorial Society —
PO Box 639   Rome City IN 46784
Ph: 260-854-3790 ▪ Fx: 260-854-9102

Gene Therapy, American Society of — www.asgt.org
611 E Wells St   Milwaukee WI 53202
Ph: 414-278-1341 ▪ Fx: 414-276-3349

Genealogical Association, Ark-La-Tex — www.rootsweb.com/~laaltga
PO Box 4463   Shreveport LA 71134
Ph: 318-746-4598

Genealogical & Biographical Society, New York — www.nygbs.org
122 E 58th St   New York NY 10022
Ph: 212-755-8532 ▪ Fx: 212-754-4218

Genealogical Society, Afro-American Historical & — www.aahgs.org
PO Box 73067   Washington DC 20056
Ph: 202-234-5350 ▪ Fx: 202-829-9280

Genealogical Society, American-Canadian — www.acgs.org
PO Box 6478   Manchester NH 03108
Ph: 603-622-1554 ▪ Fx: 603-624-8843

Genealogical Society of Flemish Americans — www.rootsweb.com/~gsfa
18740 13 Mile Rd   Roseville MI 48066
Ph: 586-776-9579

Genealogical Society, Immigrant — www.feefhs.org/igs/frg-igs.html
1310B Magnolia Blvd PO Box 7369   Burbank CA 91510
Ph: 818-848-3122 ▪ Fx: 818-716-6300

Genealogical Society International, Czechoslovak — www.cgsi.org
PO Box 16225   Saint Paul MN 55116
Ph: 952-922-1280

Genealogical Society, Jewish — www.jgsny.org
15 W 16th St   New York NY 10011
Ph: 212-294-8326

Genealogical Society, National — www.ngsgenealogy.org
4527 17th St N   Arlington VA 22207
Ph: 703-525-0050 ▪ Fx: 703-525-0052 ▪ TF: 800-473-0060

Genealogical Society, New England Historic — www.newenglandancestors.org
101 Newbury St   Boston MA 02116
Ph: 617-536-5740 ▪ Fx: 617-536-7307 ▪ TF: 888-296-3447

(Genealogy) American/Schleswig-Holstein Heritage Society — www.ashhs.org
PO Box 506   Walcott IA 52773
Ph: 563-284-4184

(Genealogy) Familia Ancestral Research Association —
PO Box 10359   Westminster CA 92685
Ph: 714-687-0390

Genealogy & Family History, International Society for British —
PO Box 3115   Salt Lake City UT 84110
Ph: 801-272-2178

(Genealogy) General Society of Mayflower Descendants — www.mayflower.org
PO Box 3297   Plymouth MA 02361
Ph: 508-746-3188 ▪ Fx: 508-746-2488

(Genealogy) Gluckstal Colonies Research Association — www.raile.com/gluckstal
611 Esplanade   Redondo Beach CA 90277
Ph: 310-540-1872 ▪ Fx: 310-792-8058

(Genealogy) Palatines to America — www.palam.org
611 E Weber Rd   Columbus OH 43211
Ph: 614-267-4700 ▪ Fx: 614-267-4888

(Genealogy) Society of the Descendants of the Schwenkfeldian Exiles 105 Seminary St Pennsburg PA 18073 www.centralschwenkfelder.com/exile
Ph: 215-679-3103 ▪ Fx: 215-679-8175

(Genealogy) Society of the Descendants of Washington's Army at Valley Forge www.valleyforgesociety.org

(Genealogy) Statue of Liberty-Ellis Island Foundation www.ellisisland.org
292 Madison Ave New York NY 10017
Ph: 212-561-4500 ▪ Fx: 212-779-1990

General Association of General Baptists www.generalbaptist.com
100 Stinson Dr Poplar Bluff MO 63901
Ph: 573-785-7746 ▪ Fx: 573-785-0564

General Association of Regular Baptist Churches www.garbc.org
1300 N Meacham Rd Schaumburg IL 60173
Ph: 847-843-1600 ▪ Fx: 847-843-3757 ▪ TF: 800-588-1600

General Aviation Manufacturers Association www.gama.aero
1400 K St NW Suite 801 Washington DC 20005
Ph: 202-393-1500 ▪ Fx: 202-842-4063

General Board of Church & Society of the United Methodist Church www.umc-gbcs.org
100 Maryland Ave NE Washington DC 20002
Ph: 202-488-5600 ▪ Fx: 202-488-5619

General Commission on Archives & History of the United Methodist Church 36 Madison Ave PO Box 127 Madison NJ 07940 www.gcah.org
Ph: 973-408-3189 ▪ Fx: 973-408-3909

General Contractors of America, Associated www.agc.org
333 John Carlyle St Suite 200 Alexandria VA 22314
Ph: 703-548-3118 ▪ Fx: 703-548-3119 ▪ TF: 800-242-1766

General Federation of Women's Clubs www.gfwc.org
1734 'N' St NW Washington DC 20036
Ph: 202-347-3168 ▪ Fx: 202-835-0246

General Grand Chapter Order of the Eastern Star www.easternstar.org/ggc/frame.html
1618 New Hampshire Ave NW Washington DC 20009
Ph: 202-667-4737 ▪ Fx: 202-462-5162 ▪ TF: 800-648-1182

General Grand Chapter of Royal Arch Masons International
PO Box 489 Danville KY 40423
Ph: 859-236-0757 ▪ Fx: 859-236-6773

General Merchandise Distributors Council www.gmdc.com
1275 Lake Plaza Dr Colorado Springs CO 80906
Ph: 719-576-4260 ▪ Fx: 719-576-2661

General Merchandise Representatives, National Association of www.nagmr.org
110 Friar Tuck Cir Denton TX 76201
Ph: 940-243-0409 ▪ Fx: 940-382-3741

General Society of Mayflower Descendants www.mayflower.org
PO Box 3297 Plymouth MA 02361
Ph: 508-746-3188 ▪ Fx: 508-746-2488

General Society Sons of the Revolution www.sr1776.org
201 W Lexington Ave Suite 1776 Independence MO 64050
Ph: 800-593-1776

General Society of the War of 1812 www.societyofthewarof1812.org
1219 Charmuth Rd Lutherville MD 21093
Ph: 410-825-3015

Generating Systems Association, Electrical www.egsa.org
1650 S Dixie Hwy Suite 500 Boca Raton FL 33432
Ph: 561-750-5575 ▪ Fx: 561-395-8557

Generations United www.gu.org
122 C St NW Suite 820 Washington DC 20001
Ph: 202-638-1263 ▪ Fx: 202-638-7555

Generic Horse Association, International www.igha.org
PO Box 6778 San Pedro CA 90734
Ph: 310-719-9094

Generic Pharmaceutical Association www.gphaonline.com
1620 I St NW Suite 800 Washington DC 20006
Ph: 202-833-9070 ▪ Fx: 202-833-9612

Genesis Institute www.genesisinstitute.org
10220 N Nevada St Suite 280 Spokane WA 99218
Ph: 509-467-7913 ▪ Fx: 509-467-0344

Genesis, Project www.torah.org/
122 Slade Ave Suite 250 Baltimore MD 21208
Ph: 410-602-1350 ▪ Fx: 410-510-1053 ▪ TF: 888-999-8672

Genetic Alliance Inc www.geneticalliance.org
4301 Connecticut Ave NW Suite 404 Washington DC 20008
Ph: 202-966-5557 ▪ Fx: 202-966-8553 ▪ TF: 800-336-4363

Genetic Association, American www.theaga.org
PO Box 257 Buckeystown MD 21717
Ph: 301-695-9292

Genetic Counseling, American Board of www.abgc.net
9650 Rockville Pike Bethesda MD 20814
Ph: 301-571-1825 ▪ Fx: 301-634-7320

Genetic Counselors, National Society of www.nsgc.org
233 Canterbury Dr Wallingford PA 19086
Ph: 610-872-7608

Genetic Diseases, Center for Jewish www.nfjgd.org
Mt Sinai Medical Center 5th Ave at 100 St New York NY 10029
Ph: 212-659-6774

(Genetic Disorders) Stickler Involved People www.sticklers.org
15 Angelina Dr Augusta KS 67010
Ph: 316-775-2993

Genetic Technologists, Association of www.agt-info.org
PO Box 15945-288 Lenexa KS 66285
Ph: 913-541-0497 ▪ Fx: 913-599-5340

Genetics, American College of Medical www.acmg.net
9650 Rockville Pike Bethesda MD 20814
Ph: 301-530-7127 ▪ Fx: 301-634-7275

Genetics, American Society of Human www.ashg.org/genetics/ashg
9650 Rockville Pike Bethesda MD 20814
Ph: 301-571-1825 ▪ Fx: 301-634-7079

Genetics Association, Behavior www.bga.org
Indiana Univ SE Dept of Psychology 4201 Grant Line Rd New Albany IN 47150
Ph: 812-941-2668 ▪ Fx: 812-941-2591

Genetics, Council for Responsible www.gene-watch.org
5 Upland Rd Suite 3 Cambridge MA 02140
Ph: 617-868-0870 ▪ Fx: 617-491-5344

Genetics Society of America www.genetics-gsa.org
9650 Rockville Pike Bethesda MD 20814
Ph: 301-634-7300 ▪ Fx: 301-530-7079

Genocide & the Holocaust, Society for the Philosophical Study of Loyola Univ Dept of Philosophy New Orleans LA 70118 www.loyno.edu/~spsgh
Ph: 504-865-3940 ▪ Fx: 504-865-3948

Geochemical Society gs.wustl.edu
Washington Univ Dept of Earth & Planetary Sciences 1 Brookings Dr Saint Louis MO 63130
Ph: 314-935-4131 ▪ Fx: 314-935-4121

Geochemistry & Health, Society for Environmental www.segh.net
4698 S Forrest Ave Springfield MO 65810
Ph: 417-885-1166 ▪ Fx: 417-881-6920

Geocosmic Research, National Council for www.geocosmic.org
8810-C Jamacha Blvd PMB 183 Spring Valley CA 91977
Ph: 619-303-9236

Geodesy & Geophysics, International Union of www.iugg.org
Univ of Colorado UCB 216 Boulder CO 80309
Ph: 303-497-5147 ▪ Fx: 303-497-3645

Geodetic Surveying, American Association for www.acsm.net/aags
6 Montgomery Village Ave Suite 403 Gaithersburg MD 20879
Ph: 240-632-9716 ▪ Fx: 240-632-1321

Geographers, Association of American www.aag.org
1710 16th St NW Washington DC 20009
Ph: 202-234-1450 ▪ Fx: 202-234-2744

Geographers, Society of Woman www.iswg.org
415 E Capital St SE Washington DC 20003
Ph: 202-546-9228 ▪ Fx: 202-546-5232

Geographic Education, National Council for www.ncge.org
Jacksonville State Univ 206A Martin Hall Jacksonville AL 36265
Ph: 256-782-5293 ▪ Fx: 256-782-5336

Geographic Information Society, Cartography & www.acsm.net/cagis
6 Montgomery Village Ave Suite 403 Gaithersburg MD 20879
Ph: 240-632-9716 ▪ Fx: 240-632-1321

Geographic Society, National www.nationalgeographic.com
1145 17th St NW Washington DC 20036
Ph: 202-857-7000 ▪ Fx: 202-775-6141 ▪ TF: 800-647-5463

Geographical Society, American www.amergeog.org
120 Wall St Suite 100 New York NY 10005
Ph: 212-422-5456 ▪ Fx: 212-422-5480

(Geography) Gamma Theta Upsilon www.gtuhonors.org
Univ of Wisconsin La Crosse Dept of Geography La Crosse WI 54601
Ph: 608-785-8333 ▪ Fx: 608-785-8332

Geological Institute, American www.agiweb.org
4220 King St Alexandria VA 22302
Ph: 703-379-2480 ▪ Fx: 703-379-7563

Geological Society of America www.geosociety.org
3300 Penrose Pl PO Box 9140 Boulder CO 80301
Ph: 303-447-2020 ▪ Fx: 303-357-1070 ▪ TF: 800-472-1988

Geologists, American Association of Petroleum www.aapg.org
1444 S Boulder Ave Tulsa OK 74119
Ph: 918-584-2555 ▪ Fx: 918-560-2694 ▪ TF: 800-364-2274

Geologists, American Institute of Professional www.aipg.org
8703 Yates Dr Suite 200 Westminster CO 80031
Ph: 303-412-6205 ▪ Fx: 303-253-9220

Geologists, American Society of Forensic www.forensicgeology.org
8401 Summerspring Ln Raleigh NC 27615
Ph: 919-618-0810

Geologists, Association of Engineering www.aegweb.org
PO Box 460518 Denver CO 80246
Ph: 303-757-2926 ▪ Fx: 303-757-2969

Geologists, Society of Economic www.segweb.org
7811 Shaffer Pkwy Littleton CO 80127
Ph: 720-981-7882 ▪ Fx: 720-981-7874

Geology, National Association of State Boards of www.asbog.org
PO Box 11591 Columbia SC 29211
Ph: 803-799-1047 ▪ Fx: 803-252-3432

Geology, Society for Sedimentary www.sepm.org
6128 E 38th St Suite 308 Tulsa OK 74135
Ph: 918-610-3361 ▪ Fx: 918-621-1685 ▪ TF: 800-865-9765

Geophysical Contractors, International Association of www.iagc.org
2550 North Loop W Suite 104 Houston TX 77092
Ph: 713-957-8080 ▪ Fx: 713-957-0008

Geophysical Society, Environmental & Engineering www.eegs.org
1720 S Bellaire St Suite 110 Denver CO 80222
Ph: 303-531-7517 ▪ Fx: 303-820-3844

Geophysical Union, American www.agu.org
2000 Florida Ave NW Washington DC 20009
Ph: 202-462-6900 ▪ Fx: 202-328-0566 ▪ TF: 800-966-2481

Geophysicists, Society of Exploration www.seg.org
8801 S Yale Ave Tulsa OK 74137
Ph: 918-493-3516 ▪ Fx: 918-497-5557

Geophysics, International Union of Geodesy & www.iugg.org
Univ of Colorado UCB 216 Boulder CO 80309
Ph: 303-497-5147 ▪ Fx: 303-497-3645

George C Marshall Foundation www.marshallfoundation.org
VMI Parade PO Drawer 1600 Lexington VA 24450
Ph: 540-463-7103

George Khoury Association of Baseball Leagues
5400 Meramec Bottom Rd Saint Louis MO 63128
Ph: 314-849-8900 ▪ Fx: 314-849-8901

George Lucas Educational Foundation www.glef.org
PO Box 3494   San Rafael CA 94912
Ph: 415-507-0399 ▪ Fx: 415-507-0499

George S & Dolores Dore Eccles Foundation
79 S Main St 12th Fl   Salt Lake City UT 84111
Ph: 801-246-5355 ▪ Fx: 801-350-3510

George Sand Association www.disls.ualr.edu/gsand

George Wright Society www.georgewright.org
PO Box 65   Hancock MI 49930
Ph: 906-487-9722 ▪ Fx: 906-487-9405

Georgia Peanut Commission www.gapeanuts.com
110 E 4th St PO Box 967   Tifton GA 31793
Ph: 229-386-3470 ▪ Fx: 229-386-3501

Georgian Association in the USA Inc www.georgianassociation.org
1224 Centre W Suite 400B   Springfield IL 62704
Ph: 217-698-7071 ▪ TF: 877-527-8854

Geoscience Information Society www.geoinfo.org

Geoscience & Remote Sensing Society, IEEE www.ewh.ieee.org/soc/grss
IEEE Operations Ctr 445 Hoes Ln   Piscataway NJ 08854
Ph: 732-981-0060 ▪ Fx: 732-981-1721

Geoscience Teachers, National Association of www.nagt.org
PO Box 5443   Bellingham WA 98227
Ph: 360-650-3587

Geoscientists, Association for Women www.awg.org
PO Box 30645   Lincoln NE 68505
Ph: 402-489-8122

Geospatial Information & Technology Association www.gita.org
14456 E Evans Ave   Aurora CO 80014
Ph: 303-337-0513 ▪ Fx: 303-337-1001

Geosynthetic Materials Association www.gmanow.com
1801 County Rd 'B' W   Roseville MN 55113
Ph: 651-222-2508 ▪ Fx: 651-631-9334 ▪ TF: 800-225-4324

Geothermal Energy Association www.geo-energy.org
209 Pennsylvania Ave SE   Washington DC 20003
Ph: 202-454-5261 ▪ Fx: 202-454-5265

Geothermal Resources Council www.geothermal.org
2001 2nd St Suite 5 PO Box 1350   Davis CA 95617
Ph: 530-758-2360 ▪ Fx: 530-758-2839

Geraldine R Dodge Foundation www.grdodge.org
163 Madison Ave   Morristown NJ 07962
Ph: 973-540-8442 ▪ Fx: 973-540-1211

Gerda Lissner Foundation members.aol.com/lissnerfdtn
135 E 55th St   New York NY 10022
Ph: 212-826-6100 ▪ Fx: 212-826-0366

Geriatric Cardiology, Society of www.sgcard.org
9111 Old Georgetown Rd   Bethesda MD 20814
Ph: 301-581-3449 ▪ Fx: 301-581-3456

Geriatric Care Managers, National Association of Professional www.caremanager.org
1604 N Country Club Rd   Tucson AZ 85716
Ph: 520-881-8008 ▪ Fx: 520-325-7925

Geriatric Dentistry, American Society for www.scdonline.org/ASGD_Index.htm
c/o Special Care Dentistry 211 E Chicago Ave Suite
740   Chicago IL 60611
Ph: 312-440-2660 ▪ Fx: 312-440-2824

Geriatric Pharmacy, Commission for Certification in www.ccgp.org
1321 Duke St   Alexandria VA 22314
Ph: 703-535-3038 ▪ Fx: 703-739-1500

Geriatric Psychiatry, American Association for www.aagpgpa.org
7910 Woodmont Ave Suite 1050   Bethesda MD 20814
Ph: 301-654-7850 ▪ Fx: 301-654-4137

Geriatrics Society, American www.americangeriatrics.org
350 5th Ave Empire State Bldg Suite 801   New York NY 10018
Ph: 212-308-1414 ▪ Fx: 212-832-8646

German Academic Exchange Service www.daad.org
871 United Nations Plaza   New York NY 10017
Ph: 212-758-3223 ▪ Fx: 212-755-5780

German, American Association of Teachers of www.aatg.org
112 Haddontowne Ct Suite 104   Cherry Hill NJ 08034
Ph: 856-795-5553 ▪ Fx: 856-795-9398

German-American Chamber of Commerce Inc www.gaccny.com
12 E 49th St 24th Fl   New York NY 10017
Ph: 212-974-8830 ▪ Fx: 212-974-8867

German-American National Congress www.dank.org
4740 N Western Ave 2nd Fl   Chicago IL 60625
Ph: 773-275-1100 ▪ Fx: 773-275-4010

German-American Studies, Society for www.ulib.iupui.edu/kade/sgasin.html
Scott Community College 500 Belmont Rd   Bettendorf IA
52722
Ph: 319-441-4319

German Descendants, American www.geocities.com/aidsociety/americanaidsociety.html
Aid Society of   6540 N Milwaukee Ave   Chicago IL 60631
Ph: 773-763-9554

German Historical Institute www.ghi-dc.org
1607 New Hampshire Ave NW   Washington DC 20009
Ph: 202-387-3355 ▪ Fx: 202-483-3430

German Shepherd Dog Club of America www.gsdca.org
PO Box 429   Applegate CA 95703
Ph: 530-878-2826

German Society of Pennsylvania www.germansociety.org
611 Spring Garden St   Philadelphia PA 19123
Ph: 215-627-2332 ▪ Fx: 215-627-5297

(German) Steuben Society of America steubensociety.org
6705 Fresh Pond Rd   Ridgewood NY 11385
Ph: 718-381-0900 ▪ Fx: 718-628-4874

German Studies, American Institute for Contemporary www.aicgs.org
1400 16th St NW Suite 420   Washington DC 20036
Ph: 202-332-9312 ▪ Fx: 202-265-9531

German-Texan Heritage Society www.gths.net
507 E 10th St PO Box 684171   Austin TX 78768
Ph: 512-482-0927 ▪ Fx: 512-482-8809 ▪ TF: 866-482-4847

Germanna Colonies in Virginia, Memorial Foundation of www.germanna.org
PO Box 279   Locust Grove VA 22508
Ph: 540-423-1700 ▪ 540-423-1747

Germans from Russia, American Historical Society of www.ahsgr.org
631 D St   Lincoln NE 68502
Ph: 402-474-3363 ▪ Fx: 402-474-7229

Germans from Russia Heritage Society www.grhs.com
1125 W Turnpike Ave   Bismarck ND 58501
Ph: 701-223-6167 ▪ Fx: 701-223-4421

Germany, American Council on www.acgusa.org
14 E 60th St Suite 606   New York NY 10022
Ph: 212-826-3636 ▪ Fx: 212-758-3445

Germany, Conference on Jewish Material Claims Against www.claimscon.org
15 E 26th St Rm 906   New York NY 10010
Ph: 646-536-9100 ▪ Fx: 212-679-2126

Gerontological Nursing Association, National www.ngna.org
7794 Grow Dr   Pensacola FL 32514
Ph: 850-473-1174 ▪ Fx: 850-484-8762 ▪ TF: 800-723-0560

Gerontological Society of America www.geron.org
1030 15th St NW Suite 250   Washington DC 20005
Ph: 202-842-1275 ▪ Fx: 202-842-1150

Gerontology, Center for Social www.tcsg.org
2307 Shelby Ave   Ann Arbor MI 48103
Ph: 734-665-1126 ▪ Fx: 734-665-2071

Gerontology in Higher Education, Association for www.aghe.org
1030 15th St NW Suite 240   Washington DC 20005
Ph: 202-289-9806 ▪ Fx: 202-289-9824

Getty J Paul Trust www.getty.edu
1200 Getty Center Dr   Los Angeles CA 90049
Ph: 310-440-7340 ▪ Fx: 310-440-7704

Gettysburg, Friends of the National Parks at www.friendsofgettysburg.org
304B York St PO Box 4622   Gettysburg PA 17325
Ph: 717-334-0772 ▪ Fx: 717-334-3118

Ghost Research Society www.ghostresearch.org
PO Box 205   Oak Lawn IL 60454
Ph: 708-425-5163

Gideons International www.gideons.org
50 Century Blvd   Nashville TN 37214
Ph: 615-564-5000 ▪ Fx: 615-564-6000

Gift Association, National Specialty www.nsgaonline.com
7238 Bucks Ford Dr   Riverview FL 33569
Ph: 813-671-4757 ▪ Fx: 813-677-5075

Gift from the Heart Foundation www.promograph.com/giftfromtheheart
2653 N Narragansett Ave   Chicago IL 60639
Ph: 773-237-4800 ▪ Fx: 773-237-1221

Gift of Life Bone Marrow Foundation www.giftoflife.org
7700 Congress Ave   Boca Raton FL 33487
Ph: 561-988-0100 ▪ Fx: 561-988-0140 ▪ TF: 800-962-7769

Gift Mission, American Scripture www.gospelcom.net/asgm/
PO Box 410280   Melbourne FL 32941
Ph: 321-255-7774 ▪ Fx: 321-255-8986 ▪ TF: 877-873-2746

Gifted Child Society www.gifted.org
190 Rock Rd   Glen Rock NJ 07452
Ph: 201-444-6530 ▪ Fx: 201-444-9099

Gifted Children, American Association for www.aagc.org
Duke University PO Box 90270   Durham NC 27708
Ph: 919-783-6152

Gifted Children, National Association for www.nagc.org
1707 L St NW Suite 550   Washington DC 20036
Ph: 202-785-4268 ▪ Fx: 202-785-4248

Gifted & Talented Children, World Council for www.worldgifted.org
18401 Hiawatha St   Northridge CA 91326
Ph: 818-368-7501 ▪ Fx: 818-368-2163

Gifted & Talented Students, Association for
PO Box 16037   Baton Rouge LA 70896
Ph: 504-388-3422 ▪ Fx: 504-388-1375 ▪ TF: 800-626-8811

Giftmakers Guild, Collectibles & www.collectiblesguild.org
77 W Washington St Suite 1716   Chicago IL 60602
Ph: 312-379-2935 ▪ Fx: 312-379-2939

Gifts In Kind International www.giftsinkind.org
333 N Fairfax St Suite 100   Alexandria VA 22314
Ph: 703-836-2121 ▪ Fx: 703-549-1481

Giftware Association, National Tabletop &
112 Adrossan Ct   Deptford NJ 08096
Ph: 856-227-6802 ▪ Fx: 856-227-6782

Gilda Radner Familial Ovarian Cancer Registry www.ovariancancer.com
Roswell Park Cancer Institute Elm & Carlton Sts   Buffalo NY
14263
Ph: 716-845-4503 ▪ Fx: 716-845-8266 ▪ TF: 800-682-7426

Giraffe Project www.giraffe.org
PO Box 759   Langley WA 98260
Ph: 360-221-7989 ▪ Fx: 360-221-7817

Girl Friends Inc
5215 Lobello Dr   Dallas TX 75229
Ph: 214-373-8513 ▪ Fx: 214-739-4691

Girl Scout Committee, National Jewish www.njgsc.org
33 Central Dr   Bronxville NY 10708
Ph: 914-738-3986 ▪ Fx: 914-738-6752

Girl Scout Executive Staff, Association of
222 S Riverside Plaza Suite 2120   Chicago IL 60606
Ph: 312-416-2500 ▪ Fx: 312-416-2932

Girl Scouts of the USA www.girlscouts.org
420 5th Ave   New York NY 10018
Ph: 212-852-8000 ▪ Fx: 212-852-6517 ▪ TF: 800-223-0624

Girls Inc www.girlsinc.org
120 Wall St 3rd Fl   New York NY 10005
Ph: 212-509-2000 ▪ Fx: 212-509-8708 ▪ TF: 800-374-4475

Girls & Boys Town www.girlsandboystown.org
14100 Crawford St   Boys Town NE 68010
Ph: 402-498-1300 ▪ Fx: 402-498-1348 ▪ TF: 800-448-3000

Girls in Education, National Coalition for Women & www.ncwge.org
c/o National Women's Law Ctr 11 Dupont Cir NW Suite
800 Washington DC 20036
Ph: 202-785-7730 ▪ Fx: 202-588-5185

Girls Nation www.legion-aux.org
American Legion Auxiliary 777 N Meridian St Indianapolis IN
46204
Ph: 317-955-3845 ▪ Fx: 317-955-3884

Girls, National Association of Principals of Schools for
41 Van Brunt Manor Rd East Setauket NY 11733
Ph: 631-751-0850 ▪ Fx: 631-689-7311

Girls' Schools, National Coalition of www.ncgs.org
57 Main St Concord MA 01742
Ph: 978-287-4485 ▪ Fx: 978-287-6014

Girls & Women in Sport, National Association for www.aahperd.org
1900 Association Dr Reston VA 20191
Ph: 703-476-3400 ▪ Fx: 703-476-4566 ▪ TF: 800-213-7193

Givat Haviva Educational Foundation Inc www.givathaviva.org
114 W 26th Suite 1001 New York NY 10001
Ph: 212-989-9272 ▪ Fx: 212-989-9840

Give Kids the World Village www.gktw.org
210 S Bass Rd Kissimmee FL 34746
Ph: 407-396-1114 ▪ Fx: 407-396-1207 ▪ TF: 800-995-5437

Giving, National Committee on Planned www.ncpg.org
233 McCrea St Suite 400 Indianapolis IN 46225
Ph: 317-269-6274 ▪ Fx: 317-269-6276

Gladiolus Council, North American www.gladworld.org
8401 SE Strawberry Ln Milwaukie OR 97267
Ph: 503-656-9270

Gladstone Equestrian Association
PO Box 119 Gladstone NJ 07934
Ph: 908-234-0151 ▪ Fx: 908-234-0863

Glaser Elizabeth Pediatric AIDS Foundation www.pedaids.org
2950 31st St Suite 125 Santa Monica CA 90405
Ph: 310-314-1459 ▪ Fx: 310-314-1469 ▪ TF: 888-499-4673

Glass Art Society www.glassart.org
1305 4th Ave Suite 711 Seattle WA 98101
Ph: 206-382-1305 ▪ Fx: 206-382-2630

Glass Association of America, Stained www.stainedglass.org
10009 E 62nd St Raytown MO 64133
Ph: 816-737-2090 ▪ Fx: 816-737-2801 ▪ TF: 800-438-9581

Glass Association, Art www.artglassassociation.com
PO Box 2537 Zanesville OH 43702
Ph: 740-454-1194 ▪ TF: 866-301-2421

Glass Association, Independent www.iga.org
54840 S Circle Dr PO Box 1762 Idyllwild CA 92549
Ph: 909-659-5972 ▪ Fx: 909-659-5002

Glass Association, International Carnival www.woodsland.com/ICGA
PO Box 306 Mentone IN 46539
Ph: 574-353-7678

Glass Association, National www.glass.org
8200 Greensboro Dr Suite 302 McLean VA 22102
Ph: 703-442-4890 ▪ Fx: 703-442-0630 ▪ TF: 866-342-5642

Glass Association of North America www.glasswebsite.com
2945 SW Wanamaker Dr Suite A Topeka KS 66614
Ph: 785-271-0208 ▪ Fx: 785-271-0166

Glass & Ceramic Decorators, Society of www.sgcd.org
47 N 4th St Zanesville OH 43702
Ph: 740-588-9882 ▪ Fx: 740-588-0245

Glass Collectors of America Inc, Fenton Art fagcainc.wirefire.com
PO Box 384 Williamstown WV 26187
Ph: 304-375-6196 ▪ Fx: 304-375-4679

Glass Collectors Club, Tiffin www.tiffinglass.org

Glass Collectors Society, National Imperial www.imperialglass.org

Glass Collectors Society, National Milk www.nmgcs.org
500 Union Cemetery Rd Greensburg PA 15601
Ph: 724-832-7968

Glass Manufacturers Alliance, Insulated www.igmaonline.org
27 Goulburn Ave Ottawa ON K1N8C7
Ph: 613-233-1510 ▪ Fx: 613-233-1929

Glass Molders Pottery Plastics & Allied Workers International Union www.gmpiu.org
608 E Baltimore Pike Media PA 19063
Ph: 610-565-5051 ▪ Fx: 610-565-0983

Glass Packaging Institute www.gpi.org
515 King St Suite 420 Alexandria VA 22314
Ph: 703-684-6359 ▪ Fx: 703-684-6048

Glass Society, National Fenton www.fentonglasssociety.org
PO Box 4008 Marietta OH 45750
Ph: 740-374-3345 ▪ Fx: 740-376-9708

Glass Technical Institute
12653 Portada Pl San Diego CA 92130
Ph: 858-481-1277 ▪ Fx: 858-481-6771

Glassblowers Society, American Scientific www.asgs-glass.org
PO Box 778 Madison NC 27025
Ph: 336-427-2406 ▪ Fx: 336-427-2496

Glasser William Institute www.wglasser.com
22024 Lassen St Suite 118 Chatsworth CA 91311
Ph: 818-700-8000 ▪ Fx: 818-700-0555 ▪ TF: 800-899-0688

Glaucoma Foundation www.glaucomafoundation.org
116 John St Suite 1605 New York NY 10038
Ph: 212-285-0080 ▪ Fx: 212-651-1888

Glaucoma Research Foundation www.glaucoma.org
490 Post St Suite 1427 San Francisco CA 94102
Ph: 415-986-3162 ▪ Fx: 415-986-3763 ▪ TF: 800-826-6693

Glazing Certification Council, Safety www.sgcc.org
PO Box 9 Henderson Harbor NY 13651
Ph: 315-646-2234 ▪ Fx: 315-646-2297

Glazing Council, Protective www.protectiveglazing.org
2945 SW Wanamaker Dr Suite A Topeka KS 66614
Ph: 785-271-0208 ▪ Fx: 785-271-0166

Gleaner Life Insurance Society www.gleanerlife.com
5200 W US Hwy 223 PO Box 1894 Adrian MI 49221
Ph: 517-263-2244 ▪ Fx: 517-265-7745 ▪ TF: 800-992-1894

Glenmary Home Missioners www.glenmary.org
PO Box 465618 Cincinnati OH 45246
Ph: 513-874-8900 ▪ Fx: 513-874-1690

Glider Pilots Association Inc, National WWII www.ww2gp.org
21 Phyllis Rd Freehold NJ 07728
Ph: 732-462-1838

Global Action International www.globalactionintl.org
PO Box 717 Carlsbad CA 92018
Ph: 760-438-3979 ▪ Fx: 760-602-0383

Global Alliance for Africa www.globalallianceafrica.org
122 S DesPlaines St Chicago IL 60661
Ph: 312-382-0607 ▪ Fx: 312-906-9930

Global Alliance for Intelligent Arts www.global-alliance.com
PO Box 403 Northampton MA 01061
Ph: 413-584-3022

Global Alliance for Women's Health www.gawh.org
823 UN Plaza Suite 712 New York NY 10017
Ph: 212-286-0424 ▪ Fx: 212-286-9561

Global Association of Risk Professionals www.garp.com
111 Pavonia Ave Suite 430 Jersey City NJ 07310
Ph: 201-222-0054 ▪ Fx: 201-222-5022

Global Automation Information Network
900 Victors Way PO Box 3724 Ann Arbor MI 48106
Ph: 734-994-6088 ▪ Fx: 734-994-3338

Global Children's Organization www.globalchild.org
PO Box 67583 Los Angeles CA 90067
Ph: 310-581-2234 ▪ Fx: 310-581-6155

Global Climate Coalition www.globalclimate.org
1275 K St NW Washington DC 20005
Ph: 202-682-9161 ▪ Fx: 202-628-3622

Global Coalition for Africa www.gca-cma.org
1919 Pennsylvania Ave NW Suite 550 Washington DC 20006
Ph: 202-458-4338 ▪ Fx: 202-522-3259

Global Communications, Institute for www.igc.org
PO Box 29904 San Francisco CA 94129
Ph: 415-561-6100 ▪ Fx: 415-561-6101

Global Community, Foundation for www.globalcommunity.org
222 High St Palo Alto CA 94301
Ph: 650-328-7756 ▪ Fx: 650-328-7785 ▪ TF: 800-707-7932

Global Coral Reef Alliance www.globalcoral.org
37 Pleasant St Cambridge MA 02139
Ph: 617-864-4226 ▪ Fx: 617-864-0433

Global Education, American Forum for www.globaled.org
120 Wall St Suite 2600 New York NY 10005
Ph: 212-624-1300 ▪ Fx: 212-624-1412 ▪ TF: 800-813-5056

Global Education Associates www.globaleduc.org
475 Riverside Dr Suite 1850 New York NY 10115
Ph: 212-870-3290 ▪ Fx: 212-870-2729

Global Exchange www.globalexchange.org
2017 Mission St Suite 303 San Francisco CA 94110
Ph: 415-255-7296 ▪ Fx: 415-255-7498 ▪ TF: 800-497-1994

Global Fund for Women www.globalfundforwomen.org
1375 Sutter St Suite 400 San Francisco CA 94109
Ph: 415-202-7640 ▪ Fx: 415-202-8604

Global Futures Foundation www.globalff.org
415 Jackson St 2nd Fl San Francisco CA 94111
Ph: 415-364-3803 ▪ Fx: 415-693-9163

Global Health Council www.globalhealth.org
1701 K St NW Suite 600 Washington DC 20006
Ph: 202-833-5900 ▪ Fx: 202-833-0075

Global Health Ministries www.ghm.org
7831 Hickory St NE Minneapolis MN 55432
Ph: 763-586-9590 ▪ Fx: 763-586-9591

Global Impact www.charity.org
66 Canal Center Plaza Suite 310 Alexandria VA 22314
Ph: 703-548-2200 ▪ Fx: 703-548-7684

Global Issues Resource Center www.global-issues.org
Cuyahoga Community College East 1 4250 Richmond
Rd Cleveland OH 44122
Ph: 216-987-2224 ▪ Fx: 216-987-2133

Global Jewish Assistance & Relief Network www.globaljewish.org
666 5th Ave Suite 246 New York NY 10103
Ph: 212-868-3636 ▪ Fx: 212-868-7878

Global Learning Inc www.globallearningnj.org
400 Union Ave Brielle NJ 08730
Ph: 732-528-0016

Global Organization of People of Indian Origin www.gopio.net
PO Box 1413 Stamford CT 06904
Ph: 203-329-8010 ▪ Fx: 203-322-2233

Global Outreach Inc www.globaloutreach.net
PO Box 25883 Alexandria VA 22313
Ph: 703-299-9551 ▪ Fx: 703-299-9557

Global Policy Forum www.globalpolicy.org
777 UN Plaza Suite 7G New York NY 10017
Ph: 212-557-3161 ▪ Fx: 212-557-3165

Global Response www.globalresponse.org
PO Box 7490 Boulder CO 80306
Ph: 303-444-0306 ▪ Fx: 303-449-9794

Global Rights www.globalrights.org
1200 18th St NW Suite 602 Washington DC 20036
Ph: 202-822-4600 ▪ Fx: 202-822-4606

Global Village Institute www.i4at.org
89 Schoolhouse Rd PO Box 90 Summertown TN 38483
Ph: 931-964-4324 ▪ Fx: 931-964-2200

Global Volunteers Partners in Development www.globalvolunteers.org
375 E Little Canada Rd Saint Paul MN 55117
Ph: 651-407-6100 ▪ Fx: 651-482-0915 ▪ TF: 800-487-1074

Global Warming International Center
PO Box 5275   Woodridge IL 60517
Ph: 630-910-1551 ▪ Fx: 630-910-1561
www.globalwarming.net

Glove Association, International
PO Box 146   Brookville PA 15825
Ph: 814-328-5208
www.iga-online.com

Glove Shippers Association
PO Box 1908   San Juan Capistrano CA 92693
Ph: 949-425-0888 ▪ Fx: 949-425-9232 ▪ TF: 877-877-8780

Glovebox Society, American
PO Box 9099   Santa Rosa CA 95405
Ph: 800-530-1022 ▪ Fx: 707-578-4406
www.gloveboxsociety.org

Gluckstal Colonies Research Association
611 Esplanade   Redondo Beach CA 90277
Ph: 310-540-1872 ▪ Fx: 310-792-8058
www.raile.com/gluckstal

Glutamate Association
PO Box 14266   Washington DC 20044
Ph: 202-783-6135 ▪ Fx: 202-637-5910
www.msgfacts.com

Gluten Association, International Wheat
9300 Metcalf Ave Suite 300   Overland Park KS 66212
Ph: 913-381-8180 ▪ Fx: 913-381-8836
www.iwga.net

Gluten Intolerance Group
15110 10th Ave SW Suite A   Seattle WA 98166
Ph: 206-246-6652 ▪ Fx: 206-246-6531
www.gluten.net

Gnathologic Orthopedics, American Academy of
2651 Oak Grove Rd   Walnut Creek CA 94598
Ph: 925-939-5024 ▪ Fx: 925-676-7678 ▪ TF: 800-510-2246
www.aago.com

Go-Kart Association, International Recreational
435 Corona St   San Antonio TX 78209
Ph: 210-824-1923 ▪ Fx: 210-824-5186

Go RVing Coalition
1896 Preston White Dr   Reston VA 20191
Ph: 703-620-6003 ▪ TF: 888-467-8464
www.gorving.com

Goat Association, American Dairy
209 W Main St PO Box 865   Spindale NC 28160
Ph: 828-286-3801 ▪ Fx: 828-287-0476
www.adga.org

Goat Association, National Pygmy
1932 149th Ave SE   Snohomish WA 98290
Ph: 425-334-6506 ▪ Fx: 425-334-5447
www.npga-pygmy.com

Goat Breeders Association, American Angora
PO Box 195   Rocksprings TX 78880
Ph: 830-683-4483

Goat Society, American
PO Box 330   Broad Run VA 20137
Ph: 540-349-4709
www.americangoatsociety.com

(Goats) Alpines International
485 McKinney Rd   Walla Walla WA 99362
Ph: 509-525-4606 ▪ Fx: 509-526-0673
www.alpinesinternationalclub.com

(Goats) National Saanen Breeders Association
PO Box 315   Santa Margarita CA 93453
Ph: 805-461-5547
nationalsaanenbreeders.com

(Goats) National Toggenburg Club
www.nationaltoggclub.com

(Goats) Oberhasli Breeders of America
www.oba-usa.org

God, National Institute for the Word of
487 Michigan Ave NE   Washington DC 20017
Ph: 202-529-0001 ▪ Fx: 202-636-4460
www.wordofgodinstitute.org

Goddess International, Re-Formed Congregation of the
PO Box 6677   Madison WI 53716
Ph: 608-226-9998
www.rcgi.org

Godparent Foundation, Liberty
PO Box 4199   Lynchburg VA 24502
Ph: 434-845-3466 ▪ TF: 800-542-4453
www.godparent.org

God's Child Project
721 Memorial Hwy PO Box 1573   Bismarck ND 58504
Ph: 701-255-7956 ▪ Fx: 701-222-0874
www.godschild.org

God's Love We Deliver
166 Ave of the Americas   New York NY 10013
Ph: 212-294-8100 ▪ Fx: 212-294-8101 ▪ TF: 800-747-2023
www.glwd.org

Goethe-Institut New York
1014 5th Ave   New York NY 10028
Ph: 212-439-8700 ▪ Fx: 212-439-8705
www.goethe.de/uk/ney

Goizueta Foundation
4401 Northside Pkwy Suite 520   Atlanta GA 30327
Ph: 404-239-0390 ▪ Fx: 404-239-0018
www.goizuetafoundation.org

Gold Coast Jazz Society
103 NW 2nd Ave   Fort Lauderdale FL 33311
Ph: 954-524-0805 ▪ Fx: 954-525-7880
www.goldcoastjazz.org

Gold Council, World
444 Madison Ave Suite 301   New York NY 10022
Ph: 212-317-3800 ▪ Fx: 212-688-0410
www.gold.org

Gold Cross, Ukrainian
6616 W Roscoe St   Chicago IL 60634
Ph: 773-736-4568 ▪ Fx: 773-736-4658

Gold Foil Operators, American Academy of
1 Woods End Rd   Etna NH 03750
Ph: 603-643-2899
www.goldfoil.org

Gold Institute
1112 16th St NW Suite 240   Washington DC 20036
Ph: 202-835-0185 ▪ Fx: 202-835-0155
www.goldinstitute.org

Gold Prospectors Association of America
PO Box 891509   Temecula CA 92589
Ph: 909-699-4749 ▪ Fx: 909-699-4062 ▪ TF: 800-551-9707
www.goldprospectors.org

Gold Star Mothers Inc, American
2128 Leroy Pl NW   Washington DC 20008
Ph: 202-265-0991 ▪ Fx: 202-265-6963
www.goldstarmoms.com

Gold Star Wives of America Inc
5510 Columbia Pike Suite 205   Arlington VA 22204
Ph: 888-479-9788
www.goldstarwives.org

Gold Wing Road Riders Association
21423 N 11th Ave   Phoenix AZ 85027
Ph: 623-581-2500 ▪ Fx: 623-581-3844 ▪ TF: 800-843-9460
www.gwrra.org

Golden Age, Catholic
PO Box 249   Olyphant PA 18447
Ph: 570-586-1091 ▪ Fx: 570-586-7721 ▪ TF: 800-836-5699
www.catholicgoldenage.org

Golden Key International Honour Society
1189 Ponce de Leon Ave   Atlanta GA 30306
Ph: 404-377-2400 ▪ Fx: 404-373-7033 ▪ TF: 800-377-2401
gknhs.gsu.edu/GKWeb

Golden Retriever Club of America
www.grca.org

Golden Rule Foundation
www.goldrule.org

Golden Rule, International Order of the
13523 Lakefront Dr   Bridgeton MO 63045
Ph: 314-209-7142 ▪ Fx: 314-209-1289 ▪ TF: 800-367-8030
www.ogr.org

Golden Threads
PO Box 1688   Demorest GA 30535
Ph: 706-776-3959
www.home.earthlink.net/~goldengurl

Golden West, Native Daughters of the
543 Baker St   San Francisco CA 94117
Ph: 415-563-9091 ▪ Fx: 415-563-5230 ▪ TF: 800-944-6349
www.ndgw.org

Golden West, Native Sons of the
414 Mason St   San Francisco CA 94102
Ph: 415-392-1223 ▪ Fx: 415-392-1230 ▪ TF: 800-337-1875
www.nsgw.org

Goldfish Growers Association, National Ornamental
6916 Blacks Mill Rd   Thurmont MD 21788
Ph: 301-271-7475 ▪ Fx: 301-271-7059

Goldsmith Horace W Foundation
375 Park Ave Rm 1602   New York NY 10152
Ph: 212-319-8700 ▪ Fx: 212-319-2881

Goldsmiths, Society of North American
4513 Lincoln Ave Suite 213   Lisle IL 60532
Ph: 630-852-6385 ▪ Fx: 630-241-0142
www.snagmetalsmith.org

Goldwater Institute
500 E Coronado Rd   Phoenix AZ 85004
Ph: 602-462-5000 ▪ Fx: 602-256-7045
www.goldwaterinstitute.org

Golf Administrators, International Association of
3740 Cahuenga Blvd   North Hollywood CA 91604
Ph: 818-980-3630 ▪ Fx: 818-980-5019
www.iaga.org

Golf Associates, International
4370 La Jolla Village Dr 4th Fl   San Diego CA 92122
Ph: 858-546-4737 ▪ Fx: 858-615-2083
www.iga-golf.com

Golf Association of America Inc, Multicultural
3 Sunset Ave PO Box 1081   Westhampton Beach NY 11978
Ph: 631-288-8255
www.mgaa.com

Golf Association, American Junior
1980 Sports Club Dr   Braselton GA 30517
Ph: 770-868-4200 ▪ Fx: 770-868-4211 ▪ TF: 877-373-2542
www.ajga.org

Golf Association, American Recreational
PO Box 35215   Chicago IL 60707
Ph: 708-453-0080 ▪ Fx: 708-453-0083
www.rentamark.com/arga

Golf Association, Executive Women's
300 Ave of the Champions Suite 140   Palm Beach Gardens FL 33418
Ph: 561-691-0096 ▪ Fx: 561-691-0012 ▪ TF: 800-407-1477
www.ewga.com

Golf Association, Ladies Professional
100 International Golf Dr   Daytona Beach FL 32124
Ph: 386-274-6200 ▪ Fx: 386-274-1099
www.lpga.com

Golf Association, National Amputee
11 Walnut Hill Rd   Amherst NH 03031
Ph: 800-633-6242
www.nagagolf.com

Golf Association, National Pan-American Junior
4813 Larcade Dr   Corpus Christi TX 78415
Ph: 361-853-6860 ▪ Fx: 361-854-7242
npaga.callernetwork.com/junior.html

Golf Association, National Senior
3672 Nottingham Way   Hamilton Square NJ 08690
Ph: 800-282-6772 ▪ Fx: 609-921-2707 ▪ TF: 800-282-6772
www.nsgatour.com

Golf Association, US
PO Box 708   Far Hills NJ 07931
Ph: 908-234-2300 ▪ Fx: 908-234-9687 ▪ TF: 800-336-4446
www.usga.org

Golf Association US, Miniature
435 Corona   San Antonio TX 78209
Ph: 210-824-7011 ▪ Fx: 210-824-5186
www.mgaus.org

Golf Association, Western
1 Briar Rd   Golf IL 60029
Ph: 847-724-4600 ▪ Fx: 847-724-7133
www.westerngolfassociation.com

Golf Coaches Association of America
1225 W Main St Suite 110   Norman OK 73069
Ph: 405-329-4222 ▪ Fx: 405-573-7888 ▪ TF: 866-422-2669
gcaa.collegiategolf.com

Golf Coaches Association, National
180 N LaSalle St Suite 1822   Chicago IL 60601
Ph: 312-551-0814 ▪ Fx: 312-551-0815
www.ngca.com

Golf Collectors' Society
PO Box 3103   Ponte Vedra Beach FL 32004
Ph: 904-825-2191 ▪ Fx: 904-810-5305
www.golfcollectors.com

Golf Course Architects, American Society of
111 E Wacker Dr 18th Fl   Chicago IL 60601
Ph: 312-372-7090 ▪ Fx: 312-372-6160
www.asgca.org

Golf Course Builders Association of America
770 'O' St   Lincoln NE 68503
Ph: 402-476-4444 ▪ Fx: 402-476-4489
www.gcbaa.org

Golf Course Owners Association, National
291 Seven Farms Dr 2nd Fl   Charleston SC 29492
Ph: 843-881-9956 ▪ Fx: 843-881-9958 ▪ TF: 800-933-4262
www.ngcoa.org

Golf Course Superintendents Association of America
1421 Research Park Dr   Lawrence KS 66049
Ph: 785-841-2240 ▪ Fx: 785-832-4455 ▪ TF: 800-472-7878
www.gcsaa.org

Golf Foundation, All-American Collegiate
555 Madison Ave 12th Fl   New York NY 10022
Ph: 212-751-5170 ▪ Fx: 212-755-3762

Golf Foundation, National   www.ngf.org
1150 S US Hwy 1 Suite 401   Jupiter FL 33477
Ph: 561-744-6006 ▪ Fx: 561-744-6107 ▪ TF: 800-733-6006

Golf Merchandisers, Association of   www.agmgolf.org
PO Box 7247   Phoenix AZ 85011
Ph: 602-604-8250 ▪ Fx: 602-604-8251

(Golf) PGA of America   www.pga.com
100 Ave of the Champions   Palm Beach Gardens FL 33418
Ph: 561-624-8400 ▪ Fx: 561-624-8439 ▪ TF: 800-477-6465

(Golf) PGA Tour Inc   www.pgatour.com
112 PGA Tour Blvd   Ponte Vedra Beach FL 32082
Ph: 904-285-3700 ▪ Fx: 904-285-7913

Golf Players Association, American   www.agpa.com
PO Box 33039   Phoenix AZ 85067
Ph: 602-279-4653 ▪ Fx: 602-241-9450 ▪ TF: 888-790-2472

Golf Range Association of America   www.golfrange.org
PO Box 1265   New Canaan CT 06840
Ph: 203-972-6201 ▪ Fx: 203-972-1667

Golf Teachers Federation, US   www.usgtf.com
1295 SE Port St Lucie Blvd   Port Saint Lucie FL 34952
Ph: 772-335-3216 ▪ Fx: 772-335-3822 ▪ TF: 888-346-3290

Golf Tournament Directors, National Association of   www.nagtd.com
212 S Henry St 2nd Fl   Alexandria VA 22314
Ph: 703-549-3543 ▪ Fx: 703-549-9074 ▪ TF: 888-899-2483

Golf Writers Association of America   www.gwaa.com
10210 Greentree Rd   Houston TX 77042
Ph: 713-782-6664 ▪ Fx: 713-781-2575

Golfers' Association, US Blind   www.blindgolf.com
3094 Shamrock St N   Tallahassee FL 32308
Ph: 850-893-4511

Golfers, National Association of Left-Handed   www.nalg.org
3249 Hazelwood Dr SW   Atlanta GA 30311
Ph: 404-696-1763 ▪ Fx: 404-691-5549 ▪ TF: 800-844-6524

Good Bears of the World   www.goodbearsoftheworld.org
PO Box 13097   Toledo OH 43613
Ph: 419-531-5365

Good News Jail & Prison Ministry   www.goodnewsjail.org
2230 E Parham Rd Suite 200   Richmond VA 23228
Ph: 804-553-4090 ▪ Fx: 804-553-4144 ▪ TF: 800-220-2202

Good Sam Recreational Vehicle Club   www.goodsamclub.com
PO Box 6888   Englewood CO 80155
Ph: 800-234-3450

Goodall Jane Institute for Wildlife Research Education &   www.janegoodall.org
  Conservation 8700 Georgia Ave Suite 500   Silver Spring MD
  20910
Ph: 301-565-0086 ▪ Fx: 301-565-3188 ▪ TF: 800-592-5263

Goodguys Rod & Custom Association   www.good-guys.com
PO Box 424   Alamo CA 94507
Ph: 925-838-9876 ▪ Fx: 925-820-8241

Goodwill Industries International Inc   www.goodwill.org
9200 Rockville Pike   Bethesda MD 20814
Ph: 301-530-6500 ▪ Fx: 301-530-1516

GOPAC   www.gopac.org
122 C St NW Suite 505   Washington DC 20001
Ph: 202-464-5170 ▪ Fx: 202-464-5177

Gorilla Foundation   www.gorilla.org
PO Box 620530   Woodside CA 94062
Ph: 650-216-6450 ▪ Fx: 650-365-7906 ▪ TF: 800-634-6273

Gorilla Fund International, Dian Fossey   www.gorillafund.org
800 Cherokee Ave SE   Atlanta GA 30315
Ph: 404-624-5881 ▪ Fx: 404-624-5999 ▪ TF: 800-851-0203

Gospel Association for the Blind   www.careministries.org/gab.html
1450 SW 10th Ave Bldg B-2   Delray Beach FL 33444
Ph: 386-586-5885

Gospel Association, Slavic   www.sga.org
6151 Commonwealth Dr   Loves Park IL 61111
Ph: 815-282-8900 ▪ Fx: 815-282-8901 ▪ TF: 800-242-5350

Gospel Fellowship, Missionary   www.mgfhq.org
PO Box 1535   Turlock CA 95381
Ph: 209-634-8575 ▪ Fx: 209-634-8472

Gospel, International Church of the Foursquare   www.foursquare.org
1910 W Sunset Blvd Suite 200   Los Angeles CA 90026
Ph: 213-989-4200 ▪ Fx: 213-989-4590 ▪ TF: 888-635-4234

Gospel Literature International   www.glint.org
PO Box 4060   Ontario CA 91761
Ph: 909-481-5222 ▪ Fx: 909-481-5216 ▪ TF: 800-434-5468

Gospel Ministry Inc, Friends of Israel   foi.org
PO Box 908   Bellmawr NJ 08099
Ph: 856-853-5590 ▪ Fx: 856-853-9565 ▪ TF: 800-257-7843

Gospel Mission, Spanish World   www.spanishworld.org
PO Box 542   Winona Lake IN 46590
Ph: 574-267-8821 ▪ Fx: 574-267-3524 ▪ TF: 800-419-3683

Gospel Mission, World   www.wgm.org
PO Box 948   Marion IN 46952
Ph: 765-664-7331 ▪ Fx: 765-671-7230

Gospel Missionary Union   www.gmu.org
10000 N Oak   Kansas City MO 64155
Ph: 816-734-8500 ▪ Fx: 816-734-4601 ▪ TF: 800-468-1892

Gospel Music Association   www.gospelmusic.org
1205 Division St   Nashville TN 37203
Ph: 615-242-0303 ▪ Fx: 615-254-9755

Gospel Music Workshop of America   www.gmwa.org
3908 W Warren Ave   Detroit MI 48208
Ph: 313-898-6900 ▪ Fx: 313-898-4520

Gospel Recordings Network   www.gospelrecordings.com
41823 Enterprise Cir N   Temecula CA 92590
Ph: 909-719-1650 ▪ Fx: 909-719-1651 ▪ TF: 888-444-7872

Gospel Rescue Missions, Association of   www.agrm.org
1045 Swift St   Kansas City MO 64116
Ph: 816-471-8020 ▪ Fx: 816-471-3718 ▪ TF: 800-624-5156

Governing Boards of Universities & Colleges, Association of www.agb.org
1 Dupont Cir NW Suite 400   Washington DC 20036
Ph: 202-296-8400 ▪ Fx: 202-223-7053 ▪ TF: 800-356-6317

Government, Academy for State & Local
444 N Capitol St NW Suite 345   Washington DC 20001
Ph: 202-434-4850 ▪ Fx: 202-434-4851

(Government Accountability) OMB Watch   www.ombwatch.org
1742 Connecticut Ave NW   Washington DC 20009
Ph: 202-234-8494 ▪ Fx: 202-234-8584

Government Accountants, Association of   www.agacgfm.org
2208 Mt Vernon Ave   Alexandria VA 22301
Ph: 703-684-6931 ▪ Fx: 703-548-9367 ▪ TF: 800-242-7211

Government Affairs Council, State   www.sgac.org
1255 23rd St NW   Washington DC 20037
Ph: 202-728-0500 ▪ Fx: 202-833-3636

Government, A Alfred Taubman Center for   www.ksg.harvard.edu/taubmancenter
  State & Local Harvard Univ John F Kennedy School of
  Government 79 JFK St   Cambridge MA 02138
Ph: 617-495-2199

Government Archives & Records Administrators, National   www.nagara.org
  Association of 48 Howard St   Albany NY 12207
Ph: 518-463-8644 ▪ Fx: 518-463-8656

Government Association, Better   bettergov.org
28 E Jackson Blvd Suite 1900   Chicago IL 60604
Ph: 312-427-8330 ▪ Fx: 312-427-8340

Government, Association for Counselors & Educators in
c/o American Counseling Assn 5999 Stevenson Ave   Alexandria
  VA 22304
Ph: 703-823-9800 ▪ Fx: 703-823-0252

Government Auditors, National Association of Local   www.nalga.org
2401 Regency Rd Suite 302   Lexington KY 40503
Ph: 859-276-0686

Government, Blacks in   www.bignet.org
1820 11th St NW   Washington DC 20001
Ph: 202-667-3280 ▪ Fx: 202-667-3705

Government, Center for Business &   www.ksg.harvard.edu/cbg/
Harvard Univ John F Kennedy School of Government Weil Hall
  79 JFK St   Cambridge MA 02138
Ph: 617-384-7329 ▪ Fx: 617-496-0063

Government, Christians in   www.christiansingovernment.org
PO Box 71654   Los Angeles CA 90071
Ph: 213-250-5016

Government Communicators, National Association of   www.nagc.com
10366 Democracy Ln Suite B   Fairfax VA 22030
Ph: 703-691-0377 ▪ Fx: 703-706-9583

Government, Council for Excellence in   www.excelgov.org
1301 K St NW Suite 450 West   Washington DC 20005
Ph: 202-728-0418 ▪ Fx: 202-728-0422

Government Defined Contribution Administrators Inc,   www.nagdca.org
  National Association of 167 W Main St Suite 600   Lexington
  KY 40507
Ph: 859-514-9161 ▪ Fx: 859-514-9166

Government Employees, American Federation of   www.afge.org
80 F St NW   Washington DC 20001
Ph: 202-737-8700 ▪ Fx: 202-639-6441

Government Employees, National Association of   www.nage.org
159 Burgin Pkwy   Quincy MA 02169
Ph: 617-376-0220 ▪ Fx: 617-376-0285

Government Environmental Professionals, National Association www.nalgep.org/
  of Local 1333 New Hampshire Ave NW Suite
  1100   Washington DC 20036
Ph: 202-638-6254 ▪ Fx: 202-393-2866

Government, Executive Women in   www.execwomeningov.org
PO Box 1046   Laurel MD 20725
Ph: 301-725-3500 ▪ Fx: 301-725-5323

Government Finance Officers Association   www.gfoa.org
203 N LaSalle St Suite 2700   Chicago IL 60601
Ph: 312-977-9700 ▪ Fx: 312-977-4806

Government Guaranteed Lenders, National Association of   www.naggl.com
424 S Squires Landing Blvd Suite 130   Stillwater OK 74074
Ph: 405-377-4022 ▪ Fx: 405-377-3931

Government Management Information Sciences   www.gmis.org
PO Box 421   Kennesaw GA 30156
Ph: 770-975-0729 ▪ Fx: 770-975-0719 ▪ TF: 800-460-7454

Government Meeting Professionals, Society of   www.sgmp.org
908 King St   Alexandria VA 22314
Ph: 703-549-0892 ▪ Fx: 703-549-0708 ▪ TF: 800-827-8916

Government, Nelson A Rockefeller Institute of   rockinst.org/
411 State St   Albany NY 12203
Ph: 518-443-5522 ▪ Fx: 518-443-5788

Government Oversight, Project on   www.pogo.org
666 11th St NW Suite 500   Washington DC 20001
Ph: 202-347-1122 ▪ Fx: 202-347-1116

Government Procurement, Coalition for   www.coalgovpro.org
1990 M St NW Suite 400   Washington DC 20036
Ph: 202-331-0975 ▪ Fx: 202-822-9788

Government & Public Affairs, Institute of   www.igpa.uiuc.edu
Univ of Illinois 1007 W Nevada St   Urbana IL 61801
Ph: 217-333-3340 ▪ Fx: 217-244-4817

Government Reform, Council for   www.govreform.org
3124 N 10th St   Arlington VA 22201
Ph: 703-243-7400 ▪ Fx: 703-243-7403

Government Relations, Women in   www.wgr.org
801 N Fairfax St Suite 211   Alexandria VA 22314
Ph: 703-299-8546 ▪ Fx: 703-299-9233

Government, Society for History in the Federal   www.shfg.org
PO Box 14139 Ben Franklin Stn   Washington DC 20044
Ph: 202-501-5350 ▪ Fx: 202-219-2176

Government Training & Development, National Association for
2516 Wertherson Ln   Raleigh NC 27613
Ph: 919-870-8496 ▪ Fx: 919-845-6922

Government Travel Professionals, Society of www.government-travel.org
6935 Wisconsin Ave Suite 200 Bethesda MD 20815
Ph: 301-654-8595 ▪ Fx: 301-654-6663

Government Waste, Citizens Against www.cagw.org
1301 Connecticut Ave NW Suite 400 Washington DC 20036
Ph: 202-467-5300 ▪ Fx: 202-467-4253 ▪ TF: 800-232-6479

Government, Women in www.womeningovernment.org
2600 Virginia Ave NW Suite 709 Washington DC 20037
Ph: 202-333-0825 ▪ Fx: 202-333-0875

Government, Women in Municipal
c/o National League of Cities 1301 Pennsylvania Ave NW Suite
550 Washington DC 20004
Ph: 202-626-3000 ▪ Fx: 202-626-3043

Governmental Ethics Laws, Council on www.cogel.org
PO Box 417 Locust Grove VA 22508
Ph: 540-972-3662 ▪ Fx: 540-972-3693

Governmental Financial Management, International Consortium on www.icgfm.org/
444 N Capitol St Suite 234 Washington DC 20001
Ph: 202-624-8461 ▪ Fx: 202-624-5473

Governmental Industrial Hygienists, American Conference of www.acgih.org
1330 Kemper Meadows Dr Cincinnati OH 45240
Ph: 513-742-2020 ▪ Fx: 513-742-3355

Governmental Labor Officials, National Association of www.naglo.org
c/o Council of State Governments 444 N Capitol St NW Suite
401 Washington DC 20001
Ph: 202-624-5460 ▪ Fx: 202-624-5452

Governmental Leasing & Finance, Association for www.aglf.org
1255 23rd St NW Suite 200 Washington DC 20037
Ph: 202-742-2453 ▪ Fx: 202-833-3636

Governmental Purchasing, National Institute of www.nigp.org
151 Spring St Suite 300 Herndon VA 20170
Ph: 703-736-8900 ▪ Fx: 703-736-9644 ▪ TF: 800-367-6447

Governmental Relations, Council on www.cogr.edu
1200 New York Ave NW Suite 320 Washington DC 20005
Ph: 202-289-6655 ▪ Fx: 202-289-6698

Governmental Research Association www.graonline.org
402 Samford Hall Birmingham AL 35229
Ph: 205-726-2482 ▪ Fx: 205-726-2900

Governments, Council of State www.csg.org
2760 Research Park Dr PO Box 11910 Lexington KY 40578
Ph: 859-244-8000 ▪ Fx: 859-244-8001 ▪ TF: 800-800-1910

Governors Association, Democratic www.democraticgovernors.org
499 S Capitol St SW Suite 422 Washington DC 20003
Ph: 202-772-5600 ▪ Fx: 202-772-5602

Governors Association, National www.nga.org
444 N Capitol St NW Hall of States Suite 267 Washington DC
20001
Ph: 202-624-5300 ▪ Fx: 202-624-5313

Governors' Association, Southern www.southerngovernors.org
444 N Capitol St NW Suite 200 Washington DC 20001
Ph: 202-624-5897 ▪ Fx: 202-624-7797

Governors Highway Safety Association www.statehighwaysafety.org
750 1st St NE Suite 720 Washington DC 20002
Ph: 202-789-0942 ▪ Fx: 202-789-0946

Grace Brethren Ministers, Association of www.fgbc.org
1909 Neal Dr Wooster OH 44691
Ph: 330-345-7826 ▪ Fx: 330-345-3348

Graduate Admissions Professionals, National Association of www.nagap.org
Iowa State Univ 10 Pearson Hall Ames IA 50011
Ph: 515-294-2682 ▪ Fx: 515-294-3003

Graduate Liberal Studies Programs, Association of www.udel.edu/aglsp
Univ of Delaware 219 McDowell Hall Newark DE 19716
Ph: 302-831-4218 ▪ Fx: 302-831-4461

Graduate Management Admission Council www.gmac.com
1600 Tyson Blvd Suite 1400 McLean VA 22102
Ph: 703-749-0131 ▪ Fx: 703-749-0169

Graduate-Professional Students, National Association of www.nagps.org
209 Pennsylvania Ave SE Washington DC 20003
Ph: 202-543-0812 ▪ Fx: 202-454-5298 ▪ TF: 888-886-2477

Graduate Record Examinations Board www.gre.org
Educational Testing Svc PO Box 6000 Princeton NJ 08541
Ph: 609-921-9000 ▪ Fx: 609-734-5410

Graduate Schools, Council of www.cgsnet.org
1 Dupont Cir NW Suite 430 Washington DC 20036
Ph: 202-223-3791 ▪ Fx: 202-331-7157

Graduate Study in Management, Consortium for www.cgsm.org
200 S Hanley Rd Suite 1102 Saint Louis MO 63105
Ph: 314-877-5500 ▪ Fx: 314-877-5505 ▪ TF: 888-658-6814

Graduate Women in Business www.gwib.org

Graduates, Jobs for America's www.jag.org
1729 King St Suite 200 Alexandria VA 22314
Ph: 703-684-9479 ▪ Fx: 703-684-9489

Graham Billy Evangelistic Association www.billygraham.org
PO Box 779 Minneapolis MN 55440
Ph: 612-338-0500 ▪ Fx: 612-335-1289 ▪ TF: 877-247-2426

Grail in the US The www.grail-us.org
932 O'Bannonville Rd Loveland OH 45140
Ph: 513-683-2340 ▪ Fx: 513-683-4752

Grain Association, North American Export
1250 I St NW Washington DC 20005
Ph: 202-682-4030 ▪ Fx: 202-682-4033

Grain Elevator & Processing Society www.geaps.com
301 4th Ave S Suite 365 PO Box 15026 Minneapolis MN
55415
Ph: 612-339-4625 ▪ Fx: 612-339-4644

Grain & Feed Association, National www.ngfa.org
1250 I St NW Suite 1003 Washington DC 20005
Ph: 202-289-0873 ▪ Fx: 202-289-5388

Grain & Feed Association, Pacific Northwest www.pnwgfa.org
200 SW Market St Suite 348 Portland OR 97201
Ph: 503-227-0234 ▪ Fx: 503-227-0059

Grain Millers International Union, Bakery Confectionery Tobacco www.bctgm.org
Workers & 10401 Connecticut Ave Kensington MD 20895
Ph: 301-933-8600 ▪ Fx: 301-946-8452

Grain Sorghum Producers, National www.sorghumgrowers.com
4201 N I-27 PO Box 5309 Lubbock TX 79408
Ph: 806-749-3478 ▪ Fx: 806-749-9002

Grain Trade Council, National ngtc.org
1300 L St NW Suite 1020 Washington DC 20005
Ph: 202-842-0400 ▪ Fx: 202-789-7223

Grains Council, US www.grains.org
1400 K St NW Suite 1200 Washington DC 20005
Ph: 202-789-0789 ▪ Fx: 202-898-0522

Grains Technology Council, Distillers www.distillersgrains.org
Lutz Hall Rm 435 Louisville KY 40292
Ph: 502-852-1575 ▪ Fx: 502-852-1577

Grand Aerie Fraternal Order of Eagles www.foe.com
1623 Gateway Cir S Grove City OH 43123
Ph: 614-883-2200 ▪ Fx: 614-883-2201

Grand Canyon Trust www.grandcanyontrust.org
2601 N Fort Valley Rd Flagstaff AZ 86001
Ph: 928-774-7488 ▪ Fx: 928-774-7570 ▪ TF: 888-428-5550

Grand Encampment of Knights Templar of the US www.knightstemplar.org
5097 N Elston Ave Suite 101 Chicago IL 60630
Ph: 773-777-3300 ▪ Fx: 773-777-8836

Grandmothers for Peace International www.grandmothersforpeace.org
PO Box 580788 Elk Grove CA 95758
Ph: 916-685-1130

Grandparent Information Center, AARP www.aarp.org/grandparents
601 'E' St NW Washington DC 20049
Ph: 202-434-2296

Grandparent Program Directors, National Association of Foster www.nafgpd.org
Foster Grandparent Program City Hall 4th Fl Kansas City MO
64106
Ph: 816-513-3221 ▪ Fx: 816-513-3212

Grandparent Program, Foster www.seniorcorps.org/joining/fgp
PO Box 70675 Washington DC 20024
Ph: 202-678-4215 ▪ Fx: 202-561-2414

Grandparenting Inc, Creative www.creativegrandparenting.org
100 W 10th St Suite 1007 Wilmington DE 19801
Ph: 302-656-2122 ▪ Fx: 302-656-2123

Grandparents Rights Organization www.grandparentsrights.org
100 W Long Lake Rd Suite 250 Bloomfield Hills MI 48304
Ph: 248-646-7177 ▪ Fx: 248-646-9722

Grandprix Association, American www.stadiumjumping.com/aga
1301 6th Ave W Suite 406 Bradenton FL 34205
Ph: 941-744-5465 ▪ Fx: 941-744-0874 ▪ TF: 800-237-8924

Grange, National www.grange.org
1616 H St NW Washington DC 20006
Ph: 202-628-3507 ▪ Fx: 202-347-1091 ▪ TF: 888-447-2643

Granite Association, Barre www.barregranite.org
51 Church St PO Box 481 Barre VT 05641
Ph: 802-476-4131 ▪ Fx: 802-476-4765

Granite Quarries Association, National Building www.nbgqa.com
1220 L St NW Suite 100-167 Washington DC 20005
Ph: 800-557-2848

Grant Ulysses S Association www.lib.siu.edu/projects/usgrant
Southern Illinois Univ Morris Library Carbondale IL 62901
Ph: 618-453-2773 ▪ Fx: 618-453-6119

Grantmakers for Children Youth & Families www.gcyf.org
1522 K St NW Suite 1100 Washington DC 20005
Ph: 202-962-3940 ▪ Fx: 202-393-4148

Grantmakers in Health www.gih.org
1100 Connecticut Ave NW Suite 1200 Washington DC 20036
Ph: 202-452-8331 ▪ Fx: 202-452-8340

Grantmakers, National Network of www.nng.org
138 Court St Suite 427 Brooklyn NY 11201
Ph: 718-643-8814 ▪ Fx: 718-643-8817

Grants Management Association, National www.ngma-grants.org
11654 Plaza America Dr Suite 609 Reston VA 20190
Ph: 703-648-9023 ▪ Fx: 703-648-9024

Grantsmanship Center www.tgci.com
PO Box 17220 Los Angeles CA 90017
Ph: 213-482-9860 ▪ Fx: 213-482-9863

Granulomatous Disease Association, Chronic home.socal.rr.com/cgda
2616 Monterey Rd San Marino CA 91108
Ph: 626-441-4118

Grape Association, Concord www.concordgrape.org
5775 Peachtree-Dunwoody Rd Bldg G Suite 500 Atlanta GA
30342
Ph: 404-252-3663 ▪ Fx: 404-252-0774

Grape Commission, California Table www.tablegrape.com
392 W Fallbrook Ave Suite 101 Fresno CA 93711
Ph: 559-447-8350 ▪ Fx: 559-447-9180

Grape Foundation, New York Wine & www.newyorkwines.org
350 Elm St Penn Yan NY 14527
Ph: 315-536-7442 ▪ Fx: 315-536-0719

Grape Growers Association, Napa Valley www.napagrowers.org
811 Jefferson St Napa CA 94559
Ph: 707-944-8311 ▪ Fx: 707-224-7836

Grape Growers Association, Sonoma County www.scgga.org
PO Box 1959 Sebastopol CA 95473
Ph: 707-829-3963

Graphic Artists Guild Inc www.gag.org
90 John St Suite 403 New York NY 10038
Ph: 212-791-3400 ▪ Fx: 212-791-0333

Graphic Artists, Society of American www.clt.astate.edu/elind/sagamain.htm
32 Union Sq Rm 214 New York NY 10003
Ph: 212-260-5706

Graphic Arts, American Institute of   www.aiga.org
164 5th Ave   New York NY 10010
Ph: 212-807-1990 ▪ Fx: 212-807-1799 ▪ TF: 800-548-1634

(Graphic Arts) Digital Distribution of Advertising for   www.ddap.org
Publications Association   PO Box 175   Marblehead MA
01945
Ph: 781-639-7785 ▪ Fx: 781-639-7786

Graphic Arts Education Association, International   www.igaea.org
1899 Preston White Dr   Reston VA 20191
Ph: 703-758-0595

Graphic Arts Employers of America
100 Daingerfield Rd   Alexandria VA 22314
Ph: 703-519-8100 ▪ Fx: 703-548-3227

Graphic Arts Industry, Research & Engineering Council of the   www.recouncil.org
PO Box 1086   White Stone VA 22578
Ph: 804-436-9922 ▪ Fx: 804-436-9511

(Graphic Arts Marketing) Graphic Arts Marketing Information Service   www.gamis.org
100 Daingerfield Rd   Alexandria VA 22314
Ph: 703-519-8179 ▪ Fx: 703-548-3227

Graphic Arts Marketing Information Service   www.gamis.org
100 Daingerfield Rd   Alexandria VA 22314
Ph: 703-519-8179 ▪ Fx: 703-548-3227

Graphic Arts Sales Foundation
113 E Evans St   West Chester PA 19380
Ph: 610-431-9780 ▪ Fx: 610-436-5238

Graphic Arts Suppliers Association, North American   www.nagasa.org
1604 New Hampshire Ave NW   Washington DC 20009
Ph: 202-328-8441 ▪ Fx: 202-328-8513

Graphic Arts, Technical Association of the   www.taga.org
68 Lomb Memorial Dr   Rochester NY 14623
Ph: 585-475-7470 ▪ Fx: 585-475-2250

Graphic Arts Technical Foundation   www.gain.net
200 Deer Run Rd   Sewickley PA 15143
Ph: 412-741-6860 ▪ Fx: 412-741-2311 ▪ TF: 800-910-4283

Graphic Arts Training, Association for   www.agatweb.org

Graphic Communications, Association of   www.agcomm.org
330 7th Ave 9th Fl   New York NY 10001
Ph: 212-279-2100 ▪ Fx: 212-279-5381

Graphic Communications International Union   www.gciu.org
1900 L St NW 9th Fl   Washington DC 20036
Ph: 202-462-1400 ▪ Fx: 202-721-0600

Graphic Design, Society for Environmental   www.segd.org
1000 Vermont Ave Suite 400   Washington DC 20005
Ph: 202-638-5555 ▪ Fx: 202-638-0891

Graphic Imaging Association, Specialty   www.sgia.org
10015 Main St   Fairfax VA 22031
Ph: 703-385-1335 ▪ Fx: 703-273-0456

(Graphic Installation) United Applications Standards Group   www.uasg.org
PO Box 1435   Des Moines IA 50305
Ph: 515-289-4467 ▪ Fx: 515-289-4468

Graphic & Product Identification Manufacturers Inc,   www.gpiweb.org
National Association of   PO Box 15466   Santa Ana CA 92735
Ph: 714-508-4915 ▪ Fx: 714-508-4904

Graphic Products Association   www.graphicspro.org
4709 N El Capitan Ave Suite 103   Fresno CA 93722
Ph: 559-276-8494 ▪ Fx: 559-276-8496 ▪ TF: 800-276-8428

Graphics Association, Banner Flag &   www.bannerflag.com
1801 County Rd 'B' W   Roseville MN 55113
Ph: 651-222-2508 ▪ Fx: 651-631-9334 ▪ TF: 800-225-4324

Graphics Association, International Engraved   www.iega.org
305 Plus Park Blvd   Nashville TN 37217
Ph: 615-366-1094 ▪ Fx: 615-366-4192 ▪ TF: 800-821-3138

Graphics, Center for the Study of Political   www.politicalgraphics.org
8124 W 3rd St Suite 211   Los Angeles CA 90048
Ph: 323-653-4662 ▪ Fx: 323-653-6991

Graphics & Imaging Systems, Association for Engineering
800 Enterprise Dr Suite 202   Oak Brook IL 60523
Ph: 630-574-8200 ▪ Fx: 630-571-4731

Graphoanalysis Society, International   www.igas.com
111 N Canal St Suite 399   Chicago IL 60606
Ph: 312-930-9446 ▪ Fx: 312-930-5903

Graphological Society, International
PO Box 793743   Dallas TX 75379
Ph: 214-351-3668 ▪ TF: 800-960-1034

Graphology, National Society for
250 W 57th St Suite 1228A   New York NY 10107
Ph: 212-265-1148 ▪ Fx: 212-307-5671

Grassland Council, American Forage &   www.afgc.org
PO Box 94   Georgetown TX 78627
Ph: 512-868-2899 ▪ Fx: 512-931-1166 ▪ TF: 800-944-2342

Grassland Heritage Foundation   www.grasslandheritage.org
PO Box 394   Shawnee Mission KS 66201
Ph: 913-262-3506

Grassroots International   www.grassrootsonline.org
179 Boylston St 4th Fl   Boston MA 02130
Ph: 617-524-1400 ▪ Fx: 617-524-5525

Gravel Association, National Stone Sand &   www.nssga.org
1605 King St   Alexandria VA 22314
Ph: 703-525-8788 ▪ Fx: 703-525-7782 ▪ TF: 800-342-1415

Graves' Disease Foundation, National   www.ngdf.org
PO Box 1969   Brevard NC 28712
Ph: 828-877-5251

Gravestone Studies, Association for   www.gravestonestudies.org
278 Main St Suite 207   Greenfield MA 01301
Ph: 413-772-0836

Gravure Association of America   www.gaa.org
1200-A Scottsville Rd   Rochester NY 14624
Ph: 585-436-2150 ▪ Fx: 585-436-7689

Gravure Education Foundation   www.gaa.org/GEF/index.htm
1200A Scottsville Rd   Rochester NY 14624
Ph: 716-436-2150 ▪ Fx: 716-436-7689

Gray Panthers   www.graypanthers.org
733 15th St NW Suite 437   Washington DC 20005
Ph: 202-737-6637 ▪ Fx: 202-737-1160 ▪ TF: 800-280-5362

Grease Institute, National Lubricating   www.nlgi.org
4635 Wyandotte St   Kansas City MO 64112
Ph: 816-931-9480 ▪ Fx: 816-753-5026

Great Bear Foundation   www.greatbear.org
802 E Front St PO Box 9383   Missoula MT 59807
Ph: 406-829-9378 ▪ Fx: 406-829-9371

Great Books Foundation   www.greatbooks.org
35 E Wacker Dr Suite 2300   Chicago IL 60601
Ph: 312-332-5870 ▪ Fx: 312-407-0334 ▪ TF: 800-222-5870

Great Lakes Booksellers Association   www.books-glba.org
208 Franklin St PO Box 901   Grand Haven MI 49417
Ph: 616-847-2460 ▪ Fx: 616-842-0051 ▪ TF: 800-745-2460

Great Lakes Colleges Association   www.glca.org
535 W William St Suite 301   Ann Arbor MI 48103
Ph: 734-761-4833 ▪ Fx: 734-761-3939

Great Lakes Commission   www.glc.org
2805 S Industrial Hwy Suite 100   Ann Arbor MI 48104
Ph: 734-971-9135 ▪ Fx: 734-971-9150

Great Lakes Historical Society   www.inlandseas.org
Inland Seas Maritime Museum 480 Main St   PO Box
435   Vermilion OH 44089
Ph: 440-967-3467 ▪ Fx: 440-967-1419 ▪ TF: 800-893-1485

Great Lakes Indian Fish & Wildlife Commission   www.glifwc.org
100 Maple St PO Box 9   Odanah WI 54861
Ph: 715-682-6619

Great Lakes Lighthouse Keepers Association   www.gllka.com
PO Box 219   Mackinaw City MI 49701
Ph: 231-436-5580 ▪ Fx: 231-436-5466

Great Lakes Maritime Institute Inc   www.glmi.org
100 Strand on Belle Isle   Detroit MI 48207
Ph: 313-852-4051

Great Lakes Research, International Association for   www.iaglr.org
2205 Commonwealth Blvd   Ann Arbor MI 48105
Ph: 734-665-5303 ▪ Fx: 734-741-2055

Great Lakes Sport Fishing Council   www.great-lakes.org
PO Box 297   Elmhurst IL 60126
Ph: 630-941-1351 ▪ Fx: 630-941-1196

Great Lakes United   www.glu.org
Buffalo State College Cassety Hall 1300 Elmwood Ave   Buffalo
NY 14222
Ph: 716-886-0142 ▪ Fx: 716-886-0303

Great Outdoors Conservancy   www.thegreatoutdoors.org
4311 Manatee Ave W Suite 210   Bradenton FL 34209
Ph: 941-708-3456 ▪ Fx: 941-708-3535

Great Plains, Institute of the   institutegreatplains.tripod.com
PO Box 68   Lawton OK 73502
Ph: 580-581-3460 ▪ Fx: 580-581-3458

Greater Blouse Skirt & Undergarment Association   www.greaterblouse.org
225 W 34th St Suite 612   New York NY 10122
Ph: 212-563-5052 ▪ Fx: 212-563-5373

Greater Independent Association of National Travel Services   www.giantstravel.com
2 Park Ave Suite 2205   New York NY 10016
Ph: 212-545-7460 ▪ Fx: 212-545-7428 ▪ TF: 800-442-6871

Greater Yellowstone Coalition   www.greateryellowstone.org
13 S Willson Ave Suite 2   Bozeman MT 59771
Ph: 406-586-1593 ▪ Fx: 406-556-2839

(Greece) Chian Federation of America   www.chianfed.org
44-01 Broadway   Astoria NY 11103
Ph: 718-204-2550 ▪ Fx: 718-278-6199

(Greece) Hellenic-American Chamber of Commerce   www.hellenicamerican.cc
960 Ave of the Americas 9th Fl   New York NY 10001
Ph: 212-629-6380 ▪ Fx: 212-564-9281

Greek Catholic Union of the USA   www.gcuusa.org
5400 Tuscarawas Rd   Beaver PA 15009
Ph: 724-495-3400 ▪ Fx: 724-495-3421 ▪ TF: 800-722-4428

Greek Food & Wine Institute
34-80 48th St   Long Island City NY 11101
Ph: 718-729-5277 ▪ Fx: 718-361-9725

Greek Orthodox Archdiocese of America   www.goarch.org
8 E 79th St   New York NY 10021
Ph: 212-570-3500 ▪ Fx: 212-570-3569

Greek Orthodox Ladies Philoptochos Society   www.philoptochos.org
345 E 74th St   New York NY 10021
Ph: 212-744-4390 ▪ Fx: 212-861-1956

Greek Philosophy, International Association for   www.hri.org/iagp

Greek Philosophy, Society for Ancient   sagp.binghamton.edu
Binghamton Univ Dept of Philosophy   Binghamton NY 13902
Ph: 607-777-2886 ▪ Fx: 607-777-2734

Greek Studies Association, Modern   www.humanities.uci.edu/classics/MGSA
PO Box 1826   New Haven CT 06508
Ph: 203-392-5668 ▪ Fx: 203-392-5670

Green Building Council, US   www.usgbc.org
1015 18th St NW Suite 805   Washington DC 20036
Ph: 202-828-7422 ▪ Fx: 202-828-5110

Green Hotels Association   www.greenhotels.com
PO Box 420212   Houston TX 77242
Ph: 713-789-8889 ▪ Fx: 713-789-9786

Green Seal   www.greenseal.org
1001 Connecticut Ave NW Suite 827   Washington DC 20036
Ph: 202-872-6400 ▪ Fx: 202-872-4324

Greenhouse Association, Hobby   www.hobbygreenhouse.org
8 Glen Terr   Bedford MA 01730
Ph: 781-275-0377

Greenhouse Manufacturers Association, National www.ngma.com
20 W Dry Creek Cir Suite 110   Littleton CO 80120
Ph: 303-798-1338 ▪ Fx: 303-798-1332 ▪ TF: 800-792-6462

Greening Earth Society www.greeningearthsociety.org
333 John Carlyle St Suite 530   Alexandria VA 22314
Ph: 703-684-4748 ▪ Fx: 703-684-6297 ▪ TF: 800-529-4503

Greenpeace Canada www.greenpeace.ca
250 Dundas St W Suite 605   Toronto ON M5T2Z5
Ph: 416-597-8408 ▪ Fx: 416-597-8422 ▪ TF: 800-320-7183

Greenpeace USA www.greenpeace.org
702 H St NW Suite 300   Washington DC 20001
Ph: 202-462-1177 ▪ Fx: 202-462-4507 ▪ TF: 800-326-0959

Greens/Green Party USA www.greenparty.org
PO Box 1406   Chicago IL 60690
Ph: 708-524-1741 ▪ Fx: 708-524-1742 ▪ TF: 866-473-3672

Greeting Card Association www.greetingcard.org
1156 15th St NW Suite 900   Washington DC 20005
Ph: 202-393-1778 ▪ Fx: 202-331-2714

Greyhound Adoption Center www.greyhoundog.org
PO Box 2433   La Mesa CA 91943
Ph: 619-443-0940 ▪ Fx: 619-443-0130 ▪ TF: 877-478-8364

Greyhound Adoption Program, National www.ngap.org
4701 Bath St   Philadelphia PA 19137
Ph: 215-331-7918 ▪ Fx: 215-331-1947 ▪ TF: 800-348-2517

Greyhound Alliance, American-European www.ameurogreyhoundalliance.org/start.html
167 Saddle Hill Rd   Hopkinton MA 01748
Ph: 508-435-5969

Greyhound Association, National www.ngagreyhounds.com
PO Box 543   Abilene KS 67410
Ph: 785-263-4660 ▪ Fx: 785-263-4689

Greyhound Friends Inc www.greyhound.org
167 Saddle Hill Rd   Hopkinton MA 01748
Ph: 508-435-5969 ▪ Fx: 508-435-0547

Greyhound Track Operators Association, American www.agtoa.com
Melbourne Greyhound Park 1100 N Wickham Rd   Melbourne
FL 32935
Ph: 321-259-1143 ▪ Fx: 321-259-3437

Grid Flooring Manufacturers Association, Bridge www.abcdpittsburgh.org/BGFMA.htm
201 Castle Dr   West Mifflin PA 15122
Ph: 412-469-3985

Gridiron Club of Washington DC www.gridironclub.org
1001 16th St NW Rm 402   Washington DC 20036
Ph: 202-639-5480

(Grief) Compassionate Friends www.compassionatefriends.com
PO Box 3696   Oak Brook IL 60522
Ph: 630-990-0010 ▪ Fx: 630-990-0246 ▪ TF: 877-969-0010

Grinding Association, International Grooving & www.igga.net
126 Mansion St PO Box 58   Coxsackie NY 12051
Ph: 518-731-7450 ▪ Fx: 518-731-7490

Grocers of America, Women www.nationalgrocers.org/WGA.html
1005 N Glebe Rd Suite 250   Arlington VA 22201
Ph: 703-516-0700 ▪ Fx: 703-516-0115

Grocers Association, Mexican American
405 N San Fernando Rd   Los Angeles CA 90031
Ph: 323-227-1565 ▪ Fx: 323-227-6935

Grocers Association, National www.nationalgrocers.org
1005 N Glebe Rd Suite 250   Arlington VA 22201
Ph: 703-516-0700 ▪ Fx: 703-516-0115

Grocery Manufacturers of America www.gmabrands.com
2401 Pennsylvania Ave NW 2nd Fl   Washington DC 20037
Ph: 202-337-9400 ▪ Fx: 202-337-4508

Grocery Manufacturers of America PAC
2401 Pennsylvania Ave NW Suite 200   Washington DC 20037
Ph: 202-337-9400 ▪ Fx: 202-337-4508

Grolier Club of New York www.grolierclub.org
47 E 60th St   New York NY 10022
Ph: 212-838-6690 ▪ Fx: 212-838-2445

Groomers Association of America Inc, National Dog www.nationaldoggroomers.com
PO Box 101   Clark PA 16113
Ph: 724-962-2711 ▪ Fx: 724-962-1919

Groomers, International Professional www.ipgcmg.org
120 Turner Ave   Elk Grove Village IL 60007
Ph: 847-758-1938 ▪ Fx: 847-758-8031

Grooving & Grinding Association, International www.igga.net
126 Mansion St PO Box 58   Coxsackie NY 12051
Ph: 518-731-7450 ▪ Fx: 518-731-7490

Grottoes of North America www.scgrotto.com
1696 Brice Rd   Reynoldsburg OH 43068
Ph: 614-860-9193 ▪ Fx: 614-860-9099

Ground Source Heat Pump Association, International www.igshpa.okstate.edu
Oklahoma State University 499 Cordell S   Stillwater OK 74078
Ph: 405-744-5175 ▪ Fx: 405-744-5283 ▪ TF: 800-626-4747

Ground Transportation Association, Airport www.agtaweb.org
UMSL Ctr for Transportation Studies 154 University Ctr 8001
Natural Bridge Rd   Saint Louis MO 63121
Ph: 314-516-7271 ▪ Fx: 314-516-7272

Ground Water Association, National www.ngwa.org
601 Dempsey Rd   Westerville OH 43081
Ph: 614-898-7791 ▪ Fx: 614-898-7786 ▪ TF: 800-551-7379

Ground Water Protection Council www.gwpc.org
13208 N MacArthur Blvd   Oklahoma City OK 73142
Ph: 405-516-4972 ▪ Fx: 405-516-4973

Ground Water Trust, American www.agwt.org
16 Centre St   Concord NH 03301
Ph: 603-228-5444 ▪ Fx: 603-228-6557 ▪ TF: 800-423-7748

Grounds Management, National Institute on Park & www.nipgm.org
PO Box 5162   De Pere WI 54115
Ph: 920-339-9057

Grounds Management Society, Professional www.pgms.org
720 Light St   Baltimore MD 21230
Ph: 410-223-2861 ▪ Fx: 410-752-8295 ▪ TF: 800-609-7467

Groundwater Foundation www.groundwater.org
PO Box 22558   Lincoln NE 68542
Ph: 402-434-2740 ▪ Fx: 402-434-2742 ▪ TF: 800-858-4844

Group Harmony Association, United in www.ugha.org
PO Box 185   Clifton NJ 07011
Ph: 973-365-0049

Group Work, Association for Specialists in www.asgw.org
Texas A&M Commerce Dept of Counseling 202 Education
N   Commerce TX 75429
Ph: 903-886-5630 ▪ Fx: 903-886-5780

Growers Association, Monterey County Vintners & www.montereywines.org
Box 1793   Monterey CA 93942
Ph: 831-375-9400 ▪ Fx: 831-375-1116

Growers Association, Napa Valley Grape www.napagrowers.org
811 Jefferson St   Napa CA 94559
Ph: 707-944-8311 ▪ Fx: 707-224-7836

Growers Association, National Ornamental Goldfish
6916 Blacks Mill Rd   Thurmont MD 21788
Ph: 301-271-7475 ▪ Fx: 301-271-7059

Growers & Industries Foundation, National Cherry www.usacherries.com
PO Box 30285   Lansing MI 48909
Ph: 517-669-4264 ▪ Fx: 517-669-3354

Growing Companies, Council of
PO Box 10863   McLean VA 22102
Ph: 703-893-5343 ▪ Fx: 703-893-5222 ▪ TF: 800-929-3165

Growth Foundation, Human www.hgfound.org
997 Glen Cove Ave   Glen Head NY 11545
Ph: 516-671-4041 ▪ Fx: 516-671-4055 ▪ TF: 800-451-6434

Grupo de Artistas Latino Americanos
21 W 112th St Unit 9J   New York NY 10026
Ph: 212-369-3401 ▪ Fx: 212-480-9734

Gruppo Esponenti Italiani www.gei-ny.com
60 E 42nd St Suite 1341, PO Box 789   New York NY 10150
Ph: 212-867-2772 ▪ Fx: 212-867-4114

Guaranty Insurers, Association of Financial www.afgi.org
c/o TowersGroup 15 W 39th St 14th Fl   New York NY 10018
Ph: 212-354-5020 ▪ Fx: 212-391-6920

Guard Association of the US Inc, State www.sgaus.org
PO Box 1416   Fayetteville GA 30214
Ph: 770-460-1215

Guard & Reserve, National Committee for Employer Support of the www.esgr.org
1555 Wilson Blvd Suite 200   Arlington VA 22209
Ph: 703-696-1386 ▪ Fx: 703-696-1411 ▪ TF: 800-336-4590

Guardian Angels, Alliance of www.guardianangels.org
982 E 89th St   Brooklyn NY 11236
Ph: 212-397-7822

Guardianship Association, National www.guardianship.org
1604 N Country Club Rd   Tucson AZ 85716
Ph: 520-881-6561 ▪ Fx: 520-325-7925

Guards Union of America, International www.amaonline.com/igua
Rt 8 Box 32-14   Amarillo TX 79118
Ph: 806-622-2424 ▪ Fx: 806-622-3500

Guatemala, Network in Solidarity with the People of www.nisgua.org
1830 Connecticut Ave NW   Washington DC 20009
Ph: 202-518-7638 ▪ Fx: 202-223-8221

Guernsey Association, American www.usguernsey.com
7614 Slate Ridge Blvd PO Box 666   Reynoldsburg OH 43068
Ph: 614-864-2409 ▪ Fx: 614-864-5614

Guest Ranch Association, Colorado Dude & www.coloradoranch.com
PO Box 2120   Granby CO 80446
Ph: 970-887-3128 ▪ Fx: 970-887-1229

Guggenheim John Simon Memorial Foundation www.gf.org
90 Park Ave 33rd Fl   New York NY 10016
Ph: 212-687-4470 ▪ Fx: 212-697-3248

Guide Dog Foundation for the Blind Inc www.guidedog.org
371 E Jericho Tkpe   Smithtown NY 11787
Ph: 631-265-2121 ▪ Fx: 631-361-5192 ▪ TF: 800-548-4337

Guide Dog Foundation, Fidelco www.fidelco.org
PO Box 142   Bloomfield CT 06002
Ph: 860-243-5200 ▪ Fx: 860-243-7215

Guide Dog Users Inc www.gdui.org
57 Grandview Ave   Watertown MA 02472
Ph: 617-926-9198 ▪ Fx: 617-923-0004 ▪ TF: 888-858-1008

Guide Dogs of America www.guidedogsofamerica.org
13445 Glenoaks Blvd   Sylmar CA 91342
Ph: 818-362-5834 ▪ Fx: 818-362-6870 ▪ TF: 800-459-4843

Guide Dogs for the Blind www.guidedogs.com
PO Box 151200   San Rafael CA 94915
Ph: 415-499-4000 ▪ Fx: 415-499-4035 ▪ TF: 800-295-4050

Guiding Eyes for the Blind guidingeyes.org
611 Granite Springs Rd   Yorktown Heights NY 10598
Ph: 914-245-4024 ▪ Fx: 914-245-1609 ▪ TF: 800-942-0149

Guild of American Luthiers www.luth.org
8222 South Park Ave   Tacoma WA 98408
Ph: 253-472-7853

Guild of American Papercutters www.papercutters.org

Guild of Book Workers
521 5th Ave 17th Fl   New York NY 10175
Ph: 212-292-4444

Guild of Italian American Actors www.nygiaa.org
31 E 32nd St 12th Fl   New York NY 10016
Ph: 212-420-6590

Guild of Natural Science Illustrators www.gnsi.org
PO Box 652   Washington DC 20044
Ph: 301-309-1514

Guillain-Barre Syndrome Foundation International www.guillain-barre.com
PO Box 262   Wynnewood PA 19096
Ph: 610-667-0131 ▪ Fx: 610-667-7036

Guinea Development Foundation www.guineadev.org
140 West End Ave Suite 17G   New York NY 10023
Ph: 212-874-2911 ■ Fx: 212-496-9549

Guitar & Accessories Marketing Association www.discoverguitar.com
PO Box 5488   Long Island City NY 11105
Ph: 718-274-3210 ■ Fx: 718-274-3214

Guitar Association, Pedal Steel www.psga.org
PO Box 20248   Floral Park NY 11002
Ph: 516-616-9214

Guitar Foundation of America www.guitarfoundation.org
PO Box 1240   Claremont CA 91711
Ph: 909-624-7730 ■ Fx: 909-624-1151

Gum Manufacturers, National Association of Chewing www.nacgm.com
17000 Commerce Pkwy Suite C   Mount Laurel NJ 08054
Ph: 856-439-0500 ■ Fx: 856-439-0525

(Gun Control) Million Mom March www.millionmommarch.org
c/o Brady Campaign to Prevent Gun Violence 1225 'I' St NW
Suite 1100   Washington DC 20005
Ph: 202-898-0792 ■ Fx: 202-371-9615

Gun Owners of America www.gunowners.org
8001 Forbes Pl Suite 102   Springfield VA 22151
Ph: 703-321-8585 ■ Fx: 703-321-8408

Gun Safety, Americans for www.americansforgunsafety.com
2000 L St NW Suite 702   Washington DC 20036
Ph: 202-775-0300 ■ Fx: 202-775-0430

Gun Violence, Brady Campaign to Prevent www.bradycampaign.org
1225 'I' St NW Suite 1100   Washington DC 20005
Ph: 202-898-0792 ■ Fx: 202-371-9615

Gun Violence, Brady Center to Prevent www.bradycenter.org
1225 'I' St NW Suite 1100   Washington DC 20005
Ph: 202-289-7319 ■ Fx: 202-408-1851

Gun Violence, Coalition to Stop www.csgv.org
1023 15th St NW Suite 600   Washington DC 20005
Ph: 202-408-0061 ■ Fx: 202-408-0062

Gungywamp Society www.gungywamp.com
PO Box 592   Colchester CT 06415
Ph: 860-537-2811

Gunmakers Guild, American Custom www.acgg.org
22 Vista View Dr   Cody WY 82414
Ph: 307-587-4297

Guns, Common Sense About Kids & www.kidsandguns.org
418 C St NE   Washington DC 20002
Ph: 202-546-0200 ■ Fx: 202-546-6250 ■ TF: 877-955-5437

Guttmacher Alan Institute www.agi-usa.org
120 Wall St 21st Fl   New York NY 10005
Ph: 212-248-1111 ■ Fx: 212-248-1951

Gymnastic Clubs Inc, US Association of Independent www.usaigc.com
22 River Terr Suite 20D   New York NY 10282
Ph: 212-227-9792 ■ Fx: 212-227-9793 ■ TF: 800-480-0201

(Gymnastics) American Sokol www.american-sokol.org
122 W 22nd St   Oak Brook IL 60523
Ph: 630-368-0771 ■ Fx: 630-368-0758

Gymnastics Association, College tigger.uic.edu/~cjgym
52 Evelyn Rd   Needham MA 02494
Ph: 781-444-3893 ■ Fx: 781-455-0782

Gymnastics Judges Association, National www.ngja.org
719 Anthony Ln   Lincoln NE 68520
Ph: 402-483-7436 ■ Fx: 402-472-4305

Gymnastics, USA www.usa-gymnastics.org
201 S Capitol Ave Suite 300   Indianapolis IN 46225
Ph: 317-237-5050 ■ Fx: 317-237-5069 ■ TF: 800-345-4719

Gynecologic Cancer Foundation www.wcn.org/gcf
230 W Monroe St Suite 2528   Chicago IL 60606
Ph: 312-578-1439 ■ Fx: 312-578-9769

Gynecologic Investigation, Society for www.sgionline.org
409 12th St SW   Washington DC 20024
Ph: 202-863-2544 ■ Fx: 202-863-0739

Gynecologic Oncologists, Society of www.sgo.org
401 N Michigan Ave   Chicago IL 60611
Ph: 312-644-6610 ■ Fx: 312-527-6959

Gynecologic Oncology Group www.gog.org
1600 JFK Blvd Suite 1020   Philadelphia PA 19103
Ph: 215-854-0770 ■ Fx: 215-854-0716 ■ TF: 800-225-3053

Gynecologic Surgery Society www.gynecologicsurgerysociety.org
2440 M St NW Suite 801   Washington DC 20037
Ph: 202-293-2046 ■ Fx: 202-778-6195

Gynecological Laparoscopists, American Association of www.aagl.com
13021 E Florence Ave   Santa Fe Springs CA 90670
Ph: 562-946-8774 ■ Fx: 562-946-0073 ■ TF: 800-554-2245

Gynecologists, American College of Obstetricians & www.acog.com
409 12th St SW PO Box 96920   Washington DC 20090
Ph: 202-638-5577 ■ Fx: 202-863-4284

Gynecologists, American College of Osteopathic Obstetricians & www.acoog.com
900 Auburn Rd   Pontiac MI 48342
Ph: 248-332-6360 ■ Fx: 248-332-4607 ■ TF: 800-875-6360

Gynecology, American Board of Obstetrics & www.abog.org
2915 Vine St   Dallas TX 75204
Ph: 214-871-1619 ■ Fx: 214-871-1943

Gynecology, Association of Physician Assistants in Obstetrics &
PO Box 1109   Madison WI 53701
Ph: 800-545-0636

Gynecology & Obstetrics, Association of Professors of www.apgo.org
2130 Priest Bridge Dr Suite 7   Crofton MD 21114
Ph: 410-451-9560 ■ Fx: 410-451-9568

Gypsum Association www.gypsum.org
810 1st St NE Suite 510   Washington DC 20002
Ph: 202-289-5440 ■ Fx: 202-289-3707

Gypsy Lore Society www.gypsyloresociety.org
5607 Greenleaf Rd   Cheverly MD 20785
Ph: 301-341-1261

Gyro International www.gyro-international.org
1019 Mentor Ave PO Box 489   Painesville OH 44077
Ph: 440-352-2501 ■ Fx: 440-352-3882

H

Haas Evelyn & Walter Jr Fund www.haasjr.org
1 Market St Suite 400   San Francisco CA 94105
Ph: 415-856-1400 ■ Fx: 415-856-1500

Haas Walter & Elise Fund www.haassr.org
1 Market St Suite 400   San Francisco CA 94105
Ph: 415-856-1400 ■ Fx: 415-856-1500

Habitat for Humanity International Inc www.habitat.org
121 Habitat St   Americus GA 31709
Ph: 229-924-6935 ■ Fx: 229-924-6541 ■ TF: 800-422-4828

Habitat Organization, Native www.nativehabitat.org/
PO Box 101071   Fort Worth TX 76185
Ph: 817-396-4370

Hackney Horse Society, American www.hackneysociety.com
4059 Iron Works Pkwy Suite 3   Lexington KY 40511
Ph: 859-255-8694 ■ Fx: 859-255-0177

Hadassah Women's Zionist Organization of America Inc www.hadassah.org
50 W 58th St   New York NY 10019
Ph: 212-355-7900 ■ Fx: 212-303-8282 ■ TF: 888-303-3640

Haemostasis, International Society on Thrombosis & www.med.unc.edu/isth
UNC Medical School CB 7035   Chapel Hill NC 27599
Ph: 919-929-3807 ■ Fx: 919-929-3935

Haflinger Breeders Organization Inc www.stallionstation.com/hbo/hbo.html
14640 State Rt 83   Coshocton OH 43812
Ph: 740-829-2790 ■ Fx: 740-829-2322

Haflinger Registry, American www.haflingerhorse.com
2746 State Rt 44   Rootstown OH 44272
Ph: 330-325-8116 ■ Fx: 330-325-8178

Hair Loss Council, American www.ahlc.org
125 7th St Suite 625   Pittsburgh PA 15222
Ph: 412-765-3666 ■ Fx: 412-765-3669

Hair Removal Inc, Society for Clinical & Medical www.scmhr.org
7600 Terrace Ave Suite 203   Middleton WI 53562
Ph: 608-831-8009 ■ Fx: 608-831-5122

Hair Restoration Surgery, American Society of www.cosmeticsurgery.org
737 N Michigan Ave Suite 820   Chicago IL 60611
Ph: 312-981-6760 ■ Fx: 312-981-6787

Hair Restoration Surgery, International Society of www.ishrs.org
13 S 2nd St   Geneva IL 60134
Ph: 630-262-5399 ■ Fx: 630-262-1520 ■ TF: 800-444-2737

Hairenik Association Inc www.hairenik.com
80 Bigelow Ave   Watertown MA 02472
Ph: 617-926-3974 ■ Fx: 617-926-1750

Haiti Philatelic Society www.haitiphilately.org
5709 Marble Arch Way   Alexandria VA 22315
Ph: 703-922-9531

Haitian Centers Council Inc www.haitiancenterscouncil.org
50 Court St Suite 1010   Brooklyn NY 11201
Ph: 718-855-7275 ■ Fx: 718-852-5377

Haitian Rights, National Coalition for www.nchr.org
275 7th Ave 17th Fl   New York NY 10001
Ph: 212-337-0005 ■ Fx: 212-741-8749

Hajji Baba Society, International
2106 Woodmont Rd   Alexandria VA 22307
Ph: 703-960-0343 ■ Fx: 703-683-7545

Hakluyt Society, American Friends of the www.hakluyt.com/hak-soc-amer-top.htm
John Carter Brown Library PO Box 1894   Providence RI 02912
Ph: 401-863-2725 ■ Fx: 401-863-3477

Half Saddlebred Registry of America www.saddlebred.com/halfsaddlebred
4093 Iron Works Pkwy   Lexington KY 40511
Ph: 859-259-2742 ■ Fx: 859-259-1628

Halfway House Alcoholism Programs of North America Inc, Association of www.ahhap.org
860 N Center St   Mesa AZ 85201
Ph: 480-610-8300 ■ Fx: 480-964-2004 ■ TF: 800-861-0599

Halibut Commission, International Pacific www.iphc.washington.edu
PO Box 95009   Seattle WA 98145
Ph: 206-634-1838 ■ Fx: 206-632-2983

Hall Family Foundation
2501 McGee St MD 323   Kansas City MO 64108
Ph: 816-274-8516 ■ Fx: 816-274-8547

Halls of Fame, International Association of Sports Museums & www.sportshalls.com
180 N LaSalle St Suite 1822   Chicago IL 60601
Ph: 312-551-0810 ■ Fx: 312-551-0815

HALT Inc www.halt.org
1612 K St NW Suite 510   Washington DC 20006
Ph: 202-887-8255 ■ Fx: 202-887-9699 ■ TF: 888-367-4258

(Ham Radio) ARRL Foundation Inc www.arrl.org/arrlf
225 Main St   Newington CT 06111
Ph: 860-594-0230

Hampshire Sheep Association, American www.countrylovin.com/ahsa/
15603 173rd Ave   Milo IA 50166
Ph: 641-942-6402 ■ Fx: 641-942-6502

Hand, American Society for Surgery of the www.assh.org
6300 N River Rd Suite 600   Rosemont IL 60018
Ph: 847-384-8300 ■ Fx: 847-384-1435 ■ TF: 888-576-2774

Hand, International Federation of Societies for Surgery of the
Duke University Medical Ctr PO Box 2912   Durham NC 27710
Ph: 919-684-5388 ■ Fx: 919-681-7378

Hand Surgery, American Association for www.handsurgery.org
20 N Michigan Ave Suite 700   Chicago IL 60602
Ph: 312-236-3307 ■ Fx: 312-782-0553

Hand Therapists, American Society of www.asht.org
401 N Michigan Ave Suite 2200   Chicago IL 60611
Ph: 312-321-6866 ■ Fx: 312-673-6670

Hand Tools Institute
25 N Broadway   Tarrytown NY 10591
Ph: 914-332-0040 ▪ Fx: 914-332-1541
www.hti.org

Handball Association, US
2333 N Tucson Blvd   Tucson AZ 85716
Ph: 520-795-0434 ▪ Fx: 520-795-0465
ushandball.org

Handball, USA Team
1 Olympic Plaza   Colorado Springs CO 80909
Ph: 719-866-4036 ▪ Fx: 719-866-4055
www.usateamhandball.org

Handbell Ringers Inc, American Guild of English
1055 E Centerville Stn Rd   Centerville OH 45459
Ph: 937-438-0085 ▪ Fx: 937-438-0434 ▪ TF: 800-878-5459
www.agehr.org

Handel Society, American
Univ of Maryland School of Music   College Park MD 20742
Ph: 301-581-9602
www.americanhandelsociety.org

Handgun Metallic Silhouette Association, International
PO Box 9   Anoka MN 55303
Ph: 763-323-3359 ▪ Fx: 763-422-1910
www.ihmsa.org

Handicapped, Adventures in Movement for the
945 Danbury Rd   Dayton OH 45420
Ph: 937-294-4611 ▪ Fx: 937-294-3783 ▪ TF: 800-332-8210
www.aimforthehandicapped.org

Handicapped Association, North American Riding for the
PO Box 33150   Denver CO 80233
Ph: 303-452-1212 ▪ Fx: 303-252-4610 ▪ TF: 800-369-7433
www.narha.org

Handicapped, Disabled & Alone/Life Services for the
352 Park Ave S 11th Fl   New York NY 10010
Ph: 212-532-6740 ▪ Fx: 212-532-3588 ▪ TF: 800-995-0066
www.disabledandalone.org

Handicapped, National Association for Visually
22 W 21st St 6th Fl   New York NY 10010
Ph: 212-889-3141 ▪ Fx: 212-727-2931
www.navh.org

Handicapped, National Foundation of Dentistry for the
1800 15th St Unit 100   Denver CO 80202
Ph: 303-534-5360 ▪ Fx: 303-534-5290 ▪ TF: 888-471-6334
www.nfdh.org

Handicapped, National Theatre Workshop of the
535 Greenwich St   New York NY 10013
Ph: 212-206-7789 ▪ Fx: 212-206-0200
www.ntwh.org

Handicapped Physicians, American Society of
3424 S Culpepper Ct   Springfield MO 65804
Ph: 417-881-1570 ▪ Fx: 417-887-9830

Handicapped Scuba Association International
1104 El Prado   San Clemente CA 92672
Ph: 949-498-4540 ▪ Fx: 949-498-6128
www.hsascuba.com

Handicapped, Skating Association for the Blind &
1200 East & West Rd   West Seneca NY 14224
Ph: 716-675-7222 ▪ Fx: 716-675-7223
www.sabahinc.org

Handicapped Travel Club
5929 Our Way   Citrus Heights CA 95610
Ph: 916-966-7090
www.handicappedtravelclub.com

Handlers Association Inc, Professional
17017 Norbrook Dr   Olney MD 20832
Ph: 301-924-0089
www.infodog.com/misc/pha/phamain.htm

Handling & Logistics Engineers, National Institute of Packaging
6902 Lyle St   Lanham MD 20706
Ph: 301-459-9105 ▪ Fx: 301-459-4925
www.niphle.com

Handoverprint Study & Research Group, Russian Zone
1108 Eureka Ave   Davis CA 95616
Ph: 530-756-1638

Handweavers Guild of America
1255 Buford Hwy Suite 211   Suwanee GA 30024
Ph: 678-730-0010
www.weavespindye.org

Handwriting Analysis Foundation, American
PO Box 6201   San Jose CA 95150
Ph: 408-377-6775 ▪ TF: 800-826-7774
iwhome.com/handwriting/applictn.htm

Handwriting Analysts, American Association of
W8871 Gossfield Ln   Beaver Dam WI 53916
Ph: 920-887-2642 ▪ Fx: 920-887-3101
www.handwriting.org/aaha

Handyman Club of America
12301 Whitewater Dr   Minnetonka MN 55343
Ph: 952-988-7402 ▪ TF: 800-243-7679
www.handymanclub.com

Hang Gliding Association Inc, US
PO Box 1330   Colorado Springs CO 80901
Ph: 719-632-8300 ▪ Fx: 719-632-6417
www.ushga.org

Hanoverian Association of American Breeders & Owners, Purebred
Box 429   Rocky Hill NJ 08553
Ph: 609-466-1383 ▪ Fx: 609-466-9543

Hanoverian Society, American
4067 Iron Works Pike Suite 1   Lexington KY 40511
Ph: 859-255-4141 ▪ Fx: 859-255-8467
www.hanoverian.org

Happy Hours Brotherhood
87 School St   Fall River MA 02720
Ph: 508-672-2082

Harabonim of America, American Board of Rabbis - VAAD
292 5th Ave 4th Fl   New York NY 10001
Ph: 212-714-3598
www.angelfire.com/ny2/abor

Harbors Cooperative, Clean
4601 Tremley Pt Rd   Linden NJ 07036
Ph: 908-862-7500 ▪ Fx: 908-862-7560

Hard Anodizing Association, International
PO Box 579   Moorestown NJ 08057
Ph: 856-234-0330 ▪ Fx: 856-727-9504
www.ihanodizing.com

Hard Hatted Women
4207 Lorain Ave   Cleveland OH 44113
Ph: 216-961-4449 ▪ Fx: 216-961-0927
www.hardhattedwomen.org

Hard of Hearing, League for the
50 Broadway   New York NY 10004
Ph: 917-305-7700 ▪ Fx: 917-305-7888
www.lhh.org

Hard of Hearing People, Self Help for
7910 Woodmont Ave Suite 1200   Bethesda MD 20814
Ph: 301-657-2248 ▪ Fx: 301-913-9413
www.hearingloss.org

Hardware Association, National Retail
5822 W 74th St   Indianapolis IN 46278
Ph: 317-290-0338 ▪ Fx: 317-328-4354 ▪ TF: 800-772-4424
www.nrha.org

Hardware Distributors Association, Security
1900 Arch St   Philadelphia PA 19103
Ph: 215-564-3484 ▪ Fx: 215-564-2175
www.shda.org

Hardware Industry Association, US
PO Box 35180   Chicago IL 60607
Ph: 773-283-3880 ▪ Fx: 708-453-0083
www.associationhardware.com

Hardware Institute, Door &
14150 Newbrook Dr Suite 200   Chantilly VA 20151
Ph: 703-222-2010 ▪ Fx: 703-222-2410
www.dhi.org

Hardware Manufacturers Association, American
801 N Plaza Dr   Schaumburg IL 60173
Ph: 847-605-1025 ▪ Fx: 847-605-1030
www.ahma.org

Hardware Manufacturers Association, Builders'
355 Lexington Ave 17th Fl   New York NY 10017
Ph: 212-297-2122 ▪ Fx: 212-370-9047
www.buildershardware.com

Hardwood Council
PO Box 525   Oakmont PA 15139
Ph: 412-281-4980 ▪ Fx: 412-323-9334
www.hardwoodcouncil.com

Hardwood Distributors Association
2559 S Damen Ave   Chicago IL 60608
Ph: 773-847-7444 ▪ Fx: 773-847-7833
www.hardwooddistributors.com

Hardwood Export Council, American
1111 19th St NW Suite 800   Washington DC 20036
Ph: 202-463-2720 ▪ Fx: 202-463-2787
www.ahec.org

Hardwood Lumber Association, National
6830 Raleigh-LaGrange Rd   Memphis TN 38184
Ph: 901-377-1818 ▪ Fx: 901-382-6419 ▪ TF: 800-933-0318
www.natlhardwood.org

Hardwood Manufacturers Inc, Appalachian
PO Box 427   High Point NC 27261
Ph: 336-885-8315 ▪ Fx: 336-886-8865
www.appalachianwood.org

Hardwood Manufacturers Association
400 Penn Center Blvd Suite 530   Pittsburgh PA 15235
Ph: 412-829-0770 ▪ Fx: 412-829-0844 ▪ TF: 800-373-9663
www.hardwood.com

Hardwood Plywood & Veneer Association
PO Box 2789   Reston VA 20195
Ph: 703-435-2900 ▪ Fx: 703-435-2537
www.hpva.org

Hardwood Preservation Society, North American
2804 Ladd Ln   Longview TX 75604
Ph: 903-759-9830

Harlem Globetrotters International Inc
400 E Van Buren St Suite 300   Phoenix AZ 85004
Ph: 602-258-0000 ▪ Fx: 602-258-5925 ▪ TF: 800-641-4667
www.harlemglobetrotters.com

Harlequin Rabbit Club, American
1299 Josie Ln   Conover NC 28613
Ph: 828-466-2274

Harley Hummer Club Inc
4517 Chase Ave   Bethesda MD 20814
Ph: 301-657-4035
www.harleyhummerclub.org

Harley Owners Group
PO Box 453   Milwaukee WI 53208
Ph: 414-343-4056 ▪ Fx: 414-343-4515 ▪ TF: 800-464-2582
www.hog.com

Harmonica, Society for the Preservation & Advancement of the
PO Box 865   Troy MI 48099
Ph: 810-984-3115
www.spah.org

Harmonious Human Being Inc, Institute for the Development of the
PO Box 370   Nevada City CA 95959
Ph: 530-272-0180 ▪ Fx: 530-272-0184
www.idhhb.org

Harmony Association, United in Group
PO Box 185   Clifton NJ 07011
Ph: 973-365-0049
www.ugha.org

Harmony Foundation Inc
7930 Sheridan Rd   Kenosha WI 53143
Ph: 262-653-8440 ▪ Fx: 262-654-5552
www.harmonyfoundation.org

Harmony, Project
5197 Main St Unit 6   Waitsfield VT 05673
Ph: 802-496-4545 ▪ Fx: 802-496-4548
www.projectharmony.org

Harness Allied Trades Association, Saddle
c/o Proleptic Inc 1101 Broad St   Oriental NC 28571
Ph: 252-249-3409 ▪ Fx: 252-249-3415
www.proleptic.net/shata.asp

Harness Horse Youth Foundation
14950 Greyhound Ct Suite 210   Carmel IN 46032
Ph: 317-848-5132 ▪ Fx: 317-848-5136
www.hhyf.org

Harness Horsemen International
14 Main St Suite C   Robbinsville NJ 08691
Ph: 609-259-3717 ▪ Fx: 609-259-3778

Harness Manufacturers Association, Wiring
7500 Flying Cloud Dr Suite 900   Eden Prairie MN 55344
Ph: 952-253-6225 ▪ Fx: 952-835-4774
www.whma.org

Harness Tracks of America
4640 E Sunrise Dr Suite 200   Tucson AZ 85718
Ph: 520-529-2525 ▪ Fx: 520-529-3235
www.harnesstracks.com

Harp Society Inc, American
PO Box 38334   Los Angeles CA 90038
Ph: 323-825-4760 ▪ Fx: 323-469-3050
www.harpsociety.org

Harp Society, Historical
631 N 3rd Ave   Saint Charles IL 60174
Ph: 630-584-5259
www.historicalharps.org

Harpers & Craftsmen, International Society of Folk
4110 Brandemere Way   Houston TX 77066
Ph: 832-249-7885
www.folkharpsociety.org

Harriet Beecher Stowe Center
77 Forest St   Hartford CT 06105
Ph: 860-522-9258 ▪ Fx: 860-522-9259
www.harrietbeecherstowecenter.org

Harrison Home Foundation, President Benjamin
1230 N Delaware St   Indianapolis IN 46202
Ph: 317-631-1888 ▪ Fx: 317-632-5488
www.presidentbenjaminharrison.org

Harry Singer Foundation
PO Box 223159   Carmel CA 93922
Ph: 831-625-4223 ▪ Fx: 831-624-7994
www.singerfoundation.org

Hashomer Hatzair USA
114 W 26th St Suite 1001   New York NY 10001
Ph: 212-627-2830 ▪ Fx: 212-989-9840
www.hashomerhatzair.org

Haskins Society
www.haskins.cornell.edu

Hastings Center
21 Malcolm Gordon Dr   Garrison NY 10524
Ph: 845-424-4040 ▪ Fx: 845-424-4545
www.thehastingscenter.org

Hatpin Society, American
20 Montecillo Dr   Rolling Hills Estates CA 90274
Ph: 310-326-2196
www.collectoronline.com/AHS/

Hauser Center for Nonprofit Organizations
Harvard Univ John F Kennedy School of Government 79 JFK
St   Cambridge MA 02138
Ph: 617-496-5675 ▪ Fx: 617-495-0996
www.ksg.harvard.edu/hauser

Havurah Committee, National
7135 Germantown Ave 2nd Fl   Philadelphia PA 19119
Ph: 215-248-1335 ▪ Fx: 215-248-9760
www.havurah.org

Hawaii Agriculture Research Center
99-193 Aiea Heights Dr Suite 300   Aiea HI 96701
Ph: 808-487-5561 ▪ Fx: 808-486-5020
www2.hawaii.edu/~jzhu/harc.html

Hawaii Foundation, Historic
PO Box 1658   Honolulu HI 96806
Ph: 808-523-2900 ▪ Fx: 808-523-0800
www.historichawaii.org

Hawaiian Farmers, Institute for the Advancement of
86-649 Puuhulu Rd   Waianae HI 96792
Ph: 808-697-3045 ▪ Fx: 808-696-7774
www.opihi.com/sovereignty

Hawk Migration Association of North America
www.hmana.org

Hawk Mountain Sanctuary Association
1700 Hawk Mountain Rd   Kempton PA 19529
Ph: 610-756-6961 ▪ Fx: 610-756-4468
www.hawkmountain.org

HawkWatch International
1800 S West Temple Suite 2262   Salt Lake City UT 84115
Ph: 801-484-6808 ▪ Fx: 801-484-6810 ▪ TF: 800-726-4295
www.hawkwatch.org

Hawthorne Nathaniel Society
Univ of Cincinnati Dept of English   Cincinnati OH 45221
Ph: 513-556-5924
asweb.artsci.uc.edu/english/HawthorneSociety/nh.html

Hay Association, National
102 Treasure Island Cswy Suite 201   Saint Petersburg FL
33706
Ph: 727-367-9702 ▪ Fx: 727-367-9608 ▪ TF: 800-707-0014
www.nationalhay.org

Hayden Charles Foundation
140 Broadway 51st Fl   New York NY 10005
Ph: 212-785-3677 ▪ Fx: 212-785-3689
fdncenter.org/grantmaker/hayden

Hazard Control Management, Board of Certified
11900 Parklawn Dr Suite 451   Rockville MD 20852
Ph: 301-770-2540 ▪ Fx: 301-770-2183
www.chcm-chsp.org

Hazardous Articles, Conference on Safe Transportation of
7803 Hill House Ct   Fairfax Station VA 22039
Ph: 703-451-4031 ▪ Fx: 703-451-4207
www.costha.com

Hazardous Materials Association, International Vessel Operators
1118 Bay Rd   Lake George NY 12845
Ph: 518-761-0263 ▪ Fx: 518-792-7781
www.vohma.com

Hazardous Materials Management, Institute of
11900 Parklawn Dr Suite 450   Rockville MD 20852
Ph: 301-984-8969 ▪ Fx: 301-984-1516
www.ihmm.org

Hazardous Materials Training & Research Institute
6301 Kirkwood Blvd SW PO Box 2068   Cedar Rapids IA 52406
Ph: 319-398-5678 ▪ Fx: 319-398-1250 ▪ TF: 800-464-6874
www.hmtri.org

HBI Global Partners
PO Box 584   Forest VA 24551
Ph: 434-525-5847 ▪ TF: 877-424-4634
hbi.gospelcom.net

Head Injury Hotline
PO Box 84151   Seattle WA 98124
Ph: 206-621-8558 ▪ Fx: 206-329-4355
www.headinjury.com

(Head Lice) National Pediculosis Association
50 Kearney   Needham MA 02494
Ph: 781-449-6487 ▪ Fx: 781-449-8129 ▪ TF: 800-446-4672
www.headlice.org

Head-Neck Nurses Inc, Society of Otorhinolaryngology &
116 Canal St Suite A   New Smyrna Beach FL 32168
Ph: 386-428-1695 ▪ Fx: 386-423-7566
www.sohnnurse.com

Head & Neck Radiology, American Society of
2210 Midwest Rd Suite 207   Oak Brook IL 60523
Ph: 630-574-0220 ▪ Fx: 630-574-0661
www.ashnr.org

Head & Neck Surgery, American Academy of Otolaryngology-
1 Prince St   Alexandria VA 22314
Ph: 703-836-4444 ▪ Fx: 703-683-5100
www.entnet.org

Head Start Association, National
1651 Prince St   Alexandria VA 22314
Ph: 703-739-0875 ▪ Fx: 703-739-0878
www.nhsa.org

Headache Education, American Council for
19 Mantua Rd   Mount Royal NJ 08061
Ph: 856-423-0258 ▪ Fx: 856-423-0082 ▪ TF: 800-255-2243
www.achenet.org

Headache Foundation, National
820 N Orleans St Suite 217   Chicago IL 60610
Ph: 888-643-5552
www.headaches.org

Headache Society, American
19 Mantua Rd   Mount Royal NJ 08061
Ph: 856-423-0043 ▪ Fx: 856-423-0082
ahsnet.org

Headwear Information Bureau
302 W 12th St PH-C   New York NY 10014
Ph: 212-627-8333 ▪ Fx: 212-627-0067

Healing the Children
PO Box 9065   Spokane WA 99209
Ph: 509-327-4281 ▪ Fx: 509-327-4284 ▪ TF: 877-432-5543
www.healingchildren.org

Healing, National Center for Jewish
850 7th Ave Suite 1201   New York NY 10019
Ph: 212-399-2685 ▪ Fx: 212-399-2475
www.jewishhealing.org

Healing, William Wendt Center for Loss &
730 11th St NW   Washington DC 20001
Ph: 202-624-0010 ▪ Fx: 202-624-0062
www.wendtcenter.org

Health, Academy
1801 K St NW Suite 701-L   Washington DC 20006
Ph: 202-292-6700 ▪ Fx: 202-292-6800
www.academyhealth.org

Health Accreditation Program Inc, Community
39 Broadway Suite 710   New York NY 10006
Ph: 212-480-8828 ▪ Fx: 212-480-8833 ▪ TF: 800-656-9656
www.chapinc.org

Health Administration, Association of University Programs in
730 11th St NW 4th Fl   Washington DC 20001
Ph: 202-638-1448 ▪ Fx: 202-638-3429
www.aupha.org

Health Administrators, National Conference of
Local Environmental   Univ of Washington Dept of
Environmental Health CB 357234   Seattle WA 98195
Ph: 206-616-2097 ▪ Fx: 206-616-8123
depts.washington.edu/clehaweb

Health Alliance, American International
1212 New York Ave NW Suite 750   Washington DC 20005
Ph: 202-789-1136 ▪ Fx: 202-789-1277
www.aiha.com

Health, American Council on Science &
1995 Broadway 2nd Fl   New York NY 10023
Ph: 212-362-7044 ▪ Fx: 212-362-4919
www.acsh.org

Health Association, American College
PO Box 28937   Baltimore MD 21240
Ph: 410-859-1500 ▪ Fx: 410-859-1510
www.acha.org

Health Association, American Holistic
PO Box 17400   Anaheim CA 92817
Ph: 714-779-6152
ahha.org

Health Association, American Public
800 'I' St NW   Washington DC 20001
Ph: 202-777-2742 ▪ Fx: 202-777-2534
www.apha.org

Health Association, American School
7263 State Rt 43   Kent OH 44240
Ph: 330-678-1601 ▪ Fx: 330-678-4526 ▪ TF: 800-445-2742
www.ashaweb.org

Health Association, American Social
PO Box 13827   Research Triangle Park NC 27709
Ph: 919-361-8400 ▪ Fx: 919-361-8425 ▪ TF: 800-277-8922
www.ashastd.org

Health Association, National
11816 Race Track Rd PO Box 30630   Tampa FL 33630
Ph: 813-855-6607 ▪ Fx: 813-855-8052
www.anhs.org

Health Association, National Environmental
720 S Colorado Blvd Suite 970S   Denver CO 80246
Ph: 303-756-9090 ▪ Fx: 303-691-9490
www.neha.org

Health Association, National Rural
1 W Armour Blvd Suite 203   Kansas City MO 64111
Ph: 816-756-3140 ▪ Fx: 816-756-3144
www.nrharural.org

Health, Association of Schools of Public
1101 15th St NW Suite 910   Washington DC 20005
Ph: 202-296-1099 ▪ Fx: 202-296-1252
www.asph.org

Health Association, Semiconductor Environmental Safety &
1313 Dolley Madison Blvd Suite 402   McLean VA 22101
Ph: 703-790-1745 ▪ Fx: 703-790-2672
seshaonline.org

Health Association of the US, Catholic
4455 Woodson Rd   Saint Louis MO 63134
Ph: 314-427-2500 ▪ Fx: 314-427-0029
www.chausa.org

Health Association, US-Mexico Border
5400 Suncrest Dr Suite C-5   El Paso TX 79912
Ph: 915-833-6450 ▪ Fx: 915-833-7840
www.usmbha.org

Health Association, World Federation of Public
800 'I' St NW   Washington DC 20001
Ph: 202-777-2486 ▪ Fx: 202-777-2530
www.wfpha.org

Health Association, Zero Balancing
801 W Main St Suite 202   Charlottesville VA 22903
Ph: 434-244-2458 ▪ Fx: 434-244-2645
www.zerobalancing.com

Health & Beauty Aids Institute, American
401 N Michigan Ave Suite 2200   Chicago IL 60611
Ph: 312-644-6610 ▪ Fx: 312-321-5194
www.proudlady.org

Health Board, National Indian
1385 S Colorado Blvd Suite A708   Denver CO 80222
Ph: 303-759-3075 ▪ Fx: 303-759-3674
www.nihb.org

Health Care, Accreditation Association for Ambulatory
3201 Old Glenview Rd Suite 300   Wilmette IL 60091
Ph: 847-853-6060 ▪ Fx: 847-853-9028
www.aaahc.org

Health Care Administrators, American College of
300 N Lee St Suite 301   Alexandria VA 22314
Ph: 703-739-7900 ▪ Fx: 703-793-7901 ▪ TF: 888-882-2422
www.achca.org

Health Care Advisors Association, National CPA
1 Valmont Plaza 4th Fl   Omaha NE 68154
Ph: 402-964-3865 ▪ Fx: 402-964-3811 ▪ TF: 888-475-4476
www.hcaa.com

Health Care Anti-Fraud Association, National
1255 23rd St NW Suite 200   Washington DC 20037
Ph: 202-659-5955 ▪ Fx: 202-785-6764
www.nhcaa.org

Health Care Association, American
1201 L St NW   Washington DC 20005
Ph: 202-842-4444 ▪ Fx: 202-842-3860 ▪ TF: 800-321-0343
www.ahca.org

Health Care Association PAC, American
1201 L St NW   Washington DC 20005
Ph: 202-842-4444 ▪ Fx: 202-842-3860 ▪ TF: 800-321-0343

Health Care Compliance Association
5780 Lincoln Dr Suite 120   Minneapolis MN 55436
Ph: 952-988-0141 ▪ Fx: 952-988-0146 ▪ TF: 888-580-8373
www.hcca-info.org

Health Care Education Association
PO Box 50603   Amarillo TX 79159
Ph: 888-298-3861 ▪ Fx: 806-354-1656
www.hcea-info.org

Health Care Executive Assistants
1 N Franklin Ave 31st Fl N   Chicago IL 60606
Ph: 312-422-3851 ▪ Fx: 312-422-4575
www.hceaonline.org

Health Care for the Homeless Council, National
HCH Clinicians' Network PO Box 60427   Nashville TN 37206
Ph: 615-226-2292 ▪ Fx: 615-226-1656
www.nhchc.org

Health Care Management Research & Educational Foundation, National Institute for 1225 19th St NW Suite 710 Washington DC 20036
Ph: 202-296-4426 ▪ Fx: 202-296-4319
www.nihcm.org

Health Care, National Coalition on
1200 G St NW Suite 750 Washington DC 20005
Ph: 202-638-7151
www.nchc.org

Health Care, National Commission on Correctional
1300 W Belmont Ave Chicago IL 60657
Ph: 773-880-1460 ▪ Fx: 773-880-2424
www.ncchc.org

Health Care, National Committee for Quality
1701 K St NW Suite 205 Washington DC 20006
Ph: 202-331-7535 ▪ Fx: 202-331-7532
www.ncqhc.org

Health Care Office Management, Professional Association of
461 E 10 Mile Rd Pensacola FL 32534
Ph: 850-474-9460 ▪ Fx: 850-474-6352 ▪ TF: 800-451-9311
www.pahcom.com

Health Care Providers in the Addictive Disorders, American Academy of 314 W Superior St Suite 702 Duluth MN 55802
Ph: 218-727-3940 ▪ Fx: 218-722-0346
www.americanacademy.org

Health Care, Society for Social Work Leadership in
1211 Locust St Philadelphia PA 19107
Ph: 215-599-6134 ▪ Fx: 215-545-8107 ▪ TF: 866-237-9542
www.sswlhc.org

Health Care Strategies Inc, Center for
PO Box 3469 Princeton NJ 08543
Ph: 609-895-8101 ▪ Fx: 609-895-9648
www.chcs.org

(Health) Case Management Society of America
8201 Cantrell Rd Suite 230 Little Rock AR 72227
Ph: 501-225-2229 ▪ Fx: 501-221-9068
www.cmsa.org

Health Centers, Association of Academic
1400 16th St NW Suite 720 Washington DC 20036
Ph: 202-265-9600 ▪ Fx: 202-265-7514
www.ahcnet.org

Health Centers, National Association of Community
7200 Wisconsin Ave Suite 210 Bethesda MD 20814
Ph: 301-347-0400 ▪ Fx: 301-347-0459
www.nachc.com

Health Charities, Community
200 N Glebe Rd Suite 801 Arlington VA 22203
Ph: 703-528-1007 ▪ Fx: 703-528-1365 ▪ TF: 800-654-0845
www.healthcharities.org

Health Club Association, National
640 Plaza Dr Suite 300 Highland Ranch CO 80129
Ph: 303-753-6422 ▪ Fx: 303-986-6813 ▪ TF: 800-765-6422

Health Coalition, International Women's
24 E 21st St New York NY 10010
Ph: 212-979-8500 ▪ Fx: 212-979-9009
www.iwhc.org

Health Coalition on Liability & Access
PO Box 19008 Washington DC 20036
Ph: 202-293-4255 ▪ Fx: 202-296-7689
www.hcla.org

Health Connection, Friends'
PO Box 114 New Brunswick NJ 08903
Ph: 732-418-1811 ▪ Fx: 732-249-9897 ▪ TF: 800-483-7436
www.friendshealthconnection.org

Health, Council on Family
1155 Connecticut Ave Suite 1200-B Washington DC 20036
Ph: 202-331-7373 ▪ Fx: 202-223-6835
www.cfhinfo.org

Health Council, Global
1701 K St NW Suite 600 Washington DC 20006
Ph: 202-833-5900 ▪ Fx: 202-833-0075
www.globalhealth.org

Health Council, National
1730 M St NW Suite 500 Washington DC 20036
Ph: 202-785-3910 ▪ Fx: 202-785-5923 ▪ TF: 800-684-6814
www.nhcouncil.org

Health Crisis, Gay Men's
119 W 24th St New York NY 10011
Ph: 212-367-1000 ▪ Fx: 212-367-1220 ▪ TF: 800-243-7692
www.gmhc.org

Health Data Organizations, National Association of
375 Chipeta Way Suite A Salt Lake City UT 84108
Ph: 801-587-9104 ▪ Fx: 801-587-9125
www.nahdo.org

Health Education, American Association for
1900 Association Dr Reston VA 20191
Ph: 703-476-3437 ▪ Fx: 703-476-6638 ▪ TF: 800-213-7193
www.aahperd.org/aahe

(Health Education) Delta Omega
www.deltaomega.org

(Health Education) Eta Sigma Gamma
2000 University Ave Muncie IN 47306
Ph: 765-285-2258 ▪ Fx: 765-285-3210 ▪ TF: 800-715-2559
www.bsu.edu/web/esg

Health Education Foundation, Comprehensive
22419 Pacific Hwy S Seattle WA 98198
Ph: 206-824-2907 ▪ Fx: 206-824-3072 ▪ TF: 800-323-2433
www.chef.org

Health Education Programs, Commission on Accreditation of Allied
35 E Wacker Dr Suite 1970 Chicago IL 60601
Ph: 312-553-9355 ▪ Fx: 312-553-9616
www.caahep.org

Health Education Resource Organization
1734 Maryland Ave Baltimore MD 21201
Ph: 410-685-1180 ▪ Fx: 410-685-3101
www.hero-mcrc.org

Health Education Schools, Accrediting Bureau of
7777 Leesburg Pike Suite 314 N Falls Church VA 22043
Ph: 703-917-9503 ▪ Fx: 703-917-4109
www.abhes.org

Health Education, Society for Public
750 1st St NE Suite 910 Washington DC 20002
Ph: 202-408-9804 ▪ Fx: 202-408-9815
www.sophe.org

Health Education & Welfare Association, Presbyterian
100 Witherspoon St Rm 3041 Louisville KY 40202
Ph: 502-569-5794 ▪ Fx: 502-569-8034 ▪ TF: 888-728-7228
www.pcusa.org/phewa

Health Employees, International Union of Industrial Service Transport
254 W 31st St New York NY 10001
Ph: 212-696-5545 ▪ Fx: 212-696-5556 ▪ TF: 800-331-1070

Health Environment & Justice, Center for
PO Box 6806 Falls Church VA 22040
Ph: 703-237-2249 ▪ Fx: 703-237-8389
www.chej.org/

Health Environment & Safety, Beach Education Advocates for Children PO Box 530702 Miami Shores FL 33153
Ph: 305-893-8838 ▪ Fx: 305-893-8823
www.beachesfoundation.org

Health Environmental & Safety Technologies, Council on Certification of 208 Burwash Ave Savoy IL 61874
Ph: 217-359-2686 ▪ Fx: 217-359-0055
www.cchest.org

Health Evaluation Association, International
846 S Hotel St Suite 301 Honolulu HI 96813
Ph: 808-524-4411 ▪ Fx: 808-524-5559
www.ihea.net

Health Federation, National
PO Box 688 Monrovia CA 91017
Ph: 626-357-2181 ▪ Fx: 626-303-0642
www.thenhf.com

Health & Fitness, National Association for
201 S Capitol Ave Suite 560 Indianapolis IN 46225
Ph: 317-237-5630 ▪ Fx: 317-237-5632
www.physicalfitness.org

Health Forum, Asian & Pacific Islander American
450 Sutter St Suite 600 San Francisco CA 94108
Ph: 415-954-9988 ▪ Fx: 415-954-9999
www.apiahf.org

Health Foundation, Child
10630 Little Patuxent Pkwy Century Plaza Suite 126 Columbia MD 21044
Ph: 301-596-4514 ▪ Fx: 410-992-5641
www.childhealthfoundation.org

Health Foundation, People-to-People
225 Carter Hall Ln Millwood VA 22646
Ph: 540-837-2100 ▪ Fx: 540-837-1813 ▪ TF: 800-544-4673
www.projhope.org

Health Freedom, American Association for
9912 Georgetown Pike Suite D-2 PO Box 458 Great Falls VA 22066
Ph: 703-759-0662 ▪ Fx: 703-759-6711 ▪ TF: 800-230-2762
www.healthfreedom.net

Health Freedom, Institute for
1825 'I' St NW Suite 400 Washington DC 20006
Ph: 202-429-6610 ▪ Fx: 202-861-1973
www.forhealthfreedom.org

Health Fund, Children's
317 E 64th St New York NY 10021
Ph: 212-535-9400 ▪ Fx: 212-535-7488
www.childrenshealthfund.org

Health, Grantmakers in
1100 Connecticut Ave NW Suite 1200 Washington DC 20036
Ph: 202-452-8331 ▪ Fx: 202-452-8340
www.gih.org

Health & Human Service Organizations, National Assembly of
1319 F St NW Suite 601 Washington DC 20004
Ph: 202-347-2080 ▪ Fx: 202-393-4517
www.nassembly.org

Health, Imagine World
105 E Dolphin Blvd Ponte Vedra Beach FL 32082
Ph: 904-285-0240
www.imagineworldhealth.org

Health Imperative, Black Women's
600 Pennsylvania Ave SE Suite 310 Washington DC 20003
Ph: 202-548-4000 ▪ Fx: 202-543-9743
www.blackwomenshealth.org

Health Industry Business Communications Council
2525 E Arizona Biltmore Cir Suite 127 Phoenix AZ 85016
Ph: 602-381-1091 ▪ Fx: 602-381-1093
www.hibcc.org

Health Industry Distributors Association
310 Mongomery St Suite 520 Alexandria VA 22314
Ph: 703-549-4432 ▪ Fx: 703-549-6495
www.hida.org

Health Industry Group Purchasing Association
1100 Wilson Blvd Suite 1200 Arlington VA 22209
Ph: 703-243-9262 ▪ Fx: 703-243-8664
www.higpa.com

Health Industry Representatives Association
6740 E Hampden Ave Suite 306 Denver CO 80224
Ph: 303-756-8115 ▪ Fx: 303-756-5699
www.hira.org

Health Information Center, National
PO Box 1133 Washington DC 20013
Ph: 301-565-4167 ▪ Fx: 301-984-4256 ▪ TF: 800-336-4797
www.health.gov/nhic

Health Information Clearinghouse, National Oral
1 NOHIC Way Bethesda MD 20892
Ph: 301-402-7364 ▪ Fx: 301-907-8830
www.nohic.nidcr.nih.gov

Health Information Coalition, National Public
986 Hidden Hollow Dr Marietta GA 30068
Ph: 770-509-5555 ▪ Fx: 770-565-8436
www.nphic.org

Health Information Management Association, American
233 N Michigan Ave Suite 2150 Chicago IL 60601
Ph: 312-233-1100 ▪ Fx: 312-233-1090 ▪ TF: 800-335-5535
www.ahima.org

Health Information Network, NEA
1201 16th St NW Suite 521 Washington DC 20036
Ph: 202-822-7570 ▪ Fx: 202-822-7775 ▪ TF: 800-718-8387
www.bocadcweb.net/healthinfo

Health Information Resource Center
1850 W Winchester Rd Suite 213 Libertyville IL 60048
Ph: 847-816-8660 ▪ Fx: 847-816-8662 ▪ TF: 800-828-8225

(Health Insurance) AAHP-HIAA
1129 20th St NW Suite 600 Washington DC 20036
Ph: 202-778-3200 ▪ Fx: 202-331-7487 ▪ TF: 877-291-2247
www.aahp.org

Health Insurance Advisors, Association of
2901 Telestar Ct Falls Church VA 22042
Ph: 703-770-8200 ▪ Fx: 703-770-8201
www.ahia.net

Health Insurance, Council for Affordable
112 S West St Suite 400 Alexandria VA 22314
Ph: 703-836-6200 ▪ Fx: 703-836-6550
www.cahi.org

Health Insurance Guaranty Associations, National Organization of Life & 13873 Park Center Rd Suite 329 Herndon VA 20171
Ph: 703-481-5206 ▪ Fx: 703-481-5209
www.nolhga.com

Health, Jacobs Institute of Women's
409 12th St SW Washington DC 20024
Ph: 202-863-4990 ▪ Fx: 202-488-4229
www.jiwh.org

Health Laboratories, Association of Public
2025 M St NW Suite 550 Washington DC 20036
Ph: 202-822-5227 ▪ Fx: 202-887-5098
www.aphl.org

Health Law Program, National
2639 S La Cienega Blvd Los Angeles CA 90034
Ph: 310-204-6010 ▪ Fx: 310-204-0891
www.healthlaw.org

Health Lawyers Association, American
1025 Connecticut Ave NW Suite 600 Washington DC 20036
Ph: 202-833-1100 ▪ Fx: 202-833-1105
www.healthlawyers.org

Health Libraries Association, Canadian — www.chla-absc.ca
3324 Yonge St   Toronto ON M4N3R1
Ph: 416-485-0377 ▪ Fx: 416-485-6877

Health Ministries, Global — www.ghm.org
7831 Hickory St NE   Minneapolis MN 55432
Ph: 763-586-9590 ▪ Fx: 763-586-9591

Health, National Alliance for Hispanic — www.hispanichealth.org
1501 16th St NW   Washington DC 20036
Ph: 202-387-5000 ▪ Fx: 202-797-4353

Health, National Association of Local Boards of — www.nalboh.org
1840 E Gypsy Lane Rd   Bowling Green OH 43402
Ph: 419-353-7714 ▪ Fx: 419-352-6278

Health, National Business Coalition on — www.nbch.org
1015 18th St NW Suite 730   Washington DC 20036
Ph: 202-775-9300 ▪ Fx: 202-775-1569

Health, National Center for Farmworker — www.ncfh.org
1770 FM 967   Buda TX 78610
Ph: 512-312-2700 ▪ Fx: 512-312-2600

Health Network, National Women's — www.nwhn.org
514 10th St NW Suite 400   Washington DC 20004
Ph: 202-347-1140 ▪ Fx: 202-347-1168

Health Network, Women's International Public
7100 Oak Forest Ln   Bethesda MD 20817
Ph: 301-469-9210 ▪ Fx: 301-469-8423

Health Nurses, American Association of Occupational — www.aaohn.org
2920 Brandywine Rd Suite 100   Atlanta GA 30341
Ph: 770-455-7757 ▪ Fx: 770-455-7271 ▪ TF: 888-646-4631

Health Nurses & Associates Inc, Consortium of Behavioral — www.cbhna.org
1733 H St Suite 330 PMB 1214   Blaine WA 98230
Ph: 800-876-2236 ▪ Fx: 360-332-2280

Health Nursing Educators, Association of Community — www.uncc.edu/achne
11 Cornell Rd   Latham NY 12110
Ph: 518-782-9400 ▪ Fx: 518-782-9530

Health Occupations Students of America — www.hosa.org
6021 Morriss Rd Suite 111   Flower Mound TX 75028
Ph: 800-321-4672 ▪ Fx: 972-874-0063

Health Officials, Association of State & Territorial — www.astho.org
1275 K St NW Suite 800   Washington DC 20005
Ph: 202-371-9090 ▪ Fx: 202-371-9797

Health Officials, National Association of County & City — www.naccho.org
1100 17th St 2nd Fl   Washington DC 20036
Ph: 202-783-5550 ▪ Fx: 202-783-1583

Health Optimizing Institute — www.year2020vision.net/hoi.htm
PO Box 1233   Del Mar CA 92014
Ph: 858-481-7751

Health Organization, National Asian Women's — www.nawho.org
250 Montgomery St Suite 900   San Francisco CA 94104
Ph: 415-989-9747 ▪ Fx: 415-989-9758

Health Organization, Pan American — www.paho.org
525 23rd St NW   Washington DC 20037
Ph: 202-974-3000 ▪ Fx: 202-974-3663

Health Organizations, Association of Asian/Pacific Community — www.aapcho.org
429 23rd St   Oakland CA 94612
Ph: 510-272-9536 ▪ Fx: 510-272-0817

Health Physical Education Recreation & Dance, American Alliance for — www.aahperd.org
1900 Association Dr   Reston VA 20191
Ph: 703-476-3400 ▪ Fx: 703-476-9527 ▪ TF: 800-213-7193

Health Physical Education Recreation Sport & Dance, International Council for — www.ichpersd.org
1900 Association Dr   Reston VA 20191
Ph: 703-476-3462 ▪ Fx: 703-476-9527 ▪ TF: 800-213-7193

Health Physics, American Academy of — www.hps1.org/aahp
1313 Dolley Madison Blvd Suite 402   McLean VA 22101
Ph: 703-790-1745 ▪ Fx: 703-790-2672

Health Physics Society — www.hps.org
1313 Dolley Madison Blvd Suite 402   McLean VA 22101
Ph: 703-790-1745 ▪ Fx: 703-790-2672

Health Planning Association, American — www.ahpanet.org
7245 Arlington Blvd Suite 300   Falls Church VA 22042
Ph: 703-573-3103 ▪ Fx: 703-573-1276

Health Plans, Alliance of Community — www.achp.org
2000 M St NW Suite 201   Washington DC 20036
Ph: 202-785-2247 ▪ Fx: 202-785-4060

Health Policy Forum, National — www.nhpf.org
2131 K St NW Suite 500   Washington DC 20037
Ph: 202-872-1390 ▪ Fx: 202-862-9837

Health Policy, Schneider Institute for — sihp.brandeis.edu
Brandeis University Heller Graduate School Box 9110 MS
   035   Waltham MA 02454
Ph: 781-736-3901 ▪ Fx: 781-736-3905

Health & Productivity Management, Institute for — www.ihpm.org
4435 Waterfront Dr Suite 101   Glen Allen VA 23060
Ph: 804-257-1905 ▪ Fx: 804-747-5316 ▪ TF: 800-722-0376

Health Professionals, Association of Occupational — www.aohp.org
109 VIP Dr   Wexford PA 15090
Ph: 800-362-4347 ▪ Fx: 724-935-1560

Health Professionals, Association of Reproductive — www.arhp.org
2401 Pennsylvania Ave NW Suite 350   Washington DC 20037
Ph: 202-466-3825 ▪ Fx: 202-466-3826

Health Professionals, Association of Rheumatology — www.rheumatology.org/arhp
1800 Century Pl Suite 250   Atlanta GA 30345
Ph: 404-633-3777 ▪ Fx: 404-633-1870

Health Professionals, National Association of Certified Natural — www.cnhp.org
714 E Winona Ave   Warsaw IN 46580
Ph: 574-267-4230 ▪ Fx: 574-268-5393 ▪ TF: 800-321-1005

Health Professions, Association of Schools of Allied — www.asahp.org
1730 M St NW Suite 500   Washington DC 20036
Ph: 202-293-4848 ▪ Fx: 202-293-4852

Health Professions, National Association of Advisors for the — www.naahp.org
PO Box 1518   Champaign IL 61824
Ph: 217-355-0063 ▪ Fx: 217-355-1287

Health Professions Schools, Association of Minority
507 Capitol Ct NE Suite 200   Washington DC 20002
Ph: 202-544-7499 ▪ Fx: 202-546-7105

Health Professions Schools Inc, Hispanic-Serving — www.hshps.com
1411 K St NW Suite 200   Washington DC 20005
Ph: 202-783-5262 ▪ Fx: 202-628-5898

Health, Program for Appropriate Technology in — www.path.org
1455 NW Leary St   Seattle WA 98107
Ph: 206-285-3500 ▪ Fx: 206-285-6619

Health Program, Physicians for a National — www.pnhp.org
29 E Madison St Suite 602   Chicago IL 60602
Ph: 312-782-6006 ▪ Fx: 312-782-6007

Health Programs, Association of Maternal & Child — www.amchp.org
1220 19th St NW Suite 801   Washington DC 20036
Ph: 202-775-0436 ▪ Fx: 202-775-0061

Health Promotion & Education, Directors of — www.dhpe.org
1101 15th St NW Suite 601   Washington DC 20005
Ph: 202-659-2230 ▪ Fx: 202-659-2339

Health Promotion Institute
c/o National Council on the Aging 300 D St SW Suite
   801   Washington DC 20024
Ph: 202-479-1200 ▪ Fx: 202-479-0735

Health Quality Association, American — www.ahqa.org
1140 Connecticut Ave NW   Washington DC 20036
Ph: 202-331-5790 ▪ Fx: 202-331-9334

Health Racquet & Sportsclub Association, International — www.ihrsa.org
263 Summer St   Boston MA 02210
Ph: 617-951-0055 ▪ Fx: 617-951-0056 ▪ TF: 800-228-4772

Health Research Group, Public Citizen — www.citizen.org/hrg
1600 20th St NW   Washington DC 20009
Ph: 202-588-1000 ▪ Fx: 202-588-7796

Health Research, Society for Women's — www.womens-health.org
1828 L St NW Suite 625   Washington DC 20036
Ph: 202-223-8224 ▪ Fx: 202-833-3472

(Health) Research!America — www.researchamerica.org
1101 King St Suite 520   Alexandria VA 22314
Ph: 703-739-2577 ▪ Fx: 703-739-2372 ▪ TF: 800-366-2873

Health Researchers, Association of International
2665 Pleasant Valley Rd   Mobile AL 36606
Ph: 251-473-3946

Health & Safety in Child Care, National Resource Center for — nrc.uchsc.edu
Univ of Colorado Health Sciences Ctr at Fitzsimons CMS F 541
   PO Box 6508   Aurora CO 80045
Ph: 303-724-0665 ▪ Fx: 303-724-0960 ▪ TF: 800-598-5437

Health & Safety Council of North America, Silicones Environmental — www.sehsc.com
11921 Freedom Dr Suite 550   Reston VA 20190
Ph: 703-904-4322 ▪ Fx: 703-925-5955

(Health & Safety) NSF International — www.nsf.org
789 N Dixboro Rd   Ann Arbor MI 48105
Ph: 734-769-8010 ▪ Fx: 734-769-0109 ▪ TF: 877-867-3435

Health Sciences, Academy — www.bemycoach.com
2578 Broadway Suite 112   New York NY 10025
Ph: 212-932-2381

Health Sciences, Archivists & Librarians in the History of the — www.alhhs.org
Virginia Commonwealth Univ Tompkins-McCaw Library Box
   980582   Richmond VA 23298
Ph: 804-828-9898 ▪ Fx: 804-828-6089

Health & Sciences, Association for Environmental — www.aehs.org
150 S Fearing St   Amherst MA 01002
Ph: 413-549-5170 ▪ Fx: 413-549-0579

Health Sciences Communications Association — www.hesca.org
39 Wedgewood Dr Suite A   Jewett City CT 06351
Ph: 860-376-5915 ▪ Fx: 860-376-6621

Health Sciences Libraries, Association of Academic — www.aahsl.org
2150 N 107th St Suite 205   Seattle WA 98133
Ph: 206-367-8704 ▪ Fx: 206-367-8777

Health Service, Commissioned Officers Association of the US Public — www.coausphs.org
8201 Corporate Dr Suite 560   Landover MD 20785
Ph: 301-731-9080 ▪ Fx: 301-731-9084

Health Services Association, American Correctional — www.corrections.com/ACHSA
250 Gatsby Pl   Alpharetta GA 30022
Ph: 877-918-1842 ▪ Fx: 770-650-5789

Health Services Executives, National Association of — www.nahse.org
8630 Fenton St Suite 126   Silver Spring MD 20910
Ph: 202-628-3953 ▪ Fx: 301-588-0011

Health Services Inc, Farm Worker — www.farmworkerhealth.org
1221 Massachusetts Ave NW Suite 5   Washington DC 20005
Ph: 202-347-7377 ▪ Fx: 202-347-6385

Health Society, Dinshah — www.dinshahhealth.org
PO Box 707   Malaga NJ 08328
Ph: 856-692-4686 ▪ Fx: 856-696-7890

Health, Society for Environmental Geochemistry & — www.segh.net
4698 S Forrest Ave   Springfield MO 65810
Ph: 417-885-1166 ▪ Fx: 417-881-6920

Health, Society for Occupational & Environmental — www.soeh.org
6728 Old McLean Village Dr   McLean VA 22101
Ph: 703-556-9222 ▪ Fx: 703-556-8729

Health Statistics & Information Systems, National Association for Public — www.naphsis.org
801 Roeder Rd Suite 650   Silver Spring MD 20910
Ph: 301-563-6001 ▪ Fx: 301-563-6012

Health Strategies, National Center for Environmental — www.ncehs.org
1100 Rural Ave   Voorhees NJ 08043
Ph: 856-429-5358

Health Studies, Academy for International — www.aihs.com
37 Aspen Dr   South Glastonbury CT 06037
Ph: 860-430-1388 ▪ Fx: 860-430-1420

Health-System Pharmacists, American Society of — www.ashp.org
7272 Wisconsin Ave   Bethesda MD 20814
Ph: 301-657-3000 ▪ Fx: 301-664-8877

Health Systems, National Association of Psychiatric
325 7th St NW Suite 625 Washington DC 20004
Ph: 202-393-6700 ▪ Fx: 202-783-6041
www.naphs.org

Health Systems, National Association of Public Hospitals &
1301 Pennsylvania Ave NW Suite 950 Washington DC 20004
Ph: 202-585-0100 ▪ Fx: 202-585-0101
www.naph.org

Health & Temperance Association, International
12501 Old Columbia Pike Silver Spring MD 20904
Ph: 301-680-6719 ▪ Fx: 301-680-6707

Health Underwriters, National Association of
2000 N 14th St Suite 450 Arlington VA 22201
Ph: 703-276-0220 ▪ Fx: 703-841-7797
www.nahu.org

Health Unit Coordinators, National Association of
1947 Madron Rd Rockford IL 61107
Ph: 815-633-4351 ▪ Fx: 815-633-4438 ▪ TF: 888-226-2482
www.nahuc.org

Health Volunteers Overseas Inc
PO Box 65157 Washington DC 20035
Ph: 202-296-0928 ▪ Fx: 202-296-8018
www.hvousa.org

Health & Welfare Ministries, United Methodist Association of
601 W Riverview Ave Dayton OH 45406
Ph: 937-227-9494 ▪ Fx: 937-222-7364 ▪ TF: 800-411-9901
www.umassociation.org

(Healthcare Access) Access Project
30 Winter St Suite 930 Boston MA 02108
Ph: 617-654-9911 ▪ Fx: 617-654-9922
www.accessproject.org

Healthcare Access Management, National Association of
2025 M St NW Suite 800 Washington DC 20036
Ph: 202-367-1125 ▪ Fx: 202-367-2125
www.naham.org

Healthcare Administrative Management, American Association of
11240 Waples Mill Rd Suite 200 Fairfax VA 22030
Ph: 703-281-4043 ▪ Fx: 703-359-7562
www.aaham.org

Healthcare, AFT
American Federation of Teachers 555 New Jersey Ave
NW Washington DC 20001
Ph: 202-879-4491 ▪ Fx: 202-393-5672
www.aft.org/healthcare

Healthcare Architects, American College of
8310 Nieman Rd PO Box 14548 Lenexa KS 66285
Ph: 913-492-4307 ▪ Fx: 913-599-5340
www.healtharchitects.org

Healthcare, Association for Ambulatory Behavioral
2301 Mt Vernon Ave Suite 100 Alexandria VA 22301
Ph: 703-836-2274 ▪ Fx: 703-836-0083
www.aabh.org

Healthcare Association, American Managed Behavioral
1101 Pennsylvania Ave NW 6th Fl Washington DC 20004
Ph: 202-756-7726 ▪ Fx: 202-756-7308
www.ambha.org

Healthcare Association, Collaborative Family
PO Box 20838 Rochester NY 14602
Ph: 716-482-8210 ▪ Fx: 716-482-2901
www.cfhcc.org

Healthcare Audit Network, Catholic
231 S Bemiston Ave Suite 300 Saint Louis MO 63105
Ph: 314-802-2000 ▪ Fx: 314-802-2020
www.chanllc.com

Healthcare Billing & Management Association
1540 S Coast Hwy Suite 203 Laguna Beach CA 92651
Ph: 877-640-4262 ▪ Fx: 949-376-3456
www.hbma.com

Healthcare Business Consultants, Institute of Certified
307 N Michigan Ave Suite 800 Chicago IL 60601
Ph: 312-360-0384 ▪ Fx: 312-360-0388 ▪ TF: 800-447-1684
www.ichbc.org

Healthcare Central Service Materiel Management, International Association of 213 W Institute Pl Suite 307 Chicago IL 60610
Ph: 312-440-0078 ▪ Fx: 312-440-9474 ▪ TF: 800-962-8274
www.iahcsmm.com

Healthcare Central Service Professionals, American Society for
1 N Franklin St Suite 280 Chicago IL 60606
Ph: 312-422-3750 ▪ Fx: 312-422-4577
www.ashcsp.org

HealthCare Commission, American Accreditation
1220 L St NW Suite 400 Washington DC 20005
Ph: 202-216-9010 ▪ Fx: 202-216-9006
www.urac.org

Healthcare Consultants, American Association of
5 Revere Dr Suite 200 Northbrook IL 60062
Ph: 847-205-2718 ▪ Fx: 847-350-2241 ▪ TF: 888-350-2242
www.aahc.net

Healthcare Consultants, National Association of
1255 23rd St NW Suite 200 Washington DC 20037
Ph: 202-452-8282 ▪ Fx: 202-833-3636
www.healthcon.org

Healthcare Consumer Advocacy, Society for
1 Franklin St 31st Fl N Chicago IL 60606
Ph: 312-422-3726 ▪ Fx: 312-422-4581
www.shca-aha.org

Healthcare Convention & Exhibitors Association
5775 Peachtree-Dunwoody Rd Bldg G Suite 500 Atlanta GA 30342
Ph: 404-252-3663 ▪ Fx: 404-252-0774
www.hcea.org

Healthcare Delivery Systems Inc, American Association of Integrated
4435 Waterfront Dr Suite 101 Glen Allen VA 23060
Ph: 804-747-5823 ▪ Fx: 804-747-5316
www.aaihds.org

Healthcare Distribution Management Association
1821 Michael Faraday Dr Suite 400 Reston VA 20190
Ph: 703-787-0000 ▪ Fx: 703-787-6930
www.healthcaredistribution.org

(Healthcare Education) CHOICE
1233 Locust St Suite 301 Philadelphia PA 19107
Ph: 215-985-3355 ▪ Fx: 215-985-2838
www.choice-phila.org

Healthcare Educators, International Alliance of
11211 Prosperity Farms Rd Suite D-325 Palm Beach Gardens FL 33410
Ph: 561-622-4334 ▪ Fx: 561-622-4771
www.iahe.com

Healthcare Engineering, American Society for
1 N Franklin St 28th Fl Chicago IL 60606
Ph: 312-422-3800 ▪ Fx: 312-422-4571
www.ashe.org

Healthcare Environmental Services, American Society for
1 N Franklin St Suite 2800 Chicago IL 60606
Ph: 312-422-3860 ▪ Fx: 312-422-4577
www.ashes.org

Healthcare Epidemiology of America, Society for
19 Mantua Rd Mount Royal NJ 08061
Ph: 856-423-0087 ▪ Fx: 856-423-3420
www.shea-online.org

Healthcare Executives, American College of
1 N Franklin St Suite 1700 Chicago IL 60606
Ph: 312-424-2800 ▪ Fx: 312-424-0023
www.ache.org

Healthcare Financial Management Association
2 Westbrook Corporate Ctr Suite 700 Westchester IL 60154
Ph: 708-531-9600 ▪ Fx: 708-531-0032 ▪ TF: 800-252-4362
www.hfma.org

Healthcare Food Service Administrators, American Society for
304 W Liberty St Suite 201 Louisville KY 40202
Ph: 800-620-6422
www.ashfsa.org

Healthcare Food Service Management, National Society for
204 'E' St NE Washington DC 20002
Ph: 202-546-7236 ▪ Fx: 202-547-6348
www.hfm.org

Healthcare Human Resources Administration, American Society for
1 N Franklin PO Box 75315 Chicago IL 60675
Ph: 312-422-3725 ▪ Fx: 312-422-4577
www.ashhra.org

Healthcare Improvement, Institute for
375 Longwood Ave 4th Fl Boston MA 02215
Ph: 617-754-4800 ▪ Fx: 617-754-4848
www.ihi.org

Healthcare Information Management Executives, College of
3300 Washtenaw Ave Suite 225 Ann Arbor MI 48104
Ph: 734-665-0000 ▪ Fx: 734-665-4922
www.cio-chime.org

Healthcare Information & Management Systems Society
230 E Ohio St Suite 500 Chicago IL 60611
Ph: 312-664-4467 ▪ Fx: 312-664-6143
www.himss.org

Healthcare Internal Auditors, Association of
PO Box 449 Onsted MI 49265
Ph: 517-467-7729 ▪ Fx: 517-467-6104 ▪ TF: 888-275-2442
www.ahia.org

Healthcare Leadership Council
1001 Pennsylvania Ave NW Suite 550 S Washington DC 20004
Ph: 202-452-8700 ▪ Fx: 202-296-9561
hlc.org

Healthcare Marketing & Communications Council
1525 Valley Ctr Pkwy Suite 150 Bethlehem PA 18017
Ph: 610-868-8299 ▪ Fx: 610-868-8387
www.hmc-council.org

HealthCare Ministries
521 W Lynn St Springfield MO 65802
Ph: 417-866-6311 ▪ Fx: 417-866-4972
www.healthcareministries.org

(Healthcare) National Academies of Practice
PO Box 1037 Edgewood MD 21040
Ph: 410-676-3390
www.nap.vcu.edu

(Healthcare) National Association of Subacute & Post Acute Care
1960 Gallows Rd Suite 210 Vienna VA 22182
Ph: 703-790-8989 ▪ Fx: 703-790-8485
www.naspac.net

Healthcare, National Council for Community Behavioral
12300 Twinbrook Pkwy Suite 320 Rockville MD 20852
Ph: 301-984-6200 ▪ Fx: 301-881-7159
www.nccbh.org

Healthcare Nurses Association, Home
228 7th St SE Washington DC 20003
Ph: 202-546-4754 ▪ Fx: 202-547-3540
www.hhna.org

Healthcare Organizations, Joint Commission on Accreditation of
1 Renaissance Blvd Oakbrook Terrace IL 60181
Ph: 630-792-5000 ▪ Fx: 630-792-5005
www.jcaho.org

Healthcare Philanthropy, Association for
313 Park Ave Suite 400 Falls Church VA 22046
Ph: 703-532-6243 ▪ Fx: 703-532-7170
www.ahp.org

Healthcare Practitioners, International Association of
11211 Prosperity Farms Rd Suite D-325 Palm Beach Gardens FL 33410
Ph: 561-622-4334 ▪ Fx: 561-622-4771 ▪ TF: 800-233-5880
www.iahp.com

Healthcare Products Association, Consumer
1150 Connecticut Ave NW Suite 1200 Washington DC 20036
Ph: 202-429-9260 ▪ Fx: 202-223-6835
www.chpa-info.org

Healthcare Quality, National Association for
4700 W Lake Ave Glenview IL 60025
Ph: 847-375-4720 ▪ Fx: 877-218-7939 ▪ TF: 800-966-9392
www.nahq.org

Healthcare Risk Management, American Society for
1 N Franklin St Chicago IL 60606
Ph: 312-422-3980 ▪ Fx: 312-422-4580
www.ashrm.org

Healthcare Security & Safety, International Association for
PO Box 5038 Glendale Heights IL 60139
Ph: 630-871-9936 ▪ Fx: 630-871-9938 ▪ TF: 888-353-0990
www.iahss.org

(Healthcare Standards) NCCLS
940 W Valley Rd Suite 1400 Wayne PA 19087
Ph: 610-688-0100 ▪ Fx: 610-688-0700
www.nccls.org

Healthcare Strategy & Market Development, Society for
American Hospital Assn 1 N Franklin St 28th Fl Chicago IL 60606
Ph: 312-422-3737 ▪ Fx: 312-422-4579 ▪ TF: 800-242-2626
www.stratsociety.org

Healthy Homes, Alliance for
227 Massachusetts Ave NE Suite 200 Washington DC 20002
Ph: 202-543-1147 ▪ Fx: 202-543-4466
www.afhh.org

Healthy Mothers Healthy Babies Coalition, National
121 N Washington St Suite 300 Alexandria VA 22314
Ph: 703-836-6110 ▪ Fx: 703-836-3470
www.hmhb.org

Hear My Voice
1100 N Main St Suite 201 Ann Arbor MI 48104
Ph: 734-747-9654 ▪ Fx: 734-747-9559 ▪ TF: 800-958-6423
www.hearmyvoice.org

Hearing Association, American Speech-Language-
10801 Rockville Pike Rockville MD 20852
Ph: 301-897-5700 ▪ Fx: 301-571-0457 ▪ TF: 800-498-2071
www.asha.org

Hearing Association, National Student Speech Language
10801 Rockville Pike Rockville MD 20852
Ph: 301-897-5700 ▪ Fx: 301-571-0481 ▪ TF: 800-498-2071
www.nsslha.org

Hearing & Balance Pathology Resource Registry, NIDCD National Temporal Bone Massachusetts Eye & Ear Infirmary 243 Charles St Boston MA 02114
Ph: 617-573-3711 ▪ Fx: 617-573-3838 ▪ TF: 800-822-1327
www.tbregistry.org

Hearing Conservation Association, National
9101 E Kenyon Ave Suite 3000 Denver CO 80237
Ph: 303-224-9022 ▪ Fx: 303-770-1812
www.hearingconservation.org

Hearing Conservation, Council for Accreditation in Occupational　　www.caohc.org
611 E Wells St　Milwaukee WI 53202
Ph: 414-276-5338　▪ Fx: 414-276-2146

Hearing Dog Inc, International　　www.ihdi.org
5901 E 89th Ave　Henderson CO 80640
Ph: 303-287-3277　▪ Fx: 303-287-3425

Hearing Impaired Hockey Association, American　　www.ahiha.org
1143 W Lake St　Chicago IL 60607
Ph: 312-226-5880　▪ Fx: 312-829-2098

Hearing Industries Association　　www.hearing.org
515 King St Suite 420　Alexandria VA 22314
Ph: 703-684-5744　▪ Fx: 703-684-6048

Hearing Institute, Better　　www.betterhearing.org
515 King St Suite 420　Alexandria VA 22314
Ph: 703-684-3391　▪ Fx: 703-684-6048　▪ TF: 888-432-7435

Hearing, League for the Hard of　　www.lhh.org
50 Broadway　New York NY 10004
Ph: 917-305-7700　▪ Fx: 917-305-7888

Hearing Research Foundation, American　　www.american-hearing.org
8 S Michigan Ave Suite 814　Chicago IL 60603
Ph: 312-726-9670　▪ Fx: 312-726-9695

Hearing Society, International　　www.ihsinfo.org
16880 Middlebelt Rd Suite 4　Livonia MI 48154
Ph: 734-522-7200　▪ Fx: 734-522-0200　▪ TF: 800-521-5247

Hearst William Randolph Foundation　　hearstfdn.org
888 7th Ave 45th Fl　New York NY 10106
Ph: 212-586-5404　▪ Fx: 212-586-1917

Heart Association, American　　www.americanheart.org
7272 Greenville Ave　Dallas TX 75231
Ph: 214-373-6300　▪ Fx: 214-706-1191　▪ TF: 800-242-8721

Heart Council, National　　www.nemahealth.org
306 W Joppa Rd　Baltimore MD 21204
Ph: 410-494-0300　▪ Fx: 410-494-0725

(Heart Disease) Mended Hearts　　www.mendedhearts.org
7272 Greenville Ave　Dallas TX 75231
Ph: 214-706-1442　▪ Fx: 214-706-5245　▪ TF: 888-432-1899

Heart Disease Research Foundation
50 Court St　Brooklyn NY 11201
Ph: 718-649-6210

Heart Foundation, InterAmerican　　www.interamericanheart.org
7272 Greenville Ave　Dallas TX 75231
Ph: 972-562-3806　▪ Fx: 972-562-3807

Heart to Heart International　　www.hearttoheart.org
401 S Clairborne Rd Suite 302　Olathe KS 66062
Ph: 913-764-5200　▪ Fx: 913-764-0809　▪ TF: 800-764-5220

Heart & Lung Transplantation, International Society for　　www.ishlt.org
14673 Midway Rd Suite 200　Addison TX 75001
Ph: 972-490-9495　▪ Fx: 972-490-9499

Heart Research, International Society for　　www.ishrworld.org
Univ of Louisville Health Science Ctr 550 S Jackson
St　Louisville KY 40292
Ph: 502-852-1837　▪ Fx: 502-852-6474

Heart Rhythm Society Inc, NASPE -　　www.naspe.org
6 Strathmore Rd　Natick MA 01760
Ph: 508-647-0100　▪ Fx: 508-647-0124

Heart Savers Association, National　　www.heartsavers.org
9140 W Dodge Rd　Omaha NE 68114
Ph: 402-398-1993　▪ Fx: 402-398-1994

Heartbeat International　　www.heartbeatinternational.org
665 E Dublin-Granville Rd Suite 440　Columbus OH 43229
Ph: 614-885-7577　▪ Fx: 614-885-8746　▪ TF: 888-550-7577

HEARTBEAT/Survivors After Suicide Inc　　www.heartbeatsurvivorsaftersuicide.org
2015 Devon St　Colorado Springs CO 80909
Ph: 719-596-2575

Hearth Patio & Barbecue Association　　www.hpba.org
1601 N Kent St Suite 1001　Arlington VA 22209
Ph: 703-522-0086　▪ Fx: 703-522-0548

Heartland Institute　　www.heartland.org
19 S LaSalle St Suite 903　Chicago IL 60603
Ph: 312-377-4000　▪ Fx: 312-377-5000

HeartLink, Children's　　www.childrensheartlink.org
5075 Arcadia Ave　Minneapolis MN 55436
Ph: 952-928-4860　▪ Fx: 952-928-4859

HeartMath, Institute of　　www.heartmath.org
14700 W Park Ave　Boulder Creek CA 95006
Ph: 831-338-8500　▪ Fx: 831-338-8504

Heartworm Society, American　　www.heartwormsociety.org
PO Box 667　Batavia IL 60510
Ph: 630-844-9676　▪ Fx: 630-208-8398

Heat Exchange Institute Inc　　www.heatexchange.org
1300 Sumner Ave　Cleveland OH 44115
Ph: 216-241-7333　▪ Fx: 216-241-0105

Heat & Frost Insulators & Asbestos Workers, International　　www.insulators.org
Association of　9602 ML King Jr Hwy　Lanham MD 20706
Ph: 301-731-9101　▪ Fx: 301-731-5058

Heat Pump Association, International Ground Source　　www.igshpa.okstate.edu
Oklahoma State University 499 Cordell S　Stillwater OK 74078
Ph: 405-744-5175　▪ Fx: 405-744-5283　▪ TF: 800-626-4747

Heat Treating Society
ASM International 9639 Kinsman Rd　Materials Park OH 44073
Ph: 440-338-5151　▪ Fx: 440-338-4634

HEATH Resource Center　　www.heath.gwu.edu
George Washington Univ 2121 K St NW Suite 220　Washington
DC 20037
Ph: 202-973-0904　▪ Fx: 202-973-0908　▪ TF: 800-544-3284

Heating Airconditioning & Refrigeration Distributors International　　www.hardinet.org
1389 Dublin Rd　Columbus OH 43215
Ph: 614-488-1835　▪ Fx: 614-488-0482　▪ TF: 888-253-2128

Heating Contractors Association, Independent
12342 Layton Ave　Greenfield WI 53228
Ph: 414-529-4702　▪ Fx: 414-529-4722

Heating Equipment Association, Industrial　　www.iea.org
1111 N 19th St Suite 425　Arlington VA 22209
Ph: 703-525-2513　▪ Fx: 703-525-2515

Heating Refrigerating & Air-Conditioning Engineers Inc, American　　www.ashrae.org
Society of　1791 Tullie Cir NE　Atlanta GA 30329
Ph: 404-636-8400　▪ Fx: 404-321-5478　▪ TF: 800-527-4723

Heavy Duty Distribution Association　　www.hdda.org
4600 East-West Hwy Suite 300　Bethesda MD 20814
Ph: 301-654-6664　▪ Fx: 301-654-3299

Heavy Duty Manufacturers Association
10 Laboratory Dr PO Box 13966　Research Triangle Park NC
27709
Ph: 919-549-4800　▪ Fx: 919-549-4824

Heavy Duty Representatives Association　　www.hdra.org
4015 Marks Rd Suite 2B　Medina OH 44256
Ph: 330-725-7160　▪ Fx: 330-722-5638　▪ TF: 800-763-5717

Heavy Equipment Claims Council, National Truck &　　www.nthecc.org

Hebrew Association, 92nd Street Young Men's & Young Women's　　www.92y.org
1395 Lexington Ave　New York NY 10128
Ph: 212-415-5765

Hebrew Catholics, Association of　　www.hebrewcatholic.org
PO Box 980280　Ypsilanti MI 48198
Ph: 734-480-4242　▪ Fx: 734-480-8990

Hebrew Congregations, Union of American　　www.uahcweb.org
633 3rd Ave　New York NY 10017
Ph: 212-650-4000　▪ Fx: 212-650-4159

Hebrew Day Schools, Torah Umesorah-National Society for
160 Broadway　New York NY 10038
Ph: 212-227-1000　▪ Fx: 212-406-6934

Hebrew Free Burial Association
224 W 35th St Rm 300　New York NY 10001
Ph: 212-239-1662　▪ Fx: 212-239-1981

(Hebrew) Histadruth Ivrith of America　　www.hebrewusa.org
520 8th Ave 15th Fl　New York NY 10018
Ph: 646-472-5390　▪ Fx: 646-472-5490　▪ TF: 866-243-2739

Hebrew Immigrant Aid Society　　www.hias.org
333 7th Ave 17th Fl　New York NY 10001
Ph: 212-967-4100　▪ Fx: 212-967-4483　▪ TF: 800-442-7714

Hebrew University, American Friends of the　　www.afhu.org
11 E 69th St　New York NY 10021
Ph: 212-472-9800　▪ Fx: 212-744-2324　▪ TF: 800-567-2348

Hedge Fund Association　　www.thehfa.org
2875 NE 191st St Suite 900　Aventura FL 33180
Ph: 202-478-2000　▪ Fx: 202-478-1999

Hedgehog Association, International　　www.hedgehogclub.com

Heidelberg Digital Imaging Association　　www.hdia.org
1 Barney Rd Suite 232　Clifton Park NY 12065
Ph: 518-373-1225　▪ Fx: 518-373-9205

Heifer Project International　　www.heifer.org
PO Box 8058　Little Rock AR 72203
Ph: 501-907-2600　▪ Fx: 501-907-2602　▪ TF: 800-422-0474

Heinz Howard Endowment　　www.heinz.org
625 Liberty Ave 30 Dominion Tower　Pittsburgh PA 15222
Ph: 412-281-5777　▪ Fx: 412-281-5788

Heinz Vira I Endowment　　www.heinz.org
625 Liberty Ave 30 Dominion Tower　Pittsburgh PA 15222
Ph: 412-281-5777　▪ Fx: 412-281-5788

Heisey Collectors of America Inc　　www.heiseymuseum.org/hca
National Heisey Glass Museum 169 W Church St　Newark OH
43055
Ph: 740-345-2932　▪ Fx: 740-345-9638

Helen Keller National Center for Deaf-Blind Youths & Adults　　hknc.org
141 Middle Neck Rd　Sands Point NY 11050
Ph: 516-944-8900　▪ Fx: 516-944-7302

Helen Keller Worldwide　　www.hkworld.org
352 Park Ave S 12th Fl　New York NY 10010
Ph: 212-532-0544　▪ Fx: 212-532-5860　▪ TF: 877-535-5374

Heliconia Society International　　www.heliconia.org
c/o Fairchild Tropical Garden 10901 Old Cutler Rd　Miami FL
33156
Ph: 305-667-1651

Helicopter Association International　　www.rotor.com
1635 Prince St　Alexandria VA 22314
Ph: 703-683-4646　▪ Fx: 703-683-4745　▪ TF: 800-435-4976

Helicopter Foundation International　　www.hfi.rotor.com
1635 Prince St　Alexandria VA 22314
Ph: 703-683-4646　▪ Fx: 703-683-4745

Helicopter Pilots Association, Vietnam　　www.vhpa.org
5530 Birdcage St Suite 200　Citrus Heights CA 95610
Ph: 916-966-7592　▪ Fx: 916-966-8743　▪ TF: 800-505-8472

Helicopter Safety Advisory Conference　　www.hsac.org

Helicopter Society International, American　　www.vtol.org
217 N Washington St　Alexandria VA 22314
Ph: 703-684-6777　▪ Fx: 703-739-9279

Hellenic American Bankers Association Inc　　www.haba.org
PO Box 48　New York NY 10008
Ph: 212-421-1057

Hellenic-American Chamber of Commerce　　www.hellenicamerican.cc
960 Ave of the Americas 9th Fl　New York NY 10001
Ph: 212-629-6380　▪ Fx: 212-564-9281

Hellenic Educational Progressive Association, American　　www.ahepa.org
1909 Q St NW Suite 500　Washington DC 20009
Ph: 202-232-6300　▪ Fx: 202-232-2140

(Hellenic) Maids of Athena　　www.ahepa.org/maids
1909 Q St NW Suite 500　Washington DC 20009
Ph: 202-232-6300　▪ Fx: 202-232-2140

Hellenic Philatelic Society of America
541 Cedar Hill Ave　Wyckoff NJ 07481
Ph: 201-447-6262　▪ Fx: 201-612-9228

Hellenic Voters of America, United
525 W Lake St   Addison IL 60101
Ph: 630-628-0820 ▪ Fx: 630-543-7001
www.smartbiz.net/uhva

Hells Canyon Preservation Council
PO Box 2768   La Grande OR 97850
Ph: 541-963-3950 ▪ Fx: 541-963-0584
www.hellscanyon.org

Helmet Safety Institute, Bicycle
4611 7th St S   Arlington VA 22204
Ph: 703-486-0100
www.helmets.org

Help the Children, World Opportunities International/
1415 Cahuenga Blvd   Hollywood CA 90028
Ph: 323-466-7187 ▪ Fx: 323-871-1546
www.helpthechildren.org

Help Desk Institute
6385 Corporate Dr Suite 311   Colorado Springs CO 80919
Ph: 719-268-0174 ▪ Fx: 719-268-0184 ▪ TF: 800-248-5667
www.thinkhdi.com

HELP USA
30 E 33rd St   New York NY 10016
Ph: 212-779-3350 ▪ Fx: 212-779-3353
www.helpusa.org

Helps International Ministries Inc
573 Fairview Rd   Asheville NC 28803
Ph: 828-277-3812 ▪ Fx: 828-274-7770
www.helpsintl.com

Hematology, American Society of
1900 M St NW Suite 200   Washington DC 20036
Ph: 202-776-0544 ▪ Fx: 202-776-0545
www.hematology.org

Hematology, International Society for Experimental
2025 M St NW Suite 800   Washington DC 20036
Ph: 202-367-1183 ▪ Fx: 202-367-2183
www.iseh.org

Hematology/Oncology, American Society of Pediatric
4700 W Lake Ave   Glenview IL 60025
Ph: 847-375-4716 ▪ Fx: 877-734-9557
www.aspho.org

Hematopathology, Society for
3643 Walton Way Ext   Augusta GA 30909
Ph: 706-733-7550 ▪ Fx: 706-733-8033
www.socforheme.org

Hemispheric Affairs, Council on
1444 'I' St NW Suite 211   Washington DC 20005
Ph: 202-216-9261 ▪ Fx: 202-216-9193 ▪ TF: 888-922-9261
www.coha.org

Hemochromatosis Foundation Inc
PO Box 8569   Albany NY 12208
Ph: 518-489-0972 ▪ Fx: 518-489-0227
www.hemochromatosis.org

Hemophilia Foundation, National
116 W 32nd St 11th Fl   New York NY 10001
Ph: 212-328-3700 ▪ Fx: 212-328-3777 ▪ TF: 800-424-2634
www.hemophilia.org

Hemp, Business Alliance for Commerce in
PO Box 1716   El Cerrito CA 94530
Ph: 510-215-8326
www.chrisconrad.com

Hemp Council, North American Industrial
PO Box 259329   Madison WI 53725
Ph: 608-258-0243 ▪ Fx: 608-835-0428
www.naihc.org

Hemp Industries Association
PO Box 1080   Occidental CA 95465
Ph: 707-874-3648 ▪ Fx: 707-874-1104
www.thehia.org

Henri Capitant, Association
Louisiana State Univ Paul M Hebert Law Ctr   Baton Rouge LA
  70803
Ph: 225-578-1126 ▪ Fx: 225-578-3677
host.law.lsu.edu/ahclouisiane

Henry Clay Memorial Foundation
120 Sycamore Rd   Lexington KY 40502
Ph: 859-266-8581 ▪ Fx: 859-268-7266
www.henryclay.org

Henry J Kaiser Family Foundation
2400 Sand Hill Rd   Menlo Park CA 94025
Ph: 650-854-9400 ▪ Fx: 650-854-4800
www.kff.org

Henry Luce Foundation Inc
111 W 50th St Suite 4601   New York NY 10020
Ph: 212-489-7700 ▪ Fx: 212-581-9541
www.hluce.org

Hepatitis C Coalition, National
PO Box 5058   Hemet CA 92544
Ph: 909-658-4414
nationalhepatitis-c.org

Hepatitis Foundation International
504 Blick Dr   Silver Spring MD 20904
Ph: 301-622-4200 ▪ Fx: 301-622-4702 ▪ TF: 800-891-0707
www.hepfi.org

Hepato-Pancreato-Biliary Association, American
11300 W Olympic Blvd Suite 600   Los Angeles CA 90064
Ph: 310-437-0557 ▪ Fx: 310-437-0585
www.ahpba.org

Herb Association, American
PO Box 1673   Nevada City CA 95959
Ph: 916-265-9552
www.ahaherb.com/

Herb Association, International
www.iherb.org

Herb Association, International Aromatherapy &
3541 W Acapulco Ln   Phoenix AZ 85053
Ph: 602-938-4439
www.aromaherbshow.com

Herb Growing & Marketing Network
PO Box 245   Silver Spring PA 17575
Ph: 717-393-3295 ▪ Fx: 717-393-9261
www.herbworld.com

Herb Research Foundation
4140 15th St   Boulder CO 80304
Ph: 303-449-2265 ▪ Fx: 303-449-7849 ▪ TF: 800-748-2617
www.herbs.org

Herb Society of America Inc
9019 Kirtland Chardon Rd   Kirtland OH 44094
Ph: 440-256-0514 ▪ Fx: 440-256-0541
www.herbsociety.org

Herbal Products Association, American
8484 Georgia Ave Suite 370   Silver Spring MD 20910
Ph: 301-588-1171 ▪ Fx: 301-588-1174
www.ahpa.org

Herbalists Guild, American
1931 Gaddis Rd   Canton GA 30115
Ph: 770-751-6021 ▪ Fx: 770-751-7472
www.americanherbalistsguild.com

Herbert H & Grace A Dow Foundation
1018 W Main St   Midland MI 48640
Ph: 989-631-3699 ▪ Fx: 989-631-0675 ▪ TF: 800-362-4849
www.hhdowfoundation.org

Herbert Hoover Presidential Library Association
PO Box 696   West Branch IA 52358
Ph: 319-643-5327 ▪ Fx: 319-643-2391 ▪ TF: 800-828-0475
www.hooverassociation.org

Hereditary Disease Foundation
1303 Pico Blvd   Santa Monica CA 90405
Ph: 310-450-9913 ▪ Fx: 310-450-9532
www.hdfoundation.org

(Hereditary Hemorrhagic Telangiectasia) HHT Foundation International Inc   PO Box 8087   New Haven CT 06530
Ph: 800-448-6389
www.hht.org

Hereford Association, American
1501 Wyandotte St   Kansas City MO 64108
Ph: 816-842-3757 ▪ Fx: 816-842-6931
www.hereford.org

Hereford Association, National Junior
PO Box 014059   Kansas City MO 64101
Ph: 816-842-3757 ▪ Fx: 816-842-6931
www.hereford.org

Hereford Hog Record Association, National
22405 480th Ave   Flandreau SD 57028
Ph: 605-997-2116

Heritage Canada Foundation
5 Blackburn Ave   Ottawa ON K1N8A2
Ph: 613-237-1066 ▪ Fx: 613-237-5987
www.heritagecanada.org

Heritage Foundation
214 Massachusetts Ave NE   Washington DC 20002
Ph: 202-546-4400 ▪ Fx: 202-546-8328
www.heritage.org

Heritage Foundation, American Indian
PO Box 6330 6051 F Arlington Blvd   Falls Church VA 22040
Ph: 703-237-7500 ▪ Fx: 703-532-1921
www.indians.org

Heritage Foundation, Chemical
315 Chestnut St   Philadelphia PA 19106
Ph: 215-925-2222 ▪ Fx: 215-925-1954
www.chemheritage.org

Heritage Foundation, Grassland
PO Box 394   Shawnee Mission KS 66201
Ph: 913-262-3506
www.grasslandheritage.org

Heritage & Recreation, Americans for Our
1615 M St NW   Washington DC 20036
Ph: 202-429-2606 ▪ Fx: 202-429-2621
www.ahrinfo.org

Heritage Roses Group
916 Union St Suite 302   Alameda CA 94501
Ph: 510-865-3242
www.thefragrantgarden.com/hrg.html

Heritage Society, Cornish American
www.cousinjack.org

Hermann in Texas, Order of the Sons of
PO Box 1941   San Antonio TX 78297
Ph: 210-226-9261 ▪ Fx: 210-226-3055 ▪ TF: 800-234-4124
www.texashermannsons.org

Hermitage Association, Ladies'
4580 Rachel's Ln   Hermitage TN 37076
Ph: 615-889-2941 ▪ Fx: 615-889-9909
www.thehermitage.com

Hernia Society, American
PO Box 536544   Orlando FL 32853
Ph: 407-898-1695 ▪ Fx: 407-894-2312
www.americanherniasociety.org

Hero Fund Commission, Carnegie
425 6th Ave Suite 1640   Pittsburgh PA 15219
Ph: 412-281-1302 ▪ Fx: 412-281-5751 ▪ TF: 800-447-8900
www.carnegiehero.org

Heroes of '76
8301 E Boulevard Dr   Alexandria VA 22308
Ph: 703-765-5000 ▪ Fx: 703-765-8390

Herpes Resource Center, National
PO Box 13827   Research Triangle Park NC 27709
Ph: 919-361-8488 ▪ Fx: 919-361-8425
www.ashastd.org/hrc

Herpetologists, American Society of Ichthyologists &
Florida International Univ Biology Dept 11200 SW 8th
  St   Miami FL 33199
Ph: 305-919-5651 ▪ Fx: 305-919-5964
www.asih.org

Hetrick-Martin Institute Inc
2 Astor Pl   New York NY 10003
Ph: 212-674-2400 ▪ Fx: 212-674-8650
www.hmi.org

Hewlett William & Flora Foundation
2121 Sand Hill Rd   Menlo Park CA 94025
Ph: 650-234-4500 ▪ Fx: 650-234-4501
www.hewlett.org

HHT Foundation International Inc
PO Box 8087   New Haven CT 06530
Ph: 800-448-6389
www.hht.org

Hibakusha, Friends of
1765 Sutter St Suite 2   San Francisco CA 94115
Ph: 415-567-7599 ▪ Fx: 415-931-6158

Hibel Edna Society
PO Box 9721   Coral Springs FL 33075
Ph: 954-731-6699
www.hibel.com/society.htm

High Frontier
2800 Shirlington Rd Suite 405   Arlington VA 22206
Ph: 703-671-4111 ▪ Fx: 703-931-6432
www.highfrontier.org

High School Associations, National Federation of State
PO Box 690   Indianapolis IN 46206
Ph: 317-972-6900 ▪ Fx: 317-822-5700 ▪ TF: 800-776-3462
www.nfhs.org

High School Rodeo Association, National
12001 Tejon St Suite 128   Denver CO 80234
Ph: 303-452-0820 ▪ Fx: 303-452-0912 ▪ TF: 800-466-4772
www.nhsra.org

High/Scope Educational Research Foundation
600 N River St   Ypsilanti MI 48198
Ph: 734-485-2000 ▪ Fx: 734-485-0704 ▪ TF: 800-407-7377
www.highscope.org

High Technology Crime Investigation Association International
1474 Freeman Dr   Amissville VA 20106
Ph: 540-937-5019 ▪ Fx: 540-937-7848
www.htcia.org

High Technology Distribution, Association for
1900 Arch St   Philadelphia PA 19103
Ph: 215-564-3484 ▪ Fx: 215-963-9784
www.ahtd.org

Higher Education Accreditation, Council for
1 Dupont Cir NW Suite 510   Washington DC 20036
Ph: 202-955-6126 ▪ Fx: 202-955-6129
www.chea.org

Higher Education, Alliance for www.allianceedu.org
2602 Rutford Ave   Richardson TX 75080
Ph: 972-883-4920 ▪ Fx: 972-713-8209

Higher Education, American Association for www.aahe.org
1 Dupont Cir NW Suite 360   Washington DC 20036
Ph: 202-293-6440 ▪ Fx: 202-293-0073

Higher Education Assistance Organizations, Coalition of www.coheao.org
1101 Vermont Ave NW Suite 400   Washington DC 20005
Ph: 202-289-3910 ▪ Fx: 202-371-0197

Higher Education, Association for Continuing www.acheinc.org
2001 Mabelene Rd   Charleston SC 29406
Ph: 843-574-6658 ▪ Fx: 843-574-6470 ▪ TF: 800-807-2243

Higher Education, Association for Gerontology in www.aghe.org
1030 15th St NW Suite 240   Washington DC 20005
Ph: 202-289-9806 ▪ Fx: 202-289-9824

Higher Education, Association for the Study of www.ashe.missouri.edu
202 Hill Hall   Columbia MO 65211
Ph: 573-882-9645 ▪ Fx: 573-884-2197

Higher Education Collaboration, Consortium for North American www.conahec.org
Univ of Arizona PO Box 210300   Tucson AZ 85721
Ph: 520-621-7761 ▪ Fx: 520-626-2675

Higher Education, Consortium for the Advancement of Private www.cic.edu/caphe
1 Dupont Cir NW Suite 320   Washington DC 20036
Ph: 202-466-7230 ▪ Fx: 202-466-7238

Higher Education Consortium, American Indian www.aihec.org
121 Oronoco St   Alexandria VA 22314
Ph: 703-838-0400 ▪ Fx: 703-838-0388

Higher Education Consortium for Urban Affairs www.hecua.org
2233 University Ave W Suite 210   Saint Paul MN 55114
Ph: 651-646-8831 ▪ Fx: 651-659-9421 ▪ TF: 800-554-1089

Higher Education, Council for the Advancement of Standards in www.cas.edu
1 Dupont Cir NW Suite 300   Washington DC 20036
Ph: 202-862-1400 ▪ Fx: 202-296-3286

Higher Education, Council on Law in www.clhe.org
111 Coconut Key Ct   Palm Beach Gardens FL 33418
Ph: 561-622-5765 ▪ Fx: 561-624-9198

Higher Education & Disability, Association on www.ahead.org
PO Box 540666   Waltham MA 02454
Ph: 781-788-0003 ▪ Fx: 781-788-0033

Higher Education Executive Officers, State www.sheeo.org
700 Broadway Suite 1200   Denver CO 80203
Ph: 303-299-3685 ▪ Fx: 303-296-9016

Higher Education, Friends Association for www.earlham.edu/~fahe
1501 Cherry St   Philadelphia PA 19102
Ph: 215-241-7116 ▪ Fx: 215-241-7278

Higher Education Loan Programs, National Council of www.nchelp.org
1100 Connecticut Ave NW 12th Fl   Washington DC 20036
Ph: 202-822-2106 ▪ Fx: 202-822-2142

Higher Education Management Systems, National Center for www.nchems.org
PO Box 9752   Boulder CO 80301
Ph: 303-497-0301 ▪ Fx: 303-497-0338

Higher Education, National Association for Equal Opportunity in www.nafeo.org
8701 Georgia Ave Suite 200   Silver Spring MD 20910
Ph: 301-650-2440 ▪ Fx: 301-495-3306

Higher Education, National Association for Physical Education in www.napehe.org
Northern Illinois Univ Dept of Kinesiology & Physical Education
Anderson Hall   DeKalb IL 60015
Ph: 815-753-1894

Higher Education, Society for Values in www.svhe.org
Portland State Univ PO Box 751   Portland OR 97207
Ph: 503-725-2575 ▪ Fx: 503-725-2577

Higher Education, United Ministries in www.umhe.org
7407 Steele Creek Rd   Charlotte NC 28217
Ph: 704-588-2182 ▪ Fx: 704-588-3652

Higher Learning Commission, North Central Association www.ncacihe.org
30 N La Salle St Suite 2400   Chicago IL 60602
Ph: 312-263-0456 ▪ Fx: 312-263-7462 ▪ TF: 800-621-7440

Highland Cattle Association, American www.highlandcattle.org
4701 Marion St 200 Livestock Exchange Bldg   Denver CO 80216
Ph: 303-292-9102 ▪ Fx: 303-292-9171

Highway & Auto Safety, Advocates for www.saferoads.org
750 1st St NE Suite 901   Washington DC 20002
Ph: 202-408-1711 ▪ Fx: 202-408-1699

Highway Engineers, American Society of www.highwayengineers.org
113 Heritage Hills Rd   Uniontown PA 15401
Ph: 724-929-2760 ▪ Fx: 724-929-2234

Highway Loss Data Institute www.carsafety.org
1005 N Glebe Rd Suite 800   Arlington VA 22201
Ph: 703-247-1600 ▪ Fx: 703-247-1595

Highway Safety Association, Governors www.statehighwaysafety.org
750 1st St NE Suite 720   Washington DC 20002
Ph: 202-789-0942 ▪ Fx: 202-789-0946

Highway Safety, Insurance Institute for www.hwysafety.org
1005 N Glebe Rd Suite 800   Arlington VA 22201
Ph: 703-247-1500 ▪ Fx: 703-247-1678

Highway Safety Leaders Inc, National Association of Women www.nawhsl.org
145 Berry Rd   Clinton MS 39056
Ph: 601-924-7815

Highway & Transportation Officials, American Association of State www.aashto.org
444 N Capitol St NW Suite 249   Washington DC 20001
Ph: 202-624-5800 ▪ Fx: 202-624-5806

Highway Users Alliance, American www.highways.org
1 Thomas Cir NW 10th Fl   Washington DC 20005
Ph: 202-857-1200 ▪ Fx: 202-857-1220

Hike Fund Inc www.missouriiojd.org/HIKE
10115 Cherry Hill Pl   Spring Hill FL 34608
Ph: 352-688-2579

(Hiking) Adirondack Forty-Sixers www.adk46r.org
PO Box 180   Cadyville NY 12918
Ph: 518-293-6401

Hiking Society, American www.americanhiking.org
1422 Fenwick Ln   Silver Spring MD 20910
Ph: 301-565-6704 ▪ Fx: 301-565-6714 ▪ TF: 800-972-8608

Hillel: Foundation for Jewish Campus Life www.hillel.org
800 8th St NW   Washington DC 20001
Ph: 202-449-6500 ▪ Fx: 202-847-6693

Hilton Conrad N Foundation www.hiltonfoundation.org
100 W Liberty St Suite 840   Reno NV 89501
Ph: 775-323-4221 ▪ Fx: 775-323-4150

Himalayan International Institute of Yoga Science & Philosophy www.himalayaninstitute.org
RR 1 Box 1127   Honesdale PA 18431
Ph: 570-253-5551 ▪ Fx: 570-253-9078 ▪ TF: 800-822-4547

Himalayan Rabbit Association, American ahra.homestead.com

Hineni International www.hineni.org
232 West End Ave   New York NY 10023
Ph: 212-496-1660 ▪ Fx: 212-496-1908

Hip & Knee Surgeons, American Association of
704 N Florence Dr   Park Ridge IL 60068
Ph: 847-698-1200 ▪ Fx: 847-825-9294

His Majesty's 10th Regiment of Foot - American Contingent www.redcoat.org
61 Ivan St   Lexington MA 02420
Ph: 781-862-2586

Hispana Leadership Institute, National www.nhli.org
1901 N Moore St Suite 206   Arlington VA 22209
Ph: 703-527-6007 ▪ Fx: 703-527-6009

Hispanic Advertising Agencies, Association of www.ahaa.org
8201 Greensboro Dr Suite 300   McLean VA 22102
Ph: 703-610-9014 ▪ Fx: 703-610-9005

Hispanic Americans, Foundation for the Advancement of
6004 Roxbury Ave   Springfield VA 22152
Ph: 703-866-1578 ▪ Fx: 703-354-2329

Hispanic Arts, Association of www.latinoarts.org
155 Ave of the Americas 14th Fl   New York NY 10013
Ph: 212-727-7227 ▪ Fx: 212-427-0549

Hispanic Assembly of the US, Republican National www.rnha.org
PO Box 1882   Washington DC 20013
Ph: 202-544-6700 ▪ Fx: 202-544-6869 ▪ TF: 877-544-6701

Hispanic Association of Colleges & Universities www.hacu.net
8415 Datapoint Dr Suite 400   San Antonio TX 78229
Ph: 210-692-3805 ▪ Fx: 210-692-0823 ▪ TF: 800-780-4228

Hispanic Association on Corporate Responsibility www.hacr.org
1444 'I' St NW Suite 850   Washington DC 20005
Ph: 202-835-9672 ▪ Fx: 202-457-0455

Hispanic Caucus Institute, Congressional www.chci.org
911 2nd St NE   Washington DC 20002
Ph: 202-543-1771 ▪ Fx: 202-546-2143 ▪ TF: 800-392-3532

Hispanic Chamber of Commerce, US www.ushcc.com
2175 K St NW Suite 100   Washington DC 20037
Ph: 202-842-1212 ▪ Fx: 202-842-3221 ▪ TF: 800-874-2286

Hispanic Corporate Council, National www.nhcc-hq.org
1530 Wilson Blvd Suite 110   Arlington VA 22209
Ph: 703-807-5137 ▪ Fx: 703-807-0567

Hispanic Council on Aging, National www.nhcoa.org
2713 Ontario Rd NW   Washington DC 20009
Ph: 202-265-1288 ▪ Fx: 202-745-2522

Hispanic Culture, Association for Puerto Rican-
83 Park Terr W   New York NY 10034
Ph: 212-942-2338

Hispanic Dental Association www.hdassoc.org
188 W Randolph St Suite 415   Chicago IL 60601
Ph: 312-577-4013 ▪ Fx: 312-577-0052 ▪ TF: 800-852-7921

Hispanic Elderly, National Association for
1452 W Temple St Suite 100   Los Angeles CA 90026
Ph: 213-202-5900 ▪ Fx: 213-202-5905

Hispanic Federal Executives, National Association of www.nahfe.org
PO Box 469   Herndon VA 20172
Ph: 703-787-0291 ▪ Fx: 703-787-4675

Hispanic Federation www.hispanicfederation.org
130 William St 9th Fl   New York NY 10038
Ph: 212-233-8655 ▪ Fx: 212-233-8996

Hispanic Foundation for the Arts, National www.hispanicarts.org
1010 Wisconsin Ave NW Suite 210   Washington DC 20007
Ph: 202-293-8330 ▪ Fx: 202-965-5252

Hispanic Health, National Alliance for www.hispanichealth.org
1501 16th St NW   Washington DC 20036
Ph: 202-387-5000 ▪ Fx: 202-797-4353

Hispanic Institute, National www.nhi-net.org
PO Box 220   Maxwell TX 78656
Ph: 512-357-6137 ▪ Fx: 512-357-2206

Hispanic Journalists, National Association of www.nahj.org
529 14th St NW National Press Bldg Suite 1000   Washington DC 20045
Ph: 202-662-7145 ▪ Fx: 202-662-7144 ▪ TF: 888-346-6245

Hispanic & Latino Studies, National Association of
PO Box 325   Biddeford ME 04005
Ph: 207-839-8004 ▪ Fx: 207-839-3776

Hispanic MBAs, National Society of www.nshmba.org
1303 Walnut Hill Ln Suite 300   Irving TX 75038
Ph: 214-596-9325 ▪ TF: 877-467-4622

Hispanic Media Coalition, National www.nhmc.org
2514 S Grand Ave   Los Angeles CA 90007
Ph: 213-746-6988 ▪ Fx: 213-746-1305

Hispanic Medical Association, National www.nhmamd.org
1411 K St NW Suite 200   Washington DC 20005
Ph: 202-628-5895 ▪ Fx: 202-628-5898

(Hispanic Men) Phi Iota Alpha Fraternity Inc www.phiota.org

Hispanic National Bar Association www.hnba.com
815 Connecticut Ave NW Suite 500   Washington DC 20006
Ph: 202-223-4777 ▪ TF: 877-221-6569

Hispanic Nurses, National Association of www.thehispanicnurses.org
1501 16th St NW   Washington DC 20036
Ph: 202-387-2477 ▪ Fx: 202-483-7183

Hispanic Organization of Latin Actors www.hellohola.org
107 Suffolk St Suite 302   New York NY 10002
Ph: 212-253-1015 ▪ Fx: 212-253-9651

Hispanic Professional Engineers, Society of www.shpe.org
5400 E Olympic Blvd Suite 210   Los Angeles CA 90022
Ph: 323-725-3970 ▪ Fx: 323-725-0316

Hispanic Public Relations Association www.hprala.org

Hispanic Publications, National Association of www.nahponline.org
529 14th St NW National Press Bldg Suite 941   Washington
DC 20045
Ph: 202-662-7250 ▪ Fx: 202-662-7254

Hispanic Publishers Federation Inc, US www.ushpf.org
c/o La Informacion 6065 Hillcroft St Suite 400-B   Houston TX
77081
Ph: 713-272-0100 ▪ Fx: 713-272-0011

Hispanic Real Estate Professionals, National Association of www.nahrep.org
404 Camino del Rio S Suite 602   San Diego CA 92108
Ph: 800-964-5373 ▪ Fx: 619-297-3229

Hispanic-Serving Health Professions Schools Inc www.hshps.com
1411 K St NW Suite 200   Washington DC 20005
Ph: 202-783-5262 ▪ Fx: 202-628-5898

Hispanic Social Workers Inc, National Association of Puerto Rican/ www.naprhsw.com
PO Box 651   Brentwood NY 11717
Ph: 631-864-1536

Hispanic Society of America www.hispanicsociety.org
613 W 155th St   New York NY 10032
Ph: 212-926-2234 ▪ Fx: 212-690-0743

(Hispanic) Willie Velasquez Institute www.wcvi.org
206 Lombard St 1st Fl   San Antonio TX 78226
Ph: 210-922-3118 ▪ Fx: 210-932-4055

(Hispanic Women) Latinas Promoviendo Communidad/Lambda www.lambdapichi.org
Pi Chi Sorority Inc

Hispano de Liturgia, Instituto Nacional
PO Box 18   Washington DC 20064
Ph: 202-319-6450 ▪ Fx: 202-319-6949

Histadruth Ivrith of America www.hebrewusa.org
520 8th Ave 15th Fl   New York NY 10018
Ph: 646-472-5390 ▪ Fx: 646-472-5490 ▪ TF: 866-243-2739

Histiocytosis Association of America www.histio.org
72 E Holly Ave Suite 101   Pitman NJ 08071
Ph: 856-589-6606 ▪ Fx: 856-589-6614 ▪ TF: 800-548-2758

Histochemistry & Cytochemistry, International Federation of www.ifshc.org
Societies for   Univ of Washington Dept of Biological Structure
PO Box 357420   Seattle WA 98195
Ph: 206-616-5894 ▪ Fx: 206-616-5842

Histocompatability & Immunogenetics, American Society for www.ashi-hla.org
17000 Commerce Pkwy Suite C   Mount Laurel NJ 08054
Ph: 856-638-0428 ▪ Fx: 856-439-0525

Historians, Academy of Accounting accounting.rutgers.edu/raw/aah
Univ of Alabama Culverhouse School of Accountancy Box
870220   Tuscaloosa AL 34587
Ph: 205-348-9784 ▪ Fx: 205-348-8453

Historians of American www.historians.org/affiliates/hisn_am_communism.htm
Communism

Historians of American Foreign Relations, Society for www.shafr.org

Historians Association, American Journalism www.berry.edu/ajha
Oklahoma Baptist Univ 500 W University St Box
61201   Shawnee OK 74804
Ph: 405-878-2221

Historians, Association of Ancient www.trentu.ca/ahc/aah
City College of New York Dept of Foreign Languages &
Literatures NAC 5-223   New York NY 10031
Ph: 212-650-6731 ▪ Fx: 718-796-4392

Historians, Association of Personal www.personalhistorians.org

Historians of the Early American Republic, Society for www.sla.purdue.edu/jer

Historians of Medieval Spain, American Academy of Research www.uca.edu/aarhms

Historians, Organization of American www.indiana.edu/~oah
112 N Bryan Ave   Bloomington IN 47408
Ph: 812-855-7311 ▪ Fx: 812-855-0696

Historians' Organization, MARHO: Radical www.historians.org/affiliates
c/o American Historical Assn 400 A St SE   Washington DC
20003
Ph: 202-544-2422 ▪ Fx: 202-544-8307

Historians, Society of American www.historians.org/affiliates
Columbia Univ 603 Fayerweather Hall MC 2538   New York NY
10027
Ph: 212-854-5943 ▪ Fx: 212-932-0602

Historians, Society of Architectural www.sah.org
1365 N Astor St   Chicago IL 60610
Ph: 312-573-1365 ▪ Fx: 312-573-1141

Historians, Society of Automotive www.autohistory.org
1102 Long Cove Rd   Gales Ferry CT 06335
Ph: 860-464-6466 ▪ Fx: 860-464-2614

Historic American Theatres, League of www.lhat.org
616 Water St Suite 320   Baltimore MD 21202
Ph: 410-659-9533 ▪ Fx: 410-837-9664 ▪ TF: 877-627-0833

Historic & Artistic Works, American Institute for Conservation of aic.stanford.edu
1717 K St NW Suite 200   Washington DC 20006
Ph: 202-452-9545 ▪ Fx: 202-452-9328

Historic Brass Society www.historicbrass.org
148 W 23rd St Unit 2A   New York NY 10011
Ph: 212-627-3820

Historic Deerfield Inc www.historic-deerfield.org
PO Box 321   Deerfield MA 01342
Ph: 413-774-5581 ▪ Fx: 413-775-7220

Historic Genealogical Society, New England www.newenglandancestors.org
101 Newbury St   Boston MA 02116
Ph: 617-536-5740 ▪ Fx: 617-536-7307 ▪ TF: 888-296-3447

Historic Hawaii Foundation www.historichawaii.org
PO Box 1658   Honolulu HI 96806
Ph: 808-523-2900 ▪ Fx: 808-523-0800

Historic Naval Ships Association www.hnsa.org

Historic Preservation, National Trust for www.nationaltrust.org
1785 Massachusetts Ave NW   Washington DC 20036
Ph: 202-588-6000 ▪ Fx: 202-588-6038 ▪ TF: 800-944-6847

Historic Preservation Officers, National Conference of State www.ncshpo.org
444 N Capitol St NW Hall of States Suite 342   Washington DC
20001
Ph: 202-624-5465 ▪ Fx: 202-624-5419

(Historic Preservation) Victorian Society in America www.victoriansociety.org
205 S Camac St   Philadelphia PA 19107
Ph: 215-545-8340 ▪ Fx: 215-545-8379

Historic Pullman Foundation www.pullmanil.org
614 E 113th St   Chicago IL 60628
Ph: 773-785-8181 ▪ Fx: 773-785-8182

Historic Racing Motorcycle Association, American www.ahrma.org
PO Box 1723   Goodlettsville TN 37070
Ph: 615-851-3674 ▪ Fx: 615-851-3678

(Historic Sites) National Temple Hill Association www.nationaltemplehill.org
PO Box 315   Vails Gate NY 12584
Ph: 914-561-5073

Historic Winslow House Association www.winslowhouse.org
644 Careswell St   Marshfield MA 02050
Ph: 781-837-5753

Historical Archaeology, Society for www.sha.org
19 Mantua Rd   Mount Royal NJ 08061
Ph: 856-224-0995 ▪ Fx: 856-423-3420

Historical Association, Adirondack
Adirondack Museum PO Box 99   Blue Mountain Lake NY
12812
Ph: 518-352-7311 ▪ Fx: 518-352-7653

Historical Association, American www.historians.org
400 A St SE   Washington DC 20003
Ph: 202-544-2422 ▪ Fx: 202-544-8307

Historical Association, American Italian www.mobilito.com/aiha
169 Country Club Rd   Chicago Heights IL 60411
Ph: 708-756-7168

Historical Association, Friends www.haverford.edu/library/fha/fha.html
Haverford College Library 370 Lancaster Ave   Haverford PA
19041
Ph: 610-896-1161 ▪ Fx: 610-896-1102

Historical Association, John Pelham
7 Carmel Tier   Hampton VA 23666
Ph: 757-838-1685

Historical Association, Norwegian-American www.naha.stolaf.edu
St Olaf College 1510 St Olaf Ave   Northfield MN 55057
Ph: 507-646-3221 ▪ Fx: 507-646-3734

Historical Association, Polish American www.polishamericanstudies.org
3535 Indian Trail   Orchard Lake MI 48324
Ph: 248-683-1743 ▪ Fx: 248-738-6736

Historical Association, Pony Express www.stjoseph.net/ponyexpress
12th & Penn Sts PO Box 1022   Saint Joseph MO 64502
Ph: 816-232-8206 ▪ Fx: 816-232-3717

Historical Center, Houdini www.foxvalleyhistory.org/houdini
330 E College Ave   Appleton WI 54911
Ph: 920-733-8445 ▪ Fx: 920-733-8636

Historical Committee, Mennonite Church USA www.mcusa-archives.org
1700 S Main St   Goshen IN 46526
Ph: 574-535-7477 ▪ Fx: 574-535-7756

Historical Conference, Lutheran www.luthhist.org
Concordia Univ 7400 Augusta St   River Forest IL 60305
Ph: 708-771-6640

Historical & Cultural Society, Portuguese www.sacramentophcs.com
PO Box 161990   Sacramento CA 95816
Ph: 916-392-1048

Historical Fire Foundation, National www.historicalharps.org
6101 E Van Buren St   Phoenix AZ 85008
Ph: 602-275-3473 ▪ Fx: 602-275-0896

Historical Foundation, Air Force www.afhistoricalfoundation.com
1535 Command Dr Suite A-122   Andrews Air Force Base MD
20762
Ph: 301-736-1959 ▪ Fx: 301-981-3574

Historical Foundation, Army www.armyhistoryfnd.org
2425 Wilson Blvd   Arlington VA 22201
Ph: 703-522-7901 ▪ Fx: 703-522-7929 ▪ TF: 800-506-2672

Historical Foundation, Naval www.navyhistory.org
1306 Dahlgren Ave SE Washington Navy Yard   Washington DC
20374
Ph: 202-678-4333 ▪ Fx: 202-889-3565

Historical & Genealogical Society, Afro-American www.aahgs.org
PO Box 73067   Washington DC 20056
Ph: 202-234-5350 ▪ Fx: 202-829-9280

Historical Harp Society www.historicalharps.org
631 N 3rd Ave   Saint Charles IL 60174
Ph: 630-584-5259

Historical Journals, Conference of
Univ of Arkansas Dept of History Old Main 416   Fayetteville AR
72701
Ph: 501-575-5884

Historical Keyboard Society, Southeastern www.sehks.org
PO Box 32022   Charlotte NC 28232
Ph: 704-334-3468 ▪ Fx: 704-334-3442

Historical Library & Archives, Southern Baptist   www.sbhla.org
901 Commerce St Suite 400   Nashville TN 37203
Ph: 615-244-0344

Historical & Museum Association, Custer Battlefield   www.cbhma.org
PO Box 902   Hardin MT 59034
Ph: 406-665-2060 ▪ Fx: 406-665-3133

Historical Organization, International Photographic   www.well.com/user/silver
PO Box 16074   San Francisco CA 94116
Ph: 415-681-4356

Historical Print Collectors Society, American   www.ahpcs.org
PO Box 201   Fairfield CT 06824
Ph: 203-255-1627

Historical Society of America, Italian   www.italianhistorical.org
111 Columbia Heights   Brooklyn NY 11201
Ph: 718-852-2929

Historical Society of America, Steamship   www.sshsa.net
300 Ray Dr Suite 4   Providence RI 02906
Ph: 401-274-0805 ▪ Fx: 401-274-0836

Historical Society of America, Theatre   www.historictheatres.org
152 N York Rd 2nd Fl   Elmhurst IL 60126
Ph: 630-782-1800 ▪ Fx: 630-782-1802

Historical Society, American Baptist   www.abc-usa.org/abhs
PO Box 851   Valley Forge PA 19482
Ph: 610-768-2269 ▪ Fx: 610-768-2266

Historical Society, American Catholic   www.amchs.org

Historical Society, American Hungarian Library &   www.hungarianhouse.org
213 E 82nd St   New York NY 10028
Ph: 212-249-9360

Historical Society, American Irish   www.aihs.org
991 5th Ave   New York NY 10028
Ph: 212-288-2263 ▪ Fx: 212-628-7927

Historical Society, American Jewish   www.ajhs.org
15 W 16th St   New York NY 10011
Ph: 212-294-6160 ▪ Fx: 212-294-6161

Historical Society, American Photographic   www.superexpo.com/APHS.htm
1150 Ave of the Americas   New York NY 10036
Ph: 212-575-0483

Historical Society, American Truck   www.aths.org
PO Box 901611   Kansas City MO 64190
Ph: 816-891-9900 ▪ Fx: 816-891-9903

Historical Society, Augustana   www.augustana.edu/Historical
Augustana College 639 38th St   Rock Island IL 61201
Ph: 309-794-7166 ▪ Fx: 309-794-7443

Historical Society, B-26 Marauder   b-26marauderarchive.org
PO Box 1786   Rockville MD 20849
Ph: 301-460-4488 ▪ Fx: 301-460-2075

Historical Society, Cherokee National   www.cherokeeheritage.org
PO Box 515   Tahlequah OK 74465
Ph: 918-456-6007 ▪ Fx: 918-456-6165 ▪ TF: 888-999-6007

Historical Society, Chesapeake & Ohio   www.cohs.org
PO Box 79   Clifton Forge VA 24422
Ph: 540-862-2210 ▪ Fx: 540-863-9159 ▪ TF: 800-453-2647

Historical Society, Congregational Christian   www.cchsonline.org
14 Beacon St   Boston MA 02108
Ph: 617-523-0470 ▪ Fx: 617-523-0491

Historical Society, Disciples of Christ   www.dishistsoc.org
1101 19th Ave S   Nashville TN 37212
Ph: 615-327-1444 ▪ Fx: 615-327-1445

Historical Society of Early American Decoration   www.hsead.org
Farmers Museum PO Box 30   Cooperstown NY 13326
Ph: 607-547-5667

Historical Society of the Episcopal Church   www.hsec-usa.org
PO Box 2247   Manchaca TX 78652
Ph: 512-282-3234 ▪ Fx: 512-280-3902 ▪ TF: 800-553-7745

Historical Society, Filipino American National   www.fanhs-national.org
810 18th Ave Rm 100   Seattle WA 98122
Ph: 206-322-0203 ▪ Fx: 206-461-4879

Historical Society of Germans from Russia, American   www.ahsgr.org
631 D St   Lincoln NE 68502
Ph: 402-474-3363 ▪ Fx: 402-474-7229

Historical Society, Great Lakes   www.inlandseas.org
Inland Seas Maritime Museum 480 Main St   PO Box 435   Vermilion OH 44089
Ph: 440-967-3467 ▪ Fx: 440-967-1419 ▪ TF: 800-893-1485

Historical Society, Huguenot   www.hhs-newpaltz.org
18 Broadhead Ave   New Paltz NY 12561
Ph: 845-255-1660 ▪ Fx: 845-255-0376

Historical Society, Illinois Central Railroad   www.icrrhistorical.org
PO Box 288   Paxton IL 60957
Ph: 217-379-2261

Historical Society, Lancaster Mennonite   www.lmhs.org
2215 Millstream Rd   Lancaster PA 17602
Ph: 717-393-9745 ▪ Fx: 717-393-8751

Historical Society, Mid-Continent Railway   www.midcontinent.org
PO Box 358   North Freedom WI 53951
Ph: 608-522-4261 ▪ Fx: 608-522-4490

Historical Society, Moravian   www.moravianhistoricalsociety.org
214 E Center St   Nazareth PA 18064
Ph: 610-759-5070 ▪ Fx: 610-759-2461

Historical Society, National Japanese American   www.njahs.org
1684 Post St   San Francisco CA 94115
Ph: 415-921-5007 ▪ Fx: 415-921-5087

Historical Society, National Railway   www.nrhs.com
PO Box 58547   Philadelphia PA 19102
Ph: 215-557-6606 ▪ Fx: 215-557-6740

Historical Society, Ontario & Western Railway   www.nyow.org

Historical Society, Organ   www.organsociety.org
PO Box 26811   Richmond VA 23261
Ph: 804-353-9226 ▪ Fx: 804-353-9266

Historical Society, Partisan Prohibition   www.prohibitionists.org
PO Box 2635   Denver CO 80201
Ph: 303-237-4947

Historical Society Inc, Railway & Locomotive   www.rrhistorical-2.com/rlhs
1610 N Vinton Rd   Anthony NM 88021
Ph: 505-882-5485

Historical Society, Rodeo
c/o National Cowboy & Western Heritage Museum 1700 NE 63rd St   Oklahoma City OK 73111
Ph: 405-478-6400 ▪ Fx: 405-478-2842

Historical Society, Seventh Day Baptist   home.inwave.com/sdbhist
PO Box 1678   Janesville WI 53547
Ph: 608-752-5055 ▪ Fx: 608-752-7711

Historical Society, Superstition Mountain   www.superstitionmountainmuseum.org
PO Box 3845   Apache Junction AZ 85217
Ph: 480-983-4888 ▪ Fx: 480-474-9410

Historical Society, Supreme Court   www.supremecourthistory.org/
224 E Capitol St NE   Washington DC 20003
Ph: 202-543-0400 ▪ Fx: 202-547-7730

Historical Society, Surveyors   www.surveyhistory.org/surveyor's_historical_society.htm
300 W High St Suite 2   Lawrenceburg IN 47025
Ph: 812-537-2000

Historical Society, Titanic   www.titanic1.org
208 Main St PO Box 51053   Indian Orchard MA 01151
Ph: 413-543-4770 ▪ Fx: 413-583-3633

Historical Society, US   www.ushs.org
1st & Main Sts   Richmond VA 23219
Ph: 804-648-4736 ▪ Fx: 804-648-0002 ▪ TF: 800-788-4478

Historical Society, US Capitol   www.uschs.org
200 Maryland Ave NE   Washington DC 20002
Ph: 202-543-8919 ▪ Fx: 202-544-8244

Historical Society of Washington DC   www.hswdc.org
801 K St NW   Washington DC 20001
Ph: 202-383-1800 ▪ Fx: 202-383-1870

Historical Society of the West, Finnish-American   www.finamhsw.com
PO Box 5522   Portland OR 97228
Ph: 503-654-0448

Historical Studies, Society for Italian   www.historians.org/affiliates
Boston College   Chestnut Hill MA 02467
Ph: 617-552-3814 ▪ Fx: 617-552-2478

Historical Studies, Society for   www.ukans.edu/~iberia/ssphs/ssphs_main.html
Spanish & Portuguese

Historical Trust, Holland   www.hollandmuseum.org
31 W 10th St   Holland MI 49423
Ph: 616-394-1362 ▪ Fx: 616-394-4756 ▪ TF: 888-200-9123

History, American Association for State & Local   www.aaslh.org
1717 Church St   Nashville TN 37203
Ph: 615-320-3203 ▪ Fx: 615-327-9013

History Associates Inc, Pearl Harbor   www.pearlharbor-history.org
PO Box 1007   Stratford CT 06615
Ph: 203-378-2353

History Association, American Printing   www.printinghistory.org

History Association, Mining   www.mininghistoryassociation.org
c/o Colorado School of Mines Library 1400 Illinois St   Golden CO 80401
Ph: 303-273-3815

History Association, Mormon   www.mhahome.org
581 S 630 East   Orem UT 84097
Ph: 801-224-0241 ▪ Fx: 801-224-5684 ▪ TF: 888-642-3678

History Association, Social Science   www.ssha.org
c/o Duke University Press Box 90660   Durham NC 27708
Ph: 919-687-3602

History, Association for the Study of African American Life &   www.asalh.org
Howard Univ CB Powell Bldg 525 Bryant St Suite C142   Washington DC 20059
Ph: 202-865-0053 ▪ Fx: 202-265-7920

History Association, World   www.thewha.org
Univ of Hawaii at Manoa Sakamaki Hall A203 2530 Dole St   Honolulu HI 96822
Ph: 808-956-7688

History of Authorship Reading & Publishing, Society for the   www.sharpweb.org
PO Box 30   Wilmington NC 28402
Ph: 910-254-0308

History of Behavioral & Social Sciences, Cheiron: www.psych.yorku.ca/orgs/cheiron
International Society for the

History, Center for Socialist   csh.gn.apc.org/
PO Box 626   Alameda CA 94501
Ph: 510-601-6460

History of Chiropractic, Association for the   www.chiroweb.com/ahc
1000 Brady St   Davenport IA 52803
Ph: 563-884-5855 ▪ Fx: 563-884-5616

History, Conference on Faith &   www.huntington.edu/cfh
Gordon College Dept of History   Wrenham MA 01984
Ph: 978-867-4415

History & Culture, Omohundro Institute of Early American   www.wm.edu/oieahc
PO Box 8781   Williamsbury VA 23187
Ph: 757-221-1110 ▪ Fx: 757-221-1047

History Day, National   www.nationalhistoryday.org
Univ of Maryland 0119 Cecil Hall   College Park MD 20742
Ph: 301-314-9739 ▪ Fx: 301-314-9767

History of Dentistry, American Academy of the
Oregon Health Sciences Univ School of Dentistry 611 SW Campus Dr   Portland OR 97239
Ph: 503-494-4316

History of Dermatology Society   www.dermato.med.br/hds
1819 John F Kennedy Blvd Suite 465   Philadelphia PA 19103
Ph: 215-563-8333 ▪ Fx: 215-563-3044

History of Discoveries, Society for the www.sochistdisc.org
5502 Laurel Ridge Dr Alpharetta GA 30005
Ph: 770-772-6366

History of Earth Sciences Society www.historyearthscience.org
PO Box 455 Poncha Springs CO 81242
Ph: 719-539-4113 ▪ Fx: 719-539-4542

History of Economics Society eh.net/HE/HisEcSoc

History Education, National Council for www.history.org/nche
26915 Westwood Rd Suite B2 Westlake OH 44145
Ph: 440-835-1776 ▪ Fx: 440-835-1295

History Education, Society for www.csulb.edu/~histeach
PO Box 1578 Borrego Springs CA 92004
Ph: 760-767-5938

History of Education Society www.sru.edu/depts/scc/hes/hes.htm
Slippery Rock Univ 220 McKay Educational Bldg Slippery Rock
PA 16057
Ph: 724-738-4557 ▪ Fx: 724-738-4548

History in the Federal Government, Society for www.shfg.org
PO Box 14139 Ben Franklin Stn Washington DC 20044
Ph: 202-501-5350 ▪ Fx: 202-219-2176

History of the Health Sciences, Archivists & Librarians in the www.alhhs.org
Virginia Commonwealth Univ Tompkins-McCaw Library Box
980582 Richmond VA 23298
Ph: 804-828-9898 ▪ Fx: 804-828-6089

History of Medicine, American Association for the www.histmed.org
East Carolina Univ School of Medicine Dept of Medical
Humanities Greenville NC 27858
Ph: 252-816-2797 ▪ Fx: 252-816-2319

History, National Coalition for www.h-net.org/~nch
400 A St SE Washington DC 20003
Ph: 202-544-2422 ▪ Fx: 202-544-8307

History, National Council on Public ncph.org
425 University Blvd Indianapolis IN 46202
Ph: 317-274-2716 ▪ Fx: 317-278-5230

History, North American Society for Oceanic www.ecu.edu/nasoh/
PO Box 18108 Washington DC 20036
Ph: 202-707-1409

History, North American Society for Sport www.nassh.org
PO Box 1026 Lemont PA 16851
Ph: 814-238-1288

History of Nursing, American Association for the www.aahn.org
PO Box 175 Lanoka Harbor NJ 08734
Ph: 609-693-7250 ▪ Fx: 609-693-1037

History & Ourselves National Foundation Inc, Facing www.facing.org
16 Hurd Rd Brookline MA 02445
Ph: 617-232-1595 ▪ Fx: 617-232-0281

History of Pharmacy, American Institute of the www.aihp.org
777 Highland Ave Madison WI 53705
Ph: 608-262-5378

(History) Phi Alpha Theta www.phialphatheta.org
Univ of South Florida 4202 E Fowler Ave SOC 107 Tampa FL
33620
Ph: 813-974-8212 ▪ Fx: 813-974-8215 ▪ TF: 800-394-8195

History Philosophy & Social Studies of Biology, International www.phil.vt.edu/ishpssb
Society for the 13423 Burma Rd SW Vashon Island WA
98070
Ph: 206-567-5839

History Project, National Women's www.nwhp.org
3343 Industrial Dr Suite 4 Santa Rosa CA 95403
Ph: 707-636-2888 ▪ Fx: 707-636-2909 ▪ TF: 800-691-8888

History of Science Society www.hssonline.org
Univ of Florida 3310 Turlington Hall PO Box
117360 Gainesville FL 32611
Ph: 352-392-1677 ▪ Fx: 352-392-2795

History, Society for the Comparative Study of www.lsa.umich.edu/history/CSSH
Society & Univ of Michigan 4418 Modern Languages Bldg
812 E Washington St Ann Arbor MI 48109
Ph: 734-764-6362 ▪ Fx: 734-647-2105

History Society, Immigration & Ethnic www.iehs.org
American Univ 4400 Massachusetts NW Washington DC
20016
Ph: 202-885-2410

History, Society for Military www.smh-hq.org
3119 Lakeview Cir Leavenworth KS 66048
Ph: 913-758-3322 ▪ Fx: 913-758-3309

History Society, Postal 8207 Daren Ct Pikesville MD 21208
Ph: 410-653-0665

History Society, Postcard 1795 Kleinfeltersville Rd Stevens PA 17578
Ph: 717-721-9273

History of Technology, Society for the shot.press.jhu.edu

Histotechnology, National Society for www.nsh.org
4201 Northview Dr Suite 502 Bowie MD 20716
Ph: 301-262-6221 ▪ Fx: 301-262-9188

Hitchhikers of America International www.hitchhikerrvclub.com
PO Box 180 Osceola IN 46561
Ph: 574-258-0591 ▪ Fx: 574-259-7105 ▪ TF: 800-262-5178

(HIV/AIDS) Damien Ministries www.damienministries.org
PO Box 10202 Washington DC 20018
Ph: 202-526-3020 ▪ Fx: 202-526-9770

(HIV/AIDS) Women Alive www.women-alive.org
1566 S Burnside Ave Los Angeles CA 90019
Ph: 323-965-1564 ▪ Fx: 323-965-9886 ▪ TF: 800-554-4876

(HIV/AIDS) WORLD www.womenhiv.org
414 13th St 2nd Fl Oakland CA 94612
Ph: 510-986-0340 ▪ Fx: 510-986-0341

Hobbit Association, American
PO Box 51 Mason OH 45040
Ph: 513-398-4742

Hobby Greenhouse Association www.hobbygreenhouse.org
8 Glen Terr Bedford MA 01730
Ph: 781-275-0377

Hobby Industry Association www.hobby.org
319 E 54th St Elmwood Park NJ 07407
Ph: 201-794-1133 ▪ Fx: 201-797-0657 ▪ TF: 800-822-0494

Hobby Stores Association, National Retail www.hobbystores.org
710 E Ogden Ave Suite 600 Naperville IL 60563
Ph: 630-579-3296 ▪ Fx: 630-629-2488

Hobby Trade Association, Radio Control www.rchta.org
PO Box 315 Butler NJ 07405
Ph: 973-283-9088 ▪ Fx: 973-838-7124

Hobie Class Association, International www.hobieclass.com
3334 Fulton Victoria BC V9C2T9
Ph: 250-474-7580

Hockey America, College info.bemidjistate.edu/sports/cha
3163 Birchmont Dr NE Bemidji MN 56601
Ph: 218-755-2767 ▪ Fx: 218-755-3898

Hockey Association, American Collegiate www.achahockey.org
PO Box 1013 Kent OH 44240
Ph: 330-221-4411

Hockey Association, American Hearing Impaired www.ahiha.org
1143 W Lake St Chicago IL 60607
Ph: 312-226-5880 ▪ Fx: 312-829-2098

Hockey Association, Central Collegiate www.ccha.com
23995 Freeway Park Dr Farmington Hills MI 48335
Ph: 248-888-0600 ▪ Fx: 248-888-0664

Hockey Association, NorthEast Collegiate www.necha.org
PO Box 58 Keene NH 03431
Ph: 603-363-4508

Hockey Association, US Field www.usfieldhockey.com
1 Olympic Plaza Colorado Springs CO 80909
Ph: 719-866-4567 ▪ Fx: 719-632-0979

Hockey Association, Western Collegiate wcha.ocsn.com
2190 S High St Denver CO 80208
Ph: 303-871-4223 ▪ Fx: 303-871-2600

Hockey Coaches Association, American www.ahcahockey.com
7 Concord St Gloucester MA 01930
Ph: 781-245-4177 ▪ Fx: 781-245-2492

Hockey East Association www.hockeyeastonline.com
591 North Ave Suite 2 Wakefield MA 01880
Ph: 781-245-2122 ▪ Fx: 781-245-2492

Hockey InLine, USA www.usahockey.com/inline
1775 Bob Johnson Dr Colorado Springs CO 80906
Ph: 719-576-8724 ▪ Fx: 719-538-1160

Hockey League, Atlantic Coast Collegiate www.acchockey.com
380 S State Rd 434 Altamonte Springs FL 32714
Ph: 407-296-5269

Hockey League, Central States Collegiate www.cschl.com
2475 Archdale West Bloomfield MI 48324
Ph: 248-366-7914 ▪ Fx: 248-366-7915

Hockey League Players Association, National www.nhlpa.com
777 Bay St Suite 2400 Toronto ON M5G2C8
Ph: 416-408-4040 ▪ Fx: 416-313-2301 ▪ TF: 800-363-4625

Hockey League, Southwest Collegiate www.schl.org
1533 Fairfield Ct Lewisville TX 75077
Ph: 972-436-1560 ▪ Fx: 972-436-1560

Hockey League, Tri-State Collegiate www.tschl.com
Purdue University West Lafayette IN 47907
Ph: 765-494-8931 ▪ Fx: 765-494-8956

Hockey North America www.theleagueoffice.com
PO Box 78 Sterling VA 20167
Ph: 703-430-8100 ▪ Fx: 703-421-9205 ▪ TF: 800-446-2539

Hockey, USA www.usahockey.com
1775 Bob Johnson Dr Colorado Springs CO 80906
Ph: 719-576-8724 ▪ Fx: 719-538-1160

Hog Record Association, National Hereford
22405 480th Ave Flandreau SD 57028
Ph: 605-997-2116

(Hogs) American Berkshire Association www.americanberkshire.com
PO Box 2436 West Lafayette IN 47996
Ph: 765-497-3618 ▪ Fx: 765-497-2959

Hoist Manufacturers Institute www.mhia.org/psc
8720 Red Oak Blvd Suite 201 Charlotte NC 28217
Ph: 704-676-1190 ▪ Fx: 704-676-1199

Hole in the Wall Gang Camps Inc www.hitwgcamps.org
265 Church St New Haven CT 06510
Ph: 203-562-1203 ▪ Fx: 203-562-1207

Holiday Inns, International Association of www.iahi.org
3 Ravinia Dr Suite 100 Atlanta GA 30346
Ph: 770-604-5555 ▪ Fx: 770-604-5684 ▪ TF: 866-826-5808

Holiday Rambler Recreational Vehicle Club www.hrrvc.org
PO Box 587 Wakarusa IN 46573
Ph: 574-862-7330 ▪ Fx: 574-862-7390 ▪ TF: 877-702-5415

Holisfic Dental Association www.holisticdental.org
PO Box 5007 Durango CO 81301
Ph: 970-259-1091

Holistic Aromatherapy, National Association for www.naha.org
4509 Interlake Ave N Suite 233 Seattle WA 98103
Ph: 206-547-2164 ▪ Fx: 206-547-2680 ▪ TF: 888-275-6242

Holistic Health Association, American ahha.org
PO Box 17400 Anaheim CA 92817
Ph: 714-779-6152

Holistic Medical Association, American www.holisticmedicine.org
12101 Menaul Blvd NE Suite C Albuquerque NM 87112
Ph: 505-292-7788 ▪ Fx: 505-293-7582

Holistic Nurses' Association, American ahna.org
PO Box 2130 Flagstaff AZ 86003
Ph: 928-526-2196 ▪ Fx: 928-526-2752 ▪ TF: 800-278-2462

Holistic Veterinary Medical Association, American   www.ahvma.org
2218 Old Emmorton Rd   Bel Air MD 21015
Ph: 410-569-0795 ▪ Fx: 410-569-2346

Holland Historical Trust   www.hollandmuseum.org
31 W 10th St   Holland MI 49423
Ph: 616-394-1362 ▪ Fx: 616-394-4756 ▪ TF: 888-200-9123

Holly Society of America   www.hollysocam.org
309 Buck St PO Box 803   Millville NJ 08332
Ph: 856-825-4300

Hollywood Foreign Press Association
646 N Robertson Blvd   West Hollywood CA 90069
Ph: 310-657-1731 ▪ Fx: 310-657-5576

Hollywood Radio & Television Society   www.hrts-iba.org
13701 Riverside Dr Suite 205   Sherman Oaks CA 91423
Ph: 818-789-1182 ▪ Fx: 818-789-1210

Holocaust Documentation & Education Center
13899 Biscayne Blvd   North Miami Beach FL 33181
Ph: 305-919-5690 ▪ Fx: 305-919-5691

(Holocaust) Simon Wiesenthal Center   www.wiesenthal.com
1399 S Roxbury Dr   Los Angeles CA 90035
Ph: 310-553-9036 ▪ Fx: 310-772-7655

Holocaust, Society for the Philosophical Study of   www.loyno.edu/~spsgh
Genocide & the   Loyola Univ   Dept of Philosophy   New
Orleans LA 70118
Ph: 504-865-3940 ▪ Fx: 504-865-3948

Holocaust Survivors, American Gathering of Jewish
122 W 30th St Suite 205   New York NY 10001
Ph: 212-239-4230 ▪ Fx: 212-279-2926

Holocaust Survivors & Friends In Pursuit of Justice
800 New Loudon Rd Suite 400   Latham NY 12110
Ph: 518-785-0035 ▪ Fx: 518-783-1557

Holstein Association USA Inc   www.holsteinusa.com
1 Holstein Pl   Brattleboro VT 05302
Ph: 802-254-4551 ▪ Fx: 802-254-8251 ▪ TF: 800-952-5200

Holstein Junior Program   www.holsteinusa.com
1 Holstein Pl   Brattleboro VT 05302
Ph: 802-254-4551 ▪ Fx: 802-254-8251 ▪ TF: 800-952-5200

Holsteiner Horse Association, American   www.holsteiner.com
222 E Main St Suite 1   Georgetown KY 40324
Ph: 502-863-4239 ▪ Fx: 502-868-0722

Holt International Children's Services   www.holtinternational.org
1195 City View PO Box 2880   Eugene OR 97402
Ph: 541-687-2202 ▪ Fx: 541-683-6175

Holy Childhood Association   www.worldmissions-catholicchurch.org
366 5th Ave   New York NY 10001
Ph: 212-563-8700 ▪ Fx: 212-563-8725

Holy Cross Family Ministries   www.familyrosary.org
518 Washington St   North Easton MA 02356
Ph: 508-238-4095 ▪ Fx: 508-238-3953 ▪ TF: 800-299-7729

Holy Face Association   www.holyface.org
PO Box 1000 Stn A   Montreal QC H3C2W9
Ph: 514-747-0357 ▪ Fx: 514-747-9147

Holy Trinity, Society of Our Lady of the Most   www.solt3.org
PO Box 152   Robstown TX 78380
Ph: 361-387-2754 ▪ Fx: 361-387-3818

Home Appliance Manufacturers, Association of   www.aham.org
1111 19th St NW Suite 402   Washington DC 20036
Ph: 202-872-5955 ▪ Fx: 202-872-9354

Home Baking Association   www.homebaking.org
2931 SW Gainsboro Rd   Topeka KS 66614
Ph: 785-478-3283 ▪ Fx: 785-478-3024

Home Based Businesses, National Association of   www.usahomebusiness.com
10451 Mill Run Cir Suite 400   Owings Mills MD 21117
Ph: 410-363-3698

Home-Based Working Moms   www.hbwm.com
PO Box 500164   Austin TX 78750
Ph: 512-266-0900 ▪ TF: 800-281-8565

Home Builders Institute   www.hbi.org
1201 15th St NW 6th Fl   Washington DC 20005
Ph: 202-371-0600 ▪ Fx: 202-266-8999

Home Builders, National Association of   www.nahb.org
1201 15th St NW   Washington DC 20005
Ph: 202-266-8200 ▪ TF: 800-368-5242

Home Care & Hospice, National Association for   www.nahc.org
228 7th St SE   Washington DC 20003
Ph: 202-547-7424 ▪ Fx: 202-547-3540

Home Care Physicians, American Academy of   www.aahcp.org
PO Box 1037   Edgewood MD 21040
Ph: 410-676-7966 ▪ Fx: 410-676-7980

Home Education Research Institute, National   www.nheri.org
PO Box 13939   Salem OR 97309
Ph: 503-364-1490 ▪ Fx: 503-364-2827

Home Equity Conversion, National Center for   www.reverse.org/nchec.htm
360 N Robert St Suite 403   Saint Paul MN 55101
Ph: 651-222-6775 ▪ Fx: 651-222-6797 ▪ TF: 800-209-8085

Home Equity Mortgage Association, National   www.nhema.org
1301 Pennsylvania Ave NW Sutie 500   Washington DC 20004
Ph: 202-347-1210 ▪ Fx: 202-347-1171 ▪ TF: 800-342-1121

Home Fashion Products Association
355 Lexington Ave 17th Fl   New York NY 10017
Ph: 212-297-2122 ▪ Fx: 212-370-9047

Home Furnishings Association, National   www.nhfa.org
PO Box 2396   High Point NC 27261
Ph: 336-886-6100 ▪ Fx: 336-801-6102 ▪ TF: 800-888-9590

Home Furnishings International Association   www.hfia.org
PO Box 420807   Dallas TX 75342
Ph: 214-741-7632 ▪ Fx: 214-742-9103 ▪ TF: 800-942-4663

Home Furnishings Marketing Authority, International   www.furnituremarket.org
PO Box 5243   High Point NC 27262
Ph: 336-869-1000 ▪ Fx: 336-869-6999

Home Furnishings Representatives Association, International   www.ihfra.org
PO Box 670   High Point NC 27261
Ph: 336-889-3920 ▪ Fx: 336-883-8245 ▪ TF: 800-889-3920

Home Healthcare Nurses Association   www.hhna.org
228 7th St SE   Washington DC 20003
Ph: 202-546-4754 ▪ Fx: 202-547-3540

Home Improvement Research Institute   www.hiri.org
3922 Coconut Palm Dr 3rd Fl   Tampa FL 33619
Ph: 813-627-6750 ▪ Fx: 813-627-7063

Home Infusion Association, National   www.nhianet.org
205 Daingerfield Rd   Alexandria VA 22314
Ph: 703-549-3740 ▪ Fx: 703-683-1484 ▪ TF: 800-544-7447

Home Inspectors, American Society of   www.ashi.com
932 Lee St Suite 101   Des Plaines IL 60016
Ph: 847-759-2820 ▪ Fx: 847-759-1620 ▪ TF: 800-743-2744

Home Inspectors, Examination Board of Professional   www.homeinspectionexam.org
932 Lee St Suite 202   Des Plaines IL 60016
Ph: 847-298-7750 ▪ Fx: 847-299-2505

Home Inspectors, National Association of   www.nahi.org
4248 Park Glen Rd   Minneapolis MN 55416
Ph: 952-928-4641 ▪ Fx: 952-929-1318 ▪ TF: 800-448-3942

Home Life International, American   www.amhomelife.com
1725 Oregon Pike   Lancaster PA 17601
Ph: 717-560-2840 ▪ Fx: 717-560-2845

Home & Office Products Association, School   www.shopa.org
3131 Elbee Rd   Dayton OH 45439
Ph: 937-297-2250 ▪ Fx: 937-297-2254 ▪ TF: 800-854-7467

Home Office Underwriters, Association of   www.alu-web.org/ahou
2300 Windy Ridge Pkwy Suite 600   Atlanta GA 30339
Ph: 770-984-3715 ▪ Fx: 770-984-6418

Home Recording Rights Coalition   www.hrrc.org
PO Box 14267   Washington DC 20044
Ph: 202-628-9212 ▪ Fx: 202-628-9227 ▪ TF: 800-282-8273

Home Safety, Institute for Business &   www.ibhs.org
4775 E Fowler Ave   Tampa FL 33617
Ph: 813-286-3400 ▪ Fx: 813-286-9960 ▪ TF: 866-675-4247

Home Safety & Security Professionals, International Association of
PO Box 2044   Erie PA 16512
Ph: 814-456-2911

Home & School Institute   www.megaskillshsi.org
1500 Massachusetts Ave NW   Washington DC 20005
Ph: 202-466-3633

Home School Legal Defense Association   www.hslda.org
PO Box 3000   Purcellville VA 20134
Ph: 540-338-5600 ▪ Fx: 540-338-2733

Home Sewing Association   www.sewing.org
PO Box 1312   Monroeville PA 15146
Ph: 412-372-5950 ▪ Fx: 412-372-5953

Home Ventilating Institute   www.hvi.org
30 W University Dr   Arlington Heights IL 60004
Ph: 847-394-0150 ▪ Fx: 847-253-0088

Home Wine & Beer Trade Association   www.hwbta.org
PO Box 1373   Valrico FL 33595
Ph: 813-685-4261 ▪ Fx: 813-681-5625

Homebrewers Association, American   www.beertown.org
736 Pearl St   Boulder CO 80302
Ph: 303-447-0816 ▪ Fx: 303-447-2825 ▪ TF: 888-822-6273

Homecare, American Association for   www.aahomecare.org
625 Slaters Ln Suite 200   Alexandria VA 22314
Ph: 703-836-6263 ▪ Fx: 703-836-6730

Homeland Security Industries Association   www.hsianet.org
666 11th St NW Suite 315   Washington DC 20001
Ph: 202-331-3096 ▪ Fx: 202-331-8191

Homeless Council, National Health Care for the   www.nhchc.org
HCH Clinicians' Network PO Box 60427   Nashville TN 37206
Ph: 615-226-2292 ▪ Fx: 615-226-1656

Homeless, Homes for the   www.homesforthehomeless.com
36 Cooper Sq 6th Fl   New York NY 10003
Ph: 212-529-5252 ▪ Fx: 212-529-7698

Homeless, National Coalition for the   www.nationalhomeless.org
1012 14th St NW Suite 600   Washington DC 20005
Ph: 202-737-6444 ▪ Fx: 202-737-6445

Homeless Veterans, National Coalition for   www.nchv.org
333 1/2 Pennsylvania Ave SE   Washington DC 20003
Ph: 202-546-1969 ▪ Fx: 202-546-2063 ▪ TF: 800-838-4357

(Homelessness) HELP USA   www.helpusa.org
30 E 33rd St   New York NY 10016
Ph: 212-779-3350 ▪ Fx: 212-779-3353

Homelessness & Mental Illness, National Resource Center on   www.nrchmi.com
345 Delaware Ave   Delmar NY 12054
Ph: 518-439-7415 ▪ Fx: 518-439-7612 ▪ TF: 800-444-7415

Homelessness, National Alliance to End   www.endhomelessness.org
1518 K St NW Suite 206   Washington DC 20005
Ph: 202-638-1526 ▪ Fx: 202-638-4664

Homelessness, National Student Campaign Against Hunger &   www.nscahh.org
233 N Pleasant St Suite 32   Amherst MA 01002
Ph: 413-253-6417 ▪ Fx: 413-256-6435 ▪ TF: 800-664-8647

Homelessness & Poverty, National Law Center on   www.nlchp.org
1411 K St NW Suite 1400   Washington DC 20005
Ph: 202-628-2535 ▪ Fx: 202-628-2737

(Homelessness) Project Renewal   www.projectrenewal.org
200 Varick St 9th Fl   New York NY 10014
Ph: 212-620-0340 ▪ Fx: 212-243-4868

Homeopathic Pharmacopoeia of the US   www.hpus.com
PO Box 2221   Southeastern PA 19399
Ph: 610-783-5124 ▪ Fx: 610-783-5180

Homeopathy, Academy of Veterinary   www.theavh.org
PO Box 9280   Wilmington DE 19809
Ph: 866-652-1590

Homeopathy, American Institute of www.homeopathyusa.org
801 N Fairfax St Suite 306   Alexandria VA 22314
Ph: 888-445-9988 ▪ Fx: 703-548-7792

Homeopathy, National Center for www.homeopathic.org
801 N Fairfax St Suite 306   Alexandria VA 22314
Ph: 703-548-7790 ▪ Fx: 703-548-7792 ▪ TF: 877-624-0613

Homeowners Association, American www.ahahome.com
1100 Summer St 1st Fl   Stamford CT 06905
Ph: 203-323-7715 ▪ Fx: 203-323-4558 ▪ TF: 800-470-2242

Homeowners Foundation, American www.americanhomeowners.org
6776 Little Falls Rd   Arlington VA 22213
Ph: 703-536-7776 ▪ Fx: 703-536-7079 ▪ TF: 800-489-7079

Homeowners' Resource Center, American www.ahrc.com
PO Box 97   San Juan Capistrano CA 92693
Ph: 949-366-2125

Homes, Alliance for Healthy www.afhh.org
227 Massachusetts Ave NE Suite 200   Washington DC 20002
Ph: 202-543-1147 ▪ Fx: 202-543-4466

Homes for the Homeless www.homesforthehomeless.com
36 Cooper Sq 6th Fl   New York NY 10003
Ph: 212-529-5252 ▪ Fx: 212-529-7698

Homes & Hospitals Association, American www.nationalministries.org/mission/abhha
Baptist   PO Box 851   Valley Forge PA 19482
Ph: 800-222-3872 ▪ Fx: 610-768-2453

Homes & Services for the Aging, American Association of www2.aahsa.org
2519 Connecticut Ave NW   Washington DC 20008
Ph: 202-783-2242 ▪ Fx: 202-783-2255 ▪ TF: 800-508-9442

Homes & Services Inc, Bethesda Lutheran www.blhs.org
600 Hoffman Dr   Watertown WI 53094
Ph: 920-261-3050 ▪ Fx: 920-261-8441 ▪ TF: 800-369-4636

Homeschoolers Associated Network, National Challenged www.nathhan.com
PO Box 39   Porthill ID 83853
Ph: 208-267-6246

Homeworkers Organized for More Employment Inc www.homecoop.net
PO Box 10   Orland ME 04472
Ph: 207-469-7961 ▪ Fx: 207-469-1023

Homiletics, Academy of www.wlu.ca/~wwwsem/ah
Lincoln Christian Seminary 100 Campus View Dr   Lincoln IL
62656
Ph: 217-732-3168 ▪ Fx: 217-732-1821

Homing Pigeon Fanciers Inc, International Federation of American www.ifpigeon.com
PO Box 374   Hicksville NY 11802
Ph: 516-794-3612 ▪ Fx: 516-794-6654

(Homosexual) Exodus International North America www.exodus-international.org
PO Box 540119   Orlando FL 32854
Ph: 407-599-6872 ▪ Fx: 407-599-0011 ▪ TF: 888-264-0877

(Homosexuality) Courage couragerc.net
210 W 31st St   New York NY 10001
Ph: 212-268-1010 ▪ Fx: 212-268-7150

(Homosexuality) Evergreen International www.evergreen-intl.org
PO Box 3   Salt Lake City UT 84110
Ph: 801-363-3837 ▪ Fx: 801-264-8641 ▪ TF: 800-391-1000

(Homosexuality) Family Pride Coalition www.familypride.org
PO Box 65327   Washington DC 20035
Ph: 202-331-5015 ▪ Fx: 202-331-0080

(Homosexuality) Golden Threads www.home.earthlink.net/~goldengurl
PO Box 1688   Demorest GA 30535
Ph: 706-776-3959

(Homosexuality) Hetrick-Martin Institute Inc www.hmi.org
2 Astor Pl   New York NY 10003
Ph: 212-674-2400 ▪ Fx: 212-674-8650

(Homosexuality) Lutherans Concerned/North America www.lcna.org

(Homosexuality) Metanoia Ministries www.metanoiaonline.com
PO Box 1353   Tacoma WA 98401
Ph: 253-627-1580 ▪ Fx: 253-627-1054

Homosexuality, National Association for Research & Therapy of www.narth.com
16633 Ventura Blvd Suite 1340   Encino CA 91436
Ph: 818-789-4440 ▪ Fx: 818-789-6452

(Homosexuality) New Ways Ministry newwaysministry.org
4012 29th St   Mount Rainier MD 20712
Ph: 301-277-5674

(Homosexuality) ONE Institute & Archives www.oneinstitute.org
909 W Adams Blvd   Los Angeles CA 90007
Ph: 213-741-0094 ▪ Fx: 213-741-0220

(Homosexuality) OutProud www.outproud.org
369 3rd St Suite B362   San Rafael CA 94901
Ph: 415-460-5452 ▪ Fx: 415-460-5451

(Homosexuality) Spring of Living www.emmanuel-baptist.org/SpringLivingWater.htm
Water Ministry   403 S Grant St   Enid OK 73703
Ph: 580-233-9345

(Homosexuality) Straight Spouse Network www.ssnetwk.org
8215 Terrace Dr   El Cerrito CA 94530
Ph: 510-525-0200 ▪ Fx: 510-525-4831

(Homosexuality) Trikone www.trikone.org
PO Box 14161   San Francisco CA 94114
Ph: 408-270-8776 ▪ Fx: 408-274-2733

Homosexuals Anonymous Fellowship Services members.aol.com/hawebpage
PO Box 7881   Reading PA 19603
Ph: 610-921-0345 ▪ Fx: 610-921-0470

Homowo African Arts & Cultures www.homowo.org
4839 NE ML King Blvd Suite 209   Portland OR 97211
Ph: 503-288-3025 ▪ Fx: 503-331-6688

Honey Board, National www.nhb.org/
390 Lashley St   Longmont CO 80501
Ph: 303-776-2337 ▪ Fx: 303-776-1177

Honey Packers & Dealers Association, National
3301 Rt 66 Bldg C Suite 205   Neptune NJ 07753
Ph: 732-922-3008 ▪ Fx: 732-922-3590

Honor Societies, Association of College www.achsnatl.org
4990 Northwind Dr Suite 140   East Lansing MI 48823
Ph: 517-351-8335 ▪ Fx: 517-351-8336

Honor Society, National www.nhs.us
1904 Association Dr   Reston VA 20191
Ph: 703-860-0200 ▪ Fx: 703-476-5432 ▪ TF: 800-253-7746

Honor Society, National Junior www.njhs.org
1904 Association Dr   Reston VA 20191
Ph: 703-860-0200 ▪ Fx: 703-476-5432

Honor Society, National Technical www.nvths.org
PO Box 1336   Flat Rock NC 28731
Ph: 828-698-8011

Honor Society of Phi Kappa Phi www.phikappaphi.org
LSU Baton Rouge PO Box 16000   Baton Rouge LA 70893
Ph: 225-388-4917 ▪ Fx: 225-388-4900 ▪ TF: 800-804-9880

Honor Society, Phi Theta Kappa International www.ptk.org
1625 Eastover Dr PO Box 13729   Jackson MS 39236
Ph: 601-984-3504 ▪ Fx: 601-984-3550

Honor Society in Psychology, Psi Chi National www.psichi.org
PO Box 709   Chattanooga TN 37401
Ph: 423-756-2044 ▪ Fx: 423-265-1529

Honor Society, Tri-M Music www.menc.org/information/trim/TriMMain1.html
c/o MENC 1806 Robert Fulton Dr   Reston VA 20191
Ph: 703-860-4000 ▪ Fx: 703-860-2652 ▪ TF: 800-336-3768

Honorable Order of the Blue Goose International www.bluegoose.org
12940 Walnut Rd   Elm Grove WI 53122
Ph: 414-221-0341 ▪ Fx: 414-782-7608

Honour Society, Golden Key International gknhs.gsu.edu/GKWeb
1189 Ponce de Leon Ave   Atlanta GA 30306
Ph: 404-377-2400 ▪ Fx: 404-373-7033 ▪ TF: 800-377-2401

Hoo-Hoo International www.hoo-hoo.org
PO Box 118   Gurdon AR 71743
Ph: 870-353-4997 ▪ Fx: 870-353-4151 ▪ TF: 800-979-9950

Hooved Animal Humane Society www.hahs.org
10804 McConnell Rd PO Box 400   Woodstock IL 60098
Ph: 815-337-5563 ▪ Fx: 815-337-5569

Hoover Herbert Presidential Library Association www.hooverassociation.org
PO Box 696   West Branch IA 52358
Ph: 319-643-5327 ▪ Fx: 319-643-2391 ▪ TF: 800-828-0475

Hoover Institution on War Revolution & Peace www-hoover.stanford.edu
434 Galvez Mall   Stanford CA 94305
Ph: 650-723-1754 ▪ Fx: 650-723-1687 ▪ TF: 877-466-8374

Hop Growers of America www.usahops.org
PO Box 9218   Yakima WA 98909
Ph: 509-248-7043 ▪ Fx: 509-248-7044

Hope Center, Kristin Brooks www.hopeline.com
201 N 23rd St Suite 100   Purcelville VA 20132
Ph: 540-338-5756 ▪ Fx: 540-338-5746 ▪ TF: 800-784-2433

Hope Foundation, New www.newhopefoundation.org
51 Throckmorton St   Freehold NJ 07728
Ph: 732-308-0113 ▪ Fx: 732-308-0115

HOPE International www.hopeinternational.net
PO Box 10001   Lancaster PA 17605
Ph: 877-982-4673 ▪ Fx: 717-464-9046

Hope International, World www.worldhope.org
8136 Old Keene Mill Rd Suite 209A   Springfield VA 22152
Ph: 703-923-9414 ▪ Fx: 703-923-9418 ▪ TF: 888-466-4673

HOPE worldwide www.hopeww.org
353 W Lancaster Ave Suite 200   Wayne PA 19087
Ph: 610-254-8800 ▪ Fx: 610-254-8989

Horace Mann League of the USA www.unocoe.unomaha.edu/mckay/int.htm

Horace W Goldsmith Foundation
375 Park Ave Rm 1602   New York NY 10152
Ph: 212-319-8700 ▪ Fx: 212-319-2881

Horatio Alger Association of Distinguished Americans www.horatioalger.com
99 Canal Center Plaza   Alexandria VA 22314
Ph: 703-684-9444 ▪ Fx: 703-684-9445

Horn Society, International www.hornsociety.org

Horror Films, Academy of Science Fiction Fantasy & www.saturnawards.org
334 W 54th St   Los Angeles CA 90037
Ph: 323-752-5811

Horror Writers Association www.horror.crg
PO Box 50577   Palo Alto CA 94303
Ph: 888-893-4008

Horse Adventure Society, Icelandic
795 Entrance Rd   Solvang CA 93463
Ph: 805-688-3869 ▪ Fx: 805-688-2651

Horse Association of America, Hungarian www.horseplaza.com/cfusion/template/hhaa
c/o Horse Plaza PO Box S-3292   Carmel CA 93921
Ph: 530-304-0140

Horse Association of America, Percheron www.horseworlddata.com
10330 Quaker Rd PO Box 141   Fredericktown OH 43019
Ph: 740-694-3602 ▪ Fx: 740-694-3604

Horse Association of America, Pinto www.pinto.org
1900 Samuels Ave   Fort Worth TX 76102
Ph: 817-336-7842 ▪ Fx: 817-336-7416

Horse Association, American Cream Draft www.americancreamdraft.org
193 Crossover Rd   Bennington VT 05201
Ph: 802-447-7612 ▪ Fx: 802-447-0711

Horse Association, American Holsteiner www.holsteiner.com
222 E Main St Suite 1   Georgetown KY 40324
Ph: 502-863-4239 ▪ Fx: 502-868-0722

Horse Association, American Miniature www.swcp.com/amha
5601 S I-35 W   Alvarado TX 76009
Ph: 817-783-5600 ▪ Fx: 817-783-6403

Horse Association, American Morgan www.morganhorse.com
PO Box 519   Shelburne VT 05482
Ph: 802-985-8430

Horse Association, American Paint www.apha.com
PO Box 961023 Fort Worth TX 76161
Ph: 817-834-2742 ▪ Fx: 817-834-3152

Horse Association, American Paso Fino
PO Box 2363 Pittsburgh PA 15230
Ph: 724-437-5170 ▪ Fx: 724-438-4471

Horse Association, American Quarter www.aqha.org
PO Box 200 Amarillo TX 79168
Ph: 806-376-4811 ▪ Fx: 806-349-6404 ▪ TF: 800-414-7433

Horse Association, American Saddlebred www.saddlebred.com
4093 Iron Works Pkwy Lexington KY 40511
Ph: 859-259-2742 ▪ Fx: 859-259-1628

Horse Association, American Shire www.shirehorse.org/
1211 Hill Harrell Rd Effingham SC 29541
Ph: 843-629-0072

Horse Association, Appaloosa Sport appaloosasport.com
3380 Saxonburg Blvd Glenshaw PA 15116
Ph: 412-767-4616

Horse Association, Arabian www.arabianhorses.org
10805 E Bethany Dr Aurora CO 80014
Ph: 303-696-4500 ▪ Fx: 303-696-4599

Horse Association, Blazer www.integrity.com/homes/lorenzo/bha.htm
820 N Can-Ada Rd Star ID 83669
Ph: 208-286-7267

Horse Association, Colorado Ranger www.coloradoranger.com
RD 1 Box 1290 Wampum PA 16157
Ph: 412-535-4841

Horse Association, International Buckskin www.ibha.net
PO Box 268 Shelby IN 46377
Ph: 219-552-1013

Horse Association, International Generic www.igha.org
PO Box 6778 San Pedro CA 90734
Ph: 310-719-9094

Horse Association, National Barrel www.nbha.com
725 Broad St PO Box 1988 Augusta GA 30903
Ph: 706-722-7223 ▪ Fx: 706-722-9575

Horse Association, National Cutting www.nchacutting.com
260 Bailey Ave Fort Worth TX 76107
Ph: 817-244-6188 ▪ Fx: 817-244-2015

Horse Association, National Morgan Reining www.nmrha.com

Horse Association, National Reining www.nrha.com
3000 NW 10th St Oklahoma City OK 73107
Ph: 405-946-7400 ▪ Fx: 405-946-8410

Horse Association, National Spotted Saddle www.nssha.com
108 N Spring St PO Box 898 Murfreesboro TN 37133
Ph: 615-890-2864

Horse Association, North American Single-footing www.singlefootinghorse.com
PO Box 1079 Three Forks MT 59752
Ph: 406-285-6826

Horse Association, Palomino www.palominohorseassoc.com
HCR 63 Box 24 Dornsife PA 17823
Ph: 570-758-3067 ▪ Fx: 570-758-5336

Horse Association, Paso Fino pasofino.org
101 N Collins St Plant City FL 33566
Ph: 813-719-7777 ▪ Fx: 813-719-7872

Horse Association Inc, Purebred Morab www.puremorab.com
PO Box 280 Sherwood WI 54169
Ph: 920-853-3086 ▪ Fx: 920-853-3114

Horse Association, Walkaloosa www.walkaloosaregistry.com
PO Box 3170 Carefree AZ 85377
Ph: 480-595-1699

Horse Breed Association Inc, Missouri Fox Trotting www.mfthba.com
PO Box 1027 Ava MO 65608
Ph: 417-683-2468 ▪ Fx: 417-683-6144

Horse Breeders of America, Palomino www.palominohba.com
15253 E Skelly Dr Tulsa OK 74116
Ph: 918-438-1234 ▪ Fx: 918-438-1232

Horse Breeders Association of America, Racking www.rackinghorse.com
67 Horse Ctr Rd Decatur AL 35603
Ph: 256-353-7225 ▪ Fx: 256-353-7266

Horse Breeders Association, Galiceno
PO Box 219 Godley TX 76044
Ph: 817-389-3547

Horse Breeders' & Exhibitors' Association, Tennessee Walking www.twhbea.com
PO Box 286 Lewisburg TN 37091
Ph: 931-359-1574 ▪ Fx: 931-359-2539 ▪ TF: 800-359-1574

Horse & Burro Program, National Wild wildhorseandburro.blm.gov
PO Box 3270 Sparks NV 89432
Ph: 775-475-2222 ▪ Fx: 775-861-6711 ▪ TF: 800-417-9647

Horse Club, Appaloosa www.appaloosa.com
2720 W Pullman Rd Moscow ID 83843
Ph: 208-882-5578 ▪ Fx: 208-882-8150

Horse Congress, US Icelandic www.icelandics.org
PO Box 1724 Santa Ynez CA 93460
Ph: 805-688-6355

Horse Corp of America, Belgian Draft www.belgiancorp.com
PO Box 335 Wabash IN 46992
Ph: 260-563-3205

Horse Council, American www.horsecouncil.org
1616 H St NW 7th Fl Washington DC 20006
Ph: 202-296-4031 ▪ Fx: 202-296-1970

Horse Council, American Youth www.ayhc.com
577 N Boyero Ave Pueblo West CO 81007
Ph: 719-547-7677 ▪ TF: 800-879-2942

Horse Guild, American Warmblood & Sport
PO Box 5512 Grants Pass OR 97527
Ph: 541-855-8942

Horse Owners Association of America, Walking www.walkinghorseowners.com
304 W Thompson Ln Murfreesboro TN 37129
Ph: 615-494-8822 ▪ Fx: 615-494-8825

Horse Owners Foundation, Arabian www.arabianhorseowners.org
4101 N Bear Canyon Rd PO Box 30924 Tucson AZ 85749
Ph: 520-760-0682 ▪ Fx: 520-749-2572 ▪ TF: 800-892-0682

Horse Protection Association, American www.americanhorseprotection.org
1000 29th St NW Suite T100 Washington DC 20007
Ph: 202-965-0500 ▪ Fx: 202-965-9621

Horse Publications, American www.americanhorsepubs.org
49 Spinnaker Cir South Daytona FL 32119
Ph: 904-760-7743 ▪ Fx: 904-760-7728

(Horse Racing) Kids to the Cup www.kidstothecup.com
120 S 1st Ave Arcadia CA 91006
Ph: 626-695-3433

Horse Registry of America, Arabian
12000 Zuni St Westminster CO 80234
Ph: 303-450-4748 ▪ Fx: 303-450-2841

Horse Registry, American Indian www.indianhorse.com
Rancho San Francisco 9028 State Park Rd Lockhart TX 78644
Ph: 512-398-6642

Horse Registry, American Part-Blooded www.apbhorseregistry.com
4120 SE River Dr Portland OR 97267
Ph: 503-654-6204

Horse Registry, American White www.whitehorseranchnebraska.com/registry.htm
Horse & American Creme 90000 Edwards Rd Naper NE
68755
Ph: 402-832-5560

Horse Registry Association, International Spotted members.tripod.com/~spottedhorses
PO Box 412 Anderson MO 64831
Ph: 417-475-6273 ▪ TF: 866-201-3098

Horse Registry, National Show www.nshregistry.org
10368 Bluegrass Pkwy Louisville KY 40299
Ph: 502-266-5100 ▪ Fx: 502-266-5806

Horse Registry of North America, Peruvian Paso www.pphrna.org
3077 Wiljan Ct Suite A Santa Rosa CA 95407
Ph: 707-579-4394 ▪ Fx: 707-579-1038

Horse Registry, Norwegian Fjord www.nfhr.com
1203 Appian Dr Webster NY 14580
Ph: 585-872-4114 ▪ Fx: 585-787-0497

(Horse Rescue) Bright Futures Farm www.brightfuturesfarm.org
44793 Harrison Rd Spartanburg PA 16434
Ph: 814-827-8270 ▪ Fx: 814-827-8278

Horse Show Commission, National
PO Box 167 Shelbyville TN 37162
Ph: 931-684-9506 ▪ Fx: 931-684-9538

Horse Society, American Hackney www.hackneysociety.com
4059 Iron Works Pkwy Suite 3 Lexington KY 40511
Ph: 859-255-8694 ▪ Fx: 859-255-0177

Horse Society of North America, Cleveland Bay www.clevelandbay.org
PO Box 483 Goshen NH 03752
Ph: 603-863-5193

Horse Trainers Association, Walking www.walkinghorsetrainers.com
PO Box 61 Shelbyville TN 37162
Ph: 931-684-5866 ▪ Fx: 931-684-5895

Horse Youth Foundation, Harness www.hhyf.org
14950 Greyhound Ct Suite 210 Carmel IN 46032
Ph: 317-848-5132 ▪ Fx: 317-848-5136

Horseless Carriage Club of America www.hcca.org
49637 Hwy 41 Oakhurst CA 93644
Ph: 559-683-8800 ▪ TF: 888-832-2374

Horsemanship Association, Certified www.cha-ahse.org
5318 Old Bullard Rd Tyler TX 75703
Ph: 903-509-2473 ▪ Fx: 903-509-2474 ▪ TF: 800-399-0138

Horsemen of America, Back Country www.backcountryhorse.com
PO Box 1367 Graham WA 98338
Ph: 360-832-2461 ▪ Fx: 360-832-2471 ▪ TF: 888-893-5161

Horsemen International, Harness
14 Main St Suite C Robbinsville NJ 08691
Ph: 609-259-3717 ▪ Fx: 609-259-3778

Horsemen's Association, North American www.arkagency-naha.com/NAHA.html
PO Box 223 Paynesville MN 56362
Ph: 320-243-7224 ▪ Fx: 320-243-7224 ▪ TF: 800-328-8894

Horsemen's Association, United Professional www.uphaonline.com
4059 Iron Works Pkwy Suite 2 Lexington KY 40511
Ph: 859-231-5070 ▪ Fx: 859-255-2774

Horsemen's Benevolent & Protective Association www.hbpa.org
4063 Iron Works Pkwy Suite B-2 Lexington KY 40511
Ph: 859-259-0451 ▪ Fx: 859-259-0452 ▪ TF: 866-245-1711

Horses, American Association of Owners & Breeders of Peruvian www.aaobpph.com
Paso PO Box 476 Wilton CA 95693
Ph: 916-687-6232 ▪ Fx: 916-687-6691

(Horses) American Bashkir Curly Registry www.abcregistry.org
PO Box 151029 Ely NV 89315
Ph: 775-289-4999 ▪ Fx: 775-289-8579

(Horses) American Buckskin Registry Association Inc www.americanbuckskin.com
1141 Hartnell Ave PO Box 3850 Redding CA 96049
Ph: 530-223-1420

(Horses) American Grandprix Association www.stadiumjumping.com/aga
1301 6th Ave W Suite 406 Bradenton FL 34205
Ph: 941-744-5465 ▪ Fx: 941-744-0874 ▪ TF: 800-237-8924

(Horses) American Haflinger Registry www.haflingerhorse.com
2746 State Rt 44 Rootstown OH 44272
Ph: 330-325-8116 ▪ Fx: 330-325-8178

(Horses) American Trakehner Association www.americantrakehner.com
1514 W Church St Newark OH 43055
Ph: 740-344-1111 ▪ Fx: 740-344-3225

(Horses) American Warmblood Registry www.americanwarmblood.com
PO Box 211735 Royal Palm Beach FL 33421
Ph: 561-333-5848

(Horses) American Warmblood Society www.americanwarmblood.org
2 Buffalo Run Center Ridge AR 72027
Ph: 501-893-2777 ▪ Fx: 501-893-2779

(Horses) Dutch Warmblood Studbook in North America   www.nawpn.org
PO Box 0   Sutherlin OR 97479
Ph: 541-459-3232 ▪ Fx: 541-459-2967

(Horses) Equine Advocates   www.equineadvocates.com
PO Box 700   Bedford NY 10506
Ph: 845-278-3095

(Horses) Equine Rescue League Inc   erl.freeyellow.com
PO Box 4366   Leesburg VA 20177
Ph: 703-771-1240

(Horses) Haflinger Breeders Organization Inc   www.stallionstation.com/hbo/hbo.html
14640 State Rt 83   Coshocton OH 43812
Ph: 740-829-2790 ▪ Fx: 740-829-2322

(Horses) International Jumper Futurity   youngjumpers.com/IJF
PO Box 757   Kirkland WA 98083
Ph: 425-827-5417

(Horses) International Morab Breeders Association   www.morab.com/imba.html
RR 3 Box 235   Ava MO 65608
Ph: 417-683-4426 ▪ Fx: 417-683-5708

(Horses) International Morab Registry   www.morab.com
RR 3 Box 235   Ava MO 65608
Ph: 417-683-4426 ▪ Fx: 417-683-5708

(Horses) International Sporthorse Registry   www.isroldenburg.org
939 Merchandise Mart   Chicago IL 60654
Ph: 312-527-6544 ▪ Fx: 312-527-6573

(Horses) International Trotting & Pacing Association Inc   www.trottingbreds.com
60 Gulf Rd   Gouverneur NY 13642
Ph: 315-287-2294 ▪ Fx: 315-287-5010

(Horses) Lipizzan Association of North America   www.lipizzan.org
PO Box 1133   Anderson IN 46015
Ph: 765-644-3904 ▪ Fx: 765-641-1205

(Horses) National Center for Therapeutic Riding   www.nctrriding.org/about
PO Box 434   Burtonsville MD 20866
Ph: 301-421-0380 ▪ Fx: 301-421-0384

(Horses) National Chincoteague Pony Association   www.pony-chincoteague.com
2595 Jensen Rd   Bellingham WA 98226
Ph: 360-671-8338 ▪ Fx: 360-671-7603

(Horses) National Hunter & Jumper Association   www.nhja.org
PO Box 1015   Riverside CT 06878
Ph: 203-869-1225

(Horses) National Snaffle Bit Association   www.nsba.com
4815 S Sheridan Suite 109   Tulsa OK 74145
Ph: 918-270-1469 ▪ Fx: 918-270-1471

(Horses) North American Riding for the Handicapped Association   www.narha.org
PO Box 33150   Denver CO 80233
Ph: 303-452-1212 ▪ Fx: 303-252-4610 ▪ TF: 800-369-7433

(Horses) North American Selle Francais Association   www.sellefrancais.org
PO Box 579   Waynesboro VA 22980
Ph: 540-932-9160 ▪ Fx: 540-932-9163

(Horses) North American Shagya-Arabian Society   www.shagya.net
9797 S Rangeline Rd   Clinton IN 47842
Ph: 765-665-3851

(Horses) North American Trail Ride Conference   www.natrc.org
PO Box 224   Sedalia CO 80135
Ph: 303-688-1677 ▪ Fx: 303-688-3022

(Horses) Oldenburg Registry NA   www.isroldenburg.org
939 Merchandise Mart   Chicago IL 60654
Ph: 312-527-6544 ▪ Fx: 312-527-6573

(Horses) Pony of the Americas Club Inc   www.poac.org
5240 Elmwood Ave   Indianapolis IN 46203
Ph: 317-788-0107 ▪ Fx: 317-788-8974

(Horses) Purebred Hanoverian Association of American Breeders & Owners
Box 429   Rocky Hill NJ 08553
Ph: 609-466-1383 ▪ Fx: 609-466-9543

(Horses) Spanish Barb Breeders Association   www.spanishbarb.com
PO Box 598   Anthony FL 32617
Ph: 352-622-5878

(Horses) Spanish Mustang Registry   www.spanishmustang.org
4970 S Kansas Settlement Rd   Willcox AZ 85643
Ph: 520-384-2886

(Horses) Swedish Gotland Breeders' Society
3240 Hinton-Webber Rd   Corinth KY 41010
Ph: 859-234-5707

(Horses) Thoroughbred Club of America
PO Box 8098   Lexington KY 40533
Ph: 859-254-4282 ▪ Fx: 859-231-6131

(Horses) Thoroughbred Owners & Breeders Association   www.toba.org
PO Box 4367   Lexington KY 40544
Ph: 859-276-2291 ▪ Fx: 859-276-2462 ▪ TF: 888-606-8622

(Horses) Thoroughbred Racing Protective Bureau   www.trpb.com
420 Fair Hill Dr Suite 2   Elkton MD 21921
Ph: 410-398-2261 ▪ Fx: 410-398-1499

(Horses) US Dressage Federation   www.usdf.org
PO Box 6669   Lincoln NE 68506
Ph: 402-434-8550 ▪ Fx: 402-434-8570

(Horses) US Lipizzan Registry   www.lipizzan-uslr.com
707 13th St SE Suite 275   Salem OR 97301
Ph: 503-589-3172 ▪ Fx: 503-362-6390

(Horses) US Pony Clubs   www.ponyclub.org
Kentucky Horse Park 4041 Iron Works Pkwy   Lexington KY 40511
Ph: 859-254-7669 ▪ Fx: 859-233-4652

(Horses) Welsh Pony & Cob Society of America   www.welshpony.org
PO Box 2977   Winchester VA 22604
Ph: 540-667-6195

Horseshoers & Allied Trades, International Union of Journeymen
2070 Jericho Tpke   Commack NY 11725
Ph: 718-658-5740

Horticultural Council, Northwest   www.nwhort.org
6 S 2nd St Suite 600   Yakima WA 98901
Ph: 509-453-3193 ▪ Fx: 509-457-7615

Horticultural Libraries Inc, Council   www2.ville.montreal.qc.ca/jardin/cbhl/cbhl.htm
on Botanical &   Carnegie Mellon Univ Hunt Institute for
Botanical Documentation   Pittsburgh PA 15213
Ph: 412-268-7301 ▪ Fx: 412-268-5677

Horticultural Research Institute   www.anla.org/research
1000 Vermont Ave NW Suite 300   Washington DC 20005
Ph: 202-789-2900 ▪ Fx: 202-789-1893

Horticultural Science, American Society for   www.ashs.org
113 South West St Suite 200   Alexandria VA 22314
Ph: 703-836-4606 ▪ Fx: 703-836-2024

Horticultural Society, American   www.ahs.org
7931 E Boulevard Dr   Alexandria VA 22308
Ph: 703-768-5700 ▪ Fx: 703-768-8700 ▪ TF: 800-777-7931

Horticultural Supply Association, North American   www.nahsa.org
1900 Arch St   Philadelphia PA 19103
Ph: 215-564-3484 ▪ Fx: 215-963-9784

Horticultural Therapy Association, American   www.ahta.org
909 York St   Denver CO 80206
Ph: 303-370-8087 ▪ Fx: 303-331-5776 ▪ TF: 800-634-1603

Hose & Accessories Distributors, National Association of   www.nahad.org
105 Eastern Ave Suite 104   Annapolis MD 21403
Ph: 410-263-1014 ▪ Fx: 410-263-1659 ▪ TF: 800-624-2227

Hosiery Association   www.hosieryassociation.com
3623 Latrobe Dr Suite 130   Charlotte NC 28211
Ph: 704-365-0913 ▪ Fx: 704-362-2056

Hospice Association of America   www.nahc.org/HAA
228 7th St SE   Washington DC 20003
Ph: 202-546-4757 ▪ Fx: 202-547-9559

Hospice Association, National Prison
PO Box 3769   Boulder CO 80307
Ph: 303-447-8051 ▪ Fx: 303-447-8055

Hospice Education Institute   www.hospiceworld.org
3 Unity Sq PO Box 98   Machiasport ME 04655
Ph: 207-255-8800 ▪ Fx: 207-255-8008 ▪ TF: 800-331-1620

Hospice Foundation of America   www.hospicefoundation.org
2001 'S' St NW Suite 300   Washington DC 20009
Ph: 202-638-5419 ▪ Fx: 202-638-5312 ▪ TF: 800-854-3402

Hospice International, Children's   www.chionline.org
901 N Pitt St Suite 230   Alexandria VA 22314
Ph: 703-684-0330 ▪ Fx: 703-684-0226 ▪ TF: 800-242-4453

Hospice, National Association for Home Care &   www.nahc.org
228 7th St SE   Washington DC 20003
Ph: 202-547-7424 ▪ Fx: 202-547-3540

Hospice & Palliative Care Organization, National   www.nhpco.org
1700 Diagonal Rd Suite 625   Alexandria VA 22314
Ph: 703-837-1500 ▪ Fx: 703-837-1233 ▪ TF: 800-658-8898

Hospice & Palliative Medicine, American Academy of   www.aahpm.org
4700 W Lake Ave   Glenview IL 60025
Ph: 847-375-4712 ▪ Fx: 877-734-8671

Hospice & Palliative Nurses Association   www.hpna.org
Penn Ctr W 1 Suite 229   Pittsburgh PA 15276
Ph: 412-787-9301 ▪ Fx: 412-787-9305

Hospital Association, Acute Long Term   www.altha.org
1055 N Fairfax Suite 201   Alexandria VA 22314
Ph: 703-299-5571 ▪ Fx: 703-299-5574

Hospital Association, American   www.aha.org
1 N Franklin St   Chicago IL 60606
Ph: 312-422-3000 ▪ Fx: 312-422-4796 ▪ TF: 800-424-4301

Hospital Association, American Surgical   www.surgicalhospital.org
PO Box 23220   San Diego CA 92193
Ph: 858-490-8085 ▪ Fx: 858-490-9016 ▪ TF: 800-237-3768

Hospital Audiences Inc   www.hospitalaudiences.org
548 Broadway 3rd Fl   New York NY 10012
Ph: 212-575-7676 ▪ Fx: 212-575-7669

Hospital Dentists, American Association of   scdonline.org/AAHD_Index.htm
211 E Chicago Ave Suite 740   Chicago IL 60611
Ph: 312-440-2660 ▪ Fx: 312-440-2824

Hospital Hospitality Houses, National Association of   www.nahhh.org
PO Box 18087   Asheville NC 28814
Ph: 828-253-1188 ▪ Fx: 828-253-8082 ▪ TF: 800-542-9730

Hospital Managers Association Inc, Veterinary   www.vhma.org
48 Howard St   Albany NY 12207
Ph: 518-433-8911 ▪ Fx: 518-463-8656

Hospital Medical Education, Association for   www.ahme.org
419 Beulah Rd   Pittsburgh PA 15235
Ph: 412-244-9302 ▪ Fx: 412-243-4693 ▪ TF: 866-617-4780

Hospitality Alliance, Multicultural Foodservice &   www.mfha.net
65 Weybosset St Suite 50   Providence RI 02903
Ph: 401-751-8883 ▪ Fx: 401-751-8333

Hospitality Association, National Park   www.nphassn.org
3701Court House Dr   Ellicott City MD 21043
Ph: 410-480-2240 ▪ Fx: 410-480-2617

Hospitality Consultants, International Society of   www.ishc.com
515 King St Suite 420   Alexandria VA 22314
Ph: 703-684-6681 ▪ Fx: 703-684-6048

Hospitality Financial & Technology Professionals   www.hftp.org
11709 Boulder Ln Suite 110   Austin TX 78726
Ph: 512-249-5333 ▪ Fx: 512-249-1533 ▪ TF: 800-856-4242

Hospitality Houses, National Association of Hospital   www.nahhh.org
PO Box 18087   Asheville NC 28814
Ph: 828-253-1188 ▪ Fx: 828-253-8082 ▪ TF: 800-542-9730

Hospitality & Information Service   www.this4diplomats.org
1630 Crescent Pl NW   Washington DC 20009
Ph: 202-232-3002 ▪ Fx: 202-667-1475

Hospitality Information Technology Association   www.hitaworld.com
www.hitaworld.org

Hospitality, Network of Executive Women in   www.newh.org
PO Box 322   Shawano WI 54166
Ph: 715-526-5267 ▪ Fx: 715-526-5979

Hospitality Network, National Interfaith   www.nihn.org
71 Summit Ave   Summit NJ 07901
Ph: 908-273-1100 ■ Fx: 908-273-0030

Hospitality Purchasers, International Society of   www.ishp.org
300 Montgomery St Suite 833   San Francisco CA 94104
Ph: 415-399-0995 ■ Fx: 415-399-0935

Hospitality Sales & Marketing Association International   www.hsmai.org
8201 Greensboro Dr Suite 300   McLean VA 22102
Ph: 703-610-9024 ■ Fx: 703-610-9005

Hospitals, American Association of Eye & Ear   www.aaeeh.org
1100 Wilson Blvd Suite 1200   Arlington VA 22209
Ph: 703-243-8848 ■ Fx: 703-243-8664

Hospitals Association, American Baptist   www.nationalministries.org/mission/abhha
Homes &   PO Box 851   Valley Forge PA 19482
Ph: 800-222-3872 ■ Fx: 610-768-2453

Hospitals, Federation of American   www.fahs.com
801 Pennsylvania Ave NW Suite 245   Washington DC 20004
Ph: 202-624-1500 ■ Fx: 202-737-6462

Hospitals & Health Systems, National Association of Public   www.naph.org
1301 Pennsylvania Ave NW Suite 950   Washington DC 20004
Ph: 202-585-0100 ■ Fx: 202-585-0101

Hospitals, National Association of Urban   www.nauh.org
10 Pidgeon Hill Dr Suite 150   Sterling VA 20165
Ph: 703-444-0989 ■ Fx: 703-444-3029

Hospitals & Related Institutions, National Association of   www.childrenshospitals.net
Children's   401 Wythe St   Alexandria VA 22314
Ph: 703-684-1355 ■ Fx: 703-684-1589

Hosta Society, American   www.hosta.org
9448 Mayfield Rd   Chesterland OH 44026
Ph: 440-729-9838 ■ Fx: 440-729-2836

Hostelling International - American Youth Hostels   www.hiusa.org
8401 Colesville Rd Suite 600   Silver Spring MD 20910
Ph: 301-495-1240 ■ Fx: 301-495-6697

Hostess Association, Armed Forces   www.army.mil/afha
The Pentagon Rm 1D110 6604 Army Pentagon   Washington
DC 20310
Ph: 703-697-3180 ■ Fx: 703-693-9510

Hot Rod Association, American   www.spokaneracewaypark.com/drags
111 N Hayford Rd   Spokane WA 99224
Ph: 509-244-2372 ■ Fx: 509-244-2472

Hot Rod Association, International   www.ihra.com
9 1/2 E Main St   Norwalk OH 44857
Ph: 419-663-6666 ■ Fx: 419-663-4472

Hotel Association, Resort   www.resorthotelinsurance.com
461 McLaws Cir Suite 4   Williamsburg VA 23185
Ph: 757-220-7194 ■ Fx: 757-253-2445

Hotel Electronic Distribution Network Association   www.hedna.org
333 John Carlyle St Suite 600   Alexandria VA 22314
Ph: 703-837-6181 ■ Fx: 703-548-5738

Hotel Employees & Restaurant Employees International Union   www.hereunion.org
1219 28th St NW   Washington DC 20007
Ph: 202-393-4373 ■ Fx: 202-333-0468

Hotel & Lodging Association, American   www.ahla.com
1201 New York Ave NW Suite 600   Washington DC 20005
Ph: 202-289-3100 ■ Fx: 202-289-3186

Hotel Owners Association, Asian American   www.aahoa.com
66 Lenox Pointe NE   Atlanta GA 30324
Ph: 404-816-5759 ■ Fx: 404-816-6260

Hotel Restaurant & Institutional Education, International Council on   www.chrie.org
2613 N Parham Rd 2nd Fl   Richmond VA 23294
Ph: 804-346-4800 ■ Fx: 804-346-5009

Hotel & Restaurant Trainers, Council of   www.chart.org
PO Box 2835   Westfield NJ 07091
Ph: 800-463-5918 ■ Fx: 800-427-5436

HotelPAC   www.ahla.com/public_hotelpac.asp
1201 New York Ave NW Suite 600   Washington DC 20005
Ph: 202-289-3124 ■ Fx: 202-289-3185

Hotels, Associated Luxury   www.alhi.com
1000 Connecticut Ave NW Suite 603   Washington DC 20036
Ph: 202-887-7020 ■ Fx: 202-887-0085

Hotels Association, Green   www.greenhotels.com
PO Box 420212   Houston TX 77242
Ph: 713-789-8889 ■ Fx: 713-789-9786

Hotels & Resorts Worldwide Inc, Preferred   www.preferredhotels.com
311 S Wacker Dr Suite 1900   Chicago IL 60606
Ph: 312-913-0400 ■ Fx: 312-913-0444 ■ TF: 800-323-7500

Hotels of the World, Small Luxury   www.slh.com
370 Lexington Ave Suite 1506   New York NY 10017
Ph: 212-953-2064 ■ Fx: 212-953-0576

Houdini Historical Center   www.foxvalleyhistory.org/houdini
330 E College Ave   Appleton WI 54911
Ph: 920-733-8445 ■ Fx: 920-733-8636

House Rabbit Society   www.rabbit.org
148 Broadway   Richmond CA 94804
Ph: 510-970-7575 ■ Fx: 510-970-9820

House of Ruth   www.houseofruth.org
5 Thomas Cir NW   Washington DC 20005
Ph: 202-745-2326 ■ Fx: 202-667-7047

Houseboat Association of America   www.houseboatassociation.org
c/o Harris Publishing 360 B St   Idaho Falls ID 83402
Ph: 208-524-7000 ■ Fx: 208-522-5241

Houseboat Industry Association
200 E Randolph Dr Suite 5100   Chicago IL 60601
Ph: 312-946-6280 ■ Fx: 312-946-0388 ■ TF: 800-669-5462

Household Goods Forwarders Association of America Inc   www.hhgfaa.org
2320 Mill Rd Suite 102   Alexandria VA 22314
Ph: 703-684-3780 ■ Fx: 703-684-3784

Household International PAC
1401 'I' St NW Suite 520   Washington DC 20005
Ph: 202-466-3561 ■ Fx: 202-466-3583

Housekeepers Association, International Executive   www.ieha.org
1001 Eastwind Dr Suite 301   Westerville OH 43081
Ph: 614-895-7166 ■ Fx: 614-895-1248 ■ TF: 800-200-6342

Housewares Association, International   www.housewares.org
6400 Shafer Ct Suite 650   Rosemont IL 60018
Ph: 847-292-4200 ■ Fx: 847-292-4211

Housewares Representatives Association, International   www.ihra.org
175 N Harbor Dr Suite 1712   Chicago IL 60601
Ph: 312-240-0822 ■ Fx: 312-240-1005

Housework Campaign, International Wages for   www.allwomencount.net
c/o Crossroad Women's Ctr PO Box 86681   Los Angeles CA
90086
Ph: 323-292-7405

Housing Agencies, National Council of State   www.ncsha.org
444 N Capitol St NW Suite 438   Washington DC 20001
Ph: 202-624-7710 ■ Fx: 202-624-5899

Housing Assistance Council   www.ruralhome.org
1025 Vermont Ave NW Suite 606   Washington DC 20005
Ph: 202-842-8600 ■ Fx: 202-347-3441 ■ TF: 800-989-4422

Housing Association, American Seniors   www.seniorshousing.org
5100 Wisconsin Ave NW Suite 307   Washington DC 20016
Ph: 202-237-0900 ■ Fx: 202-237-1616

Housing Association, National Leased   www.hudnlha.com
1818 'N' St NW Suite 405   Washington DC 20036
Ph: 202-785-8888 ■ Fx: 202-785-2008

Housing Authorities, Council of Large Public   www.clpha.org
1250 'I' St NW Suite 901A   Washington DC 20005
Ph: 202-638-1300 ■ Fx: 202-638-2364

Housing Authorities Directors Association, Public   www.phada.org
511 Capitol Ct NE   Washington DC 20002
Ph: 202-546-5445 ■ Fx: 202-546-2280

Housing Coalition, National Low Income   www.nlihc.org
1012 14th St NW Suite 610   Washington DC 20005
Ph: 202-662-1530 ■ Fx: 202-393-1973

Housing Coalition, National Rural   www.nrhcweb.org
1250 'I' St NW Suite 902   Washington DC 20005
Ph: 202-393-5229 ■ Fx: 202-393-3034

Housing Conference, National   www.nhc.org
1801 K St NW Suite M-100   Washington DC 20006
Ph: 202-466-2121 ■ Fx: 202-466-2122

Housing Cooperatives, National Association of   www.coophousing.org
1707 H St NW Suite 201   Washington DC 20006
Ph: 202-737-0797 ■ Fx: 202-783-7869

Housing, Council for Affordable & Rural   www.carh.org
121 N Washington St Suite 301   Alexandria VA 22314
Ph: 703-837-9001 ■ Fx: 703-837-8467

Housing Council, National American Indian   naihc.indian.com
900 2nd St NE Suite 305   Washington DC 20002
Ph: 202-789-1754 ■ Fx: 202-789-1758 ■ TF: 800-284-9165

Housing Council, National Multi   www.nmhc.org
1850 M St NW Suite 540   Washington DC 20036
Ph: 202-974-2300 ■ Fx: 202-775-0112

Housing Educators, American Association of
Illinois State Univ Dept of Family & Consumer Sciences CB
5060   Normal IL 61790
Ph: 309-438-5802 ■ Fx: 309-438-5307

Housing Endowment, National   www.nationalhousingendowment.com
1201 15th St NW   Washington DC 20005
Ph: 202-266-8483

Housing Finance Agencies, National Association of Local   www.nalhfa.org
2025 M St NW Suite 800   Washington DC 20036
Ph: 202-367-1197 ■ Fx: 202-367-2197

Housing & Finance, Women in   www.whfdc.org
717 Princess St   Alexandria VA 22314
Ph: 703-683-4742 ■ Fx: 703-683-0018

Housing Foundation Inc, Cooperative   www.chfhq.org
8601 Georgia Ave Suite 800   Silver Spring MD 20910
Ph: 301-587-4700 ■ Fx: 301-587-7315

(Housing) Habitat for Humanity International Inc   www.habitat.org
121 Habitat St   Americus GA 31709
Ph: 229-924-6935 ■ Fx: 229-924-6541 ■ TF: 800-422-4828

Housing Information Managers, National Association of   www.nahim.org
PO Box 67202   Lincoln NE 68506
Ph: 402-476-9424 ■ Fx: 402-420-1770 ■ TF: 800-379-3807

Housing Inspection Foundation   www.iami.org/hif.cfm
1224 N Nokomis NE   Alexandria MN 56308
Ph: 320-763-6350 ■ Fx: 320-763-9290

Housing Institute, Manufactured   www.manufacturedhousing.org
2101 Wilson Blvd Suite 610   Arlington VA 22201
Ph: 703-558-0400 ■ Fx: 703-558-0401 ■ TF: 800-505-5500

Housing Institute, National   www.nhi.org
460 Bloomfield Ave Suite 211   Montclair NJ 07042
Ph: 973-509-2888 ■ Fx: 973-509-8005

Housing Law Project, National   www.nhlp.org
614 Grand Ave Suite 320   Oakland CA 94610
Ph: 510-251-9400 ■ Fx: 510-451-2300

Housing Lenders, National Association of Affordable
1300 Connecticut Ave NW Suite 905   Washington DC 20036
Ph: 202-293-9850 ■ Fx: 202-293-9852

Housing Management Association, National Affordable   www.nahma.org
526 W King St Suite 511   Alexandria VA 22314
Ph: 703-683-8630 ■ Fx: 703-683-8634

Housing Management Association, Professional   www.phma.com
PO Box 4251   Leesburg VA 20177
Ph: 703-327-2399 ■ Fx: 703-327-4005

Housing Management, National Center for   www.nchm.org
1010 N Glebe Rd Suite 160   Arlington VA 22201
Ph: 703-516-4070 ■ Fx: 703-516-4069 ■ TF: 800-368-5625

(Housing) McAuley Institute   www.mcauley.org
8300 Colesville Rd   Silver Spring MD 20910
Ph: 301-588-8110 ■ Fx: 301-588-8154

(Housing) Neighbor to Neighbor   www.n2n.org
424 Pine St Suite 203   Fort Collins CO 80524
Ph: 970-484-7498 ▪ Fx: 970-407-7045 ▪ TF: 800-366-8289

Housing Network, National Affordable   www.nahn.com
PO Box 3706   Butte MT 59702
Ph: 406-782-8145 ▪ Fx: 406-782-5168

Housing Officers International, Association of   www.acuho.ohio-state.edu
College & University   941 Chatham Ln Suite 318   Columbus
OH 43221
Ph: 614-292-0099 ▪ Fx: 614-292-3205

Housing Preservation, Institute for Responsible   www.housingpreservation.org
401 9th St NW Suite 900   Washington DC 20004
Ph: 202-585-8739 ▪ Fx: 202-585-8080

Housing Providers Association, Corporate   www.corporatehousingproviders.org
7150 Winton Dr Suite 300   Indianapolis IN 46268
Ph: 317-328-4631 ▪ Fx: 317-280-8527

Housing & Redevelopment Officials, National Association of   www.nahro.org
630 'I' St NW   Washington DC 20001
Ph: 202-289-3500 ▪ Fx: 202-289-8181 ▪ TF: 877-866-2476

Housing & Rehabilitation Association, National   housingonline.com
1625 Massachusetts Ave NW Suite 601   Washington DC 20036
Ph: 202-939-1750 ▪ Fx: 202-265-4435

Housing Resource Center, National Shared   www.nationalsharedhousing.org
5342 Tilly Mill Rd   Dunwoody GA 30338
Ph: 770-395-2625 ▪ Fx: 770-698-2055

Housing Services of America, Neighborhood   www.nhsofamerica.org
1970 Broadway Suite 470   Oakland CA 94612
Ph: 510-832-5542 ▪ Fx: 510-444-3063

Housing Studies, Joint Center for   www.jchs.harvard.edu
Harvard Univ 1033 Massachusetts Ave 5th Fl   Cambridge MA
02138
Ph: 617-495-7908 ▪ Fx: 617-496-9957

Housing Tax Credit Coalition, Affordable   www.taxcreditcoalition.org
401 9th St NW Suite 900   Washington DC 20004
Ph: 202-585-8739 ▪ Fx: 202-585-8080

Howard Heinz Endowment   www.heinz.org
625 Liberty Ave 30 Dominion Tower   Pittsburgh PA 15222
Ph: 412-281-5777 ▪ Fx: 412-281-5788

HPV & Cervical Cancer Prevention Resource Center, National   www.ashastd.org/hpvccrc
PO Box 13827   Research Triangle Park NC 27709
Ph: 919-361-8400 ▪ Fx: 919-361-8425

HR Policy Association   www.hrpolicy.org
1015 15th St NW Suite 1200   Washington DC 20005
Ph: 202-789-8670 ▪ Fx: 202-789-0064

Hudson Institute   www.hudson.org
5395 Emerson Way   Indianapolis IN 46226
Ph: 317-545-1000 ▪ Fx: 317-545-9639 ▪ TF: 800-483-7660

Hudson River Sloop Clearwater Inc   www.clearwater.org
112 Market St   Poughkeepsie NY 12601
Ph: 845-454-7673

Hudson-Webber Foundation   www.hudson-webber.org
333 W Fort St Suite 1310   Detroit MI 48226
Ph: 313-963-7777 ▪ Fx: 313-963-2818

Hug-a-Tree & Survive   www.tbt.com/hugatree
PO Box 712739   Santee CA 92072
Ph: 619-286-7536

Hugh O'Brian Youth Leadership   www.hoby.org
10880 Wilshire Blvd Suite 410   Los Angeles CA 90024
Ph: 310-474-4370 ▪ Fx: 310-475-5426

Huguenot Historical Society   www.hhs-newpaltz.org
18 Broadhead Ave   New Paltz NY 12561
Ph: 845-255-1660 ▪ Fx: 845-255-0376

Hull Cordell Foundation for International Education   www.payson.tulane.edu/cordellhull
135 E 50th St Suite 3H   New York NY 10022
Ph: 212-759-3311

Human Anatomy & Physiology Society   www.hapsweb.org
8000 Bonhomme Ave Suite 412   Saint Louis MO 63105
Ph: 800-448-4277 ▪ Fx: 314-863-6457

Human Being Inc, Institute for the Development of the Harmonious   www.idhhb.org
PO Box 370   Nevada City CA 95959
Ph: 530-272-0180 ▪ Fx: 530-272-0184

Human & Civil Rights Organizations of America   www.hcr.org
21 Tamal Vista Blvd Suite 209   Corte Madera CA 94925
Ph: 415-924-1108 ▪ Fx: 415-924-1379 ▪ TF: 800-686-6347

Human Development, Catholic Campaign for   www.nccbuscc.org/chd
3211 4th St NE   Washington DC 20017
Ph: 202-541-3210 ▪ Fx: 202-541-3329 ▪ TF: 800-946-4243

(Human Development) Counterpart International Inc   www.counterpart.org
1200 18th St NW Suite 1100   Washington DC 20036
Ph: 202-296-9676 ▪ Fx: 202-296-9679

Human Development Resource Council   www.hdrc.org
3941 Holcomb Bridge Rd Suite 300   Norcross GA 30092
Ph: 770-447-1598 ▪ Fx: 770-447-0759

Human Ecology Action League   members.aol.com/HEALNatnl
PO Box 29629   Atlanta GA 30359
Ph: 404-248-1898 ▪ Fx: 404-248-0162

Human Ecology & Ethnology, International Council for   www.ichee.org
PO Box 7024   New York NY 10128
Ph: 212-410-6560

Human Ecology, Society for   www.societyforhumanecology.org
College of the Atlantic 105 Eden St   Bar Harbor ME 04609
Ph: 207-288-5015 ▪ Fx: 207-288-3780

Human Environment, Institute for the
2572 Acacia Ave   Sonoma CA 95476
Ph: 707-935-9335 ▪ Fx: 707-935-9593

Human Factors & Ergonomics Society   hfes.org
PO Box 1369   Santa Monica CA 90406
Ph: 310-394-1811 ▪ Fx: 310-394-2410

Human Genetics, American Society of   www.ashg.org/genetics/ashg
9650 Rockville Pike   Bethesda MD 20814
Ph: 301-571-1825 ▪ Fx: 301-634-7079

Human Growth Foundation   www.hgfound.org
997 Glen Cove Ave   Glen Head NY 11545
Ph: 516-671-4041 ▪ Fx: 516-671-4055 ▪ TF: 800-451-6434

Human Knowledge, Institute for the Study of   www.ishkbooks.com
PO Box 176   Los Altos CA 94023
Ph: 650-948-9428 ▪ Fx: 650-948-2687

(Human Knowledge) Jean Piaget Society   www.piaget.org
Harvard Univ Dept of Human Development & Psychology Larsen
Hall   Cambridge MA 02138
Ph: 617-495-3446 ▪ Fx: 617-495-3626

Human Life Foundation Inc   www.humanlifereview.com
215 Lexington Ave 4th Fl   New York NY 10016
Ph: 212-685-5210 ▪ Fx: 212-725-9793

Human Life International   www.hli.org
4 Family Life Ln   Front Royal VA 22630
Ph: 540-635-7884 ▪ Fx: 540-636-7363 ▪ TF: 800-549-5433

Human Milk & Lactation, International Society for Research in   www.isrhml.org
Meriter Hospital Perinatal Ctr 202 S Park St   Madison WI
53715
Ph: 608-262-6561 ▪ Fx: 608-267-6377

Human Needs, Coalition on   www.chn.org
1120 Connecticut Ave NW Suite 919   Washington DC 20036
Ph: 202-223-2532 ▪ Fx: 202-223-2538

Human Policy, Center on   soeweb.syr.edu/thechp
805 S Crouse Ave   Syracuse NY 13244
Ph: 315-443-3851 ▪ Fx: 315-443-4338 ▪ TF: 800-894-0826

Human Potential, Association for the Development of
PO Box 3543   Spokane WA 99220
Ph: 509-838-6652 ▪ TF: 800-251-9273

Human Potential, Institutes for the Achievement of   www.iahp.org
8801 Stenton Ave   Wyndmoor PA 19038
Ph: 215-233-2050 ▪ Fx: 215-233-9312

Human Powered Vehicle Association   www.ihpva.org/hpva
PO Box 1307   San Luis Obispo CA 93406
Ph: 805-772-5888 ▪ Fx: 805-545-9005

Human Relations Area Files Inc   www.yale.edu/hraf
Yale Univ 755 Prospect St   New Haven CT 06511
Ph: 203-764-9401 ▪ Fx: 203-764-9404 ▪ TF: 800-520-4723

Human Relations Association of America, Lutheran   lhra.org
5233 N 52st Blvd   Milwaukee WI 53218
Ph: 414-536-0585 ▪ Fx: 414-536-0690

Human Resource Certification Institute   www.hrci.org
Society for Human Resource Management 1800 Duke
St   Alexandria VA 22314
Ph: 703-548-3440

(Human Resource Development) OIC International   www.oicinternational.org
240 W Tulpehocken St   Philadelphia PA 19144
Ph: 215-842-0860 ▪ Fx: 215-849-7033 ▪ TF: 800-653-6424

Human Resource Information Management, International   www.ihrim.org
Association for   PO Box 1086   Burlington MA 01803
Ph: 800-946-6363 ▪ Fx: 781-998-8011

Human Resource Management, Society for   www.shrm.org
1800 Duke St   Alexandria VA 22314
Ph: 703-548-3440 ▪ Fx: 703-836-0367 ▪ TF: 800-283-7476

Human Resource Planning Society   www.hrps.org
317 Madison Ave Suite 1509   New York NY 10017
Ph: 212-490-6387 ▪ Fx: 212-682-6851

Human Resources Administration, American Society for Healthcare   www.ashhra.org
1 N Franklin PO Box 75315   Chicago IL 60675
Ph: 312-422-3725 ▪ Fx: 312-422-4577

Human Resources Association, Cable & Telecommunications   www.cthra.com
1755 Park St Suite 260   Naperville IL 60563
Ph: 630-416-1166 ▪ Fx: 630-416-9798

Human Resources Association, National   www.humanresources.org
PO Box 803   Pewaukee WI 53072
Ph: 414-453-7499 ▪ Fx: 414-475-5959 ▪ TF: 866-523-4417

Human Resources, College & University Professional Association for   www.cupahr.org
1233 20th St NW Suite 301   Washington DC 20036
Ph: 202-429-0311 ▪ Fx: 202-429-0149

(Human Resources) HR Policy Association   www.hrpolicy.org
1015 15th St NW Suite 1200   Washington DC 20005
Ph: 202-789-8670 ▪ Fx: 202-789-0064

Human Resources, International Public Management Association for   www.ipma-hr.org
1617 Duke St   Alexandria VA 22314
Ph: 703-549-7100 ▪ Fx: 703-684-0948 ▪ TF: 800-220-4762

Human Resources, National Association of African Americans in   www.naaahr.org

Human Resources Network, Black   www.bhrn.org
8855 Annapolis Rd Suite 301   Lanham MD 20706
Ph: 301-459-6200 ▪ Fx: 301-459-3134

Human Resources Research Organization   www.humrro.org
66 Canal Ctr Plaza Suite 400   Alexandria VA 22314
Ph: 703-549-3611 ▪ Fx: 703-549-9025

(Human Resources) TOC Management Services   www.toc.org
6825 SW Sandburg St   Tigard OR 97223
Ph: 503-620-1710 ▪ Fx: 503-620-3935

(Human Resources) WorldatWork   www.worldatwork.org
14040 N Northsight Blvd   Scottsdale AZ 85260
Ph: 480-951-9191 ▪ Fx: 480-483-8352 ▪ TF: 877-951-9191

Human Rights Agencies, International Association of Official   www.sso.org/iaohra
444 N Capitol St NW Suite 536   Washington DC 20001
Ph: 202-624-5410 ▪ Fx: 202-624-8185

(Human Rights) Amnesty International USA   www.amnestyusa.org
322 8th Ave   New York NY 10001
Ph: 212-807-8400 ▪ Fx: 212-627-1451 ▪ TF: 800-266-3789

Human Rights Campaign   www.hrc.org
919 18th St NW Suite 800   Washington DC 20006
Ph: 202-628-4160 ▪ Fx: 202-347-5323 ▪ TF: 800-777-4723

Human Rights Campaign PAC
1640 Rhode Island Ave NW   Washington DC 20036
Ph: 202-628-4160 ▪ Fx: 202-347-5323 ▪ TF: 800-777-4723

Human Rights, Center for the Advancement of   www.cahr.fsu.edu
Florida State Univ MC 1602 426 W Jefferson St Tallahassee FL 32301
Ph: 850-664-4500 ▪ Fx: 850-664-4633

Human Rights, Center for the Study of   www.columbia.edu/cu/humanrights
420 W 118th St Suite 1187 New York NY 10027
Ph: 212-854-2479 ▪ Fx: 212-316-4578

Human Rights in China   www.hrichina.org
350 5th Ave Suite 3309 New York NY 10118
Ph: 212-239-4495 ▪ Fx: 212-239-2561

Human Rights, Coalition for the Defense of   www.dhimmi.com
195 Jamestown Rd Macomb IL 61455
Ph: 309-833-6039

Human Rights Commission, International Gay & Lesbian   www.iglhrc.org
1375 Sutter St Suite 222 San Francisco CA 94109
Ph: 415-561-0633 ▪ Fx: 415-561-0619

(Human Rights) EarthRights International   www.earthrights.org
1612 K St NW Suite 401 Washington DC 20006
Ph: 202-466-5188 ▪ Fx: 202-466-5189

(Human Rights) Global Exchange   www.globalexchange.org
2017 Mission St Suite 303 San Francisco CA 94110
Ph: 415-255-7296 ▪ Fx: 415-255-7498 ▪ TF: 800-497-1994

(Human Rights) Global Rights   www.globalrights.org
1200 18th St NW Suite 602 Washington DC 20036
Ph: 202-822-4600 ▪ Fx: 202-822-4606

Human Rights, Inter-American Commission on   www.oas.org
1889 F St NW 5th Fl Washington DC 20006
Ph: 202-458-6002 ▪ Fx: 202-458-3992

Human Rights, International League for   www.ilhr.org
228 East 45th St 5th Fl New York NY 10017
Ph: 212-661-0480 ▪ Fx: 212-661-0416

(Human Rights) Madre Inc   www.madre.org
121 W 27th St Rm 301 New York NY 10001
Ph: 212-627-0444 ▪ Fx: 212-675-3704

(Human Rights) MindFreedom Support Coalition International   www.mindfreedom.org
PO Box 11284 Eugene OR 97440
Ph: 541-345-9106 ▪ Fx: 541-345-3737 ▪ TF: 877-623-7743

Human Rights Network, Vietnam   www.vnhrnet.org
4745 El Cajon Blvd Suite 104 San Diego CA 92115
Ph: 619-284-5111 ▪ Fx: 619-284-5115

Human Rights, Physicians for   www.phrusa.org
100 Boylston St Suite 702 Boston MA 02116
Ph: 617-695-0041 ▪ Fx: 617-695-0307

Human Rights Policy, Carr Center for   www.ksg.harvard.edu/cchrp
Harvard Univ John F Kennedy School of Government 79 JFK St Cambridge MA 02138
Ph: 617-495-5819 ▪ Fx: 617-495-4297

(Human Rights) Southern Christian Leadership Conference   www.sclcnational.org
591-A Edgewood Ave SE Atlanta GA 30312
Ph: 404-522-1420 ▪ Fx: 404-527-4333

Human Rights Watch   www.hrw.org
350 5th Ave 34th Fl New York NY 10118
Ph: 212-290-4700 ▪ Fx: 212-736-1300

Human Service Education, National Organization for   www.nohse.org
9001 Braddock Rd Suite 380 Springfield VA 22151
Ph: 703-323-9896 ▪ Fx: 703-426-8400

Human Service Organizations, National Assembly of Health &   www.nassembly.org
1319 F St NW Suite 601 Washington DC 20004
Ph: 202-347-2080 ▪ Fx: 202-393-4517

Human Services Association, American Public   www.aphsa.org
810 1st St NE Suite 500 Washington DC 20002
Ph: 202-682-0100 ▪ Fx: 202-289-6555

Human Services, Center for Development of   www.bsc-cdhs.org
1695 Elmwood Ave Buffalo NY 14207
Ph: 716-876-7600 ▪ Fx: 716-876-2237

(Human Services) National Association of Program Information & Performance Measurement   www.napipm.org
810 1st St NE Suite 500 Washington DC 20002
Ph: 202-682-0100 ▪ Fx: 202-289-6555

Human Services Officials, US Conference of City
1620 'I' St NW Washington DC 20006
Ph: 202-293-7330 ▪ Fx: 202-293-2352

Human Services Inc, Protestant Guild for   www.protestantguild.org
411 Waverley Oaks Rd Suite 104 Waltham MA 02452
Ph: 781-893-6000 ▪ Fx: 781-893-1171

Humane Association, American   www.americanhumane.org
63 Inverness Dr E Englewood CO 80112
Ph: 303-792-9900 ▪ Fx: 303-792-5333 ▪ TF: 800-227-4645

(Humane Education) Latham Foundation   www.latham.org
1826 Clement Ave Alameda CA 94501
Ph: 510-521-0920 ▪ Fx: 510-521-9861

Humane Education Society, American
350 S Huntington Ave Boston MA 02130
Ph: 617-522-7400 ▪ Fx: 617-522-4885

Humane Education Society, National   www.nhes.org
PO Box 340 Charles Town WV 25414
Ph: 304-725-0506 ▪ Fx: 304-725-1523

Humane & Environmental Education, National Association for   www.nahee.org
PO Box 362 East Haddam CT 06423
Ph: 860-434-8666 ▪ Fx: 860-434-9579

Humane Farming Association   www.hfa.org
PO Box 3577 San Rafael CA 94912
Ph: 415-771-2253 ▪ Fx: 415-485-0106

Humane Societies, Associated   www.petfinder.org
124 Evergreen Ave Newark NJ 07114
Ph: 973-824-7080 ▪ Fx: 973-824-2720

Humane Societies, Canadian Federation of   www.cfhs.ca
30 Concourse Gate Suite 102 Nepean ON K2E7V7
Ph: 613-224-8072 ▪ Fx: 613-723-0252 ▪ TF: 888-678-2347

Humane Society, Hooved Animal   www.hahs.org
10804 McConnell Rd PO Box 400 Woodstock IL 60098
Ph: 815-337-5563 ▪ Fx: 815-337-5569

Humane Society of the US   www.hsus.org
2100 L St NW Washington DC 20037
Ph: 202-452-1100 ▪ Fx: 202-778-6132

Humanics, American   www.humanics.org
4601 Madison Ave Kansas City MO 64112
Ph: 816-561-6415 ▪ Fx: 816-531-3527 ▪ TF: 800-343-6466

Humanism, Council for Secular   www.secularhumanism.org
PO Box 664 Amherst NY 14226
Ph: 716-636-7571 ▪ Fx: 716-636-1733

Humanist Association, American   www.americanhumanist.org
1777 T St NW Washington DC 20009
Ph: 202-238-9088 ▪ Fx: 202-238-9003 ▪ TF: 866-486-2647

Humanistic Anthropology, Society for   www.smcm.edu/sha
c/o American Anthropological Assn 2200 Wilson Blvd Suite 600 Arlington VA 22201
Ph: 703-528-1902 ▪ Fx: 703-528-3546

Humanistic Education & Development, Counseling Association for
c/o American Counseling Assn 5999 Stevenson Ave Alexandria VA 22304
Ph: 703-823-9800 ▪ Fx: 703-823-0252 ▪ TF: 800-347-6647

Humanistic Jews, International Federation of Secular   www.ifshj.org
224 W 35th St New York NY 10001
Ph: 212-564-6711 ▪ Fx: 212-564-6721

Humanistic Judaism, Society for   www.shj.org
28611 W 12-Mile Rd Farmington Hills MI 48334
Ph: 248-478-7610 ▪ Fx: 248-478-3159

Humanistic Psychology, Association for   ahpweb.org
1516 Oak St Suite 320A Alameda CA 94501
Ph: 510-769-6495 ▪ Fx: 510-769-6433

Humanistic Rabbis, Association of   www.iishj.org
28611 W 12 Mile Rd Farmington Hills MI 48334
Ph: 248-476-9532 ▪ Fx: 248-476-8509

Humanistic Sociology, Association for   www.humanistsoc.org

(Humanitarian) Air Serv International   www.airserv.org
6583 Merchant Pl Suite 100 Warrenton VA 20187
Ph: 540-428-2323 ▪ Fx: 540-428-2326

(Humanitarian) AmeriCares Foundation   www.americares.org
161 Cherry St New Canaan CT 06840
Ph: 203-966-5195 ▪ Fx: 203-966-6028 ▪ TF: 800-486-4357

(Humanitarian) Assist International   www.assistintl.org
PO Box 66396 Scotts Valley CA 95067
Ph: 831-438-4582 ▪ Fx: 831-439-9602

(Humanitarian) Bright Hope International   www.brighthope.org
2060 Stonington Ave Hoffman Estates IL 60195
Ph: 847-519-0012 ▪ Fx: 847-519-0024

(Humanitarian) CARE USA   www.care.org
151 Ellis St NE Atlanta GA 30303
Ph: 404-681-2552 ▪ Fx: 404-589-2630 ▪ TF: 800-422-7385

(Humanitarian) Carter Center   www.cartercenter.org
1 Copenhill 453 Freedom Pkwy Atlanta GA 30307
Ph: 404-331-3900 ▪ Fx: 404-331-0283

Humanitarian Foundation Inc, Israel   projects.ihf.net
276 5th Ave Suite 901 New York NY 10001
Ph: 212-683-5676 ▪ Fx: 212-213-9233 ▪ TF: 888-434-7443

(Humanitarian) God's Child Project   www.godschild.org
721 Memorial Hwy PO Box 1573 Bismarck ND 58504
Ph: 701-255-7956 ▪ Fx: 701-222-0874

(Humanitarian) Heart to Heart International   www.hearttoheart.org
401 S Clairborne Rd Suite 302 Olathe KS 66062
Ph: 913-764-5200 ▪ Fx: 913-764-0809 ▪ TF: 800-764-5220

(Humanitarian) Humanity International   www.humanityinternational.org
PO Box 8222 Gaithersburg MD 20898
Ph: 800-486-2648

(Humanitarian) Lalmba Association   webbresources.com/lalmba
7685 Quartz St Arvada CO 80007
Ph: 303-420-1810 ▪ Fx: 303-467-1232

(Humanitarian) Mercy Corps   www.mercycorps.org
3015 SW 1st Ave Portland OR 97201
Ph: 503-242-1032 ▪ Fx: 503-796-6844 ▪ TF: 800-292-3355

(Humanitarian) Operation Blessing International Relief & Development Corp   www.ob.org
977 Centerville Tpke Virginia Beach VA 23463
Ph: 757-226-3401 ▪ Fx: 757-226-3411 ▪ TF: 800-730-2537

(Humanitarian) Operation USA   www.opusa.org
8320 Melrose Ave Suite 200 Los Angeles CA 90069
Ph: 323-658-8876 ▪ Fx: 323-653-7846 ▪ TF: 800-678-7255

(Humanitarian) Pax World Service   www.paxworld.org
1730 Rhode Island Ave NW Suite 707 Washington DC 20036
Ph: 202-463-0486 ▪ Fx: 202-463-7322

(Humanitarian) Samaritan's Purse   www.samaritanspurse.org
PO Box 3000 Boone NC 28607
Ph: 828-262-1980 ▪ Fx: 828-266-1053

(Humanitarian) Ukrainian Gold Cross
6616 W Roscoe St Chicago IL 60634
Ph: 773-736-4568 ▪ Fx: 773-736-4658

(Humanitarian) Water for People   www.waterforpeople.org
6666 W Quincy Ave Denver CO 80235
Ph: 303-734-3490 ▪ Fx: 303-734-3499

(Humanitarian) World Care   www.worldcare.org
PO Box 64001 Tucson AZ 85728
Ph: 520-514-1588 ▪ Fx: 520-514-1589

(Humanitarian) World Concern   www.worldconcern.org
19303 Fremont Ave N Seattle WA 98133
Ph: 206-546-7201 ▪ Fx: 206-546-7269 ▪ TF: 800-755-5022

Humanitarians, United   www.unitedhumanitarians.com
PO Box 14587 Philadelphia PA 19115
Ph: 215-750-0171

Humanities Alliance, National www.nhalliance.org
21 Dupont Cir NW Suite 604   Washington DC 20036
Ph: 202-296-4994 ▪ Fx: 202-872-0884

Humanities, American Society for Bioethics & www.asbh.org
4700 W Lake Ave   Glenview IL 60025
Ph: 847-375-4745 ▪ Fx: 877-734-9385

Humanities Association, Community College www.ccha-assoc.org
Essex County College 303 University Ave   Newark NJ 07102
Ph: 973-877-3577 ▪ Fx: 973-877-3578

Humanities Center, National www.nhc.rtp.nc.us
7 Alexander Dr PO Box 12256   Research Triangle Park NC
27709
Ph: 919-549-0661 ▪ Fx: 919-990-8535

Humanities Centers & Institutes, Consortium of www.fas.harvard.edu/~chci
Harvard Univ Humanities Ctr 12 Quincy St   Cambridge MA
02138
Ph: 617-495-0738 ▪ Fx: 617-495-0730

Humanities Councils, Federation of State www.statehumanities.com
1600 Wilson Blvd Suite 902   Arlington VA 22209
Ph: 703-908-9700 ▪ Fx: 703-908-9706

Humanities Education, National Association for www.nahe.org
Brigham Young Univ PO Box 26100   Provo UT 84602
Ph: 801-378-2212 ▪ Fx: 801-378-2284

Humanities Institute, National www.nhinet.org
PO Box 1387   Bowie MD 20718
Ph: 301-464-4277

Humanities Institute, Packard
300 2nd St   Los Altos CA 94022
Ph: 650-948-0150 ▪ Fx: 650-948-4135

Humanities, Society for the www.arts.cornell.edu/sochum
Cornell Univ AD White House 27 East Ave   Ithaca NY 14853
Ph: 607-255-9274 ▪ Fx: 607-255-1422

Humanity International www.humanityinternational.org
PO Box 8222   Gaithersburg MD 20898
Ph: 800-486-2648

Hummer Club Inc, Harley www.harleyhummerclub.org
4517 Chase Ave   Bethesda MD 20814
Ph: 301-657-4035

Humor, Association for Applied & Therapeutic www.aath.org
1951 W Camelback Rd Suite 445   Phoenix AZ 85015
Ph: 602-995-1454 ▪ Fx: 602-995-1449

Humor Helps!
14224 SE 88th Ave   Summerfield FL 34491
Ph: 352-307-7993

Humor Project Inc www.humorproject.com
480 Broadway Suite 210   Saratoga Springs NY 12866
Ph: 518-587-8770 ▪ Fx: 800-600-4242 ▪ TF: 800-225-0330

Huna Research Inc www.huna-research.com
1760 Anna St   Cape Girardeau MO 63701
Ph: 573-334-3478

Hungarian-American Chamber of Commerce in the US Inc
205 De Anza Blvd PMB 157   San Mateo CA 94402
Ph: 650-573-7351

Hungarian/American Friendship Society www.dholmes.com/hafs.html
1035 Starbrook Dr   Galt CA 95632
Ph: 209-744-8099

Hungarian Culture, Emanuel Foundation for
97-45 Queens Blvd Suite 614   Rego Park NY 11374
Ph: 718-896-8300 ▪ Fx: 718-896-8323

Hungarian Educators' Association, American magyar.org/ahea

Hungarian Foundation, American www.ahfoundation.org
300 Somerset St PO Box 1084   New Brunswick NJ 08903
Ph: 732-846-5777 ▪ Fx: 732-249-7033

Hungarian Horse Association of America www.horseplaza.com/cfusion/template/hhaa
c/o Horse Plaza PO Box S-3292   Carmel CA 93921
Ph: 530-304-0140

Hungarian Library & Historical Society, American www.hungarianhouse.org
213 E 82nd St   New York NY 10028
Ph: 212-249-9360

Hungarian Literary Society, First www.onkepzo.com
323 E 79th St   New York NY 10021
Ph: 212-288-5002

Hungarian Reformed Federation of America www.hrfa.org
2001 Massachusetts Ave NW   Washington DC 20036
Ph: 202-328-2630 ▪ Fx: 202-328-7984 ▪ TF: 888-567-7884

Hungarian-US Business Council
c/o US Chamber of Commerce 1615 H St NW   Washington DC
20062
Ph: 202-463-5482 ▪ Fx: 202-463-3114

Hungarians, National Federation of American hungarianfed-usa.org
717 2nd St NE   Washington DC 20002
Ph: 202-204-5348 ▪ Fx: 202-544-2819

Hunger, Action Against www.aah-usa.org
247 W 37th St Suite 1201   New York NY 10018
Ph: 212-967-7800 ▪ Fx: 212-967-5480 ▪ TF: 877-777-1420

(Hunger) Bread for the World www.bread.org
50 F St NW Suite 500   Washington DC 20001
Ph: 202-639-9400 ▪ Fx: 202-639-9401 ▪ TF: 800-822-7323

Hunger Center, Congressional www.hungercenter.org
229 1/2 Pennsylvania Ave SE   Washington DC 20003
Ph: 202-547-7022 ▪ Fx: 202-547-7575

(Hunger) Chirofeed International
2627 Capital Mall Dr Suite B 3-A   Olympia WA 98502
Ph: 360-786-6322 ▪ Fx: 360-786-5677

Hunger Clearinghouse, National www.worldhungeryear.org/nhc
505 8th Ave Suite 2100   New York NY 10018
Ph: 212-629-8850 ▪ Fx: 212-465-9274 ▪ TF: 800-453-2648

Hunger, Freedom from www.freefromhunger.org
1644 DaVinci Ct   Davis CA 95616
Ph: 530-758-6200 ▪ Fx: 530-758-6241

(Hunger) God's Love We Deliver www.glwd.org
166 Ave of the Americas   New York NY 10013
Ph: 212-294-8100 ▪ Fx: 212-294-8101 ▪ TF: 800-747-2023

Hunger & Homelessness, National Student Campaign Against www.nscahh.org
233 N Pleasant St Suite 32   Amherst MA 01002
Ph: 413-253-6417 ▪ Fx: 413-256-6435 ▪ TF: 800-664-8647

Hunger Organization, Education Concerns for www.echonet.org
17391 Durrance Rd   Fort Myers FL 33917
Ph: 941-543-3246 ▪ Fx: 941-543-5317

Hunger Project The www.thp.org
15 E 26th St Suite 1401   New York NY 10010
Ph: 212-251-9100 ▪ Fx: 212-532-9785 ▪ TF: 800-228-6691

(Hunger) Senior Gleaners Inc www.seniorgleaners.org
1951 Bell Ave   Sacramento CA 95838
Ph: 916-925-3240 ▪ Fx: 916-568-1528 ▪ TF: 800-585-1530

Hunger Year Inc, World www.worldhungeryear.org
505 8th Ave Suite 2100   New York NY 10018
Ph: 212-629-8850 ▪ Fx: 212-465-9274 ▪ TF: 800-548-6479

Hungry Inc, Food for the www.fh.org
PO Box 12349   Scottsdale AZ 85267
Ph: 480-998-3100 ▪ Fx: 480-443-1420 ▪ TF: 800-248-6437

Hunter & Jumper Association, National www.nhja.com
PO Box 1015   Riverside CT 06878
Ph: 203-869-1225

Hunting Club, North American www.huntingclub.com
12301 Whitewater Dr   Minnetonka MN 55343
Ph: 800-922-4868 ▪ Fx: 952-936-9755

Hunting, Committee to Abolish Sport www.all-creatures.org/cash
PO Box 562   New Paltz NY 12561
Ph: 845-255-4227 ▪ Fx: 845-256-9113

Hunting Retriever Club Inc www.hrc-ukc.com

Huntington's Disease Society of America www.hdsa.org
158 W 29th St 7th Fl   New York NY 10001
Ph: 212-242-1968 ▪ Fx: 212-239-3430 ▪ TF: 800-345-4372

Husky Inc, Adopt a www.adoptahusky.com
PO Box 275   Salem WI 53168
Ph: 262-909-2244 ▪ Fx: 262-878-1890

Hybridizers Association, Rose www.rosehybridizers.org
21 S Wheaton Rd   Horseheads NY 14845
Ph: 607-562-8592

Hydraulic Institute www.pumps.org
9 Sylvan Way   Parsippany NJ 07054
Ph: 973-267-9700 ▪ Fx: 973-267-9055 ▪ TF: 888-786-7744

Hydrogen Association, American www.clean-air.org
1739 W 7th Ave   Mesa AZ 85202
Ph: 480-827-7915 ▪ Fx: 480-967-6601

Hydrogen Association, National www.hydrogenus.org
1800 M St NW Suite 300   Washington DC 20036
Ph: 202-223-5547 ▪ Fx: 202-223-5537

Hydrogen Energy, International Association for www.iahe.org
PO Box 248266   Coral Gables FL 33124
Ph: 305-284-4666 ▪ Fx: 305-284-4792

Hydrology, American Institute of www.aihydro.org
2499 Rice St Suite 135   Saint Paul MN 55113
Ph: 651-484-8169 ▪ Fx: 651-484-8357

Hydrolyzed Protein Council, International
555 13th St NW   Washington DC 20004
Ph: 202-637-5926 ▪ Fx: 202-637-5910

Hydronics Institute
35 Russo Pl PO Box 218   Berkeley Heights NJ 07922
Ph: 908-464-8200 ▪ Fx: 908-464-7818

Hydroponic Merchants Association www.hydromerchants.org
10210 Leatherleaf Ct   Manassas VA 20111
Ph: 703-392-5890 ▪ Fx: 703-257-0213

Hydropower Association, National www.hydro.org
1 Massachusetts Ave NW Suite 850   Washington DC 20001
Ph: 202-682-1700 ▪ Fx: 202-682-9478

Hydrotherapy, International Association for Colon www.i-act.org
PO Box 461285   San Antonio TX 78246
Ph: 210-366-2888 ▪ Fx: 210-366-2999

Hygiene, American Board of Industrial www.abih.org
6015 W St Joseph Hwy Suite 102   Lansing MI 48917
Ph: 517-321-2638 ▪ Fx: 517-321-4624

Hygiene, American Society of Tropical Medicine & www.astmh.org
60 Revere Dr Suite 500   Northbrook IL 60062
Ph: 847-480-9592 ▪ Fx: 847-480-9282

Hygiene Association, American Industrial www.aiha.org
2700 Prosperity Ave Suite 250   Fairfax VA 22031
Ph: 703-849-8888 ▪ Fx: 703-207-3561

Hygienists, American Conference of Governmental Industrial www.acgih.org
1330 Kemper Meadows Dr   Cincinnati OH 45240
Ph: 513-742-2020 ▪ Fx: 513-742-3355

Hygienists' Association, National Dental www.ndaonline.org
3517 16th St NW   Washington DC 20010
Ph: 202-588-1697 ▪ Fx: 202-588-1244

Hymn Society in the US & Canada www.thehymnsociety.org
Boston Univ School of Theology 745 Commonwealth
Ave   Boston MA 02215
Ph: 617-353-6493 ▪ Fx: 617-353-7322 ▪ TF: 800-843-4966

Hynek J Allen Center for UFO Studies www.cufos.org
2457 W Peterson Ave Suite 6   Chicago IL 60659
Ph: 773-271-3611

Hyperactivity Disorder, Children & Adults with Attention-Deficit/ www.chadd.org
8181 Professional Pl Suite 201   Landover MD 20785
Ph: 301-306-7070 ▪ Fx: 301-306-7090 ▪ TF: 800-233-4050

Hyperbaric Medical Society, Undersea & www.uhms.org
10531 Metropolitan Ave   Kensington MD 20895
Ph: 301-942-2980 ▪ Fx: 301-942-7804

Hyperlexia Association, American   www.hyperlexia.org
195 W Spangler Suite B   Elmhurst IL 60126
Ph: 630-415-2212 ▪ Fx: 630-530-5908

Hypersensitive, National Foundation for the Chemically   www.mcsrelief.com
4407 Swinson Rd   Rhodes MI 48652
Ph: 989-689-6369 ▪ Fx: 989-689-6877

Hypertension, American Society of   www.ash-us.org
148 Madison Ave 5th Fl   New York NY 10016
Ph: 212-696-9099 ▪ Fx: 212-696-0711

Hyperthermia Association of the US, Malignant   www.mhaus.org
11 E State St PO Box 1069   Sherburne NY 13460
Ph: 607-674-7901 ▪ Fx: 607-674-7910

Hypnoanalysts, American Academy of Medical   www.aamh.com
1022 Depot Hill Rd   Broomfield CO 80020
Ph: 888-454-9766 ▪ Fx: 303-465-1260

Hypnosis, American Society of Clinical   www.asch.net
140 N Bloomingdale Rd   Bloomingdale IL 60108
Ph: 630-980-4740 ▪ Fx: 630-351-8490

Hypnosis Association, American
18607 Ventura Blvd Suite 310   Tarzana CA 91356
Ph: 818-758-2730 ▪ Fx: 818-344-2262 ▪ TF: 800-990-0426

Hypnosis, Society for Clinical & Experimental   ijceh.educ.wsu.edu/sceh/scehframe.htm
Massachusetts School of Professional Psychology 221
    Rivermoor St   Boston MA 02132
Ph: 617-469-1981 ▪ Fx: 617-469-1889

Hypnotherapists, National Board of Certified Clinical   www.natboard.com
1110 Fiddler Ln Suite L-1   Silver Spring MD 20910
Ph: 301-608-0123 ▪ Fx: 301-588-9535 ▪ TF: 800-449-8144

Hypnotherapists, National Society of
1833 W Charleston Blvd   Las Vegas NV 89102
Ph: 702-384-4420 ▪ Fx: 702-386-2851

Hypnotherapy, Academy of Scientific
PO Box 12041   San Diego CA 92112
Ph: 619-427-6225 ▪ Fx: 619-427-5650

Hypnotist Examiners, American Council of   www.sonic.net/hypno/ache.html
700 S Central Ave   Glendale CA 91204
Ph: 818-242-1159 ▪ Fx: 818-247-9379 ▪ TF: 800-894-9766

Hypopigmentation, National Organization for Albinism &   www.albinism.org
PO Box 959   East Hampstead NH 03826
Ph: 603-887-2310 ▪ Fx: 603-887-6049 ▪ TF: 800-473-2310

Hysterectomy Educational Resources & Services Foundation   www.hersfoundation.com
422 Bryn Mawr Ave   Bala Cynwyd PA 19004
Ph: 610-667-7757 ▪ Fx: 610-667-8096 ▪ TF: 888-750-4377

I

I-CAR Inter-Industry Conference on Auto Collision Repair   www.i-car.com
3701 Algonquin Rd Suite 400   Rolling Meadows IL 60008
Ph: 847-590-1191 ▪ Fx: 847-590-1215 ▪ TF: 800-422-7872

I Have a Dream Foundation   www.ihad.org
330 7th Ave 20th Fl   New York NY 10001
Ph: 212-293-5480 ▪ Fx: 212-293-5478

IA International   www.iai.org
9200 S Dadeland Blvd Suite 510   Miami FL 33156
Ph: 305-670-0580 ▪ Fx: 305-670-3818

IASCA Worldwide Inc   www.iasca.com
2129 S Ridgewood Ave   South Daytona FL 32119
Ph: 386-322-1551 ▪ Fx: 386-761-1740

IATSE PAC   www.iatse-intl.org/pac/pac.html
1430 Broadway 20th Fl   New York NY 10018
Ph: 212-730-1770 ▪ Fx: 212-921-7699 ▪ TF: 800-223-6972

Ibero-American Action League Inc   www.iaal.org
817 E Main St   Rochester NY 14605
Ph: 585-256-8900 ▪ Fx: 585-256-0120

Ice Age Park & Trail Foundation   www.iceagetrail.org
207 E Buffalo St Suite 515   Milwaukee WI 53202
Ph: 414-278-8518 ▪ Fx: 414-278-8665 ▪ TF: 800-227-0046

Ice Association, International Packaged   www.packagedice.com
PO Box 1199   Tampa FL 33601
Ph: 813-258-1690 ▪ Fx: 813-251-2783 ▪ TF: 800-742-0627

Ice Carving Association, National   www.nica.org
PO Box 3593   Oak Brook IL 60522
Ph: 630-871-8431 ▪ Fx: 630-871-0839

Ice Cream Association, International
1250 H St NW Suite 900   Washington DC 20005
Ph: 202-737-4332 ▪ Fx: 202-331-7820

Ice Cream Milk & Cheese PAC
1250 H St NW Suite 900   Washington DC 20005
Ph: 202-737-4332 ▪ Fx: 202-331-7820

Ice Cream Vendors, International Association of   www.iaicv.org
1900 Arch St   Philadelphia PA 19103
Ph: 215-564-3484 ▪ Fx: 215-564-2175

Ice Cream & Yogurt Retailers Association, National   www.nicyra.org
184 Hicks Rd Suite C   Rolling Meadows IL 60008
Ph: 847-934-0926 ▪ Fx: 847-202-4791

Ice Management Association Inc, Snow &   www.sima.org
1903 W 8th St PMB 150   Erie PA 16505
Ph: 814-835-3577 ▪ Fx: 814-835-0527

Ice Screamers   www.icescreamers.com
PO Box 465   Warrington PA 18976
Ph: 215-343-2676

Ice Skating Institute   www.skateisi.org
17120 Dallas Pkwy Suite 140   Dallas TX 75248
Ph: 972-735-8800 ▪ Fx: 972-735-8815

Icelandic-American Chamber of Commerce   www.icelandnaturally.com
800 3rd Ave 36th Fl   New York NY 10022
Ph: 212-593-2700 ▪ Fx: 212-593-6269

Icelandic Horse Adventure Society
795 Entrance Rd   Solvang CA 93463
Ph: 805-688-3869 ▪ Fx: 805-688-2651

Icelandic Horse Congress, US   www.icelandics.org
PO Box 1724   Santa Ynez CA 93460
Ph: 805-688-6355

Ichthyologists & Herpetologists, American Society of   www.asih.org
Florida International Univ Biology Dept 11200 SW 8th
    St   Miami FL 33199
Ph: 305-919-5651 ▪ Fx: 305-919-5964

ICOM   www.icomagencies.com
1649 Lump Gulch Rd PO Box 490   Rollinsville CO 80474
Ph: 303-258-9511 ▪ Fx: 303-258-3090

ICU Foundation Inc, Japan   www.jicuf.org
475 Riverside Dr Suite 439   New York NY 10115
Ph: 212-870-3386 ▪ Fx: 212-870-2696

IDEA Inc   www.ideafit.com
6190 Cornerstone Ct E Suite 204   San Diego CA 92121
Ph: 858-535-8979 ▪ Fx: 858-535-8234 ▪ TF: 800-999-4332

Idealist   www.idealist.org
79 5th Ave Suite 6614   New York NY 10003
Ph: 212-843-3973 ▪ Fx: 212-564-3377

Ideas & Action, Demos: A Network for   www.demos-usa.org
220 5th Ave 5th Fl   New York NY 10001
Ph: 212-633-1405 ▪ Fx: 212-633-2015

(Identification) AIM Inc - Association for Automatic   www.aimglobal.org
Identification & Mobility   125 Warrendale-Bayne
    Rd   Warrendale PA 15086
Ph: 724-934-4470 ▪ Fx: 724-934-4495 ▪ TF: 800-338-0206

Identification Association, International Marking &   www.mdai.org
222 Wisconsin Ave Suite 1   Lake Forest IL 60045
Ph: 847-283-9810 ▪ Fx: 847-283-9808

Identification, International Association for   www.theiai.org/
2535 Pilot Knob Rd Suite 117   Mendota Heights MN 55120
Ph: 651-681-8566 ▪ Fx: 651-681-8443

Identification Manufacturers Inc, National Association of   www.gpiweb.org
Graphic & Product   PO Box 15466   Santa Ana CA 92735
Ph: 714-508-4915 ▪ Fx: 714-508-4904

Identification & Mobility, AIM Inc - Association for Automatic   www.aimglobal.org
125 Warrendale-Bayne Rd   Warrendale PA 15086
Ph: 724-934-4470 ▪ Fx: 724-934-4495 ▪ TF: 800-338-0206

IEEE Aerospace & Electronics Systems Society   www.ewh.ieee.org/soc/aes
IEEE Operations Ctr 445 Hoes Ln   Piscataway NJ 08854
Ph: 732-981-0060 ▪ Fx: 732-981-1721

IEEE Antennas & Propagation Society   www.ieeeaps.org
IEEE Operations Ctr 445 Hoes Ln   Piscataway NJ 08854
Ph: 732-981-0060 ▪ Fx: 732-981-1721

IEEE Broadcast Technology Society   www.ieee.org/organizations/society/bt
IEEE Operations Ctr 445 Hoes Ln   Piscataway NJ 08854
Ph: 732-981-0060 ▪ Fx: 732-981-1721

IEEE Circuits & Systems Society   www.ieee-cas.org
IEEE Operations Ctr 445 Hoes Ln   Piscataway NJ 08854
Ph: 732-981-0060 ▪ Fx: 732-981-1721

IEEE Communications Society   www.comsoc.org
IEEE Operations Ctr 445 Hoes Ln   Piscataway NJ 08854
Ph: 732-981-0060 ▪ Fx: 732-981-1721

IEEE Components Packaging & Manufacturing Technology Society   www.cpmt.org
445 Hoes Ln PO Box 1331   Piscataway NJ 08855
Ph: 732-562-5529 ▪ Fx: 732-981-1769

IEEE Computer Society   www.computer.org
IEEE Operations Ctr 445 Hoes Ln   Piscataway NJ 08854
Ph: 732-981-0060 ▪ Fx: 732-981-1721

IEEE Consumer Electronics Society   www.ewh.ieee.org/soc/ces
IEEE Operations Ctr 445 Hoes Ln   Piscataway NJ 08854
Ph: 732-981-0060 ▪ Fx: 732-981-1721

IEEE Control Systems Society   www.ieeecss.org
IEEE Operations Ctr 445 Hoes Ln   Piscataway NJ 08854
Ph: 732-981-0060 ▪ Fx: 732-981-1721

IEEE Dielectrics & Electrical Insulation Society   tdei.sju.edu/deis
IEEE Operations Ctr 445 Hoes Ln   Piscataway NJ 08854
Ph: 732-981-0060 ▪ Fx: 732-981-1721

IEEE Education Society   www.ewh.ieee.org/soc/es
IEEE Operations Ctr 445 Hoes Ln   Piscataway NJ 08854
Ph: 732-981-0060 ▪ Fx: 732-981-1721

IEEE Electromagnetic Compatibility Society   www.ewh.ieee.org/soc/emcs
IEEE Operations Ctr 445 Hoes Ln   Piscataway NJ 08854
Ph: 732-981-0060 ▪ Fx: 732-981-1721

IEEE Electron Devices Society   www.ieee.org/organizations/society/eds
IEEE Operations Ctr 445 Hoes Ln   Piscataway NJ 08854
Ph: 732-981-0060 ▪ Fx: 732-981-1721

IEEE Engineering Management Society   www.ewh.ieee.org/soc/ems
IEEE Operations Ctr 445 Hoes Ln   Piscataway NJ 08854
Ph: 732-981-0060 ▪ Fx: 732-981-1721

IEEE Engineering in Medicine & Biology Society   www.eng.unsw.edu.au/embs/index.html
IEEE Operations Ctr 445 Hoes Ln   Piscataway NJ 08854
Ph: 732-981-0060 ▪ Fx: 732-981-1721

IEEE Geoscience & Remote Sensing Society   www.ewh.ieee.org/soc/grss
IEEE Operations Ctr 445 Hoes Ln   Piscataway NJ 08854
Ph: 732-981-0060 ▪ Fx: 732-981-1721

IEEE Industrial Electronics Society   www.ewh.ieee.org/soc/ies
IEEE Operations Ctr 445 Hoes Ln   Piscataway NJ 08854
Ph: 732-981-0060 ▪ Fx: 732-981-1721

IEEE Industry Applications Society   www.ewh.ieee.org/soc/ias
IEEE Operations Ctr 445 Hoes Ln   Piscataway NJ 08854
Ph: 732-981-0060 ▪ Fx: 732-981-1721

IEEE Information Theory Society   golay.uvic.ca
IEEE Operations Ctr 445 Hoes Ln   Piscataway NJ 08854
Ph: 732-981-0060 ▪ Fx: 732-981-1721

IEEE Instrumentation & Measurement Society   www.ewh.ieee.org/soc/im
IEEE Operations Ctr 445 Hoes Ln   Piscataway NJ 08854
Ph: 732-981-0060 ▪ Fx: 732-981-1721

IEEE Lasers & Electro-Optics Society — www.i-LEOS.org
IEEE Operations Ctr 445 Hoes Ln Piscataway NJ 08854
Ph: 732-981-0060 ▪ Fx: 732-981-1721

IEEE Magnetics Society — www.ieeemagnetics.org
IEEE Operations Ctr 445 Hoes Ln Piscataway NJ 08854
Ph: 732-981-0060 ▪ Fx: 732-981-1721

IEEE Microwave Theory & Techniques Society — www.mtt.org
IEEE Operations Ctr 445 Hoes Ln Piscataway NJ 08854
Ph: 732-981-0060 ▪ Fx: 732-981-1721

IEEE Neural Networks Society — www.ieee-nns.org
IEEE Operations Ctr 445 Hoes Ln Piscataway NJ 08854
Ph: 732-981-0060 ▪ Fx: 732-981-1721

IEEE Nuclear & Plasma Sciences Society — ewh.ieee.org/soc/nps
IEEE Operations Ctr 445 Hoes Ln Piscataway NJ 08854
Ph: 732-981-0060 ▪ Fx: 732-981-1721

IEEE Oceanic Engineering Society — www.oceanicengineering.org
IEEE Operations Ctr 445 Hoes Ln Piscataway NJ 08854
Ph: 732-981-0060 ▪ Fx: 732-981-1721

IEEE Power Electronics Society — www.pels.org
IEEE Operations Ctr 445 Hoes Ln Piscataway NJ 08854
Ph: 732-981-0060 ▪ Fx: 732-981-1721

IEEE Power Engineering Society — www.ieee.org/portal/index.jsp?pageID=pes_home
IEEE Operations Ctr 445 Hoes Ln Piscataway NJ 08854
Ph: 732-981-0060 ▪ Fx: 732-981-1721

IEEE Product Safety Engineering Society — ewh.ieee.org/soc/pses
IEEE Operations Ctr 445 Hoes Ln Piscataway NJ 08854
Ph: 732-981-0060 ▪ Fx: 732-981-1721

IEEE Professional Communication Society — www.ieeepcs.org
IEEE Operations Ctr 445 Hoes Ln Piscataway NJ 08854
Ph: 732-981-0060 ▪ Fx: 732-981-1721

IEEE Reliability Society — www.ewh.ieee.org/soc/rs
IEEE Operations Ctr 445 Hoes Ln Piscataway NJ 08854
Ph: 732-981-0060 ▪ Fx: 732-981-1721

IEEE Robotics & Automation Society — www.ncsu.edu/IEEE-RAS
IEEE Operations Ctr 445 Hoes Ln Piscataway NJ 08854
Ph: 732-981-0060 ▪ Fx: 732-981-1721

IEEE Signal Processing Society — www.ieee.org/organizations/society/sp
IEEE Operations Ctr 445 Hoes Ln Piscataway NJ 08854
Ph: 732-981-0060 ▪ Fx: 732-981-1721

IEEE Society on Social Implications of Technology — radburn.rutgers.edu/andrews/projects/ssit
IEEE Operations Ctr 445 Hoes Ln Piscataway NJ 08854
Ph: 732-981-0060 ▪ Fx: 732-981-1721

IEEE Solid State Circuits Society — sscs.org
IEEE Operations Ctr 445 Hoes Ln Piscataway NJ 08854
Ph: 732-981-0060 ▪ Fx: 732-981-1721

IEEE Systems Man & Cybernetics Society — www.ieeesmc.org
IEEE Operations Ctr 445 Hoes Ln Piscataway NJ 08854
Ph: 732-981-0060 ▪ Fx: 732-981-1721

IEEE Ultrasonics Ferroelectrics & Frequency Control Society — www.ieee-uffc.org
IEEE Operations Ctr 445 Hoes Ln Piscataway NJ 08854
Ph: 732-981-0060 ▪ Fx: 732-981-1721

IEEE Vehicular Technology Society — www.vtsociety.org
IEEE Operations Ctr 445 Hoes Ln Piscataway NJ 08854
Ph: 732-981-0060 ▪ Fx: 732-981-1721

IFCA International — www.ifca.org
PO Box 810 Grandville MI 49468
Ph: 616-531-1840 ▪ Fx: 616-531-1814 ▪ TF: 800-347-1840

Illinois Central Railroad Historical Society — www.icrrhistorical.org
PO Box 288 Paxton IL 60957
Ph: 217-379-2261

Illness & Loss, American Institute of Life Threatening — www.lifethreat.org/
Columbia-Presbyterian Medical Ctr 630 W 168th St New York NY 10032
Ph: 718-601-4453 ▪ Fx: 718-549-7219

(Illness) Shanti — www.shanti.org
730 Polk St San Francisco CA 94109
Ph: 415-674-4700 ▪ Fx: 415-674-0371

Illuminating Companies, Association of Edison — www.aeic.org
600 N 18th St PO Box 2641 Birmingham AL 35291
Ph: 205-257-2530 ▪ Fx: 205-257-2540

Illuminating Engineering Society of North America — www.iesna.org
120 Wall St 17th Fl New York NY 10005
Ph: 212-248-5000 ▪ Fx: 212-248-5017

Illustrators, Association of Medical — www.ami.org
5475 Mark Dabling Blvd Suite 108 Colorado Springs CO 80918
Ph: 719-598-8622 ▪ Fx: 719-599-3075

Illustrators, Society of — www.societyillustrators.org
Museum of American Illustration 128 E 63rd St New York NY 10021
Ph: 212-838-2560 ▪ Fx: 212-838-2561

Illustrators, Society of Children's Book Writers & — www.scbwi.org
8271 Beverly Blvd Los Angeles CA 90048
Ph: 323-782-1010 ▪ Fx: 323-782-1892

IMACA Education Foundation — www.imaca.org
6410 Southwest Blvd Suite 212 Fort Worth TX 76109
Ph: 817-732-4600 ▪ Fx: 817-732-9610

Image Consultants International, Association of — www.aici.org
2695 Villa Creek Dr Suite 260 Dallas TX 75234
Ph: 972-755-1503 ▪ Fx: 972-755-2561 ▪ TF: 800-383-8831

Image Management, Institute for — www.image360.com
PO Box 190007 San Francisco CA 94119
Ph: 415-863-2573

Imagery Association, International — www.imagery-iia.com
18 Edgecliff Terr Yonkers NY 10705
Ph: 914-476-0781 ▪ Fx: 914-476-5796

Imagine World Health — www.imagineworldhealth.org
105 E Dolphin Blvd Ponte Vedra Beach FL 32082
Ph: 904-285-0240

Imaging Association, Automated — www.machinevisiononline.org
900 Victors Way PO Box 3724 Ann Arbor MI 48106
Ph: 734-994-6088 ▪ Fx: 734-994-3338

Imaging Association, Digital Printing & — www.dpia.org
10015 Main St Fairfax VA 22031
Ph: 703-385-1339 ▪ Fx: 703-359-1336

Imaging Association, Optical — www.opia.org
252 Reinekers Ln Suite 625 Alexandria VA 22314
Ph: 703-836-1360 ▪ Fx: 703-836-6644

Imaging Association, Specialty Graphic — www.sgia.org
10015 Main St Fairfax VA 22031
Ph: 703-385-1335 ▪ Fx: 703-273-0456

Imaging Industry Association, International — www.i3a.org
550 Mamaroneck Ave Suite 310 Harrison NY 10528
Ph: 914-698-7603 ▪ Fx: 914-698-7609

Imaging, North American Society for Cardiac — www.nasci.org
PO Box 20085 Stanford CA 94309
Ph: 650-216-6621 ▪ Fx: 650-556-1678

Imaging Science & Technology, Society for — www.imaging.org
7003 Kilworth Ln Springfield VA 22151
Ph: 703-642-9090 ▪ Fx: 703-642-9094

Imaging, Society of Atherosclerosis — www.sai.org
13140 Coit Rd Suite 320 LB 120 Dallas TX 75240
Ph: 972-233-9107 ▪ Fx: 972-490-4219

Imaging Supplies Coalition — www.isc-inc.org
1750 Alexandria Dr Suite 6 Lexington KY 40504
Ph: 859-278-3032 ▪ Fx: 859-278-1244

Imaging Systems, Association for Engineering Graphics &
800 Enterprise Dr Suite 202 Oak Brook IL 60523
Ph: 630-574-8200 ▪ Fx: 630-571-4731

Immaculata Movement, Militia of the — www.consecration.com
1600 W Park Ave Libertyville IL 60048
Ph: 847-367-7800 ▪ Fx: 847-367-7831

(Immaculate Conception) Central Association of the Miraculous Medal — www.cammonline.org
475 E Chelten Ave Philadelphia PA 19144
Ph: 215-848-1010 ▪ Fx: 215-848-1014 ▪ TF: 800-523-3674

Immigrant Aid Society, Hebrew — www.hias.org
333 7th Ave 17th Fl New York NY 10001
Ph: 212-967-4100 ▪ Fx: 212-967-4483 ▪ TF: 800-442-7714

Immigrant Genealogical Society — www.feefhs.org/igs/frg-igs.html
1310B Magnolia Blvd PO Box 7369 Burbank CA 91510
Ph: 818-848-3122 ▪ Fx: 818-716-6300

Immigrant & Refugee Rights, National Network for — www.nnirr.org
310 8th St Suite 303 Oakland CA 94607
Ph: 510-465-1984 ▪ Fx: 510-465-1885

Immigration Center of New York, Emerald Isle — www.eiic.org
59-26 Woodside Ave Woodside NY 11377
Ph: 718-478-5502 ▪ Fx: 718-446-3727

Immigration Control, Americans for — www.immigrationcontrol.com
PO Box 738 Monterey VA 24465
Ph: 540-468-2023 ▪ Fx: 540-468-2026

Immigration & Ethnic History Society — www.iehs.org
American Univ 4400 Massachusetts NW Washington DC 20016
Ph: 202-885-2410

Immigration Forum, National — www.immigrationforum.org
50 F St NW Suite 300 Washington DC 20001
Ph: 202-347-0040 ▪ Fx: 202-347-0058

Immigration Law Center, National — www.nilc.org
3435 Wilshire Blvd Suite 2850 Los Angeles CA 90010
Ph: 213-639-3900 ▪ Fx: 213-639-3911

Immigration Law Foundation, American — www.ailf.org
918 F St NW 6th Fl Washington DC 20004
Ph: 202-742-5600 ▪ Fx: 202-742-5619

Immigration Lawyers Association, American — www.aila.org
918 F St NW Washington DC 20004
Ph: 202-216-2400 ▪ Fx: 202-783-7853

Immigration Network Inc, Catholic Legal — www.cliniclegal.org
McCormick Pavilion 415 Michigan Ave NE Washington DC 20017
Ph: 202-635-2556

Immigration Reform, Federation for American — www.fairus.org
1666 Connecticut Ave NW Suite 400 Washington DC 20009
Ph: 202-328-7004 ▪ Fx: 202-387-3447 ▪ TF: 877-627-3247

Immigration & Refugee Service, Lutheran — www.lirs.org
700 Light St Baltimore MD 21230
Ph: 410-230-2700 ▪ Fx: 410-230-2890

Immigration & Refugee Services of America — www.irsa-uscr.org
1717 Massachusetts Ave NW Suite 200 Washington DC 20036
Ph: 202-797-2105 ▪ Fx: 202-797-2363

Immigration, Research Foundation for Jewish
570 7th Ave New York NY 10018
Ph: 212-921-3871 ▪ Fx: 212-575-1918

Immigration Studies, Center for — www.cis.org
1522 K St NW Suite 820 Washington DC 20005
Ph: 202-466-8185 ▪ Fx: 202-466-8076

Immune Deficiency Foundation — www.primaryimmune.org
40 W Chesapeake Ave Suite 308 Towson MD 21204
Ph: 410-321-6647 ▪ Fx: 410-321-9165 ▪ TF: 800-296-4433

(Immunization) Every Child by Two — www.ecbt.org
666 11th St NW Suite 202 Washington DC 20001
Ph: 202-783-7034 ▪ Fx: 202-783-7042

Immunization, National Coalition for Adult — www.nfid.org/ncai
4733 Bethesda Ave Suite 750 Bethesda MD 20814
Ph: 301-656-0003 ▪ Fx: 301-907-0878

Immunogenetics, American Society for Histocompatability & — www.ashi-hla.org
17000 Commerce Pkwy Suite C Mount Laurel NJ 08054
Ph: 856-638-0428 ▪ Fx: 856-439-0525

Immunologists, American Association of — www.aai.org
9650 Rockville Pike Bethesda MD 20814
Ph: 301-634-7178 ▪ Fx: 301-571-1816

Immunologists, American Association of Veterinary — www.cvm.missouri.edu/aavi

Immunology, Academy of Veterinary Allergy & Clinical — www.avaci.org
330 Waukegan Rd   Glenview IL 60025
Ph: 847-729-5200 ■ Fx: 847-729-5214

Immunology, American Academy of Allergy Asthma & — www.aaaai.org
611 E Wells St 4th Fl   Milwaukee WI 53202
Ph: 414-272-6071 ■ Fx: 414-272-6070 ■ TF: 800-822-2762

Immunology, American Board of Allergy & — www.abai.org
510 Walnut Suite 1701   Philadelphia PA 19106
Ph: 215-592-9466 ■ Fx: 215-592-9411

Immunology, American College of Allergy Asthma & — allergy.mcg.edu
85 W Algonquin Rd Suite 550   Arlington Heights IL 60005
Ph: 847-427-1200 ■ Fx: 847-427-1294 ■ TF: 800-842-7777

Immunology, American Osteopathic College of Allergy &
7025 E McDowell Rd Suite 1-B   Scottsdale AZ 85257
Ph: 480-585-1580 ■ Fx: 480-585-1581

Immunology, Joint Council of Allergy Asthma & — www.jcaai.org
50 N Brockway St Suite 3-3   Palatine IL 60067
Ph: 847-934-1918 ■ Fx: 847-934-1820

Immunology Society, Clinical — www.clinimmsoc.org
611 E Wells St   Milwaukee WI 53202
Ph: 414-224-8095 ■ Fx: 414-272-6070

Immunology, Society for Mucosal — www.socmucimm.org
4350 East West Hwy Suite 401   Bethesda MD 20814
Ph: 301-718-6515 ■ Fx: 301-656-0989

Impact Assessment, International Association for — www.iaia.org
1330 23rd St S Suite C   Fargo ND 58103
Ph: 701-297-7908 ■ Fx: 701-297-7917

Impala Association, National — www.impala.blackhills.com
2928 4th Ave PO Box 968   Spearfish SD 57783
Ph: 605-642-5864 ■ Fx: 605-642-5868

Imperial Council AAONMS — www.shrinershq.org
2900 N Rocky Point Dr   Tampa FL 33607
Ph: 813-281-0300 ■ Fx: 813-281-2519

Imperial Glass Collectors Society, National — www.imperialglass.org

Implant Association Inc, Cochlear — www.cici.org

Implant Dentistry, American Academy of — www.aaid-implant.org
211 E Chicago Ave Suite 750   Chicago IL 60611
Ph: 312-335-1550 ■ Fx: 312-335-9090 ■ TF: 877-335-2243

Implant Prosthodontics, American Academy of
709 Haddonfield-Berlin Rd   Voorhees NJ 08043
Ph: 856-782-3990 ■ Fx: 856-782-3775

Implantologists, International Congress of Oral — www.dentalimplants.com
248 Lorraine Ave 3rd Fl   Upper Montclair NJ 07043
Ph: 973-783-6300 ■ Fx: 973-783-1175 ■ TF: 800-442-0525

Import Shippers Association, American — www.aisaship.com
662 Main St   New Rochelle NY 10801
Ph: 914-633-3770 ■ Fx: 914-633-4041

Importers, American Association of Exporters & — www.aaei.org
1200 G St NW Suite 800   Washington DC 20005
Ph: 202-661-2181 ■ Fx: 202-661-2185

Importers Association of America, Cheese
460 Park Ave 11th Fl   New York NY 10022
Ph: 212-753-7500 ■ Fx: 212-688-2870

Importers Association of America, Diamond Manufacturers &
PO Box 5297   New York NY 10185
Ph: 212-944-2066

Importers & Exporters, National Council of Music
PO Box 5488   Long Island City NY 11105
Ph: 718-274-3210 ■ Fx: 718-274-3214

Importers of Textiles & Apparel, US Association of — www.usaita.com
13 E 16th St 6th Fl   New York NY 10003
Ph: 212-463-0089 ■ Fx: 212-463-0583

Improved Order of Red Men — www.redmen.org
4521 Speight Ave   Waco TX 76711
Ph: 254-756-1221 ■ Fx: 254-756-4828

In Defense of Animals — www.idausa.org
131 Camino Alto Suite E   Mill Valley CA 94941
Ph: 415-388-9641 ■ Fx: 415-388-0388

In Vitro Biology, Society for — www.sivb.org
9315 Largo Dr W Suite 255   Largo MD 20774
Ph: 301-324-5054 ■ Fx: 301-324-5057

Incentive Marketing Association — www.incentivemarketing.org
1801 N Mill St Suite R   Naperville IL 60563
Ph: 630-369-7780 ■ Fx: 630-369-3773

Incentive & Travel Executives, Society of — www.site-intl.org
401 N Michigan Ave Suite 2200   Chicago IL 60611
Ph: 312-321-5148 ■ Fx: 312-527-6783

Incentive Travel Suppliers & Agents, American Association — www.traveltran.com
of Premium   PO Box 35189   Chicago IL 60707
Ph: 708-453-0080 ■ Fx: 708-453-0083

Incest Anonymous, Survivors of — www.siawso.org
PO Box 190   Benson MD 21018
Ph: 410-893-3322

Incest National Network, Rape Abuse & — www.rainn.org
635-B Pennsylvania Ave SE   Washington DC 20003
Ph: 202-544-1034 ■ Fx: 202-544-3556 ■ TF: 800-656-4673

Incest Survivors Anonymous — www.lafn.org/medical/isa
PO Box 17245   Long Beach CA 90807
Ph: 562-428-5599

Income Analysts Society, Fixed — www.fiasi.org
151 Herricks Rd Suite 1   Garden City Park NY 11040
Ph: 516-739-2510 ■ Fx: 516-739-3803 ■ TF: 800-284-6228

Income & Wealth, International Association for Research in — www.econ.nyu.edu/iariw
New York Univ Dept of Economics 269 Mercer St Rm
700   New York NY 10003
Ph: 212-924-4386 ■ Fx: 212-366-5067

Incubation Association, National Business — www.nbia.org
20 E Circle Dr   Athens OH 45701
Ph: 740-593-4331 ■ Fx: 740-593-1996

INDA: Association of the Nonwoven Fabrics Industry — www.inda.org
1300 Crescent Green Suite 100   Cary NC 27511
Ph: 919-233-1210 ■ Fx: 919-233-1282

Independent Action Inc — www.independentaction.org
1619 13th St NW   Washington DC 20009
Ph: 202-783-2900 ■ Fx: 202-783-3477

Independent Armored Car Operators Association — www.iacoa.com
102 E Ave J   Lancaster CA 93535
Ph: 661-726-9864 ■ Fx: 661-949-7877

Independent Association of Accredited Registrars — www.iaar.org
3942 N Upland St   Arlington VA 22207
Ph: 703-533-9539 ■ Fx: 703-533-1612

Independent Association of Publishers' Employees — www.iape1096.org
14 Washington Rd Suite 521   Princeton Junction NJ 08550
Ph: 609-799-1520 ■ Fx: 609-716-0626 ■ TF: 800-325-8273

Independent Automotive Damage Appraisers Association — www.iada.org
PO Box 12291   Columbus GA 31917
Ph: 800-369-4232 ■ Fx: 888-423-2669

Independent Bakers Association — www.independentbaker.org
1223 Potomac St NW PO Box 3731   Washington DC 20007
Ph: 202-333-8190 ■ Fx: 202-337-3809

Independent Battery Manufacturers Association — www.thebatteryman.com
401 N Michigan Ave 24th Fl   Chicago IL 60611
Ph: 312-245-1074 ■ Fx: 312-527-6640 ■ TF: 800-237-6126

Independent Board for Presbyterian Foreign Missions — www.ibpfm.org
246 W Walnut Ln   Philadelphia PA 19144
Ph: 215-438-0511 ■ Fx: 215-438-0560

Independent Business, National Federation of — www.nfib.org
1201 F St NW Suite 200   Washington DC 20004
Ph: 202-554-9000 ■ Fx: 202-554-0496 ■ TF: 800-552-6342

Independent Charities of America — www.independentcharities.org
21 Tamal Vista Blvd Suite 209   Corte Madera CA 94925
Ph: 800-477-0733 ■ Fx: 415-924-1379

Independent Colleges of Art & Design, Association of — www.aicad.org
3957 2nd St   San Francisco CA 94114
Ph: 415-642-8595 ■ Fx: 415-642-8590

Independent Colleges & Schools, Accrediting Council for — www.acics.org
750 1st St NE Suite 980   Washington DC 20002
Ph: 202-336-6780 ■ Fx: 202-842-2593

Independent Colleges & Universities, National Association of — www.naicu.edu
1025 Connecticut Ave NW Suite 700   Washington DC 20036
Ph: 202-785-8866 ■ Fx: 202-835-0003

Independent Commercial Producers, Association of — www.aicp.com
3 W 18th St 5th Fl   New York NY 10010
Ph: 212-929-3000 ■ Fx: 212-929-3359

Independent Community Bankers of America — www.icba.org
1 Thomas Cir NW Suite 400   Washington DC 20005
Ph: 202-659-8111 ■ Fx: 202-659-9216 ■ TF: 800-422-8439

Independent Community Bankers of America PAC
1 Thomas Cir NW Suite 400   Washington DC 20005
Ph: 202-659-8111 ■ Fx: 202-659-9216 ■ TF: 800-422-8439

Independent Computer Consultants Association — www.icca.org
11131 S Towne Sq Suite F   Saint Louis MO 63123
Ph: 314-892-1675 ■ Fx: 314-487-1345 ■ TF: 800-774-4222

Independent Corrugated Converters, Association of — www.aiccbox.org
113 S West St PO Box 25708   Alexandria VA 22313
Ph: 703-836-2422 ■ Fx: 703-836-2795 ■ TF: 877-836-2422

Independent Cosmetic Manufacturers & Distributors Inc — www.icmad.org
1220 W Northwest Hwy   Palatine IL 60067
Ph: 847-991-4499 ■ Fx: 847-991-8161 ■ TF: 800-334-2623

Independent Crop Consultants, National Association of — www.naicc.org
349 E Nolley Dr   Collierville TN 38017
Ph: 901-861-0511 ■ Fx: 901-861-0512

Independent Curators International — www.ici-exhibitions.org
799 Broadway Suite 205   New York NY 10003
Ph: 212-254-8200 ■ Fx: 212-477-4781

Independent Distributors Association — www.idaparts.com
13370 Branch View Ln Suite 100   Dallas TX 75234
Ph: 972-241-1124 ■ Fx: 972-484-3599

Independent Education, Institute for — www.ifie.org
PO Box 42428   Washington DC 20015
Ph: 202-362-9344 ■ Fx: 202-362-0513

Independent Educational Consultants Association — www.educationalconsulting.org
3251 Old Lee Hwy Suite 510   Fairfax VA 22030
Ph: 703-591-4850 ■ Fx: 703-591-4860 ■ TF: 800-808-4322

Independent Electrical Contractors — www.ieci.org
4401 Ford Ave Suite 1100   Alexandria VA 22302
Ph: 703-549-7351 ■ Fx: 703-549-7448 ■ TF: 800-456-4324

Independent Feature Project — www.ifp.org
104 W 29th St 12th Fl   New York NY 10001
Ph: 212-465-8200 ■ Fx: 212-465-8525

(Independent Film & Television) AFMA — www.afma.com
10850 Wilshire Blvd 9th Fl   Los Angeles CA 90024
Ph: 310-446-1000 ■ Fx: 310-446-1600

(Independent Films) Sundance Institute — institute.sundance.org
PO Box 3630   Salt Lake City UT 84110
Ph: 801-328-3456 ■ Fx: 801-575-5175

Independent Free Papers of America — www.ifpa.org
107 Hemlock Dr   Rio Grande NJ 08242
Ph: 609-886-0141 ■ Fx: 609-889-8835 ■ TF: 800-441-4372

Independent Glass Association — www.iga.org
54840 S Circle Dr PO Box 1762   Idyllwild CA 92549
Ph: 909-659-5972 ■ Fx: 909-659-5002

Independent Heating Contractors Association
12342 Layton Ave   Greenfield WI 53228
Ph: 414-529-4702 ■ Fx: 414-529-4722

Independent Information Professionals, Association of www.aiip.org
8550 United Plaza Blvd Suite 1001   Baton Rouge LA 70809
Ph: 225-408-4400 ▪ Fx: 225-922-4611 ▪ TF: 888-544-2447

Independent Institute www.independent.org
100 Swan Way   Oakland CA 94621
Ph: 510-632-1366 ▪ Fx: 510-568-6040

Independent Insurance Adjusters, National Association of www.naiia.com
825 W State St Suite 117-C   Geneve IL 60134
Ph: 630-397-5012 ▪ Fx: 630-397-5013

Independent Insurance Agents & Brokers of America Inc www.iiaba.org
127 S Peyton St   Alexandria VA 22314
Ph: 703-683-4422 ▪ Fx: 703-683-7556 ▪ TF: 800-221-7917

Independent Insurance Agents & Brokers of America PAC
412 1st St SE Suite 300   Washington DC 20003
Ph: 202-863-7000 ▪ Fx: 202-863-7015

Independent Insurance Auditors & Engineers, National Association of www.naiiae.com

Independent Investor Protective League
PO Box 5031   Fort Lauderdale FL 33310
Ph: 954-749-1551 ▪ Fx: 954-749-1553

Independent Jewelers Organization www.independentjewelers.com
25 Seir Hill Rd   Norwalk CT 06850
Ph: 203-846-4215 ▪ Fx: 203-846-8571 ▪ TF: 800-624-9252

Independent Life Brokerage Agencies, National Association of www.nailba.org
12150 Monument Dr Suite 125   Fairfax VA 22033
Ph: 703-383-3081 ▪ Fx: 703-383-6942

Independent Lighting Distributors Inc, National Association of www.naild.org
2207 Elmwood Ave   Buffalo NY 14216
Ph: 716-875-3670 ▪ Fx: 716-875-0734

Independent Liquid Terminals Association www.ilta.org
1444 'I' St NW Suite 400   Washington DC 20005
Ph: 202-842-9200 ▪ Fx: 202-326-8660

Independent Living Association, National www.nilausa.org
4203 Southpoint Blvd   Jacksonville FL 32216
Ph: 904-296-1038 ▪ Fx: 904-296-1953

Independent Living, National Council on www.ncil.org
1916 Wilson Blvd Suite 209   Arlington VA 22201
Ph: 703-525-3406 ▪ Fx: 703-525-3409

Independent Living, Research & Training Center on www.rtcil.org
Univ of Kansas Dole Ctr Rm 7089 100 Sunnyside
    Ave   Lawrence KS 66045
Ph: 785-864-4095 ▪ Fx: 785-864-5063

Independent Lubricant Manufacturers Association www.ilma.org
651 S Washington St   Alexandria VA 22314
Ph: 703-684-5574 ▪ Fx: 703-836-8503

Independent Mailing Equipment Dealers, Association of www.aimedweb.org
949 Winding Brook Ln   Walnut CA 91789
Ph: 909-444-9680 ▪ Fx: 909-594-9743 ▪ TF: 888-750-6245

Independent Manufacturers'/Representatives Inc, Association of www.aimr.net
PO Box 3467   Laguna Hills CA 92654
Ph: 949-859-2884 ▪ Fx: 949-855-2973 ▪ TF: 866-729-0975

Independent Medical Distributors Association www.imda.org
414 Plaza Dr Suite 209   Westmont IL 60559
Ph: 866-463-2937 ▪ Fx: 630-655-0391

Independent Medical Examiners, American Board of www.abime.org
111 Lions Dr Suite 217   Barrington IL 60010
Ph: 847-277-7902 ▪ Fx: 847-277-7912 ▪ TF: 800-234-3490

Independent Music Publishers, Association of www.aimp.org
PO Box 69473   Los Angeles CA 90069
Ph: 818-771-7301

Independent News Distributors, American Association of www.aaind.org
900 Fox Valley Dr Suite 204   Longwood FL 32779
Ph: 407-774-9794 ▪ Fx: 407-774-6751

Independent Office Products & Furniture Dealers Association www.iopfda.org
301 N Fairfax St   Alexandria VA 22314
Ph: 703-549-9040 ▪ Fx: 703-683-7552

Independent Order of Foresters www.foresters.biz
789 Don Mills Rd   Toronto ON M3C1T9
Ph: 416-429-3000 ▪ Fx: 416-429-3896 ▪ TF: 800-828-1540

Independent Order of Odd Fellows www.ioof.org
422 Trade St   Winston-Salem NC 27101
Ph: 336-725-5955 ▪ Fx: 336-722-7317 ▪ TF: 800-235-8358

Independent Order of Svithiod
5518 W Lawrence Ave   Chicago IL 60630
Ph: 773-736-1191

Independent Order of Vikings www.iovikings.org
5250 S 6th St PO Box 5147   Springfield IL 62705
Ph: 877-241-6006 ▪ Fx: 217-241-6578

Independent Party, Committee for a Unified www.cuip.org
225 Broadway Suite 2010   New York NY 10007
Ph: 212-962-1811 ▪ Fx: 212-803-1899

Independent Pet & Animal Transportation Association International Inc www.ipata.com
745 Winding Trail   Holly Lake Ranch TX 75755
Ph: 903-769-2267 ▪ Fx: 903-769-2867

Independent Petroleum Association of America www.ipaa.org
1201 15th St NW Suite 300   Washington DC 20005
Ph: 202-857-4722 ▪ Fx: 202-857-4799 ▪ TF: 800-433-2851

Independent Press Association www.indypress.org
2729 Mission St Suite 201   San Francisco CA 94110
Ph: 415-643-4401 ▪ Fx: 415-643-4402 ▪ TF: 877-463-9624

Independent Producers & Royalty Owners Association, Texas www.tipro.org
515 Congress Ave Suite 1910   Austin TX 78701
Ph: 512-477-4452 ▪ Fx: 512-476-8070

Independent Professional Earth Scientists, Society of www.sipes.org
4925 Greenville Ave Suite 1106   Dallas TX 75206
Ph: 214-363-1780 ▪ Fx: 214-363-8195

Independent Professional Representatives Organization www.avreps.org
2700 N 29th Ave Suite 101   Hollywood FL 33020
Ph: 954-923-0233 ▪ Fx: 954-925-1549 ▪ TF: 800-420-4268

Independent Public Finance Advisors, National Association of www.naipfa.com
PO Box 304   Montgomery IL 60538
Ph: 800-624-7321

Independent Publishers, National Association of www.publishersreport.com
PO Box 430   Highland City FL 33846
Ph: 863-648-4420

Independent Publishers Representatives, National Association of www.naipr.com
111 E 14th St PMB 157   New York NY 10003
Ph: 888-624-7779 ▪ Fx: 800-416-2586

Independent Publishing, Small Press Center for www.smallpress.org
20 W 44th St   New York NY 10036
Ph: 212-764-7021 ▪ Fx: 212-354-5365

Independent Research Institutes, Association of www.airi.org
DAI Management Inc PO Box 844   Westminster MD 21158
Ph: 410-751-8900 ▪ Fx: 410-751-2662

Independent Restaurants of America, Council of www.ciraonline.org
304 W Liberty St Suite 201   Louisville KY 40202
Ph: 502-583-3783 ▪ Fx: 502-589-3602

Independent Scholars of Asia www.hypersphere.com/isa
2321 Russell St Unit 3C   Berkeley CA 94705
Ph: 510-849-3791

Independent Scholars, National Coalition of www.ncis.org
PO Box 5743   Berkeley CA 94705
Ph: 510-540-8415

Independent Schools Association of the Central States www.isacs.org
1550 N Dearborn Pkwy   Chicago IL 60610
Ph: 312-255-1244 ▪ Fx: 312-255-1278

Independent Schools, National Association of www.nais-schools.org
1620 L St NW Suite 1100   Washington DC 20036
Ph: 202-973-9700 ▪ Fx: 202-973-9790

Independent Sealing Distributors www.isd.org
105 Eastern Ave Suite 104   Annapolis MD 21403
Ph: 410-263-1014 ▪ Fx: 410-263-1659

Independent Sector www.independentsector.org
1200 18th St NW Suite 200   Washington DC 20036
Ph: 202-467-6100 ▪ Fx: 202-467-6101 ▪ TF: 888-860-8118

Independent Show Organizers, Society of www.siso.org
7000 W SW Hwy   Chicago Ridge IL 60415
Ph: 708-361-6000 ▪ Fx: 708-361-6166 ▪ TF: 877-937-7476

Independent Terminal Operators Association
1150 Connecticut NW 9th Fl   Washington DC 20036
Ph: 202-828-4130

Independent Thinking, Resources for www.rit.org
484 Lake Park Ave Suite 24   Oakland CA 94610
Ph: 925-228-0565 ▪ Fx: 866-422-7612

Independent Trust Companies, Association of www.aitco.net
710 E Ogden Ave Suite 600   Naperville IL 60563
Ph: 630-579-3290 ▪ Fx: 630-369-2488

Independent Turf & Ornamental Distributors Association www.itoda.org
526 Brittany Dr   State College PA 16803
Ph: 814-238-1573 ▪ Fx: 814-238-7051

Independent Unions, National Federation of www.nfiu.org
1166 S 11th St   Philadelphia PA 19147
Ph: 215-336-3300 ▪ Fx: 215-755-3542 ▪ TF: 888-595-6348

Independent Video & Filmmakers, Association of www.aivf.org
304 Hudson St 6th Fl   New York NY 10013
Ph: 212-807-1400 ▪ Fx: 212-463-8519

Independent Women's Forum www.iwf.org
1726 M St NW Suite 1001   Washington DC 20036
Ph: 202-419-1820 ▪ TF: 800-224-6000

Independents & Franchisees, Association for Car & Truck Rental www.actif.org
4248 Park Glen Rd   Minneapolis MN 55416
Ph: 952-928-4645 ▪ Fx: 952-929-1318 ▪ TF: 888-200-2795

Indexers, American Society of www.asindexing.org
10200 W 44th Ave Suite 304   Wheat Ridge CO 80033
Ph: 303-463-2887 ▪ Fx: 303-422-8894

India American Cultural Association
1281 Cooper Lake Rd SE   Smyrna GA 30082
Ph: 770-436-3719

India, Friends of Christ in www.foci.org
Greenfield Hill Congregational Church 1045 Old Academy
    Rd   Fairfield CT 06430
Ph: 203-259-5596

India Partners www.indiapartners.org
PO Box 5470   Eugene OR 97405
Ph: 541-683-0696 ▪ Fx: 541-683-2773 ▪ TF: 888-870-9085

India Society International, Friends of www.fisiusa.org
PO Box 73327   Houston TX 77273
Ph: 281-494-1909

India Study Circle for Philately www.indiastudycircle.org
PO Box 7326   Washington DC 20044
Ph: 202-564-6876 ▪ Fx: 202-565-2441

India Veterans Association, China-Burma-
PO Box 780676   Orlando FL 32878
Ph: 407-282-0346

Indian Affairs, Association on American www.indian-affairs.org
PO Box 268   Sisseton SD 57262
Ph: 605-698-3998 ▪ Fx: 605-698-3316

Indian American Center for Political Awareness www.iacfpa.org
1025 Connecticut Ave NW Suite 1000   Washington DC 20036
Ph: 202-955-8338 ▪ Fx: 202-327-5483

Indian American Forum for Political Education www.iafpe.org
8210 Riverside Rd   Alexandria VA 22308
Ph: 703-619-1320

Indian Arts Council, American
725 Preston Forest Shopping Ctr Suite B   Dallas TX 75230
Ph: 214-891-9640 ▪ Fx: 214-891-0221

Indian Arts & Crafts Association www.iaca.com
4010 Carlisle Blvd NE Suite C   Albuquerque NM 87107
Ph: 505-265-9149 ▪ Fx: 505-265-8251

Indian Arts, Institute for the Study of Traditional American
PO Box 66124   Portland OR 97290
Ph: 503-233-8131

Indian Association, Pan-American
8335 Sevigny Dr   North Fort Myers FL 33917
Ph: 239-543-7727

Indian Cattlemen's Association, National American
1541 Foster Rd   Toppenish WA 98948
Ph: 509-854-1329

Indian Ceremonial Association, Gallup Inter-Tribal   www.gallupnm.org/ceremonial
226 W Coal Ave   Gallup NM 87301
Ph: 505-863-3896 ▪ Fx: 505-722-5158 ▪ TF: 888-685-2564

Indian Child Welfare Association, National   www.nicwa.org
5100 SW Macadam Ave Suite 300   Portland OR 97239
Ph: 503-222-4044 ▪ Fx: 503-222-4007

Indian College Fund, American   www.collegefund.org
8333 Greenwood Blvd   Denver CO 80221
Ph: 303-426-8900 ▪ Fx: 303-426-1200 ▪ TF: 800-776-3863

Indian Council on Aging, National   www.nicoa.org
10501 Montgomery Blvd NE Suite 210   Albuquerque NM 87111
Ph: 505-292-2001 ▪ Fx: 505-292-1922

Indian Court Judges Association, National American   www.naicja.org
3618 Reder St   Rapid City SD 57702
Ph: 605-342-4804 ▪ Fx: 605-719-9357

Indian Culture Research Center, American   www.bluecloud.org/dakota.html
Blue Cloud Abbey Box 98   Marvin SD 57251
Ph: 605-398-9200 ▪ Fx: 605-398-9201

Indian Dental Association   www.dentalhealthindia.com
146-02 89th Ave   Jamaica NY 11435
Ph: 718-523-8438

Indian Development, Seventh Generation Fund for   www.7genfund.org
PO Box 4569   Arcata CA 95518
Ph: 707-825-7640 ▪ Fx: 707-825-7639

Indian Diamond & Colorstone Association
56 W 45th St Suite 705   New York NY 10036
Ph: 212-921-4488 ▪ Fx: 212-768-7935

Indian Education Association, National   www.niea.org
700 N Fairfax St Suite 210   Alexandria VA 22314
Ph: 703-838-2870 ▪ Fx: 703-838-1620

Indian Education, Council for   www.cie-mt.org
1240 Burlington Ave   Billings MT 59102
Ph: 406-652-7598 ▪ Fx: 406-652-0536

Indian Educators Federation   www.ief-aft.org
2031 Yale Blvd Suite E-1   Albuquerque NM 87106
Ph: 505-243-4088 ▪ Fx: 505-243-4098 ▪ TF: 888-433-2382

Indian Enterprise Development, National Center for American   www.ncaied.org
953 E Juanita Ave   Mesa AZ 85204
Ph: 480-545-1298 ▪ Fx: 480-545-4208

Indian Fish & Wildlife Commission, Great Lakes   www.glifwc.org
100 Maple St PO Box 9   Odanah WI 54861
Ph: 715-682-6619

Indian Gaming Association, National   www.indiangaming.org
224 2nd St SE   Washington DC 20003
Ph: 202-546-7711 ▪ Fx: 202-546-1755 ▪ TF: 800-286-6442

Indian Graduate Center, American   www.aigc.com
4520 Montgomery Blvd NE Suite 1-B   Albuquerque NM 87109
Ph: 505-881-4584 ▪ Fx: 505-884-0427 ▪ TF: 800-628-1920

Indian Health Board, National   www.nihb.org
1385 S Colorado Blvd Suite A708   Denver CO 80222
Ph: 303-759-3075 ▪ Fx: 303-759-3674

Indian Heritage Foundation, American   www.indians.org
PO Box 6330 6051 F Arlington Blvd   Falls Church VA 22040
Ph: 703-237-7500 ▪ Fx: 703-532-1921

Indian Higher Education Consortium, American   www.aihec.org
121 Oronoco St   Alexandria VA 22314
Ph: 703-838-0400 ▪ Fx: 703-838-0388

Indian Horse Registry, American   www.indianhorse.com
Rancho San Francisco 9028 State Park Rd   Lockhart TX 78644
Ph: 512-398-6642

Indian Housing Council, National American   naihc.indian.com
900 2nd St NE Suite 305   Washington DC 20002
Ph: 202-789-1754 ▪ Fx: 202-789-1758 ▪ TF: 800-284-9165

Indian Institute, American   www.ou.edu/aii
Univ of Oklahoma College of Continuing Education 555
Constitution Ave Suite 237   Norman OK 73072
Ph: 405-325-4127 ▪ Fx: 405-325-7757

Indian Law Resource Center   www.indianlaw.org
602 N Ewing St   Helena MT 59601
Ph: 406-449-2006 ▪ Fx: 406-449-2031

Indian Lore Association, American
960 Walhonding Ave   Logan OH 43138
Ph: 740-385-7136

Indian Ministries, North American   www.naim.ca
PO Box 39   Delta BC V4K3N5
Ph: 604-946-1227 ▪ Fx: 604-946-1465

Indian Missions International, United   www.uim.org
PO Box 336010   Greeley CO 80633
Ph: 970-330-7788 ▪ Fx: 970-330-2559

Indian Motorcycle Club of America   www.indian-motorcycles.com
PO Box 1743   Perris CA 92572
Ph: 909-780-0421 ▪ Fx: 909-780-0857

Indian Movement, American   www.aimovement.org
2717 Mission St Rm 303   San Francisco CA 94110
Ph: 415-552-1992

Indian Opportunity, Americans for   www.aio.org
681 Juniper Hill Rd   Santa Ana Pueblo NM 87004
Ph: 505-867-0278 ▪ Fx: 505-867-0441

Indian Origin, Global Organization of People of   www.gopio.net
PO Box 1413   Stamford CT 06904
Ph: 203-329-8010 ▪ Fx: 203-322-2233

Indian Physicians, Association of American   www.aaip.com
1225 Sovereign Row Suite 103   Oklahoma City OK 73108
Ph: 405-946-7072 ▪ Fx: 405-946-7651

Indian Professionals of North America, Network of   www.netip.org

Indian Pueblo Council, All   www.aipcinc.com
PO Box 400   Albuquerque NM 87103
Ph: 505-881-1992 ▪ Fx: 505-883-7682

Indian Research & Development Center, American
2233 W Lindsey Suite 118   Norman OK 73069
Ph: 405-364-0656 ▪ Fx: 405-364-5464

Indian Rights Center, South & Meso American   saiic.nativeweb.org
PO Box 7829   Oakland CA 94601
Ph: 510-534-4882 ▪ Fx: 510-834-4264

Indian Ritual Object Repatriation Foundation, American   www.repatriationfoundation.org
463 E 57th St   New York NY 10022
Ph: 212-980-9441 ▪ Fx: 212-421-2746

Indian Science & Engineering Society, American   www.aises.org
PO Box 9828   Albuquerque NM 87119
Ph: 505-765-1052 ▪ Fx: 505-765-5608

Indian Studies, American Institute of   www.indiastudies.org
1130 E 59th St Foster Hall   Chicago IL 60637
Ph: 773-702-8638 ▪ Fx: 773-702-6636

Indian Treaty Council, International   www.treatycouncil.org
2390 Mission St Suite 301   San Francisco CA 94110
Ph: 415-641-4482 ▪ Fx: 415-641-1298

Indian Tribal Youth, United National   www.unityinc.org
PO Box 800   Oklahoma City OK 73101
Ph: 405-236-2800 ▪ Fx: 405-971-1071

Indian Wars, Order of the   www.indianwars.com
PO Box 7401   Little Rock AR 72217
Ph: 501-225-3996

Indian Youth of America
623 Jackson St PO Box 2786   Sioux City IA 51106
Ph: 712-252-3230 ▪ Fx: 712-252-3712

Indian Youth Council, National
318 Elm St SW   Albuquerque NM 87102
Ph: 505-247-2251 ▪ Fx: 505-247-4251

Indian Youth, Running Strong for American   www.indianyouth.org
8815 Telegraph Rd   Lorton VA 22079
Ph: 703-550-2123 ▪ Fx: 703-550-2473

Indiana Limestone Institute of America Inc   www.iliai.com
400 Stone City Bank Bldg   Bedford IN 47421
Ph: 812-275-4426 ▪ Fx: 812-279-8682

Indiana Pioneers, Society of   www.indianapioneers.com
450 W Ohio St   Indianapolis IN 46202
Ph: 317-233-6588

Indians of All Tribes Foundation, United   www.unitedindians.com
PO Box 99100   Seattle WA 98199
Ph: 206-285-4425 ▪ Fx: 206-282-3640

Indians, National Congress of American   www.ncai.org
1301 Connecticut Ave NW Suite 200   Washington DC 20036
Ph: 202-466-7767 ▪ Fx: 202-466-7797

India's Development, Association for   www.aidindia.org
PO Box F   College Park MD 20741
Ph: 301-209-0508 ▪ Fx: 301-513-0565

Indigenous Environmental Network   www.ienearth.org
PO Box 485   Bemidji MN 56601
Ph: 218-751-4967 ▪ Fx: 218-751-0561

Indigenous Languages of the Americas, Society for the Study of   www.ssila.org
PO Box 555   Arcata CA 95518
Ph: 707-826-4324 ▪ Fx: 707-677-1676

Indigenous Studies, Center for World   www.cwis.org
1001 Cooper Point Rd SW Suite 140 PMB 214   Olympia WA 98502
Ph: 360-754-1990 ▪ Fx: 253-276-0084

Individual Freedom Federation
PO Box 392   Lathrup Village MI 48076
Ph: 248-738-7496

Individual Rights, Center for   www.cir-usa.org
1233 20th St NW Suite 300   Washington DC 20036
Ph: 202-833-8400 ▪ Fx: 202-833-8410

Indonesian Chamber of Commerce, American-   www.aiccusa.org
317 Madison Ave Suite 520   New York NY 10017
Ph: 212-687-4505 ▪ Fx: 212-687-5844

Indoor Soccer Association, US   www.usindoor.com

Indoor Soccer Coaches Association   www.isca.net
9606 Aero Dr   San Diego CA 92123
Ph: 858-836-4422 ▪ Fx: 858-836-4421

Industrial Accident Boards & Commissions, International   www.iaiabc.org
Association of   5610 Medical Cir Suite 14   Madison WI 53711
Ph: 608-663-6355 ▪ Fx: 608-663-1546

Industrial Archeology, Society for   www.sia-web.org
Michigan Technological Univ Dept of Social Sciences 1400
Townsend Dr   Houghton MI 49931
Ph: 906-487-1889 ▪ Fx: 906-487-2468

Industrial Areas Foundation
220 W Kinzie St 5th Fl   Chicago IL 60610
Ph: 312-245-9211 ▪ Fx: 312-245-9744

Industrial Association of Juvenile Apparel Manufacturers Inc
1430 Broadway Suite 1603   New York NY 10018
Ph: 212-244-2953 ▪ Fx: 212-221-3540

Industrial Association, National Defense   www.ndia.org
2111 Wilson Blvd Suite 400   Arlington VA 22201
Ph: 703-522-1820 ▪ Fx: 703-522-1885

Industrial Belting Association, National   www.niba.org
N19 W24400 Riverwood Dr   Waukesha WI 53188
Ph: 262-523-9090 ▪ Fx: 262-523-9091 ▪ TF: 800-488-4845

Industrial Boiler Owners, Council of — www.cibo.org
6035 Burke Center Pkwy Suite 360   Burke VA 22015
Ph: 703-250-9042 ▪ Fx: 703-239-9042

Industrial Caterers Association - International, Mobile — www.mobilecaterers.com
304 W Liberty St Suite 201   Louisville KY 40202
Ph: 502-583-3783 ▪ Fx: 502-589-3602 ▪ TF: 800-620-6422

Industrial Chaplaincy, National Institute of Business & — www.nibic.com
1770 St James Pl Suite 550   Houston TX 77056
Ph: 713-266-2456 ▪ Fx: 713-266-0845

Industrial Chiropractic Consultants, Academy of Forensic & — aficc.tripod.com
18331 Gridely Rd Suite C   Cerritos CA 90703
Ph: 562-860-3662 ▪ Fx: 562-860-4377

Industrial Designers Society of America — www.idsa.org
45195 Business Ct Suite 250   Dulles VA 20166
Ph: 703-707-6000 ▪ Fx: 703-787-8501

Industrial Diamond Association of America — www.superabrasives.org
PO Box 29460   Columbus OH 43229
Ph: 614-797-2265 ▪ Fx: 614-797-2264

Industrial Distribution Association — www.ida-assoc.org
1277 Lenox Park Blvd Suite 275   Atlanta GA 30319
Ph: 404-266-3991 ▪ Fx: 877-664-5398 ▪ TF: 877-591-6210

Industrial Education, National Association of State Supervisors of Trade & — itednt.ited.uidaho.edu/nasstie

Industrial Education, National Association of Trade & — www.skillsusa.org/NATIE
PO Box 1665   Leesburg VA 20177
Ph: 703-777-1740

Industrial Electronics Society, IEEE — www.ewh.ieee.org/soc/ies
IEEE Operations Ctr 445 Hoes Ln   Piscataway NJ 08854
Ph: 732-981-0060 ▪ Fx: 732-981-1721

(Industrial Engineering) Alpha Pi Mu — www.alphapimu.eas.pdx.edu
PO Box 773   Portland OR 97207
Ph: 503-297-3604 ▪ Fx: 503-297-3694

Industrial Engineers, Institute of — www.iienet.org
3577 Parkway Ln Suite 200   Norcross GA 30092
Ph: 770-449-0460 ▪ Fx: 770-441-3295 ▪ TF: 800-494-0460

Industrial Fabric Manufacturers, International Society of
1337 Garden Cir Dr   Newberry SC 29108
Ph: 803-276-2684

Industrial Fabrics Association International — www.ifai.com
1801 County Rd 'B' W   Roseville MN 55113
Ph: 651-222-2508 ▪ Fx: 651-631-9334 ▪ TF: 800-225-4324

Industrial Fabrics Institute, US — www.ifai.com/membership/divisions
1801 County Rd 'B' W   Roseville MN 55113
Ph: 651-222-2508 ▪ Fx: 651-631-9334

Industrial Fasteners Institute — www.industrial-fasteners.org
1717 E 9th St Suite 1105   Cleveland OH 44114
Ph: 216-241-1482 ▪ Fx: 216-241-5901

Industrial Foundation of America — www.ifa-america.com
402 E San Antonio Ave   Boerne TX 78006
Ph: 830-249-7899 ▪ Fx: 800-628-2397 ▪ TF: 800-592-1433

Industrial Heating Equipment Association — www.iea.org
1111 N 19th St Suite 425   Arlington VA 22209
Ph: 703-525-2513 ▪ Fx: 703-525-2515

Industrial Hemp Council, North American — www.naihc.org
PO Box 259329   Madison WI 53725
Ph: 608-258-0243 ▪ Fx: 608-835-0428

Industrial Hygiene, American Board of — www.abih.org
6015 W St Joseph Hwy Suite 102   Lansing MI 48917
Ph: 517-321-2638 ▪ Fx: 517-321-4624

Industrial Hygiene Association, American — www.aiha.org
2700 Prosperity Ave Suite 250   Fairfax VA 22031
Ph: 703-849-8888 ▪ Fx: 703-207-3561

Industrial Hygienists, American Conference of Governmental — www.acgih.org
1330 Kemper Meadows Dr   Cincinnati OH 45240
Ph: 513-742-2020 ▪ Fx: 513-742-3355

Industrial Management, American Association of — www.aaimnmta.com
293 Bridge St Stearns Bldg Suite 206   Springfield MA 01103
Ph: 413-737-8766 ▪ Fx: 413-737-9724 ▪ TF: 888-698-1968

Industrial Manufacturers' Representatives Association, Agricultural & — www.aimrareps.org
7500 Flying Cloud Rd Suite 900   Eden Prairie MN 55344
Ph: 952-253-6230 ▪ Fx: 952-835-4774

Industrial Microbiology, Society for — www.simhq.org
3929 Old Lee Hwy Suite 92A   Fairfax VA 22030
Ph: 703-691-3357 ▪ Fx: 703-691-7991

Industrial & Office Properties, National Association of — www.naiop.org
2201 Cooperative Way 3rd Fl   Herndon VA 20171
Ph: 703-904-7100 ▪ Fx: 703-904-7942 ▪ TF: 800-666-6780

Industrial & Office REALTORS, Society of — www.sior.com
1201 New York Ave NW Suite 350   Washington DC 20005
Ph: 202-449-8200 ▪ Fx: 202-449-8201

Industrial & Organizational Psychology, Society for — www.siop.org
PO Box 87   Bowling Green OH 43402
Ph: 419-353-0032 ▪ Fx: 419-352-2645

Industrial Organizations, American Federation of Labor & Congress of — www.aflcio.org
815 16th St NW   Washington DC 20006
Ph: 202-637-5000 ▪ Fx: 202-637-5058

Industrial Packaging Association, Reusable — www.reusablepackaging.org
8401 Corporate Dr Suite 450   Landover MD 20785
Ph: 301-577-3786 ▪ Fx: 301-577-6476 ▪ TF: 800-533-3786

Industrial Perforators Association — www.iperf.org
5157 Deerhurst Crescent Cir   Boca Raton FL 33486
Ph: 561-447-7511

Industrial Real Estate Brokers, Association of — www.aireb.org
710 E Ogden Ave Suite 600   Naperville IL 60563
Ph: 630-579-3254 ▪ Fx: 630-369-2488

Industrial Relations Association, North American Trucking
908 King St Suite 300   Alexandria VA 22314
Ph: 703-836-9400 ▪ Fx: 703-836-9410

Industrial Relations Conference, Airline — www.aircon.org
1300 19th St NW Suite 750   Washington DC 20036
Ph: 202-861-7550 ▪ Fx: 202-861-7557

Industrial Relations, Institute of Labor & — www.ilir.umich.edu
Univ of Michigan Victor Vaughan Bldg 1111 Catherine St   Ann Arbor MI 48109
Ph: 734-763-3116 ▪ Fx: 734-763-0913

Industrial Relations Research Association — www.irra.uiuc.edu
Univ of Illinois 121 Labor & Industrial Relations 504 E Armory MC-504   Champaign IL 61820
Ph: 217-333-0072 ▪ Fx: 217-265-5130

Industrial Representatives Association, North American — www.nira.org
105 Eastern Ave Suite 104   Annapolis MD 21403
Ph: 410-263-1014 ▪ Fx: 410-263-1659 ▪ TF: 800-315-7429

Industrial Research Institute Inc — www.iriinc.org
1550 M St NW Suite 1100   Washington DC 20005
Ph: 202-296-8811 ▪ Fx: 202-776-0756

Industrial Resources, National Association for the Exchange of — www.naeir.org
560 McClure St   Galesburg IL 61401
Ph: 309-343-0704 ▪ Fx: 309-343-7316 ▪ TF: 800-562-0955

Industrial Sand Association, National — www.sand.org
4041 Powder Mill Rd Suite 450   Claverton MD 20705
Ph: 301-595-5550 ▪ Fx: 301-595-3303

Industrial Service Transport Health Employees, International Union of
254 W 31st St   New York NY 10001
Ph: 212-696-5545 ▪ Fx: 212-696-5556 ▪ TF: 800-331-1070

Industrial Supply Manufacturers Association — www.asmma.com
1300 Sumner Ave   Cleveland OH 44115
Ph: 216-241-7333 ▪ Fx: 216-241-0105

Industrial Technology, National Association of — www.nait.org
3300 Washtenaw Ave Suite 220   Ann Arbor MI 48104
Ph: 734-677-0720 ▪ Fx: 734-677-0046

Industrial Telecommunications Association Inc — www.ita-relay.com
1110 N Glebe Rd Suite 500   Arlington VA 22201
Ph: 703-528-5115 ▪ Fx: 703-524-1074 ▪ TF: 800-482-8282

Industrial Trade Unions, National Organization of — www.noitu.org
148-06 Hillside Ave   Jamaica NY 11435
Ph: 718-291-3434 ▪ Fx: 718-526-2920

Industrial Transportation League, National — www.nitl.org
1700 N Moore St Suite 1900   Arlington VA 22209
Ph: 703-524-5011 ▪ Fx: 703-524-5017

Industrial Truck Association — www.indtrk.org
1750 K St NW Suite 460   Washington DC 20006
Ph: 202-296-9880 ▪ Fx: 202-296-9884

Industrial Union of Marine & Shipbuilding Workers of America
719 E Fort Ave   Baltimore MD 21230
Ph: 410-837-0056 ▪ Fx: 410-837-0058

Industrial Veterinarians, American Association of
PO Box 488   Oskaloosa KS 66066
Ph: 785-863-2389 ▪ Fx: 785-863-3141

Industrial Workers, International Union of Petroleum &
8131 E Rosecrans Ave   Paramount CA 90723
Ph: 562-630-6232 ▪ Fx: 562-408-1073 ▪ TF: 800-624-5842

Industrialization Centers of America Inc, Opportunities — www.oicofamerica.org
1415 N Broad St   Philadelphia PA 19122
Ph: 215-236-4500 ▪ Fx: 215-236-7480 ▪ TF: 800-621-4642

Industries for the Blind, National — www.nib.org
1901 N Beauregard St Suite 200   Alexandria VA 22311
Ph: 703-998-0770 ▪ Fx: 703-998-8268 ▪ TF: 800-433-2304

Industry Applications Society, IEEE — www.ewh.ieee.org/soc/ias
IEEE Operations Ctr 445 Hoes Ln   Piscataway NJ 08854
Ph: 732-981-0060 ▪ Fx: 732-981-1721

Industry Committee, ERISA — www.eric.org
1400 L St NW Suite 350   Washington DC 20005
Ph: 202-789-1400 ▪ Fx: 202-789-1120

Industry Council for Tangible Assets — www.ictaonline.org/mainindex.html
PO Box 1365   Severna Park MD 21146
Ph: 410-626-7005 ▪ Fx: 410-626-7007

Industry Council, US Business & — www.usbusiness.org
910 16th St NW Suite 300   Washington DC 20006
Ph: 202-728-1980 ▪ Fx: 202-728-1981

Industry-Education Cooperation, National Association for — www2.pcom.net/naiec/
235 Hendricks Blvd   Buffalo NY 14226
Ph: 716-834-7047

Industry for a Sound Environment, Responsible — www.pestfacts.org
1156 15th St NW Suite 400   Washington DC 20005
Ph: 202-872-3860 ▪ Fx: 202-463-0474

Indy Racing League — www.indyracingleague.com
4565 W 16th St   Indianapolis IN 46222
Ph: 317-492-6526 ▪ Fx: 317-492-6525

Infact — www.infact.org
46 Plympton St   Boston MA 02118
Ph: 617-695-2525 ▪ Fx: 617-695-2626 ▪ TF: 800-688-8797

Infant Death Resource Center, National SIDS/ — www.sidscenter.org
2070 Chain Bridge Rd Suite 450   Vienna VA 22182
Ph: 703-821-8955 ▪ Fx: 703-821-2098 ▪ TF: 866-866-7437

Infant Loss Support Inc, SHARE Pregnancy & — www.nationalshareoffice.com
St Joseph's Health Ctr 300 1st Capitol Dr   Saint Charles MO 63301
Ph: 636-947-6164 ▪ Fx: 636-947-7486 ▪ TF: 800-821-6819

Infant Massage, International Association of — www.iaim-us.com
1891 Goodyear Ave Suite 622   Ventura CA 93003
Ph: 805-644-8524 ▪ Fx: 805-644-7699 ▪ TF: 800-248-5432

(Infant & Maternal Health) Wellstart International — www.wellstart.org
PO Box 8077   San Diego CA 92138
Ph: 619-295-5192

Infant Mental Health, World Association for — www.waimh.org
Michigan State Univ Institute for Children Youth & Families Kellogg Ctr Rm 27   East Lansing MI 48824
Ph: 517-432-3793 ▪ Fx: 517-432-3694

Infant Mortality Programs, Association of SIDS &　　www.asip1.org
　Stony Brook Univ School of Social Welfare　Stony Brook NY
　　11794
　Ph: 631-444-3690　■　Fx: 631-444-6475

Infant Survival, American Guild for
　301 Eastwood Cir Suite 200　Virginia Beach VA 23454
　Ph: 757-463-3845

Infantry National Association, USS Landing Craft　www.usslci.com

Infants Assistance Resource Center, National Abandoned　aia.berkeley.edu
　UC Berkeley Family Welfare Research Group 1950 Addison St
　　Suite 104　Berkeley CA 94704
　Ph: 510-643-8390　■　Fx: 510-643-7019

Infection Control & Epidemiology Inc, Association for Professionals in　www.apic.org
　1275 K St NW Suite 1000　Washington DC 20005
　Ph: 202-789-1890　■　Fx: 202-789-1899　■　TF: 888-278-2742

Infectious Diseases, International Society for　www.isid.org
　181 Longwood Ave　Boston MA 02115
　Ph: 617-277-0551　■　Fx: 617-731-1541

Infectious Diseases, National Foundation for　www.nfid.org
　4733 Bethesda Ave Suite 750　Bethesda MD 20814
　Ph: 301-656-0003　■　Fx: 301-907-0878

Infectious Diseases Pharmacists, Society of　www.sidp.org
　502 E 11th St Suite 400　Austin TX 78701
　Ph: 512-708-0611　■　Fx: 512-708-0627

Infectious Diseases Society of America　www.idsociety.org
　66 Canal Center Plaza Suite 600　Alexandria VA 22314
　Ph: 703-299-0200　■　Fx: 703-299-0204

Infectious Diseases Society, Pediatric　www.pids.org
　66 Canal Ctr Plaza Suite 600　Alexandria VA 22314
　Ph: 703-299-6764　■　Fx: 703-299-0473

Infertility Association, RESOLVE: National　www.resolve.org
　1310 Broadway　Somerville MA 02144
　Ph: 617-623-1156　■　Fx: 617-623-0252

Infertility Network Exchange, National　www.nine-infertility.org
　PO Box 204　East Meadow NY 11554
　Ph: 516-794-5772　■　Fx: 516-794-0008

Infertility, Society for Reproductive Endocrinology &　www.socrei.org
　1209 Montgomery Hwy　Birmingham AL 35216
　Ph: 205-978-5000　■　Fx: 205-978-5005

Inflatable Advertising Dealers Association　www.inflatableads.com
　136 S Keowee St　Dayton OH 45402
　Ph: 937-222-1024　■　Fx: 937-222-5794

Inflight Food Service Association, International　www.ifsanet.com
　5775 Peachtree-Dunwoody Rd Bldg G Suite 500　Atlanta GA
　　30342
　Ph: 404-252-3663　■　Fx: 404-252-0774

Inform, Project　www.projinf.org
　205 13th St Suite 2001　San Francisco CA 94103
　Ph: 415-558-8669　■　Fx: 415-558-0684

Information Center, Freedom of　www.missouri.edu/~foiwww/
　Univ of Missouri 133 Neff Annex　Columbia MO 65211
　Ph: 573-882-4856　■　Fx: 573-884-6204

Information Center, National Soy Ink　www.soyink.com
　4454 NW 114th St　Urbandale IA 50322
　Ph: 515-251-8640　■　Fx: 515-251-8657　■　TF: 800-747-4275

Information Council of the Americas
　PO Box 53371　New Orleans LA 70153
　Ph: 985-641-2166

Information Display, Society for　www.sid.org
　610 S 2nd St　San Jose CA 95112
　Ph: 408-977-1013　■　Fx: 408-977-1531

Information & Dissemination Centers, Association of　www.asidic.org
　PO Box 3212　Maple Glen PA 19002
　Ph: 215-654-9129

Information on the Environment, American Public　www.americanpie.org
　316 Oak St PO Box 676　Northfield MN 55057
　Ph: 507-645-5616　■　Fx: 507-645-5724　■　TF: 800-320-2743

Information Inc, Essential　www.essential.org
　PO Box 19405　Washington DC 20036
　Ph: 202-387-8030　■　Fx: 202-234-5176

Information Fusion, International Society of　www.inforfusion.org/
　2393 Fieldstone Cir　Fairborn OH 45324
　Ph: 937-255-2632　■　Fx: 937-255-1100

Information Industry Association, Software &　www.siia.net
　1090 Vermont Ave NW 6th Fl　Washington DC 20005
　Ph: 202-289-7442　■　Fx: 202-289-7097

(Information Management) ARMA International　www.arma.org
　13725 W 109th St Suite 101　Lenexa KS 66215
　Ph: 913-341-3808　■　Fx: 913-341-3742　■　TF: 800-422-2762

Information Management Executives, College of Healthcare　www.cio-chime.org
　3300 Washtenaw Ave Suite 225　Ann Arbor MI 48104
　Ph: 734-665-0000　■　Fx: 734-665-9222

Information Management, Society for　www.simnet.org
　401 N Michigan Ave Suite 2400　Chicago IL 60611
　Ph: 312-527-6734

Information & Management Systems Society, Healthcare　www.himss.org
　230 E Ohio St Suite 500　Chicago IL 60611
　Ph: 312-664-4467　■　Fx: 312-664-6143

Information Media & Equipment, Association for　www.aime.org
　PO Box 9844　Cedar Rapids IA 52409
　Ph: 319-654-0608　■　Fx: 319-654-0609

Information Network, Community Learning &　www.clin.org
　1750 K St NW Suite 1200　Washington DC 20006
　Ph: 202-857-2330　■　Fx: 202-857-0643

Information Network, Global Automation
　900 Victors Way PO Box 3724　Ann Arbor MI 48106
　Ph: 734-994-6088　■　Fx: 734-994-3338

Information Officers, National Association of State Chief　www.nascio.org
　167 W Main St Suite 600　Lexington KY 40507
　Ph: 859-231-1971　■　Fx: 859-231-1928

Information Processing Society, North American Fuzzy　morden.csee.usf.edu/Nafipsf

Information Professionals, Association of Armenian
　139 Cedar St　Cliffside Park NJ 07010
　Ph: 201-941-2266　■　Fx: 201-941-5110

Information Professionals, Association of Independent　www.aiip.org
　8550 United Plaza Blvd Suite 1001　Baton Rouge LA 70809
　Ph: 225-408-4400　■　Fx: 225-922-4611　■　TF: 888-544-2447

Information & Referral Systems, Alliance of　www.airs.org
　PO Box 31668　Seattle WA 98103
　Ph: 206-632-2477　■　Fx: 206-632-0855

Information Resources Management, Association for Federal　www.affirm.org
　PO Box 2851　Washington DC 20013
　Ph: 202-208-2780

Information Resources for Nursing, Interagency Council on　www.icirn.org

Information Science Education, Association for Library &　www.alise.org
　1009 Commerce Pk Suite 150　Oak Ridge TN 37839
　Ph: 865-425-0155　■　Fx: 865-481-0390

Information Science & Technology, American Society for　www.asis.org
　1320 Fenwick Ln Suite 510　Silver Spring MD 20910
　Ph: 301-495-0900　■　Fx: 301-495-0810

Information Services on Latin America　isla.igc.org
　PO Box 6103　Albany CA 94706
　Ph: 510-869-2711　■　Fx: 510-835-3017

Information Services Management International, Professional Records &　www.prismintl.org
　605 Benson Rd Suite B　Garner NC 27529
　Ph: 919-771-0657　■　Fx: 919-771-0457　■　TF: 800-336-9793

Information Services, National Federation of Abstracting &　www.nfais.org
　1518 Walnut St Suite 307　Philadelphia PA 19102
　Ph: 215-893-1561　■　Fx: 215-893-1564

Information Specialists, Substance Abuse Librarians &　www.salis.org
　PO Box 9513　Berkeley CA 94709
　Ph: 510-642-5208　■　Fx: 510-642-7175

Information Standards Organization, National　www.niso.org
　4733 Bethesda Ave Suite 300　Bethesda MD 20814
　Ph: 301-654-2512　■　Fx: 301-654-1721

Information Storage Industry Consortium　www.insic.org
　3655 Ruffin Rd Suite 335　San Diego CA 92123
　Ph: 858-279-7230　■　Fx: 858-279-8591

Information Systems, Association for　www.aisnet.org
　PO Box 2712　Atlanta GA 30301
　Ph: 404-651-0348　■　Fx: 404-651-4938

Information Systems, Association for the Development of Religious
　PO Box 210735　Nashville TN 37221
　Ph: 615-429-8744

Information Systems Association, Urban & Regional　www.urisa.org
　1460 Renaissance Dr Suite 305　Park Ridge IL 60068
　Ph: 847-824-6300　■　Fx: 847-824-6363

Information Systems Audit & Control Association　www.isaca.org
　3701 Algonquin Rd Suite 1010　Rolling Meadows IL 60008
　Ph: 847-253-1545　■　Fx: 847-253-1443

Information Systems Security Association　www.issa.org
　7044 S 13th St　Oak Creek WI 53154
　Ph: 414-768-8000　■　Fx: 414-768-8001

Information Technologies Credit Union Association　www.itcua.org
　PO Box 160　Del Mar CA 92014
　Ph: 858-792-3883　■　Fx: 858-792-3884

(Information Technologies) Markle Foundation　www.markle.org
　10 Rockefeller Plaza 16th Fl　New York NY 10020
　Ph: 212-489-6655　■　Fx: 212-765-9690

Information Technology Administrators, National Association of County
　c/o National Assn of Counties 440 1st St NW　Washington DC
　　20001
　Ph: 202-393-6226

Information Technology Association of America　www.itaa.org
　1401 Wilson Blvd Suite 1100　Arlington VA 22209
　Ph: 703-522-5055　■　Fx: 703-525-2279

Information Technology Association, Hospitality　www.hitaworld.org

Information Technology Association, Library &　www.lita.org
　50 E Huron St　Chicago IL 60611
　Ph: 312-280-4270　■　Fx: 312-280-3257　■　TF: 800-545-2433

(Information Technology) EDUCAUSE　www.educause.edu
　1150 18th St NW Suite 1010　Washington DC 20036
　Ph: 202-872-4200　■　Fx: 202-872-4318

Information Technology Industry Council　www.itic.org
　1250 'I' St NW Suite 200　Washington DC 20005
　Ph: 202-737-8888　■　Fx: 202-638-4922

(Information Technology) Interex　www.interex.org
　PO Box 3439　Sunnyvale CA 94088
　Ph: 408-747-0227　■　Fx: 408-747-0947　■　TF: 800-468-3739

Information Technology Professionals, Association of　www.aitp.org
　401 N Michigan Ave Suite 2200　Chicago IL 60611
　Ph: 312-245-1070　■　Fx: 312-527-6636　■　TF: 800-224-9371

(Information Technology) UniForum Association　www.uniforum.org
　PO Box 3177　Annapolis MD 21043
　Ph: 410-715-9500　■　Fx: 240-465-0207　■　TF: 800-333-8649

Information Theory Society, IEEE　golay.uvic.ca
　IEEE Operations Ctr 445 Hoes Ln　Piscataway NJ 08854
　Ph: 732-981-0060　■　Fx: 732-981-1721

Infrared Data Association　www.irda.org
　PO Box 3883　Walnut Creek CA 94598
　Ph: 925-943-6546　■　Fx: 925-943-5600

Infrastructure Financing Authorities, Council of　www.cifanet.org
　805 15th St NW Suite 500　Washington DC 20005
　Ph: 202-371-9694　■　Fx: 202-371-6601

Infusion Association, National Home　www.nhianet.org
　205 Daingerfield Rd　Alexandria VA 22314
　Ph: 703-549-3740　■　Fx: 703-683-1484　■　TF: 800-544-7447

Infusion Nurses Society   www.ins1.org
220 Norwood Pk S   Norwood MA 02062
Ph: 781-440-9408 ▪ Fx: 781-440-9409

Infusion Therapy Association, Outpatient Intravenous
PO Box 1234   Tacoma WA 98491
Ph: 253-272-4581 ▪ Fx: 253-272-0360

Ingersoll-Rand Distributors, Association of   www.aird.org
1300 Sumner Ave   Cleveland OH 44115
Ph: 216-241-7333 ▪ Fx: 216-241-0105

Ingot Industry, Brass & Bronze
200 S Michigan Ave Suite 1100   Chicago IL 60604
Ph: 312-372-4000 ▪ Fx: 312-939-5617

Ingredient Marketing Specialists Inc, Network of   www.nimsgroup.com
PO Box 610   Montville NJ 07045
Ph: 973-402-4803 ▪ Fx: 973-316-6668

Inhalant Prevention Coalition, National   www.inhalants.org
2904 Kerbey Ln   Austin TX 78703
Ph: 512-480-8953 ▪ Fx: 512-477-3932 ▪ TF: 800-269-4237

Initiative for Social Action & Renewal in Eurasia   www.isar.org
1601 Connecticut Ave NW Suite 301   Washington DC 20009
Ph: 202-387-3034 ▪ Fx: 202-667-3291

Initiatives of Change   www.us.initiativesofchange.org
1156 15th St NW Suite 910   Washington DC 20005
Ph: 202-872-9077 ▪ Fx: 202-872-9137

Injection Molding Association, Metal   www.mpif.org/mima.html
105 College Rd E   Princeton NJ 08540
Ph: 609-452-7700 ▪ Fx: 609-987-8523

Injury Association, American Spinal   www.asia-spinalinjury.org
345 E Superior St Suite 1436   Chicago IL 60611
Ph: 312-238-1242 ▪ Fx: 312-238-0869

Injury Prevention Directors' Association, State & Territorial   www.stipda.org
2965 Flowers Rd S Suite 105   Atlanta GA 30341
Ph: 770-690-9000 ▪ Fx: 770-690-8996

Injury Prevention Program, Think First Foundation: National   www.thinkfirst.org
5550 Meadowbrook Dr Suite 110   Rolling Meadows IL 60008
Ph: 847-290-8600 ▪ Fx: 847-290-9005

Ink Information Center, National Soy   www.soyink.com
4454 NW 114th St   Urbandale IA 50322
Ph: 515-251-8640 ▪ Fx: 515-251-8657 ▪ TF: 800-747-4275

Ink Manufacturers, National Association of Printing   www.napim.org
581 Main St   Woodbridge NJ 07095
Ph: 732-855-1525 ▪ Fx: 732-855-1838

Inland Lake Yachting Association   www.ilya.org
W4680 Tory's Trail PO Box 311   Fontana WI 53125
Ph: 262-275-6921

Inland Marine Underwriters Association   www.imua.org
14 Wall St 8th Fl   New York NY 10005
Ph: 212-233-0550 ▪ Fx: 212-227-5102

Inland Rivers Ports & Terminals Inc   www.irpt.net
PO Box 4363   Jackson MS 39296
Ph: 601-352-4778 ▪ Fx: 601-355-1506

Inland Seas Education Association   www.schoolship.org
PO Box 218   Suttons Bay MI 49682
Ph: 231-271-3077 ▪ Fx: 231-271-3088

Inlandboatmen's Union of the Pacific   www.ibu.org
1711 W Nickerson St Suite D   Seattle WA 98119
Ph: 206-284-6001 ▪ Fx: 206-284-5043

INMED Partnerships for Children   www.inmed.org
45449 Severn Way Suite 161   Sterling VA 20166
Ph: 703-444-4477 ▪ Fx: 703-444-4471 ▪ TF: 800-521-1175

Inner Light Foundation   www.innerlight.org
PO Box 750265   Petaluma CA 94975
Ph: 707-765-2200 ▪ Fx: 707-769-9779

Inner Peace Movement Inc   www.innerpeacemovement.org
PO Box 681757   San Antonio TX 78268
Ph: 210-641-7912 ▪ Fx: 210-641-7871 ▪ TF: 877-475-7792

Innerspring Manufacturers, American   www.aiminfo.org
1918 North Pkwy   Memphis TN 38112
Ph: 901-274-9030 ▪ Fx: 901-725-0510 ▪ TF: 800-882-5634

Innkeepers International, Professional Association of   www.paii.org
PO Box 90710   Santa Barbara CA 93190
Ph: 805-569-1853 ▪ Fx: 805-682-1016

Innovation in the Community College, League for   www.league.org
4505 E Chandler Blvd Suite 250   Phoenix AZ 85048
Ph: 480-705-8200 ▪ Fx: 480-705-8201

Inns of North America, Select Registry Distinguished   www.selectregistry.com
PO Box 150   Marshall MI 49068
Ph: 269-789-0393 ▪ Fx: 269-789-0970 ▪ TF: 800-344-5244

INROADS Inc   www.inroads.org
10 S Broadway Suite 700   Saint Louis MO 63102
Ph: 314-241-7488 ▪ Fx: 314-241-9325

Insolvency & Restructuring Advisors, Association of   www.airacira.org
221 Stewart Ave Suite 207   Medford OR 97501
Ph: 541-858-1665 ▪ Fx: 541-858-9187

Inspection Agencies - Americas Committee, International Federation of   3942 N Upland St   Arlington VA 22207   www.ifia-ac.org
Ph: 703-533-9539 ▪ Fx: 703-533-1612

Inspection Cleaning & Restoration Certification, Institute of   www.iicrc.org
2715 E Mill Plain Blvd   Vancouver WA 98661
Ph: 360-693-5675 ▪ Fx: 360-693-4858

Inspection Engineers, National Academy of Building   www.nabie.org
PO Box 520   York Harbor ME 03911
Ph: 800-294-7729 ▪ Fx: 207-351-1915

Inspection Foundation, Housing   www.iami.org/hif.cfm
1224 N Nokomis NE   Alexandria MN 56308
Ph: 320-763-6350 ▪ Fx: 320-763-9290

Inspectors, American Institute of   www.inspection.org
1421 Esplanade Ave Suite 7   Klamath Falls OR 97601
Ph: 541-273-6440 ▪ Fx: 541-273-1780 ▪ TF: 800-877-4770

Inspectors, American Society of Home   www.ashi.com
932 Lee St Suite 101   Des Plaines IL 60016
Ph: 847-759-2820 ▪ Fx: 847-759-1620 ▪ TF: 800-743-2744

Inspectors, Association of Construction   www.iami.org/aci
1224 N Nokomis NE   Alexandria MN 56308
Ph: 320-763-6350 ▪ Fx: 320-763-9290

Inspectors, Examination Board of Professional Home   www.homeinspectionexam.org
932 Lee St Suite 202   Des Plaines IL 60016
Ph: 847-298-7750 ▪ Fx: 847-299-2505

Inspectors, National Association of Home   www.nahi.org
4248 Park Glen Rd   Minneapolis MN 55416
Ph: 952-928-4641 ▪ Fx: 952-929-1318 ▪ TF: 800-448-3942

Inspectors, National Association of Property   napi.lincoln-grad.org
c/o Lincoln Graduate Ctr 303 W Cypress St   San Antonio TX 78212
Ph: 210-225-2897 ▪ Fx: 210-225-8450 ▪ TF: 800-531-5333

Inspectors, National Board of Boiler & Pressure Vessel   www.nationalboard.org
1055 Crupper Ave   Columbus OH 43229
Ph: 614-888-8320 ▪ Fx: 614-847-1147

Inspiration Ministries   www.inspirationministries.org
PO Box 948   Walworth WI 53184
Ph: 262-275-6131 ▪ Fx: 262-275-3355

Installation Developers, National Association of   www.naid.org
734 15th St NW Suite 900   Washington DC 20005
Ph: 202-822-5256 ▪ Fx: 202-822-8819

Institute for Adoption Information   www.adoptioninformationinstitute.org
PO Box 4405   Bennington VT 05201
Ph: 802-442-7135

Institute of Advanced Philosophic Research
PO Box 805   Moultonborough NH 03254
Ph: 603-284-7047

Institute for Advanced Studies of World Religions   www.iaswr.org
2020 Rt 301   Carmel NY 10512
Ph: 845-225-1445 ▪ Fx: 845-225-1485

Institute for the Advanced Study of Black Family Life & Culture   www.iasbflc.org
1484 9th St   Oakland CA 94607
Ph: 510-836-3245 ▪ Fx: 510-836-3248

Institute for the Advancement of Hawaiian Farmers   www.opihi.com/sovereignty
86-649 Puuhulu Rd   Waianae HI 96792
Ph: 808-697-3045 ▪ Fx: 808-696-7774

Institute for the Advancement of Human Behavior   www.ibh.com
4370 Alpine Rd Suite 209   Portola Valley CA 94028
Ph: 650-851-8411 ▪ Fx: 650-851-0406 ▪ TF: 800-258-8411

Institute for the Advancement of Philosophy for Children   www.montclair.edu/pages/iapc
Montclair State Univ 14 Normal Ave   Upper Montclair NJ 07043
Ph: 973-655-4977

Institute for Agriculture & Trade Policy   www.iatp.org
2105 1st Ave S   Minneapolis MN 55404
Ph: 612-870-0453 ▪ Fx: 612-870-4846

Institute for Alternative Futures   www.altfutures.com
100 N Pitt St Suite 235   Alexandria VA 22314
Ph: 703-684-5880 ▪ Fx: 703-684-0640

Institute of the American Musical
121 N Detroit St   Los Angeles CA 90036
Ph: 323-934-1221

Institute for American Values   www.americanvalues.org
1841 Broadway Suite 211   New York NY 10023
Ph: 212-246-3942 ▪ Fx: 212-541-6665

Institute for Appropriate Technology   www.i4at.org
89 Schoolhouse Rd PO Box 90   Summertown TN 38483
Ph: 931-964-4324 ▪ Fx: 931-964-2200

Institute in Basic Life Principles   www.iblp.org
PO Box 1   Oak Brook IL 60522
Ph: 630-323-9800

Institute of Behavioral & Applied Management   www.ibam.com

Institute of Business Appraisers   www.go-iba.org
PO Box 17410   Plantation FL 33318
Ph: 954-584-1144 ▪ Fx: 954-584-1184 ▪ TF: 800-299-4130

Institute for Business & Home Safety   www.ibhs.org
4775 E Fowler Ave   Tampa FL 33617
Ph: 813-286-3400 ▪ Fx: 813-286-9960 ▪ TF: 866-675-4247

Institute for Cancer Prevention   www.ifcp.us
390 5th Ave   New York NY 10018
Ph: 212-953-1900 ▪ Fx: 212-687-2339

Institute of Caribbean Studies   icsdc.org
1612 7th St NW   Washington DC 20001
Ph: 202-829-1887 ▪ Fx: 202-829-1667

Institute of Caster & Wheel Manufacturers   www.mhia.org/psc
8720 Red Oak Blvd Suite 201   Charlotte NC 28217
Ph: 704-676-1190 ▪ Fx: 704-676-1199 ▪ TF: 800-345-1815

Institute for Certification of Computing Professionals   www.iccp.org
2350 E Devon Ave Suite 115   Des Plaines IL 60018
Ph: 847-299-4227 ▪ Fx: 847-299-4280 ▪ TF: 800-843-8227

Institute of Certified Healthcare Business Consultants   www.ichbc.org
307 N Michigan Ave Suite 800   Chicago IL 60601
Ph: 312-360-0384 ▪ Fx: 312-360-0388 ▪ TF: 800-447-1684

Institute of Certified Professional Managers   cob.jmu.edu/icpm
James Madison University MSC 5504   Harrisonburg VA 22807
Ph: 540-568-3247 ▪ Fx: 540-801-8650 ▪ TF: 800-568-4120

Institute of Certified Records Managers   www.icrm.org
318 Oak St   Syracuse NY 13203
Ph: 315-234-1904 ▪ Fx: 315-474-1784 ▪ TF: 877-244-3128

Institute of Certified Travel Agents   www.icta.com
PO Box 812059   Wellesley MA 02482
Ph: 781-237-0280 ▪ Fx: 781-237-3860 ▪ TF: 800-542-4282

Institute for Chemical Education   ice.chem.wisc.edu
Univ of Wisconsin-Madison Dept of Chemistry 1101 University Ave   Madison WI 53706
Ph: 608-262-3033 ▪ Fx: 608-265-8094 ▪ TF: 800-991-5534

Institute for Childhood Resources
268 Bush St   San Francisco CA 94104
Ph: 415-864-1169 ■ Fx: 510-540-0171 ■ TF: 800-551-8697

Institute of Clean Air Companies   icac.com
1660 L St NW Suite 1100   Washington DC 20036
Ph: 202-457-0911 ■ Fx: 202-331-1388

Institute for Community Economics Inc   www.iceclt.org
57 School St   Springfield MA 01105
Ph: 413-746-8660 ■ Fx: 413-746-8862

Institute for Computer Capacity Management   www.demandtech.com
1020 8th Ave S Suite 6   Naples FL 34102
Ph: 239-261-8945 ■ Fx: 239-261-5456 ■ TF: 800-531-6143

Institute for Computers in Jewish Life
7074 N Western Ave   Chicago IL 60645
Ph: 773-262-9200 ■ Fx: 773-262-9298

Institute for Conservation Leadership   www.icl.org
6930 Carroll Ave Suite 420   Takoma Park MD 20912
Ph: 301-270-2900 ■ Fx: 301-270-0610

Institute of Consumer Financial Education   www.financial-education-icfe.org
PO Box 34070   San Diego CA 92163
Ph: 619-232-8811 ■ Fx: 619-239-1401

Institute for Contemporary Studies   www.icspress.com
310 Harrison St   Oakland CA 94611
Ph: 510-238-5010 ■ Fx: 510-238-8440 ■ TF: 800-326-0263

Institute for Creation Research   www.icr.org
10946 N Woodside Ave   Santee CA 92071
Ph: 619-448-0900 ■ Fx: 619-448-3469

Institute of Cultural Affairs   www.ica-usa.org
215 NE 40th St Suite C-2   Seattle WA 98105
Ph: 206-323-2100 ■ Fx: 206-547-4057

Institute for Defense & Disarmament Studies   www.idds.org
675 Massachusetts Ave 8th Fl   Cambridge MA 02139
Ph: 617-354-4337 ■ Fx: 617-354-1450

Institute for Development of Educational Activities   www.idea.org
259 Regency Ridge   Dayton OH 45459
Ph: 937-434-6969 ■ Fx: 937-434-5203

Institute for the Development of the Harmonious Human Being Inc   www.idhhb.org
PO Box 370   Nevada City CA 95959
Ph: 530-272-0180 ■ Fx: 530-272-0184

Institute of Diving   www.diveweb.com/iod
17314 Panama City Beach Pkwy   Panama City Beach FL 32413
Ph: 850-235-4101

Institute for a Drug-Free Workplace   www.drugfreeworkplace.org
1225 'I' St NW Suite 1000   Washington DC 20005
Ph: 202-842-7400 ■ Fx: 202-842-0022

Institute for Earth Education   www.eartheducation.org
Cedar Cove   Greenville WV 24945
Ph: 304-832-6404 ■ Fx: 304-832-6077

Institute for Economic Analysis   www.iea-macro-economics.org
262 Harvard St Suite 12   Cambridge MA 02139
Ph: 617-864-9933

Institute for Educational Leadership   www.iel.org
1001 Connecticut Ave NW Suite 310   Washington DC 20036
Ph: 202-822-8405 ■ Fx: 202-872-4050

Institute of Electrical & Electronics Engineers   www.ieee.org
3 Park Ave 17th Fl   New York NY 10016
Ph: 212-419-7900 ■ Fx: 212-752-4929 ■ TF: 800-678-4333

Institute of Environmental Sciences & Technology   www.iest.org
5005 Newport Dr Suite 506   Rolling Meadows IL 60008
Ph: 847-255-1561 ■ Fx: 847-255-1699

Institute for Food & Development Policy   www.foodfirst.org
398 60th St   Oakland CA 94618
Ph: 510-654-4400 ■ Fx: 510-654-4551

Institute of Food Technologists   www.ift.org
525 W Van Buren St Suite 1000   Chicago IL 60607
Ph: 312-782-8424 ■ Fx: 312-782-8348 ■ TF: 800-438-3663

Institute for the Future   www.iftf.org
2744 Sand Hill Rd   Menlo Park CA 94025
Ph: 650-854-6322 ■ Fx: 650-854-7850

Institute of General Semantics   www.general-semantics.org
86 85th St   Brooklyn NY 11209
Ph: 718-921-7093 ■ Fx: 718-921-4276

Institute for Global Communications   www.igc.org
PO Box 29904   San Francisco CA 94129
Ph: 415-561-6100 ■ Fx: 415-561-6101

Institute of Government & Public Affairs   www.igpa.uiuc.edu
Univ of Illinois 1007 W Nevada St   Urbana IL 61801
Ph: 217-333-3340 ■ Fx: 217-244-4817

Institute of the Great Plains   institutegreatplains.tripod.com
PO Box 68   Lawton OK 73502
Ph: 580-581-3460 ■ Fx: 580-581-3458

Institute of Hazardous Materials Management   www.ihmm.org
11900 Parklawn Dr Suite 450   Rockville MD 20852
Ph: 301-984-8969 ■ Fx: 301-984-1516

Institute for Health Freedom   www.forhealthfreedom.org
1825 'I' St NW Suite 400   Washington DC 20006
Ph: 202-429-6610 ■ Fx: 202-861-1973

Institute for Health & Productivity Management   www.ihpm.org
4435 Waterfront Dr Suite 101   Glen Allen VA 23060
Ph: 804-257-1905 ■ Fx: 804-747-5316 ■ TF: 800-722-0376

Institute for Healthcare Improvement   www.ihi.org
375 Longwood Ave 4th Fl   Boston MA 02215
Ph: 617-754-4800 ■ Fx: 617-754-4848

Institute of HeartMath   www.heartmath.org
14700 W Park Ave   Boulder Creek CA 95006
Ph: 831-338-8500 ■ Fx: 831-338-8504

Institute for the Human Environment
2572 Acacia Ave   Sonoma CA 95476
Ph: 707-935-9335 ■ Fx: 707-935-9593

Institute for Image Management   www.image360.com
PO Box 190007   San Francisco CA 94119
Ph: 415-863-2573

Institute for Independent Education   www.ifie.org
PO Box 42428   Washington DC 20015
Ph: 202-362-9344 ■ Fx: 202-362-0513

Institute for Individual & World Peace   www.iiwp.org
2101 Wilshire Blvd Suite 119   Santa Monica CA 90403
Ph: 310-315-3451 ■ Fx: 310-315-3452 ■ TF: 888-848-4497

Institute of Industrial Engineers   www.iienet.org
3577 Parkway Ln Suite 200   Norcross GA 30092
Ph: 770-449-0460 ■ Fx: 770-441-3295 ■ TF: 800-494-0460

Institute of Inspection Cleaning & Restoration Certification   www.iicrc.org
2715 E Mill Plain Blvd   Vancouver WA 98661
Ph: 360-693-5675 ■ Fx: 360-693-4858

Institute for Integral Development   www.institutefortraining.com
PO Box 2172   Colorado Springs CO 80901
Ph: 719-634-7943 ■ Fx: 719-632-7025 ■ TF: 800-544-9562

Institute for Intercultural Studies   www.mead2001.org/Aboutus.htm
67-A E 77th St   New York NY 10021
Ph: 212-737-1011

Institute of Internal Auditors   www.theiia.org
249 Maitland Ave   Altamonte Springs FL 32701
Ph: 407-937-1100 ■ Fx: 407-937-1101

Institute of International Bankers   www.iib.org
299 Park Ave 17th Fl   New York NY 10171
Ph: 212-421-1611 ■ Fx: 212-421-1119

Institute of International Container Lessors   www.iicl.org
555 Pleasantville Rd Suite 140S   Briarcliff Manor NY 10510
Ph: 914-747-9100 ■ Fx: 914-747-4600

Institute for International Cooperation & Development   www.iicd-volunteer.org
PO Box 520   Williamstown MA 01267
Ph: 413-458-9828 ■ Fx: 413-458-3323

Institute for International Economics   www.iie.com
1750 Massachusetts Ave NW   Washington DC 20036
Ph: 202-328-9000 ■ Fx: 202-328-5432

Institute of International Education   www.iie.org
809 UN Plaza   New York NY 10017
Ph: 212-883-8200 ■ Fx: 212-984-5452

Institute for the International Education of Students   www.iesabroad.org
33 N LaSalle St 15th Fl   Chicago IL 60602
Ph: 312-944-1750 ■ Fx: 312-944-1448 ■ TF: 800-995-2300

Institute of International Finance   www.iif.com
2000 Pennsylvania Ave NW Suite 8500   Washington DC 20006
Ph: 202-857-3600 ■ Fx: 202-775-1430

Institute for International Mediation & Conflict Resolution   www.iimcr.org
1424 K St NW Suite 650   Washington DC 20005
Ph: 202-347-2042 ■ Fx: 202-347-2440

Institute of the Ironworking Industry   www.instituteiw.org
1750 New York Ave NW   Washington DC 20006
Ph: 202-783-3998 ■ Fx: 202-393-1507

Institute of Islamic & Arabic Sciences in America   www.iiasa.org
8500 Hilltop Rd   Fairfax VA 22031
Ph: 703-641-4890 ■ Fx: 703-641-4899

Institute of Judicial Administration
NYU School of Law 40 Washington Sq S Vanderbilt Hall   New York NY 10012
Ph: 212-998-6196 ■ Fx: 212-995-4036

Institute of Labor & Industrial Relations   www.ilir.umich.edu
Univ of Michigan Victor Vaughan Bldg 1111 Catherine St   Ann Arbor MI 48109
Ph: 734-763-3116 ■ Fx: 734-763-0913

Institute for Local Self-Reliance   www.ilsr.org
927 15th St NW 4th Fl   Washington DC 20005
Ph: 202-898-1610 ■ Fx: 202-898-1612

Institute of Makers of Explosives   www.ime.org
1120 19th St NW Suite 310   Washington DC 20036
Ph: 202-429-9280 ■ Fx: 202-293-2420

Institute of Management Accountants Inc   www.imanet.org
10 Paragon Dr   Montvale NJ 07645
Ph: 201-573-9000 ■ Fx: 201-573-8185 ■ TF: 800-638-4427

Institute of Management Consultants USA Inc   www.imcusa.org
2025 M St NW Suite 800   Washington DC 20036
Ph: 202-367-1134 ■ Fx: 202-367-2134 ■ TF: 800-221-2557

Institute of Mathematical Studies   www.imstat.org/
PO Box 22718   Beachwood OH 44122
Ph: 216-295-2340 ■ Fx: 216-921-6703

Institute for Mediation & Conflict Resolution   www.mediate.com/imcr
384 E 149th St Suite 330   Bronx NY 10455
Ph: 718-585-1190 ■ Fx: 718-585-1962

Institute of Medicine   www.iom.edu
500 5th St NW   Washington DC 20001
Ph: 202-334-2352 ■ Fx: 202-334-1412

Institute of Nautical Archaeology   ina.tamu.edu
PO Drawer HG   College Station TX 77841
Ph: 979-845-6694 ■ Fx: 979-847-9260

Institute of Navigation   www.ion.org
3975 University Dr Suite 390   Fairfax VA 22030
Ph: 703-383-9688 ■ Fx: 703-383-9689

Institute of Near Eastern & African Studies   www.ineas.org
PO Box 425125   Cambridge MA 02142
Ph: 617-864-6327

Institute of Noetic Sciences   www.noetic.org
101 San Antonio Rd   Petaluma CA 94952
Ph: 707-775-3500 ■ Fx: 707-781-7420

Institute of Nuclear Materials Management   www.inmm.org
60 Revere Dr Suite 500   Northbrook IL 60062
Ph: 847-480-9573 ■ Fx: 847-480-9282

Institute of Nuclear Power Operations   tis.eh.doe.gov/nsps/inpo/
700 Galleria Pkwy SE Suite 100   Atlanta GA 30339
Ph: 770-644-8000 ■ Fx: 770-644-8549

Institute for Operations Research & the Management Sciences   www.informs.org
901 Elkridge Landing Rd Suite 400   Linthicum MD 21090
Ph: 410-850-0300 ▪ Fx: 410-684-2963 ▪ TF: 800-446-3676

Institute of Outdoor Drama   www.unc.edu/depts/outdoor
Univ of North Carolina 1700 Airport Rd CB 3240   Chapel Hill
NC 27599
Ph: 919-962-1328 ▪ Fx: 919-962-4212

Institute of Packaging Professionals   www.iopp.org
1601 N Bond St Suite 101   Naperville IL 60563
Ph: 630-544-5050 ▪ Fx: 630-544-5055 ▪ TF: 800-432-4085

Institute for Palestine Studies   www.ipsjps.org
3501 M St NW   Washington DC 20007
Ph: 202-342-3990 ▪ Fx: 202-342-3927 ▪ TF: 800-874-3614

Institute of Paper Science & Technology   www.ipst.edu
500 10th St NW   Atlanta GA 30318
Ph: 404-894-5700 ▪ Fx: 404-894-4778 ▪ TF: 800-558-6611

Institute for Peace & Justice   www.ipj-ppj.org
4144 Lindell Blvd Suite 408   Saint Louis MO 63108
Ph: 314-533-4445 ▪ Fx: 314-715-6455

Institute for Philosophy & Public Policy   www.puaf.umd.edu/IPPP
Maryland School of Public Affairs 3111 Van Munching
Hall   College Park MD 20742
Ph: 301-405-4753 ▪ Fx: 301-314-9346

Institute for Policy Innovation   www.ipi.org
1660 S Stemmons Fwy Suite 475   Lewisville TX 75067
Ph: 972-847-5139 ▪ Fx: 972-874-5144

Institute for Policy Studies   www.ips-dc.org
733 15th St NW Suite 1020   Washington DC 20005
Ph: 202-234-9382 ▪ Fx: 202-387-7915

Institute of Politics   www.iop.harvard.edu
Harvard Univ John F Kennedy School of Government 79 JFK
St   Cambridge MA 02138
Ph: 617-495-1360

Institute for Polyacrylate Absorbents
1850 M St NW Suite 700   Washington DC 20036
Ph: 202-721-4145 ▪ Fx: 202-296-8120

Institute of Professional Environmental Practice   www.ipep.org
600 Forbes Ave 333 Fisher Hall   Pittsburgh PA 15282
Ph: 412-396-1703 ▪ Fx: 412-396-1704

Institute for Professionals in Taxation   www.ipt.org
3350 Peachtree Rd Suite 280   Atlanta GA 30326
Ph: 404-240-2300 ▪ Fx: 404-240-2315

Institute for Psychohistory   www.psychohistory.org
140 Riverside Dr   New York NY 10024
Ph: 212-799-2294 ▪ TF: 800-445-2268

Institute of Public Administration   www.theipa.org
411 N Lafayette St Suite 303   New York NY 10003
Ph: 212-992-9898 ▪ Fx: 212-995-4876

Institute for Public Relations   www.instituteforpr.com
PO Box 118400 2096 Weimer Hall   Gainesville FL 32611
Ph: 352-392-0280 ▪ Fx: 352-846-1122

Institute of Public Utilities   www.ipu.msu.edu
Michigan State Univ 240 Nisbet Bldg   East Lansing MI 48823
Ph: 517-355-1876 ▪ Fx: 517-355-1854

Institute of Real Estate Management   www.irem.org
430 N Michigan Ave   Chicago IL 60611
Ph: 312-329-6000 ▪ Fx: 800-338-4736 ▪ TF: 800-837-0706

Institute on Religion in an Age of Science Inc   www.iras.org
310 Windham Dr   Booneville MS 38829
Ph: 662-720-1241

Institute on Religion & Democracy   www.ird-renew.org
1110 Vermont Ave NW Suite 1180   Washington DC 20005
Ph: 202-969-8430 ▪ Fx: 202-969-8429

Institute for Resource & Security Studies   www.irss-usa.org
27 Ellsworth Ave   Cambridge MA 02139
Ph: 617-491-5177 ▪ Fx: 617-491-6904

Institute for Responsible Housing Preservation   www.housingpreservation.org
401 9th St NW Suite 900   Washington DC 20004
Ph: 202-585-8739 ▪ Fx: 202-585-8080

Institute for Responsive Education   www.responsiveeducation.org
Northeastern Univ 21 Lake Hall   Boston MA 02115
Ph: 617-373-2595 ▪ Fx: 617-373-8839

Institute of Scrap Recycling Industries Inc   www.isri.org
1325 G St NW Suite 1000   Washington DC 20005
Ph: 202-737-1770 ▪ Fx: 202-626-0900

Institute of Shortening & Edible Oils   www.iseo.org
1750 New York Ave NW Suite 120   Washington DC 20006
Ph: 202-783-7960 ▪ Fx: 202-393-1367

Institute for Southern Studies   www.southernstudies.org
PO Box 531   Durham NC 27702
Ph: 919-419-8311 ▪ Fx: 919-419-8315

Institute for Space & Security Studies   rmbowman.com/isss
5017 Bellflower Ct   Melbourne FL 32940
Ph: 321-752-5955

Institute of Store Planners   www.ispo.org
25 N Broadway   Tarrytown NY 10591
Ph: 914-332-1806 ▪ Fx: 914-332-1541 ▪ TF: 800-379-9912

Institute for Studies in American Music   depthome.brooklyn.cuny.edu/isam
Brooklyn College of CUNY 2900 Bedford Ave   Brooklyn NY
11210
Ph: 718-951-5655 ▪ Fx: 718-951-4858

Institute for the Study of American Cultures   www.isacnet.org
233 12th St Suite 500 PO Box 2707   Columbus GA 31902
Ph: 706-243-6218 ▪ Fx: 706-322-7747

Institute for the Study of Human Knowledge   www.ishkbooks.com
PO Box 176   Los Altos CA 94023
Ph: 650-948-9428 ▪ Fx: 650-948-2687

Institute for the Study of Traditional American Indian Arts
PO Box 66124   Portland OR 97290
Ph: 503-233-8131

Institute for Supply Management   www.ism.ws
PO Box 22160   Tempe AZ 85285
Ph: 480-752-6276 ▪ Fx: 480-752-7890 ▪ TF: 800-888-6276

Institute for Sustainable Communities   www.iscvt.org
535 Stone Cutters Way   Montpelier VT 05602
Ph: 802-229-2900 ▪ Fx: 802-229-2919

Institute of Tax Consultants   www.taxprofessionals.homestead.com/welcome.html
7500 212th St SW Suite 205   Edmonds WA 98026
Ph: 425-774-3521 ▪ Fx: 425-672-0461

Institute for Theological Encounter with Science & Technology   itest.slu.edu
3601 Lindell Blvd   Saint Louis MO 63108
Ph: 314-977-2703

Institute for Transportation & Development Policy   www.itdp.org/AccessAfrica.html
115 W 30th St Suite 1205   New York NY 10001
Ph: 212-629-8001 ▪ Fx: 212-629-8033

Institute of Transportation Engineers   www.ite.org
1099 14th St NW Suite 300W   Washington DC 20005
Ph: 202-289-0222 ▪ Fx: 202-289-7722

Institute of Turkish Studies   turkishstudies.org
Georgetown Univ Intercultural Center   Washington DC 20057
Ph: 202-687-0295 ▪ Fx: 202-687-3780

Institute for Victims of Trauma   www.microneil.com/ivt
6801 Market Square Dr   McLean VA 22101
Ph: 703-847-8456 ▪ Fx: 703-847-0470

Institute for Women & Technology   www.iwt.org
1501 Page Mill Rd MS 1105   Palo Alto CA 94304
Ph: 650-236-4756 ▪ Fx: 650-852-8172

Institute for Women in Trades Technology & Science   www.iwitts.com
1150 Ballena Blvd Suite 102   Alameda CA 94501
Ph: 510-749-0200 ▪ Fx: 510-749-0500

Institute of World Affairs   www.iwa.org
1321 Pennsylvania Ave SE   Washington DC 20003
Ph: 202-544-4141 ▪ Fx: 202-544-5115

Institutes for the Achievement of Human Potential   www.iahp.org
8801 Stenton Ave   Wyndmoor PA 19038
Ph: 215-233-2050 ▪ Fx: 215-233-9312

Institutional Cooperation, Committee on   www.cic.uiuc.edu
302 E John St Suite 1705   Champaign IL 61820
Ph: 217-333-8475 ▪ Fx: 217-244-7127

Institutional Education, International Council on Hotel Restaurant &   www.chrie.org
2613 N Parham Rd 2nd Fl   Richmond VA 23294
Ph: 804-346-4800 ▪ Fx: 804-346-5009

Institutional Furniture Manufacturers Association, Business &   www.bifma.com
2680 Horizon Dr SE Suite A-1   Grand Rapids MI 49546
Ph: 616-285-3963 ▪ Fx: 616-285-3765

Institutional & International Initiatives, Center for   www.acenet.edu/programs/ciii.cfm
American Council on Education 1 Dupont Cir NW   8th
Fl   Washington DC 20036
Ph: 202-939-9427

Institutional Linen Management, National Association of   www.nlmnet.org
2130 Lexington Rd Suite H   Richmond KY 40475
Ph: 859-624-0177 ▪ Fx: 859-624-3580 ▪ TF: 800-669-0863

Institutional Locksmiths' Association   www.ilanational.org
PO Box 4188   Trenton NJ 08610
Ph: 866-745-5625

Institutional Research, Association for   www.airweb.org
Florida State Univ 222 Stone Bldg   Tallahassee FL 32306
Ph: 850-644-4470 ▪ Fx: 850-644-8824

Institutions & Alternatives, National Center on   www.ncianet.org
7222 Ambassador Rd   Baltimore MD 21244
Ph: 410-265-1490

Instituto Nacional Hispano de Liturgia
PO Box 18   Washington DC 20064
Ph: 202-319-6450 ▪ Fx: 202-319-6949

Instruction, Association for Direct   www.adihome.org
PO Box 10252   Eugene OR 97440
Ph: 541-485-1293 ▪ Fx: 541-683-7543

Instruction, Association for Technology in Music   atmi.music.org

Instruction, World Council for Curriculum &   www.alliant.edu/gsoe/wcci
Alliant International Univ Cross Cultural Studies Institute School
of Education 10455 Pomerado Rd   San Diego CA 92131
Ph: 858-635-4719 ▪ Fx: 858-635-4714

Instructional Materials, American Association for Vocational   www.aavim.com
220 Smithonia Rd   Winterville GA 30683
Ph: 706-742-5355 ▪ Fx: 706-742-7005 ▪ TF: 800-228-4689

Instructional Systems Association   www.isaconnection.org
12427 Hedges Run Dr Suite 120   Lake Ridge VA 22192
Ph: 703-730-2838 ▪ Fx: 703-730-2857 ▪ TF: 877-533-4914

Instructional Technology, Agency for   www.ait.net
1800 N Stonelake Dr Box A   Bloomington IN 47402
Ph: 812-339-2203 ▪ Fx: 812-333-4218 ▪ TF: 800-457-4509

Instructional Technology Council   www.itcnetwork.org
1 Dupont Cir NW Suite 360   Washington DC 20036
Ph: 202-293-3110

Instructors, American Association of Snowboard   www.aasi.org
133 S Van Gordon St Suite 101   Lakewood CO 80228
Ph: 303-987-9390 ▪ Fx: 800-222-4754

Instructors Association, National Photography   www.nppa.org
1255 Hill Dr   Eagle Rock CA 90041
Ph: 323-254-1549 ▪ Fx: 323-254-2797

Instructors, National Association of Underwater   www.naui.org
1232 Tech Blvd   Tampa FL 33619
Ph: 813-628-6284 ▪ Fx: 813-628-8253 ▪ TF: 800-553-6284

Instrument Manufacturers, National Association of Band   www.nabim.com
PO Box 5488   Long Island City NY 11105
Ph: 718-274-3210 ▪ Fx: 718-274-3214

Instrument Repair Technicians, National Association of Professional Band   www.napbirt.org   PO Box 51   Normal IL 61761
Ph: 309-452-4257 ▪ Fx: 309-452-4825

Instrumentalists & Directors Association, Christian — www.cidaonline.com

Instrumentation, Association for the Advancement of Medical — www.aami.org
1110 N Glebe Rd Suite 220 Arlington VA 22201
Ph: 703-525-4890 ▪ Fx: 703-276-0793 ▪ TF: 800-332-2264

Instrumentation & Measurement Society, IEEE — www.ewh.ieee.org/soc/im
IEEE Operations Ctr 445 Hoes Ln Piscataway NJ 08854
Ph: 732-981-0060 ▪ Fx: 732-981-1721

Instrumentation Systems & Automation Society, ISA - — www.isa.org
67 Alexander Dr Research Triangle Park NC 27709
Ph: 919-549-8411 ▪ Fx: 919-549-8288

Instrumentation Testing Association — www.instrument.org
631 N Stephanie St Suite 279 Henderson NV 89014
Ph: 702-568-1445 ▪ Fx: 702-568-1446 ▪ TF: 877-236-1256

Insulated Cable Engineers Association — www.icea.net
PO Box 1568 Carrollton GA 30112
770-830-0369 ▪ Fx: 770-830-8501

Insulated Glass Manufacturers Alliance — www.igmaonline.org
27 Goulburn Ave Ottawa ON K1N8C7
Ph: 613-233-1510 ▪ Fx: 613-233-1929

Insulated Panel Association, Structural — www.sips.org
PO Box 1699 Gig Harbor WA 98335
Ph: 253-858-7472 ▪ Fx: 253-858-0272

Insulated Steel Door Institute — www.isdi.org
30200 Detroit Rd Cleveland OH 44145
Ph: 440-899-0010 ▪ Fx: 440-892-1404

Insulating Concrete Form Association — www.forms.org
1730 Dewes St Suite 2 Glenview IL 60025
Ph: 847-657-9730 ▪ Fx: 847-657-9728 ▪ TF: 888-864-4232

Insulation Association, National — www.insulation.org
99 Canal Center Plaza Suite 222 Alexandria VA 22314
Ph: 703-683-6422 ▪ Fx: 703-549-4838

Insulation Conference, Electrical — www.electricalinsulation.org
13707 Brook Hollow Ct Fort Wayne IN 46814
Ph: 219-625-5987 ▪ Fx: 219-625-3693

Insulation Contractors Association of America — www.insulate.org
1321 Duke St Suite 303 Alexandria VA 22314
Ph: 703-739-0356 ▪ Fx: 703-739-0412

Insulation Manufacturers Association, Cellulose — www.cellulose.org
136 S Keowee St Dayton OH 45402
Ph: 937-222-2462 ▪ Fx: 937-222-5794 ▪ TF: 888-881-2462

Insulation Manufacturers Association, North American — www.naima.org
44 Canal Center Plaza Suite 310 Alexandria VA 22314
Ph: 703-684-0084 ▪ Fx: 703-684-0427

Insulators & Asbestos Workers, International Association of Heat & Frost 9602 ML King Jr Hwy Lanham MD 20706 — www.insulators.org
Ph: 301-731-9101 ▪ Fx: 301-731-5058

Insurance Accounting & Systems Association — www.iasa.org
4705 University Dr Suite 280 PO Box 51340 Durham NC 27717
Ph: 919-489-0991 ▪ Fx: 919-489-1994

Insurance Adjusters, National Association of Independent — www.naiia.com
825 W State St Suite 117-C Geneve IL 60134
Ph: 630-397-5012 ▪ Fx: 630-397-5013

Insurance Adjusters, National Association of Public — www.napia.com
21165 Whitfield Pl Suite 105 Potomac Falls VA 20165
Ph: 703-433-9217 ▪ Fx: 703-433-0369

Insurance Advisors, Association of Health — www.ahia.net
2901 Telestar Ct Falls Church VA 22042
Ph: 703-770-8200 ▪ Fx: 703-770-8201

Insurance Agents & Brokers of America Inc, Independent — www.iiaba.org
127 S Peyton St Alexandria VA 22314
Ph: 703-683-4422 ▪ Fx: 703-683-7556 ▪ TF: 800-221-7917

Insurance Agents & Brokers, Council of — www.ciab.com
701 Pennsylvania Ave NW Suite 750 Washington DC 20004
Ph: 202-783-4400 ▪ Fx: 202-783-4410

Insurance Agents, National Association of Professional — www.pianet.com
400 N Washington St Alexandria VA 22314
Ph: 703-836-9340 ▪ Fx: 703-836-1279 ▪ TF: 800-742-6900

Insurance Agents Society, Certified Professional — www.cpia.com
PO Box 35718 Richmond VA 23235
Ph: 804-674-6466 ▪ Fx: 804-276-1300 ▪ TF: 877-674-2472

Insurance Association, American — www.aiadc.org
1130 Connecticut Ave NW Suite 1000 Washington DC 20036
Ph: 202-828-7100 ▪ Fx: 202-293-1219

Insurance Association, American Risk & — www.aria.org
716 Providence Rd PO Box 3028 Malvern PA 19355
Ph: 610-640-1997 ▪ Fx: 610-725-1007

Insurance Association, Aviation — www.aiaweb.org
14 W 3rd St Suite 200 Kansas City MO 64105
Ph: 816-221-8488 ▪ Fx: 816-472-2265

Insurance Association, Foreign Credit — www.fcia.com
40 Rector St 11th Fl New York NY 10006
Ph: 212-885-1500 ▪ Fx: 212-885-1535

Insurance Association, Police & Firemen's — www.pfia.net
101 E 116th St Carmel IN 46032
Ph: 317-581-1913 ▪ Fx: 317-571-5946 ▪ TF: 800-221-7342

Insurance Association, University Risk Management & — www.urmia.org
342 N Main St West Hartford CT 06117
Ph: 860-586-7565 ▪ Fx: 860-586-7550

Insurance Auditors & Engineers, National Association of Independent — www.naiiae.org

(Insurance) Blue Cross & Blue Shield Association — www.bluecares.com
225 N Michigan Ave Chicago IL 60601
Ph: 312-297-6000 ▪ Fx: 312-297-6609

(Insurance) Catholic Knights — www.catholicknights.com
1100 W Wells St Milwaukee WI 53233
Ph: 414-273-6266 ▪ Fx: 414-223-3201 ▪ TF: 800-927-2547

Insurance, Catholic Life — www.catholiclifeinsurance.com
1635 NE Loop 410 Suite 300 San Antonio TX 78209
Ph: 210-828-9921 ▪ Fx: 210-828-4629 ▪ TF: 800-262-2548

Insurance Clearing House, American Marine — www.amich.org
30 Broad St 7th Fl New York NY 10004
Ph: 212-405-2835 ▪ Fx: 212-344-1664

Insurance Commissioners, National Association of — www.naic.org
2301 McGee St Suite 800 Kansas City MO 64108
Ph: 816-842-3600 ▪ Fx: 816-783-8175

Insurance Companies of America, Mortgage — www.privatemi.com
727 15th St NW Suite 1200 Washington DC 20005
Ph: 202-393-5566 ▪ Fx: 202-393-5557

Insurance Companies, National Association of Mutual — www.namic.org
3601 Vincennes Rd Indianapolis IN 46268
Ph: 317-875-5250 ▪ Fx: 317-879-8408 ▪ TF: 800-336-2642

Insurance Compliance Professionals, Association of — www.aicp.net
12110 Sunset Hills Rd Suite 130 Reston VA 20190
Ph: 703-234-4074 ▪ Fx: 703-435-4390

Insurance Consumer Affairs Exchange — www.icae.com

Insurance, Council for Affordable Health — www.cahi.org
112 S West St Suite 400 Alexandria VA 22314
Ph: 703-836-6200 ▪ Fx: 703-836-6550

Insurance Counselors, National Association of Fraternal — www.namic.org
PO Box 357 Sheboygan WI 53082
Ph: 920-458-1996 ▪ Fx: 920-457-4661

Insurance Counselors, Society of Certified —
PO Box 27027 Austin TX 78755
Ph: 512-345-7932 ▪ Fx: 512-343-2167 ▪ TF: 800-633-2165

(Insurance) CPCU Society — www.cpcusociety.org
720 Providence Rd Kahler Hall PO Box 3009 Malvern PA 19355
Ph: 800-932-2728 ▪ Fx: 610-251-2780

Insurance Crime Bureau, National — www.nicb.org
10330 S Roberts Rd Palos Hills IL 60465
Ph: 708-430-2430 ▪ Fx: 708-430-5025 ▪ TF: 800-447-6282

Insurance Education Foundation — www.ins-ed-fdn.org
3601 Vincennes Rd PO Box 68700 Indianapolis IN 46268
Ph: 317-876-6046 ▪ Fx: 317-879-8408 ▪ TF: 800-433-4811

(Insurance) Equitable Reserve Association — www.equitablereserve.com
116 S Commercial St PO Box 448 Neenah WI 54957
Ph: 920-722-1574 ▪ Fx: 920-722-5400 ▪ TF: 800-722-1574

Insurance & Financial Advisors, National Association of — www.naifa.org
2901 Telestar Ct Falls Church VA 22042
Ph: 703-770-8100 ▪ TF: 877-866-2432

Insurance & Financial Advisors PAC, National Association of —
2901 Telestar Ct Falls Church VA 22042
Ph: 703-770-8100 ▪ Fx: 703-770-8194

Insurance Financial Management, Society of — www.sifm.org

Insurance & Financial Services, Women in — www.w-wifs.org
9101 LBJ Fwy Suite 450 Dallas TX 75243
Ph: 469-621-3525 ▪ TF: 800-753-3973

Insurance Fraud Agencies, International Association of — www.iaifa.org
PO Box 10018 Kansas City MO 64171
Ph: 816-756-5285 ▪ Fx: 816-756-5287

(Insurance) Gamma Iota Sigma — www.gammaiotasigma.org
2586 Oakstone Dr Columbus OH 43231
Ph: 614-891-4242 ▪ Fx: 614-891-7698

Insurance Guaranty Associations, National Organization of Life & Health 13873 Park Center Rd Suite 329 Herndon VA 20171 — www.nolhga.com
Ph: 703-481-5206 ▪ Fx: 703-481-5209

(Insurance) Honorable Order of the Blue Goose International — www.bluegoose.org
12940 Walnut Rd Elm Grove WI 53122
Ph: 414-221-0341 ▪ Fx: 414-782-7608

Insurance Information Institute — www.iii.org
110 William St 24th Fl New York NY 10038
Ph: 212-346-5500 ▪ Fx: 212-732-1916 ▪ TF: 800-331-9146

Insurance Institute of America, American Institute for CPCU & — www.aicpcu.org
720 Providence Rd PO Box 3016 Malvern PA 19355
Ph: 610-644-2100 ▪ Fx: 610-640-9576 ▪ TF: 800-644-2101

Insurance Institute of America Inc, Self- — www.siia.org
PO Box 1237 Simpsonville SC 29681
Ph: 864-962-2208 ▪ Fx: 864-962-2483 ▪ TF: 800-851-7789

Insurance Institute for Highway Safety — www.hwysafety.org
1005 N Glebe Rd Suite 800 Arlington VA 22201
Ph: 703-247-1500 ▪ Fx: 703-247-1678

Insurance Institute, Mass Marketing — www.mi2.org
14 W 3rd St Suite 200 Kansas City MO 64105
Ph: 816-221-7575 ▪ Fx: 816-472-7765

Insurance Legislators, National Conference of — www.ncoil.org
139 Lancaster St Albany NY 12210
Ph: 518-449-3210 ▪ Fx: 518-432-5651

Insurance Loss Control Association — www.insurancelosscontrol.org

Insurance Management Consultants, American Association of — www.aaimco.com
3925 Fenn Rd Medina OH 44256
Ph: 330-725-8946 ▪ Fx: 330-723-6270

Insurance Management Society Inc, Risk & — www.rims.org
655 3rd Ave 2nd Fl New York NY 10017
Ph: 212-286-9292 ▪ Fx: 212-986-9716 ▪ TF: 800-711-0317

Insurance Marketing Association, Professional — www.pima-assn.org
6300 Ridgelea Pl Suite 1008 Fort Worth TX 76116
Ph: 817-569-7462 ▪ Fx: 817-569-7461

Insurance Marketing Communications Association — www.imcanet.com
PO Box 473054 Charlotte NC 28247
Ph: 704-543-1776 ▪ Fx: 704-543-6345

Insurance Medicine, American Academy of — www.aaimedicine.org
174 Colonade Rd Ottawa ON K2E7J5
Ph: 613-226-9601 ▪ Fx: 613-721-3581

(Insurance) Order of the Sons of Hermann in Texas — www.texashermannsons.org
PO Box 1941 San Antonio TX 78297
Ph: 210-226-9261 ▪ Fx: 210-226-3055 ▪ TF: 800-234-4124

(Insurance) Polish Falcons of America — www.polishfalcons.org
615 Iron City Dr Pittsburgh PA 15205
Ph: 412-922-2244 ▪ Fx: 412-922-5029 ▪ TF: 800-535-2071

Insurance Premium Auditors, National Society of — www.nsipa.org
PO Box 1896 Columbus OH 43216
Ph: 614-221-9266 ▪ Fx: 614-221-2335 ▪ TF: 888-846-7472

Insurance Premium Finance Association
2890 Niagara Falls PO Box 726 Amherst NY 14226
Ph: 716-695-8757 ▪ Fx: 716-695-8758

Insurance Professionals, Association of Finance & — www.afip.com
PO Box 212003 Bedford TX 76095
Ph: 817-428-2434 ▪ Fx: 817-581-4609

Insurance Receivers, International Association of — www.iair.org
174 Grace Blvd Altamonte Springs FL 32714
Ph: 407-682-4513 ▪ Fx: 407-682-3175

Insurance Reform, Coalition for Auto-
7310 Stafford Rd Alexandria VA 22307
Ph: 703-660-0799

Insurance Research Bureau, Crop — www.cropinsurance.org
9200 Indian Creek Pkwy Suite 220 Overland Park KS 66210
Ph: 913-338-0470 ▪ Fx: 913-661-1640

Insurance Research Bureau, Liability — www.lirb.org
3025 Highland Pkwy Suite 800 Downers Grove IL 60515
Ph: 630-724-2200 ▪ Fx: 630-724-2260 ▪ TF: 888-711-7572

Insurance Research Council — www.ircweb.org
718 Providence Rd PO Box 3025 Malvern PA 19355
Ph: 610-644-2212 ▪ Fx: 610-644-5388 ▪ TF: 800-644-2101

(Insurance) Resort Hotel Association — www.resorthotelinsurance.com
461 McLaws Cir Suite 4 Williamsburg VA 23185
Ph: 757-220-7194 ▪ Fx: 757-253-2445

(Insurance) Royal Neighbors of America — www.royalneighbors.org
230 16th St Rock Island IL 61201
Ph: 309-788-4561 ▪ TF: 800-627-4762

(Insurance) Russian Brotherhood Organization of the USA — www.rbo.org
1733 Spring Garden St Philadelphia PA 19130
Ph: 215-563-2537 ▪ Fx: 215-563-8106 ▪ TF: 800-726-8721

Insurance & Securities Association, Bank — www.bisanet.org
303 W Lancaster Ave Suite 2D Wayne PA 19087
Ph: 610-989-9047 ▪ Fx: 610-989-9102

Insurance Services, American Association of — www.aais.org
1745 S Naperville Rd Wheaton IL 60187
Ph: 630-681-8347 ▪ Fx: 630-681-8356 ▪ TF: 800-564-2247

Insurance Services, National Crop — www.ag-risk.org
7201 W 129th St Suite 200 Overland Park KS 66213
Ph: 913-685-2767 ▪ Fx: 913-685-3080 ▪ TF: 800-951-6247

(Insurance) Slovene National Benefit Society — www.snpj.com
247 W Allegheny Rd Imperial PA 15126
Ph: 724-695-1100 ▪ Fx: 724-695-1555 ▪ TF: 800-843-7675

Insurance Society, Gleaner Life — www.gleanerlife.com
5200 W US Hwy 223 PO Box 1894 Adrian MI 49221
Ph: 517-263-2244 ▪ Fx: 517-265-7745 ▪ TF: 800-992-1894

Insurance Society, International — www.iisonline.org
101 Murray St New York NY 10007
Ph: 212-815-9294 ▪ Fx: 212-815-9297

Insurance Society, Luso-American Life — www.luso-american.org
7080 Donlon Way Dublin CA 94568
Ph: 925-828-4884 ▪ Fx: 925-828-4554 ▪ TF: 877-525-5876

Insurance Syndicate, Water Quality — www.wqis.org
80 Broad St 21st Fl New York NY 10004
Ph: 212-292-8700 ▪ Fx: 212-292-8716

Insurance Trainers & Educators, Society of — www.insurancetrainers.org
2120 Market St Suite 108 San Francisco CA 94114
Ph: 415-621-2830 ▪ Fx: 415-621-0889

(Insurance) US Letter Carriers Mutual Benefit Association — www.nalc.org/depart/mba
100 Indiana Ave NW Suite 510 Washington DC 20001
Ph: 202-638-4318 ▪ Fx: 202-783-6123 ▪ TF: 800-424-5184

(Insurance) William Penn Association — www.williampennassociation.org
709 Brighton Rd Pittsburgh PA 15233
Ph: 412-231-2979 ▪ Fx: 412-231-8535 ▪ TF: 800-848-7366

Insurance Women, Association of Professional — www.apiw.org
551 5th Ave Suite 1625 New York NY 10176
Ph: 212-867-0228 ▪ Fx: 212-867-2544

Insurance Women (International), National Association of — www.naiw.org
1847 E 15th St Tulsa OK 74104
Ph: 918-744-5195 ▪ Fx: 918-743-1968 ▪ TF: 800-766-6249

(Insurance) Workmen's Benefit Fund of the USA — www.wbfusa.com
99 N Broadway Hicksville NY 11801
Ph: 516-938-6060 ▪ Fx: 516-938-6882

(Insurance) Workmen's Circle/Arbeter Ring — www.circle.org
45 E 33rd St New York NY 10016
Ph: 212-889-6800 ▪ Fx: 212-532-7518 ▪ TF: 800-922-2558

Insurers of America, Property Casualty — www.allianceai.org
2600 S River Rd Des Plaines IL 60018
Ph: 847-297-7800 ▪ Fx: 847-297-5064

Insurers, American Association of Crop — users.erols.com/aaci
1 Massachusetts Ave NW Suite 800 Washington DC 20001
Ph: 202-789-4100 ▪ Fx: 202-408-7763

Insurers Association of America, Physician — www.thepiaa.org
2275 Research Blvd Suite 250 Rockville MD 20850
Ph: 301-947-9000 ▪ Fx: 301-947-9090

Insurers, Association of Financial Guaranty — www.afgi.org
c/o TowersGroup 15 W 39th St 14th Fl New York NY 10018
Ph: 212-354-5020 ▪ Fx: 212-391-6920

Insurers, Committee of Annuity — www.annuity-insurers.org
c/o Davis & Harman LLP 1455 Pennsylvania Ave NW Suite
1200 Washington DC 20004
Ph: 202-347-2230 ▪ Fx: 202-393-3310

Insurers, National Association of Bar-Related Title — www.nabrti.com
2355 S Arlington Heights Rd Suite 230 Arlington Heights IL
60005
Ph: 847-545-0500 ▪ Fx: 847-545-0550

Insurers, National Council of Self- — www.natcouncil.com
1253 Springfield Ave PMB 345 New Providence NJ 07974
Ph: 908-665-2152 ▪ Fx: 908-665-4020

Integral Development, Institute for — www.institutefortraining.com
PO Box 2172 Colorado Springs CO 80901
Ph: 719-634-7943 ▪ Fx: 719-630-7025 ▪ TF: 800-544-9562

Integral Development, Inter-American Council for — www.cidi.oas.org
1889 F St NW Rm 220I Washington DC 20006
Ph: 202-458-3783 ▪ Fx: 202-458-3526

Integrated Business Communications Alliance — www.ibacweb.org
139 E Oakland Ave Doylestown PA 18901
Ph: 215-489-1722 ▪ Fx: 215-489-1799

Integrated Waste Services Association — www.wte.org
1401 H St NW Suite 220 Washington DC 20005
Ph: 202-467-6240 ▪ Fx: 202-467-6225

Integrative Medicine, Association for — www.integrativemedicine.org
Box 1 Mont Clare PA 19453
Ph: 610-933-8145 ▪ Fx: 610-983-9162

Integrative Strategies Forum — www.isforum.org
11426 Rockville Pike Suite 306 Rockville MD 20852
Ph: 301-770-6375 ▪ Fx: 301-770-6377

Integrative Studies, Association for — www.units.muohio.edu/aisorg
Miami Univ School of Interdisciplinary Studies Oxford OH
45056
Ph: 513-529-2213

Integrity — www.integrityusa.org
1718 M St NW PMB 148 Washington DC 20036
Ph: 800-462-9498

Integrity, Center for Public — www.publicintegrity.org
910 17th St NW 7th Fl Washington DC 20006
Ph: 202-466-1300 ▪ Fx: 202-466-1101

Intel Alumni Association Inc, Defense — www.dialumni.org
PO Box 86 McLean VA 22101
Ph: 202-231-3414

Intellectual History, International Society for — www.princeton.edu/~isih
Princeton Univ Hamilton Hall Princeton NJ 08544
Ph: 609-258-3317 ▪ Fx: 609-258-2889

Intellectual Life, Association for Religion & — www.aril.org
475 Riverside Dr Suite 1945 New York NY 10115
Ph: 212-870-2544 ▪ Fx: 212-870-2539

Intellectual Property Alliance, International — www.iipa.com
1747 Pennsylvania Ave NW Suite 825 Washington DC 20006
Ph: 202-833-4198 ▪ Fx: 202-872-0546

Intellectual Property Law Association, American — www.aipla.org
2001 Jefferson Davis Hwy Suite 203 Arlington VA 22202
Ph: 703-415-0780 ▪ Fx: 703-415-0786

Intellectual Property Law Associations, National Council of — www.ipo.org
1255 23rd St NW Suite 200 Washington DC 20037
Ph: 202-466-2396 ▪ Fx: 202-466-2893

Intellectual Property Owners Association — www.ipo.org
1255 23rd St NW Suite 200 Washington DC 20037
Ph: 202-466-2396 ▪ Fx: 202-466-2893

Intellectual Property Rights, Americans for the Enforcement of — rentamark.com/aeipr
PO Box 35189 Chicago IL 60707
Ph: 773-283-3880 ▪ Fx: 708-453-0083

Intelligence Association, National Military — www.nmia.org
9200 Centerway Rd Gaithersburg MD 20879
Ph: 301-840-6642 ▪ Fx: 301-840-8502

Intelligence, Consortium for the Study of — www.intelligenceconsortium.org
1730 Rhode Island Ave NW Suite 500 Washington DC 20036
Ph: 202-429-0129 ▪ Fx: 202-659-5429

Intelligence Officers, Association of Former — www.afio.com
6723 Whittier Ave Suite 303A McLean VA 22101
Ph: 703-790-0320 ▪ Fx: 703-790-0264

Intelligence Professionals, Naval — www.navintpro.org
PO Box 9324 McLean VA 22102
Ph: 202-554-8095

Intelligence Professionals, Society of Competitive — www.scip.org
1700 Diagonal Rd Suite 600 Alexandria VA 22314
Ph: 703-739-0696 ▪ Fx: 703-739-2524

Intelligent Arts, Global Alliance for — www.global-alliance.com
PO Box 403 Northampton MA 01061
Ph: 413-584-3022

Intelligent Transportation Society of America — www.itsa.org
400 Virginia Ave SW Suite 800 Washington DC 20024
Ph: 202-484-4847 ▪ Fx: 202-484-3483 ▪ TF: 800-374-8472

Inter-American Association of Sanitary & Environmental Engineering — www.aidis-usa.org
601 Wythe St Alexandria VA 22314
Ph: 703-684-2400

Inter-American Bar Association — www.iaba.org
1211 Connecticut Ave NW Suite 202 Washington DC 20036
Ph: 202-393-1217 ▪ Fx: 202-393-1241

Inter-American Commission on Human Rights — www.oas.org
1889 F St NW 5th Fl Washington DC 20006
Ph: 202-458-6002 ▪ Fx: 202-458-3992

Inter-American Commission of Women — www.oas.org/CIM/
1889 F St NW Rm 880 Washington DC 20006
Ph: 202-458-6084 ▪ Fx: 202-458-6094

Inter-American Council for Integral Development — www.cidi.oas.org
1889 F St NW Rm 220I Washington DC 20006
Ph: 202-458-3783 ▪ Fx: 202-458-3526

Inter-American Dialogue — www.thedialogue.org
1211 Connecticut Ave NW Suite 510 Washington DC 20036
Ph: 202-822-9002 ▪ Fx: 202-822-9553

Inter American Press Association — sipiapa.org
1801 SW 3rd Ave 7th Fl Miami FL 33129
Ph: 305-634-2465 ▪ Fx: 305-635-2272 ▪ TF: 877-747-4272

Inter-American Tropical Tuna Commission — www.iattc.org
8604 La Jolla Shores Dr La Jolla CA 92037
Ph: 858-546-7100 ▪ Fx: 858-546-7133

Inter-Association Task Force on Alcohol & Other Substance Abuse Issues www.iatf.org
PO Box 100430   Denver CO 80250
Ph: 303-871-0901 ▪ Fx: 303-871-0907

Inter-Collegiate Sailing Association of North America www.collegesailing.org
Old Dominion Univ H&PE Bldg Rm 101   Norfolk VA 23529
Ph: 757-683-3387 ▪ Fx: 757-683-6124

Inter-Society Color Council www.iscc.org
11491 Sunset Hills Rd Suite 301   Reston VA 20190
Ph: 703-318-0263 ▪ Fx: 703-318-0514

Inter-University Consortium for Political & Social Research www.icpsr.umich.edu
Univ of Michigan Institute for Social Research PO Box
1248   Ann Arbor MI 48106
Ph: 734-647-5000 ▪ Fx: 734-647-8200

InterAct Ministries www.interactministries.org
31000 SE Kelso Rd   Boring OR 97009
Ph: 800-258-3464

InterAction www.interaction.org
1717 Massachusetts Ave NW Suite 701   Washington DC 20036
Ph: 202-667-8227 ▪ Fx: 202-667-8236

Interactive Advertising Bureau www.iab.net
200 Park Ave S Suite 501   New York NY 10003
Ph: 212-949-9033

Interactive Audio Special Interest Group www.iasig.org
c/o MIDI Manufacturers Assn PO Box 3173   La Habra CA
90632
Ph: 714-736-9774 ▪ Fx: 714-736-9775

Interactive Entertainment Merchants Association www.iema.org
64 Danbury Rd Suite 700   Wilton CT 06897
Ph: 203-761-6780 ▪ Fx: 203-761-6184

Interactive Marketing, Association for www.interactivehq.org
1430 Broadway 8th Fl   New York NY 10018
Ph: 212-790-1404 ▪ Fx: 212-391-9233 ▪ TF: 888-337-0008

Interactive Multimedia & Collaborative Communications Association www.imcca.org
PO Box 756   Syosset NY 11771
Ph: 516-818-8184 ▪ Fx: 516-922-2170

Interagency Council on Information Resources for Nursing www.icirn.org

Interamerican Accounting Association
275 Fountainebleau Blvd Suite 245   Miami FL 33172
Ph: 305-225-1991 ▪ Fx: 305-225-2011

Interamerican College of Physicians & Surgeons www.icps.org
915 Broadway Suite 1105   New York NY 10102
Ph: 212-777-3642 ▪ Fx: 212-777-5000

InterAmerican Heart Foundation www.interamericanheart.org
7272 Greenville Ave   Dallas TX 75231
Ph: 972-562-3806 ▪ Fx: 972-562-3807

Interamerican Travel Agents Society
248 S Alden St   Philadelphia PA 19139
Ph: 215-471-5321 ▪ Fx: 215-471-5473

Interart Center, Women's
549 W 52nd St   New York NY 10019
Ph: 212-246-1050

Intercessors for America Inc www.ifapray.org
PO Box 915   Purcellville VA 20134
Ph: 800-872-7729

Interchurch Medical Assistance Inc www.interchurch.org
500 Main St PO Box 429   New Windsor MD 21776
Ph: 410-635-8720 ▪ Fx: 410-635-8726

Intercoiffure America www.intercoiffure.bz
540 Robert E Lee Blvd   New Orleans LA 70134
Ph: 504-282-4907 ▪ Fx: 504-282-5531

Intercollegiate Athletic Association, Central www.theciaa.com
303 Butler Farm Rd Suite 102   Hampton VA 23666
Ph: 757-865-0071 ▪ Fx: 757-865-8436

Intercollegiate Athletics, National Association of www.naia.org
23500 W 105th St   Olathe KS 66051
Ph: 913-791-0044 ▪ Fx: 913-791-9555

Intercollegiate Broadcasting System Inc www.ibsradio.org
367 Windsor Hwy   New Windsor NY 12553
Ph: 845-565-0003 ▪ Fx: 845-565-7446

Intercollegiate Fencing Association ifa.ecac.org
PO Box 3   Centerville MA 02632
Ph: 508-771-5060 ▪ Fx: 508-771-9481

Intercollegiate Men's Choruses www.cco.caltech.edu/~dgc/imc.html
Kansas State Univ 109 McCain Auditorium   Manhattan KS
66506
Ph: 785-532-3824 ▪ Fx: 785-532-5709

Intercollegiate Rodeo Association, National www.collegerodeo.com
2316 Eastgate N St Suite 160   Walla Walla WA 99362
Ph: 509-529-4402 ▪ Fx: 509-525-1090

Intercollegiate Rowing Association rowing.ecac.org
PO Box 3   Centerville MA 02632
Ph: 508-771-5060 ▪ Fx: 508-771-9481

Intercollegiate Soccer Officials Association, National www.nisoa.com
541 Woodview Dr   Longwood FL 32779
Ph: 407-862-3305 ▪ Fx: 407-862-8545

Intercollegiate Studies Institute www.isi.org
3901 Centerville Rd   Wilmington DE 19807
Ph: 302-652-4600 ▪ Fx: 302-652-1760 ▪ TF: 800-526-7022

Intercollegiate Tennis Association www.itatennis.com
174 Tamarack Cir   Skillman NJ 08558
Ph: 609-497-6920 ▪ Fx: 609-497-9766

Interconnection Technology, International Institute of Connector & www.iicit.org
PO Box 665   Hudson MA 01749
Ph: 978-568-0717 ▪ Fx: 978-568-0716 ▪ TF: 800-854-4248

Intercultural Development Research Association www.idra.org
5835 Callaghan Rd Suite 350   San Antonio TX 78228
Ph: 210-444-1710 ▪ Fx: 210-444-1714

Intercultural Education Training & Research, International Society for 8835 SW Canyon Ln Suite 110   Portland OR 97225 www.sietarusa.org
Ph: 503-297-4622 ▪ Fx: 503-297-4695

(Intercultural Exchange) AFS International Inc www.afs.org
71 W 23rd St 17th Fl   New York NY 10010
Ph: 212-807-8686 ▪ Fx: 212-807-1001

(Intercultural Relations) Amizade Ltd www.amizade.org
920 William Pitt Union   Pittsburgh PA 15260
Ph: 888-973-4443 ▪ Fx: 412-648-1492

Intercultural Student Exchange, American www.aise.com
7720 Herschel Ave   La Jolla CA 92037
Ph: 858-459-9761 ▪ Fx: 858-459-5301

Intercultural Studies, Institute for www.mead2001.org/Aboutus.htm
67-A E 77th St   New York NY 10021
Ph: 212-737-1011

Interdenominational Foreign Mission Association of North America PO Box 398   Wheaton IL 60189 www.ifmamissions.org
Ph: 630-682-9270 ▪ Fx: 630-682-9278

Interdisciplinary Biblical Research Institute www.ibri.org
PO Box 423 200 N Main St   Hatfield PA 19440
Ph: 215-368-5000 ▪ Fx: 215-368-7002

Interest Compensation, National Council for Uniform www.ncuic.org
13665 Dulles Technology Dr Suite 300   Herndon VA 20171
Ph: 703-561-1100 ▪ Fx: 703-787-0996

Interex www.interex.org
PO Box 3439   Sunnyvale CA 94088
Ph: 408-747-0227 ▪ Fx: 408-747-0947 ▪ TF: 800-468-3739

InterExchange Inc www.interexchange.org
161 6th Ave   New York NY 10013
Ph: 212-924-0446 ▪ Fx: 212-924-0575

Interfaith Alliance www.interfaithalliance.org
1331 H St NW 11th Fl   Washington DC 20005
Ph: 202-639-6370 ▪ Fx: 202-639-6375

Interfaith Center on Corporate Responsibility www.iccr.org
475 Riverside Dr Rm 550   New York NY 10115
Ph: 212-870-2295 ▪ Fx: 212-870-2023

Interfaith Coalition on Aging, National www.ncoa.org
300 D St SW   Washington DC 20024
Ph: 202-479-1200 ▪ Fx: 202-479-0735 ▪ TF: 800-424-9046

Interfaith Committee for Worker Justice, National www.nicwj.org
1020 W Bryn Mawr Ave 4th Fl   Chicago IL 60660
Ph: 773-728-8400 ▪ Fx: 773-728-8409

Interfaith Council for the Protection of Animals & Nature
3691 Tuxedo Rd NW   Atlanta GA 30305
Ph: 404-814-1371

Interfaith Hospitality Network, National www.nihn.org
71 Summit Ave   Summit NJ 07901
Ph: 908-273-1100 ▪ Fx: 908-273-0030

(Interfaith) Temple of Understanding www.templeofunderstanding.org
720 5th Ave 16th Fl   New York NY 10019
Ph: 212-246-2746 ▪ Fx: 212-246-2340

Interfraternal Foundation, North American www.nif-inc.net
10023 Cedar Point Dr   Carmel IN 46032
Ph: 317-872-3304 ▪ Fx: 317-571-9686

Interfraternity Conference, National www.nicindy.org
3901 W 86th St Suite 390   Indianapolis IN 46268
Ph: 317-872-1112 ▪ Fx: 317-872-1134

Intergovernmental Relations Officials, National Association of County
c/o National Assn of Counties 440 1st St NW   Washington DC
20001
Ph: 202-393-6226

Interhemispheric Resource Center www.irc-online.org
PO Box 2178   Silver City NM 88062
Ph: 505-388-0208 ▪ Fx: 505-388-0619

Interhostel www.learn.unh.edu/interhostel
Univ of New Hampshire 6 Garrison Ave   Durham NH 03824
Ph: 603-862-1147 ▪ Fx: 603-862-1113 ▪ TF: 800-733-9753

Interior Design Association, International www.iida.org
13-122 Merchandise Mart   Chicago IL 60654
Ph: 312-467-1950 ▪ Fx: 312-467-0779 ▪ TF: 888-799-4432

Interior Design Education Research, Foundation for www.fider.org
146 Monroe Ctr NW Suite 1318   Grand Rapids MI 49503
Ph: 616-458-0400 ▪ Fx: 616-458-0460

Interior Design Educators Council www.idec.org
7150 Winton Dr Suite 300   Indianapolis IN 46268
Ph: 317-328-4437 ▪ Fx: 317-280-8527

Interior Design Qualification, National Council for www.ncidq.org
1200 18th St NW Suite 1001   Washington DC 20036
Ph: 202-721-0220 ▪ Fx: 202-721-0221

Interior Design Society www.interiordesignsociety.org
PO Box 2396   High Point NC 27261
Ph: 800-888-9590 ▪ Fx: 336-801-6110

Interior Designers, American Society of www.asid.org
608 Massachusetts Ave NE   Washington DC 20002
Ph: 202-546-3480 ▪ Fx: 202-546-3240

Interior Designers, Association of University www.auid.org

Interior Systems Construction Association, Ceilings & cisca.org
1500 Lincoln Hwy Suite 202   Saint Charles IL 60174
Ph: 630-584-1919 ▪ Fx: 630-584-2003

Interlocking Concrete Pavement Institute icpi.org
1444 'I' St NW Suite 700   Washington DC 20005
Ph: 202-712-9036 ▪ Fx: 202-408-0285 ▪ TF: 800-241-3652

Intermarket Agency Network www.intermarketnetwork.com
5307 S 92nd St   Hales Corners WI 53130
Ph: 414-425-8800 ▪ Fx: 414-425-0021

Intermediaries & Reinsurance Underwriters Association www.irua.com
971 Rt 202 N   Branchburg NJ 08876
Ph: 908-203-0211 ▪ Fx: 908-203-0213

Intermodal Association of North America www.intermodal.org
7501 Greenway Ctr Dr Suite 720   Greenbelt MD 20770
Ph: 301-982-3400 ▪ Fx: 301-982-4815

Intermodal Institute, Containerization &
195 Fairfield Ave Suite 4D   West Caldwell NJ 07006
Ph: 973-226-0160 ▪ Fx: 973-364-1212

Intermountain Forest Association www.ifia.com
3731 N Ramsey Rd Suite 110   Coeur d'Alene ID 83815
Ph: 208-667-4641 ▪ Fx: 208-664-0557

Internal Auditors, Association of Credit Union www.acuia.org
PO Box 1926   Columbus OH 43216
Ph: 614-221-9702 ▪ Fx: 614-221-2335 ▪ TF: 866-254-8128

Internal Management Consultants, Association of www.aimc.org
86 Clarendon Ave   Rutland VT 05777
Ph: 802-438-2882 ▪ Fx: 802-438-9859

Internal Medicine, American College of Veterinary www.acvim.org
1997 Wadsworth Blvd Suite A   Lakewood CO 80214
Ph: 303-231-9933 ▪ Fx: 303-231-0880 ▪ TF: 800-245-9081

Internal Medicine, Association of Program Directors in www.im.org/APDIM
2501 M St NW Suite 550   Washington DC 20037
Ph: 202-887-9450 ▪ Fx: 202-887-9447 ▪ TF: 800-622-4558

Internal Medicine, Clerkship Directors in www.im.org/cdim
2501 M St NW Suite 550   Washington DC 20037
Ph: 202-861-8600 ▪ Fx: 202-861-9731

Internal Medicine, Society of General www.sgim.org
2501 M St NW Suite 575   Washington DC 20037
Ph: 202-887-5150 ▪ Fx: 202-887-5405 ▪ TF: 800-822-3060

Internal Organs, American Society for Artificial www.asaio.com
PO Box C   Boca Raton FL 33429
Ph: 561-391-8589 ▪ Fx: 561-368-9153

International Academy of Compounding Pharmacists www.iacprx.org
PO Box 1365   Sugar Land TX 77487
Ph: 281-933-8400 ▪ Fx: 281-495-0602 ▪ TF: 800-927-4227

International Academy of Digital Arts & Sciences www.iadas.net
3515 24th St   San Francisco CA 94110
Ph: 415-824-2268 ▪ Fx: 415-826-9111

International Academy of Oral Medicine & Toxicology www.iaomt.org
8297 Championsgate Blvd Suite 193   Championsgate FL 33896
Ph: 863-420-6373 ▪ Fx: 863-420-6394

International Academy of Pathology www.iaphomepage.org
Armed Forces Institute of Pathology Walter Reed Compound
6825 16th St NW   Washington DC 20306
Ph: 202-782-2503 ▪ Fx: 202-782-7166

International Academy for Sports Dentistry www.acadsportsdent.org
118 Faye St   Farmersville IL 62533
Ph: 217-227-3431 ▪ Fx: 217-227-3438 ▪ TF: 800-273-1788

International Academy of Television Arts & Sciences www.iemmys.tv
142 W 57th St   New York NY 10019
Ph: 212-489-6969 ▪ Fx: 212-489-6557

International Academy of Trial Lawyers www.iatl.net
5041 Cedar Lake Rd Suite 204   Minneapolis MN 55416
Ph: 952-546-2364 ▪ Fx: 952-545-6073 ▪ TF: 866-823-2443

International Accounts Payable Professionals www.iappnet.org
PO Box 590373   Orlando FL 32859
Ph: 407-351-322 ▪ Fx: 407-345-8361

International Action Center www.iacenter.org
39 W 14th St Suite 206   New York NY 10011
Ph: 212-633-6646 ▪ Fx: 212-633-2889

International Advertising Association www.iaaglobal.org
521 5th Ave Suite 1807   New York NY 10175
Ph: 212-557-1133 ▪ Fx: 212-983-0455

International Aerobatic Club www.iac.org
PO Box 3086   Oshkosh WI 54903
Ph: 920-426-4800 ▪ Fx: 920-426-6865

International Affairs, Association of Professional Schools of www.apsia.org
2101 Van Munching Hall   College Park MD 20742
Ph: 301-405-7553 ▪ Fx: 301-405-4675

International Affairs, Belfer Center for Science & bcsia.ksg.harvard.edu
Harvard Univ John F Kennedy School of Government 79 JFK
St   Cambridge MA 02138
Ph: 617-495-1400

International Affairs, Carnegie Council on Ethics & www.carnegiecouncil.org
Merrill House 170 E 64th St   New York NY 10021
Ph: 212-838-4120 ▪ Fx: 212-752-2432

International Affairs, Weatherhead Center for www.wcfia.harvard.edu
Harvard Univ 1033 Massachusetts Ave   Cambridge MA 02138
Ph: 617-495-4420 ▪ Fx: 617-495-8292

International Agricultural Aviation Foundation www.agpilot.com
PO Box 1607   Mount Vernon WA 98273
Ph: 360-724-3881 ▪ TF: 888-490-8206

International Agriculture & Rural Development, Association for aiard.org
Mississippi State Univ Dept of Agricultural Economics Box
5187   Mississippi State MS 39762
Ph: 662-325-0549 ▪ Fx: 662-325-8777

International Aid Inc www.gospelcom.net/ia
17011 W Hickory St   Spring Lake MI 49456
Ph: 616-846-7490 ▪ Fx: 616-846-3842 ▪ TF: 800-968-7490

International AIDS Vaccine Initiative www.iavi.org
110 Williams St 27th Fl   New York NY 10038
Ph: 212-847-1111 ▪ Fx: 212-847-1112

International Air Cargo Association www.tiaca.org
5600 NW 36th St Suite 620   Miami FL 33159
Ph: 786-265-7011 ▪ Fx: 786-265-7012

International Air Transport Association www.iata.org
800 Pl Victoria PO Box 113   Montreal QC H4Z1M1
Ph: 514-874-0202 ▪ Fx: 514-874-9632

International Airline Passengers Association www.iapa.com
PO Box 700188   Dallas TX 75370
Ph: 972-404-9980 ▪ Fx: 972-233-5348 ▪ TF: 800-821-4272

International Airlines Travel Agent Network www.iatan.org
300 Garden City Plaza Suite 342   Garden City NY 11530
Ph: 516-663-6000 ▪ Fx: 516-747-4462 ▪ TF: 800-294-2826

International Alliance of Healthcare Educators www.iahe.com
11211 Prosperity Farms Rd Suite D-325   Palm Beach Gardens
FL 33410
Ph: 561-622-4334 ▪ Fx: 561-622-4771

International Alliance of Messianic Congregations & Synagogues iamcs.org
PO Box 20006   Sarasota FL 34276
Ph: 941-923-0193 ▪ TF: 866-426-2766

**International Alliance of Theatrical Stage Employees Moving
Picture Technicians Artists & Allied Crafts of the US Its
Territories & Canada**   1430 Broadway 20th Fl   New York www.iatse-intl.org
NY 10018
Ph: 212-730-1770 ▪ Fx: 212-921-7699 ▪ TF: 800-223-6872

International Alliance for Women www.tiaw.org
8405 Greensboro Dr Suite 800   McLean VA 22102
Ph: 703-506-3284 ▪ Fx: 703-506-3266

International Alliance for Women in Music music.acu.edu/www/iawm
Indiana University of Pennsylvania Dept of Music Rm
209   Indiana PA 15705
Ph: 724-357-7918 ▪ Fx: 724-357-9570

International Aloe Science Council www.iasc.org
415 E Airport Fwy Suite 260   Irving TX 75062
Ph: 972-258-8772 ▪ Fx: 972-258-8777

International & American Associations of Clinical Nutritionists www.iaacn.org
15280 Addison St Suite 130   Addison TX 75001
Ph: 972-407-9089 ▪ Fx: 972-250-0233

International Andalusian Lusitano Horse Association www.ialha.com
101 Carnoustie N Suite 200   Birmingham AL 35242
Ph: 205-995-8900 ▪ Fx: 205-995-8966

International Anesthesia Research Society www.iars.org
2 Summit Pk Dr Suite 140   Cleveland OH 44131
Ph: 216-642-1124 ▪ Fx: 216-642-1127

International Animated Film Society www.asifa-hollywood.org
721 S Victory Blvd   Burbank CA 91502
Ph: 818-842-8330 ▪ Fx: 818-842-5645

International Anti-Counterfeiting Coalition www.iacc.org
1725 K St NW Suite 1101   Washington DC 20006
Ph: 202-223-6667 ▪ Fx: 202-223-6668

International Aroid Society Inc www.aroid.org

International Aromatherapy & Herb Association www.aromaherbshow.com
3541 W Acapulco Ln   Phoenix AZ 85053
Ph: 602-938-4439

International Artists Network
PO Box 182   Bowdoinham ME 04008
Ph: 207-666-8453

International Assembly for Collegiate Business Education www.iacbe.org
PO Box 25217   Overland Park KS 66225
Ph: 913-631-3009 ▪ Fx: 913-631-9154

International Association of Addictions & Offender Counselors www.counseling.org
5999 Stevenson Ave   Alexandria VA 22304
Ph: 800-347-6647 ▪ Fx: 800-473-2329

International Association of Addictions & Offender Counselors
c/o American Counseling Assn 5999 Stevenson Ave   Alexandria
VA 22304
Ph: 703-823-9800 ▪ Fx: 703-823-0252 ▪ TF: 800-347-6647

International Association of Administrative Professionals www.iaap-hq.org
10502 NW Ambassador Dr   Kansas City MO 64153
Ph: 816-891-6600 ▪ Fx: 816-891-9118

International Association of Airport Duty Free Stores www.iaadfs.org
2025 M St NW Suite 800   Washington DC 20036
Ph: 202-367-1184 ▪ Fx: 202-429-5154

International Association of Amusement Parks & Attractions www.iaapa.org
1448 Duke St   Alexandria VA 22314
Ph: 703-836-4800 ▪ Fx: 703-836-9678

International Association of Approved Basketball Officials www.iaabo.org
12321 Middlebrook Rd Suite 290   Germantown MD 20875
Ph: 301-601-8013 ▪ Fx: 301-601-8018

International Association for Aquatic Animal Medicine iaaam.org

**International Association of Aquatic & Marine Science
Libraries & Information Centers**   Harbor Branch www.iamslic.org
Oceanographic Institution 5600 US 1 N   Fort Pierce FL
34946
Ph: 561-465-2400 ▪ Fx: 561-465-2446

International Association of Arson Investigators www.fire-investigators.org
12770 Boenker Rd   Bridgeton MO 63044
Ph: 314-739-4224 ▪ Fx: 314-739-4219

International Association of Asian Studies
PO Box 325   Biddeford ME 04005
Ph: 207-839-8004 ▪ Fx: 207-839-3776

International Association of Assembly Managers iaam.org
635 Fritz Dr   Coppell TX 75019
Ph: 972-906-7441 ▪ Fx: 972-906-7418 ▪ TF: 800-965-4582

International Association of Assessing Officers www.iaao.org
130 E Randolph St Suite 850   Chicago IL 60601
Ph: 312-819-6100 ▪ Fx: 312-819-6149

International Association of Association Management Companies www.iaamc.org
414 Plaza Dr Suite 209   Westmont IL 60559
Ph: 630-655-1669 ▪ Fx: 630-655-0391

**International Association of Attorneys & Executives in
Corporate Real Estate**   20106 S Sycamore Dr   Frankfort IL www.aecre.org
60423
Ph: 815-464-6019 ▪ Fx: 815-464-8334

International Association of Audio Information Services www.iaais.org

International Association of Audio Visual Communicators www.iaavc.org
57 W Palo Verde Ave PO Box 250   Ocotillo CA 92259
Ph: 760-358-7000 ▪ Fx: 760-358-7569

International Association of Auto Theft Investigators   www.iaati.org
PO Box 223   Clinton NY 13323
Ph: 315-853-1913 ▪ Fx: 315-793-0048

International Association of Avian Trainers & Educators   www.iaate.org
350 St Andrews Fairway   Memphis TN 38111
Ph: 901-685-9122 ▪ Fx: 901-685-7233

International Association of Black Professional Fire Fighters   www.iabpff.org

International Association of Bowling Lane Specialists   www.nairbowl.org
5806 W 127th St   Alsip IL 60803
Ph: 708-371-8237 ▪ Fx: 708-371-8283

International Association for Bridge & Structural Engineering   www.iabse.ethz.ch

International Association of Bridge Structural Ornamental &   www.ironworkers.org
Reinforcing Iron Workers   1750 New York Ave NW Suite
400   Washington DC 20006
Ph: 202-383-4800 ▪ Fx: 202-638-4856 ▪ TF: 800-368-0105

International Association of Broadcast Monitors   www.iabm.com
PO Box 986   Irmo SC 29063
Ph: 800-236-1741 ▪ Fx: 888-732-9004

International Association of Business Communicators   www.iabc.com
1 Hallidie Plaza Suite 600   San Francisco CA 94102
Ph: 415-544-4700 ▪ Fx: 415-544-4747 ▪ TF: 800-766-4222

International Association of Campus Law Enforcement Administrators   www.iaclea.org
342 W Main St   West Hartford CT 06117
Ph: 860-586-7517 ▪ Fx: 860-586-7550

International Association of Career Consulting Firms   www.iaccf.com
1910 Cochran Rd Suite 740   Pittsburgh PA 15220
Ph: 800-565-2182

International Association of Career Management Professionals   www.iacmp.org
204 'E' St NE   Washington DC 20002
Ph: 202-547-6377 ▪ Fx: 202-547-6348

International Association of Chiefs of Police   www.theiacp.org
515 N Washington St   Alexandria VA 22314
Ph: 703-836-6767 ▪ Fx: 703-836-4543 ▪ TF: 800-843-4227

International Association for Child & Adolescent Psychiatry &   www.iacapap.org
Allied Professions

International Association for Cold Storage Construction   www.iacsc.org
1500 King St Suite 201   Alexandria VA 22314
Ph: 703-373-4300 ▪ Fx: 703-373-4301

International Association for Colon Hydrotherapy   www.i-act.org
PO Box 461285   San Antonio TX 78246
Ph: 210-366-2888 ▪ Fx: 210-366-2999

International Association of Color Manufacturers   www.iacmcolor.org
1620 'I' St NW Suite 925   Washington DC 20006
Ph: 202-293-5800 ▪ Fx: 202-463-8998

International Association of Commercial Collectors   www.commercialcollector.com
4040 W 70th St   Minneapolis MN 55435
Ph: 952-925-0760 ▪ Fx: 952-926-1624

International Association for Computer Information Systems   www.iacis.org

International Association for Computer Systems Security   www.iacss.com
6 Swarthmore Ln   Dix Hills NY 11746
Ph: 631-499-1616 ▪ Fx: 631-462-9178

International Association of Conference Center Administrators   www.iacca.org
1685 S Colorado Blvd Unit S   Denver CO 80222
Ph: 303-757-3303 ▪ Fx: 303-753-1455

International Association of Conference Centers   www.iacconline.org
243 N Lindbergh Blvd   Saint Louis MO 63141
Ph: 314-993-8575 ▪ Fx: 314-993-8919

International Association for Continuing Education & Training   www.iacet.org
1620 'I' St NW Suite 615   Washington DC 20006
Ph: 202-463-2905 ▪ Fx: 202-463-8497

International Association of Convention & Visitor Bureaus   www.iacvb.org
2025 M St NW Suite 500   Washington DC 20036
Ph: 202-296-7888 ▪ Fx: 202-296-7889

International Association of Corporate & Professional Recruitment   www.iacpr.org
20 N Wacker Dr Suite 2262   Chicago IL 60606
Ph: 312-630-9881 ▪ Fx: 312-630-9882

International Association of Correctional Training Personnel   www.iactp.org
PO Box 11018   Albany NY 12211
Ph: 518-783-6939

International Association of Counseling Services   www.iacsinc.org
101 S Whiting St Suite 211   Alexandria VA 22304
Ph: 703-823-9840 ▪ Fx: 703-823-9843

International Association of Counselors & Therapists   www.iact.org
10915 Bonita Beach Rd SE Suite 1101   Bonita Springs FL
34135
Ph: 941-498-9710 ▪ Fx: 941-498-1215

International Association for Creative Dance   www.dancecreative.org
103 Princeton Ave   Providence RI 02907
Ph: 401-521-0546

International Association of Culinary Professionals   www.iacp.com
304 W Liberty St Suite 201   Louisville KY 40202
Ph: 502-581-9786 ▪ Fx: 502-589-3602

International Association of Defense Counsel   www.iadclaw.org
1 N Franklin St Suite 1205   Chicago IL 60606
Ph: 312-368-1494 ▪ Fx: 312-368-1854

International Association for Dental Research   www.iadr.com
1619 Duke St   Alexandria VA 22314
Ph: 703-548-0066 ▪ Fx: 703-548-1883

International Association of Diecutting & Diemaking   www.iadd.org
651 W Terra Cotta Ave Suite 132   Crystal Lake IL 60014
Ph: 815-455-7519 ▪ Fx: 815-455-7510 ▪ TF: 800-828-4233

International Association for Disability & Oral Health   www.iadh.org
Ohio State Univ College of Dentistry 305 W 12th Ave PO Box
182357   Columbus OH 43218
Ph: 614-292-1232 ▪ Fx: 614-292-4522

International Association of Dive Rescue Specialists   www.iadrs.org
201 N Link Ln   Fort Collins CO 80524
Ph: 970-482-1562 ▪ Fx: 970-482-0893 ▪ TF: 800-423-7791

International Association of Drilling Contractors   www.iadc.org
PO Box 4287   Houston TX 77210
Ph: 713-292-1945 ▪ Fx: 713-292-1946

International Association of Drilling Contractors PAC
PO Box 4287   Houston TX 77210
Ph: 281-578-7171 ▪ Fx: 281-578-0589

International Association of Eating Disorders Professionals   www.iaedp.com
PO Box 1295   Pekin IL 61555
Ph: 309-346-3341 ▪ Fx: 309-346-2874 ▪ TF: 800-800-8126

International Association of Electrical Inspectors   www.iaei.org
901 Waterfall Way Suite 602   Richardson TX 75080
Ph: 972-235-1455 ▪ Fx: 972-235-6858 ▪ TF: 800-786-4234

International Association of Electronic Keyboard Manufacturers   www.iaekm.com

International Association for Energy Economics   www.iaee.org
28790 Chagrin Blvd Suite 350   Cleveland OH 44122
Ph: 216-464-5365 ▪ Fx: 216-464-2737

International Association for the Exchange of Students Technology Experience
10400 Little Patuxent Pkwy Suite 250   Columbia MD 21044
Ph: 410-997-3069 ▪ Fx: 410-997-5186

International Association for Exhibition Management   www.iaem.org
PO Box 802425   Dallas TX 75380
Ph: 972-458-8002 ▪ Fx: 972-458-8119

International Association of Fairs & Expositions   www.iafenet.org
PO Box 985   Springfield MO 65801
Ph: 417-862-5771 ▪ Fx: 417-862-0156 ▪ TF: 800-516-0313

International Association for the Fantastic in the Arts   wiz.cath.vt.edu/iafa

International Association of Financial Crimes Investigators   www.iafci.org
873 Embarcadero Dr Suite 5   El Dorado Hills CA 95762
Ph: 916-939-5000 ▪ Fx: 916-939-0395

International Association of Fire Chiefs   www.iafc.org
4025 Fair Ridge Dr Suite 300   Fairfax VA 22033
Ph: 703-273-0911 ▪ Fx: 703-273-9363

International Association of Fire Fighters   www.iaff.org
1750 New York Ave NW 3rd Fl   Washington DC 20006
Ph: 202-737-8484 ▪ Fx: 202-737-8418

International Association of Fish & Wildlife Agencies   www.iafwa.org
444 N Capitol St NW Suite 544   Washington DC 20001
Ph: 202-624-7890 ▪ Fx: 202-624-7891

International Association of Food Industry Suppliers   www.iafis.org
1451 Dolley Madison Blvd   McLean VA 22101
Ph: 703-761-2600 ▪ Fx: 703-761-4334

International Association for Food Protection   www.foodprotection.org
6200 Aurora Ave Suite 200W   Des Moines IA 50322
Ph: 515-276-3344 ▪ Fx: 515-276-8655 ▪ TF: 800-369-6337

International Association of Forensic Toxicologists   www.tiaft.org

International Association of Gay Square Dance Clubs   www.iagsdc.org
PO Box 87507   San Diego CA 92138
Ph: 800-835-6462

International Association of Geophysical Contractors   www.iagc.org
2550 North Loop W Suite 104   Houston TX 77092
Ph: 713-957-8080 ▪ Fx: 713-957-0008

International Association of Golf Administrators   www.iaga.org
3740 Cahuenga Blvd   North Hollywood CA 91604
Ph: 818-980-3630 ▪ Fx: 818-980-5019

International Association for Great Lakes Research   www.iaglr.org
2205 Commonwealth Blvd   Ann Arbor MI 48105
Ph: 734-665-5303 ▪ Fx: 734-741-2055

International Association for Greek Philosophy   www.hri.org/iagp

International Association of Healthcare Central Service Materiel   www.iahcsmm.com
Management   213 W Institute Pl Suite 307   Chicago IL 60610
Ph: 312-440-0078 ▪ Fx: 312-440-9474 ▪ TF: 800-962-8274

International Association of Healthcare Practitioners   www.iahp.com
11211 Prosperity Farms Rd Suite D-325   Palm Beach Gardens
FL 33410
Ph: 561-622-4334 ▪ Fx: 561-622-4771 ▪ TF: 800-233-5880

International Association for Healthcare Security & Safety   www.iahss.org
PO Box 5038   Glendale Heights IL 60139
Ph: 630-871-9936 ▪ Fx: 630-871-9938 ▪ TF: 888-353-0990

International Association of Heat & Frost Insulators &   www.insulators.org
Asbestos Workers   9602 ML King Jr Hwy   Lanham MD 20706
Ph: 301-731-9101 ▪ Fx: 301-731-5058

International Association of Holiday Inns   www.iahi.org
3 Ravinia Dr Suite 100   Atlanta GA 30346
Ph: 770-604-5555 ▪ Fx: 770-604-5684 ▪ TF: 866-826-5808

International Association of Home Safety & Security Professionals
PO Box 2044   Erie PA 16512
Ph: 814-456-2911

International Association for Human Resource Information   www.ihrim.org
Management   PO Box 1086   Burlington MA 01803
Ph: 800-946-6363 ▪ Fx: 781-998-8011

International Association for Hydrogen Energy   www.iahe.org
PO Box 248266   Coral Gables FL 33124
Ph: 305-284-4666 ▪ Fx: 305-284-4792

International Association of Ice Cream Vendors   www.iaicv.org
1900 Arch St   Philadelphia PA 19103
Ph: 215-564-3484 ▪ Fx: 215-564-2175

International Association for Identification   www.theiai.org/
2535 Pilot Knob Rd Suite 117   Mendota Heights MN 55120
Ph: 651-681-8566 ▪ Fx: 651-681-8443

International Association for Impact Assessment   www.iaia.org
1330 23rd St S Suite C   Fargo ND 58103
Ph: 701-297-7908 ▪ Fx: 701-297-7917

International Association of Industrial Accident Boards & Commissions   www.iaiabc.org
5610 Medical Cir Suite 14   Madison WI 53711
Ph: 608-663-6355 ▪ Fx: 608-663-1546

International Association of Infant Massage   www.iaim-us.com
1891 Goodyear Ave Suite 622   Ventura CA 93003
Ph: 805-644-8524 ▪ Fx: 805-644-7699 ▪ TF: 800-248-5432

International Association of Insurance Fraud Agencies www.iaifa.org
PO Box 10018   Kansas City MO 64171
Ph: 816-756-5285 ▪ Fx: 816-756-5287

International Association of Insurance Receivers www.iair.org
174 Grace Blvd   Altamonte Springs FL 32714
Ph: 407-682-4513 ▪ Fx: 407-682-3175

International Association of Jazz Education www.iaje.org
PO Box 724   Manhattan KS 66505
Ph: 785-776-8744 ▪ Fx: 785-776-6190

International Association of Jazz Record Collectors rhythmsociety.net/iajrc

International Association of Jewish Vocational Services www.iajvs.org/
1845 Walnut St Suite 640   Philadelphia PA 19103
Ph: 215-854-0233 ▪ Fx: 215-854-0212

International Association of Knowledge Engineers www.iake.org
973 Russell Ave Suite D   Gaithersburg MD 20879
Ph: 301-948-5390 ▪ Fx: 301-926-4243

International Association for Language Learning Technology www.iallt.org

International Association of Laryngectomees www.larynxlink.com
PO Box 691060   Stockton CA 95269
Ph: 866-425-3678 ▪ Fx: 209-472-0516

International Association of Law Enforcement Firearms Instructors www.ialefi.com
25 Country Club Rd Suite 707   Gilford NH 03249
Ph: 603-524-8787 ▪ Fx: 603-524-8856

International Association of Law Enforcement Planners www.ialep.org
PO Box 11437   Torrance CA 90510
Ph: 310-225-5148

International Association for the Leisure & Entertainment Industry www.ialei.org
33 Henniker St   Hillsborough NH 03244
Ph: 603-464-6498 ▪ Fx: 603-464-6497 ▪ TF: 888-464-6498

International Association of Libraries & www.theatrelibrary.org/sibmas/sibmas.html
Museums of the Performing Arts-USA

International Association of Lighting Designers www.iald.org
200 World Trade Ctr Merchandise Mart Suite 9-104   Chicago IL
60654
Ph: 312-527-3677 ▪ Fx: 312-527-3680

interNational Association of Lighting Management Cos www.nalmco.org
431 E Locust St Suite 300   Des Moines IA 50309
Ph: 515-243-2360 ▪ Fx: 515-243-2049

International Association of Lions Clubs www.lionsclubs.org
300 W 22nd St   Oak Brook IL 60523
Ph: 630-571-5466 ▪ Fx: 630-571-8890

International Association of Machinists & Aerospace Workers www.iamaw.org
9000 Machinists Pl   Upper Marlboro MD 20772
Ph: 301-967-4500 ▪ Fx: 301-967-4588

International Association of Management www.aom-iaom.org
920 S Battlefield Blvd Suite 100   Chesapeake VA 23322
Ph: 757-482-2273 ▪ Fx: 757-482-0325

International Association of Marriage & Family Counselors www.iamfc.com
c/o American Counseling Assn 5999 Stevenson Ave   Alexandria
VA 22304
Ph: 703-823-9800 ▪ Fx: 703-823-0252 ▪ TF: 800-545-2223

International Association for Medical Assistance to Travellers www.iamat.org
40 Regal Rd   Guelph ON N1K1B5
Ph: 519-836-0102 ▪ Fx: 519-836-3412

International Association of Museum Facility Administrators www.iamfa.org
c/o High Museum of Art 1280 Peachtree Rd NE   Atlanta GA
30309
Ph: 404-733-4407 ▪ Fx: 404-733-4502

International Association of Music Libraries Archives & www.iaml.info
Documentation Centres

International Association of Natural Resource Pilots www.ianrp.org

International Association for Near-Death Studies www.iands.org
PO Box 502   East Windsor Hill CT 06028
Ph: 860-882-1211 ▪ Fx: 860-882-1212

International Association of Nitrox & Technical Divers www.iantd.com
9628 NE 2nd Ave Suite D   Miami Shores FL 33138
Ph: 305-751-4873 ▪ Fx: 305-751-3958

International Association of Ocular Surgeons
820 N Orleans St Suite 208   Chicago IL 60610
Ph: 312-440-0699 ▪ Fx: 312-440-0580 ▪ TF: 800-621-4002

International Association of Official Human Rights Agencies www.sso.org/iaohra
444 N Capitol St NW Suite 536   Washington DC 20001
Ph: 202-624-5410 ▪ Fx: 202-624-8185

International Association of Operative Millers www.aomillers.org
5001 College Blvd Suite 104   Leawood KS 66211
Ph: 913-338-3377 ▪ Fx: 913-338-3553

International Association for Orthodontics www.iaortho.org
750 N Lincoln Memorial Dr Suite 422   Milwaukee WI 53202
Ph: 414-272-2757 ▪ Fx: 414-272-2754

InterNational Association of Parents & Professionals for www.napsac.org
Safe Alternatives in Childbirth   Rt 4 Box 646   Marble Hill MO
63764
Ph: 573-238-2010

International Association of Personal Protection Agents www.iappa.org
PO Box 266   Arlington Heights IL 60006
Ph: 847-870-8007 ▪ Fx: 847-870-8990

International Association of Personnel in Employment Security
International Assn of Workforce Professionals 1801 Louisville
Rd   Frankfort KY 40601
Ph: 502-223-4459 ▪ Fx: 502-223-4127 ▪ TF: 888-898-9960

International Association of Pet Cemeteries www.iaopc.com
5055 Rt 11 PO Box 163   Ellenburg Depot NY 12935
Ph: 518-594-3000 ▪ Fx: 518-594-8801

International Association for Philosophy of Law & www.cirfid.unibo.it/ivr
Social Philosophy   Univ of Hawaii at Manoa Dept of
Philosophy 2530 Dole St   Honolulu HI 96822
Ph: 808-956-8954 ▪ Fx: 808-956-9228

International Association for Philosophy & Literature www.iapl.info
Stony Brook University   Stony Brook NY 11794
Ph: 631-632-7592 ▪ Fx: 631-331-0142

International Association of Physical www.rit.edu/~pjr0120/csa/iapaas/main.html
Activity Aging & Sports   706 Madison Ave   Albany NY 12208
Ph: 518-465-6927 ▪ Fx: 518-462-1339

International Association for the Physical Sciences of the Oceans www.iugg.org/iapso
PO Box 820440   Vicksburg MS 39182
Ph: 601-636-1363 ▪ Fx: 601-629-9640

International Association of Physicians in AIDS Care www.iapac.org
33 N LaSalle St Suite 1700   Chicago IL 60602
Ph: 312-795-4930 ▪ Fx: 312-795-4938

International Association of Plastics Distributors www.iapd.org
4707 College Blvd Suite 105   Leawood KS 66211
Ph: 913-345-1005 ▪ Fx: 913-345-1006

International Association of Plumbing & Mechanical Officials www.iapmo.org
5001 E Philadelphia St   Ontario CA 91761
Ph: 909-472-4100 ▪ Fx: 909-472-4150 ▪ TF: 800-854-2766

International Association of Printing House Craftsmen www.iaphc.org
7042 Brooklyn Blvd   Minneapolis MN 55429
Ph: 763-560-1620 ▪ Fx: 763-560-1350 ▪ TF: 800-466-4274

International Association of Privacy Professionals www.privacyassociation.org
1211 Locust St   Philadelphia PA 19107
Ph: 215-545-8990 ▪ Fx: 215-545-8107 ▪ TF: 800-266-6501

International Association of Professional Security Consultants www.iapsc.org
525 SW 5th St Suite A   Des Moines IA 50309
Ph: 515-282-8192 ▪ Fx: 515-282-9117

International Association for the Properties of Water & Steam www.iapws.org

International Association for Property & Evidence Inc www.iape.org
903 N San Fernando Blvd Suite 4   Burbank CA 91504
Ph: 818-846-2926 ▪ Fx: 818-846-4543 ▪ TF: 800-449-4273

International Association of Psychosocial Rehabilitation Services www.iapsrs.org
601 N Hammonds Ferry Rd Suite A   Linthicum MD 21090
Ph: 410-789-7054 ▪ Fx: 410-789-7675

International Association for Public Participation www.iap2.org
11166 Huron St Suite 27   Denver CO 80234
Ph: 303-451-9545 ▪ Fx: 303-458-0002 ▪ TF: 800-644-4273

International Association of Pupil Personnel Workers www.iappw.com
2940 N Stratham Pt   Hernando FL 34442
Ph: 352-637-0653 ▪ Fx: 352-637-0926

International Association of Railway Operating Officers www.iaroo.org
621 Peacock Cir   Pontoon City IL 62040
Ph: 618-931-8208 ▪ Fx: 618-931-8209

International Association of Refrigerated Warehouses www.iarw.org
1500 King St Suite 201   Alexandria VA 22314
Ph: 703-373-4300 ▪ Fx: 703-373-4301

International Association of Registered Financial Consultants www.iarfc.org
2507 N Venty Pkwy PO Box 42506   Middletown OH 45042
Ph: 513-424-6395 ▪ Fx: 513-424-5752 ▪ TF: 800-532-9060

International Association of Rehabilitation Professionals www.rehabpro.org
3540 Soqel Ave Suite A   Santa Cruz CA 95062
Ph: 831-464-4892 ▪ Fx: 831-576-1417 ▪ TF: 800-240-9059

International Association for Research in Income & Wealth www.econ.nyu.edu/iariw
New York Univ Dept of Economics 269 Mercer St Rm
700   New York NY 10003
Ph: 212-924-4386 ▪ Fx: 212-366-5067

International Association for Research in Vietnamese Music
2005 Willow Ridge Cir   Kent OH 44240
Ph: 330-673-3763 ▪ Fx: 330-673-4434

International Association of Reservation Executives www.iare.com
7853 Arapahoe Ct Suite 2100   Centennial CO 80112
Ph: 303-694-4728 ▪ Fx: 303-694-4869

International Association of Round Dance Teachers Inc www.roundalab.org
355 N Orchard St Suite 200   Boise ID 83706
Ph: 208-377-1232 ▪ Fx: 208-377-1236 ▪ TF: 800-346-7522

International Association of School Librarianship www.iasl-slo.org

International Association of Skateboard Companies www.skateboardiasc.org
22431 Antonio Pkwy   Rancho Santa Margarita CA 92688
Ph: 949-589-8863 ▪ Fx: 949-589-3604

International Association of Speakers Bureaus www.iasbweb.org
2780 Waterfront Pkwy E Dr Suite 120   Indianapolis IN 46214
Ph: 317-297-0872 ▪ Fx: 317-387-3387

International Association of Special Investigation Units www.iasiu.com
8015 Corporate Dr Suite A   Baltimore MD 21236
Ph: 410-931-3332 ▪ Fx: 410-931-2060

International Association of Sports Museums & Halls of Fame www.sportshalls.com
180 N LaSalle St Suite 1822   Chicago IL 60601
Ph: 312-551-0810 ▪ Fx: 312-551-0815

International Association of Structural Movers www.iasm.org
PO Box 2637   Lexington SC 29071
Ph: 803-951-9304 ▪ Fx: 803-951-9314

International Association for the Study of Common Property www.iascp.org
PO Box 2355   Gary IN 46409
Ph: 219-980-1433 ▪ Fx: 219-980-2801

International Association for the Study of Cooperation in Education www.iasce.net
PO Box 390   Readfield ME 04355
Ph: 207-685-3171 ▪ Fx: 207-685-4455

International Association for the Study of Organized Crime www.iasoc.net
c/o National Institute of Justice 810 7th St NW   Washington
DC 20531
Ph: 202-616-1960 ▪ Fx: 202-307-6256

International Association for the Study of Pain www.iasp-pain.org
909 NE 43rd St Suite 306   Seattle WA 98105
Ph: 206-547-6409 ▪ Fx: 206-547-1703

International Association of Tartan www.scottish-coalition.org/TECA/teca.htm
Studies/Tartan Educational Cultural Assn   442 Freedom Blvd
PO Box 138   Skippack PA 19474
Ph: 610-584-4220 ▪ Fx: 610-584-6456

International Association of Teachers of Czech www.language.brown.edu/NAATC/

International Association of Theatre for Children & Young People www.assitej-usa.org
724 2nd Ave S Nashville TN 37210
Ph: 615-254-5719 ▪ Fx: 615-254-3255

International Association of Theoretical & Applied Limnology www.limnology.org

International Association of Torch Clubs www.torch.org
749 Boush St Norfolk VA 23510
Ph: 757-622-3927 ▪ Fx: 757-623-9740 ▪ TF: 888-622-4101

International Association of Tour Managers www.members.aol.com/iatmone
9500 Rainier Ave S Unit 603 Seattle WA 98118
Ph: 206-725-7108 ▪ Fx: 206-725-4020

International Association of Used Equipment Dealers www.iaued.org
214 Edgewood Dr Suite 100 Wilmington DE 19809
Ph: 302-765-3571

International Association of Wildland Fire www.iawfonline.org
4025 Fair Ridge Dr Fairfax VA 22033
Ph: 785-423-1818 ▪ Fx: 785-542-3511

International Association of Women Police www.iawp.org

International Atherosclerosis Society www.athero.org
6550 Fannin St Suite 1211 Houston TX 77030
Ph: 713-797-0401 ▪ Fx: 713-796-8853

International Atlantic Economic Society www.iaes.org
4949 W Pine Blvd 2nd Fl Saint Louis MO 63108
Ph: 314-454-0100 ▪ Fx: 314-454-9109

International Aviation Women Association www.iawa.org
PO Box 4491 New York NY 10163
Ph: 212-921-5100 ▪ Fx: 212-774-7415

International B-24 Liberator Club www.bomberlegends.com/b24club.html
1672 Main St Suite E PMB 124 Ramona CA 92065
Ph: 760-788-3624 ▪ Fx: 760-789-8911

International Banana Association www.eatmorebananas.com
1901 Pennsylvania Ave NW Suite 1100 Washington DC 20006
Ph: 202-303-3400 ▪ Fx: 202-303-3433

International Barbeque Cookers Association www.ibcabbq.org
PO Box 300556 Arlington TX 76007
Ph: 817-469-1579

International Benevolent Society Inc
PO Box 1276 Columbus GA 31902
Ph: 706-322-5671

International Betta Congress www.ibcbettas.org
923 Wadsworth St Syracuse NY 13208
Ph: 315-454-4792

International Beverage Dispensing Equipment Association www.ibdea.org
4145 Amos Ave Baltimore MD 21215
Ph: 410-764-0616 ▪ Fx: 410-764-6799

International Beverage Packaging Association www.ibpa.org
631 N Stephanie St Suite 564 Henderson NV 89014
Ph: 702-566-7103 ▪ Fx: 702-566-7166

International Bible Society www.gospelcom.net/ibs
1820 Jet Stream Dr Colorado Springs CO 80921
Ph: 719-488-9200 ▪ Fx: 719-488-0810 ▪ TF: 800-524-1588

International Bicycle Fund www.ibike.org
4887 Columbia Dr S Seattle WA 98108
Ph: 206-767-0848

International Biometric Society www.tibs.org
1444 'I' St NW Suite 700 Washington DC 20005
Ph: 202-712-9049 ▪ Fx: 202-216-9646

International Bird Rescue Research Center www.ibrrc.org
4369 Cordelia Rd Fairfield CA 94534
Ph: 707-207-0380 ▪ Fx: 707-207-0395

International Black Women's Congress www.ibwc.info
555 Fenchurch St Suite 102 Norfolk VA 23510
Ph: 757-625-0500 ▪ Fx: 757-625-1905

International Black Writers & Artists Inc members.tripod.com/~IBWA
PO Box 43576 Los Angeles CA 90043
Ph: 323-964-3721

International Blade Collectors Inc
c/o Krause Publications 700 E State St Iola WI 54990
Ph: 715-445-2214 ▪ Fx: 715-445-4087

International Bluegrass Music Association www.ibma.org
2 Music Cir S Suite 100 Nashville TN 37203
Ph: 615-256-3222 ▪ Fx: 615-256-0450 ▪ TF: 888-438-4262

International Board of Jewish Missions www.ibjm.org
1928 Hamill Rd PO Box 1386 Hixson TN 37343
Ph: 423-876-8150 ▪ Fx: 423-877-8156 ▪ TF: 888-876-8150

International Bond & Share Society www.scripophily.org
15 Dyatt Pl PO Box 430 Hackensack NJ 07602
Ph: 201-489-2440 ▪ Fx: 201-592-0282

International Bone Marrow Transplant Registry www.ibmtr.org
8701 Watertown Plank Rd PO Box 26509 Milwaukee WI 53226
Ph: 414-456-8325 ▪ Fx: 414-456-6530

International Bone & Mineral Society www.ibmsonline.org
2025 M St NW Suite 800 Washington DC 20036
Ph: 202-367-1121 ▪ Fx: 202-367-2121

International Book Bank www.internationalbookbank.org
2201 Eagle St Unit D Baltimore MD 21223
Ph: 410-362-0334 ▪ Fx: 410-362-0336 ▪ TF: 877-416-4265

International Book Project www.intlbookproject.org
1440 Delaware Ave Lexington KY 40505
Ph: 859-254-6771 ▪ Fx: 859-253-2293 ▪ TF: 888-999-2665

International Bottled Water Association www.bottledwater.org
1700 Diagonal Rd Suite 650 Alexandria VA 22314
Ph: 703-683-5213 ▪ Fx: 703-683-4074 ▪ TF: 800-928-3711

International Bowling Federation www.fiq.org
1631 Mesa Ave Suite A Colorado Springs CO 80906
Ph: 719-636-2695 ▪ Fx: 719-636-3300

International Bowling Pro Shop & Instructors Association www.ibpsia.com
4337 N Golden State Blvd Suite 109 Fresno CA 93722
Ph: 559-275-9245 ▪ Fx: 559-275-9250 ▪ TF: 800-659-9444

International Boxing Federation www.ibf-usba-boxing.com
134 Evergreen Pl 9th Fl East Orange NJ 07018
Ph: 973-414-0300 ▪ Fx: 973-414-0307

International Boys' Schools Coalition www.boysschoolscoalition.org
7 Forehand Dr PO Box 117 Dennis MA 02638
Ph: 508-385-4563 ▪ Fx: 508-385-4273

International Brangus Breeders Association www.int-brangus.org
5750 Epsilon PO Box 696020 San Antonio TX 78269
Ph: 210-696-4343 ▪ Fx: 210-696-8718

International Brecht Society german.lss.wisc.edu/brecht
Georgia Southern Univ Dept of Literature & Philosophy PO Box 8023 Statesboro GA 30460
Ph: 912-681-0155 ▪ Fx: 912-681-0653

International Brick Collectors' Association
3265 Hood Ct Wichita KS 67204
Ph: 316-831-9713

International Bridge Tunnel & Turnpike Association www.ibtta.org
1146 19th St NW Suite 800 Washington DC 20036
Ph: 202-659-4620 ▪ Fx: 202-659-0500

International Brotherhood of Boilermakers Iron Shipbuilders Blacksmiths Forgers & Helpers 753 State Ave Suite 570 www.boilermakers.org
Kansas City KS 66101
Ph: 913-371-2640 ▪ Fx: 913-281-8101

International Brotherhood of Correctional Officers www.ibco.org
159 Burgin Pkwy Quincy MA 02169
Ph: 617-376-0220 ▪ Fx: 617-376-0285

International Brotherhood of DuPont Workers www.dupontworkers.com
PO Box 16333 Louisville KY 40256
Ph: 502-569-3232

International Brotherhood of Electrical Workers www.ibew.org
1125 15th St NW Washington DC 20005
Ph: 202-833-7000 ▪ Fx: 202-467-6316

International Brotherhood of Electrical Workers PAC
1125 15th St NW Washington DC 20005
Ph: 202-833-7000 ▪ Fx: 202-467-6316

International Brotherhood of Live Steamers
26062 Todd Ln Los Altos Hills CA 94022
Ph: 650-948-8555

International Brotherhood of Magicians www.magician.org
11155-C South Towne Sq Saint Louis MO 63123
Ph: 314-845-9200 ▪ Fx: 314-845-9220

International Brotherhood of Motorcycle Campers www.ibmc.org
PO Box 375 Helper UT 84526
Ph: 435-650-3290

International Brotherhood of Police Officers www.ibpo.org
159 Burgin Pkwy Quincy MA 02169
Ph: 617-376-0220 ▪ Fx: 617-376-0285

International Brotherhood of Teamsters www.teamster.org
25 Louisiana Ave NW Washington DC 20001
Ph: 202-624-6800 ▪ Fx: 202-624-6918

International Buckskin Horse Association www.ibha.net
PO Box 268 Shelby IN 46377
Ph: 219-552-1013

International Builders Exchange Executives www.ibee.org
43636 Woodward Ave Suite 300 Bloomfield Hills MI 48302
Ph: 248-409-1504 ▪ Fx: 248-409-1503

International Bulb Society Inc www.bulbsociety.com

International Business, Academy of aib.msu.edu
Michigan State Univ Eli Broad College of Business 7 Eppley Ctr East Lansing MI 48824
Ph: 517-432-1452 ▪ Fx: 517-432-1009

International Business Brokers Association Inc www.ibba.org
401 N Michigan Ave Suite 2200 Chicago IL 60611
Ph: 312-321-4097 ▪ Fx: 312-673-6599 ▪ TF: 888-686-4222

International Business Fellows, Society of www.sibf.org
191 Peachtree St NE Suite 3220 Atlanta GA 30303
Ph: 404-525-7423 ▪ Fx: 404-525-5331

International Business Music Association www.ibma.net
PO Box 940 Franklin NC 28744
Ph: 828-369-2322

International Business, US Council for www.uscib.org
1212 Ave of the Americas 18th Fl New York NY 10036
Ph: 212-354-4480 ▪ Fx: 212-944-0012

International Cadmium Association www.cadmium.org
PO Box 924 Great Falls VA 22066
Ph: 703-759-7400 ▪ Fx: 703-759-7003

International Card Manufacturers Association www.icma.com
PO Box 727 Princeton Junction NJ 08550
Ph: 609-799-4900 ▪ Fx: 609-799-7032

International Cargo Gear Bureau www.icgb.com
120 W 44th St Suite 401 New York NY 10036
Ph: 917-510-9938 ▪ Fx: 917-510-9974

International Carnival Glass Association www.woodsland.com/ICGA
PO Box 306 Mentone IN 46539
Ph: 574-353-7678

International Carwash Association www.carwashes.com
401 N Michigan Ave Chicago IL 60611
Ph: 312-321-5199 ▪ Fx: 312-245-1085

International Cast Polymer Alliance www.icpa-hq.org
1010 N Glebe Rd Suite 450 Arlington VA 22201
Ph: 703-525-0320 ▪ Fx: 703-525-0743 ▪ TF: 800-414-4272

International Castor Oil Association www.icoa.org
656 Linwood Ave Ridgewood NJ 07450
Ph: 201-652-0889 ▪ Fx: 201-652-7383

International Cat Association www.tica.org
PO Box 2684 Harlingen TX 78551
Ph: 956-428-8046 ▪ Fx: 956-428-8047

International Catacomb Society www.catacombsociety.org
3 Lewis St PO Box 130439 Boston MA 02113
Ph: 617-742-1285 ▪ Fx: 617-742-1550

International Caterers Association www.icacater.org
1200 17th St NW Washington DC 20036
Ph: 888-604-5844

International Catholic Migration Commission www.icmc.net
MRS/US Conference of Catholic Bishops 3211 4th St
NE Washington DC 20017
Ph: 202-541-3389 ▪ Fx: 202-722-8755

International Catholic Stewardship Council www.catholicstewardship.org
1275 K St NW Suite 980 Washington DC 20005
Ph: 202-289-1093 ▪ Fx: 202-682-9018

International Cemetery & Funeral Association www.icfa.org
1895 Preston White Dr Suite 220 Reston VA 20191
Ph: 703-391-8400 ▪ Fx: 703-391-8416 ▪ TF: 800-645-7700

International Center for Alcohol Policies www.icap.org
1519 New Hampshire Ave NW Washington DC 20036
Ph: 202-986-1159 ▪ Fx: 202-986-2080

International Center for the Disabled www.icdrehab.org
340 E 24th St New York NY 10010
Ph: 212-585-6000 ▪ Fx: 212-585-6161

International Center for Economic Growth www.iceg.org
777 Campus Commons Rd Suite 200 Sacramento CA 95825
Ph: 916-563-7180 ▪ Fx: 916-929-0448

International Center for the Health Sciences www.ichsciences.org
Barracks Hill PO Box 4744 Charlottesville VA 22904
Ph: 804-971-7605

International Center for Journalists www.icfj.org
1616 H St NW 3rd Fl Washington DC 20006
Ph: 202-737-3700 ▪ Fx: 202-737-0530

International Center for Law in Development
777 United Nations Plaza Suite 7E New York NY 10017
Ph: 212-687-0036 ▪ Fx: 212-370-9844

International Center of Medieval Art www.medievalart.org
The Cloisters Fort Tryon Pk New York NY 10040
Ph: 212-928-1146 ▪ Fx: 212-928-9946

International Center in New York www.intlcenter.org
50 W 23rd St 7th Fl New York NY 10010
Ph: 212-255-9555 ▪ Fx: 212-255-0177

International Center for Not-for-Profit Law www.icnl.org
733 15th St NW Suite 420 Washington DC 20005
Ph: 202-624-0766 ▪ Fx: 202-624-0767

International Center for Research on Women www.icrw.org
1717 Massachusetts Ave NW Suite 302 Washington DC 20036
Ph: 202-797-0007 ▪ Fx: 202-797-0020

International Center for Technology Assessment www.icta.org
666 Pennsylvania Ave SE Suite 302 Washington DC 20003
Ph: 202-547-9359 ▪ Fx: 202-547-9429 ▪ TF: 800-600-6664

International Centre for Settlement of Investment Disputes www.worldbank.org/icsid
1818 H St NW Washington DC 20433
Ph: 202-458-1534 ▪ Fx: 202-522-2615

International Cesarean Awareness Network Inc www.ican-online.org
1304 Kingsdale Ave Redondo Beach CA 90278
Ph: 310-542-6400 ▪ Fx: 310-542-5368 ▪ TF: 800-686-4226

International Chain Salon Association www.icsa.cc
13331 Millbank Dr Plainfield IL 60544
Ph: 815-254-7477 ▪ Fx: 815-609-3969 ▪ TF: 866-444-4272

International Chamber of Commerce www.iccwbo.org
1212 Ave of the Americas New York NY 10036
Ph: 212-354-4480 ▪ Fx: 212-575-0327

International Chemical Workers Union Council www.icwuc.org
1655 W Market St Akron OH 44313
Ph: 330-867-2444 ▪ Fx: 330-867-0544

International Child Care Inc www.gospelcom.net/icc
3620 N High St Suite 110 Columbus OH 43214
Ph: 614-447-9952 ▪ Fx: 614-447-1123 ▪ TF: 800-722-4453

International Child Resource Institute www.icrichild.org
1581 Le Roy Ave Berkeley CA 94708
Ph: 510-644-1000 ▪ Fx: 510-525-4106

International Childbirth Education Association www.icea.org
PO Box 20048 Minneapolis MN 55420
Ph: 952-854-8660 ▪ Fx: 952-854-8772 ▪ TF: 800-624-4934

International Chinese Snuff Bottle Society Inc www.snuffbottle.org
2601 N Charles St Baltimore MD 21218
Ph: 410-467-9400 ▪ Fx: 410-243-3451

International Chiropractors Association www.chiropractic.org
1110 N Glebe Rd Suite 1000 Arlington VA 22201
Ph: 703-528-5000 ▪ Fx: 703-528-5023 ▪ TF: 800-423-4690

International Chiropractors Association PAC
1110 N Glebe Rd Suite 1000 Arlington VA 22201
Ph: 703-528-5000 ▪ Fx: 703-528-5023 ▪ TF: 800-423-4690

International Christian Accrediting Association www.oru.edu/oruef/icaa
7777 S Lewis Ave Tulsa OK 74171
Ph: 918-495-6163 ▪ Fx: 918-495-6175

International Christian Concern www.persecution.org
2020 Pennsylvania Ave NW Suite 941 Washington DC 20006
Ph: 301-989-1708 ▪ Fx: 301-989-1709 ▪ TF: 800-422-5441

International Christian Cycling Club USA www.ironclad.org
PO Box 411757 Aurora CO 80044
Ph: 720-870-3707

International Christian Studies Association www.jis3.org/abouticsa.htm
1065 Pine Bluff Dr Pasadena CA 91107
Ph: 626-351-0419

International Christian Technologists Association www.gospelcom.net/icta
15455 Gleneagle Dr Suite 210 Colorado Springs CO 80921
Ph: 719-785-0120 ▪ Fx: 719-785-0117

International Church of the Foursquare Gospel www.foursquare.org
1910 W Sunset Blvd Suite 200 Los Angeles CA 90026
Ph: 213-989-4200 ▪ Fx: 213-989-4590 ▪ TF: 888-635-4234

International City/County Management Association www.icma.org
777 N Capitol St NE Suite 500 Washington DC 20002
Ph: 202-289-4262 ▪ Fx: 202-962-3500

International Civil Aviation Organization www.icao.int
999 University St Montreal QC H3C5H7
Ph: 514-954-8219 ▪ Fx: 514-954-6077

International Civil Service Commission icsc.un.org
2 United Nations Plaza 10th Fl New York NY 10017
Ph: 212-963-5465 ▪ Fx: 212-963-0159

International Claim Association www.claim.org
1225 23rd St NW Suite 200 Washington DC 20037
Ph: 202-452-0143 ▪ Fx: 202-833-3636

International Clarinet Association www.clarinet.org
PO Box 5039 Wheaton IL 60189
Ph: 630-665-3602 ▪ Fx: 630-665-3848

International Coach Federation www.coachfederation.org
1441 'I' St NW Suite 700 Washington DC 20005
Ph: 202-712-9039 ▪ Fx: 202-216-9646 ▪ TF: 888-423-3131

International Coalition for Religious Freedom www.religiousfreedom.com
7777 Leesburg Pike Suite 404 N-A Falls Church VA 22043
Ph: 703-790-1500 ▪ Fx: 703-790-5562

International Code Council www.iccsafe.org
5203 Leesburg Pike Suite 600 Falls Church VA 22041
Ph: 703-931-4533 ▪ Fx: 703-379-1546

International College of Applied Kinesiology www.icakusa.com
6405 Metcalf Ave Suite 503 Shawnee Mission KS 66202
Ph: 913-384-5336 ▪ Fx: 913-384-5112

International College of Cranio-Mandibular Orthopedics tmj-iccmo.org
619 N 35th St Suite 307 Seattle WA 98103
Ph: 206-633-4355 ▪ Fx: 206-633-4352 ▪ TF: 800-446-1763

International College of Dentists www.icd.org
51 Monroe St Suite 1400 Rockville MD 20850
Ph: 301-251-8861 ▪ Fx: 301-738-9143

International College of Prosthodontists www.icp-org.com
PO Box 99119 San Diego CA 92169
Ph: 858-270-1814 ▪ Fx: 858-272-7687

International College of Surgeons www.icsglobal.org
1516 N Lake Shore Dr Chicago IL 60610
Ph: 312-642-3555 ▪ Fx: 312-787-1624

International Collegiate Licensing Association nacda.ocsn.com/icla/nacda-icla.html
24651 Detroit Rd Westlake OH 44145
Ph: 440-892-4000 ▪ Fx: 440-892-4007

International Commission on English in the Liturgy
1522 K St NW Suite 1000 Washington DC 20005
Ph: 202-347-0800

International Commission for the Prevention of Alcoholism &
Drug Dependency 12501 Old Columbia Pike Silver Spring
MD 20904
Ph: 301-680-6719 ▪ Fx: 301-680-6707

International Commission on Radiation Units & Measurements Inc www.icru.org
7910 Woodmont Ave Suite 400 Bethesda MD 20814
Ph: 301-657-2652 ▪ Fx: 301-907-8768

International Communication Association www.icahdq.org
1730 Rhode Island Ave NW Suite 300 Washington DC 20036
Ph: 202-530-9855 ▪ Fx: 202-530-9851

International Communications Industries Association www.infocomm.org
11242 Waples Mill Rd Suite 200 Fairfax VA 22030
Ph: 703-273-7200 ▪ Fx: 703-278-8082 ▪ TF: 800-659-7469

International Community Assistance, Foundation for www.villagebanking.org
1101 14th St NW 11th Fl Washington DC 20005
Ph: 202-682-1510 ▪ Fx: 202-682-3510

International Community Corrections Association www.iccaweb.org
PO Box 1987 La Crosse WI 54602
Ph: 608-785-0200 ▪ Fx: 608-784-5335

International Compressor Remanufacturers Association
PO Box 33092 Kansas City MO 64114
Ph: 816-333-7205 ▪ Fx: 816-822-8826

International Computer Music Association www.computermusic.org
PO Box 118 Gurdon AR 71743
Ph: 870-353-4997 ▪ Fx: 870-353-4151 ▪ TF: 800-979-9950

International Concrete Repair Institute www.icri.org
3166 S River Rd Suite 132 Des Plaines IL 60018
Ph: 847-827-0830 ▪ Fx: 847-827-0832

International Confederation for Plastic Reconstructive & www.ipras.org
Aesthetic Surgery 4 Executive Park Dr Albany NY 12203
Ph: 518-438-1434 ▪ Fx: 518-489-1205

International Conference of Funeral Service Examining Boards Inc www.cfseb.org
1885 Shelby Ln Fayetteville AR 72704
Ph: 479-442-7076 ▪ Fx: 479-442-7090

International Conference of Police Chaplains www.icpc4cops.org
PO Box 5590 Destin FL 32540
Ph: 850-654-9736 ▪ Fx: 850-654-9742

International Conference of Symphony & Opera Musicians www.icsom.org
4 W 31st St Unit 921 New York NY 10001
Ph: 212-594-1636

International Congress of Oral Implantologists www.dentalimplants.com
248 Lorraine Ave 3rd Fl Upper Montclair NJ 07043
Ph: 973-783-6300 ▪ Fx: 973-783-1175 ▪ TF: 800-442-0525

International Consortium on Governmental Financial Management www.icgfm.org/
444 N Capitol St Suite 234 Washington DC 20001
Ph: 202-624-8461 ▪ Fx: 202-624-5473

International Convention of Faith Ministries www.icfm.org
5500 Woodland Park Blvd Arlington TX 76013
Ph: 817-451-9620 ▪ Fx: 817-451-9621

International Cooperation, Canadian Council for www.ccic.ca
1 Nicholas St Suite 300 Ottawa ON K1N7B7
Ph: 613-241-7007 ▪ Fx: 613-241-5302

International Cooperation & Development, Institute for — www.iicd-volunteer.org
PO Box 520   Williamstown MA 01267
Ph: 413-458-9828 ▪ Fx: 413-458-3323

International Cooperation, Foundation for — www.ficcultureswap.org
1237 S Western Ave   Park Ridge IL 60068
Ph: 847-518-0934 ▪ Fx: 847-518-8384 ▪ TF: 800-890-3543

International Coordinating Council of Aerospace — www.aia-aerospace.org
Industries Association   1250 'I' St NW Suite
1200   Washington DC 20005
Ph: 202-371-8400 ▪ Fx: 202-371-8471

International Copper Association — www.copperinfo.com
260 Madison Ave 16th Fl   New York NY 10016
Ph: 212-251-7240 ▪ Fx: 212-251-7245

International Corrugated Case Association — www.iccanet.org
2850 Golf Rd Suite 412   Rolling Meadows IL 60008
Ph: 847-364-9600 ▪ Fx: 847-364-9639

International Corrugated Packaging Foundation — icpf.corrugated.org
113 S West St PO Box 25708   Alexandria VA 22313
Ph: 703-836-2422 ▪ Fx: 703-836-2795

International Cost Engineering Council — www.icoste.org

International Cotton Advisory Committee — www.icac.org
1629 K St NW Suite 702   Washington DC 20006
Ph: 202-463-6660 ▪ Fx: 202-463-6950

International Council of Academies of Engineering & — www.caets.org
Technological Sciences Inc   500 5th St NW   Washington DC
20001
Ph: 703-527-5782 ▪ Fx: 703-526-0570

International Council of Air Shows — www.airshows.org
751 Miller Dr SE Suite F-4   Leesburg VA 20175
Ph: 703-779-8510 ▪ Fx: 703-779-8511

International Council of Aircraft Owner & Pilot Associations — www.iaopa.org
421 Aviation Way   Frederick MD 21701
Ph: 301-695-2000 ▪ Fx: 301-695-2375

International Council of Community Churches — iccc-world.org
21116 Washington Pkwy   Frankfort IL 60423
Ph: 815-464-5690 ▪ Fx: 815-464-5692

International Council for Computer Communication — www.icccgovernors.org
PO Box 9745   Washington DC 20016
Ph: 703-836-7787

International Council of Cruise Lines — www.iccl.org
2111 Wilson Blvd 8th Fl   Arlington VA 22201
Ph: 703-522-8463 ▪ Fx: 703-522-3811 ▪ TF: 800-595-9338

International Council of Cruise Lines PAC
2111 Wilson Blvd 8th Fl   Arlington VA 22201
Ph: 703-522-8463 ▪ Fx: 703-522-3811

International Council of Employers of Bricklayers & Allied — www.icebac.org
Craftworkers   1776 'I' St NW   Washington DC 20006
Ph: 202-783-3788 ▪ Fx: 202-393-0222 ▪ TF: 888-880-8222

International Council of Fine Arts Deans — www.icfad.org
Pennsylvania State Univ 111 Arts Bldg   University Park PA
16802
Ph: 814-865-2593 ▪ Fx: 814-865-2018

International Council for Health Physical Education Recreation — www.ichpersd.org
Sport & Dance   1900 Association Dr   Reston VA 20191
Ph: 703-476-3462 ▪ Fx: 703-476-9527 ▪ TF: 800-213-7193

International Council on Hotel Restaurant & Institutional Education — www.chrie.org
2613 N Parham Rd 2nd Fl   Richmond VA 23294
Ph: 804-346-4800 ▪ Fx: 804-346-5009

International Council for Human Ecology & Ethnology — www.ichee.org
PO Box 7024   New York NY 10128
Ph: 212-410-6560

International Council of Kinetography Laban — www.ickl.org

International Council of the Museum of Modern Art
11 W 53rd St   New York NY 10019
Ph: 212-708-9470 ▪ Fx: 212-708-9740

International Council of Shopping Centers — www.icsc.org
1221 Ave of the Americas 41st Fl   New York NY 10020
Ph: 646-728-3800 ▪ Fx: 212-589-5555

International Council of Shopping Centers PAC
1033 N Fairfax St Suite 404   Alexandria VA 22314
Ph: 703-549-7404 ▪ Fx: 703-549-8712

International Council for Small Business — www.icsb.org
George Washington Univ School of Business & Public
Management 2115 G St NW Suite 403   Washington DC
20052
Ph: 202-994-0704 ▪ Fx: 202-994-4930

International Council on Systems Engineering — www.incose.org
2150 N 107th St Suite 205   Seattle WA 98133
Ph: 206-361-6607 ▪ Fx: 206-367-8777 ▪ TF: 800-366-1164

International Crane Foundation — www.savingcranes.org
PO Box 447   Baraboo WI 53913
Ph: 608-356-9462 ▪ Fx: 608-356-9465

International Criminal Court, Coalition for the — www.iccnow.org
777 UN Plaza   New York NY 10017
Ph: 212-687-2176 ▪ Fx: 212-599-1332

International Customer Service Association — www.icsa.com
401 N Michigan Ave   Chicago IL 60611
Ph: 312-321-6800 ▪ Fx: 312-245-1084 ▪ TF: 800-360-4272

International Cut Flower Growers Association — www.rosesinc.org
PO Box 99   Haslett MI 48840
Ph: 517-655-3726 ▪ Fx: 517-655-3727 ▪ TF: 800-968-7673

International Cytokine Society — www.weizmann.ac.il/cytokine
119 Davis Rd Suite 5A   Augusta GA 30907
Ph: 706-722-7511 ▪ Fx: 706-228-4678

International Dairy-Deli-Bakery Association — www.iddanet.org
313 Price Pl Suite 202   Madison WI 53705
Ph: 608-238-7908 ▪ Fx: 608-238-6330

International Dairy Foods Association — www.idfa.org
1250 H St NW Suite 900   Washington DC 20005
Ph: 202-737-4332 ▪ Fx: 202-331-7820

International Dance Alliance — www.idanews.com
1120 Broderick St   San Francisco CA 94115
Ph: 415-922-0560 ▪ Fx: 415-922-0588

International Dark-Sky Association — www.darksky.org
3225 N 1st Ave   Tucson AZ 85719
Ph: 520-293-3198 ▪ Fx: 520-293-3192

International Defense Equipment Exhibitors Association — www.ideea.com
6233 Nelway Dr   McLean VA 22101
Ph: 703-760-0762 ▪ Fx: 703-760-0764

International Desalination Association — www.idadesal.org
PO Box 387   Topsfield MA 01983
Ph: 978-887-0410 ▪ Fx: 978-887-0411

(International Development) Aga Khan Foundation USA — www.akdn.org/agency/akf.html
1825 K St NW Suite 901   Washington DC 20006
Ph: 202-293-2537 ▪ Fx: 202-785-1752

International Development, Community Colleges for — www.ccid.kirkwood.cc.ia.us
6301 Kirkwood Blvd SW   Cedar Rapids IA 52406
Ph: 319-398-5653 ▪ Fx: 319-398-1255

(International Development) Concern America — www.concernamerica.org
2015 N Broadway PO Box 1790   Santa Ana CA 92702
Ph: 714-953-8575 ▪ Fx: 714-953-1242 ▪ TF: 800-266-2376

International Development at Harvard University, Center for — www.cid.harvard.edu
Harvard Univ John F Kennedy School of Government 1 Eliot St
Bldg 79 JFK St   Cambridge MA 02138
Ph: 617-496-7294 ▪ Fx: 617-496-8753

International Development - USA, Society for — www.sidint.org
1875 Connecticut Ave NW   Washington DC 20009
Ph: 202-884-8590 ▪ Fx: 202-884-8499

International Digital Enterprise Alliance — www.idealliance.org
100 Daingerfield Rd   Alexandria VA 22314
Ph: 703-837-1070 ▪ Fx: 703-837-1072

International Digital Imaging Association — pwr.com/Idia
PO Box 81261   Chamblee GA 30366
Ph: 770-452-8119 ▪ Fx: 770-234-9058

International Disaster Recovery Association — www.idra.com
c/o BWT Assoc PO Box 4515   Shrewsbury MA 01545
Ph: 508-845-6000 ▪ Fx: 508-842-9003

International Disk Drive Equipment & Materials Association — www.idema.org
470 Lakeside Dr Suite A   Sunnyvale CA 94085
Ph: 408-991-9430 ▪ Fx: 408-991-9434

International District Energy Association — www.districtenergy.org
125 Turnpike Rd Suite 4   Westborough MA 01581
Ph: 508-366-9339 ▪ Fx: 508-366-0019

International Documentary Association — www.documentary.org
1201 W 5th St Suite M320   Los Angeles CA 90017
Ph: 213-534-3600 ▪ Fx: 213-534-3610

International Doll Makers Association — www.idmadolls.com
1204 Bakers Bridge Rd   Douglasville GA 30134
Ph: 770-949-1737

International Door Association — www.doors.org
PO Box 246   West Milton OH 45383
Ph: 800-355-4432 ▪ Fx: 937-698-6153

International Double Reed Society — www.idrs.org
2423 Lawndale Rd   Finksburg MD 21048
Ph: 410-871-0658 ▪ Fx: 410-871-0659

International Downtown Association — ida-downtown.org
1250 H St NW 10th Fl   Washington DC 20005
Ph: 202-393-6801 ▪ Fx: 202-393-6869

International Drycleaners Congress — www.idcnews.org
9016 Oak Branch Dr   Apex NC 27502
Ph: 919-363-5062 ▪ Fx: 919-387-8326

International Dwarf Fruit Tree Association — www.idfta.org
14 S Main St   Middleburg PA 17842
Ph: 570-837-1551 ▪ Fx: 570-837-0090

International Dyslexia Association — www.interdys.org
8600 LaSalle Rd Chester Bldg Suite 382   Baltimore MD 21286
Ph: 410-296-0232 ▪ Fx: 410-321-5069 ▪ TF: 800-222-3123

International Economic Development, Business Alliance for — www.fintrac.com/alliance
1615 L St NW Suite 520   Washington DC 20036
Ph: 202-429-8855 ▪ Fx: 202-429-8857

International Economic Development Council — www.iedconline.org
734 15th St NW Suite 900   Washington DC 20005
Ph: 202-223-7800 ▪ Fx: 202-223-4745

International Economics, Institute for — www.iie.com
1750 Massachusetts Ave NW   Washington DC 20036
Ph: 202-328-9000 ▪ Fx: 202-328-5432

International Economy, Berkeley Roundtable on the — brie.berkeley.edu/~briewww
Univ of California Berkeley 2234 Piedmont Ave   Berkeley CA
94720
Ph: 510-642-3067 ▪ Fx: 510-643-6617

International Ecotourism Society — www.ecotourism.org
733 15th St NW Suite 1000   Washington DC 20005
Ph: 202-347-9203 ▪ Fx: 202-387-7915

International Education Administrators, Association of — wings.buffalo.edu/intled/aiea
Univ at Buffalo Office of International Education 411 Capen Hall
Box 601604   Buffalo NY 14260
Ph: 716-645-2368 ▪ Fx: 716-645-2528

International Education, Association for the Advancement of — www.aaie.org
San Diego State Univ College of Extended Studies 5250
Campanile Dr Rm 2525   San Diego CA 92182
Ph: 619-594-2877 ▪ Fx: 619-594-8566

International Education, Cordell Hull Foundation for — www.payson.tulane.edu/cordellhull
135 E 50th St Suite 3H   New York NY 10022
Ph: 212-759-3311

International Education Research Foundation — www.ierf.org
PO Box 3665   Culver City CA 90231
Ph: 310-258-9451 ▪ Fx: 310-342-7086

International Education of Students, Institute for the — www.iesabroad.org
33 N LaSalle St 15th Fl   Chicago IL 60602
Ph: 312-944-1750 ▪ Fx: 312-944-1448 ▪ TF: 800-995-2300

International Educational & Cultural Exchange, www.alliance-exchange.org
Alliance for 1776 Massachusetts Ave NW Suite
620 Washington DC 20036
Ph: 202-293-6141 ▪ Fx: 202-293-6144

International Educational Exchange, Council on www.ciee.org
3 Copley Pl 2nd Fl Boston MA 02116
Ph: 617-247-0350 ▪ Fx: 617-247-2911 ▪ TF: 888-268-6245

International Educational Travel, Council on Standards for www.csiet.org
212 S Henry St Alexandria VA 22314
Ph: 703-739-9050 ▪ Fx: 703-739-9035

InterNational Electrical Testing Association www.netaworld.org
106 Stone St PO Box 687 Morrison CO 80465
Ph: 303-697-8441 ▪ Fx: 303-697-8431 ▪ TF: 888-300-6382

International Electronic Article Surveillance Manufacturers www.ieasma.org
Association 1800 K St NW Washington DC 20006
Ph: 202-466-4212 ▪ Fx: 202-466-7414

International Embryo Transfer Society www.iets.org
1111 N Dunlap Ave Savoy IL 61874
Ph: 217-356-3182 ▪ Fx: 217-398-4119

International Energy Credit Association www.ieca.net
8325 Lantern View Ln Saint John IN 46373
Ph: 219-365-7313 ▪ Fx: 219-365-0327

International Engineering Consortium www.iec.org
549 W Randolph St Suite 600 Chicago IL 60661
Ph: 312-559-4100 ▪ Fx: 312-559-4111

International Engraved Graphics Association www.iega.org
305 Plus Park Blvd Nashville TN 37217
Ph: 615-366-1094 ▪ Fx: 615-366-4192 ▪ TF: 800-821-3138

International Entertainment Buyers Association www.ieba.org
PO Box 128376 Nashville TN 37212
Ph: 615-463-0161 ▪ Fx: 615-463-0163 ▪ TF: 888-999-4322

International Environmental Law, Center for www.ciel.org
1367 Connecticut Ave NW Suite 300 Washington DC 20036
Ph: 202-785-8700 ▪ Fx: 202-785-8701

International Erosion Control Association www.ieca.org
3001 S Lincoln Ave Suite A Steamboat Springs CO 80487
Ph: 970-879-3010 ▪ Fx: 970-879-8563 ▪ TF: 800-455-4322

International Etchells Class Association Inc www.etchells.org
PO Box 676 Jamestown RI 02835
Ph: 401-560-0022 ▪ Fx: 401-560-0013

International Exchange of Scholars, Council for www.cies.org
3007 Tilden St NW Suite 5L Washington DC 20008
Ph: 202-686-4000 ▪ Fx: 202-362-3442

International Exchange, Youth for Understanding www.yfu.org
6400 Goldsboro Rd Suite 100 Bethesda MD 20817
Ph: 240-235-2100 ▪ Fx: 240-235-2104 ▪ TF: 800-424-3691

International Executive Housekeepers Association www.ieha.org
1001 Eastwind Dr Suite 301 Westerville OH 43081
Ph: 614-895-7166 ▪ Fx: 614-895-1248 ▪ TF: 800-200-6342

International Executive Service Corps www.iesc.org
901 15th St NW Suite 350 Washington DC 20005
Ph: 202-326-0280 ▪ Fx: 202-326-0280 ▪ TF: 800-243-4372

International Eye Foundation www.iefusa.org
10801 Connecticut Ave Kensington MD 20895
Ph: 240-290-0263 ▪ Fx: 240-290-0269

International Fabricare Institute www.ifi.org
12251 Tech Rd Silver Spring MD 20904
Ph: 301-622-1900 ▪ Fx: 301-236-9320 ▪ TF: 800-638-2627

International Facility Management Association www.ifma.org
1 E Greenway Plaza Suite 1100 Houston TX 77046
Ph: 713-623-4362 ▪ Fx: 713-623-6124

International Fantasy Gaming Society www.ifgs.org
PO Box 3577 Boulder CO 80307
Ph: 303-443-1012

International Federation of Accountants www.ifac.org
535 5th Ave 14th Fl New York NY 10017
Ph: 212-286-9344 ▪ Fx: 212-286-9570

International Federation of Air Line Pilots' Associations www.ifalpa.org

International Federation of American Homing Pigeon Fanciers Inc www.ifpigeon.com
PO Box 374 Hicksville NY 11802
Ph: 516-794-3612 ▪ Fx: 516-794-6654

International Federation for Cell Biology www.ifcbiol.org

International Federation for Choral Music ifcm.net
Univ of Illinois at Chicago Dept of Performing Arts 1040 W
Harrison St MC 255 Chicago IL 60607
Ph: 312-996-8744 ▪ Fx: 312-996-0954

International Federation of Festival Organizations www.morenofidof.org
4230 Stansbury Ave Suite 105 Sherman Oaks CA 91423
Ph: 818-789-7596 ▪ Fx: 818-784-9141

International Federation of Inspection Agencies - Americas Committee www.ifia-ac.org
3942 N Upland St Arlington VA 22207
Ph: 703-533-9539 ▪ Fx: 703-533-1612

International Federation of Nonlinear Analysts www.fit.edu/AcadRes/math/ifna
Florida Institute of Technology Dept of Mathematical Studies
150 W University Blvd Melbourne FL 32901
Ph: 321-674-7412

International Federation of Nurse Anesthetists www.ifna.info
222 S Prospect Ave Park Ridge IL 60068
Ph: 847-692-7050 ▪ Fx: 847-692-6968

International Federation of Pharmaceutical Wholesalers www.ifpw.com
10569 Crestwood Dr Manassas VA 22109
Ph: 703-331-3714 ▪ Fx: 703-331-3715

International Federation of Professional & Technical Engineers www.ifpte.org
8630 Fenton St Suite 400 Silver Spring MD 20910
Ph: 301-565-9016 ▪ Fx: 301-565-0018

International Federation of Secular Humanistic Jews www.ifshj.org
224 W 35th St New York NY 10001
Ph: 212-564-6711 ▪ Fx: 212-564-6721

International Federation of Societies for Histochemistry & www.ifshc.org
Cytochemistry Univ of Washington Dept of Biological
Structure PO Box 357420 Seattle WA 98195
Ph: 206-616-5894 ▪ Fx: 206-616-5842

International Federation of Societies for Surgery of the Hand
Duke University Medical Ctr PO Box 2912 Durham NC 27710
Ph: 919-684-5388 ▪ Fx: 919-681-7378

International Federation of Women's Travel Organizations www.ifwto.org

International Fellowship of Christians & Jews www.ifcj.org
30 N LaSalle St Suite 2600 Chicago IL 60602
Ph: 312-641-7200 ▪ Fx: 312-641-7201 ▪ TF: 800-486-8844

International Feminist Approaches to Bioethics www.msu.edu/~hlnelson/fab
California State Univ - Fresno 5340 N Campus Dr MS
SS78 Fresno CA 93740
Ph: 559-278-5721

International Fertilizer Development Center www.ifdc.org
PO Box 2040 Muscle Shoals AL 35662
Ph: 256-381-6600 ▪ Fx: 256-381-7408

International Festivals & Events Association www.ifea.com
2601 Eastover Terr Boise ID 83706
Ph: 208-433-0950 ▪ Fx: 208-433-9812

International Fibrodysplasia Ossificans Progressiva Association www.ifopa.org
PO Box 196217 Winter Springs FL 32719
Ph: 407-365-4194 ▪ Fx: 407-365-3213

International Film Seminars www.flahertyseminar.org
6 E 39th St 12th Fl New York NY 10016
Ph: 212-448-0457 ▪ Fx: 212-448-0458

International Financial Services Association www.ifsa.org
9 Sylvan Way 1st Fl Parsippany NJ 07054
Ph: 973-656-1900 ▪ Fx: 973-656-1915

International Fine Print Dealers Association www.printdealer.com
15 Gramercy Park S Suite 7A New York NY 10003
Ph: 212-674-6095 ▪ Fx: 212-674-6783

International Fire Buff Associates Inc www.ifba.org
955 Regina Dr Baltimore MD 21227
Ph: 410-242-8672 ▪ Fx: 410-242-4688

International Fire Marshals Association www.nfpa.org/MemberSections/IFMA/IFMA.asp
c/o NFPA International 1 Batterymarch Park Quincy MA 02169
Ph: 617-770-3000 ▪ Fx: 617-770-0700

International Fire Photographers Association www.ifpaonline.com
143 40th St New Orleans LA 70124
Ph: 504-482-9616 ▪ Fx: 504-482-9636

International Fire Service Training Association www.ifsta.org
Fire Protection Publications Oklahoma State Univ 930 N
Willis Stillwater OK 74078
Ph: 405-744-5723 ▪ Fx: 405-744-8204 ▪ TF: 800-654-4055

International Firestop Council www.firestop.org
25 N Broadway Tarrytown NY 10591
Ph: 914-332-0040 ▪ Fx: 914-332-1541

International Flying Farmers www.flyingfarmers.org
PO Box 9124 Wichita KS 67277
Ph: 316-943-4234 ▪ Fx: 800-266-5415

International Food Additives Council
5775 Peachtree-Dunwoody Rd Bldg G Suite 500 Atlanta GA
30342
Ph: 404-252-3663 ▪ Fx: 404-252-0774

International Food Information Council www.ific.org
1100 Connecticut Ave NW Suite 430 Washington DC 20036
Ph: 202-296-6540 ▪ Fx: 202-296-6547

International Food Policy Research Institute www.ifpri.org
2033 K St NW Washington DC 20006
Ph: 202-862-5600 ▪ Fx: 202-467-4439

International Food Service Executives Association www.ifsea.org
836 San Bruno Ave Henderson NV 89015
Ph: 702-564-0997 ▪ Fx: 702-564-4836 ▪ TF: 888-234-3732

International Food Wine & Travel Writers Association www.ifwtwa.org
PO Box 8249 Calabasas CA 91372
Ph: 818-999-9959 ▪ Fx: 818-347-7545

International Foodservice Distributors Association www.ifdaonline.org
201 Park Washington Ct Falls Church VA 22046
Ph: 703-532-9400 ▪ Fx: 703-538-4673

International Foodservice Editorial Council www.ifec-is-us.com
PO Box 491 Hyde Park NY 12538
Ph: 845-229-6973 ▪ Fx: 845-229-6993

International Foodservice Manufacturers Association www.ifmaworld.com
180 N Stetson Ave 2 Prudential Plaza Suite 4400 Chicago IL
60601
Ph: 312-540-4400 ▪ Fx: 312-540-4401

International Footprint Association www.footprinter.org
PO Box 2487 Walnut Creek CA 94595
Ph: 925-944-1763 ▪ Fx: 925-944-1771 ▪ TF: 888-944-1763

International Formalwear Association www.formalwear.org
401 N Michigan Ave Chicago IL 60611
Ph: 312-644-6610 ▪ Fx: 312-321-4098

International Forum www.int-forum.org
401 N Michigan Ave Chicago IL 60611
Ph: 312-644-6610 ▪ Fx: 312-673-6594 ▪ TF: 800-499-0974

International Foundation for Art Research www.ifar.org
500 5th Ave Suite 1234 New York NY 10110
Ph: 212-391-6234 ▪ Fx: 212-391-8794

International Foundation of Doll Makers www.ifdm.org
PO Box 120187 Clermont FL 34712
Ph: 352-394-1404 ▪ Fx: 352-394-1270

International Foundation for Election Systems www.ifes.org
1101 15th NW Suite 300 Washington DC 20005
Ph: 202-828-8507 ▪ Fx: 202-466-8466

International Foundation of Employee Benefit Plans www.ifebp.org
PO Box 69 Brookfield WI 53008
Ph: 262-786-6700 ▪ Fx: 262-786-8670 ▪ TF: 888-334-3327

International Foundation for Ethical Research www.ifer.org
53 W Jackson Blvd Suite 1552 Chicago IL 60604
Ph: 312-427-6025 ▪ Fx: 312-427-6524

International Foundation for Functional Gastrointestinal Disorders www.iffgd.org
PO Box 170864 Milwaukee WI 53217
Ph: 414-964-1799 ▪ Fx: 414-964-7176 ▪ TF: 888-964-2001

International Foundation for Gender Education www.ifge.org
PO Box 540229 Waltham MA 02454
Ph: 781-899-2212 ▪ Fx: 781-899-5703

International Foundation for Protection Officers www.ifpo.org
PO Box 771329 Naples FL 34107
Ph: 941-430-0534 ▪ Fx: 941-430-0533

International Franchise Association www.franchise.org
1350 New York Ave NW Suite 900 Washington DC 20005
Ph: 202-628-8000 ▪ Fx: 202-628-0812 ▪ TF: 800-543-1038

(International Franchise Association) FRAN-PAC www.franchise.org
1350 New York Ave NW Suite 900 Washington DC 20005
Ph: 202-628-8000 ▪ Fx: 202-628-0812 ▪ TF: 800-543-1038

International Fraternity of Phi Gamma Delta www.phigam.org
1201 Red Mile Rd PO Box 1599 Lexington KY 40544
Ph: 859-255-1848 ▪ Fx: 859-253-0779

International Freeze-Dry Floral Association www.ifdfa.com
11407 N Main St Suite A High Point NC 27263
Ph: 336-861-6737 ▪ TF: 888-554-9706

International Fresh-Cut Produce Association www.fresh-cuts.org
1600 Duke St Suite 440 Alexandria VA 22314
Ph: 703-299-6282 ▪ Fx: 703-299-6288

International Friends of the London Library Inc
515 Madison Ave Suite 3702 New York NY 10022
Ph: 212-644-4858 ▪ Fx: 212-644-4859

International Frozen Food Association
2000 Corporate Ridge Suite 1000 McLean VA 22102
Ph: 703-821-0770 ▪ Fx: 703-821-1350

International Function Point Users Group www.ifpug.org
191 Clarksville Rd Princeton Junction NJ 08550
Ph: 609-799-4900 ▪ Fx: 609-799-7032

International Fund for Animal Welfare www.ifaw.org
411 Main St PO Box 193 Yarmouth Port MA 02675
Ph: 508-744-2000 ▪ Fx: 508-744-2009 ▪ TF: 800-932-4329

International Furnishings & Design Association www.ifda.com
191 Clarksville Rd Princeton Junction NJ 08550
Ph: 609-799-3423 ▪ Fx: 609-799-7023

International Furniture Rental Association www.ifra.org
9202 N Meridian St Suite 200 Indianapolis IN 46260
Ph: 317-571-5613 ▪ Fx: 317-571-5603

International Furniture & Transportation Logistics Council www.iftlc.org
PO Box 889 Gardner MA 01440
Ph: 978-632-1913 ▪ Fx: 978-630-2917

International Game Developers Association www.igda.org
600 Harrison St San Francisco CA 94107
Ph: 415-947-6235 ▪ Fx: 415-947-6090

International Game Fish Association www.igfa.org
IGFA Fishing Hall of Fame & Museum 300 Gulf Stream
Way Dania Beach FL 33004
Ph: 954-927-2628 ▪ Fx: 954-924-4299

International Gas Turbine Institute www.asme.org/igti
5775B Glenridge Dr Suite 370 Atlanta GA 30328
Ph: 404-847-0072 ▪ Fx: 404-847-0151

International Gay & Lesbian Human Rights Commission www.iglhrc.org
1375 Sutter St Suite 222 San Francisco CA 94109
Ph: 415-561-0633 ▪ Fx: 415-561-0619

International Gay & Lesbian Travel Association www.iglta.org
4331 N Federal Hwy Suite 304 Fort Lauderdale FL 33308
Ph: 954-776-2626 ▪ Fx: 954-776-3303 ▪ TF: 800-448-8550

International Gay Rodeo Association www.igra.com
900 E Colfax Ave Denver CO 80218
Ph: 303-832-4472 ▪ Fx: 303-860-9105

International Generic Horse Association www.igha.org
PO Box 6778 San Pedro CA 90734
Ph: 310-719-9094

International Glove Association www.iga-online.com
PO Box 146 Brookville PA 15825
Ph: 814-328-5208

International Golf Associates www.iga-golf.com
4370 La Jolla Village Dr 4th Fl San Diego CA 92122
Ph: 858-546-4737 ▪ Fx: 858-615-2083

International Graphic Arts Education Association www.igaea.org
1899 Preston White Dr Reston VA 20191
Ph: 703-758-0595

International Graphoanalysis Society www.igas.com
111 N Canal St Suite 399 Chicago IL 60606
Ph: 312-930-9446 ▪ Fx: 312-930-5903

International Graphological Society
PO Box 793743 Dallas TX 75379
Ph: 214-351-3668 ▪ TF: 800-960-1034

International Grooving & Grinding Association www.igga.net
126 Mansion St PO Box 58 Coxsackie NY 12051
Ph: 518-731-7450 ▪ Fx: 518-731-7490

International Ground Source Heat Pump Association www.igshpa.okstate.edu
Oklahoma State University 499 Cordell S Stillwater OK 74078
Ph: 405-744-5175 ▪ Fx: 405-744-5283 ▪ TF: 800-626-4747

International Group of Accounting Firms www.igaf.org
2250 Satellite Blvd Suite 115 Duluth GA 30097
Ph: 678-417-7730 ▪ Fx: 678-417-6977

International Guards Union of America www.amaonline.com/igua
Rt 8 Box 32-14 Amarillo TX 79118
Ph: 806-622-2424 ▪ Fx: 806-622-3500

International Guild of Miniature Artisans www.igma.org
PO Box 629 Freedom CA 95019
Ph: 831-724-7974 ▪ Fx: 831-724-8605 ▪ TF: 800-711-4462

International Guild of Professional Electrologists www.igpe.org
803 N Main St Suite 3A High Point NC 27262
Ph: 336-841-6631 ▪ Fx: 336-841-5187 ▪ TF: 800-830-3247

International Hajji Baba Society
2106 Woodmont Rd Alexandria VA 22307
Ph: 703-960-0343 ▪ Fx: 703-683-7545

International Handgun Metallic Silhouette Association www.ihmsa.org
PO Box 9 Anoka MN 55303
Ph: 763-323-3359 ▪ Fx: 763-422-1910

International Hard Anodizing Association www.ihanodizing.com
PO Box 579 Moorestown NJ 08057
Ph: 856-234-0330 ▪ Fx: 856-727-9504

International Harvester Collectors Club Inc www.ihcollectors.org
1318 W Main St Springfield OH 45504
Ph: 937-525-0000

International Health Evaluation Association www.ihea.net
846 S Hotel St Suite 301 Honolulu HI 96813
Ph: 808-524-4411 ▪ Fx: 808-524-5559

International Health Racquet & Sportsclub Association www.ihrsa.org
263 Summer St Boston MA 02210
Ph: 617-951-0055 ▪ Fx: 617-951-0056 ▪ TF: 800-228-4772

International Health & Temperance Association
12501 Old Columbia Pike Silver Spring MD 20904
Ph: 301-680-6719 ▪ Fx: 301-680-6707

International Hearing Dog Inc www.ihdi.org
5901 E 89th Ave Henderson CO 80640
Ph: 303-287-3277 ▪ Fx: 303-287-3425

International Hearing Society www.ihsinfo.org
16880 Middlebelt Rd Suite 4 Livonia MI 48154
Ph: 734-522-7200 ▪ Fx: 734-522-0200 ▪ TF: 800-521-5247

International Hedgehog Association www.hedgehogclub.com

International Herb Association www.iherb.org

International Hobie Class Association www.hobieclass.com
3334 Fulton Victoria BC V9C2T9
Ph: 250-474-7580

International Home Furnishings Marketing Authority www.furnituremarket.org
PO Box 5243 High Point NC 27262
Ph: 336-869-1000 ▪ Fx: 336-869-6999

International Home Furnishings Representatives Association www.ihfra.org
PO Box 670 High Point NC 27261
Ph: 336-889-3920 ▪ Fx: 336-883-8245 ▪ TF: 800-889-3920

International Horn Society www.hornsociety.org

International Hot Rod Association www.ihra.com
9 1/2 E Main St Norwalk OH 44857
Ph: 419-663-6666 ▪ Fx: 419-663-4472

International Housewares Association www.housewares.org
6400 Shafer Ct Suite 650 Rosemont IL 60018
Ph: 847-292-4200 ▪ Fx: 847-292-4211

International Housewares Representatives Association www.ihra.org
175 N Harbor Dr Suite 1712 Chicago IL 60601
Ph: 312-240-0822 ▪ Fx: 312-240-1005

International Hydrolyzed Protein Council
555 13th St NW Washington DC 20004
Ph: 202-637-5926 ▪ Fx: 202-637-5910

International Ice Cream Association
1250 H St NW Suite 900 Washington DC 20005
Ph: 202-737-4332 ▪ Fx: 202-331-7820

International Imagery Association www.imagery-iia.com
18 Edgecliff Terr Yonkers NY 10705
Ph: 914-476-0781 ▪ Fx: 914-476-5796

International Imaging Industry Association www.i3a.org
550 Mamaroneck Ave Suite 310 Harrison NY 10528
Ph: 914-698-7603 ▪ Fx: 914-698-7609

International Indian Treaty Council www.treatycouncil.org
2390 Mission St Suite 301 San Francisco CA 94110
Ph: 415-641-4482 ▪ Fx: 415-641-1298

International Inflight Food Service Association www.ifsanet.com
5775 Peachtree-Dunwoody Rd Bldg G Suite 500 Atlanta GA
30342
Ph: 404-252-3663 ▪ Fx: 404-252-0774

International Initiatives, Center for Institutional & www.acenet.edu/programs/ciii.cfm
American Council on Education 1 Dupont Cir NW 8th
Fl Washington DC 20036
Ph: 202-939-9427

International Institute of Ammonia Refrigeration www.iiar.org
1110 N Glebe Rd Suite 250 Arlington VA 22201
Ph: 703-312-4200 ▪ Fx: 703-312-0065

International Institute for Bau-Biologie & Ecology www.bau-biologieusa.com
1401 A Cleveland St Clearwater FL 33755
Ph: 727-461-4371 ▪ Fx: 727-441-4373

International Institute of Connector & Interconnection Technology www.iicit.org
PO Box 665 Hudson MA 01749
Ph: 978-568-0717 ▪ Fx: 978-568-0716 ▪ TF: 800-854-4248

International Institute for Energy Conservation www.iiec.org
10005 Leamoore Ln Suite 100 Vienna VA 22181
Ph: 703-281-7263 ▪ Fx: 703-968-6678

International Institute of Fisheries Economics & Trade oregonstate.edu/dept/iifet
Oregon State Univ Dept of Agricultural & Resource
Economics Corvallis OR 97331
Ph: 541-737-1416 ▪ Fx: 541-737-2563

International Institute for Frame Study www.iifs.org

International Institute of Islamic Thought www.iiit.org
500 Grove St Herndon VA 20170
Ph: 703-471-1133 ▪ Fx: 703-471-3922

International Institute for Lath & Plaster www.iilp.org
PO Box 1663 Lafayette CA 94549
Ph: 925-283-5160 ▪ Fx: 925-283-5161

International Institute of Municipal Clerks
8331 Utica Ave Suite 200   Rancho Cucamonga CA 91730
Ph: 909-944-4162 ▪ Fx: 909-944-8545 ▪ TF: 800-251-1639
www.iimc.com

International Institute of Reflexology
5650 1st Ave N   Saint Petersburg FL 33710
Ph: 727-343-4811 ▪ Fx: 727-381-2807
www.reflexology-usa.net

International Institute of Rural Reconstruction
333 E 38th St 6th Fl   New York NY 10016
Ph: 212-880-9147 ▪ Fx: 212-880-9148
www.iirr.org

International Institute of Space Law
www.iafastro-iisl.com

International Institute for the Study of Death
1000 Island Blvd Suite 512   Aventura FL 33160
Ph: 305-936-1408

International Institute of Synthetic Rubber Producers Inc
2077 S Gessner Rd Suite 133   Houston TX 77063
Ph: 713-783-7511 ▪ Fx: 713-783-7253
www.iisrp.com

International Insurance Society
101 Murray St   New York NY 10007
Ph: 212-815-9294 ▪ Fx: 212-815-9297
www.iisonline.org

International Intellectual Property Alliance
1747 Pennsylvania Ave NW Suite 825   Washington DC 20006
Ph: 202-833-4198 ▪ Fx: 202-872-0546
www.iipa.com

International Interior Design Association
13-122 Merchandise Mart   Chicago IL 60654
Ph: 312-467-1950 ▪ Fx: 312-467-0779 ▪ TF: 888-799-4432
www.iida.org

International Investigators, Council of
2150 N 107th St Suite 205   Seattle WA 98133
Ph: 206-361-8869 ▪ Fx: 206-367-8777 ▪ TF: 888-759-8884
www.cii2.org

International Investment, Organization for
1901 Pennsylvania Ave NW Suite 807   Washington DC 20006
Ph: 202-659-1903 ▪ Fx: 202-659-2293
www.ofii.org

International Iridology Practitioners Association
PO Box 3334   Escondido CA 92033
Ph: 888-682-2208 ▪ TF: 888-682-2208
www.iridologyassn.org

International Isotope Society
www.intl-isotope-soc.org

International Ivory Society
11109 Nicholas Dr   Wheaton MD 20902
Ph: 301-649-4002

International Jelly & Preserve Association
5775 Peachtree-Dunwoody Rd Bldg G Suite 500   Atlanta GA
30342
Ph: 404-252-3663 ▪ Fx: 404-252-0774
www.jelly.org

International Joint Commission
1250 23rd St NW Suite 100   Washington DC 20440
Ph: 202-736-9024 ▪ Fx: 202-736-9015
www.ijc.org

International Jugglers' Association Inc
www.juggle.org

International Jumper Futurity
PO Box 757   Kirkland WA 98083
Ph: 425-827-5417
youngjumpers.com/IJF

International Junior Brangus Breeders Association
5750 Epsilon PO Box 696020   San Antonio TX 78269
Ph: 210-696-4343 ▪ Fx: 210-696-8718
www.int-brangus.org

International Kart Federation
1609 S Grove Ave   Ontario CA 91761
Ph: 909-923-4999 ▪ Fx: 909-923-6940
www.ikfkarting.com

International Kitchen Exhaust Cleaning Association
1518 K St NW Suite 503   Washington DC 20005
Ph: 202-393-5955 ▪ Fx: 202-638-4833
www.ikeca.org

International Labor Communications Association
AFL-CIO CLC 815 16th St NW   Washington DC 20006
Ph: 202-637-5068 ▪ Fx: 202-508-6973
www.ilcaonline.org

International Labor History Association
706 Bruce Ct   Madison WI 53705
Ph: 608-231-1886

International Labor Organization - US
1828 L St NW Suite 600   Washington DC 20036
Ph: 202-653-7652 ▪ Fx: 202-653-7687
www.us.ilo.org

International Labor Rights Fund
733 15th St NW Suite 920   Washington DC 20005
Ph: 202-347-4100 ▪ Fx: 202-347-4885
www.laborrights.org

International Lactation Consultant Association
1500 Sunday Dr Suite 102   Raleigh NC 27607
Ph: 919-861-5577 ▪ Fx: 919-787-4916
www.ilca.org

International Landslide Research Group
ilrg.gndci.pg.cnr.it

International Laser Display Association
3721 SE Henry St   Portland OR 97202
Ph: 503-407-0289
www.laserist.org

International Laser Tag Association
5351 E Thompson Ave Suite 236   Indianapolis IN 46237
Ph: 317-375-9631 ▪ Fx: 317-375-9658
www.lasertag.org

International Laughter Society
16000 Glen Una Dr   Los Gatos CA 95030
Ph: 408-354-3456

International Law, American Society of
2223 Massachusetts Ave NW   Washington DC 20008
Ph: 202-939-6000 ▪ Fx: 202-797-7133
www.asil.org

International Law Institute
1055 Thomas Jefferson St NW   Washington DC 20007
Ph: 202-247-6006 ▪ Fx: 202-247-6010
www.ili.org

International Law & Practice, ABA Section of
740 15th St NW   Washington DC 20005
Ph: 202-662-1660 ▪ Fx: 202-662-1669
www.abanet.org/intlaw

International Law Students Association
25 E Jackson Blvd Suite 518   Chicago IL 60604
Ph: 312-362-5025 ▪ Fx: 312-362-5073
www.ilsa.org

International Lawrence Durrell Society
www.lawrencedurrell.org

International Lead Zinc Research Organization
PO Box 12036   Research Triangle Park NC 27709
Ph: 919-361-4647 ▪ Fx: 919-361-1957
www.ilzro.org

International League of Antiquarian Booksellers
400 Summit Ave   Saint Paul MN 55102
Ph: 651-290-0700 ▪ Fx: 651-290-0646
www.ilab-lila.com

International League of Dermatological Societies
PO Box 35069   Sarasota FL 34232
Ph: 941-346-1226 ▪ Fx: 941-927-1936
www.ilds.org

International League of Electrical Associations
2901 Metro Dr Suite 203   Bloomington MN 55425
Ph: 952-854-4405 ▪ Fx: 952-854-7076
www.ileaweb.org

International League for Human Rights
228 East 45th St 5th Fl   New York NY 10017
Ph: 212-661-0480 ▪ Fx: 212-661-0416
www.ilhr.org

International League of Professional Baseball Clubs
55 S High St Suite 202   Dublin OH 43017
Ph: 614-791-9300 ▪ Fx: 614-791-9009
www.ilbaseball.com

International Licensing Industry Merchandisers' Association
350 5th Ave Suite 1408   New York NY 10118
Ph: 212-244-1944 ▪ Fx: 212-563-6552
www.licensing.org

International Life Sciences Institute North America
1 Thomas Cir NW 9th Fl   Washington DC 20005
Ph: 202-659-0074 ▪ Fx: 202-659-3859
www.ilsina.org

International Life Services
2606 1/2 W 8th St   Los Angeles CA 90057
Ph: 213-382-2156 ▪ Fx: 213-382-4203
www.life-services.org

International Lightning Class Association
PO Box 10747   Murfreesboro TN 37129
Ph: 615-893-5274 ▪ Fx: 615-893-5205
www.lightningclass.org

International Linen Promotion Commission
PO Box 1630   New York NY 10028
Ph: 212-734-3640

International Listening Association
PO Box 744   River Falls WI 54022
Ph: 715-425-3377 ▪ Fx: 715-425-9533 ▪ TF: 800-452-4505
www.listen.org/

International Liver Transplantation Society
17000 Commerce Pkwy Suite C   Mount Laurel NJ 08054
Ph: 856-439-0500 ▪ Fx: 856-439-0525
www.ilts.org

International Livestock Identification Association
4701 Marion St Suite 201   Denver CO 80216
Ph: 303-294-0895 ▪ Fx: 303-294-0918

International Longshore & Warehouse Union
1188 Franklin St 4th Fl   San Francisco CA 94109
Ph: 415-775-0533 ▪ Fx: 415-775-1302
www.ilwu.org

International Longshoremen's Association
17 Battery Pl Rm 930   New York NY 10004
Ph: 212-425-1200 ▪ Fx: 212-425-2928
www.ila2000.org

International Loran Association
741 Cathedral Pointe Ln   Santa Barbara CA 93111
Ph: 805-967-8649 ▪ Fx: 805-967-8471
www.loran.org

International Luggage Repair Association
1425 SOM Center Rd   Mayfield Heights OH 44124
Ph: 440-442-5910 ▪ Fx: 440-442-5325

International Lutheran Laymen's League
660 Mason Ridge Ctr Dr   Saint Louis MO 63141
Ph: 314-317-4100 ▪ TF: 800-944-3450
www.lhm.org

International Magnesium Association
900 17th St NW Suite 450   Washington DC 20006
Ph: 202-466-6601 ▪ Fx: 202-466-6678
www.intlmag.org

International Magnetics Association
8 S Michigan Ave Suite 1000   Chicago IL 60603
Ph: 312-456-5590 ▪ Fx: 312-580-0165
www.intl-magnetics.org

International Maintenance Institute
PO Box 751896   Houston TX 77275
Ph: 281-481-0869 ▪ Fx: 281-481-8337
www.imionline.org/

International Manuel Ponce Society
PO Box 59152   Dallas TX 75229
Ph: 972-293-5360
www.imps.org

International Manufacturers Representatives Association
PO Box 702678   Tulsa OK 74170
Ph: 918-743-5443

International Map Trade Association
2629 Manhattan Ave PMB 281   Hermosa Beach CA 90254
Ph: 310-376-7731 ▪ Fx: 310-376-7287
www.maptrade.org

International Maple Syrup Institute
PO Box 53010   Burlington VT 05405
Ph: 802-656-5417 ▪ Fx: 802-656-5422

International Marina Institute
PO Box 7197   Jupiter FL 33468
Ph: 561-741-0626 ▪ Fx: 561-741-0676
www.imimarina.org

International Marine Transit Association
34 Otis Hill Rd   Hingham MA 02043
Ph: 781-749-0078
www.interferry.com

International Marking & Identification Association
222 Wisconsin Ave Suite 1   Lake Forest IL 60045
Ph: 847-283-9810 ▪ Fx: 847-283-9808
www.mdai.org

International Masonry Institute
James Brice House 42 East St   Annapolis MD 21401
Ph: 410-280-1305 ▪ Fx: 301-261-2855
www.imiweb.org

International Mass Retail Association
1700 N Moore St Suite 2250   Arlington VA 22209
Ph: 703-841-2300 ▪ Fx: 703-841-1184
www.imra.org

International Mediation & Conflict Resolution, Institute for
1424 K St NW Suite 650   Washington DC 20005
Ph: 202-347-2042 ▪ Fx: 202-347-2440
www.iimcr.org

International Medical Corps
1919 Santa Monica Blvd Suite 300   Santa Monica CA 90404
Ph: 310-826-7800 ▪ Fx: 310-442-6622 ▪ TF: 800-481-4462
www.imc-la.org

International Memorialization Supply Association
PO Box 663   Export PA 15632
Ph: 800-864-4174
www.imsa-online.com

International Mercury Owners Association   www.mercuryclub.com
6445 W Grand Ave   Chicago IL 60707
Ph: 773-622-6445 ▪ Fx: 773-622-3602

International Metallographic Society Inc   www.metallography.com/ims/info.htm
ASM International 9639 Kinsman Rd   Materials Park OH 44073
Ph: 440-338-5151 ▪ Fx: 440-338-4634

International Microelectronics & Packaging Society   www.imaps.org
611 2nd St NE   Washington DC 20002
Ph: 202-548-4001 ▪ Fx: 202-548-6115

International Microwave Power Institute   www.impi.org
1916 Sussex Rd   Blacksburg VA 24060
Ph: 540-552-3070 ▪ Fx: 540-961-1463

International Midas Dealers Association   www.imdaonline.org
14 W 3rd St Suite 200   Kansas City MO 64105
Ph: 816-472-6632 ▪ Fx: 816-472-7765 ▪ TF: 877-543-6203

International Military Community Executives Association   www.imcea.com
2100 E Stan Schleuter Loop Suite G   Killeen TX 76542
Ph: 254-554-6619 ▪ Fx: 254-554-6629

International Miniature Cattle Breeders Society & Registry   www.minicattle.com
25204 156th Ave SE   Covington WA 98042
Ph: 253-631-1911 ▪ Fx: 253-631-5774

International Miniature Donkey Registry   www.qis.net/~minidonk/imdr.htm
1338 Hughes Shop Rd   Westminster MD 21158
Ph: 410-875-0118 ▪ Fx: 410-857-9145

International Miniature Zebu Association   www.miniature-zebu-cattle.com
PO Box 66   Crawford NE 68339
Ph: 308-665-3919 ▪ Fx: 308-665-1931

International Mission Board   www.imb.org
PO Box 6767   Richmond VA 23230
Ph: 800-999-3113

International Model Power Boat Association   www.impba.org
2804 Woods Dr   Violet LA 70092
Ph: 504-276-4500

International Molded Pulp Environmental Packaging Association   www.impepa.org
1425 W Mequon Rd Suite A   Mequon WI 53092
Ph: 262-241-0522 ▪ Fx: 262-241-3766

International Montessori Society   trust.wdn.com/ims
912 Thayer Ave Suite 207   Silver Spring MD 20910
Ph: 301-589-1127 ▪ Fx: 301-589-0733 ▪ TF: 800-301-3131

International Morab Breeders Association   www.morab.com/imba.html
RR 3 Box 235   Ava MO 65608
Ph: 417-683-4426 ▪ Fx: 417-683-5708

International Morab Registry   www.morab.com
RR 3 Box 235   Ava MO 65608
Ph: 417-683-4426 ▪ Fx: 417-683-5708

International Motor Coach Group Inc   www.imgcoach.com
8645 College Blvd Suite 220   Overland Park KS 66210
Ph: 913-903-0111 ▪ Fx: 913-906-0115 ▪ TF: 888-447-3466

International Motor Contest Association   www.imca.com
1800 W 'D' St PO Box 921   Vinton IA 52349
Ph: 319-472-2201 ▪ Fx: 319-472-2218

International Motor Press Association   www.impa.org
4 Park St   Harrington Park NJ 07640
Ph: 201-750-3533 ▪ Fx: 201-750-2010

International Motor Sports Association   www.imsaracing.net
1394 Broadway Ave   Braselton GA 30517
Ph: 706-658-2120 ▪ Fx: 706-658-2130

International Mountain Bicycling Association   www.imba.com
207 Canyon Blvd Suite 301 PO Box 7578   Boulder CO 80306
Ph: 303-545-9011 ▪ Fx: 303-545-9026 ▪ TF: 888-442-4622

International Multimedia Teleconferencing Consortium Inc   www.imtc.org
2400 Camino Ramon Suite 275   San Ramon CA 94583
Ph: 925-275-6600 ▪ Fx: 925-275-6691

International Municipal Lawyers Association   www.imla.org
1110 Vermont Ave NW Suite 200   Washington DC 20005
Ph: 202-466-5424 ▪ Fx: 202-785-0152

International Municipal Signal Association   www.imsasafety.org
165 E Union St PO Box 539   Newark NY 14513
Ph: 315-331-2182 ▪ Fx: 315-331-8205 ▪ TF: 800-723-4672

International Museum Theatre Alliance   www.imtal.org
c/o Wildlife Theater Central Park Zoo 830 5th Ave   New York
NY 10021
Ph: 212-439-6542

International Nanny Association   www.nanny.org
191 Clarksville Rd   Princeton Junction NJ 08550
Ph: 609-799-7527 ▪ Fx: 609-799-7032 ▪ TF: 888-878-1477

International Narcotic Enforcement Officers Association   www.ineoa.org
112 State St Suite 1200   Albany NY 12207
Ph: 518-463-6232 ▪ Fx: 518-432-3378

International Natural Sausage Casing Association   www.insca.org
12339 Carroll Ave   Rockville MD 20852
Ph: 301-231-9811 ▪ Fx: 301-231-4871

International Naval Research Organization   www.warship.org
5905 Reinwood Dr   Toledo OH 43613
Ph: 419-472-1331

International Navigation Association   www.internationalnavigation.org

International Network of M&A Partners   www.imap.com
525 SW 5th St Suite A   Des Moines IA 50309
Ph: 515-282-8192 ▪ Fx: 515-282-9117

International Network of Performing & Visual Arts   www.artsschoolsnetwork.org
Schools   173 Ridge View Dr   Berkeley Springs WV 25411
Ph: 304-258-1799 ▪ Fx: 304-258-0839

International Neural Network Society   www.inns.org
7600 Terrace Ave Suite 203   Middleton WI 53562
Ph: 608-831-0584 ▪ Fx: 608-831-5122

International Neuropsychological Society   www.the-ins.org
700 Ackerman Rd Suite 625   Columbus OH 43202
Ph: 614-263-4200 ▪ Fx: 614-263-4366

International Newspaper Financial Executives   www.infe.org
21525 Ridgetop Cir Suite 200   Sterling VA 20166
Ph: 703-421-4060 ▪ Fx: 703-421-4068

International Newspaper Marketing Association   www.inma.org
10300 N Central Expy Suite 467   Dallas TX 75231
Ph: 214-373-9111 ▪ Fx: 214-373-9112

International Nortel Networks Users Group   www.innua.org
401 N Michigan Ave Suite 2200   Chicago IL 60611
Ph: 312-673-6102 ▪ Fx: 312-673-6718 ▪ TF: 877-446-6684

International Nurses Society on Addictions   www.intnsa.org
PO Box 10752   Raleigh NC 27605
Ph: 919-821-1292 ▪ Fx: 919-833-5743

International Oak Society   www.saintmarys.edu/~rjensen/iosboard.html

International Occultation Timing Association Inc   www.occultations.org

International Oceanographic Foundation   www.rsmas.miami.edu/iof
Univ of Miami Rosenstiel School of Marine & Atmospheric
   Science 4600 Rickenbacker Cswy   Miami FL 33149
Ph: 305-361-4000 ▪ Fx: 305-361-4711

International Oculoplastic Society
1018 Harmon Cove Towers   Secaucus NJ 07094
Ph: 201-392-3438

International Oil Mill Superintendents Association
1835 Edinburgh St   Prattville AL 36066
Ph: 334-491-1754 ▪ Fx: 334-491-3109

International Oil Scouts Association   www.oilscouts.org
PO Box 272949   Houston TX 77277
Ph: 512-472-8138 ▪ Fx: 512-472-1057

International Oracle Users Group   www.ioug.org
401 N Michigan Ave   Chicago IL 60611
Ph: 312-245-1579 ▪ Fx: 312-527-6785

International Order of the Armadillo
PO Box 60305   Jacksonville FL 32236
Ph: 904-384-8594 ▪ Fx: 904-387-1806

International Order of EARS Inc   www.cornislandstorytellingfestival.org
12019 Donohue Ave   Louisville KY 40243
Ph: 502-245-0643 ▪ Fx: 502-254-7542

International Order of the Golden Rule   www.ogr.org
13523 Lakefront Dr   Bridgeton MO 63045
Ph: 314-209-7142 ▪ Fx: 314-209-1289 ▪ TF: 800-367-8030

International Order of the King's Daughters & Sons   www.iokds.org
34 Vincent Ave PO Box 1017   Chautauqua NY 14722
Ph: 716-357-4951 ▪ Fx: 716-357-3762

International Order of Rainbow for Girls   www.iorg.org
PO Box 1868   McAlester OK 74502
Ph: 918-423-1328 ▪ Fx: 918-423-1329

International Order of Saint Luke the Physician   www.orderofstluke.org
PO Box 13701   San Antonio TX 78213
Ph: 210-492-5222 ▪ TF: 877-992-5222

International Organization for Chemical Sciences in Development   www.iocd.org

International Organization of Masters Mates & Pilots   www.bridgedeck.org
700 Maritime Blvd   Linthicum Heights MD 21090
Ph: 410-850-8700 ▪ Fx: 410-850-0973 ▪ TF: 877-667-5522

International Organization for Migration   www.iom.int
1752 'N' St NW Suite 700   Washington DC 20036
Ph: 202-862-1826 ▪ Fx: 202-862-1879

International Organization of Plant Biosystematists   www.iopb.org

International Organization for Septuagint & Cognate Studies   ccat.sas.upenn.edu/ioscs

International Orthodox Christian Charities   www.iocc.org
110 West Rd Suite 360   Baltimore MD 21204
Ph: 410-243-9820 ▪ Fx: 410-243-9824 ▪ TF: 877-803-4622

International Oxygen Manufacturers Association   www.iomaweb.org
1255 23rd St NW Suite 200   Washington DC 20037
Ph: 202-521-9300 ▪ Fx: 202-833-3636

International Ozone Association   www.int-ozone-assoc.org
31 Strawberry Hill Ave   Stamford CT 06902
Ph: 203-348-3542 ▪ Fx: 203-967-4845

International Pacific Halibut Commission   www.iphc.washington.edu
PO Box 95009   Seattle WA 98145
Ph: 206-634-1838 ▪ Fx: 206-632-2983

International Packaged Ice Association   www.packagedice.com
PO Box 1199   Tampa FL 33601
Ph: 813-258-1690 ▪ Fx: 813-251-2783 ▪ TF: 800-742-0627

International Packet Communications Consortium   www.packetcomm.org
2400 Camino Ramon Suite 275   San Ramon CA 94583
Ph: 925-275-6635 ▪ Fx: 925-275-6691

International Palm Society   www.palms.org
PO Box 7075   Lawrence KS 66044
Ph: 785-843-1235 ▪ Fx: 785-843-1274

International Paperweight Society   www.paperweight.com
123 Locust St   Santa Cruz CA 95060
Ph: 831-427-1177 ▪ Fx: 831-427-0111 ▪ TF: 800-538-0766

International Parking Institute   www.parking.org
PO Box 7167   Fredericksburg VA 22404
Ph: 540-371-7535 ▪ Fx: 540-371-8022

International Parrotlet Society   www.internationalparrotletsociety.org
PO Box 2428   Santa Cruz CA 95063
Ph: 831-688-5560 ▪ Fx: 831-689-9534

International Peace, Carnegie Endowment for   www.ceip.org
1779 Massachusetts Ave NW   Washington DC 20036
Ph: 202-483-7600 ▪ Fx: 202-483-1840

International Peat Society   www.peatsociety.fi/natcoms
US National Committee 10105 White City Rd   Britt MN 55710
Ph: 218-741-2813

International Pediatric Transplant Association   www.iptaonline.org
17000 Commerce Pkwy Suite C   Mount Laurel NJ 08054
Ph: 856-439-0500 ▪ Fx: 856-439-0525

International Pentecostal Holiness Church   www.iphc.org
PO Box 12609   Oklahoma City OK 73157
Ph: 405-787-7110 ▪ Fx: 405-789-3957

International Percy Grainger Society   www.percygrainger.org
7 Cromwell Pl   White Plains NY 10601
Ph: 914-948-7436

International Perfume Bottle Association   www.perfumebottles.org
1789 Maryland Ave N   Minneapolis MN 55427
Ph: 763-544-5038

International Perimetric Society   www.perimetry.org
c/o Glaucoma Consultants NW 1221 Madison St Suite
   1124   Seattle WA 98104
Ph: 206-682-3447 ▪ Fx: 206-682-8219

International Personnel, American Council on   www.acip.com
515 Madison Ave 6th Fl   New York NY 10022
Ph: 212-688-2437 ▪ Fx: 212-593-4697

International Pharmaceutical Excipients Council of the Americas   www.ipecamericas.org
1655 N Fort Myer Dr Suite 700   Arlington VA 22209
Ph: 703-875-2127 ▪ Fx: 703-525-5157

International Photographic Historical Organization   www.well.com/user/silver
PO Box 16074   San Francisco CA 94116
Ph: 415-681-4356

International Photography Art Dealers,   www.artline.com/associations/ipa/ipa.html
Association of   1609 Connecticut Ave NW Suite
   200   Washington DC 20009
Ph: 202-986-0105 ▪ Fx: 202-986-0448

International Physical Fitness Association   www.ipfa.org
415 W Court St   Flint MI 48503
Ph: 810-239-2166 ▪ Fx: 810-239-9390 ▪ TF: 877-520-4732

International Piano Guild   www.pianoguild.com
808 Rio Grande St   Austin TX 78701
Ph: 512-478-5775 ▪ Fx: 512-478-5843

International Planetarium Society   www.ips-planetarium.org
PO Box 1812   Greenville NC 27835
Ph: 252-328-6139 ▪ Fx: 252-328-6218

International Planned Parenthood Federation - Western   www.ippfwhr.org
Hemisphere Region   120 Wall St 9th Fl   New York NY 10005
Ph: 212-248-6400 ▪ Fx: 212-248-4221

International Plant Propagators Society Inc   www.ipps.org
Washington Park Arboretum 2300 Arboreton Dr   Seattle WA
   98112
Ph: 206-543-8602

International Plate Printers Die Stampers & Engravers Union of
North America   14 C St SW Rm 213-5a   Washington DC
   20228
Ph: 202-874-2554

International Poetry Forum   www.thepoetryforum.org
Grace Library 3333 5th Ave   Pittsburgh PA 15213
Ph: 412-621-9893 ▪ Fx: 412-621-9898

International Police Mountain Bike Association   www.ipmba.org
583 Fredrick Rd Suite 5B   Baltimore MD 21228
Ph: 410-744-2400 ▪ Fx: 410-744-5504 ▪ TF: 800-323-0037

International Policy, Center for   www.ciponline.org
1717 Massachusetts Ave NW Suite 801   Washington DC 20036
Ph: 202-232-3317 ▪ Fx: 202-232-3440

International Polka Association   www.internationalpolka.com
4608 S Archer Ave   Chicago IL 60632
Ph: 800-867-6552

International Practical Training, Association for   www.aipt.org
10400 Little Patuxent Pkwy Suite 250   Columbia MD 21044
Ph: 410-997-2200 ▪ Fx: 410-992-3924

International Precious Metals Institute   www.ipmi.org
4400 Bayou Blvd Suite 18   Pensacola FL 32503
Ph: 850-476-1156 ▪ Fx: 850-476-1548

International Prepaid Communications Association   www.i-pca.org
904 Massachusetts Ave NE   Washington DC 20002
Ph: 202-544-4448 ▪ Fx: 202-547-7417 ▪ TF: 800-958-7824

International Prepress Association   www.ipa.org
7200 France Ave S Suite 223   Edina MN 55435
Ph: 952-896-1908 ▪ Fx: 952-896-0181 ▪ TF: 800-255-8141

International Primate Protection League   www.ippl.org
PO Box 766   Summerville SC 29484
Ph: 843-871-2280 ▪ Fx: 843-871-7988

International Primatological Society   www.primate.wisc.edu/pin/ips.html
Univ of Georgia Psychology Dept   Athens GA 30602
Ph: 706-542-3036 ▪ Fx: 706-542-3275

International Private Enterprise, Center for   www.cipe.org
1155 15th St NW Suite 700   Washington DC 20005
Ph: 202-721-9200 ▪ Fx: 202-721-9250

International Probate Research Association   www.lostheir.com/ipra.htm
c/o Josh Butler & Co Inc 201 Commerce St Suite
   150   Youngstown OH 44503
Ph: 330-747-3000 ▪ Fx: 330-747-3006

International Professional Groomers   www.ipgcmg.org
120 Turner Ave   Elk Grove Village IL 60007
Ph: 847-758-1938 ▪ Fx: 847-758-8031

International Professional Rodeo Association   www.iprarodeo.com
PO Box 83377   Oklahoma City OK 73148
Ph: 405-235-6540 ▪ Fx: 405-235-6577

International Programs USA, Council of   www.cipusa.org
1700 E 13th St Suite 4ME   Cleveland OH 44114
Ph: 216-566-1088 ▪ Fx: 216-566-1490

International Psychogeriatric Association   www.ipa-online.org
5215 Old Orchard Rd Suite 340   Skokie IL 60077
Ph: 847-663-0574 ▪ Fx: 847-663-0591

International Psychohistorical Association   www.geocities.com/athens/acropolis/8623
266 Monroe Ave   Wyckoff NJ 07481
Ph: 201-891-4980

International Public Management Association for Human Resources   www.ipma-hr.org
1617 Duke St   Alexandria VA 22314
Ph: 703-549-7100 ▪ Fx: 703-684-0948 ▪ TF: 800-220-4762

International Public Relations Association   www.ipra.org

International Publishing Management Association   www.ipma.org
1205 W College St   Liberty MO 64068
Ph: 816-781-1111 ▪ Fx: 816-781-2790

International Quorum of Motion Picture Producers   www.iqfilm.org
c/o Film House 810 Dominican Dr   Nashville TN 37228
Ph: 615-255-4000 ▪ Fx: 615-255-4111

International Racquetball Federation   www.internationalracquetball.com
1685 W Uintah St   Colorado Springs CO 80904
Ph: 719-635-5396 ▪ Fx: 719-635-0685

International Radio & Television Society Foundation Inc   www.irts.org
420 Lexington Ave Suite 1601   New York NY 10170
Ph: 212-867-6650 ▪ Fx: 212-867-6653

International Reading Association   www.reading.org
800 Barksdale Rd   Newark DE 19714
Ph: 302-731-1600 ▪ Fx: 302-731-1057

International Real Estate Institute   www.iami.org/irei.cfm
1224 N Nokomis St NE   Alexandria MN 56308
Ph: 320-763-4648 ▪ Fx: 320-763-9290

International Reciprocal Trade Association   www.irta.com
140 Metro Park   Rochester NY 14623
Ph: 716-424-2940 ▪ Fx: 716-424-2964

International Recording Media Association   www.recordingmedia.org
182 Nassau St Suite 204   Princeton NJ 08542
Ph: 609-279-1700 ▪ Fx: 609-279-1999

International Recreational Go-Kart Association
435 Corona St   San Antonio TX 78209
Ph: 210-824-1923 ▪ Fx: 210-824-5186

International Refrigerated Transportation Association   www.irta.com
4255 S Buckley Rd Suite 118   Aurora CO 80013
Ph: 888-454-4782 ▪ Fx: 720-851-6090

International Reprographic Association   www.irga.com
401 N Michigan Ave   Chicago IL 60611
Ph: 312-245-1026 ▪ Fx: 312-527-6705 ▪ TF: 800-833-4742

International Republican Institute-USA   www.iri.org
1225 'I' St NW Suite 700   Washington DC 20005
Ph: 202-408-9450 ▪ Fx: 202-408-9462

International Rescue Committee   www.intrescom.org
122 E 42nd St 12th Fl   New York NY 10168
Ph: 212-551-3000 ▪ Fx: 212-551-3180

International Research & Exchanges Board   www.irex.org
2121 K St NW Suite 700   Washington DC 20037
Ph: 202-628-8188 ▪ Fx: 202-628-8189

International Right of Way Association   www.irwaonline.org
19750 S Vermont Ave Suite 220 \Torrance CA 90502
Ph: 310-538-0233 ▪ Fx: 310-538-1471

International Rivers Network   www.irn.org
1847 Berkeley Way   Berkeley CA 94703
Ph: 510-848-1155 ▪ Fx: 510-848-1008

International Road Federation   www.irfnet.org
1010 Massachusetts Ave NW Suite 410   Washington DC 20001
Ph: 202-371-5544 ▪ Fx: 202-371-5565

International Safe Transit Association   www.ista.org
1400 Abbott Rd Suite 160   East Lansing MI 48823
Ph: 517-333-3437 ▪ Fx: 517-333-3813

International Safety Equipment Association   www.safetyequipment.org
1901 N Moore St Suite 808   Arlington VA 22209
Ph: 703-525-1695 ▪ Fx: 703-528-2148

International Sanitary Supply Association   www.issa.com
7373 N Lincoln Ave   Lincolnwood IL 60712
Ph: 847-982-0800 ▪ Fx: 847-982-1012 ▪ TF: 800-225-4772

International Saw & Knife Association
351 'O' St   Fresno CA 93721
Ph: 559-237-0809 ▪ Fx: 559-237-8879

International Schools Services   www.iss.edu
15 Roszel Rd PO Box 5910   Princeton NJ 08543
Ph: 609-452-0990 ▪ Fx: 609-452-2690

International Security Management Association   www.ismanet.com
PO Box 623   Buffalo IA 52728
Ph: 563-381-4008 ▪ Fx: 563-381-4283 ▪ TF: 800-368-1894

International Security, Women in   wiis.georgetown.edu
Georgetown Univ Walsh School of Foreign Service Ctr for
   Peace & Security Studies 3240 Prospect St
   NW   Washington DC 20057
Ph: 202-687-3366 ▪ Fx: 202-687-3233

International Service Robot Association
900 Victors Way PO Box 3724   Ann Arbor MI 48106
Ph: 734-994-6088 ▪ Fx: 734-994-3338

International Ship Masters' Association   www.shipmaster.org

International Shooting Coaches Association
17446 SW Granada Dr   Beaverton OR 97007
Ph: 503-642-5873 ▪ Fx: 503-649-5182

International Sign Association   www.signs.org
707 N Saint Asaph St   Alexandria VA 22314
Ph: 703-836-4012 ▪ Fx: 703-836-8353

International Skeletal Society   www.internationalskeletalsociety.com

International Sled Dog Racing Association   www.isdra.org
22702 Rebel Rd   Merrifield MN 56465
Ph: 218-765-4297 ▪ Fx: 218-765-3246

International Sleep Products Association   www.sleepproducts.org
501 Wythe St   Alexandria VA 22314
Ph: 703-683-8371 ▪ Fx: 703-683-4503

International Slurry Surfacing Association   www.slurry.org
3 Church Cir PMB 250   Annapolis MD 21401
Ph: 410-267-0023 ▪ Fx: 410-267-7546

International Snow Leopard Trust   www.snowleopard.org
4649 Sunnyside Ave N Suite 325   Seattle WA 98103
Ph: 206-632-2421 ▪ Fx: 206-632-3967

International Snowmobile Manufacturers Association — www.snowmobile.org
1640 Haslett Rd Suite 170   Haslett MI 48840
Ph: 517-339-7788 ▪ Fx: 517-339-7798

International Social Service USA Branch — www.iss-usa.org
700 Light St   Baltimore MD 21230
Ph: 410-230-2734 ▪ Fx: 410-230-2741

International Society for Adolescent Psychiatry — www.isap-web.org
223 Sunset Blvd   Bronx NY 10473
Ph: 718-892-4868

International Society for Adult Congenital Cardiac Disease — www.isaccd.org
1500 Sunday Dr Suite 102   Raleigh NC 27607
Ph: 919-861-5578 ▪ Fx: 919-787-4916

International Society of Air Safety Investigators — www.isasi.org
107 E Holly Ave Suite 11   Sterling VA 20164
Ph: 703-430-9668 ▪ Fx: 703-430-4970

International Society for Analytical Cytology — www.isac-net.org
60 Revere Dr Suite 500   Northbrook IL 60062
Ph: 847-205-4722 ▪ Fx: 847-480-9282

International Society of Animal License Collectors
928 SR 2206   Clinton KY 42031
Ph: 270-653-6060 ▪ Fx: 270-653-3030

International Society for Animal Rights — www.isaronline.org
965 Griffin Pond Rd   Clarks Summit PA 18411
Ph: 570-586-2200 ▪ Fx: 570-586-9580 ▪ TF: 800-543-4727

International Society of Antique Scale Collectors — www.isasc.org
3616 Noakes St   Los Angeles CA 90023
Ph: 323-263-6878 ▪ Fx: 323-263-3147

International Society for Antiviral Research — www.georgetown.edu/research/arc/ISAR

International Society of Appraisers — www.isa-appraisers.org
1131 SW 7th St Suite 105   Renton WA 98055
Ph: 206-241-0359 ▪ Fx: 206-241-0436 ▪ TF: 888-472-5762

International Society of Arboriculture — www.isa-arbor.com
1400 W Anthony Dr PO Box 3129   Champaign IL 61826
Ph: 217-355-9411 ▪ Fx: 217-355-9516 ▪ TF: 888-472-8733

International Society of Arthroscopy Knee Surgery & Orthopaedic — www.isakos.com
Sports Medicine   2678 Bishop Dr Suite 250   San Ramon CA
94583
Ph: 925-807-1197 ▪ Fx: 925-807-1199

International Society for Astrological Research — www.isarastrology.com
PO Box 38613   Los Angeles CA 90038
Ph: 805-525-0461 ▪ Fx: 805-933-0301 ▪ TF: 800-982-1788

International Society of Bassists — www.isbworldoffice.com
13140 Coit Rd Suite 320 LB 120   Dallas TX 75240
Ph: 972-233-9107 ▪ Fx: 972-490-4219

International Society of Beverage Technologists — www.bevtech.org
8110 S Suncoast Blvd   Homosassa FL 34446
Ph: 352-382-2008 ▪ Fx: 352-382-2018

International Society of Bible Collectors — www.biblecollectors.org
2901 Pennsylvania Ave S   Saint Louis Park MN 55426
Ph: 952-929-3728

International Society for Biomedical Research on Alcoholism — www.isbra.com
PO Box 202332   Denver CO 80220
Ph: 303-355-6420 ▪ Fx: 303-355-1207

International Society of Blood Purification — www.isbp.org
Vanderbilt University Medical Ctr 1161 21st Ave S MCN
S-3301   Nashville TN 37232
Ph: 615-343-2220 ▪ Fx: 615-322-8653

International Society for British Genealogy & Family History
PO Box 3115   Salt Lake City UT 84110
Ph: 801-272-2178

International Society for Business Education — www.siec-isbe.org
PO Box 20457   Carson City NV 89721
Ph: 775-882-1445 ▪ Fx: 775-882-1449

International Society of Certified Electronics Technicians — www.iscet.org
3608 Pershing Ave   Fort Worth TX 76107
Ph: 817-921-9101 ▪ Fx: 817-921-3741 ▪ TF: 800-946-0201

International Society of Certified Employee Benefit Specialists — www.iscebs.org
18700 W Bluemond Rd PO Box 209   Brookfield WI 53008
Ph: 262-786-8771 ▪ Fx: 262-786-8650

International Society of Chemical Ecology — www.chemecol.org
North Dakota State Univ Dept of Entomology   Fargo ND 58105
Ph: 701-231-6444 ▪ Fx: 701-231-8557

International Society of Citriculture — www.lal.ufl.edu/ISC_Citrus_homepage.htm
UC Riverside Dept of Botany & Plant Sciences   Riverside CA
92521
Ph: 909-787-4412 ▪ Fx: 909-787-4437

International Society of Cleaning Technicians — www.isct.org
109 Mill Stone Dr   Dothan AL 36305
Ph: 334-702-1984 ▪ Fx: 334-792-2999

International Society for Clinical Densitometry — www.iscd.org
342 N Main St   West Hartford CT 06117
Ph: 860-586-7563 ▪ Fx: 860-586-7550

International Society of Communications Specialists — www.iscs.cc
201 Blue Sky Dr   Marietta GA 30068
Ph: 770-973-0662 ▪ Fx: 770-973-1410

International Society for the Comparative Study of Civilizations — www.iscsc.net

International Society for a Complete Earth — www.hollow-earth.org
PO Box 1952   Kapaa HI 96746
Ph: 808-245-3820

International Society of Copier Artists
759 President St Suite 2H   Brooklyn NY 11215
Ph: 718-638-3264

International Society of Cryptozoology
PO Box 43070   Tucson AZ 85733
Ph: 520-884-8369

International Society Daughters of Utah Pioneers — www.dupinternational.org
300 N Main St   Salt Lake City UT 84103
Ph: 801-538-1050 ▪ Fx: 801-538-1119

International Society of Dermatology — www.intsocdermatol.org
847 S Randall Rd Suite 412   Elgin IL 60123
Ph: 847-429-9535 ▪ Fx: 847-429-9545

International Society for Developmental Neuroscience — developmental-neuroscience.org

International Society for Ecological Economics — www.ecoeco.org
1313 Dolley Madison Blvd Suite 402   McLean VA 22101
Ph: 703-790-1745 ▪ Fx: 703-790-2672

International Society for Experimental Hematology — www.iseh.org
2025 M St NW Suite 800   Washington DC 20036
Ph: 202-367-1183 ▪ Fx: 202-367-2183

International Society of Explosives Engineers — www.isee.org
30325 Bainbridge Rd   Cleveland OH 44139
Ph: 440-349-4400 ▪ Fx: 440-349-3788

International Society of Exposure Analysis — www.iseaweb.org
c/o JSI Research & Training Institute 44 Farnsworth St   Boston
MA 02210
Ph: 617-482-9485 ▪ Fx: 617-482-0617

International Society of Facilities Executives — www.isfe.org
200 Corporate Pl 2B   Peabody MA 01960
Ph: 978-536-0108 ▪ Fx: 978-536-0199

International Society of Financiers — www.insofin.com
PO Box 398   Naples NC 28760
Ph: 828-698-7805 ▪ Fx: 828-698-7806

International Society of Fire Service Instructors — www.isfsi.org
PO Box 2320   Stafford VA 22555
Ph: 540-657-2490 ▪ Fx: 540-657-0154 ▪ TF: 800-435-0005

International Society of Folk Harpers & Craftsmen — www.folkharpsociety.org
4110 Brandemere Way   Houston TX 77066
Ph: 832-249-7885

International Society for General Semantics — www.generalsemantics.org
PO Box 728   Concord CA 94522
Ph: 925-798-0311 ▪ Fx: 925-798-0312

International Society of Hair Restoration Surgery — www.ishrs.org
13 S 2nd St   Geneva IL 60134
Ph: 630-262-5399 ▪ Fx: 630-262-1520 ▪ TF: 800-444-2737

International Society for Heart & Lung Transplantation — www.ishlt.org
14673 Midway Rd Suite 200   Addison TX 75001
Ph: 972-490-9495 ▪ Fx: 972-490-9499

International Society for Heart Research — www.ishrworld.org
Univ of Louisvillle Health Science Ctr 550 S Jackson
St   Louisville KY 40292
Ph: 502-852-1837 ▪ Fx: 502-852-6474

International Society for the History Philosophy & — www.phil.vt.edu/ishpssb
Social Studies of Biology   13423 Burma Rd SW   Vashon
Island WA 98070
Ph: 206-567-5839

International Society of Hospitality Consultants — www.ishc.com
515 King St Suite 420   Alexandria VA 22314
Ph: 703-684-6681 ▪ Fx: 703-684-6048

International Society of Hospitality Purchasers — www.ishp.org
300 Montgomery St Suite 833   San Francisco CA 94104
Ph: 415-399-0995 ▪ Fx: 415-399-0935

International Society for Individual Liberty — www.isil.org
836-B Southampton Rd Suite 299   Benicia CA 94510
Ph: 707-746-8796 ▪ Fx: 707-746-8797

International Society of Industrial Fabric Manufacturers
1337 Garden Cir Dr   Newberry SC 29108
Ph: 803-276-2684

International Society for Infectious Diseases — www.isid.org
181 Longwood Ave   Boston MA 02115
Ph: 617-277-0551 ▪ Fx: 617-731-1541

International Society of Information Fusion — www.inforfusion.org/
2393 Fieldstone Cir   Fairborn OH 45324
Ph: 937-255-2632 ▪ Fx: 937-255-1100

International Society for Intellectual History — www.princeton.edu/~isih
Princeton Univ Hamilton Hall   Princeton NJ 08544
Ph: 609-258-3317 ▪ Fx: 609-258-2889

International Society for Intercultural Education Training & — www.sietarusa.org
Research   8835 SW Canyon Ln Suite 110   Portland OR 97225
Ph: 503-297-4622 ▪ Fx: 503-297-4695

International Society of Livestock Appraisers — www.amagappraisers.com/livestok.htm
1126 Eastland Dr N Suite 100 PO Box 186   Twin Falls ID
83303
Ph: 208-733-2323 ▪ Fx: 208-733-2326 ▪ TF: 800-488-7570

International Society for Magnetic Resonance in Medicine — www.ismrm.org
2118 Millvia St Suite 201   Berkeley CA 94704
Ph: 510-841-1899 ▪ Fx: 510-841-2340

International Society of Meeting Planners — www.iami.org/ismp
1224 N Nokomis NE   Alexandria MN 56308
Ph: 320-763-4919 ▪ Fx: 320-763-9290

International Society on Metabolic Eye Disease
1125 Park Ave   New York NY 10128
Ph: 212-427-1246 ▪ Fx: 212-360-7009

International Society for Minimally Invasive Cardiac Surgery — www.ismics.org
900 Cummings Ctr Suite 221-U   Beverly MA 01915
Ph: 978-927-8330 ▪ Fx: 978-524-8890

International Society for Molecular Plant Microbe Interactions — www.ismpminet.org
3340 Pilot Knob Rd   Saint Paul MN 55121
Ph: 651-454-7250 ▪ Fx: 651-454-0766 ▪ TF: 800-481-2698

International Society of Offshore & Polar Engineers — www.isope.org
PO Box 189   Cupertino CA 95015
Ph: 650-254-1871 ▪ Fx: 650-254-2038

International Society of Parametric Analysts — www.ispa-cost.org
PO Box 9699   Canoga Park CA 91309
Ph: 818-888-3419 ▪ Fx: 818-888-8362

International Society for Performance Improvement — www.ispi.org
1400 Spring St Suite 260   Silver Spring MD 20910
Ph: 301-587-8570 ▪ Fx: 301-587-8573

International Society for the Performing Arts Foundation www.ispa.org
17 Purdy Ave PO Box 909   Rye NY 10580
Ph: 914-921-1550 ■ Fx: 914-921-1593

International Society for Peritoneal Dialysis www.ispd.org
66 Martin St   Milton ON L9T2R2
Ph: 905-875-2456 ■ Fx: 905-875-2864 ■ TF: 888-834-1001

International Society for Pharmaceutical Engineering www.ispe.org
3109 W Dr ML King Jr Blvd Suite 250   Tampa FL 33607
Ph: 813-960-2105 ■ Fx: 813-264-2816

International Society for Pharmacoeconomics & Outcomes Research www.ispor.org
3100 Princeton Pike Bldg 3 Suite E   Lawrenceville NJ 08648
Ph: 609-219-0773 ■ Fx: 609-219-0774

International Society for Pharmacoepidemiology www.pharmacoepi.org
4350 East-West Hwy Suite 401   Bethesda MD 20814
Ph: 301-718-6500 ■ Fx: 301-656-0989

International Society for Plant Molecular Biology www.uga.edu/~ispmb
Univ of Georgia Dept of Biochemistry & Molecular
Biology   Athens GA 30602
Ph: 706-542-3239 ■ Fx: 706-542-2090

International Society of Political Psychology ispp.org
Pitzer College 1050 N Mills Ave   Claremont CA 91711
Ph: 909-621-8442 ■ Fx: 909-621-8481

International Society for Preservation of the Tropical Rainforest www.isptr-pard.org
3302 N Burton Ave   Rosemead CA 91770
Ph: 626-572-0233 ■ Fx: 626-572-9521

International Society for Prosthetics & Orthotics, US Member Society of the www.usispo.org
1161 Francisco Rd   Columbus OH 43220
Ph: 614-457-4312 ■ Fx: 614-538-1914

International Society for the Protection of Mustangs & Burros www.ispmb.org
PO Box 55   Lantry SD 57636
Ph: 605-964-6866 ■ Fx: 605-365-6991

International Society of Psychiatric www.ispn-psych.org/html/ispcln.html
Consultation-Liaison Nurses   1211 Locust St   Philadelphia PA
19107
Ph: 215-545-2843 ■ Fx: 215-545-8107 ■ TF: 800-826-2950

International Society of Psychiatric-Mental Health Nurses www.ispn-psych.org
1211 Locust St   Philadelphia PA 19107
Ph: 215-545-2843 ■ Fx: 215-545-8107 ■ TF: 800-826-2950

International Society for Quality of Life Studies market1.cob.vt.edu/isqols
Virginia Polytechnic Institute Pamplin College of Business Mktg
Dept   Blacksburg VA 24061
Ph: 540-231-5110 ■ Fx: 540-231-3076

International Society of Radiology www.isradiology.org
7910 Woodmont Ave Suite 400   Bethesda MD 20814
Ph: 301-657-2652 ■ Fx: 301-907-8768

International Society of Refractive Surgery www.isrs.org
655 Beach St   San Francisco CA 94109
Ph: 415-561-8581 ■ Fx: 415-561-8575

International Society for Research on Aggression www.israsociety.com

International Society for Research in Human Milk & Lactation www.isrhml.org
Meriter Hospital Perinatal Ctr 202 S Park St   Madison WI
53715
Ph: 608-262-6561 ■ Fx: 608-267-6377

International Society for Respiratory Protection - Americas Section www.amersectisrp.org

International Society of Restaurant Association Executives www.israe.org
8525 Douglas Ave Suite 47   Des Moines IA 50322
Ph: 515-276-1454 ■ Fx: 515-276-3660

International Society of Statistical Science in Economics
536 Oasis Dr   Santa Rosa CA 95407
Ph: 707-575-3529

International Society of Stress Analysts
9 Westchester Dr   Kissimmee FL 34744
Ph: 407-933-4839 ■ Fx: 407-935-0911

International Society for the Study of Dissociation www.issd.org
60 Revere Dr Suite 500   Northbrook IL 60062
Ph: 847-480-0899 ■ Fx: 847-480-9282

International Society for the Study of Subtle Energies & www.issseem.org
Energy Medicine   11005 Ralston Rd Suite 100D   Arvada CO
80004
Ph: 303-425-4625 ■ Fx: 303-425-4685

International Society for the Systems Sciences www.isss.org/
38 Seca Pl   Salinas CA 93908
Ph: 831-375-7614

International Society for Technology in Education www.iste.org
480 Charnelton St   Eugene OR 97401
Ph: 541-302-3777 ■ Fx: 541-302-3778 ■ TF: 800-336-5191

International Society for Third-Sector Research www.istr.org
3400 N Charles St Suite 559   Baltimore MD 21218
Ph: 410-516-4678 ■ Fx: 410-516-4870

International Society on Thrombosis & Haemostasis www.med.unc.edu/isth
UNC Medical School CB 7035   Chapel Hill NC 27599
Ph: 919-929-3807 ■ Fx: 919-929-3935

International Society of Transport Aircraft Trading www.istat.org
5517 Talon Ct   Fairfax VA 22032
Ph: 703-978-8156 ■ Fx: 703-503-5964

International Society for Traumatic Stress Studies www.istss.org
60 Revere Dr Suite 500   Northbrook IL 60062
Ph: 847-480-9028 ■ Fx: 847-480-9282

International Society of Travel Medicine www.istm.org
PO Box 871089   Stone Mountain GA 30087
Ph: 770-736-7060 ■ Fx: 770-736-6732

International Society of Travel & Tourism Educators www.istte.org
23220 Edgewater   Saint Clair Shores MI 48082
Ph: 586-294-0208

International Society of Tropical Foresters www.istf-bethesda.org
5400 Grosvenor Ln   Bethesda MD 20814
Ph: 301-897-8720 ■ Fx: 301-897-3690

International Society for Vehicle Preservation
PO Box 50046   Tucson AZ 85703
Ph: 520-622-2201 ■ Fx: 520-792-8501

International Society of Weekly Newspaper Editors www.iswne.org
Missouri Southern State Univ 3950 E Newman Rd   Joplin MO
64801
Ph: 417-625-9736 ■ Fx: 417-659-4445

International Society of Weighing & Measurement www.iswm.com
15245 Shady Grove Rd Suite 130   Rockville MD 20850
Ph: 301-258-1115 ■ Fx: 301-990-9771

International Softball Federation www.internationalsoftball.com
1900 S Park Rd   Plant City FL 33566
Ph: 813-864-0100 ■ Fx: 813-864-0105

International Solid Surface Fabricators Association www.issfa.net
975 American Pacific Dr   Henderson NV 89014
Ph: 702-567-8150 ■ Fx: 702-567-8145

International Soundex Reunion Registry www.isrr.net
PO Box 2312   Carson City NV 89702
Ph: 775-882-7755

International Spa Association www.experienceispa.com
2365 Harrodsburg Rd Suite A325   Lexington KY 40504
Ph: 859-226-4326 ■ Fx: 859-226-4445 ■ TF: 888-651-4772

International Special Events Society www.ises.com
401 N Michigan Ave   Chicago IL 60611
Ph: 312-312-6853 ■ Fx: 312-673-6953 ■ TF: 800-688-4737

International Special Tooling & Machining Association
9300 Livingston Rd   Fort Washington MD 20744
Ph: 301-248-6200 ■ Fx: 301-248-7104 ■ TF: 800-248-6862

International Sporthorse Registry www.isroldenburg.org
939 Merchandise Mart   Chicago IL 60654
Ph: 312-527-6544 ■ Fx: 312-527-6573

International Sports Sciences Association www.issaonline.com
400 E Gutierrez St   Santa Barbara CA 93101
Ph: 805-884-8111 ■ Fx: 805-884-8119 ■ TF: 800-892-4772

International Spotted Horse Registry Association members.tripod.com/~spottedhorses
PO Box 412   Anderson MO 64831
Ph: 417-475-6273 ■ TF: 866-201-3098

International Sprout Growers Association www.isga-sprouts.org
2150 N 107th St Suite 205   Seattle WA 98133
Ph: 206-367-8704

International Staple Nail & Tool Association www.isanta.org
512 W Burlington Ave Suite 203   La Grange IL 60525
Ph: 708-482-8138 ■ Fx: 708-482-8186

International Star Class Yacht Racing Association www.starclass.org
1545 Waukegan Rd   Glenview IL 60025
Ph: 847-729-0630 ■ Fx: 847-729-0718

International Steel, American Institute for www.aiis.org
1325 G St NW Suite 980   Washington DC 20005
Ph: 202-628-3878 ■ Fx: 202-737-3134

International String Figure Association www.isfa.org/isfa.htm
PO Box 5134   Pasadena CA 91117
Ph: 626-398-1057

International Student Organization www.isoa.org
250 W 49th St Suite 806   New York NY 10019
Ph: 212-262-8922 ■ Fx: 212-262-8920 ■ TF: 800-244-1180

International Students Inc www.isionline.org
PO Box C   Colorado Springs CO 80901
Ph: 719-576-2700 ■ Fx: 719-576-5363 ■ TF: 800-474-4145

International Studies, American Council for www.acis.com
343 Congress St Suite 3100   Boston MA 02210
Ph: 617-236-2051 ■ Fx: 617-236-4703

International Studies Association csf.colorado.edu/isa
Univ of Arizona 324 Social Sciences   Tucson AZ 85721
Ph: 520-621-7715 ■ Fx: 520-621-5780

International Studies, Center of www.wws.princeton.edu/~cis
Princeton University Bendheim Hall   Princeton NJ 08544
Ph: 609-258-4852 ■ Fx: 609-258-3988

International Studies, Center for Strategic & www.csis.org
1800 K St NW Suite 400   Washington DC 20006
Ph: 202-887-0200 ■ Fx: 202-775-3199

International Studies, College Consortium for www.ccisabroad.org
2000 P St NW Suite 503   Washington DC 20036
Ph: 202-223-0330 ■ Fx: 202-223-0999 ■ TF: 800-453-6956

International Studies, National Council for Languages & www.languagepolicy.org
4646 40th St NW Suite 310   Washington DC 20016
Ph: 202-966-8477 ■ Fx: 202-966-8210

International Studies, World Association of wais.stanford.edu
Hoover Institution   Stanford CA 94305
Ph: 650-322-2026 ■ Fx: 650-723-1687

International Stunt Association www.isastunts.com
11331 Ventura Blvd Suite 205   Studio City CA 91604
Ph: 818-760-2072 ■ Fx: 818-760-2217

International Sunfish Class Association www.sunfishclass.org
PO Box 300128   Waterford MI 48330
Ph: 248-673-2750

International Surfing Association
5580 La Jolla Blvd PMB 145   La Jolla CA 92037
Ph: 858-551-5292 ■ Fx: 858-551-5290

International Swaps & Derivatives Association www.isda.org
360 Madison Ave 16th Fl   New York NY 10017
Ph: 212-901-6000 ■ Fx: 212-901-6001

International Tandem Users' Group www.itug.org
401 N Michigan   Chicago IL 60611
Ph: 312-321-6851 ■ Fx: 312-321-5158 ■ TF: 800-845-4884

International Tap Association www.tapdance.org
PO Box 356   Boulder CO 80306
Ph: 303-443-7989 ■ Fx: 303-443-7992

International Task Force on Euthanasia & www.internationaltaskforce.org
Assisted Suicide   PO Box 760   Steubenville OH 43952
Ph: 740-282-3810 ■ Fx: 740-282-0769 ■ TF: 800-958-5678

International Tax Education, Council for　　www.fdta-cite.org
PO Box 1012　White Plains NY 10602
Ph: 914-328-5656 ▪ Fx: 914-328-5757

International Technology Education Association　www.iteawww.org
1914 Association Dr Suite 201　Reston VA 20191
Ph: 703-860-2100 ▪ Fx: 703-860-0353

International Technology Institute　　www.itiworld.org
PO Box 23166　San Diego CA 92193
Ph: 858-279-0483 ▪ Fx: 858-279-0493

International Telecommunications Satellite Organization　www.itso.int/
3400 International Dr NW　Washington DC 20008
Ph: 202-243-5096 ▪ Fx: 202-243-5018

International Telecommunications Society　www.itsworld.org
33 Alpine Dr　Gilford NH 03249
Ph: 603-293-4094 ▪ Fx: 603-293-4095

International Telework Association & Council　www.telecommute.org
8403 Colesville Rd Suite 865　Silver Spring MD 20910
Ph: 301-650-2322

International Test & Evaluation Association　www.itea.org
4400 Fair Lakes Ct Suite 104　Fairfax VA 22033
Ph: 703-631-6220 ▪ Fx: 703-631-6221

International Textile & Apparel Association　www.itaa.org
PO Box 1360　Monument CO 80132
Ph: 719-488-3716

International Theatre Equipment Association　www.itea.com
770 Broadway 5th Fl　New York NY 10003
Ph: 646-654-7680 ▪ Fx: 646-654-7694

International Thomas Merton Society　www.merton.org

International Ticketing Association　www.intix.org
330 W 38th St Suite 605　New York NY 10018
Ph: 212-629-4036 ▪ Fx: 212-629-8532

International Tire Association
PO Box 1067　Farmington CT 06034
Ph: 860-228-2536 ▪ Fx: 860-228-9772

International Titanium Association　www.titanium.org
350 Interlocken Blvd Suite 390　Broomfield CO 80021
Ph: 303-404-2221 ▪ Fx: 303-404-9111

International Trade Associations, Federation of　www.fita.org
11800 Sunrise Valley Dr Suite 210　Reston VA 20191
Ph: 703-620-1588 ▪ Fx: 703-620-4922

International Trade Bar Association, Customs &　www.citba.org
729 15th St NW Suite 800　Washington DC 20005
Ph: 202-783-6900 ▪ Fx: 202-783-6909

International Trade Commission Trial Lawyers Association　www.itctla.org
PO Box 6186 Benjamin Franklin Stn　Washington DC 20004
Ph: 202-942-6423

International Trade Council
3114 Circle Hill Rd　Alexandria VA 22305
Ph: 703-548-1234 ▪ Fx: 703-548-6216

International Trade Development, National Council on　www.ncitd.org
818 Connecticut Ave NW 12th Fl　Washington DC 20006
Ph: 202-872-9280 ▪ Fx: 202-872-8324

International Trade, Organization of Women in　www.owit.org
1413 K St NW 1st Fl Suite 857　Washington DC 20005
Ph: 202-785-9842

International Trademark Association　www.inta.org
1133 Ave of the Americas　New York NY 10036
Ph: 212-768-9887 ▪ Fx: 212-786-7796

International Traditional Karate Federation　www.itkf.org
1930 Wilshire Blvd Suite 1208　Los Angeles CA 90057
Ph: 213-483-8261 ▪ Fx: 213-483-4060

International Training in Communication　www.itcintl.com
2519 Woodland Dr　Anaheim CA 92801
Ph: 714-995-3660 ▪ Fx: 714-995-6974

International Transactional Analysis Association　www.itaa-net.org
436 14th St Suite 1301　Oakland CA 94612
Ph: 510-625-7720 ▪ Fx: 510-625-7725

International Transplant Nurses Society　www.itns.org
1739 E Carson St Box 351　Pittsburgh PA 15203
Ph: 412-343-4867 ▪ Fx: 412-343-3959

International Trauma Anesthesia & Critical Care Society　www.itaccs.com
PO Box 4826　Baltimore MD 21211
Ph: 410-235-7697 ▪ Fx: 410-235-8084

International Trotting & Pacing Association Inc　www.trottingbreds.com
60 Gulf Rd　Gouverneur NY 13642
Ph: 315-287-2294 ▪ Fx: 315-287-5010

International Trumpet Guild　www.trumpetguild.org

International Tuba-Euphonium Association　www.tubaonline.org
2253 Downing St　Denver CO 80205
Ph: 303-832-4676 ▪ Fx: 303-832-0839

International Turf Producers Foundation　www.turfgrasssod.org
1855-A Hicks Rd　Rolling Meadows IL 60008
Ph: 847-705-9898 ▪ Fx: 847-705-8347 ▪ TF: 800-405-8873

International Understanding, Business Council for　www.bciu.org
1212 Ave of the Americas 10th Fl　New York NY 10036
Ph: 212-490-0460 ▪ Fx: 212-697-8526

International Unicycling Federation Inc　www.unicycling.org/iuf

International Union of Allied Novelty & Production Workers
1950 W Erie St　Chicago IL 60622
Ph: 312-738-0822 ▪ Fx: 312-738-3553

International Union of Bricklayers & Allied Craftworkers　www.bacweb.org
1776 'I' St NW Suite 500　Washington DC 20006
Ph: 202-783-3788 ▪ Fx: 202-393-0219 ▪ TF: 800-331-1077

International Union for Conservation of Nature & Natural Resources　www.iucn.org
USA Multilateral Office 1630 Connecticut Ave NW 3rd
　Fl　Washington DC 20009
Ph: 202-387-4826 ▪ Fx: 202-387-4823

International Union of Electronic Electrical Salaried Machine & Furniture Workers　1275 K St NW Suite 600　Washington DC 20005　www.iue-cwa.org
Ph: 202-513-6300 ▪ Fx: 202-513-6357

International Union of Elevator Constructors　www.iuec.org
7154 Columbia Gateway Dr　Columbia MD 21046
Ph: 410-953-6150 ▪ Fx: 410-953-6169

International Union of Geodesy & Geophysics　www.iugg.org
Univ of Colorado UCB 216　Boulder CO 80309
Ph: 303-497-5147 ▪ Fx: 303-497-3645

International Union of Industrial Service Transport Health Employees
254 W 31st St　New York NY 10001
Ph: 212-696-5545 ▪ Fx: 212-696-5556 ▪ TF: 800-331-1070

International Union of Journeymen Horseshoers & Allied Trades
2070 Jericho Tpke　Commack NY 11725
Ph: 718-658-5740

International Union of Operating Engineers　www.iuoe.org
1125 17th St NW　Washington DC 20036
Ph: 202-429-9100 ▪ Fx: 202-778-2616

International Union of Painters & Allied Trades　www.ibpat.org
1750 New York Ave NW 8th Fl　Washington DC 20006
Ph: 202-637-0700 ▪ Fx: 202-637-0771

International Union of Petroleum & Industrial Workers
8131 E Rosecrans Ave　Paramount CA 90723
Ph: 562-630-6232 ▪ Fx: 562-408-1073 ▪ TF: 800-624-5842

International Union of Police Associations　www.iupa.org
1421 Prince St Suite 400　Alexandria VA 22314
Ph: 703-549-7473 ▪ Fx: 703-683-9048 ▪ TF: 800-247-4872

International Union of Pure & Applied Chemistry　www.iupac.org
PO Box 13757　Research Triangle Park NC 27709
Ph: 919-485-8700 ▪ Fx: 919-485-8706

International Union of Pure & Applied Physics　www.iupap.org
c/o American Physical Society 1 Physics Ellipse　College Park
　MD 20740
Ph: 301-209-3269

International Union of Security Officers
2201 Broadway Suite 101　San Leandro CA 94612
Ph: 510-625-9913 ▪ Fx: 510-625-0998 ▪ TF: 800-772-3326

International Union Security Police & Fire Professionals of America　www.spfpa.org
25510 Kelly Rd　Roseville MI 48066
Ph: 586-772-7250 ▪ Fx: 586-772-9644 ▪ TF: 800-228-7492

International Union United Automobile Aerospace & Agricultural Implement Workers of America　8000 E Jefferson Ave　Detroit MI 48214　www.uaw.org
Ph: 313-926-5000 ▪ Fx: 313-823-6016

International University Foundation
1301 S Noland Rd　Independence MO 64055
Ph: 816-461-3633 ▪ Fx: 816-461-4925 ▪ TF: 800-369-0009

International Vessel Operators Hazardous Materials Association　www.vohma.com
1118 Bay Rd　Lake George NY 12845
Ph: 518-761-0263 ▪ Fx: 518-792-7781

International Veterinary Acupuncture Society　www.ivas.org
PO Box 271395　Fort Collins CO 80527
Ph: 970-266-0666 ▪ Fx: 970-266-0777

International Virginia Woolf Society　www.utoronto.ca/IVWS
Southern Connecticut State Univ Dept of English 501 Crescent
　St　New Haven CT 06515
Ph: 203-392-6717 ▪ Fx: 203-392-6731

International Virtual Assistants Association　www.ivaa.org/
11024 Balboa Blvd Suite 315　Los Angeles CA 91344
Ph: 877-440-2750

International Visitors, National Council for　www.nciv.org
1420 K St NW Suite 800　Washington DC 20005
Ph: 202-842-1414 ▪ Fx: 202-289-4625 ▪ TF: 800-523-8101

International Visual Literacy Association　www.ivla.org/
Navarro College 3200 W 7th Ave　Corsicana TX 75110
Ph: 903-875-7441 ▪ Fx: 903-875-4636

International Wages for Housework Campaign　www.allwomencount.net
c/o Crossroad Women's Ctr PO Box 86681　Los Angeles CA
　90086
Ph: 323-292-7405

International Warehouse Logistics Association　www.iwla.com
2800 River Rd Suite 260　Des Plaines IL 60018
Ph: 847-813-4699 ▪ Fx: 847-813-0115

International Watch Fob Association　www.watchfob.com
601 Patriot Pl　Holmen WI 54636
Ph: 608-526-2328

International Water Lily & Water Gardening Society　www.iwgs.org
6828 26th St W　Bradenton FL 34207
Ph: 941-756-0880

International Water Resources Association　www.iwra.siu.edu
Southern Illinois Univ Carbondale 4535 Faner Hall　Carbondale
　IL 62901
Ph: 618-453-5138 ▪ Fx: 618-453-6465

International Webmasters Association　www.iwanet.org
119 E Union St Suite F　Pasadena CA 91103
Ph: 626-449-3709 ▪ Fx: 626-449-8308

International Weed Science Society　www.olemiss.edu/orgs/iws/DEFAULT.HTM
PO Box 8048　University MS 38677
Ph: 662-915-1036 ▪ Fx: 662-915-1035

International Wheat Gluten Association　www.iwga.net
9300 Metcalf Ave Suite 300　Overland Park KS 66212
Ph: 913-381-8180 ▪ Fx: 913-381-8836

International Wholesale Furniture Association　www.iwfa.net
164 S Main St Suite 310 PO Box 2482　High Point NC 27261
Ph: 336-884-1566 ▪ Fx: 336-884-1350

International Wild Waterfowl Association　www.wildwaterfowl.org
PO Box 36　Scotland Neck NC 27874
Ph: 252-826-5038 ▪ Fx: 252-826-5284

International Wildfowl Carving Association — iwfca.com

International Wildlife Coalition — www.iwc.org
70 E Falmouth Hwy   East Falmouth MA 02536
Ph: 508-548-8328 ▪ Fx: 508-548-8542 ▪ TF: 800-548-8704

International Wildlife Rehabilitation Council — www.iwrc-online.org
829 Bancroft Way   Berkeley CA 94710
Ph: 707-864-1761 ▪ Fx: 707-864-3106

International Window Cleaning Association — www.iwca.org
6418 Grovedale Dr Suite 101B   Alexandria VA 22310
Ph: 703-971-7771 ▪ Fx: 703-971-7772 ▪ TF: 800-875-4922

International Window Film Association — www.iwfa.com
PO Box 3871   Martinsville VA 24115
Ph: 276-666-4932

International Wireless Telecommunications Association — www.iwta.org
200 N Glebe Rd Suite 1000   Arlington VA 22203
Ph: 202-331-7773 ▪ Fx: 202-331-9062

International Women's Forum — www.iwforum.org
1621 Connecticut Ave NW Suite 300   Washington DC 20009
Ph: 202-775-8917 ▪ Fx: 202-429-0271

International Women's Health Coalition — www.iwhc.org
24 E 21st St   New York NY 10010
Ph: 212-979-8500 ▪ Fx: 212-979-9009

International Women's Media Foundation — www.iwmf.org
1726 M St NW Suite 1002   Washington DC 20036
Ph: 202-496-1992 ▪ Fx: 202-496-1977

International Women's Writing Guild — www.iwwg.com
PO Box 810 Gracie Stn   New York NY 10028
Ph: 212-737-7536 ▪ Fx: 212-737-9469

International Wood Products Association — www.iwpawood.org
4214 King St W   Alexandria VA 22302
Ph: 703-820-6696 ▪ Fx: 703-820-8550

International Youth Foundation — www.iyfnet.org
32 South St Suite 500   Baltimore MD 21202
Ph: 410-347-1500 ▪ Fx: 410-347-1188 ▪ TF: 800-446-2700

(Internet Activism) Common Dreams — www.commondreams.org
PO Box 443   Portland ME 04112
Ph: 207-775-0488 ▪ Fx: 207-775-0489

Internet Alliance — www.internetalliance.org
1111 19th St NW Suite 1180   Washington DC 20036
Ph: 202-955-8091 ▪ Fx: 202-955-8081

Internet Assigned Numbers Authority — www.iana.org
USC ISI 4676 Admiralty Way Suite 330   Marina del Rey CA 90292
Ph: 310-823-9358 ▪ Fx: 310-823-8649

Internet Association, Cellular Telecommunications & — www.wow-com.com
1400 16th St NW Suite 600   Washington DC 20036
Ph: 202-785-0081 ▪ Fx: 202-785-0721

(Internet) Center for Digital Democracy — www.democraticmedia.org
1718 Connecticut Ave NW Suite 200   Washington DC 20009
Ph: 202-986-2220

Internet Content Rating Association — www.icra.org
1130 Connecticut Ave NW Suite 501   Washington DC 20036
Ph: 202-331-8651 ▪ Fx: 202-331-8652

Internet Corp for Assigned Names & Numbers — www.icann.org
4676 Admiralty Way Suite 330   Marina del Rey CA 90292
Ph: 310-823-9358 ▪ Fx: 310-823-8649

Internet Council, US — www.usinternetcouncil.org
503 N Roosevelt Blvd Unit A-220   Falls Church VA 22044
Ph: 703-536-5770

(Internet Development) CANARIE — www.canarie.ca
110 O'Connor St 4th Fl   Ottawa ON K1P1H1
Ph: 613-943-5454 ▪ Fx: 613-943-5443

Internet Development, University Consortium for Advanced — www.internet2.edu
3025 Boardwalk Suite 200   Ann Arbor MI 48108
Ph: 734-913-4250 ▪ Fx: 734-913-4255

Internet Engineering Task Force — www.ietf.cnri.reston.va.us
1895 Preston White Dr Suite 100   Reston VA 20191
Ph: 703-620-8990 ▪ Fx: 703-620-0913

(Internet) Federal Search Foundation — www.fed-search.org

Internet Fraud Watch — www.fraud.org/internet/intinfo.htm
c/o National Fraud Information Ctr 1701 K St NW Suite 1200   Washington DC 20006
Ph: 202-835-3323 ▪ Fx: 202-835-0747 ▪ TF: 800-876-7060

Internet Industry Association, US — www.usiia.org
5810 Kingstowne Center Dr Suite 120 PMB 212   Alexandria VA 22315
Ph: 703-924-0006 ▪ Fx: 703-924-4203

Internet Numbers, American Registry for — www.arin.net
3635 Concorde Pkwy Suite 200   Chantilly VA 20151
Ph: 703-227-9840 ▪ Fx: 703-227-0676

(Internet) Peacefire — www.peacefire.org
14615 NW 30th Pl Unit 10D   Bellevue WA 98007
Ph: 425-497-9002

Internet Scambusters — www.scambusters.com
197 New Market Ctr Suite 115   Boone NC 28607
Ph: 828-262-5885

Internet Service Providers Association, US — www.usispa.org
1330 Connecticut Ave NW   Washington DC 20036
Ph: 202-862-3816 ▪ Fx: 202-261-0604

Internet Society — www.isoc.org
1775 Wiehle Ave Suite 102   Reston VA 20190
Ph: 703-326-9880 ▪ Fx: 703-326-9881

(Internet) TRUSTe — www.truste.org
685 Market St Suite 560   San Francisco CA 94105
Ph: 415-618-3400 ▪ Fx: 415-618-3420

Internet2 — www.internet2.edu
3025 Boardwalk Suite 200   Ann Arbor MI 48108
Ph: 734-913-4250 ▪ Fx: 734-913-4255

Internists, American College of Osteopathic — www.acoi.org
3 Bethesda Metro Ctr Suite 508   Bethesda MD 20814
Ph: 301-656-8877 ▪ Fx: 301-656-7133 ▪ TF: 800-327-5183

Interns & Residents, Committee of — www.cirseiu.org
520 8th Ave Suite 1200   New York NY 10018
Ph: 212-356-8100 ▪ Fx: 212-356-8111

Internship Centers, Association of Psychology Postdoctoral & — www.appic.org
10 G St NE Suite 750   Washington DC 20002
Ph: 202-589-0600 ▪ Fx: 202-589-0603

Interoperability Association, LonMark — www.lonmark.org
550 Meridian Ave   San Jose CA 95126
Ph: 408-938-5266 ▪ Fx: 408-790-3838

(Interoperability) Open Group — www.opengroup.org
44 Montgomery St Suite 960   San Francisco CA 94104
Ph: 415-374-8280 ▪ Fx: 415-374-8293

Interpretation, National Association for — www.interpnet.com
528 S Howes St PO Box 2246   Fort Collins CO 80521
Ph: 970-484-8283 ▪ Fx: 970-484-8179 ▪ TF: 888-900-8283

Interpreters for the Deaf Inc, Registry of — www.rid.org
333 Commerce St   Alexandria VA 22314
Ph: 703-838-0030 ▪ Fx: 703-838-0454

Interpreters & Translators, National Association of Judiciary — www.najit.org
2150 N 107th St Suite 205   Seattle WA 98133
Ph: 206-367-8704 ▪ Fx: 206-367-8777

Interreligious Foundation for Community Organization — www.ifconews.org
402 W 145th St   New York NY 10031
Ph: 212-926-5757 ▪ Fx: 212-926-5842

Interreligious & International Federation for World Peace — www.iifwp.org
155 White Plains Rd   Tarrytown NY 10591
Ph: 914-631-1331 ▪ Fx: 914-631-1308

Interreligious Staff, National Association of Ecumenical &
PO Box 7093   Tacoma WA 98406
Ph: 253-759-0141 ▪ Fx: 253-759-9689

Interserve USA — www.interserve.org
PO Box 418 7000 Ludlow St   Upper Darby PA 19082
Ph: 610-352-0581 ▪ Fx: 610-352-4394 ▪ TF: 800-809-4440

Intersocietal Commission for the Accreditation of Vascular Laboratories — www.icavl.org
8840 Stanford Blvd Suite 4900   Columbia MD 21045
Ph: 410-872-0100 ▪ Fx: 410-872-0030

Intersociety Committee on Pathology Information Inc — www.pathologytraining.org
9650 Rockville Pike   Bethesda MD 20814
Ph: 301-634-7200 ▪ Fx: 301-634-7990

Interstate Council of State Boards of Cosmetology Inc, National- — www.nictesting.org
7622 Briarwood Cir   Little Rock AR 72205
Ph: 501-227-8262 ▪ Fx: 501-227-8212

Interstate Council on Water Policy — www.icwp.org
1299 Pennsylvania Ave NW 8th Fl W   Washington DC 20004
Ph: 202-218-4196 ▪ Fx: 202-478-1738

Interstate Migrant Education Council — www.migedimec.org
1 Massachusetts Ave NW Suite 700   Washington DC 20001
Ph: 202-336-7078 ▪ Fx: 202-408-8062

Interstate Milk Shipments, National Conference on — www.ncims.org
123 Buena Vista Dr   Frankfort KY 40601
Ph: 502-695-0253

Interstate Natural Gas Association of America — www.ingaa.org
10 G St NE Suite 700   Washington DC 20002
Ph: 202-216-5900 ▪ Fx: 202-216-0870 ▪ TF: 888-854-6422

Interstate Oil & Gas Compact Commission — www.iogcc.oklaosf.state.ok.us
PO Box 53127   Oklahoma City OK 73152
Ph: 405-525-3556 ▪ Fx: 405-525-3592 ▪ TF: 800-822-4015

Interstate Postgraduate Medical Association — www.ipmameded.org
PO Box 5474   Madison WI 53705
Ph: 608-231-9045 ▪ Fx: 877-292-4489

Interstate Professional Applicators Association
PO Box 1377   Milton WA 98354
Ph: 253-922-9437

Intertel — www.intertel-iq.org
PO Box 1083   Tulsa OK 74101
Ph: 918-583-2928

InterVarsity Christian Fellowship/USA — www.intervarsity.org
6400 Schroeder Rd   Madison WI 53711
Ph: 608-274-9001 ▪ Fx: 608-274-7882

Interventional Radiographers, Association of Vascular & — www.avir.org
10201 Lee Hwy Suite 500   Fairfax VA 22030
Ph: 703-691-2350 ▪ Fx: 703-691-8540

Interventional Radiology, Society of — www.sirweb.org
10201 Lee Hwy Suite 500   Fairfax VA 22030
Ph: 703-691-1805 ▪ Fx: 703-691-1855 ▪ TF: 800-488-7284

Interweave Continental Inc — www.qrd.org/qrd/www/orgs/uua/uu-interweave.html

Intestinal Disease Foundation — www.intestinalfoundation.org
100 W Station Sq Suite 525   Pittsburgh PA 15219
Ph: 412-261-5888 ▪ Fx: 412-471-2722 ▪ TF: 877-587-9606

Intimate Apparel Square Club — thehugaward.org
326 Field Rd   Clinton Corners NY 12514
Ph: 845-758-5752 ▪ Fx: 845-758-2546

Intramural-Recreational Sports Association, National — www.nirsa.org
4185 SW Research Way   Corvallis OR 97333
Ph: 541-766-8211 ▪ Fx: 541-766-8284

(Intravenous Feeding) Oley Foundation — c4isr.com/oley
Albany Medical Ctr 214 Hun Memorial MC A-28   Albany NY 12208
Ph: 518-262-5079 ▪ Fx: 518-262-5528 ▪ TF: 800-776-6539

Intravenous Infusion Therapy Association, Outpatient
PO Box 1234   Tacoma WA 98491
Ph: 253-272-4581 ▪ Fx: 253-272-0360

Invasive Cardiovascular Professionals, Society of — www.sicp.com
PO Box 61606   Virginia Beach VA 23466
Ph: 757-497-3694 ▪ Fx: 757-497-0010

Invent America!   www.inventamerica.org
PO Box 26065   Alexandria VA 22313
Ph: 703-942-7121 ▪ Fx: 703-461-0068

Inventors, American Society of   www.americaninventor.org
PO Box 58426   Philadelphia PA 19102
Ph: 215-546-6601 ▪ Fx: 215-843-4234

Inventors Assistance League   www.inventions.org
403 S Central Ave   Glendale CA 91204
Ph: 818-246-6546 ▪ Fx: 818-244-1882 ▪ TF: 877-433-2246

Inventors Association, United   www.uiausa.org
PO Box 23447   Rochester NY 14692
Ph: 585-359-9310 ▪ Fx: 585-359-1132

Inventors Clubs of America
PO Box 450261   Atlanta GA 31145
Ph: 404-816-4774 ▪ Fx: 404-846-0980

Inventors Foundation, Affiliated   www.affiliatedinventors.com
1405 Potter Dr Suite 107   Colorado Springs CO 80909
Ph: 719-380-1234 ▪ Fx: 800-380-3862 ▪ TF: 800-525-5885

Inventors Workshop International Education Foundation &   www.inventorsworkshop.org
Entrepreneurs Workshop   1029 Castillo St   Santa Barbara CA
     93101
Ph: 805-967-5722 ▪ Fx: 805-899-4927

(Invertebrate Conservation) Xerces Society   www.xerces.org
4828 SE Hawthorne Blvd   Portland OR 97215
Ph: 503-232-6639 ▪ Fx: 503-233-6794

Invertebrate Pathology, Society for   www.sipweb.org
8904 Straw Flower Dr   Knoxville TN 37922
Ph: 888-684-4682 ▪ Fx: 888-486-1505

Investigation Association International, High Technology Crime   www.htcia.org
1474 Freeman Dr   Amissville VA 20106
Ph: 540-937-5019 ▪ Fx: 540-937-7848

Investigation & Security Services, National Council of   www.nciss.org
7501 Sparrows Pointe Blvd   Baltimore MD 21219
Ph: 800-445-8408 ▪ Fx: 410-388-9746

Investigation Units, International Association of Special   www.iasiu.com
8015 Corporate Dr Suite A   Baltimore MD 21236
Ph: 410-931-3332 ▪ Fx: 410-931-2060

Investigations Committee on Unidentified Flying Objects, National   www.nicufo.org
14617 Victory Blvd Suite 4   Van Nuys CA 91411
Ph: 818-989-5942 ▪ Fx: 818-989-2165

Investigative Pathology, American Society for
9650 Rockville Pike   Bethesda MD 20814
Ph: 301-530-7130 ▪ Fx: 301-571-1879

Investigative Reporters & Editors   www.ire.org
Missouri School of Journalism 138 Neff Annex   Columbia MO
     65211
Ph: 573-882-2042 ▪ Fx: 573-882-5431

Investigative Reporting, Center for   www.muckraker.org
131 Steuart St Suite 600   San Francisco CA 94105
Ph: 415-543-1200 ▪ Fx: 415-543-8311

Investigative Specialists, National Association of   www.pimall.com/nais
PO Box 33244   Austin TX 78764
Ph: 512-719-3595 ▪ Fx: 512-719-3594

Investigator Association, National Defender   www.ndia.net
2600 Dixwell Ave Suite 7   Hamden CT 06514
Ph: 203-281-6342 ▪ Fx: 203-248-8932

Investigators, Council of International   www.cii2.org
2150 N 107th St Suite 205   Seattle WA 98133
Ph: 206-361-8869 ▪ Fx: 206-367-8777 ▪ TF: 888-759-8884

Investigators, International Association of Arson   www.fire-investigators.org
12770 Boenker Rd   Bridgeton MO 63044
Ph: 314-739-4224 ▪ Fx: 314-739-4219

Investigators, International Association of Financial Crimes   www.iafci.org
873 Embarcadero Dr Suite 5   El Dorado Hills CA 95762
Ph: 916-939-5000 ▪ Fx: 916-939-0395

Investigators, International Society of Air Safety   www.isasi.org
107 E Holly Ave Suite 11   Sterling VA 20164
Ph: 703-430-9668 ▪ Fx: 703-430-4970

Investigators, National Association of Fire   www.nafi.org
857 Tallevast Rd   Sarasota FL 34243
Ph: 941-359-2800 ▪ Fx: 941-351-5849 ▪ TF: 877-506-6234

Investigators, National Association of Legal   www.nalionline.org

Investigators Network, World   www.worldinvestigatorsnetwork.com
7501 Sparrows Point Blvd   Baltimore MD 21219
Ph: 410-477-8879 ▪ Fx: 410-388-0846 ▪ TF: 888-946-6389

Investment Association, Stable Value   www.stablevalue.org
2121 K St NW Suite 800   Washington DC 20037
Ph: 202-261-6530 ▪ Fx: 202-261-6527 ▪ TF: 800-327-2270

Investment Casting Institute   www.investmentcasting.org
136 Summit Ave   Montvale NJ 07645
Ph: 201-573-9770 ▪ Fx: 201-573-9771

Investment Communications Resources, Professional Association for   www.paicr.org
1320 19th St NW Suite 300   Washington DC 20036
Ph: 202-371-9750 ▪ Fx: 202-371-8977 ▪ TF: 800-561-0751

Investment Companies, National Association of   www.naicvc.com
1300 Pennsylvania Ave NW Suite 700   Washington DC 20004
Ph: 202-289-4336 ▪ Fx: 202-289-4329

Investment Companies, National Association of Small Business   www.nasbic.org
666 11th St NW Suite 750   Washington DC 20001
Ph: 202-628-5055 ▪ Fx: 202-628-5080

Investment Company Institute   www.ici.org
1401 H St NW 12th Fl   Washington DC 20005
Ph: 202-326-5800 ▪ Fx: 202-326-5985

Investment Company Institute PAC
1401 H St NW 12th Fl   Washington DC 20005
Ph: 202-326-5800 ▪ Fx: 202-326-5985

Investment Company Service Association, National   www.nicsa.org
36 Washington St Suite 70   Wellesley Hills MA 02481
Ph: 781-416-7200 ▪ Fx: 781-416-7065

Investment Consultants, Association of Professional   www.apic-ssb.com
1101 17th St NW Suite 703   Washington DC 20036
Ph: 202-464-4155 ▪ Fx: 202-464-4157

Investment Counsel Association of America   www.icaa.org
1050 17th St NW Suite 725   Washington DC 20036
Ph: 202-293-4222 ▪ Fx: 202-293-4223

Investment Disputes, International Centre for Settlement of   www.worldbank.org/icsid
1818 H St NW   Washington DC 20433
Ph: 202-458-1534 ▪ Fx: 202-522-2615

Investment Fiduciaries, National Council of Real Estate   www.ncreif.org
2 Prudential Plaza 180 N Stetson Ave Suite 2515   Chicago IL
     60601
Ph: 312-819-5890 ▪ Fx: 312-819-5891

Investment Management Consultants Association   www.imca.org
9101 E Kenyon Ave Suite 3000   Denver CO 80237
Ph: 303-770-3377 ▪ Fx: 303-770-1812

Investment Management & Research, Association for   www.aimr.org
560 Ray C Hunt Dr PO Box 3668   Charlottesville VA 22903
Ph: 434-951-5499 ▪ Fx: 434-951-5262 ▪ TF: 800-247-8132

Investment Management Sales Executives, Association of   www.aimse.org
1320 19th St NW Suite 300   Washington DC 20036
Ph: 202-296-3560 ▪ Fx: 202-371-8977 ▪ TF: 800-343-5659

Investment Managers, National Association of Real Estate   www.nareim.com
11755 Wilshire Blvd Suite 1380   Los Angeles CA 90025
Ph: 310-479-2219

(Investment) NASD Regulation Inc   www.nasdr.com
9509 Key West Ave   Rockville MD 20850
Ph: 301-590-6500

Investment, Organization for International   www.ofii.org
1901 Pennsylvania Ave NW Suite 807   Washington DC 20006
Ph: 202-659-1903 ▪ Fx: 202-659-2293

Investment Professionals, National Association of   www.naip.com
12664 Emmer Pl Suite 201   Saint Paul MN 55124
Ph: 952-322-4322

Investment Program Association   www.ipa-dc.org
1101 17th St NW Suite 703   Washington DC 20036
Ph: 202-775-9750 ▪ Fx: 202-331-8446

Investment Recovery Association   www.invrecovery.org
638 W 39th St   Kansas City MO 64111
Ph: 816-561-5323 ▪ Fx: 816-561-1991

Investment Trusts, National Association of Real Estate   www.nareit.com
1875 'I' St NW Suite 600   Washington DC 20006
Ph: 202-739-9400 ▪ Fx: 202-739-9401 ▪ TF: 800-362-7348

Investor Advice, Forum for   www.investoradvice.org
7200 Wisconsin Ave Suite 709   Bethesda MD 20814
Ph: 301-656-7998 ▪ Fx: 301-656-5019

Investor Protection Trust   www.investorprotection.org
1901 N Fort Meyer Dr Suite 1012   Arlington VA 22209
Ph: 703-276-1116 ▪ Fx: 703-841-9327

Investor Protective League, Independent
PO Box 5031   Fort Lauderdale FL 33310
Ph: 954-749-1551 ▪ Fx: 954-749-1553

Investor Relations Institute, National   www.niri.org
8020 Towers Crescent Dr Suite 250   Vienna VA 22182
Ph: 703-506-3570 ▪ Fx: 703-506-3571

Investor Responsibility Research Center   www.irrc.org
1350 Connecticut Ave NW Suite 700   Washington DC 20036
Ph: 202-833-0700 ▪ Fx: 202-833-3555

Investors, American Association of Individual   www.aaii.com
625 N Michigan Ave   Chicago IL 60611
Ph: 312-280-0170 ▪ Fx: 312-280-9883 ▪ TF: 800-428-2244

Investors Association, National Real Estate   www.nationalreia.com
525 W 5th St Suite 230   Covington KY 41011
Ph: 888-762-7342 ▪ Fx: 859-581-5993

Investors Corp, National Association of   www.better-investing.org
PO Box 220   Royal Oak MI 48068
Ph: 248-583-6242 ▪ Fx: 248-583-4880 ▪ TF: 877-275-6242

Investors, Council of Institutional   www.cii.org
1730 Rhode Island Ave NW Suite 512   Washington DC 20036
Ph: 202-822-0800 ▪ Fx: 202-822-0801

Investors in Real Estate, Association of Foreign   www.afire.org
1300 Pennsylvania Ave NW   Washington DC 20004
Ph: 202-312-1400 ▪ Fx: 202-312-1401

Iota Lambda Sigma
607 Park Way W   Oregon OH 43616
Ph: 419-693-6860 ▪ Fx: 419-693-6859

Iota Phi Lambda Sorority Inc   www.iota1929.org
1462 W 113th Pl   Chicago IL 60643
Ph: 773-445-1315 ▪ TF: 800-982-4682

Iota Phi Theta Fraternity Inc   www.iotaphitheta.org
3001 Hewitt Ave Suite 390   Silver Spring MD 20906
Ph: 888-835-5109

Iowa, Veteran's Association of the USS   www.ussiowa.org

IPC-Association Connecting Electronics Industries   www.ipc.org
2215 Sanders Rd   Northbrook IL 60062
Ph: 847-509-9700 ▪ Fx: 847-509-9798

Iran Freedom Foundation   www.iffmrt.org
PO Box 422   Bethesda MD 20817
Ph: 301-215-6677 ▪ Fx: 301-907-8877

Iranian Studies, Society for   www.iranian-studies.org
New York Univ Dept of Middle Eastern Studies 50 Washington
     Sq S   New York NY 10012
Ph: 212-995-4689

Iranian Trade Association   www.iraniantrade.org
PO Box 927743   San Diego CA 92192
Ph: 858-586-0560 ▪ Fx: 858-547-0823

Iraqi Jews, American Committee for Rescue & Resettlement of
1125 Park Ave   New York NY 10029
Ph: 212-427-1246 ▪ Fx: 212-360-7009

Ireland Chamber of Commerce in the US
556 Central Ave   New Providence NJ 07974
Ph: 908-286-1300 ▪ Fx: 908-286-1200

Ireland-US Council for Commerce & Industry
1156 Ave of the Americas   New York NY 10036
Ph: 212-921-1414 ▪ Fx: 212-730-2232

Iridology Practitioners Association, International   www.iridologyassn.org
PO Box 3334   Escondido CA 92033
Ph: 888-682-2208 ▪ TF: 888-682-2208

Irises, Society for Pacific Coast Native   www.pacificcoastiris.org
33450 Little Valley Rd   Fort Bragg CA 95437
Ph: 707-964-3907

Irish American Cultural Institute   www.iaci-usa.org
1 Lackawanna Pl   Morristown NJ 07960
Ph: 973-605-1991 ▪ Fx: 973-605-8875

Irish American Democrats   www.irishamericandemocrats.org
PO Box 15638   Chevy Chase MD 20825
Ph: 202-362-9064

Irish American Partnership   www.irishap.org
33 Broad St 9th Fl   Boston MA 02109
Ph: 617-723-2707 ▪ Fx: 617-723-5478 ▪ TF: 800-722-3893

Irish American Unity Conference   www.iauc.org
611 Pennsylvania Ave SE Suite 450   Washington DC 20003
Ph: 202-662-8830 ▪ Fx: 202-662-8831 ▪ TF: 800-947-4282

(Irish-Catholic) Knights of Equity   www.knightsofequity.com
229 Sample St   Pittsburgh PA 15209
Ph: 412-828-8770

Irish Family History Forum   www.ifhf.org
PO Box 67   Plainview NY 11803
Ph: 516-616-3587

Irish Historical Society, American   www.aihs.org
991 5th Ave   New York NY 10028
Ph: 212-288-2263 ▪ Fx: 212-628-7927

Irish National Caucus Inc   www.irishnationalcaucus.org
PO Box 15128   Washington DC 20003
Ph: 202-544-0568 ▪ Fx: 202-488-7537

Irish Northern Aid Inc   inac.org
363 7th Ave Suite 405   New York NY 10001
Ph: 212-736-1916 ▪ Fx: 212-279-1916 ▪ TF: 800-473-5263

Irish Studies, American Conference for   www.acisweb.com

Iron Casting Research Institute   www.ironcasting.org
2802 Fisher Rd   Columbus OH 43204
Ph: 614-275-4201 ▪ Fx: 614-275-4203

Iron Ore Association, American   www.aioa.org
302 W Superior St   Duluth MN 55802
Ph: 218-722-7724 ▪ Fx: 218-720-6707

Iron Overload Diseases Association   www.ironoverload.org
433 Westwind Dr   North Palm Beach FL 33408
Ph: 561-840-8512 ▪ Fx: 561-842-9881

Iron Pipe Research Association, Ductile   www.dipra.org
245 Riverchase Pkwy E Suite 'O'   Birmingham AL 35244
Ph: 205-402-8700 ▪ Fx: 205-402-8730

Iron & Steel Engineers, Association of   www.aise.org
3 Gateway Ctr Suite 1900   Pittsburgh PA 15222
Ph: 412-281-6323 ▪ Fx: 412-281-4657 ▪ TF: 800-966-6323

Iron & Steel Institute, American   www.steel.org
1140 Connecticut Ave NW Suite 705   Washington DC 20036
Ph: 202-452-7100 ▪ Fx: 202-463-6573

Iron & Steel Society   www.issource.org
186 Thorn Hill Rd   Warrendale PA 15086
Ph: 724-776-1535 ▪ Fx: 724-776-0430

Iron Workers, International Association of Bridge Structural   www.ironworkers.org
Ornamental & Reinforcing   1750 New York Ave NW Suite
400   Washington DC 20006
Ph: 202-383-4800 ▪ Fx: 202-638-4856 ▪ TF: 800-368-0105

Ironworkers Political Action League
1750 New York Ave NW Suite 400   Washington DC 20006
Ph: 202-383-4800 ▪ Fx: 202-383-6483 ▪ TF: 800-368-0105

Ironworking Industry, Institute of the   www.instituteiw.org
1750 New York Ave NW   Washington DC 20006
Ph: 202-783-3998 ▪ Fx: 202-393-1507

Irrigation Association   www.irrigation.org
6540 Arlington Blvd   Falls Church VA 22042
Ph: 703-536-7080 ▪ Fx: 703-536-7019

Irrigation Consultants, American Society of   www.asic.org
111 E Wacker Dr 18th Fl   Chicago IL 60601
Ph: 312-372-7090 ▪ Fx: 312-372-6160

Irrigation & Drainage, US Committee on   www.uscid.org
1616 17th St Suite 483   Denver CO 80202
Ph: 303-628-5430 ▪ Fx: 303-628-5431

IRU Inc   www.irua.com
971 Rt 202 N   Branchburg NJ 08876
Ph: 908-203-0211 ▪ Fx: 908-203-0213

Irvine James Foundation   www.irvine.org
1 Market St Steuart Tower Suite 2500   San Francisco CA
94105
Ph: 415-777-2244 ▪ Fx: 415-777-0869

ISA - Instrumentation Systems & Automation Society   www.isa.org
67 Alexander Dr   Research Triangle Park NC 27709
Ph: 919-549-8411 ▪ Fx: 919-549-8288

Isabella, Daughters of   www.daughtersofisabella.org
PO Box 9585   New Haven CT 06535
Ph: 203-865-2570 ▪ Fx: 203-865-5586

Islam, Nation of   www.noi.org
7351 S Stony Island   Chicago IL 60649
Ph: 773-324-6000 ▪ Fx: 773-324-6309

Islamic & Arabic Sciences in America, Institute of   www.iiasa.org
8500 Hilltop Rd   Fairfax VA 22031
Ph: 703-641-4890 ▪ Fx: 703-641-4899

Islamic Charitable Projects, Association of   www.aicp.org
4431 Walnut St   Philadelphia PA 19104
Ph: 215-387-8888 ▪ Fx: 215-387-3815

(Islamic) Fiqh Council of North America
750-A Miller Dr SE   Leesburg VA 20175
Ph: 703-779-7477 ▪ Fx: 703-779-7999

Islamic Information Center of America   www.iica.org
PO Box 4052   Des Plaines IL 60016
Ph: 847-541-8141 ▪ Fx: 847-824-8436

(Islamic) Makassed Foundation of America   www.makassed.org
1510 H St NW Suite 301   Washington DC 20005
Ph: 202-783-7979 ▪ Fx: 202-783-7977

Islamic Medical Association of North America   www.imana.org
950 75th St   Downers Grove IL 60516
Ph: 630-852-2122 ▪ Fx: 630-435-1429

Islamic Research Foundation   www.irf.net
7102 Shefford Ln W   Louisville KY 40242
Ph: 502-423-1988 ▪ Fx: 502-423-1933 ▪ TF: 800-484-1162

Islamic Resources, Arab World &   www.awaironline.org
PO Box 174   Abiquiu NM 87510
Ph: 505-685-4533

Islamic Thought, International Institute of   www.iiit.org
500 Grove St   Herndon VA 20170
Ph: 703-471-1133 ▪ Fx: 703-471-3922

Islamic Trust, North American   www.nait.net
745 McClintock Dr Suite 114   Burr Ridge IL 60527
Ph: 630-489-9191 ▪ Fx: 630-789-9455

Island Resources Foundation   www.irf.org
1718 P St NW Suite T-4   Washington DC 20036
Ph: 202-265-9712 ▪ Fx: 202-232-0748

Island States, Alliance of Small   www.sidsnet.org/aosis
800 2nd Ave 4th Fl   New York NY 10017
Ph: 212-599-6196 ▪ Fx: 212-599-0797

Islands International Inc, Clean   www.islands.org
8219 Elvaton Dr   Pasadena MD 21122
Ph: 410-647-2500 ▪ Fx: 410-647-4554 ▪ TF: 888-647-2501

Isotope Society, International   www.intl-isotope-soc.org

Israel Aliyah Center   www.aliyah.org
633 3rd Ave 21st Fl   New York NY 10017
Ph: 212-339-6063 ▪ Fx: 212-318-6145

Israel, American Jewish League for   www.americanjewishleague.org
130 E 59th St   New York NY 10022
Ph: 212-371-1583 ▪ Fx: 212-371-3265

Israel, American Physicians Fellowship for Medicine in   www.apfmed.org
2001 Beacon St Suite 210   Boston MA 02135
Ph: 617-232-5382 ▪ Fx: 617-739-2616

Israel, American Red Magen David for   www.armdi.org
888 7th Ave Suite 403   New York NY 10106
Ph: 212-757-1627 ▪ Fx: 212-757-4662 ▪ TF: 866-632-2763

Israel, American Society for the Protection of Nature in   www.aspni.org
28 Arrandale Ave   Great Neck NY 11024
Ph: 212-398-6750 ▪ Fx: 212-398-1665 ▪ TF: 800-411-0966

Israel, American Veterans of
136 E 39th St   New York NY 10016
Ph: 631-499-4327

Israel, Americans for a Safe   www.afsi.org
1623 3rd Ave Suite 205   New York NY 10128
Ph: 212-828-2424 ▪ Fx: 212-828-1717

(Israel) AMIT   www.amitchildren.org
817 Broadway   New York NY 10003
Ph: 212-477-4720 ▪ Fx: 212-353-2312 ▪ TF: 800-989-2648

Israel Chamber of Commerce & Industry Inc, America-   www.israeltrade.org
120 W 45th St 18th Fl   New York NY 10036
Ph: 212-819-0430 ▪ Fx: 212-819-0431

Israel, Concern for Helping Animals in   www.chai-online.org
PO Box 3341   Alexandria VA 22302
Ph: 703-658-9650 ▪ Fx: 703-941-6132

Israel Defense Forces, Friends of the   www.israelsoldiers.org
298 5th Ave 5th Fl   New York NY 10001
Ph: 212-244-3118 ▪ Fx: 212-244-3119

Israel Disabled Veterans, Friends of   fidv-bh.com
419 Park Ave S Suite 905   New York NY 10016
Ph: 212-689-3220 ▪ Fx: 212-689-3236 ▪ TF: 800-648-2125

(Israel) Emunah of America   www.emunah.org
7 Penn Plaza 7th Fl   New York NY 10001
Ph: 212-564-9045 ▪ Fx: 212-643-9731 ▪ TF: 800-368-6440

Israel Inc, Free Sons of   www.freesons.org
247-25 Jamaica Ave   Bellerose NY 11426
Ph: 718-347-1614

Israel Friendship League, America   www.aifl.org
134 E 39th St   New York NY 10016
Ph: 212-213-8630 ▪ Fx: 212-683-3475

Israel Fund, New   www.nif.org
1101 14th St NW 6th Fl   Washington DC 20005
Ph: 202-842-0900 ▪ Fx: 202-842-0991 ▪ TF: 800-988-3863

(Israel) Givat Haviva Educational Foundation Inc   www.givathaviva.org
114 W 26th Suite 1001   New York NY 10001
Ph: 212-989-9272 ▪ Fx: 212-989-9840

Israel Gospel Ministry Inc, Friends of   foi.org
PO Box 908   Bellmawr NJ 08099
Ph: 856-853-5590 ▪ Fx: 856-853-9565 ▪ TF: 800-257-7843

Israel Humanitarian Foundation Inc   projects.ihf.net
276 5th Ave Suite 901   New York NY 10001
Ph: 212-683-5676 ▪ Fx: 212-213-9233 ▪ TF: 888-434-7443

Israel International, Artists for   www.afii.org
PO Box 2056   New York NY 10163
Ph: 212-245-4188

Israel, Maccabi USA/Sports for   www.maccabiusa.com
1926 Arch St Suite 4R   Philadelphia PA 19103
Ph: 215-561-6900 ▪ Fx: 215-561-5470

Israel, Masorti Foundation for Conservative Judaism in www.masorti.org
475 Riverside Dr Suite 832   New York NY 10115
Ph: 212-870-2216 ▪ Fx: 212-870-2218 ▪ TF: 877-287-7414

Israel Museum, American Friends of the www.imj.org.il
500 5th Ave Suite 2540   New York NY 10110
Ph: 212-997-5611 ▪ Fx: 212-997-5536

(Israel) Na'Amat USA www.naamat.org
350 5th Ave Suite 4700   New York NY 10118
Ph: 212-563-5222 ▪ Fx: 212-563-5710

Israel, National Christian Leadership Conference for www.nclci.org
43422 W Oaks Dr Suite 300   Novi MI 48377
Ph: 248-557-4540 ▪ Fx: 248-557-4527

Israel, National Committee for Labor www.laborisrael.org
275 7th Ave   New York NY 10001
Ph: 212-647-0300 ▪ Fx: 212-647-0308

Israel, National Council of Young www.youngisrael.org
3 W 16th St   New York NY 10011
Ph: 212-929-1525 ▪ Fx: 212-727-9526

Israel Public Action Campaign, Christians' www.cipaconline.org
PO Box 18173   Washington DC 20036
Ph: 202-234-3600 ▪ Fx: 202-332-3221

Israel Public Affairs Committee, American www.aipac.org
440 1st St NW Suite 600   Washington DC 20001
Ph: 202-639-5200 ▪ Fx: 202-347-4918

Israel, Remnant of remnantofisrael.net
3050 Gap Knob Rd   New Hope KY 40052
Ph: 270-325-3061 ▪ Fx: 270-325-3094 ▪ TF: 888-352-7153

Israel, SEARCH for Justice & Equality in Palestine/ searchforjustice.org
PO Box 3452   Framingham MA 01705
Ph: 508-879-0777 ▪ Fx: 508-877-2611

Israel, Volunteers for www.vfi-usa.org
330 W 42nd St Suite 1618   New York NY 10036
Ph: 212-643-4848 ▪ Fx: 212-643-4855

Israel, Women's League for
160 E 56th St   New York NY 10022
Ph: 212-838-1997 ▪ Fx: 212-888-5972

Israeli-Palestinian Peace, America-Israel Council for otherisrael.home.igc.org
224 Lake Dr   Kensington CA 94708
Ph: 510-526-8449

Issue Management Council www.issuemanagement.org
207 Loudoun St SE   Leesburg VA 20175
Ph: 703-777-8450

Issues Forums, National www.nifi.org
100 Commons Rd   Dayton OH 45459
Ph: 937-434-7300 ▪ Fx: 937-439-9804 ▪ TF: 800-433-7834

Istituto Italiano di Cultura www.italcultny.org
686 Park Ave   New York NY 10021
Ph: 212-879-4242 ▪ Fx: 212-861-4018

IT Financial Management Association www.itfma.com
PO Box 30188   Santa Barbara CA 93130
Ph: 805-687-7390 ▪ Fx: 805-687-7382

Italian American Actors, Guild of www.nygiaa.org
31 E 32nd St 12th Fl   New York NY 10016
Ph: 212-420-6590

(Italian-American) Alpha Phi Delta Fraternity Inc www.apd.org
916 62nd St   Brooklyn NY 11219
Ph: 718-745-9551 ▪ Fx: 718-745-9592

Italian, American Association of Teachers of www.italianstudies.org/aati
Univ of Wisconsin Dept of French & Italian 618 Van Hise Hall
1220 Linden Dr   Madison WI 53706
Ph: 608-262-3941 ▪ Fx: 608-265-3892

Italian American Foundation, National www.niaf.org
1860 19th St NW   Washington DC 20009
Ph: 202-387-0600 ▪ Fx: 202-387-0800 ▪ TF: 800-989-6423

(Italian-American) UNICO National Inc www.unico.org
271 US Hwy 46 W Suite A-108   Fairfield NJ 07004
Ph: 973-808-0035 ▪ Fx: 973-808-0043 ▪ TF: 800-877-1492

Italian-American Women, National Organization of www.noiaw.org
445 W 59th St Rm 1248   New York NY 10019
Ph: 212-237-8574 ▪ Fx: 212-489-6130

(Italian Business Leaders) Gruppo Esponenti Italiani www.gei-ny.com
60 E 42nd St Suite 1341 PO Box 789   New York NY 10150
Ph: 212-867-2772 ▪ Fx: 212-867-4114

Italian Catholic Federation icf.org
675 Hegenberger Rd Suite 230   Oakland CA 94621
Ph: 510-633-9058 ▪ Fx: 510-633-9758 ▪ TF: 888-423-1924

Italian Charities of America
8320 Queens Blvd   Elmhurst NY 11373
Ph: 718-478-3100 ▪ Fx: 718-478-2665

Italian Folk Art Federation of America www.italian-american.com/ifafa

Italian Historical Association, American www.mobilito.com/aiha
169 Country Club Rd   Chicago Heights IL 60411
Ph: 708-756-7168

Italian Historical Society of America www.italianhistorical.org
111 Columbia Heights   Brooklyn NY 11201
Ph: 718-852-2929

Italian Historical Studies, Society for www.historians.org/affiliates
Boston College   Chestnut Hill MA 02467
Ph: 617-552-3814 ▪ Fx: 617-552-2478

Italian Migration, American Committee on www.acimimmigra.org
25 Carmine St   New York NY 10014
Ph: 212-247-7373 ▪ Fx: 212-265-5793

Italian Sons & Daughters of America, Order www.orderisda.org
419 Wood St   Pittsburgh PA 15222
Ph: 412-261-3550 ▪ Fx: 412-261-9897

Italian Wine & Food Institute www.italianwineandfoodinstitute.com
60 E 42nd St Suite 1341 PO Box 789   New York NY 10150
Ph: 212-867-4111 ▪ Fx: 212-867-4114

Italiano di Cultura, Istituto www.italcultny.org
686 Park Ave   New York NY 10021
Ph: 212-879-4242 ▪ Fx: 212-861-4018

Italic Institute of America www.italic.org
PO Box 818   Floral Park NY 11001
Ph: 516-488-7400 ▪ Fx: 516-488-4889

Italy-America Chamber of Commerce Inc www.italchambers.net
730 5th Ave Suite 600   New York NY 10019
Ph: 212-459-0044 ▪ Fx: 212-459-0090

Italy in America, Order of the Sons of www.osia.org
219 'E' St NE   Washington DC 20002
Ph: 202-547-2900 ▪ Fx: 202-546-8168 ▪ TF: 800-547-6742

Italy Inc, Boys' Towns of www.boystown.it
250 E 63rd St Suite 204   New York NY 10021
Ph: 212-980-8770 ▪ Fx: 212-644-0766

ITS America www.itsa.org
400 Virginia Ave SW Suite 800   Washington DC 20024
Ph: 202-484-4847 ▪ Fx: 202-484-3483 ▪ TF: 800-374-8472

Ives Charles Society www.charlesives.org
Indiana Univ School of Music   Bloomington IN 47405
Ph: 812-855-7097 ▪ Fx: 812-855-4936

Ivory Society, International
11109 Nicholas Dr   Wheaton MD 20902
Ph: 301-649-4002

Ivy Group Presidents, Council of www.ivyleaguesports.com
228 Alexander St 1st Fl   Princeton NJ 08544
Ph: 609-258-6426 ▪ Fx: 609-258-1690

Ivy Society Inc, American www.ivy.org

Izaak Walton League of America www.iwla.org
707 Conservation Ln   Gaithersburg MD 20878
Ph: 301-548-0150 ▪ Fx: 301-548-0146 ▪ TF: 800-453-5463

J

J Allen Hynek Center for UFO Studies www.cufos.org
2457 W Peterson Ave Suite 6   Chicago IL 60659
Ph: 773-271-3611

J Bulow Campbell Foundation
50 Hurt Plaza Suite 850   Atlanta GA 30303
Ph: 404-658-9066 ▪ Fx: 404-659-4802

J Paul Getty Trust www.getty.edu
1200 Getty Center Dr   Los Angeles CA 90049
Ph: 310-440-7340 ▪ Fx: 310-440-7704

JA & Kathryn Albertson Foundation www.jkaf.org
PO Box 70002   Boise ID 83707
Ph: 208-424-2600 ▪ Fx: 208-424-2626

Jack & Jill of America Inc www.jack-and-jill.org
1930 17th St NW   Washington DC 20009
Ph: 202-667-7010 ▪ Fx: 202-667-7133

Jack & Jill of America Foundation Inc www.jackandjillfoundation.org
PO Box 468   Pickerington OH 43147
Ph: 614-864-7085 ▪ Fx: 614-864-7093

Jack London Foundation Inc jacklondonfdn.org
14300 Arnold Dr   Glen Ellen CA 95442
Ph: 707-996-2888 ▪ Fx: 707-996-4107

Jack Russell Terrier Club of America www.terrier.com
PO Box 4527   Lutherville MD 21094
Ph: 410-561-3655 ▪ Fx: 410-560-2563

Jackie Robinson Foundation www.jackierobinson.org
3 W 35th St 11th Fl   New York NY 10001
Ph: 212-290-8600 ▪ Fx: 212-290-8081

Jackson Ruth Orthopaedic Society www.rjos.org
6300 N River Rd Suite 727   Rosemont IL 60018
Ph: 847-698-1637 ▪ Fx: 847-823-0536

Jacob Sheep Breeders Association www.jsba.org
PO Box 10427   Bozeman MT 59719
Ph: 406-388-9537

Jacob Wetterling Foundation www.jwf.org
2314 University Ave W Suite 14   Saint Paul MN 55114
Ph: 651-714-4673 ▪ Fx: 651-714-9098

Jacobs Institute of Women's Health www.jiwh.org
409 12th St SW   Washington DC 20024
Ph: 202-863-4990 ▪ Fx: 202-488-4229

(Jacques Maritain) American Maritain Association www.jacquesmaritain.org
3921 Glenview Dr   South Bend IN 46628
Ph: 574-271-1187 ▪ Fx: 574-271-1292

Jaguar Clubs of North America Inc www.jcna.com
1000 Glenbrook Rd   Anchorage KY 40223
Ph: 888-258-2524

Jail Association, American www.corrections.com/aja
1135 Professional Ct   Hagerstown MD 21740
Ph: 301-790-3930

James A Baker III Institute for Public Policy www.rice.edu/projects/baker
Rice University 6100 Main St Baker Hall Suite 120   Houston TX 77005
Ph: 713-348-4683 ▪ Fx: 713-348-5993

James A Michener Society www.unco.edu/library/jamsociety

James Beard Foundation www.jamesbeard.org
167 W 12th St   New York NY 10011
Ph: 212-675-4984 ▪ Fx: 212-645-1438 ▪ TF: 800-362-3273

James Buchanan Foundation for the Preservation www.lanccounty.com/wheatland
of Wheatland   1120 Marietta Ave   Lancaster PA 17603
Ph: 717-392-8721 ▪ Fx: 717-295-8825

James Irvine Foundation www.irvine.org
1 Market St Steuart Tower Suite 2500   San Francisco CA 94105
Ph: 415-777-2244 ▪ Fx: 415-777-0869

James Joyce Society   joycesociety.org
41 W 47th St   New York NY 10036
Ph: 212-719-4448

James K Polk Memorial Association   www.jameskpolk.com
c/o James K Polk Home PO Box 741   Columbia TN 38402
Ph: 931-388-2354 ▪ Fx: 931-388-5971

James Monroe Memorial Foundation   www.monroefoundation.org
908 1/2 Charles St   Fredericksburg VA 22401
Ph: 804-231-1827

Jamestown Foundation   www.jamestown.org
4516 43rd St NW   Washington DC 20016
Ph: 202-483-8888 ▪ Fx: 202-483-8337

Jane Austen Society of North America   www.jasna.org
106 Barlows Run   Williamsburg VA 23188
Ph: 800-836-3911

Jane Goodall Institute for Wildlife Research   www.janegoodall.org
Education & Conservation   8700 Georgia Ave Suite
500   Silver Spring MD 20910
Ph: 301-565-0086 ▪ Fx: 301-565-3188 ▪ TF: 800-592-5263

Japan Aikido Association USA   tomiki.org
5752 S Kingston Way   Englewood CO 80111
Ph: 303-740-7424 ▪ Fx: 303-337-1631

Japan-America Society of Washington DC   www.us-japan.org/dc
1020 19th St NW Lower Lobby Suite 40   Washington DC
20036
Ph: 202-833-2210 ▪ Fx: 202-833-2456

Japan-America Student Conference   www.jasc.org
606 18th St NW 2nd Fl   Washington DC 20006
Ph: 202-289-4231 ▪ Fx: 202-789-8265

Japan-American Societies, National Association of   www.us-japan.org
733 15th St NW Suite 700   Washington DC 20005
Ph: 202-783-4550 ▪ Fx: 202-783-4551

Japan Automobile Manufacturers Association   www.japanauto.com
1050 17th St NW Suite 410   Washington DC 20036
Ph: 202-296-8537 ▪ Fx: 202-872-1212

Japan Business Council, US-   www.usjbc.org
2000 L St NW Suite 515   Washington DC 20036
Ph: 202-728-0068 ▪ Fx: 202-728-0073

Japan Club, Occupied
29 Freeborn St   Newport RI 02840
Ph: 401-846-9024

Japan ICU Foundation Inc   www.jicuf.org
475 Riverside Dr Suite 439   New York NY 10115
Ph: 212-870-3386 ▪ Fx: 212-870-2696

Japan Information Access Project   www.jiaponline.org
2000 P St NW Suite 620   Washington DC 20036
Ph: 202-822-6040 ▪ Fx: 202-822-6044

Japan Society   www.japansociety.org
333 E 47th St   New York NY 10017
Ph: 212-832-1155 ▪ Fx: 212-755-6752

Japanese American Citizens League   www.jacl.org
1765 Sutter St   San Francisco CA 94115
Ph: 415-921-5225 ▪ Fx: 415-931-4671

Japanese-American Cultural Trade Association
PO Box 4804   Panorama City CA 91412
Ph: 818-780-0815 ▪ Fx: 818-780-8501

Japanese American Historical Society, National   www.njahs.org
1684 Post St   San Francisco CA 94115
Ph: 415-921-5007 ▪ Fx: 415-921-5087

Japanese, Association of Teachers of   www.colorado.edu/ealld/atj
Univ of Colorado-Boulder 279 UCB   Boulder CO 80309
Ph: 303-492-5487 ▪ Fx: 303-492-5856

Japanese Sword Society of the US   www.jssus.org

Jar Collectors, Society of Tobacco   www.tobaccojarsociety.com
1705 Chanticleer   Cherry Hill NJ 08003
Ph: 856-489-8363 ▪ Fx: 856-489-8364

Jargon Society   www.jargonbooks.com
8 3rd St Suite 565   Winston-Salem NC 27101
Ph: 336-724-7619

Jay & Betty Van Andel Foundation   www.vai.org
333 Bostwick Ave NE   Grand Rapids MI 49503
Ph: 616-234-5000 ▪ Fx: 616-234-5001

Jayco Travel Club   www.jaycorvclub.com
PO Box 192   Osceola IN 46561
Ph: 574-258-0591 ▪ Fx: 574-259-7105 ▪ TF: 800-262-5178

(Jazz) Bix Beiderbecke Memorial Society   www.bixsociety.org
PO Box 3688   Davenport IA 52808
Ph: 563-324-7170 ▪ Fx: 563-326-1732 ▪ TF: 888-249-5487

Jazz Club, New Orleans   www.nojazzclub.com
828 Royal St Suite 265   New Orleans LA 70116
Ph: 504-455-6847

Jazz Education, International Association of   www.iaje.org
PO Box 724   Manhattan KS 66505
Ph: 785-776-8744 ▪ Fx: 785-776-6190

Jazz Record Collectors, International Association of   rhythmsociety.net/iajrc

Jazz Society, Gold Coast   www.goldcoastjazz.org
103 NW 2nd Ave   Fort Lauderdale FL 33311
Ph: 954-524-0805 ▪ Fx: 954-525-7880

JCC Association   www.jcca.org
15 E 26th St 10th Fl   New York NY 10010
Ph: 212-532-4949 ▪ Fx: 212-481-4174

JE & LE Mabee Foundation Inc   www.mabeefoundation.com
401 S Boston Ave 30th Fl   Tulsa OK 74103
Ph: 918-584-4286

Jean-Jacques Rousseau, North American Association   www.wabash.edu/Rousseau
for the Study of   Wabash College Dept of Political Science 301
W Wabash Ave   Crawfordsville IN 47933
Ph: 765-361-6312

Jean Piaget Society   www.piaget.org
Harvard Univ Dept of Human Development & Psychology Larsen
Hall   Cambridge MA 02138
Ph: 617-495-3446 ▪ Fx: 617-495-3626

JEDEC Solid State Technology Association   www.jedec.org
2500 Wilson Blvd   Arlington VA 22201
Ph: 703-907-7534 ▪ Fx: 703-907-7583

Jefferson Thomas Center for the Protection of Free Expression   www.tjcenter.org
400 Worrell Dr   Charlottesville VA 22911
Ph: 434-295-4784 ▪ Fx: 434-296-3621

Jefferson Thomas Foundation   www.monticello.org
PO Box 316   Charlottesville VA 22902
Ph: 434-984-9808 ▪ Fx: 434-977-7757

Jefferson's Poplar Forest, Corporation for   www.poplarforest.org
PO Box 419   Forest VA 24551
Ph: 434-525-1806 ▪ Fx: 434-525-7252

Jehovah's Witnesses   www.watchtower.org
25 Columbia Heights   Brooklyn NY 11201
Ph: 718-560-5000

(Jehovah's Witnesses) Free Minds Inc   www.freeminds.org
PO Box 3818   Manhattan Beach CA 90266
Ph: 310-545-7831 ▪ Fx: 310-545-0068

Jelly & Preserve Association, International   www.jelly.org
5775 Peachtree-Dunwoody Rd Bldg G Suite 500   Atlanta GA
30342
Ph: 404-252-3663 ▪ Fx: 404-252-0774

Jersey Cattle Association, American   www.usjersey.com
6486 E Main St   Reynoldsburg OH 43068
Ph: 614-861-3636 ▪ Fx: 614-861-8040

Jersey Cattle Registry, American Miniature
PO Box 942   Rochester WA 98579
Ph: 360-273-7789

Jerusalem Foundation of America, Boys Town   www.boystownjerusalem.com
12 W 31st St Suite 300   New York NY 10001
Ph: 212-244-2766 ▪ Fx: 212-244-2052 ▪ TF: 800-469-2697

Jesse Smith Noyes Foundation   www.noyes.org
6 E 39th St 12th Fl   New York NY 10016
Ph: 212-684-6577 ▪ Fx: 212-689-6549

Jesse Stuart Foundation Inc   www.jsfbooks.com
1645 Winchester Ave PO Box 669   Ashland KY 41105
Ph: 606-326-1667 ▪ Fx: 606-325-2519

(Jesuit) Alpha Sigma Nu   www.marquette.edu/dept/ASN
Marquette Univ 707 Bldg Rm 330 PO Box 1881   Milwaukee WI
53201
Ph: 414-288-7542 ▪ Fx: 414-288-3259

Jesuit Association of Student Personnel Administrators   jaspa.creighton.edu
1 Dupont Cir NW Suite 405   Washington DC 20036
Ph: 202-862-9893

Jesuit Colleges & Universities, Association of   www.ajcunet.edu
1 Dupont Cir NW Suite 405   Washington DC 20036
Ph: 202-862-9893 ▪ Fx: 202-862-8523

Jesuit Conference, US   www.jesuit.org
1616 P St NW Suite 300   Washington DC 20036
Ph: 202-462-5200 ▪ Fx: 202-328-9212

Jesuit Refugee Service - North America   www.jesref.org
1616 P St NW Suite 400   Washington DC 20036
Ph: 202-462-0400 ▪ Fx: 202-328-9212

Jesuit Secondary Education Association   www.jsea.org
1616 P St NW Suite 400   Washington DC 20036
Ph: 202-667-3888 ▪ Fx: 202-387-6305

Jesuit Volunteers International   www.jesuitvolunteers.org
PO Box 3756   Washington DC 20027
Ph: 202-687-1132 ▪ Fx: 202-687-5082

Jesus Christ of Latter-Day Saints, Church of   www.lds.org
50 E North Temple St   Salt Lake City UT 84150
Ph: 801-240-1000 ▪ Fx: 801-240-2033 ▪ TF: 800-453-3860

Jesus, Jews for   www.jfjonline.org
60 Haight St   San Francisco CA 94102
Ph: 415-864-2600 ▪ Fx: 415-552-8325

Jesus, Saints Alive in   www.saintsalive.com
PO Box 1347   Issaquah WA 98027
Ph: 425-888-3904 ▪ TF: 800-961-9888

Jewelers of America   www.jewelers.org
52 Vanderbilt Ave 19th Fl   New York NY 10017
Ph: 646-658-0246 ▪ Fx: 646-658-0256 ▪ TF: 800-223-0673

Jewelers Board of Trade   www.jewelersboard.com
95 Jefferson Blvd   Warwick RI 02888
Ph: 401-467-0055 ▪ Fx: 401-467-1199

Jewelers Guild, Leading   www.love-story.com/ljgstory.htm
PO Box 69604   Los Angeles CA 90069
Ph: 310-820-3386 ▪ Fx: 310-820-3530

Jewelers Organization, Independent   www.independentjewelers.com
25 Seir Hill Rd   Norwalk CT 06850
Ph: 203-846-4215 ▪ Fx: 203-846-8571 ▪ TF: 800-624-9252

Jewelers Security Alliance   www.jewelerssecurity.org
6 E 45th St   New York NY 10017
Ph: 212-687-0328 ▪ Fx: 212-808-9168

Jewelers Shipping Association
125 Carlsbad St   Cranston RI 02920
Ph: 401-943-6490 ▪ Fx: 401-943-1490 ▪ TF: 800-688-4572

Jewelers & Suppliers of America, Manufacturing   www.mjsainc.com
45 Royal Little Dr   Providence RI 02904
Ph: 401-274-3840 ▪ Fx: 401-274-0265 ▪ TF: 800-444-6572

Jewelers Vigilance Committee   www.jvclegal.org
25 W 45th St Suite 400   New York NY 10036
Ph: 212-997-2002 ▪ Fx: 212-997-9148 ▪ TF: 800-564-6582

Jewelry Appraisers, National Association of
PO Box 6558   Annapolis MD 21401
Ph: 410-897-0889

Jewelry Association, Women's   www.womensjewelry.org
373 US Hwy 46 W Suite E-215   Fairfield NJ 07004
Ph: 973-575-7190 ▪ Fx: 973-575-1445

Jewelry Club, Vintage Fashion & Costume   www.lizjewel.com/vf
PO Box 265   Glen Oaks NY 11004
Ph: 718-939-3095 ▪ Fx: 718-939-7988

Jewelry Industry Distributors Association
11812-A N 56th St   Tampa FL 33617
Ph: 813-914-8756 ▪ Fx: 813-988-5837

Jewelry Information Center   www.jewelryinfo.org
52 Vanderbilt Ave 19th Fl   New York NY 10017
Ph: 646-658-0240 ▪ Fx: 646-658-0245 ▪ TF: 800-459-0130

Jewelry Manufacturers Guild
PO Box 46099   Los Angeles CA 90046
Ph: 909-769-1820 ▪ Fx: 909-769-1920 ▪ TF: 800-359-0340

Jewelry Salesman's Association, Costume
403 Charles St   Providence RI 02904
Ph: 401-272-3090 ▪ Fx: 401-274-5114 ▪ TF: 800-225-2452

Jewish Aging Services, Association of   www.ajas.org
316 Pennsylvania Ave SE Suite 402   Washington DC 20003
Ph: 202-543-7500 ▪ Fx: 202-543-4090

Jewish Alcoholics Chemically Dependent Persons & Significant   www.jacsweb.org
Others   850 7th Ave Suite 1201   New York NY 10019
Ph: 212-397-4197 ▪ Fx: 212-399-3525

Jewish Alliance of America, Messianic   www.mjaa.org
PO Box 274   Springfield PA 19064
Ph: 610-338-0451 ▪ Fx: 610-338-0471 ▪ TF: 800-225-6552

(Jewish) Alpha Epsilon Phi Sorority   www.aephi.org
111 Prospect St 2nd Fl   Stamford CT 06901
Ph: 203-358-8744 ▪ Fx: 203-357-7975

(Jewish) Alpha Epsilon Pi Fraternity Inc   www.aepi.org
8815 Wesleyan Rd   Indianapolis IN 46268
Ph: 317-876-1913 ▪ Fx: 317-876-1057 ▪ TF: 800-223-2374

Jewish Archives, American   huc.edu/aja
3101 Clifton Ave   Cincinnati OH 45220
Ph: 513-221-1875 ▪ Fx: 513-221-7812

(Jewish) ARZA/World Union North America   arza.org
633 3rd Ave   New York NY 10017
Ph: 212-650-4280 ▪ Fx: 212-650-4289

Jewish Assistance & Relief Network, Global   www.globaljewish.org
666 5th Ave Suite 246   New York NY 10103
Ph: 212-868-3636 ▪ Fx: 212-868-7878

Jewish Association for Services for the Aged   www.jasa.org
132 W 31st St 15th Fl   New York NY 10001
Ph: 212-273-5227

Jewish Board of Family & Children Services   www.jbfcs.org
120 W 57th St   New York NY 10019
Ph: 212-582-9100 ▪ Fx: 212-956-5676 ▪ TF: 888-523-2769

Jewish Book Council   www.jewishbookcouncil.org
15 E 26th St 10th Fl   New York NY 10010
Ph: 212-532-4949 ▪ Fx: 212-481-4174

Jewish Braille Institute of America   www.jbilibrary.org
110 E 30th St   New York NY 10016
Ph: 212-889-2525 ▪ Fx: 212-689-3692 ▪ TF: 800-433-1531

(Jewish) Brith Sholom   www.brithsholom.com
6410 N Broad St   Philadelphia PA 19126
Ph: 215-878-5696 ▪ Fx: 215-878-5699

Jewish Brotherhood of America, Sephardic   www.sephardicstudies.org/brotherhood.html
9745 Queens Blvd Suite 610   Rego Park NY 11374
Ph: 718-459-1600

Jewish Campus Life, Hillel: Foundation for   www.hillel.org
800 8th St NW   Washington DC 20001
Ph: 202-449-6500 ▪ Fx: 202-847-6693

Jewish Center for Learning & Leadership, CLAL - National   www.clal.org
440 Park Ave S 4th Fl   New York NY 10016
Ph: 212-779-3300 ▪ Fx: 212-779-1009

Jewish Center Professionals, Association of   www.ajcp.org
15 E 26th St 10th Fl   New York NY 10010
Ph: 212-532-4949 ▪ Fx: 212-481-4174

Jewish Chaplains Council, JWB   www.jcca.org/JWB
15 E 26th St   New York NY 10010
Ph: 212-532-4949 ▪ Fx: 212-481-4174

Jewish Chautauqua Society   www.nftb.org/jcs.html
633 3rd Ave   New York NY 10017
Ph: 212-650-4100 ▪ Fx: 212-650-4189 ▪ TF: 800-765-6200

Jewish Children's Adoption Network   www.users.qwest.net/~jcan
PO Box 147016   Denver CO 80214
Ph: 303-573-8113 ▪ Fx: 303-893-1447

(Jewish-Christian) AMF International   www.amfi.org
PO Box 5470   Lansing IL 60438
Ph: 708-418-0020 ▪ Fx: 708-418-0132

Jewish Committee, American   www.ajc.org
165 E 56th St   New York NY 10022
Ph: 212-751-4000 ▪ Fx: 212-319-0975

Jewish Committee on Scouting, National   www.jewishscouting.org
1325 W Walnut Hill Ln PO Box 152079   Irving TX 75015
Ph: 972-580-2295 ▪ Fx: 972-580-7870

Jewish Communities, United   www.ujc.org
111 8th Ave Suite 11E   New York NY 10011
Ph: 212-284-6500 ▪ Fx: 212-284-6835

Jewish Community Centers Association of North America   www.jcca.org
15 E 26th St 10th Fl   New York NY 10010
Ph: 212-532-4949 ▪ Fx: 212-481-4174

Jewish Congress, American   www.ajcongress.org
15 E 84th St   New York NY 10028
Ph: 212-879-4500 ▪ Fx: 212-249-3672

Jewish Congress, World   www.wjc.org.il
501 Madison Ave 17th Fl   New York NY 10022
Ph: 212-755-5770 ▪ Fx: 212-755-5883 ▪ TF: 800-755-5883

Jewish Council for Public Affairs   www.jewishpublicaffairs.org
443 Park Ave S 11th Fl   New York NY 10016
Ph: 212-684-6950 ▪ Fx: 212-686-1353

Jewish Culture, Congress for
25 E 21st St   New York NY 10010
Ph: 212-505-8040 ▪ Fx: 212-505-8044

Jewish Culture, Memorial Foundation for   www.mfjc.org
50 Broadway 34th Fl   New York NY 10004
Ph: 212-425-6606 ▪ Fx: 212-425-6602

Jewish Culture, National Foundation for   www.jewishculture.org
330 7th Ave 21st Fl   New York NY 10001
Ph: 212-629-0500 ▪ Fx: 212-629-0508

Jewish Defense Organization   www.jdo.org
PO Box 159 FDR Stn   New York NY 10150
Ph: 212-252-3383

Jewish Democratic Council, National   www.njdc.org
PO Box 75308   Washington DC 20013
Ph: 202-216-9060 ▪ Fx: 202-216-9061

Jewish Education, Coalition for the Advancement of   www.caje.org
261 W 35th St 12th Fl   New York NY 10001
Ph: 212-268-4210 ▪ Fx: 212-268-4214

Jewish Education Service of North America   www.jesna.org
111 8th Ave Suite 11-E   New York NY 10011
Ph: 212-284-6950 ▪ Fx: 212-284-6951

Jewish Educators Assembly   www.jewisheducators.org
300 Forest Dr   East Hills NY 11548
Ph: 516-484-9585 ▪ Fx: 516-484-9586

Jewish Family & Children's Agencies, Association of   www.ajfca.org
557 Cranbury Rd Suite 2   East Brunswick NJ 08816
Ph: 732-432-7120 ▪ Fx: 732-432-7127 ▪ TF: 800-634-7346

Jewish Film, National Center for   www.jewishfilm.org
Brandeis Univ Lown 102 MS 053   Waltham MA 02454
Ph: 781-899-7044 ▪ Fx: 781-736-2070

Jewish Foundation for the Righteous   www.jfr.org
305 7th Ave 19th Fl   New York NY 10001
Ph: 212-727-9955 ▪ Fx: 212-727-9956 ▪ TF: 888-421-1221

Jewish Free Loan Association   www.jfla.org
6505 Wilshire Blvd Suite 715   Los Angeles CA 90048
Ph: 323-761-8830 ▪ Fx: 323-761-8841

Jewish Fund for Justice   www.jfjustice.org
260 5th Ave Suite 701   New York NY 10001
Ph: 212-213-2113 ▪ Fx: 212-213-2233

Jewish Funeral Directors of America   www.jfda.org
150 Lynnway Suite 506   Lynn MA 01902
Ph: 781-477-9300 ▪ Fx: 781-477-9393

Jewish Genealogical Society   www.jgsny.org
15 W 16th St   New York NY 10011
Ph: 212-294-8326

Jewish Genetic Diseases, Center for   www.nfjgd.org
Mt Sinai Medical Center 5th Ave at 100 St   New York NY 10029
Ph: 212-659-6774

Jewish Girl Scout Committee, National   www.njgsc.org
33 Central Dr   Bronxville NY 10708
Ph: 914-738-3986 ▪ Fx: 914-738-6752

Jewish Guild for the Blind   www.jgb.org
15 W 65th St   New York NY 10023
Ph: 212-769-6200 ▪ Fx: 212-769-6266 ▪ TF: 800-284-4422

Jewish Healing, National Center for   www.jewishhealing.org
850 7th Ave Suite 1201   New York NY 10019
Ph: 212-399-2685 ▪ Fx: 212-399-2475

(Jewish) Hineni International   www.hineni.org
232 West End Ave   New York NY 10023
Ph: 212-496-1660 ▪ Fx: 212-496-1908

Jewish Historical Society, American   www.ajhs.org
15 W 16th St   New York NY 10011
Ph: 212-294-6160 ▪ Fx: 212-294-6161

Jewish Holocaust Survivors, American Gathering of
122 W 30th St Suite 205   New York NY 10001
Ph: 212-239-4230 ▪ Fx: 212-279-2926

Jewish Immigration, Research Foundation for
570 7th Ave   New York NY 10018
Ph: 212-921-3871 ▪ Fx: 212-575-1918

Jewish Joint Distribution Committee, American   www.jdc.org
711 3rd Ave 10th Fl   New York NY 10017
Ph: 212-687-6200 ▪ Fx: 212-370-5467

Jewish Labor Committee
25 E 21st St 2nd Fl   New York NY 10010
Ph: 212-477-0707 ▪ Fx: 212-477-1918

Jewish Law Students Association, National
154 Stuart St   Boston MA 02116
Ph: 617-451-0010 ▪ Fx: 617-353-7214

Jewish League for Israel, American   www.americanjewishleague.org
130 E 59th St   New York NY 10022
Ph: 212-371-1583 ▪ Fx: 212-371-3265

(Jewish) Leo Baeck Institute   www.lbi.org
15 W 16th St   New York NY 10011
Ph: 212-744-6400 ▪ Fx: 212-988-1305

Jewish Libraries, Association of   www.jewishlibraries.org
15 E 26th St Rm 1034   New York NY 10010
Ph: 212-725-5359

Jewish Life, Institute for Computers in
7074 N Western Ave   Chicago IL 60645
Ph: 773-262-9200 ▪ Fx: 773-262-9298

(Jewish) Lubavitch Movement   www.lubavitch.com
770 Eastern Pkwy   Brooklyn NY 11213
Ph: 718-774-4000 ▪ Fx: 718-774-2718

Jewish Material Claims Against Germany, Conference on   www.claimscon.org
15 E 26th St Rm 906   New York NY 10010
Ph: 646-536-9100 ▪ Fx: 212-679-2126

Jewish Men's Clubs, Federation of — fjmc.org
475 Riverside Dr Suite 832   New York NY 10115
Ph: 212-749-8100 ▪ Fx: 212-316-4271 ▪ TF: 800-288-3562

Jewish Ministries, Messianic — www.messianicjewish.net
6204 Park Heights Ave   Baltimore MD 21215
Ph: 410-358-6471 ▪ Fx: 410-764-1376

Jewish Missions, International Board of — www.ibjm.org
1928 Hamill Rd PO Box 1386   Hixson TN 37343
Ph: 423-876-8150 ▪ Fx: 423-876-8156 ▪ TF: 888-876-8150

Jewish Movement International, Messianic — www.mjmi.org
PO Box 1212   Chandler AZ 85244
Ph: 480-786-6564 ▪ TF: 800-493-7482

Jewish Music Alliance
1133 Broadway Rm 820   New York NY 10010
Ph: 212-243-1304 ▪ Fx: 212-243-1305

Jewish National Fund — www.jnf.org
42 E 69th St   New York NY 10021
Ph: 212-879-9300 ▪ TF: 888-563-0099

(Jewish) National Havurah Committee — www.havurah.org
7135 Germantown Ave 2nd Fl   Philadelphia PA 19119
Ph: 215-248-1335 ▪ Fx: 215-248-9760

(Jewish) National Ramah Commission — www.campramah.org
3080 Broadway   New York NY 10027
Ph: 212-678-8881 ▪ Fx: 212-749-8251

Jewish Organizations, Conference of Presidents — www.conferenceofpresidents.org
of Major American   633 3rd Ave 21st Fl   New York NY 10017
Ph: 212-318-6111 ▪ Fx: 212-644-4135

Jewish Organizations, Congress of Secular — www.csjo.org
19657 Villa Dr N   Southfield MI 48076
Ph: 248-569-8127 ▪ Fx: 248-569-5222

(Jewish) Orthodox Union — www.ou.org
11 Broadway   New York NY 10004
Ph: 212-563-4000 ▪ Fx: 212-564-9058

Jewish Outreach, Central Organization for
770 Eastern Pkwy   Brooklyn NY 11213
Ph: 718-953-2353

(Jewish) Ozar Hatorah — www.shemayisrael.co.il/orgs/ozar
625 Broadway 5th Fl   New York NY 10012
Ph: 212-253-7245 ▪ Fx: 212-473-4773

Jewish Peace Fellowship — www.jewishpeacefellowship.org
PO Box 271   Nyack NY 10960
Ph: 914-358-4601 ▪ Fx: 914-358-4924

Jewish Press Association, American — www.ajpa.org
1828 L St NW Suite 1000   Washington DC 20036
Ph: 202-785-2282 ▪ Fx: 202-785-2307

Jewish Reconstructionist Federation — www.jrf.org
7804 Montgomery Ave Suite 9   Elkins Park PA 19027
Ph: 215-782-8500 ▪ Fx: 215-782-8805

Jewish Renewal, ALEPH: Alliance for — www.aleph.org
7000 Lincoln Dr Suite B2   Philadelphia PA 19119
Ph: 215-247-9700 ▪ Fx: 215-247-9703

Jewish Research, YIVO Institute for — www.yivoinstitute.org
15 W 16th St   New York NY 10011
Ph: 212-246-6080 ▪ Fx: 212-292-1892

Jewish Restitution Successor Organization
15 E 26th St Rm 906   New York NY 10010
Ph: 212-696-4944 ▪ Fx: 212-679-2126

Jewish Scientists, Association of Orthodox — www.aojs.org
25 W 45th St Suite 1405   New York NY 10036
Ph: 212-840-1166 ▪ Fx: 212-840-1514

(Jewish) Sigma Alpha Mu Fraternity — www.sam.org
9245 N Meridian St Suite 105   Indianapolis IN 46260
Ph: 317-846-0600 ▪ Fx: 317-846-9462 ▪ TF: 888-369-9361

(Jewish) Sigma Delta Tau — www.sigmadeltatau.com
111 Congressional Blvd Suite 110   Carmel IN 46032
Ph: 317-846-7747 ▪ Fx: 317-575-5562

Jewish Society for Service, American — www.ajss.org
15 E 26th St Rm 1029   New York NY 10010
Ph: 212-683-6178 ▪ Fx: 212-481-4174

Jewish Sponsored Camps, Association of — www.jewishcamps.org
130 E 59th St   New York NY 10022
Ph: 212-751-0477 ▪ Fx: 212-755-9183

Jewish Storytelling Coalition — users.rcn.com/jewish.ma.ultranet
63 Gould Rd   Waban MA 02468
Ph: 617-244-2884

Jewish Studies, Association for — www.brandeis.edu/ajs
Center for Jewish History 15 W 16th St   New York NY 10011
Ph: 917-606-8249 ▪ Fx: 917-606-8282

Jewish Teachers, Association of Orthodox
1577 Coney Island Dr   Brooklyn NY 11230
Ph: 718-258-3585 ▪ Fx: 718-258-3586

(Jewish) Tzivos Hashem — www.tzivos-hashem.org
332 Kingston   Brooklyn NY 11213
Ph: 718-467-6630 ▪ Fx: 718-467-8527

Jewish Understanding, Center for Christian- — www.ccju.org
Sacred Heart Univ 5151 Park Ave   Fairfield CT 06432
Ph: 203-365-7592 ▪ Fx: 203-365-4815

Jewish Vegetarians of North America — www.jewishveg.com

Jewish Vocational Services, International Association of — www.iajvs.org/
1845 Walnut St Suite 640   Philadelphia PA 19103
Ph: 215-854-0233 ▪ Fx: 215-854-0212

Jewish War Veterans of the USA — www.jwv.org
1811 R St NW   Washington DC 20009
Ph: 202-265-6280 ▪ Fx: 202-234-5662

Jewish War Veterans of the USA - National Ladies Auxiliary
1811 R St NW   Washington DC 20009
Ph: 202-667-9061 ▪ Fx: 202-667-6689

Jewish Women International — www.jewishwomen.org
2000 M St NW Suite 720   Washington DC 20036
Ph: 202-847-1300 ▪ Fx: 202-857-1380 ▪ TF: 800-343-2823

Jewish Women, National Council of — www.ncjw.org
53 W 23rd St 6th Fl   New York NY 10010
Ph: 212-645-4048 ▪ Fx: 212-645-7466 ▪ TF: 800-829-6259

Jewish World Service, American — www.jws.org
45 W 36th St 10th Fl   New York NY 10018
Ph: 212-736-2597 ▪ Fx: 212-736-3463 ▪ TF: 800-889-7146

(Jewish) Zeta Beta Tau Fraternity Inc — www.zbt.org
3905 Vincennes Rd Suite 300   Indianapolis IN 46268
Ph: 317-334-1898 ▪ Fx: 317-334-1899

Jewry, North American Conference on Ethiopian — www.nacoej.org
132 Nassau St Suite 412   New York NY 10038
Ph: 212-233-5200 ▪ Fx: 212-233-5243

Jewry, Struggle to Save Ethiopian — www.studentstruggle.org
2472 Broadway Suite 316   New York NY 10025
Ph: 866-376-7735

Jews, American Committee for Rescue & Resettlement of Iraqi
1125 Park Ave   New York NY 10029
Ph: 212-427-1246 ▪ Fx: 212-360-7009

Jews for Animal Rights — www.micahbooks.com/JAR.html
255 Humphrey St   Marblehead MA 01945
Ph: 617-631-7601

Jews from Central Europe, American Federation of
570 7th Ave   New York NY 10018
Ph: 212-921-3871 ▪ Fx: 212-575-1918

Jews in the Former Soviet Union, Union of Councils for — www.ucsj.com
PO Box 11676   Washington DC 20008
Ph: 202-237-8262 ▪ Fx: 202-237-2236

Jews, International Federation of Secular Humanistic — www.ifshj.org
224 W 35th St   New York NY 10001
Ph: 212-564-6711 ▪ Fx: 212-564-6721

Jews, International Fellowship of Christians & — www.ifcj.org
30 N LaSalle St Suite 2600   Chicago IL 60602
Ph: 312-641-7200 ▪ Fx: 312-641-7201 ▪ TF: 800-486-8844

Jews for Jesus — www.jfjonline.org
60 Haight St   San Francisco CA 94102
Ph: 415-864-2600 ▪ Fx: 415-552-8325

Jews for Morality — www.jewsformorality.org
PO Box 230262 Gravesend Stn   Brooklyn NY 11223
Ph: 718-336-0053 ▪ Fx: 718-645-0556

Jews in Russia Ukraine the Baltic States & Eurasia, NCSJ: Advocates — www.ncsj.org
on Behalf of   2020 K St NW Suite 7800   Washington DC 20036
Ph: 202-898-2500 ▪ Fx: 202-898-0822

Jimmy Ryce Center for Victims of Predatory Abduction — www.jimmyryce.org
5050 Collins Ave Suite 1036   Miami Beach FL 33140
Ph: 305-864-1344 ▪ Fx: 305-864-4161 ▪ TF: 800-546-7923

Jimmy Swaggart Ministries — www.jsm.org
8919 World Ministry Blvd   Baton Rouge LA 70810
Ph: 225-768-8300 ▪ Fx: 225-769-2244 ▪ TF: 800-288-8350

JN 'Ding' Darling Foundation — www.ding-darling.org
785 Crandon Blvd Suite 1206   Key Biscayne FL 33149
Ph: 305-361-9788 ▪ Fx: 305-361-9789

Joan Shorenstein Center on the Press Politics & — www.ksg.harvard.edu/presspol
Public Policy   Harvard Univ John F Kennedy School of
Government 79 John F Kennedy St   Cambridge MA 02138
Ph: 617-495-8269 ▪ Fx: 617-495-8696

Job Accommodation Network — www.jan.wvu.edu
PO Box 6080   Morgantown WV 26506
Ph: 304-293-7186 ▪ Fx: 304-293-5407 ▪ TF: 800-526-7234

Jobs for America's Graduates — www.jag.org
1729 King St Suite 200   Alexandria VA 22314
Ph: 703-684-9479 ▪ Fx: 703-684-9489

Job's Daughters International — www.iojd.org
233 W 6th St   Papillon NE 68046
Ph: 402-592-7987 ▪ Fx: 402-592-2177

Jobs for the Future — www.jff.org
88 Broad St 8th Fl   Boston MA 02110
Ph: 617-728-4446 ▪ Fx: 617-728-4857

Jobs for Progress National Inc, SER - — www.ser-national.org
1925 W John Carpenter Fwy Suite 575   Irving TX 75063
Ph: 972-506-7815 ▪ Fx: 972-506-7832 ▪ TF: 800-427-2306

Jockey Club — www.jockeyclub.com
40 E 52nd St 15th Fl   New York NY 10022
Ph: 212-371-5970 ▪ Fx: 212-371-6123

Jockey Club, Arabian — www.arabianracing.org
10805 E Bethany Dr   Aurora CO 80014
Ph: 303-696-4500 ▪ Fx: 303-696-4599

Jockeys' Guild Inc
250 W Main St Suite 1820   Lexington KY 40507
Ph: 859-259-3211 ▪ Fx: 859-252-0938 ▪ TF: 866-465-6257

John Birch Society — www.jbs.org
PO Box 8040   Appleton WI 54912
Ph: 920-749-3780 ▪ Fx: 920-749-5062

John Burroughs Association Inc — www.johnburroughs.org
15 W 77th St   New York NY 10024
Ph: 212-769-5169

John D & Catherine T MacArthur Foundation — www.macfound.org
140 S Dearborn St Suite 1100   Chicago IL 60603
Ph: 312-726-8000 ▪ Fx: 312-920-6284 ▪ TF: 800-662-8004

(John Deere Tractors) Two-Cylinder Club — www.two-cylinder.com
PO Box 430   Grundy Center IA 50638
Ph: 319-345-6060 ▪ Fx: 319-345-2662 ▪ TF: 888-782-2582

John Dewey Society — johndeweysociety.org

John Elton AIDS Foundation — www.ejaf.org
PO Box 17139   Beverly Hills CA 90209
Ph: 310-535-1775

John F Kennedy Library Foundation — www.jfklibrary.org/fn_menu.htm
Columbia Pt   Boston MA 02125
Ph: 617-929-1200 ▪ Fx: 617-436-3395 ▪ TF: 877-616-4599

John Howard Association   www.johnhowardassociation.org
300 W Adams St Suite 617   Chicago IL 60606
Ph: 312-782-1901 ▪ Fx: 312-782-1902
John Marshall Foundation   www.vba.org/jmfinfo.htm
c/o Virginia Bar Assn 701 E Franklin St Suite 1120   Richmond
VA 23219
Ph: 804-644-0041 ▪ Fx: 804-644-0052
John Pelham Historical Association
7 Carmel Tier   Hampton VA 23666
Ph: 757-838-1685
John S & James L Knight Foundation   www.knightfdn.org
200 S Biscayne Blvd Suite 3300   Miami FL 33131
Ph: 305-908-2600 ▪ Fx: 305-908-2698 ▪ TF: 800-711-2004
John Simon Guggenheim Memorial Foundation   www.gf.org
90 Park Ave 33rd Fl   New York NY 10016
Ph: 212-687-4470 ▪ Fx: 212-697-3248
John Templeton Foundation   www.templeton.org
100 Matsonford Rd 5 Radnor Corporate Ctr Suite 100   Radnor
PA 19087
Ph: 610-687-8942 ▪ Fx: 610-687-8961
Johns Hopkins Center for Alternatives to Animal Testing   altweb.jhsph.edu
111 Market Pl Suite 840   Baltimore MD 21202
Ph: 410-223-1612 ▪ Fx: 410-223-1603
Johnson Magic Foundation Inc   www.magicjohnson.com
9100 Wilshire Blvd East Tower Suite 700   Beverly Hills CA
90212
Ph: 310-246-4400 ▪ Fx: 310-246-1106 ▪ TF: 888-624-4205
Johnson Robert Wood Foundation   www.rwjf.org
PO Box 2316   Princeton NJ 08543
Ph: 609-452-8701 ▪ Fx: 609-627-6701
Joiners of America, United Brotherhood of Carpenters &   www.carpenters.org
101 Constitution Ave NW   Washington DC 20001
Ph: 202-546-6206 ▪ Fx: 202-543-5724
Joint Action in Community Service Inc   www.jacsinc.org
5225 Wisconsin Ave NW Suite 404   Washington DC 20015
Ph: 202-537-0996 ▪ Fx: 202-363-0239 ▪ TF: 800-522-7773
Joint Center for Housing Studies   www.jchs.harvard.edu
Harvard Univ 1033 Massachusetts Ave 5th Fl   Cambridge MA
02138
Ph: 617-495-7908 ▪ Fx: 617-496-9957
Joint Center for Political & Economic Studies   www.jointcenter.org
1090 Vermont Ave NW Suite 1100   Washington DC 20005
Ph: 202-789-3500 ▪ Fx: 202-789-6390
Joint Commission on Accreditation of Healthcare Organizations   www.jcaho.org
1 Renaissance Blvd   Oakbrook Terrace IL 60181
Ph: 630-792-5000 ▪ Fx: 630-792-5005
Joint Commission, International   www.ijc.org
1250 23rd St NW Suite 100   Washington DC 20440
Ph: 202-736-9024 ▪ Fx: 202-736-9015
Joint Council of Allergy Asthma & Immunology   www.jcaai.org
50 N Brockway St Suite 3-3   Palatine IL 60067
Ph: 847-934-1918 ▪ Fx: 847-934-1820
Joint Custody Association   www.jointcustody.org
10606 Wilkins Ave   Los Angeles CA 90024
Ph: 310-475-5352 ▪ Fx: 310-475-6541
Joint Industry Group   www.jig.org
1620 'I' St NW Suite 615   Washington DC 20006
Ph: 202-466-5490 ▪ Fx: 202-463-8497
Joint Labor Management Committee of the Retail Food Industry
3720 Farragut Ave Suite 301   Kensington MD 20895
Ph: 301-942-5400 ▪ Fx: 301-942-5409
Joint Manufacturers Association, Expansion   www.ejma.org
25 N Broadway   Tarrytown NY 10591
Ph: 914-332-0040 ▪ Fx: 914-332-1541
Joint National Committee for Languages   www.languagepolicy.org
4646 40th St NW   Washington DC 20016
Ph: 202-966-8477 ▪ Fx: 202-966-8310
Joint Review Committee on Education in Radiologic Technology   www.jrcert.org
20 N Wacker Dr Suite 900   Chicago IL 60606
Ph: 312-704-5300 ▪ Fx: 312-704-5304
Joint Surgeons, Association of Bone &   www.abjs.org
6300 N River Rd Suite 727   Rosemont IL 60018
Ph: 847-698-1636 ▪ Fx: 847-823-4921
Joist Institute, Steel   www.steeljoist.org
3127 10th Ave Ext N   Myrtle Beach SC 29577
Ph: 843-626-1995 ▪ Fx: 843-626-5565
Joplin Scott International Ragtime Foundation   www.scottjoplin.org
321 S Ohio Ave   Sedalia MO 65301
Ph: 660-826-2271 ▪ Fx: 660-826-5054 ▪ TF: 866-218-6258
Joseph Campbell Foundation   www.jcf.org
PO Box 36   San Anselmo CA 94979
Ph: 800-330-6984
Joseph Conrad Society of America   www.engl.unt.edu/~jgpeters/Conrad
Joshua Slocum Society International   www.joshuaslocumsocietyintl.org
15 Codfish Hill Rd Ext   Bethel CT 06801
Ph: 203-790-6616 ▪ Fx: 203-790-6617
Journalism Association of Community Colleges   www.jaccoline.org
Journalism Education Association   www.jea.org
Kansas State Univ 103 Kedzie Hall   Manhattan KS 66506
Ph: 785-532-5532 ▪ Fx: 785-532-5563
Journalism Historians Association, American   www.berry.edu/ajha
Oklahoma Baptist Univ 500 W University St Box
61201   Shawnee OK 74804
Ph: 405-878-2221
Journalism & Mass Communication, Association for Education in   www.aejmc.org/
234 Outlet Pointe Blvd Suite A   Columbia SC 29210
Ph: 803-798-0271 ▪ Fx: 803-772-3509
Journalism & Mass Communication, Association of Schools of   www.aejmc.org
234 Outlet Pointe Blvd   Columbia SC 29210
Ph: 803-798-0271 ▪ Fx: 803-772-3509

Journalism & Mass Communications, Accrediting Council on Education in   www.ukans.edu/~acejmc
Univ of Kansas School of Journalism Stauffer-Flint Hall   Lawrence KS 66045
Ph: 785-864-3973 ▪ Fx: 785-864-5225
(Journalism) Panos Institute   www.panosinst.org
1322 18th St NW Suite 26   Washington DC 20006
Ph: 202-429-0730
(Journalism) Quill & Scroll Society   www.uiowa.edu/~quill-sc
Univ of Iowa School of Journalism   Iowa City IA 52242
Ph: 319-335-5795 ▪ Fx: 319-335-5210
Journalists of America, Chess   www.correspondencechess.com/cja
22 Budd St   Morristown NJ 07960
Ph: 973-984-3832
Journalists Association, Asian American   www.aaja.org
1182 Market St Suite 320   San Francisco CA 94102
Ph: 415-346-2051 ▪ Fx: 415-346-6343
Journalists Association, National Lesbian & Gay   www.nlgja.org
1420 K St NW Suite 910   Washington DC 20005
Ph: 202-588-9888 ▪ Fx: 202-588-1818
Journalists Association, Native American   www.naja.com
Univ of South Dakota 414 E Clark St   Vermillion SD 57069
Ph: 605-677-5282 ▪ Fx: 866-694-4264
Journalists Association, North American Snowsports   www.nasja.org
11738 SE Madison St   Portland OR 97216
Ph: 503-255-3771
Journalists Association, North American Travel   www.natja.org
531 Main St Suite 902   El Segundo CA 90245
Ph: 310-836-8712 ▪ Fx: 310-836-8769
Journalists Association, South Asian   www.saja.org
Columbia Graduate School of Journalism 2950 Broadway   New York NY 10027
Ph: 212-854-5979 ▪ Fx: 212-854-7318
Journalists, Association for Women   www.awjdfw.org/
PO Box 2199   Fort Worth TX 76113
Ph: 817-685-3876
Journalists & Authors, American Society of   www.asja.org
1501 Broadway Suite 302   New York NY 10036
Ph: 212-997-0947 ▪ Fx: 212-768-7414
Journalists, Committee to Protect   www.cpj.org
330 7th Ave 12th Fl   New York NY 10001
Ph: 212-465-1004 ▪ Fx: 212-465-9568
Journalists, International Center for   www.icfj.org
1616 H St NW 3rd Fl   Washington DC 20006
Ph: 202-737-3700 ▪ Fx: 202-737-0530
Journalists, National Association of Black   www.nabj.org
Univ of Maryland 8701-A Adelphi Rd   Adelphi MD 20783
Ph: 301-445-7100 ▪ Fx: 301-445-7101
Journalists, National Association of Hispanic   www.nahj.org
529 14th St NW National Press Bldg Suite 1000   Washington DC 20045
Ph: 202-662-7145 ▪ Fx: 202-662-7144 ▪ TF: 888-346-6245
Journalists, Society of Environmental   www.sej.org
321 Old York Rd Suite 200   Jenkintown PA 19046
Ph: 215-884-8174 ▪ Fx: 215-884-8175
Journalists, Society of Professional   www.spj.org
3909 Meridian St   Indianapolis IN 46208
Ph: 317-927-8000 ▪ Fx: 317-920-4789
Journals, Conference of Historical
Univ of Arkansas Dept of History Old Main 416   Fayetteville AR 72701
Ph: 501-575-5884
Journeymen & Apprentices of the Plumbing Pipe Fitting Sprinkler Fitting Industry of the US & Canada, United Association of   www.ua.org
901 Massachusetts Ave NW   Washington DC 20001
Ph: 202-628-5823 ▪ Fx: 202-628-5024
Joyce Foundation   www.joycefdn.org
70 W Madison St Suite 2750   Chicago IL 60602
Ph: 312-782-2464 ▪ Fx: 312-782-4160
Joyce James Society   joycesociety.org
41 W 47th St   New York NY 10036
Ph: 212-719-4448
Jozef Pilsudski Institute of America   www.pilsudski.org
180 2nd Ave   New York NY 10003
Ph: 212-505-9077 ▪ Fx: 212-505-9052
Judaea, Young   www.youngjudaea.org
50 W 58th St   New York NY 10019
Ph: 212-303-8014 ▪ Fx: 212-303-4572
Judaic Needlework, Pomegranate Guild of   www.pomegranateguild.org
34 Summit Ave   Sharon MA 02067
Ph: 781-784-2668
Judaism, American Council for   www.acjna.org
PO Box 9009   Alexandria VA 22304
Ph: 703-836-2546
Judaism in Israel, Masorti Foundation for Conservative   www.masorti.org
475 Riverside Dr Suite 832   New York NY 10115
Ph: 212-870-2216 ▪ Fx: 212-870-2218 ▪ TF: 877-287-7414
Judaism, Society for the Advancement of   www.thesaj.org
15 W 86th St   New York NY 10024
Ph: 212-724-7000
Judaism, Society for Humanistic   www.shj.org
28611 W 12-Mile Rd   Farmington Hills MI 48334
Ph: 248-478-7610 ▪ Fx: 248-478-3159
Judaism, Union for Traditional   www.utj.org
811 Palisade Ave   Teaneck NJ 07666
Ph: 201-801-0707 ▪ Fx: 201-801-0449
Judaism, United Synagogue of Conservative   www.uscj.org
155 5th Ave   New York NY 10010
Ph: 212-533-7800 ▪ Fx: 212-353-9439
Judaism, Women of Reform - Federation of Temple Sisterhoods   www.rj.org/wrj
633 3rd Ave   New York NY 10017
Ph: 212-650-4050 ▪ Fx: 212-650-4059

Judaism, Women's League for Conservative www.wlcj.org
475 Riverside Dr   New York NY 10015
Ph: 212-870-1260 ▪ Fx: 212-870-1261 ▪ TF: 800-628-5083

Judge Advocates Association www.jaa.org
720 7th St NW 3rd Fl   Washington DC 20001
Ph: 202-448-1712 ▪ Fx: 202-628-0080

Judges Association, American aja.ncsc.dni.us
300 Newport Ave   Williamsburg VA 23185
Ph: 757-259-1841 ▪ Fx: 757-259-1520 ▪ TF: 800-616-6165

Judges Association, Federal www.federaljudgesassoc.org
111 W Washington St Suite 1100   Chicago IL 60602
Ph: 312-641-1441 ▪ Fx: 312-641-1288

Judges Association, National www.nationaljudgesassociation.org
PO Box 160   Maud OK 74854
Ph: 405-374-1213 ▪ Fx: 405-374-2316 ▪ TF: 888-366-3652

Judges Association, National American Indian Court www.naicja.org
3618 Reder St   Rapid City SD 57702
Ph: 605-342-4804 ▪ Fx: 605-719-9357

Judges Association, National Gymnastics www.ngja.org
719 Anthony Ln   Lincoln NE 68520
Ph: 402-483-7436 ▪ Fx: 402-472-4305

Judges Conference, Federal Administrative Law www.faljc.org
2000 Pennsylvania Ave NW Suite 260   Washington DC 20006
Ph: 202-675-3065 ▪ Fx: 202-219-3289

Judges, National Association of Women www.nawj.org
1112 16th St NW Suite 520   Washington DC 20036
Ph: 202-393-0222 ▪ Fx: 202-393-0125

Judges, National Conference of Bankruptcy www.ncbj.org
235 Secret Cove Dr   Lexington SC 29072
Ph: 803-957-6225

Judges, National Conference of Federal Trial www.abanet.org/jd/ncftjweb.html
541 N Fairbanks Ct   Chicago IL 60611
Ph: 312-988-5689 ▪ Fx: 312-988-5709

Judges, National Conference of Specialized Court www.abanet.org/jd/ncscj
541 N Fairbanks Ct MS 13.2   Chicago IL 60611
Ph: 312-988-5705 ▪ Fx: 312-988-5709

Judges, National Council of Juvenile & Family Court www.ncjfcj.org
Univ of Nevada PO Box 8970   Reno NV 89507
Ph: 775-784-6012 ▪ Fx: 775-784-6628

Judicature Society, American www.ajs.org
Drake Univ Opperman Ctr 2700 University Ave   Des Moines IA
50311
Ph: 515-271-2281 ▪ Fx: 515-279-3090

Judicial Accountability Inc, Center for www.judgewatch.org
PO Box 69 Gedney Stn   White Plains NY 10605
Ph: 914-421-1200 ▪ Fx: 914-428-4994

Judicial Administration, Institute of
NYU School of Law 40 Washington Sq S Vanderbilt Hall   New
York NY 10012
Ph: 212-998-6196 ▪ Fx: 212-995-4036

Judicial College, National www.judges.org
Univ of Nevada Judicial College Bldg MS 358   Reno NV 89557
Ph: 775-784-6747 ▪ Fx: 775-784-4234 ▪ TF: 800-255-8343

Judicial Decisions, Association of Reporters of arjd.washlaw.edu
5711 Nevada St   College Park MD 20740
Ph: 202-479-3194 ▪ Fx: 202-479-3240

Judicial Watch Inc www.judicialwatch.org
PO Box 44444   Washington DC 20026
Ph: 202-646-5172 ▪ Fx: 202-646-5199 ▪ TF: 888-593-8442

Judiciary Interpreters & Translators, National Association of www.najit.org
2150 N 107th St Suite 205   Seattle WA 98133
Ph: 206-367-8704 ▪ Fx: 206-367-8777

Judo Association, US www.usja-judo.org
21 N Union Blvd   Colorado Springs CO 80909
Ph: 719-633-7750 ▪ Fx: 719-633-4041

Judo Federation, US www.usjf.com
PO Box 338   Ontario OR 97914
Ph: 541-889-8753

Judo & Jujitsu Federation, American www.ajjf.org

Judo Inc, USA www.usjudo.org
1 Olympic Plaza Suite 202   Colorado Springs CO 80909
Ph: 719-866-4730 ▪ Fx: 719-866-4733

Jugglers' Association Inc, International www.juggle.org

Juice Products Association www.juiceproducts.org
1156 15th St NW Suite 900   Washington DC 20005
Ph: 202-785-3232 ▪ Fx: 202-223-9741

Jujitsu Federation, American Judo & www.ajjf.org

(Jump Rope) American Double Dutch League www.usaddl.org
4220 Eads St NE   Washington DC 20019
Ph: 800-982-2335

Jump Rope Federation, US Amateur www.usajrf.org

Jumper Association, National Hunter & www.nhja.com
PO Box 1015   Riverside CT 06878
Ph: 203-869-1225

Jumper Futurity, International youngjumpers.com/IJF
PO Box 757   Kirkland WA 98083
Ph: 425-827-5417

Junior Achievement Inc www.ja.org
1 Education Way   Colorado Springs CO 80906
Ph: 719-540-8000 ▪ Fx: 719-540-6113

Junior Achievement of Canada www.jacan.org
2275 Lakeshore Blvd W Suite 306   Toronto ON M8V3Y3
Ph: 416-622-4602 ▪ Fx: 416-622-6861 ▪ TF: 800-265-0699

Junior Achievement International www.jaintl.org
460 Abernathy Rd NE   Atlanta GA 30328
Ph: 404-257-4620 ▪ Fx: 404-257-4621

Junior Angus Association, National www.njaa.info
3201 Frederick Ave   Saint Joseph MO 64506
Ph: 816-383-5100 ▪ Fx: 816-233-9703

Junior Auxiliaries Inc, National Association of www.najanet.org
845 S Main St PO Box 1873   Greenville MS 38702
Ph: 662-332-3000 ▪ Fx: 662-332-3076

Junior Brangus Breeders Association, International www.int-brangus.org
5750 Epsilon PO Box 696020   San Antonio TX 78269
Ph: 210-696-4343 ▪ Fx: 210-696-8718

Junior Chamber of Commerce, US www.usjaycees.org
PO Box 7   Tulsa OK 74102
Ph: 918-584-2481 ▪ Fx: 918-584-4422 ▪ TF: 800-529-2337

Junior Chamber International www.juniorchamber.org
16120 Chesterfield Pkwy W Suite 250   Chesterfield MO 63017
Ph: 636-449-3100 ▪ Fx: 636-449-3107 ▪ TF: 800-905-5499

Junior Classical League, National www.njcl.org
Miami Univ 422 Wells Mill Dr   Oxford OH 45056
Ph: 513-529-7741 ▪ Fx: 513-529-7742

Junior College Athletic Association, National www.njcaa.org
PO Box 7305   Colorado Springs CO 80933
Ph: 719-590-9788 ▪ Fx: 719-590-7324

Junior Daughters of Peter Claver www.knightsofpeterclaver.com
1825 Orleans Ave   New Orleans LA 70116
Ph: 504-821-4225 ▪ Fx: 504-821-4253

Junior Engineering Technical Society www.jets.org
1420 King St Suite 405   Alexandria VA 22314
Ph: 703-548-5387 ▪ Fx: 703-548-0769

Junior Golf Association, American www.ajga.org
1980 Sports Club Dr   Braselton GA 30517
Ph: 770-868-4200 ▪ Fx: 770-868-4211 ▪ TF: 877-373-2542

Junior Golf Association, National Pan-American npaga.callernetwork.com/junior.html
4813 Larcade Dr   Corpus Christi TX 78415
Ph: 361-853-6860 ▪ Fx: 361-854-7242

Junior Hereford Association, National www.hereford.org
PO Box 014059   Kansas City MO 64101
Ph: 816-842-3757 ▪ Fx: 816-842-6931

Junior Honor Society, National www.njhs.org
1904 Association Dr   Reston VA 20191
Ph: 703-860-0200 ▪ Fx: 703-476-5432

Junior Knights of Peter Claver www.knightsofpeterclaver.com
1825 Orleans Ave   New Orleans LA 70116
Ph: 504-821-4225 ▪ Fx: 504-821-4253

Junior Leagues International Inc, Association of www.ajli.org
132 W 31st St 11th Fl   New York NY 10001
Ph: 212-683-1515 ▪ Fx: 212-481-7196 ▪ TF: 800-955-3248

Junior Limousin Association, North American www.nalf.org/programs/juniors.html
7383 S Alton Way Suite 100   Englewood CO 80112
Ph: 303-220-1693 ▪ Fx: 303-220-1884

Junior Optimist Octagon International www.optimist.org
4494 Lindell Blvd   Saint Louis MO 63108
Ph: 314-371-6000 ▪ Fx: 314-371-6006 ▪ TF: 800-500-8130

Junior Order Knights of Pythias www.pythias.org/jr-order
59 Coddington St Suite 202   Quincy MA 02169
Ph: 617-472-8800

Junior Philatelists of America www.jpastamps.org
PO Box 2625   Albany OR 97321
Ph: 541-967-7043 ▪ Fx: 541-967-9515

Junior Rodeo Association, American home1.gte.net/ajra
4501 Armstrong St   San Angelo TX 76903
Ph: 915-658-8009

Junior Santa Gertrudis Association, National www.santagertrudis.ws/jrwelcome.html
PO Box 1257   Kingsville TX 78364
Ph: 361-592-9357 ▪ Fx: 361-592-8572

Junior State of America www.jsa.org
400 S El Camino Real Suite 300   San Mateo CA 94402
Ph: 650-347-1600 ▪ Fx: 650-347-7200 ▪ TF: 800-334-5353

Junior Statesmen Foundation www.jsa.org/foundation
400 S El Camino Real Suite 300   San Mateo CA 94402
Ph: 650-347-1600 ▪ Fx: 650-347-7200 ▪ TF: 800-334-5353

Jurist Association, World www.worldjurist.org
1000 Connecticut Ave NW Suite 202   Washington DC 20036
Ph: 202-466-5428 ▪ Fx: 202-452-8540

Jury Association, Fully Informed www.fija.org
PO Box 5570   Helena MT 59604
Ph: 406-442-7800 ▪ Fx: 406-442-9332 ▪ TF: 800-835-5879

Just Act: Youth Action for Global Justice www.justact.org
333 Valencia St Suite 325   San Francisco CA 94103
Ph: 415-431-4204 ▪ Fx: 415-431-5953

Just for the Kids www.just4kids.org
4030-2 W Braker Ln   Austin TX 78759
Ph: 512-232-0770 ▪ Fx: 512-232-0777 ▪ TF: 800-762-4645

Just One Break Inc www.justonebreak.com
120 Wall St   New York NY 10005
Ph: 212-785-7300 ▪ Fx: 212-785-4513

Justice, Alliance for www.afj.org
11 Dupont Cir NW 2nd Fl   Washington DC 20036
Ph: 202-822-6070 ▪ Fx: 202-822-6068

Justice, American Center for Law & www.aclj.org
PO Box 64429   Virginia Beach VA 23467
Ph: 757-226-2489 ▪ Fx: 757-226-2836 ▪ TF: 800-296-4529

Justice Association, American Criminal www.acjalae.org
PO Box 601047   Sacramento CA 95860
Ph: 916-484-6553 ▪ Fx: 916-488-2227

Justice Association, National Criminal www.ncja.org
720 7th St NW 3rd Fl   Washington DC 20001
Ph: 202-628-8550 ▪ Fx: 202-628-0080

Justice Inc, Black Veterans for Social www.bvsj.org
665 Willoughby Ave   Brooklyn NY 11221
Ph: 718-852-6004 ▪ Fx: 718-852-4805

Justice, Brennan Center for www.brennancenter.org
NYU School of Law 161 Ave of the Americas 12th Fl   New
York NY 10013
Ph: 212-998-6730 ▪ Fx: 212-995-4550

Justice, Center for Health Environment &   www.chej.org/
PO Box 6806 Falls Church VA 22040
Ph: 703-237-2249 ▪ Fx: 703-237-8389

Justice, Center for Public   www.cpjustice.org
2444 Solomons Island Rd Suite 201 Annapolis MD 21401
Ph: 410-571-6300 ▪ Fx: 410-571-6365 ▪ TF: 866-275-8784

Justice, Citizens for Impartial   www.cijonline.com
     www.cij.org

Justice, Coalition for International   www.cij.org
2001 'S' St NW Suite 740 Washington DC 20009
Ph: 202-483-9234 ▪ Fx: 202-483-9263

Justice, Coalition for Juvenile   www.juvjustice.org/
1211 Conncecticut Ave NW Suite 414 Washington DC 20036
Ph: 202-467-0864 ▪ Fx: 202-887-0738

Justice, Counselors For Social   www.counselorsforsocialjustice.org
c/o American Counseling Assn 5999 Stevenson Ave Alexandria VA 22304
Ph: 703-823-9800 ▪ Fx: 703-823-0252 ▪ TF: 800-347-6647

Justice & Equality in Palestine/Israel, SEARCH for   searchforjustice.org
PO Box 3452 Framingham MA 01705
Ph: 508-879-0777 ▪ Fx: 508-877-2611

Justice Foundation, US   www.usjf.net
2091 E Valley Pkwy Suite 1-C Escondido CA 92027
Ph: 760-741-8086 ▪ Fx: 760-741-9548 ▪ TF: 800-367-8753

Justice Fund, Farmworker   www.fwjustice.org
1010 Vermont Ave NW Suite 915 Washington DC 20005
Ph: 202-783-2628 ▪ Fx: 202-783-2561

Justice, Holocaust Survivors & Friends In Pursuit of
800 New Loudon Rd Suite 400 Latham NY 12110
Ph: 518-785-0035 ▪ Fx: 518-783-1557

Justice Information & Statistics, SEARCH - National Consortium for   www.search.org
7311 Greenhaven Dr Suite 145 Sacramento CA 95831
Ph: 916-392-2550 ▪ Fx: 916-392-8440

Justice, Institute for Peace &   www.ipj-ppj.org
4144 Lindell Blvd Suite 408 Saint Louis MO 63108
Ph: 314-533-4445 ▪ Fx: 314-715-6455

Justice, Jewish Fund for   www.jfjustice.org
260 5th Ave Suite 701 New York NY 10001
Ph: 212-213-2113 ▪ Fx: 212-213-2233

Justice, Just Act: Youth Action for Global   www.justact.org
333 Valencia St Suite 325 San Francisco CA 94103
Ph: 415-431-4204 ▪ Fx: 415-431-5953

Justice, Lawyers for Civil   www.lfcj.com
1140 Connecticut Ave NW Suite 503 Washington DC 20036
Ph: 202-429-0045 ▪ Fx: 202-429-6892

Justice Legal Foundation, Criminal   www.cjlf.org
PO Box 1199 Sacramento CA 95812
Ph: 916-446-0345 ▪ Fx: 916-446-1194

Justice & the Media, Leadership Council for Mental Health   www.leadershipcouncil.org
191 Presidential Blvd Suite C132 Bala Cynwyd PA 19004
Ph: 610-664-5007 ▪ Fx: 610-664-5279

Justice, National Association of Blacks in Criminal   www.nabcj.org
North Carolina Central Univ PO Box 19788 Durham NC 27707
Ph: 919-683-1801 ▪ Fx: 919-683-1903

Justice, National Conference for Community &   www.nccj.org
475 Park Ave S 19th Fl New York NY 10016
Ph: 212-545-1300 ▪ Fx: 212-545-8053

Justice, National Interfaith Committee for Worker   www.nicwj.org
1020 W Bryn Mawr Ave 4th Fl Chicago IL 60660
Ph: 773-728-8400 ▪ Fx: 773-728-8409

Justice Network, Africa Faith &   afjn.cua.edu
3035 4th St NE Washington DC 20017
Ph: 202-832-3412 ▪ Fx: 202-832-9051

Justice, No Peace Without   www.npwj.org
866 UN Plaza Suite 408 New York NY 10017
Ph: 212-980-2558 ▪ Fx: 212-980-1072

Justice Policy Foundation, Criminal   www.cjpf.org
8730 Georgia Ave Suite 400 Silver Spring MD 20910
Ph: 301-589-6020 ▪ Fx: 301-589-5056

Justice Project, Battered Women's   www.bwjp.org
2104 4th Ave S Suite B Minneapolis MN 55404
Ph: 612-824-8768 ▪ Fx: 612-824-8965 ▪ TF: 800-903-0111

Justice Research & Statistics Association   www.jrsainfo.org
777 N Capitol St NE Suite 801 Washington DC 20002
Ph: 202-842-9330 ▪ Fx: 202-842-9329

Justice Sciences, Academy of Criminal   www.acjs.org
7319 Hanover Pkwy Suite C Greenbelt MD 20770
Ph: 301-446-6300 ▪ Fx: 301-446-2819 ▪ TF: 800-757-2257

Justice Studies Association, Peace &   www.peacejusticestudies.org
Evergreen State College MS Seminar 3127 Olympia WA 98505
Ph: 360-867-6196 ▪ Fx: 360-867-6553

Justice, Trial Lawyers for Public   www.tlpj.org
1717 Massachusetts Ave NW Suite 800 Washington DC 20036
Ph: 202-797-8600 ▪ Fx: 202-232-7203

Justice, Vera Institute of   www.vera.org
233 Broadway 12th Fl New York NY 10279
Ph: 212-334-1300 ▪ Fx: 212-941-9407

Justice & Witness Ministries, United Church of Christ   www.ucc.org/justice/index.html
700 Prospect Ave Cleveland OH 44115
Ph: 216-736-3704 ▪ Fx: 216-736-3703

Justices, Conference of Chief   ccj.ncsc.dni.us
300 Newport Ave Williamsburg VA 23185
Ph: 757-259-1841 ▪ Fx: 757-259-1520

Juvenile Apparel Manufacturers, Industrial Association of
1430 Broadway Suite 1603 New York NY 10018
Ph: 212-244-2953 ▪ Fx: 212-221-3540

Juvenile Arthritis Organization, American   www.arthritis.org/communities
1330 W Peachtree St Atlanta GA 30309
Ph: 404-965-7514 ▪ Fx: 404-872-0457

Juvenile Detention Association, National   www.njda.com
Eastern Kentucky Univ 301 Perkins Bldg 521 Lancaster Ave Richmond KY 40475
Ph: 859-622-6259 ▪ Fx: 859-622-2333

Juvenile Diabetes Research Foundation International   www.jdf.org
120 Wall St New York NY 10005
Ph: 212-785-9500 ▪ Fx: 212-785-9595 ▪ TF: 800-533-2873

Juvenile & Family Court Judges, National Council of   www.ncjfcj.org
Univ of Nevada PO Box 8970 Reno NV 89507
Ph: 775-784-6012 ▪ Fx: 775-784-6628

Juvenile Justice, Coalition for   www.juvjustice.org/
1211 Conncecticut Ave NW Suite 414 Washington DC 20036
Ph: 202-467-0864 ▪ Fx: 202-887-0738

Juvenile Justice, National Center for   www.ncjj.org
710 5th Ave 3rd Fl Pittsburgh PA 15219
Ph: 412-227-6950 ▪ Fx: 412-227-6955 ▪ TF: 800-577-6903

Juvenile Products Manufacturers Association   www.jpma.org
17000 Commerce Pkwy Suite C Mount Laurel NJ 08054
Ph: 856-638-0420 ▪ Fx: 856-439-0525

Juvenile Scleroderma Network Inc   www.jsdn.org
1204 W 13th St San Pedro CA 90731
Ph: 310-519-9511

JWB Jewish Chaplains Council   www.jcca.org/JWB
15 E 26th St New York NY 10010
Ph: 212-532-4949 ▪ Fx: 212-481-4174

K

KaBOOM! Inc   www.kaboom.org
2213 M St NW Suite 300 Washington DC 20037
Ph: 202-659-0215 ▪ Fx: 202-659-0210

Kaiser Henry J Family Foundation   www.kff.org
2400 Sand Hill Rd Menlo Park CA 94025
Ph: 650-854-9400 ▪ Fx: 650-854-4800

Kampground Owners Association Inc   www.koaowners.org
3416 Primm Ln Birmingham AL 35216
Ph: 205-824-0022 ▪ Fx: 205-823-2760 ▪ TF: 800-678-9976

Kamut Association of North America   www.kamut.com
PO Box 6447 Great Falls MT 59406
Ph: 800-644-6450 ▪ Fx: 406-452-7175

Kant Society, North American   naks.ucsd.edu
Columbia Univ Dept of Philosophy 1150 Amsterdam Ave MC 4971 New York NY 10027
Ph: 212-854-3196

Kappa Alpha Order   www.kappaalphaorder.org
7 Courthouse Sq PO Box 1865 Lexington VA 24450
Ph: 540-463-1865 ▪ Fx: 540-463-2140

Kappa Alpha Psi Fraternity Inc   www.kappaalphapsi.com
2322-24 N Broad St Philadelphia PA 19132
Ph: 215-228-7184 ▪ Fx: 215-228-7181

Kappa Alpha Theta Fraternity   www.kappaalphatheta.org
8740 Founders Rd Indianapolis IN 46268
Ph: 317-876-1870 ▪ Fx: 317-876-1925 ▪ TF: 800-526-1870

Kappa Delta Epsilon   www.kappadeltaepsilon.org
2561 Rocky Ridge Rd Birmingham AL 35243
Ph: 800-779-4106 ▪ Fx: 205-822-4106

Kappa Delta Pi   www.kdp.org
3707 Woodview Trace Indianapolis IN 46268
Ph: 317-871-4900 ▪ Fx: 317-704-2323 ▪ TF: 800-284-3167

Kappa Delta Rho, National Fraternity of   www.kdr.com
331 S Main St Greensburg PA 15601
Ph: 724-838-7100 ▪ Fx: 724-838-7101 ▪ TF: 800-536-5371

Kappa Delta Sorority   www.kappadelta.org
3205 Players Ln Memphis TN 38125
Ph: 901-748-1897 ▪ Fx: 901-748-0949 ▪ TF: 800-536-1897

Kappa Gamma Pi   www.kappagammapi.org
10215 Chardon Rd Chardon OH 44024
Ph: 440-286-3764 ▪ Fx: 440-286-4379

Kappa Kappa Gamma   www.kappakappagamma.org
530 E Town St PO Box 38 Columbus OH 43216
Ph: 614-228-6515 ▪ Fx: 614-228-7809 ▪ TF: 866-554-1870

Kappa Kappa Iota   www.kappakappaiota.org
1875 E 15th St Tulsa OK 74104
Ph: 918-744-0389 ▪ Fx: 918-744-0578 ▪ TF: 800-678-0389

Kappa Kappa Psi National Honorary Band Fraternity   www.kkytbs.org/kky
PO Box 849 Stillwater OK 74076
Ph: 405-372-2333 ▪ Fx: 405-372-2363 ▪ TF: 800-543-6505

Kappa Omicron Nu Honor Society   www.kon.org
4990 Northwind Dr Suite 140 East Lansing MI 48823
Ph: 517-351-8335 ▪ Fx: 517-351-8336

Kappa Phi Gamma Sorority Inc   www.kappaphigamma.org

Kappa Psi Pharmaceutical Fraternity   www.kappa-psi.org
100 Campus Dr Weatherford OK 73096
Ph: 580-774-7170 ▪ Fx: 580-774-7125

Kappa Sigma Fraternity   www.kappasigma.org
PO Box 5066 Charlottesville VA 22905
Ph: 434-295-3193 ▪ Fx: 434-296-9557

Karakul Sheep Registry, American   www.karakulsheep.com
11500 Hwy 5 Boonville MO 65233
Ph: 660-838-6340 ▪ Fx: 660-838-6322

Karate Association, American Shorin Kempo   www.americanblackbeltacademy.com
1587 York St Colorado Springs CO 80918
Ph: 719-598-0398 ▪ Fx: 719-268-2733

Karate Federation, American Amateur   www.aakf.org
1930 Wilshire Blvd Suite 1208 Los Angeles CA 90057
Ph: 213-483-8261 ▪ Fx: 213-483-4060

Karate Federation, International Traditional   www.itkf.org
1930 Wilshire Blvd Suite 1208 Los Angeles CA 90057
Ph: 213-483-8261 ▪ Fx: 213-483-4060

Karate Federation, USA   www.usakarate.org
1300 Kenmore Blvd   Akron OH 44314
Ph: 330-753-3114   Fx: 330-753-6888

Karate International, American Kenpo   www.akki.com
PO Box 768   Evanston WY 82931
Ph: 307-789-4124

Karate Union, Feminist   www.geocities.com/wellesley/5466
1426 S Jackson St 3rd Fl   Seattle WA 98107
Ph: 206-325-3878

Karen Inc, Friends of   www.friendsofkaren.org
118 Titicus Rd   Purdys NY 10578
Ph: 914-277-4547   Fx: 914-277-4967   TF: 800-637-2774

Kart Federation, International   www.ikfkarting.com
1609 S Grove Ave   Ontario CA 91761
Ph: 909-923-4999   Fx: 909-923-6940

Kashmiri American Council   www.kashmiri.com
733 15th St NW Suite 100   Washington DC 20005
Ph: 202-628-6789   Fx: 202-393-0062

Katalysis Partnership   www.katalysis.org
1331 N Commerce St   Stockton CA 95202
Ph: 209-943-6165   Fx: 209-943-7046

Kate B Reynolds Charitable Trust   www.kbr.org
128 Reynolda Village   Winston-Salem NC 27106
Ph: 336-723-1456   Fx: 336-723-7765

Kauffman Ewing Marion Foundation   www.emkf.org
4801 Rockhill Rd   Kansas City MO 64110
Ph: 816-932-1000   Fx: 816-932-1100   TF: 800-489-4900

Keats-Shelley Association of America   www.rc.umd.edu/ksaa/ksaa.html
New York Public Library 476 5th Ave Rm 226   New York NY
    10018
Ph: 212-764-0655

Keck WM Foundation   www.wmkeck.org
550 S Hope St Suite 2500   Los Angeles CA 90071
Ph: 213-680-3833   Fx: 213-614-0934

Keep America Beautiful Inc   www.kab.org
1010 Washington Blvd   Stamford CT 06901
Ph: 203-323-8987   Fx: 203-325-9199

KEEP Inc, American Committee for   www.keep.or.jp/indexe.html
825 Green Bay Rd Suite 122   Wilmette IL 60091
Ph: 847-853-2500   Fx: 847-853-8901   TF: 800-368-5337

Keller Helen International   www.hkworld.org
352 Park Ave S 12th Fl   New York NY 10010
Ph: 212-532-0544   Fx: 212-532-5860   TF: 877-535-5374

Keller Helen National Center for Deaf-Blind Youths & Adults   hknc.org
141 Middle Neck Rd   Sands Point NY 11050
Ph: 516-944-8900   Fx: 516-944-7302

Kellogg WK Foundation   www.wkkf.org
1 Michigan Ave E   Battle Creek MI 49017
Ph: 269-968-1611   Fx: 269-968-0413

Kempe Children's Center   www.kempecenter.org
1825 Marion St   Denver CO 80218
Ph: 303-864-5300   Fx: 303-864-5179

Kennedy Center Alliance for Arts   www.kennedy-center.org/education/kcaaen
   Education Network   John F Kennedy Ctr for the Performing
    Arts 2700 F St NW   Washington DC 20566
Ph: 202-416-8845   Fx: 202-416-8802   TF: 800-444-1324

Kennedy Center, Friends of the   www.kennedy-center.org/support/volunteers
Kennedy Ctr for the Performing Arts 2700 F St
    NW   Washington DC 20566
Ph: 202-416-4600   Fx: 202-416-8076   TF: 800-444-1324

Kennedy John F Library Foundation   www.jfklibrary.org/fn_menu.htm
Columbia Pt   Boston MA 02125
Ph: 617-929-1200   Fx: 617-436-3395   TF: 877-616-4599

Kennedy Robert F Memorial   www.rfkmemorial.org
1367 Connecticut Ave NW Suite 200   Washington DC 20036
Ph: 202-463-7575   Fx: 202-463-6606   TF: 800-558-1880

Kennel Club, American   www.akc.org
260 Madison Ave   New York NY 10016
Ph: 212-696-8200   Fx: 212-696-8299

Kennel Club Ltd, Worldwide   www.worldwidekennel.qpg.com
530 5th Ave   Pelham NY 10803
Ph: 914-654-8574   Fx: 914-654-0364

Kennel Club Inc, United   www.ukcdogs.com
100 E Kilgore Rd   Kalamazoo MI 49002
Ph: 269-343-9020   Fx: 269-343-7037

Kennel Club, Westminster   www.westminsterkennelclub.org
149 Madison Ave Suite 803   New York NY 10016
Ph: 212-213-3165

Kennels Association, American Boarding   abka.com
1702 E Pikes Peak Ave   Colorado Springs CO 80909
Ph: 719-667-1600   Fx: 719-667-0116

Kenpo Karate International, American   www.akki.com
PO Box 768   Evanston WY 82931
Ph: 307-789-4124

Keramos National Professional Ceramic Engineering   www.ceramics.org/keramos
   Fraternity   c/o Seagate Technology 389 Disc Dr MS
    COL-MW1   Longmont CO 80503
Ph: 720-684-2034   Fx: 720-684-2677

Keren-Or Inc   www.keren-or.org
350 7th Ave Suite 200   New York NY 10001
Ph: 212-279-4070   Fx: 212-279-4043

Kerosene Heater Association, National   www.space-heating.com
1816 Old Natchez Trace   Franklin TN 37069
Ph: 615-790-0770   Fx: 615-790-6700

Kerouac! Inc, Lowell Celebrates   ecommunity.uml.edu/lck
PO Box 1111   Lowell MA 01853
Ph: 978-970-0755   TF: 877-537-6822

Kerry Blue Terrier Club, US   www.uskbtc.com
2458 Eastridge Dr   Hamilton OH 45011
Ph: 513-863-5041

Key Club International   www.keyclub.org
3636 Woodview Trace   Indianapolis IN 46268
Ph: 317-875-8755   Fx: 317-879-0204

Keyboard Manufacturers, International Association of Electronic   www.iaekm.org

Keyboard Society, Southeastern Historical   www.sehks.org
PO Box 32022   Charlotte NC 28232
Ph: 704-334-3468   Fx: 704-334-3442

Keystone Center   www.keystone.org
1628 St John Rd   Keystone CO 80435
Ph: 970-513-5800   Fx: 970-262-0152

Khoury George Association of Baseball Leagues
5400 Meramec Bottom Rd   Saint Louis MO 63128
Ph: 314-849-8900   Fx: 314-849-8901

Kid, Adopt a Special   www.adoptaspecialkid.org
7700 Edgewater Dr Suite 320   Oakland CA 94621
Ph: 510-553-1748   Fx: 510-553-1747   TF: 888-680-7349

Kidney Foundation, National   www.kidney.org
30 E 33rd St Suite 1100   New York NY 10016
Ph: 212-889-2210   Fx: 212-689-9261   TF: 800-622-9010

Kidney Fund, American   www.akfinc.org
6110 Executive Blvd Suite 1010   Rockville MD 20852
Ph: 301-881-3052   Fx: 301-881-0898   TF: 800-638-8299

Kids, Athletes & Entertainers for   www.aefk.org
3337 Colorado St   Long Beach CA 90814
Ph: 562-438-5905   Fx: 562-438-9175

Kids for a Clean Environment   www.kidsface.org
PO Box 158254   Nashville TN 37215
Ph: 615-331-7381   Fx: 615-333-9879   TF: 800-952-3223

Kids, Connect For   www.connectforkids.org
1625 K St NW Suite 1100   Washington DC 20006
Ph: 202-638-5770   Fx: 202-638-5771   TF: 877-236-8666

Kids to the Cup   www.kidstothecup.com
120 S 1st Ave   Arcadia CA 91006
Ph: 626-695-3433

Kids In Distressed Situations Inc   www.kidsdonations.org
350 5th Ave Suite 3801   New York NY 10118
Ph: 212-279-5493   Fx: 212-279-5917   TF: 800-266-3314

Kids FACE   www.kidsface.org
PO Box 158254   Nashville TN 37215
Ph: 615-331-7381   Fx: 615-333-9879   TF: 800-952-3223

Kids, Farm Safety 4 Just   www.fs4jk.org
PO Box 458   Earlham IA 50072
Ph: 515-758-2827   Fx: 515-758-2517   TF: 800-423-5437

Kids Foundation Inc, Rosie's For All   www.forallkids.org
PO Box 225   Allendale NJ 07401
Ph: 201-934-5567

Kids & Guns, Common Sense About   www.kidsandguns.org
418 C St NE   Washington DC 20002
Ph: 202-546-0200   Fx: 202-546-6250   TF: 877-955-5437

Kids at Hope   www.kidsathope.org
11811 N Tatum Blvd Suite 3031   Phoenix AZ 85028
Ph: 602-953-7862   Fx: 602-953-7863   TF: 866-275-4673

Kids, Just for   www.just4kids.org
4030-2 W Braker Ln   Austin TX 78759
Ph: 512-232-0770   Fx: 512-232-0777   TF: 800-762-4645

Kids Korps USA   www.kidskorps.org
265 Santa Helena Suite 110A   Solana Beach CA 92075
Ph: 858-259-3602   Fx: 858-259-3603

Kids Meeting Kids   kidsmeetingkids.org
380 Riverside Dr Box 8H   New York NY 10025
Ph: 212-662-2327   Fx: 212-222-1416

Kids, Miracle Flights for   www.miracleflights.org
2756 N Green Valley Pkwy Suite 115   Green Valley NV 89014
Ph: 702-261-0494   Fx: 702-261-0497   TF: 800-358-1711

Kids for Saving Earth   www.kidsforsavingearth.org
PO Box 421118   Minneapolis MN 55442
Ph: 763-559-1234   Fx: 763-559-6980

Kids the World Village, Give   www.gktw.org
210 S Bass Rd   Kissimmee FL 34746
Ph: 407-396-1114   Fx: 407-396-1207   TF: 800-995-5437

Kiewit Peter Foundation
8805 Indian Hills Dr Suite 225   Omaha NE 68114
Ph: 402-344-7890   Fx: 402-344-8099

Killifish Association, American   www.aka.org
280 Cold Springs Dr   Manchester PA 17345
Ph: 610-566-2098

Kiln Drying Association, New England   www.macgregormillsystems.com/nekda.htm
15 Main St PO Box 401   Belfast ME 04915
Ph: 207-338-4377   Fx: 207-338-2692

Kiln Recycling Coalition, Cement   www.ckrc.org
1730 K St NW Suite 710   Washington DC 20006
Ph: 202-466-6802   Fx: 202-466-5009

Kinesiology Association, Touch for Health   www.tfhka.org
PO Box 392   New Carlisle OH 45344
Ph: 937-845-3404   Fx: 937-845-3909   TF: 800-466-8342

Kinesiology, International College of Applied   www.icakusa.com
6405 Metcalf Ave Suite 503   Shawnee Mission KS 66202
Ph: 913-384-5336   Fx: 913-384-5112

Kinesiology & Physical Education, American Academy of   www.aakpe.org
c/o Human Kinetics Publishers Inc PO Box 5076   Champaign IL
    61820
Ph: 217-351-5076   Fx: 217-351-2674   TF: 800-747-4457

Kinetography Laban, International Council of   www.ickl.org

King Charles the Martyr, Society of   www.skcm-usa.org
291 Bacon St   Waltham MA 02451
Ph: 781-899-3165

King Martin Luther Jr Center for Nonviolent Social Change Inc   www.thekingcenter.com
449 Auburn Ave NE   Atlanta GA 30312
Ph: 404-524-1956   Fx: 404-526-8969

King's Daughters & Sons, International Order of the www.iokds.org
34 Vincent Ave PO Box 1017 Chautauqua NY 14722
Ph: 716-357-4951 Fx: 716-357-3762

Kitchen & Bath Association, National www.nkba.org
687 Willow Grove St Hackettstown NJ 07840
Ph: 908-852-0033 Fx: 908-852-1695 TF: 800-843-6522

Kitchen & Bathroom Designers, Society of Certified
687 Willow Grove St Hackettstown NJ 07840
Ph: 908-852-0033 Fx: 908-852-1695 TF: 800-843-6522

Kitchen Cabinet Manufacturers Association www.kcma.org
1899 Preston White Dr Reston VA 20191
Ph: 703-264-1690 Fx: 703-620-6530

Kitchen Exhaust Cleaning Association, International www.ikeca.org
1518 K St NW Suite 503 Washington DC 20005
Ph: 202-393-5955 Fx: 202-638-4833

Kite Trade Association International www.kitetrade.com
PO Box 115 Rose Lodge OR 97372
Ph: 541-994-3453 Fx: 541-994-3459 TF: 800-243-8548

Kitefliers Association, American www.aka.kite.org
PO Box 1614 Walla Walla WA 99362
Ph: 509-529-9171 TF: 800-252-2550

Kiwanis International www.kiwanis.org
3636 Woodview Trace Indianapolis IN 46268
Ph: 317-875-8755 Fx: 317-879-0204 TF: 800-549-2647

Kiwanis International Foundation kif.kiwanis.org
3636 Woodview Trace Indianapolis IN 46268
Ph: 317-875-8755

Kiwifruit Commission, California www.kiwifruit.org
9845 Horn Rd Suite 160 Sacramento CA 95827
Ph: 916-362-7490 Fx: 916-362-7993

Klaas Kids Foundation www.klaaskids.org
PO Box 925 Sausalito CA 94966
Ph: 415-331-6867 Fx: 415-331-5633

Klinefelter Syndrome Information & Support, American Association for www.aaksis.org
2945 W Farwell Ave Chicago IL 60645
Ph: 773-761-5298

Knee Surgeons, American Association of Hip &
704 N Florence Dr Park Ridge IL 60068
Ph: 847-698-1200 Fx: 847-825-9294

Knee Surgery & Orthopaedic Sports Medicine, International Society of Arthroscopy www.isakos.com 2678 Bishop Dr Suite 250 San Ramon CA 94583
Ph: 925-807-1197 Fx: 925-807-1199

Knife Association, International Saw &
351 'O' St Fresno CA 93721
Ph: 559-237-0809 Fx: 559-237-8879

Knife Association, Machine www.mka.org
30200 Detroit Rd Cleveland OH 44145
Ph: 440-899-0010 Fx: 440-892-1404

Knife Collectors Association, National www.nationalknife.org
5924 Shallowford Rd PO Box 21070 Chattanooga TN 37424
Ph: 423-892-5007 Fx: 423-899-9456

Knife & Tool Institute, American www.akti.org
22 Vista View Cody WY 82414
Ph: 307-587-8296

Knifemakers Guild www.knifemakersguild.com
13950 NE 20th St Williston FL 32696
Ph: 352-528-6124

Knight John S & James L Foundation www.knightfdn.org
200 S Biscayne Blvd Suite 3300 Miami FL 33131
Ph: 305-908-2600 Fx: 305-908-2698 TF: 800-711-2004

Knights of Columbus www.kofc.org
1 Columbus Plaza New Haven CT 06510
Ph: 203-752-4000 Fx: 203-773-3000

Knights of Equity www.knightsofequity.com
229 Sample St Pittsburgh PA 15209
Ph: 412-828-8770

Knights of Malta, Ancient & Illustrious Order
2632 Skylark Dr Wilmington DE 19808
Ph: 302-996-0800

Knights of the Mystic Light, Aladdin www.aladdinknights.org
3935 Kelley Rd Kevil KY 42053
Ph: 270-488-2116 Fx: 270-488-2055

Knights of Peter Claver www.knightsofpeterclaver.com
1825 Orleans Ave New Orleans LA 70116
Ph: 504-821-4225 Fx: 504-821-4253

Knights of Pythias, Order of www.pythias.org
59 Coddington St Suite 202 Quincy MA 02169
Ph: 617-472-8800 Fx: 617-376-0363

Knights of Saint John International home.fuse.net/ksji
89 S Pine Ave Albany NY 12208
Ph: 518-453-5675

Knights Templar of the US, Grand Encampment of www.knightstemplar.org
5097 N Elston Ave Suite 101 Chicago IL 60630
Ph: 773-777-3300 Fx: 773-777-8836

Knights of the Vine, Brotherhood of the www.kov.org
2210 Northpoint Pkwy Santa Rosa CA 95407
Ph: 707-579-3781 Fx: 707-579-3996

Knitwear Designers Guild, Professional
W3090 County Rd Y Lomira WI 53048
Ph: 920-583-4298

(Knives) Case Collectors Club www.casesales.com/ccc
PO Box 4000 Bradford PA 16701
Ph: 814-368-4123 Fx: 814-368-1736 TF: 800-523-6350

Knowledge Engineers, International Association of www.iake.org
973 Russell Ave Suite D Gaithersburg MD 20879
Ph: 301-948-5390 Fx: 301-926-4243

Knowledge Industry Association, National Education www.nekia.org
1718 Connecticut Ave NW Suite 700 Washington DC 20009
Ph: 202-518-0847 Fx: 202-785-3849

Koala Foundation, Friends of the Australian www.savethekoala.com
c/o Nolan/Lehr Group Inc 224 W 29th St 15th Fl New York NY 10001
Ph: 212-967-8200 Fx: 212-967-7292 TF: 800-695-6252

Koch Foundation Inc www.kochenterprises.com/corporate/foundation.htm
4421 NW 39th Ave Suite 1 Gainesville FL 32606
Ph: 352-373-7491

Kodaly Educators, Organization of American www.oake.org
1612 29th Ave S Moorhead MN 56560
Ph: 218-227-6253 Fx: 218-277-6254

Koi Clubs of America, Associated www.akca.org
258 Sherwood St Costa Mesa CA 92627
Ph: 949-548-3690

Kolel Chibas Jerusalem - Reb Meyer Baal Haness Charity www.chibasjerusalem.com
4802-A 12th Ave Brooklyn NY 11219
Ph: 718-633-7112 Fx: 718-633-5783

Kolping Society of America, Catholic www.kolping.org
PO Box 4907 Clifton NJ 07015
Ph: 973-478-8635 Fx: 973-478-8049 TF: 877-659-7237

Komen Susan G Breast Cancer Foundation www.komen.org
5005 LBJ Fwy Suite 250 Dallas TX 75244
Ph: 972-855-1600 Fx: 972-855-1605 TF: 800-462-9273

Korean, American Association of Teachers of www.fsu.edu/~aatk
Florida State Univ Dept of Modern Languages & Linguistics Tallahassee FL 32306
Ph: 850-644-3728 Fx: 850-644-0524

Korean American Coalition
3727 W 6th St Suite 505 Los Angeles CA 90020
Ph: 213-380-6175 Fx: 213-380-7990

Korean-American Scientists & Engineers Association www.ksea.org
1952 Gallows Rd Suite 300 Vienna VA 22182
Ph: 703-748-1221 Fx: 703-748-1331

Korean Chamber of Commerce & Industry in USA Inc www.kocham.org
460 Park Ave Suite 410 New York NY 10022
Ph: 212-644-0140 Fx: 212-644-9106

(Korean War) Chosin Few home.hawaii.rr.com/chosin
238 Cornwall Cir Chalfont PA 18914
Ph: 215-822-9093 Fx: 215-822-0163 TF: 888-999-7819

Korean War Project www.koreanwar.org
PO Box 180190 Dallas TX 75218
Ph: 214-320-0342

Korean War Veterans Association www.kwva.org
PO Box 10806 Arlington VA 22210
Ph: 703-522-9629

Koret Foundation www.koretfoundation.org
33 New Montgomery St Suite 1090 San Francisco CA 94105
Ph: 415-882-7740 Fx: 415-882-7775

Kosciuszko Foundation www.kosciuszkofoundation.org
15 E 65th St New York NY 10021
Ph: 212-734-2130 Fx: 212-628-4552

Kresge Foundation www.kresge.org
3215 W Big Beaver Rd Troy MI 48084
Ph: 248-643-9630 Fx: 248-643-0588

Krishnamurti Foundation of America www.kfa.org
PO Box 1560 Ojai CA 93024
Ph: 805-646-2726 Fx: 805-646-6674

Kristin Brooks Hope Center www.hopeline.com
201 N 23rd St Suite 100 Purcellville VA 20132
Ph: 540-338-5756 Fx: 540-338-5746 TF: 800-784-2433

Kroeber Anthropological Society sscl.berkeley.edu/~kas
UC Berkeley Dept of Anthropology 232 Kroeber Hall Berkeley CA 94720
Ph: 510-642-3391 Fx: 510-643-8557

Kurdish Heritage Foundation of America
345 Park Pl Brooklyn NY 11238
Ph: 718-783-7930 Fx: 718-398-4365

Kurdish Information Network, American www.kurdistan.org
2600 Connecticut Ave NW Suite 1 Washington DC 20008
Ph: 202-483-6444 Fx: 202-483-6476

Kurt Weill Foundation for Music www.kwf.org
7 E 20th St New York NY 10003
Ph: 212-505-5240 Fx: 212-353-9663

L

La Leche League International Inc www.lalecheleague.org
1400 N Meacham Rd Schaumburg IL 60173
Ph: 847-519-7730 Fx: 847-519-0035 TF: 800-525-3243

La Raza, National Council of www.nclr.org
1111 19th St NW Suite 1000 Washington DC 20036
Ph: 202-785-1670 Fx: 202-776-1792 TF: 800-311-6257

La Raza Unida, Partido Nacional www.pnlru.org
11663 Herrick Ave PO Box 13 San Fernando CA 91340
Ph: 818-365-6534

La Societe des Quarante Hommes at Huit Chevaux fortyandeight.org
777 N Meridian St Rm 204 Indianapolis IN 46204
Ph: 317-634-1804 Fx: 317-632-9365

Laban/Bartenieff Institute of Movement Studies www.limsonline.org
520 8th Ave Suite 304 New York NY 10018
Ph: 212-643-8888 Fx: 212-643-8388

Laban, International Council of Kinetography www.ickl.org

Label Manufacturers Institute, Tag & www.tlmi.com
40 Shuman Blvd Suite 295 Naperville IL 60563
Ph: 630-357-9222 Fx: 630-357-0192 TF: 800-533-8564

Label Printing Industries of America www.gain.net/PIA_GATF/LPIA/main.html
100 Daingerfield Rd Alexandria VA 22314
Ph: 703-519-8100 Fx: 703-548-3227

Label Society, Citrus   www.citruslabelsociety.com
131 Miramonte Dr   Fullerton CA 92835
Ph: 714-871-2864 ▪ Fx: 714-871-0249

Labor Alliance, Asian Pacific American   www.apalanet.org
815 16th St NW   Washington DC 20006
Ph: 202-974-8051 ▪ Fx: 202-974-8056

Labor Association of the USA, Christian
405 Centerstone Ct PO Box 65   Zeeland MI 49464
Ph: 616-772-9164 ▪ Fx: 616-772-9830

Labor Committee, Jewish
25 E 21st St 2nd Fl   New York NY 10010
Ph: 212-477-0707 ▪ Fx: 212-477-1918

Labor Committee, National   www.nlcnet.org
540 W 48th St   New York NY 10036
Ph: 212-242-3002 ▪ Fx: 212-242-3821

Labor Communications Association, International   www.ilcaonline.org
AFL-CIO CLC 815 16th St NW   Washington DC 20006
Ph: 202-637-5068 ▪ Fx: 202-508-6973

Labor & Community Research, Center for   www.clcr.org
3411 W Diversey Ave Suite 10   Chicago IL 60647
Ph: 773-278-5418 ▪ Fx: 773-278-5918

Labor Conference, National Railway
1901 L St NW Suite 500   Washington DC 20036
Ph: 202-862-7200 ▪ Fx: 202-862-7230

Labor Council for Latin American Advancement   www.lclaa.org
888 16th St NW Suite 640   Washington DC 20006
Ph: 202-347-4223 ▪ Fx: 202-347-5095

Labor Education in the Americas Project, US   www.usleap.org
PO Box 268-290   Chicago IL 60626
Ph: 773-262-6502 ▪ Fx: 773-262-6602

Labor Education Center, American
2000 P St NW Suite 300   Washington DC 20036
Ph: 202-828-5170 ▪ Fx: 202-785-3862

Labor Heritage Foundation   www.laborheritage.org
888 16th St NW Suite 680   Washington DC 20006
Ph: 202-974-8040 ▪ Fx: 202-974-8043

Labor History Association, International
706 Bruce Ct   Madison WI 53705
Ph: 608-231-1886

Labor & Industrial Relations, Institute of   www.ilir.umich.edu
Univ of Michigan Victor Vaughan Bldg 1111 Catherine St   Ann
Arbor MI 48109
Ph: 734-763-3116 ▪ Fx: 734-763-0913

Labor Israel, National Committee for   www.laborisrael.org
275 7th Ave   New York NY 10001
Ph: 212-647-0300 ▪ Fx: 212-647-0308

Labor Management Association, National   www.nlma.org
PO Box 819   Jamestown NY 14702
Ph: 716-665-3654 ▪ Fx: 716-665-8060 ▪ TF: 800-967-2687

Labor Management Committee of the Retail Food Industry, Joint
3720 Farragut Ave Suite 301   Kensington MD 20895
Ph: 301-942-5400 ▪ Fx: 301-942-5409

Labor Management Maritime Committee Inc
1150 17th St NW Suite 700   Washington DC 20036
Ph: 202-955-5662 ▪ Fx: 202-872-0912

Labor Officials, National Association of Governmental   www.naglo.org
c/o Council of State Governments 444 N Capitol St NW Suite
401   Washington DC 20001
Ph: 202-624-5460 ▪ Fx: 202-624-5452

Labor Organization - US, International   www.us.ilo.org
1828 L St NW Suite 600   Washington DC 20036
Ph: 202-653-7652 ▪ Fx: 202-653-7687

Labor Organizing Committee AFL-CIO, Farm   floc.com
1221 Broadway St   Toledo OH 43609
Ph: 419-243-3456 ▪ Fx: 419-243-5655

Labor Policy, Center on National
5211 Port Royal Rd Suite 103   North Springfield VA 22151
Ph: 703-321-9180 ▪ Fx: 703-321-9325

Labor Project for Working Families   www.laborproject.org
2521 Channing Way Suite 5555   Berkeley CA 94720
Ph: 510-643-7088 ▪ Fx: 510-642-6432

Labor Relations Agencies, Association of   www.alra.org

Labor Relations Association, National Public Employer   www.npelra.org
1617 Duke St   Alexandria VA 22314
Ph: 703-836-9626 ▪ Fx: 703-836-9628 ▪ TF: 800-296-2230

Labor Relations Professionals, Society of Federal
PO Box 25112   Arlington VA 22202
Ph: 703-685-4130 ▪ Fx: 703-685-1144

Labor Research Fund Inc, National Council on Agricultural Life &   www.ncall.org
20 E Division St PO Box 1092   Dover DE 19903
Ph: 302-678-9400 ▪ Fx: 302-678-9058

Labor Rights Fund, International   www.laborrights.org
733 15th St NW Suite 920   Washington DC 20005
Ph: 202-347-4100 ▪ Fx: 202-347-4885

Labor Union Women Center for Education &   www.cluw.org/programs-edresearch.html
Research, Coalition of   1925 K St NW Suite 402   Washington
DC 20006
Ph: 202-223-8360 ▪ Fx: 202-776-0537

Labor Union Women, Coalition of   www.cluw.org
1925 K St NW Suite 402   Washington DC 20006
Ph: 202-223-8360 ▪ Fx: 202-776-0537

Labor Zionist Alliance   www.laborzionist.org
275 7th Ave 17th Fl   New York NY 10001
Ph: 212-366-1194 ▪ Fx: 212-675-7685

Laboratories, American Council of Independent   www.acil.org
1629 K St NW Suite 400   Washington DC 20006
Ph: 202-887-5872 ▪ Fx: 202-887-0021

Laboratories, Association of Cinema & Video   www.acvl.org

Laboratories Association, Optical   www.ola-labs.org
11096-B Lee Hwy Suite 102   Fairfax VA 22030
Ph: 703-359-2830 ▪ Fx: 703-359-2834 ▪ TF: 800-477-5652

Laboratories, Association of Public Health   www.aphl.org
2025 M St NW Suite 550   Washington DC 20036
Ph: 202-822-5227 ▪ Fx: 202-887-5098

Laboratories, Intersocietal Commission for the Accreditation of   www.icavl.org
Vascular   8840 Stanford Blvd Suite 4900   Columbia MD
21045
Ph: 410-872-0100 ▪ Fx: 410-872-0030

Laboratory Accreditation, American Association for   www.a2la.org
5301 Buckeystown Pike Suite 350   Frederick MD 21704
Ph: 301-644-3248 ▪ Fx: 301-662-2974

Laboratory Accreditation, Commission on Office   www.cola.org
9881 Broken Land Pkwy Suite 200   Columbia MD 21046
Ph: 410-381-6581 ▪ Fx: 410-381-8611 ▪ TF: 800-981-9883

Laboratory Animal Care International, Association for Assessment &   www.aaalac.org
Accreditation of   11300 Rockville Pike Suite 1211   Rockville
MD 20852
Ph: 301-231-5353 ▪ Fx: 301-231-8282 ▪ TF: 800-926-0066

Laboratory Animal Medicine, American College of   www.aclam.org
Univ of Houston   Houston TX 77204
Ph: 713-743-9191 ▪ Fx: 713-743-9200

Laboratory Animal Practitioners, American Society of   www.aslap.org
11300 Rockville Pike   Rockville MD 20852
Ph: 301-231-6349 ▪ Fx: 301-231-6071

Laboratory Animal Science, American Association for   www.aalas.org
9190 Crestwyn Hills Dr   Memphis TN 38125
Ph: 901-754-8620 ▪ Fx: 901-753-0046

Laboratory Association, American Clinical
1250 H St NW Suite 880   Washington DC 20005
Ph: 202-637-9466 ▪ Fx: 202-637-2050

Laboratory Directors, American Society of Crime   www.ascld.org
PO Box 2710   Largo FL 33779
Ph: 727-549-6067 ▪ Fx: 727-549-6070

Laboratory Education, Association for Biology   www.zoo.toronto.edu/able
Univ of California Irvine Dept of Ecology & Evolutionary
Biology   Irvine CA 92697
Ph: 949-824-5573 ▪ Fx: 949-824-2181

Laboratory Management Association, Clinical   www.clma.org
989 Old Eagle School Rd Suite 815   Wayne PA 19087
Ph: 610-995-9580 ▪ Fx: 610-995-9568

Laboratory Managers Association, Analytical   www.labmanagers.org
2019 Galisteo St Bldg I   Santa Fe NM 87505
Ph: 505-989-4683 ▪ Fx: 505-989-1073

Laboratory Personnel Inc, National Credentialing Agency for   www.nca-info.org
PO Box 15945-289   Lenexa KS 66285
Ph: 913-438-5110 ▪ Fx: 913-599-5340

Laboratory Physicians & Scientists, Academy of Clinical   depts.washington.edu/lmaclps
Univ of Chicago Dept of Pathology MC 0006 5841 S Maryland
Ave   Chicago IL 60637
Ph: 773-702-1878 ▪ Fx: 773-702-9082

Laboratory Products Association   www.lpanet.org
225 Reinekers Ln Suite 625   Alexandria VA 22314
Ph: 703-836-1360 ▪ Fx: 703-836-6644

Laboratory Science, American Society for Clinical   www.ascls.org
6701 Democracy Blvd Suite 300   Bethesda MD 20817
Ph: 301-657-2768 ▪ Fx: 301-657-2909

Laborers' International Union of North America   www.liuna.org
905 16th St NW   Washington DC 20006
Ph: 202-737-8320 ▪ Fx: 202-737-2754

Labrador Foundation - Atlantic Center for the Environment, Quebec-   www.qlf.org
55 S Main St   Ipswich MA 01938
Ph: 978-356-0038 ▪ Fx: 978-356-7322

Lacrosse Players' Association, Professional   www.plpa.com
97 Rhode Island Ave   Newport RI 02840
Ph: 401-845-6263

Lacrosse Inc, US   www.lacrosse.org
113 University Pkwy   Baltimore MD 21210
Ph: 410-235-6882 ▪ Fx: 410-366-6735

Lactation Consultant Association, International   www.ilca.org
1500 Sunday Dr Suite 102   Raleigh NC 27607
Ph: 919-861-5577 ▪ Fx: 919-787-4916

Lactation, International Society for Research in Human Milk &   www.isrhml.org
Meriter Hospital Perinatal Ctr 202 S Park St   Madison WI
53715
Ph: 608-262-6561 ▪ Fx: 608-267-6377

Ladder Institute, American   www.americanladderinstitute.org
401 N Michigan Ave   Chicago IL 60611
Ph: 312-644-6610 ▪ Fx: 312-527-6705

Ladies Apparel Contractors Association
147 W 36th St 15th Fl   New York NY 10001
Ph: 212-564-6161 ▪ Fx: 212-564-6166

Ladies Auxiliary VFW   www.ladiesauxvfw.com
406 W 34th St   Kansas City MO 64111
Ph: 816-561-8655 ▪ Fx: 816-931-4753

Ladies of Charity USA   www.famvin.org/LCUSA
PO Box 31697   Saint Louis MO 63131
Ph: 314-344-1184 ▪ Fx: 314-344-2989

Ladies' Hermitage Association   www.thehermitage.com
4580 Rachel's Ln   Hermitage TN 37076
Ph: 615-889-2941 ▪ Fx: 615-889-9909

Ladies Professional Golf Association   www.lpga.com
100 International Golf Dr   Daytona Beach FL 32124
Ph: 386-274-6200 ▪ Fx: 386-274-1099

Ladyslipper Inc   www.ladyslipper.org
3205 Hillsborough Rd PO Box 3124   Durham NC 27715
Ph: 919-383-8773 ▪ Fx: 919-383-3525 ▪ TF: 800-634-6044

Lafayette, American Friends of www.friendsoflafayette.org
Lafayette College 316 Markle Hall Easton PA 18042
Ph: 610-330-5200 ▪ Fx: 610-330-5700

Lake Carriers' Association www.lcaships.com
614 W Superior Ave Suite 915 Cleveland OH 44113
Ph: 216-621-1107 ▪ Fx: 216-241-8262

Lake Management Society, North American www.nalms.org
4513 Vernon Blvd Suite 100 Madison WI 53705
Ph: 608-233-2836 ▪ Fx: 608-233-3186

Lake Tahoe, League to Save www.keeptahoeblue.org
955 Emerald Bay Rd South Lake Tahoe CA 96150
Ph: 530-541-5388 ▪ Fx: 530-541-5454

Lalmba Association webbresources.com/lalmba
7685 Quartz St Arvada CO 80007
Ph: 303-420-1810 ▪ Fx: 303-467-1232

LAM Foundation lam.uc.edu
10105 Beacon Hills Dr Cincinnati OH 45241
Ph: 513-777-6889 ▪ Fx: 513-777-4109

Lama Foundation lamafoundation.org
PO Box 240 San Cristobal NM 87564
Ph: 505-586-1269 ▪ Fx: 505-758-8648

Lamaze International www.lamaze-childbirth.com
2025 M St NW Suite 800 Washington DC 20036
Ph: 202-367-1128 ▪ Fx: 202-367-2128 ▪ TF: 800-368-4404

Lamb Council, American www.sheepusa.org
9875 Maroon Cir Suite 360 Centennial CO 80112
Ph: 303-771-3500 ▪ Fx: 303-771-8200

Lambda Alpha www.lambdaalpha.com
Ball State Univ Dept of Anthropology Muncie IN 47306
Ph: 765-285-1575

Lambda Chi Alpha International Fraternity www.lambdachi.org
8741 Founders Rd Indianapolis IN 46268
Ph: 317-872-8000 ▪ Fx: 317-875-3828 ▪ TF: 800-209-6837

Lambda Iota Tau www.bsu.edu/csh/english/undergraduate/lit
Ball State Univ Dept of English Muncie IN 47306
Ph: 765-285-8456 ▪ Fx: 765-285-3765

Lambda Kappa Sigma www.lks.org
20110 Glenoaks Dr Brookfield WI 53045
Ph: 800-557-1913 ▪ Fx: 414-784-8406

Lambda Legal Defense & Education Fund www.lambdalegal.org
120 Wall St Suite 1500 New York NY 10005
Ph: 212-809-8585 ▪ Fx: 212-809-0055

Lambda Pi Chi Sorority Inc, Latinas Promoviendo Communidad/ www.lambdapichi.org

Laminating Materials Association www.lma.org
116 Lawrence St Hillsdale NJ 07642
Ph: 201-664-2700 ▪ Fx: 201-666-5665

Laminators, Association of Industrial Metallizers Coaters & aimcal.org
2166 Gold Hill Rd Fort Mill SC 29708
Ph: 803-802-7820 ▪ Fx: 803-802-7821

Lancaster Mennonite Historical Society www.lmhs.org
2215 Millstream Rd Lancaster PA 17602
Ph: 717-393-9745 ▪ Fx: 717-393-8751

Land Assistance Fund, Federation of Southern www.federationsoutherncoop.com
Cooperatives/ 2769 Church St East Point GA 30344
Ph: 404-765-0991 ▪ Fx: 404-765-9178

Land Grant Colleges, National Association of State Universities & www.nasulgc.org
1307 New York Ave NW Suite 400 Washington DC 20005
Ph: 202-478-6040 ▪ Fx: 202-478-6046

Land Improvement Contractors of America www.licanational.com
3060 Ogden Ave Suite 304 Lisle IL 60532
Ph: 630-548-1984 ▪ Fx: 630-548-9189

Land Institute www.landinstitute.org
2440 E Water Well Rd Salina KS 67401
Ph: 785-823-5376 ▪ Fx: 785-823-8728

Land Institute, Realtors www.rliland.com
430 N Michigan Ave Chicago IL 60611
Ph: 312-329-8440 ▪ Fx: 312-329-8633 ▪ TF: 800-441-5263

Land Institute, Urban www.uli.org
1025 Thomas Jefferson St NW Suite 500W Washington DC 20007
Ph: 202-624-7000 ▪ Fx: 202-624-7140 ▪ TF: 800-321-5011

Land Mobile Communications Council www.lmcc.org
1110 N Glebe Rd Suite 500 Arlington VA 22201
Ph: 202-331-7773 ▪ Fx: 202-331-9062

Land Reclamationists, National Association of State www.crc.siu.edu/naslr.htm
Southern Illinois Univ Coal Research Ctr Carbondale IL 62901
Ph: 618-536-5521

Land Rights Association, American www.landrights.org
30218 NE 82nd Ave PO Box 400 Battle Ground WA 98604
Ph: 360-687-3087 ▪ Fx: 360-687-2973

(Land Stewardship) Tall Timbers www.talltimbers.org
13093 Henry Beadel Dr Tallahassee FL 32312
Ph: 850-893-4153 ▪ Fx: 850-893-6470

Land Title Association, American www.alta.org
1828 L St NW Suite 705 Washington DC 20036
Ph: 202-296-3671 ▪ Fx: 202-223-5843 ▪ TF: 800-787-2582

Land Trust Alliance www.lta.org
1331 H St NW Suite 400 Washington DC 20005
Ph: 202-638-4725 ▪ Fx: 202-638-4730

Land, Trust for Public www.tpl.org
116 New Montgomery St 4th Fl San Francisco CA 94105
Ph: 415-495-4014 ▪ Fx: 415-495-4103 ▪ TF: 800-729-6428

Landing Craft Infantry National Association, USS www.usslci.com

Landmark Volunteers www.volunteers.com
PO Box 455 Sheffield MA 02157
Ph: 413-229-0255 ▪ Fx: 413-229-2050

Landmen, American Association of Professional www.landman.org
4100 Fossil Creek Blvd Fort Worth TX 76137
Ph: 817-847-7700 ▪ Fx: 817-847-7704 ▪ TF: 888-566-2275

Landmine Survivors Network www.landminesurvivors.org
1420 K St NW Suite 650 Washington DC 20005
Ph: 202-464-0007 ▪ Fx: 202-464-0011

Landmines, Physicians Against www.banmines.org
351 E Huron St Suite 225 Chicago IL 60611
Ph: 312-926-0030 ▪ Fx: 312-926-7662

Landowners Association, Forest www.forestlandowners.com
PO Box 450209 Atlanta GA 31145
Ph: 404-325-2954 ▪ Fx: 404-325-2955 ▪ TF: 800-325-2954

Lands Alliance, American www.americanlands.org
726 7th St SE Washington DC 20002
Ph: 202-547-9400 ▪ Fx: 202-547-9213

Lands Council, Public hill.beef.org/plc
1301 Pennsylvania Ave NW Suite 300 Washington DC 20004
Ph: 202-347-5355 ▪ Fx: 202-638-0607

Lands Foundation, Public www.publicland.org
PO Box 7226 Arlington VA 22207
Ph: 703-790-1988 ▪ Fx: 703-821-3490

Landscape Architects, American Society of www.asla.org
636 'I' St NW Washington DC 20001
Ph: 202-898-2444 ▪ Fx: 202-898-1185 ▪ TF: 800-787-2752

Landscape Architectural Registration Boards, Council of www.clarb.org
144 Church St NW Suite 201 Vienna VA 22180
Ph: 703-319-8380 ▪ Fx: 703-319-8290

Landscape Architecture Foundation www.laprofession.org
818 18th St NW Suite 810 Washington DC 20006
Ph: 202-331-7070 ▪ Fx: 202-331-7079

Landscape Association, American Nursery & www.anla.org
1000 Vermont Ave NW Suite 300 Washington DC 20005
Ph: 202-789-2900 ▪ Fx: 202-789-1893

Landscape Contractors of America, Associated www.alca.org
150 Elden St Suite 270 Herndon VA 20170
Ph: 703-736-9666 ▪ Fx: 703-736-9668 ▪ TF: 800-395-2522

Landscape Designers, Association of Professional www.apld.org
1924 N 2nd St Harrisburg PA 17102
Ph: 717-238-9780 ▪ Fx: 717-238-9985

Landscape Nursery Council
1611 Creekview Dr Florence KY 41042
Ph: 859-525-1809 ▪ Fx: 859-525-9114

Landslide Research Group, International ilrg.gndci.pg.cnr.it

Langshan Club, American
18077 S Hwy 88 Claremore OK 74017
Ph: 918-341-2238

Language Association of America, Modern www.mla.org
26 Broadway 3rd FL New York NY 10004
Ph: 646-576-5000 ▪ Fx: 646-458-0030

Language Association, College www.clascholars.org

Language Group, Logical www.lojban.org
2904 Beau Ln Fairfax VA 22031
Ph: 703-385-0273

Language-Hearing Association, American Speech- www.asha.org
10801 Rockville Pike Rockville MD 20852
Ph: 301-897-5700 ▪ Fx: 301-571-0457 ▪ TF: 800-498-2071

Language Instruction Consortium, Computer Assisted www.calico.org
601 University Dr 214 Centennial Hall San Marcos TX 78666
Ph: 512-245-2360 ▪ Fx: 512-245-8298

Language Instruction Educational Programs, National www.ncela.gwu.edu
Clearinghouse for English Language Acquisition & George
Washington Univ 2121 K St NW Suite 260 Washington
DC 20037
Ph: 202-467-0867 ▪ Fx: 800-531-9347 ▪ TF: 800-321-6223

Language Learning Technology, International Association for www.iallt.org

Language & Literacy, National Conference on Research in www.coe.uga.edu/ncrll
Colorado State Univ English Dept 359 Eddy Bldg Fort Collins
CO 80523
Ph: 970-491-5161 ▪ Fx: 970-491-5601

Language Programs, National Association of Self-Instructional www.nasilp.org
Univ of Arizona 1717 E Speedway Blvd Suite 3312 Tucson AZ
85721
Ph: 520-626-5258 ▪ Fx: 520-626-8205

Language Schools, Canadian Association of Private www.capls.com
12880 54A Ave Surrey BC V3X3C9
Ph: 604-507-2577 ▪ Fx: 604-502-0373

Language Teachers Association, Chinese clta.deall.ohio-state.edu
Univ of Hawaii Center for Chinese Studies 416 Moore
Hall Honolulu HI 96822
Ph: 808-956-2692

Language Therapy Association, Academic www.altaread.org
13140 Coit Rd Suite 320 LB 120 Dallas TX 75240
Ph: 972-233-9107 ▪ Fx: 972-490-4219

Languages, American Association of Teachers of Slavic & www.aatseel.org
East European PO Box 7039 Berkeley CA 94707
Ph: 510-526-6614

Languages, American Association of Teachers www.princeton.edu/~ehgilson/aatt.html
of Turkic Princeton Univ Near Eastern Studies 110 Jones
Hall Princeton NJ 08544
Ph: 609-258-1435 ▪ Fx: 609-258-1242

Languages, American Council on the Teaching of Foreign www.actfl.org
6 Executive Plaza Yonkers NY 10701
Ph: 914-963-8830 ▪ Fx: 914-963-1275

Languages of the Americas, Society for the Study of Indigenous www.ssila.org
PO Box 555 Arcata CA 95518
Ph: 707-826-4324 ▪ Fx: 707-677-1676

Languages, Association of Departments of Foreign www.adfl.org
26 Broadway 3rd Fl New York NY 10004
Ph: 646-576-5140 ▪ Fx: 646-458-0030

Languages & International Studies, National Council for www.languagepolicy.org
4646 40th St NW Suite 310 Washington DC 20016
Ph: 202-966-8477 ▪ Fx: 202-966-8210

Languages, Joint National Committee for　　www.languagepolicy.org
4646 40th St NW　Washington DC 20016
Ph: 202-966-8477　■　Fx: 202-966-8310

Languages, National Council of Less Commonly Taught　　www.councilnet.org
Univ of Wisconsin　National Foreign Language Ctr 4231
　　Humanities Bldg　455 N Park St　Madison WI 53706
Ph: 608-265-7905　■　Fx: 608-265-7904

Languages, Northeast Conference on the Teaching of　　www.dickinson.edu/nectfl
Foreign　Dickinson College PO Box 1773　Carlisle PA 17013
Ph: 717-245-1977　■　Fx: 717-245-1976

Languages, Teachers of English to Speakers of Other　　www.tesol.org
700 S Washington St Suite 200　Alexandria VA 22314
Ph: 703-836-0774　■　Fx: 703-836-7864

Laparoendoscopic Surgeons, Society of　　www.sls.org
7330 SW 62nd Pl Suite 410　South Miami FL 33143
Ph: 305-665-9959　■　Fx: 305-667-4123　■　TF: 800-446-2659

Laparoscopists, American Association of Gynecological　　www.aagl.com
13021 E Florence Ave　Santa Fe Springs CA 90670
Ph: 562-946-8774　■　Fx: 562-946-0073　■　TF: 800-554-2245

Lapidary Dealers Association, Gem &　　www.glda.org
PO Box 2391　Tucson AZ 85702
Ph: 520-792-9431　■　Fx: 520-882-2836

Largesse Network for Size Esteem　　www.largesse.net
PO Box 9404　New Haven CT 06534
Ph: 203-787-1624

Laryngectomees, International Association of　　www.larynxlink.com
PO Box 691060　Stockton CA 95269
Ph: 866-425-3678　■　Fx: 209-472-0516

Laryngological Association, American　　www.alahns.org

Laryngological Rhinological & Otological Society Inc, American　　www.triological.org
555 N 30th St　Omaha NE 68131
Ph: 402-346-5500　■　Fx: 402-346-5300

Lasalle Club, Cadillac-　　www.cadillaclasalleclub.org
PO Box 360835　Columbus OH 43236
Ph: 614-478-4622　■　Fx: 614-472-3222

Lasallian Volunteers　　www.cbconf.org/cbc.nsf/pages/volunteers
4351 Garden City Dr Suite 200　Landover MD 20785
Ph: 301-459-9410　■　Fx: 301-459-8056

Laser Dentistry, Academy of　　www.laserdentistry.org
PO Box 8667　Coral Springs FL 33075
Ph: 954-346-3776　■　Fx: 954-757-2598

Laser Display Association, International　　www.laserist.org
3721 SE Henry St　Portland OR 97202
Ph: 503-407-0289

Laser & Electro-Optics Manufacturers' Association　　www.leoma.com
123 Kent Rd　Pacifica CA 94044
Ph: 650-738-1492　■　Fx: 650-738-1769

Laser Institute of America　　www.laserinstitute.org
13501 Ingenuity Dr Suite 128　Orlando FL 32826
Ph: 407-380-1553　■　Fx: 407-380-5588　■　TF: 800-345-2737

Laser Medicine & Surgery, American Society for　　www.aslms.org
2404 Stewart Ave　Wausau WI 54401
Ph: 715-845-9283　■　Fx: 715-848-2493

Laser Tag Association, International　　www.lasertag.org
5351 E Thompson Ave Suite 236　Indianapolis IN 46237
Ph: 317-375-9631　■　Fx: 317-375-9658

Lasers & Electro-Optics Society, IEEE　　www.i-LEOS.org
IEEE Operations Ctr 445 Hoes Ln　Piscataway NJ 08854
Ph: 732-981-0060　■　Fx: 732-981-1721

LASPAU: Academic & Professional Programs for the Americas　　www.laspau.harvard.edu
25 Mount Auburn St　Cambridge MA 02138
Ph: 617-495-5255　■　Fx: 617-495-8990

Last Chance for Animals　　www.lcanimal.org
8033 Sunset Blvd Suite 835　Los Angeles CA 90046
Ph: 310-271-6096　■　Fx: 310-271-1890

Last Chance Forever　　www.lastchanceforever.org
PO Box 460993　San Antonio TX 78246
Ph: 210-499-4080　■　Fx: 210-499-4305

Late Great Chevrolet Association　　www.lategreatchevy.com
2166 S Orange Blossom Trail　Apopka FL 32703
Ph: 407-886-1963　■　Fx: 407-886-7571　■　TF: 800-683-1961

Late-Onset Tay-Sachs Foundation　　www.lotsf.org
PO Box 5　Flourtown PA 19031
Ph: 800-672-2022

Latex Council, SB　　www.regnet.com/sblc
1250 Connecticut Ave NW Suite 700　Washington DC 20036
Ph: 202-419-1500　■　Fx: 202-659-8037

Lath & Plaster, International Institute for　　www.iilp.org
PO Box 1663　Lafayette CA 94549
Ph: 925-283-5160　■　Fx: 925-283-5161

Latham Foundation　　www.latham.org
1826 Clement Ave　Alameda CA 94501
Ph: 510-521-0920　■　Fx: 510-521-9861

Latin Actors, Hispanic Organization of　　www.hellohola.org
107 Suffolk St Suite 302　New York NY 10002
Ph: 212-253-1015　■　Fx: 212-253-9651

Latin America, Association of American Chambers of Commerce in　　www.aaccla.org
1615 H St NW 3rd Fl　Washington DC 20062
Ph: 202-463-5485　■　Fx: 202-463-3126

Latin America, Community Action on　　www.sit.wisc.edu/~omsuarez/cala.html
731 State St　Madison WI 53703
Ph: 608-251-3241　■　Fx: 608-251-3267

Latin America, Consortium of Physicians from　　www.cophyla.org
1850 E 17th St Suite 219　Santa Ana CA 92705
Ph: 714-836-1116　■　Fx: 714-245-1664

Latin America, Information Services on　　isla.igc.org
PO Box 6103　Albany CA 94706
Ph: 510-869-2711　■　Fx: 510-835-3017

Latin America Mission　　www.lam.org
PO Box 52-7900　Miami FL 33152
Ph: 305-884-8400　■　Fx: 305-885-8649

Latin America, North American Congress on　　www.nacla.org
475 Riverside Dr Suite 454　New York NY 10115
Ph: 212-870-3146　■　Fx: 212-870-3305

Latin America, Washington Office on　　www.wola.org
1630 Connecticut Ave NW Suite 200　Washington DC 20009
Ph: 202-797-2171　■　Fx: 202-797-2172

Latin America Working Group　　www.lawg.org
110 Maryland Ave NE PO Box 15　Washington DC 20002
Ph: 202-546-7010　■　Fx: 202-543-7647

Latin American Advancement, Labor Council for　　www.lclaa.org
888 16th St NW Suite 640　Washington DC 20006
Ph: 202-347-4223　■　Fx: 202-347-5095

Latin American Anthropology, Society for　　www.aaanet.org/slaa/Slaa1.htm
c/o American Anthropological Assn 2200 Wilson Blvd Suite
　　600　Arlington VA 22201
Ph: 703-528-1902　■　Fx: 703-528-3546

Latin American Citizens, League of United　　www.lulac.org
2000 L St NW Suite 610　Washington DC 20036
Ph: 202-833-6130

Latin American Education Foundation　　www.laef.org
924 W Colfax Ave Suite 103　Denver CO 80204
Ph: 303-446-0541　■　Fx: 303-446-0526

Latin American Management Association
419 New Jersey Ave SE　Washington DC 20003
Ph: 202-546-3803　■　Fx: 202-546-3807

Latin American Studies Association　　lasa.international.pitt.edu
Univ of Pittsburgh 946 William Pitt Union　Pittsburgh PA
　　15260
Ph: 412-648-7929　■　Fx: 412-624-7145

Latin Business Association　　www.lbausa.com
5400 E Olympic Blvd Suite 130　Los Angeles CA 90022
Ph: 323-721-4000　■　Fx: 323-722-5050　■　TF: 800-371-4522

Latin Chamber of Commerce of the US　　www.camacol.org
1417 W Flagler St　Miami FL 33135
Ph: 305-642-3870　■　Fx: 305-642-0653

Latin Liturgy Association　　www.latinliturgy.com
34 Dumont Ave　Staten Island NY 10305
Ph: 718-979-6685　■　Fx: 718-667-7128

Latin Sorority Inc, Corazones Unidos Siempre/Chi Upsilon　　www.justbecus.org
Sigma National　99 Park Ave Suite 278A　New York NY 10016
Ph: 212-969-0793　■　Fx: 212-867-7904

Latina Institute for Reproductive Health, National　　www.latinainstitute.org
162 Montague St 3rd Fl　Brooklyn NY 11201
Ph: 718-260-8811　■　Fx: 718-260-9941

Latina/o Lesbian Gay Bisexual & Transgender Organization,　　www.llego.org
LLEGO - National　1420 K St NW Suite 400　Washington DC
　　20005
Ph: 202-408-5380　■　Fx: 202-408-8478　■　TF: 888-633-8320

Latina Organization, MANA - National　　www.hermana.org
1725 K St NW Suite 501　Washington DC 20006
Ph: 202-833-0060　■　Fx: 202-496-0588

Latinas Promoviendo Communidad/Lambda Pi Chi Sorority Inc　　www.lambdapichi.org

Latino Americanos, Grupo de Artistas
21 W 112th St Unit 9J　New York NY 10026
Ph: 212-369-3401　■　Fx: 212-480-9734

Latino Anthropologists, Association of Latina &　　sbsi.csumb.edu/ALLA
c/o American Anthropological Assn 2200 Wilson Blvd Suite
　　600　Arlington VA 22201
Ph: 703-528-1902　■　Fx: 703-528-3546

Latino Elected & Appointed Officials, National Association of　　www.naleo.org
1122 W Washington Blvd 3rd Fl　Los Angeles CA 90015
Ph: 213-747-7606　■　Fx: 213-747-7664

Latino Issues Forum　　www.lif.org
785 Market St 3rd Fl　San Francisco CA 94103
Ph: 415-284-7220　■　Fx: 415-284-7222

Latino Professionals in Finance & Accounting, Association of　　www.alpfa.org
510 W 6th St Suite 400　Los Angeles CA 90014
Ph: 213-243-0004　■　Fx: 213-243-0006

Latino Studies, National Association of Hispanic &
PO Box 325　Biddeford ME 04005
Ph: 207-839-8004　■　Fx: 207-839-3776

Latinos & the Spanish-Speaking, REFORMA National Association　　www.reforma.org
to Promote Library Services to　PO Box 25963　Scottsdale AZ
　　85255
Ph: 480-471-7452　■　Fx: 480-471-7442

Latter-Day Saints, Church of Jesus Christ of　　www.lds.org
50 E North Temple St　Salt Lake City UT 84150
Ph: 801-240-1000　■　Fx: 801-240-2033　■　TF: 800-453-3860

Latvian Association in the US, American　　www.alausa.org
400 Hurley Ave　Rockville MD 20850
Ph: 301-340-1914　■　Fx: 301-340-8732

Latvian Choir Association of the US
7886 Anita Dr　Philadelphia PA 19111
Ph: 215-725-6953

Latvians, World Federation of Free　　www.pbla.lv
400 Hurley Ave　Rockville MD 20850
Ph: 301-340-7646　■　Fx: 301-762-5438

Laughter Society, International
16000 Glen Una Dr　Los Gatos CA 95030
Ph: 408-354-3456

Laundry Association, Coin　　www.coinlaundry.org
1315 Butterfield Rd Suite 212　Downers Grove IL 60515
Ph: 630-963-5547　■　Fx: 630-963-5864　■　TF: 800-570-5629

Laundry Association, Multi-Housing　　www.mhla.com
1500 Sunday Dr Suite 102　Raleigh NC 27607
Ph: 919-861-5579　■　Fx: 919-787-4916　■　TF: 800-380-3652

Laundry & Dry Cleaning International Union
307 4th Ave Suite 405   Pittsburgh PA 15222
Ph: 412-471-4829 ▪ Fx: 412-471-1840

Laura Ingalls Wilder Memorial Society Inc   www.liwms.com
PO Box 426   DeSmet SD 57231
Ph: 800-880-3383 ▪ Fx: 605-854-3064

Law, ABA Center on Children & the   www.abanet.org/child
740 15th St NW 9th Fl   Washington DC 20005
Ph: 202-662-1720 ▪ Fx: 202-662-1755

Law Administrators, National Association of State Boating   www.nasbla.org
1500 Leestown Rd Suite 330   Lexington KY 40511
Ph: 859-225-9487 ▪ Fx: 859-231-6403

Law & Aging, ABA Commission on   www.abanet.org/aging
740 15th St NW 8th Fl   Washington DC 20005
Ph: 202-662-8690 ▪ Fx: 202-662-8698

Law Alliance Worldwide, Environmental   www.elaw.org
1877 Garden Ave   Eugene OR 97403
Ph: 541-687-8454 ▪ Fx: 541-687-0535

Law, American Academy of Psychiatry & the   www.aapl.org
1 Regency Dr PO Box 30   Bloomfield CT 06002
Ph: 860-242-5450 ▪ Fx: 860-286-0787 ▪ TF: 800-331-1389

(Law) American Inns of Court   www.innsofcourt.org
1229 King St 2nd Fl   Alexandria VA 22314
Ph: 703-684-3590 ▪ Fx: 703-684-3607

Law, American Society of International   www.asil.org
2223 Massachusetts Ave NW   Washington DC 20008
Ph: 202-939-6000 ▪ Fx: 202-797-7133

Law Association, American Agricultural   www.aglaw-assn.org
415 S Duff Ave Suite C   Ames IA 50010
Ph: 515-956-4255 ▪ Fx: 515-233-3101

Law Association, American Intellectual Property   www.aipla.org
2001 Jefferson Davis Hwy Suite 203   Arlington VA 22202
Ph: 703-415-0780 ▪ Fx: 703-415-0786

Law Association, Christian   www.christianlaw.org
PO Box 4010   Seminole FL 33775
Ph: 727-399-8300 ▪ Fx: 727-398-3907

Law Association, Computer   www.cla.org
3028 Javier Rd Suite 402   Fairfax VA 22031
Ph: 703-560-7747 ▪ Fx: 703-207-7028

Law Association, Education   www.educationlaw.org
300 College Pk MD 0528   Dayton OH 45469
Ph: 937-229-3589 ▪ Fx: 937-229-3845

Law Association, National Lesbian & Gay   www.nlgla.org
200 E Lexington St Suite 1511   Baltimore MD 21202
Ph: 508-892-8290 ▪ Fx: 410-244-0775

Law Association of the US, Maritime   www.mlaus.org
c/o Hill Rivkins & Hayden LLP 45 Broadway Suite 1500   New
   York NY 10006
Ph: 212-669-0600 ▪ Fx: 212-669-0699

Law Associations, National Council of Intellectual Property   www.ipo.org
1255 23rd St NW Suite 200   Washington DC 20037
Ph: 202-466-2396 ▪ Fx: 202-466-2893

Law Attorneys, National Academy of Elder   www.naela.com
1604 N Country Club Rd   Tucson AZ 85716
Ph: 520-881-4005 ▪ Fx: 520-325-7925

Law Center for Children & Families, National   www.nationallawcenter.org
3819 Plaza Dr   Fairfax VA 22030
Ph: 703-691-4626

Law Center on Homelessness & Poverty, National   www.nlchp.org
1411 K St NW Suite 1400   Washington DC 20005
Ph: 202-628-2535 ▪ Fx: 202-628-2737

Law, Center for International Environmental   www.ciel.org
1367 Connecticut Ave NW Suite 300   Washington DC 20036
Ph: 202-785-8700 ▪ Fx: 202-785-8701

Law Center, National Consumer   www.consumerlaw.org
77 Summer St 10th Fl   Boston MA 02110
Ph: 617-542-8010 ▪ Fx: 617-542-8028

Law Center, National Economic Development &   www.nedlc.org
2201 Broadway Suite 815   Oakland CA 94612
Ph: 510-251-2600 ▪ Fx: 510-251-0600

Law Center, National Immigration   www.nilc.org
3435 Wilshire Blvd Suite 2850   Los Angeles CA 90010
Ph: 213-639-3900 ▪ Fx: 213-639-3911

Law Center, National Senior Citizens   www.nsclc.org
1101 14th St NW Suite 400   Washington DC 20005
Ph: 202-289-6976 ▪ Fx: 202-289-7224

Law Center, National Women's   www.nwlc.org
11 Dupont Cir NW Suite 800   Washington DC 20036
Ph: 202-588-5180 ▪ Fx: 202-588-5185

Law Center, Southern Poverty   www.splcenter.org
400 Washington Ave   Montgomery AL 36104
Ph: 334-956-8200 ▪ Fx: 334-956-8483

Law, Center for Study of Responsive   www.csrl.org
PO Box 19367   Washington DC 20036
Ph: 202-387-8030 ▪ Fx: 202-234-5176

Law Center, Welfare   www.welfarelaw.org
275 7th Ave Suite 1205   New York NY 10001
Ph: 212-633-6967 ▪ Fx: 212-633-6371

Law, Conference on Consumer Finance   www.theccfl.com
Oklahoma City Univ School of Law 2501 N Blackwelder
   Ave   Oklahoma City OK 73106
Ph: 405-521-5363 ▪ Fx: 405-521-5089

Law, Council on Ocean
1600 H St NW 2nd Fl   Washington DC 20006
Ph: 202-347-3766

(Law) Delta Theta Phi   www.deltathetaphi.org
38640 Butternut Ridge Rd   Elyria OH 44035
Ph: 440-458-4381 ▪ Fx: 440-458-4380 ▪ TF: 800-783-2600

Law in Development, International Center for
777 United Nations Plaza Suite 7E   New York NY 10017
Ph: 212-687-0036 ▪ Fx: 212-370-9844

Law & Education, Center for   www.cleweb.org
1875 Connecticut Ave NW Suite 510   Washington DC 20009
Ph: 202-986-3000 ▪ Fx: 202-986-6648

Law Education Fund, Peace Through   www.ptlef.org
PO Box 44354   Washington DC 20026
Ph: 202-686-4600

Law Enforcement Administrators, International Association of Campus   www.iaclea.org
342 W Main St   West Hartford CT 06117
Ph: 860-586-7517 ▪ Fx: 860-586-7550

Law Enforcement Agencies, Commission on Accreditation for   www.calea.org
10306 Eaton Pl Suite 320   Fairfax VA 22030
Ph: 703-352-4225 ▪ Fx: 703-591-2206 ▪ TF: 800-368-3757

Law Enforcement Alliance of America   www.leaa.org
7700 Leesburg Pike Suite 421   Falls Church VA 22043
Ph: 703-847-2677 ▪ Fx: 703-556-6485 ▪ TF: 800-766-8578

Law Enforcement, Americans for Effective   www.aele.org
841 W Touhy Ave   Park Ridge IL 60068
Ph: 847-685-0700 ▪ Fx: 847-685-9700

Law Enforcement Association, Airborne   www.alea.org
PO Box 3683   Tulsa OK 74101
Ph: 918-599-0705 ▪ Fx: 918-583-2353

Law Enforcement Executives, National Association of Women   www.nawlee.com

Law Enforcement Executives, National Organization of Black   www.noblenatl.org
4609 Pinecrest Office Park Dr Suite F   Alexandria VA 22312
Ph: 703-658-1529 ▪ Fx: 703-658-9479

Law Enforcement Firearms Instructors, International Association of   www.ialefi.com
25 Country Club Rd Suite 707   Gilford NH 03249
Ph: 603-524-8787 ▪ Fx: 603-524-8856

(Law Enforcement) International Footprint Association   www.footprinter.org
PO Box 2487   Walnut Creek CA 94595
Ph: 925-944-1763 ▪ Fx: 925-944-1771 ▪ TF: 888-944-1763

Law Enforcement Memorial Association   www.forgottenheroes-lema.org
PO Box 72835   Roselle IL 60172
Ph: 312-623-1391

Law Enforcement Motorcycle Club Inc, Blue Knights   www.blueknights.org
International   38 Alden St   Bangor ME 04401
Ph: 207-947-4600 ▪ Fx: 207-947-5814

Law Enforcement Officers Association, Federal   www.fleoa.org
PO Box 326   Lewisberry PA 17339
Ph: 717-938-2300 ▪ Fx: 717-932-2262

Law Enforcement Officers Memorial Fund, National   www.nleomf.org
605 'E' St NW   Washington DC 20004
Ph: 202-737-3400 ▪ Fx: 202-737-3405

Law Enforcement Officers, National Association of School Safety &   www.nassleo.org
PO Box 3147   Oswego NY 13126
Ph: 315-529-4858 ▪ Fx: 315-343-2935

Law Enforcement Planners, International Association of   www.ialep.org
PO Box 11437   Torrance CA 90510
Ph: 310-225-5148

Law Enforcement Training, American Society for   www.aslet.org
121 N Court St   Frederick MD 21701
Ph: 301-668-9466 ▪ Fx: 301-668-9482

Law Firm Group, State Capital Global   www.statecapitallaw.com
1250 24th St NW Suite 700   Washington DC 20037
Ph: 202-659-6601 ▪ Fx: 202-659-6641

Law Firm Services Association   www.lawfirmcpas.com
1 Valmont Plaza 4th Fl   Omaha NE 68154
Ph: 402-964-3865 ▪ Fx: 402-964-3811 ▪ TF: 800-475-4476

Law Foundation, American Immigration   www.ailf.org
918 F St NW 6th Fl   Washington DC 20004
Ph: 202-742-5600 ▪ Fx: 202-742-5619

Law Foundation, Energy & Mineral   www.emlf.org
Univ of Kentucky Mineral Law Ctr Rm 21 Law Bldg   Lexington
   KY 40507
Ph: 859-257-7140 ▪ Fx: 859-257-2884

Law Fraternity International, Phi Alpha Delta   www.pad.org
345 N Charles St   Baltimore MD 21201
Ph: 410-347-3118 ▪ Fx: 410-347-3119

Law in Higher Education, Council on   www.clhe.org
111 Coconut Key Ct   Palm Beach Gardens FL 33418
Ph: 561-622-5765 ▪ Fx: 561-624-9198

Law Institute, American   www.ali.org
4025 Chestnut St   Philadelphia PA 19104
Ph: 215-243-1600 ▪ Fx: 215-243-1664 ▪ TF: 800-253-6397

Law Institute - American Bar Association, American   www.ali-aba.org
4025 Chestnut St   Philadelphia PA 19104
Ph: 215-243-1600 ▪ Fx: 215-243-1664 ▪ TF: 800-253-6397

Law Institute, Environmental   www.eli.org
1616 P St NW Suite 200   Washington DC 20036
Ph: 202-939-3800 ▪ Fx: 202-939-3868 ▪ TF: 800-433-5120

Law Institute, Food & Drug   www.fdli.org
1000 Vermont Ave NW Suite 200   Washington DC 20005
Ph: 202-371-1420 ▪ Fx: 202-371-0649 ▪ TF: 800-956-6293

Law Institute, International   www.ili.org
1055 Thomas Jefferson St NW   Washington DC 20007
Ph: 202-247-6006 ▪ Fx: 202-247-6010

Law Institute, Practising   www.pli.edu
810 7th Ave 26th Fl   New York NY 10019
Ph: 212-824-5700 ▪ Fx: 800-321-0093 ▪ TF: 800-260-4754

Law, International Center for Not-for-Profit   www.icnl.org
733 15th St NW Suite 420   Washington DC 20005
Ph: 202-624-0766 ▪ Fx: 202-624-0767

Law, International Institute of Space   www.iafastro-iisl.com

Law Judges Conference, Federal Administrative   www.faljc.org
2000 Pennsylvania Ave NW Suite 260   Washington DC 20006
Ph: 202-675-3065 ▪ Fx: 202-219-3289

Law & Justice, American Center for   www.aclj.org
PO Box 64429   Virginia Beach VA 23467
Ph: 757-226-2489 ▪ Fx: 757-226-2836 ▪ TF: 800-296-4529

Law League of America, Commercial
150 N Michigan Ave Suite 600   Chicago IL 60601
Ph: 312-781-2000 ▪ Fx: 312-781-2010 ▪ TF: 800-978-2552
www.clla.org

Law Libraries, American Association of
53 W Jackson Blvd Suite 940   Chicago IL 60604
Ph: 312-939-4764 ▪ Fx: 312-431-1097
www.aallnet.org

Law Libraries, Canadian Association of
PO Box 1570   Kingston ON K7L5C8
Ph: 613-531-9338 ▪ Fx: 613-531-0626
www.callacbd.ca

Law Logistics & Policy, Association for Transportation
3 Church Cir PMB 250   Annapolis MD 21401
Ph: 410-267-0023 ▪ Fx: 410-267-7546
www.atllp.com

Law Medicine & Ethics, American Society of
765 Commonwealth Ave 16th Fl   Boston MA 02215
Ph: 617-262-4990 ▪ Fx: 617-437-7596
www.aslme.org

Law, National Center for Preservation
1333 Connecticut Ave NW Suite 300   Washington DC 20036
Ph: 202-338-0392 ▪ Fx: 202-775-9038

Law, National Center for Youth
405 14th St Suite 1500   Oakland CA 94612
Ph: 510-835-8098 ▪ Fx: 510-835-8099
www.youthlaw.org

Law & Order Inc, Citizens for
PO Box 412   Carlsbad CA 92018
Ph: 760-631-2028
www.cloinc.org

Law Placement, National Association for
1025 Connecticut Ave NW Suite 1110   Washington DC 20036
Ph: 202-835-1001 ▪ Fx: 202-835-1112
www.nalp.org

Law & Policy, Center for Oceans
Univ of Virginia School of Law 580 Massie Rd   Charlottesville VA 22903
Ph: 804-924-7441 ▪ Fx: 804-924-7362
www.virginia.edu/colp

Law & Policy Inc, Center for Reproductive
120 Wall St 14th Fl   New York NY 10005
Ph: 917-637-3600 ▪ Fx: 917-637-3666
www.crlp.org

Law & Poverty, Western Center on
3701 Wilshire Blvd Suite 208   Los Angeles CA 90010
Ph: 213-487-7211 ▪ Fx: 213-487-0242
www.wclp.org

Law & Practice, ABA Section of International
740 15th St NW   Washington DC 20005
Ph: 202-662-1660 ▪ Fx: 202-662-1669
www.abanet.org/intlaw

Law Professors, World Association of
1000 Connecticut Ave NW Suite 202   Washington DC 20036
Ph: 202-466-5428 ▪ Fx: 202-452-8540

Law Program, National Health
2639 S La Cienega Blvd   Los Angeles CA 90034
Ph: 310-204-6010 ▪ Fx: 310-204-0891
www.healthlaw.org

Law Project, National Employment
55 John St 7th Fl   New York NY 10038
Ph: 212-285-3025 ▪ Fx: 212-285-3044
www.nelp.org

Law Project, National Housing
614 Grand Ave Suite 320   Oakland CA 94610
Ph: 510-251-9400 ▪ Fx: 510-451-2300
www.nhlp.org

Law in the Public Interest, Center for
10951 W Pico Blvd 3rd Fl   Los Angeles CA 90064
Ph: 310-470-3000 ▪ Fx: 310-474-7083
www.clipi.org

Law & Public Policy, National Institute for
Science 1400 16th St NW Suite 330   Washington DC 20036
Ph: 202-462-8800 ▪ Fx: 202-265-6564
www.swankin-turner.com/nislapp.html

Law & Public Policy Studies, Federalist Society for
1015 18th St NW Suite 425   Washington DC 20036
Ph: 202-822-8138 ▪ Fx: 202-296-8061
www.fed-soc.org

Law & Religious Freedom, Center for
4208 Evergreen Ln Suite 222   Annandale VA 22003
Ph: 703-642-1070 ▪ Fx: 703-642-1075
www.clsnet.org

Law Resource Center, Indian
602 N Ewing St   Helena MT 59601
Ph: 406-449-2006 ▪ Fx: 406-449-2031
www.indianlaw.org

Law, Sargent Shriver National Center on Poverty
111 N Wabash Ave Suite 500   Chicago IL 60602
Ph: 312-263-3830 ▪ Fx: 312-263-3846 ▪ TF: 800-621-3256
www.povertylaw.org

Law School Admission Council Inc
PO Box 40   Newtown PA 18940
Ph: 215-968-1101 ▪ Fx: 215-968-1169
www.lsac.org

Law Schools, Association of American
1201 Connecticut Ave NW Suite 800   Washington DC 20036
Ph: 202-296-8851 ▪ Fx: 202-296-8869
www.aals.org

Law & Social Philosophy, International Association
for Philosophy of Univ of Hawaii at Manoa Dept of Philosophy
2530 Dole St   Honolulu HI 96822
Ph: 808-956-8954 ▪ Fx: 808-956-9228
www.cirfid.unibo.it/ivr

Law & Social Policy, Center for
1015 15th St NW Suite 400   Washington DC 20005
Ph: 202-906-8000 ▪ Fx: 202-842-2885
www.clasp.org

Law Societies, National Association of Environmental
www.naels.org

Law & Society Association
Univ of Massachusetts 131 County Cir 205 Hampshire House   Amherst MA 01003
Ph: 413-545-4617 ▪ Fx: 413-545-1640
www.lawandsociety.org

Law Society, Tau Epsilon Rho
1951 Old Cuthbert Rd Suite 413   Cherry Hill NJ 08034
Ph: 856-429-3901
www.ter-law.org

Law Student Association, National Asian Pacific American
www.napalsa.org

Law Students Association, International
25 E Jackson Blvd Suite 518   Chicago IL 60604
Ph: 312-362-5025 ▪ Fx: 312-362-5073
www.ilsa.org

Law Students Association, National Black
www.nblsa.org

Law Students Association, National Jewish
154 Stuart St   Boston MA 02216
Ph: 617-451-0010 ▪ Fx: 617-353-7214

Law Students Association, National Women
www.nwlsa.com

Law Task Force, Military
1168 Union St Suite 302   San Diego CA 92101
Ph: 619-233-1701 ▪ Fx: 619-233-6314
www.nlg.org/mltf

Law Teachers, Society of American
www.saltlaw.org

Lawman History Inc, National Association for Outlaw &
1917 Sutton Pl Trail   Harker Heights TX 76548
Ph: 254-698-6518
www.outlawlawman.com

Lawn Care Association of America, Professional
1000 Johnson Ferry Rd NE Suite C-135   Marietta GA 30068
Ph: 770-977-5222 ▪ Fx: 770-578-6071 ▪ TF: 800-458-3466
www.plcaa.org

Lawn & Garden Dealers Association
2411 E Skelly Dr Suite 105   Tulsa OK 74105
Ph: 800-752-5296 ▪ Fx: 918-749-1718
www.lgda.org

Lawn & Garden Marketing & Distribution Association
1900 Arch St   Philadelphia PA 19103
Ph: 215-564-3484 ▪ Fx: 215-564-2175
www.lgmda.org

Lawrence Delos Miles Value Foundation
5505 Connecticut Ave NW Suite 149   Washington DC 20015
Ph: 703-237-2050 ▪ Fx: 703-237-2113
www.valuefoundation.org

Lawrence DH Society of North America
www.wsu.edu/~hydev/dhlsna.htm

Lawrence Durrell Society, International
www.lawrencedurrell.org

Laws, Council on Governmental Ethics
PO Box 417   Locust Grove VA 22508
Ph: 540-972-3662 ▪ Fx: 540-972-3693
www.cogel.org

Laws, National Conference of Commissioners on Uniform State
211 E Ontario St Suite 1300   Chicago IL 60611
Ph: 312-915-0195 ▪ Fx: 312-915-0187
www.nccusl.org

Laws & Ordinances, National Committee on Uniform Traffic
107 S West St Suite 110   Alexandria VA 22314
Ph: 540-465-4701 ▪ Fx: 540-465-5383 ▪ TF: 800-807-5290
www.ncutlo.org

Lawyer-Pilots Bar Association
PO Box 685   Poolesville MD 20837
Ph: 301-972-7700 ▪ Fx: 301-972-7727
www.lpba.org/

Lawyers of America, Association of Trial
1050 31st St NW   Washington DC 20007
Ph: 202-965-3500 ▪ Fx: 202-625-7313 ▪ TF: 800-424-2725
www.atlanet.org

Lawyers, American Academy of Appellate
15245 Shady Grove Rd Suite 130   Rockville MD 20850
Ph: 301-258-9210 ▪ Fx: 301-990-9771
www.appellateacademy.org

Lawyers, American Academy of Matrimonial
150 N Michigan Ave Suite 2040   Chicago IL 60601
Ph: 312-263-6477 ▪ Fx: 312-263-7682
www.aaml.org

Lawyers, American College of Real Estate
11300 Rockville Pike Suite 903   Rockville MD 20852
Ph: 301-816-9811 ▪ Fx: 301-816-9786
www.acrel.org

Lawyers, American College of Trial
19900 MacArthur Blvd Suite 610   Irvine CA 92612
Ph: 949-752-1801 ▪ Fx: 949-752-1674
www.actl.com

Lawyers Association, American Blind
c/o American Council of the Blind 1155 15th St NW Suite 1004   Washington DC 20005
Ph: 202-467-5081 ▪ Fx: 202-467-5085 ▪ TF: 800-424-8666

Lawyers Association, American Health
1025 Connecticut Ave NW Suite 600   Washington DC 20036
Ph: 202-833-1100 ▪ Fx: 202-833-1105
www.healthlawyers.org

Lawyers Association, American Immigration
918 F St NW   Washington DC 20004
Ph: 202-216-2400 ▪ Fx: 202-783-7853
www.aila.org

Lawyers Association, Black Entertainment & Sports
PO Box 441485   Fort Washington MD 20749
Ph: 301-248-1818 ▪ Fx: 301-248-0700
www.besla.org

Lawyers Association, First Amendment
200 S Wacker Dr Suite 3100   Chicago IL 60606
Ph: 312-236-0606 ▪ Fx: 312-332-6008
www.fala.org

Lawyers Association, International Municipal
1110 Vermont Ave NW Suite 200   Washington DC 20005
Ph: 202-466-5424 ▪ Fx: 202-785-0152
www.imla.org

Lawyers Association, International Trade Commission Trial
PO Box 6186 Benjamin Franklin Stn   Washington DC 20004
Ph: 202-942-6423
www.itctla.org

Lawyers Association, National Employment
44 Montgomery St Suite 2080   San Francisco CA 94104
Ph: 415-296-7629 ▪ Fx: 415-677-9445
www.nela.org

Lawyers Association, Transportation
PO Box 15122   Lenexa KS 66285
Ph: 913-541-9077 ▪ Fx: 913-599-5340
www.translaw.org

Lawyers Auxiliary, American
541 N Fairbanks 15th Fl   Chicago IL 60611
Ph: 312-988-5522 ▪ TF: 800-285-2221
www.abanet.org/publiced/ala/

Lawyers for Civil Justice
1140 Connecticut Ave NW Suite 503   Washington DC 20036
Ph: 202-429-0045 ▪ Fx: 202-429-6892
www.lfcj.com

Lawyers' Committee for Civil Rights Under Law
1401 New York Ave NW Suite 400   Washington DC 20005
Ph: 202-662-8600 ▪ Fx: 202-783-0857
www.lawyerscommittee.org

Lawyers' Committee on Nuclear Policy Inc
211 E 43rd St   New York NY 10017
Ph: 212-818-1861 ▪ Fx: 212-818-1857
www.lcnp.org

Lawyers, Decalogue Society of
39 S LaSalle St Suite 410   Chicago IL 60603
Ph: 312-263-6493 ▪ Fx: 312-263-6512

Lawyers Div, ABA Young
750 N Lake Shore Dr   Chicago IL 60611
Ph: 312-988-5000 ▪ Fx: 312-988-6231
www.abanet.org/yld

Lawyers Guild, National
143 Madison Ave 4th Fl   New York NY 10016
Ph: 212-679-5100 ▪ Fx: 212-679-2811
www.nlg.org

Lawyers, International Academy of Trial   www.iatl.net
5041 Cedar Lake Rd Suite 204   Minneapolis MN 55416
Ph: 952-546-2364 ▪ Fx: 952-545-6073 ▪ TF: 866-823-2443

Lawyers, National Association of Bond   www.nabl.org
250 S Wacker Dr Suite 1550   Chicago IL 60606
Ph: 312-648-9590 ▪ Fx: 312-648-9588

Lawyers, National Association of Women   www.abanet.org/nawl
750 N Lake Shore Dr   Chicago IL 60611
Ph: 312-988-6186 ▪ Fx: 312-988-6281

Lawyers, National Conference of Black   www.ncbl.org
PO Box 80043   Lansing MI 48908
Ph: 866-266-5091

Lawyers PAC, Association of Trial
1050 31st St NW   Washington DC 20007
Ph: 202-965-3500 ▪ Fx: 202-333-2861

Lawyers for Public Justice, Trial   www.tlpj.org
1717 Massachusetts Ave NW Suite 800   Washington DC 20036
Ph: 202-797-8600 ▪ Fx: 202-232-7203

Lay Carmelite Order of the Blessed Virgin Mary of   carmelnet.org/toc/toc.htm
Mount Carmel   8501 Bailey Rd   Darien IL 60561
Ph: 630-969-5050 ▪ Fx: 630-969-7519

Lay Mission-Helpers Association   www.laymissionhelpers.org
3424 Wilshire Blvd   Los Angeles CA 90010
Ph: 213-637-7222 ▪ Fx: 213-637-6223

Lay Missionaries, SMA   www.smafathers.org
256 N Manor Cir   Takoma Park MD 20912
Ph: 301-891-2037 ▪ Fx: 301-270-6370

Laymen, National Committee of Catholic
215 Lexington Ave 4th Fl   New York NY 10016
Ph: 212-685-6666 ▪ Fx: 212-725-9793

Lead Burning Association, National
c/o NELCO Inc 98 Baldwin Ave   Woburn MA 01801
Ph: 781-933-1940 ▪ Fx: 781-933-4763

Lead Poisoning, Coalition to End Childhood   www.leadsafe.org
2714 Hudson St   Baltimore MD 21224
Ph: 410-534-6447 ▪ Fx: 410-534-6475 ▪ TF: 800-370-5323

Lead Zinc Research Organization, International   www.ilzro.org
PO Box 12036   Research Triangle Park NC 27709
Ph: 919-361-4647 ▪ Fx: 919-361-1957

Leader Dogs for the Blind   www.leaderdog.org
PO Box 5000   Rochester MI 48308
Ph: 248-651-9011 ▪ Fx: 248-651-5812 ▪ TF: 888-777-5332

Leadership Abroad, Coalition for American   www.colead.org
2101 'E' St NW   Washington DC 20037
Ph: 202-944-5519 ▪ Fx: 202-338-6820

Leadership America   www.leadershipamerica.com
3001 Maple Ave Suite 100   Dallas TX 75201
Ph: 214-397-0900 ▪ Fx: 214-954-0712

Leadership Association, Community   www.communityleadership.org
200 S Meridian St Suite 250   Indianapolis IN 46225
Ph: 317-637-7408 ▪ Fx: 317-637-7413

Leadership, Association for Consortium   www.acl.odu.edu
1417 43rd St   Norfolk VA 23529
Ph: 757-683-3183 ▪ Fx: 757-683-4515

Leadership, Center for Public   www.ksg.harvard.edu/leadership
Harvard Univ John F Kennedy School of Government 79 JFK
St   Cambridge MA 02138
Ph: 617-496-8866 ▪ Fx: 617-496-3337

Leadership, CLAL - National Jewish Center for Learning &   www.clal.org
440 Park Ave S 4th Fl   New York NY 10016
Ph: 212-779-3300 ▪ Fx: 212-779-1009

Leadership Conference on Civil Rights   www.civilrights.org/lccr/index.html
1629 K St NW Suite 1000   Washington DC 20006
Ph: 202-466-3311 ▪ Fx: 202-466-3435

Leadership Conference of Women Religious   www.lcwr.org
8808 Cameron St   Silver Spring MD 20910
Ph: 301-588-4955 ▪ Fx: 301-587-4575

(Leadership) Coro Foundation   www.coro.org
1010 W 39th St   Kansas City MO 64111
Ph: 816-931-0751 ▪ Fx: 816-756-0924

Leadership Council for Mental Health Justice & the Media   www.leadershipcouncil.org
191 Presidential Blvd Suite C132   Bala Cynwyd PA 19004
Ph: 610-664-5007 ▪ Fx: 610-664-5279

Leadership Council, National Youth   www.nylc.org
1667 Snelling Ave N   Saint Paul MN 55108
Ph: 651-631-3672 ▪ Fx: 651-631-2955

Leadership Education for Asian Pacifics   www.leap.org
327 E 2nd St Suite 226   Los Angeles CA 90012
Ph: 213-485-1422 ▪ Fx: 213-485-0050

Leadership in Education, Association for Gender Equity   www.agele.org
317 S Division St PMB 54   Ann Arbor MI 48104
Ph: 734-449-5066

Leadership Education Network, Public   www.plen.org
1001 Connecticut Ave NW Suite 900   Washington DC 20036
Ph: 202-872-1585 ▪ Fx: 202-872-0141

Leadership Forum, American   www.alfnational.org
PO Box 20089   Stanford CA 94309
Ph: 650-723-6127 ▪ Fx: 650-723-6131

Leadership Institute   www.lead-inst.org
1101 N Highland St   Arlington VA 22201
Ph: 703-247-2000 ▪ Fx: 703-247-2001 ▪ TF: 800-827-5323

(Leadership) Omicron Delta Kappa Society   www.odk.org
Univ of Kentucky 118 Bradley Hall   Lexington KY 40506
Ph: 859-257-2110 ▪ Fx: 859-323-1014

Leading Jewelers Guild   www.love-story.com/ljgstory.htm
PO Box 69604   Los Angeles CA 90069
Ph: 310-820-3386 ▪ Fx: 310-820-3530

Leaf Tobacco Exporters Association
3716 National Dr Suite 114   Raleigh NC 27612
Ph: 919-782-5151 ▪ Fx: 919-781-0915

Leafy Greens Council   www.leafy-greens.org
33 Pheasant Ln   Saint Paul MN 55127
Ph: 651-484-3321 ▪ Fx: 651-484-1098

League of American Bicyclists   www.bikeleague.org
1612 K St NW Suite 800   Washington DC 20006
Ph: 202-822-1333 ▪ Fx: 202-822-1334

League of American Theatres & Producers   www.broadway.com
226 W 47th St   New York NY 10036
Ph: 212-764-1122 ▪ Fx: 212-719-4389

League of Conservation Voters   www.lcv.org
1920 L St NW Suite 800   Washington DC 20036
Ph: 202-785-8683 ▪ Fx: 202-835-0491

League for the Hard of Hearing   www.lhh.org
50 Broadway   New York NY 10004
Ph: 917-305-7700 ▪ Fx: 917-305-7888

League of Historic American Theatres   www.lhat.org
616 Water St Suite 320   Baltimore MD 21202
Ph: 410-659-9533 ▪ Fx: 410-837-9664 ▪ TF: 877-627-0833

League for Innovation in the Community College   www.league.org
4505 E Chandler Blvd Suite 250   Phoenix AZ 85048
Ph: 480-705-8200 ▪ Fx: 480-705-8201

League of Private Property Voters   www.landrights.org/_private/lppvhome.htm
PO Box 423   Battle Ground WA 98604
Ph: 360-687-2471 ▪ Fx: 360-687-2973

League of Resident Theatres   www.lort.org
c/o Glick & Weintraub PC 1501 Broadway Suite 2401   New
York NY 10036
Ph: 212-944-1501 ▪ Fx: 212-768-0785

League to Save Lake Tahoe   www.keeptahoeblue.org
955 Emerald Bay Rd   South Lake Tahoe CA 96150
Ph: 530-541-5388 ▪ Fx: 530-541-5454

League of United Latin American Citizens   www.lulac.org
2000 L St NW Suite 610   Washington DC 20036
Ph: 202-833-6130

League of Women Voters   www.lwv.org
1730 M St NW Suite 1000   Washington DC 20036
Ph: 202-429-1965 ▪ Fx: 202-429-0854 ▪ TF: 800-249-8683

League for Yiddish Inc   www.ibiblio.org/yiddish/YidLeague
200 W 72nd St Suite 40   New York NY 10023
Ph: 212-787-6675

Learned Societies, American Council of   www.acls.org
633 3rd Ave   New York NY 10017
Ph: 212-697-1505 ▪ Fx: 212-949-8058

Learning, Center for Lifelong   www.acenet.edu/clll
1 Dupont Cir NW Suite 250   Washington DC 20036
Ph: 202-939-9475 ▪ Fx: 202-833-4760

Learning Center Inc, Trichotillomania   www.trich.org
303 Potrero St Suite 51   Santa Cruz CA 95060
Ph: 831-457-1004 ▪ Fx: 831-426-4383

Learning Disabilities Association of America   www.ldanatl.org
4156 Library Rd   Pittsburgh PA 15234
Ph: 412-341-1515 ▪ Fx: 412-344-0224 ▪ TF: 888-300-6710

Learning Disabilities, Council for   www.cldinternational.org
PO Box 4014   Leesburg VA 20177
Ph: 571-258-1010 ▪ Fx: 571-258-1011

Learning Disabilities, National Center for   www.ncld.org
381 Park Ave S Suite 1401   New York NY 10016
Ph: 212-545-7510 ▪ Fx: 212-545-9665 ▪ TF: 888-575-7373

Learning & Information Network, Community   www.clin.org
1750 K St NW Suite 1200   Washington DC 20006
Ph: 202-857-2330 ▪ Fx: 202-857-0643

Learning for International Development, World   www.worldlearning.org
1015 15th St NW Suite 750   Washington DC 20005
Ph: 202-408-5420 ▪ Fx: 202-408-5397

Learning Light Foundation   www.learninglight.org
1212 E Lincoln Ave   Anaheim CA 92805
Ph: 714-533-2311 ▪ Fx: 714-533-1458

Learning, National Institute for Work &   www.niwl.org
1825 Connecticut Ave NW 7th Fl   Washington DC 20009
Ph: 202-884-8186 ▪ Fx: 202-884-8422

Learning Needs, National Association for Adults With Special   www.naasln.org
c/o Correctional Education Assn 4380 Forbes Blvd   Lanham MD
20706
Ph: 800-496-9222

Learning Resources Network   www.lern.org
208 S Main St Suite 2 PO Box 9   River Falls WI 54022
Ph: 715-426-9777 ▪ Fx: 715-426-9558 ▪ TF: 800-678-5376

Learning, Schwab   www.schwablearning.org
1650 S Amphlett Blvd Suite 300   San Mateo CA 94402
Ph: 650-655-2410 ▪ Fx: 650-655-2411 ▪ TF: 800-230-0988

Learning Technology, Society for Applied   www.salt.org
50 Culpepper St   Warrenton VA 20186
Ph: 540-347-0055 ▪ Fx: 540-349-3169

LearnWell Resources Inc   www.learnwell.org
3967 Valley Vista Dr PO Box 944   Camino CA 95709
Ph: 530-644-2123 ▪ Fx: 530-604-2810

Leased Housing Association, National   www.hudnlha.com
1818 'N' St NW Suite 405   Washington DC 20036
Ph: 202-785-8888 ▪ Fx: 202-785-2008

Leasing Association of America, Equipment   www.elaonline.com
4301 N Fairfax Dr Suite 550   Arlington VA 22203
Ph: 703-527-8655 ▪ Fx: 703-527-2649

Leasing Association, American Automotive   www.aalafleet.com
675 N Washington Ave Suite 410   Alexandria VA 22314
Ph: 703-548-0777 ▪ Fx: 703-236-1949

Leasing Association, Automotive Fleet &   www.aflaonline.org
21061 S Western Ave   Torrance CA 90501
Ph: 310-533-2520 ▪ Fx: 310-533-2506

Leasing Brokers, National Association of Equipment   www.naelb.org
5024-R Campbell Blvd   Baltimore MD 21236
Ph: 410-931-8100 ▪ Fx: 410-931-8111 ▪ TF: 800-996-2352

Leasing & Finance, Association for Governmental   www.aglf.org
  1255 23rd St NW Suite 200   Washington DC 20037
  Ph: 202-742-2453   ▪ Fx: 202-833-3636
Leasing, United Association of Equipment   www.uael.org
  78120 Calle Estado Suite 201   La Quinta CA 92253
  Ph: 760-564-2227   ▪ Fx: 760-564-2206
Leather Apparel Association   www.leatherassociation.com
  19 W 21st St Suite 403   New York NY 10010
  Ph: 212-924-8895   ▪ Fx: 212-727-1218
Leather Chemists Association, American   www.leatherchemists.org
  1314 50th St Suite 103   Lubbock TX 79412
  Ph: 806-744-1798   ▪ Fx: 806-744-1785
Leather Industries of America   www.leatherusa.com
  1900 L St NW Suite 710   Washington DC 20036
  Ph: 202-296-4806   ▪ Fx: 202-296-7892
Leave No Trace Center for Outdoor Ethics Inc   www.lnt.org
  PO Box 997   Boulder CO 80306
  Ph: 303-442-8222   ▪ Fx: 303-442-8217   ▪ TF: 800-332-4100
Lebanese American Organizations, Council of   www.clao.com
  PO Box 181116   Cleveland OH 44118
  Ph: 216-932-9936
Lebanese Engineering Society, American
  PO Box 690785   Orlando FL 32869
  Ph: 407-422-6761   ▪ Fx: 407-422-9664
Lebanese Syrian Associated Charities, American   www.stjude.org
  501 St Jude Pl   Memphis TN 38105
  Ph: 901-578-2000   ▪ Fx: 901-578-2805   ▪ TF: 800-822-6344
Lebanon of North America, Tall Cedars of   www.mastermason.com/tcl
  2609 N Front St   Harrisburg PA 17110
  Ph: 717-232-5991   ▪ Fx: 717-232-5997
Lee Robert E Memorial Association   www.stratfordhall.org
  Stratford Hall Plantation   Stratford VA 22558
  Ph: 804-493-8038   ▪ Fx: 804-493-0333
Left-Handed Golfers, National Association of   www.nalg.org
  3249 Hazelwood Dr SW   Atlanta GA 30311
  Ph: 404-696-1763   ▪ Fx: 404-691-5549   ▪ TF: 800-844-6524
Lefthanders International
  PO Box 8249   Topeka KS 66608
  Ph: 913-234-2177   ▪ Fx: 913-232-3999
LEGACY   www.legacyonline.org
  PO Box 37   Lower Waterford VT 05848
  Ph: 802-748-8538   ▪ Fx: 802-748-4742
Legacy International   www.legacyintl.org
  1020 Legacy Dr   Bedford VA 24523
  Ph: 540-297-5982   ▪ Fx: 540-297-1860
Legal Action Program, Migrant   www.mlap.org
  1001 Connecticut Ave NW Suite 915   Washington DC 20036
  Ph: 202-775-7780   ▪ Fx: 202-775-7784
Legal Action for Women   www.legalactionforwomen.org
Legal Administrators, Association of   www.alanet.org
  175 E Hawthorn Pkwy Suite 325   Vernon Hills IL 60061
  Ph: 847-816-1212   ▪ Fx: 847-816-1213
Legal Aid & Defender Association, National   www.nlada.org
  1140 Connecticut Ave NW Suite 900   Washington DC 20036
  Ph: 202-452-0620   ▪ Fx: 202-872-1031
Legal Anthropology, Association for Political &   www.aaanet.org/apla
  c/o American Anthropological Assn 2200 Wilson Blvd Suite
    600   Arlington VA 22201
  Ph: 703-528-1902   ▪ Fx: 703-528-3546
Legal Assistant Management Association   www.lamanet.org
  PO Box 659   Avondale Estates GA 30002
  Ph: 404-292-2976   ▪ Fx: 404-292-2931
Legal Assistants, National Association of   www.nala.org
  1516 S Boston Ave Suite 200   Tulsa OK 74119
  Ph: 918-587-6828   ▪ Fx: 918-582-6772
Legal Center for the Medically Dependent & Disabled, National
  1 S 6th St   Terre Haute IN 47808
  Ph: 812-232-2434   ▪ Fx: 812-235-3658
Legal Center for the Public Interest, National   www.nlcpi.org
  1600 K St NW Suite 800   Washington DC 20006
  Ph: 202-466-9360   ▪ Fx: 202-466-9366
Legal Consortium, National Asian Pacific American   www.napalc.org
  1140 Connecticut Ave NW Suite 1200   Washington DC 20036
  Ph: 202-296-2300   ▪ Fx: 202-296-2318
Legal Counsel for the Elderly
  601 'E' St NW Bldg A 4th Fl   Washington DC 20049
  Ph: 202-434-2170   ▪ Fx: 202-434-6464
Legal Defense Association, Home School   www.hslda.org
  PO Box 3000   Purcellville VA 20134
  Ph: 540-338-5600   ▪ Fx: 540-338-2733
Legal Defense & Education Fund, Asian American   www.aaldef.org
  99 Hudson St 12th Fl   New York NY 10013
  Ph: 212-966-5932   ▪ Fx: 212-966-4303
Legal Defense & Education Fund, Lambda   www.lambdalegal.org
  120 Wall St Suite 1500   New York NY 10005
  Ph: 212-809-8585   ▪ Fx: 212-809-0055
Legal Defense & Education Fund, Minority Business Enterprise   www.mbeldef.org
  419 New Jersey Ave SE   Washington DC 20003
  Ph: 202-289-1700   ▪ Fx: 202-289-1701
Legal Defense Foundation Inc, National Right to Work   www.nrtw.org
  8001 Braddock Rd Suite 600   Springfield VA 22160
  Ph: 703-321-8510   ▪ Fx: 703-321-9613   ▪ TF: 800-325-7892
Legal Defense Fund, Animal   www.aldf.org
  127 4th St   Petaluma CA 94952
  Ph: 707-769-7771   ▪ Fx: 707-769-0785
Legal Defense Fund, Sierra   www.sierralegal.org
  131 Water St Suite 214   Vancouver BC V6B4M3
  Ph: 604-685-5618   ▪ Fx: 604-685-7813   ▪ TF: 800-926-7744

Legal Defense Network, Servicemembers   www.sldn.org
  PO Box 65301   Washington DC 20035
  Ph: 202-328-3244   ▪ Fx: 202-797-1635
Legal & Economic Public Policy Studies, Phoenix Center   www.phoenix-center.org
  for Advanced   5335 Wisconsin Ave NW Suite
    440   Washington DC 20015
  Ph: 202-274-0235
Legal Education, Association for Continuing   www.aclea.org
  PO Box 4646   Austin TX 78765
  Ph: 512-453-4340   ▪ Fx: 512-451-2911
Legal Environmental Assistance Foundation   www.leaflaw.org
  1114 Thomasville Rd Suite E   Tallahassee FL 32303
  Ph: 850-681-2591   ▪ Fx: 850-224-1275
Legal Foundation, Atlantic   www.atlanticlegal.org
  205 E 42nd St 9th Fl   New York NY 10017
  Ph: 212-571-1960   ▪ Fx: 212-573-1959
Legal Foundation, Criminal Justice   www.cjlf.org
  PO Box 1199   Sacramento CA 95812
  Ph: 916-446-0345   ▪ Fx: 916-446-1194
Legal Foundation, National   www.nlf.net
  PO Box 64427   Virginia Beach VA 23467
  Ph: 757-463-6133   ▪ Fx: 757-463-6055
Legal Foundation, Pacific   www.pacificlegal.org
  10360 Old Placerville Rd Suite 100   Sacramento CA 95827
  Ph: 916-362-2833   ▪ Fx: 916-362-2932
Legal Foundation, Washington   www.wlf.org
  2009 Massachusetts Ave NW   Washington DC 20036
  Ph: 202-588-0302   ▪ Fx: 202-588-0386
Legal Fraternity, Phi Delta Phi International   www.phideltaphi.org
  1426 21st St NW   Washington DC 20036
  Ph: 202-223-6801   ▪ Fx: 202-223-6808   ▪ TF: 800-368-5606
Legal History, American Society for   www.acls.org/asleghis.htm
  Univ of Notre Dame PO Box R   Notre Dame IN 46556
  Ph: 219-631-6984
Legal Immigration Network Inc, Catholic   www.cliniclegal.org
  McCormick Pavilion 415 Michigan Ave NE   Washington DC
    20017
  Ph: 202-635-2556
Legal Instruction, Center for Computer-Assisted   www.cali.org
  1313 5th Ave SE   Minneapolis MN 55414
  Ph: 612-625-3419   ▪ Fx: 612-379-3875
Legal Investigators, National Association of   www.nalionline.org
Legal Marketing Association   www.legalmarketing.org
  1926 Waukegan Rd Suite 1   Glenview IL 60025
  Ph: 847-657-6717   ▪ Fx: 847-657-6819
Legal Medicine, American College of   www.aclm.org
  1111 N Plaza Dr Suite 550   Schaumburg IL 60173
  Ph: 847-969-0283   ▪ Fx: 847-517-7229
Legal Nurse Consultants, American Association of   www.aalnc.org
  401 N Michigan Ave   Chicago IL 60611
  Ph: 312-321-5177   ▪ Fx: 312-673-6655   ▪ TF: 877-402-2562
Legal Professionals, NALS - Association for   www.nals.org
  314 E 3rd St Suite 210   Tulsa OK 74120
  Ph: 918-582-5188   ▪ Fx: 918-582-5907
(Legal Reform) HALT Inc   www.halt.org
  1612 K St NW Suite 510   Washington DC 20006
  Ph: 202-887-8255   ▪ Fx: 202-887-9699   ▪ TF: 888-367-4258
Legal Research, Center for Social &   www.privacyexchange.org
  2 University Plaza Suite 414   Hackensack NJ 07601
  Ph: 201-996-1154   ▪ Fx: 201-996-1883
(Legal Scholarship) Order of the Coif   www.orderofthecoif.org
  Univ of North Carolina Law Library CB 3385   Chapel Hill NC
    27599
  Ph: 919-962-1321   ▪ Fx: 919-962-1193
Legal Search Consultants, National Association of   www.nalsc.org
  The Biltmore 817 W Peachtree St Suite 208   Atlanta GA 30308
  Ph: 404-879-5080   ▪ Fx: 404-879-5075   ▪ TF: 866-394-9347
Legal Secretaries International Inc   www.legalsecretaries.org
Legal Services Corp   www.lsc.gov
  3333 K St NW 3rd Fl   Washington DC 20007
  Ph: 202-295-1500   ▪ Fx: 202-337-6797
Legal Services Institute, American Prepaid   www.aplsi.org
  541 N Fairbanks Ct   Chicago IL 60611
  Ph: 312-988-5751   ▪ Fx: 312-988-5710
Legal Services Workers, National Organization of   www.nolsw.org
  113 University Pl 5th Fl   New York NY 10003
  Ph: 212-228-0992   ▪ Fx: 212-228-0097   ▪ TF: 800-829-2320
Legal Society, Christian   www.clsnet.org
  4208 Evergreen Ln Suite 222   Annandale VA 22003
  Ph: 703-642-1070   ▪ Fx: 703-642-1075
Legal Subjects, SCRIBES - American Society of Writers on   www.scribes.org
  Barry Univ School of Law 6441 E Colonial Dr   Orlando FL
    32807
  Ph: 407-275-2000   ▪ Fx: 407-275-6142
Legal Support of Alternative Schools, National Association for
  PO Box 2823   Santa Fe NM 87504
  Ph: 505-471-6928
Legatus   www.legatus.org
  24 Frank Lloyd Wright Dr PO Box 511   Ann Arbor MI 48106
  Ph: 734-930-3854   ▪ Fx: 734-668-2448
Legion of Honor, American Society of the French
  22 E 60th St Rm 53   New York NY 10022
  Ph: 212-751-8537   ▪ Fx: 212-755-7061
Legion of Valor of the USA   www.legionofvalor.com
  4706 Calle Reina   Santa Barbara CA 93110
  Ph: 805-692-2244
Legion of Young Polish Women
  Copernicus Ctr 5216 W Lawrence Ave   Chicago IL 60630
  Ph: 773-777-9037   ▪ Fx: 773-763-4069

Legionarios del Trabajo in America
2154 S San Joaquin St Stockton CA 95206
Ph: 209-463-6516

Legislation, Friends Committee on National   www.fcnl.org
245 2nd St NE Washington DC 20002
Ph: 202-547-6000 ▪ Fx: 202-547-6019

Legislative Council, Small Business   www.sblc.org
1010 Massachusetts Ave NW Suite 400 Washington DC 20001
Ph: 202-639-8500 ▪ Fx: 202-296-5333

Legislative Exchange Council, American   www.alec.org
1129 20th St NW Suite 500 Washington DC 20036
Ph: 202-466-3800 ▪ Fx: 202-466-3801

Legislative Improvement Committee, Carpenter's
101 Constitution Ave NW 10th Fl Washington DC 20001
Ph: 202-546-6206 ▪ Fx: 202-547-8979

Legislators from Gaming States, National Council of
139 Lancaster St Albany NY 12210
Ph: 518-449-4699 ▪ Fx: 518-432-5651

Legislators, National Black Caucus of State   www.nbcsl.com
444 N Capitol St NW Suite 622 Washington DC 20001
Ph: 202-624-5457 ▪ Fx: 202-508-3826

Legislators, National Conference of Insurance   www.ncoil.org
139 Lancaster St Albany NY 12210
Ph: 518-449-3210 ▪ Fx: 518-432-5651

Legislators, National Foundation for Women   www.womenlegislators.org
910 16th St NW Suite 100 Washington DC 20006
Ph: 202-293-3040 ▪ Fx: 202-293-5430

Legislators, National Order of Women   www.womenlegislators.org/nowl
910 16th St NW Suite 100 Washington DC 20006
Ph: 202-337-3565

Legislatures, National Conference of State   www.ncsl.org
7700 E 1st Pl Denver CO 80230
Ph: 303-364-7700 ▪ Fx: 303-364-7800

Leisure & Entertainment Industry, International Association for the   www.ialei.org
33 Henniker St Hillsborough NH 03244
Ph: 603-464-6498 ▪ Fx: 603-464-6497 ▪ TF: 888-464-6498

Leisure & Recreation, American Association for   www.aahperd.org/aalr
1900 Association Dr Reston VA 20191
Ph: 703-476-3400 ▪ Fx: 703-476-9527 ▪ TF: 800-213-7193

Lemans America   www.lemansamerica.com

Lenders, National Association of Affordable Housing
1300 Connecticut Ave NW Suite 905 Washington DC 20036
Ph: 202-293-9850 ▪ Fx: 202-293-9852

Lenders, National Association of Government Guaranteed   www.naggl.com
424 S Squires Landing Blvd Suite 130 Stillwater OK 74074
Ph: 405-377-4022 ▪ Fx: 405-377-3931

Lentil Council, USA Dry Pea &   www.pea-lentil.com
2780 W Pullman Rd Moscow ID 83843
Ph: 208-882-3023 ▪ Fx: 208-882-6406

Leo Baeck Institute   www.lbi.org
15 W 16th St New York NY 10011
Ph: 212-744-6400 ▪ Fx: 212-988-1305

Leonard Peltier Defense Committee Inc   www.leonardpeltier.org
PO Box 583 Lawrence KS 66044
Ph: 785-842-5774 ▪ Fx: 785-842-5796

Leonardo - International Society for the Arts   mitpress2.mit.edu/e-journals/Leonardo
Sciences & Technology 425 Market St 2nd Fl San Francisco
CA 94105
Ph: 415-405-3335 ▪ Fx: 415-405-7758

Leopard Trust, International Snow   www.snowleopard.org
4649 Sunnyside Ave N Suite 325 Seattle WA 98103
Ph: 206-632-2421 ▪ Fx: 206-632-3967

Lepidoptera, Association for Tropical   www.troplep.org
PO Box 141210 Gainesville FL 32614
Ph: 352-392-5894 ▪ Fx: 352-373-3249

Leprosy Missions, American   www.leprosy.org
1 ALM Way Greenville SC 29601
Ph: 864-271-7040 ▪ Fx: 864-271-7062 ▪ TF: 800-543-3135

Les Dames D'Escoffier   www.ldei.org

Lesbian Alliance Against Defamation, Gay &   www.glaad.org
248 W 35th St 8th Fl New York NY 10001
Ph: 212-629-3322 ▪ Fx: 212-629-3225

Lesbian & Bisexual Issues in Counseling, Association for Gay   www.aglbic.org
c/o American Counseling Assn 5999 Stevenson Ave Alexandria
VA 22304
Ph: 703-823-9800 ▪ Fx: 703-823-0252 ▪ TF: 800-347-6647

Lesbian/Gay Addiction Professionals, National Association of   www.nalgap.org
901 N Washington St Suite 600 Alexandria VA 22314
Ph: 703-465-0539 ▪ Fx: 703-741-6989

Lesbian & Gay Anthropologists, Society of   www.solga.org
c/o American Anthropological Assn 2200 Wilson Blvd Suite
600 Arlington VA 22201
Ph: 703-528-1902 ▪ Fx: 703-528-3546

Lesbian & Gay Bands of America   www.gaybands.org
PO Box 14874 San Francisco CA 94114
Ph: 415-554-0402 ▪ Fx: 415-621-4637

Lesbian Gay Bisexual & Transgender Organization, LLEGO -   www.llego.org
National Latina/o 1420 K St NW Suite 400 Washington DC
20005
Ph: 202-408-5380 ▪ Fx: 202-408-8478 ▪ TF: 888-633-8320

Lesbian & Gay History, Committee on   www.usc.edu/clgh
College of William & Mary PO Box 8795 Williamsburg VA
23187
Ph: 757-221-2453 ▪ Fx: 757-221-3737

Lesbian & Gay Journalists Association, National   www.nlgja.org
1420 K St NW Suite 910 Washington DC 20005
Ph: 202-588-9888 ▪ Fx: 202-588-1818

Lesbian & Gay Law Association, National   www.nlgla.org
200 E Lexington St Suite 1511 Baltimore MD 21202
Ph: 508-892-8290 ▪ Fx: 410-244-0775

Lesbian & Gay Studies, Center for   www.clags.org
City Univ of New York 365 5th Ave Rm 7115 New York NY
10016
Ph: 212-817-1955 ▪ Fx: 212-817-2985

Lesbian Human Rights Commission, International Gay &   www.iglhrc.org
1375 Sutter St Suite 222 San Francisco CA 94109
Ph: 415-561-0633 ▪ Fx: 415-561-0619

Lesbian National Hotline, Gay &   www.glnh.org
2261 Market St PMB 296 San Francisco CA 94114
Ph: 415-355-0999 ▪ Fx: 415-552-5498 ▪ TF: 888-415-3022

Lesbian Psychiatrists, Association of Gay &   www.aglp.org
4514 Chester Ave Philadelphia PA 19143
Ph: 215-222-2800 ▪ Fx: 215-222-3881

Lesbian Rights, National Center for   www.nclrights.org
870 Market St Suite 570 San Francisco CA 94102
Ph: 415-392-6257 ▪ Fx: 415-392-8442

Lesbian Task Force, National Gay &   www.ngltf.org
1325 Massachusetts Ave NW Suite 600 Washington DC 20005
Ph: 202-393-5177 ▪ Fx: 202-393-2241

Lesbian Travel Association, International Gay &   www.iglta.org
4331 N Federal Hwy Suite 304 Fort Lauderdale FL 33308
Ph: 954-776-2626 ▪ Fx: 954-776-3303 ▪ TF: 800-448-8550

Lesbian Victory Fund, Gay &   www.victoryfund.org
1705 DeSales St NW Suite 500 Washington DC 20036
Ph: 202-842-8679 ▪ Fx: 202-289-3863

Lesbians Inc, Conference for Catholic   www.catholicwomenl2l.org

Lesbians & Gays Everywhere, Children of   www.colage.org
3543 18th St Suite 1 San Francisco CA 94110
Ph: 415-861-5437 ▪ Fx: 415-255-8345

Lesbians & Gays, Parents Families & Friends of   www.pflag.org
1726 M St NW Suite 400 Washington DC 20036
Ph: 202-467-8180 ▪ Fx: 202-467-8194

Lesbians, Pro-Life Alliance of Gays &   www.plagal.org
PO Box 33292 Washington DC 20033
Ph: 202-223-6697 ▪ Fx: 202-265-9737

Leschetizky Association   www.leschetizky.org
884 West End Ave New York NY 10025
Ph: 212-222-2733

Leslie-Lohman Gay Art Foundation   www.leslielohman.org
127-B Prince St New York NY 10012
Ph: 212-673-7007 ▪ Fx: 212-260-0363

Lessors, National Council of Coal
300 Summers St Suite 1050 Charleston WV 25301
Ph: 304-346-0569 ▪ Fx: 304-346-6516

Let's Face It USA   www.faceit.org
PO Box 29972 Bellingham WA 98228
Ph: 360-676-7325

Letter Carriers' Association, National Rural   www.nrlca.org
1630 Duke St 4th Fl Alexandria VA 22314
Ph: 703-684-5545 ▪ Fx: 703-548-8735

Letter Carriers Mutual Benefit Association, US   www.nalc.org/depart/mba
100 Indiana Ave NW Suite 510 Washington DC 20001
Ph: 202-638-4318 ▪ Fx: 202-783-6123 ▪ TF: 800-424-5184

Letter Carriers, National Association of   www.nalc.org
100 Indiana Ave NW Washington DC 20001
Ph: 202-393-4695 ▪ Fx: 202-737-1540

Letter Carriers Political Education, Committee on
100 Indiana Ave NW Washington DC 20001
Ph: 202-393-4695 ▪ Fx: 202-737-1540

Letter Exchange, Student   www.pen-pal.com
211 Broadway Suite 201 Lynbrook NY 11563
Ph: 516-887-8628 ▪ Fx: 516-887-8631

Leukemia Foundation, Friends of the Jose   www.carrerasfoundation.org
Carreras International 1100 Fairview Ave N D5-100 PO Box
19024 Seattle WA 98109
Ph: 206-667-7108 ▪ Fx: 206-667-6498

Leukemia & Lymphoma Society   www.leukemia-lymphoma.org
475 Park Ave S 8th Fl New York NY 10016
Ph: 212-448-9206 ▪ Fx: 212-448-9214 ▪ TF: 800-955-4572

Leukemia Research Association, Children's   www.childrensleukemia.org
585 Stewart Ave Suite 18 Garden City NY 11530
Ph: 516-222-1944 ▪ Fx: 516-222-0457

Leukocyte Biology, Society for   www.leukocytebiology.org
9650 Rockville Pike Bethesda MD 20814
Ph: 301-634-7810 ▪ Fx: 301-634-7813

Levy Economics Institute of Bard College   www.levy.org
Blithewood Annandale-on-Hudson NY 12504
Ph: 845-758-7700 ▪ Fx: 845-758-1149

Lewis & Clark Trail Heritage Foundation   www.lewisandclark.org
PO Box 3434 Great Falls MT 59404
Ph: 406-454-1234 ▪ Fx: 406-771-9237 ▪ TF: 888-701-3434

Lex Mundi   www.lexmundi.com
2100 West Loop S Suite 1000 Houston TX 77027
Ph: 713-626-9393 ▪ Fx: 713-626-9933

Liability & Access, Health Coalition on   www.hcla.org
PO Box 19008 Washington DC 20036
Ph: 202-293-4255 ▪ Fx: 202-296-7689

Liability Agents Network, Professional   www.plan.org
PO Box 1632 Monterey CA 93942
Ph: 877-960-7526 ▪ Fx: 831-372-6647

Liability Attorneys, American Board of Professional   www.abpla.org
5712 244th St Douglaston NY 11362
Ph: 718-631-1400 ▪ Fx: 718-631-1456

Liability Insurance Research Bureau   www.lirb.org
3025 Highland Pkwy Suite 800 Downers Grove IL 60515
Ph: 630-724-2200 ▪ Fx: 630-724-2260 ▪ TF: 888-711-7572

Liability Underwriters, Mutual Atomic Energy
3158 River Rd Suite 103 Des Plaines IL 60018
Ph: 312-467-0003 ▪ Fx: 312-467-0774

Liability Underwriting Society, Professional   www.plusweb.org
5353 Wayzata Blvd Suite 600   Minneapolis MN 55416
Ph: 952-746-2580 ▪ Fx: 952-746-2599 ▪ TF: 800-845-0778

Liaison Committee on Medical Education   www.lcme.org
American Medical Assn 515 N State St   Chicago IL 60610
Ph: 312-464-4933 ▪ Fx: 312-464-5830

Libel Defense Resource Center   www.ldrc.com
80 8th Ave Suite 200   New York NY 10011
Ph: 212-337-0200 ▪ Fx: 212-337-9893

Liberal Education, American Academy for   www.aale.org
1710 Rhode Island Ave NW 4th Fl   Washington DC 20036
Ph: 202-452-8611 ▪ Fx: 202-452-8620

Liberal Studies Programs, Association of Graduate   www.udel.edu/aglsp
Univ of Delaware 219 McDowell Hall   Newark DE 19716
Ph: 302-831-4218 ▪ Fx: 302-831-4461

Liberator Club, International B-24   www.bomberlegends.com/b24club.html
1672 Main St Suite E PMB 124   Ramona CA 92065
Ph: 760-788-3624 ▪ Fx: 760-789-8911

Libertarian Party   www.lp.org
2600 Virginia Ave NW Suite 100   Washington DC 20037
Ph: 202-333-0008 ▪ Fx: 202-333-0072 ▪ TF: 800-682-1776

Libertarian Studies, Center for   www.libertarianstudies.org
851 Burlway Rd Suite 202   Burlingame CA 94010
Ph: 800-325-7257 ▪ Fx: 650-401-5530

(Libertarianism) Reason Foundation   www.reason.org
3415 S Sepulveda Blvd Suite 400   Los Angeles CA 90034
Ph: 310-391-2245 ▪ Fx: 310-391-4395

Libertarians for Life   www.l4l.org
13424 Hathaway Dr   Wheaton MD 20906
Ph: 301-460-4141 ▪ Fx: 301-871-8552

Liberty, Acton Institute for the Study of Religion &   www.acton.org
161 Ottawa NW Suite 301   Grand Rapids MI 49503
Ph: 616-454-3080 ▪ Fx: 616-454-9454

Liberty, Becket Fund for Religious   www.becketfund.org
1350 Connecticut Ave NW Suite 605   Washington DC 20036
Ph: 202-955-0095 ▪ Fx: 202-955-0090

Liberty Godparent Foundation   www.godparent.org
PO Box 4199   Lynchburg VA 24502
Ph: 434-845-3466 ▪ TF: 800-542-4453

Liberty, International Society for Individual   www.isil.org
836-B Southampton Rd Suite 299   Benicia CA 94510
Ph: 707-746-8796 ▪ Fx: 707-746-8797

Liberty Matters   www.libertymatters.org
PO Box 1207   Taylor TX 76574
Ph: 800-847-0227

Liberty Veterans Association, USS   www.ussliberty.org/
Librarians, American Association of School   www.ala.org/aasl
50 E Huron St   Chicago IL 60611
Ph: 312-280-4386 ▪ Fx: 312-664-7459 ▪ TF: 800-545-2433

Librarians Association, Chinese-American   www.cala-web.org
PO Box 4992   Irvine CA 92616
Ph: 949-824-6832 ▪ Fx: 949-857-1988

Librarians, Association of Christian   www.acl.org
PO Box 4   Cedarville OH 45314
Ph: 937-766-2255 ▪ Fx: 937-766-2337

Librarians' Association, Major Orchestra   www.mola-inc.org
c/o National Arts Centre Orchestra PO Box 1534 Stn B   Ottawa
ON K1P5W1
Ph: 613-947-7000 ▪ Fx: 613-947-8623

Librarians Association, Middle East   depts.washington.edu/wsx9/melahp.html
Univ of Washington Libraries Cataloging CB 352900   Seattle
WA 98195
Ph: 206-543-1642 ▪ Fx: 206-685-8787

Librarians, Association of Seventh-day Adventist   www.asdal.org
Librarians, Canadian Association of Children's   www.cla.ca/divisions/capl/cacl.htm
328 Frank St   Ottawa ON K2P0X8
Ph: 613-232-9625 ▪ Fx: 613-563-9895

Librarians in the History of the Health Sciences, Archivists &   www.alhhs.org
Virginia Commonwealth Univ Tompkins-McCaw Library Box
980582   Richmond VA 23298
Ph: 804-828-9898 ▪ Fx: 804-828-6089

Librarians & Information Specialists, Substance Abuse   www.salis.org
PO Box 9513   Berkeley CA 94709
Ph: 510-642-5208 ▪ Fx: 510-642-7175

Librarianship, International Association of School   www.iasl-slo.org
Libraries, American Association of Law   www.aallnet.org
53 W Jackson Blvd Suite 940   Chicago IL 60604
Ph: 312-939-4764 ▪ Fx: 312-431-1097

Libraries Archives & Documentation Centres, International Association of Music   www.iaml.info
Libraries, Association of Academic Health Sciences   www.aahsl.org
2150 N 107th St Suite 205   Seattle WA 98133
Ph: 206-367-8704 ▪ Fx: 206-367-8777

Libraries Association, Canadian Health   www.chla-absc.ca
3324 Yonge St   Toronto ON M4N3R1
Ph: 416-485-0377 ▪ Fx: 416-485-6877

Libraries, Association of College & Research   www.ala.org/acrl.html
50 E Huron St   Chicago IL 60611
Ph: 312-280-2519 ▪ Fx: 312-280-2520 ▪ TF: 800-545-2433

Libraries, Association of Jewish   www.jewishlibraries.org
15 E 26th St Rm 1034   New York NY 10010
Ph: 212-725-5359

Libraries, Association of Research   arl.cni.org
21 Dupont Cir NW Suite 800   Washington DC 20036
Ph: 202-296-2296 ▪ Fx: 202-872-0884

Libraries Association, Special   www.sla.org
1700 18th St NW   Washington DC 20009
Ph: 202-234-4700 ▪ Fx: 202-265-9317

Libraries, Canadian Association of College & University   www.cla.ca/divisions/cacul/cacul.htm
328 Frank St   Ottawa ON K2P0X8
Ph: 613-232-9625 ▪ Fx: 613-563-9895

Libraries, Canadian Association of Law   www.callacbd.ca
PO Box 1570   Kingston ON K7L5C8
Ph: 613-531-9338 ▪ Fx: 613-531-0626

Libraries, Canadian Association of Public   www.cla.ca/divisions/capl/capl.htm
328 Frank St   Ottawa ON K2P0X8
Ph: 613-232-9625 ▪ Fx: 613-563-9895

Libraries, Center for Research   wwwcrl.uchicago.edu
6050 S Kenwood Ave   Chicago IL 60637
Ph: 773-955-4545 ▪ Fx: 773-955-4339 ▪ TF: 800-621-6044

Libraries Inc, Council on Botanical &   www2.ville.montreal.qc.ca/jardin/cbhl/cbhl.htm
Horticultural   Carnegie Mellon Univ Hunt Institute for Botanical
Documentation   Pittsburgh PA 15213
Ph: 412-268-7301 ▪ Fx: 412-268-5677

Libraries Council, Urban   www.urbanlibraries.org
1603 Orrington Ave Suite 1080   Evanston IL 60201
Ph: 847-866-9999 ▪ Fx: 847-866-9989

Libraries for the Future   www.iff.org/
27 Union Sq W Suite 204   New York NY 10003
Ph: 646-336-6236 ▪ Fx: 646-336-6318 ▪ TF: 800-542-1918

Libraries Group Inc, Research   www.rlg.org
2029 Stierlin Ct Suite 100   Mountain View CA 94043
Ph: 650-962-9951 ▪ Fx: 650-964-0943 ▪ TF: 800-537-7546

Libraries & Information Centers, International Association of Aquatic & Marine Science   Harbor Branch Oceanographic   www.iamslic.org
Institution 5600 US 1 N   Fort Pierce FL 34946
Ph: 561-465-2400 ▪ Fx: 561-465-2446

Libraries & Information Centers International, Association for Population/Family Planning   c/o Family Health International   www.aplici.org
Library PO Box 13950   Research Triangle Park NC 27709
Ph: 919-405-1433 ▪ Fx: 919-544-7261

Libraries & Information Services, Canadian Association of Special   328 Frank St   Ottawa ON K2P0X8   www.cla.ca/caslis/index.htm
Ph: 613-232-9625 ▪ Fx: 613-563-9895

Libraries & Museums of the Performing Arts-USA, International Association of   www.theatrelibrary.org/sibmas/sibmas.html
Libraries Society of North America, Art   www.arlisna.org
329 March Rd Suite 232 Box 11   Kanata ON K2K2E1
Ph: 800-817-0621 ▪ Fx: 613-599-7027

Libraries USA, Friends of   www.folusa.com
1420 Walnut St Suite 450   Philadelphia PA 19102
Ph: 215-790-1674 ▪ Fx: 215-545-3821 ▪ TF: 800-936-5872

Library Administration & Management Association   www.ala.org/lama
50 E Huron St   Chicago IL 60611
Ph: 312-280-5036 ▪ Fx: 312-280-5033 ▪ TF: 800-545-2433

Library Agencies, Association of Specialized & Cooperative   www.ala.org/ascla
50 E Huron St   Chicago IL 60611
Ph: 312-280-4395 ▪ Fx: 312-944-8085 ▪ TF: 800-545-2433

Library Agencies, Chief Officers of State   www.cosla.org
167 W Main St Suite 600   Lexington KY 40507
Ph: 859-514-9151 ▪ Fx: 859-514-9166

Library & Archives, Southern Baptist Historical   www.sbhla.org
901 Commerce St Suite 400   Nashville TN 37203
Ph: 615-244-0344

Library Association, American   www.ala.org
50 E Huron St   Chicago IL 60611
Ph: 312-944-6780 ▪ Fx: 312-944-2641 ▪ TF: 800-545-2433

Library Association, American Merchant Marine   www.uss-ammla.com
20 Exchange Pl Suite 2901   New York NY 10005
Ph: 212-269-0711 ▪ Fx: 212-432-5492

Library Association, American Theological   www.atla.com
250 S Wacker Dr Suite 1600   Chicago IL 60606
Ph: 312-454-5100 ▪ Fx: 312-454-5005 ▪ TF: 888-665-2852

Library Association, Canadian   www.cla.ca
328 Frank St   Ottawa ON K2P0X8
Ph: 613-232-9625 ▪ Fx: 613-563-9895

Library Association, Canadian School   www.cla.ca/divisions/csla
328 Frank St   Ottawa ON K2P0X8
Ph: 613-232-9625 ▪ Fx: 613-563-9895

Library Association, Catholic   www.cathla.org
100 North St Suite 224   Pittsfield MA 01201
Ph: 413-443-2252

Library Association, Church & Synagogue   www.worldaccessnet.com/~csla
PO Box 19357   Portland OR 97280
Ph: 503-244-6919 ▪ Fx: 503-977-3734 ▪ TF: 800-542-2752

Library Association, Evangelical Church   www.eclibraries.org
PO Box 353   Glen Ellyn IL 60138
Ph: 630-681-7591 ▪ Fx: 630-681-7592 ▪ TF: 800-223-0001

Library Association, Herbert Hoover Presidential   www.hooverassociation.org
PO Box 696   West Branch IA 52358
Ph: 319-643-5327 ▪ Fx: 319-643-2391 ▪ TF: 800-828-0475

Library Association, Lutheran Church   www.lclahq.org
216 W Myrtle St   Stillwater MN 55082
Ph: 651-430-0770

Library Association, Medical   www.mlanet.org
65 E Wacker Pl Suite 1900   Chicago IL 60601
Ph: 312-419-9094 ▪ Fx: 312-419-8950

Library Association Inc, Music   www.musiclibraryassoc.com
8551 Research Way Suite 180   Middleton WI 53562
Ph: 608-836-5825 ▪ Fx: 608-831-8200

Library Association, Public   www.pla.org
50 E Huron St   Chicago IL 60611
Ph: 312-280-5752 ▪ Fx: 312-280-5029 ▪ TF: 800-545-2433

Library Association, Theatre   tla.library.unt.edu
149 W 45th St   New York NY 10036
Ph: 212-944-3895 ▪ Fx: 212-944-4139

Library Binding Institute www.lbibinders.org
70 E Lake St Suite 300   Chicago IL 60601
Ph: 312-704-5020 ▪ Fx: 312-704-5025

Library Cat Society www.ironfrog.com/libcats/lcs.html
PO Box 274   Moorhead MN 56560
Ph: 218-236-7205

Library Center Inc, Online Computer www.oclc.org
6565 Frantz Rd   Dublin OH 43017
Ph: 614-764-6000 ▪ Fx: 614-764-6096 ▪ TF: 800-848-5878

Library Collections & Technical Services, Association for www.ala.org/alcts
50 E Huron St   Chicago IL 60611
Ph: 312-280-5038 ▪ Fx: 312-280-5033 ▪ TF: 800-545-2433

Library Foundation, John F Kennedy www.jfklibrary.org/fn_menu.htm
Columbia Pt   Boston MA 02125
Ph: 617-929-1200 ▪ Fx: 617-436-3395 ▪ TF: 877-616-4599

Library & Historical Society, American Hungarian www.hungarianhouse.org
213 E 82nd St   New York NY 10028
Ph: 212-249-9360

Library & Information Resources, Council on www.clir.org
1775 Massachusetts Ave NW Suite 500   Washington DC 20036
Ph: 202-939-4750 ▪ Fx: 202-939-4765

Library & Information Science Education, Association for www.alise.org
1009 Commerce Pk Suite 150   Oak Ridge TN 37839
Ph: 865-425-0155 ▪ Fx: 865-481-0390

Library & Information Technology Association www.lita.org
50 E Huron St   Chicago IL 60611
Ph: 312-280-4270 ▪ Fx: 312-280-3257 ▪ TF: 800-545-2433

Library Inc, International Friends of the London
515 Madison Ave Suite 3702   New York NY 10022
Ph: 212-644-4858 ▪ Fx: 212-644-4859

Library Media Technicians Inc, Council on colt.ucr.edu
Daniel Boone Regional Library 100 W Broadway   Columbia MO 65203
Ph: 573-443-3161 ▪ Fx: 573-874-0862

Library of Medicine, Friends of the National www.fnlm.org
1555 Connecticut Ave NW Suite 200   Washington DC 20036
Ph: 202-462-0992 ▪ Fx: 202-462-9043

(Library Science) Beta Phi Mu www.beta-phi-mu.org
Florida State Univ School of Information Studies   Tallahassee FL 32306
Ph: 850-644-3907 ▪ Fx: 850-644-9763

Library Service to Children, Association for www.ala.org/alsc
50 E Huron St   Chicago IL 60611
Ph: 312-280-2163 ▪ Fx: 312-944-7671 ▪ TF: 800-545-2433

Library Services Association, Young Adult www.ala.org/yalsa
50 E Huron St   Chicago IL 60611
Ph: 312-280-4390 ▪ Fx: 312-664-7459 ▪ TF: 800-545-2433

Library Services to Latinos & the Spanish-Speaking, REFORMA National Association to Promote   PO Box 25963   Scottsdale AZ 85255 www.reforma.org
Ph: 480-471-7452 ▪ Fx: 480-471-7442

Library Trustees & Advocates, Association for www.ala.org/alta
50 E Huron St   Chicago IL 60611
Ph: 312-280-2161 ▪ Fx: 312-280-3256 ▪ TF: 800-545-2433

Library Trustees Association, Canadian www.cla.ca/divisions/clta/clta.htm
328 Frank St   Ottawa ON K2P0X8
Ph: 613-232-9625 ▪ Fx: 613-563-9895

Library Users of America libraryusers.tripod.com
127 June St   Worcester MA 01602
Ph: 508-363-3866

License Collectors, International Society of Animal
928 SR 2206   Clinton KY 42031
Ph: 270-653-6060 ▪ Fx: 270-653-3030

License Law Officials, Association of Real Estate www.arello.org
PO Box 230159   Montgomery AL 36123
Ph: 334-260-2902 ▪ Fx: 334-260-2903

Licensing Association, International Collegiate nacda.ocsn.com/icla/nacda-icla.html
24651 Detroit Rd   Westlake OH 44145
Ph: 440-892-4000 ▪ Fx: 440-892-4007

Licensing Boards, Federation of Chiropractic www.fclb.org
901 54th Ave Suite 101   Greeley CO 80634
Ph: 970-356-3500 ▪ Fx: 970-356-3599

Licensing Executives Society www.usa-canada.les.org
1800 Diagonal Rd Suite 280   Alexandria VA 22314
Ph: 703-836-3106 ▪ Fx: 703-836-3107

Licensing Industry Merchandisers' Association, International www.licensing.org
350 5th Ave Suite 1408   New York NY 10118
Ph: 212-244-1944 ▪ Fx: 212-563-6552

Licensure Enforcement & Regulation, Council on www.clearhq.org
403 Marquis Ave Suite 100   Lexington KY 40502
Ph: 859-269-1289 ▪ Fx: 859-231-1943

Lichenological Society, American Bryological & www.unomaha.edu/~abls/
Univ of Nevada Dept of Biological Sciences 4505 Maryland Pkwy Box 454004   Las Vegas NV 89154
Ph: 702-895-3119 ▪ Fx: 702-895-3956

Liederkranz Foundation www.liederkranznycity.org
6 E 87th St   New York NY 10128
Ph: 212-534-0880 ▪ Fx: 212-828-5372

Life Action Ministries www.lifeaction.org
PO Box 31   Buchanan MI 49107
Ph: 269-684-5905 ▪ Fx: 269-684-0923

Life After Assault League
1336 W Lindbergh St   Appleton WI 54914
Ph: 920-739-4489 ▪ Fx: 920-739-1990

Life Brokerage Agencies, National Association of Independent www.nailba.org
12150 Monument Dr Suite 125   Fairfax VA 22033
Ph: 703-383-3081 ▪ Fx: 703-383-6942

Life Coalition International www.lifecoalition.com
PO Box 360221   Melbourne FL 32936
Ph: 321-726-0444 ▪ Fx: 321-726-0509

Life, Consistent www.consistent-life.org
PO Box 792   Garner NC 27529
Ph: 919-779-8766 ▪ Fx: 919-779-1912

Life & Environment, Center for Respect of www.crle.org
2100 L St NW   Washington DC 20037
Ph: 202-778-6133 ▪ Fx: 202-778-6138

Life Fellowship Inc, Word of www.wol.org
PO Box 600   Schroon Lake NY 12870
Ph: 518-494-6000 ▪ Fx: 518-494-6306 ▪ TF: 800-331-9673

Life & Health Insurance Guaranty Associations, National Organization of   13873 Park Center Rd Suite 329   Herndon VA 20171 www.nolhga.com
Ph: 703-481-5206 ▪ Fx: 703-481-5209

Life Insurance, Catholic www.catholiclifeinsurance.com
1635 NE Loop 410 Suite 300   San Antonio TX 78209
Ph: 210-828-9921 ▪ Fx: 210-828-4629 ▪ TF: 800-262-2548

(Life Insurance) International Forum www.int-forum.org
401 N Michigan Ave   Chicago IL 60611
Ph: 312-644-6610 ▪ Fx: 312-673-6594 ▪ TF: 800-499-0974

Life Insurance Society, Gleaner www.gleanerlife.com
5200 W US Hwy 223 PO Box 1894   Adrian MI 49221
Ph: 517-263-2244 ▪ Fx: 517-265-7745 ▪ TF: 800-992-1894

Life Insurance Society, Luso-American www.luso-american.org
7080 Donlon Way   Dublin CA 94568
Ph: 925-828-4884 ▪ Fx: 925-828-4554 ▪ TF: 877-525-5876

Life Insurers, American Council of www.acli.com
101 Constitution Ave NW Suite 700 W   Washington DC 20001
Ph: 202-624-2000 ▪ Fx: 202-624-2319

Life League, American www.all.org
PO Box 1350   Stafford VA 22555
Ph: 540-659-4171 ▪ Fx: 540-659-2586 ▪ TF: 888-546-2580

Life & Liberty for Women www.lifeandlibertyforwomen.org
1015 S Taft Hill Rd PMB 213   Fort Collins CO 80521
Ph: 970-416-6872

Life Ministries, Alliance for www.alliance4lifemin.org
PO Box 5468   Madison WI 53705
Ph: 608-833-7363

Life Outreach International www.lifetoday.org
PO Box 982000   Fort Worth TX 76182
Ph: 817-267-4211 ▪ Fx: 817-685-1971 ▪ TF: 800-947-5433

Life Science Systems Association, Analytical & www.alssa.org
225 Reinekers Ln Suite 625   Alexandria VA 22314
Ph: 703-836-1360 ▪ Fx: 703-836-6644

Life Sciences, Coalition for Education in the www.wisc.edu/cbe/cels

Life Sciences Institute North America, International www.ilsina.org
1 Thomas Cir NW 9th Fl   Washington DC 20005
Ph: 202-659-0074 ▪ Fx: 202-659-3859

Life Sciences, Society for Chaos Theory in Psychology &   Univ of Oregon Dept of Psychology CMB 1227   Eugene OR 97403 www.societyforchaostheory.org
Ph: 541-346-1996 ▪ Fx: 541-346-4911

Life Services, International www.life-services.org
2606 1/2 W 8th St   Los Angeles CA 90057
Ph: 213-382-2156 ▪ Fx: 213-382-4203

Life Settlement Association of America, Viatical & www.viatical.org
800 Mayfair Cir   Orlando FL 32803
Ph: 407-894-3797 ▪ Fx: 407-897-1325 ▪ TF: 800-842-9811

Life Underwriting, Association for Advanced www.aalu.org
2901 Telestar Ct   Falls Church VA 22042
Ph: 703-641-9400 ▪ Fx: 703-641-9885 ▪ TF: 888-275-0092

Lifelong Learning, Center for www.acenet.edu/clll
1 Dupont Cir NW Suite 250   Washington DC 20036
Ph: 202-939-9475 ▪ Fx: 202-833-4760

Lifesaver Inc, Operation www.oli.org
1420 King St Suite 401   Alexandria VA 22314
Ph: 703-739-0308 ▪ Fx: 703-519-8267 ▪ TF: 800-537-6224

Lifesaving Association, US www.usla.org

Lifespire www.lifespire.org
345 Hudson St 3rd Fl   New York NY 10014
Ph: 212-741-0100 ▪ Fx: 212-463-9814

Lifetime Institute for Family Education
9 Old Kings Hwy S 4th Fl   Darien CT 06820
Ph: 203-656-3600 ▪ Fx: 203-656-2221 ▪ TF: 800-832-0277

Lift Institute, Automotive www.autolift.org
PO Box 33116   Indialantic FL 32903
Ph: 321-722-9993 ▪ Fx: 321-722-9931

LIGA International Inc liga.blytheco.com
1464 N Fitzgerald Ave Hangar 2   Rialto CA 92376
Ph: 909-875-6300 ▪ Fx: 909-875-6900

Ligand Assay Society, Clinical www.clas.org
3139 S Wayne Rd   Wayne MI 48184
Ph: 734-722-6290 ▪ Fx: 734-722-7006

Light for Life Foundation International www.yellowribbon.org
PO Box 644   Westminster CO 80036
Ph: 303-429-3530 ▪ Fx: 303-426-4496

Light Treatment & Biological Rhythms, Society for www.websciences.org/sltbr
174 Cook St PO Box 591687   San Francisco CA 94159
Ph: 415-876-0716 ▪ Fx: 415-751-2758

Lighter Association Inc www.lighterassociation.org
1920 'N' St NW Suite 800   Washington DC 20036
Ph: 202-973-2709 ▪ Fx: 202-331-8330

LightHawk www.lighthawk.org
PO Box 653   Lander WY 82520
Ph: 307-332-3242

Lighthouse International www.lighthouse.org
111 E 59th St   New York NY 10022
Ph: 212-821-9200 ▪ Fx: 212-821-9708 ▪ TF: 800-829-0500

Lighthouse Keepers Association, Great Lakes www.gllka.com
PO Box 219   Mackinaw City MI 49701
Ph: 231-436-5580 ▪ Fx: 231-436-5466

Lighthouse Society, US
244 Kearny St 5th Fl   San Francisco CA 94108
Ph: 415-362-7255   Fx: 415-362-7464   www.uslhs.org

Lighting Association, American   www.americanlightingassoc.com
2050 Stemmons Fwy Suite 10046   Dallas TX 75207
Ph: 214-698-9898   Fx: 214-698-9899   TF: 800-605-4448

Lighting Bureau, National   www.nlb.org
8811 Colesville Rd Suite G106   Silver Spring MD 20910
Ph: 301-587-9572   Fx: 301-589-2017

Lighting Designers, International Association of   www.iald.org
200 World Trade Ctr Merchandise Mart Suite 9-104   Chicago IL
60654
Ph: 312-527-3677   Fx: 312-527-3680

Lighting Distributors Inc, National Association of Independent   www.naild.org
2207 Elmwood Ave   Buffalo NY 14216
Ph: 716-875-3670   Fx: 716-875-0734

Lighting Professions, National Council on Qualifications for the   www.ncqlp.org
526 King St Suite 405   Alexandria VA 22314
Ph: 703-518-4370   Fx: 703-706-9583

Lighting Research Office   www.epri.com/LRO
3574 Atherstone Rd   Cleveland Heights OH 44121
Ph: 216-291-1884   Fx: 216-382-6424

Lightning Class Association, International   www.lightningclass.org
PO Box 10747   Murfreesboro TN 37129
Ph: 615-893-5274   Fx: 615-893-5205

Lightning Protection Institute   www.lightning.org
3335 N Arlington Heights Rd Suite E   Arlington Heights IL
60004
Ph: 847-577-7200   Fx: 847-577-7276   TF: 800-488-6864

Lignin Institute   www.lignin.info
5775 Peachtree-Dunwoody Rd Bldg G Suite 500   Atlanta GA
30342
Ph: 404-252-3663   Fx: 404-252-0774

Lignite Energy Council   www.lignite.com
1016 E Owens Ave Suite 200   Bismarck ND 58502
Ph: 701-258-7117   Fx: 701-258-2755

Lilac Rabbit Club of America, National   www.geocities.com/nlrca2002
N3650 Oak Ridge Rd   Waupaca WI 54981
Ph: 715-258-3106

Lilliputian Bottle Club
5626 Corning Ave   Los Angeles CA 90056
Ph: 323-294-3231

Lilly Endowment Inc   www.lillyendowment.org
2801 N Meridian St   Indianapolis IN 46208
Ph: 317-924-5471   Fx: 317-926-4431

Lily Society, North American   www.lilies.org
PO Box 272   Owatonna MN 55060
Ph: 507-451-2170

Lily & Water Gardening Society, International Water   www.iwgs.org
6828 26th St W   Bradenton FL 34207
Ph: 941-756-0880

Lime Association, National   www.lime.org
200 N Glebe Rd Suite 800   Arlington VA 22203
Ph: 703-243-5463   Fx: 703-243-5489

Limestone Institute of America Inc, Indiana   www.iliai.com
400 Stone City Bank Bldg   Bedford IN 47421
Ph: 812-275-4426   Fx: 812-279-8682

Limited Edition Dealers, National Association of   www.naled.org
332 Hurst Mill N   Bremen GA 30110
Ph: 770-537-1970   TF: 800-446-2533

Limited Partners, American Association of
4224 Montgomery Ave Suite 102   Bethesda MD 20814
Ph: 301-652-5066   Fx: 301-913-9146

Limnology, International Association of Theoretical & Applied   www.limnology.org

Limnology & Oceanography, American Society of   aslo.org
5400 Bosque Blvd Suite 680   Waco TX 76710
Ph: 254-399-9635   Fx: 254-776-3767   TF: 800-929-2756

Limousin Association, North American Junior   www.nalf.org/programs/juniors.html
7383 S Alton Way Suite 100   Englewood CO 80112
Ph: 303-220-1693   Fx: 303-220-1884

Limousin Foundation, North American   www.nalf.org
7383 S Alton Way Suite 100   Englewood CO 80112
Ph: 303-220-1693   Fx: 303-220-1884

Limousine Association, National   www.limo.org
49 S Maple Ave   Marlton NJ 08053
Ph: 856-596-3344   Fx: 856-596-2145   TF: 800-652-7007

Limousine & Paratransit Association, Taxicab   www.tlpa.org
3849 Farragut Ave   Kensington MD 20895
Ph: 301-946-5701   Fx: 301-946-4641

LIMRA International Inc   www.limra.com
300 Day Hill Rd   Windsor CT 06095
Ph: 860-688-3358   Fx: 860-298-9555   TF: 800-285-7792

Lincoln Abraham Association   www.alincolnassoc.com
1 Old State Capitol Plaza   Springfield IL 62701
Ph: 217-782-2118   Fx: 217-785-7937

Lincoln Abraham National Cemetery Support Committee
28 Kansas St   Frankfort IL 60423
Ph: 815-469-2176   Fx: 815-469-0295

Lincoln Brigade, Veterans of the Abraham   www.alba-valb.org
799 Broadway Rm 227   New York NY 10003
Ph: 212-674-5552

Lincoln Cent Collectors, Society of   www.slcc.nasc.net
13515 Magnolia Blvd   Sherman Oaks CA 91423
Ph: 818-789-7805

Lincoln Highway Association   www.lincolnhighwayassoc.com
PO Box 308   Franklin Grove IL 61031
Ph: 815-456-3030   Fx: 815-456-2140

Lincoln Institute of Public Opinion Research Inc   www.lincolninstitute.org
453 Springlake Rd   Harrisburg PA 17112
Ph: 717-671-0776   Fx: 717-671-1176

Lincoln Museum, Friends of the Abraham
Lincoln Memorial Univ Box 2006   Harrogate TN 37752
Ph: 423-869-6235   Fx: 423-869-6350

Lincoln Sheep Breeders Association, National   www.lincolnsheep.org
15603 173rd Ave   Milo IA 50166
Ph: 641-942-6402

(Lindbergh, Charles) CAL/N-X-211 Collectors Society   www.isoc.net/astuder/calnx211

Lindbergh Foundation   www.lindberghfoundation.org
2150 3rd Ave N Suite 310   Anoka MN 55303
Ph: 763-576-1596   Fx: 763-576-1664

Lindenwald, Friends of
1013 Old Post Rd PO Box 64   Kinderhook NY 12106
Ph: 518-758-9689   Fx: 518-758-6986

Linen Management, National Association of Institutional   www.nlmnet.org
2130 Lexington Rd Suite H   Richmond KY 40475
Ph: 859-624-0177   Fx: 859-624-3580   TF: 800-669-0863

Linen Promotion Commission, International
PO Box 1630   New York NY 10028
Ph: 212-734-3640

Linguistic Anthropology, Society for   www.aaanet.org/sla
c/o American Anthropological Assn 2200 Wilson Blvd Suite
600   Arlington VA 22201
Ph: 703-528-1902   Fx: 703-528-3546

Linguistic Association of Canada & the US   www.lacus.org

Linguistic Fellowship, Elvish   www.elvish.org

Linguistic Society of America   www.lsadc.org
1325 18th St NW Suite 211   Washington DC 20036
Ph: 202-835-1714   Fx: 202-835-1717

Linguistics, American Association for Applied   www.aaal.org
PO Box 361806   Birmingham AL 35236
Ph: 205-824-7700   Fx: 205-823-2760   TF: 866-821-7700

Linguistics, Association for Computational   www.aclweb.org
3 Landmark Ctr   East Stroudsburg PA 18301
Ph: 570-476-8006   Fx: 570-476-0860

Linguistics, Center for Applied   www.cal.org
4646 40th St NW   Washington DC 20016
Ph: 202-362-0700   Fx: 202-362-3740

Links Inc   www.linksinc.org
1200 Massachusetts Ave NW   Washington DC 20005
Ph: 202-842-8686   Fx: 202-842-4020   TF: 800-574-3720

Linkup The - Survivors of Clergy Abuse   www.thelinkup.org
291 N Hubbards Ln Suite B26   Louisville KY 40207
Ph: 502-290-4055   Fx: 502-290-4056

Lion Foundation, Mountain   www.mountainlion.org
PO Box 1896   Sacramento CA 95812
Ph: 916-442-2666   Fx: 916-442-2871

Lions, American Council of Blind   www.acb.org/affiliates
1155 15th St NW Suite 1004   Washington DC 20005
Ph: 202-467-5081   TF: 800-424-8666

Lions Clubs International   www.lionsclubs.org
300 W 22nd St   Oak Brook IL 60523
Ph: 630-571-5466   Fx: 630-571-8890

Lions Clubs, International Association of   www.lionsclubs.org
300 W 22nd St   Oak Brook IL 60523
Ph: 630-571-5466   Fx: 630-571-8890

Lipid Association, National   www.lipid.org
8833 Perimeter Park Blvd Suite 301   Jacksonville FL 32216
Ph: 904-998-0854   Fx: 904-998-0855

Lipizzan Association of North America   www.lipizzan.org
PO Box 1133   Anderson IN 46015
Ph: 765-644-3904   Fx: 765-641-1205

Lipizzan Registry, US   www.lipizzan-uslr.com
707 13th St SE Suite 275   Salem OR 97301
Ph: 503-589-3172   Fx: 503-362-6390

Lipo-Suction Surgery, American Society of   www.cosmeticsurgery.org
737 N Michigan Ave Suite 820   Chicago IL 60611
Ph: 312-981-6760   Fx: 312-981-6787

Liquid Terminals Association, Independent   www.ilta.org
1444 'I' St NW Suite 400   Washington DC 20005
Ph: 202-842-9200   Fx: 202-326-8660

Liquor Administrators, National Conference of State   www.ncsla.org
8325 Horseshoe Dr   Lincoln NE 68516
Ph: 402-486-1774

Lisle Fellowship   www.lisleinternational.org
900 County Rd 269   Leander TX 78641
Ph: 512-259-7612   Fx: 512-259-3902   TF: 800-477-1538

Lissner Gerda Foundation   members.aol.com/lissnerfdtn
135 E 55th St   New York NY 10022
Ph: 212-826-6100   Fx: 212-826-0366

Listening Association, International   www.listen.org/
PO Box 744   River Falls WI 54022
Ph: 715-425-3377   Fx: 715-425-9533   TF: 800-452-4505

Liszt Society, American   www.americanlisztsociety.org
Hog Mountain Rd   Fleishmanns NY 12430
Ph: 845-586-4457

Literacy Association, International Visual   www.ivla.org/
Navarro College 3200 W 7th Ave   Corsicana TX 75110
Ph: 903-875-7441   Fx: 903-875-4636

Literacy, Barbara Bush Foundation for Family   www.barbarabushfoundation.com
1201 15th St SW Suite 420   Washington DC 20005
Ph: 202-955-6183   Fx: 202-955-5492

Literacy Council, American   www.americanliteracy.com
148 W 117th St   New York NY 10026
Ph: 212-663-4200   TF: 800-781-9985

Literacy & Evangelism International   www.literacyevangelism.org
1800 S Jackson Ave   Tulsa OK 74107
Ph: 918-585-3826   Fx: 918-585-3224   TF: 800-266-7139

Literacy Initiative, Children's   www.cliontheweb.org
2314 Market St   Philadelphia PA 19103
Ph: 215-561-4676 ▪ Fx: 215-561-4677 ▪ TF: 888-408-3388

Literacy, National Center for Family   www.famlit.org
325 W Main St Suite 300   Louisville KY 40202
Ph: 502-584-1133 ▪ Fx: 502-584-0172 ▪ TF: 877-326-5481

Literacy, National Coalition for
50 E Huron   Chicago IL 60611
Ph: 800-228-8813

Literacy, National Conference on Research in Language &   www.coe.uga.edu/ncrll
Colorado State Univ English Dept 359 Eddy Bldg   Fort Collins
  CO 80523
Ph: 970-491-5161 ▪ Fx: 970-491-5601

Literacy Worldwide, Pro   www.proliteracy.org
1320 Jamesville Ave   Syracuse NY 13210
Ph: 315-422-9121 ▪ Fx: 315-422-6369 ▪ TF: 800-448-8878

Literary Guild, Numismatic   www.numismaticliteraryguild.org
12 Abbington Terr   Glen Rock NJ 07452
Ph: 201-612-0482

Literary Magazines & Presses, Council of   www.clmp.org
154 Christopher St Suite 3C   New York NY 10014
Ph: 212-741-9110 ▪ Fx: 212-741-9112

Literary Managers & Dramaturgs of the Americas   www.lmda.org
Village Stn PO Box 728   New York NY 10014
Ph: 212-561-0315

Literary Scholars & Critics, Association of   www.bu.edu/literary
Boston Univ 650 Beacon St Suite 510   Boston MA 02215
Ph: 617-358-1990 ▪ Fx: 617-358-1995

Literary Society, Confederate Memorial   www.moc.org
1201 E Clay St   Richmond VA 23219
Ph: 804-649-1861 ▪ Fx: 804-644-7150

Literary Society, First Hungarian   www.onkepzo.org
323 E 79th St   New York NY 10021
Ph: 212-288-5002

Literary Translators Association, American   www.literarytranslators.org
Univ of Texas at Dallas PO Box 830688 MC35   Richardson TX
  75083
Ph: 972-883-2093 ▪ Fx: 972-883-6303

Literature Association, American Comparative   www.acla.org
Univ of Texas at Austin Program in Comparative Literature 1
   University Stn B5003   Austin TX 78712
Ph: 512-471-8020

Literature Association, Children's   www.childlitassn.org
PO Box 138   Battle Creek MI 49016
Ph: 269-965-8180 ▪ Fx: 269-965-3568

Literature & Environment, Association for the Study of   www.asle.umn.edu
Davidson College English Dept Box 7056   Davidson NC 28036
Ph: 704-894-2487

Literature Foundation, Organ
45 Norfolk Rd   Braintree MA 02184
Ph: 781-848-1388 ▪ Fx: 781-848-7655

Literature, International Association for Philosophy &   www.iapl.info
Stony Brook University   Stony Brook NY 11794
Ph: 631-632-7592 ▪ Fx: 631-331-0142

Literature International, Gospel   www.glint.org
PO Box 4060   Ontario CA 91761
Ph: 909-481-5222 ▪ Fx: 909-481-5216 ▪ TF: 800-434-5468

(Literature) Lambda Iota Tau   www.bsu.edu/csh/english/undergraduate/lit
Ball State Univ Dept of English   Muncie IN 47306
Ph: 765-285-8456 ▪ Fx: 765-285-3765

Literature, Society of Biblical   www.sbl-site.org
825 Houston Mill Rd Suite 350   Atlanta GA 30329
Ph: 404-727-3100 ▪ Fx: 404-727-3101

Literature, Society for the Preservation of English Language &   www.spellorg.com
PO Box 321   Braselton GA 30517
Ph: 770-586-0184 ▪ Fx: 770-868-0578

Literature, Society for the Study of Midwestern   writing.msu.edu:16080/ssml
Michigan State Univ Bessey Hall   East Lansing MI 48824
Ph: 517-355-3507 ▪ Fx: 517-353-5250

Literatures, Council on National   annehenrypaolucci.homestead.com/CNL1.html
68-02 Metropolitan Ave   Middle Village NY 11379
Ph: 718-821-3916

Litho Clubs, National Association of   www.graphicarts.org
PO Box 6190   Shallotte NC 28470
Ph: 910-575-0399

Lithotripsy Society, American   www.lithotripsy.org
305 2nd Ave Suite 200   Waltham MA 02451
Ph: 781-895-9098 ▪ Fx: 781-895-9088

Lithuanian Alliance of America
307 W 30th St   New York NY 10001
Ph: 212-563-2210

Lithuanian-American Community Inc   www.lithuanian-american.org
11876 Sunrise Valley Dr Suite 200C   Reston VA 20191
Ph: 703-390-0498 ▪ Fx: 703-390-0497

Lithuanian American Council   www.altcenter.org
6500 S Pulaski Rd Suite 200   Chicago IL 60629
Ph: 773-735-6677 ▪ Fx: 773-735-3946

Lithuanian Catholic Alliance
71-73 S Washington St   Wilkes-Barre PA 18701
Ph: 570-823-8876

Lithuanian Catholic Press Society
4545 W 63rd St   Chicago IL 60629
Ph: 773-585-9500 ▪ Fx: 773-585-8284

Lithuanian Relief Fund of America, United
4545 W 63rd St   Chicago IL 60629
Ph: 773-767-3401 ▪ Fx: 773-767-3402

Lithuanian Society of America, National
9136 55th Ct   Oak Lawn IL 60453
Ph: 708-423-7871

Lithuanian-US Business Council
c/o US Chamber of Commerce 1615 H St NW   Washington DC
  20062
Ph: 202-463-5601 ▪ Fx: 202-463-3114

Litigation Center, National Chamber   www.uschamber.com/ncl
c/o US Chamber of Commerce 1615 H St NW   Washington DC
  20062
Ph: 202-659-6000

Little Big Horn Associates   www.lbha.org

Little Britches Rodeo Association, National   www.nlbra.org
1045 W Rio Grande St   Colorado Springs CO 80906
Ph: 719-389-0333 ▪ Fx: 719-578-1367 ▪ TF: 800-763-3694

Little Brothers - Friends of the Elderly   www.littlebrothers.org
954 W Washington Blvd 5th Fl   Chicago IL 60607
Ph: 312-829-3055 ▪ Fx: 312-829-3077

Little City Foundation   www.littlecity.org
1760 W Algonquin Rd   Palatine IL 60067
Ph: 847-358-5510 ▪ Fx: 847-358-3291

Little Flower, Society of the   www.littleflower.org
1313 Frontage Rd   Darien IL 60561
Ph: 630-968-9400 ▪ Fx: 630-968-9542 ▪ TF: 800-621-2806

Little League Baseball Inc   www.littleleague.org
PO Box 3485   Williamsport PA 17701
Ph: 570-326-1921 ▪ Fx: 570-326-1074

Little People of America   www.lpaonline.org
5289 NE Elam Young Pkwy Suite F-700   Hillsboro OR 97124
Ph: 503-846-1562 ▪ Fx: 503-846-1590 ▪ TF: 888-572-2001

Little Scholars Inc, Pop Warner   www.popwarner.com
586 Middletown Blvd Suite C-100   Langhorne PA 19047
Ph: 215-752-2691 ▪ Fx: 215-752-2879

Littoral Society, American   www.littoralsociety.org
Sandy Hook Bldg 18   Highlands NJ 07732
Ph: 732-291-0055 ▪ Fx: 732-872-8041

Liturgica, Societas
800 S 9th St   Louisville KY 40203
Ph: 502-569-5759 ▪ Fx: 502-582-3763

Liturgical Commissions, Federation of Diocesan   www.fdlc.org
415 Michigan Ave NE Suite 70   Washington DC 20017
Ph: 202-635-6990 ▪ Fx: 202-529-2452

Liturgy Association, Latin   www.latinliturgy.com
34 Dumont Ave   Staten Island NY 10305
Ph: 718-979-6685 ▪ Fx: 718-667-7128

Liturgy, International Commission on English in the
1522 K St NW Suite 1000   Washington DC 20005
Ph: 202-347-0800

Liturgy & Mission, Associated Parishes for   www.associatedparishes.org
PO Box 27141   Baltimore MD 21230
Ph: 410-752-0877

Liturgy, North American Academy of   www.naal-liturgy.org
Univ of Portland 5000 N Willamette Blvd   Portland OR 97203
Ph: 503-943-7380 ▪ Fx: 503-943-7803

Livable Communities, Partners for   www.livable.com
1429 21st St NW   Washington DC 20036
Ph: 202-887-5990 ▪ Fx: 202-466-4845

Live Oak Society   www.louisianagardenclubs.org/pages/oak.htm
3609 Purdue Dr   Metairie LA 70003
Ph: 504-887-1800

Live Steamers, International Brotherhood of
26062 Todd Ln   Los Altos Hills CA 94022
Ph: 650-948-8555

Livebearer Association, American   www.livebearers.org
5 Zerbe St   Cressona PA 17929
Ph: 570-385-0573 ▪ Fx: 570-385-2781

Liver Diseases, American Association for the Study of   www.aasld.org
1729 King St Suite 200   Alexandria VA 22314
Ph: 703-299-9766 ▪ Fx: 703-299-9622

Liver Foundation, American   www.liverfoundation.org
75 Maiden Ln Suite 603   New York NY 10038
Ph: 212-668-1000 ▪ Fx: 212-483-8179 ▪ TF: 800-465-4837

Liver Transplantation Society, International   www.ilts.org
17000 Commerce Pkwy Suite C   Mount Laurel NJ 08054
Ph: 856-439-0500 ▪ Fx: 856-439-0525

Livestock Appraisers, International Society of   www.amagappraisers.com/livestok.htm
1126 Eastland Dr N Suite 100 PO Box 186   Twin Falls ID
  83303
Ph: 208-733-2323 ▪ Fx: 208-733-2326 ▪ TF: 800-488-7570

Livestock Association, United Producers   www.uproducers.com
210 Landmark Dr Suite D   Normal IL 61761
Ph: 309-888-9907

Livestock Breeds Conservancy, American   www.albc-usa.org
PO Box 477   Pittsboro NC 27312
Ph: 919-542-5704 ▪ Fx: 919-545-0022

Livestock Council, National Pedigreed   nplc.net
177 Palermo Pl   The Villages FL 32159
Ph: 352-259-6005

Livestock Identification Association, International
4701 Marion St Suite 201   Denver CO 80216
Ph: 303-294-0895 ▪ Fx: 303-294-0918

Livestock Marketing Association   www.lmaweb.com
10510 NW Ambassador Dr   Kansas City MO 64153
Ph: 816-891-0502 ▪ Fx: 816-891-7926 ▪ TF: 800-821-2048

Livestock Marketing Association, Producers   www.producerslivestock.com
PO Box 540477   North Salt Lake UT 84054
Ph: 801-936-2424

Livestock Producers Association, National   www.nlpa.org
660 Southpoint Ct Suite 314   Colorado Springs CO 80906
Ph: 719-538-8843 ▪ Fx: 719-538-8847 ▪ TF: 800-237-7193

Livestock Publications Council   www.livestockpublications.com
910 Currie St   Fort Worth TX 76107
Ph: 817-336-1130 ▪ Fx: 817-232-4820

(Livestock) United Producers Inc www.uproducers.com
5909 Cleveland Ave   Columbus OH 43231
Ph: 614-890-6666 ▪ Fx: 614-890-4776 ▪ TF: 800-456-3276

Living Bank www.livingbank.org
PO Box 6725   Houston TX 77625
Ph: 713-961-9431 ▪ Fx: 713-961-0979 ▪ TF: 800-528-2971

Living Classrooms Foundation www.livingclassrooms.org
802 S Caroline St   Baltimore MD 21230
Ph: 410-396-3453 ▪ Fx: 410-396-3393

Living/Dying Project www.livingdying.org
PO Box 357   Fairfax CA 94978
Ph: 415-456-3915

Living History Farm & Agricultural Museums, Association for www.alhfam.org
8774 Rt 45 NW   North Bloomfield OH 44450
Ph: 440-685-4410

Llama Association of North America www.llamainfo.org
1800 S Obenchain Rd   Eagle Point OR 97524
Ph: 541-830-5262

LLEGO - National Latina/o Lesbian Gay Bisexual & Transgender www.llego.org
Organization   1420 K St NW Suite 400   Washington DC
20005
Ph: 202-408-5380 ▪ Fx: 202-408-8478 ▪ TF: 888-633-8320

Lloyd Shaw Foundation www.lloydshaw.org
1620 Los Alamos SW   Albuquerque NM 87104
Ph: 505-247-3921

Loan Association, Jewish Free www.jfla.org
6505 Wilshire Blvd Suite 715   Los Angeles CA 90048
Ph: 323-761-8830 ▪ Fx: 323-761-8841

Loan Programs, National Council of Higher Education www.nchelp.org
1100 Connecticut Ave NW 12th Fl   Washington DC 20036
Ph: 202-822-2106 ▪ Fx: 202-822-2142

(Lobbying) Common Cause www.commoncause.org
1250 Connecticut Ave NW Suite 600   Washington DC 20036
Ph: 202-833-1200 ▪ Fx: 202-659-3716 ▪ TF: 800-926-1064

Lobbyists, American League of www.alldc.org
PO Box 30005   Alexandria VA 22310
Ph: 703-960-3011 ▪ Fx: 703-960-4070

Lobstermen's Association, Atlantic Offshore www.offshorelobster.org
114 Adams Rd   Candia NH 03034
Ph: 603-483-3030 ▪ Fx: 603-483-4862

Lobstermen's Association, Maine www.mainelobstermen.org
1 High St Suite 5   Kennebunk ME 04043
Ph: 207-985-4544 ▪ Fx: 207-985-8099

Local Air Pollution Control Officials, Association of www.cleanairworld.org
444 N Capitol St NW Suite 307   Washington DC 20001
Ph: 202-624-7864 ▪ Fx: 202-624-7863

Local Boards of Health, National Association of www.nalboh.org
1840 E Gypsy Lane Rd   Bowling Green OH 43402
Ph: 419-353-7714 ▪ Fx: 419-352-6278

Local Elected Officials, National Black Caucus of www.nbc-leo.org
1301 Pennsylvania Ave NW Suite 550   Washington DC 20004
Ph: 202-626-3000 ▪ Fx: 202-626-3043

Local Environmental Health Administrators, National depts.washington.edu/clehaweb
Conference of   Univ of Washington Dept of Environmental
Health CB 357234   Seattle WA 98195
Ph: 206-616-2097 ▪ Fx: 206-616-8123

Local Government, Academy for State &
444 N Capitol St NW Suite 345   Washington DC 20001
Ph: 202-434-4850 ▪ Fx: 202-434-4851

Local Government Auditors, National Association of www.nalga.org
2401 Regency Rd Suite 302   Lexington KY 40503
Ph: 859-276-0686

Local Government Environmental Professionals, National www.nalgep.org/
Association of   1333 New Hampshire Ave NW Suite
1100   Washington DC 20036
Ph: 202-638-6254 ▪ Fx: 202-393-2866

Local Initiatives Support Corp www.liscnet.org
733 3rd Ave 8th Fl   New York NY 10017
Ph: 212-455-9800 ▪ Fx: 212-682-5929

Local Self-Reliance, Institute for www.ilsr.org
927 15th St NW 4th Fl   Washington DC 20005
Ph: 202-898-1610 ▪ Fx: 202-898-1612

Local Telecommunications Services, Association for www.alts.org
888 17th St NW 12th Fl   Washington DC 20006
Ph: 202-969-2587 ▪ Fx: 202-969-2581

Locknut Manufacturers Association, Aircraft www.almanet.org
994 Old Eagle School Rd Suite 1019   Wayne PA 19087
Ph: 610-971-4850 ▪ Fx: 610-971-4859

Locks of Love www.locksoflove.org
2925 10th Ave N Suite 102   Lake Worth FL 33461
Ph: 561-963-1677 ▪ Fx: 561-963-9914 ▪ TF: 888-896-1588

Locksmiths of America, Associated aloa.org
3003 Live Oak St   Dallas TX 75204
Ph: 214-827-1701 ▪ Fx: 214-827-1810 ▪ TF: 800-532-2562

Locksmiths' Association, Institutional www.ilanational.org
PO Box 4188   Trenton NJ 08610
Ph: 866-745-5625

Locomotive Engineers & Trainmen, Brotherhood of www.ble.org
1370 Ontario St Mezzanine Level   Cleveland OH 44113
Ph: 216-241-2630 ▪ Fx: 216-241-6516

Locomotive Historical Society Inc, Railway & www.rrhistorical-2.com/rlhs
1610 N Vinton Rd   Anthony NM 88021
Ph: 505-882-5485

Log Cabin Republicans www.lcr.org
1607 17th St NW   Washington DC 20009
Ph: 202-347-5306 ▪ Fx: 202-347-5224

Log Home Builder's Association of North America www.loghomebuilders.org
22203 State Rt 203   Monroe WA 98272
Ph: 360-794-4469

Log Homes Council www.loghomes.org
1201 W 15th St NW   Washington DC 20005
Ph: 202-266-8577 ▪ Fx: 202-266-8141 ▪ TF: 800-368-5242

Logging Congress, Pacific www.pacificloggingcongress.com
20816 SE 22nd St PO Box 1281   Maple Valley WA 98038
Ph: 425-413-2808 ▪ Fx: 425-413-1359

Logic, Association for Symbolic www.aslonline.org
Vassar College PO Box 742   Poughkeepsie NY 12604
Ph: 845-437-7080 ▪ Fx: 845-437-7830

Logic & Critical Thinking, Association for Informal ailact.mcmaster.ca

Logical Language Group www.lojban.org
2904 Beau Ln   Fairfax VA 22031
Ph: 703-385-0273

Logistics, American Society of Transportation & www.astl.org
1700 N Moore St Suite 1900   Arlington VA 22209
Ph: 703-524-5011 ▪ Fx: 703-524-5017

Logistics Association, American www.ala-national.org
1133 15th St NW Suite 640   Washington DC 20005
Ph: 202-466-2520 ▪ Fx: 202-296-4419

Logistics Association, International Warehouse www.iwla.com
2800 River Rd Suite 260   Des Plaines IL 60018
Ph: 847-813-4699 ▪ Fx: 847-813-0115

Logistics Engineers, National Institute of Packaging Handling & www.niphle.com
6902 Lyle St   Lanham MD 20706
Ph: 301-459-9105 ▪ Fx: 301-459-4925

Logistics Management, Council of www.clm1.org
2805 Butterfield Rd Suite 200   Oak Brook IL 60523
Ph: 630-574-0985 ▪ Fx: 630-574-0989

Logistics Organization, World Food www.wflo.org
1500 King St Suite 201   Alexandria VA 22314
Ph: 703-373-4300 ▪ Fx: 703-373-4301

Logistics & Policy, Association for Transportation Law www.atllp.com
3 Church Cir PMB 250   Annapolis MD 21401
Ph: 410-267-0023 ▪ Fx: 410-267-7546

Logistics, SOLE - International Society of www.sole.org
8100 Professional Pl Suite 111   Hyattsville MD 20785
Ph: 301-459-8446 ▪ Fx: 301-459-1522

Logoi www.logoi.org
14540 SW 136th St Suite 200   Miami FL 33186
Ph: 305-232-5880

Lois Pope LIFE Foundation www.life-edu.org
6274 Linton Blvd Suite 103   Delray Beach FL 33484
Ph: 561-865-0955 ▪ Fx: 561-865-0938

LOMA www.loma.org
2300 Windy Ridge Pkwy Suite 600   Atlanta GA 30339
Ph: 770-984-6432 ▪ Fx: 770-984-6420 ▪ TF: 800-275-5662

London Jack Foundation Inc jacklondonfdn.org
14300 Arnold Dr   Glen Ellen CA 95442
Ph: 707-996-2888 ▪ Fx: 707-996-4107

London Library Inc, International Friends of the
515 Madison Ave Suite 3702   New York NY 10022
Ph: 212-644-4858 ▪ Fx: 212-644-4859

Loners on Wheels www.lonersonwheels.com
PO Box 1060-WB   Cape Girardeau MO 63702
Ph: 888-569-4478 ▪ Fx: 573-651-8601

Long Term Care Administrators, National Association of Boards www.nabweb.org
of Examiners of   1444 'I' St NW Suite 700   Washington DC
20005
Ph: 202-712-9040 ▪ Fx: 202-216-9646

(Long-Term Care) Eden Alternative www.edenalt.com
742 Turnpike Rd   Sherburne NY 13460
Ph: 607-674-5232 ▪ Fx: 607-674-6723

Long Term Care, National Association of Directors of Nursing www.nadona.org
Administration in   10101 Alliance Rd Suite 140   Cincinnati OH
45242
Ph: 513-791-3679 ▪ Fx: 513-791-3699 ▪ TF: 800-222-0539

Long Term Care, National Association for the Support of www.nasl.org
1321 Duke St Suite 304   Alexandria VA 22314
Ph: 703-549-8500 ▪ Fx: 703-549-8342

Long-Term Care, National Institute on Community-Based www.ncoa.org
c/o National Council on the Aging 300 D St SW Suite
801   Washington DC 20024
Ph: 202-479-1200 ▪ Fx: 202-479-0735

Long Term Hospital Association, Acute www.altha.org
1055 N Fairfax Suite 201   Alexandria VA 22314
Ph: 703-299-5571 ▪ Fx: 703-299-5574

Longfellow Society www.dlstewart.com/longfellow
PO Box 138   Sherborn MA 01770
Ph: 508-653-1111 ▪ Fx: 508-655-7000

Longhorn Breeders Association of America, Texas www.tlbaa.org
2315 N Main St Suite 402   Fort Worth TX 76106
Ph: 817-625-6241 ▪ Fx: 817-625-1388

Longrifle Collectors, Association of Ohio
23003 State Rt 339   Beverly OH 45715
Ph: 740-984-4896

Longshore & Warehouse Union, International www.ilwu.org
1188 Franklin St 4th Fl   San Francisco CA 94109
Ph: 415-775-0533 ▪ Fx: 415-775-1302

Longshoremen's Association, International www.ila2000.org
17 Battery Pl Rm 930   New York NY 10004
Ph: 212-425-1200 ▪ Fx: 212-425-2928

Longwave Club of America www.lwca.org
45 Wildflower Rd   Levittown PA 19057
Ph: 215-945-0543

Longwood Foundation Inc
100 W 10th St Suite 1109   Wilmington DE 19801
Ph: 302-654-2477 ▪ Fx: 302-654-2323

LonMark Interoperability Association www.lonmark.org
550 Meridian Ave   San Jose CA 95126
Ph: 408-938-5266 ▪ Fx: 408-790-3838

Loon Fund, North American   www.loonfund.org

Lop Rabbit Club of America   www.lrca.net
PO Box 8367   Fremont CA 94537
Ph: 510-793-4977

Loran Association, International   www.loran.org
741 Cathedral Pointe Ln   Santa Barbara CA 93111
Ph: 805-967-8649 ▪ Fx: 805-967-8471

Lord Ruthven Assembly   ebbs.english.vt.edu/LRA/lra.html

Los Ninos   www.losninosinternational.org
287 G St   Chula Vista CA 91910
Ph: 619-426-9110 ▪ Fx: 619-426-6664 ▪ TF: 866-567-6466

Loss Control Association, Insurance   www.insurancelosscontrol.org

Loss Data Institute, Highway   www.carsafety.org
1005 N Glebe Rd Suite 800   Arlington VA 22201
Ph: 703-247-1600 ▪ Fx: 703-247-1595

Loss & Healing, William Wendt Center for   www.wendtcenter.org
730 11th St NW   Washington DC 20001
Ph: 202-624-0010 ▪ Fx: 202-624-0062

Loss Prevention Management Council, Safety &   www.truckline.com/cc/councils/slpmc
American Trucking Assns 2200 Mill Rd   Alexandria VA 22314
Ph: 703-838-1919 ▪ Fx: 703-838-8468

Lotteries, North American Association of State & Provincial   www.naspl.org
2775 Bishop Rd Suite B   Willoughby Hills OH 44092
Ph: 216-241-2310 ▪ Fx: 216-241-4350

(Lou Gehrig's Disease) ALS Association   www.alsa.org
27001 Agoura Rd Suite 150   Calabasas Hills CA 91301
Ph: 818-880-9007 ▪ Fx: 818-880-9006 ▪ TF: 800-782-4747

Loudspeaker Association, ALMA - International   www.almainternational.org
191 Clarksville Rd   Princeton Junction NJ 08550
Ph: 609-799-8440 ▪ Fx: 609-799-7032

Louisa May Alcott Memorial Association   www.louisamayalcott.org
PO Box 343   Concord MA 01742
Ph: 978-369-4118 ▪ Fx: 978-369-1367

Love in Action   www.loveinaction.org
PO Box 171444   Memphis TN 38187
Ph: 901-751-8468 ▪ Fx: 901-751-1927

Low Income Housing Coalition, National   www.nlihc.org
1012 14th St NW Suite 610   Washington DC 20005
Ph: 202-662-1530 ▪ Fx: 202-393-1973

Lowe Syndrome Association   www.lowesyndrome.org
222 Lincoln St   West Lafayette IN 47906
Ph: 765-743-3634

Lowell Celebrates Kerouac! Inc   ecommunity.uml.edu/lck
PO Box 1111   Lowell MA 01853
Ph: 978-970-0755 ▪ TF: 877-537-6822

Loyal Christian Benefit Association   www.lcba.com
PO Box 13005   Erie PA 16514
Ph: 814-453-4331 ▪ Fx: 814-453-3211 ▪ TF: 800-234-5222

Loyal Christian Benefit Association OSA Div   www.lcba.com/aboutosa.htm
PO Box 13005   Erie PA 16514
Ph: 814-453-4331 ▪ Fx: 814-453-3211 ▪ TF: 800-234-5222

Loyal Order of Moose   www.mooseintl.org
Rt 31   Mooseheart IL 60539
Ph: 630-859-2000 ▪ Fx: 630-859-6618

LTL Carriers Association, Distribution &   www.dltlca.com
2200 Mill Rd Suite 600   Alexandria VA 22314
Ph: 703-838-1806 ▪ Fx: 703-684-8143

Lubavitch Movement   www.lubavitch.com
770 Eastern Pkwy   Brooklyn NY 11213
Ph: 718-774-4000 ▪ Fx: 718-774-2718

Lubavitch Women's Organization
325 Kingston Ave   Brooklyn NY 11213
Ph: 718-493-1773 ▪ Fx: 718-604-0594

Lubavitch Youth Organization   www.lubavitch.qpg.com
305 Kingston Ave   Brooklyn NY 11213
Ph: 718-953-1000 ▪ Fx: 718-493-1000

Lubricant Manufacturers Association, Independent   www.ilma.org
651 S Washington St   Alexandria VA 22314
Ph: 703-684-5574 ▪ Fx: 703-836-8503

Lubricating Grease Institute, National   www.nlgi.org
4635 Wyandotte St   Kansas City MO 64112
Ph: 816-931-9480 ▪ Fx: 816-753-5026

Lubrication Engineers, Society of Tribologists &   www.stle.org
840 Busse Hwy   Park Ridge IL 60068
Ph: 847-825-5536 ▪ Fx: 847-825-1456

Lucas George Educational Foundation   www.glef.org
PO Box 3494   San Rafael CA 94912
Ph: 415-507-0399 ▪ Fx: 415-507-0499

Luce Henry Foundation Inc   www.hluce.org
111 W 50th St Suite 4601   New York NY 10020
Ph: 212-489-7700 ▪ Fx: 212-581-9541

Luge Association, US   www.usaluge.org
35 Church St   Lake Placid NY 12946
Ph: 518-523-2071 ▪ Fx: 518-523-4106

Luggage Dealers Association, American   www.luggagedealers.com
1114 State St   Santa Barbara CA 93101
Ph: 805-966-6909 ▪ Fx: 805-966-5710

Luggage Dealers Association, National   www.nlda.com
1817 Elmdale Ave   Glenview IL 60025
Ph: 847-998-6869 ▪ Fx: 847-998-6884

Luggage Repair Association, International
1425 SOM Center Rd   Mayfield Heights OH 44124
Ph: 440-442-5910 ▪ Fx: 440-442-5325

Luis Palau Evangelistic Association   www.palau.org
PO Box 50   Portland OR 97207
Ph: 503-614-1500 ▪ Fx: 503-614-1599

Lum & Abner Society, National   home.inu.net/stemple
81 Sharon Blvd   Dora AL 35062
Ph: 205-674-0101 ▪ Fx: 205-674-0190

Lumber Association, National Hardwood   www.natlhardwood.org
6830 Raleigh-LaGrange Rd   Memphis TN 38184
Ph: 901-377-1818 ▪ Fx: 901-382-6419 ▪ TF: 800-933-0318

Lumber Association, North American Wholesale   www.lumber.org
3601 Algonquin Rd Suite 400   Rolling Meadows IL 60008
Ph: 847-870-7470 ▪ Fx: 847-870-0201 ▪ TF: 800-527-8258

Lumber Association, Northeastern Retail   www.nrla.org
585 N Greenbush Rd   Rensselaer NY 12144
Ph: 518-286-1010 ▪ Fx: 518-286-1755 ▪ TF: 800-292-6752

Lumber Association, Western Red Cedar   www.wrcla.org
1501-700 W Pender St   Vancouver BC V6C1G8
Ph: 604-684-0266 ▪ Fx: 604-687-4930

Lumber & Building Material Dealers Association, National   www.dealer.org
40 Ivy St SE   Washington DC 20003
Ph: 202-547-2230 ▪ Fx: 202-547-7640 ▪ TF: 800-634-8645

Lumber Imports, Coalition for Fair   www.fairlumbercoalition.org
1775 Pennsylvania Ave NW Suite 600   Washington DC 20006
Ph: 202-862-4505 ▪ Fx: 202-862-1093

Lumber Manufacturers Association, Northeastern   www.nelma.org
272 Tuttle Rd PO Box 87A   Cumberland ME 04021
Ph: 207-829-6901 ▪ Fx: 207-829-4293

Lumber Manufacturers Association, Southeastern   www.slma.org
671 Forest Pkwy   Forest Park GA 30297
Ph: 404-361-1445 ▪ Fx: 404-361-5963

Lumber Standard Committee Inc, American   www.alsc.org
PO Box 210   Germantown MD 20875
Ph: 301-972-1700 ▪ Fx: 301-540-8004

Lumina Foundation for Education   www.luminafoundation.org
30 S Meridian St Suite 700   Indianapolis IN 46204
Ph: 317-951-5704 ▪ Fx: 317-951-5063 ▪ TF: 800-834-5756

Luminescence Microscopy & Spectroscopy, Society for   www.ruf.rice.edu/~jinnys/slms/SLMS.html

Lung Association, American   www.lungusa.org
61 Broadway 6th Fl   New York NY 10006
Ph: 212-315-8700 ▪ Fx: 212-315-8872 ▪ TF: 800-586-4872

Lung Transplantation, International Society for Heart &   www.ishlt.org
14673 Midway Rd Suite 200   Addison TX 75001
Ph: 972-490-9495 ▪ Fx: 972-490-9499

Lupus Foundation of America Inc   www.lupus.org
1300 Piccard Dr Suite 200   Rockville MD 20850
Ph: 301-670-9292 ▪ Fx: 301-670-9486 ▪ TF: 800-558-0121

Lupus Research, Alliance for   www.lupusresearch.org
28 W 44th St Suite 1217   New York NY 10036
Ph: 212-218-2840 ▪ Fx: 212-218-2848

Luso-American Education Foundation   www.luso-american.org/laef
PO Box 2967   Dublin CA 94568
Ph: 925-828-3883

Luso-American Life Insurance Society   www.luso-american.org
7080 Donlon Way   Dublin CA 94568
Ph: 925-828-4884 ▪ Fx: 925-828-4554 ▪ TF: 877-525-5876

Lute Society of America   www.cs.dartmouth.edu/~lsa/
PO Box 1328   Lexington VA 24450
Ph: 540-463-5812 ▪ Fx: 540-463-8073

(Lutheran) Augustana Historical Society   www.augustana.edu/Historical
Augustana College 639 38th St   Rock Island IL 61201
Ph: 309-794-7166 ▪ Fx: 309-794-7443

Lutheran Bible Translators   www.gospelcom.net/lbt
303 N Lake St PO Box 2050   Aurora IL 60507
Ph: 630-897-0660 ▪ Fx: 630-897-3567 ▪ TF: 800-532-4253

Lutheran Braille Workers   www.lbwinc.org
13471 California St   Yucaipa CA 92399
Ph: 909-795-8977 ▪ Fx: 909-795-8970

Lutheran Church in America, Evangelical   www.elca.org
8765 W Higgins Rd   Chicago IL 60631
Ph: 773-380-2700 ▪ Fx: 773-380-1465 ▪ TF: 800-638-3522

Lutheran Church Library Association   www.lclahq.org
216 W Myrtle St   Stillwater MN 55082
Ph: 651-430-0770

Lutheran Church Missouri Synod   www.lcms.org
1333 S Kirkwood Rd   Saint Louis MO 63122
Ph: 314-965-9000 ▪ Fx: 888-526-7329 ▪ TF: 888-843-5267

Lutheran Deaconess Association   www.valpo.edu/lda
1304 La Porte Ave   Valparaiso IN 46383
Ph: 219-464-6925 ▪ Fx: 219-464-6928

Lutheran Disaster Response   www.ldr.org
8765 W Higgins Rd   Chicago IL 60631
Ph: 773-380-2822 ▪ Fx: 773-380-2493 ▪ TF: 800-638-3522

Lutheran Education Association   www.lea.org
7400 Augusta St   River Forest IL 60305
Ph: 708-209-3343 ▪ Fx: 708-209-3458

Lutheran Educational Conference of North America   www.lutherancolleges.org
110 S Phillips Ave Suite 306   Sioux Falls SD 57104
Ph: 605-782-4003 ▪ Fx: 605-782-4008

Lutheran Fraternities of America   www.gbu.org/lutheran.htm
45163 Cass Ave   Utica MI 48317
Ph: 586-991-0166 ▪ Fx: 586-991-0601 ▪ TF: 800-400-6955

Lutheran Fraternity, Beta Sigma Psi National   www.betasigmapsi.org
2408 Lebanon Ave   Belleville IL 62221
Ph: 618-235-0014 ▪ Fx: 618-235-0051

Lutheran Girl Pioneers   www.lgp.org
1611 Caledonia St   La Crosse WI 54603
Ph: 608-781-5232 ▪ Fx: 608-781-5233

Lutheran Historical Conference   www.luthhist.org
Concordia Univ 7400 Augusta St   River Forest IL 60305
Ph: 708-771-6640

Lutheran Homes & Services Inc, Bethesda   www.blhs.org
600 Hoffman Dr   Watertown WI 53094
Ph: 920-261-3050 ▪ Fx: 920-261-8441 ▪ TF: 800-369-4636

Lutheran Human Relations Association of America   lhra.org
5233 N 52st Blvd   Milwaukee WI 53218
Ph: 414-536-0585 ▪ Fx: 414-536-0690

Lutheran Immigration & Refugee Service   www.lirs.org
700 Light St   Baltimore MD 21230
Ph: 410-230-2700 ▪ Fx: 410-230-2890

Lutheran Laymen's League, International   www.lhm.org
660 Mason Ridge Ctr Dr   Saint Louis MO 63141
Ph: 314-317-4100 ▪ TF: 800-944-3450

Lutheran Men in Mission   www.elca.org/lmm
8765 W Higgins Rd   Chicago IL 60631
Ph: 773-380-2566 ▪ Fx: 773-380-2588 ▪ TF: 800-638-3522

Lutheran Outdoors Ministry Association, National   www.nloma.org
2016 Camp Lone Star Rd   La Grange TX 78945
Ph: 979-247-4128 ▪ Fx: 979-247-4120

Lutheran Peace Fellowship   www.lutheranpeace.org
1710 11th Ave   Seattle WA 98122
Ph: 206-720-0313

Lutheran Publicity Bureau, American   www.alpb.org
PO Box 327   Delhi NY 13753
Ph: 607-746-7511

Lutheran Services in America   www.lutheranservices.org
700 Light St   Baltimore MD 21230
Ph: 410-230-2702 ▪ Fx: 410-230-2710 ▪ TF: 800-664-3848

Lutheran Society, United
PO Box 947   Ligonier PA 15658
Ph: 724-238-9505 ▪ Fx: 724-238-9506 ▪ TF: 800-235-0857

Lutheran Student Movement USA   www.lsm-usa.org
8765 W Higgins Rd   Chicago IL 60631
Ph: 773-380-2852 ▪ Fx: 773-380-2750 ▪ TF: 800-638-3522

Lutheran Synod, Wisconsin Evangelical   www.wels.net
2929 N Mayfair Rd   Milwaukee WI 53222
Ph: 414-256-3888 ▪ Fx: 414-256-3899

Lutheran Volunteer Corps   www.lvchome.org
1226 Vermont Ave NW   Washington DC 20005
Ph: 202-387-3222 ▪ Fx: 202-667-0037

Lutheran Women's Missionary League   www.lwml.org
PO Box 411993   Saint Louis MO 63141
Ph: 314-268-1531 ▪ Fx: 314-268-1532 ▪ TF: 800-252-5965

Lutheran World Relief   www.lwr.org
700 Light St   Baltimore MD 21230
Ph: 410-230-2700 ▪ Fx: 410-230-2882

Lutherans Concerned/North America   www.lcna.org

Lutherans for Life   www.lutheransforlife.org
1120 S 'G' Ave   Nevada IA 50201
Ph: 515-382-2077 ▪ Fx: 515-382-3020 ▪ TF: 888-364-5433

Luthiers, Guild of American   www.luth.org
8222 South Park Ave   Tacoma WA 98408
Ph: 253-472-7853

Luxembourg-American Chamber of Commerce   www.luxembourgbusiness.org
17 Beekman Pl   New York NY 10022
Ph: 212-888-6701 ▪ Fx: 212-935-5896

Luxury Hotels, Associated   www.alhi.com
1000 Connecticut Ave NW Suite 603   Washington DC 20036
Ph: 202-887-7020 ▪ Fx: 202-887-0085

Lyme Disease Foundation Inc   www.lyme.org
1 Financial Plaza 18th Fl   Hartford CT 06103
Ph: 860-525-2000 ▪ Fx: 860-525-8425 ▪ TF: 800-886-5963

Lyme Disease Foundation Inc, American   www.aldf.com
293 Rt 100   Somers NY 10589
Ph: 914-277-6970 ▪ Fx: 914-277-6974 ▪ TF: 800-876-5963

(Lymphangioleiomyomatosis) LAM Foundation   lam.uc.edu
10105 Beacon Hills Dr   Cincinnati OH 45241
Ph: 513-777-6889 ▪ Fx: 513-777-4109

Lymphoma Research Foundation   www.lymphoma.org
8800 Venice Blvd Suite 207   Los Angeles CA 90034
Ph: 310-204-7040 ▪ Fx: 310-204-7043 ▪ TF: 800-500-9976

Lymphoma Society, Leukemia &   www.leukemia-lymphoma.org
475 Park Ave S 8th Fl   New York NY 10016
Ph: 212-448-9206 ▪ Fx: 212-448-9214 ▪ TF: 800-955-4572

Lynde & Harry Bradley Foundation Inc   www.bradleyfdn.org
1241 N Franklin Pl   Milwaukee WI 53202
Ph: 414-291-9915 ▪ Fx: 414-291-9991

Lyndhurst Foundation   www.lyndhurstfoundation.org
517 E 5th St   Chattanooga TN 37403
Ph: 423-756-0767 ▪ Fx: 423-756-0770

Lyricists, Society of Composers &   www.thescl.com
400 S Beverly Dr Suite 214   Beverly Hills CA 90212
Ph: 310-281-2812 ▪ Fx: 310-284-4861

M

M&A Partners, International Network of   www.imap.com
525 SW 5th St Suite A   Des Moines IA 50309
Ph: 515-282-8192 ▪ Fx: 515-282-9117

Mabee JE & LE Foundation Inc   www.mabeefoundation.com
401 S Boston Ave 30th Fl   Tulsa OK 74103
Ph: 918-584-4286

MacArthur John D & Catherine T Foundation   www.macfound.org
140 S Dearborn St Suite 1100   Chicago IL 60603
Ph: 312-726-8000 ▪ Fx: 312-920-6284 ▪ TF: 800-662-8004

Maccabi USA/Sports for Israel   www.maccabiusa.com
1926 Arch St Suite 4R   Philadelphia PA 19103
Ph: 215-561-6900 ▪ Fx: 215-561-5470

Macedonian Outreach   www.macedonianoutreach.org
PO Box 398   Danville CA 94526
Ph: 925-820-4107

Machine & Furniture Workers, International Union of Electronic Electrical Salaried   www.iue-cwa.org
1275 K St NW Suite 600   Washington DC 20005
Ph: 202-513-6300 ▪ Fx: 202-513-6357

Machine Knife Association   www.mka.org
30200 Detroit Rd   Cleveland OH 44145
Ph: 440-899-0010 ▪ Fx: 440-892-1404

Machine Printers & Engravers Association of the US
690 Warren Ave   Providence RI 02914
Ph: 401-438-5849

Machine Tool Distributors' Association, American   www.amtda.org
1445 Research Blvd Suite 450   Rockville MD 20850
Ph: 301-738-1200 ▪ Fx: 301-738-9499 ▪ TF: 800-878-2683

Machine Workers of America, United Electrical Radio &   www.ranknfile-ue.org
1 Gateway Ctr Suite 1400   Pittsburgh PA 15222
Ph: 412-471-8919 ▪ Fx: 412-471-8999

Machinery Dealers National Association   www.mdna.org
315 S Patrick St   Alexandria VA 22314
Ph: 703-836-9300 ▪ Fx: 703-836-9303 ▪ TF: 800-872-7807

Machinery & Equipment Appraisers, Association of   www.amea.org
315 S Patrick St   Alexandria VA 22314
Ph: 703-836-7900 ▪ Fx: 703-836-9303 ▪ TF: 800-537-8629

Machining Association, International Special Tooling &
9300 Livingston Rd   Fort Washington MD 20744
Ph: 301-248-6200 ▪ Fx: 301-248-7104 ▪ TF: 800-248-6862

Machining Association, National Tooling &   www.ntma.org
9300 Livingston Rd   Fort Washington MD 20744
Ph: 301-248-6200 ▪ Fx: 301-248-7104 ▪ TF: 800-248-6862

Machining Institute, Photo-Chemical   www.pcmi.org
38 Strawberry Ln PO Box 739   East Dennis MA 02641
Ph: 508-385-0085 ▪ Fx: 508-385-0086

Machinists & Aerospace Workers, International Association of   www.iamaw.org
9000 Machinists Pl   Upper Marlboro MD 20772
Ph: 301-967-4500 ▪ Fx: 301-967-4588

Machinists Non-Partisan Political League   www.goiam.org/politics.asp?n=87
9000 Machinists Pl   Upper Marlboro MD 20772
Ph: 301-967-4500

Macro Society   www.macrosociety.com

Macrocosm USA Inc   www.macronet.org
PO Box 185   Cambria CA 93428
Ph: 805-927-2515

Macula Foundation Inc   www.macula.org
210 E 64th St 8th Fl   New York NY 10021
Ph: 212-605-3777 ▪ Fx: 212-605-3795

Macular Diseases Inc, Association for   www.macula.org/association/about.html
210 E 64th St 8th Fl   New York NY 10021
Ph: 212-605-3719 ▪ Fx: 212-628-0695

Madre Inc   www.madre.org
121 W 27th St Rm 301   New York NY 10001
Ph: 212-627-0444 ▪ Fx: 212-675-3704

Magazine Association, City & Regional   www.citymag.org
4929 Wilshire Blvd Suite 428   Los Angeles CA 90010
Ph: 323-937-5514 ▪ Fx: 323-937-0959

Magazine Book & Film Carriers, National   www.nmbfc.com
100 Daingerfield Rd   Alexandria VA 22314
Ph: 703-837-1070 ▪ Fx: 703-837-1072

Magazine Editors, American Society of   www.magazine.org/Editorial
810 7th Ave   New York NY 10022
Ph: 212-872-3737 ▪ Fx: 212-906-0128

Magazine Publishers of America   www.magazine.org
810 7th Ave 24th Fl   New York NY 10019
Ph: 212-872-3700 ▪ Fx: 212-888-4217 ▪ TF: 888-567-3228

Magazine Publishers of America PAC
1211 Connecticut Ave NW Suite 610   Washington DC 20036
Ph: 202-296-7277 ▪ Fx: 202-296-0343

Magazines Associated, Engineering College   www.ecmaweb.org
Univ of Minnesota Institute of Technology 1701 University Ave SE   Minneapolis MN 55414
Ph: 612-626-7959

Magazines & Presses, Council of Literary   www.clmp.org
154 Christopher St Suite 3C   New York NY 10014
Ph: 212-741-9110 ▪ Fx: 212-741-9112

Maghrib Studies, American Institute for   www.la.utexas.edu/research/mena/aims
Univ of Arizona Center for Middle Eastern Studies PO Box 210080   Tucson AZ 85721
Ph: 520-626-6498

Magic Collectors' Association
PO Box 511   Glenwood IL 60425
Ph: 708-757-4950

Magic Johnson Foundation Inc   www.magicjohnson.org
9100 Wilshire Blvd East Tower Suite 700   Beverly Hills CA 90212
Ph: 310-246-4400 ▪ Fx: 310-246-1106 ▪ TF: 888-624-4205

Magicians, Fellowship of Christian   www.gospelcom.net/fcm

Magicians, International Brotherhood of   www.magician.org
11155-C South Towne Sq   Saint Louis MO 63123
Ph: 314-845-9200 ▪ Fx: 314-845-9220

Magicians, Society of American   www.magicsam.com
PO Box 510260   Saint Louis MO 63151
Ph: 314-846-5659

Magna Charta, Baronial Order of   www.magnacharta.com

Magnesium Association, International   www.intlmag.org
900 17th St NW Suite 450   Washington DC 20006
Ph: 202-466-6601 ▪ Fx: 202-466-6678

Magnetic Resonance in Medicine, International Society for   www.ismrm.org
2118 Millvia St Suite 201   Berkeley CA 94704
Ph: 510-841-1899 ▪ Fx: 510-841-2340

Magnetic Resonance, Society for Cardiovascular   www.scmr.org
19 Mantua Rd   Mount Royal NJ 08061
Ph: 856-423-8955 ▪ Fx: 856-423-3420

Magnetic Resonance Society, Clinical   www.cmrs.com
4550 Post Oak Pl Suite 342   Houston TX 77027
Ph: 713-623-8336 ▪ Fx: 713-960-0488 ▪ TF: 877-841-2522

Magnetic Resonance, Society of Computed Body Tomography &   www.scbtmr.org
PO Box 1026   Rochester MN 55903
Ph: 507-288-5620 ▪ Fx: 507-288-0014

Magnetics Association, International   www.intl-magnetics.org
8 S Michigan Ave Suite 1000   Chicago IL 60603
Ph: 312-456-5590 ▪ Fx: 312-580-0165

Magnetics Society, IEEE   www.ieeemagnetics.org
IEEE Operations Ctr 445 Hoes Ln   Piscataway NJ 08854
Ph: 732-981-0060 ▪ Fx: 732-981-1721

Magnolia Society   www.magnoliasociety.org
6616 81st St   Cabin John MD 20818
Ph: 301-320-4296

Mahayana Tradition, Foundation for the Preservation of the   www.fpmt.org
PO Box 888   Taos NM 87571
Ph: 505-758-7766 ▪ Fx: 505-758-7765

Maids of Athena   www.ahepa.org/maids
1909 Q St NW Suite 500   Washington DC 20009
Ph: 202-232-6300 ▪ Fx: 202-232-2140

Mail Contractors Association, National Star Route   www.starroutecontractors.org
324 E Capitol St   Washington DC 20003
Ph: 202-543-1661 ▪ Fx: 202-543-8863

Mail Handlers Union, National Postal   www.npmhu.org
1101 Connecticut Ave NW Suite 500   Washington DC 20036
Ph: 202-833-9095 ▪ Fx: 202-833-0008

Mail Order Association, National   www.nmoa.org
2807 Polk St NE   Minneapolis MN 55418
Ph: 612-788-1673 ▪ Fx: 612-788-1147

Mailbox Club Inc   www.mailboxclub.org
404 Eager Rd   Valdosta GA 31602
Ph: 229-244-6812

Mailers, Alliance of Nonprofit   www.nonprofitmailers.org
1211 Connecticut Ave NW Suite 620   Washington DC 20036
Ph: 202-462-5132

Mailing Equipment Dealers, Association of Independent   www.aimedweb.org
949 Winding Brook Ln   Walnut CA 91789
Ph: 909-444-9680 ▪ Fx: 909-594-9743 ▪ TF: 888-750-6245

Mailing & Fulfillment Service Association   www.mfsanet.org
1421 Prince St Suite 410   Alexandria VA 22314
Ph: 703-836-9200 ▪ Fx: 703-548-8204 ▪ TF: 800-333-6272

Mailorder Gardening Association   www.mailordergardening.com
5836 Rockburn Woods Way   Elkridge MD 21075
Ph: 410-540-9830 ▪ Fx: 410-540-9827

Maine-Anjou Association, American   www.maine-anjou.org
204 Marshall Rd PO Box 1100   Platte City MO 64079
Ph: 816-431-9950 ▪ Fx: 816-431-9951

Maine Lobstermen's Association   www.mainelobstermen.org
1 High St Suite 5   Kennebunk ME 04043
Ph: 207-985-4544 ▪ Fx: 207-985-8099

Maintenance Institute, International   www.imionline.org/
PO Box 751896   Houston TX 77275
Ph: 281-481-0869 ▪ Fx: 281-481-8337

Maintenance & Reliability Professionals, Society for   www.smrp.org
PO Box 51787   Knoxville TN 37950
Ph: 865-212-0111 ▪ Fx: 865-558-3060 ▪ TF: 800-950-7354

Maintenance of Way Employees, Brotherhood of   www.bmwe.org
20300 Civic Ctr Dr Suite 320   Southfield MI 48076
Ph: 248-948-1010 ▪ Fx: 248-948-7150

Major Indoor Soccer League   www.misl.net
1175 Post Rd E   Westport CT 06880
Ph: 203-222-4900 ▪ Fx: 203-221-7300 ▪ TF: 866-647-5638

Major League Baseball Players Association   bigleaguers.yahoo.com
12 E 49th St 24th Fl   New York NY 10017
Ph: 212-826-0808 ▪ Fx: 212-752-4378

Major Orchestra Librarians' Association   www.mola-inc.org
c/o National Arts Centre Orchestra PO Box 1534 Stn B   Ottawa
ON K1P5W1
Ph: 613-947-7000 ▪ Fx: 613-947-8623

Major Superiors of Men, Conference of   www.cmsm.org
8808 Cameron St   Silver Spring MD 20910
Ph: 301-588-4030 ▪ Fx: 301-587-4575

Makassed Foundation of America   www.makassed.org
1510 H St NW Suite 301   Washington DC 20005
Ph: 202-783-7979 ▪ Fx: 202-783-7977

Make-A-Wish Foundation of America   www.wish.org
3550 N Central Ave Suite 300   Phoenix AZ 85012
PO Box 279-9474 ▪ Fx: 602-279-0855 ▪ TF: 800-722-9474

Make Today Count
1235 E Cherokee St   Springfield MO 65804
Ph: 417-885-3324 ▪ Fx: 417-888-7426 ▪ TF: 800-432-2273

Malcolm Wiener Center for Social Policy   www.ksg.harvard.edu/socpol
John F Kennedy School of Government Harvard University 79
John F Kennedy St   Cambridge MA 02138
Ph: 617-495-1461 ▪ Fx: 617-496-9053

Male Psychology & Physiology, Society for the Study of
321 Iuka Rd   Montpelier OH 43543
Ph: 419-485-3602

Male Survivor   www.malesurvivor.org
5505 Connecticut Ave NW PMB 103   Washington DC 20015
Ph: 800-738-4181

Males, National Organization to Halt the Abuse & Routine   www.noharmm.org
Mutilation of   PO Box 460795   San Francisco CA 94146
Ph: 415-826-9351

Malignant Hyperthermia Association of the US   www.mhaus.org
11 E State St PO Box 1069   Sherburne NY 13460
Ph: 607-674-7901 ▪ Fx: 607-674-7910

Malinois Club, American Belgian   www.breedclub.org/ABMC.htm
21710 Cove Point Farm Rd   Tilghman MD 21671
Ph: 410-886-2232

Malta, Ancient & Illustrious Order Knights of
2632 Skylark Dr   Wilmington DE 19808
Ph: 302-996-0800

Maltase Deficiency Association, Acid   www.amda-pompe.org
PO Box 700248   San Antonio TX 78270
Ph: 210-494-6144 ▪ Fx: 210-497-3810

Maltese-American Benevolent Society Inc
1832 Michigan Ave   Detroit MI 48216
Ph: 313-961-8393 ▪ Fx: 313-961-2050

Malting Barley Association, American   www.ambainc.org
740 N Plankinton Ave Suite 830   Milwaukee WI 53203
Ph: 414-272-4640

Mamie Doud Eisenhower Birthplace Foundation Inc   www.booneiowa.com
PO Box 55   Boone IA 50036
Ph: 515-432-1896 ▪ Fx: 515-432-3097

Mammalogists, American Society of   www.mammalsociety.org
810 E 10th St   Lawrence KS 66044
Ph: 785-843-1235 ▪ Fx: 785-843-1274 ▪ TF: 800-627-0629

Man, Research Institute for the Study of   www.rism.org
162 E 78th St   New York NY 10021
Ph: 212-535-8448 ▪ Fx: 212-535-0084

MANA - National Latina Organization   www.hermana.org
1725 K St NW Suite 501   Washington DC 20006
Ph: 202-833-0060 ▪ Fx: 202-496-0588

Managed Behavioral Healthcare Association, American   www.ambha.org
1101 Pennsylvania Ave NW 6th Fl   Washington DC 20004
Ph: 202-756-7726 ▪ Fx: 202-756-7308

Managed Care Administrators, American College of   www.aameda.org
701 Lee St Suite 600   Des Plaines IL 60016
Ph: 847-759-8601 ▪ Fx: 847-759-8602

Managed Care Dentists, Association of   www.amcd.org
1223 Wilshire Blvd Suite 483   Santa Monica CA 90403
Ph: 310-453-3439 ▪ Fx: 310-453-7895 ▪ TF: 800-864-6848

Managed Care Medicine, American College of   www.acmcm.org
4435 Waterfront Dr Suite 101   Glen Allen VA 23060
Ph: 804-527-1906 ▪ Fx: 804-747-5316

Managed Care Nurses, American Association of   www.aamcn.org
4435 Waterfront Dr Suite 101   Glen Allen VA 23060
Ph: 804-527-9698 ▪ Fx: 804-747-5316

Managed Care Nursing, American Board of   www.abmcn.org
4435 Waterfront Dr Suite 101   Glen Allen VA 23060
Ph: 804-527-1905 ▪ Fx: 804-747-5316

Managed Care Pharmacy, Academy of   www.amcp.org
100 N Pitt St Suite 400   Alexandria VA 22314
Ph: 703-683-8416 ▪ Fx: 703-683-8417 ▪ TF: 800-827-2627

Managed Care Physicians, National Association of   www.namcp.com
4435 Waterfront Dr Suite 101 PO Box 4765   Glen Allen VA
23058
Ph: 804-527-1905 ▪ Fx: 804-747-5316 ▪ TF: 800-722-0376

Managed Care Providers, Academy of   www.academymcp.org
1945 Palo Verde Ave Suite 202   Long Beach CA 90815
Ph: 562-682-3559 ▪ Fx: 562-799-3355 ▪ TF: 800-297-2627

Managed Care Inc, Women in   www.wimc.org
4435 Waterfront Dr Suite 101 PO Box 6026   Glen Allen VA
23058
Ph: 804-527-1905 ▪ Fx: 804-747-5316

Managed Funds Association   www.mfainfo.org
2025 M St NW Suite 800   Washington DC 20036
Ph: 202-367-1140 ▪ Fx: 202-367-2140

Management, Academy of   www.aomonline.org
PO Box 3020   Briarcliff Manor NY 10510
Ph: 914-923-2607 ▪ Fx: 914-923-2615

Management Admission Council, Graduate   www.gmac.com
1600 Tyson Blvd Suite 1400   McLean VA 22102
Ph: 703-749-0131 ▪ Fx: 703-749-0169

Management, American Academy of Podiatric Practice   www.aappm.com
707 Turnpike St   North Andover MA 01845
Ph: 978-686-6185 ▪ Fx: 978-685-9410

Management Assistance Group   www.managementassistance.org
1555 Connecticut Ave NW 3rd Fl   Washington DC 20036
Ph: 202-659-1963 ▪ Fx: 202-659-3105

Management, Association of   www.aom-iaom.org
920 S Battlefield Blvd Suite 100   Chesapeake VA 23322
Ph: 757-482-2273 ▪ Fx: 757-482-0325

Management Association, American   www.amanet.org
1601 Broadway   New York NY 10019
Ph: 212-586-8100 ▪ Fx: 212-903-8168 ▪ TF: 800-262-6969

Management Association, Christian   www.christianity.com/cma
PO Box 4090   San Clemente CA 92674
Ph: 949-487-0900 ▪ Fx: 949-487-0927

Management Association, International City/County   www.icma.org
777 N Capitol St NE Suite 500   Washington DC 20002
Ph: 202-289-4262 ▪ Fx: 202-962-3500

Management Association, Latin American
419 New Jersey Ave SE   Washington DC 20003
Ph: 202-546-3803 ▪ Fx: 202-546-3807

Management Association Inc, MRA -   www.mranet.org
N19 W24400 Riverwood Dr   Waukesha WI 53188
Ph: 262-523-9090 ▪ Fx: 262-523-9091 ▪ TF: 800-488-4845

Management Association, National   www.nma1.org
2210 Arbor Blvd   Dayton OH 45439
Ph: 937-294-0421 ▪ Fx: 937-294-2374

Management Association for Private Photogrammetric Surveyors   www.mapps.org/
1760 Reston Pkwy Suite 515   Reston VA 20190
Ph: 703-787-6996 ▪ Fx: 703-787-7550

Management, Association for Women in   www.womens.org
927 15th St NW Suite 1000   Washington DC 20005
Ph: 202-659-6364 ▪ Fx: 202-371-1467

Management Committee of the Retail Food Industry, Joint Labor
3720 Farragut Ave Suite 301   Kensington MD 20895
Ph: 301-942-5400 ▪ Fx: 301-942-5409

Management, Consortium for Graduate Study in   www.cgsm.org
200 S Hanley Rd Suite 1102   Saint Louis MO 63105
Ph: 314-877-5500 ▪ Fx: 314-877-5505 ▪ TF: 888-658-6814

Management Consultants, Association of Internal   www.aimc.org
86 Clarendon Ave   Rutland VT 05777
Ph: 802-438-2882 ▪ Fx: 802-438-9859

Management Consultants USA Inc, Institute of   www.imcusa.org
2025 M St NW Suite 800   Washington DC 20036
Ph: 202-367-1134 ▪ Fx: 202-367-2134 ▪ TF: 800-221-2557

Management Consulting Firms, Association of   www.amcf.org
380 Lexington Ave Suite 1700   New York NY 10168
Ph: 212-551-7887 ▪ Fx: 212-551-7934

Management Effectiveness, Center for   www.cmeinc.org
PO Box 1202   Pacific Palisades CA 90272
Ph: 310-459-6052 ▪ Fx: 310-459-9307 ▪ TF: 888-819-0200

Management Information in Financial Services, Association for   www.amifs.org
3895 Fairfax Ct   Atlanta GA 30339
Ph: 770-444-3557 ▪ Fx: 770-444-9084

Management Information Sciences, Government   www.gmis.org
PO Box 421   Kennesaw GA 30156
Ph: 770-975-0729 ▪ Fx: 770-975-0719 ▪ TF: 800-460-7454

Management Information Systems Group Inc   www.misg.com
10 Laboratory Dr PO Box 13966   Research Triangle Park NC
27709
Ph: 919-549-8700 ▪ Fx: 919-549-8733

Management Professionals, International Association of Career   www.iacmp.org
204 'E' St NE   Washington DC 20002
Ph: 202-547-6377 ▪ Fx: 202-547-6348

Management Sciences, Center for Mathematical   www.kellogg.nwu.edu/research/math
Studies in Economics &   Northwestern University 2001
Sheridan Rd Leverone Hall Rm 580   Evanston IL 60208
Ph: 847-491-3527 ▪ Fx: 847-491-2530

(Management) Sigma Iota Epsilon   sienational.colostate.edu
Colorado State Univ 312 Rockwell Hall   Fort Collins CO 80523
Ph: 970-491-6265 ▪ Fx: 970-491-7200

Management, Society for Advancement of   www.cob.tamucc.edu/sam
Texas A&M Univ Corpus Christi College of Business 6300 Ocean
Dr FC111   Corpus Christi TX 78412
Ph: 361-825-6045 ▪ Fx: 361-825-2725 ▪ TF: 888-827-6077

Management Systems, National Center for Higher Education   www.nchems.org
PO Box 9752   Boulder CO 80301
Ph: 303-497-0301 ▪ Fx: 303-497-0338

Management, Women in   www.wimonline.org
PO Box 9560   Springfield IL 62791
Ph: 877-946-6285 ▪ Fx: 847-683-3751

Managers Association, Federal   www.fedmanagers.org
1641 Prince St   Alexandria VA 22314
Ph: 703-683-8700 ▪ Fx: 703-683-8707

Managers Association, Professional   www.promanager.org
PO Box 77235   Washington DC 20013
Ph: 202-874-1508 ▪ Fx: 202-874-1739

Managers, Institute of Certified Professional   cob.jmu.edu/icpm
James Madison University MSC 5504   Harrisonburg VA 22807
Ph: 540-568-3247 ▪ Fx: 540-801-8650 ▪ TF: 800-568-4120

Managing General Agents, American Association of   www.aamga.org
150 S Warner Rd Suite 156   King of Prussia PA 19406
Ph: 610-225-1999 ▪ Fx: 610-225-1996

Manatee Club, Save the   www.savethemanatee.org
500 N Maitland Ave   Maitland FL 32751
Ph: 407-539-0990 ▪ Fx: 407-539-0871 ▪ TF: 800-432-5646

Mandala Society   www.year2020vision.net/mandala.htm
PO Box 1233   Del Mar CA 92014
Ph: 858-481-7751

Mandatory Minimums, Families Against   www.famm.org
1612 K St NW Suite 700   Washington DC 20006
Ph: 202-822-6700 ▪ Fx: 202-822-6704

Mandibular Orthopedics, International College of Cranio-   tmj-iccmo.org
619 N 35th St Suite 307   Seattle WA 98103
Ph: 206-633-4355 ▪ Fx: 206-633-4352 ▪ TF: 800-446-1763

Manhattan Institute for Policy Research   www.manhattan-institute.org
52 Vanderbilt Ave 2nd Fl   New York NY 10017
Ph: 212-599-7000 ▪ Fx: 212-599-3494

Manhattan Ryegrass Growers Association
PO Box 250   Hubbard OR 97032
Ph: 503-651-2130 ▪ Fx: 503-651-2351

Maniilaq Association   www.maniilaq.org
PO Box 256   Kotzebue AK 99752
Ph: 800-478-3312

ManKind Project   www.mkp.org
PO Box 230   Malone NY 12953
Ph: 800-870-4611

Mann Horace League of the USA   www.unocoe.unomaha.edu/mckay/int.htm

Manpower Demonstration Research Corp   www.mdrc.org
16 E 34th St 19th Fl   New York NY 10016
Ph: 212-532-3200 ▪ Fx: 212-684-0832 ▪ TF: 800-221-3165

Manpower Education Institute   www.manpower-education.org
715 Ladd Rd   Bronx NY 10471
Ph: 718-548-4200 ▪ Fx: 718-548-4202

Manpower Franchise Owners, Association of
1123 N Water St   Milwaukee WI 53202
Ph: 414-276-2651 ▪ Fx: 414-276-7704

Manuel Ponce Society, International   www.imps.org
PO Box 59152   Dallas TX 75229
Ph: 972-293-5360

Manufactured Home Owners, National Foundation of   www.manhousingfoundation.org
62 Hawthorne Cir   Willow Street PA 17584
Ph: 717-284-4520

Manufactured Housing Association for Regulatory Reform
1331 Pennsylvania Ave NW Suite 508   Washington DC 20004
Ph: 202-783-4087 ▪ Fx: 202-783-4075

Manufactured Housing Institute   www.manufacturedhousing.org
2101 Wilson Blvd Suite 610   Arlington VA 22201
Ph: 703-558-0400 ▪ Fx: 703-558-0401 ▪ TF: 800-505-5500

Manufactured Housing Institute PAC   www.mfghome.org/GA_pac.html
2101 Wilson Blvd Suite 610   Arlington VA 22201
Ph: 703-558-0400 ▪ Fx: 703-558-0401 ▪ TF: 800-505-5500

Manufactured Housing Research Alliance   www.mhrahome.org
2109 Broadway Suite 200   New York NY 10023
Ph: 212-496-0900 ▪ Fx: 212-496-5389

Manufacturers' Agents Association for the Foodservice Industry   www.mafsi.org
2814 Spring Rd Suite 211   Atlanta GA 30339
Ph: 770-433-9844 ▪ Fx: 770-433-2450

Manufacturers' Agents National Association   www.manaonline.org
PO Box 3467   Laguna Hills CA 92654
Ph: 949-859-4040 ▪ Fx: 949-855-2973 ▪ TF: 877-626-2776

Manufacturers Alliance/MAPI Inc   www.mapi.net
1525 Wilson Blvd Suite 900   Arlington VA 22209
Ph: 703-841-9000 ▪ Fx: 703-841-9514

Manufacturers Association, Converting Equipment   www.cema-converting.org
2166 Gold Hill Rd   Fort Mill SC 29708
Ph: 803-802-7820 ▪ Fx: 803-802-7821

Manufacturers, Association of Defensive Spray   www.pepperspray.org
917 Locust St Suite 1100   Saint Louis MO 63101
Ph: 314-241-1445 ▪ Fx: 314-241-1449

Manufacturers, Association of Equipment   www.aem.org
111 E Wisconsin Ave Suite 1000   Milwaukee WI 53202
Ph: 414-272-0943 ▪ Fx: 414-272-1170

Manufacturers Association International, Fabricators &   www.fmametalfab.org
833 Featherstone Rd   Rockford IL 61107
Ph: 815-399-8700 ▪ Fx: 815-484-7700 ▪ TF: 800-432-2832

Manufacturers Council, Nail   www.abbies.org/nmc.html
401 N Michigan Ave   Chicago IL 60611
Ph: 312-245-1575 ▪ Fx: 312-245-1080 ▪ TF: 800-868-4265

Manufacturers of Emission Controls Association   meca.org
1660 L St NW Suite 1100   Washington DC 20036
Ph: 202-296-4797 ▪ Fx: 202-331-1388

Manufacturers, National Association of   www.nam.org
1331 Pennsylvania Ave NW Suite 600   Washington DC 20004
Ph: 202-637-3000 ▪ Fx: 202-637-3182 ▪ TF: 800-814-8468

Manufacturers Radio Frequency Advisory Committee   www.mrfac.com
899-A Harrison St SE   Leesburg VA 20175
Ph: 703-669-0320 ▪ Fx: 703-318-9209 ▪ TF: 800-262-9206

Manufacturers Representatives of America   www.mra-reps.com
PO Box 150229   Arlington TX 76015
Ph: 817-561-7272 ▪ Fx: 817-561-7275

Manufacturers' Representatives Association, Agricultural &   www.aimrareps.com
Industrial   7500 Flying Cloud Rd Suite 900   Eden Prairie MN
55344
Ph: 952-253-6230 ▪ Fx: 952-835-4774

Manufacturers'/Representatives Inc, Association of Independent   www.aimr.net
PO Box 3467   Laguna Hills CA 92654
Ph: 949-859-2884 ▪ Fx: 949-855-2973 ▪ TF: 866-729-0975

Manufacturers Representatives Association, International
PO Box 702678   Tulsa OK 74170
Ph: 918-743-5443

Manufacturers Representatives Educational Research Foundation   www.mrerf.org
PO Box 247   Geneva IL 60134
Ph: 630-208-1466 ▪ Fx: 630-208-1475 ▪ TF: 800-346-7373

Manufacturers' Representatives, United Association   www.uamr.com
PO Box 986   Dana Point CA 92629
Ph: 949-240-4966 ▪ Fx: 949-240-7001

Manufacturers Standardization Society of the Valve & Fittings   www.mss-hq.com
Industry Inc   127 Park St NE   Vienna VA 22180
Ph: 703-281-6613 ▪ Fx: 703-281-6671

Manufacturing Associations, Council of   www.nam.org/ac
National Assn of Manufacturers 1331 Pennsylvania Ave
NW   Washington DC 20004
Ph: 202-637-3000 ▪ Fx: 202-637-3182

Manufacturing Engineers, Society of   www.sme.org
1 SME Dr   Dearborn MI 48121
Ph: 313-271-1500 ▪ Fx: 313-425-3400 ▪ TF: 800-733-4763

Manufacturing Excellence, Association for   www.trainingforum.com/ASN/AME
380 W Palatine Rd Suite 7   Wheeling IL 60090
Ph: 847-520-3282 ▪ Fx: 847-520-0163

Manufacturing - International, Consortium for Advanced   www.cam-i.com
6737 Brentwood Stair Rd Suite 214   Fort Worth TX 76112
Ph: 817-496-4644 ▪ Fx: 817-496-4674

Manufacturing Jewelers & Suppliers of America   www.mjsainc.com
45 Royal Little Dr   Providence RI 02904
Ph: 401-274-3840 ▪ Fx: 401-274-0265 ▪ TF: 800-444-6572

Manufacturing, National Coalition for Advanced   www.nacfam.org
2000 L St NW Suite 807   Washington DC 20036
Ph: 202-429-2220 ▪ Fx: 202-429-2422 ▪ TF: 800-622-3260

Manufacturing & Packaging Association, Contract   www.contractpackaging.org
519 N Highland Ave   Jackson TN 38301
Ph: 731-422-7994 ▪ Fx: 731-427-2430

Manufacturing Research Institution of SME, North American   www.sme.org/namri
1 SME Dr PO Box 930   Dearborn MI 48121
Ph: 313-271-1500 ▪ Fx: 313-425-3400 ▪ TF: 800-733-4763

Manufacturing Technology, Association for   www.amtonline.org
7901 Westpark Dr   McLean VA 22102
Ph: 703-893-2900 ▪ Fx: 703-893-1151 ▪ TF: 800-524-0475

Manufacturing Trade Action Coalition, American   www.amtacdc.org
910 16th St NW Suite 410   Washington DC 20006
Ph: 202-452-0866 ▪ Fx: 202-452-0739

MAP International   www.map.org
PO Box 215000   Brunswick GA 31521
Ph: 912-265-6010 ▪ Fx: 912-265-6170 ▪ TF: 800-225-8550

Map Trade Association, International   www.maptrade.org
2629 Manhattan Ave PMB 281   Hermosa Beach CA 90254
Ph: 310-376-7731 ▪ Fx: 310-376-7287

MAPI Inc, Manufacturers Alliance/   www.mapi.net
1525 Wilson Blvd Suite 900   Arlington VA 22209
Ph: 703-841-9000 ▪ Fx: 703-841-9514

Maple Flooring Manufacturers Association   www.maplefloor.org
60 Revere Dr Suite 500   Northbrook IL 60062
Ph: 847-480-9138 ▪ Fx: 847-480-9282

Maple Industry Council, Vermont
655 Spear St   Burlington VT 05405
Ph: 802-656-5433 ▪ Fx: 802-656-5422

Maple Syrup Institute, International
PO Box 53010   Burlington VT 05405
Ph: 802-656-5417 ▪ Fx: 802-656-5422

Mapping, American Congress on Surveying &   www.acsm.net
6 Montgomery Village Ave Suite 403   Gaithersburg MD 20879
Ph: 240-632-9716 ▪ Fx: 240-632-1321

Marathon Cycling Association Inc, Ultra   www.ultracycling.com
PO Box 18028   Boulder CO 80308
Ph: 303-545-9566 ▪ Fx: 303-545-9619

Marble Collectors Society of America
PO Box 222   Trumbull CT 06611
Ph: 203-261-3223 ▪ Fx: 203-261-7033

Marble Institute of America   www.marble-institute.com
28901 Clemens Rd Suite 100   Westlake OH 44145
Ph: 440-250-9222 ▪ Fx: 440-250-9223

Marcel Gabriel Society   www.lemoyne.edu/gms
Loyola Univ Philosophy Dept 6363 St Charles Ave   New
    Orleans LA 70118
Ph: 504-865-3940 ▪ Fx: 504-865-3347

March of Dimes Birth Defects Foundation   www.modimes.org
1275 Mamaroneck Ave   White Plains NY 10605
Ph: 914-428-7100 ▪ Fx: 914-428-8203 ▪ TF: 888-663-4637

Marchigiana Society, American International   www.marchigiana.org
PO Box 198   Walton KS 67151
Ph: 316-837-3303 ▪ Fx: 316-283-8379

Marfan Foundation, National   www.marfan.org
22 Manhasset Ave   Port Washington NY 11050
Ph: 516-883-8712 ▪ Fx: 516-883-8040 ▪ TF: 800-862-7326

Margaret Sanger Center International   www.ppnyc.org/services/msci.html
26 Bleecker St   New York NY 10012
Ph: 212-274-7315 ▪ Fx: 212-274-7299

Margarine Manufacturers, National Association of   www.margarine.org/namm.html
1156 15th St NW Suite 900   Washington DC 20005
Ph: 202-785-3232 ▪ Fx: 202-223-9741

MARHO: Radical Historians' Organization   www.historians.org/affiliates
c/o American Historical Assn 400 A St SE   Washington DC
    20003
Ph: 202-544-2422 ▪ Fx: 202-544-8307

Maria Mitchell Association   www.mmo.org
4 Vestal St   Nantucket MA 02554
Ph: 508-288-9198 ▪ Fx: 508-228-1031

Marian Movement of Priests   www.mmp-usa.net
PO Box 8   Saint Francis ME 04774
Ph: 207-398-3375

Marijuana Anonymous World Services   www.marijuana-anonymous.org
PO Box 2912   Van Nuys CA 91404
Ph: 800-766-6779

Marijuana Laws, National Organization for the Reform of   www.norml.org
1600 K St NW Suite 501   Washington DC 20006
Ph: 202-483-5500 ▪ Fx: 202-483-0057

Marina Institute, International   www.imimarina.org
PO Box 7197   Jupiter FL 33468
Ph: 561-741-0626 ▪ Fx: 561-741-0676

Marina Operators Association of America   www.moaa.com
1819 L St NW Suite 700   Washington DC 20036
Ph: 202-721-1630 ▪ Fx: 202-721-1635

Marine Artists, American Society of   www.americansocietyofmarineartists.com
PO Box 369   Ambler PA 19002
Ph: 215-283-0888 ▪ Fx: 215-646-1581

Marine Bankers Association, National   www.marinebankers.org
200 E Randolph Dr Suite 5100   Chicago IL 60601
Ph: 312-946-6260

Marine Conservation, National Coalition for   www.savethefish.org
3 N King St   Leesburg VA 20176
Ph: 703-777-0037 ▪ Fx: 703-777-1107

Marine Corps Association   www.mca-marines.org
PO Box 1775   Quantico VA 22134
Ph: 703-640-6161 ▪ Fx: 703-640-0823 ▪ TF: 800-336-0291

Marine Corps Aviation Association   www.flymcaa.org
715 Broadway St PO Box 296   Quantico VA 22134
Ph: 703-630-1903 ▪ Fx: 703-630-2713 ▪ TF: 800-280-3001

Marine Corps Combat Correspondents Association, US   www.usmccca.org
238 Cornwall Cir   Chalfont PA 18914
Ph: 215-822-6898 ▪ Fx: 215-822-0163 ▪ TF: 888-999-7819

Marine Corps Heritage Foundation   www.usmcmuseum.org
307 5th Ave PO Box 420   Quantico VA 22134
Ph: 703-640-7961 ▪ Fx: 703-640-9546 ▪ TF: 800-397-7585

Marine Corps League   www.mcleague.org
PO Box 3070   Merrifield VA 22116
Ph: 703-207-9588 ▪ Fx: 703-207-0047 ▪ TF: 800-625-1775

Marine Corps League Auxiliary   www.nationalmcla.org
8626 Lee Hwy Suite 207   Fairfax VA 22031
Ph: 703-207-0626 ▪ Fx: 703-207-0264

Marine Corps Relief Society, Navy-   www.nmcrs.org
4015 Wilson Blvd 10th Fl   Arlington VA 22203
Ph: 703-696-4759 ▪ Fx: 703-696-0144 ▪ TF: 800-654-8364

Marine Corps Reserve Association   www.mcrassn.org
337 Potomac Ave   Quantico VA 22134
Ph: 703-630-3772 ▪ Fx: 703-630-1904 ▪ TF: 800-927-6270

Marine Distributors Association, National   www.nmdaonline.com
37 Pratt St   Essex CT 06426
Ph: 860-767-7898 ▪ Fx: 860-797-7932

Marine Electronics Association, National   www.nmea.org
7 Riggs Ave   Severna Park MD 21146
Ph: 410-975-9425 ▪ Fx: 410-975-9450

Marine Engineers' Beneficial Association   www.d1meba.org
444 N Capitol St NW Suite 800   Washington DC 20001
Ph: 202-638-5355 ▪ Fx: 202-638-5369

Marine Engineers, Society of Naval Architects &   www.sname.org
601 Pavonia Ave 4th Fl   Jersey City NJ 07306
Ph: 201-798-4800 ▪ Fx: 201-798-4975

Marine Fabricators Association   www.marinecanvas.com
1801 County Rd 'B' W   Roseville MN 55113
Ph: 651-222-2508 ▪ Fx: 651-631-9334 ▪ TF: 800-225-4324

Marine Fisheries Commission, Atlantic States   www.asmfc.org
1444 'I' St NW 6th Fl   Washington DC 20005
Ph: 202-289-6400 ▪ Fx: 202-289-6051

Marine Fisheries Commission, Pacific States   www.psmfc.org
205 SE Spokane St Suite 100   Portland OR 97027
Ph: 503-595-3100 ▪ Fx: 503-595-3232

Marine Insurance Clearing House, American   www.amich.com
30 Broad St 7th Fl   New York NY 10004
Ph: 212-405-2835 ▪ Fx: 212-344-1664

Marine Mammal Center, Friends of the Sea Lion   www.fslmmc.org
20612 Laguna Canyon Rd   Laguna Beach CA 92651
Ph: 949-494-3050 ▪ Fx: 949-494-2802

Marine Manufacturers Association, Canadian   www.cmma.ca
243 North Service Rd W Suite 106   Oakville ON L6M3E5
Ph: 905-845-4999 ▪ Fx: 905-845-1701

Marine Manufacturers Association, National   www.nmma.org
200 E Randolph Dr Suite 5100   Chicago IL 60601
Ph: 312-946-6200 ▪ Fx: 312-946-0388

Marine Port Engineers, Society of   www.smpe.org
PO Box 466   Avenel NJ 07001
Ph: 732-381-7673 ▪ Fx: 732-381-2046

Marine Representatives Association, National   www.nmraonline.org
1333 Delany Rd Suite 500   Gurnee IL 60031
Ph: 847-662-3167 ▪ Fx: 847-336-7126

Marine Retailers Association of America   www.mraa.com
PO Box 1127   Oak Park IL 60304
Ph: 708-763-9120 ▪ Fx: 708-763-9236

Marine Safety Association, US   www.usmsa.org
5050 Industrial Rd   Farmingdale NJ 07727
Ph: 732-751-0102 ▪ Fx: 732-751-0508

Marine Science Libraries & Information Centers, International   www.iamslic.org
Association of Aquatic &   Harbor Branch Oceanographic
    Institution 5600 US 1 N   Fort Pierce FL 34946
Ph: 561-465-2400 ▪ Fx: 561-465-2446

Marine Service Association, Offshore   www.offshoremarine.org
990 N Corporate Dr Suite 210   Harahan LA 70123
Ph: 504-734-7622 ▪ Fx: 504-734-7134

Marine Services, National Association of   www.namsshipchandler.com
5458 Wagon Master Dr   Colorado Springs CO 80917
Ph: 719-573-5946 ▪ Fx: 719-573-5952

Marine & Shipbuilding Workers of America, Industrial Union of
719 E Fort Ave   Baltimore MD 21230
Ph: 410-837-0056 ▪ Fx: 410-837-0058

Marine Surveyors, National Association of   www.nams-cms.org
PO Box 9306   Chesapeake VA 23321
Ph: 757-488-9538 ▪ Fx: 757-488-0584 ▪ TF: 800-822-6267

Marine Surveyors, Society of Accredited   www.marinesurvey.org
4605 Cardina Blvd   Jacksonville FL 32210
Ph: 904-384-1494 ▪ Fx: 904-388-3958

Marine Technicians, Association of   www.am-tech.org
455 Knollwood Terr   Roswell GA 30075
Ph: 770-587-2432 ▪ Fx: 770-993-8982 ▪ TF: 800-467-0982

Marine Technology Society   www.mtsociety.org
5565 Sterrett Pl Suite 108   Columbia MD 21044
Ph: 410-884-5330 ▪ Fx: 410-884-9060

Marine Toys for Tots Foundation   www.toysfortots.org
715 Broadway St   Quantico VA 22134
Ph: 703-640-9433 ▪ Fx: 703-640-0917

Marine Trade Association, Northwest   www.nmta.net
1900 N Northlake Way Suite 233   Seattle WA 98103
Ph: 206-634-0911 ▪ Fx: 206-632-0078

Marine Transit Association, International   www.interferry.com
34 Otis Hill Rd   Hingham MA 02043
Ph: 781-749-0078

Marine Underwriters, American Institute of   www.aimu.org
14 Wall St 8th Fl   New York NY 10005
Ph: 212-233-0550 ▪ Fx: 212-227-5102

Marine Underwriters Association, Inland   www.imua.org
14 Wall St 8th Fl   New York NY 10005
Ph: 212-233-0550 ▪ Fx: 212-227-5102

Mariners, Council of American Master   www.mastermariner.org
2700 Broening Hwy Dunmar Bldg Suite 115   Baltimore MD
    21222
Ph: 410-285-7800

Marionnette, Union Internationale de la   www.unima-usa.org
Center for Puppetry Arts   Atlanta GA 30309
Ph: 404-873-3089 ▪ Fx: 404-873-9907

Marist Missionary Sisters   www.maristmissionarysmsm.org
349 Grove St   Waltham MA 02453
Ph: 781-893-0149 ▪ Fx: 781-899-6838

Maritain Association, American   www.jacquesmaritain.org
3921 Glenview Dr   South Bend IN 46628
Ph: 574-271-1187 ▪ Fx: 574-271-1292

Marital & Date Rape, National Clearinghouse on   www.ncmdr.org
2325 Oak St   Berkeley CA 94708
Ph: 510-524-1582

Maritime Association of the Port of New York/New Jersey   www.nymaritime.org
17 Battery Pl Suite 913   New York NY 10004
Ph: 212-425-5704 ■ Fx: 212-635-9498

Maritime Committee Inc, Labor Management
1150 17th St NW Suite 700   Washington DC 20036
Ph: 202-955-5662 ■ Fx: 202-872-0912

Maritime Congress, American   www.us-flag.org
1300 'I' St NW Suite 250-W   Washington DC 20005
Ph: 202-842-4900 ■ Fx: 202-842-3492

Maritime Educators, National Association of
124 N Van Ave   Houma LA 70363
Ph: 985-879-3866 ■ Fx: 985-879-3911

Maritime Institute, Great Lakes   www.glmi.org
100 Strand on Belle Isle   Detroit MI 48207
Ph: 313-852-4051

Maritime Law Association of the US   www.mlaus.org
c/o Hill Rivkins & Hayden LLP 45 Broadway Suite 1500   New
   York NY 10006
Ph: 212-669-0600 ■ Fx: 212-669-0699

Maritime Ministry Association, North American   www.maritimeministry.org
3257 Post Rd   Warwick RI 02886
Ph: 401-739-5257 ■ Fx: 401-737-4148

Maritime Museums, Council of American   www.councilofamericanmaritimemuseums.org
c/o Maine Maritime Museum 243 Washington St   Bath ME
   04530
Ph: 207-443-1316 ■ Fx: 207-443-1663

Maritime National Park Association, San Francisco   www.maritime.org
PO Box 470310   San Francisco CA 94147
Ph: 415-561-6662 ■ Fx: 415-561-6660

Maritime Officers Service, American
490 L'Enfant Plaza E SW Suite 7204   Washington DC 20024
Ph: 202-479-1133 ■ Fx: 202-479-1136

Maritime Services, Radio Technical Commission for   www.rtcm.org
1800 N Kent St Suite 1060   Arlington VA 22209
Ph: 703-527-2000 ■ Fx: 703-351-9932

Maritime Union of America, National
1150 17th St NW Suite 700   Washington DC 20036
Ph: 202-466-7060 ■ Fx: 202-872-0912

Mark Twain Home Foundation   www.marktwainmuseum.org
208 Hill St   Hannibal MO 63401
Ph: 573-221-9010 ■ Fx: 573-221-7975

Mark Twain Research Foundation
c/o Mark Twain Memorial Shrine Museum 37352 Shrine
   Rd   Florida MO 65283
Ph: 573-565-3449 ■ Fx: 573-565-3718

Marketers Association Inc, American Wholesale   www.awmanet.org
2750 Prosperity Ave Suite 550   Fairfax VA 22031
Ph: 703-208-3358 ■ Fx: 703-573-5738 ■ TF: 800-482-2962

Marketing Administrators, National Association of Collegiate   nacda.ocsn.com/nacma
PO Box 16428   Cleveland OH 44116
Ph: 440-892-4000 ■ Fx: 440-892-4007

Marketing & Advertising Global Network   www.magnetglobal.org
464 Walnut St Suite 2-D   Pittsburgh PA 15238
Ph: 412-828-4031 ■ Fx: 412-828-4057

Marketing Agencies Association Worldwide   www.maaw.org
94 Valley Rd   Montclair NJ 07042
Ph: 973-746-2555 ■ Fx: 973-746-5563

Marketing Association, American   www.marketingpower.com
311 S Wacker Dr Suite 5800   Chicago IL 60606
Ph: 312-542-9000 ■ Fx: 312-542-9001 ■ TF: 800-262-1150

Marketing Association, Biomedical   www.bmaonline.org
10293 N Meridian St Suite 175   Indianapolis IN 46290
Ph: 317-816-1640 ■ Fx: 317-816-1633

Marketing Association, Business   www.marketing.org
400 N Michigan Ave 15th Fl   Chicago IL 60611
Ph: 312-409-4262 ■ Fx: 312-409-4266 ■ TF: 800-664-4262

Marketing Association, Communications   www.commktga.com
PO Box 36275   Denver CO 02365
Ph: 303-988-3515 ■ Fx: 303-988-3517

Marketing Association Inc, Direct   www.the-dma.org
1120 Ave of the Americas   New York NY 10036
Ph: 212-768-7277 ■ Fx: 202-302-6714

Marketing, Association of Directory   www.admworks.org
1187 Thorn Run Rd Suite 630   Moon Township PA 15108
Ph: 412-269-0663 ■ Fx: 412-269-0655

Marketing Association, Incentive   www.incentivemarketing.org
1801 N Mill St Suite R   Naperville IL 60563
Ph: 630-369-7780 ■ Fx: 630-369-3773

Marketing, Association for Interactive   www.interactivehq.org
1430 Broadway 8th Fl   New York NY 10018
Ph: 212-790-1404 ■ Fx: 212-391-9233 ■ TF: 888-337-0008

Marketing Association, International Newspaper   www.inma.org
10300 N Central Expy Suite 467   Dallas TX 75231
Ph: 214-373-9111 ■ Fx: 214-373-9112

Marketing Association, Legal   www.legalmarketing.org
1926 Waukegan Rd Suite 1   Glenview IL 60025
Ph: 847-657-6717 ■ Fx: 847-657-6819

Marketing Association, Livestock   www.lmaweb.com
10510 NW Ambassador Dr   Kansas City MO 64153
Ph: 816-891-0502 ■ Fx: 816-891-7926 ■ TF: 800-821-2048

Marketing Association, Medical   www.mmanet.org
74 New Montgomery St Suite 230   San Francisco CA 94105
Ph: 415-764-4807 ■ Fx: 415-927-5734 ■ TF: 800-551-2173

Marketing Association, North American Farmers' Direct   www.nafdma.com
62 White Loaf Rd   Southampton MA 01073
Ph: 413-529-0386

Marketing Association Inc, Promotion   www.pmalink.org
257 Park Ave S Suite 1102   New York NY 10010
Ph: 212-420-1100 ■ Fx: 212-533-7622 ■ TF: 877-762-5465

Marketing Association, Publishers   www.pma-online.org
627 Aviation Way   Manhattan Beach CA 90266
Ph: 310-372-2732 ■ Fx: 310-374-3342

Marketing Association, Retail Advertising &   www.rama-nrf.org
325 7th St NW Suite 1100   Washington DC 20004
Ph: 202-661-3052 ■ Fx: 202-661-3049

Marketing Authority, International Home Furnishings   www.furnituremarket.org
PO Box 5243   High Point NC 27262
Ph: 336-869-1000 ■ Fx: 336-869-6999

(Marketing) Distributive Education Clubs of America   www.deca.org
1908 Association Dr   Reston VA 20191
Ph: 703-860-5000 ■ Fx: 703-860-4013

Marketing Education Association   www.nationalmea.org
PO Box 27473   Tempe AZ 85285
Ph: 602-750-6735

Marketing Educational Foundation, Direct   www.the-dma.org/dmef
1120 Ave of the Americas   New York NY 10036
Ph: 212-768-7277 ■ Fx: 212-302-6714

Marketing Executives International Inc, Sales &   www.smei.org
PO Box 1390   Sumas WA 98295
Ph: 312-893-0751 ■ Fx: 604-855-0165

Marketing Fundraisers Association, Direct   www.dmfa.org
224 7th St   Garden City NY 11530
Ph: 516-746-6700 ■ Fx: 516-294-8141

Marketing Information Service, Graphic Arts   www.gamis.org
100 Daingerfield Rd   Alexandria VA 22314
Ph: 703-519-8179 ■ Fx: 703-548-3227

Marketing International Association, Multi-Level   www.mlmia.com
119 Stanford Ct   Irvine CA 92612
Ph: 949-854-0484 ■ Fx: 949-854-7687

(Marketing) LIMRA International Inc   www.limra.com
300 Day Hill Rd   Windsor CT 06095
Ph: 860-688-3358 ■ Fx: 860-298-9555 ■ TF: 800-285-7792

Marketing Network, ABA   www.aba.com/MarketingNetwork
1120 Connecticut Ave NW   Washington DC 20036
Ph: 202-663-5268 ■ Fx: 202-828-4540 ■ TF: 800-433-9013

Marketing Network, Herb Growing &   www.herbworld.com
PO Box 245   Silver Spring PA 17575
Ph: 717-393-3295 ■ Fx: 717-393-9261

Marketing & Opinion Research, Council for   www.cmor.org
4147-U Crossgate Dr   Cincinnati OH 45236
Ph: 513-985-0001 ■ Fx: 513-985-0119 ■ TF: 800-887-2667

(Marketing) Pi Sigma Epsilon   www.pse.org
427 E Stewart St   Milwaukee WI 53207
Ph: 414-328-1952 ■ Fx: 414-328-1953 ■ TF: 800-761-9350

Marketing Professional Services, Society for   www.smps.org
99 Canal Center Plaza Suite 330   Alexandria VA 22314
Ph: 703-549-6117 ■ Fx: 703-549-2498 ■ TF: 800-292-7677

(Marketing) PROMAX   www.promax.org
2029 Century Park E Suite 555   Los Angeles CA 90067
Ph: 310-788-7600 ■ Fx: 310-788-7616

Marketing & Public Relations, National Council for   www.ncmpr.org
PO Box 336039   Greeley CO 80633
Ph: 970-330-0771 ■ Fx: 970-330-0769

Marketing Research Association   www.mra-net.org
1344 Silas Deane Hwy Suite 306   Rocky Hill CT 06067
Ph: 860-257-4008 ■ Fx: 860-257-3990

Marketing Science Institute   www.msi.org
1000 Massachusetts Ave   Cambridge MA 02138
Ph: 617-491-2060 ■ Fx: 617-491-2065

Marketing Services, Association of Retail   www.goarms.com
244 Broad St   Red Bank NJ 07701
Ph: 732-842-5070 ■ Fx: 732-219-1938

Marketing Services, National Association for Retail   www.narms.com
PO Box 906   Plover WI 54467
Ph: 715-342-0948 ■ Fx: 715-342-1943 ■ TF: 888-526-2767

Marketing Training, Professional Society for Sales &   www.smt.org
180 N LaSalle St Suite 1822   Chicago IL 60601
Ph: 312-551-0768 ■ Fx: 312-551-0815

Marking & Identification Association, International   www.mdai.org
222 Wisconsin Ave Suite 1   Lake Forest IL 60045
Ph: 847-283-9810 ■ Fx: 847-283-9808

Markle Foundation   www.markle.org
10 Rockefeller Plaza 16th Fl   New York NY 10020
Ph: 212-489-6655 ■ Fx: 212-765-9690

Marksman Association, Police   www.policemarksman.com
PO Box 241387   Montgomery AL 36124
Ph: 334-271-2010 ■ Fx: 334-279-9267

Marky Cattle Association   www.marchigiana.org
PO Box 198   Walton KS 67151
Ph: 316-837-3303 ■ Fx: 316-283-8379

Marlowe Society of America   web.ics.purdue.edu/~pwhite/marlowe
23 Dockerel Rd   Toland CT 06084
Ph: 860-768-4137 ■ Fx: 860-768-4940

Marriage Encounter USA, United Worldwide   www.uwwme.org

Marriage Enrichment, Association for Couples in   www.bettermarriages.org
PO Box 10596   Winston-Salem NC 27108
Ph: 336-724-1526 ■ Fx: 336-721-4746 ■ TF: 800-634-8325

Marriage & Family Counselors, International Association of   www.iamfc.com
c/o American Counseling Assn 5999 Stevenson Ave   Alexandria
   VA 22304
Ph: 703-823-9800 ■ Fx: 703-823-0252 ■ TF: 800-545-2223

Marriage & Family Therapy, American Association for   www.aamft.org
112 S Alfred St   Alexandria VA 22314
Ph: 703-838-9808 ■ Fx: 703-838-9805

Marroquin, Foundation Francisco   www.ffmnet.org
PO Box 2422   Stuart FL 34995
Ph: 772-286-6450 ■ Fx: 772-280-0670

Marrow Donor Program, National   www.marrow.org
3001 Broadway St NE Suite 500   Minneapolis MN 55413
Ph: 612-627-5800 ▪ Fx: 612-627-8125 ▪ TF: 800-526-7809

Marrow Foundation   www.themarrowfoundation.org
400 7th St NW Suite 206   Washington DC 20004
Ph: 202-638-6601 ▪ Fx: 202-638-0641

Marrow Transplantation, American Society for Blood &   www.asbmt.org
85 W Algonquin Rd Suite 550   Arlington Heights IL 60005
Ph: 847-427-0224 ▪ Fx: 847-427-9656

Mars Society   www.marssociety.org
PO Box 273   Indian Hills CO 80454
Ph: 303-697-0315 ▪ Fx: 303-697-7033

Marshall George C Foundation   www.marshallfoundation.org
VMI Parade PO Drawer 1600   Lexington VA 24450
Ph: 540-463-7103

Marshall John Foundation   www.vba.org/jmfinfo.htm
c/o Virginia Bar Assn 701 E Franklin St Suite 1120   Richmond
VA 23219
Ph: 804-644-0041 ▪ Fx: 804-644-0052

Marshall Thurgood Scholarship Fund   www.thurgoodmarshallfund.org
60 E 42nd St Suite 833   New York NY 10165
Ph: 212-573-8888 ▪ Fx: 212-573-8497

Marten Rabbit Club, Silver   www.silvermarten.com
2113 Sommer St   Napa CA 94559
Ph: 707-255-2821

Martial Arts International, Zen-Do Kai   www.superior.net/~zendokai
PO Box 186   Johnstown NY 12095
Ph: 518-762-4723

Martin Luther King Jr Center for Nonviolent Social Change Inc   www.thekingcenter.com
449 Auburn Ave NE   Atlanta GA 30312
Ph: 404-524-1956 ▪ Fx: 404-526-8969

Martyr, Society of King Charles the   www.skcm-usa.org
291 Bacon St   Waltham MA 02451
Ph: 781-899-3165

Martyrs, Voice of the   www.persecution.com
PO Box 443   Bartlesville OK 74005
Ph: 918-337-8015 ▪ Fx: 918-338-0189 ▪ TF: 800-747-0085

Marxism, Society for the Philosophical   www.pages.drexel.edu/~pa34/spsm_website.htm
Study of   Univ at Buffalo Dept of Philosophy 135 Park
Hall   Buffalo NY 14260
Ph: 716-645-2444 ▪ Fx: 716-645-6139

Mary Magdalene, Society of Saint   www.st-mary-magdalene.org
PO Box 352   Fountain Inn SC 29644
Ph: 864-409-0077

Mary, Missionary Sisters of the Society of   www.maristmissionarysmsm.org
349 Grove St   Waltham MA 02453
Ph: 781-893-0149 ▪ Fx: 781-899-6838

Maryknoll Mission Association of the Faithful   home.maryknoll.org
PO Box 307   Maryknoll NY 10545
Ph: 914-762-6364 ▪ Fx: 914-762-7031 ▪ TF: 800-818-5276

(Masculinity) ManKind Project   www.mkp.org
PO Box 230   Malone NY 12953
Ph: 800-870-4611

Maserati Club   www.themaseraticlub.com

Mason Contractors Association of America   www.masonryshowcase.com
33 S Roselle Rd   Schaumburg IL 60193
Ph: 847-301-0001 ▪ Fx: 847-301-1110 ▪ TF: 800-536-2225

(Masonic) Acacia International Fraternity   www.acacia.org
8777 Purdue Rd Suite 130   Indianapolis IN 46268
Ph: 317-872-8210 ▪ Fx: 317-872-8213 ▪ TF: 888-345-1904

Masonic Clubs Inc, National League of
2244 Locust Ln   York PA 17404
Ph: 717-764-6768

(Masonic) Grottoes of North America   www.scgrotto.com
1696 Brice Rd   Reynoldsburg OH 43068
Ph: 614-860-9193 ▪ Fx: 614-860-9099

(Masonic) Heroes of '76
8301 E Boulevard Dr   Alexandria VA 22308
Ph: 703-765-5000 ▪ Fx: 703-765-8390

(Masonic) National Sojourners Inc   www.nationalsojourners.org
8301 E Boulevard Dr   Alexandria VA 22308
Ph: 703-765-5000 ▪ Fx: 703-765-8390

(Masonic) Philalethes Society   www.freemasonry.org/psoc
5266 Mary Ball Rd   Lancaster VA 22503
Ph: 804-737-4498 ▪ Fx: 804-328-2386

Masonic Service Association of North America   www.msana.com
8120 Fenton St   Silver Spring MD 20910
Ph: 301-588-4010 ▪ Fx: 301-608-3457

(Masonic) Tall Cedars of Lebanon of North America   www.mastermason.com/tcl
2609 N Front St   Harrisburg PA 17110
Ph: 717-232-5991 ▪ Fx: 717-232-5997

Masonry Association, National Concrete   www.ncma.org
13750 Sunrise Valley Dr   Herndon VA 20171
Ph: 703-713-1900 ▪ Fx: 703-713-1910

Masonry Institute, International   www.imiweb.org
James Brice House 42 East St   Annapolis MD 21401
Ph: 410-280-1305 ▪ Fx: 301-261-2855

Masonry Society   www.masonrysociety.org
3970 Broadway Suite 201-D   Boulder CO 80304
Ph: 303-939-9700 ▪ Fx: 303-541-9215

Masons' International Association of the US & Canada,   www.opcmia.org
Operative Plasterers' & Cement   14405 Laurel Pl Suite
300   Laurel MD 20707
Ph: 301-470-4200 ▪ Fx: 301-470-2502

Masons International, General Grand Chapter of Royal Arch
PO Box 489   Danville KY 40423
Ph: 859-236-0757 ▪ Fx: 859-236-6773

Masons of the World, Federation of
1017 E 11th St   Austin TX 78702
Ph: 512-477-5380 ▪ Fx: 512-477-5313

Masons of the World Inc, Modern Free & Accepted   www.modernfree.com
627 5th Ave PO Box 1072   Columbus GA 31902
Ph: 706-322-3326 ▪ Fx: 706-322-3805

Masorti Foundation for Conservative Judaism in Israel   www.masorti.org
475 Riverside Dr Suite 832   New York NY 10115
Ph: 212-870-2216 ▪ Fx: 212-870-2218 ▪ TF: 877-287-7414

(Mass Cards) Assumption Guild   www.masscardsaa.com
PO Box 35190   Brighton MA 02135
Ph: 617-783-0495 ▪ Fx: 617-783-8030

Mass Communication, Association for Education in Journalism &   www.aejmc.org/
234 Outlet Pointe Blvd Suite C   Columbia SC 29210
Ph: 803-798-0271 ▪ Fx: 803-772-3509

Mass Communication, Association of Schools of Journalism &   www.aejmc.org
234 Outlet Pointe Blvd   Columbia SC 29210
Ph: 803-798-0271 ▪ Fx: 803-772-3509

Mass Finishing Job Shops Association   www.mfjsa.com
808 13th St   Moline IL 61244
Ph: 309-755-1101 ▪ Fx: 309-755-1121

Mass Marketing Insurance Institute   www.mi2.org
14 W 3rd St Suite 200   Kansas City MO 64105
Ph: 816-221-7575 ▪ Fx: 816-472-7765

Mass Retail Association, International   www.imra.org
1700 N Moore St Suite 2250   Arlington VA 22209
Ph: 703-841-2300 ▪ Fx: 703-841-1184

Mass Spectometry, American Society for   www.asms.org
2019 Galisteo St Bldg 1   Santa Fe NM 87505
Ph: 505-989-4517 ▪ Fx: 505-989-1073

Massachusetts, Colonial Society of   www.colonialsociety.org
87 Mt Vernon St   Boston MA 02108
Ph: 617-227-2782

Massage Federation, US Sports
2156 Newport Blvd   Costa Mesa CA 92627
Ph: 949-642-0735 ▪ Fx: 949-642-1729

Massage, International Association of Infant   www.iaim-us.com
1891 Goodyear Ave Suite 622   Ventura CA 93003
Ph: 805-644-8524 ▪ Fx: 805-644-7699 ▪ TF: 800-248-5432

Massage Professionals, Associated Bodywork &   www.abmp.com
1271 Sugarbush Dr   Evergreen CO 80439
Ph: 303-674-8478 ▪ Fx: 303-674-0859 ▪ TF: 800-458-2267

Massage Therapy Inc, American Institute of   www.aimtinc.com
1570 Brookhollow Dr Suite 200   Santa Ana CA 92705
Ph: 714-432-7879 ▪ Fx: 714-210-3199

Massage Therapy Association, American   www.amtamassage.org
820 Davis St Suite 100   Evanston IL 60201
Ph: 847-864-0123 ▪ Fx: 847-864-1178

Master Brewers Association of the Americas   www.mbaa.com
3340 Pilot Knob Rd   Saint Paul MN 55121
Ph: 651-454-7250 ▪ Fx: 651-454-0766

Master Drawings Association Inc   www.masterdrawings.org
29 E 36th St   New York NY 10016
Ph: 212-685-0008 ▪ Fx: 212-685-4740

Master Mariners, Council of American   www.mastermariner.org
2700 Broening Hwy Dunmar Bldg Suite 115   Baltimore MD
21222
Ph: 410-285-7800

Master Printers of America   www.masterprinters.org
100 Daingerfield Rd   Alexandria VA 22314
Ph: 703-519-8100 ▪ Fx: 703-548-3227 ▪ TF: 800-742-2666

Masters of Foxhounds Association of America   www.mfha.com
PO Box 363   Millwood VA 22646
Ph: 540-955-5680 ▪ Fx: 540-955-5682

Masters Mates & Pilots, International Organization of   www.bridgedeck.org
700 Maritime Blvd   Linthicum Heights MD 21090
Ph: 410-850-8700 ▪ Fx: 410-850-0973 ▪ TF: 877-667-5522

Master's Men   www.nafwb.org/mm
PO Box 5002   Antioch TN 37011
Ph: 615-760-6141 ▪ Fx: 615-731-0049 ▪ TF: 877-767-8039

Masters Swimming, US   www.usms.org
PO Box 185   Londonderry NH 03053
Ph: 603-537-0203 ▪ Fx: 603-537-0204 ▪ TF: 800-550-7946

Mastiff Club of America Inc   mastiff.org
PO Box 609   Fruitland Park FL 34731
Ph: 352-787-8549

Mastitis Council, National   www.nmconline.org
5944 Seminole Centre Ct Suite C   Madison WI 53711
Ph: 608-663-1255 ▪ Fx: 608-663-1249

Material Handling Consultants, Association of Professional   www.mhia.org/apmhc
8720 Red Oak Blvd Suite 201   Charlotte NC 28217
Ph: 704-676-1184 ▪ Fx: 704-676-1199

Material Handling Equipment Distributors Association   www.mheda.org
201 US Hwy 45   Vernon Hills IL 60061
Ph: 847-680-3500 ▪ Fx: 847-362-6989

Material Handling Industry of America   www.mhia.org
8720 Red Oak Blvd Suite 201   Charlotte NC 28217
Ph: 704-676-1190 ▪ Fx: 704-676-1199 ▪ TF: 800-345-1815

Material & Process Engineering, Society for the Advancement of   org.et.byu.edu/sampe
PO Box 2459   Covina CA 91722
Ph: 626-331-0616 ▪ Fx: 626-332-8929 ▪ TF: 800-562-7360

(Materials) ASM International   www.asm-intl.org
9639 Kinsman Rd   Materials Park OH 44073
Ph: 440-338-5151 ▪ Fx: 440-338-4634 ▪ TF: 800-336-5152

Materials Handling & Management Society   www.mhia.org/mhms
8720 Red Oak Blvd Suite 201   Charlotte NC 28217
Ph: 704-676-1183 ▪ Fx: 704-676-1199

Materials Managers, National Association of Scientific   www.naosmm.org

Materials Properties Council   www.forengineers.org/mpc/index.html
3 Park Ave 27th Fl   New York NY 10016
Ph: 212-591-7693 ▪ Fx: 212-591-7183

Materials Research Society www.mrs.org
506 Keystone Dr   Warrendale PA 15086
Ph: 724-779-3003 ▪ Fx: 724-779-8313

Materials Societies, Federation of www.materialsocieties.org
910 17th St NW Suite 800   Washington DC 20006
Ph: 202-296-9282 ▪ Fx: 202-833-3014

Materials Society, Minerals Metals & www.tms.org
184 Thorn Hill Rd   Warrendale PA 15086
Ph: 724-776-9000 ▪ Fx: 724-776-3770 ▪ TF: 800-966-4867

Materials Technology Institute of the Chemical Process Industry Inc www.mti-link.org
1215 Fern Ridge Pkwy Suite 206   Saint Louis MO 63141
Ph: 314-576-7712 ▪ Fx: 314-576-6078

Materiel Management, International Association of Healthcare www.iahcsmm.com
Central Service   213 W Institute Pl Suite 307   Chicago IL 60610
Ph: 312-440-0078 ▪ Fx: 312-440-9474 ▪ TF: 800-962-8274

Maternal & Child Health Programs, Association of www.amchp.org
1220 19th St NW Suite 801   Washington DC 20036
Ph: 202-775-0436 ▪ Fx: 202-775-0061

Maternal Fetal Medicine, Society for www.smfm.org
409 12th St SW   Washington DC 20024
Ph: 202-863-2476 ▪ Fx: 202-554-1132

Mates & Pilots, International Organization of Masters www.bridgedeck.org
700 Maritime Blvd   Linthicum Heights MD 21090
Ph: 410-850-8700 ▪ Fx: 410-850-0973 ▪ TF: 877-667-5522

Mathematical Association of America www.maa.org
1529 18th St NW   Washington DC 20036
Ph: 202-387-5200 ▪ Fx: 202-265-2384 ▪ TF: 800-741-9415

Mathematical Association of Two-Year Colleges, American www.amatyc.org
Southwest Tennessee Community College 5983 Macon Cove   Memphis TN 38134
Ph: 901-333-4643 ▪ Fx: 901-383-4651

Mathematical Sciences, Conference Board of the www.cbmsweb.org
1529 18th St NW   Washington DC 20036
Ph: 202-293-1170 ▪ Fx: 202-293-3412

Mathematical Society, American www.ams.org
PO Box 6248   Providence RI 02940
Ph: 401-455-4000 ▪ Fx: 401-331-3842 ▪ TF: 800-321-4267

Mathematical Studies in Economics & www.kellogg.nwu.edu/research/math
Management Sciences, Center for   Northwestern University
2001 Sheridan Rd Leverone Hall Rm 580   Evanston IL 60208
Ph: 847-491-3527 ▪ Fx: 847-491-2530

Mathematical Studies, Institute of www.imstat.org/
PO Box 22718   Beachwood OH 44122
Ph: 216-295-2340 ▪ Fx: 216-921-6703

Mathematics, Association for Women in www.awm-math.org
Univ of Maryland 4114 Computer & Space Science Bldg   College Park MD 20742
Ph: 301-405-7892 ▪ Fx: 301-314-9363

(Mathematics) Mu Alpha Theta www.mualphatheta.org
601 Elm Ave Rm 423   Norman OK 73019
Ph: 405-325-4489 ▪ Fx: 405-325-7184

Mathematics, National Council of Supervisors of www.ncsmonline.org
PO Box 10667   Golden CO 80401
Ph: 303-274-5932

Mathematics, National Council of Teachers of www.nctm.org
1906 Association Dr   Reston VA 20191
Ph: 703-620-9840 ▪ Fx: 703-476-2970 ▪ TF: 800-235-7566

Mathematics, Society for Industrial & Applied www.siam.org
3600 University City Science Ctr 6th Fl   Philadelphia PA 19104
Ph: 215-382-9800 ▪ Fx: 215-386-7999 ▪ TF: 800-447-7426

Matrimonial Lawyers, American Academy of www.aaml.org
150 N Michigan Ave Suite 2040   Chicago IL 60601
Ph: 312-263-6477 ▪ Fx: 312-263-7682

Maxillofacial Pathology, American Academy of Oral & aaomp.org
710 E Ogden Ave Suite 600   Naperville IL 60563
Ph: 888-552-2667 ▪ Fx: 630-369-2488

Maxillofacial Prosthetics, American Academy of www.maxillofacialprosth.org
Univ of Florida College of Dentistry Dept of Prosthodontics Box 100435   Gainesville FL 32610
Ph: 352-846-2684 ▪ Fx: 352-846-2683

Maxillofacial Radiology, American Academy of Oral & www.aaomr.org
PO Box 1010   Evans GA 30809
Ph: 706-721-2607

Maxillofacial Surgeons, American Association of Oral & www.aaoms.org
9700 W Bryn Mawr Ave   Rosemont IL 60018
Ph: 847-678-6200 ▪ Fx: 847-678-6286 ▪ TF: 800-822-6637

Maxillofacial Surgeons, American College of Oral & www.acoms.org
1100 NW Loop 410 Suite 420   San Antonio TX 78213
Ph: 210-344-5674 ▪ Fx: 210-344-9754 ▪ TF: 800-522-6676

Maxillofacial Surgeons, American Society of www.maxface.org
444 E Algonquin Rd   Arlington Heights IL 60005
Ph: 847-228-3338

Maxillofacial Surgery, American Board of Oral & www.aboms.org
625 N Michigan Ave Suite 1820   Chicago IL 60611
Ph: 312-642-0070 ▪ Fx: 312-642-8584

Mayflower Descendants, General Society of www.mayflower.org
PO Box 3297   Plymouth MA 02361
Ph: 508-746-3188 ▪ Fx: 508-746-2488

Mayors, National Conference of Black www.blackmayors.org
1151 Cleveland Ave Suite D   East Point GA 30344
Ph: 404-765-6444 ▪ Fx: 404-765-6430

Mayors, US Conference of www.usmayors.org
1620 'I' St NW Suite 400   Washington DC 20006
Ph: 202-293-7330 ▪ Fx: 202-293-2352

MBA Association, National Black www.nbmbaa.org
180 N Michigan Ave Suite 1400   Chicago IL 60601
Ph: 312-236-2622 ▪ Fx: 312-236-4131

MBAs, National Society of Hispanic www.nshmba.org
1303 Walnut Hill Ln Suite 300   Irving TX 75038
Ph: 214-596-9325 ▪ TF: 877-467-4622

McAuley Institute www.mcauley.org
8300 Colesville Rd   Silver Spring MD 20910
Ph: 301-588-8110 ▪ Fx: 301-588-8154

McCormick Robert R Tribune Foundation www.mccormicktribune.org
435 N Michigan Ave Suite 770   Chicago IL 60611
Ph: 312-222-3512 ▪ Fx: 312-222-3523

McCune Foundation www.mccune.org
6 PPG Pl Suite 750   Pittsburgh PA 15222
Ph: 412-644-8779 ▪ Fx: 412-644-8059

McDonald's Operators Association, National Black www.nbmoa.org
PO Box 8204   Los Angeles CA 90008
Ph: 323-296-5495 ▪ Fx: 323-296-6134

McKnight Foundation www.mcknight.org
710 2nd St S Suite 400   Minneapolis MN 55401
Ph: 612-333-4220 ▪ Fx: 612-332-3833

MCS Referral & Resources Inc www.mcsrr.org
508 Westgate Rd   Baltimore MD 21229
Ph: 410-362-6400 ▪ Fx: 410-362-6401

MDS International Foundation Inc, Aplastic Anemia & www.aamds.org
PO Box 613   Annapolis MD 21404
Ph: 410-867-0242 ▪ Fx: 410-867-0240 ▪ TF: 800-747-2820

Meadows Foundation Inc www.mfi.org
3003 Swiss Ave   Dallas TX 75204
Ph: 214-826-9431 ▪ Fx: 214-827-7042 ▪ TF: 800-826-9431

Meal & Oil Association, National Fish
1901 N Fort Myer Dr Suite 700   Arlington VA 22209
Ph: 703-524-8884 ▪ Fx: 703-524-4619

Meals on Wheels Association of America www.mowaa.org
1414 Prince St Suite 302   Alexandria VA 22314
Ph: 703-548-5558 ▪ Fx: 703-548-8024

Measurement Control & Automation Association www.measure.org
PO Box 3698   Williamsburg VA 23187
Ph: 757-258-3100 ▪ Fx: 757-258-9066

Measurement in Education, National Council on www.ncme.org
1230 17th St NW   Washington DC 20036
Ph: 202-223-9318 ▪ Fx: 202-775-1824

Measurement Group, Computer www.cmg.org
151 Fries Mill Rd Suite 104   Turnersville NJ 08012
Ph: 856-401-1700 ▪ Fx: 856-401-1708 ▪ TF: 800-436-7264

Measurement, International Society of Weighing & www.iswm.org
15245 Shady Grove Rd Suite 130   Rockville MD 20850
Ph: 301-258-1115 ▪ Fx: 301-990-9771

Measurement Society, IEEE Instrumentation & www.ewh.ieee.org/soc/im
IEEE Operations Ctr 445 Hoes Ln   Piscataway NJ 08854
Ph: 732-981-0060 ▪ Fx: 732-981-1721

Measurement Techniques Association, Antenna www.amta.org

Measures, National Conference on Weights & www.ncwm.net
15245 Shady Grove Rd Suite 130   Rockville MD 20850
Ph: 240-632-9454 ▪ Fx: 301-990-9771

Measuring Tool Manufacturers Association, American www.amtma.org
1300 Sumner Ave   Cleveland OH 44115
Ph: 216-241-7333 ▪ Fx: 216-241-0105

Meat Association, National www.nmaonline.org
1970 Broadway Suite 825   Oakland CA 94612
Ph: 510-763-1533 ▪ Fx: 510-763-6186

Meat Canners Association, National www.meatami.com/content/AboutAMI/canners.htm
1700 N Moore St Suite 1600   Arlington VA 22209
Ph: 703-841-2400 ▪ Fx: 703-527-0938

Meat Export Federation Inc, US www.usmef.org
1050 17th St Suite 2200   Denver CO 80265
Ph: 303-623-6328 ▪ Fx: 303-623-0297

Meat Importers Council of America www.micausa.org
1901 N Fort Myer Dr   Arlington VA 22209
Ph: 703-522-1910 ▪ Fx: 703-524-6039

Meat Industry Suppliers Association
Food Processing Machinery Assn 200 Dangerfield Rd 1st Fl   Alexandria VA 22314
Ph: 703-684-1080 ▪ Fx: 703-548-6563 ▪ TF: 800-331-8816

Meat Institute, American www.meatami.com
1700 N Moore St Suite 1600   Arlington VA 22209
Ph: 703-841-2400 ▪ Fx: 703-527-0938

Meat Processors, American Association of www.aamp.com
PO Box 269   Elizabethtown PA 17022
Ph: 717-367-1168 ▪ Fx: 717-367-9096

Meat Processors Association, North American www.namp.com
1910 Association Dr   Reston VA 20191
Ph: 703-758-1900 ▪ Fx: 703-758-8001

Meat Science Association, American www.meatscience.org
1111 N Dunlap Ave   Savoy IL 61874
Ph: 217-356-3182 ▪ Fx: 217-398-4119

Mechanical Association Railcar Technical Services www.marts-rail.org
5 Berkshire Dr   Saint Charles MO 63301
Ph: 636-723-9947 ▪ Fx: 636-947-3750

Mechanical Bank Collectors of America www.mechanicalbanks.org
PO Box 13323   Pittsburgh PA 15242
Ph: 412-343-8733 ▪ Fx: 412-344-5273

Mechanical Contractors Association of America www.mcaa.org
1385 Piccard Dr   Rockville MD 20850
Ph: 301-869-5800 ▪ Fx: 301-990-9690 ▪ TF: 800-556-3653

Mechanical Contractors Association of America PAC
1385 Piccard Dr   Rockville MD 20850
Ph: 301-869-5800 ▪ Fx: 301-990-9690 ▪ TF: 800-556-3653

Mechanical Engineers, American Society of www.asme.org
3 Park Ave   New York NY 10016
Ph: 212-591-7722 ▪ Fx: 212-591-7739 ▪ TF: 800-843-2763

Mechanical Officials, International Association of Plumbing & www.iapmo.org
5001 E Philadelphia St   Ontario CA 91761
Ph: 909-472-4100 ▪ Fx: 909-472-4150 ▪ TF: 800-854-2766

Mechanical Power Transmission Association www.mpta.org
6724 Lone Oak Blvd   Naples FL 34109
Ph: 239-514-3441 ▪ Fx: 239-514-3470

Mechanical Service Contractors of America www.mcaa.org/msca
1385 Piccard Dr   Rockville MD 20850
Ph: 301-869-5800 ▪ Fx: 301-990-9690

Mechanics, Championship Association of www.racecrews.org
8435 Georgetown Rd Suite 200   Indianapolis IN 46268
Ph: 317-802-0001 ▪ Fx: 317-802-0003

Mechanics Fraternal Association, Aircraft www.amfa2000.org
PO Box 51955   Indianapolis IN 46251
Ph: 317-244-4413 ▪ Fx: 317-244-4418

Mechanics Inc, Society for Experimental www.sem.org
7 School St   Bethel CT 06801
Ph: 203-790-6373 ▪ Fx: 203-790-4472

Mechanics, US Association for Computational www.usacm.org
Scientific Computation Research Ctr 7011 CIL Bldg   Troy NY
12180
Ph: 518-276-3590 ▪ Fx: 518-276-4886

Medal, Central Association of the Miraculous www.cammonline.org
475 E Chelten Ave   Philadelphia PA 19144
Ph: 215-848-1010 ▪ Fx: 215-848-1014 ▪ TF: 800-523-3674

Medal of Honor Society, Congressional www.cmohs.org
40 Patriots Point Rd   Mount Pleasant SC 29464
Ph: 843-884-8862 ▪ Fx: 843-884-1471

Medal Society Inc, Token & www.money.org/clubs/tams

Medecins Sans Frontieres www.doctorswithoutborders.org
6 E 39th St 8th Fl   New York NY 10016
Ph: 212-679-6800 ▪ Fx: 212-679-7016 ▪ TF: 888-392-0392

Media Access Project www.mediaaccess.org
1625 K St NW   Washington DC 20006
Ph: 202-232-4300 ▪ Fx: 202-466-7656

Media Inc, Accuracy in www.aim.org
4455 Connecticut Ave NW Suite 330   Washington DC 20008
Ph: 202-364-4401 ▪ Fx: 202-364-4098 ▪ TF: 800-787-4567

Media Advisers, College www.collegemedia.org
Univ of Memphis Dept of Journalism   Memphis TN 38152
Ph: 901-678-2403 ▪ Fx: 901-678-4798

Media Alliance www.media-alliance.org
942 Market St Suite 503   San Francisco CA 94102
Ph: 415-546-6491 ▪ Fx: 415-546-6218

Media, Alliance for Community www.alliancecm.org
666 11th St NW Suite 740   Washington DC 20001
Ph: 202-393-2650 ▪ Fx: 202-393-2653

Media, American Business www.americanbusinessmedia.com
675 3rd Ave Suite 415   New York NY 10017
Ph: 212-661-6360 ▪ Fx: 212-370-0736

Media Arts & Culture, National Alliance for www.namac.org
145 9th St Suite 250   San Francisco CA 94103
Ph: 415-431-1391 ▪ Fx: 415-431-1392

Media Associates International www.littworld.org
130 N Bloomingdale Rd Suite 101   Bloomingdale IL 60108
Ph: 630-893-1977 ▪ Fx: 630-893-1141

Media, Association for Women in Sports www.awsmonline.org

Media Association, World www.wmassociation.com
3600 New York Ave NE 3rd Fl   Washington DC 20002
Ph: 202-636-3124 ▪ Fx: 202-635-9227

Media Association, Yellow Pages Integrated www.ypima.org
820 Kirts Blvd Suite 100   Troy MI 48084
Ph: 248-244-6200 ▪ Fx: 248-244-0700 ▪ TF: 800-841-0639

Media Centers, Consortium of College & University www.ccumc.org
Iowa State Univ Instructional Technology Ctr 1200
Communications Bldg   Ames IA 50011
Ph: 515-294-1811 ▪ Fx: 515-294-8089

Media Coalition Inc www.mediacoalition.org
139 Fulton St Suite 302   New York NY 10038
Ph: 212-587-4025 ▪ Fx: 212-587-2436

Media Coalition, National Hispanic www.nhmc.org
2514 S Grand Ave   Los Angeles CA 90007
Ph: 213-746-6988 ▪ Fx: 213-746-1305

Media Communications Association International www.mca-i.org
401 N Michigan Ave   Chicago IL 60611
Ph: 312-321-5171 ▪ Fx: 312-673-6716

Media Education, Center for www.cme.org
2120 L St NW Suite 200   Washington DC 20037
Ph: 202-331-7833 ▪ Fx: 202-331-7841

Media Executives, National Association of Minority www.namme.org
1921 Gallows Rd Suite 600   Vienna VA 22182
Ph: 703-893-2410 ▪ Fx: 703-893-2414 ▪ TF: 888-968-7658

Media Foundation, International Women's www.iwmf.org
1726 M St NW Suite 1002   Washington DC 20036
Ph: 202-496-1992 ▪ Fx: 202-496-1977

Media Foundation, Public www.scribblingwomen.org
100 Boylston St Suite 230   Boston MA 02116
Ph: 617-357-5835

Media Guilds International www.mediaguilds.com
10020 Benjamin Nicholas Pl Suite 103   Las Vegas NV 89144
Ph: 888-898-4298

Media, Leadership Council for Mental Health Justice & the www.leadershipcouncil.org
191 Presidential Blvd Suite C132   Bala Cynwyd PA 19004
Ph: 610-664-5007 ▪ Fx: 610-664-5279

Media Management Association, Communications www.cmma.net
PO Box 227   Wheaton IL 60189
Ph: 630-653-2772 ▪ Fx: 630-653-2882

Media Measurement, Traffic Audit Bureau for www.tabonline.com
420 Lexington Ave Room 2520   New York NY 10170
Ph: 212-972-8075 ▪ Fx: 212-972-8928

Media Inc, Morality in www.moralityinmedia.org
475 Riverside Dr Suite 239   New York NY 10115
Ph: 212-870-3222 ▪ Fx: 212-870-2765

Media, National Information Center for Educational www.nicem.com
PO Box 8640   Albuquerque NM 87198
Ph: 505-998-0800 ▪ Fx: 505-256-1080 ▪ TF: 800-926-8328

Media Photographers, American Society of www.asmp.org
150 N 2nd St   Philadelphia PA 19106
Ph: 215-451-2767 ▪ Fx: 215-451-0880

Media & Public Affairs, Center for www.cmpa.com
2100 L St NW Suite 300   Washington DC 20037
Ph: 202-223-2942

Media Rating Council www.mrc.com
200 W 57th St Suite 204   New York NY 10019
Ph: 212-765-0200 ▪ Fx: 212-765-1868

Media Research Center www.mediaresearch.org
325 S Patrick St   Alexandria VA 22314
Ph: 703-683-9733 ▪ Fx: 703-683-9736 ▪ TF: 800-672-1423

Media Resource Service www.mediaresource.org
99 Alexander Dr PO Box 13975   Research Triangle Park NC
27709
Ph: 919-547-5259 ▪ Fx: 919-549-0090

Media Studies, Society for Cinema & www.cinemastudies.org
Univ of Texas Press PO Box 7819   Austin TX 78713
Ph: 512-471-4531

Media Technicians Inc, Council on Library colt.ucr.edu
Daniel Boone Regional Library 100 W Broadway   Columbia MO
65203
Ph: 573-443-3161 ▪ Fx: 573-874-0862

Media Watch www.mediawatch.com
PO Box 618   Santa Cruz CA 95061
Ph: 831-423-6355 ▪ TF: 800-631-6355

**Media Workers Sector, Communications Workers of America Printing
Publishing &**   501 3rd St NW Suite 950   Washington DC
20001
Ph: 202-434-1238 ▪ Fx: 202-434-1245

Mediation, Center for Medical Ethics & www.cmem.org
PO Box 86110   San Diego CA 92138
Ph: 619-296-7268

Mediation & Conflict Resolution, Institute for www.mediate.com/imcr
384 E 149th St Suite 330   Bronx NY 10455
Ph: 718-585-1190 ▪ Fx: 718-585-1962

Mediation & Conflict Resolution, Institute for International www.iimcr.org
1424 K St NW Suite 650   Washington DC 20005
Ph: 202-347-2042 ▪ Fx: 202-347-2440

Mediation Education, National Center for
1160 Spa Rd Suite 1B   Annapolis MD 21403
Ph: 410-974-8888 ▪ Fx: 410-295-9190 ▪ TF: 800-781-7500

Mediation, National Association for Community www.nafcm.org
1527 New Hampshire Ave NW 4th Fl   Washington DC 20036
Ph: 202-667-9700 ▪ Fx: 202-667-8629

Mediators, Association of Attorney- www.attorney-mediators.org
PO Box 741955   Dallas TX 75374
Ph: 972-669-8101 ▪ Fx: 972-669-8180 ▪ TF: 800-280-1368

Medical Acupuncture, American Academy of www.medicalacupuncture.org
4929 Wilshire Blvd Suite 428   Los Angeles CA 90010
Ph: 323-937-5514 ▪ Fx: 323-937-0959

Medical Administrators, American Academy of www.aameda.org
701 Lee St Suite 600   Des Plaines IL 60016
Ph: 847-759-8601 ▪ Fx: 847-759-8602

Medical Airlift Service, American Veterans
931 Flanders Rd PO Box 1065   La Canada Flintridge CA 91011
Ph: 818-952-6212

Medical Ambassadors International www.medicalambassadors.org
PO Box 576645   Modesto CA 95357
Ph: 209-524-0600 ▪ Fx: 209-571-3538 ▪ TF: 888-403-0660

Medical Anthropology, Society for www.medanthro.net
c/o American Anthropological Assn 2200 Wilson Blvd Suite
600   Arlington VA 22201
Ph: 703-528-1902 ▪ Fx: 703-528-3546

Medical Assistance Inc, Interchurch www.interchurch.org
500 Main St PO Box 429   New Windsor MD 21776
Ph: 410-635-8720 ▪ Fx: 410-635-8726

(Medical Assistance) MAP International www.map.org
PO Box 215000   Brunswick GA 31521
Ph: 912-265-6010 ▪ Fx: 912-265-6170 ▪ TF: 800-225-8550

Medical Assistance to Travellers, International Association for www.iamat.org
40 Regal Rd   Guelph ON N1K1B5
Ph: 519-836-0102 ▪ Fx: 519-836-3412

Medical Assistants, American Association of www.aama-ntl.org
20 N Wacker Dr Suite 1575   Chicago IL 60606
Ph: 312-899-1500 ▪ Fx: 312-899-1259 ▪ TF: 800-228-2262

Medical Assistants, American Registry of
69 Southwick Rd   Westfield MA 01085
Ph: 413-562-7336 ▪ Fx: 413-562-9021 ▪ TF: 800-527-2762

Medical Assistants, American Society of Podiatric www.aspma.org
2124 S Austin Blvd   Cicero IL 60804
Ph: 708-863-6303 ▪ Fx: 708-863-5375 ▪ TF: 888-882-7762

Medical Association, Aerospace www.asma.org
320 S Henry St   Alexandria VA 22314
Ph: 703-739-2240 ▪ Fx: 703-739-9652

Medical Association, American www.ama-assn.org
515 N State St   Chicago IL 60610
Ph: 312-464-5000 ▪ Fx: 312-464-4184 ▪ TF: 800-621-8335

Medical Association, American Holistic www.holisticmedicine.org
12101 Menaul Blvd NE Suite C   Albuquerque NM 87112
Ph: 505-292-7788 ▪ Fx: 505-293-7582

Medical Association, American Holistic Veterinary www.ahvma.org
2218 Old Emmorton Rd   Bel Air MD 21015
Ph: 410-569-0795 ▪ Fx: 410-569-2346

Medical Association, American Naturopathic　　　www.anma.com
PO Box 96273　Las Vegas NV 89193
Ph: 702-897-7053 ▪ Fx: 702-897-7140

Medical Association, American Podiatric　　　www.apma.org
9312 Old Georgetown Rd　Bethesda MD 20814
Ph: 301-571-9200 ▪ Fx: 301-634-2752 ▪ TF: 800-275-2762

Medical Association, Canadian　　　　　www.cma.ca
1867 Alta Vista Dr　Ottawa ON K1G3Y6
Ph: 613-731-9331 ▪ Fx: 613-731-7314

Medical Association, Catholic　　　　www.cathmed.org
159 Washington St Suite 3　Boston MA 02135
Ph: 617-782-3356 ▪ Fx: 617-782-3362

Medical Association, Civil Aviation　　　www.civilavmed.com
PO Box 23864　Oklahoma City OK 73123
Ph: 405-840-0199 ▪ Fx: 405-848-1053

Medical Association Foundation,　　www.ama-assn.org/ama/pub/category/3119.html
American　515 N State St　Chicago IL 60610
Ph: 312-464-4543 ▪ Fx: 312-464-5973

Medical Association, Interstate Postgraduate　　www.ipmameded.org
PO Box 5474　Madison WI 53705
Ph: 608-231-9045 ▪ Fx: 877-292-4489

Medical Association, National　　　　www.nmanet.org
1012 10th St NW　Washington DC 20001
Ph: 202-347-1895 ▪ Fx: 202-842-3293 ▪ TF: 800-662-0554

Medical Association, National Arab American　　www.naama.com
801 S Adams Rd Suite 208　Birmingham MI 48009
Ph: 248-646-3661 ▪ Fx: 248-646-0617

Medical Association, National Hispanic　　www.nhmamd.org
1411 K St NW Suite 200　Washington DC 20005
Ph: 202-628-5895 ▪ Fx: 202-628-5898

Medical Association, National Podiatric
1706 E 87th St　Chicago IL 60617
Ph: 773-374-1616 ▪ Fx: 773-374-5860

Medical Association of North America, Islamic　　www.imana.org
950 75th St　Downers Grove IL 60516
Ph: 630-852-2122 ▪ Fx: 630-435-1429

Medical Association PAC, American
1101 Vermont Ave NW 12th Fl　Washington DC 20005
Ph: 202-789-7400 ▪ Fx: 202-789-7485

Medical Association, Southern　　　　www.sma.org
35 Lakeshore Dr　Birmingham AL 35209
Ph: 205-945-1840 ▪ Fx: 205-942-0642 ▪ TF: 800-423-4992

Medical Association, Student National　　　www.snma.org
5113 Georgia Ave NW　Washington DC 20011
Ph: 202-882-2881 ▪ Fx: 202-882-2886

Medical Association, Student Osteopathic　　www.studentdo.com
142 E Ontario St 6th Fl　Chicago IL 60611
Ph: 800-621-1772

Medical & Biological Engineering, American Institute for　www.aimbe.org
1901 Pennsylvania Ave NW Suite 401　Washington DC 20006
Ph: 202-496-9660 ▪ Fx: 202-466-8489

Medical Boards, Federation of Podiatric　　www.fpmb.org
PO Box 880187　Boca Raton FL 33474
Ph: 561-477-3060

Medical Boards of the US Inc, Federation of State　　www.fsmb.org
400 Fuller Wiser Rd Suite 300　Euless TX 76039
Ph: 817-868-4000 ▪ Fx: 817-868-4099 ▪ TF: 800-876-5396

Medical Care Development Inc　　　　www.mcd.org
1742 R St NW　Washington DC 20009
Ph: 202-462-1920 ▪ Fx: 202-265-4078

Medical Colleges, Association of American　　www.aamc.org
2450 'N' St NW　Washington DC 20037
Ph: 202-828-0400 ▪ Fx: 202-828-1125

Medical Consultants to the Armed Forces, Society of　www.smcaf.org

Medical Consumers, Center for　　　www.medicalconsumers.org
130 MacDougal St　New York NY 10012
Ph: 212-674-7105 ▪ Fx: 212-674-7100

Medical Corps, International　　　　www.imc-la.com
1919 Santa Monica Blvd Suite 300　Santa Monica CA 90404
Ph: 310-826-7800 ▪ Fx: 310-442-6622 ▪ TF: 800-481-4462

Medical Decision Making, Society for　　www.smdm.org
1211 Locust St　Philadelphia PA 19107
Ph: 215-545-7697 ▪ Fx: 215-545-8107

Medical & Dental Association, National　　www.polishnmda.com
72-41 Grand Ave　Maspeth NY 11378
Ph: 718-478-3333

Medical & Dental Associations, Christian　　www.cmdahome.org
PO Box 7500　Bristol TN 37620
Ph: 423-844-1000 ▪ Fx: 423-844-1005

Medical-Dental Management Consultants, Society of　www.smdmc.org
125 Strafford Ave Suite 300　Wayne PA 19087
Ph: 800-826-2264 ▪ Fx: 610-687-7702

Medical Device Manufacturers Association　　www.medicaldevices.org
1900 K St NW Suite 300　Washington DC 20006
Ph: 202-496-7150 ▪ Fx: 202-496-7756

Medical Diagnostics Manufacturers, Association of　www.amdm.org
555 13th St NW Suite 7W-404　Washington DC 20004
Ph: 202-637-6837 ▪ Fx: 202-637-5910

Medical Directors Association, American　　www.amda.com
10480 Little Patuxent Pkwy Suite 760　Columbia MD 21044
Ph: 410-740-9743 ▪ Fx: 410-740-4572 ▪ TF: 800-876-2632

Medical Distributors Association, Independent　　www.imda.org
414 Plaza Dr Suite 209　Westmont IL 60559
Ph: 866-463-2937 ▪ Fx: 630-655-0391

Medical Education, Accreditation Council for Graduate　www.acgme.org
515 N State St Suite 2000　Chicago IL 60610
Ph: 312-755-5000 ▪ Fx: 312-755-7498

Medical Education, Alliance for Continuing　　www.acme-assn.org
1025 Montgomery Hwy Suite 105　Birmingham AL 35216
Ph: 205-824-1355 ▪ Fx: 205-824-1357

Medical Education, Association for the Behavioral Sciences &　www.absame.org
1460 N Center Rd　Burton MI 48509
Ph: 810-715-4365 ▪ Fx: 810-715-4371

Medical Education, Association for Hospital　　www.ahme.org
419 Beulah Rd　Pittsburgh PA 15235
Ph: 412-244-9302 ▪ Fx: 412-243-4693 ▪ TF: 866-617-4780

Medical Education, Fund for Podiatric　　www.apma.org/fpme/fundmain.htm
9312 Old Georgetown Rd　Bethesda MD 20814
Ph: 301-581-9200 ▪ Fx: 301-530-2752

Medical Education, Liaison Committee on　　www.lcme.org
American Medical Assn 515 N State St　Chicago IL 60610
Ph: 312-464-4933 ▪ Fx: 312-464-5830

Medical Education & Research in Substance Abuse, Association of　www.amersa.org
125 Whipple St Suite 300　Providence RI 02908
Ph: 401-349-0000 ▪ Fx: 877-418-8769

Medical Education for South African Blacks　　www.mesab.org/
120 Albany St Suite 810　New Brunswick NJ 08901
Ph: 732-745-1292 ▪ Fx: 732-745-9794

Medical Educators, Association of Osteopathic Directors &　www.aodme.org
142 E Ontario St　Chicago IL 60611
Ph: 312-202-8211 ▪ Fx: 312-202-8224

Medical Equestrian Association, American　　www.ameaonline.org
PO Box 130848　Birmingham AL 35213
Ph: 866-441-2632

Medical Ethics & Mediation, Center for　　www.cmem.org
PO Box 86110　San Diego CA 92138
Ph: 619-296-7268

Medical Evangelism, Fellowship of Associates of　www.fameworld.org
PO Box 33548　Indianapolis IN 46203
Ph: 317-358-2480 ▪ Fx: 317-358-2483

Medical Examiners, American Board of Independent　www.abime.org
111 Lions Dr Suite 217　Barrington IL 60010
Ph: 847-277-7902 ▪ Fx: 847-277-7912 ▪ TF: 800-234-3490

Medical Examiners, National Association of　　www.thename.org
430 Pryor St SW　Atlanta GA 30312
Ph: 404-730-4781 ▪ Fx: 404-730-4420

Medical Examiners, National Board of Podiatric　www.nbpme.info
PO Box 510　Bellefonte PA 16823
Ph: 814-357-0487 ▪ Fx: 814-357-0581

Medical Fellowships, National　　　www.nmfonline.org
5 Hanover Sq 15th Fl　New York NY 10004
Ph: 212-483-8880 ▪ Fx: 212-483-8897

Medical Foundation, Ellison　　　www.ellisonfoundation.org
4710 Bethesda Ave Suite 204　Bethesda MD 20814
Ph: 301-657-1830 ▪ Fx: 301-657-1828

Medical Fraternity, Phi Chi　　　　www.phi-chi.org
2039 Ridgewood Dr　Floyds Knobs IN 47119
Ph: 812-948-0581 ▪ Fx: 812-941-8850 ▪ TF: 800-800-7442

Medical Fraternity, Phi Delta Epsilon　　　www.phide.org
2228 E Solana Dr　Phoenix AZ 85016
Ph: 800-347-3713 ▪ Fx: 602-956-3983

Medical Friends of Wine, Society of　　medicalfriendsofwine.org
511 Jones Pl　Walnut Creek CA 94597
Ph: 925-933-9691 ▪ Fx: 925-939-5224

Medical Genetics, American College of　　www.acmg.net
9650 Rockville Pike　Bethesda MD 20814
Ph: 301-530-7127 ▪ Fx: 301-634-7275

Medical Group Association, American　　www.amga.org
1422 Duke St　Alexandria VA 22314
Ph: 703-838-0033 ▪ Fx: 703-548-1890

Medical Group Management Association　　www.mgma.com
104 Inverness Terr E　Englewood CO 80112
Ph: 303-799-1111 ▪ Fx: 303-643-4439 ▪ TF: 877-275-6462

Medical Hypnoanalysts, American Academy of　www.aamh.com
1022 Depot Hill Rd　Broomfield CO 80020
Ph: 888-454-9766 ▪ Fx: 303-465-1260

Medical Illustrators, Association of　　www.ami.org
5475 Mark Dabling Blvd Suite 108　Colorado Springs CO 80918
Ph: 719-598-8622 ▪ Fx: 719-599-3075

Medical Impression, American Military　　www.ww2medicine.org
PO Box 2026　Columbia MD 21045
Ph: 410-381-4293

Medical Informatics Association, American　　www.amia.org
4915 Saint Elmo Ave Suite 401　Bethesda MD 20814
Ph: 301-657-1291 ▪ Fx: 301-657-1296

Medical Instrumentation, Association for the Advancement of　www.aami.org
1110 N Glebe Rd Suite 220　Arlington VA 22201
Ph: 703-525-4890 ▪ Fx: 703-276-0793 ▪ TF: 800-332-2264

Medical Library Association　　　　www.mlanet.org
65 E Wacker Pl Suite 1900　Chicago IL 60601
Ph: 312-419-9094 ▪ Fx: 312-419-8950

Medical Management, American Academy of　www.mlanet.org
6855 Jimmy Carter Blvd Suite 2100　Norcross GA 30071
Ph: 770-734-9904 ▪ Fx: 770-734-9709

Medical Management Association, Biotech　　www.bmma.org
10592 Perry Hwy Suite 300　Wexford PA 15090
Ph: 724-934-8440 ▪ Fx: 724-934-8449 ▪ TF: 888-990-2662

Medical Marketing Association　　　　www.mmanet.org
74 New Montgomery St Suite 230　San Francisco CA 94105
Ph: 415-764-4807 ▪ Fx: 415-927-5734 ▪ TF: 800-551-2173

Medical Milk Commissions Inc, American Association of
1824 N Hillhurst Ave　Los Angeles CA 90027
Ph: 323-664-1977 ▪ Fx: 323-664-0870

Medical Ministries, Children's　　　www.childmed.org
PO Box 3382　Crofton MD 21114
Ph: 301-261-3211 ▪ Fx: 301-721-4647

Medical Minority Educators Inc, National Association of   www.namme-hpe.org

Medical Mission Board, Catholic   www.cmmb.org
10 W 17th St   New York NY 10011
Ph: 212-242-7757 ▪ Fx: 212-807-9161 ▪ TF: 800-678-5659

Medical Mission Sisters   www.medicalmissionsisters.org
8400 Pine Rd   Philadelphia PA 19111
Ph: 215-742-6100 ▪ Fx: 215-342-3948

Medical Physics, American College of   www.acmp.org
12100 Sunset Hills Rd Suite 130   Reston VA 20190
Ph: 703-481-5001 ▪ Fx: 703-435-4390

Medical Practice Executives, American College of   www.mgma.com/acmpe
104 Inverness Terr E   Englewood CO 80112
Ph: 303-799-1111 ▪ Fx: 303-643-4427 ▪ TF: 888-608-5601

Medical Publishers Association, American   www.ampaonline.org
14 Fort Hill Rd   Huntington NY 11743
Ph: 631-423-0075

Medical Quality, American College of   www.acmq.org
4334 Montgomery Ave 2nd Fl   Bethesda MD 20814
Ph: 301-913-9149 ▪ Fx: 301-913-9142 ▪ TF: 800-924-2149

Medical Records Institute   www.medrecinst.com
255 Washington St 2 Newton Pl Suite 180   Newton MA 02458
Ph: 617-964-3923 ▪ Fx: 617-964-3926

Medical Rehabilitation Providers Association, American   www.amrpa.org
1710 'N' St NW   Washington DC 20036
Ph: 202-223-1920 ▪ Fx: 202-223-1925 ▪ TF: 888-346-4624

Medical Relief Inc, World   www.worldmedicalrelief.com
11745 Rosa Parks Blvd   Detroit MI 48206
Ph: 313-866-5333 ▪ Fx: 313-866-5588

Medical Research, American Federation for   www.afmr.org
900 Cummings Ctr Suite 221-U   Beverly MA 01915
Ph: 978-927-8330 ▪ Fx: 978-524-8890

Medical & Research Foundation, African   www.amref.org
19 W 44th St Suite 710   New York NY 10036
Ph: 212-768-2440 ▪ Fx: 212-768-4230

Medical Research Foundation, Dystonia   www.dystonia-foundation.org
1 E Wacker Dr Suite 2430   Chicago IL 60601
Ph: 312-755-0198 ▪ Fx: 312-803-0138 ▪ TF: 800-377-3978

Medical Research, Paul G Allen Foundation for   www.pgafoundations.com/med.asp
505 5th Ave S Suite 900   Seattle WA 98104
Ph: 206-342-2000 ▪ Fx: 206-342-3000

Medical Review Officers, American Association of   www.aamro.com
PO Box 12873   Research Triangle Park NC 27709
Ph: 919-489-5407 ▪ Fx: 919-490-1010 ▪ TF: 800-489-1839

Medical School Pediatric Department Chairs, Association of
111 Silver Cedar Ct   Chapel Hill NC 27514
Ph: 919-942-1993 ▪ Fx: 919-929-9255

Medical Services, Association of Air   www.aams.org
526 King St Suite 415   Alexandria VA 22314
Ph: 703-836-8732 ▪ Fx: 703-836-8920

Medical Society, Alpha Omega Alpha Honor   www.alphaomegaalpha.org
525 Middlefield Rd Suite 130   Menlo Park CA 94025
Ph: 650-329-0291 ▪ Fx: 650-329-1618

Medical Society Executives, American Association of   www.aamse.org
611 E Wells St   Milwaukee WI 53202
Ph: 414-221-9275 ▪ Fx: 414-276-3349

Medical Society, Phi Rho Sigma   www.phirhosigma.org
PO Box 90264   Indianapolis IN 46290
Ph: 317-334-8720 ▪ Fx: 317-334-8721

Medical Society for Sports Medicine, American   www.amssm.org
11639 Earnshaw St   Overland Park KS 66210
Ph: 913-327-1415 ▪ Fx: 913-327-1491

Medical Society, Undersea & Hyperbaric   www.uhms.org
10531 Metropolitan Ave   Kensington MD 20895
Ph: 301-942-2980 ▪ Fx: 301-942-7804

Medical Society, Wilderness   www.wms.org
5390 N Academy Blvd Suite 310   Colorado Springs CO 80910
Ph: 719-572-9255 ▪ Fx: 719-572-1514

Medical Sonographers, American Registry of Diagnostic   www.ardms.org
51 Monroe St Plaza East 1   Rockville MD 20850
Ph: 301-738-8401 ▪ Fx: 301-738-0312 ▪ TF: 800-541-9754

Medical Sonography, Society of Diagnostic   www.sdms.org
2745 N Dallas Pkwy Suite 350   Plano TX 75093
Ph: 214-473-8057 ▪ Fx: 214-473-8563 ▪ TF: 800-229-9506

Medical Specialties, American Board of   www.abms.org
1007 Church St Suite 404   Evanston IL 60201
Ph: 847-491-9091 ▪ Fx: 847-328-3596

Medical Specialty Societies, Council of   www.cmss.org
51 Sherwood Terr Suite M   Lake Bluff IL 60044
Ph: 847-295-3456 ▪ Fx: 847-295-3759

Medical Staff Services, National Association   www.namss.org
8317 Cross Park Dr Suite 150   Austin TX 78754
Ph: 512-454-7928 ▪ Fx: 512-454-3036

Medical Student Association, American   www.amsa.org
1902 Association Dr   Reston VA 20191
Ph: 703-620-6600 ▪ Fx: 703-620-5873 ▪ TF: 800-767-2266

Medical Students' Association, American Podiatric   www.apmsa.org
9312 Old Georgetown Rd   Bethesda MD 20814
Ph: 301-493-9667 ▪ Fx: 301-530-2752

Medical Studies in Female Health, World Foundation for   www.wffh.org
405 Main St Suite 8   Port Washington NY 11050
Ph: 516-944-8655 ▪ Fx: 516-944-8663

Medical-Surgical Nurses, Academy of   www.medsurgnurse.org
PO Box 56   Pitman NJ 08071
Ph: 856-256-2323 ▪ Fx: 856-589-7463

Medical Teams International, Northwest   www.nwmti.com
PO Box 10   Portland OR 97207
Ph: 503-624-1000 ▪ Fx: 503-624-1001 ▪ TF: 800-959-4325

Medical Technicians, National Association of Emergency   www.naemt.org
PO Box 1400   Clinton MS 39060
Ph: 800-346-2368

Medical Technologists, American   www.amt1.com
710 Higgins Rd   Park Ridge IL 60068
Ph: 847-823-5169 ▪ Fx: 847-823-0458 ▪ TF: 800-275-1268

Medical Technology Association, Advanced   www.advamed.org
1200 G St NW Suite 400   Washington DC 20005
Ph: 202-783-8700 ▪ Fx: 202-783-8750

Medical Tennis Association, American   www.mdtennis.org
1803 Cobbleston Dr   Provo UT 84604
Ph: 800-326-2682 ▪ Fx: 801-374-0135

Medical Toxicology, American College of   www.acmt.net
11240 Waples Mill Rd Suite 200   Fairfax VA 22030
Ph: 703-934-1223 ▪ Fx: 703-359-7562

Medical Transcription, American Association for   www.aamt.org
100 Sycamore Ave   Modesto CA 95354
Ph: 209-527-9620 ▪ Fx: 209-527-9633 ▪ TF: 800-982-2182

Medical Transcription Industry Alliance   www.mtia.com
711 Broadway E Suite 7   Seattle WA 98102
Ph: 800-543-6842 ▪ Fx: 206-628-3333

Medical War Memorial Project, National   www.medicalwarmemorial.org
PO Box 14492   Kansas City MO 64152
Ph: 816-452-0606 ▪ Fx: 816-454-0897

Medical Women's Association, American   www.amwa-doc.org
801 N Fairfax St Suite 400   Alexandria VA 22314
Ph: 703-838-0500 ▪ Fx: 703-549-3864

Medical Writers Association, American   www.amwa.org
40 W Gude Dr Suite 101   Rockville MD 20850
Ph: 301-294-5303 ▪ Fx: 301-294-9006

Medical Writers Association, American Podiatric
104-20 Queens Blvd Suite 17B   Forest Hills NY 11375
Ph: 718-897-9700 ▪ Fx: 718-896-5747

MedicAlert Foundation International   www.medicalert.org
2323 Colorado Ave   Turlock CA 95382
Ph: 209-668-3333 ▪ Fx: 209-669-2495 ▪ TF: 800-432-5378

Medically Dependent & Disabled, National Legal Center for the
1 S 6th St   Terre Haute IN 47808
Ph: 812-232-2434 ▪ Fx: 812-235-3658

Medicare, National Committee to Preserve Social Security &   www.ncpssm.org
10 G St NE Suite 600   Washington DC 20002
Ph: 202-216-0420 ▪ Fx: 202-216-0451 ▪ TF: 800-966-1935

Medicare Rights Center   www.medicarerights.org
1460 Broadway 17th Fl   New York NY 10036
Ph: 212-869-3850 ▪ Fx: 212-869-3532 ▪ TF: 800-333-4114

Medicine, Academy of Breastfeeding   www.bfmed.org
191 Clarksville Rd   Princeton Junction NJ 08550
Ph: 609-799-6327 ▪ Fx: 609-799-7032 ▪ TF: 877-836-9947

Medicine, Academy of Dental Sleep   www.dentalsleepmed.org
1 Westbrook Corporate Ctr Suite 920   Westchester IL 60154
Ph: 708-273-9335 ▪ Fx: 708-492-0943

Medicine, Academy of Psychosomatic   www.apm.org
5824 N Magnolia Ave   Chicago IL 60660
Ph: 773-784-2025 ▪ Fx: 773-784-1304

Medicine Alliance, Acupuncture & Oriental   www.aomalliance.org
6405 43rd Avenue Ct NW Suite B   Gig Harbor WA 98335
Ph: 253-851-6896 ▪ Fx: 253-851-6883

Medicine, American Academy of Anti-Aging   www.worldhealth.net
2415 N Greenview Ave   Chicago IL 60614
Ph: 773-528-4333 ▪ Fx: 773-528-5390

Medicine, American Academy of Emergency   www.aaem.org
611 E Wells St   Milwaukee WI 53202
Ph: 800-884-2236 ▪ Fx: 414-276-3349

Medicine, American Academy of Environmental   www.aaem.com
7701 E Kellogg Dr Suite 625   Wichita KS 67207
Ph: 316-684-5500 ▪ Fx: 316-684-5709

Medicine, American Academy of Hospice & Palliative   www.aahpm.org
4700 W Lake Ave   Glenview IL 60025
Ph: 847-375-4712 ▪ Fx: 877-734-8671

Medicine, American Academy of Insurance   www.aaimedicine.org
174 Colonade Rd   Ottawa ON K2E7J5
Ph: 613-226-9601 ▪ Fx: 613-721-3581

Medicine, American Academy of Podiatric Sports   www.aapsm.org
PO Box 723   Rockville MD 20848
Ph: 301-845-9887 ▪ Fx: 301-845-9888 ▪ TF: 800-438-3338

Medicine, American Academy of Sleep   www.aasmnet.org
1 Westbrook Corporate Ctr Suite 920   Westchester IL 60154
Ph: 708-492-0930 ▪ Fx: 708-492-0943

Medicine, American Academy of Tropical
PO Box 24224   Detroit MI 48224
Ph: 313-882-0641 ▪ Fx: 313-882-5110

Medicine, American Association for the History of   www.histmed.org
East Carolina Univ School of Medicine Dept of Medical
Humanities   Greenville NC 27858
Ph: 252-816-2797 ▪ Fx: 252-816-2319

Medicine, American Association of Orthopaedic   www.aaomed.org
PO Box 4997   Buena Vista CO 81211
Ph: 719-475-0032 ▪ Fx: 719-395-5615 ▪ TF: 800-922-2063

Medicine, American Association of Physicists in   www.aapm.org
1 Physics Ellipse   College Park MD 20740
Ph: 301-209-3350 ▪ Fx: 301-209-0862

Medicine, American Board of Emergency   www.abem.org
3000 Coolidge Rd   East Lansing MI 48823
Ph: 517-332-4800 ▪ Fx: 517-332-2234

Medicine, American Board of Environmental   www.americanboardofenvironmentalmedicine.org
65 Wehrle Dr   Buffalo NY 14225
Ph: 716-833-2213 ▪ Fx: 716-833-2244

Medicine, American Board of Preventive   www.abprevmed.org
330 S Wells St Suite 1018   Chicago IL 60606
Ph: 312-939-2276 ▪ Fx: 312-939-2218

Medicine, American College for Advancement in   www.acam.com
23121 Verdugo Dr Suite 204   Laguna Hills CA 92653
Ph: 949-583-7666 ▪ Fx: 949-455-9679 ▪ TF: 800-532-3688

Medicine, American College of Laboratory Animal www.aclam.org
Univ of Houston Houston TX 77204
Ph: 713-743-9191 ▪ Fx: 713-743-9200

Medicine, American College of Legal www.aclm.org
1111 N Plaza Dr Suite 550 Schaumburg IL 60173
Ph: 847-969-0283 ▪ Fx: 847-517-7229

Medicine, American College of Managed Care www.acmcm.org
4435 Waterfront Dr Suite 101 Glen Allen VA 23060
Ph: 804-527-1906 ▪ Fx: 804-747-5316

Medicine, American College of Nuclear www.acnucmed.org
PO Box 175 Landisville PA 17538
Ph: 717-898-5008 ▪ Fx: 717-898-2555

Medicine, American College of Occupational & Environmental www.acoem.org
1114 N Arlington Heights Rd Arlington Heights IL 60004
Ph: 847-818-1800 ▪ Fx: 847-818-9266

Medicine, American College of Sports www.acsm.org
401 W Michigan St Indianapolis IN 46206
Ph: 317-637-9200 ▪ Fx: 317-634-7817

Medicine, American College of Veterinary Internal www.acvim.org
1997 Wadsworth Blvd Suite A Lakewood CO 80214
Ph: 303-231-9933 ▪ Fx: 303-231-0880 ▪ TF: 800-245-9081

Medicine, American Congress of Rehabilitation www.acrm.org
6801 Lake Plaza Dr Suite B-205 Indianapolis IN 46220
Ph: 317-915-2250 ▪ Fx: 317-915-2245

Medicine, American Institute of Ultrasound in www.aium.org
14750 Sweitzer Ln Suite 100 Laurel MD 20707
Ph: 301-498-4100 ▪ Fx: 301-498-4450 ▪ TF: 800-638-5352

Medicine, American Orthopaedic Society for Sports www.sportsmed.org
6300 N River Rd Suite 500 Rosemont IL 60018
Ph: 847-292-4900 ▪ Fx: 847-292-4905 ▪ TF: 877-321-3500

Medicine, American Osteopathic Academy for Addiction
142 E Ontario St Chicago IL 60611
Ph: 312-202-8163 ▪ Fx: 312-202-8463

Medicine, American Osteopathic Academy of Sports www.aoasm.org
7600 Terrace Ave Suite 203 Middleton WI 53562
Ph: 608-831-4400 ▪ Fx: 608-831-5185

Medicine, American Osteopathic Board of Emergency www.aobem.org
142 E Ontario St 8th Fl Chicago IL 60611
Ph: 312-335-1065 ▪ Fx: 312-335-5489

Medicine, American Osteopathic College of Occupational & Preventive www.aocopm.org
PO Box 2606 Leesburg VA 20177
Ph: 800-558-8686 ▪ Fx: 703-443-0567

Medicine, American Society of Addiction www.asam.org
4601 N Park Ave Upper Arcade Suite 101 Chevy Chase MD 20815
Ph: 301-656-3920 ▪ Fx: 301-656-3815

Medicine, American Society of Podiatric
1111 Lane Concourse Dr Suite 111 Bay Harbor FL 33152
Ph: 305-866-9608 ▪ Fx: 305-866-1750

Medicine, American Society for Reproductive www.asrm.org
1209 Montgomery Hwy Birmingham AL 35216
Ph: 205-978-5000 ▪ Fx: 205-978-5005

Medicine, Association for the Advancement of Automotive www.carcrash.org
PO Box 4176 Barrington IL 60011
Ph: 847-844-3880 ▪ Fx: 847-844-3884

Medicine, Association for Integrative www.integrativemedicine.org
Box 1 Mont Clare PA 19453
Ph: 610-933-8145 ▪ Fx: 610-983-9162

Medicine, Association of Professors of www.im.org/apm
2501 M St NW Suite 550 Washington DC 20037
Ph: 202-861-7700 ▪ Fx: 202-861-9731

Medicine, Association of Program Directors in Internal www.im.org/APDIM
2501 M St NW Suite 550 Washington DC 20037
Ph: 202-887-9450 ▪ Fx: 202-887-9447 ▪ TF: 800-622-4558

Medicine, Association for Psychoanalytic www.theapm.org
4560 Delafield Ave Riverdale NY 10471
Ph: 718-548-6088 ▪ Fx: 718-548-8302

Medicine, Canadian Academy of Sport www.casm-acms.org
1010 Polytek St Unit 14 Suite 100 Ottawa ON K1J9H9
Ph: 613-748-5851 ▪ Fx: 613-748-5792 ▪ TF: 877-585-2394

Medicine, Clerkship Directors in Internal www.im.org/cdim
2501 M St NW Suite 550 Washington DC 20037
Ph: 202-861-8600 ▪ Fx: 202-861-9731

Medicine, Council of Colleges of Acupuncture & Oriental www.ccaom.org
7501 Greenway Ctr Dr Suite 820 Greenbelt MD 20770
Ph: 301-313-0868 ▪ Fx: 301-313-0869

Medicine & Ethics, American Society of Law www.aslme.org
765 Commonwealth Ave 16th Fl Boston MA 02215
Ph: 617-262-4990 ▪ Fx: 617-437-7596

Medicine, Friends of the National Library of www.fnlm.org
1555 Connecticut Ave NW Suite 200 Washington DC 20036
Ph: 202-462-0992 ▪ Fx: 202-462-9043

Medicine & Hygiene, American Society of Tropical www.astmh.org
60 Revere Dr Suite 500 Northbrook IL 60062
Ph: 847-480-9592 ▪ Fx: 847-480-9282

Medicine, Institute of www.iom.edu
500 5th St NW Washington DC 20001
Ph: 202-334-2352 ▪ Fx: 202-334-1412

Medicine, International Association for Aquatic Animal iaaam.org

Medicine, International Society for Magnetic Resonance in www.ismrm.org
2118 Millvia St Suite 201 Berkeley CA 94704
Ph: 510-841-1899 ▪ Fx: 510-841-2340

Medicine, International Society for the Study of Subtle Energies & Energy www.issseem.org
11005 Ralston Rd Suite 100D Arvada CO 80004
Ph: 303-425-4625 ▪ Fx: 303-425-4685

Medicine, International Society of Travel www.istm.org
PO Box 871089 Stone Mountain GA 30087
Ph: 770-736-7060 ▪ Fx: 770-736-6732

Medicine in Israel, American Physicians Fellowship for www.apfmed.org
2001 Beacon St Suite 210 Boston MA 02135
Ph: 617-232-5382 ▪ Fx: 617-739-2616

Medicine, New York Academy of www.nyam.org
1216 5th Ave New York NY 10029
Ph: 212-822-7200

Medicine, North American College of Botanical www.nacbm.org
1116 Park Ave SW Albuquerque NM 87102
Ph: 505-873-8107 ▪ Fx: 505-873-4530

Medicine, Physicians Association for Anthroposophical www.paam.net
1923 Geddes Ave Ann Arbor MI 48104
Ph: 734-930-9462 ▪ Fx: 734-662-1727

Medicine, Physicians' Committee for Responsible www.pcrm.org
5100 Wisconsin Ave NW Suite 400 Washington DC 20016
Ph: 202-686-2210 ▪ Fx: 202-686-2216

Medicine Program, Women in www.aamc.org/members/wim
Association of American Medical Colleges 2450 'N' St NW Washington DC 20037
Ph: 202-828-0521 ▪ Fx: 202-828-1125

Medicine & Rehabilitation, American Academy of Physical www.aapmr.org
1 IBM Plaza Suite 2500 Chicago IL 60611
Ph: 312-464-9700 ▪ Fx: 312-464-0227

Medicine & Rehabilitation, American Board of Physical www.abpmr.org
3015 Allegro Park Ln SW Rochester MN 55902
Ph: 507-282-1776 ▪ Fx: 507-282-9242

Medicine & Rehabilitation, American Osteopathic College of Physical www.aocpmr.org
314 S Knight Ave Park Ridge IL 60068
Ph: 847-825-2515 ▪ Fx: 847-825-2509

Medicine & Science, Foundation for Advances in www.scanning.org
PO Box 832 Mahwah NJ 07430
Ph: 201-818-1010 ▪ Fx: 201-818-0086 ▪ TF: 800-443-0263

Medicine, Society for Adolescent www.adolescenthealth.org
1916 NW Copper Oaks Cir Blue Springs MO 64015
Ph: 816-224-8010 ▪ Fx: 816-224-8009

Medicine, Society of Critical Care www.sccm.org
701 Lee St Suite 200 Des Plaines IL 60016
Ph: 847-827-6869 ▪ Fx: 847-827-6886

Medicine, Society for Experimental Biology & www.sebm.org
197 W Spring Valley Ave Maywood NJ 07607
Ph: 201-291-9080 ▪ Fx: 201-291-2988

Medicine, Society for Free Radical Biology & www.sfrbm.org
2950 Buskirk Ave Suite 170 Walnut Creek CA 94597
Ph: 925-472-5904 ▪ Fx: 925-472-5901

Medicine, Society of General Internal www.sgim.org
2501 M St NW Suite 575 Washington DC 20037
Ph: 202-887-5150 ▪ Fx: 202-887-5405 ▪ TF: 800-822-3060

Medicine, Society for Maternal Fetal www.smfm.org
409 12th St SW Washington DC 20024
Ph: 202-863-2476 ▪ Fx: 202-554-1132

Medicine, Society of Nuclear www.snm.org
1850 Samuel Morse Dr Reston VA 20190
Ph: 703-708-9000 ▪ Fx: 703-708-9015

Medicine, Society for Physical Regulation in Biology & www.sprbm.org
2412 Cobblestone Way Frederick MD 21702
Ph: 301-663-4556 ▪ Fx: 301-694-4948

Medicine, Society of Teachers of Family www.stfm.org
11400 Tomahawk Creek Pkwy Suite 540 Leawood KS 66211
Ph: 913-906-6000 ▪ Fx: 913-906-6096

Medicine & Surgery, American Society for Laser www.aslms.org
2404 Stewart Ave Wausau WI 54401
Ph: 715-845-9283 ▪ Fx: 715-848-2493

Medicine Surgery & Ophthalmology, American Society of Contemporary
820 N Orleans St Suite 208 Chicago IL 60610
Ph: 312-440-0699 ▪ Fx: 312-440-0580 ▪ TF: 800-621-4002

Medicine & Toxicology, International Academy of Oral www.iaomt.org
8297 Championsgate Blvd Suite 193 Championsgate FL 33896
Ph: 863-420-6373 ▪ Fx: 863-420-6394

Medicines, National Association of Alternative www.rentamark.com/naam
PO Box 35189 Chicago IL 60707
Ph: 708-453-0080 ▪ Fx: 708-453-0083

Medieval Academy of America www.medievalacademy.org
104 Mount Auburn St 5th Fl Cambridge MA 02138
Ph: 617-491-1622 ▪ Fx: 617-492-3303

Medieval Art, International Center of www.medievalart.org
The Cloisters Fort Tryon Pk New York NY 10040
Ph: 212-928-1146 ▪ Fx: 212-928-9946

Medieval Spain, American Academy of Research Historians of www.uca.edu/aarhms

Meet the Composer www.meetthecomposer.org
75 9th Ave 3R Suite C New York NY 10011
Ph: 212-645-6949 ▪ Fx: 212-645-9669

Meeting Planners, International Society of www.iami.org/ismp
1224 N Nokomis NE Alexandria MN 56308
Ph: 320-763-4919 ▪ Fx: 320-763-9290

Meeting Planners, National Coalition of Black www.ncbmp.com
8630 Fenton St Suite 126 Silver Spring MD 20910
Ph: 202-628-3952 ▪ Fx: 301-588-0011

Meeting Professionals, Association of www.ampsweb.org
2025 M St NW Suite 800 Washington DC 20036
Ph: 202-973-8686 ▪ Fx: 202-973-8722

Meeting Professionals Association, Connected International www.cimpa.org
9200 Bayard Pl Fairfax VA 22032
Ph: 703-978-6287 ▪ Fx: 703-978-5524

Meeting Professionals International www.mpiweb.org
4455 LBJ Fwy Suite 1200 Dallas TX 75244
Ph: 972-702-3000 ▪ Fx: 972-702-3070

Meeting Professionals, Society of Corporate www.scmp.org
217 Ridgemont Ave San Antonio TX 78209
Ph: 210-822-6522 ▪ Fx: 210-882-9838

Meeting Professionals, Society of Government   www.sgmp.org
908 King St   Alexandria VA 22314
Ph: 703-549-0892 ▪ Fx: 703-549-0708 ▪ TF: 800-827-8916

Meiklejohn Civil Liberties Institute   www.sfsu.edu/~mclicfc
PO Box 673   Berkeley CA 94701
Ph: 510-848-0599 ▪ Fx: 510-848-6008

Mellon Andrew W Foundation   www.mellon.org
140 E 62nd St   New York NY 10021
Ph: 212-838-8400 ▪ Fx: 212-888-4172

Mellon Richard King Foundation   www.fdncenter.org/grantmaker/rkmellon
500 Grant St Suite 4106   Pittsburgh PA 15219
Ph: 412-392-2800 ▪ Fx: 412-392-2837

Melpomene Institute   www.melpomene.org
1010 Universitiy Ave W   Saint Paul MN 55104
Ph: 651-642-1951 ▪ Fx: 651-642-1871

Melville Society   people.hofstra.edu/faculty/John_L_Bryant/Melville
Univ of Minnesota 140 Appleby Hall   Minneapolis MN 55455
Ph: 612-625-0855 ▪ Fx: 612-625-0709

Membrane Society, North American   www.membranes.org
Univ of Toledo Chemical & Environmental Engineering Dept MS
305   Toledo OH 43606
Ph: 419-530-3469 ▪ Fx: 419-530-8086

Memorial Foundation of Germanna Colonies in Virginia   www.germanna.org
PO Box 279   Locust Grove VA 22508
Ph: 540-423-1700 ▪ Fx: 540-423-1747

Memorial Foundation for Jewish Culture   www.mfjc.org
50 Broadway 34th Fl   New York NY 10004
Ph: 212-425-6606 ▪ Fx: 212-425-6602

Memorial Fund, Vietnam Veterans   www.vvmf.org
1023 15th St NW 2nd Fl   Washington DC 20005
Ph: 202-393-0090 ▪ Fx: 202-393-0029

Memorialization Supply Association, International   www.imsa-online.com
PO Box 663   Export PA 15632
Ph: 800-864-4174

Memory Card International Association, Personal Computer   www.pc-card.com
2635 N 1st St Suite 209   San Jose CA 95134
Ph: 408-433-2273 ▪ Fx: 408-433-9558

Men, American Union of   groups.yahoo.com/group/aum
PO Box 80131   Santa Barbara CA 93117
Ph: 805-968-8068

Men & Fathers Resource Center   www.fathers.org
807 Brazos St Suite 315   Austin TX 78701
Ph: 512-472-3237 ▪ Fx: 512-499-8056

Men International
17854 Lyons St   Forest Lake MN 55025
Ph: 651-464-7663 ▪ Fx: 651-464-7135

Men in Mission, Lutheran   www.elca.org/lmm
8765 W Higgins Rd   Chicago IL 60631
Ph: 773-380-2566 ▪ Fx: 773-380-2588 ▪ TF: 800-638-3522

Men, National Coalition of Free   www.ncfm.org
PO Box 129   Manhasset NY 11030
Ph: 516-482-6378 ▪ TF: 888-223-1280

Men, National Organization of Restoring   www.norm.org
3205 Northwood Dr Suite 209   Concord CA 94520
Ph: 925-827-4077 ▪ Fx: 925-827-4119

Men, National Trust for the Development of African American
6811 Kenilworth Ave Suite 501   Riverdale MD 20737
Ph: 301-887-0100 ▪ Fx: 301-887-0405

Men in Nursing, American Assembly for   www.aamn.org
c/o NY State Nurses Assn 11 Cornell Rd   Latham NY 12110
Ph: 518-782-9400 ▪ Fx: 518-782-9530

MENC: National Association for Music Education   www.menc.org
1806 Robert Fulton Dr   Reston VA 20191
Ph: 703-860-4000 ▪ Fx: 703-860-1531 ▪ TF: 800-336-3768

Mencken Society   www.mencken.org
PO Box 16218   Baltimore MD 21210
Ph: 410-857-2431 ▪ Fx: 410-561-0238

Mended Hearts   www.mendedhearts.org
7272 Greenville Ave   Dallas TX 75231
Ph: 214-706-1442 ▪ Fx: 214-706-5245 ▪ TF: 888-432-1899

Mennonite Central Committee   www.mcc.org
21 S 12th St PO Box 500   Akron PA 17501
Ph: 717-859-1151 ▪ Fx: 717-859-2171 ▪ TF: 888-563-4676

Mennonite Church USA Historical Committee   www.mcusa-archives.org
1700 S Main St   Goshen IN 46526
Ph: 574-535-7477 ▪ Fx: 574-535-7756

Mennonite Disaster Service   mds.mennonite.net
1018 Main St   Akron PA 17501
Ph: 717-859-2210 ▪ Fx: 717-859-4910

Mennonite Economic Development Associates   www.meda.org
1821 Oregon Pike Suite 201   Lancaster PA 17601
Ph: 717-560-6546 ▪ Fx: 717-560-6549 ▪ TF: 800-665-7026

Mennonite Historical Society, Lancaster   www.lmhs.org
2215 Millstream Rd   Lancaster PA 17602
Ph: 717-393-9745 ▪ Fx: 717-393-8751

Mennonite Missions, Rosedale   www.rosedalemennonitemissions.org
9920 Rosedale-Milford Ctr Rd   Irwin OH 43029
Ph: 740-857-1366 ▪ Fx: 740-857-1605

Mennonite Voluntary Service   www.mennonitemission.net/Work/Service/MVS
722 Main St Box 347   Newton KS 67114
Ph: 316-283-5155 ▪ Fx: 316-283-0454

Menopause Foundation Inc, American   www.americanmenopause.org
350 5th Ave Suite 2822   New York NY 10118
Ph: 212-714-2398 ▪ Fx: 212-714-1252

Menopause Society, North American   www.menopause.org
5900 Landerbrook Dr Suite 195   Mayfield Heights OH 44124
Ph: 440-442-7550 ▪ Fx: 440-442-2660 ▪ TF: 800-774-5342

Men's Choruses Inc, Intercollegiate   www.cco.caltech.edu/~dgc/imc.html
Kansas State Univ 109 McCain Auditorium   Manhattan KS
66506
Ph: 785-532-3824 ▪ Fx: 785-532-5709

Men's Defense Association   www.mensdefense.org
17854 Lyons St   Forest Lake MN 55025
Ph: 651-464-7887 ▪ Fx: 651-464-7135

Men's International Peace Exchange   www.peaceexchange.org
PO Box 36   Swarthmore PA 19081
Ph: 610-872-8178 ▪ Fx: 610-872-3642

Men's Studies Association, American   www.mensstudies.org
382 W Coyote Ln SE   Albuquerque NM 87123
Ph: 505-323-2386 ▪ Fx: 505-323-3634

Mensa Ltd, American   www.us.mensa.org
1229 Corporate Dr W   Arlington TX 76006
Ph: 817-607-0060 ▪ Fx: 817-649-5232 ▪ TF: 800-666-3672

Menstrual Cycle Research, Society for   www.pop.psu.edu/smcr
10559 N 104th Pl   Scottsdale AZ 85258
Ph: 480-451-9731

Menswear Association, Young
47 W 34th St   New York NY 10001
Ph: 212-594-6422 ▪ Fx: 212-594-9349

Mental Disease, Association for Research in Nervous &   www.arnmd.org/arnmd

Mental Health Administration, American College of   www.acmha.org
324 Freeport Rd   Pittsburgh PA 15238
Ph: 412-820-0670 ▪ Fx: 412-820-0669

Mental Health Association, National   www.nmha.org
1021 Prince St   Alexandria VA 22311
Ph: 703-684-7722 ▪ Fx: 703-684-5968 ▪ TF: 800-969-6642

Mental Health Consumers' Self-Help Clearinghouse, National   www.mhselfhelp.org
1211 Chestnut St Suite 1207   Philadelphia PA 19107
Ph: 215-751-1810 ▪ Fx: 215-636-6312 ▪ TF: 800-553-4539

Mental Health Counselors Association, American   www.amhca.org
801 N Fairfax St Suite 304   Alexandria VA 22314
Ph: 703-548-6002 ▪ Fx: 703-548-4775 ▪ TF: 800-326-2642

Mental Health, Federation of Families for Children's   www.ffcmh.org
1101 King St Suite 420   Alexandria VA 22314
Ph: 703-684-7710 ▪ Fx: 703-836-1040

Mental Health Justice & the Media, Leadership Council for   www.leadershipcouncil.org
191 Presidential Blvd Suite C132   Bala Cynwyd PA 19004
Ph: 610-664-5007 ▪ Fx: 610-664-5279

(Mental Health) National Association for the Dually Diagnosed   www.thenadd.org
132 Fair St   Kingston NY 12401
Ph: 845-331-4336 ▪ Fx: 845-331-4569 ▪ TF: 800-331-5362

Mental Health, National Association for Rural   www.narmh.org
3700 W Division St Suite 105   Saint Cloud MN 56301
Ph: 320-202-1820 ▪ Fx: 320-202-1833 ▪ TF: 800-809-5879

Mental Health Nurses, International Society of Psychiatric-   www.ispn-psych.org
1211 Locust St   Philadelphia PA 19107
Ph: 215-545-2843 ▪ Fx: 215-545-8107 ▪ TF: 800-826-2950

Mental Health Professionals in Corrections, American Association of
PO Box 160208   Sacramento CA 95816
Ph: 916-323-8305 ▪ Fx: 916-649-1070

Mental Health Program Directors, National Association of State   www.nasmhpd.org
66 Canal Center Plaza Suite 302   Alexandria VA 22314
Ph: 703-739-9333 ▪ Fx: 703-548-9517

(Mental Health) Recovery Inc   www.recovery-inc.com
802 N Dearborn St   Chicago IL 60610
Ph: 312-337-5661 ▪ Fx: 312-337-5756

Mental Health, World Association for Infant   www.waimh.org
Michigan State Univ Institute for Children Youth & Families
Kellogg Ctr Rm 27   East Lansing MI 48824
Ph: 517-432-3793 ▪ Fx: 517-432-3694

Mental Illness, National Resource Center on Homelessness &   www.nrchmi.com
345 Delaware Ave   Delmar NY 12054
Ph: 518-439-7415 ▪ Fx: 518-439-7612 ▪ TF: 800-444-7415

Mental Retardation, American Association on   www.aamr.org
444 N Capitol St NW Suite 846   Washington DC 20001
Ph: 202-387-1968 ▪ Fx: 202-387-2193 ▪ TF: 800-424-3688

(Mental Retardation) Order of Alhambra   www.orderalhambra.org
4200 Leeds Ave   Baltimore MD 21229
Ph: 410-242-0660 ▪ Fx: 410-536-5729

(Mentally Disabled) Arc of the US The   www.thearc.org
1010 Wayne Ave Suite 650   Silver Spring MD 20910
Ph: 301-565-3842 ▪ Fx: 301-565-3843 ▪ TF: 800-433-5255

(Mentally Disabled) Little City Foundation   www.littlecity.org
1760 W Algonquin Rd   Palatine IL 60067
Ph: 847-358-5510 ▪ Fx: 847-358-3291

Mentally Ill, National Alliance for the   www.nami.org
2107 Wilson Blvd Suite 300   Arlington VA 22201
Ph: 703-524-7600 ▪ Fx: 703-524-9094 ▪ TF: 800-950-6264

MENTOR/National Mentoring Partnership   www.mentoring.org
1600 Duke St Suite 300   Alexandria VA 22314
Ph: 703-224-2200 ▪ Fx: 703-226-2581

Mentoring USA   www.mentoringusa.org
113 E 13th St   New York NY 10003
Ph: 212-253-1194 ▪ Fx: 212-253-1267

MERCAZ USA   www.mercazusa.org
155 5th Ave   New York NY 10010
Ph: 212-533-7800 ▪ Fx: 212-533-2601

Mercedes-Benz Club of America   www.mbca.org
1907 Lelaray St   Colorado Springs CO 80909
Ph: 719-633-6427 ▪ Fx: 719-633-9283 ▪ TF: 800-637-2360

Merchandise Distributors Council, General   www.gmdc.com
1275 Lake Plaza Dr   Colorado Springs CO 80906
Ph: 719-576-4260 ▪ Fx: 719-576-2661

Merchandise Representatives, National Association of General   www.nagmr.org
110 Friar Tuck Cir   Denton TX 76201
Ph: 940-243-0409 ▪ Fx: 940-382-3741

Merchandisers' Association, International Licensing Industry   www.licensing.org
350 5th Ave Suite 1408   New York NY 10118
Ph: 212-244-1944 ▪ Fx: 212-563-6552

Merchandising Association, National Automatic
20 N Wacker Dr Suite 3500   Chicago IL 60606
Ph: 312-346-0370 ▪ Fx: 312-704-4140
www.vending.org

Merchant Marine Library Association, American
20 Exchange Pl Suite 2901   New York NY 10005
Ph: 212-269-0711 ▪ Fx: 212-432-5492
www.uss-ammla.com

Mercury Owners Association, International
6445 W Grand Ave   Chicago IL 60707
Ph: 773-622-6445 ▪ Fx: 773-622-3602
www.mercuryclub.com

Mercury Policy Project
1420 North St   Montpelier VT 05602
Ph: 802-223-9000
www.mercurypolicy.org

Mercy Corps
3015 SW 1st Ave   Portland OR 97201
Ph: 503-242-1032 ▪ Fx: 503-796-6844 ▪ TF: 800-292-3355
www.mercycorps.org

Mercy Fund, World
PO Box 227   Waterford VA 20197
Ph: 540-882-4425 ▪ Fx: 540-882-3226
www.worldmercyfund.ie

Mercy-USA for Aid & Development Inc
44450 Pinetree Dr Suite 201   Plymouth MI 48170
Ph: 734-454-0011 ▪ Fx: 734-454-0303 ▪ TF: 800-556-3729
www.mercyusa.org

Meridian International Center
1630 Crescent Pl NW   Washington DC 20009
Ph: 202-667-6800 ▪ Fx: 202-667-1475
www.meridian.org

Merino Record Association, American Delaine &
59419 Walters Rd   Jacobsburg OH 43933
Ph: 740-686-2172
www.admra.org

Merleau-Ponty Circle
Binghamton Univ Dept of Philosophy   Binghamton NY 13902
Ph: 607-777-2443 ▪ Fx: 607-777-2734
m-pc.binghamton.edu

Mershon Center
1501 Neil Ave   Columbus OH 43201
Ph: 614-292-1681 ▪ Fx: 614-292-2407
www.mershon.ohio-state.edu

(Merton, Thomas) International Thomas Merton Society
www.merton.org

Meso American Indian Rights Center, South &
PO Box 7829   Oakland CA 94601
Ph: 510-534-4882 ▪ Fx: 510-834-4264
saiic.nativeweb.org

Messenger Courier Association of the Americas
1156 15th St NW Suite 900   Washington DC 20005
Ph: 202-785-3298 ▪ Fx: 202-223-9741
www.mcaa.com

Messianic Congregations & Synagogues, International Alliance of
PO Box 20006   Sarasota FL 34276
Ph: 941-923-0193 ▪ TF: 866-426-2766
iamcs.org

Messianic Jewish Alliance of America
PO Box 274   Springfield PA 19064
Ph: 610-338-0451 ▪ Fx: 610-338-0471 ▪ TF: 800-225-6552
www.mjaa.org

Messianic Jewish Ministries
6204 Park Heights Ave   Baltimore MD 21215
Ph: 410-358-6471 ▪ Fx: 410-764-1376
www.messianicjewish.net

Messianic Jewish Movement International
PO Box 1212   Chandler AZ 85244
Ph: 480-786-6564 ▪ TF: 800-493-7482
www.mjmi.org

Metabolic Eye Disease, International Society on
1125 Park Ave   New York NY 10128
Ph: 212-427-1246 ▪ Fx: 212-360-7009

Metal Building Contractors & Erectors Association
28 Lowry Dr PO Box 117   West Milton OH 45383
Ph: 937-698-4127 ▪ Fx: 937-698-6153 ▪ TF: 800-866-6722
www.mbcea.org

Metal Building Manufacturers Association
1300 Sumner Ave   Cleveland OH 44115
Ph: 216-241-7333 ▪ Fx: 216-241-0105
www.mbma.com

Metal Construction Association
4700 W Lake Ave   Glenview IL 60025
Ph: 847-375-4718 ▪ Fx: 877-665-2235
www.metalconstruction.org

Metal Decorators Association, National
9616 Deereco Rd   Timonium MD 21093
Ph: 410-252-5205 ▪ Fx: 410-628-8079
www.nmda.org

Metal Detecting Association, American
www.amdaonline.net

Metal Finishers, National Association of
12644 Research Parkway Suite 105   Orlando FL 32826
Ph: 407-281-6445 ▪ Fx: 407-281-7345
www.namf.org

Metal Finishing Suppliers' Association
112 J Elden St   Herndon VA 20170
Ph: 703-709-5729 ▪ Fx: 703-709-1036
www.mfsa.org

Metal Framing Manufacturers Association
401 N Michigan Ave   Chicago IL 60611
Ph: 312-644-6610 ▪ Fx: 312-321-4098
www.metalframingmfg.org

Metal Industries, Association of Women in the
515 King St Suite 420   Alexandria VA 22314
Ph: 703-739-8335 ▪ Fx: 703-684-6048
www.awmi.com

Metal Injection Molding Association
105 College Rd E   Princeton NJ 08540
Ph: 609-452-7700 ▪ Fx: 609-987-8523
www.mpif.org/mima.html

Metal Manufacturers, National Association of Architectural
8 S Michigan Ave Suite 1000   Chicago IL 60603
Ph: 312-332-0405 ▪ Fx: 312-332-0706
www.naamm.org

Metal Powder Industries Federation
105 College Rd E   Princeton NJ 08540
Ph: 609-452-7700 ▪ Fx: 609-987-8523
www.mpif.org

Metal Powder Producers Association
105 College Rd E   Princeton NJ 08540
Ph: 609-452-7700 ▪ Fx: 609-987-8523
www.mpif.org/mppa.html

Metal Products Manufacturers Association, Plastic &
225 W 39th St   New York NY 10018
Ph: 212-398-5400 ▪ Fx: 212-398-3141

Metal Statistics, American Bureau of
PO Box 805   Chatham NJ 07928
Ph: 973-701-2299 ▪ Fx: 973-701-2152
www.abms.com

Metal Treating Institute
1550 Roberts Dr   Jacksonville Beach FL 32250
Ph: 904-249-0448 ▪ Fx: 904-249-0459
www.metaltreat.com

Metalcasting Consortium, American
5300 International Blvd   Charleston SC 29418
Ph: 843-760-3219 ▪ Fx: 843-767-3354
amc.aticorp.org

Metalforming Association, Precision
6363 Oak Tree Blvd   Independence OH 44131
Ph: 216-901-8800 ▪ Fx: 216-901-9190
www.metalforming.com

Metallic Silhouette Association, International Handgun
PO Box 9   Anoka MN 55303
Ph: 763-323-3359 ▪ Fx: 763-422-1910
www.ihmsa.org

Metallizers Coaters & Laminators, Association of Industrial
2166 Gold Hill Rd   Fort Mill SC 29708
Ph: 803-802-7820 ▪ Fx: 803-802-7821
aimcal.org

Metallographic Society Inc, International
ASM International 9639 Kinsman Rd   Materials Park OH 44073
Ph: 440-338-5151 ▪ Fx: 440-338-4634
www.metallography.com/ims/info.htm

Metallurgical & Petroleum Engineers, American Institute of Mining
8307 Shaffer Pkwy PO Box 270728   Littleton CO 80127
Ph: 303-948-4255 ▪ Fx: 303-948-4260
www.aimehq.org

Metallurgical Society of America, Mining &
476 Wilson Ave   Novato CA 94947
Ph: 415-897-4236 ▪ Fx: 415-899-0262
www.mmsa.net

Metallurgy & Exploration Inc, Society for Mining
8307 Shaffer Pkwy   Littleton CO 80127
Ph: 303-973-9550 ▪ Fx: 303-973-3845 ▪ TF: 800-763-3132
www.smenet.org

Metals Association, National Ornamental & Miscellaneous
532-A Forest Pkwy   Forest Park GA 30297
Ph: 404-363-4009 ▪ Fx: 404-366-1852
www.nomma.org

Metals & Materials Society, Minerals
184 Thorn Hill Rd   Warrendale PA 15086
Ph: 724-776-9000 ▪ Fx: 724-776-3770 ▪ TF: 800-966-4867
www.tms.org

Metals Service Center Institute
8550 Bryn Mawr Ave Suite 550   Chicago IL 60631
Ph: 773-867-1300 ▪ Fx: 773-867-8750
www.msci.org

Metanoia Ministries
PO Box 1353   Tacoma WA 98401
Ph: 253-627-1580 ▪ Fx: 253-627-1054
www.metanoiaonline.org

Metaphysical Society of America
Univ of Alabama Dept of Philosophy   Huntsville AL 35899
Ph: 205-895-6555 ▪ Fx: 205-895-6949
www.acls.org/metaphys.htm

Metaphysics, School of
163 Moon Valley Rd   Windyville MO 65783
Ph: 417-345-8411 ▪ Fx: 417-345-6668
www.som.org

Meteoritical Society
Univ of Arizona Lunar & Planetary Lab   Tucson AZ 85721
Ph: 520-621-4128 ▪ Fx: 520-621-4933
www.meteoriticalsociety.org

Meteorological Society, American
45 Beacon St   Boston MA 02108
Ph: 617-227-2425 ▪ Fx: 617-742-8718
www.ametsoc.org

Methanol Institute
4100 N Fairfax Dr Suite 470   Arlington VA 22203
Ph: 703-248-3636 ▪ Fx: 703-248-3997 ▪ TF: 888-275-0768
www.methanol.org

Methodist Association of Health & Welfare Ministries, United
601 W Riverview Ave   Dayton OH 45406
Ph: 937-227-9494 ▪ Fx: 937-222-7364 ▪ TF: 800-411-9901
www.umassociation.org

Methodist Church, General Board of Church & Society of the United   100 Maryland Ave NE   Washington DC 20002
Ph: 202-488-5600 ▪ Fx: 202-488-5619
www.umc-gbcs.org

Methodist Church, General Commission on Archives & History of the United   36 Madison Ave PO Box 127   Madison NJ 07940
Ph: 973-408-3189 ▪ Fx: 973-408-3909
www.gcah.org

Methodist Church, National Association of Schools Colleges & Universities of the United   PO Box 340007   Nashville TN 37203
Ph: 615-340-7399 ▪ Fx: 615-340-7379

Methodist Committee on Relief, United
475 Riverside Dr Suite 330   New York NY 10115
Ph: 212-870-3816 ▪ Fx: 212-870-3624 ▪ TF: 800-554-8583
gbgm-umc.org/umcor

Methodist Council, World
PO Box 518   Lake Junaluska NC 28745
Ph: 828-456-9432 ▪ Fx: 828-456-9433
www.worldmethodistcouncil.org

Methodist Federation for Social Action
212 E Capitol St NE   Washington DC 20003
Ph: 202-546-8806 ▪ Fx: 202-546-6811
www.mfsaweb.org

Methodist Historical Society, World
36 Madison Ave PO Box 127   Madison NJ 07940
Ph: 973-408-3789 ▪ Fx: 973-408-3909
www.gcah.org/WMHS.htm

(Methodist) Reconciling Ministries Network
3801 N Keeler Ave   Chicago IL 60641
Ph: 773-736-5526 ▪ Fx: 773-736-5475
www.rmnetwork.org

Methodist Youth Organization, United
1001 19th Ave S PO Box 340003   Nashville TN 37203
Ph: 615-340-7184 ▪ Fx: 615-340-1764 ▪ TF: 877-899-2780
umyouth.org

Methodists for Church Renewal, Black
601 W Riverview Ave   Dayton OH 45406
Ph: 937-227-9460 ▪ Fx: 937-227-9463
www.bmcr-umc.org

Methodists, Mission Society for United
6234 Crooked Creek Rd   Norcross GA 30092
Ph: 770-446-1381 ▪ Fx: 770-446-3044
www.msum.org

Methodists in Music & Worship Arts, Fellowship of United
PO Box 24787   Nashville TN 37202
Ph: 615-749-6875 ▪ Fx: 615-749-6874 ▪ TF: 800-952-8977
www.fummwa.org

Methyl Chloride Industry Association
555 11th St NW Suite 1000   Washington DC 20004
Ph: 202-637-2230 ▪ Fx: 202-637-2201

Metric Association Inc, US
10245 S Andasol Ave   Northridge CA 91325
Ph: 818-363-5606
lamar.colostate.edu/~hillger

Metro Atlantic Athletic Conference www.maacsports.com
712 Amboy Ave   Edison NJ 08837
Ph: 732-738-5455 ▪ Fx: 732-738-8366

Metropolitan Community Churches, Universal Fellowship of www.mccchurch.org
8704 Santa Monica Blvd 2nd Fl   West Hollywood CA 90069
Ph: 310-360-8640 ▪ Fx: 310-360-8680

Metropolitan Opera Association www.metopera.org
Lincoln Ctr   New York NY 10023
Ph: 212-362-6000 ▪ Fx: 212-874-2659

Metropolitan Opera Guild www.metopera.org/guild
70 Lincoln Ctr Plaza 6th Fl   New York NY 10023
Ph: 212-769-7000 ▪ Fx: 212-769-7007 ▪ TF: 800-829-2525

Metropolitan Sewerage Agencies, Association of www.amsa-cleanwater.org
1816 Jefferson Pl NW   Washington DC 20036
Ph: 202-833-2672 ▪ Fx: 202-833-4657

Metropolitan Water Agencies, Association of www.amwa.net
1717 K St NW Suite 801   Washington DC 20036
Ph: 202-331-2820 ▪ Fx: 202-785-1845

Mexican American Cultural Center www.maccsa.org
3115 W Ashby Pl PO Box 28185   San Antonia TX 78228
Ph: 210-732-2156 ▪ Fx: 210-732-9072

Mexican American Grocers Association
405 N San Fernando Rd   Los Angeles CA 90031
Ph: 323-227-1565 ▪ Fx: 323-227-6935

Mexican-American Opportunity Foundation www.maof.org
401 N Garfield Ave   Montebello CA 90640
Ph: 323-890-9600 ▪ Fx: 323-890-9637

Mexican American Unity Council
2300 W Commerce Suite 300   San Antonio TX 78207
Ph: 210-978-0500 ▪ Fx: 210-978-0547

Mexico Border Health Association, US- www.usmbha.org
5400 Suncrest Dr Suite C-5   El Paso TX 79912
Ph: 915-833-6450 ▪ Fx: 915-833-7840

Mexico Chamber of Commerce, US- www.usmcoc.org
1300 Pennsylvania Ave NW Suite 0003   Washington DC 20004
Ph: 202-312-1520 ▪ Fx: 202-312-1530

Meyer Memorial Trust www.mmt.org
425 NW 10th Ave Suite 400   Portland OR 97209
Ph: 503-228-5512 ▪ Fx: 503-228-5840

MHE Coalition www.mhecoalition.com
8838 Holly Ln   Olmsted Falls OH 44138
Ph: 440-235-6325

Michael E DeBakey International Surgical Society www.mediss.org
1 Baylor Plaza   Houston TX 77030
Ph: 713-798-4557 ▪ Fx: 713-796-9605

Michael J Fox Foundation for Parkinson's Research www.michaeljfox.org
PO Box 4777 Grand Central Stn   New York NY 10163
Ph: 800-708-7644

Michener James A Society www.unco.edu/library/jamsociety

Michigan/Canadian Bigfoot Information Center
152 W Sherman   Caro MI 48723
Ph: 989-673-2715

Microbe Interactions, International Society for Molecular Plant www.ismpminet.org
3340 Pilot Knob Rd   Saint Paul MN 55121
Ph: 651-454-7250 ▪ Fx: 651-454-0766 ▪ TF: 800-481-2698

Microbeam Analysis Society www.microbeamanalysis.org

Microbiology, American Society for www.asm.org
1752 'N' St NW   Washington DC 20036
Ph: 202-737-3600

Microbiology, Society for Industrial www.simhq.org
3929 Old Lee Hwy Suite 92A   Fairfax VA 22030
Ph: 703-691-3357 ▪ Fx: 703-691-7991

Microbiology, Waksman Foundation for www.waksmanfoundation.org
Univ of Michigan Medical School Dept of Microbiology &
Immunology Medical Sciences Bldg II Box 620   Ann
Arbor MI 48109
Ph: 734-995-2951 ▪ Fx: 734-995-9071

Microelectronics & Packaging Society, International www.imaps.org
611 2nd St NE   Washington DC 20002
Ph: 202-548-4001 ▪ Fx: 202-548-6115

Microscopical Society, American www.amicros.org
Bryn Mawr College Dept of Biology 101 N Merion Ave   Bryn
Mawr PA 19010
Ph: 610-526-5094 ▪ Fx: 610-526-5086

Microscopy Society of America www.msa.microscopy.org
230 E Ohio St Suite 400   Chicago IL 60611
Ph: 312-644-1527 ▪ Fx: 312-644-8557 ▪ TF: 800-538-3672

Microscopy & Spectroscopy, Society for www.ruf.rice.edu/~jinnys/slms/SLMS.html
Luminescence

Microsurgery, American Society for Reconstructive www.microsurg.org
20 N Michigan Ave Suite 700   Chicago IL 60602
Ph: 312-456-9579 ▪ Fx: 312-782-0553

Microtonal Music Inc, American Festival of www.afmm.org
318 E 70th St Suite 5FW   New York NY 10021
Ph: 212-517-3550 ▪ Fx: 212-517-5495

Microwave Power Institute, International www.impi.org
1916 Sussex Rd   Blacksburg VA 24060
Ph: 540-552-3070 ▪ Fx: 540-961-1463

Microwave Theory & Techniques Society, IEEE www.mtt.org
IEEE Operations Ctr 445 Hoes Ln   Piscataway NJ 08854
Ph: 732-981-0060 ▪ Fx: 732-981-1721

Mid Atlantic Fiber Association www.mafafiber.org
PO Box 701   Scranton PA 18501
Ph: 570-961-2304 ▪ Fx: 570-961-5110

Mid-Continent Railway Historical Society www.midcontinent.org
PO Box 358   North Freedom WI 53951
Ph: 608-522-4261 ▪ Fx: 608-522-4490

Mid-West Truckers Association Inc www.mid-westtruckers.com
2727 N Dirksen Pkwy   Springfield IL 62702
Ph: 217-525-0310 ▪ Fx: 217-525-0342

Midas Dealers Association, International www.imdaonline.org
14 W 3rd St Suite 200   Kansas City MO 64105
Ph: 816-472-6632 ▪ Fx: 816-472-7765 ▪ TF: 877-543-6203

Middle Atlantic Fisheries Association
7 Dey St Suite 801   New York NY 10007
Ph: 212-732-4340 ▪ Fx: 212-732-6644

Middle East, Committee on the www.middleeast.org/archives/come.htm
PO Box 18367   Washington DC 20036
Ph: 202-362-5266 ▪ Fx: 202-362-6965

Middle East Information Network www.mideastinfo.com
197 Fairmont Ave Unit 2   Boston MA 02136
Ph: 617-507-5844

Middle East Institute www.mideasti.org
1761 'N' St NW   Washington DC 20036
Ph: 202-785-1141 ▪ Fx: 202-331-8861

Middle East Librarians Association depts.washington.edu/wsx9/melahp.html
Univ of Washington Libraries Cataloging CB 352900   Seattle
WA 98195
Ph: 206-543-1642 ▪ Fx: 206-685-8787

(Middle East) National US-Arab Chamber of Commerce www.nusacc.org
1023 15th St NW Suite 400   Washington DC 20005
Ph: 202-289-5920 ▪ Fx: 202-289-5938

Middle East Peace, Foundation for www.fmep.org
1761 'N' St NW   Washington DC 20036
Ph: 202-835-3650 ▪ Fx: 202-835-3651

Middle East Policy Council www.mepc.org
1730 M St NW Suite 512   Washington DC 20036
Ph: 202-296-6767 ▪ Fx: 202-296-5791

Middle East Reporting in America, Committee for Accuracy in www.camera.org
PO Box 35040   Boston MA 02135
Ph: 617-789-3672 ▪ Fx: 617-787-7853

Middle East Research & Information Project www.merip.org
1500 Massachusetts Ave NW Suite 119   Washington DC 20005
Ph: 202-223-3677 ▪ Fx: 202-223-3604

Middle East Studies Association of North America fp.arizona.edu/mesassoc
Univ of Arizona 1219 N Santa Rita Ave   Tucson AZ 85721
Ph: 520-621-5850 ▪ Fx: 520-626-9095

Middle East Understanding, www.cafearabica.com/organizations/org12/orgameu1.html
Americans for   475 Riverside Dr Suite 245   New York NY
10115
Ph: 212-870-2053 ▪ Fx: 212-870-2050

Middle School Association, National www.nmsa.org
4151 Executive Pkwy Suite 300   Westerville OH 43081
Ph: 614-895-4730 ▪ Fx: 614-895-4750 ▪ TF: 800-528-6672

Middle States Association of Colleges & Schools www.msache.org
3624 Market St   Philadelphia PA 19104
Ph: 215-662-5600 ▪ Fx: 215-662-5950 ▪ TF: 800-355-1258

Mideast Educational & Training Services, America- www.amideast.org
1730 M St NW Suite 1100   Washington DC 20036
Ph: 202-776-9600 ▪ Fx: 202-776-7000

MIDI Manufacturers Association Inc www.midi.org
PO Box 3173   La Habra CA 90632
Ph: 714-736-9774 ▪ Fx: 714-736-9775

Midwest, Associated Colleges of the www.acm.edu
205 W Wacker Dr Suite 1300   Chicago IL 60606
Ph: 312-263-5000 ▪ Fx: 312-263-5879

Midwest Bioethics Center www.midbio.org
1021-1025 Jefferson St   Kansas City MO 64105
Ph: 816-221-1100 ▪ Fx: 816-221-2002 ▪ TF: 800-344-3829

Midwest Decoy Collectors Association www.midwestdecoy.com
6 E Scott St Suite 3   Chicago IL 60610
Ph: 312-337-7957 ▪ Fx: 312-337-9679

Midwest Fish & Wildlife Agencies, Association of
c/o Nebraska Game & Parks Commission 2200 N 33rd St   PO
Box 30370   Lincoln NE 68503
Ph: 402-471-5539 ▪ Fx: 402-471-5528

Midwest Institute, Northeast- www.nemw.org
218 D St SE   Washington DC 20003
Ph: 202-544-5200 ▪ Fx: 202-544-0043

Midwest Old Settlers & Threshers Association www.oldthreshers.org
405 E Threshers Rd   Mount Pleasant IA 52641
Ph: 319-385-8937 ▪ Fx: 319-385-0563

Midwestern Literature, Society for the Study of writing.msu.edu:16080/ssml
Michigan State Univ Bessey Hall   East Lansing MI 48824
Ph: 517-355-3507 ▪ Fx: 517-353-5250

Midwives Alliance of North America www.mana.org
4805 Lawrenceville Hwy Suite 116-279   Lilburn GA 30047
Ph: 888-923-6262 ▪ Fx: 801-720-3026

Midwives, American College of Community www.collegeofmidwives.org
3889 Middlefield Rd   Palo Alto CA 94303
Ph: 650-328-8491

Migraine Awareness Group: A National Understanding for www.migraines.org
Migraineurs   113 S Saint Asaph St Suite 300   Alexandria VA
22314
Ph: 703-739-9384 ▪ Fx: 703-739-2432

Migrant Education Council, Interstate www.migedimec.org
1 Massachusetts Ave NW Suite 700   Washington DC 20001
Ph: 202-336-7078 ▪ Fx: 202-408-8062

Migrant Education, National Association of State Directors of www.nasdme.org
500 Mero St Rm 832   Frankfort KY 40601
Ph: 502-564-3791

Migrant Legal Action Program www.mlap.org
1001 Connecticut Ave NW Suite 915   Washington DC 20036
Ph: 202-775-7780 ▪ Fx: 202-775-7784

Migration, American Committee on Italian www.acimimmigra.org
25 Carmine St   New York NY 10014
Ph: 212-247-7373 ▪ Fx: 212-265-5793

Migration Commission, International Catholic   www.icmc.net
MRS/US Conference of Catholic Bishops 3211 4th St
NE   Washington DC 20017
Ph: 202-541-3389 ▪ Fx: 202-722-8755

Migration, International Organization for   www.iom.int
1752 'N' St NW Suite 700   Washington DC 20036
Ph: 202-862-1826 ▪ Fx: 202-862-1879

Migration Ministries, Episcopal   demo.episcopalchurch.org/emm
815 2nd Ave   New York NY 10017
Ph: 212-716-6252 ▪ Fx: 212-972-0860 ▪ TF: 800-334-7626

Migration & Refugee Services   www.nccbuscc.org/mrs
US Conference of Catholic Bishops 3211 4th St
NE   Washington DC 20017
Ph: 202-541-3000 ▪ Fx: 202-541-3351

Migration Studies of New York Inc, Center for   www.cmsny.org
209 Flagg Pl   Staten Island NY 10304
Ph: 718-351-8800 ▪ Fx: 718-667-4598

Miles Lawrence Delos Value Foundation   www.valuefoundation.org
5505 Connecticut Ave NW Suite 149   Washington DC 20015
Ph: 703-237-2050 ▪ Fx: 703-237-2113

Militarism & the Draft, Committee Opposed to   www.comdsd.org
PO Box 15195   San Diego CA 92175
Ph: 760-753-7518

Military Active Retired Travel Club, Special   www.smartrving.net
600 University Office Blvd Suite 1A   Pensacola FL 32504
Ph: 800-354-7681

Military Aviation Preservation Society & Museum   www.mapsairmuseum.org
2260 International Pkwy   North Canton OH 44720
Ph: 330-896-6332

Military Banks of America, Association of
7417 Jenna Rd   Springfield VA 22153
Ph: 703-569-5163 ▪ Fx: 703-455-2110

Military Benefit Association   www.militarybenefit.org
PO Box 221110   Chantilly VA 20153
Ph: 703-968-6200 ▪ Fx: 703-968-6423 ▪ TF: 800-336-0100

Military Chaplains Association of the USA   www.mca-usa.org
PO Box 7056   Arlington VA 22207
Ph: 703-276-2189

Military Colleges & Schools of the US, Association of   www.amcsus.org
9429 Garden Ct   Potomac MD 20854
Ph: 301-765-0695 ▪ Fx: 301-983-0583

Military Community Executives Association, International   www.imcea.com
2100 E Stan Schleuter Loop Suite G   Killeen TX 76542
Ph: 254-554-6619 ▪ Fx: 254-554-6629

Military Comptrollers, American Society of   www.asmconline.org
2034 Eisenhower Ave Suite 145   Alexandria VA 22314
Ph: 703-549-0360 ▪ Fx: 703-549-3181 ▪ TF: 800-462-5637

Military Engineers, Society of American   www.same.org
607 Prince St   Alexandria VA 22314
Ph: 703-549-3800 ▪ Fx: 703-684-0231 ▪ TF: 800-336-3097

Military Family Association, National   www.nmfa.org
2500 N Van Dorn St Suite 102   Alexandria VA 22302
Ph: 703-931-6632 ▪ Fx: 703-931-4600

Military Fellowship, Christian   www.cmfhq.org
PO Box 1207   Englewood CO 80150
Ph: 303-761-1959 ▪ Fx: 303-761-4577 ▪ TF: 800-798-7875

Military Fish & Wildlife Association, National   www.nmfwa.org
6300 Somerset Way   Cambria CA 93428
Ph: 805-238-8265

Military Food & Packaging Systems Inc, Research &   www.militaryfood.org
Development Associates for   16607 Blanco Rd Suite
1506   San Antonio TX 78232
Ph: 210-493-8024 ▪ Fx: 210-493-8036

Military History, Society for   www.smh-hq.org
3119 Lakeview Cir   Leavenworth KS 66048
Ph: 913-758-3322 ▪ Fx: 913-758-3309

Military Impacted Schools Association   www.esu3.org/districts/bellevue/misa
1600 Hwy 370   Bellevue NE 68005
Ph: 402-293-4005 ▪ TF: 800-291-6472

Military Intelligence Association, National   www.nmia.org
9200 Centerway Rd   Gaithersburg MD 20879
Ph: 301-840-6642 ▪ Fx: 301-840-8502

Military Law Task Force   www.nlg.org/mltf
1168 Union St Suite 302   San Diego CA 92101
Ph: 619-233-1701 ▪ Fx: 619-233-6314

Military Madness, Women Against   www.worldwidewamm.org
310 E 38th St Suite 222   Minneapolis MN 55409
Ph: 612-827-5364 ▪ Fx: 612-827-6433

Military Medical Impression, American   www.ww2medicine.org
PO Box 2026   Columbia MD 21045
Ph: 410-381-4293

Military Officers Association of America   www.moaa.org
201 N Washington St   Alexandria VA 22314
Ph: 703-549-2311 ▪ Fx: 703-838-8173 ▪ TF: 800-234-6622

Military Operations Research Society   www.mors.org
1703 N Beauregard St Suite 450   Alexandria VA 22311
Ph: 703-933-9070 ▪ Fx: 703-933-9066

Military Order of the Purple Heart of the USA   www.purpleheart.org
5413-B Backlick Rd   Springfield VA 22151
Ph: 703-642-5360 ▪ Fx: 703-642-2054

Military Order of the Stars & Bars   www.mosbihq.org
PO Box 59   Columbia TN 38402
Ph: 800-380-1896

Military Orthopaedic Surgeons, Society of   www.somos.org
810 North St   Belgium WI 53004
Ph: 262-285-4280 ▪ Fx: 262-285-4231

Military Past, Council on America's   www.campjamp.org
PO Box 1151   Fort Myer VA 22211
Ph: 703-912-6124 ▪ Fx: 703-912-5666 ▪ TF: 800-398-4693

(Military Pilots) Order of Daedalians   www.daedalians.org
PO Box 249   Randolph AFB TX 78148
Ph: 210-945-2111 ▪ Fx: 210-945-2112

Military Service for America Memorial Foundation,   www.womensmemorial.org
Women in   Dept 560   Washington DC 20042
Ph: 703-533-1155 ▪ Fx: 703-931-4208 ▪ TF: 800-222-2294

Military Surgeons of the US, Association of   www.amsus.org
9320 Old Georgetown Rd   Bethesda MD 20814
Ph: 301-897-8800 ▪ Fx: 301-530-5446 ▪ TF: 800-761-9320

Military Uniform Collectors, Association of American   www.naples.net/clubs/aamuc
PO Box 1876   Elyria OH 44036
Ph: 440-365-5321

Military Vehicle Preservation Association   www.mvpa.org
PO Box 520378   Independence MO 64052
Ph: 816-833-6872 ▪ Fx: 816-833-5115

(Military Widows) Gold Star Wives of America Inc   www.goldstarwives.org
5510 Columbia Pike Suite 205   Arlington VA 22204
Ph: 888-479-9788

Military Widows, Society of   www.nous.org
5535 Hempstead Way   Springfield VA 22151
Ph: 703-750-1342 ▪ Fx: 703-354-4380 ▪ TF: 800-842-3451

Militia of the Immaculata Movement   www.consecration.com
1600 W Park Ave   Libertyville IL 60048
Ph: 847-367-7800 ▪ Fx: 847-367-7831

Milk Commissions Inc, American Association of Medical
1824 N Hillhurst Ave   Los Angeles CA 90027
Ph: 323-664-1977 ▪ Fx: 323-664-0870

Milk Glass Collectors Society, National   www.nmgcs.org
500 Union Cemetery Rd   Greensburg PA 15601
Ph: 724-832-7968

Milk Industry Foundation
1250 H St NW Suite 900   Washington DC 20005
Ph: 202-737-4332 ▪ Fx: 202-331-7820

Milk & Lactation, International Society for Research in Human   www.isrhml.org
Meriter Hospital Perinatal Ctr 202 S Park St   Madison WI
53715
Ph: 608-262-6561 ▪ Fx: 608-267-6377

Milk Producers Association of America, Certified
8300 Pine Ave   Chino CA 91710
Ph: 909-399-3560 ▪ Fx: 909-399-3627

Milk Producers Federation, National   www.nmpf.org
2101 Wilson Blvd Suite 400   Arlington VA 22201
Ph: 703-243-6111 ▪ Fx: 703-841-9328 ▪ TF: 888-549-7600

Milk Shipments, National Conference on Interstate   www.ncims.org
123 Buena Vista Dr   Frankfort KY 40601
Ph: 502-695-0253

Milken Family Foundation   www.mff.org
1250 4th St   Santa Monica CA 90401
Ph: 310-570-4800 ▪ Fx: 310-570-4801

Milken Institute   www.milkeninstitute.org
1250 4th St   Santa Monica CA 90401
Ph: 310-570-4600 ▪ Fx: 310-570-4601

Milking Devon Association, American   www.milkingdevons.org
135 Old Bay Rd   New Durham NH 03855
Ph: 603-859-6611

Milking Shorthorn Junior Society, American   www.milkingshorthorn.com/juniors.html
800 Pleasant St   Beloit WI 53511
Ph: 608-365-3332 ▪ Fx: 608-365-6644

Milking Shorthorn Society, American   www.milkingshorthorn.com
800 Pleasant St   Beloit WI 53511
Ph: 608-365-3332

Millers Association, North American   www.namamillers.org
600 Maryland Ave SW Suite 305-W   Washington DC 20024
Ph: 202-484-2200 ▪ Fx: 202-488-7416

Millers, International Association of Operative   www.aomillers.org
5001 College Blvd Suite 104   Leawood KS 66211
Ph: 913-338-3377 ▪ Fx: 913-338-3553

Million Dollar Round Table   www.mdrt.org
325 W Touhy Ave   Park Ridge IL 60068
Ph: 847-692-6378 ▪ Fx: 847-518-8921 ▪ TF: 800-879-6378

Million Mom March   www.millionmommarch.org
c/o Brady Campaign to Prevent Gun Violence 1225 'I' St NW
Suite 1100   Washington DC 20005
Ph: 202-898-0792 ▪ Fx: 202-371-9615

Mills, Society for the Preservation of Old   www.spoom.org

Millwork Distributors, Association of   www.nsdja.com
10047 Robert Trent Jones Pkwy   New Port Richey FL 34655
Ph: 727-372-3665 ▪ Fx: 727-372-2879

Millwork Producers Association, Wood Moulding &   wmmpa.com
507 First St   Woodland CA 95695
Ph: 530-661-9591 ▪ Fx: 530-661-9586 ▪ TF: 800-550-7889

Milton H Erickson Foundation Inc   www.erickson-foundation.org
3606 N 24th St   Phoenix AZ 85016
Ph: 602-956-6196 ▪ Fx: 602-956-0519

Milton Society of America   www.richmond.edu/~creamer/milton
Duquesne Univ English Dept   Pittsburgh PA 15282
Ph: 412-396-6420 ▪ Fx: 412-396-4792

Mind Science Foundation   www.mindscience.org
117 W El Prado Dr   San Antonio TX 78212
Ph: 210-821-6094 ▪ Fx: 210-821-6199

MindFreedom Support Coalition International   www.mindfreedom.org
PO Box 11284   Eugene OR 97440
Ph: 541-345-9106 ▪ Fx: 541-345-3737 ▪ TF: 877-623-7743

Mindszenty Foundation, Cardinal   www.mindszenty.org
PO Box 11321   Saint Louis MO 63105
Ph: 314-727-6279 ▪ Fx: 314-727-5897

Mine Rescue Association, National   www.miningorganizations.org/nmra.htm
RR 1 Box 736   Hunker PA 15639
Ph: 724-925-5150 ▪ Fx: 724-925-6190

Mine Workers of America, United　www.umwa.org
8315 Lee Hwy　Fairfax VA 22031
Ph: 703-208-7200　▪　Fx: 703-208-7227

MinePAC
101 Constitution Ave NW Suite 500E　Washington DC 20001
Ph: 202-463-2625　▪　Fx: 202-463-6152

Mineral Economics & Management Society　www.minecon.com
PO Box 721　Houghton MI 49931
Ph: 906-487-2771　▪　Fx: 906-487-2944

Mineral Information Institute　www.mii.org
501 Violet St　Golden CO 80401
Ph: 303-277-9190　▪　Fx: 303-277-9198

Mineral Law Foundation, Energy &　www.emlf.org
Univ of Kentucky Mineral Law Ctr Rm 21 Law Bldg　Lexington
　KY 40507
Ph: 859-257-7140　▪　Fx: 859-257-2884

Mineral Law Foundation, Rocky Mountain　www.rmmlf.org
9191 Sheridan Blvd Suite 203　Westminster CO 80031
Ph: 303-321-8100　▪　Fx: 303-321-7657

Mineral Policy Center　www.mineralpolicy.org
1612 K St NW Suite 808　Washington DC 20006
Ph: 202-887-1872　▪　Fx: 202-887-1875

Mineral Research, American Society for Bone &　www.asbmr.org
2025 M St NW Suite 800　Washington DC 20036
Ph: 202-367-1161　▪　Fx: 202-367-2161

Mineral Resources, Circum-Pacific Council for Energy &　www.circum-pacificcouncil.org
345 Middlefield Rd MS 973　Menlo Park CA 94025
Ph: 650-329-5430　▪　Fx: 650-329-4936

Mineral Society, Fluorescent　www.uvminerals.org
PO Box 572694　Tarzana CA 91357
Ph: 818-343-6637

Mineral Society, International Bone &　www.ibmsonline.org
2025 M St NW Suite 800　Washington DC 20036
Ph: 202-367-1121　▪　Fx: 202-367-2121

Mineralogical Societies, American Federation of　www.amfed.org/
2706 Lascassas Pike　Murfreesboro TN 37130
Ph: 615-893-8270

Mineralogical Society of America　www.minsocam.org
1015 18th St NW Suite 601　Washington DC 20036
Ph: 202-775-4344　▪　Fx: 202-775-0018

Minerals Institute, Sorptive　www.sorptive.org
1 Thomas Cir NW 10th Fl　Washington DC 20005
Ph: 202-289-2760　▪　Fx: 202-530-0659

Minerals Metals & Materials Society　www.tms.org
184 Thorn Hill Rd　Warrendale PA 15086
Ph: 724-776-9000　▪　Fx: 724-776-3770　▪　TF: 800-966-4867

Minerals Society, Clay　cms.lanl.gov
PO Box 460130　Aurora CO 80046
Ph: 303-680-9002　▪　Fx: 303-680-9003

Mini Lop Rabbit Club of America　www.miniloprabbit.com

Miniature Arms Collectors & Makers Society Ltd　www.miniaturearms.com
2502 Fresno Ln　Plainfield IL 60544
Ph: 815-254-8692　▪　TF: 800-847-6788

Miniature Artisans, International Guild of　www.igma.org
PO Box 629　Freedom CA 95019
Ph: 831-724-7974　▪　Fx: 831-724-8605　▪　TF: 800-711-4462

Miniature Book Society　www.mbs.org
620 Clinton Springs Ave　Cincinnati OH 45229
Ph: 513-556-1964

Miniature Cattle Breeders Society & Registry, International　www.minicattle.com
25204 156th Ave SE　Covington WA 98042
Ph: 253-631-1911　▪　Fx: 253-631-5774

Miniature Donkey Association, National
6450 Dewey Rd　Rome NY 13440
Ph: 315-336-0154　▪　Fx: 315-339-4414

Miniature Donkey Registry, International　www.qis.net/~minidonk/imdr.htm
1338 Hughes Shop Rd　Westminster MD 21158
Ph: 410-875-0118　▪　Fx: 410-857-9145

Miniature Enthusiasts, National Association of　www.miniatures.org
130 N Rangeline Rd PO Box 69　Carmel IN 46032
Ph: 317-571-8094　▪　Fx: 317-571-8105

Miniature Golf Association US　www.mgaus.org
435 Corona　San Antonio TX 78209
Ph: 210-824-7011　▪　Fx: 210-824-5186

Miniature Horse Association, American　www.swcp.com/amha
5601 S I-35 W　Alvarado TX 76009
Ph: 817-783-5600　▪　Fx: 817-783-6403

Miniature Jersey Cattle Registry, American
PO Box 942　Rochester WA 98579
Ph: 360-273-7789

Miniature Zebu Association, International　www.miniature-zebu-cattle.com
PO Box 66　Crawford NE 68339
Ph: 308-665-3919　▪　Fx: 308-665-1931

Miniaturists Trade Association Inc, Cottage Industry　www.cimta.org/cimta.htm
PO Box 42849　Evergreen Park IL 60805
Ph: 773-233-5522　▪　Fx: 773-233-5506

Mining Association, National　www.nma.org
101 Constitution Ave NW Suite 500-E　Washington DC 20001
Ph: 202-463-2600　▪　Fx: 202-463-2666

Mining History Association　www.mininghistoryassociation.org
c/o Colorado School of Mines Library 1400 Illinois St　Golden
　CO 80401
Ph: 303-273-3815

Mining Metallurgical & Petroleum Engineers, American Institute of　www.aimehq.org
8307 Shaffer Pkwy PO Box 270728　Littleton CO 80127
Ph: 303-948-4255　▪　Fx: 303-948-4260

Mining & Metallurgical Society of America　www.mmsa.net
476 Wilson Ave　Novato CA 94947
Ph: 415-897-4236　▪　Fx: 415-899-0262

Mining Metallurgy & Exploration Inc, Society for　www.smenet.org
8307 Shaffer Pkwy　Littleton CO 80127
Ph: 303-973-9550　▪　Fx: 303-973-3845　▪　TF: 800-763-3132

Mining & Reclamation, American Society of　ces.ca.uky.edu/asmr
3134 Montavesta Rd　Lexington KY 40502
Ph: 859-335-6529

Mining Research Institute, Solution　www.solutionmining.org
3336 Lone Hill Ln　Encinitas CA 92024
Ph: 858-759-7532　▪　Fx: 858-759-7542

Mining, Women in　www.womeninmining.org
PO Box 260246　Lakewood CO 80226
Ph: 303-298-1535

Ministers, Association of Grace Brethren　www.fgbc.org
1909 Neal Dr　Wooster OH 44691
Ph: 330-345-7826　▪　Fx: 330-345-3348

Ministers, Association of Southern Baptist Campus
PO Box 25118　Baton Rouge LA 70894
Ph: 225-343-0408　▪　Fx: 225-343-0424

Ministers Association, Unitarian Universalist　www.uuma.org
25 Beacon St　Boston MA 02108
Ph: 617-848-0498　▪　Fx: 617-848-0973

Ministries Abroad USA, Sharing of　www.episcopalian.org/soma
5290 Saratoga Ln　Woodbridge VA 22193
Ph: 703-878-7667　▪　Fx: 703-878-7015

Ministries, Alliance for Life　www.alliance4lifemin.org
PO Box 5468　Madison WI 53705
Ph: 608-833-7363

Ministries, Children's Medical　www.childmed.org
PO Box 3382　Crofton MD 21114
Ph: 301-261-3211　▪　Fx: 301-721-4647

Ministries in Higher Education, United　www.umhe.org
7407 Steele Creek Rd　Charlotte NC 28217
Ph: 704-588-2182　▪　Fx: 704-588-3652

Ministries, Holy Cross Family　www.familyrosary.org
518 Washington St　North Easton MA 02356
Ph: 508-238-4095　▪　Fx: 508-238-3953　▪　TF: 800-299-7729

(Ministries Support) Religious Formation Conference　www.relforcon.org
8820 Cameron St　Silver Spring MD 20910
Ph: 301-588-4938

Ministries USA, Chi Alpha Campus　www.chialpha.com
3728 W Chestnut Expy　Springfield MO 65802
Ph: 417-862-2781　▪　Fx: 417-865-9947

Ministries, Wheat Ridge　www.wheatridge.org
1 Pierce Pl Suite 250E　Itasca IL 60143
Ph: 630-766-9066　▪　Fx: 630-766-9622　▪　TF: 800-762-6748

Ministries, Wider Church　www.ucc.org/wcm
700 Prospect Ave NE 7th Fl　Cleveland OH 44115
Ph: 216-736-3200　▪　Fx: 216-736-3203

Ministry, American Academy of　www.ministry.org
PO Box 681868　Franklin TN 37068
Ph: 615-599-9889　▪　Fx: 615-599-8985　▪　TF: 800-288-9673

Ministry, American Baptist Women in　www.abwim.org
PO Box 851　Valley Forge PA 19482
Ph: 610-768-2000　▪　Fx: 610-768-2275　▪　TF: 800-222-3872

Ministry to the Armed Forces, National Conference on　www.ncmaf.org
4141 N Henderson Rd Suite 13　Arlington VA 22203
Ph: 703-276-7905　▪　Fx: 703-276-7906

Ministry Inc, Friends of Israel Gospel　foi.org
PO Box 908　Bellmawr NJ 08099
Ph: 856-853-5590　▪　Fx: 856-853-9565　▪　TF: 800-257-7843

Minorities in Communications, National Association of　www.namic.com
600 Anton Blvd Suite 1100　Costa Mesa CA 92625
Ph: 714-371-4077　▪　Fx: 714-371-2103

Minorities in Engineering, National Action Council for　www.nacme.org
440 Hamilton Ave Suite 302　White Planes NY 10601
Ph: 914-539-4010　▪　Fx: 914-539-4032

Minorities Network, Quality Education for　qemnetwork.qem.org
1818 'N' St NW Suite 350　Washington DC 20036
Ph: 202-659-1818　▪　Fx: 202-659-5408

Minority AIDS Council, National　www.nmac.org
1931 13th St NW　Washington DC 20009
Ph: 202-483-6622　▪　Fx: 202-483-1135

Minority Architects, National Organization of　www.noma.net
Howard Univ School of Architecture & Design 2366 6th St NW
　Rm 100　Washington DC 20059
Ph: 202-686-2780

Minority Automobile Dealers, National Association of　www.namad.com/
8401 Corporate Dr Suite 404　Lanham MD 20785
Ph: 301-306-1614　▪　Fx: 301-306-1493

Minority Business Council Inc, National　www.nmbc.org
25 W 45th St Suite 301　New York NY 10036
Ph: 212-997-4753　▪　Fx: 212-997-5102

Minority Business Enterprise Legal Defense & Education Fund　www.mbeldef.org
419 New Jersey Ave SE　Washington DC 20003
Ph: 202-289-1700　▪　Fx: 202-289-1701

Minority Contractors, National Association of　www.namconline.org
666 11th St NW Suite 520　Washington DC 20001
Ph: 202-347-8259　▪　Fx: 202-628-1876

Minority Dealers Association, Ford Motor　www.fmmda.org
16000 W Nine-Mile Rd Suite 603　Southfield MI 48075
Ph: 248-557-2500　▪　Fx: 248-557-2882　▪　TF: 800-247-0293

Minority Educators Inc, National Association of Medical　www.namme-hpe.org

Minority Engineering Program Administrators, National Association of　www.namepa.org
1133 W Morse Blvd Suite 201　Winter Park
　FL 32789
Ph: 407-647-8839　▪　Fx: 407-629-2502

Minority Health Professions Schools, Association of
507 Capitol Ct NE Suite 200　Washington DC 20002
Ph: 202-544-7499　▪　Fx: 202-546-7105

Minority Media Executives, National Association of   www.namme.org
1921 Gallows Rd Suite 600   Vienna VA 22182
Ph: 703-893-2410 ▪ Fx: 703-893-2414 ▪ TF: 888-968-7658

Minority Professors, Research Association of   www.rampresearch.org

Minority Public Administrators, Conference of   www.natcompa.org
1120 G St NW Suite 700   Washington DC 20005
Ph: 202-393-7878 ▪ Fx: 202-638-4952

Minority Supplier Development Council, National   www.nmsdcus.org
1040 Ave of the Americas 2nd Fl   New York NY 10018
Ph: 212-944-2430 ▪ Fx: 212-719-9611

Minority Transportation Officials, Conference of   www.comto.com
1725 DeSales St NW Suite 808   Washington DC 20036
Ph: 202-289-0567 ▪ Fx: 202-289-1214

Miracle Flights for Kids   www.miracleflights.org
2756 N Green Valley Pkwy Suite 115   Green Valley NV 89014
Ph: 702-261-0494 ▪ Fx: 702-261-0497 ▪ TF: 800-358-1711

Miracles, Foundation for A Course in   www.facim.org
41397 Buecking Dr   Temecula CA 92590
Ph: 909-296-6261 ▪ Fx: 909-296-9117

Miraculous Medal, Association of the   www.amm.org
1811 W St Joseph St   Perryville MO 63775
Ph: 573-547-2508 ▪ Fx: 573-547-1389 ▪ TF: 800-264-6279

Miraculous Medal, Central Association of the   www.cammonline.org
475 E Chelten Ave   Philadelphia PA 19144
Ph: 215-848-1010 ▪ Fx: 215-848-1014 ▪ TF: 800-523-3674

Missileers, Association of Air Force   www.afmissileers.org
PO Box 5693   Breckenridge CO 80424
Ph: 970-453-0500

Missing Children Association Inc, North America   www.namca.com
136 Rt 420 Hwy   South Esk NB E1V4N8
Ph: 506-627-1209 ▪ Fx: 506-622-3515

Missing & Exploited Children, Commission on   www.comec.org
616 Adams Ave   Memphis TN 38105
Ph: 901-405-8441 ▪ Fx: 901-575-8856

Missing & Exploited Children, National Center for   www.missingkids.com
699 Prince St   Alexandria VA 22314
Ph: 703-274-3900 ▪ Fx: 703-274-2095 ▪ TF: 800-843-5678

Missing in Southeast Asia, National League of Families of American Prisoners &   www.pow-miafamilies.org
1005 N Glebe Rd Suite 170   Arlington VA 22201
Ph: 703-465-7432 ▪ Fx: 703-465-7433

Missiological Society, Evangelical   www.missiology.org/EMS
PO Box 794   Wheaton IL 60189
Ph: 630-752-5533 ▪ Fx: 630-752-5916

Missiology, American Society of   www.asmweb.org
64 Mercer St CN 821   Princeton NJ 08542
Ph: 609-497-3639 ▪ Fx: 609-430-0316

Mission Agencies, Evangelical Fellowship of
4201 N Peachtree Rd Suite 300   Atlanta GA 30341
Ph: 770-457-6677 ▪ Fx: 770-457-0037

Mission, Associated Parishes for Liturgy &   www.associatedparishes.org
PO Box 27141   Baltimore MD 21230
Ph: 410-752-0877

Mission Association of North America, Interdenominational Foreign   www.ifmamissions.org
PO Box 398   Wheaton IL 60189
Ph: 630-682-9270 ▪ Fx: 630-682-9278

Mission, Association of Professors of   www.asmweb.org/apm
1443 N Euclid Ave   Dayton OH 45406
Ph: 937-274-0821 ▪ Fx: 937-278-6237

Mission Aviation Fellowship   www.maf.org
1849 N Wabash Ave   Redlands CA 92374
Ph: 909-794-1151 ▪ Fx: 909-794-3016 ▪ TF: 800-359-7623

Mission Board, Catholic Medical   www.cmmb.org
10 W 17th St   New York NY 10011
Ph: 212-242-7757 ▪ Fx: 212-807-9161 ▪ TF: 800-678-5659

Mission Board, International   www.imb.org
PO Box 6767   Richmond VA 23230
Ph: 800-999-3113

Mission Doctors Association   www.missiondoctors.org
3424 Wilshire Blvd   Los Angeles CA 90010
Ph: 626-285-8868 ▪ Fx: 626-309-1716

Mission, Evangelical Free Church   www.efcm.org
901 E 78th St   Bloomington MN 55420
Ph: 952-854-1300 ▪ Fx: 952-853-8474 ▪ TF: 800-745-2202

Mission, Fellowship International   www.gospelcom.net/fim/
555 S 24th St   Allentown PA 18104
Ph: 610-435-9099 ▪ Fx: 610-435-1641 ▪ TF: 888-346-9099

Mission-Helpers Association, Lay   www.laymissionhelpers.org
3424 Wilshire Blvd   Los Angeles CA 90010
Ph: 213-637-7222 ▪ Fx: 213-637-6223

Mission of Mercy   www.missionofmercy.org
15475 Gleneagle Dr PO Box 62600   Colorado Springs CO 80962
Ph: 719-481-0400 ▪ Fx: 719-481-4649 ▪ TF: 800-864-0200

Mission: Moving Mountains   www.movingmountains.org
PO Box 1168   Burnsville MN 55337
Ph: 952-440-9100 ▪ Fx: 952-440-9104 ▪ TF: 800-545-7980

Mission Services Association   www.missionservices.org
7545 Hodges Ferry Rd PO Box 13111   Knoxville TN 37920
Ph: 865-577-9740

Mission Society for United Methodists   www.msum.org
6234 Crooked Creek Rd   Norcross GA 30092
Ph: 770-446-1381 ▪ Fx: 770-446-3044

Mission Training International   www.mti.org
PO Box 1220   Palmer Lake CO 80133
Ph: 719-487-0111 ▪ Fx: 719-487-9350 ▪ TF: 800-896-3710

Mission: Wolf   www.missionwolf.com
PO Box 211   Silver Cliff CO 81252
Ph: 719-859-2157

Mission to the World   www.mtw.org
1600 N Brown Rd   Lawrenceville GA 30043
Ph: 678-823-0004 ▪ Fx: 678-823-0027

Missionaries of Africa, Society of   www.missionariesofafrica.org/policies.php
1624 21st St NW   Washington DC 20009
Ph: 202-232-5154 ▪ Fx: 202-332-8640

Missionaries of the Assumption, Associate
914 Main St Suite 5   Worcester MA 01610
Ph: 508-767-1356 ▪ Fx: 508-791-2936

Missionaries, SMA Lay   www.smafathers.org
256 N Manor Cir   Takoma Park MD 20912
Ph: 301-891-2037 ▪ Fx: 301-270-6370

Missionary Alliance, Christian &   www.cmalliance.org
PO Box 35000   Colorado Springs CO 80935
Ph: 719-599-5999 ▪ Fx: 719-593-8692

(Missionary) AMG International
6815 Shallowford Rd   Chattanooga TN 37421
Ph: 423-894-6060 ▪ Fx: 423-894-6863 ▪ TF: 800-241-7206

Missionary Association of America, Armenian   www.amaa.org
31 W Century Rd   Paramus NJ 07652
Ph: 201-265-2607 ▪ Fx: 201-265-6015

Missionary Association of America, Baptist   www.bmaam.com
PO Box 30910   Little Rock AR 72206
Ph: 501-455-4977 ▪ Fx: 501-455-3636

(Missionary) Bethany Fellowship Missions   www.bethfel.org
6820 Auto Club Rd Suite M   Minneapolis MN 55438
Ph: 952-829-2492 ▪ TF: 800-323-3417

(Missionary) Brethren in Christ World Missions   www.bic-church.org/wm
431 Grantham Rd PO Box 390   Grantham PA 17027
Ph: 717-697-2634 ▪ Fx: 717-691-6053

(Missionary) Cabrini Mission Corps   cabrini-missioncorps.org
610 King of Prussia Rd   Radnor PA 19087
Ph: 610-971-0821 ▪ Fx: 610-971-0396

(Missionary) CAM International   caminternational.gospelcom.net
8625 La Prada Dr   Dallas TX 75228
Ph: 214-327-8206 ▪ Fx: 214-327-8201 ▪ TF: 800-366-2264

(Missionary) CBInternational   www.cbi.org
1501 W Mineral Ave   Littleton CO 80120
Ph: 720-283-2000 ▪ Fx: 720-283-2111 ▪ TF: 800-487-4224

(Missionary) Christar   www.christar.org
PO Box 14866   Reading PA 19612
Ph: 610-375-0300 ▪ Fx: 610-375-6862 ▪ TF: 800-755-7955

Missionary Church Inc   www.mcusa.org
3811 Vanguard Dr PO Box 9127   Fort Wayne IN 46899
Ph: 219-747-2027 ▪ Fx: 219-747-5331

(Missionary) Claretians The   www.claretians.org
205 W Monroe St   Chicago IL 60606
Ph: 312-236-7782 ▪ Fx: 312-236-7230

Missionary Community, Episcopal Church   www.episcopalian.org/ecmc
PO Box 278   Ambridge PA 15003
Ph: 724-266-2810 ▪ Fx: 724-266-6773

(Missionary) Engineering Ministries International   www.emiusa.org
110 S Weber St Suite 104   Colorado Springs CO 80903
Ph: 719-633-2078 ▪ Fx: 719-633-2970

Missionary Evangelism, Committee on   www.comemissions.com
PO Box 88085   Grand Rapids MI 49518
Ph: 616-455-8228

Missionary Fellowship, American   www.americanmissionary.org
672 Conestoga Rd PO Box 370   Villanova PA 19085
Ph: 610-527-4439 ▪ Fx: 610-527-4720

Missionary Fellowship, Christian   www.cmfi.org
5525 E 82nd St PO Box 501020   Indianapolis IN 46250
Ph: 317-578-2700 ▪ Fx: 317-578-2827

Missionary Fellowship, Overseas   www.us.omf.org
10 W Dry Creek Cir   Littleton CO 80120
Ph: 303-730-4160 ▪ Fx: 303-730-4165 ▪ TF: 800-993-2751

Missionary Gospel Fellowship   www.mgfhq.org
PO Box 1535   Turlock CA 95381
Ph: 209-634-8575 ▪ Fx: 209-634-8472

(Missionary) Helps International Ministries Inc   www.helpsintl.com
573 Fairview Rd   Asheville NC 28803
Ph: 828-277-3812 ▪ Fx: 828-274-7770

(Missionary) InterAct Ministries   www.interactministries.org
31000 SE Kelso Rd   Boring OR 97009
Ph: 800-258-3464

Missionary League, Lutheran Women's   www.lwml.org
PO Box 411993   Saint Louis MO 63141
Ph: 314-268-1531 ▪ Fx: 314-268-1532 ▪ TF: 800-252-5965

(Missionary) Life Outreach International   www.lifetoday.org
PO Box 982000   Fort Worth TX 76182
Ph: 817-267-4211 ▪ Fx: 817-685-1971 ▪ TF: 800-947-5433

Missionary Ministries, Brethren Church   www.brethrenchurch.org
524 College Ave   Ashland OH 44805
Ph: 419-289-1708 ▪ Fx: 419-281-0450

Missionary Movement, Volunteer   www.vmmusa.org
5980 W Loomis   Greendale WI 53129
Ph: 414-423-8660 ▪ Fx: 414-423-8964

(Missionary) New Tribes Mission   www.ntm.org
1000 E 1st St   Sanford FL 32771
Ph: 407-323-3430 ▪ Fx: 407-330-0376 ▪ TF: 866-547-2460

(Missionary) OC International   www.gospelcom.net/oci
PO Box 36900   Colorado Springs CO 80936
Ph: 719-592-9292 ▪ Fx: 719-592-0693

(Missionary) Red Sea Team International   www.rsmt.u-net.com
PO Box 2047   Lexington SC 29071
Ph: 803-358-2330

(Missionary) Salesian Missions   salesianmissions.org
2 Lefevre Ln PO Box 30   New Rochelle NY 10802
Ph: 914-633-8344 ▪ Fx: 914-633-7404

Missionary Sisters of the Society of Mary   www.maristmissionarysmsm.org
349 Grove St   Waltham MA 02453
Ph: 781-893-0149 ▪ Fx: 781-899-6838

Missionary Society - AME Church, Women's   www.amecnet.org/wms/main_fr.htm
1134 11th St NW   Washington DC 20001
Ph: 202-371-8886 ▪ Fx: 202-371-8820

Missionary Society, Romanian   www.rmsonline.org
1415 Hill Ave PO Box 527   Wheaton IL 60189
Ph: 630-665-6503 ▪ Fx: 630-665-6538

Missionary Society of Saint Columban   www.columban.org
PO Box 10   Saint Columbans NE 68056
Ph: 402-291-1920 ▪ Fx: 402-291-4984

Missionary Society of Saint Paul the Apostle   www.paulist.org
86-11 Midland Pkwy   Jamaica Estates NY 11432
Ph: 718-291-5995 ▪ Fx: 718-291-6646

Missionary Society, Seventh Day Baptist   sdbmissoc.home.mindspring.com
119 Main St   Westerly RI 02891
Ph: 401-596-4326 ▪ Fx: 401-348-9494

Missionary Society, South American   www.sams-usa.org
PO Box 399   Ambridge PA 15003
Ph: 724-266-0669 ▪ Fx: 724-266-2681

Missionary Society, Voice of China & Asia   www.vocamissionarysociety.org
183 E Glenarm St PO Box 150   Pasadena CA 91102
Ph: 626-441-0640 ▪ Fx: 626-441-8124

(Missionary) South America Mission   www.southamericamission.org
5217 S Military Trail   Lake Worth FL 33463
Ph: 561-965-1833 ▪ Fx: 561-439-8950

(Missionary) TEAM   www.teamworld.org
PO Box 969   Wheaton IL 60189
Ph: 630-653-5300 ▪ Fx: 630-653-1826 ▪ TF: 800-343-3144

Missionary TECH Team   www.techteam.org
25 FRJ Dr   Longview TX 75602
Ph: 903-757-4530 ▪ Fx: 903-758-2799

(Missionary) Teen Missions International   www.teenmissions.org
885 E Hall Rd   Merritt Island FL 32953
Ph: 321-453-0350 ▪ Fx: 321-452-7988

(Missionary) UFM International   www.ufm.org
306 Bala Ave PO Box 306   Bala Cynwyd PA 19004
Ph: 610-667-7660 ▪ Fx: 610-660-9068

Missionary Union, Gospel   www.gmu.org
10000 N Oak   Kansas City MO 64155
Ph: 816-734-8500 ▪ Fx: 816-734-4601 ▪ TF: 800-468-1892

Missionary Union, Woman's   www.wmu.com
100 Missionary Ridge   Birmingham AL 35242
Ph: 205-991-8100 ▪ Fx: 205-991-4990 ▪ TF: 800-968-7301

(Missionary) World Team USA   www.worldteam.org
1431 Stuckert Rd   Warrington PA 18976
Ph: 215-491-4900 ▪ Fx: 215-491-4910 ▪ TF: 800-967-7109

(Missions Assistance) World Salt Foundation Inc   www.angelfire.com/fl3/worldsalt
PO Box 851   Lake Wales FL 33859
Ph: 863-638-0557

Missions, Association of North American   www.anamissions.org
PO Box 8667   Longview TX 75607
Ph: 903-234-2075

Missions, Evangelistic Faith   www.efm-missions.org
PO Box 609   Bedford IN 47421
Ph: 812-275-7531 ▪ Fx: 812-275-7532 ▪ TF: 877-864-7480

Missions, Fellowship of   www.fellowshipofmissions.org
140 Jacqueline Dr   Berea OH 44017
Ph: 440-243-0156

Missions, Independent Board for Presbyterian Foreign   www.ibpfm.org
246 W Walnut Ln   Philadelphia PA 19144
Ph: 215-438-0511 ▪ Fx: 215-438-0560

Missions Information Service, Evangelism &   bgc.gospelcom.net/emis
500 College Ave   Wheaton IL 60187
Ph: 630-752-7158 ▪ Fx: 630-752-7155

Mississippi River Conservation Committee, Upper   www.mississippi-river.com/umrcc
4469 48th Ave Ct   Rock Island IL 61201
Ph: 309-793-5800 ▪ Fx: 309-793-5804

Missouri Fox Trotting Horse Breed Association Inc   www.mfthba.com
PO Box 1027   Ava MO 65608
Ph: 417-683-2468 ▪ Fx: 417-683-6144

Missouri Synod, Lutheran Church   www.lcms.org
1333 S Kirkwood Rd   Saint Louis MO 63122
Ph: 314-965-9000 ▪ Fx: 888-526-7329 ▪ TF: 888-843-5267

Mitchell Maria Association   www.mmo.org
4 Vestal St   Nantucket MA 02554
Ph: 508-288-9198 ▪ Fx: 508-228-1031

Mitochondrial Disease Foundation, United   www.umdf.org
8085 Saltsburg Rd Suite 201   Pittsburgh PA 15239
Ph: 412-793-8077 ▪ Fx: 412-793-6477

MJ Murdock Charitable Trust   www.murdock-trust.org
703 Broadway St Suite 710   Vancouver WA 98660
Ph: 360-694-8415 ▪ Fx: 360-694-1819

(Mobile Air Conditioning) IMACA Education Foundation   www.imaca.org
6410 Southwest Blvd Suite 212   Fort Worth TX 76109
Ph: 817-732-4600 ▪ Fx: 817-732-9610

Mobile Air Conditioning Society Worldwide   www.macsw.org
225 S Broad St   Lansdale PA 19446
Ph: 215-631-7020 ▪ Fx: 215-631-7017

Mobile Alliance, Open   www.openmobilealliance.org
4275 Executive Sq Suite 240   La Jolla CA 92037
Ph: 858-623-0740 ▪ Fx: 858-623-0743

Mobile Communications Council, Land   www.lmcc.org
1110 N Glebe Rd Suite 500   Arlington VA 22201
Ph: 202-331-7773 ▪ Fx: 202-331-9062

(Mobile Electronics) IASCA Worldwide Inc   www.iasca.com
2129 S Ridgewood Ave   South Daytona FL 32119
Ph: 386-322-1551 ▪ Fx: 386-761-1740

Mobile Industrial Caterers Association - International   www.mobilecaterers.com
304 W Liberty St Suite 201   Louisville KY 40202
Ph: 502-583-3783 ▪ Fx: 502-589-3602 ▪ TF: 800-620-6422

Mobile Post Office Society   www.eskimo.com/~rkunz/mposhome.html
PO Box 427   Marston Mills MA 02648
Ph: 508-428-9132

Mobile Telecommunications Association, American   www.amtausa.org
200 N Glebe Rd Suite 1000   Arlington VA 22203
Ph: 202-835-7819 ▪ Fx: 202-331-9062

Mobility, AIM Inc - Association for Automatic Identification &   www.aimglobal.org
125 Warrendale-Bayne Rd   Warrendale PA 15086
Ph: 724-934-4470 ▪ Fx: 724-934-4495 ▪ TF: 800-338-0206

Mobility Equipment Dealers Association, National   www.nmeda.org
11211 N Nebraska Ave Suite A-5   Tampa FL 33612
Ph: 813-977-6603 ▪ Fx: 813-977-6402 ▪ TF: 800-833-0427

Mobility International USA   www.miusa.org
PO Box 10767   Eugene OR 97440
Ph: 541-343-1284 ▪ Fx: 541-343-6812

Model Aeronautics, Academy of   www.modelaircraft.org
5161 E Memorial Dr   Muncie IN 47302
Ph: 765-287-1256 ▪ Fx: 765-289-4248 ▪ TF: 800-435-9262

Model Boat Association, North American   www.namba.com
1815 Halley St   San Diego CA 92154
Ph: 619-424-6380 ▪ Fx: 619-424-8845

Model A Ford Club of America   www.mafca.org
250 S Cypress St   La Habra CA 90631
Ph: 562-697-2712 ▪ Fx: 562-690-7452

Model A Restorers Club   www.modelaford.com
24800 Michigan Ave   Dearborn MI 48124
Ph: 313-278-1455

Model Kit Collecting, Society for the Preservation & Encouragement
of Scale   3213 Hardy Dr   Edmond OK 73013
Ph: 405-341-4640

Model Pilots Association, Precision Aerobatics   www.control-line.org
158 Flying Cloud Isle   Foster City CA 94404
Ph: 650-345-0130 ▪ Fx: 650-578-8454

Model Power Boat Association, International   www.impba.org
2804 Woods Dr   Violet LA 70092
Ph: 504-276-4500

Model Railroad Association, National   www.nmra.org
4121 Cromwell Rd   Chattanooga TN 37421
Ph: 423-892-2846 ▪ Fx: 423-899-4869

Model Railroad Industry Association   www.mria.org
PO Box 3269   Renton WA 98056
Ph: 425-271-2609 ▪ Fx: 425-271-3834

(Model Railroads) International Brotherhood of Live Steamers
26062 Todd Ln   Los Altos Hills CA 94022
Ph: 650-948-8555

Model T Ford Club of America   www.mtfca.com
PO Box 126   Centerville IN 47330
Ph: 765-855-5248 ▪ Fx: 765-855-3428

Modelers, Society of Antique   www.antiquemodeler.org
203 N Brockfield Dr   Sun City Center FL 33573
Ph: 813-634-7749

Modeling & Simulation International, Society for   www.scs.org
4838 Ronson Ct Suite L PO Box 17900   San Diego CA 92111
Ph: 858-277-3888 ▪ Fx: 858-277-3930

Moderation Management Network Inc   www.moderation.org
22 W 27th St 5th Fl   New York NY 10001
Ph: 212-871-0974 ▪ Fx: 212-213-6582

Modern Art, International Council of the Museum of   11 W 53rd St   New York NY 10019
Ph: 212-708-9470 ▪ Fx: 212-708-9740

Modern Free & Accepted Masons of the World Inc   www.modernfree.com
627 5th Ave PO Box 1072   Columbus GA 31902
Ph: 706-322-3326 ▪ Fx: 706-322-3805

Modern Greek Studies Association   www.humanities.uci.edu/classics/MGSA
PO Box 1826   New Haven CT 06508
Ph: 203-392-5668 ▪ Fx: 203-392-5670

Modern Language Association of America   www.mla.org
26 Broadway 3rd FL   New York NY 10004
Ph: 646-576-5000 ▪ Fx: 646-458-0030

Modern Painters & Sculptors, Federation of
234 W 21st St   New York NY 10011
Ph: 212-255-4858

Modern Poetry Association   www.poetrymagazine.org
1030 N Clark St Suite 420   Chicago IL 60610
Ph: 312-787-7070

Modular Building Institute   www.mbinet.org
413 Park St   Charlottesville VA 22902
Ph: 804-296-3288 ▪ Fx: 804-296-3361 ▪ TF: 888-811-3288

Mohair Council of America   www.mohairusa.com
233 W Twohig Rd PO Box 5337   San Angelo TX 76902
Ph: 915-655-3161 ▪ Fx: 915-655-4761 ▪ TF: 800-583-3161

Mohs College   www.mohscollege.org
611 E Wells St   Milwaukee WI 53202
Ph: 414-347-1103 ▪ Fx: 414-272-6070 ▪ TF: 800-500-7224

Mohs Micrographic Surgery & Cutaneous Oncology, American   www.mohscollege.org
College of   611 E Wells St   Milwaukee WI 53202
Ph: 414-347-1103 ▪ Fx: 414-272-6070 ▪ TF: 800-500-7224

Mold Builders Association, American   www.amba.org
701 E Irving Park Rd Suite 207   Roselle IL 60172
Ph: 630-980-7667 ▪ Fx: 630-980-9714

Molders Association, EPS   www.epsmolders.org
1298 Cronson Blvd Suite 201   Crofton MD 21114
Ph: 410-451-8341 ▪ Fx: 410-451-8343 ▪ TF: 800-607-3772

Molders, Association of Rotational   www.rotomolding.org
2000 Spring Rd Suite 511   Oak Brook IL 60523
Ph: 630-571-0611 ▪ Fx: 630-571-0616

Molding Association, Metal Injection www.mpif.org/mima.html
105 College Rd E Princeton NJ 08540
Ph: 609-452-7700 ▪ Fx: 609-987-8523

Mole Day Foundation, National www.moleday.org
1220 S 5th St Prairie du Chien WI 53821
Ph: 608-326-6036

Molecular Biology, American Society for Biochemistry & www.asbmb.org
9650 Rockville Pike Bethesda MD 20814
Ph: 301-634-7145 ▪ Fx: 301-634-7126

Molecular Biology, International Society for Plant www.uga.edu/~ispmb
Univ of Georgia Dept of Biochemistry & Molecular
Biology Athens GA 30602
Ph: 706-542-3239 ▪ Fx: 706-542-2090

Molecular Pathology, Association for www.ampweb.org
9650 Rockville Pike Bethesda MD 20814
Ph: 301-634-7939 ▪ Fx: 301-634-7990

Molecular Plant Microbe Interactions, International Society for www.ismpminet.org
3340 Pilot Knob Rd Saint Paul MN 55121
Ph: 651-454-7250 ▪ Fx: 651-454-0766 ▪ TF: 800-481-2698

Moms, Home-Based Working www.hbwm.com
PO Box 500164 Austin TX 78750
Ph: 512-266-0900 ▪ TF: 800-281-8565

Moms in Touch International www.momsintouch.org
PO Box 1120 Poway CA 92074
Ph: 800-949-6667 ▪ Fx: 858-486-5132

Monetary Education, Foundation for the Advancement of www.fame.org
PO Box 625 FDR Stn New York NY 10150
Ph: 212-818-1206 ▪ Fx: 212-754-6543

Money Collectors, Dedicated Wooden
2084 N Brook Cir York PA 17403
Ph: 717-845-4295

Money Management International www.moneymanagement.org
9009 W Loop S 7th Fl Houston TX 77096
Ph: 888-889-9347

Money Managers, American Association of Daily www.aadmm.com
PO Box 8857 Gaithersburg MD 20898
Ph: 301-593-5462 ▪ Fx: 301-668-5760

Mongolia Society www.indiana.edu/~mongsoc
Indiana Univ 322 Goodbody Hall 1011 E 3rd St Bloomington
IN 47405
Ph: 812-855-4078 ▪ Fx: 812-855-7500

Monitors, International Association of Broadcast www.iabm.com
PO Box 986 Irmo SC 29063
Ph: 800-236-1741 ▪ Fx: 888-732-9004

Monomer Manufacturers Inc, Basic Acrylic www.bamm.net
941 Rhonda Pl SE Leesburg VA 20175
Ph: 703-669-5688 ▪ Fx: 703-669-5689

Monorail Manufacturers Association Inc www.mhia.org/psc
8720 Red Oak Blvd Suite 201 Charlotte NC 28217
Ph: 704-676-1190 ▪ Fx: 704-676-1199

Monroe Institute www.MonroeInstitute.org
62 Roberts Mountain Rd Faber VA 22938
Ph: 434-361-1252 ▪ Fx: 434-361-1237

Monroe James Memorial Foundation www.monroefoundation.org
908 1/2 Charles St Fredericksburg VA 22401
Ph: 804-231-1827

Montadale Sheep Breeders Association www.countrylovin.com/msba
2514 Willow Rd E Fargo ND 58102
Ph: 701-297-9199

Monterey County Vintners & Growers Association www.montereywines.org
Box 1793 Monterey CA 93942
Ph: 831-375-9400 ▪ Fx: 831-375-1116

Montessori Foundation www.montessori.org
1001 Bern Creek Loop Sarasota FL 34240
Ph: 941-379-6626 ▪ Fx: 941-379-6671

Montessori Internationale-USA, Association www.montessori-ami.org
410 Alexander St Rochester NY 14607
Ph: 716-461-5920 ▪ Fx: 716-461-0075 ▪ TF: 800-872-2643

Montessori Society, American www.amshq.org
281 Park Ave S 6th Fl New York NY 10010
Ph: 212-358-1250 ▪ Fx: 212-358-1256

Montessori Society, International trust.wdn.com/ims
912 Thayer Ave Suite 207 Silver Spring MD 20910
Ph: 301-589-1127 ▪ Fx: 301-589-0733 ▪ TF: 800-301-3131

(Monticello) Thomas Jefferson Foundation www.monticello.org
PO Box 316 Charlottesville VA 22902
Ph: 434-984-9808 ▪ Fx: 434-977-7757

Monument Association, American www.imsa-online.com/ammonas.htm
30 Eden Alley Suite 301 Columbus OH 43215
Ph: 614-461-5852 ▪ Fx: 614-461-1497

Monument Builders of North America www.monumentbuilders.org
401 N Michigan Ave Suite 2200 Chicago IL 60611
Ph: 312-321-5143 ▪ Fx: 312-673-6732 ▪ TF: 800-233-4472

Monuments & Sites, US Committee of the International www.icomos.org/usicomos
Council on National Building Museum 401 F St NW Rm
331 Washington DC 20001
Ph: 202-842-1866 ▪ Fx: 202-842-1861

Moody Foundation www.moodyf.org
2302 Post Office St Suite 704 Galveston TX 77550
Ph: 409-763-5333 ▪ Fx: 409-763-5564

Moose International Inc www.mooseintl.org
Rt 31 Mooseheart IL 60539
Ph: 630-859-2000 ▪ Fx: 630-859-6618

Morab Breeders Association, International www.morab.com/imba.html
RR 3 Box 235 Ava MO 65608
Ph: 417-683-4426 ▪ Fx: 417-683-5708

Morab Horse Association Inc, Purebred www.puremorab.com
PO Box 280 Sherwood WI 54169
Ph: 920-853-3086 ▪ Fx: 920-853-3114

Morab Registry, International www.morab.com
RR 3 Box 235 Ava MO 65608
Ph: 417-683-4426 ▪ Fx: 417-683-5708

Moral Restoration, Foundation for
PO Box 1009 Ashburn VA 20146
Ph: 703-724-4141

Morality, Jews for www.jewsformorality.org
PO Box 230262 Gravesend Stn Brooklyn NY 11223
Ph: 718-336-0053 ▪ Fx: 718-645-0556

Morality in Media Inc www.moralityinmedia.org
475 Riverside Dr Suite 239 New York NY 10115
Ph: 212-870-3222 ▪ Fx: 212-870-2765

Moravian Historical Society www.moravianhistoricalsociety.org
214 E Center St Nazareth PA 18064
Ph: 610-759-5070 ▪ Fx: 610-759-2461

Moravian Music Foundation www.moravianmusic.org
457 S Church St PO Box L Winston-Salem NC 27108
Ph: 336-725-0651 ▪ Fx: 336-725-4514

Morgan Horse Association, American www.morganhorse.com
PO Box 519 Shelburne VT 05482
Ph: 802-985-8430

Morgan Pony Registry, National www.bulldancers.com/morganpony

Morgan Reining Horse Association, National www.nmrha.com

Mormon History Association www.mhahome.org
581 S 630 East Orem UT 84097
Ph: 801-224-0241 ▪ Fx: 801-224-5684 ▪ TF: 888-642-3678

Moroccan American Business Council Ltd www.usa-morocco.org
1085 Commonwealth Ave Suite 194 Boston MA 02215
Ph: 617-319-3400 ▪ Fx: 508-230-9943

Morocco, Friends of morocco.home.att.net
PO Box 2579 Washington DC 20013
Ph: 703-660-9292

MORPAC
1919 Pennsylvania Ave Washington DC 20006
Ph: 202-557-2700 ▪ Fx: 202-721-0249

Morris Animal Foundation www.morrisanimalfoundation.org
45 Inverness Dr E Englewood CO 80112
Ph: 303-790-2345 ▪ Fx: 303-790-4066 ▪ TF: 800-243-2345

Morris & Gwendolyn Cafritz Foundation www.cafritzfoundation.org
1825 K St NW 14th Fl Washington DC 20006
Ph: 202-223-3100 ▪ Fx: 202-296-7567

Morris Pratt Institute www.morrispratt.org
11811 Watertown Plank Rd Milwaukee WI 53226
Ph: 414-774-2994 ▪ Fx: 414-774-2964

Mortar Board Inc www.mortarboard.org
1200 Chambers Rd Suite 201 Columbus OH 43212
Ph: 614-488-4094 ▪ Fx: 614-488-4095 ▪ TF: 800-989-6266

Mortgage Association, American Credit Union www.acuma.org
3419 Via Lido PMB 135 Newport Beach CA 92663
Ph: 949-645-5288 ▪ Fx: 949-645-5297

Mortgage Association, National Home Equity www.nhema.org
1301 Pennsylvania Ave NW Sutie 500 Washington DC 20004
Ph: 202-347-1210 ▪ Fx: 202-347-1171 ▪ TF: 800-342-1121

Mortgage Attorneys, American College of www.acmaatty.org
15245 Shady Grove Rd Suite 130 Rockville MD 20850
Ph: 301-990-9075 ▪ Fx: 301-990-9771

Mortgage Bankers Association www.mortgagebankers.org
1919 Pennsylvania Ave NW Washington DC 20006
Ph: 202-557-2700 ▪ Fx: 202-721-0247 ▪ TF: 800-793-6222

(Mortgage Bankers Association of America) MORPAC
1919 Pennsylvania Ave Washington DC 20006
Ph: 202-557-2700 ▪ Fx: 202-721-0249

Mortgage Banking Attorneys, USFN - America's www.usfn.org
14471 Chambers Rd Suite 260 Tustin CA 92780
Ph: 714-838-7167 ▪ Fx: 714-573-2650 ▪ TF: 800-635-6128

Mortgage Brokers, National Association of www.namb.org
8201 Greensboro Dr Suite 300 McLean VA 22102
Ph: 703-610-9009 ▪ Fx: 703-610-9005

Mortgage Coalition, Consumer
801 N Pennsylvania Ave NW Suite 625 Washington DC 20004
Ph: 202-544-3550 ▪ Fx: 202-543-1438

Mortgage Insurance Companies of America www.privatemi.com
727 15th St NW Suite 1200 Washington DC 20005
Ph: 202-393-5566 ▪ Fx: 202-393-5557

Mortgage Securities Association, Commercial www.cmbs.org
30 Broad St 28th Fl New York NY 10004
Ph: 212-509-1844 ▪ Fx: 212-509-1895

Mortgage Underwriters, National Association of Review www.iami.org/nara.html
Appraisers & 1224 N Nokomis NE Alexandria MN 56308
Ph: 320-763-6870 ▪ Fx: 320-763-9290

Mortgage Women, National Association of Professional www.napmw.org
PO Box 2016 Edmonds WA 98020
Ph: 425-778-6162 ▪ Fx: 425-771-9588 ▪ TF: 800-827-3034

Morticians Association, National Funeral Directors & www.nfdma.com
3951 Snapfinger Pkwy Suite 570 Decatur GA 30035
Ph: 404-286-6680 ▪ Fx: 404-286-6573 ▪ TF: 800-434-0958

Mosaic Association, National Terrazzo & www.ntma.com
201 N Maple Ave Suite 208 Purcellville VA 20132
Ph: 540-751-0930 ▪ Fx: 540-751-0935 ▪ TF: 800-323-9736

Mosquito Control Association, American www.mosquito.org
PO Box 234 Eatontown NJ 07727
Ph: 732-544-4645 ▪ Fx: 732-542-3267

Mossberg Collectors Association, National www.mossbergcollectors.org
PO Box 487 Festus MO 63028
Ph: 636-937-6401

Mother & Child Rights Inc, Committee for
6536 Colgate Ave Los Angeles CA 90048
Ph: 323-634-0543 ▪ Fx: 323-936-7762

Mothers Against Drunk Driving   www.madd.org
511 E John Carpenter Fwy Suite 700   Irving TX 75062
Ph: 214-744-6233 ▪ Fx: 972-869-2207 ▪ TF: 800-438-6233

Mothers Inc, American   www.americanmothers.org
15 Dupont Cir NW   Washington DC 20036
Ph: 202-234-7375 ▪ Fx: 202-234-7390 ▪ TF: 877-242-4264

Mothers, Archconfraternity of Christian   www.capuchin.com/christia.htm
220 37th St   Pittsburgh PA 15201
Ph: 412-683-2400 ▪ Fx: 412-683-7155

Mothers' Centers, National Association of   www.motherscenter.org
64 Division Ave   Levittown NY 11756
Ph: 516-520-2929 ▪ Fx: 516-520-1639 ▪ TF: 800-645-3828

Mothers by Choice Inc, Single   mattes.home.pipeline.com
PO Box 1642 Gracie Square Stn   New York NY 10028
Ph: 212-988-0993

Mothers & More   www.mothersandmore.org
PO Box 31   Elmhurst IL 60126
Ph: 630-941-3553 ▪ Fx: 630-941-3551

Mothers, National Association of At-Home   www.athomemothers.com
406 E Buchanan Ave   Fairfield IA 52556
Ph: 515-472-3202 ▪ Fx: 515-469-3068

Mothers, National Organization of Single   singlemothers.org
PO Box 68   Midland NC 28107
Ph: 704-888-5437

Mothers Supporting Daughters with Breast Cancer   www.mothersdaughters.org
21710 Bayshore Rd   Chestertown MD 21620
Ph: 410-778-1982 ▪ Fx: 410-778-1411

Mothers of Twins Clubs Inc, National Organization of   www.nomotc.org
PO Box 438   Thompsons Station TN 37179
Ph: 615-595-0936 ▪ TF: 877-540-2200

Motility Society, American   motilitysociety.org
45685 Harmony Ln   Belleville MI 48111
Ph: 734-699-1130 ▪ Fx: 734-699-1136

Motion Association, Motor & - SMMA   www.smma.org
PO Box P182   South Dartmouth MA 02748
Ph: 508-979-5935 ▪ Fx: 508-979-5845

Motion Picture Arts & Sciences, Academy of   www.oscars.org
8949 Wilshire Blvd   Beverly Hills CA 90211
Ph: 310-247-3000 ▪ Fx: 310-859-9619

Motion Picture Association   www.mpaa.org
15503 Ventura Blvd   Encino CA 91436
Ph: 818-995-6600 ▪ Fx: 818-382-1799 ▪ TF: 800-662-6797

Motion Picture Association of America   www.mpaa.org
15503 Ventura Blvd   Encino CA 91436
Ph: 818-995-6600 ▪ TF: 800-662-6797

Motion Picture Association of America PAC
1600 'I' St NW   Washington DC 20006
Ph: 202-293-1966 ▪ Fx: 202-293-7674

Motion Picture Industry International, Women of the   www.wompi.org
c/o Twentieth Century Fox PO Box 900   Beverly Hills CA 90213
Ph: 310-369-4083 ▪ Fx: 310-369-8903

Motion Picture Producers, International Quorum of   www.iqfilm.com
c/o Film House 810 Dominican Dr   Nashville TN 37228
Ph: 615-255-4000 ▪ Fx: 615-255-4111

Motion Picture & Television Engineers, Society of   www.smpte.org
595 W Hartsdale Ave   White Plains NY 10607
Ph: 914-761-1100 ▪ Fx: 914-761-3115

Motion Picture & Television Fund   www.mptvfund.org
23388 Mulholland Dr   Woodland Hills CA 91364
Ph: 818-876-1888 ▪ Fx: 818-876-1436

Motion Picture & Television Producers, Alliance of   www.amptp.org
15503 Ventura Blvd   Encino CA 91436
Ph: 818-995-3600 ▪ Fx: 818-382-1793

Motion Pictures, Stuntmen's Association of   www.stuntmen.com
10660 Riverside Dr 2nd Fl Suite E   Toluca Lake CA 91602
Ph: 818-766-4334 ▪ Fx: 818-766-5943

Motion Pictures, Stuntwomen's Association of   www.stuntwomen.com
12457 Ventura Blvd Suite 208   Studio City CA 91604
Ph: 818-762-0907 ▪ Fx: 818-762-9534

Motion Technology Representatives Association, Power-   www.ptra.org
PO Box 150229   Arlington TX 76015
Ph: 817-561-7272 ▪ Fx: 817-561-7275 ▪ TF: 888-817-7872

Motor Car Club of America, Veteran   www.vmcca.org
4441 W Altadena Ave   Glendale AZ 85304
Ph: 800-428-7327

Motor Coach Association, Family   www.fmca.org
8291 Clough Pike   Cincinnati OH 45244
Ph: 513-474-3622 ▪ Fx: 513-474-2332 ▪ TF: 800-543-3622

Motor Coach Group Inc, International   www.imgcoach.com
8645 College Blvd Suite 220   Overland Park KS 66210
Ph: 913-903-0111 ▪ Fx: 913-906-0115 ▪ TF: 888-447-3466

Motor Contest Association, International   www.imca.com
1800 W 'D' St PO Box 921   Vinton IA 52349
Ph: 319-472-2201 ▪ Fx: 319-472-2218

Motor & Equipment Manufacturers Association   www.mema.org
10 Laboratory Dr PO Box 13966   Research Triangle Park NC 27709
Ph: 919-549-4800 ▪ Fx: 919-549-4824 ▪ TF: 800-227-4655

Motor Freight Carriers Association   www.mfca.org
499 S Capitol St SW Suite 502A   Washington DC 20003
Ph: 202-554-3060 ▪ Fx: 202-554-3160

Motor Freight Traffic Association, National   www.nmfta.org
2200 Mill Rd   Alexandria VA 22314
Ph: 703-838-1810 ▪ Fx: 703-683-1094

Motor Press Association, International   www.impa.org
4 Park St   Harrington Park NJ 07640
Ph: 201-750-3533 ▪ Fx: 201-750-2010

(Motor Scooters) Cushman Club of America   cushmanclubofamerica.com
PO Box 661   Union Springs AL 36089
Ph: 334-738-3874

Motor Sports Association, International   www.imsaracing.net
1394 Broadway Ave   Braselton GA 30517
Ph: 706-658-2120 ▪ Fx: 706-658-2130

Motor Vehicle Administrators, American Association of   www.aamva.org
4301 Wilson Blvd Suite 400   Arlington VA 22203
Ph: 703-522-4200 ▪ Fx: 703-522-1553 ▪ TF: 800-515-8881

Motorcoach Association, United   www.uma.org
113 S West St 4th Fl   Alexandria VA 22314
Ph: 703-838-2929 ▪ Fx: 703-838-2950 ▪ TF: 800-424-8262

Motorcycle Association, American Historic Racing   www.ahrma.org
PO Box 1725   Goodlettsville TN 37070
Ph: 615-851-3674 ▪ Fx: 615-851-3678

Motorcycle Association, Wheelchair
101 Torrey St   Brockton MA 02301
Ph: 508-583-8614

Motorcycle Association, Women on Wheels   www.womenonwheels.org
PO Box 14180   Saint Paul MN 55114
Ph: 651-647-4344

Motorcycle Campers, International Brotherhood of   www.ibmc.org
PO Box 375   Helper UT 84526
Ph: 435-650-3290

Motorcycle Club of America, Indian   www.indian-motorcycles.com
PO Box 1743   Perris CA 92572
Ph: 909-780-0421 ▪ Fx: 909-780-0857

**Motorcycle Club Inc, Blue Knights International Law
Enforcement**   38 Alden St   Bangor ME 04401   www.blueknights.org
Ph: 207-947-4600 ▪ Fx: 207-947-5814

Motorcycle Events Association Inc   www.motorcycle-events.com
303 E Sioux Ave PO Box 100   Pierre SD 57501
Ph: 605-224-9999 ▪ Fx: 605-224-2063 ▪ TF: 888-675-4656

Motorcycle Heritage Foundation, American
Motorcycle Hall of Fame Museum 13515 Yarmouth
   Dr   Pickerington OH 43147
Ph: 614-856-2222 ▪ Fx: 614-856-2221

Motorcycle Industry Council   www.mic.org
2 Jenner St Suite 150   Irvine CA 92618
Ph: 949-727-4211 ▪ Fx: 949-727-3313

Motorcycle Owners of America, BMW   www.bmwmoa.org
PO Box 3982   Ballwin MO 63022
Ph: 636-394-7277 ▪ Fx: 636-537-9848

Motorcycle Owners Ltd, Vintage BMW   www.vintagebmw.org
PO Box 67   Exeter NH 03833
Ph: 603-772-9799

Motorcycle Riders Foundation   www.mrf.org
PO Box 1808   Washington DC 20013
Ph: 202-546-0983 ▪ Fx: 202-546-0986

Motorcycle Safety Foundation   www.msf-usa.org
2 Jenner St Suite 150   Irvine CA 92618
Ph: 949-727-3227

Motorcycle Touring Association   www.mtariders.com
11539 Village Place Dr   Houston TX 77077
Ph: 281-752-9406 ▪ Fx: 281-752-9507 ▪ TF: 877-833-3687

(Motorcycles) BMW Riders Association International   www.bmwra.org
PO Box 120430   West Melbourne FL 32912
Ph: 321-984-7800

(Motorcycles) Harley Hummer Club Inc   www.harleyhummerclub.org
4517 Chase Ave   Bethesda MD 20814
Ph: 301-657-4035

(Motorcycles) Harley Owners Group   www.hog.com
PO Box 453   Milwaukee WI 53208
Ph: 414-343-4056 ▪ Fx: 414-343-4515 ▪ TF: 800-464-2582

(Motorcycles) Lemans America   www.lemansamerica.com

(Motorcycles) Triumph International Owners Club   members.aol.com/JohnTIOC/tioc.htm
PO Box 158   Plympton MA 02367
Ph: 508-946-1144 ▪ Fx: 508-946-1145

(Motorcycles) Women in the Wind Inc   www.womeninthewind.org

(Motorcycles) Yamaha 650 Society   www.yamaha650society.com

Motorcyclist Association, American   www.ama-cycle.org
13515 Yarmouth Dr   Pickerington OH 43147
Ph: 614-856-1900 ▪ Fx: 614-856-1920 ▪ TF: 800-262-5646

Motorcyclist Foundation Inc, Women's   www.ponyexpressrides.org
7 Lent Ave   Le Roy NY 14482
Ph: 800-442-3550

Motorcyclists, American Federation of   www.afmracing.org
6167 Jarvis Ave Suite 333   Newark CA 94560
Ph: 510-796-7005

Motorcyclists Association, Christian   www.cmausa.org
PO Box 9   Hatfield AR 71945
Ph: 870-389-6196 ▪ Fx: 870-389-6199

Motorists Association, National   www.motorists.org
402 W 2nd St   Waunakee WI 53597
Ph: 608-849-6000 ▪ Fx: 608-849-8697 ▪ TF: 800-882-2785

MotorMaids Inc   www.motormaids.org

Motorsport International, American
7963 Depew St   Arvada CO 80003
Ph: 303-428-8760 ▪ Fx: 303-428-1070

Motorsports Ministries, Christian   www.christianmotorsports.com
PO Box 129   Mansfield PA 16933
Ph: 570-549-2282 ▪ Fx: 570-549-3366

Mott Charles Stewart Foundation   www.mott.org
503 S Saginaw St Suite 1200   Flint MI 48502
Ph: 810-238-5651 ▪ Fx: 810-766-1753

Moulding & Millwork Producers Association, Wood   wmmpa.com
507 First St   Woodland CA 95695
Ph: 530-661-9591 ▪ Fx: 530-661-9586 ▪ TF: 800-550-7889

Mount Diablo Peace Center   www.mtdpc.org
55 Eckley Ln   Walnut Creek CA 94596
Ph: 925-933-7850 ▪ Fx: 925-934-3136

Mount Rushmore National Memorial Society
PO Box 1524   Rapid City SD 57709
Ph: 605-341-8883 ▪ Fx: 605-341-0433

Mount Vernon Ladies' Association — www.mountvernon.org
3200 Mt Vernon Memorial Hwy PO Box 110   Mount Vernon VA 22121
Ph: 703-780-2000

Mountain Bicycling Association, International — www.imba.com
207 Canyon Blvd Suite 301 PO Box 7578   Boulder CO 80306
Ph: 303-545-9011 ▪ Fx: 303-545-9026 ▪ TF: 888-442-4622

Mountain Bike Association, International Police — www.ipmba.org
583 Fredrick Rd Suite 5B   Baltimore MD 21228
Ph: 410-744-2400 ▪ Fx: 410-744-5504 ▪ TF: 800-323-0037

Mountain Bike & Tea Society, Women's — www.wombats.org
PO Box 757   Fairfax CA 94978
Ph: 415-459-0980

Mountain Club, Appalachian — www.outdoors.org
5 Joy St   Boston MA 02108
Ph: 617-523-0636 ▪ Fx: 617-523-0722 ▪ TF: 800-262-4455

Mountain Institute — www.mountain.org
1828 L St NW Suite 725   Washington DC 20036
Ph: 202-452-1636 ▪ Fx: 202-452-1635

Mountain Lion Foundation — www.mountainlion.org
PO Box 1896   Sacramento CA 95812
Ph: 916-442-2666 ▪ Fx: 916-442-2871

Mountaineers — www.mountaineers.org
300 3rd Ave W   Seattle WA 98119
Ph: 206-284-6310 ▪ Fx: 206-284-4977

Mouse Association, American Fancy Rat & — www.afrma.org
9230 64th St   Riverside CA 92509
Ph: 626-966-0350

Mouse Club of America, Rat & — www.rmca.org

Movement Disorder Society — www.movementdisorders.org
611 E Wells St   Milwaukee WI 53202
Ph: 414-276-2145 ▪ Fx: 414-276-3349

Movement Studies, Laban/Bartenieff Institute of — www.limsonline.org
520 8th Ave Suite 304   New York NY 10018
Ph: 212-643-8888 ▪ Fx: 212-643-8388

Movement Theatre Association, National
3112 17th Ave S   Minneapolis MN 55407
Ph: 612-722-2333

Movement Theatre International
50 Bernard Dr   Yardley PA 19067
Ph: 215-337-9100

Movement Writing, Center for Sutton — www.dancewriting.org
PO Box 517   La Jolla CA 92038
Ph: 858-456-0098 ▪ Fx: 858-456-0020

Movers, International Association of Structural — www.iasm.org
PO Box 2637   Lexington SC 29071
Ph: 803-951-9304 ▪ Fx: 803-951-9314

Movies, Women Make — www.wmm.com
462 Broadway Rm 500   New York NY 10013
Ph: 212-925-0606 ▪ Fx: 212-925-2052

Moving Image Archivists, Association of — www.amianet.org
1313 N Vine St   Hollywood CA 90028
Ph: 323-463-1500 ▪ Fx: 323-463-1506

Moving Picture Technicians Artists & Allied Crafts of the US Its Territories & Canada, International Alliance of Theatrical Stage Employees — www.iatse-intl.org
1430 Broadway 20th Fl   New York NY 10018
Ph: 212-730-1770 ▪ Fx: 212-921-7699 ▪ TF: 800-223-6872

Moving & Storage Association, American — www.amconf.org
1611 Duke St   Alexandria VA 22314
Ph: 703-683-7410 ▪ Fx: 703-683-7527

Mr Holland's Opus Foundation — www.mhopus.org
15125 Ventura Blvd Suite 204   Sherman Oaks CA 91403
Ph: 818-784-6787 ▪ Fx: 818-784-6788

(Mr Peanut) Peanut Pals — www.peanutpals.org
PO Box 4465   Huntsville AL 35815
Ph: 256-881-9198

MRA - Management Association Inc — www.mranet.org
N19 W24400 Riverwood Dr   Waukesha WI 53188
Ph: 262-523-9090 ▪ Fx: 262-523-9091 ▪ TF: 800-488-4845

MRFAC Inc — www.mrfac.com
899-A Harrison St SE   Leesburg VA 20175
Ph: 703-669-0320 ▪ Fx: 703-318-9209 ▪ TF: 800-262-9206

Ms Foundation for Women — www.ms.foundation.org
120 Wall St 33rd Fl   New York NY 10005
Ph: 212-742-2300 ▪ Fx: 212-742-1653

MTM Association for Standards & Research — www.mtm.org
1111 E Touhy Ave Suite 280   Des Plaines IL 60018
Ph: 847-299-1111 ▪ Fx: 847-299-3509

Mu Alpha Theta — www.mualphatheta.org
601 Elm Ave Rm 423   Norman OK 73019
Ph: 405-325-4489 ▪ Fx: 405-325-7184

Mu Phi Epsilon International Music Fraternity — home.muphiepsilon.org
4202 Atlantic Ave Suite 202   Long Beach CA 90807
Ph: 562-424-9799 ▪ Fx: 562-424-9778 ▪ TF: 888-259-1471

Mucosal Immunology, Society for — www.socmucimm.org
4350 East West Hwy Suite 401   Bethesda MD 20814
Ph: 301-718-6515 ▪ Fx: 301-656-0989

Mujeres Activas en Letras y Cambio Social — malcs.chicanas.com

Mulch & Soil Council — www.mulchandsoilcouncil.org
10210 Leatherleaf Ct   Manassas VA 20111
Ph: 703-257-0111 ▪ Fx: 703-257-0213

Mule Association, American
264 Clovis Ave   Clovis CA 93612
Ph: 559-324-6583

Mule Society, American Donkey & — www.lovelongears.com
PO Box 1210   Lewisville TX 75067
Ph: 972-219-0781 ▪ Fx: 972-420-9980

Multi Housing Council, National — www.nmhc.org
1850 M St NW Suite 540   Washington DC 20036
Ph: 202-974-2300 ▪ Fx: 202-775-0112

Multi-Housing Laundry Association — www.mhla.com
1500 Sunday Dr Suite 102   Raleigh NC 27607
Ph: 919-861-5579 ▪ Fx: 919-787-4916 ▪ TF: 800-380-3652

Multi-Level Marketing International Association — www.mlmia.com
119 Stanford Ct   Irvine CA 92612
Ph: 949-854-0484 ▪ Fx: 949-854-7687

Multicultural Counseling & Development, Association for
c/o American Counseling Assn 5999 Stevenson Ave   Alexandria VA 22304
Ph: 703-823-9800 ▪ Fx: 703-823-0252

Multicultural Foodservice & Hospitality Alliance — www.mfha.net
65 Weybosset St Suite 50   Providence RI 02903
Ph: 401-751-8883 ▪ Fx: 401-751-8333

Multicultural Golf Association of America Inc — www.mgaa.com
3 Sunset Ave PO Box 1081   Westhampton Beach NY 11978
Ph: 631-288-8255

MultiCultural Institute, National — www.nmci.org
3000 Connecticut Ave NW Suite 438   Washington DC 20008
Ph: 202-483-0700 ▪ Fx: 202-483-5233

MultiEthnic Americans Inc, Association of — www.ameasite.org/
PO Box 341304   Los Angeles CA 90034
Ph: 877-954-2632

Multimedia & Collaborative Communications Association, Interactive — www.imcca.org
PO Box 756   Syosset NY 11771
Ph: 516-818-8184 ▪ Fx: 516-922-2170

Multimedia Teleconferencing Consortium Inc, International — www.imtc.org
2400 Camino Ramon Suite 275   San Ramon CA 94583
Ph: 925-275-6600 ▪ Fx: 925-275-6691

Multiple Birth, Center for Loss in — www.climb-support.org
PO Box 91377   Anchorage AK 99509
Ph: 907-222-5321 ▪ Fx: 907-274-7029

Multiple Sclerosis Association of America — www.msaa.com
706 Haddonfield Rd   Cherry Hill NJ 08002
Ph: 800-532-7667 ▪ Fx: 856-661-9797

Multiple Sclerosis Foundation — www.msfacts.org
6350 N Andrews Ave   Fort Lauderdale FL 33309
Ph: 954-776-6805 ▪ Fx: 954-938-8708 ▪ TF: 800-225-6495

Multiple Sclerosis Society, National — www.nmss.org
733 3rd Ave   New York NY 10017
Ph: 212-986-3240 ▪ Fx: 212-986-7981 ▪ TF: 800-344-4867

Multiservice Switching Forum — www.msforum.org
39355 California St Suite 307   Fremont CA 94538
Ph: 510-608-5922 ▪ Fx: 510-608-5917

Multistate Tax Commission — www.mtc.gov
444 N Capitol St NW Suite 425   Washington DC 20001
Ph: 202-624-8699 ▪ Fx: 202-624-8819

MultiTechnology Association, Asia America — www.aamasv.com
3300 Zanker Rd MD SJ2F8   San Jose CA 95134
Ph: 408-955-4505 ▪ Fx: 408-955-4516

Multivariate Experimental Psychology, Society of — www.smep.org
Univ of Oklahoma Psychology Dept   Norman OK 73019
Ph: 405-325-4511 ▪ Fx: 405-325-4737

Municipal Analysts, National Federation of — www.nfma.org
PO Box 14893   Pittsburgh PA 15234
Ph: 412-341-4898 ▪ Fx: 412-341-4894

Municipal Arborists, Society of — www.urban-forestry.com
PO Box 641   Watkinsville GA 30677
Ph: 706-769-7412 ▪ Fx: 706-769-7307

Municipal Clerks, International Institute of — www.iimc.org
8331 Utica Ave Suite 200   Rancho Cucamonga CA 91730
Ph: 909-944-4162 ▪ Fx: 909-944-8545 ▪ TF: 800-251-1639

Municipal Employees, American Federation of State County & — www.afscme.org
1625 L St NW   Washington DC 20036
Ph: 202-452-4800 ▪ Fx: 202-429-1293

Municipal Government, Women in
c/o National League of Cities 1301 Pennsylvania Ave NW   Suite 550   Washington DC 20004
Ph: 202-626-3000 ▪ Fx: 202-626-3043

Municipal Lawyers Association, International — www.imla.org
1110 Vermont Ave NW Suite 200   Washington DC 20005
Ph: 202-466-5424 ▪ Fx: 202-785-0152

Municipal Securities Rulemaking Board — www.msrb.org
1900 Duke St Suite 600   Alexandria VA 22314
Ph: 703-797-6600 ▪ Fx: 703-797-6700

Municipal Signal Association, International — www.imsasafety.org
165 E Union St PO Box 539   Newark NY 14513
Ph: 315-331-2182 ▪ Fx: 315-331-8205 ▪ TF: 800-723-4672

Municipal Waste Management Association — www.usmayors.org/uscm/mwma
1620 'I' St NW Suite 300   Washington DC 20006
Ph: 202-293-7330 ▪ Fx: 202-293-2352

Mural Painters, National Society of
c/o American Fine Arts Society 215 W 57th St   New York NY 10019
Ph: 212-941-0130 ▪ Fx: 212-941-0138

Murdered Children, Parents of — www.pomc.com
100 E 8th St Suite B-41   Cincinnati OH 45202
Ph: 513-721-5683 ▪ Fx: 513-345-4489 ▪ TF: 888-818-7662

Murdock MJ Charitable Trust — www.murdock-trust.org
703 Broadway St Suite 710   Vancouver WA 98660
Ph: 360-694-8415 ▪ Fx: 360-694-1819

Murray Grey Association, American — www.murraygreybeefcattle.com
PO Box 224   New Bethlehem PA 16242
Ph: 814-275-2515 ▪ Fx: 814-275-2506

Muscular Dystrophy Association   www.mdausa.org
3300 E Sunrise Dr   Tucson AZ 85718
Ph: 520-529-2000 ▪ Fx: 520-529-5300 ▪ TF: 800-572-1717

Musculoskeletal Tumor Society   msts.org
Vanderbilt University Medical Ctr 1161 21st Ave S D-4216
    Medical Ctr N   Nashville TN 37232
Ph: 615-343-4400 ▪ Fx: 615-343-1028

Museum of America, Polish   pma.prcua.org
984 N Milwaukee Ave   Chicago IL 60622
Ph: 773-384-3352 ▪ Fx: 773-384-3799

Museum Anthropology, Council for   www.nmnh.si.edu/cma
c/o American Anthropological Assn 2200 Wilson Blvd Suite
    600   Arlington VA 22201
Ph: 703-528-1902 ▪ Fx: 703-528-3546

Museum Association, Custer Battlefield Historical &   www.cbhma.org
PO Box 902   Hardin MT 59034
Ph: 406-665-2060 ▪ Fx: 406-665-3133

Museum Association, Steamtown
350 Cliff St   Scranton PA 18503
Ph: 570-963-6590 ▪ Fx: 570-346-7093

Museum Computer Network   www.mcn.edu
329 March Rd Suite 232 Box 11   Ottawa ON K2K2E1
Ph: 888-211-1477 ▪ Fx: 613-599-7027

Museum Directors, Association of Art   www.aamd.org
41 E 65th St   New York NY 10021
Ph: 212-249-4423 ▪ Fx: 212-535-5039

Museum Education Roundtable   www.mer-online.org
621 Pennsylvania Ave SE   Washington DC 20003
Ph: 202-547-8378 ▪ Fx: 202-547-8344

Museum Facility Administrators, International Association of   www.iamfa.org
c/o High Museum of Art 1280 Peachtree Rd NE   Atlanta GA
    30309
Ph: 404-733-4407 ▪ Fx: 404-733-4502

Museum of Modern Art, International Council of the
11 W 53rd St   New York NY 10019
Ph: 212-708-9470 ▪ Fx: 212-708-9740

Museum Store Association   www.museumdistrict.com
4100 E Mississippi Ave Suite 800   Denver CO 80246
Ph: 303-504-9223 ▪ Fx: 303-504-9585

Museum Theatre Alliance, International   www.imtal.org
c/o Wildlife Theater Central Park Zoo 830 5th Ave   New York
    NY 10021
Ph: 212-439-6542

Museum Trustee Association   www.mta-hq.org
2025 M St NW Suite 800   Washington DC 20036
Ph: 202-367-1180 ▪ Fx: 202-367-2180

Museum Volunteers, American Association for   www.aamv.org
1575 'I' St NW Suite 400   Washington DC 20005
Ph: 202-289-1818 ▪ Fx: 202-289-6578

Museums, American Association of   www.aam-us.org
1575 'I' St NW Suite 400   Washington DC 20005
Ph: 202-289-1818 ▪ Fx: 202-289-6578

Museums, Association of African American   www.blackmuseums.org

Museums, Association of Children's   www.childrensmuseums.org
1300 L St NW Suite 975   Washington DC 20005
Ph: 202-898-1080 ▪ Fx: 202-898-1086

Museums, Association for Living History Farm & Agricultural   www.alhfam.org
8774 Rt 45 NW   North Bloomfield OH 44450
Ph: 440-685-4410

Museums, Association of Railway   www.railwaymuseums.org
PO Box 370   Tujunga CA 91043
Ph: 818-951-9151

Museums, Council of American Maritime   www.councilofamericanmaritimemuseums.org
c/o Maine Maritime Museum 243 Washington St   Bath ME
    04530
Ph: 207-443-1316 ▪ Fx: 207-443-1663

Museums & Galleries, Association of College & University   www.acumg.org
Ursinus College 601 E Main St   Collegeville PA 19426
Ph: 610-409-3500 ▪ Fx: 610-409-3664

Museums & Halls of Fame, International Association of Sports   www.sportshalls.com
180 N LaSalle St Suite 1822   Chicago IL 60601
Ph: 312-551-0810 ▪ Fx: 312-551-0815

Museums of the Performing Arts-USA,   www.theatrelibrary.org/sibmas/sibmas.html
International Association of Libraries &

Mushroom Council   www.mushroomcouncil.org
11875 Dublin Rd Suite D262   Dublin CA 94568
Ph: 925-558-2749 ▪ Fx: 925-558-2740

Mushroom Institute, American   www.americanmushroom.org
1 Massachusetts Ave NW Suite 800   Washington DC 20001
Ph: 202-842-4344 ▪ Fx: 202-408-7763

Music, Academy of Country   www.acmcountry.com
4100 W Alameda Ave Suite 208   Burbank CA 91505
Ph: 818-842-8400 ▪ Fx: 818-842-8535

Music, African Heritage Center for African Dance &
4018 Minnesota Ave NE   Washington DC 20019
Ph: 202-399-5252

Music, Allen Foundation for   www.pgafoundations.com/music.asp
505 5th Ave S Suite 900   Seattle WA 98104
Ph: 206-342-2000 ▪ Fx: 206-342-3000

Music Alliance, Jewish
1133 Broadway Rm 820   New York NY 10010
Ph: 212-243-1304 ▪ Fx: 212-243-1305

Music America, Chamber   www.chamber-music.org
305 7th Ave 5th Fl   New York NY 10001
Ph: 212-242-2022 ▪ Fx: 212-242-7955

Music America, Early   www.earlymusic.org
11421 1/2 Bellflower Rd   Cleveland OH 44106
Ph: 216-229-1685 ▪ Fx: 216-229-1688 ▪ TF: 888-722-5288

Music Inc, American Festival of Microtonal   www.afmm.org
318 E 70th St Suite 5FW   New York NY 10021
Ph: 212-517-3550 ▪ Fx: 212-517-5495

Music, American Guild of   www.americanguild.org
PO Box 599   Warren MI 48090
Ph: 248-336-9388

Music Arrangers & Composers, American Society of   www.asmac.org
PO Box 17840   Encino CA 91416
Ph: 818-994-4661 ▪ Fx: 818-994-6181

Music Association of America, Church   www.musicasacra.com
Christendom College 134 Christendom Dr   Front Royal VA
    22630
Ph: 540-636-2900 ▪ Fx: 540-636-1655

Music Association, Blues   www.bluesmusicassociation.org
PO Box 3122   Memphis TN 38173
Ph: 901-572-3843

Music Association, Country   www.cmaworld.com
1 Music Cir S   Nashville TN 37203
Ph: 615-244-2840 ▪ Fx: 615-726-0314 ▪ TF: 800-998-4636

Music Association, Gospel   www.gospelmusic.org
1205 Division St   Nashville TN 37203
Ph: 615-242-0303 ▪ Fx: 615-254-9755

Music, Association for Independent   www.afim.org
PO Box 16754   Rocky River OH 44116
Ph: 440-333-2208 ▪ Fx: 440-333-2280

Music Association, International Bluegrass   www.ibma.org
2 Music Cir S Suite 100   Nashville TN 37203
Ph: 615-256-3222 ▪ Fx: 615-256-0450 ▪ TF: 888-438-4262

Music Association, International Business   www.ibma.net
PO Box 940   Franklin NC 28744
Ph: 828-369-2322

Music Association, International Computer   www.computermusic.org

Music Association, National Traditional Country   www.oldtimemusic.bigstep.com/
PO Box 492   Anita IA 50020
Ph: 712-762-4363

Music Association, NFHS   www.nfhs.org/nfma.htm
PO Box 690   Indianapolis IN 46206
Ph: 317-972-6900 ▪ Fx: 317-822-5700

Music Association, World Folk   www.wfma.net
PO Box 40553   Washington DC 20016
Ph: 202-362-2225 ▪ Fx: 202-244-1543 ▪ TF: 800-779-2226

(Music) Balalaika & Domra Association of America   www.bdaa.com
2801 Warner St   Madison WI 53713
Ph: 608-259-9440

Music Inc, Broadcast   www.bmi.com
320 W 57th St   New York NY 10019
Ph: 212-586-2000 ▪ Fx: 212-489-2368

Music Center, American   www.amc.net
30 W 26th St Suite 1001   New York NY 10010
Ph: 212-366-5260 ▪ Fx: 212-366-5265

Music Circle, Philatelic   www.philatelicmusic.com
PO Box 1781   Sequim WA 98382
Ph: 360-683-6373

Music Clubs, National Federation of   www.nfmc-music.org
1336 N Delaware St   Indianapolis IN 46202
Ph: 317-638-4003 ▪ Fx: 317-638-0503

Music Composers, Christian Fellowship of Art   www.cfamc.org
Houghton College Greatbatch School of Music   Houghton NY
    14744
Ph: 585-567-9424

Music Conference, American   www.amc-music.com
5790 Armada Dr   Carlsbad CA 92008
Ph: 760-431-9124 ▪ Fx: 760-438-7237

Music Council, National   www.musiccouncil.org
425 Park St   Upper Montclair NJ 07043
Ph: 973-655-7974 ▪ Fx: 973-655-5432

Music Critics Association of North America   www.mcana.org
722 Dulaney Valley Rd Suite 259   Baltimore MD 21204
Ph: 410-435-3881

Music Dealers Association, Retail Print   www.printmusic.org
13140 Coit Rd Suite 320 LB 120   Dallas TX 75240
Ph: 972-233-9107 ▪ Fx: 972-490-4219

Music Dealers, National Association of School   www.nasmd.com
13140 Coit Rd Suite 320 LB 120   Dallas TX 75240
Ph: 972-233-9107 ▪ Fx: 972-490-4219

(Music) Delta Omicron   www.delta-omicron.org

Music Distributors Association   www.musicdistributors.org
PO Box 5488   Long Island City NY 11105
Ph: 718-274-3210 ▪ Fx: 718-274-3214

Music Education, MENC: National Association for   www.menc.org
1806 Robert Fulton Dr   Reston VA 20191
Ph: 703-860-4000 ▪ Fx: 703-860-1531 ▪ TF: 800-336-3768

Music & Entertainment Industry Educators Association   www.meiea.org
6363 St Charles Ave PO Box 83   New Orleans LA 70118
Ph: 504-865-3975

Music Festival Association, American
PO Box 2987   Anaheim CA 92814
Ph: 562-948-2281 ▪ Fx: 562-948-4575

Music Foundation Inc, Country
222 5th Ave S   Nashville TN 37203
Ph: 615-416-2001 ▪ Fx: 615-255-2245

Music Foundation Inc, Creative   www.creativemusicstudio.org
PO Box 671   Woodstock NY 12498
Ph: 845-679-8847

Music Foundation, Moravian   www.moravianmusic.org
457 S Church St PO Box L   Winston-Salem NC 27108
Ph: 336-725-0651 ▪ Fx: 336-725-4514

Music Fraternity, Mu Phi Epsilon International   home.muphiepsilon.org
4202 Atlantic Ave Suite 202   Long Beach CA 90807
Ph: 562-424-9799 ▪ Fx: 562-424-9778 ▪ TF: 888-259-1471

Music Honor Society, Tri-M www.menc.org/information/trim/TriMMain1.html
c/o MENC 1806 Robert Fulton Dr   Reston VA 20191
Ph: 703-860-4000 ▪ Fx: 703-860-2652 ▪ TF: 800-336-3768

Music Importers & Exporters, National Council of
PO Box 5488   Long Island City NY 11105
Ph: 718-274-3210 ▪ Fx: 718-274-3214

Music, Institute for Studies in American depthome.brooklyn.cuny.edu/isam
Brooklyn College of CUNY 2900 Bedford Ave   Brooklyn NY
11210
Ph: 718-951-5655 ▪ Fx: 718-951-4858

Music Instruction, Association for Technology in atmi.music.org

Music, International Alliance for Women in music.acu.edu/www/iawm
Indiana University of Pennsylvania Dept of Music Rm
209   Indiana PA 15705
Ph: 724-357-7918 ▪ Fx: 724-357-9570

Music, International Association for Research in Vietnamese
2005 Willow Ridge Cir   Kent OH 44240
Ph: 330-673-3763 ▪ Fx: 330-673-4434

Music, International Federation for Choral ifcm.net
Univ of Illinois at Chicago Dept of Performing Arts 1040 W
Harrison St MC 255   Chicago IL 60607
Ph: 312-996-8744 ▪ Fx: 312-996-0954

(Music) International Percy Grainger Society www.percygrainger.org
7 Cromwell Pl   White Plains NY 10601
Ph: 914-948-7436

Music, Kurt Weill Foundation for www.kwf.org
7 E 20th St   New York NY 10003
Ph: 212-505-5240 ▪ Fx: 212-353-9663

Music Libraries Archives & Documentation Centres, International www.iaml.info
Association of

Music Library Association Inc www.musiclibraryassoc.org
8551 Research Way Suite 180   Middleton WI 53562
Ph: 608-836-5825 ▪ Fx: 608-831-8200

Music, National Academy of Popular
330 W 58th St Suite 411   New York NY 10019
Ph: 212-957-9230 ▪ Fx: 212-957-9227

Music, National Association of Schools of nasm.arts-accredit.org
11250 Roger Bacon Dr Suite 21   Reston VA 20190
Ph: 703-437-0700 ▪ Fx: 703-437-6312

Music, National Association for the Study & Performance of www.naspaam.org
African-American

Music National Network, Women in www.womeninmusic.com
31121 Mission Blvd Suite 300   Hayward CA 94544
Ph: 510-232-3897 ▪ Fx: 510-215-2846

Music Notation Modernization Association www.speechskript.com/mnma.htm
PO Box 241   Kirksville MO 63501
Ph: 660-665-8098

Music Operators Association, Amusement & www.amoa.com
1145 N Arlington Heights Rd Suite 300   Itasca IL 60143
Ph: 630-250-1430 ▪ Fx: 630-250-3533 ▪ TF: 800-937-2662

Music Performance Trust Funds www.mptf.org
1501 Broadway Suite 518   New York NY 10036
Ph: 212-391-3950 ▪ Fx: 212-221-2604

(Music) Pi Kappa Lambda
Northwestern Univ School of Music 711 Elgin Rd   Evanston IL
60208
Ph: 847-491-5737

Music Players, Amateur Chamber www.acmp.net
1123 Broadway Rm 304   New York NY 10010
Ph: 212-645-7424 ▪ Fx: 212-741-2678

Music Products Association, NAMM - International www.namm.com
5790 Armada Dr   Carlsbad CA 92008
Ph: 760-438-8001 ▪ Fx: 760-438-7327 ▪ TF: 800-767-6266

Music Publishers Association, Church www.cmpamusic.org
PO Box 158992   Nashville TN 37215
Ph: 615-791-0273 ▪ Fx: 615-790-8847

Music Publishers, Association of Independent www.aimp.org
PO Box 69473   Los Angeles CA 90069
Ph: 818-771-7301

Music Publishers Association, National www.nmpa.org
475 Park Ave S 29th Fl   New York NY 10016
Ph: 646-742-1651 ▪ Fx: 646-742-1779

Music Publishers' Association of the US www.mpa.org
1562 1st Ave PMB 246   New York NY 10028
Ph: 212-327-4044

(Music) Roger Sessions Society www.uncwil.edu/music/Sessionssociety
Univ of North Carolina at Wilmington 601 S College
Rd   Wilmington NC 28403
Ph: 910-962-3390 ▪ Fx: 910-962-7106

Music Scholarship Association, American www.amsa-wpc.org
441 Vine St Suite 1030   Cincinnati OH 45202
Ph: 513-421-5342 ▪ Fx: 513-421-2672

Music Showcase International, Country www.cmshowcase.org
PO Box 368   Carlisle IA 50047
Ph: 515-989-3748 ▪ Fx: 515-989-0235

(Music) Sigma Alpha Iota www.sai-national.org
34 Wall St Suite 515   Asheville NC 28801
Ph: 828-251-0606 ▪ Fx: 828-251-0644

Music Society, African-American
PO Box 2522   Springfield MA 01101
Ph: 413-734-2555 ▪ Fx: 413-731-9587

Music, Society for American www.american-music.org
Univ of Pittsburgh Stephen Foster Memorial 405 Bellefield
Hall   Pittsburgh PA 15260
Ph: 412-624-3031 ▪ Fx: 412-624-7447

Music, Society for Asian www.skidmore.edu/academics/asianmusic
Cornell Univ Dept of Music Lincoln Hall   Ithaca NY 14853
Ph: 607-255-5049 ▪ Fx: 607-254-2877

Music Society, College www.music.org
312 E Pine St   Missoula MT 59802
Ph: 406-721-9616 ▪ Fx: 406-721-9419

Music Society, Film www.filmmusicsociety.org
15125 Ventura Blvd Suite 201   Sherman Oaks CA 91403
Ph: 818-789-6404 ▪ Fx: 818-789-6414

Music Society of North America, Chinese www.chinesemusic.net
PO Box 5275   Woodridge IL 60517
Ph: 630-910-1551 ▪ Fx: 630-910-1561

Music Society, Villa-Lobos www.rdpl.red-deer.ab.ca/villa/society.html
153 E 92nd St Unit 4R   New York NY 10128
Ph: 212-427-5103

Music Teachers National Association www.mtna.org
441 Vine St Suite 505   Cincinnati OH 45202
Ph: 513-421-1420 ▪ Fx: 513-421-2503 ▪ TF: 888-512-5278

Music Theatre Network, National www.nmtn.org
1697 Broadway Suite 902   New York NY 10019
Ph: 212-664-0979 ▪ Fx: 212-664-0978

Music Therapy Association, American www.musictherapy.org
8455 Colesville Rd Suite 1000   Silver Spring MD 20910
Ph: 301-589-3300 ▪ Fx: 301-589-5175

Music & Video Association, United Catholic www.ucmva.com
PO Box 230   Donnellson IA 52625
Ph: 319-835-9340 ▪ Fx: 319-835-9071 ▪ TF: 877-668-2682

Music Workshop of America, Gospel www.gmwa.org
3908 W Warren Ave   Detroit MI 48208
Ph: 313-898-6900 ▪ Fx: 313-898-4520

Music & Worship Arts, Fellowship of United Methodists in www.fummwa.org
PO Box 24787   Nashville TN 37202
Ph: 615-749-6875 ▪ Fx: 615-749-6874 ▪ TF: 800-952-8977

Musical Artists, American Guild of www.musicalartists.org
1430 Broadway 14th Fl   New York NY 10018
Ph: 212-265-3687 ▪ Fx: 212-262-9088 ▪ TF: 800-543-2462

Musical Box Society International www.mbsi.org

Musical, Institute of the American
121 N Detroit St   Los Angeles CA 90036
Ph: 323-934-1221

Musical Instrument Society, American www.amis.org/
389 Main St Siote 202   Malden MA 02148
Ph: 781-397-8870

Musical Studies, American Institute of www.aimsgraz.org
6621 Snider Plaza   Dallas TX 75205
Ph: 214-363-2683 ▪ Fx: 214-363-6474

Musical Theatre, National Alliance for www.namt.net
520 8th Ave Suite 301   New York NY 10018
Ph: 212-714-6668 ▪ Fx: 212-714-0469

Musicians, American College of www.pianoguild.com
808 Rio Grande St   Austin TX 78701
Ph: 512-478-5775 ▪ Fx: 512-478-5843

Musicians, Association for the Advancement www.aacmchicago.org/aacmgoals.html
of Creative   PO Box 5757   Chicago IL 60680
Ph: 312-752-2212 ▪ Fx: 312-752-2226

Musicians, Association of Anglican www.anglicanmusicians.org
28 Ashton Rd   Fort Mitchell KY 41017
Ph: 859-344-9308

Musicians Coalition, Creative www.aimcmc.com
1024 W Wilcox Ave   Peoria IL 61604
Ph: 309-685-4843 ▪ Fx: 309-685-4878 ▪ TF: 800-882-4262

Musicians Foundation Inc www.musiciansfoundation.org
875 6th Ave Suite 2303   New York NY 10001
Ph: 212-239-9137 ▪ Fx: 212-239-9138

Musicians, International Conference of Symphony & Opera www.icsom.org
4 W 31st St Unit 921   New York NY 10001
Ph: 212-594-1636

Musicians, National Association of Negro www.nanm.8m.com
11551 S Laflin St PO Box 43053   Chicago IL 60643
Ph: 773-568-3818 ▪ Fx: 773-779-1325

Musicians, National Association of Pastoral www.npm.org
962 Wayne Ave Suite 210   Silver Spring MD 20910
Ph: 240-247-3000

Musicians, National Fraternity of Student
808 Rio Grande PO Box 1807   Austin TX 78767
Ph: 512-478-5775 ▪ Fx: 512-478-5843

Musicians' Network, Unitarian Universalist www.uua.org/uumn
2208 Henery Tuckers Ct   Charlotte NC 28270
Ph: 800-969-8866

Musicians, Presbyterian Association of horeb.pcusa.org/pam
100 Witherspoon St   Louisville KY 40202
Ph: 502-569-5288 ▪ Fx: 502-569-8465 ▪ TF: 888-728-7228

Musicians Union, American
8 Tobin Ct   Dumont NJ 07628
Ph: 201-384-5378

Musicians of the US & Canada, American Federation of www.afm.org
1501 Broadway Suite 600   New York NY 10036
Ph: 212-869-1330 ▪ Fx: 212-764-6134 ▪ TF: 800-762-3444

Musicological Society, American www.sas.upenn.edu/music/ams/
201 S 34th St   Philadelphia PA 19104
Ph: 215-898-8698 ▪ Fx: 215-573-2106

Musicological Society, American Accordion
334 S Broadway   Pitman NJ 08071
Ph: 856-854-6628

Muslim Scientists & Engineers, Association of www.amse.net
PO Box 38   Plainfield IN 46168
Ph: 517-947-6338

Muslim Social Scientists, Association of www.amss.net
PO Box 669   Herndon VA 20172
Ph: 703-471-1133 ▪ Fx: 703-471-3922

Muslim Students' Association of the US & Canada www.msa-natl.org
PO Box 18612   Washington DC 20036
Ph: 703-820-7900 ▪ Fx: 703-820-7888

Muslim Youth, World Assembly of www.wamyusa.org
PO Box 8096   Falls Church VA 22041
Ph: 703-783-8410 ▪ Fx: 703-783-8409

Mustang Association & Registry, North American
PO Box 850906   Mesquite TX 75185
Ph: 972-289-9344

Mustang & Burro Association Inc, American www.bardalisa.com
PO Box 788   Lincoln CA 95648
Ph: 530-633-9271 ▪ TF: 800-874-8453

Mustang Registry, Spanish www.spanishmustang.org
4970 S Kansas Settlement Rd   Willcox AZ 85643
Ph: 520-384-2886

Mustangs & Burros, International Society for the Protection of www.ispmb.org
PO Box 55   Lantry SD 57636
Ph: 605-964-6866 ▪ Fx: 605-365-6991

Mustard Seed Foundation www.msfdn.org
3330 N Washington Blvd Suite 100   Arlington VA 22201
Ph: 703-524-5620 ▪ Fx: 703-524-5643

Mutagen Society, Environmental www.ems-us.org
1821 Michael Faraday Dr Suite 330   Reston VA 20190
Ph: 703-438-8220 ▪ Fx: 703-438-3113

Mutilation of Males, National Organization to Halt the www.noharmm.org
Abuse & Routine   PO Box 460795   San Francisco CA 94146
Ph: 415-826-9351

Mutual Aid Association, Navy www.navymutual.org
29 Carpenter Rd Henderson Hall   Arlington VA 22212
Ph: 703-614-1638 ▪ Fx: 703-695-4635 ▪ TF: 800-628-6011

Mutual Aid Society of USA, Russian Orthodox Catholic www.rocmas.org
10 Downs Dr   Wilkes-Barre PA 18705
Ph: 570-822-8591 ▪ Fx: 570-821-7060 ▪ TF: 877-476-2627

Mutual Atomic Energy Liability Underwriters
3158 River Rd Suite 103   Des Plaines IL 60018
Ph: 312-467-0003 ▪ Fx: 312-467-0774

Mutual Benefit Association, Armed Services www.asmba.com
PO Box 160384   Nashville TN 37216
Ph: 615-851-0800 ▪ Fx: 615-851-9484 ▪ TF: 800-251-8434

Mutual Fund Education Alliance www.mfea.com
100 NW Englewood Rd Suite 130   Kansas City MO 64118
Ph: 816-454-9422 ▪ Fx: 816-454-9322

Mutual Help Association Inc, Southern www.southernmutualhelp.org
3602 Old Jeanerette Rd   New Iberia LA 70563
Ph: 337-367-3277 ▪ Fx: 337-367-3279

Mutual Insurance Companies, National Association of www.namic.org
3601 Vincennes Rd   Indianapolis IN 46268
Ph: 317-875-5250 ▪ Fx: 317-879-8408 ▪ TF: 800-336-2642

Mutual UFO Network www.mufon.org
PO Box 369   Morrison CO 80465
Ph: 303-932-7709 ▪ Fx: 303-932-9279

Muzzle Loading Rifle Association, National www.nmlra.org
PO Box 67   Friendship IN 47021
Ph: 812-667-5131 ▪ Fx: 812-667-5136

Myasthenia Gravis Foundation of America www.myasthenia.org
1821 University Ave W Suite S256   Saint Paul MN 55104
Ph: 651-917-6256 ▪ Fx: 651-917-1835 ▪ TF: 800-541-5454

Mycological Association, North American www.namyco.org
6615 Tudor Ct   Gladstone OR 97027
Ph: 503-657-7358

Mycological Society of America www.msafungi.org
810 E 10th St   Lawrence KS 66044
Ph: 785-843-1235 ▪ Fx: 785-843-1274 ▪ TF: 800-527-0529

Mystery Shopping Providers Association www.mysteryshop.org
12300 Ford Rd Suite 135   Dallas TX 75234
Ph: 972-406-1104 ▪ Fx: 972-755-2561

Mystery Writers of America Inc www.mysterywriters.org
17 E 47th St 6th Fl   New York NY 10017
Ph: 212-888-8171 ▪ Fx: 212-888-8107

Mystic Shrine, Ancient Egyptian Arabic Order Nobles www.aeaonms.org
2239 Democrat Rd   Memphis TN 38132
Ph: 901-395-0150 ▪ Fx: 901-395-0115

Mystic Valley Railway Society www.mysticvalleyrs.org
PO Box 365468   Hyde Park MA 02136
Ph: 617-361-4445

Myth & Tradition, Society for the Study of www.parabola.org
656 Broadway   New York NY 10012
Ph: 212-505-6200 ▪ Fx: 212-979-7325 ▪ TF: 800-560-6984

Myvesta.org Inc www.myvesta.org
6 Taft Ct Suite 200   Rockville MD 20850
Ph: 301-762-5270 ▪ TF: 800-698-3782

N

NAADAC - Association for Addiction Professionals www.naadac.org
901 N Washington St Suite 600   Alexandria VA 22314
Ph: 703-741-7686 ▪ Fx: 800-377-1136 ▪ TF: 800-548-0497

NAADAC PAC
901 N Washington St Suite 600   Alexandria VA 22314
Ph: 703-741-7686 ▪ Fx: 703-741-7689 ▪ TF: 800-548-0497

Na'Amat USA www.naamat.org
350 5th Ave Suite 4700   New York NY 10118
Ph: 212-563-5222 ▪ Fx: 212-563-5710

NACE International: Corrosion Society www.nace.org
1440 S Creek Dr   Houston TX 77084
Ph: 281-228-6200 ▪ Fx: 281-228-6300

Nacel Open Door www.nacelopendoor.org
1536 Hewitt Ave Box 268   Saint Paul MN 55104
Ph: 651-686-0080 ▪ Fx: 651-686-9601 ▪ TF: 800-622-3553

NACHA - Electronic Payments Association www.nacha.org
13665 Dulles Technology Dr Suite 300   Herndon VA 20171
Ph: 703-561-1100 ▪ Fx: 703-787-0996 ▪ TF: 800-487-9180

NAFSA: Association of International Educators www.nafsa.org
1307 New York Ave NW 8th Fl   Washington DC 20005
Ph: 202-737-3699 ▪ Fx: 202-737-3657

Nail & Beauty Association, World International
1221 N Lake View Ave   Anaheim CA 92807
Ph: 714-779-9883 ▪ Fx: 714-779-9971 ▪ TF: 800-624-5777

Nail Manufacturers Council www.abbies.org/nmc.html
401 N Michigan Ave   Chicago IL 60611
Ph: 312-245-1575 ▪ Fx: 312-245-1080 ▪ TF: 800-868-4265

Nail & Tool Association, International Staple www.isanta.org
512 W Burlington Ave Suite 203   La Grange IL 60525
Ph: 708-482-8138 ▪ Fx: 708-482-8186

NAIR: National Association of Independent Resurfacers Inc www.nairbowl.org
5806 W 127th St   Alsip IL 60803
Ph: 708-371-8237 ▪ Fx: 708-371-8283

NALS - Association for Legal Professionals www.nals.org
314 E 3rd St Suite 210   Tulsa OK 74120
Ph: 918-582-5188 ▪ Fx: 918-582-5907

NAMDRC www.namdrc.org
5454 Wisconsin Ave Suite 1270   Chevy Chase MD 20815
Ph: 301-718-2975 ▪ Fx: 301-718-2976

Name Society, American www.wtsn.binghamton.edu/ANS

Names & Numbers, Internet Corp for Assigned www.icann.org
4676 Admiralty Way Suite 330   Marina del Rey CA 90292
Ph: 310-823-9358 ▪ Fx: 310-823-8649

NAMES Project Foundation/AIDS Memorial Quilt www.aidsquilt.org
101 Krog St   Atlanta GA 30307
Ph: 404-688-5500 ▪ Fx: 404-688-5552

NAMM - International Music Products Association www.namm.com
5790 Armada Dr   Carlsbad CA 92008
Ph: 760-438-8001 ▪ Fx: 760-438-7327 ▪ TF: 800-767-6266

NANDA International www.nanda.org
1211 Locust St   Philadelphia PA 19107
Ph: 215-545-8105 ▪ Fx: 215-545-8107 ▪ TF: 800-647-9002

Nanny Association, International www.nanny.org
191 Clarksville Rd   Princeton Junction NJ 08550
Ph: 609-799-7527 ▪ Fx: 609-799-7032 ▪ TF: 888-878-1477

(Nanotechnology) Foresight Institute www.foresight.org
PO Box 61058   Palo Alto CA 94306
Ph: 650-917-1122 ▪ Fx: 650-917-1123

Napa Valley Grape Growers Association www.napagrowers.org
811 Jefferson St   Napa CA 94559
Ph: 707-944-8311 ▪ Fx: 707-224-7836

Napa Valley Vintners Association www.napavintners.com
PO Box 141   Saint Helena CA 94574
Ph: 707-963-3388 ▪ Fx: 707-963-3488 ▪ TF: 800-982-1371

Napoleonic Society of America www.napoleonic-society.com
1115 Ponce de Leon Blvd   Clearwater FL 33756
Ph: 610-581-0400

Naprapathic Association, American www.naprapathy.org
164 Division St Suite 202   Elgin IL 60120
Ph: 847-214-8642 ▪ Fx: 847-214-8645

Nar-Anon World Service Office www.naranon.com
22527 Crenshaw Blvd Suite 200B   Torance CA 90505
Ph: 310-547-5800

NARAL Pro-Choice America www.naral.org
1156 15th St NW Suite 700   Washington DC 20005
Ph: 202-973-3000 ▪ Fx: 202-973-3096

NARAL Pro-Choice America PAC
1156 15th St NW Suite 700   Washington DC 20005
Ph: 202-973-3000 ▪ Fx: 202-973-3096

Narcolepsy Network Inc www.narcolepsynetwork.org
10921 Reed Hartman Hwy Suite 119   Cincinnati OH 45242
Ph: 513-891-3522 ▪ Fx: 513-891-3836

Narcotic Enforcement Officers Association, International www.ineoa.org
112 State St Suite 1200   Albany NY 12207
Ph: 518-463-6232 ▪ Fx: 518-432-3378

Narcotics Anonymous World Services www.na.org
PO Box 9999   Van Nuys CA 91409
Ph: 818-773-9999 ▪ Fx: 818-700-0700

Narrow Fabrics Institute www.narrowfabrics.org
1801 County Rd 'B' W   Roseville MN 55113
Ph: 651-222-2508 ▪ Fx: 651-631-9334 ▪ TF: 800-225-4324

NASAO Center for Aviation Research & www.nasao.org/center/Center_Home_Page.htm
Education   1010 Wayne Ave Suite 930   Silver Spring MD 20910
Ph: 301-495-2848 ▪ Fx: 301-585-1803

NASBIC PAC www.nasbic.org/resources
666 11th St NW Suite 750   Washington DC 20001
Ph: 202-628-5055 ▪ Fx: 202-628-5080

NASD Regulation Inc www.nasdr.com
9509 Key West Ave   Rockville MD 20850
Ph: 301-590-6500

Nash Car Club of America www.nashcarclub.org
1N274 Prarie   Glen Ellyn IL 60137
Ph: 630-469-5848

Nashville Songwriters Association International www.nashvillesongwriters.com
1701 West End Ave 3rd Fl   Nashville TN 37203
Ph: 615-256-3354 ▪ Fx: 615-256-0034 ▪ TF: 800-321-6008

NASPE - Heart Rhythm Society Inc www.naspe.org
6 Strathmore Rd   Natick MA 01760
Ph: 508-647-0100 ▪ Fx: 508-647-0124

NASSCO www.nassco.org
1314 Bedford Ave Suite 201   Baltimore MD 21208
Ph: 410-486-3500 ▪ Fx: 410-486-6838

Nast Thomas Society www.jfpl.org/nast.htm
c/o Morristown-Morris Township Library 1 Miller Rd   Morristown NJ 07960
Ph: 973-538-3473 ▪ Fx: 973-267-4064

Nathaniel Hawthorne Society   asweb.artsci.uc.edu/english/HawthorneSociety/nh.html
Univ of Cincinnati Dept of English   Cincinnati OH 45221
Ph: 513-556-5924

Nation of Islam   www.noi.org
7351 S Stony Island   Chicago IL 60649
Ph: 773-324-6000 ▪ Fx: 773-324-6309

National 4-H Council   www.fourhcouncil.edu
7100 Connecticut Ave   Chevy Chase MD 20815
Ph: 301-961-2800 ▪ Fx: 301-961-2848

National Abandoned Infants Assistance Resource Center   aia.berkeley.edu
UC Berkeley Family Welfare Research Group 1950 Addison St
   Suite 104   Berkeley CA 94704
Ph: 510-643-8390 ▪ Fx: 510-643-7019

National Ability Center   www.nac1985.org
PO Box 682799   Park City UT 84068
Ph: 435-649-3991 ▪ Fx: 435-658-3992

National Abortion Federation   www.prochoice.org
1755 Massachusetts Ave NW Suite 600   Washington DC 20036
Ph: 202-667-5881 ▪ Fx: 202-667-5890 ▪ TF: 800-772-9100

National Academic Advising Association   www.nacada.ksu.edu
Kansas State Univ 2323 Anderson Ave Suite 225   Manhattan
   KS 66502
Ph: 785-532-5717 ▪ Fx: 785-532-7732

National Academies of Practice   www.nap.vcu.edu
PO Box 1037   Edgewood MD 21040
Ph: 410-676-3390

National Academy on an Aging Society   agingsociety.org
1030 15th St NW Suite 250   Washington DC 20005
Ph: 202-842-1275 ▪ Fx: 202-842-1150

National Academy of American Scholars   www.naas.org
1249 S Diamond Bar Blvd PMB 325   Diamond Bar CA 91765
Ph: 909-621-6856

National Academy of Arbitrators   www.naarb.org
1 N Main St Suite 412   Cortland NY 13045
Ph: 607-756-8363 ▪ Fx: 607-756-8365

National Academy of Building Inspection Engineers   www.nabie.org
PO Box 520   York Harbor ME 03911
Ph: 800-294-7729 ▪ Fx: 207-351-1915

National Academy of Education   www.nae.nyu.edu
New York Univ School of Education 726 Broadway Rm
   509   New York NY 10003
Ph: 212-998-9035 ▪ Fx: 212-995-4435

National Academy of Elder Law Attorneys   www.naela.com
1604 N Country Club Rd   Tucson AZ 85716
Ph: 520-881-4005 ▪ Fx: 520-325-7925

National Academy of Engineering   www.nae.edu
2101 Constitution Ave NW   Washington DC 20418
Ph: 202-334-3200 ▪ Fx: 202-334-1563

National Academy of Neuropsychology   www.nanonline.org
2121 S Oneida St Suite 550   Denver CO 80224
Ph: 303-691-3694 ▪ Fx: 303-691-5983

National Academy of Opticianry   www.nao.org
8401 Corporate Dr Suite 605   Landover MD 20785
Ph: 301-577-4828 ▪ Fx: 301-577-3880 ▪ TF: 800-229-4828

National Academy of Popular Music
330 W 58th St Suite 411   New York NY 10019
Ph: 212-957-9230 ▪ Fx: 212-957-9227

National Academy of Public Administration   www.napawash.org
1100 New York Ave NW Suite 1090 E   Washington DC 20005
Ph: 202-347-3190 ▪ Fx: 202-393-0993 ▪ TF: 800-883-3190

National Academy of Recording Arts & Sciences   www.grammy.com
3402 Pico Blvd   Santa Monica CA 90405
Ph: 310-392-3777 ▪ Fx: 310-392-2306 ▪ TF: 800-423-2017

National Academy of Sciences   www.nas.edu
500 5th St NW   Washington DC 20001
Ph: 202-334-2138 ▪ Fx: 202-334-2229

National Academy of Television Arts & Sciences   www.emmyonline.org
111 W 57th St Suite 600   New York NY 10019
Ph: 212-586-8424 ▪ Fx: 212-246-8129

National Accessible Apartment Clearinghouse   www.forrent.com/naac
201 N Union St Suite 200   Alexandria VA 22314
Ph: 703-518-6141 ▪ Fx: 703-518-6191 ▪ TF: 800-421-1221

National Accounting & Finance Council   truckline.com/cc/councils/nafc
American Trucking Assns 2200 Mill Rd   Alexandria VA 22314
Ph: 703-838-1915 ▪ Fx: 703-836-0751

National Accrediting Agency for Clinical Laboratory Sciences   www.naacls.org
8410 W Bryn Mawr Ave Suite 670   Chicago IL 60631
Ph: 773-714-8880 ▪ Fx: 773-714-8886

National Accrediting Commission of Cosmetology Arts & Sciences   www.naccas.org
4401 Ford Ave Suite 1300   Alexandria VA 22302
Ph: 703-600-7600 ▪ Fx: 703-379-2200

National Action Council for Minorities in Engineering   www.nacme.org
440 Hamilton Ave Suite 302   White Planes NY 10601
Ph: 914-539-4010 ▪ Fx: 914-539-4032

National Acupuncture Detoxification Association   www.acudetox.com
PO Box 1927   Vancouver WA 98668
Ph: 360-254-0186 ▪ Fx: 360-260-8620 ▪ TF: 888-765-6232

National Adoption Center   www.adopt.org
1500 Walnut St Suite 701   Philadelphia PA 19102
Ph: 215-735-9988 ▪ Fx: 215-735-9410

National Adoption Information Clearinghouse   naic.acf.hhs.gov
330 C St SW   Washington DC 20447
Ph: 703-352-3488 ▪ Fx: 703-385-3206 ▪ TF: 888-251-0075

National Adrenal Diseases Foundation   www.medhelp.org/nadf
505 Northern Blvd   Great Neck NY 11021
Ph: 516-487-4992

National Adult Day Services Association   www.nadsa.org
8201 Greensboro Dr Suite 300   McLean VA 22102
Ph: 703-610-9000 ▪ Fx: 703-610-9005 ▪ TF: 800-424-9046

National Adult Education Professional Development Consortium   www.naepdc.org/
444 N Capitol St NW Suite 422   Washington DC 20001
Ph: 202-624-5250 ▪ Fx: 202-624-1497

National Advertising Div, Council of Better Business Bureaus Inc   www.nadreview.org
70 W 36th St 13th Fl   New York NY 10018
Ph: 212-705-0114

National Aeronautic Association   www.naa-usa.org
1815 N Fort Myer Dr Suite 500   Arlington VA 22209
Ph: 703-527-0226 ▪ Fx: 703-527-0229 ▪ TF: 800-644-9777

National Affordable Housing Management Association   www.nahma.org
526 W King St Suite 511   Alexandria VA 22314
Ph: 703-683-8630 ▪ Fx: 703-683-8634

National Affordable Housing Network   www.nahn.com
PO Box 3706   Butte MT 59702
Ph: 406-782-8145 ▪ Fx: 406-782-5168

National African American Speakers Association   www.4naasa.org
3033 Western Ave   Park Forest IL 60466
Ph: 708-747-2219 ▪ TF: 877-866-2272

National Agri-Marketing Association   www.nama.org
11020 King St Suite 205   Overland Park KS 66210
Ph: 913-491-6500 ▪ Fx: 913-491-6502 ▪ TF: 800-530-5646

National Agricultural Aviation Association   www.agaviation.org
1005 'E' St SE   Washington DC 20003
Ph: 202-546-5722 ▪ Fx: 202-546-5726

National Agricultural Communicators of Tomorrow   nact.okstate.edu

National Air Carrier Association   www.naca.cc
1000 Wilson Blvd Suite 1700   Arlington VA 22209
Ph: 703-358-8060 ▪ Fx: 703-358-8070

National Air Duct Cleaners Association   www.nadca.com
1518 K St Suite 503   Washington DC 20005
Ph: 202-737-2926 ▪ Fx: 202-347-8847

National Air Filtration Association   www.nafahq.org
PO Box 68639 Suite 503   Virginia Beach VA 23471
Ph: 757-313-7400 ▪ Fx: 757-497-1895

National Air Traffic Controllers Association   www.natca.org
1325 Massachusetts Ave NW   Washington DC 20005
Ph: 202-628-5451 ▪ Fx: 202-628-5767 ▪ TF: 800-266-0895

National Air Traffic Controllers Association PAC
1325 Massachusetts Ave NW   Washington DC 20005
Ph: 202-628-5451 ▪ Fx: 202-628-5767

National Air Transportation Association   www.nata-online.org
4226 King St   Alexandria VA 22302
Ph: 703-845-9000 ▪ Fx: 703-845-8176 ▪ TF: 800-808-6282

National Aircraft Finance Association   www.nafa-us.org
PO Box 85   Poolesville MD 20837
Ph: 301-349-2070 ▪ Fx: 301-972-7727

National Aircraft Resale Association   www.nara-dealers.com/
4226 King St   Alexandria VA 22302
Ph: 703-671-8273 ▪ Fx: 703-671-5848

National Alarm Association of America   www.naaa.org
PO Box 3409   Dayton OH 45401
Ph: 800-283-6285 ▪ Fx: 513-461-4759

National Alcohol Beverage Control Association   www.nabca.org
4216 King St W   Alexandria VA 22302
Ph: 703-578-4200 ▪ Fx: 703-820-3551

National Alfalfa Alliance   www.alfalfa.org
100 N Fruitland St Suite B   Kennewick WA 99336
Ph: 509-585-5460 ▪ Fx: 509-585-2671

National Allergy Bureau   www.aaaai.org/nab
611 E Wells St 4th Fl   Milwaukee WI 53202
Ph: 414-272-6071 ▪ Fx: 414-272-6070

National Alliance for Autism Research   www.naar.org
99 Wall St Research Park   Princeton NJ 08540
Ph: 609-430-9160 ▪ Fx: 609-430-9163 ▪ TF: 888-777-6227

National Alliance of Black School Educators   www.nabse.org
310 Pennsylvania Ave SE   Washington DC 20003
Ph: 202-608-6310 ▪ Fx: 202-608-6319 ▪ TF: 800-221-2654

National Alliance of Blind Students Inc   www.blindstudents.org
1155 15th St NW Suite 1004   Washington DC 20005
Ph: 202-467-5081 ▪ Fx: 202-467-5085 ▪ TF: 800-424-8666

National Alliance of Breast Cancer Organizations   www.nabco.org
9 E 37th St 10th Fl   New York NY 10016
Ph: 212-889-0606 ▪ Fx: 212-689-1213 ▪ TF: 888-806-2226

National Alliance for Caregiving   www.caregiving.org
4720 Montgomery Ln Suite 642   Bethesda MD 20814
Ph: 301-718-8444 ▪ Fx: 301-652-7711

National Alliance to End Homelessness   www.endhomelessness.org
1518 K St NW Suite 206   Washington DC 20005
Ph: 202-638-1526 ▪ Fx: 202-638-4664

National Alliance for Hispanic Health   www.hispanichealth.org
1501 16th St NW   Washington DC 20036
Ph: 202-387-5000 ▪ Fx: 202-797-4353

National Alliance for Media Arts & Culture   www.namac.org
145 9th St Suite 250   San Francisco CA 94103
Ph: 415-431-1391 ▪ Fx: 415-431-1392

National Alliance for the Mentally Ill   www.nami.org
2107 Wilson Blvd Suite 300   Arlington VA 22201
Ph: 703-524-7600 ▪ Fx: 703-524-9094 ▪ TF: 800-950-6264

National Alliance for Musical Theatre   www.namt.net
520 8th Ave Suite 301   New York NY 10018
Ph: 212-714-6668 ▪ Fx: 212-714-0469

National Alliance of Nurse Practitioners
PO Box 40326   Washington DC 20016
Ph: 202-675-6350

National Alliance of Postal & Federal Employees   www.napfe.com
1628 11th St NW   Washington DC 20001
Ph: 202-939-6325 ▪ Fx: 202-939-6389

National Alliance of Preservation Commissions   www.arches.uga.edu/~napc
PO Box 1605   Athens GA 30603
Ph: 706-542-4731 ▪ Fx: 706-583-0320

National Alliance of State & Territorial AIDS Directors   www.nastad.org
444 N Capitol St NW Suite 339   Washington DC 20001
Ph: 202-434-8090 ▪ Fx: 202-434-8092
National Alliance of Statewide Preservation Organizations
c/o Historic Landmarks Foundation of Indiana 340 W Michigan
St   Indianapolis IN 46202
Ph: 317-639-4534 ▪ TF: 800-450-4534
National Alliance for Youth Sports   www.nays.org
2050 Vista Pkwy   West Palm Beach FL 33411
Ph: 561-684-1141 ▪ Fx: 561-684-2546 ▪ TF: 800-729-2057
National Alopecia Areata Foundation   www.naaf.org
PO Box 150760   San Rafael CA 94915
Ph: 415-456-4644 ▪ Fx: 415-472-5343
National Alpha Lambda Delta   www.mercer.edu/ald
PO Box 4403   Macon GA 31208
Ph: 478-744-9595 ▪ Fx: 478-744-9924
National Amateur Baseball Federation   www.nabf.com
PO Box 705   Bowie MD 20718
Ph: 301-262-5005
National AMBUCS Inc   www.ambucs.com
3315 N Main St   High Point NC 27265
Ph: 336-869-2166 ▪ Fx: 336-887-8451
National American Indian Cattlemen's Association
1541 Foster Rd   Toppenish WA 98948
Ph: 509-854-1329
National American Indian Court Judges Association   www.naicja.org
3618 Reder St   Rapid City SD 57702
Ph: 605-342-4804 ▪ Fx: 605-719-9357
National American Indian Housing Council   naihc.indian.com
900 2nd St NE Suite 305   Washington DC 20002
Ph: 202-789-1754 ▪ Fx: 202-789-1758 ▪ TF: 800-284-9165
National American Legion Press Association   www.nalpa.legion.org
National American Motors Drivers & Racers Association   www.namdra.org
PO Box 987   Twin Lakes WI 53181
Ph: 262-396-9552
National Amputation Foundation   www.nationalamputation.org
40 Church St   Malverne NY 11565
Ph: 516-887-3600 ▪ Fx: 516-887-3667
National Amputee Golf Association   www.nagagolf.org
11 Walnut Hill Rd   Amherst NH 03031
Ph: 800-633-6242
National Animal Control Association   www.nacanet.org
132 S Cherry St   Olathe KS 66061
Ph: 913-768-1319 ▪ Fx: 913-768-1378
National Animal Damage Control Association   nadca.unl.edu
PO Box 2180   Ardmore OK 73402
Ph: 580-223-5810
National Animal Interest Alliance   www.naiaonline.org
PO Box 66579   Portland OR 97290
Ph: 503-761-1139 ▪ Fx: 503-761-1289
National Anti-Vivisection Society   www.navs.org
53 W Jackson Blvd Suite 1552   Chicago IL 60604
Ph: 312-427-6065 ▪ Fx: 312-427-6524 ▪ TF: 800-888-6287
National Antique & Art Dealers Association of America   naadaa.org
220 E 57th St   New York NY 10022
Ph: 212-826-9707 ▪ Fx: 212-832-9493
National Antique Oldsmobile Club Inc   www.antiqueolds.org
National Anxiety Center   www.anxietycenter.com
9 Brookside Rd   Maplewood NJ 07040
Ph: 973-763-6392 ▪ Fx: 973-763-4287
National Apartment Association   www.naahq.org
201 N Union St Suite 200   Alexandria VA 22314
Ph: 703-518-6141 ▪ Fx: 703-518-6191 ▪ TF: 800-842-4054
National Aphasia Association   www.aphasia.org
29 John St Suite 1103   New York NY 10038
Ph: 212-267-2814 ▪ Fx: 212-267-2812 ▪ TF: 800-922-4622
National Apostolate for Inclusion Ministry   www.nafim.org
PO Box 218   Riverdale MD 20738
Ph: 301-699-9500 ▪ TF: 800-736-1280
National Appliance Parts Suppliers Association   www.napsaweb.org
PO Box 87907   Vancouver WA 98687
Ph: 360-834-3805 ▪ Fx: 360-834-3507
National Appliance Service Association   www.nasa1.org
PO Box 2514   Kokomo IN 46904
Ph: 765-453-1820 ▪ Fx: 765-453-1895
National Arab American Medical Association   www.naama.com
801 S Adams Rd Suite 208   Birmingham MI 48009
Ph: 248-646-3661 ▪ Fx: 248-646-0617
National Arbor Day Foundation   www.arborday.org
211 N 12th St   Lincoln NE 68508
Ph: 402-474-5655 ▪ Fx: 402-474-0820 ▪ TF: 888-448-7337
National Arboretum, Friends of the   www.fona.org
3501 New York Ave NE   Washington DC 20002
Ph: 202-544-8733 ▪ Fx: 202-544-5398
National Architectural Accrediting Board   www.naab.org
1735 New York Ave NW   Washington DC 20006
Ph: 202-783-2007 ▪ Fx: 202-783-2822
National Armored Car Association
1730 M St NW   Washington DC 20036
Ph: 202-296-3522 ▪ Fx: 202-296-7713
National Art Education Association   www.naea-reston.org
1916 Association Dr   Reston VA 20191
Ph: 703-860-8000 ▪ Fx: 703-860-2960
National Art Materials Trade Association   www.namta.org
15806 Brookway Dr Suite 300   Huntersville NC 28078
Ph: 704-892-6244 ▪ Fx: 704-892-6247
National Arts Foundation   www.nafgallery.com
444 Oakton St   Skokie IL 60077
Ph: 847-674-7990 ▪ Fx: 847-675-8116

National Asian American Telecommunications Association   www.naatanet.org
145 9th St Suite 350   San Francisco CA 94103
Ph: 415-863-0814 ▪ Fx: 415-863-7428
National Asian Pacific American Bar Association   www.napaba.org
733 15th St NW Suite 315   Washington DC 20005
Ph: 202-367-0796 ▪ Fx: 202-393-0995
National Asian Pacific American Families Against Substance Abuse   www.napafasa.org
340 E Second St Suite 409   Los Angeles CA 90012
Ph: 213-625-5795 ▪ Fx: 213-625-5796
National Asian Pacific American Law Student Association   www.napalsa.org
National Asian Pacific American Legal Consortium   www.napalc.org
1140 Connecticut Ave NW Suite 1200   Washington DC 20036
Ph: 202-296-2300 ▪ Fx: 202-296-2318
National Asian Pacific American Women's Forum   www.napawf.org
1112 16th St NW Suite 110   Washington DC 20036
Ph: 202-293-2688 ▪ Fx: 202-463-2119
National Asian Pacific Center on Aging   www.napca.org/
PO Box 21668   Seattle WA 98101
Ph: 206-624-1221 ▪ Fx: 206-624-1023
National Asian Women's Health Organization   www.nawho.org
250 Montgomery St Suite 900   San Francisco CA 94104
Ph: 415-989-9747 ▪ Fx: 415-989-9758
National Asphalt Pavement Association   www.hotmix.org
5100 Forbes Blvd   Lanham MD 20706
Ph: 301-731-4748 ▪ Fx: 301-731-4621 ▪ TF: 888-468-6499
National Assembly of Health & Human Service Organizations   www.nassembly.org
1319 F St NW Suite 601   Washington DC 20004
Ph: 202-347-2080 ▪ Fx: 202-393-4517
National Assembly of State Arts Agencies   www.nasaa-arts.org
1029 Vermont Ave NW 2nd Fl   Washington DC 20005
Ph: 202-347-6352 ▪ Fx: 202-737-0526
National Assistance League   www.nal.org
PO Box 6637   Burbank CA 91510
Ph: 818-846-3777 ▪ Fx: 818-846-3535
National Associated Certified Public Accounting Firms   www.nacpaf.com
136 S Keowee St   Dayton OH 45402
Ph: 937-222-1024 ▪ Fx: 937-222-5794
National Association of Academic Advisors for Athletics   www.nfoura.org
14606 Woodlake Terr   Louisville KY 40245
Ph: 502-253-9530 ▪ Fx: 502-253-9533
National Association of Accompanists & Coaches
395 Riverside Dr Apt 13A   New York NY 10025
Ph: 212-316-6164 ▪ Fx: 212-663-1900
National Association of Addiction Treatment Providers   www.naatp.org
313 West Liberty Suite 129   Lancaster PA 17603
Ph: 717-392-8480 ▪ Fx: 717-392-8481
National Association for Adults With Special Learning Needs   www.naasln.org
c/o Correctional Education Assn 4380 Forbes Blvd   Lanham MD 20706
Ph: 800-496-9222
National Association to Advance Fat Acceptance   www.naafa.org
PO Box 188620   Sacramento CA 95818
Ph: 916-558-6880 ▪ Fx: 916-558-6881
National Association for the Advancement of Colored People   www.naacp.org
4805 Mount Hope Dr   Baltimore MD 21215
Ph: 410-358-8900 ▪ Fx: 410-486-9255 ▪ TF: 877-622-2798
National Association for the Advancement of Psychoanalysis   www.naap.org
80 8th Ave Suite 1501   New York NY 10011
Ph: 212-741-0515 ▪ Fx: 212-366-4347
National Association of Advisors for the Health Professions   www.naahp.org
PO Box 1518   Champaign IL 61824
Ph: 217-355-0063 ▪ Fx: 217-355-1287
National Association of Affordable Housing Lenders
1300 Connecticut Ave NW Suite 905   Washington DC 20036
Ph: 202-293-9850 ▪ Fx: 202-293-9852
National Association of African-American Sportswriters & Broadcasters
308A Deer Park Ave   Dix Hills NY 11746
Ph: 631-462-3933
National Association of African-American Studies & Affiliates   www.naaas.org
PO Box 325   Biddeford ME 04005
Ph: 207-839-8004 ▪ Fx: 207-839-3776
National Association of African Americans in Human Resources   www.naaahr.org
National Association of Agricultural Educators   www.naae.org
Univ of Kentucky 300 Garrigus Bldg   Lexington KY 40546
Ph: 859-257-2224 ▪ Fx: 859-323-3919 ▪ TF: 800-509-0204
National Association of Air Traffic Specialists   www.naats.org
11303 Amherst Ave Suite 4   Wheaton MD 20902
Ph: 301-933-6228 ▪ Fx: 301-933-3902
National Association on Alcohol Drugs & Disability   www.naadd.org
2165 Bunker Hill Dr   San Mateo CA 94402
Ph: 650-578-8047 ▪ Fx: 650-286-9205
(National Association of Alcoholism & Drug Abuse Council)
NAADAC PAC   901 N Washington St Suite 600   Alexandria VA 22314
Ph: 703-741-7686 ▪ Fx: 703-741-7689 ▪ TF: 800-548-0497
National Association of Alternative Medicines   www.rentamark.com/naam
PO Box 35189   Chicago IL 60707
Ph: 708-453-0080 ▪ Fx: 708-453-0083
National Association of Amusement Ride Safety Officials   www.naarso.com
PO Box 638   Brandon FL 33509
Ph: 813-661-2779 ▪ Fx: 813-685-5117 ▪ TF: 800-669-9053
National Association of Animal Breeders   www.naab-css.org
PO Box 1033   Columbia MO 65205
Ph: 573-445-4406 ▪ Fx: 573-446-2279
National Association of Anorexia Nervosa & Associated Disorders   www.anad.org
PO Box 7   Highland Park IL 60035
Ph: 847-831-3438 ▪ Fx: 847-433-4632
National Association of Antique Malls   www.antiqueandcollectible.com
PO Box 4389   Davidson NC 28036
Ph: 704-895-9088 ▪ Fx: 704-895-0230 ▪ TF: 800-287-7127

National Association of Architectural Metal Manufacturers www.naamm.org
8 S Michigan Ave Suite 1000 Chicago IL 60603
Ph: 312-332-0405 ▪ Fx: 312-332-0706

National Association of Area Agencies on Aging www.n4a.org
927 15th St NW 6th Fl Washington DC 20005
Ph: 202-296-8130 ▪ Fx: 202-296-8134

National Association for Armenian www.commercemarketplace.com/home/naasr
Studies & Research 395 Concord Ave Belmont MA 02478
Ph: 617-489-1610 ▪ Fx: 617-484-1759

National Association of Asian American Professionals www.naaap.org

National Association of Assistant US Attorneys www.naausa.org
9001 Braddock Rd Suite 380 Springfield VA 22151
Ph: 703-426-4266 ▪ Fx: 800-528-3492 ▪ TF: 800-455-5661

National Association of Attorneys General www.naag.org
750 1st St NE Suite 1100 Washington DC 20002
Ph: 202-326-6000 ▪ Fx: 202-408-7014 ▪ TF: 888-245-6224

National Association of Band Instrument Manufacturers www.nabim.org
PO Box 5488 Long Island City NY 11105
Ph: 718-274-3210 ▪ Fx: 718-274-3214

National Association of Bankruptcy Trustees www.nabt.com
1 Windsor Cove Suite 305 Columbia SC 29223
Ph: 803-252-5646 ▪ Fx: 803-765-0860

National Association of Bankshot Operators www.nabo-assn.com
785F Rockville Pike PMB 504 Rockville MD 20852
Ph: 301-309-0260 ▪ Fx: 301-309-0263 ▪ TF: 800-933-0140

National Association of Baptist Professors of Religion www.cssr.org/soc_nabpr.htm
Mercer University Macon GA 31207
Ph: 478-301-2758 ▪ Fx: 478-301-2384

National Association of Bar Executives www.abanet.org/nabe
541 N Fairbanks Ct Chicago IL 60611
Ph: 312-988-6008 ▪ Fx: 312-988-5492

National Association of Bar-Related Title Insurers www.nabrti.org
2355 S Arlington Heights Rd Suite 230 Arlington Heights IL
60005
Ph: 847-545-0500 ▪ Fx: 847-545-0550

National Association of Basketball Coaches nabc.ocsn.com
9300 W 110th St Suite 640 Overland Park KS 66210
Ph: 913-469-1001 ▪ Fx: 913-469-1390

National Association for Bilingual Education www.nabe.org
1030 15th St NW Suite 470 Washington DC 20005
Ph: 202-898-1829 ▪ Fx: 202-789-2866

National Association of Biology Teachers www.nabt.org
12030 Sunrise Valley Dr Suite 110 Reston VA 20191
Ph: 703-264-9696 ▪ Fx: 703-264-7778 ▪ TF: 800-406-0775

National Association for Biomedical Research www.nabr.org
818 Connecticut Ave NW 2nd Fl Washington DC 20006
Ph: 202-857-0540 ▪ Fx: 202-659-1902

National Association of Black Accountants www.nabainc.org
7249-A Hanover Pkwy Greenbelt MD 20770
Ph: 301-474-6222 ▪ Fx: 301-474-3114

National Association of Black County Officials
440 1st St NW Suite 410 Washington DC 20001
Ph: 202-347-6953 ▪ Fx: 202-393-6596

National Association of Black Journalists www.nabj.org
Univ of Maryland 8701-A Adelphi Rd Adelphi MD 20783
Ph: 301-445-7100 ▪ Fx: 301-445-7101

National Association of Black Owned Broadcasters www.nabob.org
1155 Connecticut Ave NW 6th Fl Washington DC 20036
Ph: 202-463-8970 ▪ Fx: 202-429-0657

National Association of Black Scuba Divers www.nabsdivers.org

National Association of Black Social Workers www.nabsw.org
1220 11th St NW Washington DC 20001
Ph: 202-589-1850 ▪ Fx: 202-589-1853

National Association of Black Storytellers www.nabsnet.org
PO Box 67722 Baltimore MD 21215
Ph: 410-947-1117

National Association of Blacks in Criminal Justice www.nabcj.org
North Carolina Central Univ PO Box 19788 Durham NC 27707
Ph: 919-683-1801 ▪ Fx: 919-683-1903

National Association of Boards Commissions & www.ncea.org/departments/nabccce
Councils of Catholic Education National Catholic Educational
Assn 1077 30th St NW Suite 100 Washington DC 20007
Ph: 202-337-6232 ▪ Fx: 202-333-6706

National Association of Boards of Examiners of Long Term Care www.nabweb.org
Administrators 1444 'I' St NW Suite 700 Washington DC
20005
Ph: 202-712-9040 ▪ Fx: 202-216-9646

National Association of Boards of Pharmacy www.nabp.net
700 Busse Hwy Park Ridge IL 60068
Ph: 847-698-6227 ▪ Fx: 847-698-6238

National Association of Bond Lawyers www.nabl.org
250 S Wacker Dr Suite 1550 Chicago IL 60606
Ph: 312-648-9590 ▪ Fx: 312-648-9588

National Association Breweriana Advertising www.nababrew.org

National Association of Broadcast Employees & Technicians- www.nabetcwa.org
Communications Workers of America 501 3rd St NW Suite
880 Washington DC 20001
Ph: 202-434-1254 ▪ Fx: 202-434-1426

National Association of Broadcasters www.nab.org
1771 'N' St NW Washington DC 20036
Ph: 202-429-5300 ▪ Fx: 202-429-5406

(National Association of Broadcasters) Television & Radio PAC
1771 'N' St NW Washington DC 20036
Ph: 202-429-5300 ▪ Fx: 202-429-5406

National Association for Business Economics www.nabe.com
1233 20th St NW Suite 505 Washington DC 20036
Ph: 202-463-6223 ▪ Fx: 202-463-6239

National Association of Business Leaders www.nabl.com/
4132 Shoreline Dr Suite J Earth City MO 63045
Ph: 314-344-1111 ▪ Fx: 314-928-9110

National Association for Business Organizations
10451 Mill Run Cir Suite 400 Owings Mills MD 21117
Ph: 410-581-1373

National Association of Business Political Action Committees www.nabpac.org
1133 21st St NW Suite M-100 Washington DC 20036
Ph: 202-572-6279 ▪ Fx: 202-546-4243

National Association for Business Teacher Education www.nbea.org
1914 Association Dr Reston VA 20191
Ph: 703-860-8300 ▪ Fx: 703-620-4483

National Association of Business Travel Agents
3699 Wilshire Blvd Suite 700 Los Angeles CA 90010
Ph: 213-382-3335

National Association for Campus Activities www.naca.org
13 Harbison Way Columbia SC 29212
Ph: 803-732-6222 ▪ Fx: 803-749-1047 ▪ TF: 800-845-2338

National Association of Case Management www.yournacm.addr.com

National Association of Casino & Theme Party Operators www.casinoparties.com
18946 Des Moines Memorial Dr Bldg 5 SeaTac WA 98146
Ph: 206-241-4777 ▪ Fx: 206-241-6956 ▪ TF: 800-355-8299

National Association of Catastrophe Adjusters www.nacatadj.org
PO Box 821864 North Richland Hills TX 76180
Ph: 817-498-3466 ▪ Fx: 817-498-0480

National Association of Catering Executives www.nace.net
5565 Sterrett Pl Suite 328 Columbia MD 21044
Ph: 410-997-9055 ▪ Fx: 410-997-8834

National Association of Catholic Chaplains www.nacc.org
PO Box 070473 Milwaukee WI 53207
Ph: 414-483-4898 ▪ Fx: 414-483-6712

National Association of Catholic Family Life Ministers www.nacflm.org
300 College Park Dayton OH 45469
Ph: 937-229-3324 ▪ Fx: 937-229-4902

National Association of Catholic School Teachers www.nacst.com
1700 Sansom St Suite 903 Philadelphia PA 19103
Ph: 215-665-0993 ▪ Fx: 215-568-8270 ▪ TF: 800-996-2278

National Association for Cave Diving www.safecavediving.com
PO Box 14492 Gainesville FL 32604
Ph: 352-331-7666 ▪ TF: 888-565-6223

National Association of Certified Natural Health Professionals www.cnhp.org
714 E Winona Ave Warsaw IN 46580
Ph: 574-267-4230 ▪ Fx: 574-268-5393 ▪ TF: 800-321-1005

National Association of Certified Valuation Analysts www.nacva.com
1111 E Brickyard Rd Suite 200 Salt Lake City UT 84106
Ph: 801-486-0600 ▪ Fx: 801-486-7500 ▪ TF: 800-677-2009

National Association of Chain Drug Stores www.nacds.org
413 N Lee St Alexandria VA 22314
Ph: 703-549-3001 ▪ Fx: 703-836-4869 ▪ TF: 800-678-6223

National Association of Chain Drug Stores PAC
413 N Lee St Alexandria VA 22314
Ph: 703-549-3001 ▪ Fx: 703-836-4869 ▪ TF: 800-678-6223

National Association of Chapter 13 Trustees www.nactt.com
1 Windsor Cove Suite 305 Columbia SC 29205
Ph: 803-252-5646 ▪ Fx: 803-765-0860 ▪ TF: 800-445-8629

National Association of Chemical Distributors www.nacd.com
1560 Wilson Blvd Suite 1250 Arlington VA 22209
Ph: 703-527-6223 ▪ Fx: 703-527-7747

National Association of Chewing Gum Manufacturers www.nacgm.org
17000 Commerce Pkwy Suite C Mount Laurel NJ 08054
Ph: 856-439-0500 ▪ Fx: 856-439-0525

National Association for Chicana & Chicano Studies www.naccs.org

National Association of Chiefs of Police www.aphf.org/nacop.html
6350 Horizon Dr Titusville FL 32780
Ph: 321-264-0911 ▪ Fx: 321-264-0033

National Association of Child Care Professionals www.naccp.org
7610 Hwy 71 W Suite E Austin TX 78735
Ph: 512-301-5557 ▪ Fx: 512-301-5080 ▪ TF: 800-537-1118

National Association of Child Care Resource & Referral Agencies www.naccrra.org
1319 F St NW Suite 500 Washington DC 20004
Ph: 202-393-5501 ▪ Fx: 202-393-1109 ▪ TF: 800-424-2246

National Association of Childbearing Centers www.birthcenters.org
3123 Gottschall Rd Perkiomenville PA 18074
Ph: 215-234-8068 ▪ Fx: 215-234-8829

National Association of Children's Hospitals & Related www.childrenshospitals.net
Institutions 401 Wythe St Alexandria VA 22314
Ph: 703-684-1355 ▪ Fx: 703-684-1589

National Association of Church Business Administration www.nacba.net
100 N Central Expy Suite 914 Richardson TX 75080
Ph: 972-699-7555 ▪ Fx: 972-699-7617 ▪ TF: 800-898-8085

National Association of Church Food Service www.nacfs.org
PO Box 550413 Atlanta GA 30355
Ph: 404-261-1794 ▪ Fx: 404-240-8276

National Association of Church Personnel Administrators www.nacpa.org
100 E 8th St Cincinnati OH 45202
Ph: 513-421-3134 ▪ Fx: 513-421-3085

National Association of Citizens Crime Commissions www.crimecom.org/naccc
125 N Market Suite 115 Wichita KS 67202
Ph: 316-267-1235

National Association of Civil Service Employees
6829 Park Ridge Blvd San Diego CA 92120
Ph: 619-466-3150

National Association of Civilian Conservation Corps Alumni www.cccalumni.org
16 Hancock Ave PO Box 16429 Saint Louis MO 63125
Ph: 314-487-8666 ▪ Fx: 314-487-9488

National Association of Clinical Nurse Specialists www.nacns.org
3969 Green St Harrisburg PA 17110
Ph: 717-234-6799 ▪ Fx: 717-234-6798

National Association of Collectors   www.collectors.org/NAC
18222 Flower Hill Way Suite 299   Gaithersburg MD 20879
Ph: 301-926-8663 ▪ Fx: 301-926-7648

National Association for College Admission Counseling   www.nacac.com
1631 Prince St   Alexandria VA 22314
Ph: 703-836-2222 ▪ Fx: 703-836-8015 ▪ TF: 800-822-6285

National Association of College Auxiliary Services   www.nacas.org
7 Boars Head Ln   Charlottesville VA 22903
Ph: 434-245-8425 ▪ Fx: 434-245-8453

National Association of College Deans Registrars & Admissions Officers   www.vsu.edu/nacdrao
Albany State Univ 504 College Dr   Albany GA 31705
Ph: 229-430-4638 ▪ Fx: 229-430-2953

National Association of College Stores   www.nacs.org
500 E Lorain St   Oberlin OH 44074
Ph: 440-775-7777 ▪ Fx: 440-775-4769 ▪ TF: 800-622-7498

National Association of College & University Attorneys   www.nacua.org
1 Dupont Cir NW Suite 620   Washington DC 20036
Ph: 202-833-8390 ▪ Fx: 202-296-8379

National Association of College & University Business Officers   www.nacubo.org
2501 M St NW Suite 400   Washington DC 20037
Ph: 202-861-2500 ▪ Fx: 202-861-2583

National Association of College & University Food Services   www.nacufs.org
1405 S Harrison Rd Suite 305   East Lansing MI 48824
Ph: 517-332-2494 ▪ Fx: 517-332-8144

National Association of Colleges & Employers   www.naceweb.org
62 Highland Ave   Bethlehem PA 18017
Ph: 610-868-1421 ▪ Fx: 610-868-0208 ▪ TF: 800-544-5272

National Association of Collegiate Directors of Athletics   nacda.ocsn.com
24651 Detroit Rd   Westlake OH 44145
Ph: 440-892-4000 ▪ Fx: 440-892-4007

National Association of Collegiate Marketing Administrators   nacda.ocsn.com/nacma
PO Box 16428   Cleveland OH 44116
Ph: 440-892-4000 ▪ Fx: 440-892-4007

National Association of Collegiate Women Athletic Administrators   www.nacwaa.org
4701 Wrightsville Ave Oak Park D-1   Wilmington NC 28403
Ph: 910-793-8244 ▪ Fx: 910-793-8246

National Association of Colored Women's Clubs Inc
1601 R St NW   Washington DC 20009
Ph: 202-667-4080 ▪ Fx: 202-667-4113

National Association of Commissioned Travel Agents   www.nacta.org
1101 King St Suite 200   Alexandria VA 22314
Ph: 703-739-6826 ▪ Fx: 703-739-6861

National Association of Commissions for Women   www.nacw.org
8630 Fenton St Suite 934   Silver Spring MD 20910
Ph: 301-585-8101 ▪ Fx: 301-585-3445 ▪ TF: 800-338-9267

National Association of Community Health Centers   www.nachc.com
7200 Wisconsin Ave Suite 210   Bethesda MD 20814
Ph: 301-347-0400 ▪ Fx: 301-347-0459

National Association for Community Mediation   www.nafcm.org
1527 New Hampshire Ave NW 4th Fl   Washington DC 20036
Ph: 202-667-9700 ▪ Fx: 202-667-8629

National Association of Composers USA   www.music-usa.org/nacusa
PO Box 49256   Los Angeles CA 90049
Ph: 310-838-4465 ▪ Fx: 310-373-3244

National Association of Computer Consultant Businesses   www.naccb.org
1800 Diagonal Rd Suite 520   Alexandria VA 22314
Ph: 703-838-2050 ▪ Fx: 703-838-3610

National Association of Concessionaires   www.naconline.org
35 E Wacker Dr Suite 1816   Chicago IL 60601
Ph: 312-236-3858 ▪ Fx: 312-236-7809

National Association of Congregational Christian Churches   www.naccc.org
8473 S Howell Ave   Oak Creek WI 53154
Ph: 414-764-1620 ▪ Fx: 414-764-0319 ▪ TF: 800-262-1620

National Association of Conservation Districts   www.nacdnet.org
509 Capitol Ct NE   Washington DC 20002
Ph: 202-547-6223 ▪ Fx: 202-547-6450

National Association of Consumer Advocates   www.naca.net
1730 Rhode Island NW Suite 805   Washington DC 20036
Ph: 202-452-1989 ▪ Fx: 202-452-0099

National Association of Consumer Agency Administrators   www.nacaanet.org
750 Old Hickory Blvd Bldg 2 Suite 150   Brentwood TN 37027
Ph: 615-371-6125

National Association of Consumer Credit Administrators   www.naccaonline.org
PO Box 20871   Columbus OH 43220
Ph: 614-326-1165 ▪ Fx: 614-326-1162

National Association of Consumer Shows   www.publicshows.com
147 SE 102nd St   Portland OR 97216
Ph: 503-253-0832 ▪ Fx: 503-253-9172 ▪ TF: 800-728-6227

National Association of Container Distributors   www.nacd.net
1900 Arch St   Philadelphia PA 19103
Ph: 215-564-3484 ▪ Fx: 215-564-2175

National Association for Continence   www.nafc.org
PO Box 1019   Charleston SC 29402
Ph: 843-377-0900 ▪ Fx: 843-377-0905 ▪ TF: 800-252-3337

National Association of Convenience Stores   www.nacsonline.com
1600 Duke St   Alexandria VA 22314
Ph: 703-684-3600 ▪ Fx: 703-836-4564 ▪ TF: 800-966-6227

National Association of Convenience Stores PAC
1600 Duke St Suite 700   Alexandria VA 22314
Ph: 703-684-3600 ▪ Fx: 703-836-4564

National Association of Corporate Directors   www.nacdonline.org
1828 L St NW Suite 801   Washington DC 20036
Ph: 202-775-0509 ▪ Fx: 202-775-4857

National Association of Corporate Treasurers   www.nact.org
12100 Sunset Hills Rd Suite 130   Reston VA 20190
Ph: 703-437-4377 ▪ Fx: 703-435-4390

National Association of Councils on Developmental Disabilities   www.nacdd.org
1234 Massachusetts Ave NW Suite 103   Washington DC 20005
Ph: 202-347-1234 ▪ Fx: 202-347-4023

National Association of Counsel for Children   www.naccchildlaw.org
1825 Marion St Suite 340   Denver CO 80218
Ph: 888-828-6222

National Association of Counselors   nac.lincoln-grad.org
c/o Lincoln Graduate Ctr 303 W Cypress St   San Antonio TX 78212
Ph: 210-271-0781 ▪ Fx: 210-225-8450

National Association of Counties   www.naco.org
440 1st St NW   Washington DC 20001
Ph: 202-393-6226 ▪ Fx: 202-393-2630

National Association of County Administrators   www.countyadministrators.org
777 N Capitol St NE Suite 500   Washington DC 20002
Ph: 301-469-7460

National Association of County Aging Programs   www.naco.org
440 1st St NW 8th Fl   Washington DC 20001
Ph: 202-942-4235 ▪ Fx: 202-393-2630

National Association of County Agricultural Agents   www.nacaa.com
252 N Park St   Decatur IL 62523
Ph: 217-876-1220 ▪ Fx: 217-877-5382

National Association of County Behavioral Health Directors   www.nacbhd.org
440 1st St NW   Washington DC 20001
Ph: 202-661-8816

National Association of County & City Health Officials   www.naccho.org
1100 17th St 2nd Fl   Washington DC 20036
Ph: 202-783-5550 ▪ Fx: 202-783-1583

National Association of County Civil Attorneys
c/o National Assn of Counties 440 1st St NW   Washington DC 20001
Ph: 202-393-6226

National Association for County Community & Economic Development   www.nacced.org
2025 M St NW Suite 800   Washington DC 20036
Ph: 202-367-1149 ▪ Fx: 202-367-2149

National Association of County Engineers   www.countyengineers.org
c/o National Assn of Counties 440 1st St NW   Washington DC 20001
Ph: 202-393-6226

National Association of County Information Technology Administrators
c/o National Assn of Counties 440 1st St NW   Washington DC 20001
Ph: 202-393-6226

National Association of County Intergovernmental Relations Officials
c/o National Assn of Counties 440 1st St NW   Washington DC 20001
Ph: 202-393-6226

National Association of County Park & Recreation Officials   www.nacpro.org
c/o Harris County Public Infrastructure Dept 1001 Preston Ave 7th Fl   Houston TX 77002
Ph: 713-755-5583

National Association of County Planners
c/o National Assn of Counties 440 1st St NW   Washington DC 20001
Ph: 202-393-6226

National Association of County Recorders Election Officials & Clerks   www.nacrc.org
PO Box 3159   Durham NC 27715
Ph: 919-384-8446 ▪ Fx: 919-383-0035

National Association of County Surveyors   www.naco.org/nacs/index.html
c/o National Assn of Counties 440 1st St NW   Washington DC 20001
Ph: 202-393-6226 ▪ Fx: 202-393-2630

National Association of County Treasurers & Finance Officers   www.nactfo.org
c/o National Assn of Counties 440 1st St NW   Washington DC 20001
Ph: 202-393-6226

National Association for Court Management   www.nacmnet.org
National Ctr for State Courts 300 Newport Ave   Williamsburg VA 23185
Ph: 757-259-1841 ▪ Fx: 757-259-1520

National Association of Credential Evaluation Services   www.naces.org
c/o International Education Research Foundation PO Box 3665   Culver City CA 90231
Ph: 310-258-9451 ▪ Fx: 310-342-7086

National Association of Credit Management   www.nacm.org
8840 Columbia 100 Pkwy   Columbia MD 21045
Ph: 410-740-5560 ▪ Fx: 410-740-5574 ▪ TF: 800-955-8815

National Association of Credit Union Chairmen   www.nacuc.org
PO Box 160   Del Mar CA 92014
Ph: 858-792-3883 ▪ Fx: 858-792-3884 ▪ TF: 888-987-4247

National Association of Credit Union Services Organizations   www.nacuso.org
3419 Via Lido PMB 135   Newport Beach CA 92663
Ph: 949-645-5296 ▪ Fx: 949-645-5297 ▪ TF: 888-462-2870

National Association of Credit Union Supervisory & Auditing Committees   www.nacusac.org
PO Box 160   Del Mar CA 92014
Ph: 858-792-3883 ▪ Fx: 858-792-3884 ▪ TF: 800-287-5949

National Association of Crime Victim Compensation Boards   www.nacvcb.org
PO Box 16003   Alexandria VA 22302
Ph: 703-313-9500

National Association of Criminal Defense Lawyers   www.nacdl.org
1150 18th St NW Suite 950   Washington DC 20036
Ph: 202-872-8600 ▪ Fx: 202-872-8690

National Association of Cruise Oriented Agencies   www.nacoaonline.com
7600 Red Rd Suite 128   Miami FL 33143
Ph: 305-663-5626 ▪ Fx: 305-663-5625

National Association of Cuban American Women of the USA
308 38th St   Union City NJ 07087
Ph: 201-864-4879

National Association of the Deaf   www.nad.org
814 Thayer Ave Suite 250   Silver Spring MD 20910
Ph: 301-587-1788 ▪ Fx: 301-587-1791

National Association of Decorative Fabric Distributors   www.nadfd.org
1 Windsor Cove Suite 305   Columbia SC 29223
Ph: 803-252-5646 ▪ Fx: 803-765-0860 ▪ TF: 800-445-8629

National Association of Demolition Contractors — www.demolitionassociation.com
16 N Franklin St Suite 203 Doylestown PA 18901
Ph: 215-348-4949 ▪ Fx: 215-348-8422 ▪ TF: 800-541-2412

National Association of Dental Laboratories — www.nadl.org
1530 Metropolitan Blvd Tallahassee FL 32308
Ph: 850-205-5626 ▪ Fx: 850-222-0053 ▪ TF: 800-950-1150

National Association of Dental Plans — www.nadp.org
8111 LBJ Fwy Suite 935 Dallas TX 75251
Ph: 972-458-6998 ▪ Fx: 972-458-2258

National Association of Dental Plans PAC — www.nadp.org
8111 LBJ Fwy Suite 935 Dallas TX 75251
Ph: 972-458-6998 ▪ Fx: 972-458-2258

National Association of Development Companies — www.nadco.org
6764 Old McLean Village Dr McLean VA 22101
Ph: 703-748-2575 ▪ Fx: 703-748-2582

National Association of Development Organizations — www.nado.org
400 N Capitol St NW Suite 390 Washington DC 20001
Ph: 202-624-7806 ▪ Fx: 202-624-8813

National Association of Developmental Disabilities Councils — www.naddc.org
1234 Massachusetts Ave NW Suite 103 Washington DC 20005
Ph: 202-347-1234 ▪ Fx: 202-347-4023

National Association for Developmental Education — www.nade.net
2447 Tissin Ave Suite 207 Findlay OH 45840
Ph: 419-424-9360 ▪ Fx: 419-423-9078 ▪ TF: 877-881-9876

National Association of Diaper Services — www.diapernet.com
994 Old Eagle School Rd Suite 1019 Wayne PA 19087
Ph: 610-971-4850 ▪ Fx: 610-971-4859

National Association of Diocesan Ecumenical Officers — www.nadeo.com
8003 Mobud Dr Houston TX 77036
Ph: 713-774-0097 ▪ Fx: 713-774-0320

National Association of Directors of Nursing Administration in Long Term Care — www.nadona.org
10101 Alliance Rd Suite 140 Cincinnati OH 45242
Ph: 513-791-3679 ▪ Fx: 513-791-3699 ▪ TF: 800-222-0539

National Association of Disability Evaluating Professionals — www.nadep.com
PO Box 13801 Midlothian VA 23113
Ph: 804-378-7275

National Association of Division Order Analysts — www.nadoa.org
9794 Forest Ln PMB 1012 Dallas TX 75243
Ph: 972-715-4489 ▪ Fx: 972-715-6446

National Association of Document Examiners — www.documentexaminers.org
3490 US Rt 1 Suite 3B Princeton NJ 08540
Ph: 866-569-0833

National Association for Down Syndrome — www.nads.org
PO Box 4542 Oak Brook IL 60522
Ph: 630-325-9112 ▪ Fx: 630-325-8842

National Association for Drama Therapy — www.nadt.org
15 Post Side Ln Pittsford NY 14534
Ph: 585-381-5618 ▪ Fx: 585-383-1474

National Association on Drug Abuse Problems Inc — www.nadap.org
355 Lexington Ave 2nd Fl New York NY 10017
Ph: 212-986-1170 ▪ Fx: 212-697-2939

National Association for the Dually Diagnosed — www.thenadd.org
132 Fair St Kingston NY 12401
Ph: 845-331-4336 ▪ Fx: 845-331-4569 ▪ TF: 800-331-5362

National Association of Early Childhood Teacher Educators — www.naecte.org

National Association of Ecumenical & Interreligious Staff
PO Box 7093 Tacoma WA 98406
Ph: 253-759-0141 ▪ Fx: 253-759-9689

National Association for the Education of Young Children — www.naeyc.org
1509 16th St NW Washington DC 20036
Ph: 202-232-8777 ▪ Fx: 202-328-1846 ▪ TF: 800-424-2460

National Association of Educational Buyers — www.naeb.org
450 Wireless Blvd Hauppauge NY 11788
Ph: 631-273-2600 ▪ Fx: 631-952-3660

National Association of Educational Office Professionals — www.naeop.org
PO Box 12619 Wichita KS 67277
Ph: 316-942-4822 ▪ Fx: 316-942-7100

National Association of Electrical Distributors Inc — www.naed.org
1100 Corporate Sq Dr Suite 100 Saint Louis MO 63132
Ph: 314-991-9000 ▪ Fx: 314-991-3060 ▪ TF: 888-791-2512

National Association of Elementary School Principals — www.naesp.org
1615 Duke St Alexandria VA 22314
Ph: 703-684-3345 ▪ Fx: 703-548-6021 ▪ TF: 800-386-2377

National Association of Elevator Contractors — www.naec.org
1298 Wellbrook Cir NE Suite A Conyers GA 30012
Ph: 770-760-9660 ▪ Fx: 770-760-9714

National Association of Elevator Safety Authorities International — www.naesai.org
4541 N 12th St Phoenix AZ 85014
Ph: 602-266-9701 ▪ Fx: 602-265-0093

National Association of Emergency Medical Technicians — www.naemt.org
PO Box 1400 Clinton MS 39060
Ph: 800-346-2368

National Association of EMS Educators — www.naemse.org
700 N Bell Ave Suite 260 Carnegie PA 15106
Ph: 412-429-9550 ▪ Fx: 412-429-9554

National Association of EMS Physicians — www.naemsp.org
PO Box 15945-281 Lenexa KS 66214
Ph: 913-492-5858 ▪ Fx: 913-599-5340 ▪ TF: 800-228-3677

National Association of Energy Service Companies — www.naesco.org
1615 M St SW Suite 800 Washington DC 20036
Ph: 202-822-0950 ▪ Fx: 202-822-0955

National Association of Enrolled Agents — www.naea.org
200 Orchard Ridge Dr Suite 302 Gaithersburg MD 20878
Ph: 301-212-9608 ▪ Fx: 301-990-1611 ▪ TF: 800-424-4339

National Association of Entrepreneurial Parents — www.en-parent.com/NAEP.htm
PO Box 320722 Fairfield CT 06432
Ph: 203-371-6212

National Association of Environmental Law Societies — www.naels.org

National Association for Environmental Management — www.naem.org
1612 K St NW Suite 1102 Washington DC 20006
Ph: 202-986-6616 ▪ Fx: 202-530-4408 ▪ TF: 800-391-6236

National Association of Environmental Professionals — www.naep.org
PO Box 2086 Bowie MD 20718
Ph: 301-860-1140 ▪ Fx: 301-860-1141 ▪ TF: 888-251-9902

National Association of Episcopal Schools — www.episcopalschools.org
815 2nd Ave Suite 313 New York NY 10017
Ph: 212-716-6134 ▪ Fx: 212-286-9366 ▪ TF: 800-334-7626

National Association for Equal Opportunity in Higher Education — www.nafeo.org
8701 Georgia Ave Suite 200 Silver Spring MD 20910
Ph: 301-650-2440 ▪ Fx: 301-495-3306

National Association of Equipment Leasing Brokers — www.naelb.org
5024-R Campbell Blvd Baltimore MD 21236
Ph: 410-931-8100 ▪ Fx: 410-931-8111 ▪ TF: 800-996-2352

National Association of Equity Source Banks
10451 Mill Run Cir Suite 400 Owings Mills MD 21117
Ph: 410-581-1373

National Association of Estate Planners & Councils — www.naepc.org
1120 Chester Ave Suite 470 Cleveland OH 44114
Ph: 866-226-2224 ▪ Fx: 216-696-2582

National Association for Ethnic Studies — www.ethnicstudies.org
Arizona State Univ College of Arts & Sciences 4701 W
Thunderbird Rd MC 3051 Glendale AZ 85306
Ph: 602-543-4111 ▪ Fx: 602-965-3451

National Association of Evangelicals — www.nae.net
701 G St SW Washington DC 20024
Ph: 202-789-1011 ▪ Fx: 202-842-0392

National Association for the Exchange of Industrial Resources — www.naeir.org
560 McClure St Galesburg IL 61401
Ph: 309-343-0704 ▪ Fx: 309-343-7316 ▪ TF: 800-562-0955

National Association of Exclusive Buyer Agents — www.naeba.org
191 Clarksville Rd Princeton Junction NJ 08550
Ph: 609-799-4382 ▪ Fx: 609-799-7032

National Association of Executive Recruiters — www.naer.org
1320 Tower Rd Suite 2262 Schaumburg IL 60173
Ph: 847-598-3680 ▪ Fx: 847-885-5681

National Association of Executive Secretaries & Administrative Assistants — www.naesaa.com
900 S Washington St Suite G-13 Falls Church VA 22046
Ph: 703-237-8616 ▪ Fx: 703-533-1153

National Association of Export Companies — www.nexco.org
PO Box 3949 Grand Central Stn New York NY 10163
Ph: 877-291-4901 ▪ Fx: 646-349-9628

National Association for Family Child Care — www.nafcc.org
5202 Pinemont Dr Salt Lake City UT 84123
Ph: 801-269-9338 ▪ Fx: 801-268-9507 ▪ TF: 800-359-3817

National Association for Family & Community Education — www.nafce.org
73 Cavalier Blvd Suite 106 Florence KY 41042
Ph: 877-712-4477 ▪ Fx: 859-525-6496

National Association of Farm Broadcasters — www.nafb.com
700 Branch St Suite 8 PO Box 500 Platte City MO 64079
Ph: 816-431-4032 ▪ Fx: 816-431-4087

National Association of Federal Credit Unions — www.nafcunet.org
3138 10th St N Arlington VA 22201
Ph: 703-522-4770 ▪ Fx: 703-524-1082 ▪ TF: 800-336-4644

National Association of Federal Education Program Administrators — www.nafepa.org
830 Virginia Ave Sheybogan WI 53081
Ph: 920-459-6718 ▪ Fx: 920-803-7761

National Association of Federal Veterinarians — users.erols.com/nafv
1101 Vermont Ave NW Suite 710 Washington DC 20005
Ph: 202-289-6334 ▪ Fx: 202-842-4360

National Association of Federally Impacted Schools — www.sso.org/nafis
444 N Capitol St NW Suite 419 Washington DC 20001
Ph: 202-624-5455 ▪ Fx: 202-624-5468

National Association of Federally Licensed Firearms Dealers
150 SE 12th St Suite 200 Fort Lauderdale FL 33316
Ph: 954-467-9994 ▪ Fx: 954-463-2501

National Association for Female Executives — www.nafe.com
260 Madison Ave 3rd Fl New York NY 10016
Ph: 212-351-6400 ▪ TF: 800-927-6233

National Association of Financial & Estate Planning — www.nafep.com
525 E 4500 S Suite F-100 Salt Lake City UT 84107
Ph: 801-266-9900 ▪ Fx: 801-266-1019

National Association of Fire Equipment Distributors — www.nafed.org
104 S Michigan Ave Suite 300 Chicago IL 60603
Ph: 312-263-8100 ▪ Fx: 312-263-8111

National Association of Fire Investigators — www.nafi.org
857 Tallevast Rd Sarasota FL 34243
Ph: 941-359-2800 ▪ Fx: 941-351-5849 ▪ TF: 877-506-6234

National Association of Flavors & Food-Ingredient Systems Inc — www.naffs.org
3301 Rt 66 Bldg C Suite 205 Neptune NJ 07753
Ph: 732-922-3218 ▪ Fx: 732-922-3590

National Association of Fleet Administrators — www.nafa.org
100 Wood Ave S Suite 310 Iselin NJ 08830
Ph: 732-494-8100 ▪ Fx: 732-494-6789

National Association of Flight Instructors — www.nafinet.org
EAA Aviation Ctr PO Box 3086 Oshkosh WI 54903
Ph: 920-426-6801 ▪ Fx: 920-426-4881

National Association of Floor Covering Distributors — www.nafcd.org
401 N Michigan Ave Suite 2400 Chicago IL 60611
Ph: 312-321-6836 ▪ Fx: 312-673-6962

National Association of Flour Distributors
PO Box 165067 Little Rock AR 72216
Ph: 501-372-0636 ▪ Fx: 501-372-2468

National Association of Food & Stormwater Management Agencies — www.nafsma.org
1299 Pennsylvania Ave NW 8th Fl W Washington DC 20004
Ph: 202-218-4122 ▪ Fx: 202-478-1734

National Association of Foreign-Trade Zones
1000 Connecticut Ave NW Suite 1001   Washington DC 20036
Ph: 202-331-1950 ▪ Fx: 202-331-1994   www.naftz.org

National Association of Forensic Accountants
2455 E Sunrise Blvd Suite 1201   Fort Lauderdale FL 33304
Ph: 954-535-5556 ▪ Fx: 954-537-4942 ▪ TF: 800-523-3680   www.nafanet.com

National Association of Forensic Economics
PO Box 30067   Kansas City MO 64112
Ph: 816-235-2833 ▪ Fx: 816-235-5263   www.nafe.net

National Association of Foster Grandparent Program Directors
Foster Grandparent Program City Hall 4th Fl   Kansas City MO 64106
Ph: 816-513-3221 ▪ Fx: 816-513-3212   www.nafgpd.org

National Association of Fraternal Insurance Counselors
PO Box 357   Sheboygan WI 53082
Ph: 920-458-1996 ▪ Fx: 920-457-4661

National Association of Free Will Baptists
5233 Mt View Rd   Antioch TN 37013
Ph: 615-731-6812 ▪ Fx: 615-731-0771 ▪ TF: 877-767-7659   www.nafwb.org

National Association of Friendship Centres
275 MacLaren St   Ottawa ON K2P0L9
Ph: 613-563-4844 ▪ Fx: 613-563-1819   www.nafc-aboriginal.com

National Association of Fundraising Ticket Manufacturers
1885 University Ave W Suite 246   Saint Paul MN 55104
Ph: 651-644-4710   www.naftm.org

National Association of Gas Chlorinators
21939 Camille Dr   Nuevo CA 92567
Ph: 949-364-1990 ▪ Fx: 949-364-2009

National Association of General Merchandise Representatives
110 Friar Tuck Cir   Denton TX 76201
Ph: 940-243-0409 ▪ Fx: 940-382-3741   www.nagmr.org

National Association of Geoscience Teachers
PO Box 5443   Bellingham WA 98227
Ph: 360-650-3587   www.nagt.org

National Association for Gifted Children
1707 L St NW Suite 550   Washington DC 20036
Ph: 202-785-4268 ▪ Fx: 202-785-4248   www.nagc.org

National Association for Girls & Women in Sport
1900 Association Dr   Reston VA 20191
Ph: 703-476-3400 ▪ Fx: 703-476-4566 ▪ TF: 800-213-7193   www.aahperd.org

National Association of Golf Tournament Directors
212 S Henry St 2nd Fl   Alexandria VA 22314
Ph: 703-549-3543 ▪ Fx: 703-549-9074 ▪ TF: 888-899-2483   www.nagtd.com

National Association of Government Archives & Records Administrators   48 Howard St   Albany NY 12207
Ph: 518-463-8644 ▪ Fx: 518-463-8656   www.nagara.org

National Association of Government Communicators
10366 Democracy Ln Suite B   Fairfax VA 22030
Ph: 703-691-0377 ▪ Fx: 703-706-9583   www.nagc.com

National Association of Government Defined Contribution Administrators Inc   167 W Main St Suite 600   Lexington KY 40507
Ph: 859-514-9161 ▪ Fx: 859-514-9166   www.nagdca.org

National Association of Government Employees
159 Burgin Pkwy   Quincy MA 02169
Ph: 617-376-0220 ▪ Fx: 617-376-0285   www.nage.org

National Association of Government Guaranteed Lenders
424 S Squires Landing Blvd Suite 130   Stillwater OK 74074
Ph: 405-377-4022 ▪ Fx: 405-377-3931   www.naggl.com

National Association for Government Training & Development
2516 Wertherson Ln   Raleigh NC 27613
Ph: 919-870-8496 ▪ Fx: 919-845-6922

National Association of Governmental Labor Officials
c/o Council of State Governments 444 N Capitol St NW Suite 401   Washington DC 20001
Ph: 202-624-5460 ▪ Fx: 202-624-5452   www.naglo.org

National Association of Graduate Admissions Professionals
Iowa State Univ 10 Pearson Hall   Ames IA 50011
Ph: 515-294-2682 ▪ Fx: 515-294-3003   www.nagap.org

National Association of Graduate-Professional Students
209 Pennsylvania Ave SE   Washington DC 20003
Ph: 202-543-0812 ▪ Fx: 202-454-5298 ▪ TF: 888-886-2477   www.nagps.org

National Association of Graphic & Product Identification Manufacturers Inc   PO Box 15466   Santa Ana CA 92735
Ph: 714-508-4915 ▪ Fx: 714-508-4904   www.gpiweb.org

National Association of Health Data Organizations
375 Chipeta Way Suite A   Salt Lake City UT 84108
Ph: 801-587-9104 ▪ Fx: 801-587-9125   www.nahdo.org

National Association for Health & Fitness
201 S Capitol Ave Suite 560   Indianapolis IN 46225
Ph: 317-237-5630 ▪ Fx: 317-237-5632   www.physicalfitness.org

National Association of Health Services Executives
8630 Fenton St Suite 126   Silver Spring MD 20910
Ph: 202-628-3953 ▪ Fx: 301-588-0011   www.nahse.org

National Association of Health Underwriters
2000 N 14th St Suite 450   Arlington VA 22201
Ph: 703-276-0220 ▪ Fx: 703-841-7797   www.nahu.org

National Association of Health Unit Coordinators
1947 Madron Rd   Rockford IL 61107
Ph: 815-633-4351 ▪ Fx: 815-633-4438 ▪ TF: 888-226-2482   www.nahuc.org

National Association of Healthcare Access Management
2025 M St NW Suite 800   Washington DC 20036
Ph: 202-367-1125 ▪ Fx: 202-367-2125   www.naham.org

National Association of Healthcare Consultants
1255 23rd St NW Suite 200   Washington DC 20037
Ph: 202-452-8282 ▪ Fx: 202-833-3636   www.healthcon.org

National Association for Healthcare Quality
4700 W Lake Ave   Glenview IL 60025
Ph: 847-375-4720 ▪ Fx: 877-218-7939 ▪ TF: 800-966-9392   www.nahq.org

National Association for Hispanic Elderly
1452 W Temple St Suite 100   Los Angeles CA 90026
Ph: 213-202-5900 ▪ Fx: 213-202-5905

National Association of Hispanic Federal Executives Inc
PO Box 469   Herndon VA 20172
Ph: 703-787-0291 ▪ Fx: 703-787-4675   www.nahfe.org

National Association of Hispanic Journalists
529 14th St NW National Press Bldg Suite 1000   Washington DC 20045
Ph: 202-662-7145 ▪ Fx: 202-662-7144 ▪ TF: 888-346-6245   www.nahj.org

National Association of Hispanic & Latino Studies
PO Box 325   Biddeford ME 04005
Ph: 207-839-8004 ▪ Fx: 207-839-3776

National Association of Hispanic Nurses
1501 16th St NW   Washington DC 20036
Ph: 202-387-2477 ▪ Fx: 202-483-7183   www.thehispanicnurses.org

National Association of Hispanic Publications
529 14th St NW National Press Bldg Suite 941   Washington DC 20045
Ph: 202-662-7250 ▪ Fx: 202-662-7254   www.nahponline.org

National Association of Hispanic Real Estate Professionals
404 Camino del Rio S Suite 602   San Diego CA 92108
Ph: 800-964-5373 ▪ Fx: 619-297-3229   www.nahrep.org

National Association for Holistic Aromatherapy
4509 Interlake Ave N Suite 233   Seattle WA 98103
Ph: 206-547-2164 ▪ Fx: 206-547-2680 ▪ TF: 888-275-6242   www.naha.org

National Association of Home Based Businesses
10451 Mill Run Cir Suite 400   Owings Mills MD 21117
Ph: 410-363-3698   www.usahomebusiness.com

National Association of Home Builders
1201 15th St NW   Washington DC 20005
Ph: 202-266-8200 ▪ TF: 800-368-5242   www.nahb.org

National Association for Home Care & Hospice
228 7th St SE   Washington DC 20003
Ph: 202-547-7424 ▪ Fx: 202-547-3540   www.nahc.org

National Association for Home Care & Hospice PAC
228 7th St SE   Washington DC 20003
Ph: 202-547-7424 ▪ Fx: 202-547-3540

National Association of Home Inspectors
4248 Park Glen Rd   Minneapolis MN 55416
Ph: 952-928-4641 ▪ Fx: 952-929-1318 ▪ TF: 800-448-3942   www.nahi.org

National Association of At-Home Mothers
406 E Buchanan Ave   Fairfield IA 52556
Ph: 515-472-3202 ▪ Fx: 515-469-3068   www.athomemothers.com

National Association of Hose & Accessories Distributors
105 Eastern Ave Suite 104   Annapolis MD 21403
Ph: 410-263-1014 ▪ Fx: 410-263-1659 ▪ TF: 800-624-2227   www.nahad.org

National Association of Hospital Hospitality Houses
PO Box 18087   Asheville NC 28814
Ph: 828-253-1188 ▪ Fx: 828-253-8082 ▪ TF: 800-542-9730   www.nahhh.org

National Association of Housing Cooperatives
1707 H St NW Suite 201   Washington DC 20006
Ph: 202-737-0797 ▪ Fx: 202-783-7869   www.coophousing.org

National Association of Housing Information Managers
PO Box 67202   Lincoln NE 68506
Ph: 402-476-9424 ▪ Fx: 402-420-1770 ▪ TF: 800-379-3807   www.nahim.org

National Association of Housing & Redevelopment Officials
630 'I' St NW   Washington DC 20001
Ph: 202-289-3500 ▪ Fx: 202-289-8181 ▪ TF: 877-866-2476   www.nahro.org

National Association for Humane & Environmental Education
PO Box 362   East Haddam CT 06423
Ph: 860-434-8666 ▪ Fx: 860-434-9579   www.nahee.org

National Association for Humanities Education
Brigham Young Univ PO Box 26100   Provo UT 84602
Ph: 801-378-2212 ▪ Fx: 801-378-2284   www.nahe.org

National Association of Independent Colleges & Universities
1025 Connecticut Ave NW Suite 700   Washington DC 20036
Ph: 202-785-8866 ▪ Fx: 202-835-0003   www.naicu.edu

National Association of Independent Crop Consultants
349 E Nolley Dr   Collierville TN 38017
Ph: 901-861-0511 ▪ Fx: 901-861-0512   www.naicc.org

National Association of Independent Fee Appraisers
7501 Murdoch St   Saint Louis MO 63119
Ph: 314-781-6688 ▪ Fx: 314-781-2872   www.naifa.com

National Association of Independent Insurance Adjusters
825 W State St Suite 117-C   Geneve IL 60134
Ph: 630-397-5012 ▪ Fx: 630-397-5013   www.naiia.com

National Association of Independent Insurance Auditors & Engineers   www.naiiae.org

National Association of Independent Life Brokerage Agencies
12150 Monument Dr Suite 125   Fairfax VA 22033
Ph: 703-383-3081 ▪ Fx: 703-383-6942   www.nailba.org

National Association of Independent Lighting Distributors Inc
2207 Elmwood Ave   Buffalo NY 14216
Ph: 716-875-3670 ▪ Fx: 716-875-0734   www.naild.org

National Association of Independent Public Finance Advisors
PO Box 304   Montgomery IL 60538
Ph: 800-624-7321   www.naipfa.com

National Association of Independent Publishers
PO Box 430   Highland City FL 33846
Ph: 863-648-4420   www.publishersreport.com

National Association of Independent Publishers Representatives
111 E 14th St PMB 157   New York NY 10003
Ph: 888-624-7779 ▪ Fx: 800-416-2586   www.naipr.com

National Association of Independent Schools
1620 L St NW Suite 1100   Washington DC 20036
Ph: 202-973-9700 ▪ Fx: 202-973-9790   www.nais-schools.org

National Association of Industrial & Office Properties
2201 Cooperative Way 3rd Fl   Herndon VA 20171
Ph: 703-904-7100 ▪ Fx: 703-904-7942 ▪ TF: 800-666-6780   www.naiop.org

National Association of Industrial Technology www.nait.org
3300 Washtenaw Ave Suite 220 Ann Arbor MI 48104
Ph: 734-677-0720 ▪ Fx: 734-677-0046

National Association for Industry-Education Cooperation www2.pcom.net/naiec/
235 Hendricks Blvd Buffalo NY 14226
Ph: 716-834-7047

National Association of Installation Developers www.naid.org
734 15th St NW Suite 900 Washington DC 20005
Ph: 202-822-5256 ▪ Fx: 202-822-8819

National Association of Institutional Linen Management www.nlmnet.org
2130 Lexington Rd Suite H Richmond KY 40475
Ph: 859-624-0177 ▪ Fx: 859-624-3580 ▪ TF: 800-669-0863

National Association of Insurance Commissioners www.naic.org
2301 McGee St Suite 800 Kansas City MO 64108
Ph: 816-842-3600 ▪ Fx: 816-783-8175

National Association of Insurance & Financial Advisors www.naifa.org
2901 Telestar Ct Falls Church VA 22042
Ph: 703-770-8100 ▪ TF: 877-866-2432

National Association of Insurance & Financial Advisors PAC
2901 Telestar Ct Falls Church VA 22042
Ph: 703-770-8100 ▪ Fx: 703-770-8194

National Association of Insurance Women (International) www.naiw.org
1847 E 15th St Tulsa OK 74104
Ph: 918-744-5195 ▪ Fx: 918-743-1968 ▪ TF: 800-766-6249

National Association of Intercollegiate Athletics www.naia.org
23500 W 105th St Olathe KS 66051
Ph: 913-791-0044 ▪ Fx: 913-791-9555

National Association for Interpretation www.interpnet.com
528 S Howes St PO Box 2246 Fort Collins CO 80521
Ph: 970-484-8283 ▪ Fx: 970-484-8179 ▪ TF: 888-900-8283

National Association of Investigative Specialists www.pimall.com/nais
PO Box 33244 Austin TX 78764
Ph: 512-719-3595 ▪ Fx: 512-719-3594

National Association of Investment Companies www.naicvc.com
1300 Pennsylvania Ave NW Suite 700 Washington DC 20004
Ph: 202-289-4336 ▪ Fx: 202-289-4329

National Association of Investment Professionals www.naip.com
12664 Emmer Pl Suite 201 Saint Paul MN 55124
Ph: 952-322-4322

National Association of Investors Corp www.better-investing.org
PO Box 220 Royal Oak MI 48068
Ph: 248-583-6242 ▪ Fx: 248-583-4880 ▪ TF: 877-275-6242

National Association of Japan-American Societies www.us-japan.org
733 15th St NW Suite 700 Washington DC 20005
Ph: 202-783-4550 ▪ Fx: 202-783-4551

National Association of Jewelry Appraisers
PO Box 6558 Annapolis MD 21401
Ph: 410-897-0889

National Association of Judiciary Interpreters & Translators www.najit.org
2150 N 107th St Suite 205 Seattle WA 98133
Ph: 206-367-8704 ▪ Fx: 206-367-8777

National Association of Junior Auxiliaries Inc www.najanet.org
845 S Main St PO Box 1873 Greenville MS 38702
Ph: 662-332-3000 ▪ Fx: 662-332-3076

National Association of Latino Elected & Appointed Officials www.naleo.org
1122 W Washington Blvd 3rd Fl Los Angeles CA 90015
Ph: 213-747-7606 ▪ Fx: 213-747-7664

National Association for Law Placement www.nalp.org
1025 Connecticut Ave NW Suite 1110 Washington DC 20036
Ph: 202-835-1001 ▪ Fx: 202-835-1112

National Association of Left-Handed Golfers www.nalg.org
3249 Hazelwood Dr SW Atlanta GA 30311
Ph: 404-696-1763 ▪ Fx: 404-691-5549 ▪ TF: 800-844-6524

National Association of Legal Assistants www.nala.org
1516 S Boston Ave Suite 200 Tulsa OK 74119
Ph: 918-587-6828 ▪ Fx: 918-582-6772

National Association of Legal Investigators www.nalionline.org

National Association of Legal Search Consultants www.nalsc.org
The Biltmore 817 W Peachtree St Suite 208 Atlanta GA 30308
Ph: 404-879-5080 ▪ Fx: 404-879-5075 ▪ TF: 866-394-9347

National Association for Legal Support of Alternative Schools
PO Box 2823 Santa Fe NM 87504
Ph: 505-471-6928

National Association of Lesbian/Gay Addiction Professionals www.nalgap.org
901 N Washington St Suite 600 Alexandria VA 22314
Ph: 703-465-0539 ▪ Fx: 703-741-6989

National Association of Letter Carriers www.nalc.org
100 Indiana Ave NW Washington DC 20001
Ph: 202-393-4695 ▪ Fx: 202-737-1540

National Association of Limited Edition Dealers www.naled.org
332 Hurst Mill N Bremen GA 30110
Ph: 770-537-1970 ▪ TF: 800-446-2533

National Association of Litho Clubs www.graphicarts.org
PO Box 6190 Shallotte NC 28470
Ph: 910-575-0399

National Association of Local Boards of Health www.nalboh.org
1840 E Gypsy Lane Rd Bowling Green OH 43402
Ph: 419-353-7714 ▪ Fx: 419-352-6278

National Association of Local Government Auditors www.nalga.org
2401 Regency Rd Suite 302 Lexington KY 40503
Ph: 859-276-0686

National Association of Local Government Environmental Professionals www.nalgep.org/
1333 New Hampshire Ave NW Suite 1100 Washington DC 20036
Ph: 202-638-6254 ▪ Fx: 202-393-2866

National Association of Local Housing Finance Agencies www.nalhfa.org
2025 M St NW Suite 800 Washington DC 20036
Ph: 202-367-1197 ▪ Fx: 202-367-2197

National Association of Managed Care Physicians www.namcp.com
4435 Waterfront Dr Suite 101 PO Box 4765 Glen Allen VA 23058
Ph: 804-527-1905 ▪ Fx: 804-747-5316 ▪ TF: 800-722-0376

National Association of Manufacturers www.nam.org
1331 Pennsylvania Ave NW Suite 600 Washington DC 20004
Ph: 202-637-3000 ▪ Fx: 202-637-3182 ▪ TF: 800-814-8468

National Association of Margarine Manufacturers www.margarine.org/namm.html
1156 15th St NW Suite 900 Washington DC 20005
Ph: 202-785-3232 ▪ Fx: 202-223-9741

National Association of Marine Services www.namsshipchandler.com
5458 Wagon Master Dr Colorado Springs CO 80917
Ph: 719-573-5946 ▪ Fx: 719-573-5952

National Association of Marine Surveyors Inc www.nams-cms.org
PO Box 9306 Chesapeake VA 23321
Ph: 757-488-9538 ▪ Fx: 757-488-0584 ▪ TF: 800-822-6267

National Association of Maritime Educators
124 N Van Ave Houma LA 70363
Ph: 985-879-3866 ▪ Fx: 985-879-3911

National Association of Master Appraisers www.masterappraisers.org
303 W Cypress St San Antonio TX 78212
Ph: 210-271-0781 ▪ Fx: 210-225-8450 ▪ TF: 800-229-6262

National Association of Medical Examiners www.thename.org
430 Pryor St SW Atlanta GA 30312
Ph: 404-730-4781 ▪ Fx: 404-730-4420

National Association of Medical Minority Educators Inc www.namme-hpe.org

National Association Medical Staff Services www.namss.org
8317 Cross Park Dr Suite 150 Austin TX 78754
Ph: 512-454-7928 ▪ Fx: 512-454-3036

National Association of Metal Finishers www.namf.org
12644 Research Parkway Suite 105 Orlando FL 32826
Ph: 407-281-6445 ▪ Fx: 407-281-7345

National Association of Miniature Enthusiasts www.miniatures.org
130 N Rangeline Rd PO Box 69 Carmel IN 46032
Ph: 317-571-8094 ▪ Fx: 317-571-8105

National Association of Minorities in Communications www.namic.com
600 Anton Blvd Suite 1100 Costa Mesa CA 92625
Ph: 714-371-4077 ▪ Fx: 714-371-2103

National Association of Minority Automobile Dealers www.namad.com/
8401 Corporate Dr Suite 404 Lanham MD 20785
Ph: 301-306-1614 ▪ Fx: 301-306-1493

National Association of Minority Contractors www.namconline.org
666 11th St NW Suite 520 Washington DC 20001
Ph: 202-347-8259 ▪ Fx: 202-628-1876

National Association of Minority Engineering Program Administrators www.namepa.org
1133 W Morse Blvd Suite 201 Winter Park FL 32789
Ph: 407-647-8839 ▪ Fx: 407-629-2502

National Association of Minority Media Executives www.namme.org
1921 Gallows Rd Suite 600 Vienna VA 22182
Ph: 703-893-2410 ▪ Fx: 703-893-2414 ▪ TF: 888-968-7658

National Association of Mortgage Brokers www.namb.org
8201 Greensboro Dr Suite 300 McLean VA 22102
Ph: 703-610-9009 ▪ Fx: 703-610-9005

National Association of Mothers' Centers www.motherscenter.org
64 Division Ave Levittown NY 11756
Ph: 516-520-2929 ▪ Fx: 516-520-1639 ▪ TF: 800-645-3828

National Association of Mutual Insurance Companies www.namic.org
3601 Vincennes Rd Indianapolis IN 46268
Ph: 317-875-5250 ▪ Fx: 317-879-8408 ▪ TF: 800-336-2642

National Association of Native American Studies
PO Box 325 Biddeford ME 04005
Ph: 207-839-8004 ▪ Fx: 207-839-3776

National Association of Negro Business & Professional Women's Clubs Inc www.nanbpwc.com
1806 New Hampshire Ave NW Washington DC 20009
Ph: 202-483-4206 ▪ Fx: 202-462-7253

National Association of Negro Musicians www.nanm.8m.com
11551 S Laflin St PO Box 43053 Chicago IL 60643
Ph: 773-568-3818 ▪ Fx: 773-779-1325

National Association for Neighborhood Schools www.nans.org
3905 Muriel Ave Cleveland OH 44109
Ph: 216-398-4667

National Association of Neighborhoods www.nanworld.org
1300 Pennsylvania Ave NW Suite 700 NW Washington DC 20004
Ph: 202-332-7766 ▪ Fx: 202-332-2314

National Association of Neonatal Nurses www.nann.org
4700 W Lake Ave Glenview IL 60025
Ph: 847-375-3660 ▪ Fx: 888-477-6266 ▪ TF: 800-451-3795

National Association of Nephrology Technologists/Technicians www.dialysistech.org
PO Box 2307 Dayton OH 45401
Ph: 937-586-3705 ▪ Fx: 937-586-3699 ▪ TF: 877-607-6268

National Association of Nurse Practitioners in Women's Health www.npwh.org
503 Capitol Ct NE Suite 300 Washington DC 20002
Ph: 202-543-9693 ▪ Fx: 202-543-9858

National Association of Nutrition & Aging Services Programs www.nanasp.org
1612 K St NW Suite 400 Washington DC 20006
Ph: 202-682-6899 ▪ Fx: 202-223-2099

National Association for Olmsted Parks www.olmsted.org
84 Parkside Ave Buffalo NY 14214
Ph: 866-666-6905 ▪ Fx: 716-835-1300

National Association of Orthopaedic Nurses www.orthonurse.org
401 N Michigan Ave Chicago IL 60611
Ph: 800-289-6266 ▪ Fx: 312-527-6658

National Association of Orthopaedic Technologists www.naot.org
2950 Buskirk Ave Suite 170 Walnut Creek CA 94597
Ph: 925-472-5822 ▪ Fx: 925-472-5901

National Association for Outlaw & Lawman History Inc www.outlawlawman.com
1917 Sutton Pl Trail Harker Heights TX 76548
Ph: 254-698-6518

National Association for Parents of Children with Visual Impairments PO Box 317 Watertown MA 02471 www.spedex.com/napvi
Ph: 617-972-7441 ▪ Fx: 617-972-7444 ▪ TF: 800-562-6265

National Association of Parliamentarians www.parliamentarians.org
213 S Main St Independence MO 64050
Ph: 816-833-3892 ▪ Fx: 816-833-3893 ▪ TF: 888-627-2929

National Association of Partners In Education www.napehq.org
901 N Pitt St Suite 320 Alexandria VA 22314
Ph: 703-836-4880 ▪ Fx: 703-836-6941

National Association of Pastoral Musicians www.npm.org
962 Wayne Ave Suite 210 Silver Spring MD 20910
Ph: 240-247-3000

National Association of Pediatric Nurse Practitioners www.napnap.org
20 Brace Rd Suite 200 Cherry Hill NJ 08034
Ph: 856-857-9700 ▪ Fx: 856-857-1600 ▪ TF: 877-662-7627

National Association of People with AIDS www.napwa.org
1413 K St NW 7th Fl Washington DC 20005
Ph: 202-898-0414 ▪ Fx: 202-898-0435

National Association of Personal Financial Advisors www.napfa.org
3250 N Arlington Suite 109 Arlington Heights IL 60004
Ph: 847-537-7722 ▪ Fx: 847-483-5415 ▪ TF: 800-366-2732

National Association of Personnel Services www.napsweb.org
10905 Ft Washington Rd Suite 400 Fort Washington MD 20744
Ph: 301-203-6700 ▪ Fx: 301-203-4346

National Association for PET Container Resources www.napcor.com
10800 Sikes Pl Suite 240 Charlotte NC 28277
Ph: 704-845-5070 ▪ Fx: 704-845-5276

National Association of Photo Equipment Technicians napet.pmai.org
3000 Picture Pl Jackson MI 49201
Ph: 517-788-8100 ▪ Fx: 517-788-8371

National Association for Physical Education in Higher Education www.napehe.org
Northern Illinois Univ Dept of Kinesiology & Physical Education
  Anderson Hall DeKalb IL 60015
Ph: 815-753-1894

National Association of Physician Recruiters www.napr.org
PO Box 150127 Altamonte Springs FL 32715
Ph: 407-774-7880 ▪ Fx: 407-774-6440 ▪ TF: 800-726-5613

National Association of Pipe Coating Applicators www.napca.com
333 Texas St Suite 717 Shreveport LA 71101
Ph: 318-227-2769 ▪ Fx: 318-222-0482

National Association of Pizzeria Operators www.napo.com
908 S 8th St Suite 200 Louisville KY 40203
Ph: 502-736-9500 ▪ Fx: 502-736-9501 ▪ TF: 800-489-8324

National Association of Plant Patent Owners www.anla.org/industry/patents
1000 Vermont Ave NW Suite 300 Washington DC 20005
Ph: 202-789-2900 ▪ Fx: 202-789-1893

National Association for Poetry Therapy www.poetrytherapy.org
16861 SW 6th St Pembroke Pines FL 33027
Ph: 954-499-4333 ▪ Fx: 954-499-4324 ▪ TF: 866-844-6278

National Association of Police Athletic Leagues www.nationalpal.org
618 US Hwy 1 Suite 201 North Palm Beach FL 33408
Ph: 561-844-1823 ▪ Fx: 561-863-6120

National Association of Police Organizations www.napo.org
750 1st St NW Suite 920 Washington DC 20002
Ph: 202-842-4420 ▪ Fx: 202-842-4396

National Association of Postal Supervisors www.naps.org
1727 King St Suite 400 Alexandria VA 22314
Ph: 703-836-9660 ▪ Fx: 703-836-9665

National Association of Postmasters of the US www.napus.org
8 Herbert St Alexandria VA 22305
Ph: 703-683-9027 ▪ Fx: 703-683-6820

National Association of Postpartum Care Services www.napcs.org
800 Detroit St Denver CO 80206
Ph: 800-453-6852 ▪ Fx: 303-321-4058

National Association of Power Engineers Inc www.powerengineers.com
1 Springfield St Chicopee MA 01013
Ph: 413-592-6273 ▪ Fx: 413-592-1998

National Association for Practical Nurse Education & Service www.napnes.org
8607 2nd Ave Suite 404-A Silver Spring MD 20910
Ph: 301-588-2491

National Association for the Practice of Anthropology www.practicinganthropology.org
c/o American Anthropological Assn 2200 Wilson Blvd Suite
  600 Arlington VA 22201
Ph: 703-528-1902 ▪ Fx: 703-528-3546

National Association of Precollege Directors www.jhuapl.edu/NAPD/aboutNAPD.htm
45 Wintonbury Ave Bloomfield CT 06002
Ph: 860-769-5283 ▪ Fx: 860-769-5287

National Association of Presbyterian Scouters www.presbyterianscouters.org
8520 MacKenzie Rd Box 6900 Saint Louis MO 63123
Ph: 314-638-1017 ▪ Fx: 314-638-7250 ▪ TF: 800-933-7729

National Association of Principals of Schools for Girls
41 Van Brunt Manor Rd East Setauket NY 11733
Ph: 631-751-0850 ▪ Fx: 631-689-7311

National Association of Printing Ink Manufacturers www.napim.org
581 Main St Woodbridge NJ 07095
Ph: 732-855-1525 ▪ Fx: 732-855-1838

National Association for Printing Leadership www.napl.org
75 W Century Rd Paramus NJ 07652
Ph: 201-634-9600 ▪ Fx: 201-634-0324 ▪ TF: 800-642-6275

National Association of Private Catholic & Independent Schools www.napcis.org
24 Frank Lloyd Wright Dr PO Box 501 Ann Arbor MI 48106
Ph: 734-930-4535

National Association of Private Nontraditional Schools & Colleges www.napnsc.org
182 Thompson Rd Grand Junction CO 81503
Ph: 970-243-5441 ▪ Fx: 970-242-4392

National Association of Private Special Education Centers www.napsec.org
1522 K St NW Suite 1032 Washington DC 20005
Ph: 202-408-3338 ▪ Fx: 202-408-3340

National Association of Probation Executives www.napehome.org
Sam Houston State Univ Correctional Management Institute of
  Texas Huntsville TX 77341
Ph: 936-294-3757 ▪ Fx: 936-294-1671

National Association of Professional Accident Reconstruction Specialists Inc PO Box 65 Brandywine MD 20613 www.napars.org
Ph: 301-843-0048

National Association of Professional Band Instrument Repair Technicians PO Box 51 Normal IL 61761 www.napbirt.org
Ph: 309-452-4257 ▪ Fx: 309-452-4825

National Association of Professional Baseball Leagues www.minorleaguebaseball.com
201 Bayshore Dr SE Saint Petersburg FL 33701
Ph: 727-822-6937 ▪ Fx: 727-821-5819

National Association of Professional Educators www.teacherspet.com/napeindx.htm
900 17th St Suite 300 Washington DC 20006
Ph: 202-848-8969

National Association of Professional Employer Organizations www.napeo.org
901 N Pitt St Suite 150 Alexandria VA 22314
Ph: 703-836-0466 ▪ Fx: 703-836-0976

National Association of Professional Geriatric Care Managers www.caremanager.org
1604 N Country Club Rd Tucson AZ 85716
Ph: 520-881-8008 ▪ Fx: 520-325-7925

National Association of Professional Insurance Agents www.pianet.com
400 N Washington St Alexandria VA 22314
Ph: 703-836-9340 ▪ Fx: 703-836-1279 ▪ TF: 800-742-6900

National Association of Professional Mortgage Women www.napmw.org
PO Box 2016 Edmonds WA 98020
Ph: 425-778-6162 ▪ Fx: 425-771-9588 ▪ TF: 800-827-3034

National Association of Professional Organizers www.napo.net
35 Technology Pkwy Suite 150 Norcross GA 30092
Ph: 770-325-3440 ▪ Fx: 770-325-8825

National Association of Professional Pet Sitters www.petsitters.org
17000 Commerce Pkwy Suite C Mount Laurel NJ 08054
Ph: 856-439-0500 ▪ Fx: 856-439-0525 ▪ TF: 800-296-7387

National Association of Professional Process Servers www.napps.org
PO Box 4547 Portland OR 97208
Ph: 503-222-4180 ▪ Fx: 503-222-3950 ▪ TF: 800-477-8211

National Association of Professional Surplus Lines Offices www.napslo.org
6405 N Cosby Ave Suite 201 Kansas City MO 64151
Ph: 816-741-3910 ▪ Fx: 816-741-5409

National Association of the Professions www.nap-assn.com
350 Fairway Dr Suite 200 Deerfield Beach FL 33441
Ph: 954-571-1877 ▪ Fx: 954-571-8582 ▪ TF: 800-221-2168

National Association of Program Information & Performance Measurement 810 1st St NE Suite 500 Washington DC www.napipm.org
  20002
Ph: 202-682-0100 ▪ Fx: 202-289-6555

National Association for Promotional & Advertising Allowances Inc www.napaa.org
13771 N Fountain Hills Blvd Suite 114 Fountain Hills AZ 85268
Ph: 480-837-9704 ▪ Fx: 602-296-0277

National Association of Property Inspectors napi.lincoln-grad.org
c/o Lincoln Graduate Ctr 303 W Cypress St San Antonio TX
  78212
Ph: 210-225-2897 ▪ Fx: 210-225-8450 ▪ TF: 800-531-5333

National Association of Protection & Advocacy Systems 900 2nd St NE Suite 211 Washington DC 20002 www.protectionandadvocacy.com
Ph: 202-408-9514 ▪ Fx: 202-408-9520

National Association for Pseudoxanthoma Elasticum Inc www.pxenape.org
8764 Manchester Rd Suite 200 Saint Louis MO 63144
Ph: 314-962-0100

National Association of Psychiatric Health Systems www.naphs.org
325 7th St NW Suite 625 Washington DC 20004
Ph: 202-393-6700 ▪ Fx: 202-783-6041

National Association of Public Child Welfare Administrators
810 1st St NE Suite 500 Washington DC 20002
Ph: 202-682-0100 ▪ Fx: 202-289-6555

National Association for Public Health Statistics & Information Systems 801 Roeder Rd Suite 650 Silver Spring MD 20910 www.naphsis.org
Ph: 301-563-6001 ▪ Fx: 301-563-6012

National Association of Public Hospitals & Health Systems www.naph.org
1301 Pennsylvania Ave NW Suite 950 Washington DC 20004
Ph: 202-585-0100 ▪ Fx: 202-585-0101

National Association of Public Insurance Adjusters www.napia.com
21165 Whitfield Pl Suite 105 Potomac Falls VA 20165
Ph: 703-433-9217 ▪ Fx: 703-433-0369

National Association Publications, Society of www.snaponline.org
8405 Greensboro Dr Suite 800 McLean VA 22102
Ph: 703-506-3285 ▪ Fx: 703-506-3266

National Association of Puerto Rican/Hispanic Social Workers Inc www.naprhsw.com
PO Box 651 Brentwood NY 11717
Ph: 631-446-1536

National Association of Pupil Service Administrators www.napsa.com
PO Box 783 Pittsford NY 14534
Ph: 585-223-2018 ▪ Fx: 585-223-1497

National Association for Pupil Transportation www.napt.org
1840 Western Ave Albany NY 12203
Ph: 518-452-3611 ▪ Fx: 518-218-0867 ▪ TF: 800-989-6278

National Association of Radiation Survivors www.radiationsurvivors.org
PO Box 1587 Marysville CA 95901
Ph: 530-741-6954 ▪ TF: 800-798-5102

National Association of Radio & Telecommunications Engineers www.narte.org
167 Village St Medway MA 02053
Ph: 508-533-8333 ▪ Fx: 508-533-3815 ▪ TF: 800-896-2783

National Association of Railroad Passengers www.narprail.org
900 2nd St NE Suite 308 Washington DC 20002
Ph: 202-408-8362 ▪ Fx: 202-408-8287

National Association of Railroad Trial Counsel www.usnartc.org
881 Alma Real Dr Suite 218 Pacific Palisades CA 90272
Ph: 310-459-7659 ▪ Fx: 310-459-6603

National Association of Real Estate Appraisers   www.iami.org/narea
1224 N Nokomis NE   Alexandria MN 56308
Ph: 320-763-7626 ▪ Fx: 320-763-9290

National Association of Real Estate Brokers   www.nareb.com
9831 Greenbelt Rd Suite 309   Lanham MD 20706
Ph: 301-552-9340 ▪ Fx: 301-552-9216 ▪ TF: 800-838-3075

National Association of Real Estate Companies   www.narec.org
PO Box 958   Columbia MD 21044
Ph: 410-992-6476 ▪ Fx: 410-992-6363

National Association of Real Estate Editors   www.naree.org
1003 NW 6th Terr   Boca Raton FL 33486
Ph: 561-391-3599

National Association of Real Estate Investment Managers   www.nareim.org
11755 Wilshire Blvd Suite 1380   Los Angeles CA 90025
Ph: 310-479-2219

National Association of Real Estate Investment Trusts   www.nareit.com
1875 'I' St NW Suite 600   Washington DC 20006
Ph: 202-739-9400 ▪ Fx: 202-739-9401 ▪ TF: 800-362-7348

(National Association of Real Estate Investment Trusts) REITPAC
1875 'I' St NW Suite 600   Washington DC 20006
Ph: 202-739-9400 ▪ Fx: 202-739-9401

National Association of REALTORS   www.realtor.org
430 N Michigan Ave   Chicago IL 60611
Ph: 312-329-8200 ▪ Fx: 312-329-8390 ▪ TF: 800-874-6500

National Association of REALTORS PAC
700 11th St NW   Washington DC 20001
Ph: 202-383-1000 ▪ Fx: 202-383-1035

National Association of Recording Merchandisers   www.narm.com
9 Eves Dr Suite 120   Marlton NJ 08053
Ph: 856-596-2221 ▪ Fx: 856-596-3268

National Association of Recreation Resource Planners   www.narrp.org

National Association of Regional Councils   www.narc.org
1666 Connecticut Ave NW Suite 300   Washington DC 20009
Ph: 202-986-1032 ▪ Fx: 202-986-1038

National Association of Regulatory Utility Commissioners   www.naruc.org
1101 Vermont Ave NW Suite 200   Washington DC 20005
Ph: 202-898-2200 ▪ Fx: 202-898-2213

National Association of Rehabilitation   www.nationalrehab.org/website/divs/nari.html
Instructors 633 S Washington St   Alexandria VA 22314
Ph: 703-836-0850 ▪ Fx: 703-836-0848 ▪ TF: 800-671-6840

National Association of Rehabilitation Providers & Agencies   www.naranet.org
12100 Sunset Hills Rd Suite 130   Reston VA 20190
Ph: 703-437-4377 ▪ Fx: 703-435-4390

National Association of Reinforcing Steel Contractors   www.narsc.com
10382 Main St Suite 200 PO Box 280   Fairfax VA 22030
Ph: 703-591-1870 ▪ Fx: 703-591-1895

National Association of Relay Manufacturers   www.ec-central.org/NARM
9549 N Broadmoor Rd   Milwaukee WI 53217
Ph: 414-351-4548 ▪ Fx: 414-351-4897

National Association of the Remodeling Industry   www.nari.org
780 Lee St Suite 200   Des Plaines IL 60016
Ph: 847-298-9200 ▪ Fx: 847-298-9225 ▪ TF: 800-611-6274

National Association of Republican Attorneys
PO Box 656513   Fresh Meadows NY 11365
Ph: 718-357-7075

National Association of Resale & Thrift Shops   www.narts.org
PO Box 80707   Saint Clair Shores MI 48080
Ph: 800-544-0751 ▪ Fx: 810-294-6776

National Association for Research in Science Teaching   www.educ.sfu.ca/narstsite
Univ of Missouri-Columbia 303 Townsend Hall   Columbia MO
65211
Ph: 573-884-1401 ▪ Fx: 573-884-2917

National Association for Research & Therapy of Homosexuality   www.narth.com
16633 Ventura Blvd Suite 1340   Encino CA 91436
Ph: 818-789-4440 ▪ Fx: 818-789-6452

National Association of Residential Property Managers   www.narpm.org
PO Box 140647   Austin TX 78714
Ph: 512-381-6091 ▪ Fx: 512-454-3036 ▪ TF: 800-782-3452

National Association of Retail Collection Attorneys   www.narca.org
1620 'I' St NW Suite 165   Washington DC 20006
Ph: 202-861-0706 ▪ Fx: 202-463-8498 ▪ TF: 800-633-6069

National Association for Retail Marketing Services   www.narms.com
PO Box 906   Plover WI 54467
Ph: 715-342-0948 ▪ Fx: 715-342-1943 ▪ TF: 888-526-2767

National Association of Retired Federal Employees   www.narfe.org
606 N Washington St   Alexandria VA 22314
Ph: 703-838-7760 ▪ Fx: 703-838-7785 ▪ TF: 800-627-3394

National Association of Retired Senior Volunteer Program Directors
12388 Warwick Blvd   Newport News VA 23601
Ph: 757-595-9037 ▪ Fx: 757-595-9047

National Association of Retired & Veteran Railway Employees   www.narvre.com
300 Cedar Blvd Suite 201A   Pittsburgh PA 15228
Ph: 412-563-5611 ▪ Fx: 412-563-5612

National Association of Reunion Managers   www.reunions.com
PO Box 23211   Tampa FL 33623
Ph: 800-654-2776

National Association of Review Appraisers & Mortgage   www.iami.org/nara.html
Underwriters 1224 N Nokomis NE   Alexandria MN 56308
Ph: 320-763-6870 ▪ Fx: 320-763-9290

National Association of Rocketry   www.nar.org
PO Box 177   Altoona WI 54720
Ph: 715-832-1946 ▪ Fx: 715-832-6432 ▪ TF: 800-262-4872

National Association of Royalty Owners   www.naro-us.org
PO Box 5779   Norman OK 73070
Ph: 405-573-2972 ▪ Fx: 405-364-3082 ▪ TF: 800-558-0557

National Association for Rural Mental Health   www.narmh.org
3700 W Division St Suite 105   Saint Cloud MN 56301
Ph: 320-202-1820 ▪ Fx: 320-202-1833 ▪ TF: 800-809-5879

National Association of RV Parks & Campgrounds   www.arvc.org
113 Park Ave   Falls Church VA 22046
Ph: 703-241-8801 ▪ Fx: 703-241-1004

National Association of Sales Professionals   www.nasp.com
11000 N 130th Pl   Scottsdale AZ 85259
Ph: 480-951-4311 ▪ Fx: 480-483-2860

National Association of Scholars   www.nas.org
221 Witherspoon St 2nd Fl   Princeton NJ 08542
Ph: 609-683-7878 ▪ Fx: 609-683-0316

National Association of School Music Dealers Inc   www.nasmd.com
13140 Coit Rd Suite 320 LB 120   Dallas TX 75240
Ph: 972-233-9107 ▪ Fx: 972-490-4219

National Association of School Nurses   www.nasn.org
PO Box 1300   Scarborough ME 04070
Ph: 207-883-2117 ▪ Fx: 207-883-2683 ▪ TF: 877-627-6476

National Association of School Psychologists   www.nasponline.org
4340 East West Hwy Suite 402   Bethesda MD 20814
Ph: 301-657-0270 ▪ Fx: 301-657-0275

National Association of School Resource Officers   www.nasro.org
PO Box 39   Osprey FL 34229
Ph: 888-316-2776 ▪ Fx: 941-918-8231

National Association of School Safety & Law Enforcement Officers   www.nassleo.org
PO Box 3147   Oswego NY 13126
Ph: 315-529-4858 ▪ Fx: 315-343-2935

National Association of Schools of Art & Design   nasad.arts-accredit.org
11250 Roger Bacon Dr Suite 21   Reston VA 20190
Ph: 703-437-0700 ▪ Fx: 703-437-6312

**National Association of Schools Colleges & Universities of the
United Methodist Church**   PO Box 340007   Nashville TN
37203
Ph: 615-340-7399 ▪ Fx: 615-340-7379

National Association of Schools of Dance   nasd.arts-accredit.org
11250 Roger Bacon Dr Suite 21   Reston VA 20190
Ph: 703-437-0700 ▪ Fx: 703-437-6312

National Association of Schools of Music   nasm.arts-accredit.org
11250 Roger Bacon Dr Suite 21   Reston VA 20190
Ph: 703-437-0700 ▪ Fx: 703-437-6312

National Association of Schools of Public Affairs & Administration   www.naspaa.org
1120 G St NW Suite 730   Washington DC 20005
Ph: 202-628-8965 ▪ Fx: 202-626-4978

National Association of Schools of Theatre   nast.arts-accredit.org
11250 Roger Bacon Dr Suite 21   Reston VA 20190
Ph: 703-437-0700 ▪ Fx: 703-437-6312

National Association of Science Writers   www.nasw.org
PO Box 890   Hedgesville WV 25427
Ph: 304-754-5077 ▪ Fx: 304-754-5076

National Association of Scientific Materials Managers   www.naosmm.org

National Association of Screening Agencies   www.n-a-s-a.com
2020 Pennsylvania Ave NW   Washington DC 20006
Ph: 202-955-6272 ▪ Fx: 202-492-2852

National Association for Search & Rescue   www.nasar.org
4500 Southgate Pl Suite 100   Chantilly VA 20151
Ph: 703-222-6277 ▪ Fx: 703-222-6283

National Association of Secondary School Principals   www.principals.org
1904 Association Dr   Reston VA 20191
Ph: 703-860-0200 ▪ Fx: 703-476-5432

National Association of Secretaries of State   www.nass.org
444 N Capitol St NW Hall of States Suite 401   Washington DC
20001
Ph: 202-624-3525 ▪ Fx: 202-624-3527

National Association of Securities Dealers Inc   www.nasd.com
1735 K St NW   Washington DC 20006
Ph: 202-728-8000 ▪ TF: 800-289-9999

National Association of Securities Professionals   www.nasphq.com
1212 New York Ave NW Suite 210   Washington DC 20005
Ph: 202-371-5535 ▪ Fx: 202-371-5536

National Association of Security Companies   www.nasco.org
1625 Prince St   Alexandria VA 22314
Ph: 703-518-1477

National Association for the Self-Employed   www.nase.org
PO Box 612067 DFW Airport   Dallas TX 75261
Ph: 800-232-6273 ▪ Fx: 800-551-4446

National Association of Self-Instructional Language Programs   www.nasilp.org
Univ of Arizona 1717 E Speedway Blvd Suite 3312   Tucson AZ
85721
Ph: 520-626-5258 ▪ Fx: 520-626-8205

National Association of Service & Conservation Corps   www.nascc.org
666 11th St NW Suite 1000   Washington DC 20001
Ph: 202-737-6272 ▪ Fx: 202-737-6277 ▪ TF: 800-666-2722

National Association of Service Managers   www.nasm.org
12603 224th Ave PMB 17   Bristol WI 53104
Ph: 262-857-7227

National Association of Settlement Purchasers   www.setcap.com/Gov_Nasp.asp
14755 Preston Rd Suite 130   Dallas TX 75254
Ph: 800-959-0006 ▪ Fx: 800-959-0028

National Association of Seventh-day Adventist Dentists   www.llu.edu/llu/dentistry/nasdad
PO Box 101   Loma Linda CA 92354
Ph: 909-558-8187 ▪ Fx: 909-558-4607

National Association for Sick Child Daycare   www.nascd.com
1716 5th Ave N   Birmingham AL 35203
Ph: 205-324-8447 ▪ Fx: 205-324-8050

National Association of Sign Supply Distributors Inc   www.nassd.org
5024 Campbell Blvd Suite R   Baltimore MD 21236
Ph: 410-931-8100 ▪ Fx: 410-931-8111

National Association of Small Business Investment Companies   www.nasbic.org
666 11th St NW Suite 750   Washington DC 20001
Ph: 202-628-5055 ▪ Fx: 202-628-5080

National Association of Special Needs State Administrators
c/o Illinois State Board of Education 100 N 1st St Suite
C-421   Springfield IL 62777
Ph: 217-782-3370 ▪ Fx: 217-782-9224

National Association for the Specialty Food Trade Inc   www.specialtyfoodmarket.com
120 Wall St 27th Fl   New York NY 10005
Ph: 212-482-6440 ▪ Fx: 212-482-6459 ▪ TF: 800-627-3869

National Association for Sport & Physical Education   www.aahperd.org
1900 Association Dr   Reston VA 20191
Ph: 703-476-3410 ▪ Fx: 703-476-8316 ▪ TF: 800-213-7193

National Association of Sporting Goods Wholesalers   www.nasgw.org
400 E Randolph St Suite 700   Chicago IL 60601
Ph: 312-565-0233 ▪ Fx: 312-565-2654

National Association of Sports Officials   www.naso.org
2017 Lathrop Ave   Racine WI 53405
Ph: 262-632-5448 ▪ Fx: 262-632-5460 ▪ TF: 800-733-6100

National Association of State Agencies for Surplus Property   nasasp.org
2221 Forster St Rm G-49   Harrisburg PA 17105
Ph: 717-787-9724 ▪ Fx: 717-772-2491

National Association of State Alcohol & Drug Abuse Directors   www.nasadad.org
808 17th St NW Suite 410   Washington DC 20006
Ph: 202-293-0090 ▪ Fx: 202-293-1250

National Association of State Archaeologists   www.uiowa.edu/~osa/nasa

National Association of State Auditors Comptrollers & Treasurers   www.nasact.org
2401 Regency Rd Suite 302   Lexington KY 40503
Ph: 859-276-1147 ▪ Fx: 859-278-0507

National Association of State Aviation Officials   www.nasao.org
1010 Wayne Ave Suite 930   Silver Spring MD 20910
Ph: 301-588-0587 ▪ Fx: 301-585-1803

National Association of State Boards of Accountancy   www.nasba.org
150 4th Ave N Suite 700   Nashville TN 37219
Ph: 615-880-4200 ▪ Fx: 615-880-4290 ▪ TF: 800-272-3926

National Association of State Boards of Education   www.nasbe.org
277 S Washington St Suite 100   Alexandria VA 22314
Ph: 703-684-4000 ▪ Fx: 703-836-2313 ▪ TF: 800-368-5023

National Association of State Boards of Geology   www.asbog.org
PO Box 11591   Columbia SC 29211
Ph: 803-799-1047 ▪ Fx: 803-252-3432

National Association of State Boating Law Administrators   www.nasbla.org
1500 Leestown Rd Suite 330   Lexington KY 40511
Ph: 859-225-9487 ▪ Fx: 859-231-6403

National Association of State Budget Officers   www.nasbo.org
444 N Capitol St NW Suite 642   Washington DC 20001
Ph: 202-624-5382 ▪ Fx: 202-624-7745

National Association of State Catholic Conference Directors   www.nasccd.org
1042 Burlington Ln   Frankfort KY 40601
Ph: 502-875-4345 ▪ Fx: 502-875-2841

National Association of State Chief Administrators   www.nasca.org
167 W Main St Suite 600   Lexington KY 40507
Ph: 859-231-1931 ▪ Fx: 859-514-9188

National Association of State Chief Information Officers   www.nascio.org
167 W Main St Suite 600   Lexington KY 40507
Ph: 859-231-1971 ▪ Fx: 859-231-1928

National Association for State Community Services Programs   www.nascsp.org
400 N Capitol St NW   Washington DC 20001
Ph: 202-624-5866 ▪ Fx: 202-624-8472

National Association of State Controlled Substance Authorities   www.nascsa.org
72 Brook St   Quincy MA 02170
Ph: 617-472-0520 ▪ Fx: 617-472-0521

National Association of State Credit Union Supervisors   www.nascus.org
1655 N Fort Myer Dr Suite 300   Arlington VA 22209
Ph: 703-528-8351 ▪ Fx: 703-528-3248

National Association of State Departments of Agriculture   www.nasda.org
1156 15th St NW Suite 1020   Washington DC 20005
Ph: 202-296-9680 ▪ Fx: 202-296-9686

National Association of State Development Agencies   www.nasda.com
12884 Harbor Dr   Woodbridge VA 22192
Ph: 703-490-6777 ▪ Fx: 703-492-4404

National Association of State Directors of Career Technical   www.careertech.org
Education Consortium   444 N Capitol St NW Suite
830   Washington DC 20001
Ph: 202-737-0303 ▪ Fx: 202-737-1106

National Association of State Directors of Developmental   www.nasddds.org
Disabilities Services   113 Oronoco St   Alexandria VA 22314
Ph: 703-683-4202 ▪ Fx: 703-684-1395

National Association of State Directors of Migrant Education   www.nasdme.org
500 Mero St Rm 832   Frankfort KY 40601
Ph: 502-564-3791

National Association of State Directors of Special Education   www.nasdse.org
1800 Diagonal Rd Suite 320   Alexandria VA 22314
Ph: 703-519-3800 ▪ Fx: 703-519-3808

National Association of State Directors of Teacher Education &   www.nasdtec.org
Certification   39 Nathan Ellis Hwy PMB 134   Mashpee MA
02649
Ph: 508-539-8844 ▪ Fx: 508-539-8868

National Association of State Directors of Veterans Affairs   www.nasdva.com

National Association of State Election Directors   www.nased.org
Council of State Governments 444 N Capitol St NW Suite
401   Washington DC 20001
Ph: 202-624-5460 ▪ Fx: 202-624-5452

National Association of State EMS Directors   www.nasemsd.org
201 Park Washington Ct   Falls Church VA 22046
Ph: 703-538-1799 ▪ Fx: 703-241-5603

National Association of State Energy Officials   www.naseo.org
1414 Prince St Suite 200   Alexandria VA 22314
Ph: 703-299-8800 ▪ Fx: 703-299-6208

National Association of State Facilities Administrators   www.nasfa.net
2760 Research Park Dr PO Box 11910   Lexington KY 40578
Ph: 859-244-8181 ▪ Fx: 859-244-8001

National Association of State Fire Marshals   www.firemarshals.org
PO Box 4127   Clifton Park NY 12065
Ph: 518-317-0018 ▪ Fx: 518-383-9647 ▪ TF: 877-996-2736

National Association of State Foresters   www.stateforesters.org
444 N Capitol St NW Suite 540   Washington DC 20001
Ph: 202-624-5415 ▪ Fx: 202-624-5407

National Association of State Land Reclamationists   www.crc.siu.edu/naslr.htm
Southern Illinois Univ Coal Research Ctr   Carbondale IL 62901
Ph: 618-536-5521

National Association of State Mental Health Program Directors   www.nasmhpd.org
66 Canal Center Plaza Suite 302   Alexandria VA 22314
Ph: 703-739-9333 ▪ Fx: 703-548-9517

National Association of State Outdoor Recreation Liaison Officers
3116 Woodbrook Pl   Boise ID 83706
Ph: 208-384-5421

National Association of State Park Directors   naspd.indstate.edu
9894 E Holden Pl   Tucson AZ 85748
Ph: 520-298-4924 ▪ Fx: 520-298-6515

National Association of State Personnel Executives   www.naspe.net
2760 Research Park Dr PO Box 11910   Lexington KY 40578
Ph: 859-244-8182 ▪ Fx: 859-244-8001

National Association of State Procurement Officials   www.naspo.org
167 W Main St Suite 600   Lexington KY 40507
Ph: 859-231-1877 ▪ Fx: 859-514-9166

National Association of State Radio Networks   www.statenets.com

National Association of State Retirement Administrators   www.nasra.org
444 N Capitol St NW Suite 234   Washington DC 20001
Ph: 202-624-1417

National Association of State Supervisors of Trade &   itednt.ited.uidaho.edu/nasstie
Industrial Education

National Association of State Telecommunications Directors   www.nastd.org
2760 Research Park Dr PO Box 11910   Lexington KY 40578
Ph: 859-244-8186 ▪ Fx: 859-244-8001

National Association of State Trail Administrators
701 Ivanhoe St   Denver CO 80220
Ph: 720-308-0567 ▪ Fx: 303-321-8082

National Association of State Treasurers   www.nast.net
2760 Research Park Dr PO Box 11910   Lexington KY 40578
Ph: 859-244-8175 ▪ Fx: 859-244-8053

National Association of State Units on Aging   www.nasua.org
1201 15th St NW Sutie 350   Washington DC 20005
Ph: 202-898-2578 ▪ Fx: 202-898-2583

National Association of State Universities & Land Grant Colleges   www.nasulgc.org
1307 New York Ave NW Suite 400   Washington DC 20005
Ph: 202-478-6040 ▪ Fx: 202-478-6046

National Association of State Utility Consumer Advocates   www.nasuca.org
8300 Colesville Rd Suite 101   Silver Spring MD 20910
Ph: 301-589-6313 ▪ Fx: 301-589-6380

National Association of State Workforce Agencies   www.naswa.org
444 N Capitol St NW Suite 142   Washington DC 20001
Ph: 202-434-8020 ▪ Fx: 202-434-8033

National Association of Steel Pipe Distributors   www.naspd.org
14760 Memorial Dr Suite 302   Houston TX 77079
Ph: 281-531-7473 ▪ Fx: 281-531-7475

National Association for Stock Car Auto Racing   www.nascar.com
1801 W International Speedway Blvd   Daytona Beach FL 32114
Ph: 386-253-0611 ▪ Fx: 386-947-6712

National Association of Stock Plan Professionals   naspp.com
PO Box 21639   Concord CA 94521
Ph: 925-685-9271 ▪ Fx: 925-685-5402

National Association of Store Fixture Manufacturers   www.nasfm.org
3595 Sheridan St Suite 200   Hollywood FL 33021
Ph: 954-893-7300 ▪ Fx: 954-893-7500

National Association of Student Activity Advisors
1904 Association Dr   Reston VA 20191
Ph: 703-860-0200 ▪ Fx: 703-476-5432

National Association of Student Affairs Professionals   www.nasap.net
Tuskegee Univ Tompkins Hall Rm 100   Tuskegee AL 36088
Ph: 334-727-8837 ▪ Fx: 334-724-3758

National Association of Student Anthropologists   www.aaanet.org/nasa
c/o American Anthropological Assn 2200 Wilson Blvd Suite
600   Arlington VA 22201
Ph: 703-528-1902 ▪ Fx: 703-528-3546

National Association of Student Assistance Professionals   www.nasap.org
4200 Wisconsin Ave NW Suite 106-118   Washington DC 20016
Ph: 800-257-6310 ▪ Fx: 215-257-6997

National Association of Student Financial Aid Administrators   www.nasfaa.org
1129 20th St NW Suite 400   Washington DC 20036
Ph: 202-785-0453 ▪ Fx: 202-785-1487

National Association of Student Personnel Administrators   www.naspa.org
1875 Connecticut Ave NW Suite 418   Washington DC 20009
Ph: 202-265-7500 ▪ Fx: 202-797-1157

National Association for the Study & Performance of   www.naspaam.org
African-American Music

National Association of Subacute & Post Acute Care   www.naspac.net
1960 Gallows Rd Suite 210   Vienna VA 22182
Ph: 703-790-8989 ▪ Fx: 703-790-8485

National Association of Subrogation Professionals   www.subrogation.org
4248 Park Glen Rd   Minneapolis MN 55416
Ph: 952-928-4661 ▪ Fx: 952-929-1318 ▪ TF: 888-828-8186

National Association of Substance Abuse   www.preventionpartners.samhsa.gov/partner
Trainers & Educators   1521 Hillary St   New Orleans LA 70118
Ph: 504-286-5234

National Association for the Support of Long Term Care   www.nasl.org
1321 Duke St Suite 304   Alexandria VA 22314
Ph: 703-549-8500 ▪ Fx: 703-549-8342

National Association of Surety Bond Producers   www.nasbp.org
5225 Wisconsin Ave NW Suite 600   Washington DC 20015
Ph: 202-686-3700 ▪ Fx: 202-686-3656

National Association of Tax Professionals www.natptax.com
720 Association Dr Appleton WI 54914
Ph: 920-749-1040 ▪ Fx: 800-747-0001 ▪ TF: 800-558-3402

National Association of Teachers' Agencies www.jobsforteachers.com
797 Kings Hwy Fairfield CT 06825
Ph: 203-333-0611 ▪ Fx: 203-334-7224

National Association of Teachers of Singing Inc www.nats.org
4745 Sutton Park Ct Suite 201 Jacksonville FL 32224
Ph: 904-992-9101 ▪ Fx: 904-992-9326

National Association of Telecommunications Officers & Advisors www.natoa.org
8405 Greensboro Dr Suite 800 McLean VA 22102
Ph: 703-506-3275 ▪ Fx: 703-506-3266

National Association of Television Program Executives www.natpe.org
2425 Olympic Blvd Suite 600-E Santa Monica CA 90404
Ph: 310-453-4440 ▪ Fx: 310-453-5258

National Association of Temple Administrators rj.org/nata
PO Box 936 Ridgefield WA 98642
Ph: 360-887-0464 ▪ TF: 800-966-6282

National Association of Temple Educators rj.org/nate
633 3rd Ave 7th Fl New York NY 10017
Ph: 212-452-6510 ▪ Fx: 212-452-6512

National Association of Test Directors www.natd.org
c/o Fenton Research 8520 N Coral Ridge Loop Tucson AZ
85704
Ph: 520-229-8687

National Association of Theatre Owners www.natoonline.org
4605 Lankershim Blvd Suite 340 North Hollywood CA 91602
Ph: 818-506-1778 ▪ Fx: 818-506-0269

National Association of Ticket Brokers www.natb.org
1666 K St NW Suite 5000 Washington DC 20006
Ph: 202-887-1400

National Association of Tower Erectors www.natehome.com
8 2nd St SE Watertown SD 57201
Ph: 605-882-5865 ▪ Fx: 605-886-5184 ▪ TF: 888-882-5865

National Association of Town Watch www.nationaltownwatch.org
1 E Wynnewood Rd Suite 102 Wynnewood PA 19096
Ph: 610-649-7055 ▪ Fx: 610-649-5456 ▪ TF: 800-648-3688

National Association of Towns & Townships www.natat.org
444 N Capitol St NW Suite 397 Washington DC 20001
Ph: 202-624-3550 ▪ Fx: 202-624-3554

National Association of Trade Exchanges www.nate.org
8836 Tyler Blvd Mentor OH 44060
Ph: 440-205-5378 ▪ Fx: 440-205-5379

National Association of Trade & Industrial Education www.skillsusa.org/NATIE
PO Box 1665 Leesburg VA 20177
Ph: 703-777-1740

National Association of Trailer Manufacturers www.natm.com
2951 SW Wanamaker Dr Suite A Topeka KS 66614
Ph: 785-272-4433 ▪ Fx: 785-272-4455

National Association for Treasurers of Religious Institutes Inc www.natri.org
8824 Cameron St Silver Spring MD 20910
Ph: 301-587-7776 ▪ Fx: 301-589-2897

National Association of Unclaimed Property Administrators www.unclaimed.org
PO Box 11910 Lexington KY 40578
Ph: 859-244-8150 ▪ Fx: 859-244-8053

National Association of Underwater Instructors www.naui.org
1232 Tech Blvd Tampa FL 33619
Ph: 813-628-6284 ▪ Fx: 813-628-8253 ▪ TF: 800-553-6284

National Association of Uniform Manufacturers & Distributors www.naumd.com
16 E 41st St Suite 700 New York NY 10017
Ph: 212-869-0670 ▪ Fx: 212-575-2847

National Association for Uniformed Services www.naus.org
5535 Hempstead Way Springfield VA 22151
Ph: 703-750-1342 ▪ Fx: 703-354-4380 ▪ TF: 800-842-3451

National Association of University www.ag.iastate.edu/departments/aecl/naufwp
Fisheries & Wildlife Programs Univ of Montana 310 Lewis
Hall Box 173460 Bozeman MT 59717
Ph: 406-994-2270 ▪ Fx: 406-994-3190

National Association of University Women www.nauw.org
1001 'E' St SE Washington DC 20003
Ph: 202-547-3967 ▪ Fx: 202-547-5226

National Association of Urban Hospitals www.nauh.org
10 Pidgeon Hill Dr Suite 150 Sterling VA 20165
Ph: 703-444-0989 ▪ Fx: 703-444-3029

National Association of VA Physicians & Dentists www.navapd.org
11 Canal Ctr Plaza Suite 110 Alexandria VA 22314
Ph: 703-548-0280 ▪ Fx: 703-683-7939

National Association for Variable Annuities www.navanet.org
11710 Plaza America Dr Suite 100 Reston VA 20190
Ph: 703-707-8830 ▪ Fx: 703-707-8831

National Association of Vascular Access Networks www.navannet.org
11441 S State St Suite A113 Draper UT 84020
Ph: 801-576-1824 ▪ Fx: 801-553-9137 ▪ TF: 888-576-2826

National Association of Vertical Transportation Professionals www.navtp.org
PO Box 636 Bowie Bowie MD 20718
Ph: 301-262-3150 ▪ Fx: 301-262-3194

National Association of Veterans Program Administrators www.navpa.org

National Association of Veterans' Research & Education Foundations www.navref.org
5018 Sangamore Rd Suite 300 Bethesda MD 20816
Ph: 301-229-1048 ▪ Fx: 301-229-0442

National Association for Visually Handicapped www.navh.org
22 W 21st St 6th Fl New York NY 10010
Ph: 212-889-3141 ▪ Fx: 212-727-2931

National Association of Waste Transporters www.nawt.org
PO Box 70 Edgewater MD 21037
Ph: 410-798-0842 ▪ TF: 800-236-6298

National Association of Watch & Clock Collectors www.nawcc.org
514 Poplar St Columbia PA 17512
Ph: 717-684-8261 ▪ Fx: 717-684-0878

National Association of Water Companies www.nawc.com
1725 K St NW Suite 1212 Washington DC 20006
Ph: 202-833-8383 ▪ Fx: 202-331-7442

National Association of Water Companies PAC www.nawc.com
1725 K St NW Suite 1212 Washington DC 20006
Ph: 202-833-8383 ▪ Fx: 202-331-7442

National Association of Waterfront Employers
2011 Pennsylvania Ave NW Suite 301 Washington DC 20006
Ph: 202-296-2810 ▪ Fx: 202-331-7479

National Association of Waterproofing & Structural Repair www.nawsrc.org
Contractors 8015 Corporate Dr Suite A Baltimore MD 21236
Ph: 410-931-3332 ▪ Fx: 410-931-2060 ▪ TF: 800-245-6292

National Association of Wheat Growers www.wheatworld.org
415 2nd St NE Suite 300 Washington DC 20002
Ph: 202-547-7800 ▪ Fx: 202-546-2638

National Association of Wheat Weavers www.geocities.com/nawwstrawart

National Association of Wholesaler-Distributors www.naw.org
1725 K St NW Suite 300 Washington DC 20006
Ph: 202-872-0885 ▪ Fx: 202-785-0586

National Association of Women Artists www.nawanet.org
80 5th Ave Suite 1405 New York NY 10011
Ph: 212-675-1616

National Association of Women Business Owners www.nawbo.org
8405 Greensboro Dr Suite 800 McLean VA 22102
Ph: 703-506-3268 ▪ Fx: 703-506-3266 ▪ TF: 800-556-2926

National Association of Women in Construction www.nawic.org
327 S Adams St Fort Worth TX 76104
Ph: 817-877-5551 ▪ Fx: 817-877-0324 ▪ TF: 800-552-3506

National Association of Women Highway Safety Leaders Inc www.nawhsl.org
145 Berry Rd Clinton MS 39056
Ph: 601-924-7815

National Association of Women Judges www.nawj.org
1112 16th St NW Suite 520 Washington DC 20036
Ph: 202-393-0222 ▪ Fx: 202-393-0125

National Association of Women Law Enforcement Executives www.nawlee.com
750 N Lake Shore Dr Chicago IL 60611

National Association of Women Lawyers www.abanet.org/nawl
750 N Lake Shore Dr Chicago IL 60611
Ph: 312-988-6186 ▪ Fx: 312-988-6281

National Association for Women Writers www.naww.org
PO Box 183812 Arlington TX 76096
Ph: 866-821-5829

National Association of Workforce Boards www.nawb.org
1701 K St NW Suite 1000 Washington DC 20006
Ph: 202-775-0960 ▪ Fx: 202-775-0330

National Association of Workforce Development Professionals www.nawdp.org
810 1st St NE Suite 525 Washington DC 20002
Ph: 202-589-1790 ▪ Fx: 202-589-1799

National Association for Year-Round Education www.nayre.org
PO Box 711386 San Diego CA 92171
Ph: 619-276-5298 ▪ Fx: 858-571-5754

National Association of Youth Clubs
1601 R St NW Washington DC 20009
Ph: 202-667-4080 ▪ Fx: 202-667-4113

National Athletic Trainers Association www.nata.org
2952 Stemmons Fwy Suite 200 Dallas TX 75247
Ph: 214-637-6282 ▪ Fx: 214-637-2206 ▪ TF: 800-879-6282

National Attention Deficit Disorder Association www.add.org
1788 2nd St Suite 200 Highland Park IL 60035
Ph: 847-432-2332 ▪ Fx: 847-432-5874

National Auctioneers Association www.auctioneers.org
8880 Ballentine St Overland Park KS 66214
Ph: 913-541-8084 ▪ Fx: 913-894-5281 ▪ TF: 888-541-8084

National Audubon Society www.audubon.org
700 Broadway New York NY 10003
Ph: 212-979-3000 ▪ Fx: 212-979-3188

National Auto Auction Association www.naaa.com
5320-D Spectrum Dr Frederick MD 21703
Ph: 301-696-0400 ▪ Fx: 301-631-1359

National Auto Body Council www.autobodycouncil.org
PO Box 4489 West Richland WA 99352
Ph: 509-545-3399 ▪ Fx: 509-545-4222 ▪ TF: 888-667-7443

National Automated Clearing House Association www.nacha.org
13665 Dulles Technology Dr Suite 300 Herndon VA 20171
Ph: 703-561-1100 ▪ Fx: 703-787-0996 ▪ TF: 800-487-9180

National Automatic Merchandising Association www.vending.org
20 N Wacker Dr Suite 3500 Chicago IL 60606
Ph: 312-346-0370 ▪ Fx: 312-704-4140

National Automatic Pistol Collectors Association napca.net
PO Box 15738 Saint Louis MO 63163
Ph: 314-638-6505

National Automobile Dealers Association www.nada.org
8400 Westpark Dr McLean VA 22102
Ph: 703-821-7000 ▪ Fx: 703-821-7075 ▪ TF: 800-252-6232

National Automotive Finance Association www.nafassociation.com
217 St Charles Pl Pittsburgh PA 15215
Ph: 412-781-5601 ▪ Fx: 412-781-5607

National Automotive Radiator Service Association www.narsa.org
PO Box 97 East Greenville PA 18041
Ph: 215-541-4500 ▪ Fx: 215-679-4977

National Automotive Technicians Education Foundation www.natef.org
101 Blue Seal Dr SE Suite 101 Leesburg VA 20175
Ph: 703-669-6650 ▪ Fx: 703-669-6125

National Ballroom & Entertainment Association www.nbea.com
2799 Locust Rd Decorah IA 52101
Ph: 563-382-3871

National Band Association www.nationalbandassociation.org
PO Box 5032 Hattiesburg MS 39406
Ph: 601-297-8168 ▪ Fx: 601-266-6185

National Bankers Association   www.nationalbankers.org
1513 P St NW Washington DC 20005
Ph: 202-588-5432 ▪ Fx: 202-588-5443

National Baptist Convention of America Inc   www.nbcamerica.net
1320 Pierre Ave Shreveport LA 71103
Ph: 318-221-3701 ▪ Fx: 318-222-7512

National Baptist Convention USA Inc   www.nationalbaptist.com
1700 Baptist World Ctr Dr Nashville TN 37207
Ph: 615-228-6292 ▪ Fx: 615-226-8757 ▪ TF: 866-531-3054

National Bar Association   www.nationalbar.org
1225 11th St NW Washington DC 20001
Ph: 202-842-3900 ▪ Fx: 202-289-6170 ▪ TF: 800-621-2988

National Barbecue Association   www.nbbqa.org
PO Box 9685 Kansas City MO 64134
Ph: 816-767-8311 ▪ Fx: 816-765-5860 ▪ TF: 888-909-2121

National Barrel Horse Association   www.nbha.com
725 Broad St PO Box 1988 Augusta GA 30903
Ph: 706-722-7223 ▪ Fx: 706-722-9575

National Baseball Congress   www.nbcbaseball.com
PO Box 1420 Wichita KS 67201
Ph: 316-267-3372 ▪ Fx: 316-267-3382

National Basketball Players Association   www.nbpa.com
2 Penn Plaza Suite 2430 New York NY 10121
Ph: 212-655-0880 ▪ Fx: 212-655-0881

National Basketball Trainers Association
400 Colony Sq Suite 1750 Atlanta GA 30361
Ph: 404-875-4000 ▪ Fx: 404-892-8560

National Baton Twirling Association
PO Box 266 Janesville WI 53547
Ph: 608-754-2238 ▪ Fx: 608-754-1986

National Beauty Culturists' League Inc   www.nbcl.org
25 Logan Cir NW Washington DC 20005
Ph: 202-332-2695 ▪ Fx: 202-332-0940

National Bed & Breakfast Association   www.nbba.com
PO Box 332 Norwalk CT 06852
Ph: 203-847-6196 ▪ Fx: 203-847-0469

National Beep Baseball Association   www.nbba.org
2231 W 1st Ave Topeka KS 66606
Ph: 785-234-2156

National Beer Wholesalers Association   www.nbwa.org
1101 King St Suite 600 Alexandria VA 22314
Ph: 703-683-4300 ▪ Fx: 703-683-8965 ▪ TF: 800-300-6417

National Beer Wholesalers Association PAC
1101 King St Suite 600 Alexandria VA 22314
Ph: 703-683-4300 ▪ Fx: 703-683-8965

National Bench Rest Shooters Association   nbrsa.benchrest.com
2835 Guilford Ln Oklahoma City OK 73120
Ph: 405-842-9585 ▪ Fx: 405-842-9575

National Benevolent Association   www.nbacares.org
11780 Borman Dr Saint Louis MO 63146
Ph: 314-993-9000 ▪ Fx: 314-993-9018

National Beta Club   www.betaclub.org
151 Beta Club Way Spartanburg SC 29306
Ph: 864-583-4553 ▪ Fx: 864-542-9300 ▪ TF: 800-845-8281

National Beverage Packaging Association
200 Dangerfield Rd Alexandria VA 22314
Ph: 800-331-8816 ▪ Fx: 703-548-6563

National Bible Association   www.nationalbible.org
1865 Broadway New York NY 10023
Ph: 212-408-1390 ▪ Fx: 212-408-1448

National Bicycle Dealers Association   nbda.com
777 W 19th St Suite O Costa Mesa CA 92627
Ph: 949-722-6909 ▪ Fx: 949-722-1747

National Bicycle League   www.nbl.org
3958 Brown Park Dr Suite D Hilliard OH 43026
Ph: 614-777-1625 ▪ Fx: 614-777-1680 ▪ TF: 800-866-2691

National Biodiesel Board   www.biodiesel.org
3337-A Emerald Ln PO Box 104898 Jefferson City MO 65110
Ph: 800-841-5849 ▪ Fx: 573-635-7913

National Bison Association   www.bisoncentral.com
4100 W 122nd Ave Suite 106 Westminster CO 80234
Ph: 303-292-2833 ▪ Fx: 303-292-2564

National Black Catholic Congress   www.nbccongress.org
320 Cathedral St Baltimore MD 21201
Ph: 410-547-8496 ▪ Fx: 410-752-3958

National Black Caucus of Local Elected Officials   www.nbc-leo.org
1301 Pennsylvania Ave NW Suite 550 Washington DC 20004
Ph: 202-626-3000 ▪ Fx: 202-626-3043

National Black Caucus of State Legislators   www.nbcsl.com
444 N Capitol St NW Suite 622 Washington DC 20001
Ph: 202-624-5457 ▪ Fx: 202-508-3826

National Black Chamber of Commerce   www.nationalbcc.org
1350 Connecticut Ave NW Suite 825 Washington DC 20036
Ph: 202-466-6888 ▪ Fx: 202-466-4918

National Black Child Development Institute   www.nbcdi.org
1101 15th St NW Suite 900 Washington DC 20005
Ph: 202-833-2220 ▪ Fx: 202-833-8222

National Black Law Students Association   www.nblsa.org

National Black MBA Association   www.nbmbaa.org
180 N Michigan Ave Suite 1400 Chicago IL 60601
Ph: 312-236-2622 ▪ Fx: 312-236-4131

National Black McDonald's Operators Association   www.nbmoa.org
PO Box 8204 Los Angeles CA 90008
Ph: 323-296-5495 ▪ Fx: 323-296-6134

National Black Nurses Association
8630 Fenton St Suite 330 Silver Spring MD 20910
Ph: 301-589-3200 ▪ Fx: 301-589-3223

National Black Police Association   www.blackpolice.org
3251 Mt Pleasant St NW Washington DC 20010
Ph: 202-986-2070 ▪ Fx: 202-986-0410

National Black Public Relations Society   www.nbprs.org
6565 Sunset Blvd Suite 425 Hollywood CA 90028
Ph: 323-466-8221 ▪ Fx: 323-856-9510

National Black Sisters' Conference   nbsc68.tripod.com
101 Q St NE Washington DC 20002
Ph: 202-529-9250 ▪ Fx: 202-529-9370

National Black State Troopers Coalition Inc   www.nbstc.com
PO Box 70059 Nashville TN 37207
Ph: 877-996-2782

National Black United Federation of Charities
1212 New York Ave NW Suite 550 Washington DC 20005
Ph: 202-289-7888 ▪ Fx: 202-289-5950

National Black United Fund Inc   www.nbuf.org
40 Clinton St 5th Fl Newark NJ 07102
Ph: 973-643-5122 ▪ Fx: 973-648-8350 ▪ TF: 800-223-0866

National Blacksmiths & Weldors Association Inc   blacksmithing.tripod.com
PO Box 123 Arnold NE 69120
Ph: 308-848-2913

National Block & Bridle Club   www.blockandbridle.org
Colorado State Univ Dept of Dairy & Animal Science University Park PA 16802
Ph: 814-863-0734 ▪ Fx: 814-863-6042

National Blue Crab Industry Association   www.nfi.org
1901 N Fort Myer Dr Suite 700 Arlington VA 22209
Ph: 703-524-8883 ▪ Fx: 703-524-4619

National Board of Boiler & Pressure Vessel Inspectors   www.nationalboard.org
1055 Crupper Ave Columbus OH 43229
Ph: 614-888-8320 ▪ Fx: 614-847-1147

National Board for Certification in Occupational Therapy Inc   www.nbcot.org
800 S Frederick Ave Suite 200 Gaithersburg MD 20877
Ph: 301-990-7979 ▪ Fx: 301-869-8492

National Board of Certified Clinical Hypnotherapists   www.natboard.com
1110 Fiddler Ln Suite L-1 Silver Spring MD 20910
Ph: 301-608-0123 ▪ Fx: 301-588-9535 ▪ TF: 800-449-8144

National Board for Certified Counselors Inc   www.nbcc.org
3 Terrace Way Suite D Greensboro NC 27403
Ph: 336-547-0607 ▪ Fx: 336-547-0017 ▪ TF: 800-398-5389

National Board of Chiropractic Examiners   www.nbce.org
901 54th Ave Greeley CO 80634
Ph: 970-356-9100

National Board of Podiatric Medical Examiners   www.nbpme.info
PO Box 510 Bellefonte PA 16823
Ph: 814-357-0487 ▪ Fx: 814-357-0581

National Board for Professional Teaching Standards   www.nbpts.org
1525 Wilson Blvd Suite 500 Arlington VA 22209
Ph: 703-465-2700

National Board for Respiratory Care Inc   www.nbrc.org
8310 Nieman Rd Lenexa KS 66214
Ph: 913-599-4200 ▪ Fx: 913-541-0156

National Book Critics Circle   www.bookcritics.org

National Border Patrol Council   www.nbpc.net

National Bowhunter Education Foundation   www.nbef.org
101 1/2 N Front St Townsend MT 59644
Ph: 406-266-3236 ▪ Fx: 406-266-3239

National Bowling Association   www.tnbainc.org
377 Park Ave S 7th Fl New York NY 10016
Ph: 212-689-8308 ▪ Fx: 212-725-5063

National Brachial Plexus/Erb's Palsy Association Inc   www.nbpepa.org
PO Box 23 Larsen WI 54947
Ph: 920-836-2151

National Breast Cancer Coalition   www.stopbreastcancer.org
1707 L St NW Suite 1060 Washington DC 20036
Ph: 202-296-7477 ▪ Fx: 202-265-6854 ▪ TF: 800-622-2838

National Broadcast Association for Community Affairs
13502 Whittier Blvd Suite H Box 341 Whittier CA 90605
Ph: 562-698-6280 ▪ Fx: 562-698-9912

National Brotherhood of Skiers   www.nbs.org
1525 E 53rd St Suite 418 Chicago IL 60615
Ph: 773-955-4100

National Building Granite Quarries Association Inc   www.nbgqa.com
1220 L St NW Suite 100-167 Washington DC 20005
Ph: 800-557-2848

National Bulk Vendors Association   www.nbva.org
191 N Wacker Dr Suite 1800 Chicago IL 60606
Ph: 312-521-2400 ▪ Fx: 312-521-2300

National Bureau of Certified Consultants Inc   www.national-bureau.com
1850 5th Ave San Diego CA 92101
Ph: 619-239-7076 ▪ Fx: 619-296-3580 ▪ TF: 800-543-1114

National Burglar & Fire Alarm Association   www.alarm.org
8300 Colesville Rd Suite 750 Silver Spring MD 20910
Ph: 301-585-1855 ▪ Fx: 301-585-1866

National Burn Victim Foundation   www.nbvf.org
PO Box 409 Basking Ridge NJ 07920
Ph: 908-953-9091 ▪ Fx: 908-953-9099

National Bus Traffic Association   www.bustraffic.org
700 13th St NE Suite 575 Washington DC 20005
Ph: 202-898-2700 ▪ Fx: 202-842-0850

National Business Association   www.nationalbusiness.org
5151 Beltline Rd Suite 1150 Dallas TX 75240
Ph: 972-458-0900 ▪ Fx: 972-960-9149 ▪ TF: 800-456-0440

National Business Aviation Association   www.nbaa.org
1200 18th St NW Suite 400 Washington DC 20036
Ph: 202-783-9000 ▪ Fx: 202-331-8364

National Business Coalition on Health   www.nbch.org
1015 18th St NW Suite 730 Washington DC 20036
Ph: 202-775-9300 ▪ Fx: 202-775-1569

National Business Education Association   www.nbea.org
1914 Association Dr Reston VA 20191
Ph: 703-860-8300 ▪ Fx: 703-620-4483

National Business Incubation Association   www.nbia.org
20 E Circle Dr   Athens OH 45701
Ph: 740-593-4331 ▪ Fx: 740-593-1996

National Business Officers' Association   www.nboa.net
PO Box 4576   Boulder CO 80306
Ph: 720-564-0475 ▪ Fx: 720-564-4951

National Business Travel Association   www.nbta.org
110 N Royal St 4th Fl   Alexandria VA 22314
Ph: 703-684-0836 ▪ Fx: 703-684-0263

National Cable & Telecommunications Association   www.ncta.com
1724 Massachusetts Ave NW   Washington DC 20036
Ph: 202-775-3550 ▪ Fx: 202-775-1055

National Cable & Telecommunications Association PAC
1724 Massachusetts Ave NW   Washington DC 20036
Ph: 202-775-3550 ▪ Fx: 202-775-3675

National Cable Television Cooperative Inc   www.cabletvco-op.org
11200 Corporate Ave   Lenexa KS 66219
Ph: 913-599-5900 ▪ Fx: 913-599-5903

National Californian Rabbit Specialty Club   home.woh.rr.com/crsc
22162 S Hunter Rd   Colton OR 97017
Ph: 503-824-2138

National Camp Association   www.summercamp.org
610 5th Ave PO Box 5371   New York NY 10185
Ph: 845-354-5504 ▪ Fx: 845-354-5501 ▪ TF: 800-966-2267

National Campaign To Prevent Teen Pregnancy   www.teenpregnancy.org
1776 Massachusetts Ave NW Suite 200   Washington DC 20036
Ph: 202-478-8500 ▪ Fx: 202-478-8588

National Campaign for Radioactive Waste Safety   www.sric.org
105 Stanford SE PO Box 4524   Albuquerque NM 87106
Ph: 505-262-1862 ▪ Fx: 505-262-1864

National Campus Ministry Association   www.campusministry.net
2 Ocean Dune Cir   Palm Coast FL 32137
Ph: 386-446-8066

National Cancer Registrars Association   www.ncra-usa.org
1340 Braddock Pl Suite 203   Alexandria VA 22314
Ph: 703-299-6640 ▪ Fx: 703-299-6620

National Candle Association   www.candles.org
1156 15th St Suite 900   Washington DC 20005
Ph: 202-393-2210 ▪ Fx: 202-393-0336

National CAPACD   www.nationalcapacd.org
1001 Connecticut Ave NW Suite 730   Washington DC 20036
Ph: 202-223-2442 ▪ Fx: 202-223-4144

National Captive Nations Committee
PO Box 1171   Washington DC 20013
Ph: 202-547-0018 ▪ Fx: 202-543-5502

National Career Development Association   www.ncda.org
10820 E 45th St Suite 210   Tulsa OK 74146
Ph: 918-663-7060 ▪ Fx: 918-663-7058 ▪ TF: 866-367-6232

National Caregiving Foundation   www.caregivingfoundation.org
801 N Pitt St Suite 116   Alexandria VA 22314
Ph: 703-299-9300 ▪ Fx: 703-299-9304 ▪ TF: 800-930-1357

National Cargo Bureau Inc   www.natcargo.org
17 Battery Pl Suite 1232   New York NY 10004
Ph: 212-785-8300 ▪ Fx: 212-785-8333

National Cargo Security Council   www.cargosecurity.com
3 Church Cir Suite 292   Annapolis MD 21401
Ph: 410-956-0941 ▪ Fx: 410-956-0679 ▪ TF: 800-976-0403

National Catalog Managers Association   www.ncmacat.org
4600 East-West Hwy Suite 300   Bethesda MD 20814
Ph: 301-654-6664 ▪ Fx: 301-654-3299

National Cathedral Association   www.cathedral.org/cathedral
Washington National Cathedral 3101 Wisconsin Ave
NW   Washington DC 20016
Ph: 202-537-6243 ▪ Fx: 202-364-6600 ▪ TF: 800-622-6304

National Catholic AIDS Network   www.ncan.org
1400 W Devon Ave Suite 502   Chicago IL 60660
Ph: 773-508-7080 ▪ Fx: 773-508-7083

National Catholic Band Association   www.catholicbands.org
3334 N Normandy Ave   Chicago IL 60634
Ph: 773-282-9153

National Catholic Cemetery Conference   www.ntriplec.org
710 N River Rd   Des Plaines IL 60016
Ph: 847-824-8131 ▪ Fx: 847-824-9608

National Catholic Committee on Scouting   www.nccs-bsa.org
PO Box 152079   Irving TX 75015
Ph: 972-580-2114 ▪ Fx: 972-580-7870

National Catholic Council on Alcoholism & Related Drug   www.nccatoday.org
Problems Inc   PO Box 248   Lafayette IN 47902
Ph: 765-420-0129 ▪ Fx: 765-420-0189

National Catholic Development Conference   www.ncdcusa.org
80 Front St   Hempstead NY 11550
Ph: 516-481-6000 ▪ Fx: 516-489-9287 ▪ TF: 888-879-6232

National Catholic Educational Association   www.ncea.org
1077 30th St NW Suite 100   Washington DC 20007
Ph: 202-337-6232 ▪ Fx: 202-333-6706

National Catholic Office for the Deaf   www.ncod.org
7202 Buchanan St   Hyattsville MD 20784
Ph: 301-577-1684 ▪ Fx: 301-577-1690

National Catholic Partnership on Disability   www.ncpd.org
415 Michigan Ave NE Suite 240   Washington DC 20017
Ph: 202-529-2933 ▪ Fx: 202-529-4678

National Catholic Pharmacists Guild of the US
1012 Surrey Hills Dr   Saint Louis MO 63117
Ph: 314-645-0085

National Catholic Rural Life Conference   www.ncrlc.com
4625 Beaver Ave   Des Moines IA 50310
Ph: 515-270-2634 ▪ Fx: 515-270-9447

National Catholic Society of Foresters   www.ncsf.com
320 S School St   Mount Prospect IL 60056
Ph: 800-344-0273

National Cattlemen's Beef Association   www.beef.org
9110 E Nichols Ave Suite 300   Centennial CO 80112
Ph: 303-694-0305 ▪ Fx: 303-694-2851

National Cattlemen's Beef Association PAC   hill.beef.org
1301 Pennsylvania Ave NW Suite 300   Washington DC 20004
Ph: 202-347-0228 ▪ Fx: 202-638-0607

National Caucus & Center on Black Aged Inc   www.ncba-aged.org
1220 L St NW Suite 800   Washington DC 20005
Ph: 202-637-8400 ▪ Fx: 202-347-0895

National Caves Association   www.cavern.com
PO Box 280   Park City KY 42160
Ph: 270-749-2228 ▪ Fx: 270-749-2428 ▪ TF: 866-552-2837

National Center of Afro-American Artists   www.ncaaa.org
300 Walnut Ave   Boston MA 02119
Ph: 617-442-8614 ▪ Fx: 617-445-5525

National Center for American Indian Enterprise Development   www.ncaied.org
953 E Juanita Ave   Mesa AZ 85204
Ph: 480-545-1298 ▪ Fx: 480-545-4208

National Center for the American Revolution   www.valleyforgemuseum.org
435 Devon Park Dr Bldg 800   Wayne PA 19087
Ph: 610-975-4939 ▪ Fx: 610-917-3188

National Center for Appropriate Technology   www.ncat.org
PO Box 3838   Butte MT 59702
Ph: 406-494-4572 ▪ Fx: 406-494-2905 ▪ TF: 800-275-6228

National Center for Assault Prevention   www.ncap.org
606 Delsea Dr   Sewell NJ 08080
Ph: 856-582-7000 ▪ Fx: 856-582-3588 ▪ TF: 800-582-4206

National Center for Bicycling & Walking   www.bikewalk.org
1506 21st St NW Suite 200   Washington DC 20036
Ph: 202-463-6622 ▪ Fx: 202-463-6625

National Center for Charitable Statistics   nccsdataweb.urban.org
Urban Institute 2100 M St NW   Washington DC 20037
Ph: 202-833-7200 ▪ TF: 866-518-3874

National Center for Children in Poverty   cpmcnet.columbia.edu/dept/nccp
215 W 125th St 3rd Fl   New York NY 10027
Ph: 646-284-9600 ▪ Fx: 646-284-9623

National Center for Community Education   www.nccenet.org
1017 Avon St   Flint MI 48503
Ph: 810-238-0463 ▪ Fx: 810-238-9211 ▪ TF: 800-811-1105

National Center for Construction Education & Research   www.nccer.org
3600 NW 43rd St Bldg G PO Box 141104   Gainesville FL
32606
Ph: 352-334-0911 ▪ Fx: 352-334-0932

National Center for Disability Services   www.ncds.org
201 IU Willets Rd   Albertson NY 11507
Ph: 516-747-5400 ▪ Fx: 516-393-2668

National Center for Economic & Security Alternatives   www.ncesa.org
2000 P St NW Suite 330   Washington DC 20036
Ph: 202-986-1373 ▪ Fx: 202-986-7938

National Center on Education & the Economy   www.ncee.org
555 13th St NW Suite 500 W   Washington DC 20004
Ph: 202-783-3668 ▪ Fx: 202-783-3672

National Center for Education Information   www.ncei.org
1901 Pennsylvania Ave NW Suite 207   Washington DC 20006
Ph: 202-822-8280 ▪ Fx: 202-822-8284

National Center for Educational Accountability   www.nc4ea.org
4030-2 W Braker Ln   Austin TX 78759
Ph: 512-232-0770 ▪ Fx: 512-232-0777

National Center on Elder Abuse   www.elderabusecenter.org
1225 'I' St NW Suite 725   Washington DC 20005
Ph: 202-898-2586 ▪ Fx: 202-898-2583

National Center for Employee Ownership   www.nceo.org
1736 Franklin St 8th Fl   Oakland CA 94612
Ph: 510-208-1300 ▪ Fx: 510-272-9510

National Center for Environmental Health Strategies   www.ncehs.org
1100 Rural Ave   Voorhees NJ 08043
Ph: 856-429-5358

National Center for Fair & Open Testing   www.fairtest.org
342 Broadway   Cambridge MA 02139
Ph: 617-864-4810 ▪ Fx: 617-497-2224

National Center for Family Literacy   www.famlit.org
325 W Main St Suite 300   Louisville KY 40202
Ph: 502-584-1133 ▪ Fx: 502-584-0172 ▪ TF: 877-326-5481

National Center for Farmworker Health   www.ncfh.org
1770 FM 967   Buda TX 78610
Ph: 512-312-2700 ▪ Fx: 512-312-2600

National Center for Fathering   www.fathers.com
PO Box 413888   Kansas City MO 64141
Ph: 913-384-4661 ▪ Fx: 913-384-4665 ▪ TF: 800-593-3237

National Center for Film & Video Preservation
c/o American Film Institute 2021 N Western Ave   Los Angeles
CA 90027
Ph: 323-856-7708 ▪ Fx: 323-586-7616

National Center for Food Safety & Technology   www.iit.edu/~ncfs
6502 S Archer Rd   Summit IL 60501
Ph: 708-563-1576 ▪ Fx: 708-563-1873

National Center for Higher Education Management Systems   www.nchems.org
PO Box 9752   Boulder CO 80301
Ph: 303-497-0301 ▪ Fx: 303-497-0338

National Center for Home Equity Conversion   www.reverse.org/nchec.htm
360 N Robert St Suite 403   Saint Paul MN 55101
Ph: 651-222-6775 ▪ Fx: 651-222-6797 ▪ TF: 800-209-8085

National Center for Homeopathy   www.homeopathic.org
801 N Fairfax St Suite 306   Alexandria VA 22314
Ph: 703-548-7790 ▪ Fx: 703-548-7792 ▪ TF: 877-624-0613

National Center for Housing Management   www.nchm.org
1010 N Glebe Rd Suite 160   Arlington VA 22201
Ph: 703-516-4070 ▪ Fx: 703-516-4069 ▪ TF: 800-368-5625

National Center on Institutions & Alternatives   www.ncianet.org
7222 Ambassador Rd   Baltimore MD 21244
Ph: 410-265-1490

National Center for Jewish Film   www.jewishfilm.org
Brandeis Univ Lown 102 MS 053   Waltham MA 02454
Ph: 781-899-7044 ▪ Fx: 781-736-2070

National Center for Jewish Healing   www.jewishhealing.org
850 7th Ave Suite 1201   New York NY 10019
Ph: 212-399-2685 ▪ Fx: 212-399-2475

National Center for Juvenile Justice   www.ncjj.org
710 5th Ave 3rd Fl   Pittsburgh PA 15219
Ph: 412-227-6950 ▪ Fx: 412-227-6955 ▪ TF: 800-577-6903

National Center for Learning Disabilities   www.ncld.org
381 Park Ave S Suite 1401   New York NY 10016
Ph: 212-545-7510 ▪ Fx: 212-545-9665 ▪ TF: 888-575-7373

National Center for Lesbian Rights   www.nclrights.org
870 Market St Suite 570   San Francisco CA 94102
Ph: 415-392-6257 ▪ Fx: 415-392-8442

National Center for Mediation Education
1160 Spa Rd Suite 1B   Annapolis MD 21403
Ph: 410-974-8888 ▪ Fx: 410-295-9190 ▪ TF: 800-781-7500

National Center for Missing & Exploited Children   www.missingkids.com
699 Prince St   Alexandria VA 22314
Ph: 703-274-3900 ▪ Fx: 703-274-2095 ▪ TF: 800-843-5678

National Center for Neighborhood Enterprise   www.ncne.com
1424 16th St NW Suite 300   Washington DC 20036
Ph: 202-518-6500 ▪ Fx: 202-588-0314

National Center for Policy Analysis   www.ncpa.org
12655 N Central Expy Suite 720   Dallas TX 75243
Ph: 972-386-6272 ▪ Fx: 972-386-0924 ▪ TF: 800-859-1154

National Center on Poverty Law, Sargent Shriver   www.povertylaw.org
111 N Wabash Ave Suite 500   Chicago IL 60602
Ph: 312-263-3830 ▪ Fx: 312-263-3846 ▪ TF: 800-621-3256

National Center for Preservation Law
1333 Connecticut Ave NW Suite 300   Washington DC 20036
Ph: 202-338-0392 ▪ Fx: 202-775-9038

National Center for Prosecution of Child Abuse   www.ndaa-apri.org
99 Canal Ctr Plaza Suite 510   Alexandria VA 22314
Ph: 703-739-0321 ▪ Fx: 703-549-6259

National Center for Public Policy Research   www.nationalcenter.org
777 N Capitol St NE Suite 803   Washington DC 20002
Ph: 202-371-1400 ▪ Fx: 202-408-7773

National Center for Science Education   www.ncseweb.org
420 40th St Suite 2   Oakland CA 94609
Ph: 510-601-7203 ▪ Fx: 510-601-7204 ▪ TF: 800-290-6006

National Center for State Courts   www.ncsconline.org
300 Newport Ave   Williamsburg VA 23185
Ph: 757-253-2000 ▪ Fx: 757-564-2022 ▪ TF: 800-616-6164

National Center for the Study of   www.temple.edu/education/ncscpa/ncscpa.html
Corporal Punishment & Alternatives   Temple Univ 253 Ritter
     Annex   Philadelphia PA 19122
Ph: 215-204-6091 ▪ Fx: 215-204-6013

National Center for Stuttering   www.stuttering.com
200 E 33rd St   New York NY 10016
Ph: 212-532-1460 ▪ Fx: 212-683-1372 ▪ TF: 800-221-2483

National Center for Therapeutic Riding   www.nctrriding.org/about
PO Box 434   Burtonsville MD 20866
Ph: 301-421-0380 ▪ Fx: 301-421-0384

National Center for Tobacco-Free Kids   www.tobaccofreekids.org
1400 'I' St NW Suite 1200   Washington DC 20005
Ph: 202-296-5469 ▪ Fx: 202-296-5427 ▪ TF: 800-284-5437

National Center for Urban Ethnic Affairs
PO Box 20 Cardinal Stn   Washington DC 20064
Ph: 202-319-5129 ▪ Fx: 202-319-6289

National Center for Victims of Crime   www.ncvc.org
2000 M St NW Suite 480   Washington DC 20036
Ph: 202-467-8700 ▪ Fx: 202-467-8701 ▪ TF: 800-394-2255

National Center on Women & Aging   heller.brandeis.edu/national/ind.html
Brandeis University Heller Graduate School MS 035   Waltham
     MA 02454
Ph: 781-736-3866 ▪ Fx: 781-736-3865 ▪ TF: 800-929-1995

National Center for Youth Law   www.youthlaw.org
405 14th St Suite 1500   Oakland CA 94612
Ph: 510-835-8098 ▪ Fx: 510-835-8099

National Certification Commission   pages.zdnet.com/washdc/certification
PO Box 15282   Chevy Chase MD 20825
Ph: 301-847-0102 ▪ Fx: 301-847-0103

National Certification Council for Activity Professionals   www.nccap.org
PO Box 62589   Virginia Beach VA 23466
Ph: 757-552-0653 ▪ Fx: 757-552-0491

National Certified Pipe Welding Bureau   www.mcaa.org/ncpwb
1385 Piccard Dr   Rockville MD 20850
Ph: 301-869-5800 ▪ Fx: 301-990-9690

National Challenged Homeschoolers Associated Network   www.nathhan.com
PO Box 39   Porthill ID 83853
Ph: 208-267-6246

National Chamber Foundation   www.uschamber.com/ncf
1615 H St NW   Washington DC 20062
Ph: 202-463-5500 ▪ Fx: 202-463-3129 ▪ TF: 800-638-6582

National Chamber Litigation Center   www.uschamber.com/nclc
c/o US Chamber of Commerce 1615 H St NW   Washington DC
     20062
Ph: 202-659-6000

National Cheese Institute
1250 H St NW Suite 900   Washington DC 20005
Ph: 202-737-4332 ▪ Fx: 202-331-7820

National Chemical Credit Association   www.ncca1.org
1100 Main St   Buffalo NY 14209
Ph: 716-878-2894 ▪ Fx: 716-878-2866

National Cherry Growers & Industries Foundation   www.usacherries.com
PO Box 30285   Lansing MI 48909
Ph: 517-669-4264 ▪ Fx: 517-669-3354

National Chicken Council   www.eatchicken.com/about_sponsors
1015 15th St NW Suite 930   Washington DC 20005
Ph: 202-296-2622 ▪ Fx: 202-293-4005

National Chicken Council PAC
1015 15th St NW Suite 930   Washington DC 20005
Ph: 202-296-2622 ▪ Fx: 202-293-4005

National Chief Petty Officers' Association   www.members.tripod.com/NCPOA/main.html
106 Waring Welfare Rd   Boerne TX 78006
Ph: 830-537-4899

National Child Abuse Defense & Resource Center   www.falseallegation.org
PO Box 638   Holland OH 43528
Ph: 419-865-0513 ▪ Fx: 419-865-0526

National Child Abuse Hotline   www.childhelpusa.org
15757 N 78th St   Scottsdale AZ 85260
Ph: 480-922-8212 ▪ Fx: 480-922-7061 ▪ TF: 800-422-4453

National Child Care Association   www.nccanet.org
1016 Rosser St   Conyers GA 30012
Ph: 770-922-8198 ▪ Fx: 770-388-7772 ▪ TF: 800-543-7161

National Child Safety Council
PO Box 1368   Jackson MI 49204
Ph: 517-764-6070 ▪ Fx: 517-764-3068 ▪ TF: 800-222-1464

National Child Support Enforcement Association   www.ncsea.org
444 N Capitol St NW Suite 414   Washington DC 20001
Ph: 202-624-8180 ▪ Fx: 202-624-8828

National Children's Advocacy Center   www.nationalcac.org
210 Pratt Ave   Huntsville AL 35801
Ph: 256-533-5437 ▪ Fx: 256-534-6883

National Children's Cancer Society   www.children-cancer.org
1015 Locust St Suite 600   Saint Louis MO 63101
Ph: 314-241-1600 ▪ Fx: 314-241-6949 ▪ TF: 800-532-6459

National Children's Eye Care Foundation   www.mentalhealth.about.com
PO Box 795069   Dallas TX 75379
Ph: 972-407-0404 ▪ Fx: 972-407-0616

National Chimney Sweep Guild   www.ncsg.org
2155 Commercial Dr   Plainfield IN 46168
Ph: 317-837-1500 ▪ Fx: 317-837-5365

National Chincoteague Pony Association   www.pony-chincoteague.com
2595 Jensen Rd   Bellingham WA 98226
Ph: 360-671-8338 ▪ Fx: 360-671-7603

National Christ Child Society Inc   www.nationalchristchildsoc.org
5105 Wisconsin Ave NW Suite 304   Washington DC 20016
Ph: 202-363-9516 ▪ Fx: 202-966-2880 ▪ TF: 800-814-2149

National Christian Choir   nationalchristianchoir.org
983-A Russell Ave   Gaithersburg MD 20879
Ph: 301-670-6331 ▪ Fx: 301-330-7299 ▪ TF: 800-599-4710

National Christian College Athletic Association   www.thenccaa.org
302 W Washington St   Greenville SC 29601
Ph: 864-250-1199 ▪ Fx: 864-250-1141

National Christian Leadership Conference for Israel   www.nclci.org
43422 W Oaks Dr Suite 300   Novi MI 48377
Ph: 248-557-4540 ▪ Fx: 248-557-4527

National Christian Life Community of the USA   www.clc-usa.org
3691 Lindell Blvd   Saint Louis MO 63108
Ph: 314-977-7370

National Christmas Tree Association   www.realchristmastrees.org
1000 Executive Pkwy Suite 220   Saint Louis MO 63141
Ph: 314-205-0944 ▪ Fx: 314-576-7989

National Chronic Care Consortium   www.nccconline.org
801 Pennsylvania Ave Suite 245   Washington DC 20004
Ph: 202-624-1516

National Chronic Pain Outreach Association   www.chronicpain.org
PO Box 274   Millboro VA 24460
Ph: 540-862-9437 ▪ Fx: 540-862-9485

National Chrysanthemum Society   www.mums.org
10107 Homar Pond Dr   Fairfax Station VA 22039
Ph: 703-978-7981

National Church Goods Association   www.ncgaweb.com
800 Roosevelt Rd Bldg C Suite 20   Glen Ellyn IL 60137
Ph: 630-942-6599 ▪ Fx: 630-790-3095

National Circus Project
56 Lion Ln   Westbury NY 11590
Ph: 516-334-2123 ▪ Fx: 516-334-2249

National Citizens' Coalition for Nursing Home Reform   www.nursinghomeaction.org
1424 16th St NW Suite 202   Washington DC 20036
Ph: 202-332-2275 ▪ Fx: 202-332-2949

National Civic League   www.ncl.org
1445 Market St Suite 300   Denver CO 80202
Ph: 303-571-4343 ▪ Fx: 303-571-4404

National Classification Management Society   www.classmgmt.com
994 Old Eagle School Rd Suite 1019   Wayne PA 19087
Ph: 610-971-4856 ▪ Fx: 610-971-4859

National Clay Pipe Institute   www.ncpi.org
PO Box 759   Lake Geneva WI 53147
Ph: 262-248-9094

National Cleaners Association   www.nca-i.com
252 W 29th St 2nd Fl   New York NY 10001
Ph: 212-967-3002 ▪ Fx: 212-967-2240

National Clearinghouse for Commuter Programs   www.cacs.umd.edu/NCCP
Univ of Maryland 1120 Stamp Student Union   College Park MD
     20742
Ph: 301-314-5274 ▪ Fx: 301-314-9874

National Clearinghouse for English Language Acquisition &   www.ncela.gwu.edu
Language Instruction Educational Programs   George
     Washington Univ 2121 K St NW Suite 260   Washington
     DC 20037
Ph: 202-467-0867 ▪ Fx: 800-531-9347 ▪ TF: 800-321-6223

National Clearinghouse on Marital & Date Rape   www.ncmdr.org
2325 Oak St   Berkeley CA 94708
Ph: 510-524-1582

National Club Association
1201 15th St NW Suite 450   Washington DC 20005
Ph: 202-822-9822 ▪ Fx: 202-822-9808 ▪ TF: 800-625-6221
www.natlclub.org

National Coalition of 100 Black Women
38 W 32nd St Suite 1610   New York NY 10001
Ph: 212-947-2196 ▪ Fx: 212-947-2477
www.ncbw.org

National Coalition to Abolish Corporal Punishment in Schools   155 W Main St Suite 1603   Columbus OH 43215
Ph: 614-221-8829 ▪ Fx: 614-221-2110
www.stophitting.com/disatschool

National Coalition to Abolish the Death Penalty
920 Pennsylvania Ave SE   Washington DC 20003
Ph: 202-543-9577 ▪ Fx: 202-543-7798 ▪ TF: 888-286-2237
www.ncadp.org

National Coalition of Abortion Providers
908 King St Suite 400W   Alexandria VA 22314
Ph: 703-684-0055 ▪ Fx: 703-684-5051
www.ncap.com

National Coalition for Adult Immunization
4733 Bethesda Ave Suite 750   Bethesda MD 20814
Ph: 301-656-0003 ▪ Fx: 301-907-0878
www.nfid.org/ncai

National Coalition for Advanced Manufacturing
2000 L St NW Suite 807   Washington DC 20036
Ph: 202-429-2220 ▪ Fx: 202-429-2422 ▪ TF: 800-622-3260
www.nacfam.org

National Coalition of Advocates for Students
100 Boylston St Suite 808   Boston MA 02116
Ph: 617-357-8507 ▪ Fx: 617-357-9549
www.ncasboston.org

National Coalition Against Censorship
275 7th Ave 9th Fl   New York NY 10001
Ph: 212-807-6222 ▪ Fx: 212-807-6245
www.ncac.org

National Coalition Against Domestic Violence
1201 E Colfax Ave Suite 385   Denver CO 80218
Ph: 303-839-1852 ▪ Fx: 303-831-9251 ▪ TF: 800-799-7233
www.ncadv.org

National Coalition of Alternative Community Schools
1289 Jewett   Ann Arbor MI 48104
Ph: 734-668-9171 ▪ TF: 888-771-9171
www.ncacs.org

National Coalition for Asian Pacific American Community Development   1001 Connecticut Ave NW Suite 730   Washington DC 20036
Ph: 202-223-2442 ▪ Fx: 202-223-4144
www.nationalcapacd.org

National Coalition on Black Civic Participation Inc
1025 Vermont Ave NW Suite 1010   Washington DC 20005
Ph: 202-659-4929 ▪ Fx: 202-659-5025
www.bigvote.org

National Coalition of Black Meeting Planners
8630 Fenton St Suite 126   Silver Spring MD 20910
Ph: 202-628-3952 ▪ Fx: 301-588-0011
www.ncbmp.com

National Coalition of Blacks for Reparations in America
PO Box 90604   Washington DC 20090
Ph: 202-291-8400 ▪ Fx: 202-291-4600
www.ncobra.com

National Coalition for Campus Children's Centers
Univ of Northern Iowa 119 Schindler Education Ctr   Cedar Falls IA 50614
Ph: 319-273-3113 ▪ Fx: 319-273-3109 ▪ TF: 800-813-8207
www.campuschildren.org

National Coalition for Cancer Survivorship
1010 Wayne Ave Suite 770   Silver Spring MD 20910
Ph: 301-650-9127 ▪ Fx: 301-565-9670
www.canceradvocacy.org

National Coalition of Education Activists
1420 Walnut St Suite 720   Philadelphia PA 19102
Ph: 215-735-2418
www.nceaonline.org

National Coalition of Free Men
PO Box 129   Manhasset NY 11030
Ph: 516-482-6378 ▪ TF: 888-223-1280
www.ncfm.org

National Coalition of Girls' Schools
57 Main St   Concord MA 01742
Ph: 978-287-4485 ▪ Fx: 978-287-6014
www.ncgs.org

National Coalition for Haitian Rights
275 7th Ave 17th Fl   New York NY 10001
Ph: 212-337-0005 ▪ Fx: 212-741-8749
www.nchr.org

National Coalition on Health Care
1200 G St NW Suite 750   Washington DC 20005
Ph: 202-638-7151
www.nchc.org

National Coalition for History
400 A St SE   Washington DC 20003
Ph: 202-544-2422 ▪ Fx: 202-544-8307
www.h-net.org/~nch

National Coalition for the Homeless
1012 14th St NW Suite 600   Washington DC 20005
Ph: 202-737-6444 ▪ Fx: 202-737-6445
www.nationalhomeless.org

National Coalition for Homeless Veterans
333 1/2 Pennsylvania Ave SE   Washington DC 20003
Ph: 202-546-1969 ▪ Fx: 202-546-2063 ▪ TF: 800-838-4357
www.nchv.org

National Coalition of Independent Scholars
PO Box 5743   Berkeley CA 94705
Ph: 510-540-8415
www.ncis.org

National Coalition for Literacy
50 E Huron   Chicago IL 60611
Ph: 800-228-8813

National Coalition for Marine Conservation
3 N King St   Leesburg VA 20176
Ph: 703-777-0037 ▪ Fx: 703-777-1107
www.savethefish.org

National Coalition for the Protection of Children & Families
800 Compton Rd Suite 9224   Cincinnati OH 45231
Ph: 513-521-6227 ▪ Fx: 513-521-6337
www.eos.net/ncpcf

National Coalition for Students with Disabilities
1413 K St NW 9th Fl   Washington DC 20005
Ph: 202-347-8772 ▪ Fx: 202-393-5886
www.ncsd.org

National Coalition for Women & Girls in Education
c/o National Women's Law Ctr 11 Dupont Cir NW Suite 800   Washington DC 20036
Ph: 202-785-7730 ▪ Fx: 202-588-5185
www.ncwge.org

National Coffee Association of USA Inc
15 Maiden Ln Suite 1405   New York NY 10038
Ph: 212-766-4007 ▪ Fx: 212-766-5815
www.ncausa.org

National Coil Coating Association
1300 Sumner Ave   Cleveland OH 44115
Ph: 216-241-7333 ▪ Fx: 216-241-0105
www.coilcoating.org

National College of District Attorneys
Univ of South Carolina Plaza 937 Assembly St   Columbia SC 29208
Ph: 803-544-5005 ▪ Fx: 803-544-5301
www.law.sc.edu/ncda/

National Collegiate Athletic Association
700 W Washington St PO Box 6222   Indianapolis IN 46206
Ph: 317-917-6222 ▪ Fx: 317-917-6888
www.ncaa.org

National Collegiate Roller Hockey Association
www.ncrha.org

National Collegiate Wrestling Association
11411 N Central Expy Suite 100W   Dallas TX 75243
Ph: 214-378-8700 ▪ Fx: 214-378-9900
www.ncwa.net

National Commission for Cooperative Education
360 Huntington Ave 384 CP   Boston MA 02115
Ph: 617-373-3770 ▪ Fx: 617-373-3463
www.co-op.edu

National Commission on Correctional Health Care
1300 W Belmont Ave   Chicago IL 60657
Ph: 773-880-1460 ▪ Fx: 773-880-2424
www.ncchc.org

National Committee for Amish Religious Freedom
30650 6 Mile Rd   Livonia MI 48152
Ph: 734-427-1414 ▪ Fx: 734-427-1419
www.holycrosslivonia.org/amish

National Committee of Catholic Laymen
215 Lexington Ave 4th Fl   New York NY 10016
Ph: 212-685-6666 ▪ Fx: 212-725-9793

National Committee for an Effective Congress
122 C St NW Suite 650   Washington DC 20001
Ph: 202-639-8300 ▪ Fx: 202-639-5038
www.ncec.org

National Committee for Employer Support of the Guard & Reserve
1555 Wilson Blvd Suite 200   Arlington VA 22209
Ph: 703-696-1386 ▪ Fx: 703-696-1411 ▪ TF: 800-336-4590
www.esgr.org

National Committee for Labor Israel
275 7th Ave   New York NY 10001
Ph: 212-647-0300 ▪ Fx: 212-647-0308
www.laborisrael.org

National Committee on Planned Giving
233 McCrea St Suite 400   Indianapolis IN 46225
Ph: 317-269-6274 ▪ Fx: 317-269-6276
www.ncpg.org

National Committee to Preserve Social Security & Medicare
10 G St NE Suite 600   Washington DC 20002
Ph: 202-216-0420 ▪ Fx: 202-216-0451 ▪ TF: 800-966-1935
www.ncpssm.org

National Committee for the Prevention of Alcoholism & Drug Dependency
12501 Old Columbia Pike   Silver Spring MD 20904
Ph: 301-680-6733 ▪ Fx: 301-680-6707

National Committee for the Prevention of Elder Abuse
1612 K St NW Suite 400   Washington DC 20006
Ph: 202-682-4140 ▪ Fx: 202-682-3984
www.preventelderabuse.org

National Committee for Quality Assurance
2000 L St NW Suite 500   Washington DC 20036
Ph: 202-955-3500 ▪ Fx: 202-955-3599 ▪ TF: 800-236-5903
www.ncqa.org

National Committee for Quality Health Care
1701 K St NW Suite 205   Washington DC 20006
Ph: 202-331-7535 ▪ Fx: 202-331-7532
www.ncqhc.org

National Committee for Responsive Philanthropy
2001 'S' St NW Suite 620   Washington DC 20009
Ph: 202-387-9177 ▪ Fx: 202-332-5084
www.ncrp.org

National Committee on Uniform Traffic Laws & Ordinances
107 S West St Suite 110   Alexandria VA 22314
Ph: 540-465-4701 ▪ Fx: 540-465-5383 ▪ TF: 800-807-5290
www.ncutlo.org

National Committee on US-China Relations
71 W 23rd St Suite 1901   New York NY 10010
Ph: 212-645-9677 ▪ Fx: 212-645-1695
www.ncuscr.org

National Committees on Potbellied Pigs
www.ncopp.com

National Communication Association
1765 'N' St NW   Washington DC 20036
Ph: 202-464-4622 ▪ Fx: 202-464-4600
www.natcom.org

National Community Action Foundation
810 1st St NE Suite 530   Washington DC 20002
Ph: 202-842-2092 ▪ Fx: 202-842-2095
www.ncaf.org

National Community Capital Association
620 Chestnut St Suite 572   Philadelphia PA 19106
Ph: 215-923-4754 ▪ Fx: 215-923-4755
www.communitycapital.org

National Community Development Association
522 21st St NW Suite 120   Washington DC 20006
Ph: 202-293-7587 ▪ Fx: 202-887-5546
www.ncdaonline.org

National Community Education Association
3929 Old Lee Hwy Suite 91-A   Fairfax VA 22030
Ph: 703-359-8973 ▪ Fx: 703-359-0972
www.ncea.com

National Community Pharmacists Association
205 Daingerfield Rd   Alexandria VA 22314
Ph: 703-683-8200 ▪ Fx: 703-683-3619 ▪ TF: 800-544-7447
www.ncpanet.org

National Community Reinvestment Coalition
733 15th St NW Suite 540   Washington DC 20005
Ph: 202-628-8866 ▪ Fx: 202-628-9800
www.ncrc.org

National Concrete Burial Vault Association
900 Fox Valley Dr Suite 204   Longwood FL 32779
Ph: 407-788-1996 ▪ Fx: 407-774-6751 ▪ TF: 800-538-1423
ncbva.org

National Concrete Masonry Association
13750 Sunrise Valley Dr   Herndon VA 20171
Ph: 703-713-1900 ▪ Fx: 703-713-1910
www.ncma.org

National Confectioners Association PAC
8320 Old Courthouse Rd Suite 300   Vienna VA 22182
Ph: 703-790-5750 ▪ Fx: 703-790-5752 ▪ TF: 800-433-1200

National Confectioners Association of the US
8320 Old Courthouse Rd Suite 300   Vienna VA 22182
Ph: 703-790-5750 ▪ Fx: 703-790-5752 ▪ TF: 800-433-1200
www.candyusa.org

National Confectionery Sales Association
10225 Berea Rd Suite B   Cleveland OH 44102
Ph: 216-631-8200 ▪ Fx: 216-631-8210
www.candyhalloffame.com

National Conference of Appellate Court Clerks ncacc.ncsconline.org
300 Newport Ave   Williamsburg VA 23185
Ph: 757-259-1841 ▦ Fx: 757-259-1520

National Conference of Bankruptcy Judges www.ncbj.org
235 Secret Cove Dr   Lexington SC 29072
Ph: 803-957-6225

National Conference of Bar Examiners www.ncbex.org
402 W Wilson St   Madison WI 53703
Ph: 608-280-8550 ▦ Fx: 608-280-8552

National Conference of Bar Foundations www.ncbf.org
541 N Fairbanks Ct Suite 1400   Chicago IL 60611
Ph: 312-988-5343 ▦ Fx: 312-988-5492

National Conference of Bar Presidents www.ncbp.org
541 N Fairbanks Ct Suite 1400   Chicago IL 60611
Ph: 312-988-5345 ▦ Fx: 312-988-5492

National Conference of Black Lawyers www.ncbl.org
PO Box 80043   Lansing MI 48908
Ph: 866-266-5091

National Conference of Black Mayors www.blackmayors.org
1151 Cleveland Ave Suite D   East Point GA 30344
Ph: 404-765-6444 ▦ Fx: 404-765-6430

National Conference of Black Political Scientists www.poli.ncat.edu/ncobps
3695-F Cascade Rd SW Suite 212   Atlanta GA 30331
Ph: 404-880-8240

National Conference for Catechetical Leadership www.nccl.org
3021 4th St NE   Washington DC 20017
Ph: 202-636-3826 ▦ Fx: 202-832-2712

National Conference on Citizenship www.ncoc.net
1300 19th St NW Suite 800   Washington DC 20036
Ph: 202-778-0448

National Conference of Commissioners on Uniform State Laws www.nccusl.org
211 E Ontario St Suite 1300   Chicago IL 60611
Ph: 312-915-0195 ▦ Fx: 312-915-0187

National Conference for Community & Justice www.nccj.org
475 Park Ave S 19th Fl   New York NY 10016
Ph: 212-545-1300 ▦ Fx: 212-545-8053

National Conference of CPA Practitioners www.nccpap.org
50 Jericho Tpke Suite 106   Jericho NY 11753
Ph: 516-333-8282 ▦ Fx: 516-333-4099 ▦ TF: 888-488-5400

National Conference of Diocesan Vocation Directors www.ncdvd.org
PO Box 1570   Little River SC 29566
Ph: 843-280-7191 ▦ Fx: 843-280-0681

National Conference of Editorial Writers www.ncew.org
3899 N Front St   Harrisburg PA 17110
Ph: 717-703-3015 ▦ Fx: 717-703-3014

National Conference of Federal Trial Judges www.abanet.org/jd/ncftjweb.html
541 N Fairbanks Ct   Chicago IL 60611
Ph: 312-988-5689 ▦ Fx: 312-988-5709

National Conference of Firemen & Oilers www.ncfo.org
1023 15th St NW 10th Fl   Washington DC 20005
Ph: 202-962-0981 ▦ Fx: 202-872-1222

National Conference of Insurance Legislators www.ncoil.org
139 Lancaster St   Albany NY 12210
Ph: 518-449-3210 ▦ Fx: 518-432-5651

National Conference on Interstate Milk Shipments www.ncims.org
123 Buena Vista Dr   Frankfort KY 40601
Ph: 502-695-0253

National Conference of Local Environmental Health depts.washington.edu/clehaweb
Administrators   Univ of Washington Dept of Environmental
Health CB 357234   Seattle WA 98195
Ph: 206-616-2097 ▦ Fx: 206-616-8123

National Conference on Ministry to the Armed Forces www.ncmaf.org
4141 N Henderson Rd Suite 13   Arlington VA 22203
Ph: 703-276-7905 ▦ Fx: 703-276-7906

National Conference on Peacemaking & Conflict Resolution www.apeacemaker.net
3070 Bristol Pike Bldg 1 Suite 116   Bensalem PA 19020
Ph: 215-245-6993 ▦ Fx: 215-245-6994 ▦ TF: 877-397-3223

National Conference on Public Employee Retirement Systems www.ncpers.org
444 N Capitol St NW Suite 221   Washington DC 20001
Ph: 202-624-1456 ▦ Fx: 202-624-1439 ▦ TF: 877-202-5706

National Conference on Research in Language & Literacy www.coe.uga.edu/ncrll
Colorado State Univ English Dept 359 Eddy Bldg   Fort Collins
CO 80523
Ph: 970-491-5161 ▦ Fx: 970-491-5601

National Conference of Shomrim Societies
45 E 33rd St Rm 601   New York NY 10016
Ph: 212-689-2015 ▦ Fx: 212-447-1633

National Conference of Specialized Court Judges www.abanet.org/jd/ncscj
541 N Fairbanks Ct MS 13.2   Chicago IL 60611
Ph: 312-988-5705 ▦ Fx: 312-988-5709

National Conference of State Fleet Administrators ncsfa.state.ut.us
PO Box 159   Litchfield Park AZ 85340
Ph: 623-772-9096 ▦ Fx: 623-772-9098

National Conference of State Historic Preservation Officers www.ncshpo.org
444 N Capitol St NW Hall of States Suite 342   Washington DC
20001
Ph: 202-624-5465 ▦ Fx: 202-624-5419

National Conference of State Legislatures www.ncsl.org
7700 E 1st Pl   Denver CO 80230
Ph: 303-364-7700 ▦ Fx: 303-364-7800

National Conference of State Liquor Administrators www.ncsla.org
8325 Horseshoe Dr   Lincoln NE 68516
Ph: 402-486-1774

National Conference of States on Building Codes & Standards www.ncsbcs.org
505 Huntmar Park Dr Suite 210   Herndon VA 20170
Ph: 703-437-0100 ▦ Fx: 703-481-3596

National Conference of Synagogue Youth www.ou.org/ncsy
11 Broadway   New York NY 10004
Ph: 212-613-8232 ▦ Fx: 212-613-0633

National Conference on Weights & Measures www.ncwm.net
15245 Shady Grove Rd Suite 130   Rockville MD 20850
Ph: 240-632-9454 ▦ Fx: 301-990-9771

National Conference of Women's Bar Associations www.ncwba.org
PO Box 82366   Portland OR 97282
Ph: 503-775-4396 ▦ Fx: 503-657-3932

National Conference of Yeshiva Principals
160 Broadway   New York NY 10038
Ph: 212-227-1000 ▦ Fx: 212-406-6934

National Conferences on Undergraduate Research www.ncur.org
Univ of Minnesota Duluth 10 University Dr 140 Engineering
Bldg   Duluth MN 55812
Ph: 218-726-7807 ▦ Fx: 218-726-6360

National Congress of American Indians www.ncai.org
1301 Connecticut Ave NW Suite 200   Washington DC 20036
Ph: 202-466-7767 ▦ Fx: 202-466-7797

National Congress of Black Women Inc www.npcbw.org
8484 Georgia Ave Suite 420   Silver Spring MD 20910
Ph: 301-562-8000 ▦ Fx: 301-562-8303 ▦ TF: 877-274-1198

National Congress for Community Economic Development www.ncced.org
1030 15th St NW Suite 325   Washington DC 20005
Ph: 202-289-9020 ▦ Fx: 202-289-7051 ▦ TF: 877-446-2233

National Congress for Fathers & Children www.ncfc.net
9454 Wilshire Blvd Suite 907   Beverly Hills CA 90212
Ph: 310-247-6051 ▦ TF: 800-733-3237

National Congress of Neighborhood Women
249 Manhattan Ave   Brooklyn NY 11211
Ph: 718-388-8915 ▦ Fx: 718-388-0285

National Congress of Parents & Teachers www.pta.org
330 N Wabash Ave Suite 2100   Chicago IL 60611
Ph: 312-670-6782 ▦ Fx: 312-670-6783 ▦ TF: 800-307-4782

National Congress of State Games www.stategames.org
290 Roberts St   East Hartford CT 06108
Ph: 860-528-4588 ▦ Fx: 860-291-8032

National Consumer Law Center www.consumerlaw.org
77 Summer St 10th Fl   Boston MA 02110
Ph: 617-542-8010 ▦ Fx: 617-542-8028

National Consumers League www.natlconsumersleague.org
1701 K St NW Suite 1200   Washington DC 20006
Ph: 202-835-3323 ▦ Fx: 202-835-0747 ▦ TF: 800-876-7060

National Contact Lens Examiners www.abo-ncle.org
6506 Loisdale Rd Suite 209   Springfield VA 22150
Ph: 703-719-5800 ▦ Fx: 703-719-9144 ▦ TF: 800-296-1379

National Contract Management Association www.ncmahq.org
8260 Greensboro Dr Suite 200   McLean VA 22102
Ph: 571-382-0082 ▦ Fx: 703-448-0939 ▦ TF: 800-344-8096

National Cooperative Business Association www.ncba.org
1401 New York Ave NW Suite 1100   Washington DC 20005
Ph: 202-638-6222 ▦ Fx: 202-638-1374

National Corn Growers Association www.ncga.com
632 Cepi Dr   Chesterfield MO 63005
Ph: 636-733-9004 ▦ Fx: 636-733-9005

National Corporate Theatre Fund www.nctf.org
1 E 53rd St 3rd Fl   New York NY 10022
Ph: 212-750-6895 ▦ Fx: 212-750-6977

National Corrugated Steel Pipe Association www.ncspa.org
13140 Coit Rd Suite 320 LB 120   Dallas TX 75240
Ph: 972-850-9107 ▦ Fx: 972-490-4219

National Corvette Restorers Society www.ncrs.org
6291 Day Rd   Cincinnati OH 45252
Ph: 513-385-8526 ▦ Fx: 513-385-8554

National Cosmetology Association www.behindthechair.com/ncacares
401 N Michigan Ave Suite 2200   Chicago IL 60611
Ph: 312-644-6610 ▦ Fx: 312-464-6118

National Costumers Association www.costumers.org
6914 Upper Trail Cir   Mesa AZ 85207
Ph: 800-622-1321 ▦ Fx: 480-654-6223

National Cotton Batting Institute www.natbat.com
1918 N Parkway PO Box 820287   Memphis TN 38182
Ph: 901-274-9030 ▦ Fx: 901-725-0510

National Cotton Council of America www.cotton.org
1918 North Pkwy   Memphis TN 38112
Ph: 901-274-9030 ▦ Fx: 901-725-0510 ▦ TF: 800-377-9030

National Cotton Ginners' Association
PO Box 820285   Memphis TN 38182
Ph: 901-274-9030 ▦ Fx: 901-725-0510

National Cottonseed Products Association www.cottonseed.com
104 Timber Creek Dr Suite 200   Cordova TN 38108
Ph: 901-682-0800 ▦ Fx: 901-682-2856

National Council for Accreditation of Teacher Education www.ncate.org
2010 Massachusetts Ave NW Suite 500   Washington DC 20036
Ph: 202-466-7496 ▦ Fx: 202-296-6620

National Council of Acoustical Consultants www.ncac.com
66 Morris Ave Suite 1A   Springfield NJ 07081
Ph: 973-564-5859 ▦ Fx: 973-564-7480

National Council for Adoption www.adoptioncouncil.org
225 N Washington St   Alexandria VA 22314
Ph: 703-299-6633 ▦ Fx: 703-299-6004

National Council on the Aging www.ncoa.org
300 D St SW Suite 801   Washington DC 20024
Ph: 202-479-1200 ▦ Fx: 202-479-0735 ▦ TF: 800-424-9046

National Council for Agricultural Education www.teamaged.org/councilindex.cfm
1410 King St Suite 400   Alexandria VA 22314
Ph: 703-838-5881 ▦ Fx: 703-838-5888 ▦ TF: 800-772-0939

National Council of Agricultural Employers www.ncaeonline.org
1112 16th St NW Suite 920   Washington DC 20036
Ph: 202-728-0300 ▦ Fx: 202-728-0303

National Council on Agricultural Life & Labor Research Fund Inc www.ncall.org
20 E Division St PO Box 1092   Dover DE 19903
Ph: 302-678-9400 ▦ Fx: 302-678-9058

National Council for Air & Stream Improvement Inc
PO Box 13318   Research Triangle Park NC 27709
Ph: 919-941-6400 ▪ Fx: 919-941-6401
www.ncasi.org

National Council on Alcoholism & Drug Dependence
20 Exchange Pl Suite 2902   New York NY 10005
Ph: 212-269-7797 ▪ Fx: 212-269-7510 ▪ TF: 800-622-2255
www.ncadd.org

National Council on Architectural Registration Boards
1801 K St NW Suite 1100   Washington DC 20006
Ph: 202-783-6500 ▪ Fx: 202-783-0290
www.ncarb.org

National Council of Arts Administrators
Univ of Kentucky College of Fine Arts   Lexington KY 40506
Ph: 606-257-1707

National Council on Bible Curriculum In Public Schools
PO Box 9743   Greensboro NC 27429
Ph: 336-272-3799
www.bibleinschools.net

National Council of Black Engineers & Scientists
1525 Aviation Blvd Suite C424   Redondo Beach CA 90278
Ph: 213-896-9779
www.ncbes.org

National Council of Catholic Women
200 N Glebe Rd Suite 703   Arlington VA 22203
Ph: 703-224-0990 ▪ Fx: 703-224-0991 ▪ TF: 800-506-9407
www.nccw.org

National Council of Chain Restaurants
325 7th St NW Suite 1100   Washington DC 20004
Ph: 202-626-8183 ▪ Fx: 202-626-8185
www.nccr.net

National Council on Child Abuse & Family Violence
1025 Connecticut Ave NW Suite 1012   Washington DC 20036
Ph: 202-429-6695
www.nccafv.org

National Council of the Churches of Christ in the USA
475 Riverside Dr 8th Fl   New York NY 10115
Ph: 212-870-2227 ▪ Fx: 212-870-2030
www.ncccusa.org

National Council of Coal Lessors
300 Summers St Suite 1050   Charleston WV 25301
Ph: 304-346-0569 ▪ Fx: 304-346-6516

National Council for Community Behavioral Healthcare
12300 Twinbrook Pkwy Suite 320   Rockville MD 20852
Ph: 301-984-6200 ▪ Fx: 301-881-7159
www.nccbh.org

National Council for Continuing Education & Training
PO Box 130623   Carlsbad CA 92013
Ph: 760-753-8375 ▪ Fx: 760-942-7296
www.nccet.org

National Council of County Association Executives
440 1st St NW 8th Fl   Washington DC 20001
Ph: 202-942-4291 ▪ Fx: 202-942-4203

National Council on Crime & Delinquency
1970 Broadway Suite 500   Oakland CA 94612
Ph: 510-208-0500 ▪ Fx: 510-208-0511
www.nccd-crc.org

National Council on Economic Education
1140 6th Ave 2nd Fl   New York NY 10036
Ph: 212-730-7007 ▪ Fx: 212-730-1793 ▪ TF: 800-338-1192
www.ncee.net

National Council on Education for the Ceramic Arts
77 Erie Village Sq Suite 280   Erie CO 80516
Ph: 303-828-2811 ▪ Fx: 303-828-0911 ▪ TF: 866-266-2322
www.nceca.net

National Council of Erectors Fabricators & Riggers
10382 Main St Suite 200 PO Box 280   Fairfax VA 22030
Ph: 703-591-1870 ▪ Fx: 703-591-1895

National Council for Eurasian & East European Research
910 17th St NW Suite 300   Washington DC 20006
Ph: 202-822-6950 ▪ Fx: 202-822-6955
www.nceeer.org

National Council of Examiners for Engineering & Surveying
280 Seneca Creek Rd   Clemson SC 29633
Ph: 864-654-6824 ▪ Fx: 864-654-6033 ▪ TF: 800-250-3196
www.ncees.org

National Council of Exchangors
PO Box 668   Morro Bay CA 93443
Ph: 800-324-1031 ▪ Fx: 866-332-3004
www.infoville.com/nce

National Council on Family Relations
3989 Central Ave NE Suite 550   Minneapolis MN 55421
Ph: 763-781-9331 ▪ Fx: 763-781-9348 ▪ TF: 888-781-9331
www.ncfr.com

National Council of Farmer Cooperatives
50 F St NW Suite 900   Washington DC 20001
Ph: 202-626-8700 ▪ Fx: 202-626-8722
www.ncfc.org

National Council on Gene Resources
1738 Thousand Oaks Blvd   Berkeley CA 94707
Ph: 510-524-8973 ▪ Fx: 510-526-3092

National Council for Geocosmic Research Inc
8810-C Jamacha Blvd PMB 183   Spring Valley CA 91977
Ph: 619-303-9236
www.geocosmic.org

National Council for Geographic Education
Jacksonville State Univ 206A Martin Hall   Jacksonville AL 36265
Ph: 256-782-5293 ▪ Fx: 256-782-5336
www.ncge.org

National Council of Higher Education Loan Programs
1100 Connecticut Ave NW 12th Fl   Washington DC 20036
Ph: 202-822-2106 ▪ Fx: 202-822-2142
www.nchelp.org

National Council for History Education
26915 Westwood Rd Suite B2   Westlake OH 44145
Ph: 440-835-1776 ▪ Fx: 440-835-1295
www.history.org/nche

National Council on Independent Living
1916 Wilson Blvd Suite 209   Arlington VA 22201
Ph: 703-525-3406 ▪ Fx: 703-525-3409
www.ncil.org

National Council of Intellectual Property Law Associations
1255 23rd St NW Suite 200   Washington DC 20037
Ph: 202-466-2396 ▪ Fx: 202-466-2893
www.ipo.org

National Council for Interior Design Qualification
1200 18th St NW Suite 1001   Washington DC 20036
Ph: 202-721-0220 ▪ Fx: 202-721-0221
www.ncidq.org

National Council on International Trade Development
818 Connecticut Ave NW 12th Fl   Washington DC 20006
Ph: 202-872-9280 ▪ Fx: 202-872-8324
www.ncitd.org

National Council for International Visitors
1420 K St NW Suite 800   Washington DC 20005
Ph: 202-842-1414 ▪ Fx: 202-289-4625 ▪ TF: 800-523-8101
www.nciv.org

National Council of Investigation & Security Services
7501 Sparrows Pointe Blvd   Baltimore MD 21219
Ph: 800-445-8408 ▪ Fx: 410-388-9746
www.nciss.org

National Council of Jewish Women
53 W 23rd St 6th Fl   New York NY 10010
Ph: 212-645-4048 ▪ Fx: 212-645-7466 ▪ TF: 800-829-6259
www.ncjw.org

National Council of Juvenile & Family Court Judges
Univ of Nevada PO Box 8970   Reno NV 89507
Ph: 775-784-6012 ▪ Fx: 775-784-6628
www.ncjfcj.org

National Council of La Raza
1111 19th St NW Suite 1000   Washington DC 20036
Ph: 202-785-1670 ▪ Fx: 202-776-1792 ▪ TF: 800-311-6257
www.nclr.org

National Council for Languages & International Studies
4646 40th St NW Suite 310   Washington DC 20016
Ph: 202-966-8477 ▪ Fx: 202-966-8210
www.languagepolicy.org

National Council of Legislators from Gaming States
139 Lancaster St   Albany NY 12210
Ph: 518-449-4699 ▪ Fx: 518-432-5651

National Council of Less Commonly Taught Languages
Univ of Wisconsin National Foreign Language Ctr 4231 Humanities Bldg 455 N Park St   Madison WI 53706
Ph: 608-265-7905 ▪ Fx: 608-265-7904
www.councilnet.org

National Council for Marketing & Public Relations
PO Box 336039   Greeley CO 80633
Ph: 970-330-0771 ▪ Fx: 970-330-0769
www.ncmpr.org

National Council on Measurement in Education
1230 17th St NW   Washington DC 20036
Ph: 202-223-9318 ▪ Fx: 202-775-1824
www.ncme.org

National Council of Music Importers & Exporters
PO Box 5488   Long Island City NY 11105
Ph: 718-274-3210 ▪ Fx: 718-274-3214

National Council of Negro Women Inc
633 Pennsylvania Ave NW   Washington DC 20004
Ph: 202-737-0120 ▪ Fx: 202-737-0476
www.ncnw.org

National Council of Nonprofit Associations
1030 15th St NW Suite 870   Washington DC 20005
Ph: 202-962-0322 ▪ Fx: 202-962-0321
www.ncna.org

National Council of Postal Credit Unions
PO Box 160   Del Mar CA 92014
Ph: 858-792-3883 ▪ Fx: 858-792-3884
www.ncpcu.org

National Council for Prescription Drug Programs
9240 E Raintree Dr   Scottsdale AZ 85260
Ph: 480-477-1000 ▪ Fx: 480-767-1042
www.ncpdp.org

National Council on Private Forests
5400 Grosvenor Ln   Bethesda MD 20814
Ph: 301-897-8720 ▪ Fx: 301-897-3690
www.ncpf.org

National Council on Problem Gambling Inc
208 G St NE 1st Fl   Washington DC 20002
Ph: 202-547-9204 ▪ Fx: 202-547-9206 ▪ TF: 800-522-4700
www.ncpgambling.org

National Council on Public History
425 University Blvd   Indianapolis IN 46202
Ph: 317-274-2716 ▪ Fx: 317-278-5230
ncph.org

National Council on Public Polls
150 River St   Hackensack NJ 07601
Ph: 201-646-4379 ▪ Fx: 201-646-4772
www.ncpp.org

National Council for Public-Private Partnerships
1660 L St NW Suite 510   Washington DC 20036
Ph: 202-467-6800 ▪ Fx: 202-467-6312
www.ncppp.org

National Council on Qualifications for the Lighting Professions
526 King St Suite 405   Alexandria VA 22314
Ph: 703-518-4370 ▪ Fx: 703-706-9583
www.ncqlp.org

National Council on Radiation Protection & Measurements
7910 Woodmont Ave Suite 400   Bethesda MD 20814
Ph: 301-657-2652 ▪ Fx: 301-907-8768 ▪ TF: 800-229-2652
www.ncrp.com

National Council of Real Estate Investment Fiduciaries
2 Prudential Plaza 180 N Stetson Ave Suite 2515   Chicago IL 60601
Ph: 312-819-5890 ▪ Fx: 312-819-5891
www.ncreif.org

National Council on Rehabilitation Education
CSU Fresno School of Education & Human Development 5005 N Maple Ave MS 3 Fresno CA 93740
Ph: 559-278-0325 ▪ Fx: 559-278-0098
www.rehabeducators.org

National Council for Research & Planning
www.nmsu.edu/~NCRP

National Council of Self-Insurers
1253 Springfield Ave PMB 345   New Providence NJ 07974
Ph: 908-665-2152 ▪ Fx: 908-665-4020
www.natcouncil.com

National Council of Social Security Management Associations
22 Sussex St   Hackensack NJ 07601
Ph: 201-489-3515 ▪ Fx: 201-487-2254
www.ncssma.org/

National Council for the Social Studies
8555 16th St Suite 500   Silver Spring MD 20910
Ph: 301-588-1800 ▪ Fx: 301-588-2049 ▪ TF: 800-296-7840
www.ncss.org

National Council of State Agencies for the Blind
PO Box 25380   Washington DC 20027
Ph: 202-298-8468 ▪ Fx: 202-333-5881
www.ncsab.org

National Council of State Boards of Nursing
111 E Wacker Dr Suite 2900   Chicago IL 60601
Ph: 312-525-3600 ▪ Fx: 312-279-1032
www.ncsbn.org

National Council of State Directors of Community Colleges
1 Dupont Cir NW Suite 410   Washington DC 20036
Ph: 202-728-0200 ▪ Fx: 202-833-2467
www.statedirectors.org

National Council of State Education Associations
1201 16th St NW Suite 817   Washington DC 20036
Ph: 202-822-7745 ▪ Fx: 202-822-7113

National Council of State Emergency Medical Services Training Coordinators   201 Park Washington Ct   Falls Church VA 22046
Ph: 703-538-1794 ▪ Fx: 703-241-5603
www.ncsemstc.org

National Council of State Housing Agencies   www.ncsha.org
444 N Capitol St NW Suite 438   Washington DC 20001
Ph: 202-624-7710 ▪ Fx: 202-624-5899

National Council of State Pharmacy Association Executives   www.ncspae.org
c/o Virginia Pharmacists Assn 5501 Patterson Ave Suite
200   Richmond VA 23226
Ph: 804-285-4145 ▪ Fx: 804-285-4227

National Council of State Supervisors of Foreign Languages   www.ncssfl.org

National Council of State Tourism Directors   www.tia.org/councils/ncstd.asp
1100 New York Ave NW Suite 450   Washington DC 20005
Ph: 202-408-8422 ▪ Fx: 202-408-1255

National Council of Structural Engineers Associations   dwp.bigplanet.com/engineers
203 N Wabash Ave Suite 2010   Chicago IL 60601
Ph: 312-372-8035 ▪ Fx: 312-372-5673

National Council on Student Development   www.nationalcouncilstudentdevelopment.org
Univ of Illinois 51 Gerty Dr Rm 129   Champaign IL 61820
Ph: 217-333-9230 ▪ Fx: 217-244-0851

National Council of Supervisors of Mathematics   www.ncsmonline.org
PO Box 10667   Golden CO 80401
Ph: 303-274-5932

National Council on Teacher Retirement   www.nctr.org
7600 Greenhaven Dr Suite 302   Sacramento CA 95831
Ph: 916-394-2075 ▪ Fx: 916-392-0295

National Council of Teachers of English   www.ncte.org
1111 W Kenyon Rd   Urbana IL 61801
Ph: 217-328-3870 ▪ Fx: 217-328-0977 ▪ TF: 800-369-6283

National Council of Teachers of Mathematics   www.nctm.org
1906 Association Dr   Reston VA 20191
Ph: 703-620-9840 ▪ Fx: 703-476-2970 ▪ TF: 800-235-7566

National Council for Therapeutic Recreation Certification Inc   www.nctrc.org
7 Elmwood Dr   New City NY 10956
Ph: 845-639-1439 ▪ Fx: 845-639-1471

National Council for the Traditional Arts   www.NCTA.net
1320 Fenwick Ln Suite 200   Silver Spring MD 20910
Ph: 301-565-0654 ▪ Fx: 301-565-0472

National Council for Uniform Interest Compensation   www.ncuic.org
13665 Dulles Technology Dr Suite 300   Herndon VA 20171
Ph: 703-561-1100 ▪ Fx: 703-787-0996

National Council of University Research Administrators   www.ncura.edu
1 Dupont Cir NW Suite 220   Washington DC 20036
Ph: 202-466-3894 ▪ Fx: 202-223-5573

National Council of Urban Education Associations   www.nea.org/ncuea
1201 16th St NW Suite 410   Washington DC 20036
Ph: 202-822-7376 ▪ Fx: 202-822-7624

National Council on US-Arab Relations   www.ncusar.org
1140 Connecticut Ave NW Suite 1210   Washington DC 20036
Ph: 202-293-0801 ▪ Fx: 202-293-0903

National Council of Women of the US Inc   www.ncw-usa.org
777 UN Plaza   New York NY 10017
Ph: 212-697-1278 ▪ Fx: 212-972-0164

National Council of Women's Organizations   www.womensorganizations.org
733 15th St NW Suite 1011   Washington DC 20005
Ph: 202-393-7122 ▪ Fx: 202-387-7915

National Council for Workforce Education   www.ncwe.org
PO Box 3188   Dublin OH 43016
Ph: 614-659-0196 ▪ Fx: 614-336-8596

National Council of Young Israel   www.youngisrael.org
3 W 16th St   New York NY 10011
Ph: 212-929-1525 ▪ Fx: 212-727-9526

National Council of Youth Sports   www.ncys.org
7185 SE Seagate Ln   Stuart FL 34997
Ph: 772-781-1452 ▪ Fx: 772-781-7298

National Court Appointed Special Advocate Association   www.nationalcasa.org
100 W Harrison St North Tower Suite 500   Seattle WA 98119
Ph: 206-270-0072 ▪ Fx: 206-270-0078 ▪ TF: 800-628-3233

National Court Reporters Association   www.ncraonline.org
8224 Old Courthouse Rd   Vienna VA 22182
Ph: 703-556-6272 ▪ Fx: 703-556-6291 ▪ TF: 800-272-6272

National Court Reporters Association PAC
8224 Old Courthouse Rd   Vienna VA 22182
Ph: 703-556-6272 ▪ Fx: 703-556-6291 ▪ TF: 800-272-6272

National CPA Health Care Advisors Association   www.hcaa.com
1 Valmont Plaza 4th Fl   Omaha NE 68154
Ph: 402-964-3865 ▪ Fx: 402-964-3811 ▪ TF: 888-475-4476

National Craft Association   www.craftassoc.com
2012 Ridge Rd E Suite 120   Rochester NY 14622
Ph: 585-266-5472 ▪ Fx: 585-785-3231 ▪ TF: 800-715-9594

National Credentialing Agency for Laboratory Personnel Inc   www.nca-info.org
PO Box 15945-289   Lenexa KS 66285
Ph: 913-438-5110 ▪ Fx: 913-599-5340

National Credit Reporting Association   www.ncrainc.org
125 E Lake St Suite 200   Bloomingdale IL 60108
Ph: 630-539-1525 ▪ Fx: 630-539-1526

National Credit Union Management Association
4989 Rebel Trail NW   Atlanta GA 30327
Ph: 404-255-6828 ▪ Fx: 404-851-1752

National Crime Prevention Council   www.ncpc.org
1000 Connecticut Ave NW 13th Fl   Washington DC 20036
Ph: 202-466-6272 ▪ Fx: 202-296-1356

National Criminal Justice Association   www.ncja.org
720 7th St NW 3rd Fl   Washington DC 20001
Ph: 202-628-8550 ▪ Fx: 202-628-0080

National Cristina Foundation   www.cristina.org
500 W Putnam Ave   Greenwich CT 06830
Ph: 203-863-9100 ▪ Fx: 203-863-9230

National Crop Insurance Services   www.ag-risk.org
7201 W 129th St Suite 200   Overland Park KS 66213
Ph: 913-685-2767 ▪ Fx: 913-685-3080 ▪ TF: 800-951-6247

National Crossbowmen of the US Inc   www.usarchery.org/divisions/crossbow/xbow.htm
3731 SW 144th Ave   Miramar FL 33027
Ph: 954-704-0770 ▪ Fx: 954-704-9566

National Cued Speech Association   www.cuedspeech.org
23970 Hermitage Rd   Cleveland OH 44122
Ph: 216-292-6213 ▪ TF: 800-459-3529

National Cursillo Movement   www.natl-cursillo.org
PO Box 210226   Dallas TX 75211
Ph: 214-339-6321 ▪ Fx: 214-339-6322

National Customs Brokers & Forwarders Association of America Inc   www.ncbfaa.org
1200 18th St NW Suite 901   Washington DC 20036
Ph: 202-466-0222 ▪ Fx: 202-466-0226

National Cutting Horse Association   www.nchacutting.com
260 Bailey Ave   Fort Worth TX 76107
Ph: 817-244-6188 ▪ Fx: 817-244-2015

National Dairy Council   www.nationaldairycouncil.org
10255 W Higgins Rd Suite 900   Rosemont IL 60018
Ph: 847-803-2000 ▪ Fx: 847-803-2077

National Dairy Herd Improvement Association Inc   www.dhia.org
3021 E Dublin Granville Rd Suite 102   Columbus OH 43231
Ph: 614-890-3630 ▪ Fx: 614-890-3667

National Dairy Shrine   dairyshrine.org
1224 Alton Darby Creek Rd   Columbus OH 43228
Ph: 614-878-5333 ▪ Fx: 614-870-2622

National Dance Association   www.aahperd.org/nda
1900 Association Dr   Reston VA 20191
Ph: 703-476-3421 ▪ Fx: 703-476-9527 ▪ TF: 800-213-7193

National Dance Education Association   www.ndea.org
4948 St Elmo Ave Suite 301   Bethesda MD 20814
Ph: 301-657-2880 ▪ Fx: 301-657-2882

National Dance Institute   www.nationaldance.org/
594 Broadway Rm 805   New York NY 10012
Ph: 212-226-0083 ▪ Fx: 212-226-0761 ▪ TF: 877-634-4255

National Dart Association   www.ndadarts.com
5613 W 74th St   Indianapolis IN 46278
Ph: 317-387-1299 ▪ Fx: 317-387-0999 ▪ TF: 800-808-9884

National Deaf Education Center   clerccenter.gallaudet.edu
800 Florida Ave NE   Washington DC 20002
Ph: 202-651-5051 ▪ Fx: 202-651-5054

National Defender Investigator Association   www.ndia.net
2600 Dixwell Ave Suite 7   Hamden CT 06514
Ph: 203-281-6342 ▪ Fx: 203-248-8932

National Defense Council Foundation   www.ndcf.org
1220 King St Suite 1   Alexandria VA 22314
Ph: 703-836-3443 ▪ Fx: 703-836-5402

National Defense Industrial Association   www.ndia.org
2111 Wilson Blvd Suite 400   Arlington VA 22201
Ph: 703-522-1820 ▪ Fx: 703-522-1885

National Defense Transportation Association   www.ndtahq.org
50 S Pickett St Suite 220   Alexandria VA 22304
Ph: 703-751-5011 ▪ Fx: 703-823-8761

National Defined Contribution Council   www.ndcconline.org
9101 E Kenyon Ave Suite 3000   Denver CO 80237
Ph: 303-770-5353 ▪ Fx: 303-770-1812

National Democratic Club   www.natdemclub.org
30 Ivy St SE   Washington DC 20003
Ph: 202-543-2035 ▪ Fx: 202-479-4273

National Dental Assistants Association   www.ndaonline.org
3517 16th St NW   Washington DC 20010
Ph: 202-588-1697 ▪ Fx: 202-588-1244

National Dental Association   www.ndaonline.org
3517 16th St NW   Washington DC 20010
Ph: 202-588-1697 ▪ Fx: 202-588-1244

National Dental Hygienists' Association   www.ndaonline.org
3517 16th St NW   Washington DC 20010
Ph: 202-588-1697 ▪ Fx: 202-588-1244

National Denturist Association   www.nationaldenturist.com
PO Box 308   Towanda PA 18848
Ph: 570-265-0238 ▪ Fx: 570-265-0239 ▪ TF: 888-599-7958

National Derby Rallies Inc   www.ndr.org
6644 Switzer St   Shawnee KS 66203
Ph: 913-962-0706

National Development Council   www.ndc-online.org
51 E 42nd St Suite 300   New York NY 10017
Ph: 212-682-1106 ▪ Fx: 212-573-6118

National Disability Sports Alliance   www.ndsaonline.org
25 W Independence Way   Kingston RI 02881
Ph: 401-792-7130 ▪ Fx: 401-792-7132

National Disaster Search Dog Foundation   www.ndsdf.org
206 N Signal St Suite R   Ojai CA 93023
Ph: 805-646-1015 ▪ Fx: 805-640-1848

National Dissemination Center for Children with Disabilities   www.nichcy.org
PO Box 1492   Washington DC 20013
Ph: 202-884-8200 ▪ Fx: 202-884-8441 ▪ TF: 800-695-0285

National District Attorneys Association   www.ndaa.org
99 Canal Center Plaza Suite 510   Alexandria VA 22314
Ph: 703-549-9222 ▪ Fx: 703-836-3195

National Dog Groomers Association of America Inc   www.nationaldoggroomers.com
PO Box 101   Clark PA 16113
Ph: 724-962-2711 ▪ Fx: 724-962-1919

National Dog Registry   www.natldogregistry.com
PO Box 116   Woodstock NY 12498
Ph: 845-679-2355 ▪ TF: 800-637-3647

National Domestic Violence Hotline   www.ndvh.org
PO Box 161810   Austin TX 78716
Ph: 800-799-7233

National Down Syndrome Congress   www.ndsccenter.org
1370 Center Dr Suite 102   Atlanta GA 30338
Ph: 770-604-9500 ▪ Fx: 770-604-9898 ▪ TF: 800-232-6372

National Down Syndrome Society — www.ndss.org
666 Broadway 8th Fl   New York NY 10012
Ph: 212-460-9330 ▪ Fx: 212-979-2873 ▪ TF: 800-221-4602

National Drilling Association — www.nda4u.com
10901D Roosevelt Blvd N Suite 100   Saint Petersburg FL
33716
Ph: 727-577-5006 ▪ Fx: 727-577-5012

National Dropout Prevention Center — www.dropoutprevention.org
Clemson Univ 209 Martin St   Clemson SC 29631
Ph: 864-656-2599 ▪ Fx: 864-656-0136

National Dry Bean Council
8233 Old Courthouse Rd Suite 210   Vienna VA 22182
Ph: 703-556-9305 ▪ Fx: 703-556-9301

National Duckpin Bowling Congress — ndbc.org
4991 Fairview Ave   Linthicum Heights MD 21090
Ph: 410-636-2695 ▪ Fx: 410-636-3256

National Eagle Scout Association — www.scouting.org/nesa
1325 W Walnut Hill Ln PO Box 152079   Irving TX 75015
Ph: 972-580-2000 ▪ Fx: 972-580-2399

National Earth Science Teachers Association — www.nestanet.org

National Eating Disorders Association — www.nationaleatingdisorders.org
603 Stewart St Suite 803   Seattle WA 98101
Ph: 206-382-3587 ▪ Fx: 206-829-8501 ▪ TF: 800-931-2237

National Economic Development & Law Center — www.nedlc.org
2201 Broadway Suite 815   Oakland CA 94612
Ph: 510-251-2600 ▪ Fx: 510-251-0600

National Economists Club — www.national-economists.org
PO Box 19281   Washington DC 20036
Ph: 703-739-9042 ▪ Fx: 703-739-9405

National Education for Assistance Dog Services — www.neads.org
PO Box 213   West Boylston MA 01583
Ph: 978-422-9064 ▪ Fx: 978-422-3255

National Education Association — www.nea.org
1201 16th St NW   Washington DC 20036
Ph: 202-833-4000 ▪ Fx: 202-822-7974

National Education Knowledge Industry Association — www.nekia.org
1718 Connecticut Ave NW Suite 700   Washington DC 20009
Ph: 202-518-0847 ▪ Fx: 202-785-3849

National Electrical Contractors Association — www.necanet.org
3 Bethesda Metro Ctr Suite 1100   Bethesda MD 20814
Ph: 301-657-3110 ▪ Fx: 301-215-4500

National Electrical Manufacturers Association — www.nema.org
1300 N 17th St Suite 1847   Rosslyn VA 22209
Ph: 703-841-3200 ▪ Fx: 703-841-5900

National Electrical Manufacturers Representatives Association — www.nemra.org
660 White Plains Rd   Tarrytown NY 10591
Ph: 914-524-8650 ▪ Fx: 914-524-8655

National Electronic Distributors Association — www.nedassoc.org
1111 Alderman Dr Suite 400   Alpharetta GA 30005
Ph: 678-393-9990 ▪ Fx: 678-393-9998 ▪ TF: 800-347-6332

National Electronics Manufacturers Initiative — www.nemi.org
2214 Rock Hill Rd Suite 110   Herndon VA 20170
Ph: 703-834-0330 ▪ Fx: 703-834-2735

National Electronics Service Dealers Association — www.nesda.com
3608 Pershing Ave   Fort Worth TX 76107
Ph: 817-921-9061 ▪ Fx: 817-921-3741

National Elevator Industry Inc — www.neii.org
1677 County Rd 64 PO Box 838   Salem NY 12865
Ph: 518-854-3100 ▪ Fx: 518-854-3257

National Emergency Equipment Dealers Association — www.needa.org
8421 Frost Way   Annandale VA 22003
Ph: 703-280-4622 ▪ Fx: 703-280-0942

National Emergency Management Association — www.nemaweb.org
PO Box 11910   Lexington KY 40578
Ph: 859-244-8000 ▪ Fx: 859-244-8239

National Emergency Number Association — www.nena9-1-1.org
4350 N Fairfax Dr Suite 750   Arlington VA 22203
Ph: 703-812-4600 ▪ Fx: 703-812-4675 ▪ TF: 800-332-3911

National Employment Counseling Association — www.employmentcounseling.org
5999 Stevenson Ave   Alexandria VA 22304
Ph: 703-823-0252 ▪ Fx: 800-473-2329 ▪ TF: 800-347-6647

National Employment Counseling Association — www.employmentcounseling.org
c/o American Counseling Assn 5999 Stevenson Ave   Alexandria
VA 22304
Ph: 703-823-9800 ▪ Fx: 703-461-9260 ▪ TF: 800-347-6647

National Employment Law Project — www.nelp.org
55 John St 7th Fl   New York NY 10038
Ph: 212-285-3025 ▪ Fx: 212-285-3044

National Employment Lawyers Association — www.nela.org
44 Montgomery St Suite 2080   San Francisco CA 94104
Ph: 415-296-7629 ▪ Fx: 415-677-9445

National EMS Pilots Association — www.nemspa.org
526 King St Suite 415   Alexandria VA 22314
Ph: 703-836-8930 ▪ Fx: 703-836-8920

National Endangered Species Act Reform Coalition — www.nesarc.org
1050 Thomas Jefferson St 7th Fl   Washington DC 20007
Ph: 202-333-7481 ▪ Fx: 202-338-2416

National Endowment for Democracy — www.ned.org
1101 15th St NW Suite 700   Washington DC 20005
Ph: 202-293-9072 ▪ Fx: 202-223-6042

National Energy Assistance Directors' Association — www.neada.org
1615 M St NW Suite 800   Washington DC 20036
Ph: 202-237-5199 ▪ Fx: 202-237-7316

National Energy Foundation — www.nef1.org
3676 California Ave Suite A117   Salt Lake City UT 84104
Ph: 801-908-5800 ▪ Fx: 801-908-5400

National Energy Management Institute — www.nemionline.org
601 N Fairfax St Suite 250   Alexandria VA 22314
Ph: 703-739-7100 ▪ Fx: 703-683-7615 ▪ TF: 800-458-6525

National Energy Services Association — www.nesanet.org
6430 FM 1960 W Suite 213   Houston TX 77069
Ph: 713-856-6525 ▪ Fx: 713-856-6199

National Engine Parts Manufacturers Association
4012 E Harbor Rd Suite 141   Port Clinton OH 43452
Ph: 419-734-2501

National Enthronement Center — communications.sscc.org/enthronement
PO Box 111   Fairhaven MA 02719
Ph: 508-999-2680 ▪ Fx: 508-993-8233

National Environmental Balancing Bureau — www.nebb.org
8575 Grovemont Cir   Gaithersburg MD 20877
Ph: 301-977-3698 ▪ Fx: 301-977-9589

National Environmental Education & Training Foundation — www.neetf.org
1707 H St NW Suite 900   Washington DC 20006
Ph: 202-833-2933 ▪ Fx: 202-261-6464

National Environmental Health Association — www.neha.org
720 S Colorado Blvd Suite 970S   Denver CO 80246
Ph: 303-756-9090 ▪ Fx: 303-691-9490

National Environmental Training Association — www.ehs-training.org
5320 N 16th St Suite 114   Phoenix AZ 85016
Ph: 602-956-6099 ▪ Fx: 602-956-6399

National Environmental Trust — www.net.org
1200 18th St NW 5th Fl   Washington DC 20036
Ph: 202-887-8800 ▪ Fx: 202-887-8877

National Episcopal AIDS Coalition — www.neac.org
520 Clinton Ave   Brooklyn NY 11238
Ph: 718-857-9445 ▪ Fx: 718-638-3039 ▪ TF: 800-588-6628

National Exchange Club — www.nationalexchangeclub.com
3050 W Central Ave   Toledo OH 43606
Ph: 419-535-3232 ▪ Fx: 419-535-1989 ▪ TF: 800-924-2643

National Executive Service Corps — www.nesc.org
120 Wall St 16th Fl   New York NY 10005
Ph: 212-269-1234 ▪ Fx: 212-269-0959

National Extension Association of Family & Consumer Sciences — www.neafcs.org
PO Box 239   Great Falls VA 22066
Ph: 703-759-1040 ▪ Fx: 703-759-4801 ▪ TF: 800-808-9133

National Families in Action — www.nationalfamilies.org
2957 Clairmont Rd NE Suite 50   Atlanta GA 30329
Ph: 404-248-9676 ▪ Fx: 404-248-1312

National Family Association — www.familyassociation.org

National Family Caregivers Association — www.nfcacares.org
10400 Connecticut Ave Suite 500   Kensington MD 20895
Ph: 301-942-6430 ▪ Fx: 301-942-2302 ▪ TF: 800-896-3650

National Family Farm Coalition — www.nffc.net
110 Maryland Ave NE Suite 307   Washington DC 20002
Ph: 202-543-5675 ▪ Fx: 202-543-0978 ▪ TF: 800-639-3276

National Family Planning & Reproductive Health Association — www.nfprha.org
1627 K St NW 12th Fl   Washington DC 20006
Ph: 202-293-3114 ▪ Fx: 202-293-1990

National Farm-City Council — www.farmcity.org
225 Touhy Ave   Park Ridge IL 60068
Ph: 847-685-8764 ▪ Fx: 847-685-8969

National Farm Worker Ministry — www.nfwm.org
438 N Skinker Blvd   Saint Louis MO 63130
Ph: 314-726-6470 ▪ Fx: 314-726-6427

National Farmers Organization — www.nfo.org
528 Billy Sunday Rd Suite 100   Ames IA 50010
Ph: 515-292-2000 ▪ Fx: 515-292-7106 ▪ TF: 800-247-2110

National Farmers Union — www.nfu.org
11900 E Cornell Ave   Aurora CO 80014
Ph: 303-337-5500 ▪ Fx: 303-368-1390 ▪ TF: 800-347-1961

National Fashion Accessories Association Inc — www.accessoryweb.com
350 5th Ave Suite 2030   New York NY 10118
Ph: 212-947-3424 ▪ Fx: 212-629-0361

National Fastener Distributors Association — www.nfda-fastener.org
1717 E 9th St Suite 1185   Cleveland OH 44114
Ph: 216-579-1571 ▪ Fx: 216-579-1531

National Federation of Abstracting & Information Services — www.nfais.org
1518 Walnut St Suite 307   Philadelphia PA 19102
Ph: 215-893-1561 ▪ Fx: 215-893-1564

National Federation of American Hungarians — hungarianfed-usa.org
717 2nd St NE   Washington DC 20002
Ph: 202-204-5348 ▪ Fx: 202-544-2819

National Federation of the Blind — www.nfb.org
1800 Johnson St   Baltimore MD 21230
Ph: 410-659-9314 ▪ Fx: 410-685-5653

National Federation for Catholic Youth Ministry — www.nfcym.org
415 Michigan Ave NE Suite 40   Washington DC 20017
Ph: 202-636-3825 ▪ Fx: 202-526-7544

National Federation of Community Broadcasters — www.nfcb.org
970 Broadway Suite 1000   Oakland CA 94612
Ph: 510-451-8200 ▪ Fx: 510-451-8208

National Federation of Community Development Credit Unions — www.natfed.org
120 Wall St 10th Fl   New York NY 10005
Ph: 212-809-1850 ▪ Fx: 212-809-3274 ▪ TF: 800-437-8711

National Federation of Democratic Women — www.nfdw.org
19432 Burlington Dr   Detroit MI 48203
Ph: 313-892-6199 ▪ Fx: 313-892-8424

National Federation of Federal Employees — www.nffe.org
1016 16th St NW Suite 300   Washington DC 20036
Ph: 202-862-4400 ▪ Fx: 202-862-4432

National Federation of Filipino American Associations — www.naffaa.org
1444 'N' St NW   Washington DC 20005
Ph: 202-986-9330 ▪ Fx: 202-478-5109

National Federation of Flemish Giant Rabbit Breeders — www.nffgrb.com
2259 Barbara Dr   Camarillo CA 93012
Ph: 805-491-2029

National Federation of the Grand Order of Pachyderm Clubs — www.pachyderms.org
511 Central Ave PO Box 1602   Great Falls MT 59403
Ph: 888-467-2249 ▪ Fx: 406-771-3941

National Federation of Independent Business www.nfib.com
1201 F St NW Suite 200   Washington DC 20004
Ph: 202-554-9000 ▪ Fx: 202-554-0496 ▪ TF: 800-552-6342

National Federation of Independent Business SAFE Trust
1201 F St NW Suite 200   Washington DC 20004
Ph: 202-554-9000 ▪ Fx: 202-554-0496 ▪ TF: 800-552-6342

National Federation of Independent Unions www.nfiu.com
1166 S 11th St   Philadelphia PA 19147
Ph: 215-336-3300 ▪ Fx: 215-755-3542 ▪ TF: 888-595-6348

National Federation of Licensed Practical Nurses www.nflpn.com
605 Poole Dr   Garner NC 27529
Ph: 919-779-0046 ▪ Fx: 919-779-5642 ▪ TF: 800-948-2511

National Federation of Municipal Analysts www.nfma.org
PO Box 14893   Pittsburgh PA 15234
Ph: 412-341-4898 ▪ Fx: 412-341-4894

National Federation of Music Clubs www.nfmc-music.org
1336 N Delaware St   Indianapolis IN 46202
Ph: 317-638-4003 ▪ Fx: 317-638-0503

National Federation of Nonpublic School State Accrediting www.nfnssaa.org
Associations   6300 Father Tribou St   Little Rock AR 72205
Ph: 501-664-0340 ▪ Fx: 501-664-9075

National Federation of Paralegal Associations www.paralegals.org
2517 Eastlake Ave E Suite 200   Seattle WA 98102
Ph: 206-652-4120 ▪ Fx: 206-652-4122

National Federation of Press Women www.nfpw.org
PO Box 5556   Arlington VA 22205
Ph: 703-534-2500 ▪ Fx: 703-534-5751 ▪ TF: 800-780-2715

National Federation of Priests' Councils www.nfpc.org
1337 W Ohio St   Chicago IL 60622
Ph: 312-226-3334 ▪ Fx: 312-829-8915

National Federation of Professional Trainers www.nfpt.com
PO Box 4579   Lafayette IN 47903
Ph: 765-471-4514 ▪ Fx: 765-471-7369 ▪ TF: 800-729-6378

National Federation of Republican Women www.nfrw.org
124 N Alfred St   Alexandria VA 22314
Ph: 703-548-9688 ▪ Fx: 703-548-9836

National Federation of State High School Associations www.nfhs.org
PO Box 690   Indianapolis IN 46206
Ph: 317-972-6900 ▪ Fx: 317-822-5700 ▪ TF: 800-776-3462

National Fellowship of Child Care Executives www.nfcce.org/fset.htm
1101 Hartman St   McKeesport PA 15132
Ph: 412-673-1992 ▪ Fx: 412-673-1996

National Fenton Glass Society www.fentonglasssociety.org
PO Box 4008   Marietta OH 45750
Ph: 740-374-3345 ▪ Fx: 740-376-9708

National FFA Organization www.ffa.org
6060 FFA Dr   Indianapolis IN 46268
Ph: 317-802-6060 ▪ Fx: 317-802-6061 ▪ TF: 800-772-0939

National Fibromyalgia Partnership Inc www.fmpartnership.org
140 Zinn Way PO Box 160   Linden VA 22642
Ph: 866-725-4404 ▪ Fx: 866-666-2727

National Field Archery Association www.nfaa-archery.org
31407 Outer I-10   Redlands CA 92373
Ph: 909-794-2133 ▪ Fx: 909-794-8512 ▪ TF: 800-811-2331

National Field Selling Association www.nfsa.com
1900 Arch St   Philadelphia PA 19103
Ph: 215-564-1627 ▪ Fx: 215-564-2175

National Finance Adjusters www.nfa.org
1370 W North Ave   Baltimore MD 21217
Ph: 410-728-2400 ▪ Fx: 410-523-8336

National Fire Sprinkler Association www.nfsa.org
40 Jon Barrett Rd PO Box 1000   Patterson NY 12563
Ph: 845-878-4200 ▪ Fx: 845-878-4215

National Fireworks Association www.nationalfireworks.org
8224 NW Bradford Ct   Kansas City MO 64151
Ph: 816-505-3589 ▪ Fx: 816-741-4058

National Fish Meal & Oil Association
1901 N Fort Myer Dr Suite 700   Arlington VA 22209
Ph: 703-524-8884 ▪ Fx: 703-524-4619

National Fish & Wildlife Foundation www.nfwf.org
1120 Connecticut Ave NW Rm 900   Washington DC 20036
Ph: 202-857-0166 ▪ Fx: 202-857-0162

National Fisheries Institute Inc www.nfi.org
1901 N Fort Myer Dr Suite 700   Arlington VA 22209
Ph: 703-524-8880 ▪ Fx: 703-524-4619

National Fisheries Institute PAC
1901 N Fort Myer Dr Suite 700   Arlington VA 22209
Ph: 703-524-8880 ▪ Fx: 703-524-4619

National Flag Foundation www.americanflags.org
Flag Plaza 1275 Bedford Ave   Pittsburgh PA 15219
Ph: 412-261-1776 ▪ Fx: 412-261-9132 ▪ TF: 800-615-1776

National Flight Nurses Association www.astna.org
9101 E Kenyon Ave Suite 3000   Denver CO 80237
Ph: 800-897-6362 ▪ Fx: 303-770-1812

National Flight Paramedics Association www.flightparamedic.org
383 F St   Salt Lake City UT 84103
Ph: 800-381-6372

National Fluid Power Association www.nfpa.com
3333 N Mayfair Rd Suite 101   Milwaukee WI 53222
Ph: 414-778-3344 ▪ Fx: 414-778-3361

National Food & Energy Council www.nfec.org
601 Business Loop 70W Suite 216D   Columbia MO 65203
Ph: 573-875-7155 ▪ Fx: 573-449-5322

National Food Processors Association www.nfpa-food.org
1350 'I' St NW Suite 300   Washington DC 20005
Ph: 202-639-5900 ▪ Fx: 202-639-5932 ▪ TF: 800-355-0983

National Food Processors Association PAC
1350 'I' St NW Suite 300   Washington DC 20005
Ph: 202-639-5900 ▪ Fx: 202-639-5932

National Food Service Management Institute www.nfsmi.org
PO Drawer 188   University MS 38677
Ph: 662-915-7658 ▪ Fx: 662-915-5615 ▪ TF: 800-321-3054

National Football League Players Association www.nflpa.org
2021 L St NW Suite 600   Washington DC 20036
Ph: 202-463-2200 ▪ Fx: 202-857-0380 ▪ TF: 800-372-2000

National Foreign Trade Council www.nftc.org
1625 K St NW Suite 200   Washington DC 20006
Ph: 202-887-0278 ▪ Fx: 202-452-8160

National Forensic League www.nflonline.org
125 Watson St   Ripon WI 54971
Ph: 920-748-6206 ▪ Fx: 920-748-9478

National Forest Foundation www.natlforests.org/
2715 M St NW Suite 410   Washington DC 20007
Ph: 202-298-6740 ▪ Fx: 202-298-6758

National Forest Recreation Association www.nfra.org
PO Box 488   Woodlake CA 93286
Ph: 559-564-2365 ▪ Fx: 559-564-2048

National Forum for Black Public Administrators www.nfbpa.org
777 N Capitol St NE Suite 807   Washington DC 20002
Ph: 202-408-9300 ▪ Fx: 202-408-8558

National Foster Parent Association www.nfpainc.org
7512 Stanich Ave Suite 6   Gig Harbor WA 98335
Ph: 253-853-4000 ▪ Fx: 253-853-4001 ▪ TF: 800-557-5238

National Foundation for Advancement in the Arts www.nfaa.org
800 Brickell Ave Suite 500   Miami FL 33131
Ph: 305-377-1140 ▪ Fx: 305-377-1149 ▪ TF: 800-970-2787

National Foundation for the Chemically Hypersensitive www.mcsrelief.com
4407 Swinson Rd   Rhodes MI 48652
Ph: 989-689-6369 ▪ Fx: 989-689-6877

National Foundation for Credit Counseling www.nfcc.org
801 Roeder Rd Suite 900   Silver Spring MD 20910
Ph: 301-589-5600 ▪ Fx: 301-495-5623 ▪ TF: 800-388-2227

National Foundation of Dentistry for the Handicapped www.nfdh.org
1800 15th St Unit 100   Denver CO 80202
Ph: 303-534-5360 ▪ Fx: 303-534-5290 ▪ TF: 888-471-6334

National Foundation for Depressive Illness Inc www.depression.org
PO Box 2257   New York NY 10116
Ph: 800-239-1265

National Foundation for Facial Reconstruction www.nffr.org
317 E 34th St   New York NY 10016
Ph: 212-263-6656 ▪ Fx: 212-263-7534

National Foundation for Infectious Diseases www.nfid.org
4733 Bethesda Ave Suite 750   Bethesda MD 20814
Ph: 301-656-0003 ▪ Fx: 301-907-0878

National Foundation for Jewish Culture www.jewishculture.org
330 7th Ave 21st Fl   New York NY 10001
Ph: 212-629-0500 ▪ Fx: 212-629-0508

National Foundation of Manufactured Home Owners www.manhousingfoundation.org
62 Hawthorne Cir   Willow Street PA 17584
Ph: 717-284-4520

National Foundation for Transplants www.transplants.org
1102 Brookfield Rd Suite 200   Memphis TN 38119
Ph: 901-684-1697 ▪ Fx: 901-684-1128 ▪ TF: 800-489-3863

National Foundation for Women Legislators www.womenlegislators.org
910 16th St NW Suite 100   Washington DC 20006
Ph: 202-293-3040 ▪ Fx: 202-293-5430

National Fragile X Foundation www.fragilex.org
PO Box 190488   San Francisco CA 94119
Ph: 925-938-9300 ▪ Fx: 925-938-9315 ▪ TF: 800-688-8765

National Frame Builders Association nfba.org
4840 W 15th St Suite 1000   Lawrence KS 66049
Ph: 785-843-2444 ▪ Fx: 785-843-7555 ▪ TF: 800-557-6957

National Franchisee Association www.nfabk.org
3901 Roswell NE Suite 312   Marietta GA 30062
Ph: 770-971-0808 ▪ Fx: 770-971-3799

National Fraternal Congress of America www.nfcanet.org
1240 Iroquois Ave Suite 300   Naperville IL 60563
Ph: 630-355-6633 ▪ Fx: 630-355-0042

National Fraternal Society of the Deaf www.nfsd.com
1118 S 6th St   Springfield IL 62703
Ph: 217-789-7429 ▪ Fx: 217-289-7489

National Fraternity of Kappa Delta Rho www.kdr.com
331 S Main St   Greensburg PA 15601
Ph: 724-838-7100 ▪ Fx: 724-838-7101 ▪ TF: 800-536-5371

National Fraternity of Phi Mu Delta www.phimudelta.org
PO Box 4633   Chapel Hill NC 27515
Ph: 888-401-2213 ▪ Fx: 919-929-9053

National Fraternity of Student Musicians
808 Rio Grande PO Box 1807   Austin TX 78767
Ph: 512-478-5775 ▪ Fx: 512-478-5843

National Fraud Information Center www.fraud.org
1701 K St NW Suite 1200   Washington DC 20006
Ph: 202-835-3323 ▪ Fx: 202-835-0747 ▪ TF: 800-876-7060

National Freight Transportation Association www.nftahq.org
PO Box 1321   Exton PA 19341
Ph: 610-363-7747 ▪ Fx: 610-363-2971

National Frozen Pizza Institute www.affi.com/nfpi/nfpihomepage.htm
2000 Corporate Ridge Suite 1000   McLean VA 22102
Ph: 703-821-0770 ▪ Fx: 703-821-1350

National Frozen & Refrigerated Foods Association www.nfraweb.org
4755 Linglestown Rd Suite 300   Harrisburg PA 17112
Ph: 717-657-8601 ▪ Fx: 717-657-9862

National Funeral Directors Association www.nfda.org
13625 Bishop's Dr   Brookfield WI 53005
Ph: 262-789-1880 ▪ Fx: 262-789-6977 ▪ TF: 800-228-6332

National Funeral Directors Association PAC
400 C St NE   Washington DC 20002
Ph: 202-547-0441 ▪ Fx: 202-547-0726

National Funeral Directors & Morticians Association www.nfdma.com
3951 Snapfinger Pkwy Suite 570   Decatur GA 30035
Ph: 404-286-6680 ■ Fx: 404-286-6573 ■ TF: 800-434-0958

National Futures Association www.nfa.futures.org
200 W Madison St   Chicago IL 60606
Ph: 312-781-1300 ■ Fx: 312-781-1467 ■ TF: 800-366-6321

National Garden Clubs Inc www.gardenclub.org
4401 Magnolia Ave Suite 1600   Saint Louis MO 63110
Ph: 314-776-7574 ■ Fx: 314-776-5108 ■ TF: 800-550-6007

National Gardening Association www.garden.org
1100 Dorset St   South Burlington VT 05403
Ph: 802-863-5251 ■ Fx: 802-864-6889 ■ TF: 800-538-7476

National Gaucher Foundation www.gaucherdisease.org
5410 Edson Ln Suite 260   Rockville MD 20852
Ph: 301-816-1515 ■ Fx: 301-816-1516 ■ TF: 800-428-2437

National Gay & Lesbian Task Force www.ngltf.org
1325 Massachusetts Ave NW Suite 600   Washington DC 20005
Ph: 202-393-5177 ■ Fx: 202-393-2241

National Genealogical Society www.ngsgenealogy.org
4527 17th St N   Arlington VA 22207
Ph: 703-525-0050 ■ Fx: 703-525-0052 ■ TF: 800-473-0060

National Geographic Society www.nationalgeographic.com
1145 17th St NW   Washington DC 20036
Ph: 202-857-7000 ■ Fx: 202-775-6141 ■ TF: 800-647-5463

National Geographic Society Education www.nationalgeographic.com/foundation
Foundation   1145 17th St NW   Washington DC 20036
Ph: 202-857-7310 ■ Fx: 202-429-5701

National Gerontological Nursing Association www.ngna.org
7794 Grow Dr   Pensacola FL 32514
Ph: 850-473-1174 ■ Fx: 850-484-8762 ■ TF: 800-723-0560

National Glass Association www.glass.org
8200 Greensboro Dr Suite 302   McLean VA 22102
Ph: 703-442-4890 ■ Fx: 703-442-0630 ■ TF: 866-342-5642

National Golf Coaches Association www.ngca.org
180 N LaSalle St Suite 1822   Chicago IL 60601
Ph: 312-551-0814 ■ Fx: 312-551-0815

National Golf Course Owners Association www.ngcoa.org
291 Seven Farms Dr 2nd Fl   Charleston SC 29492
Ph: 843-881-9956 ■ Fx: 843-881-9958 ■ TF: 800-933-4262

National Golf Foundation www.ngf.org
1150 S US Hwy 1 Suite 401   Jupiter FL 33477
Ph: 561-744-6006 ■ Fx: 561-744-6107 ■ TF: 800-733-6006

National Governors Association www.nga.org
444 N Capitol St NW Hall of States Suite 267   Washington DC 20001
Ph: 202-624-5300 ■ Fx: 202-624-5313

National Grain & Feed Association www.ngfa.org
1250 I St NW Suite 1003   Washington DC 20005
Ph: 202-289-0873 ■ Fx: 202-289-5388

National Grain & Feed Association PAC
1250 'I' St NW Suite 1003   Washington DC 20005
Ph: 202-289-0873 ■ Fx: 202-289-5388

National Grain Sorghum Producers www.sorghumgrowers.com
4201 N I-27 PO Box 5309   Lubbock TX 79408
Ph: 806-749-3478 ■ Fx: 806-749-9002

National Grain Trade Council ngtc.org
1300 L St NW Suite 1020   Washington DC 20005
Ph: 202-842-0400 ■ Fx: 202-789-7223

National Grange www.grange.org
1616 H St NW   Washington DC 20006
Ph: 202-628-3507 ■ Fx: 202-347-1091 ■ TF: 888-447-2643

National Grants Management Association www.ngma-grants.org
11654 Plaza America Dr Suite 609   Reston VA 20190
Ph: 703-648-9023 ■ Fx: 703-648-9024

National Graves' Disease Foundation www.ngdf.org
PO Box 1969   Brevard NC 28712
Ph: 828-877-5251

National Greenhouse Manufacturers Association www.ngma.com
20 W Dry Creek Cir Suite 110   Littleton CO 80120
Ph: 303-798-1338 ■ Fx: 303-798-1332 ■ TF: 800-792-6462

National Greyhound Adoption Program www.ngap.org
4701 Bath St   Philadelphia PA 19137
Ph: 215-331-7918 ■ Fx: 215-331-1947 ■ TF: 800-348-2517

National Greyhound Association www.ngagreyhounds.com
PO Box 543   Abilene KS 67410
Ph: 785-263-4660 ■ Fx: 785-263-4689

National Grocers Association www.nationalgrocers.org
1005 N Glebe Rd Suite 250   Arlington VA 22201
Ph: 703-516-0700 ■ Fx: 703-516-0115

National Ground Water Association www.ngwa.org
601 Dempsey Rd   Westerville OH 43081
Ph: 614-898-7791 ■ Fx: 614-898-7786 ■ TF: 800-551-7379

National Ground Water Association PAC
601 Dempsey Rd   Westerville OH 43081
Ph: 614-898-7791 ■ Fx: 614-898-7786 ■ TF: 800-551-7379

National Guard Association of the US www.ngaus.org
1 Massachusetts Ave NW Suite 200   Washington DC 20001
Ph: 202-789-0031 ■ Fx: 202-682-9358 ■ TF: 888-226-4287

National Guard Executive Directors Association
PO Box 10045   Austin TX 78766
Ph: 512-454-7300 ■ Fx: 512-467-6803

National Guard of the US, Enlisted Association of the www.eangus.org
3133 Mt Vernon Ave   Alexandria VA 22305
Ph: 703-519-3846 ■ Fx: 703-519-3849 ■ TF: 800-234-3264

National Guardianship Association www.guardianship.org
1604 N Country Club Rd   Tucson AZ 85716
Ph: 520-881-6561 ■ Fx: 520-325-7925

National Guild of Churchmen
PO Box 34548   San Diego CA 92163
Ph: 619-542-8660 ■ Fx: 619-542-8585

National Guild of Community Schools of the Arts www.nationalguild.org
520 8th Ave Suite 302   New York NY 10018
Ph: 212-268-3337 ■ Fx: 212-268-3995

National Guild of Piano Teachers www.pianoguild.com
PO Box 1807   Austin TX 78767
Ph: 512-478-5775 ■ Fx: 512-478-5843

National Guild of Professional Paperhangers www.ngpp.org
136 S Keowee St   Dayton OH 45402
Ph: 937-222-6477 ■ Fx: 937-222-5794 ■ TF: 800-254-6477

National Gymnastics Judges Association www.ngja.org
719 Anthony Ln   Lincoln NE 68520
Ph: 402-483-7436 ■ Fx: 402-472-4305

National Hardwood Lumber Association www.natlhardwood.org
6830 Raleigh-LaGrange Rd   Memphis TN 38184
Ph: 901-377-1818 ■ Fx: 901-382-6419 ■ TF: 800-933-0318

National Havurah Committee www.havurah.org
7135 Germantown Ave 2nd Fl   Philadelphia PA 19119
Ph: 215-248-1335 ■ Fx: 215-248-9760

National Hay Association www.nationalhay.org
102 Treasure Island Cswy Suite 201   Saint Petersburg FL 33706
Ph: 727-367-9702 ■ Fx: 727-367-9608 ■ TF: 800-707-0014

National Head Start Association www.nhsa.org
1651 Prince St   Alexandria VA 22314
Ph: 703-739-0875 ■ Fx: 703-739-0878

National Headache Foundation www.headaches.org
820 N Orleans St Suite 217   Chicago IL 60610
Ph: 888-643-5552

National Health Association www.anhs.org
11816 Race Track Rd PO Box 30630   Tampa FL 33630
Ph: 813-855-6607 ■ Fx: 813-855-8052

National Health Care Anti-Fraud Association www.nhcaa.org
1255 23rd St NW Suite 200   Washington DC 20037
Ph: 202-659-5955 ■ Fx: 202-785-6764

National Health Care for the Homeless Council www.nhchc.org
HCH Clinicians' Network PO Box 60427   Nashville TN 37206
Ph: 615-226-2292 ■ Fx: 615-226-1656

National Health Club Association
640 Plaza Dr Suite 300   Highland Ranch CO 80129
Ph: 303-753-6422 ■ Fx: 303-986-6813 ■ TF: 800-765-6422

National Health Council www.nhcouncil.org
1730 M St NW Suite 500   Washington DC 20036
Ph: 202-785-3910 ■ Fx: 202-785-5923 ■ TF: 800-684-6814

National Health Federation www.thenhf.com
PO Box 688   Monrovia CA 91017
Ph: 626-357-2181 ■ Fx: 626-303-0642

National Health Information Center www.health.gov/nhic
PO Box 1133   Washington DC 20013
Ph: 301-565-4167 ■ Fx: 301-984-4256 ■ TF: 800-336-4797

National Health Law Program www.healthlaw.org
2639 S La Cienega Blvd   Los Angeles CA 90034
Ph: 310-204-6010 ■ Fx: 310-204-0891

National Health Policy Forum www.nhpf.org
2131 K St NW Suite 500   Washington DC 20037
Ph: 202-872-1390 ■ Fx: 202-862-9837

National Healthy Mothers Healthy Babies Coalition www.hmhb.org
121 N Washington St Suite 300   Alexandria VA 22314
Ph: 703-836-6110 ■ Fx: 703-836-3470

National Hearing Conservation Association www.hearingconservation.org
9101 E Kenyon Ave Suite 3000   Denver CO 80237
Ph: 303-224-9022 ■ Fx: 303-770-1812

National Heart Council www.nemahealth.org
306 W Joppa Rd   Baltimore MD 21204
Ph: 410-494-0300 ■ Fx: 410-494-0725

National Heart Savers Association www.heartsavers.org
9140 W Dodge Rd   Omaha NE 68114
Ph: 402-398-1993 ■ Fx: 402-398-1994

National Hemophilia Foundation www.hemophilia.org
116 W 32nd St 11th Fl   New York NY 10001
Ph: 212-328-3700 ■ Fx: 212-328-3777 ■ TF: 800-424-2634

National Hepatitis C Coalition nationalhepatitis-c.org
PO Box 5058   Hemet CA 92544
Ph: 909-658-4414

National Hereford Hog Record Association
22405 480th Ave   Flandreau SD 57028
Ph: 605-997-2116

National Herpes Resource Center www.ashastd.org/hrc
PO Box 13827   Research Triangle Park NC 27709
Ph: 919-361-8488 ■ Fx: 919-361-8425

National High School Rodeo Association www.nhsra.org
12001 Tejon St Suite 128   Denver CO 80234
Ph: 303-452-0820 ■ Fx: 303-452-0912 ■ TF: 800-466-4772

National Hispana Leadership Institute www.nhli.org
1901 N Moore St Suite 206   Arlington VA 22209
Ph: 703-527-6007 ■ Fx: 703-527-6009

National Hispanic Corporate Council www.nhcc-hq.org
1530 Wilson Blvd Suite 110   Arlington VA 22209
Ph: 703-807-5137 ■ Fx: 703-807-0567

National Hispanic Council on Aging www.nhcoa.org
2713 Ontario Rd NW   Washington DC 20009
Ph: 202-265-1288 ■ Fx: 202-745-2522

National Hispanic Foundation for the Arts www.hispanicarts.org
1010 Wisconsin Ave NW Suite 210   Washington DC 20007
Ph: 202-293-8330 ■ Fx: 202-965-5252

National Hispanic Institute www.nhi-net.org
PO Box 220   Maxwell TX 78656
Ph: 512-357-6137 ■ Fx: 512-357-2206

National Hispanic Media Coalition www.nhmc.org
2514 S Grand Ave   Los Angeles CA 90007
Ph: 213-746-6988 ■ Fx: 213-746-1305

National Hispanic Medical Association   www.nhmamd.org
1411 K St NW Suite 200   Washington DC 20005
Ph: 202-628-5895 ▪ Fx: 202-628-5898

National Historic Route 66 Federation   www.national66.com
PO Box 423   Tujunga CA 91043
Ph: 818-352-7232

National Historical Fire Foundation
6101 E Van Buren St   Phoenix AZ 85008
Ph: 602-275-3473 ▪ Fx: 602-275-0896

National History Day   www.nationalhistoryday.org
Univ of Maryland 0119 Cecil Hall   College Park MD 20742
Ph: 301-314-9739 ▪ Fx: 301-314-9767

National Hockey League Players Association   www.nhlpa.com
777 Bay St Suite 2400   Toronto ON M5G2C8
Ph: 416-408-4040 ▪ Fx: 416-313-2301 ▪ TF: 800-363-4625

National Home Education Research Institute   www.nheri.org
PO Box 13939   Salem OR 97309
Ph: 503-364-1490 ▪ Fx: 503-364-2827

National Home Equity Mortgage Association   www.nhema.org
1301 Pennsylvania Ave NW Sutie 500   Washington DC 20004
Ph: 202-347-1210 ▪ Fx: 202-347-1171 ▪ TF: 800-342-1121

National Home Furnishings Association   www.nhfa.org
PO Box 2396   High Point NC 27261
Ph: 336-886-6100 ▪ Fx: 336-801-6102 ▪ TF: 800-888-9590

National Home Gardening Club   www.gardeningclub.com
12301 Whitewater Dr   Minnetonka MN 55343
Ph: 952-988-7404 ▪ TF: 800-324-8454

National Home Infusion Association   www.nhianet.org
205 Daingerfield Rd   Alexandria VA 22314
Ph: 703-549-3740 ▪ Fx: 703-683-1484 ▪ TF: 800-544-7447

National Honey Board   www.nhb.org/
390 Lashley St   Longmont CO 80501
Ph: 303-776-2337 ▪ Fx: 303-776-1177

National Honey Packers & Dealers Association
3301 Rt 66 Bldg C Suite 205   Neptune NJ 07753
Ph: 732-922-3008 ▪ Fx: 732-922-3590

National Honor Society   www.nhs.us
1904 Association Dr   Reston VA 20191
Ph: 703-860-0200 ▪ Fx: 703-476-5432 ▪ TF: 800-253-7746

National Honor Society in Psychology, Psi Chi   www.psichi.org
PO Box 709   Chattanooga TN 37401
Ph: 423-756-2044 ▪ Fx: 423-265-1529

National Hopeline Network   www.hopeline.com
201 N 23rd St Suite 100   Purcellville VA 20132
Ph: 540-338-5756 ▪ Fx: 540-338-5746 ▪ TF: 800-784-2433

National Horse Show Commission
PO Box 167   Shelbyville TN 37162
Ph: 931-684-9506 ▪ Fx: 931-684-9538

National Hospice & Palliative Care Organization   www.nhpco.org
1700 Diagonal Rd Suite 625   Alexandria VA 22314
Ph: 703-837-1500 ▪ Fx: 703-837-1233 ▪ TF: 800-658-8898

National Housing Conference   www.nhc.org
1801 K St NW Suite M-100   Washington DC 20006
Ph: 202-466-2121 ▪ Fx: 202-466-2122

National Housing Endowment   www.nationalhousingendowment.com
1201 15th St NW   Washington DC 20005
Ph: 202-266-8483

National Housing Institute   www.nhi.org
460 Bloomfield Ave Suite 211   Montclair NJ 07042
Ph: 973-509-2888 ▪ Fx: 973-509-8005

National Housing Law Project   www.nhlp.org
614 Grand Ave Suite 320   Oakland CA 94610
Ph: 510-251-9400 ▪ Fx: 510-451-2300

National Housing & Rehabilitation Association   housingonline.com
1625 Massachusetts Ave NW Suite 601   Washington DC 20036
Ph: 202-939-1750 ▪ Fx: 202-265-4435

National HPV & Cervical Cancer Prevention Resource   www.ashastd.org/hpvccrc
Center   PO Box 13827   Research Triangle Park NC 27709
Ph: 919-361-8400 ▪ Fx: 919-361-8425

National Human Resources Association   www.humanresources.org
PO Box 803   Pewaukee WI 53072
Ph: 414-453-7499 ▪ Fx: 414-457-5959 ▪ TF: 866-523-4417

National Humane Education Society   www.nhes.org
PO Box 340   Charles Town WV 25414
Ph: 304-725-0506 ▪ Fx: 304-725-1523

National Humanities Alliance   www.nhalliance.org
21 Dupont Cir NW Suite 604   Washington DC 20036
Ph: 202-296-4994 ▪ Fx: 202-872-0884

National Humanities Center   www.nhc.rtp.nc.us
7 Alexander Dr PO Box 12256   Research Triangle Park NC 27709
Ph: 919-549-0661 ▪ Fx: 919-990-8535

National Humanities Institute   www.nhinet.org
PO Box 1387   Bowie MD 20718
Ph: 301-464-4277

National Hunger Clearinghouse   www.worldhungeryear.org/nhc
505 8th Ave Suite 2100   New York NY 10018
Ph: 212-629-8850 ▪ Fx: 212-465-9274 ▪ TF: 800-453-2648

National Hunter & Jumper Association   www.nhja.org
PO Box 1015   Riverside CT 06878
Ph: 203-869-1225

National Hydrogen Association   www.hydrogenus.org
1800 M St NW Suite 300   Washington DC 20036
Ph: 202-223-5547 ▪ Fx: 202-223-5537

National Hydropower Association   www.hydro.org
1 Massachusetts Ave NW Suite 850   Washington DC 20001
Ph: 202-682-1700 ▪ Fx: 202-682-9478

National Ice Carving Association   www.nica.org
PO Box 3593   Oak Brook IL 60522
Ph: 630-871-8431 ▪ Fx: 630-871-0839

National Ice Cream & Yogurt Retailers Association   www.nicyra.org
184 Hicks Rd Suite C   Rolling Meadows IL 60008
Ph: 847-934-0926 ▪ Fx: 847-202-4791

National Immigration Forum   www.immigrationforum.org
50 F St NW Suite 300   Washington DC 20001
Ph: 202-347-0040 ▪ Fx: 202-347-0058

National Immigration Law Center   www.nilc.org
3435 Wilshire Blvd Suite 2850   Los Angeles CA 90010
Ph: 213-639-3900 ▪ Fx: 213-639-3911

National Impala Association   www.impala.blackhills.com
2928 4th Ave PO Box 968   Spearfish SD 57783
Ph: 605-642-5864 ▪ Fx: 605-642-5868

National Imperial Glass Collectors Society   www.imperialglass.org

National Independent Automobile Dealers Association   www.niada.com
2521 Brown Blvd   Arlington TX 76006
Ph: 817-640-3838 ▪ Fx: 817-649-5866 ▪ TF: 800-682-3837

National Independent Bank Equipment & Systems Association   nibesa.com
5300 Sequoia Rd NW Suite 205   Albuquerque NM 87120
Ph: 505-839-7958 ▪ Fx: 505-839-0017 ▪ TF: 800-843-6082

National Independent Fire Alarm Distributors   www.nifad.org
1001 Office Park Rd Suite 105   West Des Moines IA 50625
Ph: 515-440-6057 ▪ Fx: 515-440-6055

National Independent Flag Dealers Association   www.flaginfo.com
710 E Ogden Ave Suite 600   Naperville IL 60563
Ph: 630-579-3274 ▪ Fx: 630-369-2488 ▪ TF: 877-544-3524

National Independent Living Association   www.nilausa.org
4203 Southpoint Blvd   Jacksonville FL 32216
Ph: 904-296-1038 ▪ Fx: 904-296-1953

National Independent Nursery Furniture Retailers   www.babyexpressstores.com
Association   12302 Hart Ranch   San Antonio TX 78249
Ph: 210-699-1133 ▪ Fx: 210-699-3232

National Indian Child Welfare Association   www.nicwa.org
5100 SW Macadam Ave Suite 300   Portland OR 97239
Ph: 503-222-4044 ▪ Fx: 503-222-4007

National Indian Council on Aging   www.nicoa.org
10501 Montgomery Blvd NE Suite 210   Albuquerque NM 87111
Ph: 505-292-2001 ▪ Fx: 505-292-1922

National Indian Education Association   www.niea.org
700 N Fairfax St Suite 210   Alexandria VA 22314
Ph: 703-838-2870 ▪ Fx: 703-838-1620

National Indian Gaming Association   www.indiangaming.org
224 2nd St SE   Washington DC 20003
Ph: 202-546-7711 ▪ Fx: 202-546-1755 ▪ TF: 800-286-6442

National Indian Health Board   www.nihb.org
1385 S Colorado Blvd Suite A708   Denver CO 80222
Ph: 303-759-3075 ▪ Fx: 303-759-3674

National Indian Youth Council
318 Elm St SW   Albuquerque NM 87102
Ph: 505-247-2251 ▪ Fx: 505-247-4251

National Industrial Belting Association   www.niba.org
N19 W24400 Riverwood Dr   Waukesha WI 53188
Ph: 262-523-9090 ▪ Fx: 262-523-9091 ▪ TF: 800-488-4845

National Industrial Sand Association   www.sand.org
4041 Powder Mill Rd Suite 450   Claverton MD 20705
Ph: 301-595-5550 ▪ Fx: 301-595-3303

National Industrial Transportation League   www.nitl.org
1700 N Moore St Suite 1900   Arlington VA 22209
Ph: 703-524-5011 ▪ Fx: 703-524-5017

National Industries for the Blind   www.nib.org
1901 N Beauregard St Suite 200   Alexandria VA 22311
Ph: 703-998-0770 ▪ Fx: 703-998-8268 ▪ TF: 800-433-2304

National Industries for the Severely Handicapped   www.nish.org
8401 Old Courthouse Rd   Vienna VA 22182
Ph: 703-560-6800 ▪ Fx: 703-849-8916

National Infertility Network Exchange   www.nine-infertility.org
PO Box 204   East Meadow NY 11554
Ph: 516-794-5772 ▪ Fx: 516-794-0008

National Information Center for Educational Media   www.nicem.com
PO Box 8640   Albuquerque NM 87198
Ph: 505-998-0800 ▪ Fx: 505-256-1080 ▪ TF: 800-926-8328

National Information Service for Earthquake Engineering   nisee.berkeley.edu
Univ of California Berkeley 1301 S 46th St RFS 453   Richmond CA 94804
Ph: 510-231-9403 ▪ Fx: 510-231-9461

National Information Standards Organization   www.niso.org
4733 Bethesda Ave Suite 300   Bethesda MD 20814
Ph: 301-654-2512 ▪ Fx: 301-654-1721

National Inhalant Prevention Coalition   www.inhalants.org
2904 Kerbey Ln   Austin TX 78703
Ph: 512-480-8953 ▪ Fx: 512-477-3932 ▪ TF: 800-269-4237

National Initiative for Democracy   ni4d.us
1600 N Oak St Suite 1412   Arlington VA 22209
Ph: 703-516-4056 ▪ Fx: 703-516-4057

National Institute of American Doll Artists   www.niada.org

National Institute for Animal Agriculture   www.animalagriculture.org
1910 Lyda Ave   Bowling Green KY 42104
Ph: 270-782-9798 ▪ Fx: 270-782-0188

National Institute for Automotive Service Excellence   www.asecert.org
101 Blue Seal Dr SE   Leesburg VA 20175
Ph: 703-669-6600 ▪ Fx: 703-713-0727 ▪ TF: 877-273-8324

National Institute of Building Sciences   www.nibs.org
1090 Vermont Ave NW Suite 700   Washington DC 20005
Ph: 202-289-7800 ▪ Fx: 202-289-1092

National Institute of Business & Industrial Chaplaincy   www.nibic.com
1770 St James Pl Suite 550   Houston TX 77056
Ph: 713-266-2456 ▪ Fx: 713-266-0845

National Institute of Ceramic Engineers
PO Box 6136   Westerville OH 43086
Ph: 614-890-4700

National Institute for Certification in Engineering Technologies www.nicet.org
1420 King St Alexandria VA 22314
Ph: 703-548-1518 Fx: 703-682-2756 TF: 888-476-4238

National Institute for Chemical Studies www.nicsinfo.org
2300 MacCorkle Ave SE Charleston WV 25304
Ph: 304-346-6264 Fx: 304-346-6349

National Institute on Community-Based Long-Term Care www.ncoa.org
c/o National Council on the Aging 300 D St SW Suite
801 Washington DC 20024
Ph: 202-479-1200 Fx: 202-479-0735

National Institute for Farm Safety www.ag.ohio-state.edu/~agsafety/NIFS/nifs.htm
Univ of Wisconsin 460 Henry Mall Madison WI 53706
Ph: 608-265-0568 Fx: 608-262-1228

National Institute of Governmental Purchasing www.nigp.org
151 Spring St Suite 300 Herndon VA 20170
Ph: 703-736-8900 Fx: 703-736-9644 TF: 800-367-6447

National Institute for Health Care Management Research & www.nihcm.org
Educational Foundation 1225 19th St NW Suite
710 Washington DC 20036
Ph: 202-296-4426 Fx: 202-296-4319

National Institute of Oilseed Products www.oilseed.org
1156 15th St NW Suite 900 Washington DC 20005
Ph: 202-785-3232 Fx: 202-223-9741

National Institute of Packaging Handling & Logistics Engineers www.niphle.com
6902 Lyle St Lanham MD 20706
Ph: 301-459-9105 Fx: 301-459-4925

National Institute on Park & Grounds Management www.nipgm.org
PO Box 5162 De Pere WI 54115
Ph: 920-339-9057

National Institute of Pension Administrators www.nipa.org
401 N Michigan Ave Suite 2200 Chicago IL 60611
Ph: 800-999-6472 Fx: 312-245-1085

National Institute for Public Policy www.nipp.org
3031 Javier Rd Suite 300 Fairfax VA 22031
Ph: 703-698-0563 Fx: 703-698-0566

National Institute for Rehabilitation Engineering www.angelfire.com/nj/nire2
PO Box T Hewitt NJ 07421
Ph: 973-853-6585 TF: 800-736-2216

National Institute for Science Law & Public www.swankin-turner.com/nislapp.html
Policy 1400 16th St NW Suite 330 Washington DC 20036
Ph: 202-462-8800 Fx: 202-265-6564

National Institute of Senior Centers www.ncoa.org
c/o National Council on the Aging 300 D St SW Suite
801 Washington DC 20024
Ph: 202-479-1200 Fx: 202-479-0735

National Institute of Statistical Sciences www.niss.org
19 T W Alexander Dr PO Box 14006 Research Triangle Park
NC 27709
Ph: 919-685-9300 Fx: 919-685-9310

National Institute of Steel Detailing www.nisd.org
7700 Edgewater Dr Suite 670 Oakland CA 94621
Ph: 510-568-3741 Fx: 510-568-3781

National Institute for Trial Advocacy www.nd.edu/~nita
PO Box 6500 Notre Dame IN 46556
Ph: 574-271-8370 Fx: 574-271-8375 TF: 800-225-6482

National Institute for the Word of God www.wordofgodinstitute.org
487 Michigan Ave NE Washington DC 20017
Ph: 202-529-0001 Fx: 202-636-4460

National Institute for Work & Learning www.niwl.org
1825 Connecticut Ave NW 7th Fl Washington DC 20009
Ph: 202-884-8186 Fx: 202-884-8422

National Insulation Association www.insulation.org
99 Canal Center Plaza Suite 222 Alexandria VA 22314
Ph: 703-683-6422 Fx: 703-549-4838

National Insurance Crime Bureau www.nicb.org
10330 S Roberts Rd Palos Hills IL 60465
Ph: 708-430-2430 Fx: 708-430-5025 TF: 800-447-6282

National Intercollegiate Rodeo Association www.collegerodeo.com
2316 Eastgate N St Suite 160 Walla Walla WA 99362
Ph: 509-529-4402 Fx: 509-525-1090

National Intercollegiate Soccer Officials Association www.nisoa.org
541 Woodview Dr Longwood FL 32779
Ph: 407-862-3305 Fx: 407-862-8545

National Interest, Council for the www.cnionline.org
1250 4th St SW Suite WG-1 Washington DC 20024
Ph: 202-863-2951 Fx: 202-863-2952 TF: 800-296-6958

National Interfaith Coalition on Aging www.ncoa.org
300 D St SW Washington DC 20024
Ph: 202-479-1200 Fx: 202-479-0735 TF: 800-424-9046

National Interfaith Committee for Worker Justice www.nicwj.org
1020 W Bryn Mawr Ave 4th Fl Chicago IL 60660
Ph: 773-728-8400 Fx: 773-728-8409

National Interfaith Hospitality Network www.nihn.org
71 Summit Ave Summit NJ 07901
Ph: 908-273-1100 Fx: 908-273-0030

National Interfraternity Conference www.nicindy.org
3901 W 86th St Suite 390 Indianapolis IN 46268
Ph: 317-872-1112 Fx: 317-872-1134

National-Interstate Council of State Boards of Cosmetology Inc www.nictesting.org
7622 Briarwood Cir Little Rock AR 72205
Ph: 501-227-8262 Fx: 501-227-8212

National Intramural-Recreational Sports Association www.nirsa.org
4185 SW Research Way Corvallis OR 97333
Ph: 541-766-8211 Fx: 541-766-8284

National Investigations Committee on Unidentified Flying Objects www.nicufo.org
14617 Victory Blvd Suite 4 Van Nuys CA 91411
Ph: 818-989-5942 Fx: 818-989-2165

National Investment Company Service Association www.nicsa.org
36 Washington St Suite 70 Wellesley Hills MA 02481
Ph: 781-416-7200 Fx: 781-416-7065

National Investor Relations Institute www.niri.org
8020 Towers Crescent Dr Suite 250 Vienna VA 22182
Ph: 703-506-3570 Fx: 703-506-3571

National Issues Forums www.nifi.org
100 Commons Rd Dayton OH 45459
Ph: 937-434-7300 Fx: 937-439-9804 TF: 800-433-7834

National Italian American Foundation www.niaf.org
1860 19th St NW Washington DC 20009
Ph: 202-387-0600 Fx: 202-387-0800 TF: 800-989-6423

National Japanese American Historical Society www.njahs.org
1684 Post St San Francisco CA 94115
Ph: 415-921-5007 Fx: 415-921-5087

National Jewish Committee on Scouting www.jewishscouting.org
1325 W Walnut Hill Ln PO Box 152079 Irving TX 75015
Ph: 972-580-2295 Fx: 972-580-7870

National Jewish Democratic Council www.njdc.org
PO Box 75308 Washington DC 20013
Ph: 202-216-9060 Fx: 202-216-9061

National Jewish Girl Scout Committee www.njgsc.org
33 Central Dr Bronxville NY 10708
Ph: 914-738-3986 Fx: 914-738-6752

National Jewish Law Students Association
154 Stuart St Boston MA 02216
Ph: 617-451-0010 Fx: 617-353-7214

National Judges Association www.nationaljudgesassociation.org
PO Box 160 Maud OK 74854
Ph: 405-374-1213 Fx: 405-374-2316 TF: 888-366-3652

National Judicial College www.judges.org
Univ of Nevada Judicial College Bldg MS 358 Reno NV 89557
Ph: 775-784-6747 Fx: 775-784-4234 TF: 800-255-8343

National Junior Angus Association www.njaa.info
3201 Frederick Ave Saint Joseph MO 64506
Ph: 816-383-5100 Fx: 816-233-9703

National Junior Classical League www.njcl.org
Miami Univ 422 Wells Mill Dr Oxford OH 45056
Ph: 513-529-7741 Fx: 513-529-7742

National Junior College Athletic Association www.njcaa.org
PO Box 7305 Colorado Springs CO 80933
Ph: 719-590-9788 Fx: 719-590-7324

National Junior Hereford Association www.hereford.org
PO Box 014059 Kansas City MO 64101
Ph: 816-842-3757 Fx: 816-842-6931

National Junior Honor Society www.njhs.org
1904 Association Dr Reston VA 20191
Ph: 703-860-0200 Fx: 703-476-5432

National Junior Santa Gertrudis Association www.santagertrudis.ws/jrwelcome.html
PO Box 1257 Kingsville TX 78364
Ph: 361-592-9357 Fx: 361-592-8572

National Juvenile Detention Association www.njda.com
Eastern Kentucky Univ 301 Perkins Bldg 521 Lancaster
Ave Richmond KY 40475
Ph: 859-622-6259 Fx: 859-622-2333

National Kerosene Heater Association www.space-heating.com
1816 Old Natchez Trace Franklin TN 37069
Ph: 615-790-0770 Fx: 615-790-6700

National Kidney Foundation www.kidney.org
30 E 33rd St Suite 1100 New York NY 10016
Ph: 212-889-2210 Fx: 212-689-9261 TF: 800-622-9010

National Kitchen & Bath Association www.nkba.org
687 Willow Grove St Hackettstown NJ 07840
Ph: 908-852-0033 Fx: 908-852-1695 TF: 800-843-6522

National Knife Collectors Association www.nationalknife.org
5924 Shallowford Rd PO Box 21070 Chattanooga TN 37424
Ph: 423-892-5007 Fx: 423-899-9456

National Labor Committee www.nlcnet.org
540 W 48th St New York NY 10036
Ph: 212-242-3002 Fx: 212-242-3821

National Labor Management Association www.nlma.org
PO Box 819 Jamestown NY 14702
Ph: 716-665-3654 Fx: 716-665-8060 TF: 800-967-2687

National Lamb Feeders Association www.nlfa-sheep.org
1270 Chemeketa St NE Salem OR 97301
Ph: 503-370-7024 Fx: 503-585-1921

National Latina Institute for Reproductive Health www.latinainstitute.org
162 Montague St 3rd Fl Brooklyn NY 11201
Ph: 718-260-8811 Fx: 718-260-9941

National Law Center for Children & Families www.nationallawcenter.org
3819 Plaza Dr Fairfax VA 22030
Ph: 703-691-4626

National Law Center on Homelessness & Poverty www.nlchp.org
1411 K St NW Suite 1400 Washington DC 20005
Ph: 202-628-2535 Fx: 202-628-2737

National Law Enforcement Officers Memorial Fund Inc www.nleomf.com
605 'E' St NW Washington DC 20004
Ph: 202-737-3400 Fx: 202-737-3405

National Lawyers Guild www.nlg.org
143 Madison Ave 4th Fl New York NY 10016
Ph: 212-679-5100 Fx: 212-679-2811

National Lead Burning Association
c/o NELCO Inc 98 Baldwin Ave Woburn MA 01801
Ph: 781-933-1940 Fx: 781-933-4763

National League of American Pen Women Inc www.americanpenwomen.org
1300 17th St NW Washington DC 20036
Ph: 202-785-1997 Fx: 202-452-6868

National League of Cities www.nlc.org
1301 Pennsylvania Ave NW Suite 550 Washington DC 20004
Ph: 202-626-3000 Fx: 202-626-3043

National League of Families of American Prisoners & www.pow-miafamilies.org
Missing in Southeast Asia 1005 N Glebe Rd Suite
170 Arlington VA 22201
Ph: 703-465-7432 Fx: 703-465-7433

National League of Masonic Clubs Inc
2244 Locust Ln   York PA 17404
Ph: 717-764-6768

National League for Nursing www.nln.org
61 Broadway   New York NY 10006
Ph: 212-363-5555 ▪ Fx: 212-812-0393 ▪ TF: 800-669-1656

National League for Nursing Accrediting Commission Inc www.nlnac.org
61 Broadway 33rd Fl   New York NY 10006
Ph: 212-363-5555 ▪ Fx: 212-812-0390 ▪ TF: 800-669-1656

National League of Postmasters of the US www.postmasters.org
1023 N Royal St   Alexandria VA 22314
Ph: 703-548-5922 ▪ Fx: 703-836-8937

National Leased Housing Association www.hudnlha.com
1818 'N' St NW Suite 405   Washington DC 20036
Ph: 202-785-8888 ▪ Fx: 202-785-2008

National Legal Aid & Defender Association www.nlada.org
1140 Connecticut Ave NW Suite 900   Washington DC 20036
Ph: 202-452-0620 ▪ Fx: 202-872-1031

National Legal Center for the Medically Dependent & Disabled
1 S 6th St   Terre Haute IN 47808
Ph: 812-232-2434 ▪ Fx: 812-235-3658

National Legal Center for the Public Interest www.nlcpi.org
1600 K St NW Suite 800   Washington DC 20006
Ph: 202-466-9360 ▪ Fx: 202-466-9366

National Legal Foundation www.nlf.net
PO Box 64427   Virginia Beach VA 23467
Ph: 757-463-6133 ▪ Fx: 757-463-6055

National Lesbian & Gay Journalists Association www.nlgja.org
1420 K St NW Suite 910   Washington DC 20005
Ph: 202-588-9888 ▪ Fx: 202-588-1818

National Lesbian & Gay Law Association www.nlgla.org
200 E Lexington St Suite 1511   Baltimore MD 21202
Ph: 508-892-8290 ▪ Fx: 410-244-0775

National Lighting Bureau www.nlb.org
8811 Colesville Rd Suite G106   Silver Spring MD 20910
Ph: 301-587-9572 ▪ Fx: 301-589-2017

National Lilac Rabbit Club of America www.geocities.com/nlrca2002
N3650 Oak Ridge Rd   Waupaca WI 54981
Ph: 715-258-3106

National Lime Association www.lime.org
200 N Glebe Rd Suite 800   Arlington VA 22203
Ph: 703-243-5463 ▪ Fx: 703-243-5489

National Limousine Association www.limo.org
49 S Maple Ave   Marlton NJ 08053
Ph: 856-596-3344 ▪ Fx: 856-596-2145 ▪ TF: 800-652-7007

National Lincoln Sheep Breeders Association www.lincolnsheep.org
15603 173rd Ave   Milo IA 50166
Ph: 641-942-6402

National Lipid Association www.lipid.org
8833 Perimeter Park Blvd Suite 301   Jacksonville FL 32216
Ph: 904-998-0854 ▪ Fx: 904-998-0855

National Literatures, Council on annehenrypaolucci.homestead.com/CNL1.html
68-02 Metropolitan Ave   Middle Village NY 11379
Ph: 718-821-3916

National Lithuanian Society of America
9136 55th Ct   Oak Lawn IL 60453
Ph: 708-423-7871

National Little Britches Rodeo Association www.nlbra.org
1045 W Rio Grande St   Colorado Springs CO 80906
Ph: 719-389-0333 ▪ Fx: 719-578-1367 ▪ TF: 800-763-3694

National Livestock Producers Association www.nlpa.org
660 Southpoint Ct Suite 314   Colorado Springs CO 80906
Ph: 719-538-8843 ▪ Fx: 719-538-8847 ▪ TF: 800-237-7193

National Low Income Housing Coalition www.nlihc.org
1012 14th St NW Suite 610   Washington DC 20005
Ph: 202-662-1530 ▪ Fx: 202-393-1973

National Lubricating Grease Institute www.nlgi.com
4635 Wyandotte St   Kansas City MO 64112
Ph: 816-931-9480 ▪ Fx: 816-753-5026

National Luggage Dealers Association www.nlda.com
1817 Elmdale Ave   Glenview IL 60025
Ph: 847-998-6869 ▪ Fx: 847-998-6884

National Lum & Abner Society home.inu.net/stemple
81 Sharon Blvd   Dora AL 35062
Ph: 205-674-0101 ▪ Fx: 205-674-0190

National Lumber & Building Material Dealers Association www.dealer.org
40 Ivy St SE   Washington DC 20003
Ph: 202-547-2230 ▪ Fx: 202-547-7640 ▪ TF: 800-634-8645

National Lutheran Outdoors Ministry Association www.nloma.org
2016 Camp Lone Star Rd   La Grange TX 78945
Ph: 979-247-4128 ▪ Fx: 979-247-4120

National Magazine Book & Film Carriers www.nmbfc.com
100 Daingerfield Rd   Alexandria VA 22314
Ph: 703-837-1070 ▪ Fx: 703-837-1072

National Mail Order Association www.nmoa.org
2807 Polk St NE   Minneapolis MN 55418
Ph: 612-788-1673 ▪ Fx: 612-788-1147

National Management Association www.nma1.org
2210 Arbor Blvd   Dayton OH 45439
Ph: 937-294-0421 ▪ Fx: 937-294-2374

National Marfan Foundation www.marfan.org
22 Manhasset Ave   Port Washington NY 11050
Ph: 516-883-8712 ▪ Fx: 516-883-8040 ▪ TF: 800-862-7326

National Marine Bankers Association www.marinebankers.org
200 E Randolph Dr Suite 5100   Chicago IL 60601
Ph: 312-946-6260

National Marine Distributors Association www.nmdaonline.com
37 Pratt St   Essex CT 06426
Ph: 860-767-7898 ▪ Fx: 860-797-7932

National Marine Electronics Association www.nmea.org
7 Riggs Ave   Severna Park MD 21146
Ph: 410-975-9425 ▪ Fx: 410-975-9450

National Marine Manufacturers Association www.nmma.org
200 E Randolph Dr Suite 5100   Chicago IL 60601
Ph: 312-946-6200 ▪ Fx: 312-946-0388

National Marine Representatives Association www.nmraonline.org
1333 Delany Rd Suite 500   Gurnee IL 60031
Ph: 847-662-3167 ▪ Fx: 847-336-7126

National Maritime Union of America
1150 17th St NW Suite 700   Washington DC 20036
Ph: 202-466-7060 ▪ Fx: 202-872-0912

National Marrow Donor Program www.marrow.org
3001 Broadway St NE Suite 500   Minneapolis MN 55413
Ph: 612-627-5800 ▪ Fx: 612-627-8125 ▪ TF: 800-526-7809

National Mastitis Council www.nmconline.org
5944 Seminole Centre Ct Suite C   Madison WI 53711
Ph: 608-663-1255 ▪ Fx: 608-663-1249

National Meat Association www.nmaonline.org
1970 Broadway Suite 825   Oakland CA 94612
Ph: 510-763-1533 ▪ Fx: 510-763-6186

National Meat Canners Association www.meatami.com/content/AboutAMI/canners.htm
1700 N Moore St Suite 1600   Arlington VA 22209
Ph: 703-841-2400 ▪ Fx: 703-527-0938

National Medical Association www.nmanet.org
1012 10th St NW   Washington DC 20001
Ph: 202-347-1895 ▪ Fx: 202-842-3293 ▪ TF: 800-662-0554

National Medical & Dental Association www.polishnmda.com
72-41 Grand Ave   Maspeth NY 11378
Ph: 718-478-3333

National Medical Fellowships www.nmfonline.org
5 Hanover Sq 15th Fl   New York NY 10004
Ph: 212-483-8880 ▪ Fx: 212-483-8897

National Medical War Memorial Project www.medicalwarmemorial.org
PO Box 14492   Kansas City MO 64152
Ph: 816-452-0606 ▪ Fx: 816-454-0897

National Mental Health Association www.nmha.org
1021 Prince St   Alexandria VA 22311
Ph: 703-684-7722 ▪ Fx: 703-684-5968 ▪ TF: 800-969-6642

National Mental Health Consumers' Self-Help Clearinghouse www.mhselfhelp.org
1211 Chestnut St Suite 1207   Philadelphia PA 19107
Ph: 215-751-1810 ▪ Fx: 215-636-6312 ▪ TF: 800-553-4539

National Metal Decorators Association www.nmda.org
9616 Deereco Rd   Timonium MD 21093
Ph: 410-252-5205 ▪ Fx: 410-628-8079

National Middle School Association www.nmsa.org
4151 Executive Pkwy Suite 300   Westerville OH 43081
Ph: 614-895-4730 ▪ Fx: 614-895-4750 ▪ TF: 800-528-6672

National Military Family Association www.nmfa.org
2500 N Van Dorn St Suite 102   Alexandria VA 22302
Ph: 703-931-6632 ▪ Fx: 703-931-4600

National Military Fish & Wildlife Association www.nmfwa.org
6300 Somerset Way   Cambria CA 93428
Ph: 805-238-8265

National Military Intelligence Association www.nmia.org
9200 Centerway Rd   Gaithersburg MD 20879
Ph: 301-840-6642 ▪ Fx: 301-840-8502

National Milk Glass Collectors Society www.nmgcs.org
500 Union Cemetery Rd   Greensburg PA 15601
Ph: 724-832-7968

National Milk Producers Federation www.nmpf.org
2101 Wilson Blvd Suite 400   Arlington VA 22201
Ph: 703-243-6111 ▪ Fx: 703-841-9328 ▪ TF: 888-549-7600

National Milk Producers Federation PAC
2101 Wilson Blvd Suite 400   Arlington VA 22201
Ph: 703-243-6111 ▪ Fx: 703-841-9328

National Mine Rescue Association www.miningorganizations.org/nmra.htm
RR 1 Box 736   Hunker PA 15639
Ph: 724-925-5150 ▪ Fx: 724-925-6190

National Miniature Donkey Association
6450 Dewey Rd   Rome NY 13440
Ph: 315-336-0154 ▪ Fx: 315-339-4414

National Mining Association www.nma.org
101 Constitution Ave NW Suite 500-E   Washington DC 20001
Ph: 202-463-2600 ▪ Fx: 202-463-2666

(National Mining Association) COALPAC
101 Constitution Ave NW Suite 500E   Washington DC 20001
Ph: 202-463-2625 ▪ Fx: 202-463-6152

National Minority AIDS Council www.nmac.org
1931 13th St NW   Washington DC 20009
Ph: 202-483-6622 ▪ Fx: 202-483-1135

National Minority Business Council Inc www.nmbc.org
25 W 45th St Suite 301   New York NY 10036
Ph: 212-997-4753 ▪ Fx: 212-997-5102

National Minority Supplier Development Council www.nmsdcus.org
1040 Ave of the Americas 2nd Fl   New York NY 10018
Ph: 212-944-2430 ▪ Fx: 212-719-9611

National Mobility Equipment Dealers Association www.nmeda.org
11211 N Nebraska Ave Suite A-5   Tampa FL 33612
Ph: 813-977-6603 ▪ Fx: 813-977-6402 ▪ TF: 800-833-0427

National Model Railroad Association www.nmra.org
4121 Cromwell Rd   Chattanooga TN 37421
Ph: 423-892-2846 ▪ Fx: 423-899-4869

National Mole Day Foundation Inc www.moleday.org
1220 S 5th St   Prairie du Chien WI 53821
Ph: 608-326-6036

National Morgan Pony Registry www.bulldancers.com/morganpony

National Morgan Reining Horse Association www.nmrha.com

National Mossberg Collectors Association www.mossbergcollectors.org
PO Box 487 Festus MO 63028
Ph: 636-937-6401

National Motor Freight Traffic Association www.nmfta.org
2200 Mill Rd Alexandria VA 22314
Ph: 703-838-1810 ▪ Fx: 703-683-1094

National Motorists Association www.motorists.org
402 W 2nd St Waunakee WI 53597
Ph: 608-849-6000 ▪ Fx: 608-849-8697 ▪ TF: 800-882-2785

National Movement Theatre Association
3112 17th Ave S Minneapolis MN 55407
Ph: 612-722-2333

National Multi Housing Council www.nmhc.org
1850 M St NW Suite 540 Washington DC 20036
Ph: 202-974-2300 ▪ Fx: 202-775-0112

National Multi Housing Council PAC
1850 M St NW Suite 540 Washington DC 20036
Ph: 202-974-2300 ▪ Fx: 202-775-0112

National MultiCultural Institute www.nmci.org
3000 Connecticut Ave NW Suite 438 Washington DC 20008
Ph: 202-483-0700 ▪ Fx: 202-483-5233

National Multiple Sclerosis Society www.nmss.org
733 3rd Ave New York NY 10017
Ph: 212-986-3240 ▪ Fx: 212-986-7981 ▪ TF: 800-344-4867

National Music Council www.musiccouncil.org
425 Park St Upper Montclair NJ 07043
Ph: 973-655-7974 ▪ Fx: 973-655-5432

National Music Publishers Association www.nmpa.org
475 Park Ave S 29th Fl New York NY 10016
Ph: 646-742-1651 ▪ Fx: 646-742-1779

National Music Theatre Network www.nmtn.org
1697 Broadway Suite 902 New York NY 10019
Ph: 212-664-0979 ▪ Fx: 212-664-0978

National Muzzle Loading Rifle Association www.nmlra.org
PO Box 67 Friendship IN 47021
Ph: 812-667-5131 ▪ Fx: 812-667-5136

National Native American AIDS Prevention Center www.nnaapc.org
436 14th St Suite 1020 Oakland CA 94610
Ph: 510-444-2051 ▪ Fx: 510-444-1593 ▪ TF: 800-283-6880

National Native American Cooperative www.usaindianinfo.org
PO Box 27626 Tucson AZ 85726
Ph: 520-622-4900

National Naval Officers Association www.nnoa.org
PO Box 10871 Alexandria VA 22310
Ph: 703-757-4808

National Needlework Association www.tnna.org
PO Box 3388 Zanesville OH 43702
Ph: 740-455-6773 ▪ Fx: 740-452-2552 ▪ TF: 800-889-8662

National Neighborhood Coalition www.neighborhoodcoalition.org
1030 15th St NW Suite 325 Washington DC 20005
Ph: 202-408-8553 ▪ Fx: 202-408-8551

National Network of Abortion Funds www.nnaf.org
c/o CLPP Hampshire College Amherst MA 01002
Ph: 413-559-5645 ▪ Fx: 413-559-6045

National Network to End Domestic Violence www.nnedv.org
660 Pennsylvania Ave SE Suite 303 Washington DC 20003
Ph: 202-543-5566 ▪ Fx: 202-543-5626

National Network of Estate Planning Attorneys Inc www.netplanning.com
1 Valmont Plaza 4th Fl Omaha NE 68154
Ph: 402-964-3700 ▪ Fx: 402-964-3800 ▪ TF: 888-837-4090

National Network of Grantmakers www.nng.org
138 Court St Suite 427 Brooklyn NY 11201
Ph: 718-643-8814 ▪ Fx: 718-643-8817

National Network for Immigrant & Refugee Rights www.nnirr.org
310 8th St Suite 303 Oakland CA 94607
Ph: 510-465-1984 ▪ Fx: 510-465-1885

National Network for Social Work Managers www.socialworkmanager.org
Jane Adams College of Social Work MC 309 1040 W Harrison
St 4th Fl Chicago IL 60607
Ph: 312-413-2302 ▪ Fx: 312-996-2770

National Network for Youth www.nn4youth.org
1319 F St NW Suite 401 Washington DC 20004
Ph: 202-783-7949 ▪ Fx: 202-783-7955

National Neurofibromatosis Foundation www.nf.org
95 Pine St 16th Fl New York NY 10005
Ph: 212-344-6633 ▪ Fx: 212-747-0004 ▪ TF: 800-323-7938

National New Deal Preservation Association www.newdeallegacy.org/
PO Box 602 Santa Fe NM 87504
Ph: 505-473-2089 ▪ Fx: 505-473-3985

National Newspaper Association www.nna.org
Univ of Missouri 127-129 Neff Annex PO Box 7540 Columbia
MO 65211
Ph: 573-882-5800 ▪ Fx: 573-884-5490 ▪ TF: 800-829-4662

National Newspaper Association Foundation www.nna.org/Partners/NNAF.htm
127-129 Neff Annex PO Box 7540 Columbia MO 65211
Ph: 573-882-5800 ▪ Fx: 573-884-5490 ▪ TF: 800-829-4662

National Newspaper Publishers Association www.nnpa.org
3200 13th St NW Washington DC 20010
Ph: 202-588-8764 ▪ Fx: 202-588-5302

National Niemann-Pick Disease Foundation www.nnpdf.org
415 Madison Ave Fort Atkinson WI 53538
Ph: 920-563-0930 ▪ Fx: 920-563-0931 ▪ TF: 877-287-3672

National Nostalgic Nova www.nnnova.com
PO Box 2344 York PA 17405
Ph: 717-252-4192 ▪ Fx: 717-252-1666

National Notary Association www.nationalnotary.org
9350 DeSoto Ave Chatsworth CA 91313
Ph: 818-739-4000 ▪ Fx: 818-700-1830 ▪ TF: 800-876-6827

National Nurses in Business Association Inc www.nnba.net
867 Levitt Pkwy Rockledge FL 32955
Ph: 321-633-4610 ▪ TF: 877-353-8888

National Nursing Staff Development Organization www.nnsdo.org
7794 Grow Dr Pensacola FL 32514
Ph: 850-474-0995 ▪ Fx: 850-484-8762 ▪ TF: 800-489-1995

National Nutrition Alliance www.am-coll-nutr.org/nna/nna.htm
300 S Duncan Ave Suite 225 Clearwater FL 33755
Ph: 727-446-6086 ▪ Fx: 727-446-6202

National Nutritional Foods Association www.nnfa.org
3931 MacArthur Blvd Suite 101 Newport Beach CA 92660
Ph: 949-622-6272 ▪ Fx: 949-622-6266 ▪ TF: 800-966-6632

National Ocean Industries Association www.noia.org
1120 G St NW Suite 900 Washington DC 20005
Ph: 202-347-6900 ▪ Fx: 202-347-8650

National Odd Shoe Exchange www.oddshoe.org
PO Box 1120 Chandler AZ 85244
Ph: 480-892-3484 ▪ Fx: 480-892-3568

National Off-Highway Vehicle Conservation Council Inc www.nohvcc.org
4718 S Taylor Dr Sheboygan WI 53081
Ph: 800-348-6487 ▪ Fx: 920-458-3446

National Office Products Alliance www.nopanet.org
301 N Fairfax St Alexandria VA 22314
Ph: 703-549-9040 ▪ Fx: 703-683-7552

National Oil & Acrylic Painters Society www.noaps.org
PO Box 676 Osage Beach MO 65049
Ph: 417-533-7550

National Oilseed Processors Association www.nopa.org
1300 L St NW Suite 1020 Washington DC 20005
Ph: 202-842-0463 ▪ Fx: 202-842-9126

National Older Worker Partnership
c/o National Council on the Aging 300 D St SW Suite
801 Washington DC 20024
Ph: 202-479-1200 ▪ Fx: 202-479-0735

National Oldtime Fiddlers' Association
309 State St Weiser ID 83672
Ph: 800-437-1280 ▪ Fx: 208-414-0255

National Onion Association www.onions-usa.org
822 7th St Suite 510 Greeley CO 80631
Ph: 970-353-5895 ▪ Fx: 970-353-5897

National Onsite Wastewater Recycling Association www.nowra.org
PO Box 1270 Edgewater MD 21037
Ph: 410-798-1697 ▪ Fx: 410-798-5741

National Opera Association www.noa.org
PO Box 60869 Canyon TX 79016
Ph: 806-651-2857 ▪ Fx: 806-651-2958

National Operating Committee on Standards for Athletic Equipment www.nocsae.org
PO Box 12290 Overland Park KS 66282
Ph: 913-888-1340 ▪ Fx: 913-888-1065

National Oral Health Information Clearinghouse www.nohic.nidcr.nih.gov
1 NOHIC Way Bethesda MD 20892
Ph: 301-402-7364 ▪ Fx: 301-907-8830

National Order of Battlefield Commissions www.battlefieldcommissions.org
4 Meadowlark Ln Pinehurst NC 28374
Ph: 910-235-0007 ▪ Fx: 910-235-0579

National Order of Women Legislators www.womenlegislators.org/nowl
910 16th St NW Suite 100 Washington DC 20006
Ph: 202-337-3565

National Organization on Adolescent Pregnancy Parenting & Prevention Inc www.noappp.org
2401 Pennsylvania Ave NW Suite
350 Washington DC 20037
Ph: 202-293-8370 ▪ Fx: 202-293-8805 ▪ TF: 888-766-2777

National Organization for Albinism & Hypopigmentation www.albinism.org
PO Box 959 East Hampstead NH 03826
Ph: 603-887-2310 ▪ Fx: 603-887-6049 ▪ TF: 800-473-2310

National Organization of Bar Counsel www.nobc.org
515 5th St NW Bldg A Rm 127 Washington DC 20001
Ph: 202-638-1501 ▪ Fx: 202-638-0862

National Organization of Black Law Enforcement Executives www.noblenatl.org
4609 Pinecrest Office Park Dr Suite F Alexandria VA 22312
Ph: 703-658-1529 ▪ Fx: 703-658-9479

National Organization of Circumcision Information Resource Centers www.nocirc.org
PO Box 2512 San Anselmo CA 94979
Ph: 415-488-9883 ▪ Fx: 415-488-9660

National Organization for Competency Assurance www.noca.org
2025 M St NW Suite 800 Washington DC 20036
Ph: 202-367-1165 ▪ Fx: 202-367-2165

National Organization for Continuing Education of Roman Catholic Clergy www.nocercc.org
1337 W Ohio St Chicago IL 60622
Ph: 312-226-1890 ▪ Fx: 312-829-8915

National Organization on Disability www.nod.org
910 16th St NW Suite 600 Washington DC 20006
Ph: 202-293-5960 ▪ Fx: 202-293-7999

National Organization of Gay & Lesbian Scientists & Technical Professionals www.noglstp.org/
PO Box 91803 Pasadena CA 91109
Ph: 626-791-7689

National Organization to Halt the Abuse & Routine Mutilation of Males www.noharmm.org
PO Box 460795 San Francisco CA 94146
Ph: 415-826-9351

National Organization for Human Service Education www.nohse.org
9001 Braddock Rd Suite 380 Springfield VA 22151
Ph: 703-323-9896 ▪ Fx: 703-426-8400

National Organization of Industrial Trade Unions www.noitu.org
148-06 Hillside Ave Jamaica NY 11435
Ph: 718-291-3434 ▪ Fx: 718-526-2920

National Organization of Italian-American Women www.noiaw.com
445 W 59th St Rm 1248 New York NY 10019
Ph: 212-237-8574 ▪ Fx: 212-489-6130

National Organization of Legal Services Workers www.nolsw.org
113 University Pl 5th Fl New York NY 10003
Ph: 212-228-0992 ▪ Fx: 212-228-0097 ▪ TF: 800-829-2320

National Organization of Life & Health Insurance Guaranty Associations   13873 Park Center Rd Suite 329   Herndon VA 20171   www.nolhga.com
Ph: 703-481-5206 ▪ Fx: 703-481-5209

National Organization of Minority Architects   www.noma.net
Howard Univ School of Architecture & Design 2366 6th St NW Rm 100   Washington DC 20059
Ph: 202-686-2780

National Organization of Mothers of Twins Clubs Inc   www.nomotc.org
PO Box 438   Thompsons Station TN 37179
Ph: 615-595-0936 ▪ TF: 877-540-2200

National Organization of Nurse Practitioner Faculties   www.nonpf.com
1522 K St NW Suite 702   Washington DC 20005
Ph: 202-289-8044 ▪ Fx: 202-289-8046

National Organization of Parents of Blind Children   www.nfb.org/nopbc/nopbc_what.htm
1800 Johnson St   Baltimore MD 21230
Ph: 410-659-9314

National Organization for the Professional Advancement of Black Chemists & Chemical Engineers   PO Box 77040   Washington DC 20013   www.nobcche.org
Ph: 202-667-1699 ▪ Fx: 202-667-1705 ▪ TF: 800-776-1419

National Organization for Rare Disorders   www.rarediseases.org
55 Kenosia Ave PO Box 1968   Danbury CT 06813
Ph: 203-744-0100 ▪ Fx: 203-798-2291 ▪ TF: 800-999-6673

National Organization for Raw Materials   www.normeconomics.org
680 E 5 Point Hwy   Charlotte MI 48813
Ph: 517-543-0111

National Organization for the Reform of Marijuana Laws   www.norml.org
1600 K St NW Suite 501   Washington DC 20006
Ph: 202-483-5500 ▪ Fx: 202-483-0057

National Organization of Restoring Men   www.norm.org
3205 Northwood Dr Suite 209   Concord CA 94520
Ph: 925-827-4077 ▪ Fx: 925-827-4119

National Organization for Rivers   www.nationalrivers.org
212 W Cheyenne Mountain Blvd   Colorado Springs CO 80906
Ph: 719-579-8759 ▪ Fx: 719-576-6238

National Organization of Single Mothers   singlemothers.org
PO Box 68   Midland NC 28107
Ph: 704-888-5437

National Organization of Social Security Claimants' Representatives   www.nosscr.org
6 Prospect St   Midland Park NJ 07432
Ph: 201-444-1415 ▪ Fx: 201-444-1823 ▪ TF: 800-431-2804

National Organization Taunting Safety & Fairness Everywhere   www.notsafe.org
PO Box 5743   Santa Barbara CA 93150
Ph: 805-966-0611

National Organization of Test Research & Training Reactors   www.trtr.org

National Organization for Victim Assistance   www.try-nova.org
1730 Park Rd NW   Washington DC 20010
Ph: 202-232-6682 ▪ Fx: 202-462-2255 ▪ TF: 800-879-6682

National Organization for Women   www.now.org
733 15th St NW 2nd Fl   Washington DC 20005
Ph: 202-628-8669 ▪ Fx: 202-785-8576

National Organization for Women PAC   www.nowpacs.org
733 15th St NW 2nd Fl   Washington DC 20005
Ph: 202-331-0066 ▪ Fx: 202-785-8576

National Orientation Directors Association   www.nodaweb.org
Univ of Michigan-Flint 375 University Ctr   Flint MI 48502
Ph: 810-424-5513 ▪ Fx: 810-762-3023

National Ornamental Goldfish Growers Association
6916 Blacks Mill Rd   Thurmont MD 21788
Ph: 301-271-7475 ▪ Fx: 301-271-7059

National Ornamental & Miscellaneous Metals Association   www.nomma.org
532-A Forest Pkwy   Forest Park GA 30297
Ph: 404-363-4009 ▪ Fx: 404-366-1852

National Osteoporosis Foundation   www.nof.org
1232 22nd St NW   Washington DC 20037
Ph: 202-223-2226 ▪ Fx: 202-223-2237 ▪ TF: 800-223-9994

National Ovarian Cancer Coalition   www.ovarian.org
500 NE Spanish River Blvd Suite 14   Boca Raton FL 33431
Ph: 561-393-0005 ▪ Fx: 561-393-7275 ▪ TF: 888-682-7426

National PACE Association   www.natlpaceassn.com
801 N Fairfax St Suite 309   Alexandria VA 22314
Ph: 703-535-1565 ▪ Fx: 703-535-1566

National Paddleball Association   www.paddleball.org
7642 Kingston Dr   Portage MI 49002
Ph: 616-323-0011 ▪ Fx: 616-279-6275

National Paideia Center   www.paideia.org
400 Silver Cedar Ct Suite 200   Chapel Hill NC 27514
Ph: 919-962-3128 ▪ Fx: 919-962-3139

National Paint & Coatings Association   www.paint.org
1500 Rhode Island Ave NW   Washington DC 20005
Ph: 202-462-6272 ▪ Fx: 202-462-8549

National Pan-American Junior Golf Association   npaga.callernetwork.com/junior.html
4813 Larcade Dr   Corpus Christi TX 78415
Ph: 361-853-6860 ▪ Fx: 361-854-7242

National Panhellenic Conference   www.npcwomen.org
3905 Vincennes Rd Suite 105   Indianapolis IN 46268
Ph: 317-872-3185 ▪ Fx: 317-872-3192

National Paperbox Association   www.paperbox.org
113 S West St 3rd Fl   Alexandria VA 22313
Ph: 703-684-2212 ▪ Fx: 703-683-6920

National Paralegal Association   www.nationalparalegal.org
PO Box 406   Solebury PA 18963
Ph: 215-297-8333 ▪ Fx: 215-297-8358

National Parenting Association   www.parentsunite.org
PO Box 77   New York NY 10113
Ph: 212-229-5990 ▪ Fx: 212-679-3127 ▪ TF: 800-709-8795

National Parents Association   www.bixxo.com/npa
603 E Lincoln Way Ave Main Stn Box 1993   Valparaiso IN 46383
Ph: 219-462-9996 ▪ Fx: 219-464-3538

National Park Academy of the Arts   www.artsfortheparks.com
PO Box 608   Jackson Hole WY 83001
Ph: 307-733-2787 ▪ Fx: 307-739-1199 ▪ TF: 800-553-2787

National Park Foundation   www.nationalparks.org
11 Dupont Cir NW Suite 600   Washington DC 20036
Ph: 202-785-4200 ▪ Fx: 202-785-3103 ▪ TF: 888-407-2757

National Park Hospitality Association   www.nphassn.com
3701 Court House Dr   Ellicott City MD 21043
Ph: 410-480-2240 ▪ Fx: 410-480-2617

National Park Trust   www.parktrust.org
415-2nd St NE Suite 210   Washington DC 20002
Ph: 202-548-0500 ▪ Fx: 202-548-0595

National Parking Association   www.npapark.org
1112 16th St NW Suite 300   Washington DC 20036
Ph: 202-296-4336 ▪ Fx: 202-331-8523 ▪ TF: 800-647-7275

National Parking Association PAC
1112 16th St NW Suite 300   Washington DC 20036
Ph: 202-296-4336 ▪ Fx: 202-331-8523 ▪ TF: 800-647-7275

National Parkinson Foundation   www.parkinson.org
1501 NW 9th Ave   Miami FL 33136
Ph: 305-547-6666 ▪ Fx: 305-243-4403 ▪ TF: 800-327-4545

National Parks, A Christian Ministry in the   www.acmnp.com
10 Justins Way   Freeport ME 04032
Ph: 207-865-6436 ▪ Fx: 207-865-6852 ▪ TF: 800-786-3450

National Parks Conservation Association   www.npca.org
1300 19th St NW Suite 300   Washington DC 20036
Ph: 202-223-6722 ▪ Fx: 202-659-0650 ▪ TF: 800-628-7275

National Parks at Gettysburg, Friends of the   www.friendsofgettysburg.org
304B York St PO Box 4622   Gettysburg PA 17325
Ph: 717-334-0772 ▪ Fx: 717-334-3118

National Partnership for Women & Families   www.nationalpartnership.org
1875 Connecticut Ave NW Suite 650   Washington DC 20009
Ph: 202-986-2600 ▪ Fx: 202-986-2539

National Party Boat Owners Alliance
181 Thames St   Groton CT 06340
Ph: 860-535-2066 ▪ Fx: 860-535-8389

National Pasta Association   www.ilovepasta.org
1156 15th St NW Suite 900   Washington DC 20005
Ph: 202-637-5888 ▪ Fx: 202-223-9741

National Patio Enclosure Association
12625 Frederick St Suite 1-5 315   Moreno Valley CA 92553
Ph: 909-485-8881 ▪ Fx: 909-924-3078

National Pawnbrokers Association   www.nationalpawnbrokers.org
611 Dallas Dr Suite 109   Roanoke TX 76262
Ph: 817-491-4554 ▪ Fx: 817-491-6770

National Peace Corps Association   www.rpcv.org
1900 L St NW Suite 205   Washington DC 20036
Ph: 202-293-7728 ▪ Fx: 202-293-7554 ▪ TF: 800-424-8580

National Peace Foundation   www.nationalpeace.org
666 11th St NW Suite 202   Washington DC 20001
Ph: 202-783-7030 ▪ Fx: 202-783-7040 ▪ TF: 800-237-3223

National Peace Garden Foundation   www.peacefront.org
1 Grumman Hill Rd   Wilton CT 06897
Ph: 203-762-7917 ▪ Fx: 203-762-9053 ▪ TF: 877-467-3223

National Peach Council   www.nationalpeach.org
12 Nicklaus Ln Suite 101   Columbia SC 29229
Ph: 803-788-7101 ▪ Fx: 803-865-8090

National Peanut Buying Points Association
PO Box 314   Tifton GA 31793
Ph: 229-386-1716 ▪ Fx: 229-386-8757

National Peanut Festival Association   www.nationalpeanutfestival.com
5622 U S Hwy 231 S   Dothan AL 36301
Ph: 334-793-4323 ▪ Fx: 334-793-3247

National Pecan Shellers Association   www.ilovepecans.org
5775 Peachtree-Dunwoody Rd Bldg G Suite 500   Atlanta GA 30342
Ph: 404-252-3663 ▪ Fx: 404-252-0774

National Pediculosis Association   www.headlice.org
50 Kearney   Needham MA 02494
Ph: 781-449-6487 ▪ Fx: 781-449-8129 ▪ TF: 800-446-4672

National Pedigreed Livestock Council   nplc.net
177 Palermo Pl   The Villages FL 32159
Ph: 352-259-6005

National Peer Helpers Association   www.peerhelping.org
PO Box 32272   Kansas City MO 64171
Ph: 877-314-7337 ▪ Fx: 866-314-7337

National People's Action   www.npa-us.org
810 N Milwaukee Ave   Chicago IL 60622
Ph: 312-243-3038 ▪ Fx: 312-243-7044

National Performance Network   www.npnweb.org/
225 Baronne St Suite 1712   New Orleans LA 70112
Ph: 504-595-8008 ▪ Fx: 504-595-8006

National Perinatal Association   www.nationalperinatal.org
3500 E Fletcher Ave Suite 205   Tampa FL 33613
Ph: 813-971-1008 ▪ Fx: 813-971-9306 ▪ TF: 888-971-3295

National Pest Management Association Inc   www.pestworld.org
8100 Oak St   Dunn Loring VA 22027
Ph: 703-573-8330 ▪ Fx: 703-573-4116

National Pest Management Association PAC
8100 Oak St   Dunn Loring VA 22027
Ph: 703-573-8330 ▪ Fx: 703-573-4116

National Pesticide Information Center   npic.orst.edu
333 Weniger Hall   Corvallis OR 97331
Ph: 800-858-7378 ▪ Fx: 541-737-0761

National Petrochemical & Refiners Association   www.npradc.org
1899 L St NW Suite 1000   Washington DC 20036
Ph: 202-457-0480 ▪ Fx: 202-457-0486

National Petroleum Council www.npc.org
1625 K St NW Suite 600 Washington DC 20006
Ph: 202-393-6100 ■ Fx: 202-331-8539

National Pharmaceutical Association www.npha.net
107 Kilmayne Dr Suite C Cary NC 27511
Ph: 800-944-6742 ■ Fx: 919-469-5870

National Pharmaceutical Council www.npcnow.org
1894 Preston White Dr Reston VA 20191
Ph: 703-620-6390 ■ Fx: 703-476-0904

National Pharmacy Technicians Association www.pharmacytechnician.org
3920 FM 1960 W Suite 380 Houston TX 77068
Ph: 281-866-7900 ■ Fx: 281-895-7320 ■ TF: 888-247-8700

National Phlebotomy Association www.nationalphlebotomy.org
1901 Brightseat Rd Landover MD 20785
Ph: 301-386-4200 ■ Fx: 301-386-4203

National Photography Instructors Association
1255 Hill Dr Eagle Rock CA 90041
Ph: 323-254-1549 ■ Fx: 323-254-2797

National Piano Foundation www.pianonet.com
13140 Coit Rd Suite 320 LB 120 Dallas TX 75240
Ph: 972-233-9107 ■ Fx: 972-490-4219

National Plant Board www.aphis.usda.gov/npb
California Dept of Food & Agriculture 1220 'N' St Sacramento CA 95814
Ph: 916-654-1022 ■ Fx: 916-654-1018

National Plasterers Council www.npconline.org
2811-D Tamiami Trail Port Charlotte FL 33952
Ph: 866-483-4672 ■ Fx: 800-279-1729 ■ TF: 866-483-4672

National Podiatric Medical Association
1706 E 87th St Chicago IL 60617
Ph: 773-374-1616 ■ Fx: 773-374-5860

National Police Bloodhound Association
RR2 Box 1165 Milton PA 17847
Ph: 570-742-7310 ■ Fx: 570-742-7319

National Policy Association www.npa1.org
1424 16th St NW Suite 700 Washington DC 20036
Ph: 202-884-7623 ■ Fx: 202-797-5516

National Policy, Center for www.cnponline.org
1 Massachusetts Ave NW Suite 333 Washington DC 20001
Ph: 202-682-1800 ■ Fx: 202-682-1818

National Policy & Resource Center on Nutrition & Aging www.fiu.edu/~nutreldr
Florida International Univ University Park OE200 Miami FL 33199
Ph: 305-348-1517 ■ Fx: 305-348-1518

National Pollution Prevention Roundtable www.p2.org
11 Dupont Cir NW Suite 201 Washington DC 20036
Ph: 202-299-9701 ■ Fx: 202-299-9704 ■ TF: 888-748-7272

National Pop Can Collectors www.one-mans-junk.com/npcc/npcc.htm

National Pork Producers Council www.nppc.org
122 C St NW Suite 875 Washington DC 20001
Ph: 202-347-3600 ■ Fx: 202-347-5265

National Pork Producers Council PAC
122 C St NW Suite 875 Washington DC 20001
Ph: 202-347-3600 ■ Fx: 202-347-5265 ■ TF: 866-701-6388

National Postal Forum www.npf.org
50 W Corporate Ctr 3998 Fair Ridge Dr Suite 300 Fairfax VA 22033
Ph: 703-218-5015 ■ Fx: 703-218-5020

National Postal Mail Handlers Union www.npmhu.org
1101 Connecticut Ave NW Suite 500 Washington DC 20036
Ph: 202-833-9095 ■ Fx: 202-833-0008

National Postsecondary Agricultural Student Organization www.nationalpas.org
6060 FFA Dr PO Box 68960 Indianapolis IN 46268
Ph: 317-802-4220 ■ Fx: 317-802-5220

National Potato Council www.nationalpotatocouncil.org
1300 L St NW Suite 910 Washington DC 20005
Ph: 202-682-9456 ■ Fx: 202-682-0333

National Poultry & Food Distributors Association www.npfda.org
958 McEver Rd Ext Unit B-8 Gainesville GA 30504
Ph: 770-535-9901 ■ Fx: 770-535-7385 ■ TF: 877-845-1545

National Precast Concrete Association www.precast.org
10333 N Meridian St Suite 272 Indianapolis IN 46290
Ph: 317-571-9500 ■ Fx: 317-571-0041 ■ TF: 800-366-7731

National Preservation Institute www.npi.org
PO Box 1702 Alexandria VA 22313
Ph: 703-765-0100

National Press Club npc.press.org
529 14th St NW National Press Bldg Washington DC 20045
Ph: 202-662-7500 ■ Fx: 202-662-7569

National Press Foundation www.nationalpress.org
1211 Connecticut Ave NW Suite 310 Washington DC 20036
Ph: 202-663-7280 ■ Fx: 202-530-2855

National Press Photographers Association www.nppa.org
3200 Croasdaile Dr Suite 306 Durham NC 27705
Ph: 919-383-7246 ■ Fx: 919-383-7261

National Pressure Ulcer Advisory Panel www.npuap.org
12100 Sunset Hills Rd Suite 130 Reston VA 20190
Ph: 703-464-4849 ■ Fx: 703-435-4390

National Prison Hospice Association
PO Box 3769 Boulder CO 80307
Ph: 303-447-8051 ■ Fx: 303-447-8055

National Private Truck Council www.nptc.org
2200 Mill Rd Suite 350 Alexandria VA 22314
Ph: 703-683-1300 ■ Fx: 703-683-1217

National Professional Soccer League www.allsports.com/npsl
115 Dewalt Ave NW 5th Fl Canton OH 44702
Ph: 330-454-4625 ■ Fx: 330-455-3885

National Propane Gas Association www.npga.org
1150 17th St NW Suite 310 Washington DC 20036
Ph: 202-466-7200 ■ Fx: 202-466-7205

National Propane Gas Association PAC
1150 17th St NW Suite 310 Washington DC 20036
Ph: 202-466-7200 ■ Fx: 202-466-7205

National Property Management Association www.npma.org
1108 Pinehurst Rd Dunedin FL 34698
Ph: 727-736-3788 ■ Fx: 727-736-6707

National Psoriasis Foundation www.psoriasis.org
6600 SW 92nd Ave Suite 300 Portland OR 97223
Ph: 503-244-7404 ■ Fx: 503-245-0626 ■ TF: 800-723-9166

National Psychological Association for Psychoanalysis www.npap.org
150 W 13th St New York NY 10011
Ph: 212-924-7440 ■ Fx: 212-989-7543

National PTA www.pta.org
330 N Wabash Ave Suite 2100 Chicago IL 60611
Ph: 312-670-6782 ■ Fx: 312-670-6783 ■ TF: 800-307-4782

National Public Employer Labor Relations Association www.npelra.org
1617 Duke St Alexandria VA 22314
Ph: 703-836-9626 ■ Fx: 703-836-9628 ■ TF: 800-296-2230

National Public Health Information Coalition www.nphic.org
986 Hidden Hollow Dr Marietta GA 30068
Ph: 770-509-5555 ■ Fx: 770-565-8436

National Public Parks Tennis Association
1001 W 98th St Suite 101 Bloomington MN 55431
Ph: 952-887-5001 ■ Fx: 952-887-5061 ■ TF: 800-536-6982

National Public Radio www.npr.org
635 Massachusetts Ave NW Washington DC 20001
Ph: 202-513-2000 ■ Fx: 202-513-3329

National Public Records Research Association www.nprra.org
PO Box 3159 Durham NC 27705
Ph: 919-384-0434 ■ Fx: 919-383-0035

National Puerto Rican Coalition Inc www.bateylink.org/overview.htm
1900 L St NW Suite 802 Washington DC 20006
Ph: 202-223-3915 ■ Fx: 202-429-2223

National Puerto Rican Forum www.nprf.org
1946 Webster Ave 3rd Fl Bronx NY 10457
Ph: 646-792-1010 ■ Fx: 646-792-1020

National Purchasing Institute www.nationalpurchasinginstitute.com
701 N Green Valley Pkwy Suite 200 Henderson NV 89053
Ph: 702-260-7114 ■ Fx: 702-260-7052

National Pygmy Goat Association www.npga-pygmy.com
1932 149th Ave SE Snohomish WA 98290
Ph: 425-334-6506 ■ Fx: 425-334-5447

National Radio Heritage Association
15347 Nall Rd Council Bluffs IA 51503
Ph: 712-388-9088

National Railroad Construction & Maintenance Association Inc www.nrcma.org
122 C St NW Suite 850 Washington DC 20001
Ph: 202-638-7790 ■ Fx: 202-638-1045 ■ TF: 800-883-1557

National Railway Historical Society www.nrhs.com
PO Box 58547 Philadelphia PA 19102
Ph: 215-557-6606 ■ Fx: 215-557-6740

National Railway Labor Conference
1901 L St NW Suite 500 Washington DC 20036
Ph: 202-862-7200 ■ Fx: 202-862-7230

National Ramah Commission www.campramah.org
3080 Broadway New York NY 10027
Ph: 212-678-8881 ■ Fx: 212-749-8251

National Reading Conference www.nrconline.org
7044 S 13th St Oak Creek WI 53154
Ph: 414-768-8000 ■ Fx: 414-768-8001

National Ready Mixed Concrete Association www.nrmca.org
900 Spring St Silver Spring MD 20910
Ph: 301-587-1400 ■ Fx: 301-585-4219

National Real Estate Investors Association www.nationalreia.com
525 W 5th St Suite 230 Covington KY 41011
Ph: 888-762-7342 ■ Fx: 859-581-5993

National Recreation & Park Association www.nrpa.org
22377 Belmont Ridge Rd Ashburn VA 20148
Ph: 703-858-0784 ■ Fx: 703-858-0794 ■ TF: 800-626-6772

National Recreational Vehicle Owners Club www.nrvoc.com
PO Box 520 Gonzalez FL 32560
Ph: 850-937-8354 ■ Fx: 850-937-8356 ■ TF: 800-281-9186

National Recycling Coalition www.nrc-recycle.org
1325 G St NW Suite 1025 Washington DC 20005
Ph: 202-347-0450 ■ Fx: 202-347-0449

National REGAP Network www.regap.org
PO Box 4454 Cary IL 60013
Ph: 847-217-1836

National Registration Center for Study Abroad www.nrcsa.com
PO Box 1393 Milwaukee WI 53201
Ph: 414-278-0631 ■ Fx: 414-271-8884

National Registry of Certified Chemists www.nrcc6.org
927 S Walter Reed Dr Suite 11 Arlington VA 22204
Ph: 703-979-9001

National Registry of Emergency Medical Technicians www.nremt.org
6610 Bush Blvd PO Box 29233 Columbus OH 43229
Ph: 614-888-4484 ■ Fx: 614-888-8920

National Registry of Environmental Professionals www.nrep.org
PO Box 2099 Glenview IL 60025
Ph: 847-724-6631 ■ Fx: 847-724-4223

National Rehabilitation Administration Association www.rehabadmin.org
1020 W 5th St Dickinson ND 58601
Ph: 701-227-7415

National Rehabilitation Association www.nationalrehab.org
633 S Washington St Alexandria VA 22314
Ph: 703-836-0850 ■ Fx: 703-836-0848 ■ TF: 888-258-4295

National Rehabilitation Counseling Association nrca-net.org
8807 Sudley Rd Suite 102 Manassas VA 20110
Ph: 703-361-2077 ■ Fx: 703-361-2489

National Rehabilitation Information Center   www.naric.com
4200 Forbes Blvd Suite 202   Lanham MD 20706
Ph: 301-459-5900 ▪ Fx: 301-459-4263 ▪ TF: 800-346-2742

National Reining Horse Association   www.nrha.com
3000 NW 10th St   Oklahoma City OK 73107
Ph: 405-946-7400 ▪ Fx: 405-946-8410

National Religious Broadcasters   www.nrb.org
9510 Technology Dr   Manassas VA 20110
Ph: 703-330-7000 ▪ Fx: 703-330-7100

National Religious Vocation Conference   www.nrvc.net
5420 S Cornell Ave Suite 105   Chicago IL 60615
Ph: 773-363-5454 ▪ Fx: 773-363-5530

National Remotivation Therapy Organization Inc   www.remotivation.com
103 McDonald St   West Nanticoke PA 18634
Ph: 570-735-7079 ▪ Fx: 570-735-2997

National Renal Administrators Association   www.nraa.org
1904 Naomi Pl   Prescot AZ 86303
Ph: 928-717-2772 ▪ Fx: 928-441-3857

National Renderers Association   www.renderers.org
801 N Fairfax St Suite 207   Alexandria VA 22314
Ph: 703-683-0155 ▪ Fx: 703-683-2626

National Renewal, Alliance for   www.ncl.org
National Civic League 1319 F ST NW Suite 204   Washington
DC 20004
Ph: 202-783-2961 ▪ Fx: 202-347-2161

National Republican Club of Capitol Hill   www.capitolhillclub.com
300 1st St SE   Washington DC 20003
Ph: 202-484-4590 ▪ Fx: 202-479-9110

National Republican Congressional Committee   nrcc.org
320 1st St SE   Washington DC 20003
Ph: 202-479-7000 ▪ Fx: 202-863-0693

National Republican Senatorial Committee   www.nrsc.org
425 2nd St NE   Washington DC 20002
Ph: 202-675-6000 ▪ Fx: 202-675-6058

National Resident Matching Program   www.nrmp.org
2501 'N' St NW   Washington DC 20037
Ph: 202-828-0566 ▪ Fx: 202-828-4797

National Residential Appraisers Institute   www.nraiappraisers.com
2001 Cooper Foster Pk Rd   Amherst OH 44001
Ph: 440-282-7925 ▪ Fx: 440-282-8027

National Resource Center on Domestic Violence   www.nrcdv.org
6400 Flank Dr Suite 1300   Harrisburg PA 17112
Ph: 717-545-6400 ▪ Fx: 717-545-9456 ▪ TF: 800-537-2238

National Resource Center for Health & Safety in Child Care   nrc.uchsc.edu
Univ of Colorado Health Sciences Ctr at Fitzsimons CMS F 541
PO Box 6508   Aurora CO 80045
Ph: 303-724-0665 ▪ Fx: 303-724-0960 ▪ TF: 800-598-5437

National Resource Center on Homelessness & Mental Illness   www.nrchmi.com
345 Delaware Ave   Delmar NY 12054
Ph: 518-439-7415 ▪ Fx: 518-439-7612 ▪ TF: 800-444-7415

National Resource Center on Native   www.med.und.nodak.edu/depts/rural//nrcnaa
American Aging   PO Box 9037   Grand Forks ND 58202
Ph: 701-777-3437 ▪ Fx: 701-777-2389 ▪ TF: 800-896-7628

National Resource Center for Paraprofessionals   www.nrcpara.org
Utah State Univ 6526 Old Main Hill   Logan UT 84322
Ph: 435-797-7272

National Resource Center for Special Needs Adoptions   www.spaulding.org
16250 Northland Dr Suite 120   Southfield MI 48075
Ph: 248-443-7080 ▪ Fx: 248-443-7099 ▪ TF: 877-767-5437

National Resource Center for Youth Services   www.nrcys.ou.edu
4502 E 41st St Bldg 4 W   Tulsa OK 74135
Ph: 918-660-3700 ▪ Fx: 918-660-3737

National Restaurant Association   www.restaurant.org
1200 17th St NW   Washington DC 20036
Ph: 202-331-5900 ▪ Fx: 202-331-2429 ▪ TF: 800-424-5156

National Restaurant Association Educational Foundation   www.nraef.org
175 W Jackson Blvd Suite 1500   Chicago IL 60604
Ph: 312-715-1010 ▪ TF: 800-765-2122

National Restaurant Association PAC   www.restaurant.org/government/nrapac.html
1200 17th St NW   Washington DC 20036
Ph: 202-331-5900 ▪ Fx: 202-331-2429 ▪ TF: 800-424-5156

National Retail Federation   www.nrf.com
325 7th St NW Suite 1100   Washington DC 20004
Ph: 202-783-7971 ▪ Fx: 202-737-2849 ▪ TF: 800-673-4692

National Retail Hardware Association   www.nrha.org
5822 W 74th St   Indianapolis IN 46278
Ph: 317-290-0338 ▪ Fx: 317-328-4354 ▪ TF: 800-772-4424

National Retail Hobby Stores Association   www.hobbystores.org
710 E Ogden Ave Suite 600   Naperville IL 60563
Ph: 630-579-3296 ▪ Fx: 630-629-2488

National Retired Teachers Association   www.aarp.org/nrta
601 'E' St NW   Washington DC 20049
Ph: 202-434-2277 ▪ Fx: 202-434-2320 ▪ TF: 800-424-3410

National Retriever Club   www.working-retriever.com/nrc
4379 S Howell Ave Suite 17   Milwaukee WI 53207
Ph: 414-481-2760 ▪ Fx: 414-481-2743

National Rex Rabbit Club   www.nationalrexrc.com
21840 S 116th Ave   New Lenox IL 60451
Ph: 815-469-5150

National Reye's Syndrome Foundation   www.reyessyndrome.org
PO Box 829   Bryan OH 43506
Ph: 419-636-2679 ▪ Fx: 419-636-9897 ▪ TF: 800-233-7393

National Rifle Association of America   www.nra.org
11250 Waples Mill Rd   Fairfax VA 22030
Ph: 703-267-1000 ▪ Fx: 703-267-3957 ▪ TF: 800-672-3888

National Right to Life Committee Inc   www.nrlc.org
512 10th St NW   Washington DC 20004
Ph: 202-626-8800

National Right to Life PAC
512 10th St NW   Washington DC 20004
Ph: 202-626-8808 ▪ Fx: 202-393-2874

National Right to Read Foundation   www.nrrf.org

National Right to Work Committee   www.right-to-work.org
8001 Braddock Rd Suite 500   Springfield VA 22160
Ph: 703-321-8510 ▪ Fx: 703-321-7342 ▪ TF: 800-336-3600

National Right to Work Legal Defense Foundation Inc   www.nrtw.org
8001 Braddock Rd Suite 600   Springfield VA 22160
Ph: 703-321-8510 ▪ Fx: 703-321-9613 ▪ TF: 800-325-7892

National Risk Retention Association   www.nrra-usa.org
4248 Park Glen Rd   Minneapolis MN 55416
Ph: 952-928-4656 ▪ Fx: 952-929-1318 ▪ TF: 800-999-4505

National Roadside Vegetation Management Association   www.nrvma.org
6402 Betty Cook Dr   Austin TX 78723
Ph: 512-933-9930 ▪ Fx: 512-933-9971

National Roof Deck Contractors Association   nrdca.org
PO Box 1582   Westford MA 01886
Ph: 800-217-7944 ▪ Fx: 978-250-9788

National Roofing Contractors Association   www.nrca.net
10255 W Higgins Rd Suite 600   Rosemont IL 60018
Ph: 847-299-9070 ▪ Fx: 847-299-1183 ▪ TF: 800-323-9545

National Roofing Contractors Association PAC   www.nrca.net/government
324 4th St NE   Washington DC 20002
Ph: 202-546-7584 ▪ Fx: 202-546-9289

National Rosacea Society   www.rosacea.org
800 S Northwest Hwy Suite 200   Barrington IL 60010
Ph: 847-382-8971 ▪ Fx: 847-382-5567 ▪ TF: 888-662-5874

National Rowing Foundation   www.natrowing.org
67 Mystic Rd   North Stonington CT 06359
Ph: 860-535-0634 ▪ Fx: 860-535-0637

National Runaway Switchboard   www.nrscrisisline.org
3080 N Lincoln Ave   Chicago IL 60657
Ph: 773-880-9860 ▪ Fx: 773-929-5150 ▪ TF: 800-621-4000

National Rural Economic Developers Association   www.nreda.org
431 E Locust Suite 300   Des Moines IA 50309
Ph: 515-284-1421 ▪ Fx: 515-243-2049

National Rural Education Association   www.nrea.net
Univ of Oklahoma 820 Van Vleet Oval Rm 227   Norman OK
73109
Ph: 405-324-7959

National Rural Electric Cooperative Association   www.nreca.org
4301 Wilson Blvd   Arlington VA 22203
Ph: 703-907-5500 ▪ Fx: 703-907-5528

National Rural Health Association   www.nrharural.org
1 W Armour Blvd Suite 203   Kansas City MO 64111
Ph: 816-756-3140 ▪ Fx: 816-756-3144

National Rural Housing Coalition   www.nrhcweb.org
1250 'I' St NW Suite 902   Washington DC 20005
Ph: 202-393-5229 ▪ Fx: 202-393-3034

National Rural Letter Carriers' Association   www.nrlca.org
1630 Duke St 4th Fl   Alexandria VA 22314
Ph: 703-684-5545 ▪ Fx: 703-548-8735

National Rural Water Association   www.nrwa.org
2915 S 13th St   Duncan OK 73533
Ph: 580-252-0629 ▪ Fx: 580-255-4476

National Saanen Breeders Association   nationalsaanenbreeders.com
PO Box 315   Santa Margarita CA 93453
Ph: 805-461-5547

National SAFE KIDS Campaign   www.safekids.org
1301 Pennsylvania Ave NW Suite 1000   Washington DC 20004
Ph: 202-662-0600 ▪ Fx: 202-393-2072

National Safe Skies Alliance   sskies.org
McGhee Tyson Airport 2057 Alcoa Hwy   Alcoa TN 37701
Ph: 865-970-0515 ▪ Fx: 865-970-0506

National Safety Council   www.nsc.org
1121 Spring Lake Dr   Itasca IL 60143
Ph: 630-285-1121 ▪ Fx: 630-285-1315 ▪ TF: 800-621-7619

National Safety Management Society   www.safetyhealthmanager.org
2004 Hatton Ct   Columbia MO 65203
Ph: 800-321-2910

National Sales Network   www.salesnetwork.org
1075 Easton Ave Suite 11 PMB 316   Somerset NJ 08873
Ph: 732-246-5236

National Scholarship Service   www.nssfns.com
2001 ML King Jr Dr Suite 501 PO Box 11409   Atlanta GA
30310
Ph: 404-752-7277 ▪ Fx: 404-752-9280

National Scholastic Press Association   www.studentpress.org/nspa
2221 University Ave SE Suite 121   Minneapolis MN 55414
Ph: 612-625-8335 ▪ Fx: 612-626-0720

National Scholastic Surfing Association   www.nssa.org
PO Box 495   Huntington Beach CA 92648
Ph: 714-536-0445 ▪ Fx: 714-960-4380

National School-Age Care Alliance   www.nsaca.org
1137 Washington Ave   Boston MA 02124
Ph: 617-298-5012 ▪ Fx: 617-298-5022

National School Boards Association   www.nsba.org
1680 Duke St   Alexandria VA 22314
Ph: 703-838-6722 ▪ Fx: 703-683-7590

National School Development Council   www.casdany.org/nsdc.html
28 Lord Rd Suite 210   Marlborough MA 01752
Ph: 508-481-9444 ▪ Fx: 508-481-5655

National School Public Relations Association   www.nspra.org
15948 Derwood Rd   Rockville MD 20855
Ph: 301-519-0496 ▪ Fx: 301-519-0494

National School Safety Center   www.nssc1.org
141 Duesenberg Dr Suite 11   Westlake Village CA 91362
Ph: 805-373-9977 ▪ Fx: 805-373-9277

National School Supply & Equipment Association   www.nssea.org
8380 Colesville Rd Suite 250   Silver Spring MD 20910
Ph: 301-495-0240 ▪ Fx: 301-495-3330 ▪ TF: 800-395-5550

National School Transportation Association   www.schooltrans.com
625 Slaters Ln Suite 205   Alexandria VA 22314
Ph: 703-684-3200 ▪ Fx: 703-684-3212

National Schools Committee for Economic Education   www.nscee.org
30 S Broadway   Irvington-on-Hudson NY 10533
Ph: 914-591-7230 ▪ Fx: 914-591-8910

National Science Education Leadership Association   www.nsela.org
PO Box 99381   Raleigh NC 27624
Ph: 919-848-1871 ▪ Fx: 919-848-0496

National Science Teachers Association   www.nsta.org
1840 Wilson Blvd   Arlington VA 22201
Ph: 703-243-7100 ▪ Fx: 703-243-7177 ▪ TF: 800-722-6782

National Science & Technology Education Partnership   www.nationalstep.org
2500 Wilson Blvd Suite 210   Arlington VA 22201
Ph: 703-907-7400 ▪ Fx: 703-907-7401

National Science & Technology Medals Foundation   www.asee.org/nstmf
1818 'N' St NW Suite 600   Washington DC 20036
Ph: 202-331-3506

National Scoliosis Foundation   www.scoliosis.org
5 Cabot Pl   Stoughton MA 02072
Ph: 781-341-6333 ▪ Fx: 781-341-8333 ▪ TF: 800-673-6922

National Scrabble Association   www.scrabble-assoc.com
403 Front St PO Box 700   Greenport NY 11944
Ph: 631-477-0033 ▪ Fx: 631-477-0294

National Sculpture Society   www.nationalsculpture.org
237 Park Ave   New York NY 10017
Ph: 212-764-5645 ▪ Fx: 212-764-5651

National Seafood Educators
PO Box 60006   Richmond Beach WA 98160
Ph: 206-546-6410 ▪ Fx: 206-546-6411

National Seasoning Manufacturers Association
8905 Maxwell Dr Suite 200   Potomac MD 20854
Ph: 301-765-9675 ▪ Fx: 301-299-7523

National Secretarial Association   rentamark.com/nsa
7300 W Fullerton Ave PO Box 35189   Chicago IL 60707
Ph: 708-453-0080 ▪ Fx: 708-453-0083

National Security, Business Executives for   www.bens.org
1717 Pennsylvania Ave NW Suite 350   Washington DC 20006
Ph: 202-296-2125 ▪ Fx: 202-296-2490 ▪ TF: 800-296-2125

(National Security) Mershon Center   www.mershon.ohio-state.edu
1501 Neil Ave   Columbus OH 43201
Ph: 614-292-1681 ▪ Fx: 614-292-2407

National Self-Help Clearinghouse   www.selfhelpweb.org
365 5th Ave Suite 3300   New York NY 10016
Ph: 212-817-1822 ▪ Fx: 212-817-1561

National Senior Citizens Law Center   www.nsclc.org
1101 14th St NW Suite 400   Washington DC 20005
Ph: 202-289-6976 ▪ Fx: 202-289-7224

National Senior Games Association   www.nsga.com/
PO Box 82059   Baton Rouge LA 70884
Ph: 225-766-6800 ▪ Fx: 225-766-9115

National Senior Golf Association   www.nsgatour.com
3672 Nottingham Way   Hamilton Square NJ 08690
Ph: 800-282-6772 ▪ Fx: 609-921-2707 ▪ TF: 800-282-6772

National Senior Women's Tennis Association   www.nswta.com
PO Box 142   Lake Oswego OR 97034
Ph: 503-636-9292 ▪ Fx: 503-636-9660

National Service Dog Center   www.deltasociety.org/dsb000.htm
c/o Delta Society   580 Naches Ave SW Suite 101   Renton WA 98055
Ph: 425-226-7357 ▪ Fx: 425-235-1076

National Shared Housing Resource Center   www.nationalsharedhousing.org
5342 Tilly Mill Rd   Dunwoody GA 30338
Ph: 770-395-2625 ▪ Fx: 770-698-2055

National Shaving Mug Collectors Association   www.nsmca.org
320 S Glenwood St   Allentown PA 18104
Ph: 610-437-2534

National Shellfisheries Association   www.shellfish.org

National Sheriffs' Association   www.sheriffs.org
1450 Duke St   Alexandria VA 22314
Ph: 703-836-7827 ▪ Fx: 703-683-6541 ▪ TF: 800-424-7827

National Shiba Club of America   www.shibas.org
4360 Deer Spring Rd   Middletown MD 21769
Ph: 301-371-7815

National Shoe Retailers Association   nsra.org
7150 Columbia Gateway Dr Suite G   Columbia MD 21046
Ph: 410-381-8282 ▪ Fx: 410-381-1167 ▪ TF: 800-673-8446

National Shooting Sports Foundation   www.nssf.org
11 Mile Hill Rd   Newtown CT 06470
Ph: 203-426-1320 ▪ Fx: 203-426-1087

National Show Horse Registry   www.nshregistry.org
10368 Bluegrass Pkwy   Louisville KY 40299
Ph: 502-266-5100 ▪ Fx: 502-266-5806

National SIDS/Infant Death Resource Center   www.sidscenter.org
2070 Chain Bridge Rd Suite 450   Vienna VA 22182
Ph: 703-821-8955 ▪ Fx: 703-821-2098 ▪ TF: 866-866-7437

National Skeet Shooting Association   www.mynssa.com
5931 Roft Rd   San Antonio TX 78257
Ph: 210-688-3371 ▪ Fx: 210-688-3014 ▪ TF: 800-877-5338

National Ski Areas Association   www.nsaa.org
133 S Van Gordon St Suite 300   Lakewood CO 80228
Ph: 303-987-1111 ▪ Fx: 303-986-2345

National Ski Patrol System Inc   www.nsp.org
133 S Van Gordon St Suite 100   Lakewood CO 80228
Ph: 303-988-1111 ▪ Fx: 303-988-3005

National Ski & Snowboard Retailers Association   www.nssra.com
1601 Feehanville Dr Suite 300   Mount Prospect IL 60056
Ph: 847-391-9825 ▪ Fx: 847-391-9827

National Slag Association   www.nationalslagassoc.org
25 Stevens Ave Bldg A   West Lawn PA 19609
Ph: 610-670-0701 ▪ Fx: 610-670-0702

National Sleep Foundation   www.sleepfoundation.org
1522 K St NW Suite 500   Washington DC 20005
Ph: 202-347-3471 ▪ Fx: 202-347-3472

National Slovak Society of the USA   www.nsslife.com
351 Valley Brook Rd   McMurray PA 15317
Ph: 724-873-1890 ▪ Fx: 724-873-0145 ▪ TF: 800-488-1890

National Small Business Association   www.nsba.biz
1156 15th St NW Suite 1100   Washington DC 20005
Ph: 202-393-8830 ▪ Fx: 202-872-8543 ▪ TF: 800-345-6728

National Small Shipment Traffic Conference   www.nasstrac.org
758 Quail Run   Waconia MN 55387
Ph: 952-442-8858 ▪ Fx: 952-442-3941

National Snaffle Bit Association   www.nsba.com
4815 S Sheridan Suite 109   Tulsa OK 74145
Ph: 918-270-1469 ▪ Fx: 918-270-1471

National Soccer Coaches Association of America   www.nscaa.com
6700 Squibb Rd Suite 215   Mission KS 66202
Ph: 913-362-1747 ▪ Fx: 913-362-3439 ▪ TF: 800-458-0678

National Society of Accountants   www.nsacct.org
1010 N Fairfax St   Alexandria VA 22314
Ph: 703-549-6400 ▪ Fx: 703-549-2984 ▪ TF: 800-966-6679

National Society of Accountants for Cooperatives   www.nsacoop.org
6320 Augusta Dr Suite 800   Springfield VA 22150
Ph: 703-569-3088 ▪ Fx: 703-569-0235

National Society of Appraiser Specialists   pcb.lincoln-grad.org
303 W Cypress St PO Box 12617   San Antonio TX 78212
Ph: 210-271-0781 ▪ Fx: 210-225-8450 ▪ TF: 800-531-5333

National Society of Artists   www.nsartists.org
PO Box 150   Santa Fe TX 77510
Ph: 409-425-3381

National Society of Arts & Letters   www.arts-nsal.org
4227 46th St NW   Washington DC 20016
Ph: 202-363-5443

National Society of Black Engineers   www.nsbe.org
1454 Duke St   Alexandria VA 22314
Ph: 703-549-2207 ▪ Fx: 703-683-5312

National Society of Black Physicists   www.nsbp.org
6704 Lee Hwy Suite G   Arlington VA 22205
Ph: 703-536-4207 ▪ Fx: 703-536-4203

National Society of the Children of the American Revolution   www.nscar.org
1776 D St NW   Washington DC 20006
Ph: 202-638-3153 ▪ Fx: 202-737-3162

National Society of the Colonial Dames of America   www.nscda.org
2715 Q St NW   Washington DC 20007
Ph: 202-337-0972 ▪ Fx: 202-337-0348

National Society Colonial Dames XVII Century   www.colonialdames17c.net
1300 New Hampshire Ave NW   Washington DC 20036
Ph: 202-293-1700 ▪ Fx: 202-466-6099

National Society of Compliance Professionals Inc   www.nscp.org
22 Kent Rd   Cornwall Bridge CT 06754
Ph: 860-672-0843 ▪ Fx: 860-672-3005

National Society Daughters of the American Revolution   www.dar.org
1776 D St NW   Washington DC 20006
Ph: 202-628-1776 ▪ Fx: 202-879-3252

National Society of Environmental Consultants   nsec.lincoln-grad.org
303 W Cypress St   San Antonio TX 78212
Ph: 210-271-0781 ▪ Fx: 210-225-8450 ▪ TF: 800-486-3676

National Society for Experiential Education   www.nsee.org
9001 Braddock Rd Suite 380   Springfield VA 22151
Ph: 703-426-4268 ▪ Fx: 703-426-8400 ▪ TF: 800-803-4170

National Society of Genetic Counselors   www.nsgc.org
233 Canterbury Dr   Wallingford PA 19086
Ph: 610-872-7608

National Society for Graphology
250 W 57th St Suite 1228A   New York NY 10107
Ph: 212-265-1148 ▪ Fx: 212-307-5671

National Society for Healthcare Food Service Management   www.hfm.org
204 'E' St NE   Washington DC 20002
Ph: 202-546-7236 ▪ Fx: 202-547-6348

National Society for Hebrew Day Schools, Torah Umesorah-
160 Broadway   New York NY 10038
Ph: 212-227-1000 ▪ Fx: 212-406-6934

National Society of Hispanic MBAs   www.nshmba.org
1303 Walnut Hill Ln Suite 300   Irving TX 75038
Ph: 214-596-9325 ▪ TF: 877-467-4622

National Society for Histotechnology   www.nsh.org
4201 Northview Dr Suite 502   Bowie MD 20716
Ph: 301-262-6221 ▪ Fx: 301-262-9188

National Society of Hypnotherapists
1833 W Charleston Blvd   Las Vegas NV 89102
Ph: 702-384-4420 ▪ Fx: 702-386-2851

National Society of Insurance Premium Auditors   www.nsipa.org
PO Box 1896   Columbus OH 43216
Ph: 614-221-9266 ▪ Fx: 614-221-2335 ▪ TF: 888-846-7472

National Society of Mural Painters
c/o American Fine Arts Society 215 W 57th St   New York NY 10019
Ph: 212-941-0130 ▪ Fx: 212-941-0138

National Society of Newspaper Columnists   www.columnists.com
1410 Stiener St Suite 709   San Francisco CA 94115
Ph: 415-563-5403

National Society for Park Resources
c/o National Recreation & Park Assn 22377 Belmont Ridge Rd   Ashburn VA 20148
Ph: 703-858-0784 ▪ Fx: 703-858-0794

National Society of Pershing Rifles   nhq.pershingrifles.com/
200 Nebraska Union Box 240 PO Box 880456   Lincoln NE 68588
Ph: 402-472-2472 ▪ Fx: 402-472-2478

National Society for the Preservation of   www.vermontbridges.com/nspcb1st.htm
Covered Bridges   44 Cleveland Ave   Worcester MA 01603
Ph: 508-756-4516

National Society of Professional Engineers   www.nspe.org
1420 King St   Alexandria VA 22314
Ph: 703-684-2800 ▪ Fx: 703-836-4875

National Society of Professional Surveyors   www.acsm.net/nsps
6 Montgomery Village Ave Suite 403   Gaithersburg MD 20879
Ph: 240-632-9716 ▪ Fx: 240-632-1321

National Society of the Sons of the American Revolution   www.sar.org
1000 S 4th St   Louisville KY 40203
Ph: 502-589-1776 ▪ Fx: 502-589-1671

National Society Sons of Colonial New England   www.nsscne.org

National Society for the Study of Education   www.uic.edu/educ/nsse
Univ of Illinois College of Education 1040 W Harrison St   M/C 147   Chicago IL 60607
Ph: 312-996-4529 ▪ Fx: 312-996-6400

National Society of Tax Professionals   www.nstp.org
10818 NE Coxley Dr Suite A   Vancouver WA 98662
Ph: 360-695-8309 ▪ Fx: 360-695-7115 ▪ TF: 800-367-8130

National Society US Daughters of 1812   www.iaw.on.ca/~jsek/usd1812.htm
1461 Rhode Island Ave NW   Washington DC 20005
Ph: 202-745-1812

National Soft Drink Association   www.nsda.org
1101 16th St NW   Washington DC 20036
Ph: 202-463-6732 ▪ Fx: 202-463-8178

(National Soft Drink Association) Soft Drink PAC
1101 16th St NW   Washington DC 20036
Ph: 202-463-6732 ▪ Fx: 202-463-8178

National Softball Association   www.playnsa.com
PO Box 7   Nicholasville KY 40340
Ph: 859-887-4114 ▪ Fx: 859-887-4874

National Sojourners Inc   www.nationalsojourners.org
8301 E Boulevard Dr   Alexandria VA 22308
Ph: 703-765-5000 ▪ Fx: 703-765-8390

National Solid Wastes Management Association   www.nswma.org
4301 Connecticut Ave NW Suite 300   Washington DC 20008
Ph: 202-244-4700 ▪ Fx: 202-966-4818 ▪ TF: 800-424-2869

National Soy Ink Information Center   www.soyink.com
4454 NW 114th St   Urbandale IA 50322
Ph: 515-251-8640 ▪ Fx: 515-251-8657 ▪ TF: 800-747-4275

National Spa & Pool Institute   www.nspi.org
2111 Eisenhower Ave   Alexandria VA 22314
Ph: 703-838-0083 ▪ Fx: 703-549-0493 ▪ TF: 800-323-3996

National Space Society   www.nss.org
600 Pennsylvania Ave SE Suite 201   Washington DC 20003
Ph: 202-543-1900 ▪ Fx: 202-546-4189

National Speakers Association   www.nsaspeaker.org
1500 S Priest Dr   Tempe AZ 85281
Ph: 480-968-2552 ▪ Fx: 480-968-0911

National Specialty Gift Association   www.nsgaonline.com
7238 Bucks Ford Dr   Riverview FL 33569
Ph: 813-671-4757 ▪ Fx: 813-677-5075

National Speleological Society   www.caves.org
2813 Cave Ave   Huntsville AL 35810
Ph: 256-852-1300 ▪ Fx: 256-851-9241

National Spinal Cord Injury Association   www.spinalcord.org
6701 Democracy Blvd Suite 300-9   Bethesda MD 20817
Ph: 800-962-9629 ▪ Fx: 301-564-9619

National Spiritual Alliance of the USA   www.thenationalspiritualallianceinc.org
2 Montague Ave PO Box 88   Lake Pleasant MA 01347
Ph: 413-367-0138

National Spiritual Assembly of the Baha'is of the US   www.us.bahai.org
1233 Central St   Evanston IL 60201
Ph: 847-869-9039 ▪ TF: 800-999-9019

National Spiritualist Association of Churches   www.nsac.org
PO Box 217   Lily Dale NY 14752
Ph: 716-595-2000 ▪ Fx: 716-595-2020

National Sporting Clays Association   www.mynsca.com
5931 Roft Rd   San Antonio TX 78253
Ph: 210-688-3371 ▪ Fx: 210-688-3014 ▪ TF: 800-877-5338

National Sporting Goods Association   www.nsga.org
1601 Feehanville Dr Suite 300   Mount Prospect IL 60056
Ph: 847-296-6742 ▪ Fx: 847-391-9827

National Spotted Saddle Horse Association   www.nssha.com
108 N Spring St PO Box 898   Murfreesboro TN 37133
Ph: 615-890-2864

National Spotted Swine Record
PO Box 9758   Peoria IL 61612
Ph: 309-693-1804 ▪ Fx: 309-691-0168

National Staff Development Council   www.nsdc.org
PO Box 240   Oxford OH 45056
Ph: 513-523-6029 ▪ Fx: 513-523-0638 ▪ TF: 800-727-7288

National Standard Plumbing Code Committee   www.phccweb.org/technical/code.cfm
180 S Washington St PO Box 6808   Falls Church VA 22046
Ph: 703-237-8100 ▪ Fx: 703-237-7442 ▪ TF: 800-533-7694

National Star Route Mail Contractors Association   www.starroutecontractors.org
324 E Capitol St   Washington DC 20003
Ph: 202-543-1661 ▪ Fx: 202-543-8863

National Steeplechase Association   www.nationalsteeplechase.com
400 Fair Hill Dr   Elkton MD 21921
Ph: 410-392-0700 ▪ Fx: 410-392-0706

National Stone Sand & Gravel Association   www.nssga.com
1605 King St   Alexandria VA 22314
Ph: 703-525-8788 ▪ Fx: 703-525-7782 ▪ TF: 800-342-1415

National Stone Sand & Gravel Association PAC
1605 King St   Alexandria VA 22314
Ph: 703-525-8788 ▪ Fx: 703-525-7782

National Stonewall Democrats   www.stonewalldemocrats.org
PO Box 9330   Washington DC 20005
Ph: 202-625-1382 ▪ Fx: 202-625-1383

National Story League
1630 Country Club Cir   Las Cruces NM 88001
Ph: 505-526-8377

National Storytelling Network   www.storynet.org
101 Courthouse Sq   Jonesborough TN 37659
Ph: 423-913-8201 ▪ Fx: 423-753-9331 ▪ TF: 800-525-4514

National Strategy Information Center
1730 Rhode Island Ave NW Suite 500   Washington DC 20036
Ph: 202-429-0129 ▪ Fx: 202-659-5429

National Street Rod Association   www.nsra-usa.com
4030 Park Ave   Memphis TN 38111
Ph: 901-452-4030 ▪ Fx: 901-452-6772

National Strength & Conditioning Association   www.nsca-lift.org
PO Box 9908   Colorado Springs CO 80932
Ph: 719-632-6722 ▪ Fx: 719-632-6367 ▪ TF: 800-815-6826

National Stripper Well Association
302 N Independence St   Enid OK 73702
Ph: 580-233-8955

National Stroke Association   www.stroke.org
9707 E Easter Ln   Englewood CO 80112
Ph: 303-649-9299 ▪ Fx: 303-649-1328 ▪ TF: 800-787-6537

National Structured Settlements Trade Association   www.nssta.com
1800 K St NW Suite 718   Washington DC 20006
Ph: 202-466-2714 ▪ Fx: 202-466-7414

National Student Campaign Against Hunger & Homelessness   www.nscahh.com
233 N Pleasant St Suite 32   Amherst MA 01002
Ph: 413-253-6417 ▪ Fx: 413-256-6435 ▪ TF: 800-664-8647

National Student Campaign for Voter Registration
1533 Market St 2nd Fl   Denver CO 80202
Ph: 303-573-5885 ▪ Fx: 303-573-5999

National Student Employment Association   nseastudemp.org
PO Box 23606   Eugene OR 97402
Ph: 541-484-6935

National Student Exchange   www.nse.org
4656 W Jefferson Blvd Suite 140   Fort Wayne IN 46804
Ph: 260-436-2634 ▪ Fx: 260-436-5676

National Student Nurses Association   www.nsna.org
45 Main St Suite 606   Brooklyn NY 11201
Ph: 718-210-0705 ▪ Fx: 718-210-0710

National Student Speech Language Hearing Association   www.nsslha.org
10801 Rockville Pike   Rockville MD 20852
Ph: 301-897-5700 ▪ Fx: 301-571-0481 ▪ TF: 800-498-2071

National Stuttering Association   www.nsastutter.org
119 W 40th St 14th Fl   New York NY 10018
Ph: 212-944-4050 ▪ Fx: 212-944-8244 ▪ TF: 800-364-1677

National Submetering & Utility Allocation Association   www.nsuaa.org
1866 Sheridan Rd Suite 201   Highland Park IL 60035
Ph: 847-681-8475 ▪ Fx: 847-681-1869

National Sugar Brokers Association
3000 Chestnut Ave Suite 100A   Baltimore MD 21211
Ph: 410-366-7400 ▪ Fx: 410-467-9552

National Sunflower Association   www.sunflowernsa.com
4023 State St   Bismarck ND 58501
Ph: 701-328-5100 ▪ Fx: 701-328-5101 ▪ TF: 888-718-7033

National Sunflower Association PAC
4023 State St   Bismarck ND 58503
Ph: 701-328-5100 ▪ Fx: 701-328-5101 ▪ TF: 888-718-7033

National Sunroom Association   www.nationalsunroom.org
2945 SW Wanamaker Dr Suite A   Topeka KS 66614
Ph: 785-271-0208 ▪ Fx: 785-271-0166

National Suppliers to Food Processors Association
PO Box 59149   Minneapolis MN 55459
Ph: 612-341-9600 ▪ Fx: 612-341-9648

National Surgical Assistant Association   www.nsaa.net
3024 W Shangri-La Rd   Phoenix AZ 85029
Ph: 602-212-0479 ▪ Fx: 602-212-9692 ▪ TF: 888-633-0479

National Swim School Association   www.nationalswimschools.com
8300 N Hayden Rd Suite 207   Scottsdale AZ 85258
Ph: 480-467-0283 ▪ Fx: 480-467-0204

National Swimming Pool Foundation   www.nspf.org
224 E Cheyenne Mountain Blvd   Colorado Springs CO 80906
Ph: 719-540-9119 ▪ Fx: 719-540-2787

National Swine Improvement Federation   www.nsif.org
Iowa State Univ Dept of Animal Science 109 Kildee Hall   Ames IA 50011
Ph: 515-294-4683 ▪ Fx: 515-294-5698

National Swine Registry   www.nationalswine.com
PO Box 2417   West Lafayette IN 47996
Ph: 765-463-3594 ▪ Fx: 765-497-2959

National Systems Contractors Association   www.nsca.org
625 1st St SE Suite 420   Cedar Rapids IA 52401
Ph: 319-366-6722 ▪ Fx: 319-366-4164 ▪ TF: 800-446-6722

National Tabletop & Giftware Association
112 Adrossan Ct   Deptford NJ 08096
Ph: 856-227-6802 ▪ Fx: 856-227-6782

National Tank Truck Carriers Inc   www.tanktruck.org
2200 Mill Rd Suite 620   Alexandria VA 22314
Ph: 703-838-1960 ▪ Fx: 703-684-5753

National Tattoo Association   www.nationaltattooassociation.com
485 Business Pk Ln   Allentown PA 18109
Ph: 610-433-7261 ▪ Fx: 610-433-7294

National Tax Association   www.ntanet.org
725 15th St NW Suite 600   Washington DC 20005
Ph: 202-737-3325 ▪ Fx: 202-737-7308

National Tax Lien Association — www.ntlainfo.org
220 W Gadsden St Suite 600   Pensacola FL 32501
Ph: 850-470-9974 ▪ Fx: 850-470-9522

National Taxidermists Association — www.nationaltaxidermists.com
108 Branch Dr   Slidell LA 70461
Ph: 985-641-4682 ▪ Fx: 985-641-9463

National Taxpayers Union — www.ntu.org
108 N Alfred St   Alexandria VA 22314
Ph: 703-683-5700 ▪ Fx: 703-683-5722 ▪ TF: 800-829-4258

National Tay-Sachs & Allied Diseases Association — www.ntsad.org
2001 Beacon St Suite 204   Brighton MA 02135
Ph: 617-277-4463 ▪ Fx: 617-277-0134 ▪ TF: 800-906-8723

National Technical Association — www.ntaonline.org
1761 E 30th St Suite 100 A   Cleveland OH 44114
Ph: 216-298-4425 ▪ Fx: 216-289-3015

National Technical Honor Society — www.nvths.org
PO Box 1336   Flat Rock NC 28731
Ph: 828-698-8011

National Technical Services Association — www.ntsa.org
2121 Eisenhower Ave Suite 604   Alexandria VA 22314
Ph: 703-684-4722 ▪ Fx: 703-684-7627

National Telecommunications Cooperative Association — www.ntca.org
4121 Wilson Blvd Suite 1000   Arlington VA 22203
Ph: 703-351-2000 ▪ Fx: 703-351-2001

National Telemedia Council — www.danenet.wicip.org/ntc/
120 E Wilson St   Madison WI 53703
Ph: 608-257-7712 ▪ Fx: 608-257-7714

National Temple Hill Association — www.nationaltemplehill.org
PO Box 315   Vails Gate NY 12584
Ph: 914-561-5073

National Terrazzo & Mosaic Association — www.ntma.com
201 N Maple Suite 208   Purcellville VA 20132
Ph: 540-751-0930 ▪ Fx: 540-751-0935 ▪ TF: 800-323-9736

National Textile Association — www.nationaltextile.org
6 Beacon St Suite 1125   Boston MA 02108
Ph: 617-542-8220 ▪ Fx: 617-542-2199

National Textile Center — www.ntcresearch.org
1121 N Bethlehem Pike Suite 60   Spring House PA 19477
Ph: 215-540-0760 ▪ Fx: 215-689-4835

National Theatre of the Deaf — ntd.org
55 Van Dyke Ave Suite 312   Hartford CT 06106
Ph: 860-724-5179 ▪ Fx: 860-550-7974 ▪ TF: 800-300-5179

National Theatre Institute — nti.conncoll.edu
305 Great Neck Rd   Waterford CT 06385
Ph: 860-443-7139 ▪ Fx: 860-443-1212

National Theatre Workshop of the Handicapped — www.ntwh.org
535 Greenwich St   New York NY 10013
Ph: 212-206-7789 ▪ Fx: 212-206-0200

National Therapeutic Recreation Society
c/o National Recreation & Park Assn 22377 Belmont Ridge
   Rd   Ashburn VA 20148
Ph: 703-858-2151 ▪ Fx: 703-858-0794 ▪ TF: 800-626-6772

National Thoroughbred Racing Association — www.ntra.com
2525 Harrodsburg Rd   Lexington KY 40504
Ph: 859-223-5444 ▪ Fx: 859-223-3945

National Threshers Association Inc — www.nationalthreshers.com

National Tile Contractors Association — www.tile-assn.com
626 Lakeland East Dr PO Box 13629   Jackson MS 39236
Ph: 601-939-2071 ▪ Fx: 601-932-6117

National Time Equipment Association — www.thentea.com
PO Box 27399   Memphis TN 38167
Ph: 800-235-6832 ▪ Fx: 901-358-2139

National Toggenburg Club — www.nationaltoggclub.org

National Tooling & Machining Association — www.ntma.org
9300 Livingston Rd   Fort Washington MD 20744
Ph: 301-248-6200 ▪ Fx: 301-248-7104 ▪ TF: 800-248-6862

National Toothpick Holder Collectors Society — www.collectoronline.com/NTHCS

National Tour Association Inc — www.ntaonline.com
546 E Main St   Lexington KY 40508
Ph: 859-226-4444 ▪ Fx: 859-226-4404 ▪ TF: 800-682-8886

National Tour Association PAC
546 E Main St   Lexington KY 40508
Ph: 859-226-4250 ▪ Fx: 859-226-4263

National Tractor Parts Dealer Association — www.ntpda.com
PO Box 1181   Gainesville TX 76241
Ph: 940-668-0900 ▪ Fx: 940-668-1627

National Tractor Pullers Association — www.ntpapull.com
6155-B Huntley Rd   Columbus OH 43229
Ph: 614-436-1761 ▪ Fx: 614-436-0964

National Trade Circulation Foundation Inc — www.ntcfi.org

National Traditional Country Music Association — www.oldtimemusic.bigstep.com/
PO Box 492   Anita IA 50020
Ph: 712-762-4363

National Trailer Dealers Association — www.ntda.org
37400 Hills Tech Dr   Farmington Hills MI 48331
Ph: 800-800-4552 ▪ Fx: 248-489-8590

National Training & Information Center — www.ntic-us.org
810 N Milwaukee Ave   Chicago IL 60622
Ph: 312-243-3035 ▪ Fx: 312-243-7044

National Training Systems Association — www.trainingsystems.org
2111 Wilson Blvd Suite 400   Arlington VA 22201
Ph: 703-347-9471 ▪ Fx: 703-243-1659 ▪ TF: 800-677-6897

National Translator Association — www.tvfmtranslators.com
5611 Kendell Ct Suite 2   Arvada CO 80002
Ph: 303-465-5742 ▪ Fx: 303-465-4067

National Trappers Association — www.nationaltrappers.com
4111 E Starr Ave   Nacogdoches TX 75961
Ph: 936-569-6444 ▪ Fx: 936-569-9805

National Treasury Employees Union — www.nteu.org
1750 H St NW 10th Fl   Washington DC 20006
Ph: 202-572-5500 ▪ Fx: 202-572-5643

National Tribal Environmental Council — www.ntec.org
2501 Rio Grande Blvd NW Suite A   Albuquerque NM 87104
Ph: 505-242-2175 ▪ Fx: 505-242-2654

National Truck Equipment Association — www.ntea.com
37400 Hills Tech Dr   Farmington Hills MI 48331
Ph: 248-489-7090 ▪ Fx: 248-489-8590 ▪ TF: 800-441-6832

National Truck & Heavy Equipment Claims Council — www.nthecc.org

National Trust for the Development of African American Men
6811 Kenilworth Ave Suite 501   Riverdale MD 20737
Ph: 301-887-0100 ▪ Fx: 301-887-0405

National Trust for Historic Preservation — www.nationaltrust.org
1785 Massachusetts Ave NW   Washington DC 20036
Ph: 202-588-6000 ▪ Fx: 202-588-6038 ▪ TF: 800-944-6847

National Tuberculosis Controllers Association
2951 Flowers Rd S Suite 102   Atlanta GA 30341
Ph: 770-455-0801 ▪ Fx: 770-455-4221 ▪ TF: 888-455-0801

National Tunis Sheep Registry Inc — www.tunissheep.org
819 Lyons St   Ludlow MA 01056
Ph: 413-589-9653

National Turkey Federation — www.eatturkey.com
1225 New York Ave NW Suite 400   Washington DC 20005
Ph: 202-898-0100 ▪ Fx: 202-898-0203

National Turkey Federation PAC
1225 New York Ave NW Suite 400   Washington DC 20005
Ph: 202-898-0100 ▪ Fx: 202-898-0203

National Tutoring Association — www.ntatutor.org/
3719 Washington Blvd   Indianapolis IN 46205
Ph: 317-926-9671 ▪ TF: 866-311-6630

National United Merchants Beverage Association — www.numba.org
609 S Ann St   Homestead PA 15120
Ph: 412-636-3120 ▪ Fx: 412-636-3107

National Urban Agriculture Council — www.nuac.org
1015 18th St NW Suite 600   Washington DC 20036
Ph: 202-429-4344 ▪ Fx: 202-429-4342

National Urban League Inc — www.nul.org
120 Wall St 8th Fl   New York NY 10005
Ph: 212-558-5300 ▪ Fx: 212-344-5332

National Urban Technology Center — www.urbantech.org
55 John St Suite 300   New York NY 10038
Ph: 212-528-7350 ▪ Fx: 212-528-7355 ▪ TF: 800-998-3212

National US-Arab Chamber of Commerce — www.nusacc.org
1023 15th St NW Suite 400   Washington DC 20005
Ph: 202-289-5920 ▪ Fx: 202-289-5938

National Utility Contractors Association — www.nuca.org
4301 N Fairfax Dr Suite 360   Arlington VA 22203
Ph: 703-358-9300 ▪ Fx: 703-358-9307 ▪ TF: 800-662-6822

National Vaccine Information Center — www.909shot.com
421-E Church St   Vienna VA 22180
Ph: 703-938-3783 ▪ Fx: 703-938-5768 ▪ TF: 800-909-7468

National Valedictorian Society — www.valedictorian.org
PO Box 250   Louviers CO 80131
Ph: 303-343-4000 ▪ Fx: 303-343-4300

National Valentine Collectors' Association
PO Box 1404   Santa Ana CA 92702
Ph: 714-547-1355

National Vehicle Leasing Association — www.nvla.org
1900 Arch St   Philadelphia PA 19103
Ph: 215-564-3484 ▪ Fx: 215-963-9785

National Venture Capital Association — www.nvca.org
1655 N Fort Myer Dr Suite 850   Arlington VA 22209
Ph: 703-524-2549 ▪ Fx: 703-524-3940

(National Venture Capital Association) Venture PAC
1655 N Fort Myer Dr Suite 850   Arlington VA 22209
Ph: 703-524-2549 ▪ Fx: 703-524-3940

National Verbatim Reporters Association — www.nvra.org
207 3rd Ave   Hattiesburg MS 39401
Ph: 601-582-4345 ▪ Fx: 601-582-3354

National Veterans Organization of America — www.nvo.org/
7700 Alabama St PO Box 640064   El Paso TX 79904
Ph: 915-759-8387 ▪ Fx: 915-587-3028

National Visiting Teachers Association — www.nvta4parents.org
650 Howe Ave Suite 1014   Sacramento CA 95825
Ph: 916-921-6882 ▪ Fx: 916-921-1460

National Vitiligo Foundation — www.vitiligofoundation.org
611 S Fleishel Ave   Tyler TX 75701
Ph: 903-531-0074 ▪ Fx: 903-525-1234

National Voluntary Organizations Active in Disaster — www.nvoad.org
14253 Ballinger Terr   Burtonsville MD 20866
Ph: 301-890-2119

National Volunteer Fire Council — www.nvfc.org
1050 17th St NW Suite 490   Washington DC 20036
Ph: 202-887-5700 ▪ Fx: 202-887-5291 ▪ TF: 888-275-6832

National Vulvodynia Association — www.nva.org
PO Box 4491   Silver Spring MD 20914
Ph: 301-299-0775 ▪ Fx: 301-299-3999

National Water Resources Association — www.nwra.org
3800 N Fairfax Dr Suite 4   Arlington VA 22203
Ph: 703-524-1544 ▪ Fx: 703-524-1548

National Water Safety Congress — www.watersafetycongress.org
PO Box 1632   Mentor OH 44061
Ph: 440-209-9805

National Watercolor Society — www.nws-online.org
915 S Pacific Ave   San Pedro CA 90731
Ph: 800-486-8670

National Waterways Conference Inc — www.waterways.org
1130 17th St NW Suite 200   Washington DC 20036
Ph: 202-296-4415 ▪ Fx: 202-835-3861

National Weather Association　　www.nwas.org
1697 Capri Way　Charlottesville VA 22911
Ph: 434-296-9966

National Weather Service Employees Organization
601 Pennsylvania Ave Suite 900　Washington DC 20004
Ph: 703-293-9651 ▪ Fx: 703-293-9653

National Wellness Institute　www.nationalwellness.org
1300 College Ct PO Box 827　Stevens Point WI 54481
Ph: 715-342-2969 ▪ Fx: 715-342-2979 ▪ TF: 800-243-8694

National Welsh-American Foundation　www.wales-usa.org
301 Stone Ave　Clarks Summit PA 18411
Ph: 570-587-4131 ▪ Fx: 570-586-4901

National Wetlands Coalition　www.thenwc.org
1050 Thomas Jefferson St NW Suite 700　Washington DC
20007
Ph: 202-298-1800

National Wheel & Rim Association　nationalwheelandrim.com
5121 Bowden Rd Suite 303　Jacksonville FL 32216
Ph: 904-737-2900 ▪ Fx: 904-636-9881

National Wheelchair Softball Association　www.wheelchairsoftball.com
1616 Todd Ct　Hastings MN 55033
Ph: 612-437-1792 ▪ Fx: 612-437-3889

National Whistleblower Center　www.whistleblowers.org
3238 P St NW　Washington DC 20007
Ph: 202-342-1902 ▪ Fx: 202-342-1904

National WIC Association　www.nwica.org
2001 'S' St NW Suite 580　Washington DC 20009
Ph: 202-232-5492 ▪ Fx: 202-387-5281

National Wild Horse & Burro Program　wildhorseandburro.blm.gov
PO Box 3270　Sparks NV 89432
Ph: 775-475-2222 ▪ Fx: 775-861-6711 ▪ TF: 800-417-9647

National Wild Turkey Federation　www.nwtf.org
770 Augusta Rd PO Box 530　Edgefield SC 29824
Ph: 803-637-3106 ▪ Fx: 803-637-0034 ▪ TF: 800-843-6983

National Wilderness Institute　www.nwi.org
PO Box 25766　Washington DC 20007
Ph: 703-836-7404 ▪ Fx: 703-836-7405

National Wildlife Federation　www.nwf.org
11100 Wildlife Center Dr　Reston VA 20190
Ph: 703-438-6000 ▪ Fx: 703-438-3570 ▪ TF: 800-822-9919

National Wildlife Refuge Association　www.refugenet.org
1010 Wisconsin Ave NW Suite 200　Washington DC 20007
Ph: 202-333-9075 ▪ Fx: 202-333-9077 ▪ TF: 877-396-6972

National Wildlife Rehabilitators Association　www.nwrawildlife.org
14 N 7th Ave　Saint Cloud MN 56303
Ph: 320-259-4086

National Woman's Party　www.sewallbelmont.org
144 Constitution Ave NE　Washington DC 20002
Ph: 202-546-1210 ▪ Fx: 202-546-3997

National Women Bowling Writers Association　www.nwbw.freeservers.com
3001 21st St　Lubbock TX 79410
Ph: 806-795-3830

National Women Law Students Association　www.nwlsa.com

National Women's Business Council　www.nwbc.gov
409 3rd St SW Suite 210　Washington DC 20024
Ph: 202-205-3850 ▪ Fx: 202-205-6825

National Women's Health Network　www.nwhn.org
514 10th St NW Suite 400　Washington DC 20004
Ph: 202-347-1140 ▪ Fx: 202-347-1168

National Women's History Project　www.nwhp.org
3343 Industrial Dr Suite 4　Santa Rosa CA 95403
Ph: 707-636-2888 ▪ Fx: 707-636-2909 ▪ TF: 800-691-8888

National Women's Law Center　www.nwlc.org
11 Dupont Cir NW Suite 800　Washington DC 20036
Ph: 202-588-5180 ▪ Fx: 202-588-5185

National Women's Political Caucus　www.nwpc.org
1634 'I' St NW Suite 310　Washington DC 20006
Ph: 202-785-1100 ▪ Fx: 202-785-3605

National Women's Studies Association　www.nwsa.org
7100 Baltimore Ave Suite 500　College Park MD 20740
Ph: 301-403-0525 ▪ Fx: 301-403-4137

National Wood Carvers Association　www.chipchats.org
7424 Miami Ave　Cincinnati OH 45243
Ph: 513-561-9051

National Wood Flooring Association　www.woodfloors.org
111 Chesterfield Industrial Blvd　Chesterfield MO 63005
Ph: 636-519-9663 ▪ Fx: 636-519-9664 ▪ TF: 800-422-4556

National Wood Tank Institute
PO Box 2755　Philadelphia PA 19120
Ph: 215-329-9022 ▪ Fx: 215-329-1177

National Wooden Pallet & Container Association　www.nwpca.com
329 S Patrick St　Alexandria VA 22314
Ph: 703-519-6104 ▪ Fx: 703-519-4720

National Woodland Owners Association　www.nationalwoodlands.org
374 Maple Ave E Suite 310　Vienna VA 22180
Ph: 703-255-2700 ▪ Fx: 703-281-9200 ▪ TF: 800-476-8733

National Wrestling Coaches　www.nwcaadmin.bluestep.net/my/shared/home.jsp
Association　PO Box 254　Manheim PA 17545
Ph: 717-653-8009 ▪ Fx: 717-653-8270

National Write Your Congressman Inc　www.nwyc.com
9696 Skillman St Suite 170　Dallas TX 75243
Ph: 214-342-0299 ▪ Fx: 214-342-9186 ▪ TF: 800-872-8683

National Writers Association　www.nationalwriters.com
3140 S Peoria St Suite 295　Aurora CO 80014
Ph: 303-841-0246 ▪ Fx: 303-841-2607

National Writers Union　www.nwu.org
113 University Pl 6th Fl　New York NY 10003
Ph: 212-254-0279 ▪ Fx: 212-254-0673

National Writing Centers Association
Univ of Toledo 2801 W Bancroft　Toledo OH 43606
Ph: 419-530-4913 ▪ Fx: 419-530-4752

National WWII Glider Pilots Association Inc　www.ww2gp.org
21 Phyllis Rd　Freehold NJ 07728
Ph: 732-462-1838

National Yiddish Book Center　www.yiddishbookcenter.org
1021 West St　Amherst MA 01002
Ph: 413-256-4900 ▪ Fx: 413-256-4700

National Yogurt Association
2000 Corporate Ridge Suite 1000　McLean VA 22102
Ph: 703-821-0770 ▪ Fx: 703-821-1350

National Young Farmer Educational Association　www.nyfea.org
PO Box 20326　Montgomery AL 36120
Ph: 334-288-0097

National Youth Advocacy Coalition　www.nyacyouth.org
1638 R St NW Suite 300　Washington DC 20009
Ph: 202-319-7596 ▪ Fx: 202-319-7365 ▪ TF: 800-541-6922

National Youth Employment Coalition　www.nyec.org
1836 Jefferson Pl NW　Washington DC 20036
Ph: 202-659-1064 ▪ Fx: 202-659-0339

National Youth Leadership Council　www.nylc.org
1667 Snelling Ave N　Saint Paul MN 55108
Ph: 651-631-3672 ▪ Fx: 651-631-2955

National Youth Sports Coaches Association　www.nays.org
2050 Vista Pkwy　West Palm Beach FL 33411
Ph: 561-684-1141 ▪ Fx: 561-684-2546 ▪ TF: 800-729-2057

National Youth Sports Safety Foundation　www.nyssf.org
1 Beacon St Suite 3333　Boston MA 02108
Ph: 617-367-6677 ▪ Fx: 617-722-9999

National Zoo, Friends of the　www.fonz.org
National Zoological Pk　Washington DC 20008
Ph: 202-673-4973 ▪ Fx: 202-673-4890

Nationalist Foundation
227 E Petros Rd　Pearl MS 39208
Ph: 601-936-3636

Nationalist Union, American　www.anu.org

Nationalities, Association for the Study of　www.nationalities.org
Columbia Univ 1216 IAB 420 W 118th St　New York NY 10027
Ph: 212-854-8487 ▪ Fx: 212-666-3481

Native American Aging, National　www.med.und.nodak.edu/depts/rural//nrcnaa
Resource Center on　PO Box 9037　Grand Forks ND 58202
Ph: 701-777-3437 ▪ Fx: 701-777-2389 ▪ TF: 800-896-7628

Native American AIDS Prevention Center, National　www.nnaapc.org
436 14th St Suite 1020　Oakland CA 94610
Ph: 510-444-2051 ▪ Fx: 510-444-1593 ▪ TF: 800-283-6880

(Native American) Amerind Foundation Inc　www.amerind.org
2100 N Amerind Rd PO Box 400　Dragoon AZ 85609
Ph: 520-586-3666 ▪ Fx: 520-586-4679

Native American Cancer Research　natamcancer.org
3022 S Nova Rd　Pine CO 80470
Ph: 303-838-9359 ▪ Fx: 303-838-7629

Native American Community Board　www.nativeshop.org
PO Box 572　Lake Andes SD 57356
Ph: 605-487-7072 ▪ Fx: 605-487-7964

(Native American) First Nations Development Institute　www.firstnations.org
11917 Main St　Fredericksburg VA 22408
Ph: 540-371-5615 ▪ Fx: 540-371-3505 ▪ TF: 800-682-5384

(Native American) Gathering of Nations Ltd　www.gatheringofnations.com
3301 Coors Blvd NW Suite R300　Albuquerque NM 87120
Ph: 505-836-2810 ▪ Fx: 505-839-0475

Native American Journalists Association　www.naja.com
Univ of South Dakota 414 E Clark St　Vermillion SD 57069
Ph: 605-677-5282 ▪ Fx: 866-694-4264

(Native American) Native Seeds/SEARCH　www.nativeseeds.org
526 N 4th Ave　Tucson AZ 85705
Ph: 520-622-5561 ▪ Fx: 520-622-5591

(Native American) Oyate　www.oyate.org
2702 Mathews St　Berkeley CA 94702
Ph: 510-848-6700 ▪ Fx: 510-848-4815

Native American Public Telecommunications　www.nativetelecom.org
1800 N 33rd St　Lincoln NE 68583
Ph: 402-472-3522 ▪ Fx: 402-472-8675

Native American Rights Fund　www.narf.org
1506 Broadway St　Boulder CO 80302
Ph: 303-447-8760 ▪ Fx: 303-443-7776

Native American Studies, National Association of
PO Box 325　Biddeford ME 04005
Ph: 207-839-8004 ▪ Fx: 207-839-3776

(Native American) Tekakwitha Conference National Center　www.tekconf.org
PO Box 6768　Great Falls MT 59406
Ph: 406-727-0147 ▪ Fx: 406-452-9845 ▪ TF: 800-842-9635

(Native American) United South & Eastern Tribes Inc　usetinc.org
711 Stewarts Ferry Pike Suite 100　Nashville TN 37214
Ph: 615-872-7900 ▪ Fx: 615-872-7417

(Native American) White Bison Inc　www.whitebison.org
6145 Lehman Dr Suite 200　Colorado Springs CO 80918
Ph: 719-548-1000 ▪ Fx: 719-548-9407

Native Americans in Science, Society for Advancement of　www.sacnas.org
Chicanos &　PO Box 8526　Santa Cruz CA 95061
Ph: 831-459-0170 ▪ Fx: 831-459-0194

Native Daughters of the Golden West　www.ndgw.org
543 Baker St　San Francisco CA 94117
Ph: 415-563-9091 ▪ Fx: 415-563-5230 ▪ TF: 800-944-6349

Native Fish Society　www.nativefishsociety.org
PO Box 19570　Portland OR 97280
Ph: 503-977-0287 ▪ Fx: 503-977-0026

Native Fishes Association, North American　www.nanfa.org
1107 Argonne Dr　Baltimore MD 21218
Ph: 410-243-9050

Native Forest Council — www.forestcouncil.org
PO Box 2190   Eugene OR 97402
Ph: 541-431-2600 ▪ Fx: 541-461-2156

Native Forest Network — www.nativeforest.org/
PO Box 8251   Missoula MT 59807
Ph: 406-542-7343 ▪ Fx: 406-542-7347

Native Habitat Organization — www.nativehabitat.org/
PO Box 101071   Fort Worth TX 76185
Ph: 817-396-4370

Native Seeds/SEARCH — www.nativeseeds.org
526 N 4th Ave   Tucson AZ 85705
Ph: 520-622-5561 ▪ Fx: 520-622-5591

Native Sons of the Golden West — www.nsgw.org
414 Mason St   San Francisco CA 94102
Ph: 415-392-1223 ▪ Fx: 415-392-1230 ▪ TF: 800-337-1875

Native Writers' Circle of the Americas — www.ou.edu/cas/nas/writers.html
Univ of Oklahoma 216 Ellison Hall 633 Elm Ave   Norman OK
73019
Ph: 405-325-2312 ▪ Fx: 405-325-0842

NATSO Inc — www.natso.com
1199 N Fairfax St Suite 801   Alexandria VA 22314
Ph: 703-549-2100 ▪ Fx: 703-684-4525 ▪ TF: 888-275-2876

NATSO Foundation — www.natsofoundation.org
1199 N Fairfax St Suite 801   Alexandria VA 22314
Ph: 703-549-2100 ▪ Fx: 703-684-4525 ▪ TF: 888-275-6287

NATSO PAC
1199 N Fairfax St Suite 801   Alexandria VA 22314
Ph: 703-549-2100 ▪ Fx: 703-684-4525

Natural Areas Association — www.naturalarea.org
PO Box 1504   Bend OR 97709
Ph: 541-317-0199

Natural Casing Association, North American — www.nanca.org
666 11th St NW   Washington DC 20001
Ph: 202-331-8234 ▪ Fx: 202-331-8191

Natural Colored Wool Growers Association — www.ncwga.org
429 W US 30   Valparaiso IN 46385
Ph: 219-759-9665

(Natural Family Planning) Couple to Couple League International — www.ccli.org
PO Box 111184   Cincinnati OH 45211
Ph: 513-471-2000 ▪ Fx: 513-557-2449

Natural Gas Association of America, Interstate — www.ingaa.org
10 G St NE Suite 700   Washington DC 20002
Ph: 202-216-5900 ▪ Fx: 202-216-0870 ▪ TF: 888-854-6422

Natural Gas Supply Association — www.ngsa.org
805 15th St NW Suite 510   Washington DC 20005
Ph: 202-326-9300 ▪ Fx: 202-326-9330

Natural Gas Vehicle Coalition — www.ngvc.org
400 N Capitol St NW   Washington DC 20001
Ph: 202-824-7360 ▪ Fx: 202-824-7367

(Natural Hazards) Crowding the Rim — www.crowdingtherim.org
345 Middlefield Rd MS 973   Menlo Park CA 94025
Ph: 650-329-5430 ▪ Fx: 650-329-4936

Natural Health Professionals, National Association of Certified — www.cnhp.org
714 E Winona Ave   Warsaw IN 46580
Ph: 574-267-4230 ▪ Fx: 574-268-5393 ▪ TF: 800-321-1005

Natural History Association, Big Bend — www.nps.gov/bibe/BBNHA/bbnha.htm
PO Box 196   Big Bend National Park TX 79834
Ph: 432-477-2236 ▪ Fx: 432-477-2234

Natural History Collections, Society for the Preservation of — www.spnhc.org

(Natural History) John Burroughs Association Inc — www.johnburroughs.org
15 W 77th St   New York NY 10024
Ph: 212-769-5169

Natural Law Party of the USA — www.naturallaw.org
PO Box 1900   Fairfield IA 52556
Ph: 641-472-2040 ▪ Fx: 641-472-2011 ▪ TF: 800-332-0000

Natural Medicine Pharmacists, Association of — www.anmp.org
PO Box 150727   San Rafael CA 94915
Ph: 415-479-1512 ▪ Fx: 415-472-2559

Natural Resource Enforcement Trainers, Association of — www.anret.org
402 W Washington St IGCS Rm W255D   Indianapolis IN 46204
Ph: 317-232-4014 ▪ Fx: 317-232-8035

Natural Resources Council of America — www.naturalresourcescouncil.org
1025 Thomas Jefferson St NW Suite 109   Washington DC
20007
Ph: 202-333-0411 ▪ Fx: 202-333-0412

Natural Resources Defense Council — www.nrdc.org
40 W 20th St   New York NY 10011
Ph: 212-727-2700 ▪ Fx: 212-727-1773

Natural Resources Foundation, Renewable — www.rnrf.org
5430 Grosvenor Ln   Bethesda MD 20814
Ph: 301-493-9101 ▪ Fx: 301-493-6148

Natural Resources Information Council — www.quinneylibrary.usu.edu/NRIC

(Natural Resources) Resources for the Future — www.rff.org
1616 P St NW   Washington DC 20036
Ph: 202-328-5000 ▪ Fx: 202-939-3460

Natural Sausage Casing Association, International — www.insca.org
12339 Carroll Ave   Rockville MD 20852
Ph: 301-231-9811 ▪ Fx: 301-231-4871

Natural Science Collections Alliance — www.nscalliance.org
1725 K St NW Suite 601   Washington DC 20006
Ph: 202-835-9050 ▪ Fx: 202-835-7334

Natural Science Illustrators, Guild of — www.gnsi.org
PO Box 652   Washington DC 20044
Ph: 301-309-1514

Natural Science for Youth Foundation
130 Azalea Dr   Roswell GA 30075
Ph: 770-594-9367 ▪ Fx: 770-594-7738

Natural Sciences, Academy of — www.acnatsci.org
1900 Benjamin Franklin Pkwy   Philadelphia PA 19103
Ph: 215-299-1000 ▪ Fx: 215-299-1028

Naturalist Society, Audubon — www.audubonnaturalist.org
8940 Jones Mill Rd   Chevy Chase MD 20815
Ph: 301-652-9188 ▪ Fx: 301-951-7179

Naturalists, American Society of — www.amnat.org
Univ of Chicago Press PO Box 37005   Chicago IL 60637
Ph: 773-753-3347 ▪ Fx: 773-753-0811

Nature Conservancy — nature.org
4245 N Fairfax Dr Suite 100   Arlington VA 22203
Ph: 703-841-5300 ▪ Fx: 703-841-1283 ▪ TF: 800-628-6860

Nature Conservancy of Canada — www.natureconservancy.ca
110 Eglinton Ave W Suite 400   Toronto ON M4R1A3
Ph: 416-932-3202 ▪ Fx: 416-932-3208 ▪ TF: 800-465-0029

Nature & Environmental Writers - College & University Educators — www.new-cue.org
Saint Thomas Aquinas College   Sparkill NY 10976
Ph: 845-398-4247 ▪ Fx: 845-398-4224

Nature Federation, Canadian — www.cnf.ca
1 Nicholas St Suite 606   Ottawa ON K1N7B7
Ph: 613-562-3447 ▪ Fx: 613-562-3371 ▪ TF: 800-267-4088

Nature, Interfaith Council for the Protection of Animals &
3691 Tuxedo Rd NW   Atlanta GA 30305
Ph: 404-814-1371

Nature in Israel, American Society for the Protection of — www.aspni.org
28 Arrandale Ave   Great Neck NY 11024
Ph: 212-398-6750 ▪ Fx: 212-398-1665 ▪ TF: 800-411-0966

Nature & Natural Resources, International Union for Conservation of — www.iucn.org
USA Multilateral Office 1630 Connecticut Ave NW 3rd
Fl   Washington DC 20009
Ph: 202-387-4826 ▪ Fx: 202-387-4823

Nature Photography Association, North American — www.nanpa.org
10200 W 44th Ave Suite 304   Wheat Ridge CO 80033
Ph: 303-422-8527 ▪ Fx: 303-422-8894

Nature Study Society, American — www.nature-study.org
Pocono Environmental Education Ctr RR 2 Box
1010   Dingmans Ferry PA 18328
Ph: 570-828-9692 ▪ Fx: 570-828-9695

Naturist Society — www.naturistsociety.com
PO Box 132   Oshkosh WI 54903
Ph: 920-426-5009 ▪ Fx: 920-426-5184 ▪ TF: 800-558-8250

Naturopathic Medical Association, American — www.anma.com
PO Box 96273   Las Vegas NV 89193
Ph: 702-897-7053 ▪ Fx: 702-897-7140

Naturopathic Physicians, American Association of — www.naturopathic.org
3201 New Mexico Ave NW Suite 350   Washington DC 20016
Ph: 202-895-1392 ▪ Fx: 202-274-1992 ▪ TF: 866-538-2267

Nautical Archaeology, Institute of — ina.tamu.edu
PO Drawer HG   College Station TX 77841
Ph: 979-845-6694 ▪ Fx: 979-847-9260

Navajo-Churro Sheep Association — www.navajo-churrosheep.com
PO Box 94   Ojo Caliente NM 87549
Ph: 505-737-0488

Naval Airship Association — www.naval-airships.org/
2 Maryhill Dr   Saint Louis MO 63124
Ph: 314-991-3901 ▪ Fx: 314-991-9621

Naval Architects & Marine Engineers, Society of — www.sname.org
601 Pavonia Ave 4th Fl   Jersey City NJ 07306
Ph: 201-798-4800 ▪ Fx: 201-798-4975

Naval Aviation, Association of — www.anahq.org
2550 Huntington Ave Suite 201   Alexandria VA 22303
Ph: 703-960-2490 ▪ Fx: 703-960-4490

Naval Civilian Managers Association — www.ncmanational.org
PO Box 215   Portsmouth VA 23705
Ph: 757-396-3862 ▪ Fx: 757-396-3170

Naval Engineers, American Society of — www.navalengineers.org
1452 Duke St   Alexandria VA 22314
Ph: 703-836-6727 ▪ Fx: 703-836-7491

Naval Enlisted Reserve Association — www.nera.org
6703 Farragut Ave   Falls Church VA 22042
Ph: 703-534-1329 ▪ Fx: 703-534-3617 ▪ TF: 800-776-9020

Naval Historical Foundation — www.navyhistory.org
1306 Dahlgren Ave SE Washington Navy Yard   Washington DC
20374
Ph: 202-678-4333 ▪ Fx: 202-889-3565

Naval Institute, US — www.usni.org
291 Wood Rd   Annapolis MD 21402
Ph: 410-268-6110 ▪ Fx: 410-269-7940 ▪ TF: 800-233-8764

Naval Intelligence Professionals — www.navintpro.org
PO Box 9324   McLean VA 22102
Ph: 202-554-8095

Naval Officers Association, National — www.nnoa.org
PO Box 10871   Alexandria VA 22310
Ph: 703-757-4808

Naval Research Organization, International — www.warship.org
5905 Reinwood Dr   Toledo OH 43613
Ph: 419-472-1331

Naval Reserve Association — www.navy-reserve.org
1619 King St   Alexandria VA 22314
Ph: 703-548-5800 ▪ Fx: 866-683-3647 ▪ TF: 866-672-4968

Naval Sea Cadet Corps — www.seacadets.org
2300 Wilson Blvd   Arlington VA 22201
Ph: 703-243-6910 ▪ Fx: 703-243-3985

Naval Ships Association, Historic — www.hnsa.org

Naval Submarine League — www.navalsubleague.com
5025-D Backlick Rd Suite D   Annandale VA 22003
Ph: 703-256-0891 ▪ Fx: 703-642-5815

Navigation Association, International — www.internationalnavigation.org

Navigation, Institute of — www.ion.org
3975 University Dr Suite 390   Fairfax VA 22030
Ph: 703-383-9688 ▪ Fx: 703-383-9689

Navigators
PO Box 6000   Colorado Springs CO 80934   home.navigators.org/us
Ph: 719-598-1212 ▪ Fx: 719-260-0479

Navy Anesthesia Society   www.geocities.com/Vienna/2209/nas.html
Naval Medical Ctr Dept of Anesthesiology   San Diego CA 92134
Ph: 619-532-8943 ▪ Fx: 619-532-8945

Navy Club of the USA   www.navyclubusa.org
5473 S Jones Blvd Suite 1099   Las Vegas NV 89118
Ph: 702-897-8729 ▪ Fx: 702-897-1939 ▪ TF: 800-628-7265

Navy League of the US   www.navyleague.org
2300 Wilson Blvd   Arlington VA 22201
Ph: 703-528-1775 ▪ Fx: 703-528-2333 ▪ TF: 800-356-5760

Navy-Marine Corps Relief Society   www.nmcrs.org
4015 Wilson Blvd 10th Fl   Arlington VA 22203
Ph: 703-696-4904 ▪ Fx: 703-696-0144 ▪ TF: 800-654-8364

Navy Mutual Aid Association   www.navymutual.org
29 Carpenter Rd Henderson Hall   Arlington VA 22212
Ph: 703-614-1638 ▪ Fx: 703-695-4635 ▪ TF: 800-628-6011

Navy Union USA, Army &   www.armynavy.net
2002 Tallmadge Ave   Kent OH 44240
Ph: 330-343-9015

Nazarene, Church of the   www.nazarene.org
6401 The Paseo   Kansas City MO 64131
Ph: 816-333-7000

Nazarene Compassionate Ministries International   www.nazcompassion.org
6401 The Paseo   Kansas City MO 64131
Ph: 816-333-7000 ▪ Fx: 816-333-2948 ▪ TF: 877-626-4145

Nazarene World Mission   www.nazareneworldmission.org
6401 The Paseo   Kansas City MO 64131
Ph: 816-333-7000 ▪ Fx: 816-822-8296

NCALL Research Inc   www.ncall.org
20 E Division St PO Box 1092   Dover DE 19903
Ph: 302-678-9400 ▪ Fx: 302-678-9058

NCCLS   www.nccls.org
940 W Valley Rd Suite 1400   Wayne PA 19087
Ph: 610-688-0100 ▪ Fx: 610-688-0700

NCSJ: Advocates on Behalf of Jews in Russia Ukraine the Baltic   www.ncsj.org
States & Eurasia   2020 K St NW Suite 7800   Washington DC
20036
Ph: 202-898-2500 ▪ Fx: 202-898-0822

NCSL International   www.ncsli.org
2995 Wilderness Pl Suite 107   Boulder CO 80301
Ph: 303-440-3339 ▪ Fx: 303-440-3384

NEA - Association of Union Constructors   www.nea-online.org
1501 Lee Hwy Suite 202   Arlington VA 22209
Ph: 703-524-3336 ▪ Fx: 703-524-3364

NEA Foundation for the Improvement of Education   www.nfie.org
1201 16th St NW   Washington DC 20036
Ph: 202-822-7840 ▪ Fx: 202-822-7779

NEA Fund for Children & Public Education
1201 16th St NW   Washington DC 20036
Ph: 202-833-4000 ▪ Fx: 202-822-7974

NEA Health Information Network   www.bocadcweb.net/healthinfo
1201 16th St NW Suite 521   Washington DC 20036
Ph: 202-822-7570 ▪ Fx: 202-822-7775 ▪ TF: 800-718-8387

Near-Death Studies, International Association for   www.iands.org
PO Box 502   East Windsor Hill CT 06028
Ph: 860-882-1211 ▪ Fx: 860-882-1212

Near East Archaeological Society   www.neasweb.org
Horn Archaeological Museum Andrews Univ   Berrien Springs
MI 49104
Ph: 269-471-3273 ▪ Fx: 269-471-3619

Near East Foundation   www.neareast.org
420 Lexington Ave Suite 2516   New York NY 10170
Ph: 212-867-0064 ▪ Fx: 212-867-0169

Near East Welfare Association, Catholic   www.cnewa.org
1011 1st Ave   New York NY 10022
Ph: 212-826-1480 ▪ Fx: 212-838-1344 ▪ TF: 800-442-6392

Near Eastern & African Studies, Institute of   www.ineas.org
PO Box 425125   Cambridge MA 02142
Ph: 617-864-6327

Neck Radiology, American Society of Head &   www.ashnr.org
2210 Midwest Rd Suite 207   Oak Brook IL 60523
Ph: 630-574-0220 ▪ Fx: 630-574-0661

Neckwear Association of America
151 Lexington Ave 2nd Fl   New York NY 10016
Ph: 212-683-8454 ▪ Fx: 212-686-7382

Needlepoint Guild, American   www.needlepoint.org
PO Box 1027   Cordova TN 38088
Ph: 901-755-3728 ▪ Fx: 901-755-3803

Needletrades Industrial & Textile Employees, Union of   www.uniteunion.org
275 7th Ave   New York NY 10001
Ph: 212-265-7000 ▪ Fx: 212-265-3415 ▪ TF: 800-238-6483

Needlework Association, National   www.tnna.org
PO Box 3388   Zanesville OH 43702
Ph: 740-455-6773 ▪ Fx: 740-452-2552 ▪ TF: 800-889-8662

Needlework, Pomegranate Guild of Judaic   www.pomegranateguild.org
34 Summit Ave   Sharon MA 02067
Ph: 781-784-2668

Negative Population Growth   www.npg.org
1717 Massachusetts Ave NW Suite 101   Washington DC 20036
Ph: 202-667-8950 ▪ Fx: 202-667-8953

Negev, American Associates Ben-Gurion University of the www.aabgu.org
1430 Broadway 8th Fl   New York NY 10018
Ph: 212-687-7721 ▪ Fx: 212-302-6443 ▪ TF: 800-962-2248

Negotiators, North American Association of Educational   www.naen.org
6678 County Rd 32   Norwich NY 13815
Ph: 503-588-2800

Negro American Mission Board, Catholic
2021 H St NW   Washington DC 20006
Ph: 202-331-8542 ▪ Fx: 202-331-8544

Negro Business & Professional Women's Clubs Inc,   www.nanbpwc.org
National Association of   1806 New Hampshire Ave
NW   Washington DC 20009
Ph: 202-483-4206 ▪ Fx: 202-462-7253

Negro College Fund Inc, United   www.uncf.org
8260 Willow Oaks Corporate Dr   Fairfax VA 22031
Ph: 703-205-3400 ▪ Fx: 703-205-3597 ▪ TF: 800-331-2244

Negro Musicians, National Association of   www.nanm.8m.com
11551 S Laflin St PO Box 43053   Chicago IL 60643
Ph: 773-568-3818 ▪ Fx: 773-779-1325

Negro Women Inc, National Council of   www.ncnw.org
633 Pennsylvania Ave NW   Washington DC 20004
Ph: 202-737-0120 ▪ Fx: 202-737-0476

Neighbor to Neighbor   www.n2n.org
424 Pine St Suite 203   Fort Collins CO 80524
Ph: 970-484-7498 ▪ Fx: 970-407-7045 ▪ TF: 800-366-8289

Neighborhood Bible Studies   www.neighborhoodbiblestudies.org
56 Main St   Dobbs Ferry NY 10522
Ph: 914-693-3273 ▪ Fx: 914-693-4345 ▪ TF: 800-369-0307

Neighborhood Centers of America Inc, United   www.unca.org
3631 Perkins Ave 4th Fl   Cleveland OH 44114
Ph: 216-391-3028 ▪ Fx: 216-391-6206

Neighborhood Coalition, National   www.neighborhoodcoalition.org
1030 15th St NW Suite 325   Washington DC 20005
Ph: 202-408-8553 ▪ Fx: 202-408-8551

Neighborhood Enterprise, National Center for   www.ncne.com
1424 16th St NW Suite 300   Washington DC 20036
Ph: 202-518-6500 ▪ Fx: 202-588-0314

Neighborhood Housing Services of America   www.nhsofamerica.org
1970 Broadway Suite 470   Oakland CA 94612
Ph: 510-832-5542 ▪ Fx: 510-444-3063

Neighborhood Schools, National Association for   www.nans.org
3905 Muriel Ave   Cleveland OH 44109
Ph: 216-398-4667

Neighborhood Technology, Center for   www.cnt.org
2125 W North Ave   Chicago IL 60647
Ph: 773-278-4800 ▪ Fx: 773-278-3840

Neighborhood Women, National Congress of
249 Manhattan Ave   Brooklyn NY 11211
Ph: 718-388-8915 ▪ Fx: 718-388-0285

Neighborhoods, National Association of   www.nanworld.org
1300 Pennsylvania Ave NW Suite 700 NW   Washington DC
20004
Ph: 202-332-7766 ▪ Fx: 202-332-2314

Neighbors Inc, World   www.wn.org
4127 NW 122nd St   Oklahoma City OK 73120
Ph: 405-752-9700 ▪ Fx: 405-752-9393 ▪ TF: 800-242-6387

Nellie Mae Education Foundation   www.nmefdn.org
1250 Hancock St Suite 205N   Quincy MA 02169
Ph: 781-348-4200 ▪ Fx: 781-348-4299 ▪ TF: 877-635-5436

Nelson A Rockefeller Institute of Government   rockinst.org/
411 State St   Albany NY 12203
Ph: 518-443-5522 ▪ Fx: 518-443-5788

Neonatal Nurses, Association of Women's Health Obstetric & www.awhonn.org
2000 L St NW Suite 740   Washington DC 20036
Ph: 202-261-2400 ▪ Fx: 202-728-0575 ▪ TF: 800-673-8499

Neonatal Nurses, National Association of   www.nann.org
4700 W Lake Ave   Glenview IL 60025
Ph: 847-375-3660 ▪ Fx: 888-477-6266 ▪ TF: 800-451-3795

Neot-Kedumim, American Friends of   www.neot-kedumim.org.il
813 Rt 3   Halcott Center NY 12430
Ph: 845-254-5031 ▪ Fx: 845-254-9836

Nephrology, American Society of   www.asn-online.com
1725 'I' St NW Suite 510   Washington DC 20006
Ph: 202-659-0599 ▪ Fx: 202-659-0709

Nephrology, American Society of Pediatric   www.aspneph.com
JW Riley Hospital for Children 702 Barnhill Dr Wells Research
Ctr Rm 2600-A   Indianapolis IN 46202
Ph: 317-278-0854 ▪ Fx: 317-278-3599

Nephrology Nurses' Association, American   anna.inurse.com
E Holly Ave Box 56   Pitman NJ 08071
Ph: 856-256-2320 ▪ Fx: 856-589-7463 ▪ TF: 888-600-2662

Nephrology Technologists/Technicians, National Association of www.dialysistech.org
PO Box 2307   Dayton OH 45401
Ph: 937-586-3705 ▪ Fx: 937-586-3699 ▪ TF: 877-607-6268

Nervous & Mental Disease, Association for Research in   www.arnmd.org/arnmd

Net PAC
1401 Wilson Blvd Suite 1100   Arlington VA 22209
Ph: 703-522-5055 ▪ Fx: 703-525-2279

NetAction   www.netaction.org
PO Box 6739   Santa Barbara CA 93160
Ph: 415-215-9392

Netherlands Chamber of Commerce in the US Inc   www.netherlands.org
1 Rockefeller Plaza Suite 1420   New York NY 10020
Ph: 212-265-6460 ▪ Fx: 212-265-6402

Network Against Coercive Psychiatry   www.sethfarber.com
172 W 79th St Suite 2E   New York NY 10024
Ph: 212-560-7288 ▪ Fx: 212-799-9026

Network of Alternatives for Publishers Retailers & Artists www.napra.com
PO Box 9   Eastsound WA 98245
Ph: 360-376-2702 ▪ Fx: 360-376-2704 ▪ TF: 800-367-1907

Network of Executive Women in Hospitality   www.newh.org
PO Box 322   Shawano WI 54166
Ph: 715-526-5267 ▪ Fx: 715-526-5979

Network of Indian Professionals of North America   www.netip.org

Network of Ingredient Marketing Specialists Inc   www.nimsgroup.com
PO Box 610   Montville NJ 07045
Ph: 973-402-4803 ▪ Fx: 973-316-6668

Network Professional Association
1405 Warner Ave   Tustin CA 92780
Ph: 714-258-8381 ■ Fx: 714-258-8391
www.npanet.org

Network & Services Inc, Advanced
200 Business Park Dr   Armonk NY 10504
Ph: 914-765-1100 ■ Fx: 914-273-1809
www.advanced.org

Network in Solidarity with the People of Guatemala
1830 Connecticut Ave NW   Washington DC 20009
Ph: 202-518-7638 ■ Fx: 202-223-8221
www.nisgua.org

Network & Systems Professionals Association Inc
7044 S 13th St   Oak Creek WI 53154
Ph: 414-768-8000 ■ Fx: 414-768-8001
www.naspa.com

Networked Information, Coalition for
21 Dupont Cir NW Euram Bldg Suite 800   Washington DC 20036
Ph: 202-296-5098 ■ Fx: 202-872-0884
www.cni.org

Networking, Consortium for School
1710 Rhode Island Ave NW Suite 900   Washington DC 20036
Ph: 202-861-2676 ■ Fx: 202-861-0888 ■ TF: 866-267-8747
www.cosn.org

Neural Network Society, International
7600 Terrace Ave Suite 203   Middleton WI 53562
Ph: 608-831-0584 ■ Fx: 608-831-5122
www.inns.org

Neural Networks Society, IEEE
IEEE Operations Ctr 445 Hoes Ln   Piscataway NJ 08854
Ph: 732-981-0060 ■ Fx: 732-981-1721
www.ieee-nns.org

Neuro-Developmental Treatment Association
1550 S Coast Hwy Suite 201   Laguna Beach CA 92651
Ph: 714-497-9007 ■ TF: 800-869-9295
www.ndta.org

Neuro-Ophthalmology Society, North American
342 N Main St   West Hartford CT 06117
Ph: 860-558-7507 ■ Fx: 860-586-7550
www.nanosweb.org

Neuro-Psychopharmacologicum, Collegium Internationale
2014 Broadway Suite 320   Nashville TN 37203
Ph: 615-343-2068 ■ Fx: 615-343-2069
www.cinp.org

Neurochemistry, American Society for
9037 Ron Den Ln   Windermere FL 34786
Ph: 407-876-0750
www.ASNeurochem.org

Neurofibromatosis Foundation, National
95 Pine St 16th Fl   New York NY 10005
Ph: 212-344-6633 ■ Fx: 212-747-0004 ■ TF: 800-323-7938
www.nf.org

Neuroimaging, American Society of
5841 Cedar Lake Rd Suite 204   Minneapolis MN 55416
Ph: 952-545-6291 ■ Fx: 952-545-6073
www.asnweb.org

Neurological Association, American
5841 Cedar Lake Rd Suite 204   Minneapolis MN 55416
Ph: 952-545-6204 ■ Fx: 952-545-6073
www.aneuroa.org

Neurological & Orthopaedic Surgeons, American Academy of
2300 S Rancho Dr Suite 202   Las Vegas NV 89102
Ph: 702-388-7390 ■ Fx: 702-388-7395
www.aanos.org

Neurological Surgeons, American Association of
5550 Meadowbrook Dr   Rolling Meadows IL 60068
Ph: 847-378-0500 ■ Fx: 847-378-0600 ■ TF: 888-566-2267
www.aans.org

Neurological Surgeons, Congress of
10 N Martingale Rd Suite 190   Schaumburg IL 60173
Ph: 847-240-2500 ■ Fx: 847-240-0804 ■ TF: 877-517-1267
www.neurosurgeon.org

Neurological Surgeons, Society of
600 Highland Ave   Madison WI 53792
Ph: 608-263-0170 ■ Fx: 608-263-1728
www.societyns.org

Neurology, American Academy of
1080 Montreal Ave   Saint Paul MN 55116
Ph: 651-695-2717 ■ Fx: 651-695-2791 ■ TF: 800-879-1960
www.aan.com

Neurology Society, Child
1000 W County Rd   Saint Paul MN 55126
Ph: 651-486-9447 ■ Fx: 651-486-9436
www.childneurologysociety.org

Neuroma Association, Acoustic
600 Peachtree Pkwy Suite 108   Cumming GA 30041
Ph: 770-205-8211 ■ Fx: 770-205-0239
anausa.org

Neuromodulation Society, North American
4700 W Lake Ave   Glenview IL 60025
Ph: 847-375-4714 ■ Fx: 877-594-6704
www.neuromodulation.org

Neuropathologists, American Association of
2095 Adelbert Rd   Cleveland OH 44106
Ph: 216-368-2488 ■ Fx: 216-368-8964
www.aanp-jnen.org

Neurophysiology, American Academy of Clinical
104 13th St   Hudson WI 54016
Ph: 715-381-3440 ■ Fx: 715-381-3442
www.aacnonline.com

Neurophysiology Society, American Clinical
PO Box 30   Bloomfield CT 06002
Ph: 860-243-3977 ■ Fx: 860-286-0787
www.acns.org

Neuropsychiatric Association, American
700 Ackerman Rd Suite 550   Columbus OH 43202
Ph: 614-447-2077 ■ Fx: 614-263-4366
www.neuropsychiatry.com/ANPA/

Neuropsychological Society, International
700 Ackerman Rd Suite 625   Columbus OH 43202
Ph: 614-263-4200 ■ Fx: 614-263-4366
www.the-ins.org

Neuropsychology, National Academy of
2121 S Oneida St Suite 550   Denver CO 80224
Ph: 303-691-3694 ■ Fx: 303-691-5983
www.nanonline.org

Neuropsychopharmacology, American College of
2014 Broadway Suite 320   Nashville TN 37203
Ph: 615-322-2075 ■ Fx: 615-343-0662
www.acnp.org

Neuroradiological Societies, World Federation of
2210 Midwest Rd Suite 207   Oak Brook IL 60523
Ph: 630-574-0220 ■ Fx: 630-574-0661
www.wfnrs.org

Neuroradiology, American Society of
2210 Midwest Rd Suite 207   Oak Brook IL 60523
Ph: 630-574-0220 ■ Fx: 630-574-0661
www.asnr.org

Neuroradiology, American Society of Interventional & Therapeutic
2210 Midwest Rd Suite 207   Oak Brook IL 60523
Ph: 630-574-0220 ■ Fx: 630-574-0661
www.asitn.org

Neuroradiology, American Society of Pediatric
2210 Midwest Rd Suite 207   Oak Brook IL 60523
Ph: 630-574-0220 ■ Fx: 630-574-0661
www.asnr.org/aspnr

Neurorehabilitation, American Society of
5841 Cedar Lake Rd Suite 204   Minneapolis MN 55416
Ph: 952-545-6324 ■ Fx: 952-545-6073
www.asnr.com

Neuroscience, International Society for Developmental
developmental-neuroscience.org

Neuroscience Nurses, American Association of
4700 W Lake Ave   Glenview IL 60025
Ph: 847-375-4733 ■ Fx: 877-734-8677 ■ TF: 888-557-2266
www.aann.org

Neuroscience, Society for
11 Dupont Cir NW Suite 500   Washington DC 20036
Ph: 202-462-6688 ■ Fx: 202-462-9740
web.sfn.org

Neurosurgery, American Society for Pediatric
James Whitcomb Riley Hospital For Children 1 Children's Sq Suite 1730   Indianapolis IN 46202
Ph: 317-274-8852 ■ Fx: 317-274-8895
www.aspn.org

Neurosurgery, American Society for Stereotactic & Functional
Presbyterian Hospital 200 Lothrop St Suite B-400   Pittsburgh PA 15213
Ph: 412-647-6782 ■ Fx: 412-647-5559

Neurosurgical Society of America
PO Box 208082   New Haven CT 06520
Ph: 203-785-2791
www.neurosurgicalsociety.com

NeuroTherapeutics, American Society for Experimental
611 E Wells St   Milwaukee WI 53202
Ph: 414-273-8290 ■ Fx: 414-276-2146
www.asent.org

Nevada Desert Experience
PO Box 46645   Las Vegas NV 89114
Ph: 702-646-4814
www.nevadadesertexperience.org

Nevus Network
PO Box 305   West Salem OH 44287
Ph: 419-853-4525
www.nevusnetwork.org

New Age Citizen
PO Box 419   Dearborn Heights MI 48127
Ph: 313-563-3192
www.newagecitizen.com

New America Foundation
1630 Connecticut Ave NW 7th Fl   Washington DC 20009
Ph: 202-986-2700 ■ Fx: 202-986-3696
www.newamerica.net

New Canaan Historical Society
13 Oenoke Ridge   New Canaan CT 06840
Ph: 203-966-1776 ■ Fx: 203-972-5917
nchistory.org

NEW-CUE Inc
Saint Thomas Aquinas College   Sparkill NY 10976
Ph: 845-398-4247 ■ Fx: 845-398-4224
www.new-cue.org

New Deal Preservation Association, National
PO Box 602   Santa Fe NM 87504
Ph: 505-473-2089 ■ Fx: 505-473-3985
www.newdeallegacy.org/

New Democrat Network
777 N Capitol St NE Suite 410   Washington DC 20002
Ph: 202-544-9200 ■ Fx: 202-547-2929
www.newdem.org

New Dramatists
424 W 44th St   New York NY 10036
Ph: 212-757-6960 ■ Fx: 212-265-4738
newdramatists.org

New England Antiquities Research Association
www.neara.org

New England Antiquities, Society for the Preservation of
141 Cambridge St   Boston MA 02114
Ph: 617-227-3956 ■ Fx: 617-227-9204
www.spnea.org

New England Association of Schools & Colleges
209 Burlington Rd   Bedford MA 01730
Ph: 781-271-0022 ■ Fx: 781-271-0950
www.neasc.org

New England Fisheries Development Association
197 8th St Suite 600A   Charlestown MA 02129
Ph: 617-886-0793 ■ Fx: 617-886-0173
www.fishfacts.com

New England Historic Genealogical Society
101 Newbury St   Boston MA 02116
Ph: 617-536-5740 ■ Fx: 617-536-7307 ■ TF: 888-296-3447
www.newenglandancestors.org

New England Kiln Drying Association
15 Main St PO Box 401   Belfast ME 04915
Ph: 207-338-4377 ■ Fx: 207-338-2692
www.macgregormillsystems.com/nekda.htm

New England, National Society Sons of Colonial
www.nsscne.org

New England Wild Flower Society
180 Hemenway Rd   Framingham MA 01701
Ph: 617-877-7630 ■ Fx: 617-877-3658
www.newfs.org

New Environment Association
270 Fenway Dr   Syracuse NY 13224
Ph: 315-446-8009
web.syr.edu/~hs38/neaindex.htm

New Eyes for the Needy
549 Millburn Ave PO Box 332   Short Hills NJ 07078
Ph: 973-376-4903 ■ Fx: 973-376-3807

New Forest Pony Association Inc
PO Box 206   Pascoag RI 02859
Ph: 401-568-8238 ■ Fx: 401-567-0311
www.newforestpony.net

New Hope Foundation
51 Throckmorton St   Freehold NJ 07728
Ph: 732-308-0113 ■ Fx: 732-308-0115
www.newhopefoundation.org

New Humanity, Alliance for the
www.anhglobal.org

New Israel Fund
1101 14th St NW 6th Fl   Washington DC 20005
Ph: 202-842-0900 ■ Fx: 202-842-0991 ■ TF: 888-988-3863
www.nif.org

New Jersey, Descendants of Founders of
109 Christopher St   Montclair NJ 07042
Ph: 973-744-2926
www.njfounders.org

New Orleans Jazz Club
828 Royal St Suite 265   New Orleans LA 70116
Ph: 504-455-6847
www.nojazzclub.com

New Parents Network   www.npn.org
PO Box 64237   Tucson AZ 85728
Ph: 520-327-1451 ▪ Fx: 520-844-1854

New Party   www.newparty.org
88 3rd Ave Suite 313   Brooklyn NY 11217
Ph: 800-200-1294

New Road Map Foundation   www.newroadmap.org
PO Box 15981   Seattle WA 98115
Ph: 206-527-0437

New Tribes Mission   www.ntm.org
1000 E 1st St   Sanford FL 32771
Ph: 407-323-3430 ▪ Fx: 407-330-0376 ▪ TF: 866-547-2460

New Uses Council   www.newuses.org
7777 Walnut Grove Rd Suite B4   Box 50   Memphis TN 38120
Ph: 901-309-1668 ▪ Fx: 901-309-3823

New Ways Ministry   newwaysministry.org
4012 29th St   Mount Rainier MD 20712
Ph: 301-277-5674

New Ways to Work Inc   www.nww.org
103 Morris St Suite A   Sebastopol CA 95472
Ph: 707-824-4000 ▪ Fx: 707-824-4410

New York Academy of Medicine   www.nyam.org
1216 5th Ave   New York NY 10029
Ph: 212-822-7200

New York Academy of Sciences   www.nyas.org
2 E 63rd St   New York NY 10021
Ph: 212-838-0230 ▪ Fx: 212-888-2894 ▪ TF: 800-843-6927

New York Arm Wrestling Association   www.nycarms.com
PO Box 670952   Flushing NY 11367
Ph: 718-544-4592 ▪ Fx: 718-261-8111 ▪ TF: 877-692-2767

New York Celebrity Assistants   www.nycelebrityassistants.org
459 Columbus Ave Suite 216   New York NY 10024
Ph: 212-803-5444

New York Financial Writers' Association   www.nyfwa.org
PO Box 338   Ridgewood NJ 07451
Ph: 201-612-0100 ▪ Fx: 201-612-9915

New York Genealogical & Biographical Society   www.nygbs.org
122 E 58th St   New York NY 10022
Ph: 212-755-8532 ▪ Fx: 212-754-4218

New York, International Center in   www.intlcenter.org
50 W 23rd St 7th Fl   New York NY 10010
Ph: 212-255-9555 ▪ Fx: 212-255-0177

New York Society of Security Analysts   www.nyssa.org
1601 Broadway 11 Fl   New York NY 10019
Ph: 212-541-4530 ▪ Fx: 212-541-4677 ▪ TF: 800-248-0108

New York State, Canal Society of   www.canalsnys.org

New York Turtle & Tortoise Society Inc   nytts.org

New York Wine & Grape Foundation   www.newyorkwines.org
350 Elm St   Penn Yan NY 14527
Ph: 315-536-7442 ▪ Fx: 315-536-0719

New Zealand American Chambers of Commerce,   www.austemb.org/chambers.htm
Australian   c/o Embassy of Australia 1601 Massachusetts Ave
NW   Washington DC 20036
Ph: 202-797-3028 ▪ Fx: 202-797-3457

New Zealand Council, US-   www.usnzcouncil.org
DACOR Bacon House 1801 F St NW   Washington DC 20006
Ph: 202-842-0772 ▪ Fx: 202-842-0749

New Zealand Rabbit Breeders, American   www.geocities.com/newzealandrba
Federation of   PO Box 171   Honeoye NY 14471
Ph: 585-229-5760

Newcomen Society of the US   www.newcomen.org
211 Welsh Pool Rd Suite 240   Exton PA 19341
Ph: 610-363-6600 ▪ Fx: 610-363-0612

Newport Restoration Foundation   www.newportrestoration.com
51 Touro St   Newport RI 02840
Ph: 401-849-7300 ▪ Fx: 401-849-0125

News Design, Society for   www.snd.org
1130 Ten Rod Rd Suite F-104   North Kingstown RI 02852
Ph: 401-294-5233 ▪ Fx: 401-294-5238

News Directors Association, Radio-Television   www.rtnda.org
1600 K St NW Suite 700   Washington DC 20006
Ph: 202-659-6510 ▪ Fx: 202-223-4007 ▪ TF: 800-807-8632

News Directors, Public Radio   www.prndi.org
Wisconsin Public Radio 821 University Ave   Madison WI 53706
Ph: 608-265-3378 ▪ Fx: 608-263-5838

News Distributors, American Association of Independent   www.aaind.org
900 Fox Valley Dr Suite 204   Longwood FL 32779
Ph: 407-774-9794 ▪ Fx: 407-774-6751

News Media, Center for War Peace & the   www.nyu.edu/cwpnm
New York Univ 418 Lafayette Suite 554   New York NY 10003
Ph: 212-998-7960 ▪ Fx: 212-995-4143

News Media Guild   www.newsmediaguild.org
1501 Broadway Rm 708   New York NY 10036
Ph: 212-869-9290 ▪ Fx: 212-840-0687

News Ombudsmen, Organization of   www.newsombudsmen.org
PO Box 120191   San Diego CA 92112
Ph: 619-293-1525

News Photographers' Association, White House   www.whnpa.org
PO Box 7119 Ben Franklin Stn   Washington DC 20044
Ph: 202-785-5230

News Women's Club, American   www.anwc.org
1607 22nd St NW   Washington DC 20008
Ph: 202-332-6770 ▪ Fx: 202-265-6092

Newsletter & Electronic Publishers Association   www.newsletters.org
1501 Wilson Blvd Suite 509   Arlington VA 22209
Ph: 703-527-2333 ▪ Fx: 703-841-0629 ▪ TF: 800-356-9302

Newspaper Association of America   www.naa.org
1921 Gallows Rd Suite 600   Vienna VA 22182
Ph: 703-902-1600 ▪ Fx: 703-917-0636

Newspaper Association Foundation, National   www.nna.org/Partners/NNAF.htm
127-129 Neff Annex PO Box 7540   Columbia MO 65211
Ph: 573-882-5800 ▪ Fx: 573-884-5490 ▪ TF: 800-829-4662

Newspaper Association, National   www.nna.org
Univ of Missouri 127-129 Neff Annex PO Box 7540   Columbia
MO 65211
Ph: 573-882-5800 ▪ Fx: 573-884-5490 ▪ TF: 800-829-4662

Newspaper Columnists, National Society of   www.columnists.com
1410 Stiener St Suite 709   San Francisco CA 94115
Ph: 415-563-5403

Newspaper Editors, American Society of   www.asne.org
11690-B Sunrise Valley Dr   Reston VA 20191
Ph: 703-453-1122 ▪ Fx: 703-453-1133

Newspaper Editors, International Society of Weekly   www.iswne.org
Missouri Southern State Univ 3950 E Newman Rd   Joplin MO
64801
Ph: 417-625-9736 ▪ Fx: 417-659-4445

Newspaper Features Council   www.nfccouncil.com
PO Box 7421   Greenwich CT 06830
Ph: 203-661-3386 ▪ Fx: 203-661-7337

Newspaper Financial Executives, International   www.infe.org
21525 Ridgetop Cir Suite 200   Sterling VA 20166
Ph: 703-421-4060 ▪ Fx: 703-421-4068

Newspaper Fund Inc, Dow Jones   djnewspaperfund.dowjones.com
4300 Rt 1 N PO Box 300   Princeton NJ 08543
Ph: 609-452-2820 ▪ Fx: 609-520-5804 ▪ TF: 800-639-7386

Newspaper Guild   www.newsguild.org
501 3rd St NW Suite 250   Washington DC 20001
Ph: 202-434-7177 ▪ Fx: 202-434-1472 ▪ TF: 800-585-5864

Newspaper Marketing Association, International   www.inma.org
10300 N Central Expy Suite 467   Dallas TX 75231
Ph: 214-373-9111 ▪ Fx: 214-373-9112

Newspaper Publishers Association, National   www.nnpa.org
3200 13th St NW   Washington DC 20010
Ph: 202-588-8764 ▪ Fx: 202-588-5302

Newspaper Purchasing Management Association   site.netopia.com/npma/door/
101 W Main St Suite 7000   Norfolk VA 23510
Ph: 757-628-2079

Newspapers of America, Suburban   www.suburban-news.org
116 Cass St   Traverse City MI 49684
Ph: 888-486-2466 ▪ Fx: 231-932-2985

Newsweeklies, Association of Alternative   aan.org
1020 16th St NW 4th Fl   Washington DC 20036
Ph: 202-822-1955 ▪ Fx: 202-822-0929

Newswomen's Club of New York   www.newswomensclubnewyork.com
15 Gramercy Pk S   New York NY 10003
Ph: 212-777-1610 ▪ Fx: 212-353-9569

Newswriters Association, Religion   www.religionwriters.com
PO Box 2037   Westerville OH 43086
Ph: 614-891-9001 ▪ Fx: 614-981-9774

NewTithing Group   www.newtithing.org
1 Market Stewart Tower Suite 2105   San Francisco CA 94105
Ph: 415-274-2765 ▪ Fx: 415-274-2756

NFHS Coaches Association   www.nfhs.org/nfca.htm
PO Box 690   Indianapolis IN 46206
Ph: 317-972-6900 ▪ Fx: 317-822-5700

NFHS Music Association   www.nfhs.org/nfma.htm
PO Box 690   Indianapolis IN 46206
Ph: 317-972-6900 ▪ Fx: 317-822-5700

NFHS Officials Association   www.nfhs.org/nfoa.htm
PO Box 690   Indianapolis IN 46206
Ph: 317-972-6900 ▪ Fx: 317-822-5700

NFHS Speech Debate & Theatre Association   www.nfhs.org/sdta.htm
PO Box 690   Indianapolis IN 46206
Ph: 317-972-6900 ▪ Fx: 317-822-5700

NFHS Spirit Association
PO Box 690   Indianapolis IN 46206
Ph: 317-972-6900 ▪ Fx: 317-822-5700

NFL Alumni Inc   www.nflalumni.org
3696 N Federal Hwy Suite 202   Fort Lauderdale FL 33308
Ph: 954-630-2100 ▪ Fx: 954-630-2535 ▪ TF: 800-878-5437

NFPA International   www.nfpa.org
1 Batterymarch Pk   Quincy MA 02169
Ph: 617-770-3000 ▪ Fx: 617-770-0700 ▪ TF: 800-344-3555

NGA   www.nga-inc.org
820 Newtown Rd   Warminster PA 18974
Ph: 215-682-9183 ▪ Fx: 215-682-9185 ▪ TF: 866-295-9974

NGO Committee on Disarmament Peace & Security   disarm.igc.org
777 United Nations Plaza Rm 3-B   New York NY 10017
Ph: 212-687-5340 ▪ Fx: 212-687-1643

Nicaragua Network   www.nicanet.org
1247 'E' St SE   Washington DC 20003
Ph: 202-544-9355 ▪ Fx: 202-544-9359

Nicaraguan-American Chamber of Commerce   www.nacc-miami.com
PO Box 527723   Miami FL 33152
Ph: 305-599-2737 ▪ Fx: 305-220-1841

Nicotine Anonymous World Services   nicotine-anonymous.org
419 Main St PMB 370   Huntington Beach CA 92648
Ph: 415-750-0328

Nicotine & Tobacco, Society for Research on   www.srnt.org
7600 Terrace Ave Suite 203   Middleton WI 53562
Ph: 608-836-3787 ▪ Fx: 608-831-5485

NIDCD National Temporal Bone Hearing & Balance Pathology   www.tbregistry.org
Resource Registry   Massachusetts Eye & Ear Infirmary 243
Charles St   Boston MA 02114
Ph: 617-573-3711 ▪ Fx: 617-573-3838 ▪ TF: 800-822-1327

Nieman Foundation for Journalism   www.nieman.harvard.edu
Harvard Univ 1 Francis Ave   Cambridge MA 02138
Ph: 617-495-2237 ▪ Fx: 617-495-8976

Niemann-Pick Disease Foundation, National   www.nnpdf.org
415 Madison Ave   Fort Atkinson WI 53538
Ph: 920-563-0930 ▪ Fx: 920-563-0931 ▪ TF: 877-287-3672

Nigeria Inc, Friends of   friendsofnigeria.org
1203 Cambria Ct   Iowa City IA 52246
Ph: 319-351-3375

NIH Black Scientists Association   bsa.od.nih.gov
PO Box 2262   Kensington MD 20891
Ph: 301-402-6425

Nile, Daughters of the   www.daughtersofthenile.com
2001 Broadway PO Box 1322   Helena MT 59601
Ph: 406-443-4949

Ninety-Nines Inc   www.ninety-nines.org
4300 Amelia Earhart Rd   Oklahoma City OK 73159
Ph: 405-685-7969 ▪ Fx: 405-685-7985 ▪ TF: 800-944-1929

Nippon Club   www.jcciny.org/jpg/nipponclub/index2.htm
145 W 57th St   New York NY 10019
Ph: 212-581-2223 ▪ Fx: 212-581-3332

NISH   www.nish.org
8401 Old Courthouse Rd   Vienna VA 22182
Ph: 703-560-6800 ▪ Fx: 703-849-8916

Nitrox & Technical Divers, International Association of   www.iantd.com
9628 NE 2nd Ave Suite D   Miami Shores FL 33138
Ph: 305-751-4873 ▪ Fx: 305-751-3958

Nixon Center   www.nixoncenter.org
1615 L St NW Suite 1250   Washington DC 20036
Ph: 202-887-1000 ▪ Fx: 202-887-5222

No Greater Love   www.ngl.org
1750 New York Ave NW   Washington DC 20006
Ph: 202-637-0776 ▪ Fx: 202-783-1168

No Peace Without Justice   www.npwj.org
866 UN Plaza Suite 408   New York NY 10017
Ph: 212-980-2558 ▪ Fx: 212-980-1072

Noah Worcester Dermatological Society   www.noahw.org
61 Donna Rd   Newton MA 02459
Ph: 617-641-9761 ▪ Fx: 617-527-4423

Noble Samuel Roberts Foundation   www.noble.org
PO Box 2180   Ardmore OK 73402
Ph: 580-223-5810 ▪ Fx: 580-224-6217

Nocturnal Adoration Society   www.sjbrcc.org/nas.html
Saint Jean Baptiste Catholic Church 184 E 76th St   New York
NY 10021
Ph: 212-288-5082 ▪ Fx: 212-717-8397

NOEL   www.noelforlife.org
405 Frederick Ave   Sewickley PA 15143
Ph: 412-749-0455 ▪ Fx: 412-749-0422 ▪ TF: 800-707-6635

Noer OJ Research Foundation   www.noerfoundation.org
PO Box 1494   Milwaukee WI 53201
Ph: 414-258-7337

Noetic Sciences, Institute of   www.noetic.org
101 San Antonio Rd   Petaluma CA 94952
Ph: 707-775-3500 ▪ Fx: 707-781-7420

NOFMA: Wood Flooring Manufacturers Association   www.nofma.org
PO Box 3009   Memphis TN 38173
Ph: 901-526-5016 ▪ Fx: 901-526-7022

Nomenclature, American Association for Zoological   www.iczn.org/aazn.htm
c/o Smithsonian Institution Dept of Zoology MRC
159   Washington DC 20013
Ph: 202-633-9786 ▪ Fx: 202-357-2986

Non-Commissioned Officers Association   www.ncoausa.org
10635 IH-35 N   San Antonio TX 78233
Ph: 210-653-6161 ▪ Fx: 210-637-3337 ▪ TF: 800-662-2620

Non-Ferrous Founders Society   www.nffs.org
1480 Renaissance Dr Suite 310   Park Ridge IL 60068
Ph: 847-299-0950 ▪ Fx: 847-299-3598

(Non-profit) Independent Sector   www.independentsector.org
1200 18th St NW Suite 200   Washington DC 20036
Ph: 202-467-6100 ▪ Fx: 202-467-6101 ▪ TF: 888-860-8118

Non-Traditional Casting Project   www.ntcp.org
1560 Broadway Suite 1600   New York NY 10036
Ph: 212-730-4750 ▪ Fx: 212-730-4820

Non-Violence, Community for Creative   users.erols.com/ccnv
425 2nd St NW   Washington DC 20001
Ph: 202-393-1909 ▪ Fx: 202-783-3254

Nondestructive Testing Inc, American Society for   www.asnt.org
1711 Arlingate Ln   Columbus OH 43228
Ph: 614-274-6003 ▪ Fx: 614-274-6899 ▪ TF: 800-222-2768

Nonlinear Analysts, International Federation of   www.fit.edu/AcadRes/math/ifna
Florida Institute of Technology Dept of Mathematical Studies
150 W University Blvd   Melbourne FL 32901
Ph: 321-674-7412

Nonprescription Drug Manufacturers Association of Canada   www.ndmac.ca
1111 Prince of Wales Dr Suite 406   Ottawa ON K2C3T2
Ph: 613-723-0777 ▪ Fx: 613-723-0779

Nonprofit Associations, National Council of   www.ncna.org
1030 15th St NW Suite 870   Washington DC 20005
Ph: 202-962-0322 ▪ Fx: 202-962-0321

Nonprofit Mailers, Alliance of   www.nonprofitmailers.org
1211 Connecticut Ave NW Suite 620   Washington DC 20036
Ph: 202-462-5132

Nonprofit Management, Alliance for   www.allianceonline.org
1899 L St NW 6th Fl   Washington DC 20036
Ph: 202-955-8406

Nonprofit Organizations, Hauser Center for   www.ksg.harvard.edu/hauser
Harvard Univ John F Kennedy School of Government 79 JFK
St   Cambridge MA 02138
Ph: 617-496-5675 ▪ Fx: 617-495-0996

Nonprofit Organizations, Society for   www.snpo.org
5820 Canton Center Rd Suite 165   Canton MI 48187
Ph: 734-451-3582 ▪ Fx: 734-451-5935 ▪ TF: 800-424-7367

Nonproliferation Studies, Center for   www.cns.miis.edu
460 Pierce St   Monterey CA 93940
Ph: 831-647-4154 ▪ Fx: 831-546-3518

Nonpublic School State Accrediting Associations, National   www.nfnssaa.org
Federation of   6300 Father Tribou St   Little Rock AR 72205
Ph: 501-664-0340 ▪ Fx: 501-664-9075

Nonsmokers' Rights, Americans for   www.no-smoke.org
2530 San Pablo Ave Suite J   Berkeley CA 94702
Ph: 510-841-3032 ▪ Fx: 510-841-3071

(Nonviolence) Albert Einstein Institution   www.aeinstein.org
427 Newbury St   Boston MA 02115
Ph: 617-247-4882 ▪ Fx: 617-247-4035

Nonviolence International   www.members.tripod.com/nviusa
PO Box 39127 Friendship Stn NW   Washington DC 20016
Ph: 202-244-0951

Nonviolence, Resource Center for   www.rcnv.org
515 Broadway   Santa Cruz CA 95060
Ph: 831-423-1626 ▪ Fx: 831-423-8716

Nonviolent Communication, Center for   cnvc.org
2428 Foothill Blvd Suite E   La Crescenta CA 91214
Ph: 818-957-9393 ▪ Fx: 818-957-1424 ▪ TF: 800-255-7696

Nonviolent Social Change Inc, Martin Luther King Jr   www.thekingcenter.com
Center for   449 Auburn Ave NE   Atlanta GA 30312
Ph: 404-524-1956 ▪ Fx: 404-526-8969

Nonwoven Fabrics Industry, INDA: Association of the   www.inda.org
1300 Crescent Green Suite 100   Cary NC 27511
Ph: 919-233-1210 ▪ Fx: 919-233-1282

NORA: Association of Responsible Recyclers   www.noranews.org
5965 Amber Ridge Rd   Haymarket VA 20169
Ph: 703-753-4277 ▪ Fx: 703-753-2445

Norcross Wildlife Foundation   www.norcrossws.org
250 W 88th St Suite 806   New York NY 10024
Ph: 212-362-4831

Normande Association, North American   www.normandeassociation.com
30698 Ottoman Ave   Elroy WI 53929
Ph: 866-685-8491

Nortel Networks Users Group, International   www.innua.org
401 N Michigan Ave Suite 2200   Chicago IL 60611
Ph: 312-673-6102 ▪ Fx: 312-673-6718 ▪ TF: 877-446-6684

(North Africa) American Institute for   www.la.utexas.edu/research/mena/aims
Maghrib Studies   Univ of Arizona Center for Middle Eastern
Studies PO Box 210080   Tucson AZ 85721
Ph: 520-626-6498

North America Missing Children Association Inc   www.namca.com
136 Rt 420 Hwy   South Esk NB E1V4N8
Ph: 506-627-1209 ▪ Fx: 506-622-3515

North America, Society for the   faculty.kutztown.edu/ehrensal/sana2.html
Anthropology of   c/o American Anthropological Assn 2200
Wilson Blvd Suite 600   Arlington VA 22201
Ph: 703-528-1902 ▪ Fx: 703-528-3546

North American Academy of Ecumenists   www.naae.net
211 Easton Dr   Lakeland FL 33803
Ph: 863-682-8415

North American Academy of Liturgy   www.naal-liturgy.org
Univ of Portland 5000 N Willamette Blvd   Portland OR 97203
Ph: 503-943-7380 ▪ Fx: 503-943-7803

North American Araucanian Royalist Society   www.geocities.com/tourtoirac

North American Association for Ambulatory Care   www.nafac.com
18870 Rutledge Rd   Minneapolis MN 55391
Ph: 952-476-0015 ▪ Fx: 952-456-0646

North American Association of Christians in Social Work   www.nacsw.org
PO Box 121   Botsford CT 06404
Ph: 203-270-8780 ▪ TF: 888-426-4712

North American Association of Educational Negotiators   www.naen.org
6678 County Rd 32   Norwich NY 13815
Ph: 503-588-2800

North American Association for Environmental Education   www.naaee.org
1707 H St NW Suite 900   Washington DC 20006
Ph: 202-261-6481 ▪ Fx: 202-261-6464

North American Association of Food Equipment Manufacturers   www.nafem.org
161 N Clark Suite 2020   Chicago IL 60601
Ph: 312-821-0201 ▪ Fx: 312-821-0202

North American Association of State & Provincial Lotteries   www.naspl.org
2775 Bishop Rd Suite B   Willoughby Hills OH 44092
Ph: 216-241-2310 ▪ Fx: 216-241-4350

North American Association for the Study of   www.wabash.edu/Rousseau
Jean-Jacques Rousseau   Wabash College Dept of Political
Science 301 W Wabash Ave   Crawfordsville IN 47933
Ph: 765-361-6312

North American Association of Summer Sessions   www.naass.org
43 Belanger St   Dover NH 03820
Ph: 603-740-9880 ▪ Fx: 603-742-7085

North American Association of Telecommunications Dealers   www.natd.com
131 NW 1st Ave   Delray Beach FL 33444
Ph: 561-266-9440 ▪ Fx: 561-266-9017

North American Association of Ventriloquists   www.maherstudios.com
PO Box 420   Littleton CO 80160
Ph: 800-250-5125 ▪ Fx: 720-344-2907

North American Association of Wardens & Superintendents   corrections.com/naaws
PO Box 11037   Albany NY 12211
Ph: 518-786-6801

North American Bear Society   www.nonprofitnet.com/nabs
4061 E Hartford Ave PO Box 55774   Phoenix AZ 85078
Ph: 602-971-2338 ▪ Fx: 602-971-2100

North American Benthological Society   www.benthos.org
PO Box 1897   Lawrence KS 66044
Ph: 785-843-1235 ▪ Fx: 785-843-1274 ▪ TF: 800-627-0629

North American Blueberry Council   www.blueberry.org
4995 Golden Foothill Pkwy Suite 2   El Dorado Hills CA 95762
Ph: 916-933-9399 ▪ Fx: 916-933-9777

North American Bluebird Society www.nabluebirdsociety.org
PO Box 244   Wilmot OH 44689
Ph: 330-359-5511 ▪ Fx: 330-359-5455 ▪ TF: 888-235-1331
North American Boxing Federation www.nabfnews.com
North American Bramble Growers Association www.nabga.com
13006 Mason Rd NE   Cumberland MD 21502
Ph: 301-724-4085 ▪ Fx: 301-724-3020
North American Brass Band Association www.nabba.com
North American Building Material Distribution Association www.nbmda.org
401 N Michigan Ave Suite 2400   Chicago IL 60611
Ph: 312-644-6610 ▪ Fx: 312-321-6869 ▪ TF: 888-747-7862
North American Butterfly Association www.naba.org
4 Delaware Rd   Morristown NJ 07960
Ph: 973-285-0907 ▪ Fx: 973-285-0936
North American Canon Law Society www.rbsocc.org/organizations.html
North American Cartographic Information Society www.nacis.org/
PO Box 399   Milwaukee WI 53201
Ph: 414-229-6282 ▪ Fx: 414-229-3624 ▪ TF: 800-558-8993
North American Catalysis Society www.nacatsoc.org
c/o DuPont Co PO Box 80262   Wilmington DE 19880
Ph: 302-695-2488 ▪ Fx: 302-695-8347
North American Center For Emergency Communications www.nacec.org
PO Box 174   Aurora MN 55705
Ph: 218-229-2887
North American Christian Convention www.nacctheconnectingplace.org
110 Boggs Ln Suite 330   Cincinnati OH 45246
Ph: 513-772-9970 ▪ Fx: 513-772-9980
North American Clun Forest Association www.clunforestsheep.org
Bramble Hill 21777 Randall Dr   Houston MN 55943
Ph: 507-864-7585
North American Coalition for Christianity & Ecology www.nacce.org
PO Box 40011   Saint Paul MN 55104
Ph: 612-698-0349
North American Coalition on Religion & Ecology
5 Thomas Cir NW   Washington DC 20005
Ph: 202-462-2591 ▪ Fx: 202-462-6534
North American College of Botanical Medicine www.nacbm.org
1116 Park Ave SW   Albuquerque NM 87102
Ph: 505-873-8107 ▪ Fx: 505-873-4530
North American Conference on British Studies www.nacbs.org
North American Conference on Ethiopian Jewry www.nacoej.org
132 Nassau St Suite 412   New York NY 10038
Ph: 212-233-5200 ▪ Fx: 212-233-5243
North American Conference of Separated & Divorced Catholics Inc www.nacsdc.org
PO Box 360   Richland OR 97870
Ph: 541-893-6089
North American Congress on Latin America www.nacla.org
475 Riverside Dr Suite 454   New York NY 10115
Ph: 212-870-3146 ▪ Fx: 212-870-3305
North American Contractors Association
1702 W Market St   Greensboro NC 27403
Ph: 336-370-4979 ▪ Fx: 336-370-4946
North American Corriente Association www.corrientecattle.org
PO Box 12359   North Kansas City MO 64116
Ph: 816-421-1992 ▪ Fx: 816-421-1991
North American Council on Adoptable Children www.nacac.org
970 Raymond Ave Suite 106   Saint Paul MN 55114
Ph: 651-644-3036 ▪ Fx: 651-644-9848
North American Council of Automotive Teachers www.nacat.com
11956 Bernardo Plaza Dr Dept 436   San Diego CA 92128
Ph: 858-487-8126 ▪ Fx: 858-487-3617
North American Crane Working Group www.nacwg.org
341 W Olympic Pl   Seattle WA 98119
Ph: 206-286-8607
North American Deer Farmers Association www.nadefa.org
1720 W Wisconsin Ave   Appleton WI 54914
Ph: 920-734-0934 ▪ Fx: 920-734-0955
North American Die Casting Association www.diecasting.org
9701 W Higgins Rd Suite 880   Rosemont IL 60018
Ph: 847-292-3600 ▪ Fx: 847-292-3620
North American Economics & Finance Association www.naefa.org
Ohio Univ Dept of Economics   Athens OH 45701
Ph: 740-593-2034 ▪ Fx: 740-593-0181
North American Electric Reliability Council www.nerc.com
116-390 Village Blvd   Princeton NJ 08540
Ph: 609-452-8060 ▪ Fx: 609-452-9550
North American Elk Breeders Association www.naelk.org
PO Box 1640   Platte City MO 64079
Ph: 816-431-3605 ▪ Fx: 816-431-2705
North American Equipment Dealers Association www.naeda.com
1195 Smizer Mill Rd   Fenton MO 63026
Ph: 636-349-5000 ▪ Fx: 636-349-5443
North American Export Grain Association
1250 I St NW   Washington DC 20005
Ph: 202-682-4030 ▪ Fx: 202-682-4033
North American Family Campers Association www.nafca.org
PO Box 318   Lunenburg MA 01462
Ph: 978-345-7267
North American Farm Show Council www.ag.ohio-state.edu/~farmshow
North American Farmers' Direct Marketing Association www.nafdma.com
62 White Loaf Rd   Southampton MA 01073
Ph: 413-529-0386
North American Federation of Temple Brotherhoods www.nftb.org
633 3rd Ave   New York NY 10017
Ph: 212-650-4100 ▪ Fx: 212-650-4189 ▪ TF: 800-765-6200
North American Fishing Club www.fishingclub.com
12301 Whitewater Dr   Minnetonka MN 55343
Ph: 800-843-6232 ▪ Fx: 952-936-9755

North American Forum on the Catechumenate www.naforum.org
3033 4th St NE   Washington DC 20017
Ph: 202-529-9493 ▪ Fx: 202-529-9497
North American Fruit Explorers Inc www.nafex.org
1716 Apples Rd   Chapin IL 62628
Ph: 217-245-7589
North American Fuzzy Information Processing Society morden.csee.usf.edu/Nafipsf
North American Gamebird Association
1214 Brooks Ave   Raleigh NC 27607
Ph: 919-782-6758
North American Gaming Regulators Association www.nagra.org
26 E Exchange St Suite 500   Saint Paul MN 55101
Ph: 651-203-7244 ▪ Fx: 651-290-2266
North American Gladiolus Council www.gladworld.org
8401 SE Strawberry Ln   Milwaukie OR 97267
Ph: 503-656-9270
North American Graphic Arts Suppliers Association www.nagasa.org
1604 New Hampshire Ave NW   Washington DC 20009
Ph: 202-328-8441 ▪ Fx: 202-328-8513
North American Guild of Change Ringers www.nagcr.org
829 N 25th St   Philadelphia PA 19130
Ph: 215-765-8736 ▪ Fx: 215-276-5238
North American Hardwood Preservation Society
2804 Ladd Ln   Longview TX 75604
Ph: 903-759-9830
North American Higher Education Collaboration, Consortium for www.conahec.org
Univ of Arizona PO Box 210300   Tucson AZ 85721
Ph: 520-621-7761 ▪ Fx: 520-626-2675
North American Horsemen's Association www.arkagency-naha.com/NAHA.html
PO Box 223   Paynesville MN 56362
Ph: 320-243-7250 ▪ Fx: 320-243-7224 ▪ TF: 800-328-8894
North American Horticultural Supply Association www.nahsa.org
1900 Arch St   Philadelphia PA 19103
Ph: 215-564-3484 ▪ Fx: 215-963-9784
North American Hunting Club www.huntingclub.com
12301 Whitewater Dr   Minnetonka MN 55343
Ph: 800-922-4868 ▪ Fx: 952-936-9755
North American Indian Ministries www.naim.ca
PO Box 39   Delta BC V4K3N5
Ph: 604-946-1227 ▪ Fx: 604-946-1465
North American Industrial Hemp Council www.naihc.org
PO Box 259329   Madison WI 53725
Ph: 608-258-0243 ▪ Fx: 608-835-0428
North American Industrial Representatives Association www.nira.org
105 Eastern Ave Suite 104   Annapolis MD 21403
Ph: 410-263-1014 ▪ Fx: 410-263-1659 ▪ TF: 800-315-7429
North American Insulation Manufacturers Association www.naima.org
44 Canal Center Plaza Suite 310   Alexandria VA 22314
Ph: 703-684-0084 ▪ Fx: 703-684-0427
North American Interfraternal Foundation www.nif-inc.net
10023 Cedar Point Dr   Carmel IN 46032
Ph: 317-872-3304 ▪ Fx: 317-571-9686
North American Islamic Trust www.nait.net
745 McClintock Dr Suite 114   Burr Ridge IL 60527
Ph: 630-489-9191 ▪ Fx: 630-789-9455
North American Junior Limousin Association www.nalf.org/programs/juniors.html
7383 S Alton Way Suite 100   Englewood CO 80112
Ph: 303-220-1693 ▪ Fx: 303-220-1884
North American Kant Society naks.ucsd.edu
Columbia Univ Dept of Philosophy 1150 Amsterdam Ave MC
    4971   New York NY 10027
Ph: 212-854-3196
North American Lake Management Society www.nalms.org
4513 Vernon Blvd Suite 100   Madison WI 53705
Ph: 608-233-2836 ▪ Fx: 608-233-3186
North American Lily Society www.lilies.org
PO Box 272   Owatonna MN 55060
Ph: 507-451-2170
North American Limousin Foundation www.nalf.org
7383 S Alton Way Suite 100   Englewood CO 80112
Ph: 303-220-1693 ▪ Fx: 303-220-1884
North American Loon Fund www.loonfund.org
North American Manufacturing Research Institution of SME www.sme.org/namri
1 SME Dr PO Box 930   Dearborn MI 48121
Ph: 313-271-1500 ▪ Fx: 313-425-3400 ▪ TF: 800-733-4763
North American Maritime Ministry Association www.maritimeministry.org
3257 Post Rd   Warwick RI 02886
Ph: 401-739-5257 ▪ Fx: 401-737-4148
North American Meat Processors Association www.namp.com
1910 Association Dr   Reston VA 20191
Ph: 703-758-1900 ▪ Fx: 703-758-8001
North American Membrane Society www.membranes.org
Univ of Toledo Chemical & Environmental Engineering Dept MS
    305   Toledo OH 43606
Ph: 419-530-3469 ▪ Fx: 419-530-8086
North American Menopause Society www.menopause.org
5900 Landerbrook Dr Suite 195   Mayfield Heights OH 44124
Ph: 440-442-7550 ▪ Fx: 440-442-2660 ▪ TF: 800-774-5342
North American Millers Association www.namamillers.org
600 Maryland Ave SW Suite 305-W   Washington DC 20024
Ph: 202-484-2200 ▪ Fx: 202-488-7416
North American Model Boat Association www.namba.com
1815 Halley St   San Diego CA 92154
Ph: 619-424-6380 ▪ Fx: 619-424-8845
North American Mustang Association & Registry
PO Box 850906   Mesquite TX 75185
Ph: 972-289-9344
North American Mycological Association www.namyco.org
6615 Tudor Ct   Gladstone OR 97027
Ph: 503-657-7358

North American Native Fishes Association www.nanfa.org
1107 Argonne Dr   Baltimore MD 21218
Ph: 410-243-9050

North American Natural Casing Association www.nanca.org
666 11th St NW   Washington DC 20001
Ph: 202-331-8234 ▪ Fx: 202-331-8191

North American Nature Photography Association www.nanpa.org
10200 W 44th Ave Suite 304   Wheat Ridge CO 80033
Ph: 303-422-8527 ▪ Fx: 303-422-8894

North American Neuro-Ophthalmology Society www.nanosweb.org
342 N Main St   West Hartford CT 06117
Ph: 860-558-7507 ▪ Fx: 860-586-7550

North American Neuromodulation Society www.neuromodulation.org
4700 W Lake Ave   Glenview IL 60025
Ph: 847-375-4714 ▪ Fx: 877-594-6704

North American Normande Association www.normandeassociation.com
30698 Ottoman Ave   Elroy WI 53929
Ph: 866-685-8491

North American Nursing Diagnosis Association www.nanda.org
1211 Locust St   Philadelphia PA 19107
Ph: 215-545-8105 ▪ Fx: 215-545-8107 ▪ TF: 800-647-9002

North American Olive Oil Association www.naooa.org
3301 Rt 66 Bldg C Suite 205   Neptune NJ 07753
Ph: 732-922-3008 ▪ Fx: 732-922-3590

North American Performing Arts Managers & Agents www.napama.org
459 Columbus Ave   New York NY 10024
Ph: 888-745-8759

North American Plant Preservation Council
HC 67 Box 539B   Renick WV 24966
Ph: 304-497-2208 ▪ Fx: 304-497-2698

North American Police Work Dog Association www.napwda.com
4222 Manchester Ave   Perry OH 44081
Ph: 440-259-3169 ▪ Fx: 440-259-3170 ▪ TF: 888-422-6463

North American Potbellied Pig Association www.petpigs.com
304 County Rd 438   Rocheport MO 65279
Ph: 573-698-3030

North American Professors of Christian Education www.napce.org
c/o Cook Communications Ministries 4050 Lee Vance
     View   Colorado Springs CO 80918
Ph: 719-536-0100

North American Punch Manufacturers Association www.napma.org
7402 Chestnut Ridge Rd   Lockport NY 14094
Ph: 716-433-2917

North American Rail Shippers Association www.railshippers.com
2115 Portsmouth Dr   Richardson TX 75082
Ph: 972-690-4740 ▪ Fx: 972-644-8208

North American Retail Dealers Association www.narda.com
10 E 22nd St Suite 310   Lombard IL 60148
Ph: 630-953-8950 ▪ Fx: 630-953-8957 ▪ TF: 800-621-0298

North American Riding for the Handicapped Association www.narha.org
PO Box 33150   Denver CO 80233
Ph: 303-452-1212 ▪ Fx: 303-252-4610 ▪ TF: 800-369-7433

North American Rock Garden Society www.nargs.org
PO Box 67   Millwood NY 10546
Ph: 914-762-2948

North American Roller Hockey Championships Inc www.narch.com
521 Hidden Ridge Ct Suite B   Encinitas CA 92024
Ph: 760-943-0049

North American Sawing Association www.sawingassociation.com
1300 Sumner Ave   Cleveland OH 44115
Ph: 216-241-7333 ▪ Fx: 216-241-0105

North American Securities Administrators Association www.nasaa.org
10 G St NE Suite 710   Washington DC 20002
Ph: 202-737-0900 ▪ Fx: 202-783-3571 ▪ TF: 888-846-2722

North American Selle Francais Association www.sellefrancais.org
PO Box 579   Waynesboro VA 22980
Ph: 540-932-9160 ▪ Fx: 540-932-9163

North American Shagya-Arabian Society www.shagya.net
9797 S Rangeline Rd   Clinton IN 47842
Ph: 765-665-3851

North American Sheep Dog Society
Rt 3 Box 107   McLeansboro IL 62859
Ph: 618-757-2238

North American Shetland Sheepbreeders Association www.shetland-sheep.org

North American Shippers Association www.nasaships.com
1600 St Georges Ave Suite 310 PO Box 249   Rahway NJ
     07065
Ph: 732-388-6256 ▪ Fx: 732-388-6580 ▪ TF: 800-524-1186

North American Shortwave Association www.anarc.org/naswa
45 Wildflower Rd   Levittown PA 19057
Ph: 215-945-0543

North American Simulation & Gaming Association www.nasaga.org
PO Box 78636   Indianapolis IN 46278
Ph: 317-387-1424 ▪ Fx: 317-387-1921 ▪ TF: 888-432-4263

North American Singers Association
13550 Ann Dr   North Huntingdon PA 15642
Ph: 724-863-0984

North American Single-footing Horse Association www.singlefootinghorse.com
PO Box 1079   Three Forks MT 59752
Ph: 406-285-6826

North American Skull Base Society www.nasbs.org
12100 Sunset Hills Rd Suite 130   Reston VA 12100
Ph: 703-234-4149 ▪ Fx: 703-435-4390

North American Small Business International Trade Educators www.nasbite.org
Wright State Univ 120 Rike Hall 3640 Colonel Glenn
     Hwy   Dayton OH 45435
Ph: 937-775-3524 ▪ Fx: 937-775-3545

North American Snowsports Journalists Association www.nasja.org
11738 SE Madison St   Portland OR 97216
Ph: 503-255-3771

North American Society of Adlerian Psychology www.alfredadler.org
50 Northeast Dr   Hershey PA 17033
Ph: 717-579-8795 ▪ Fx: 717-533-8616

North American Society for Cardiac Imaging www.nasci.org
PO Box 20085   Stanford CA 94309
Ph: 650-216-6621 ▪ Fx: 650-556-1678

North American Society for Dialysis & Transplantation www.nasdat.org
4010 Bentley Dr   Pearland TX 77584
Ph: 281-997-1944

North American Society for Oceanic History www.ecu.edu/nasoh/
PO Box 18108   Washington DC 20036
Ph: 202-707-1409

**North American Society for Pediatric Gastroenterology
Hepatology & Nutrition**   PO Box 6   Flourtown PA 19031 www.naspghan.org
Ph: 215-233-0808 ▪ Fx: 215-233-3918

**North American Society for the Psychology of Sport &
Physical Activity**   Univ of Nevada Dept of Kinesiology 4505 www.naspspa.org
     Maryland Pkwy   Las Vegas NV 89154
Ph: 702-895-0938

North American Society for Social Philosophy www.pitt.edu/~nassp/nassp.html
c/o Philosophy Documentation Ctr PO Box 7147   Charlottesville
     VA 22906
Ph: 434-220-3300 ▪ Fx: 434-220-3301 ▪ TF: 800-444-2419

North American Society for the www.uwm.edu/~aycock/nasss/nasss.html
Sociology of Sport   Bowling Green State Univ Dept of
     Sociology   Bowling Green OH 43403
Ph: 419-372-8306 ▪ Fx: 419-372-8360

North American Society for Sport History www.nassh.org
PO Box 1026   Lemont PA 16851
Ph: 814-238-1288

North American Society for Sport Management www.nassm.org
Slippery Rock Univ NASSM Business Office West Gym
     014   Slippery Rock PA 16057
Ph: 724-738-4812 ▪ Fx: 724-738-4858

North American Society for Trenchless Technology www.nastt.org
1655 N Fort Myer Dr Suite 700   Arlington VA 22209
Ph: 703-739-6671 ▪ Fx: 703-739-6672

North American South Devon Association www.southdevon.com
2514 Ave 'S'   Santa Fe TX 77510
Ph: 409-927-4445

North American Spine Society www.spine.org
22 Calendar Ct 2nd Fl   La Grange IL 60525
Ph: 708-588-8080 ▪ Fx: 708-588-1080 ▪ TF: 877-774-6337

North American Strawberry Growers Association www.nasga.org
526 Brittany Dr   State College PA 16803
Ph: 814-238-8863 ▪ Fx: 814-238-7051

North American Students of Cooperation www.umich.edu/~nasco
PO Box 7715   Ann Arbor MI 48107
Ph: 734-663-0889 ▪ Fx: 734-663-5072

North American Swiss Alliance
7650 Chippewa Rd Rm 214   Brecksville OH 44141
Ph: 440-526-2257

North American Technician Excellence www.natex.org
4100 N Fairfax Dr 210   Arlington VA 22203
Ph: 703-276-7247 ▪ Fx: 703-527-2316 ▪ TF: 877-420-6283

North American Trail Ride Conference www.natrc.org
PO Box 224   Sedalia CO 80135
Ph: 303-688-1677 ▪ Fx: 303-688-3022

North American Transplant Coordinators Organization www.natco1.org
PO Box 15384   Lenexa KS 66285
Ph: 913-492-3600 ▪ Fx: 913-599-5340

North American Transportation Management Institute www.truckline.com/cc/natmi
9769 W 119th Dr Suite 1   Broomfield CO 80021
Ph: 720-887-0835 ▪ Fx: 303-404-0725

North American Trap Collector Association
PO Box 94   Galloway OH 43119
Ph: 614-878-6011

North American Travel Journalists Association www.natja.org
531 Main St Suite 902   El Segundo CA 90245
Ph: 310-836-8712 ▪ Fx: 310-836-8769

North American Trucking Industrial Relations Association
908 King St Suite 300   Alexandria VA 22314
Ph: 703-836-9400 ▪ Fx: 703-836-9410

North American Vegetarian Society www.navs-online.org
PO Box 72   Dolgeville NY 13329
Ph: 518-568-7970 ▪ Fx: 518-568-7979

North American Vexillological Association www.nava.org

North American Wensleydale Sheep Association www.wensleydalesheep.org
4589 Fruitland Rd   Loma Rica CA 95901
Ph: 530-743-5262

North American Wholesale Lumber Association www.lumber.org
3601 Algonquin Rd Suite 400   Rolling Meadows IL 60008
Ph: 847-870-7470 ▪ Fx: 847-870-0201 ▪ TF: 800-527-8258

North American Wild Sheep, Foundation for www.fnaws.org
PO Box 146   Douglas WY 82633
Ph: 307-358-3693 ▪ Fx: 307-358-3262

North American Youth Sport Institute www.naysi.com
4985 Oak Garden Dr   Kernersville NC 27284
Ph: 336-784-4926 ▪ Fx: 336-784-5546 ▪ TF: 800-767-4916

North Carolina Battleship Association, USS www.battleshipnc.com
PO Box 480   Wilmington NC 28402
Ph: 910-251-5797 ▪ Fx: 910-251-5807

**North Central Association Commission on Accreditation &
School Improvement**   Arizona State Univ PO Box www.ncacasi.org
     873011   Tempe AZ 85287
Ph: 480-965-8700 ▪ TF: 800-525-9517

North Central Association Higher Learning Commission www.ncacihe.org
30 N La Salle St Suite 2400   Chicago IL 60602
Ph: 312-263-0456 ▪ Fx: 312-263-7462 ▪ TF: 800-621-7440

North Central Conference on Summer Schools www.nccss.org
Univ of Wisconsin-River Falls 317 Agricultural Science Bldg
410 S 3rd St River Falls WI 54022
Ph: 715-425-3851 ▪ Fx: 715-425-3785
North Country Trail Association www.northcountrytrail.org
229 E Main St Lowell MI 49331
Ph: 616-897-5987 ▪ Fx: 616-897-6605 ▪ TF: 888-454-6282
North-South Skirmish Association Inc www.n-ssa.org
PO Box 361 Bloomfield Hills MI 48303
Ph: 248-447-5909 ▪ Fx: 248-447-5944
North Star Fund Inc www.northstarfund.org
305 7th Ave 5th Fl New York NY 10001
Ph: 212-620-9110 ▪ Fx: 212-620-8178
NorthEast Collegiate Hockey Association www.necha.org
PO Box 58 Keene NH 03431
Ph: 603-363-4508
Northeast Conference on the Teaching of Foreign www.dickinson.edu/nectfl
Languages Dickinson College PO Box 1773 Carlisle PA
17013
Ph: 717-245-1977 ▪ Fx: 717-245-1976
Northeast-Midwest Institute www.nemw.org
218 D St SE Washington DC 20003
Ph: 202-544-5200 ▪ Fx: 202-544-0043
Northeastern Lumber Manufacturers Association www.nelma.org
272 Tuttle Rd PO Box 87A Cumberland ME 04021
Ph: 207-829-6901 ▪ Fx: 207-829-4293
Northeastern Retail Lumber Association www.nrla.org
585 N Greenbush Rd Rensselaer NY 12144
Ph: 518-286-1010 ▪ Fx: 518-286-1755 ▪ TF: 800-292-6752
Northern Nut Growers Association Inc www.northernnutgrowers.org
648 Oak Hill School Rd PO Box 427 Townsend DE 19734
Ph: 302-659-1731 ▪ Fx: 302-659-1732
Northwest Association of Accredited Schools www2.boisestate.edu/NASC
1910 University Dr Boise ID 83725
Ph: 208-426-5727 ▪ Fx: 208-334-3228
Northwest Coalition for Alternatives to Pesticides www.pesticide.org
PO Box 1393 Eugene OR 97440
Ph: 541-344-5044 ▪ Fx: 541-344-6923
Northwest Ecosystem Alliance www.ecosystem.org
1208 Bay St Suite 201 Bellingham WA 98225
Ph: 360-671-9950 ▪ Fx: 360-671-8429
Northwest Fisheries Association www.northwestfisheries.org
2208 SW Market St Suite 318 Seattle WA 98107
Ph: 206-789-6197 ▪ Fx: 206-789-8147
Northwest Fruit Exporters
105 S 18th St Suite 227 Yakima WA 98901
Ph: 509-576-8004 ▪ Fx: 509-576-3646
Northwest Horticultural Council www.nwhort.org
6 S 2nd St Suite 600 Yakima WA 98901
Ph: 509-453-3193 ▪ Fx: 509-457-7615
Northwest Marine Trade Association www.nmta.net
1900 N Northlake Way Suite 233 Seattle WA 98103
Ph: 206-634-0911 ▪ Fx: 206-632-0078
Northwest Medical Teams International www.nwmti.org
PO Box 10 Portland OR 97207
Ph: 503-624-1000 ▪ Fx: 503-624-1001 ▪ TF: 800-959-4325
Northwest Regional Spinners Association www.nwrsa.org
12410 9th Dr SE Everett WA 98208
Ph: 425-385-2138
Northwest Steam Society www.northweststeamsociety.org
PO Box 9639 Seattle WA 98109
Ph: 206-789-0287
Northwest Steelheaders, Association of www.nwsteelheaders.org
PO Box 22065 Milwaukie OR 97269
Ph: 503-653-4176 ▪ Fx: 503-653-8769
Northwestern University Center for Public Safety server.traffic.northwestern.edu
600 Foster Evanston IL 60204
Ph: 847-491-5476 ▪ Fx: 847-491-5270 ▪ TF: 800-323-4011
Norway, Sons of www.sofn.com
1455 W Lake St Minneapolis MN 55408
Ph: 612-827-3611 ▪ Fx: 612-827-0658 ▪ TF: 800-945-8851
Norwegian-American Chamber of Commerce www.nacc.no
800 3rd Ave 23rd Fl New York NY 10022
Ph: 212-421-1655 ▪ Fx: 212-838-0374
Norwegian-American Historical Association www.naha.stolaf.edu
St Olaf College 1510 St Olaf Ave Northfield MN 55057
Ph: 507-646-3221 ▪ Fx: 507-646-3734
Norwegian Elkhound Association of America www.neaa.net
21738 Hampton Ct Kildeer IL 60047
Ph: 847-438-3670
Norwegian Fjord Horse Registry www.nfhr.com
1203 Appian Dr Webster NY 14580
Ph: 585-872-4114 ▪ Fx: 585-787-0497
Nose & Throat Advances in Children, Society for Ear www.sentac.org
3333 Burnet Ave Cincinnati OH 45229
Ph: 513-636-2287
Nostalgic Nova, National www.nnnova.com
PO Box 2344 York PA 17405
Ph: 717-252-4192 ▪ Fx: 717-252-1666
Not-for-Profit Law, International Center for www.icnl.org
733 15th St NW Suite 420 Washington DC 20005
Ph: 202-624-0766 ▪ Fx: 202-624-0767
Not-for-Profit Services Association www.nonprofitcpas.com
1 Valmont Plaza 4th Fl Omaha NE 68154
Ph: 402-964-3865 ▪ Fx: 402-964-3811 ▪ TF: 888-475-4476
Notaries, American Society of www.notaries.com
PO Box 940489 Maitland FL 32314
Ph: 800-422-1555 ▪ Fx: 800-224-6368
Notary Association, National www.nationalnotary.org
9350 DeSoto Ave Chatsworth CA 91313
Ph: 818-739-4000 ▪ Fx: 818-700-1830 ▪ TF: 800-876-6827

Nova, National Nostalgic www.nnnova.com
PO Box 2344 York PA 17405
Ph: 717-252-4192 ▪ Fx: 717-252-1666
Novelties Trade Association, Souvenir &
10 E Athens Ave Suite 208 Ardmore PA 19003
Ph: 610-645-6940 ▪ Fx: 610-645-6943 ▪ TF: 800-284-5451
Novelty & Production Workers, International Union of Allied
1950 W Erie St Chicago IL 60622
Ph: 312-738-0822 ▪ Fx: 312-738-3553
Novelty Salt & Pepper Shakers Club members.aol.com/spclub1234
PO Box 416 Gladstone OR 97027
Ph: 503-650-8499
Noyes Jesse Smith Foundation www.noyes.org
6 E 39th St 12th Fl New York NY 10016
Ph: 212-684-6577 ▪ Fx: 212-689-6549
NPES: Association for Suppliers of Printing Publishing & www.npes.org
Converting Technologies 1899 Preston White Dr Reston VA
20191
Ph: 703-264-7200 ▪ Fx: 703-620-0994
NPTA Alliance www.gonpta.com
500 Bi-County Blvd Suite 200E Farmingdale NY 11735
Ph: 631-777-2223 ▪ Fx: 631-777-2224 ▪ TF: 800-355-6782
NRA Institute for Legislative Action www.nraila.org
11250 Waples Mill Rd Fairfax VA 22030
Ph: 703-267-1000 ▪ Fx: 703-267-3907 ▪ TF: 800-672-3888
NSF International www.nsf.org
789 N Dixboro Rd Ann Arbor MI 48105
Ph: 734-769-8010 ▪ Fx: 734-769-0109 ▪ TF: 877-867-3435
Nuclear Accountability, Alliance for www.ananuclear.org
1914 N 34th St Suite 407 Seattle WA 98103
Ph: 206-547-3175 ▪ Fx: 206-547-7158
Nuclear Age Peace Foundation www.wagingpeace.org
1187 Coast Village Rd Suite 1 PMB 121 Santa Barbara CA
93108
Ph: 805-965-3443 ▪ Fx: 805-568-0466
Nuclear Cardiology, American Society of www.asnc.org
9111 Old Georgetown Rd Bethesda MD 20814
Ph: 301-493-2360 ▪ Fx: 301-493-2376
Nuclear Control Institute www.nci.org
1000 Connecticut Ave NW Suite 410 Washington DC 20036
Ph: 202-822-8444 ▪ Fx: 202-452-0892
Nuclear Energy Information Service www.neis.org
PO Box 1637 Evanston IL 60204
Ph: 847-869-7650 ▪ Fx: 847-869-7658
Nuclear Energy Institute www.nei.org
1776 'I' St NW Suite 400 Washington DC 20006
Ph: 202-739-8000 ▪ Fx: 202-785-4019
Nuclear Energy Institute Federal PAC
1776 'I' St NW Suite 400 Washington DC 20006
Ph: 202-739-8000 ▪ Fx: 202-785-4019
Nuclear Information & Records Management Association www.nirma.org
10 Almas Rd Windham NH 03087
Ph: 603-432-6476 ▪ Fx: 603-432-3024
Nuclear Information & Resource Service www.nirs.org
1424 16th St NW Suite 404 Washington DC 20036
Ph: 202-328-0002 ▪ Fx: 202-462-2183
Nuclear Insurers, American www.amnucins.com
29 S Main St Suite 300-S West Hartford CT 06107
Ph: 860-561-3433 ▪ Fx: 860-561-4655 ▪ TF: 888-561-3433
Nuclear Materials Management, Institute of www.inmm.org
60 Revere Dr Suite 500 Northbrook IL 60062
Ph: 847-480-9573 ▪ Fx: 847-480-9282
Nuclear Medicine, American College of www.acnucmed.org
PO Box 175 Landisville PA 17538
Ph: 717-898-5008 ▪ Fx: 717-898-2555
Nuclear Medicine, Society of www.snm.org
1850 Samuel Morse Dr Reston VA 20190
Ph: 703-708-9000 ▪ Fx: 703-708-9015
Nuclear Physicians, American College of www.acnponline.org
1850 Samuel Morse Dr Reston VA 20190
Ph: 703-326-1190 ▪ Fx: 703-708-9015
Nuclear & Plasma Sciences Society, IEEE ewh.ieee.org/soc/nps
IEEE Operations Ctr 445 Hoes Ln Piscataway NJ 08854
Ph: 732-981-0060 ▪ Fx: 732-981-1721
Nuclear Policy Inc, Lawyers' Committee on www.lcnp.org
211 E 43rd St New York NY 10017
Ph: 212-818-1861 ▪ Fx: 212-818-1857
Nuclear Power Operations, Institute of tis.eh.doe.gov/nsps/inpo/
700 Galleria Pkwy SE Suite 100 Atlanta GA 30339
Ph: 770-644-8000 ▪ Fx: 770-644-8549
(Nuclear Power) Three Mile Island Alert Inc www.tmia.com
315 Peffer St Harrisburg PA 17102
Ph: 717-233-7897 ▪ Fx: 717-233-3261
Nuclear Resister www.serve.com/nukeresister
PO Box 43383 Tucson AZ 85733
Ph: 520-323-8697
Nuclear Responsibility, Committee for www.ratical.org/radiation/CNR
PO Box 421993 San Francisco CA 94142
Ph: 415-776-8299
Nuclear Science, Educational Foundation for www.thebulletin.org/nuclear/efns.html
6042 S Kimbark Ave Chicago IL 60637
Ph: 773-702-2555 ▪ Fx: 773-702-0725
Nuclear Society, American www.ans.org
555 N Kensington Ave La Grange Park IL 60526
Ph: 708-352-6611 ▪ Fx: 708-352-0499 ▪ TF: 800-323-3044
Nuclear Suppliers Association www.nuclearsuppliers.org
PO Box 2038 Springfield VA 22152
Ph: 703-451-1912 ▪ Fx: 703-451-2334
(Nuclear Testing) Nevada Desert Experience www.nevadadesertexperience.org
PO Box 46645 Las Vegas NV 89114
Ph: 702-646-4814

Nude Recreation, American Association for   www.aanr.com
1703 N Main St Suite E   Kissimmee FL 34744
Ph: 407-933-2064

Nuestros Pequenos Hermanos   www.nphamigos.org
1210 Hillside Terr   Alexandria VA 22302
Ph: 703-836-1233 ▪ Fx: 703-836-3554

Nukewatch   www.nukewatch.com
c/o Progressive Foundation PO Box 649   Luck WI 54853
Ph: 715-472-4185 ▪ Fx: 715-472-4184

Numbers Authority, Internet Assigned   www.iana.org
USC ISI 4676 Admiralty Way Suite 330   Marina del Rey CA 90292
Ph: 310-823-9358 ▪ Fx: 310-823-8649

Numbers, Internet Corp for Assigned Names &   www.icann.org
4676 Admiralty Way Suite 330   Marina del Rey CA 90292
Ph: 310-823-9358 ▪ Fx: 310-823-8649

Numismatic Association, American   www.money.org
818 N Cascade Ave   Colorado Springs CO 80903
Ph: 719-632-2646 ▪ Fx: 719-634-4085 ▪ TF: 800-367-9723

Numismatic Literary Guild   www.numismaticliteraryguild.org
12 Abbington Terr   Glen Rock NJ 07452
Ph: 201-612-0482

Numismatic Society, Armenian
8511 Beverly Park Pl   Pico Rivera CA 90660
Ph: 562-695-0380

Numismatic Society, Russian   www.russiannumismaticsociety.org
PO Box 3684   Santa Rosa CA 95402
Ph: 707-527-1007 ▪ Fx: 707-527-1204

Numismatics, Society of Private & Pioneer
98 Main St Suite 201   Tiburon CA 94920
Ph: 415-435-2601 ▪ Fx: 415-435-1627 ▪ TF: 888-852-4467

(Numismatics) Token & Medal Society Inc   www.money.org/clubs/tams

Numismatics, Women in   www.money.org/sum-baber.html

Numismatists Guild, Professional   www.pngdealers.com
3950 Concordia Ln   Fallbrook CA 92028
Ph: 760-728-1300 ▪ Fx: 760-728-8507

Nurse Anesthetists, American Association of   www.aana.com
222 S Prospect Ave   Park Ridge IL 60068
Ph: 847-692-7050 ▪ Fx: 847-692-6968

Nurse Anesthetists, International Federation of   www.ifna.info
222 S Prospect Ave   Park Ridge IL 60068
Ph: 847-692-7050 ▪ Fx: 847-692-6968

Nurse Associations of America, Visiting   www.vnaa.org
99 Summer St Suite 1700   Boston MA 02110
Ph: 617-737-3200 ▪ Fx: 617-737-1144 ▪ TF: 800-426-2547

Nurse Attorneys, American Association of   www.taana.org
7794 Grow Dr   Pensacola FL 32514
Ph: 850-474-3646 ▪ Fx: 850-484-8762 ▪ TF: 877-538-2262

Nurse Consultants, American Association of Legal   www.aalnc.org
401 N Michigan Ave   Chicago IL 60611
Ph: 312-321-5177 ▪ Fx: 312-673-6655 ▪ TF: 877-402-2562

Nurse Education & Service, National Association for Practical   www.napnes.org
8607 2nd Ave Suite 404-A   Silver Spring MD 20910
Ph: 301-588-2491

Nurse Executives, American Organization of   www.aone.org
1 N Franklin St 32nd Fl   Chicago IL 60606
Ph: 312-422-2800 ▪ Fx: 312-422-4503

Nurse Healers - Professional Associates International   www.therapeutic-touch.org
3760 Highland Dr Suite 418   Salt Lake City UT 84106
Ph: 801-273-3399

Nurse-Midwives, American College of   www.midwife.org
818 Connecticut Ave NW Suite 900   Washington DC 20006
Ph: 202-728-9860 ▪ Fx: 202-728-9897

Nurse Practitioner Faculties, National Organization of   www.nonpf.com
1522 K St NW Suite 702   Washington DC 20005
Ph: 202-289-8044 ▪ Fx: 202-289-8046

Nurse Practitioners, American Academy of   www.aanp.org
PO Box 10729   Glendale AZ 85318
Ph: 623-376-9467 ▪ Fx: 623-376-0369

Nurse Practitioners, American College of   www.nurse.org/acnp/
1111 19th St NW Suite 404   Washington DC 20036
Ph: 202-659-2190 ▪ Fx: 202-659-2191

Nurse Practitioners, National Alliance of
PO Box 40326   Washington DC 20016
Ph: 202-675-6350

Nurse Practitioners, National Association of Pediatric   www.napnap.org
20 Brace Rd Suite 200   Cherry Hill NJ 08034
Ph: 856-857-9700 ▪ Fx: 856-857-1600 ▪ TF: 877-662-7627

Nurse Practitioners in Women's Health, National Association of   www.npwh.org
503 Capitol Ct NE Suite 300   Washington DC 20002
Ph: 202-543-9693 ▪ Fx: 202-543-9858

Nurse Specialists, National Association of Clinical   www.nacns.org
3969 Green St   Harrisburg PA 17110
Ph: 717-234-6799 ▪ Fx: 717-234-6798

Nursery Association Executives of North America
457 Ashpoint Dr   Owls Head ME 04854
Ph: 207-594-5657

Nursery Council, Landscape
1611 Creekview Dr   Florence KY 41042
Ph: 859-525-1809 ▪ Fx: 859-525-9114

Nursery Furniture Retailers Association, National Independent   www.babyexpressstores.com
12302 Hart Ranch   San Antonio TX 78249
Ph: 210-699-1133 ▪ Fx: 210-699-3232

Nursery & Landscape Association, American   www.anla.org
1000 Vermont Ave NW Suite 300   Washington DC 20005
Ph: 202-789-2900 ▪ Fx: 202-789-1893

Nurses, Academy of Medical-Surgical   www.medsurgnurse.org
PO Box 56   Pitman NJ 08071
Ph: 856-256-2323 ▪ Fx: 856-589-7463

Nurses in AIDS Care, Association of   www.anacnet.org
3538 Ridgewood Rd   Akron OH 44333
Ph: 330-670-0101 ▪ Fx: 330-670-0109 ▪ TF: 800-260-6780

Nurses, American Association of Critical-Care   www.aacn.org
101 Columbia   Aliso Viejo CA 92656
Ph: 949-362-2000 ▪ Fx: 949-362-2020 ▪ TF: 800-809-2273

Nurses, American Association of Managed Care   www.aamcn.org
4435 Waterfront Dr Suite 101   Glen Allen VA 23060
Ph: 804-747-9698 ▪ Fx: 804-747-5316

Nurses, American Association of Neuroscience   www.aann.org
4700 W Lake Ave   Glenview IL 60025
Ph: 847-375-4733 ▪ Fx: 877-734-8677 ▪ TF: 888-557-2266

Nurses, American Association of Occupational Health   www.aaohn.org
2920 Brandywine Rd Suite 100   Atlanta GA 30341
Ph: 770-455-7757 ▪ Fx: 770-455-7271 ▪ TF: 888-646-4631

Nurses, American Association of Office   www.aaon.org
109 Kinderkamack Rd   Montvale NJ 07645
Ph: 201-391-2600 ▪ Fx: 201-573-8543 ▪ TF: 800-457-7504

Nurses, American Society of Ophthalmic Registered   www.asorn.org
PO Box 193030   San Francisco CA 94109
Ph: 415-561-8513 ▪ Fx: 415-561-8531

Nurses, American Society of Pain Management   www.aspmn.org
7794 Grow Dr   Pensacola FL 32514
Ph: 850-473-0233 ▪ Fx: 850-484-8762 ▪ TF: 888-342-7766

Nurses, American Society of PeriAnesthesia   www.aspan.org
10 Melrose Ave Suite 110   Cherry Hill NJ 08003
Ph: 856-616-9600 ▪ Fx: 856-616-9601 ▪ TF: 877-737-9696

Nurses, American Society of Plastic Surgical   www.aspsn.org
3220 Pointe Pkwy Suite 500   Atlanta GA 30092
Ph: 678-291-0011 ▪ Fx: 678-291-9731

Nurses & Associates Inc, Consortium of Behavioral Health   www.cbhna.org
1733 H St Suite 330 PMB 1214   Blaine WA 98230
Ph: 800-876-2236 ▪ Fx: 360-332-2280

Nurses & Associates Inc, Society of Gastroenterology   www.sgna.org
401 N Michigan Ave   Chicago IL 60611
Ph: 312-321-5165 ▪ Fx: 312-527-6658 ▪ TF: 800-245-7462

Nurses & Associates, Society of Urologic   www.suna.org
PO Box 56   Pitman NJ 08071
Ph: 856-256-2335 ▪ Fx: 856-589-7463 ▪ TF: 888-827-7862

Nurses Association, Air & Surface Transport   www.astna.org
9101 E Kenyon Ave Suite 3000   Denver CO 80237
Ph: 800-897-6362 ▪ Fx: 303-770-1812

Nurses Association, American   www.ana.org
600 Maryland Ave SW Suite 100-W   Washington DC 20024
Ph: 202-651-7000 ▪ Fx: 202-651-7001 ▪ TF: 800-274-4262

Nurses' Association, American Holistic   ahna.org
PO Box 2130   Flagstaff AZ 86003
Ph: 928-526-2196 ▪ Fx: 928-526-2752 ▪ TF: 800-278-2462

Nurses Association, American Licensed Practical
1090 Vermont Ave NW Suite 800   Washington DC 20005
Ph: 202-682-9000 ▪ Fx: 202-682-0168

Nurses Association, American Practical
1090 Vermont Ave NW Suite 800   Washington DC 20005
Ph: 202-682-9000 ▪ Fx: 202-682-9298

Nurses Association, American Psychiatric   www.apna.org
1555 Wilson Blvd Suite 515   Arlington VA 22209
Ph: 703-243-2443 ▪ Fx: 703-243-3390

Nurses Association, American Radiological   www.arna.net
7794 Grow Dr   Pensacola FL 32514
Ph: 850-474-7292 ▪ Fx: 850-484-8762 ▪ TF: 866-486-2762

Nurses, Association of Camp   www.campnurse.org
8630 Thorsonveien Rd NE   Bemidji MN 56601
Ph: 218-586-2633 ▪ Fx: 218-586-3661

Nurses Association, Dermatology   www.dnanurse.org
PO Box 56   Pitman NJ 08071
Ph: 856-256-2330 ▪ Fx: 856-589-7463 ▪ TF: 800-454-4362

Nurses Association, Developmental Disabilities   www.ddna.org
1733 H St Suite 330 PMB 1214   Blaine WA 98230
Ph: 800-888-6733 ▪ Fx: 360-332-2280

Nurses Association, Emergency   www.ena.org
915 Lee St   Des Plaines IL 60016
Ph: 847-460-4000 ▪ Fx: 847-460-4001 ▪ TF: 800-900-9659

Nurses Association, Home Healthcare   www.hhna.org
228 7th St SE   Washington DC 20003
Ph: 202-546-4754 ▪ Fx: 202-547-3540

Nurses Association, Hospice & Palliative   www.hpna.org
Penn Ctr W 1 Suite 229   Pittsburgh PA 15276
Ph: 412-787-9301 ▪ Fx: 412-787-9305

Nurses Association, National Black
8630 Fenton St Suite 330   Silver Spring MD 20910
Ph: 301-589-3200 ▪ Fx: 301-589-3223

Nurses Association, National Student   www.nsna.org
45 Main St Suite 606   Brooklyn NY 11201
Ph: 718-210-0705 ▪ Fx: 718-210-0710

Nurses, Association of Pediatric Oncology   www.apon.org
4700 W Lake Ave   Glenview IL 60025
Ph: 847-375-4724 ▪ Fx: 877-734-8755

Nurses, Association of Rehabilitation   www.rehabnurse.org
4700 W Lake Ave   Glenview IL 60025
Ph: 847-375-4710 ▪ Fx: 877-734-9384

Nurses, Association of Women's Health Obstetric & Neonatal   www.awhonn.org
2000 L St NW Suite 740   Washington DC 20036
Ph: 202-261-2400 ▪ Fx: 202-728-0575 ▪ TF: 800-673-8499

Nurses in Business Association Inc, National   www.nnba.net
867 Levitt Pkwy   Rockledge FL 32955
Ph: 321-633-4610 ▪ Fx: 877-353-8888

Nurses Certification Board, Orthopaedic   www.orthonurse.org/certification/oncb.cfm
401 N Michigan Ave Suite 2200   Chicago IL 60611
Ph: 800-289-6266 ▪ Fx: 312-527-6658

Nurses Christian Fellowship www.intervarsity.org/ncf
PO Box 7895   Madison WI 53707
Ph: 608-274-9001

Nurses, International Society of Psychiatric www.ispn-psych.org/html/ispcln.html
Consultation-Liaison   1211 Locust St   Philadelphia PA 19107
Ph: 215-545-2843 ▪ Fx: 215-545-8107 ▪ TF: 800-826-2950

Nurses, International Society of Psychiatric-Mental Health www.ispn-psych.org
1211 Locust St   Philadelphia PA 19107
Ph: 215-545-2843 ▪ Fx: 215-545-8107 ▪ TF: 800-826-2950

Nurses, National Association of Hispanic www.thehispanicnurses.org
1501 16th St NW   Washington DC 20036
Ph: 202-387-2477 ▪ Fx: 202-483-7183

Nurses, National Association of Neonatal www.nann.org
4700 W Lake Ave   Glenview IL 60025
Ph: 847-375-3660 ▪ Fx: 888-477-6266 ▪ TF: 800-451-3795

Nurses, National Association of Orthopaedic www.orthonurse.org
401 N Michigan Ave   Chicago IL 60611
Ph: 800-289-6266 ▪ Fx: 312-527-6658

Nurses, National Association of School www.nasn.org
PO Box 1300   Scarborough ME 04070
Ph: 207-883-2117 ▪ Fx: 207-883-2683 ▪ TF: 877-627-6476

Nurses, National Federation of Licensed Practical www.nflpn.org
605 Poole Dr   Garner NC 27529
Ph: 919-779-0046 ▪ Fx: 919-779-5642 ▪ TF: 800-948-2511

Nurses Organization of Veterans Affairs www.vanurse.org
1726 M St NW Suite 1101   Washington DC 20036
Ph: 202-296-0888 ▪ Fx: 202-833-1577

Nurses for the Rights of the Child nurses.cirp.org
369 Montezuma Ave Suite 354   Santa Fe NM 87501
Ph: 505-989-7377

Nurses Society on Addictions, International www.intnsa.org
PO Box 10752   Raleigh NC 27605
Ph: 919-821-1292 ▪ Fx: 919-833-5743

Nurses Society, Infusion www.ins1.org
220 Norwood Pk S   Norwood MA 02062
Ph: 781-440-9408 ▪ Fx: 781-440-9409

Nurses Inc, Society of Otorhinolaryngology & Head-Neck www.sohnnurse.com
116 Canal St Suite A   New Smyrna Beach FL 32168
Ph: 386-428-1695 ▪ Fx: 386-423-7566

Nurses, Society of Pediatric www.pedsnurses.org
7794 Grow Dr   Pensacola FL 32514
Ph: 850-484-9987 ▪ Fx: 850-484-8762 ▪ TF: 800-723-2902

Nurses, Society of Trauma www.traumanursesoc.org
223 N Guadalupe St PMB 300   Santa Fe NM 87501
Ph: 505-983-4923 ▪ Fx: 505-983-5109

Nurses Society, Wound Ostomy & Continence www.wocn.org
4700 W Lake Ave   Glenview IL 60025
Ph: 888-224-9626 ▪ Fx: 866-615-8560

Nursing Accrediting Commission Inc, National League for www.nlnac.org
61 Broadway 33rd Fl   New York NY 10006
Ph: 212-363-5555 ▪ Fx: 212-812-0390 ▪ TF: 800-669-1656

Nursing Administration in Long Term Care, National Association www.nadona.org
of Directors of   10101 Alliance Rd Suite 140   Cincinnati OH
45242
Ph: 513-791-3679 ▪ Fx: 513-791-3699 ▪ TF: 800-222-0539

Nursing, American Academy of www.nursingworld.org/aan
600 Maryland Ave SW Suite 100 W   Washington DC 20024
Ph: 202-651-7238 ▪ Fx: 202-554-2641

Nursing, American Academy of Ambulatory Care www.aaacn.org
E Holly Ave Box 56   Pitman NJ 08071
Ph: 856-256-2350 ▪ Fx: 856-589-7463 ▪ TF: 800-262-6877

Nursing, American Assembly for Men in www.aamn.org
c/o NY State Nurses Assn 11 Cornell Rd   Latham NY 12110
Ph: 518-782-9400 ▪ Fx: 518-782-9530

Nursing, American Association of Colleges of www.aacn.nche.edu
1 Dupont Cir NW Suite 530   Washington DC 20036
Ph: 202-463-6930 ▪ Fx: 202-785-8320

Nursing, American Association for the History of www.aahn.org
PO Box 175   Lanoka Harbor NJ 08734
Ph: 609-693-7250 ▪ Fx: 609-693-1037

Nursing, American Board of Managed Care www.abmcn.org
4435 Waterfront Dr Suite 101   Glen Allen VA 23060
Ph: 804-527-1905 ▪ Fx: 804-747-5316

(Nursing) AORN Inc www.aorn.org
2170 S Parker Rd Suite 300   Denver CO 80231
Ph: 303-755-6300 ▪ Fx: 303-750-3212 ▪ TF: 800-755-2676

Nursing Association, National Gerontological www.ngna.org
7794 Grow Dr   Pensacola FL 32514
Ph: 850-473-1174 ▪ Fx: 850-484-8762 ▪ TF: 800-723-0560

Nursing, Association of State & Territorial Directors of www.astdn.org

Nursing Educators, Association of Community Health www.uncc.edu/achne
11 Cornell Rd   Latham NY 12110
Ph: 518-782-9400 ▪ Fx: 518-782-9530

Nursing Home Reform, National Citizens' Coalition for www.nursinghomeaction.org
1424 16th St NW Suite 202   Washington DC 20036
Ph: 202-332-2275 ▪ Fx: 202-332-2949

Nursing, Interagency Council on Information Resources for www.icirn.org

(Nursing) NANDA International www.nanda.org
1211 Locust St   Philadelphia PA 19107
Ph: 215-545-8105 ▪ Fx: 215-545-8107 ▪ TF: 800-647-9002

Nursing, National Council of State Boards of www.ncsbn.org
111 E Wacker Dr Suite 2900   Chicago IL 60601
Ph: 312-525-3600 ▪ Fx: 312-279-1032

Nursing, National League for www.nln.org
61 Broadway   New York NY 10006
Ph: 212-363-5555 ▪ Fx: 212-812-0393 ▪ TF: 800-669-1656

(Nursing) Sigma Theta Tau International www.nursingsociety.org
550 W North St   Indianapolis IN 46202
Ph: 317-634-8171 ▪ Fx: 317-634-8188 ▪ TF: 888-634-7575

Nursing Society, Oncology www.ons.org
125 Enterprise Dr   Pittsburgh PA 15275
Ph: 412-859-6100 ▪ Fx: 877-369-5497 ▪ TF: 866-257-4667

Nursing Society, Respiratory www.respiratorynursingsociety.org
c/o NY State Nurses Assn 11 Cornell Rd   Latham NY 12110
Ph: 518-782-9400

Nursing, Society for Vascular www.svnnet.org
7794 Grow Dr   Pensacola FL 32514
Ph: 888-536-4786 ▪ Fx: 850-484-8762

Nursing Specialties, American Board of www.nursingcertification.org
610 Thornhill Ln   Aurora OH 44202
Ph: 330-995-9172 ▪ Fx: 330-995-9743

Nursing Staff Development Organization, National www.nnsdo.org
7794 Grow Dr   Pensacola FL 32514
Ph: 850-474-0995 ▪ Fx: 850-484-8762 ▪ TF: 800-489-1995

NURTUREart Non-Profit Inc www.nurtureart.org
160 Cabrini Blvd PH 134   New York NY 10033
Ph: 212-795-5566

Nut Growers Association Inc, Northern www.northernnutgrowers.org
648 Oak Hill School Rd PO Box 427   Townsend DE 19734
Ph: 302-659-1731 ▪ Fx: 302-659-1732

Nutrition & Aging, National Policy & Resource Center on www.fiu.edu/~nutreldr
Florida International Univ University Park OE200   Miami FL
33199
Ph: 305-348-1517 ▪ Fx: 305-348-1518

Nutrition & Aging Services Programs, National Association of www.nanasp.org
1612 K St NW Suite 400   Washington DC 20006
Ph: 202-682-6899 ▪ Fx: 202-223-2099

Nutrition Alliance, National am-coll-nutr.org/nna/nna.htm
300 S Duncan Ave Suite 225   Clearwater FL 33755
Ph: 727-446-6086 ▪ Fx: 727-446-6202

Nutrition, American Academy of www.nutritioneducation.com
1204-D Kenesaw Ave   Knoxville TN 37919
Ph: 865-524-8079 ▪ Fx: 865-524-8339 ▪ TF: 800-290-4226

Nutrition, American Board of www.uab.edu/nusc/abn.htm
Univ of Alabama Birmingham Dept of Nutrition Sciences 1675
University Blvd WEBB 232   Birmingham AL 35194
Ph: 205-975-5564 ▪ Fx: 205-934-7049

Nutrition, American College of www.am-coll-nutr.org
300 S Duncan Ave Suite 225   Clearwater FL 33755
Ph: 727-446-6086 ▪ Fx: 727-446-6202

Nutrition, American Society for Clinical www.ascn.org
9650 Rockville Pike   Bethesda MD 20814
Ph: 301-634-7110 ▪ Fx: 301-571-1863

Nutrition, American Society for Parenteral & Enteral www.clinnutr.org
8630 Fenton St Suite 412   Silver Spring MD 20910
Ph: 301-587-6315 ▪ Fx: 301-587-2365 ▪ TF: 800-727-4567

Nutrition, Council for Responsible www.crnusa.org
1875 'I' St NW Suite 400   Washington DC 20006
Ph: 202-872-1488 ▪ Fx: 202-872-9594

Nutrition Directors, Association of State & Territorial Public Health www.astphnd.org

Nutrition Education, Society for www.sne.org
7150 Winton Dr Suite 300   Indianapolis IN 46268
Ph: 317-328-4627 ▪ Fx: 317-280-8527 ▪ TF: 800-235-6690

Nutrition, Foundation for Digestive Health & www.fdhn.org
4930 Del Ray Ave   Bethesda MD 20814
Ph: 301-222-4002 ▪ Fx: 301-222-4010

Nutrition Institute of America
1524 Crystal St   Kansas City MO 64126
Ph: 816-241-8315 ▪ Fx: 816-231-6423

(Nutrition) National WIC Association www.nwica.org
2001 'S' St NW Suite 580   Washington DC 20009
Ph: 202-232-5492 ▪ Fx: 202-387-5281

Nutrition, North American Society for Pediatric www.naspghan.org
Gastroenterology Hepatology &   PO Box 6   Flourtown PA
19031
Ph: 215-233-0808 ▪ Fx: 215-233-3918

Nutrition Specialists, Certification Board for www.cert-nutrition.org
300 S Duncan Ave Suite 225   Clearwater FL 33755
Ph: 727-446-6086 ▪ Fx: 727-446-6202

Nutritional Anthropology, Council on www.aaanet.org/cna
c/o American Anthropological Assn 2200 Wilson Blvd Suite
600   Arlington VA 22201
Ph: 703-528-1902 ▪ Fx: 703-528-3546

Nutritional Consultants, American Association of www.aanc.net
400 Oak Hill Dr   Winona Lake IN 46590
Ph: 574-269-6165 ▪ Fx: 574-269-4060 ▪ TF: 888-828-2262

Nutritional Foods Association, National www.nnfa.org
3931 MacArthur Blvd Suite 101   Newport Beach CA 92660
Ph: 949-622-6272 ▪ Fx: 949-622-6266 ▪ TF: 800-966-6632

Nutritional Sciences, American Society for www.nutrition.org
9650 Rockville Pike   Bethesda MD 20814
Ph: 301-530-7050 ▪ Fx: 301-571-1892

Nutritionists, International & American Associations of Clinical www.iaacn.org
15280 Addison St Suite 130   Addison TX 75001
Ph: 972-407-9089 ▪ Fx: 972-250-0233

Nutritionists, Sports Cardiovascular & Wellness www.scandpg.org
PO Box 60820   Colorado Springs CO 80960
Ph: 719-635-6005 ▪ Fx: 719-635-3587

Nuttall Ornithological Club
c/o Museum of Comparative Zoology 26 Oxford St   Cambridge
MA 02138
Ph: 617-495-2471

O

O-Anon
General Service Office PO Box 1314   North Fork CA 93643
Ph: 559-877-3615 ▪ Fx: 559-877-3015

Oak Ridge Associated Universities www.orau.org
130 Badger Ave PO Box 117   Oak Ridge TN 37831
Ph: 865-576-3000 ▪ Fx: 865-576-3643

Oak Society, International www.saintmarys.edu/~rjensen/iosboard.html

Oberhasli Breeders of America www.oba-usa.org

Obesity Association, American www.obesity.org
1250 24th St NW Suite 300   Washington DC 20037
Ph: 202-776-7711 ▪ Fx: 202-776-7712 ▪ TF: 800-986-2373

Object Management Group www.omg.org
250 1st Ave Suite 100   Needham MA 02494
Ph: 781-444-0404 ▪ Fx: 781-444-0320

Objectivism, Ayn Rand Institute: The Center for the www.aynrand.org
Advancement of   2121 Alton Pkwy Suite 250   Irvine CA
92606
Ph: 949-222-6550 ▪ Fx: 949-222-6558

Objectivist Center www.objectivistcenter.org
11 Raymond Ave Suite 31   Poughkeepsie NY 12603
Ph: 845-471-6100 ▪ Fx: 845-471-6195 ▪ TF: 800-374-1776

O'Brian Hugh Youth Leadership www.hoby.org
10880 Wilshire Blvd Suite 410   Los Angeles CA 90024
Ph: 310-474-4370 ▪ Fx: 310-475-5426

Obsessive-Compulsive Anonymous hometown.aol.com/_ht_a/west24th
PO Box 215   New Hyde Park NY 11040
Ph: 516-739-0662

Obsessive Compulsive Foundation www.ocfoundation.org
PO Box 9573   New Haven CT 06535
Ph: 203-315-2190 ▪ Fx: 203-315-2196

Obstetric Anesthesia & Perinatology, Society for www.soap.org
2 Summit Park Dr Suite 140   Cleveland OH 44131
Ph: 216-447-7863 ▪ Fx: 216-642-1127

Obstetric & Neonatal Nurses, Association of Women's Health www.awhonn.org
2000 L St NW Suite 740   Washington DC 20036
Ph: 202-261-2400 ▪ Fx: 202-728-0575 ▪ TF: 800-673-8499

Obstetricians & Gynecologists, American College of www.acog.com
409 12th St SW PO Box 96920   Washington DC 20090
Ph: 202-638-5577 ▪ Fx: 202-863-4284

Obstetricians & Gynecologists, American College of Osteopathic www.acoog.com
900 Auburn Rd   Pontiac MI 48342
Ph: 248-332-6360 ▪ Fx: 248-332-4607 ▪ TF: 800-875-6360

Obstetrics, Association of Professors of Gynecology & www.apgo.org
2130 Priest Bridge Dr Suite 7   Crofton MD 21114
Ph: 410-451-9560 ▪ Fx: 410-451-9568

Obstetrics & Gynecology, American Board of www.abog.org
2915 Vine St   Dallas TX 75204
Ph: 214-871-1619 ▪ Fx: 214-871-1943

Obstetrics & Gynecology, Association of Physician Assistants in
PO Box 1109   Madison WI 53701
Ph: 800-545-0636

OC International www.gospelcom.net/oci
PO Box 36900   Colorado Springs CO 80936
Ph: 719-592-9292 ▪ Fx: 719-592-0693

Occultation Timing Association Inc, International www.occultations.org

Occupant Restraints Council, Automotive www.aorc.org
1081 Dove Run Rd Suite 403   Lexington KY 40502
Ph: 859-269-4240 ▪ Fx: 859-269-4241

Occupational Education, Council on www.council.org
41 Perimeter Ctr East NE Suite 640   Atlanta GA 30346
Ph: 770-396-3898 ▪ Fx: 770-396-3790 ▪ TF: 800-917-2081

Occupational & Environmental Clinics, Association of www.aoec.org
1010 Vermont Ave NW Suite 513   Washington DC 20005
Ph: 202-347-4976 ▪ Fx: 202-347-4950 ▪ TF: 888-347-2632

Occupational & Environmental Health, Society for www.soeh.org
6728 Old McLean Village Dr   McLean VA 22101
Ph: 703-556-9222 ▪ Fx: 703-556-8729

Occupational & Environmental Medicine, American College of www.acoem.org
1114 N Arlington Heights Rd   Arlington Heights IL 60004
Ph: 847-818-1800 ▪ Fx: 847-818-9266

Occupational Health Institute Trust, Sheet Metal www.smohit.org
601 N Fairfax St Suite 250   Alexandria VA 22314
Ph: 703-739-7130 ▪ Fx: 703-739-7134

Occupational Health Nurses, American Association of www.aaohn.org
2920 Brandywine Rd Suite 100   Atlanta GA 30341
Ph: 770-455-7757 ▪ Fx: 770-455-7271 ▪ TF: 888-646-4631

Occupational Health Professionals, Association of www.aohp.org
109 VIP Dr   Wexford PA 15090
Ph: 800-362-4347 ▪ Fx: 724-935-1560

Occupational Hearing Conservation, Council for Accreditation in www.caohc.org
611 E Wells St   Milwaukee WI 53202
Ph: 414-276-5338 ▪ Fx: 414-276-2146

Occupational & Preventive Medicine, American Osteopathic www.aocopm.org
College of   PO Box 2606   Leesburg VA 20177
Ph: 800-558-8686 ▪ Fx: 703-443-0567

Occupational Psychiatry, Academy of Organizational & www.aoop.org
717 Princess St   Alexandria VA 22314
Ph: 877-789-2667 ▪ Fx: 877-789-6050

Occupational Therapy Association Inc, American www.aota.org
4720 Montgomery Ln PO Box 31220   Bethesda MD 20824
Ph: 301-652-2682 ▪ Fx: 301-652-7711

Occupational Therapy Inc, National Board for Certification in www.nbcot.org
800 S Frederick Ave Suite 200   Gaithersburg MD 20877
Ph: 301-990-7979 ▪ Fx: 301-869-8492

Occupied Japan Club
29 Freeborn St   Newport RI 02840
Ph: 401-846-9024

Ocean Coalition, Antarctic & Southern www.asoc.org
1630 Connecticut Ave Fl 3   Washington DC 20009
Ph: 202-234-2480 ▪ Fx: 202-387-4823

Ocean Conservancy www.oceanconservancy.org
1725 DeSales St NW Suite 600   Washington DC 20036
Ph: 202-429-5609 ▪ Fx: 202-872-0619

Ocean & Cruise Liner Society, World www.oceancruisenews.com
PO Box 4850   Stamford CT 06907
Ph: 203-329-2787

Ocean Futures Society www.oceanfutures.org
325 Chapala St   Santa Barbara CA 93101
Ph: 805-899-8899 ▪ Fx: 805-899-8898

Ocean Industries Association, National www.noia.org
1120 G St NW Suite 900   Washington DC 20005
Ph: 202-347-6900 ▪ Fx: 202-347-8650

Ocean Law, Council on
1600 H St NW 2nd Fl   Washington DC 20006
Ph: 202-347-3766

Ocean Research Foundation, Pacific www.holoholo.org/porf
74-381 Kealakehe Pkwy Suite C   Kailua Kona HI 96740
Ph: 808-329-6105 ▪ Fx: 808-329-1148

Ocean Society www.oceansociety.org
441 Ridgewater Dr   Marietta GA 30068
Ph: 770-977-1838 ▪ Fx: 770-971-9419 ▪ TF: 877-616-2326

Oceana www.oceana.org
2501 M St NW Suite 300   Washington DC 20037
Ph: 202-833-3900 ▪ Fx: 202-833-2070 ▪ TF: 877-762-3262

Oceanic Engineering Society, IEEE www.oceanicengineering.org
IEEE Operations Ctr 445 Hoes Ln   Piscataway NJ 08854
Ph: 732-981-0060 ▪ Fx: 732-981-1721

Oceanic History, North American Society for www.ecu.edu/nasoh/
PO Box 18108   Washington DC 20036
Ph: 202-707-1409

Oceanic Society www.oceanic-society.org
Fort Mason Ctr   San Francisco CA 94123
Ph: 415-441-1106 ▪ Fx: 415-474-3395 ▪ TF: 800-326-7491

Oceanographic Foundation, International www.rsmas.miami.edu/iof
Univ of Miami Rosenstiel School of Marine & Atmospheric
Science 4600 Rickenbacker Cswy   Miami FL 33149
Ph: 305-361-4000 ▪ Fx: 305-361-4711

Oceanography, American Society of Limnology & aslo.org
5400 Bosque Blvd Suite 680   Waco TX 76710
Ph: 254-399-9635 ▪ Fx: 254-776-3767 ▪ TF: 800-929-2756

Oceanography Society www.tos.org
PO Box 1931   Rockville MD 20849
Ph: 301-251-7708 ▪ Fx: 301-251-7709

Oceans, International Association for the Physical Sciences www.iugg.org/iapso
of the   PO Box 820440   Vicksburg MS 39182
Ph: 601-636-1363 ▪ Fx: 601-629-9640

Oceans Law & Policy, Center for www.virginia.edu/colp
Univ of Virginia School of Law 580 Massie Rd   Charlottesville
VA 22903
Ph: 804-924-7441 ▪ Fx: 804-924-7362

Octagon International, Junior Optimist www.optimist.org
4494 Lindell Blvd   Saint Louis MO 63108
Ph: 314-371-6000 ▪ Fx: 314-371-6006 ▪ TF: 800-500-8130

Ocular Surgeons, International Association of www.
820 N Orleans St Suite 208   Chicago IL 60610
Ph: 312-440-0699 ▪ Fx: 312-440-0580 ▪ TF: 800-621-4002

Oculoplastic Society, International
1018 Harmon Cove Towers   Secaucus NJ 07094
Ph: 201-392-3438

Odd Fellows, Independent Order of www.ioof.org
422 Trade St   Winston-Salem NC 27101
Ph: 336-725-5955 ▪ Fx: 336-722-7317 ▪ TF: 800-235-8358

Oddities Collector's Club, Errors Freaks & www.efoers.org
955 S Grove Blvd Suite 65   Kingsland GA 31548
Ph: 912-729-1573 ▪ Fx: 912-729-1585

Odontology, American Society of Forensic www.asfo.org
11 Tiffany Pl   Saratoga Springs NY 12866
Ph: 518-584-2342 ▪ Fx: 518-584-9706

Off-Highway Vehicle Conservation Council Inc, National www.nohvcc.org
4718 S Taylor Dr   Sheboygan WI 53081
Ph: 800-348-6487 ▪ Fx: 920-458-3446

Office Business Center Association International www.officebusinesscenters.com
200 E Campus View Blvd Suite 200   Columbus OH 43235
Ph: 614-985-3633 ▪ Fx: 614-985-3601 ▪ TF: 800-237-4741

Office Furniture Distribution Association www.theofda.org
6 Main St PO Box 326   Petersham MA 01366
Ph: 978-724-3267 ▪ Fx: 978-724-3507

Office Laboratory Accreditation, Commission on www.cola.org
9881 Broken Land Pkwy Suite 200   Columbia MD 21046
Ph: 410-381-6581 ▪ Fx: 410-381-8611 ▪ TF: 800-981-9883

Office Management, Professional Association of Health Care www.pahcom.com
461 E 10 Mile Rd   Pensacola FL 32534
Ph: 850-474-9460 ▪ Fx: 850-474-6352 ▪ TF: 800-451-9311

Office Products Alliance, National www.nopanet.org
301 N Fairfax St   Alexandria VA 22314
Ph: 703-549-9040 ▪ Fx: 703-683-7552

Office Products Association, School Home & www.shopa.org
3131 Elbee Rd   Dayton OH 45439
Ph: 937-297-2250 ▪ Fx: 937-297-2254 ▪ TF: 800-854-7467

Office Products & Furniture Dealers Association, Independent www.iopfda.org
301 N Fairfax St   Alexandria VA 22314
Ph: 703-549-9040 ▪ Fx: 703-683-7552

Office Products Representatives Advisory Group www.oprareps.com
3131 Elbee Rd   Dayton OH 45439
Ph: 937-297-2250 ▪ TF: 800-854-7467

Office Products Wholesalers Association www.opwa.org
5024-R Campbell Blvd   Baltimore MD 21236
Ph: 410-931-8100 ▪ Fx: 410-931-8111

Office & Professional Employees International Union www.opeiu.org
265 W 14th St Suite 610   New York NY 10011
Ph: 212-675-3210 ▪ Fx: 212-727-3466 ▪ TF: 800-346-7348

Office Professionals, National Association of Educational www.naeop.org
PO Box 12619 Wichita KS 67277
Ph: 316-942-4822 ■ Fx: 316-942-7100

Office Properties, National Association of Industrial & www.naiop.org
2201 Cooperative Way 3rd Fl Herndon VA 20171
Ph: 703-904-7100 ■ Fx: 703-904-7942 ■ TF: 800-666-6780

Office REALTORS, Society of Industrial & www.sior.com
1201 New York Ave NW Suite 350 Washington DC 20005
Ph: 202-449-8200 ■ Fx: 202-449-8201

Officers Association, Non-Commissioned www.ncoausa.org
10635 IH-35 N San Antonio TX 78233
Ph: 210-653-6161 ■ Fx: 210-637-3337 ■ TF: 800-662-2620

Officers' Christian Fellowship www.gospelcom.net/ocf
3784 S Inca St Englewood CO 80110
Ph: 800-424-1984

Officials Association, National Intercollegiate Soccer www.nisoa.com
541 Woodview Dr Longwood FL 32779
Ph: 407-862-3305 ■ Fx: 407-862-8545

Officials Association, NFHS www.nfhs.org/nfoa.htm
PO Box 690 Indianapolis IN 46206
Ph: 317-972-6900 ■ Fx: 317-822-5700

Offshore Lobstermen's Association, Atlantic www.offshorelobster.org
114 Adams Rd Candia NH 03034
Ph: 603-483-3030 ■ Fx: 603-483-4862

Offshore Marine Service Association www.offshoremarine.org
990 N Corporate Dr Suite 210 Harahan LA 70123
Ph: 504-734-7622 ■ Fx: 504-734-7134

Offshore & Polar Engineers, International Society of www.isope.org
PO Box 189 Cupertino CA 95015
Ph: 650-254-1871 ■ Fx: 650-254-2038

Offshore Rescue & Towing, Committee for Private www.c-port.org
1600 Duke St Suite 220 Alexandria VA 22314
Ph: 703-519-1713 ■ Fx: 703-519-1716

Ohio Historical Society, Chesapeake & www.cohs.org
PO Box 79 Clifton Forge VA 24422
Ph: 540-862-2210 ■ Fx: 540-863-9159 ■ TF: 800-453-2647

Ohio Longrifle Collectors, Association of
23003 State Rt 339 Beverly OH 45715
Ph: 740-984-4896

OIC International www.oicinternational.org
240 W Tulpehocken St Philadelphia PA 19144
Ph: 215-842-0860 ■ Fx: 215-849-7033 ■ TF: 800-653-6424

Oil & Acrylic Painters Society, National www.noaps.org
PO Box 676 Osage Beach MO 65049
Ph: 417-533-7550

Oil Association, National Fish Meal &
1901 N Fort Myer Dr Suite 700 Arlington VA 22209
Ph: 703-524-8884 ■ Fx: 703-524-4619

Oil Association, North American Olive www.naooa.org
3301 Rt 66 Bldg C Suite 205 Neptune NJ 07753
Ph: 732-922-3008 ■ Fx: 732-922-3590

Oil Change Association, Automotive www.aoca.org
12810 Hillcrest Rd Suite 221 Dallas TX 75230
Ph: 972-458-9468 ■ Fx: 972-458-9539 ■ TF: 800-331-0329

Oil Chemists Society, American www.aocs.org
2211 W Bradley Ave Champaign IL 61821
Ph: 217-359-2344 ■ Fx: 217-351-8091 ■ TF: 800-336-2627

Oil & Gas Association, US
901 F St NW Suite 601 Washington DC 20004
Ph: 202-638-4400 ■ Fx: 202-638-5967

Oil & Gas Compact Commission, Interstate www.iogcc.oklaosf.state.ok.us
PO Box 53127 Oklahoma City OK 73152
Ph: 405-525-3556 ■ Fx: 405-525-3592 ■ TF: 800-822-4015

Oil Mill Superintendents Association, International
1835 Edinburgh St Prattville AL 36066
Ph: 334-491-1754 ■ Fx: 334-491-3109

Oil Pastel Association International Ltd www.opai.org

Oil Pipe Lines, Association of www.aopl.org
1101 Vermont Ave NW Suite 604 Washington DC 20005
Ph: 202-408-7970 ■ Fx: 202-408-7983

Oil Saves Energy), Project ROSE (Recycled www.eng.ua.edu/~prose
PO Box 870203 Tuscaloosa AL 35487
Ph: 205-348-4878 ■ Fx: 205-348-7558

Oil Scouts Association, International www.oilscouts.org
PO Box 272949 Houston TX 77277
Ph: 512-472-8138 ■ Fx: 512-472-1057

Oilers, National Conference of Firemen & www.ncfo.org
1023 15th St NW 10th Fl Washington DC 20005
Ph: 202-962-0981 ■ Fx: 202-872-1222

Oils, Institute of Shortening & Edible www.iseo.org
1750 New York Ave NW Suite 120 Washington DC 20006
Ph: 202-783-7960 ■ Fx: 202-393-1367

Oilseed Processors Association, National www.nopa.org
1300 L St NW Suite 1020 Washington DC 20005
Ph: 202-842-0463 ■ Fx: 202-842-9126

Oilseed Products, National Institute of www.oilseed.org
1156 15th St NW Suite 900 Washington DC 20005
Ph: 202-785-3232 ■ Fx: 202-223-9741

OJ Noer Research Foundation www.noerfoundation.org
PO Box 1494 Milwaukee WI 53201
Ph: 414-258-7337

Old Crows, Association of www.crows.org
1000 N Payne St Alexandria VA 22314
Ph: 703-549-1600 ■ Fx: 703-549-2589 ■ TF: 888-653-2769

Old English Sheepdog Club of America Inc www.oldenglishsheepdogclubofamerica.org
N 64 W 20708 Mill Rd Suite 1015 Menomonee Falls WI 53501
Ph: 262-252-3936

Old Mills, Society for the Preservation of www.spoom.org

Old Settlers & Threshers Association, Midwest www.oldthreshers.org
405 E Threshers Rd Mount Pleasant IA 52641
Ph: 319-385-8937 ■ Fx: 319-385-0563

Old-Time Radio, Friends of
PO Box 4321 Hamden CT 06514
Ph: 203-248-2887 ■ Fx: 203-281-1322

Oldenburg Registry NA www.isroldenburg.org
939 Merchandise Mart Chicago IL 60654
Ph: 312-527-6544 ■ Fx: 312-527-6573

Older Women's League www.owl-national.org
1750 New York Ave NW Suite 350 Washington DC 20006
Ph: 202-783-6686 ■ Fx: 202-628-0458 ■ TF: 800-825-3695

Older Worker Partnership, National
c/o National Council on the Aging 300 D St SW Suite
  801 Washington DC 20024
Ph: 202-479-1200 ■ Fx: 202-479-0735

Oldtime Barbell & Strongmen, Association of
33-30 150th St Flushing NY 11354
Ph: 718-661-3195

Oldsmobile Club Inc, National Antique www.antiqueolds.org

Oldtime Fiddlers' Association, National
309 State St Weiser ID 83672
Ph: 800-437-1280 ■ Fx: 208-414-0255

Oley Foundation c4isr.com/oley
Albany Medical Ctr 214 Hun Memorial MC A-28 Albany NY
  12208
Ph: 518-262-5079 ■ Fx: 518-262-5528 ■ TF: 800-776-6539

Olive Oil Association, North American www.naooa.org
3301 Rt 66 Bldg C Suite 205 Neptune NJ 07753
Ph: 732-922-3008 ■ Fx: 732-922-3590

Olmsted Parks, National Association for www.olmsted.org
84 Parkside Ave Buffalo NY 14214
Ph: 866-666-6905 ■ Fx: 716-835-1300

Olympic Committee, US www.olympic-usa.org
1 Olympic Plaza Colorado Springs CO 80909
Ph: 719-632-5551 ■ Fx: 719-866-4654 ■ TF: 888-866-8687

Olympics Inc, Special www.specialolympics.org
1325 G St NW Suite 500 Washington DC 20005
Ph: 202-628-3630 ■ Fx: 202-824-0200

OMB Watch www.ombwatch.org
1742 Connecticut Ave NW Washington DC 20009
Ph: 202-234-8494 ■ Fx: 202-234-8584

Ombudsman Association www.ombuds-toa.org
203 Towne Centre Dr Hillsborough NJ 08844
Ph: 908-359-1184 ■ Fx: 908-359-7619

Ombudsmen, Organization of News www.newsombudsmen.org
PO Box 120191 San Diego CA 92112
Ph: 619-293-1525

Omega Delta
Southern College of Optometry 245 Madison Ave Memphis TN
  38104
Ph: 901-722-3200

Omega Psi Phi Fraternity Inc www.oppf.org
3951 Snapfinger Pkwy Decatur GA 30035
Ph: 404-284-5533 ■ Fx: 404-284-0333

Omega Tau Sigma www.cvm.uiuc.edu/ots
9947 E Bloomfield Hills Dr Effingham IL 62401
Ph: 217-868-5095

Omicron Delta Epsilon www.cba.ua.edu/~ode
PO Box 1486 Hattiesburg MS 39403
Ph: 601-264-3115 ■ Fx: 601-264-3669 ■ TF: 800-584-5514

Omicron Delta Kappa Society www.odk.org
Univ of Kentucky 118 Bradley Hall Lexington KY 40506
Ph: 859-257-2110 ■ Fx: 859-323-1014

Omicron Kappa Upsilon www.oku.org
Univ of Nebraska Medical Ctr College of Dentistry Lincoln NE
  68583
Ph: 402-472-1339 ■ Fx: 402-472-5290

Omohundro Institute of Early American History & Culture www.wm.edu/oieahc
PO Box 8781 Williamsbury VA 23187
Ph: 757-221-1110 ■ Fx: 757-221-1047

OMS International www.omsinternational.org
941 Fry Rd Box A Greenwood IN 46142
Ph: 317-881-6751 ■ Fx: 317-888-5275

Oncologists, Society of Gynecologic www.sgo.org
401 N Michigan Ave Chicago IL 60611
Ph: 312-644-6610 ■ Fx: 312-527-6959

Oncology Administrators, Society for Radiation www.sroa.org
PO Box 51687 Albuquerque NM 87181
Ph: 866-458-7762 ■ Fx: 505-298-5063

Oncology, American College of Mohs Micrographic Surgery & www.mohscollege.org
Cutaneous 611 E Wells St Milwaukee WI 53202
Ph: 414-347-1103 ■ Fx: 414-272-6070 ■ TF: 800-500-7224

Oncology, American College of Radiation www.acro.org
4350 East-West Hwy Suite 401 Bethesda MD 20814
Ph: 301-718-6515 ■ Fx: 301-656-0989

Oncology, American Society of Clinical www.asco.org
1900 Duke St Suite 200 Alexandria VA 22314
Ph: 703-299-0150 ■ Fx: 703-299-1044 ■ TF: 888-282-2552

Oncology, American Society of Pediatric Hematology/ www.aspho.org
4700 W Lake Ave Glenview IL 60025
Ph: 847-375-4716 ■ Fx: 877-734-9557

Oncology, American Society of Preventive www.aspo.org
610 Walnut St Suite 256 Madison WI 53726
Ph: 608-263-9515 ■ Fx: 608-263-4497

Oncology, American Society for Therapeutic Radiology & www.astro.org
12500 Fair Lakes Cir Suite 375 Fairfax VA 22033
Ph: 703-502-1550 ■ Fx: 703-502-7852 ■ TF: 800-962-7876

Oncology, Association of Residents in Radiation   www.arro.org
12500 Fair Lakes Cir Suite 375 Fairfax VA 22033
Ph: 703-502-1550 ▪ Fx: 703-502-7852 ▪ TF: 800-962-7876

Oncology Centers, Association of Freestanding Radiation   www.afroc.org
1875 'I' St NW 12th Fl Washington DC 20006
Ph: 888-334-4542 ▪ Fx: 202-466-5938

Oncology Group, Gynecologic   www.gog.org
1600 JFK Blvd Suite 1020 Philadelphia PA 19103
Ph: 215-854-0770 ▪ Fx: 215-854-0716 ▪ TF: 800-225-3053

Oncology Group, Radiation Therapy   www.rtog.org
1101 Market St 14th Fl Philadelphia PA 19107
Ph: 215-574-3189 ▪ Fx: 215-923-1737

Oncology Nurses, Association of Pediatric   www.apon.org
4700 W Lake Ave Glenview IL 60025
Ph: 847-375-4724 ▪ Fx: 877-734-8755

Oncology Nursing Society   www.ons.org
125 Enterprise Dr Pittsburgh PA 15275
Ph: 412-859-6100 ▪ Fx: 877-369-5497 ▪ TF: 866-257-4667

Oncology Social Work, Association of   www.aosw.org
1211 Locust St Philadelphia PA 19107
Ph: 215-599-6093 ▪ Fx: 215-545-8107

Oncology Inc, Society of Surgical   www.surgonc.org
85 W Algonquin Rd Suite 550 Arlington Heights IL 60005
Ph: 847-427-1400 ▪ Fx: 847-427-9656

ONE Institute & Archives   www.oneinstitute.org
909 W Adams Blvd Los Angeles CA 90007
Ph: 213-741-0094 ▪ Fx: 213-741-0220

O'Neill Eugene Society
PO Box 402 Danville CA 94526
Ph: 925-820-1818 ▪ Fx: 925-828-0265

O'Neill Eugene Theater Center   www.oneilltheatercenter.org
305 Great Neck Rd Waterford CT 06385
Ph: 860-443-5378 ▪ Fx: 860-443-9653

Onion Association, National   www.onions-usa.org
822 7th St Suite 510 Greeley CO 80631
Ph: 970-353-5895 ▪ Fx: 970-353-5897

Online Audiovisual Catalogers   www.olacinc.org
Minnesota State Univ Memorial Library 3097 PO Box
8419 Mankato MN 56001
Ph: 507-389-5952

Online Computer Library Center Inc   www.oclc.org
6565 Frantz Rd Dublin OH 43017
Ph: 614-764-6000 ▪ Fx: 614-764-6096 ▪ TF: 800-848-5878

Online Privacy Alliance   www.privacyalliance.org
c/o Hogan & Hartson LLP 555 13th St NW Washington DC
20004
Ph: 202-637-5600 ▪ Fx: 202-637-5710

Online Publishers Association   www.online-publishers.org
500 7th Ave 8th Fl New York NY 10018
Ph: 646-698-8071 ▪ Fx: 646-698-8081

Online Scholarship, Communication Institute for   www.cios.org
PO Box 57 Rotterdam Junction NY 12150
Ph: 518-887-2443 ▪ Fx: 518-887-5186

Onsite Wastewater Recycling Association, National   www.nowra.org
PO Box 1270 Edgewater MD 21037
Ph: 410-798-1697 ▪ Fx: 410-798-5741

Ontario & Western Railway Historical Society   www.nyow.org

Open Air Campaigners USA   www.oacusa.org
PO Box D Nazareth PA 18064
Ph: 610-746-0508 ▪ Fx: 610-746-0509

Open Applications Group Inc   www.openapplications.org
1950 Spectrum Cir Suite 400 Marietta GA 30067
Ph: 770-980-3418

Open Group   www.opengroup.org
44 Montgomery St Suite 960 San Francisco CA 94104
Ph: 415-374-8280 ▪ Fx: 415-374-8293

Open Mobile Alliance   www.openmobilealliance.org
4275 Executive Sq Suite 240 La Jolla CA 92037
Ph: 858-623-0740 ▪ Fx: 858-623-0743

OPEN Society, Fund for an   www.opensoc.org
1315 Walnut St Suite 1708 Philadelphia PA 19107
Ph: 215-546-0511 ▪ Fx: 215-546-0514

Open Society Institute   www.soros.org
400 W 59th St New York NY 10019
Ph: 212-548-0600 ▪ Fx: 212-548-4679

Open Space Institute   www.openspaceinstitute.org
1350 Broadway Suite 201 New York NY 10018
Ph: 212-629-3981 ▪ Fx: 212-244-3441

Opening Door Inc   www.travelguides.org
8049 Ornesby Ln Woodford VA 22580
Ph: 804-633-6752

OPERA America   www.operaam.org
1156 15th St NW Suite 810 Washington DC 20005
Ph: 202-293-4466 ▪ Fx: 202-393-0735

Opera Association, Metropolitan   www.metopera.org
Lincoln Ctr New York NY 10023
Ph: 212-362-6000 ▪ Fx: 212-874-2659

Opera Association, National   www.noa.org
PO Box 60869 Canyon TX 79016
Ph: 806-651-2857 ▪ Fx: 806-651-2958

Opera & Ballet, American Friends of the Paris
972 5th Ave New York NY 10021
Ph: 212-439-1426 ▪ Fx: 212-439-1455

Opera, Center for Contemporary   www.conopera.org
PO Box 258 New York NY 10044
Ph: 212-785-2757 ▪ Fx: 212-758-0389

Opera Guild, Metropolitan   www.metopera.org/guild
70 Lincoln Ctr Plaza 6th Fl New York NY 10023
Ph: 212-769-7000 ▪ Fx: 212-769-7007 ▪ TF: 800-829-2525

Opera Musicians, International Conference of Symphony &   www.icsom.org
4 W 31st St Unit 921 New York NY 10001
Ph: 212-594-1636

Operating Engineers, International Union of   www.iuoe.org
1125 17th St NW Washington DC 20036
Ph: 202-429-9100 ▪ Fx: 202-778-2616

Operation Blessing International Relief & Development Corp   www.ob.org
977 Centerville Tpke Virginia Beach VA 23463
Ph: 757-226-3401 ▪ Fx: 757-226-3411 ▪ TF: 800-730-2537

Operation Crossroads Africa   oca.igc.org
PO Box 5570 New York NY 10027
Ph: 212-289-1949 ▪ Fx: 212-289-2526

Operation K9 Rescue Inc   www.operationk9rescue.com
PO Box 235207 Encinitas CA 92023
Ph: 760-497-7764

Operation Lifesaver Inc   www.oli.org
1420 King St Suite 401 Alexandria VA 22314
Ph: 703-739-0308 ▪ Fx: 703-519-8267 ▪ TF: 800-537-6224

Operation Smile   www.operationsmile.org
6435 Tidewater Dr Norfolk VA 23509
Ph: 757-321-7645 ▪ Fx: 757-321-7660 ▪ TF: 888-677-6453

Operation USA   www.opusa.org
8320 Melrose Ave Suite 200 Los Angeles CA 90069
Ph: 323-658-8876 ▪ Fx: 323-653-7846 ▪ TF: 800-678-7255

Operations Management Society, Production &   www.poms.org
Florida International Univ College of Engineering EAS 2460
10555 W Flagler St Miami FL 33174
Ph: 305-348-1413 ▪ Fx: 305-348-6890

Operations Research & the Management Sciences, Institute for   www.informs.org
901 Elkridge Landing Rd Suite 400 Linthicum MD 21090
Ph: 410-850-0300 ▪ Fx: 410-684-2963 ▪ TF: 800-446-3676

Operative Plasterers' & Cement Masons' International Association of the US & Canada   www.opcmia.org
14405 Laurel Pl Suite 300 Laurel MD 20707
Ph: 301-470-4200 ▪ Fx: 301-470-2502

Ophthalmic Administrators, American Society of   www.asoa.org
4000 Legato Rd Suite 850 Fairfax VA 22033
Ph: 703-591-2222 ▪ Fx: 703-591-0614 ▪ TF: 800-451-1339

Ophthalmic Photographers' Society   www.opsweb.org
1869 Ranch Rd Nixa MO 65714
Ph: 417-725-0181 ▪ Fx: 417-724-8450 ▪ TF: 800-403-1677

Ophthalmic Plastic & Reconstructive Surgery, American Society of   www.asoprs.org
1133 W Morse Blvd Suite 201 Winter Park FL 32789
Ph: 407-647-8839 ▪ Fx: 407-629-2502

Ophthalmic Registered Nurses, American Society of   www.asorn.org
PO Box 193030 San Francisco CA 94109
Ph: 415-561-8513 ▪ Fx: 415-561-8531

Ophthalmic Surgery Society, Outpatient   www.ooss.org
793-A Foothill Blvd PMB 119 San Luis Obispo CA 93405
Ph: 877-720-3585

Ophthalmologists, American College of Veterinary   www.acvo.com
PO Box 1311 Meridian ID 83680
Ph: 208-466-7624 ▪ Fx: 208-466-7693

Ophthalmologists, Contact Lens Association of   www.clao.org
721 Papworth Ave Suite 205 Metairie LA 70005
Ph: 504-835-3937 ▪ Fx: 504-833-5884

Ophthalmology, American Academy of   www.aao.org
655 Beach St San Francisco CA 94120
Ph: 415-561-8500 ▪ Fx: 415-561-8533 ▪ TF: 800-222-3937

Ophthalmology, American Osteopathic College of   www.aocoohns.org/aoco.htm
405 W Grand Ave Dayton OH 45405
Ph: 937-222-8820 ▪ Fx: 937-222-8840 ▪ TF: 800-455-9404

Ophthalmology, American Society of Contemporary Medicine Surgery &   820 N Orleans St Suite 208 Chicago IL 60610
Ph: 312-440-0699 ▪ Fx: 312-440-0580 ▪ TF: 800-621-4002

Ophthalmology, Association for Research in Vision &   www.arvo.org
12300 Twinbrook Pkwy Suite 250 Rockville MD 20852
Ph: 240-221-2900 ▪ Fx: 240-221-0370

Ophthalmology, Association of University Professors of
PO Box 420369 San Francisco CA 94142
Ph: 415-561-8548 ▪ Fx: 415-561-8531

Ophthalmology Society, North American Neuro-   www.nanosweb.org
342 N Main St West Hartford CT 06117
Ph: 860-558-7507 ▪ Fx: 860-586-7550

Ophthalmology & Strabismus, American Association for Pediatric   www.aapos.org
PO Box 193832 San Francisco CA 94119
Ph: 415-561-8505 ▪ Fx: 415-561-8531

Opinion Research, American Association for Public   www.aapor.org
PO Box 14263 Lenexa KS 66285
Ph: 913-310-0118 ▪ Fx: 913-599-5340

Opinion Research, Council for Marketing &   www.cmor.org
4147-U Crossgate Dr Cincinnati OH 45236
Ph: 513-985-0001 ▪ Fx: 513-985-0119 ▪ TF: 800-887-2667

Opinion Research, World Association for Public   www.unl.edu/wapor
UNL Gallup Research Ctr Univ of Nebraska - Lincoln 200 N 11th
St Lincoln NE 68588
Ph: 402-458-2030 ▪ Fx: 402-458-2038

Opportunities Industrialization Centers of America Inc   www.oicofamerica.org
1415 N Broad St Philadelphia PA 19122
Ph: 215-236-4500 ▪ Fx: 215-236-7480 ▪ TF: 800-621-4642

Opportunity in Education, Council for   www.trioprograms.org
1025 Vermont Ave NW Suite 900 Washington DC 20005
Ph: 202-347-7430 ▪ Fx: 202-347-0786

Opportunity International-USA   www.opportunity.org
2122 York Rd Oak Brook IL 60523
Ph: 630-645-4100 ▪ Fx: 630-645-1458 ▪ TF: 800-793-9455

Optical Engineering, SPIE - International Society for   www.spie.org
1000 20th St Bellingham WA 98225
Ph: 360-676-3290 ▪ Fx: 360-647-1445

Optical Imaging Association   www.opia.org
    252 Reinekers Ln Suite 625   Alexandria VA 22314
    Ph: 703-836-1360 ▪ Fx: 703-836-6644
Optical Laboratories Association   www.ola-labs.org
    11096-B Lee Hwy Suite 102   Fairfax VA 22030
    Ph: 703-359-2830 ▪ Fx: 703-359-2834 ▪ TF: 800-477-5652
Optical Society of America   www.osa.org
    2010 Massachusetts Ave NW   Washington DC 20036
    Ph: 202-223-8130 ▪ Fx: 202-223-1096 ▪ TF: 800-762-6960
Opticianry Accreditation, Commission on   www.coaccreditation.com
    PO Box 3073   Merrifield VA 22116
    Ph: 703-766-1600 ▪ Fx: 703-766-2834
Opticianry, American Board of   www.abo.org
    6506 Loisdale Rd Suite 209   Springfield VA 22150
    Ph: 703-719-5800 ▪ Fx: 703-719-9144 ▪ TF: 800-296-1379
Opticianry, National Academy of   www.nao.org
    8401 Corporate Dr Suite 605   Landover MD 20785
    Ph: 301-577-4828 ▪ Fx: 301-577-3880 ▪ TF: 800-229-4828
Opticians Association of America   www.opticians.org
    12100 Sunset Hills Rd Suite 130   Reston VA 20190
    Ph: 703-437-4377 ▪ Fx: 703-435-4390 ▪ TF: 800-443-8997
Optimist Dinghy Association, US   www.usoda.org
Optimist International   www.optimist.org
    4494 Lindell Blvd   Saint Louis MO 63108
    Ph: 314-371-6000 ▪ Fx: 314-371-6006 ▪ TF: 800-500-8130
Optimist International Canada   www.optimist.org
    4559 E Metropolitan Blvd   Saint-Leonard QC H1R1Z4
    Ph: 514-593-4401 ▪ Fx: 514-721-1104 ▪ TF: 800-363-7151
Optimist Octagon International, Junior   www.optimist.org
    4494 Lindell Blvd   Saint Louis MO 63108
    Ph: 314-371-6000 ▪ Fx: 314-371-6006 ▪ TF: 800-500-8130
Optometric Association, American   www.aoanet.org
    243 N Lindbergh Blvd   Saint Louis MO 63141
    Ph: 314-991-4100 ▪ Fx: 314-991-4101
Optometric Society, Armed Forces   www.afos2020.org
    411 Sweetgrass Ct   Great Falls MT 59405
    Ph: 406-452-5688 ▪ Fx: 406-452-5740
Optometric Student Association, American   www.theaosa.org
    243 N Lindbergh Blvd   Saint Louis MO 63141
    Ph: 314-991-4100 ▪ Fx: 314-991-4101
Optometrists in Vision Development, College of   www.covd.org
    243 N Lindbergh Blvd Suite 310   Saint Louis MO 63141
    Ph: 314-991-4007 ▪ Fx: 314-991-1167 ▪ TF: 888-268-3770
Optometry, American Academy of   www.aaopt.org
    6110 Executive Blvd Suite 506   Rockville MD 20852
    Ph: 301-984-1441 ▪ Fx: 301-984-4737
Optometry, Association of Regulatory Boards of   www.arbo.org
    1750 S Brentwood Blvd Suite 503   Saint Louis MO 63144
    Ph: 314-785-6000 ▪ Fx: 314-785-6002
Optometry, Association of Schools & Colleges of   www.opted.org
    6110 Executive Blvd Suite 510   Rockville MD 20852
    Ph: 301-231-5944 ▪ Fx: 301-770-1828
(Optometry) Omega Delta
    Southern College of Optometry 245 Madison Ave   Memphis TN
        38104
    Ph: 901-722-3200
Opus Dei Foundation   www.opusdei.org
    524 North Ave Suite 203   New Rochelle NY 10801
    Ph: 914-235-1201 ▪ Fx: 914-235-7805
Oracle Users Group, International   www.ioug.org
    401 N Michigan Ave   Chicago IL 60611
    Ph: 312-245-1579 ▪ Fx: 312-527-6785
Oral Biology, American Institute of   www.aiob.org
    PO Box 7184   Loma Linda CA 92354
    Ph: 909-558-4671 ▪ Fx: 909-558-0285
Oral Cancer Foundation   www.oralcancerfoundation.org
    3419 Via Lido Suite 205   Newport Beach CA 92663
    Ph: 949-646-8000 ▪ Fx: 949-496-3331
Oral Health America   www.oralhealthamerica.org
    410 N Michigan Ave Suite 352   Chicago IL 60611
    Ph: 312-836-9900 ▪ Fx: 312-836-9986 ▪ TF: 800-523-3438
Oral Health Information Clearinghouse, National   www.nohic.nidcr.nih.gov
    1 NOHIC Way   Bethesda MD 20892
    Ph: 301-402-7364 ▪ Fx: 301-907-8830
Oral Health, International Association for Disability &   www.iadh.org
    Ohio State Univ College of Dentistry 305 W 12th Ave PO Box
        182357   Columbus OH 43218
    Ph: 614-292-1232 ▪ Fx: 614-292-4522
Oral History Association   www.dickinson.edu/oha
    Dickinson College PO Box 1773   Carlisle PA 17013
    Ph: 717-245-1036 ▪ Fx: 717-245-1046
Oral Implantologists, International Congress of   www.dentalimplants.com
    248 Lorraine Ave 3rd Fl   Upper Montclair NJ 07043
    Ph: 973-783-6300 ▪ Fx: 973-783-1175 ▪ TF: 800-442-0525
Oral & Maxillofacial Pathology, American Academy of   aaomp.org
    710 E Ogden Ave Suite 600   Naperville IL 60563
    Ph: 888-552-2667 ▪ Fx: 630-369-2488
Oral & Maxillofacial Radiology, American Academy of   www.aaomr.org
    PO Box 1010   Evans GA 30809
    Ph: 706-721-2607
Oral & Maxillofacial Surgeons, American Association of   www.aaoms.org
    9700 W Bryn Mawr Ave   Rosemont IL 60018
    Ph: 847-678-6200 ▪ Fx: 847-678-6286 ▪ TF: 800-822-6637
Oral & Maxillofacial Surgeons, American College of   www.acoms.org
    1100 NW Loop 410 Suite 420   San Antonio TX 78213
    Ph: 210-344-5674 ▪ Fx: 210-344-9754 ▪ TF: 800-522-6676
Oral & Maxillofacial Surgery, American Board of   www.aboms.org
    625 N Michigan Ave Suite 1820   Chicago IL 60611
    Ph: 312-642-0070 ▪ Fx: 312-642-8584

Oral Medicine, American Academy of   www.aaom.com
    2910 Lightfoot Dr   Baltimore MD 21209
    Ph: 410-602-8585
Oral Medicine & Toxicology, International Academy of   www.iaomt.org
    8297 Championsgate Blvd Suite 193   Championsgate FL 33896
    Ph: 863-420-6373 ▪ Fx: 863-420-6394
Oral Roberts University Educational Fellowship   www.oru.edu/oruef
    7777 S Lewis Ave   Tulsa OK 74171
    Ph: 918-495-6163 ▪ Fx: 918-495-6175
ORBIS International Inc   www.orbis.org
    520 8th Ave 11th Fl   New York NY 10018
    Ph: 646-674-5500 ▪ Fx: 646-674-5599 ▪ TF: 800-672-4787
Orchestra League, American Symphony   www.symphony.org
    33 W 60th St 5th Fl   New York NY 10023
    Ph: 212-262-5161 ▪ Fx: 212-262-5198
Orchestra Librarians' Association, Major   www.mola-inc.org
    c/o National Arts Centre Orchestra PO Box 1534 Stn B   Ottawa
        ON K1P5W1
    Ph: 613-947-7000 ▪ Fx: 613-947-8623
Orchid Society, American   www.orchidweb.org
    16700 AOS Ln   Delray Beach FL 33446
    Ph: 561-404-2000 ▪ Fx: 561-404-2100
Orchid Society of Hawaii, Pacific   honoluluorchsoc.tripod.com/pos.html
    PO Box 1091   Honolulu HI 96808
    Ph: 808-237-8672
Order of Alhambra   www.orderalhambra.org
    4200 Leeds Ave   Baltimore MD 21229
    Ph: 410-242-0660 ▪ Fx: 410-536-5729
Order of Americans of Armorial Ancestry
    PO Box 453   Abingdon MD 21009
    Ph: 410-515-1824
Order Analysts, National Association of Division   www.nadoa.org
    9794 Forest Ln PMB 1012   Dallas TX 75243
    Ph: 972-715-4489 ▪ Fx: 972-715-6446
Order of the Arrow   www.oa-bsa.org
    1325 W Walnut Hill Ln PO Box 152079   Irving TX 75015
    Ph: 972-580-2438 ▪ Fx: 972-580-2399
Order of the Coif   www.orderofthecoif.org
    Univ of North Carolina Law Library CB 3385   Chapel Hill NC
        27599
    Ph: 919-962-1321 ▪ Fx: 919-962-1193
Order of Daedalians   www.daedalians.org
    PO Box 249   Randolph AFB TX 78148
    Ph: 210-945-2111 ▪ Fx: 210-945-2112
Order of the Daughters of the King   www.dok-national.org
    Margaret J Franklin Ctr 101 Weatherstone Dr Suite
        870   Woodstock GA 30188
    Ph: 770-517-8552 ▪ Fx: 770-517-8066
Order of Descendants of Colonial Physicians & Chirurgiens
    9317 Bent Tree Cir   Wichita KS 67226
    Ph: 316-634-1930
Order of the Indian Wars   www.indianwars.com
    PO Box 7401   Little Rock AR 72217
    Ph: 501-225-3996
Order Italian Sons & Daughters of America   www.orderisda.org
    419 Wood St   Pittsburgh PA 15222
    Ph: 412-261-3550 ▪ Fx: 412-261-9897
Order of Knights of Pythias   www.pythias.org
    59 Coddington St Suite 202   Quincy MA 02169
    Ph: 617-472-8800 ▪ Fx: 617-376-0363
Order of the Sons of Hermann in Texas   www.texashermannsons.org
    PO Box 1941   San Antonio TX 78297
    Ph: 210-226-9261 ▪ Fx: 210-226-3055 ▪ TF: 800-234-4124
Order of the Sons of Italy in America   www.osia.org
    219 'E' St NE   Washington DC 20002
    Ph: 202-547-2900 ▪ Fx: 202-546-8168 ▪ TF: 800-547-6742
Order of United Commercial Travelers of America   www.uct.org
    632 N Park St PO Box 159019   Columbus OH 43215
    Ph: 614-228-3276 ▪ Fx: 614-228-1898 ▪ TF: 800-848-0123
Oregon-California Trails Association   www.octa-trails.org
    PO Box 1019   Independence MO 64051
    Ph: 816-252-2276 ▪ Fx: 816-836-0989
Oregon Pioneers, Sons & Daughters of   www.webtrail.com/sdop
    PO Box 6685   Portland OR 97228
    Ph: 503-786-9804
Orff-Schulwerk Association, American   www.aosa.org
    PO Box 391089   Cleveland OH 44139
    Ph: 440-543-5366 ▪ Fx: 440-543-2687
Organ Builders of America, Associated Pipe   www.apoba.com
    PO Box 155   Chicago Ridge IL 60415
    Ph: 800-473-5270
(Organ Donor Education) Living Bank   www.livingbank.org
    PO Box 6725   Houston TX 77265
    Ph: 713-961-9431 ▪ Fx: 713-961-0979 ▪ TF: 800-528-2971
Organ Historical Society   www.organsociety.org
    PO Box 26861   Richmond VA 23261
    Ph: 804-353-9226 ▪ Fx: 804-353-9266
Organ Literature Foundation
    45 Norfolk Rd   Braintree MA 02184
    Ph: 781-848-1388 ▪ Fx: 781-848-7655
Organ Recovery & Education, Center for   www.core.org
    204 Sigma Dr   Pittsburgh PA 15238
    Ph: 800-366-6777 ▪ Fx: 412-963-3563
Organ Sharing, United Network for   www.unos.org
    700 N 4th St   Richmond VA 23219
    Ph: 804-330-8500 ▪ Fx: 804-782-4817 ▪ TF: 888-894-6361
Organ Society Inc, American Theatre   atos.org
Organ Transplant Association, American   www.a-o-t-a.org
    PO Box 41766   Houston TX 77244
    Ph: 281-493-2047 ▪ Fx: 281-493-2099

Organ Transplant Association, Children's　www.cota.org
2501 Cota Dr　Bloomington IN 47403
Ph: 812-336-8872　Fx: 812-336-8885　TF: 800-366-2682

Organbuilders, American Institute of　www.pipeorgan.org
PO Box 130982　Houston TX 77219
Ph: 713-529-2212

Organic Acidemia Association　www.oaanews.org
13210 35th Ave N　Plymouth MN 55441
Ph: 763-559-1797　Fx: 763-694-0017

Organic Chemical Manufacturers Association, Synthetic　www.socma.com
1850 M St NW Suite 700　Washington DC 20036
Ph: 202-721-4100　Fx: 202-296-8120

Organic Crop Improvement Association　www.ocia.org
6400 Cornhusker Hwy Suite 125　Lincoln NE 68507
Ph: 402-477-2323　Fx: 402-477-4325

Organic Reactions Catalysis Society　www.orcs.org

Organic Trade Association　www.ota.com
60 Wells St PO Box 547　Greenfield MA 01302
Ph: 413-774-7511　Fx: 413-774-6432

Organists, American Guild of　www.agohq.org
475 Riverside Dr Suite 1260　New York NY 10115
Ph: 212-870-2310　Fx: 212-870-2163　TF: 800-246-5115

Organization of American Historians　www.indiana.edu/~oah
112 N Bryan Ave　Bloomington IN 47408
Ph: 812-855-7311　Fx: 812-855-0696

Organization of American Kodaly Educators　www.oake.org
1612 29th Ave S　Moorhead MN 56560
Ph: 218-227-6253　Fx: 218-277-6254

Organization of American States　www.oas.org
1889 F St NW　Washington DC 20006
Ph: 202-458-3000　Fx: 202-458-3967

Organization of Biological Field Stations　www.obfs.org
Santa Margarita Ecological Reserve 2648 N Stagecoach
Ln　Fallbrook CA 92028
Ph: 760-728-9306　Fx: 760-451-0769

Organization of Black Airline Pilots　www.obap.org
8630 Fenton St Suite 126　Silver Spring MD 20910
Ph: 800-538-6227

Organization of Black Designers　www.core77.com/OBD
300 M St SW Suite N110　Washington DC 20024
Ph: 202-659-3918　Fx: 202-488-3838

Organization of Chinese Americans　www.ocanatl.org
1001 Connecticut Ave NW Suite 601　Washington DC 20036
Ph: 202-223-5500　Fx: 202-296-0540

Organization Development Institute　www.odinstitute.org
11234 Walnut Ridge Rd　Chesterland OH 44026
Ph: 440-729-7419　Fx: 440-729-9319

Organization Development Network　www.odnetwork.org
71 Valley St Suite 301　South Orange NJ 07079
Ph: 973-763-7337　Fx: 973-763-7448

Organization for Flora Neotropica　www.nybg.org/bsci/ofn
New York Botanical Garden　Bronx NY 10458
Ph: 718-817-8625　Fx: 718-817-8648

Organization for International Investment　www.ofii.org
1901 Pennsylvania Ave NW Suite 807　Washington DC 20006
Ph: 202-659-1903　Fx: 202-659-2293

Organization of News Ombudsmen　www.newsombudsmen.org
PO Box 120191　San Diego CA 92112
Ph: 619-293-1525

Organization of Parents Through Surrogacy　www.opts.com
PO Box 611　Gurnee IL 60031
Ph: 847-782-0224　Fx: 847-782-0240

Organization of Professional Acting Coaches & Teachers
3968 Eureka Dr　Studio City CA 91604
Ph: 323-877-4988

Organization for the Promotion & Advancement of Small Telecommunications Companies　www.opastco.org
21 Dupont Cir NW Suite 700　Washington DC 20036
Ph: 202-659-5990　Fx: 202-659-4619　TF: 800-828-1726

Organization of Regulatory & Clinical Associates　www.orcanw.org
PO Box 3490　Redmond WA 98052
Ph: 206-464-0825

Organization for Safety & Asepsis Procedures　www.osap.org
PO Box 6297　Annapolis MD 21401
Ph: 410-571-0003　Fx: 410-571-0028　TF: 800-298-6727

Organization for Tropical Studies　www.ots.duke.edu
410 Swift Ave　Durham NC 27708
Ph: 919-684-5774　Fx: 919-684-5661

Organization of Wildlife Planners　www.owpweb.org
402 W Washington St Rm W273　Indianapolis IN 46204
Ph: 317-232-4080　Fx: 317-232-8150

Organization of Women in International Trade　www.owit.org
1413 K St NW 1st Fl Suite 857　Washington DC 20005
Ph: 202-785-9842

Organizational Behavior Teaching Society　obtsweb.pitzer.edu

Organizational Psychology, Society for Industrial &　www.siop.org
PO Box 87　Bowling Green OH 43402
Ph: 419-353-0032　Fx: 419-352-2645

Organizational Systems Research Association　www.osra.org
Morehead State Univ UPO 2478　Morehead KY 40351
Ph: 606-783-2718　Fx: 606-783-5025

Organized Adoption Search Information Services
PO Box 53-0761　Miami Shores FL 33153
Ph: 305-947-8788

Organized Crime, International Association for the Study of　www.iasoc.net
c/o National Institute of Justice 810 7th St NW　Washington DC 20531
Ph: 202-616-1960　Fx: 202-307-6256

Organized Flying Adjusters Inc　www.ofainc.com
1501 Bluff Dr　Round Rock TX 78681
Ph: 512-255-2740　Fx: 512-246-1066

Organizers, National Association of Professional　www.napo.net
35 Technology Pkwy Suite 150　Norcross GA 30092
Ph: 770-325-3440　Fx: 770-325-8825

Organs, American Society for Artificial Internal　www.asaio.com
PO Box C　Boca Raton FL 33429
Ph: 561-391-8589　Fx: 561-368-9153

Orgonomy, American College of　www.orgonomy.org
PO Box 490　Princeton NJ 08542
Ph: 732-821-1144　Fx: 732-821-0174

Oriental Medicine Alliance, Acupuncture &　www.aomalliance.org
6405 43rd Avenue Ct NW Suite B　Gig Harbor WA 98335
Ph: 253-851-6896　Fx: 253-851-6883

Oriental Medicine, American Association of　www.aaom.org
5530 Wisconsin Ave Suite 1210　Chevy Chase MD 20815
Ph: 301-941-1064　Fx: 301-986-9313　TF: 888-500-7999

Oriental Medicine, Council of Colleges of Acupuncture &　www.ccaom.org
7501 Greenway Ctr Dr Suite 820　Greenbelt MD 20770
Ph: 301-313-0868　Fx: 301-313-0869

Oriental Research, American Schools of　www.asor.org
656 Beacon St 5th Fl　Boston MA 02215
Ph: 617-353-6570　Fx: 617-353-6575

Oriental Rug Retailers of America Inc　www.orrainc.com
PO Box 1191　Milwaukee WI 53201
Ph: 414-224-0448　Fx: 414-224-0480

Oriental Society, American　www.umich.edu/~aos
Univ of Michigan Hatcher Graduate Library　Ann Arbor MI 48109
Ph: 734-647-4760

Orientation Directors Association, National　www.nodaweb.org
Univ of Michigan-Flint 375 University Ctr　Flint MI 48502
Ph: 810-424-5513　Fx: 810-762-3023

Orienteering Federation, US　www.us.orienteering.org
PO Box 1444　Forest Park GA 30298
Ph: 404-363-2110

Original Doll Artists Council of America　www.odaca.org
2917 SW Fairview Blvd　Portland OR 97201
Ph: 503-222-5809

Original Equipment Suppliers Association　www.oesa.org
2950 W Square Lake Rd Suite 101　Troy MI 48098
Ph: 248-952-6401　Fx: 248-952-6404

Original Paper Doll Artists Guild　www.opdag.org
PO Box 14　Kingfield ME 04947
Ph: 207-265-2500

Ormoc Bay Association, Battle of　www.ormocbattle.com/veteran.htm
117 Tuscarora St　Harrisburg PA 17104
Ph: 717-238-0907

Ornamental Communicators Association, Turf &　www.toca.org
120 W Main St PO Box 156　New Prague MN 56071
Ph: 952-758-6340　Fx: 952-758-5813

Ornamental Concrete Producers Association　www.ornamentalconcrete.org
502 Kay Ave SE　Bemidji MN 56601
Ph: 218-751-1982　Fx: 218-751-2186

Ornamental Distributors Association, Independent Turf &　www.itoda.org
526 Brittany Dr　State College PA 16803
Ph: 814-238-1573　Fx: 814-238-7051

Ornamental Goldfish Growers Association, National
6916 Blacks Mill Rd　Thurmont MD 21788
Ph: 301-271-7475　Fx: 301-271-7059

Ornamental & Miscellaneous Metals Association, National　www.nomma.org
532-A Forest Pkwy　Forest Park GA 30297
Ph: 404-363-4009　Fx: 404-366-1852

Ornithological Club, Nuttall
c/o Museum of Comparative Zoology 26 Oxford St　Cambridge MA 02138
Ph: 617-495-2471

Ornithological Societies of North America　osna.allenmm.com
PO Box 11897　Lawrence KS 66044
Ph: 800-627-0629　Fx: 785-843-1274

Ornithological Society, Cooper　www.cooper.org
PO Box 1897　Lawrence KS 66044
Ph: 800-627-0629　Fx: 785-843-1274

Ornithologists, Association of Field　www.afonet.org
PO Box 1897　Lawrence KS 66044
Ph: 785-843-1221　Fx: 785-843-1274

Ornithologists' Union, American　www.aou.org
1313 Dolley Madison Blvd Suite 402　McLean VA 22101
Ph: 703-790-1745　Fx: 703-790-2672

Orofacial Pain, American Academy of　www.aaop.org
19 Mantua Rd　Mount Royal NJ 08061
Ph: 856-423-3629　Fx: 856-423-3420

Orphan Foundation of America　www.orphan.org
12020-D N Shore Dr　Reston VA 20190
Ph: 571-203-0270　Fx: 571-203-0203　TF: 800-950-4673

Orphan Train Heritage Society of America　www.orphantrainriders.com
614 E Emma Ave Suite 115　Springdale AR 72764
Ph: 479-756-2780

Orphanage, Wild Animal　www.wildanimalorphanage.org
9626 Leslie Rd PO Box 690422　San Antonio TX 78269
Ph: 210-688-9038　Fx: 210-688-9514

(Orphans) Nuestros Pequenos Hermanos　www.nphamigos.org
1210 Hillside Terr　Alexandria VA 22302
Ph: 703-836-1233　Fx: 703-836-3554

Orphans Support Association, Coptic　www.copticorphans.org
PO Box 2881　Merrifield VA 22116
Ph: 703-641-8910　Fx: 703-641-8787　TF: 800-499-2989

ORT, American　www.aort.org
817 Broadway 10th Fl　New York NY 10003
Ph: 212-353-5800　Fx: 212-353-5888　TF: 800-364-9678

ORT, Women's American   www.waort.org
315 Park Ave S   New York NY 10010
Ph: 212-505-7700   Fx: 212-674-3057   TF: 800-519-2678

Orthodontic Education & Research Foundation
3320 Rutger St   Saint Louis MO 63104
Ph: 314-577-8189   Fx: 314-268-5673

Orthodontics, American Association for Functional   www.aafo.org
106 S Kent St   Winchester VA 22601
Ph: 540-662-2200   Fx: 540-665-8910   TF: 800-441-3850

Orthodontics, American Board of   www.americanboardortho.com
401 N Lindbergh Blvd Suite 308   Saint Louis MO 63141
Ph: 314-432-6130   Fx: 314-432-8170

Orthodontics, College of Diplomates of the American Board of   www.cdabo.org
8005 W 110 St Suite 214   Overland Park KS 66210
Ph: 913-451-1443   Fx: 913-451-1453

Orthodontics, International Association for   www.iaortho.org
750 N Lincoln Memorial Dr Suite 422   Milwaukee WI 53202
Ph: 414-272-2757   Fx: 414-272-2754

Orthodontists, American Association of   www.aaomembers.org
401 N Lindbergh Blvd   Saint Louis MO 63141
Ph: 314-993-1700   Fx: 314-997-1745   TF: 800-424-2841

Orthodontists PAC, American Association of
401 N Lindbergh Blvd   Saint Louis MO 63141
Ph: 314-993-1700   Fx: 314-997-1745   TF: 800-424-2841

Orthodontists, World Federation of   www.wfo.org
401 N Lindbergh Blvd   Saint Louis MO 63141
Ph: 314-993-1700   Fx: 314-993-5208

Orthodox Bishops in the Americas, Standing Conference of Canonical   8 E 79th St   New York NY 10021   www.scoba.us
Ph: 212-570-3500   Fx: 212-570-3569

Orthodox Christian Charities, International   www.iocc.org
110 West Rd Suite 360   Baltimore MD 21204
Ph: 410-243-9820   Fx: 410-243-9824   TF: 877-803-4622

Orthodox Christians in America, Fellowship of   www.orthodoxfellowship.org
10 Downs Dr   Wilkes-Barre PA 18705
Ph: 570-825-3158   Fx: 570-825-0136

Orthodox Christians for Life   www.oclife.org
PO Box 805   Melville NY 11747
Ph: 631-271-4408

Orthodox Jewish Scientists, Association of   www.aojs.org
25 W 45th St Suite 1405   New York NY 10036
Ph: 212-840-1166   Fx: 212-840-1514

Orthodox Jewish Teachers, Association of
1577 Coney Island Dr   Brooklyn NY 11230
Ph: 718-258-3585   Fx: 718-258-3586

Orthodox Rabbis of the US & Canada, Union of
235 E Broadway   New York NY 10002
Ph: 212-964-6337

Orthodox Society of America   www.lcba.com/aboutsa.htm
PO Box 13005   Erie PA 16514
Ph: 814-453-4331   Fx: 814-453-3211   TF: 800-234-5222

Orthodox Theological Society in America   www.otsamerica.org
50 Goddard Ave   Brookline MA 02445
Ph: 617-731-3500

Orthodox Union   www.ou.org
11 Broadway   New York NY 10004
Ph: 212-563-4000   Fx: 212-564-9058

Orthopaedic Association, American   www.aoassn.org
6300 N River Rd Suite 505   Rosemont IL 60018
Ph: 847-318-7330   Fx: 847-318-7339

Orthopaedic Foot & Ankle Society, American   www.aofas.org
2517 Eastlake Ave E Suite 200   Seattle WA 98102
Ph: 206-223-1120   Fx: 206-223-1178   TF: 800-235-4855

Orthopaedic Medicine, American Association of   www.aaomed.org
PO Box 4997   Buena Vista CO 81211
Ph: 719-475-0032   Fx: 719-395-5615   TF: 800-922-2063

Orthopaedic Nurses Certification Board   www.orthonurse.org/certification/oncb.cfm
401 N Michigan Ave Suite 2200   Chicago IL 60611
Ph: 800-289-6266   Fx: 312-527-6658

Orthopaedic Nurses, National Association of   www.orthonurse.org
401 N Michigan Ave   Chicago IL 60611
Ph: 800-289-6266   Fx: 312-527-6658

Orthopaedic Physician's Assistants, American Society of   www.asopa.org
6300 N River Rd Suite 727   Rosemont IL 60018
Ph: 847-823-7186   Fx: 847-823-0536   TF: 800-998-6022

Orthopaedic Research & Education Foundation   www.oref.org/
6300 N River Rd Suite 700   Rosemont IL 60018
Ph: 847-698-9980   Fx: 847-698-7806

Orthopaedic Society, Academic   www.a-o-s.org
6300 N River Rd Suite 505   Rosemont IL 60018
Ph: 847-318-7330   Fx: 847-318-7339

Orthopaedic Society, Clinical   www.cosociety.org
PO Box 531823   Indianapolis IN 46253
Ph: 317-388-0329   Fx: 317-388-8984   TF: 800-843-9735

Orthopaedic Society, Ruth Jackson   www.rjos.org
6300 N River Rd Suite 727   Rosemont IL 60018
Ph: 847-698-1637   Fx: 847-823-0536

Orthopaedic Society for Sports Medicine, American   www.sportsmed.org
6300 N River Rd Suite 500   Rosemont IL 60018
Ph: 847-292-4900   Fx: 847-292-4905   TF: 877-321-3500

Orthopaedic Sports Medicine, International Society of Arthroscopy Knee Surgery &   2678 Bishop Dr Suite 250   San Ramon CA 94583   www.isakos.com
Ph: 925-807-1197   Fx: 925-807-1199

Orthopaedic Surgeons, American Academy of   www.aaos.org
6300 N River Rd   Rosemont IL 60018
Ph: 847-823-7186   Fx: 847-823-8125

Orthopaedic Surgeons, American Academy of Neurological &   www.aaanos.org
2300 S Rancho Dr Suite 202   Las Vegas NV 89102
Ph: 702-388-7390   Fx: 702-388-7395

Orthopaedic Surgeons, Society of Military   www.somos.org
810 North St   Belgium WI 53004
Ph: 262-285-4280   Fx: 262-285-4231

Orthopaedic Surgery, American Board of   www.abos.org
400 Silver Cedar Ct   Chapel Hill NC 27514
Ph: 919-929-7103   Fx: 919-942-8988

Orthopaedic Technologists, National Association of   www.naot.org
2950 Buskirk Ave Suite 170   Walnut Creek CA 94597
Ph: 925-472-5822   Fx: 925-472-5901

Orthopaedic Trauma Association   www.ota.org
6300 N River Rd Suite 727   Rosemont IL 60018
Ph: 847-698-1631   Fx: 847-823-0536

Orthopedic Foundation for Animals   www.offa.org
2300 E Nifong Blvd   Columbia MO 65201
Ph: 573-442-0418   Fx: 573-875-5073

Orthopedic Society of North America, Pediatric   www.posna.org
6300 N River Rd Suite 727   Rosemont IL 60018
Ph: 847-698-1692   Fx: 847-823-0536

Orthopedic Society, Veterinary   www.vet.ohio-state.edu/docs/vos
PO Box 313   Newmarket NH 03857
Ph: 603-659-7989

Orthopedic Surgical Manufacturers Association   www.osma.cc/
1962 Deep Valley Cove   Germantown TN 38138
Ph: 901-754-8097

Orthopedics, American Academy of Gnathologic   www.aago.com
2651 Oak Grove Rd   Walnut Creek CA 94598
Ph: 925-939-5024   Fx: 925-676-7678   TF: 800-510-2246

Orthopedics, American Osteopathic Academy of   www.aoao.org
PO Box 291690   Davie FL 33329
Ph: 954-262-1700   Fx: 954-262-1748   TF: 800-741-2626

Orthopedics, International College of Cranio-Mandibular   tmj-iccmo.org
619 N 35th St Suite 307   Seattle WA 98103
Ph: 206-633-4355   Fx: 206-633-4352   TF: 800-446-1763

Orthopedics & Medicine, American College of Foot & Ankle   www.acfaom.org
3525 Ellicott Mills Dr Suite N   Ellicott City MD 21043
Ph: 800-265-8263   Fx: 410-418-4805

Orthopedics & Primary Podiatric Medicine, American Board of Podiatric   22910 Crenshaw Blvd Suite B   Torrance CA 90505   www.abpoppm.org
Ph: 310-891-0100   Fx: 310-891-0500

Orthopedists, American College of Chiropractic   www.accoweb.org
1030 Broadway Suite 101   El Centro CA 92243
Ph: 760-370-9106   Fx: 760-352-3966

Orthopsychiatric Association, American   www.amerortho.org
2001 N Beauregard St 12th Fl   Alexandria VA 22311
Ph: 703-797-2584   Fx: 703-684-5968

Orthotic & Prosthetic Association, American   www.aopanet.org
330 John Carlyle St Suite 200   Alexandria VA 22314
Ph: 571-431-0876   Fx: 571-431-0899

Orthotics, US Member Society of the International Society for Prosthetics &   1161 Francisco Rd   Columbus OH 43220   www.usispo.org
Ph: 614-457-4312   Fx: 614-538-1914

Orthotists & Prosthetists, American Academy of   www.oandp.org
526 King St Suite 201   Alexandria VA 22314
Ph: 703-836-0788   Fx: 703-836-0737

Osborne Association   www.osborneny.org
36-31 38th St   Long Island City NY 11101
Ph: 718-707-2600   Fx: 718-707-3103

OSI Special Agents Inc, Association of Former   www.afosisa-ncc.org
PO Box 52315   Springfield VA 22152
Ph: 703-978-6198

Osseointegration, Academy of   www.osseo.org
85 W Algonquin Rd Suite 550   Arlington Heights IL 60005
Ph: 847-439-1919   Fx: 847-439-1569   TF: 800-656-7736

OsteoArthritis Research Society International   www.oarsi.org
17000 Commerce Pkwy Suite C   Mount Laurel NJ 08054
Ph: 856-439-1385   Fx: 856-439-0525

Osteogenesis Imperfecta Foundation   www.oif.org
804 W Diamond Ave Suite 210   Gaithersburg MD 20878
Ph: 301-947-0083   Fx: 301-947-0456   TF: 800-981-2663

Osteopathic Academy for Addiction Medicine, American
142 E Ontario St   Chicago IL 60611
Ph: 312-202-8163   Fx: 312-202-8463

Osteopathic Academy of Orthopedics, American   www.aoao.org
PO Box 291690   Davie FL 33329
Ph: 954-262-1700   Fx: 954-262-1748   TF: 800-741-2626

Osteopathic Academy of Sports Medicine, American   www.aoasm.org
7600 Terrace Ave Suite 203   Middleton WI 53562
Ph: 608-831-4400   Fx: 608-831-5185

Osteopathic Association, American   www.aoa-net.org
142 E Ontario St   Chicago IL 60611
Ph: 312-202-8000   Fx: 312-202-8200   TF: 800-621-1773

Osteopathic Board of Emergency Medicine, American   www.aobem.org
142 E Ontario St 8th Fl   Chicago IL 60611
Ph: 312-335-1065   Fx: 312-335-5489

Osteopathic Board of Family Physicians, American   www.aobfp.org
330 E Algonquin Rd Suite 6   Arlington Heights IL 60005
Ph: 847-640-8477

Osteopathic Board of Pediatrics, American   www.aobp.org
142 E Ontario St 6th Fl   Chicago IL 60611
Ph: 312-202-8267

Osteopathic College of Allergy & Immunology, American
7025 E McDowell Rd Suite 1-B   Scottsdale AZ 85257
Ph: 480-585-1580   Fx: 480-585-1581

Osteopathic College of Dermatology, American   www.aocd.org
1501 E Illinois St PO Box 7525   Kirksville MO 63501
Ph: 660-665-2184   Fx: 660-627-2623   TF: 800-449-2623

Osteopathic College of Occupational & Preventive Medicine, American   PO Box 2606   Leesburg VA 20177   www.aocopm.org
Ph: 800-558-8686   Fx: 703-443-0567

Osteopathic College of Ophthalmology, American www.aocoohns.org/aoco.htm
405 W Grand Ave   Dayton OH 45405
Ph: 937-222-8820 ▪ Fx: 937-222-8840 ▪ TF: 800-455-9404

Osteopathic College of Otolaryngology - Head & www.aocoohns.org/aocohns.htm
Neck Surgery, American   405 W Grand Ave   Dayton OH
45405
Ph: 937-222-8820 ▪ Fx: 937-222-8840 ▪ TF: 800-455-9404

Osteopathic College of Pathologists Inc, American www.aocp-net.org
142 E Ontario St   Chicago IL 60611
Ph: 312-202-8197 ▪ Fx: 312-202-8224

Osteopathic College of Physical Medicine & Rehabilitation, www.aocpmr.org
American   314 S Knight Ave   Park Ridge IL 60068
Ph: 847-825-2515 ▪ Fx: 847-825-2509

Osteopathic College of Radiology, American www.aocr.org
119 E 2nd St   Milan MO 63556
Ph: 660-265-4011 ▪ Fx: 660-265-3494 ▪ TF: 800-258-2627

Osteopathic College of Rheumatology, American
193 Monroe Ave   Edison NJ 08820
Ph: 732-494-6688 ▪ Fx: 732-494-6689

Osteopathic Directors & Medical Educators, Association of www.aodme.org
142 E Ontario St   Chicago IL 60611
Ph: 312-202-8211 ▪ Fx: 312-202-8224

Osteopathic Emergency Physicians, American College of www.acoep.org
142 E Ontario St Suite 1250   Chicago IL 60611
Ph: 312-587-3709 ▪ Fx: 312-587-9951 ▪ TF: 800-521-3709

Osteopathic Family Physicians, American College of www.acofp.org
330 E Algonquin Rd Suite 1   Arlington Heights IL 60005
Ph: 847-228-6090 ▪ Fx: 847-228-9755 ▪ TF: 800-323-0794

Osteopathic Internists, American College of www.acoi.org
3 Bethesda Metro Ctr Suite 508   Bethesda MD 20814
Ph: 301-656-8877 ▪ Fx: 301-656-7133 ▪ TF: 800-327-5183

Osteopathic Medical Association, Student www.studentdo.com
142 E Ontario St 6th Fl   Chicago IL 60611
Ph: 800-621-1772

Osteopathic Medicine, American Association of Colleges of www.aacom.org
5550 Friendship Blvd Suite 310   Chevy Chase MD 20815
Ph: 301-968-4100 ▪ Fx: 301-968-4101

Osteopathic Obstetricians & Gynecologists, American College of www.acoog.com
900 Auburn Rd   Pontiac MI 48342
Ph: 248-332-6360 ▪ Fx: 248-332-4607 ▪ TF: 800-875-6360

Osteopathic Pediatricians, American College of www.acopeds.org
142 E Ontario St   Chicago IL 60611
Ph: 312-202-8174 ▪ Fx: 312-202-8224 ▪ TF: 877-231-2267

Osteopathic Sclerotherapeutic Pain Management Inc, www.acopms.com
American College of   303 S Ingram Ct   Middletown DE 19709
Ph: 302-376-8080 ▪ Fx: 302-376-8081 ▪ TF: 800-471-6114

Osteopathic State Executive Directors, Association of
2007 Apalachee Pkwy   Tallahassee FL 32301
Ph: 850-878-7364 ▪ Fx: 850-942-7538

Osteopathic Surgeons, American College of www.facos.org
123 N Henry St   Alexandria VA 22314
Ph: 703-684-0416 ▪ Fx: 703-684-3280

Osteopathy, American Academy of www.academyofosteopathy.org
3500 DePauw Blvd Suite 1080   Indianapolis IN 46268
Ph: 317-879-1881 ▪ Fx: 317-879-0563

Osteoporosis Foundation, National www.nof.org
1232 22nd St NW   Washington DC 20037
Ph: 202-223-2226 ▪ Fx: 202-223-2237 ▪ TF: 800-223-9994

Ostomy Association, United www.uoa.org
19772 MacArthur Blvd Suite 200   Irvine CA 92612
Ph: 949-660-8624 ▪ Fx: 949-660-9262 ▪ TF: 800-826-0826

Ostomy & Continence Nurses Society, Wound www.wocn.org
4700 W Lake Ave   Glenview IL 60025
Ph: 888-224-9626 ▪ Fx: 866-615-8560

Ostrich Association, American www.ostriches.org
PO Box 163   Ranger TX 76470
Ph: 254-647-1645

Otolaryngic Allergy, American Academy of www.aaoaf.org
1900 M St NW Suite 680   Washington DC 20036
Ph: 202-955-5010 ▪ Fx: 202-955-5016

Otolaryngology Administrators, Association of www.oto-online.org
1805 Ardmore Blvd   Pittsburgh PA 15221
Ph: 412-243-5156 ▪ Fx: 412-243-5160

Otolaryngology, American Board of www.aboto.org
3050 Post Oak Blvd Suite 1700   Houston TX 77056
Ph: 713-850-0399 ▪ Fx: 713-850-1104

Otolaryngology, Association for Research in www.aro.org
19 Mantua Rd   Mount Royal NJ 08061
Ph: 856-423-0041 ▪ Fx: 856-423-3420

Otolaryngology-Head & Neck Surgery, American Academy of www.entnet.org
1 Prince St   Alexandria VA 22314
Ph: 703-836-4444 ▪ Fx: 703-683-5100

Otolaryngology - Head & Neck Surgery, American www.aocoohns.org/aocohns.htm
Osteopathic College of   405 W Grand Ave   Dayton OH 45405
Ph: 937-222-8820 ▪ Fx: 937-222-8840 ▪ TF: 800-455-9404

Otological Society, American otology-neurotology.org/AOS/AOS-home.html
2720 Tartan Way   Springfield IL 62707
Ph: 217-483-6966

Otological Society Inc, American Laryngological Rhinological & www.triological.org
555 N 30th St   Omaha NE 68131
Ph: 402-346-5500 ▪ Fx: 402-346-5300

Otorhinolaryngology & Head-Neck Nurses Inc, Society of www.sohnnurse.com
116 Canal St Suite A   New Smyrna Beach FL 32168
Ph: 386-428-1695 ▪ Fx: 386-423-7566

Otter, Friends of the Sea www.seaotters.org
2150 Garden Rd Suite A-3   Monterey CA 93940
Ph: 831-373-2747 ▪ Fx: 831-373-2749

Otterhound Club of America clubs.akc.org/ohca
2185 Seeman St SW   East Sparta OH 44626
Ph: 330-484-4845

Oughtred Society www.oughtred.org
2160 Middlefield Rd   Palo Alto CA 94301
Ph: 650-324-1821

Our Bodies Ourselves www.ourbodiesourselves.org
34 Plympton St   Boston MA 02118
Ph: 617-451-3666 ▪ Fx: 617-451-3664

Our Developing World www.magiclink.net/~odw
13004 Paseo Presada   Saratoga CA 95070
Ph: 408-379-4431 ▪ Fx: 408-376-0755

Our Lady of the Most Holy Trinity, Society of www.solt3.org
PO Box 152   Robstown TX 78380
Ph: 361-387-2754 ▪ Fx: 361-387-3818

(Outdoor Adventure) Outward Bound USA www.outwardbound.org
100 Mystery Point Rd   Garrison NY 10524
Ph: 845-424-4000 ▪ Fx: 845-424-4121 ▪ TF: 800-243-8520

Outdoor Advertising Association of America www.oaaa.org
1850 M St NW Suite 1040   Washington DC 20036
Ph: 202-833-5566 ▪ Fx: 202-833-1522

Outdoor Advertising Association of America PAC
1850 M St NW Suite 1040   Washington DC 20036
Ph: 202-833-5566 ▪ Fx: 202-833-1522

Outdoor Amusement Business Association www.oaba.org
1035 S Semoran Blvd Suite 1045A   Winter Park FL 32792
Ph: 407-681-9444 ▪ Fx: 407-681-9445 ▪ TF: 800-517-6222

Outdoor Amusement Business Association PAC www.oaba.org/pac.htm
1035 S Semoran Blvd Suite 1045A   Winter Park FL 32792
Ph: 407-681-9444 ▪ Fx: 407-681-9445

Outdoor Drama, Institute of www.unc.edu/depts/outdoor
Univ of North Carolina 1700 Airport Rd CB 3240   Chapel Hill
NC 27599
Ph: 919-962-1328 ▪ Fx: 919-962-4212

(Outdoor Enthusiasts) Prairie Club www.prairieclub.org
533 W North Ave Suite 10   Elmhurst IL 60126
Ph: 630-516-7277 ▪ Fx: 630-516-1278

Outdoor Ethics Inc, Leave No Trace Center for www.lnt.org
PO Box 997   Boulder CO 80306
Ph: 303-442-8222 ▪ Fx: 303-442-8217 ▪ TF: 800-332-4100

Outdoor Industry Association www.outdoorindustry.org
4909 Pearl East Cir Suite 200   Boulder CO 80301
Ph: 303-444-3353 ▪ Fx: 303-444-3284

Outdoor Power Equipment Aftermarket Association www.opeaa.org
1726 M St NW Suite 1101   Washington DC 20036
Ph: 202-775-8605 ▪ Fx: 202-833-1577

Outdoor Power Equipment & Engine Service Association www.opeesa.com
210 Allen Dr   Exton PA 19341
Ph: 610-363-3844 ▪ Fx: 610-363-3817

Outdoor Power Equipment Institute Inc opei.mow.org
341 S Patrick St   Alexandria VA 22314
Ph: 703-549-7600 ▪ Fx: 703-549-7604

Outdoor Recreation & Education, Association of www.aore.org
2705 Robin St   Bloomington IL 61704
Ph: 309-829-9189

Outdoor Recreation Liaison Officers, National Association of State
3116 Woodbrook Pl   Boise ID 83706
Ph: 208-384-5421

Outdoor Writers Association of America www.owaa.org
121 Hickory St Suite 1   Missoula MT 59801
Ph: 406-728-7434 ▪ Fx: 406-728-7445

Outdoors, America www.americaoutdoors.org
PO Box 10847   Knoxville TN 37939
Ph: 865-558-3595 ▪ Fx: 865-558-3598

Outdoors Conservancy, Great www.thegreatoutdoors.org
4311 Manatee Ave W Suite 210   Bradenton FL 34209
Ph: 941-708-3456 ▪ Fx: 941-708-3535

Outdoors Ministry Association, National Lutheran www.nloma.org
2016 Camp Lone Star Rd   La Grange TX 78945
Ph: 979-247-4128 ▪ Fx: 979-247-4120

Outer Critics Circle
101 W 57th St   New York NY 10019
Ph: 212-765-8557 ▪ Fx: 212-765-7979

OUTFEST www.outfest.org
3470 Wilshire Blvd Suite 1022   Los Angeles CA 90010
Ph: 213-480-7088 ▪ Fx: 213-180-7099

Outlaw & Lawman History Inc, National Association for www.outlawlawman.com
1917 Sutton Pl Trail   Harker Heights TX 76548
Ph: 254-698-6518

Outpatient Intravenous Infusion Therapy Association
PO Box 1234   Tacoma WA 98491
Ph: 253-272-4581 ▪ Fx: 253-272-0360

Outpatient Ophthalmic Surgery Society www.ooss.org
793-A Foothill Blvd PMB 119   San Luis Obispo CA 93405
Ph: 877-720-3585

OutProud www.outproud.org
369 3rd St Suite B362   San Rafael CA 94901
Ph: 415-460-5452 ▪ Fx: 415-460-5451

Outreach Association, American www.americanoutreach.org
PO Box 25042   Colorado Springs CO 80936
Ph: 719-592-1134

Outreach International www.outreach-international.org
PO Box 210   Independence MO 64051
Ph: 816-833-0883 ▪ Fx: 816-833-0103 ▪ TF: 888-833-1235

Outward Bound USA www.outwardbound.org
100 Mystery Point Rd   Garrison NY 10524
Ph: 845-424-4000 ▪ Fx: 845-424-4121 ▪ TF: 800-243-8520

Ovarian Cancer Coalition, National www.ovarian.org
500 NE Spanish River Blvd Suite 14   Boca Raton FL 33431
Ph: 561-393-0005 ▪ Fx: 561-393-7275 ▪ TF: 888-682-7426

Ovarian Cancer National Alliance www.ovariancancer.org
910 17th St NW Suite 413   Washington DC 20006
Ph: 202-331-1332 ▪ Fx: 202-292-2292

Ovarian Cancer Registry, Gilda Radner Familial www.ovariancancer.com
Roswell Park Cancer Institute Elm & Carlton Sts   Buffalo NY 14263
Ph: 716-845-4503 ▪ Fx: 716-845-8266 ▪ TF: 800-682-7426

Over the Hill Gang International www.othgi.com
1820 W Colorado Ave   Colorado Springs CO 80904
Ph: 719-389-0022 ▪ Fx: 719-389-0024

Overeaters Anonymous Inc www.oa.org
PO Box 44020   Rio Rancho NM 87174
Ph: 505-891-2664 ▪ Fx: 505-891-4320

(Overeaters) O-Anon
General Service Office PO Box 1314   North Fork CA 93643
Ph: 559-877-3615 ▪ Fx: 559-877-3015

Overseas Automotive Council www.oac-intl.org
10 Laboratory Dr PO Box 13966   Research Triangle Park NC 27709
Ph: 919-406-8810 ▪ Fx: 919-549-4824

Overseas Brats www.overseasbrats.com
PO Box 47112   Wichita KS 67201
Ph: 316-269-9610

Overseas Missionary Fellowship www.us.omf.org
10 W Dry Creek Cir   Littleton CO 80120
Ph: 303-730-4160 ▪ Fx: 303-730-4165 ▪ TF: 800-993-2751

Overseas Press Club of America www.opcofamerica.org
40 W 45th St   New York NY 10036
Ph: 212-626-9220 ▪ Fx: 212-626-9210

Overseas Research Centers, Council of American www.caorc.org
Smithsonian Institution PO Box 37012 NHB Rm CE-123 MRC 178   Washington DC 20013
Ph: 202-842-8636 ▪ Fx: 202-786-2430

Ovulation Method Association - USA, Billings www.boma-usa.org
PO Box 16206   Saint Paul MN 55116
Ph: 651-699-8139 ▪ Fx: 651-699-8144

Owner-Operator Independent Drivers Association www.ooida.com
1 NW OOIDA Dr   Grain Valley MO 64029
Ph: 816-229-5791 ▪ TF: 800-444-5791

Owners & Developers, Associated www.constructionchannel.net/aod
PO Box 4163   McLean VA 22103
Ph: 703-734-2397 ▪ Fx: 703-734-2908 ▪ TF: 888-999-2536

Oxfam America www.oxfamamerica.org
26 West St   Boston MA 02111
Ph: 617-482-1211 ▪ Fx: 617-728-2594 ▪ TF: 800-776-9326

Oxford Sheep Association, American
1960 E 2100 N Rd   Stonington IL 62567
Ph: 217-325-3515

Oxford Society, Shakespeare www.shakespeare-oxford.com
1556 Connecticut Ave NW Suite 200   Washington DC 20036
Ph: 202-207-0281

Oxygen Manufacturers Association, International www.iomaweb.org
1255 23rd St NW Suite 200   Washington DC 20037
Ph: 202-521-9300 ▪ Fx: 202-833-3636

Oxygenated Fuels Association www.ofa.net
1401 New York Ave NW Suite 520   Washington DC 20005
Ph: 202-393-6190 ▪ Fx: 202-393-6199

Oyate www.oyate.org
2702 Mathews St   Berkeley CA 94702
Ph: 510-848-6700 ▪ Fx: 510-848-4815

Ozar Hatorah www.shemayisrael.co.il/orgs/ozar
625 Broadway 5th Fl   New York NY 10012
Ph: 212-253-7245 ▪ Fx: 212-473-4773

Ozark Society www.ozarksociety.net
PO Box 2914   Little Rock AR 72203
Ph: 501-847-3738

Ozone Association, International www.int-ozone-assoc.org
31 Strawberry Hill Ave   Stamford CT 06902
Ph: 203-348-3542 ▪ Fx: 203-967-4845

P

PACE Association, National www.natlpaceassn.org
801 N Fairfax St Suite 309   Alexandria VA 22314
Ph: 703-535-1565 ▪ Fx: 703-535-1566

PACE International Union www.paceunion.org
3340 Perimeter Hill Dr   Nashville TN 37211
Ph: 615-834-8590 ▪ Fx: 615-834-7741

Pacer Club, AMC clubs.hemmings.com/amcpacer
2628 Queenston Rd   Cleveland Heights OH 44118
Ph: 216-371-0226

Pachyderm Clubs, National Federation of the Grand Order of www.pachyderms.org
511 Central Ave PO Box 1602   Great Falls MT 59403
Ph: 888-467-2249 ▪ Fx: 406-771-3941

Pacific 10 Conference www.pac-10.org
800 S Broadway Suite 400   Walnut Creek CA 94596
Ph: 925-932-4411 ▪ Fx: 925-932-4601

Pacific American Labor Alliance, Asian www.apalanet.org
815 16th St NW   Washington DC 20006
Ph: 202-974-8051 ▪ Fx: 202-974-8056

Pacific American Legal Consortium, National Asian www.napalc.org
1140 Connecticut Ave NW Suite 1200   Washington DC 20036
Ph: 202-296-2300 ▪ Fx: 202-296-2318

Pacific Asia Travel Association www.pata.org
1611 Telegraph Ave Suite 1515   Oakland CA 94612
Ph: 510-625-2055 ▪ Fx: 510-625-2044

Pacific Basin Development Council
711 Kapiolana Blvd Suite 1075   Honolulu HI 96813
Ph: 808-596-7229 ▪ Fx: 808-596-7249

Pacific Coast Federation of Fishermen's Associations www.pcffa.org
PO Box 29370   San Francisco CA 94159
Ph: 415-561-5080 ▪ Fx: 415-561-5464

Pacific Coast Shellfish Growers Association www.pcsga.org
120 State Ave NE PMB 142   Olympia WA 98501
Ph: 360-754-2744 ▪ Fx: 360-754-2743

Pacific Crest Trail Association www.pcta.org
5325 Elkhorn Blvd PMB 256   Sacramento CA 95842
Ph: 916-349-2109 ▪ Fx: 916-349-1268 ▪ TF: 888-728-7245

Pacific Dance, Foundation for home.att.net/~pacificdance
PO Box 621435   Littleton CO 80162
Ph: 303-933-2157

Pacific Dermatologic Association www.pacificderm.org
2950 Buskirk Ave Suite 170   Walnut Creek CA 94597
Ph: 925-472-5910 ▪ Fx: 925-472-5901

Pacific Dragon Boat Association www.pdbausa.org
PO Box 23693   Portland OR 97281
Ph: 503-639-2799 ▪ Fx: 503-670-1003

Pacific Fishery Management Council www.pcouncil.org
7700 NE Ambassador Pl Suite 200   Portland OR 97220
Ph: 503-820-2280 ▪ Fx: 503-820-2299 ▪ TF: 866-806-7204

Pacific Halibut Commission, International www.iphc.washington.edu
PO Box 95009   Seattle WA 98145
Ph: 206-634-1838 ▪ Fx: 206-632-2983

Pacific Institute for Studies in Development Environment & Security www.pacinst.org
654 13th St   Oakland CA 94612
Ph: 510-251-1600 ▪ Fx: 510-251-2203

Pacific Islander American Health Forum, Asian & www.apiahf.org
450 Sutter St Suite 600   San Francisco CA 94108
Ph: 415-954-9988 ▪ Fx: 415-954-9999

Pacific Islanders' Cultural Association www.pica-org.org
1016 Lincoln Blvd Suite 5   San Francisco CA 94131
Ph: 415-281-0221

Pacific Legal Foundation www.pacificlegal.org
10360 Old Placerville Rd Suite 100   Sacramento CA 95827
Ph: 916-362-2833 ▪ Fx: 916-362-2932

Pacific Logging Congress www.pacificloggingcongress.com
20816 SE 22nd St PO Box 1281   Maple Valley WA 98038
Ph: 425-413-2808 ▪ Fx: 425-413-1359

Pacific Northwest Grain & Feed Association www.pnwgfa.org
200 SW Market St Suite 348   Portland OR 97201
Ph: 503-227-0234 ▪ Fx: 503-227-0059

Pacific Northwest Trail Association www.pnt.org
PO Box 1817   Mount Vernon WA 98273
Ph: 877-854-9415

Pacific Ocean Research Foundation www.holoholo.org/porf
74-381 Kealakehe Pkwy Suite C   Kailua Kona HI 96740
Ph: 808-329-6105 ▪ Fx: 808-329-1148

Pacific Orchid Society of Hawaii honoluluorchsoc.tripod.com/pos.html
PO Box 1091   Honolulu HI 96808
Ph: 808-237-8672

Pacific Railroad Society www.pacificrailroadsociety.org
PO Box 80726   San Marino CA 91118
Ph: 213-283-0087

Pacific Research Institute for Public Policy www.pacificresearch.org
755 Sansome St Suite 450   San Francisco CA 94111
Ph: 415-989-0833 ▪ Fx: 415-989-2411

Pacific Rivers Council www.pacrivers.org
PO Box 10798   Eugene OR 97440
Ph: 541-345-0119 ▪ Fx: 541-345-0710

Pacific Rocket Society www.translunar.org/prs
PO Box 662   Mojave CA 93502
Ph: 661-824-1662

Pacific Seafood Processors Association www.pspafish.net
1900 W Emerson Pl Suite 205   Seattle WA 98119
Ph: 206-281-1667 ▪ Fx: 206-283-2387

Pacific States Marine Fisheries Commission www.psmfc.org
205 SE Spokane St Suite 100   Portland OR 97027
Ph: 503-595-3100 ▪ Fx: 503-595-3232

Pacific Telecommunications Council www.ptc.org/
2454 S Beretania St 3rd Fl   Honolulu HI 96826
Ph: 808-941-3789 ▪ Fx: 808-944-4874

Pacific Whale Foundation www.pacificwhale.org
300 Maalaea Rd Suite 211   Wailuku HI 96793
Ph: 808-879-8811 ▪ Fx: 808-243-9021 ▪ TF: 800-942-5311

Pacifica Radio Foundation www.pacifica.org
2390 Champlain St NW 2nd Fl   Washington DC 20009
Ph: 202-588-0999

Pacifist Party, US www.uspacifistparty.org
5729 S Dorchester Ave   Chicago IL 60637
Ph: 773-324-0654 ▪ Fx: 773-324-6426

Pacing Association Inc, International Trotting & www.trottingbreds.com
60 Gulf Rd   Gouverneur NY 13642
Ph: 315-287-2294 ▪ Fx: 315-287-5010

Packaged Ice Association, International www.packagedice.com
PO Box 1199   Tampa FL 33601
Ph: 813-258-1690 ▪ Fx: 813-251-2783 ▪ TF: 800-742-0627

Packaging Association, Contract Manufacturing & www.contractpackaging.org
519 N Highland Ave   Jackson TN 38301
Ph: 731-422-7994 ▪ Fx: 731-427-2430

Packaging Association, Flexible www.flexpack.org
971 Corporate Blvd Suite 403   Linthicum MD 21090
Ph: 410-694-0800 ▪ Fx: 410-694-0900

Packaging Association, International Molded Pulp Environmental www.impepa.org
1425 W Mequon Rd Suite A   Mequon WI 53092
Ph: 262-241-0522 ▪ Fx: 262-241-3766

Packaging Association, National Beverage
200 Dangerfield Rd   Alexandria VA 22314
Ph: 800-331-8816 ▪ Fx: 703-548-6563

Packaging Association, Reusable Industrial www.reusablepackaging.org
8401 Corporate Dr Suite 450   Landover MD 20785
Ph: 301-577-3786 ▪ Fx: 301-577-6476 ▪ TF: 800-533-3786

Packaging Council, Paperboard
201 N Union St Suite 220   Alexandria VA 22314
Ph: 703-836-3300 ▪ Fx: 703-836-3290
www.ppcnet.org

Packaging Council, Petroleum
111 E Avenida San Gabriel   San Clemente CA 92672
Ph: 949-369-7102 ▪ Fx: 949-366-1057
www.ppcouncil.org

Packaging Council, Polystyrene
1300 Wilson Blvd   Arlington VA 22209
Ph: 703-741-5000 ▪ Fx: 703-741-6000
www.polystyrene.org

Packaging Education Forum
4350 N Fairfax Dr Suite 600   Arlington VA 22203
Ph: 703-243-5717 ▪ Fx: 703-524-8691
www.packagingeducation.org

Packaging Foundation, International Corrugated
113 S West St PO Box 25708   Alexandria VA 22313
Ph: 703-836-2422 ▪ Fx: 703-836-2795
icpf.corrugated.org

Packaging Handling & Logistics Engineers, National Institute of
6902 Lyle St   Lanham MD 20706
Ph: 301-459-9105 ▪ Fx: 301-459-4925
www.niphle.com

Packaging Institute, Foodservice &
150 S Washington St Suite 204   Falls Church VA 22046
Ph: 703-538-2800 ▪ Fx: 703-538-2187
www.fpi.org

Packaging Institute, Glass
515 King St Suite 420   Alexandria VA 22314
Ph: 703-684-6359 ▪ Fx: 703-684-6048
www.gpi.org

Packaging Machinery Manufacturers Institute
4350 N Fairfax Dr Suite 600   Arlington VA 22203
Ph: 703-243-8555 ▪ Fx: 703-243-8556 ▪ TF: 800-275-7664
www.pmmi.org

Packaging Manufacturers Association, Retail
PO Box 17656   Covington KY 41017
Ph: 859-341-9623 ▪ Fx: 859-341-6211
www.retailpackaging.org

Packaging Professionals, Institute of
1601 N Bond St Suite 101   Naperville IL 60563
Ph: 630-544-5050 ▪ Fx: 630-544-5055 ▪ TF: 800-432-4085
www.iopp.org

Packaging Society, International Microelectronics &
611 2nd St NE   Washington DC 20002
Ph: 202-548-4001 ▪ Fx: 202-548-6115
www.imaps.org

Packaging Systems Inc, Research & Development Associates for Military Food &   16607 Blanco Rd Suite 1506   San Antonio TX 78232
Ph: 210-493-8024 ▪ Fx: 210-493-8036
www.militaryfood.org

Packaging, Women in
4290 Bells Ferry Rd Suite 106-17   Kennesaw GA 30144
Ph: 770-924-3563 ▪ Fx: 770-928-2338
womeninpackaging.org

Packard Club
PO Box 360806   Columbus OH 43236
Ph: 614-478-4946 ▪ Fx: 614-472-3222 ▪ TF: 800-478-0012
www.packardclub.org

Packard David & Lucile Foundation
300 2nd St Suite 200   Los Altos CA 94022
Ph: 650-948-7658 ▪ Fx: 650-948-5793
www.packard.org

Packard Humanities Institute
300 2nd St   Los Altos CA 94022
Ph: 650-948-0150 ▪ Fx: 650-948-4135

Packet Communications Consortium, International
2400 Camino Ramon Suite 275   San Ramon CA 94583
Ph: 925-275-6635 ▪ Fx: 925-275-6691
www.packetcomm.org

Paddleball Association, National
7642 Kingston Dr   Portage MI 49002
Ph: 616-323-0011 ▪ Fx: 616-279-6275
www.paddleball.org

Paddlesports Association, Professional
7432 Alban Stn Blvd Suite B232   Springfield VA 22150
Ph: 703-451-3864 ▪ Fx: 703-451-1015
www.propaddle.com

Paddlesports, Trade Association of
PO Box 6353   Olympia WA 98507
Ph: 360-352-0764 ▪ Fx: 360-352-0784 ▪ TF: 800-755-5228
www.gopaddle.com

Paget Foundation for Paget's Disease of Bone & Related Disorders
120 Wall St Suite 1602   New York NY 10005
Ph: 212-509-5335 ▪ Fx: 212-509-8492 ▪ TF: 800-237-2438
www.paget.org

Paideia Center, National
400 Silver Cedar Ct Suite 200   Chapel Hill NC 27514
Ph: 919-962-3128 ▪ Fx: 919-962-3139
www.paideia.org

Pain, American Academy of Craniofacial
516 W Pipeline Rd   Hurst TX 76053
Ph: 817-282-1501 ▪ Fx: 817-282-8012 ▪ TF: 800-322-8651
www.aacfp.org

Pain, American Academy of Orofacial
19 Mantua Rd   Mount Royal NJ 08061
Ph: 856-423-3629 ▪ Fx: 856-423-3420
www.aaop.org

Pain Association, American Chronic
PO Box 850   Rocklin CA 95677
Ph: 916-632-0922 ▪ Fx: 916-632-3208 ▪ TF: 800-533-3231
www.theacpa.org

Pain, International Association for the Study of
909 NE 43rd St Suite 306   Seattle WA 98105
Ph: 206-547-6409 ▪ Fx: 206-547-1703
www.iasp-pain.org

Pain Management, American Academy of
13947 Mono Way Suite A   Sonora CA 95370
Ph: 209-533-9744 ▪ Fx: 209-533-9750
www.aapainmanage.org

Pain Management Inc, American College of Osteopathic Sclerotheraputic   303 S Ingram Ct   Middletown DE 19709
Ph: 302-376-8080 ▪ Fx: 302-376-8081 ▪ TF: 800-471-6114
www.acopms.com

Pain Management Nurses, American Society of
7794 Grow Dr   Pensacola FL 32514
Ph: 850-473-0233 ▪ Fx: 850-484-8762 ▪ TF: 888-342-7766
www.aspmn.org

Pain Medicine, American Academy of
4700 W Lake Ave   Glenview IL 60025
Ph: 847-375-4731 ▪ Fx: 847-375-6331 ▪ TF: 877-734-8750
www.painmed.org

Pain Medicine, American Society of Regional Anesthesia &
PO Box 11086   Richmond VA 23230
Ph: 804-282-0010 ▪ Fx: 804-282-0090
www.asra.com

Pain Outreach Association, National Chronic
PO Box 274   Millboro VA 24460
Ph: 540-862-9437 ▪ Fx: 540-862-9485
www.chronicpain.org

Pain Society, American
4700 W Lake Ave   Glenview IL 60025
Ph: 847-375-4715 ▪ Fx: 847-375-4777
www.ampainsoc.org

Paint & Coatings Association, National
1500 Rhode Island Ave NW   Washington DC 20005
Ph: 202-462-6272 ▪ Fx: 202-462-8549
www.paint.org

Paint & Decorating Retailers Association
403 Axminister Dr   Fenton MO 63026
Ph: 636-326-2636 ▪ Fx: 636-326-1823 ▪ TF: 800-737-0107
www.pdra.org

Paint Horse Association, American
PO Box 961023   Fort Worth TX 76161
Ph: 817-834-2742 ▪ Fx: 817-834-3152
www.apha.com

Paint Horse Association, American Junior
PO Box 961023   Fort Worth TX 76161
Ph: 817-834-2746 ▪ Fx: 817-834-3152
www.ajpha.com

Painters & Allied Trades, International Union of
1750 New York Ave NW 8th Fl   Washington DC 20006
Ph: 202-637-0700 ▪ Fx: 202-637-0771
www.ibpat.org

Painters, National Society of Mural
c/o American Fine Arts Society 215 W 57th St   New York NY 10019
Ph: 212-941-0130 ▪ Fx: 212-941-0138

Painters & Sculptors, Federation of Modern
234 W 21st St   New York NY 10011
Ph: 212-255-4858

Painters, Society of Decorative
393 N McLean Blvd   Wichita KS 67203
Ph: 316-269-9300 ▪ Fx: 316-269-9191
www.decorativepainters.org

Painters Society, National Oil & Acrylic
PO Box 676   Osage Beach MO 65049
Ph: 417-533-7550
www.noaps.org

Painters, World Organization of China
2641 NW 10th St   Oklahoma City OK 73107
Ph: 405-521-1234 ▪ Fx: 405-521-1265
www.theshop.net/wocporg

Painting & Decorating Contractors of America
11960 Westline Industrial Dr Suite 201   Saint Louis MO 63146
Ph: 314-514-7322 ▪ Fx: 314-514-9417 ▪ TF: 800-332-7322
www.pdca.com

(Painting) Sumi-e Society of America
5321 Long Sky Ct   Columbia MD 21045
Ph: 410-730-7597
www.sumiesociety.org

Pakistani Physicians of North America, Association of
6414 S Cass Ave   Westmont IL 60559
Ph: 630-968-8585 ▪ Fx: 630-968-8677
www.appna.com

Palatines to America
611 E Weber Rd   Columbus OH 43211
Ph: 614-267-4700 ▪ Fx: 614-267-4888
www.palam.org

Palau Luis Evangelistic Association
PO Box 50   Portland OR 97207
Ph: 503-614-1500 ▪ Fx: 503-614-1599
www.palau.org

Paleontological Research Institution
1259 Trumansburg Rd   Ithaca NY 14850
Ph: 607-273-6623 ▪ Fx: 607-273-6620
www.priweb.org

Paleontological Society
www.paleosoc.org

Palestine, Center for Policy Analysis on
2425-35 Virginia Ave NW   Washington DC 20037
Ph: 202-338-1290 ▪ Fx: 202-338-7742
www.palestinecenter.org

Palestine/Israel, SEARCH for Justice & Equality in
PO Box 3452   Framingham MA 01705
Ph: 508-879-0777 ▪ Fx: 508-877-2611
searchforjustice.org

Palestine Liberation Organization
1320 18th St NW Suite 200   Washington DC 20036
Ph: 202-974-6360

Palestine Studies, Institute for
3501 M St NW   Washington DC 20007
Ph: 202-342-3990 ▪ Fx: 202-342-3927 ▪ TF: 800-874-3614
www.ipsjps.org

Palestinian Peace, America-Israel Council for Israeli-
224 Lake Dr   Kensington CA 94708
Ph: 510-526-8449
otherisrael.home.igc.org

Pallet & Container Association, National Wooden
329 S Patrick St   Alexandria VA 22314
Ph: 703-519-6104 ▪ Fx: 703-519-4720
www.nwpca.com

Palliative Care Organization, National Hospice &
1700 Diagonal Rd Suite 625   Alexandria VA 22314
Ph: 703-837-1500 ▪ Fx: 703-837-1233 ▪ TF: 800-658-8898
www.nhpco.org

Palliative Medicine, American Academy of Hospice &
4700 W Lake Ave   Glenview IL 60025
Ph: 847-375-4712 ▪ Fx: 877-734-8671
www.aahpm.org

Palliative Nurses Association, Hospice &
Penn Ctr W 1 Suite 229   Pittsburgh PA 15276
Ph: 412-787-9301 ▪ Fx: 412-787-9305
www.hpna.org

Pallotti Center for Apostolic Development, Saint Vincent
415 Michigan Ave NE   Washington DC 20017
Ph: 202-529-3330 ▪ Fx: 202-529-0911 ▪ TF: 877-865-5465
www.pallotticenter.org

Palm Society, International
PO Box 7075   Lawrence KS 66044
Ph: 785-843-1235 ▪ Fx: 785-843-1274
www.palms.org

Palomino Horse Association
HCR 63 Box 24   Dornsife PA 17823
Ph: 570-758-3067 ▪ Fx: 570-758-5336
www.palominohorseassoc.com

Palomino Horse Breeders of America
15253 E Skelly Dr   Tulsa OK 74116
Ph: 918-438-1234 ▪ Fx: 918-438-1232
www.palominohba.com

Palsy Association Inc, National Brachial Plexus/Erb's
PO Box 23   Larsen WI 54947
Ph: 920-836-2151
www.nbpepa.org

Palsy, Society for Progressive Supranuclear
1838 Greene Tree Rd   Baltimore MD 21208
Ph: 410-486-3330 ▪ Fx: 410-486-4283 ▪ TF: 800-457-4777
www.psp.org

Palynologists, American Association of Stratigraphic — www.palynology.org
600 N Dairy Ashford PO Box 2197   Houston TX 77252
Ph: 281-293-3189 ▪ Fx: 281-293-3833

Pan American Development Foundation — www.padf.org
2600 16th St NW 4th Fl   Washington DC 20009
Ph: 202-458-3969 ▪ Fx: 202-458-6316

Pan American Health Organization — www.paho.org
525 23rd St NW   Washington DC 20037
Ph: 202-974-3000 ▪ Fx: 202-974-3663

Pan-American Indian Association
8335 Sevigny Dr   North Fort Myers FL 33917
Ph: 239-543-7727

Pan-American Junior Golf Association, National — npaga.callernetwork.com/junior.html
4813 Larcade Dr   Corpus Christi TX 78415
Ph: 361-853-6860 ▪ Fx: 361-854-7242

Pan American Taekwondo Union — www.patu.org
440 S Washington St   Falls Church VA 22046
Ph: 703-534-3737 ▪ Fx: 703-536-3223

Pan Arcadian Federation of America — www.panarcadian.org
880 N York Rd   Elmhurst IL 60126
Ph: 630-833-1900 ▪ Fx: 630-833-1956

Pancreatic Association, American
UCLA School of Medicine 10833 LeConte Ave CHS72-259   Los Angeles CA 90095
Ph: 310-825-4976 ▪ Fx: 310-206-2472

Pancreato-Biliary Association, American Hepato- — www.ahpba.org
11300 W Olympic Blvd Suite 600   Los Angeles CA 90064
Ph: 310-437-0557 ▪ Fx: 310-437-0585

Panel Association, Composite — www.pbmdf.com
18922 Premiere Ct   Gaithersburg MD 20879
Ph: 301-670-0604 ▪ Fx: 301-840-1252

Panel Association, Structural Insulated — www.sips.org
PO Box 1699   Gig Harbor WA 98335
Ph: 253-858-7472 ▪ Fx: 253-858-0272

Panhellenic Conference, National — www.npcwomen.org
3905 Vincennes Rd Suite 105   Indianapolis IN 46268
Ph: 317-872-3185 ▪ Fx: 317-872-3192

Panos Institute — www.panosinst.org
1322 18th St NW Suite 26   Washington DC 20006
Ph: 202-429-0730

Paper Association, American Forest & — www.afandpa.org
1111 19th St NW Suite 800   Washington DC 20036
Ph: 202-463-2700 ▪ Fx: 202-463-2785 ▪ TF: 800-878-8878

Paper Doll Artists Guild, Original — www.opdag.com
PO Box 14   Kingfield ME 04947
Ph: 207-265-2500

Paper Industry, Association of Suppliers to the — www.aspinet.org
201 Park Washington Ct   Falls Church VA 22046
Ph: 703-538-1787 ▪ Fx: 703-241-5603

Paper Industry Management Association — pima-online.org
PO Box 3781   Oak Brook IL 60025
Ph: 847-375-6860 ▪ Fx: 877-527-5973

Paper Industry, Technical Association of the Pulp & — www.tappi.org
15 Technology Pkwy S   Norcross GA 30092
Ph: 770-446-1400 ▪ Fx: 770-446-6947 ▪ TF: 800-332-8686

(Paper & Packaging) NPTA Alliance — www.gonpta.com
500 Bi-County Blvd Suite 200E   Farmingdale NY 11735
Ph: 631-777-2223 ▪ Fx: 631-777-2224 ▪ TF: 800-355-6782

Paper & Plastic Representatives Management Council — www.pprmc.com
PO Box 150229   Arlington TX 76015
Ph: 817-561-7272 ▪ Fx: 817-561-7275

Paper Science & Technology, Institute of — www.ipst.edu
500 10th St NW   Atlanta GA 30318
Ph: 404-894-5700 ▪ Fx: 404-894-4778 ▪ TF: 800-558-6611

Paper Shipping Sack Manufacturers' Association — www.pssma.org
520 E Oxford St   Coopersburg PA 19036
Ph: 610-282-6845 ▪ Fx: 610-282-6921

Paper Workers, Association of Western Pulp & — www.awppw.org
PO Box 4566   Portland OR 97208
Ph: 503-228-7486 ▪ Fx: 503-228-1346

Paperback Association, Educational — www.edupaperback.org
PO Box 1399   East Hampton NY 11937
Ph: 212-879-6850

Paperboard Packaging Council — www.ppcnet.org
201 N Union St Suite 220   Alexandria VA 22314
Ph: 703-836-3300 ▪ Fx: 703-836-3290

Paperboard Technical Association, Recycled
920 Davis Rd Suite 306   Elgin IL 60123
Ph: 847-622-2544 ▪ Fx: 847-622-2546

Paperbox Association, National — www.paperbox.org
113 S West St 3rd Fl   Alexandria VA 22313
Ph: 703-684-2212 ▪ Fx: 703-683-6920

Papercutters, Guild of American — www.papercutters.org

Paperhangers, National Guild of Professional — www.ngpp.org
136 S Keowee St   Dayton OH 45402
Ph: 937-222-6477 ▪ Fx: 937-222-5794 ▪ TF: 800-254-6477

Papers of America, Independent Free — www.ifpa.com
107 Hemlock Dr   Rio Grande NJ 08242
Ph: 609-886-0141 ▪ Fx: 609-889-8835 ▪ TF: 800-441-4372

Papers, Association of Free Community — www.afcp.org
1634 Miner St PO Box 1989   Idaho Springs CO 80452
Ph: 877-203-2327

Papers, Association of State Baptist
c/o The Alabama Baptist Newspaper 3310 Independence Dr   Birmingham AL 35209
Ph: 205-870-4720 ▪ Fx: 205-870-8957

Paperweight Society, International — www.paperweight.com
123 Locust St   Santa Cruz CA 95060
Ph: 831-427-1177 ▪ Fx: 831-427-0111 ▪ TF: 800-538-0766

Paperworkers International Union, United
PO Box 1475   Nashville TN 37202
Ph: 615-834-8590 ▪ Fx: 615-831-6791

Papyrologists, American Society of — www.papyrology.org

Parachute Association, US — www.uspa.org
1440 Duke St   Alexandria VA 22314
Ph: 703-836-3495 ▪ Fx: 703-836-2843 ▪ TF: 800-371-8772

Paraffins Industry Association, Chlorinated — www.regnet.com/cpia
1250 Connecticut Ave NW Suite 700   Washington DC 20036
Ph: 202-637-9040 ▪ Fx: 202-637-9178

Paralegal Association, National — www.nationalparalegal.org
PO Box 406   Solebury PA 18963
Ph: 215-297-8333 ▪ Fx: 215-297-8358

Paralegal Associations, National Federation of — www.paralegals.org
2517 Eastlake Ave E Suite 200   Seattle WA 98102
Ph: 206-652-4120 ▪ Fx: 206-652-4122

Paralegal Educators, American Association for — www.aafpe.org
407 Wekiva Springs Rd Suite 241   Longwood FL 32779
Ph: 407-834-6688 ▪ Fx: 407-834-4747

Paralysis Foundation, Christopher Reeve — www.christopherreeve.org
500 Morris Ave   Springfield NJ 07081
Ph: 973-379-2690 ▪ Fx: 973-912-9433 ▪ TF: 800-225-0292

Paralyzed Veterans of America — www.pva.org
801 18th St NW   Washington DC 20006
Ph: 202-872-1300 ▪ Fx: 202-416-7641 ▪ TF: 800-424-8200

Paramedics Association, National Flight — www.flightparamedic.org
383 F St   Salt Lake City UT 84103
Ph: 800-381-6372

Parametric Analysts, International Society of — www.ispa-cost.org
PO Box 9699   Canoga Park CA 91309
Ph: 818-888-3419 ▪ Fx: 818-888-8362

Paranormal, Committee for the Scientific Investigation of Claims of the — www.csicop.org
PO Box 703   Amherst NY 14226
Ph: 716-636-1425 ▪ Fx: 716-636-1733 ▪ TF: 800-634-1610

Paraplegia Society, American — www.apssci.org
75-20 Astoria Blvd   Jackson Heights NY 11370
Ph: 718-803-3782 ▪ Fx: 718-803-0414

Paraprofessionals, National Resource Center for — www.nrcpara.org
Utah State Univ 6526 Old Main Hill   Logan UT 84322
Ph: 435-797-7272

Parapsychological Association — www.parapsych.org

Parapsychology Foundation — www.parapsychology.org
228 E 71st St   New York NY 10021
Ph: 212-628-1550 ▪ Fx: 212-628-1559

Parasitologists, American Association of Veterinary — www.aavp.org
2001 W Main St MS GL52 PO Box 708   Greenfield IN 46140
Ph: 317-277-4439 ▪ Fx: 317-651-4532

Parasitologists, American Society of — asp.unl.edu

Paratransit Association, Taxicab Limousine & — www.tlpa.org
3849 Farragut Ave   Kensington MD 20895
Ph: 301-946-5701 ▪ Fx: 301-946-4641

Parcel Shippers Association — www.parcelshippers.org
1211 Connecticut Ave NW Suite 610   Washington DC 20036
Ph: 202-296-3690 ▪ Fx: 202-296-0343

Parent Association, National Foster — www.nfpainc.org
7512 Stanich Ave Suite 6   Gig Harbor WA 98335
Ph: 253-853-4000 ▪ Fx: 253-853-4001 ▪ TF: 800-557-5238

Parent Cooperative Preschools International — preschools.coop
1401 New York Ave NW Suite 1100   Washington DC 20005
Ph: 800-636-6222 ▪ Fx: 202-347-1968

Parent Network — www.tma-el.org/Parentnetwork.htm
530 E Day Rd   Mishawaka IN 46545
Ph: 574-256-5313 ▪ Fx: 574-256-5493

Parent Resource Center, Single — singleparentusa.com
31 E 28th St Fl 2   New York NY 10016
Ph: 212-951-7030 ▪ Fx: 212-951-7037

Parent Support Group, Freeman-Sheldon — www.fspsg.org
509 E Northmont Way   Salt Lake City UT 84103
Ph: 801-364-7060

Parenteral & Enteral Nutrition, American Society for — www.clinnutr.org
8630 Fenton St Suite 412   Silver Spring MD 20910
Ph: 301-587-6315 ▪ Fx: 301-587-2365 ▪ TF: 800-727-4567

Parenthood Federation of America, Planned — www.plannedparenthood.org
810 7th Ave   New York NY 10019
Ph: 212-541-7800 ▪ Fx: 212-245-1845 ▪ TF: 800-829-7732

Parenthood Federation - Western Hemisphere Region, International Planned — www.ippfwhr.org
120 Wall St 9th Fl   New York NY 10005
Ph: 212-248-6400 ▪ Fx: 212-248-4221

Parenting Association, National — www.parentsunite.org
PO Box 77   New York NY 10113
Ph: 212-229-5990 ▪ Fx: 212-679-3127 ▪ TF: 800-709-8795

Parenting & Prevention Inc, National Organization on Adolescent Pregnancy — www.noappp.org
2401 Pennsylvania Ave NW Suite 350   Washington DC 20037
Ph: 202-293-8370 ▪ Fx: 202-293-8805 ▪ TF: 888-766-2777

Parenting Publications of America — www.parentingpublications.org
4929 Wilshire Blvd Suite 428   Los Angeles CA 90010
Ph: 323-937-5514 ▪ Fx: 323-937-0959

Parents Active for Vision Education — www.pavevision.org
4135 54th Pl   San Diego CA 92105
Ph: 619-287-0081 ▪ Fx: 619-287-0084 ▪ TF: 800-728-3988

Parents of America, College — www.collegeparents.org
8300 Boone Blvd Suite 500   Vienna VA 22182
Ph: 703-761-6702 ▪ TF: 888-256-4627

Parents Anonymous Inc — www.parentsanonymous.org
675 W Foothill Blvd Suite 220   Claremont CA 91711
Ph: 909-621-6184 ▪ Fx: 909-625-6304

Parents Association, National www.bixxo.com/npa
603 E Lincoln Way Ave Main Stn Box 1993 Valparaiso IN 46383
Ph: 219-462-9996 ▪ Fx: 219-464-3538

Parents of Blind Children, National Organization of www.nfb.org/nopbc/nopbc_what.htm
1800 Johnson St Baltimore MD 21230
Ph: 410-659-9314

Parents of Children with Visual Impairments, National Association for PO Box 317 Watertown MA 02471 www.spedex.com/napvi
Ph: 617-972-7441 ▪ Fx: 617-972-7444 ▪ TF: 800-562-6265

Parents of Children Who Are Deaf or Hard of Hearing Inc, BEGINNINGS for PO Box 17646 Raleigh NC 27619 www.ncbegin.org
Ph: 919-850-2746 ▪ Fx: 919-850-2804 ▪ TF: 800-541-4327

Parents' Choice Foundation www.parents-choice.org
201 W Padonia Rd Suite 303 Timonium MD 21093
Ph: 410-308-3858 ▪ Fx: 410-308-3877

Parents in Control www.parentsincontrol.org
PO Box 2232 Olathe KS 66051
Ph: 877-426-4742 ▪ Fx: 913-764-4492

Parents Families & Friends of Lesbians & Gays www.pflag.org
1726 M St NW Suite 400 Washington DC 20036
Ph: 202-467-8180 ▪ Fx: 202-467-8194

Parents & Friends of Ex-Gays www.pfox.org
PO Box 561 Fort Belvoir VA 22060
Ph: 703-739-8220

Parents Helping Parents www.php.com
3041 Olcott St Santa Clara CA 95054
Ph: 408-727-5775 ▪ Fx: 408-727-0182

Parents of Murdered Children www.pomc.com
100 E 8th St Suite B-41 Cincinnati OH 45202
Ph: 513-721-5683 ▪ Fx: 513-345-4489 ▪ TF: 888-818-7662

Parents, National Association of Entrepreneurial www.en-parent.com/NAEP.htm
PO Box 320722 Fairfield CT 06432
Ph: 203-371-6212

Parents Network, New www.npn.org
PO Box 64237 Tucson AZ 85728
Ph: 520-327-1451 ▪ Fx: 520-844-1854

Parents Organization, Adoptees & Natural
949 Lacon Dr Newport News VA 23608
Ph: 757-874-9091

Parents Rights Organization
12571 Northwinds Dr Saint Louis MO 63146
Ph: 314-434-4171 ▪ Fx: 314-997-6321

Parents & Teachers Against Violence in Education www.nospank.net
PO Box 1033 Alamo CA 94507
Ph: 925-831-1661 ▪ Fx: 925-838-8914

Parents & Teachers, National Congress of www.pta.org
330 N Wabash Ave Suite 2100 Chicago IL 60611
Ph: 312-670-6782 ▪ Fx: 312-670-6783 ▪ TF: 800-307-4782

Parents Television Council www.parentstv.org
707 Wilshire Blvd Suite 2075 Los Angeles CA 90017
Ph: 213-629-9255 ▪ Fx: 213-629-9254 ▪ TF: 800-882-6868

Parents Through Surrogacy, Organization of www.opts.com
PO Box 611 Gurnee IL 60031
Ph: 847-782-0224 ▪ Fx: 847-782-0240

Parents Without Partners www.parentswithoutpartners.org
1650 S Dixie Hwy Suite 510 Boca Raton FL 33432
Ph: 561-391-8833 ▪ Fx: 561-395-8557 ▪ TF: 800-637-7974

Parents, World Association for Children & www.wacap.org
315 S 2nd St Renton WA 98055
Ph: 206-575-4550 ▪ Fx: 206-575-4148

Paris Opera & Ballet, American Friends of the
972 5th Ave New York NY 10021
Ph: 212-439-1426 ▪ Fx: 212-439-1455

Parish Clergy, Academy of www.apclergy.org
1851 King James Pkwy Suite 322 Westlake OH 44145
Ph: 440-835-0931

Parishes for Liturgy & Mission, Associated www.associatedparishes.org
PO Box 27141 Baltimore MD 21230
Ph: 410-752-0877

Park Academy of the Arts, National www.artsfortheparks.com
PO Box 608 Jackson Hole WY 83001
Ph: 307-733-2787 ▪ Fx: 307-739-1199 ▪ TF: 800-553-2787

Park Association, National Recreation & www.nrpa.org
22377 Belmont Ridge Rd Ashburn VA 20148
Ph: 703-858-0784 ▪ Fx: 703-858-0794 ▪ TF: 800-626-6772

Park Association, San Francisco Maritime National www.maritime.org
PO Box 470310 San Francisco CA 94147
Ph: 415-561-6662 ▪ Fx: 415-561-6660

Park Association, Shenandoah National www.snpbooks.org
3655 US Hwy 211 E Luray VA 22835
Ph: 540-999-3582 ▪ Fx: 540-999-3583

Park Directors, National Association of State naspd.indstate.edu
9894 E Holden Pl Tucson AZ 85748
Ph: 520-298-4924 ▪ Fx: 520-298-6515

Park Foundation, National www.nationalparks.org
11 Dupont Cir NW Suite 600 Washington DC 20036
Ph: 202-785-4200 ▪ Fx: 202-785-3103 ▪ TF: 888-407-2757

Park & Grounds Management, National Institute on www.nipgm.org
PO Box 5162 De Pere WI 54115
Ph: 920-339-9057

Park Hospitality Association, National www.nphassn.org
3701 Court House Dr Ellicott City MD 21043
Ph: 410-480-2240 ▪ Fx: 410-480-2617

Park & Recreation Educators, Society of www.nrpa.org
c/o National Recreation & Park Assn 22377 Belmont Ridge Rd Ashburn VA 20148
Ph: 703-858-0784 ▪ Fx: 703-858-0794

Park & Recreation Officials, National Association of County www.nacpro.org
c/o Harris County Public Infrastructure Dept 1001 Preston Ave 7th Fl Houston TX 77002
Ph: 713-755-5583

Park & Recreation Society, American
c/o National Recreation & Park Assn 22377 Belmont Ridge Rd Ashburn VA 20148
Ph: 703-858-4741 ▪ Fx: 703-858-0794

Park Resources, National Society for
c/o National Recreation & Park Assn 22377 Belmont Ridge Rd Ashburn VA 20148
Ph: 703-858-0784 ▪ Fx: 703-858-0794

Park & Trail Foundation, Ice Age www.iceagetrail.org
207 E Buffalo St Suite 515 Milwaukee WI 53202
Ph: 414-278-8518 ▪ Fx: 414-278-8665 ▪ TF: 800-227-0046

Park Trust, National www.parktrust.org
415-2nd St NE Suite 210 Washington DC 20002
Ph: 202-548-0500 ▪ Fx: 202-548-0595

Parking Association, National www.npapark.org
1112 16th St NW Suite 300 Washington DC 20036
Ph: 202-296-4336 ▪ Fx: 202-331-8523 ▪ TF: 800-647-7275

Parking Institute, International www.parking.org
PO Box 7167 Fredericksburg VA 22404
Ph: 540-371-7535 ▪ Fx: 540-371-8022

Parkinson Disease Association, American www.apdaparkinson.com
1250 Hyland Blvd Suite 4B Staten Island NY 10305
Ph: 718-981-8001 ▪ Fx: 718-981-4399 ▪ TF: 800-223-2732

Parkinson Foundation, National www.parkinson.org
1501 NW 9th Ave Miami FL 33136
Ph: 305-547-6666 ▪ Fx: 305-243-4403 ▪ TF: 800-327-4545

Parkinson's Disease Foundation www.parkinsons-foundation.org
710 W 168th St New York NY 10032
Ph: 212-923-4700 ▪ Fx: 212-923-4778 ▪ TF: 800-457-6676

Parkinson's Research, Michael J Fox Foundation for www.michaeljfox.org
PO Box 4777 Grand Central Stn New York NY 10163
Ph: 800-708-7644

Parks Association, Western National www.wnpa.org
12880 N Vistoso Village Dr Tucson AZ 85737
Ph: 520-622-1999 ▪ Fx: 520-623-9519

Parks, A Christian Ministry in the National www.acmnp.com
10 Justins Way Freeport ME 04032
Ph: 207-865-6436 ▪ Fx: 207-865-6852 ▪ TF: 800-786-3450

Parks Conservation Association, National www.npca.org
1300 19th St NW Suite 300 Washington DC 20036
Ph: 202-223-6722 ▪ Fx: 202-659-0650 ▪ TF: 800-628-7275

(Parks) George Wright Society www.georgewright.org
PO Box 65 Hancock MI 49930
Ph: 906-487-9722 ▪ Fx: 906-487-9405

Parks, National Association for Olmsted www.olmsted.org
84 Parkside Ave Buffalo NY 14214
Ph: 866-666-6905 ▪ Fx: 716-835-1300

Parks, Partners in www.partnersinparks.org
205 E 3rd St PO Box 130 Paonia CO 81428
Ph: 970-527-6691 ▪ Fx: 970-527-7297

Parks & Recreation Association, Canadian www.cpra.ca
2197 Riverside Dr Suite 404 Ottawa ON K1H7X3
Ph: 613-523-5315 ▪ Fx: 613-523-1182

Parks Tennis Association, National Public
1001 W 98th St Suite 101 Bloomington MN 55431
Ph: 952-887-5001 ▪ Fx: 952-887-5061 ▪ TF: 800-536-6982

Parks & Wilderness Society, Canadian www.cpaws.org
880 Wellington St Suite 506 Ottawa ON K1R6K7
Ph: 613-569-7226 ▪ Fx: 613-569-7098 ▪ TF: 800-333-9453

Parliament Association, World Constitution & www.wcpa.biz

Parliamentarians, American Institute of www.parliamentaryprocedure.org
PO Box 2173 Wilmington DE 19899
Ph: 302-762-1811 ▪ Fx: 302-762-2170 ▪ TF: 888-664-0428

Parliamentarians, National Association of www.parliamentarians.org
213 S Main St Independence MO 64050
Ph: 816-833-3892 ▪ Fx: 816-833-3893 ▪ TF: 888-627-2929

Parole Association, American Probation & www.appa-net.org
2760 Research Park Dr Lexington KY 40511
Ph: 859-244-8203 ▪ Fx: 859-244-8001

Paroling Authorities International, Association of www.apaintl.org
1941 Jefferson Davis Hwy CCM4 2nd Fl Rm 222 Arlington VA 22202
Ph: 703-607-1504 ▪ Fx: 703-607-2047

Parrot Society, African www.wingscc.com/aps
PO Box 204 Clarinda IA 51632
Ph: 712-542-4190

Parrotlet Society, International www.internationalparrotletsociety.org
PO Box 2428 Santa Cruz CA 95063
Ph: 831-688-5560 ▪ Fx: 831-689-9534

Part-Blooded Horse Registry, American www.apbhorseregistry.com
4120 SE River Dr Portland OR 97267
Ph: 503-654-6204

Parthenais Cattle Breeders Association www.parthenaiscattle.org/
PO Box 550 Bells TX 75414
Ph: 903-965-4259 ▪ Fx: 903-965-5452 ▪ TF: 800-762-0164

Partido Nacional La Raza Unida www.pnlru.org
11663 Herrick Ave PO Box 13 San Fernando CA 91340
Ph: 818-365-6534

Partisan Prohibition Historical Society www.prohibitionists.org
PO Box 2635 Denver CO 80201
Ph: 303-237-4947

Partners of the Americas www.partners.net
1424 K St NW Suite 700 Washington DC 20005
Ph: 202-628-3300 ▪ Fx: 202-628-3306

Partners In Education, National Association of   www.napehq.org
901 N Pitt St Suite 320   Alexandria VA 22314
Ph: 703-836-4880 ▪ Fx: 703-836-6941

Partners for Livable Communities   www.livable.com
1429 21st St NW   Washington DC 20036
Ph: 202-887-5990 ▪ Fx: 202-466-4845

Partners in Parks   www.partnersinparks.org
205 E 3rd St PO Box 130   Paonia CO 81428
Ph: 970-527-6691 ▪ Fx: 970-527-7297

Partnership for Caring Inc   www.partnershipforcaring.org
1620 'I' St NW Suite 202   Washington DC 20006
Ph: 202-296-8071 ▪ Fx: 202-296-8352 ▪ TF: 800-989-9455

Partnership for a Drug-Free America   www.drugfreeamerica.org
405 Lexington Ave Suite 1601   New York NY 10174
Ph: 212-922-1560 ▪ Fx: 212-922-1570 ▪ TF: 888-575-3115

Partnership for Patient Safety   www.p4ps.org
1 W Superior St Suite 2410   Chicago IL 60610
Ph: 312-274-9695 ▪ Fx: 312-274-9696

Partnership in Print Production   www.p3-ny.org
276 Bowery   New York NY 10012
Ph: 212-334-2106 ▪ Fx: 212-431-5786

Partnerships, National Council for Public-Private   www.ncppp.org
1660 L St NW Suite 510   Washington DC 20036
Ph: 202-467-6800 ▪ Fx: 202-467-6312

Party Boat Owners Alliance, National
181 Thames St   Groton CT 06340
Ph: 860-535-2066 ▪ Fx: 860-535-8389

Party Operators, National Association of Casino & Theme   www.casinoparties.com
18946 Des Moines Memorial Dr Bldg 5   SeaTac WA 98146
Ph: 206-241-4777 ▪ Fx: 206-241-6956 ▪ TF: 800-355-8299

Pasadena Tournament of Roses Association   www.tournamentofroses.com
391 S Orange Grove Blvd   Pasadena CA 91184
Ph: 626-449-4100 ▪ Fx: 626-449-9066

Paso Fino Horse Association   pasofino.org
101 N Collins St   Plant City FL 33566
Ph: 813-719-7777 ▪ Fx: 813-719-7872

Paso Fino Horse Association, American
PO Box 2363   Pittsburgh PA 15230
Ph: 724-437-5170 ▪ Fx: 724-438-4471

Paso Horse Registry of North America, Peruvian   www.pphrna.org
3077 Wiljan Ct Suite A   Santa Rosa CA 95407
Ph: 707-579-4394 ▪ Fx: 707-579-1038

Paso Horses, American Association of Owners & Breeders   www.aaobpph.org
of Peruvian   PO Box 476   Wilton CA 95693
Ph: 916-687-6232 ▪ Fx: 916-687-6691

Passenger Vessel Association   www.passengervessel.com
801 N Quincy St Suite 200   Arlington VA 22203
Ph: 703-807-0100 ▪ Fx: 703-807-0103 ▪ TF: 800-807-8360

Passengers, National Association of Railroad   www.narprail.org
900 2nd St NE Suite 308   Washington DC 20002
Ph: 202-408-8362 ▪ Fx: 202-408-8287

Pasta Association, National   www.ilovepasta.org
1156 15th St NW Suite 900   Washington DC 20005
Ph: 202-637-5888 ▪ Fx: 202-223-9741

Pastel Association International Ltd, Oil   www.opai.org

Pastel Society of America   www.pastelsocietyofamerica.org
15 Gramercy Park S   New York NY 10003
Ph: 212-533-6931 ▪ Fx: 212-353-8140

Pastoral Counseling, American Board of Examiners in
13014 N Dale Mabry Hwy Suite 363   Tampa FL 33618
Ph: 813-926-5446

Pastoral Counselors, American Association of   www.aapc.org
9504-A Lee Hwy   Fairfax VA 22031
Ph: 703-385-6967 ▪ Fx: 703-352-7725

Pastoral Education, Association for Clinical   www.acpe.edu
1549 Clairmont Rd Suite 103   Decatur GA 30033
Ph: 404-320-1472 ▪ Fx: 404-320-0849

Pastoral Musicians, National Association of   www.npm.org
962 Wayne Ave Suite 210   Silver Spring MD 20910
Ph: 240-247-3000

Patent Office Professional Association   www.popa.org
PO Box 2745   Arlington VA 22202
Ph: 703-305-3000 ▪ Fx: 703-308-0818

Patent Owners, National Association of Plant   www.anla.org/industry/patents
1000 Vermont Ave NW Suite 300   Washington DC 20005
Ph: 202-789-2900 ▪ Fx: 202-789-1893

Pathfinder International   www.pathfind.org
9 Galen St Suite 217   Watertown MA 02472
Ph: 617-924-7200 ▪ Fx: 617-924-3833

Pathologists, American Association of Avian   www.aaap.info
953 College Station Rd   Athens GA 30602
Ph: 706-542-5645 ▪ Fx: 706-542-0249

Pathologists, American College of Veterinary   www.acvp.org
7600 Terrace Ave Suite 203   Middleton WI 53562
Ph: 608-833-8725 ▪ Fx: 608-831-5122

Pathologists Inc, American Osteopathic College of   www.aocp-net.org
142 E Ontario St   Chicago IL 60611
Ph: 312-202-8197 ▪ Fx: 312-202-8224

Pathologists' Assistants, American Association of   www.pathologistsassistants.org
1711 W County Rd B   Roseville MN 55113
Ph: 651-697-9264 ▪ Fx: 651-635-0307 ▪ TF: 800-532-2272

Pathologists, College of American   www.cap.org
325 Waukegan Rd   Northfield IL 60093
Ph: 847-832-7000 ▪ Fx: 847-832-8000 ▪ TF: 800-323-4040

Pathologists, Society of Toxicologic   www.toxpath.org
1821 Michael Faraday Dr Suite 300   Reston VA 20190
Ph: 703-438-7508 ▪ Fx: 703-438-3113

Pathology, American Academy of Oral & Maxillofacial   aaomp.org
710 E Ogden Ave Suite 600   Naperville IL 60563
Ph: 888-552-2667 ▪ Fx: 630-369-2488

Pathology, American Board of   www.abpath.org
PO Box 25915   Tampa FL 33622
Ph: 813-286-2444 ▪ Fx: 813-289-5279

Pathology, American Society for Clinical   www.ascp.org
2100 W Harrison St   Chicago IL 60612
Ph: 312-738-1336 ▪ Fx: 312-738-1619 ▪ TF: 800-621-4142

Pathology, American Society for Colposcopy & Cervical   www.asccp.org
20 W Washington St Suite 1   Hagerstown MD 21740
Ph: 301-733-3640 ▪ Fx: 301-733-5775 ▪ TF: 800-787-7227

Pathology, American Society for Investigative
9650 Rockville Pike   Bethesda MD 20814
Ph: 301-530-7130 ▪ Fx: 301-571-1879

Pathology, Association for Molecular   www.ampweb.org
9650 Rockville Pike   Bethesda MD 20814
Ph: 301-634-7939 ▪ Fx: 301-634-7990

Pathology Chairs, Association of   www.apcprods.org
9650 Rockville Pike   Bethesda MD 20814
Ph: 301-634-7880 ▪ Fx: 301-634-7990

Pathology Foundation, American   www.americanpathologyfoundation.org
1202 Allanson Rd   Mundelein IL 60060
Ph: 847-949-6055 ▪ Fx: 847-566-4580 ▪ TF: 877-993-9935

Pathology Information Inc, Intersociety Committee on   www.pathologytraining.org
9650 Rockville Pike   Bethesda MD 20814
Ph: 301-634-7200 ▪ Fx: 301-634-7990

Pathology, International Academy of   www.iaphomepage.org
Armed Forces Institute of Pathology Walter Reed Compound
   6825 16th St NW   Washington DC 20306
Ph: 202-782-2503 ▪ Fx: 202-782-7166

Pathology, Society for Invertebrate   www.sipweb.org
8904 Straw Flower Dr   Knoxville TN 37922
Ph: 888-684-4682 ▪ Fx: 888-486-1505

Pathology, Society for Pediatric   www.spponline.org
3643 Walton Way Ext   Augusta GA 30909
Ph: 706-364-3375 ▪ Fx: 706-733-8033

Pathology Society, Renal   www.renalpathsoc.org
LSU Medical Center Dept of Pathology 1501 Kings
   Hwy   Shreveport LA 71103
Ph: 318-675-5878 ▪ Fx: 318-675-7662

Pathology, US & Canadian Academy of   www.uscap.org
3643 Walton Way Ext   Augusta GA 30909
Ph: 706-733-7550 ▪ Fx: 706-733-8033

Patient Advocacy, Center for   www.patientadvocacy.org
1350 Beverly Rd Suite 108   McLean VA 22101
Ph: 703-748-0400 ▪ Fx: 703-748-0402 ▪ TF: 800-846-7444

Patient Advocates for Advanced Cancer Treatment   www.paactusa.org
1143 Parmelee NW   Grand Rapids MI 49504
Ph: 616-453-1477 ▪ Fx: 616-453-1846

Patient, American Academy on Physician &   www.physicianpatient.org
1000 Executive Pkwy Suite 220   Saint Louis MO 63141
Ph: 314-576-5333 ▪ Fx: 314-576-7989

Patient Safety, Partnership for   www.p4ps.org
1 W Superior St Suite 2410   Chicago IL 60610
Ph: 312-274-9695 ▪ Fx: 312-274-9696

Patio & Barbecue Association, Hearth   www.hpba.org
1601 N Kent St Suite 1001   Arlington VA 22209
Ph: 703-522-0086 ▪ Fx: 703-522-0548

Patio Enclosure Association, National
12625 Frederick St Suite 1-5 315   Moreno Valley CA 92553
Ph: 909-485-8881 ▪ Fx: 909-924-3078

Patriotic Order Sons of America   www.posofa.org
PO Box 1847   Valley Forge PA 19482
Ph: 610-783-0626

Patrol Craft Sailors Association   www.ww2pcsa.org
11610 Paso Robles Ave   Granada Hills CA 91344
Ph: 818-363-2917

Pattern Recognition Society   pir.georgetown.edu/nbrf/pr.html
c/o National Biomedical Research Foundation Georgetown Univ
   Medical Ctr 3900 Reservoir Rd NW   Washington DC
   20007
Ph: 202-687-2121 ▪ Fx: 202-687-1662

Patton Society   www.pattonhq.com
3116 Thorn St   San Diego CA 92104
Ph: 619-282-4201

Paul G Allen Charitable Foundation   www.pgafoundations.com
505 5th Ave S Suite 900   Seattle WA 98104
Ph: 206-342-2000 ▪ Fx: 206-342-3000

Paul G Allen Forest Protection Foundation   www.pgafoundations.com/forest.asp
505 5th Ave S Suite 900   Seattle WA 98104
Ph: 206-342-2000 ▪ Fx: 206-342-3000

Paul G Allen Foundation for Medical Research   www.pgafoundations.com/med.asp
505 5th Ave S Suite 900   Seattle WA 98104
Ph: 206-342-2000 ▪ Fx: 206-342-3000

Paul G Allen Virtual Education Foundation   www.pgafoundations.com/edu.asp
505 5th Ave S Suite 900   Seattle WA 98104
Ph: 206-342-2000 ▪ Fx: 206-342-3000

Paul & Lisa Program Inc   www.paulandlisa.org
PO Box 348   Westbrook CT 06498
Ph: 860-767-7660 ▪ Fx: 860-767-3122

Paul VI Institute for the Arts
619 10th St NW   Washington DC 20001
Ph: 202-347-1450 ▪ Fx: 202-347-1401

Pavement Association, American Concrete   www.pavement.com
5420 Old Orchard Rd Suite A-100   Skokie IL 60077
Ph: 847-966-2272 ▪ Fx: 847-966-9970

Pavement Association, National Asphalt   www.hotmix.org
5100 Forbes Blvd   Lanham MD 20706
Ph: 301-731-4748 ▪ Fx: 301-731-4621 ▪ TF: 888-468-6499

Pavement Institute, Interlocking Concrete   icpi.org
1444 'I' St NW Suite 700   Washington DC 20005
Ph: 202-712-9036 ▪ Fx: 202-408-0285 ▪ TF: 800-241-3652

Pavement Marking Manufacturers Association, Thermoplastic
1747 Pennsylvania Ave NW Suite 1000   Washington DC 20006
Ph: 800-221-2574 ▪ Fx: 202-835-0243

Pavement Preservation, Foundation for   www.fp2.org
PO Box 23093   Lansing MI 48909
Ph: 517-381-0549

Pavements Association, Rubber   www.rubberpavements.org
1801 S Jentilly Ln Suite A2   Tempe AZ 85281
Ph: 480-517-9944 ▪ Fx: 480-517-9959

Paving Technologists, Association of Asphalt   www.asphalttechnology.org
4711 Clark Ave Suite G   White Bear Lake MN 55110
Ph: 651-293-9188 ▪ Fx: 651-293-9193

Paw Paw Foundation   www.pawpaw.kysu.edu/ppf
Kentucky State Univ 147 Atwood Research Facility   Frankfort
   KY 40601
Ph: 502-597-6174

Pawnbrokers Association, National   www.nationalpawnbrokers.org
611 Dallas Dr Suite 109   Roanoake TX 76262
Ph: 817-491-4554 ▪ Fx: 817-491-6770

Paws With a Cause   www.pawswithacause.org
4646 S Division St   Wayland MI 49348
Ph: 616-877-7297 ▪ Fx: 616-877-0248 ▪ TF: 800-253-7297

Pax Christi - USA   www.paxchristiusa.org
532 W 8th St   Erie PA 16502
Ph: 814-453-4955 ▪ Fx: 814-452-4784

Pax World Service   www.paxworld.org
1730 Rhode Island Ave NW Suite 707   Washington DC 20036
Ph: 202-463-0486 ▪ Fx: 202-463-7322

Payment Systems Association, Check   www.cpsa-checks.org
2025 M St NW Suite 800   Washington DC 20036
Ph: 202-857-1144 ▪ Fx: 202-223-4579

Payroll Association, American   www.americanpayroll.org
30 E 33rd St 5th Fl   New York NY 10016
Ph: 212-686-2030 ▪ Fx: 212-686-4080

PC/104 Consortium   www.pc104.org
490 2nd St Suite 301   San Francisco CA 94107
Ph: 415-243-2104 ▪ Fx: 415-836-9094

PCIA - Wireless Infrastructure Association   www.pcia.com
500 Montgomery St Suite 700   Alexandria VA 22314
Ph: 703-739-0300 ▪ Fx: 703-836-1608 ▪ TF: 800-759-0300

PDA   www.pda.org
PO Box 79465   Baltimore MD 21279
Ph: 301-986-0293 ▪ Fx: 301-986-1093

Pea & Lentil Council, USA Dry   www.pea-lentil.com
2780 W Pullman Rd   Moscow ID 83843
Ph: 208-882-3023 ▪ Fx: 208-882-6406

Peace Action   www.peace-action.org
1100 Wayne Ave Suite 1020   Silver Spring MD 20910
Ph: 301-565-4050 ▪ Fx: 301-565-0850

(Peace) Advocacy Project   www.advocacynet.org
1326 14th St NW   Washington DC 20005
Ph: 202-332-3900

Peace, America-Israel Council for Israeli-Palestinian   otherisrael.home.igc.org
224 Lake Dr   Kensington CA 94708
Ph: 510-526-8449

Peace, Benedictines for   www.mountosb.org/bfp.html
Mount St Benedict Monastery 6101 E Lake Rd   Erie PA 16511
Ph: 814-899-0614 ▪ Fx: 814-898-4004

Peace Brigades International - US   www.peacebrigades.org
428 8th St SE 2nd Fl   Washington DC 20003
Ph: 202-544-3765 ▪ Fx: 202-544-3766

Peace, Carnegie Endowment for International   www.ceip.org
1779 Massachusetts Ave NW   Washington DC 20036
Ph: 202-483-7600 ▪ Fx: 202-483-1840

Peace Center, Mount Diablo   www.mtdpc.org
55 Eckley Ln   Walnut Creek CA 94596
Ph: 925-933-7850 ▪ Fx: 925-934-3136

Peace Corps Association, National   www.rpcv.org
1900 L St NW Suite 205   Washington DC 20036
Ph: 202-293-7728 ▪ Fx: 202-293-7554 ▪ TF: 800-424-8580

Peace Development Fund   www.peacefund.org
44 N Prospect St PO Box 1280   Amherst MA 01004
Ph: 413-256-8306 ▪ Fx: 413-256-8871

(Peace) Earthstewards Network   www.earthstewards.org
PO Box 10697   Bainbridge Island WA 98110
Ph: 206-842-7986 ▪ Fx: 206-842-8918

Peace Education Foundation   www.peace-ed.org
1900 Biscayne Blvd   Miami FL 33132
Ph: 305-576-5075 ▪ Fx: 305-576-3106 ▪ TF: 800-749-8838

Peace in El Salvador, Christians for   www.crispaz.org
122 Dewitt Dr   Boston MA 02120
Ph: 617-445-5115 ▪ Fx: 617-249-0769

Peace Exchange, Men's International   www.peaceexchange.org
PO Box 36   Swarthmore PA 19081
Ph: 610-872-8178 ▪ Fx: 610-872-3642

Peace Fellowship, Brethren
PO Box 455   New Windsor MD 21776
Ph: 410-848-5631

Peace Fellowship, Buddhist   www.bpf.org
PO Box 3470   Berkeley CA 94703
Ph: 510-655-6169 ▪ Fx: 510-655-1369

Peace Fellowship, Catholic   www.catholicpeacefellowship.org
PO Box 41   Notre Dame IN 46556
Ph: 574-631-7666

Peace Fellowship, Disciples   www.homelandministries.org/DPF
PO Box 1986   Indianapolis IN 46206
Ph: 317-713-2679 ▪ Fx: 317-635-4426 ▪ TF: 888-346-2631

Peace Fellowship, Jewish   www.jewishpeacefellowship.org
PO Box 271   Nyack NY 10960
Ph: 914-358-4601 ▪ Fx: 914-358-4924

Peace Fellowship, Lutheran   www.lutheranpeace.org
1710 11th Ave   Seattle WA 98122
Ph: 206-720-0313

Peace Fellowship of North America, Baptist   www.bpfna.org
4800 Wedgewood Dr   Charlotte NC 28210
Ph: 704-521-6051 ▪ Fx: 704-521-6053

Peace Fellowship, Presbyterian
PO Box 271   Nyack NY 10960
Ph: 845-358-4601 ▪ Fx: 845-358-4924

PEACE, Foundation for
PO Box 98381   Raleigh NC 27624
Ph: 919-850-9696 ▪ Fx: 919-876-3621

Peace, Foundation for Middle East   www.fmep.org
1761 'N' St NW   Washington DC 20036
Ph: 202-835-3650 ▪ Fx: 202-835-3651

Peace Foundation, National   www.nationalpeace.org
666 11th St NW Suite 202   Washington DC 20001
Ph: 202-783-7030 ▪ Fx: 202-783-7040 ▪ TF: 800-237-3223

Peace Foundation, Nuclear Age   www.wagingpeace.org
1187 Coast Village Rd Suite 1 PMB 121   Santa Barbara CA
   93108
Ph: 805-965-3443 ▪ Fx: 805-568-0466

Peace Foundation, War &   www.warpeace.org
777 United Nations Plaza   New York NY 10017
Ph: 212-557-2501 ▪ Fx: 212-557-2515

Peace Foundation, World   www.worldpeacefoundation.org
79 John F Kennedy St   Cambridge MA 02138
Ph: 617-491-5085 ▪ Fx: 617-491-8588

Peace & Freedom-US Section, Women's International League for   www.wilpf.org
1213 Race St   Philadelphia PA 19107
Ph: 215-563-7110 ▪ Fx: 215-563-5527

Peace, Fund for   www.fundforpeace.org
1701 K St NW 11th Fl   Washington DC 20006
Ph: 202-223-7940 ▪ Fx: 202-223-7947

Peace Garden Foundation, National   www.peacefront.org
1 Grumman Hill Rd   Wilton CT 06897
Ph: 203-762-7917 ▪ Fx: 203-762-9053 ▪ TF: 877-467-3223

Peace, Hoover Institution on War Revolution &   www-hoover.stanford.edu
434 Galvez Mall   Stanford CA 94305
Ph: 650-723-1754 ▪ Fx: 650-723-1687 ▪ TF: 877-466-8374

Peace, Institute for Individual & World   www.iiwp.org
2101 Wilshire Blvd Suite 119   Santa Monica CA 90403
Ph: 310-315-3451 ▪ Fx: 310-315-3452 ▪ TF: 888-848-4497

Peace International, Grandmothers for   www.grandmothersforpeace.org
PO Box 580788   Elk Grove CA 95758
Ph: 916-685-1130

Peace, Interreligious & International Federation for World   www.iifwp.org
155 White Plains Rd   Tarrytown NY 10591
Ph: 914-631-1331 ▪ Fx: 914-631-1308

Peace & Justice, Institute for   www.ipj-ppj.org
4144 Lindell Blvd Suite 408   Saint Louis MO 63108
Ph: 314-533-4445 ▪ Fx: 314-715-6455

Peace & Justice Studies Association   www.peacejusticestudies.org
Evergreen State College MS Seminar 3127   Olympia WA 98505
Ph: 360-867-6196 ▪ Fx: 360-867-6553

Peace Mission, COAR
4395 Rocky River Dr   Cleveland OH 44135
Ph: 216-252-5572 ▪ Fx: 216-252-5573

Peace Movement Inc, Inner   www.innerpeacemovement.org
PO Box 681757   San Antonio TX 78268
Ph: 210-641-7912 ▪ Fx: 210-641-7871 ▪ TF: 877-475-7792

Peace & the News Media, Center for War   www.nyu.edu/cwpnm
New York Univ 418 Lafayette Suite 554   New York NY 10003
Ph: 212-998-7960 ▪ Fx: 212-995-4143

Peace Now, Americans for   www.peacenow.org
1101 14th St NW 6th Fl   Washington DC 20005
Ph: 202-728-1893 ▪ Fx: 202-728-1895

Peace Officers for Christ International   www.pofci.org
3000 W MacArthur Blvd Suite 426   Santa Ana CA 92704
Ph: 714-426-7632 ▪ Fx: 714-426-0792

Peace Officers USA, Fellowship of Christian   www.fcpo.org
PO Box 3686   Chattanooga TN 37404
Ph: 423-622-1234 ▪ Fx: 423-622-9725

Peace PAC
322 4th St NE   Washington DC 20002
Ph: 202-543-4100 ▪ Fx: 202-543-6297

(Peace) Pax Christi - USA   www.paxchristiusa.org
532 W 8th St   Erie PA 16502
Ph: 814-453-4955 ▪ Fx: 814-452-4784

Peace Pilgrim, Friends of   www.peacepilgrim.org/FoPP
7350 Dorado Canyon Rd   Somerset CA 95684
Ph: 530-620-0333 ▪ Fx: 530-620-7085

(Peace) Plowshares Institute   www.plowsharesinstitute.org
809 Hopmeadow St PO Box 243   Simsbury CT 06070
Ph: 203-651-4304 ▪ Fx: 203-651-4305

Peace Prayer Society, World   www.worldpeace.org
26 Benton Rd   Wassaic NY 12592
Ph: 845-877-6093 ▪ Fx: 845-877-6862

Peace, Promoting Enduring   www.pepeace.org
112 Beach Ave   Milford CT 06460
Ph: 203-878-4769

Peace, Quest for   www.quixote.org/quest
Quixote Center PO Box 5206   Hyattsville MD 20782
Ph: 301-699-0042 ▪ Fx: 301-864-2182

Peace Quilt Project, Boise   www.boisepeacequilt.org
PO Box 6469   Boise ID 83707
Ph: 208-343-3035 ▪ Fx: 208-323-0848

Peace Science Society (International)   pss.la.psu.edu
Pennsylvania State Univ Dept of Political Science   University
   Park PA 16802
Ph: 814-865-7515 ▪ Fx: 814-863-8979

Peace & Security, NGO Committee on Disarmament   disarm.igc.org
777 United Nations Plaza Rm 3-B   New York NY 10017
Ph: 212-687-5340 ※ Fx: 212-687-1643

Peace Studies Association   www.earlham.edu/~psa
Earlham College Drawer 105   Richmond IN 47374
Ph: 765-983-1386 ※ Fx: 765-983-1229

Peace Studies, Center for War/   www.cwps.org
180 W 80th St Suite 211   New York NY 10024
Ph: 212-579-4206 ※ Fx: 212-579-4362

Peace Through Law Education Fund   www.ptlef.org
PO Box 44354   Washington DC 20026
Ph: 202-686-4600

Peace Through Technology Organization, World   www.peacetour.org
150 Folsom St   San Francisco CA 94105
Ph: 415-371-8706 ※ Fx: 415-348-0762

Peace Inc, Veterans for   www.veteransforpeace.org
438 N Skinker Blvd   Saint Louis MO 63130
Ph: 314-725-6005

Peace, Volunteers for   www.vfp.org
1034 Tiffany Rd   Belmont VT 05730
Ph: 802-259-2759 ※ Fx: 802-259-2922

Peace Without Justice, No   www.npwj.org
866 UN Plaza Suite 408   New York NY 10017
Ph: 212-980-2558 ※ Fx: 212-980-1072

Peace, Witness for   www.witnessforpeace.org
1229 15th St NW   Washington DC 20005
Ph: 202-588-1471 ※ Fx: 202-588-1472

Peace, Women Strike for
110 Maryland Ave NE Suite 102   Washington DC 20002
Ph: 202-543-2660

Peace, World Conference of Religions for   www.wcrp.org
777 United Nations Plaza   New York NY 10017
Ph: 212-687-2163 ※ Fx: 212-983-0566

Peacefire   www.peacefire.org
14615 NW 30th Pl Unit 10D   Bellevue WA 98007
Ph: 425-497-9002

Peacemakers, World   www.worldpeacemakers.org
11427 Scottsbury Terr   Germantown MD 20876
Ph: 301-972-4041 ※ Fx: 301-916-5335

Peacemaking & Conflict Resolution, National Conference on   www.apeacemaker.net
3070 Bristol Pike Bldg 1 Suite 116   Bensalem PA 19020
Ph: 215-245-6993 ※ Fx: 215-245-6994 ※ TF: 877-397-3223

Peach Council, National   www.nationalpeach.org
12 Nicklaus Ln Suite 101   Columbia SC 29229
Ph: 803-788-7101 ※ Fx: 803-865-8090

Peale Center for Christian Living
66 E Main St   Pawling NY 12564
Ph: 845-855-5000 ※ Fx: 845-855-1036 ※ TF: 800-431-2344

Peanut Advisory Board   www.peanutbutterlovers.com
1025 Sugar Mill Rd   Canton GA 30115
Ph: 770-998-7311 ※ Fx: 770-998-5962

Peanut Buying Points Association, National
PO Box 314   Tifton GA 31793
Ph: 229-386-1716 ※ Fx: 229-386-8757

Peanut Commission, Georgia   www.gapeanuts.com
110 E 4th St PO Box 967   Tifton GA 31793
Ph: 229-386-3470 ※ Fx: 229-386-3501

Peanut Council, American   www.peanutsusa.com
1500 King St Suite 301   Alexandria VA 22314
Ph: 703-838-9500 ※ Fx: 703-838-9508

Peanut Festival Association, National   www.nationalpeanutfestival.com
5622 U S Hwy 231 S   Dothan AL 36301
Ph: 334-793-4323 ※ Fx: 334-793-3247

Peanut Growers Association, Southwestern   www.swpga.com
304 SE Lubbock PO Box 338   Gorman TX 76454
Ph: 254-734-2222 ※ Fx: 254-734-2288

Peanut Institute   www.peanut-institute.org
PO Box 70157   Albany GA 31708
Ph: 229-888-0216 ※ Fx: 229-888-5150 ※ TF: 888-873-2688

Peanut Pals   www.peanutpals.org
PO Box 4465   Huntsville AL 35815
Ph: 256-881-9198

Peanut Research & Education Society   www.agr.okstate.edu/apres/welcome.htm
Inc, American   Oklahoma State Univ 376 Agriculture
   Hall   Stillwater OK 74078
Ph: 405-372-3052 ※ Fx: 405-744-0354

Peanut Shellers Association, American   www.peanut-shellers.org
PO Box 70157   Albany GA 31708
Ph: 229-888-2508 ※ Fx: 229-888-5150

Peanut & Tree Nut Processors Association   www.ptnpa.org
PO Box 59811   Potomac MD 20859
Ph: 301-365-2521 ※ Fx: 301-365-7705

Pear Bureau Northwest   www.usapears.com
4382 SE International Way Suite A   Milwaukie OR 97222
Ph: 503-652-9720 ※ Fx: 503-652-9721

Pearl Harbor History Associates Inc   www.pearlharbor-history.org
PO Box 1007   Stratford CT 06615
Ph: 203-378-2353

Pearl Harbor Survivors Association   members.aol.com/phsasecy97
PO Box 701   Menomonee Falls WI 53052
Ph: 262-251-0787 ※ Fx: 262-251-8035

Pearl S Buck International   www.pearl-s-buck.org/psbi
520 Dublin Rd   Perkasie PA 18944
Ph: 215-249-0100 ※ Fx: 215-249-9657 ※ TF: 800-220-2825

Peat Society, International   www.peatsociety.fi/natcoms
US National Committee 10105 White City Rd   Britt MN 55710
Ph: 218-741-2813

Pecan Shellers Association, National   www.ilovepecans.com
5775 Peachtree-Dunwoody Rd Bldg G Suite 500   Atlanta GA
   30342
Ph: 404-252-3663 ※ Fx: 404-252-0774

Pedal Steel Guitar Association   www.psga.org
PO Box 20248   Floral Park NY 11002
Ph: 516-616-9214

Pediatric AIDS Foundation, Elizabeth Glaser   www.pedaids.org
2950 31st St Suite 125   Santa Monica CA 90405
Ph: 310-314-1459 ※ Fx: 310-314-1469 ※ TF: 888-499-4673

Pediatric Anesthesia, Society for   www.pedsanesthesia.org
PO Box 11086   Richmond VA 23230
Ph: 804-282-9780 ※ Fx: 804-282-0090

Pediatric Association, Ambulatory   www.ambpeds.org
6728 Old McLean Village Dr   McLean VA 22101
Ph: 703-556-9222 ※ Fx: 703-556-8729

Pediatric Dentistry, American Academy of   www.aapd.org
211 E Chicago Ave Suite 700   Chicago IL 60611
Ph: 312-337-2169 ※ Fx: 312-337-6329

Pediatric Dentistry, American Board of   www.abpd.org
325 E Washington St Suite 101   Iowa City IA 52240
Ph: 319-341-9499

Pediatric Department Chairs, Association of Medical School
111 Silver Cedar Ct   Chapel Hill NC 27514
Ph: 919-942-1993 ※ Fx: 919-929-9255

Pediatric Dermatology, Society for   www.pedsderm.net
5422 N Bernard St   Chicago IL 60625
Ph: 773-583-9780 ※ Fx: 773-583-9765

Pediatric Gastroenterology Hepatology & Nutrition, North   www.naspghan.org
American Society for   PO Box 6   Flourtown PA 19031
Ph: 215-233-0808 ※ Fx: 215-233-3918

Pediatric Hematology/Oncology, American Society of   www.aspho.org
4700 W Lake Ave   Glenview IL 60025
Ph: 847-375-4716 ※ Fx: 877-734-9557

Pediatric Infectious Diseases Society   www.pids.org
66 Canal Ctr Plaza Suite 600   Alexandria VA 22314
Ph: 703-299-6764 ※ Fx: 703-299-0473

Pediatric Nephrology, American Society of   www.aspneph.com
JW Riley Hospital for Children 702 Barnhill Dr Wells Research
   Ctr Rm 2600-A   Indianapolis IN 46202
Ph: 317-278-0854 ※ Fx: 317-278-3599

Pediatric Neuroradiology, American Society of   www.asnr.org/aspnr
2210 Midwest Rd Suite 207   Oak Brook IL 60523
Ph: 630-574-0220 ※ Fx: 630-574-0661

Pediatric Neurosurgery, American Society for   www.aspn.org
James Whitcomb Riley Hospital for Children 1 Children's Sq
   Suite 1730   Indianapolis IN 46202
Ph: 317-274-8852 ※ Fx: 317-274-8895

Pediatric Nurse Practitioners, National Association of   www.napnap.org
20 Brace Rd Suite 200   Cherry Hill NJ 08034
Ph: 856-857-9700 ※ Fx: 856-857-1600 ※ TF: 877-662-7627

Pediatric Nurses, Society of   www.pedsnurses.org
7794 Grow Dr   Pensacola FL 32514
Ph: 850-484-9987 ※ Fx: 850-484-8762 ※ TF: 800-723-2902

Pediatric Oncology Nurses, Association of   www.apon.org
4700 W Lake Ave   Glenview IL 60025
Ph: 847-375-4724 ※ Fx: 877-734-8755

Pediatric Ophthalmology & Strabismus, American Association for   www.aapos.org
PO Box 193832   San Francisco CA 94119
Ph: 415-561-8505 ※ Fx: 415-561-8531

Pediatric Orthopedic Society of North America   www.posna.org
6300 N River Rd Suite 727   Rosemont IL 60018
Ph: 847-698-1692 ※ Fx: 847-823-0536

Pediatric Pathology, Society for   www.spponline.org
3643 Walton Way Ext   Augusta GA 30909
Ph: 706-364-3375 ※ Fx: 706-733-8033

Pediatric Program Directors, Association of   www.appd.org
6728 Old McLean Village Dr   McLean VA 22101
Ph: 703-556-9222 ※ Fx: 703-556-8729

Pediatric Radiology, Society for   www.pedrad.org
4550 Post Oak Pl Suite 342   Houston TX 77027
Ph: 713-965-0566 ※ Fx: 713-960-0488

Pediatric Research, Society for   www.aps-spr.org
3400 Research Forest Dr Suite B-7   The Woodlands TX 77381
Ph: 281-419-0052 ※ Fx: 281-419-0082

Pediatric Society, American   www.aps-spr.org
3400 Research Forest Dr Suite B7   The Woodlands TX 77381
Ph: 281-419-0052 ※ Fx: 281-419-0082

Pediatric Surgical Association, American   www.eapsa.org
60 Revere Dr Suite 500   Northbrook IL 60062
Ph: 847-480-9576 ※ Fx: 847-480-9282

Pediatric Transplant Association, International   www.iptaonline.org
17000 Commerce Pkwy Suite C   Mount Laurel NJ 08054
Ph: 856-439-0500 ※ Fx: 856-439-0525

Pediatricians, American College of Osteopathic   www.acopeds.org
142 E Ontario St   Chicago IL 60611
Ph: 312-202-8174 ※ Fx: 312-202-8224 ※ TF: 877-231-2267

Pediatrics, American Academy of   www.aap.org
141 Northwest Point Blvd   Elk Grove Village IL 60007
Ph: 847-434-4000 ※ Fx: 847-434-8000 ※ TF: 800-433-9016

Pediatrics, American Board of   www.abp.org
111 Silver Cedar Ct   Chapel Hill NC 27514
Ph: 919-929-0461 ※ Fx: 919-929-9255

Pediatrics, American College of Foot & Ankle
6477 Auburn Dr   Virginia Beach VA 23464
Ph: 757-523-0414 ※ Fx: 757-523-2047

Pediatrics, American Osteopathic Board of   www.aobp.org
142 E Ontario St 6th Fl   Chicago IL 60611
Ph: 312-202-8267

Pediatrics, Society for Developmental & Behavioral   www.sdbp.org
17000 Commerce Pkwy Suite C   Mount Laurel NJ 08054
Ph: 856-439-0500 ※ Fx: 856-439-0525

Pediatrics, Society for Physician Assistants in   www.aapa.org/spec/SPAP
950 N Washington St   Alexandria VA 22314
Ph: 800-596-4398

Pediculosis Association, National www.headlice.org
50 Kearney   Needham MA 02494
Ph: 781-449-6487 ▪ Fx: 781-449-8129 ▪ TF: 800-446-4672

Pedigreed Livestock Council, National nplc.net
177 Palermo Pl   The Villages FL 32159
Ph: 352-259-6005

Pedorthic Footwear Association www.pedorthics.org
7150 Columbia Gateway Dr Suite G   Columbia MD 21046
Ph: 410-381-7278 ▪ Fx: 410-381-1167 ▪ TF: 800-673-8447

Peer Education Network, BACCHUS & GAMMA bacchusgamma.org
2130 S University Blvd   Denver CO 80210
Ph: 303-871-0901 ▪ Fx: 303-871-0907

Peer Helpers Association, National www.peerhelping.org
PO Box 32272   Kansas City MO 64171
Ph: 877-314-7337 ▪ Fx: 866-314-7337

Pelham John Historical Association
7 Carmel Tier   Hampton VA 23666
Ph: 757-838-1685

Pellet Fuels Institute www.pelletheat.org
1601 N Kent St Suite 1001   Arlington VA 22209
Ph: 703-522-6778 ▪ Fx: 703-522-0548

Peltier Leonard Defense Committee www.leonardpeltier.org
PO Box 583   Lawrence KS 66044
Ph: 785-842-5774 ▪ Fx: 785-842-5796

Pembroke Welsh Corgi Club of America www.pembrokecorgi.org
PO Box 2141   Duxbury MA 02331
Ph: 781-934-0110 ▪ Fx: 781-934-6597

PEN American Center www.pen.org
568 Broadway   New York NY 10012
Ph: 212-334-1660 ▪ Fx: 212-334-2181

Pen & Brush Inc www.penandbrush.org
16 E 10th St   New York NY 10003
Ph: 212-475-3669 ▪ Fx: 212-475-6018

PEN Center USA www.penusa.org
672 S Lafayette Park Pl Suite 42   Los Angeles CA 90057
Ph: 213-365-8500 ▪ Fx: 213-365-9616

(Pen Pals) Student Letter Exchange www.pen-pal.com
211 Broadway Suite 201   Lynbrook NY 11563
Ph: 516-887-8628 ▪ Fx: 516-887-8631

Pen Pals, World www.world-pen-pals.com
PO Box 337   Saugerties NY 12477
Ph: 845-246-7828

Pen Women Inc, National League of American www.americanpenwomen.org
1300 17th St NW   Washington DC 20036
Ph: 202-785-1997 ▪ Fx: 202-452-6868

Pencil Collectors Society, American www.pencilcollector.org

Penelope, Daughters of www.ahepa.org/dop
1909 Q St NW Suite 500   Washington DC 20009
Ph: 202-234-9741 ▪ Fx: 202-483-6983

Penitents, Confraternity of www.penitents.org
520 Oliphant Ln   Middletown RI 02842
Ph: 401-849-5421

Penn William Association www.williampennassociation.org
709 Brighton Rd   Pittsburgh PA 15233
Ph: 412-231-2979 ▪ Fx: 412-231-8535 ▪ TF: 800-848-7366

Penn William Foundation www.wpennfdn.org
100 N 18th St 2 Logan Sq 11th Fl   Philadelphia PA 19103
Ph: 215-988-1830 ▪ Fx: 215-988-1823

Pennsylvania, German Society of www.germansociety.org
611 Spring Garden St   Philadelphia PA 19123
Ph: 215-627-2332 ▪ Fx: 215-627-5297

Pension Actuaries, American Society of www.aspa.org
4245 N Fairfax Dr Suite 750   Arlington VA 22203
Ph: 703-516-9300 ▪ Fx: 703-516-9308

Pension Administrators, National Institute of www.nipa.org
401 N Michigan Ave Suite 2200   Chicago IL 60611
Ph: 800-999-6472 ▪ Fx: 312-245-1085

Pension Group, Church www.cpg.org
445 5th Ave   New York NY 10016
Ph: 212-592-1800 ▪ Fx: 212-779-3370 ▪ TF: 800-223-6602

Pension Real Estate Association www.prea.org
100 Pearl St 13th Fl   Hartford CT 06103
Ph: 860-692-6341 ▪ Fx: 860-692-6351

Pension Research Council prc.wharton.upenn.edu/prc/prc.html
Univ of Pennsylvania Wharton School 641 Locust Walk 304
Colonial Penn Ctr   Philadelphia PA 19104
Ph: 215-898-7620 ▪ Fx: 215-898-0310

Pension Rights Center www.pensionrights.org
1140 19th St NW Suite 602   Washington DC 20036
Ph: 202-296-3776 ▪ Fx: 202-833-2472

Penstemon Society, American
1569 S Holland Ct   Lakewood CO 80232
Ph: 303-986-8096

Pentathlon Association, US Modern usmpa.home.texas.net
305 E Ramsey   San Antonio TX 78216
Ph: 210-229-2004 ▪ Fx: 210-340-4970

Pentecostal Assemblies of the World www.pawinc.org
3939 Meadows Dr   Indianapolis IN 46205
Ph: 317-547-9541 ▪ Fx: 317-543-0513

Pentecostal Church International, United www.upci.org
8855 Dunn Rd   Hazelwood MO 63042
Ph: 314-837-7300 ▪ Fx: 314-837-4503

Pentecostal Holiness Church, International www.iphc.org
PO Box 12609   Oklahoma City OK 73157
Ph: 405-787-7110 ▪ Fx: 405-789-3957

Pentecostal World Fellowship www.pentecostalworldconf.org
1445 Boonville Ave   Springfield MO 65804
Ph: 417-862-2781 ▪ Fx: 417-863-6614

PEO Sisterhood www.peointernational.org
3700 Grand Ave   Des Moines IA 50312
Ph: 515-255-3153 ▪ Fx: 515-255-3820

People Against Cancer www.peopleagainstcancer.com
604 East St PO Box 10   Otho IA 50569
Ph: 515-972-4444 ▪ Fx: 515-972-4415

People Against Rape Inc www.people-against-rape.org
2148 Dorchester Rd   North Charleston SC 29405
Ph: 843-745-0144 ▪ Fx: 843-745-0119 ▪ TF: 800-877-7252

People for the American Way www.pfaw.org
2000 M St NW Suite 400   Washington DC 20036
Ph: 202-467-4999 ▪ Fx: 202-293-2672 ▪ TF: 800-326-7329

People-Animals-Love www.peopleanimalslove.com
3201 New Mexico Ave NW Suite 350   Washington DC 20016
Ph: 202-895-1395 ▪ Fx: 202-274-1995

People for the Ethical Treatment of Animals www.peta-online.org
501 Front St   Norfolk VA 23510
Ph: 757-622-7382 ▪ Fx: 757-628-0782 ▪ TF: 800-483-4366

People-to-People Health Foundation www.projhope.org
225 Carter Hall Ln   Millwood VA 22646
Ph: 540-837-2100 ▪ Fx: 540-837-1813 ▪ TF: 800-544-4673

People to People International www.ptpi.org
501 E Armour Blvd   Kansas City MO 64109
Ph: 816-531-4701 ▪ Fx: 816-561-7502

People to People Sports Ambassadors Program www.sportsambassadors.org
110 S Ferrall St   Spokane WA 99202
Ph: 509-534-0430 ▪ Fx: 509-534-5245

People-Plant Council www.hort.vt.edu/human/PPC.html
Virginia Polytechnic Institute 407 Saunders Hall   Blacksburg VA
24061
Ph: 540-231-6254 ▪ Fx: 540-231-3083

Pepper Institute on Aging & Public Policy www.pepperinstitute.org
Florida State Univ 207 Pepper Ctr 636 W Call St   Tallahassee
FL 32306
Ph: 850-644-2831 ▪ Fx: 850-644-2304

Pepper Shakers Club, Novelty Salt & members.aol.com/spclub1234
PO Box 416   Gladstone OR 97027
Ph: 503-650-8499

Peptide Society Inc, American www.ampepsoc.org
2033 San Elijo Ave Suite 421   Cardiff by the Sea CA 92007
Ph: 858-455-4752

Per Scholas www.perscholas.org
1231 Lafayette Ave   Bronx NY 10474
Ph: 718-991-8400 ▪ Fx: 718-991-0362 ▪ TF: 800-877-4068

Percheron Horse Association of America www.horseworlddata.com
10330 Quaker Rd PO Box 141   Fredericktown OH 43019
Ph: 740-694-3602 ▪ Fx: 740-694-3604

Percussive Arts Society www.pas.org
701 NW Ferris Ave   Lawton OK 73507
Ph: 580-353-1455 ▪ Fx: 580-353-1456

Percy Grainger Society, International www.percygrainger.org
7 Cromwell Pl   White Plains NY 10601
Ph: 914-948-7436

Peregrine Foundation, Canadian www.peregrine-foundation.ca
250 Merton St Suite 104   Toronto ON M4S1B1
Ph: 416-481-1233 ▪ Fx: 416-481-7158 ▪ TF: 888-709-3944

Peregrine Fund www.peregrinefund.org
5668 W Flying Hawk Ln   Boise ID 83709
Ph: 208-362-3716 ▪ Fx: 208-362-2376

Perennial Plant Association www.perennialplant.org
3383 Schirtzinger Rd   Hilliard OH 43026
Ph: 614-771-8431 ▪ Fx: 614-876-5238

Perfins Club Inc www.perfins.com/perfclub.htm
10 Clarridge Cir   Milford MA 01757
Ph: 508-478-7303

Perforators Association, Industrial www.iperf.org
5157 Deerhurst Crescent Cir   Boca Raton FL 33486
Ph: 561-447-7511

Performance Improvement, International Society for www.ispi.org
1400 Spring St Suite 260   Silver Spring MD 20910
Ph: 301-587-8570 ▪ Fx: 301-587-8573

Performance Management, College of www.cpm-pmi.org
101 S Whiting St Suite 320   Alexandria VA 22304
Ph: 703-370-7885 ▪ Fx: 703-370-1757

Performance Network, National www.npnweb.org/
225 Baronne St Suite 1712   New Orleans LA 70112
Ph: 504-595-8008 ▪ Fx: 504-595-8006

Performance Warehouse Association www.pwa-par.org
41-701 Corporate Way Suite 1   Palm Desert CA 92260
Ph: 760-346-5647 ▪ Fx: 760-346-5847

Performing Animal Welfare Society www.pawsweb.org
PO Box 849   Galt CA 95632
Ph: 209-745-2606 ▪ Fx: 209-745-1809

Performing Arts Foundation, International Society for the www.ispa.org
17 Purdy Ave PO Box 909   Rye NY 10580
Ph: 914-921-1550 ▪ Fx: 914-921-1593

Performing Arts Managers & Agents, North American www.napama.org
459 Columbus Ave   New York NY 10024
Ph: 888-745-8759

Performing Arts Presenters, Association of www.artspresenters.org
1112 16th St NW Suite 400   Washington DC 20036
Ph: 202-833-2787 ▪ Fx: 202-833-1543

Performing Arts-USA, International www.theatrelibrary.org/sibmas/sibmas.html
Association of Libraries & Museums of the

(Performing Rights) SESAC Inc www.sesac.com
55 Music Sq E   Nashville TN 37203
Ph: 615-320-0055 ▪ Fx: 615-329-9627 ▪ TF: 800-826-9996

Performing & Visual Arts Schools, International www.artsschoolsnetwork.org
Network of   173 Ridge View Dr   Berkeley Springs WV 25411
Ph: 304-258-1799 ▪ Fx: 304-258-0839

Perfume Bottle Association, International　　www.perfumebottles.org
1789 Maryland Ave N　Minneapolis MN 55427
Ph: 763-544-5038

Perfumers, American Society of　　www.perfumers.org
PO Box 1551　West Caldwell NJ 07007
Ph: 201-991-0040　Fx: 201-991-0073

PeriAnesthesia Nurses, American Society of　　www.aspan.org
10 Melrose Ave Suite 110　Cherry Hill NJ 08003
Ph: 856-616-9600　Fx: 856-616-9601　TF: 877-737-9696

Perimetric Society, International　　www.perimetry.org
c/o Glaucoma Consultants NW 1221 Madison St Suite
1124　Seattle WA 98104
Ph: 206-682-3447　Fx: 206-682-8219

Perinatal Association, National　　www.nationalperinatal.org
3500 E Fletcher Ave Suite 205　Tampa FL 33613
Ph: 813-971-1008　Fx: 813-971-9306　TF: 888-971-3295

Perinatology, Society for Obstetric Anesthesia &　　www.soap.org
2 Summit Park Dr Suite 140　Cleveland OH 44131
Ph: 216-447-7863　Fx: 216-642-1127

Periodical & Book Association of America　　www.pbaa.net
481 8th Ave Suite 826　New York NY 10001
Ph: 212-563-6502　Fx: 212-563-4098

Periodical Club, Church　　arc.episcopalchurch.org/cpc
815 2nd Ave　New York NY 10017
Ph: 800-334-7626　Fx: 212-867-0395

Periodical Publications Association
PO Box 10669　Rockville MD 20849
Ph: 301-260-1646　Fx: 301-260-1647

Periodicals, Research Society for Victorian　　www.aztecfreenet.org/rsvp/
Univ of South Florida FA 0209　Tampa FL 33620
Ph: 813-974-3365　Fx: 813-974-0810

Periodontology, American Academy of　　www.perio.org
737 N Michigan Ave Suite 800　Chicago IL 60611
Ph: 312-787-5518　Fx: 312-787-3670　TF: 800-282-4867

Periodontology, American Board of　　www.perio.org/amboard/amboard.html
737 N Michigan Ave Suite 800　Chicago IL 60611
Ph: 312-787-5518　Fx: 312-787-3670

Peritoneal Dialysis, International Society for　　www.ispd.org
66 Martin St　Milton ON L9T2R2
Ph: 905-875-2456　Fx: 905-875-2864　TF: 888-834-1001

Perlite Institute Inc　　www.perlite.org
1924 N 2nd St　Harrisburg PA 17102
Ph: 717-238-9723　Fx: 717-238-9985

Permanent Cosmetic Professionals, Society of　　www.spcp.org
69 N Broadway St　Des Plaines IL 60016
Ph: 847-635-1330　Fx: 847-635-1326

Pershing Rifles, National Society of　　nhq.pershingrifles.com/
200 Nebraska Union Box 240 PO Box 880456　Lincoln NE
68588
Ph: 402-472-2472　Fx: 402-472-2478

Personal Assistants, Association of Celebrity　　www.celebrityassistants.org
914 Westwood Blvd PMB 507　Los Angeles CA 90024
Ph: 310-322-7755

Personal Chef Association, US　　uspca.com
481 Rio Rancho Blvd NE　Rio Rancho NM 87124
Ph: 505-896-3522　Fx: 505-994-6399　TF: 800-995-2138

Personal Computer Memory Card International Association　　www.pc-card.com
2635 N 1st St Suite 209　San Jose CA 95134
Ph: 408-433-2273　Fx: 408-433-9558

Personal Computer User Groups, Association of　　www.apcug.org
3150 Payne Ave Suite 12　Cleveland OH 44114
Ph: 301-423-1618

Personal Flotation Device Manufacturers Association　　www.pfdma.org
200 E Randolph Dr Suite 510　Chicago IL 60601
Ph: 312-946-6280　Fx: 312-946-0388

Personal Freedom Outreach　　www.pfo.org
PO Box 26062　Saint Louis MO 63136
Ph: 314-921-9800

Personal Historians, Association of　　www.personalhistorians.org

Personal Protection Agents, International Association of　　www.iappa.org
PO Box 266　Arlington Heights IL 60006
Ph: 847-870-8007　Fx: 847-870-8990

Personal Watercraft Industry Association　　www.pwia.org
1819 L St NW Suite 700　Washington DC 20036
Ph: 202-721-1621　Fx: 202-721-1626

Personality Assessment, Society for　　www.personality.org
6109H Arlington Blvd　Falls Church VA 22044
Ph: 703-534-4772

Personnel Administrators, Jesuit Association of Student　　jaspa.creighton.edu
1 Dupont Cir NW Suite 405　Washington DC 20036
Ph: 202-862-9893

Personnel Administrators, National Association of Church　　www.nacpa.org
100 E 8th St　Cincinnati OH 45202
Ph: 513-421-3134　Fx: 513-421-3085

Personnel Administrators, National Association of Student　　www.naspa.org
1875 Connecticut Ave NW Suite 418　Washington DC 20009
Ph: 202-265-7500　Fx: 202-797-1157

Personnel Association, American College　　www.acpa.nche.edu
1 Dupont Cir NW Suite 300　Washington DC 20036
Ph: 202-835-2272　Fx: 202-296-3286

Personnel Executives, National Association of State　　www.naspe.net
2760 Research Park Dr PO Box 11910　Lexington KY 40578
Ph: 859-244-8182　Fx: 859-244-8001

Personnel Services, National Association of　　www.napsweb.org
10905 Ft Washington Rd Suite 400　Fort Washington MD
20744
Ph: 301-203-6700　Fx: 301-203-4346

Personnel Workers, International Association of Pupil　　www.iappw.org
2940 N Stratham Pt　Hernando FL 34442
Ph: 352-637-0653　Fx: 352-637-0926

Peru, Committee to Support the Revolution in　　www.csrp.org
PO Box 1246　Berkeley CA 94701
Ph: 415-252-5786　Fx: 415-252-7414

Peruvian American Chamber of Commerce　　www.peruvianchamber.org
9737 NW 41st St PMB 348　Doral FL 33178
Ph: 305-471-9434　Fx: 305-471-9605

Peruvian Paso Horse Registry of North America　　www.pphrna.org
3077 Wiljan Ct Suite A　Santa Rosa CA 95407
Ph: 707-579-4394　Fx: 707-579-1038

**Peruvian Paso Horses, American Association of
Owners & Breeders of**　PO Box 476　Wilton CA 95693　www.aaobpph.org
Ph: 916-687-6232　Fx: 916-687-6691

**(Pest Control) United Product Formulators & Distributors
Association**　2034 Beaver Run Rd　Norcross GA 30071　www.pestworld.org/upfda
Ph: 770-417-1418　Fx: 770-417-1419

Pest Management Association Inc, National　　www.pestworld.org
8100 Oak St　Dunn Loring VA 22027
Ph: 703-573-8330　Fx: 703-573-4116

Pesticide Action Network North America　　www.panna.org
49 Powell St Suite 500　San Francisco CA 94102
Ph: 415-981-1771　Fx: 415-981-1991

Pesticide Applicators Professional Association　　www.papaseminars.com
PO Box 80095　Salinas CA 93912
Ph: 831-442-3536　Fx: 831-442-2351

Pesticide Control Officials, Association of American　　aapco.ceris.purdue.edu
PO Box 1249　Hardwick VT 05843
Ph: 802-472-6956　Fx: 802-472-6957

Pesticide Information Center, National　　npic.orst.edu
333 Weniger Hall　Corvallis OR 97331
Ph: 800-858-7378　Fx: 541-737-0761

Pesticides, Beyond　　www.beyondpesticides.org
701 'E' St SE Suite 200　Washington DC 20003
Ph: 202-543-5450　Fx: 202-543-4791

Pesticides, Northwest Coalition for Alternatives to　　www.pesticide.org
PO Box 1393　Eugene OR 97440
Ph: 541-344-5044　Fx: 541-344-6923

(Pesticides) Rachel Carson Council Inc　　members.aol.com/rccouncil/ourpage
PO Box 10779　Silver Spring MD 20914
Ph: 301-593-7507　Fx: 301-593-6251

(Pet Adoption) Bide-A-Wee Association　　www.bideawee.org
410 E 38th St　New York NY 10016
Ph: 212-532-6395　Fx: 212-532-4210

**Pet & Animal Transportation Association International Inc,
Independent**　745 Winding Trail　Holly Lake Ranch TX 75755　www.ipata.com
Ph: 903-769-2267　Fx: 903-769-2867

Pet Boarding Association, American
22096 N Pet Ln　Prairie View IL 60069
Ph: 847-634-9444　Fx: 847-634-9460

Pet Care Trust　　www.petcaretrust.org
3951 Leland Valley Rd W　Quilcene WA 98376
Ph: 360-765-3311　Fx: 360-765-3399

Pet Cemeteries, International Association of　　www.iaopc.org
5055 Rt 11 PO Box 163　Ellenburg Depot NY 12935
Ph: 518-594-3000　Fx: 518-594-8801

Pet Cemetery Society, Accredited　　www.accreditedpetcemeterysociety.org
3426 Brush Rd　Richfield OH 44286
Ph: 330-659-4270　Fx: 330-659-4254

PET Container Resources, National Association for　　www.napcor.com
10800 Sikes Pl Suite 240　Charlotte NC 28277
Ph: 704-845-5070　Fx: 704-845-5276

Pet Dog Trainers, Association of　　www.apdt.com
PO Box 1781　Hobbs NM 88241
Ph: 800-738-3647

Pet Food Institute　　www.petfoodinstitute.org
2025 M St NW Suite 800　Washington DC 20036
Ph: 202-367-1120　Fx: 202-367-2120

Pet Industry Distributors Association　　www.pida.org
2105 Laurel Bush Rd Suite 200　Bel Air MD 21015
Ph: 443-640-1060　Fx: 443-640-1031

Pet Industry Joint Advisory Council　　www.pijac.org
1220 19th St NW Suite 400　Washington DC 20036
Ph: 202-452-1525　Fx: 202-293-4377　TF: 800-553-7387

Pet Lovers Association
PO Box 145　Joppa MD 21085
Ph: 410-679-0978

Pet Pride　　www.petpride.org
PO Box 1055　Pacific Palisades CA 90272
Ph: 310-836-5427

Pet Products Manufacturers Association Inc, American　　www.appma.org
255 Glenville Rd　Greenwich CT 06831
Ph: 203-532-0000　Fx: 203-532-0551

Pet Savers Foundation　　www.petsavers.org
59 S Bayles Ave　Port Washington NY 11050
Ph: 516-944-5025

Pet Sitters International　　www.petsit.com
201 E King St　King NC 27021
Ph: 336-983-9222　Fx: 336-983-5266

Pet Sitters, National Association of Professional　　www.petsitters.org
17000 Commerce Pkwy Suite C　Mount Laurel NJ 08054
Ph: 856-439-0500　Fx: 856-439-0525　TF: 800-296-7387

Pet Supply Association Inc, World Wide　　www.wwpsa.org
406 S 1st Ave　Arcadia CA 91006
Ph: 626-447-2222　Fx: 626-447-8350　TF: 800-999-7295

Pet, Tattoo-a-　　www.tattoo-a-pet.com
6571 SW 20th Ct　Fort Lauderdale FL 33317
Ph: 954-581-5834　Fx: 954-581-0056　TF: 800-828-8667

Peter Claver, Junior Daughters of　　www.knightsofpeterclaver.com
1825 Orleans Ave　New Orleans LA 70116
Ph: 504-821-4225　Fx: 504-821-4253

Peter Claver, Junior Knights of   www.knightsofpeterclaver.com
1825 Orleans Ave   New Orleans LA 70116
Ph: 504-821-4225 ▪ Fx: 504-821-4253

Peter Claver, Knights of   www.knightsofpeterclaver.com
1825 Orleans Ave   New Orleans LA 70116
Ph: 504-821-4225 ▪ Fx: 504-821-4253

Peter Kiewit Foundation
8805 Indian Hills Dr Suite 225   Omaha NE 68114
Ph: 402-344-7890 ▪ Fx: 402-344-8099

Petrochemical & Refiners Association, National   www.npradc.org
1899 L St NW Suite 1000   Washington DC 20036
Ph: 202-457-0480 ▪ Fx: 202-457-0486

**Petroglyphs & Pictographs, American Committee to Advance
the Study of**   PO Box 158   Shepherdstown WV 25443
Ph: 304-876-3208

Petroleum Accountants Societies, Council of   www.copas.org
PO Box 1190   Denison TX 75021
Ph: 903-463-5463 ▪ Fx: 903-463-5473

Petroleum Association of America, Independent   www.ipaa.org
1201 15th St NW Suite 300   Washington DC 20005
Ph: 202-857-4722 ▪ Fx: 202-857-4799 ▪ TF: 800-433-2851

Petroleum Council, National   www.npc.org
1625 K St NW Suite 600   Washington DC 20006
Ph: 202-393-6100 ▪ Fx: 202-331-8539

Petroleum Engineers, American Institute of Mining Metallurgical &   www.aimehq.org
8307 Shaffer Pkwy PO Box 270728   Littleton CO 80127
Ph: 303-948-4255 ▪ Fx: 303-948-4260

Petroleum Engineers, Society of   www.spe.org
222 Palisades Creek Dr   Richardson TX 75080
Ph: 972-952-9300 ▪ Fx: 972-952-9435

Petroleum Equipment Institute   www.peinet.org
PO Box 2380   Tulsa OK 74101
Ph: 918-494-9696 ▪ Fx: 918-491-9895

Petroleum Equipment Suppliers Association   www.pesa.org
9225 Katy Fwy Suite 310   Houston TX 77024
Ph: 713-932-0168 ▪ Fx: 713-932-0497

Petroleum Evaluation Engineers, Society of   www.spee.org
1001 McKinney St Suite 801   Houston TX 77002
Ph: 713-651-1639 ▪ Fx: 713-951-9659

Petroleum Geologists, American Association of   www.aapg.org
1444 S Boulder Ave   Tulsa OK 74119
Ph: 918-584-2555 ▪ Fx: 918-560-2694 ▪ TF: 800-364-2274

Petroleum & Industrial Workers, International Union of
8131 E Rosecrans Ave   Paramount CA 90723
Ph: 562-630-6232 ▪ Fx: 562-408-1073 ▪ TF: 800-624-5842

Petroleum Industry Research Foundation Inc   pirinc.org
3 Park Ave 26th Fl   New York NY 10016
Ph: 212-686-6470 ▪ Fx: 212-686-6558

Petroleum Institute, American   api-ec.api.org
1220 L St NW   Washington DC 20005
Ph: 202-682-8000 ▪ Fx: 202-682-8029

Petroleum Marketers Association of America   www.pmaa.org
1901 N Fort Myer Dr Suite 500   Arlington VA 22209
Ph: 703-351-8000 ▪ Fx: 703-351-9160 ▪ TF: 800-300-7622

Petroleum Marketers Association of America's Small Business Community
1901 N Fort Myer Dr Suite 5000   Arlington VA 22209
Ph: 703-351-8000 ▪ Fx: 703-351-9160 ▪ TF: 800-300-7622

Petroleum Packaging Council   www.ppcouncil.org
111 E Avenida San Gabriel   San Clemente CA 92672
Ph: 949-369-7102 ▪ Fx: 949-366-1057

Petroleum, Society of Professional Women in   www.spwp.org
13511 Queensbury Ln   Houston TX 77079
Ph: 713-461-2898

Petroleum Technology Transfer Council   www.pttc.org
16010 Barkers Point Ln Suite 220   Houston TX 77079
Ph: 281-921-1720 ▪ Fx: 281-921-1723 ▪ TF: 888-843-7882

Petrophysicists & Well Log Analysts, Society of   www.spwla.org
8866 Gulf Fwy Suite 320   Houston TX 77017
Ph: 713-947-8727 ▪ Fx: 713-947-7181

Petty Officers' Association, National Chief   www.members.tripod.com/NCPOA/main.html
106 Waring Welfare Rd   Boerne TX 78006
Ph: 830-537-4899

Petty Officers Association, US Coast Guard Chief   www.uscgcpoa.org
5520-G Hempstead Way   Springfield VA 22151
Ph: 703-941-0395 ▪ Fx: 703-941-0397

Pew Charitable Trusts   www.pewtrusts.org
2005 Market St 1 Commerce Sq Suite 1700   Philadelphia PA
19103
Ph: 215-575-9050 ▪ Fx: 215-575-4939 ▪ TF: 800-634-4850

Pewter Guild, American
c/o Fischer Pewter 11940 Old Buckingham Rd   Midlothian VA
23113
Ph: 804-379-3282 ▪ Fx: 804-897-1593

Peyote Way Church   www.peyoteway.org
30800 W Klondyke Rd   Klondyke AZ 85643
Ph: 928-828-3444 ▪ Fx: 928-828-3417

PGA of America   www.pga.com
100 Ave of the Champions   Palm Beach Gardens FL 33418
Ph: 561-624-8400 ▪ Fx: 561-624-8439 ▪ TF: 800-477-6465

PGA Tour Inc   www.pgatour.com
112 PGA Tour Blvd   Ponte Vedra Beach FL 32082
Ph: 904-285-3700 ▪ Fx: 904-285-7913

Phantom Friends, Society of   www.nancydrewsleuth.com/tww.html
PO Box 1437   North Highlands CA 95660
Ph: 916-331-7435

Pharmaceutical Association, Generic   www.gphaonline.com
1620 I St NW Suite 800   Washington DC 20006
Ph: 202-833-9070 ▪ Fx: 202-833-9612

Pharmaceutical Association, National   www.npha.net
107 Kilmayne Dr Suite C   Cary NC 27511
Ph: 800-944-6742 ▪ Fx: 919-469-5870

Pharmaceutical & Biotech Trainers, Society of   www.spbt.org
4423 Pheasant Ridge Rd Suite 100   Roanoke VA 24014
Ph: 540-725-3859 ▪ Fx: 540-989-7482

Pharmaceutical Care Management Association   www.pcmanet.org
601 Pennsylvania Ave Suite 740   Washington DC 20004
Ph: 202-207-3610 ▪ Fx: 202-207-3623

Pharmaceutical Companies, Canada's Research-Based   www.canadapharma.org
55 Metcalfe St Suite 1220   Ottawa ON K1P6L5
Ph: 613-236-0455 ▪ Fx: 613-236-6756

Pharmaceutical Council, National   www.npcnow.org
1894 Preston White Dr   Reston VA 20191
Ph: 703-620-6390 ▪ Fx: 703-476-0904

Pharmaceutical Education, American Council on   www.acpe-accredit.org
20 N Clark St Suite 2500   Chicago IL 60602
Ph: 312-664-3575 ▪ Fx: 312-664-4652

Pharmaceutical Education, American Foundation for
1 Church St Suite 202   Rockville MD 20850
Ph: 301-738-2160 ▪ Fx: 301-738-2161

Pharmaceutical Engineering, International Society for   www.ispe.org
3109 W Dr ML King Jr Blvd Suite 250   Tampa FL 33607
Ph: 813-960-2105 ▪ Fx: 813-264-2816

**Pharmaceutical Excipients Council of the Americas,
International**   1655 N Fort Myer Dr Suite 700   Arlington VA
22209   www.ipecamericas.org
Ph: 703-875-2127 ▪ Fx: 703-525-5157

Pharmaceutical Fraternity, Alpha Zeta Omega   www.azo.org/
4422 Porpoise Dr   Tampa FL 33617
Ph: 813-988-5338

Pharmaceutical Fraternity, Kappa Psi   www.kappa-psi.org
100 Campus Dr   Weatherford OK 73096
Ph: 580-774-7170 ▪ Fx: 580-774-7125

Pharmaceutical Physicians, American Academy of   aapp.org
1031 Pemberton Hill Rd Suite 101   Apex NC 27502
Ph: 919-355-1000 ▪ Fx: 919-355-1010

Pharmaceutical Printed Literature Association   www.pplaonline.org
252 N Washington St   Falls Church VA 22046
Ph: 703-538-5799 ▪ Fx: 703-538-6305

Pharmaceutical Research & Manufacturers of America   www.phrma.org
1100 15th St NW   Washington DC 20005
Ph: 202-835-3400 ▪ Fx: 202-835-3414

Pharmaceutical Scientists, American Association of   www.aaps.org
2107 Wilson Blvd Suite 700   Arlington VA 22201
Ph: 703-243-2800 ▪ Fx: 703-243-9650

Pharmaceutical Specialties, Board of   www.bpsweb.org
2215 Constitution Ave NW   Washington DC 20037
Ph: 202-429-7591 ▪ Fx: 202-429-6304

(Pharmaceutical Technology) PDA   www.pda.org
PO Box 79465   Baltimore MD 21279
Ph: 301-986-0293 ▪ Fx: 301-986-1093

Pharmaceutical Wholesalers, International Federation of   www.ifpw.com
10569 Crestwood Dr   Manassas VA 22109
Ph: 703-331-3714 ▪ Fx: 703-331-3715

(Pharmaceuticals) Blessings International   www.blessing.org
PO Box 35292   Tulsa OK 74146
Ph: 918-250-8101 ▪ Fx: 918-250-1281 ▪ TF: 877-250-8101

Pharmacists, American Society of Consultant   www.ascp.com
1321 Duke St   Alexandria VA 22314
Ph: 703-739-1300 ▪ Fx: 703-739-1321 ▪ TF: 800-355-2727

Pharmacists, American Society of Health-System   www.ashp.org
7272 Wisconsin Ave   Bethesda MD 20814
Ph: 301-657-3000 ▪ Fx: 301-664-8877

(Pharmacists) APhA Foundation   www.aphafoundation.org
2215 Constitution Ave NW   Washington DC 20037
Ph: 202-429-7565 ▪ Fx: 202-429-6300

Pharmacists Association, American   www.aphanet.org
2215 Constitution Ave NW   Washington DC 20037
Ph: 202-628-4410 ▪ Fx: 202-783-2351

Pharmacists Association, National Community   www.ncpanet.org
205 Daingerfield Rd   Alexandria VA 22314
Ph: 703-683-8200 ▪ Fx: 703-683-3619 ▪ TF: 800-544-7447

Pharmacists, Association of Natural Medicine   www.anmp.org
PO Box 150727   San Rafael CA 94915
Ph: 415-479-1512 ▪ Fx: 415-472-2559

Pharmacists Guild of the US, National Catholic
1012 Surrey Hills Dr   Saint Louis MO 63117
Ph: 314-645-0085

Pharmacists, International Academy of Compounding   www.iacprx.org
PO Box 1365   Sugar Land TX 77487
Ph: 281-933-8400 ▪ Fx: 281-495-0602 ▪ TF: 800-927-4227

Pharmacists, Society of Infectious Diseases   www.sidp.org
502 E 11th St Suite 400   Austin TX 78701
Ph: 512-708-0611 ▪ Fx: 512-708-0627

Pharmacoeconomics & Outcomes Research, International Society for   www.ispor.org
3100 Princeton Pike Bldg 3 Suite E   Lawrenceville NJ 08648
Ph: 609-219-0773 ▪ Fx: 609-219-0774

Pharmacoepidemiology, International Society for   www.pharmacoepi.org
4350 East-West Hwy Suite 401   Bethesda MD 20814
Ph: 301-718-6500 ▪ Fx: 301-656-0989

Pharmacognosy, American Society of   www.phcog.org
PO Box 28665   Scottsdale AZ 85255
Ph: 623-202-3500 ▪ Fx: 623-572-3510

Pharmacology Inc, American Board of Clinical   www.abcp.net
PO Box 40278   San Antonio TX 78229
Ph: 210-567-8505 ▪ Fx: 210-567-8509

Pharmacology, American College of Clinical   www.accp1.org
3 Ellinwood Ct   New Hartford NY 13413
Ph: 315-768-6117 ▪ Fx: 315-768-6119

Pharmacology & Experimental Therapeutics, American Society for   www.aspet.org
9650 Rockville Pike   Bethesda MD 20814
Ph: 301-634-7060 ▪ Fx: 301-634-7061

(Pharmacology) Lambda Kappa Sigma   www.lks.org
20110 Glenoaks Dr Brookfield WI 53045
Ph: 800-557-1913 Fx: 414-784-8406

Pharmacology & Therapeutics, American Academy of Veterinary   www.aavpt.org
621 W Hill St Champaign IL 61820
Ph: 217-359-0661 Fx: 217-244-1652

Pharmacology & Therapeutics, American Society for Clinical   www.ascpt.org
528 N Washington St Alexandria VA 22314
Ph: 703-836-6981 Fx: 703-836-5223

Pharmacopeia, US   www.usp.org
12601 Twinbrook Pkwy Rockville MD 20852
Ph: 301-881-0666 Fx: 301-816-8525 TF: 800-877-6209

Pharmacopoeia of the US, Homeopathic   www.hpus.com
PO Box 2221 Southeastern PA 19399
Ph: 610-783-5124 Fx: 610-783-5180

Pharmacy, Academy of Managed Care   www.amcp.org
100 N Pitt St Suite 400 Alexandria VA 22314
Ph: 703-683-8416 Fx: 703-683-8417 TF: 800-827-2627

Pharmacy, Academy of Students of   www.aphanet.org/students/studentsnew.htm
American Pharmacists Assn 2215 Constitution Ave NW Washington DC 20037
Ph: 202-628-4410 Fx: 202-783-2351

Pharmacy, American Association of Colleges of   www.aacp.org
1426 Prince St Alexandria VA 22314
Ph: 703-739-2330 Fx: 703-836-8982

Pharmacy, American College of Clinical   www.accp.com
3101 Broadway Suite 650 Kansas City MO 64111
Ph: 816-531-2177 Fx: 816-531-4990

Pharmacy, American Institute of the History of   www.aihp.org
777 Highland Ave Madison WI 53705
Ph: 608-262-5378

Pharmacy, American Society for Automation in   www.asapnet.org
492 Norristown Rd Suite 160 Blue Bell PA 19422
Ph: 610-825-7783 Fx: 610-825-7641

Pharmacy Association Executives, National Council of State   www.ncspae.org
c/o Virginia Pharmacists Assn 5501 Patterson Ave Suite 200 Richmond VA 23226
Ph: 804-285-4145 Fx: 804-285-4227

Pharmacy, Commission for Certification in Geriatric   www.ccgp.org
1321 Duke St Alexandria VA 22314
Ph: 703-535-3038 Fx: 703-739-1500

Pharmacy, National Association of Boards of   www.nabp.net
700 Busse Hwy Park Ridge IL 60068
Ph: 847-698-6227 Fx: 847-698-6238

Pharmacy Practice & Management, Academy of   www.aphanet.org/APPMIntro.html
American Pharmacists Assn 2215 Constitution Ave NW Washington DC 20037
Ph: 202-628-4410 Fx: 202-783-2351

Pharmacy Technician Certification Board   www.ptcb.org
2215 Constitution Ave NW Washington DC 20037
Ph: 202-429-7576 Fx: 202-429-7596

Pharmacy Technicians Association, National   www.pharmacytechnician.org
3920 FM 1960 W Suite 380 Houston TX 77068
Ph: 281-866-7900 Fx: 281-895-7320 TF: 888-247-8700

Pharmacy Technicians, Canadian Association of   www.capt.ca
PO Box 1271 Stn F Toronto ON M4Y2V8
Ph: 416-410-1142

Pheasant & Waterfowl Society, American   www3.upatsix.com/apws
W2270 US Hwy 10 Granton WI 54436
Ph: 715-238-7291 Fx: 715-238-7623

Phelps-Stokes Fund   www.psfdc.org
1420 K St NW Washington DC 20005
Ph: 202-371-9344 TF: 800-874-7797

Phenomenology & Existential Philosophy, Society for   www.spep.org
Seattle Univ Dept of Philosophy 900 Broadway Seattle WA 98122
Ph: 206-296-5473 Fx: 206-296-5997

Phenomenology Institute, World   www.phenomenology.org
1 Ivy Pointe Way Hanover NH 03755
Ph: 802-295-3487 Fx: 802-295-5963

Phi Alpha Delta Law Fraternity International   www.pad.org
345 N Charles St Baltimore MD 21201
Ph: 410-347-3118 Fx: 410-347-3119

Phi Alpha Theta   www.phialphatheta.org
Univ of South Florida 4202 E Fowler Ave SOC 107 Tampa FL 33620
Ph: 813-974-8212 Fx: 813-974-8215 TF: 800-394-8195

Phi Beta Fraternity   www.phibeta.com
2110 Manor Green Dr Madison WI 53711
Ph: 608-288-0561

Phi Beta Kappa Society   www.pbk.org
1606 New Hampshire Ave NW Washington DC 20009
Ph: 202-265-3808 Fx: 202-986-1601

Phi Beta Lambda Inc, Future Business Leaders of America -   www.fbla-pbl.org
1912 Association Dr Reston VA 20191
Ph: 703-860-3334 Fx: 703-758-0749 TF: 800-325-2946

Phi Beta Sigma Fraternity Inc   www.pbs1914.org
145 Kennedy St NW Washington DC 20011
Ph: 202-726-5434 Fx: 202-882-1681

Phi Chi Medical Fraternity   www.phi-chi.org
2039 Ridgewood Dr Floyds Knobs IN 47119
Ph: 812-948-0581 Fx: 812-941-8850 TF: 800-800-7442

Phi Chi Theta   www.phichitheta.org
5215 N O'Connor Blvd Suite 200 Irving TX 75039
Ph: 972-443-9889 Fx: 214-350-8011

Phi Delta Epsilon Medical Fraternity   www.phide.org
2228 E Solana Dr Phoenix AZ 85016
Ph: 800-347-3713 Fx: 602-956-3983

Phi Delta Kappa International   www.pdkintl.org
408 N Union St Bloomington IN 47402
Ph: 812-339-1156 Fx: 812-339-0018 TF: 800-766-1156

Phi Delta Phi International Legal Fraternity   www.phideltaphi.org
1426 21st St NW Washington DC 20036
Ph: 202-223-6801 Fx: 202-223-6808 TF: 800-368-5606

Phi Delta Theta   www.phideltatheta.org
2 S Campus Ave Oxford OH 45056
Ph: 513-523-6345 Fx: 513-523-9200

Phi Epsilon Kappa   www2.truman.edu/pek
901 W New York St Indianapolis IN 46202
Ph: 317-637-8431

Phi Eta Sigma   www.phietasigma.org
Western Kentucky University 525 Grise Hall 1 Big Red Way Bowling Green KY 42101
Ph: 270-745-6540 Fx: 270-745-3893

Phi Gamma Delta, International Fraternity of   www.phigam.org
1201 Red Mile Rd PO Box 1599 Lexington KY 40544
Ph: 859-255-1848 Fx: 859-253-0779

Phi Iota Alpha Fraternity Inc   www.phiota.org

Phi Kappa Phi, Honor Society of   www.phikappaphi.org
LSU Baton Rouge PO Box 16000 Baton Rouge LA 70893
Ph: 225-388-4917 Fx: 225-388-4900 TF: 800-804-9880

Phi Kappa Psi   www.phikappapsi.com
510 Lockerbie St Indianapolis IN 46202
Ph: 317-632-1852 Fx: 317-637-1898 TF: 800-486-1852

Phi Kappa Sigma International Fraternity Inc   www.pks.org
2 Timber Dr Chester Springs PA 19425
Ph: 610-469-3282 Fx: 610-469-3286

Phi Kappa Tau   www.phikappatau.org
5221 Morning Sun Rd Oxford OH 45056
Ph: 513-523-4193 Fx: 513-523-9325 TF: 800-758-1906

Phi Kappa Theta National Fraternity   www.phikaps.org
9640 N Augusta Dr Suite 420 Carmel IN 46032
Ph: 317-872-9934 Fx: 317-879-1889

Phi Kappa Upsilon Fraternity   www.phikappaupsilon.com
21000 W Nine-Mile Rd Southfield MI 48075
Ph: 248-356-9591

Phi Lambda Upsilon   www.cpac.washington.edu/~campbell/plu
Univ of Washington Chemistry Dept Box 351700 Seattle WA 98195
Ph: 206-616-6085

Phi Mu Alpha Sinfonia Fraternity of America Inc   www.sinfonia.org
10600 Old State Rd Evansville IN 47711
Ph: 812-867-2433 Fx: 812-867-0633

Phi Mu Fraternity   www.phimu.org
3558 Habersham at Northlake Tucker GA 30084
Ph: 770-496-5582 Fx: 770-496-0833 TF: 888-744-6836

Phi Rho Sigma Medical Society   www.phirhosigma.org
PO Box 90264 Indianapolis IN 46290
Ph: 317-334-8720 Fx: 317-334-8721

Phi Sigma Biological Sciences Honor Society   www.phisigmasociety.org
Eastern Illinois Univ 2029 Life Science Bldg Charleston IL 61920
Ph: 217-581-3126 Fx: 217-581-7141

Phi Sigma Iota   www.phisigmaiota.org
Univ of South Florida World Language Education 4202 E Fowler Ave Tampa FL 33620
Ph: 813-974-2746 Fx: 813-974-6944 TF: 800-673-5599

Phi Sigma Kappa   www.phisigmakappa.org
2925 E 96th St Indianapolis IN 46240
Ph: 317-573-5420 Fx: 317-573-5430

Phi Sigma Phi National Fraternity Inc   www.phisigmaphi.org
PO Box 9089 Appleton WI 54911
Ph: 920-788-4295 Fx: 920-788-4322

Phi Sigma Pi National Honor Fraternity Inc   www.phisigmapi.org
2119 Ambassador Cir Lancaster PA 17603
Ph: 717-299-4710 Fx: 717-390-3054

Phi Sigma Sigma Fraternity Inc   www.phisigmasigma.org
23123 SR 7 Suite 250 Boca Raton FL 33428
Ph: 561-451-4415 Fx: 561-451-4576

Phi Sigma Tau
Marquette Univ Dept of Philosophy Milwaukee WI 53201
Ph: 414-288-6857 Fx: 414-288-3010

Phi Theta Kappa International Honor Society   www.ptk.org
1625 Eastover Dr PO Box 13729 Jackson MS 39236
Ph: 601-984-3504 Fx: 601-984-3550

Phi Theta Pi Fraternity   www.phithetapi.org
2103 Cortez Rd Jacksonville FL 32246
Ph: 888-608-9841 Fx: 904-641-9006

Phi Upsilon Omicron Inc   phiu.unl.edu

Philalethes Society   www.freemasonry.org/psoc
5266 Mary Ball Rd Lancaster VA 22503
Ph: 804-737-4498 Fx: 804-328-2386

Philanthropic Research Inc   www.guidestar.org
427 Scotland St Williamsburg VA 23185
Ph: 757-229-4631 Fx: 757-229-8912 TF: 800-784-9378

Philanthropique, Societe Culinaire   www.societeculinaire.com
305 E 47th St Suite 11B New York NY 10017
Ph: 212-308-0628 Fx: 212-308-0588

Philanthropy, AAFRC Trust for   www.aafrc.org/philanthropy/
10293 N Meridian St Suite 175 Indianapolis IN 46290
Ph: 317-816-1613 Fx: 317-816-1633 TF: 800-462-2372

(Philanthropy) Adolph Coors Foundation   www.acoorsfdn.org
4100 E Mississippi Ave Suite 1850 Denver CO 80246
Ph: 303-388-1636 Fx: 303-388-1684

(Philanthropy) Ahmanson Foundation
9215 Wilshire Blvd Beverly Hills CA 90210
Ph: 310-278-0770

(Philanthropy) Alfred P Sloan Foundation   www.sloan.org
630 5th Ave Suite 2550 New York NY 10111
Ph: 212-649-1649 Fx: 212-757-5117

(Philanthropy) Allen Foundation for the Arts
505 5th Ave S Suite 900   Seattle WA 98104
Ph: 206-342-2000 ▩ Fx: 206-342-3000
www.pgafoundations.com/arts.asp

(Philanthropy) Allen Foundation for Music
505 5th Ave S Suite 900   Seattle WA 98104
Ph: 206-342-2000 ▩ Fx: 206-342-3000
www.pgafoundations.com/music.asp

Philanthropy, American Institute of
3450 N Lake Shore Dr Suite 2802E   Chicago IL 60657
Ph: 773-529-2300 ▩ Fx: 773-529-0024
www.charitywatch.org

(Philanthropy) Amon G Carter Foundation
PO Box 1036   Fort Worth TX 76101
Ph: 817-332-2783 ▩ Fx: 817-332-2787
www.agcf.org

(Philanthropy) Andrew W Mellon Foundation
140 E 62nd St   New York NY 10021
Ph: 212-838-8400 ▩ Fx: 212-888-4172
www.mellon.org

(Philanthropy) Annenberg Foundation
150 N Radnor-Chester Rd Suite 200   Radnor PA 19087
Ph: 610-341-9066 ▩ Fx: 610-964-8688
www.whannenberg.org

(Philanthropy) Annie E Casey Foundation
701 Saint Paul St   Baltimore MD 21202
Ph: 410-547-6600 ▩ Fx: 410-547-6624 ▩ TF: 800-222-1099
www.aecf.org

(Philanthropy) Archibald Bush Foundation
332 Minnesota St Suite E-900   Saint Paul MN 55101
Ph: 651-227-0891 ▩ Fx: 651-297-6485
www.bushfoundation.org

(Philanthropy) Arison Foundation
3655 NW 87th Ave   Miami FL 33178
Ph: 305-599-2600 ▩ Fx: 305-406-4700

(Philanthropy) Arthur DeMoss Foundation
777 S Flagler Dr Suite 1600   West Palm Beach FL 33401
Ph: 561-804-9000 ▩ Fx: 561-804-9025

(Philanthropy) Arthur Vining Davis Foundations
225 Water St Suite 1510   Jacksonville FL 32202
Ph: 904-359-0670 ▩ Fx: 904-359-0675
www.jvm.com/davis

Philanthropy, Association for Healthcare
313 Park Ave Suite 400   Falls Church VA 22046
Ph: 703-532-6243 ▩ Fx: 703-532-7170
www.ahp.org

(Philanthropy) Barr Foundation
136 NE Olive Way   Boca Raton FL 33432
Ph: 561-394-6514 ▩ Fx: 561-391-7601
www.oandp.com/barr

(Philanthropy) Bill & Melinda Gates Foundation
PO Box 23350   Seattle WA 98102
Ph: 206-709-3100 ▩ Fx: 206-709-3180 ▩ TF: 888-452-6352
www.gatesfoundation.org

(Philanthropy) Brown Foundation Inc
PO Box 130646   Houston TX 77219
Ph: 713-523-6867 ▩ Fx: 713-523-2917
www.brownfoundation.org

(Philanthropy) Carnegie Corp of New York
437 Madison Ave 26th Fl   New York NY 10022
Ph: 212-371-3200 ▩ Fx: 212-754-4073
www.carnegie.org

(Philanthropy) Champlin Foundations
300 Centerville Rd Suite 300S   Warwick RI 02886
Ph: 401-736-0370 ▩ Fx: 401-736-7248
fdncenter.org/grantmaker/champlin

(Philanthropy) Charles Hayden Foundation
140 Broadway 51st Fl   New York NY 10005
Ph: 212-785-3677 ▩ Fx: 212-785-3689
fdncenter.org/grantmaker/hayden

(Philanthropy) Charles & Helen Schwab Foundation
1650 S Amphlett Blvd Suite 300   San Mateo CA 94402
Ph: 650-655-2412 ▩ Fx: 650-655-2411
www.schwabfoundation.org

(Philanthropy) Charles Stewart Mott Foundation
503 S Saginaw St Suite 1200   Flint MI 48502
Ph: 810-238-5651 ▩ Fx: 810-766-1753
www.mott.org

(Philanthropy) Chatlos Foundation
PO Box 915048   Longwood FL 32791
Ph: 407-862-5077
www.chatlos.org

(Philanthropy) Commonwealth Fund
1 E 75th St   New York NY 10021
Ph: 212-606-3800 ▩ Fx: 212-249-1276
www.cmwf.org

(Philanthropy) Conrad N Hilton Foundation
100 W Liberty St Suite 840   Reno NV 89501
Ph: 775-323-4221 ▩ Fx: 775-323-4150
www.hiltonfoundation.org

(Philanthropy) David & Lucile Packard Foundation
300 2nd St Suite 200   Los Altos CA 94022
Ph: 650-948-7658 ▩ Fx: 650-948-5793
www.packard.org

(Philanthropy) Donald W Reynolds Foundation
1701 Village Ctr Cir   Las Vegas NV 89134
Ph: 702-804-6000 ▩ Fx: 702-804-6099
www.dwreynolds.org

(Philanthropy) Doris Duke Charitable Foundation
650 5th Ave 19th Fl   New York NY 10019
Ph: 212-974-7000 ▩ Fx: 212-974-7095
fdncenter.org/grantmaker/dorisduke

(Philanthropy) Duke Endowment
100 N Tryon St Suite 3500   Charlotte NC 28202
Ph: 704-376-0291 ▩ Fx: 704-376-9336
www.dukeendowment.org

(Philanthropy) Edna McConnell Clark Foundation
250 Park Ave Suite 900   New York NY 10177
Ph: 212-551-9100 ▩ Fx: 212-986-4558
www.emcf.org

(Philanthropy) Educational Foundation of America
35 Church Ln   Westport CT 06880
Ph: 203-226-6498 ▩ Fx: 203-227-0424
www.efaw.org

(Philanthropy) EL Wiegand Foundation
165 W Liberty St Suite 200 Wiegand Ctr   Reno NV 89501
Ph: 775-333-0310 ▩ Fx: 775-333-0314

(Philanthropy) Evelyn & Walter Haas Jr Fund
1 Market St Suite 400   San Francisco CA 94105
Ph: 415-856-1400 ▩ Fx: 415-856-1500
www.haasjr.org

(Philanthropy) Ewing Marion Kauffman Foundation
4801 Rockhill Rd   Kansas City MO 64110
Ph: 816-932-1000 ▩ Fx: 816-932-1100 ▩ TF: 800-489-4900
www.emkf.org

(Philanthropy) Ford Family Foundation
1600 NW Stewart Pkwy   Roseburg OR 97470
Ph: 541-957-5574 ▩ Fx: 541-957-5720
www.tfff.org

(Philanthropy) Ford Foundation
320 E 43rd St   New York NY 10017
Ph: 212-573-5000 ▩ Fx: 212-351-3677
www.fordfound.org

(Philanthropy) Foundation Center
79 5th Ave 2nd Fl   New York NY 10003
Ph: 212-620-4230 ▩ Fx: 212-807-3691 ▩ TF: 800-424-9836
fdncenter.org

(Philanthropy) Gates Family Foundation
3575 Cherry Creek North Dr Suite 100   Denver CO 80209
Ph: 303-722-1881 ▩ Fx: 303-316-3038
www.gatesfamilyfoundation.org

(Philanthropy) George S & Dolores Dore Eccles Foundation
79 S Main St 12th Fl   Salt Lake City UT 84111
Ph: 801-246-5355 ▩ Fx: 801-350-3510

(Philanthropy) Geraldine R Dodge Foundation
163 Madison Ave   Morristown NJ 07962
Ph: 973-540-8442 ▩ Fx: 973-540-1211
www.grdodge.org

(Philanthropy) Goizueta Foundation
4401 Northside Pkwy Suite 520   Atlanta GA 30327
Ph: 404-239-0390 ▩ Fx: 404-239-0018
www.goizuetafoundation.org

(Philanthropy) Hall Family Foundation
2501 McGee St MD 323   Kansas City MO 64108
Ph: 816-274-8516 ▩ Fx: 816-274-8547

(Philanthropy) Henry J Kaiser Family Foundation
2400 Sand Hill Rd   Menlo Park CA 94025
Ph: 650-854-9400 ▩ Fx: 650-854-4800
www.kff.org

(Philanthropy) Henry Luce Foundation Inc
111 W 50th St Suite 4601   New York NY 10020
Ph: 212-489-7700 ▩ Fx: 212-581-9541
www.hluce.org

(Philanthropy) Herbert H & Grace A Dow Foundation
1018 W Main St   Midland MI 48640
Ph: 989-631-3699 ▩ Fx: 989-631-0675 ▩ TF: 800-362-4849
www.hhdowfoundation.org

(Philanthropy) Horace W Goldsmith Foundation
375 Park Ave Rm 1602   New York NY 10152
Ph: 212-319-8700 ▩ Fx: 212-319-2881

(Philanthropy) Howard Heinz Endowment
625 Liberty Ave 30 Dominion Tower   Pittsburgh PA 15222
Ph: 412-281-5777 ▩ Fx: 412-281-5788
www.heinz.org

(Philanthropy) Hudson-Webber Foundation
333 W Fort St Suite 1310   Detroit MI 48226
Ph: 313-963-7777 ▩ Fx: 313-963-2818
www.hudson-webber.org

(Philanthropy) J Bulow Campbell Foundation
50 Hurt Plaza Suite 850   Atlanta GA 30303
Ph: 404-658-9066 ▩ Fx: 404-659-4802

(Philanthropy) J Paul Getty Trust
1200 Getty Center Dr   Los Angeles CA 90049
Ph: 310-440-7340 ▩ Fx: 310-440-7704
www.getty.edu

(Philanthropy) JA & Kathryn Albertson Foundation
PO Box 70002   Boise ID 83707
Ph: 208-424-2600 ▩ Fx: 208-424-2626
www.jkaf.org

(Philanthropy) James Irvine Foundation
1 Market St Steuart Tower Suite 2500   San Francisco CA 94105
Ph: 415-777-2244 ▩ Fx: 415-777-0869
www.irvine.org

(Philanthropy) Jay & Betty Van Andel Foundation
333 Bostwick Ave NE   Grand Rapids MI 49503
Ph: 616-234-5000 ▩ Fx: 616-234-5001
www.vai.org

(Philanthropy) JE & LE Mabee Foundation Inc
401 S Boston Ave 30th Fl   Tulsa OK 74103
Ph: 918-584-4286
www.mabeefoundation.com

(Philanthropy) John D & Catherine T MacArthur Foundation
140 S Dearborn St Suite 1100   Chicago IL 60603
Ph: 312-726-8000 ▩ Fx: 312-920-6284 ▩ TF: 800-662-8004
www.macfound.org

(Philanthropy) John S & James L Knight Foundation
200 S Biscayne Blvd Suite 3300   Miami FL 33131
Ph: 305-908-2600 ▩ Fx: 305-908-2698 ▩ TF: 800-711-2004
www.knightfdn.org

(Philanthropy) John Templeton Foundation
100 Matsonford Rd 5 Radnor Corporate Ctr Suite 100   Radnor PA 19087
Ph: 610-687-8942 ▩ Fx: 610-687-8961
www.templeton.org

(Philanthropy) Joyce Foundation
70 W Madison St Suite 2750   Chicago IL 60602
Ph: 312-782-2464 ▩ Fx: 312-782-4160
www.joycefdn.org

(Philanthropy) Kate B Reynolds Charitable Trust
128 Reynolda Village   Winston-Salem NC 27106
Ph: 336-723-1456 ▩ Fx: 336-723-7765
www.kbr.org

(Philanthropy) Kiwanis International Foundation
3636 Woodview Trace   Indianapolis IN 46268
Ph: 317-875-8755
kif.kiwanis.org

(Philanthropy) Koret Foundation
33 New Montgomery St Suite 1090   San Francisco CA 94105
Ph: 415-882-7740 ▩ Fx: 415-882-7775
www.koretfoundation.org

(Philanthropy) Kresge Foundation
3215 W Big Beaver Rd   Troy MI 48084
Ph: 248-643-9630 ▩ Fx: 248-643-0588
www.kresge.org

(Philanthropy) Lilly Endowment Inc
2801 N Meridian St   Indianapolis IN 46208
Ph: 317-924-5471 ▩ Fx: 317-926-4431
www.lillyendowment.org

(Philanthropy) Lois Pope LIFE Foundation
6274 Linton Blvd Suite 103   Delray Beach FL 33484
Ph: 561-865-0955 ▩ Fx: 561-865-0938
www.life-edu.org

(Philanthropy) Longwood Foundation Inc
100 W 10th St Suite 1109   Wilmington DE 19801
Ph: 302-654-2477 ▩ Fx: 302-654-2323

(Philanthropy) Lynde & Harry Bradley Foundation Inc
1241 N Franklin Pl   Milwaukee WI 53202
Ph: 414-291-9915 ▩ Fx: 414-291-9991
www.bradleyfdn.org

(Philanthropy) Lyndhurst Foundation
517 E 5th St   Chattanooga TN 37403
Ph: 423-756-0767 ▩ Fx: 423-756-0770
www.lyndhurstfoundation.org

(Philanthropy) Magic Johnson Foundation Inc   www.magicjohnson.org
9100 Wilshire Blvd East Tower Suite 700   Beverly Hills CA 90212
Ph: 310-246-4400 ▪ Fx: 310-246-1106 ▪ TF: 888-624-4205

(Philanthropy) McCune Foundation   www.mccune.org
6 PPG Pl Suite 750   Pittsburgh PA 15222
Ph: 412-644-8779 ▪ Fx: 412-644-8059

(Philanthropy) McKnight Foundation   www.mcknight.org
710 2nd St S Suite 400   Minneapolis MN 55401
Ph: 612-333-4220 ▪ Fx: 612-332-3833

(Philanthropy) Meadows Foundation Inc   www.mfi.org
3003 Swiss Ave   Dallas TX 75204
Ph: 214-826-9431 ▪ Fx: 214-827-7042 ▪ TF: 800-826-9431

(Philanthropy) Meyer Memorial Trust   www.mmt.org
425 NW 10th Ave Suite 400   Portland OR 97209
Ph: 503-228-5512 ▪ Fx: 503-228-5840

(Philanthropy) Milken Family Foundation   www.mff.org
1250 4th St   Santa Monica CA 90401
Ph: 310-570-4800 ▪ Fx: 310-570-4801

(Philanthropy) MJ Murdock Charitable Trust   www.murdock-trust.org
703 Broadway St Suite 710   Vancouver WA 98660
Ph: 360-694-8415 ▪ Fx: 360-694-1819

(Philanthropy) Moody Foundation   www.moodyf.org
2302 Post Office St Suite 704   Galveston TX 77550
Ph: 409-763-5333 ▪ Fx: 409-763-5564

(Philanthropy) Morris & Gwendolyn Cafritz Foundation   www.cafritzfoundation.org
1825 K St NW 14th Fl   Washington DC 20006
Ph: 202-223-3100 ▪ Fx: 202-296-7567

Philanthropy, National Committee for Responsive   www.ncrp.org
2001 'S' St NW Suite 620   Washington DC 20009
Ph: 202-387-9177 ▪ Fx: 202-332-5084

(Philanthropy) Nellie Mae Education Foundation   www.nmefdn.org
1250 Hancock St Suite 205N   Quincy MA 02169
Ph: 781-348-4200 ▪ Fx: 781-348-4299 ▪ TF: 877-635-5436

(Philanthropy) Open Society Institute   www.soros.org
400 W 59th St   New York NY 10019
Ph: 212-548-0600 ▪ Fx: 212-548-4679

(Philanthropy) Paul G Allen Charitable Foundation   www.pgafoundations.com
505 5th Ave S Suite 900   Seattle WA 98104
Ph: 206-342-2000 ▪ Fx: 206-342-3000

(Philanthropy) Paul G Allen Forest Protection   www.pgafoundations.com/forest.asp
Foundation   505 5th Ave S Suite 900   Seattle WA 98104
Ph: 206-342-2000 ▪ Fx: 206-342-3000

(Philanthropy) Paul G Allen Foundation for   www.pgafoundations.com/med.asp
Medical Research   505 5th Ave S Suite 900   Seattle WA 98104
Ph: 206-342-2000 ▪ Fx: 206-342-3000

(Philanthropy) Paul G Allen Virtual Education   www.pgafoundations.com/edu.asp
Foundation   505 5th Ave S Suite 900   Seattle WA 98104
Ph: 206-342-2000 ▪ Fx: 206-342-3000

(Philanthropy) Peter Kiewit Foundation
8805 Indian Hills Dr Suite 225   Omaha NE 68114
Ph: 402-344-7890 ▪ Fx: 402-344-8099

(Philanthropy) Pew Charitable Trusts   www.pewtrusts.org
2005 Market St 1 Commerce Sq Suite 1700   Philadelphia PA 19103
Ph: 215-575-9050 ▪ Fx: 215-575-4939 ▪ TF: 800-634-4850

(Philanthropy) Pritzker Foundation
200 W Madison St 38th Fl   Chicago IL 60606
Ph: 312-750-8400 ▪ Fx: 312-750-8545

(Philanthropy) Research Corp   www.rescorp.org
4703 E Camp Lowell Dr Suite 201   Tucson AZ 85712
Ph: 520-571-1111 ▪ Fx: 520-571-1119

(Philanthropy) Retirement Research Foundation   www.rrf.org
8765 W Higgins Rd Suite 430   Chicago IL 60631
Ph: 773-714-8080 ▪ Fx: 773-714-8089

(Philanthropy) Richard King Mellon   www.fdncenter.org/grantmaker/rkmellon
Foundation   500 Grant St Suite 4106   Pittsburgh PA 15219
Ph: 412-392-2800 ▪ Fx: 412-392-2837

(Philanthropy) Robert R McCormick Tribune Foundation   www.mccormicktribune.org
435 N Michigan Ave Suite 770   Chicago IL 60611
Ph: 312-222-3512 ▪ Fx: 312-222-3523

(Philanthropy) Robert W Woodruff Foundation Inc   www.woodruff.org
50 Hurt Plaza Suite 1200   Atlanta GA 30303
Ph: 404-522-6755 ▪ Fx: 404-522-7026

(Philanthropy) Robert A Welch Foundation   www.welch1.org
5555 San Felipe St Suite 1900   Houston TX 77056
Ph: 713-961-9884 ▪ Fx: 713-961-5168

(Philanthropy) Robert Wood Johnson Foundation   www.rwjf.org
PO Box 2316   Princeton NJ 08543
Ph: 609-452-8701 ▪ Fx: 609-627-6701

(Philanthropy) Rockefeller Brothers Fund   www.rbf.org
437 Madison Ave 37th Fl   New York NY 10022
Ph: 212-812-4200 ▪ Fx: 212-812-4299

(Philanthropy) Rockefeller Foundation   www.rockfound.org
420 5th Ave   New York NY 10018
Ph: 212-869-8500 ▪ Fx: 212-764-3468 ▪ TF: 800-645-1133

(Philanthropy) Rosie's For All Kids Foundation Inc   www.forallkids.org
PO Box 225   Allendale NJ 07401
Ph: 201-934-5567

Philanthropy Roundtable   www.philanthropyroundtable.org
1150 17th St NW Suite 503   Washington DC 20036
Ph: 202-822-8333 ▪ Fx: 202-822-8325

(Philanthropy) Roy J Carver Charitable Trust   www.carvertrust.org
202 Iowa Ave   Muscatine IA 52761
Ph: 563-263-4010 ▪ Fx: 563-263-1547

(Philanthropy) Skillman Foundation   www.skillman.org
600 Rennissance Ctr Suite 1700   Detroit MI 48243
Ph: 313-393-1185 ▪ Fx: 313-393-1187

(Philanthropy) Spencer Foundation   www.spencer.org
875 N Michigan Ave Suite 3930   Chicago IL 60611
Ph: 312-337-7000 ▪ Fx: 312-337-0282

(Philanthropy) Starr Foundation   fdncenter.org/grantmaker/starr
70 Pine St 14th Fl   New York NY 10270
Ph: 212-770-6883 ▪ Fx: 212-425-6261

(Philanthropy) Sunshine Lady Foundation Inc   www.sunshineladyfdn.org
PO Box 1074   Morehead City NC 28557
Ph: 252-240-2788 ▪ Fx: 252-240-2933

(Philanthropy) Surdna Foundation Inc   www.surdna.org
330 Madison Ave 30th Fl   New York NY 10017
Ph: 212-557-0010 ▪ Fx: 212-557-0003

(Philanthropy) Tinker Foundation   fdncenter.org/grantmaker/tinker
55 E 59th St   New York NY 10022
Ph: 212-421-6858 ▪ Fx: 212-223-3326

(Philanthropy) Turner Foundation Inc   www.turnerfoundation.org
133 Luckie St NW 2nd Fl   Atlanta GA 30303
Ph: 404-681-9900 ▪ Fx: 404-681-0172

(Philanthropy) Vira I Heinz Endowment   www.heinz.org
625 Liberty Ave 30 Dominion Tower   Pittsburgh PA 15222
Ph: 412-281-5777 ▪ Fx: 412-281-5788

(Philanthropy) Wallace Foundation   www.wallacefoundation.org
2 Park Ave 23rd Fl   New York NY 10016
Ph: 212-251-9700 ▪ Fx: 212-679-6990 ▪ TF: 800-771-9701

(Philanthropy) Walter & Elise Haas Fund   www.haassr.org
1 Market St Suite 400   San Francisco CA 94105
Ph: 415-856-1400 ▪ Fx: 415-856-1500

(Philanthropy) Walton Family Foundation Inc   www.wffhome.com
PO Box 2030   Bentonville AR 72712
Ph: 479-464-1570 ▪ Fx: 479-464-1580

(Philanthropy) Wayne & Gladys Valley Foundation
1939 Harrison St Suite 510   Oakland CA 94612
Ph: 510-466-6060 ▪ Fx: 510-466-6067

(Philanthropy) Weingart Foundation   www.weingartfnd.org
1055 W 7th St Suite 3050   Los Angeles CA 90017
Ph: 213-688-7799 ▪ Fx: 213-688-1515

(Philanthropy) Whitaker Foundation   www.whitaker.org
1700 N Moore St Suite 2200   Arlington VA 22209
Ph: 703-528-2430 ▪ Fx: 703-528-2431

(Philanthropy) Whitehall Foundation Inc   www.whitehall.org
380 South County Rd PO Box 3423   Palm Beach FL 33480
Ph: 561-655-4474 ▪ Fx: 561-659-4978

(Philanthropy) William & Flora Hewlett Foundation   www.hewlett.org
2121 Sand Hill Rd   Menlo Park CA 94025
Ph: 650-234-4500 ▪ Fx: 650-234-4501

(Philanthropy) William K Warren Foundation
6585 S Yale Ave Suite 900   Tulsa OK 74136
Ph: 918-492-8100 ▪ Fx: 918-481-7935

(Philanthropy) William Penn Foundation   www.wpennfdn.org
100 N 18th St 2 Logan Sq 11th Fl   Philadelphia PA 19103
Ph: 215-988-1830 ▪ Fx: 215-988-1823

(Philanthropy) William Randolph Hearst Foundation   hearstfdn.org
888 7th Ave 45th Fl   New York NY 10106
Ph: 212-586-5404 ▪ Fx: 212-586-1917

(Philanthropy) WK Kellogg Foundation   www.wkkf.org
1 Michigan Ave E   Battle Creek MI 49017
Ph: 269-968-1611 ▪ Fx: 269-968-0413

(Philanthropy) WM Keck Foundation   www.wmkeck.org
550 S Hope St Suite 2500   Los Angeles CA 90071
Ph: 213-680-3833 ▪ Fx: 213-614-0934

Philatelic Association, Brazil
462 W Walnut St   Long Beach NY 11561
Ph: 516-431-3412

Philatelic Association, Eire   www.eirephilatelicassoc.org
PO Box 704   Bernardsville NJ 07924
Ph: 908-766-2728 ▪ Fx: 908-766-7783

Philatelic Foundation   www.philatelicfoundation.org
70 W 40th St 15th Fl   New York NY 10018
Ph: 212-221-6555 ▪ Fx: 212-221-6208

Philatelic Music Circle   www.philatelicmusic.com
PO Box 1781   Sequim WA 98382
Ph: 360-683-6373

Philatelic Research Library,   www.stamps.org/TheLibrary/lib_AbouttheAPRL.htm
American   PO Box 8000   State College PA 16803
Ph: 814-237-3803 ▪ Fx: 814-237-6128

Philatelic Society of America, Hellenic
541 Cedar Hill Ave   Wyckoff NJ 07481
Ph: 201-447-6262 ▪ Fx: 201-612-9228

Philatelic Society, American   www.stamps.org
100 Oakwood Ave PO Box 8000   State College PA 16803
Ph: 814-237-3803 ▪ Fx: 814-237-6128

Philatelic Society, Christopher Columbus
11258 Goodnight Ln Suite 105   Dallas TX 75229
Ph: 972-241-2326 ▪ Fx: 972-243-4381

Philatelic Society, Croatian   www.croatianstamps.com
PO Box 696   Fritch TX 79036
Ph: 806-857-0129

Philatelic Society, Haiti   www.haitiphilately.org
5709 Marble Arch Way   Alexandria VA 22315
Ph: 703-922-9531

Philatelic Specialist Society, Ryukyu   users.netmdc.com/~rpss
PO Box 381   Clayton CA 94517
Ph: 925-672-0960

Philatelists of America, Junior   www.jpastamps.org
PO Box 2625   Albany OR 97321
Ph: 541-967-7043 ▪ Fx: 541-967-9515

Philatelists, American Society of Polar   www.polarphilatelists.org
PO Box 39   Exton PA 19341
Ph: 610-321-0740 ▪ Fx: 610-321-0219

(Philately) American First Day Cover Society   www.afdcs.org
PO Box 65960   Tucson AZ 85728
Ph: 520-321-0880 ▨ Fx: 520-321-0879

(Philately) American Topical Association   www.americantopicalassn.org
PO Box 57   Arlington TX 76004
Ph: 817-274-1181 ▨ Fx: 817-274-1184

(Philately) Collectors Club   www.collectorsclub.org
22 E 35th St   New York NY 10016
Ph: 212-683-0559 ▨ Fx: 212-481-1269

(Philately) Disabled Collectors' Correspondence   www.members.aol.com/disabledcc
Club

Philately, India Study Circle for   www.indiastudycircle.org
PO Box 7326   Washington DC 20044
Ph: 202-564-6876 ▨ Fx: 202-565-2441

(Philately) Mobile Post Office Society   www.eskimo.com/~rkunz/mposhome.html
PO Box 427   Marston Mills MA 02648
Ph: 508-428-9132

(Philately) Perfins Club Inc   www.perfins.com/perfclub.htm
10 Clarridge Cir   Milford MA 01757
Ph: 508-478-7303

(Philately) Universal Ship Cancellation Society   www.uscs.org

(Philately) Western Cover Society   www.westerncoversociety.org

Philippine American Chamber of Commerce Inc   www.philamchamber.org
317 Madison Ave Suite 520   New York NY 10017
Ph: 212-972-9326 ▨ Fx: 212-687-5844

Philippine American Chambers of Commerce Inc, US Federation of   www.fpacc.com
2887 College Ave Suite 1 Box 106   Berkeley CA 94705
Ph: 510-548-7952 ▨ Fx: 510-845-9901

Philolexian Society   www.columbia.edu/cu/philo
Columbia Univ 521 W 114th St   New York NY 10027
Ph: 212-854-4909 ▨ Fx: 212-854-3434

Philological Association, American   www.apaclassics.org
Univ of Pennsylvania 292 Logan Hall   249 S 36th
St   Philadelphia PA 19104
Ph: 215-898-4975 ▨ Fx: 215-573-7874

Philoptochos Society, Greek Orthodox Ladies   www.philoptochos.org
345 E 74th St   New York NY 10021
Ph: 212-744-4390 ▨ Fx: 212-861-1956

Philosophers, Society of Christian   www.siu.edu/~scp
Calvin College Dept of Philosophy 3201 Burton St SE   Grand
Rapids MI 49546
Ph: 616-526-6421

Philosophic Research, Institute of Advanced
PO Box 805   Moultonborough NH 03254
Ph: 603-284-7047

Philosophical Association, American   www.apa.udel.edu/apa
Univ of Delaware 31 Amstel Ave   Newark DE 19716
Ph: 302-831-1112 ▨ Fx: 302-831-8690

Philosophical Research Society   www.prs.org
3910 Los Feliz Blvd   Los Angeles CA 90027
Ph: 323-663-2167 ▨ Fx: 323-663-9443 ▨ TF: 800-548-4062

Philosophical Societies, Conference of
D'Youville College Div of Liberal Arts   Buffalo NY 14201
Ph: 716-881-7786

Philosophical Society, American   www.amphilsoc.org
104 S 5th St   Philadelphia PA 19106
Ph: 215-440-3400 ▨ Fx: 215-440-3436

Philosophical Society, Evangelical   www.epsociety.org
Biola Univ McNally 66 13800 Biola Ave   La Mirada CA 90639
Ph: 562-906-4570 ▨ Fx: 562-906-4592

Philosophical Study of Genocide & the Holocaust, Society   www.loyno.edu/~spsgh
for the   Loyola Univ Dept of Philosophy   New Orleans LA
70118
Ph: 504-865-3940 ▨ Fx: 504-865-3948

Philosophical Study of Marxism,   www.pages.drexel.edu/~pa34/spsm_website.htm
Society for the   Univ at Buffalo Dept of Philosophy 135 Park
Hall   Buffalo NY 14260
Ph: 716-645-2444 ▨ Fx: 716-645-6139

Philosophy for Children, Institute for the Advancement   www.montclair.edu/pages/iapc
of   Montclair State Univ 14 Normal Ave   Upper Montclair NJ
07043
Ph: 973-655-4977

Philosophy, Council for Research in Values &   www.crvp.org
PO Box 261 Cardinal Stn   Washington DC 20064
Ph: 202-319-6089

Philosophy Documentation Center   www.pdcnet.org
706 Forest St   Charlottesville VA 22903
Ph: 434-220-3300 ▨ Fx: 434-220-3301 ▨ TF: 800-444-2419

Philosophy of Education Society   cuip.net/pes
Southern Illinois Univ College of Education   Carbondale IL
62901
Ph: 618-536-4434

Philosophy, International Association for Greek   www.hri.org/iagp

Philosophy of Law & Social Philosophy, International   www.cirfid.unibo.it/ivr
Association for   Univ of Hawaii at Manoa Dept of Philosophy
2530 Dole St   Honolulu HI 96822
Ph: 808-956-8954 ▨ Fx: 808-956-9228

Philosophy & Literature, International Association for   www.iapl.info
Stony Brook University   Stony Brook NY 11794
Ph: 631-632-7592 ▨ Fx: 631-331-0142

Philosophy, North American Society for Social   www.pitt.edu/~nassp/nassp.html
c/o Philosophy Documentation Ctr PO Box 7147   Charlottesville
VA 22906
Ph: 434-220-3300 ▨ Fx: 434-220-3301 ▨ TF: 800-444-2419

(Philosophy) Phi Sigma Tau
Marquette Univ Dept of Philosophy   Milwaukee WI 53201
Ph: 414-288-6857 ▨ Fx: 414-288-3010

Philosophy & Public Policy, Institute for   www.puaf.umd.edu/IPPP
Maryland School of Public Affairs 3111 Van Munching
Hall   College Park MD 20742
Ph: 301-405-4753 ▨ Fx: 301-314-9346

Philosophy of Religion, Society for
Univ of Georgia Dept of Philosophy Peabody Hall   Athens GA
30602
Ph: 706-542-2823 ▨ Fx: 706-542-2839

Philosophy & Social Studies of Biology, International   www.phil.vt.edu/ishpssb
Society for the History   13423 Burma Rd SW   Vashon Island
WA 98070
Ph: 206-567-5839

Philosophy, Society for the Advancement of American   www.american-philosophy.org
Southern Illinois Univ Dept of Philosophy MC 4505   Carbondale
IL 62901
Ph: 618-536-6641

Philosophy, Society for Ancient Greek   sagp.binghamton.edu
Binghamton Univ Dept of Philosophy   Binghamton NY 13902
Ph: 607-777-2886 ▨ Fx: 607-777-2734

Philosophy, Society for Exact   web.phil.ufl.edu/SEP

Philosophy, Society for Natural   tam.cornell.edu/SNP/society.htm
Cornell Univ Kimball Hall - TAM   Ithaca NY 14853
Ph: 607-255-3738 ▨ Fx: 607-255-2011

Philosophy, Society for Phenomenology & Existential   www.spep.org
Seattle Univ Dept of Philosophy 900 Broadway   Seattle WA
98122
Ph: 206-296-5473 ▨ Fx: 206-296-5997

Philosophy & Technology, Society for   www.spt.org
San Jose Univ Dept of Philosophy 1 Washington Sq   San Jose
CA 95192
Ph: 408-924-4526

Phlebology Society of America
5 Daremy Ct   Nesconset NY 11767
Ph: 631-366-1429 ▨ Fx: 631-366-3609

Phlebotomy Association, National   www.nationalphlebotomy.org
1901 Brightseat Rd   Landover MD 20785
Ph: 301-386-4200 ▨ Fx: 301-386-4203

Phoenix Center for Advanced Legal & Economic Public   www.phoenix-center.org
Policy Studies   5335 Wisconsin Ave NW Suite
440   Washington DC 20015
Ph: 202-274-0235

Phoenix Society for Burn Survivors   www.phoenix-society.org
2153 Wealthy St SE Suite 215   East Grand Rapids MI 49506
Ph: 616-458-2773 ▨ Fx: 616-458-2831 ▨ TF: 800-888-2876

Phonograph Collectors Club, Antique
502 E 17th St   Brooklyn NY 11226
Ph: 718-941-6835 ▨ Fx: 718-941-1408

Phosphate Chemicals Export Association   www.phoschem.com
100 S Saunders Rd Suite 300   Lake Forest IL 60045
Ph: 847-739-1200

Photo-Chemical Machining Institute   www.pcmi.org
38 Strawberry Ln PO Box 739   East Dennis MA 02641
Ph: 508-385-0085 ▨ Fx: 508-385-0086

Photo Equipment Technicians, National Association of   napet.pmai.org
3000 Picture Pl   Jackson MI 49201
Ph: 517-788-8100 ▨ Fx: 517-788-8371

Photo Finishing Engineers, Society of   spfe.pmai.org
3000 Picture Pl   Jackson MI 49201
Ph: 517-788-8100 ▨ Fx: 517-788-8371

Photo Imaging Education Association   piea.pmai.org
3000 Picture Pl   Jackson MI 49201
Ph: 517-788-8100 ▨ Fx: 517-788-8371

Photo Marketing Association International   www.pmai.org
3000 Picture Pl   Jackson MI 49201
Ph: 517-788-8100 ▨ Fx: 517-788-8371

Photo-Technologists, Society of   www.spt.info
11112 Spotted Rd S   Cheney WA 99004
Ph: 509-624-9621 ▨ Fx: 509-624-5320 ▨ TF: 888-662-7678

Photobiology, American Society for   www.photobiology.org
PO Box 1897   Lawrence KS 66044
Ph: 785-843-1235 ▨ Fx: 785-843-1287

Photogrammetric Surveyors, Management Association for Private   www.mapps.org/
1760 Reston Pkwy Suite 515   Reston VA 20190
Ph: 703-787-6996 ▨ Fx: 703-787-7550

Photogrammetry & Remote Sensing, American Society for   www.asprs.org
5410 Grosvenor Ln Suite 210   Bethesda MD 20814
Ph: 301-493-0290 ▨ Fx: 301-493-0208

Photographers of America, Advertising   www.apanational.org
PO Box 361309   Los Angeles CA 90036
Ph: 800-272-6264

Photographers of America, Pictorial   www.ppa-photoclub.org
299 W 12th St Suite 11G   New York NY 10014
Ph: 212-242-1117

Photographers of America Inc, Professional   www.ppa.com
229 Peachtree St NE Suite 2200   Atlanta GA 30303
Ph: 404-522-8600 ▨ Fx: 404-614-6400 ▨ TF: 800-786-6277

Photographers, American Society of
PO Box 316   Willimantic CT 06226
Ph: 860-423-1402 ▨ Fx: 860-423-9402 ▨ TF: 800-638-9609

Photographers, American Society of Media   www.asmp.org
150 N 2nd St   Philadelphia PA 19106
Ph: 215-451-2767 ▨ Fx: 215-451-0880

Photographers Association, International Fire   www.ifpaonline.com
143 40th St   New Orleans LA 70124
Ph: 504-482-9616 ▨ Fx: 504-482-9636

Photographers Association, National Press   www.nppa.org
3200 Croasdaile Dr Suite 306   Durham NC 27705
Ph: 919-383-7246 ▨ Fx: 919-383-7261

Photographers' Association, White House News   www.whnpa.org
PO Box 7119 Ben Franklin Stn   Washington DC 20044
Ph: 202-785-5230

Photographers International, Antique & Amusement   www.oldtimephotos.org
37 W Broad St Suite 480   Columbus OH 43215
Ph: 614-358-2828 ▪ Fx: 614-241-2215

Photographers International Council, Evidence   www.epic-photo.org
600 Main St   Honesdale PA 18431
Ph: 570-253-5450 ▪ Fx: 570-253-5011 ▪ TF: 800-356-3742

Photographers International, Professional School   pspa.pmai.org
3000 Picture Pl   Jackson MI 49201
Ph: 517-788-8100 ▪ Fx: 517-788-8371

Photographers International, Wedding & Portrait   www.wppinow.com/index2.tml
1312 Lincoln Blvd   Santa Monica CA 90406
Ph: 310-451-0090 ▪ Fx: 310-395-9058

Photographers' Society, Ophthalmic   www.opsweb.org
1869 Ranch Rd   Nixa MO 65714
Ph: 417-725-0181 ▪ Fx: 417-724-8450 ▪ TF: 800-403-1677

Photographic Art & Science Foundation
2100 NE 52nd St   Oklahoma City OK 73111
Ph: 405-424-4055 ▪ Fx: 405-424-4058

Photographic Artisans Guild, American   apag.net

Photographic Education, Society for   www.spenational.org
Miami Univ 110 Art Bldg   Oxford OH 45056
Ph: 513-529-8328 ▪ Fx: 513-529-1532

Photographic Historical Organization, International   www.well.com/user/silver
PO Box 16074   San Francisco CA 94116
Ph: 415-681-4356

Photographic Historical Society, American   www.superexpo.com/APHS.htm
1150 Ave of the Americas   New York NY 10036
Ph: 212-575-0483

Photographic Society of America   www.psa-photo.org
3000 United Founders Blvd Suite 103   Oklahoma City OK 73112
Ph: 405-843-1437 ▪ Fx: 405-843-1438

Photography Art Dealers, Association of International   www.artline.com/associations/ipa/ipa.html
1609 Connecticut Ave NW Suite 200   Washington DC 20009
Ph: 202-986-0105 ▪ Fx: 202-986-0448

Photography Association, North American Nature   www.nanpa.org
10200 W 44th Ave Suite 304   Wheat Ridge CO 80033
Ph: 303-422-8527 ▪ Fx: 303-422-8894

Photography Instructors Association, National
1255 Hill Dr   Eagle Rock CA 90041
Ph: 323-254-1549 ▪ Fx: 323-254-2797

Photoimaging Manufacturers & Distributors Association
109 White Oak Ln Suite 72F   Old Bridge NJ 08857
Ph: 732-679-3460 ▪ Fx: 732-679-2294

Phycological Society of America   www.psaalgae.org

Physiatric Association of Spine Sports & Occupational Rehabilitation   www.aapmr.org/passor.htm
1 IBM Plaza Suite 2500   Chicago IL 60611
Ph: 312-464-9700 ▪ Fx: 312-464-0227

Physical Activity Aging & Sports, International Association of   www.rit.edu/~pjr0120/csa/iapaas/main.html
706 Madison Ave   Albany NY 12208
Ph: 518-465-6927 ▪ Fx: 518-462-1339

Physical Activity, North American Society for the Psychology of Sport &   www.naspspa.org
Univ of Nevada Dept of Kinesiology 4505 Maryland Pkwy   Las Vegas NV 89154
Ph: 702-895-0938

Physical Education, American Academy of Kinesiology &   www.aakpe.org
c/o Human Kinetics Publishers Inc PO Box 5076   Champaign IL 61820
Ph: 217-351-5076 ▪ Fx: 217-351-2674 ▪ TF: 800-747-4457

Physical Education in Higher Education, National Association for   www.napehe.org
Northern Illinois Univ Dept of Kinesiology & Physical Education Anderson Hall   DeKalb IL 60015
Ph: 815-753-1894

Physical Education, National Association for Sport &   www.aahperd.org
1900 Association Dr   Reston VA 20191
Ph: 703-476-3410 ▪ Fx: 703-476-8316 ▪ TF: 800-213-7193

(Physical Education) Phi Epsilon Kappa   www2.truman.edu/pek
901 W New York St   Indianapolis IN 46202
Ph: 317-637-8431

Physical Education Recreation & Dance, American Alliance for Health   www.aahperd.org
1900 Association Dr   Reston VA 20191
Ph: 703-476-3400 ▪ Fx: 703-476-9527 ▪ TF: 800-213-7193

Physical Fitness Association, International   www.ipfa.org
415 W Court St   Flint MI 48503
Ph: 810-239-2166 ▪ Fx: 810-239-9390 ▪ TF: 877-520-4732

(Physical Fitness) Sigma Delta Psi
The Citadel 171 Moultrie DEAS Hall   Charleston SC 29409
Ph: 843-953-7778 ▪ Fx: 843-953-6978

Physical Medicine & Rehabilitation, American Academy of   www.aapmr.org
1 IBM Plaza Suite 2500   Chicago IL 60611
Ph: 312-464-9700 ▪ Fx: 312-464-0227

Physical Regulation in Biology & Medicine, Society for   www.sprbm.org
2412 Cobblestone Way   Frederick MD 21702
Ph: 301-663-4556 ▪ Fx: 301-694-4948

Physical Sciences of the Oceans, International Association for the   www.iugg.org/iapso
PO Box 820440   Vicksburg MS 39182
Ph: 601-636-1363 ▪ Fx: 601-629-9640

Physical Society, American   www.aps.org
1 Physics Ellipse   College Park MD 20740
Ph: 301-209-3200 ▪ Fx: 301-209-0865

Physical Therapy Association, American   www.apta.org
1111 N Fairfax St   Alexandria VA 22314
Ph: 703-684-2782 ▪ Fx: 703-684-7343 ▪ TF: 800-999-2782

Physical Therapy, Federation of State Boards of   www.fsbpt.org
509 Wythe St   Alexandria VA 22314
Ph: 703-299-3100 ▪ Fx: 703-299-3110 ▪ TF: 800-881-1430

Physical Therapy, Foundation for   www.apta.org/Foundation
1111 Fairfax St   Alexandria VA 22314
Ph: 800-875-1378 ▪ Fx: 703-683-6743

Physically Challenged Bowhunters of America Inc   www.pcba-inc.org
RD 1 Box 470   New Alexandria PA 15670
Ph: 724-668-7439

Physician Assistant Inc, Accreditation Review Commission on Education for the   www.arc-pa.org
1000 N Oak Ave   Marshfield WI 54449
Ph: 715-389-3785 ▪ Fx: 715-387-5163

Physician Assistant Programs, Association of   www.apap.org
950 N Washington St   Alexandria VA 22314
Ph: 703-548-5538 ▪ Fx: 703-684-1924

Physician Assistant Programs, Association of Postgraduate   www.appap.org
PO Box 2128ABC   Philippi WV 26416
Ph: 304-457-6356 ▪ Fx: 304-457-6308

Physician Assistants, American Academy of   www.aapa.org
950 N Washington St   Alexandria VA 22314
Ph: 703-836-2272 ▪ Fx: 703-684-1924

Physician Assistants, American Association of Surgical   www.aaspa.com
PO Box 867   Bernardsville NJ 07924
Ph: 732-560-8378 ▪ Fx: 732-805-9582 ▪ TF: 888-882-2772

Physician Assistants in Cardiovascular Surgery, Association of   www.apacvs.org
PO Box 4834   Englewood CO 80155
Ph: 303-221-5651 ▪ Fx: 303-771-2550 ▪ TF: 877-221-5651

Physician Assistants in Obstetrics & Gynecology, Association of
PO Box 1109   Madison WI 53701
Ph: 800-545-0636

Physician Assistants in Pediatrics, Society for   www.aapa.org/spec/SPAP
950 N Washington St   Alexandria VA 22314
Ph: 800-596-4398

Physician Assistants, Society of Army   www.sapa.org
6762 Candlewood Dr   Fort Myers FL 33919
Ph: 941-482-2162

Physician Assistants, Society of Emergency Medicine   www.sempa.org
950 N Washington St   Alexandria VA 22314
Ph: 703-519-7334 ▪ Fx: 703-684-1924

Physician Association, Air Medical   www.ampa.org
383 F St   Salt Lake City UT 84103
Ph: 801-408-3699 ▪ Fx: 801-408-1668

Physician Executives, American College of   www.acpe.org
4890 W Kennedy Blvd Suite 200   Tampa FL 33609
Ph: 813-287-2000 ▪ Fx: 813-287-8993 ▪ TF: 800-562-8088

Physician Insurers Association of America   www.thepiaa.org
2275 Research Blvd Suite 250   Rockville MD 20850
Ph: 301-947-9000 ▪ Fx: 301-947-9090

Physician, International Order of Saint Luke the   www.orderofstluke.org
PO Box 13701   San Antonio TX 78213
Ph: 210-492-5222 ▪ TF: 877-992-5222

Physician & Patient, American Academy on   www.physicianpatient.org
1000 Executive Pkwy Suite 220   Saint Louis MO 63141
Ph: 314-576-5333 ▪ Fx: 314-576-7989

Physician Recruiters, Association of Staff   www.aspr.org
1711 W County Rd B Suite 300N   Roseville MN 55113
Ph: 651-635-0359 ▪ Fx: 651-635-0307 ▪ TF: 800-830-2777

Physician Recruiters, National Association of   www.napr.org
PO Box 150127   Altamonte Springs FL 32715
Ph: 407-774-7880 ▪ Fx: 407-774-6440 ▪ TF: 800-726-5613

Physician Specialists, American Association of   www.aapsga.org
2296 Henderson Mill Rd Suite 206   Atlanta GA 30345
Ph: 770-939-8555 ▪ Fx: 770-939-8559 ▪ TF: 800-447-9397

Physicians Against Landmines   www.banmines.org
351 E Huron St Suite 225   Chicago IL 60611
Ph: 312-926-0030 ▪ Fx: 312-926-7662

Physicians in AIDS Care, International Association of   www.iapac.org
33 N LaSalle St Suite 1700   Chicago IL 60602
Ph: 312-795-4930 ▪ Fx: 312-795-4938

Physicians, American Academy of Disability Evaluating   www.aadep.org
150 N Wacker Dr Suite 1420   Chicago IL 60606
Ph: 312-658-1171 ▪ Fx: 312-658-1175 ▪ TF: 800-456-6095

Physicians, American Academy of Family   www.aafp.org
11400 Tomahawk Creek Pkwy   Leawood KS 66211
Ph: 913-906-6000 ▪ Fx: 913-906-6075 ▪ TF: 800-274-2237

Physicians, American Academy of Home Care   www.aahcp.org
PO Box 1037   Edgewood MD 21040
Ph: 410-676-7966 ▪ Fx: 410-676-7980

Physicians, American Academy of Pharmaceutical   aapp.org
1031 Pemberton Hill Rd Suite 101   Apex NC 27502
Ph: 919-355-1000 ▪ Fx: 919-355-1010

Physicians, American Academy of Sports
17445 Oak Creek Ct   Encino CA 91316
Ph: 818-501-4433 ▪ Fx: 818-501-8855

Physicians, American Association of Naturopathic   www.naturopathic.org
3201 New Mexico Ave NW Suite 350   Washington DC 20016
Ph: 202-895-1392 ▪ Fx: 202-274-1992 ▪ TF: 866-538-2267

Physicians, American College of   www.acponline.org
190 N Independence Mall W   Philadelphia PA 19106
Ph: 215-351-2400 ▪ Fx: 215-351-2594 ▪ TF: 800-523-1546

Physicians, American College of Emergency   www.acep.org
PO Box 619911   Dallas TX 75261
Ph: 972-550-0911 ▪ Fx: 972-580-2816 ▪ TF: 800-798-1822

Physicians, American College of International   www.acip.org
9323 Old Mount Vernon Rd   Alexandria VA 22309
Ph: 703-221-1500

Physicians, American College of Nuclear   www.acnponline.org
1850 Samuel Morse Dr   Reston VA 20190
Ph: 703-326-1190 ▪ Fx: 703-708-9015

Physicians, American College of Osteopathic Emergency www.acoep.org
142 E Ontario St Suite 1250   Chicago IL 60611
Ph: 312-587-3709 ▪ Fx: 312-587-9951 ▪ TF: 800-521-3709

Physicians, American College of Osteopathic Family www.acofp.org
330 E Algonquin Rd Suite 1   Arlington Heights IL 60005
Ph: 847-228-6090 ▪ Fx: 847-228-9755 ▪ TF: 800-323-0794

Physicians, American Society of Handicapped
3424 S Culpepper Ct   Springfield MO 65804
Ph: 417-881-1570 ▪ Fx: 417-887-9830

Physician's Assistants, American Society of Orthopaedic www.asopa.org
6300 N River Rd Suite 727   Rosemont IL 60018
Ph: 847-823-7186 ▪ Fx: 847-823-0536 ▪ TF: 800-998-6022

Physicians, Association of American www.aap-online.org
Harvard Univ Dept of Medicine Channing Lab 181 Longwood
   Ave   Boston MA 02115
Ph: 617-277-0551 ▪ Fx: 617-731-1541

Physicians, Association of American Indian www.aaip.com
1225 Sovereign Row Suite 103   Oklahoma City OK 73108
Ph: 405-946-7072 ▪ Fx: 405-946-7651

Physicians Association for Anthroposophical Medicine www.paam.net
1923 Geddes Ave   Ann Arbor MI 48104
Ph: 734-930-9462 ▪ Fx: 734-662-1727

Physicians Association, Federal www.fedphy.org
9001 Braddock Rd Suite 380   Springfield VA 22151
Ph: 703-323-9888 ▪ Fx: 703-426-8400 ▪ TF: 800-403-3374

Physicians Association, Flying www.fpadrs.org
PO Box 677427   Orlando FL 32867
Ph: 407-359-1423 ▪ Fx: 407-359-1167

Physicians Association, Renal www.renalmd.org
1700 Rockville Pike Suite 220   Rockville MD 20852
Ph: 301-468-3515 ▪ Fx: 301-468-3511

Physicians & Chirurgiens, Order of Descendants of Colonial
9317 Bent Tree Cir   Wichita KS 67226
Ph: 316-634-1930

Physicians' Committee for Responsible Medicine www.pcrm.org
5100 Wisconsin Ave NW Suite 400   Washington DC 20016
Ph: 202-686-2210 ▪ Fx: 202-686-2216

Physicians & Dentists, National Association of VA www.navapd.org
11 Canal Ctr Plaza Suite 110   Alexandria VA 22314
Ph: 703-548-0280 ▪ Fx: 703-683-7939

Physicians & Dentists, Union of American www.uapd.com
1330 Broadway Suite 730   Oakland CA 94612
Ph: 510-839-0193 ▪ Fx: 510-763-8756

Physicians Fellowship for Medicine in Israel, American www.apfmed.org
2001 Beacon St Suite 210   Boston MA 02135
Ph: 617-232-5382 ▪ Fx: 617-739-2616

Physicians for Human Rights www.phrusa.org
100 Boylston St Suite 702   Boston MA 02116
Ph: 617-695-0041 ▪ Fx: 617-695-0307

Physicians from Latin America, Consortium of www.cophyla.org
1850 E 17th St Suite 219   Santa Ana CA 92705
Ph: 714-836-1116 ▪ Fx: 714-245-1664

Physicians, National Association of EMS www.naemsp.org
PO Box 15945-281   Lenexa KS 66214
Ph: 913-492-5858 ▪ Fx: 913-599-5340 ▪ TF: 800-228-3677

Physicians, National Association of Managed Care www.namcp.com
4435 Waterfront Dr Suite 101 PO Box 4765   Glen Allen VA
   23058
Ph: 804-527-1905 ▪ Fx: 804-747-5316 ▪ TF: 800-722-0376

Physicians for a National Health Program www.pnhp.org
29 E Madison St Suite 602   Chicago IL 60602
Ph: 312-782-6006 ▪ Fx: 312-782-6007

Physicians of North America, Association of Pakistani www.appna.org
6414 S Cass Ave   Westmont IL 60559
Ph: 630-968-8585 ▪ Fx: 630-968-8677

Physicians & Scientists, Academy of Clinical depts.washington.edu/lmaclps
   Laboratory   Univ of Chicago Dept of Pathology MC 0006 5841
   S Maryland Ave   Chicago IL 60637
Ph: 773-702-1878 ▪ Fx: 773-702-9082

Physicians for Social Responsibility www.psr.org
1875 Connecticut Ave NW Suite 1012   Washington DC 20009
Ph: 202-667-4260 ▪ Fx: 202-667-4201

Physicians & Surgeons, American Association of Podiatric
1328 Southern Ave SE Suite 200   Washington DC 20032
Ph: 202-562-2777 ▪ Fx: 202-562-5351

Physicians & Surgeons Inc, Association of American www.aapsonline.org
1601 N Tucson Blvd Suite 9   Tucson AZ 85716
Ph: 520-327-4885 ▪ Fx: 520-325-4230 ▪ TF: 800-635-1196

Physicians & Surgeons, Interamerican College of www.icps.org
915 Broadway Suite 1105   New York NY 10102
Ph: 212-777-3642 ▪ Fx: 212-777-5000

Physicians, Uniformed Services Academy of Family www.usafp.org
2301 N Parham Rd Suite 4   Richmond VA 23229
Ph: 804-968-4436 ▪ Fx: 804-968-4418

Physicians for a Violence-Free Society www.pvs.org
160 14th St   San Francisco CA 94103
Ph: 415-621-3582 ▪ Fx: 415-621-3438

Physicists in Medicine, American Association of www.aapm.org
1 Physics Ellipse   College Park MD 20740
Ph: 301-209-3350 ▪ Fx: 301-209-0862

Physicists, National Society of Black www.nsbp.org
6704 Lee Hwy Suite G   Arlington VA 22205
Ph: 703-536-4207 ▪ Fx: 703-536-4203

Physics, American Academy of Health www.hps1.org/aahp
1313 Dolley Madison Blvd Suite 402   McLean VA 22101
Ph: 703-790-1745 ▪ Fx: 703-790-2672

Physics, American College of Medical www.acmp.org
12100 Sunset Hills Rd Suite 130   Reston VA 20190
Ph: 703-481-5001 ▪ Fx: 703-435-4390

Physics, American Institute of www.aip.org
1 Physics Ellipse   College Park MD 20740
Ph: 301-209-3100 ▪ Fx: 301-209-0843

Physics, International Union of Pure & Applied www.iupap.org
c/o American Physical Society 1 Physics Ellipse   College Park
   MD 20740
Ph: 301-209-3269

Physics Society, Health www.hps.org
1313 Dolley Madison Blvd Suite 402   McLean VA 22101
Ph: 703-790-1745 ▪ Fx: 703-790-2672

Physics Students, Society of www.aip.org/education/sps/index.html
1 Physics Ellipse   College Park MD 20740
Ph: 301-209-3007 ▪ Fx: 301-209-0839

Physics Teachers, American Association of www.aapt.org
1 Physics Ellipse   College Park MD 20740
Ph: 301-209-3300 ▪ Fx: 301-209-0845

Physiological Society, American www.the-aps.org
9650 Rockville Pike   Bethesda MD 20814
Ph: 301-634-7164 ▪ Fx: 301-634-7241

Physiologists, Society of General www.sgpweb.org
PO Box 257   Woods Hole MA 02543
Ph: 508-540-6719 ▪ Fx: 508-540-0155

Physiology Society, Human Anatomy & www.hapsweb.org
8000 Bonhomme Ave Suite 412   Saint Louis MO 63105
Ph: 314-448-4277 ▪ Fx: 314-863-6457

Physiology, Society for the Study of Male Psychology &
321 Iuka Rd   Montpelier OH 43543
Ph: 419-485-3602

Phytopathological Society, American www.apsnet.org
3340 Pilot Knob Rd   Saint Paul MN 55121
Ph: 651-454-7250 ▪ Fx: 651-454-0766

Pi Alpha Alpha www.naspaa.org/initiatives/honor.asp
1120 G St NW Suite 730   Washington DC 20005
Ph: 202-628-8965 ▪ Fx: 202-626-4978

Pi Beta Phi Fraternity for Women www.pibetaphi.org
1154 Town & Country Commons Dr   Town and Country MO
   63017
Ph: 636-256-0680 ▪ Fx: 636-256-8124

Pi Delta Phi
Sam Houston State Univ Box 2147   Huntsville TX 77341
Ph: 936-294-1442 ▪ Fx: 936-294-1408

Pi Kappa Alpha Fraternity www.pka.com
8347 W Range Cove   Memphis TN 38125
Ph: 901-748-1868 ▪ Fx: 901-748-3100

Pi Kappa Lambda
Northwestern Univ School of Music 711 Elgin Rd   Evanston IL
   60208
Ph: 847-491-5737

Pi Kappa Phi Fraternity www.pikapp.org
2102 Cambridge Beltway Dr Suite A PO Box 240526   Charlotte
   NC 28273
Ph: 704-504-0888 ▪ Fx: 704-504-0880

Pi Lambda Phi Fraternity Inc www.pilambdaphi.org
304 Federal Rd Suite 113   Brookfield CT 06804
Ph: 203-740-1044 ▪ Fx: 203-740-1644 ▪ TF: 800-394-7573

Pi Lambda Theta www.pilambda.org
PO Box 6626   Bloomington IN 47407
Ph: 800-487-3411 ▪ Fx: 812-339-3462

Pi Sigma Alpha www.apsanet.org/~psa
1527 New Hampshire Ave NW   Washington DC 20036
Ph: 202-483-2512 ▪ Fx: 202-483-2657

Pi Sigma Epsilon www.pse.org
427 E Stewart St   Milwaukee WI 53207
Ph: 414-328-1952 ▪ Fx: 414-328-1953 ▪ TF: 800-761-9350

Piaget Jean Society www.piaget.org
Harvard Univ Dept of Human Development & Psychology Larsen
   Hall   Cambridge MA 02138
Ph: 617-495-3446 ▪ Fx: 617-495-3626

Piano Foundation, National www.pianonet.com
13140 Coit Rd Suite 320 LB 120   Dallas TX 75240
Ph: 972-233-9107 ▪ Fx: 972-490-4219

Piano Guild, International www.pianoguild.com
808 Rio Grande St   Austin TX 78701
Ph: 512-478-5775 ▪ Fx: 512-478-5843

Piano Manufacturers Association International
13140 Coit Rd Suite 320 LB 120   Dallas TX 75240
Ph: 972-233-9107 ▪ Fx: 972-490-4219

Piano Teachers, National Guild of www.pianoguild.com
PO Box 1807   Austin TX 78767
Ph: 512-478-5775 ▪ Fx: 512-478-5843

Piano Technicians Guild www.ptg.org
3930 Washington St   Kansas City MO 64111
Ph: 816-753-7747 ▪ Fx: 816-531-0070

Pickard Collectors Club
300 E Grove St   Bloomington IL 61701
Ph: 309-828-5533 ▪ Fx: 309-829-2266

Pickle Packers International Inc www.ilovepickles.org
1 Pickle & Pepper Plaza PO Box 606   Saint Charles IL 60174
Ph: 630-584-8950 ▪ Fx: 630-584-0759

Pictographs, American Committee to Advance the Study of
   Petroglyphs &   PO Box 158   Shepherdstown WV 25443
Ph: 304-876-3208

Pictorial Photographers of America www.ppa-photoclub.org
299 W 12th St Suite 11G   New York NY 10014
Ph: 212-242-1117

Picture Framers Association, Professional www.ppfa.com
3000 Picture Pl   Jackson MI 49201
Ph: 517-788-8100 ▪ Fx: 517-788-8371

Picture Professionals, American Society of www.aspp.com
409 S Washington St   Alexandria VA 22314
Ph: 703-229-0219 ▪ Fx: 703-299-0219

Pie Council, American　　　　www.piecouncil.org
PO Box 368　Lake Forest IL 60045
Ph: 847-374-0170　■　Fx: 847-371-0199

Piedmontese Association of the US　　　　pauscattle.org
343 Barrett Rd　Elsberry MO 63343
Ph: 573-384-5685　■　Fx: 573-384-5567

Piercers, Association of Professional　　　www.safepiercing.org
5446 Peachtree Industrial Blvd PMB 286　Chamblee GA 30341
Ph: 888-888-1277

Pierre Fauchard Academy　　　　www.fauchard.org
PO Box 80330　Las Vegas NV 89180
Ph: 702-651-5013　■　Fx: 702-651-5537　■　TF: 800-232-0099

Pig Association, North American Potbellied　　www.petpigs.com
304 County Rd 438　Rocheport MO 65279
Ph: 573-698-3030

Pigeon Fanciers Inc, International Federation of American　www.ifpigeon.com
Homing　PO Box 374　Hicksville NY 11802
Ph: 516-794-3612　■　Fx: 516-794-6654

Pigeon Union, American Racing　　　　www.pigeon.org
PO Box 18465　Oklahoma City OK 73154
Ph: 405-848-5801　■　Fx: 405-848-5888　■　TF: 800-755-2778

Pigments Manufacturers Association, Color　　www.cpma.com
PO Box 20839　Alexandria VA 22320
Ph: 703-684-4044　■　Fx: 703-684-1795

Pigs, National Committees on Potbellied　　www.ncopp.com

PIGS - A Sanctuary　　　　www.pigs.org
RR 1 Box 604　Shepherdstown WV 25443
Ph: 304-262-0080

Pilot Associations, International Council of Aircraft Owner &　www.iaopa.org
421 Aviation Way　Frederick MD 21701
Ph: 301-695-2000　■　Fx: 301-695-2375

Pilot Dogs Inc　　　　www.pilotdogs.org
625 W Town St　Columbus OH 43215
Ph: 614-221-6367　■　Fx: 614-221-1577

Pilot International　　　www.pilotinternational.org
244 College St PO Box 4844　Macon GA 31208
Ph: 478-743-7403　■　Fx: 478-743-2173

Pilots Association, Air Line　　　　www.alpa.org
535 Herndon Pkwy　Herndon VA 20170
Ph: 703-689-2270　■　Fx: 703-689-4177

Pilots Association, Aircraft Owners &　　www.aopa.org
421 Aviation Way　Frederick MD 21701
Ph: 301-695-2000　■　Fx: 301-695-2375　■　TF: 800-872-2672

Pilots Association, Allied　　　www.alliedpilots.org
14600 Trinity Blvd Suite 500　Fort Worth TX 76155
Ph: 817-302-2250　■　Fx: 817-302-2119　■　TF: 800-323-1470

Pilots Association, American
499 S Capitol St SW Suite 409　Washington DC 20003
Ph: 202-484-0700　■　Fx: 202-484-9320

Pilots Association, Cessna　　　　www.cessna.org
3409 Corsair Cir PO Box 5817　Santa Maria CA 93456
Ph: 805-922-2580　■　Fx: 805-922-7249

Pilots Association, Christian　　　www.christianpilots.org
PO Box 90452　Los Angeles CA 90009
Ph: 562-208-2912

Pilots Association, National EMS　　　www.nemspa.org
526 King St Suite 415　Alexandria VA 22314
Ph: 703-836-8930　■　Fx: 703-836-8920

Pilots Association Inc, National WWII Glider　　www.ww2gp.org
21 Phyllis Rd　Freehold NJ 07728
Ph: 732-462-1838

Pilots Association PAC, Air Line　　　www.alpa.org
1625 Massachusetts Ave NW　Washington DC 20036
Ph: 202-797-4033　■　Fx: 202-797-4030

Pilots Association, Precision Aerobatics Model　www.control-line.org
158 Flying Cloud Isle　Foster City CA 94404
Ph: 650-345-0130　■　Fx: 650-578-8454

Pilots Association, Retired Airline　　　www.rapa.org
PO Box 293443　Sacramento CA 95829
Ph: 650-368-0200

Pilots Association, Seaplane　　　www.seaplanes.org
4315 Highland Park Blvd Suite C　Lakeland FL 33813
Ph: 863-701-7979　■　Fx: 863-701-7588　■　TF: 888-772-8923

Pilots Association, US　　　　www.uspilots.org
483 S Kirkwood Rd Suite 10　Saint Louis MO 63122
Ph: 314-849-8772

Pilots Association, Vietnam Helicopter　　www.vhpa.org
5530 Birdcage St Suite 200　Citrus Heights CA 95610
Ph: 916-966-7592　■　Fx: 916-966-8743　■　TF: 800-505-8472

Pilots Bar Association, Lawyer-　　　www.lpba.org/
PO Box 685　Poolesville MD 20837
Ph: 301-972-7700　■　Fx: 301-972-7727

Pilots, International Association of Natural Resource　www.ianrp.org

Pilots, International Organization of Masters Mates &　www.bridgedeck.org
700 Maritime Blvd　Linthicum Heights MD 21090
Ph: 410-850-8700　■　Fx: 410-850-0973　■　TF: 877-667-5522

Pilots, Organization of Black Airline　　www.obap.org
8630 Fenton St Suite 126　Silver Spring MD 20910
Ph: 800-538-6227

Pilots, Society of Experimental Test　　　www.setp.org
PO Box 986　Lancaster CA 93584
Ph: 661-942-9574　■　Fx: 661-940-0398

Pilsudski Jozef Institute of America　　www.pilsudski.org
180 2nd Ave　New York NY 10003
Ph: 212-505-9077　■　Fx: 212-505-9052

Pine Chemicals Association　　　www.pinechemicals.org
3350 Riverwood Pkwy SE Suite 1900　Atlanta GA 30339
Ph: 770-984-5340　■　Fx: 770-984-5341

Pineapple Growers Association of Hawaii
1116 Whitmore Ave　Wahiawa HI 96786
Ph: 808-621-1220　■　Fx: 808-621-7410

Pinto Horse Association of America　　　www.pinto.org
1900 Samuels Ave　Fort Worth TX 76102
Ph: 817-336-7842　■　Fx: 817-336-7416

Pinzgauer Association, American　　　www.pinzgauers.org
PO Box 147　Bethany MO 64424
Ph: 660-425-8617　■　Fx: 660-425-8374　■　TF: 800-914-9883

Pioneer Clubs　　　　www.pioneerclubs.org
PO Box 788　Wheaton IL 60189
Ph: 630-293-1600　■　Fx: 630-293-3053　■　TF: 800-694-2582

Pioneer Memorial & Educational Foundation, Willa Cather　www.willacather.org
413 N Webster　Red Cloud NE 68970
Ph: 402-746-2653　■　Fx: 402-746-2652

Pioneers, Society of California　　　www.californiapioneers.org
300 4th St　San Francisco CA 94107
Ph: 415-957-1849　■　Fx: 415-957-9858

Pioneers, Society of Indiana　　　www.indianapioneers.com
450 W Ohio St　Indianapolis IN 46202
Ph: 317-233-6588

Pioneers, Sons & Daughters of Oregon　　www.webtrail.com/sdop
PO Box 6685　Portland OR 97228
Ph: 503-786-9804

Pipe Association, American Concrete　　www.concrete-pipe.org
222 W Las Colinas Blvd Suite 641　Irving TX 75039
Ph: 972-506-7216　■　Fx: 972-506-7682

Pipe Association International, Tube &　www.tpatube.org/TPA/TPA_Homepage.htm
833 Featherstone Rd　Rockford IL 61107
Ph: 815-399-8775　■　Fx: 815-484-7701

Pipe Association, National Corrugated Steel　　www.ncspa.org
13140 Coit Rd Suite 320 LB 120　Dallas TX 75240
Ph: 972-850-9107　■　Fx: 972-490-4219

Pipe Coating Applicators, National Association of　www.napca.com
333 Texas St Suite 717　Shreveport LA 71101
Ph: 318-227-2769　■　Fx: 318-222-0482

Pipe Distributors, National Association of Steel　www.naspd.com
14760 Memorial Dr Suite 302　Houston TX 77079
Ph: 281-531-7473　■　Fx: 281-531-7475

Pipe Fabrication Institute　　　www.pfi-institute.org
655 32nd Ave Suite 201　Lachine QC H8T3G6
Ph: 514-634-3434　■　Fx: 514-634-9736

Pipe Fittings Association, American　　www.apfa.org
201 Park Washington Ct　Falls Church VA 22046
Ph: 703-538-1786　■　Fx: 703-538-5603

Pipe & Fittings Association, Plastic　　www.ppfahome.org
800 Roosevelt Rd Bldg C Suite 20　Glen Ellyn IL 60137
Ph: 630-858-6540　■　Fx: 630-790-3095

Pipe Institute, Cast Iron Soil　　　www.cispi.org
5959 Shallowford Rd Suite 419　Chattanooga TN 37421
Ph: 423-892-0137　■　Fx: 423-892-0817

Pipe Institute, Fiberglass Tank &　www.fiberglasstankandpipe.com
11150 Wilcrest Dr Suite 101　Houston TX 77099
Ph: 281-568-4100　■　Fx: 281-568-4500

Pipe Institute, National Clay　　　www.ncpi.org
PO Box 759　Lake Geneva WI 53147
Ph: 262-248-9094

Pipe Institute, Plastics　　　www.plasticpipe.org
1825 Connecticut Ave NW Suite 680　Washington DC 20009
Ph: 202-462-9607　■　Fx: 202-462-9779　■　TF: 888-314-6774

Pipe Line Contractors Association　　www.plca.org
1700 Pacific Ave Suite 4100　Dallas TX 75201
Ph: 214-969-2700　■　Fx: 214-969-2705

Pipe Lines, Association of Oil　　　www.aopl.org
1101 Vermont Ave NW Suite 604　Washington DC 20005
Ph: 202-408-7970　■　Fx: 202-408-7983

Pipe Organ Builders of America, Associated　www.apoba.com
PO Box 155　Chicago Ridge IL 60415
Ph: 800-473-5270

Pipe Research Association, Ductile Iron　　www.dipra.org
245 Riverchase Pkwy E Suite 'O'　Birmingham AL 35244
Ph: 205-402-8700　■　Fx: 205-402-8730

Pipe Tobacco Council
1707 H St NW Suite 800　Washington DC 20006
Ph: 202-223-8207　■　Fx: 202-833-0379

Pipe Welding Bureau, National Certified　www.mcaa.org/ncpwb
1385 Piccard Dr　Rockville MD 20850
Ph: 301-869-5800　■　Fx: 301-990-9690

Pipeline Research Council International　　www.prci.org
1401 Wilson Blvd Suite 1101　Arlington VA 22209
Ph: 703-387-0190　■　Fx: 703-387-0192

Piper Owner Society　　　www.piperowner.org
N7450 Aanstad Rd PO Box 5000　Iola WI 54945
Ph: 715-445-5000　■　Fx: 715-445-4053　■　TF: 866-697-4737

Piping Engineers & Designers, Society of　www.spedweb.org
1 Main St Suite 719　Houston TX 77002
Ph: 713-221-8089　■　Fx: 713-226-5230

Pirandello Society of America
592 7th St　Brooklyn NY 11215
Ph: 212-222-9803

Pistachio Commission, California　　　www.pistachios.org
1318 E Shaw Ave Suite 420　Fresno CA 93710
Ph: 559-221-8294　■　Fx: 559-221-8044

Pistol Collectors Association, National Automatic　napca.net
PO Box 15738　Saint Louis MO 63163
Ph: 314-638-6505

Pituitary Network Association　　　www.pituitary.org
PO Box 1958　Thousand Oaks CA 91358
Ph: 805-499-9973　■　Fx: 805-499-1523

Pizza Institute, National Frozen www.affi.com/nfpi/nfpihomepage.htm
2000 Corporate Ridge Suite 1000 McLean VA 22102
Ph: 703-821-0770 ▪ Fx: 703-821-1350

Pizzeria Operators, National Association of www.napo.com
908 S 8th St Suite 200 Louisville KY 40203
Ph: 502-736-9500 ▪ Fx: 502-736-9501 ▪ TF: 800-489-8324

PKF North American Network www.pkfnan.org
3700 Crestwood Pkwy Suite 350 Duluth GA 30096
Ph: 770-279-4560 ▪ Fx: 770-279-4566

Plains Cotton Growers Inc www.plainscotton.org
4517 W Loop 289 Lubbock TX 79414
Ph: 806-792-4904 ▪ Fx: 806-792-4906

Plan International USA www.childreach.org
155 Plan Way Warwick RI 02886
Ph: 401-738-5600 ▪ Fx: 401-738-5608 ▪ TF: 800-556-7918

Planet Drum Foundation www.planetdrum.org
PO Box 31251 San Francisco CA 94131
Ph: 415-285-6556 ▪ Fx: 415-285-6563

Planetarium Society, International www.ips-planetarium.org
PO Box 1812 Greenville NC 27835
Ph: 252-328-6139 ▪ Fx: 252-328-6218

Planetary Society www.planetary.org
65 N Catalina Ave Pasadena CA 91106
Ph: 626-793-5100 ▪ Fx: 626-793-5528

Planned Giving, National Committee on www.ncpg.org
233 McCrea St Suite 400 Indianapolis IN 46225
Ph: 317-269-6274 ▪ Fx: 317-269-6276

Planned Parenthood Action Fund Inc www.plannedparenthoodvotes.org
1780 Massachusetts Ave NW Washington DC 20036
Ph: 202-785-3351 ▪ Fx: 202-296-3763

Planned Parenthood Federation of America www.plannedparenthood.org
810 7th Ave New York NY 10019
Ph: 212-541-7800 ▪ Fx: 212-245-1845 ▪ TF: 800-829-7732

Planned Parenthood Federation, International - Western www.ippfwhr.org
Hemisphere Region 120 Wall St 9th Fl New York NY 10005
Ph: 212-248-6400 ▪ Fx: 212-248-4221

(Planned Parenthood) Margaret Sanger Center www.ppnyc.org/services/msci.html
International 26 Bleecker St New York NY 10012
Ph: 212-274-7315 ▪ Fx: 212-274-7299

Planners, American Institute of Certified www.planning.org/aicp
1776 Massachusetts Ave NW Suite 400 Washington DC 20036
Ph: 202-872-0611 ▪ Fx: 202-872-0643

Planners International, Association of Contingency www.acp-international.com
7044 S 13th St Oak Creek WI 53154
Ph: 414-768-8000 ▪ Fx: 414-768-8001

Planners, International Society of Meeting www.iami.org/ismp
1224 N Nokomis NE Alexandria MN 56308
Ph: 320-763-4919 ▪ Fx: 320-763-9290

Planners, National Association of County
c/o National Assn of Counties 440 1st St NW Washington DC
20001
Ph: 202-393-6226

Planners Network www.plannersnetwork.org
379 DeKalb Ave Brooklyn NY 11205
Ph: 718-636-3461 ▪ Fx: 718-636-3709

Planning Association, American www.planning.org
1776 Massachusetts Ave NW Washington DC 20036
Ph: 202-872-0611 ▪ Fx: 202-872-0643

Planning, Association of Collegiate Schools of www.acsp.org
6311 Mallard Trace Tallahassee FL 32312
Ph: 850-385-2054 ▪ Fx: 850-385-2084

Planning, National Council for Research & www.nmsu.edu/~NCRP

Planning, Society for College & University www.scup.org
339 E Liberty St Suite 300 Ann Arbor MI 48104
Ph: 734-998-7832 ▪ Fx: 734-998-6532

Planning & Visual Education Partnership www.visualstore.com/pave
3368A Oxford Ave Saint Louis MO 63143
Ph: 314-645-0701

Plant Association, Perennial www.perennialplant.org
3383 Schirtzinger Rd Hilliard OH 43026
Ph: 614-771-8431 ▪ Fx: 614-876-5238

Plant Biologists, American Society of www.aspb.org
15501 Monona Dr Rockville MD 20855
Ph: 301-251-0560 ▪ Fx: 301-279-2996

Plant Biosystematists, International Organization of www.iopb.org

Plant Board, National www.aphis.usda.gov/npb
California Dept of Food & Agriculture 1220 'N' St Sacramento
CA 95814
Ph: 916-654-1022 ▪ Fx: 916-654-1018

Plant Conservation, Center for www.mobot.org/CPC
PO Box 299 Saint Louis MO 63166
Ph: 314-577-9450 ▪ Fx: 314-577-9465

Plant Council, People- www.hort.vt.edu/human/PPC.html
Virginia Polytechnic Institute 407 Saunders Hall Blacksburg VA
24061
Ph: 540-231-6254 ▪ Fx: 540-231-3083

Plant Food Control Officials, Association of American www.aapfco.org
Univ of Kentucky 103 Regulatory Services Bldg Lexington KY
40546
Ph: 859-257-2668 ▪ Fx: 859-257-9478

Plant Growth Regulation Society of America www.griffin.peachnet.edu/pgrsa
PO Box 2945 La Grange GA 30241
Ph: 706-845-9085 ▪ Fx: 706-883-8215

Plant Management Society, Aquatic www.apms.org
PO Box 821265 Vicksburg MS 39182
Ph: 601-634-2656

Plant Manufacturers Bureau, Concrete www.cpmb.org
900 Spring St Silver Spring MD 20910
Ph: 301-587-1400 ▪ Fx: 301-587-1605

Plant Microbe Interactions, International Society for Molecular www.ismpminet.org
3340 Pilot Knob Rd Saint Paul MN 55121
Ph: 651-454-7250 ▪ Fx: 651-454-0766 ▪ TF: 800-481-2698

Plant Molecular Biology, International Society for www.uga.edu/~ispmb
Univ of Georgia Dept of Biochemistry & Molecular
Biology Athens GA 30602
Ph: 706-542-3239 ▪ Fx: 706-542-2090

Plant Patent Owners, National Association of www.anla.org/industry/patents
1000 Vermont Ave NW Suite 300 Washington DC 20005
Ph: 202-789-2900 ▪ Fx: 202-789-1893

Plant Preservation Council, North American
HC 67 Box 539B Renick WV 24966
Ph: 304-497-2208 ▪ Fx: 304-497-2698

Plant Propagators Society, International www.ipps.org
Washington Park Arboretum 2300 Arboreton Dr Seattle WA
98112
Ph: 206-543-8602

Plant Taxonomists, American Society of www.sysbot.org
Univ of Wyoming Dept of Botany 3165 1000 E University
Ave Laramie WY 82071
Ph: 307-766-2556 ▪ Fx: 307-766-2851

Plasma Protein Therapeutics Association www.pptaglobal.org
147 Old Solomon's Island Rd Suite 100 Annapolis MD 21401
Ph: 410-263-8296 ▪ Fx: 410-263-2298

Plaster, International Institute for Lath & www.iilp.org
PO Box 1663 Lafayette CA 94549
Ph: 925-283-5160 ▪ Fx: 925-283-5161

Plasterers' & Cement Masons' International Association of the US & www.opcmia.org
Canada, Operative 14405 Laurel Pl Suite 300 Laurel MD
20707
Ph: 301-470-4200 ▪ Fx: 301-470-2502

Plasterers Council, National www.npconline.org
2811-D Tamiami Trail Port Charlotte FL 33952
Ph: 866-483-4672 ▪ Fx: 800-279-1729 ▪ TF: 866-483-4672

Plastic & Metal Products Manufacturers Association
225 W 39th St New York NY 10018
Ph: 212-398-5400 ▪ Fx: 212-398-3141

Plastic Pipe & Fittings Association www.ppfahome.org
800 Rossevelt Rd Bldg C Suite 20 Glen Ellyn IL 60137
Ph: 630-858-6540 ▪ Fx: 630-790-3095

Plastic Reconstructive & Aesthetic Surgery, International www.ipras.org
Confederation for 4 Executive Park Dr Albany NY 12203
Ph: 518-438-1434 ▪ Fx: 518-489-1205

Plastic & Reconstructive Surgery, American Academy www.facial-plastic-surgery.org
of Facial 310 S Henry St Alexandria VA 22314
Ph: 703-299-9291 ▪ Fx: 703-299-8898 ▪ TF: 800-332-3223

Plastic & Reconstructive Surgery, American Society of Ophthalmic www.asoprs.org
1133 W Morse Blvd Suite 201 Winter Park FL 32789
Ph: 407-647-8839 ▪ Fx: 407-629-2502

Plastic Representatives Management Council, Paper & www.pprmc.com
PO Box 150229 Arlington TX 76015
Ph: 817-561-7272 ▪ Fx: 817-561-7275

Plastic Shipping Container Institute www.pscionline.org
1920 'N' St NW Suite 800 Washington DC 20036
Ph: 202-973-2709 ▪ Fx: 202-331-8330

Plastic Surgeons, American Association of www.aaps1921.org
4900B S 31st St Arlington VA 22206
Ph: 703-820-7400 ▪ Fx: 703-931-4520

Plastic Surgeons, American Society of www.plasticsurgery.org
444 E Algonquin Rd Arlington Heights IL 60005
Ph: 847-228-9900 ▪ Fx: 847-228-9131 ▪ TF: 888-475-2784

Plastic Surgery Inc, American Board of www.abplsurg.org
1635 Market St 7 Penn Ctr Suite 400 Philadelphia PA 19103
Ph: 215-587-9322 ▪ Fx: 215-587-9622

Plastic Surgery, American Society for Aesthetic www.surgery.org
11081 Winners Cir Los Alamitos CA 90720
Ph: 562-799-2356 ▪ Fx: 562-799-1098 ▪ TF: 800-364-2147

Plastic Surgery, Association of Academic Chairmen of www.aacplasticsurgery.org
4900 B South 31st St Arlington VA 22206
Ph: 703-820-7400 ▪ Fx: 703-931-4520

Plastic Surgery Educational Foundation www.plasticsurgery.org
444 E Algonquin Rd Arlington Heights IL 60005
Ph: 847-228-9900 ▪ Fx: 847-228-9131 ▪ TF: 888-4PL-ASTI

Plastic Surgery Research Council www.ps-rc.org
45 Lyme Rd Suite 304 Hanover NH 03755
Ph: 603-643-2325 ▪ Fx: 603-643-1444

Plastic Surgical Nurses, American Society of www.aspsn.org
3220 Pointe Pkwy Suite 500 Atlanta GA 30092
Ph: 678-291-0011 ▪ Fx: 678-291-9731

Plastics & Allied Workers International Union, Glass Molders Pottery www.gmpiu.org
608 E Baltimore Pike Media PA 19063
Ph: 610-565-5051 ▪ Fx: 610-565-0983

Plastics Council, American www.americanplasticscouncil.org
1300 Wilson Blvd Arlington VA 22209
Ph: 703-253-0700 ▪ Fx: 703-253-0710

Plastics Distributors, International Association of www.iapd.org
4707 College Blvd Suite 105 Leawood KS 66211
Ph: 913-345-1005 ▪ Fx: 913-345-1006

Plastics Engineers, Society of www.4spe.org
14 Fairfield Dr Brookfield CT 06804
Ph: 203-775-0471 ▪ Fx: 203-775-8490

Plastics Industry Conference, United Steelworkers of America Rubber/
5 Gateway Ctr 7th Fl Pittsburgh PA 15222
Ph: 412-562-6971 ▪ Fx: 412-562-6963

Plastics Industry Inc, Society of the www.plasticsindustry.org
1801 K St NW Suite 600-K Washington DC 20006
Ph: 202-974-5200 ▪ Fx: 202-296-7005

Plastics Institute of America www.plasticsinstitute.org
333 Aiken St Lowell MA 01854
Ph: 978-934-3130 ▪ Fx: 978-459-9420

Plastics Packaging Institute, Rigid　　　www.rigidplasticpackaging.org
179 S Kenilworth Ave　Elmhurst IL 60126
Ph: 630-833-5894　▪ Fx: 630-833-5896

Plastics Pipe Institute　　　www.plasticpipe.org
1825 Connecticut Ave NW Suite 680　Washington DC 20009
Ph: 202-462-9607　▪ Fx: 202-462-9779　▪ TF: 888-314-6774

Plasticulture, American Society for　　　www.plasticulture.org
526 Brittany Dr　State College PA 16803
Ph: 814-238-7045　▪ Fx: 814-238-7051

Plate Printers Die Stampers & Engravers Union of North America, International　14 C St SW Rm 213-5a　Washington DC 20228
Ph: 202-874-2554

Platemakers Association, Flexographic Prepress　　　www.fppa.net
2105 Laurel Bush Rd Suite 200　Bel Air MD 21015
Ph: 443-640-1045　▪ Fx: 443-640-1031

Platform Tennis Association, American　　　www.platformtennis.org
PO Box 43336　Upper Montclair NJ 07043
Ph: 973-744-1190　▪ Fx: 973-783-4407　▪ TF: 888-744-9490

Play, Association for the Study of　　　www.csuchico.edu/phed/tasp

Play Therapy, Association for　　　www.a4pt.org
2050 N Winery Ave Suite 101　Fresno CA 93703
Ph: 559-252-2278　▪ Fx: 559-252-2297

Players The　　　www.theplayersnyc.org
16 Gramercy Park　New York NY 10003
Ph: 212-475-6116　▪ Fx: 212-473-2701

Players of America, Association of Professional Ball　　　www.apbpa.org
1820 W Orangewood Ave Suite 206　Orange CA 92868
Ph: 714-935-9993　▪ Fx: 714-935-0431

Players Association, Major League Baseball　　　bigleaguers.yahoo.com
12 E 49th St 24th Fl　New York NY 10017
Ph: 212-826-0808　▪ Fx: 212-752-4378

Players Association, National Basketball　　　www.nbpa.com
2 Penn Plaza Suite 2430　New York NY 10121
Ph: 212-655-0880　▪ Fx: 212-655-0881

Players Association, National Football League　　　www.nflpa.org
2021 L St NW Suite 600　Washington DC 20036
Ph: 202-463-2200　▪ Fx: 202-857-0380　▪ TF: 800-372-2000

Players Association, National Hockey League　　　www.nhlpa.com
777 Bay St Suite 2400　Toronto ON M5G2C8
Ph: 416-408-4040　▪ Fx: 416-313-2301　▪ TF: 800-363-4625

Playing2Win Inc　　　www.playing2win.org
1330 5th Ave　New York NY 10026
Ph: 212-369-4077　▪ Fx: 212-369-7046

Pleaters Stitchers & Embroiderers Association
225 W 39th St　New York NY 10018
Ph: 212-398-5400　▪ Fx: 212-398-3141

Plenty International　　　www.plenty.org
PO Box 394　Summertown TN 38483
Ph: 931-964-4864

Plowing Organization, USA
7660 Burns Rd　Versailles OH 45380
Ph: 937-526-3525　▪ Fx: 937-526-3100

Plowshares Institute　　　www.plowsharesinstitute.org
809 Hopmeadow St PO Box 243　Simsbury CT 06070
Ph: 203-651-4304　▪ Fx: 203-651-4305

Plumbing Contractors of America　　　www.mcaa.org/pca
1385 Piccard Dr　Rockville MD 20850
Ph: 301-869-5800　▪ Fx: 301-990-9690

Plumbing & Drainage Institute　　　www.pdionline.org
800 Turnpike St Suite 300　North Andover MA 01845
Ph: 978-557-0720　▪ Fx: 978-557-0721　▪ TF: 800-589-8956

Plumbing Engineers, American Society of　　　www.aspe.org
8614 W Catalpa Ave Suite 1007　Chicago IL 60656
Ph: 773-693-2773

Plumbing-Heating-Cooling Contractors National Association　　　www.phccweb.org
180 S Washington St　Falls Church VA 22040
Ph: 703-237-8100　▪ Fx: 703-237-7442　▪ TF: 800-533-7694

Plumbing Manufacturers Institute　　　www.pmihome.org
1340 Remington Rd Suite A　Schaumburg IL 60173
Ph: 847-884-9764　▪ Fx: 847-884-9775

Plumbing & Mechanical Officials, International Association of　　　www.iapmo.org
5001 E Philadelphia St　Ontario CA 91761
Ph: 909-472-4100　▪ Fx: 909-472-4150　▪ TF: 800-854-2766

Plumbing Pipe Fitting Sprinkler Fitting Industry of the US & Canada, United Association of Journeymen & Apprentices of the　901 Massachusetts Ave NW　Washington DC 20001　　　www.ua.org
Ph: 202-628-5823　▪ Fx: 202-628-5024

Plumeria Society of America
PO Box 22791　Houston TX 77227
Ph: 713-529-7041

Plymouth Owners Club Inc　　　www.plymouthbulletin.com
PO Box 416　Cavalier ND 58220
Ph: 701-549-3746　▪ Fx: 701-549-3744

Plymouth Rock Foundation　　　www.plymrock.org
1120 Long Pond Rd　Plymouth MA 02360
Ph: 508-833-1189　▪ Fx: 508-833-2481　▪ TF: 800-210-1620

Plywood & Veneer Association, Hardwood　　　www.hpva.org
PO Box 2789　Reston VA 20195
Ph: 703-435-2900　▪ Fx: 703-435-2537

Pocket Testament League USA　　　www.readcarryshare.org
11 Toll Gate Rd PO Box 800　Lititz PA 17543
Ph: 717-626-1919　▪ Fx: 717-626-5553　▪ TF: 800-636-8785

Podiatric Medical Assistants, American Society of　　　www.aspma.org
2124 S Austin Blvd　Cicero IL 60804
Ph: 708-863-6303　▪ Fx: 708-863-5375　▪ TF: 888-882-7762

Podiatric Medical Association, American　　　www.apma.org
9312 Old Georgetown Rd　Bethesda MD 20814
Ph: 301-571-9200　▪ Fx: 301-634-2752　▪ TF: 800-275-2762

Podiatric Medical Association, National
1706 E 87th St　Chicago IL 60617
Ph: 773-374-1616　▪ Fx: 773-374-5860

Podiatric Medical Boards, Federation of　　　www.fpmb.org
PO Box 880187　Boca Raton FL 33474
Ph: 561-477-3060

Podiatric Medical Education, Fund for　　　www.apma.org/fpme/fundmain.htm
9312 Old Georgetown Rd　Bethesda MD 20814
Ph: 301-581-9200　▪ Fx: 301-530-2752

Podiatric Medical Examiners, National Board of　　　www.nbpme.info
PO Box 510　Bellefonte PA 16823
Ph: 814-357-0487　▪ Fx: 814-357-0581

Podiatric Medical Students' Association, American　　　www.apmsa.org
9312 Old Georgetown Rd　Bethesda MD 20814
Ph: 301-493-9667　▪ Fx: 301-530-2752

Podiatric Medical Writers Association, American
104-20 Queens Blvd Suite 17B　Forest Hills NY 11375
Ph: 718-897-9700　▪ Fx: 718-896-5747

Podiatric Medicine, American Association of Colleges of　　　www.aacpm.org
1350 Piccard Dr Suite 322　Rockville MD 20850
Ph: 301-990-7400　▪ Fx: 301-990-2807　▪ TF: 800-922-9266

Podiatric Medicine, American Society of
1111 Lane Concourse Dr Suite 111　Bay Harbor FL 33152
Ph: 305-866-9608　▪ Fx: 305-866-1750

Podiatric Orthopedics & Primary Podiatric Medicine, American Board of　22910 Crenshaw Blvd Suite B　Torrance CA 90505　　　www.abpoppm.org
Ph: 310-891-0100　▪ Fx: 310-891-0500

Podiatric Physicians & Surgeons, American Association of
1328 Southern Ave SE Suite 200　Washington DC 20032
Ph: 202-562-2777　▪ Fx: 202-562-5351

Podiatric Practice Management, American Academy of　　　www.aappm.org
707 Turnpike St　North Andover MA 01845
Ph: 978-686-6185　▪ Fx: 978-685-9410

Podiatric Sports Medicine, American Academy of　　　www.aapsm.org
PO Box 723　Rockville MD 20848
Ph: 301-845-9887　▪ Fx: 301-845-9888　▪ TF: 800-438-3338

Podiatrists Inc, American Association for Women　　　www.aawpinc.com
PO Box 593　Pleasanton CA 94566
Ph: 925-785-8285　▪ Fx: 925-426-5617

Poe Edgar Allan Society of Baltimore　　　www.eapoe.org

Poe Foundation　　　www.poemuseum.org
1914-16 Main St　Richmond VA 23223
Ph: 804-648-5523　▪ Fx: 804-648-8729　▪ TF: 888-213-2763

Poetry Association, Modern　　　www.poetrymagazine.org
1030 N Clark St Suite 420　Chicago IL 60610
Ph: 312-787-7070

Poetry Forum, International　　　www.thepoetryforum.org
Grace Library 3333 5th Ave　Pittsburgh PA 15213
Ph: 412-621-9893　▪ Fx: 412-621-9898

Poetry Project　　　www.poetryproject.com
Saint Mark's Church 131 E 10th St　New York NY 10003
Ph: 212-674-0910　▪ Fx: 212-529-2318

Poetry Society of America　　　www.poetrysociety.org
15 Gramercy Pk　New York NY 10003
Ph: 212-254-9628　▪ Fx: 212-673-2352　▪ TF: 888-872-7636

Poetry Therapy, National Association for　　　www.poetrytherapy.org
16861 SW 6th St　Pembroke Pines FL 33027
Ph: 954-499-4333　▪ Fx: 954-499-4324　▪ TF: 866-844-6278

Poets, Academy of American　　　www.poets.org
588 Broadway Suite 604　New York NY 10012
Ph: 212-274-0343　▪ Fx: 212-274-9427

Poets Cooperative, Unitarian Universalist　　　www.puddinghouse.com/unitarian.htm
c/o Pudding House Publications 81 Shadymere Ln　Columbus OH 43210
Ph: 614-986-1881

Poets, World Congress of
3146 Buckeye Ct　Placerville CA 95667
Ph: 530-626-4166　▪ Fx: 530-344-9427

Poets & Writers Inc　　　www.pw.org
72 Spring St　New York NY 10012
Ph: 212-226-3586　▪ Fx: 212-226-3963

Point-of-Purchase Advertising International　　　www.popai.com
1660 L St NW 10th Fl　Washington DC 20036
Ph: 202-530-3000　▪ Fx: 202-530-3030

Points of Light Foundation & Volunteer Center National Network　1400 'I' St NW Suite 800　Washington DC 20005　　　www.pointsoflight.org
Ph: 202-729-8000　▪ Fx: 202-729-8100　▪ TF: 800-750-7653

Poison Control Center, ASPCA Animal　　　www.apcc.aspca.org
1717 S Philo Rd Suite 36　Urbana IL 61802
Ph: 217-337-5030　▪ Fx: 217-337-0599　▪ TF: 888-426-4435

Poison Control Centers, American Association of　　　www.aapcc.org
3201 New Mexico Ave Suite 330　Washington DC 20016
Ph: 202-362-7217　▪ TF: 800-222-1222

Poisoning, Coalition to End Childhood Lead　　　www.leadsafe.org
2714 Hudson St　Baltimore MD 21224
Ph: 410-534-6447　▪ Fx: 410-534-6475　▪ TF: 800-370-5323

Poland, Association of the Sons of　　　www.sonsofpoland.com
333 Hackensack St　Carlstadt NJ 07072
Ph: 201-935-2807　▪ Fx: 201-935-2752

Polanyi Society　　　www.mwsc.edu/orgs/polanyi

Polar Engineers, International Society of Offshore &　　　www.isope.org
PO Box 189　Cupertino CA 95015
Ph: 650-254-1871　▪ Fx: 650-254-2038

Polar Philatelists, American Society of　　　www.polarphilatelists.org
PO Box 39　Exton PA 19341
Ph: 610-321-0740　▪ Fx: 610-321-0219

Polar Society, American — www.oaedks.net/amerpolr.html

Polarity Therapy Association, American — www.polaritytherapy.org
PO Box 19858   Boulder CO 80308
Ph: 303-545-2080 ■ Fx: 303-545-2161 ■ TF: 800-359-5620

Pole Association, Western Red Cedar — www.preservedwood.com/wrcpa/main.html
2405 61st Ave SE   Mercer Island WA 98040
Ph: 800-410-1917 ■ Fx: 206-275-4755

Poles of America, Alliance of — www.allianceofpoles.com
6966 Broadway   Cleveland OH 44105
Ph: 216-883-3131

Poles in America, Union of — www.unionofpoles.com
9999 Grainger Rd   Garfield Heights OH 44125
Ph: 216-478-0120 ■ Fx: 216-478-0122

Police Association, National Black — www.blackpolice.org
3251 Mt Pleasant St NW   Washington DC 20010
Ph: 202-986-2070 ■ Fx: 202-986-0410

Police Associations, International Union of — www.iupa.org
1421 Prince St Suite 400   Alexandria VA 22314
Ph: 703-549-7473 ■ Fx: 703-683-9048 ■ TF: 800-247-4872

Police Athletic Leagues, National Association of — www.nationalpal.org
618 US Hwy 1 Suite 201   North Palm Beach FL 33408
Ph: 561-844-1823 ■ Fx: 561-863-6120

Police Bloodhound Association, National
RR2 Box 1165   Milton PA 17847
Ph: 570-742-7310 ■ Fx: 570-742-7319

Police Canine Association, US — www.uspcak9.com
PO Box 80   Springboro OH 45066
Ph: 800-531-1614

Police Chaplains, International Conference of — www.icpc4cops.org
PO Box 5590   Destin FL 32540
Ph: 850-654-9736 ■ Fx: 850-654-9742

Police & Concerned Citizens, American Federation of — www.aphf.org/afp_cc.html
6350 Horizon Dr   Titusville FL 32780
Ph: 321-264-0911 ■ Fx: 321-264-0033

Police & Criminal Psychology, Society for — cep.jmu.edu/spcp/
Southwest Texas State Univ Dept of Criminal Justice   San
    Marcos TX 78666
Ph: 512-530-8211

Police Executive Research Forum — www.policeforum.org
1120 Connecticut Ave NW Suite 930   Washington DC 20036
Ph: 202-466-7820 ■ Fx: 202-466-7826 ■ TF: 888-202-4563

Police & Fire Professionals of America, International Union Security — www.spfpa.org
25510 Kelly Rd   Roseville MI 48066
Ph: 586-772-7250 ■ Fx: 586-772-9644 ■ TF: 800-228-7492

Police & Firemen's Insurance Association — www.pfia.net
101 E 116th St   Carmel IN 46032
Ph: 317-581-1913 ■ Fx: 317-571-5946 ■ TF: 800-221-7342

Police Foundation — www.policefoundation.org
1201 Connecticut Ave NW Suite 200   Washington DC 20036
Ph: 202-833-1460 ■ Fx: 202-659-9149

Police, Fraternal Order of — www.grandlodgefop.org
1410 Donelson Pike Suite A-17   Nashville TN 37217
Ph: 615-399-0900 ■ Fx: 615-399-0400 ■ TF: 800-451-2711

Police, International Association of Chiefs of — www.theiacp.org
515 N Washington St   Alexandria VA 22314
Ph: 703-836-6767 ■ Fx: 703-836-4543 ■ TF: 800-843-4227

Police, International Association of Women — www.iawp.org

Police Marksman Association — www.policemarksman.com
PO Box 241387   Montgomery AL 36124
Ph: 334-271-2010 ■ Fx: 334-279-9267

Police Mountain Bike Association, International — www.ipmba.org
583 Fredrick Rd Suite 5B   Baltimore MD 21228
Ph: 410-744-2400 ■ Fx: 410-744-5504 ■ TF: 800-323-0037

Police, National Association of Chiefs of — www.aphf.org/nacop.html
6350 Horizon Dr   Titusville FL 32780
Ph: 321-264-0911 ■ Fx: 321-264-0033

Police Officers, International Brotherhood of — www.ibpo.org
159 Burgin Pkwy   Quincy MA 02169
Ph: 617-376-0220 ■ Fx: 617-376-0285

Police Officers, United Federation of
540 N State Rd   Briarcliff Manor NY 10510
Ph: 914-941-4103 ■ Fx: 914-941-4472

Police Organizations, National Association of — www.napo.org
750 1st St NW Suite 920   Washington DC 20002
Ph: 202-842-4420 ■ Fx: 202-842-4396

Police Polygraphists, American Association of — www.wordnet.net/aapp/
18160 Cottonwood Rd Suite 253   Sunriver OR 97707
Ph: 541-598-7332 ■ Fx: 541-593-1021 ■ TF: 888-743-5479

Police Security & Correction Officers, Federation of — www.fopsco-afspa.org
71 E Cherry St   Rahway NJ 07065
Ph: 732-388-3323 ■ Fx: 732-388-5620

Police Work Dog Association, North American — www.napwda.com
4222 Manchester Ave   Perry OH 44081
Ph: 440-259-3169 ■ Fx: 440-259-3170 ■ TF: 888-422-6463

Policy Alternatives, Center for — www.cfpa.org
1875 Connecticut Ave NW Suite 710   Washington DC 20009
Ph: 202-387-6030 ■ Fx: 202-387-8529 ■ TF: 800-935-0699

Policy Analysis, National Center for — www.ncpa.org
12655 N Central Expy Suite 720   Dallas TX 75243
Ph: 972-386-6272 ■ Fx: 972-386-0924 ■ TF: 800-859-1154

Policy Analysis on Palestine, Center for — www.palestinecenter.org
2425-35 Virginia Ave NW   Washington DC 20037
Ph: 202-338-1290 ■ Fx: 202-338-7742

Policy Association, Foreign — www.fpa.org
470 Park Ave S 2nd Fl   New York NY 10016
Ph: 212-481-8100 ■ Fx: 212-481-9275 ■ TF: 800-628-5754

Policy Association, National — www.npa1.org
1424 16th St NW Suite 700   Washington DC 20036
Ph: 202-884-7623 ■ Fx: 202-797-5516

Policy, Center for International — www.ciponline.org
1717 Massachusetts Ave NW Suite 801   Washington DC 20036
Ph: 202-232-3317 ■ Fx: 202-232-3440

Policy, Center for Law & Social — www.clasp.org
1015 15th St NW Suite 400   Washington DC 20005
Ph: 202-906-8000 ■ Fx: 202-842-2885

Policy, Center for National — www.cnponline.org
1 Massachusetts Ave NW Suite 333   Washington DC 20001
Ph: 202-682-1800 ■ Fx: 202-682-1818

Policy, Center for Oceans Law & — www.virginia.edu/colp
Univ of Virginia School of Law 580 Massie Rd   Charlottesville
    VA 22903
Ph: 804-924-7441 ■ Fx: 804-924-7362

Policy Forum, Global — www.globalpolicy.org
777 UN Plaza Suite 7G   New York NY 10017
Ph: 212-557-3161 ■ Fx: 212-557-3165

Policy Innovation, Institute for — www.ipi.org
1660 S Stemmons Fwy Suite 475   Lewisville TX 75067
Ph: 972-847-5139 ■ Fx: 972-874-5144

Policy Institute, Cascade — www.cascadepolicy.org
813 SW Alder St Suite 450   Portland OR 97205
Ph: 503-242-0900 ■ Fx: 503-242-3822

Policy Institute, Progressive — www.ppionline.org
600 Pennsylvania Ave SE Suite 400   Washington DC 20003
Ph: 202-547-0001 ■ Fx: 202-544-5014 ■ TF: 800-546-0027

Policy Institute, World — worldpolicy.org
66 5th Ave 9th Fl   New York NY 10011
Ph: 212-229-5808 ■ Fx: 212-229-5579

Policy Priorities, Center on Budget & — www.cbpp.org
820 1st St NE Suite 510   Washington DC 20002
Ph: 202-408-1080 ■ Fx: 202-408-1056

Policy Research, Center for — www-cpr.maxwell.syr.edu
Syracuse University Eggers Hall Rm 426   Syracuse NY 13244
Ph: 315-443-3114 ■ Fx: 315-443-1081

Policy Research, Manhattan Institute for — www.manhattan-institute.org
52 Vanderbilt Ave 2nd Fl   New York NY 10017
Ph: 212-599-7000 ■ Fx: 212-599-3494

Policy Studies, Institute for — www.ips-dc.org
733 15th St NW Suite 1020   Washington DC 20005
Ph: 202-234-9382 ■ Fx: 202-387-7915

Polio Health International, Post- — www.post-polio.org
4207 Lindell Blvd Suite 110   Saint Louis MO 63108
Ph: 314-534-0475 ■ Fx: 314-534-5070

Polish American Congress — www.polamcon.org
5711 N Milwaukee Ave   Chicago IL 60646
Ph: 773-763-9944 ■ Fx: 773-763-7114

Polish American Historical Association — www.polishamericanstudies.org
3535 Indian Trail   Orchard Lake MI 48324
Ph: 248-683-1743 ■ Fx: 248-738-6736

Polish-American Travel Agents, Society of — www.spata.org
2297 E Main St   Bridgeport CT 06610
Ph: 203-336-9960 ■ Fx: 203-335-5319

Polish Beneficial Association
2595 Orthodox St   Philadelphia PA 19137
Ph: 215-535-2626 ■ Fx: 215-535-0169

Polish Culture, American Council for — www.polishcultureacpc.org
35 Fernridge Rd   West Hartford CT 06107
Ph: 860-521-7621

Polish Culture, American Institute of — www.ampolinstitute.org
1440 79th St Cswy Suite 117   Miami FL 33141
Ph: 305-864-2349 ■ Fx: 305-865-5150

Polish Falcons of America — www.polishfalcons.org
615 Iron City Dr   Pittsburgh PA 15205
Ph: 412-922-2244 ■ Fx: 412-922-5029 ■ TF: 800-535-2071

Polish Institute of Arts & Sciences of America Inc — www.piasa.org
208 E 30th St   New York NY 10016
Ph: 212-686-4164 ■ Fx: 212-545-1130

Polish Museum of America — pma.prcua.org
984 N Milwaukee Ave   Chicago IL 60622
Ph: 773-384-3352 ■ Fx: 773-384-3799

Polish National Alliance — www.pna-znp.org
6100 N Cicero Ave   Chicago IL 60646
Ph: 773-286-0500 ■ Fx: 773-286-9148 ■ TF: 800-621-3723

Polish National Union of America — www.pnu.org
1002 Pittston Ave   Scranton PA 18505
Ph: 570-344-1513 ■ Fx: 570-961-5961 ■ TF: 800-724-6352

Polish Roman Catholic Union of America — www.prcua.org
984 N Milwaukee Ave   Chicago IL 60622
Ph: 773-782-2600 ■ Fx: 773-278-4595 ■ TF: 800-772-8632

Polish Singers Alliance of America — www.polishsingersalliance.org

Polish Union of America — www.polishunion.com
745 Center Rd PO Box 288   West Seneca NY 14224
Ph: 716-677-0220 ■ Fx: 716-677-0246 ■ TF: 800-724-0246

Polish-US Business Council
c/o US Chamber of Commerce 1615 H St NW   Washington DC
    20062
Ph: 202-463-5482 ■ Fx: 202-463-3114

Polish Women, Legion of Young
Copernicus Ctr 5216 W Lawrence Ave   Chicago IL 60630
Ph: 773-777-9037 ■ Fx: 773-763-4069

Polish Women's Alliance of America — www.pwaa.org
205 S Northwest Hwy   Park Ridge IL 60068
Ph: 847-384-1200 ■ Fx: 847-384-1222 ■ TF: 888-522-1898

Political Action Committees, National Association of Business — www.nabpac.org
1133 21st St NW Suite M-100   Washington DC 20036
Ph: 202-572-6279 ■ Fx: 202-546-4243

Political Awareness, Indian American Center for — www.iacfpa.org
1025 Connecticut Ave NW Suite 1000   Washington DC 20036
Ph: 202-955-8338 ■ Fx: 202-327-5483

Political Caucus, National Women's   www.nwpc.org
1634 'I' St NW Suite 310   Washington DC 20006
Ph: 202-785-1100 ▪ Fx: 202-785-3605

Political Consultants, American Association of   www.theaapc.org
600 Pennsylvania Ave SE Suite 330   Washington DC 20003
Ph: 202-544-9815 ▪ Fx: 202-544-9816

Political & Economic Studies, Joint Center for   www.jointcenter.org
1090 Vermont Ave NW Suite 1100   Washington DC 20005
Ph: 202-789-3500 ▪ Fx: 202-789-6390

Political Economics, Union for Radical   www.urpe.org
37 Howe St   New Haven CT 06511
Ph: 203-777-4605

Political Economy Research Center   www.perc.org
2048 Analysis Dr Suite A   Bozeman MT 59718
Ph: 406-578-9591 ▪ Fx: 406-586-7555

Political Education, AFL-CIO Committee on
815 16th St NW   Washington DC 20006
Ph: 202-637-5000 ▪ Fx: 202-637-5058

Political Education, American Federation of Teachers Committee on
555 New Jersey Ave NW   Washington DC 20001
Ph: 202-879-4400 ▪ Fx: 202-879-4556 ▪ TF: 800-238-1133

Political Education, Committee on Letter Carriers
100 Indiana Ave NW   Washington DC 20001
Ph: 202-393-4695 ▪ Fx: 202-737-1540

Political Education, Indian American Forum for   www.iafpe.org
8210 Riverside Rd   Alexandria VA 22308
Ph: 703-619-1320

Political Graphics, Center for the Study of   www.politicalgraphics.org
8124 W 3rd St Suite 211   Los Angeles CA 90048
Ph: 323-653-4662 ▪ Fx: 323-653-6991

Political Leaders, American Council of Young   www.acypl.org
1612 K St NW Suite 300   Washington DC 20006
Ph: 202-857-0999 ▪ Fx: 202-857-0027

Political League, Machinists Non-Partisan   www.goiam.org/politics.asp?n=87
9000 Machinists Pl   Upper Marlboro MD 20772
Ph: 301-967-4500

Political & Legal Anthropology, Association for   www.aaanet.org/apla
c/o American Anthropological Assn 2200 Wilson Blvd Suite
    600   Arlington VA 22201
Ph: 703-528-1902 ▪ Fx: 703-528-3546

Political Products Manufacturers Association
60 State St   Liberty NY 12754
Ph: 845-292-7677 ▪ Fx: 845-292-2695

Political Psychology, International Society of   ispp.org
Pitzer College 1050 N Mills Ave   Claremont CA 91711
Ph: 909-621-8442 ▪ Fx: 909-621-8481

Political Research Associates   www.publiceye.org
1310 Broadway Suite 201   Somerville MA 02144
Ph: 617-666-5300 ▪ Fx: 617-666-6622

Political Science, Academy of   www.epn.org/psq/psaops.html
475 Riverside Dr Suite 1274   New York NY 10115
Ph: 212-870-2500 ▪ Fx: 212-870-2202

Political Science Association, American   www.apsanet.org
1527 New Hampshire Ave NW   Washington DC 20036
Ph: 202-483-2512 ▪ Fx: 202-483-2657

(Political Science) Pi Sigma Alpha   www.apsanet.org/~psa
1527 New Hampshire Ave NW   Washington DC 20036
Ph: 202-483-2512 ▪ Fx: 202-483-2657

Political Scientists, National Conference of Black   www.poli.ncat.edu/ncobps
3695-F Cascade Rd SW Suite 212   Atlanta GA 30331
Ph: 404-880-8240

Political & Social Research, Inter-University Consortium for   www.icpsr.umich.edu
Univ of Michigan Institute for Social Research PO Box
    1248   Ann Arbor MI 48106
Ph: 734-647-5000 ▪ Fx: 734-647-8200

Political & Social Science, American Academy of   www.aapss.org
3814 Walnut St   Philadelphia PA 19104
Ph: 215-746-6500 ▪ Fx: 215-898-1202

(Politics) Ballot Initiative Strategy Center   www.ballot.org
1025 Connecticut Ave NW Suite 205   Washington DC 20036
Ph: 202-223-2373 ▪ Fx: 202-289-1530

Politics, Center for Responsive   www.opensecrets.org
1101 14th St NW Suite 1030   Washington DC 20005
Ph: 202-857-0044 ▪ Fx: 202-857-7809

(Politics) EMILY's List   www.emilyslist.org
1120 Connecticut Ave NW Suite 1100   Washington DC 20036
Ph: 202-326-1400 ▪ Fx: 202-326-1415 ▪ TF: 800-683-6459

Politics, Institute of   www.iop.harvard.edu
Harvard Univ John F Kennedy School of Government 79 JFK
    St   Cambridge MA 02138
Ph: 617-495-1360

(Politics) New Party   www.newparty.org
88 3rd Ave Suite 313   Brooklyn NY 11217
Ph: 800-200-1294

Politics & Public Policy, Joan Shorenstein Center   www.ksg.harvard.edu/presspol
on the Press   Harvard Univ John F Kennedy School of
    Government 79 John F Kennedy St   Cambridge MA 02138
Ph: 617-495-8269 ▪ Fx: 617-495-8696

Politics, Robert J Dole Institute of   www.doleinstitute.org
704 W 12th St   Lawrence KS 66044
Ph: 785-749-3911 ▪ Fx: 785-749-3907

(Politics) WISH List   www.thewishlist.org
499 S Capitol St SW Suite 408   Washington DC 20003
Ph: 202-479-1230 ▪ Fx: 202-479-1231 ▪ TF: 800-756-9474

Polk James K Memorial Association   www.jameskpolk.com
c/o James K Polk Home PO Box 741   Columbia TN 38402
Ph: 931-388-2354 ▪ Fx: 931-388-5971

Polka Association, International   www.internationalpolka.com
4608 S Archer Ave   Chicago IL 60632
Ph: 800-867-6552

Polls, National Council on Public   www.ncpp.org
150 River St   Hackensack NJ 07601
Ph: 201-646-4379 ▪ Fx: 201-646-4772

Pollution Control Administrators, Association of State &   www.asiwpca.org
Interstate Water   750 1st St NE Suite 1010   Washington DC
    20002
Ph: 202-898-0905 ▪ Fx: 202-898-0929

Pollution Prevention Roundtable, National   www.p2.org
11 Dupont Cir NW Suite 201   Washington DC 20036
Ph: 202-299-9701 ▪ Fx: 202-299-9704 ▪ TF: 888-748-7272

Pollution Probe   www.pollutionprobe.org
625 Church St Suite 402   Toronto ON M4Y2G1
Ph: 416-926-1907 ▪ Fx: 416-926-1601

Pollution Program Administrators, State & Territorial Air   www.cleanairworld.org
444 N Capitol St NW Suite 307   Washington DC 20001
Ph: 202-624-7864 ▪ Fx: 202-624-7863

Polo Association, US   www.us-polo.org
777 Corporate Dr Suite 505   Lexington KY 40503
Ph: 859-219-1000 ▪ Fx: 859-219-0520 ▪ TF: 800-232-8772

Polyacrylate Absorbents, Institute for
1850 M St NW Suite 700   Washington DC 20036
Ph: 202-721-4145 ▪ Fx: 202-296-8120

Polygraph Association, American   www.polygraph.org
PO Box 8037   Chattanooga TN 37414
Ph: 423-892-3992 ▪ Fx: 423-894-5435 ▪ TF: 800-272-8037

Polygraphists, American Association of Police   www.wordnet.net/aapp/
18160 Cottonwood Rd Suite 253   Sunriver OR 97707
Ph: 541-598-7332 ▪ Fx: 541-593-1021 ▪ TF: 888-743-5479

Polyisocyanurate Insulation Manufacturers Association   www.pima.org
515 King St Suite 420   Alexandria VA 22314
Ph: 703-684-1136 ▪ Fx: 703-684-6048

Polymer Alliance, International Cast   www.icpa-hq.org
1010 N Glebe Rd Suite 450   Arlington VA 22201
Ph: 703-525-0320 ▪ Fx: 703-525-0743 ▪ TF: 800-414-4272

Polypay Sheep Association, American   www.countrylovin.com/polypay/
15603 173rd Ave   Milo IA 50166
Ph: 641-942-6402 ▪ Fx: 641-942-6502

Polysomnographic Technologists, Association of   www.aptweb.org
1 Westbrook Corporate Ctr Suite 920   Westchester IL 60154
Ph: 708-492-0796 ▪ Fx: 708-273-9344

Polystyrene Packaging Council   www.polystyrene.org
1300 Wilson Blvd   Arlington VA 22209
Ph: 703-741-5000 ▪ Fx: 703-741-6000

Polystyrene Resin Suppliers Council, Expandable
1300 Wilson Blvd   Arlington VA 22209
Ph: 703-253-0649 ▪ Fx: 703-253-0651

Polyurethane Foam Association   www.pfa.org
PO Box 1459   Wayne NJ 07474
Ph: 973-633-9044 ▪ Fx: 973-628-8986

Polyurethane Manufacturers Association   www.pmahome.org
800 Roosevelt Rd Bldg C Suite 20   Glen Ellyn IL 60137
Ph: 630-858-2670 ▪ Fx: 630-790-3095

Polyurethanes Industry, Alliance for the   www.polyurethane.org
1300 Wilson Blvd   Arlington VA 22209
Ph: 703-741-5656 ▪ Fx: 703-741-5655

Pomegranate Guild of Judaic Needlework   www.pomegranateguild.org
34 Summit Ave   Sharon MA 02067
Ph: 781-784-2668

Pomological Society, American   hortweb.cas.psu.edu/aps/
103 Tyson Bldg   University Park PA 16802
Ph: 814-863-6163 ▪ Fx: 814-863-6139

Pony of the Americas Club Inc   www.poac.org
5240 Elmwood Ave   Indianapolis IN 46203
Ph: 317-788-0107 ▪ Fx: 317-788-8974

Pony Association, American Walking
PO Box 5282   Macon GA 31208
Ph: 478-743-2321 ▪ Fx: 478-742-6021

Pony Association, National Chincoteague   www.pony-chincoteague.com
2595 Jensen Rd   Bellingham WA 98226
Ph: 360-671-8338 ▪ Fx: 360-671-7603

Pony Association Inc, New Forest   www.newforestpony.net
PO Box 206   Pascoag RI 02859
Ph: 401-568-8238 ▪ Fx: 401-567-0311

PONY Baseball/Softball Inc   www.pony.org
300 Clare Dr   Washington PA 15301
Ph: 724-225-1060 ▪ Fx: 724-225-9852

Pony Clubs, US   www.ponyclub.org
Kentucky Horse Park 4041 Iron Works Pkwy   Lexington KY
    40511
Ph: 859-254-7669 ▪ Fx: 859-233-4652

Pony Express Historical Association   www.stjoseph.net/ponyexpress
12th & Penn Sts PO Box 1022   Saint Joseph MO 64502
Ph: 816-232-8206 ▪ Fx: 816-232-3717

Pony Registry, National Morgan   www.bulldancers.com/morganpony

Pony Society, American Connemara   www.acps.org
2360 Hunting Ridge Rd   Winchester VA 22603
Ph: 540-662-5953 ▪ Fx: 540-722-2277

Pony Society, American Welara   www.WelaraRegistry.com/
PO Box 401   Yucca Valley CA 92286
Ph: 760-364-2048

Pool Foundation, National Swimming   www.nspf.com
224 E Cheyenne Mountain Blvd   Colorado Springs CO 80906
Ph: 719-540-9119 ▪ Fx: 719-540-2787

Pool Institute, National Spa &   www.nspi.org
2111 Eisenhower Ave   Alexandria VA 22314
Ph: 703-838-0083 ▪ Fx: 703-549-0493 ▪ TF: 800-323-3996

Poolplayers Association, American   www.poolplayers.com
1000 Lake St Louis Blvd Suite 325   Lake Saint Louis MO
    63367
Ph: 636-625-8611 ▪ Fx: 636-625-2975 ▪ TF: 800-372-2536

Poor Inc, Food for the www.foodforthepoor.com
550 SW 12th Ave Bldg 4 Deerfield Beach FL 33442
Ph: 954-427-2222 ▪ Fx: 954-570-7654 ▪ TF: 800-282-7667

Pop Can Collectors, National www.one-mans-junk.com/npcc/npcc.htm

Pop Warner Little Scholars Inc www.popwarner.com
586 Middletown Blvd Suite C-100 Langhorne PA 19047
Ph: 215-752-2691 ▪ Fx: 215-752-2879

Popcorn Board www.popcorn.org
401 N Michigan Ave Chicago IL 60611
Ph: 312-644-6610 ▪ Fx: 312-527-6658

Popcorn Institute www.popcorn.org
401 N Michigan Ave Chicago IL 60611
Ph: 312-644-6610 ▪ Fx: 312-527-6658

Pope Lois LIFE Foundation www.life-edu.org
6274 Linton Blvd Suite 103 Delray Beach FL 33484
Ph: 561-865-0955 ▪ Fx: 561-865-0938

Pope & Young Club www.pope-young.org
273 Mill Creek Rd PO Box 548 Chatfield MN 55923
Ph: 507-867-4144

Poplar Forest, Corporation for Jefferson's www.poplarforest.org
PO Box 419 Forest VA 24551
Ph: 434-525-1806 ▪ Fx: 434-525-7252

Popular Music, National Academy of
330 W 58th St Suite 411 New York NY 10019
Ph: 212-957-9230 ▪ Fx: 212-957-9227

Population Action International www.populationaction.org
1300 19th St NW 2nd Fl Washington DC 20036
Ph: 202-557-3400 ▪ Fx: 202-728-4177

Population Activities, Centre for Development & www.cedpa.org
1400 16th St NW Suite 100 Washington DC 20036
Ph: 202-667-1142 ▪ Fx: 202-332-4496

Population Association of America www.popassoc.org
8630 Fenton St Suite 722 Silver Spring MD 20910
Ph: 301-565-6710 ▪ Fx: 301-565-7850

Population Communication
1250 E Walnut St Suite 220 Pasadena CA 91106
Ph: 626-793-4750 ▪ Fx: 626-793-4791

Population Communications International Inc www.population.org
777 United Nations Plaza 5th Fl New York NY 10017
Ph: 212-687-3366 ▪ Fx: 212-661-4188 ▪ TF: 877-724-7627

Population Connection www.populationconnection.org
1400 16th St NW Suite 320 Washington DC 20036
Ph: 202-332-2200 ▪ Fx: 202-332-2302 ▪ TF: 800-767-1956

Population-Environment Balance Inc www.balance.org
2000 P St NW Suite 600 Washington DC 20036
Ph: 202-955-5700 ▪ Fx: 202-955-6161 ▪ TF: 800-866-6269

Population/Family Planning Libraries & Information Centers www.aplici.org
International, Association for c/o Family Health International
Library PO Box 13950 Research Triangle Park NC 27709
Ph: 919-405-1433 ▪ Fx: 919-544-7261

Population Growth, Negative www.npg.org
1717 Massachusetts Ave NW Suite 101 Washington DC 20036
Ph: 202-667-8950 ▪ Fx: 202-667-8953

Population Institute www.populationinstitute.org
107 2nd St NE Washington DC 20002
Ph: 202-544-3300 ▪ Fx: 202-544-0068 ▪ TF: 800-787-0038

Population Reference Bureau www.prb.org
1875 Connecticut Ave NW Suite 520 Washington DC 20009
Ph: 202-483-1100 ▪ Fx: 202-328-3937 ▪ TF: 800-877-9881

Population Resource Center www.prcdc.org
15 Roszel Rd Princeton NJ 08540
Ph: 609-452-2822 ▪ Fx: 609-452-0010

Porcelain Enamel Institute www.porcelainenamel.com
PO Box 920220 Norcross GA 30010
Ph: 770-281-8980 ▪ Fx: 770-625-4923

Pork Producers Council, National www.nppc.org
122 C St NW Suite 875 Washington DC 20001
Ph: 202-347-3600 ▪ Fx: 202-347-5265

Porsche Club of America www.pca.org
PO Box 5900 Springfield VA 22150
Ph: 703-451-9000 ▪ Fx: 703-451-0145

Port Authorities, American Association of www.aapa-ports.org
1010 Duke St Alexandria VA 22314
Ph: 703-684-5700 ▪ Fx: 703-684-6321

Port Engineers, Society of Marine www.smpe.org
PO Box 466 Avenel NJ 07001
Ph: 732-381-7673 ▪ Fx: 732-381-2046

Port of New York/New Jersey, Maritime Association of the www.nymaritime.org
17 Battery Pl Suite 913 New York NY 10004
Ph: 212-425-5704 ▪ Fx: 212-635-9498

Portable Computer & Communications Association www.pcca.org
PO Box 680 Hood River OR 97031
Ph: 541-490-5140

Portable Rechargeable Battery Association www.prba.org
1000 Parkwood Cir Suite 430 Atlanta GA 30339
Ph: 770-612-8826 ▪ Fx: 770-612-8841

Portable Sanitation Association International www.psai.org
7800 Metro Pkwy Suite 104 Bloomington MN 55425
Ph: 952-854-8300 ▪ Fx: 952-854-7560 ▪ TF: 800-822-3020

Portland Cement Association www.cement.org
5420 Old Orchard Rd Skokie IL 60077
Ph: 847-966-6200 ▪ Fx: 847-966-9781

Portrait Artists, American Society of www.asopa.com
PO Box 230216 Montgomery AL 36106
Ph: 334-270-9020 ▪ Fx: 334-270-0150 ▪ TF: 800-622-7672

Portrait Photographers International, Wedding & www.wppinow.com/index2.tml
1312 Lincoln Blvd Santa Monica CA 90406
Ph: 310-451-0090 ▪ Fx: 310-395-9058

Ports & Terminals Inc, Inland Rivers www.irpt.net
PO Box 4363 Jackson MS 39296
Ph: 601-352-4778 ▪ Fx: 601-355-1506

Portugal-US Chamber of Commerce portugal-us.com
590 5th Ave 4th Fl New York NY 10036
Ph: 212-354-4627 ▪ Fx: 212-575-4737

Portuguese, American Association of Teachers of Spanish & www.aatsp.org
423 Exton Commons Exton PA 19341
Ph: 610-363-7005 ▪ Fx: 610-363-7116

(Portuguese-Americans) Luso-American Education www.luso-american.org/laef
Foundation PO Box 2967 Dublin CA 94568
Ph: 925-828-3883

Portuguese Historical & Cultural Society www.sacramentophcs.com
PO Box 161990 Sacramento CA 95816
Ph: 916-392-1048

Portuguese Historical Studies, Society www.ukans.edu/~iberia/ssphs/ssphs_main.html
for Spanish &

Post Acute Care, National Association of Subacute & www.naspac.net
1960 Gallows Rd Suite 210 Vienna VA 22182
Ph: 703-790-8989 ▪ Fx: 703-790-8485

Post Card & Souvenir Distributors Association www.postcardcentral.org
2105 Laurel Bush Rd Suite 200 Bel Air MD 21015
Ph: 443-640-1055 ▪ Fx: 443-640-1031

Post Office Society, Mobile www.eskimo.com/~rkunz/mposhome.html
PO Box 427 Marston Mills MA 02648
Ph: 508-428-9132

Post-Polio Health International www.post-polio.org
4207 Lindell Blvd Suite 110 Saint Louis MO 63108
Ph: 314-534-0475 ▪ Fx: 314-534-5070

Post-Tensioning Institute post-tensioning.org
8601 N Black Canyon Hwy Suite 103 Phoenix AZ 85021
Ph: 602-870-7540 ▪ Fx: 602-870-7541

Postal Chess Club, All Service chessaspc.com
1805 S Van Buren St Amarillo TX 79102
Ph: 806-374-5991

Postal Chess Tournaments, American www.correspondencechess.com/apct
PO Box 305 Western Springs IL 60558
Ph: 630-663-0688 ▪ Fx: 630-663-0689

Postal Commemorative Society
47 Richards Ave Norwalk CT 06857
Ph: 203-838-6600 ▪ Fx: 203-853-6690 ▪ TF: 800-641-8026

Postal Commerce, Association for www.postcom.org
1901 N Fort Myer Dr Suite 401 Arlington VA 22209
Ph: 703-524-0096 ▪ Fx: 703-524-1871

Postal Credit Unions, National Council of www.ncpcu.org
PO Box 160 Del Mar CA 92014
Ph: 858-792-3883 ▪ Fx: 858-792-3884

Postal & Federal Employees, National Alliance of www.napfe.com
1628 11th St NW Washington DC 20001
Ph: 202-939-6325 ▪ Fx: 202-939-6389

Postal Forum, National www.npf.org
50 W Corporate Ctr 3998 Fair Ridge Dr Suite 300 Fairfax VA
22033
Ph: 703-218-5015 ▪ Fx: 703-218-5020

Postal History Society
8207 Daren Ct Pikesville MD 21208
Ph: 410-653-0665

Postal Mail Handlers Union, National www.npmhu.org
1101 Connecticut Ave NW Suite 500 Washington DC 20036
Ph: 202-833-9095 ▪ Fx: 202-833-0008

Postal Supervisors, National Association of www.naps.org
1727 King St Suite 400 Alexandria VA 22314
Ph: 703-836-9660 ▪ Fx: 703-836-9665

Postal Systems Inc, Association of Alternate www.aapsinc.org
1725 Oaks Way Oklahoma City OK 73131
Ph: 405-478-0161

Postal Workers Union, American www.apwu.org
1300 L St NW Washington DC 20005
Ph: 202-842-4200 ▪ Fx: 202-842-8500

Postal Workers Union Committee on www.apwu.org/departments/legis/legisframe.htm
Political Action, American 1300 L St NW Washington DC
20005
Ph: 202-842-4200

Postcard History Society
1795 Kleinfeltersville Rd Stevens PA 17578
Ph: 717-721-9273

PostCom www.postcom.org
1901 N Fort Myer Dr Suite 401 Arlington VA 22209
Ph: 703-524-0096 ▪ Fx: 703-524-1871

Postdoctoral & Internship Centers, Association of Psychology www.appic.org
10 G St NE Suite 750 Washington DC 20002
Ph: 202-589-0600 ▪ Fx: 202-589-0603

Postgraduate Medical Association, Interstate www.ipmameded.org
PO Box 5474 Madison WI 53705
Ph: 608-231-9045 ▪ Fx: 877-292-4489

Postgraduate Physician Assistant Programs, Association of www.appap.org
PO Box 2128ABC Philippi WV 26416
Ph: 304-457-6356 ▪ Fx: 304-457-6308

Postmasters of the US, National Association of www.napus.org
8 Herbert St Alexandria VA 22305
Ph: 703-683-9027 ▪ Fx: 703-683-6820

Postmasters of the US, National League of www.postmasters.org
1023 N Royal St Alexandria VA 22314
Ph: 703-548-5922 ▪ Fx: 703-836-8937

Postpartum Care Services, National Association of www.napcs.org
800 Detroit St Denver CO 80206
Ph: 800-453-6852 ▪ Fx: 303-321-4058

Postsecondary Agricultural Student Organization, National www.nationalpas.org
6060 FFA Dr PO Box 68960 Indianapolis IN 46268
Ph: 317-802-4220 ▪ Fx: 317-802-5220

(Posture) American Center for the Alexander Technique Inc   www.acatnyc.org
39 W 14th St Rm 507   New York NY 10011
Ph: 212-633-2229

(Posture) American Society for the Alexander Technique   www.alexandertech.com
PO Box 60008   Florence MA 01062
Ph: 413-584-2359 ▪ Fx: 413-584-3097 ▪ TF: 800-473-0620

Pot Belly Pig Rescue   www.jojoba-ksa.com/p2.htm
19025 Parthenia St   Northridge CA 91324
Ph: 818-701-1534 ▪ Fx: 818-993-0194

Potato Association of America   www.ume.maine.edu/PAA
Univ of Maine 5715 Coburn Hall Rm 6   Orono ME 04469
Ph: 207-581-3042 ▪ Fx: 207-581-3015

Potato Board, US   www.uspotatoes.com
7555 E Hampden Ave Suite 412   Denver CO 80231
Ph: 303-369-7783 ▪ Fx: 303-369-7718

Potato Council, National   www.nationalpotatocouncil.org
1300 L St NW Suite 910   Washington DC 20005
Ph: 202-682-9456 ▪ Fx: 202-682-0333

Potbellied Pig Association, North American   www.petpigs.com
304 County Rd 438   Rocheport MO 65279
Ph: 573-698-3030

Potbellied Pigs, National Committees on   www.ncopp.org

Potential, Association for the Development of Human
PO Box 3543   Spokane WA 99220
Ph: 509-838-6652 ▪ TF: 800-251-9273

Pottery Association, American Art   www.amartpot.org
17736 Hwy 442   Independence LA 70443
Ph: 985-878-8640

(Pottery) Belleek Collector's International Society   www.belleek.ie
PO Box 1498   Great Falls VA 22066
Ph: 800-235-5335 ▪ Fx: 703-272-6271

Pottery Plastics & Allied Workers International Union,   www.gmpiu.org
Glass Molders   608 E Baltimore Pike   Media PA 19063
Ph: 610-565-5051 ▪ Fx: 610-565-0983

(Pottery) Red Wing Collectors Society Inc   www.redwingcollectors.org
PO Box 50   Red Wing MN 55066
Ph: 651-388-4004 ▪ TF: 800-977-7927

(Poultry) American Langshan Club
18077 S Hwy 88   Claremore OK 74017
Ph: 918-341-2238

Poultry Association, American   www.ampltya.com
133 Millville St   Mendon MA 01756
Ph: 508-473-8769

Poultry Breeders of America
1530 Cooledge Rd   Tucker GA 30084
Ph: 770-493-9401 ▪ Fx: 770-493-9257

Poultry Concerns Inc, United   www.upc-online.org
12325 Seaside Rd PO Box 150   Machipongo VA 23405
Ph: 757-678-7875 ▪ Fx: 757-678-5070

Poultry & Egg Association, US   www.poultryegg.com
1530 Cooledge Rd   Tucker GA 30084
Ph: 770-493-9401 ▪ Fx: 770-493-9257

Poultry & Egg Export Council, USA   www.usapeec.com
2300 W Park Place Blvd Suite 100   Stone Mountain GA 30087
Ph: 770-413-0006 ▪ Fx: 770-413-0007

Poultry & Food Distributors Association, National   www.npfda.org
958 McEver Rd Ext Unit B-8   Gainesville GA 30504
Ph: 770-535-9901 ▪ Fx: 770-535-7385 ▪ TF: 877-845-1545

Poultry International Inc, American
5420 I-55 N Suite B   Jackson MS 39211
Ph: 601-956-1715 ▪ Fx: 601-956-1755

Poultry Science Association   www.poultryscience.org
111 N Dunlap Ave   Savoy IL 61874
Ph: 217-398-4119

(Poverty) ANGELCARE   www.angelcare.org
PO Box 600370   San Diego CA 92160
Ph: 619-593-1222 ▪ Fx: 619-593-0222 ▪ TF: 888-264-5227

(Poverty) Children Inc   www.children-inc.org
PO Box 5381   Richmond VA 23220
Ph: 804-359-4562 ▪ Fx: 804-353-7541 ▪ TF: 800-538-5381

(Poverty) Concern Worldwide US Inc   www.concernusa.org
104 E 40th St Suite 903   New York NY 10016
Ph: 212-557-8000 ▪ Fx: 212-557-8004

(Poverty) EnterpriseWorks Worldwide Inc   www.enterpriseworks.org
1828 L St NW Suite 1000   Washington DC 20036
Ph: 202-293-4600 ▪ Fx: 202-293-4598

(Poverty) Floresta USA   www.floresta.org
4903 Morena Blvd Suite 1215   San Diego CA 92117
Ph: 858-274-3718 ▪ Fx: 858-274-3728 ▪ TF: 800-633-5319

Poverty Law, Sargent Shriver National Center on   www.povertylaw.org
111 N Wabash Ave Suite 500   Chicago IL 60602
Ph: 312-263-3830 ▪ Fx: 312-263-3846 ▪ TF: 800-621-3256

Poverty, National Center for Children in   cpmcnet.columbia.edu/dept/nccp
215 W 125th St 3rd Fl   New York NY 10027
Ph: 646-284-9600 ▪ Fx: 646-284-9623

Poverty, National Law Center on Homelessness &   www.nlchp.org
1411 K St NW Suite 1400   Washington DC 20005
Ph: 202-628-2535 ▪ Fx: 202-628-2737

(Poverty) Opportunity International-USA   www.opportunity.org
2122 York Rd   Oak Brook IL 60523
Ph: 630-645-4100 ▪ Fx: 630-645-1458 ▪ TF: 800-793-9455

(Poverty) Outreach International   www.outreach-international.org
PO Box 210   Independence MO 64051
Ph: 816-833-0883 ▪ Fx: 816-833-0103 ▪ TF: 888-833-1235

(Poverty) Oxfam America   www.oxfamamerica.org
26 West St   Boston MA 02111
Ph: 617-482-1211 ▪ Fx: 617-728-2594 ▪ TF: 800-776-9326

(Poverty) Phelps-Stokes Fund   www.psfdc.com
1420 K St NW   Washington DC 20005
Ph: 202-371-9344 ▪ TF: 800-874-7797

(Poverty) Private Agencies Collaborating Together   www.pactworld.org
1200 18th St NW Suite 350   Washington DC 20036
Ph: 202-466-5666 ▪ Fx: 202-466-5669

Poverty & Race Research Action Council   www.prrac.org
3000 Connecticut Ave NW Suite 200   Washington DC 20008
Ph: 202-387-9887 ▪ Fx: 202-387-0764

(Poverty) RESULTS   www.results.org
440 1st St NW Suite 450   Washington DC 20001
Ph: 202-783-7100 ▪ Fx: 202-783-2818

(Poverty) Share Our Strength   www.strength.org
733 15th St NW Suite 640   Washington DC 20005
Ph: 202-393-2925 ▪ Fx: 202-347-5868 ▪ TF: 800-969-4767

(Poverty) Synergos Institute Inc   www.synergos.org
9 E 69th St   New York NY 10021
Ph: 212-517-4900 ▪ Fx: 212-517-4815

(Poverty) TechnoServe   www.technoserve.org
49 Day St   Norwalk CT 06854
Ph: 203-852-0377 ▪ Fx: 203-838-6717 ▪ TF: 800-999-6757

(Poverty) Trickle Up Program Inc   www.trickleup.org
104 W 27th St 12th Fl   New York NY 10001
Ph: 212-255-9980 ▪ Fx: 212-255-9974 ▪ TF: 866-246-9980

Poverty, Western Center on Law &   www.wclp.org
3701 Wilshire Blvd Suite 208   Los Angeles CA 90010
Ph: 213-487-7211 ▪ Fx: 213-487-0242

(Poverty) World Vision Inc   www.worldvision.org
PO Box 9716   Federal Way WA 98063
Ph: 253-815-1000 ▪ Fx: 253-815-3240 ▪ TF: 800-777-5777

POW Network   www.pownetwork.org
PO Box 68   Skidmore MO 64487
Ph: 660-928-3304 ▪ Fx: 660-928-3303

Powder Actuated Tool Manufacturers Institute   www.patmi.org
1603 Boonslick Rd   Saint Charles MO 63301
Ph: 636-947-6610 ▪ Fx: 636-946-3336

Powder Coating Institute   www.powdercoating.org
2121 Eisenhower Ave Suite 401   Alexandria VA 22314
Ph: 703-684-1770 ▪ Fx: 703-684-1771 ▪ TF: 800-988-2628

Powder Producers Association, Metal   www.mpif.org/mppa.html
105 College Rd E   Princeton NJ 08540
Ph: 609-452-7700 ▪ Fx: 609-987-8523

Power Association, American Public   www.appanet.org
2301 M St NW   Washington DC 20037
Ph: 202-467-2900 ▪ Fx: 202-467-2910

Power Boat Association, American   apba-racing.com
17640 Nine Mile Rd   Eastpointe MI 48021
Ph: 586-773-9700 ▪ Fx: 586-773-6490

Power Boat Association, International Model   www.impba.com
2804 Woods Dr   Violet LA 70092
Ph: 504-276-4500

Power & Communication Contractors Association   www.pccaweb.org
103 Orinoco St Suite 200   Alexandria VA 22314
Ph: 703-212-7734 ▪ Fx: 703-548-3733 ▪ TF: 800-542-7222

Power Distributors Association, Fluid   www.fpda.org
PO Box 1420   Cherry Hill NJ 08034
Ph: 856-424-8998 ▪ Fx: 856-424-9248

Power Electronics Society, IEEE   www.pels.org
IEEE Operations Ctr 445 Hoes Ln   Piscataway NJ 08854
Ph: 732-981-0060 ▪ Fx: 732-981-1721

Power Engineering Society, IEEE   www.ieee.org/portal/index.jsp?pageID=pes_home
IEEE Operations Ctr 445 Hoes Ln   Piscataway NJ 08854
Ph: 732-981-0060 ▪ Fx: 732-981-1721

Power Engineers, National Association of   www.powerengineers.com
1 Springfield St   Chicopee MA 01013
Ph: 413-592-6273 ▪ Fx: 413-592-1998

Power Equipment Aftermarket Association, Outdoor   www.opeaa.org
1726 M St NW Suite 1101   Washington DC 20036
Ph: 202-775-8605 ▪ Fx: 202-833-1577

Power Equipment & Engine Service Association, Outdoor   www.opeesa.com
210 Allen Dr   Exton PA 19341
Ph: 610-363-3844 ▪ Fx: 610-363-3817

Power Equipment Institute Inc, Outdoor   opei.mow.org
341 S Patrick St   Alexandria VA 22314
Ph: 703-549-7600 ▪ Fx: 703-549-7604

Power-Motion Technology Representatives Association   www.ptra.org
PO Box 150229   Arlington TX 76015
Ph: 817-561-7272 ▪ Fx: 817-561-7275 ▪ TF: 888-817-7872

Power Source Manufacturers Association   www.psma.com
PO Box 418   Mendham NJ 07945
Ph: 973-543-9660 ▪ Fx: 973-543-6207

Power Squadrons, US   www.usps.org
PO Box 30423   Raleigh NC 27622
Ph: 919-821-0281 ▪ Fx: 888-304-0813 ▪ TF: 888-367-8777

Power Supply Association, Electric   www.epsa.org
1401 New York Ave 11th Fl   Washington DC 20005
Ph: 202-628-8200 ▪ Fx: 202-628-8260

Power Tool Institute Inc   www.powertoolinstitute.com
1300 Sumner Ave   Cleveland OH 44115
Ph: 216-241-7333 ▪ Fx: 216-241-0105

Power Transmission Association, Mechanical   www.mpta.org
6724 Lone Oak Blvd   Naples FL 34109
Ph: 239-514-3441 ▪ Fx: 239-514-3470

Power Transmission Distributors Association   www.ptda.org
250 S Wacker Dr Suite 300   Chicago IL 60606
Ph: 312-876-9461 ▪ Fx: 312-876-9490

Power Washers of North America   www.pwna.org
6418 Grovedale Dr Suite 101B   Alexandria VA 22310
Ph: 703-971-4011 ▪ Fx: 703-971-7772 ▪ TF: 800-393-7962

Powys Society   www.powys-society.org

Practical Allergy Research Foundation   www.drapp.com
PO Box 60   Buffalo NY 14223
Ph: 716-875-5578 ▪ Fx: 716-875-5399

Practical Nurse Education & Service, National Association for
8607 2nd Ave Suite 404-A Silver Spring MD 20910
Ph: 301-588-2491
www.napnes.org

Practice Management Association, Emergency Department
8405 Greensboro Dr Suite 800 McLean VA 22102
Ph: 703-506-3292 ▪ Fx: 703-506-3266
www.edpma.org

Practising Law Institute
810 7th Ave 26th Fl New York NY 10019
Ph: 212-824-5700 ▪ Fx: 800-321-0093 ▪ TF: 800-260-4754
www.pli.edu

Prader-Willi Syndrome Association (USA)
5700 Midnight Pass Rd Suite 6 Sarasota FL 34242
Ph: 941-312-0400 ▪ Fx: 941-312-0142 ▪ TF: 800-926-4797
www.pwsausa.org

(Prairie Chickens) Society of Tympanuchus Cupido Pinnatus Ltd
1977 Hidden Reserve Ct Mequon WI 53092
Ph: 262-512-9107

Prairie Club
533 W North Ave Suite 10 Elmhurst IL 60126
Ph: 630-516-1277 ▪ Fx: 630-516-1278
www.prairieclub.org

Pratt Morris Institute
11811 Watertown Plank Rd Milwaukee WI 53226
Ph: 414-774-2994 ▪ Fx: 414-774-2964
www.morrispratt.org

Prayer, Anglican Fellowship of
3801 Appleton Way Orlando FL 32806
Ph: 407-438-3166 ▪ Fx: 407-856-1578 ▪ TF: 800-711-6399
www.afp.org

Prayer, Fellowship in
291 Witherspoon St Princeton NJ 08540
Ph: 609-924-6863 ▪ Fx: 609-924-6910
www.sacredjourney.org

(Prayer) Intercessors for America Inc
PO Box 915 Purcellville VA 20134
Ph: 800-872-7729
www.ifapray.org

Prayer International Committee, World Day of
475 Riverside Dr Rm 560 New York NY 10115
Ph: 212-870-3049 ▪ Fx: 212-864-8648
www.worlddayofprayer.net

Prayer League, World Mission
232 Clifton Ave Minneapolis MN 55403
Ph: 612-871-6843 ▪ Fx: 612-871-6844
www.wmpl.org

Prayer Society, World Peace
26 Benton Rd Wassaic NY 12592
Ph: 845-877-6093 ▪ Fx: 845-877-6862
www.worldpeace.org

Prayers for Life
Salve Regina University Newport RI 02840
Ph: 401-849-5421

Precast Association, Architectural
6710 Winkler Rd Suite 8 Fort Myers FL 33919
Ph: 239-454-6989 ▪ Fx: 239-454-6787
www.archprecast.org

Precast Concrete Association, National
10333 N Meridian St Suite 272 Indianapolis IN 46290
Ph: 317-571-9500 ▪ Fx: 317-571-0041 ▪ TF: 800-366-7731
www.precast.org

Precast/Prestressed Concrete Institute
209 W Jackson Blvd Suite 500 Chicago IL 60606
Ph: 312-786-0300 ▪ Fx: 312-786-0353
www.pci.org

Precious Metals Institute, International
4400 Bayou Blvd Suite 18 Pensacola FL 32503
Ph: 850-476-1156 ▪ Fx: 850-476-1548
www.ipmi.org

Precious Stone Association of America, Diamond Trade &
11 W 47th St New York NY 10036
Ph: 212-790-3806 ▪ Fx: 212-869-5511

Precision Aerobatics Model Pilots Association
158 Flying Cloud Isle Foster City CA 94404
Ph: 650-345-0130 ▪ Fx: 650-578-8454
www.control-line.org

Precision Engineering, American Society for
PO Box 10826 Raleigh NC 27605
Ph: 919-839-8444 ▪ Fx: 919-839-8039
www.aspe.net

Precision Machined Products Association
6700 W Snowville Rd Brecksville OH 44141
Ph: 440-526-0300 ▪ Fx: 440-526-5803
www.pmpa.org

Precision Metalforming Association
6363 Oak Tree Blvd Independence OH 44131
Ph: 216-901-8800 ▪ Fx: 216-901-9190
www.metalforming.com

Precollege Directors, National Association of
45 Wintonbury Ave Bloomfield CT 06002
Ph: 860-769-5283 ▪ Fx: 860-769-5287
www.jhuapl.edu/NAPD/aboutNAPD.htm

Predator Conservation Alliance
PO Box 6733 Bozeman MT 59771
Ph: 406-587-3389 ▪ Fx: 406-587-3178
www.predatorconservation.org

Preferred Funeral Directors International
PO Box 335 Indian Rocks Beach FL 33785
Ph: 727-524-8100 ▪ Fx: 727-524-8200 ▪ TF: 888-655-1566
www.pfdi.org

Preferred Hotels & Resorts Worldwide Inc
311 S Wacker Dr Suite 1900 Chicago IL 60606
Ph: 312-913-0400 ▪ Fx: 312-913-0444 ▪ TF: 800-323-7500
www.preferredhotels.com

Preferred Provider Organizations, American Association of
PO Box 429 Jeffersonville IN 47131
Ph: 812-246-4376 ▪ Fx: 812-246-4630
www.aappo.org

(Pregnancy) Heartbeat International
665 E Dublin-Granville Rd Suite 440 Columbus OH 43229
Ph: 614-885-7577 ▪ Fx: 614-885-8746 ▪ TF: 888-550-7577
www.heartbeatinternational.org

Pregnancy & Infant Loss Support Inc, SHARE
St Joseph's Health Ctr 300 1st Capitol Dr Saint Charles MO 63301
Ph: 636-947-6164 ▪ Fx: 636-947-7486 ▪ TF: 800-821-6819
www.nationalshareoffice.com

Pregnancy, National Campaign To Prevent Teen
1776 Massachusetts Ave NW Suite 200 Washington DC 20036
Ph: 202-478-8500 ▪ Fx: 202-478-8588
www.teenpregnancy.org

Pregnancy Parenting & Prevention Inc, National Organization on Adolescent 2401 Pennsylvania Ave NW Suite 350 Washington DC 20037
Ph: 202-293-8370 ▪ Fx: 202-293-8805 ▪ TF: 888-766-2777
www.noappp.org

(Premedical) Alpha Epsilon Delta
James Madison University 701 Carrier Dr MSC 4307 Harrisonburg VA 22807
Ph: 540-568-2594 ▪ Fx: 540-568-2595
www.jmu.edu/orgs/nationalaed

Premium Finance Association, Insurance
2890 Niagara Falls PO Box 726 Amherst NY 14226
Ph: 716-695-8757 ▪ Fx: 716-695-8758

Premium Incentive Travel Suppliers & Agents, American Association of PO Box 35189 Chicago IL 60707
Ph: 708-453-0080 ▪ Fx: 708-453-0083
www.traveltran.com

Prepaid Communications Association, International
904 Massachusetts Ave NE Washington DC 20002
Ph: 202-544-4448 ▪ Fx: 202-547-7417 ▪ TF: 800-958-7824
www.i-pca.org

Prepaid Legal Services Institute, American
541 N Fairbanks Ct Chicago IL 60611
Ph: 312-988-5751 ▪ Fx: 312-988-5710
www.aplsi.org

Prepress Association, International
7200 France Ave S Suite 223 Edina MN 55435
Ph: 952-896-1908 ▪ Fx: 952-896-0181 ▪ TF: 800-255-8141
www.ipa.org

Prepress Platemakers Association, Flexographic
2105 Laurel Bush Rd Suite 200 Bel Air MD 21015
Ph: 443-640-1045 ▪ Fx: 443-640-1031
www.fppa.net

Presbyterian Association of Musicians
100 Witherspoon St Louisville KY 40202
Ph: 502-569-5288 ▪ Fx: 502-569-8465 ▪ TF: 888-728-7228
horeb.pcusa.org/pam

Presbyterian Church in America
1700 N Brown Rd Lawrenceville GA 30043
Ph: 678-825-1000 ▪ Fx: 678-825-1004 ▪ TF: 800-700-3221
www.pcanet.org

Presbyterian Church (USA)
100 Witherspoon St Louisville KY 40202
Ph: 502-569-5000 ▪ Fx: 502-569-5018 ▪ TF: 888-728-7228
www.pcusa.org

Presbyterian Church World Witness, Associate Reformed
1 Cleveland St Suite 220 Greenville SC 29601
Ph: 864-233-5226 ▪ Fx: 864-233-5326
worldwitness.org

Presbyterian Colleges & Universities, Association of
100 Witherspoon St Louisville KY 40202
Ph: 502-569-5364 ▪ Fx: 502-569-8766 ▪ TF: 888-728-7228
www.apcu.net

Presbyterian Disaster Assistance
100 Witherspoon St Louisville KY 40202
Ph: 502-569-5839 ▪ Fx: 502-569-8039 ▪ TF: 888-728-7228
www.pcusa.org/pda

Presbyterian Evangelistic Fellowship
4211 Flat Shoals Pkwy Decatur GA 30034
Ph: 404-244-0740 ▪ Fx: 404-244-0914 ▪ TF: 800-225-5733
www.pefministry.org

Presbyterian Foreign Missions, Independent Board for
246 W Walnut Ln Philadelphia PA 19144
Ph: 215-438-0511 ▪ Fx: 215-438-0560
www.ibpfm.org

Presbyterian Frontier Fellowship
574 Prairie Center Dr Suite 135-313 Eden Prairie MN 55344
Ph: 952-903-9733 ▪ Fx: 952-942-9675 ▪ TF: 800-720-4733
www.pff.net

Presbyterian Health Education & Welfare Association
100 Witherspoon St Rm 3041 Louisville KY 40202
Ph: 502-569-5794 ▪ Fx: 502-569-8034 ▪ TF: 888-728-7228
www.pcusa.org/phewa

Presbyterian Lay Committee
PO Box 2210 Lenoir NC 28645
Ph: 828-758-8716 ▪ Fx: 828-758-0920 ▪ TF: 800-368-0110
www.layman.org

Presbyterian Peace Fellowship
PO Box 271 Nyack NY 10960
Ph: 845-358-4601 ▪ Fx: 845-358-4924

Presbyterian-Reformed Ministries International
PO Box 429 Black Mountain NC 28711
Ph: 828-669-7373 ▪ Fx: 828-669-4880
www.prmi.org

Presbyterian Scouters, National Association of
8520 MacKenzie Rd Box 6900 Saint Louis MO 63123
Ph: 314-638-1017 ▪ Fx: 314-638-7250 ▪ TF: 800-933-7729
www.presbyterianscouters.org

Presbyterians Pro-Life
PO Box 11130 Burke VA 22009
Ph: 703-569-9474 ▪ Fx: 703-644-5708
www.ppl.org

Presbyterians for Renewal
8134 New LaGrange Rd Suite 227 Louisville KY 40222
Ph: 502-425-4630 ▪ Fx: 502-423-8329
www.pfrenewal.org

Preschools International, Parent Cooperative
1401 New York Ave NW Suite 1100 Washington DC 20005
Ph: 800-636-6222 ▪ Fx: 202-347-1968
preschools.coop

Prescription Drug Programs, National Council for
9240 E Raintree Dr Scottsdale AZ 85260
Ph: 480-477-1000 ▪ Fx: 480-767-1042
www.ncpdp.org

Presenters, Association of Performing Arts
1112 16th St NW Suite 400 Washington DC 20036
Ph: 202-833-2787 ▪ Fx: 202-833-1543
www.artspresenters.org

Preservation Action
1054 31st St NW Suite 526 Washington DC 20007
Ph: 202-298-6180 ▪ Fx: 202-298-6182
www.preservationaction.org

Preservation of Cape Cod, Association for the
PO Box 398 Barnstable MA 02630
Ph: 508-362-4226 ▪ Fx: 508-362-4227 ▪ TF: 877-955-4142
www.apcc.org

Preservation Charities of America, Conservation &
21 Tamal Vista Blvd Suite 209 Corte Madera CA 94925
Ph: 800-626-6685
www.conservenow.org

Preservation Commissions, National Alliance of
PO Box 1605 Athens GA 30603
Ph: 706-542-4731 ▪ Fx: 706-583-0320
www.arches.uga.edu/~napc

Preservation Council, Ethnic Cultural
6500 S Pulaski Rd Chicago IL 60629
Ph: 773-582-5143 ▪ Fx: 773-582-5133

Preservation Institute, National
PO Box 1702 Alexandria VA 22313
Ph: 703-765-0100
www.npi.org

Preservation Law, National Center for
1333 Connecticut Ave NW Suite 300 Washington DC 20036
Ph: 202-338-0392 ▪ Fx: 202-775-9038

Preservation Organizations, National Alliance of Statewide
c/o Historic Landmarks Foundation of Indiana 340 W Michigan
St   Indianapolis IN 46202
Ph: 317-639-4534 ▪ TF: 800-450-4534

(Preservation) Royal Oak Foundation   www.royal-oak.org
26 Broadway Suite 950   New York NY 10004
Ph: 212-480-2889 ▪ Fx: 212-785-7234 ▪ TF: 800-913-6565

Preservation Society & Museum, Military Aviation   www.mapsairmuseum.org
2260 International Pkwy   North Canton OH 44720
Ph: 330-896-6332

Preservation Technology International, Association for   apti.org
4513 Lincoln Ave Suite 213   Lisle IL 60532
Ph: 630-968-6400 ▪ Fx: 888-723-4242

Preserve Association, International Jelly &   www.jelly.org
5775 Peachtree-Dunwoody Rd Bldg G Suite 500   Atlanta GA
30342
Ph: 404-252-3663 ▪ Fx: 404-252-0774

Presidency, Center for the Study of the   www.thepresidency.org
1020 19th NW Suite 250   Washington DC 20036
Ph: 202-872-9800 ▪ Fx: 202-872-9811

President Benjamin Harrison Home Foundation   www.presidentbenjaminharrison.org
1230 N Delaware St   Indianapolis IN 46202
Ph: 317-631-1888 ▪ Fx: 317-632-5488

Presidential Center, Clinton   www.clintonpresidentialcenter.org
55 W 125th St   New York NY 10027
Ph: 212-348-8882 ▪ Fx: 212-348-9245

Presidential Debates, Commission on   www.debates.org
1200 New Hampshire Ave NW PO Box 445   Washington DC
20036
Ph: 202-872-1020 ▪ Fx: 202-783-5923

Presidential Library Association, Herbert Hoover   www.hooverassociation.org
PO Box 696   West Branch IA 52358
Ph: 319-643-5327 ▪ Fx: 319-643-2391 ▪ TF: 800-828-0475

Presidential Task Force, Republican   www.nrsc.org/memberprograms/taskforce
Ronald Reagan Republican Ctr 425 2nd St NE   Washington DC
20002
Ph: 202-675-6772 ▪ TF: 800-877-6775

Presidents' Organization, World   www.wpo.org
110 S Union St Suite 200   Alexandria VA 22314
Ph: 703-684-4900 ▪ Fx: 703-684-4955

Presidents' Organization, Young   www.ypo.org
451 S Decker Dr Suite 200   Irving TX 75062
Ph: 972-650-4600 ▪ Fx: 972-650-4777 ▪ TF: 800-773-7976

Press Advisers Association, Columbia   www.columbia.edu/cu/cspa/CSPAA.html
Scholastic   Columbia Univ MC 5711   New York NY 10027
Ph: 212-854-9400 ▪ Fx: 212-854-9401

Press Agents & Managers, Association of Theatrical
165 W 46th St Suite 700   New York NY 10036
Ph: 212-719-3666 ▪ Fx: 212-302-1585 ▪ TF: 800-858-3667

Press, Associated Church   www.theacp.org
1410 Vernon St   Stoughton WI 53589
Ph: 608-877-0011 ▪ Fx: 608-877-0062

Press, Associated Collegiate   studentpress.journ.umn.edu
2221 University Ave SE Suite 121   Minneapolis MN 55414
Ph: 612-625-8335 ▪ Fx: 612-626-0720

Press Association, American Amateur   members.aol.com/aapa96
535 Kickerillo Dr   Houston TX 77079
Ph: 281-497-8493

Press Association, American Jewish   www.ajpa.org
1828 L St NW Suite 1000   Washington DC 20036
Ph: 202-785-2282 ▪ Fx: 202-785-2307

Press Association, Catholic   www.catholicpress.org
3555 Veterans Memorial Hwy Unit 0   Ronkonkoma NY 11779
Ph: 631-471-4730 ▪ Fx: 631-471-4804

Press Association, Columbia Scholastic   www.columbia.edu/cu/cspa
Columbia University MC 5711   New York NY 10027
Ph: 212-854-9400 ▪ Fx: 212-854-9401

Press Association, Evangelical   www.gospelcom.net/epa
PO Box 28129   Crystal MN 55428
Ph: 763-535-4793 ▪ Fx: 763-535-4794

Press Association, Foreign   www.foreignpressnewyork.com
333 E 46th St Suite 1K   New York NY 10017
Ph: 212-370-1054 ▪ Fx: 212-370-1058

Press Association, Hollywood Foreign
646 N Robertson Blvd   West Hollywood CA 90069
Ph: 310-657-1731 ▪ Fx: 310-657-5576

Press Association, Independent   www.indypress.org
2729 Mission St Suite 201   San Francisco CA 94110
Ph: 415-643-4401 ▪ Fx: 415-643-4402 ▪ TF: 877-463-9624

Press Association, Inter American   sipiapa.org
1801 SW 3rd Ave 7th Fl   Miami FL 33129
Ph: 305-634-2465 ▪ Fx: 305-635-2272 ▪ TF: 877-747-4272

Press Association, International Motor   www.impa.org
4 Park St   Harrington Park NJ 07640
Ph: 201-750-3533 ▪ Fx: 201-750-2010

Press Association, National American Legion   www.nalpa.legion.org

Press Association, National Scholastic   www.studentpress.org/nspa
2221 University Ave SE Suite 121   Minneapolis MN 55414
Ph: 612-625-8335 ▪ Fx: 612-626-0720

Press Center, Alternative   www.altpress.org
PO Box 33109   Baltimore MD 21218
Ph: 410-243-2471 ▪ Fx: 410-235-5325

Press Center for Independent Publishing, Small   www.smallpress.org
20 W 44th St   New York NY 10036
Ph: 212-764-7021 ▪ Fx: 212-354-5365

Press Club of America, Overseas   www.opcofamerica.org
40 W 45th St   New York NY 10036
Ph: 212-626-9220 ▪ Fx: 212-626-9210

Press Club, Capital   www.cpcomm.org
PO Box 19403   Washington DC 20036
Ph: 202-628-1122

Press Club, National   npc.press.org
529 14th St NW National Press Bldg   Washington DC 20045
Ph: 202-662-7500 ▪ Fx: 202-662-7569

Press Foundation, National   www.nationalpress.org
1211 Connecticut Ave NW Suite 310   Washington DC 20036
Ph: 202-663-7280 ▪ Fx: 202-530-2855

Press Guild, Arab-American
13313 Debell St   Arleta CA 91331
Ph: 818-896-5860

Press Institute, American   www.americanpressinstitute.org
11690 Sunrise Valley Dr   Reston VA 20191
Ph: 703-620-3611 ▪ Fx: 703-620-5814

Press Photographers Association, National   www.nppa.org
3200 Croasdaile Dr Suite 306   Durham NC 27705
Ph: 919-383-7246 ▪ Fx: 919-383-7261

Press Politics & Public Policy, Joan Shorenstein   www.ksg.harvard.edu/presspol
Center on the   Harvard Univ John F Kennedy School of
Government 79 John F Kennedy St   Cambridge MA 02138
Ph: 617-495-8269 ▪ Fx: 617-495-8696

Press Society, Lithuanian Catholic
4545 W 63rd St   Chicago IL 60629
Ph: 773-585-9500 ▪ Fx: 773-585-8284

Press Women, National Federation of   www.nfpw.org
PO Box 5556   Arlington VA 22205
Ph: 703-534-2500 ▪ Fx: 703-534-5751 ▪ TF: 800-780-2715

Presses, Council of Literary Magazines &   www.clmp.org
154 Christopher St Suite 3C   New York NY 10014
Ph: 212-741-9110 ▪ Fx: 212-741-9112

Pressure Pipe Association, American Concrete   www.acppa.org
11800 Sunrise Valley Dr Suite 309   Reston VA 20191
Ph: 703-391-9135 ▪ Fx: 703-391-9136

Pressure Sensitive Tape Council   www.pstc.org
2514 Stonebridge Ln PO Box 609   Northbrook IL 60062
Ph: 847-562-2630 ▪ Fx: 847-562-2631 ▪ TF: 877-523-7782

Pressure Ulcer Advisory Panel, National   www.npuap.org
12100 Sunset Hills Rd Suite 130   Reston VA 20190
Ph: 703-464-4849 ▪ Fx: 703-435-4390

Pressure Vessel Inspectors, National Board of Boiler &   www.nationalboard.org
1055 Crupper Ave   Columbus OH 43229
Ph: 614-888-8320 ▪ Fx: 614-847-1147

Pressure Vessel Manufacturers Association   www.pvma.org
8 S Michigan Ave Suite 1000   Chicago IL 60603
Ph: 312-456-5590 ▪ Fx: 312-580-0165

Pressure Washer Manufacturers Association   www.pwma.org
1300 Sumner Ave   Cleveland OH 44115
Ph: 216-241-7333 ▪ Fx: 216-241-0105

Pretrial Officers Association, Federal Probation &   www.fppoa.org
350 S Main St Suite 160   Salt Lake City UT 84101
Ph: 801-524-6943

Pretrial Services Resource Center   www.pretrial.org/
1010 Vermont Ave NW Suite 300   Washington DC 20005
Ph: 202-638-3080 ▪ Fx: 202-347-0493

Prevent Blindness America   www.preventblindness.org
500 E Remington Rd Suite 200   Schaumburg IL 60173
Ph: 847-843-2020 ▪ Fx: 847-843-8458 ▪ TF: 800-331-2020

Prevent Child Abuse America   www.preventchildabuse.org
200 S Michigan Ave 17th Fl   Chicago IL 60604
Ph: 312-663-3520 ▪ Fx: 312-939-8962 ▪ TF: 800-244-5373

Prevention Probation Prisons, Volunteers in   www.vipmentoring.org
220 Bagley St 1020 Michigan Bldg   Detroit MI 48226
Ph: 313-964-1110 ▪ Fx: 313-964-1145

Preventive Medicine, American Board of   www.abprevmed.org
330 S Wells St Suite 1018   Chicago IL 60606
Ph: 312-939-2276 ▪ Fx: 312-939-2218

Preventive Medicine, American College of   www.acpm.org
1307 New York Ave NW Suite 200   Washington DC 20005
Ph: 202-466-2044 ▪ Fx: 202-466-2662

Priesthood, Corpus - National Association for an Inclusive   www.corpus.org
PO Box 104   High Bridge NJ 08829
Ph: 908-638-6877 ▪ Fx: 908-638-8220

Priests' Councils, National Federation of   www.nfpc.org
1337 W Ohio St   Chicago IL 60622
Ph: 312-226-3334 ▪ Fx: 312-829-8915

Priests for Life   www.priestsforlife.org
PO Box 141172   Staten Island NY 10314
Ph: 718-980-4400 ▪ Fx: 718-980-6515 ▪ TF: 888-735-3448

Priests, Marian Movement of   www.mmp-usa.net
PO Box 8   Saint Francis ME 04774
Ph: 207-398-3375

Priests, Survivors Network of Those Abused by   www.snapnetwork.org
PO Box 6416   Chicago IL 60680
Ph: 312-409-2720

Primarily Primates Inc   www.primarilyprimates.org
PO Box 207   San Antonio TX 78291
Ph: 830-755-4616 ▪ Fx: 830-755-2435

Primate Protection League, International   www.ippl.org
PO Box 766   Summerville SC 29484
Ph: 843-871-2280 ▪ Fx: 843-871-7988

Primates Inc, Primarily   www.primarilyprimates.org
PO Box 207   San Antonio TX 78291
Ph: 830-755-4616 ▪ Fx: 830-755-2435

Primatological Society, International   www.primate.wisc.edu/pin/ips.html
Univ of Georgia Psychology Dept   Athens GA 30602
Ph: 706-542-3036 ▪ Fx: 706-542-3275

Primatologists, American Society of   www.asp.org
Loyola Univ Psychology Dept   New Orleans LA 70118
Ph: 504-865-3255 ▪ Fx: 504-865-3970

Prince Hall Grand Masters, Conference of
PO Box 1588   Muskogee OK 74402
Ph: 918-683-3123 ▪ Fx: 918-687-4845

Principals, National Association of Elementary School   www.naesp.org
1615 Duke St   Alexandria VA 22314
Ph: 703-684-3345 ▪ Fx: 703-548-6021 ▪ TF: 800-386-2377

Principals, National Association of Secondary School   www.principals.org
1904 Association Dr   Reston VA 20191
Ph: 703-860-0200 ▪ Fx: 703-476-5432

Principals, National Conference of Yeshiva
160 Broadway   New York NY 10038
Ph: 212-227-1000 ▪ Fx: 212-406-6934

Principals of Schools for Girls, National Association of
41 Van Brunt Manor Rd   East Setauket NY 11733
Ph: 631-751-0850 ▪ Fx: 631-689-7311

Print Collectors Society, American Historical   www.ahpcs.org
PO Box 201   Fairfield CT 06824
Ph: 203-255-1627

Print Council of America   www.printcouncil.org
Univ of Kansas Spencer Museum of Art   Lawrence KS 66045
Ph: 785-864-4710 ▪ Fx: 785-864-3112

Print Dealers Association, International Fine   www.printdealter.com
15 Gramercy Park S Suite 7A   New York NY 10003
Ph: 212-674-6095 ▪ Fx: 212-674-6783

Print Music Dealers Association, Retail   www.printmusic.org
13140 Coit Rd Suite 320 LB 120   Dallas TX 75240
Ph: 972-233-9107 ▪ Fx: 972-490-4219

Print Production, Partnership in   www.p3-ny.org
276 Bowery   New York NY 10012
Ph: 212-334-2106 ▪ Fx: 212-431-5786

Printers of America, Master   www.masterprinters.org
100 Daingerfield Rd   Alexandria VA 22314
Ph: 703-519-8100 ▪ Fx: 703-548-3227 ▪ TF: 800-742-2666

Printers & Engravers Association of the US, Machine
690 Warren Ave   Providence RI 02914
Ph: 401-438-5849

PrintImage International   www.printimage.org
70 E Lake St Suite 333   Chicago IL 60601
Ph: 312-726-8015 ▪ Fx: 312-726-8113 ▪ TF: 800-234-0040

Printing History Association, American   www.printinghistory.org

Printing House for the Blind, American   www.aph.org
1839 Frankfort Ave PO Box 6085   Louisville KY 40206
Ph: 502-895-2405 ▪ Fx: 502-899-2274 ▪ TF: 800-223-1839

Printing House Craftsmen, International Association of   www.iaphc.org
7042 Brooklyn Blvd   Minneapolis MN 55429
Ph: 763-560-1620 ▪ Fx: 763-560-1350 ▪ TF: 800-466-4274

Printing & Imaging Association, Digital   www.dpia.org
10015 Main St   Fairfax VA 22031
Ph: 703-385-1339 ▪ Fx: 703-359-1336

Printing Industries of America Inc   www.gain.net
100 Daingerfield Rd   Alexandria VA 22314
Ph: 703-519-8100 ▪ Fx: 703-548-3227 ▪ TF: 800-742-2666

Printing Industries of America, Label   www.gain.net/PIA_GATF/LPIA/main.html
100 Daingerfield Rd   Alexandria VA 22314
Ph: 703-519-8100 ▪ Fx: 703-548-3227

Printing Industries of America Inc PAC   www.gain.net/gov_affairs/printpac.html
100 Daingerfield Rd   Alexandria VA 22314
Ph: 703-519-8100 ▪ Fx: 703-548-3227 ▪ TF: 800-742-2666

Printing Ink Manufacturers, National Association of   www.napim.org
581 Main St   Woodbridge NJ 07095
Ph: 732-855-1525 ▪ Fx: 732-855-1838

Printing Leadership, National Association for   www.napl.org
75 W Century Rd   Paramus NJ 07652
Ph: 201-634-9600 ▪ Fx: 201-634-0324 ▪ TF: 800-642-6275

Printing Publishing & Converting Technologies, NPES: Association   www.npes.org
for Suppliers of   1899 Preston White Dr   Reston VA 20191
Ph: 703-264-7200 ▪ Fx: 703-620-0994

Printing Publishing & Media Workers Sector, Communications
Workers of America   501 3rd St NW Suite 950   Washington
DC 20001
Ph: 202-434-1238 ▪ Fx: 202-434-1245

Printing, Society for Service Professionals in   www.sspp.org
433 E Monroe Ave   Alexandria VA 22301
Ph: 703-684-0044 ▪ Fx: 703-548-9137 ▪ TF: 877-777-7398

Printing Technical Foundation, Screen   www.sgia.org/sptf/
10015 Main St   Fairfax VA 22031
Ph: 703-385-1335 ▪ Fx: 703-273-0456 ▪ TF: 888-385-3588

Printing Thermographers Association, Worldwide   www.thermographers.org
1156 15th St NW Suite 900   Washington DC 20005
Ph: 202-393-2818 ▪ Fx: 202-223-9741

PRISM International   www.prismintl.org
605 Benson Rd Suite B   Garner NC 27529
Ph: 919-771-0657 ▪ Fx: 919-771-0457 ▪ TF: 800-336-9793

Prison-Ashram Project   www.humankindness.org/project.html
PO Box 61619   Durham NC 27715
Ph: 919-304-2220 ▪ Fx: 919-304-3220

Prison Association, Women's   www.wpa.org
110 2nd Ave   New York NY 10003
Ph: 212-674-1163 ▪ Fx: 212-677-1981

Prison Fellowship International   www.pfi.org
PO Box 17434   Washington DC 20041
Ph: 703-481-0000 ▪ Fx: 703-481-0003

Prison Fellowship Ministries   www.pfm.org
PO Box 1550   Merrifield VA 22116
Ph: 703-478-0100 ▪ Fx: 703-478-2709 ▪ TF: 877-497-0122

Prison Hospice Association, National
PO Box 3769   Boulder CO 80307
Ph: 303-447-8051 ▪ Fx: 303-447-8055

Prison Ministry, Good News Jail &   www.goodnewsjail.org
2230 E Parham Rd Suite 200   Richmond VA 23228
Ph: 804-553-4090 ▪ Fx: 804-553-4144 ▪ TF: 800-220-2202

Prison Mission Association   www.pmabcf.org
PO Box 2300   Port Orchard WA 98366
Ph: 360-876-0918 ▪ Fx: 360-876-0972

(Prison Reform) John Howard Association   www.johnhowardassociation.org
300 W Adams St Suite 617   Chicago IL 60606
Ph: 312-782-1901 ▪ Fx: 312-782-1902

Prisoner Rape, Stop   www.spr.org
6303 Wilshire Blvd Suite 204   Los Angeles CA 90048
Ph: 323-653-7867 ▪ Fx: 323-653-7870

Prisoners & Missing in Southeast Asia, National League of   www.pow-miafamilies.org
Families of American   1005 N Glebe Rd Suite 170   Arlington
VA 22201
Ph: 703-465-7432 ▪ Fx: 703-465-7433

Prisoners of War, American Ex-   www.axpow.org
3201 E Pioneer Pkwy Suite 40   Arlington TX 76010
Ph: 817-649-2979 ▪ Fx: 817-649-0109

(Prisons) Fortune Society   www.fortunesociety.org
53 W 23rd St 8th Fl   New York NY 10010
Ph: 212-691-7554 ▪ Fx: 212-255-4948

Prisons, Volunteers in Prevention Probation   www.vipmentoring.org
220 Bagley St 1020 Michigan Bldg   Detroit MI 48226
Ph: 313-964-1110 ▪ Fx: 313-964-1145

(Prisons) We Care Program   www.wecareprogram.org
5825 Hwy 21   Atmore AL 36502
Ph: 334-368-8818 ▪ Fx: 334-368-0932

Pritzker Foundation
200 W Madison St 38th Fl   Chicago IL 60606
Ph: 312-750-8400 ▪ Fx: 312-750-8545

Privacy Alliance, Online   www.privacyalliance.org
c/o Hogan & Hartson LLP 555 13th St NW   Washington DC
20004
Ph: 202-637-5600 ▪ Fx: 202-637-5710

Privacy, Americans for Computer   www.computerprivacy.org
1275 Pennsylvania Ave NW 10th Fl   Washington DC 20004
Ph: 202-393-5222 ▪ Fx: 202-467-0810

Privacy Council, US
PO Box 302   Cabin John MD 20818
Ph: 301-229-7002 ▪ Fx: 301-229-8011

Privacy Information Center, Electronic   epic.org
1718 Connecticut Ave NW Suite 200   Washington DC 20009
Ph: 202-483-1140 ▪ Fx: 202-483-1248

Privacy Professionals, International Association of   www.privacyassociation.org
1211 Locust St   Philadelphia PA 19107
Ph: 215-545-8990 ▪ Fx: 215-545-8107 ▪ TF: 800-266-6501

Privacy Rights Clearinghouse   www.privacyrights.org
3100 5th Ave Suite B   San Diego CA 92103
Ph: 619-298-3396 ▪ Fx: 619-298-5681

Private Agencies Collaborating Together   www.pactworld.org
1200 18th St NW Suite 350   Washington DC 20036
Ph: 202-466-5666 ▪ Fx: 202-466-5669

Private Art Dealers Association   www.pada.net
PO Box 872   New York NY 10021
Ph: 212-572-0772 ▪ Fx: 212-572-8398

Private Citizen Inc   privatecitizen.com
PO Box 233   Naperville IL 60566
Ph: 630-393-2370 ▪ TF: 800-288-5865

Private Education, Council for American   www.capenet.org
13017 Wisteria Dr PMB 457   Germantown MD 20874
Ph: 301-916-8460 ▪ Fx: 301-916-8485

Private Enterprise, Center for International   www.cipe.org
1155 15th St NW Suite 700   Washington DC 20005
Ph: 202-721-9200 ▪ Fx: 202-721-9250

Private Enterprise Education, Association of   www.apee.org
Univ of Tennessee at Chattanooga 313 Fletcher Hall 615
McCallie Ave   Chattanooga TN 37403
Ph: 423-755-4118 ▪ Fx: 423-755-5218

Private Enterprise Research Center   www.tamu.edu/perc
Texas A&M Univ MS 4231   College Station TX 77843
Ph: 979-845-7722 ▪ Fx: 979-845-6636

Private Enterprise Studies, Smith Center for   thesmithcenter.org
California State Univ Hayward College of Business &
Economics   Hayward CA 94542
Ph: 510-885-2640 ▪ Fx: 510-885-4222

Private Higher Education, Consortium for the Advancement of   www.cic.edu/caphe
1 Dupont Cir NW Suite 320   Washington DC 20036
Ph: 202-466-7230 ▪ Fx: 202-466-7238

Private Label Manufacturers Association   www.plma.com
369 Lexington Ave 3rd Fl   New York NY 10017
Ph: 212-972-3131 ▪ Fx: 212-983-1382

Private Nontraditional Schools & Colleges, National Association of   www.napnsc.org
182 Thompson Rd   Grand Junction CO 81503
Ph: 970-243-5441 ▪ Fx: 970-242-4392

Private Partnerships, National Council for Public-   www.ncppp.org
1660 L St NW Suite 510   Washington DC 20036
Ph: 202-467-6800 ▪ Fx: 202-467-6312

Private Property Voters, League of   www.landrights.org/_private/lppvhome.htm
PO Box 423   Battle Ground WA 98604
Ph: 360-687-2471 ▪ Fx: 360-687-2973

Private Railroad Car Owners Inc, American Association of   www.aaprco.com
630-B Constitution Ave NE   Washington DC 20002
Ph: 202-547-5696 ▪ Fx: 202-547-5623

Private Sector Council   www.privsect.org
1101 16th St NW Suite 300   Washington DC 20036
Ph: 202-822-3910 ▪ Fx: 202-822-0638

Private Special Education Centers, National Association of   www.napsec.org
1522 K St NW Suite 1032   Washington DC 20005
Ph: 202-408-3338 ▪ Fx: 202-408-3340

Private Truck Council, National   www.nptc.org
2200 Mill Rd Suite 350   Alexandria VA 22314
Ph: 703-683-1300 ▪ Fx: 703-683-1217

Privatization Center   www.privatization.org
Reason Public Policy Institute 3415 S Sepulveda Blvd Suite
    400   Los Angeles CA 90034
Ph: 310-391-2245 ▪ Fx: 310-391-4395

Pro-Choice America, NARAL   www.naral.org
1156 15th St NW Suite 700   Washington DC 20005
Ph: 202-973-3000 ▪ Fx: 202-973-3096

Pro-Choice Coalition, Republican   www.gopchoice.org
57 W 57th St Suite 1101   New York NY 10019
Ph: 212-207-8266 ▪ Fx: 212-207-8629 ▪ TF: 877-467-2464

Pro-Life Action League   www.prolifeaction.org
6160 N Cicero Ave Suite 600   Chicago IL 60646
Ph: 773-777-2900 ▪ Fx: 773-777-3061

Pro-Life Alliance of Gays & Lesbians   www.plagal.org
PO Box 33292   Washington DC 20033
Ph: 202-223-6697 ▪ Fx: 202-265-9737

(Pro-Life) American Collegians for Life   www.aclife.org
PO Box 1112   Washington DC 20013
Ph: 202-737-1007 ▪ Fx: 202-347-3245

(Pro-Life) Americans United for Life   www.unitedforlife.org
310 S Peoria St Suite 300   Chicago IL 60607
Ph: 312-492-7234 ▪ Fx: 312-492-7235 ▪ TF: 800-626-6149

(Pro-Life) Baptists for Life   www.bfl.org
PO Box 3158   Grand Rapids MI 49501
Ph: 616-257-6800 ▪ Fx: 616-257-6805 ▪ TF: 800-968-6086

(Pro-Life) Life Coalition International   www.lifecoalition.com
PO Box 360221   Melbourne FL 32936
Ph: 321-726-0444 ▪ Fx: 321-726-0509

(Pro-Life) Lutherans for Life   www.lutheransforlife.org
1120 S 'G' Ave   Nevada IA 50201
Ph: 515-382-2077 ▪ Fx: 515-382-3020 ▪ TF: 888-364-5433

(Pro-Life) Orthodox Christians for Life   www.oclife.org
PO Box 805   Melville NY 11747
Ph: 631-271-4408

(Pro-Life) Prayers for Life
Salve Regina University   Newport RI 02840
Ph: 401-849-5421

Pro-Life, Presbyterians   www.ppl.org
PO Box 11130   Burke VA 22009
Ph: 703-569-9474 ▪ Fx: 703-644-5708

(Pro-Life) Priests for Life   www.priestsforlife.org
PO Box 141172   Staten Island NY 10314
Ph: 718-980-4400 ▪ Fx: 718-980-6515 ▪ TF: 888-735-3448

(Pro-Life) Sisters of Life   www.sistersoflife.org
198 Hollywood Ave   Bronx NY 10465
Ph: 718-863-2264 ▪ Fx: 718-792-9645

(Pro-Life) Women Affirming Life   www.affirmlife.com
PO Box 35532   Brighton MA 02135
Ph: 617-254-2277 ▪ Fx: 617-254-2299

Pro Sanctity Movement   www.prosanctity.org
205 S Pine Dr   Fullerton CA 92833
Ph: 714-956-1020 ▪ Fx: 714-525-8948

Probate Research Association, International   www.lostheir.com/ipra.htm
c/o Josh Butler & Co Inc 201 Commerce St Suite
    150   Youngstown OH 44503
Ph: 330-747-3000 ▪ Fx: 330-747-3006

Probation Executives, National Association of   www.napehome.org
Sam Houston State Univ Correctional Management Institute of
    Texas   Huntsville TX 77341
Ph: 936-294-3757 ▪ Fx: 936-294-1671

Probation & Parole Association, American   www.appa-net.org
2760 Research Park Dr   Lexington KY 40511
Ph: 859-244-8203 ▪ Fx: 859-244-8001

Probation & Pretrial Officers Association, Federal   www.fppoa.org
350 S Main St Suite 160   Salt Lake City UT 84101
Ph: 801-524-6943

Probation Prisons, Volunteers in Prevention   www.vipmentoring.org
220 Bagley St 1020 Michigan Bldg   Detroit MI 48226
Ph: 313-964-1110 ▪ Fx: 313-964-1145

Probe Ministries International   www.probe.org
1900 Firman Dr Suite 100   Richardson TX 75081
Ph: 972-480-0240

Problem Solving Program, Future   www.fpsp.org
2028 Regency Rd   Lexington KY 40503
Ph: 859-276-4336 ▪ Fx: 859-276-4306 ▪ TF: 800-256-1499

Process Engineering, Society for the Advancement of   org.et.byu.edu/sampe
Material &   PO Box 2459   Covina CA 91722
Ph: 626-331-0616 ▪ Fx: 626-332-8929 ▪ TF: 800-562-7360

Process Equipment Manufacturers Association   www.pemanet.org
201 Park Washington Ct   Falls Church VA 22046
Ph: 703-538-1796 ▪ Fx: 703-241-5603

Process Servers, National Association of Professional   www.napps.org
PO Box 4547   Portland OR 97208
Ph: 503-222-4180 ▪ Fx: 503-222-3950 ▪ TF: 800-477-8211

Process Studies, Center for   www.ctr4process.org
Claremont School of Theology 1325 N College Ave   Claremont
    CA 91711
Ph: 909-621-5330 ▪ Fx: 909-621-2760

Processors Association, At-sea   www.atsea.org
4039 21st Ave W Suite 400   Seattle WA 98199
Ph: 206-285-5139 ▪ Fx: 206-285-1841

Procrastinators' Club of America   www.geocities.com/procrastinators_club_of_america
PO Box 712   Bryn Athyn PA 19009
Ph: 215-947-9020 ▪ Fx: 215-947-7210

Procurement Officials, National Association of State   www.naspo.org
167 W Main St Suite 600   Lexington KY 40507
Ph: 859-231-1877 ▪ Fx: 859-514-9166

Produce Association of the Americas, Fresh   www.fpaota.org
30 N Huggins St PO Box 848   Nogales AZ 85628
Ph: 520-287-2707 ▪ Fx: 520-287-2948

Produce Association, International Fresh-Cut   www.fresh-cuts.org
1600 Duke St Suite 440   Alexandria VA 22314
Ph: 703-299-6282 ▪ Fx: 703-299-6288

Produce & Floral Council, Fresh   www.fpfc.org
6301 Beach Blvd Suite 150   Buena Park CA 90621
Ph: 714-739-0177 ▪ Fx: 714-739-0226

Produce Marketing Association   www.pma.com
PO Box 6036x   Newark DE 19714
Ph: 302-738-7100 ▪ Fx: 302-731-2409

Producers, Alliance of Motion Picture & Television   www.amptp.org
15503 Ventura Blvd   Encino CA 91436
Ph: 818-995-3600 ▪ Fx: 818-382-1793

Producers Guild of America Inc   www.producersguild.org
8530 Wilshire Blvd Suite 450   Beverly Hills CA 90211
Ph: 310-358-9020 ▪ Fx: 310-358-9520

Producers, International Quorum of Motion Picture   www.iqfilm.org
c/o Film House 810 Dominican Dr   Nashville TN 37228
Ph: 615-255-4000 ▪ Fx: 615-255-4111

Producers, League of American Theatres &   www.broadway.org
226 W 47th St   New York NY 10036
Ph: 212-764-1122 ▪ Fx: 212-719-4389

Producers Livestock Marketing Association   www.producerslivestock.com
PO Box 540477   North Salt Lake UT 84054
Ph: 801-936-2424

Producers Inc, United   www.uproducers.com
5909 Cleveland Ave   Columbus OH 43231
Ph: 614-890-6666 ▪ Fx: 614-890-4776 ▪ TF: 800-456-3276

Product Development & Management Association   www.pdma.org
17000 Commerce Pkwy Suite C   Mount Laurel NJ 08054
Ph: 856-439-0500 ▪ Fx: 856-439-0525

Product Formulators & Distributors Association, United   www.pestworld.org/upfda
2034 Beaver Run Rd   Norcross GA 30071
Ph: 770-417-1418 ▪ Fx: 770-417-1419

Product Identification Manufacturers Inc, National Association   www.gpiweb.org
of Graphic &   PO Box 15466   Santa Ana CA 92735
Ph: 714-508-4915 ▪ Fx: 714-508-4904

Product Safety Engineering Society, IEEE   ewh.ieee.org/soc/pses
IEEE Operations Ctr 445 Hoes Ln   Piscataway NJ 08854
Ph: 732-981-0060 ▪ Fx: 732-981-1721

Production Engine Remanufacturers Association   www.pera.org
14160 Newbrook Dr Suite 210   Chantilly VA 20151
Ph: 703-968-2772 ▪ Fx: 703-968-2878

Production Equipment Rental Association   www.productionequipment.com
PO Box 55515   Sherman Oaks CA 91413
Ph: 818-906-2467 ▪ Fx: 818-906-1720

Production & Operations Management Society   www.poms.org
Florida International Univ College of Engineering EAS 2460
    10555 W Flagler St   Miami FL 33174
Ph: 305-348-1413 ▪ Fx: 305-348-6890

Productivity Management, Institute for Health &   www.ihpm.org
4435 Waterfront Dr Suite 101   Glen Allen VA 23060
Ph: 804-257-1905 ▪ Fx: 804-747-5316 ▪ TF: 800-722-0376

Productivity & Quality Center, American   www.apqc.org
123 Post Oak Ln 3rd Fl   Houston TX 77024
Ph: 713-681-4020 ▪ Fx: 713-681-8578 ▪ TF: 800-776-9676

Productivity Specialists, Association of   www.a-p-s.org
New York NY 10175
Ph: 212-286-0943

Professional Airways Systems Specialists   www.passnational.org
1150 17th St NW Suite 702   Washington DC 20036
Ph: 202-293-7277 ▪ Fx: 202-293-7727

Professional Apparel Association   www.proapparel.com
994 Old Eagle School Rd Suite 1019   Wayne PA 19087
Ph: 610-971-4850 ▪ Fx: 610-971-4859 ▪ TF: 800-722-7712

Professional Association for Childhood Education   www.pacenet.org
1290 Sutter St Suite 200   San Francisco CA 94109
Ph: 415-749-6851 ▪ Fx: 415-749-6861 ▪ TF: 800-924-2460

Professional Association of Christian Educators   www.gospelcom.net/paceinc
PO Box 140284   Dallas TX 75214
Ph: 214-841-3566 ▪ Fx: 214-841-3773 ▪ TF: 800-829-9410

Professional Association of Diving Instructors International   www.padi.com
30151 Tomas St   Rancho Santa Margarita CA 92688
Ph: 949-858-7234 ▪ Fx: 949-858-0106 ▪ TF: 800-729-7234

Professional Association of Health Care Office Management   www.pahcom.com
461 E 10 Mile Rd   Pensacola FL 32534
Ph: 850-474-9460 ▪ Fx: 850-474-6352 ▪ TF: 800-451-9311

Professional Association of Innkeepers International   www.paii.org
PO Box 90710   Santa Barbara CA 93190
Ph: 805-569-1853 ▪ Fx: 805-682-1016

Professional Association for Investment Communications Resources   www.paicr.org
1320 19th St NW Suite 300   Washington DC 20036
Ph: 202-371-9750 ▪ Fx: 202-371-8977 ▪ TF: 800-561-0751

Professional Association of Resume Writers & Career Coaches   www.parw.com
1388 Brightwaters Blvd NE   Saint Petersburg FL 33704
Ph: 727-821-2274 ▪ Fx: 727-894-1277 ▪ TF: 800-822-7279

Professional Association for SQL Server   www.sqlpass.org
401 N Michigan Ave   Chicago IL 60611
Ph: 312-527-6742 ▪ Fx: 312-245-1081

Professional Association of Volleyball Officials   www.pavo.org
PO Box 780   Oxford KS 67119
Ph: 888-791-2074 ▪ Fx: 620-455-3800

Professional Associations on Federal Statistics, Council of   www.copafs.org
1429 Duke St Suite 402   Alexandria VA 22314
Ph: 703-836-0404 ▪ Fx: 703-684-3410

Professional Athletes Outreach   www.pao.org
72 E Sunset Way PO Box 1044   Issaquah WA 98027
Ph: 425-392-6300 ▪ Fx: 425-392-7640

Professional Audiovideo Retailers Association www.paralink.org
10 E 22nd St Suite 310   Lombard IL 60148
Ph: 630-268-1500 ▪ Fx: 630-953-8957

Professional Aviation Maintenance Association www.pama.org
717 Princess St   Alexandria VA 22314
Ph: 703-683-3171 ▪ Fx: 703-683-0018 ▪ TF: 866-865-7262

Professional Awning Manufacturers Association www.awninginfo.com
1801 County Rd 'B' W   Roseville MN 55113
Ph: 651-222-2508 ▪ Fx: 651-631-9334 ▪ TF: 800-225-4324

Professional Bowhunters Society www.bowsite.com/pbs
PO Box 246   Terrell NC 28682
Ph: 704-664-2534 ▪ Fx: 704-664-7471

Professional Bowlers Association www.pba.com
719 2nd Ave Suite 701   Seattle WA 98104
Ph: 206-332-9688 ▪ Fx: 206-332-9722

Professional Car Society www.professionalcar.org
5405 Heritage Ln   Kingsport TN 37664
Ph: 423-288-3454

Professional Clubmakers Society www.proclubmakers.org
70 Persimmon Ridge Dr   Louisville KY 40245
Ph: 502-241-2816 ▪ Fx: 502-241-2817 ▪ TF: 800-548-6094

Professional Communication Society, IEEE www.ieeepcs.org
IEEE Operations Ctr 445 Hoes Ln   Piscataway NJ 08854
Ph: 732-981-0060 ▪ Fx: 732-981-1721

Professional Construction Estimators Association of America www.pcea.org
PO Box 680336   Charlotte NC 28216
Ph: 704-987-9978 ▪ Fx: 704-987-9979 ▪ TF: 877-521-7232

Professional Convention Management Association www.pcma.org
2301 S Lake Shore Dr Suite 1001   Chicago IL 60616
Ph: 312-423-7262 ▪ Fx: 312-423-7222 ▪ TF: 877-827-7262

Professional Dance Teachers Association www.dancecaravan.com/PDTA/PDTA.html
PO Box 38   Waldwick NJ 07463
Ph: 201-652-7767 ▪ Fx: 201-652-2599 ▪ TF: 800-462-8679

Professional Development Consortium, National Adult Education www.naepdc.org/
444 N Capitol St NW Suite 422   Washington DC 20001
Ph: 202-624-5250 ▪ Fx: 202-624-1497

Professional Drivers Association www.stuntplayers.com/links
5235 Mission Oaks Blvd   Camarillo CA 93012
Ph: 818-774-3889 ▪ Fx: 805-491-0708

Professional Electrical Apparatus Recyclers League www.pearl1.org
6257 Lakepoint Pl   Parker CO 80134
Ph: 303-840-1059 ▪ Fx: 720-851-6090

Professional Employees International Union, Office & www.opeiu.org
265 W 14th St Suite 610   New York NY 10011
Ph: 212-675-3210 ▪ Fx: 212-727-3466 ▪ TF: 800-346-7348

Professional Employer Organizations, National Association of www.napeo.org
901 N Pitt St Suite 150   Alexandria VA 22314
Ph: 703-836-0466 ▪ Fx: 703-836-0976

Professional Engineers in Private Practice www.nspe.org/pepp
1420 King St   Alexandria VA 22314
Ph: 703-684-2804 ▪ Fx: 703-836-4875

Professional Football Researchers Association www.footballresearch.com/
12870 Rt 30   North Huntingdon PA 15642
Ph: 724-863-6345

Professional Fraternity Association Inc www.profraternity.org
345 N Charles St 3rd Fl   Baltimore MD 21201
Ph: 888-771-4732

Professional Golfer's Association www.pga.com
100 Ave of the Champions   Palm Beach Gardens FL 33418
Ph: 561-624-8400 ▪ Fx: 561-624-8439 ▪ TF: 800-477-6465

Professional Grounds Management Society www.pgms.org
720 Light St   Baltimore MD 21230
Ph: 410-223-2861 ▪ Fx: 410-752-8295 ▪ TF: 800-609-7467

Professional Handlers Association Inc www.infodog.com/misc/pha/phamain.htm
17017 Norbrook Dr   Olney MD 20832
Ph: 301-924-0089

Professional Housing Management Association www.phma.com
PO Box 4251   Leesburg VA 20177
Ph: 703-327-2399 ▪ Fx: 703-327-4005

Professional Insurance Marketing Association www.pima-assn.org
6300 Ridgelea Pl Suite 1008   Fort Worth TX 76116
Ph: 817-569-7462 ▪ Fx: 817-569-7461

Professional Knitwear Designers Guild
W3090 County Rd Y   Lomira WI 53048
Ph: 920-583-4298

Professional Lacrosse Players' Association www.plpa.com
97 Rhode Island Ave   Newport RI 02840
Ph: 401-845-6263

Professional Lawn Care Association of America www.plcaa.org
1000 Johnson Ferry Rd NE Suite C-135   Marietta GA 30068
Ph: 770-977-5222 ▪ Fx: 770-578-6071 ▪ TF: 800-458-3466

Professional Liability Agents Network www.plan.org
PO Box 1632   Monterey CA 93942
Ph: 877-960-7526 ▪ Fx: 831-372-6647

Professional Liability Attorneys, American Board of www.abpla.org
5712 244th St   Douglaston NY 11362
Ph: 718-631-1400 ▪ Fx: 718-631-1456

Professional Liability Underwriting Society www.plusweb.org
5353 Wayzata Blvd Suite 600   Minneapolis MN 55416
Ph: 952-746-2580 ▪ Fx: 952-746-2599 ▪ TF: 800-845-0778

Professional Managers Association www.promanager.org
PO Box 77235   Washington DC 20013
Ph: 202-874-1508 ▪ Fx: 202-874-1739

Professional Numismatists Guild www.pngdealers.com
3950 Concordia Ln   Fallbrook CA 92028
Ph: 760-728-1300 ▪ Fx: 760-728-8507

Professional Paddlesports Association www.propaddle.com
7432 Alban Stn Blvd Suite B232   Springfield VA 22150
Ph: 703-451-3864 ▪ Fx: 703-451-1015

Professional Photographers of America Inc www.ppa.com
229 Peachtree St NE Suite 2200   Atlanta GA 30303
Ph: 404-522-8600 ▪ Fx: 404-614-6400 ▪ TF: 800-786-6277

Professional Picture Framers Association www.ppfa.com
3000 Picture Pl   Jackson MI 49201
Ph: 517-788-8100 ▪ Fx: 517-788-8371

Professional Practice Association, American www.appa-assn.com
350 Fairway Dr Suite 200   Deerfield Beach FL 33441
Ph: 954-571-1877 ▪ Fx: 954-571-8582 ▪ TF: 800-221-2168

Professional Programs for the Americas, LASPAU: www.laspau.harvard.edu
Academic &   25 Mount Auburn St   Cambridge MA 02138
Ph: 617-495-5255 ▪ Fx: 617-495-8990

Professional Putters Association www.proputters.com
PO Box 35237   Fayetteville NC 28303
Ph: 910-485-7131 ▪ Fx: 910-485-1122

Professional Recognition, Council for www.cdacouncil.org
2460 16th St NW   Washington DC 20009
Ph: 202-265-9090 ▪ Fx: 202-265-9161 ▪ TF: 800-424-4310

Professional Records & Information Services Management www.prismintl.org
International   605 Benson Rd Suite B   Garner NC 27529
Ph: 919-771-0657 ▪ Fx: 919-771-0457 ▪ TF: 800-336-9793

Professional Representatives Organization, Independent www.avreps.org
2700 N 29th Ave Suite 101   Hollywood FL 33020
Ph: 954-923-0233 ▪ Fx: 954-925-1549 ▪ TF: 800-420-4268

Professional Responsibility, American Bar Association Center for www.abanet.org/cpr
541 N Fairbanks Ct 14th Fl   Chicago IL 60611
Ph: 312-988-5522 ▪ Fx: 312-988-5491

Professional Rodeo Cowboys Association www.prorodeo.com
101 Pro Rodeo Dr   Colorado Springs CO 80919
Ph: 719-593-8840 ▪ Fx: 719-548-4876

Professional School Photographers International pspa.pmai.org
3000 Picture Pl   Jackson MI 49201
Ph: 517-788-8100 ▪ Fx: 517-788-8371

Professional Schools of International Affairs, Association of www.apsia.org
2101 Van Munching Hall   College Park MD 20742
Ph: 301-405-7553 ▪ Fx: 301-405-4675

Professional Service Association www.psaworld.com
71 Columbia St   Cohoes NY 12047
Ph: 518-237-7777 ▪ Fx: 518-237-0418

Professional Services Council www.pscouncil.org
2101 Wilson Blvd Suite 750   Arlington VA 22201
Ph: 703-875-8059 ▪ Fx: 703-875-8922

Professional Services Management Association www.psmanet.org
99 Canal Ctr Plaza Suite 330   Alexandria VA 22314
Ph: 703-739-0277 ▪ Fx: 703-549-2498 ▪ TF: 800-292-7677

Professional Show Managers Association Inc www.psmashows.org
1 Regency Dr PO Box 30   Bloomfield CT 06002
Ph: 860-243-3977 ▪ Fx: 860-286-0787

Professional Skaters Association skatepsa.com
3006 Allegro Park Ln SW   Rochester MN 55902
Ph: 507-281-5122 ▪ Fx: 507-281-5491

Professional Ski Instructors of America www.psia.org
133 S Van Gordon St Suite 101   Lakewood CO 80228
Ph: 303-987-9390 ▪ Fx: 303-988-3005

Professional Soccer Reporters Association
6700 Squibb Rd Suite 215   Mission KS 66202
Ph: 913-362-1747 ▪ Fx: 913-362-3439

Professional Society for Sales & Marketing Training www.smt.org
180 N LaSalle St Suite 1822   Chicago IL 60601
Ph: 312-551-0768 ▪ Fx: 312-551-0815

Professional Surveyors, National Society of www.acsm.net/nsps
6 Montgomery Village Ave Suite 403   Gaithersburg MD 20879
Ph: 240-632-9716 ▪ Fx: 240-632-1321

Professional Tattoo Artists Guild
27 Mt Vernon Ave PO Box 1374   Mount Vernon NY 10550
Ph: 914-668-2300 ▪ Fx: 914-668-5200

Professional & Technical Consultants Association www.patca.org
543 Vista Mar Ave   Pacifica CA 94044
Ph: 408-971-5902 ▪ Fx: 650-359-3089 ▪ TF: 800-747-2822

Professional Tennis Registry www.ptrtennis.org
PO Box 4739   Hilton Head Island SC 29938
Ph: 843-785-7244 ▪ Fx: 843-686-2033 ▪ TF: 800-421-6289

Professional Truck Driver Institute Inc www.ptdi.org
2200 Mill Rd   Alexandria VA 22314
Ph: 703-838-8842 ▪ Fx: 703-836-6610

Professional Well-Being, Center for www.cpwb.org
21 W Colony Pl Suite 150   Durham NC 27705
Ph: 919-489-9167 ▪ Fx: 919-419-0011

Professional Women in Construction www.pwcusa.org
315 E 56th St   New York NY 10022
Ph: 212-486-7745 ▪ Fx: 212-486-0228

Professional Women Singers Association www.womensingers.org
PO Box 884   New York NY 10024
Ph: 212-969-0590

Professional Women's Appraisal Association
1224 N Nokomis NE   Alexandria MN 56308
Ph: 320-763-7626 ▪ Fx: 320-763-9290

Professional Women's Bowling Association pwba.com
7171 Cherryvale Blvd   Rockford IL 61112
Ph: 815-332-5756 ▪ Fx: 815-332-9636

Professionals International, Association of Career www.acpinternational.org
204 'E' St NE   Washington DC 20002
Ph: 202-547-6377 ▪ Fx: 202-547-6348

Professionals, National Association of Asian American www.naaap.org

Professions, National Association of the www.nap-assn.com
350 Fairway Dr Suite 200   Deerfield Beach FL 33441
Ph: 954-571-1877 ▪ Fx: 954-571-8582 ▪ TF: 800-221-2168

Professors, Association of Environmental Engineering & Science www.aeesp.org

Professors of Cardiology, Association of www.cardiologyprofessors.org
9111 Old Georgetown Rd   Bethesda MD 20814
Ph: 301-493-2330 ▪ Fx: 301-897-9745

Professors of Christian Education, North American www.napce.org
c/o Cook Communications Ministries 4050 Lee Vance
View   Colorado Springs CO 80918
Ph: 719-536-0100

Professors of Gynecology & Obstetrics, Association of www.apgo.org
2130 Priest Bridge Dr Suite 7   Crofton MD 21114
Ph: 410-451-9560 ▪ Fx: 410-451-9568

Professors of Medicine, Association of www.im.org/apm
2501 M St NW Suite 550   Washington DC 20037
Ph: 202-861-7700 ▪ Fx: 202-861-9731

Professors of Mission, Association of www.asmweb.org/apm
1443 N Euclid Ave   Dayton OH 45406
Ph: 937-274-0821 ▪ Fx: 937-278-6237

Professors of Ophthalmology, Association of University
PO Box 420369   San Francisco CA 94142
Ph: 415-561-8548 ▪ Fx: 415-561-8531

Professors of Religion, National Association of Baptist www.cssr.org/soc_nabpr.htm
Mercer University   Macon GA 31207
Ph: 478-301-2758 ▪ Fx: 478-301-2384

Professors, Research Association of Minority www.ramresearch.org

Professors & Researchers in Religious Education, www.mtso.edu/aprre
Association of   3081 Columbus Pike PO Box 80004   Delaware
OH 43015
Ph: 740-362-3364 ▪ Fx: 740-362-5890

Professors, World Association of Law
1000 Connecticut Ave NW Suite 202   Washington DC 20036
Ph: 202-466-5428 ▪ Fx: 202-452-8540

Profit Sharing/401(k) Council of America www.psca.org
10 S Riverside Plaza Suite 1610   Chicago IL 60606
Ph: 312-441-8550 ▪ Fx: 312-441-8559

Program Analysis, American Association for Budget & www.aabpa.org
PO Box 1157   Falls Church VA 22041
Ph: 703-941-4300 ▪ Fx: 703-941-1535

Program for Appropriate Technology in Health www.path.org
1455 NW Leary St   Seattle WA 98107
Ph: 206-285-3500 ▪ Fx: 206-285-6619

Program Directors in Internal Medicine, Association of www.im.org/APDIM
2501 M St NW Suite 550   Washington DC 20037
Ph: 202-887-9450 ▪ Fx: 202-887-9447 ▪ TF: 800-622-4558

Program Directors in Radiology, Association of www.apdr.org
820 Jorie Blvd   Oak Brook IL 60523
Ph: 630-368-3737 ▪ Fx: 630-571-7837

Program Directors in Surgery, Association of www.apds.org
4900-B S 31st St   Arlington VA 22206
Ph: 703-820-7400 ▪ Fx: 703-931-4520

Programmer's Association, Public Radio www.prpd.org
517 Ocean Front Walk Suite 10   Venice CA 90291
Ph: 310-664-1591 ▪ Fx: 310-664-1592

Progress & Freedom Foundation www.pff.org
1401 H St NW Suite 1075   Washington DC 20005
Ph: 202-289-8928 ▪ Fx: 202-289-6079

Progressive National Baptist Convention Inc www.pnbc.org
601 50th St NE   Washington DC 20019
Ph: 202-396-0558 ▪ Fx: 202-398-4998 ▪ TF: 800-876-7622

Progressive Policy Institute www.ppionline.org
600 Pennsylvania Ave SE Suite 400   Washington DC 20003
Ph: 202-547-0001 ▪ Fx: 202-544-5014 ▪ TF: 800-546-0027

Prohibition Historical Society, Partisan www.prohibitionists.org
PO Box 2635   Denver CO 80201
Ph: 303-237-4947

Prohibition National Committee www.prohibition.org
PO Box 2635   Denver CO 80201
Ph: 303-237-4947 ▪ Fx: 303-233-2099

Project Appleseed: National Campaign for Public School www.projectappleseed.org
Improvement   7209 Dorset Ave   Saint Louis MO 63130
Ph: 314-726-0536 ▪ Fx: 314-725-2319

Project Censored www.projectcensored.org
1801 E Cotati Ave   Rohnert Park CA 94928
Ph: 707-664-2500 ▪ Fx: 707-664-2108

Project Children www.interwebinc.com/children/
PO Box 933   Greenwood Lake NY 10925
Ph: 845-477-3472 ▪ Fx: 845-477-2334

Project Concern International www.projectconcern.org
3550 Afton Rd   San Diego CA 92123
Ph: 858-279-9690 ▪ Fx: 858-694-0294

Project Cuddle Inc www.projectcuddle.org
2973 Harbor Blvd Suite 326   Costa Mesa CA 92626
Ph: 714-432-9681 ▪ Fx: 714-433-6815 ▪ TF: 888-628-3353

Project Equality Inc www.projectequality.org
7132 Main St   Kansas City MO 64114
Ph: 816-361-9222 ▪ Fx: 816-361-8997

Project Equus www.projectequus.org
PO Box 18030   Boulder CO 80308
Ph: 720-565-2889

Project Genesis www.torah.org/
122 Slade Ave Suite 250   Baltimore MD 21208
Ph: 410-602-1350 ▪ Fx: 410-510-1053 ▪ TF: 888-999-8672

Project on Government Oversight www.pogo.org
666 11th St NW Suite 500   Washington DC 20001
Ph: 202-347-1122 ▪ Fx: 202-347-1116

Project Harmony www.projectharmony.org
5197 Main St Unit 6   Waitsfield VT 05673
Ph: 802-496-4545 ▪ Fx: 802-496-4548

Project HOPE www.projhope.org
225 Carter Hall Ln   Millwood VA 22646
Ph: 540-837-2100 ▪ Fx: 540-837-1813 ▪ TF: 800-544-4673

Project Inform www.projinf.org
205 13th St Suite 2001   San Francisco CA 94103
Ph: 415-558-8669 ▪ Fx: 415-558-0684

Project Management Institute www.pmi.org
4 Campus Blvd   Newtown Square PA 19073
Ph: 610-356-4600 ▪ Fx: 610-356-4647

Project NoSpank www.nospank.net
PO Box 1033   Alamo CA 94507
Ph: 925-831-1661 ▪ Fx: 925-838-8914

Project for Public Spaces pps.org
153 Waverly Pl 4th Fl   New York NY 10014
Ph: 212-620-5660 ▪ Fx: 212-620-3821

Project Renewal www.projectrenewal.org
200 Varick St 9th Fl   New York NY 10014
Ph: 212-620-0340 ▪ Fx: 212-243-4868

Project ROSE (Recycled Oil Saves Energy) www.eng.ua.edu/~prose
PO Box 870203   Tuscaloosa AL 35487
Ph: 205-348-4878 ▪ Fx: 205-348-7558

Project Vote www.projectvote.org
6805 Oak Creek Dr   Columbus OH 43229
Ph: 614-523-2560 ▪ Fx: 614-523-2720 ▪ TF: 800-546-8683

Project Vote Smart www.vote-smart.org
1 Common Ground   Philipsburg MT 59858
Ph: 406-859-8686 ▪ Fx: 406-859-8680 ▪ TF: 888-868-3762

ProLiteracy Worldwide www.proliteracy.org
1320 Jamesville Ave   Syracuse NY 13210
Ph: 315-422-9121 ▪ Fx: 315-422-6369 ▪ TF: 800-448-8878

PROMAX www.promax.org
2029 Century Park E Suite 555   Los Angeles CA 90067
Ph: 310-788-7600 ▪ Fx: 310-788-7616

Promise Keepers www.promisekeepers.org
PO Box 103001   Denver CO 80250
Ph: 303-964-7600 ▪ Fx: 303-433-1036 ▪ TF: 800-888-7595

Promoting Enduring Peace www.pepeace.org
112 Beach Ave   Milford CT 06460
Ph: 203-878-4769

Promotion Marketing Association Inc www.pmalink.org
257 Park Ave S Suite 1102   New York NY 10010
Ph: 212-420-1100 ▪ Fx: 212-533-7622 ▪ TF: 877-762-5465

Promotional & Advertising Allowances Inc, National Association for www.napaa.org
13771 N Fountain Hills Blvd Suite 114   Fountain Hills AZ 85268
Ph: 480-837-9704 ▪ Fx: 602-296-0277

Promotional Products Association International www.ppa.org
3125 Skyway Cir N   Irving TX 75038
Ph: 972-252-0404 ▪ Fx: 972-258-3004 ▪ TF: 888-492-6891

Propane Gas Association, National www.npga.org
1150 17th St NW Suite 310   Washington DC 20036
Ph: 202-466-7200 ▪ Fx: 202-466-7205

Propeller Club of the US www.propellerclubhq.com
3927 Old Lee Hwy Suite 101-A   Fairfax VA 22030
Ph: 703-691-2777 ▪ Fx: 703-691-4173

Properties, National Association of Industrial & Office www.naiop.org
2201 Cooperative Way 3rd Fl   Herndon VA 20171
Ph: 703-904-7100 ▪ Fx: 703-904-7942 ▪ TF: 800-666-6780

Property Administrators, National Association of Unclaimed www.unclaimed.org
PO Box 11910   Lexington KY 40578
Ph: 859-244-8150 ▪ Fx: 859-244-8053

Property, American Society for the Defense of Tradition Family & www.tfp.org
PO Box 341   Hanover PA 17331
Ph: 717-225-7147 ▪ Fx: 717-225-7382

Property Casualty Insurers of America www.allianceai.org
2600 S River Rd   Des Plaines IL 60018
Ph: 847-297-7800 ▪ Fx: 847-297-5064

Property & Evidence Inc, International Association for www.iape.org
903 N San Fernando Blvd Suite 4   Burbank CA 91504
Ph: 818-846-2926 ▪ Fx: 818-846-4543 ▪ TF: 800-449-4273

Property Inspectors, National Association of napi.lincoln-grad.org
c/o Lincoln Graduate Ctr 303 W Cypress St   San Antonio TX
78212
Ph: 210-225-2897 ▪ Fx: 210-225-8450 ▪ TF: 800-531-5333

Property, International Association for the Study of Common www.iascp.org
PO Box 2355   Gary IN 46409
Ph: 219-980-1433 ▪ Fx: 219-980-2801

Property Loss Research Bureau www.plrb.org
3025 Highland Pkwy Suite 800   Downers Grove IL 60515
Ph: 630-724-2200 ▪ Fx: 630-724-2260

Property Management Association www.pma-dc.org
7900 Wisconsin Ave Suite 204   Bethesda MD 20814
Ph: 301-657-9200 ▪ Fx: 301-907-9326

Property Management Association, National www.npma.org
1108 Pinehurst Rd   Dunedin FL 34698
Ph: 727-736-3788 ▪ Fx: 727-736-6707

Property Managers, National Association of Residential www.narpm.org
PO Box 140647   Austin TX 78714
Ph: 512-381-6091 ▪ Fx: 512-454-3036 ▪ TF: 800-782-3452

Property, National Association of State Agencies for Surplus nasasp.org
2221 Forster St Rm G-49   Harrisburg PA 17105
Ph: 717-787-9724 ▪ Fx: 717-772-2491

Property Owners Association
121 Main St   Whitehouse Station NJ 08889
Ph: 908-534-7887 ▪ Fx: 908-534-8383

Property Owners Association, Intellectual www.ipo.org
1255 23rd St NW Suite 200   Washington DC 20037
Ph: 202-466-2396 ▪ Fx: 202-466-2893

Property Rights, Americans for the Enforcement of Intellectual rentamark.com/aeipr
PO Box 35189   Chicago IL 60707
Ph: 773-283-3880 ▪ Fx: 708-453-0083

Property Rights, Defenders of www.yourpropertyrights.org
1350 Connecticut Ave Suite 410   Washington DC 20036
Ph: 202-822-6770 ▪ Fx: 202-822-6774

(Property Rights) Stewards of the Range www.stewardsoftherange.org
PO Box 490 Meridian ID 83680
Ph: 208-855-0707 ▪ Fx: 208-855-0763

Prophecy Study Association, Bible netministries.org/see/charmin/CM00407
339 E Laguna Dr Tempe AZ 85282
Ph: 480-967-3066

(Prophetic Ministry) Confessing Synod Ministries www.confessingsynod.com
East Liberty Lutheran Church 5707 Penn Ave Pittsburgh PA
15206
Ph: 412-362-1712

Proposal Management Professionals, Association of www.apmp.org
PO Box 668 Dana Point CA 92629
Ph: 949-493-9398 ▪ Fx: 949-240-4844

Prosecution of Child Abuse, National Center for www.ndaa-apri.org
99 Canal Ctr Plaza Suite 510 Alexandria VA 22314
Ph: 703-739-0321 ▪ Fx: 703-549-6259

Prosecutors Research Institute, American www.ndaa-apri.org/apri/
99 Canal Center Plaza Suite 510 Alexandria VA 22314
Ph: 703-549-9222 ▪ Fx: 703-836-3195

Prostate Society, American www.ameripros.org
7188 Ridge Rd PO Box 870 Hanover MD 21076
Ph: 410-859-3735 ▪ Fx: 410-850-0818 ▪ TF: 800-308-1106

Prosthetic Association, American Orthotic & www.aopanet.org
330 John Carlyle St Suite 200 Alexandria VA 22314
Ph: 571-431-0876 ▪ Fx: 571-431-0899

Prosthetic-Orthotic Clinics, Association of Children's www.acpoc.org
6300 N River Rd Suite 727 Rosemont IL 60018
Ph: 847-698-1637 ▪ Fx: 847-823-0536

Prosthetics, American Academy of Maxillofacial www.maxillofacialprosth.org
Univ of Florida College of Dentistry Dept of Prosthodontics Box
100435 Gainesville FL 32610
Ph: 352-846-2684 ▪ Fx: 352-846-2683

Prosthetics & Orthotics, US Member Society of the International www.usispo.org
Society for 1161 Francisco Rd Columbus OH 43220
Ph: 614-457-4312 ▪ Fx: 614-538-1914

Prosthetists, American Academy of Orthotists & www.oandp.org
526 King St Suite 201 Alexandria VA 22314
Ph: 703-836-0788 ▪ Fx: 703-836-0737

Prosthodontic Society, American www.prostho.org
426 Hudson St Hackensack NJ 07601
Ph: 201-440-7699 ▪ Fx: 201-440-7963 ▪ TF: 877-499-3500

Prosthodontics, Academy of www.academyprosthodontics.org
6177 Orchard Lake Rd Suite 120 West Bloomfield MI 48322
Ph: 248-855-6655 ▪ Fx: 248-855-0803

Prosthodontics, American Academy of Fixed
PO Box 1409 Bodega Bay CA 94923
Ph: 707-875-3040 ▪ Fx: 707-875-2927 ▪ TF: 800-880-5184

Prosthodontics, American Academy of Implant
709 Haddonfield-Berlin Rd Voorhees NJ 08043
Ph: 856-782-3990 ▪ Fx: 856-782-3775

Prosthodontists, American College of www.prosthodontics.org
211 E Chicago Ave Suite 1000 Chicago IL 60611
Ph: 312-573-1260 ▪ Fx: 312-573-1257 ▪ TF: 800-378-1260

Prosthodontists, International College of www.icp-org.com
PO Box 99119 San Diego CA 92169
Ph: 858-270-1814 ▪ Fx: 858-272-7687

(Prostitution) Children of the Night www.childrenofthenight.org
14530 Sylvan St Van Nuys CA 91411
Ph: 818-908-4474 ▪ Fx: 818-908-1468 ▪ TF: 800-551-1300

(Prostitution) Emmaus Ministries www.streets.org
921 W Wilson Ave Chicago IL 60640
Ph: 773-334-6063 ▪ Fx: 773-334-8638 ▪ TF: 800-378-4445

Protection & Advocacy Systems, National www.protectionandadvocacy.com
Association of 900 2nd St NE Suite 211 Washington DC
20002
Ph: 202-408-9514 ▪ Fx: 202-408-9520

Protection Agents, International Association of Personal www.iappa.org
PO Box 266 Arlington Heights IL 60006
Ph: 847-870-8007 ▪ Fx: 847-870-8990

Protection Association Inc, American Self www.americanselfprotection.org
825 Greengate Oval Ave Sagamore Hills OH 44067
Ph: 330-467-1750

Protection Officers, International Foundation for www.ifpo.org
PO Box 771329 Naples FL 34107
Ph: 941-430-0534 ▪ Fx: 941-430-0533

Protective Association, Degree of Honor www.degreeofhonor.com
445 Minnesota St Suite 1600 Saint Paul MN 55101
Ph: 651-228-7600 ▪ Fx: 651-224-7446

Protective Coatings, SSPC: Society for www.sspc.org
40 24th St Pittsburgh PA 15222
Ph: 412-281-2331 ▪ Fx: 412-281-9995

Protective Glazing Council www.protectiveglazing.org
2945 SW Wanamaker Dr Suite A Topeka KS 66614
Ph: 785-271-0208 ▪ Fx: 785-271-0166

Protein Council, International Hydrolyzed
555 13th St NW Washington DC 20004
Ph: 202-637-5926 ▪ Fx: 202-637-5910

Protein Council, Soy www.spcouncil.org
1255 23rd St NW Washington DC 20037
Ph: 202-467-6610 ▪ Fx: 202-833-3636

Protein Society www.proteinsociety.org
9650 Rockville Pike Bethesda MD 20814
Ph: 301-634-7277 ▪ Fx: 301-634-7271 ▪ TF: 800-992-6466

Proteins Research Foundation Inc, Fats & www.fprf.org
16551 Old Colonial Rd Bloomington IL 61704
Ph: 309-829-7744 ▪ Fx: 309-829-5147

Protestant Guild for Human Services Inc www.protestantguild.org
411 Waverley Oaks Rd Suite 104 Waltham MA 02452
Ph: 781-893-6000 ▪ Fx: 781-893-1171

(Protestant Reformation) American Waldensian Society www.waldensian.org
102 Vultee St Allentown PA 18103
Ph: 866-825-3373 ▪ Fx: 610-797-9723

Protestant Welfare Agencies, Federation of www.fpwa.org
281 Park Ave S New York NY 10010
Ph: 212-777-4800 ▪ Fx: 212-673-4085

Protocol Executives, Council of
101 W 12th St PH-H New York NY 10011
Ph: 212-633-6934

Protozoologists, Society of www.uga.edu/~protozoa
PO Box 1897 Lawrence KS 66044
Ph: 785-843-1235 ▪ Fx: 785-843-1274

Proutist Universal North America www.prout.org/ny
PO Box 56533 Washington DC 20040
Ph: 301-231-0110

Providence Association of Ukrainian Catholics in America
817 N Franklin St Philadelphia PA 19123
Ph: 215-627-4984 ▪ Fx: 215-238-1933

Pseudoxanthoma Elasticum Inc, National Association for www.pxenape.org
8764 Manchester Rd Suite 200 Saint Louis MO 63144
Ph: 314-962-0100

Psi Beta www.psibeta.org
1027 Westbridge Ln Chattanooga TN 37405
Ph: 423-645-8205 ▪ Fx: 423-265-0033 ▪ TF: 888-774-2382

Psi Chi National Honor Society in Psychology www.psichi.org
PO Box 709 Chattanooga TN 37401
Ph: 423-756-2044 ▪ Fx: 423-265-1529

Psi Omega Dental Fraternity
1040 Savannah Hwy Charleston SC 29407
Ph: 843-556-0573 ▪ Fx: 843-556-6311

Psi Upsilon Fraternity www.psiu.org
3003 E 96th St Indianapolis IN 46240
Ph: 317-571-1833 ▪ Fx: 317-844-5170 ▪ TF: 800-394-1833

Psoriasis Foundation, National www.psoriasis.org
6600 SW 92nd Ave Suite 300 Portland OR 97223
Ph: 503-244-7404 ▪ Fx: 503-245-0626 ▪ TF: 800-723-9166

PSRC of America www.psrc-of-america.org
200 Madison Ave Suite 2108 New York NY 10016
Ph: 212-686-9147 ▪ Fx: 212-779-9307

Psychiatric Association, American www.psych.org
1000 Wilson Blvd Suite 1825 Arlington VA 22209
Ph: 703-907-7300 ▪ Fx: 703-907-1085 ▪ TF: 888-357-7924

Psychiatric Consultation-Liaison Nurses, www.ispn-psych.org/html/ispcln.html
International Society of 1211 Locust St Philadelphia PA
19107
Ph: 215-545-2843 ▪ Fx: 215-545-8107 ▪ TF: 800-826-2950

Psychiatric Health Systems, National Association of www.naphs.org
325 7th St NW Suite 625 Washington DC 20004
Ph: 202-393-6700 ▪ Fx: 202-783-6041

Psychiatric-Mental Health Nurses, International Society of www.ispn-psych.org
1211 Locust St Philadelphia PA 19107
Ph: 215-545-2843 ▪ Fx: 215-545-8107 ▪ TF: 800-826-2950

Psychiatric Nurses Association, American www.apna.org
1555 Wilson Blvd Suite 515 Arlington VA 22209
Ph: 703-243-2443 ▪ Fx: 703-243-3390

Psychiatric Residency Training, American Association of Directors of www.aadprt.org
Univ of Connecticut Health Ctr Dept of Psychiatry 263
Farmington Ave LG066 Farmington CT 06030
Ph: 860-679-8112 ▪ Fx: 860-679-1246

Psychiatrists of America, Black
24361 Greenfield Suite 300 Southfield MI 48075
Ph: 248-569-9344

Psychiatrists, American Academy of Clinical www.aacp.com
PO Box 458 Glastonbury CT 06033
Ph: 860-633-5045 ▪ Fx: 860-633-6023

Psychiatrists, American Association of Community www.wpic.pitt.edu/aacp/
PO Box 570218 Dallas TX 75228
Ph: 972-613-0985 ▪ Fx: 972-613-5532

Psychiatrists, American College of www.acpsych.org
732 Addison St Suite C Berkeley CA 94710
Ph: 510-704-8020 ▪ Fx: 510-704-0113

Psychiatrists, Association of Gay & Lesbian www.aglp.org
4514 Chester Ave Philadelphia PA 19143
Ph: 215-222-2800 ▪ Fx: 215-222-3881

Psychiatry, Academy of Organizational & Occupational www.aoop.org
717 Princess St Alexandria VA 22314
Ph: 877-789-2667 ▪ Fx: 877-789-6050

Psychiatry, Administrators in Academic www.adminpsych.org
Univ of Michigan Dept of Psychiatry UH9C 9151 Ann Arbor MI
48109
Ph: 734-936-4860 ▪ Fx: 734-936-9983

Psychiatry & Allied Professions, International Association for www.iacapap.org
Child & Adolescent

Psychiatry, American Academy of Addiction www.aaap.org
7301 Mission Rd Suite 252 Prairie Village KS 66208
Ph: 913-262-6161 ▪ Fx: 913-262-4311

Psychiatry, American Academy of Child & Adolescent www.aacap.org
3615 Wisconsin Ave NW Washington DC 20016
Ph: 202-966-7300 ▪ Fx: 202-966-2891 ▪ TF: 800-333-7636

Psychiatry, American Association for Geriatric www.aagpgpa.org
7910 Woodmont Ave Suite 1050 Bethesda MD 20814
Ph: 301-654-7850 ▪ Fx: 301-654-4137

Psychiatry, American College of Forensic www.forensicpsychiatry.cc
PO Box 5870 Balboa Island CA 92662
Ph: 949-673-7773 ▪ Fx: 949-673-7710

Psychiatry, American Society for Adolescent www.adolpsych.org
PO Box 570218 Dallas TX 75357
Ph: 972-686-6166 ▪ Fx: 972-613-5532

Psychiatry, International Society for Adolescent www.isap-web.org
223 Sunset Blvd   Bronx NY 10473
Ph: 718-892-4868

Psychiatry & the Law, American Academy of www.aapl.org
1 Regency Dr PO Box 30   Bloomfield CT 06002
Ph: 860-242-5450 ▪ Fx: 860-286-0787 ▪ TF: 800-331-1389

(Psychiatry) Milton H Erickson Foundation Inc www.erickson-foundation.org
3606 N 24th St   Phoenix AZ 85016
Ph: 602-956-6196 ▪ Fx: 602-956-0519

Psychiatry, Network Against Coercive www.sethfarber.com
172 W 79th St Suite 2E   New York NY 10024
Ph: 212-560-7288 ▪ Fx: 212-799-9026

Psychiatry, Society of Biological www.sobp.org
4500 San Pablo Rd Mayo Clinic   Jacksonville FL 32224
Ph: 904-953-2842 ▪ Fx: 904-953-7117

Psychiatry, Society of Professors of Child & Adolescent
3615 Wisconsin Ave NW   Washington DC 20016
Ph: 202-966-7300 ▪ Fx: 202-966-2891

Psychical Research, Academy of Religion & www.lightlink.com/arpr
PO Box 614   Bloomfield CT 06002
Ph: 860-242-4593

Psychical Research, American Society for www.aspr.com
5 W 73rd St   New York NY 10023
Ph: 212-799-5050 ▪ Fx: 212-496-2497

Psychoanalysis, National Association for the Advancement of www.naap.org
80 8th Ave Suite 1501   New York NY 10011
Ph: 212-741-0515 ▪ Fx: 212-366-4347

Psychoanalysis, National Psychological Association for www.npap.org
150 W 13th St   New York NY 10011
Ph: 212-924-7440 ▪ Fx: 212-989-7543

Psychoanalysts, American College of
434 Fox Run Ln   Hampshire IL 60140
Ph: 847-683-7517 ▪ Fx: 847-683-3130

Psychoanalytic Association, American www.apsa.org
309 E 49th St   New York NY 10017
Ph: 212-752-0450 ▪ Fx: 212-593-0571

Psychoanalytic Medicine, Association for www.theapm.org
4560 Delafield Ave   Riverdale NY 10471
Ph: 718-548-6088 ▪ Fx: 718-548-8302

Psychodrama, American Society of Group Psychotherapy & www.asgpp.org
301 N Harrison St Suite 508   Princeton NJ 08540
Ph: 609-452-1339 ▪ Fx: 609-936-1659

Psychodrama Sociometry & Group Psychotherapy, American Board of Examiners of   PO Box 15572   Washington DC 20003
Ph: 202-483-0514

(Psychodynamics) Unarius Academy of Science www.unarius.org
145 S Magnolia Ave   El Cajon CA 92020
Ph: 619-444-7062 ▪ Fx: 619-444-9637

Psychogeriatric Association, International www.ipa-online.org
5215 Old Orchard Rd Suite 340   Skokie IL 60077
Ph: 847-663-0574 ▪ Fx: 847-663-0591

Psychohistorical Association, International www.geocities.com/athens/acropolis/8623
266 Monroe Ave   Wyckoff NJ 07481
Ph: 201-891-4980

Psychohistory, Institute for www.psychohistory.org
140 Riverside Dr   New York NY 10024
Ph: 212-799-2294 ▪ TF: 800-445-2268

Psychological Anthropology, Society for www.aaanet.org/SPA
c/o American Anthropological Assn 2200 Wilson Blvd Suite 600   Arlington VA 22201
Ph: 703-528-1902 ▪ Fx: 703-528-3546

Psychological Association, American www.apa.org
750 1st St NE   Washington DC 20002
Ph: 202-336-5500 ▪ Fx: 202-336-5502 ▪ TF: 800-374-2721

Psychological Association for Psychoanalysis, National www.npap.org
150 W 13th St   New York NY 10011
Ph: 212-924-7440 ▪ Fx: 212-989-7543

Psychological & Cognitive Sciences, Federation of Behavioral   750 1st NE Suite 5007   Washington DC 20002 www.thefederationonline.org
Ph: 202-336-5920 ▪ Fx: 202-336-5953

Psychological Society, American www.psychologicalscience.org
1010 Vermont Ave NW Suite 1100   Washington DC 20005
Ph: 202-783-2077 ▪ Fx: 202-783-2083

Psychological Study of Social Issues, Society for the www.spssi.org
208 'I' St NE   Washington DC 20002
Ph: 202-675-6956 ▪ Fx: 202-675-6902

Psychological Type, Association for www.aptcentral.org
4700 W Lake Ave   Glenview IL 60025
Ph: 847-375-4717 ▪ Fx: 877-734-9374

Psychological Type, Center for Applications of www.capt.org
2815 NW 13th St Suite 401   Gainesville FL 32609
Ph: 352-375-0160 ▪ Fx: 352-378-0503 ▪ TF: 800-777-2278

Psychologists, Association of Black www.abpsi.org
PO Box 55999   Washington DC 20040
Ph: 202-722-0808 ▪ Fx: 202-722-5941

Psychologists for the Ethical Treatment of Animals www.psyeta.org
PO Box 1297   Washington Grove MD 20880
Ph: 301-963-4751

Psychologists, National Association of School www.nasponline.org
4340 East West Hwy Suite 402   Bethesda MD 20814
Ph: 301-657-0270 ▪ Fx: 301-657-0275

Psychologists & Social Workers, American Association of Spinal Cord Injury   75-20 Astoria Blvd   Jackson Heights NY 11370 www.aascipsw.org
Ph: 718-803-3782 ▪ Fx: 718-803-0414

Psychology, American Association for Correctional www.eaacp.org
897 Oak Park Blvd Suite 124   Pismo Beach CA 93449
Ph: 805-489-0665

Psychology Inc, American Board of Forensic www.abfp.com
2815 Eastlake Ave E Suite 220   Seattle WA 98102
Ph: 206-320-0044 ▪ Fx: 206-320-7733

Psychology, American Board of Professional www.abpp.org
300 Drayton St 3rd Fl   Savannah GA 31401
Ph: 800-255-7792 ▪ Fx: 912-644-5655

Psychology, Association for the Advancement of www.aapnet.org
PO Box 38129   Colorado Springs CO 80937
Ph: 800-869-6595 ▪ Fx: 719-520-0375

Psychology, Association for the Advancement of Applied Sport www.aaasponline.org
801 Main St Suite 010   Louisville CO 80027
Ph: 303-494-5931

Psychology, Association for Astrological www.aaperry.com
360 Quietwood Dr   San Rafael CA 94903
Ph: 415-479-5812

Psychology, Association for Comprehensive Energy www.energypsych.org
PO Box 910244   San Diego CA 92191
Ph: 858-748-5963 ▪ Fx: 858-270-0370

Psychology, Association for Humanistic ahpweb.org
1516 Oak St Suite 320A   Alameda CA 94501
Ph: 510-769-6495 ▪ Fx: 510-769-6433

Psychology, Association for Transpersonal www.atpweb.org
PO Box 50187   Palo Alto CA 94303
Ph: 650-424-8764 ▪ Fx: 650-618-1851

Psychology Boards, Association of State & Provincial www.asppb.org
PO Box 241245   Montgomery AL 36124
Ph: 334-832-4580 ▪ Fx: 334-269-6379 ▪ TF: 800-448-4069

Psychology, International Society of Political ispp.org
Pitzer College 1050 N Mills Ave   Claremont CA 91711
Ph: 909-621-8442 ▪ Fx: 909-621-8481

Psychology & Life Sciences, Society for Chaos Theory in   Univ of Oregon Dept of Psychology CMB 1227   Eugene OR 97403 www.societyforchaostheory.org
Ph: 541-346-1996 ▪ Fx: 541-346-4911

Psychology, North American Society of Adlerian www.alfredadler.org
50 Northeast Dr   Hershey PA 17033
Ph: 717-579-8795 ▪ Fx: 717-533-8616

Psychology & Physiology, Society for the Study of Male
321 Iuka Rd   Montpelier OH 43543
Ph: 419-485-3602

Psychology Postdoctoral & Internship Centers, Association of www.appic.org
10 G St NE Suite 750   Washington DC 20002
Ph: 202-589-0600 ▪ Fx: 202-589-0603

(Psychology) Psi Beta www.psibeta.org
1027 Westbridge Ln   Chattanooga TN 37405
Ph: 423-645-8205 ▪ Fx: 423-265-0033 ▪ TF: 888-774-2382

Psychology, Psi Chi National Honor Society in www.psichi.org
PO Box 709   Chattanooga TN 37401
Ph: 423-756-2044 ▪ Fx: 423-265-1529

Psychology Society
100 Beekman St   New York NY 10038
Ph: 212-285-1872

Psychology, Society for Industrial & Organizational www.siop.org
PO Box 87   Bowling Green OH 43402
Ph: 419-353-0032 ▪ Fx: 419-352-2645

Psychology, Society of Multivariate Experimental www.smep.org
Univ of Oklahoma Psychology Dept   Norman OK 73019
Ph: 405-325-4511 ▪ Fx: 405-325-4737

Psychology, Society for Police & Criminal cep.jmu.edu/spcp/
Southwest Texas State Univ Dept of Criminal Justice   San Marcos TX 78666
Ph: 512-530-8211

Psychology of Sport & Physical Activity, North American Society for the   Univ of Nevada Dept of Kinesiology 4505 Maryland Pkwy   Las Vegas NV 89154 www.naspspa.org
Ph: 702-895-0938

Psychometric Society www.psychometricsociety.org
Univ of North Carolina 207 Curry Bldg PO Box 26171   Greensboro NC 27402
Ph: 336-334-3474 ▪ Fx: 336-334-4120

Psychonomic Society www.psychonomic.com
1710 Fortview Rd   Austin TX 78704
Ph: 512-462-2442 ▪ Fx: 512-462-1101

Psychopathology of Expression, American Society of
74 Lawton St   Brookline MA 02446
Ph: 617-738-9821 ▪ Fx: 617-975-0411

Psychopharmacology Inc, American Society of Clinical www.ascpp.org
PO Box 2257   New York NY 10116
Ph: 212-696-1088 ▪ Fx: 212-696-0563

Psychophysiological Research, Society for www.sprweb.org
7600 Terrace Ave Suite 203   Middleton WI 53562
Ph: 608-831-0274

Psychophysiology & Biofeedback, Association for Applied www.aapb.org
10200 W 44th Ave Suite 304   Wheat Ridge CO 80033
Ph: 303-422-8436 ▪ Fx: 303-422-8894 ▪ TF: 800-477-8892

Psychosocial Rehabilitation Services, International Association of www.iapsrs.org
601 N Hammonds Ferry Rd Suite A   Linthicum MD 21090
Ph: 410-789-7054 ▪ Fx: 410-789-7675

Psychosomatic Medicine, Academy of www.apm.org
5824 N Magnolia Ave   Chicago IL 60660
Ph: 773-784-2025 ▪ Fx: 773-784-1304

Psychosomatic Society, American www.psychosomatic.org
6728 Old McLean Village Dr   McLean VA 22101
Ph: 703-556-9222 ▪ Fx: 703-556-8729

Psychotherapists, American Academy of www.coe.iup.edu/aap
PO Box 10589   Oakland CA 94610
Ph: 510-268-1786 ▪ Fx: 510-268-1787

Psychotherapy, American Board of Examiners of Psychodrama Sociometry & Group   PO Box 15572   Washington DC 20003
Ph: 202-483-0514

Psychotherapy, Association for the Advancement of www.ajp.org
1300 Morris Park Ave Berfer Bldg Rm 406 Bronx NY 10461
Ph: 718-430-3503 ▪ Fx: 718-430-8907

Psychotherapy Association, American www.americanpsychotherapy.com
2750 E Sunshine St Springfield MO 65804
Ph: 417-823-0173 ▪ Fx: 417-823-9959 ▪ TF: 800-205-9165

Psychotherapy Association, American Group www.agpa.org
25 E 21st St 6th Fl New York NY 10010
Ph: 212-477-2677 ▪ Fx: 212-979-6627 ▪ TF: 877-668-2472

Psychotherapy Integration, Society for the Exploration of www.cyberpsych.org/sepi
Adelphi Univ Dener Institute Garden City NY 11530
Ph: 516-877-4803 ▪ Fx: 516-877-4805

Psychotherapy & Psychodrama, American Society of Group www.asgpp.org
301 N Harrison St Suite 508 Princeton NJ 08540
Ph: 609-452-1339 ▪ Fx: 609-936-1659

Psychotronics Association, US www.psychotronics.org
PO Box 45 Elkhorn WI 53121
Ph: 262-742-4790 ▪ Fx: 262-742-3670

PT Boats Inc www.ptboats.org
PO Box 38070 Germantown TN 38183
Ph: 901-755-8440

PTPAC
1111 N Fairfax St Alexandria VA 22314
Ph: 703-684-2782 ▪ Fx: 703-684-7343

Public Administration, American Society for www.aspanet.org
1120 G St NW Suite 700 Washington DC 20005
Ph: 202-393-7878 ▪ Fx: 202-638-4952

Public Administration Education Foundation, Southern www.spaef.com
2103 Fairway Ln Harrisburg PA 17112
Ph: 717-540-5477 ▪ Fx: 215-893-1763

Public Administration, Institute of www.theipa.org
411 N Lafayette St Suite 303 New York NY 10003
Ph: 212-992-9898 ▪ Fx: 212-995-4876

Public Administration, National Academy of www.napawash.org
1100 New York Ave NW Suite 1090 E Washington DC 20005
Ph: 202-347-3190 ▪ Fx: 202-393-0993 ▪ TF: 800-883-3190

(Public Administration) Pi Alpha Alpha www.naspaa.org/initiatives/honor.asp
1120 G St NW Suite 730 Washington DC 20005
Ph: 202-628-8965 ▪ Fx: 202-626-4978

Public Administrators, Conference of Minority www.natcompa.org
1120 G St NW Suite 700 Washington DC 20005
Ph: 202-393-7878 ▪ Fx: 202-638-4952

Public Administrators, National Forum for Black www.nfbpa.org
777 N Capitol St NE Suite 807 Washington DC 20002
Ph: 202-408-9300 ▪ Fx: 202-408-8558

Public Affairs & Administration, National Association of Schools of www.naspaa.org
1120 G St NW Suite 730 Washington DC 20005
Ph: 202-628-8965 ▪ Fx: 202-626-4978

Public Affairs Association, Cable Television www.ctpaa.org
PO Box 33697 Washington DC 20033
Ph: 202-775-1081 ▪ Fx: 202-955-1134 ▪ TF: 800-210-3396

Public Affairs, Center for Media & www.cmpa.com
2100 L St NW Suite 300 Washington DC 20037
Ph: 202-223-2942

Public Affairs Council www.pac.org
2033 K St NW Suite 700 Washington DC 20006
Ph: 202-872-1790 ▪ Fx: 202-835-8343

Public Affairs, Institute of Government & www.igpa.uiuc.edu
Univ of Illinois 1007 W Nevada St Urbana IL 61801
Ph: 217-333-3340 ▪ Fx: 217-244-4817

Public Affairs, Jewish Council for www.jewishpublicaffairs.org
443 Park Ave S 11th Fl New York NY 10016
Ph: 212-684-6950 ▪ Fx: 212-686-1353

Public Agencies, Worldwide Assurance for Employees of www.waepa.org
7651 Leesburg Pike Falls Church VA 22043
Ph: 703-790-8010 ▪ Fx: 703-790-4606 ▪ TF: 800-368-3484

Public Agency Risk Managers Association www.parma.com
6067 Marla Ct Suite 201 San Jose CA 95124
Ph: 408-979-8030 ▪ Fx: 408-723-2423 ▪ TF: 888-907-2762

Public Agenda www.publicagenda.org
6 E 39th St New York NY 10016
Ph: 212-686-6610 ▪ Fx: 212-889-3461

Public Art Fund www.publicartfund.org
1 E 53rd St 11th Fl New York NY 10022
Ph: 212-980-4575 ▪ Fx: 212-980-3610

Public Broadcasting, Corporation for www.cpb.org
401 9th St NW Washington DC 20004
Ph: 202-879-9600 ▪ Fx: 202-879-9700 ▪ TF: 800-272-2190

Public Broadcasting Management Association www.pbma.org
PO Box 50008 Columbia SC 29250
Ph: 803-799-5517 ▪ Fx: 803-771-4831

Public Broadcasting Service www.pbs.org
1320 Braddock Pl Alexandria VA 22314
Ph: 703-739-5000 ▪ Fx: 703-739-0775

Public Campaign www.publiccampaign.org
1320 19th St NW Suite M-1 Washington DC 20036
Ph: 202-293-0222 ▪ Fx: 202-293-0202

Public Citizen www.citizen.org
1600 20th St NW Washington DC 20009
Ph: 202-588-1000 ▪ Fx: 202-588-7796

Public Citizen Health Research Group www.citizen.org/hrg
1600 20th St NW Washington DC 20009
Ph: 202-588-1000 ▪ Fx: 202-588-7796

Public Dialogue, Center for
10615 Brunswick Ave Kensington MD 20895
Ph: 301-933-3535

(Public Discourse) Public Forum Institute www.publicforuminstitute.org
2300 M St NW Suite 900 Washington DC 20037
Ph: 202-467-2774 ▪ Fx: 202-293-5717

Public Education, Center for Commercial-Free
1714 Franklin St Oakland CA 94612
Ph: 510-268-1100 ▪ Fx: 510-268-1277 ▪ TF: 800-867-5841

Public Education Network www.publiceducation.org
601 13th St NW Suite 900 N Washington DC 20005
Ph: 202-628-7460 ▪ Fx: 202-628-1893

Public Employee Retirement Systems, National Conference on www.ncpers.org
444 N Capitol St NW Suite 221 Washington DC 20001
Ph: 202-624-1456 ▪ Fx: 202-624-1439 ▪ TF: 877-202-5706

Public Employees Roundtable www.theroundtable.org
PO Box 75248 Washington DC 20013
Ph: 202-927-4926 ▪ Fx: 202-927-4920

Public Employer Labor Relations Association, National www.npelra.org
1617 Duke St Alexandria VA 22314
Ph: 703-836-9626 ▪ Fx: 703-836-9628 ▪ TF: 800-296-2230

Public Finance Advisors, National Association of Independent www.naipfa.com
PO Box 304 Montgomery IL 60538
Ph: 800-624-7321

Public Forum Institute www.publicforuminstitute.org
2300 M St NW Suite 900 Washington DC 20037
Ph: 202-467-2774 ▪ Fx: 202-293-5717

Public Gas Association, American www.apga.org
11094D Lee Hwy Suite 102 Fairfax VA 22030
Ph: 703-352-3890 ▪ Fx: 703-352-1271 ▪ TF: 800-927-4204

Public Health Association, American www.apha.org
800 'I' St NW Washington DC 20001
Ph: 202-777-2742 ▪ Fx: 202-777-2534

Public Health, Association of Schools of www.asph.org
1101 15th St NW Suite 910 Washington DC 20005
Ph: 202-296-1099 ▪ Fx: 202-296-1252

Public Health Association, World Federation of www.wfpha.org
800 'I' St NW Washington DC 20001
Ph: 202-777-2486 ▪ Fx: 202-777-2530

Public Health Education, Society for www.sophe.org
750 1st St NE Suite 910 Washington DC 20002
Ph: 202-408-9804 ▪ Fx: 202-408-9815

Public Health Information Coalition, National www.nphic.org
986 Hidden Hollow Dr Marietta GA 30068
Ph: 770-509-5555 ▪ Fx: 770-565-8436

Public Health Laboratories, Association of www.aphl.org
2025 M St NW Suite 550 Washington DC 20036
Ph: 202-822-5227 ▪ Fx: 202-887-5098

Public Health Network, Women's International
7100 Oak Forest Ln Bethesda MD 20817
Ph: 301-469-9210 ▪ Fx: 301-469-8423

Public Health Nutrition Directors, Association of www.astphnd.org
State & Territorial

Public Health Service, Commissioned Officers Association www.coausphs.org
of the US 8201 Corporate Dr Suite 560 Landover MD 20785
Ph: 301-731-9080 ▪ Fx: 301-731-9084

Public Health Statistics & Information Systems, National www.naphsis.org
Association for 801 Roeder Rd Suite 650 Silver Spring MD
20910
Ph: 301-563-6001 ▪ Fx: 301-563-6012

Public Hospitals & Health Systems, National Association of www.naph.org
1301 Pennsylvania Ave NW Suite 950 Washington DC 20004
Ph: 202-585-0100 ▪ Fx: 202-585-0101

Public Housing Authorities, Council of Large www.clpha.org
1250 'I' St NW Suite 901A Washington DC 20005
Ph: 202-638-1300 ▪ Fx: 202-638-2364

Public Housing Authorities Directors Association www.phada.org
511 Capitol Ct NE Washington DC 20002
Ph: 202-546-5445 ▪ Fx: 202-546-2280

Public Information on the Environment, American www.americanpie.org
316 Oak St PO Box 676 Northfield MN 55057
Ph: 507-645-5616 ▪ Fx: 507-645-5724 ▪ TF: 800-320-2743

Public Interest, Accountants for the www.geocities.com/api_woods/api/apihome.html
1420 N Charles St Suite 519 Baltimore MD 21201
Ph: 410-837-6533 ▪ Fx: 410-837-6532

Public Interest, Center for Law in the www.clipi.org
10951 W Pico Blvd 3rd Fl Los Angeles CA 90064
Ph: 310-470-3000 ▪ Fx: 310-474-7083

Public Interest, Center for Science in the www.cspinet.org
1875 Connecticut Ave NW Suite 300 Washington DC 20009
Ph: 202-332-9110 ▪ Fx: 202-265-4954

Public Interest, National Legal Center for the www.nlcpi.org
1600 K St NW Suite 800 Washington DC 20006
Ph: 202-466-9360 ▪ Fx: 202-466-9366

(Public Interest) Public Citizen www.citizen.org
1600 20th St NW Washington DC 20009
Ph: 202-588-1000 ▪ Fx: 202-588-7796

Public Justice, Center for www.cpjustice.org
2444 Solomons Island Rd Suite 201 Annapolis MD 21401
Ph: 410-571-6300 ▪ Fx: 410-571-6365 ▪ TF: 866-275-8784

Public Land, Trust for www.tpl.org
116 New Montgomery St 4th Fl San Francisco CA 94105
Ph: 415-495-4014 ▪ Fx: 415-495-4103 ▪ TF: 800-729-6428

Public Lands, Association of Partners for www.appl.org
2401 Blueridge Ave Suite 303 Wheaton MD 20902
Ph: 301-946-9475 ▪ Fx: 301-946-9478

Public Lands Council hill.beef.org/plc
1301 Pennsylvania Ave NW Suite 300 Washington DC 20004
Ph: 202-347-5355 ▪ Fx: 202-638-0607

Public Lands Foundation www.publicland.org
PO Box 7226 Arlington VA 22207
Ph: 703-790-1988 ▪ Fx: 703-821-3490

Public Lands Interpretive Association www.publiclands.org
6501 4th St NW Suite 1 Albuquerque NM 87107
Ph: 877-851-8946 ▪ Fx: 505-345-9498

Public Leadership Education Network   www.plen.org
1001 Connecticut Ave NW Suite 900   Washington DC 20036
Ph: 202-872-1585 ▪ Fx: 202-872-0141

Public Libraries, Canadian Association of   www.cla.ca/divisions/capl/capl.htm
328 Frank St   Ottawa ON K2P0X8
Ph: 613-232-9625 ▪ Fx: 613-563-9895

Public Library Association   www.pla.org
50 E Huron St   Chicago IL 60611
Ph: 312-280-5752 ▪ Fx: 312-280-5029 ▪ TF: 800-545-2433

Public Management Association for Human Resources,   www.ipma-hr.org
International   1617 Duke St   Alexandria VA 22314
Ph: 703-549-7100 ▪ Fx: 703-684-0948 ▪ TF: 800-220-4762

Public Media Foundation   www.scribblingwomen.org
100 Boylston St Suite 230   Boston MA 02116
Ph: 617-357-5835

Public Opinion Research, American Association for   www.aapor.org
PO Box 14263   Lenexa KS 66285
Ph: 913-310-0118 ▪ Fx: 913-599-5340

Public Participation, International Association for   www.iap2.org
11166 Huron St Suite 27   Denver CO 80234
Ph: 303-451-9545 ▪ Fx: 303-458-0002 ▪ TF: 800-644-4273

(Public Policy) 2030 Center   www.2030.org
1025 Connecticut Ave NW Suite 205   Washington DC 20036
Ph: 202-822-6526 ▪ Fx: 202-955-5606 ▪ TF: 877-203-0674

Public Policy, Allegheny Institute for   www.alleghenyinstitute.org
305 Mt Lebanon Blvd Suite 208   Pittsburgh PA 15234
Ph: 412-440-0079 ▪ Fx: 412-440-0085

(Public Policy) American Assembly   www.columbia.edu/cu/amassembly
475 Riverside Dr Suite 456   New York NY 10115
Ph: 212-870-3500 ▪ Fx: 212-870-3555

(Public Policy) American Freedom Center   www.homestead.com/americanfreedom
2002-A Guadalupe St Suite 284   Austin TX 78705
Ph: 512-453-7989 ▪ Fx: 512-453-7990

Public Policy Analysis & Management, Association for   www.appam.org
PO Box 18766   Washington DC 20036
Ph: 202-496-0130 ▪ Fx: 202-496-0134

(Public Policy) Aspen Institute   www.aspeninstitute.org
1 DuPont Cir NW Suite 700   Washington DC 20036
Ph: 202-736-5800 ▪ Fx: 202-467-0790

(Public Policy) Atlantic Council of the United States   www.acus.org
910 17th St NW Suite 1000   Washington DC 20006
Ph: 202-463-7226 ▪ Fx: 202-463-7241

(Public Policy) Benton Foundation   www.benton.org
1625 K St NW 11th Fl   Washington DC 20006
Ph: 202-638-5770 ▪ Fx: 202-638-5771

(Public Policy) Cato Institute   www.cato.org
1000 Massachusetts Ave NW   Washington DC 20001
Ph: 202-842-0200 ▪ Fx: 202-842-3490

Public Policy, Center for Advancement of   www.capponline.org
1735 'S' St NW   Washington DC 20009
Ph: 202-797-0606 ▪ Fx: 202-265-6245

Public Policy Center, Ethics &   www.eppc.org
1015 15th St NW Suite 900   Washington DC 20005
Ph: 202-682-1200 ▪ Fx: 202-408-0632

(Public Policy) Century Foundation   www.tcf.org
41 E 70th St   New York NY 10021
Ph: 212-535-4441 ▪ Fx: 212-535-7534

Public Policy, Churches' Center for Theology &   www.cctpp.org
4500 Massachusetts Ave NW   Washington DC 20016
Ph: 202-885-8659 ▪ Fx: 202-885-8585 ▪ TF: 800-882-4987

(Public Policy) Commonwealth Institute   www.comw.org
PO Box 398105   Cambridge MA 02139
Ph: 617-547-4474 ▪ Fx: 617-868-1267

(Public Policy) Discovery Institute   www.discovery.org
1511 3rd Ave Suite 808   Seattle WA 98101
Ph: 206-629-2041 ▪ Fx: 206-682-5320

(Public Policy) EastWest Institute   www.iews.org
700 Broadway 2nd Fl   New York NY 10003
Ph: 212-824-4100 ▪ Fx: 212-824-4149

(Public Policy) Goldwater Institute   www.goldwaterinstitute.org
500 E Coronado Rd   Phoenix AZ 85004
Ph: 602-462-5000 ▪ Fx: 602-256-7045

(Public Policy) Harry Singer Foundation   www.singerfoundation.org
PO Box 223159   Carmel CA 93922
Ph: 831-625-4223 ▪ Fx: 831-624-7994

(Public Policy) Heartland Institute   www.heartland.org
19 S LaSalle St Suite 903   Chicago IL 60603
Ph: 312-377-4000 ▪ Fx: 312-377-5000

(Public Policy) Heritage Foundation   www.heritage.org
214 Massachusetts Ave NE   Washington DC 20002
Ph: 202-546-4400 ▪ Fx: 202-546-8328

(Public Policy) Hudson Institute   www.hudson.org
5395 Emerson Way   Indianapolis IN 46226
Ph: 317-545-1000 ▪ Fx: 317-545-9639 ▪ TF: 800-483-7660

(Public Policy) Independent Institute   www.independent.org
100 Swan Way   Oakland CA 94621
Ph: 510-632-1366 ▪ Fx: 510-568-6040

Public Policy Institute, AARP   www.aarp.org/ppi
601 'E' St NW   Washington DC 20049
Ph: 202-434-2277 ▪ Fx: 202-434-2588 ▪ TF: 800-424-3410

Public Policy, Institute for Philosophy &   www.puaf.umd.edu/IPPP
Maryland School of Public Affairs 3111 Van Munching
Hall   College Park MD 20742
Ph: 301-405-4753 ▪ Fx: 301-314-9346

Public Policy Institute, Reason   www.rppi.org
3415 S Sepulveda Blvd Suite 400   Los Angeles CA 90034
Ph: 310-391-2245 ▪ Fx: 310-391-4395

(Public Policy) Inter-American Dialogue   www.thedialogue.org
1211 Connecticut Ave NW Suite 510   Washington DC 20036
Ph: 202-822-9002 ▪ Fx: 202-822-9553

Public Policy, James A Baker III Institute for   www.rice.edu/projects/baker
Rice University 6100 Main St Baker Hall Suite 120   Houston TX
77005
Ph: 713-348-4683 ▪ Fx: 713-348-5993

Public Policy, Joan Shorenstein Center on the   www.ksg.harvard.edu/presspol
Press Politics &   Harvard Univ John F Kennedy School of
Government 79 John F Kennedy St   Cambridge MA 02138
Ph: 617-495-8269 ▪ Fx: 617-495-8696

(Public Policy) Keystone Center   www.keystone.org
1628 St John Rd   Keystone CO 80435
Ph: 970-513-5800 ▪ Fx: 970-262-0152

Public Policy, National Institute for   www.nipp.org
3031 Javier Rd Suite 300   Fairfax VA 22031
Ph: 703-698-0563 ▪ Fx: 703-698-0566

Public Policy, National Institute for Science Law &   www.swankin-turner.com/nislapp.html
1400 16th St NW Suite 330   Washington DC 20036
Ph: 202-462-8800 ▪ Fx: 202-265-6564

(Public Policy) New America Foundation   www.newamerica.net
1630 Connecticut Ave NW 7th Fl   Washington DC 20009
Ph: 202-986-2700 ▪ Fx: 202-986-3696

(Public Policy) Nixon Center   www.nixoncenter.org
1615 L St NW Suite 1250   Washington DC 20036
Ph: 202-887-1000 ▪ Fx: 202-887-5222

(Public Policy) Northeast-Midwest Institute   www.nemw.org
218 D St SE   Washington DC 20003
Ph: 202-544-5200 ▪ Fx: 202-544-0043

Public Policy, Pacific Research Institute for   www.pacificresearch.org
755 Sansome St Suite 450   San Francisco CA 94111
Ph: 415-989-0833 ▪ Fx: 415-989-2411

Public Policy, Pepper Institute on Aging &   www.pepperinstitute.org
Florida State Univ 207 Pepper Ctr 636 W Call St   Tallahassee
FL 32306
Ph: 850-644-2831 ▪ Fx: 850-644-2304

Public Policy Program, Science &   www.ou.edu/spp
Univ of Oklahoma Sarkeys Energy Ctr 100 E Boyd St Rm
510   Norman OK 73019
Ph: 405-325-3821 ▪ Fx: 405-325-3180

(Public Policy) Progress & Freedom Foundation   www.pff.org
1401 H St NW Suite 1075   Washington DC 20005
Ph: 202-289-8928 ▪ Fx: 202-289-6079

(Public Policy) Public Agenda   www.publicagenda.org
6 E 39th St   New York NY 10016
Ph: 212-686-6610 ▪ Fx: 212-889-3461

Public Policy Research, American Enterprise Institute for   www.aei.org
1150 17th St NW Suite 1100   Washington DC 20036
Ph: 202-862-5800 ▪ Fx: 202-862-7177 ▪ TF: 800-862-5801

Public Policy Research, National Center for   www.nationalcenter.org
777 N Capitol St NE Suite 803   Washington DC 20002
Ph: 202-371-1400 ▪ Fx: 202-408-7773

(Public Policy) Rockford Institute   www.rockfordinstitute.org
928 N Main St   Rockford IL 61103
Ph: 815-964-5053 ▪ Fx: 815-964-9403 ▪ TF: 800-383-0680

Public Policy, School of   policy.gmu.edu
George Mason University 4400 University Dr   Fairfax VA 22030
Ph: 703-993-2280 ▪ Fx: 703-993-2284

Public Policy Studies, Federalist Society for Law &   www.fed-soc.org
1015 18th St NW Suite 425   Washington DC 20036
Ph: 202-822-8138 ▪ Fx: 202-296-8061

Public Policy Studies, Phoenix Center for Advanced   www.phoenix-center.org
Legal & Economic   5335 Wisconsin Ave NW Suite
440   Washington DC 20015
Ph: 202-274-0235

Public Policy, Tufts Center for Animals &   www.tufts.edu/vet/cfa
Tufts Univ School of Veterinary Medicine 200 Westboro
Rd   North Grafton MA 01536
Ph: 508-839-7920 ▪ Fx: 508-839-2953

(Public Policy) Urban Institute   www.urban.org
2100 M St NW   Washington DC 20037
Ph: 202-833-7200 ▪ Fx: 202-223-3043

(Public Policy) Worldwatch Institute   www.worldwatch.org
1776 Massachusetts Ave NW   Washington DC 20036
Ph: 202-452-1999 ▪ Fx: 202-296-7365 ▪ TF: 800-555-2028

Public Power Association, American   www.appanet.org
2301 M St NW   Washington DC 20037
Ph: 202-467-2900 ▪ Fx: 202-467-2910

Public-Private Partnerships, National Council for   www.ncppp.org
1660 L St NW Suite 510   Washington DC 20036
Ph: 202-467-6800 ▪ Fx: 202-467-6312

Public Radio, National   www.npr.org
635 Massachusetts Ave NW   Washington DC 20001
Ph: 202-513-2000 ▪ Fx: 202-513-3329

Public Radio News Directors Inc   www.prndi.org
Wisconsin Public Radio 821 University Ave   Madison WI 53706
Ph: 608-265-3378 ▪ Fx: 608-263-5838

Public Radio Programmer's Association Inc   www.prpd.org
517 Ocean Front Walk Suite 10   Venice CA 90291
Ph: 310-664-1591 ▪ Fx: 310-664-1592

Public Records Research Association, National   www.nprra.org
PO Box 3159   Durham NC 27705
Ph: 919-384-0434 ▪ Fx: 919-383-0035

Public Relations Association, Hispanic   www.hprala.org

Public Relations Association, International   www.ipra.org

Public Relations Association, National School   www.nspra.org
15948 Derwood Rd   Rockville MD 20855
Ph: 301-519-0496 ▪ Fx: 301-519-0494

Public Relations Firms, Council of   www.prfirms.org
27 Jefferson Plaza 2nd Fl   Princeton NJ 08540
Ph: 201-444-4457 ▪ Fx: 877-773-2937 ▪ TF: 877-773-4767

Public Relations, Institute for
PO Box 118400 2096 Weimer Hall   Gainesville FL 32611
Ph: 352-392-0280 ▪ Fx: 352-846-1122
www.instituteforpr.com

Public Relations, National Council for Marketing &
PO Box 336039   Greeley CO 80633
Ph: 970-330-0771 ▪ Fx: 970-330-0769
www.ncmpr.org

Public Relations Society of America
33 Irving Pl 3rd Fl   New York NY 10003
Ph: 212-995-2230 ▪ Fx: 212-995-0757 ▪ TF: 800-937-7772
www.prsa.org

Public Relations Society, National Black
6565 Sunset Blvd Suite 425   Hollywood CA 90028
Ph: 323-466-8221 ▪ Fx: 323-856-9510
www.nbprs.org

Public Relations Student Society of America
33 Irving Pl 3rd Fl   New York NY 10003
Ph: 212-460-1474 ▪ Fx: 212-995-0757
www.prssa.org

Public Risk Management Association
500 Montgomery St Suite 750   Alexandria VA 22314
Ph: 703-528-7701 ▪ Fx: 703-739-0200
www.primacentral.org

Public-Safety Communications Officials International Inc, Association of   351 N Williamson Blvd   Daytona Beach FL 32114
Ph: 386-322-2500 ▪ Fx: 386-322-2501 ▪ TF: 888-272-6911
www.apcointl.org

Public Safety, Northwestern University Center for
600 Foster   Evanston IL 60204
Ph: 847-491-5476 ▪ Fx: 847-491-5270 ▪ TF: 800-323-4011
server.traffic.northwestern.edu

Public School Improvement, Project Appleseed: National Campaign for   7209 Dorset Ave   Saint Louis MO 63130
Ph: 314-726-0536 ▪ Fx: 314-725-2319
www.projectappleseed.org

Public Schools, National Council on Bible Curriculum In
PO Box 9743   Greensboro NC 27429
Ph: 336-272-3799
www.bibleinschools.net

Public Service, American Institute for
100 W 10th St Suite 215   Wilmington DE 19801
Ph: 302-622-9101 ▪ Fx: 302-622-9108
www.jeffersonawards.org

Public Service Research Council
320-D Maple Ave E   Vienna VA 22180
Ph: 703-242-3575 ▪ Fx: 703-242-3579

Public Spaces, Project for
153 Waverly Pl 4th Fl   New York NY 10014
Ph: 212-620-5660 ▪ Fx: 212-620-3821
pps.org

Public Technology Inc
1301 Pennsylvania Ave NW Suite 800   Washington DC 20004
Ph: 202-626-2400 ▪ Fx: 202-626-2498 ▪ TF: 800-852-4934
www.pti.org

Public Technology, Alliance for
919 18th St NW Suite 900   Washington DC 20006
Ph: 202-263-2970 ▪ Fx: 202-263-2960
apt.org

Public Television Stations, Association of
666 11th St NW 11th Fl   Washington DC 20001
Ph: 202-654-4200 ▪ Fx: 202-654-4236
www.apts.org

Public Transportation Association, American
1666 K St NW   Washington DC 20006
Ph: 202-496-4800 ▪ Fx: 202-496-4321
www.apta.com

Public Utilities, Institute of
Michigan State Univ 240 Nisbet Bldg   East Lansing MI 48823
Ph: 517-355-1876 ▪ Fx: 517-355-1854
www.ipu.msu.edu

Public Welfare Foundation Inc
1200 U St NW   Washington DC 20009
Ph: 202-965-1800 ▪ Fx: 202-265-8852 ▪ TF: 800-275-7934
www.publicwelfare.org

Public Works Association, American
2345 Grand Blvd Suite 500   Kansas City MO 64108
Ph: 816-472-6100 ▪ Fx: 816-472-1610
www.apwa.net

Publication Designers Inc, Society of
60 E 42nd St Suite 721   New York NY 10165
Ph: 212-983-8585 ▪ Fx: 212-983-2308
www.spd.org

Publication Editors, American Society of Business
710 E Ogden Ave Suite 600   Naperville IL 60563
Ph: 630-579-3288 ▪ Fx: 630-369-2488
www.asbpe.org

Publications of America, Women's Regional
729 Bates St   Saint Louis MO 63111
Ph: 314-997-6262 ▪ Fx: 314-567-7849
www.womensyellowpages.org

Publications, Association of Area Business
4929 Wilshire Blvd Suite 428   Los Angeles CA 90010
Ph: 323-937-5514 ▪ Fx: 323-937-0959
www.bizpubs.org

Publications Association, Periodical
PO Box 10669   Rockville MD 20849
Ph: 301-260-1646 ▪ Fx: 301-260-1647

Publications Council, Livestock
910 Currie St   Fort Worth TX 76107
Ph: 817-336-1130 ▪ Fx: 817-232-4820
www.livestockpublications.com

Publications, National Association of Hispanic
529 14th St NW National Press Bldg Suite 941   Washington DC 20045
Ph: 202-662-7250 ▪ Fx: 202-662-7254
www.nahponline.org

Publications, Society of National Association
8405 Greensboro Dr Suite 800   McLean VA 22102
Ph: 703-506-3285 ▪ Fx: 703-506-3266
www.snaponline.org

Publicity Association, Publishers
www.publisherspublicity.org

Publicly Traded Partnerships, Coalition of
805 15th St NW Suite 500   Washington DC 20005
Ph: 202-371-9770 ▪ Fx: 202-371-6601
www.ptpcoalition.org

Publishers of America, Magazine
810 7th Ave 24th Fl   New York NY 10019
Ph: 212-872-3700 ▪ Fx: 212-888-4217 ▪ TF: 888-567-3228
www.magazine.org

Publishers, American Society of Composers Authors &
1 Lincoln Plaza   New York NY 10023
Ph: 212-621-6000 ▪ Fx: 212-724-9064 ▪ TF: 800-952-7227
www.ascap.com

Publishers Artists & Writers Network, Small
323 E Matilija St Suite 110   Ojai CA 93023
Ph: 818-886-4281 ▪ Fx: 818-886-3120
www.spawn.org

Publishers Inc, Association of American
71 5th Ave   New York NY 10003
Ph: 212-255-0200 ▪ Fx: 212-255-7007
www.publishers.org

Publishers Association, American Medical
14 Fort Hill Rd   Huntington NY 11743
Ph: 631-423-0075
www.ampaonline.org

Publishers Association, Art
3000 Picture Pl   Jackson MI 49201
Ph: 517-788-8100 ▪ Fx: 517-788-8371
apa.pmai.org

Publishers Association, Audio
8405 Greensboro Dr Suite 800   McLean VA 22102
Ph: 703-556-7172 ▪ Fx: 703-556-3236
www.audiopub.org

Publishers Association, Catholic Book
8404 Jamesport Dr   Rockford IL 61108
Ph: 815-332-3245
www.cbpa.org

Publishers Association, Church Music
PO Box 158992   Nashville TN 37215
Ph: 615-791-0273 ▪ Fx: 615-790-8847
www.cmpamusic.org

Publishers Association, Classroom
5335 Wisconsin Ave NW Suite 920   Washington DC 20015
Ph: 202-965-2650 ▪ Fx: 202-244-5167

Publishers, Association of Directory
116 Cass St   Traverse City MI 49684
Ph: 800-267-9002 ▪ Fx: 231-486-2182
www.adp.org

Publishers, Association of Educational
510 Heron Dr Suite 309   Logan Township NJ 08085
Ph: 856-241-7772 ▪ Fx: 856-241-0709
www.edpress.org

Publishers Association, Evangelical Christian
1969 E Broadway Rd Suite 2   Tempe AZ 85282
Ph: 480-966-3998 ▪ Fx: 480-966-1944
www.ecpa.org

Publishers, Association of Independent Music
PO Box 69473   Los Angeles CA 90069
Ph: 818-771-7301
www.aimp.org

Publishers Association, National Music
475 Park Ave S 29th Fl   New York NY 10016
Ph: 646-742-1651 ▪ Fx: 646-742-1779
www.nmpa.org

Publishers Association, National Newspaper
3200 13th St NW   Washington DC 20010
Ph: 202-588-8764 ▪ Fx: 202-588-5302
www.nnpa.org

Publishers Association, Newsletter & Electronic
1501 Wilson Blvd Suite 509   Arlington VA 22209
Ph: 703-527-2333 ▪ Fx: 703-841-0629 ▪ TF: 800-356-9302
www.newsletters.org

Publishers Association of North America, Small
PO Box 1306   Buena Vista CO 81211
Ph: 719-395-4790 ▪ Fx: 719-395-8374
www.spannet.org

Publishers Association, Online
500 7th Ave 8th Fl   New York NY 10018
Ph: 646-698-8071 ▪ Fx: 646-698-8081
www.online-publishers.org

Publishers, Association of Test
1201 Pennsylvania Ave Suite 300   Washington DC 20004
Ph: 866-240-7909
www.testpublishers.org

Publishers' Association of the US, Music
1562 1st Ave PMB 246   New York NY 10028
Ph: 212-327-4044
www.mpa.org

Publishers' Employees, Independent Association of
14 Washington Rd Suite 521   Princeton Junction NJ 08550
Ph: 609-799-1520 ▪ Fx: 609-716-0626 ▪ TF: 800-325-8273
www.iape1096.org

Publishers Federation Inc, US Hispanic
c/o La Informacion 6065 Hillcroft St Suite 400-B   Houston TX 77081
Ph: 713-272-0100 ▪ Fx: 713-272-0011
www.ushpf.org

Publishers Marketing Association
627 Aviation Way   Manhattan Beach CA 90266
Ph: 310-372-2732 ▪ Fx: 310-374-3342
www.pma-online.org

Publishers, National Association of Independent
PO Box 430   Highland City FL 33846
Ph: 863-648-4420
www.publishersreport.com

Publishers Publicity Association
www.publisherspublicity.org

Publishers Representatives, National Association of Independent
111 E 14th St PMB 157   New York NY 10003
Ph: 888-624-7779 ▪ Fx: 800-416-2586
www.naipr.com

Publishers Retailers & Artists, Network of Alternatives for
PO Box 9   Eastsound WA 98245
Ph: 360-376-2702 ▪ Fx: 360-376-2704 ▪ TF: 800-367-1907
www.napra.com

Publishing & Converting Technologies, NPES: Association for Suppliers of Printing   1899 Preston White Dr   Reston VA 20191
Ph: 703-264-7200 ▪ Fx: 703-620-0994
www.npes.org

Publishing Management Association, International
1205 W College St   Liberty MO 64068
Ph: 816-781-1111 ▪ Fx: 816-781-2790
www.ipma.org

Publishing & Media Workers Sector, Communications Workers of America Printing   501 3rd St NW Suite 950   Washington DC 20001
Ph: 202-434-1238 ▪ Fx: 202-434-1245

Publishing, Small Press Center for Independent
20 W 44th St   New York NY 10036
Ph: 212-764-7021 ▪ Fx: 212-354-5365
www.smallpress.org

Publishing, Society for the History of Authorship Reading &
PO Box 30   Wilmington NC 28402
Ph: 910-254-0308
www.sharpweb.org

Publishing, Society for Scholarly
10200 W 44th Ave Suite 304   Wheat Ridge CO 80033
Ph: 303-422-3914 ▪ Fx: 303-422-8894
www.sspnet.org

Pueblo Council, All Indian
PO Box 400   Albuquerque NM 87103
Ph: 505-881-1992 ▪ Fx: 505-883-7682
www.aipcinc.com

Puerto Rican Coalition Inc, National
1900 L St NW Suite 802   Washington DC 20006
Ph: 202-223-3915 ▪ Fx: 202-429-2223
www.bateylink.org/overview.htm

Puerto Rican Forum, National www.nprf.org
1946 Webster Ave 3rd Fl Bronx NY 10457
Ph: 646-792-1010 ▪ Fx: 646-792-1020

Puerto Rican-Hispanic Culture, Association for
83 Park Terr W New York NY 10034
Ph: 212-942-2338

Puerto Rican/Hispanic Social Workers Inc, National Association of www.naprhsw.com
PO Box 651 Brentwood NY 11717
Ph: 631-864-1536

(Puerto Rican & Latino) ASPIRA Association Inc www.aspira.org
1444 'I' St NW Suite 800 Washington DC 20005
Ph: 202-835-3600 ▪ Fx: 202-835-3613

Puerto Rico USA Citizenship Foundation www.puertoricousa.com
600 13th St NW Washington DC 20005
Ph: 202-756-8213 ▪ Fx: 202-756-8087

Pull-Thru Network www.pullthrough.org
2312 Savoy St Hoover AL 35226
Ph: 205-978-2930

Pullman Foundation, Historic www.pullmanil.org
614 E 113th St Chicago IL 60628
Ph: 773-785-8181 ▪ Fx: 773-785-8182

Pulmonary Rehabilitation, American Association of Cardiovascular & www.aacvpr.org
401 N Michigan Ave Suite 2200 Chicago IL 60611
Ph: 312-321-5146 ▪ Fx: 312-527-6635

Pulp Environmental Packaging Association, International Molded www.impepa.org
1425 W Mequon Rd Suite A Mequon WI 53092
Ph: 262-241-0522 ▪ Fx: 262-241-3766

Pulp & Paper Industry, Technical Association of the www.tappi.org
15 Technology Pkwy S Norcross GA 30092
Ph: 770-446-1400 ▪ Fx: 770-446-6947 ▪ TF: 800-332-8686

Pulp & Paper Workers, Association of Western www.awppw.org
PO Box 4566 Portland OR 97208
Ph: 503-228-7486 ▪ Fx: 503-228-1346

Pump Association, Submersible Wastewater www.swpa.org
1866 Sheridan Rd Suite 201 Highland Park IL 60035
Ph: 847-681-1868 ▪ Fx: 847-681-1869

Pumping Association, American Concrete www.concretepumpers.com
676 Enterprise Dr Lewis Center OH 43035
Ph: 614-431-5618 ▪ Fx: 614-431-6944

Pumpkin Confederation, World www.pandpseed.com/wpc.htm
56 E Union St Hamburg NY 14075
Ph: 716-648-7982

Punch Manufacturers Association, North American www.napma.org
7402 Chestnut Ridge Rd Lockport NY 14094
Ph: 716-433-2917

Punishment & Alternatives, National www.temple.edu/education/ncscpa/ncscpa.html
Center for the Study of Corporal Temple Univ 253 Ritter
Annex Philadelphia PA 19122
Ph: 215-204-6091 ▪ Fx: 215-204-6013

Punishment in Schools, National Coalition to www.stophitting.com/disatschool
Abolish Corporal 155 W Main St Suite 1603 Columbus OH
43215
Ph: 614-221-8829 ▪ Fx: 614-221-2110

Pupil Personnel Workers, International Association of www.iappw.org
2940 N Stratham Pt Hernando FL 34442
Ph: 352-637-0653 ▪ Fx: 352-637-0926

Pupil Service Administrators, National Association of www.napsa.org
PO Box 783 Pittsford NY 14534
Ph: 585-223-2018 ▪ Fx: 585-223-1497

Pupil Transportation, National Association for www.napt.org
1840 Western Ave Albany NY 12203
Ph: 518-452-3611 ▪ Fx: 518-218-0867 ▪ TF: 800-989-6278

(Puppetry) Union Internationale de la Marionnette www.unima-usa.org
Center for Puppetry Arts Atlanta GA 30309
Ph: 404-873-3089 ▪ Fx: 404-873-9907

Purchasers, International Society of Hospitality www.ishp.org
300 Montgomery St Suite 833 San Francisco CA 94104
Ph: 415-399-0995 ▪ Fx: 415-399-0935

Purchasing Association, Health Industry Group www.higpa.com
1100 Wilson Blvd Suite 1200 Arlington VA 22209
Ph: 703-243-9262 ▪ Fx: 703-243-8664

Purchasing Institute, National www.nationalpurchasinginstitute.com
701 N Green Valley Pkwy Suite 200 Henderson NV 89053
Ph: 702-260-7114 ▪ Fx: 702-260-7052

Purchasing, National Institute of Governmental www.nigp.org
151 Spring St Suite 300 Herndon VA 20170
Ph: 703-736-8900 ▪ Fx: 703-736-9644 ▪ TF: 800-367-6447

Purchasing Society, American www.american-purchasing.com
8 E Galena Blvd Suite 203 Aurora IL 60506
Ph: 630-859-0250 ▪ Fx: 630-859-0270

Purebred Hanoverian Association of American Breeders & Owners
Box 429 Rocky Hill NJ 08553
Ph: 609-466-1383 ▪ Fx: 609-466-9543

Purebred Morab Horse Association Inc www.puremorab.com
PO Box 280 Sherwood WI 54169
Ph: 920-853-3086 ▪ Fx: 920-853-3114

Purple Heart of the USA, Military Order of the www.purpleheart.org
5413-B Backlick Rd Springfield VA 22151
Ph: 703-642-5360 ▪ Fx: 703-642-2054

Purple Martin Conservation Association www.purplemartin.org
Edinboro Univ of Pennsylvania Edinboro PA 16444
Ph: 814-734-4420 ▪ Fx: 814-734-5803

Putters Association, Professional www.proputters.com
PO Box 35237 Fayetteville NC 28303
Ph: 910-485-7131 ▪ Fx: 910-485-1122

Puzzle Buffs International www.puzzlebuffs.com
41 Park Dr Port Clinton OH 43452
Ph: 419-734-2600 ▪ Fx: 419-734-2868

Pygmy Goat Association, National www.npga-pygmy.com
1932 149th Ave SE Snohomish WA 98290
Ph: 425-334-6506 ▪ Fx: 425-334-5447

Pyrotechnic Signal Manufacturers Association
28320 St Michael Rd Easton MD 21601
Ph: 410-822-0318 ▪ Fx: 410-822-7759

Pyrotechnics Association, American www.americanpyro.com
PO Box 30438 Bethesda MD 20824
Ph: 301-907-8181 ▪ Fx: 301-907-9148

Pythias, Junior Order Knights of www.pythias.org/jr-order
59 Coddington St Suite 202 Quincy MA 02169
Ph: 617-472-8800

Pythias, Order of Knights of www.pythias.org
59 Coddington St Suite 202 Quincy MA 02169
Ph: 617-472-8800 ▪ Fx: 617-376-0363

Q

Quail Unlimited www.qu.org
31 Quail Run Edgefield SC 29824
Ph: 803-637-5731 ▪ Fx: 803-637-0037

Quaker Fellowship, Wider quaker.org/fwcc/Americas/wqf.html
1506 Race St Philadelphia PA 19102
Ph: 215-241-7293 ▪ Fx: 215-241-7285

Qualitative Research Consultants Association Inc www.qrca.org
PO Box 967 Camden TN 30320
Ph: 731-584-8080 ▪ Fx: 731-584-7882 ▪ TF: 888-674-7722

Quality, American College of Medical www.acmq.org
4334 Montgomery Ave 2nd Fl Bethesda MD 20814
Ph: 301-913-9149 ▪ Fx: 301-913-9142 ▪ TF: 800-924-2149

Quality, American Society for www.asq.org
600 N Plankinton Ave Milwaukee WI 53201
Ph: 414-272-8575 ▪ Fx: 414-272-1734 ▪ TF: 800-248-1946

Quality Assurance, National Committee for www.ncqa.org
2000 L St NW Suite 500 Washington DC 20036
Ph: 202-955-3500 ▪ Fx: 202-955-3599 ▪ TF: 800-236-5903

Quality Assurance, Society of www.sqa.org
2365 Hunters Way Charlottesville VA 22911
Ph: 434-297-4772 ▪ Fx: 434-977-0899

Quality Assurance & Utilization Review Physicians, American www.abqaurp.org
Board of 2120 Range Rd Clearwater FL 33765
Ph: 727-298-8777 ▪ Fx: 727-449-0555 ▪ TF: 800-998-6030

Quality Bakers of America Inc www.qba.com
70 Riverdale Ave Greenwich CT 06831
Ph: 203-531-7100 ▪ Fx: 203-531-1406

Quality Center, American Productivity & www.apqc.org
123 Post Oak Ln 3rd Fl Houston TX 77024
Ph: 713-681-4020 ▪ Fx: 713-681-8578 ▪ TF: 800-776-9676

Quality Chekd Dairies www.qchekd.com
1733 Park St Naperville IL 60563
Ph: 630-717-1110 ▪ Fx: 630-717-1126

Quality Education for Minorities Network qemnetwork.qem.org
1818 'N' St NW Suite 350 Washington DC 20036
Ph: 202-659-1818 ▪ Fx: 202-659-5408

Quality of Life Studies, International Society for market1.cob.vt.edu/isqols
Virginia Polytechnic Institute Pamplin College of Business Mktg
Dept Blacksburg VA 24061
Ph: 540-231-5110 ▪ Fx: 540-231-3076

Quality & Participation, Association for www.aqp.org
PO Box 2005 Milwaukee WI 53201
Ph: 414-765-7219 ▪ Fx: 414-272-1247 ▪ TF: 800-733-3310

Quantitative Analyses of Behavior, Society for sqab.psychology.org
234 Huron Ave Cambridge MA 02139
Ph: 617-497-5270

Quantitative Analysts, Society of www.sqa-us.org
151 Herricks Rd Suite 1 Garden City Park NY 11040
Ph: 516-739-2510 ▪ Fx: 516-739-3803 ▪ TF: 800-284-6228

Quarries Association, National Building Granite www.nbgqa.com
1220 L St NW Suite 100-167 Washington DC 20005
Ph: 800-557-2848

Quarter Century Wireless Association www.qcwa.org
159 E 16th Ave Eugene OR 97401
Ph: 541-683-0987 ▪ Fx: 541-683-4181

Quarter Horse Association, American www.aqha.org
PO Box 200 Amarillo TX 79168
Ph: 806-376-4811 ▪ Fx: 806-349-6404 ▪ TF: 800-414-7433

Quarter Horse Youth Association, American www.aqha.com/youth
1600 Quarter Horse Dr PO Box 200 Amarillo TX 79168
Ph: 806-376-4811 ▪ Fx: 806-349-6409

Quarter Pony Association, American www.aqpa.org
PO Box 30 New Sharon IA 50207
Ph: 641-675-3669 ▪ Fx: 641-675-3969

Quartus Foundation for Spiritual Research www.quartus.org
PO Box 1768 Boerne TX 78006
Ph: 830-249-3985 ▪ Fx: 830-249-3318

Quartzite Rock Association www.quartzite.com/
PO Box 661 Sioux Falls SD 57101
Ph: 605-339-1520 ▪ Fx: 605-334-3656

Quaternary Association, American www4.nau.edu/amqua
Univ of Arkansas Dept of Geosciences Fayetteville AR 72701
Ph: 501-575-3354 ▪ Fx: 501-575-3846

Quebec-Labrador Foundation - Atlantic Center for the Environment www.qlf.org
55 S Main St Ipswich MA 01938
Ph: 978-356-0038 ▪ Fx: 978-356-7322

Quest for Peace www.quixote.org/quest
Quixote Center PO Box 5206 Hyattsville MD 20782
Ph: 301-699-0042 ▪ Fx: 301-864-2182

Questioned Document Examiners, American Society of www.asqde.org
PO Box 382684 Germantown TN 38183
Ph: 901-759-0729 ▪ Fx: 901-737-2643

Quill & Scroll Society   www.uiowa.edu/~quill-sc
Univ of Iowa School of Journalism   Iowa City IA 52242
Ph: 319-335-5795 ▪ Fx: 319-335-5210

Quilt, NAMES Project Foundation/AIDS Memorial   www.aidsquilt.org
101 Krog St   Atlanta GA 30307
Ph: 404-688-5500 ▪ Fx: 404-688-5552

Quilt Project, Boise Peace   www.boisepeacequilt.org
PO Box 6469   Boise ID 83707
Ph: 208-343-3035 ▪ Fx: 208-323-0848

Quilt Study Group, American   www.h-net.org/~aqsg/
PO Box 4737   Lincoln NE 68504
Ph: 402-472-5361 ▪ Fx: 402-472-5428

Quilter's Society, American   www.aqsquilt.com
PO Box 3290   Paducah KY 42003
Ph: 270-898-7903 ▪ Fx: 270-898-1173

Quilts, ABC   www.abcquilts.org
569 First New Hampshire Tpke Suite 3   Northwood NH 03261
Ph: 603-942-9211

Quota International   www.quota.org
1420 21st St NW   Washington DC 20036
Ph: 202-331-9694 ▪ Fx: 202-331-4395

R

RA Bloch Cancer Foundation   www.blochcancer.org
4400 Main St   Kansas City MO 64111
Ph: 816-932-8453 ▪ Fx: 816-931-7486 ▪ TF: 800-433-0464

Rabbinical Alliance of America
3 W 16th St 4th Fl   New York NY 10011
Ph: 212-242-6420 ▪ Fx: 212-255-8313

Rabbinical Assembly   www.rabassembly.org
3080 Broadway   New York NY 10027
Ph: 212-280-6000 ▪ Fx: 212-749-9166

Rabbinical Association, Reconstructionist   www.therra.org
1299 Church Rd   Wyncote PA 19095
Ph: 215-576-5210 ▪ Fx: 215-576-8051

Rabbinical Congress of the USA & Canada, Central
85 Division Ave   Brooklyn NY 11211
Ph: 718-384-6765 ▪ Fx: 718-486-5574

Rabbinical Council of America   www.rabbis.org
305 7th Ave   New York NY 10001
Ph: 212-807-7888 ▪ Fx: 212-727-8452

Rabbinical & Talmudic Schools, Association of Advanced
11 Broadway   New York NY 10004
Ph: 212-363-1991 ▪ Fx: 212-533-5335

Rabbis, Association of Humanistic   www.iishj.org
28611 W 12 Mile Rd   Farmington Hills MI 48334
Ph: 248-476-9532 ▪ Fx: 248-476-8509

Rabbis, Central Conference of American   www.ccarnet.org
355 Lexington Ave 18th Fl   New York NY 10017
Ph: 212-972-3636 ▪ Fx: 212-692-0819 ▪ TF: 800-935-2227

Rabbis of the US & Canada, Union of Orthodox
235 E Broadway   New York NY 10002
Ph: 212-964-6337

Rabbit Association, American Himalayan   ahra.homestead.com

Rabbit Breeders, American Federation of   www.geocities.com/newzealandrba
New Zealand   PO Box 171   Honeoye NY 14471
Ph: 585-229-5760

Rabbit Breeders Association, American   www.arba.net
PO Box 426   Bloomington IL 61702
Ph: 309-664-7500 ▪ Fx: 309-664-0941

Rabbit Breeders' Association, American Satin   www.asrba.org
1895 Wilson Ave   Wilton IA 52778
Ph: 563-785-6365

Rabbit Breeders, National Federation of Flemish Giant   www.nffgrb.com
2259 Barbara Dr   Camarillo CA 93012
Ph: 805-491-2029

Rabbit Club of America, Lop   www.lrca.net
PO Box 8367   Fremont CA 94537
Ph: 510-793-4977

Rabbit Club of America, Mini Lop   www.miniloprabbit.com

Rabbit Club of America, National Lilac   www.geocities.com/nlrca2002
N3650 Oak Ridge Rd   Waupaca WI 54981
Ph: 715-258-3106

Rabbit Club of America, Rhinelander   www.hop.to/Rhinelanders
1560 Vine St   El Centro CA 92243
Ph: 760-352-6525

Rabbit Club, American Harlequin
1299 Josie Ln   Conover NC 28613
Ph: 828-466-2274

Rabbit Club, National Rex   www.nationalrexrc.com
21840 S 116th Ave   New Lenox IL 60451
Ph: 815-469-5150

Rabbit Club, Silver Marten   www.silvermarten.com
2113 Sommer St   Napa CA 94559
Ph: 707-255-2821

Rabbit Federation, Champagne D'Argent
1704 Heisel Ave   Pekin IL 61554
Ph: 309-347-1347

Rabbit Society, House   www.rabbit.org
148 Broadway   Richmond CA 94804
Ph: 510-970-7575 ▪ Fx: 510-970-9820

Rabbit Specialty Club, National Californian   home.woh.rr.com/crsc
22162 S Hunter Rd   Colton OR 97017
Ph: 503-824-2138

Race Research Action Council, Poverty &   www.prrac.org
3000 Connecticut Ave NW Suite 200   Washington DC 20008
Ph: 202-387-9887 ▪ Fx: 202-387-0764

Racers Association, National American Motors Drivers &   www.namdra.org
PO Box 987   Twin Lakes WI 53181
Ph: 262-396-9552

Racers Association, United Drag   www.udra.org
18823 High Point   Chagrin Falls OH 44023
Ph: 440-543-4272

Rachel Carson Council Inc   members.aol.com/rccouncil/ourpage
PO Box 10779   Silver Spring MD 20914
Ph: 301-593-7507 ▪ Fx: 301-593-6251

Rachel Carson Homestead Association   www.rachelcarsonhomestead.org
613 Marion Ave Box 46   Springdale PA 15144
Ph: 724-274-5459 ▪ Fx: 724-275-1259

Racial Equality, Congress of   www.core-online.org
817 Broadway 3rd Fl   New York NY 10003
Ph: 212-598-4000 ▪ Fx: 212-982-0184

Racing Association, International Sled Dog   www.isdra.org
22702 Rebel Rd   Merrifield MN 56465
Ph: 218-765-4297 ▪ Fx: 218-765-3246

Racing Association, International Star Class Yacht   www.starclass.org
1545 Waukegan Rd   Glenview IL 60025
Ph: 847-729-0630 ▪ Fx: 847-729-0718

Racing Association, National Thoroughbred   www.ntra.com
2525 Harrodsburg Rd   Lexington KY 40504
Ph: 859-223-5444 ▪ Fx: 859-223-3945

Racing Association, Sportscar Vintage   www.svra.com
257 Dekalb Industrial Way   Decatur GA 30030
Ph: 404-298-3323 ▪ Fx: 404-298-3325

Racing Associations, Thoroughbred   www.tra-online.com
420 Fair Hill Dr Suite 1   Elkton MD 21921
Ph: 410-392-9200 ▪ Fx: 410-398-1366

Racing Chemists, Association of Official
PO Box 8400 Stn T   Ottawa ON K1G3H8
Ph: 613-731-7137 ▪ Fx: 613-731-7984

Racing Commissioners International, Association of   www.arci.com
2343 Alexandria Dr Suite 200   Lexington KY 40504
Ph: 859-224-7070 ▪ Fx: 859-224-7071

Racing Motorcycle Association, American Historic   www.ahrma.org
PO Box 1725   Goodlettsville TN 37070
Ph: 615-851-3674 ▪ Fx: 615-851-3678

Racing, National Association for Stock Car Auto   www.nascar.com
1801 W International Speedway Blvd   Daytona Beach FL 32114
Ph: 386-253-0611 ▪ Fx: 386-947-6712

Racing Pigeon Union, American   www.pigeon.org
PO Box 18465   Oklahoma City OK 73154
Ph: 405-848-5801 ▪ Fx: 405-848-5888 ▪ TF: 800-755-2778

Racing Protective Bureau, Thoroughbred   www.trpb.com
420 Fair Hill Dr Suite 2   Elkton MD 21921
Ph: 410-398-2261 ▪ Fx: 410-398-1499

Rack Manufacturers Institute   www.mhia.org/psc
8720 Red Oak Blvd Suite 201   Charlotte NC 28217
Ph: 704-676-1190 ▪ Fx: 704-676-1199

Racking Horse Breeders Association of America   www.rackinghorse.com
67 Horse Ctr Rd   Decatur AL 35603
Ph: 256-353-7225 ▪ Fx: 256-353-7266

Racquet & Sportsclub Association, International Health   www.ihrsa.org
263 Summer St   Boston MA 02210
Ph: 617-951-0055 ▪ Fx: 617-951-0056 ▪ TF: 800-228-4772

Racquet Stringers Association, US   www.racquettech.com
330 Main St   Vista CA 92084
Ph: 760-536-1177 ▪ Fx: 760-536-1171 ▪ TF: 888-900-3545

Racquetball Association, US   www.usra.org
1685 W Uintah St   Colorado Springs CO 80904
Ph: 719-635-5396 ▪ Fx: 719-635-0685

Racquetball Federation, International   www.internationalracquetball.com
1685 W Uintah St   Colorado Springs CO 80904
Ph: 719-635-5396 ▪ Fx: 719-635-0685

Radiant Panel Association   www.radiantpanelassociation.org
PO Box 717   Loveland CO 80539
Ph: 970-613-0100 ▪ Fx: 970-613-0098 ▪ TF: 800-660-7187

Radiation Control Program Directors, Conference of   www.crcpd.org
205 Capitol Ave   Frankfort KY 40601
Ph: 502-227-4543 ▪ Fx: 502-227-7862

Radiation Oncology Administrators, Society for   www.sroa.org
PO Box 51687   Albuquerque NM 87181
Ph: 866-458-7762 ▪ Fx: 505-298-5063

Radiation Oncology, American College of   www.acro.org
4350 East-West Hwy Suite 401   Bethesda MD 20814
Ph: 301-718-6515 ▪ Fx: 301-656-0989

Radiation Oncology, Association of Residents in   www.arro.org
12500 Fair Lakes Cir Suite 375   Fairfax VA 22033
Ph: 703-502-1550 ▪ Fx: 703-502-7852 ▪ TF: 800-962-7876

Radiation Oncology Centers, Association of Freestanding   www.afroc.org
1875 'I' St NW 12th Fl   Washington DC 20006
Ph: 888-334-4542 ▪ Fx: 202-466-5938

Radiation Protection & Measurements, National Council on   www.ncrp.com
7910 Woodmont Ave Suite 400   Bethesda MD 20814
Ph: 301-657-2652 ▪ Fx: 301-907-8768 ▪ TF: 800-229-2652

Radiation Survivors, National Association of   www.radiationsurvivors.org
PO Box 1587   Marysville CA 95901
Ph: 530-741-6954 ▪ TF: 800-798-5102

Radiation Therapy Oncology Group   www.rtog.org
1101 Market St 14th Fl   Philadelphia PA 19107
Ph: 215-574-3189 ▪ Fx: 215-923-1737

Radiation Units & Measurements, International Commission on   www.icru.org
7910 Woodmont Ave Suite 400   Bethesda MD 20814
Ph: 301-657-2652 ▪ Fx: 301-907-8768

Radiator Service Association, National Automotive   www.narsa.org
PO Box 97   East Greenville PA 18041
Ph: 215-541-4500 ▪ Fx: 215-679-4977

Radical Historians' Organization, MARHO: www.historians.org/affiliates
c/o American Historical Assn 400 A St SE   Washington DC 20003
Ph: 202-544-2422 ■ Fx: 202-544-8307

Radical Political Economics, Union for www.urpe.org
37 Howe St   New Haven CT 06511
Ph: 203-777-4605

Radio Advertising Bureau www.rab.com
261 Madison Ave 23rd Fl   New York NY 10016
Ph: 212-681-7200 ■ Fx: 212-681-7223 ■ TF: 800-252-7234

Radio Amateur Satellite Corp www.amsat.org
850 Sligo Ave Suite 600   Silver Spring MD 20910
Ph: 301-589-6062 ■ Fx: 301-608-3410

Radio Artists, American Federation of Television & www.aftra.com
260 Madison Ave 7th Fl   New York NY 10016
Ph: 212-532-0800 ■ Fx: 212-532-2242

Radio Association, American home.earthlink.net/~araplans
360 W 31st St 3rd Fl   New York NY 10001
Ph: 212-594-3600 ■ Fx: 212-594-7422

Radio, Black College www.blackcollegeradio.com
PO Box 3191   Atlanta GA 30302
Ph: 404-523-6136 ■ Fx: 404-523-5467

Radio Broadcasters Inc, Country www.crb.org
819 18th Ave S   Nashville TN 37203
Ph: 615-327-4487 ■ Fx: 615-329-4492

Radio Clubs Inc, Association of North American www.anarc.org

Radio Collectors of America
15 Walden Dr   Walpole MA 02081
Ph: 508-660-0923

Radio Control Hobby Trade Association www.rchta.org
PO Box 315   Butler NJ 07405
Ph: 973-283-9088 ■ Fx: 973-838-7124

Radio Foundation, Pacifica www.pacifica.org
2390 Champlain St NW 2nd Fl   Washington DC 20009
Ph: 202-588-0999

Radio Free Europe/Radio Liberty www.rferl.org
1201 Connecticut Ave NW 4th Fl   Washington DC 20036
Ph: 202-457-6900 ■ Fx: 202-457-6997

(Radio Frequency) MRFAC Inc www.mrfac.com
899-A Harrison St SE   Leesburg VA 20175
Ph: 703-669-0320 ■ Fx: 703-318-9209 ■ TF: 800-262-9206

Radio, Friends of Old-Time
PO Box 4321   Hamden CT 06514
Ph: 203-248-2887 ■ Fx: 203-281-1322

Radio Heritage Association, National
15347 Nall Rd   Council Bluffs IA 51503
Ph: 712-388-9088

Radio & Machine Workers of America, United Electrical www.ranknfile-ue.org
1 Gateway Ctr Suite 1400   Pittsburgh PA 15222
Ph: 412-471-8919 ■ Fx: 412-471-8999

(Radio) National Lum & Abner Society home.inu.net/stemple
81 Sharon Blvd   Dora AL 35062
Ph: 205-674-0101 ■ Fx: 205-674-0190

Radio, National Public www.npr.org
635 Massachusetts Ave NW   Washington DC 20001
Ph: 202-513-2000 ■ Fx: 202-513-3329

Radio Networks, National Association of State www.statenets.com

Radio News Directors, Public www.prndi.org
Wisconsin Public Radio 821 University Ave   Madison WI 53706
Ph: 608-265-3378 ■ Fx: 608-263-5838

Radio Programmer's Association, Public www.prpd.org
517 Ocean Front Walk Suite 10   Venice CA 90291
Ph: 310-664-1591 ■ Fx: 310-664-1592

Radio Relay League, American www.arrl.org
225 Main St   Newington CT 06111
Ph: 860-594-0200 ■ Fx: 860-594-0259

(Radio Signals) Longwave Club of America www.lwca.org
45 Wildflower Rd   Levittown PA 19057
Ph: 215-945-0543

Radio Technical Commission for Maritime Services www.rtcm.org
1800 N Kent St Suite 1060   Arlington VA 22209
Ph: 703-527-2000 ■ Fx: 703-351-9932

Radio & Telecommunications Engineers, National Association of www.narte.org
167 Village St   Medway MA 02053
Ph: 508-533-8333 ■ Fx: 508-533-3815 ■ TF: 800-896-2783

Radio & Television, American Women in www.awrt.org
8405 Greensboro Dr Suite 800   McLean VA 22102
Ph: 703-506-3290 ■ Fx: 703-506-3266

Radio-Television Correspondents Association
c/o Senate Radio-TV Gallery US Capitol Rm S-325   Washington DC 20510
Ph: 202-224-6421 ■ Fx: 202-224-4882

Radio-Television News Directors Association www.rtnda.org
1600 K St NW Suite 700   Washington DC 20006
Ph: 202-659-6510 ■ Fx: 202-223-4007 ■ TF: 800-807-8632

Radio & Television Research Council
234 5th Ave Suite 417   New York NY 10001
Ph: 212-481-3038 ■ Fx: 212-481-3071

Radio & Television Society Foundation Inc, International www.irts.org
420 Lexington Ave Suite 1601   New York NY 10170
Ph: 212-867-6650 ■ Fx: 212-867-6653

Radio & Television Society, Hollywood www.hrts-iba.org
13701 Riverside Dr Suite 205   Sherman Oaks CA 91423
Ph: 818-789-1182 ■ Fx: 818-789-1210

Radio, Trans World www.gospelcom.net/twr
PO Box 8700   Cary NC 27512
Ph: 919-460-3700 ■ Fx: 919-460-3702 ■ TF: 800-456-7897

Radioactive Waste Safety, National Campaign for www.sric.org
105 Stanford SE PO Box 4524   Albuquerque NM 87106
Ph: 505-262-1862 ■ Fx: 505-262-1864

Radiographers, Association of Vascular & Interventional www.avir.org
10201 Lee Hwy Suite 500   Fairfax VA 22030
Ph: 703-691-2350 ■ Fx: 703-691-8540

Radiologic Technologists, American Chiropractic Registry of
2330 Gull Rd   Kalamazoo MI 49048
Ph: 269-343-6666 ■ Fx: 269-343-7236

Radiologic Technologists, American Registry of www.arrt.org
1255 Northland Dr   Saint Paul MN 55120
Ph: 651-687-0048 ■ Fx: 651-687-0349

Radiologic Technologists, American Society of www.asrt.org
15000 Central Ave SE   Albuquerque NM 87123
Ph: 505-298-4500 ■ Fx: 505-298-5063 ■ TF: 800-444-2778

Radiologic Technology, Joint Review Committee on Education in www.jrcert.org
20 N Wacker Dr Suite 900   Chicago IL 60606
Ph: 312-704-5300 ■ Fx: 312-704-5304

Radiological Nurses Association, American www.arna.net
7794 Grow Dr   Pensacola FL 32514
Ph: 850-474-7292 ■ Fx: 850-484-8762 ■ TF: 866-486-2762

Radiological Sciences, Association of Educators in www.aers.org
PO Box 90204   Albuquerque NM 87199
Ph: 505-823-4740

Radiological Society of North America www.rsna.org
820 Jorie Blvd   Oak Brook IL 60523
Ph: 630-571-2670 ■ Fx: 630-571-7837

Radiologists, American Association for Women www.aawr.org
4550 Post Oak Pl Suite 342   Houston TX 77027
Ph: 713-623-8335 ■ Fx: 713-960-0488

Radiologists, Association of University www.aur.org
820 Jorie Blvd   Oak Brook IL 60523
Ph: 630-368-3730 ■ Fx: 630-571-7837

Radiologists, Society of Gastrointestinal www.sgr.org
4550 Post Oak Pl Suite 342   Houston TX 77027
Ph: 713-965-0566 ■ Fx: 713-960-0488

Radiologists in Ultrasound, Society of www.sru.org
44211 Slatestone Ct   Leesburg VA 20176
Ph: 703-858-9210 ■ Fx: 703-729-4839

Radiology Administrators, American Healthcare www.ahraonline.org
490-B Boston Post Rd Suite 101   Sudbury MA 01776
Ph: 978-443-7591 ■ Fx: 978-443-8046 ■ TF: 800-334-2472

Radiology, American Academy of Oral & Maxillofacial www.aaomr.org
PO Box 1010   Evans GA 30809
Ph: 706-721-2607

Radiology, American Board of www.theabr.org
5441 E Williams Blvd Suite 200   Tucson AZ 85711
Ph: 520-790-2900 ■ Fx: 520-790-3200

Radiology, American Chiropractic College of www.accr.org
PO Box 3053   La Habra CA 90632
Ph: 562-947-8755

Radiology, American College of www.acr.org
1891 Preston White Dr   Reston VA 20191
Ph: 703-648-8900 ■ Fx: 703-295-6772 ■ TF: 800-227-5463

Radiology, American College of Veterinary www.acvr.ucdavis.edu
777 E Park Dr PO Box 8820   Harrisburg PA 17105
Ph: 717-558-7865 ■ Fx: 717-558-7841

Radiology, American Osteopathic College of www.aocr.org
119 E 2nd St   Milan MO 63556
Ph: 660-265-4011 ■ Fx: 660-265-3494 ■ TF: 800-258-2627

Radiology, American Society of Emergency www.erad.org
4550 Post Oak Pl Suite 342   Houston TX 77027
Ph: 713-965-0566 ■ Fx: 713-960-0488

Radiology, American Society of Head & Neck www.ashnr.org
2210 Midwest Rd Suite 207   Oak Brook IL 60523
Ph: 630-574-0220 ■ Fx: 630-574-0661

Radiology, American Society of Spine www.theassr.org
2210 Midwest Rd Suite 207   Oak Brook IL 60523
Ph: 630-574-0220 ■ Fx: 630-574-0661

Radiology, Association of Program Directors in www.apdr.org
820 Jorie Blvd   Oak Brook IL 60523
Ph: 630-368-3737 ■ Fx: 630-571-7837

Radiology Business Management Association www.rbma.org
8001 Irvine Center Dr Suite 1060   Irvine CA 92618
Ph: 949-340-5000 ■ Fx: 949-340-5001 ■ TF: 888-224-7262

Radiology Departments, Society of Chairmen of Academic www.scardonline.org
820 Jorie Blvd   Oak Brook IL 60523
Ph: 630-368-3731 ■ Fx: 630-571-7837

(Radiology) Fleischner Society www.fleischner.org
c/o Intelligent Meeting Managers 4550 Post Oak Pl Suite 342   Houston TX 77027
Ph: 713-965-0566 ■ Fx: 713-960-0488

Radiology, International Society of www.isradiology.org
7910 Woodmont Ave Suite 400   Bethesda MD 20814
Ph: 301-657-2652 ■ Fx: 301-907-8768

Radiology & Oncology, American Society for Therapeutic www.astro.org
12500 Fair Lakes Cir Suite 375   Fairfax VA 22033
Ph: 703-502-1550 ■ Fx: 703-502-7852 ■ TF: 800-962-7876

Radiology Research, Academy of www.acadrad.org
1029 Vermont Ave NW Suite 505   Washington DC 20005
Ph: 202-347-5872 ■ Fx: 202-347-5876

Radiology, Society for Computer Applications in www.scarnet.org
10105 Cottesmore Ct   Great Falls VA 22066
Ph: 703-757-0054 ■ Fx: 703-757-0454

Radiology, Society of Interventional www.sirweb.org
10201 Lee Hwy Suite 500   Fairfax VA 22030
Ph: 703-691-1805 ■ Fx: 703-691-1855 ■ TF: 800-488-7284

Radiology, Society for Pediatric www.pedrad.org
4550 Post Oak Pl Suite 342   Houston TX 77027
Ph: 713-965-0566 ■ Fx: 713-960-0488

Radiology, Society of Thoracic www.thoracicrad.org
1711 Walden Ln SW   Rochester MN 55902
Ph: 507-288-5260 ■ Fx: 507-288-0014

Radium Society, American www.americanradiumsociety.org
150485 S Cicero Ave   Oak Forest IL 60452
Ph: 708-687-1034 ▪ Fx: 708-687-1072

Radner Gilda Familial Ovarian Cancer Registry www.ovariancancer.com
Roswell Park Cancer Institute Elm & Carlton Sts   Buffalo NY
14263
Ph: 716-845-4503 ▪ Fx: 716-845-8266 ▪ TF: 800-682-7426

Radon Scientists & Technologists, American Association of www.aarst.org
2502 S 5th Ave   Lebanon PA 17042
Ph: 717-949-3198 ▪ Fx: 717-949-3192 ▪ TF: 866-772-2778

RadTech International North America www.radtech.org
6935 Wisconsin Ave Suite 207   Chevy Chase MD 20815
Ph: 240-497-1243 ▪ Fx: 240-209-2337

Ragtime Foundation, Scott Joplin International www.scottjoplin.org
321 S Ohio Ave   Sedalia MO 65301
Ph: 660-826-2271 ▪ Fx: 660-826-5054 ▪ TF: 866-218-6258

Ragtime Society, Bohemia www.ragtimer.com
5059 Picket Dr   Colorado Springs CO 80918
Ph: 719-528-1547

Rail Competition, Alliance for www.railcompetition.org
499 S Capitol St SW Suite 608   Washington DC 20036
Ph: 202-216-9210 ▪ Fx: 202-216-9662

Rail Equity, Consumers United for www.railcure.org
1050 Thomas Jefferson St NW 7th Fl   Washington DC 20007
Ph: 202-298-1800 ▪ Fx: 202-338-2416

Rail Shippers Association, North American www.railshippers.com
2115 Portsmouth Dr   Richardson TX 75082
Ph: 972-690-4740 ▪ Fx: 972-644-8208

Railcar Technical Services, Mechanical Association www.marts-rail.org
5 Berkshire Dr   Saint Charles MO 63301
Ph: 636-723-9947 ▪ Fx: 636-947-3750

Railroad Association, American Short Line & Regional www.aslrra.org
50 F St NW Suite 7020   Washington DC 20005
Ph: 202-628-4500 ▪ Fx: 202-628-6430

Railroad Association, National Model www.nmra.org
4121 Cromwell Rd   Chattanooga TN 37421
Ph: 423-892-2846 ▪ Fx: 423-899-4869

Railroad Car Owners Inc, American Association of Private www.aaprco.com
630-B Constitution Ave NE   Washington DC 20002
Ph: 202-547-5696 ▪ Fx: 202-547-5623

Railroad Construction & Maintenance Association, National www.nrcma.org
122 C St NW Suite 850   Washington DC 20001
Ph: 202-638-7790 ▪ Fx: 202-638-1045 ▪ TF: 800-883-1557

Railroad Historical Society, Illinois Central www.icrrhistorical.org
PO Box 288   Paxton IL 60957
Ph: 217-379-2261

Railroad Industry Association, Model www.mria.org
PO Box 3269   Renton WA 98056
Ph: 425-271-2609 ▪ Fx: 425-271-3834

Railroad Passengers, National Association of www.narprail.org
900 2nd St NE Suite 308   Washington DC 20002
Ph: 202-408-8362 ▪ Fx: 202-408-8287

Railroad Signalmen, Brotherhood of www.brs.org
601 W Golf Rd Box U   Mount Prospect IL 60056
Ph: 847-439-3732 ▪ Fx: 847-439-3743

Railroad Society, Pacific www.pacificrailroadsociety.org
PO Box 80726   San Marino CA 91118
Ph: 213-283-0087

Railroad Superintendents, American Association of www.supt.org
PO Box 456   Tinley Park IL 60477
Ph: 708-342-0210 ▪ Fx: 708-342-0257

Railroad Trial Counsel, National Association of www.usnartc.org
881 Alma Real Dr Suite 218   Pacific Palisades CA 90272
Ph: 310-459-7659 ▪ Fx: 310-459-6603

Railroaders' Association, Electric www.electricrailroaders.org
PO Box 3323   New York NY 10163
Ph: 212-986-4482

Railroadiana Collectors Association Inc www.railroadcollectors.org
550 Veronica Pl   Escondido CA 92027
Ph: 760-746-9392

Railroads, Association of American www.aar.org
50 F St NW   Washington DC 20001
Ph: 202-639-2100 ▪ Fx: 202-639-2466 ▪ TF: 800-544-7245

Rails-to-Trails Conservancy www.railtrails.org
1100 17th St NW 10th Fl   Washington DC 20036
Ph: 202-331-9696 ▪ Fx: 202-331-9680 ▪ TF: 800-888-7747

Railway Development Association, American www.amraildev.org
PO Box 44369   Eden Prairie MN 55344
Ph: 952-828-9750 ▪ Fx: 952-828-9751

Railway Employees, National Association of Retired & Veteran www.narvre.com
300 Cedar Blvd Suite 201A   Pittsburgh PA 15228
Ph: 412-563-5611 ▪ Fx: 412-563-5612

Railway Engineering-Maintenance Suppliers Association www.remsa.org
210 Little Falls St Suite 100   Falls Church VA 22046
Ph: 703-241-8514 ▪ Fx: 703-241-8589 ▪ TF: 888-337-3672

Railway Engineering & Maintenance-of-Way Association, American   8201 Corporate Dr Suite 1125   Landover MD www.arema.org
20785
Ph: 301-459-3200 ▪ Fx: 301-459-8077

Railway Historical Society, Mid-Continent www.midcontinent.org
PO Box 358   North Freedom WI 53951
Ph: 608-522-4261 ▪ Fx: 608-522-4490

Railway Historical Society, National www.nrhs.com
PO Box 58547   Philadelphia PA 19102
Ph: 215-557-6606 ▪ Fx: 215-557-6740

Railway Historical Society, Ontario & Western www.nyow.org

Railway Industrial Clearance Association www.rica.org
c/o TTX Corp 101 N Wacker Dr   Chicago IL 60606
Ph: 312-984-3770 ▪ Fx: 312-984-3781

Railway Labor Conference, National
1901 L St NW Suite 500   Washington DC 20036
Ph: 202-862-7200 ▪ Fx: 202-862-7230

Railway & Locomotive Historical Society Inc www.rrhistorical-2.com/rlhs
1610 N Vinton Rd   Anthony NM 88021
Ph: 505-882-5485

Railway Museums, Association of www.railwaymuseums.org
PO Box 370   Tujunga CA 91043
Ph: 818-951-9151

Railway Operating Officers, International Association of www.iaroo.org
621 Peacock Cir   Pontoon City IL 62040
Ph: 618-931-8208 ▪ Fx: 618-931-8209

Railway Society, Mystic Valley www.mysticvalleyrs.org
PO Box 365468   Hyde Park MA 02136
Ph: 617-361-4445

Railway Supply Institute Inc www.rsiweb.org
50 F St NW Suite 7030   Washington DC 20001
Ph: 202-347-4664 ▪ Fx: 202-347-0047

Railway Systems Suppliers Inc www.rssi.org
9304 New LaGrange Rd Suite 200   Louisville KY 40242
Ph: 502-327-7774 ▪ Fx: 502-327-0541

Railway Tie Association www.rta.org
115 Commerce Dr Suite C   Fayetteville GA 30214
Ph: 770-460-5553 ▪ Fx: 770-460-5573

Rainbow Division Veterans Memorial Foundation Inc www.rainbowvets.org
16916 George Franklyn Dr   Independence MO 64055
Ph: 816-373-5041

Rainbow for Girls, International Order of www.iorg.org
PO Box 1868   McAlester OK 74502
Ph: 918-423-1328 ▪ Fx: 918-423-1329

Rainbow/PUSH Coalition Inc www.rainbowpush.org
930 E 50th St   Chicago IL 60615
Ph: 773-373-3366 ▪ Fx: 773-373-3571

Rainbows www.rainbows.org
2100 Golf Rd Suite 370   Rolling Meadows IL 60008
Ph: 847-952-1770 ▪ Fx: 847-952-1774 ▪ TF: 800-266-3206

Rainforest Action Network www.ran.org
221 Pine St Suite 500   San Francisco CA 94104
Ph: 415-398-4404 ▪ Fx: 415-398-2732 ▪ TF: 800-989-7246

Rainforest, International Society for Preservation of the Tropical www.isptr-pard.org
3302 N Burton Ave   Rosemead CA 91770
Ph: 626-572-0233 ▪ Fx: 626-572-9521

Raisin Administrative Committee www.raisins.org
3445 N 1st St Suite 101 PO Box 5217   Fresno CA 93726
Ph: 559-225-0520 ▪ Fx: 559-225-0652

Ralph Waldo Emerson Memorial Association
3 Post Office Sq 10th Fl   Boston MA 02109
Ph: 617-423-5705 ▪ Fx: 617-423-6656

Ramah Commission, National www.campramah.org
3080 Broadway   New York NY 10027
Ph: 212-678-8881 ▪ Fx: 212-749-8251

Rambler Club, AMC clubs.hemmings.com
2645 Ashton Rd   Cleveland Heights OH 44118
Ph: 216-371-5946

Rambouillet Sheep Breeders' Association, American www.rambouilletsheep.org
1610 S State Rd 3261   Levelland TX 79336
Ph: 806-894-3081 ▪ Fx: 806-894-5531 ▪ TF: 877-929-4414

Ranch Association, Colorado Dude & Guest www.coloradoranch.com
PO Box 2120   Granby CO 80446
Ph: 970-887-3128 ▪ Fx: 970-887-1229

Ranchers' Association, Dude www.duderanch.org
PO Box 2307   Cody WY 82414
Ph: 307-587-2339 ▪ Fx: 307-587-2776

Ranching Heritage Association www.ttu.edu/ranchingheritagecenter
PO Box 43200   Lubbock TX 79409
Ph: 806-742-2498 ▪ Fx: 806-742-0612

Rand Ayn Institute: The Center for the Advancement of Objectivism   2121 Alton Pkwy Suite 250   Irvine CA 92606 www.aynrand.org
Ph: 949-222-6550 ▪ Fx: 949-222-6558

RAND Corp www.rand.org
1700 Main St PO Box 2138   Santa Monica CA 90407
Ph: 310-393-0411 ▪ Fx: 310-393-4818

Randolph A Philip Institute www.apri.org
1444 'I' St NW Suite 300   Washington DC 20005
Ph: 202-289-2774 ▪ Fx: 202-289-5289

Random Acts of Kindness Foundation www.actsofkindness.org
1727 Tremont Pl   Denver CO 80202
Ph: 303-297-1964 ▪ Fx: 303-297-2919 ▪ TF: 800-660-2811

Range Management, Society for www.rangelands.org
445 Union Blvd Suite 230   Lakewood CO 80228
Ph: 303-986-3309 ▪ Fx: 303-986-3892

Rangers Youth Program, Woodmen www.woodmen.com/about/rangers.cfm
Woodmen of the World/Omaha Woodmen Life Insurance Society
1700 Farnam St   Omaha NE 68102
Ph: 402-271-7258 ▪ Fx: 402-449-7733

Rape Abuse & Incest National Network www.rainn.org
635-B Pennsylvania Ave SE   Washington DC 20003
Ph: 202-544-1034 ▪ Fx: 202-544-3556 ▪ TF: 800-656-4673

Rape, National Clearinghouse on Marital & Date www.ncmdr.org
2325 Oak St   Berkeley CA 94708
Ph: 510-524-1582

Rape Inc, People Against www.people-against-rape.org
2148 Dorchester Rd   North Charleston SC 29405
Ph: 843-745-0144 ▪ Fx: 843-745-0119 ▪ TF: 800-877-7252

Rape, Stop Prisoner www.spr.org
6303 Wilshire Blvd Suite 204   Los Angeles CA 90048
Ph: 323-653-7867 ▪ Fx: 323-653-7870

Raptor Education Foundation www.usaref.org
PO Box 200400   Denver CO 80220
Ph: 303-680-8500 ▪ Fx: 303-680-8502

Raptor Research Foundation   biology.boisestate.edu/raptor
PO Box 1897   Lawrence KS 66044
Ph: 800-627-0629 ▪ Fx: 785-843-1274

Rare   www.rarecenter.org
1840 Wilson Blvd Suite 204   Arlington VA 22201
Ph: 703-522-5070 ▪ Fx: 703-522-5027

Rare Breed Association, American   www.arba.org
PO Box 757   Blooming Prairie MN 55917
Ph: 507-583-7718

Rare Disorders, National Organization for   www.rarediseases.org
55 Kenosia Ave PO Box 1968   Danbury CT 06813
Ph: 203-744-0100 ▪ Fx: 203-798-2291 ▪ TF: 800-999-6673

Raskob Foundation for Catholic Activities   www.rfca.org
PO Box 4019   Wilmington DE 19807
Ph: 302-655-4440

Rat & Mouse Association, American Fancy   www.afrma.org
9230 64th St   Riverside CA 92509
Ph: 626-966-0350

Rat & Mouse Club of America   www.rmca.org

Rating Association, Internet Content   www.icra.org
1130 Connecticut Ave NW Suite 501   Washington DC 20036
Ph: 202-331-8651 ▪ Fx: 202-331-8652

Rating Council, Media   www.mrc.com
200 W 57th St Suite 204   New York NY 10019
Ph: 212-765-0200 ▪ Fx: 212-765-1868

Rational Recovery   www.rational.org
PO Box 800   Lotus CA 95651
Ph: 530-621-2667 ▪ Fx: 530-622-4296 ▪ TF: 800-303-2873

Raw Materials, National Organization for   www.normeconomics.org
680 E 5 Point Hwy   Charlotte MI 48813
Ph: 517-543-0111

RBA - Retailer's Bakery Association   www.rbanet.com
14239 Park Center Dr   Laurel MD 20707
Ph: 301-725-2149 ▪ Fx: 301-725-2187 ▪ TF: 800-638-0924

Re-Formed Congregation of the Goddess International   www.rcgi.org
PO Box 6677   Madison WI 53716
Ph: 608-226-9998

Reach-Out International   www.reach-out-international.org
1968 Wooddale Ct   Baton Rouge LA 70806
Ph: 225-928-3123 ▪ Fx: 225-924-1512

REACT International Inc   www.reactintl.org
5210 Auth Rd Suite 403   Suitland MD 20746
Ph: 301-316-2900 ▪ Fx: 301-316-2903

Reactors, National Organization of Test Research & Training   www.trtr.org

Read Foundation, National Right to   www.nrrf.org

Readers USA, Rolling   www.rollingreaders.org
4007 Camino Del Rio S Suite 203   San Diego CA 92108
Ph: 619-516-4095 ▪ Fx: 619-516-4096

Reading Association, International   www.reading.org
800 Barksdale Rd   Newark DE 19714
Ph: 302-731-1600 ▪ Fx: 302-731-1057

Reading Conference, National   www.nrconline.org
7044 S 13th St   Oak Creek WI 53154
Ph: 414-768-8000 ▪ Fx: 414-768-8001

Reading Is Fundamental   www.rif.org
1825 Connecticut Ave NW Suite 400   Washington DC 20009
Ph: 202-673-0020 ▪ Fx: 202-287-3196 ▪ TF: 877-743-7323

Reading & Learning Association, College   www.crla.net
PO Box 6251   Auburn CA 95604
Ph: 530-823-1076 ▪ Fx: 530-823-6331

Ready Mixed Concrete Association, National   www.nrmca.org
900 Spring St   Silver Spring MD 20910
Ph: 301-587-1400 ▪ Fx: 301-585-4219

Real Estate Appraisers, National Association of   www.iami.org/narea
1224 N Nokomis NE   Alexandria MN 56308
Ph: 320-763-7626 ▪ Fx: 320-763-9290

Real Estate Association, AIR Commercial   www.airea.com
700 S Flower St Suite 600   Los Angeles CA 90017
Ph: 213-687-8777 ▪ Fx: 213-687-8616

Real Estate, Association of Foreign Investors in   www.afire.org
1300 Pennsylvania Ave NW   Washington DC 20004
Ph: 202-312-1400 ▪ Fx: 202-312-1401

Real Estate Association, Pension   www.prea.org
100 Pearl St 13th Fl   Hartford CT 06103
Ph: 860-692-6341 ▪ Fx: 860-692-6351

Real Estate Brokerage Managers, Council of   www.crb.com
430 N Michigan Ave Suite 300   Chicago IL 60611
Ph: 312-321-4400 ▪ Fx: 312-329-8882 ▪ TF: 800-621-8738

Real Estate Brokers, Association of Industrial   www.aireb.org
710 E Ogden Ave Suite 600   Naperville IL 60563
Ph: 630-579-3254 ▪ Fx: 630-369-2488

Real Estate Brokers, National Association of   www.nareb.com
9831 Greenbelt Rd Suite 309   Lanham MD 20706
Ph: 301-552-9340 ▪ Fx: 301-552-9216 ▪ TF: 800-838-3075

Real Estate Buyer's Agent Council   www.rebac.net
430 N Michigan Ave   Chicago IL 60611
Ph: 312-329-8656 ▪ Fx: 312-329-8632 ▪ TF: 800-648-6224

(Real Estate) CCIM Institute   www.ccim.com
430 N Michigan Ave Suite 800   Chicago IL 60611
Ph: 312-321-4460

Real Estate Companies, National Association of   www.narec.org
PO Box 958   Columbia MD 21044
Ph: 410-992-6476 ▪ Fx: 410-992-6363

(Real Estate) CoreNet Global Inc   www.corenetglobal.org
260 Peachtree St NW Suite 1500   Atlanta GA 30303
Ph: 404-589-3200 ▪ Fx: 404-589-3201 ▪ TF: 800-726-8111

Real Estate, Counselors of   www.cre.org
430 N Michigan Ave 2nd Fl   Chicago IL 60611
Ph: 312-329-8427 ▪ Fx: 312-329-8881

Real Estate Editors, National Association of   www.naree.org
1003 NW 6th Terr   Boca Raton FL 33486
Ph: 561-391-3599

Real Estate Educators Association   www.reea.org
407 Wekiva Springs Rd Suite 241   Longwood FL 32779
Ph: 407-834-6688 ▪ Fx: 407-834-4747

(Real Estate) FIABCI-USA   www.fiabci-usa.com
2000 N 15th St Suite 101   Arlington VA 22201
Ph: 703-524-4279

Real Estate Information Professionals Association   www.reipa.org
PO Box 3159   Durham NC 27715
Ph: 919-383-0044 ▪ Fx: 919-383-0035

Real Estate Institute, International   www.iami.org/irei.cfm
1224 N Nokomis St NE   Alexandria MN 56308
Ph: 320-763-4648 ▪ Fx: 320-763-9290

Real Estate, International Association of Attorneys & Executives in Corporate   www.aecre.org
20106 S Sycamore Dr   Frankfort IL 60423
Ph: 815-464-6019 ▪ Fx: 815-464-8334

Real Estate Investment Fiduciaries, National Council of   www.ncreif.org
2 Prudential Plaza 180 N Stetson Ave Suite 2515   Chicago IL 60601
Ph: 312-819-5890 ▪ Fx: 312-819-5891

Real Estate Investment Managers, National Association of   www.nareim.org
11755 Wilshire Blvd Suite 1380   Los Angeles CA 90025
Ph: 310-479-2219

Real Estate Investment Trusts, National Association of   www.nareit.com
1875 'I' St NW Suite 600   Washington DC 20006
Ph: 202-739-9400 ▪ Fx: 202-739-9401 ▪ TF: 800-362-7348

Real Estate Investors Association, National   www.nationalreia.com
525 W 5th St Suite 230   Covington KY 41011
Ph: 888-762-7342 ▪ Fx: 859-581-5993

Real Estate Lawyers, American College of   www.acrel.org
11300 Rockville Pike Suite 903   Rockville MD 20852
Ph: 301-816-9811 ▪ Fx: 301-816-9786

Real Estate License Law Officials, Association of   www.arello.org
PO Box 230159   Montgomery AL 36123
Ph: 334-260-2902 ▪ Fx: 334-260-2903

Real Estate Management, Institute of   www.irem.org
430 N Michigan Ave   Chicago IL 60611
Ph: 312-329-6000 ▪ Fx: 800-338-4736 ▪ TF: 800-837-0706

(Real Estate) National Association of Counselors   nac.lincoln-grad.org
c/o Lincoln Graduate Ctr 303 W Cypress St   San Antonio TX 78212
Ph: 210-271-0781 ▪ Fx: 210-225-8450

Real Estate Professionals, National Association of Hispanic   www.nahrep.org
404 Camino del Rio S Suite 602   San Diego CA 92108
Ph: 800-964-5373 ▪ Fx: 619-297-3229

Real Estate Roundtable   www.rer.org
1420 New York Ave NW Suite 1100   Washington DC 20005
Ph: 202-639-8400 ▪ Fx: 202-639-8442

Real Estate Service Advisors, Corporate   www.cresa.com
405 Lexington Ave 47th Fl   New York NY 10174
Ph: 212-758-3131 ▪ Fx: 212-980-1977

Real Estate & Urban Economics Association, American   www.areuea.org
PO Box 1148   Portage MI 49081
Ph: 866-273-8321 ▪ Fx: 313-731-0174

Real Estate Women, Association of   www.arew.org
551 5th Ave Suite 3025   New York NY 10176
Ph: 212-599-6181 ▪ Fx: 212-687-4016

Realism Foundation, Aesthetic   www.aestheticrealism.org
141 Greene St   New York NY 10012
Ph: 212-777-4490 ▪ Fx: 212-777-4426

Realtors Land Institute   www.rliland.com
430 N Michigan Ave   Chicago IL 60611
Ph: 312-329-8440 ▪ Fx: 312-329-8633 ▪ TF: 800-441-5263

REALTORS, National Association of   www.realtor.org
430 N Michigan Ave   Chicago IL 60611
Ph: 312-329-8200 ▪ Fx: 312-329-8390 ▪ TF: 800-874-6500

REALTORS, Society of Industrial & Office   www.sior.com
1201 New York Ave NW Suite 350   Washington DC 20005
Ph: 202-449-8200 ▪ Fx: 202-449-8201

REALTORS, Women's Council of   www.wcr.org
430 N Michigan Ave   Chicago IL 60611
Ph: 312-329-8483 ▪ Fx: 312-329-3290

Reason Foundation   www.reason.org
3415 S Sepulveda Blvd Suite 400   Los Angeles CA 90034
Ph: 310-391-2245 ▪ Fx: 310-391-4395

Reason Public Policy Institute   www.rppi.org
3415 S Sepulveda Blvd Suite 400   Los Angeles CA 90034
Ph: 310-391-2245 ▪ Fx: 310-391-4395

Reasons to Believe   www.reasons.org
PO Box 5978   Pasadena CA 91117
Ph: 626-335-1480 ▪ Fx: 626-852-0178 ▪ TF: 800-482-7836

Reb Meyer Baal Haness Charity, Kolel Chibas Jerusalem -   www.chibasjerusalem.com
4802-A 12th Ave   Brooklyn NY 11219
Ph: 718-633-7112 ▪ Fx: 718-633-5783

Rebuilding Together   www.rebuildingtogether.org
1536 16th St NW   Washington DC 20036
Ph: 202-483-9083 ▪ Fx: 202-483-9081 ▪ TF: 800-473-4229

Receptive Services Association   www.rsana.com
17000 Commerce Pkwy Suite C   Mount Laurel NJ 08054
Ph: 856-638-0423 ▪ Fx: 856-439-0525

Reciprocal Trade Association, International   www.irta.com
140 Metro Park   Rochester NY 14623
Ph: 716-424-2940 ▪ Fx: 716-424-2964

Reclamation, American Society of Mining &   ces.ca.uky.edu/asmr
3134 Montavesta Rd   Lexington KY 40502
Ph: 859-335-6529

Reclamationists, National Association of State Land   www.crc.siu.edu/naslr.htm
Southern Illinois Univ Coal Research Ctr   Carbondale IL 62901
Ph: 618-536-5521

Reconciliation, Fellowship of www.forusa.org
PO Box 271 Nyack NY 10960
Ph: 845-358-4601 ▪ Fx: 845-358-4924

Reconciling Ministries Network www.rmnetwork.org
3801 N Keeler Ave Chicago IL 60641
Ph: 773-736-5526 ▪ Fx: 773-736-5475

Reconstruction, National Foundation for Facial www.nffr.org
317 E 34th St New York NY 10016
Ph: 212-263-6656 ▪ Fx: 212-263-7534

Reconstruction Specialists Inc, National Association of www.napars.org
Professional Accident PO Box 65 Brandywine MD 20613
Ph: 301-843-0048

Reconstructionist Federation, Jewish www.jrf.org
7804 Montgomery Ave Suite 9 Elkins Park PA 19027
Ph: 215-782-8500 ▪ Fx: 215-782-8805

Reconstructionist Rabbinical Association www.therra.org
1299 Church Rd Wyncote PA 19095
Ph: 215-576-5210 ▪ Fx: 215-576-8051

Reconstructive Microsurgery, American Society for www.microsurg.org
20 N Michigan Ave Suite 700 Chicago IL 60602
Ph: 312-456-9579 ▪ Fx: 312-782-0553

Reconstructive Surgery, American Academy of www.facial-plastic-surgery.org
Facial Plastic & 310 S Henry St Alexandria VA 22314
Ph: 703-299-9291 ▪ Fx: 703-299-8898 ▪ TF: 800-332-3223

Record Collectors, International Association of Jazz rhythmsociety.net/iajrc

Record Services, Christian www.christianrecord.org
4444 S 52nd St Lincoln NE 68516
Ph: 402-488-0981 ▪ Fx: 402-488-7582

Recorded Sound Collections, Association for www.arsc-audio.org
PO Box 543 Annapolis MD 21404
Ph: 410-757-0488 ▪ Fx: 410-349-0175

Recorder Society, American ourworld.compuserve.com/homepages/recorder/
PO Box 631 Littleton CO 80160
Ph: 303-347-1120 ▪ Fx: 303-347-1181

Recorders Election Officials & Clerks, National Association www.nacrc.org
of County PO Box 3159 Durham NC 27715
Ph: 919-384-8446 ▪ Fx: 919-383-0035

Recording Academy www.grammy.com
3402 Pico Blvd Santa Monica CA 90405
Ph: 310-392-3777 ▪ Fx: 310-392-2306 ▪ TF: 800-423-2017

(Recording Artists) Ladyslipper Inc www.ladyslipper.org
3205 Hillsborough Rd PO Box 3124 Durham NC 27715
Ph: 919-383-8773 ▪ Fx: 919-383-3525 ▪ TF: 800-634-6044

Recording Arts & Sciences, National Academy of www.grammy.com
3402 Pico Blvd Santa Monica CA 90405
Ph: 310-392-3777 ▪ Fx: 310-392-2306 ▪ TF: 800-423-2017

Recording for the Blind & Dyslexic www.rfbd.org
20 Roszel Rd Princeton NJ 08540
Ph: 609-452-0606 ▪ Fx: 609-520-7990 ▪ TF: 800-221-4792

Recording Industry Association of America Inc www.riaa.com
1330 Connecticut Ave NW Suite 300 Washington DC 20036
Ph: 202-775-0101 ▪ Fx: 202-775-7253 ▪ TF: 800-223-2328

Recording Industry Association PAC
1330 Connecticut Ave NW Suite 300 Washington DC 20036
Ph: 202-775-0101 ▪ Fx: 202-775-7253

Recording Media Association, International www.recordingmedia.org
182 Nassau St Suite 204 Princeton NJ 08542
Ph: 609-279-1700 ▪ Fx: 609-279-1999

Recording Merchandisers, National Association of www.narm.com
9 Eves Dr Suite 120 Marlton NJ 08053
Ph: 856-596-2221 ▪ Fx: 856-596-3268

Recording Rights Coalition, Home www.hrrc.org
PO Box 14267 Washington DC 20044
Ph: 202-628-9212 ▪ Fx: 202-628-9227 ▪ TF: 800-282-8273

Recording Services, Society of Professional Audio www.spars.com
PO Box 770845 Memphis TN 38177
Ph: 901-747-3111 ▪ Fx: 800-771-7727

Recordings Network, Gospel www.gospelrecordings.com
41823 Enterprise Cir N Temecula CA 92590
Ph: 909-719-1650 ▪ Fx: 909-719-1651 ▪ TF: 888-444-7872

Records Administrators, National Association of Government www.nagara.org
Archives & 48 Howard St Albany NY 12207
Ph: 518-463-8644 ▪ Fx: 518-463-8656

Records & Information Services Management International, www.prismintl.org
Professional 605 Benson Rd Suite B Garner NC 27529
Ph: 919-771-0657 ▪ Fx: 919-771-0457 ▪ TF: 800-336-9793

Records Managers, Institute of Certified www.icrm.org
318 Oak St Syracuse NY 13203
Ph: 315-234-1904 ▪ Fx: 315-474-1784 ▪ TF: 877-244-3128

Records Research Association, National Public www.nprra.org
PO Box 3159 Durham NC 27705
Ph: 919-384-0434 ▪ Fx: 919-383-0035

Recovery Inc www.recovery-inc.com
802 N Dearborn St Chicago IL 60610
Ph: 312-337-5661 ▪ Fx: 312-337-5756

Recovery Association, American www.repo.org
PO Box 231565 New Orleans LA 70183
Ph: 504-738-6404 ▪ Fx: 504-738-7910

Recovery, Rational www.rational.org
PO Box 800 Lotus CA 95651
Ph: 530-621-2667 ▪ Fx: 530-622-4296 ▪ TF: 800-303-2873

Recovery, SMART www.smartrecovery.org
7537 Mentor Ave Suite 306 Mentor OH 44060
Ph: 440-951-5357 ▪ Fx: 440-951-5358

Recreation, American Association for Leisure & www.aahperd.org/aalr
1900 Association Dr Reston VA 20191
Ph: 703-476-3400 ▪ Fx: 703-476-9527 ▪ TF: 800-213-7193

Recreation, Americans for Our Heritage & www.ahrinfo.org
1615 M St NW Washington DC 20036
Ph: 202-429-2606 ▪ Fx: 202-429-2621

Recreation, Americans for Responsible www.arra-access.com

Recreation Association, American Therapeutic www.atra-tr.org
1414 Prince St Suite 204 Alexandria VA 22314
Ph: 703-683-9420 ▪ Fx: 703-683-9431

Recreation Association, Canadian Parks & www.cpra.ca
2197 Riverside Dr Suite 404 Ottawa ON K1H7X3
Ph: 613-523-5315 ▪ Fx: 613-523-1182

Recreation Association, National Forest www.nfra.org
PO Box 488 Woodlake CA 93286
Ph: 559-564-2365 ▪ Fx: 559-564-2048

Recreation Association, Resort & Commercial www.r-c-r-a.org
PO Box 2437 Aurora IL 60507
Ph: 630-892-2175 ▪ Fx: 630-801-4202

Recreation Certification Inc, National Council for Therapeutic www.nctrc.org
7 Elmwood Dr New City NY 10956
Ph: 845-639-1439 ▪ Fx: 845-639-1471

Recreation Coalition, American www.funoutdoors.com
1225 New York Ave NW Suite 450 Washington DC 20005
Ph: 202-682-9530 ▪ Fx: 202-682-9529

Recreation & Education, Association of Outdoor www.aore.org
2705 Robin St Bloomington IL 61704
Ph: 309-829-9189

Recreation Liaison Officers, National Association of State Outdoor
3116 Woodbrook Pl Boise ID 83706
Ph: 208-384-5421

Recreation & Park Association, National www.nrpa.org
22377 Belmont Ridge Rd Ashburn VA 20148
Ph: 703-858-0784 ▪ Fx: 703-858-0794 ▪ TF: 800-626-6772

Recreation Resource Planners, National Association of www.narrp.org

Recreation Society, American Park &
c/o National Recreation & Park Assn 22377 Belmont Ridge
   Rd Ashburn VA 20148
Ph: 703-858-4741 ▪ Fx: 703-858-0794

Recreation Society, National Therapeutic
c/o National Recreation & Park Assn 22377 Belmont Ridge
   Rd Ashburn VA 20148
Ph: 703-858-2151 ▪ Fx: 703-858-0794 ▪ TF: 800-626-6772

Recreation Vehicle Dealers Association www.rvda.org
3930 University Dr Suite 200 Fairfax VA 22030
Ph: 703-591-7130 ▪ Fx: 703-591-0734 ▪ TF: 800-336-0355

Recreation Vehicle Industry Association www.rvia.org
1896 Preston White Dr Reston VA 20191
Ph: 703-620-6003 ▪ Fx: 703-620-5071 ▪ TF: 800-336-0154

Recreation Vehicle Rental Association www.rvra.org
3930 University Dr Fairfax VA 22030
Ph: 703-591-7130 ▪ Fx: 703-591-0734

Recreational Boating & Fishing Foundation www.rbff.org
601 N Fairfax St Suite 140 Alexandria VA 22314
Ph: 703-519-0013 ▪ Fx: 703-519-9565

Recreational Golf Association, American www.rentamark.com/arga
PO Box 35215 Chicago IL 60707
Ph: 708-453-0080 ▪ Fx: 708-453-0083

Recreational Park Trailer Industry Association Inc www.rptia.com
30 Greenville St 2nd Fl Newnan GA 30263
Ph: 770-251-2672 ▪ Fx: 770-251-0025

Recreational Sports Association, National Intramural- www.nirsa.org
4185 SW Research Way Corvallis OR 97333
Ph: 541-766-8211 ▪ Fx: 541-766-8284

Recreational Vehicle Aftermarket Association www.rvaftermarket.org
54 Westerly Rd Camp Hill PA 17011
Ph: 717-730-7330 ▪ Fx: 717-730-0544

Recreational Vehicle Club, Good Sam www.goodsamclub.com
PO Box 6888 Englewood CO 80155
Ph: 800-234-3450

Recreational Vehicle Club, Holiday Rambler www.hrrvc.org
PO Box 587 Wakarusa IN 46573
Ph: 574-862-7330 ▪ Fx: 574-862-7390 ▪ TF: 877-702-5415

Recreational Vehicle Owners Club, National www.nrvoc.org
PO Box 520 Gonzalez FL 32560
Ph: 850-937-8354 ▪ Fx: 850-937-8356 ▪ TF: 800-281-9186

(Recreational Vehicles) Loners on Wheels www.lonersonwheels.com
PO Box 1060-WB Cape Girardeau MO 63702
Ph: 888-569-4478 ▪ Fx: 573-651-8601

(Recreationists) BlueRibbon Coalition www.sharetrails.org
4555 Burley Dr Pocatello ID 83202
Ph: 208-237-1008 ▪ Fx: 208-237-9424 ▪ TF: 800-258-3742

Recruiters, Association of Staff Physician www.aspr.org
1711 W County Rd B Suite 300N Roseville MN 55113
Ph: 651-635-0359 ▪ Fx: 651-635-0307 ▪ TF: 800-830-2777

Recruiters, National Association of Executive www.naer.org
1320 Tower Rd Suite 2262 Schaumburg IL 60173
Ph: 847-598-3680 ▪ Fx: 847-885-5681

Recruiters, National Association of Physician www.napr.org
PO Box 150127 Altamonte Springs FL 32715
Ph: 407-774-7880 ▪ Fx: 407-774-6440 ▪ TF: 800-726-5613

Recruitment, International Association of Corporate & Professional www.iacpr.org
20 N Wacker Dr Suite 2262 Chicago IL 60606
Ph: 312-630-9881 ▪ Fx: 312-630-9882

Rectal Surgeons, American Society of Colon & www.fascrs.org
85 W Algonquin Rd Suite 550 Arlington Heights IL 60005
Ph: 847-290-9184 ▪ Fx: 847-290-9203

Rectal Surgery, American Board of Colon & www.abcrs.org
20600 Eureka Rd Suite 600 Taylor MI 48180
Ph: 734-282-9400 ▪ Fx: 734-282-9402

(Recycled Oil Saves Energy), Project ROSE www.eng.ua.edu/~prose
PO Box 870203 Tuscaloosa AL 35487
Ph: 205-348-4878 ▪ Fx: 205-348-7558

Recycled Paperboard Technical Association
920 Davis Rd Suite 306 Elgin IL 60123
Ph: 847-622-2544 ▪ Fx: 847-622-2546

Recycled Textile Association, Secondary Materials &
7910 Woodmont Ave Suite 1130 Bethesda MD 20814
Ph: 301-656-1077 ▪ Fx: 301-656-1079
www.smartasn.org

Recycled Textiles Inc, Shippers of
7910 Woodmont Ave Suite 1130 Bethesda MD 20814
Ph: 301-656-1077 ▪ Fx: 301-656-1079
www.smartasn.org

Recyclers, Alliance of Foam Packaging
1298 Cronson Blvd Suite 201 Crofton MD 21114
Ph: 410-451-8340 ▪ Fx: 410-451-8343 ▪ TF: 800-944-8448
www.epspackaging.org

Recyclers Association, Automotive
3975 Fair Ridge Dr Suite 20N Fairfax VA 22033
Ph: 703-385-1001 ▪ Fx: 703-385-1494
www.autorecyc.org

Recyclers, Association of Battery
PO Box 290286 Tampa FL 33687
Ph: 813-626-6151 ▪ Fx: 813-622-8388

Recyclers League, Professional Electrical Apparatus
6257 Lakepoint Pl Parker CO 80134
Ph: 303-840-1059 ▪ Fx: 720-851-6090
www.pearl1.org

Recyclers, NORA: Association of Responsible
5965 Amber Ridge Rd Haymarket VA 20169
Ph: 703-753-4277 ▪ Fx: 703-753-2445
www.noranews.org

Recycling Association, National Onsite Wastewater
PO Box 1270 Edgewater MD 21037
Ph: 410-798-1697 ▪ Fx: 410-798-5741
www.nowra.org

Recycling Coalition, Cement Kiln
1730 K St NW Suite 710 Washington DC 20006
Ph: 202-466-6802 ▪ Fx: 202-466-5009
www.ckrc.org

Recycling Coalition, National
1325 G St NW Suite 1025 Washington DC 20005
Ph: 202-347-0450 ▪ Fx: 202-347-0449
www.nrc-recycle.org

Recycling, Council for Textile
7910 Woodmont Ave Suite 1130 Bethesda MD 20814
Ph: 301-718-0671 ▪ Fx: 301-656-1079
www.smartasn.org

Recycling Industries Inc, Institute of Scrap
1325 G St NW Suite 1000 Washington DC 20005
Ph: 202-737-1770 ▪ Fx: 202-626-0900
www.isri.org

Recycling & Reclaiming Association, Asphalt
3 Church Cir PMB 250 Annapolis MD 21401
Ph: 410-267-0023 ▪ Fx: 410-267-7546
www.arra.org

Red Angus Association of America
4201 N I-35 Denton TX 76207
Ph: 940-387-3502 ▪ Fx: 940-383-4036
www.redangus.org

Red Cedar Lumber Association, Western
1501-700 W Pender St Vancouver BC V6C1G8
Ph: 604-684-0266 ▪ Fx: 604-687-4930
www.wrcla.org

Red Cedar Pole Association, Western
2405 61st Ave SE Mercer Island WA 98040
Ph: 800-410-1917 ▪ Fx: 206-275-4755
www.preservedwood.com/wrcpa/main.html

Red Cross, American
2025 'E' St NW Washington DC 20006
Ph: 202-303-4498 ▪ Fx: 202-639-3711 ▪ TF: 800-842-2200
www.redcross.org

Red Cross International Services, American
1730 'E' St NW Washington DC 20006
Ph: 202-942-2506 ▪ Fx: 202-728-6404
www.redcross.org/services/intl

Red Cross Overseas Association, American
200 S Lebanon Rd Loveland OH 45140
Ph: 513-683-1377

Red Magen David for Israel, American
888 7th Ave Suite 403 New York NY 10106
Ph: 212-757-1627 ▪ Fx: 212-757-4662 ▪ TF: 866-632-2763
www.armdi.org

Red Men, Improved Order of
4521 Speight Ave Waco TX 76711
Ph: 254-756-1221 ▪ Fx: 254-756-4828
www.redmen.org

Red Poll Association, American
PO Box 147 Bethany MO 64424
Ph: 660-425-7318 ▪ Fx: 660-425-8374
www.redpollusa.org

Red Sea Team International
PO Box 2047 Lexington SC 29071
Ph: 803-358-2330
www.rsmt.u-net.com

Red & White Dairy Cattle Association
3085 S Valley Rd Crystal Spring PA 15536
Ph: 814-735-4221 ▪ Fx: 814-735-3473
www.redandwhitecattle.com

Red Wing Collectors Society Inc
PO Box 50 Red Wing MN 55066
Ph: 651-388-4004 ▪ TF: 800-977-7927
www.redwingcollectors.org

Redevelopment Officials, National Association of Housing &
630 'I' St NW Washington DC 20001
Ph: 202-289-3500 ▪ Fx: 202-289-8181 ▪ TF: 877-866-2476
www.nahro.org

Redwood Association, California
405 Enfrente Dr Suite 200 Novato CA 94949
Ph: 415-382-0662 ▪ Fx: 415-382-8531 ▪ TF: 888-225-7339
www.calredwood.org

Redwood Region Logging Conference
PO Box 7127 Eureka CA 95502
Ph: 707-443-4091 ▪ Fx: 707-443-0926
www.rrlc.net

Redwoods League, Save-the-
114 Sansome St Rm 1200 San Francisco CA 94104
Ph: 415-362-2352 ▪ Fx: 415-362-7017 ▪ TF: 888-836-0005
www.savetheredwoods.org

Reed Society, International Double
2423 Lawndale Rd Finksburg MD 21048
Ph: 410-871-0658 ▪ Fx: 410-871-0659
www.idrs.org

Reengineering International Association, Workflow &
2436 N Federal Hwy Suite 374 Lighthouse Point FL 33064
Ph: 954-782-3376 ▪ Fx: 954-782-6365 ▪ TF: 800-749-2742
www.waria.com

Reeve Christopher Paralysis Foundation
500 Morris Ave Springfield NJ 07081
Ph: 973-379-2690 ▪ Fx: 973-912-9433 ▪ TF: 800-225-0292
www.christopherreeve.org

Reference & User Services Association
50 E Huron St Chicago IL 60611
Ph: 312-280-4398 ▪ Fx: 312-944-8085 ▪ TF: 800-545-2433
www.ala.org/rusa

Referral Agencies, National Association of Child Care Resource &
1319 F St NW Suite 500 Washington DC 20004
Ph: 202-393-5501 ▪ Fx: 202-393-1109 ▪ TF: 800-424-2246
www.naccrra.org

Referral Systems, Alliance of Information &
PO Box 31668 Seattle WA 98103
Ph: 206-632-2477 ▪ Fx: 206-632-0855
www.airs.org

Refiners Association, National Petrochemical &
1899 L St NW Suite 1000 Washington DC 20036
Ph: 202-457-0480 ▪ Fx: 202-457-0486
www.npradc.org

Reflexology, International Institute of
5650 1st Ave N Saint Petersburg FL 33710
Ph: 727-343-4811 ▪ Fx: 727-381-2807
www.reflexology-usa.net

Reform, Council for Government
3124 N 10th St Arlington VA 22201
Ph: 703-243-7400 ▪ Fx: 703-243-7403
www.govreform.org

Reform Judaism - Federation of Temple Sisterhoods, Women of
633 3rd Ave New York NY 10017
Ph: 212-650-4050 ▪ Fx: 212-650-4059
www.rj.org/wrj

Reform, Manufactured Housing Association for Regulatory
1331 Pennsylvania Ave NW Suite 508 Washington DC 20004
Ph: 202-783-4087 ▪ Fx: 202-783-4075

Reform Now, Association of Community Organizations for
739 8th St SE Washington DC 20003
Ph: 202-547-2500 ▪ Fx: 202-547-2483 ▪ TF: 877-552-2676
www.acorn.org

REFORMA National Association to Promote Library Services to Latinos & the Spanish-Speaking PO Box
25963 Scottsdale AZ 85255
Ph: 480-471-7452 ▪ Fx: 480-471-7442
www.reforma.org

Reformation Research, Society for
Hope College Dept of History PO Box 900 Holland MI 49422
Ph: 616-395-7591
www.reformationresearch.org

Reformed Church in America
475 Riverside Dr 18th Fl New York NY 10115
Ph: 212-870-3071 ▪ Fx: 212-870-2499 ▪ TF: 800-722-9977
www.rca.org

Reformed Ecumenical Council
2050 Breton Rd SE Suite 102 Grand Rapids MI 49546
Ph: 616-949-2910

Refractive Surgery, American Society of Cataract &
4000 Legato Rd Suite 850 Fairfax VA 22033
Ph: 703-591-2220 ▪ Fx: 703-591-0614 ▪ TF: 800-451-1339
www.ascrs.org

Refractive Surgery, International Society of
655 Beach St San Francisco CA 94109
Ph: 415-561-8581 ▪ Fx: 415-561-8575
www.isrs.org

Refractories Institute
650 Smithfield St Suite 1160 Pittsburgh PA 15222
Ph: 412-281-6787 ▪ Fx: 412-281-6881
www.refractoriesinstitute.org

Refractory Ceramic Fibers Coalition
1133 Connecticut Ave NW Suite 1200 Washington DC 20036
Ph: 202-775-2388 ▪ Fx: 202-833-8491
www.rcfc.net

Refrigerated Foods Association
2971 Flowers Rd S Suite 266 Atlanta GA 30341
Ph: 770-452-0660 ▪ Fx: 770-455-3879 ▪ TF: 800-719-1309
www.refrigeratedfoods.org

Refrigerated Foods Association, National Frozen &
4755 Linglestown Rd Suite 300 Harrisburg PA 17112
Ph: 717-657-8601 ▪ Fx: 717-657-9862
www.nfraweb.org

Refrigerated Transportation Association, International
4255 S Buckley Rd Suite 118 Aurora CO 80013
Ph: 888-454-4782 ▪ Fx: 720-851-6090
www.irta.org

Refrigerated Warehouses, International Association of
1500 King St Suite 201 Alexandria VA 22314
Ph: 703-373-4300 ▪ Fx: 703-373-4301
www.iarw.org

Refrigerating & Air-Conditioning Engineers Inc, American Society of Heating 1791 Tullie Cir NE Atlanta GA 30329
Ph: 404-636-8400 ▪ Fx: 404-321-5478 ▪ TF: 800-527-4723
www.ashrae.org

Refrigerating Engineers & Technicians Association
4700 W Lake Ave Glenview IL 60025
Ph: 847-375-4738 ▪ Fx: 877-218-8369
www.reta.com

Refrigeration Distributors International, Heating Airconditioning &
1389 Dublin Rd Columbus OH 43215
Ph: 614-488-1835 ▪ Fx: 614-488-0482 ▪ TF: 888-253-2128
www.hardinet.org

Refrigeration Institute, Air-Conditioning &
4100 N Fairfax Dr Suite 200 Arlington VA 22203
Ph: 703-524-8800 ▪ Fx: 703-528-3816
www.ari.org

Refrigeration Products Institute, Automotive
PO Box 9000 Fort Worth TX 76147
Ph: 817-732-4600 ▪ Fx: 817-732-9610

Refrigeration Service Engineers Society
1666 Rand Rd Des Plaines IL 60016
Ph: 847-297-6464 ▪ Fx: 847-297-5038 ▪ TF: 800-297-5660
www.rses.org

Refugee Aid, American Near East
1522 K St NW Suite 202 Washington DC 20005
Ph: 202-347-2558 ▪ Fx: 202-682-1637
www.anera.org

Refugee Committee, American
430 Oak Grove St Suite 204 Minneapolis MN 55403
Ph: 612-872-7060 ▪ Fx: 612-607-6499
www.archq.org

Refugee Rights, National Network for Immigrant &
310 8th St Suite 303 Oakland CA 94607
Ph: 510-465-1984 ▪ Fx: 510-465-1885
www.nnirr.org

Refugee Service, Lutheran Immigration &
700 Light St Baltimore MD 21230
Ph: 410-230-2700 ▪ Fx: 410-230-2890
www.lirs.org

Refugee Service, Jesuit - North America
1616 P St NW Suite 400 Washington DC 20036
Ph: 202-462-0400 ▪ Fx: 202-328-9212
www.jesref.org

Refugee Services of America, Immigration &
1717 Massachusetts Ave NW Suite 200 Washington DC 20036
Ph: 202-797-2105 ▪ Fx: 202-797-2363
www.irsa-uscr.org

Refugee Services, Migration &
US Conference of Catholic Bishops 3211 4th St
NE Washington DC 20017
Ph: 202-541-3000 ▪ Fx: 202-541-3351
www.nccbuscc.org/mrs

Refugee Women in Development Inc www.refwid.org
5501 Seminary Rd Suite 1606-S Falls Church VA 22041
Ph: 703-931-6442 ▪ Fx: 703-931-5906

Refugees International www.refugeesinternational.org
1705 'N' St NW Washington DC 20036
Ph: 202-828-0110 ▪ Fx: 202-828-0819 ▪ TF: 800-733-8433

Refugees, US Committee for www.irsa-uscr.org
1717 Massachusetts Ave NW Suite 200 Washington DC 20036
Ph: 202-347-3507 ▪ Fx: 202-347-3418

(Refugees) USA for UNHCR www.usaforunhcr.org
1775 K St NW Suite 290 Washington DC 20006
Ph: 202-296-1115 ▪ Fx: 202-296-1081 ▪ TF: 800-770-1100

Refuse & Resist! www.refuseandresist.org
305 Madison Ave Suite 166 New York NY 10165
Ph: 212-713-5657

REGAP Network, National www.regap.org
PO Box 4454 Cary IL 60013
Ph: 847-217-1836

Regional Airline Association www.raa.org
2025 M St NW Suite 800 Washington DC 20036
Ph: 202-367-1100 ▪ Fx: 202-367-2100

Regional Councils, National Association of www.narc.org
1666 Connecticut Ave NW Suite 300 Washington DC 20009
Ph: 202-986-1032 ▪ Fx: 202-986-1038

Regional Information Systems Association, Urban & www.urisa.org
1460 Renaissance Dr Suite 305 Park Ridge IL 60068
Ph: 847-824-6300 ▪ Fx: 847-824-6363

Regional Magazine Association, City & www.citymag.org
4929 Wilshire Blvd Suite 428 Los Angeles CA 90010
Ph: 323-937-5514 ▪ Fx: 323-937-0959

Regional Reporters Association www.rra.org
PO Box 254 Washington DC 20044
Ph: 202-662-8731 ▪ Fx: 202-662-8996

Regional Science Association International www.regionalscience.org
Univ of Illinois Bevier Hall Rm 83 905 S Goodwin Urbana IL 61801
Ph: 217-333-8904 ▪ Fx: 217-333-3065

Regis System Users Group
11 Spring St Hallowell ME 04347
Ph: 207-395-4837

Register of Professional Archaeologists www.rpanet.org
5024-R Campbell Blvd Baltimore MD 21236
Ph: 410-933-3486 ▪ Fx: 410-931-8111

Registered Financial Planners Institute www.rfpi.com
2001 Cooper Foster Park Rd Amherst OH 44001
Ph: 440-282-7176 ▪ Fx: 440-282-8027

Registrars & Admissions Officers, American Association www.aacrao.org
of Collegiate 1 Dupont Cir NW Suite 520 Washington DC 20036
Ph: 202-293-9161 ▪ Fx: 202-872-8857

Registrars & Admissions Officers, National Association of www.vsu.edu/nacdrao
College Deans Albany State Univ 504 College Dr Albany GA 31705
Ph: 229-430-4638 ▪ Fx: 229-430-2953

Registrars, Independent Association of Accredited www.iaar.org
3942 N Upland St Arlington VA 22207
Ph: 703-533-9539 ▪ Fx: 703-533-1612

Registration Boards, Council of Landscape Architectural www.clarb.org
144 Church St NW Suite 201 Vienna VA 22180
Ph: 703-319-8380 ▪ Fx: 703-319-8290

Registration Center for Study Abroad, National www.nrcsa.com
PO Box 1393 Milwaukee WI 53201
Ph: 414-278-0631 ▪ Fx: 414-271-8884

Registry of Interpreters for the Deaf Inc www.rid.org
333 Commerce St Alexandria VA 22314
Ph: 703-838-0030 ▪ Fx: 703-838-0454

Regulatory Affairs Professionals Society www.raps.org
11300 Rockville Pike Suite 1000 Rockville MD 20852
Ph: 301-770-2920 ▪ Fx: 301-770-2924

Regulatory Boards, Federation of Associations of www.farb.org
1603 Orrington Ave Suite 2080-F Evanston IL 60201
Ph: 847-328-7909 ▪ Fx: 847-864-0588

Regulatory & Clinical Associates, Organization of www.orcanw.org
PO Box 3490 Redmond WA 98052
Ph: 206-464-0825

Regulatory Reform, Manufactured Housing Association for
1331 Pennsylvania Ave NW Suite 508 Washington DC 20004
Ph: 202-783-4087 ▪ Fx: 202-783-4075

Rehabilitation Administration Association, National www.rehabadmin.org
1020 W 5th St Dickinson ND 58601
Ph: 701-227-7415

Rehabilitation, American Academy of Physical Medicine & www.aapmr.org
1 IBM Plaza Suite 2500 Chicago IL 60611
Ph: 312-464-9700 ▪ Fx: 312-464-0227

Rehabilitation, American Association of Cardiovascular & www.aacvpr.org
Pulmonary 401 N Michigan Ave Suite 2200 Chicago IL 60611
Ph: 312-321-5146 ▪ Fx: 312-527-6635

Rehabilitation, American Board of Physical Medicine & www.abpmr.org
3015 Allegro Park Ln SW Rochester MN 55902
Ph: 507-282-1776 ▪ Fx: 507-282-9242

Rehabilitation, American Osteopathic College of Physical www.aocpmr.org
Medicine & 314 S Knight Ave Park Ridge IL 60068
Ph: 847-825-2515 ▪ Fx: 847-825-2509

Rehabilitation Association, National www.nationalrehab.org
633 S Washington St Alexandria VA 22314
Ph: 703-836-0850 ▪ Fx: 703-836-0848 ▪ TF: 888-258-4295

Rehabilitation Association, National Housing & housingonline.com
1625 Massachusetts Ave NW Suite 601 Washington DC 20036
Ph: 202-939-1750 ▪ Fx: 202-265-4435

Rehabilitation, Council on Chiropractic Physiological Therapeutics & www.ccptr.org
312 Courtyard Dr Hillsborough NJ 08844
Ph: 908-722-9075 ▪ Fx: 908-722-1144

Rehabilitation Council, International Wildlife www.iwrc-online.org
829 Bancroft Way Berkeley CA 94710
Ph: 707-864-1761 ▪ Fx: 707-864-3106

Rehabilitation Counseling Association, American www.nchrtm.okstate.edu/arca
c/o American Counseling Assn 5999 Stevenson Ave Alexandria VA 22304
Ph: 703-823-9800 ▪ Fx: 703-823-0252 ▪ TF: 800-545-2223

Rehabilitation Counseling Association, National nrca-net.org
8807 Sudley Rd Suite 102 Manassas VA 20110
Ph: 703-361-2077 ▪ Fx: 703-361-2489

Rehabilitation Counselor Certification, Commission on www.crccertification.com
1835 Rohlwing Rd Suite E Rolling Meadows IL 60008
Ph: 847-394-2104 ▪ Fx: 847-394-2172

(Rehabilitation) Delancey Street Foundation
600 Embarcadero San Francisco CA 94107
Ph: 415-957-9800 ▪ Fx: 415-512-5141

Rehabilitation Education, National Council on www.rehabeducators.org
CSU Fresno School of Education & Human Development 5005 N Maple Ave MS 3 Fresno CA 93740
Ph: 559-278-0325 ▪ Fx: 559-278-0098

Rehabilitation Engineering & Assistive Technology Society of www.resna.org
North America 1700 N Moore St Suite 1540 Arlington VA 22209
Ph: 703-524-6686 ▪ Fx: 703-524-6630

Rehabilitation Engineering, National Institute for www.angelfire.com/nj/nire2
PO Box T Hewitt NJ 07421
Ph: 973-853-6585 ▪ TF: 800-736-2216

Rehabilitation of Errants, Citizens United for www.curenational.org
PO Box 2310 Washington DC 20013
Ph: 202-789-2126

Rehabilitation Facilities, Commission on Accreditation of www.carf.org
4891 E Grant Rd Tucson AZ 85712
Ph: 520-325-1044 ▪ Fx: 520-318-1129

Rehabilitation Information Center, National www.naric.com
4200 Forbes Blvd Suite 202 Lanham MD 20706
Ph: 301-459-5900 ▪ Fx: 301-459-4263 ▪ TF: 800-346-2742

Rehabilitation Instructors, National www.nationalrehab.org/website/divs/nari.html
Association of 633 S Washington St Alexandria VA 22314
Ph: 703-836-0850 ▪ Fx: 703-836-0848 ▪ TF: 800-671-6840

Rehabilitation International www.rehab-international.org
25 E 21st St 4th Fl New York NY 10010
Ph: 212-420-1500 ▪ Fx: 212-505-0871

Rehabilitation Medicine, American Congress of www.acrm.org
6801 Lake Plaza Dr Suite B-205 Indianapolis IN 46220
Ph: 317-915-2250 ▪ Fx: 317-915-2245

Rehabilitation Nurses, Association of www.rehabnurse.org
4700 W Lake Ave Glenview IL 60025
Ph: 847-375-4710 ▪ Fx: 877-734-9384

Rehabilitation, Physiatric Association of Spine www.aapmr.org/passor.htm
Sports & Occupational 1 IBM Plaza Suite 2500 Chicago IL 60611
Ph: 312-464-9700 ▪ Fx: 312-464-0227

Rehabilitation Professionals, International Association of www.rehabpro.org
3540 Soqel Ave Suite A Santa Cruz CA 95062
Ph: 831-464-4892 ▪ Fx: 831-576-1417 ▪ TF: 800-240-9059

Rehabilitation Programs in Computer Technology, Association of www.arpct.org
503 S York St Denver CO 80209
Ph: 303-733-2111 ▪ Fx: 303-733-2225

Rehabilitation Providers & Agencies, National Association of www.naranet.org
12100 Sunset Hills Rd Suite 130 Reston VA 20190
Ph: 703-437-4377 ▪ Fx: 703-435-4390

Rehabilitation Providers Association, American Medical www.amrpa.org
1710 'N' St NW Washington DC 20036
Ph: 202-223-1920 ▪ Fx: 202-223-1925 ▪ TF: 888-346-4624

Rehabilitation Services, International Association of Psychosocial www.iapsrs.org
601 N Hammonds Ferry Rd Suite A Linthicum MD 21090
Ph: 410-789-7054 ▪ Fx: 410-789-7675

Rehabilitative Audiology, Academy of www.audrehab.org
PO Box 26532 Minneapolis MN 55426
Ph: 952-920-0484 ▪ Fx: 952-920-6098

Reiki Alliance www.reikialliance.com
204 Chestnut Kellogg ID 83837
Ph: 208-783-3535 ▪ Fx: 208-783-4848

Reinforced Concrete Research Council
Texas A&M Univ Dept of Civil Engineering MS 3136 College Station TX 77843
Ph: 979-845-1940 ▪ Fx: 979-845-6554

Reinforcing Steel Contractors, National Association of www.narsc.com
10382 Main St Suite 200 PO Box 280 Fairfax VA 22030
Ph: 703-591-1870 ▪ Fx: 703-591-1895

Reining Horse Association, National www.nrha.com
3000 NW 10th St Oklahoma City OK 73107
Ph: 405-946-7400 ▪ Fx: 405-946-8410

Reining Horse Association, National Morgan www.nmrha.com

Reinsurance Association of America www.reinsurance.org
1301 Pennsylvania Ave NW Suite 900 Washington DC 20004
Ph: 202-638-3690 ▪ Fx: 202-638-0936 ▪ TF: 800-638-3651

Reinsurance Exchange, American Cargo War Risk www.amich.org/acwHome.htm
30 Broad St 7th Fl New York NY 10004
Ph: 212-405-2835 ▪ Fx: 212-240-0654

Reinsurance Underwriters Association, Intermediaries & www.irua.com
971 Rt 202 N Branchburg NJ 08876
Ph: 908-203-0211 ▪ Fx: 908-203-0213

Reinvestment Coalition, National Community www.ncrc.org
733 15th St NW Suite 540 Washington DC 20005
Ph: 202-628-8866 ▪ Fx: 202-628-9800

REITPAC
1875 'I' St NW Suite 600   Washington DC 20006
Ph: 202-739-9400 ▪ Fx: 202-739-9401

Relais & Chateaux Association   www.relaischateaux.com
11 E 44th St Suite 707   New York NY 10017
Ph: 212-856-0115 ▪ Fx: 212-856-0193 ▪ TF: 800-735-2478

Relay Manufacturers, National Association of   www.ec-central.org/NARM
9549 N Broadmoor Rd   Milwaukee WI 53217
Ph: 414-351-4548 ▪ Fx: 414-351-4897

Released Time Ministries, Fellowship of Christian   www.rtce.org
5722 Lime Ave   Long Beach CA 90805
Ph: 562-428-7733 ▪ Fx: 562-728-7633 ▪ TF: 800-360-7943

Reliability Engineers, Society of   www.sre.org

Reliability Professionals, Society for Maintenance &   www.smrp.org
PO Box 51787   Knoxville TN 37950
Ph: 865-212-0111 ▪ Fx: 865-558-3060 ▪ TF: 800-950-7354

Reliability Society, IEEE   www.ewh.ieee.org/soc/rs
IEEE Operations Ctr 445 Hoes Ln   Piscataway NJ 08854
Ph: 732-981-0060 ▪ Fx: 732-981-1721

Reliant Energy Inc PAC
PO Box 4567   Houston TX 77210
Ph: 713-207-8057

Relief Agency International, Adventist Development &   www.adra.org
12501 Old Columbia Pike   Silver Spring MD 20904
Ph: 301-680-6380 ▪ Fx: 301-680-6370 ▪ TF: 800-424-2372

Relief, Army Emergency   www.aerhq.org
200 Stovall St   Alexandria VA 22332
Ph: 703-328-0000 ▪ Fx: 703-325-7183

Relief Association, Egyptians   www.egyptiansrelief.org
6121 Winnepeg Dr   Burke VA 22015
Ph: 703-818-2573 ▪ Fx: 703-503-8816

Relief Committee, Christian Reformed World   www.crwrc.org
2850 Kalamazoo Ave SE   Grand Rapids MI 49560
Ph: 616-224-0740 ▪ Fx: 616-224-0806 ▪ TF: 800-552-7972

Relief Committee Inc, Estonian
243 E 34th St   New York NY 10016
Ph: 212-685-7467 ▪ Fx: 212-683-4418

Relief Committee Inc, United Ukrainian American   www.uuarc.org
1206 Cottman Ave   Philadelphia PA 19111
Ph: 215-728-1630 ▪ Fx: 215-728-1631

Relief & Development, Episcopal   www.er-d.org
815 2nd Ave   New York NY 10017
Ph: 212-867-8400 ▪ Fx: 212-983-6377 ▪ TF: 800-334-7626

Relief Fund of America, United Lithuanian
4545 W 63rd St   Chicago IL 60629
Ph: 773-767-3401 ▪ Fx: 773-767-3402

Relief Interactive   www.reliefinteractive.org
9902 Chase Hill Ct   Vienna VA 22182
Ph: 703-585-3614 ▪ Fx: 703-321-7407

Relief International, Direct   www.directrelief.org
27 S La Patera Ln   Santa Barbara CA 93117
Ph: 805-964-4767 ▪ Fx: 805-681-4838 ▪ TF: 800-676-1638

Relief, Lutheran World   www.lwr.org
700 Light St   Baltimore MD 21230
Ph: 410-230-2700 ▪ Fx: 410-230-2882

Relief Network, Global Jewish Assistance &   www.globaljewish.org
666 5th Ave Suite 246   New York NY 10103
Ph: 212-868-3636 ▪ Fx: 212-868-7878

Relief Services, Catholic   www.catholicrelief.org
209 W Fayette St   Baltimore MD 21201
Ph: 410-625-2220 ▪ Fx: 410-685-1635 ▪ TF: 800-235-2772

Relief Services, Christian   www.christianrelief.org
8815 Telegraph Rd   Lorton VA 22079
Ph: 703-550-2472 ▪ Fx: 703-550-2473 ▪ TF: 800-337-3543

Relief Society Eastern US, Armenian   www.arseastus.com
80 Bigelow Ave   Watertown MA 02472
Ph: 617-926-3801 ▪ Fx: 617-924-7238

Relief Society, Navy-Marine Corps   www.nmcrs.org
4015 Wilson Blvd 10th Fl   Arlington VA 22203
Ph: 703-696-4904 ▪ Fx: 703-696-0144 ▪ TF: 800-654-8364

Relief, Southern Baptist Disaster   www.namb.net/dr
4200 North Point Pkwy   Alpharetta GA 30022
Ph: 770-410-6442 ▪ Fx: 770-410-6014

Relief, United Methodist Committee on   gbgm-umc.org/umcor
475 Riverside Dr Suite 330   New York NY 10115
Ph: 212-870-3816 ▪ Fx: 212-870-3624 ▪ TF: 800-554-8583

Relief, World   www.wr.org
7 E Baltimore St   Baltimore MD 21202
Ph: 443-451-1900

Relief, World Emergency   www.worldemergency.org
2270 Camino Vida Roble Suite D   Carlsbad CA 92009
Ph: 760-930-8001 ▪ Fx: 760-930-9085 ▪ TF: 888-484-2543

Relief Inc, World Medical   www.worldmedicalrelief.com
11745 Rosa Parks Blvd   Detroit MI 48206
Ph: 313-866-5333 ▪ Fx: 313-866-5588

Religion in an Age of Science Inc, Institute on   www.iras.org
310 Windham Dr   Booneville MS 38829
Ph: 662-720-1241

Religion, American Academy of   www.aarweb.org
825 Houston Mill Rd Suite 300   Atlanta GA 30329
Ph: 404-727-3049 ▪ Fx: 404-727-7959

Religion, Association for the Sociology of   www.sociologyofreligion.com
3520 Wiltshire Dr   Holiday FL 34691
Ph: 727-844-5990 ▪ Fx: 727-844-7332

Religion Communicators Council   www.religioncommunicators.org
475 Riverside Dr Rm 1948A   New York NY 10115
Ph: 212-870-2985 ▪ Fx: 212-870-3578

Religion & Contemporary Culture, Society for the Arts www.sarcc.org
15811 Kutztown Rd Box 15   Maxatawny PA 19538
Ph: 610-683-7581

Religion, Council of Societies for the Study of   www.cssr.org
Valparaiso Univ   Valparaiso IN 46383
Ph: 219-464-5515 ▪ Fx: 219-464-6714 ▪ TF: 888-422-2777

Religion & Democracy, Institute on   www.ird-renew.org
1110 Vermont Ave NW Suite 1180   Washington DC 20005
Ph: 202-969-8430 ▪ Fx: 202-969-8429

Religion & Ecology, North American Coalition on
5 Thomas Cir NW   Washington DC 20005
Ph: 202-462-2591 ▪ Fx: 202-462-6534

Religion & Intellectual Life, Association for   www.aril.org
475 Riverside Dr Suite 1945   New York NY 10115
Ph: 212-870-2544 ▪ Fx: 212-870-2539

Religion & Liberty, Acton Institute for the Study of   www.acton.org
161 Ottawa NW Suite 301   Grand Rapids MI 49503
Ph: 616-454-3080 ▪ Fx: 616-454-9454

Religion, National Association of Baptist Professors of www.cssr.org/soc_nabpr.htm
Mercer University   Macon GA 31207
Ph: 478-301-2758 ▪ Fx: 478-301-2384

Religion Newswriters Association   www.religionwriters.com
PO Box 2037   Westerville OH 43086
Ph: 614-891-9001 ▪ Fx: 614-981-9774

Religion & Psychical Research, Academy of   www.lightlink.com/arpr
PO Box 614   Bloomfield CT 06002
Ph: 860-242-4593

Religion, Society for the Anthropology of   www.uwgb.edu/sar
c/o American Anthropological Assn 2200 Wilson Blvd Suite
   600   Arlington VA 22201
Ph: 703-528-1902 ▪ Fx: 703-528-3546

Religion & Society, Center for the   puffin.creighton.edu/human/csrs/centerhome.html
Study of   Creighton Univ   Omaha NE 68178
Ph: 402-280-2504

Religion, Society for Philosophy of
Univ of Georgia Dept of Philosophy Peabody Hall   Athens GA
   30602
Ph: 706-542-2823 ▪ Fx: 706-542-2839

Religion, Society for the Scientific Study of   www.sssrweb.org
Alfred Univ Div of Social Sciences 1 Saxon Dr   Alfred NY
   14802
Ph: 607-871-2215 ▪ Fx: 607-871-2085

Religion on Stamps, Collectors of
425 N Linwood Ave Suite 110   Appleton WI 54914
Ph: 920-734-2417 ▪ Fx: 920-734-6711

Religions, Council for a Parliament of the World's   www.cpwr.org
PO Box 1630   Chicago IL 60690
Ph: 312-629-2990 ▪ Fx: 312-629-2991

Religions, Institute for Advanced Studies of World   www.iaswr.org
2020 Rt 301   Carmel NY 10512
Ph: 845-225-1445 ▪ Fx: 845-225-1485

Religions for Peace, World Conference of   www.wcrp.org
777 United Nations Plaza   New York NY 10017
Ph: 212-687-2163 ▪ Fx: 212-983-0566

Religious Affairs, Association for College &   www.upenn.edu/chaplain/acura
University   Northwestern Univ Chaplain 1870 Sheridan
   Rd   Evanston IL 60208
Ph: 847-491-7256 ▪ Fx: 847-491-7353

Religious Broadcasters, National   www.nrb.org
9510 Technology Dr   Manassas VA 20110
Ph: 703-330-7000 ▪ Fx: 703-330-7100

Religious Brothers Conference   www.brothersonline.org
1337 W Ohio St   Chicago IL 60622
Ph: 773-493-2306 ▪ Fx: 773-493-2356 ▪ TF: 866-276-8437

Religious & Civil Rights, Catholic League for   www.catholicleague.org
450 7th Ave   New York NY 10123
Ph: 212-371-3191 ▪ Fx: 212-371-3394

Religious Coalition for Reproductive Choice   www.rcrc.org
1025 Vermont Ave NW Suite 1130   Washington DC 20005
Ph: 202-628-7700 ▪ Fx: 202-628-7716

Religious Conference Management Association Inc   www.rcmaweb.org
1 RCA Dome Suite 120   Indianapolis IN 46225
Ph: 317-632-1888 ▪ Fx: 317-632-7909

Religious Education Association   www.religiouseducation.net
c/o Interdenomination Theological Ctr 700 ML King Jr Dr
   SW   Atlanta GA 30314
Ph: 404-527-7739 ▪ Fx: 404-527-0901

Religious Education, Association of Professors &   www.mtso.edu/aprre
Researchers in   3081 Columbus Pike PO Box
   80004   Delaware OH 43015
Ph: 740-362-3364 ▪ Fx: 740-362-5890

Religious Formation Conference   www.relforcon.org
8820 Cameron St   Silver Spring MD 20910
Ph: 301-588-4938

Religious Freedom, Center for Law &   www.clsnet.org
4208 Evergreen Ln Suite 222   Annandale VA 22003
Ph: 703-642-1070 ▪ Fx: 703-642-1075

Religious Freedom Coalition   www.rfcnet.org
PO Box 77511   Washington DC 20013
Ph: 202-543-0300 ▪ Fx: 202-543-8447

Religious Freedom, International Coalition for   www.religiousfreedom.com
7777 Leesburg Pike Suite 404 N-A   Falls Church VA 22043
Ph: 703-790-1500 ▪ Fx: 703-790-5562

Religious Freedom, National Committee for Amish   www.holycrosslivonia.org/amish
30650 6 Mile Rd   Livonia MI 48152
Ph: 734-427-1414 ▪ Fx: 734-427-1419

Religious Information Systems, Association for the Development of
PO Box 210735   Nashville TN 37221
Ph: 615-429-8744

Religious Institutes Inc, National Association for Treasurers of   www.natri.org
8824 Cameron St   Silver Spring MD 20910
Ph: 301-587-7776 ▪ Fx: 301-589-2897

Religious, Leadership Conference of Women — www.lcwr.org
8808 Cameron St   Silver Spring MD 20910
Ph: 301-588-4955 ▪ Fx: 301-587-4575

Religious Liberty, Americans for — www.arlinc.org
PO Box 6656   Silver Spring MD 20916
Ph: 301-260-2988 ▪ Fx: 301-260-2989

Religious Liberty, Becket Fund for — www.becketfund.org
1350 Connecticut Ave NW Suite 605   Washington DC 20036
Ph: 202-955-0095 ▪ Fx: 202-955-0090

Religious Liberty Commission of the Southern Baptist Convention, Ethics & — www.erlc.com
901 Commerce St   Nashville TN 37203
Ph: 615-244-2495 ▪ Fx: 615-242-0065

(Religious Literacy) Westar Institute — www.westarinstitute.org
PO Box 6144   Santa Rosa CA 95406
Ph: 707-523-1323 ▪ Fx: 707-523-1350

Religious Research Association — rra.hartsem.edu
3520 Wiltshire Dr   Holiday FL 34691
Ph: 727-844-5990 ▪ Fx: 727-844-7332

Religious Research & Education, Community for
St Francis Univ Dept of Religious Studies   Loretto PA 15940
Ph: 814-472-3396 ▪ Fx: 814-472-2776

Religious Science International — www.rsintl.org
901 E 2nd Ave Suite 301   Spokane WA 99202
Ph: 509-624-7000 ▪ Fx: 509-624-9322 ▪ TF: 800-662-1348

Religious Unitarian Universalists, Young — www.uua.org/YRUU
25 Beacon St   Boston MA 02108
Ph: 617-948-4350 ▪ Fx: 617-367-4798

Religious Vocation Conference, National — www.nrvc.net
5420 S Cornell Ave Suite 105   Chicago IL 60615
Ph: 773-363-5454 ▪ Fx: 773-363-5530

(Religious Zionism) Bnei Akiva of the US & Canada — www.bneiakiva.org
7 Penn Plaza   New York NY 10010
Ph: 212-465-9536 ▪ Fx: 212-465-2155

Relocation Council, Employee — www.erc.org
1717 Pennsylvania Ave NW Suite 800   Washington DC 20006
Ph: 202-857-0857 ▪ Fx: 202-467-4012 ▪ TF: 888-372-2255

Relocation Directors Council Inc — relocationdirectorscouncil.org
8 S Michigan Ave Suite 1000   Chicago IL 60603
Ph: 312-726-7410 ▪ Fx: 312-580-0165

Remanufacturing Institute — www.reman.org
14160 Newbrook Dr Suite 210   Chantilly VA 20151
Ph: 703-968-2772 ▪ Fx: 703-968-2878

Remnant of Israel — remnantofisrael.net
3050 Gap Knob Rd   New Hope KY 40052
Ph: 270-325-3061 ▪ Fx: 270-325-3094 ▪ TF: 888-352-7153

Remodeling Contractors Association — www.rcact.com
17 S Main St   East Granby CT 06026
Ph: 860-653-6751 ▪ Fx: 860-653-7359 ▪ TF: 800-937-4722

Remodeling Industry, National Association of the — www.nari.org
780 Lee St Suite 200   Des Plaines IL 60016
Ph: 847-298-9200 ▪ Fx: 847-298-9225 ▪ TF: 800-611-6274

Remote Sensing, American Society for Photogrammetry & — www.asprs.org
5410 Grosvenor Ln Suite 210   Bethesda MD 20814
Ph: 301-493-0290 ▪ Fx: 301-493-0208

Remotivation Therapy Organization Inc, National — www.remotivation.com
103 McDonald St   West Nanticoke PA 18634
Ph: 570-735-7079 ▪ Fx: 570-735-2997

Renaissance Artists & Writers Association — rawa.ru.org
c/o Ananda Marga New York Sectorial Office 97-38 42nd Ave   Corona NY 11368
Ph: 718-898-1603

Renal Administrators Association, National — www.nraa.org
1904 Naomi Pl   Prescot AZ 86303
Ph: 928-717-2772 ▪ Fx: 928-441-3857

Renal Pathology Society — www.renalpathsoc.org
LSU Medical Center Dept of Pathology 1501 Kings Hwy   Shreveport LA 71103
Ph: 318-675-5878 ▪ Fx: 318-675-7662

Renal Physicians Association — www.renalmd.org
1700 Rockville Pike Suite 220   Rockville MD 20852
Ph: 301-468-3515 ▪ Fx: 301-468-3511

Renderers Association, National — www.renderers.org
801 N Fairfax St Suite 207   Alexandria VA 22314
Ph: 703-683-0155 ▪ Fx: 703-683-2626

Renewable Energy Clearinghouse, Energy Efficiency & — www.eere.energy.gov/consumerinfo
US Dept of Energy PO Box 3048   Merrifield VA 22116
Ph: 800-363-3732 ▪ Fx: 703-893-0400

Renewable Fuels Association — www.ethanolrfa.org
1 Massachusetts Ave NW Suite 820   Washington DC 20001
Ph: 202-289-3835 ▪ Fx: 202-289-7519

Renewable Natural Resources Foundation — www.rnrf.org
5430 Grosvenor Ln   Bethesda MD 20814
Ph: 301-493-9101 ▪ Fx: 301-493-6148

Renewable Technologies, Center for Energy Efficiency &
1100 11th St Suite 311   Sacramento CA 95814
Ph: 916-442-7785 ▪ Fx: 916-447-2940 ▪ TF: 877-758-4462

Renewal, Alliance for National — www.ncl.org
National Civic League 1319 F ST NW Suite 204   Washington DC 20004
Ph: 202-783-2961 ▪ Fx: 202-347-2161

Rental Association, American — www.ararental.org
1900 19th St   Moline IL 61265
Ph: 309-764-2475 ▪ Fx: 309-764-1533 ▪ TF: 800-334-2177

Rental Organizations, Association of Progressive — www.apro-rto.com
1504 Robin Hood Trail   Austin TX 78703
Ph: 512-794-0095 ▪ Fx: 512-794-0097 ▪ TF: 800-204-2776

Rental Services Association, Textile — www.trsa.org
1800 Diagonal Rd Suite 200   Alexandria VA 22314
Ph: 703-519-0029 ▪ Fx: 703-519-0026 ▪ TF: 800-868-8772

REO Club of America — clubs.hemmings.com/frameset.cfm?club=reo
7971 Vernon Rd   Cicero NY 13039
Ph: 315-458-4721

Repair Contractors, National Association of Waterproofing & Structural — www.nawsrc.org
8015 Corporate Dr Suite A   Baltimore MD 21236
Ph: 410-931-3332 ▪ Fx: 410-931-2060 ▪ TF: 800-245-6292

Reparations in America, National Coalition of Blacks for — www.ncobra.com
PO Box 90604   Washington DC 20090
Ph: 202-291-8400 ▪ Fx: 202-291-4600

Repatriation Foundation, American Indian Ritual Object — www.repatriationfoundation.org
463 E 57th St   New York NY 10022
Ph: 212-980-9441 ▪ Fx: 212-421-2746

Reporters Association, National Verbatim — www.nvra.org
207 3rd Ave   Hattiesburg MS 39401
Ph: 601-582-4345 ▪ Fx: 601-582-3354

Reporters Association, Professional Soccer
6700 Squibb Rd Suite 215   Mission KS 66202
Ph: 913-362-1747 ▪ Fx: 913-362-3439

Reporters Association, Regional — www.rra.org
PO Box 254   Washington DC 20044
Ph: 202-662-8731 ▪ Fx: 202-662-8996

Reporters of Judicial Decisions, Association of — arjd.washlaw.edu
5711 Nevada St   College Park MD 20740
Ph: 202-479-3194 ▪ Fx: 202-479-3240

Reporting in America, Committee for Accuracy in Middle East — www.camera.org
PO Box 35040   Boston MA 02135
Ph: 617-789-3672 ▪ Fx: 617-787-7853

Reporting, Center for Investigative — www.muckraker.org
131 Steuart St Suite 600   San Francisco CA 94105
Ph: 415-543-1200 ▪ Fx: 415-543-8311

Reporting, Fairness & Accuracy in — www.fair.org
112 W 27th St 6th Fl   New York NY 10001
Ph: 212-633-6700 ▪ Fx: 212-727-7668

Reproduction, Society for the Study of — www.ssr.org
1619 Monroe St   Madison WI 53711
Ph: 608-256-2777 ▪ Fx: 608-256-4610

Reproductive Choice, Religious Coalition for — www.rcrc.org
1025 Vermont Ave NW Suite 1130   Washington DC 20005
Ph: 202-628-7700 ▪ Fx: 202-628-7716

Reproductive Endocrinology & Infertility, Society for — www.socrei.org
1209 Montgomery Hwy   Birmingham AL 35216
Ph: 205-978-5000 ▪ Fx: 205-978-5005

Reproductive Health Association, National Family Planning & — www.nfprha.org
1627 K St NW 12th Fl   Washington DC 20006
Ph: 202-293-3114 ▪ Fx: 202-293-1990

(Reproductive Health) EngenderHealth — www.engenderhealth.org
440 9th Ave 3rd Fl   New York NY 10001
Ph: 212-561-8000 ▪ Fx: 212-561-8067 ▪ TF: 800-564-2872

Reproductive Health, National Latina Institute for — www.latinainstitute.org
162 Montague St 3rd Fl   Brooklyn NY 11201
Ph: 718-260-8811 ▪ Fx: 718-260-9941

Reproductive Health Professionals, Association of — www.arhp.org
2401 Pennsylvania Ave NW Suite 350   Washington DC 20037
Ph: 202-466-3825 ▪ Fx: 202-466-3826

Reproductive Law & Policy Inc, Center for — www.crlp.org
120 Wall St 14th Fl   New York NY 10005
Ph: 917-637-3600 ▪ Fx: 917-637-3666

Reproductive Medicine, American Society for — www.asrm.org
1209 Montgomery Hwy   Birmingham AL 35216
Ph: 205-978-5000 ▪ Fx: 205-978-5005

Reproductive Surgeons, Society of — www.reprodsurgery.org
1209 Montgomery Hwy   Birmingham AL 35216
Ph: 205-978-5000 ▪ Fx: 205-978-5005

Reproductive Technology, Society for Assisted — www.sart.org
1209 Montgomery Hwy   Birmingham AL 35216
Ph: 205-978-5000 ▪ Fx: 205-978-5015

Reprographic Association, International — www.irga.com
401 N Michigan Ave   Chicago IL 60611
Ph: 312-245-1026 ▪ Fx: 312-527-6705 ▪ TF: 800-833-4742

Reprographic Services Association — www.rsacorporation.com
1 Windsor Cove Suite 306   Columbia SC 29205
Ph: 803-252-5647 ▪ Fx: 803-765-0860 ▪ TF: 800-445-8629

Reptiles, Society for the Study of Amphibians & — www.ssarherps.org
PO Box 253   Marceline MO 64658
Ph: 660-256-3252

Republican Attorneys, National Association of
PO Box 656513   Fresh Meadows NY 11365
Ph: 718-357-7075

Republican Club of Capitol Hill, National — www.capitolhillclub.com
300 1st St SE   Washington DC 20003
Ph: 202-484-4590 ▪ Fx: 202-479-9110

Republican Club, Women's National — www.wnrc.org
3 W 51st St   New York NY 10019
Ph: 212-582-5454 ▪ Fx: 212-265-5633

Republican Congressional Committee, National — nrcc.org
320 1st St SE   Washington DC 20003
Ph: 202-479-7000 ▪ Fx: 202-863-0693

Republican Institute-USA, International — www.iri.org
1225 'I' St NW Suite 700   Washington DC 20005
Ph: 202-408-9450 ▪ Fx: 202-408-9462

Republican National Committee — www.gop.org
310 1st St SE   Washington DC 20003
Ph: 202-863-8500 ▪ Fx: 202-863-8820 ▪ TF: 800-445-5768

Republican National Committee, College — www.crnc.org
600 Pennsylvania Ave SE Suite 215   Washington DC 20003
Ph: 202-608-1411 ▪ Fx: 202-608-1429 ▪ TF: 888-765-3564

Republican National Federation, Young
PO Box 65337   Washington DC 20035
Ph: 202-608-1417

Republican National Hispanic Assembly of the US   www.rnha.org
PO Box 1882   Washington DC 20013
Ph: 202-544-6700 ▪ Fx: 202-544-6869 ▪ TF: 877-544-6701

Republican Presidential Task Force   www.nrsc.org/memberprograms/taskforce
Ronald Reagan Republican Ctr 425 2nd St NE   Washington DC
20002
Ph: 202-675-6772 ▪ TF: 800-877-6775

Republican Pro-Choice Coalition   www.gopchoice.org
57 W 57th St Suite 1101   New York NY 10019
Ph: 212-207-8266 ▪ Fx: 212-207-8629 ▪ TF: 877-467-2464

(Republican) Ripon Society   www.riponsoc.org
1300 L St NW Suite 900   Washington DC 20005
Ph: 202-216-1008 ▪ Fx: 202-216-0036

Republican Senatorial Committee, National   www.nrsc.org
425 2nd St NE   Washington DC 20002
Ph: 202-675-6000 ▪ Fx: 202-675-6058

Republican Women, National Federation of   www.nfrw.org
124 N Alfred St   Alexandria VA 22314
Ph: 703-548-9688 ▪ Fx: 703-548-9836

Republicans Abroad International   www.republicansabroad.org
209 Pennsylvania Ave SE   Washington DC 20003
Ph: 202-608-1423 ▪ Fx: 202-608-1431

Republicans for Choice   www.republicansforchoice.com/
2760 Eisenhower Ave Suite 260   Alexandria VA 22314
Ph: 703-960-9882 ▪ Fx: 703-329-2411

Republicans, Log Cabin   www.lcr.org
1607 17th St NW   Washington DC 20009
Ph: 202-347-5306 ▪ Fx: 202-347-5224

Republicans, Teen Age   www.teenagerepublicans.org
PO Box 1896   Manassas VA 20108
Ph: 703-368-4214 ▪ Fx: 703-368-0830

Resale Association, National Aircraft   www.nara-dealers.com/
4226 King St   Alexandria VA 22302
Ph: 703-671-8273 ▪ Fx: 703-671-5848

Resale & Thrift Shops, National Association of   www.narts.org
PO Box 80707   Saint Clair Shores MI 48080
Ph: 800-544-0751 ▪ Fx: 810-294-6776

Rescue America Inc, English Springer   www.springerrescue.org
2721 Walker Lee Rd   Los Alamitos CA 90720
Ph: 800-921-1047

Rescue Association, National Mine   www.miningorganizations.org/nmra.htm
RR 1 Box 736   Hunker PA 15639
Ph: 724-925-5150 ▪ Fx: 724-925-6190

Rescue Committee, International   www.intrescom.org
122 E 42nd St 12th Fl   New York NY 10168
Ph: 212-551-3000 ▪ Fx: 212-551-3180

Rescue Dog Association, American   www.ardainc.org
PO Box 151   Chester NY 10918
Ph: 845-469-4173 ▪ Fx: 845-774-1054

Rescue League Inc, Equine   erl.freeyellow.com
PO Box 4366   Leesburg VA 20177
Ph: 703-771-1240

Rescue Missions, Association of Gospel   www.agrm.org
1045 Swift St   Kansas City MO 64116
Ph: 816-471-8020 ▪ Fx: 816-471-3718 ▪ TF: 800-624-5156

Rescue, National Association for Search &   www.nasar.org
4500 Southgate Pl Suite 100   Chantilly VA 20151
Ph: 703-222-6277 ▪ Fx: 703-222-6283

Rescue & Resettlement of Iraqi Jews, American Committee for
1125 Park Ave   New York NY 10029
Ph: 212-427-1246 ▪ Fx: 212-360-7009

Rescue Specialists, International Association of Dive   www.iadrs.org
201 N Link Ln   Fort Collins CO 80524
Ph: 970-482-1562 ▪ Fx: 970-482-0893 ▪ TF: 800-423-7791

Rescue Team International, American   www.amerrescue.org
PO Box 534   Albuquerque NM 87103
Ph: 505-281-7977

Rescue & Towing, Committee for Private Offshore   www.c-port.org
1600 Duke St Suite 220   Alexandria VA 22314
Ph: 703-519-1713 ▪ Fx: 703-519-1716

Rescue Workers Inc, American   www.arwus.com
643 Elmira St   Williamsport PA 17701
Ph: 570-323-8401 ▪ Fx: 570-323-0980

Research, Academy of Surgical   www.surgicalresearch.org
7500 Flying Cloud Rd Suite 900   Eden Prairie MN 55344
Ph: 952-253-6240 ▪ Fx: 952-835-4774

Research & Action Center, Food   www.frac.org
1875 Connecticut Ave NW Suite 540   Washington DC 20009
Ph: 202-986-2200 ▪ Fx: 202-986-2525

Research Administrators, National Council of University   www.ncura.edu
1 Dupont Cir NW Suite 220   Washington DC 20036
Ph: 202-466-3894 ▪ Fx: 202-223-5573

Research Administrators, Society of   www.srainternational.org
1901 N Moore St Suite 1004   Arlington VA 22209
Ph: 703-741-0140 ▪ Fx: 703-741-0142

Research, Association for Institutional   www.airweb.org
Florida State Univ 222 Stone Bldg   Tallahassee FL 32306
Ph: 850-644-4470 ▪ Fx: 850-644-8824

Research Association of Minority Professors   www.rampresearch.org

Research Association Inc, Universities   www.ura-hq.org
1111 19th St NW Suite 400   Washington DC 20036
Ph: 202-293-1382 ▪ Fx: 202-293-5012

Research-Based Pharmaceutical Companies, Canada's   www.canadapharma.org
55 Metcalfe St Suite 1220   Ottawa ON K1P6L5
Ph: 613-236-0455 ▪ Fx: 613-236-6756

Research, Center for Labor & Community   www.clcr.org
3411 W Diversey Ave Suite 10   Chicago IL 60647
Ph: 773-278-5418 ▪ Fx: 773-278-5918

Research, Center for Social & Legal   www.privacyexchange.org
2 University Plaza Suite 414   Hackensack NJ 07601
Ph: 201-996-1154 ▪ Fx: 201-996-1883

Research Centers, Council of American Overseas   www.caorc.org
Smithsonian Institution PO Box 37012 NHB Rm CE-123 MRC
178   Washington DC 20013
Ph: 202-842-8636 ▪ Fx: 202-786-2430

Research Chefs Association   www.culinology.com
5775 Peachtree-Dunwoody Rd Bldg G Suite 500   Atlanta GA
30342
Ph: 404-252-3663 ▪ Fx: 404-252-0774

Research Consultants Association Inc, Qualitative   www.qrca.org
PO Box 967   Camden TN 30320
Ph: 731-584-8080 ▪ Fx: 731-584-7882 ▪ TF: 888-674-7722

Research Corp   www.rescorp.org
4703 E Camp Lowell Dr Suite 201   Tucson AZ 85712
Ph: 520-571-1111 ▪ Fx: 520-571-1119

Research Council of America, Consumers'   www.consumersresearchcncl.org
2020 Pennsylvania Ave NW Suite 300A   Washington DC 20006
Ph: 202-835-9698 ▪ Fx: 202-835-9739

Research Council Inc, Coordinating   www.crcao.com
3650 Mansell Rd Suite 140   Alpharetta GA 30022
Ph: 678-795-0506 ▪ Fx: 678-795-0509

Research & Development Associates for Military Food &   www.militaryfood.org
Packaging Systems Inc   16607 Blanco Rd Suite 1506   San
Antonio TX 78232
Ph: 210-493-8024 ▪ Fx: 210-493-8036

Research Directors, Association of
Alabama A&M Univ School of Agriculture &
Environmental   Normal AL 35762
Ph: 256-851-5781 ▪ Fx: 256-851-5906

Research on Economics & the Environment, Foundation for   www.free-eco.org
945 Technology Blvd Suite 101F   Bozeman MT 59718
Ph: 406-585-1776 ▪ Fx: 406-585-3000

Research & Education Institute, Women's   www.wrei.org
1750 New York Ave NW Suite 350   Washington DC 20006
Ph: 202-628-0444 ▪ Fx: 202-628-0458

Research & Educational Networking, Corporation for   www.cren.net
1150 18th St NW Suite 1030   Washington DC 20036
Ph: 202-293-5909 ▪ Fx: 202-293-2853

Research & Engineering Council of the Graphic Arts Industry   www.recouncil.org
PO Box 1086   White Stone VA 22578
Ph: 804-436-9922 ▪ Fx: 804-436-9511

Research & Enlightenment, Association for   www.are-cayce.com
215 67th St   Virginia Beach VA 23451
Ph: 757-428-3588 ▪ Fx: 757-422-6921 ▪ TF: 800-333-4499

Research Ethics National Association, Applied   www.primr.org/arena.html
132 Boylston St 4th Fl   Boston MA 02116
Ph: 617-423-4112 ▪ Fx: 617-423-1185

Research & Exchanges Board, International   www.irex.org
2121 K St NW Suite 700   Washington DC 20037
Ph: 202-628-8188 ▪ Fx: 202-628-8189

Research Foundation, African Medical &   www.amref.org
19 W 44th St Suite 710   New York NY 10036
Ph: 212-768-2440 ▪ Fx: 212-768-4230

Research Foundation for Jewish Immigration
570 7th Ave   New York NY 10018
Ph: 212-921-3871 ▪ Fx: 212-575-1918

Research Foundation, World   www.wrf.org
41 Bell Rock Plaza   Sedona AZ 86351
Ph: 928-284-3300 ▪ Fx: 928-284-3530

Research & Information Center, Southwest   www.sric.org
PO Box 4524   Albuquerque NM 87106
Ph: 505-262-1862 ▪ Fx: 505-262-1864

Research Initiatives, Corporation for National   www.cnri.reston.va.us
1895 Preston White Dr Suite 100   Reston VA 20191
Ph: 703-620-8990 ▪ Fx: 703-620-0913

Research Institute, Christian   www.equip.org
PO Box 7000   Rancho Santa Margarita CA 92688
Ph: 949-858-6100 ▪ Fx: 949-858-6111 ▪ TF: 800-700-6274

Research Institute for Small & Emerging Business   www.riseb.org
722 12th St NW   Washington DC 20005
Ph: 202-628-8382 ▪ Fx: 202-628-8392

Research Institute for the Study of Man   www.rism.org
162 E 78th St   New York NY 10021
Ph: 212-535-8448 ▪ Fx: 212-535-0084

Research Institutes, Association of Independent   www.airi.org
DAI Management Inc PO Box 844   Westminster MD 21158
Ph: 410-751-8900 ▪ Fx: 410-751-2662

Research, Inter-University Consortium for Political & Social   www.icpsr.umich.edu
Univ of Michigan Institute for Social Research PO Box
1248   Ann Arbor MI 48106
Ph: 734-647-5000 ▪ Fx: 734-647-8200

Research in Language & Literacy, National Conference on   www.coe.uga.edu/ncrll
Colorado State Univ English Dept 359 Eddy Bldg   Fort Collins
CO 80523
Ph: 970-491-5161 ▪ Fx: 970-491-5601

Research Libraries, Association of   arl.cni.org
21 Dupont Cir NW Suite 800   Washington DC 20036
Ph: 202-296-2296 ▪ Fx: 202-872-0884

Research Libraries, Association of College &   www.ala.org/acrl.html
50 E Huron St   Chicago IL 60611
Ph: 312-280-2519 ▪ Fx: 312-280-2520 ▪ TF: 800-545-2433

Research Libraries, Center for   wwwcrl.uchicago.edu
6050 S Kenwood Ave   Chicago IL 60637
Ph: 773-955-4545 ▪ Fx: 773-955-4339 ▪ TF: 800-621-6044

Research Libraries Group Inc   www.rlg.org
2029 Stierlin Ct Suite 100   Mountain View CA 94043
Ph: 650-962-9951 ▪ Fx: 650-964-0943 ▪ TF: 800-537-7546

Research Materials on Southeast Asia, Committee on — www.library.wisc.edu/guides/SEAasia/cormosea

Research, National Conferences on Undergraduate — www.ncur.org
Univ of Minnesota Duluth 10 University Dr 140 Engineering Bldg   Duluth MN 55812
Ph: 218-726-7807 ▪ Fx: 218-726-6360

Research, National Council for Eurasian & East European — www.nceeer.org
910 17th St NW Suite 300   Washington DC 20006
Ph: 202-822-6950 ▪ Fx: 202-822-6955

Research, National Council for Geocosmic — www.geocosmic.org
8810-C Jamacha Blvd PMB 183   Spring Valley CA 91977
Ph: 619-303-9236

Research Parks, Association of University — www.aurrp.org
12100 Sunset Hills Rd Suite 130   Reston VA 20190
Ph: 703-234-4088 ▪ Fx: 703-435-4390

Research & Planning, National Council for — www.nmsu.edu/~NCRP

Research to Prevent Blindness Inc — www.rpbusa.org
645 Madison Ave 21st Fl   New York NY 10022
Ph: 212-752-4333 ▪ Fx: 212-688-6231 ▪ TF: 800-621-0026

Research Professionals, Association of Clinical — www.acrpnet.org
500 Montgomery St Suite 800   Alexandria VA 22314
Ph: 703-254-8100 ▪ Fx: 703-254-8101

(Research) RAND Corp — www.rand.org
1700 Main St PO Box 2138   Santa Monica CA 90407
Ph: 310-393-0411 ▪ Fx: 310-393-4818

Research in Science Teaching, National Association for — www.educ.sfu.ca/narstsite
Univ of Missouri-Columbia 303 Townsend Hall   Columbia MO 65211
Ph: 573-884-1401 ▪ Fx: 573-884-2917

Research Society on Alcoholism — www.rsoa.org
7801 N Lamar Blvd Suite D-89   Austin TX 78752
Ph: 512-454-0022 ▪ Fx: 512-454-0812

Research Society for Victorian Periodicals — www.aztecfreenet.org/rsvp/
Univ of South Florida FA 0209   Tampa FL 33620
Ph: 813-974-3365 ▪ Fx: 813-974-0810

Research Inc, SOL Association for — www.solarpress.com
PO Box 2276   North Canton OH 44720
Ph: 330-497-9645

Research & Training Center on Independent Living — www.rtcil.org
Univ of Kansas Dole Ctr Rm 7089 100 Sunnyside Ave   Lawrence KS 66045
Ph: 785-864-4095 ▪ Fx: 785-864-5063

Research in Values & Philosophy, Council for — www.crvp.org
PO Box 261 Cardinal Stn   Washington DC 20064
Ph: 202-319-6089

Research in Vietnamese Music, International Association for
2005 Willow Ridge Cir   Kent OH 44240
Ph: 330-673-3763 ▪ Fx: 330-673-4434

Research!America — www.researchamerica.org
1101 King St Suite 520   Alexandria VA 22314
Ph: 703-739-2577 ▪ Fx: 703-739-2372 ▪ TF: 800-366-2873

Researchers for Advancement, Association of Professional — www.aprahome.org
40 Shuman Blvd Suite 325   Naperville IL 60563
Ph: 630-717-8160 ▪ Fx: 630-717-8354

Researchers, Association of International Health
2665 Pleasant Valley Rd   Mobile AL 36606
Ph: 251-473-3946

Researchers in Religious Education, Association of Professors & — www.mtso.edu/aprre
3081 Columbus Pike PO Box 80004   Delaware OH 43015
Ph: 740-362-3364 ▪ Fx: 740-362-5890

Reservation Executives, International Association of — www.iare.com
7853 Arapahoe Ct Suite 2100   Centennial CO 80112
Ph: 303-694-4728 ▪ Fx: 303-694-4869

Reserve Association, Naval — www.navy-reserve.org
1619 King St   Alexandria VA 22314
Ph: 703-548-5800 ▪ Fx: 866-683-3647 ▪ TF: 866-672-4968

Reserve Association, Naval Enlisted — www.nera.org
6703 Farragut Ave   Falls Church VA 22042
Ph: 703-534-1329 ▪ Fx: 703-534-3617 ▪ TF: 800-776-9020

Reserve Officers Association of the US — www.roa.org
1 Constitution Ave NE   Washington DC 20002
Ph: 202-479-2200 ▪ Fx: 202-479-0416 ▪ TF: 800-809-9448

Residency Directors, Association of Family Practice — www.afprd.org
c/o Allen Press 11400 Tomahawk Creek Pkwy Suite 670   Leawood KS 66211
Ph: 913-906-6000 ▪ Fx: 913-906-6105 ▪ TF: 800-274-2237

Resident Matching Program, National — www.nrmp.org
2501 'N' St NW   Washington DC 20037
Ph: 202-828-0566 ▪ Fx: 202-828-4797

Resident Theatres, League of — www.lort.org
c/o Glick & Weintraub PC 1501 Broadway Suite 2401   New York NY 10036
Ph: 212-944-1501 ▪ Fx: 212-768-0785

Residential Appraisers Institute, National — www.nraiappraisers.com
2001 Cooper Foster Pk Rd   Amherst OH 44001
Ph: 440-282-7925 ▪ Fx: 440-282-8027

Residential Centers, American Association of Children's — www.aacrc-dc.org
2020 Pennsylvania Ave NW Suite 745   Washington DC 20006
Ph: 877-332-2272 ▪ Fx: 877-362-2272

Residential Construction Employers Council — www.aboutrcec.org
2000 Spring Rd Suite 502   Oak Brook IL 60523
Ph: 630-990-3536 ▪ Fx: 630-990-3537

Residential Property Managers, National Association of — www.narpm.org
PO Box 140647   Austin TX 78714
Ph: 512-381-6091 ▪ Fx: 512-454-3036 ▪ TF: 800-782-3452

Residential Space Planners International
PO Box 14393   Scottsdale AZ 85267
Ph: 480-473-0986 ▪ Fx: 480-473-0757 ▪ TF: 800-548-0945

Residential Specialists, Council of — www.crs.com
430 N Michigan Ave Suite 300   Chicago IL 60611
Ph: 312-321-4400 ▪ Fx: 312-329-8882 ▪ TF: 800-462-8841

Residents' Association, Emergency Medicine — www.emra.org
1125 Executive Cir   Irving TX 75038
Ph: 972-550-0920 ▪ Fx: 972-580-2829 ▪ TF: 800-798-1822

Residents, Committee of Interns & — www.cirseiu.org
520 8th Ave Suite 1200   New York NY 10018
Ph: 212-356-8100 ▪ Fx: 212-356-8111

Residents in Radiation Oncology, Association of — www.arro.org
12500 Fair Lakes Cir Suite 375   Fairfax VA 22033
Ph: 703-502-7852 ▪ Fx: 703-502-7852 ▪ TF: 800-962-7876

Resilient Floor Covering Institute — www.rfci.com
401 E Jefferson St Suite 102   Rockville MD 20850
Ph: 301-340-8580 ▪ Fx: 301-340-7283

Resist Inc — www.resistinc.org
259 Elm St   Somerville MA 02144
Ph: 617-623-5110

Resist!, Refuse & — www.refuseandresist.org
305 Madison Ave Suite 166   New York NY 10165
Ph: 212-713-5657

Resistance Welder Manufacturers' Association — www.rwma.org
1900 Arch St   Philadelphia PA 19103
Ph: 215-564-3484 ▪ Fx: 215-564-2175

RESOLVE: National Infertility Association — www.resolve.org
1310 Broadway   Somerville MA 02144
Ph: 617-623-1156 ▪ Fx: 617-623-0252

Resort & Commercial Recreation Association — www.r-c-r-a.org
PO Box 2437   Aurora IL 60507
Ph: 630-892-2175 ▪ Fx: 630-801-4202

Resort Development Association, American — www.arda.org
1201 15th St NW Suite 400   Washington DC 20005
Ph: 202-371-6700 ▪ Fx: 202-289-8544

Resort Hotel Association — www.resorthotelinsurance.com
461 McLaws Cir Suite 4   Williamsburg VA 23185
Ph: 757-220-7194 ▪ Fx: 757-253-2445

Resorts Worldwide Inc, Preferred Hotels & — www.preferredhotels.com
311 S Wacker Dr Suite 1900   Chicago IL 60606
Ph: 312-913-0400 ▪ Fx: 312-913-0444 ▪ TF: 800-323-7500

Resource Action Center, Southeast Asia — www.searac.org
1628 16th St NW 3rd Fl   Washington DC 20009
Ph: 202-667-4690 ▪ Fx: 202-667-6449 ▪ TF: 800-600-9188

Resource Center for Nonviolence — www.rcnv.org
515 Broadway   Santa Cruz CA 95060
Ph: 831-423-1626 ▪ Fx: 831-423-8716

Resource Development, Council for — www.crdnet.org
1 Dupont Cir NW Suite 410   Washington DC 20036
Ph: 202-822-9700 ▪ Fx: 202-822-5014

Resource Foundation — www.resourcefnd.org
PO Box 3006   Larchmont NY 10538
Ph: 914-834-5810

Resource Institute Inc, College-University — www.curi-inc.org
4953 'W' St NW   Washington DC 20007
Ph: 202-337-0889

Resource Management, APICS - Educational Society for — www.apics.org
5301 Shawnee Rd   Alexandria VA 22312
Ph: 703-354-8851 ▪ Fx: 703-354-8106 ▪ TF: 800-444-2742

Resource Management, Center for — www.crminc.com
2 Highland Rd S   Hampton NH 03842
Ph: 603-394-7040 ▪ Fx: 603-394-7483

(Resource Management) Winrock International — www.winrock.org
38 Winrock Dr   Morrilton AR 72110
Ph: 501-727-5435 ▪ Fx: 501-727-5242

Resourceful Women — www.rw.org
340 Pine St Suite 302   San Francisco CA 94104
Ph: 415-956-3023 ▪ Fx: 415-837-1144

Resources for the Future — www.rff.org
1616 P St NW   Washington DC 20036
Ph: 202-328-5000 ▪ Fx: 202-939-3460

Resources for Independent Thinking — www.rit.org
484 Lake Park Ave Suite 24   Oakland CA 94610
Ph: 925-228-0565 ▪ Fx: 866-422-7612

Resources Institute, World — www.wri.org
10 G St NE Suite 800   Washington DC 20002
Ph: 202-729-7600 ▪ Fx: 202-729-7610

Respect of Life & Environment, Center for — www.crle.org
2100 L St NW   Washington DC 20037
Ph: 202-778-6133 ▪ Fx: 202-778-6138

Respiratory Care, American Association for — www.aarc.org
11030 Ables Ln   Dallas TX 75229
Ph: 972-243-2272 ▪ Fx: 972-484-2720

(Respiratory Care) NAMDRC — www.namdrc.org
5454 Wisconsin Ave Suite 1270   Chevy Chase MD 20815
Ph: 301-718-2975 ▪ Fx: 301-718-2976

Respiratory Care Inc, National Board for — www.nbrc.org
8310 Nieman Rd   Lenexa KS 66214
Ph: 913-599-4200 ▪ Fx: 913-541-0156

Respiratory Nursing Society — www.respiratorynursingsociety.org
c/o NY State Nurses Assn 11 Cornell Rd   Latham NY 12110
Ph: 518-782-9400

Respiratory Protection, International Society for - Americas Section — www.amersectisrp.org

Responsible Industry for a Sound Environment — www.pestfacts.org
1156 15th St NW Suite 400   Washington DC 20005
Ph: 202-872-3860 ▪ Fx: 202-463-0474

Responsible Medicine, Physicians' Committee for — www.pcrm.org
5100 Wisconsin Ave NW Suite 400   Washington DC 20016
Ph: 202-686-2210 ▪ Fx: 202-686-2216

Responsive Education, Institute for www.responsiveeducation.org
Northeastern Univ 21 Lake Hall   Boston MA 02115
Ph: 617-373-2595 ▪ Fx: 617-373-8839

Restaurant Association Educational Foundation, National www.nraef.org
175 W Jackson Blvd Suite 1500   Chicago IL 60604
Ph: 312-715-1010 ▪ TF: 800-765-2122

Restaurant Association Executives, International Society of www.israe.org
8525 Douglas Ave Suite 47   Des Moines IA 50322
Ph: 515-276-1454 ▪ Fx: 515-276-3660

Restaurant Association, National www.restaurant.org
1200 17th St NW   Washington DC 20036
Ph: 202-331-5900 ▪ Fx: 202-331-2429 ▪ TF: 800-424-5156

Restaurant Employees International Union, Hotel Employees & www.hereunion.org
1219 28th St NW   Washington DC 20007
Ph: 202-393-4373 ▪ Fx: 202-333-0468

Restaurant & Institutional Education, International Council on Hotel www.chrie.org
2613 N Parham Rd 2nd Fl   Richmond VA 23294
Ph: 804-346-4800 ▪ Fx: 804-346-5009

Restaurant Trainers, Council of Hotel & www.chart.org
PO Box 2835   Westfield NJ 07091
Ph: 800-463-5918 ▪ Fx: 800-427-5436

Restaurants of America, Council of Independent www.ciraonline.org
304 W Liberty St Suite 201   Louisville KY 40202
Ph: 502-583-3783 ▪ Fx: 502-589-3602

Restaurants, National Council of Chain www.nccr.net
325 7th St NW Suite 1100   Washington DC 20004
Ph: 202-626-8183 ▪ Fx: 202-626-8185

Restaurateurs, Women Chefs & www.womenchefs.org
304 W Liberty St Suite 201   Louisville KY 40202
Ph: 502-581-0300 ▪ Fx: 502-589-3602 ▪ TF: 877-927-7787

Restitution Successor Organization, Jewish
15 E 26th St Rm 906   New York NY 10010
Ph: 212-696-4944 ▪ Fx: 212-679-2126

Restless Legs Syndrome Foundation Inc www.rls.org
819 2nd St SW   Rochester MN 55902
Ph: 507-287-6465 ▪ Fx: 507-287-6312 ▪ TF: 877-463-6757

Restoration, Association of Specialists in Cleaning & www.ascr.org
8229 Cloverleaf Dr Suite 460   Millersville MD 21108
Ph: 410-729-9900 ▪ Fx: 410-729-3603 ▪ TF: 800-272-7012

Restoration Certification, Institute of Inspection Cleaning & www.iicrc.org
2715 E Mill Plain Blvd   Vancouver WA 98661
Ph: 360-693-5675 ▪ Fx: 360-693-4858

Restoration Foundation, Newport www.newportrestoration.com
51 Touro St   Newport RI 02840
Ph: 401-849-7300 ▪ Fx: 401-849-0125

Restoration Institute, Sealant Waterproofing & www.swrionline.org
14 W 3rd St Suite 200   Kansas City MO 64105
Ph: 816-472-7974 ▪ Fx: 816-472-7765

Restoration Society, Capitol Hill www.chrs.org
420 10th St NE PO Box 15264   Washington DC 20003
Ph: 202-543-0425

Restorative Dentistry, American Academy of www.restorativeacademy.com
985 Fuller Rd   Colorado Springs CO 80920
Ph: 719-633-1060 ▪ Fx: 719-953-7926

Restorers, Association of www.assoc-restorers.com
8 Medford Pl   New Hartford NY 13413
Ph: 315-733-1952

Restraints Council, Automotive Occupant www.aorc.org
1081 Dove Run Rd Suite 403   Lexington KY 40502
Ph: 859-269-4240 ▪ Fx: 859-269-4241

Restructuring Advisors, Association of Insolvency & www.airacira.org
221 Stewart Ave Suite 207   Medford OR 97501
Ph: 541-858-1665 ▪ Fx: 541-858-9187

RESULTS www.results.org
440 1st St NW Suite 450   Washington DC 20001
Ph: 202-783-7100 ▪ Fx: 202-783-2818

Resume Writers & Career Coaches, Professional Association of www.parw.com
1388 Brightwaters Blvd NE   Saint Petersburg FL 33704
Ph: 727-821-2274 ▪ Fx: 727-894-1277 ▪ TF: 800-822-7279

Retail Action Group, Black www.bragusa.org
PO Box 1192 Rockefeller Center Stn   New York NY 10185
Ph: 212-319-7751

Retail Advertising & Marketing Association www.rama-nrf.org
325 7th St NW Suite 1100   Washington DC 20004
Ph: 202-661-3052 ▪ Fx: 202-661-3049

Retail Association, International Mass www.imra.org
1700 N Moore St Suite 2250   Arlington VA 22209
Ph: 703-841-2300 ▪ Fx: 703-841-1184

Retail Collection Attorneys, National Association of www.narca.org
1620 'I' St NW Suite 165   Washington DC 20006
Ph: 202-861-0706 ▪ Fx: 202-463-8498 ▪ TF: 800-633-6069

Retail Confectioners International www.retailconfectioners.org
1807 Glenview Rd Suite 204   Glenview IL 60025
Ph: 847-724-6120 ▪ Fx: 847-724-2719 ▪ TF: 800-545-5381

Retail Dealers Association, North American www.narda.com
10 E 22nd St Suite 310   Lombard IL 60148
Ph: 630-953-8950 ▪ Fx: 630-953-8957 ▪ TF: 800-621-0298

Retail Federation, National www.nrf.com
325 7th St NW Suite 1100   Washington DC 20004
Ph: 202-783-7971 ▪ Fx: 202-737-2849 ▪ TF: 800-673-4692

Retail Lumber Association, Northeastern www.nrla.org
585 N Greenbush Rd   Rensselaer NY 12144
Ph: 518-286-1010 ▪ Fx: 518-286-1755 ▪ TF: 800-292-6752

Retail Marketing Services, Association of www.goarms.com
244 Broad St   Red Bank NJ 07701
Ph: 732-842-5070 ▪ Fx: 732-219-1938

Retail Marketing Services, National Association for www.narms.com
PO Box 906   Plover WI 54467
Ph: 715-342-0948 ▪ Fx: 715-342-1943 ▪ TF: 888-526-2767

Retail Packaging Manufacturers Association www.retailpackaging.org
PO Box 17656   Covington KY 41017
Ph: 859-341-9623 ▪ Fx: 859-341-6211

Retail Print Music Dealers Association www.printmusic.org
13140 Coit Rd Suite 320 LB 120   Dallas TX 75240
Ph: 972-233-9107 ▪ Fx: 972-490-4219

Retail Solutions Providers Association www.icrda.org
415 Taggart Creek Rd   Charlotte NC 28208
Ph: 704-357-3124 ▪ Fx: 704-357-3127

Retail Technology Standards, Association for www.nrf-arts.org
325 7th St NW Suite 1100   Washington DC 20004
Ph: 202-626-8140

Retail Tobacco Dealers of America www.rtda.org
12 Galloway Ave Suite 1B   Cockeysville MD 21030
Ph: 410-628-1674 ▪ Fx: 410-628-1679

Retail Wholesale & Department Store Union www.rwdsu.org
30 E 29th St   New York NY 10016
Ph: 212-684-5300 ▪ Fx: 212-779-2809

Retailers of America Inc, Oriental Rug www.orrainc.com
PO Box 1191   Milwaukee WI 53201
Ph: 414-224-0448 ▪ Fx: 414-224-0480

Retailers & Artists, Network of Alternatives for Publishers www.napra.org
PO Box 9   Eastsound WA 98245
Ph: 360-376-2702 ▪ Fx: 360-376-2704 ▪ TF: 800-367-1907

Retailing Association, American Collegiate www.acraretail.org

Retailing Association, Electronic www.retailing.org
2101 Wilson Blvd Suite 1002   Arlington VA 22201
Ph: 703-841-1751 ▪ Fx: 703-841-1860 ▪ TF: 800-987-6462

Retardation, American Association on Mental www.aamr.org
444 N Capitol St NW Suite 846   Washington DC 20001
Ph: 202-387-1968 ▪ Fx: 202-387-2193 ▪ TF: 800-424-3688

Retarded, Association for the Advancement of the Blind & www.aabr.org
1508 College Pt Blvd   College Point NY 11356
Ph: 718-321-3800 ▪ Fx: 718-321-8688

Retarded, Voice of the www.vor.net
5005 Newport Dr Suite 108   Rolling Meadows IL 60008
Ph: 847-253-6020 ▪ Fx: 847-253-6054

Retinitis Pigmentosa International www.rpinternational.org
PO Box 900   Woodland Hills CA 91365
Ph: 818-992-0500 ▪ Fx: 818-992-3265

Retired Airline Pilots Association www.rapa.org
PO Box 293443   Sacramento CA 95829
Ph: 650-368-0200

Retired Americans, Alliance for www.retiredamericans.org
888 16th St NW Suite 520   Washington DC 20006
Ph: 202-974-8222 ▪ Fx: 202-974-8256 ▪ TF: 888-373-6497

Retired Americans, Association of www.ara-usa.org
6505 E 82nd St Suite 130   Indianapolis IN 46250
Ph: 800-806-6160 ▪ Fx: 317-915-2510

Retired Dentists, American Society of
1 W Camino Real Blvd Suite 207   Boca Raton FL 33432
Ph: 561-395-2773 ▪ TF: 800-495-2773

Retired Enlisted Association www.trea.org
13130 E Colfax Ave   Aurora CO 80011
Ph: 303-340-3939 ▪ Fx: 303-340-4516

Retired Federal Employees, National Association of www.narfe.org
606 N Washington St   Alexandria VA 22314
Ph: 703-838-7760 ▪ Fx: 703-838-7785 ▪ TF: 800-627-3394

(Retired Persons) AARP www.aarp.org
601 'E' St NW   Washington DC 20049
Ph: 202-434-2277 ▪ Fx: 202-434-2588 ▪ TF: 800-424-3410

Retired Persons, Canadian Association of www.50plus.com
1304-27 Queen St E   Toronto ON M5C2M6
Ph: 416-363-8748 ▪ Fx: 416-363-8747 ▪ TF: 800-363-9736

Retired Senior Volunteer Program Directors, National Association of
12388 Warwick Blvd   Newport News VA 23601
Ph: 757-595-9037 ▪ Fx: 757-595-9047

Retired Teachers Association, National www.aarp.org/nrta
601 'E' St NW   Washington DC 20049
Ph: 202-434-2277 ▪ Fx: 202-434-2320 ▪ TF: 800-424-3410

Retired Travel Club, Special Military Active www.smartrving.net
600 University Office Blvd Suite 1A   Pensacola FL 32504
Ph: 800-354-7681

Retired & Veteran Railway Employees, National Association of www.narvre.com
300 Cedar Blvd Suite 201A   Pittsburgh PA 15228
Ph: 412-563-5611 ▪ Fx: 412-563-5612

Retirement Administrators, National Association of State www.nasra.org
444 N Capitol St NW Suite 234   Washington DC 20001
Ph: 202-624-1417

Retirement Communities, American Association of www.the-aarc.org
700 Pelham Rd N   Jacksonville AL 36265
Ph: 256-782-5700 ▪ Fx: 256-782-5179

Retirement Foundation, Standardbred www.adoptahorse.org
PO Box 763   Freehold NJ 07728
Ph: 732-462-8773 ▪ Fx: 732-431-9503

Retirement, Fund for Assuring an Independent
100 Indiana Ave NW Suite 813   Washington DC 20001
Ph: 202-662-2833 ▪ Fx: 202-756-7400

Retirement Industry Trust Association
4424 Montgomery Ave Suite 202   Bethesda MD 20814
Ph: 301-652-5066 ▪ Fx: 301-913-9146

Retirement, National Council on Teacher www.nctr.org
7600 Greenhaven Dr Suite 302   Sacramento CA 95831
Ph: 916-394-2075 ▪ Fx: 916-392-0295

Retirement Research Foundation www.rrf.org
8765 W Higgins Rd Suite 430   Chicago IL 60631
Ph: 773-714-8080 ▪ Fx: 773-714-8089

Retirement Systems, National Conference on Public Employee www.ncpers.org
444 N Capitol St NW Suite 221   Washington DC 20001
Ph: 202-624-1456 ▪ Fx: 202-624-1439 ▪ TF: 877-202-5706

Retreats International
PO Box 1067   Notre Dame IN 46556
Ph: 219-631-5320 ▪ Fx: 219-631-4546 ▪ TF: 800-556-4532
www.retreatsintl.org

Retriever Club, National
4379 S Howell Ave Suite 17   Milwaukee WI 53207
Ph: 414-481-2760 ▪ Fx: 414-481-2743
www.working-retriever.com/nrc

Reunion Managers, National Association of
PO Box 23211   Tampa FL 33623
Ph: 800-654-2776
www.reunions.com

Reunion Registry, International Soundex
PO Box 2312   Carson City NV 89702
Ph: 775-882-7755
www.isrr.net

Reusable Industrial Packaging Association
8401 Corporate Dr Suite 450   Landover MD 20785
Ph: 301-577-3786 ▪ Fx: 301-577-6476 ▪ TF: 800-533-3786
www.reusablepackaging.org

Reusable Textile Association, American
PO Box 1053   Mulberry FL 33860
Ph: 863-660-5350
www.arta1.com

Revenue Association, American
PO Box 728   Leesport PA 19533
Ph: 610-926-6200
www.revenuer.org

Revenue Communication Advancement, Council for Electronic
600 Cameron St Suite 309   Alexandria VA 22314
Ph: 703-340-1655
www.cerca.org/

Review Appraisers Council, Accredited
c/o Lincoln Graduate Ctr 303 W Cypress St   San Antonio TX
78212
Ph: 210-225-2897 ▪ Fx: 210-225-8450 ▪ TF: 800-531-5333
arac.lincoln-grad.org

Revolution, General Society Sons of the
201 W Lexington Ave Suite 1776   Independence MO 64050
Ph: 800-593-1776
www.sr1776.org

Revolution, National Society of the Children of the American
1776 D St NW   Washington DC 20006
Ph: 202-638-3153 ▪ Fx: 202-737-3162
www.nscar.org

Revolution, National Society Daughters of the American
1776 D St NW   Washington DC 20006
Ph: 202-628-1776 ▪ Fx: 202-879-3252
www.dar.org

Revolution, National Society of the Sons of the American
1000 S 4th St   Louisville KY 40203
Ph: 502-589-1776 ▪ Fx: 502-589-1671
www.sar.org

Revolution & Peace, Hoover Institution on War
434 Galvez Mall   Stanford CA 94305
Ph: 650-723-1754 ▪ Fx: 650-723-1687 ▪ TF: 877-466-8374
www-hoover.stanford.edu

Revolution Round Table, American
6 Grovedale Rd   Niantic CT 06357
Ph: 860-739-6859 ▪ Fx: 860-786-8230
eve.kean.edu/~leew/arrt

Revolutionary Federation, Armenian
80 Bigelow Ave   Watertown MA 02472
Ph: 617-926-3685 ▪ Fx: 617-926-5525
www.arf.am/English/

Rex Rabbit Club, National
21840 S 116th Ave   New Lenox IL 60451
Ph: 815-469-5150
www.nationalrexrc.com

Reye's Syndrome Foundation, National
PO Box 829   Bryan OH 43506
Ph: 419-636-2679 ▪ Fx: 419-636-9897 ▪ TF: 800-233-7393
www.reyessyndrome.org

Reynolds Donald W Foundation
1701 Village Ctr Cir   Las Vegas NV 89134
Ph: 702-804-6000 ▪ Fx: 702-804-6099
www.dwreynolds.org

Reynolds Kate B Charitable Trust
128 Reynolda Village   Winston-Salem NC 27106
Ph: 336-723-1456 ▪ Fx: 336-723-7765
www.kbr.org

Rheology, Society of
c/o American Institute of Physics 2 Huntington Quadrangle Suite
1N01   Melville NY 11747
Ph: 516-576-2403 ▪ Fx: 516-576-2223
www.rheology.org

Rhetoric Society of America
Univ of Nevada PO Box 455007   Las Vegas NV 89154
Ph: 702-895-3030 ▪ Fx: 702-895-4805
rhetoricsociety.org

Rheumatology, American College of
1800 Century Pl Suite 250   Atlanta GA 30345
Ph: 404-633-3777 ▪ Fx: 404-633-1870
www.rheumatology.org

Rheumatology, American Osteopathic College of
193 Monroe Ave   Edison NJ 08820
Ph: 732-494-6688 ▪ Fx: 732-494-6689

Rheumatology Health Professionals, Association of
1800 Century Pl Suite 250   Atlanta GA 30345
Ph: 404-633-3777 ▪ Fx: 404-633-1870
www.rheumatology.org/arhp

Rhinelander Rabbit Club of America
1560 Vine St   El Centro CA 92243
Ph: 760-352-6525
www.hop.to/Rhinelanders

Rhinologic Society, American
3400 Bainbridge Ave 3rd Fl   Bronx NY 10467
Ph: 718-920-2991 ▪ Fx: 718-652-5194
www.american-rhinologic.org

**Rhinological & Otological Society Inc, American
Laryngological**   555 N 30th St   Omaha NE 68131
Ph: 402-346-5500 ▪ Fx: 402-346-5300
www.triological.org

Rho Chi Society
UNC School of Pharmacy 3210 Kerr Hall CB 7360   Chapel Hill
NC 27599
Ph: 919-843-9001 ▪ Fx: 919-843-9255
www.rhochi.org

Rhodes Scholars, Association of American
2717 Lincoln St   Evanston IL 60201
Ph: 847-869-5950 ▪ Fx: 847-869-6993
www.americanrhodes.org

Rhododendron Society, American
11 Pinecrest Dr   Fortuna CA 95540
Ph: 707-725-3043 ▪ Fx: 707-725-1217
www.rhododendron.org

Rhododendron Species Foundation
2525 S 336th St PO Box 3798   Federal Way WA 98063
Ph: 253-838-4646 ▪ Fx: 253-838-4686
www.rhodygarden.org

Rhythms, Society for Light Treatment & Biological
174 Cook St PO Box 591687   San Francisco CA 94159
Ph: 415-876-0716 ▪ Fx: 415-751-2758
www.websciences.org/sltbr

Rice Council, USA
9800 Richmond Ave Suite 235   Houston TX 77042
Ph: 713-270-6699 ▪ Fx: 713-270-9021

Rice Federation, USA
9800 Richmond Ave Suite 235   Houston TX 77042
Ph: 713-270-6699 ▪ Fx: 713-270-9021
www.usarice.com

Rice Producers Association, US
2900 Wilcrest Dr Suite 180   Houston TX 77042
Ph: 713-974-7423 ▪ Fx: 713-974-7696
www.usriceproducers.com

Richard III Society - American Branch
www.r3.org/welcome.html

Richard King Mellon Foundation
500 Grant St Suite 4106   Pittsburgh PA 15219
Ph: 412-392-2800 ▪ Fx: 412-392-2837
www.fdncenter.org/grantmaker/rkmellon

Richard Wagner Society of New York
PO Box 230949 Ansonia Stn   New York NY 10023
Ph: 212-749-4561 ▪ Fx: 212-749-1542
www.wagnersocietyny.org

Richardson Smith Foundation Inc
60 Jesup Rd   Westport CT 06880
Ph: 203-222-6222 ▪ Fx: 203-222-6282
www.srf.org

RID-USA Inc
PO Box 520   Schenectady NY 12301
Ph: 518-372-0034 ▪ Fx: 518-370-4917
www.rid-usa.org

Rider's Association, American Sport Touring
PO Box 672015   Marietta GA 30006
Ph: 770-222-0380

Riders Association, Gold Wing Road
21423 N 11th Ave   Phoenix AZ 85027
Ph: 623-581-2500 ▪ Fx: 623-581-3844 ▪ TF: 800-843-9460
www.gwrra.org

Riding for the Handicapped Association, North American
PO Box 33150   Denver CO 80233
Ph: 303-452-1212 ▪ Fx: 303-252-4610 ▪ TF: 800-369-7433
www.narha.org

Riding, National Center for Therapeutic
PO Box 434   Burtonsville MD 20866
Ph: 301-421-0380 ▪ Fx: 301-421-0384
www.nctrriding.org/about

Rifle Association of America, National
11250 Waples Mill Rd   Fairfax VA 22030
Ph: 703-267-1000 ▪ Fx: 703-267-3957 ▪ TF: 800-672-3888
www.nra.org

Rifle Association, American Single Shot
PO Box 362   Delphos OH 45833
Ph: 419-692-3866 ▪ Fx: 419-695-3756
www.assra.com

Rifle Association, National Muzzle Loading
PO Box 67   Friendship IN 47021
Ph: 812-667-5131 ▪ Fx: 812-667-5136
www.nmlra.org

Rifles, National Society of Pershing
200 Nebraska Union Box 240 PO Box 880456   Lincoln NE
68588
Ph: 402-472-2472 ▪ Fx: 402-472-2478
nhq.pershingrifles.com/

Riggers, National Council of Erectors Fabricators &
10382 Main St Suite 200 PO Box 280   Fairfax VA 22030
Ph: 703-591-1870 ▪ Fx: 703-591-1895

Rigging Association, Specialized Carriers &
2750 Prosperity Ave Suite 620   Fairfax VA 22031
Ph: 703-698-0291 ▪ Fx: 703-698-0297
www.scranet.org

Right to Life Committee Inc, National
512 10th St NW   Washington DC 20004
Ph: 202-626-8800
www.nrlc.org

Right to Life PAC, National
512 10th St NW   Washington DC 20004
Ph: 202-626-8808 ▪ Fx: 202-393-2874

Right of Way Association, International
19750 S Vermont Ave Suite 220   Torrance CA 90502
Ph: 310-538-0233 ▪ Fx: 310-538-1471
www.irwaonline.org

Right to Work Committee, National
8001 Braddock Rd Suite 500   Springfield VA 22160
Ph: 703-321-8510 ▪ Fx: 703-321-7342 ▪ TF: 800-336-3600
www.right-to-work.org

Right to Work Legal Defense Foundation Inc, National
8001 Braddock Rd Suite 600   Springfield VA 22160
Ph: 703-321-8510 ▪ Fx: 703-321-9613 ▪ TF: 800-325-7892
www.nrtw.org

Righteous, Jewish Foundation for the
305 7th Ave 19th Fl   New York NY 10001
Ph: 212-727-9955 ▪ Fx: 212-727-9956 ▪ TF: 888-421-1221
www.jfr.org

Rights Action
1830 Connecticut Ave NW   Washington DC 20009
Ph: 202-783-1123 ▪ Fx: 202-483-6730
www.rightsaction.org

Rights, Center for Economic & Social
162 Montague St 2nd Fl   Brooklyn NY 11201
Ph: 718-237-9145 ▪ Fx: 718-237-9147
www.cesr.org

Rights, Center for Individual
1233 20th St NW Suite 300   Washington DC 20036
Ph: 202-833-8400 ▪ Fx: 202-833-8410
www.cir-usa.org

Rights Coalition, American
7510 Lee Hwy   Chattanooga TN 37421
Ph: 423-893-7801 ▪ Fx: 423-893-7511 ▪ TF: 800-634-2224
www.tenlaws.com

Rights Coalition, Home Recording
PO Box 14267   Washington DC 20044
Ph: 202-628-9212 ▪ Fx: 202-628-9227 ▪ TF: 800-282-8273
www.hrrc.org

Rights, Coalition for Student & Academic
PO Box 491   Solebury PA 18963
Ph: 215-862-9096 ▪ Fx: 215-862-9097
www.co-star.org

Rights Inc, Committee for Mother & Child
6536 Colgate Ave   Los Angeles CA 90048
Ph: 323-634-0543 ▪ Fx: 323-936-7762

Rights Fund, Native American
1506 Broadway St   Boulder CO 80302
Ph: 303-447-8760 ▪ Fx: 303-443-7776
www.narf.org

Rigid Plastics Packaging Institute
179 S Kenilworth Ave   Elmhurst IL 60126
Ph: 630-833-5894 ▪ Fx: 630-833-5896
www.rigidplasticpackaging.org

Rim Association, National Wheel &
5121 Bowden Rd Suite 303   Jacksonville FL 32216
Ph: 904-737-2900 ▪ Fx: 904-636-9881
nationalwheelandrim.org

Ringers, North American Guild of Change
829 N 25th St   Philadelphia PA 19130
Ph: 215-765-8736 ▪ Fx: 215-276-5238
www.nagcr.org

Ripon Society
1300 L St NW Suite 900   Washington DC 20005
Ph: 202-216-1008 ▪ Fx: 202-216-0036
www.riponsoc.org

Risk Analysis, Society for
1313 Dolley Madison Blvd Suite 402   McLean VA 22101
Ph: 703-790-1745 ▪ Fx: 703-790-2672
www.sra.org

Risk & Insurance Association, American
716 Providence Rd PO Box 3028   Malvern PA 19355
Ph: 610-640-1997 ▪ Fx: 610-725-1007
www.aria.org

Risk & Insurance Management Society Inc
655 3rd Ave 2nd Fl   New York NY 10017
Ph: 212-286-9292 ▪ Fx: 212-986-9716 ▪ TF: 800-711-0317
www.rims.org

Risk Management, American Society for Healthcare
1 N Franklin St   Chicago IL 60606
Ph: 312-422-3980 ▪ Fx: 312-422-4580
www.ashrm.org

Risk Management Association, Fiduciary &
PO Box 48297   Athens GA 30604
Ph: 706-354-0083 ▪ Fx: 706-353-3994
www.thefirma.org

Risk Management Association, Public
500 Montgomery St Suite 750   Alexandria VA 22314
Ph: 703-528-7701 ▪ Fx: 703-739-0200
www.primacentral.org

Risk Management Association, RMA -
1650 Market St 1 Liberty Pl Suite 2300   Philadelphia PA 19103
Ph: 215-446-4000 ▪ Fx: 215-446-4101 ▪ TF: 800-677-7621
www.rmahq.org

Risk Management Association, Telecommunications
10 Sylvan Way   Parsippany NJ 07054
Ph: 973-631-8000 ▪ Fx: 973-631-6221
www.trmanet.org

Risk Management Association, Weather
1156 15th St NW Suite 900   Washington DC 20005
Ph: 202-289-3800 ▪ Fx: 202-393-0336
www.wrma.org

Risk Management & Insurance Association, University
342 N Main St   West Hartford CT 06117
Ph: 860-586-7565 ▪ Fx: 860-586-7550
www.urmia.org

Risk Managers Association, Public Agency
6067 Marla Ct Suite 201   San Jose CA 95124
Ph: 408-979-8030 ▪ Fx: 408-723-2423 ▪ TF: 888-907-2762
www.parma.com

Risk Managers International, Associated
2 Pierce Pl   Itasca IL 60143
Ph: 630-285-4186 ▪ Fx: 630-285-3590
www.armnet.com

Risk Professionals, Global Association of
111 Pavonia Ave Suite 430   Jersey City NJ 07310
Ph: 201-222-0054 ▪ Fx: 201-222-5022
www.garp.com

Risk Retention Association, National
4248 Park Glen Rd   Minneapolis MN 55416
Ph: 952-928-4656 ▪ Fx: 952-929-1318 ▪ TF: 800-999-4505
www.nrra-usa.org

Ritual, Women's Alliance for Theology Ethics &
8035 13th St   Silver Spring MD 20910
Ph: 301-589-2509 ▪ Fx: 301-589-3150
www.his.com/~mhunt

River, Friends of the
915 20th St   Sacramento CA 95814
Ph: 916-442-3155 ▪ Fx: 916-442-3396
www.friendsoftheriver.org

River Management Society
PO Box 9048   Missoula MT 59807
Ph: 406-549-0514 ▪ Fx: 406-542-6208
www.river-management.org

River Network
520 SW 6th Ave Suite 1130   Portland OR 97204
Ph: 503-241-3506 ▪ Fx: 503-241-9256 ▪ TF: 800-423-6747
www.rivernetwork.org

River Touring Association Inc, American
20400 Casa Loma Rd   Groveland CA 95321
Ph: 209-962-7873 ▪ TF: 800-323-2782
www.arta.org

Rivers, American
1025 Vermont Ave NW Suite 720   Washington DC 20005
Ph: 202-347-7550 ▪ Fx: 202-347-9240 ▪ TF: 800-296-6900
www.amrivers.org

Rivers Council, Pacific
PO Box 10798   Eugene OR 97440
Ph: 541-345-0119 ▪ Fx: 541-345-0710
www.pacrivers.org

Rivers, National Organization for
212 W Cheyenne Mountain Blvd   Colorado Springs CO 80906
Ph: 719-579-8759 ▪ Fx: 719-576-6238
www.nationalrivers.org

Rivers Network, International
1847 Berkeley Way   Berkeley CA 94703
Ph: 510-848-1155 ▪ Fx: 510-848-1008
www.irn.org

Rivers Ports & Terminals Inc, Inland
PO Box 4363   Jackson MS 39296
Ph: 601-352-4778 ▪ Fx: 601-355-1506
www.irpt.net

Riveter Association, American Rosie the
2561 Rocky Ridge Rd   Birmingham AL 35243
Ph: 205-822-4106
www.rosietheriveter.net

RMA - Risk Management Association
1650 Market St 1 Liberty Pl Suite 2300   Philadelphia PA 19103
Ph: 215-446-4000 ▪ Fx: 215-446-4101 ▪ TF: 800-677-7621
www.rmahq.org

RNA Society
9650 Rockville Pike   Bethesda MD 20814
Ph: 301-530-7120 ▪ Fx: 301-530-7049
rnasociety.org

Road Federation, International
1010 Massachusetts Ave NW Suite 410   Washington DC 20001
Ph: 202-371-5544 ▪ Fx: 202-371-5565
www.irfnet.org

Road Information Program, TRIP
1726 M St NW Suite 401   Washington DC 20036
Ph: 202-466-6706 ▪ Fx: 202-785-4772
www.tripnet.org

Road Map Foundation, New
PO Box 15981   Seattle WA 98115
Ph: 206-527-0437
www.newroadmap.org

Road Riders Association, Gold Wing
21423 N 11th Ave   Phoenix AZ 85027
Ph: 623-581-2500 ▪ Fx: 623-581-3844 ▪ TF: 800-843-9460
www.gwrra.org

Road Runners Club of America
510 N Washington St   Alexandria VA 22314
Ph: 703-836-0558 ▪ Fx: 703-836-4430
www.rrca.org

Road & Transportation Builders Association, American
1010 Massachusetts Ave NW   Washington DC 20001
Ph: 202-289-4434 ▪ Fx: 202-289-4435
www.artba-hq.org

Road Travel, Association for Safe International
11769 Gainsborough Rd   Potomac MD 20854
Ph: 301-983-5252 ▪ Fx: 301-983-3663
www.asirt.org

Roadside Vegetation Management Association, National
6402 Betty Cook Dr   Austin TX 78723
Ph: 512-933-9930 ▪ Fx: 512-933-9971
www.nrvma.org

Roadway Safety Foundation
1 Thomas Cir NW 10th Fl   Washington DC 20005
Ph: 202-857-1200
www.roadwaysafety.org

Robert E Lee Memorial Association
Stratford Hall Plantation   Stratford VA 22558
Ph: 804-493-8038 ▪ Fx: 804-493-0333
www.stratfordhall.org

Robert F Kennedy Memorial
1367 Connecticut Ave NW Suite 200   Washington DC 20036
Ph: 202-463-7575 ▪ Fx: 202-463-6606 ▪ TF: 800-558-1880
www.rfkmemorial.org

Robert J Dole Institute of Politics
704 W 12th St   Lawrence KS 66044
Ph: 785-749-3911 ▪ Fx: 785-749-3907
www.doleinstitute.org

Robert R McCormick Tribune Foundation
435 N Michigan Ave Suite 770   Chicago IL 60611
Ph: 312-222-3512 ▪ Fx: 312-222-3523
www.mccormicktribune.org

Robert W Woodruff Foundation Inc
50 Hurt Plaza Suite 1200   Atlanta GA 30303
Ph: 404-522-6755 ▪ Fx: 404-522-7026
www.woodruff.org

Robert A Welch Foundation
5555 San Felipe St Suite 1900   Houston TX 77056
Ph: 713-961-9884 ▪ Fx: 713-961-5168
www.welch1.org

Robert Wood Johnson Foundation
PO Box 2316   Princeton NJ 08543
Ph: 609-452-8701 ▪ Fx: 609-627-6701
www.rwjf.org

Robinson Jackie Foundation
3 W 35th St 11th Fl   New York NY 10001
Ph: 212-290-8600 ▪ Fx: 212-290-8081
www.jackierobinson.org

Robot Association, International Service
900 Victors Way PO Box 3724   Ann Arbor MI 48106
Ph: 734-994-6088 ▪ Fx: 734-994-3338

Robotic Industries Association
PO Box 3724   Ann Arbor MI 48106
Ph: 734-994-6088 ▪ Fx: 734-994-3338
www.roboticsonline.com

Robotics & Automation Society, IEEE
IEEE Operations Ctr 445 Hoes Ln   Piscataway NJ 08854
Ph: 732-981-0060 ▪ Fx: 732-981-1721
www.ncsu.edu/IEEE-RAS

Rock Art Research Association, American
PO Box 210026   Tucson AZ 85721
Ph: 888-668-0052
www.arara.org

Rock Association, Quartzite
PO Box 661   Sioux Falls SD 57101
Ph: 605-339-1520 ▪ Fx: 605-334-3656
www.quartzite.com/

Rock Coalition, Black
PO Box 1054 Cooper Stn   New York NY 10276
Ph: 212-713-5097 ▪ Fx: 212-226-6707
www.blackrockcoalition.org

Rock Garden Society, North American
PO Box 67   Millwood NY 10546
Ph: 914-762-2948
www.nargs.org

Rock Mechanics Association, American
600 Woodland Terr   Alexandria VA 22302
Ph: 703-683-1808 ▪ Fx: 703-683-1815
www.armarocks.org

Rock the Vote
10635 Santa Monica Blvd Suite 150   Los Angeles CA 90025
Ph: 310-234-0665 ▪ Fx: 310-234-0666
www.rockthevote.com

Rockefeller Brothers Fund
437 Madison Ave 37th Fl   New York NY 10022
Ph: 212-812-4200 ▪ Fx: 212-812-4299
www.rbf.org

Rockefeller Foundation
420 5th Ave   New York NY 10018
Ph: 212-869-8500 ▪ Fx: 212-764-3468 ▪ TF: 800-645-1133
www.rockfound.org

Rockefeller Nelson A Institute of Government
411 State St   Albany NY 12203
Ph: 518-443-5522 ▪ Fx: 518-443-5788
rockinst.org/

Rocket Society, Pacific
PO Box 662   Mojave CA 93502
Ph: 661-824-1662
www.translunar.org/prs

Rocketry Association Inc, Tripoli
PO Box 970010   Orem UT 84097
Ph: 801-225-9306 ▪ Fx: 801-225-9307
www.tripoli.org

Rocketry, National Association of
PO Box 177   Altoona WI 54720
Ph: 715-832-1946 ▪ Fx: 715-832-6432 ▪ TF: 800-262-4872
www.nar.org

Rockette Alumnae Association
908 N Broadway Unit 62E   Yonkers NY 10701
Ph: 914-423-3636

Rockford Institute
928 N Main St   Rockford IL 61103
Ph: 815-964-5053 ▪ Fx: 815-964-9403 ▪ TF: 800-383-0680
www.rockfordinstitute.org

Rocky Mountain Elk Foundation
PO Box 8249   Missoula MT 59807
Ph: 406-523-4500 ▪ Fx: 406-523-4550 ▪ TF: 800-225-5355
www.rmef.org

Rocky Mountain Mineral Law Foundation   www.rmmlf.org
9191 Sheridan Blvd Suite 203   Westminster CO 80031
Ph: 303-321-8100 ▪ Fax: 303-321-7657

Rod Association, National Street   www.nsra-usa.com
4030 Park Ave   Memphis TN 38111
Ph: 901-452-4030 ▪ Fax: 901-452-6772

Rod & Custom Association, Goodguys   www.good-guys.com
PO Box 424   Alamo CA 94507
Ph: 925-838-9876 ▪ Fax: 925-820-8241

Rodeo Association, American Junior   home1.gte.net/ajra
4501 Armstrong St   San Angelo TX 76903
Ph: 915-658-8009

Rodeo Association, International Gay   www.igra.com
900 E Colfax Ave   Denver CO 80218
Ph: 303-832-4472 ▪ Fax: 303-860-9105

Rodeo Association, International Professional   www.iprarodeo.com
PO Box 83377   Oklahoma City OK 73148
Ph: 405-235-6540 ▪ Fax: 405-235-6577

Rodeo Association, National High School   www.nhsra.com
12001 Tejon St Suite 128   Denver CO 80234
Ph: 303-452-0820 ▪ Fax: 303-452-0912 ▪ TF: 800-466-4772

Rodeo Association, National Intercollegiate   www.collegerodeo.com
2316 Eastgate N St Suite 160   Walla Walla WA 99362
Ph: 509-529-4402 ▪ Fax: 509-525-1090

Rodeo Association, National Little Britches   www.nlbra.com
1045 W Rio Grande St   Colorado Springs CO 80906
Ph: 719-389-0333 ▪ Fax: 719-578-1367 ▪ TF: 800-763-3694

Rodeo Association, Women's Professional   www.wpra.com
1235 Lake Plaza Dr Suite 127   Colorado Springs CO 80906
Ph: 719-576-0900 ▪ Fax: 719-576-1386

Rodeo Cowboys Association, Professional   www.prorodeo.com
101 Pro Rodeo Dr   Colorado Springs CO 80919
Ph: 719-593-8840 ▪ Fax: 719-548-4876

Rodeo Historical Society
c/o National Cowboy & Western Heritage Museum 1700 NE
63rd St   Oklahoma City OK 73111
Ph: 405-478-6400 ▪ Fax: 405-478-2842

Roentgen Ray Society, American   www.arrs.org
44211 Slatestone Ct   Leesburg VA 20176
Ph: 703-729-3353 ▪ Fax: 703-729-4839 ▪ TF: 800-438-2777

Roger Sessions Society   www.uncwil.edu/music/Sessionssociety
Univ of North Carolina at Wilmington 601 S College
Rd   Wilmington NC 28403
Ph: 910-962-3390 ▪ Fax: 910-962-7106

Rolf Institute of Structural Integration   www.rolf.org
205 Canyon Rd   Boulder CO 80302
Ph: 303-449-5903 ▪ Fax: 303-449-5978 ▪ TF: 800-530-8875

Roll Forming Institute, Custom   www.metalforming.com/division/crfid
Precision Metal Forming Assn 6363 Oak Tree Blvd   Cleveland
OH 44131
Ph: 216-901-8800 ▪ Fax: 216-901-9190

(Roller Coasters) American Coaster Enthusiasts   www.aceonline.org
7700 Shawnee Mission Pkwy Suite 201   Overland Park KS
66202
Ph: 913-262-4512 ▪ Fax: 913-262-4513

Roller Hockey Association, National Collegiate   www.ncrha.org

Roller Hockey Championships Inc, North American   www.narch.com
521 Hidden Ridge Ct Suite B   Encinitas CA 92024
Ph: 760-943-0049

(Roller Hockey) USA Hockey InLine   www.usahockey.com/inline
1775 Bob Johnson Dr   Colorado Springs CO 80906
Ph: 719-576-8724 ▪ Fax: 719-538-1160

Roller Skating Association International   www.rollerskating.org
6905 Corporate Dr   Indianapolis IN 46278
Ph: 317-347-2626 ▪ Fax: 317-347-2636

Roller Skating Teachers of America, Society of
6905 Corporate Dr   Indianapolis IN 46278
Ph: 317-347-2626 ▪ Fax: 317-347-2636

Roller Sports, USA   www.usarollersports.org
4730 South St   Lincoln NE 68506
Ph: 402-483-7551 ▪ Fax: 402-483-1465

Rolling Readers USA   www.rollingreaders.org
4007 Camino Del Rio S Suite 203   San Diego CA 92108
Ph: 619-516-4095 ▪ Fax: 619-516-4096

Rolls-Royce Owners' Club   www.rroc.org
191 Hempt Rd   Mechanicsburg PA 17050
Ph: 717-697-4671 ▪ Fax: 717-697-7820

Romagnola Association, American   www.americanromagnola.com
3815 Touzalin Ave Suite 104   Lincoln NE 68507
Ph: 402-466-3334 ▪ Fax: 402-466-3338

Roman Catholic Union of America, Polish   www.prcua.org
984 N Milwaukee Ave   Chicago IL 60622
Ph: 773-782-2600 ▪ Fax: 773-278-4595 ▪ TF: 800-772-8632

Romance Writers of America   www.rwanational.org
16000 Stuebner Airline Rd Suite 140   Spring TX 77379
Ph: 832-717-5200 ▪ Fax: 832-717-5210

Romania, American Friends of
4600 Connecticut Ave NW Unit 723   Washington DC 20008
Ph: 202-966-1922

Romanian-American Chamber of Commerce   www.racc.ro
5530 Wisconsin Ave Suite 1110   Chevy Chase MD 20815
Ph: 301-656-9022 ▪ Fax: 301-656-9008

Romanian Missionary Society   www.rmsonline.org
1415 Hill Ave PO Box 527   Wheaton IL 60189
Ph: 630-665-6503 ▪ Fax: 630-665-6538

Romanian Orthodox Episcopate of America   www.roea.org
2535 Grey Tower Rd   Jackson MI 49201
Ph: 517-522-4800

Romanian Orthodox Youth, American   www.aroy.org
Romanian Orthodox Episcopate of America 2535 Grey Tower
Rd   Jackson MI 49201
Ph: 517-522-4800

Romanian Societies of America, Union & League of   www.romaniansocieties.com
23203 Lorain Rd   North Olmsted OH 44070
Ph: 440-779-9913 ▪ Fax: 440-779-9151

Romanian-US Business Council
c/o US Chamber of Commerce 1615 H St NW   Washington DC
20062
Ph: 202-463-5482 ▪ Fax: 202-463-3114

Romney Breeders' Association, American   www.americanromney.org
744 Riverbanks Rd   Grants Pass OR 97527
Ph: 541-476-6428

Ronald McDonald House Charities   www.rmhc.org
1 Kroc Dr   Oak Brook IL 60523
Ph: 630-623-7048 ▪ Fax: 630-623-7488

Roof Coatings Manufacturers Association   www.roofcoatings.org
1156 15th St NW Suite 900   Washington DC 20005
Ph: 202-207-0919 ▪ Fax: 202-223-9741

Roof Consultants Institute   www.rci-online.org
1500 Sunday Dr Suite 204   Raleigh NC 27607
Ph: 919-859-0742 ▪ Fax: 919-859-1328 ▪ TF: 800-828-1902

Roof Deck Contractors Association, National   nrdca.org
PO Box 1582   Westford MA 01886
Ph: 800-217-7944 ▪ Fax: 978-250-9788

Roof Tile Institute   www.rooftile.org
230 E Ohio St Suite 400   Chicago IL 60611
Ph: 312-670-4177 ▪ Fax: 312-644-8557

Roofers Waterproofers & Allied Workers, United Union of www.unionroofers.com
1660 L St NW Suite 800   Washington DC 20036
Ph: 202-463-7663 ▪ Fax: 202-463-6906

Roofing Contractors Association, National   www.nrca.net
10255 W Higgins Rd Suite 600   Rosemont IL 60018
Ph: 847-299-9070 ▪ Fax: 847-299-1183 ▪ TF: 800-323-9545

Roofing Industry Educational Institute   www.nrca.net/riei
10255 W Higgins Rd Suite 600   Rosemont IL 60018
Ph: 847-299-9070 ▪ Fax: 847-299-1183

Roofing, Single Ply   www.spri.org
77 Rumford Ave Suite 3B   Waltham MA 02453
Ph: 781-647-7026 ▪ Fax: 781-647-7222

Roofing Manufacturers Association, Asphalt   www.asphaltroofing.org
1156 15th St NW Suite 900   Washington DC 20005
Ph: 202-207-0917 ▪ Fax: 202-223-9741

Roosevelt Franklin & Eleanor Institute   www.feri.org
4079 Albany Post Rd   Hyde Park NY 12538
Ph: 212-259-1259

Roosevelt Theodore Association   www.theodoreroosevelt.org
PO Box 719   Oyster Bay NY 11771
Ph: 516-921-6319 ▪ Fax: 516-921-6481

Rosacea Society, National   www.rosacea.org
800 S Northwest Hwy Suite 200   Barrington IL 60010
Ph: 847-382-8971 ▪ Fax: 847-382-5567 ▪ TF: 888-662-5874

Roscoe Pound Institute   www.roscoepound.org
1050 31st St NW   Washington DC 20007
Ph: 202-965-3500 ▪ Fax: 202-965-0355

Rose Hybridizers Association   www.rosehybridizers.org
21 S Wheaton Rd   Horseheads NY 14845
Ph: 607-562-8592

ROSE (Recycled Oil Saves Energy), Project   www.eng.ua.edu/~prose
PO Box 870203   Tuscaloosa AL 35487
Ph: 205-348-4878 ▪ Fax: 205-348-7558

Rose Selections, All-America   www.rose.org
111 E Wacker Dr 18th Fl   Chicago IL 60601
Ph: 312-372-7090

Rose Society, American   www.ars.org
8877 Jefferson Paige Rd PO Box 30   Shreveport LA 71119
Ph: 318-938-5402 ▪ Fax: 318-938-5405 ▪ TF: 800-637-6534

Rosedale Mennonite Missions   www.rosedalemennonitemissions.org
9920 Rosedale-Milford Ctr Rd   Irwin OH 43029
Ph: 740-857-1366 ▪ Fax: 740-857-1605

Roses Association, Pasadena Tournament of   www.tournamentofroses.com
391 S Orange Grove Blvd   Pasadena CA 91184
Ph: 626-449-4100 ▪ Fax: 626-449-9066

Roses Group, Heritage   www.thefragrantgarden.com/hrg.html
916 Union St Suite 302   Alameda CA 94501
Ph: 510-865-3242

Rosicrucian Fellowship   www.rosicrucianfellowship.org
2222 Mission Ave PO Box 713   Oceanside CA 92049
Ph: 760-757-6600 ▪ Fax: 760-721-3806

Rosicrucian Order AMORC   www.rosicrucian.org
1342 Naglee Ave   San Jose CA 95191
Ph: 408-947-3600 ▪ Fax: 408-947-3677

Rosie the Riveter Association, American   www.rosietheriveter.net
2561 Rocky Ridge Rd   Birmingham AL 35243
Ph: 205-822-4106

Rosie's For All Kids Foundation Inc   www.forallkids.org
PO Box 225   Allendale NJ 07401
Ph: 201-934-5567

Rotary Foundation   www.rotary.org/foundation
1560 Sherman Ave   Evanston IL 60201
Ph: 847-866-3000 ▪ Fax: 847-328-4101

Rotary International   www.rotary.org
1560 Sherman Ave   Evanston IL 60201
Ph: 847-866-3000 ▪ Fax: 847-328-8554

Rotational Molders, Association of   www.rotomolding.org
2000 Spring Rd Suite 511   Oak Brook IL 60523
Ph: 630-571-0611 ▪ Fax: 630-571-0616

Rotisseurs, Confrerie de la Chaine des   www.chaineus.org
444 Park Ave S Suite 301   New York NY 10016
Ph: 212-683-3770 ▪ Fax: 212-683-3882

Round Dance Teachers, International Association of www.roundalab.org
355 N Orchard St Suite 200   Boise ID 83706
Ph: 208-377-1232 ▪ Fx: 208-377-1236 ▪ TF: 800-346-7522

Rousseau Association www.wabash.edu/Rousseau
Wabash College Dept of Political Science 301 W Wabash
Ave   Crawfordsville IN 47933
Ph: 765-361-6312

Rousseau, North American Association for the Study www.wabash.edu/Rousseau
of Jean-Jacques   Wabash College Dept of Political Science
301 W Wabash Ave   Crawfordsville IN 47933
Ph: 765-361-6312

Route 66 Federation, National Historic www.national66.com
PO Box 423   Tujunga CA 91043
Ph: 818-352-7232

Rowing Association, Intercollegiate rowing.ecac.org
PO Box 3   Centerville MA 02632
Ph: 508-771-5060 ▪ Fx: 508-771-9481

Rowing Association, US www.usrowing.org
201 S Capitol Ave Suite 400   Indianapolis IN 46225
Ph: 317-237-5656 ▪ Fx: 317-237-5646 ▪ TF: 800-314-4769

Rowing Foundation, National www.natrowing.org
67 Mystic Rd   North Stonington CT 06359
Ph: 860-535-0634 ▪ Fx: 860-535-0637

Roy J Carver Charitable Trust www.carvertrust.org
202 Iowa Ave   Muscatine IA 52761
Ph: 563-263-4010 ▪ Fx: 563-263-1547

Royal Arcanum, Supreme Council of the www.royalarcanum.com
61 Batterymarch St PO Box 392   Boston MA 02110
Ph: 617-426-4135 ▪ Fx: 617-426-2322 ▪ TF: 888-272-2686

Royal Association, American www.americanroyal.com
1701 American Royal Ct   Kansas City MO 64102
Ph: 816-221-9800 ▪ Fx: 816-221-8189 ▪ TF: 800-821-5857

Royal Neighbors of America www.royalneighbors.org
230 16th St   Rock Island IL 61201
Ph: 309-788-4561 ▪ TF: 800-627-4762

Royal Oak Foundation www.royal-oak.org
26 Broadway Suite 950   New York NY 10004
Ph: 212-480-2889 ▪ Fx: 212-785-7234 ▪ TF: 800-913-6565

Royalist Society, North American Araucanian www.geocities.com/tourtoirac

Royalty Owners Association, Texas Independent Producers & www.tipro.org
515 Congress Ave Suite 1910   Austin TX 78701
Ph: 512-477-4452 ▪ Fx: 512-476-8070

Royalty Owners, National Association of www.naro-us.org
PO Box 5779   Norman OK 73070
Ph: 405-573-2972 ▪ Fx: 405-364-3082 ▪ TF: 800-558-0557

Royalty, Society of American
PO Box 190313   Dallas TX 75219
Ph: 972-224-6881

Roycrofters-at-Large Association www.roycrofter.com/rala/rala.html
21 S Grove St Suite 110   East Aurora NY 14052
Ph: 716-457-3565

RP International www.rpinternational.org
PO Box 900   Woodland Hills CA 91365
Ph: 818-992-0500 ▪ Fx: 818-992-3265

RTCA Inc www.rtca.org
1828 L St NW Suite 805   Washington DC 20036
Ph: 202-833-9339 ▪ Fx: 202-833-9434

Rubber Div, American Chemical Society www.rubber.org
250 S Forge St 4th Fl   Akron OH 44309
Ph: 330-972-7814 ▪ Fx: 330-972-5269

Rubber Manufacturers Association www.rma.org
1400 K St NW Suite 900   Washington DC 20005
Ph: 202-682-4800 ▪ Fx: 202-682-4854

Rubber Pavements Association www.rubberpavements.org
1801 S Jentilly Ln Suite A2   Tempe AZ 85281
Ph: 480-517-9944 ▪ Fx: 480-517-9959

Rubber/Plastics Industry Conference of the United Steelworkers
of America   5 Gateway Ctr 7th Fl   Pittsburgh PA 15222
Ph: 412-562-6971 ▪ Fx: 412-562-6963

Rubber Producers Inc, International Institute of Synthetic www.iisrp.com
2077 S Gessner Rd Suite 133   Houston TX 77063
Ph: 713-783-7511 ▪ Fx: 713-783-7253

Rubber Trade Association of North America
220 Maple Ave PO Box 196   Rockville Centre NY 11571
Ph: 516-536-7228 ▪ Fx: 516-536-3771

Ruffed Grouse Society www.ruffedgrousesociety.org
451 McCormick Rd   Coraopolis PA 15108
Ph: 412-262-4044 ▪ Fx: 412-262-9207 ▪ TF: 888-564-6747

Rug Institute, Carpet & www.carpet-rug.com
310 S Holiday Ave   Dalton GA 30720
Ph: 706-278-3176 ▪ Fx: 706-278-8835 ▪ TF: 800-882-8846

Rug Retailers of America Inc, Oriental www.orrainc.com
PO Box 1191   Milwaukee WI 53201
Ph: 414-224-0448 ▪ Fx: 414-224-0480

Rugby, USA www.usarugby.org
3595 E Fountain Blvd   Colorado Springs CO 80910
Ph: 719-637-1022 ▪ Fx: 719-637-1315 ▪ TF: 800-280-6302

Ruminant Practitioners, American Association of Small www.aasrp.org
1910 Lyda Ave Suite 200   Bowling Green KY 42104
Ph: 270-793-0781 ▪ Fx: 270-782-0188

Runaway Switchboard, National www.nrscrisisline.org
3080 N Lincoln Ave   Chicago IL 60657
Ph: 773-880-9860 ▪ Fx: 773-929-5150 ▪ TF: 800-621-4000

(Runaway Youth) Covenant House www.covenanthouse.org
346 W 17th St   New York NY 10011
Ph: 212-727-4000 ▪ Fx: 212-727-6516 ▪ TF: 800-999-9999

Runners Club of America, Road www.rrca.org
510 N Washington St   Alexandria VA 22314
Ph: 703-836-0558 ▪ Fx: 703-836-4430

Running Association, American www.americanrunning.org
4405 East-West Hwy Suite 405   Bethesda MD 20814
Ph: 301-913-9517 ▪ Fx: 301-913-9520 ▪ TF: 800-776-2732

Running Strong for American Indian Youth www.indianyouth.org
8815 Telegraph Rd   Lorton VA 22079
Ph: 703-550-2123 ▪ Fx: 703-550-2473

Rural Advancement Foundation International-USA www.rafiusa.org
PO Box 640   Pittsboro NC 27312
Ph: 919-542-1396 ▪ Fx: 919-542-0069

Rural Affairs, Center for www.cfra.org
PO Box 406   Walthill NE 68067
Ph: 402-846-5428 ▪ Fx: 402-846-5420

Rural Appraisers, American Society of Farm Managers & www.asfmra.org
950 S Cherry St Suite 508   Denver CO 80246
Ph: 303-758-3513 ▪ Fx: 303-758-0190

Rural Community Assistance Program www.rcap.org
1522 K St NW Suite 400   Washington DC 20005
Ph: 202-408-1273 ▪ Fx: 202-408-8165 ▪ TF: 888-321-7227

Rural Development, Association for International Agriculture & aiard.org
Mississippi State Univ Dept of Agricultural Economics Box
5187   Mississippi State MS 39762
Ph: 662-325-0549 ▪ Fx: 662-325-8777

Rural Economic Developers Association, National www.nreda.org
431 E Locust Suite 300   Des Moines IA 50309
Ph: 515-284-1421 ▪ Fx: 515-243-2049

Rural Education Association, National www.nrea.net
Univ of Oklahoma 820 Van Vleet Oval Rm 227   Norman OK
73109
Ph: 405-324-7959

Rural Electric Cooperative Association, National www.nreca.org
4301 Wilson Blvd   Arlington VA 22203
Ph: 703-907-5500 ▪ Fx: 703-907-5528

Rural Health Association, National www.nrharural.org
1 W Armour Blvd Suite 203   Kansas City MO 64111
Ph: 816-756-3140 ▪ Fx: 816-756-3144

Rural Housing Coalition, National www.nrhcweb.org
1250 'I' St NW Suite 902   Washington DC 20005
Ph: 202-393-5229 ▪ Fx: 202-393-3034

Rural Housing, Council for Affordable & www.carh.org
121 N Washington St Suite 301   Alexandria VA 22314
Ph: 703-837-9001 ▪ Fx: 703-837-8467

Rural Letter Carriers' Association, National www.nrlca.org
1630 Duke St 4th Fl   Alexandria VA 22314
Ph: 703-684-5545 ▪ Fx: 703-548-8735

Rural Life Conference, National Catholic www.ncrlc.com
4625 Beaver Ave   Des Moines IA 50310
Ph: 515-270-2634 ▪ Fx: 515-270-9447

Rural Mental Health, National Association for www.narmh.org
3700 W Division St Suite 105   Saint Cloud MN 56301
Ph: 320-202-1820 ▪ Fx: 320-202-1833 ▪ TF: 800-809-5879

Rural Reconstruction, International Institute of www.iirr.org
333 E 38th St 6th Fl   New York NY 10016
Ph: 212-880-9147 ▪ Fx: 212-880-9148

Rural Sociological Society www.ruralsociology.org
Univ of Missouri 104 Gentry Hall   Columbia MO 65211
Ph: 573-882-9065 ▪ Fx: 573-882-1473

Rural Special Education, American Council on extension.usu.edu/acres
Utah State Univ 2865 Old Main Hill   Logan UT 84322
Ph: 435-797-3911

Rural Water Association, National www.nrwa.org
2915 S 13th St   Duncan OK 73533
Ph: 580-252-0629 ▪ Fx: 580-255-4476

Ruritan National www.ruritan.org
PO Box 487   Dublin VA 24084
Ph: 540-674-5431 ▪ Fx: 540-674-2304 ▪ TF: 877-787-8727

Russell Sage Foundation www.russellsage.org
112 E 64th St   New York NY 10021
Ph: 212-750-6000 ▪ Fx: 212-371-4761

Russia, American Historical Society of Germans from www.ahsgr.org
631 D St   Lincoln NE 68502
Ph: 402-474-3363 ▪ Fx: 402-474-7229

Russia Business Council, US- www.usrbc.org
1701 Pennsylvania Ave NW Suite 520   Washington DC 20006
Ph: 202-739-9180 ▪ Fx: 202-659-5920

Russia, Children of www.leahi.net/russia
4117 Kahala Ave   Honolulu HI 96816
Ph: 808-737-5248 ▪ Fx: 808-737-7806

Russia Heritage Society, Germans from www.grhs.com
1125 W Turnpike Ave   Bismarck ND 58501
Ph: 701-223-6167 ▪ Fx: 701-223-4421

Russia House www.russiahouse.org
1800 Connecticut Ave NW   Washington DC 20009
Ph: 202-986-6010 ▪ Fx: 202-667-4244

Russia Ukraine the Baltic States & Eurasia, NCSJ: Advocates on www.ncsj.org
Behalf of Jews in   2020 K St NW Suite 7800   Washington DC
20036
Ph: 202-898-2500 ▪ Fx: 202-898-0822

Russian-American Center
2670 Leavenworth St   San Francisco CA 94133
Ph: 415-563-4731 ▪ Fx: 415-563-1566

Russian-American Chamber of Commerce www.russianamericanchamber.org
1552 Pennsylvania St   Denver CO 80203
Ph: 303-831-0829 ▪ Fx: 303-831-0830

Russian-American Economic Cooperation, Foundation for www.fraec.org
2601 4th Ave Suite   310   Seattle WA 98121
Ph: 206-443-1935 ▪ Fx: 206-443-0954

Russian-American Scholars in the USA, Association of
PO Box 180035   Richmond Hill NY 11418
Ph: 518-785-6780

Russian-Americans, Congress of   www.russian-americans.org
2460 Sutter St   San Francisco CA 94115
Ph: 415-928-5841   Fx: 415-928-5831

Russian Brotherhood Organization of the USA   www.rbo.org
1733 Spring Garden St   Philadelphia PA 19130
Ph: 215-563-2537   Fx: 215-563-8106   TF: 800-726-8721

Russian Chamber of Commerce & Industry, American-   www.arcci.org
1101 Pennsylvania Ave NW 6th Fl   Washington DC 20004
Ph: 202-756-4943   Fx: 202-362-4634

Russian Children's Welfare Society Inc   www.rcws.org
200 Park Ave S Suite 1617   New York NY 10003
Ph: 212-473-6263   Fx: 212-473-6301   TF: 888-732-7297

Russian Numismatic Society   www.russiannumismaticsociety.org
PO Box 3684   Santa Rosa CA 95402
Ph: 707-527-1007   Fx: 707-527-1204

Russian Orthodox Catholic Mutual Aid Society of USA   www.rocmas.org
10 Downs Dr   Wilkes-Barre PA 18705
Ph: 570-822-8591   Fx: 570-821-7060   TF: 877-476-2627

Russian Zone Handoverprint Study & Research Group
1108 Eureka Ave   Davis CA 95616
Ph: 530-756-1638

Ruth, House of   www.houseofruth.org
5 Thomas Cir NW   Washington DC 20005
Ph: 202-745-2326   Fx: 202-667-7047

Ruth Jackson Orthopaedic Society   www.rjos.org
6300 N River Rd Suite 727   Rosemont IL 60018
Ph: 847-698-1637   Fx: 847-823-0536

Rutherford Institute   www.rutherford.org
PO Box 7482   Charlottesville VA 22906
Ph: 434-978-3888   Fx: 434-978-1789

Ruthven Assembly, Lord   ebbs.english.vt.edu/LRA/lra.html

RV Club, Escapees   www.escapees.com
100 Rainbow Dr   Livingston TX 77351
Ph: 936-327-8873   Fx: 936-327-4388   TF: 888-757-2582

RV Manufacturers Clubs Association
PO Box 587   Wakarusa IN 46573
Ph: 574-862-7330   Fx: 574-862-7390   TF: 877-702-5415

RV Parks & Campgrounds, National Association of   www.arvc.org
113 Park Ave   Falls Church VA 22046
Ph: 703-241-8801   Fx: 703-241-1004

RVers, Family Campers &   www.fcrv.org
4808 Transit Rd Bldg 2   Depew NY 14043
Ph: 716-668-6242   TF: 800-245-9755

RVing Coalition, Go   www.gorving.com
1896 Preston White Dr   Reston VA 20191
Ph: 703-620-6003   TF: 888-467-8464

RVing Women   www.rvingwomen.org
PO Box 1940   Apache Junction AZ 85217
Ph: 480-671-6226   Fx: 480-671-6230   TF: 888-557-8464

Rwanda Association, Friends of
8391 Red Fox Way   Elk Grove CA 95758
Ph: 916-683-3356   Fx: 916-688-7295

Ryce Jimmy Center For Victims of Predatory Abduction   www.jimmyryce.org
5050 Collins Ave Suite 1036   Miami Beach FL 33140
Ph: 305-864-1344   Fx: 305-864-4161   TF: 800-546-7923

Ryegrass Growers Association, Manhattan
PO Box 250   Hubbard OR 97032
Ph: 503-651-2130   Fx: 503-651-2351

Ryukyu Philatelic Specialist Society   users.netmdc.com/~rpss
PO Box 381   Clayton CA 94517
Ph: 925-672-0960

S

Saanen Breeders Association, National   nationalsaanenbreeders.com
PO Box 315   Santa Margarita CA 93453
Ph: 805-461-5547

Sabbath Association, Bible   www.biblesabbath.org
HC 60 Box 8   Fairview OK 73737
Ph: 580-227-4494   Fx: 580-227-3200   TF: 888-687-5191

Sabre Foundation Inc   www.sabre.org
872 Massachusetts Ave Suite 2-1   Cambridge MA 02139
Ph: 617-868-3510   Fx: 617-868-7916

Sack Manufacturers' Association, Paper Shipping   www.pssma.com
520 E Oxford St   Coopersburg PA 19036
Ph: 610-282-6845   Fx: 610-282-6921

Sacrament, Congregation of the Blessed   www.blessedsacrament.com
5384 Wilson Mills Rd   Cleveland OH 44143
Ph: 440-449-2103   Fx: 440-449-3862

Sacred Dance Guild   www.sacreddanceguild.org
305 Townsend Ave   New Haven CT 06512
Ph: 203-469-4277

Sacred Earth Network   www.sacredearthnetwork.org
592 Main St   Amherst MA 01002
Ph: 413-253-6998   Fx: 413-253-1657

Saddle Harness Allied Trades Association   www.proleptic.net/shata.asp
c/o Proleptic Inc 1101 Broad St   Oriental NC 28571
Ph: 252-249-3409   Fx: 252-249-3415

Saddle Horse Association, National Spotted   www.nssha.com
108 N Spring St PO Box 898   Murfreesboro TN 37133
Ph: 615-890-2864

Saddlebred Horse Association, American   www.saddlebred.com
4093 Iron Works Pkwy   Lexington KY 40511
Ph: 859-259-2742   Fx: 859-259-1628

SAFE Association   www.safeassociation.com
PO Box 130   Creswell OR 97426
Ph: 541-895-3012   Fx: 541-895-3014

Safe Deposit Association, American   www.tasda.com
98 W Madison St   Franklin IN 46131
Ph: 317-738-4432   Fx: 317-738-5267

Safe International Road Travel, Association for   www.asirt.org
11769 Gainsborough Rd   Potomac MD 20854
Ph: 301-983-5252   Fx: 301-983-3663

SAFE KIDS Campaign, National   www.safekids.org
1301 Pennsylvania Ave NW Suite 1000   Washington DC 20004
Ph: 202-662-0600   Fx: 202-393-2072

(Safe Playgrounds) KaBOOM! Inc   www.kaboom.org
2213 M St NW Suite 300   Washington DC 20037
Ph: 202-659-0215   Fx: 202-659-0210

Safe Skies Alliance, National   sskies.org
McGhee Tyson Airport 2057 Alcoa Hwy   Alcoa TN 37701
Ph: 865-970-0515   Fx: 865-970-0506

Safe Tables Our Priority, STOP -   www.safetables.org
PO Box 4352   Burlington VT 05406
Ph: 802-863-0555   Fx: 802-863-3733   TF: 800-350-7867

Safe Transit Association, International   www.ista.org
1400 Abbott Rd Suite 160   East Lansing MI 48823
Ph: 517-333-3437   Fx: 517-333-3813

Safe Transportation of Hazardous Articles, Conference on   www.costha.com
7803 Hill House Ct   Fairfax Station VA 22039
Ph: 703-451-4031   Fx: 703-451-4207

Safe & Vault Technicians Association   www.savta.org
3003 Live Oak St   Dallas TX 75204
Ph: 214-827-7233   Fx: 214-827-1810

Safer Society Foundation Inc   www.safersociety.org
PO Box 340   Brandon VT 05733
Ph: 802-247-3132   Fx: 802-247-4233

Safety, AAA Foundation for Traffic   www.aaafoundation.org
607 14th St NW Suite 201   Washington DC 20005
Ph: 202-638-5944   Fx: 202-638-5943

Safety Advisory Conference, Helicopter   www.hsac.org

Safety, Advocates for Highway & Auto   www.saferoads.org
750 1st St NE Suite 901   Washington DC 20002
Ph: 202-408-1711   Fx: 202-408-1699

Safety Alliance, Commercial Vehicle   www.cvsa.org
1101 17th St NW Suite 803   Washington DC 20036
Ph: 202-775-1623   Fx: 202-775-1624

Safety, Arts Crafts & Theatre   www.caseweb.com/ACTS
181 Thompson St Suite 23   New York NY 10012
Ph: 212-777-0062   Fx: 212-673-4403

Safety & Asepsis Procedures, Organization for   www.osap.org
PO Box 6297   Annapolis MD 21401
Ph: 410-571-0003   Fx: 410-571-0028   TF: 800-298-6727

Safety Association, American Biological   www.absa.org
1202 Allanson Rd   Mundelein IL 60060
Ph: 847-949-1517   Fx: 847-566-4580

Safety Association, Exercise   www.exercisesafety.com
PO Box 3340   Spring Hill FL 34611
Ph: 352-683-5246   Fx: 352-666-7862

Safety Association, Governors Highway   www.statehighwaysafety.org
750 1st St NE Suite 720   Washington DC 20002
Ph: 202-789-0942   Fx: 202-789-0946

Safety Association, US Marine   www.usmsa.org
5050 Industrial Rd   Farmingdale NJ 07727
Ph: 732-751-0102   Fx: 732-751-0508

Safety Authorities International, National Association of Elevator   www.naesai.org
4541 N 12th St   Phoenix AZ 85014
Ph: 602-266-9701   Fx: 602-265-0093

Safety, Beach Education Advocates for Culture Health   www.beachesfoundation.org
Environment &   PO Box 530702   Miami Shores FL 33153
Ph: 305-893-8838   Fx: 305-893-8823

Safety, Center for Auto   www.autosafety.org
1825 Connecticut Ave NW Suite 330   Washington DC 20009
Ph: 202-328-7700

Safety, Center for Chemical Process   www.aiche.org/ccps/index.htm
3 Park Ave   New York NY 10016
Ph: 212-591-7319   Fx: 212-591-8895

Safety Center, National School   www.nssc1.org
141 Duesenberg Dr Suite 11   Westlake Village CA 91362
Ph: 805-373-9977   Fx: 805-373-9277

Safety in Child Care, National Resource Center for Health &   nrc.uchsc.edu
Univ of Colorado Health Sciences Ctr at Fitzsimons CMS F 541
  PO Box 6508   Aurora CO 80045
Ph: 303-724-0665   Fx: 303-724-0960   TF: 800-598-5437

Safety Communications Officials International Inc, Association   www.apcointl.org
of Public-   351 N Williamson Blvd   Daytona Beach FL 32114
Ph: 386-322-2500   Fx: 386-322-2501   TF: 888-272-6911

Safety Congress, National Water   www.watersafetycongress.org
PO Box 1632   Mentor OH 44061
Ph: 440-209-9805

Safety Council, National   www.nsc.org
1121 Spring Lake Dr   Itasca IL 60143
Ph: 630-285-1121   Fx: 630-285-1315   TF: 800-621-7619

Safety Council, National Child
PO Box 1368   Jackson MI 49204
Ph: 517-764-6070   Fx: 517-764-3068   TF: 800-222-1464

Safety Council of North America, Silicones Environmental Health &   www.sehsc.com
11921 Freedom Dr Suite 550   Reston VA 20190
Ph: 703-904-4322   Fx: 703-925-5955

Safety Council, Window Covering   www.windowcoverings.org
355 Lexington Ave Suite 1700   New York NY 10017
Ph: 800-506-4636

Safety Education, American Academy of   www.veteransofsafety.org
Central Missouri State Univ Humphreys Bldg   Warrensburg MO 64093
Ph: 660-543-4281   Fx: 660-543-4482

Safety Engineering Society, IEEE Product — ewh.ieee.org/soc/pses
IEEE Operations Ctr 445 Hoes Ln　Piscataway NJ 08854
Ph: 732-981-0060　Fx: 732-981-1721

Safety Engineers, American Society of — www.asse.org
1800 E Oakton St　Des Plaines IL 60018
Ph: 847-699-2929　Fx: 847-768-3434

Safety Equipment Association, International — www.safetyequipment.org
1901 N Moore St Suite 808　Arlington VA 22209
Ph: 703-525-1695　Fx: 703-528-2148

Safety Equipment Distributors Association — www.safetycentral.org
2105 Laurel Bush Rd Suite 200　Bel Air MD 21015
Ph: 443-640-1065　Fx: 443-640-1031

Safety Equipment Institute — www.seinet.org
1307 Dolley Madison Blvd Suite 3A　McLean VA 22101
Ph: 703-442-5732　Fx: 703-442-5756

Safety Equipment Manufacturers Agents Association — www.nira.org/semaa.html
105 Eastern Ave Suite 104　Annapolis MD 21403
Ph: 410-263-1014　Fx: 410-263-1659　TF: 800-315-7429

Safety & Fairness Everywhere, National Organization Taunting — www.notsafe.org
PO Box 5743　Santa Barbara CA 93150
Ph: 805-966-0611

Safety Foundation, Elevator Escalator — www.eesf.org
362 Pinehill Dr　Mobile AL 36606
Ph: 334-479-2199　TF: 888-743-3723

Safety Foundation, Flight — www.flightsafety.org
601 Madison St Suite 300　Alexandria VA 22314
Ph: 703-739-6700　Fx: 703-739-6708

Safety Foundation, Motorcycle — www.msf-usa.org
2 Jenner St Suite 150　Irvine CA 92618
Ph: 949-727-3227

Safety Foundation, National Youth Sports — www.nyssf.org
1 Beacon St Suite 3333　Boston MA 02108
Ph: 617-367-6677　Fx: 617-722-9999

Safety Foundation, Roadway — www.roadwaysafety.org
1 Thomas Cir NW 10th Fl　Washington DC 20005
Ph: 202-857-1200

Safety Glazing Certification Council — www.sgcc.org
PO Box 9　Henderson Harbor NY 13651
Ph: 315-646-2234　Fx: 315-646-2297

Safety & Health Association, Semiconductor Environmental — seshaonline.org
1313 Dolley Madison Blvd Suite 402　McLean VA 22101
Ph: 703-790-1745　Fx: 703-790-2672

(Safety & Health) Voluntary Protection Programs Participants' Association — www.vpppa.org
7600-E Leesburg Pike Suite 440　Falls Church VA 22043
Ph: 703-761-1146　Fx: 703-761-1148

Safety Institute, All-Terrain Vehicle — www.atvsafety.org
2 Jenner St Suite 150　Irvine CA 92618
Ph: 949-727-3727　Fx: 949-786-3323　TF: 800-887-2887

Safety Institute of America, Chimney — www.csia.org
2155 Commercial Dr　Plainfield IN 46168
Ph: 317-837-5362　Fx: 317-837-5365　TF: 800-536-0118

Safety Institute, Aviation — www.aero-farm.com/asi/asi.htm
PO Box 690　Worthington OH 43085
Ph: 614-793-1679　Fx: 614-793-1708

Safety Institute, Bicycle Helmet — www.helmets.org
4611 7th St S　Arlington VA 22204
Ph: 703-486-0100

Safety, Institute for Business & Home — www.ibhs.org
4775 E Fowler Ave　Tampa FL 33617
Ph: 813-286-3400　Fx: 813-286-9960　TF: 866-675-4247

Safety, Insurance Institute for Highway — www.hwysafety.org
1005 N Glebe Rd Suite 800　Arlington VA 22201
Ph: 703-247-1500　Fx: 703-247-1678

Safety, International Association for Healthcare Security & — www.iahss.org
PO Box 5038　Glendale Heights IL 60139
Ph: 630-871-9936　Fx: 630-871-9938　TF: 888-353-0990

Safety Investigators, International Society of Air — www.isasi.org
107 E Holly Ave Suite 11　Sterling VA 20164
Ph: 703-430-9668　Fx: 703-430-4970

Safety & Law Enforcement Officers, National Association of School — www.nassleo.org
PO Box 3147　Oswego NY 13126
Ph: 315-529-4858　Fx: 315-343-2935

Safety Leaders Inc, National Association of Women Highway — www.nawhsl.org
145 Berry Rd　Clinton MS 39056
Ph: 601-924-7815

Safety & Loss Prevention Management Council — www.truckline.com/cc/councils/slpmc
American Trucking Assns 2200 Mill Rd　Alexandria VA 22314
Ph: 703-838-1919　Fx: 703-838-8468

Safety Management Society, National — www.safetyhealthmanager.org
2004 Hatton Ct　Columbia MO 65203
Ph: 800-321-2910

Safety, National Campaign for Radioactive Waste — www.sric.org
105 Stanford SE PO Box 4524　Albuquerque NM 87106
Ph: 505-262-1862　Fx: 505-262-1864

Safety, National Institute for Farm — www.ag.ohio-state.edu/~agsafety/NIFS/nifs.htm
Univ of Wisconsin 460 Henry Mall　Madison WI 53706
Ph: 608-265-0568　Fx: 608-262-1228

Safety, Northwestern University Center for Public — server.traffic.northwestern.edu
600 Foster　Evanston IL 60204
Ph: 847-491-5476　Fx: 847-491-5270　TF: 800-323-4011

Safety Officers Association, Fire Department — www.fdsoa.org
30 Main St Suite 6 PO Box 149　Ashland MA 01721
Ph: 508-881-3114　Fx: 508-881-1128

Safety Officials, Association of State Dam — www.damsafety.org
450 Old Vine　Lexington KY 40507
Ph: 859-257-5140　Fx: 859-323-1958

Safety Officials, National Association of Amusement Ride — www.naarso.com
PO Box 638　Brandon FL 33509
Ph: 813-661-2779　Fx: 813-685-5117　TF: 800-669-9053

(Safety) Operation Lifesaver Inc — www.oli.org
1420 King St Suite 401　Alexandria VA 22314
Ph: 703-739-0308　Fx: 703-519-8267　TF: 800-537-6224

Safety, Partnership for Patient — www.p4ps.org
1 W Superior St Suite 2410　Chicago IL 60610
Ph: 312-274-9695　Fx: 312-274-9696

Safety Professionals, Board of Certified — www.bcsp.org
208 Burwash Ave　Savoy IL 61874
Ph: 217-359-9263　Fx: 217-359-0055

Safety & Security Professionals, International Association of Home
PO Box 2044　Erie PA 16512
Ph: 814-456-2911

Safety Services Association, American Traffic — www.atssa.com
15 Riverside Pkwy Suite 100　Fredericksburg VA 22406
Ph: 540-368-1701　Fx: 540-368-1717　TF: 800-272-8772

Safety Society, System — www.system-safety.org
PO Box 70　Unionville VA 22567
Ph: 540-854-8630　Fx: 540-854-4561

Safety, Veterans of — www.veteransofsafety.org
Central Missouri State Univ Safety Ctr Humphreys Bldg Rm 201　Warrensburg MO 64093
Ph: 660-543-4281　Fx: 660-543-4482

Sage Russell Foundation — www.russellsage.org
112 E 64th St　New York NY 10021
Ph: 212-750-6000　Fx: 212-371-4761

Saharan People's Support Committee
217 E Lehr Ave　Ada OH 45810
Ph: 419-634-3666

Sail America — www.sailamerica.com
850 Aquidneck Ave Unit B4　Middletown RI 02842
Ph: 401-841-0900　Fx: 401-847-2044　TF: 800-817-7245

Sail Training Association, American — tallships.sailtraining.org
PO Box 1459　Newport RI 02840
Ph: 401-846-1775　Fx: 401-849-5400

Sailing Association of North America, Inter-Collegiate — www.collegesailing.org
Old Dominion Univ H&PE Bldg　Rm 101　Norfolk VA 23529
Ph: 757-683-3387　Fx: 757-683-6124

Sailing Association, US — www.ussailing.org
15 Maritime Dr PO Box 1260　Portsmouth RI 02871
Ph: 401-683-0800　Fx: 401-683-0840　TF: 800-877-2451

Sailing Associations, Council of — www.ussailing.org/csa
PO Box 1260　Portsmouth RI 02871
Ph: 401-683-0800　Fx: 401-683-0840

Sailors Association, Patrol Craft — www.ww2pcsa.org
11610 Paso Robles Ave　Granada Hills CA 91344
Ph: 818-363-2917

Sailors, Tin Can — www.destroyers.org
PO Box 100　Somerset MA 02726
Ph: 508-677-0515　Fx: 508-676-9740　TF: 800-223-5535

Sailors' Union of the Pacific — www.sailors.org
450 Harrison St Rm 108　San Francisco CA 94105
Ph: 415-777-3400　Fx: 415-777-5088

Sailplane Association, Vintage — www.vintagesailplane.org

Saint Agnes, Congregation of Sisters of — www.csasisters.org/
330 County Rd K　Fond du Lac WI 54935
Ph: 920-923-2121　Fx: 920-823-3194

Saint Andrew, Brotherhood of — www.brotherhoodstandrew.org
PO Box 632　Ambridge PA 15003
Ph: 724-266-4810　Fx: 724-266-5810

Saint Andrew, Society of — www.endhunger.org
3383 Sweet Hollow Rd　Big Island VA 24526
Ph: 434-299-5956　Fx: 434-299-5949　TF: 800-333-4597

Saint Anthony's Guild — www.anthonian.org
158 W 27th St 6th Fl　New York NY 10001
Ph: 212-924-1451　Fx: 212-924-1994

Saint Boniface Society, American
PO Box 1352　Bronx NY 10466
Ph: 718-994-0989　Fx: 718-994-6119

Saint Columban, Missionary Society of — www.columban.org
PO Box 10　Saint Columbans NE 68056
Ph: 402-291-1920　Fx: 402-291-4984

Saint David's Cathedral, American Friends of — www.afsdc.org
1001 Wilson Blvd Suite 405　Arlington VA 22209
Ph: 703-528-8192　Fx: 703-528-6186

Saint Francis Desales, Secular Institute of — www.secularinstitutes.org/sfs.htm
87 Gerrish Ave Suite T-2　East Haven CT 06512
Ph: 203-469-3277　Fx: 203-469-2094

Saint James, Fellowship of
PO Box 410788　Chicago IL 60641
Ph: 773-481-1090　Fx: 773-481-1095

Saint Joan's International Alliance US Section
1545 W Armour Ave　Milwaukee WI 53221
Ph: 414-282-6943

Saint John the Divine, Fellowship of — www.antiochian.org/Fellowship
Antiochian Orthodox Christian Archdiocese 358 Mountain Rd　Englewood NJ 07631
Ph: 201-871-1355　Fx: 201-871-7954

Saint John International, Knights of — home.fuse.net/ksji
89 S Pine Ave　Albany NY 12208
Ph: 518-453-5675

Saint Jude League — www.stjudeleague.org
205 W Monroe St　Chicago IL 60606
Ph: 312-236-7782　Fx: 312-236-7230

Saint Luke the Physician, International Order of — www.orderofstluke.org
PO Box 13701　San Antonio TX 78213
Ph: 210-492-5222　TF: 877-992-5222

Saint Martin De Porres Guild
141 E 65th St　New York NY 10021
Ph: 212-744-2410　Fx: 212-737-3875　TF: 800-850-5228

Saint Mary Magdalene, Society of
www.st-mary-magdalene.org
PO Box 352   Fountain Inn SC 29644
Ph: 864-409-0077

Saint Paul the Apostle, Missionary Society of
www.paulist.org
86-11 Midland Pkwy   Jamaica Estates NY 11432
Ph: 718-291-5995 ▪ Fx: 718-291-6646

Saint Peter Apostle, Society of
www.worldmissions-catholicchurch.org
366 5th Ave   New York NY 10001
Ph: 212-563-8700 ▪ Fx: 212-563-8725 ▪ TF: 800-431-2222

Saint Vincent Pallotti Center for Apostolic Development
www.pallotticenter.org
415 Michigan Ave NE   Washington DC 20017
Ph: 202-529-3330 ▪ Fx: 202-529-0911 ▪ TF: 877-865-5465

Saint Vincent de Paul, US Council of Society of
www.svdpusa.org
58 Progress Pkwy   Maryland Heights MO 63043
Ph: 314-576-3993 ▪ Fx: 314-576-6755

Saints Alive in Jesus
www.saintsalive.com
PO Box 1347   Issaquah WA 98027
Ph: 425-888-3904 ▪ TF: 800-961-9888

Salers Association, American
www.salersusa.org
19590 E Main St Suite 202   Parker CO 80138
Ph: 303-770-9292 ▪ Fx: 303-770-9302

Salers Junior Association, American
www.salersusa.org
7383 Alton Way Suite 103   Englewood CO 80112
Ph: 303-770-9292 ▪ Fx: 303-770-9302

Sales Association of the Chemical Industry
66 Morris Ave Suite 2A   Springfield NJ 07081
Ph: 973-379-1100 ▪ Fx: 973-379-6507

Sales Association, National Confectionery
www.candyhalloffame.com
10225 Berea Rd Suite B   Cleveland OH 44102
Ph: 216-631-8200 ▪ Fx: 216-631-8210

Sales Executives, Association of Investment Management
www.aimse.com
1320 19th St NW Suite 300   Washington DC 20036
Ph: 202-296-3560 ▪ Fx: 202-371-8977 ▪ TF: 800-343-5659

Sales & Marketing Executives International Inc
www.smei.org
PO Box 1390   Sumas WA 98295
Ph: 312-893-0751 ▪ Fx: 604-855-0165

Sales & Marketing Training, Professional Society for
www.smt.org
180 N LaSalle St Suite 1822   Chicago IL 60601
Ph: 312-551-0768 ▪ Fx: 312-551-0815

Sales Professionals, National Association of
www.nasp.com
11000 N 130th Pl   Scottsdale AZ 85259
Ph: 480-951-4311 ▪ Fx: 480-483-2860

Sales Professionals - USA
www.salesprofessionals-usa.com
PO Box 149   Arvada CO 80001
Ph: 303-534-4937 ▪ TF: 888-763-7767

Sales Representatives, Bureau of Wholesale
www.bwsr.com
1100 Spring St NW Suite 700   Atlanta GA 30309
Ph: 404-870-7600 ▪ Fx: 404-870-7601 ▪ TF: 800-877-1808

Salesian Missions
salesianmissions.org
2 Lefevre Ln PO Box 30   New Rochelle NY 10802
Ph: 914-633-8344 ▪ Fx: 914-633-7404

Salmagundi Club
www.salmagundi.org
47 5th Ave   New York NY 10003
Ph: 212-255-7740 ▪ Fx: 212-229-0172

Salmon Federation, Atlantic
www.asf.ca
PO Box 5200   Saint Andrews NB E5B3S8
Ph: 506-529-1033 ▪ Fx: 506-529-4438

Salmon Unlimited
cdma95.tripod.com
4548 N Milwaukee Ave   Chicago IL 60630
Ph: 773-736-5757 ▪ Fx: 773-736-8900

Salon Association
www.salons.org/index2.html
15825 N 71st St Suite 100   Scottsdale AZ 85254
Ph: 480-281-0429 ▪ Fx: 480-905-0708 ▪ TF: 800-211-4872

Salt Foundation Inc, World
www.angelfire.com/fl3/worldsalt
PO Box 851   Lake Wales FL 33859
Ph: 863-638-0557

Salt Institute
www.saltinstitute.org
700 N Fairfax St Suite 600   Alexandria VA 22314
Ph: 703-549-4648 ▪ Fx: 703-548-2194

Salt & Pepper Shakers Club, Novelty
members.aol.com/spclub1234
PO Box 416   Gladstone OR 97027
Ph: 503-650-8499

Salvage Pool Association, American
www.aspa.com
PO Box 6749   Glendale AZ 85312
Ph: 602-547-0052 ▪ Fx: 602-547-0246

Salvation Army
www.salvationarmyusa.org
PO Box 269   Alexandria VA 22313
Ph: 703-684-5500 ▪ Fx: 703-684-3478 ▪ TF: 800-725-2769

Salzburg Seminar
www.salzburgseminar.org
c/o The Marble Works 152 Maple St Suite 104   Middlebury VT 05753
Ph: 802-388-0007 ▪ Fx: 802-388-1030

Samaritans, Foundation of Compassionate American
www.focas-us.org
PO Box 428760   Cincinnati OH 45242
Ph: 513-621-5300 ▪ Fx: 513-621-5307

Samaritan's Purse
www.samaritanspurse.org
PO Box 3000   Boone NC 28607
Ph: 828-262-1980 ▪ Fx: 828-266-1053

Samuel Roberts Noble Foundation
www.noble.org
PO Box 2180   Ardmore OK 73402
Ph: 580-223-5810 ▪ Fx: 580-224-6217

San Francisco Camerawork
www.sfcamerawork.org
1246 Folsom St   San Francisco CA 94103
Ph: 415-863-1001 ▪ Fx: 415-863-1015

San Francisco Maritime National Park Association
www.maritime.org
PO Box 470310   San Francisco CA 94147
Ph: 415-561-6662 ▪ Fx: 415-561-6660

San Joaquin Valley Wine Growers Association
PO Box 2908   Fresno CA 93745
Ph: 559-834-2525 ▪ Fx: 559-834-1348

Sanctuary Association, Hawk Mountain
www.hawkmountain.org
1700 Hawk Mountain Rd   Kempton PA 19529
Ph: 610-756-6961 ▪ Fx: 610-756-4468

Sanctuary Network, Circle
www.circlesanctuary.org
PO Box 219   Mount Horeb WI 53572
Ph: 608-924-2216 ▪ Fx: 608-924-5961

Sand Association, American Slow
PO Box 330   Ilion NY 13357
Ph: 315-895-7711 ▪ Fx: 315-895-7196

Sand Association, National Industrial
www.sand.org
4041 Powder Mill Rd Suite 450   Claverton MD 20705
Ph: 301-595-5550 ▪ Fx: 301-595-3303

Sand & Gravel Association, National Stone
www.nssga.org
1605 King St   Alexandria VA 22314
Ph: 703-525-8788 ▪ Fx: 703-525-7782 ▪ TF: 800-342-1415

Sanger Margaret Center International
www.ppnyc.org/services/msci.html
26 Bleecker St   New York NY 10012
Ph: 212-274-7315 ▪ Fx: 212-274-7299

Sanitarians Inc, American Academy of
www.sanitarians.org
720 S Colorado Blvd Suite 960-S   Denver CO 80246
Ph: 678-584-4912

Sanitary Engineering, American Society of
www.asse-plumbing.org
901 Canterbury Rd Suite A   Westlake OH 44145
Ph: 440-835-3040 ▪ Fx: 440-835-3488

Sanitary & Environmental Engineering, Inter-American Association of   601 Wythe St   Alexandria VA 22314
www.aidis-usa.org
Ph: 703-684-2400

Sanitary Supply Association, International
www.issa.com
7373 N Lincoln Ave   Lincolnwood IL 60712
Ph: 847-982-0800 ▪ Fx: 847-982-1012 ▪ TF: 800-225-4772

Sanitation Association International, Portable
www.psai.org
7800 Metro Pkwy Suite 104   Bloomington MN 55425
Ph: 952-854-8300 ▪ Fx: 952-854-7560 ▪ TF: 800-822-3020

Santa Fe Trail Association
www.santafetrail.org
Santa Fe Trail Ctr RR 3   Larned KS 67550
Ph: 620-285-2054 ▪ Fx: 620-285-7491

Santa Gertrudis Association, National Junior
www.santagertrudis.ws/jrwelcome.html
PO Box 1257   Kingsville TX 78364
Ph: 361-592-9357 ▪ Fx: 361-592-8572

Santa Gertrudis Breeders International
www.santagertrudis.ws
PO Box 1257   Kingsville TX 78364
Ph: 361-592-9357 ▪ Fx: 361-592-8572

Sargent Shriver National Center on Poverty Law
www.povertylaw.org
111 N Wabash Ave Suite 500   Chicago IL 60602
Ph: 312-263-3830 ▪ Fx: 312-263-3846 ▪ TF: 800-621-3256

Satellite Broadcasting & Communications Association
www.sbca.com
225 Reinekers Ln Suite 600   Alexandria VA 22314
Ph: 703-549-6990 ▪ Fx: 703-549-7640 ▪ TF: 800-541-5981

Satellite Corp, Radio Amateur
www.amsat.org
850 Sligo Ave Suite 600   Silver Spring MD 20910
Ph: 301-589-6062 ▪ Fx: 301-608-3410

Satellite Organization, International Telecommunications
www.itso.int/
3400 International Dr NW   Washington DC 20008
Ph: 202-243-5096 ▪ Fx: 202-243-5018

Satellite Professionals International, Society of
www.sspi.org
55 Broad St 14th Fl   New York NY 10004
Ph: 212-809-5199 ▪ Fx: 212-825-0075

Satin Rabbit Breeders' Association, American
www.asrba.com
1895 Wilson Ave   Wilton IA 52778
Ph: 563-785-6365

Sauces, Association for Dressings &
www.dressings-sauces.org
5775 Peachtree-Dunwoody Rd Bldg G Suite 500   Atlanta GA 30342
Ph: 404-252-3663 ▪ Fx: 404-252-0774

Saudi Arabian Business Council, US-
www.us-saudi-business.org
1401 New York Ave NW Suite 720   Washington DC 20005
Ph: 202-638-1212 ▪ Fx: 202-638-2894

Sauna Society of America
PO Box 19001   Washington DC 20036
Ph: 202-331-1363

Sausage Casing Association, International Natural
www.insca.org
12339 Carroll Ave   Rockville MD 20852
Ph: 301-231-9811 ▪ Fx: 301-231-4871

Save America's Forests
www.saveamericasforests.org
4 Library Ct SE   Washington DC 20003
Ph: 202-544-9219 ▪ Fx: 202-544-7462

Save the Battlefield Coalition
PO Box 110   Catharpin VA 20143
Ph: 703-754-4260

Save the Children
www.savethechildren.org
54 Wilton Rd   Westport CT 06880
Ph: 203-221-4000 ▪ Fx: 203-227-5667 ▪ TF: 800-243-5075

Save a Family Plan
www.safp.org
PO Box 3622   London ON N6A4L4
Ph: 519-672-1115 ▪ Fx: 519-672-6379

SAVE International
www.value-eng.org
136 S Keowee St   Dayton OH 45402
Ph: 937-224-7283 ▪ Fx: 937-222-5794

Save the Manatee Club
www.savethemanatee.org
500 N Maitland Ave   Maitland FL 32751
Ph: 407-539-0990 ▪ Fx: 407-539-0871 ▪ TF: 800-432-5646

Save-the-Redwoods League
www.savetheredwoods.org
114 Sansome St Rm 1200   San Francisco CA 94104
Ph: 415-362-2352 ▪ Fx: 415-362-7017 ▪ TF: 888-836-0005

SAVE - Suicide Awareness Voices of Education
www.save.org
7317 Cahill Rd Suite 207   Minneapolis MN 55439
Ph: 952-946-7998 ▪ Fx: 952-829-0841 ▪ TF: 888-511-7283

Save the Whales
www.savethewhales.org
PO Box 2397   Venice CA 90291
Ph: 831-899-9957 ▪ Fx: 831-394-5555

Savings Education Council, American   www.asec.org
2121 K St NW Suite 600   Washington DC 20037
Ph: 202-659-0670   Fx: 202-775-6360

Saw & Knife Association, International
351 'O' St   Fresno CA 93721
Ph: 559-237-0809   Fx: 559-237-8879

Sawing Association, North American   www.sawingassociation.com
1300 Sumner Ave   Cleveland OH 44115
Ph: 216-241-7333   Fx: 216-241-0105

Sawing & Drilling Association, Concrete   www.csda.org
10901 D Roosevelt Blvd N Suite 100A   Saint Petersburg FL 33716
Ph: 727-577-5004   Fx: 727-577-5012

Saxons, Alliance of Transylvanian   www.atsaxons.com
5393 Pearl Rd   Cleveland OH 44129
Ph: 440-842-8442

SB Latex Council   www.regnet.com/sblc
1250 Connecticut Ave NW Suite 700   Washington DC 20036
Ph: 202-419-1500   Fx: 202-659-8037

Scaffold Industry Association   www.scaffold.org
20335 Ventura Blvd Suite 420   Woodland Hills CA 91364
Ph: 818-610-0320   Fx: 818-610-0323

Scaffolding Shoring & Forming Institute Inc   www.ssfi.org
1300 Sumner Ave   Cleveland OH 44115
Ph: 216-241-7333   Fx: 216-241-0105

Scale Collectors, International Society of Antique   www.isasc.org
3616 Noakes St   Los Angeles CA 90023
Ph: 323-263-6878   Fx: 323-263-3147

Scale Manufacturers Association   www.scalemanufacturers.org
6724 Lone Oak Blvd   Naples FL 34109
Ph: 239-514-3441   Fx: 239-514-3470

Scale Model Kit Collecting, Society for the Preservation & Encouragement of   3213 Hardy Dr   Edmond OK 73013
Ph: 405-341-4640

Scambusters, Internet   www.scambusters.com
197 New Market Ctr Suite 115   Boone NC 28607
Ph: 828-262-5885

Scandinavia, Thanks to   www.thankstoscandinavia.org
165 E 56th St   New York NY 10022
Ph: 212-751-4000   Fx: 212-891-1450

Scandinavian Collectors Club   www.scc-online.org/
PO Box 13196   El Cajon CA 92020
Ph: 619-447-8559   Fx: 619-447-8558

Scandinavian Foundation, American   www.amscan.org
58 Park Ave   New York NY 10016
CN 212-879-9779   Fx: 212-249-3444

Scandinavian Seminar   www.scandinavianseminar.org
24 Dickinson St   Amherst MA 01002
Ph: 413-253-9736   Fx: 413-253-5282

Scenic America   www.scenic.org
801 Pennsylvania Ave SE Suite 300   Washington DC 20003
Ph: 202-543-6200   Fx: 202-543-9130

Scenic Artists, United   www.usa829.org
29 W 38th St 15th Fl   New York NY 10018
Ph: 212-581-0300   Fx: 212-977-2011   TF: 877-728-5635

Schechter Solomon Day School Association
155 5th Ave   New York NY 10010
Ph: 212-533-7800   Fx: 212-353-9439

Schleswig-Holstein Heritage Society, American/   www.ashhs.org
PO Box 506   Walcott IA 52773
Ph: 563-284-4184

Schneider Institute for Health Policy   sihp.brandeis.edu
Brandeis University Heller Graduate School Box 9110 MS 035   Waltham MA 02454
Ph: 781-736-3901   Fx: 781-736-3905

Scholarly Publishing, Society for   www.sspnet.org
10200 W 44th Ave Suite 304   Wheat Ridge CO 80033
Ph: 303-422-3914   Fx: 303-422-8894

Scholars of Asia, Independent   www.hypersphere.com/isa
2321 Russell St Unit 3C   Berkeley CA 94705
Ph: 510-849-3791

Scholars Association, Catalogue Raisonne
15 Lawrence Hall Dr Suite 2   Williamstown MA 01267
Ph: 413-597-2335

Scholars, Council for International Exchange of   www.cies.org
3007 Tilden St NW Suite 5L   Washington DC 20008
Ph: 202-686-4000   Fx: 202-362-3442

Scholars & Critics, Association of Literary   www.bu.edu/literary
Boston Univ 650 Beacon St Suite 510   Boston MA 02215
Ph: 617-358-1990   Fx: 617-358-1995

Scholars, Dollars for   www.scholarshipamerica.org/dfs
Scholarship America 1 Scholarship Way   Saint Peter MN 56082
Ph: 507-931-1682   Fx: 507-931-9168   TF: 800-537-4180

Scholars, Fellowship of Catholic   www.catholicscholars.org
916 S Wolcott St   Chicago IL 60612
Ph: 312-355-3336

Scholars, National Academy of American   www.naas.org
1249 S Diamond Bar Blvd PMB 325   Diamond Bar CA 91765
Ph: 909-621-6856

Scholars, National Association of   www.nas.org
221 Witherspoon St 2nd Fl   Princeton NJ 08542
Ph: 609-683-7878   Fx: 609-683-0316

Scholars, National Coalition of Independent   www.ncis.org
PO Box 5743   Berkeley CA 94705
Ph: 510-540-8415

Scholars Inc, Society of Dance History   www.sdhs.org
3416 Primm Ln   Birmingham AL 35216
Ph: 205-978-1404   Fx: 205-823-2760

Scholars in the USA, Association of Russian-American
PO Box 180035   Richmond Hill NY 11418
Ph: 518-785-6780

Scholars, Woodrow Wilson International Center for   wwics.si.edu
1 Woodrow Wilson Plaza 1300 Pennsylvania Ave NW   Washington DC 20004
Ph: 202-691-4000   202-691-4001

Scholarship America   www.scholarshipamerica.org
1 Scholarship Way   Saint Peter MN 56082
Ph: 507-931-1682   Fx: 507-931-9168   TF: 800-537-4180

Scholarship in Art History, Association for Textual   www.uml.edu/Dept/History/ArtHistory/ATSAH
112 Charles St Beacon Hill   Boston MA 02114
Ph: 617-367-1679   Fx: 617-557-2962

Scholarship Association, American Music   www.amsa-wpc.org
441 Vine St Suite 1030   Cincinnati OH 45202
Ph: 513-421-5342   Fx: 513-421-2672

Scholarship, Communication Institute for Online   www.cios.org
PO Box 57   Rotterdam Junction NY 12150
Ph: 518-887-2443   Fx: 518-887-5186

Scholarship Service, National   www.nssfns.com
2001 ML King Jr Dr Suite 501 PO Box 11409   Atlanta GA 30310
Ph: 404-752-7277   Fx: 404-752-9280

(Scholarships) Jackie Robinson Foundation   www.jackierobinson.org
3 W 35th St 11th Fl   New York NY 10001
Ph: 212-290-8600   Fx: 212-290-8081

Scholastic Associates International, American   www.asainternational.com
29256 Old US 20 W   Elkhart IN 46514
Ph: 574-389-0237   Fx: 574-522-3831   TF: 866-301-5515

Scholastic Press Advisers Association, Columbia   www.columbia.edu/cu/cspa/CSPAA.html
Columbia Univ MC 5711   New York NY 10027
Ph: 212-854-9400   Fx: 212-854-9401

Scholastic Press Association, Columbia   www.columbia.edu/cu/cspa
Columbia University MC 5711   New York NY 10027
Ph: 212-854-9400   Fx: 212-854-9401

Scholastic Press Association, National   www.studentpress.org/nspa
2221 University Ave SE Suite 121   Minneapolis MN 55414
Ph: 612-625-8335   Fx: 612-626-0720

Scholastic Surfing Association, National   www.nssa.org
PO Box 495   Huntington Beach CA 92648
Ph: 714-536-0445   Fx: 714-960-4380

School Administrators, American Association of   www.aasa.org
801 N Quincy St Suite 700   Arlington VA 22203
Ph: 703-528-0700   Fx: 703-841-1543   TF: 800-771-1162

School Administrators, American Federation of   www.admin.org
1729 21st St NW   Washington DC 20009
Ph: 202-986-4209   Fx: 202-986-4211   TF: 800-354-2372

School Admission Test Board, Secondary   www.ssat.org
CN 5339   Princeton NJ 08543
Ph: 609-683-4440   Fx: 800-442-7728

School-Age Care Alliance, National   www.nsaca.org
1137 Washington Ave   Boston MA 02124
Ph: 617-298-5012   Fx: 617-298-5022

School of the Americas Watch   www.soaw.org
PO Box 4566   Washington DC 20017
Ph: 202-234-3440   Fx: 202-636-4505

School Association, National Middle   www.nmsa.org
4151 Executive Pkwy Suite 300   Westerville OH 43081
Ph: 614-895-4730   Fx: 614-895-4750   TF: 800-528-6672

School Band Directors' Association, American   www.asbda.com
PO Box 696   Guttenberg IA 52052
Ph: 319-252-2500

School Boards Association, National   www.nsba.org
1680 Duke St   Alexandria VA 22314
Ph: 703-838-6722   Fx: 703-683-7590

School Business Officials International, Association of   asbointl.org
11401 N Shore Dr   Reston VA 20190
Ph: 703-478-0405   Fx: 703-478-0205

School Counselor Association, American   www.schoolcounselor.org
1101 King St Suite 625   Alexandria VA 22314
Ph: 703-683-2722   Fx: 703-683-1619   TF: 800-306-4722

School Development Council, National   www.casdany.org/nsdc.html
28 Lord Rd Suite 210   Marlborough MA 01752
Ph: 508-481-9444   Fx: 508-481-5655

School Educators, National Alliance of Black   www.nabse.org
310 Pennsylvania Ave SE   Washington DC 20003
Ph: 202-608-6310   Fx: 202-608-6319   TF: 800-221-2654

School Employees, American Association of Classified   www.aacse.org
7140 SW Childs Rd   Lake Oswego OR 97035
Ph: 503-620-5663   Fx: 503-684-4597

School Food Service Association, American   www.asfsa.org
700 S Washington St Suite 300   Alexandria VA 22314
Ph: 703-739-3900   Fx: 703-739-3915   TF: 800-877-8822

School Health Association, American   www.ashaweb.org
7263 State Rt 43   Kent OH 44240
Ph: 330-678-1601   Fx: 330-678-4526   TF: 800-445-2742

School Home & Office Products Association   www.shopa.org
3131 Elbee Rd   Dayton OH 45439
Ph: 937-297-2250   Fx: 937-297-2254   TF: 800-854-7467

School Improvement, North Central Association Commission on Accreditation &   www.ncacasi.org
Arizona State Univ PO Box 873011   Tempe AZ 85287
Ph: 480-965-8700   TF: 800-525-9517

School Improvement, Project Appleseed: National Campaign for Public   www.projectappleseed.org
7209 Dorset Ave   Saint Louis MO 63130
Ph: 314-726-0536   Fx: 314-725-2319

School Institute, Home &   www.megaskillshsi.org
1500 Massachusetts Ave NW   Washington DC 20005
Ph: 202-466-3633

School Legal Defense Association, Home   www.hslda.org
PO Box 3000   Purcellville VA 20134
Ph: 540-338-5600   Fx: 540-338-2733

School Librarians, American Association of www.ala.org/aasl
50 E Huron St   Chicago IL 60611
Ph: 312-280-4386 ▪ Fx: 312-664-7459 ▪ TF: 800-545-2433

School Librarianship, International Association of www.iasl-slo.org

School Library Association, Canadian www.cla.ca/divisions/csla
328 Frank St   Ottawa ON K2P0X8
Ph: 613-232-9625 ▪ Fx: 613-563-9895

School of Metaphysics www.som.org
163 Moon Valley Rd   Windyville MO 65783
Ph: 417-345-8411 ▪ Fx: 417-345-6668

School Music Dealers, National Association of www.nasmd.com
13140 Coit Rd Suite 320 LB 120   Dallas TX 75240
Ph: 972-233-9107 ▪ Fx: 972-490-4219

School Networking, Consortium for www.cosn.org
1710 Rhode Island Ave NW Suite 900   Washington DC 20036
Ph: 202-861-2676 ▪ Fx: 202-861-0888 ▪ TF: 866-267-8747

School Nurses, National Association of www.nasn.org
PO Box 1300   Scarborough ME 04070
Ph: 207-883-2117 ▪ Fx: 207-883-2683 ▪ TF: 877-627-6476

School Officers, Council of Chief State www.ccsso.org
1 Massachusetts Ave NW Suite 700   Washington DC 20001
Ph: 202-408-5505 ▪ Fx: 202-408-8072

School Photographers International, Professional pspa.pmai.org
3000 Picture Pl   Jackson MI 49201
Ph: 517-788-8100 ▪ Fx: 517-788-8371

School Principals, National Association of Elementary www.naesp.org
1615 Duke St   Alexandria VA 22314
Ph: 703-684-3345 ▪ Fx: 703-548-6021 ▪ TF: 800-386-2377

School Principals, National Association of Secondary www.principals.org
1904 Association Dr   Reston VA 20191
Ph: 703-860-0200 ▪ Fx: 703-476-5432

School Psychologists, National Association of www.nasponline.org
4340 East West Hwy Suite 402   Bethesda MD 20814
Ph: 301-657-0270 ▪ Fx: 301-657-0275

School of Public Policy policy.gmu.edu
George Mason University 4400 University Dr   Fairfax VA 22030
Ph: 703-993-2280 ▪ Fx: 703-993-2284

School Public Relations Association, National www.nspra.org
15948 Derwood Rd   Rockville MD 20855
Ph: 301-519-0496 ▪ Fx: 301-519-0494

School Resource Officers, National Association of www.nasro.org
PO Box 39   Osprey FL 34229
Ph: 888-316-2776 ▪ Fx: 941-918-8231

School Safety Center, National www.nssc1.org
141 Duesenberg Dr Suite 11   Westlake Village CA 91362
Ph: 805-373-9977 ▪ Fx: 805-373-9277

School Safety & Law Enforcement Officers, National Association of www.nassleo.org
PO Box 3147   Oswego NY 13126
Ph: 315-529-4858 ▪ Fx: 315-343-2935

School State Accrediting Associations, National Federation of Nonpublic www.nfnssaa.org
6300 Father Tribou St   Little Rock AR 72205
Ph: 501-664-0340 ▪ Fx: 501-664-9075

School Supply & Equipment Association, National www.nssea.org
8380 Colesville Rd Suite 250   Silver Spring MD 20910
Ph: 301-495-0240 ▪ Fx: 301-495-3330 ▪ TF: 800-395-5550

School Teachers, National Association of Catholic www.nacst.com
1700 Sansom St Suite 903   Philadelphia PA 19103
Ph: 215-665-0993 ▪ Fx: 215-568-8270 ▪ TF: 800-996-2278

School Transportation Association, National www.schooltrans.com
625 Slaters Ln Suite 205   Alexandria VA 22314
Ph: 703-684-3200 ▪ Fx: 703-684-3212

School of Wicca, Church & www.wicca.org
PO Box 297-IN   Hinton WV 25951
Ph: 304-466-2613 ▪ Fx: 304-466-1353

Schools, Accrediting Bureau of Health Education www.abhes.org
7777 Leesburg Pike Suite 314 N   Falls Church VA 22043
Ph: 703-917-9503 ▪ Fx: 703-917-4109

Schools, Accrediting Council for Independent Colleges & www.acics.org
750 1st St NE Suite 980   Washington DC 20002
Ph: 202-336-6780 ▪ Fx: 202-842-2593

Schools of Allied Health Professions, Association of www.asahp.org
1730 M St NW Suite 500   Washington DC 20036
Ph: 202-293-4848 ▪ Fx: 202-293-4852

Schools, American Association of Christian www.aacs.org
PO Box 1097   Independence MO 64051
Ph: 816-252-9900 ▪ Fx: 816-252-6700

Schools, American Association of Cosmetology www.beautyschools.org/index2.html
15825 N 71st St Suite 100   Scottsdale AZ 85254
Ph: 480-281-0431 ▪ Fx: 480-905-0993 ▪ TF: 800-831-1086

Schools of Art & Design, National Association of nasad.arts-accredit.org
11250 Roger Bacon Dr Suite 21   Reston VA 20190
Ph: 703-437-0700 ▪ Fx: 703-437-6312

Schools of the Arts, National Guild of Community www.nationalguild.org
520 8th Ave Suite 302   New York NY 10018
Ph: 212-268-3337 ▪ Fx: 212-268-3995

Schools, Association of Advanced Rabbinical & Talmudic
11 Broadway   New York NY 10004
Ph: 212-363-1991 ▪ Fx: 212-533-5335

Schools Association, American www.asaceu.com
PO Box 14260   Chicago IL 60614
Ph: 773-782-0046 ▪ Fx: 773-782-0113 ▪ TF: 800-230-2263

Schools, Association of American Law www.aals.org
1201 Connecticut Ave NW Suite 800   Washington DC 20036
Ph: 202-296-8851 ▪ Fx: 202-296-8869

Schools, Association of Boarding www.schools.com
4455 Connecticut Ave NW Suite A-200   Washington DC 20008
Ph: 202-966-8705 ▪ Fx: 202-966-8708 ▪ TF: 800-541-5908

Schools Association of the Central States, Independent www.isacs.org
1550 N Dearborn Pkwy   Chicago IL 60610
Ph: 312-255-1244 ▪ Fx: 312-255-1278

Schools, Association of Community Tribal
616 4th Ave W   Sisseton SD 57262
Ph: 605-698-3953 ▪ Fx: 605-698-7686

Schools Association, Military Impacted www.esu3.org/districts/bellevue/misa
1600 Hwy 370   Bellevue NE 68005
Ph: 402-293-4005 ▪ TF: 800-291-6472

Schools, Association of Minority Health Professions
507 Capitol Ct NE Suite 200   Washington DC 20002
Ph: 202-544-7499 ▪ Fx: 202-546-7105

Schools, Chess in the www.chessintheschools.org
520 8th Ave Fl 2   New York NY 10018
Ph: 212-643-0225 ▪ Fx: 212-564-3083

Schools, Coalition of Essential www.essentialschools.org/
1814 Franklin St Suite 700   Oakland CA 94612
Ph: 510-433-1451 ▪ Fx: 510-433-1455

Schools Coalition, International Boys' www.boysschoolscoalition.org
7 Forehand Dr PO Box 117   Dennis MA 02638
Ph: 508-385-4563 ▪ Fx: 508-385-4273

Schools & Colleges, National Association of Private Nontraditional www.napnsc.org
182 Thompson Rd   Grand Junction CO 81503
Ph: 970-243-5441 ▪ Fx: 970-242-4392

Schools & Colleges, New England Association of www.neasc.org
209 Burlington Rd   Bedford MA 01730
Ph: 781-271-0022 ▪ Fx: 781-271-0950

Schools & Colleges of Optometry, Association of www.opted.org
6110 Executive Blvd Suite 510   Rockville MD 20852
Ph: 301-231-5944 ▪ Fx: 301-770-1828

Schools & Colleges of Technology, Accrediting Commission of Career www.accsct.org
2101 Wilson Blvd Suite 302   Arlington VA 22201
Ph: 703-247-4212 ▪ Fx: 703-247-4533

Schools Colleges & Universities of the United Methodist Church, National Association of   PO Box 340007   Nashville TN 37203
Ph: 615-340-7399 ▪ Fx: 615-340-7379

Schools & Colleges, Western Association of www.wascweb.org
985 Atlantic Ave Suite 100   Alameda CA 94501
Ph: 510-748-9001 ▪ Fx: 510-748-9797

Schools Committee for Economic Education, National www.nscee.org
30 S Broadway   Irvington-on-Hudson NY 10533
Ph: 914-591-7230 ▪ Fx: 914-591-8910

Schools Inc, Communities in www.cisnet.org
277 S Washington St Suite 210   Alexandria VA 22314
Ph: 703-519-8999 ▪ Fx: 703-519-7537 ▪ TF: 800-247-4543

Schools, Council of Graduate www.cgsnet.org
1 Dupont Cir NW Suite 430   Washington DC 20036
Ph: 202-223-3791 ▪ Fx: 202-331-7157

Schools of Dance, National Association of nasd.arts-accredit.org
11250 Roger Bacon Dr Suite 21   Reston VA 20190
Ph: 703-437-0700 ▪ Fx: 703-437-6312

Schools for Girls, National Association of Principals of
41 Van Brunt Manor Rd   East Setauket NY 11733
Ph: 631-751-0850 ▪ Fx: 631-689-7311

Schools Inc, Hispanic-Serving Health Professions www.hshps.com
1411 K St NW Suite 200   Washington DC 20005
Ph: 202-783-5262 ▪ Fx: 202-628-5898

Schools of International Affairs, Association of Professional www.apsia.org
2101 Van Munching Hall   College Park MD 20742
Ph: 301-405-7553 ▪ Fx: 301-405-4675

Schools International, Association of Christian www.acsi.org
731 Chapel Hills Dr   Colorado Springs CO 80920
Ph: 719-528-6906 ▪ Fx: 719-531-0631 ▪ TF: 800-367-0798

Schools International, Christian www.gospelcom.net/csi
3350 E Paris Ave SE   Grand Rapids MI 49512
Ph: 616-957-1070 ▪ Fx: 616-957-5022 ▪ TF: 800-635-8288

Schools, International Network of Performing & Visual Arts   173 Ridge View Dr   Berkeley Springs WV 25411 www.artsschoolsnetwork.org
Ph: 304-258-1799 ▪ Fx: 304-258-0839

Schools of Journalism & Mass Communication, Association of www.aejmc.org
234 Outlet Pointe Blvd   Columbia SC 29210
Ph: 803-798-0271 ▪ Fx: 803-772-3509

Schools, Middle States Association of Colleges & www.msache.org
3624 Market St   Philadelphia PA 19104
Ph: 215-662-5600 ▪ Fx: 215-662-5950 ▪ TF: 800-355-1258

Schools of Music, National Association of nasm.arts-accredit.org
11250 Roger Bacon Dr Suite 21   Reston VA 20190
Ph: 703-437-0700 ▪ Fx: 703-437-6312

Schools, National Association of Episcopal www.episcopalschools.org
815 2nd Ave Suite 313   New York NY 10017
Ph: 212-716-6134 ▪ Fx: 212-286-9366 ▪ TF: 800-334-7626

Schools, National Association of Federally Impacted www.sso.org/nafis
444 N Capitol St NW Suite 419   Washington DC 20001
Ph: 202-624-5455 ▪ Fx: 202-624-5468

Schools, National Association of Independent www.nais-schools.org
1620 L St NW Suite 1100   Washington DC 20036
Ph: 202-973-9700 ▪ Fx: 202-973-9790

Schools, National Association for Legal Support of Alternative
PO Box 2823   Santa Fe NM 87504
Ph: 505-471-6928

Schools, National Association for Neighborhood www.nans.org
3905 Muriel Ave   Cleveland OH 44109
Ph: 216-398-4667

Schools, National Coalition to Abolish Corporal Punishment in   155 W Main St Suite 1603   Columbus OH 43215 www.stophitting.com/disatschool
Ph: 614-221-8829 ▪ Fx: 614-221-2110

Schools, National Coalition of Alternative Community www.ncacs.org
1289 Jewett   Ann Arbor MI 48104
Ph: 734-668-9171 ▪ TF: 888-771-9171

Schools, National Coalition of Girls' www.ncgs.org
57 Main St   Concord MA 01742
Ph: 978-287-4485 ▪ Fx: 978-287-6014

Schools, North Central Conference on Summer   www.nccss.org
Univ of Wisconsin-River Falls 317 Agricultural Science Bldg
    410 S 3rd St   River Falls WI 54022
Ph: 715-425-3851 ▪ Fx: 715-425-3785

Schools, Northwest Association of Accredited   www2.boisestate.edu/NASC
1910 University Dr   Boise ID 83725
Ph: 208-426-5727 ▪ Fx: 208-334-3228

Schools of Oriental Research, American   www.asor.org
656 Beacon St 5th Fl   Boston MA 02215
Ph: 617-353-6570 ▪ Fx: 617-353-6575

Schools of Public Affairs & Administration, National Association of   www.naspaa.org
1120 G St NW Suite 730   Washington DC 20005
Ph: 202-628-8965 ▪ Fx: 202-626-4978

Schools of Public Health, Association of   www.asph.org
1101 15th St NW Suite 910   Washington DC 20005
Ph: 202-296-1099 ▪ Fx: 202-296-1252

Schools Services, International   www.iss.edu
15 Roszel Rd PO Box 5910   Princeton NJ 08543
Ph: 609-452-0990 ▪ Fx: 609-452-2690

Schools in South America, Association of American   www.aassa.com
14750 NW 77th Ct Suite 210   Miami Lakes FL 33016
Ph: 305-821-0345 ▪ Fx: 305-821-4244

Schools, Southern Association of Colleges &   www.sacs.org
1866 Southern Ln   Decatur GA 30033
Ph: 404-679-4500 ▪ Fx: 404-679-4556 ▪ TF: 800-248-7701

Schools of Theatre, National Association of   nast.arts-accredit.org
11250 Roger Bacon Dr Suite 21   Reston VA 20190
Ph: 703-437-0700 ▪ Fx: 703-437-6312

Schools, Torah Umesorah-National Society for Hebrew Day
160 Broadway   New York NY 10038
Ph: 212-227-1000 ▪ Fx: 212-406-6934

Schools & Universities Club of New York, British   www.bsuc.org
24 E 39th St   New York NY 10016
Ph: 212-713-5713

Schools & Universities Foundation, British   www.bsuf.org
575 Madison Ave Suite 1006   New York NY 10022
Ph: 212-662-5576

Schools in the US & Canada, Association of Theological   www.ats.edu
10 Summit Park Dr   Pittsburgh PA 15275
Ph: 412-788-6505 ▪ Fx: 412-788-6510

Schumacher EF Society   www.smallisbeautiful.org
140 Jug End Rd   Great Barrington MA 01230
Ph: 413-528-1737 ▪ Fx: 413-528-4472

Schutzhund Clubs of America, United   www.germanshepherddog.com
3810 Paule Ave   Saint Louis MO 63125
Ph: 314-638-9686 ▪ Fx: 314-683-0609

Schwab Charles & Helen Foundation   www.schwabfoundation.org
1650 S Amphlett Blvd Suite 300   San Mateo CA 94402
Ph: 650-655-2412 ▪ Fx: 650-655-2411

Schwab Learning   www.schwablearning.org
1650 S Amphlett Blvd Suite 300   San Mateo CA 94402
Ph: 650-655-2410 ▪ Fx: 650-655-2411 ▪ TF: 800-230-0988

Schweitzer Albert Fellowship   www.schweitzerfellowship.org
330 Brookline Ave   Boston MA 02215
Ph: 617-667-5111 ▪ Fx: 617-667-7989

Schwenkfeldian Exiles, Society of the   www.centralschwenkfelder.com/exile
Descendants of the   105 Seminary St   Pennsburg PA 18073
Ph: 215-679-3103 ▪ Fx: 215-679-8175

Science, American Association for the Advancement of   www.aaas.org
1200 New York Ave NW   Washington DC 20005
Ph: 202-326-6400 ▪ Fx: 202-682-0816 ▪ TF: 800-731-4939

Science & Art Foundation, Filipinas Americas
1209 Park Ave   New York NY 10128
Ph: 212-427-6930 ▪ Fx: 212-427-6931

Science, Association for the Education of Teachers of   aets.chem.pitt.edu
East Carolina Univ College of Education Austin
    324-A   Greenville NC 27858
Ph: 252-328-6736 ▪ Fx: 252-328-6218

Science Association International, Regional   www.regionalscience.org
Univ of Illinois Bevier Hall Rm 83 905 S Goodwin   Urbana IL
    61801
Ph: 217-333-8904 ▪ Fx: 217-333-3065

Science Inc, Association for Women in   www.awis.org
1200 New York Ave NW Suite 650   Washington DC 20005
Ph: 202-326-8940 ▪ Fx: 202-326-8960 ▪ TF: 800-886-2947

Science Collections Alliance, Natural   www.nscalliance.org
1725 K St NW Suite 601   Washington DC 20006
Ph: 202-835-9050 ▪ Fx: 202-835-7334

Science Editors, Council of   www.councilofscienceeditors.org
12100 Sunset Hills Rd Suite 130   Reston VA 20190
Ph: 703-437-4377 ▪ Fx: 703-435-4399

Science Education Leadership Association, National   www.nsela.org
PO Box 99381   Raleigh NC 27624
Ph: 919-848-1871 ▪ Fx: 919-848-0496

Science Education, National Center for   www.ncseweb.org
420 40th St Suite 2   Oakland CA 94609
Ph: 510-601-7203 ▪ Fx: 510-601-7204 ▪ TF: 800-290-6006

Science & Engineering Society, American Indian   www.aises.org
PO Box 9828   Albuquerque NM 87119
Ph: 505-765-1052 ▪ Fx: 505-765-5608

Science & Environmental Policy Project   www.sepp.org
1600 S Eads St Suite 712-S   Arlington VA 22202
Ph: 703-920-2744

Science Fiction & Fantasy Artists, Association of   www.asfa-art.org

Science Fiction Fantasy & Horror Films, Academy of   www.saturnawards.com
334 W 54th St   Los Angeles CA 90037
Ph: 323-752-5811

Science Fiction & Fantasy Writers of America Inc   www.sfwa.org
PO Box 877   Chestertown MD 21620
Ph: 410-778-3052

Science Fiction Research Association   www.sfra.org

Science Fiction Society, World   worldcon.org

Science, Foundation for Advances in Medicine &   www.scanning.org
PO Box 832   Mahwah NJ 07430
Ph: 201-818-1010 ▪ Fx: 201-818-0086 ▪ TF: 800-443-0263

Science Foundation, Photographic Art &
2100 NE 52nd St   Oklahoma City OK 73111
Ph: 405-424-4055 ▪ Fx: 405-424-4058

Science & Health, American Council on   www.acsh.org
1995 Broadway 2nd Fl   New York NY 10023
Ph: 212-362-7044 ▪ Fx: 212-362-4919

Science & International Affairs, Belfer Center for   bcsia.ksg.harvard.edu
Harvard Univ John F Kennedy School of Government 79 JFK
    St   Cambridge MA 02138
Ph: 617-495-1400

Science International, Council for Elementary   unr.edu/homepage/crowther/cesi.html
511 Marion Dr   Columbia MO 65203
Ph: 573-874-1038

Science Law & Public Policy, National   www.swankin-turner.com/nislapp.html
Institute for   1400 16th St NW Suite 330   Washington DC
    20036
Ph: 202-462-8800 ▪ Fx: 202-265-6564

(Science & Mathematics) Sigma Zeta   www.sigmazeta.org
Milliken Univ 1184 W Main   Decatur IL 62522
Ph: 217-424-6233 ▪ Fx: 217-362-6408

Science in the Public Interest, Center for   www.cspinet.org
1875 Connecticut Ave NW Suite 300   Washington DC 20009
Ph: 202-332-9110 ▪ Fx: 202-265-4954

Science & Public Policy Program   www.ou.edu/spp
Univ of Oklahoma Sarkeys Energy Ctr 100 E Boyd St Rm
    510   Norman OK 73019
Ph: 405-325-3821 ▪ Fx: 405-325-3180

Science Service   www.sciserv.org
1719 'N' St NW   Washington DC 20036
Ph: 202-785-2255 ▪ Fx: 202-331-1121

Science, Society for Advancement of Chicanos & Native   www.sacnas.org
Americans in   PO Box 8526   Santa Cruz CA 95061
Ph: 831-459-0170 ▪ Fx: 831-459-0194

Science Society, History of   www.hssonline.org
Univ of Florida 3310 Turlington Hall PO Box
    117360   Gainesville FL 32611
Ph: 352-392-1677 ▪ Fx: 352-392-2795

Science, Society for Social Studies of   www.lsu.edu/ssss
Louisiana State Univ Dept of Sociology   Baton Rouge LA 70803
Ph: 225-578-5311 ▪ Fx: 225-578-5102

Science Supervisors, Council of State   csss.enc.org

Science Teachers Association, National   www.nsta.org
1840 Wilson Blvd   Arlington VA 22201
Ph: 703-243-7100 ▪ Fx: 703-243-7177 ▪ TF: 800-722-6782

Science Teaching, National Association for Research in   www.educ.sfu.ca/narstsite
Univ of Missouri-Columbia 303 Townsend Hall   Columbia MO
    65211
Ph: 573-884-1401 ▪ Fx: 573-884-2917

Science-Technology Centers Inc, Association of   www.astc.org
1025 Vermont Ave NW Suite 500   Washington DC 20005
Ph: 202-783-7200 ▪ Fx: 202-783-7207

Science & Technology, Commission on Professionals in   www.cpst.org
1200 New York Ave NW Suite 390   Washington DC 20005
Ph: 202-326-7080 ▪ Fx: 202-842-1603

Science & Technology, Council for Agricultural   www.cast-science.org
4420 W Lincoln Way   Ames IA 50014
Ph: 515-292-2125 ▪ Fx: 515-292-4512

Science & Technology Education Partnership, National   www.nationalstep.org
2500 Wilson Blvd Suite 210   Arlington VA 22201
Ph: 703-907-7400 ▪ Fx: 703-907-7401

(Science & Technology) FIRST   www.usfirst.org
200 Bedford St   Manchester NH 03101
Ph: 603-666-3906 ▪ Fx: 603-666-3907 ▪ TF: 800-871-8326

Science & Technology, Institute for Theological Encounter with   itest.slu.edu
3601 Lindell Blvd   Saint Louis MO 63108
Ph: 314-977-2703

Science & Technology Society, AVS   www.avs.org
120 Wall St 32nd Fl   New York NY 10005
Ph: 212-248-0200 ▪ Fx: 212-248-0245

Science, Unarius Academy of   www.unarius.org
145 S Magnolia Ave   El Cajon CA 92020
Ph: 619-444-7062 ▪ Fx: 619-444-9637

Science, World Academy of Art &   www.worldacademy.org/
301 19th Ave S   Minneapolis MN 55455
Ph: 612-624-5592 ▪ Fx: 612-625-3513

Science Writers, National Association of   www.nasw.org
PO Box 890   Hedgesville WV 25427
Ph: 304-754-5077 ▪ Fx: 304-754-5076

Science for Youth Foundation, Natural
130 Azalea Dr   Roswell GA 30075
Ph: 770-594-9367 ▪ Fx: 770-594-7738

Sciences of America Inc, Polish Institute of Arts &   www.piasa.org
208 E 30th St   New York NY 10016
Ph: 212-686-4164 ▪ Fx: 212-545-1130

Sciences, American Academy of Arts &   www.amacad.org
136 Irving St   Cambridge MA 02138
Ph: 617-576-5000 ▪ Fx: 617-576-5050

Sciences, Association for Environmental Health &   www.aehs.com
150 S Fearing St   Amherst MA 01002
Ph: 413-549-5170 ▪ Fx: 413-549-0579

Sciences, Council of Colleges of Arts &   www.ccas.net
PO Box 873108   Tempe AZ 85287
Ph: 480-727-6064 ▪ Fx: 480-727-6078

Sciences, Foundation for Advanced Education in the www.faes.org
1 Cloister Ct Suite 230   Bethesda MD 20814
Ph: 301-496-7976 ▪ Fx: 301-402-0174

Sciences Honor Society, Phi Sigma Biological www.phisigmasociety.org
Eastern Illinois Univ 2029 Life Science Bldg   Charleston IL
61920
Ph: 217-581-3126 ▪ Fx: 217-581-7141

Sciences Libraries, Association of Academic Health www.aahsl.org
2150 N 107th St Suite 205   Seattle WA 98133
Ph: 206-367-8704 ▪ Fx: 206-367-8777

Sciences, National Academy of www.nas.edu
500 5th St NW   Washington DC 20001
Ph: 202-334-2138 ▪ Fx: 202-334-2229

Sciences, New York Academy of www.nyas.org
2 E 63rd St   New York NY 10021
Ph: 212-838-0230 ▪ Fx: 212-888-2894 ▪ TF: 800-843-6927

Sciences & Technology, Leonardo - International mitpress2.mit.edu/e-journals/Leonardo
Society for the Arts   425 Market St 2nd Fl   San Francisco CA
94105
Ph: 415-405-3335 ▪ Fx: 415-405-7758

Sciences in the US, Ukrainian Academy of Arts &
206 W 100th St   New York NY 10025
Ph: 212-222-1866 ▪ Fx: 212-864-3977

Scientific Equipment & Furniture Association www.sefalabs.com
1205 Franklin Ave   Garden City NY 11530
Ph: 516-294-5424 ▪ Fx: 516-294-2758

Scientific Glassblowers Society, American www.asgs-glass.org
PO Box 778   Madison NC 27025
Ph: 336-427-2406 ▪ Fx: 336-427-2496

Scientific Institute, African www.asi-org.net
PO Box 12153   Oakland CA 94604
Ph: 510-653-7027 ▪ Fx: 510-547-0387

Scientific Investigation of Claims of the Paranormal, Committee www.csicop.org
for the   PO Box 703   Amherst NY 14226
Ph: 716-636-1425 ▪ Fx: 716-636-1733 ▪ TF: 800-634-1610

Scientific Materials Managers, National Association of www.naosmm.org

Scientific Research Society, Sigma Xi www.sigmaxi.org
PO Box 13975   Research Triangle Park NC 27709
Ph: 919-549-4691 ▪ Fx: 919-549-0090 ▪ TF: 800-243-6534

Scientific Society Presidents, Council of cssp.us
1155 16th St NW   Washington DC 20036
Ph: 202-872-4452

Scientific Society Inc, Shevchenko www.shevchenko.org
63 4th Ave   New York NY 10003
Ph: 212-254-5130 ▪ Fx: 212-254-5239

Scientists, Academy of Clinical Laboratory depts.washington.edu/lmaclps
Physicians &   Univ of Chicago Dept of Pathology MC 0006
5841 S Maryland Ave   Chicago IL 60637
Ph: 773-702-1878 ▪ Fx: 773-702-9082

Scientists of America, Armenian Engineers & www.aesa.org
417 W Arden Ave Suite 112C   Glendale CA 91203
Ph: 818-547-3372

Scientists, Association of Clinical www.clinicalscience.org
PO Box 1287   Middlebury VT 05753
Ph: 802-462-2507 ▪ Fx: 802-462-2673

Scientists Association, NIH Black bsa.od.nih.gov
PO Box 2262   Kensington MD 20891
Ph: 301-402-6425

Scientists, Association of Orthodox Jewish www.aojs.org
25 W 45th St Suite 1405   New York NY 10036
Ph: 212-840-1166 ▪ Fx: 212-840-1514

Scientists Center for Animal Welfare www.scaw.com
7833 Walker Dr Suite 410   Greenbelt MD 20770
Ph: 301-345-3500 ▪ Fx: 301-345-3503

Scientists, Committee of Concerned www.libertynet.org/ccs
53-34 208th St   Bayside NY 11364
Ph: 718-229-2813 ▪ Fx: 718-229-7540

Scientists & Engineers Association, Korean-American www.ksea.org
1952 Gallows Rd Suite 300   Vienna VA 22182
Ph: 703-748-1221 ▪ Fx: 703-748-1331

Scientists & Engineers, Association of Muslim www.amse.net
PO Box 38   Plainfield IN 46168
Ph: 517-947-6338

Scientists, Federation of American www.fas.org
1717 K St NW Suite 209   Washington DC 20036
Ph: 202-546-3300 ▪ Fx: 202-675-1010

Scientists, National Council of Black Engineers & www.ncbes.org
1525 Aviation Blvd Suite C424   Redondo Beach CA 90278
Ph: 213-896-9779

Scientists Organizations, Council of Engineers & www.cesounions.org/
15205 52nd Ave S   Seattle WA 98188
Ph: 206-433-0991

Scientists, Society of Independent Professional Earth www.sipes.org
4925 Greenville Ave Suite 1106   Dallas TX 75206
Ph: 214-363-1780 ▪ Fx: 214-363-8195

Scientists Inc, Society of Turkish Architects Engineers & www.m-l-m.org
821 United Nations Plaza 2nd Fl   New York NY 10017
Ph: 212-682-7688 ▪ Fx: 212-687-3026

Scientists & Technical Professionals, National Organization of www.noglstp.org/
Gay & Lesbian   PO Box 91803   Pasadena CA 91109
Ph: 626-791-7689

Scientists, Union of Concerned www.ucsusa.org
2 Brattle Sq   Cambridge MA 02238
Ph: 617-547-5552 ▪ Fx: 617-864-9405

Sciots, Ancient Egyptian Order of www.sciots.org
PO Box 501801   San Diego CA 92150
Ph: 858-755-0931

Scleroderma Foundation www.scleroderma.org
12 Kent Way Suite 101   Byfield MA 01922
Ph: 978-463-5843 ▪ Fx: 978-463-5809 ▪ TF: 800-722-4673

Scleroderma Network Inc, Juvenile www.jsdn.org
1204 W 13th St   San Pedro CA 90731
Ph: 310-519-9511

Scleroderma Research Foundation www.srfcure.org
2320 Bath St Suite 315   Santa Barbara CA 93105
Ph: 805-563-9133 ▪ Fx: 805-563-2402 ▪ TF: 800-441-2873

Sclerotherapeutic Pain Management Inc, American College www.acopms.com
of Osteopathic   303 S Ingram Ct   Middletown DE 19709
Ph: 302-376-8080 ▪ Fx: 302-376-8081 ▪ TF: 800-471-6114

Scoliosis Association Inc www.scoliosis-assoc.org
PO Box 811705   Boca Raton FL 33481
Ph: 561-994-4435 ▪ Fx: 561-994-2455 ▪ TF: 800-800-0669

Scoliosis Foundation, National www.scoliosis.org
5 Cabot Pl   Stoughton MA 02072
Ph: 781-341-6333 ▪ Fx: 781-341-8333 ▪ TF: 800-673-6922

Scoliosis Research Society www.srs.org
611 E Wells St   Milwaukee WI 53202
Ph: 414-289-9107 ▪ Fx: 414-276-3349

SCORE Association www.score.org
409 3rd St SW 6th Fl   Washington DC 20024
Ph: 202-205-6762 ▪ Fx: 202-205-7636 ▪ TF: 800-634-0245

Scotia, Daughters of www.daughtersofscotia.org
7595 Carter Rd   Sagamore Hills OH 44067
Ph: 330-467-6387 ▪ Fx: 330-724-9307

Scott Joplin International Ragtime Foundation www.scottjoplin.org
321 S Ohio Ave   Sedalia MO 65301
Ph: 660-826-2271 ▪ Fx: 660-826-5054 ▪ TF: 866-218-6258

Scottish Clans & Associations Inc, Council of www.cosca.net
PO Box 2828   Moultrie GA 31776
Ph: 229-985-6540 ▪ Fx: 229-985-0936

Scottish Fiddling Revival Ltd www.scottishfiddling.org
1938 Rose Villa St   Pasadena CA 91107
Ph: 626-792-6323 ▪ Fx: 626-793-9401

Scottish Foundation, American www.americanscottishfoundation.com
575 Madison Ave Suite 1006   New York NY 10022
Ph: 212-605-0338 ▪ Fx: 212-605-0222

Scottish Games & Festivals, Association of www.asgf.org
3000 Walnut Ave   Altoona PA 16601
Ph: 412-851-9900 ▪ Fx: 412-854-5963

Scottish Heritage USA www.sandhillsonline.com/shusa
PO Box 457   Pinehurst NC 28370
Ph: 910-295-4448 ▪ Fx: 910-295-3147

Scottish Studies Society, Eighteenth-Century www.ecsss.org
New Jersey Institute of Technology   Newark NJ 07102
Ph: 973-596-3377 ▪ Fx: 973-642-4689

Scout Association, National Eagle www.scouting.org/nesa
1325 W Walnut Hill Ln PO Box 152079   Irving TX 75015
Ph: 972-580-2000 ▪ Fx: 972-580-2399

Scout Committee, National Jewish Girl www.njgsc.org
33 Central Dr   Bronxville NY 10708
Ph: 914-738-3986 ▪ Fx: 914-738-6752

Scouters, National Association of Presbyterian www.presbyterianscouters.org
8520 MacKenzie Rd   Box 6900   Saint Louis MO 63123
Ph: 314-638-1017 ▪ Fx: 314-638-7250 ▪ TF: 800-933-7729

Scouting, Association of Baptists for www.bsa.net/abs
PO Box 152079   Irving TX 75015
Ph: 254-799-4696

Scouting, National Catholic Committee on www.nccs-bsa.org
PO Box 152079   Irving TX 75015
Ph: 972-580-2114 ▪ Fx: 972-580-7870

Scouting, National Jewish Committee on www.jewishscouting.org
1325 W Walnut Hill Ln PO Box 152079   Irving TX 75015
Ph: 972-580-2295 ▪ Fx: 972-580-7870

Scrabble Association, National www.scrabble-assoc.com
403 Front St PO Box 700   Greenport NY 11944
Ph: 631-477-0033 ▪ Fx: 631-477-0294

Scrap Recycling Industries Inc, Institute of www.isri.org
1325 G St NW Suite 1000   Washington DC 20005
Ph: 202-737-1770 ▪ Fx: 202-626-0900

Scrap Tire Management Council www.scraptire.org
1400 K St NW Suite 900   Washington DC 20005
Ph: 202-682-4880 ▪ Fx: 202-682-4854

Screen Actors Guild www.sag.org
5757 Wilshire Blvd   Los Angeles CA 90036
Ph: 323-954-1600 ▪ Fx: 323-549-6656

Screen Manufacturers Association www.smacentral.org
2850 S Ocean Blvd Suite 114   Palm Beach FL 33480
Ph: 561-533-0991 ▪ Fx: 561-533-7466

Screen Printing Technical Foundation www.sgia.org/sptf/
10015 Main St   Fairfax VA 22031
Ph: 703-385-1335 ▪ Fx: 703-273-0456 ▪ TF: 888-385-3588

Screening Agencies, National Association of www.n-a-s-a.com
2020 Pennsylvania Ave NW   Washington DC 20006
Ph: 202-955-6272 ▪ Fx: 202-492-2852

Screening, Society for Biomolecular www.sbsonline.org
36 Tamarack Ave Suite 348   Danbury CT 06811
Ph: 203-743-1336 ▪ Fx: 203-748-7557

SCRIBES - American Society of Writers on Legal Subjects www.scribes.org
Barry Univ School of Law 6441 E Colonial Dr   Orlando FL
32807
Ph: 407-275-2000 ▪ Fx: 407-275-6142

Scribes, Society of www.societyofscribes.org
PO Box 933   New York NY 10150
Ph: 212-452-0139

Scriptural Christianity, Forum for
308 E Main St PO Box 150   Wilmore KY 40390
Ph: 606-858-4661 ▪ Fx: 606-858-4972 ▪ TF: 800-487-7784

Scripture Gift Mission, American www.gospelcom.net/asgm/
PO Box 410280   Melbourne FL 32941
Ph: 321-255-7774 ▪ Fx: 321-255-8986 ▪ TF: 877-873-2746

Scrollsaw Association of the World   www.saw-online.com
610 Daisy Ln   Round Lake Beach IL 60073
Ph: 847-546-1319

SCSI Trade Association   www.scsita.org
Presidio of San Francisco PO Box 29920   San Francisco CA 94129
Ph: 415-561-6273 ▪ Fx: 415-561-6120

Scuba Association International, Handicapped   www.hsascuba.com
1104 El Prado   San Clemente CA 92672
Ph: 949-498-4540 ▪ Fx: 949-498-6128

Scuba Divers, National Association of Black   www.nabsdivers.org

Sculptors, Federation of Modern Painters &
234 W 21st St   New York NY 10011
Ph: 212-255-4858

Sculptors Guild   www.sculptorsguild.org
110 Greene St Suite 601   New York NY 10012
Ph: 212-431-5669

Sculpture Society, National   www.nationalsculpture.org
237 Park Ave   New York NY 10017
Ph: 212-764-5645 ▪ Fx: 212-764-5651

Sea Cadet Corps, Naval   www.seacadets.org
2300 Wilson Blvd   Arlington VA 22201
Ph: 703-243-6910 ▪ Fx: 703-243-3985

Sea Education Association   www.sea.edu
PO Box 6   Woods Hole MA 02543
Ph: 508-540-3954 ▪ Fx: 508-457-4673 ▪ TF: 800-552-3633

Sea Grant Association   www.sga.seagrant.org
1755 Massachusetts Ave NW Suite 800   Washington DC 20036
Ph: 202-448-1240 ▪ Fx: 202-332-8887

Sea Lion Marine Mammal Center, Friends of the   www.fslmmc.org
20612 Laguna Canyon Rd   Laguna Beach CA 92651
Ph: 949-494-3050 ▪ Fx: 949-494-2802

Sea Otter, Friends of the   www.seaotters.org
2150 Garden Rd Suite A-3   Monterey CA 93940
Ph: 831-373-2747 ▪ Fx: 831-373-2749

Sea Shepherd Conservation Society   www.seashepherd.org
PO Box 2616   Friday Harbor WA 98250
Ph: 360-370-5650 ▪ Fx: 360-370-5651

Sea Turtle Survival League   www.cccturtle.org
4424 NW 13th St Suite A1   Gainesville FL 32609
Ph: 352-373-6441 ▪ Fx: 352-375-2449 ▪ TF: 800-678-7853

Seafarers & International House   www.sihnyc.org
123 E 15th St   New York NY 10003
Ph: 212-677-4800 ▪ Fx: 212-353-0526

Seafarers International Union   www.seafarers.org
5201 Auth Way   Camp Springs MD 20746
Ph: 301-899-0675 ▪ Fx: 301-899-7355 ▪ TF: 800-252-4674

Seafarers' Rights, Center for   www.seamenschurch.org
241 Water St   New York NY 10038
Ph: 212-349-9090 ▪ Fx: 212-349-8342

Seafood Distributors Association, American   www.freetradeinseafood.org
1901 N Fort Myer Dr Suite 700   Arlington VA 22209
Ph: 703-524-8880 ▪ Fx: 703-524-4619

Seafood Educators, National
PO Box 60006   Richmond Beach WA 98160
Ph: 206-546-6410 ▪ Fx: 206-546-6411

Seafood Processors Association, Pacific   www.pspafish.net
1900 W Emerson Pl Suite 205   Seattle WA 98119
Ph: 206-281-1667 ▪ Fx: 206-283-2387

Sealant Council Inc, Adhesive &   www.ascouncil.org
7979 Old Georgetown Rd Suite 500   Bethesda MD 20814
Ph: 301-986-9700 ▪ Fx: 301-986-9795

Sealant Waterproofing & Restoration Institute   www.swrionline.org
14 W 3rd St Suite 200   Kansas City MO 64105
Ph: 816-472-7974 ▪ Fx: 816-472-7765

Sealing Association, Fluid   www.fluidsealing.com
994 Old Eagle School Rd Suite 1019   Wayne PA 19087
Ph: 610-971-4850 ▪ Fx: 610-971-4859

Sealing Distributors, Independent   www.isd.org
105 Eastern Ave Suite 104   Annapolis MD 21403
Ph: 410-263-1014 ▪ Fx: 410-263-1659

Seamen's Church Institute   www.seamenschurch.org
241 Water St   New York NY 10038
Ph: 212-349-9090 ▪ Fx: 212-349-8342

Seaplane Pilots Association   www.seaplanes.org
4315 Highland Park Blvd Suite C   Lakeland FL 33813
Ph: 863-701-7979 ▪ Fx: 863-701-7588 ▪ TF: 888-772-8923

Search Consultants, National Association of Legal   www.nalsc.org
The Biltmore 817 W Peachtree St Suite 208   Atlanta GA 30308
Ph: 404-879-5080 ▪ Fx: 404-879-5075 ▪ TF: 866-394-9347

Search Dog Foundation, National Disaster   www.ndsdf.org
206 N Signal St Suite R   Ojai CA 93023
Ph: 805-646-1015 ▪ Fx: 805-640-1848

SEARCH for Justice & Equality in Palestine/Israel   searchforjustice.org
PO Box 3452   Framingham MA 01705
Ph: 508-879-0777 ▪ Fx: 508-877-2611

SEARCH - National Consortium for Justice Information & Statistics   www.search.org
7311 Greenhaven Dr Suite 145   Sacramento CA 95831
Ph: 916-392-2550 ▪ Fx: 916-392-8440

Search & Rescue, National Association for   www.nasar.org
4500 Southgate Pl Suite 100   Chantilly VA 20151
Ph: 703-222-6277 ▪ Fx: 703-222-6283

Search Roundtable Inc, Executive   www.esroundtable.org

Seas Education Association, Inland   www.schoolship.org
PO Box 218   Suttons Bay MI 49682
Ph: 231-271-3077 ▪ Fx: 231-271-3088

Seasoning Manufacturers Association, National
8905 Maxwell Dr Suite 200   Potomac MD 20854
Ph: 301-765-9675 ▪ Fx: 301-299-7523

Seat of the Soul Foundation   www.seatofthesoul.org
1257 Siskiyou Blvd Suite 57   Ashland OR 97520
Ph: 541-482-8999 ▪ Fx: 541-482-9176 ▪ TF: 888-440-7685

Second Amendment Foundation   www.saf.org
12500 NE 10th Pl   Bellevue WA 98005
Ph: 425-454-7012 ▪ Fx: 425-451-3959

Second Harvest, America's   www.secondharvest.org
35 E Wacker Dr Suite 2000   Chicago IL 60601
Ph: 312-263-2303 ▪ Fx: 312-263-5626 ▪ TF: 800-771-2303

Second Nature   www.secondnature.org
PO Box 120007   Boston MA 02112
Ph: 617-876-3534 ▪ Fx: 617-292-0150

Secondary Education Association, Jesuit   www.jsea.org
1616 P St NW Suite 400   Washington DC 20036
Ph: 202-667-3888 ▪ Fx: 202-387-6305

Secondary Materials & Recycled Textile Association   www.smartasn.org
7910 Woodmont Ave Suite 1130   Bethesda MD 20814
Ph: 301-656-1077 ▪ Fx: 301-656-1079

Secondary School Admission Test Board   www.ssat.org
CN 5339   Princeton NJ 08543
Ph: 609-683-4440 ▪ Fx: 800-442-7728

Secondary School Principals, National Association of   www.principals.org
1904 Association Dr   Reston VA 20191
Ph: 703-860-0200 ▪ Fx: 703-476-5432

Secretarial Association, National   rentamark.com/nsa
7300 W Fullerton Ave PO Box 35189   Chicago IL 60707
Ph: 708-453-0080 ▪ Fx: 708-453-0083

Secretaries & Administrative Assistants, National Association of Executive   www.naesaa.com
900 S Washington St Suite G-13   Falls Church VA 22046
Ph: 703-237-8616 ▪ Fx: 703-533-1153

Secretaries, American Society of Corporate   ascs.org
521 5th Ave   New York NY 10175
Ph: 212-681-2000 ▪ Fx: 212-681-2005

Secretaries International Inc, Legal   www.legalsecretaries.org

Secretaries of State, National Association of   www.nass.org
444 N Capitol St NW Hall of States Suite 401   Washington DC 20001
Ph: 202-624-3525 ▪ Fx: 202-624-3527

Secular Humanism, Council for   www.secularhumanism.org
PO Box 664   Amherst NY 14226
Ph: 716-636-7571 ▪ Fx: 716-636-1733

Secular Humanistic Jews, International Federation of   www.ifshj.org
224 W 35th St   New York NY 10001
Ph: 212-564-6711 ▪ Fx: 212-564-6721

Secular Institute of Saint Francis Desales   www.secularinstitutes.org/sfs.htm
87 Gerrish Ave Suite T-2   East Haven CT 06512
Ph: 203-469-3277 ▪ Fx: 203-469-2094

Secular Jewish Organizations, Congress of   www.csjo.org
19657 Villa Dr N   Southfield MI 48076
Ph: 248-569-8127 ▪ Fx: 248-569-5222

Securities Administrators Association, North American   www.nasaa.org
10 G St NE Suite 710   Washington DC 20002
Ph: 202-737-0900 ▪ Fx: 202-783-3571 ▪ TF: 888-846-2722

Securities Association, Bank Insurance &   www.bisanet.org
303 W Lancaster Ave Suite 2D   Wayne PA 19087
Ph: 610-989-9047 ▪ Fx: 610-989-9102

Securities Association, Commercial Mortgage   www.cmbs.org
30 Broad St 28th Fl   New York NY 10004
Ph: 212-509-1844 ▪ Fx: 212-509-1895

Securities Dealers Inc, National Association of   www.nasd.com
1735 K St NW   Washington DC 20006
Ph: 202-728-8000 ▪ TF: 800-289-9999

Securities Industry Association   www.sia.com
120 Broadway 35th Fl   New York NY 10271
Ph: 212-608-1500 ▪ Fx: 212-608-1604

Securities Industry Association PAC   www.sia.com/political_action
1401 'I' St NW Suite 1000   Washington DC 20005
Ph: 202-296-9410 ▪ Fx: 202-408-1914

Securities Professionals, National Association of   www.nasphq.com
1212 New York Ave NW Suite 210   Washington DC 20005
Ph: 202-371-5535 ▪ Fx: 202-371-5536

Securities Rulemaking Board, Municipal   www.msrb.org
1900 Duke St Suite 600   Alexandria VA 22314
Ph: 703-797-6600 ▪ Fx: 703-797-6700

Securities Transfer Association   www.stai.org
PO Box 5067   Hazlet NJ 07730
Ph: 732-888-6040 ▪ Fx: 732-888-2121

Security Alliance, Jewelers   www.jewelerssecurity.org
6 E 45th St   New York NY 10017
Ph: 212-687-0328 ▪ Fx: 212-808-9168

Security Alternatives, National Center for Economic &   www.ncesa.org
2000 P St NW Suite 330   Washington DC 20036
Ph: 202-986-1373 ▪ Fx: 202-986-7938

Security Analysts, New York Society of   www.nyssa.org
1601 Broadway 11 Fl   New York NY 10019
Ph: 212-541-4530 ▪ Fx: 212-541-4677 ▪ TF: 800-248-0108

(Security) ASIS International   www.asisonline.org
1625 Prince St   Alexandria VA 22314
Ph: 703-519-6200 ▪ Fx: 703-519-6299

Security Association, Information Systems   www.issa.org
7044 S 13th St   Oak Creek WI 53154
Ph: 414-768-8000 ▪ Fx: 414-768-8001

Security, Business Executives for National   www.bens.org
1717 Pennsylvania Ave NW Suite 350   Washington DC 20006
Ph: 202-296-2125 ▪ Fx: 202-296-2490 ▪ TF: 800-296-2125

Security on Campus Inc   www.securityoncampus.org
649 S Henderson Rd Suite 6   King of Prussia PA 19406
Ph: 610-768-9330 ▪ Fx: 610-768-0646 ▪ TF: 888-251-7959

Security Companies, National Association of   www.nasco.org
1625 Prince St   Alexandria VA 22314
Ph: 703-518-1477

Security Consultants, International Association of Professional   www.iapsc.org
525 SW 5th St Suite A   Des Moines IA 50309
Ph: 515-282-8192 ▪ Fx: 515-282-9117

Security & Correction Officers, Federation of Police   www.fopsco-afspa.org
71 E Cherry St   Rahway NJ 07065
Ph: 732-388-3323 ▪ Fx: 732-388-5620

Security Council, Energy   www.energysecuritycouncil.org
5555 San Felipe Rd Suite 101   Houston TX 77056
Ph: 713-296-1893 ▪ Fx: 713-296-1895

Security Council Foundation, American   www.ascfusa.org/asc_home.htm
201A N Main St   Culpeper VA 22701
Ph: 540-547-1776 ▪ Fx: 540-547-9737

Security Council, National Cargo   www.cargosecurity.com
3 Church Cir Suite 292   Annapolis MD 21401
Ph: 410-956-0491 ▪ Fx: 410-956-0679 ▪ TF: 800-976-0403

Security Educators & Trainers, Academy of   www.personalprotection.com/aset
PO Box 802   Berryville VA 22611
Ph: 540-554-2241 ▪ Fx: 540-554-2558

Security Hardware Distributors Association   www.shda.org
1900 Arch St   Philadelphia PA 19103
Ph: 215-564-3484 ▪ Fx: 215-564-2175

Security Industry Association   www.siaonline.org
635 Slaters Ln Suite 110   Alexandria VA 22314
Ph: 703-683-2075 ▪ Fx: 703-683-2469

Security Institute, Computer   www.gocsi.com
600 Harrison St   San Francisco CA 94107
Ph: 415-947-6000 ▪ Fx: 415-905-2218

Security, International Association for Computer Systems   www.iacss.org
6 Swarthmore Ln   Dix Hills NY 11746
Ph: 631-499-1616 ▪ Fx: 631-462-9178

Security, International Association of Personnel in Employment
International Assn of Workforce Professionals 1801 Louisville
Rd   Frankfort KY 40601
Ph: 502-223-4459 ▪ Fx: 502-223-4127 ▪ TF: 888-898-9960

Security Management Association, International   www.ismanet.com
PO Box 623   Buffalo IA 52728
Ph: 563-381-4008 ▪ Fx: 563-381-4283 ▪ TF: 800-368-1894

Security, NGO Committee on Disarmament Peace &   disarm.igc.org
777 United Nations Plaza Rm 3-B   New York NY 10017
Ph: 212-687-5340 ▪ Fx: 212-687-1643

Security Officers, International Union of
2201 Broadway Suite 101   San Leandro CA 94612
Ph: 510-625-9913 ▪ Fx: 510-625-0998 ▪ TF: 800-772-3326

Security, Pacific Institute for Studies in Development Environment &   www.pacinst.org
654 13th St   Oakland CA 94612
Ph: 510-251-1600 ▪ Fx: 510-251-2203

Security Police & Fire Professionals of America, International Union   www.spfpa.org
25510 Kelly Rd   Roseville MI 48066
Ph: 586-772-7250 ▪ Fx: 586-772-9644 ▪ TF: 800-228-7492

Security Professionals, International Association of Home Safety &
PO Box 2044   Erie PA 16512
Ph: 814-456-2911

Security & Safety, International Association for Healthcare   www.iahss.org
PO Box 5038   Glendale Heights IL 60139
Ph: 630-871-9936 ▪ Fx: 630-871-9938 ▪ TF: 888-353-0990

Security Services, National Council of Investigation &   www.nciss.org
7501 Sparrows Pointe Blvd   Baltimore MD 21219
Ph: 800-445-8408 ▪ Fx: 410-388-9746

Security Studies, Institute for Resource &   www.irss-usa.org
27 Ellsworth Ave   Cambridge MA 02139
Ph: 617-491-5177 ▪ Fx: 617-491-6904

Security Studies, Institute for Space &   rmbowman.com/isss
5017 Bellflower Ct   Melbourne FL 32940
Ph: 321-752-5955

Security Traders Association   www.securitytraders.org
420 Lexington Ave Suite 2334   New York NY 10170
Ph: 212-867-7002 ▪ Fx: 212-867-7030

Security, Women in International   wiis.georgetown.edu
Georgetown Univ Walsh School of Foreign Service Ctr for
Peace & Security Studies 3240 Prospect St
NW   Washington DC 20057
Ph: 202-687-3366 ▪ Fx: 202-687-3233

Sedation in Dentistry, American Society for the   www.sedation4dentists.com
Advancement of Anesthesia &   6 E Union Ave   Bound Brook
NJ 08805
Ph: 732-469-9050 ▪ Fx: 732-271-1985

Sedimentary Geology, Society for   www.sepm.org
6128 E 38th St Suite 308   Tulsa OK 74135
Ph: 918-610-3361 ▪ Fx: 918-621-1685 ▪ TF: 800-865-9765

SEE (Signing Exact English) Center for the Advancement of   www.seecenter.org
Deaf Children   PO Box 1181   Los Alamitos CA 90720
Ph: 562-430-1467 ▪ Fx: 562-795-6614

Seed Analysts, Association of Official   www.aosaseed.com
1763 E University Ave Suite A PMB 411   Las Cruces NM
88001
Ph: 505-522-1437

Seed Certifying Agencies, Association of Official   www.aosca.org
55 SW 5th Ave Suite 150   Meridian ID 83642
Ph: 208-884-2493 ▪ Fx: 208-884-4201

Seed Research Foundation, American   www.amseed.org/asrf
225 Reinekers Ln Suite 650   Alexandria VA 22314
Ph: 703-837-8140 ▪ Fx: 703-837-9365

Seed Trade Association, American   www.amseed.com
225 Reinekers Ln Suite 650   Alexandria VA 22314
Ph: 703-837-8140 ▪ Fx: 703-837-9365 ▪ TF: 888-890-7333

Seeds/SEARCH, Native   www.nativeseeds.org
526 N 4th Ave   Tucson AZ 85705
Ph: 520-622-5561 ▪ Fx: 520-622-5591

Seeing Eye   www.seeingeye.org
PO Box 375   Morristown NJ 07963
Ph: 973-539-4425 ▪ Fx: 973-539-0922

Segmental Bridge Institute, American   www.asbi-assoc.org
9201 N 25th Ave Suite 150B   Phoenix AZ 85021
Ph: 602-997-9964 ▪ Fx: 602-997-9965

Seismological Society of America   www.seismosoc.org
Plaza Professional Bldg Suite 201   El Cerrito CA 94530
Ph: 510-525-5474 ▪ Fx: 510-525-7204

Select Registry Distinguished Inns of North America   www.selectregistry.com
PO Box 150   Marshall MI 49068
Ph: 269-789-0393 ▪ Fx: 269-789-0970 ▪ TF: 800-344-5244

Selected Independent Funeral Homes   www.selectedfuneralhomes.com
500 Lake Cook Rd Suite 205   Deerfield IL 60015
Ph: 847-236-9401 ▪ Fx: 847-236-9968 ▪ TF: 800-323-4219

(Self-Development) Aloha International   www.alohainternational.org
4504 Kukui St Suite 11   Kapaa HI 96746
Ph: 808-823-8381

Self-Employed, Communicating for Agriculture & the   www.selfemployedcountry.org
112 E Lincoln Ave   Fergus Falls MN 56537
Ph: 218-739-3241 ▪ Fx: 218-739-3832 ▪ TF: 800-432-3276

Self-Employed, National Association for the   www.nase.org
PO Box 612067 DFW Airport   Dallas TX 75261
Ph: 800-232-6273 ▪ Fx: 800-551-4446

Self-Government, Advocates for   www.self-gov.org
213 S Erwin St   Cartersville GA 30120
Ph: 770-386-8372 ▪ Fx: 770-386-8373

(Self-Government) Institute for Contemporary Studies   www.icspress.com
310 Harrison St   Oakland CA 94611
Ph: 510-238-5010 ▪ Fx: 510-238-8440 ▪ TF: 800-326-0263

Self-Help Clearinghouse, National   www.selfhelpweb.org
365 5th Ave Suite 3300   New York NY 10016
Ph: 212-817-1822 ▪ Fx: 212-817-1561

Self-Help Clearinghouse, National Mental Health Consumers'   www.mhselfhelp.org
1211 Chestnut St Suite 1207   Philadelphia PA 19107
Ph: 215-751-1810 ▪ Fx: 215-636-6312 ▪ TF: 800-553-4539

(Self-Help Development) Resource Foundation   www.resourcefnd.org
PO Box 3006   Larchmont NY 10538
Ph: 914-834-5810

Self-Help Group Clearinghouse, American   www.mentalhelp.net/selfhelp
Saint Claires Health Services 100 E Hanover Ave Suite
202   Cedar Knolls NJ 07927
Ph: 973-326-8853 ▪ Fx: 973-326-9467

Self Help for Hard of Hearing People   www.hearingloss.org
7910 Woodmont Ave Suite 1200   Bethesda MD 20814
Ph: 301-657-2248 ▪ Fx: 301-913-9413

Self Help International   www.selfhelpinternational.org
805 W Bremer Ave   Waverly IA 50677
Ph: 319-352-4040 ▪ Fx: 319-352-4820

Self-Instructional Language Programs, National Association of   www.nasilp.org
Univ of Arizona 1717 E Speedway Blvd Suite 3312   Tucson AZ
85721
Ph: 520-626-5258 ▪ Fx: 520-626-8205

Self-Insurance Institute of America Inc   www.siia.org
PO Box 1237   Simpsonville SC 29681
Ph: 864-962-2208 ▪ Fx: 864-962-2483 ▪ TF: 800-851-7789

Self-Insurers, National Council of   www.natcouncil.com
1253 Springfield Ave PMB 345   New Providence NJ 07974
Ph: 908-665-2152 ▪ Fx: 908-665-4020

Self Protection Association Inc, American   www.americanselfprotection.org
825 Greengate Oval St   Sagamore Hills OH 44067
Ph: 330-467-1750

Self-Realization Fellowship   www.yogananda-srf.org
3880 San Rafael Ave   Los Angeles CA 90065
Ph: 323-225-2471 ▪ Fx: 323-225-5088

Self-Reliance, Institute for Local   www.ilsr.org
927 15th St NW 4th Fl   Washington DC 20005
Ph: 202-898-1610 ▪ Fx: 202-898-1612

(Self-Reliance) Windward Foundation   www.windward.org
55 Windward Ln   Klickitat WA 98628
Ph: 509-369-2000

Self Storage Association   www.selfstorage.org
6506 Louisdale Rd Suite 315   Springfield VA 22150
Ph: 703-921-9123 ▪ Fx: 703-921-9105 ▪ TF: 888-735-3784

Self Winding Clock Association
1161 E Marcellus St   Long Beach CA 90807
Ph: 562-422-5158

Selle Francais Association, North American   www.sellefrancais.org
PO Box 579   Waynesboro VA 22980
Ph: 540-932-9160 ▪ Fx: 540-932-9163

Selling Association, Direct   www.dsa.org
1275 Pennsylvania Ave NW Suite 800   Washington DC 20004
Ph: 202-347-8866 ▪ Fx: 202-347-0055

Selling Association, National Field   www.nfsa.com
1900 Arch St   Philadelphia PA 19103
Ph: 215-564-1627 ▪ Fx: 215-564-2175

Selling Associations, World Federation of Direct   www.wfdsa.org
1275 Pennsylvania Ave NW Suite 800   Washington DC 20004
Ph: 202-347-8866 ▪ Fx: 202-347-0055

Selling Education Foundation, Direct   www.dsef.org
1275 Pennsylvania Ave NW Suite 800   Washington DC 20004
Ph: 202-347-8866 ▪ Fx: 202-347-8401

Semantics, Institute of General   www.general-semantics.org
86 85th St   Brooklyn NY 11209
Ph: 718-921-7093 ▪ Fx: 718-921-4276

Semantics, International Society for General   www.generalsemantics.org
PO Box 728   Concord CA 94522
Ph: 925-798-0311 ▪ Fx: 925-798-0312

Semiconductor Environmental Safety & Health Association   seshaonline.org
1313 Dolley Madison Blvd Suite 402   McLean VA 22101
Ph: 703-790-1745 ▪ Fx: 703-790-2672

Semiconductor Equipment & Materials International   www.semi.org
3081 Zenker Rd   San Jose CA 95134
Ph: 408-943-6900 ▪ Fx: 408-428-9600

Semiconductor Industry Association   www.semichips.org
181 Metro Dr Suite 450   San Jose CA 95110
Ph: 408-436-6600 ▪ Fx: 408-436-6646

Seminar Leaders Association, American   www.asla.com
2405 E Washington Blvd   Pasadena CA 91104
Ph: 626-791-1211 ▪ Fx: 626-798-0701 ▪ TF: 800-735-0511

Semiotic Society of America   com.pp.asu.edu/semiotics/ssa.htm

Senatorial Committee, National Republican   www.nrsc.org
425 2nd St NE   Washington DC 20002
Ph: 202-675-6000 ▪ Fx: 202-675-6058

Senior Action in a Gay Environment   www.sageusa.org
305 7th Ave 16th Fl   New York NY 10001
Ph: 212-741-2247 ▪ Fx: 212-366-1947

Senior Centers, National Institute of   www.ncoa.org
c/o National Council on the Aging 300 D St SW Suite
801   Washington DC 20024
Ph: 202-479-1200 ▪ Fx: 202-479-0735

(Senior Citizens) 60 Plus Association Inc   www.60plus.org
1600 Wilson Blvd Suite 960   Arlington VA 22209
Ph: 703-807-2070 ▪ Fx: 703-807-2073

Senior Citizens Association, American   www.ncseniorcitizens.com
PO Box 41   Fayetteville NC 28302
Ph: 910-323-3641 ▪ Fx: 910-323-4343 ▪ TF: 800-323-6525

(Senior Citizens) Catholic Golden Age   www.catholicgoldenage.org
PO Box 249   Olyphant PA 18447
Ph: 570-586-1091 ▪ Fx: 570-586-7721 ▪ TF: 800-836-5699

(Senior Citizens) Experience Works Inc   www.experienceworks.org
2200 Clarendon Blvd Suite 1000   Arlington VA 22201
Ph: 703-522-7272 ▪ Fx: 703-522-0141 ▪ TF: 866-397-9757

Senior Citizens Law Center, National   www.nsclc.org
1101 14th St NW Suite 400   Washington DC 20005
Ph: 202-289-6976 ▪ Fx: 202-289-7224

(Senior Citizens) Over the Hill Gang International   www.othgi.com
1820 W Colorado Ave   Colorado Springs CO 80904
Ph: 719-389-0022 ▪ Fx: 719-389-0024

Senior Companion Program   www.seniorcorps.org/joining/scp
2900 Newton St NE   Washington DC 20018
Ph: 202-529-8701 ▪ Fx: 202-832-0127

Senior Executives Association   www.seniorexecs.org
PO Box 44808   Washington DC 20026
Ph: 202-927-7000 ▪ Fx: 202-927-5192

Senior Fitness Association, American   www.seniorfitness.net
PO Box 2575   New Smyrna Beach FL 32170
Ph: 386-423-6634 ▪ Fx: 386-427-0613 ▪ TF: 800-243-1478

Senior Games Association, National   www.nsga.com/
PO Box 82059   Baton Rouge LA 70884
Ph: 225-766-6800 ▪ Fx: 225-766-9115

Senior Gleaners Inc   www.seniorgleaners.org
1951 Bell Ave   Sacramento CA 95838
Ph: 916-925-3240 ▪ Fx: 916-568-1528 ▪ TF: 800-585-1530

Senior Golf Association, National   www.nsgatour.com
3672 Nottingham Way   Hamilton Square NJ 08690
Ph: 800-282-6772 ▪ Fx: 609-921-2707 ▪ TF: 800-282-6772

Senior Involvement, Environmental Alliance for   www.easi.org
PO Box 250   Catlett VA 20119
Ph: 540-788-3274 ▪ Fx: 540-788-9301

Senior Softball USA   www.seniorsoftball.com
2701 K St Suite 101A   Sacramento CA 95816
Ph: 916-236-5303 ▪ Fx: 916-326-5304

Senior Volunteer Program Directors, National Association of Retired
12388 Warwick Blvd   Newport News VA 23601
Ph: 757-595-9037 ▪ Fx: 757-595-9047

Senior Women's Tennis Association, National   www.nswta.com
PO Box 142   Lake Oswego OR 97034
Ph: 503-636-9292 ▪ Fx: 503-636-9660

Seniors Against Federal Extravagance   www.s-a-f-e.org
413 Delaware Ave   Wilmington DE 19803
Ph: 302-478-0676

Seniors Association, United   www.unitedseniors.org
3900 Jermantown Rd Suite 450   Fairfax VA 22030
Ph: 703-359-6500 ▪ Fx: 703-359-6510 ▪ TF: 800-887-2872

Seniors Coalition   www.senior.org
9001 Braddock Rd Suite 200   Springfield VA 22151
Ph: 703-239-1960 ▪ Fx: 703-239-1985

Seniors Housing Association, American   www.seniorshousing.org
5100 Wisconsin Ave NW Suite 307   Washington DC 20016
Ph: 202-237-0900 ▪ Fx: 202-237-1616

Sense of Smell Institute   www.senseofsmell.org
145 E 32nd St   New York NY 10016
Ph: 212-725-2755 ▪ Fx: 212-779-9058

Sentencing Project   www.sentencingproject.org
514 10th St NW Suite 1000   Washington DC 20004
Ph: 202-628-0871 ▪ Fx: 202-628-1091

Separated & Divorced Catholics Inc, North American Conference of   www.nacsdc.org
PO Box 360   Richland OR 97870
Ph: 541-893-6089

Separation of Church & State, Americans United for   www.au.org
518 C St NE   Washington DC 20002
Ph: 202-466-3234 ▪ Fx: 202-466-2587 ▪ TF: 800-875-3707

Separations Society, American Filtration &   www.afssociety.org
Univ of Houston Dept of Chemical Engineering 4800 Calhoun
Rd   Houston TX 77204
Ph: 713-743-3671 ▪ Fx: 713-743-3679

Sephardi Federation, American   www.asfonline.org
15 W 16th St   New York NY 10011
Ph: 212-294-8350 ▪ Fx: 212-294-8348

Sephardic Jewish Brotherhood of America   www.sephardicstudies.org/brotherhood.html
9745 Queens Blvd Suite 610   Rego Park NY 11374
Ph: 718-459-1600

Sephardic Studies & Culture, Foundation for the Advancement of   www.sephardicstudies.org
34 W 15th St 3rd Fl   New York NY 10011
Ph: 212-960-5492 ▪ Fx: 212-960-0067

Septuagint & Cognate Studies, International Organization for   ccat.sas.upenn.edu/ioscs

Sequella Global Tuberculosis Foundation   www.sequellafoundation.org
9610 Medical Ctr Dr Suite 220   Rockville MD 20850
Ph: 301-762-3100 ▪ Fx: 301-762-2122

SER - Jobs for Progress National Inc   www.ser-national.org
1925 W John Carpenter Fwy Suite 575   Irving TX 75063
Ph: 972-506-7815 ▪ Fx: 972-506-7832 ▪ TF: 800-427-2306

Serb National Federation   www.serbnatlfed.org/
1 5th Ave 7th Fl   Pittsburgh PA 15222
Ph: 412-642-7372 ▪ Fx: 412-642-1372 ▪ TF: 800-538-7372

Serbian National Defense Council of America   www.snd-us.com
5782 N Elston Ave   Chicago IL 60646
Ph: 773-775-7772 ▪ Fx: 773-775-7779

Sergeants Association, Air Force   www.afsahq.org
5211 Auth Rd   Suitland MD 20746
Ph: 301-899-3500 ▪ Fx: 301-899-8136 ▪ TF: 800-638-0594

Sertoma International   www.sertoma.org
1912 E Meyer Blvd   Kansas City MO 64132
Ph: 816-333-8300 ▪ Fx: 816-333-4320 ▪ TF: 800-593-5646

Servants in Faith & Technology   www.sifat.org
2944 County Rd 113   Lineville AL 36266
Ph: 256-396-2017 ▪ Fx: 256-396-2501

(Service) Active 20-30 US & Canada Inc   www.active20-30.com
915 L St Suite 1000   Sacramento CA 95814
Ph: 916-447-3217 ▪ Fx: 916-442-0382

(Service) American Legion Auxiliary   www.legion-aux.org
777 N Meridian St 3rd Fl   Indianapolis IN 46204
Ph: 317-955-3845 ▪ Fx: 317-955-3884

Service Association of North America, Masonic   www.msana.com
8120 Fenton St   Silver Spring MD 20910
Ph: 301-588-4010 ▪ Fx: 301-608-3457

(Service) Campus Compact   www.compact.org
Brown Univ Box 1970   Providence RI 02912
Ph: 401-867-3950 ▪ Fx: 401-867-3925

(Service) Christophers The   www.christophers.org
12 E 48th St   New York NY 10017
Ph: 212-759-4050 ▪ Fx: 212-838-5073 ▪ TF: 888-298-4050

(Service) Circle K International   www.circlek.org
3636 Woodview Trace   Indianapolis IN 46268
Ph: 317-875-8755 ▪ Fx: 317-879-0204 ▪ TF: 800-549-2647

(Service) Civitan International   www.civitan.org
1 Civitan Pl PO Box 130744   Birmingham AL 35213
Ph: 205-591-8910 ▪ Fx: 205-592-6307 ▪ TF: 800-248-4826

Service & Conservation Corps, National Association of   www.nascc.org
666 11th St NW Suite 1000   Washington DC 20001
Ph: 202-737-6272 ▪ Fx: 202-737-6277 ▪ TF: 800-666-2722

Service Contract Industry Council   www.go-scic.com
204 S Monroe St   Tallahassee FL 32302
Ph: 850-681-1058 ▪ Fx: 850-681-6713

Service Corps, National Executive   www.nesc.org
120 Wall St 16th Fl   New York NY 10005
Ph: 212-269-1234 ▪ Fx: 212-269-0959

Service Corps of Retired Executives Association   www.score.org
409 3rd St SW 6th Fl   Washington DC 20024
Ph: 202-205-6762 ▪ Fx: 202-205-7636 ▪ TF: 800-634-0245

(Service) CRISTA Ministries   www.crista.org
19303 Fremont Ave N   Seattle WA 98133
Ph: 206-546-7200 ▪ Fx: 206-546-7484 ▪ TF: 800-442-4003

Service & Development Agency Inc   www.amecnet.org/sada/sada.htm
1134 11th St NW Suite 214   Washington DC 20001
Ph: 202-371-8722 ▪ Fx: 202-371-0981

(Service) Do Something   www.dosomething.org
423 W 55th St 8th Fl   New York NY 10019
Ph: 212-523-1175 ▪ Fx: 212-582-1307

Service Employees International Union   www.seiu.org
1313 L St NW   Washington DC 20005
Ph: 202-898-3200 ▪ Fx: 202-898-3491 ▪ TF: 800-424-8592

Service Industries, Coalition of   www.uscsi.org
1090 Vermont Ave NW Suite 420   Washington DC 20005
Ph: 202-289-7460 ▪ Fx: 202-775-1726

Service Industry Association   www.servicenetwork.org
2164 Decatur Rd Villa 19   San Diego CA 92106
Ph: 619-221-9200 ▪ Fx: 619-221-8201

(Service) Job's Daughters International   www.iojd.org
233 W 6th St   Papillon NE 68046
Ph: 402-592-7987 ▪ Fx: 402-592-2177

(Service) Key Club International   www.keyclub.org
3636 Woodview Trace   Indianapolis IN 46268
Ph: 317-875-8755 ▪ Fx: 317-879-0204

(Service) Kiwanis International   www.kiwanis.org
3636 Woodview Trace   Indianapolis IN 46268
Ph: 317-875-8755 ▪ Fx: 317-879-0204 ▪ TF: 800-549-2647

(Service) Landmark Volunteers   www.volunteers.com
PO Box 455   Sheffield MA 02157
Ph: 413-229-0255 ▪ Fx: 413-229-2050

Service Managers, National Association of   www.nasm.com
12603 224th Ave PMB 17   Bristol WI 53104
Ph: 262-857-7227

Service Organizations, United   www.uso.org
1008 Eberle Pl SE Suite 301   Washington Navy Yard DC 20374
Ph: 202-610-5700 ▪ Fx: 202-610-5699

(Service) Pilot International · www.pilotinternational.org
244 College St PO Box 4844   Macon GA 31208
Ph: 478-743-7403 ■ Fx: 478-743-2173

Service Professionals in Printing, Society for · www.sspp.org
433 E Monroe Ave   Alexandria VA 22301
Ph: 703-684-0044 ■ Fx: 703-548-9137 ■ TF: 877-777-7398

(Service) Quota International · www.quota.org
1420 21st St NW   Washington DC 20036
Ph: 202-331-9694 ■ Fx: 202-331-4395

Service Research Council, Public
320-D Maple Ave E   Vienna VA 22180
Ph: 703-242-3575 ■ Fx: 703-242-3579

Service Robot Association, International
900 Victors Way PO Box 3724   Ann Arbor MI 48106
Ph: 734-994-6088 ■ Fx: 734-994-3338

(Service) Rotary International · www.rotary.org
1560 Sherman Ave   Evanston IL 60201
Ph: 847-866-3000 ■ Fx: 847-328-8554

(Service) Ruritan National · www.ruritan.org
PO Box 487   Dublin VA 24084
Ph: 540-674-5431 ■ Fx: 540-674-2304 ■ TF: 877-787-8727

(Service) Sertoma International · www.sertoma.org
1912 E Meyer Blvd   Kansas City MO 64132
Ph: 816-333-8300 ■ Fx: 816-333-4320 ■ TF: 800-593-5646

(Service) Seva Foundation · www.seva.org
1786 5th St   Berkeley CA 94710
Ph: 510-845-7382 ■ Fx: 510-845-7410 ■ TF: 800-223-7382

(Service) Soroptimist International of the Americas · www.soroptimist.org
2 Penn Ctr Plaza Suite 1000   Philadelphia PA 19102
Ph: 215-557-9300 ■ Fx: 215-568-5200

Service Specialists Association · www.truckservice.org
4015 Marks Rd Suite 2B   Medina OH 44256
Ph: 330-725-7160 ■ Fx: 330-722-5638 ■ TF: 800-763-5717

Service Station Dealers of America · www.ssda-at.org
1532 Pointer Ridge Pl Suite E   Bowie MD 20716
Ph: 301-390-0900 ■ Fx: 301-390-3161

(Service & Support Industry) Help Desk Institute · www.thinkhdi.com
6385 Corporate Dr Suite 311   Colorado Springs CO 80919
Ph: 719-268-0174 ■ Fx: 719-268-0184 ■ TF: 800-248-5667

Servicemembers Legal Defense Network · www.sldn.org
PO Box 65301   Washington DC 20035
Ph: 202-328-3244 ■ Fx: 202-797-1635

Services, American Council for Trade in · www.acts-talks.com
1030 15th St NW   Washington DC 20005
Ph: 202-842-1030 ■ Fx: 202-842-1225

Services Association of America, Contract · www.csa-dc.org
1000 Wilson Blvd Suite 1800   Arlington VA 22209
Ph: 703-243-2020 ■ Fx: 703-243-3601

Services Council, Professional · www.pscouncil.org
2101 Wilson Blvd Suite 750   Arlington VA 22201
Ph: 703-875-8059 ■ Fx: 703-875-8922

Services Management International, Association for · www.afsmi.org
1342 Colonial Blvd Suite 25   Fort Myers FL 33907
Ph: 239-275-7887 ■ Fx: 239-275-0794 ■ TF: 800-333-9786

SESAC Inc · www.sesac.com
55 Music Sq E   Nashville TN 37203
Ph: 615-320-0055 ■ Fx: 615-329-9627 ■ TF: 800-826-9996

Sesame Workshop · www.sesameworkshop.org
1 Lincoln Plaza   New York NY 10023
Ph: 212-595-3456 ■ Fx: 212-875-6111

Sessions Roger Society · www.uncwil.edu/music/Sessionssociety
Univ of North Carolina at Wilmington 601 S College
   Rd   Wilmington NC 28403
Ph: 910-962-3390 ■ Fx: 910-962-7106

SETI League Inc · www.setileague.org
PO Box 555   Little Ferry NJ 07643
Ph: 201-641-1770 ■ Fx: 201-641-1771 ■ TF: 800-828-7384

Setting Priorities for Retirement Years Foundation · www.spry.org
10 G St NE Suite 600   Washington DC 20002
Ph: 202-216-0401 ■ Fx: 202-216-0779

Settlement Association of America, Viatical & Life · www.viatical.org
800 Mayfair Cir   Orlando FL 32803
Ph: 407-894-3797 ■ Fx: 407-897-1325 ■ TF: 800-842-9811

Settlement Purchasers, National Association of · www.setcap.com/Gov_Nasp.asp
14755 Preston Rd Suite 130   Dallas TX 75254
Ph: 800-959-0006 ■ Fx: 800-959-0028

Settlements Trade Association, National Structured · www.nssta.com
1800 K St NW Suite 718   Washington DC 20006
Ph: 202-466-2714 ■ Fx: 202-466-7414

Settlers & Threshers Association, Midwest Old · www.oldthreshers.org
405 E Threshers Rd   Mount Pleasant IA 52641
Ph: 319-385-8937 ■ Fx: 319-385-0563

Seva Foundation · www.seva.org
1786 5th St   Berkeley CA 94710
Ph: 510-845-7382 ■ Fx: 510-845-7410 ■ TF: 800-223-7382

Seven Seas Cruising Association · www.ssca.org
1525 S Andrews Ave Suite 217   Fort Lauderdale FL 33316
Ph: 954-463-2431 ■ Fx: 954-463-7183

Seventh-day Adventist Dentists, National · www.llu.edu/llu/dentistry/nasdad
Association of   PO Box 101   Loma Linda CA 92354
Ph: 909-558-8187 ■ Fx: 909-558-4607

Seventh-day Adventist Dietetic Association · www.sdada.org
6100 Leoni Rd   Grizzly Flats CA 95636
Ph: 530-626-3610 ■ Fx: 530-626-8524

Seventh-day Adventist Kinship International · www.sdakinship.org
PO Box 7320   Laguna Niguel CA 92607
Ph: 949-248-1299

Seventh-day Adventist Librarians, Association of · www.asdal.org

Seventh-day Adventist World Church · www.adventist.org
12501 Old Columbia Pike   Silver Spring MD 20904
Ph: 301-680-6000 ■ Fx: 301-680-6307

Seventh Day Baptist General Conference of the · www.seventhdaybaptist.org
US & Canada   PO Box 1678   Janesville WI 53547
Ph: 608-752-5055 ■ Fx: 608-752-7711

Seventh Day Baptist Historical Society · home.inwave.com/sdbhist
PO Box 1678   Janesville WI 53547
Ph: 608-752-5055 ■ Fx: 608-752-7711

Seventh Day Baptist Missionary Society · sdbmissoc.home.mindspring.com
119 Main St   Westerly RI 02891
Ph: 401-596-4326 ■ Fx: 401-348-9494

Seventh Day Baptist World Federation · www.seventhdaybaptist.org
PO Box 1678   Janesville WI 53547
Ph: 608-752-5055 ■ Fx: 608-752-7711

Seventh Generation Fund for Indian Development · www.7genfund.org
PO Box 4569   Arcata CA 95518
Ph: 707-825-7640 ■ Fx: 707-825-7639

Sewer Distributors of America, Water & · www.wasda.com
1900 Arch St   Philadelphia PA 19103
Ph: 215-564-3484 ■ Fx: 215-564-2175

(Sewer Systems) NASSCO · www.nassco.org
1314 Bedford Ave Suite 201   Baltimore MD 21208
Ph: 410-486-3500 ■ Fx: 410-486-6838

Sewerage Agencies, Association of Metropolitan · www.amsa-cleanwater.org
1816 Jefferson Pl NW   Washington DC 20036
Ph: 202-833-2672 ■ Fx: 202-833-4657

Sewing Association, Home · www.sewing.org
PO Box 1312   Monroeville PA 15146
Ph: 412-372-5950 ■ Fx: 412-372-5953

Sewing Guild, American · www.asg.org
9660 Hillcroft Suite 516   Houston TX 77096
Ph: 713-729-3000 ■ Fx: 713-721-9230 ■ TF: 877-422-6739

Sewn Products Equipment Suppliers Association · www.spesa.org
5107 Falls of the Neuse Suite B15   Raleigh NC 27609
Ph: 919-872-8909 ■ Fx: 919-872-1915 ■ TF: 888-447-7372

Sex Addicts Anonymous · www.saa-recovery.org
PO Box 70949   Houston TX 77270
Ph: 713-869-4902 ■ Fx: 713-869-4176 ■ TF: 800-477-8191

Sex & Love Addicts Anonymous · www.slaafws.org
PO Box 338   Norwood MA 02062
Ph: 781-255-8825 ■ Fx: 781-255-9190

Sex Therapy & Research, Society for · www.sstarnet.org
409 12th St NW PO Box 96920   Washington DC 20090
Ph: 202-863-1646 ■ Fx: 202-554-0453

Sexaholics Anonymous · www.sa.org
PO Box 3565   Brentwood TN 37024
Ph: 615-370-6062 ■ Fx: 615-370-0882

Sexology, American Board of · www.sexologist.org
2431 Aloma Ave Suite 277   Winter Park FL 32792
Ph: 407-645-1641

(Sexual Abuse) VOICES in Action · www.voices-action.org

(Sexual Abuse) Wings Foundation · www.wingsfound.org
8725 W 14th Ave Suite 150   Lakewood CO 80215
Ph: 303-238-8660 ■ TF: 800-373-8671

Sexual Abusers, Association for the Treatment of · www.atsa.com
4900 SW Griffith Dr Suite 274   Beaverton OR 97005
Ph: 503-643-1023 ■ Fx: 503-643-5084

(Sexual Addiction) COSA · www.cosa-recovery.org
PO Box 14537   Minneapolis MN 55414
Ph: 763-537-6904

(Sexual Exploitation) Paul & Lisa Program Inc · www.paulandlisa.org
PO Box 348   Westbrook CT 06498
Ph: 860-767-7660 ■ Fx: 860-767-3122

(Sexual & Reproductive Health) Alan Guttmacher Institute · www.agi-usa.org
120 Wall St 21st Fl   New York NY 10005
Ph: 212-248-1111 ■ Fx: 212-248-1951

(Sexual Victimization) Male Survivor · www.malesurvivor.org
5505 Connecticut Ave NW PMB 103   Washington DC 20015
Ph: 800-738-4181

(Sexuality & Health Education) ETR Associates · www.etr.org
4 Carbonero Way   Scotts Valley CA 95066
Ph: 831-438-4060

Sexuality Information & Education Council of the US · www.siecus.org
130 W 42nd St Suite 350   New York NY 10036
Ph: 212-819-9770 ■ Fx: 212-819-9776

Sexuality, Society for the Scientific Study of · www.sexscience.org
PO Box 416   Allentown PA 18105
Ph: 610-530-2483 ■ Fx: 610-530-2485

SFI Foundation Inc · www.sfifoundation.com
15708 Pomerado Rd Suite N208   Poway CA 92064
Ph: 858-451-8868 ■ Fx: 858-451-9268

SGMA International · www.sgma.com
200 Castlewood Dr   North Palm Beach FL 33408
Ph: 561-842-4100 ■ Fx: 561-863-8984

SHAEF/ETOUSA Veterans Association · www.shaef.org
2301 Broadway   San Francisco CA 94115
Ph: 415-921-8322

Shagya-Arabian Society, North American · www.shagya.net
9797 S Rangeline Rd   Clinton IN 47842
Ph: 765-665-3851

Shake & Shingle Bureau, Cedar · www.cedarbureau.org
PO Box 1178   Sumas WA 98295
Ph: 604-820-7700 ■ Fx: 604-820-0266 ■ TF: 800-843-3578

Shakers, Friends of the · www.maineshakers.com/friends.html
707 Shaker Rd   New Gloucester ME 04260
Ph: 207-926-4597

Shakespeare Birthplace Trust, American Friends of the
625 Slaters Ln Suite 103   Alexandria VA 22314
Ph: 703-684-7703 ▪ Fx: 703-684-7594

Shakespeare Oxford Society   www.shakespeare-oxford.com
1556 Connecticut Ave NW Suite 200   Washington DC 20036
Ph: 202-207-0281

Shakespeare Society of America   www.shakespearesociety.org
45 E 78th St   New York NY 10021
Ph: 212-327-3399 ▪ Fx: 212-327-3377

Shale Clay & Slate Institute, Expanded   www.escsi.org
2225 E Murray Holladay Rd Suite 102   Salt Lake City UT 84117
Ph: 801-272-7070 ▪ Fx: 801-272-3377

Shamanic Studies, Foundation for   www.shamanism.org
PO Box 1939   Mill Valley CA 94942
Ph: 415-380-8282

Shamanism Network, Cross-Cultural
PO Box 270   Williams OR 97544
Ph: 541-846-1313 ▪ Fx: 541-846-1204

Shanti   www.shanti.org
730 Polk St   San Francisco CA 94109
Ph: 415-674-4700 ▪ Fx: 415-674-0371

Shape Up America!   www.shapeup.org
15757 Crabbs Branch Way   Rockville MD 20855
Ph: 301-258-0540 ▪ Fx: 301-258-0541

SHARE Foundation   www.share-elsalvador.org
598 Bosworth St Suite 1   San Francisco CA 94131
Ph: 415-239-2595 ▪ Fx: 415-239-0785

Share Our Strength   www.strength.org
733 15th St NW Suite 640   Washington DC 20005
Ph: 202-393-2925 ▪ Fx: 202-347-5868 ▪ TF: 800-969-4767

SHARE Pregnancy & Infant Loss Support Inc   www.nationalshareoffice.com
St Joseph's Health Ctr 300 1st Capitol Dr   Saint Charles MO
   63301
Ph: 636-947-6164 ▪ Fx: 636-947-7486 ▪ TF: 800-821-6819

Shareware Professionals, Association of   www.asp-shareware.org
PO Box 1522   Martinsville IN 46151
Ph: 765-349-4740 ▪ Fx: 765-349-4744

Sharing of Ministries Abroad USA   www.episcopalian.org/soma
5290 Saratoga Ln   Woodbridge VA 22193
Ph: 703-878-7667 ▪ Fx: 703-878-7015

Sharkhunters International   www.sharkhunters.com
PO Box 1539   Hernando FL 34442
Ph: 352-637-2917 ▪ Fx: 352-637-6289

Shaving Mug Collectors Association, National   www.nsmca.org
320 S Glenwood St   Allentown PA 18104
Ph: 610-437-2534

Shaw Lloyd Foundation   www.lloydshaw.org
1620 Los Alamos SW   Albuquerque NM 87104
Ph: 505-247-3921

(Sheep) American Border Leicester Association   www.ablasheep.org
PO Box 947   Canby OR 97013
Ph: 503-266-7156

(Sheep) American Corriedale Association Inc   www.americancorriedale.com
PO Box 391   Clay City IL 62824
Ph: 618-676-1046 ▪ Fx: 618-676-1133

(Sheep) American Cotswold Record Association
PO Box 59   Plympton MA 02367
Ph: 781-585-2026

(Sheep) American Delaine & Merino Record Association   www.admra.org
59419 Walters Rd   Jacobsburg OH 43933
Ph: 740-686-2172

(Sheep) American Romney Breeders' Association   www.americanromney.org
744 Riverbanks Rd   Grants Pass OR 97527
Ph: 541-476-6428

(Sheep) American Shropshire Registry Association   www.shropshires.org
PO Box 635   Harvard IL 60033
Ph: 815-943-2034 ▪ Fx: 815-945-2034

(Sheep) American Southdown Breeders' Association   www.southdownsheep.org
HCR 13 Box 220   Fredonia TX 76842
Ph: 915-429-6226 ▪ Fx: 915-429-6225

Sheep Association, American Cormo   www.cormosheep.com
Rt 59 Box 25   Broadus MT 59317
Ph: 406-427-5449

Sheep Association, American Hampshire   www.countrylovin.com/ahsa/
15603 173rd Ave   Milo IA 50166
Ph: 641-942-6402 ▪ Fx: 641-942-6502

Sheep Association, American North Country Cheviot
8708 S County Rd 500 W   Reelsville IN 46171
Ph: 765-672-8205 ▪ Fx: 765-672-4275

Sheep Association, American Oxford
1960 E 2100 N Rd   Stonington IL 62567
Ph: 217-325-3515

Sheep Association, American Polypay   www.countrylovin.com/polypay/
15603 173rd Ave   Milo IA 50166
Ph: 641-942-6402 ▪ Fx: 641-942-6502

Sheep Association, Navajo-Churro   www.navajo-churrosheep.com
PO Box 94   Ojo Caliente NM 87549
Ph: 505-737-0488

Sheep Association, North American Wensleydale   www.wensleydalesheep.org
4589 Fruitland Rd   Loma Rica CA 95901
Ph: 530-743-5262

Sheep Association, United Suffolk   www.u-s-s-a.org
PO Box 256   Newton UT 84327
Ph: 435-563-6105 ▪ Fx: 435-563-9356

Sheep Breeders Association of America, Columbia   www.columbiasheep.org
PO Box 272   Upper Sandusky OH 43351
Ph: 740-482-2608

Sheep Breeders' Association, American Rambouillet   www.rambouilletsheep.org
1610 S State Rd 3261   Levelland TX 79336
Ph: 806-894-3081 ▪ Fx: 806-894-5531 ▪ TF: 877-929-4414

Sheep Breeders Association, Jacob   www.jsba.org
PO Box 10427   Bozeman MT 59719
Ph: 406-388-9537

Sheep Breeders Association, Montadale   www.countrylovin.com/msba
2514 Willow Rd E   Fargo ND 58102
Ph: 701-297-9199

Sheep Breeders Association, National Lincoln   www.lincolnsheep.org
15603 173rd Ave   Milo IA 50166
Ph: 641-942-6402

(Sheep) Continental Dorset Club   www.dorsets.homestead.com
PO Box 506   North Scituate RI 02857
Ph: 401-647-4676 ▪ Fx: 401-647-4679

Sheep Dog Society, North American
Rt 3 Box 107   McLeansboro IL 62859
Ph: 618-757-2238

(Sheep) Finnsheep Breeders Association   www.finnsheep.org
143 Gravel Ln   Lexington VA 24450
Ph: 540-463-4594

Sheep, Foundation for North American Wild   www.fnaws.org
PO Box 146   Douglas WY 82633
Ph: 307-358-3693 ▪ Fx: 307-358-3262

Sheep Industry Association, American   www.sheepusa.org
9785 Maroon Cir Suite 360   Centennial CO 80112
Ph: 303-771-3500 ▪ Fx: 303-771-8200

Sheep Registry, American Karakul   www.karakulsheep.com
11500 Hwy 5   Boonville MO 65233
Ph: 660-838-6340 ▪ Fx: 660-838-6322

Sheep Registry, National Tunis   www.tunissheep.org
819 Lyons St   Ludlow MA 01056
Ph: 413-589-9653

Sheep Society, American Cheviot   members.aol.com/culhamef/bcheviots/cheviot.htm
Rt 1 Box 120   New Richland MN 56072
Ph: 507-465-8474

Sheepbreeders Association, North American Shetland   www.shetland-sheep.org

Sheepdog Association, American Shetland   www.assa.org
7274 S Chase Way   Littleton CO 80128
Ph: 303-979-8998

Sheepdog Club of America Inc, Old English   www.oldenglishsheepdogclubofamerica.org
N 64 W 20708 Mill Rd Suite 1015   Menomonee Falls WI 53501
Ph: 262-252-3936

Sheet Metal & Air Conditioning Contractors' National Association   www.smacna.org
4201 Lafayette Center Dr   Chantilly VA 20151
Ph: 703-803-2980 ▪ Fx: 703-803-3732

Sheet Metal Occupational Health Institute Trust   www.smohit.org
601 N Fairfax St Suite 250   Alexandria VA 22314
Ph: 703-739-7130 ▪ Fx: 703-739-7134

Sheet Metal Workers International Association   www.smwia.org
1750 New York Ave NW 6th Fl   Washington DC 20006
Ph: 202-783-5880 ▪ Fx: 202-662-0894 ▪ TF: 800-457-7694

Shelley Association of America, Keats-   www.rc.umd.edu/ksaa/ksaa.html
New York Public Library 476 5th Ave Rm 226   New York NY
   10018
Ph: 212-764-0655

Shellfish Growers Association, Pacific Coast   www.pcsga.org
120 State Ave NE PMB 142   Olympia WA 98501
Ph: 360-754-2744 ▪ Fx: 360-754-2743

Shellfisheries Association, National   www.shellfish.org

Shelter Now International   www.shelter.org
502 E New York Ave PO Box 1306   Oshkosh WI 54903
Ph: 920-426-1207 ▪ Fx: 920-426-4321

Shema Yisrael, Congregation   www.shema.com
28600 Lahser Rd PO Box 804   Southfield MI 48037
Ph: 248-593-5150

Shenandoah National Park Association   www.snpbooks.org
3655 US Hwy 211 E   Luray VA 22835
Ph: 540-999-3582 ▪ Fx: 540-999-3583

Sheriffs' Association, National   www.sheriffs.org
1450 Duke St   Alexandria VA 22314
Ph: 703-836-7827 ▪ Fx: 703-683-6541 ▪ TF: 800-424-7827

Shetland Pony Club, American   www.shetlandminiature.com
81-B E Queenwood Rd   Morton IL 61550
Ph: 309-263-4044 ▪ Fx: 309-263-5113

Shetland Sheepbreeders Association, North American   www.shetland-sheep.org

Shetland Sheepdog Association, American   www.assa.org
7274 S Chase Way   Littleton CO 80128
Ph: 303-979-8998

Shevchenko Scientific Society Inc   www.shevchenko.org
63 4th Ave   New York NY 10003
Ph: 212-254-5130 ▪ Fx: 212-254-5239

Shiba Club of America, National   www.shibas.org
4360 Deer Spring Rd   Middletown MD 21769
Ph: 301-371-7815

Shingle Bureau, Cedar Shake &   www.cedarbureau.org
PO Box 1178   Sumas WA 98295
Ph: 604-820-7700 ▪ Fx: 604-820-0266 ▪ TF: 800-843-3578

Ship Brokers & Agents (USA) Inc, Association of   www.asba.org
510 Sylvan Ave Suite 201   Englewood Cliffs NJ 07632
Ph: 201-569-2882 ▪ Fx: 201-569-9082

Ship Cancellation Society, Universal   www.uscs.org

Ship Masters' Association, International   www.shipmaster.org

Shipbuilders Blacksmiths Forgers & Helpers, International   www.boilermakers.org
   Brotherhood of Boilermakers Iron   753 State Ave Suite
   570   Kansas City KS 66101
Ph: 913-371-2640 ▪ Fx: 913-281-8101

Shipbuilders Council of America   www.shipbuilders.org
1455 F St NW Suite 225   Washington DC 20005
Ph: 202-347-5462 ▪ Fx: 202-347-5464

Shipbuilding Association, American www.americanshipbuilding.com
600 Pennsylvania Ave SE Suite 305   Washington DC 20003
Ph: 202-544-8170 ▪ Fx: 202-544-8252

Shipbuilding Workers of America, Industrial Union of Marine &
719 E Fort Ave   Baltimore MD 21230
Ph: 410-837-0056 ▪ Fx: 410-837-0058

Shipment Traffic Conference, National Small www.nasstrac.org
758 Quail Run   Waconia MN 55387
Ph: 952-442-8858 ▪ Fx: 952-442-3941

Shipowners Claims Bureau www.american-club.com
60 Broad St 37th Fl   New York NY 10004
Ph: 212-847-4500 ▪ Fx: 212-847-4599 ▪ TF: 800-730-2535

Shippers of America, Food www.foodshippersofamerica.org
6166 Booror Rd   Grove City OH 43123
Ph: 614-875-3955

Shippers Association, American Cotton www.acsa-cotton.org
88 Union Ave Suite 1204   Memphis TN 38103
Ph: 901-525-2272 ▪ Fx: 901-527-6527

Shippers Association, American Import www.aisaship.com
662 Main St   New Rochelle NY 10801
Ph: 914-633-3770 ▪ Fx: 914-633-4041

Shippers Association Inc, Fashion Accessories www.accessoryweb.com
350 5th Ave Suite 2030   New York NY 10118
Ph: 212-947-3424 ▪ Fx: 212-629-0361

Shippers Association, North American www.nasaships.com
1600 St Georges Ave Suite 310 PO Box 249   Rahway NJ 07065
Ph: 732-388-6256 ▪ Fx: 732-388-6580 ▪ TF: 800-524-1186

Shippers Association, North American Rail www.railshippers.com
2115 Portsmouth Dr   Richardson TX 75082
Ph: 972-690-4740 ▪ Fx: 972-644-8208

Shippers Association, Parcel www.parcelshippers.org
1211 Connecticut Ave NW Suite 610   Washington DC 20036
Ph: 202-296-3690 ▪ Fx: 202-296-0343

Shippers Association, Sporting Goods www.sgsa.net
9237 Dove Ct   Gilroy CA 95020
Ph: 408-846-9592 ▪ Fx: 408-846-9213

Shippers' Associations, American Institute for www.shippers.org
PO Box 33457   Washington DC 20033
Ph: 202-628-0933 ▪ Fx: 202-296-7374

Shippers of Recycled Textiles Inc www.smartasn.org
7910 Woodmont Ave Suite 1130   Bethesda MD 20814
Ph: 301-656-1077 ▪ Fx: 301-656-1079

Shipping of America, Chamber of
1730 M St NW Suite 407   Washington DC 20036
Ph: 202-775-4399 ▪ Fx: 202-659-3795

Shipping, American Bureau of www.eagle.org
16855 Northchase Dr   Houston TX 77060
Ph: 281-877-6000 ▪ Fx: 281-877-6001

Shipping Association, Jewelers
125 Carlsbad St   Cranston RI 02920
Ph: 401-943-6490 ▪ Fx: 401-943-1490 ▪ TF: 800-688-4572

Shipping Container Institute, Plastic www.pscionline.org
1920 'N' St NW Suite 800   Washington DC 20036
Ph: 202-973-2709 ▪ Fx: 202-331-8330

Shipping Container Institute, Steel www.steelcontainers.com
1101 14th St NW Suite 1020   Washington DC 20005
Ph: 202-408-1900 ▪ Fx: 202-408-1972

Shipping Sack Manufacturers' Association, Paper www.pssma.org
520 E Oxford St   Coopersburg PA 19036
Ph: 610-282-6845 ▪ Fx: 610-282-6921

Ships Association, Historic Naval www.hnsa.org

Ships-in-Bottles Association of America www.shipsinbottles.org
PO Box 180550   Coronado CA 92178
Ph: 619-435-3555

Ships on Stamps Unit www.shipsonstamps.org

Shire Horse Association, American www.shirehorse.org/
1211 Hill Harrell Rd   Effingham SC 29541
Ph: 843-629-0072

Shoe & Allied Craftsmen, Brotherhood of
PO Box 390   East Bridgewater MA 02333
Ph: 508-378-9300 ▪ Fx: 508-588-9735

Shoe Association, World www.wsashow.com
20281 SW Birch St Suite 100   Newport Beach CA 92660
Ph: 949-851-8451 ▪ Fx: 949-851-8523

Shoe Exchange, National Odd www.oddshoe.org
PO Box 1120   Chandler AZ 85244
Ph: 480-892-3484 ▪ Fx: 480-892-3568

Shoe Retailers Association, National nsra.org
7150 Columbia Gateway Dr Suite G   Columbia MD 21046
Ph: 410-381-8282 ▪ Fx: 410-381-1167 ▪ TF: 800-673-8446

Shoe Service Institute of America www.ssia.info
18 School St   North Brookfield MA 01535
Ph: 508-867-7731 ▪ Fx: 508-867-4600

Shomrim Societies, National Conference of
45 E 33rd St Rm 601   New York NY 10016
Ph: 212-689-2015 ▪ Fx: 212-447-1633

Shooters Association, National Bench Rest nbrsa.benchrest.com
2835 Guilford Ln   Oklahoma City OK 73120
Ph: 405-842-9585 ▪ Fx: 405-842-9575

Shooting Association, National Skeet www.mynssa.com
5931 Roft Rd   San Antonio TX 78257
Ph: 210-688-3371 ▪ Fx: 210-688-3014 ▪ TF: 800-877-5338

Shooting Coaches Association, International
17446 SW Granada Dr   Beaverton OR 97007
Ph: 503-642-5873 ▪ Fx: 503-649-5182

(Shooting) National Sporting Clays Association www.mynsca.com
5931 Roft Rd   San Antonio TX 78253
Ph: 210-688-3371 ▪ Fx: 210-688-3014 ▪ TF: 800-877-5338

Shooting Sports Foundation, National www.nssf.org
11 Mile Hill Rd   Newtown CT 06470
Ph: 203-426-1320 ▪ Fx: 203-426-1087

(Shooting) United Sportsmen's Association of North America www.usanamtc.com
224 Sandbridge Rd   Pittsgrove NJ 08318
Ph: 856-358-4891

Shooting, USA www.usashooting.com
1 Olympic Plaza   Colorado Springs CO 80909
Ph: 719-578-4670

Shopping Centers, International Council of www.icsc.org
1221 Ave of the Americas 41st Fl   New York NY 10020
Ph: 646-728-3800 ▪ Fx: 212-589-5555

Shopping Providers Association, Mystery www.mysteryshop.org
12300 Ford Rd Suite 135   Dallas TX 75234
Ph: 972-406-1104 ▪ Fx: 972-755-2561

Shore & Beach Preservation Association, American www.asbpa.org
1724 Indian Way   Oakland CA 94611
Ph: 510-339-2818 ▪ Fx: 510-339-6710

Shorenstein Center on the Press Politics & www.ksg.harvard.edu/presspol
Public Policy   Harvard Univ John F Kennedy School of
Government 79 John F Kennedy St   Cambridge MA 02138
Ph: 617-495-8269 ▪ Fx: 617-495-8696

Shorin Kempo Karate Association, American www.americanblackbeltacademy.com
1587 York St   Colorado Springs CO 80918
Ph: 719-598-0398 ▪ Fx: 719-268-2733

Shoring & Forming Institute Inc, Scaffolding www.ssfi.org
1300 Sumner Ave   Cleveland OH 44115
Ph: 216-241-7333 ▪ Fx: 216-241-0105

Short Line & Regional Railroad Association, American www.aslrra.org
50 F St NW Suite 7020   Washington DC 20005
Ph: 202-628-4500 ▪ Fx: 202-628-6430

Shortening & Edible Oils, Institute of www.iseo.org
1750 New York Ave NW Suite 120   Washington DC 20006
Ph: 202-783-7960 ▪ Fx: 202-393-1367

Shorthorn Association, American www.beefshorthornusa.com
8288 Hascall St   Omaha NE 68124
Ph: 402-393-7200 ▪ Fx: 402-393-7203

Shorthorn Association, American Junior www.beefshorthornusa.com
8288 Hascall St   Omaha NE 68124
Ph: 402-393-7200 ▪ Fx: 402-393-7203

Shorthorn Junior Society, American Milking www.milkingshorthorn.com/juniors.html
800 Pleasant St   Beloit WI 53511
Ph: 608-365-3332 ▪ Fx: 608-365-6644

Shorthorn Society, American Milking www.milkingshorthorn.com
800 Pleasant St   Beloit WI 53511
Ph: 608-365-3332

Shortwave Association, North American www.anarc.org/naswa
45 Wildflower Rd   Levittown PA 19057
Ph: 215-945-0543

Shortwave Listeners Club, American
16182 Ballad Ln   Huntington Beach CA 92649
Ph: 714-846-1685

Shotcrete Association, American www.shotcrete.org
38800 Country Club Dr   Farmington Hills MI 48331
Ph: 248-848-3780 ▪ Fx: 248-848-3740

Shoulder & Elbow Surgeons, American www.ases-assn.org
6300 N River Rd Suite 727   Rosemont IL 60018
Ph: 847-698-1629 ▪ Fx: 847-823-0536

Show Horse Registry, National www.nshregistry.org
10368 Bluegrass Pkwy   Louisville KY 40299
Ph: 502-266-5100 ▪ Fx: 502-266-5806

Show Managers Association Inc, Professional www.psmashows.com
1 Regency Dr PO Box 30   Bloomfield CT 06002
Ph: 860-243-3977 ▪ Fx: 860-286-0787

Show Organizers, Society of Independent www.siso.org
7000 W SW Hwy   Chicago Ridge IL 60415
Ph: 708-361-6000 ▪ Fx: 708-361-6166 ▪ TF: 877-937-7476

Show Promoters Association, Antique & Collectible www.antiqueandcollectible.com
PO Box 4389   Davidson NC 28036
Ph: 704-895-9088 ▪ Fx: 704-895-0230 ▪ TF: 800-287-7127

Showmen's League of America www.showmensleague.org
300 W Randolph St   Chicago IL 60606
Ph: 312-332-6236 ▪ Fx: 312-332-6237 ▪ TF: 800-350-9906

Shrimp Processors Association, American
PO Box 50774   New Orleans LA 70150
Ph: 504-368-1571 ▪ Fx: 504-368-1573

Shrine of North America www.shrinershq.org
2900 N Rocky Point Dr   Tampa FL 33607
Ph: 813-281-0300 ▪ Fx: 813-281-2519

Shriver Sargent National Center on Poverty Law www.povertylaw.org
111 N Wabash Ave Suite 500   Chicago IL 60602
Ph: 312-263-3830 ▪ Fx: 312-263-3846 ▪ TF: 800-621-3256

Shropshire Registry Association, American www.shropshires.org
PO Box 635   Harvard IL 60033
Ph: 815-943-2034 ▪ Fx: 815-945-2034

(Sicily) Arba Sicula www.arbasicula.org
St Johns Univ Modern Foreign Languages Dept 8000 Utopia
Pkwy   Jamaica NY 11439
Ph: 718-990-5203 ▪ Fx: 718-990-5954

Sick Child Daycare, National Association for www.nascd.org
1716 5th Ave N   Birmingham AL 35203
Ph: 205-324-8447 ▪ Fx: 205-324-8050

Sick & Disabled, CUSA - An Apostolate of the Chronically www.cusan.org
176 W 8th St   Bayonne NJ 07002
Ph: 201-437-0412

Sickle Cell Anemia Association, American www.ascaa.org
10300 Carnegie Ave   Cleveland OH 44106
Ph: 216-229-8600 ▪ Fx: 216-229-4500

Sickle Cell Disease Association of America www.sicklecelldisease.org
200 Corporate Pointe Suite 495   Culver City CA 90230
Ph: 310-216-6363 ▪ Fx: 310-215-3722 ▪ TF: 800-421-8453

Sidecar Association, United   www.sidecar.com
130 S Michigan Ave   Villa Park IL 60181
Ph: 630-833-6732

Sidesaddle Federation, World   www.sidesaddle.org
PO Box 1104   Bucyrus OH 44820
Ph: 419-284-3176

Siding Institute, Vinyl   www.vinylsiding.org
1801 K St NW Suite 600K   Washington DC 20006
Ph: 202-974-5200 ▪ Fx: 202-296-7005 ▪ TF: 888-367-8741

Sidran Institute   www.sidran.org
200 E Joppa Rd Suite 207   Baltimore MD 21286
Ph: 410-825-8888 ▪ Fx: 410-337-0747 ▪ TF: 888-825-8249

SIDS Alliance, First Candle/   www.firstcandle.org
1314 Bedford Ave Suite 210   Baltimore MD 21208
Ph: 410-653-8226 ▪ Fx: 410-653-8709 ▪ TF: 800-221-7437

SIDS/Infant Death Resource Center, National   www.sidscenter.org
2070 Chain Bridge Rd Suite 450   Vienna VA 22182
Ph: 703-821-8955 ▪ Fx: 703-821-2098 ▪ TF: 866-866-7437

SIDS & Infant Mortality Programs, Association of   www.asip1.org
Stony Brook Univ School of Social Welfare   Stony Brook NY 11794
Ph: 631-444-3690 ▪ Fx: 631-444-6475

SIDS Institute, American   www.sids.org
2480 Windy Hill Rd Suite 380   Marietta GA 30067
Ph: 770-612-1030 ▪ Fx: 770-612-8277 ▪ TF: 800-232-7437

SIDS.org, Stop   www.stopsids.org
1673 Rt 9 Suite 2   Clifton Park NY 12065
Ph: 888-521-9499

Sierra Club   www.sierraclub.org
85 2nd St 2nd Fl   San Francisco CA 94105
Ph: 415-977-5500 ▪ Fx: 415-977-5799

Sierra Club of Canada   www.sierraclub.ca
1 Nicholas St Suite 412   Ottawa ON K1N7B7
Ph: 613-241-4611 ▪ Fx: 613-241-2292

(Sierra Club) Earthjustice   www.earthjustice.org
426 17th St 6th Fl   Oakland CA 94612
Ph: 510-550-6700 ▪ Fx: 510-550-6740

Sierra Club Foundation   www.sierraclub.org/foundation
85 2nd St Suite 750   San Francisco CA 94105
Ph: 415-995-1780 ▪ Fx: 415-995-1791 ▪ TF: 800-216-2110

Sierra Club Political Committee
85 2nd St 2nd Fl   San Francisco CA 94105
Ph: 415-977-5500 ▪ Fx: 415-977-5797

Sierra Legal Defense Fund   www.sierralegal.org
131 Water St Suite 214   Vancouver BC V6B4M3
Ph: 604-685-5618 ▪ Fx: 604-685-7813 ▪ TF: 800-926-7744

Sierra Student Coalition   www.ssc.org
408 C St NE   Washington DC 20002
Ph: 202-548-4593 ▪ Fx: 202-675-6277 ▪ TF: 888-564-6772

Sighthound Field Association, American   www.asfa.org

Sightseeing International, American   www.americansightseeing.org
490 Post St Suite 1701   San Francisco CA 94102
Ph: 415-332-7916 ▪ Fx: 415-332-7980

Sigma Alpha Epsilon Fraternity   www.saefraternity.org
1856 Sheridan Rd   Evanston IL 60201
Ph: 847-475-1856 ▪ Fx: 847-475-2250 ▪ TF: 800-233-1856

Sigma Alpha Iota   www.sai-national.org
34 Wall St Suite 515   Asheville NC 28801
Ph: 828-251-0606 ▪ Fx: 828-251-0644

Sigma Alpha Mu Fraternity   www.sam.org
9245 N Meridian St Suite 105   Indianapolis IN 46260
Ph: 317-846-0600 ▪ Fx: 317-846-9462 ▪ TF: 888-369-9361

Sigma Chi Fraternity   www.sigmachi.org
1714 Hinman Ave PO Box 469   Evanston IL 60201
Ph: 847-869-3655 ▪ Fx: 847-869-4906

Sigma Delta Psi
The Citadel 171 Moultrie DEAS Hall   Charleston SC 29409
Ph: 843-953-7778 ▪ Fx: 843-953-6978

Sigma Delta Tau   www.sigmadeltatau.com
111 Congressional Blvd Suite 110   Carmel IN 46032
Ph: 317-846-7747 ▪ Fx: 317-575-5562

Sigma Gamma Epsilon   www.earth.uni.edu/SGE
Univ of Oklahoma 100 E Boyd Rm N-131   Norman OK 73019
Ph: 405-325-3031 ▪ Fx: 405-325-7069

Sigma Gamma Rho Sorority Inc   www.sgrho1922.org
8800 S Stony Island   Chicago IL 60617
Ph: 773-873-9000 ▪ Fx: 773-731-9642

Sigma Gamma Tau   www.engr.twsu.edu/ae/sgt/sgthome.html
Wichita State Univ Dept of Aerospace Engineering   Wichita KS 67260
Ph: 316-978-6327 ▪ Fx: 316-978-3307

Sigma Iota Epsilon   sienational.colostate.edu
Colorado State Univ 312 Rockwell Hall   Fort Collins CO 80523
Ph: 970-491-6265 ▪ Fx: 970-491-7200

Sigma Kappa Sorority   www.sigmakappa.org
8733 Founders Rd   Indianapolis IN 46268
Ph: 317-872-3275 ▪ Fx: 317-872-0716

Sigma Nu Fraternity Inc   www.sigmanu.org
9 Lewis St PO Box 1869   Lexington VA 24450
Ph: 540-463-1869 ▪ Fx: 540-463-1669

Sigma Phi Alpha   www.sigmaphialpha.org
Univ of Texas Health Science Ctr Dental Branch PO Box 20068   Houston TX 77225
Ph: 713-500-4085

Sigma Phi Epsilon Fraternity   www.sigep.org
310 S Boulevard   Richmond VA 23220
Ph: 804-353-1901 ▪ Fx: 804-359-8160 ▪ TF: 800-313-1901

Sigma Pi Fraternity   www.sigmapi.org
PO Box 1897   Brentwood TN 37024
Ph: 888-744-6274 ▪ Fx: 615-373-8949

Sigma Sigma Sigma Sorority   www.sigmasigmasigma.org
225 N Muhlenberg St   Woodstock VA 22664
Ph: 540-459-4212 ▪ Fx: 540-459-2361

Sigma Tau Delta   www.english.org
Northern Illinois Univ Dept of English   DeKalb IL 60115
Ph: 815-753-1612

Sigma Tau Gamma Fraternity Inc   www.sigmataugamma.org
PO Box 54   Warrensburg MO 64093
Ph: 660-747-2222 ▪ Fx: 660-747-9599

Sigma Theta Tau International   www.nursingsociety.org
550 W North St   Indianapolis IN 46202
Ph: 317-634-8171 ▪ Fx: 317-634-8188 ▪ TF: 888-634-7575

Sigma Xi Scientific Research Society   www.sigmaxi.org
PO Box 13975   Research Triangle Park NC 27709
Ph: 919-549-4691 ▪ Fx: 919-549-0090 ▪ TF: 800-243-6534

Sigma Zeta   www.sigmazeta.org
Milliken Univ 1184 W Main   Decatur IL 62522
Ph: 217-424-6233 ▪ Fx: 217-362-6408

Sign Associates, World
8774 Yates Dr Suite 120   Westminster CO 80031
Ph: 303-427-7252 ▪ Fx: 303-427-7090

Sign Association, International   www.signs.org
707 N Saint Asaph St   Alexandria VA 22314
Ph: 703-836-4012 ▪ Fx: 703-836-8353

Sign Supply Distributors, National Association of   www.nassd.org
5024 Campbell Blvd Suite R   Baltimore MD 21236
Ph: 410-931-8100 ▪ Fx: 410-931-8111

Signal Association, International Municipal   www.imsasafety.org
165 E Union St PO Box 539   Newark NY 14513
Ph: 315-331-2182 ▪ Fx: 315-331-8205 ▪ TF: 800-723-4672

Signal Manufacturers Association, Pyrotechnic
28320 St Michael Rd   Easton MD 21601
Ph: 410-822-0318 ▪ Fx: 410-822-7759

Signal Processing Society, IEEE   www.ieee.org/organizations/society/sp
IEEE Operations Ctr 445 Hoes Ln   Piscataway NJ 08854
Ph: 732-981-0060 ▪ Fx: 732-981-1721

Signalmen, Brotherhood of Railroad   www.brs.org
601 W Golf Rd Box U   Mount Prospect IL 60056
Ph: 847-439-3732 ▪ Fx: 847-439-3743

(Signing Exact English) Center for the Advancement of Deaf Children, SEE   PO Box 1181   Los Alamitos CA 90720   www.seecenter.org
Ph: 562-430-1467 ▪ Fx: 562-795-6614

Silhouette Association, International Handgun Metallic   www.ihmsa.org
PO Box 9   Anoka MN 55303
Ph: 763-323-3359 ▪ Fx: 763-422-1910

Silica & Silicates Industry Association, Synthetic Amorphous
1 PPG Pl   Pittsburgh PA 15272
Ph: 412-434-2801 ▪ Fx: 412-434-3193

Silicones Environmental Health & Safety Council of North America   www.sehsc.com
11921 Freedom Dr Suite 550   Reston VA 20190
Ph: 703-904-4322 ▪ Fx: 703-925-5955

Silky Terrier Club of America   www.silky-terrier-club.com

Silver Fanciers, United   www.unitedsilverfanciers.com

Silver Institute   www.silverinstitute.org
1200 G St NW Suite 800   Washington DC 20005
Ph: 202-835-0185 ▪ Fx: 202-835-0155

Silver Marten Rabbit Club   www.silvermarten.com
2113 Sommer St   Napa CA 94559
Ph: 707-255-2821

Silver Users Association
1730 M St NW Suite 911   Washington DC 20036
Ph: 202-785-3050 ▪ Fx: 202-659-5760 ▪ TF: 800-245-6999

Simmental Association, American   www.simmental.org
1 Simmental Way   Bozeman MT 59718
Ph: 406-587-4531 ▪ Fx: 406-587-9301

Simmental Association, American Junior   www.simmental.org/ajsainfo.html
1 Simmental Way   Bozeman MT 59715
Ph: 406-587-4531

Simon Foundation for Continence   www.simonfoundation.org
PO Box 815   Wilmette IL 60091
Ph: 847-864-3913 ▪ Fx: 847-864-9758 ▪ TF: 800-237-4666

Simon Wiesenthal Center   www.wiesenthal.com
1399 S Roxbury Dr   Los Angeles CA 90035
Ph: 310-553-9036 ▪ Fx: 310-772-7655

Simply Love Foundation   www.simplylove.net
PO Box 8888   Albuquerque NM 87198
Ph: 505-833-5025

Simulation & Gaming Association, North American   www.nasaga.org
PO Box 78636   Indianapolis IN 46278
Ph: 317-387-1424 ▪ Fx: 317-387-1921 ▪ TF: 888-432-4263

Simulation International, Society for Modeling &   www.scs.org
4838 Ronson Ct Suite L PO Box 17900   San Diego CA 92111
Ph: 858-277-3888 ▪ Fx: 858-277-3930

Singer Harry Foundation   www.singerfoundation.org
PO Box 223159   Carmel CA 93922
Ph: 831-625-4223 ▪ Fx: 831-624-7994

Singers Alliance of America, Polish   www.polishsingersalliance.org

Singers Association, North American
13550 Ann Dr   North Huntingdon PA 15642
Ph: 724-863-0984

Singers Association, Professional Women   www.womensingers.org
PO Box 884   New York NY 10024
Ph: 212-969-0590

Singing in America, Society for the Preservation & Encouragement of Barber Shop Quartet   7930 Sheridan Rd   Kenosha WI 53143   www.spebsqsa.org
Ph: 262-653-8440 ▪ Fx: 262-654-5552

Singing, National Association of Teachers of
4745 Sutton Park Ct Suite 201   Jacksonville FL 32224
Ph: 904-992-9101 ▪ Fx: 904-992-9326
www.nats.org

(Singing) Sweet Adelines International
9110 S Toledo Ave   Tulsa OK 74137
Ph: 918-622-1444 ▪ Fx: 918-665-0894 ▪ TF: 800-992-7464
www.sweetadelineintl.org

(Singing) United in Group Harmony Association
PO Box 185   Clifton NJ 07011
Ph: 973-365-0049
www.ugha.org

Single-footing Horse Association, North American
PO Box 1079   Three Forks MT 59752
Ph: 406-285-6826
www.singlefootinghorse.com

Single Mothers by Choice Inc
PO Box 1642 Gracie Square Stn   New York NY 10028
Ph: 212-988-0993
mattes.home.pipeline.com

Single Mothers, National Organization of
PO Box 68   Midland NC 28107
Ph: 704-888-5437
singlemothers.org

Single Parent Resource Center
31 E 28th St Fl 2   New York NY 10016
Ph: 212-951-7030 ▪ Fx: 212-951-7037
singleparentusa.com

Single Ply Roofing Institute
77 Rumford Ave Suite 3B   Waltham MA 02453
Ph: 781-647-7026 ▪ Fx: 781-647-7222
www.spri.org

Single Shot Rifle Association, American
PO Box 362   Delphos OH 45833
Ph: 419-692-3866 ▪ Fx: 419-695-3756
www.assra.com

Sino-American Amity Fund
86 Riverside Dr   New York NY 10024
Ph: 212-787-6969 ▪ Fx: 212-787-0260

Sino American Cooperative Organization
7471 Thunderbird Rd   Liverpool NY 13088
Ph: 315-457-7751

Sinsinawa Dominicans
585 County Rd Z   Sinsinawa WI 53824
Ph: 608-748-4411 ▪ Fx: 608-748-4491
www.sinsinawa.org

Sister Cities International
1301 Pennsylvania Ave NW Suite 850   Washington DC 20004
Ph: 202-347-8630 ▪ Fx: 202-393-6524
www.sister-cities.org

Sisterhood Agenda
1721 Chapel Hill Rd   Durham NC 27707
Ph: 919-493-8358 ▪ Fx: 919-493-2524
www.sisterhoodagenda.com

Sisters of Charity of the Incarnate Word
4503 Broadway   San Antonio TX 78209
Ph: 210-828-2224 ▪ Fx: 210-828-9741
www.ccvisanantonio.org

Sisters' Conference, National Black
101 Q St NE   Washington DC 20002
Ph: 202-529-9250 ▪ Fx: 202-529-9370
nbsc68.tripod.com

Sisters of Life
198 Hollywood Ave   Bronx NY 10465
Ph: 718-863-2264 ▪ Fx: 718-792-9645
www.sistersoflife.org

Sisters of Mercy of the Americas
8380 Colesville Rd Suite 300   Silver Spring MD 20910
Ph: 301-587-0423 ▪ Fx: 301-587-0533
www.sistersofmercy.org

Sisters Network
8787 Woodway Dr Suite 4206   Houston TX 77063
Ph: 713-781-0255 ▪ Fx: 713-780-8998
sistersnetworkinc.org

Size Esteem, Largesse Network for
PO Box 9404   New Haven CT 06534
Ph: 203-787-1624
www.largesse.net

Size & Weight Discrimination, Council on
PO Box 305   Mount Marion NY 12456
Ph: 845-679-1209 ▪ Fx: 845-679-1206
www.cswd.org

Sjogren's Syndrome Foundation Inc
8120 Woodmont Ave Suite 530   Bethesda MD 20814
Ph: 301-718-0300 ▪ Fx: 301-718-0322 ▪ TF: 800-475-6473
www.sjogrens.org

Skateboard Companies, International Association of
22431 Antonio Pkwy   Rancho Santa Margarita CA 92688
Ph: 949-589-8863 ▪ Fx: 949-589-3604
www.skateboardiasc.org

Skaters Association, Professional
3006 Allegro Park Ln SW   Rochester MN 55902
Ph: 507-281-5122 ▪ Fx: 507-281-5491
skatepsa.com

Skating Association for the Blind & Handicapped
1200 East & West Rd   West Seneca NY 14224
Ph: 716-675-7222 ▪ Fx: 716-675-7223
www.sabahinc.org

Skating Association International, Roller
6905 Corporate Dr   Indianapolis IN 46278
Ph: 317-347-2626 ▪ Fx: 317-347-2636
www.rollerskating.org

Skating Association, US Figure
20 1st St   Colorado Springs CO 80906
Ph: 719-635-5200 ▪ Fx: 719-635-9548
www.usfsa.org

Skating Institute, Ice
17120 Dallas Pkwy Suite 140   Dallas TX 75248
Ph: 972-735-8800 ▪ Fx: 972-735-8815
www.skateisi.com

Skating Teachers of America, Society of Roller
6905 Corporate Dr   Indianapolis IN 46278
Ph: 317-347-2626 ▪ Fx: 317-347-2636

Skeet Shooting Association, National
5931 Roft Rd   San Antonio TX 78257
Ph: 210-688-3371 ▪ Fx: 210-688-3014 ▪ TF: 800-877-5338
www.mynssa.com

Skeletal Society, International
www.internationalskeletalsociety.com

Skeleton Federation, US Bobsled &
421 Old Military Rd   Lake Placid NY 12946
Ph: 518-523-1842 ▪ Fx: 518-523-9491 ▪ TF: 800-262-7533
www.usbsf.com

Skeptics Society
2761 N Marengo Ave   Altadena CA 91001
Ph: 626-794-3119 ▪ Fx: 626-794-1301
www.skeptic.com

Ski Areas Association, Cross Country
259 Bolton Rd   Winchester NH 03470
Ph: 603-239-4341 ▪ Fx: 603-239-6387 ▪ TF: 877-779-2754
www.xcski.org

Ski Areas Association, National
133 S Van Gordon St Suite 300   Lakewood CO 80228
Ph: 303-987-1111 ▪ Fx: 303-986-2345
www.nsaa.org

Ski Instructors of America, Professional
133 S Van Gordon St Suite 101   Lakewood CO 80228
Ph: 303-987-9390 ▪ Fx: 303-988-3005
www.psia.org

Ski for Light Inc
1455 W Lake St   Minneapolis MN 55408
Ph: 612-827-3232 ▪ Fx: 612-779-0211
www.sfl.org

Ski Patrol System Inc, National
133 S Van Gordon St Suite 100   Lakewood CO 80228
Ph: 303-988-1111 ▪ Fx: 303-988-3005
www.nsp.org

Ski & Snowboard Association, US
PO Box 10045   Park City UT 84060
Ph: 435-649-9090 ▪ Fx: 435-649-3613
www.usskiteam.com

Ski & Snowboard Retailers Association, National
1601 Feehanville Dr Suite 300   Mount Prospect IL 60056
Ph: 847-391-9825 ▪ Fx: 847-391-9827
www.nssra.com

Skiers, American Cross Country
PO Box 604   Bend OR 97709
Ph: 541-317-0217
www.xcskiworld.com

Skiers, National Brotherhood of
1525 E 53rd St Suite 418   Chicago IL 60615
Ph: 773-955-4100
www.nbs.org

Skillman Foundation
600 Rennissance Ctr Suite 1700   Detroit MI 48243
Ph: 313-393-1185 ▪ Fx: 313-393-1187
www.skillman.org

SkillsUSA-VICA Inc
PO Box 3000   Leesburg VA 20177
Ph: 703-777-8810 ▪ Fx: 703-777-8999 ▪ TF: 800-321-8422
www.skillsusa.org

Skin Association, American
346 Park Ave S 4th Fl   New York NY 10010
Ph: 212-889-4858 ▪ Fx: 212-889-4959 ▪ TF: 800-499-7546
www.skinassn.org

Skin Cancer Foundation
245 5th Ave Suite 1403   New York NY 10016
Ph: 212-725-5176 ▪ Fx: 212-725-5751 ▪ TF: 800-754-6490
www.skincancer.org

Skirt & Undergarment Association, Greater Blouse
225 W 34th St Suite 612   New York NY 10122
Ph: 212-563-5052 ▪ Fx: 212-563-5373
www.greaterblouse.org

Skull Base Society, North American
12100 Sunset Hills Rd Suite 130   Reston VA 12100
Ph: 703-234-4149 ▪ Fx: 703-435-4390
www.nasbs.org

Skye Terrier Club of America
11567 Sutters Mill Cir   Gold River CA 95670
Ph: 916-631-8716
clubs.akc.org/skye

Slag Association, National
25 Stevens Ave Bldg A   West Lawn PA 19609
Ph: 610-670-0701 ▪ Fx: 610-670-0702
www.nationalslagassoc.org

Slate Institute, Expanded Shale Clay &
2225 E Murray Holladay Rd Suite 102   Salt Lake City UT 84117
Ph: 801-272-7070 ▪ Fx: 801-272-3377
www.escsi.org

Slavery Group Inc, American Anti-
198 Tremont St Suite 421   Boston MA 02116
Ph: 617-426-8161 ▪ Fx: 617-507-8257 ▪ TF: 800-884-0719
www.iabolish.com

**Slavic & East European Languages, American Association of
Teachers of**   PO Box 7039   Berkeley CA 94707
Ph: 510-526-6614
www.aatseel.org

Slavic Gospel Association
6151 Commonwealth Dr   Loves Park IL 61111
Ph: 815-282-8900 ▪ Fx: 815-282-8901 ▪ TF: 800-242-5350
www.sga.org

**Slavic Studies, American Association for the
Advancement of**   Harvard Univ 8 Story St 3rd Fl Box
14   Cambridge MA 02138
Ph: 617-495-0677 ▪ Fx: 617-495-0680
www.fas.harvard.edu/~aaass

Sled Dog Racing Association, International
22702 Rebel Rd   Merrifield MN 56465
Ph: 218-765-4297 ▪ Fx: 218-765-3246
www.isdra.org

Sleep Apnea Association, American
1424 K St NW Suite 302   Washington DC 20005
Ph: 202-293-3650 ▪ Fx: 202-293-3656
www.sleepapnea.org

Sleep Council, Better
501 Wythe St   Alexandria VA 22314
Ph: 703-683-8371 ▪ Fx: 703-683-4503
www.bettersleep.org

Sleep Foundation, National
1522 K St NW Suite 500   Washington DC 20005
Ph: 202-347-3471 ▪ Fx: 202-347-3472
www.sleepfoundation.org

Sleep Medicine, Academy of Dental
1 Westbrook Corporate Ctr Suite 920   Westchester IL 60154
Ph: 708-273-9335 ▪ Fx: 708-492-0943
www.dentalsleepmed.org

Sleep Medicine, American Academy of
1 Westbrook Corporate Ctr Suite 920   Westchester IL 60154
Ph: 708-492-0930 ▪ Fx: 708-492-0943
www.aasmnet.org

Sleep Products Association, International
501 Wythe St   Alexandria VA 22314
Ph: 703-683-8371 ▪ Fx: 703-683-4503
www.sleepproducts.org

Sleep Research Society
www.sleepresearchsociety.org

Sleep Societies, Associated Professional
1 Westbrook Corporate Ctr Suite 920   Westchester IL 60154
Ph: 708-492-0930 ▪ Fx: 708-492-0943
www.apss.org

(Slide Rules) Oughtred Society
2160 Middlefield Rd   Palo Alto CA 94301
Ph: 650-324-1821
www.oughtred.org

Sloan Alfred P Foundation
630 5th Ave Suite 2550   New York NY 10111
Ph: 212-649-1649 ▪ Fx: 212-757-5117
www.sloan.org

Slocum Joshua Society International
15 Codfish Hill Rd Ext   Bethel CT 06801
Ph: 203-790-6616 ▪ Fx: 203-790-6617
www.joshuaslocumsocietyintl.org

Sloop Clearwater Inc, Hudson River www.clearwater.org
112 Market St Poughkeepsie NY 12601
Ph: 845-454-7673

Slovak Catholic Federation
St John the Baptist Rectory 108 N Main St Taylor PA 18517
Ph: 570-562-1341 ▪ Fx: 570-562-2807

Slovak Catholic Sokol www.slovakcatholicsokol.org
205 Madison St PO Box 899 Passaic NJ 07055
Ph: 800-886-7656

Slovak Ladies Association, First Catholic www.fcsla.com
24950 Chagrin Blvd Beachwood OH 44122
Ph: 216-464-8015 ▪ Fx: 216-464-9260 ▪ TF: 800-464-4642

Slovak League of America
205 Madison St Passaic NJ 07055
Ph: 973-472-8993 ▪ Fx: 973-669-8483

Slovak Society of the USA, National www.nsslife.com
351 Valley Brook Rd McMurray PA 15317
Ph: 724-873-1890 ▪ Fx: 724-873-0145 ▪ TF: 800-488-1890

Slovak Union of the US & Canada, First Catholic www.fcsu.com
6611 Rockside Rd Independence OH 44131
Ph: 216-642-9406 ▪ Fx: 216-642-4310 ▪ TF: 800-533-6682

Slovene National Benefit Society www.snpj.com
247 W Allegheny Rd Imperial PA 15126
Ph: 724-695-1100 ▪ Fx: 724-695-1555 ▪ TF: 800-843-7675

Slovenian Research Center of America
29227 Eddy Rd Willoughby Hills OH 44092
Ph: 440-944-7237 ▪ Fx: 440-944-0461

Slovenian Women's Union of America www.swua.org
431 N Chicago St Joliet IL 60432
Ph: 815-727-1926

Slow Sand Association, American
PO Box 330 Ilion NY 13357
Ph: 315-895-7711 ▪ Fx: 315-895-7196

Slurry Surfacing Association, International www.slurry.org
3 Church Cir PMB 250 Annapolis MD 21401
Ph: 410-267-0023 ▪ Fx: 410-267-7546

SMA Lay Missionaries www.smafathers.org
256 N Manor Cir Takoma Park MD 20912
Ph: 301-891-2037 ▪ Fx: 301-270-6370

Small Business Association, National www.nsba.biz
1156 15th St NW Suite 1100 Washington DC 20005
Ph: 202-393-8830 ▪ Fx: 202-872-8543 ▪ TF: 800-345-6728

Small Business Council of America www.sbca.net
800 Delaware Ave 7th Fl Wilmington DE 19899
Ph: 302-691-7222 ▪ Fx: 877-404-1329

Small Business Development Centers, Association of www.asbdc-us.org
8990 Burke Lake Rd Burke VA 22015
Ph: 703-764-9850 ▪ Fx: 703-764-1234

Small Business Exporters Association www.sbea.org
1156 15th St NW Suite 1100 Washington DC 20005
Ph: 202-659-9320 ▪ Fx: 202-872-5843

Small Business, International Council for www.icsb.org
George Washington Univ School of Business & Public
    Management 2115 G St NW Suite 403 Washington DC
    20052
Ph: 202-994-0704 ▪ Fx: 202-994-4930

Small Business International Trade Educators, North American www.nasbite.org
Wright State Univ 120 Rike Hall 3640 Colonel Glenn
    Hwy Dayton OH 45435
Ph: 937-775-3524 ▪ Fx: 937-775-3545

Small Business Investment Companies, National Association of www.nasbic.org
666 11th St NW Suite 750 Washington DC 20001
Ph: 202-628-5055 ▪ Fx: 202-628-5080

Small Business Legislative Council www.sblc.org
1010 Massachusetts Ave NW Suite 400 Washington DC 20001
Ph: 202-639-8500 ▪ Fx: 202-296-5333

Small Business Survival Committee www.sbsc.org
1920 L St NW Suite 200 Washington DC 20036
Ph: 202-785-0238 ▪ Fx: 202-822-8118

Small Businesses Association, American www.asbaonline.org
206 E College St Suite 201B Grapevine TX 76051
Ph: 817-488-8770 ▪ Fx: 817-251-8578

Small Craft Association, Traditional www.tsca.net
PO Box 350 Mystic CT 06355
Ph: 860-572-0711

Small & Emerging Business, Research Institute for www.riseb.org
722 12th St NW Washington DC 20005
Ph: 202-628-8382 ▪ Fx: 202-628-8392

Small Luxury Hotels of the World www.slh.com
370 Lexington Ave Suite 1506 New York NY 10017
Ph: 212-953-2064 ▪ Fx: 212-953-0576

Small Press Center for Independent Publishing www.smallpress.org
20 W 44th St New York NY 10036
Ph: 212-764-7021 ▪ Fx: 212-354-5365

Small Publishers Artists & Writers Network www.spawn.org
323 E Matilija St Suite 110 Ojai CA 93023
Ph: 818-886-4281 ▪ Fx: 818-886-3120

Small Publishers Association of North America www.spannet.org
PO Box 1306 Buena Vista CO 81211
Ph: 719-395-4790 ▪ Fx: 719-395-8374

Smart Card Alliance www.smartcardalliance.org
191 Clarkville Rd Princeton Junction NJ 08550
Ph: 609-799-5654 ▪ Fx: 609-799-7032 ▪ TF: 800-848-7242

SMART Recovery www.smartrecovery.org
7537 Mentor Ave Suite 306 Mentor OH 44060
Ph: 440-951-5357 ▪ Fx: 440-951-5358

Smell Institute, Sense of www.senseofsmell.org
145 E 32nd St New York NY 10016
Ph: 212-725-2755 ▪ Fx: 212-779-9058

Smile, Operation www.operationsmile.org
6435 Tidewater Dr Norfolk VA 23509
Ph: 757-321-7645 ▪ Fx: 757-321-7660 ▪ TF: 888-677-6453

Smith Center for Private Enterprise Studies thesmithcenter.org
California State Univ Hayward College of Business &
    Economics Hayward CA 94542
Ph: 510-885-2640 ▪ Fx: 510-885-4222

Smith Richardson Foundation Inc www.srf.org
60 Jesup Rd Westport CT 06880
Ph: 203-222-6222 ▪ Fx: 203-222-6282

() Smith Richardson Foundation Inc www.srf.org
60 Jesup Rd Westport CT 06880
Ph: 203-222-6222 ▪ Fx: 203-222-6282

Smithsonian Archives of American Art artarchives.si.edu
750 9th St NW Suite 2200 Washington DC 20560
Ph: 202-275-2156 ▪ Fx: 202-275-1955

SMMA - Motor & Motion Association www.smma.org
PO Box P182 South Dartmouth MA 02748
Ph: 508-979-5935 ▪ Fx: 508-979-5845

Smoke Containment & Control, Alliance for Fire & www.afscc.org
25 N Broadway Tarrytown NY 10591
Ph: 914-332-0040 ▪ Fx: 914-332-1541

Smokeless Tobacco Council
1627 K St NW Suite 700 Washington DC 20006
Ph: 202-452-1252 ▪ Fx: 202-452-0118 ▪ TF: 800-272-7144

Smoking & Health, Action on www.ash.org
2013 H St NW Washington DC 20006
Ph: 202-659-4310 ▪ Fx: 202-833-3921

Snack Bakers Association, Cookie &
1128 Maple Dr NW Cleveland TN 37312
Ph: 423-472-5856 ▪ Fx: 423-478-1273

Snack Food Association www.sfa.org
1711 King St Suite 1 Alexandria VA 22314
Ph: 703-836-4500 ▪ Fx: 703-836-8262 ▪ TF: 800-628-1334

Snaffle Bit Association, National www.nsba.com
4815 S Sheridan Suite 109 Tulsa OK 74145
Ph: 918-270-1469 ▪ Fx: 918-270-1471

Snow & Ice Management Association Inc www.sima.org
1903 W 8th St PMB 150 Erie PA 16505
Ph: 814-835-3577 ▪ Fx: 814-835-0527

Snow Leopard Trust, International www.snowleopard.org
4649 Sunnyside Ave N Suite 325 Seattle WA 98103
Ph: 206-632-2421 ▪ Fx: 206-632-3967

Snowboard Association, US Ski & www.usskiteam.com
PO Box 10045 Park City UT 84060
Ph: 435-649-9090 ▪ Fx: 435-649-3613

Snowboard Instructors, American Association of www.aasi.org
133 S Van Gordon St Suite 101 Lakewood CO 80228
Ph: 303-987-9390 ▪ Fx: 800-222-4754

Snowboard Retailers Association, National Ski & www.nssra.com
1601 Feehanville Dr Suite 300 Mount Prospect IL 60056
Ph: 847-391-9825 ▪ Fx: 847-391-9827

Snowmobile Associations, American Council of www.snowmobileacsa.org
271 Woodland Pass Suite 216 East Lansing MI 48823
Ph: 517-351-4362 ▪ Fx: 517-351-1363

Snowmobile Manufacturers Association, International www.snowmobile.org
1640 Haslett Rd Suite 170 Haslett MI 48840
Ph: 517-339-7788 ▪ Fx: 517-339-7798

Snowshoe Association, US www.snowshoeracing.com
678 County Rt 25 Corinth NY 12822
Ph: 518-654-7648 ▪ Fx: 518-643-8806

SnowSports Industries America www.thesnowtrade.org/sia
8377-B Greensboro Dr McLean VA 22102
Ph: 703-556-9020 ▪ Fx: 703-821-8276

Snowsports Journalists Association, North American www.nasja.org
11738 SE Madison St Portland OR 97216
Ph: 503-255-3771

Snuff Bottle Society Inc, International Chinese www.snuffbottle.org
2601 N Charles St Baltimore MD 21218
Ph: 410-467-9400 ▪ Fx: 410-243-3451

SOA Watch www.soaw.org
PO Box 4566 Washington DC 20017
Ph: 202-234-3440 ▪ Fx: 202-636-4505

Soap & Detergent Association www.cleaning101.com
1500 K St NW Suite 300 Washington DC 20005
Ph: 202-347-2900 ▪ Fx: 202-347-4110

Soaring Society of America Inc www.ssa.org
PO Box 2100 Hobbs NM 88241
Ph: 505-392-1177 ▪ Fx: 505-392-8154

Sobriety Inc, Women for www.womenforsobriety.org
PO Box 618 Quakertown PA 18951
Ph: 215-536-8026 ▪ Fx: 215-538-9026

SOCAP International www.socap.org
675 N Washington St Suite 200 Alexandria VA 22314
Ph: 703-519-3700 ▪ Fx: 703-549-4886

(Soccer) America Scores www.americascores.org
1327 14th St NW Suite 100 Washington DC 20005
Ph: 202-234-4112 ▪ Fx: 202-234-4119

Soccer Association, US Indoor www.usindoor.com

Soccer Association, US Youth usysa.org
899 Presidential Dr Suite 117 Richardson TX 75081
Ph: 972-235-4499 ▪ Fx: 972-235-4480 ▪ TF: 800-476-2237

Soccer Association for Youth www.saysoccer.org
1 N Commerce Park Dr Suite 320 Cincinnati OH 45215
Ph: 513-769-3800 ▪ Fx: 513-769-0500 ▪ TF: 800-233-7291

Soccer Coaches Association of America, National www.nscaa.com
6700 Squibb Rd Suite 215 Mission KS 66202
Ph: 913-362-1747 ▪ Fx: 913-362-3439 ▪ TF: 800-458-0678

Soccer Coaches Association, Indoor www.isca.net
9606 Aero Dr   San Diego CA 92123
Ph: 858-836-4422 ▪ Fx: 858-836-4421

Soccer Federation, US www.ussoccer.com
1801-1811 S Prairie Ave   Chicago IL 60616
Ph: 312-808-1300 ▪ Fx: 312-808-1301 ▪ TF: 800-759-9636

Soccer League, Major Indoor www.misl.net
1175 Post Rd E   Westport CT 06880
Ph: 203-222-4900 ▪ Fx: 203-221-7300 ▪ TF: 866-647-5638

Soccer League, National Professional www.allsports.com/npsl
115 Dewalt Ave NW 5th Fl   Canton OH 44702
Ph: 330-455-4625 ▪ Fx: 330-455-3885

Soccer Officials Association, National Intercollegiate www.nisoa.com
541 Woodview Dr   Longwood FL 32779
Ph: 407-862-3305 ▪ Fx: 407-862-8545

Soccer Organization, American Youth soccer.org
12501 S Isis Ave   Hawthorne CA 90250
Ph: 310-643-6455 ▪ Fx: 310-643-5310 ▪ TF: 800-872-2976

Soccer Reporters Association, Professional
6700 Squibb Rd Suite 215   Mission KS 66202
Ph: 913-362-1747 ▪ Fx: 913-362-3439

Social Action, Evangelicals for www.esa-online.org
10 E Lancaster Ave   Wynnewood PA 19096
Ph: 610-645-9390 ▪ Fx: 610-649-8090 ▪ TF: 800-650-6600

Social Action, Methodist Federation for www.mfsaweb.org
212 E Capitol St NE   Washington DC 20003
Ph: 202-546-8806 ▪ Fx: 202-546-6811

Social Action & Renewal in Eurasia, Initiative for www.isar.org
1601 Connecticut Ave NW Suite 301   Washington DC 20009
Ph: 202-387-3034 ▪ Fx: 202-387-3291

Social Administration, Association for Community Organization & www.acosa.org
20560 Bensley Ave   Lynwood IL 60411
Ph: 708-757-4187 ▪ Fx: 708-757-4234

Social Biology, Society for the Study of www-rcf.usc.edu/~crimmin/sssb
USC Andrus Gerontology Ctr 3715 McClintock Ave   Los
Angeles CA 90089
Ph: 213-740-5156 ▪ Fx: 213-740-0792

Social Change Inc, Martin Luther King Jr Center for www.thekingcenter.com
Nonviolent   449 Auburn Ave NE   Atlanta GA 30312
Ph: 404-524-1956 ▪ Fx: 404-526-8969

(Social Change) North Star Fund Inc www.northstarfund.org
305 7th Ave 5th Fl   New York NY 10001
Ph: 212-620-9110 ▪ Fx: 212-620-8178

(Social Change) Partido Nacional La Raza Unida www.pnlru.org
11663 Herrick Ave PO Box 13   San Fernando CA 91340
Ph: 818-365-6534

(Social Change) Rainbow/PUSH Coalition Inc www.rainbowpush.org
930 E 50th St   Chicago IL 60615
Ph: 773-373-3366 ▪ Fx: 773-373-3571

(Social Change) Resist Inc www.resistinc.org
259 Elm St   Somerville MA 02144
Ph: 617-623-5110

Social Democrats USA www.socialdemocrats.org
PO Box 18865   Washington DC 20036
Ph: 202-467-0028 ▪ Fx: 202-457-0029

(Social Entrepreneurship) Ashoka USA/Canada www.ashoka.org/us-canada
1700 N Moore St Suite 2000   Arlington VA 22209
Ph: 703-527-8300 ▪ Fx: 703-527-8383

Social Gerontology, Center for www.tcsg.org
2307 Shelby Ave   Ann Arbor MI 48103
Ph: 734-665-1126 ▪ Fx: 734-665-2071

Social Health Association, American www.ashastd.org
PO Box 13827   Research Triangle Park NC 27709
Ph: 919-361-8400 ▪ Fx: 919-361-8425 ▪ TF: 800-277-8922

Social Ideas, Foundation for the Study of Independent
310 Riverside Dr Suite 1201   New York NY 10025
Ph: 212-316-3120 ▪ Fx: 212-316-3145

Social Implications of Technology, IEEE radburn.rutgers.edu/andrews/projects/ssit
Society on   IEEE Operations Ctr 445 Hoes Ln   Piscataway NJ
08854
Ph: 732-981-0060 ▪ Fx: 732-981-1721

Social Issues, Society for the Psychological Study of www.spssi.org
208 'I' St NE   Washington DC 20002
Ph: 202-675-6956 ▪ Fx: 202-675-6902

(Social Justice) Advocacy Institute www.advocacy.org
1629 K St NW Suite 200   Washington DC 20006
Ph: 202-777-7575 ▪ Fx: 202-777-7577

Social Justice Inc, Black Veterans for www.bvsj.org
665 Willoughby Ave   Brooklyn NY 11221
Ph: 718-852-6004 ▪ Fx: 718-852-4805

Social Justice, Counselors For www.counselorsforsocialjustice.org
c/o American Counseling Assn 5999 Stevenson Ave   Alexandria
VA 22304
Ph: 703-823-9800 ▪ Fx: 703-823-0252 ▪ TF: 800-347-6647

(Social Justice) DataCenter www.datacenter.org
1904 Franklin St Suite 900   Oakland CA 94612
Ph: 510-835-4692 ▪ Fx: 510-835-3017 ▪ TF: 800-735-3741

Social & Legal Research, Center for www.privacyexchange.org
2 University Plaza Suite 414   Hackensack NJ 07601
Ph: 201-996-1154 ▪ Fx: 201-996-1883

Social Philosophy, International Association for Philosophy www.cirfid.unibo.it/ivr
of Law &   Univ of Hawaii at Manoa Dept of Philosophy 2530
Dole St   Honolulu HI 96822
Ph: 808-956-8954 ▪ Fx: 808-956-9228

Social Philosophy, North American Society for www.pitt.edu/~nassp/nassp.html
c/o Philosophy Documentation Ctr PO Box 7147   Charlottesville
VA 22906
Ph: 434-220-3300 ▪ Fx: 434-220-3301 ▪ TF: 800-444-2419

Social Policy, Center for Law & www.clasp.org
1015 15th St NW Suite 400   Washington DC 20005
Ph: 202-906-8000 ▪ Fx: 202-842-2885

Social Policy, Center for the Study of www.cssp.org
1575 'I' St NW Suite 500   Washington DC 20005
Ph: 202-371-1565 ▪ Fx: 202-371-1472

Social Policy, Malcolm Wiener Center for www.ksg.harvard.edu/socpol
John F Kennedy School of Government Harvard University 79
John F Kennedy St   Cambridge MA 02138
Ph: 617-495-1461 ▪ Fx: 617-496-9053

Social Problems, Society for the Study of www.sssp1.org
Univ of Tennessee 901 McClung Tower   Knoxville TN 37996
Ph: 865-974-3620 ▪ Fx: 865-689-1534

Social Research, Inter-University Consortium for Political & www.icpsr.umich.edu
Univ of Michigan Institute for Social Research PO Box
1248   Ann Arbor MI 48106
Ph: 734-647-5000 ▪ Fx: 734-647-8200

Social Responsibility, Business for www.bsr.org
111 Sutter St 12th Fl   San Francisco CA 94104
Ph: 415-984-3200 ▪ Fx: 415-984-3201

Social Responsibility, Computer Professionals for www.cpsr.org
PO Box 717   Palo Alto CA 94302
Ph: 650-322-3778 ▪ Fx: 650-322-4748

Social Responsibility, Educators for www.esrnational.org
23 Garden St   Cambridge MA 02138
Ph: 617-492-1764 ▪ Fx: 617-864-5164 ▪ TF: 800-370-2515

Social Responsibility, Physicians for www.psr.org
1875 Connecticut Ave NW Suite 1012   Washington DC 20009
Ph: 202-667-4260 ▪ Fx: 202-667-4201

Social Rights, Center for Economic & www.cesr.org
162 Montague St 2nd Fl   Brooklyn NY 11201
Ph: 718-237-9145 ▪ Fx: 718-237-9147

Social Science, American Academy of Political & www.aapss.org
3814 Walnut St   Philadelphia PA 19104
Ph: 215-746-6500 ▪ Fx: 215-898-1202

Social Science Associations, Allied www.vanderbilt.edu/AEA
2014 Broadway Suite 305   Nashville TN 37203
Ph: 615-322-3509 ▪ Fx: 615-343-2986

Social Science Associations, Consortium of www.cossa.org
1522 K St NW Suite 836   Washington DC 20005
Ph: 202-842-3525 ▪ Fx: 202-842-2788

Social Science History Association www.ssha.org
c/o Duke University Press Box 90660   Durham NC 27708
Ph: 919-687-3602

Social Science Research Council www.ssrc.org
810 7th Ave   New York NY 10019
Ph: 212-377-2700 ▪ Fx: 212-377-2727

Social Science Research Institute www.ssri.niu.edu
Northern Illinois University 148 N 3rd St   DeKalb IL 60115
Ph: 815-753-1901 ▪ Fx: 815-753-2305

Social Sciences, Cheiron: International Society for www.psych.yorku.ca/orgs/cheiron
the History of Behavioral &

(Social Sciences) Russell Sage Foundation www.russellsage.org
112 E 64th St   New York NY 10021
Ph: 212-750-6000 ▪ Fx: 212-371-4761

Social Sciences Services & Resources
PO Box 153   Wasco IL 60183
Ph: 630-897-5345 ▪ Fx: 630-896-4654

Social Scientists, Association of Muslim www.amss.net
PO Box 669   Herndon VA 20172
Ph: 703-471-1133 ▪ Fx: 703-471-3922

Social Security Claimants' Representatives, National www.nosscr.org
Organization of   6 Prospect St   Midland Park NJ 07432
Ph: 201-444-1415 ▪ Fx: 201-444-1823 ▪ TF: 800-431-2804

Social Security Management Associations, National Council of www.ncssma.org/
22 Sussex St   Hackensack NJ 07601
Ph: 201-489-3515 ▪ Fx: 201-487-2254

Social Security & Medicare, National Committee to Preserve www.ncpssm.org
10 G St NE Suite 600   Washington DC 20002
Ph: 202-216-0420 ▪ Fx: 202-216-0451 ▪ TF: 800-966-1935

Social Service USA Branch, International www.iss-usa.org
700 Light St   Baltimore MD 21230
Ph: 410-230-2734 ▪ Fx: 410-230-2741

Social Studies Education, Center for
901 Old Hickory Rd   Pittsburgh PA 15243
Ph: 412-341-1967 ▪ Fx: 412-341-6533

Social Studies, National Council for the www.ncss.org
8555 16th St Suite 500   Silver Spring MD 20910
Ph: 301-588-1800 ▪ Fx: 301-588-2049 ▪ TF: 800-296-7840

Social Studies of Science, Society for www.lsu.edu/ssss
Louisiana State Univ Dept of Sociology   Baton Rouge LA 70803
Ph: 225-578-5311 ▪ Fx: 225-578-5102

Social Work, Association of Oncology www.aosw.org
1211 Locust St   Philadelphia PA 19107
Ph: 215-599-6093 ▪ Fx: 215-545-8107

Social Work Boards, Association of www.aswb.org
400 South Ridge Pkwy Suite B   Culpeper VA 22701
Ph: 540-829-6880 ▪ Fx: 540-829-0142 ▪ TF: 800-225-6880

Social Work Education, Council on www.cswe.org
1725 Duke St Suite 500   Alexandria VA 22314
Ph: 703-683-8080 ▪ Fx: 703-683-8099

Social Work Federation, Clinical www.cswf.org
PO Box 3740   Arlington VA 22203
Ph: 703-522-3866 ▪ Fx: 703-522-9441 ▪ TF: 800-270-9739

Social Work Leadership in Health Care, Society for www.sswlhc.org
1211 Locust St   Philadelphia PA 19107
Ph: 215-599-6134 ▪ Fx: 215-545-8107 ▪ TF: 866-237-9542

Social Work Managers, National Network for www.socialworkmanager.org
Jane Adams College of Social Work MC 309 1040 W Harrison
St 4th Fl   Chicago IL 60607
Ph: 312-413-2302 ▪ Fx: 312-996-2770

Social Work, North American Association of Christians in www.nacsw.org
PO Box 121   Botsford CT 06404
Ph: 203-270-8780 ▪ TF: 888-426-4712

Social Workers, American Association of Spinal Cord www.aascipsw.org
Injury Psychologists &   75-20 Astoria Blvd   Jackson Heights
NY 11370
Ph: 718-803-3782 ▪ Fx: 718-803-0414

Social Workers, National Association of Black www.nabsw.org
1220 11th St NW   Washington DC 20001
Ph: 202-589-1850 ▪ Fx: 202-589-1853

Social Workers Inc, National Association of Puerto www.naprhsw.com
Rican/Hispanic   PO Box 651   Brentwood NY 11717
Ph: 631-864-1536

Socialist History, Center for csh.gn.apc.org/
PO Box 626   Alameda CA 94501
Ph: 510-601-6460

Socialist Labor Party of America www.slp.org
PO Box 218   Mountain View CA 94042
Ph: 408-280-7266 ▪ Fx: 408-280-6964

Socialist Party of the US, World www.worldsocialism.org
PO Box 440247   Somerville MA 02144
Ph: 617-628-9096 ▪ Fx: 617-628-5239

Socialist Party USA sp-usa.org
339 Lafayette St Suite 303   New York NY 10012
Ph: 212-982-4586 ▪ Fx: 212-982-4586

Societas Liturgica
800 S 9th St   Louisville KY 40203
Ph: 502-569-5759 ▪ Fx: 502-582-3763

Societe de Chimie Industrielle American Section www.societe.org
PO Box 873 Grand Central Stn   New York NY 10163
Ph: 212-725-9539

Societe Culinaire Philanthropique www.societeculinaire.com
305 E 47th St Suite 11B   New York NY 10017
Ph: 212-308-0628 ▪ Fx: 212-308-0588

Society for Academic Emergency Medicine www.saem.org
901 N Washington Ave   Lansing MI 48906
Ph: 517-485-5484 ▪ Fx: 517-485-0801

Society of Accredited Marine Surveyors Inc www.marinesurvey.org
4605 Cardina Blvd   Jacksonville FL 32210
Ph: 904-384-1494 ▪ Fx: 904-388-3958

Society of Actuaries www.soa.org
475 N Martingale Rd Suite 800   Schaumburg IL 60173
Ph: 847-706-3500 ▪ Fx: 847-706-3599

Society for Adolescent Medicine www.adolescenthealth.org
1916 NW Copper Oaks Cir   Blue Springs MO 64015
Ph: 816-224-8010 ▪ Fx: 816-224-8009

Society for the Advancement of American Philosophy www.american-philosophy.org
Southern Illinois Univ Dept of Philosophy MC 4505   Carbondale
IL 62901
Ph: 618-536-6641

Society for the Advancement of Behavior Analysis www.abainternational.org/saba
1219 S Park St   Kalamazoo MI 49001
Ph: 269-492-9310 ▪ Fx: 269-492-9316

Society for Advancement of Chicanos & Native Americans www.sacnas.org
in Science   PO Box 8526   Santa Cruz CA 95061
Ph: 831-459-0170 ▪ Fx: 831-459-0194

Society for the Advancement of Economic Theory
Univ of Illinois 330 Wohlerr Hall 1206 S 6th St   Champaign IL
61802
Ph: 217-333-0120 ▪ Fx: 217-244-6678

Society for the Advancement of Excellence in Education www.excellenceineducation.ca
1889 Springfield Rd Suite 225   Kelowna BC V1Y5V5
Ph: 250-717-1163 ▪ Fx: 250-717-1134

Society for the Advancement of Judaism www.thesaj.org
15 W 86th St   New York NY 10024
Ph: 212-724-7000

Society for Advancement of Management www.cob.tamucc.edu/sam
Texas A&M Univ Corpus Christi College of Business 6300 Ocean
Dr FC111   Corpus Christi TX 78412
Ph: 361-825-6045 ▪ Fx: 361-825-2725 ▪ TF: 888-827-6077

Society for the Advancement of Material & Process Engineering org.et.byu.edu/sampe
PO Box 2459   Covina CA 91722
Ph: 626-331-0616 ▪ Fx: 626-332-8929 ▪ TF: 800-562-7360

Society for the Advancement of Socio-Economics www.sase.org
PO Box 39008   Baltimore MD 21212
Ph: 410-435-6617 ▪ Fx: 410-377-7965

Society of African Missions www.smafathers.org
23 Bliss Ave   Tenafly NJ 07670
Ph: 201-567-0450

Society of Allied Weight Engineers www.sawe.org
204 Hubbard St   Glastonbury CT 06033
Ph: 860-633-0850 ▪ Fx: 860-633-8971

Society for American Archaeology www.saa.org
900 2nd St NE Suite 12   Washington DC 20002
Ph: 202-789-8200 ▪ Fx: 202-789-0284

Society of American Archivists www.archivists.org
527 S Wells St 5th Fl   Chicago IL 60607
Ph: 312-922-0140 ▪ Fx: 312-347-1452

Society for American Baseball Research www.sabr.org
812 Huron Rd E Suite 719   Cleveland OH 44115
Ph: 216-575-0500 ▪ Fx: 216-575-0502

Society of American Business Editors & Writers Inc www.sabew.org
Missouri School of Journalism 134A Neff Annex   Columbia MO
65211
Ph: 573-882-7862 ▪ Fx: 573-884-1372

Society of American Fight Directors www.safd.org
350 W 51st St Suite 3A   New York NY 10019
Ph: 212-315-3956 ▪ TF: 800-659-6579

Society of American Florists www.safnow.org
1601 Duke St   Alexandria VA 22314
Ph: 703-836-8700 ▪ Fx: 703-836-8705 ▪ TF: 800-336-4743

Society of American Florists PAC
1601 Duke St   Alexandria VA 22314
Ph: 703-836-8700 ▪ Fx: 703-836-8705 ▪ TF: 800-336-4743

Society of American Foresters www.safnet.org
5400 Grosvenor Ln   Bethesda MD 20814
Ph: 301-897-8720 ▪ Fx: 301-897-3690

Society of American Gastrointestinal Endoscopic Surgeons www.sages.org
11300 W Olympic Blvd Suite 600   Los Angeles CA 90064
Ph: 310-437-0544 ▪ Fx: 310-437-0585

Society of American Graphic Artists www.clt.astate.edu/elind/sagamain.htm
32 Union Sq Rm 214   New York NY 10003
Ph: 212-260-5706

Society of American Historians www.historians.org/affiliates
Columbia Univ 603 Fayerweather Hall MC 2538   New York NY
10027
Ph: 212-854-5943 ▪ Fx: 212-932-0602

Society of American Law Teachers www.saltlaw.org

Society of American Magicians www.magicsam.com
PO Box 510260   Saint Louis MO 63151
Ph: 314-846-5659

Society of American Military Engineers www.same.org
607 Prince St   Alexandria VA 22314
Ph: 703-549-3800 ▪ Fx: 703-684-0231 ▪ TF: 800-336-3097

Society for American Music www.american-music.org
Univ of Pittsburgh Stephen Foster Memorial 405 Bellefield
Hall   Pittsburgh PA 15260
Ph: 412-624-3031 ▪ Fx: 412-624-7447

Society of American Registered Architects www.sara-national.org

Society of American Royalty
PO Box 190313   Dallas TX 75219
Ph: 972-224-6881

Society for Analytical Feminism www.ukans.edu/~acudd/safhomepage.htm
Univ of Kentucky Dept of Philosophy Suite 1415   Lexington KY
40506
Ph: 859-257-1861

Society for Ancient Greek Philosophy sagp.binghamton.edu
Binghamton Univ Dept of Philosophy   Binghamton NY 13902
Ph: 607-777-2886 ▪ Fx: 607-777-2734

Society of Animal Artists Inc www.societyofanimalartists.com
47 5th Ave   New York NY 10003
Ph: 212-741-2880 ▪ Fx: 212-471-2262

Society for Animal Protective Legislation www.saplonline.org
PO Box 3719   Washington DC 20027
Ph: 703-836-4300 ▪ Fx: 703-836-0400

Society for Anthropology in Community Colleges ccanthro.bizland.com
c/o American Anthropological Assn 2200 Wilson Blvd Suite
600   Arlington VA 22201
Ph: 703-528-1902 ▪ Fx: 703-528-3545

Society for the Anthropology of Consciousness www.sacaaa.org
c/o American Anthropological Assn 2200 Wilson Blvd Suite
600   Arlington VA 22201
Ph: 703-528-1902 ▪ Fx: 703-528-3546

Society for the Anthropology of Europe www.h-net.org/~sae/sae
c/o American Anthropological Assn 2200 Wilson Blvd Suite
600   Arlington VA 22201
Ph: 703-528-1902 ▪ Fx: 703-528-3546

Society for the Anthropology of North faculty.kutztown.edu/ehrensal/sana2.html
America   c/o American Anthropological Assn 2200 Wilson Blvd
Suite 600   Arlington VA 22201
Ph: 703-528-1902 ▪ Fx: 703-528-3546

Society for the Anthropology of Religion www.uwgb.edu/sar
c/o American Anthropological Assn 2200 Wilson Blvd Suite
600   Arlington VA 22201
Ph: 703-528-1902 ▪ Fx: 703-528-3546

Society for the Anthropology of Work www.aaanet.org/saw
c/o American Anthropological Assn 2200 Wilson Blvd Suite
600   Arlington VA 22201
Ph: 703-528-1902 ▪ Fx: 703-528-3546

Society of Antique Modelers www.antiquemodeler.org
203 N Brockfield Dr   Sun City Center FL 33573
Ph: 813-634-7749

Society for Applied Anthropology www.sfaa.net
PO Box 2436   Oklahoma City OK 73101
Ph: 405-843-5113 ▪ Fx: 405-843-8553

Society for Applied Learning Technology www.salt.org
50 Culpepper St   Warrenton VA 20186
Ph: 540-347-0055 ▪ Fx: 540-349-3169

Society for Applied Sociology www.appliedsoc.org
Bowling Green State Univ Dept of Sociology   Bowling Green
OH 43403
Ph: 419-372-2217

Society for Applied Spectroscopy www.s-a-s.org
201B Broadway St   Frederick MD 21701
Ph: 301-694-8122 ▪ Fx: 301-694-6860

Society of Architectural Historians www.sah.org
1365 N Astor St   Chicago IL 60610
Ph: 312-573-1365 ▪ Fx: 312-573-1141

Society of Armenian Studies Inc armenianstudies.csufresno.edu/sas
California State Univ - Fresno 5245 N Backer Ave PB 4   Fresno
CA 93740
Ph: 559-278-4930 ▪ Fx: 559-278-2129

Society of Army Physician Assistants www.sapa.org
6762 Candlewood Dr   Fort Myers FL 33919
Ph: 941-482-2162

Society for the Arts Religion & Contemporary Culture www.sarcc.org
15811 Kutztown Rd Box 15   Maxatawny PA 19538
Ph: 610-683-7581

Society for Asian Music Inc www.skidmore.edu/academics/asianmusic
Cornell Univ Dept of Music Lincoln Hall   Ithaca NY 14853
Ph: 607-255-5049 ▪ Fx: 607-254-2877

Society for Assisted Reproductive Technology   www.sart.org
1209 Montgomery Hwy   Birmingham AL 35216
Ph: 205-978-5000 ▪ Fx: 205-978-5015

Society of Atherosclerosis Imaging   www.sai.org
13140 Coit Rd Suite 320 LB 120   Dallas TX 75240
Ph: 972-233-9107 ▪ Fx: 972-490-4219

Society of Automotive Analysts   www.cybersaa.org
3300 Washtenaw Ave Suite 220   Ann Arbor MI 48104
Ph: 734-677-3518 ▪ Fx: 734-677-2407

Society of Automotive Engineers Inc   www.sae.org
400 Commonwealth Dr   Warrendale PA 15096
Ph: 724-776-4841 ▪ Fx: 724-776-5760 ▪ TF: 877-606-7323

Society of Automotive Historians   www.autohistory.org
1102 Long Cove Rd   Gales Ferry CT 06335
Ph: 860-464-6466 ▪ Fx: 860-464-2614

Society of Basque Studies in America   www.basque.ws
19 Colonial Gardens   Brooklyn NY 11209
Ph: 718-745-1141 ▪ Fx: 718-745-2503

Society of Behavioral Medicine   www.sbm.org
7600 Terrace Ave Suite 203   Middleton WI 53562
Ph: 608-827-7267 ▪ Fx: 608-831-5485

Society of Biblical Literature   www.sbl-site.org
825 Houston Mill Rd Suite 350   Atlanta GA 30329
Ph: 404-727-3100 ▪ Fx: 404-727-3101

Society of Biological Psychiatry   www.sobp.org
4500 San Pablo Rd Mayo Clinic   Jacksonville FL 32224
Ph: 904-953-2842 ▪ Fx: 904-953-7117

Society for Biomaterials   www.biomaterials.org
17000 Commerce Pkwy Suite C   Mount Laurel NJ 08054
Ph: 856-439-0826 ▪ Fx: 856-439-0525

Society for Biomolecular Screening   www.sbsonline.org
36 Tamarack Ave Suite 348   Danbury CT 06811
Ph: 203-743-1336 ▪ Fx: 203-748-7557

Society, Black Women in Church &   www.itc.edu/WSP/WSPBWCS.htm
700 ML King Jr Dr   Atlanta GA 30314
Ph: 404-527-5713 ▪ Fx: 404-527-5715

Society of Broadcast Engineers   www.sbe.org
9247 N Meridian St Suite 305   Indianapolis IN 46260
Ph: 317-846-9000 ▪ Fx: 317-846-9120

Society for Business Ethics   www.societyforbusinessethics.org
Loyola Univ of Chicago School of Business Administration 820
   N Michigan Ave   Chicago IL 60611
Ph: 312-915-6994 ▪ Fx: 312-915-6988

Society of Cable Telecommunications Engineers   www.scte.org
140 Philips Rd   Exton PA 19341
Ph: 610-363-6888 ▪ Fx: 610-363-5898 ▪ TF: 800-542-5040

Society of California Pioneers   www.californiapioneers.org
300 4th St   San Francisco CA 94107
Ph: 415-957-1849 ▪ Fx: 415-957-9858

Society for Calligraphy   www.societyforcalligraphy.org
PO Box 64174   Los Angeles CA 90064
Ph: 323-931-6146

Society of Carbide & Tool Engineers   www.scte10.org
ASM International 9639 Kinsman Rd   Materials Park OH 44072
Ph: 440-338-5151 ▪ Fx: 440-338-4634

Society for Cardiac Angiography & Interventions   www.scai.org
9111 Old Georgetown Rd   Bethesda MD 20814
Ph: 301-581-3450 ▪ Fx: 301-581-3408 ▪ TF: 800-992-7224

Society of Cardiovascular Anesthesiologists   www.scahq.org
2209 Dickens Rd   Richmond VA 23230
Ph: 804-282-0084 ▪ Fx: 804-282-0090

Society for Cardiovascular Magnetic Resonance   www.scmr.org
19 Mantua Rd   Mount Royal NJ 08061
Ph: 856-423-8955 ▪ Fx: 856-423-3420

Society of Certified Insurance Counselors
PO Box 27027   Austin TX 78755
Ph: 512-345-7932 ▪ Fx: 512-343-2167 ▪ TF: 800-633-2165

Society of Certified Kitchen & Bathroom Designers
687 Willow Grove St   Hackettstown NJ 07840
Ph: 908-852-0033 ▪ Fx: 908-852-1695 ▪ TF: 800-843-6522

Society of Chairmen of Academic Radiology Departments   www.scardonline.org
820 Jorie Blvd   Oak Brook IL 60523
Ph: 630-368-3731 ▪ Fx: 630-571-7837

Society for Chaos Theory in Psychology &   www.societyforchaostheory.org
Life Sciences   Univ of Oregon Dept of Psychology CMB
1227   Eugene OR 97403
Ph: 541-346-1996 ▪ Fx: 541-346-4911

Society of Chemical Industry - American Section   www.soci.org/SCI
15 W 72nd St Suite 12N   New York NY 10023
Ph: 212-873-4449 ▪ Fx: 212-873-4446

Society of Children's Book Writers & Illustrators   www.scbwi.org
8271 Beverly Blvd   Los Angeles CA 90048
Ph: 323-782-1010 ▪ Fx: 323-782-1892

Society of Christian Ethics   www.scethics.org
St Johns University PO Box 5633   Collegeville MN 56321
Ph: 320-363-3525 ▪ Fx: 320-363-3145

Society of Christian Philosophers   www.siu.edu/~scp
Calvin College Dept of Philosophy 3201 Burton St SE   Grand
   Rapids MI 49546
Ph: 616-526-6421

Society of the Cincinnati   members.tripod.com/~Historic_Trust/cincinna.htm
2118 Massachusetts Ave NW   Washington DC 20008
Ph: 202-785-2040 ▪ Fx: 202-785-0729

Society for Cinema & Media Studies   www.cinemastudies.org
Univ of Texas Press PO Box 7819   Austin TX 78713
Ph: 512-471-4531

Society for Cinephiles/Cinecon Inc   www.cinecon.org
3405 Glendale Blvd Suite 251   Los Angeles CA 90039
Ph: 800-411-0455

Society for Clinical & Experimental   ijceh.educ.wsu.edu/sceh/scehframe.htm
Hypnosis   Massachusetts School of Professional Psychology
221 Rivermoor St   Boston MA 02132
Ph: 617-469-1981 ▪ Fx: 617-469-1889

Society for Clinical & Medical Hair Removal Inc   www.scmhr.org
7600 Terrace Ave Suite 203   Middleton WI 53562
Ph: 608-831-8009 ▪ Fx: 608-831-5122

Society for Clinical Trials   www.sctweb.org
600 Wyndhurst Ave Suite 112   Baltimore MD 21210
Ph: 410-433-4722 ▪ Fx: 410-435-8631

Society for Clinical Vascular Surgery   scvs.vascularweb.org
900 Cummings Ctr Suite 221-U   Beverly MA 01915
Ph: 978-927-8330 ▪ Fx: 978-927-4018

Society for College & University Planning   www.scup.org
339 E Liberty St Suite 300   Ann Arbor MI 48104
Ph: 734-998-7832 ▪ Fx: 734-998-6532

Society of Collision Repair Specialists   www.scrs.com
PO Box 4519   West Richland WA 99353
Ph: 509-943-8919 ▪ Fx: 509-943-8942 ▪ TF: 877-841-0660

Society for Commercial Archeology   www.sca-roadside.org
Bowling Green State Univ Dept of Popular Culture   Bowling
   Green OH 43403
Ph: 419-372-2136

Society for the Comparative Study of Society &   www.lsa.umich.edu/history/CSSH
History   Univ of Michigan 4418 Modern Languages Bldg 812 E
   Washington St   Ann Arbor MI 48109
Ph: 734-764-6362 ▪ Fx: 734-647-2105

Society of Competitive Intelligence Professionals   www.scip.org
1700 Diagonal Rd Suite 600   Alexandria VA 22314
Ph: 703-739-0696 ▪ Fx: 703-739-2524

Society of Composers & Lyricists   www.thescl.com
400 S Beverly Dr Suite 214   Beverly Hills CA 90212
Ph: 310-281-2812 ▪ Fx: 310-284-4861

Society of Computed Body Tomography & Magnetic Resonance   www.scbtmr.org
PO Box 1026   Rochester MN 55903
Ph: 507-288-5620 ▪ Fx: 507-288-0014

Society for Computer Applications in Radiology   www.scarnet.org
10105 Cottesmore Ct   Great Falls VA 22066
Ph: 703-757-0054 ▪ Fx: 703-757-0454

Society for Conservation Biology   www.conservationbiology.org
4245 N Fairfax Dr Suite 400   Arlington VA 22203
Ph: 703-276-2384 ▪ Fx: 703-995-4633

Society of Corporate Meeting Professionals   www.scmp.org
217 Ridgemont Ave   San Antonio TX 78209
Ph: 210-822-6522 ▪ Fx: 210-882-9838

Society of Cosmetic Chemists   www.scconline.org
120 Wall St Suite 2400   New York NY 10005
Ph: 212-668-1500 ▪ Fx: 212-668-1504

Society of Cost Estimating & Analysis   www.sceaonline.net
101 S Whiting St Suite 201   Alexandria VA 22304
Ph: 703-751-8069 ▪ Fx: 703-461-7328

Society of Craft Designers   www.craftdesigners.org
PO Box 3388   Zanesville OH 43702
Ph: 740-452-4541 ▪ Fx: 740-454-2552

Society for Creative Anachronism   www.sca.org
PO Box 360789   Milpitas CA 95036
Ph: 408-263-9305 ▪ Fx: 408-263-0641

Society of Critical Care Medicine   www.sccm.org
701 Lee St Suite 200   Des Plaines IL 60016
Ph: 847-827-6869 ▪ Fx: 847-827-6886

Society for Cross-Cultural Research   www.sccr.org
Western Connecticut State Univ 233 N Quaker Ln   West
   Hartford CT 06119
Ph: 203-837-8678

Society for Cultural Anthropology   www.aaanet.org/sca
c/o American Anthropological Assn 2200 Wilson Blvd Suite
   600   Arlington VA 22201
Ph: 703-528-1902 ▪ Fx: 703-528-3546

Society for Dance History Scholars Inc   www.sdhs.org
3416 Primm Ln   Birmingham AL 35216
Ph: 205-978-1404 ▪ Fx: 205-823-2760

Society of Decorative Painters   www.decorativepainters.org
393 N McLean Blvd   Wichita KS 67203
Ph: 316-269-9300 ▪ Fx: 316-269-9191

Society of Depreciation Professionals   www.depr.org
8100-M4 Wyoming Blvd NE Suite 228   Albuquerque NM 87113
Ph: 505-792-4604 ▪ Fx: 505-922-1495

Society of the Descendants of the   www.centralschwenkfelder.com/exile
Schwenkfeldian Exiles   105 Seminary St   Pennsburg PA
   18073
Ph: 215-679-3103 ▪ Fx: 215-679-8175

Society of the Descendants of Washington's Army   www.valleyforgesociety.org
at Valley Forge

Society for Developmental & Behavioral Pediatrics   www.sdbp.org
17000 Commerce Pkwy Suite C   Mount Laurel NJ 08054
Ph: 856-439-0500 ▪ Fx: 856-439-0525

Society for Developmental Biology   sdb.bio.purdue.edu
9650 Rockville Pike   Bethesda MD 20814
Ph: 301-571-0647 ▪ Fx: 301-571-5704

Society of Diagnostic Medical Sonography   www.sdms.org
2745 N Dallas Pkwy Suite 350   Plano TX 75093
Ph: 214-473-8057 ▪ Fx: 214-473-8563 ▪ TF: 800-229-9506

Society for Disability Studies   www.uic.edu/orgs/sds
Univ of Chicago Dept of Disability & Human Development 1640
   W Roosevelt Rd Suite 236   Chicago IL 60608
Ph: 312-996-4664 ▪ Fx: 312-996-7743

Society for Ear Nose & Throat Advances in Children   www.sentac.org
3333 Burnet Ave   Cincinnati OH 45229
Ph: 513-636-2287

Society for Ecological Restoration International   www.ser.org
1955 W Grant Rd Suite 150 Tucson AZ 85745
Ph: 520-622-5485 ▪ Fx: 520-622-5491

Society for Economic Botany   www.econbot.org
PO Box 1897 Lawrence KS 66044
Ph: 785-843-1235 ▪ Fx: 785-843-1274 ▪ TF: 800-627-0629

Society of Economic Geologists   www.segweb.org
7811 Shaffer Pkwy Littleton CO 80127
Ph: 720-981-7882 ▪ Fx: 720-981-7874

Society for Education in Anesthesia   www.seahq.org
520 N Northwest Hwy Park Ridge IL 60068
Ph: 847-825-5586 ▪ Fx: 847-825-5658

Society of Emergency Medicine Physician Assistants   www.sempa.org
950 N Washington St Alexandria VA 22314
Ph: 703-519-7334 ▪ Fx: 703-684-1924

Society of Engineering Science Inc   www.sesinc.org
Texas A & M University 701 HR Bright Bldg 3141
TAMU College Station TX 77843
Ph: 979-845-1604

Society for Environmental Geochemistry & Health   www.segh.net
4698 S Forrest Ave Springfield MO 65810
Ph: 417-885-1166 ▪ Fx: 417-881-6920

Society for Environmental Graphic Design   www.segd.org
1000 Vermont Ave Suite 400 Washington DC 20005
Ph: 202-638-5555 ▪ Fx: 202-638-0891

Society of Environmental Journalists   www.sej.org
321 Old York Rd Suite 200 Jenkintown PA 19046
Ph: 215-884-8174 ▪ Fx: 215-884-8175

Society of Environmental Toxicology & Chemistry   www.setac.org
1010 N 12th Ave Pensacola FL 32501
Ph: 850-469-1500 ▪ Fx: 850-469-9778 ▪ TF: 888-899-2088

Society for Epidemiologic Research   www.epiresearch.org
PO Box 990 Clearfield UT 84098
Ph: 801-525-0231 ▪ Fx: 801-774-9211

Society of Ethnobiology   www.ethnobiology.org
Univ of North Carolina Dept of Anthropology CB 3115 Alumni
Bldg Chapel Hill NC 27599
Ph: 919-962-3841 ▪ Fx: 919-962-1613

Society for Ethnomusicology   www.ethnomusicology.org
Indiana University 1165 E 3rd St Morrison Hall
005 Bloomington IN 47405
Ph: 812-855-0389 ▪ Fx: 812-855-6673

Society for Exact Philosophy   web.phil.ufl.edu/SEP

Society for Excellence in Eyecare Inc   www.excellenteyesurgery.com
2850 Countrybrook Dr Suite F16 Palm Harbor FL 34684
Ph: 630-699-1929 ▪ Fx: 727-786-6622

Society for Experimental Biology & Medicine   www.sebm.org
197 W Spring Valley Ave Maywood NJ 07607
Ph: 201-291-9080 ▪ Fx: 201-291-2988

Society for Experimental Mechanics Inc   www.sem.org
7 School St Bethel CT 06801
Ph: 203-790-6373 ▪ Fx: 203-790-4472

Society of Experimental Test Pilots   www.setp.org
PO Box 986 Lancaster CA 93584
Ph: 661-942-9574 ▪ Fx: 661-940-0398

Society of Exploration Geophysicists   www.seg.org
8801 S Yale Ave Tulsa OK 74137
Ph: 918-493-3516 ▪ Fx: 918-497-5557

Society for the Exploration of Psychotherapy Integration   www.cyberpsych.org/sepi
Adelphi Univ Dener Institute Garden City NY 11530
Ph: 516-877-4803 ▪ Fx: 516-877-4805

Society of Eye Surgeons
10801 Connecticut Ave Kensington MD 20814
Ph: 240-290-0263 ▪ Fx: 240-290-0269

Society Farsarotul   www.farsarotul.org
466 Silver Ln PO Box 753 Trumbull CT 06611
Ph: 203-375-0600 ▪ Fx: 203-375-5003

Society of Federal Labor Relations Professionals
PO Box 25112 Arlington VA 22202
Ph: 703-685-4130 ▪ Fx: 703-685-1144

Society of Financial Examiners   www.sofe.org
174 Grace Blvd Altamonte Springs FL 32714
Ph: 407-682-4930 ▪ Fx: 407-682-3175 ▪ TF: 800-787-7633

Society of Financial Service Professionals   www.financialpro.org
270 S Bryn Mawr Ave Bryn Mawr PA 19010
Ph: 610-526-2500 ▪ Fx: 610-527-4010 ▪ TF: 800-392-6900

Society of Fire Protection Engineers   www.sfpe.org
7315 Wisconsin Ave Suite 1225W Bethesda MD 20814
Ph: 301-718-2910 ▪ Fx: 301-718-2242

Society of Flavor Chemists   www.flavorchemist.org
86 Watertower Plaza Suite 343 Leominster MA 01453
Ph: 978-840-4596 ▪ Fx: 978-383-0580

Society for Folk Arts Preservation   www.societyforfolkarts.com
69 Timberhill Ln South Fallsburg NY 12779
Ph: 845-436-7314

Society for Foodservice Management   www.sfm-online.org
304 W Liberty St Suite 201 Louisville KY 40202
Ph: 502-583-3783 ▪ Fx: 502-589-3602

Society of Former Special Agents of the FBI Inc   www.socxfbi.org
PO Box 1027 Quantico VA 22134
Ph: 703-640-6469 ▪ Fx: 703-640-6537

Society for Free Radical Biology & Medicine   www.sfrbm.org
2950 Buskirk Ave Suite 170 Walnut Creek CA 94597
Ph: 925-472-5904 ▪ Fx: 925-472-5901

Society for French American Cultural Services & Educational Aid   www.facsea.org
972 5th Ave New York NY 10021
Ph: 212-439-1439 ▪ Fx: 212-439-1455 ▪ TF: 800-937-3624

Society of Gastroenterology Nurses & Associates Inc   www.sgna.org
401 N Michigan Ave Chicago IL 60611
Ph: 312-321-5165 ▪ Fx: 312-527-6658 ▪ TF: 800-245-7462

Society of Gastrointestinal Radiologists   www.sgr.org
4550 Post Oak Pl Suite 342 Houston TX 77027
Ph: 713-965-0566 ▪ Fx: 713-960-0488

Society of General Internal Medicine   www.sgim.org
2501 M St NW Suite 575 Washington DC 20037
Ph: 202-887-5150 ▪ Fx: 202-887-5405 ▪ TF: 800-822-3060

Society of General Physiologists   www.sgpweb.org
PO Box 257 Woods Hole MA 02543
Ph: 508-540-6719 ▪ Fx: 508-540-0155

Society of Geriatric Cardiology   www.sgcard.org
9111 Old Georgetown Rd Bethesda MD 20814
Ph: 301-581-3449 ▪ Fx: 301-581-3456

Society for German-American Studies   www.ulib.iupui.edu/kade/sgasin.html
Scott Community College 500 Belmont Rd Bettendorf IA
52722
Ph: 319-441-4319

Society of Glass & Ceramic Decorators   www.sgcd.org
47 N 4th St Zanesville OH 43702
Ph: 740-588-9882 ▪ Fx: 740-588-0245

Society of Government Meeting Professionals   www.sgmp.org
908 King St Alexandria VA 22314
Ph: 703-549-0892 ▪ Fx: 703-549-0708 ▪ TF: 800-827-8916

Society of Government Travel Professionals   www.government-travel.org
6935 Wisconsin Ave Suite 200 Bethesda MD 20815
Ph: 301-654-8595 ▪ Fx: 301-654-6663

Society for Gynecologic Investigation   www.sgionline.org
409 12th St SW Washington DC 20024
Ph: 202-863-2544 ▪ Fx: 202-863-0739

Society of Gynecologic Oncologists   www.sgo.org
401 N Michigan Ave Chicago IL 60611
Ph: 312-644-6610 ▪ Fx: 312-527-6959

Society for Healthcare Consumer Advocacy   www.shca-aha.org
1 Franklin St 31st Fl N Chicago IL 60606
Ph: 312-422-3726 ▪ Fx: 312-422-4581

Society for Healthcare Epidemiology of America   www.shea-online.org
19 Mantua Rd Mount Royal NJ 08061
Ph: 856-423-0087 ▪ Fx: 856-423-3420

Society for Healthcare Strategy & Market Development   www.stratsociety.org
American Hospital Assn 1 N Franklin St 28th Fl Chicago IL
60606
Ph: 312-422-3737 ▪ Fx: 312-422-4579 ▪ TF: 800-242-2626

Society for Hematopathology   www.socforheme.org
3643 Walton Way Ext Augusta GA 30909
Ph: 706-733-7550 ▪ Fx: 706-733-8033

Society of Hispanic Professional Engineers   www.shpe.org
5400 E Olympic Blvd Suite 210 Los Angeles CA 90022
Ph: 323-725-3970 ▪ Fx: 323-725-0316

Society for Historians of American Foreign Relations   www.shafr.org

Society for Historians of the Early American Republic   www.sla.purdue.edu/jer

Society for Historical Archaeology   www.sha.org
19 Mantua Rd Mount Royal NJ 08061
Ph: 856-224-0995 ▪ Fx: 856-423-3420

Society for the History of Authorship Reading & Publishing   www.sharpweb.org
PO Box 30 Wilmington NC 28402
Ph: 910-254-0308

Society for the History of Discoveries   www.sochistdisc.org
5502 Laurel Ridge Dr Alpharetta GA 30005
Ph: 770-772-6366

Society for History Education   www.csulb.edu/~histeach
PO Box 1578 Borrego Springs CA 92004
Ph: 760-767-5938

Society for History in the Federal Government   www.shfg.org
PO Box 14139 Ben Franklin Stn Washington DC 20044
Ph: 202-501-5350 ▪ Fx: 202-219-2176

Society & History, Society for the Comparative   www.lsa.umich.edu/history/CSSH
Study of Univ of Michigan 4418 Modern Languages Bldg 812
E Washington St Ann Arbor MI 48109
Ph: 734-764-6362 ▪ Fx: 734-647-2105

Society for the History of Technology   shot.press.jhu.edu

Society for Human Ecology   www.societyforhumanecology.org
College of the Atlantic 105 Eden St Bar Harbor ME 04609
Ph: 207-288-5015 ▪ Fx: 207-288-3780

Society for Human Resource Management   www.shrm.org
1800 Duke St Alexandria VA 22314
Ph: 703-548-3440 ▪ Fx: 703-836-0367 ▪ TF: 800-283-7476

Society for Humanistic Anthropology   www.smcm.edu/sha
c/o American Anthropological Assn 2200 Wilson Blvd Suite
600 Arlington VA 22201
Ph: 703-528-1902 ▪ Fx: 703-528-3546

Society for Humanistic Judaism   www.shj.org
28611 W 12-Mile Rd Farmington Hills MI 48334
Ph: 248-478-7610 ▪ Fx: 248-478-3159

Society for the Humanities   www.arts.cornell.edu/sochum
Cornell Univ AD White House 27 East Ave Ithaca NY 14853
Ph: 607-255-9274 ▪ Fx: 607-255-1422

Society of Illustrators   www.societyillustrators.org
Museum of American Illustration 128 E 63rd St New York NY
10021
Ph: 212-838-2560 ▪ Fx: 212-838-2561

Society for Imaging Science & Technology   www.imaging.org
7003 Kilworth Ln Springfield VA 22151
Ph: 703-642-9090 ▪ Fx: 703-642-9094

Society for In Vitro Biology   www.sivb.org
9315 Largo Dr W Suite 255 Largo MD 20774
Ph: 301-324-5054 ▪ Fx: 301-324-5057

Society of Incentive & Travel Executives   www.site-intl.org
401 N Michigan Ave Suite 2200 Chicago IL 60611
Ph: 312-321-5148 ▪ Fx: 312-527-6783

Society of Independent Gasoline Marketers of America   www.sigma.org
11911 Freedom Dr Suite 590   Reston VA 20190
Ph: 703-709-7000 ▪ Fx: 703-709-7007

Society of Independent Professional Earth Scientists   www.sipes.org
4925 Greenville Ave Suite 1106   Dallas TX 75206
Ph: 214-363-1780 ▪ Fx: 214-363-8195

Society of Independent Show Organizers   www.siso.org
7000 W SW Hwy   Chicago Ridge IL 60415
Ph: 708-361-6000 ▪ Fx: 708-361-6166 ▪ TF: 877-937-7476

Society of Indiana Pioneers   www.indianapioneers.com
450 W Ohio St   Indianapolis IN 46202
Ph: 317-233-6588

Society for Industrial & Applied Mathematics   www.siam.org
3600 University City Science Ctr 6th Fl   Philadelphia PA 19104
Ph: 215-382-9800 ▪ Fx: 215-386-7999 ▪ TF: 800-447-7426

Society for Industrial Archeology   www.sia-web.org
Michigan Technological Univ Dept of Social Sciences 1400
   Townsend Dr   Houghton MI 49931
Ph: 906-487-1889 ▪ Fx: 906-487-2468

Society for Industrial Microbiology   www.simhq.org
3929 Old Lee Hwy Suite 92A   Fairfax VA 22030
Ph: 703-691-3357 ▪ Fx: 703-691-7991

Society of Industrial & Office REALTORS   www.sior.com
1201 New York Ave NW Suite 350   Washington DC 20005
Ph: 202-449-8200 ▪ Fx: 202-449-8201

Society for Industrial & Organizational Psychology   www.siop.org
PO Box 87   Bowling Green OH 43402
Ph: 419-353-0032 ▪ Fx: 419-352-2645

Society of Infectious Diseases Pharmacists   www.sidp.org
502 E 11th St Suite 400   Austin TX 78701
Ph: 512-708-0611 ▪ Fx: 512-708-0627

Society for Information Display   www.sid.org
610 S 2nd St   San Jose CA 95112
Ph: 408-977-1013 ▪ Fx: 408-977-1531

Society for Information Management   www.simnet.org
401 N Michigan Ave Suite 2400   Chicago IL 60611
Ph: 312-527-6734

Society of Insurance Financial Management   www.sifm.org

Society of Insurance Trainers & Educators   www.insurancetrainers.org
2120 Market St Suite 108   San Francisco CA 94114
Ph: 415-621-2830 ▪ Fx: 415-621-0889

Society for Integrative & Comparative Biology   www.sicb.org
1313 Dolley Madison Blvd Suite 402   McLean VA 22101
Ph: 703-790-1745 ▪ Fx: 703-790-2672 ▪ TF: 800-955-1236

Society of International Business Fellows   www.sibf.org
191 Peachtree St NE Suite 3220   Atlanta GA 30303
Ph: 404-525-7423 ▪ Fx: 404-525-5331

Society for International Development - USA   www.sidint.org
1875 Connecticut Ave NW   Washington DC 20009
Ph: 202-884-8590 ▪ Fx: 202-884-8499

Society of Interventional Radiology   www.sirweb.org
10201 Lee Hwy Suite 500   Fairfax VA 22030
Ph: 703-691-1805 ▪ Fx: 703-691-1855 ▪ TF: 800-488-7284

Society of Invasive Cardiovascular Professionals   www.sicp.com
PO Box 61606   Virginia Beach VA 23466
Ph: 757-497-3694 ▪ Fx: 757-497-0010

Society for Invertebrate Pathology   www.sipweb.org
8904 Straw Flower Dr   Knoxville TN 37922
Ph: 888-684-4682 ▪ Fx: 888-486-1505

Society for Investigative Dermatology Inc   www.sidnet.org
820 W Superior Ave 7th Fl   Cleveland OH 44113
Ph: 216-579-9300 ▪ Fx: 216-579-9333

Society for Iranian Studies   www.iranian-studies.org
New York Univ Dept of Middle Eastern Studies 50 Washington
   Sq S   New York NY 10012
Ph: 212-995-4689

Society for Italian Historical Studies   www.historians.org/affiliates
Boston College   Chestnut Hill MA 02467
Ph: 617-552-3814 ▪ Fx: 617-552-2478

Society of King Charles the Martyr   www.skcm-usa.org
291 Bacon St   Waltham MA 02451
Ph: 781-899-3165

Society of Laparoendoscopic Surgeons   www.sls.org
7330 SW 62nd Pl Suite 410   South Miami FL 33143
Ph: 305-665-9959 ▪ Fx: 305-667-4123 ▪ TF: 800-446-2659

Society for Latin American Anthropology   www.aaanet.org/slaa/Slaa1.htm
c/o American Anthropological Assn 2200 Wilson Blvd Suite
   600   Arlington VA 22201
Ph: 703-528-1902 ▪ Fx: 703-528-3546

Society of Lesbian & Gay Anthropologists   www.solga.org
c/o American Anthropological Assn 2200 Wilson Blvd Suite
   600   Arlington VA 22201
Ph: 703-528-1902 ▪ Fx: 703-528-3546

Society for Leukocyte Biology   www.leukocytebiology.org
9650 Rockville Pike   Bethesda MD 20814
Ph: 301-634-7810 ▪ Fx: 301-634-7813

Society for Light Treatment & Biological Rhythms   www.websciences.org/sltbr
174 Cook St PO Box 591687   San Francisco CA 94159
Ph: 415-876-0716 ▪ Fx: 415-751-2758

Society of Lincoln Cent Collectors   www.slcc.nasc.net
13515 Magnolia Blvd   Sherman Oaks CA 91423
Ph: 818-789-7805

Society for Linguistic Anthropology   www.aaanet.org/sla
c/o American Anthropological Assn 2200 Wilson Blvd Suite
   600   Arlington VA 22201
Ph: 703-528-1902 ▪ Fx: 703-528-3546

Society of the Little Flower   www.littleflower.org
1313 Frontage Rd   Darien IL 60561
Ph: 630-968-9400 ▪ Fx: 630-968-9542 ▪ TF: 800-621-2806

Society for Luminescence Microscopy &   www.ruf.rice.edu/~jinnys/slms/SLMS.html
Spectroscopy

Society for Maintenance & Reliability Professionals   www.smrp.org
PO Box 51787   Knoxville TN 37950
Ph: 865-212-0111 ▪ Fx: 865-558-3060 ▪ TF: 800-950-7354

Society of Manufacturing Engineers   www.sme.org
1 SME Dr   Dearborn MI 48121
Ph: 313-271-1500 ▪ Fx: 313-425-3400 ▪ TF: 800-733-4763

Society of Marine Port Engineers   www.smpe.org
PO Box 466   Avenel NJ 07001
Ph: 732-381-7673 ▪ Fx: 732-381-2046

Society for Marketing Professional Services   www.smps.org
99 Canal Center Plaza Suite 330   Alexandria VA 22314
Ph: 703-549-6117 ▪ Fx: 703-549-2498 ▪ TF: 800-292-7677

Society for Maternal Fetal Medicine   www.smfm.org
409 12th St SW   Washington DC 20024
Ph: 202-863-2476 ▪ Fx: 202-554-1132

Society for Medical Anthropology   www.medanthro.net
c/o American Anthropological Assn 2200 Wilson Blvd Suite
   600   Arlington VA 22201
Ph: 703-528-1902 ▪ Fx: 703-528-3546

Society of Medical Consultants to the Armed Forces   www.smcaf.org

Society for Medical Decision Making   www.smdm.org
1211 Locust St   Philadelphia PA 19107
Ph: 215-545-7697 ▪ Fx: 215-545-8107

Society of Medical-Dental Management Consultants   www.smdmc.org
125 Strafford Ave Suite 300   Wayne PA 19087
Ph: 800-826-2264 ▪ Fx: 610-687-7702

Society of Medical Friends of Wine   medicalfriendsofwine.org
511 Jones Pl   Walnut Creek CA 94597
Ph: 925-933-9691 ▪ Fx: 925-939-5224

Society for Menstrual Cycle Research   www.pop.psu.edu/smcr
10559 N 104th Pl   Scottsdale AZ 85258
Ph: 480-451-9731

Society for Military History   www.smh-hq.org
3119 Lakeview Cir   Leavenworth KS 66048
Ph: 913-758-3322 ▪ Fx: 913-758-3309

Society of Military Orthopaedic Surgeons   www.somos.org
810 North St   Belgium WI 53004
Ph: 262-285-4280 ▪ Fx: 262-285-4231

Society of Military Widows   www.nous.org
5535 Hempstead Way   Springfield VA 22151
Ph: 703-750-1342 ▪ Fx: 703-354-4380 ▪ TF: 800-842-3451

Society for Mining Metallurgy & Exploration Inc   www.smenet.org
8307 Shaffer Pkwy   Littleton CO 80127
Ph: 303-973-9550 ▪ Fx: 303-973-3845 ▪ TF: 800-763-3132

Society of Missionaries of Africa   www.missionariesofafrica.org/policies.php
1624 21st St NW   Washington DC 20009
Ph: 202-232-5154 ▪ Fx: 202-332-8640

Society for Modeling & Simulation International   www.scs.org
4838 Ronson Ct Suite L PO Box 17900   San Diego CA 92111
Ph: 858-277-3888 ▪ Fx: 858-277-3930

Society of Motion Picture & Television Engineers   www.smpte.org
595 W Hartsdale Ave   White Plains NY 10607
Ph: 914-761-1100 ▪ Fx: 914-761-3115

Society for Mucosal Immunology   www.socmucimm.org
4350 East West Hwy Suite 401   Bethesda MD 20814
Ph: 301-718-6515 ▪ Fx: 301-656-0989

Society of Multivariate Experimental Psychology   www.smep.org
Univ of Oklahoma Psychology Dept   Norman OK 73019
Ph: 405-325-4511 ▪ Fx: 405-325-4737

Society of Municipal Arborists   www.urban-forestry.com
PO Box 641   Watkinsville GA 30677
Ph: 706-769-7412 ▪ Fx: 706-769-7307

Society of National Association Publications   www.snaponline.org
8405 Greensboro Dr Suite 800   McLean VA 22102
Ph: 703-506-3285 ▪ Fx: 703-506-3266

Society for Natural Philosophy   tam.cornell.edu/SNP/society.htm
Cornell Univ Kimball Hall - TAM   Ithaca NY 14853
Ph: 607-255-3738 ▪ Fx: 607-255-2011

Society of Naval Architects & Marine Engineers   www.sname.org
601 Pavonia Ave 4th Fl   Jersey City NJ 07306
Ph: 201-798-4800 ▪ Fx: 201-798-4975

Society of Neurological Surgeons   www.societyns.org
600 Highland Ave   Madison WI 53792
Ph: 608-263-0170 ▪ Fx: 608-263-1728

Society for Neuroscience   web.sfn.org
11 Dupont Cir NW Suite 500   Washington DC 20036
Ph: 202-462-6688 ▪ Fx: 202-462-9740

Society for News Design   www.snd.org
1130 Ten Rod Rd Suite F-104   North Kingstown RI 02852
Ph: 401-294-5233 ▪ Fx: 401-294-5238

Society for Nonprofit Organizations   www.snpo.org
5820 Canton Center Rd Suite 165   Canton MI 48187
Ph: 734-451-3582 ▪ Fx: 734-451-5935 ▪ TF: 800-424-7367

Society of North American Goldsmiths   www.snagmetalsmith.org
4513 Lincoln Ave Suite 213   Lisle IL 60532
Ph: 630-852-6385 ▪ Fx: 630-241-0142

Society of Nuclear Medicine   www.snm.org
1850 Samuel Morse Dr   Reston VA 20190
Ph: 703-708-9000 ▪ Fx: 703-708-9015

Society for Nutrition Education   www.sne.org
7150 Winton Dr Suite 300   Indianapolis IN 46268
Ph: 317-328-4627 ▪ Fx: 317-280-8527 ▪ TF: 800-235-6690

Society for Obstetric Anesthesia & Perinatology   www.soap.org
2 Summit Park Dr Suite 140   Cleveland OH 44131
Ph: 216-447-7863 ▪ Fx: 216-642-1127

Society for Occupational & Environmental Health   www.soeh.org
6728 Old McLean Village Dr   McLean VA 22101
Ph: 703-556-9222 ▪ Fx: 703-556-8729

Society of Otorhinolaryngology & Head-Neck Nurses Inc   www.sohnnurse.com
116 Canal St Suite A   New Smyrna Beach FL 32168
Ph: 386-428-1695 ▪ Fx: 386-423-7566

Society of Our Lady of the Most Holy Trinity   www.solt3.org
PO Box 152   Robstown TX 78380
Ph: 361-387-2754 ▪ Fx: 361-387-3818

Society for Pacific Coast Native Irises   www.pacificcoastiris.org
33450 Little Valley Rd   Fort Bragg CA 95437
Ph: 707-964-3907

Society of Park & Recreation Educators   www.nrpa.org
c/o National Recreation & Park Assn 22377 Belmont Ridge
Rd   Ashburn VA 20148
Ph: 703-858-0784 ▪ Fx: 703-858-0794

Society for Pediatric Anesthesia   www.pedsanesthesia.org
PO Box 11086   Richmond VA 23230
Ph: 804-282-9780 ▪ Fx: 804-282-0090

Society for Pediatric Dermatology   www.pedsderm.net
5422 N Bernard St   Chicago IL 60625
Ph: 773-583-9780 ▪ Fx: 773-583-9765

Society of Pediatric Nurses   www.pedsnurses.org
7794 Grow Dr   Pensacola FL 32514
Ph: 850-484-9987 ▪ Fx: 850-484-8762 ▪ TF: 800-723-2902

Society for Pediatric Pathology   www.spponline.org
3643 Walton Way Ext   Augusta GA 30909
Ph: 706-364-3375 ▪ Fx: 706-733-8033

Society for Pediatric Radiology   www.pedrad.org
4550 Post Oak Pl Suite 342   Houston TX 77027
Ph: 713-965-0566 ▪ Fx: 713-960-0488

Society for Pediatric Research   www.aps-spr.org
3400 Research Forest Dr Suite B-7   The Woodlands TX 77381
Ph: 281-419-0052 ▪ Fx: 281-419-0082

Society of Permanent Cosmetic Professionals   www.spcp.org
69 N Broadway St   Des Plaines IL 60016
Ph: 847-635-1330 ▪ Fx: 847-635-1326

Society for Personality Assessment   www.personality.org
6109H Arlington Blvd   Falls Church VA 22044
Ph: 703-534-4772

Society of Petroleum Engineers   www.spe.org
222 Palisades Creek Dr   Richardson TX 75080
Ph: 972-952-9300 ▪ Fx: 972-952-9435

Society of Petroleum Evaluation Engineers   www.spee.org
1001 McKinney St Suite 801   Houston TX 77002
Ph: 713-651-1639 ▪ Fx: 713-951-9659

Society of Petrophysicists & Well Log Analysts   www.spwla.org
8866 Gulf Fwy Suite 320   Houston TX 77017
Ph: 713-947-8727 ▪ Fx: 713-947-7181

Society of Phantom Friends   www.nancydrewsleuth.com/tww.html
PO Box 1437   North Highlands CA 95660
Ph: 916-331-7435

Society of Pharmaceutical & Biotech Trainers   www.spbt.org
4423 Pheasant Ridge Rd Suite 100   Roanoke VA 24014
Ph: 540-725-3859 ▪ Fx: 540-989-7482

Society for Phenomenology & Existential Philosophy   www.spep.org
Seattle Univ Dept of Philosophy 900 Broadway   Seattle WA
98122
Ph: 206-296-5473 ▪ Fx: 206-296-5997

Society for the Philosophical Study of Genocide &   www.loyno.edu/~spsgh
the Holocaust   Loyola Univ Dept of Philosophy   New Orleans
LA 70118
Ph: 504-865-3940 ▪ Fx: 504-865-3948

Society for the Philosophical Study   www.pages.drexel.edu/~pa34/spsm_website.htm
of Marxism   Univ at Buffalo Dept of Philosophy 135 Park
Hall   Buffalo NY 14260
Ph: 716-645-2444 ▪ Fx: 716-645-6139

Society for Philosophy of Religion
Univ of Georgia Dept of Philosophy Peabody Hall   Athens GA
30602
Ph: 706-542-2823 ▪ Fx: 706-542-2839

Society for Philosophy & Technology   www.spt.org
San Jose Univ Dept of Philosophy 1 Washington Sq   San Jose
CA 95192
Ph: 408-924-4526

Society of Photo Finishing Engineers   spfe.pmai.org
3000 Picture Pl   Jackson MI 49201
Ph: 517-788-8100 ▪ Fx: 517-788-8371

Society of Photo-Technologists   www.spt.info
11112 Spotted Rd S   Cheney WA 99004
Ph: 509-624-9621 ▪ Fx: 509-624-5320 ▪ TF: 888-662-7678

Society for Photographic Education   www.spenational.org
Miami Univ 110 Art Bldg   Oxford OH 45056
Ph: 513-529-8328 ▪ Fx: 513-529-1532

Society for Physical Regulation in Biology & Medicine   www.sprbm.org
2412 Cobblestone Way   Frederick MD 21702
Ph: 301-663-4556 ▪ Fx: 301-694-4948

Society for Physician Assistants in Pediatrics   www.aapa.org/spec/SPAP
950 N Washington St   Alexandria VA 22314
Ph: 800-596-4398

Society of Physics Students   www.aip.org/education/sps/index.html
1 Physics Ellipse   College Park MD 20740
Ph: 301-209-3007 ▪ Fx: 301-209-0839

Society of Piping Engineers & Designers   www.spedweb.org
1 Main St Suite 719   Houston TX 77002
Ph: 713-221-8089 ▪ Fx: 713-226-5230

Society of Plastics Engineers   www.4spe.org
14 Fairfield Dr   Brookfield CT 06804
Ph: 203-775-0471 ▪ Fx: 203-775-8490

Society of the Plastics Industry Inc   www.plasticsindustry.org
1801 K St NW Suite 600-K   Washington DC 20006
Ph: 202-974-5200 ▪ Fx: 202-296-7005

Society for Police & Criminal Psychology   cep.jmu.edu/spcp/
Southwest Texas State Univ Dept of Criminal Justice   San
Marcos TX 78666
Ph: 512-530-8211

Society of Polish-American Travel Agents   www.spata.org
2297 E Main St   Bridgeport CT 06610
Ph: 203-336-9960 ▪ Fx: 203-335-5319

Society for the Preservation & Advancement of the Harmonica   www.spah.org
PO Box 865   Troy MI 48099
Ph: 810-984-3115

Society for the Preservation & Encouragement of Barber Shop   www.spebsqsa.org
Quartet Singing in America   7930 Sheridan Rd   Kenosha WI
53143
Ph: 262-653-8440 ▪ Fx: 262-654-5552

Society for the Preservation & Encouragement of Scale Model
Kit Collecting   3213 Hardy Dr   Edmond OK 73013
Ph: 405-341-4640

Society for the Preservation of English Language & Literature   www.spellorg.com
PO Box 321   Braselton GA 30517
Ph: 770-586-0184 ▪ Fx: 770-868-0578

Society for the Preservation of Natural History Collections   www.spnhc.org

Society for the Preservation of New England Antiquities   www.spnea.org
141 Cambridge St   Boston MA 02114
Ph: 617-227-3956 ▪ Fx: 617-227-9204

Society for the Preservation of Old Mills   www.spoom.org

Society of Private & Pioneer Numismatics
98 Main St Suite 201   Tiburon CA 94920
Ph: 415-435-2601 ▪ Fx: 415-435-1627 ▪ TF: 888-852-4467

Society of Professional Audio Recording Services   www.spars.com
PO Box 770845   Memphis TN 38177
Ph: 901-747-3111 ▪ TF: 800-771-7727

Society of Professional Benefit Administrators   users.erols.com/spba
2 Wisconsin Cir Suite 670   Chevy Chase MD 20815
Ph: 301-718-7722 ▪ Fx: 301-718-9440

Society of Professional Journalists   www.spj.org
3909 Meridian St   Indianapolis IN 46208
Ph: 317-927-8000 ▪ Fx: 317-920-4789

Society of Professional Women in Petroleum   www.spwp.org
13511 Queensbury Ln   Houston TX 77079
Ph: 713-461-2898

Society of Professors of Child & Adolescent Psychiatry
3615 Wisconsin Ave NW   Washington DC 20016
Ph: 202-966-7300 ▪ Fx: 202-966-2891

Society for Progressive Supranuclear Palsy   www.psp.org
1838 Greene Tree Rd   Baltimore MD 21208
Ph: 410-486-3330 ▪ Fx: 410-486-4283 ▪ TF: 800-457-4777

Society Promoting Environmental Conservation   www.spec.bc.ca
2150 Maple St   Vancouver BC V6J3T3
Ph: 604-736-7732 ▪ Fx: 604-736-7115

Society for the Propagation of the Faith   www.worldmissions-catholicchurch.org
366 5th Ave   New York NY 10001
Ph: 212-563-8700 ▪ Fx: 212-563-8725 ▪ TF: 800-431-2222

Society of Protozoologists   www.uga.edu/~protozoa
PO Box 1897   Lawrence KS 66044
Ph: 785-843-1235 ▪ Fx: 785-843-1274

Society for Psychological Anthropology   www.aaanet.org/SPA
c/o American Anthropological Assn 2200 Wilson Blvd Suite
600   Arlington VA 22201
Ph: 703-528-1902 ▪ Fx: 703-528-3546

Society for the Psychological Study of Social Issues   www.spssi.org
208 'I' St NE   Washington DC 20002
Ph: 202-675-6956 ▪ Fx: 202-675-6902

Society for Psychophysiological Research   www.sprweb.org
7600 Terrace Ave Suite 203   Middleton WI 53562
Ph: 608-831-0274

Society for Public Health Education   www.sophe.org
750 1st St NE Suite 910   Washington DC 20002
Ph: 202-408-9804 ▪ Fx: 202-408-9815

Society of Publication Designers Inc   www.spd.org
60 E 42nd St Suite 721   New York NY 10165
Ph: 212-983-8585 ▪ Fx: 212-983-2308

Society of Quality Assurance   www.sqa.org
2365 Hunters Way   Charlottesville VA 22911
Ph: 434-297-4772 ▪ Fx: 434-977-0899

Society for Quantitative Analyses of Behavior   sqab.psychology.org
234 Huron Ave   Cambridge MA 02139
Ph: 617-497-5270

Society of Quantitative Analysts Inc   www.sqa-us.org
151 Herricks Rd Suite 1   Garden City Park NY 11040
Ph: 516-739-2510 ▪ Fx: 516-739-3803 ▪ TF: 800-284-6228

Society for Radiation Oncology Administrators   www.sroa.org
PO Box 51687   Albuquerque NM 87181
Ph: 866-458-7762 ▪ Fx: 505-298-5063

Society of Radiologists in Ultrasound   www.sru.org
44211 Slatestone Ct   Leesburg VA 20176
Ph: 703-858-9210 ▪ Fx: 703-729-4839

Society for Range Management   www.rangelands.org
445 Union Blvd Suite 230   Lakewood CO 80228
Ph: 303-986-3309 ▪ Fx: 303-986-3892

Society for Reformation Research   www.reformationresearch.org
Hope College Dept of History PO Box 900   Holland MI 49422
Ph: 616-395-7591

Society of Reliability Engineers   www.sre.org

Society for Reproductive Endocrinology & Infertility   www.socrei.org
1209 Montgomery Hwy   Birmingham AL 35216
Ph: 205-978-5000 ▪ Fx: 205-978-5005

Society of Reproductive Surgeons   www.reprodsurgery.org
1209 Montgomery Hwy   Birmingham AL 35216
Ph: 205-978-5000 ▪ Fx: 205-978-5005

Society of Research Administrators www.srainternational.org
1901 N Moore St Suite 1004   Arlington VA 22209
Ph: 703-741-0140 ■ Fx: 703-741-0142

Society for Research on Adolescence www.s-r-a.org
3131 S State St Suite 302   Ann Arbor MI 48108
Ph: 734-998-6567 ■ Fx: 734-998-9586

Society for Research in Child Development www.srcd.org
3131 S State St Suite 302   Ann Arbor MI 48108
Ph: 734-998-6578 ■ Fx: 734-998-6569

Society for Research on Nicotine & Tobacco www.srnt.org
7600 Terrace Ave Suite 203   Middleton WI 53562
Ph: 608-836-3787 ■ Fx: 608-831-5485

Society for Rheology www.rheology.org
c/o American Institute of Physics 2 Huntington Quadrangle Suite
   1N01   Melville NY 11747
Ph: 516-576-2403 ■ Fx: 516-576-2223

Society for Risk Analysis www.sra.org
1313 Dolley Madison Blvd Suite 402   McLean VA 22101
Ph: 703-790-1745 ■ Fx: 703-790-2672

Society of Roller Skating Teachers of America
6905 Corporate Dr   Indianapolis IN 46278
Ph: 317-347-2626 ■ Fx: 317-347-2636

Society of Saint Andrew www.endhunger.org
3383 Sweet Hollow Rd   Big Island VA 24526
Ph: 434-299-5956 ■ Fx: 434-299-5949 ■ TF: 800-333-4597

Society of Saint Mary Magdalene www.st-mary-magdalene.org
PO Box 352   Fountain Inn SC 29644
Ph: 864-409-0077

Society of Saint Peter Apostle www.worldmissions-catholicchurch.org
366 5th Ave   New York NY 10001
Ph: 212-563-8700 ■ Fx: 212-563-8725 ■ TF: 800-431-2222

Society of Satellite Professionals International www.sspi.org
55 Broad St 14th Fl   New York NY 10004
Ph: 212-809-5199 ■ Fx: 212-825-0075

Society for Scholarly Publishing www.sspnet.org
10200 W 44th Ave Suite 304   Wheat Ridge CO 80033
Ph: 303-422-3914 ■ Fx: 303-422-8894

Society for the Scientific Study of Religion www.sssrweb.org
Alfred Univ Div of Social Sciences 1 Saxon Dr   Alfred NY
   14802
Ph: 607-871-2215 ■ Fx: 607-871-2085

Society for the Scientific Study of Sexuality www.sexscience.org
PO Box 416   Allentown PA 18105
Ph: 610-530-2483 ■ Fx: 610-530-2485

Society of Scribes www.societyofscribes.org
PO Box 933   New York NY 10150
Ph: 212-452-0139

Society for Sedimentary Geology www.sepm.org
6128 E 38th St Suite 308   Tulsa OK 74135
Ph: 918-610-3361 ■ Fx: 918-621-1685 ■ TF: 800-865-9765

Society for Service Professionals in Printing www.sspp.org
433 E Monroe Ave   Alexandria VA 22301
Ph: 703-684-0044 ■ Fx: 703-548-9137 ■ TF: 877-777-7398

Society for Sex Therapy & Research www.sstarnet.org
409 12th St NW PO Box 96920   Washington DC 20090
Ph: 202-863-1646 ■ Fx: 202-554-0453

Society for Social Studies of Science www.lsu.edu/ssss
Louisiana State Univ Dept of Sociology   Baton Rouge LA 70803
Ph: 225-578-5311 ■ Fx: 225-578-5102

Society for Social Work Leadership in Health Care www.sswlhc.org
1211 Locust St   Philadelphia PA 19107
Ph: 215-599-6134 ■ Fx: 215-545-8107 ■ TF: 866-237-9542

Society for Software Quality www.ssq.org
PO Box 86958   San Diego CA 92138
Ph: 619-571-3112

Society for Spanish & Portuguese www.ukans.edu/~iberia/ssphs/ssphs_main.html
Historical Studies

Society of Spanish & Spanish-American Studies www.colorado.edu/spanish/sssas
Univ of Colorado at Boulder Dept of Spanish & Portuguese 134
   McKenna Languages Bldg UCB 278   Boulder CO 80309
Ph: 303-492-7308 ■ Fx: 303-492-3699

Society of Stage Directors & Choreographers www.ssdc.org
1501 Broadway Suite 1701   New York NY 10036
Ph: 212-391-1070 ■ Fx: 212-302-6195

Society for the Study of Amphibians & Reptiles www.ssarherps.org
PO Box 253   Marceline MO 64658
Ph: 660-256-3252

Society for the Study of Evolution lsul.la.asu.edu/evolution
810 E 10th St PO Box 1897   Lawrence KS 66044
Ph: 785-843-1235

Society for the Study of Indigenous Languages of the Americas www.ssila.org
PO Box 555   Arcata CA 95518
Ph: 707-826-4324 ■ Fx: 707-677-1676

Society for the Study of Male Psychology & Physiology
321 Iuka Rd   Montpelier OH 43543
Ph: 419-485-3602

Society for the Study of Midwestern Literature writing.msu.edu:16080/ssml
Michigan State Univ Bessey Hall   East Lansing MI 48824
Ph: 517-355-3507 ■ Fx: 517-353-5250

Society for the Study of Myth & Tradition www.parabola.org
656 Broadway   New York NY 10012
Ph: 212-505-6200 ■ Fx: 212-979-7325 ■ TF: 800-560-6984

Society for the Study of Reproduction www.ssr.org
1619 Monroe St   Madison WI 53711
Ph: 608-256-2777 ■ Fx: 608-256-4610

Society for the Study of Social Biology www-rcf.usc.edu/~crimmin/sssb
USC Andrus Gerontology Ctr 3715 McClintock Ave   Los
   Angeles CA 90089
Ph: 213-740-5156 ■ Fx: 213-740-0792

Society for the Study of Social Problems www.sssp1.org
Univ of Tennessee 901 McClung Tower   Knoxville TN 37996
Ph: 865-974-3620 ■ Fx: 865-689-1534

Society for Surgery of the Alimentary Tract www.ssat.com
900 Cummings Ctr Suite 221-U   Beverly MA 01915
Ph: 978-927-8330 ■ Fx: 978-524-8890

Society of Surgical Oncology Inc www.surgonc.org
85 W Algonquin Rd Suite 550   Arlington Heights IL 60005
Ph: 847-427-1400 ■ Fx: 847-427-9656

Society of Teachers of Family Medicine www.stfm.org
11400 Tomahawk Creek Pkwy Suite 540   Leawood KS 66211
Ph: 913-906-6000 ■ Fx: 913-906-6096

Society for Technical Communication www.stc.org
901 N Stuart St Suite 904   Arlington VA 22203
Ph: 703-522-4114 ■ Fx: 703-522-2075

Society of Telecommunications Consultants www.stcconsultants.org
PO Box 416   Fall River Mills CA 96028
Ph: 530-336-7070 ■ Fx: 530-336-7060 ■ TF: 800-782-7670

Society for Textual Scholarship www.textual.org

Society for Theriogenology www.therio.org
PO Box 3007   Montgomery AL 36109
Ph: 334-395-4666 ■ Fx: 334-270-3399

Society of Thoracic Radiology www.thoracicrad.org
1711 Walden Ln SW   Rochester MN 55902
Ph: 507-288-5260 ■ Fx: 507-288-0014

Society of Thoracic Surgeons www.sts.org
633 N Saint Clair St Suite 2320   Chicago IL 60611
Ph: 312-202-5800 ■ Fx: 312-202-5801

Society of Tobacco Jar Collectors www.tobaccojarsociety.com
1705 Chanticleer   Cherry Hill NJ 08003
Ph: 856-489-8363 ■ Fx: 856-489-8364

Society of Toxicologic Pathologists www.toxpath.org
1821 Michael Faraday Dr Suite 300   Reston VA 20190
Ph: 703-438-7508 ■ Fx: 703-438-3113

Society of Toxicology www.toxicology.org
1821 Michael Faraday Dr Suite 300   Reston VA 20190
Ph: 703-438-3115 ■ Fx: 703-438-3113

Society of Trauma Nurses www.traumanursesoc.org
223 N Guadalupe St PMB 300   Santa Fe NM 87501
Ph: 505-983-4923 ■ Fx: 505-983-5109

Society of Tribologists & Lubrication Engineers www.stle.org
840 Busse Hwy   Park Ridge IL 60068
Ph: 847-825-5536 ■ Fx: 847-825-1456

Society of Turkish Architects Engineers & Scientists Inc www.m-l-m.org
821 United Nations Plaza 2nd Fl   New York NY 10017
Ph: 212-682-7688 ■ Fx: 212-687-3026

Society of Tympanuchus Cupido Pinnatus Ltd
1977 Hidden Reserve Ct   Mequon WI 53092
Ph: 262-512-9107

Society of University Surgeons www.susweb.org
1133 W Morse Blvd Suite 201   Winter Park FL 32789
Ph: 407-647-7714 ■ Fx: 407-629-2502

Society of Urban National & Transnational/Global Anthropology www.sunta.org
c/o American Anthropological Assn 2200 Wilson Blvd Suite
   600   Arlington VA 22201
Ph: 703-528-1902 ■ Fx: 703-528-3546

Society of Urologic Cryosurgeons
1950 Old Tustin Ave   Santa Ana CA 92705
Ph: 714-550-9155 ■ Fx: 714-550-9234

Society of Urologic Nurses & Associates www.suna.org
PO Box 56   Pitman NJ 08071
Ph: 856-256-2335 ■ Fx: 856-589-7463 ■ TF: 888-827-7862

Society for Uroradiology www.uroradiology.org
4550 Post Oak Pl Suite 342   Houston TX 77027
Ph: 713-965-0566 ■ Fx: 713-960-0488

Society of US Air Force Flight Surgeons www.sousaffs.org
PO Box 35387   Brooks AFB TX 78235
Ph: 210-536-2845 ■ Fx: 210-536-1779

Society for Utopian Studies www.utoronto.ca/utopia
Univ of Texas at Arlington English Dept   Arlington TX 76019
Ph: 817-272-2729

Society of Vacuum Coaters www.svc.org
71 Pinon Hill Pl NE   Albuquerque NM 87122
Ph: 505-856-7188 ■ Fx: 505-856-6716

Society for Values in Higher Education www.svhe.org
Portland State Univ PO Box 751   Portland OR 97207
Ph: 503-725-2575 ■ Fx: 503-725-2577

Society for Vascular Nursing www.svnnet.org
7794 Grow Dr   Pensacola FL 32514
Ph: 888-536-4786 ■ Fx: 850-484-8762

Society for Vascular Surgery svs.vascularweb.org
900 Cummings Ctr Suite 221-U   Beverly MA 01915
Ph: 978-526-8330 ■ Fx: 978-526-4018

Society for Vascular Ultrasound www.svunet.org
4601 Presidents Dr Suite 260   Lanham MD 20706
Ph: 301-459-7550 ■ Fx: 301-459-5651 ■ TF: 800-788-8346

Society for Vector Ecology www.sove.org/
1966 Compton Ave   Corona CA 92881
Ph: 909-340-9792 ■ Fx: 909-340-2515

Society for Visual Anthropology www.societyforvisualanthropology.org
c/o American Anthropological Assn 2200 Wilson Blvd Suite
   600   Arlington VA 22201
Ph: 703-528-1902 ■ Fx: 703-528-3546

Society of Wetland Scientists www.sws.org
1313 Dolley Madison Blvd Suite 402   McLean VA 22101
Ph: 703-790-1745 ■ Fx: 703-790-2672

Society of Wine Educators www.wine.gurus.com
1200 G St NW Suite 360   Washington DC 20005
Ph: 202-347-5677 ■ Fx: 202-347-5667

Society of Wireless Pioneers   www.sowp.org
PO Box 86   Geyserville CA 95441
Ph: 707-545-0766

Society of Woman Geographers   www.iswg.org
415 E Capital St SE   Washington DC 20003
Ph: 202-546-9228 ▪ Fx: 202-546-5232

Society of Women Engineers   www.societyofwomenengineers.org
230 E Ohio St Suite 400   Chicago IL 60611
Ph: 312-596-5223 ▪ Fx: 312-596-5252

Society of Women in Urology   www.swiu.org
1111 N Plaza Dr Suite 550   Schaumburg IL 60173
Ph: 847-517-7225 ▪ Fx: 847-517-7229

Society for Women's Health Research   www.womens-health.org
1828 L St NW Suite 625   Washington DC 20036
Ph: 202-223-8224 ▪ Fx: 202-833-3472

Society of Wood Science & Technology   www.swst.org
1 Gifford Pinchot Dr   Madison WI 53726
Ph: 608-231-9347 ▪ Fx: 608-231-9592

Socio-Economics, Society for the Advancement of   www.sase.org
PO Box 39008   Baltimore MD 21212
Ph: 410-435-6617 ▪ Fx: 410-377-7965

Sociological Association, American   www.asanet.org
1307 New York Ave NW Suite 700   Washington DC 20005
Ph: 202-383-9005 ▪ Fx: 202-638-0882

Sociological Practice Association   www.socpractice.org

Sociological Society, Christian   www.christiansociology.com

Sociological Society, Rural   www.ruralsociology.org
Univ of Missouri 104 Gentry Hall   Columbia MO 65211
Ph: 573-882-9065 ▪ Fx: 573-882-1473

Sociologists, Association of Black   www.blacksociologists.org
4200 Wisconsin Ave NW PMB 106-257   Washington DC 20016
Ph: 202-365-1759

(Sociology) Alpha Kappa Delta International   www.alpha-kappa-delta.org
PO Box U-1147   Mobile AL 36688
Ph: 251-461-1700 ▪ Fx: 251-460-7925

Sociology, Association for Humanistic   www.humanistsoc.org

Sociology of Education Association   lmri.ucsb.edu/profdev/2/sea

Sociology of Religion, Association for the   www.sociologyofreligion.com
3520 Wiltshire Dr   Holiday FL 34691
Ph: 727-844-5990 ▪ Fx: 727-844-7332

Sociology, Society for Applied   www.appliedsoc.org
Bowling Green State Univ Dept of Sociology   Bowling Green
OH 43403
Ph: 419-372-2217

Sociology of Sport, North American   www.uwm.edu/~aycock/nasss/nasss.html
Society for the   Bowling Green State Univ Dept of
Sociology   Bowling Green OH 43403
Ph: 419-372-8306 ▪ Fx: 419-372-8360

**Sociometry & Group Psychotherapy, American Board of Examiners
of Psychodrama**   PO Box 15572   Washington DC 20003
Ph: 202-483-0514

Soft Drink Association, National   www.nsda.org
1101 16th St NW   Washington DC 20036
Ph: 202-463-6732 ▪ Fx: 202-463-8178

Soft Drink PAC
1101 16th St NW   Washington DC 20036
Ph: 202-463-6732 ▪ Fx: 202-463-8178

Softball Association of America Inc, Amateur   www.softball.org
2801 NE 50th St   Oklahoma City OK 73111
Ph: 405-424-5266 ▪ Fx: 405-424-3855 ▪ TF: 800-654-8337

Softball Association, National   www.playnsa.com
PO Box 7   Nicholasville KY 40340
Ph: 859-887-4114 ▪ Fx: 859-887-4874

Softball Association, National Wheelchair   www.wheelchairsoftball.com
1616 Todd Ct   Hastings MN 55033
Ph: 612-437-1792 ▪ Fx: 612-437-3889

Softball Federation, International   www.internationalsoftball.com
1900 S Park Rd   Plant City FL 33566
Ph: 813-864-0100 ▪ Fx: 813-864-0105

Softball Inc, PONY Baseball/   www.pony.org
300 Clare Dr   Washington PA 15301
Ph: 724-225-1060 ▪ Fx: 724-225-9852

Softball USA, Senior   www.seniorsoftball.com
2701 K St Suite 101A   Sacramento CA 95816
Ph: 916-236-5303 ▪ Fx: 916-326-5304

Software Alliance, Business   www.bsa.org
1150 18th St Suite 700   Washington DC 20036
Ph: 202-872-5500 ▪ Fx: 202-872-5501 ▪ TF: 888-667-4722

Software Association, Entertainment   www.theesa.com
1211 Connecticut Ave NW Suite 600   Washington DC 20036
Ph: 202-223-2400 ▪ Fx: 202-223-2401

Software Dealers Association, Video   www.vsda.org
16530 Ventura Blvd Suite 400   Encino CA 91436
Ph: 818-385-1500 ▪ Fx: 818-385-0567 ▪ TF: 800-955-8732

(Software Development) Open Applications Group Inc   www.openapplications.org
1950 Spectrum Cir Suite 400   Marietta GA 30067
Ph: 770-980-3418

Software Foundation, Free   www.gnu.org/fsf/fsf.html
59 Temple Pl Suite 330   Boston MA 02111
Ph: 617-542-5942 ▪ Fx: 617-542-2652

Software & Information Industry Association   www.siia.net
1090 Vermont Ave NW 6th Fl   Washington DC 20005
Ph: 202-289-7442 ▪ Fx: 202-289-7097

Software Productivity Consortium   www.software.org
2214 Rock Hill Rd SPC Bldg   Herndon VA 20170
Ph: 703-742-8877 ▪ Fx: 703-742-7200

Software Quality, Society for   www.ssq.org
PO Box 86958   San Diego CA 92138
Ph: 619-571-3112

Softwood Export Council   www.softwood.org
520 SW 6th Ave Suite 810   Portland OR 97204
Ph: 503-248-0406 ▪ Fx: 503-248-0402

Soil Council, Mulch &   www.mulchandsoilcouncil.org
10210 Leatherleaf Ct   Manassas VA 20111
Ph: 703-257-0111 ▪ Fx: 703-257-0213

Soil Pipe Institute, Cast Iron   www.cispi.org
5959 Shallowford Rd Suite 419   Chattanooga TN 37421
Ph: 423-892-0137 ▪ Fx: 423-892-0817

Soil Science Society of America   www.soils.org
677 S Segoe Rd   Madison WI 53711
Ph: 608-273-8080 ▪ Fx: 608-273-2021

Soil & Water Conservation Society   www.swcs.org
945 SW Ankeny Rd   Ankeny IA 50021
Ph: 515-289-2331 ▪ Fx: 515-289-1227 ▪ TF: 800-843-7645

Sojourners   www.sojo.net
2401 15th St NW   Washington DC 20009
Ph: 202-328-8842 ▪ Fx: 202-328-8757 ▪ TF: 800-714-7474

Sojourners Inc, National   www.nationalsojourners.org
8301 E Boulevard Dr   Alexandria VA 22308
Ph: 703-765-5000 ▪ Fx: 703-765-8390

Soka Gakkai International-USA   www.sgi-usa.org
606 Wilshire Blvd   Santa Monica CA 90401
Ph: 310-260-8900 ▪ Fx: 310-260-8917 ▪ TF: 800-626-1313

Sokol, American   www.american-sokol.org
122 W 22nd St   Oak Brook IL 60523
Ph: 630-368-0771 ▪ Fx: 630-368-0758

Sokol, Slovak Catholic   www.slovakcatholicsokol.org
205 Madison St PO Box 899   Passaic NJ 07055
Ph: 800-886-7656

SOL Association for Research Inc   www.solarpress.com
PO Box 2276   North Canton OH 44720
Ph: 330-497-9645

Solar Cookers International   solarcookers.org
1919 21st St Suite 101   Sacramento CA 95814
Ph: 916-455-4499 ▪ Fx: 916-455-4498

Solar Energy Industries Association   www.seia.org
1616 H St NW 8th Fl   Washington DC 20006
Ph: 202-628-7745 ▪ Fx: 202-628-7779

Solar Energy Society, American   www.ases.org
2400 Central Ave Suite A   Boulder CO 80301
Ph: 303-443-3130 ▪ Fx: 303-443-3212

Solar Rating & Certification Corp   www.solar-rating.org
c/o Florida Solar Energy Ctr 1679 Clearlake Rd   Cocoa FL
32922
Ph: 321-638-1537 ▪ Fx: 321-638-1010

SOLE - International Society of Logistics   www.sole.org
8100 Professional Pl Suite 111   Hyattsville MD 20785
Ph: 301-459-8446 ▪ Fx: 301-459-1522

Solid State Circuits Society, IEEE   sscs.org
IEEE Operations Ctr 445 Hoes Ln   Piscataway NJ 08854
Ph: 732-981-0060 ▪ Fx: 732-981-1721

Solid State Technology Association, JEDEC   www.jedec.org
2500 Wilson Blvd   Arlington VA 22201
Ph: 703-907-7534 ▪ Fx: 703-907-7583

Solid Surface Fabricators Association, International   www.issfa.net
975 American Pacific Dr   Henderson NV 89014
Ph: 702-567-8150 ▪ Fx: 702-567-8145

Solid Waste Association of North America   www.swana.org
PO Box 7219   Silver Spring MD 20907
Ph: 301-585-2898 ▪ Fx: 301-589-7068 ▪ TF: 800-467-9262

Solid Waste Management Officials, Association of   www.astswmo.org
State & Territorial   444 N Capitol St NW Suite
315   Washington DC 20001
Ph: 202-624-5828 ▪ Fx: 202-624-7875

Solid Wastes Management Association, National   www.nswma.org
4301 Connecticut Ave NW Suite 300   Washington DC 20008
Ph: 202-244-4700 ▪ Fx: 202-966-4818 ▪ TF: 800-424-2869

Solidarity Alliance, Workers   www.workersolidarity.org
339 Lafayette St Rm 202   New York NY 10012
Ph: 212-979-8353

Solomon Schechter Day School Association
155 5th Ave   New York NY 10010
Ph: 212-533-7800 ▪ Fx: 212-353-9439

Solution Mining Research Institute   www.solutionmining.org
3336 Lone Hill Ln   Encinitas CA 92024
Ph: 858-759-7532 ▪ Fx: 858-759-7542

Solvents Committee, Brominated
1250 Connecticut Ave NE Suite 700   Washington DC 20036
Ph: 202-637-9040 ▪ Fx: 202-637-9178

Somatics Society   somaticsed.com/somSociety.html
1516 Grant Ave Suite 212   Novato CA 94945
Ph: 415-892-0617 ▪ Fx: 415-892-4388

Sommelier Society of America   www.sommeliersocietyofamerica.org
PO Box 20080 West Village Stn   New York NY 10014
Ph: 212-679-4190 ▪ Fx: 212-255-8959

Somnology, American Academy of
PO Box 27077   Las Vegas NV 89126
Ph: 702-222-6463 ▪ Fx: 702-384-3264

Song Society, Country Dance &   www.cdss.org
132 Main St PO Box 338   Haydenville MA 01039
Ph: 413-268-7426 ▪ Fx: 413-268-7471

Songwriters Association International, Nashville   www.nashvillesongwriters.com
1701 West End Ave 3rd Fl   Nashville TN 37203
Ph: 615-256-3354 ▪ Fx: 615-256-0034 ▪ TF: 800-321-6008

Songwriters Guild of America   www.songwriters.org
1500 Harbor Blvd   Weehawken NJ 07087
Ph: 201-867-7603 ▪ Fx: 201-867-7535

Sonographers, American Registry of Diagnostic Medical   www.ardms.org
51 Monroe St Plaza East 1   Rockville MD 20850
Ph: 301-738-8401 ▪ Fx: 301-738-0312 ▪ TF: 800-541-9754

Sonography, Society of Diagnostic Medical
2745 N Dallas Pkwy Suite 350   Plano TX 75093
Ph: 214-473-8057 ▪ Fx: 214-473-8563 ▪ TF: 800-229-9506
www.sdms.org

Sonoma County Grape Growers Association
PO Box 1959   Sebastopol CA 95473
Ph: 707-829-3963
www.scgga.org

Sonoma County Wineries Association
5000 Roberts Lake Rd Suite A   Rohnert Park CA 94928
Ph: 707-586-3795 ▪ Fx: 707-586-1383 ▪ TF: 800-939-7666
www.sonomawine.com

Sons of the American Legion
PO Box 1055   Indianapolis IN 46206
Ph: 317-630-1200 ▪ Fx: 317-630-1413
www.sal.legion.org

Sons of the American Revolution, National Society of the
1000 S 4th St   Louisville KY 40203
Ph: 502-589-1776 ▪ Fx: 502-589-1671
www.sar.org

Sons of Confederate Veterans
PO Box 59   Columbia TN 38402
Ph: 800-380-1896 ▪ Fx: 931-381-6712
www.scv.org

Sons & Daughters of Oregon Pioneers
PO Box 6685   Portland OR 97228
Ph: 503-786-9804
www.webtrail.com/sdop

Sons of Italy in America, Order of the
219 'E' St NE   Washington DC 20002
Ph: 202-547-2900 ▪ Fx: 202-546-8168 ▪ TF: 800-547-6742
www.osia.org

Sons of Norway
1455 W Lake St   Minneapolis MN 55408
Ph: 612-827-3611 ▪ Fx: 612-827-0658 ▪ TF: 800-945-8851
www.sofn.com

Sons of Poland, Association of the
333 Hackensack St   Carlstadt NJ 07072
Ph: 201-935-2807 ▪ Fx: 201-935-2752
www.sonsofpoland.com

Sons of Spanish American War Veterans
32028 Mt Vernon   Rockwood MI 48173
Ph: 734-379-4996
www.spanamwar.com/SSAWV.htm

Sons of Union Veterans of the Civil War, Auxiliary to
2449 Center Ave   Alliance OH 44601
Ph: 330-823-6919

Sorghum Producers, National Grain
4201 N I-27 PO Box 5309   Lubbock TX 79408
Ph: 806-749-3478 ▪ Fx: 806-749-9002
www.sorghumgrowers.com

Soroptimist International of the Americas
2 Penn Ctr Plaza Suite 1000   Philadelphia PA 19102
Ph: 215-557-9300 ▪ Fx: 215-568-5200
www.soroptimist.org

Sorptive Minerals Institute
1 Thomas Cir NW 10th Fl   Washington DC 20005
Ph: 202-289-2760 ▪ Fx: 202-530-0659
www.sorptive.org

SOS Children's Villages-USA
1317 F St NW Suite 550   Washington DC 20004
Ph: 202-347-7920 ▪ Fx: 202-347-7334 ▪ TF: 800-886-5767
www.soschildrensvillages.org

Sotos Syndrome Support Association
3 Danada Sq E Suite 235   Wheaton IL 60187
Ph: 888-246-7772
www.well.com/user/sssa

Sound Collections, Association for Recorded
PO Box 543   Annapolis MD 21404
Ph: 410-757-0488 ▪ Fx: 410-349-0175
www.arsc-audio.org

Soundex Reunion Registry, International
PO Box 2312   Carson City NV 89702
Ph: 775-882-7755
www.isrr.net

South African Blacks, Medical Education for
120 Albany St Suite 810   New Brunswick NJ 08901
Ph: 732-745-1292 ▪ Fx: 732-745-9794
www.mesab.org/

South America, Association of American Schools in
14750 NW 77th Ct Suite 210   Miami Lakes FL 33016
Ph: 305-821-0345 ▪ Fx: 305-821-4244
www.aassa.com

South America Mission
5217 S Military Trail   Lake Worth FL 33463
Ph: 561-965-1833 ▪ Fx: 561-439-8950
www.southamericamission.org

South American Explorers
126 Indian Creek Rd   Ithaca NY 14850
Ph: 607-277-0488 ▪ Fx: 607-277-6122 ▪ TF: 800-274-0568
www.saexplorers.org

South American Missionary Society
PO Box 399   Ambridge PA 15003
Ph: 724-266-0669 ▪ Fx: 724-266-2681
www.sams-usa.org

(South Asian) Indian American Center for Political Awareness
1025 Connecticut Ave NW Suite 1000   Washington DC 20036
Ph: 202-955-8338 ▪ Fx: 202-327-5483
www.iacfpa.org

South Asian Journalists Association
Columbia Graduate School of Journalism 2950 Broadway   New York NY 10027
Ph: 212-854-5979 ▪ Fx: 212-854-7318
www.saja.org

(South Asian) Network of Indian Professionals of North America
www.netip.org

(South Asian Women) Kappa Phi Gamma Sorority Inc
www.kappaphigamma.org

South Devon Association, North American
2514 Ave 'S'   Santa Fe TX 77510
Ph: 409-927-4445
www.southdevon.com

South & Meso American Indian Rights Center
PO Box 7829   Oakland CA 94601
Ph: 510-534-4882 ▪ Fx: 510-834-4264
saiic.nativeweb.org

Southdown Breeders' Association, American
HCR 13 Box 220   Fredonia TX 76842
Ph: 915-429-6226 ▪ Fx: 915-429-6225
www.southdownsheep.com

Southeast Asia, Committee on Research Materials on
www.library.wisc.edu/guides/SEAasia/cormosea

Southeast Asia Resource Action Center
1628 16th St NW 3rd Fl   Washington DC 20009
Ph: 202-667-4690 ▪ Fx: 202-667-6449 ▪ TF: 800-600-9188
www.searac.org

Southeast Asian Languages, Council of Teachers of
www.cotseal.org

Southeastern Apparel Manufacturers Suppliers
4921-C Broad River Rd   Columbia SC 29212
Ph: 803-772-5861 ▪ Fx: 803-731-7709
www.seams.org

Southeastern Association of Fish & Wildlife Agencies
8500 Freshwater Farms Rd   Tallahassee FL 32309
Ph: 850-893-1204 ▪ Fx: 850-893-6204
www.seafwa.org

Southeastern Composers' League
6812 Dina Leigh Ct   Springfield VA 22153
Ph: 540-463-8852
www.runet.edu/~scl-web/

Southeastern Conference
2201 Richard Arrington Blvd N   Birmingham AL 35203
Ph: 205-458-3000 ▪ Fx: 205-458-3031
www.secsports.com

Southeastern Fisheries Association Inc
1118-B Thomasville Rd   Tallahassee FL 32303
Ph: 850-224-0612 ▪ Fx: 850-222-3663
www.southeasternfish.org

Southeastern Historical Keyboard Society
PO Box 32022   Charlotte NC 28232
Ph: 704-334-3468 ▪ Fx: 704-334-3442
www.sehks.org

Southeastern Lumber Manufacturers Association
671 Forest Pkwy   Forest Park GA 30297
Ph: 404-361-1445 ▪ Fx: 404-361-5963
www.slma.org

Southeastern Theatre Conference
PO Box 9868   Greensboro NC 27429
Ph: 336-272-3645 ▪ Fx: 336-272-8810
www.setc.org

Southern Association of Colleges & Schools
1866 Southern Ln   Decatur GA 30033
Ph: 404-679-4500 ▪ Fx: 404-679-4556 ▪ TF: 800-248-7701
www.sacs.org

Southern Baptist Campus Ministers, Association of
PO Box 25118   Baton Rouge LA 70894
Ph: 225-343-0408 ▪ Fx: 225-343-0424

Southern Baptist Colleges & Schools, Association of
PO Box 11655   Jackson TN 38308
Ph: 731-660-3497 ▪ Fx: 731-664-6459
www.baptistschools.org

Southern Baptist Convention
901 Commerce St Suite 750   Nashville TN 37203
Ph: 615-244-2355 ▪ Fx: 615-742-8919
www.sbc.net

Southern Baptist Convention, Ethics & Religious Liberty Commission of the   901 Commerce St   Nashville TN 37203
Ph: 615-244-2495 ▪ Fx: 615-242-0065
www.erlc.com

Southern Baptist Disaster Relief
4200 North Point Pkwy   Alpharetta GA 30022
Ph: 770-410-6442 ▪ Fx: 770-410-6014
www.namb.net/dr

Southern Baptist Foundation
901 Commerce St Suite 600   Nashville TN 37203
Ph: 615-254-8823 ▪ Fx: 615-255-1832
www.sbfdn.org

Southern Baptist Historical Library & Archives
901 Commerce St Suite 400   Nashville TN 37203
Ph: 615-244-0344
www.sbhla.org

Southern Christian Leadership Conference
591-A Edgewood Ave SE   Atlanta GA 30312
Ph: 404-522-1420 ▪ Fx: 404-527-4333
www.sclcnational.org

Southern Conference
905 E Main St   Spartanburg SC 29302
Ph: 864-591-5100
www.soconsports.com

Southern Cooperatives/Land Assistance Fund, Federation of   2769 Church St   East Point GA 30344
Ph: 404-765-0991 ▪ Fx: 404-765-9178
www.federationsoutherncoop.com

Southern Cotton Association
88 Union Ave Suite 1204   Memphis TN 38103
Ph: 901-525-2272 ▪ Fx: 901-527-8303
www.southerncottonassociation.com

Southern Cotton Ginners Association
874 Cotton Gin Pl   Memphis TN 38106
Ph: 901-947-3104 ▪ Fx: 901-947-3103
www.southerncottonginners.org

Southern Cypress Manufacturers Association
400 Penn Center Blvd Suite 530   Pittsburgh PA 15235
Ph: 412-829-0770 ▪ Fx: 412-829-0844 ▪ TF: 877-607-7262
www.cypressinfo.org

Southern Early Childhood Association
PO Box 55930   Little Rock AR 72215
Ph: 501-221-1648 ▪ Fx: 501-227-5297 ▪ TF: 800-305-7322
www.southernearlychildhood.org

Southern Economic Association
Oklahoma State Univ College of Business Admin   Stillwater OK 74078
Ph: 405-744-7645 ▪ Fx: 405-744-5180
www.okstate.edu/economics/journal/south1.html

Southern Forest Products Association
PO Box 641700   Kenner LA 70064
Ph: 504-443-4464 ▪ Fx: 504-443-6612
www.sfpa.org

Southern Governors' Association
444 N Capitol St NW Suite 200   Washington DC 20001
Ph: 202-624-5897 ▪ Fx: 202-624-7797
www.southerngovernors.org

Southern Medical Association
35 Lakeshore Dr   Birmingham AL 35209
Ph: 205-945-1840 ▪ Fx: 205-942-0642 ▪ TF: 800-423-4992
www.sma.org

Southern Mutual Help Association Inc
3602 Old Jeanerette Rd   New Iberia LA 70563
Ph: 337-367-3277 ▪ Fx: 337-367-3279
www.southernmutualhelp.org

Southern Ocean Coalition, Antarctic &
1630 Connecticut Ave Fl 3   Washington DC 20009
Ph: 202-234-2480 ▪ Fx: 202-387-4823
www.asoc.org

Southern Poverty Law Center
400 Washington Ave   Montgomery AL 36104
Ph: 334-956-8200 ▪ Fx: 334-956-8483
www.splcenter.org

Southern Public Administration Education Foundation Inc
2103 Fairway Ln   Harrisburg PA 17112
Ph: 717-540-5477 ▪ Fx: 215-893-1763
www.spaef.com

Southern Regional Council
133 Carnegie Way NW Suite 1030   Atlanta GA 30303
Ph: 404-522-8764 ▪ Fx: 404-522-8791
www.southerncouncil.org

Southern Studies, Institute for
PO Box 531   Durham NC 27702
Ph: 919-419-8311 ▪ Fx: 919-419-8315
www.southernstudies.org

Southern Textile Association Inc
PO Box 66   Gastonia NC 28053
Ph: 704-824-3522 ▪ Fx: 704-824-0630
www.southerntextile.org

Southern US Trade Association
2 Canal St World Trade Ctr Suite 2515   New Orleans LA 70130
Ph: 504-568-5986 ▪ Fx: 504-568-6010
www.susta.org

Southern Utah Wilderness Alliance
1471 S 1100 East   Salt Lake City UT 84105
Ph: 801-486-3161 ▪ Fx: 801-486-4233
www.suwa.org

Southwest Collegiate Hockey League
1533 Fairfield Ct   Lewisville TX 75077
Ph: 972-436-1560 ▪ Fx: 972-436-1560
www.schl.org

Southwest Research & Information Center
PO Box 4524   Albuquerque NM 87106
Ph: 505-262-1862 ▪ Fx: 505-262-1864
www.sric.org

Southwest Voter Registration Education Project
206 Lombard St 2nd Fl   San Antonio TX 78226
Ph: 210-922-0225 ▪ Fx: 210-932-4055 ▪ TF: 800-404-8683
www.svrep.org

Southwestern Athletic Conference
1527 5th Ave N   Birmingham AL 35204
Ph: 205-251-7573 ▪ Fx: 205-297-9820
www.swac.org

Southwestern Peanut Growers Association
304 SE Lubbock PO Box 338   Gorman TX 76454
Ph: 254-734-2222 ▪ Fx: 254-734-2288
www.swpga.com

Souvenir Distributors Association, Post Card &
2105 Laurel Bush Rd Suite 200   Bel Air MD 21015
Ph: 443-640-1055 ▪ Fx: 443-640-1031
www.postcardcentral.org

Souvenir & Novelties Trade Association
10 E Athens Ave Suite 208   Ardmore PA 19003
Ph: 610-645-6940 ▪ Fx: 610-645-6943 ▪ TF: 800-284-5451

Soviet Union, Union of Councils for Jews in the Former
PO Box 11676   Washington DC 20008
Ph: 202-237-8262 ▪ Fx: 202-237-2236
www.ucsj.org

Soy Ink Information Center, National
4454 NW 114th St   Urbandale IA 50322
Ph: 515-251-8640 ▪ Fx: 515-251-8657 ▪ TF: 800-747-4275
www.soyink.com

Soy Protein Council
1255 23rd St NW   Washington DC 20037
Ph: 202-467-6610 ▪ Fx: 202-833-3636
www.spcouncil.org

Soybean Association, American
12125 Woodcrest Executive Dr Suite 100   Saint Louis MO 63141
Ph: 314-576-1770 ▪ Fx: 314-576-2786 ▪ TF: 800-688-7692
www.amsoy.org

Soybean Board, United
16640 Chesterfield Grove Rd Suite 130   Chesterfield MO 63005
Ph: 636-530-1777 ▪ Fx: 636-530-1560 ▪ TF: 800-989-8721
www.unitedsoybean.org

Soyfoods Association of North America
PO Box 234   Lafayette CA 94549
Ph: 925-283-2991
www.soyfoods.org

Spa Association, International
2365 Harrodsburg Rd Suite A325   Lexington KY 40504
Ph: 859-226-4326 ▪ Fx: 859-226-4445 ▪ TF: 888-651-4772
www.experienceispa.com

Spa & Pool Institute, National
2111 Eisenhower Ave   Alexandria VA 22314
Ph: 703-838-0083 ▪ Fx: 703-549-0493 ▪ TF: 800-323-3996
www.nspi.org

Space Explorers, Association of
1150 Gemini Ave   Houston TX 77058
Ph: 281-280-8172 ▪ Fx: 281-280-8173
www.space-explorers.org

Space Foundation
310 S 14th St   Colorado Springs CO 80908
Ph: 719-576-8000 ▪ Fx: 719-576-8801 ▪ TF: 800-691-4000
www.spacefoundation.org

Space Industry Association, Council of Defense &
1000 Wilson Blvd Suite 1800   Arlington VA 22209
Ph: 703-243-2020 ▪ Fx: 703-243-8539
www.codsia.org

Space Law, International Institute of
www.iafastro-iisl.com

Space Planners International, Residential
PO Box 14393   Scottsdale AZ 85267
Ph: 480-473-0986 ▪ Fx: 480-473-0757 ▪ TF: 800-548-0945

Space Research Association, Universities
10227 Wincopin Cir American City Bldg Suite 212   Columbia MD 21044
Ph: 410-730-2656 ▪ Fx: 410-730-3496
www.usra.edu

Space Science Education, Challenger Center for
1250 N Pitt St   Alexandria VA 22314
Ph: 703-683-9740 ▪ Fx: 703-683-7546 ▪ TF: 800-987-8277
www.challenger.org

Space & Security Studies, Institute for
5017 Bellflower Ct   Melbourne FL 32940
Ph: 321-752-5955
rmbowman.com/isss

Space Society, National
600 Pennsylvania Ave SE Suite 201   Washington DC 20003
Ph: 202-543-1900 ▪ Fx: 202-546-4189
www.nss.org

Space Studies Institute
PO Box 82   Princeton NJ 08542
Ph: 609-921-0377 ▪ Fx: 609-921-0389
www.ssi.org

SPACES - Saving & Preserving Arts & Cultural Environments
1804 N Van Ness Blvd   Los Angeles CA 90028
Ph: 323-463-1629

Spain, American Academy of Research Historians of Medieval
www.uca.edu/aarhms

Spain-US Chamber of Commerce
350 5th Ave Suite 2029   New York NY 10118
Ph: 212-967-2170 ▪ Fx: 212-564-1415
www.spainuscc.org

Spaniel Club, American
30 Cardinal Loop   Crossville TN 38555
Ph: 931-456-6690 ▪ Fx: 931-707-8504
www.asc-cockerspaniel.org

Spaniel Club USA, Cavalier King Charles
PO Box 330   Conway NH 03818
Ph: 603-447-5218 ▪ Fx: 603-447-5419
www.ckcsc.org

Spanish American Committee
4407 Lorain Ave   Cleveland OH 44113
Ph: 216-961-2100 ▪ Fx: 216-961-3305
span-am.tripod.com/Start.htm

Spanish American War Veterans, Sons of
32028 Mt Vernon   Rockwood MI 48173
Ph: 734-379-4996
www.spanamwar.com/SSAWV.htm

Spanish Barb Breeders Association
PO Box 598   Anthony FL 32617
Ph: 352-622-5878
www.spanishbarb.com

Spanish Institute
684 Park Ave   New York NY 10021
Ph: 212-628-0420 ▪ Fx: 212-734-4177
www.spanishinstitute.org/default.htm

Spanish Mustang Registry
4970 S Kansas Settlement Rd   Willcox AZ 85643
Ph: 520-384-2886
www.spanishmustang.org

Spanish & Portuguese, American Association of Teachers of
423 Exton Commons   Exton PA 19341
Ph: 610-363-7005 ▪ Fx: 610-363-7116
www.aatsp.org

Spanish & Portuguese Historical Studies, Society for
www.ukans.edu/~iberia/ssphs/ssphs_main.html

Spanish & Spanish-American Studies, Society of
Univ of Colorado at Boulder Dept of Spanish & Portuguese 134 McKenna Languages Bldg UCB 278   Boulder CO 80309
Ph: 303-492-7308 ▪ Fx: 303-492-3699
www.colorado.edu/spanish/sssas

Spanish-Speaking, REFORMA National Association to Promote Library Services to Latinos & the   PO Box 25963   Scottsdale AZ 85255
Ph: 480-471-7452 ▪ Fx: 480-471-7442
www.reforma.org

Spanish World Gospel Mission
PO Box 542   Winona Lake IN 46590
Ph: 574-267-8821 ▪ Fx: 574-267-3524 ▪ TF: 800-419-3683
www.spanishworld.org

Spaulding for Children
16250 Northland Dr Suite 120   Southfield MI 48075
Ph: 248-443-7080 ▪ Fx: 248-443-7099 ▪ TF: 877-767-5437
www.spaulding.org

SPEAK Inc - Society for Promoting & Encouraging Arts & Knowledge of the Church   805 County Rd 102   Eureka Springs AR 72632
Ph: 479-253-9701 ▪ Fx: 479-253-1277
www.speakinc.org

Speakers Association, National
1500 S Priest Dr   Tempe AZ 85281
Ph: 480-968-2552 ▪ Fx: 480-968-0911
www.nsaspeaker.org

Speakers Association, National African American
3033 Western Ave   Park Forest IL 60466
Ph: 708-747-2219 ▪ Fx: 877-866-2272
www.4naasa.org

Speakers Bureaus, International Association of
2780 Waterfront Pkwy E Dr Suite 120   Indianapolis IN 46214
Ph: 317-297-0872 ▪ Fx: 317-387-3387
www.iasbweb.org

Special Care Dentistry
211 E Chicago Ave Suite 740   Chicago IL 60611
Ph: 312-440-2660 ▪ Fx: 312-440-2824
scdonline.org

Special Education, American Council on Rural
Utah State Univ 2865 Old Main Hill   Logan UT 84322
Ph: 435-797-3911
extension.usu.edu/acres

Special Education Centers, National Association of Private
1522 K St NW Suite 1032   Washington DC 20005
Ph: 202-408-3338 ▪ Fx: 202-408-3340
www.napsec.org

Special Education, Council of Administrators of
Fort Valley State Univ 1005 State University Dr   Fort Valley GA 31030
Ph: 478-825-7667 ▪ Fx: 478-825-7811
www.casecec.org

Special Education, National Association of State Directors of
1800 Diagonal Rd Suite 320   Alexandria VA 22314
Ph: 703-519-3800 ▪ Fx: 703-519-3808
www.nasdse.org

Special Events Society, International
401 N Michigan Ave   Chicago IL 60611
Ph: 312-312-6853 ▪ Fx: 312-673-6953 ▪ TF: 800-688-4737
www.ises.com

Special Investigation Units, International Association of
8015 Corporate Dr Suite A   Baltimore MD 21236
Ph: 410-931-3332 ▪ Fx: 410-931-2060
www.iasiu.com

Special Learning Needs, National Association for Adults With
c/o Correctional Education Assn 4380 Forbes Blvd   Lanham MD 20706
Ph: 800-496-9222
www.naasln.org

Special Libraries Association
1700 18th St NW   Washington DC 20009
Ph: 202-234-4700 ▪ Fx: 202-265-9317
www.sla.org

Special Libraries & Information Services, Canadian Association of   328 Frank St   Ottawa ON K2P0X8
Ph: 613-232-9625 ▪ Fx: 613-563-9895
www.cla.ca/caslis/index.htm

Special Military Active Retired Travel Club
600 University Office Blvd Suite 1A   Pensacola FL 32504
Ph: 800-354-7681
www.smartrving.net

(Special Needs) Elwyn Inc
111 Elwyn Rd   Elwyn PA 19063
Ph: 610-891-2000 ▪ Fx: 610-891-2458
www.elwyn.org

Special Needs, Federation for Children with
1135 Tremont St Suite 420   Boston MA 02120
Ph: 617-236-7210 ▪ Fx: 617-572-2094 ▪ TF: 800-331-0688
www.fcsn.org

Special Needs State Administrators, National Association of
c/o Illinois State Board of Education 100 N 1st St Suite C-421   Springfield IL 62777
Ph: 217-782-3370 ▪ Fx: 217-782-9224

Special Olympics Inc
1325 G St NW Suite 500   Washington DC 20005
Ph: 202-628-3630 ▪ Fx: 202-824-0200
www.specialolympics.org

Special Tooling & Machining Association, International
9300 Livingston Rd   Fort Washington MD 20744
Ph: 301-248-6200 ▪ Fx: 301-248-7104 ▪ TF: 800-248-6862

Special Wish Foundation Inc
5340 E Main St Suite 208   Columbus OH 43213
Ph: 614-575-9474 ▪ Fx: 614-575-1866 ▪ TF: 800-486-9474
www.spwish.org

Specialists Inc, American Association of Physician
2296 Henderson Mill Rd Suite 206   Atlanta GA 30345
Ph: 770-939-8555 ▪ Fx: 770-939-8559 ▪ TF: 800-447-9397
www.aapsga.org

Specialists in Group Work, Association for   www.asgw.org
Texas A&M Commerce Dept of Counseling 202 Education
    N   Commerce TX 75429
Ph: 903-886-5630 ▪ Fx: 903-886-5780

Specialized Carriers & Rigging Association   www.scranet.org
2750 Prosperity Ave Suite 620   Fairfax VA 22031
Ph: 703-698-0291 ▪ Fx: 703-698-0297

Specialized Court Judges, National Conference of   www.abanet.org/jd/ncscj
541 N Fairbanks Ct MS 13.2   Chicago IL 60611
Ph: 312-988-5705 ▪ Fx: 312-988-5709

Specialty Coffee Association of America   www.scaa.org
330 Golden Shore Suite 50   Long Beach CA 90802
Ph: 562-624-4100 ▪ Fx: 562-624-4101

Specialty Contractors, Associated   www.assoc-spec-con.org
3 Bethesda Metro Ctr Suite 1100   Bethesda MD 20814
Ph: 301-657-3110 ▪ Fx: 301-215-4500

Specialty Cut Flower Growers, Association of   www.ascfg.org
PO Box 268   Oberlin OH 44074
Ph: 440-774-2887 ▪ Fx: 440-774-2435

Specialty Equipment Market Association   www.sema.org
1575 S Valley Vista Dr   Diamond Bar CA 91765
Ph: 909-396-0289 ▪ Fx: 909-860-0184

Specialty Food Trade Inc, National Association   www.specialtyfoodmarket.com
for the   120 Wall St 27th Fl   New York NY 10005
Ph: 212-482-6440 ▪ Fx: 212-482-6459 ▪ TF: 800-627-3869

Specialty Gift Association, National   www.nsgaonline.com
7238 Bucks Ford Dr   Riverview FL 33569
Ph: 813-671-4757 ▪ Fx: 813-677-5075

Specialty Graphic Imaging Association   www.sgia.org
10015 Main St   Fairfax VA 22031
Ph: 703-385-1335 ▪ Fx: 703-273-0456

Specialty Sports Association, US   www.usssa.com
3935 S Crater Rd   Petersburg VA 23805
Ph: 804-732-4099 ▪ Fx: 804-732-1704 ▪ TF: 800-635-0468

Specialty Tobacco Council Inc
204 Northgate Park Dr   Winston-Salem NC 27106
Ph: 336-759-0391 ▪ Fx: 336-759-0965

Specialty Tools & Fasteners Distributors Association   www.stafda.org
PO Box 44   Elm Grove WI 53122
Ph: 262-784-4774 ▪ Fx: 262-784-5059 ▪ TF: 800-352-2981

Specialty Toy Retailing Association, American   www.astratoy.org
4700 W Lake Ave   Glenview IL 60025
Ph: 847-375-4727 ▪ Fx: 888-840-2650

Specialty Vehicle Institute of America   www.atvsafety.org
2 Jenner St Suite 150   Irvine CA 92618
Ph: 949-727-3727 ▪ Fx: 949-727-4216 ▪ TF: 800-887-2887

Spectroscopy Societies, Federation of Analytical Chemistry &   www.facss.org
PO Box 24379   Sante Fe NM 87502
Ph: 505-820-1648 ▪ Fx: 505-989-1073

Spectroscopy, Society for Applied   www.s-a-s.org
201B Broadway St   Frederick MD 21701
Ph: 301-694-8122 ▪ Fx: 301-694-6860

Spectroscopy, Society for Luminescence   www.ruf.rice.edu/~jinnys/slms/SLMS.html
Microscopy &

Speech Association, National Cued   www.cuedspeech.org
23970 Hermitage Rd   Cleveland OH 44122
Ph: 216-292-6213 ▪ TF: 800-459-3529

Speech Debate & Theatre Association, NFHS   www.nfhs.org/sdta.htm
PO Box 690   Indianapolis IN 46206
Ph: 317-972-6900 ▪ Fx: 317-822-5700

Speech-Language-Hearing Association, American   www.asha.org
10801 Rockville Pike   Rockville MD 20852
Ph: 301-897-5700 ▪ Fx: 301-571-0457 ▪ TF: 800-498-2071

Speech Language Hearing Association, National Student   www.nsslha.org
10801 Rockville Pike   Rockville MD 20852
Ph: 301-897-5700 ▪ Fx: 301-571-0481 ▪ TF: 800-498-2071

Speedskating, US   www.usspeedskating.org
PO Box 450639   Westlake OH 44145
Ph: 440-899-0128 ▪ Fx: 440-899-0109

Speleological Society, National   www.caves.org
2813 Cave Ave   Huntsville AL 35810
Ph: 256-852-1300 ▪ Fx: 256-851-9241

Spencer Foundation   www.spencer.org
875 N Michigan Ave Suite 3930   Chicago IL 60611
Ph: 312-337-7000 ▪ Fx: 312-337-0282

Spice Trade Association, American   www.astaspice.org
2025 M St NW Suite 800   Washington DC 20036
Ph: 202-367-1127 ▪ Fx: 202-367-2127

SPIE - International Society for Optical Engineering   www.spie.org
1000 20th St   Bellingham WA 98225
Ph: 360-676-3290 ▪ Fx: 360-647-1445

Spill Control Association of America   www.scaa-spill.org
8631 W Jefferson Ave   Detroit MI 48209
Ph: 313-849-2649 ▪ Fx: 313-849-1623

Spina Bifida Association of America   www.sbaa.org
4590 MacArthur Blvd NW Suite 250   Washington DC 20007
Ph: 202-944-3285 ▪ Fx: 202-944-3295 ▪ TF: 800-621-3141

Spinal Cord Injury Association, National   www.spinalcord.org
6701 Democracy Blvd Suite 300-9   Bethesda MD 20817
Ph: 800-962-9629 ▪ Fx: 301-564-9619

Spinal Cord Injury Psychologists & Social Workers, American   www.aascipsw.org
Association of   75-20 Astoria Blvd   Jackson Heights NY
    11370
Ph: 718-803-3782 ▪ Fx: 718-803-0414

Spinal Cord Society   members.aol.com/scsweb
19051 County Hwy 1   Fergus Falls MN 56537
Ph: 218-739-5252 ▪ Fx: 218-739-5262

Spinal Injury Association, American   www.asia-spinalinjury.org
345 E Superior St Suite 1436   Chicago IL 60611
Ph: 312-238-1242 ▪ Fx: 312-238-0869

Spine Radiology, American Society of   www.theassr.org
2210 Midwest Rd Suite 207   Oak Brook IL 60523
Ph: 630-574-0220 ▪ Fx: 630-574-0661

Spine Research Society, Cervical   www.csrs.org
6300 N River Rd Suite 727   Rosemont IL 60018
Ph: 847-698-1628 ▪ Fx: 847-823-0536

Spine Society, North American   www.spine.org
22 Calendar Ct 2nd Fl   La Grange IL 60525
Ph: 708-588-8080 ▪ Fx: 708-588-1080 ▪ TF: 877-774-6337

Spine Sports & Occupational Rehabilitation, Physiatric   www.aapmr.org/passor.htm
Association of   1 IBM Plaza Suite 2500   Chicago IL 60611
Ph: 312-464-9700 ▪ Fx: 312-464-0227

Spinners Association, Northwest Regional   www.nwrsa.org
12410 9th Dr SE   Everett WA 98208
Ph: 425-385-2138

Spirits Council of the US Inc, Distilled   www.discus.org
1250 'I' St NW Suite 400   Washington DC 20005
Ph: 202-628-3544 ▪ Fx: 202-682-8888 ▪ TF: 888-862-7597

Spiritual Alliance of the USA, National   www.thenationalspiritualallianceinc.org
2 Montague Ave PO Box 88   Lake Pleasant MA 01347
Ph: 413-367-0138

(Spiritual) Ananda Marga New York Sector   www.anandamarga.org
97-38 42nd Ave Suite 1F   Corona NY 11368
Ph: 718-898-1603 ▪ Fx: 718-898-1604

Spiritual Assembly of the Baha'is of the US, National   www.us.bahai.org
1233 Central St   Evanston IL 60201
Ph: 847-869-9039 ▪ TF: 800-999-9019

Spiritual Counterfeits Project   www.scp-inc.org
PO Box 4308   Berkeley CA 94704
Ph: 510-540-0300 ▪ Fx: 510-540-1107

Spiritual & Ethical Education, Council for   www.csee.org
1465 Northside Dr Suite 220   Atlanta GA 30318
Ph: 404-355-4460 ▪ Fx: 404-355-4435 ▪ TF: 800-298-4599

Spiritual Ethical & Religious Values in Counseling, Association for   www.aservic.org
c/o American Counseling Assn 5999 Stevenson Ave   Alexandria
    VA 22304
Ph: 703-823-9800 ▪ Fx: 703-823-0252 ▪ TF: 800-347-6647

(Spiritual) Huna Research Inc   www.huna-research.com
1760 Anna St   Cape Girardeau MO 63701
Ph: 573-334-3478

Spiritual Life Institute of America   www.spirituallifeinstitute.org
PO Box 219   Crestone CO 81131
Ph: 719-256-4778 ▪ Fx: 719-256-4719

(Spiritual) Mandala Society   www.year2020vision.net/mandala.htm
PO Box 1233   Del Mar CA 92014
Ph: 858-481-7751

Spiritual Research, Quartus Foundation for   www.quartus.org
PO Box 1768   Boerne TX 78006
Ph: 830-249-3985 ▪ Fx: 830-249-3318

(Spiritual) Rosicrucian Order AMORC   www.rosicrucian.org
1342 Naglee Ave   San Jose CA 95191
Ph: 408-947-3600 ▪ Fx: 408-947-3677

(Spiritual) Seat of the Soul Foundation   www.seatofthesoul.org
1257 Siskiyou Blvd Suite 57   Ashland OR 97520
Ph: 541-482-8999 ▪ Fx: 541-482-9176 ▪ TF: 888-440-7685

(Spiritual) Sri Aurobindo Association of America   www.collaboration.org
PO Box 163237   Sacramento CA 95816
Ph: 209-339-3710 ▪ Fx: 209-339-3715

(Spiritual) Stelle Group   www.thestellegroup.org
127 Sun St   Stelle IL 60919
Ph: 815-256-2200 ▪ Fx: 815-256-2220

(Spiritual) SUBUD USA   www.subudusa.org
14019 NE 8th St Suite A   Bellevue WA 98007
Ph: 425-643-1904 ▪ Fx: 425-643-2725

(Spiritual) Teleos Institute   www.consciousnesswork.com
7119 E Shea Blvd Suite 109 PMB 418   Scottsdale AZ 85254
Ph: 480-948-1800 ▪ Fx: 480-948-1870

Spiritual Unity of Nations   www.spiritualunityofnations.org
PO Box 9553   Wyoming MI 49509
Ph: 616-531-1339 ▪ Fx: 616-531-2294 ▪ TF: 800-704-2324

(Spiritualism) Morris Pratt Institute   www.morrispratt.org
11811 Watertown Plank Rd   Milwaukee WI 53226
Ph: 414-774-2994 ▪ Fx: 414-774-2964

Spiritualist Association of Churches, National   www.nsac.org
PO Box 217   Lily Dale NY 14752
Ph: 716-595-2000 ▪ Fx: 716-595-2020

(Spirituality) Supreme Master Ching Hai International Association   www.chinghai.com
PO Box 730247   San Jose CA 95173
Ph: 408-998-2342

Spondylitis Association of America   www.spondylitis.org
14827 Ventura Blvd Suite 222 PO Box 5872   Sherman Oaks CA
    91403
Ph: 818-981-1616 ▪ TF: 800-777-8189

Spoon Collectors, American   www.campanian.org/americanspoon.html
PO Box 243   Rhinecliff NY 12574
Ph: 845-876-0303 ▪ Fx: 845-876-2037

Sport & Dance, International Council for Health Physical   www.ichpersd.org
Education Recreation   1900 Association Dr   Reston VA
    20191
Ph: 703-476-3462 ▪ Fx: 703-476-9527 ▪ TF: 800-213-7193

Sport Fishing Council, Great Lakes   www.great-lakes.org
PO Box 297   Elmhurst IL 60126
Ph: 630-941-1351 ▪ Fx: 630-941-1196

Sport History, North American Society for   www.nassh.org
PO Box 1026   Lemont PA 16851
Ph: 814-238-1288

Sport Horse Association, Appaloosa   www.appaloosasport.com
3380 Saxonburg Blvd   Glenshaw PA 15116
Ph: 412-767-4616

Sport Horse Guild, American Warmblood &
PO Box 5512   Grants Pass OR 97527
Ph: 541-855-8942

Sport Hunting, Committee to Abolish   www.all-creatures.org/cash
PO Box 562   New Paltz NY 12561
Ph: 845-255-4227 ▪ Fx: 845-256-9113

Sport Institute, North American Youth   www.naysi.com
4985 Oak Garden Dr   Kernersville NC 27284
Ph: 336-784-4926 ▪ Fx: 336-784-5546 ▪ TF: 800-767-4916

Sport Management, North American Society for   www.nassm.org
Slippery Rock Univ NASSM Business Office West Gym
   014   Slippery Rock PA 16057
Ph: 724-738-4812 ▪ Fx: 724-738-4858

Sport Medicine, Canadian Academy of   www.casm-acms.org
1010 Polytek St Unit 14   Suite 100   Ottawa ON K1J9H9
Ph: 613-748-5851 ▪ Fx: 613-748-5792 ▪ TF: 877-585-2394

Sport, National Association for Girls & Women in   www.aahperd.org
1900 Association Dr   Reston VA 20191
Ph: 703-476-3400 ▪ Fx: 703-476-4566 ▪ TF: 800-213-7193

Sport, North American Society for the   www.uwm.edu/~aycock/nasss/nasss.html
   Sociology of   Bowling Green State Univ Dept of
   Sociology   Bowling Green OH 43403
Ph: 419-372-8306 ▪ Fx: 419-372-8360

Sport & Physical Activity, North American Society for   www.naspspa.org
the Psychology of   Univ of Nevada Dept of Kinesiology 4505
   Maryland Pkwy   Las Vegas NV 89154
Ph: 702-895-0938

Sport & Physical Education, National Association for   www.aahperd.org
1900 Association Dr   Reston VA 20191
Ph: 703-476-3410 ▪ Fx: 703-476-8316 ▪ TF: 800-213-7193

Sport Psychology, Association for the Advancement of Applied   www.aaasponline.org
801 Main St Suite 010   Louisville CO 80027
Ph: 303-494-5931

Sport Touring Rider's Association, American
PO Box 672015   Marietta GA 30006
Ph: 770-222-0380

Sportfishing Association, American   www.asafishing.org
225 Reinekers Ln Suite 420   Alexandria VA 22314
Ph: 703-519-9691 ▪ Fx: 703-519-1872

Sportfishing Association PAC, American   www.asafishing.org
225 Reinekers Ln Suite 420   Alexandria VA 22314
Ph: 703-519-9691 ▪ Fx: 703-519-1872

Sporthorse Registry, International   www.isroldenburg.org
939 Merchandise Mart   Chicago IL 60654
Ph: 312-527-6544 ▪ Fx: 312-527-6573

Sporting Clays Association, National   www.mynsca.com
5931 Roft Rd   San Antonio TX 78253
Ph: 210-688-3371 ▪ Fx: 210-688-3014 ▪ TF: 800-877-5338

Sporting Goods Agents Association   www.r-sports.com/SGAA
PO Box 998   Morton Grove IL 60053
Ph: 847-296-3670 ▪ Fx: 847-827-0196

Sporting Goods Association, National   www.nsga.org
1601 Feehanville Dr Suite 300   Mount Prospect IL 60056
Ph: 847-296-6742 ▪ Fx: 847-391-9827

Sporting Goods Shippers Association   www.sgsa.net
9237 Dove Ct   Gilroy CA 95020
Ph: 408-846-9592 ▪ Fx: 408-846-9213

Sporting Goods Wholesalers, National Association of   www.nasgw.org
400 E Randolph St Suite 700   Chicago IL 60601
Ph: 312-565-0233 ▪ Fx: 312-565-2654

Sports Academy, US   www.ussa.edu
1 Academy Dr   Daphne AL 36526
Ph: 251-626-3303 ▪ Fx: 251-625-1035 ▪ TF: 800-223-2668

Sports Alliance, National Disability   www.ndsaonline.org
25 W Independence Way   Kingston RI 02881
Ph: 401-792-7130 ▪ Fx: 401-792-7132

Sports Ambassadors Program, People to People   www.sportsambassadors.org
110 S Ferrall St   Spokane WA 99202
Ph: 509-534-0430 ▪ Fx: 509-534-5245

Sports Association, Adaptive   www.asadurango.org
PO Box 1884   Durango CO 81302
Ph: 970-259-0374 ▪ Fx: 970-259-2175

Sports Association, Diabetes Exercise &   www.diabetes-exercise.org
8001 Montcastle Dr   Nashville TN 37221
Ph: 800-898-4322

Sports Association, National Intramural-Recreational   www.nirsa.org
4185 SW Research Way   Corvallis OR 97333
Ph: 541-766-8211 ▪ Fx: 541-766-8284

Sports Association, US Specialty   www.usssa.com
3935 S Crater Rd   Petersburg VA 23805
Ph: 804-732-4099 ▪ Fx: 804-732-1704 ▪ TF: 800-635-0468

Sports Car Club of America   www.scca.com
PO Box 19400   Topeka KS 66619
Ph: 785-357-7222 ▪ Fx: 785-232-7228 ▪ TF: 800-770-2055

Sports Cardiovascular & Wellness Nutritionists   www.scandpg.org
PO Box 60820   Colorado Springs CO 80960
Ph: 719-635-6005 ▪ Fx: 719-635-3587

Sports Coaches Association, National Youth   www.nays.org
2050 Vista Pkwy   West Palm Beach FL 33411
Ph: 561-684-1141 ▪ Fx: 561-684-2546 ▪ TF: 800-729-2057

Sports, Coalition of Americans to Protect
200 Castlewood Dr   North Palm Beach FL 33408
Ph: 561-842-4225 ▪ Fx: 561-863-8984

Sports Dentistry, International Academy for   www.acadsportsdent.org
118 Faye St   Farmersville IL 62533
Ph: 217-227-3431 ▪ Fx: 217-227-3438 ▪ TF: 800-273-1788

Sports Federation, USA Deaf   www.usadsf.org
102 N Krohn Pl   Sioux Falls SD 57103
Ph: 605-367-5760 ▪ Fx: 605-367-5958

Sports Field Contractors Association
1027 S 3rd St   Council Bluffs IA 51503
Ph: 712-366-2669 ▪ Fx: 712-366-9119

Sports Foundation, National Shooting   www.nssf.org
11 Mile Hill Rd   Newtown CT 06470
Ph: 203-426-1320 ▪ Fx: 203-426-1087

Sports Foundation, Women's   www.womenssportsfoundation.org
Eisenhower Pk   East Meadow NY 11554
Ph: 516-542-4700 ▪ Fx: 516-542-4716 ▪ TF: 800-227-3988

Sports Information Directors of America, College   www.cosida.com
202 Tudor Rd   Ithaca NY 14850
Ph: 607-273-5891

Sports Injuries & Physical Fitness, American Chiropractic   www.acasc.org
Association Council on   PO Box 400 380 Wright Rd   Norwalk
   IA 52011
Ph: 515-981-9340 ▪ Fx: 515-981-9427 ▪ TF: 800-261-1495

Sports Institute, American   www.amersports.org
PO Box 1837   Mill Valley CA 94942
Ph: 415-383-5750 ▪ Fx: 415-383-5785

Sports, International Association of   www.rit.edu/~pjr0120/csa/iapaas/main.html
Physical Activity Aging &   706 Madison Ave   Albany NY
   12208
Ph: 518-465-6927 ▪ Fx: 518-462-1339

Sports for Israel, Maccabi USA/   www.maccabiusa.com
1926 Arch St Suite 4R   Philadelphia PA 19103
Ph: 215-561-6900 ▪ Fx: 215-561-5470

Sports Lawyers Association, Black Entertainment &   www.besla.org
PO Box 441485   Fort Washington MD 20749
Ph: 301-248-1818 ▪ Fx: 301-248-0700

Sports Massage Federation, US
2156 Newport Blvd   Costa Mesa CA 92627
Ph: 949-642-0735 ▪ Fx: 949-642-1729

Sports Media, Association for Women in   www.awsmonline.org

Sports Medicine, American Academy of Podiatric   www.aapsm.org
PO Box 723   Rockville MD 20848
Ph: 301-845-9887 ▪ Fx: 301-845-9888 ▪ TF: 800-438-3338

Sports Medicine, American College of   www.acsm.org
401 W Michigan St   Indianapolis IN 46206
Ph: 317-637-9200 ▪ Fx: 317-634-7817

Sports Medicine, American Medical Society for   www.amssm.org
11639 Earnshaw St   Overland Park KS 66210
Ph: 913-327-1415 ▪ Fx: 913-327-1491

Sports Medicine, American Orthopaedic Society for   www.sportsmed.org
6300 N River Rd Suite 500   Rosemont IL 60018
Ph: 847-292-4900 ▪ Fx: 847-292-4905 ▪ TF: 877-321-3500

Sports Medicine, American Osteopathic Academy of   www.aoasm.org
7600 Terrace Ave Suite 203   Middleton WI 53562
Ph: 608-831-4400 ▪ Fx: 608-831-5185

Sports Museums & Halls of Fame, International Association of   www.sportshalls.com
180 N LaSalle St Suite 1822   Chicago IL 60601
Ph: 312-551-0810 ▪ Fx: 312-551-0815

Sports, National Alliance for Youth   www.nays.org
2050 Vista Pkwy   West Palm Beach FL 33411
Ph: 561-684-1141 ▪ Fx: 561-684-2546 ▪ TF: 800-729-2057

Sports, National Council of Youth   www.ncys.org
7185 SE Seagate Ln   Stuart FL 34997
Ph: 772-781-1452 ▪ Fx: 772-781-7298

Sports & Occupational Rehabilitation, Physiatric   www.aapmr.org/passor.htm
Association of Spine   1 IBM Plaza Suite 2500   Chicago IL
   60611
Ph: 312-464-9700 ▪ Fx: 312-464-0227

Sports Officials, National Association of   www.naso.org
2017 Lathrop Ave   Racine WI 53405
Ph: 262-632-5448 ▪ Fx: 262-632-5460 ▪ TF: 800-733-6100

Sports Physicians, American Academy of
17445 Oak Creek Ct   Encino CA 91316
Ph: 818-501-4433 ▪ Fx: 818-501-8855

Sports Safety Foundation, National Youth   www.nyssf.org
1 Beacon St Suite 3333   Boston MA 02108
Ph: 617-367-6677 ▪ Fx: 617-722-9999

Sports Sciences Association, International   www.issaonline.com
400 E Gutierrez St   Santa Barbara CA 93101
Ph: 805-884-8111 ▪ Fx: 805-884-8119 ▪ TF: 800-892-4772

(Sports) SGMA International   www.sgma.com
200 Castlewood Dr   North Palm Beach FL 33408
Ph: 561-842-4100 ▪ Fx: 561-863-8984

Sports Turf Managers Association   www.sportsturfmanager.com
1027 S 3rd St   Council Bluffs IA 51503
Ph: 712-322-7862 ▪ Fx: 712-366-9119 ▪ TF: 800-323-3875

Sports USA, Disabled   www.dsusa.org
451 Hungerford Dr Suite 100   Rockville MD 20850
Ph: 301-217-0960 ▪ Fx: 301-217-0968

Sports USA, Wheelchair   www.wsusa.org
10 Lake Cir Suite G19   Colorado Springs CO 80906
Ph: 719-574-1150 ▪ Fx: 719-574-9840

Sportscar Vintage Racing Association   www.svra.com
257 Dekalb Industrial Way   Decatur GA 30030
Ph: 404-298-3323 ▪ Fx: 404-298-3325

Sportscasters Association, American   www.americansportscasters.com
225 Broadway Suite 2030   New York NY 10007
Ph: 212-227-8080 ▪ Fx: 212-571-0556

Sportsclub Association, International Health Racquet &   www.ihrsa.org
263 Summer St   Boston MA 02210
Ph: 617-951-0055 ▪ Fx: 617-951-0056 ▪ TF: 800-228-4772

Sportsmen's Foundation, Congressional   www.sportsmenslink.org
110 North Carolina Ave SE   Washington DC 20003
Ph: 202-543-6850 ▪ Fx: 202-543-6853

Sportsmen's Alliance, US   www.ussportsmen.org
801 Kingsmill Pkwy   Columbus OH 43229
Ph: 614-888-4868 ▪ Fx: 614-888-0326

Sportsmen's Association of North America, United　www.usanamtc.com
224 Sandbridge Rd　Pittsgrove NJ 08318
Ph: 856-358-4891

Sportsplex Operators & Developers Association　www.sportsplexoperators.com
PO Box 24617　Rochester NY 14624
Ph: 585-426-2215　Fx: 585-247-3112

Sportswriters & Broadcasters, National Association of African-American　308A Deer Park Ave　Dix Hills NY 11746
Ph: 631-462-3933

Spotted Asses, American Council of　www.spottedass.com
PO Box 121　New Melle MO 63365
Ph: 636-828-5430　Fx: 636-828-5431

Spotted Horse Registry Association, International　members.tripod.com/~spottedhorses
PO Box 412　Anderson MO 64831
Ph: 417-475-6273　TF: 866-201-3098

Spotted Saddle Horse Association, National　www.nssha.com
108 N Spring St PO Box 898　Murfreesboro TN 37133
Ph: 615-890-2864

Spotted Swine Record, National
PO Box 9758　Peoria IL 61612
Ph: 309-693-1804　Fx: 309-691-0168

Spouse Foundation, Well　www.wellspouse.org
63 W Main St Suite H　Freehold NJ 07728
Ph: 732-577-8899　Fx: 732-577-8644　TF: 800-838-0879

Spray Manufacturers, Association of Defensive　www.pepperspray.org
917 Locust St Suite 1100　Saint Louis MO 63101
Ph: 314-241-1445　Fx: 314-241-1449

Spring of Living Water Ministry　www.emmanuel-baptist.org/SpringLivingWater.htm
403 S Grant St　Enid OK 73703
Ph: 580-233-9345

Spring Manufacturers Institute　www.smihq.org
2001 Midwest Rd Suite 106　Oak Brook IL 60523
Ph: 630-495-8588　Fx: 630-495-8595

Spring Research Institute　www.springresearch.com
3034 N Fleming Cir　Shelbyville IN 46176
Ph: 317-398-3822　Fx: 317-392-6997

Springer Rescue America Inc, English　www.springerrescue.com
2721 Walker Lee Rd　Los Alamitos CA 90720
Ph: 800-921-1047

Sprout Growers Association, International　www.isga-sprouts.org
2150 N 107th St Suite 205　Seattle WA 98133
Ph: 206-367-8704

SPRY Foundation　www.spry.org
10 G St NE Suite 600　Washington DC 20002
Ph: 202-216-0401　Fx: 202-216-0779

SQL Server, Professional Association for　www.sqlpass.org
401 N Michigan Ave　Chicago IL 60611
Ph: 312-527-6742　Fx: 312-245-1081

Square Dance Callers, Callerlab - International Association of　www.callerlab.org
467 Forrest Ave Suite 118　Cocoa FL 32922
Ph: 321-639-0039　Fx: 321-639-0851

Square Dance Clubs, International Association of Gay　www.iagsdc.org
PO Box 87507　San Diego CA 92138
Ph: 800-835-6462

(Square Dancing) LEGACY　www.legacyonline.org
PO Box 37　Lower Waterford VT 05848
Ph: 802-748-8538　Fx: 802-748-4742

Squash Racquets Association, US　www.us-squash.org/squash
PO Box 1216　Bala Cynwyd PA 19004
Ph: 610-667-4006　Fx: 610-667-6539

Sri Aurobindo Association of America　www.collaboration.org
PO Box 163237　Sacramento CA 95816
Ph: 209-339-3710　Fx: 209-339-3715

SSPC: Society for Protective Coatings　www.sspc.org
40 24th St　Pittsburgh PA 15222
Ph: 412-281-2331　Fx: 412-281-9995

Stable Value Investment Association　www.stablevalue.org
2121 K St NW Suite 800　Washington DC 20037
Ph: 202-261-6530　Fx: 202-261-6527　TF: 800-327-2270

Staff Development Council, National　www.nsdc.org
PO Box 240　Oxford OH 45056
Ph: 513-523-6029　Fx: 513-523-0638　TF: 800-727-7288

Staffing Association, American　www.staffingtoday.net
277 S Washington St Suite 200　Alexandria VA 22314
Ph: 703-253-2020　Fx: 703-253-2053

Staffordshire Terrier Club of America　www.amstaff.org

Stage Directors & Choreographers, Society of　www.ssdc.org
1501 Broadway Suite 1701　New York NY 10036
Ph: 212-391-1070　Fx: 212-302-6195

Stained Glass Association of America　www.stainedglass.org
10009 E 62nd St　Raytown MO 64133
Ph: 816-737-2090　Fx: 816-737-2801　TF: 800-438-9581

Stamp Dealers Association Inc, American　www.asdaonline.com
3 School St Suite 205　Glen Cove NY 11542
Ph: 516-759-7000　Fx: 516-759-7014

Stamping & Embossing Association, Foil　www.fsea.com
536 NW Tyler Ct Suite 204　Topeka KS 66608
Ph: 785-232-8776　Fx: 785-232-8747

Stamps, Collectors of Religion on
425 N Linwood Ave Suite 110　Appleton WI 54914
Ph: 920-734-2417　Fx: 920-734-6711

Stamps Study Unit, Dogs on　www.dossu.org
202A Newport Rd　Monroe Township NJ 08831
Ph: 609-655-7411

Stamps Unit, Ships on　www.shipsonstamps.org

Stand For Children　www.astand.org
516 SE Morrison St Suite 206　Portland OR 97214
Ph: 503-235-2305　Fx: 503-963-9517　TF: 800-663-4032

Standardbred Retirement Foundation　www.adoptahorse.org
PO Box 763　Freehold NJ 07728
Ph: 732-462-8773　Fx: 732-431-9503

Standardization Society of the Valve & Fittings Industry Inc, Manufacturers　127 Park St NE　Vienna VA 22180　www.mss-hq.com
Ph: 703-281-6613　Fx: 703-281-6671

(Standards) ACORD　www.acord.org
PO Box 1529　Pearl River NY 10965
Ph: 845-620-1700　Fx: 845-620-3600　TF: 800-444-3341

Standards Association, Data Interchange　www.disa.org
7600 Leesburg Pike Suite 430　Falls Church VA 22043
Ph: 703-970-4480　Fx: 703-970-4488

Standards Association, Gaming　www.gamingstandards.com
39355 California St Suite 307　Fremont CA 94538
Ph: 510-744-4007

Standards Association, Video Electronics　www.vesa.org
920 Hillview Ct Suite 140　Milpitas CA 95035
Ph: 408-957-9270

(Standards) ASTM International　www.astm.org
100 Barr Harbor Dr PO Box C700　West Conshohocken PA 19428
Ph: 610-832-9500　Fx: 610-832-9555

Standards for Athletic Equipment, National Operating Committee on　www.nocsae.org
PO Box 12290　Overland Park KS 66282
Ph: 913-888-1340　Fx: 913-888-1065

Standards Board, Financial Accounting　www.fasb.org
401 Merritt 7 PO Box 5116　Norwalk CT 06856
Ph: 203-847-0700　Fx: 203-849-9714

Standards Inc, Certified Financial Planner Board of　www.cfp-board.org
1700 Broadway Suite 2100　Denver CO 80290
Ph: 303-830-7500　Fx: 303-860-7388　TF: 888-237-6275

Standards Engineering Society　www.ses-standards.org
13340 SW 96th Ave　Miami FL 33176
Ph: 305-971-4798　Fx: 305-971-4799

Standards Group, United Applications　www.uasg.org
PO Box 1435　Des Moines IA 50305
Ph: 515-289-4467　Fx: 515-289-4468

Standards in Higher Education, Council for the Advancement of　www.cas.edu
1 Dupont Cir NW Suite 300　Washington DC 20036
Ph: 202-862-1400　Fx: 202-296-3286

Standards Institute, American National　www.ansi.org
25 W 43rd St 4th Fl　New York NY 10036
Ph: 212-642-4900　Fx: 212-398-0023

Standards Institute, Friction Materials　www.fmsi.org
588 Monroe Tpke　Monroe CT 06468
Ph: 203-452-1877　Fx: 203-452-7951

Standards for International Educational Travel, Council on　www.csiet.org
212 S Henry St　Alexandria VA 22314
Ph: 703-739-9050　Fx: 703-739-9035

Standards, National Board for Professional Teaching　www.nbpts.org
1525 Wilson Blvd Suite 500　Arlington VA 22209
Ph: 703-465-2700

Standards, National Conference of States on Building Codes &　www.ncsbcs.org
505 Huntmar Park Dr Suite 210　Herndon VA 20170
Ph: 703-437-0100　Fx: 703-481-3596

Standards Organization, National Information　www.niso.org
4733 Bethesda Ave Suite 300　Bethesda MD 20814
Ph: 301-654-2512　Fx: 301-654-1721

(Standards) PSRC of America　www.psrc-of-america.org
200 Madison Ave Suite 2108　New York NY 10016
Ph: 212-686-9147　Fx: 212-779-9307

Standards & Research, MTM Association for　www.mtm.org
1111 E Touhy Ave Suite 280　Des Plaines IL 60018
Ph: 847-299-1111　Fx: 847-299-3509

(Standards) RTCA Inc　www.rtca.org
1828 L St NW Suite 805　Washington DC 20036
Ph: 202-833-9339　Fx: 202-833-9434

Standards & Traditions, Foundation for Academic
545 Madison Ave 4th Fl　New York NY 10022
Ph: 212-486-1711

(Standards) Uniform Code Council Inc　www.uc-council.org
1009 Lenox Dr Suite 202　Lawrenceville NJ 08648
Ph: 609-620-0200　Fx: 609-620-1200

Standing Conference of Canonical Orthodox Bishops in the Americas　www.scoba.us
8 E 79th St　New York NY 10021
Ph: 212-570-3500　Fx: 212-570-3569

Staple Nail & Tool Association, International　www.isanta.org
512 W Burlington Ave Suite 203　La Grange IL 60525
Ph: 708-482-8138　Fx: 708-482-8186

Star Class Yacht Racing Association, International　www.starclass.org
1545 Waukegan Rd　Glenview IL 60025
Ph: 847-729-0630　Fx: 847-729-0718

Star Observers, American Association of Variable　www.aavso.org
25 Birch St　Cambridge MA 02138
Ph: 617-354-0484　Fx: 617-354-0665　TF: 800-223-0138

Star Route Mail Contractors Association, National　www.starroutecontractors.org
324 E Capitol St　Washington DC 20003
Ph: 202-543-1661　Fx: 202-543-8863

Starlight Children's Foundation　www.starlight.org
5900 Wilshire Blvd Suite 2530　Los Angeles CA 90036
Ph: 323-634-0080　Fx: 323-634-0090　TF: 800-274-7827

Starr Foundation　fdncenter.org/grantmaker/starr
70 Pine St 14th Fl　New York NY 10270
Ph: 212-770-6883　Fx: 212-425-6261

Stars & Bars, Military Order of the　www.mosbihq.org
PO Box 59　Columbia TN 38402
Ph: 800-380-1896

State Administrators, National Association of Special Needs
c/o Illinois State Board of Education 100 N 1st St Suite C-421　Springfield IL 62777
Ph: 217-782-3370　Fx: 217-782-9224

State Administrators of Vocational Rehabilitation, Council of   www.rehabnetwork.org
4733 Bethesda Ave Suite 330 Bethesda MD 20814
Ph: 301-654-8414 ▪ Fx: 301-654-5542

State Agencies for the Blind, National Council of   www.ncsab.org
PO Box 25380 Washington DC 20027
Ph: 202-298-8468 ▪ Fx: 202-333-5881

State Agencies for Surplus Property, National Association of   nasasp.org
2221 Forster St Rm G-49 Harrisburg PA 17105
Ph: 717-787-9724 ▪ Fx: 717-772-2491

State, Americans United for Separation of Church &   www.au.org
518 C St NE Washington DC 20002
Ph: 202-466-3234 ▪ Fx: 202-466-2587 ▪ TF: 800-875-3707

State Archaeologists, National Association of   www.uiowa.edu/~osa/nasa

State Association Presidents, Council of   www.csap.org
800 Perry Hwy Suite 3 Pittsburgh PA 15229
Ph: 412-366-1177 ▪ Fx: 412-366-8804

State Bank Supervisors, Conference of   www.csbs.org
1015 18th St NW 11th Fl Washington DC 20036
Ph: 202-296-2840 ▪ Fx: 202-296-1928 ▪ TF: 800-886-2727

State Baptist Papers, Association of
c/o The Alabama Baptist Newspaper 3310 Independence
   Dr Birmingham AL 35209
Ph: 205-870-4720 ▪ Fx: 205-870-8957

State Boards, American Association of Veterinary   www.aavsb.org
4106 Central St Kansas City MO 64111
Ph: 816-931-1504 ▪ Fx: 816-931-1604 ▪ TF: 877-698-8482

State Boards of Cosmetology Inc, National-Interstate Council of   www.nictesting.org
7622 Briarwood Cir Little Rock AR 72205
Ph: 501-227-8262 ▪ Fx: 501-227-8212

State Boards of Geology, National Association of   www.asbog.org
PO Box 11591 Columbia SC 29211
Ph: 803-799-1047 ▪ Fx: 803-252-3432

State Boards of Physical Therapy, Federation of   www.fsbpt.org
509 Wythe St Alexandria VA 22314
Ph: 703-299-3100 ▪ Fx: 703-299-3110 ▪ TF: 800-881-1430

State Boating Law Administrators, National Association of   www.nasbla.org
1500 Leestown Rd Suite 330 Lexington KY 40511
Ph: 859-225-9487 ▪ Fx: 859-231-6403

State Capital Global Law Firm Group   www.statecapitallaw.org
1250 24th St NW Suite 700 Washington DC 20037
Ph: 202-659-6601 ▪ Fx: 202-659-6641

State Catholic Conference Directors, National Association of   www.nasccd.org
1042 Burlington Ln Frankfort KY 40601
Ph: 502-875-4345 ▪ Fx: 502-875-2841

State Certified Appraisers, American Academy of
1438 W Main St Ephrata PA 17522
Ph: 717-721-3500 ▪ Fx: 717-721-3515 ▪ TF: 800-640-7601

State Chief Administrators, National Association of   www.nasca.org
167 W Main St Suite 600 Lexington KY 40507
Ph: 859-231-1931 ▪ Fx: 859-514-9188

State Chief Information Officers, National Association of   www.nascio.org
167 W Main St Suite 600 Lexington KY 40507
Ph: 859-231-1971 ▪ Fx: 859-231-1928

State Climatologists, American Association of   www.ncdc.noaa.gov/oa/climate/aasc.html

State Colleges & Universities, American Association of   www.aascu.org
1307 New York Ave NW 5th Fl Washington DC 20005
Ph: 202-293-7070 ▪ Fx: 202-296-5819

State Community Development Agencies, Council of   www.coscda.org
1825 K St NW Suite 515 Washington DC 20006
Ph: 202-293-5820 ▪ Fx: 202-293-2820

State Community Services Programs, National Association for   www.nascsp.org
400 N Capitol St NW Washington DC 20001
Ph: 202-624-5866 ▪ Fx: 202-624-8472

State Controlled Substance Authorities, National Association of   www.nascsa.org
72 Brook St Quincy MA 02170
Ph: 617-472-0520 ▪ Fx: 617-472-0521

State Correctional Administrators, Association of   www.asca.net
213 Court St 6th Fl Middletown CT 06457
Ph: 860-704-6410 ▪ Fx: 860-704-6420

State County & Municipal Employees, American Federation of   www.afscme.org
1625 L St NW Washington DC 20036
Ph: 202-452-4800 ▪ Fx: 202-429-1293

State Court Administrators, Conference of   cosca.ncsc.dni.us
National Ctr for State Courts 300 Newport Ave PO Box
   8798 Williamsburg VA 23187
Ph: 757-259-1841 ▪ Fx: 757-259-1520 ▪ TF: 800-877-1233

State Courts, National Center for   www.ncsconline.org
300 Newport Ave Williamsburg VA 23185
Ph: 757-253-2000 ▪ Fx: 757-564-2022 ▪ TF: 800-616-6164

State Credit Union Supervisors, National Association of   www.nascus.org
1655 N Fort Myer Dr Suite 300 Arlington VA 22209
Ph: 703-528-8351 ▪ Fx: 703-528-3248

State Dam Safety Officials, Association of   www.damsafety.org
450 Old Vine Lexington KY 40507
Ph: 859-257-5140 ▪ Fx: 859-323-1958

State Democratic Chairs, Association of
430 S Capitol St SE Washington DC 20003
Ph: 202-479-5121 ▪ Fx: 202-479-5123

State Development Agencies, National Association of   www.nasda.com
12884 Harbor Dr Woodbridge VA 22192
Ph: 703-490-6777 ▪ Fx: 703-492-4404

State Directors of Career Technical Education Consortium, National Association of   www.careertech.org   444 N Capitol St NW Suite
   830 Washington DC 20001
Ph: 202-737-0303 ▪ Fx: 202-737-1106

State Directors of Community Colleges, National Council of   www.statedirectors.org
1 Dupont Cir NW Suite 410 Washington DC 20036
Ph: 202-728-0200 ▪ Fx: 202-833-2467

State Directors of Developmental Disabilities Services, National Association of   www.nasddds.org   113 Oronoco St Alexandria VA
   22314
Ph: 703-683-4202 ▪ Fx: 703-684-1395

State Directors of Teacher Education & Certification, National Association of   www.nasdtec.org   39 Nathan Ellis Hwy PMB
   134 Mashpee MA 02649
Ph: 508-539-8844 ▪ Fx: 508-539-8868

State Directors of Veterans Affairs, National Association of   www.nasdva.com

State Drinking Water Administrators, Association of   www.asdwa.org
1025 Connecticut Ave NW Suite 903 Washington DC 20036
Ph: 202-293-7655 ▪ Fx: 202-293-7656

State Education Associations, National Council of
1201 16th St NW Suite 817 Washington DC 20036
Ph: 202-822-7745 ▪ Fx: 202-822-7113

State Election Directors, National Association of   www.nased.org
Council of State Governments 444 N Capitol St NW Suite
   401 Washington DC 20001
Ph: 202-624-5460 ▪ Fx: 202-624-5452

State Emergency Medical Services Training Coordinators, National Council of   www.ncsemstc.org   201 Park Washington Ct Falls Church
   VA 22046
Ph: 703-538-1794 ▪ Fx: 703-241-5603

State Energy Officials, National Association of   www.naseo.org
1414 Prince St Suite 200 Alexandria VA 22314
Ph: 703-299-8800 ▪ Fx: 703-299-6208

State Executive Directors, Association of Osteopathic
2007 Apalachee Pkwy Tallahassee FL 32301
Ph: 850-878-7364 ▪ Fx: 850-942-7538

State Facilities Administrators, National Association of   www.nasfa.net
2760 Research Park Dr PO Box 11910 Lexington KY 40578
Ph: 859-244-8181 ▪ Fx: 859-244-8001

State Fleet Administrators, National Conference of   ncsfa.state.ut.us
PO Box 159 Litchfield Park AZ 85340
Ph: 623-772-9096 ▪ Fx: 623-772-9098

State Floodplain Managers, Association of   www.floods.org
2809 Fish Hatchery Rd Suite 04 Madison WI 53713
Ph: 608-274-0123 ▪ Fx: 608-274-0696

State Games, National Congress of   www.stategames.org
290 Roberts St East Hartford CT 06108
Ph: 860-528-4588 ▪ Fx: 860-291-8032

State Government Affairs Council   www.sgac.org
1255 23rd St NW Washington DC 20037
Ph: 202-728-0500 ▪ Fx: 202-833-3636

State Governments, Council of   www.csg.org
2760 Research Park Dr PO Box 11910 Lexington KY 40578
Ph: 859-244-8000 ▪ Fx: 859-244-8001 ▪ TF: 800-800-1910

State Guard Association of the US Inc   www.sgaus.org
PO Box 1416 Fayetteville GA 30214
Ph: 770-460-1215

State Higher Education Executive Officers   www.sheeo.org
700 Broadway Suite 1200 Denver CO 80203
Ph: 303-299-3685 ▪ Fx: 303-296-9016

State Highway & Transportation Officials, American Association of   www.aashto.org
444 N Capitol St NW Suite 249 Washington DC 20001
Ph: 202-624-5800 ▪ Fx: 202-624-5806

State Humanities Councils, Federation of   www.statehumanities.com
1600 Wilson Blvd Suite 902 Arlington VA 22209
Ph: 703-908-9700 ▪ Fx: 703-908-9706

State Land Reclamationists, National Association of   www.crc.siu.edu/naslr.htm
Southern Illinois Univ Coal Research Ctr Carbondale IL 62901
Ph: 618-536-5521

State Laws, National Conference of Commissioners on Uniform   www.nccusl.org
211 E Ontario St Suite 1300 Chicago IL 60611
Ph: 312-915-0195 ▪ Fx: 312-915-0187

State Legislators, National Black Caucus of   www.nbcsl.com
444 N Capitol St NW Suite 622 Washington DC 20001
Ph: 202-624-5457 ▪ Fx: 202-508-3826

State Legislatures, National Conference of   www.ncsl.org
7700 E 1st Pl Denver CO 80230
Ph: 303-364-7700 ▪ Fx: 303-364-7800

State Library Agencies, Chief Officers of   www.cosla.org
167 W Main St Suite 600 Lexington KY 40507
Ph: 859-514-9151 ▪ Fx: 859-514-9166

State Liquor Administrators, National Conference of   www.ncsla.org
8325 Horseshoe Dr Lincoln NE 68516
Ph: 402-486-1774

State & Local Government, Academy for
444 N Capitol St NW Suite 345 Washington DC 20001
Ph: 202-434-4850 ▪ Fx: 202-434-4851

State & Local Government, A Alfred Taubman Center for   www.ksg.harvard.edu/taubmancenter   Harvard Univ John F Kennedy School of
   Government 79 JFK St Cambridge MA 02138
Ph: 617-495-2199

State, National Association of Secretaries of   www.nass.org
444 N Capitol St NW Hall of States Suite 401 Washington DC
   20001
Ph: 202-624-3525 ▪ Fx: 202-624-3527

State Outdoor Recreation Liaison Officers, National Association of
3116 Woodbrook Pl Boise ID 83706
Ph: 208-384-5421

State Park Directors, National Association of   naspd.indstate.edu
9894 E Holden Pl Tucson AZ 85748
Ph: 520-298-4924 ▪ Fx: 520-298-6515

State Personnel Executives, National Association of   www.naspe.net
2760 Research Park Dr PO Box 11910 Lexington KY 40578
Ph: 859-244-8182 ▪ Fx: 859-244-8001

State Pharmacy Association Executives, National Council of
c/o Virginia Pharmacists Assn 5501 Patterson Ave Suite
200   Richmond VA 23226
Ph: 804-285-4145 ▪ Fx: 804-285-4227
www.ncspae.org

State Radio Networks, National Association of
www.statenets.com

State Retirement Administrators, National Association of
444 N Capitol St NW Suite 234   Washington DC 20001
Ph: 202-624-1417
www.nasra.org

State School Officers, Council of Chief
1 Massachusetts Ave NW Suite 700   Washington DC 20001
Ph: 202-408-5505 ▪ Fx: 202-408-8072
www.ccsso.org

State Science Supervisors, Council of
csss.enc.org

State Supervisors of Trade & Industrial Education,
National Association of
itednt.ited.uidaho.edu/nasstie

State Taxation, Council on
122 C St NW Suite 330   Washington DC 20001
Ph: 202-484-5222 ▪ Fx: 202-484-5229
www.statetax.org

State Telecommunications Directors, National Association of
2760 Research Park Dr PO Box 11910   Lexington KY 40578
Ph: 859-244-8186 ▪ Fx: 859-244-8001
www.nastd.org

State & Territorial AIDS Directors, National Alliance of
444 N Capitol St NW Suite 339   Washington DC 20001
Ph: 202-434-8090 ▪ Fx: 202-434-8092
www.nastad.org

State & Territorial Air Pollution Program Administrators
444 N Capitol St NW Suite 307   Washington DC 20001
Ph: 202-624-7864 ▪ Fx: 202-624-7863
www.cleanairworld.org

State & Territorial Chronic Disease Program Directors,
Association of   8201 Greensboro Dr Suite 300   McLean VA
22102
Ph: 703-610-9033 ▪ Fx: 703-610-9005
www.chronicdisease.org

State & Territorial Dental Directors, Association of
322 Cannondale Rd   Jefferson City MO 65109
Ph: 573-636-0453 ▪ Fx: 573-636-0454
www.astdd.org

State & Territorial Injury Prevention Directors' Association
2965 Flowers Rd S Suite 105   Atlanta GA 30341
Ph: 770-690-9000 ▪ Fx: 770-690-8996
www.stipda.org

State Treasurers, National Association of
2760 Research Park Dr PO Box 11910   Lexington KY 40578
Ph: 859-244-8175 ▪ Fx: 859-244-8053
www.nast.net

State Troopers Coalition Inc, National Black
PO Box 70059   Nashville TN 37207
Ph: 877-996-2782
www.nbstc.com

State Universities & Land Grant Colleges, National Association of
1307 New York Ave NW Suite 400   Washington DC 20005
Ph: 202-478-6040 ▪ Fx: 202-478-6046
www.nasulgc.org

Statesmen Foundation, Junior
400 S El Camino Real Suite 300   San Mateo CA 94402
Ph: 650-347-1600 ▪ Fx: 650-347-7200 ▪ TF: 800-334-5353
www.jsa.org/foundation

Statewide Preservation Organizations, National Alliance of
c/o Historic Landmarks Foundation of Indiana 340 W Michigan
St   Indianapolis IN 46202
Ph: 317-639-4534 ▪ TF: 800-450-4534

Stationery Manufacturers Association, Engraved
305 Plus Park Blvd   Nashville TN 37217
Ph: 615-366-1094 ▪ Fx: 615-366-4192

Statistical Association, American
1429 Duke St   Alexandria VA 22314
Ph: 703-684-1221 ▪ Fx: 703-684-2037 ▪ TF: 888-231-3473
www.amstat.org

Statistical Process Control Society
5908 Toole Dr Suite C   Knoxville TN 37919
Ph: 865-584-5005 ▪ Fx: 865-588-9440 ▪ TF: 800-545-8602
www.spcpress.com

Statistical Science in Economics, International Society of
536 Oasis Dr   Santa Rosa CA 95407
Ph: 707-575-3529

Statistical Sciences, National Institute of
19 T W Alexander Dr PO Box 14006   Research Triangle Park
NC 27709
Ph: 919-685-9300 ▪ Fx: 919-685-9310
www.niss.org

Statistics, American Bureau of Metal
PO Box 805   Chatham NJ 07928
Ph: 973-701-2299 ▪ Fx: 973-701-2152
www.abms.com

Statistics, Council of Professional Associations on Federal
1429 Duke St Suite 402   Alexandria VA 22314
Ph: 703-836-0404 ▪ Fx: 703-684-3410
www.copafs.org

Statistics & Information Systems, National Association for
Public Health   801 Roeder Rd Suite 650   Silver Spring MD
20910
Ph: 301-563-6001 ▪ Fx: 301-563-6012
www.naphsis.org

Statistics, National Center for Charitable
Urban Institute 2100 M St NW   Washington DC 20037
Ph: 202-833-7200 ▪ TF: 866-518-3874
nccsdataweb.urban.org

Statue of Liberty-Ellis Island Foundation
292 Madison Ave   New York NY 10017
Ph: 212-561-4500 ▪ Fx: 212-779-1990
www.ellisisland.org

Steam, International Association for the Properties of Water &
www.iapws.org

Steam Society, Northwest
PO Box 9639   Seattle WA 98109
Ph: 206-789-0287
www.northweststeamsociety.org

Steamers, International Brotherhood of Live
26062 Todd Ln   Los Altos Hills CA 94022
Ph: 650-948-8555

Steamship Historical Society of America
300 Ray Dr Suite 4   Providence RI 02906
Ph: 401-274-0805 ▪ Fx: 401-274-0836
www.sshsa.net

Steamtown Museum Association
350 Cliff St   Scranton PA 18503
Ph: 570-963-6590 ▪ Fx: 570-346-7093

Steel, American Institute for International
1325 G St NW Suite 980   Washington DC 20005
Ph: 202-628-3878 ▪ Fx: 202-737-3134
www.aiis.org

Steel Bar Institute, Cold Finished
201 Park Washington Ct   Falls Church VA 22046
Ph: 703-538-3543 ▪ Fx: 703-241-5603
www.cfsbi.com

Steel Construction, American Institute of
1 E Wacker Dr Suite 3100   Chicago IL 60601
Ph: 312-670-2400 ▪ Fx: 312-670-5403
www.aisc.org

Steel Contractors, National Association of Reinforcing
10382 Main St Suite 200 PO Box 280   Fairfax VA 22030
Ph: 703-591-1870 ▪ Fx: 703-591-1895
www.narsc.com

Steel Detailing, National Institute of
7700 Edgewater Dr Suite 670   Oakland CA 94621
Ph: 510-568-3741 ▪ Fx: 510-568-3781
www.nisd.com

Steel Distributors, Association of
401 N Michigan Ave   Chicago IL 60611
Ph: 312-644-6610 ▪ Fx: 312-527-6705
www.steeldistributors.org

Steel Door Institute
30200 Detroit Rd   Cleveland OH 44145
Ph: 440-899-0010 ▪ Fx: 440-892-1404
www.steeldoor.org

Steel Door Institute, Insulated
30200 Detroit Rd   Cleveland OH 44145
Ph: 440-899-0010 ▪ Fx: 440-892-1404
www.isdi.com

Steel Engineers, Association of Iron &
3 Gateway Ctr Suite 1900   Pittsburgh PA 15222
Ph: 412-281-6323 ▪ Fx: 412-281-4657 ▪ TF: 800-966-6323
www.aise.org

Steel Founders' Society of America
780 McArdle Dr Suite G   Crystal Lake IL 60014
Ph: 815-455-8240 ▪ Fx: 815-455-8241
www.sfsa.org

Steel Guitar Association, Pedal
PO Box 20248   Floral Park NY 11002
Ph: 516-616-9214
www.psga.org

Steel Institute, American Iron &
1140 Connecticut Ave NW Suite 705   Washington DC 20036
Ph: 202-452-7100 ▪ Fx: 202-463-6573
www.steel.org

Steel Institute, Concrete Reinforcing
933 N Plum Grove Rd   Schaumburg IL 60173
Ph: 847-517-1200 ▪ Fx: 847-517-1206
www.crsi.org

Steel Joist Institute
3127 10th Ave Ext N   Myrtle Beach SC 29577
Ph: 843-626-1995 ▪ Fx: 843-626-5565
www.steeljoist.org

Steel Manufacturers Association
1150 Connecticut Ave NW Suite 715   Washington DC 20036
Ph: 202-296-1515 ▪ Fx: 202-296-2506
www.steelnet.org

Steel Pipe Association, National Corrugated
13140 Coit Rd Suite 320 LB 120   Dallas TX 75240
Ph: 972-850-9107 ▪ Fx: 972-490-4219
www.ncspa.org

Steel Pipe Distributors, National Association of
14760 Memorial Dr Suite 302   Houston TX 77079
Ph: 281-531-7473 ▪ Fx: 281-531-7475
www.naspd.org

Steel Shipping Container Institute
1101 14th St NW Suite 1020   Washington DC 20005
Ph: 202-408-1900 ▪ Fx: 202-408-1972
www.steelcontainers.com

Steel Society, Iron &
186 Thorn Hill Rd   Warrendale PA 15086
Ph: 724-776-1535 ▪ Fx: 724-776-0430
www.issource.org

Steel Tank Institute
570 Oakwood Rd   Lake Zurich IL 60047
Ph: 847-438-8265 ▪ Fx: 847-438-8766 ▪ TF: 800-275-1300
www.steeltank.com

Steel Window Institute
1300 Sumner Ave   Cleveland OH 44115
Ph: 216-241-7333 ▪ Fx: 216-241-0105
www.steelwindows.com

Steelheaders, Association of Northwest
PO Box 22065   Milwaukie OR 97269
Ph: 503-653-4176 ▪ Fx: 503-653-8769
www.nwsteelheaders.org

Steelworkers of America PAC, United
5 Gateway Ctr   Pittsburgh PA 15222
Ph: 412-562-2400 ▪ Fx: 412-562-2445

Steelworkers of America Rubber/Plastics Industry Conference, United
5 Gateway Ctr 7th Fl   Pittsburgh PA 15222
Ph: 412-562-6971 ▪ Fx: 412-562-6963

Steelworkers of America, United
5 Gateway Ctr Rm 802   Pittsburgh PA 15222
Ph: 412-562-2400 ▪ Fx: 412-562-2445 ▪ TF: 800-248-8792
www.uswa.org

Steeplechase Association, National
400 Fair Hill Dr   Elkton MD 21921
Ph: 410-392-0700 ▪ Fx: 410-392-0706
www.nationalsteeplechase.com

STEER Inc
PO Box 1236   Bismarck ND 58502
Ph: 701-258-4911 ▪ Fx: 701-258-7684
www.steerinc.com

Stein Edith Guild
Church of Saint John the Baptist 210 W 31st St   New York NY
10001
Ph: 212-564-9070 ▪ Fx: 212-279-2823

Stelle Group
127 Sun St   Stelle IL 60919
Ph: 815-256-2200 ▪ Fx: 815-256-2220
www.thestellegroup.org

Stepfamily Association of America
650 J St Suite 205   Lincoln NE 68508
Ph: 402-477-7837 ▪ Fx: 402-477-8317 ▪ TF: 800-735-0329
www.saafamilies.org

Stepfamily Foundation
333 West End Ave Suite 11C   New York NY 10023
Ph: 212-877-3244 ▪ Fx: 212-362-7030 ▪ TF: 800-759-7837
www.stepfamily.org

Stereotactic & Functional Neurosurgery, American Society for
Presbyterian Hospital 200 Lothrop St Suite B-400   Pittsburgh
PA 15213
Ph: 412-647-6782 ▪ Fx: 412-647-5559

Sterilization Association, Ethylene Oxide
1815 H St NW Suite 500   Washington DC 20006
Ph: 202-296-6300 ▪ Fx: 202-775-5929
www.eosa.org

Steuben Society of America   steubensociety.org
6705 Fresh Pond Rd   Ridgewood NY 11385
Ph: 718-381-0900 ▪ Fx: 718-628-4874

Stewards of the Range   www.stewardsoftherange.org
PO Box 490   Meridian ID 83680
Ph: 208-855-0707 ▪ Fx: 208-855-0763

Stewardship Council, International Catholic   www.catholicstewardship.org
1275 K St NW Suite 980   Washington DC 20005
Ph: 202-289-1093 ▪ Fx: 202-682-9018

Stickler Involved People   www.sticklers.org
15 Angelina Dr   Augusta KS 67010
Ph: 316-775-2993

Still Bank Collectors Club of America   www.stillbankclub.com

Stitchers & Embroiderers Association, Pleaters
225 W 39th St   New York NY 10018
Ph: 212-398-5400 ▪ Fx: 212-398-3141

Stock Car Auto Racing, National Association for   www.nascar.com
1801 W International Speedway Blvd   Daytona Beach FL 32114
Ph: 386-253-0611 ▪ Fx: 386-947-6712

Stock Plan Professionals, National Association of   naspp.com
PO Box 21639   Concord CA 94521
Ph: 925-685-9271 ▪ Fx: 925-685-5402

Stone Industries, Allied   www.alliedstone.com
PO Box 5133   Kansas City KS 66119
Ph: 913-371-7757 ▪ Fx: 913-371-7764

Stone Institute, Building   www.buildingstone.org
PO Box 507   Purdys NY 10578
Ph: 914-232-5725 ▪ Fx: 914-232-5259

Stone Institute, Cast   www.caststone.org
10 W Kimball St   Winder GA 30680
Ph: 770-868-5909 ▪ Fx: 770-868-5910

Stone Sand & Gravel Association, National   www.nssga.org
1605 King St   Alexandria VA 22314
Ph: 703-525-8788 ▪ Fx: 703-525-7782 ▪ TF: 800-342-1415

Stonewall Democrats, National   www.stonewalldemocrats.org
PO Box 9330   Washington DC 20005
Ph: 202-625-1382 ▪ Fx: 202-625-1383

Stop it Now!   www.stopitnow.com
PO Box 495   Haydenville MA 01039
Ph: 413-268-3096 ▪ Fx: 413-268-3098 ▪ TF: 888-773-8368

Stop Prisoner Rape   www.spr.org
6303 Wilshire Blvd Suite 204   Los Angeles CA 90048
Ph: 323-653-7867 ▪ Fx: 323-653-7870

STOP - Safe Tables Our Priority   www.safetables.org
PO Box 4352   Burlington VT 05406
Ph: 802-863-0555 ▪ Fx: 802-863-3733 ▪ TF: 800-350-7867

StopSIDS.org   www.stopsids.org
1673 Rt 9 Suite 2   Clifton Park NY 12065
Ph: 888-521-9499

Storage Association, American Moving &   www.amconf.org
1611 Duke St   Alexandria VA 22314
Ph: 703-683-7410 ▪ Fx: 703-683-7527

Storage Association, Self   www.selfstorage.org
6506 Louisdale Rd Suite 315   Springfield VA 22150
Ph: 703-921-9123 ▪ Fx: 703-921-9105 ▪ TF: 888-735-3784

Storage Construction, International Association for Cold   www.iacsc.org
1500 King St Suite 201   Alexandria VA 22314
Ph: 703-373-4300 ▪ Fx: 703-373-4301

Store Association, Museum   www.museumdistrict.com
4100 E Mississippi Ave Suite 800   Denver CO 80246
Ph: 303-504-9223 ▪ Fx: 303-504-9585

Store Fixture Manufacturers, National Association of   www.nasfm.org
3595 Sheridan St Suite 200   Hollywood FL 33021
Ph: 954-893-7300 ▪ Fx: 954-893-7500

Store Planners, Institute of   www.ispo.org
25 N Broadway   Tarrytown NY 10591
Ph: 914-332-1806 ▪ Fx: 914-332-1541 ▪ TF: 800-379-9912

Stormwater Management Agencies, National Association of   www.nafsma.org
Food   1299 Pennsylvania Ave NW 8th Fl W   Washington DC
20004
Ph: 202-218-4122 ▪ Fx: 202-478-1734

Story League, National
1630 Country Club Cir   Las Cruces NM 88001
Ph: 505-526-8377

Storytellers, National Association of Black   www.nabsnet.org
PO Box 67722   Baltimore MD 21215
Ph: 410-947-1117

Storytelling Coalition, Jewish   users.rcn.com/jewish.ma.ultranet
63 Gould Rd   Waban MA 02468
Ph: 617-244-2884

Storytelling Guild, By Word of Mouth   shorock.com/folk/bwom
PO Box 56   Frankford MO 63441
Ph: 573-784-2589 ▪ Fx: 573-784-2364

(Storytelling) International Order of EARS Inc   www.cornislandstorytellingfestival.org
12019 Donohue Ave   Louisville KY 40243
Ph: 502-245-0643 ▪ Fx: 502-254-7542

Storytelling Network, National   www.storynet.org
101 Courthouse Sq   Jonesborough TN 37659
Ph: 423-913-8201 ▪ Fx: 423-753-9331 ▪ TF: 800-525-4514

Stowe Harriet Beecher Center   www.harrietbeecherstowecenter.org
77 Forest St   Hartford CT 06105
Ph: 860-522-9258 ▪ Fx: 860-522-9259

Strabismus, American Association for Pediatric Ophthalmology &   www.aapos.org
PO Box 193832   San Francisco CA 94119
Ph: 415-561-8505 ▪ Fx: 415-561-8531

Straight Chiropractors & Organizations, Federation of   www.straightchiropractic.com
2276 Wassergass Rd   Hellertown PA 18055
Ph: 610-838-3030 ▪ Fx: 610-838-3031 ▪ TF: 800-521-9856

Straight Spouse Network   www.ssnetwk.org
8215 Terrace Dr   El Cerrito CA 94530
Ph: 510-525-0200 ▪ Fx: 510-525-4831

Straight Talk America   www.straighttalkamerica.com
900 2nd St NE Suite 114   Washington DC 20002
Ph: 202-789-2626

Strategic Account Management Association   www.strategicaccounts.org
150 N Wacker Dr Suite 2222   Chicago IL 60606
Ph: 312-251-3131 ▪ Fx: 312-251-3132

Strategic & International Studies, Center for   www.csis.org
1800 K St NW Suite 400   Washington DC 20006
Ph: 202-887-0200 ▪ Fx: 202-775-3199

Strategy Gaming Society   www.gametableonline.com/StrategyGamingSociety.htm
87-6 Park Ave   Worcester MA 01605
Ph: 508-831-5334

Strategy Information Center, National
1730 Rhode Island Ave NW Suite 500   Washington DC 20036
Ph: 202-429-0129 ▪ Fx: 202-659-5429

Stratigraphic Palynologists, American Association of   www.palynology.org
600 N Dairy Ashford PO Box 2197   Houston TX 77252
Ph: 281-293-3189 ▪ Fx: 281-293-3833

Stratton-Porter Gene Memorial Society
PO Box 639   Rome City IN 46784
Ph: 260-854-3790 ▪ Fx: 260-854-9102

Strawberry Commission, California   www.calstrawberry.com
PO Box 269   Watsonville CA 95077
Ph: 831-724-1301 ▪ Fx: 831-724-5973

Strawberry Growers Association, North American   www.nasga.org
526 Brittany Dr   State College PA 16803
Ph: 814-238-8863 ▪ Fx: 814-238-7051

Street Machine Association Inc, United   www.usmacarshows.com
430 N Batchewana St   Clawson MI 48017
Ph: 248-280-0342

Street Rod Association, National   www.nsra-usa.com
4030 Park Ave   Memphis TN 38111
Ph: 901-452-4030 ▪ Fx: 901-452-6772

Strength & Conditioning Association, National   www.nsca-lift.org
PO Box 9908   Colorado Springs CO 80932
Ph: 719-632-6722 ▪ Fx: 719-632-6367 ▪ TF: 800-815-6826

Stress, American Institute of   www.stress.org
124 Park Ave   Yonkers NY 10703
Ph: 914-963-1200 ▪ Fx: 914-965-6267

Stress Analysts, International Society of
9 Westchester Dr   Kissimmee FL 34744
Ph: 407-933-4839 ▪ Fx: 407-935-0911

Stress Studies, International Society for Traumatic   www.istss.org
60 Revere Dr Suite 500   Northbrook IL 60062
Ph: 847-480-9028 ▪ Fx: 847-480-9282

Strike for Peace, Women
110 Maryland Ave NE Suite 102   Washington DC 20002
Ph: 202-543-2660

String Figure Association, International   www.isfa.org/isfa.htm
PO Box 5134   Pasadena CA 91117
Ph: 626-398-1057

String Teachers Association, American   www.astaweb.com
4153 Chain Bridge Rd   Fairfax VA 22030
Ph: 703-279-2113 ▪ Fx: 703-279-2114

Stripper Well Association, National
302 N Independence St   Enid OK 73702
Ph: 580-233-8955

Stroke Association, National   www.stroke.org
9707 E Easter Ln   Englewood CO 80112
Ph: 303-649-9299 ▪ Fx: 303-649-1328 ▪ TF: 800-787-6537

Strongmen, Association of Oldetime Barbell &
33-30 150th St   Flushing NY 11354
Ph: 718-661-3195

Structural Board Association   www.osbguide.com
25 Valleywood Dr Unit 27   Markham ON L3R5L9
Ph: 905-475-1100 ▪ Fx: 905-475-1101

Structural Engineers Associations, National Council of   dwp.bigplanet.com/engineers
203 N Wabash Ave Suite 2010   Chicago IL 60601
Ph: 312-372-8035 ▪ Fx: 312-372-5673

Structural Insulated Panel Association   www.sips.org
PO Box 1699   Gig Harbor WA 98335
Ph: 253-858-7472 ▪ Fx: 253-858-0272

Structural Integration, Rolf Institute of   www.rolf.org
205 Canyon Rd   Boulder CO 80302
Ph: 303-449-5903 ▪ Fx: 303-449-5978 ▪ TF: 800-530-8875

Structural Movers, International Association of   www.iasm.org
PO Box 2637   Lexington SC 29071
Ph: 803-951-9304 ▪ Fx: 803-951-9314

Structural Repair Contractors, National Association of   www.nawsrc.org
Waterproofing &   8015 Corporate Dr Suite A   Baltimore MD
21236
Ph: 410-931-3332 ▪ Fx: 410-931-2060 ▪ TF: 800-245-6292

Structural Stability Research Council   www.stabilitycouncil.org
Univ of Missouri - Rolla 301 Butler Carlton Hall   Rolla MO
65409
Ph: 573-341-6610 ▪ Fx: 573-341-4476

Structured Settlements Trade Association, National   www.nssta.org
1800 K St NW Suite 718   Washington DC 20006
Ph: 202-466-2714 ▪ Fx: 202-466-7414

Struggle to Save Ethiopian Jewry   www.studentstruggle.org
2472 Broadway Suite 316   New York NY 10025
Ph: 866-376-7735

Stuart Jesse Foundation Inc   www.jsfbooks.com
1645 Winchester Ave PO Box 669   Ashland KY 41105
Ph: 606-326-1667 ▪ Fx: 606-325-2519

Studbook in North America, Dutch Warmblood   www.nawpn.org
PO Box 0   Sutherlin OR 97479
Ph: 541-459-3232 ▪ Fx: 541-459-2967

Studebaker Driver's Club Inc   www.studebakerdriversclub.com
PO Box 1743   Maple Grove MN 55311
Ph: 763-420-7829 ▪ Fx: 763-420-7849

Student & Academic Rights, Coalition for   www.co-star.org
PO Box 491   Solebury PA 18963
Ph: 215-862-9096 ▪ Fx: 215-862-9097

Student Activity Advisors, National Association of
1904 Association Dr   Reston VA 20191
Ph: 703-860-0200 ▪ Fx: 703-476-5432

Student Affairs Professionals, National Association of   www.nasap.net
Tuskegee Univ Tompkins Hall Rm 100   Tuskegee AL 36088
Ph: 334-727-8837 ▪ Fx: 334-724-3758

Student Anthropologists, National Association of   www.aaanet.org/nasa
c/o American Anthropological Assn 2200 Wilson Blvd Suite
    600   Arlington VA 22201
Ph: 703-528-1902 ▪ Fx: 703-528-3546

Student Assistance Professionals, National Association of   www.nasap.org
4200 Wisconsin Ave NW Suite 106-118   Washington DC 20016
Ph: 800-257-6310 ▪ Fx: 215-257-6997

Student Association of Community Colleges, American   www.asacc.org
2250 N University Pkwy Suite 4865   Provo UT 84604
Ph: 801-863-8620 ▪ Fx: 801-764-7229

Student Association, Technology   www.tsaweb.org
1914 Association Dr   Reston VA 20191
Ph: 703-860-9000 ▪ Fx: 703-758-4852

Student Association, US   www.usstudents.org
1413 K St NW 9th Fl   Washington DC 20005
Ph: 202-347-8772 ▪ Fx: 202-393-5886 ▪ TF: 877-877-2669

Student Campaign Against Hunger & Homelessness, National   www.nscahh.org
233 N Pleasant St Suite 32   Amherst MA 01002
Ph: 413-253-6417 ▪ Fx: 413-256-6435 ▪ TF: 800-664-8647

Student Campaign for Voter Registration, National
1533 Market St 2nd Fl   Denver CO 80202
Ph: 303-573-5885 ▪ Fx: 303-573-5999

Student Coalition, Sierra   www.ssc.org
408 C St NE   Washington DC 20002
Ph: 202-548-4593 ▪ Fx: 202-675-6277 ▪ TF: 888-564-6772

Student Communication, Foundation for   www.businesstoday.org
48 University Pl   Princeton NJ 08544
Ph: 609-258-1111 ▪ Fx: 609-258-1222

Student Conservation Association   www.thesca.org
PO Box 550   Charlestown NH 03603
Ph: 603-543-1700 ▪ Fx: 603-543-1828 ▪ TF: 888-722-9675

Student Dental Association, American   www.asdanet.org
211 E Chicago Ave Suite 1160   Chicago IL 60611
Ph: 312-440-2795 ▪ Fx: 312-440-2820 ▪ TF: 800-621-8099

Student Development, National   www.nationalcouncilstudentdevelopment.org
Council on   Univ of Illinois 51 Gerty Dr Rm 129   Champaign
    IL 61820
Ph: 217-333-9230 ▪ Fx: 217-244-0851

Student Employment Association, National   nseastudemp.org
PO Box 23606   Eugene OR 97402
Ph: 541-484-6935

Student Empowerment Training Project   www.trainings.org
119 Somerset St 2nd Fl   New Brunswick NJ 08901
Ph: 732-247-2197

Student Environmental Action Coalition   www.seac.org
PO Box 31909   Philadelphia PA 19104
Ph: 215-222-4711

Student Exchange, American Intercultural   www.aise.com
7720 Herschel Ave   La Jolla CA 92037
Ph: 858-459-9761 ▪ Fx: 858-459-5301

Student Exchange, National   www.nse.org
4656 W Jefferson Blvd Suite 140   Fort Wayne IN 46804
Ph: 260-436-2634 ▪ Fx: 260-436-5676

Student Financial Aid Administrators, National Association of   www.nasfaa.org
1129 20th St NW Suite 400   Washington DC 20036
Ph: 202-785-0453 ▪ Fx: 202-785-1487

Student Letter Exchange   www.pen-pal.com
211 Broadway Suite 201   Lynbrook NY 11563
Ph: 516-887-8628 ▪ Fx: 516-887-8631

Student Movement USA, Lutheran   www.lsm-usa.org
8765 W Higgins Rd   Chicago IL 60631
Ph: 773-380-2852 ▪ Fx: 773-380-2750 ▪ TF: 800-638-3522

Student Musicians, National Fraternity of
808 Rio Grande PO Box 1807   Austin TX 78767
Ph: 512-478-5775 ▪ Fx: 512-478-5843

Student National Medical Association   www.snma.org
5113 Georgia Ave NW   Washington DC 20011
Ph: 202-882-2881 ▪ Fx: 202-882-2886

Student Nurses Association, National   www.nsna.org
45 Main St Suite 606   Brooklyn NY 11201
Ph: 718-210-0705 ▪ Fx: 718-210-0710

Student Organization, International   www.isoa.org
250 W 49th St Suite 806   New York NY 10019
Ph: 212-262-8922 ▪ Fx: 212-262-8920 ▪ TF: 800-244-1180

Student Organization, National Postsecondary Agricultural   www.nationalpas.org
6060 FFA Dr PO Box 68960   Indianapolis IN 46268
Ph: 317-802-4220 ▪ Fx: 317-802-5220

Student Osteopathic Medical Association   www.studentdo.com
142 E Ontario St 6th Fl   Chicago IL 60611
Ph: 800-621-1772

Student Personnel Administrators, Jesuit Association of   jaspa.creighton.edu
1 Dupont Cir NW Suite 405   Washington DC 20036
Ph: 202-862-9893

Student Personnel Administrators, National Association of   www.naspa.org
1875 Connecticut Ave NW Suite 418   Washington DC 20009
Ph: 202-265-7500 ▪ Fx: 202-797-1157

Student Service Council, Foreign
1930 18th St NW Suite 21   Washington DC 20009
Ph: 202-232-4979 ▪ Fx: 202-667-9305

Student Society of America, Public Relations   www.prssa.org
33 Irving Pl 3rd Fl   New York NY 10003
Ph: 212-460-1474 ▪ Fx: 212-995-0757

Student Speech Language Hearing Association, National   www.nsslha.org
10801 Rockville Pike   Rockville MD 20852
Ph: 301-897-5700 ▪ Fx: 301-571-0481 ▪ TF: 800-498-2071

Students Against Destructive Decisions   www.saddonline.com
255 Main St   Marlborough MA 01752
Ph: 508-481-3568 ▪ Fx: 508-481-5759 ▪ TF: 877-723-3462

Students' Association, American Podiatric Medical   www.apmsa.org
9312 Old Georgetown Rd   Bethesda MD 20814
Ph: 301-493-9667 ▪ Fx: 301-530-2752

Students, Association for, Armenian   www.asainc.org
333 Atlantic Ave   Warwick RI 02888
Ph: 401-461-6114 ▪ Fx: 401-461-6112

Students, Association for Gifted & Talented
PO Box 16037   Baton Rouge LA 70896
Ph: 504-388-2469 ▪ Fx: 504-388-1375 ▪ TF: 800-626-8811

Students for Change   www.studentsforchange.org
PO Box 398   Paradise CA 95969
Ph: 530-872-3733

Students of Cooperation, North American   www.umich.edu/~nasco
PO Box 7715   Ann Arbor MI 48107
Ph: 734-663-0889 ▪ Fx: 734-663-5072

Students with Disabilities, National Coalition for   www.ncsd.org
1413 K St NW 9th Fl   Washington DC 20005
Ph: 202-347-8772 ▪ Fx: 202-393-5886

Students in Free Enterprise   www.sife.org
1959 E Kerr St   Springfield MO 65803
Ph: 417-831-9505 ▪ Fx: 417-831-6165 ▪ TF: 800-677-7433

Students Inc, International   www.isionline.org
PO Box C   Colorado Springs CO 80901
Ph: 719-576-2700 ▪ Fx: 719-576-5363 ▪ TF: 800-474-4145

Students, National Coalition of Advocates for   www.ncasboston.org
100 Boylston St Suite 808   Boston MA 02116
Ph: 617-357-8507 ▪ Fx: 617-357-9549

Students of Pharmacy, Academy of   www.aphanet.org/students/studentsnew.htm
American Pharmacists Assn 2215 Constitution Ave
    NW   Washington DC 20037
Ph: 202-628-4410 ▪ Fx: 202-783-2351

Students Technology Experience, International Association for
the Exchange of   10400 Little Patuxent Pkwy Suite
    250   Columbia MD 21044
Ph: 410-997-3069 ▪ Fx: 410-997-5186

Studies, Association for General & Liberal   www.bsu.edu/web/agls
Ball State Univ English Dept RB 2109   Muncie IN 47306
Ph: 765-285-8406

Studies Association, International   csf.colorado.edu/isa
Univ of Arizona 324 Social Sciences   Tucson AZ 85721
Ph: 520-621-7715 ▪ Fx: 520-621-5780

Studies, Fund for American   www.dcinternships.org
1706 New Hampshire Ave NW   Washington DC 20009
Ph: 800-741-6964 ▪ Fx: 202-318-0441

Studies Programs, Association of Graduate Liberal   www.udel.edu/aglsp
Univ of Delaware 219 McDowell Hall   Newark DE 19716
Ph: 302-831-4218 ▪ Fx: 302-831-4461

Study Abroad, National Registration Center for   www.nrcsa.com
PO Box 1393   Milwaukee WI 53201
Ph: 414-278-0631 ▪ Fx: 414-271-8884

Study Circles Resource Center   www.studycircles.org
697 Pomfret St Box 203   Pomfret CT 06258
Ph: 860-928-2616 ▪ Fx: 860-928-3713

Stuntmen's Association of Motion Pictures   www.stuntmen.com
10660 Riverside Dr 2nd Fl Suite E   Toluca Lake CA 91602
Ph: 818-766-4334 ▪ Fx: 818-766-5943

Stunts Unlimited   www.stuntsunlimited.com
4421 Riverside Dr Suite 210   Toluca Lake CA 91505
Ph: 818-841-3555 ▪ Fx: 818-841-1655

Stuntwomen's Association of Motion Pictures   www.stuntwomen.com
12457 Ventura Blvd Suite 208   Studio City CA 91604
Ph: 818-762-0907 ▪ Fx: 818-762-9534

Stuttering Association, National   www.nsastutter.org
119 W 40th St 14th Fl   New York NY 10018
Ph: 212-944-4050 ▪ Fx: 212-944-8244 ▪ TF: 800-364-1677

Stuttering Foundation of America   www.stuttersfa.org
3100 Walnut Grove Rd Suite 603   Memphis TN 38111
Ph: 901-452-7343 ▪ Fx: 901-452-3931 ▪ TF: 800-992-9392

Stuttering, National Center for   www.stuttering.com
200 E 33rd St   New York NY 10016
Ph: 212-532-1460 ▪ Fx: 212-683-1372 ▪ TF: 800-221-2483

Styrene Information & Research Center   www.styrene.org
1300 Wilson Blvd Suite 1200   Arlington VA 22209
Ph: 703-741-5010 ▪ Fx: 703-741-6010

Subacute & Post Acute Care, National Association of   www.naspac.net
1960 Gallows Rd Suite 210   Vienna VA 22182
Ph: 703-790-8989 ▪ Fx: 703-790-8485

Subcontractors Association Inc, American   www.asaonline.com
1004 Duke St   Alexandria VA 22314
Ph: 703-684-3450 ▪ Fx: 703-836-3482

Subcontractors Trade Association   www.stanyc.com
570 7th Ave Suite 1100   New York NY 10018
Ph: 212-398-6220 ▪ Fx: 212-398-6224

Submarine League, Naval   www.navalsubleague.com
5025-D Backlick Rd Suite D   Annandale VA 22003
Ph: 703-256-0891 ▪ Fx: 703-642-5815

Submarine Veterans of World War II, US   www.ussubvetsofworldwarii.org

Submersible Wastewater Pump Association   swww.swpa.org
1866 Sheridan Rd Suite 201   Highland Park IL 60035
Ph: 847-681-1868 ▪ Fx: 847-681-1869

Associations USA

Submetering & Utility Allocation Association, National
www.nsuaa.org
1866 Sheridan Rd Suite 201   Highland Park IL 60035
Ph: 847-681-8475 ■ Fx: 847-681-1869

Subrogation Professionals, National Association of
www.subrogation.org
4248 Park Glen Rd   Minneapolis MN 55416
Ph: 952-928-4661 ■ Fx: 952-929-1318 ■ TF: 888-828-8186

Substance Abuse, Association of Medical Education & Research in
www.amersa.org
125 Whipple St Suite 300   Providence RI 02908
Ph: 401-349-0000 ■ Fx: 877-418-8769

Substance Abuse Issues, Inter-Association Task Force on
www.iatf.org
Alcohol & Other   PO Box 100430   Denver CO 80250
Ph: 303-871-0901 ■ Fx: 303-871-0907

Substance Abuse Librarians & Information Specialists
www.salis.org
PO Box 9513   Berkeley CA 94709
Ph: 510-642-5208 ■ Fx: 510-642-7175

Substance Abuse, National Asian Pacific American Families
www.napafasa.org
Against   340 E Second St Suite 409   Los Angeles CA 90012
Ph: 213-625-5795 ■ Fx: 213-625-5796

Substance Abuse Program Administrators Association
www.sapaa.com
12 Cottage Field Ct   Germantown MD 20874
Ph: 301-540-2783 ■ Fx: 301-540-1756

Substance Abuse Trainers & Educators,   www.preventionpartners.samhsa.gov/partner
National Association of   1521 Hillary St   New Orleans LA
70118
Ph: 504-286-5234

Subtle Energies & Energy Medicine, International Society
www.issseem.org
for the Study of   11005 Ralston Rd Suite 100D   Arvada CO
80004
Ph: 303-425-4625 ■ Fx: 303-425-4685

SUBUD USA
www.subudusa.org
14019 NE 8th St Suite A   Bellevue WA 98007
Ph: 425-643-1904 ■ Fx: 425-643-2725

Suburban Newspapers of America
www.suburban-news.org
116 Cass St   Traverse City MI 49684
Ph: 888-486-2466 ■ Fx: 231-932-2985

Succulent Research, Arizona Cactus &
www.arizonacactus.com
8 S Cactus Ln   Bisbee AZ 85603
Ph: 520-432-7040 ■ Fx: 520-432-7001

Succulent Society of America, Cactus &
www.cssainc.org
6811 S 230th East Ave   Broken Arrow OK 74014
Ph: 918-357-2401

Sudden Arrythmia Death Syndromes Foundation
www.sads.org
508 E South Temple Suite 20   Salt Lake City UT 84102
Ph: 801-531-0937 ■ Fx: 801-531-0945 ■ TF: 800-786-7723

Suffolk Sheep Association, United
www.u-s-s-a.org
PO Box 256   Newton UT 84327
Ph: 435-563-6105 ■ Fx: 435-563-9356

Sugar Alliance, American
www.sugaralliance.org
2111 Wilson Blvd Suite 600   Arlington VA 22201
Ph: 703-351-5055 ■ Fx: 703-351-6698

Sugar Association
www.sugar.org
1101 15th St NW Suite 600   Washington DC 20005
Ph: 202-785-1122 ■ Fx: 202-785-5019

Sugar Association, US Beet
1156 15th St NW Suite 1019   Washington DC 20005
Ph: 202-296-4820 ■ Fx: 202-331-2065

Sugar Brokers Association, National
3000 Chestnut Ave Suite 100A   Baltimore MD 21211
Ph: 410-366-7400 ■ Fx: 410-467-9552

Sugar Cane League, American
www.amscl.org
PO Box 938   Thibodaux LA 70302
Ph: 985-448-3707 ■ Fx: 985-448-3722

Sugar Development Foundation, Beet
www.bsdf-assbt.org
800 Grant St Suite 300   Denver CO 80203
Ph: 303-832-4460 ■ Fx: 303-832-4468

Sugar Industry Technologists Inc
sucrose.com/sit
164 N Hall Dr   Sugar Land TX 77478
Ph: 281-494-2046 ■ Fx: 281-494-2304

Sugarbeet Growers Association, American
members.aol.com/asga
1156 15th St NW Suite 1101   Washington DC 20005
Ph: 202-833-2398 ■ Fx: 202-833-2962

Suicide Awareness Voices of Education, SAVE -
www.save.org
7317 Cahill Rd Suite 207   Minneapolis MN 55439
Ph: 952-946-7998 ■ Fx: 952-829-0841 ■ TF: 888-511-7283

Suicide Inc, HEARTBEAT/Survivors After
www.heartbeatsurvivorsaftersuicide.org
2015 Devon St   Colorado Springs CO 80909
Ph: 719-596-2575

Suicide, International Task Force on Euthanasia &
www.internationaltaskforce.org
Assisted   PO Box 760   Steubenville OH 43952
Ph: 740-282-3810 ■ Fx: 740-282-0769 ■ TF: 800-958-5678

(Suicide) Kristin Brooks Hope Center
www.hopeline.com
201 N 23rd St Suite 100   Purcelville VA 20132
Ph: 540-338-5756 ■ Fx: 540-338-5746 ■ TF: 800-784-2433

(Suicide) Light for Life Foundation International
www.yellowribbon.org
PO Box 644   Westminster CO 80036
Ph: 303-429-3530 ■ Fx: 303-426-4496

Suicide Prevention, American Foundation for
www.afsp.org
120 Wall St 22nd Fl   New York NY 10005
Ph: 212-363-3500 ■ Fx: 212-363-6237 ■ TF: 888-333-2377

Suicidology, American Association of
www.suicidology.org
4201 Connecticut Ave NW Suite 408   Washington DC 20008
Ph: 202-237-2280 ■ Fx: 202-237-2282

Sulphur Institute
www.sulphurinstitute.org
1140 Connecticut Ave NW Suite 612   Washington DC 20036
Ph: 202-331-9660 ■ Fx: 202-293-2940

Sumi-e Society of America
www.sumiesociety.org
5321 Long Sky Ct   Columbia MD 21045
Ph: 410-730-7597

Summer & Casual Furniture Manufacturers Association
PO Box HP-7   High Point NC 27261
Ph: 336-884-5000 ■ Fx: 336-884-5303

Summer Schools, North Central Conference on
www.nccss.org
Univ of Wisconsin-River Falls 317 Agricultural Science Bldg
410 S 3rd St   River Falls WI 54022
Ph: 715-425-3851 ■ Fx: 715-425-3785

Summer Sessions, North American Association of
www.naass.org
43 Belanger Dr   Dover NH 03820
Ph: 603-740-9880 ■ Fx: 603-742-7085

Sundance Institute
institute.sundance.org
PO Box 3630   Salt Lake City UT 84110
Ph: 801-328-3456 ■ Fx: 801-575-5175

Sunday & Feature Editors, American Association of
www.aasfe.org
Univ of Maryland Merrill College of Journalism 1117 Journalism
Bldg   College Park MD 20742
Ph: 301-314-2631 ■ Fx: 301-314-9166

Sunfish Class Association, International
www.sunfishclass.org
PO Box 300128   Waterford MI 48330
Ph: 248-673-2750

Sunflower Association, National
www.sunflowernsa.com
4023 State St   Bismarck ND 58501
Ph: 701-328-5100 ■ Fx: 701-328-5101 ■ TF: 888-718-7033

Sunroom Association, National
www.nationalsunroom.org
2945 SW Wanamaker Dr Suite A   Topeka KS 66614
Ph: 785-271-0208 ■ Fx: 785-271-0166

Sunshine Foundation
www.sunshinefoundation.org
1041 Mill Creek Dr   Feasterville PA 19053
Ph: 215-396-4770 ■ Fx: 215-396-4774 ■ TF: 800-767-1976

Sunshine Lady Foundation Inc
www.sunshineladyfdn.org
PO Box 1074   Morehead City NC 28557
Ph: 252-240-2788 ■ Fx: 252-240-2933

Superintendents, North American Association of Wardens &
corrections.com/naaws
PO Box 11037   Albany NY 12211
Ph: 518-786-6801

Superstition Mountain Historical Society
www.superstitionmountainmuseum.org
PO Box 3845   Apache Junction AZ 85217
Ph: 480-983-4888 ■ Fx: 480-474-9410

Supervision & Curriculum Development, Association for
www.ascd.org
1703 N Beauregard St   Alexandria VA 22311
Ph: 703-578-9600 ■ Fx: 703-575-5400 ■ TF: 800-933-2723

Supima
www.supima.com
4141 E Broadway Rd   Phoenix AZ 85040
Ph: 602-437-1364 ■ Fx: 602-437-0143

Supplier Development Council, National Minority
www.nmsdcus.org
1040 Ave of the Americas 2nd Fl   New York NY 10018
Ph: 212-944-2430 ■ Fx: 212-719-9611

Supplier Institute, American
www.amsup.com
38701 Seven Mile Rd Suite 355   Livonia MI 48152
Ph: 734-464-1395 ■ Fx: 734-464-1399 ■ TF: 800-462-4500

Suppliers to Food Processors Association, National
PO Box 59149   Minneapolis MN 55459
Ph: 612-341-9600 ■ Fx: 612-341-9648

Supply Association, American
www.asa.net
222 Merchandise Mart Plaza Suite 1400   Chicago IL 60654
Ph: 312-464-0090 ■ Fx: 312-464-0091

Supply Chain Council
www.supply-chain.org
1150 Freeport Rd   Pittsburgh PA 15238
Ph: 412-781-4101 ■ Fx: 412-781-2871

Supply Management, Institute for
www.ism.ws
PO Box 22160   Tempe AZ 85285
Ph: 480-752-6276 ■ Fx: 480-752-7890 ■ TF: 800-888-6276

Support Dogs Inc
www.supportdogs.org
9510 Page Ave   Saint Louis MO 63132
Ph: 314-423-1988 ■ Fx: 314-423-5564

Support Enforcement Association, National Child
www.ncsea.org
444 N Capitol St NW Suite 414   Washington DC 20001
Ph: 202-624-8180 ■ Fx: 202-624-8828

Support Organization for Trisomy 18/13 & Other Related Disorders
www.trisomy.org
2982 S Union St   Rochester NY 14624
Ph: 585-594-4621 ■ Fx: 585-594-1957 ■ TF: 800-716-7638

Support Professionals, Association of
www.asponline.com
122 Barnard Ave   Watertown MA 02472
Ph: 617-924-3944 ■ Fx: 617-924-7288

Supreme Council of the Royal Arcanum
www.royalarcanum.com
61 Batterymarch St PO Box 392   Boston MA 02110
Ph: 617-426-4135 ■ Fx: 617-426-2322 ■ TF: 888-272-2686

Supreme Court Historical Society
www.supremecourthistory.org/
224 E Capitol St NE   Washington DC 20003
Ph: 202-543-0400 ■ Fx: 202-547-7730

Supreme Master Ching Hai International Association
www.chinghai.com
PO Box 730247   San Jose CA 95173
Ph: 408-998-2342

Surdna Foundation Inc
www.surdna.org
330 Madison Ave 30th Fl   New York NY 10017
Ph: 212-557-0010 ■ Fx: 212-557-0003

Surety Association of America
www.surety.org
1101 Connecticut Ave NW Suite 800   Washington DC 20036
Ph: 202-463-0600 ■ Fx: 202-463-0606

Surety Bond Producers, National Association of
www.nasbp.org
5225 Wisconsin Ave NW Suite 600   Washington DC 20015
Ph: 202-686-3700 ■ Fx: 202-686-3656

Surface Design Association
www.surfacedesign.org
PO Box 360   Sebastopol CA 95473
Ph: 707-829-3110 ■ Fx: 707-829-3285

Surface Engineering Coating Association
1300 Sumner Ave   Cleveland OH 44115
Ph: 216-241-7333 ■ Fx: 216-241-0105

Surface Mount Technology Association
www.smta.org
5200 Wilson Rd Suite 215   Edina MN 55424
Ph: 952-920-7682 ■ Fx: 952-926-1819

Surfaces in Biomaterials Foundation
www.surfaces.org
13355 10th Ave N Suite 108   Minneapolis MN 55441
Ph: 763-512-9103 ■ Fx: 763-765-2329

Surfing Association, International
5580 La Jolla Blvd PMB 145   La Jolla CA 92037
Ph: 858-551-5292 ▪ Fx: 858-551-5290

Surfing Association, National Scholastic   www.nssa.org
PO Box 495   Huntington Beach CA 92648
Ph: 714-536-0445 ▪ Fx: 714-960-4380

Surfing Professionals, Association of   www.aspworldtour.com
PO Box 309   Huntington Beach CA 92648
Ph: 714-848-8851 ▪ Fx: 714-848-8861

Surfrider Foundation USA   www.surfrider.org
122 S El Camino Real Suite 67   San Clemente CA 92672
Ph: 949-492-8170 ▪ Fx: 949-492-8142 ▪ TF: 800-743-7873

Surgeons, American Academy of Neurological & Orthopaedic   www.aanos.org
2300 S Rancho Dr Suite 202   Las Vegas NV 89102
Ph: 702-388-7390 ▪ Fx: 702-388-7395

Surgeons, American Association of Hip & Knee
704 N Florence Dr   Park Ridge IL 60068
Ph: 847-698-1200 ▪ Fx: 847-825-9294

Surgeons, American Association of Neurological   www.aans.org
5550 Meadowbrook Dr   Rolling Meadows IL 60068
Ph: 847-378-0500 ▪ Fx: 847-378-0600 ▪ TF: 888-566-2267

Surgeons, American Association of Oral & Maxillofacial   www.aaoms.org
9700 W Bryn Mawr Ave   Rosemont IL 60018
Ph: 847-678-6200 ▪ Fx: 847-678-6286 ▪ TF: 800-822-6637

Surgeons, American Association of Plastic   www.aaps1921.org
4900B S 31st St   Arlington VA 22206
Ph: 703-820-7400 ▪ Fx: 703-931-4520

Surgeons, American Association of Podiatric Physicians &
1328 Southern Ave SE Suite 200   Washington DC 20032
Ph: 202-562-2777 ▪ Fx: 202-562-5351

Surgeons, American College of   www.facs.org
633 N Saint Clair St   Chicago IL 60611
Ph: 312-202-5000 ▪ Fx: 312-202-5001 ▪ TF: 800-621-4111

Surgeons, American College of Eye   www.aces-abes.org
2665 Oak Ridge Ct Suite A   Fort Myers FL 33901
Ph: 239-275-8881 ▪ Fx: 239-275-9969 ▪ TF: 888-335-0077

Surgeons, American College of Foot & Ankle   www.acfas.org
515 Busse Hwy   Park Ridge IL 60068
Ph: 847-292-2237 ▪ Fx: 847-292-2022 ▪ TF: 800-421-2237

Surgeons, American College of Oral & Maxillofacial   www.acoms.org
1100 NW Loop 410 Suite 420   San Antonio TX 78213
Ph: 210-344-5674 ▪ Fx: 210-344-9754 ▪ TF: 800-522-6676

Surgeons, American College of Osteopathic   www.facos.org
123 N Henry St   Alexandria VA 22314
Ph: 703-684-0416 ▪ Fx: 703-684-3280

Surgeons, American College of Veterinary   www.acvs.org
4401 East-West Hwy Suite 205   Bethesda MD 20814
Ph: 301-913-9550 ▪ Fx: 301-913-2034

Surgeons, American Shoulder & Elbow   www.ases-assn.org
6300 N River Rd Suite 727   Rosemont IL 60018
Ph: 847-698-1629 ▪ Fx: 847-823-0536

Surgeons, American Society of Abdominal   www.abdominalsurg.org
675 Main St   Melrose MA 02176
Ph: 781-665-6102 ▪ Fx: 781-665-4127

Surgeons, American Society of Colon & Rectal   www.fascrs.org
85 W Algonquin Rd Suite 550   Arlington Heights IL 60005
Ph: 847-290-9184 ▪ Fx: 847-290-9203

Surgeons, American Society of General   www.theasgs.org
4200 Commercial Way   Glenview IL 60025
Ph: 847-391-9770 ▪ Fx: 847-391-9711 ▪ TF: 800-998-8322

Surgeons, American Society of Maxillofacial   www.maxface.org
444 E Algonquin Rd   Arlington Heights IL 60005
Ph: 847-228-3338

Surgeons, American Society of Plastic   www.plasticsurgery.org
444 E Algonquin Rd   Arlington Heights IL 60005
Ph: 847-228-9900 ▪ Fx: 847-228-9131 ▪ TF: 888-475-2784

Surgeons, American Society of Transplant   www.asts.org
1020 N Fairfax St Suite 200   Alexandria VA 22314
Ph: 703-684-5990 ▪ Fx: 703-684-6303 ▪ TF: 888-990-2787

Surgeons Inc, Association of American Physicians &   www.aapsonline.org
1601 N Tucson Blvd Suite 9   Tucson AZ 85716
Ph: 520-327-4885 ▪ Fx: 520-325-4230 ▪ TF: 800-635-1196

Surgeons, Association of Bone & Joint   www.abjs.org
6300 N River Rd Suite 727   Rosemont IL 60018
Ph: 847-698-1636 ▪ Fx: 847-823-4921

Surgeons, Association of Women   www.womensurgeons.org
414 Plaza Dr Suite 209   Westmont IL 60559
Ph: 630-655-0392 ▪ Fx: 630-655-0391

Surgeons, Congress of Neurological   www.neurosurgeon.org
10 N Martingale Rd Suite 190   Schaumburg IL 60173
Ph: 847-240-2500 ▪ Fx: 847-240-0804 ▪ TF: 877-517-1267

Surgeons, Interamerican College of Physicians &   www.icps.org
915 Broadway Suite 1105   New York NY 10102
Ph: 212-777-3642 ▪ Fx: 212-777-5000

Surgeons, International Association of Ocular
820 N Orleans St Suite 208   Chicago IL 60610
Ph: 312-440-0699 ▪ Fx: 312-440-0580 ▪ TF: 800-621-4002

Surgeons, International College of   www.icsglobal.org
1516 N Lake Shore Dr   Chicago IL 60610
Ph: 312-642-3555 ▪ Fx: 312-787-1624

Surgeons, Society of American Gastrointestinal Endoscopic   www.sages.org
11300 W Olympic Blvd Suite 600   Los Angeles CA 90064
Ph: 310-437-0544 ▪ Fx: 310-437-0585

Surgeons, Society of Eye
10801 Connecticut Ave   Kensington MD 20814
Ph: 240-290-0263 ▪ Fx: 240-290-0269

Surgeons, Society of Laparoendoscopic   www.sls.org
7330 SW 62nd Pl Suite 410   South Miami FL 33143
Ph: 305-665-9959 ▪ Fx: 305-667-4123 ▪ TF: 800-446-2659

Surgeons, Society of Military Orthopaedic   www.somos.org
810 North St   Belgium WI 53004
Ph: 262-285-4280 ▪ Fx: 262-285-4231

Surgeons, Society of Neurological   www.societyns.org
600 Highland Ave   Madison WI 53792
Ph: 608-263-0170 ▪ Fx: 608-263-1728

Surgeons, Society of Reproductive   www.reprodsurgery.org
1209 Montgomery Hwy   Birmingham AL 35216
Ph: 205-978-5000 ▪ Fx: 205-978-5005

Surgeons, Society of Thoracic   www.sts.org
633 N Saint Clair St Suite 2320   Chicago IL 60611
Ph: 312-202-5800 ▪ Fx: 312-202-5801

Surgeons, Society of University   www.susweb.org
1133 W Morse Blvd Suite 201   Winter Park FL 32789
Ph: 407-647-7714 ▪ Fx: 407-629-2502

Surgeons, Society of US Air Force Flight   www.sousaffs.org
PO Box 35387   Brooks AFB TX 78235
Ph: 210-536-2845 ▪ Fx: 210-536-1779

Surgeons of the US, Association of Military   www.amsus.org
9320 Old Georgetown Rd   Bethesda MD 20814
Ph: 301-897-8800 ▪ Fx: 301-530-5446 ▪ TF: 800-761-9320

Surgery, Academy of Ambulatory Foot & Ankle   www.academy-afs.org
1601 Walnut St Suite 1005   Philadelphia PA 19102
Ph: 215-569-3303 ▪ Fx: 215-569-3310 ▪ TF: 800-433-4892

Surgery of the Alimentary Tract, Society for   www.ssat.com
900 Cummings Ctr Suite 221-U   Beverly MA 01915
Ph: 978-927-8330 ▪ Fx: 978-524-8890

Surgery, American Academy of Cosmetic   www.cosmeticsurgery.org
737 N Michigan Ave Suite 820   Chicago IL 60611
Ph: 312-981-6760 ▪ Fx: 312-981-6787

Surgery, American Academy of Otolaryngology-Head & Neck   www.entnet.org
1 Prince St   Alexandria VA 22314
Ph: 703-836-4444 ▪ Fx: 703-683-5100

Surgery, American Association for Hand   www.handsurgery.org
20 N Michigan Ave Suite 700   Chicago IL 60602
Ph: 312-236-3307 ▪ Fx: 312-782-0553

Surgery, American Association for Thoracic   www.aats.org
900 Cummings Ctr Suite 221-U   Beverly MA 01915
Ph: 978-927-8330 ▪ Fx: 978-524-8890

Surgery, American Board of   www.absurgery.org
1617 John F Kennedy Blvd Suite 860   Philadelphia PA 19103
Ph: 215-568-4000 ▪ Fx: 215-563-5718

Surgery, American Board of Colon & Rectal   www.abcrs.org
20600 Eureka Rd Suite 600   Taylor MI 48180
Ph: 734-282-9400 ▪ Fx: 734-282-9402

Surgery, American Board of Oral & Maxillofacial   www.aboms.org
625 N Michigan Ave Suite 1820   Chicago IL 60611
Ph: 312-642-0070 ▪ Fx: 312-642-8584

Surgery, American Board of Orthopaedic   www.abos.org
400 Silver Cedar Ct   Chapel Hill NC 27514
Ph: 919-929-7103 ▪ Fx: 919-942-8988

Surgery Inc, American Board of Plastic   www.abplsurg.org
1635 Market St 7 Penn Ctr Suite 400   Philadelphia PA 19103
Ph: 215-587-9322 ▪ Fx: 215-587-9622

Surgery, American Board of Thoracic   www.abts.org
1560 Sherman Ave Suite 803   Evanston IL 60201
Ph: 847-475-1520 ▪ Fx: 847-475-6240

Surgery, American Society for Bariatric   www.asbs.org
7328 W University Ave Suite F   Gainesville FL 32607
Ph: 352-331-4900 ▪ Fx: 352-331-4975

Surgery, American Society of Cataract & Refractive   www.ascrs.org
4000 Legato Rd Suite 850   Fairfax VA 22033
Ph: 703-591-2220 ▪ Fx: 703-591-0614 ▪ TF: 800-451-1339

Surgery, American Society of Hair Restoration   www.cosmeticsurgery.org
737 N Michigan Ave Suite 820   Chicago IL 60611
Ph: 312-981-6760 ▪ Fx: 312-981-6787

Surgery, American Society for Laser Medicine &   www.aslms.org
2404 Stewart Ave   Wausau WI 54401
Ph: 715-845-9283 ▪ Fx: 715-848-2493

Surgery, American Society of Lipo-Suction   www.cosmeticsurgery.org
737 N Michigan Ave Suite 820   Chicago IL 60611
Ph: 312-981-6760 ▪ Fx: 312-981-6787

Surgery, American Society of Ophthalmic Plastic & Reconstructive   www.asoprs.org
1133 W Morse Blvd Suite 201   Winter Park FL 32789
Ph: 407-647-8839 ▪ Fx: 407-629-2502

Surgery, Association for Academic   www.aasurg.org
11300 W Olympic Blvd Suite 600   Los Angeles CA 90064
Ph: 310-437-0555 ▪ Fx: 310-437-0585

Surgery, Association of Academic Chairmen of Plastic   www.aacplasticsurgery.org
4900 B South 31st St   Arlington VA 22206
Ph: 703-820-7400 ▪ Fx: 703-931-4520

Surgery Association, Federated Ambulatory   www.fasa.org
700 N Fairfax St Suite 306   Alexandria VA 22314
Ph: 703-836-8808 ▪ Fx: 703-549-0976

Surgery, Association of Physician Assistants in Cardiovascular   www.apacvs.org
PO Box 4834   Englewood CO 80155
Ph: 303-221-5651 ▪ Fx: 303-771-2550 ▪ TF: 877-221-5651

Surgery, Association of Program Directors in   www.apds.org
4900-B S 31st St   Arlington VA 22206
Ph: 703-820-7400 ▪ Fx: 703-931-4520

Surgery Centers, American Association of Ambulatory   www.aaasc.org
PO Box 5271   Johnson City TN 37602
Ph: 423-915-1001 ▪ Fx: 423-282-9712 ▪ TF: 800-237-3768

Surgery & Cutaneous Oncology, American College of   www.mohscollege.org
Mohs Micrographic   611 E Wells St   Milwaukee WI 53202
Ph: 414-347-1103 ▪ Fx: 414-272-6070 ▪ TF: 800-500-7224

Surgery Facilities Inc, American Association for Accreditation   www.aaaasf.org
of Ambulatory   5101 Washington St Suite 2F PO Box
9500   Gurnee IL 60031
Ph: 888-545-5222 ▪ Fx: 847-775-1985

Surgery of the Hand, American Society for www.assh.org
6300 N River Rd Suite 600 Rosemont IL 60018
Ph: 847-384-8300 ▪ Fx: 847-384-1435 ▪ TF: 888-576-2774

Surgery of the Hand, International Federation of Societies for
Duke University Medical Ctr PO Box 2912 Durham NC 27710
Ph: 919-684-5388 ▪ Fx: 919-681-7378

Surgery, International Confederation for Plastic www.ipras.org
Reconstructive & Aesthetic 4 Executive Park Dr Albany NY
12203
Ph: 518-438-1434 ▪ Fx: 518-489-1205

Surgery, International Society of Hair Restoration www.ishrs.org
13 S 2nd St Geneva IL 60134
Ph: 630-262-5399 ▪ Fx: 630-262-1520 ▪ TF: 800-444-2737

Surgery, International Society for Minimally Invasive Cardiac www.ismics.org
900 Cummings Ctr Suite 221-U Beverly MA 01915
Ph: 978-927-8330 ▪ Fx: 978-524-8890

Surgery, International Society of Refractive www.isrs.org
655 Beach St San Francisco CA 94109
Ph: 415-561-8581 ▪ Fx: 415-561-8575

Surgery & Ophthalmology, American Society of Contemporary Medicine
820 N Orleans St Suite 208 Chicago IL 60610
Ph: 312-440-0699 ▪ Fx: 312-440-0580 ▪ TF: 800-621-4002

Surgery, Society for Clinical Vascular scvs.vascularweb.org
900 Cummings Ctr Suite 221-U Beverly MA 01915
Ph: 978-927-8330 ▪ Fx: 978-927-4018

Surgery Society, Outpatient Ophthalmic www.ooss.org
793-A Foothill Blvd PMB 119 San Luis Obispo CA 93405
Ph: 877-720-3585

Surgery, Society for Vascular svs.vascularweb.org
900 Cummings Ctr Suite 221-U Beverly MA 01915
Ph: 978-526-8330 ▪ Fx: 978-526-4018

Surgery of Trauma, American Association for the www.aast.org
Presbyterian Hospital Dept of Surgery 200 Lothrop St
MS-F1264 Pittsburgh PA 15213
Ph: 412-647-0635 ▪ Fx: 412-647-1448

Surgical Aid International, Children's www.csaintl.org
37 St Paul's Pl Hempstead NY 11550
Ph: 516-485-7909 ▪ Fx: 516-481-5393

Surgical Assistant Association, National www.nsaa.net
3024 W Shangri-La Rd Phoenix AZ 85029
Ph: 602-212-0479 ▪ Fx: 602-212-9692 ▪ TF: 888-633-0479

Surgical Association, American www.americansurgical.info
900 Cummings Ctr Suite 221-U Beverly MA 01915
Ph: 978-927-8330 ▪ Fx: 978-524-8890

Surgical Association, American Pediatric www.eapsa.org
60 Revere Dr Suite 500 Northbrook IL 60062
Ph: 847-480-9576 ▪ Fx: 847-480-9282

Surgical Education, Association for www.surgicaleducation.com
SIU School of Medicine Dept of Surgery PO Box
19655 Springfield IL 62794
Ph: 217-545-3835

Surgical Eye Expeditions International Inc www.seeintl.org
27 E de La Guerra St Suite C-2 Santa Barbara CA 93101
Ph: 805-963-3303 ▪ Fx: 805-965-3564 ▪ TF: 800-208-6733

Surgical Hospital Association, American www.surgicalhospital.org
PO Box 23220 San Diego CA 92193
Ph: 858-490-8085 ▪ Fx: 858-490-9016 ▪ TF: 800-237-3768

Surgical Manufacturers Association, Orthopedic www.osma.cc/
1962 Deep Valley Cove Germantown TN 38138
Ph: 901-754-8097

Surgical Nurses, Academy of Medical- www.medsurgnurse.org
PO Box 56 Pitman NJ 08071
Ph: 856-256-2323 ▪ Fx: 856-589-7463

Surgical Nurses, American Society of Plastic www.aspsn.org
3220 Pointe Pkwy Suite 500 Atlanta GA 30092
Ph: 678-291-0011 ▪ Fx: 678-291-9731

Surgical Oncology Inc, Society of www.surgonc.org
85 W Algonquin Rd Suite 550 Arlington Heights IL 60005
Ph: 847-427-1400 ▪ Fx: 847-427-9656

Surgical Physician Assistants, American Association of www.aaspa.com
PO Box 867 Bernardsville NJ 07924
Ph: 732-560-8378 ▪ Fx: 732-805-9582 ▪ TF: 888-882-2772

Surgical Research, Academy of www.surgicalresearch.org
7500 Flying Cloud Rd Suite 900 Eden Prairie MN 55344
Ph: 952-253-6240 ▪ Fx: 952-835-4774

Surgical Society, Michael E DeBakey International www.mediss.org
1 Baylor Plaza Houston TX 77030
Ph: 713-798-4557 ▪ Fx: 713-796-9605

Surgical Technologists, Association of www.ast.org
7108 S Alton Way Bldg C Englewood CO 80112
Ph: 303-694-9130 ▪ Fx: 303-694-9169

Surplus Lines Offices, National Association of Professional www.napslo.org
6405 N Cosby Ave Suite 201 Kansas City MO 64151
Ph: 816-741-3910 ▪ Fx: 816-741-5409

Surplus Property, National Association of State Agencies for nasasp.org
2221 Forster St Rm G-49 Harrisburg PA 17105
Ph: 717-787-9724 ▪ Fx: 717-772-2491

Surratt Society www.surratt.org/su_scty.html
PO Box 427 Clinton MD 20735
Ph: 301-868-1121 ▪ Fx: 301-868-8177

Surrogacy, Organization of Parents Through www.opts.com
PO Box 611 Gurnee IL 60031
Ph: 847-782-0224 ▪ Fx: 847-782-0240

Surveillance Manufacturers Association, International Electronic www.ieasma.org
Article 1800 K St NW Washington DC 20006
Ph: 202-466-4212 ▪ Fx: 202-466-7414

Survey Research Organizations, Council of American www.casro.org
3 Upper Devon Rd Port Jefferson NY 11777
Ph: 631-928-6954 ▪ Fx: 631-928-6041

Surveying, American Association for Geodetic www.acsm.net/aags
6 Montgomery Village Ave Suite 403 Gaithersburg MD 20879
Ph: 240-632-9716 ▪ Fx: 240-632-1321

Surveying & Mapping, American Congress on www.acsm.net
6 Montgomery Village Ave Suite 403 Gaithersburg MD 20879
Ph: 240-632-9716 ▪ Fx: 240-632-1321

Surveying, National Council of Examiners for Engineering & www.ncees.org
280 Seneca Creek Rd Clemson SC 29633
Ph: 864-654-6824 ▪ Fx: 864-654-6033 ▪ TF: 800-250-3196

Surveyors Association, US www.navsurvey.com
13430 McGregor Blvd Fort Myers FL 33919
Ph: 800-245-4425 ▪ Fx: 941-481-5150

Surveyors Historical Society www.surveyhistory.org/surveyor's_historical_society.htm
300 W High St Suite 2 Lawrenceburg IN 47025
Ph: 812-537-2000

Surveyors, Management Association for Private Photogrammetric www.mapps.org/
1760 Reston Pkwy Suite 515 Reston VA 20190
Ph: 703-787-6996 ▪ Fx: 703-787-7550

Surveyors, National Association of County www.naco.org/nacs/index.html
c/o National Assn of Counties 440 1st St NW Washington DC
20001
Ph: 202-393-6226 ▪ Fx: 202-393-2630

Surveyors, National Association of Marine www.nams-cms.org
PO Box 9306 Chesapeake VA 23321
Ph: 757-488-9538 ▪ Fx: 757-488-0584 ▪ TF: 800-822-6267

Surveyors, National Society of Professional www.acsm.net/nsps
6 Montgomery Village Ave Suite 403 Gaithersburg MD 20879
Ph: 240-632-9716 ▪ Fx: 240-632-1321

Surveyors, Society of Accredited Marine www.marinesurvey.org
4605 Cardina Blvd Jacksonville FL 32210
Ph: 904-384-1494 ▪ Fx: 904-388-3958

Survival Research Foundation
1000 Island Blvd Suite 512 Aventura FL 33160
Ph: 305-936-1408

Survivors of Clergy Abuse, Linkup The - www.thelinkup.org
291 N Hubbards Ln Suite B26 Louisville KY 40207
Ph: 502-290-4055 ▪ Fx: 502-290-4056

Survivors of Incest Anonymous www.siawso.org
PO Box 190 Benson MD 21018
Ph: 410-893-3322

Survivors Network of Those Abused by Priests www.snapnetwork.org
PO Box 6416 Chicago IL 60680
Ph: 312-409-2720

Susan G Komen Breast Cancer Foundation www.komen.org
5005 LBJ Fwy Suite 250 Dallas TX 75244
Ph: 972-855-1600 ▪ Fx: 972-855-1605 ▪ TF: 800-462-9273

Sustainability, Alliance for www.afs.nonprofitoffice.com
Univ of Minnesota Hillel Center 1521 University Ave
SE Minneapolis MN 55414
Ph: 612-331-1099 ▪ Fx: 612-379-1527

Sustainability, Federal Network for www.federalsustainability.org
1331 H St NW Suite 1000 Washington DC 20005
Ph: 202-628-6100 ▪ Fx: 202-393-5043

Sustainable Buildings Industry Council www.sbicouncil.org
1331 H St NW Suite 1000 Washington DC 20005
Ph: 202-628-7400 ▪ Fx: 202-393-5043

Sustainable Communities, Institute for www.iscvt.org
535 Stone Cutters Way Montpelier VT 05602
Ph: 802-229-2900 ▪ Fx: 802-229-2919

Sustainable Development, Citizens Network for www.citnet.org
11426 Rockville Pike Suite 306 Rockville MD 20852
Ph: 301-770-6375 ▪ Fx: 301-770-6377

Sustainable Energy, Business Council for www.bcse.org
1200 18th St NW 9th Fl Washington DC 20036
Ph: 202-785-0507 ▪ Fx: 202-785-0514

Sutton Movement Writing, Center for www.dancewriting.org
PO Box 517 La Jolla CA 92038
Ph: 858-456-0098 ▪ Fx: 858-456-0020

Suzuki Association of the Americas www.suzukiassociation.org
PO Box 17310 Boulder CO 80308
Ph: 303-444-0948 ▪ Fx: 303-444-0984

Svithiod, Independent Order of
5518 W Lawrence Ave Chicago IL 60630
Ph: 773-736-1191

Swaggart Jimmy Ministries www.jsm.org
8919 World Ministry Blvd Baton Rouge LA 70810
Ph: 225-768-8300 ▪ Fx: 225-769-2244 ▪ TF: 800-288-8350

Swan Society, Trumpeter trumpeterswansociety.org
3800 County Rd 24 Maple Plain MN 55359
Ph: 763-476-4663 ▪ Fx: 763-476-1514

Swaps & Derivatives Association, International www.isda.org
360 Madison Ave 16th Fl New York NY 10017
Ph: 212-901-6000 ▪ Fx: 212-901-6001

Swedenborg Association www.swedenborg.net
278-A Meeting St Charleston SC 29401
Ph: 843-853-6211

Swedenborg Foundation www.swedenborg.com
320 N Church St West Chester PA 19380
Ph: 610-430-3222 ▪ Fx: 610-430-7982 ▪ TF: 800-355-3222

Swedish-American Chamber of Commerce of the USA Inc www.sacc-usa.org
1403 King St Alexandria VA 22314
Ph: 703-836-6560 ▪ Fx: 703-836-6561

(Swedish American) Vasa Order of America www.vasaorder.com

Swedish Council of America www.swedishcouncil.org
2600 Park Ave Minneapolis MN 55407
Ph: 612-871-0593 ▪ Fx: 612-872-1452

Swedish Engineers, American Society of www.asse-usa.org
780 3rd Ave King of Prussia PA 19406
Ph: 610-265-4352 ▪ Fx: 610-265-4608

Swedish Gotland Breeders' Society
3240 Hinton-Webber Rd   Corinth KY 41010
Ph: 859-234-5707

Sweet Adelines International   www.sweetadelineintl.org
9110 S Toledo Ave   Tulsa OK 74137
Ph: 918-622-1444 ▪ Fx: 918-665-0894 ▪ TF: 800-992-7464

Swim School Association, National   www.nationalswimschools.com
8300 N Hayden Rd Suite 207   Scottsdale AZ 85258
Ph: 480-467-0283 ▪ Fx: 480-467-0204

Swimming Coaches Association of America, College   www.cscaa.org
PO Box 63285   Colorado Springs CO 80962
Ph: 719-266-0064 ▪ Fx: 719-266-6844

Swimming Coaches Association, American   www.swimmingcoach.org
2101 N Andrews Ave Suite 107   Fort Lauderdale FL 33311
Ph: 954-563-4930 ▪ Fx: 954-563-9813 ▪ TF: 800-356-2722

Swimming Pool Foundation, National   www.nspf.org
224 E Cheyenne Mountain Blvd   Colorado Springs CO 80906
Ph: 719-540-9119 ▪ Fx: 719-540-2787

Swimming, US Masters   www.usms.org
PO Box 185   Londonderry NH 03053
Ph: 603-537-0203 ▪ Fx: 603-537-0204 ▪ TF: 800-550-7946

Swimming, US Synchronized   www.usasynchro.org
201 S Capitol Ave Suite 901   Indianapolis IN 46225
Ph: 317-237-5700 ▪ Fx: 317-237-5705

Swimming, USA   www.usa-swimming.org
1 Olympic Plaza   Colorado Springs CO 80909
Ph: 719-866-4578 ▪ Fx: 719-866-4669

Swine Improvement Federation, National   www.nsif.org
Iowa State Univ Dept of Animal Science 109 Kildee Hall   Ames
   IA 50011
Ph: 515-294-4683 ▪ Fx: 515-294-5698

Swine Record, National Spotted
PO Box 9758   Peoria IL 61612
Ph: 309-693-1804 ▪ Fx: 309-691-0168

Swine Registry, National   www.nationalswine.com
PO Box 2417   West Lafayette IN 47996
Ph: 765-463-3594 ▪ Fx: 765-497-2959

Swine Veterinarians, American Association of   www.aasv.org
902 1st Ave   Perry IA 50220
Ph: 515-465-5255 ▪ Fx: 515-465-3832

Swiss Alliance, North American
7650 Chippewa Rd Rm 214   Brecksville OH 44141
Ph: 440-526-2257

Swiss-American Chamber of Commerce   www.amcham.ch
608 5th Ave Rm 309   New York NY 10020
Ph: 212-246-7789 ▪ Fx: 212-246-1366

Swiss Foundation, American   www.americanswiss.org
232 E 66th St   New York NY 10021
Ph: 212-754-0130 ▪ Fx: 212-754-4512

Switching Forum, Multiservice   www.msforum.org
39355 California St Suite 307   Fremont CA 94538
Ph: 510-608-5922 ▪ Fx: 510-608-5917

Sword Society of the US, Japanese   www.jssus.org

Symbolic Logic, Association for   www.aslonline.org
Vassar College PO Box 742   Poughkeepsie NY 12604
Ph: 845-437-7080 ▪ Fx: 845-437-7830

Symphony & Opera Musicians, International Conference of   www.icsom.org
4 W 31st St Unit 921   New York NY 10001
Ph: 212-594-1636

Symphony Orchestra League, American   www.symphony.org
33 W 60th St 5th Fl   New York NY 10023
Ph: 212-262-5161 ▪ Fx: 212-262-5198

Synagogue of Conservative Judaism, United   www.uscj.org
155 5th Ave   New York NY 10010
Ph: 212-533-7800 ▪ Fx: 212-353-9439

Synagogue Library Association, Church &   www.worldaccessnet.com/~csla
PO Box 19357   Portland OR 97280
Ph: 503-244-6919 ▪ Fx: 503-977-3734 ▪ TF: 800-542-2752

Synagogue Youth, National Conference of   www.ou.org/ncsy
11 Broadway   New York NY 10004
Ph: 212-613-8232 ▪ Fx: 212-613-0633

Synagogue Youth, United   www.usy.org
155 5th Ave   New York NY 10010
Ph: 212-533-7800 ▪ Fx: 212-353-9439

Synagogues, International Alliance of Messianic Congregations &   iamcs.org
PO Box 20006   Sarasota FL 34276
Ph: 941-923-0193 ▪ TF: 866-426-2766

Synchronized Swimming, US   www.usasynchro.org
201 S Capitol Ave Suite 901   Indianapolis IN 46225
Ph: 317-237-5700 ▪ Fx: 317-237-5705

Synergos Institute Inc   www.synergos.org
9 E 69th St   New York NY 10021
Ph: 212-517-4900 ▪ Fx: 212-517-4815

Synthetic Amorphous Silica & Silicates Industry Association
1 PPG Pl   Pittsburgh PA 15272
Ph: 412-434-2801 ▪ Fx: 412-434-3193

Synthetic Organic Chemical Manufacturers Association   www.socma.com
1850 M St NW Suite 700   Washington DC 20036
Ph: 202-721-4100 ▪ Fx: 202-296-8120

Synthetic Rubber Producers Inc, International Institute of   www.iisrp.com
2077 S Gessner Rd Suite 133   Houston TX 77063
Ph: 713-783-7511 ▪ Fx: 713-783-7253

Syrian Associated Charities, American Lebanese   www.stjude.org
501 St Jude Pl   Memphis TN 38105
Ph: 901-578-2000 ▪ Fx: 901-578-2805 ▪ TF: 800-822-6344

Syrup Institute, International Maple
PO Box 53010   Burlington VT 05405
Ph: 802-656-5417 ▪ Fx: 802-656-5422

System Safety Society   www.system-safety.org
PO Box 70   Unionville VA 22567
Ph: 540-854-8630 ▪ Fx: 540-854-4561

Systems Association, Insurance Accounting &   www.iasa.org
4705 University Dr Suite 280 PO Box 51340   Durham NC
   27717
Ph: 919-489-0991 ▪ Fx: 919-489-1994

Systems Client Network, Applied   www.ascnet.org
801 Douglas Ave Suite 205   Altamonte Springs FL 32714
Ph: 407-869-0404 ▪ Fx: 407-869-0418

Systems Contractors Association, National   www.nsca.org
625 1st St SE Suite 420   Cedar Rapids IA 52401
Ph: 319-366-6722 ▪ Fx: 319-366-4164 ▪ TF: 800-446-6722

Systems Engineering, International Council on   www.incose.org
2150 N 107th St Suite 205   Seattle WA 98133
Ph: 206-361-6607 ▪ Fx: 206-367-8777 ▪ TF: 800-366-1164

Systems Man & Cybernetics Society, IEEE   www.ieeesmc.org
IEEE Operations Ctr 445 Hoes Ln   Piscataway NJ 08854
Ph: 732-981-0060 ▪ Fx: 732-981-1721

Systems Professionals Association Inc, Network &   www.naspa.com
7044 S 13th St   Oak Creek WI 53154
Ph: 414-768-8000 ▪ Fx: 414-768-8001

Systems Sciences, International Society for the   www.isss.org/
38 Seca Pl   Salinas CA 93908
Ph: 831-375-7614

Szyk Arthur Society   www.szyk.org
1200 Edgehill Dr   Burlingame CA 94010
Ph: 650-343-9588 ▪ Fx: 650-579-6014

T

Table Tennis, USA   www.usatt.org
1 Olympic Plaza   Colorado Springs CO 80909
Ph: 719-866-4583 ▪ Fx: 719-632-6071

Taekwondo Union, Pan American   www.patu.org
440 S Washington St   Falls Church VA 22046
Ph: 703-534-3737 ▪ Fx: 703-536-3223

Taekwondo Union, US   www.ustu.org
1 Olympic Plaza Suite 104C   Colorado Springs CO 80909
Ph: 719-866-4632 ▪ Fx: 719-866-4642

Tag & Label Manufacturers Institute   www.tlmi.com
40 Shuman Blvd Suite 295   Naperville IL 60563
Ph: 630-357-9222 ▪ Fx: 630-357-0192 ▪ TF: 800-533-8564

Tailhook Association   www.tailhook.org
9696 Businesspark Ave   San Diego CA 92131
Ph: 858-689-9223 ▪ Fx: 858-578-8839 ▪ TF: 800-322-4665

Tailors & Designers Association of America, Custom   www.ctda.com
PO Box 53052   Washington DC 20009
Ph: 202-387-7220 ▪ Fx: 202-387-7713

Taiwan Business Council, US-   www.us-taiwan.org
1700 N Moore St Suite 703   Arlington VA 22209
Ph: 703-465-2930 ▪ Fx: 703-465-2937

Take Pounds Off Sensibly   www.tops.org
4575 S 5th St   Milwaukee WI 53207
Ph: 414-482-4620 ▪ TF: 800-932-8677

Talent Agents, Association of   www.agentassociation.com
9255 Sunset Blvd Suite 930   Los Angeles CA 90069
Ph: 310-274-0628 ▪ Fx: 310-274-5063

Talented Children, World Council for Gifted &   www.worldgifted.org
18401 Hiawatha St   Northridge CA 91326
Ph: 818-368-7501 ▪ Fx: 818-368-2163

Talented Students, Association for Gifted &
PO Box 16037   Baton Rouge LA 70896
Ph: 504-388-2469 ▪ Fx: 504-388-1375 ▪ TF: 800-626-8811

Tall Buildings & Urban Habitat, Council on   www.ctbuh.com
Illinois Institute of Technology SR Crown Hall 3360 S State
   St   Chicago IL 60616
Ph: 312-909-0253

Tall Cedars of Lebanon of North America   www.mastermason.com/tcl
2609 N Front St   Harrisburg PA 17110
Ph: 717-232-5991 ▪ Fx: 717-232-5997

Tall Timbers   www.talltimbers.org
13093 Henry Beadel Dr   Tallahassee FL 32312
Ph: 850-893-4153 ▪ Fx: 850-893-6470

TallGrass Writers Guild   www.outriderpress.com/guildinfo.html
c/o Outrider Press 937 Patricia Ln   Crete IL 60417
Ph: 708-672-6630 ▪ Fx: 708-672-5820 ▪ TF: 800-933-4680

Talmudic Schools, Association of Advanced Rabbinical &
11 Broadway   New York NY 10004
Ph: 212-363-1991 ▪ Fx: 212-533-5335

Tandem Club of America   www.tandemclub.org
2220 Vanessa Dr   Birmingham AL 35242
Ph: 205-991-7766

Tandem Users' Group, International   www.itug.org
401 N Michigan   Chicago IL 60611
Ph: 312-321-6851 ▪ Fx: 312-321-5158 ▪ TF: 800-845-4884

Tangible Assets, Industry Council for   www.ictaonline.org/mainindex.html
PO Box 1365   Severna Park MD 21146
Ph: 410-626-7005 ▪ Fx: 410-626-7007

Tangier American Legation Museum Society   www.maroc.net/legation

Tank Institute, National Wood
PO Box 2755   Philadelphia PA 19120
Ph: 215-329-9022 ▪ Fx: 215-329-1177

Tank & Pipe Institute, Fiberglass   www.fiberglasstankandpipe.com
11150 Wilcrest Dr Suite 101   Houston TX 77099
Ph: 281-568-4100 ▪ Fx: 281-568-4500

Tank Truck Carriers Inc, National   www.tanktruck.org
2200 Mill Rd Suite 620   Alexandria VA 22314
Ph: 703-838-1960 ▪ Fx: 703-684-5753

Tanker Association, Airlift/   www.atalink.org
9312 Convento Terr   Fairfax VA 22031
Ph: 703-385-2802 ▪ Fx: 703-385-2803

Tap Association, International   www.tapdance.org
PO Box 356   Boulder CO 80306
Ph: 303-443-7989 ▪ Fx: 303-443-7992

Tape Council, Pressure Sensitive   www.pstc.org
2514 Stonebridge Ln PO Box 609   Northbrook IL 60062
Ph: 847-562-2630 ▪ Fx: 847-562-2631 ▪ TF: 877-523-7782

Tarentaise Association, American   www.usa-tarentaise.com
PO Box 34705   Kansas City MO 64116
Ph: 816-421-1993 ▪ Fx: 816-421-1991

Tarp Association, Truck Cover &   www.truckcover-tarp.org
1801 County Rd 'B' W   Roseville MN 55113
Ph: 651-225-6959

Tartan Studies/Tartan Educational Cultural   www.scottish-coalition.org/TECA/teca.htm
Association, International Assn of   442 Freedom Blvd PO Box
     138   Skippack PA 19474
Ph: 610-584-4220 ▪ Fx: 610-584-6456

TASH   www.tash.org
29 W Susquehanna Ave Suite 210   Baltimore MD 21204
Ph: 410-828-8274 ▪ Fx: 410-828-6706

Tasters Guild International   www.tastersguild.com
1451 W Cypress Creek Rd Suite 300   Fort Lauderdale FL
     33309
Ph: 954-928-2823 ▪ Fx: 954-928-2824

Tattoo Artists Guild, Professional
27 Mt Vernon Ave PO Box 1374   Mount Vernon NY 10550
Ph: 914-668-2300 ▪ Fx: 914-668-5200

Tattoo Association, Christian   www.xtat.org
2815 Gull Rd   Kalamazoo MI 49048
Ph: 269-998-7738

Tattoo Association, National   www.nationaltattooassociation.com
485 Business Pk Ln   Allentown PA 18109
Ph: 610-433-7261 ▪ Fx: 610-433-7294

Tattoo-a-Pet   www.tattoo-a-pet.com
6571 SW 20th Ct   Fort Lauderdale FL 33317
Ph: 954-581-5834 ▪ Fx: 954-581-0056 ▪ TF: 800-828-8667

Tau Alpha Chi   www.taualphachi.org
82 Thompson St   Alpharetta GA 30004
Ph: 770-475-4253 ▪ Fx: 770-475-4408

Tau Alpha Pi   www.taualphapi.org

Tau Beta Pi Association   www.tbp.org
PO Box 2697   Knoxville TN 37901
Ph: 865-546-4578 ▪ Fx: 865-546-4579 ▪ TF: 800-828-2382

Tau Beta Sigma National Honorary Band Sorority   www.kkytbs.org/tbs
PO Box 849   Stillwater OK 74076
Ph: 405-372-2333 ▪ Fx: 405-372-2363 ▪ TF: 800-543-6505

Tau Epsilon Phi National Fraternity   www.tephq.org
1000 White Horse Rd Suite 512   Voorhees NJ 08043
Ph: 856-782-9837 ▪ Fx: 856-782-9849

Tau Epsilon Rho Law Society   www.ter-law.org
1951 Old Cuthbert Rd Suite 413   Cherry Hill NJ 08034
Ph: 856-429-3901

Tau Kappa Epsilon   www.tke.org
8645 Founders Rd   Indianapolis IN 46268
Ph: 317-872-6533 ▪ Fx: 317-875-8353

Taubman Center for State & Local Government   www.ksg.harvard.edu/taubmancenter
Harvard Univ John F Kennedy School of Government 79 JFK
     St   Cambridge MA 02138
Ph: 617-495-2199

Taunting Safety & Fairness Everywhere, National Organization   www.notsafe.org
PO Box 5743   Santa Barbara CA 93150
Ph: 805-966-0611

Tavern Keepers, Flagon & Trencher Society: nctimes.net/~churchyj/fandt_home.html
Descendants of Colonial   7916 Quill Point Dr   Bowie MD
     20720
Ph: 301-352-2919

Tax Administrators, Federation of   www.taxadmin.org
444 N Capitol St NW Suite 348   Washington DC 20001
Ph: 202-624-5890 ▪ Fx: 202-624-7888

Tax Association, National   www.ntanet.org
725 15th St NW Suite 600   Washington DC 20005
Ph: 202-737-3325 ▪ Fx: 202-737-7308

Tax Commission, Multistate   www.mtc.gov
444 N Capitol St NW Suite 425   Washington DC 20001
Ph: 202-624-8699 ▪ Fx: 202-624-8819

Tax Consultants, Institute of   www.taxprofessionals.homestead.com/welcome.html
7500 212th St SW Suite 205   Edmonds WA 98026
Ph: 425-774-3521 ▪ Fx: 425-672-0461

Tax Council   www.thetaxcouncil.org
1301 K St NW Suite 800 W   Washington DC 20005
Ph: 202-822-8062 ▪ Fx: 202-414-1460

Tax Counsel, American College of
1156 15th St NW Suite 900   Washington DC 20005
Ph: 202-637-3243 ▪ Fx: 202-393-0336

Tax Credit Coalition, Affordable Housing   www.taxcreditcoalition.org
401 9th St NW Suite 900   Washington DC 20004
Ph: 202-585-8739 ▪ Fx: 202-585-8080

Tax Education, Council for International   www.fdta-cite.org
PO Box 1012   White Plains NY 10602
Ph: 914-328-5656 ▪ Fx: 914-328-5757

Tax Executives Institute   www.tei.org
1200 G St NW Suite 300   Washington DC 20005
Ph: 202-638-5601 ▪ Fx: 202-638-5607

Tax Free America, Alliance for a
PO Box 476   Leonia NJ 07605
Ph: 201-947-7449 ▪ Fx: 201-947-1503

Tax Lien Association, National   www.ntlainfo.org
220 W Gadsden St Suite 600   Pensacola FL 32501
Ph: 850-470-9974 ▪ Fx: 850-470-9522

Tax Professionals, National Association of   www.natptax.com
720 Association Dr   Appleton WI 54914
Ph: 920-749-1040 ▪ Fx: 800-747-0001 ▪ TF: 800-558-3402

Tax Professionals, National Society of   www.nstp.org
10818 NE Coxley Dr Suite A   Vancouver WA 98662
Ph: 360-695-8309 ▪ Fx: 360-695-7115 ▪ TF: 800-367-8130

Tax Reform, Americans for   www.atr.org
1920 L St NW Suite 200   Washington DC 20036
Ph: 202-785-0266 ▪ Fx: 202-785-0261

Tax Token Society, American
12 Pheasant Dr   Asheville NC 28803
Ph: 828-684-1808

Taxation, Accreditation Council for Accountancy &   www.acatcredentials.org
1010 N Fairfax St   Alexandria VA 22314
Ph: 703-549-2228 ▪ Fx: 703-549-2984 ▪ TF: 888-289-7763

Taxation, Americans for Fair   www.fairtax.org
PO Box 27487   Houston TX 77227
Ph: 713-963-9023 ▪ Fx: 713-963-8403 ▪ TF: 800-324-7829

Taxation Association, American   www.atasection.org
c/o American Accounting Assn 5717 Bessie Dr   Sarasota FL
     34233
Ph: 941-921-7747 ▪ Fx: 941-923-4093

(Taxation) CapitolWatch   www.capitolwatch.org
PO Box 71   Great Falls VA 22066
Ph: 202-544-2600 ▪ Fx: 703-430-6378

Taxation, Council on State   www.statetax.org
122 C St NW Suite 330   Washington DC 20001
Ph: 202-484-5222 ▪ Fx: 202-484-5229

Taxation, Institute for Professionals in   www.ipt.org
3350 Peachtree Rd Suite 280   Atlanta GA 30326
Ph: 404-240-2300 ▪ Fx: 404-240-2315

(Taxation) Tau Alpha Chi   www.taualphachi.org
82 Thompson St   Alpharetta GA 30004
Ph: 770-475-4253 ▪ Fx: 770-475-4408

Taxicab Limousine & Paratransit Association   www.tlpa.org
3849 Farragut Ave   Kensington MD 20895
Ph: 301-946-5701 ▪ Fx: 301-946-4641

Taxidermists Association, National   www.nationaltaxidermists.com
108 Branch Dr   Slidell LA 70461
Ph: 985-641-4682 ▪ Fx: 985-641-9463

Taxonomists, American Society of Plant   www.sysbot.org
Univ of Wyoming Dept of Botany 3165 1000 E University
     Ave   Laramie WY 82071
Ph: 307-766-2556 ▪ Fx: 307-766-2851

Taxpayers Against Fraud Education Fund   www.taf.org
1220 19th St NW Suite 501   Washington DC 20036
Ph: 202-296-4826 ▪ Fx: 202-296-4838 ▪ TF: 800-873-2573

Taxpayers Union, National   www.ntu.org
108 N Alfred St   Alexandria VA 22314
Ph: 703-683-5700 ▪ Fx: 703-683-5722 ▪ TF: 800-829-4258

Tay-Sachs & Allied Diseases Association, National   www.ntsad.org
2001 Beacon St Suite 204   Brighton MA 02135
Ph: 617-277-4463 ▪ Fx: 617-277-0134 ▪ TF: 800-906-8723

Tay-Sachs Foundation, Late-Onset   www.lotsf.org
PO Box 5   Flourtown PA 19031
Ph: 800-672-2022

Tea Association of the USA Inc   www.teausa.com
420 Lexington Ave Suite 825   New York NY 10170
Ph: 212-986-9415 ▪ Fx: 212-697-8658

Tea Ceremony Society, Urasenke
153 E 69th St   New York NY 10021
Ph: 212-988-6611 ▪ Fx: 212-517-7594

Tea Council of the USA Inc   www.teausa.com
420 Lexington Ave Suite 825   New York NY 10170
Ph: 212-986-6998 ▪ Fx: 212-697-8658

Tea Leaf Club International   www.tealeafclub.com
PO Box 377   Belton MO 64012
Ph: 816-331-5546

Tea Society, Women's Mountain Bike &   www.wombats.org
PO Box 757   Fairfax CA 94978
Ph: 415-459-0980

Teach For America   www.teachforamerica.org
315 W 36th St 6th Fl   New York NY 10018
Ph: 212-279-2080 ▪ Fx: 212-279-2081

Teacher Education, American Association of Colleges for   www.aacte.org
1307 New York Ave NW Suite 300   Washington DC 20005
Ph: 202-293-2450 ▪ Fx: 202-457-8095

Teacher Education & Certification, National Association of   www.nasdtec.org
State Directors of   39 Nathan Ellis Hwy PMB 134   Mashpee
     MA 02649
Ph: 508-539-8844 ▪ Fx: 508-539-8868

Teacher Education, Council on Technology   teched.vt.edu/ctte
International Technology Education Assn 1914 Association
     Dr   Reston VA 20191
Ph: 703-860-2100 ▪ Fx: 703-860-0353

Teacher Education, National Association for Business   www.nbea.org
1914 Association Dr   Reston VA 20191
Ph: 703-860-8300 ▪ Fx: 703-620-4483

Teacher Education, National Council for Accreditation of   www.ncate.org
2010 Massachusetts Ave NW Suite 500   Washington DC 20036
Ph: 202-466-7496 ▪ Fx: 202-296-6620

Teacher Educators, National Association of Early Childhood   www.naecte.org

Teacher Retirement, National Council on   www.nctr.org
7600 Greenhaven Dr Suite 302   Sacramento CA 95831
Ph: 916-394-2075 ▪ Fx: 916-392-0295

Teachers Against Violence in Education, Parents &   www.nospank.net
PO Box 1033 Alamo CA 94507
Ph: 925-831-1661 ▪ Fx: 925-838-8914

Teachers' Agencies, National Association of   www.jobsforteachers.com
797 Kings Hwy Fairfield CT 06825
Ph: 203-333-0611 ▪ Fx: 203-334-7224

Teachers of America, Society of Roller Skating
6905 Corporate Dr Indianapolis IN 46278
Ph: 317-347-2626 ▪ Fx: 317-347-2636

Teachers, American Association of Physics   www.aapt.org
1 Physics Ellipse College Park MD 20740
Ph: 301-209-3300 ▪ Fx: 301-209-0845

Teachers, American Federation of   www.aft.org
555 New Jersey Ave NW Washington DC 20001
Ph: 202-879-4400 ▪ Fx: 202-879-4556 ▪ TF: 800-238-1133

Teachers of Arabic, American Association of   www.wm.edu/aata
College of William & Mary PO Box 8795 Williamsburg VA 23187
Ph: 757-221-3145 ▪ Fx: 757-221-3637

Teachers Association, American String   www.astaweb.com
4153 Chain Bridge Rd Fairfax VA 22030
Ph: 703-279-2113 ▪ Fx: 703-279-2114

Teachers Association, Chinese Language   clta.deall.ohio-state.edu
Univ of Hawaii Center for Chinese Studies 416 Moore Hall Honolulu HI 96822
Ph: 808-956-2692

Teachers Association, National Earth Science   www.nestanet.org

Teachers Association, National Retired   www.aarp.org/nrta
601 'E' St NW Washington DC 20049
Ph: 202-434-2277 ▪ Fx: 202-434-2320 ▪ TF: 800-424-3410

Teachers Association, National Science   www.nsta.org
1840 Wilson Blvd Arlington VA 22201
Ph: 703-243-7100 ▪ Fx: 703-243-7177 ▪ TF: 800-722-6782

Teachers Association, National Visiting   www.nvta4parents.org
650 Howe Ave Suite 1014 Sacramento CA 95825
Ph: 916-921-6882 ▪ Fx: 916-921-1460

Teachers, Association of Orthodox Jewish
1577 Coney Island Dr Brooklyn NY 11230
Ph: 718-258-3585 ▪ Fx: 718-258-3586

Teachers Committee on Political Education, American Federation of
555 New Jersey Ave NW Washington DC 20001
Ph: 202-879-4400 ▪ Fx: 202-879-4556 ▪ TF: 800-238-1133

Teachers of Czech, International Association of   www.language.brown.edu/NAATC/

Teachers of English, National Council of   www.ncte.org
1111 W Kenyon Rd Urbana IL 61801
Ph: 217-328-3870 ▪ Fx: 217-328-0977 ▪ TF: 800-369-6283

Teachers of English to Speakers of Other Languages   www.tesol.org
700 S Washington St Suite 200 Alexandria VA 22314
Ph: 703-836-0774 ▪ Fx: 703-836-7864

Teachers of Esperanto, American Association of
5140 San Lorenzo Dr Santa Barbara CA 93111
Ph: 805-967-5241

Teachers of Family Medicine, Society of   www.stfm.org
11400 Tomahawk Creek Pkwy Suite 540 Leawood KS 66211
Ph: 913-906-6000 ▪ Fx: 913-906-6096

Teachers Federation, US Golf   www.usgtf.com
1295 SE Port St Lucie Blvd Port Saint Lucie FL 34952
Ph: 772-335-3216 ▪ Fx: 772-335-3822 ▪ TF: 888-346-3290

Teachers of French, American Association of   www.frenchteachers.org
Southern Illinois Univ MC 4510 Carbondale IL 62901
Ph: 618-453-5731 ▪ Fx: 618-453-5733

Teachers of German, American Association of   www.aatg.org
112 Haddontowne Ct Suite 104 Cherry Hill NJ 08034
Ph: 856-795-5553 ▪ Fx: 856-795-9398

Teachers of Italian, American Association of   www.italianstudies.org/aati
Univ of Wisconsin Dept of French & Italian 618 Van Hise Hall 1220 Linden Dr Madison WI 53706
Ph: 608-262-3941 ▪ Fx: 608-265-3892

Teachers of Japanese, Association of   www.colorado.edu/ealld/atj
Univ of Colorado-Boulder 279 UCB Boulder CO 80309
Ph: 303-492-5487 ▪ Fx: 303-492-5856

Teachers of Korean, American Association of   www.fsu.edu/~aatk
Florida State Univ Dept of Modern Languages & Linguistics Tallahassee FL 32306
Ph: 850-644-3728 ▪ Fx: 850-644-0524

Teachers of Mathematics, National Council of   www.nctm.org
1906 Association Dr Reston VA 20191
Ph: 703-620-9840 ▪ Fx: 703-476-2970 ▪ TF: 800-235-7566

Teachers, National Association of Biology   www.nabt.org
12030 Sunrise Valley Dr Suite 110 Reston VA 20191
Ph: 703-264-9696 ▪ Fx: 703-264-7778 ▪ TF: 800-406-0775

Teachers, National Association of Catholic School   www.nacst.com
1700 Sansom St Suite 903 Philadelphia PA 19103
Ph: 215-665-0993 ▪ Fx: 215-568-8270 ▪ TF: 800-996-2278

Teachers, National Association of Geoscience   www.nagt.org
PO Box 5443 Bellingham WA 98227
Ph: 360-650-3587

Teachers National Association, Music   www.mtna.org
441 Vine St Suite 505 Cincinnati OH 45202
Ph: 513-421-1420 ▪ Fx: 513-421-2503 ▪ TF: 888-512-5278

Teachers, National Congress of Parents &   www.pta.org
330 N Wabash Ave Suite 2100 Chicago IL 60611
Ph: 312-670-6782 ▪ Fx: 312-670-6783 ▪ TF: 800-307-4782

Teachers, National Guild of Piano   www.pianoguild.com
PO Box 1807 Austin TX 78767
Ph: 512-478-5775 ▪ Fx: 512-478-5843

Teachers, North American Council of Automotive   www.nacat.com
11956 Bernardo Plaza Dr Dept 436 San Diego CA 92128
Ph: 858-487-8126 ▪ Fx: 858-487-3617

Teachers, Organization of Professional Acting Coaches &
3968 Eureka Dr Studio City CA 91604
Ph: 323-877-4988

Teachers of Science, Association for the Education of   aets.chem.pitt.edu
East Carolina Univ College of Education Austin 324-A Greenville NC 27858
Ph: 252-328-6736 ▪ Fx: 252-328-6218

Teachers of Singing, National Association of   www.nats.org
4745 Sutton Park Ct Suite 201 Jacksonville FL 32224
Ph: 904-992-9101 ▪ Fx: 904-992-9326

Teachers of Slavic & East European Languages, American Association of   www.aatseel.org
PO Box 7039 Berkeley CA 94707
Ph: 510-526-6614

Teachers, Society of American Law   www.saltlaw.org

Teachers of Southeast Asian Languages, Council of   www.cotseal.org

Teachers of Spanish & Portuguese, American Association of   www.aatsp.org
423 Exton Commons Exton PA 19341
Ph: 610-363-7005 ▪ Fx: 610-363-7116

Teachers of Turkic Languages, American Association of   www.princeton.edu/~ehgilson/aatt.html
Princeton Univ Near Eastern Studies 110 Jones Hall Princeton NJ 08544
Ph: 609-258-1435 ▪ Fx: 609-258-1242

Teachers & Writers Collaborative   www.twc.org
5 Union Sq W New York NY 10003
Ph: 212-691-6590 ▪ Fx: 212-675-0171 ▪ TF: 888-266-5789

Teaching, Carnegie Foundation for the Advancement of   www.carnegiefoundation.org
555 Middlefield Rd Menlo Park CA 94025
Ph: 650-566-5100 ▪ Fx: 650-326-0278

Teaching for Change   www.teachingforchange.org
PO Box 73038 Washington DC 20056
Ph: 202-588-7204 ▪ Fx: 202-238-0109 ▪ TF: 800-763-9131

Teaching Economics, Foundation for   www.fte.org
260 Russell Blvd Suite B Davis CA 95616
Ph: 530-757-4630 ▪ Fx: 530-757-4636

Teaching Family Association   www.teaching-family.org
4356 Bonney Rd Suite 103 Virginia Beach VA 23452
Ph: 757-497-3023 ▪ Fx: 757-497-0010

Teaching of Foreign Languages, American Council on the   www.actfl.org
6 Executive Plaza Yonkers NY 10701
Ph: 914-963-8830 ▪ Fx: 914-963-1275

Teaching of Foreign Languages, Northeast Conference on the   www.dickinson.edu/nectfl
Dickinson College PO Box 1773 Carlisle PA 17013
Ph: 717-245-1977 ▪ Fx: 717-245-1976

Teaching, National Association for Research in Science   www.educ.sfu.ca/narstsite
Univ of Missouri-Columbia 303 Townsend Hall Columbia MO 65211
Ph: 573-884-1401 ▪ Fx: 573-884-2917

Teaching Society, Organizational Behavior   obtsweb.pitzer.edu

Teaching Standards, National Board for Professional   www.nbpts.org
1525 Wilson Blvd Suite 500 Arlington VA 22209
Ph: 703-465-2700

TEAM   www.teamworld.org
PO Box 969 Wheaton IL 60189
Ph: 630-653-5300 ▪ Fx: 630-653-1826 ▪ TF: 800-343-3144

Team Handball, USA   www.usateamhandball.org
1 Olympic Plaza Colorado Springs CO 80909
Ph: 719-866-4036 ▪ Fx: 719-866-4055

Team USA, World   www.worldteam.org
1431 Stuckert Rd Warrington PA 18976
Ph: 215-491-4900 ▪ Fx: 215-491-4910 ▪ TF: 800-967-7109

Teamsters for a Democratic Union   www.tdu.org
PO Box 10128 Detroit MI 48210
Ph: 313-842-2600 ▪ Fx: 313-842-0227

Teamsters, International Brotherhood of   www.teamster.org
25 Louisiana Ave NW Washington DC 20001
Ph: 202-624-6800 ▪ Fx: 202-624-6918

TEC International Inc   www.teconline.com
11452 El Camino Real Suite 400 San Diego CA 92130
Ph: 858-627-4050 ▪ Fx: 800-934-4540 ▪ TF: 800-274-2367

Tech Corps   www.techcorps.org
2 Clock Tower Pl Suite 340 Maynard MA 01754
Ph: 978-897-8282 ▪ Fx: 978-897-4204

TECH Team, Missionary   www.techteam.org
25 FRJ Dr Longview TX 75602
Ph: 903-757-4530 ▪ Fx: 903-758-2799

Technical Assistance, Volunteers in   www.vita.org
1600 Wilson Blvd Suite 1030 Arlington VA 22209
Ph: 703-276-1800 ▪ Fx: 703-243-1865

Technical Association of the Graphic Arts   www.taga.org
68 Lomb Memorial Dr Rochester NY 14623
Ph: 585-475-7470 ▪ Fx: 585-475-2250

Technical Association, National   www.ntaonline.org
1761 E 30th St Suite 100 A Cleveland OH 44114
Ph: 216-298-4425 ▪ Fx: 216-289-3015

Technical Association of the Pulp & Paper Industry   www.tappi.org
15 Technology Pkwy S Norcross GA 30092
Ph: 770-446-1400 ▪ Fx: 770-446-6947 ▪ TF: 800-332-8686

Technical Communication, Society for   www.stc.org
901 N Stuart St Suite 904 Arlington VA 22203
Ph: 703-522-4114 ▪ Fx: 703-522-2075

Technical Consultants Association, Professional &   www.patca.org
543 Vista Mar Ave Pacifica CA 94044
Ph: 650-359-9502 ▪ Fx: 650-359-3089 ▪ TF: 800-747-2822

Technical Education Association, American   www.ateaonline.org
North Dakota State College of Science 800 N 6th St Wahpeton ND 58076
Ph: 701-671-2240 ▪ Fx: 701-671-2260

Technical Education, Association for Career &   www.acteonline.org
1410 King St   Alexandria VA 22314
Ph: 703-683-3111 ▪ Fx: 703-683-7424 ▪ TF: 800-826-9972

Technical Education Consortium, National Association of   www.careertech.org
State Directors of Career   444 N Capitol St NW Suite
830   Washington DC 20001
Ph: 202-737-0303 ▪ Fx: 202-737-1106

Technical Engineers, International Federation of Professional &   www.ifpte.org
8630 Fenton St Suite 400   Silver Spring MD 20910
Ph: 301-565-9016 ▪ Fx: 301-565-0018

Technical Honor Society, National   www.nvths.org
PO Box 1336   Flat Rock NC 28731
Ph: 828-698-8011

Technical Professionals, National Organization of Gay &   www.noglstp.org/
Lesbian Scientists &   PO Box 91803   Pasadena CA 91109
Ph: 626-791-7689

Technical Services Association, National   www.ntsa.com
2121 Eisenhower Ave Suite 604   Alexandria VA 22314
Ph: 703-684-4722 ▪ Fx: 703-684-7627

(Technical Studies) Alpha Sigma Kappa   www.tc.umn.edu/~ask
1009 University Ave SE   Minneapolis MN 55414
Ph: 612-378-4759

Technician Education Council, Aviation   www.atec-amt.org/
2090 Wexford Ct   Harrisburg PA 17112
Ph: 717-540-7121

Technician Excellence, North American   www.natex.org
4100 N Fairfax Dr 210   Arlington VA 22203
Ph: 703-276-7247 ▪ Fx: 703-527-2316 ▪ TF: 877-420-6283

Technicians, Association of Civilian   www.actnat.com
12620 Lake Ridge Dr   Woodbridge VA 22192
Ph: 703-494-4845 ▪ Fx: 703-494-0961

Technicians Association, Refrigerating Engineers &   www.reta.com
4700 W Lake Ave   Glenview IL 60025
Ph: 847-375-4738 ▪ Fx: 877-218-8369

Technicians Inc, Council on Library Media   colt.ucr.edu
Daniel Boone Regional Library 100 W Broadway   Columbia MO
65203
Ph: 573-443-3161 ▪ Fx: 573-874-0862

Technicians, National Association of Photo Equipment   napet.pmai.org
3000 Picture Pl   Jackson MI 49201
Ph: 517-788-8100 ▪ Fx: 517-788-8371

Technological Sciences Inc, International Council of Academies   www.caets.org
of Engineering &   500 5th St NW   Washington DC 20001
Ph: 703-527-5782 ▪ Fx: 703-526-0570

Technologies, Center for Waste Reduction   www.aiche.org/cwrt
3 Park Ave   New York NY 10016
Ph: 212-591-7462 ▪ Fx: 212-591-8895

Technologists, American Association of Candy   www.aactcandy.org
175 Rock Rd   Glen Rock NJ 07452
Ph: 201-652-2655 ▪ Fx: 201-652-3419

Technologists, American Chiropractic Registry of Radiologic
2330 Gull Rd   Kalamazoo MI 49048
Ph: 269-343-6666 ▪ Fx: 269-343-7236

Technologists, American Society of Radiologic   www.asrt.org
15000 Central Ave SE   Albuquerque NM 87123
Ph: 505-298-4500 ▪ Fx: 505-298-5063 ▪ TF: 800-444-2778

Technologists, Association of Genetic   www.agt-info.org
PO Box 15945-288   Lenexa KS 66285
Ph: 913-541-0497 ▪ Fx: 913-599-5340

Technologists, International Christian   www.gospelcom.net/icta
15455 Gleneagle Dr Suite 210   Colorado Springs CO 80921
Ph: 719-785-0120 ▪ Fx: 719-785-0117

Technologists Inc, Sugar Industry   sucrose.com/sit
164 N Hall Dr   Sugar Land TX 77478
Ph: 281-494-2046 ▪ Fx: 281-494-2304

Technology Inc, Accreditation Board for Engineering &   www.abet.org
111 Market Pl Suite 1050   Baltimore MD 21202
Ph: 410-347-7700 ▪ Fx: 410-625-2238

Technology, Accrediting Commission of Career Schools &   www.accsct.org
Colleges of   2101 Wilson Blvd Suite 302   Arlington VA 22201
Ph: 703-247-4212 ▪ Fx: 703-247-4533

Technology, AeA: Advancing the Business of   www.aeanet.org
5201 Great America Pkwy Suite 520   Santa Clara CA 95054
Ph: 408-987-4200 ▪ Fx: 408-970-8565 ▪ TF: 800-284-4232

Technology, American Council for   www.actgov.org
11350 Random Hills Rd Suite 120   Fairfax VA 22030
Ph: 703-218-1955 ▪ Fx: 703-218-1960

Technology, American Society of Extra-Corporeal   www.amsect.org
503 Carlisle Dr Suite 125   Herndon VA 20170
Ph: 703-435-8556 ▪ Fx: 703-435-0056

Technology Assessment, International Center for   www.icta.org
666 Pennsylvania Ave SE Suite 302   Washington DC 20003
Ph: 202-547-9359 ▪ Fx: 202-547-9429 ▪ TF: 800-600-6664

Technology Association, Business   www.bta.org
12411 Wornall Rd   Kansas City MO 64145
Ph: 816-941-0100 ▪ Fx: 816-941-2829 ▪ TF: 800-316-9721

Technology, Association for Competitive   www.actonline.org
1413 K St NW 12th Fl   Washington DC 20005
Ph: 202-331-2130 ▪ Fx: 202-331-2139

Technology, Association for Educational Communications &   www.aect.org
1800 N Stonelake Dr Suite 2   Bloomington IN 47408
Ph: 812-335-7675 ▪ Fx: 812-335-7678 ▪ TF: 877-677-2328

Technology Association, Entertainment Services &   www.esta.org
875 Sixth Ave Suite 1005   New York NY 10001
Ph: 212-244-1505 ▪ Fx: 212-244-1502

Technology, Association for Financial   www.fitech.org
5828 Zarley St Suite C   New Albany OH 43054
Ph: 614-895-1208 ▪ Fx: 614-895-3466

Technology Association, JEDEC Solid State   www.jedec.org
2500 Wilson Blvd   Arlington VA 22201
Ph: 703-907-7534 ▪ Fx: 703-907-7583

Technology, Center for Democracy &   www.cdt.org
1634 'I' St NW 11th Fl   Washington DC 20006
Ph: 202-637-9800 ▪ Fx: 202-637-0968

Technology, Center for Neighborhood   www.cnt.org
2125 W North Ave   Chicago IL 60647
Ph: 773-278-4800 ▪ Fx: 773-278-3840

Technology Consortium, Financial Services   www.fstc.org
44 Wall St 12th Fl   New York NY 10005
Ph: 212-461-7116 ▪ Fx: 646-349-3629

Technology, Consumer Project on   www.cptech.org
PO Box 19367   Washington DC 20036
Ph: 202-387-8030 ▪ Fx: 202-234-5176

Technology Council, Applied   www.atcouncil.org
201 Redwood Shores Pkwy Suite 240   Redwood City CA 94065
Ph: 650-595-1542 ▪ Fx: 650-593-2320

Technology Distribution, Association for High   www.ahtd.org
1900 Arch St   Philadelphia PA 19103
Ph: 215-564-3484 ▪ Fx: 215-963-9784

Technology Education Association, International   www.iteawww.org
1914 Association Dr Suite 201   Reston VA 20191
Ph: 703-860-2100 ▪ Fx: 703-860-0353

Technology in Education, International Society for   www.iste.org
480 Charnelton St   Eugene OR 97401
Ph: 541-302-3777 ▪ Fx: 541-302-3778 ▪ TF: 800-336-5191

Technology Education Partnership, National Science &   www.nationalstep.org
2500 Wilson Blvd Suite 210   Arlington VA 22201
Ph: 703-907-7400 ▪ Fx: 703-907-7401

Technology Experience, International Association for the Exchange
of Students   10400 Little Patuxent Pkwy Suite 250   Columbia
MD 21044
Ph: 410-997-3069 ▪ Fx: 410-997-5186

Technology, IEEE Society on Social   radburn.rutgers.edu/andrews/projects/ssit
Implications of   IEEE Operations Ctr 445 Hoes Ln   Piscataway
NJ 08854
Ph: 732-981-0060 ▪ Fx: 732-981-1721

Technology Industry Association, Assistive   www.atia.org
401 N Michigan Ave   Chicago IL 60611
Ph: 312-321-5172 ▪ Fx: 312-673-6659 ▪ TF: 877-687-2842

Technology Institute, International   www.itiworld.org
PO Box 23166   San Diego CA 92193
Ph: 858-279-0483 ▪ Fx: 858-279-0493

Technology, Institute for Theological Encounter with Science &   itest.slu.edu
3601 Lindell Blvd   Saint Louis MO 63108
Ph: 314-977-2703

Technology, International Association for Language Learning   www.iallt.org

Technology International, Compatible   www.compatibletechnology.org
Hamline Univ Box 109 1536 Hewitt Ave   Saint Paul MN 55104
Ph: 651-632-3912 ▪ Fx: 651-632-3913

Technology International, Women in   www.witi.com
13351 Riverside Dr Suite 441   Sherman Oaks CA 91423
Ph: 818-788-9484 ▪ Fx: 818-896-4746 ▪ TF: 800-334-9484

Technology, Leonardo - International Society   mitpress2.mit.edu/e-journals/Leonardo
for the Arts Sciences &   425 Market St 2nd Fl   San Francisco
CA 94105
Ph: 415-405-3335 ▪ Fx: 415-405-7758

Technology & Maintenance Council   www.trucking.org/cc/councils/tmc
American Trucking Assns 2200 Mill Rd   Alexandria VA 22314
Ph: 703-838-1761 ▪ TF: 888-333-1759

Technology Managers, Association of University   www.autm.net
60 Revere Dr Suite 500   Northbrook IL 60062
Ph: 847-559-0846 ▪ Fx: 847-480-9282

Technology in Music Instruction, Association for   atmi.music.org

Technology, National Association of Industrial   www.nait.org
3300 Washtenaw Ave Suite 220   Ann Arbor MI 48104
Ph: 734-996-6000 ▪ Fx: 734-677-0048

Technology, National Center for Appropriate   www.ncat.org
PO Box 3838   Butte MT 59702
Ph: 406-494-4572 ▪ Fx: 406-494-2905 ▪ TF: 800-275-6228

Technology Organization, World Peace Through   www.peacetour.org
150 Folsom St   San Francisco CA 94105
Ph: 415-371-8706 ▪ Fx: 415-348-0762

Technology Procurement Professionals, Caucus - Association of   www.caucusnet.com
PO Drawer 2970   Winter Park FL 32790
Ph: 407-740-5600 ▪ Fx: 407-740-0368

Technology Inc, Public   www.pti.org
1301 Pennsylvania Ave NW Suite 800   Washington DC 20004
Ph: 202-626-2400 ▪ Fx: 202-626-2498 ▪ TF: 800-852-4934

Technology, Servants in Faith &   www.sifat.org
2944 County Rd 113   Lineville AL 36266
Ph: 256-396-2017 ▪ Fx: 256-396-2501

Technology, Society for Applied Learning   www.salt.org
50 Culpepper St   Warrenton VA 20186
Ph: 540-347-0055 ▪ Fx: 540-349-3169

Technology Society, AVS Science &   www.avs.org
120 Wall St 32nd Fl   New York NY 10005
Ph: 212-248-0200 ▪ Fx: 212-248-0245

Technology, Society for the History of   shot.press.jhu.edu

Technology Society, IEEE Vehicular   www.vtsociety.org
IEEE Operations Ctr 445 Hoes Ln   Piscataway NJ 08854
Ph: 732-981-0060 ▪ Fx: 732-981-1721

Technology, Society for Philosophy &   www.spt.org
San Jose Univ Dept of Philosophy 1 Washington Sq   San Jose
CA 95192
Ph: 408-924-4526

Technology Standards, Association for Retail   www.nrf-arts.com
325 7th St NW Suite 1100   Washington DC 20004
Ph: 202-626-8140

Technology Student Association   www.tsaweb.org
1914 Association Dr   Reston VA 20191
Ph: 703-860-9000 ▪ Fx: 703-758-4852

Technology Teacher Education, Council on   teched.vt.edu/ctte
International Technology Education Assn 1914 Association
Dr   Reston VA 20191
Ph: 703-860-2100 ▪ Fx: 703-860-0353

Technology Transfer Council, Petroleum   www.pttc.org
16010 Barkers Point Ln Suite 220   Houston TX 77079
Ph: 281-921-1720 ▪ Fx: 281-921-1723 ▪ TF: 888-843-7882

Technology Inc, US Institute for Theatre   www.usitt.org
6443 Ridings Rd   Syracuse NY 13206
Ph: 315-463-6463 ▪ Fx: 315-463-6525 ▪ TF: 800-938-7488

TechnoServe   www.technoserve.org
49 Day St   Norwalk CT 06854
Ph: 203-852-0377 ▪ Fx: 203-838-6717 ▪ TF: 800-999-6757

(Teddy Bears) Good Bears of the World   www.goodbearsoftheworld.org
PO Box 13097   Toledo OH 43613
Ph: 419-531-5365

Teen Age Republicans   www.teenagerepublicans.org
PO Box 1896   Manassas VA 20108
Ph: 703-368-4214 ▪ Fx: 703-368-0830

Teen AIDS Prevention, American Institute for
PO Box 395   Oberlin OH 44074
Ph: 440-774-5411 ▪ Fx: 440-233-6455

Teen Challenge International   www.teenchallenge.com
3728 W Chestnut Expy   Springfield MO 65802
Ph: 417-862-6969 ▪ Fx: 417-862-8209 ▪ TF: 800-814-5729

Teen Missions International   www.teenmissions.org
885 E Hall Rd   Merritt Island FL 32953
Ph: 321-453-0350 ▪ Fx: 321-452-7988

Teen Pregnancy, National Campaign To Prevent   www.teenpregnancy.org
1776 Massachusetts Ave NW Suite 200   Washington DC 20036
Ph: 202-478-8500 ▪ Fx: 202-478-8588

Tekakwitha Conference National Center   www.tekconf.org
PO Box 6768   Great Falls MT 59406
Ph: 406-727-0147 ▪ Fx: 406-452-9845 ▪ TF: 800-842-9635

Tel Aviv University: American Council   www.tauac.org
39 Broadway 15th Fl   New York NY 10006
Ph: 212-742-9070 ▪ Fx: 212-742-9071

Telecom Association, US   www.usta.org
1401 H St NW Suite 600   Washington DC 20005
Ph: 202-326-7300 ▪ Fx: 202-326-7333

Telecom Council, United   www.utc.org
1901 Pennsylvania Ave NW 5th Fl   Washington DC 20006
Ph: 202-872-0030 ▪ Fx: 202-872-1331

Telecommunications Association, American Mobile   www.amtausa.org
200 N Glebe Rd Suite 1000   Arlington VA 22203
Ph: 202-835-7819 ▪ Fx: 202-331-9062

Telecommunications Association Inc, Industrial   www.ita-relay.com
1110 N Glebe Rd Suite 500   Arlington VA 22201
Ph: 703-528-5115 ▪ Fx: 703-524-1074 ▪ TF: 800-482-8282

Telecommunications Association, International Wireless   www.iwta.org
200 N Glebe Rd Suite 1000   Arlington VA 22203
Ph: 202-331-7773 ▪ Fx: 202-331-9062

Telecommunications Association for Marketing, Cable &   www.ctam.com
201 N Union St Suite 440   Alexandria VA 22314
Ph: 703-549-4200 ▪ Fx: 703-684-1167

Telecommunications Association, National Asian American   www.naatanet.org
145 9th St Suite 350   San Francisco CA 94103
Ph: 415-863-0814 ▪ Fx: 415-863-7428

Telecommunications Association, National Cable &   www.ncta.com
1724 Massachusetts Ave NW   Washington DC 20036
Ph: 202-775-3550 ▪ Fx: 202-775-1055

Telecommunications Companies, Organization for the Promotion & Advancement of Small   www.opastco.org
21 Dupont Cir NW Suite 700   Washington DC 20036
Ph: 202-659-5990 ▪ Fx: 202-659-4619 ▪ TF: 800-828-1726

Telecommunications Consultants, Society of   www.stcconsultants.org
PO Box 416   Fall River Mills CA 96028
Ph: 530-336-7070 ▪ Fx: 530-336-7060 ▪ TF: 800-782-7670

Telecommunications Cooperative Association, National   www.ntca.org
4121 Wilson Blvd Suite 1000   Arlington VA 22203
Ph: 703-351-2000 ▪ Fx: 703-351-2001

Telecommunications Council, Pacific   www.ptc.org/
2454 S Beretania St 3rd Fl   Honolulu HI 96826
Ph: 808-941-3789 ▪ Fx: 808-944-4874

Telecommunications for the Deaf Inc   www.tdi-online.org
8630 Fenton St Suite 604   Silver Spring MD 20910
Ph: 301-589-3006 ▪ Fx: 301-589-3797

Telecommunications Dealers, North American Association of   www.natd.com
131 NW 1st Ave   Delray Beach FL 33444
Ph: 561-266-9440 ▪ Fx: 561-266-9017

Telecommunications Directors, National Association of State   www.nastd.com
2760 Research Park Dr PO Box 11910   Lexington KY 40578
Ph: 859-244-8186 ▪ Fx: 859-244-8001

Telecommunications & Electrical Association, Energy   www.entelec.com
14015 Park Dr Suite 206   Tomball TX 77375
Ph: 281-357-8700 ▪ Fx: 281-357-8777 ▪ TF: 888-503-8700

Telecommunications Engineers, National Association of Radio &   www.narte.org
167 Village St   Medway MA 02053
Ph: 508-533-8333 ▪ Fx: 508-533-3815 ▪ TF: 800-896-2783

Telecommunications Engineers, Society of Cable   www.scte.org
140 Philips Rd   Exton PA 19341
Ph: 610-363-6888 ▪ Fx: 610-363-5898 ▪ TF: 800-542-5040

Telecommunications, Forest Industries   www.landmobile.com
871 Country Club Rd Suite A   Eugene OR 97401
Ph: 541-485-8441 ▪ Fx: 541-485-7556

Telecommunications Human Resources Association, Cable &   www.cthra.com
1755 Park St Suite 260   Naperville IL 60563
Ph: 630-416-1166 ▪ Fx: 630-416-9798

Telecommunications Industry Association   www.tiaonline.org
2500 Wilson Blvd Suite 300   Arlington VA 22201
Ph: 703-907-7700 ▪ Fx: 703-907-7727 ▪ TF: 800-799-6682

Telecommunications Industry Forum   www.atis.org/atis/tcif
1200 G St NW Suite 500   Washington DC 20005
Ph: 202-434-8844 ▪ Fx: 202-393-5453 ▪ TF: 800-387-2199

Telecommunications Industry Solutions, Alliance for   www.atis.org
1200 G St NW Suite 500   Washington DC 20005
Ph: 202-628-6380 ▪ Fx: 202-393-5453

Telecommunications & Internet Association, Cellular   www.wow-com.com
1400 16th St NW Suite 600   Washington DC 20036
Ph: 202-785-0081 ▪ Fx: 202-785-0721

Telecommunications, Native American Public   www.nativetelecom.org
1800 N 33rd St   Lincoln NE 68583
Ph: 402-472-3522 ▪ Fx: 402-472-8675

Telecommunications Officers & Advisors, National Association of   www.natoa.org
8405 Greensboro Dr Suite 800   McLean VA 22102
Ph: 703-506-3275 ▪ Fx: 703-506-3266

Telecommunications Research Action Center   www.trac.org
PO Box 27279   Washington DC 20005
Ph: 202-263-2950 ▪ Fx: 202-263-2962

Telecommunications Risk Management Association   www.trmanet.org
10 Sylvan Way   Parsippany NJ 07054
Ph: 973-631-8000 ▪ Fx: 973-631-6221

Telecommunications Satellite Organization, International   www.itso.int/
3400 International Dr NW   Washington DC 20008
Ph: 202-243-5096 ▪ Fx: 202-243-5018

Telecommunications Services, Association for Local   www.alts.org
888 17th St NW 12th Fl   Washington DC 20006
Ph: 202-969-2587 ▪ Fx: 202-969-2581

Telecommunications Society, International   www.itsworld.org
33 Alpine Dr   Gilford NH 03249
Ph: 603-293-4094 ▪ Fx: 603-293-4095

Telecommunications, Women in Cable &   www.wict.org
14555 Avion Pkwy Suite 250   Chantilly VA 20151
Ph: 703-234-9810 ▪ Fx: 703-817-1595

TelecomPioneers   www.telecompioneers.org
PO Box 13888   Denver CO 80201
Ph: 303-571-1200 ▪ Fx: 303-572-0520

Teleconferencing Consortium Inc, International Multimedia   www.imtc.org
2400 Camino Ramon Suite 275   San Ramon CA 94583
Ph: 925-275-6600 ▪ Fx: 925-275-6691

TeleManagement Forum   www.tmforum.org
89 Headquarters Plaza N Suite 350   Morristown NJ 07960
Ph: 973-292-1901 ▪ Fx: 973-993-3131

Telemarketing & Electronic Commerce, Alliance Against Fraud in   www.fraud.org/aaft/aaftinfo.htm
1701 K St NW Suite 1200   Washington DC 20006
Ph: 202-835-3323 ▪ Fx: 202-835-0747

Telemedia Council, National   www.danenet.wicip.org/ntc/
120 E Wilson St   Madison WI 53703
Ph: 608-257-7712 ▪ Fx: 608-257-7714

Telemedicine Association, American   www.americantelemed.org
910 17th St NW Suite 314   Washington DC 20006
Ph: 202-223-3333 ▪ Fx: 202-223-2787

Teleos Institute   www.consciousnesswork.com
7119 E Shea Blvd Suite 109 PMB 418   Scottsdale AZ 85254
Ph: 480-948-1800 ▪ Fx: 480-948-1870

Telephone Collectors Association, Antique   www.atcaonline.com
PO Box 1252   McPherson KS 67460
Ph: 620-245-9555

Telephone Collectors International   www.telephonecollectors.org
3207 E Bend Dr   Algonquin IL 60102
Ph: 847-658-7844 ▪ Fx: 847-658-9360

Telephone Preference Service, Direct Marketing Association Inc   www.dmaconsumers.org/offtelephonelist.html
PO Box 1559   Carmel NY 10512
Ph: 212-768-7277

Teleport Association, World   www.worldteleport.org
55 Broad St 14th Fl   New York NY 10004
Ph: 212-825-0218 ▪ Fx: 212-825-0075

Teleservices Association, American   www.ataconnect.org
3815 River Crossing Pkwy Suite 20   Indianapolis IN 46240
Ph: 317-816-9336 ▪ Fx: 317-218-0323

Teleservices International, Association of   www.atsi.org
12 Academy Ave   Atkinson NH 03811
Ph: 603-362-9489 ▪ Fx: 603-362-9486

Television, American Women in Radio &   www.awrt.org
8405 Greensboro Dr Suite 800   McLean VA 22102
Ph: 703-506-3290 ▪ Fx: 703-506-3266

Television Arts & Sciences, Academy of   www.emmys.tv
5220 Lankershim Blvd   North Hollywood CA 91601
Ph: 818-754-2800 ▪ Fx: 818-761-2827

Television Arts & Sciences, International Academy of   www.iemmys.tv
142 W 57th St   New York NY 10019
Ph: 212-489-6969 ▪ Fx: 212-489-6557

Television Arts & Sciences, National Academy of   www.emmyonline.org
111 W 57th St Suite 600   New York NY 10019
Ph: 212-586-8424 ▪ Fx: 212-246-8129

Television, Association for Maximum Service   www.mstv.org
PO Box 9897   Washington DC 20016
Ph: 202-966-1956 ▪ Fx: 202-966-9617

Television Bureau of Advertising   www.tvb.org
3 E 54th St 10th Fl   New York NY 10022
Ph: 212-486-1111 ▪ Fx: 212-935-5631

Television Cooperative Inc, National Cable   www.cabletvco-op.org
11200 Corporate Ave   Lenexa KS 66219
Ph: 913-599-5900 ▪ Fx: 913-599-5903

Television Correspondents Association, Radio-
c/o Senate Radio-TV Gallery US Capitol Rm S-325   Washington DC 20510
Ph: 202-224-6421 ▪ Fx: 202-224-4882

Television Council, Parents   www.parentstv.org
707 Wilshire Blvd Suite 2075   Los Angeles CA 90017
Ph: 213-629-9255   Fx: 213-629-9254   TF: 800-882-6868

Television Engineers, Society of Motion Picture &   www.smpte.org
595 W Hartsdale Ave   White Plains NY 10607
Ph: 914-761-1100   Fx: 914-761-3115

Television Fund, Motion Picture &   www.mptvfund.org
23388 Mulholland Dr   Woodland Hills CA 91364
Ph: 818-876-1888   Fx: 818-876-1436

Television Laboratories Inc, Cable   www.cablelabs.com
400 Centennial Pkwy   Louisville CO 80027
Ph: 303-661-9100   Fx: 303-661-9199

Television News Directors Association, Radio-   www.rtnda.org
1600 K St NW Suite 700   Washington DC 20006
Ph: 202-659-6510   Fx: 202-223-4007   TF: 800-807-8632

Television Operators Caucus
1776 K St NW   Washington DC 20006
Ph: 202-719-7090   Fx: 202-719-7546

Television Producers, Alliance of Motion Picture &   www.amptp.org
15503 Ventura Blvd   Encino CA 91436
Ph: 818-995-3600   Fx: 818-382-1793

Television Program Executives, National Association of   www.natpe.org
2425 Olympic Blvd Suite 600-E   Santa Monica CA 90404
Ph: 310-453-4440   Fx: 310-453-5258

Television & Radio Artists, American Federation of   www.aftra.com
260 Madison Ave 7th Fl   New York NY 10016
Ph: 212-532-0800   Fx: 212-532-2242

Television & Radio PAC
1771 'N' St NW   Washington DC 20036
Ph: 202-429-5300   Fx: 202-429-5406

Television Research Council, Radio &
234 5th Ave Suite 417   New York NY 10001
Ph: 212-481-3038   Fx: 212-481-3071

Television Society Foundation Inc, International Radio &   www.irts.org
420 Lexington Ave Suite 1601   New York NY 10170
Ph: 212-867-6650   Fx: 212-867-6653

Television Society, Hollywood Radio &   www.hrts-iba.org
13701 Riverside Dr Suite 205   Sherman Oaks CA 91423
Ph: 818-789-1182   Fx: 818-789-1210

Television Stations, Association of Public   www.apts.org
666 11th St NW 11th Fl   Washington DC 20001
Ph: 202-654-4200   Fx: 202-654-4236

Television Systems Committee, Advanced   www.atsc.org
1750 K St NW Suite 1200   Washington DC 20006
Ph: 202-872-9160   Fx: 202-872-9161

Telework Association & Council, International   www.telecommute.org
8403 Colesville Rd Suite 865   Silver Spring MD 20910
Ph: 301-650-2322

Telluride Association   www.tellurideassociation.org
217 West Ave   Ithaca NY 14850
Ph: 607-273-5011   Fx: 607-272-2667

Temperance Association, International Health &
12501 Old Columbia Pike   Silver Spring MD 20904
Ph: 301-680-6719   Fx: 301-680-6707

Temple Administrators, National Association of   rj.org/nata
PO Box 936   Ridgefield WA 98642
Ph: 360-887-0464   TF: 800-966-6282

Temple Brotherhoods, North American Federation of   www.nftb.org
633 3rd Ave   New York NY 10017
Ph: 212-650-4100   Fx: 212-650-4189   TF: 800-765-6200

Temple Educators, National Association of   rj.org/nate
633 3rd Ave 7th Fl   New York NY 10017
Ph: 212-452-6510   Fx: 212-452-6512

Temple Hill Association, National   www.nationaltemplehill.org
PO Box 315   Vails Gate NY 12584
CN: 914-561-5073

Temple Sisterhoods, Women of Reform Judaism - Federation of   www.rj.org/wrj
633 3rd Ave   New York NY 10017
Ph: 212-650-4050   Fx: 212-650-4059

Temple of Understanding   www.templeofunderstanding.org
720 5th Ave 16th Fl   New York NY 10019
Ph: 212-246-2746   Fx: 212-246-2340

**Temporal Bone Hearing & Balance Pathology Resource
Registry, NIDCD National**   Massachusetts Eye & Ear Infirmary   www.tbregistry.org
243 Charles St   Boston MA 02114
Ph: 617-573-3711   Fx: 617-573-3838   TF: 800-822-1327

Tennessee Folklore Society   www.middleenglish.org/tennfolk
Box 201   Murfreesboro TN 37132
Ph: 615-898-2573   Fx: 615-898-5098

Tennessee Walking Horse Breeders' & Exhibitors' Association   www.twhbea.com
PO Box 286   Lewisburg TN 37091
Ph: 931-359-1574   Fx: 931-359-2539   TF: 800-359-1574

Tennis Academy, US National   www.usnta.com
1014 Ferris Ave Suite 1042-E   Waxahachie TX 75165
Ph: 972-937-0311   Fx: 972-937-0450   TF: 800-452-8519

Tennis Association, American   www.atanational.com
4640 Forbes Blvd Suite 200   Lanham MD 20706
Ph: 301-306-3193

Tennis Association, American Medical   www.mdtennis.org
1803 Cobbleston Dr   Provo UT 84604
Ph: 800-326-2682   Fx: 801-374-0135

Tennis Association, American Platform   www.platformtennis.org
PO Box 43336   Upper Montclair NJ 07043
Ph: 973-744-1190   Fx: 973-783-4407   TF: 888-744-9490

Tennis Association, Intercollegiate   www.itatennis.com
174 Tamarack Cir   Skillman NJ 08558
Ph: 609-497-6920   Fx: 609-497-9766

Tennis Association, National Public Parks
1001 W 98th St Suite 101   Bloomington MN 55431
Ph: 952-887-5001   Fx: 952-887-5061   TF: 800-536-6982

Tennis Association, National Senior Women's   www.nswta.com
PO Box 142   Lake Oswego OR 97034
Ph: 503-636-9292   Fx: 503-636-9660

Tennis Association, US   www.usta.com
70 W Red Oak Ln   White Plains NY 10604
Ph: 914-696-7000   Fx: 914-696-7167   TF: 800-990-8782

Tennis Association, US Dental   www.dentaltennis.org
2180 Briarcliff Dr   Idaho Falls ID 83404
Ph: 800-445-2524   Fx: 208-523-9004

Tennis Association, US Professional   www.uspta.org
3535 Briarpark Dr Suite 1   Houston TX 77042
Ph: 713-978-7782   Fx: 713-978-7780   TF: 800-877-8248

(Tennis) ATP Tour Inc   www.atptennis.com
201 ATP Tour Blvd   Ponte Vedra Beach FL 32082
Ph: 904-285-8000   Fx: 904-285-5966   TF: 800-527-4811

Tennis Court & Track Builders Association, US   www.ustctba.com
3525 Ellicott Mills Dr Suite N   Ellicott City MD 21043
Ph: 410-418-4875   Fx: 410-418-4805

Tennis Industry Association   www.tennisindustry.org
19 Pope Ave Suite 107   Hilton Head Island SC 29928
Ph: 843-686-3036   Fx: 843-686-3078

Tennis Registry, Professional   www.ptrtennis.org
PO Box 4739   Hilton Head Island SC 29938
Ph: 843-785-7244   Fx: 843-686-2033   TF: 800-421-6289

(Tennis) WTA Tour Inc   www.wtatour.com
1 Progress Pl Suite 1500   Saint Petersburg FL 33701
Ph: 727-895-5000   Fx: 727-894-1982

Teratology Society   www.teratology.org
1821 Michael Faraday Dr Suite 300   Reston VA 20190
Ph: 703-438-3104   Fx: 703-438-3113

Term Limits Foundation, US   www.termlimits.org
10 G St NE Suite 410   Washington DC 20002
Ph: 202-379-3000   Fx: 202-379-3010   TF: 800-733-6440

Terminal Operators Association, Independent
1150 Connecticut NW 9th Fl   Washington DC 20036
Ph: 202-828-4100   Fx: 202-828-4130

Terminals Association, Independent Liquid   www.ilta.org
1444 'I' St NW Suite 400   Washington DC 20005
Ph: 202-842-9200   Fx: 202-326-8660

Terminals Inc, Inland Rivers Ports &   www.irpt.net
PO Box 4363   Jackson MS 39296
Ph: 601-352-4778   Fx: 601-355-1506

Terra Cotta, Friends of   www.preserve.org/fotc
771 West End Ave Suite 10E   New York NY 10025
Ph: 212-662-0768

Terrazzo & Mosaic Association, National   www.ntma.com
201 N Maple Suite 208   Purcellville VA 20132
Ph: 540-751-0930   Fx: 540-751-0935   TF: 800-323-9736

Terrier Club of America, Jack Russell   www.terrier.com
PO Box 4527   Lutherville MD 21094
Ph: 410-561-3655   Fx: 410-560-2563

Terrier Club of America, Silky   www.silky-terrier-club.com

Terrier Club of America, Skye   clubs.akc.org/skye
11567 Sutters Mill Cir   Gold River CA 95670
Ph: 916-631-8716

Terrier Club of America, Staffordshire   www.amstaff.org

Terrier Club, US Kerry Blue   www.uskbtc.com
2458 Eastridge Dr   Hamilton OH 45011
Ph: 513-863-5041

Tesla Memorial Society Inc   www.teslamemorialsociety.org
21 Maddaket   Scotch Plains NJ 07076
Ph: 732-396-8852

Test Board, Secondary School Admission   www.ssat.org
CN 5339   Princeton NJ 08543
Ph: 609-683-4440   Fx: 800-442-7728

Test Directors, National Association of   www.natd.org
c/o Fenton Research 8520 N Coral Ridge Loop   Tucson AZ
85704
Ph: 520-229-8687

Test & Evaluation Association, International   www.itea.org
4400 Fair Lakes Ct Suite 104   Fairfax VA 22033
Ph: 703-631-6220   Fx: 703-631-6221

Test Pilots, Society of Experimental   www.setp.org
PO Box 986   Lancaster CA 93584
Ph: 661-942-9574   Fx: 661-940-0398

Test Publishers, Association of   www.testpublishers.org
1201 Pennsylvania Ave Suite 300   Washington DC 20004
Ph: 866-240-7909

Test Research & Training Reactors, National Organization of   www.trtr.org

Testament League USA, Pocket   www.readcarryshare.com
11 Toll Gate Rd PO Box 800   Lititz PA 17543
Ph: 717-626-1919   Fx: 717-626-5553   TF: 800-636-8785

Testing Inc, American Society for Nondestructive   www.asnt.org
1711 Arlingate Ln   Columbus OH 43228
Ph: 614-274-6003   Fx: 614-274-6899   TF: 800-222-2768

Testing Association, Controlled Environment   www.cetainternational.org
1500 Sunday Dr Suite 102   Raleigh NC 27607
Ph: 919-787-5576   Fx: 919-787-4916

Testing Association, Instrumentation   www.instrument.org
631 N Stephanie St Suite 279   Henderson NV 89014
Ph: 702-568-1445   Fx: 702-568-1446   TF: 877-236-1256

Testing Association, InterNational Electrical   www.netaworld.org
106 Stone St PO Box 687   Morrison CO 80465
Ph: 303-697-8441   Fx: 303-697-8431   TF: 888-300-6382

Testing, National Center for Fair & Open   www.fairtest.org
342 Broadway   Cambridge MA 02139
Ph: 617-864-4810   Fx: 617-497-2224

Texan Heritage Society, German-   www.gths.net
507 E 10th St PO Box 684171   Austin TX 78768
Ph: 512-482-0927 ▪ Fx: 512-482-8809 ▪ TF: 866-482-4847

Texas Inc, Daughters of the Republic of   www.drtl.org/DRTInc
510 E Anderson Ln   Austin TX 78752
Ph: 512-339-1997 ▪ Fx: 512-339-1998

Texas Independent Producers & Royalty Owners Association   www.tipro.org
515 Congress Ave Suite 1910   Austin TX 78701
Ph: 512-477-4452 ▪ Fx: 512-476-8070

Texas Longhorn Breeders Association of America   www.tlbaa.org
2315 N Main St Suite 402   Fort Worth TX 76106
Ph: 817-625-6241 ▪ Fx: 817-625-1388

Texas, Order of the Sons of Hermann in   www.texashermannsons.org
PO Box 1941   San Antonio TX 78297
Ph: 210-226-9261 ▪ Fx: 210-226-3055 ▪ TF: 800-234-4124

Text & Academic Authors Association   www.taaonline.net
PO Box 76477   Saint Petersburg FL 33734
Ph: 727-821-7277 ▪ Fx: 727-821-7271

Textbook Council, American   www.historytextbooks.org
475 Riverside Dr Rm 448   New York NY 10115
Ph: 212-870-2760 ▪ Fx: 212-870-3454

Textile & Apparel Association, International   www.itaa.org
PO Box 1360   Monument CO 80132
Ph: 719-488-3716

Textile Association, American Reusable   www.arta1.com
PO Box 1053   Mulberry FL 33860
Ph: 863-660-5350

Textile Association, National   www.nationaltextile.org
6 Beacon St Suite 1125   Boston MA 02108
Ph: 617-542-8220 ▪ Fx: 617-542-2199

Textile Association, Secondary Materials & Recycled   www.smartasn.org
7910 Woodmont Ave Suite 1130   Bethesda MD 20814
Ph: 301-656-1077 ▪ Fx: 301-656-1079

Textile Association, Southern   www.southerntextile.org
PO Box 66   Gastonia NC 28053
Ph: 704-824-3522 ▪ Fx: 704-824-0630

Textile Care Allied Trades Association   www.tcata.org
271 Rt 46 W Suite D-203   Fairfield NJ 07004
Ph: 973-244-1790 ▪ Fx: 973-244-4455

Textile Center, National   www.ntcresearch.org
1121 N Bethlehem Pike Suite 60   Spring House PA 19477
Ph: 215-540-0760 ▪ Fx: 215-689-4835

Textile Chemists & Colorists, American Association of   www.aatcc.org
1 Davis Dr PO Box 12215   Research Triangle Park NC 27709
Ph: 919-549-8141 ▪ Fx: 919-549-8933

Textile Design Association, Computer Integrated   www.citda.org/
405 Battleground Ave Suite 204   Greensboro NC 27401
Ph: 336-379-0603 ▪ Fx: 336-379-0851

Textile Employees, Union of Needletrades Industrial &   www.uniteunion.org
275 7th Ave   New York NY 10001
Ph: 212-265-7000 ▪ Fx: 212-265-3415 ▪ TF: 800-238-6483

Textile Fibers & By-Products Association   www.tfbpa.org
1531 Industrial Dr PO Box D   Griffin GA 30224
Ph: 770-412-2325 ▪ Fx: 770-227-6321

Textile & Garment Council, UFCW
4207 Lebanon Pike Suite 200   Hermitage TN 37076
Ph: 615-889-9221 ▪ Fx: 615-885-3102

Textile Institute   www.textileinstitute.org
2207 Concord Pike   Wilmington DE 19803
Ph: 302-478-4744 ▪ Fx: 302-478-0213

Textile Machinery Association, American   www.atmanet.org
201 Park Washington Ct   Falls Church VA 22046
Ph: 703-538-1789 ▪ Fx: 703-241-5603

Textile Manufacturers Institute, American   www.atmi.org
1130 Connecticut Ave NW Suite 1200   Washington DC 20036
Ph: 202-862-0500 ▪ Fx: 202-862-0570

Textile Recycling, Council for   www.smartasn.org
7910 Woodmont Ave Suite 1130   Bethesda MD 20814
Ph: 301-718-0671 ▪ Fx: 301-656-1079

Textile Rental Services Association   www.trsa.org
1800 Diagonal Rd Suite 200   Alexandria VA 22314
Ph: 703-519-0029 ▪ Fx: 703-519-0026 ▪ TF: 800-868-8772

Textile Research Institute   www.triprinceton.org
PO Box 625   Princeton NJ 08542
Ph: 609-924-3150 ▪ Fx: 609-683-7836

Textile Service Association, Uniform &   www.utsa.com
1300 N 17th St Suite 750   Arlington VA 22209
Ph: 703-247-2600 ▪ Fx: 703-841-4750 ▪ TF: 800-486-6745

Textiles & Apparel, US Association of Importers of   www.usaita.com
13 E 16th St 6th Fl   New York NY 10003
Ph: 212-463-0089 ▪ Fx: 212-463-0583

Textiles Inc, Shippers of Recycled   www.smartasn.org
7910 Woodmont Ave Suite 1130   Bethesda MD 20814
Ph: 301-656-1077 ▪ Fx: 301-656-1079

Textual Scholarship in Art History,   www.uml.edu/Dept/History/ArtHistory/ATSAH
Association for   112 Charles St Beacon Hill   Boston MA
02114
Ph: 617-367-1679 ▪ Fx: 617-557-2962

Textual Scholarship, Society for
www.textual.

Textured Yarn Association of America   www.tyaa.org
PO Box 66   Gastonia NC 28053
Ph: 704-824-3522 ▪ Fx: 704-824-0630

Thailand Business Council, US-   www.ustbc.org
3050 K St NW Suite 205   Washington DC 20007
Ph: 202-337-5973 ▪ Fx: 202-337-0039

Thanks to Scandinavia   www.thankstoscandinavia.org
165 E 56th St   New York NY 10022
Ph: 212-751-4000 ▪ Fx: 212-891-1450

Thanksgiving, Center for World   www.thanksgiving.org
c/o Thanks-Giving Square PO Box 131770   Dallas TX 75313
Ph: 214-969-1977 ▪ Fx: 214-754-0152 ▪ TF: 888-305-1205

(Theater) Alpha Psi Omega   www.alphapsiomega.org
Wabash College Theater Dept   Crawfordsville IN 47933
Ph: 765-361-6394 ▪ Fx: 765-361-6341

Theater Center, Eugene O'Neill   www.oneilltheatercenter.org
305 Great Neck Rd   Waterford CT 06385
Ph: 860-443-5378 ▪ Fx: 860-443-9653

Theater Workshop, Dance   www.dtw.org
219 W 19th St   New York NY 10011
Ph: 212-691-6500 ▪ Fx: 212-633-1974

Theatre Alliance, International Museum   www.imtal.org
c/o Wildlife Theater Central Park Zoo 830 5th Ave   New York
NY 10021
Ph: 212-439-6542

Theatre, American Association of Community   www.aact.org
8402 BriarWood Cir   Lago Vista TX 78645
Ph: 512-267-0711 ▪ Fx: 512-267-0712 ▪ TF: 866-687-2228

Theatre Arts for Youth, American   www.atafy.org
1429 Walnut St   Philadelphia PA 19102
Ph: 215-563-3501 ▪ Fx: 215-563-1588 ▪ TF: 800-523-4540

Theatre Association, Educational   www.etassoc.org
2343 Auburn Ave   Cincinnati OH 45219
Ph: 513-421-3900 ▪ Fx: 513-421-7077

Theatre Association, National Movement
3112 17th Ave S   Minneapolis MN 55407
Ph: 612-722-2333

Theatre Association, NFHS Speech Debate &   www.nfhs.org/sdta.htm
PO Box 690   Indianapolis IN 46206
Ph: 317-972-6900 ▪ Fx: 317-822-5700

Theatre Association, University/Resident   www.urta.com
1560 Broadway Suite 712   New York NY 10036
Ph: 212-221-1130 ▪ Fx: 212-869-2752

Theatre for Children & Young People, International Association   www.assitej-usa.org
of   724 2nd Ave S   Nashville TN 37210
Ph: 615-254-5719 ▪ Fx: 615-254-3255

Theatre Conference Inc, Southeastern   www.setc.org
PO Box 9868   Greensboro NC 27429
Ph: 336-272-3645 ▪ Fx: 336-272-8810

Theatre Consultants, American Society of   www.theatreconsultants.org
12226 Mentz Hill Rd   Saint Louis MO 63128
Ph: 314-843-9218 ▪ Fx: 314-843-4955

Theatre Critics Association, American   www.americantheatrecritics.org
c/o THEatre SERVICE PO Box 15282   Evansville IN 47716
Ph: 812-474-0549 ▪ Fx: 812-476-4168

Theatre of the Deaf, National   ntd.org
55 Van Dyke Ave Suite 312   Hartford CT 06106
Ph: 860-724-5179 ▪ Fx: 860-550-7974 ▪ TF: 800-300-5179

Theatre & Education, American Alliance for   www.aate.com
7475 Wisconsin Ave Suite 300A   Bethesda MD 20814
Ph: 301-951-7977

Theatre Equipment Association, International   www.itea.com
770 Broadway 5th Fl   New York NY 10003
Ph: 646-654-7680 ▪ Fx: 646-654-7694

Theatre Foundation, Ballet   www.abt.org
American Ballet Theatre 890 Broadway 3rd Fl   New York NY
10003
Ph: 212-477-3030 ▪ Fx: 212-254-5938

Theatre Fund, National Corporate   www.nctf.org
1 E 53rd St 3rd Fl   New York NY 10022
Ph: 212-750-6895 ▪ Fx: 212-750-6977

Theatre Guild   www.theatreatsea.com
135 Central Park W Suite 4-S   New York NY 10023
Ph: 212-873-0676 ▪ Fx: 212-873-5972

Theatre Historical Society of America   www.historictheatres.org
152 N York Rd 2nd Fl   Elmhurst IL 60126
Ph: 630-782-1800 ▪ Fx: 630-782-1802

Theatre Institute, National   nti.conncoll.edu
305 Great Neck Rd   Waterford CT 06385
Ph: 860-443-7139 ▪ Fx: 860-443-1212

Theatre International, Movement
50 Bernard Dr   Yardley PA 19067
Ph: 215-337-9100

Theatre Library Association   tla.library.unt.edu
149 W 45th St   New York NY 10036
Ph: 212-944-3895 ▪ Fx: 212-944-4139

Theatre Movement Educators, Association of   www.asu.edu/cfa/atme

Theatre, National Alliance for Musical   www.namt.net
520 8th Ave Suite 301   New York NY 10018
Ph: 212-714-6668 ▪ Fx: 212-714-0469

Theatre, National Association of Schools of   nast.arts-accredit.org
11250 Roger Bacon Dr Suite 21   Reston VA 20190
Ph: 703-437-0700 ▪ Fx: 703-437-6312

Theatre Network, National Music   www.nmtn.org
1697 Broadway Suite 902   New York NY 10019
Ph: 212-664-0979 ▪ Fx: 212-664-0978

Theatre Organ Society Inc, American   atos.org

Theatre Owners, National Association of   www.natoonline.org
4605 Lankershim Blvd Suite 340   North Hollywood CA 91602
Ph: 818-506-1778 ▪ Fx: 818-506-0269

Theatre Research, American Society for
Brown Univ Dept of Theatre PO Box 1897   Providence RI
02912
Ph: 401-863-3289 ▪ Fx: 401-863-7529

Theatre Safety, Arts Crafts &   www.caseweb.com/ACTS
181 Thompson St Suite 23   New York NY 10012
Ph: 212-777-0062 ▪ Fx: 212-673-4403

Theatre Technology Inc, US Institute for   www.usitt.org
6443 Ridings Rd   Syracuse NY 13206
Ph: 315-463-6463 ▪ Fx: 315-463-6525 ▪ TF: 800-938-7488

Theatre Workshop of the Handicapped, National   www.ntwh.org
535 Greenwich St   New York NY 10013
Ph: 212-206-7789 ▪ Fx: 212-206-0200

Theatres, League of Historic American   www.lhat.org
616 Water St Suite 320   Baltimore MD 21202
Ph: 410-659-9533 ▪ Fx: 410-837-9664 ▪ TF: 877-627-0833

Theatres, League of Resident   www.lort.org
c/o Glick & Weintraub PC 1501 Broadway Suite 2401   New
York NY 10036
Ph: 212-944-1501 ▪ Fx: 212-768-0785

Theatres & Producers, League of American   www.broadway.org
226 W 47th St   New York NY 10036
Ph: 212-764-1122 ▪ Fx: 212-719-4389

Theatrical Press Agents & Managers, Association of
165 W 46th St Suite 700   New York NY 10036
Ph: 212-719-3666 ▪ Fx: 212-302-1585 ▪ TF: 800-858-3667

Theatrical Stage Employees Moving Picture Technicians   www.iatse-intl.org
Artists & Allied Crafts of the US Its Territories & Canada,
International Alliance of   1430 Broadway 20th Fl   New
York NY 10018
Ph: 212-730-1770 ▪ Fx: 212-921-7699 ▪ TF: 800-223-6872

Theme Party Operators, National Association of Casino &   www.casinoparties.com
18946 Des Moines Memorial Dr Bldg 5   SeaTac WA 98146
Ph: 206-241-4777 ▪ Fx: 206-241-6956 ▪ TF: 800-355-8299

Theodore Roosevelt Association   www.theodoreroosevelt.org
PO Box 719   Oyster Bay NY 11771
Ph: 516-921-6319 ▪ Fx: 516-921-6481

Theological Encounter with Science & Technology, Institute for   itest.slu.edu
3601 Lindell Blvd   Saint Louis MO 63108
Ph: 314-977-2703

Theological Institute, Boston   www.bostontheological.org
Farwell Hall 210 Herrick Rd   Newton Centre MA 02459
Ph: 617-527-4880 ▪ Fx: 617-527-1073

Theological Library Association, American   www.atla.com
250 S Wacker Dr Suite 1600   Chicago IL 60606
Ph: 312-454-5100 ▪ Fx: 312-454-5505 ▪ TF: 888-665-2852

Theological Schools in the US & Canada, Association of   www.ats.edu
10 Summit Park Dr   Pittsburgh PA 15275
Ph: 412-788-6505 ▪ Fx: 412-788-6510

Theological Seminary, Ecumenical   www.etseminary.org
2930 Woodward Ave   Detroit MI 48201
Ph: 313-831-5200 ▪ Fx: 313-831-1353

Theological Society of America, Catholic   www.jcu.edu/ctsa
John Carroll Univ 20700 North Park Blvd   University Heights
OH 44118
Ph: 216-397-1631 ▪ Fx: 216-397-1804

Theological Society in America, Orthodox   www.otsamerica.org
50 Goddard Ave   Brookline MA 02445
Ph: 617-731-3500

Theological Society, Evangelical   www.etsjets.org
200 Russell Woods Dr   Lynchburg VA 24502
Ph: 434-237-5309

Theology Ethics & Ritual, Women's Alliance for   www.his.com/~mhunt
8035 13th St   Silver Spring MD 20910
Ph: 301-589-2509 ▪ Fx: 301-589-3150

Theology & Public Policy, Churches' Center for   www.cctpp.org
4500 Massachusetts Ave NW   Washington DC 20016
Ph: 202-885-8659 ▪ Fx: 202-885-8585 ▪ TF: 800-882-4987

Theosophy Company   www.theosophycompany.org
245 W 33rd St   Los Angeles CA 90007
Ph: 213-748-7244 ▪ Fx: 213-748-0634

Therapeutic Communities of America   www.therapeuticcommunitiesofamerica.org
1601 Connecticut Ave NW Suite 803   Washington DC 20009
Ph: 202-296-3503 ▪ Fx: 202-518-5475

Therapeutic Humor, Association for Applied &   www.aath.org
1951 W Camelback Rd Suite 445   Phoenix AZ 85015
Ph: 602-995-1454 ▪ Fx: 602-995-1449

Therapeutic Recreation Association, American   www.atra-tr.org
1414 Prince St Suite 204   Alexandria VA 22314
Ph: 703-683-9420 ▪ Fx: 703-683-9431

Therapeutic Recreation Certification Inc, National Council for   www.nctrc.org
7 Elmwood Dr   New City NY 10956
Ph: 845-639-1439 ▪ Fx: 845-639-1471

Therapeutic Recreation Society, National
c/o National Recreation & Park Assn 22377 Belmont Ridge
Rd   Ashburn VA 20148
Ph: 703-858-2151 ▪ Fx: 703-858-0794 ▪ TF: 800-626-6772

Therapeutic Riding, National Center for   www.nctrriding.org/about
PO Box 434   Burtonsville MD 20866
Ph: 301-421-0380 ▪ Fx: 301-421-0384

Therapeutics, American Academy of Veterinary Pharmacology &   www.aavpt.org
621 W Hill St   Champaign IL 61820
Ph: 217-359-0661 ▪ Fx: 217-244-1652

Therapeutics, American Society for Clinical Pharmacology &   www.ascpt.org
528 N Washington St   Alexandria VA 22314
Ph: 703-836-6981 ▪ Fx: 703-836-5223

Therapeutics, American Society for Pharmacology & Experimental   www.aspet.org
9650 Rockville Pike   Bethesda MD 20814
Ph: 301-634-7060 ▪ Fx: 301-634-7061

Therapeutics Association, Plasma Protein   www.pptaglobal.org
147 Old Solomon's Island Rd Suite 100   Annapolis MD 21401
Ph: 410-263-8296 ▪ Fx: 410-263-2298

Therapeutics & Rehabilitation, Council on Chiropractic Physiological   www.ccptr.org
312 Courtyard Dr   Hillsborough NJ 08844
Ph: 908-722-9075 ▪ Fx: 908-722-1401

Therapies of Asia, American Organization for Bodywork   www.aobta.org
1010 Haddonfield-Berlin Rd Suite 408   Voorhees NJ 08043
Ph: 856-782-1616 ▪ Fx: 856-782-1653

Therapists, American Society of Alternative   www.asat.org
PO Box 703   Rockport MA 01966
Ph: 978-281-4400 ▪ Fx: 978-282-1144

Therapists, American Society of Hand   www.asht.org
401 N Michigan Ave Suite 2200   Chicago IL 60611
Ph: 312-321-6866 ▪ Fx: 312-673-6670

Therapists, Association of Christian   www.actheals.org
6728 Old McLean Village Dr   McLean VA 22101
Ph: 703-556-9222 ▪ Fx: 703-556-8729

Therapists, Association of Educational   www.aetonline.org
1804 W Burbank Blvd   Burbank CA 91506
Ph: 818-843-1183 ▪ Fx: 818-843-7423

Therapists, International Association of Counselors &   www.iact.org
10915 Bonita Beach Rd SE Suite 1101   Bonita Springs FL
34135
Ph: 941-498-9710 ▪ Fx: 941-498-1215

Therapy Academy Inc, American Family   www.afta.org
1608 20th St NW 4th Fl   Washington DC 20009
Ph: 202-333-3690 ▪ Fx: 202-333-3692

Therapy, American Association for Marriage & Family   www.aamft.org
112 S Alfred St   Alexandria VA 22314
Ph: 703-838-9808 ▪ Fx: 703-838-9805

Therapy Inc, American Institute of Massage   www.aimtinc.com
1570 Brookhollow Dr Suite 200   Santa Ana CA 92705
Ph: 714-432-7879 ▪ Fx: 714-210-3199

Therapy Association, Academic Language   www.altaread.org
13140 Coit Rd Suite 320 LB 120   Dallas TX 75240
Ph: 972-233-9107 ▪ Fx: 972-490-4219

Therapy Association, American CranioSacral   www.acsta.com
11211 Prosperity Farms Rd Suite D-325   Palm Beach Gardens
FL 33410
Ph: 561-622-4334 ▪ Fx: 561-622-4771 ▪ TF: 800-233-5880

Therapy Association, American Dance   www.adta.org
10632 Little Patuxent Pkwy Suite 108   Columbia MD 21044
Ph: 410-997-4040 ▪ Fx: 410-997-4048

Therapy Association, American Horticultural   www.ahta.org
909 York St   Denver CO 80206
Ph: 303-370-8087 ▪ Fx: 303-331-5776 ▪ TF: 800-634-1603

Therapy Association, American Music   www.musictherapy.org
8455 Colesville Rd Suite 1000   Silver Spring MD 20910
Ph: 301-589-3300 ▪ Fx: 301-589-5175

Therapy Association Inc, American Occupational   www.aota.org
4720 Montgomery Ln PO Box 31220   Bethesda MD 20824
Ph: 301-652-2682 ▪ Fx: 301-652-7711

Therapy Association, American Physical   www.apta.org
1111 N Fairfax St   Alexandria VA 22314
Ph: 703-684-2782 ▪ Fx: 703-684-7343 ▪ TF: 800-999-2782

Therapy Association, American Polarity   www.polaritytherapy.org
PO Box 19858   Boulder CO 80308
Ph: 303-545-2080 ▪ Fx: 303-545-2161 ▪ TF: 800-359-5620

Therapy, Association for Play   www.a4pt.org
2050 N Winery Ave Suite 101   Fresno CA 93703
Ph: 559-252-2278 ▪ Fx: 559-252-2297

Therapy Credentials Board, Art   www.atcb.org
3 Terrace Way Suite B   Greensboro NC 27403
Ph: 877-213-2822 ▪ Fx: 336-547-0017

Therapy Dogs International Inc   www.tdi-dog.org
88 Bartley Rd   Flanders NJ 07836
Ph: 973-252-9800 ▪ Fx: 973-252-7171

Therapy, Federation of State Boards of Physical   www.fsbpt.org
509 Wythe St   Alexandria VA 22314
Ph: 703-299-3100 ▪ Fx: 703-299-3110 ▪ TF: 800-881-1430

Therapy, Foundation for Advancement in Cancer   www.fact-ltd.org
PO Box 1242 Old Chelsea Stn   New York NY 10113
Ph: 212-741-2790

Therapy, Foundation for Physical   www.apta.org/Foundation
1111 Fairfax St   Alexandria VA 22314
Ph: 800-875-1378 ▪ Fx: 703-683-6743

Therapy, National Association for Drama   www.nadt.org
15 Post Side Ln   Pittsford NY 14534
Ph: 585-381-5618 ▪ Fx: 585-383-1474

Therapy, National Association for Poetry   www.poetrytherapy.org
16861 SW 6th St   Pembroke Pines FL 33027
Ph: 954-499-4333 ▪ Fx: 954-499-4324 ▪ TF: 866-844-6278

Therapy Organization Inc, National Remotivation   www.remotivation.com
103 McDonald St   West Nanticoke PA 18634
Ph: 570-735-7079 ▪ Fx: 570-735-2997

Theriogenologists, American College of   www.theriogenology.org
PO Box 3065   Montgomery AL 36109
Ph: 334-395-4666 ▪ Fx: 334-395-3399

Theriogenology, Society for   www.therio.org
PO Box 3007   Montgomery AL 36109
Ph: 334-395-4666 ▪ Fx: 334-270-3399

Thermal Spray Society
ASM International 9639 Kinsman Rd   Materials Park OH 44073
Ph: 440-338-5151 ▪ Fx: 440-338-4634

Thermographers Association, Worldwide Printing   www.thermographers.org
1156 15th St NW Suite 900   Washington DC 20005
Ph: 202-393-2818 ▪ Fx: 202-223-9741

Thermometer Collectors Club of America
6130 Rampart Dr   Carmichael CA 95608
Ph: 916-966-3490

Thermoplastic Pavement Marking Manufacturers Association
1747 Pennsylvania Ave NW Suite 1000   Washington DC 20006
Ph: 800-221-2574 ▪ Fx: 202-835-0243

Theta Chi Fraternity   www.thetachi.org
3330 Founders Rd   Indianapolis IN 46268
Ph: 317-824-1881 ▪ Fx: 317-824-1908

Theta Delta Chi Inc   www.tdx.org
214 Lewis Wharf   Boston MA 02110
Ph: 617-742-8886 ▪ Fx: 617-742-8868 ▪ TF: 800-999-1847

Theta Phi Alpha Fraternity Inc — www.thetaphialpha.org
27025 Knickerbocker Rd   Bay Village OH 44140
Ph: 440-899-9282 ▪ Fx: 440-899-9293 ▪ TF: 877-843-8274

Theta Tau Professional Engineering Fraternity — www.thetatau.org
815 Brazos St Suite 710   Austin TX 78701
Ph: 512-472-1904 ▪ Fx: 512-472-4820 ▪ TF: 800-264-1904

Theta Xi Fraternity — www.thetaxi.org
PO Box 411134   Saint Louis MO 63141
Ph: 314-993-6294 ▪ Fx: 314-993-8760 ▪ TF: 800-783-6294

Thimble Collectors International — www.thimblecollectors.com

Think First Foundation: National Injury Prevention Program — www.thinkfirst.org
5550 Meadowbrook Dr Suite 110   Rolling Meadows IL 60008
Ph: 847-290-8600 ▪ Fx: 847-290-9005

Thinking, Center for Critical — www.criticalthinking.org
PO Box 220   Dillon Beach CA 94929
Ph: 707-878-9100 ▪ Fx: 707-878-9111 ▪ TF: 800-833-3645

Third-Sector Research, International Society for — www.istr.org
3400 N Charles St Suite 559   Baltimore MD 21218
Ph: 410-516-4678 ▪ Fx: 410-516-4870

Third World Conference Foundation — www.twcfinternational.org
1525 E 53rd St Suite 435   Chicago IL 60615
Ph: 773-241-6688 ▪ Fx: 773-241-7898

Third World, Friends of the — www.friendsofthethirdworld.org
611 W Wayne St   Fort Wayne IN 46802
Ph: 219-422-6821 ▪ Fx: 219-422-1650

Third World Organizing, Center for — www.ctwo.org
1218 E 21st St   Oakland CA 94606
Ph: 510-533-7583 ▪ Fx: 510-533-0923

Third World Studies Inc, Association of — itc.gsw.edu/atws
Mississippi State Univ Dept of History   Mississippi State MS 39762
Ph: 662-325-4020

Thirkell Angela Society — www.angelathirkell.org
PO Box 7109   San Diego CA 92167
Ph: 619-222-8143 ▪ Fx: 619-255-3612

Thomas Dave Foundation for Adoption — www.davethomasfoundationforadoption.org
4288 W Dublin Granville Rd   Dublin OH 43017
Ph: 614-764-8454 ▪ Fx: 614-766-3871 ▪ TF: 800-275-3832

Thomas Jefferson Center for the Protection of Free Expression — www.tjcenter.org
400 Worrell Dr   Charlottesville VA 22911
Ph: 434-295-4784 ▪ Fx: 434-296-3621

Thomas Jefferson Foundation — www.monticello.org
PO Box 316   Charlottesville VA 22902
Ph: 434-984-9808 ▪ Fx: 434-977-7757

Thomas Merton Society, International — www.merton.org

Thomas Nast Society — www.jfpl.org/nast.htm
c/o Morristown-Morris Township Library 1 Miller Rd   Morristown NJ 07960
Ph: 973-538-3473 ▪ Fx: 973-267-4064

Thoracic Radiology, Society of — www.thoracicrad.org
1711 Walden Ln SW   Rochester MN 55902
Ph: 507-288-5260 ▪ Fx: 507-288-0014

Thoracic Society, American — www.thoracic.org
61 Broadway 4th Fl   New York NY 10006
Ph: 212-315-8600 ▪ Fx: 212-315-6498

Thoracic Surgeons, Society of — www.sts.org
633 N Saint Clair St Suite 2320   Chicago IL 60611
Ph: 312-202-5800 ▪ Fx: 312-202-5801

Thoracic Surgery, American Association for — www.aats.org
900 Cummings Ctr Suite 221-U   Beverly MA 01915
Ph: 978-927-8330 ▪ Fx: 978-524-8890

Thoracic Surgery, American Board of — www.abts.org
1560 Sherman Ave Suite 803   Evanston IL 60201
Ph: 847-475-1520 ▪ Fx: 847-475-6240

Thoreau Society — www.walden.org/
44 Baker Farm   Lincoln MA 01773
Ph: 781-259-4750 ▪ Fx: 781-259-4760

Thorne Ecological Institute — www.thorne-eco.org
PO Box 19107   Boulder CO 80308
Ph: 303-499-3647 ▪ Fx: 720-565-3873

Thornton W Burgess Society — www.thorntonburgess.org
6 Discovery Hill Rd   East Sandwich MA 02537
Ph: 508-888-6870 ▪ Fx: 508-888-1919

Thoroughbred Club of America
PO Box 8098   Lexington KY 40533
Ph: 859-254-4282 ▪ Fx: 859-231-6131

Thoroughbred Owners & Breeders Association — www.toba.org
PO Box 4367   Lexington KY 40544
Ph: 859-276-2291 ▪ Fx: 859-276-2462 ▪ TF: 888-606-8622

Thoroughbred Racing Association, National — www.ntra.com
2525 Harrodsburg Rd   Lexington KY 40504
Ph: 859-223-5444 ▪ Fx: 859-223-3945

Thoroughbred Racing Associations — www.tra-online.com
420 Fair Hill Dr Suite 1   Elkton MD 21921
Ph: 410-392-9200 ▪ Fx: 410-398-1366

Thoroughbred Racing Protective Bureau — www.trpb.com
420 Fair Hill Dr Suite 2   Elkton MD 21921
Ph: 410-398-2261 ▪ Fx: 410-398-1499

Thoroughbred Trainers of America, United
PO Box 7065   Louisville KY 40257
Ph: 502-893-0025 ▪ Fx: 502-893-0026 ▪ TF: 800-325-3487

Three Mile Island Alert Inc — www.tmia.com
315 Peffer St   Harrisburg PA 17102
Ph: 717-233-7897 ▪ Fx: 717-233-3261

Threefold Educational Foundation — www.threefold.org
260 Hungry Hollow Rd   Chestnut Ridge NY 10977
Ph: 845-352-5020 ▪ Fx: 845-352-5071

Threshers Association, Midwest Old Settlers & — www.oldthreshers.org
405 E Threshers Rd   Mount Pleasant IA 52641
Ph: 319-385-8937 ▪ Fx: 319-385-0563

Threshers Association, National — www.nationalthreshers.com

Thrift Shops, National Association of Resale & — www.narts.org
PO Box 80707   Saint Clair Shores MI 48080
Ph: 800-544-0751 ▪ Fx: 810-294-6776

Thrombosis & Haemostasis, International Society on — www.med.unc.edu/isth
UNC Medical School CB 7035   Chapel Hill NC 27599
Ph: 919-929-3807 ▪ Fx: 919-929-3935

Thunderbird Club International, Classic — www.ctci.org
1308 E 29th St   Signal Hill CA 90806
Ph: 562-426-2709 ▪ Fx: 562-426-7023

Thunderbird Club International, Vintage — www.vintagethunderbirdclub.org

Thurgood Marshall Scholarship Fund — www.thurgoodmarshallfund.org
60 E 42nd St Suite 833   New York NY 10165
Ph: 212-573-8888 ▪ Fx: 212-573-8497

Thyroid Association, American — www.thyroid.org
6066 Leesburg Pike Suite 650   Falls Church VA 22041
Ph: 703-998-8890 ▪ Fx: 703-998-8893

Thyroid Foundation of America Inc — www.tsh.org
410 Stuart St   Boston MA 02116
Ph: 617-534-1500 ▪ Fx: 617-534-1515 ▪ TF: 800-832-8321

Tibet Fund — www.tibetfund.org
241 E 32nd St   New York NY 10016
Ph: 212-213-5011 ▪ Fx: 212-213-1219

Tibetan Aid Project — www.tibetanaidproject.org
2910 San Pablo Ave   Berkeley CA 94702
Ph: 510-848-4238 ▪ Fx: 510-548-2230 ▪ TF: 800-338-4238

Ticket Brokers, National Association of — www.natb.org
1666 K St NW Suite 5000   Washington DC 20006
Ph: 202-887-1400

Ticket Manufacturers, National Association of Fundraising — www.naftm.org
1885 University Ave W Suite 246   Saint Paul MN 55104
Ph: 651-644-4710

Ticketing Association, International — www.intix.org
330 W 38th St Suite 605   New York NY 10018
Ph: 212-629-4036 ▪ Fx: 212-629-8532

Tie Down Association, Web Sling & — www.wstda.com
2105 Laurel Bush Rd Suite 200   Bel Air MD 21015
Ph: 443-640-1070 ▪ Fx: 443-640-1031

Tiffin Glass Collectors Club — www.tiffinglass.org

Tiger Foundation — www.tigers.ca
1177 W Hastings St Suite 2007   Vancouver BC V6E2K3
Ph: 604-893-8718 ▪ Fx: 604-687-3797

Tile Contractors' Association of America — www.tcaainc.org
4 E 113th Terr   Kansas City MO 64114
Ph: 816-941-7063 ▪ Fx: 816-767-0194 ▪ TF: 800-655-8453

Tile Contractors Association, National — www.tile-assn.com
626 Lakeland East Dr PO Box 13629   Jackson MS 39236
Ph: 601-939-2071 ▪ Fx: 601-932-6117

Tile Council of America Inc — www.tileusa.com
100 Clemson Research Blvd   Anderson SC 29625
Ph: 864-646-8453 ▪ Fx: 864-646-2821

Tile Institute, Roof — www.rooftile.org
230 E Ohio St Suite 400   Chicago IL 60611
Ph: 312-670-4177 ▪ Fx: 312-644-8557

Tilt-up Concrete Association — www.tilt-up.org
113 1st St W PO Box 204   Mount Vernon IA 52314
Ph: 319-895-6911 ▪ Fx: 319-895-8830

Timber Construction, American Institute of — www.aitc-glulam.org
7012 S Revere Pkwy Suite 140   Englewood CO 80112
Ph: 303-792-9559 ▪ Fx: 303-792-0669

Timber Frame Business Council — www.timberframe.org
217 Main St   Hamilton MT 59840
Ph: 406-375-0713 ▪ Fx: 406-375-6401 ▪ TF: 888-560-9251

Timber Framers Guild — www.tfguild.org
PO Box 60   Beckett MA 01223
Ph: 413-623-9926 ▪ Fx: 888-453-0879 ▪ TF: 888-453-0879

Timber Products Manufacturers — www.tpmrs.com
951 E 3rd Ave   Spokane WA 99202
Ph: 509-535-4646 ▪ Fx: 509-534-6106

Timbers, Tall — www.talltimbers.org
13093 Henry Beadel Dr   Tallahassee FL 32312
Ph: 850-893-4153 ▪ Fx: 850-893-6470

Time Equipment Association, National — www.thentea.com
PO Box 27399   Memphis TN 38167
Ph: 800-235-6832 ▪ Fx: 901-358-2139

Timing Association Inc, International Occultation — www.occultations.org

Tin Can Sailors — www.destroyers.org
PO Box 100   Somerset MA 02726
Ph: 508-677-0515 ▪ Fx: 508-676-9740 ▪ TF: 800-223-5535

Tin Stabilizers Association — www.tinstabilizers.org
1900 Arch St   Philadelphia PA 19103
Ph: 215-564-3484 ▪ Fx: 215-564-2175

Tinker Foundation — fdncenter.org/grantmaker/tinker
55 E 59th St   New York NY 10022
Ph: 212-421-6858 ▪ Fx: 212-223-3326

Tinnitus Association, American — www.ata.org
PO Box 5   Portland OR 97207
Ph: 503-248-9985 ▪ Fx: 503-248-0024 ▪ TF: 800-634-8978

Tip Inc, We — www.wetip.com
PO Box 1296   Rancho Cucamonga CA 91729
Ph: 909-987-5005 ▪ Fx: 909-987-2477 ▪ TF: 800-782-7463

Tire Association, International
PO Box 1067   Farmington CT 06034
Ph: 860-228-2536 ▪ Fx: 860-228-9772

Tire Industry Association — www.tireindustry.org
1532 Pointer Ridge Pl Suite E   Bowie MD 20716
Ph: 301-430-7280 ▪ Fx: 301-430-7283 ▪ TF: 800-876-8372

Tire Management Council, Scrap
1400 K St NW Suite 900   Washington DC 20005
Ph: 202-682-4880 ▪ Fx: 202-682-4854
www.scraptire.org

Tire Retread Information Bureau
900 Weldon Grove Pl   Pacific Grove CA 93950
Ph: 831-372-1917 ▪ Fx: 831-372-9210 ▪ TF: 888-473-8732
www.retread.org

Tire & Rim Association Inc
175 Montrose Ave W Suite 150   Copley OH 44321
Ph: 330-666-8121 ▪ Fx: 330-666-8340
www.us-tra.org

Tissue Banks, American Association of
1350 Beverly Rd Suite 220-A   McLean VA 22101
Ph: 703-827-9582 ▪ Fx: 703-356-2198
www.aatb.org

Tissue Banks International
815 Park Ave   Baltimore MD 21201
Ph: 410-752-3800 ▪ Fx: 410-783-0183
www.tbionline.org

Titanic Historical Society Inc
208 Main St PO Box 51053   Indian Orchard MA 01151
Ph: 413-543-4770 ▪ Fx: 413-583-3633
www.titanic1.org

Titanium Association, International
350 Interlocken Blvd Suite 390   Broomfield CO 80021
Ph: 303-404-2221 ▪ Fx: 303-404-9111
www.titanium.org

Tithing Group, New
1 Market Stewart Tower Suite 2105   San Francisco CA 94105
Ph: 415-274-2765 ▪ Fx: 415-274-2756
www.newtithing.org

Title Association, American Land
1828 L St NW Suite 705   Washington DC 20036
Ph: 202-296-3671 ▪ Fx: 202-223-5843 ▪ TF: 800-787-2582
www.alta.org

Title Industry PAC
1828 L St NW Suite 705   Washington DC 20036
Ph: 202-296-3671 ▪ Fx: 202-223-5843

Title Insurers, National Association of Bar-Related
2355 S Arlington Heights Rd Suite 230   Arlington Heights IL 60005
Ph: 847-545-0500 ▪ Fx: 847-545-0550
www.nabrti.com

Toastmasters International
PO Box 9052   Mission Viejo CA 92690
Ph: 949-858-8255 ▪ Fx: 949-858-1207
www.toastmasters.org

Tobacco Associates Inc
1725 K St NW Suite 512   Washington DC 20006
Ph: 202-828-9144 ▪ Fx: 202-828-9149
www.tobaccoassociatesinc.org

Tobacco Association of the US
3716 National Dr Suite 114   Raleigh NC 27612
Ph: 919-782-5151 ▪ Fx: 919-781-0915

(Tobacco) Bright Belt Warehouse Association
PO Box 12004   Raleigh NC 27605
Ph: 919-828-8988

Tobacco Control Resource Center
102 The Fenway Cushing Hall Suite 117   Boston MA 02115
Ph: 617-373-2026 ▪ Fx: 617-373-3672
www.tobacco.neu.edu

Tobacco Council, Pipe
1707 H St NW Suite 800   Washington DC 20006
Ph: 202-223-8207 ▪ Fx: 202-833-0379

Tobacco Council, Smokeless
1627 K St NW Suite 700   Washington DC 20006
Ph: 202-452-1252 ▪ Fx: 202-452-0118 ▪ TF: 800-272-7144

Tobacco Council Inc, Specialty
204 Northgate Park Dr   Winston-Salem NC 27106
Ph: 336-759-0391 ▪ Fx: 336-759-0965

Tobacco Dealers of America, Retail
12 Galloway Ave Suite 1B   Cockeysville MD 21030
Ph: 410-628-1674 ▪ Fx: 410-628-1679
www.rtda.org

Tobacco Exporters Association, Leaf
3716 National Dr Suite 114   Raleigh NC 27612
Ph: 919-782-5151 ▪ Fx: 919-781-0915

Tobacco-Free Kids, National Center for
1400 'I' St NW Suite 1200   Washington DC 20005
Ph: 202-296-5469 ▪ Fx: 202-296-5427 ▪ TF: 800-284-5437
www.tobaccofreekids.org

Tobacco Growers Association, Eastern Dark-Fried
1109 S Main St PO Box 517   Springfield TN 37172
Ph: 615-384-4543 ▪ Fx: 615-384-4545

Tobacco Growers Cooperative Association, Burley
620 S Broadway   Lexington KY 40508
Ph: 859-252-3561 ▪ Fx: 859-231-9804
www.burleytobacco.com

Tobacco Jar Collectors, Society of
1705 Chanticleer   Cherry Hill NJ 08003
Ph: 856-489-8363 ▪ Fx: 856-489-8364
www.tobaccojarsociety.com

Tobacco Merchants Association
PO Box 8019   Princeton NJ 08543
Ph: 609-275-4900 ▪ Fx: 609-275-8379
www.tma.org

Tobacco, Society for Research on Nicotine &
7600 Terrace Ave Suite 203   Middleton WI 53562
Ph: 608-836-3787 ▪ Fx: 608-831-5485
www.srnt.org

Tobacco Workers & Grain Millers International Union, Bakery Confectionery   10401 Connecticut Ave   Kensington MD 20895
Ph: 301-933-8600 ▪ Fx: 301-946-8452
www.bctgm.org

Tobago-USA Chamber of Commerce, Trinidad &
2900 University Dr   Coral Springs FL 33065
Ph: 954-340-5868 ▪ Fx: 954-340-5869

TOC Management Services
6825 SW Sandburg St   Tigard OR 97223
Ph: 503-620-1710 ▪ Fx: 503-620-3935
www.toc.org

Toggenburg Club, National
www.nationaltoggclub.org

Toiletry & Fragrance Association Inc, Cosmetic
1101 17th St NW Suite 300   Washington DC 20036
Ph: 202-331-1770 ▪ Fx: 202-331-1969
www.ctfa.org

Token & Medal Society Inc
www.money.org/clubs/tams

Token Society, American Tax
12 Pheasant Dr   Asheville NC 28803
Ph: 828-684-1808

(Tolerance) Anne Frank Center USA
38 Crosby St Suite 5R   New York NY 10013
Ph: 212-431-7993 ▪ Fx: 212-431-8375
www.annefrank.com

Tolstoy Foundation Inc
104 Lake Rd   Valley Cottage NY 10989
Ph: 845-268-6722 ▪ Fx: 845-268-6937
www.tolstoyfoundation.org

Tomography & Magnetic Resonance, Society of Computed Body
PO Box 1026   Rochester MN 55903
Ph: 507-288-5620 ▪ Fx: 507-288-0014
www.scbtmr.org

Tongass Conservation Society
PO Box 23377   Ketchikan AK 99901
Ph: 907-225-5827
www.ptialaska.net/~tongass

Tool Association, International Staple Nail &
512 W Burlington Ave Suite 203   La Grange IL 60525
Ph: 708-482-8138 ▪ Fx: 708-482-8186
www.isanta.org

Tool Engineers, Society of Carbide &
ASM International 9639 Kinsman Rd   Materials Park OH 44072
Ph: 440-338-5151 ▪ Fx: 440-338-4634
www.scte10.org

Tool Institute, American Knife &
22 Vista View   Cody WY 82414
Ph: 307-587-8296
www.akti.org

Tool Institute, Equipment &
10 Laboratory Dr   Research Triangle Park NC 27709
Ph: 919-406-8844 ▪ Fx: 919-406-1306
www.etools.org

Tool Institute, Power
1300 Sumner Ave   Cleveland OH 44115
Ph: 216-241-7333 ▪ Fx: 216-241-0105
www.powertoolinstitute.com

Tool Institute, US Cutting
1300 Sumner Ave   Cleveland OH 44115
Ph: 216-241-7333 ▪ Fx: 216-241-0105
www.uscti.com

Tool Manufacturers Institute, Powder Actuated
1603 Boonslick Rd   Saint Charles MO 63301
Ph: 636-947-6610 ▪ Fx: 636-946-3336
www.patmi.org

Tool Mark Examiners, Association of Firearm &
www.afte.org

Tooling & Machining Association, International Special
9300 Livingston Rd   Fort Washington MD 20744
Ph: 301-248-6200 ▪ Fx: 301-248-7104 ▪ TF: 800-248-6862

Tooling & Machining Association, National
9300 Livingston Rd   Fort Washington MD 20744
Ph: 301-248-6200 ▪ Fx: 301-248-7104 ▪ TF: 800-248-6862
www.ntma.org

Tooling & Manufacturing Association
1177 S Dee Rd   Park Ridge IL 60068
Ph: 847-825-1120 ▪ Fx: 847-825-0041
www.tmanet.com

Tools & Fasteners Distributors Association, Specialty
PO Box 44   Elm Grove WI 53122
Ph: 262-784-4774 ▪ Fx: 262-784-5059 ▪ TF: 800-352-2981
www.stafda.org

Toothpick Holder Collectors Society, National
www.collectoronline.com/NTHCS

Topical Association, American
PO Box 57   Arlington TX 76004
Ph: 817-274-1181 ▪ Fx: 817-274-1184
www.americantopicalassn.org

TOPS Club Inc
4575 S 5th St   Milwaukee WI 53207
Ph: 414-482-4620 ▪ TF: 800-932-8677
www.tops.org

Torah Umesorah-National Society for Hebrew Day Schools
160 Broadway   New York NY 10038
Ph: 212-227-1000 ▪ Fx: 212-406-6934

Torch Clubs, International Association of
749 Boush St   Norfolk VA 23510
Ph: 757-622-3927 ▪ Fx: 757-623-9740 ▪ TF: 888-622-4101
www.torch.org

Tort Reform Association, American
1101 Connecticut Ave NW Suite 400   Washington DC 20036
Ph: 202-682-1163 ▪ Fx: 202-682-1022
www.atra.org

Tortilla Industry Association
3340 Pilot Knob Rd   Eagan MN 55121
Ph: 651-994-3881 ▪ Fx: 651-454-0766
www.tortilla-info.com

Tortoise Preserve Committee, Desert
4067 Mission Inn Ave   Riverside CA 92501
Ph: 909-683-3872 ▪ Fx: 909-683-6949
www.tortoise-tracks.org

Tortoise Society, New York Turtle &
nytts.org

Touch for Health Kinesiology Association
PO Box 392   New Carlisle OH 45344
Ph: 937-845-3404 ▪ Fx: 937-845-3909 ▪ TF: 800-466-8342
www.tfhka.org

TOUGHLOVE International
100 Mechanics St   Doylestown PA 18901
Ph: 215-348-7090 ▪ Fx: 215-348-9874 ▪ TF: 800-333-1069
www.toughlove.com

Tour Association Inc, National
546 E Main St   Lexington KY 40508
Ph: 859-226-4444 ▪ Fx: 859-226-4404 ▪ TF: 800-682-8886
www.ntaonline.com

Tour Managers, International Association of
9500 Rainier Ave S Unit 603   Seattle WA 98118
Ph: 206-725-7108 ▪ Fx: 206-725-4020
www.members.aol.com/iatmone

Tour Operators Association, US
275 Madison Ave Suite 2014   New York NY 10016
Ph: 212-599-6599 ▪ Fx: 212-599-6744
www.ustoa.com

Tourette Syndrome Association Inc
42-40 Bell Blvd Suite 205   Bayside NY 11361
Ph: 718-224-2999 ▪ Fx: 718-279-9596 ▪ TF: 888-486-8738
www.tsa-usa.org

Touring Rider's Association, American Sport
PO Box 672015   Marietta GA 30006
Ph: 770-222-0380

Tourism Directors, National Council of State
1100 New York Ave NW Suite 450   Washington DC 20005
Ph: 202-408-8422 ▪ Fx: 202-408-1255
www.tia.org/councils/ncstd.asp

Tourism Educators, International Society of Travel &
23220 Edgewater   Saint Clair Shores MI 48082
Ph: 586-294-0208
www.istte.org

Tourism Research Association, Travel &
PO Box 2133   Boise ID 83701
Ph: 208-429-9511 ▪ Fx: 208-429-9512
www.ttra.org

Tournament of Roses Association, Pasadena — www.tournamentofroses.com
391 S Orange Grove Blvd   Pasadena CA 91184
Ph: 626-449-4100 ▪ Fx: 626-449-9066

Touro Synagogue Foundation — www.tourosynagogue.org
85 Touro St   Newport RI 02840
Ph: 401-847-4794 ▪ Fx: 401-845-6790

Tower Erectors, National Association of — www.natehome.com
8 2nd St SE   Watertown SD 57201
Ph: 605-882-5865 ▪ Fx: 605-886-5184 ▪ TF: 888-882-5865

Towing, Committee for Private Offshore Rescue & — www.c-port.org
1600 Duke St Suite 220   Alexandria VA 22314
Ph: 703-519-1713 ▪ Fx: 703-519-1716

Towing & Recovery Association of America — www.towserver.net
2121 Eisenhower Ave Suite 200   Alexandria VA 22314
Ph: 703-684-7734 ▪ Fx: 703-684-6720 ▪ TF: 800-728-0136

Town Watch, National Association of — www.nationaltownwatch.com
1 E Wynnewood Rd Suite 102   Wynnewood PA 19096
Ph: 610-649-7055 ▪ Fx: 610-649-5456 ▪ TF: 800-648-3688

Towns & Townships, National Association of — www.natat.org
444 N Capitol St NW Suite 397   Washington DC 20001
Ph: 202-624-3550 ▪ Fx: 202-624-3554

Toxicologic Pathologists, Society of — www.toxpath.org
1821 Michael Faraday Dr Suite 300   Reston VA 20190
Ph: 703-438-7508 ▪ Fx: 703-438-3113

Toxicologists, International Association of Forensic — www.tiaft.org

Toxicology, American Academy of Clinical — www.clintox.org
777 E Park Dr PO Box 8820   Harrisburg PA 17105
Ph: 717-558-7847 ▪ Fx: 717-558-7841

Toxicology, American Academy of Veterinary & Comparative
Murray State Univ Breathitt Veterinary Ctr 715 North Dr PO Box
2000   Hopkinsville KY 42240
Ph: 270-886-3959 ▪ Fx: 270-886-4295

Toxicology, American Board of — www.abtox.org
PO Box 30054   Raleigh NC 27612
Ph: 919-841-5022 ▪ Fx: 919-841-5042

Toxicology, American College of — actox.org
9650 Rockville Pike   Bethesda MD 20814
Ph: 301-634-7840 ▪ Fx: 301-634-7852

Toxicology, American College of Medical — www.acmt.net
11240 Waples Mill Rd Suite 200   Fairfax VA 22030
Ph: 703-934-1223 ▪ Fx: 703-359-7562

Toxicology & Chemistry, Society of Environmental — www.setac.org
1010 N 12th Ave   Pensacola FL 32501
Ph: 850-469-1500 ▪ Fx: 850-469-9778 ▪ TF: 888-899-2088

Toxicology Forum — www.toxforum.org
1575 'I' St NW Suite 325   Washington DC 20005
Ph: 202-659-0030 ▪ Fx: 202-789-0905

Toxicology, International Academy of Oral Medicine & — www.iaomt.org
8297 Championsgate Blvd Suite 193   Championsgate FL 33896
Ph: 863-420-6373 ▪ Fx: 863-420-6394

Toxicology, Society of — www.toxicology.org
1821 Michael Faraday Dr Suite 300   Reston VA 20190
Ph: 703-438-3115 ▪ Fx: 703-438-3113

Toy Association, Antique Engine Tractor &
5731 Paradise Rd   Slatington PA 18080
Ph: 610-767-4768

Toy Car Collectors Association — www.toynutz.com/TCCA.html
PO Box 1824   Bend OR 97709
Ph: 541-318-7176

Toy Industry Association Inc — www.toy-tia.org
1115 Broadway Suite 400   New York NY 10010
Ph: 212-675-1141 ▪ Fx: 212-633-1429

Toy Library Association, USA — usatla.deltacollege.org
1326 Wilmette Ave   Wilmette IL 60091
Ph: 847-920-9030 ▪ Fx: 847-920-9032

Toy Retailing Association, American Specialty — www.astratoy.org
4700 W Lake Ave   Glenview IL 60025
Ph: 847-375-4727 ▪ Fx: 888-840-2650

Toys for Tots Foundation — www.toysfortots.org
715 Broadway St   Quantico VA 22134
Ph: 703-640-9433 ▪ Fx: 703-640-0917

Trabajo in America, Legionarios del
2154 S San Joaquin St   Stockton CA 95206
Ph: 209-463-6516

Track Builders Association, US Tennis Court & — www.ustctba.com
3525 Ellicott Mills Dr Suite N   Ellicott City MD 21043
Ph: 410-418-4875 ▪ Fx: 410-418-4805

Track Club, Achilles — www.achillestrackclub.org
42 W 38th St 4th Fl   New York NY 10018
Ph: 212-354-0300 ▪ Fx: 212-354-3978

Track Coaches Association, US Women's
7263 Heartcrest Ln   Centerville OH 45458
Ph: 937-434-0383

Track & Field, USA — www.usatf.org
1 RCA Dome Suite 140   Indianapolis IN 46225
Ph: 317-261-0500 ▪ Fx: 317-261-0481

Tract Society, American — www.atstracts.org
1624 N 1st St   Garland TX 75046
Ph: 972-276-9408 ▪ Fx: 972-272-9642 ▪ TF: 800-548-7228

Tractor Club, Fordson
250 Robinson Rd   Cave Junction OR 97523
Ph: 541-592-3203

Tractor Parts Dealer Association, National — www.ntpda.com
PO Box 1181   Gainesville TX 76241
Ph: 940-668-0900 ▪ Fx: 940-668-1627

Tractor Pullers Association, National — www.ntpapull.com
6155-B Huntley Rd   Columbus OH 43229
Ph: 614-436-1761 ▪ Fx: 614-436-0964

Tractor & Toy Association, Antique Engine
5731 Paradise Rd   Slatington PA 18080
Ph: 610-767-4768

Trade Action Coalition, American Manufacturing — www.amtacdc.org
910 16th St NW Suite 410   Washington DC 20006
Ph: 202-452-0866 ▪ Fx: 202-452-0739

Trade Association Executives, Automotive
8400 Westpark Dr   McLean VA 22102
Ph: 703-821-7072 ▪ Fx: 703-556-8581

Trade Association, International Reciprocal — www.irta.com
140 Metro Park   Rochester NY 14623
Ph: 716-424-2940 ▪ Fx: 716-424-2964

Trade Association, Japanese-American Cultural
PO Box 4804   Panorama City CA 91412
Ph: 818-780-0815 ▪ Fx: 818-780-8501

Trade Association, National Structured Settlements — www.nssta.com
1800 K St NW Suite 718   Washington DC 20006
Ph: 202-466-2714 ▪ Fx: 202-466-7414

Trade Association of Paddlesports — www.gopaddle.org
PO Box 6353   Olympia WA 98507
Ph: 360-352-0764 ▪ Fx: 360-352-0784 ▪ TF: 800-755-5228

Trade Association, Southern US — www.susta.org
2 Canal St World Trade Ctr Suite 2515   New Orleans LA 70130
Ph: 504-568-5986 ▪ Fx: 504-568-6010

Trade Association, Western-English — www.wetaonline.org
451 E 58th Ave Suite 4323   Denver CO 80216
Ph: 303-295-2001 ▪ Fx: 303-295-6108

Trade Association, Western US Agricultural — www.wusata.org
2500 Main St Suite 110   Vancouver WA 98660
Ph: 360-693-3373 ▪ Fx: 360-693-3464

Trade Associations, Federation of International — www.fita.org
11800 Sunrise Valley Dr Suite 210   Reston VA 20191
Ph: 703-620-1588 ▪ Fx: 703-620-4922

Trade, Bankers' Association for Finance & — www.baft.org
1120 Connecticut Ave NW   Washington DC 20036
Ph: 202-663-7575 ▪ Fx: 202-663-5538

Trade Bar Association, Customs & International — www.citba.org
729 15th St NW Suite 800   Washington DC 20005
Ph: 202-783-6900 ▪ Fx: 202-783-6909

Trade Centers Association, World — iserve.wtca.org
60 E 42nd St Suite 1901   New York NY 10165
Ph: 212-432-2626 ▪ Fx: 212-488-0064

Trade Circulation Foundation Inc, National — www.ntcfi.org

Trade Commission Trial Lawyers Association, International — www.itctla.org
PO Box 6186 Benjamin Franklin Stn   Washington DC 20004
Ph: 202-942-6423

Trade, Consumers for World — www.cwt.org
1001 Connecticut Ave NW Suite 1110   Washington DC 20006
Ph: 202-293-2944 ▪ Fx: 202-293-0495

Trade Council, International
3114 Circle Hill Rd   Alexandria VA 22305
Ph: 703-548-1234 ▪ Fx: 703-548-6216

Trade Council, National Foreign — www.nftc.org
1625 K St NW Suite 200   Washington DC 20006
Ph: 202-887-0278 ▪ Fx: 202-452-8160

Trade Council, National Grain — ngtc.org
1300 L St NW Suite 1020   Washington DC 20005
Ph: 202-842-0400 ▪ Fx: 202-789-7223

Trade Development, National Council on International — www.ncitd.org
818 Connecticut Ave NW 12th Fl   Washington DC 20006
Ph: 202-872-9280 ▪ Fx: 202-872-8324

Trade Educators, North American Small Business International — www.nasbite.org
Wright State Univ 120 Rike Hall 3640 Colonel Glenn
Hwy   Dayton OH 45435
Ph: 937-775-3524 ▪ Fx: 937-775-3545

Trade, Emergency Committee for American — www.ecattrade.com
1211 Connecticut Ave NW Suite 801   Washington DC 20036
Ph: 202-659-5147 ▪ Fx: 202-659-1347

Trade Exchanges, National Association of — www.nate.org
8836 Tyler Blvd   Mentor OH 44060
Ph: 440-205-5378 ▪ Fx: 440-205-5379

Trade & Industrial Education, National Association of — www.skillsusa.org/NATIE
PO Box 1665   Leesburg VA 20177
Ph: 703-777-1740

Trade & Industrial Education, National Association of State Supervisors of — itednt.ited.uidaho.edu/nasstie

Trade, Organization of Women in International — www.owit.org
1413 K St NW 1st Fl Suite 857   Washington DC 20005
Ph: 202-785-9842

Trade Policy, Institute for Agriculture & — www.iatp.org
2105 1st Ave S   Minneapolis MN 55404
Ph: 612-870-0453 ▪ Fx: 612-870-4846

Trade Show Exhibitors Association — www.tsea.org
2301 S Lake Shore Dr Suite 1005   Chicago IL 60616
Ph: 312-842-8732 ▪ Fx: 312-842-8744

Trade Zones, National Association of Foreign- — www.naftz.org
1000 Connecticut Ave NW Suite 1001   Washington DC 20036
Ph: 202-331-1950 ▪ Fx: 202-331-1994

Trademark Association, International — www.inta.org
1133 Ave of the Americas   New York NY 10036
Ph: 212-768-9887 ▪ Fx: 212-786-7796

Traders Association, Emerging Markets — www.emta.org
360 Madison Ave 18th Fl   New York NY 10017
Ph: 646-637-9100 ▪ Fx: 646-637-9128

Traders Association, Security — www.securitytraders.org
420 Lexington Ave Suite 2334   New York NY 10170
Ph: 212-867-7002 ▪ Fx: 212-867-7030

Trades Technology & Science, Institute for Women in — www.iwitts.com
1150 Ballena Blvd Suite 102   Alameda CA 94501
Ph: 510-749-0200 ▪ Fx: 510-749-0500

Tradeswomen Inc   www.tradeswomen.org
PO Box 882103   San Francisco CA 94188
Ph: 415-487-6419

Tradition Family & Property, American Society for the Defense of   www.tfp.org
PO Box 341   Hanover PA 17331
Ph: 717-225-7147   Fx: 717-225-7382

Tradition, Society for the Study of Myth &   www.parabola.org
656 Broadway   New York NY 10012
Ph: 212-505-6200   Fx: 212-979-7325   TF: 800-560-6984

Traditional Arts, National Council for the   www.NCTA.net
1320 Fenwick Ln Suite 200   Silver Spring MD 20910
Ph: 301-565-0654   Fx: 301-565-0472

Traditional Country Music Association, National   www.oldtimemusic.bigstep.com/
PO Box 492   Anita IA 50020
Ph: 712-762-4363

Traditional Small Craft Association   www.tsca.net
PO Box 350   Mystic CT 06355
Ph: 860-572-0711

Traffic Association, Energy   www.energytraffic.org
3303 Main St Suite 207   Houston TX 77002
Ph: 713-827-1199   Fx: 713-464-0702

Traffic Association, National Bus   www.bustraffic.org
700 13th St NE Suite 575   Washington DC 20005
Ph: 202-898-2700   Fx: 202-842-0850

Traffic Association, National Motor Freight   www.nmfta.org
2200 Mill Rd   Alexandria VA 22314
Ph: 703-838-1810   Fx: 703-683-1094

Traffic Audit Bureau for Media Measurement   www.tabonline.com
420 Lexington Ave Room 2520   New York NY 10170
Ph: 212-972-8075   Fx: 212-972-8928

Traffic Control Association, Air   www.atca.org
2300 Clarendon Blvd Suite 711   Arlington VA 22201
Ph: 703-522-5717   Fx: 703-527-7251

Traffic Laws & Ordinances, National Committee on Uniform   www.ncutlo.org
107 S West St Suite 110   Alexandria VA 22314
Ph: 540-465-4701   Fx: 540-465-5383   TF: 800-807-5290

TRAFFIC North America   www.traffic.org
1250 24th St NW Suite 500   Washington DC 20037
Ph: 202-293-4800   Fx: 202-775-8287

Traffic Safety, AAA Foundation for   www.aaafoundation.org
607 14th St NW Suite 201   Washington DC 20005
Ph: 202-638-5944   Fx: 202-638-5943

Traffic Safety Education Association, American Driver &   www.adtsea.iup.edu
Indiana Univ of Pennsylvania Highway Safety Ctr R&P
   Bldg   Indiana PA 15705
Ph: 724-357-4051   Fx: 724-357-7595   TF: 800-896-7703

Traffic Safety Services Association, American   www.atssa.com
15 Riverside Pkwy Suite 100   Fredericksburg VA 22406
Ph: 540-368-1701   Fx: 540-368-1717   TF: 800-272-8772

Trail Administrators, National Association of State
701 Ivanhoe St   Denver CO 80220
Ph: 720-308-0567   Fx: 303-321-8082

Trail Association, Florida   www.florida-trail.org
5415 SW 13th St   Gainesville FL 32608
Ph: 352-378-8823   Fx: 352-378-4550   TF: 877-445-3352

Trail Association, North Country   www.northcountrytrail.org
229 E Main St   Lowell MI 49331
Ph: 616-897-5987   Fx: 616-897-6605   TF: 888-454-6282

Trail Association, Pacific Crest   www.pcta.org
5325 Elkhorn Blvd PMB 256   Sacramento CA 95842
Ph: 916-349-2109   Fx: 916-349-1268   TF: 888-728-7245

Trail Association, Pacific Northwest   www.pnt.org
PO Box 1817   Mount Vernon WA 98273
Ph: 877-854-9415

Trail Association, Santa Fe   www.santafetrail.org
Santa Fe Trail Ctr RR 3   Larned KS 67550
Ph: 620-285-2054   Fx: 620-285-7491

Trail Conference, Appalachian   www.appalachiantrail.org
799 Washington St   Harpers Ferry WV 25425
Ph: 304-535-6331   Fx: 304-535-2667

Trail Foundation, Ice Age Park &   www.iceagetrail.org
207 E Buffalo St Suite 515   Milwaukee WI 53202
Ph: 414-278-8518   Fx: 414-278-8665   TF: 800-227-0046

Trail Heritage Foundation, Lewis & Clark   www.lewisandclark.org
PO Box 3434   Great Falls MT 59404
Ph: 406-454-1234   Fx: 406-771-9237   TF: 888-701-3434

Trail Improvement Society, Adirondack
PO Box 565   Keene Valley NY 12943
Ph: 518-576-9157   Fx: 518-576-9949

Trail Ride Conference, North American   www.natrc.org
PO Box 224   Sedalia CO 80135
Ph: 303-688-1677   Fx: 303-688-3022

Trail Society, Continental Divide   www.cdtsociety.org
3704 N Charles St Suite 601 B   Baltimore MD 21218
Ph: 410-235-9610   Fx: 410-243-1960

Trailer Dealers Association, National   www.ntda.org
37400 Hills Tech Dr   Farmington Hills MI 48331
Ph: 800-800-4552   Fx: 248-489-8590

Trailer Industry Association Inc, Recreational Park   www.rptia.org
30 Greenville St 2nd Fl   Newnan GA 30263
Ph: 770-251-2672   Fx: 770-251-0025

Trailer Manufacturers Association
200 N Randolph Dr Suite 5100   Chicago IL 60601
Ph: 312-946-6280   Fx: 312-946-0388

Trailer Manufacturers, National Association of   www.natm.com
2951 SW Wanamaker Dr Suite A   Topeka KS 66614
Ph: 785-272-4433   Fx: 785-272-4455

Trails, American   www.americantrails.org
PO Box 491797   Redding CA 96049
Ph: 530-547-2060   Fx: 530-547-2035

Trails Association, Oregon-California   www.octa-trails.org
PO Box 1019   Independence MO 64051
Ph: 816-252-2276   Fx: 816-836-0989

Trails Association, Washington   www.wta.org
1305 4th Ave Suite 512   Seattle WA 98101
Ph: 206-625-1367   Fx: 206-625-9249

Train Collectors Association   www.traincollectors.org
PO Box 248   Strasburg PA 17579
Ph: 717-687-8623   Fx: 717-687-0742

Train Dispatchers Association, American   atdd.homestead.com/atddpg1.html
1370 Ontario St Suite 1040   Cleveland OH 44113
Ph: 216-241-2770   Fx: 216-241-6286

Trainers, Academy of Security Educators &   www.personalprotection.com/aset
PO Box 802   Berryville VA 22611
Ph: 540-554-2540   Fx: 540-554-2558

Trainers of America, United Thoroughbred
PO Box 7065   Louisville KY 40257
Ph: 502-893-0025   Fx: 502-893-0026   TF: 800-325-3487

Trainers Association, National Athletic   www.nata.org
2952 Stemmons Fwy Suite 200   Dallas TX 75247
Ph: 214-637-6282   Fx: 214-637-2206   TF: 800-879-6282

Trainers Association, National Basketball
400 Colony Sq Suite 1750   Atlanta GA 30361
Ph: 404-875-4000   Fx: 404-892-8560

Trainers, Association of Natural Resource Enforcement   www.anret.org
402 W Washington St IGCS Rm W255D   Indianapolis IN 46204
Ph: 317-232-4014   Fx: 317-232-8035

Trainers, Association of Pet Dog   www.apdt.org
PO Box 1781   Hobbs NM 88241
Ph: 800-738-3647

Trainers Association, Walking Horse   www.walkinghorsetrainers.com
PO Box 61   Shelbyville TN 37162
Ph: 931-684-5866   Fx: 931-684-5895

Trainers, Council of Hotel & Restaurant   www.chart.org
PO Box 2835   Westfield NJ 07091
Ph: 800-463-5918   Fx: 800-427-5436

Trainers & Educators, National Association   www.preventionpartners.samhsa.gov/partner
of Substance Abuse   1521 Hillary St   New Orleans LA 70118
Ph: 504-286-5234

Trainers & Educators, Society of Insurance   www.insurancetrainers.org
2120 Market St Suite 108   San Francisco CA 94114
Ph: 415-621-2830   Fx: 415-621-0289

Trainers, National Federation of Professional   www.nfpt.com
PO Box 4579   Lafayette IN 47903
Ph: 765-471-4514   Fx: 765-471-7369   TF: 800-729-6378

Trainers, Society of Pharmaceutical & Biotech   www.spbt.org
4423 Pheasant Ridge Rd Suite 100   Roanoke VA 24014
Ph: 540-725-3859   Fx: 540-989-7482

Training, American Association of Directors of Psychiatric   www.aadprt.org
Residency   Univ of Connecticut Health Ctr Dept of Psychiatry
   263 Farmington Ave LG066   Farmington CT 06030
Ph: 860-679-8112   Fx: 860-679-1246

Training, American Society for Law Enforcement   www.aslet.org
121 N Court St   Frederick MD 21701
Ph: 301-668-9466   Fx: 301-668-9482

Training Association, American Sail   tallships.sailtraining.org
PO Box 1459   Newport RI 02840
Ph: 401-846-1775   Fx: 401-849-5400

Training, Association for Graphic Arts   www.agatweb.org

Training Association, International Fire Service   www.ifsta.org
Fire Protection Publications Oklahoma State Univ 930 N
   Willis   Stillwater OK 74078
Ph: 405-744-5723   Fx: 405-744-8204   TF: 800-654-4055

Training, Association for International Practical   www.aipt.org
10400 Little Patuxent Pkwy Suite 250   Columbia MD 21044
Ph: 410-997-2200   Fx: 410-992-3924

Training Association, National Environmental   www.ehs-training.org
5320 N 16th St Suite 114   Phoenix AZ 85016
Ph: 602-956-6099   Fx: 602-956-6399

Training in the Behavioral Sciences, Association for Advanced   www.aatbs.com
5126 Ralston St   Ventura CA 93003
Ph: 805-676-3030   Fx: 805-676-3033   TF: 800-472-1931

(Training) CDS International Inc   www.cdsintl.org
871 United Nations Plaza 15th Fl   New York NY 10017
Ph: 212-497-3500   Fx: 212-497-3535

Training in Communication, International   www.itcintl.org
2519 Woodland Dr   Anaheim CA 92801
Ph: 714-995-3660   Fx: 714-995-6974

Training Coordinators, National Council of State Emergency   www.ncsemstc.org
Medical Services   201 Park Washington Ct   Falls Church VA
   22046
Ph: 703-538-1794   Fx: 703-241-5603

Training & Development, American Society for   www.astd.org
1640 King St Box 1443   Alexandria VA 22313
Ph: 703-683-8100   Fx: 703-683-1523   TF: 800-628-2783

Training & Development, National Association for Government
2516 Wertherson Ln   Raleigh NC 27613
Ph: 919-870-8496   Fx: 919-845-6922

Training Directors' Forum   www.trainingdirectorsforum.com
PO Box 3867   Federick MD 21705
Ph: 301-696-1006   Fx: 301-694-5124   TF: 888-578-7371

Training & Information Center, National   www.ntic-us.org
810 N Milwaukee Ave   Chicago IL 60622
Ph: 312-243-3035   Fx: 312-243-7044

Training, International Association for Continuing Education &   www.iacet.org
1620 'I' St NW Suite 615   Washington DC 20006
Ph: 202-463-2905   Fx: 202-463-8497

Training International, Mission   www.mti.org
PO Box 1220   Palmer Lake CO 80133
Ph: 719-487-0111   Fx: 719-487-9350   TF: 800-896-3710

Training Managers Council, Automotive www.atmc.org
101 Blue Seal Dr SE Suite 101   Leesburg VA 20175
Ph: 703-669-6670 ▪ Fx: 703-669-6126

Training, National Council for Continuing Education & www.nccet.org
PO Box 130623   Carlsbad CA 92013
Ph: 760-753-8375 ▪ Fx: 760-942-7296

Training Officers Conference www.trainingofficers.org
2025 M St NW Suite 800   Washington DC 20036
Ph: 202-973-8683 ▪ Fx: 202-331-0111

Training Personnel, International Association of Correctional www.iactp.org
PO Box 11018   Albany NY 12211
Ph: 518-783-6939

Training, Professional Society for Sales & Marketing www.smt.org
180 N LaSalle St Suite 1822   Chicago IL 60601
Ph: 312-551-0768 ▪ Fx: 312-551-0815

Training Project, Student Empowerment www.trainings.org
119 Somerset St 2nd Fl   New Brunswick NJ 08901
Ph: 732-247-2197

Training & Research Institute, Hazardous Materials www.hmtri.org
6301 Kirkwood Blvd SW PO Box 2068   Cedar Rapids IA 52406
Ph: 319-398-5678 ▪ Fx: 319-398-1250 ▪ TF: 800-464-6874

Training & Research, International Society for Intercultural www.sietarusa.org
Education   8835 SW Canyon Ln Suite 110   Portland OR
97225
Ph: 503-297-4622 ▪ Fx: 503-297-4695

Training Systems Association, National www.trainingsystems.org
2111 Wilson Blvd Suite 400   Arlington VA 22201
Ph: 703-347-9471 ▪ Fx: 703-243-1659 ▪ TF: 800-677-6897

Trainmen, Brotherhood of Locomotive Engineers & www.ble.org
1370 Ontario St Mezzanine Level   Cleveland OH 44113
Ph: 216-241-2630 ▪ Fx: 216-241-6516

Trakehner Association, American www.americantrakehner.com
1514 W Church St   Newark OH 43055
Ph: 740-344-1111 ▪ Fx: 740-344-3225

Trans World Radio www.gospelcom.net/twr
PO Box 8700   Cary NC 27512
Ph: 919-460-3700 ▪ Fx: 919-460-3702 ▪ TF: 800-456-7897

Transaction Processing Performance Council www.tpc.org
PO Box 29920   San Francisco CA 94129
Ph: 415-561-6272 ▪ Fx: 415-561-6120

Transactional Analysis Association, International www.itaa-net.org
436 14th St Suite 1301   Oakland CA 94612
Ph: 510-625-7720 ▪ Fx: 510-625-7725

Transafrica Forum www.transafricaforum.org
1426 21st NW 2nd Fl   Washington DC 20036
Ph: 202-223-1960 ▪ Fx: 202-223-1966

Transcription, American Association for Medical www.aamt.org
100 Sycamore Ave   Modesto CA 95354
Ph: 209-527-9620 ▪ Fx: 209-527-9633 ▪ TF: 800-982-2182

Transcription Industry Alliance, Medical www.mtia.org
711 Broadway E Suite 7   Seattle WA 98102
Ph: 800-543-6842 ▪ Fx: 206-628-3333

Transformer Association www.transformer-assn.org
PO Box P182   South Dartmouth MA 02748
Ph: 508-979-5935 ▪ Fx: 508-979-5845

Transgender Organization, LLEGO - National Latina/o Lesbian Gay www.llego.org
Bisexual &   1420 K St NW Suite 400   Washington DC 20005
Ph: 202-408-5380 ▪ Fx: 202-408-8478 ▪ TF: 888-633-8320

Transit Association, Advanced www.advancedtransit.org

Transit Association, International Marine www.interferry.com
34 Otis Hill Rd   Hingham MA 02043
Ph: 781-749-0078

Transit Association, International Safe www.ista.org
1400 Abbott Rd Suite 160   East Lansing MI 48823
Ph: 517-333-3437 ▪ Fx: 517-333-3813

Transit Service Council, American www.transitatsc.org
1090 Vermont Ave NW Suite 1225   Washington DC 20005
Ph: 202-842-2818 ▪ Fx: 202-789-4328

Transit Union, Amalgamated www.atu.org
5025 Wisconsin Ave NW 3rd Fl   Washington DC 20016
Ph: 202-537-1645 ▪ Fx: 202-244-7824

Translator Association, National www.tvfmtranslators.com
5611 Kendell Ct Suite 2   Arvada CO 80002
Ph: 303-465-5742 ▪ Fx: 303-465-4067

Translators Association, American www.atanet.org
225 Reinekers Ln Suite 590   Alexandria VA 22314
Ph: 703-683-6100 ▪ Fx: 703-683-6122

Translators Association, American Literary www.literarytranslators.org
Univ of Texas at Dallas PO Box 830688 MC35   Richardson TX
75083
Ph: 972-883-2093 ▪ Fx: 972-883-6303

Translators, National Association of Judiciary Interpreters & www.najit.org
2150 N 107th St Suite 205   Seattle WA 98133
Ph: 206-367-8704 ▪ Fx: 206-367-8777

Translators, Wycliffe Bible www.wycliffe.org
PO Box 628200   Orlando FL 32862
Ph: 407-852-3600 ▪ Fx: 407-852-3601 ▪ TF: 800-992-5433

Transmission Rebuilders Association, Automatic www.atra-gears.com
2400 Latigo Ave   Oxnard CA 93030
Ph: 805-604-2000 ▪ Fx: 805-604-2003

Transpersonal Psychology, Association for www.atpweb.org
PO Box 50187   Palo Alto CA 94303
Ph: 650-424-8764 ▪ Fx: 650-618-1851

Transplant Association, American www.americantransplant.org
980 N Michigan Ave Suite 1400   Chicago IL 60611
Ph: 800-494-4527

Transplant Association, American Organ www.a-o-t-a.org
PO Box 41766   Houston TX 77244
Ph: 281-493-2047 ▪ Fx: 281-493-2099

Transplant Association, Children's Organ www.cota.org
2501 Cota Dr   Bloomington IN 47403
Ph: 812-336-8872 ▪ Fx: 812-336-8885 ▪ TF: 800-366-2682

Transplant Association, International Pediatric www.iptaonline.org
17000 Commerce Pkwy Suite C   Mount Laurel NJ 08054
Ph: 856-439-0500 ▪ Fx: 856-439-0525

Transplant Coordinators Organization, North American www.natco1.org
PO Box 15384   Lenexa KS 66285
Ph: 913-492-3600 ▪ Fx: 913-599-5340

Transplant Nurses Society, International www.itns.org
1739 E Carson St Box 351   Pittsburgh PA 15203
Ph: 412-343-4867 ▪ Fx: 412-343-3959

Transplant Registry, International Bone Marrow www.ibmtr.org
8701 Watertown Plank Rd PO Box 26509   Milwaukee WI
53226
Ph: 414-456-8325 ▪ Fx: 414-456-6530

Transplant Surgeons, American Society of www.asts.org
1020 N Fairfax St Suite 200   Alexandria VA 22314
Ph: 703-684-5990 ▪ Fx: 703-684-6303 ▪ TF: 888-990-2787

Transplantation, American Society of www.a-s-t.org
17000 Commerce Pkwy Suite C   Mount Laurel NJ 08054
Ph: 856-439-9986 ▪ Fx: 856-439-9982

Transplantation, American Society for Blood & Marrow www.asbmt.org
85 W Algonquin Rd Suite 550   Arlington Heights IL 60005
Ph: 847-427-0224 ▪ Fx: 847-427-9656

Transplantation, International Society for Heart & Lung www.ishlt.org
14673 Midway Rd Suite 200   Addison TX 75001
Ph: 972-490-9495 ▪ Fx: 972-490-9499

Transplantation, North American Society for Dialysis & www.nasdat.org
4010 Bentley Dr   Pearland TX 77584
Ph: 281-997-1944

Transplantation Society www.transplantation-soc.org
205 Viger Ave W Suite 201   Montreal QC H2Z1G2
Ph: 514-874-1998 ▪ Fx: 514-874-1580

Transplantation Society, International Liver www.ilts.org
17000 Commerce Pkwy Suite C   Mount Laurel NJ 08054
Ph: 856-439-0500 ▪ Fx: 856-439-0525

Transplants, National Foundation for www.transplants.org
1102 Brookfield Rd Suite 200   Memphis TN 38119
Ph: 901-684-1697 ▪ Fx: 901-684-1128 ▪ TF: 800-489-3863

Transport Aircraft Trading, International Society of www.istat.org
5517 Talon Ct   Fairfax VA 22032
Ph: 703-978-8156 ▪ Fx: 703-503-5964

Transport Association of America, Air www.air-transport.org
1301 Pennsylvania Ave NW Suite 1100   Washington DC 20004
Ph: 202-626-4000 ▪ Fx: 202-626-4181

Transport for Christ International www.transportforchrist.org
PO Box 303   Denver PA 17517
Ph: 717-859-4870 ▪ Fx: 717-859-4798

Transport Health Employees, International Union of Industrial Service
254 W 31st St   New York NY 10001
Ph: 212-696-5545 ▪ Fx: 212-696-5556 ▪ TF: 800-331-1070

Transport Nurses Association, Air & Surface www.astna.org
9101 E Kenyon Ave Suite 3000   Denver CO 80237
Ph: 800-897-6362 ▪ Fx: 303-770-1812

Transport Workers Union of America www.twu.com
80 West End Ave 6th Fl   New York NY 10023
Ph: 212-873-6000 ▪ Fx: 212-721-1431

Transportation Association, Airport Ground www.agtaweb.org
UMSL Ctr for Transportation Studies 154 University Ctr 8001
Natural Bridge Rd   Saint Louis MO 63121
Ph: 314-516-7271 ▪ Fx: 314-516-7272

Transportation Association of America, Community www.ctaa.org
1341 G St NW Suite 1000   Washington DC 20005
Ph: 202-628-1480 ▪ Fx: 202-737-9197 ▪ TF: 800-527-8279

Transportation Association, American Public www.apta.com
1666 K St NW   Washington DC 20006
Ph: 202-496-4800 ▪ Fx: 202-496-4321

Transportation Association, Animal www.aata-animaltransport.org
1111 East Loop N   Houston TX 77029
Ph: 713-532-2177 ▪ Fx: 713-532-2166

Transportation, Association for Commuter www.actweb.org
PO Box 15542   Washington DC 20003
Ph: 202-393-3497 ▪ Fx: 202-546-2196

Transportation Association, Electric Drive www.evaa.org
701 Pennsylvania Ave NW 3rd Fl   Washington DC 20004
Ph: 202-408-0774 ▪ Fx: 202-508-5924

Transportation Association, International Refrigerated www.irta.org
4255 S Buckley Rd Suite 118   Aurora CO 80013
Ph: 888-454-4782 ▪ Fx: 720-851-6090

Transportation Association, National Air www.nata-online.org
4226 King St   Alexandria VA 22302
Ph: 703-845-9000 ▪ Fx: 703-845-8176 ▪ TF: 800-808-6282

Transportation Association, National Defense www.ndtahq.com
50 S Pickett St Suite 220   Alexandria VA 22304
Ph: 703-751-5011 ▪ Fx: 703-823-8761

Transportation Association, National Freight www.nftahq.org
PO Box 1321   Exton PA 19341
Ph: 610-363-7747 ▪ Fx: 610-363-2971

Transportation Association, National School www.schooltrans.com
625 Slaters Ln Suite 205   Alexandria VA 22314
Ph: 703-684-3200 ▪ Fx: 703-684-3212

Transportation Builders Association, American Road & www.artba-hq.org
1010 Massachusetts Ave NW   Washington DC 20001
Ph: 202-289-4434 ▪ Fx: 202-289-4435

Transportation Communications International Union www.tcunion.org
3 Research Pl   Rockville MD 20850
Ph: 301-948-4910 ▪ Fx: 301-948-1369

Transportation Consultants Association, Freight www.transportpros.org
PO Box 53087   Albuquerque NM 87153
Ph: 505-299-0615

Transportation Consumer Protection Council Inc   transportlaw.com/tcpc
120 Main St   Huntington NY 11743
Ph: 631-427-0100 ▪ Fx: 631-549-8962

Transportation Development Association   www.tdawisconsin.org
131 W Wilson St Suite 302   Madison WI 53703
Ph: 608-256-7044 ▪ Fx: 608-256-7079

Transportation & Development Policy, Institute for   www.itdp.org/AccessAfrica.html
115 W 30th St Suite 1205   New York NY 10001
Ph: 212-629-8001 ▪ Fx: 212-629-8033

Transportation Engineers, Institute of   www.ite.org
1099 14th St NW Suite 300W   Washington DC 20005
Ph: 202-289-0222 ▪ Fx: 202-289-7722

Transportation Foundation, Eno   www.enotrans.com
1634 'I' St NW Suite 500   Washington DC 20006
Ph: 202-879-4700 ▪ Fx: 202-879-4719

Transportation Fraternity, Delta Nu Alpha   www.deltanualpha.org
1451 Elm Hill Pike Suite 205   Nashville TN 37210
Ph: 615-360-6863 ▪ Fx: 615-360-1891

Transportation of Hazardous Articles, Conference on Safe   www.costha.com
7803 Hill House Ct   Fairfax Station VA 22039
Ph: 703-451-4031 ▪ Fx: 703-451-4207

Transportation Institute   www.trans-inst.org
5201 Auth Way   Camp Springs MD 20746
Ph: 301-423-3335 ▪ Fx: 301-423-0634

Transportation Institute, Armored
PO Box 333   Baltimore MD 21203
Ph: 410-229-1929 ▪ Fx: 410-229-1930 ▪ TF: 800-888-2129

Transportation Intermediaries Association   www.tianet.org
1625 Prince St Suite 200   Alexandria VA 22314
Ph: 703-299-5700 ▪ Fx: 703-836-0123

Transportation Law Logistics & Policy, Association for   www.atllp.com
3 Church Cir PMB 250   Annapolis MD 21401
Ph: 410-267-0023 ▪ Fx: 410-267-7546

Transportation Lawyers Association   www.translaw.org
PO Box 15122   Lenexa KS 66285
Ph: 913-541-9077 ▪ Fx: 913-599-5340

Transportation League, National Industrial   www.nitl.org
1700 N Moore St Suite 1900   Arlington VA 22209
Ph: 703-524-5011 ▪ Fx: 703-524-5017

Transportation & Logistics, American Society of   www.astl.org
1700 N Moore St Suite 1900   Arlington VA 22209
Ph: 703-524-5011 ▪ Fx: 703-524-5017

Transportation Logistics Council, International Furniture &   www.iftlc.org
PO Box 889   Gardner MA 01440
Ph: 978-632-1913 ▪ Fx: 978-630-2917

Transportation Management Institute, North American   www.truckline.com/cc/natmi
9769 W 119th Dr Suite 1   Broomfield CO 80021
Ph: 720-887-0835 ▪ Fx: 303-404-0725

Transportation, National Association for Pupil   www.napt.org
1840 Western Ave   Albany NY 12203
Ph: 518-452-3611 ▪ Fx: 518-218-0867 ▪ TF: 800-989-6278

Transportation Officials, American Association of State Highway &   www.aashto.org
444 N Capitol St NW Suite 249   Washington DC 20001
Ph: 202-624-5800 ▪ Fx: 202-624-5806

Transportation Officials, Conference of Minority   www.comto.com
1725 DeSales St NW Suite 808   Washington DC 20036
Ph: 202-289-0567 ▪ Fx: 202-289-1214

Transportation Professionals, National Association of Vertical   www.navtp.org
PO Box 636 Bowie   Bowie MD 20718
Ph: 301-262-3150 ▪ Fx: 301-262-3194

Transportation Research Board   www.trb.org
500 5th St NW   Washington DC 20001
Ph: 202-334-2934 ▪ Fx: 202-334-2519 ▪ TF: 800-424-9818

(Transportation Security) National Safe Skies Alliance   sskies.org
McGhee Tyson Airport 2057 Alcoa Hwy   Alcoa TN 37701
Ph: 865-970-0515 ▪ Fx: 865-970-0506

Transportation Society of America, Intelligent   www.itsa.org
400 Virginia Ave SW Suite 800   Washington DC 20024
Ph: 202-484-4847 ▪ Fx: 202-484-3483 ▪ TF: 800-374-8472

Transportation Union, United   www.utu.org
14600 Detroit Ave   Lakewood OH 44107
Ph: 216-228-9400 ▪ Fx: 216-228-5755

Transporters Conference, Agricultural & Food   www.truckline.com/cc/conferences/atc
2200 Mill Rd   Alexandria VA 22314
Ph: 703-838-7999 ▪ Fx: 703-519-1866

Transporters, National Association of Waste   www.nawt.org
PO Box 70   Edgewater MD 21037
Ph: 410-798-0842 ▪ TF: 800-236-6298

Transworld Advertising Agency Network   www.taan.org
7920 Summer Lake Ct   Fort Myers FL 33907
Ph: 239-433-0669 ▪ Fx: 239-433-1366

Transylvanian Saxons, Alliance of   www.atsaxons.com
5393 Pearl Rd   Cleveland OH 44129
Ph: 440-842-8442

Trap Collector Association, North American
PO Box 94   Galloway OH 43119
Ph: 614-878-6011

Trappers Association, National   www.nationaltrappers.com
4111 E Starr Ave   Nacogdoches TX 75961
Ph: 936-569-6444 ▪ Fx: 936-569-9805

Trapshooting Association, Amateur   www.shootata.com
601 W National Rd   Vandalia OH 45377
Ph: 937-898-4638 ▪ Fx: 937-898-5472

Trauma, American Association for the Surgery of   www.aast.org
Presbyterian Hospital Dept of Surgery 200 Lothrop St
MS-F1264   Pittsburgh PA 15213
Ph: 412-647-0635 ▪ Fx: 412-647-1448

Trauma Anesthesia & Critical Care Society, International   www.itaccs.com
PO Box 4826   Baltimore MD 21211
Ph: 410-235-7697 ▪ Fx: 410-235-8084

Trauma Association, Orthopaedic   www.ota.org
6300 N River Rd Suite 727   Rosemont IL 60018
Ph: 847-698-1631 ▪ Fx: 847-823-0536

Trauma, Institute for Victims of   www.microneil.com/ivt
6801 Market Square Dr   McLean VA 22101
Ph: 703-847-8456 ▪ Fx: 703-847-0470

Trauma Nurses, Society of   www.traumanursesoc.org
223 N Guadalupe St PMB 300   Santa Fe NM 87501
Ph: 505-983-4923 ▪ Fx: 505-983-5109

Trauma Society, American   www.amtrauma.org
8903 Presidential Pkwy Suite 512   Upper Marlboro MD 20772
Ph: 301-420-4189 ▪ Fx: 301-420-0617 ▪ TF: 800-556-7890

(Traumatic Stress) Sidran Institute   www.sidran.org
200 E Joppa Rd Suite 207   Baltimore MD 21286
Ph: 410-825-8888 ▪ Fx: 410-337-0747 ▪ TF: 888-825-8249

Traumatic Stress Studies, International Society for   www.istss.org
60 Revere Dr Suite 500   Northbrook IL 60062
Ph: 847-480-9028 ▪ Fx: 847-480-9282

Travel Adventure Cinema Society   www.travelfilms.org
765 Beverly Park Pl   Jackson MI 49203
Ph: 877-279-7604

Travel Agent Network, International Airlines   www.iatan.org
300 Garden City Plaza Suite 342   Garden City NY 11530
Ph: 516-663-6000 ▪ Fx: 516-747-4462 ▪ TF: 800-294-2826

Travel Agents, American Society of   www.astanet.com
1101 King St Suite 200   Alexandria VA 22314
Ph: 703-739-2782 ▪ Fx: 703-684-8319 ▪ TF: 800-440-2782

Travel Agents, Association of Retail   www.artaonline.com
3161 Custer Dr Suite 8   Lexington KY 40517
Ph: 859-269-9739 ▪ Fx: 859-266-9396

Travel Agents, Institute of Certified   www.icta.com
PO Box 812059   Wellesley MA 02482
Ph: 781-237-0280 ▪ Fx: 781-237-3860 ▪ TF: 800-542-4282

Travel Agents, National Association of Business
3699 Wilshire Blvd Suite 700   Los Angeles CA 90010
Ph: 213-382-3335

Travel Agents, National Association of Commissioned   www.nacta.org
1101 King St Suite 200   Alexandria VA 22314
Ph: 703-739-6826 ▪ Fx: 703-739-6861

Travel Agents Society, Interamerican
248 S Alden St   Philadelphia PA 19139
Ph: 215-471-5321 ▪ Fx: 215-471-5473

Travel Agents, Society of Polish-American   www.spata.org
2297 E Main St   Bridgeport CT 06610
Ph: 203-336-9960 ▪ Fx: 203-335-5319

Travel Association, Africa   www.africa-ata.org
347 5th Ave Suite 610   New York NY 10016
Ph: 212-447-1926 ▪ Fx: 212-725-8253

Travel Association, International Gay & Lesbian   www.iglta.org
4331 N Federal Hwy Suite 304   Fort Lauderdale FL 33308
Ph: 954-776-2626 ▪ Fx: 954-776-3303 ▪ TF: 800-448-8550

Travel Association, National Business   www.nbta.org
110 N Royal St 4th Fl   Alexandria VA 22314
Ph: 703-684-0836 ▪ Fx: 703-684-0263

Travel Association, Pacific Asia   www.pata.org
1611 Telegraph Ave Suite 1515   Oakland CA 94612
Ph: 510-625-2055 ▪ Fx: 510-625-2044

Travel, Association for Safe International Road   www.asirt.org
11769 Gainsborough Rd   Potomac MD 20854
Ph: 301-983-5252 ▪ Fx: 301-983-3663

Travel Club, Alpenlite   www.alpenlite.com/html/alpen_club_about.html
PO Box 1726   Clackamas OR 97015
Ph: 503-698-4461 ▪ Fx: 503-698-5521

Travel Club, Handicapped   www.handicappedtravelclub.com
5929 Our Way   Citrus Heights CA 95610
Ph: 916-966-7090

Travel Club, Jayco   www.jaycorvclub.com
PO Box 192   Osceola IN 46561
Ph: 574-258-0591 ▪ Fx: 574-259-7105 ▪ TF: 800-262-5178

Travel Club, Special Military Active Retired   www.smartrving.net
600 University Office Blvd Suite 1A   Pensacola FL 32504
Ph: 800-354-7681

Travel Club, Vagabundos del Mar Boat &   www.vagabundos.com
190 Main St   Rio Vista CA 94571
Ph: 707-374-5511 ▪ Fx: 707-374-6843 ▪ TF: 800-474-2252

Travel Commission, European   www.visiteurope.com
1 Rockefeller Plaza Suite 214   New York NY 10020
Ph: 212-218-1200 ▪ Fx: 212-218-1205

Travel Companion Exchange   www.travelcompanions.com
PO Box 833   Amityville NY 11701
Ph: 631-454-0880 ▪ Fx: 631-454-0170

Travel, Council on Standards for International Educational   www.csiet.org
212 S Henry St   Alexandria VA 22314
Ph: 703-739-9050 ▪ Fx: 703-739-9035

Travel Exchange, Association for World   www.international-counselors.org
38 W 88th St   New York NY 10024
Ph: 212-787-7706 ▪ Fx: 212-580-9283

Travel Executives, Association of Corporate   www.acte.org
515 King St Suite 340   Alexandria VA 22314
Ph: 703-683-5322 ▪ Fx: 703-683-2720 ▪ TF: 800-228-3669

Travel Executives, Society of Incentive &   www.site-intl.org
401 N Michigan Ave Suite 2200   Chicago IL 60611
Ph: 312-321-5148 ▪ Fx: 312-527-6783

Travel Food & Wine Writers, TravelJourno - North American Association of   866 Oneonta Dr   Los Angeles CA 90065   www.traveljourno.com
Ph: 323-257-6269

Travel Goods Association   www.travel-goods.org
5 Vaughn Dr Suite 105   Princeton NJ 08540
Ph: 609-720-1200 ▪ Fx: 609-720-0620

Travel Industry Association of America   www.tia.org
1100 New York Ave NW Suite 450   Washington DC 20005
Ph: 202-408-8422 ▪ Fx: 202-408-1255

Travel Journalists Association, North American   www.natja.org
531 Main St Suite 902   El Segundo CA 90245
Ph: 310-836-8712 ▪ Fx: 310-836-8769

Travel Marketing Executives, Association of   www.atme.org
2005 Palmer Ave Suite 193   Larchmont NY 10538
Ph: 914-834-9110 ▪ Fx: 914-576-2831 ▪ TF: 800-525-3087

Travel Medicine, International Society of   www.istm.org
PO Box 871089   Stone Mountain GA 30087
Ph: 770-736-7060 ▪ Fx: 770-736-6732

(Travel) Opening Door Inc   www.travelguides.org
8049 Ornesby Ln   Woodford VA 22580
Ph: 804-633-6752

Travel Organizations, International Federation of Women's   www.ifwto.org

(Travel Plazas & Truckstops) NATSO Inc   www.natso.com
1199 N Fairfax St Suite 801   Alexandria VA 22314
Ph: 703-549-2100 ▪ Fx: 703-684-4525 ▪ TF: 888-275-2876

Travel Professionals, Society of Government   www.government-travel.org
6935 Wisconsin Ave Suite 200   Bethesda MD 20815
Ph: 301-654-8595 ▪ Fx: 301-654-6663

(Travel) Relais & Chateaux Association   www.relaischateaux.com
11 E 44th St Suite 707   New York NY 10017
Ph: 212-856-0115 ▪ Fx: 212-856-0193 ▪ TF: 800-735-2478

Travel Services, Greater Independent Association of National   www.giantstravel.com
2 Park Ave Suite 2205   New York NY 10016
Ph: 212-545-7460 ▪ Fx: 212-545-7428 ▪ TF: 800-442-6871

Travel Suppliers & Agents, American Association of Premium Incentive   PO Box 35189   Chicago IL 60707   www.traveltran.com
Ph: 708-453-0080 ▪ Fx: 708-453-0083

Travel & Tourism Educators, International Society of   www.istte.org
23220 Edgewater   Saint Clair Shores MI 48082
Ph: 586-294-0208

Travel & Tourism Research Association   www.ttra.org
PO Box 2133   Boise ID 83701
Ph: 208-429-9511 ▪ Fx: 208-429-9512

Travel Trade Association, Adventure   www.adventuretravelbusiness.com
332 1/2 W Sackett St   Salida CO 81201
Ph: 719-530-0171 ▪ Fx: 719-530-0172

Travel Writers Association, International Food Wine &   www.ifwtwa.org
PO Box 8249   Calabasas CA 91372
Ph: 818-999-9959 ▪ Fx: 818-347-7545

Travelcade Club, Avion   www.avionclub.org
PO Box 624259   South Lake Tahoe CA 96154
Ph: 530-544-8285

Travelers Aid International   www.travelersaid.org
1612 K St NW Suite 206   Washington DC 20006
Ph: 202-546-1127 ▪ Fx: 202-546-9112

Travelers of America, Order of United Commercial   www.uct.org
632 N Park St PO Box 159019   Columbus OH 43215
Ph: 614-228-3276 ▪ Fx: 614-228-1898 ▪ TF: 800-848-0123

Travelers' Century Club   travelerscenturyclub.org
PO Box 7050   Santa Monica CA 90406
Ph: 310-393-7419 ▪ Fx: 310-395-9511

Travelers Club, Winnebago-Itasca   www.winnebagoind.com/html/lifestyle/wit/wit.html
PO Box 152   Forest City IA 50436
Ph: 641-585-3535 ▪ Fx: 641-585-6966 ▪ TF: 800-643-4892

Travelers Protective Association of America   travelersprotectiveasn.com
3755 Lindell Blvd   Saint Louis MO 63108
Ph: 314-371-0533 ▪ Fx: 314-371-0537

Traveling Companions, Environmental   www.etctrips.org
Fort Mason Ctr Landmark Bldg C   San Francisco CA 94123
Ph: 415-474-7662 ▪ Fx: 415-474-3919

TravelJourno - North American Association of Travel Food & Wine Writers   866 Oneonta Dr   Los Angeles CA 90065   www.traveljourno.com
Ph: 323-257-6269

Travellers, International Association for Medical Assistance to   www.iamat.org
40 Regal Rd   Guelph ON N1K1B5
Ph: 519-836-0102 ▪ Fx: 519-836-3412

Treasure Association, Beale Cipher &
8A Hobart Ave   Bayonne NJ 07002
Ph: 201-339-0442

Treasurers & Finance Officers, National Association of County   www.nactfo.org
c/o National Assn of Counties 440 1st St NW   Washington DC 20001
Ph: 202-393-6226

Treasurers, National Association of Corporate   www.nact.org
12100 Sunset Hills Rd Suite 130   Reston VA 20190
Ph: 703-437-4377 ▪ Fx: 703-435-4390

Treasurers, National Association of State   www.nast.net
2760 Research Park Dr PO Box 11910   Lexington KY 40578
Ph: 859-244-8175 ▪ Fx: 859-244-8053

Treasurers, National Association of State Auditors Comptrollers &   www.nasact.org
2401 Regency Rd Suite 302   Lexington KY 40503
Ph: 859-276-1147 ▪ Fx: 859-278-0507

Treasurers of Religious Institutes Inc, National Association for   www.natri.org
8824 Cameron St   Silver Spring MD 20910
Ph: 301-587-7776 ▪ Fx: 301-589-2897

Treasurers of the US & Canada, Association of Public   www.aptusc.org
1029 Vermont NW Suite 710   Washington DC 20005
Ph: 202-737-0660 ▪ Fx: 202-737-0662

Treasures for Little Children   www.treasuresforlittlechildren.com
8201 Pleasant Ave S   Bloomington MN 55420
Ph: 952-888-1079

Treasury Employees Union, National   www.nteu.org
1750 H St NW 10th Fl   Washington DC 20006
Ph: 202-572-5500 ▪ Fx: 202-572-5643

Treatment Action Group   www.aidsinfonyc.org/tag
611 Broadway Suite 612   New York NY 10012
Ph: 212-253-7922 ▪ Fx: 212-253-7923

Treatment Association, Neuro-Developmental   www.ndta.org
1550 S Coast Hwy Suite 201   Laguna Beach CA 92651
Ph: 714-497-9007 ▪ TF: 800-869-9295

Treaty Council, International Indian   www.treatycouncil.org
2390 Mission St Suite 301   San Francisco CA 94110
Ph: 415-641-4482 ▪ Fx: 415-641-1298

Tree Care Industry Association   www.treecareindustry.org
3 Perimeter Rd Unit 1   Manchester NH 03103
Ph: 603-314-5380 ▪ Fx: 603-314-5386 ▪ TF: 800-733-2622

Tree Musketeers   www.treemusketeers.org
136 Main St Suite A   El Segundo CA 90245
Ph: 310-322-0263 ▪ Fx: 310-322-4482 ▪ TF: 800-473-0263

Tree-Ring Society   www.treeringsociety.org
Univ of Arizona Tree-Ring Research Lab 105 W Stadium Bldg   Tucson AZ 85721
Ph: 520-621-1608 ▪ Fx: 520-621-8229

TreePeople   www.treepeople.org
12601 Mulholland Dr   Beverly Hills CA 90210
Ph: 818-753-4600 ▪ Fx: 818-753-4635

Trees for the Future   www.treesftf.org
9000 16th St PO Box 7027   Silver Spring MD 20907
Ph: 301-565-0630 ▪ Fx: 301-565-5012 ▪ TF: 800-643-0001

Trees for Life   www.treesforlife.org
3006 Saint Louis St   Witchita KS 67203
Ph: 316-945-6929 ▪ Fx: 316-945-0909 ▪ TF: 800-873-3736

Trees For Tomorrow   www.treesfortomorrow.com
519 Sheridan St E PO Box 609   Eagle River WI 54521
Ph: 715-479-6456 ▪ Fx: 715-479-2318 ▪ TF: 800-838-9472

Trenchless Technology, North American Society for   www.nastt.org
1655 N Fort Myer Dr Suite 700   Arlington VA 22209
Ph: 703-739-6671 ▪ Fx: 703-739-6672

Tri-M Music Honor Society   www.menc.org/information/trim/TriMMain1.html
c/o MENC 1806 Robert Fulton Dr   Reston VA 20191
Ph: 703-860-4000 ▪ Fx: 703-860-2652 ▪ TF: 800-336-3768

TRI/Princeton   www.triprinceton.org
PO Box 625   Princeton NJ 08542
Ph: 609-924-3150 ▪ Fx: 609-683-7836

Tri-State Collegiate Hockey League   www.tschl.com
Purdue University   West Lafayette IN 47907
Ph: 765-494-8931 ▪ Fx: 765-494-8956

Trial Advocacy, National Institute for   www.nd.edu/~nita
PO Box 6500   Notre Dame IN 46556
Ph: 574-271-8370 ▪ Fx: 574-271-8375 ▪ TF: 800-225-6482

Trial Advocates, American Board of   www.abota.org
2001 Bryan St Suite 3000   Dallas TX 75201
Ph: 214-871-7523 ▪ Fx: 214-871-6025 ▪ TF: 800-932-2682

Trial Advocates, Foundation of the American Board of   www.abota.org/foundation
2001 Bryan St Bryan Tower Suite 3000   Dallas TX 75201
Ph: 214-871-7523 ▪ Fx: 214-871-6025 ▪ TF: 800-932-2682

Trial Consultants, American Society of   www.astcweb.org
1941 Greenspring Dr   Timonium MD 21093
Ph: 410-560-7949 ▪ Fx: 410-560-2563

Trial Counsel, National Association of Railroad   www.usnartc.org
881 Alma Real Dr Suite 218   Pacific Palisades CA 90272
Ph: 310-459-7659 ▪ Fx: 310-459-6603

Trial Judges, National Conference of Federal   www.abanet.org/jd/ncftjweb.html
541 N Fairbanks Ct   Chicago IL 60611
Ph: 312-988-5689 ▪ Fx: 312-988-5709

(Trial Law) Roscoe Pound Institute   www.roscoepound.org
1050 31st St NW   Washington DC 20007
Ph: 202-965-3500 ▪ Fx: 202-965-0355

Trial Lawyers of America, Association of   www.atlanet.org
1050 31st St NW   Washington DC 20007
Ph: 202-965-3500 ▪ Fx: 202-625-7313 ▪ TF: 800-424-2725

Trial Lawyers, American College of   www.actl.com
19900 MacArthur Blvd Suite 610   Irvine CA 92612
Ph: 949-752-1801 ▪ Fx: 949-752-1674

Trial Lawyers Association, International Trade Commission   www.itctla.org
PO Box 6186 Benjamin Franklin Stn   Washington DC 20004
Ph: 202-942-6423

Trial Lawyers, International Academy of   www.iatl.net
5041 Cedar Lake Rd Suite 204   Minneapolis MN 55416
Ph: 952-546-2364 ▪ Fx: 952-545-6073 ▪ TF: 866-823-2443

Trial Lawyers PAC, Association of
1050 31st St NW   Washington DC 20007
Ph: 202-965-3500 ▪ Fx: 202-333-2861

Trial Lawyers for Public Justice   www.tlpj.org
1717 Massachusetts Ave NW Suite 800   Washington DC 20036
Ph: 202-797-8600 ▪ Fx: 202-232-7203

Triangle Club   www.triangleclub.org
2030 P St NW   Washington DC 20036
Ph: 202-659-8641

Triathlon, USA   www.usatriathlon.org
616 W Monument St   Colorado Springs CO 80904
Ph: 719-597-9090 ▪ Fx: 719-597-2121

Tribal Environmental Council, National   www.ntec.org
2501 Rio Grande Blvd NW Suite A   Albuquerque NM 87104
Ph: 505-242-2175 ▪ Fx: 505-242-2654

Tribal Schools, Association of Community
616 4th Ave W   Sisseton SD 57262
Ph: 605-698-3953 ▪ Fx: 605-698-7686

Tribal Youth, United National Indian   www.unityinc.org
PO Box 800   Oklahoma City OK 73101
Ph: 405-236-2800 ▪ Fx: 405-971-1071

Tribes Inc, United South & Eastern   usetinc.org
711 Stewarts Ferry Pike Suite 100   Nashville TN 37214
Ph: 615-872-7900 ▪ Fx: 615-872-7417

Tribologists & Lubrication Engineers, Society of   www.stle.org
840 Busse Hwy   Park Ridge IL 60068
Ph: 847-825-5536 ▪ Fx: 847-825-1456

Trichotillomania Learning Center Inc   www.trich.org
303 Potrero St Suite 51   Santa Cruz CA 95060
Ph: 831-457-1004 ▪ Fx: 831-426-4383

Trickle Up Program Inc   www.trickleup.org
104 W 27th St 12th Fl   New York NY 10001
Ph: 212-255-9980 ▪ Fx: 212-255-9974 ▪ TF: 866-246-9980

Trikone   www.trikone.org
PO Box 14161   San Francisco CA 94114
Ph: 408-270-8776 ▪ Fx: 408-274-2733

Trilateral Commission   www.trilateral.org
1156 15th St NW Suite 505   Washington DC 20005
Ph: 202-467-5410 ▪ Fx: 202-467-5415

Trinidad & Tobago-USA Chamber of Commerce
2900 University Dr   Coral Springs FL 33065
Ph: 954-340-5868 ▪ Fx: 954-340-5869

TRIP Road Information Program   www.tripnet.org
1726 M St NW Suite 401   Washington DC 20036
Ph: 202-466-6706 ▪ Fx: 202-785-4772

Triplet Connection   www.tripletconnection.org
PO Box 99571   Stockton CA 95209
Ph: 209-474-0885 ▪ Fx: 209-474-9243

Tripoli Rocketry Association Inc   www.tripoli.org
PO Box 970010   Orem UT 84097
Ph: 801-225-9306 ▪ Fx: 801-225-9307

Trireme Trust USA   www.atm.ox.ac.uk/rowing/trireme
803 S Main St   Geneva NY 14456
Ph: 315-789-7716 ▪ Fx: 315-789-2215

Trisomy 18/13 & Other Related Disorders, Support Organization for   www.trisomy.org
2982 S Union St   Rochester NY 14624
Ph: 585-594-4621 ▪ Fx: 585-594-1957 ▪ TF: 800-716-7638

Triumph International Owners Club   members.aol.com/JohnTIOC/tioc.htm
PO Box 158   Plympton MA 02367
Ph: 508-946-1144 ▪ Fx: 508-946-1145

Troopers Coalition Inc, National Black State   www.nbstc.com
PO Box 70059   Nashville TN 37207
Ph: 877-996-2782

Tropical Biology, Association for   www.atbio.org
US National Herbarium National Museum of Natural History
    Botany MRC-166   Washington DC 20013
Ph: 202-357-2534 ▪ Fx: 202-786-2563

Tropical Fish Farms Association, Florida   www.ftffa.com
PO Box 1519   Winter Haven FL 33882
Ph: 863-293-5710 ▪ Fx: 863-299-5154

Tropical Forest Foundation   www.tropicalforestfoundation.org
2121 Eisenhower Ave Suite 200   Alexandria VA 22314
Ph: 703-518-8834 ▪ Fx: 703-518-8974

Tropical Foresters, International Society of   www.istf-bethesda.org
5400 Grosvenor Ln   Bethesda MD 20814
Ph: 301-897-8720 ▪ Fx: 301-897-3690

Tropical Lepidoptera, Association for   www.troplep.org
PO Box 141210   Gainesville FL 32614
Ph: 352-392-5894 ▪ Fx: 352-373-3249

Tropical Medicine, American Academy of
PO Box 24224   Detroit MI 48224
Ph: 313-882-0641 ▪ Fx: 313-882-5110

Tropical Medicine & Hygiene, American Society of   www.astmh.org
60 Revere Dr Suite 500   Northbrook IL 60062
Ph: 847-480-9592 ▪ Fx: 847-480-9282

Tropical Rainforest, International Society for Preservation of the   www.isptr-pard.org
3302 N Burton Ave   Rosemead CA 91770
Ph: 626-572-0233 ▪ Fx: 626-572-9521

Tropical Studies, Organization for   www.ots.duke.edu
410 Swift Ave   Durham NC 27708
Ph: 919-684-5774 ▪ Fx: 919-684-5661

Tropical Tuna Commission, Inter-American   www.iattc.org
8604 La Jolla Shores Dr   La Jolla CA 92037
Ph: 858-546-7100 ▪ Fx: 858-546-7133

Trotting Association, US   www.ustrotting.com
750 Michigan Ave   Columbus OH 43215
Ph: 614-224-2291 ▪ Fx: 614-224-4575 ▪ TF: 800-887-8782

Trotting & Pacing Association Inc, International   www.trottingbreds.com
60 Gulf Rd   Gouverneur NY 13642
Ph: 315-287-2294 ▪ Fx: 315-287-5010

Trout Farmers Association, US   www.ustfa.org
111 W Washington St Suite 1   Charles Town WV 25414
Ph: 304-728-2189 ▪ Fx: 304-728-2196

Trout Unlimited   www.tu.org
1500 Wilson Blvd Suite 310   Arlington VA 22209
Ph: 703-522-0200 ▪ Fx: 703-284-9400 ▪ TF: 800-834-2419

Truck Association, Industrial   www.indtrk.org
1750 K St NW Suite 460   Washington DC 20006
Ph: 202-296-9880 ▪ Fx: 202-296-9884

Truck Association, Used   www.uta.org
7355 N Woodland Dr   Indianapolis IN 46278
Ph: 800-827-7468

Truck Carriers Inc, National Tank   www.tanktruck.org
2200 Mill Rd Suite 620   Alexandria VA 22314
Ph: 703-838-1960 ▪ Fx: 703-684-5753

Truck Club of America, Antique   www.atca-inc.net/
PO Box 9639   Apollo PA 15613
Ph: 724-727-9768

Truck Council, National Private   www.nptc.org
2200 Mill Rd Suite 350   Alexandria VA 22314
Ph: 703-683-1300 ▪ Fx: 703-683-1217

Truck Cover & Tarp Association   www.truckcover-tarp.org
1801 County Rd 'B' W   Roseville MN 55113
Ph: 651-225-6959

Truck Dealers, American   www.nada.org
8400 Westpark Dr   McLean VA 22102
Ph: 703-821-7230 ▪ Fx: 703-749-4700 ▪ TF: 800-252-6232

Truck Driver Institute, Professional   www.ptdi.org
2200 Mill Rd   Alexandria VA 22314
Ph: 703-838-8842 ▪ Fx: 703-836-6610

Truck Equipment Association, National   www.ntea.com
37400 Hills Tech Dr   Farmington Hills MI 48331
Ph: 248-489-7090 ▪ Fx: 248-489-8590 ▪ TF: 800-441-6832

Truck & Heavy Equipment Claims Council, National   www.nthecc.org

Truck Historical Society, American   www.aths.org
PO Box 901611   Kansas City MO 64190
Ph: 816-891-9900 ▪ Fx: 816-891-9903

Truck Manufacturers Association   www.truckmanufacturersassociation.org
1225 New York Ave NW Suite 300   Washington DC 20005
Ph: 202-638-7825 ▪ Fx: 202-737-3742

Truck PAC
430 1st St SE   Washington DC 20003
Ph: 202-544-6245 ▪ Fx: 202-675-6568

Truck Renting & Leasing Association   www.trala.org
675 N Washington St Suite 410   Alexandria VA 22314
Ph: 703-299-9120 ▪ Fx: 703-299-9115

Truck Trailer Manufacturers Association   www.ttmanet.org
1020 Princess St   Alexandria VA 22314
Ph: 703-549-3010 ▪ Fx: 703-549-3014

Truckers Association Inc, Mid-West   www.mid-westtruckers.com
2727 N Dirksen Pkwy   Springfield IL 62702
Ph: 217-525-0310 ▪ Fx: 217-525-0342

Truckers for Christ   www.truckersforchrist.org
PO Box 1311   Taylorsville NC 28681
Ph: 828-632-8842

(Truckers) Transport for Christ International   www.transportforchrist.org
PO Box 303   Denver PA 17517
Ph: 717-859-4870 ▪ Fx: 717-859-4798

Trucking Associations, American   www.trucking.org
2200 Mill Rd   Alexandria VA 22314
Ph: 703-838-1700 ▪ Fx: 703-684-5751 ▪ TF: 800-282-5463

Trucking Industrial Relations Association, North American
908 King St Suite 300   Alexandria VA 22314
Ph: 703-836-9400 ▪ Fx: 703-836-9410

(Trucking) National Accounting & Finance Council   truckline.com/cc/councils/nafc
American Trucking Assns 2200 Mill Rd   Alexandria VA 22314
Ph: 703-838-1915 ▪ Fx: 703-836-0751

(Trucking) Owner-Operator Independent Drivers Association   www.ooida.com
1 NW OOIDA Dr   Grain Valley MO 64029
Ph: 816-229-5791 ▪ TF: 800-444-5791

(Trucking) Safety & Loss Prevention   www.truckline.com/cc/councils/slpmc
Management Council   American Trucking Assns 2200 Mill
    Rd   Alexandria VA 22314
Ph: 703-838-1919 ▪ Fx: 703-838-8468

(Trucking) Technology & Maintenance Council   www.trucking.org/cc/councils/tmc
American Trucking Assns 2200 Mill Rd   Alexandria VA 22314
Ph: 703-838-1761 ▪ TF: 888-333-1759

Truckload Carriers Association   www.truckload.org
2200 Mill Rd 3rd Fl   Alexandria VA 22314
Ph: 703-838-1950 ▪ Fx: 703-836-6610

True Sisters Inc, United Order   www.uots.org
100 State St Suite 1020   Albany NY 12207
Ph: 518-436-1670 ▪ Fx: 518-436-1573

Trumpet Guild, International   www.trumpetguild.org

Trumpeter Swan Society   trumpeterswansociety.org
3800 County Rd 24   Maple Plain MN 55359
Ph: 763-476-4663 ▪ Fx: 763-476-1514

Truss Council of America, Wood   www.woodtruss.com
6300 Enterprise Ln   Madison WI 53719
Ph: 608-274-4849 ▪ Fx: 608-274-3329

Truss Plate Institute Inc   www.tpinst.org
583 D'Onofrio Dr Suite 200   Madison WI 53719
Ph: 608-833-5900 ▪ Fx: 608-833-4360

Trust Companies, Association of Independent   www.aitco.net
710 E Ogden Ave Suite 600   Naperville IL 60563
Ph: 630-579-3290 ▪ Fx: 630-369-2488

Trust & Estate Counsel, American College of   www.actec.org
3415 S Sepulveda Blvd Suite 330   Los Angeles CA 90034
Ph: 310-398-1888 ▪ Fx: 310-572-7280

Trust for Mutual Understanding   www.tmuny.org
30 Rockefeller Plaza Rm 5600   New York NY 10112
Ph: 212-632-3405 ▪ Fx: 212-632-3409

Trust for Public Land   www.tpl.org
116 New Montgomery St 4th Fl   San Francisco CA 94105
Ph: 415-495-4014 ▪ Fx: 415-495-4103 ▪ TF: 800-729-6428

TRUSTe   www.truste.org
685 Market St Suite 560   San Francisco CA 94105
Ph: 415-618-3400 ▪ Fx: 415-618-3420

Trustee Association, Museum   www.mta-hq.org
2025 M St NW Suite 800   Washington DC 20036
Ph: 202-367-1180 ▪ Fx: 202-367-2180

Trustees & Alumni, American Council of   www.goacta.org
1726 M St NW Suite 800   Washington DC 20036
Ph: 202-467-6787 ▪ Fx: 202-467-6784 ▪ TF: 888-258-6648

Trustees, Association of Community College   www.acct.org
1233 20th St NW Suite 605   Washington DC 20036
Ph: 202-775-4667 ▪ Fx: 202-223-1297

Tuba-Euphonium Association, International   www.tubaonline.org
2253 Downing St   Denver CO 80205
Ph: 303-832-4676 ▪ Fx: 303-832-0839

Tube Council of North America   www.tube.org
26 Park St Suite 2031   Montclair NJ 07042
Ph: 973-744-4551 ▪ Fx: 973-744-5568

Tube Institute, Composite Can &　　　　www.cctiwdc.org
　50 S Pickett St　Alexandria VA 22310
　Ph: 703-823-7234　Fx: 703-823-7237
Tube & Pipe Association International　www.tpatube.org/TPA/TPA_Homepage.htm
　833 Featherstone Rd　Rockford IL 61107
　Ph: 815-399-8775　Fx: 815-484-7701
Tuberculosis Controllers Association, National
　2951 Flowers Rd S Suite 102　Atlanta GA 30341
　Ph: 770-455-0801　Fx: 770-455-4221　TF: 888-455-0801
Tuberculosis Foundation, Sequella Global　www.sequellafoundation.org
　9610 Medical Ctr Dr Suite 220　Rockville MD 20850
　Ph: 301-762-3100　Fx: 301-762-2122
Tuberous Sclerosis Alliance　　　　www.tsalliance.org
　801 Roeder Rd Suite 750　Silver Spring MD 20910
　Ph: 301-562-9890　Fx: 301-562-9870　TF: 800-225-6872
Tubular Exchanger Manufacturers Association　www.tema.org
　25 N Broadway　Tarrytown NY 10591
　Ph: 914-332-0040　Fx: 914-332-1541
Tufts Center for Animals & Public Policy　www.tufts.edu/vet/cfa
　Tufts Univ School of Veterinary Medicine 200 Westboro
　　Rd　North Grafton MA 01536
　Ph: 508-839-7920　Fx: 508-839-2953
Tumor Association, American Brain　　www.abta.org
　2720 River Rd　Des Plaines IL 60018
　Ph: 847-827-9910　Fx: 847-827-9918　TF: 800-886-2282
Tumor Society, Brain　　　　　　　www.tbts.org
　124 Watertown St Suite 3-H　Watertown MA 02472
　Ph: 617-924-9997　Fx: 617-924-9998　TF: 800-770-8287
Tumor Society, Musculoskeletal　　　msts.org
　Vanderbilt University Medical Ctr 1161 21st Ave S D-4216
　　Medical Ctr N　Nashville TN 37232
　Ph: 615-343-4400　Fx: 615-343-1028
Tuna Commission, Inter-American Tropical　www.iattc.org
　8604 La Jolla Shores Dr　La Jolla CA 92037
　Ph: 858-546-7100　Fx: 858-546-7133
Tuna Foundation, US　　　　　　　www.ustuna.org
　1101 17th St NW Suite 609　Washington DC 20036
　Ph: 202-857-0610　Fx: 202-331-9686
Tune-Up Manufacturers Council　　　www.tune-up.org
　10 Laboratory Dr PO Box 13966　Research Triangle Park NC
　　27709
　Ph: 919-549-4800　Fx: 919-549-4824
Tunis Sheep Registry, National　　　www.tunissheep.org
　819 Lyons St　Ludlow MA 01056
　Ph: 413-589-9653
Tunnel & Turnpike Association, International Bridge　www.ibtta.org
　1146 19th St NW Suite 800　Washington DC 20036
　Ph: 202-659-4620　Fx: 202-659-0500
Turbine Institute, International Gas　www.asme.org/igti
　5775B Glenridge Dr Suite 370　Atlanta GA 30328
　Ph: 404-847-0072　Fx: 404-847-0151
Turf Managers Association, Sports　www.sportsturfmanager.com
　1027 S 3rd St　Council Bluffs IA 51503
　Ph: 712-322-7862　Fx: 712-366-9119　TF: 800-323-3875
Turf & Ornamental Communicators Association　www.toca.org
　120 W Main St PO Box 156　New Prague MN 56071
　Ph: 952-758-6340　Fx: 952-758-5813
Turf & Ornamental Distributors Association, Independent　www.itoda.org
　526 Brittany Dr　State College PA 16803
　Ph: 814-238-1573　Fx: 814-238-7051
Turf Producers Foundation, International　www.turfgrasssod.org
　1855-A Hicks Rd　Rolling Meadows IL 60008
　Ph: 847-705-9898　Fx: 847-705-8347　TF: 800-405-8873
(Turfgrass) OJ Noer Research Foundation　www.noerfoundation.org
　PO Box 1494　Milwaukee WI 53201
　Ph: 414-258-7337
Turfgrass Producers International　www.turfgrasssod.org
　1855-A Hicks Rd　Rolling Meadows IL 60008
　Ph: 847-705-9898　Fx: 847-705-8347　TF: 800-405-8873
Turkey Federation, National　　　　www.eatturkey.com
　1225 New York Ave NW Suite 400　Washington DC 20005
　Ph: 202-898-0100　Fx: 202-898-0203
Turkey Federation, National Wild　　www.nwtf.com
　770 Augusta Rd PO Box 530　Edgefield SC 29824
　Ph: 803-637-3106　Fx: 803-637-0034　TF: 800-843-6983
Turkic Languages, American Association　www.princeton.edu/~ehgilson/aatt.html
　of Teachers of　Princeton Univ Near Eastern Studies 110
　　Jones Hall　Princeton NJ 08544
　Ph: 609-258-1435　Fx: 609-258-1242
Turkish American Associations, Assembly of　www.ataa.org
　1526 18th St NW　Washington DC 20036
　Ph: 202-483-9090　Fx: 202-483-9092
Turkish-American Associations Inc, Federation of　www.ftaa.org
　821 United Nations Plaza 2nd Fl　New York NY 10017
　Ph: 212-682-7688　Fx: 212-687-3026
Turkish Architects Engineers & Scientists Inc, Society of　www.m-l-m.org
　821 United Nations Plaza 2nd Fl　New York NY 10017
　Ph: 212-682-7688　Fx: 212-687-3026
Turkish Society, American　　　www.americanturkishsociety.org
　305 E 47th St 8th Fl　New York NY 10017
　Ph: 212-583-7614　Fx: 212-583-7615
Turkish Studies, Institute of　　　turkishstudies.org
　Georgetown Univ Intercultural Center　Washington DC 20057
　Ph: 202-687-0295　Fx: 202-687-3780
Turner Foundation Inc　　　　　www.turnerfoundation.org
　133 Luckie St NW 2nd Fl　Atlanta GA 30303
　Ph: 404-681-9900　Fx: 404-681-0172
Turner Syndrome Society of the US　www.turner-syndrome-us.org
　14450 TC Jester Suite 260　Houston TX 77014
　Ph: 832-249-9988　Fx: 832-249-9987　TF: 800-365-9944

Turning Point Ministries　　　www.turningpointministries.org
　6101 Preservation Dr PO Box 22127　Chattanooga TN 37422
　Ph: 423-899-4770　Fx: 423-899-4547　TF: 800-879-4770
Turnpike Association, International Bridge Tunnel &　www.ibtta.org
　1146 19th St NW Suite 800　Washington DC 20036
　Ph: 202-659-4620　Fx: 202-659-0500
Turtle Survival League, Sea　　　www.cccturtle.org
　4424 NW 13th St Suite A1　Gainesville FL 32609
　Ph: 352-373-6441　Fx: 352-375-2449　TF: 800-678-7853
Turtle & Tortoise Society, New York　nytts.org
Tutoring Association, National　　www.ntatutor.org/
　3719 Washington Blvd　Indianapolis IN 46205
　Ph: 317-926-9671　TF: 866-311-6630
TV-Turnoff Network　　　　　　www.tvturnoff.org
　1200 29th St NW Lower Level 1　Washington DC 20007
　Ph: 202-333-9220　Fx: 202-333-9221
Twinless Twins Support Group International　www.twinlesstwins.org
　PO Box 980481　Ypsilanti MI 48198
　Ph: 888-205-8962
Twins Clubs Inc, National Organization of Mothers of　www.nomotc.org
　PO Box 438　Thompsons Station TN 37179
　Ph: 615-595-0936　TF: 877-540-2200
Twins Foundation　　　　　　www.twinsfoundation.com
　PO Box 6043　Providence RI 02940
　Ph: 401-751-8946
Twirling Association, National Baton
　PO Box 266　Janesville WI 53547
　Ph: 608-754-2238　Fx: 608-754-1986
Twirling Association, US　　　　www.ustwirling.com
　44 Drexel Dr PO Box 390　Copiague NY 11726
　Ph: 631-231-7434　Fx: 208-474-9067
Two-Cylinder Club　　　　　　www.two-cylinder.com
　PO Box 430　Grundy Center IA 50638
　Ph: 319-345-6060　Fx: 319-345-2662　TF: 888-782-2582
Two Ten Footwear Foundation　　www.twoten.org
　1466 Main St　Waltham MA 02451
　Ph: 781-736-1500　Fx: 781-736-1555　TF: 800-346-3210
Tympanuchus Cupido Pinnatus Ltd, Society of
　1977 Hidden Reserve Ct　Mequon WI 53092
　Ph: 262-512-9107
Type Directors Club　　　　　www.tdc.org
　127 W 25th St 8th Fl　New York NY 10001
　Ph: 212-633-8943　Fx: 212-633-8944
Typecasting Fellowship, American
　PO Box 263　Terra Alta WV 26764
　Ph: 304-789-2455
Typewriter Collectors Association, Early　www.home.earthlink.net/~dcrehr/etc.html
　PO Box 641824　Los Angeles CA 90064
　Ph: 310-477-5229
Tzivos Hashem　　　　　　　www.tzivos-hashem.org
　332 Kingston　Brooklyn NY 11213
　Ph: 718-467-6630　Fx: 718-467-8527

U

UAW Voluntary Community Action Program
　8000 E Jefferson Ave　Detroit MI 48214
　Ph: 313-926-5531　Fx: 313-926-5691
UCP National　　　　　　　　www.ucp.org
　1660 L St NW Suite 700　Washington DC 20036
　Ph: 202-776-0406　Fx: 202-776-0414　TF: 800-872-5827
UFCW International Union Distillery Wine & Allied Workers Div
　219 Paterson Ave　Little Falls NJ 07424
　Ph: 973-237-1241　Fx: 973-890-1956
UFCW Textile & Garment Council
　4207 Lebanon Pike Suite 200　Hermitage TN 37076
　Ph: 615-889-9221　Fx: 615-885-3102
UFM International　　　　　　www.ufm.org
　306 Bala Ave PO Box 306　Bala Cynwyd PA 19004
　Ph: 610-667-7660　Fx: 610-660-9068
UFO Information Retrieval Center　www.ufohelp.com
　3131 W Cochise Dr Unit 158　Phoenix AZ 85051
　Ph: 602-997-1523　Fx: 602-870-3178
UFO Network, Mutual　　　　　www.mufon.com
　PO Box 369　Morrison CO 80465
　Ph: 303-932-7709　Fx: 303-932-9279
UFO Research Inc, Fund for　　　fufor.com
UFO Studies, J Allen Hynek Center for　www.cufos.org
　2457 W Peterson Ave Suite 6　Chicago IL 60659
　Ph: 773-271-3611
Ukrainian Academy of Arts & Sciences in the US
　206 W 100th St　New York NY 10025
　Ph: 212-222-1866　Fx: 212-864-3977
Ukrainian American Relief Committee Inc, United　www.uuarc.org
　1206 Cottman Ave　Philadelphia PA 19111
　Ph: 215-728-1630　Fx: 215-728-1631
Ukrainian Catholics in America, Providence Association of
　817 N Franklin St　Philadelphia PA 19123
　Ph: 215-627-4984　Fx: 215-238-1933
Ukrainian Engineers Society of America　www.uesa.org
Ukrainian Fraternal Association　members.tripod.com/~ufa_home
　1327 Wyoming Ave　Scranton PA 18509
　Ph: 570-342-0937　Fx: 570-347-5649
Ukrainian Gold Cross
　6616 W Roscoe St　Chicago IL 60634
　Ph: 773-736-4568　Fx: 773-736-4658

Ukrainian Institute of America www.ukrainianinstitute.org
2 E 79th St   New York NY 10021
Ph: 212-288-8660 ▪ Fx: 212-288-2918

Ukrainian National Association www.unamember.com
PO Box 280   Parsippany NJ 07054
Ph: 973-292-9800 ▪ Fx: 973-292-0900 ▪ TF: 800-253-9862

Ukrainian National Women's League of America www.unwla.org
203 2nd Ave   New York NY 10003
Ph: 212-533-4646 ▪ Fx: 212-533-5237

Ulcer Advisory Panel, National Pressure www.npuap.org
12100 Sunset Hills Rd Suite 130   Reston VA 20190
Ph: 703-464-4849 ▪ Fx: 703-435-4390

Ultimate Players Association www.upa.org
714 Pearl St Side Suite   Boulder CO 80302
Ph: 303-447-3472 ▪ Fx: 303-447-3483 ▪ TF: 800-872-4384

Ultra Marathon Cycling Association Inc www.ultracycling.com
PO Box 18028   Boulder CO 80308
Ph: 303-545-9566 ▪ Fx: 303-545-9619

Ultralight Association, US www.usua.org
PO Box 667   Frederick MD 21705
Ph: 301-695-9100 ▪ Fx: 301-695-0763

Ultrasonic Industry Association www.ultrasonics.org
1111 N Dunlap Ave   Savoy IL 61874
Ph: 217-356-3182 ▪ Fx: 217-398-4119

Ultrasonics Ferroelectrics & Frequency Control Society, IEEE www.ieee-uffc.org
IEEE Operations Ctr 445 Hoes Ln   Piscataway NJ 08854
Ph: 732-981-0060 ▪ Fx: 732-981-1721

Ultrasound in Medicine, American Institute of www.aium.org
14750 Sweitzer Ln Suite 100   Laurel MD 20707
Ph: 301-498-4100 ▪ Fx: 301-498-4450 ▪ TF: 800-638-5352

Ultrasound, Society of Radiologists in www.sru.org
44211 Slatestone Ct   Leesburg VA 20176
Ph: 703-858-9210 ▪ Fx: 703-729-4839

Ultrasound, Society for Vascular www.svunet.org
4601 Presidents Dr Suite 260   Lanham MD 20706
Ph: 301-459-7550 ▪ Fx: 301-459-5651 ▪ TF: 800-788-8346

Ulysses S Grant Association www.lib.siu.edu/projects/usgrant
Southern Illinois Univ Morris Library   Carbondale IL 62901
Ph: 618-453-2773 ▪ Fx: 618-453-6119

Unarius Academy of Science www.unarius.org
145 S Magnolia Ave   El Cajon CA 92020
Ph: 619-444-7062 ▪ Fx: 619-444-9637

Unclaimed Property Administrators, National Association of www.unclaimed.org
PO Box 11910   Lexington KY 40578
Ph: 859-244-8150 ▪ Fx: 859-244-8053

Underage, American Veterans that Enlisted www.avteu.com
100 Village Ln   Philadelphia PA 19154
Ph: 215-632-2332 ▪ Fx: 215-637-9566 ▪ TF: 800-595-1006

Undergarment Association, Greater Blouse Skirt & www.greaterblouse.org
225 W 34th St Suite 612   New York NY 10122
Ph: 212-563-5052 ▪ Fx: 212-563-5373

Undergraduate Research, Council on www.cur.org
734 15th St NW Suite 550   Washington DC 20005
Ph: 202-783-4810 ▪ Fx: 202-783-4811

Undergraduate Research, National Conferences on www.ncur.org
Univ of Minnesota Duluth 10 University Dr 140 Engineering
Bldg   Duluth MN 55812
Ph: 218-726-7807 ▪ Fx: 218-726-6360

Underground Construction Association, American www.auaonline.com
3001 Hennepin Ave S Suite D202   Minneapolis MN 55408
Ph: 612-825-8933 ▪ Fx: 612-825-8944

Undersea & Hyperbaric Medical Society www.uhms.org
10531 Metropolitan Ave   Kensington MD 20895
Ph: 301-942-2980 ▪ Fx: 301-942-7804

Understanding, Temple of www.templeofunderstanding.org
720 5th Ave 16th Fl   New York NY 10019
Ph: 212-246-2746 ▪ Fx: 212-246-2340

Underwater Instructors, National Association of www.naui.org
1232 Tech Blvd   Tampa FL 33619
Ph: 813-628-6284 ▪ Fx: 813-628-8253 ▪ TF: 800-553-6284

Underwater Society of America www.underwater-society.org
PO Box 628   Daly City CA 94017
Ph: 650-583-8492 ▪ Fx: 650-583-0614

Underwriters, American Institute of Marine www.aimu.org
14 Wall St 8th Fl   New York NY 10005
Ph: 212-233-0550 ▪ Fx: 212-227-5102

Underwriters, Association of Home Office www.alu-web.org/ahou
2300 Windy Ridge Pkwy Suite 600   Atlanta GA 30339
Ph: 770-984-3715 ▪ Fx: 770-984-6418

Underwriters Association, Inland Marine www.imua.org
14 Wall St 8th Fl   New York NY 10005
Ph: 212-233-0550 ▪ Fx: 212-227-5102

Underwriters, Mutual Atomic Energy Liability
3158 River Rd Suite 103   Des Plaines IL 60018
Ph: 312-467-0003 ▪ Fx: 312-467-0774

Underwriters, National Association of Health www.nahu.org
2000 N 14th St Suite 450   Arlington VA 22201
Ph: 703-276-0220 ▪ Fx: 703-841-7797

Underwriters, National Association of Review www.iami.org/nara.html
Appraisers & Mortgage   1224 N Nokomis NE   Alexandria MN
56308
Ph: 320-763-6870 ▪ Fx: 320-763-9290

Underwriting, Association for Advanced Life www.aalu.org
2901 Telestar Ct   Falls Church VA 22042
Ph: 703-641-9400 ▪ Fx: 703-641-9885 ▪ TF: 888-275-0092

Underwriting Society, Professional Liability www.plusweb.org
5353 Wayzata Blvd Suite 600   Minneapolis MN 55416
Ph: 952-746-2580 ▪ Fx: 952-746-2599 ▪ TF: 800-845-0778

Unemployment & Workers' Compensation, UWC - Strategic www.uwcstrategy.org
Services on   1331 Pennsylvania Ave NW Suite
600   Washington DC 20004
Ph: 202-637-3464 ▪ Fx: 202-783-1616

Unfinished Furniture Association www.unfinishedfurniture.org
17000 Commerce Pkwy Suite C   Mount Laurel NJ 08054
Ph: 856-439-0500 ▪ Fx: 856-439-0525 ▪ TF: 800-487-8321

UNHCR, USA for www.usaforunhcr.org
1775 K St NW Suite 290   Washington DC 20006
Ph: 202-296-1115 ▪ Fx: 202-296-1081 ▪ TF: 800-770-1100

UNICEF, US Fund for www.unicefusa.org
333 E 38th St 6th Fl   New York NY 10016
Ph: 212-922-2649 ▪ Fx: 212-779-1679 ▪ TF: 800-367-5437

UNICO National Inc www.unico.org
271 US Hwy 46 W Suite A-108   Fairfield NJ 07004
Ph: 973-808-0035 ▪ Fx: 973-808-0043 ▪ TF: 800-877-1492

Unicycling Federation Inc, International www.unicycling.org/iuf

Unicycling Society of America www.unicycling.org/usa
PO Box 40534   Redford MI 48240
Ph: 248-661-0334

Unidentified Flying Objects, National Investigations Committee on www.nicufo.org
14617 Victory Blvd Suite 4   Van Nuys CA 91411
Ph: 818-989-5942 ▪ Fx: 818-989-2165

Unified Abrasives Manufacturers' Association www.uama.org
30200 Detroit Rd   Cleveland OH 44145
Ph: 440-899-0010 ▪ Fx: 440-892-1404

Uniform Code Council Inc www.uc-council.org
1009 Lenox Dr Suite 202   Lawrenceville NJ 08648
Ph: 609-620-0200 ▪ Fx: 609-620-1200

Uniform Collectors, Association of American Military www.naples.net/clubs/aamuc
PO Box 1876   Elyria OH 44036
Ph: 440-365-5321

Uniform Interest Compensation, National Council for www.ncuic.org
13665 Dulles Technology Dr Suite 300   Herndon VA 20171
Ph: 703-561-1100 ▪ Fx: 703-787-0996

Uniform Manufacturers & Distributors, National Association of www.naumd.org
16 E 41st St Suite 700   New York NY 10017
Ph: 212-869-0670 ▪ Fx: 212-575-2847

Uniform State Laws, National Conference of Commissioners on www.nccusl.org
211 E Ontario St Suite 1300   Chicago IL 60611
Ph: 312-915-0195 ▪ Fx: 312-915-0187

Uniform & Textile Service Association www.utsa.org
1300 N 17th St Suite 750   Arlington VA 22209
Ph: 703-247-2600 ▪ Fx: 703-841-4750 ▪ TF: 800-486-6745

Uniform Traffic Laws & Ordinances, National Committee on www.ncutlo.org
107 S West St Suite 110   Alexandria VA 22314
Ph: 540-465-4701 ▪ Fx: 540-465-5383 ▪ TF: 800-807-5290

Uniformed Services Academy of Family Physicians www.usafp.org
2301 N Parham Rd Suite 4   Richmond VA 23229
Ph: 804-968-4436 ▪ Fx: 804-968-4418

Uniformed Services, National Association for www.naus.org
5535 Hempstead Way   Springfield VA 22151
Ph: 703-750-1342 ▪ Fx: 703-354-4380 ▪ TF: 800-842-3451

UniForum Association www.uniforum.org
PO Box 3177   Annapolis MD 21043
Ph: 410-715-9500 ▪ Fx: 240-465-0207 ▪ TF: 800-333-8649

Union of American Hebrew Congregations www.uahcweb.org
633 3rd Ave   New York NY 10017
Ph: 212-650-4000 ▪ Fx: 212-650-4159

Union of American Physicians & Dentists www.uapd.org
1330 Broadway Suite 730   Oakland CA 94612
Ph: 510-839-0193 ▪ Fx: 510-763-8756

Union of Concerned Scientists www.ucsusa.org
2 Brattle Sq   Cambridge MA 02238
Ph: 617-547-5552 ▪ Fx: 617-864-9405

Union Constructors, NEA - Association of www.nea-online.org
1501 Lee Hwy Suite 202   Arlington VA 22209
Ph: 703-524-3336 ▪ Fx: 703-524-3364

Union of Councils for Jews in the Former Soviet Union www.ucsj.org
PO Box 11676   Washington DC 20008
Ph: 202-237-8262 ▪ Fx: 202-237-2236

Union Democracy, Association for www.uniondemocracy.org
104 Montgomery St   Brooklyn NY 11225
Ph: 718-855-6650 ▪ Fx: 718-855-6799

Union-Free Environment, Council on www.cueinc.com
825 W Bitters Rd Suite 103   San Antonio TX 78216
Ph: 866-409-4283 ▪ Fx: 210-545-4284

Union Internationale de la Marionnette www.unima-usa.org
Center for Puppetry Arts   Atlanta GA 30309
Ph: 404-873-3089 ▪ Fx: 404-873-9907

Union & League of Romanian Societies of America www.romaniansocieties.com
23203 Lorain Rd   North Olmsted OH 44070
Ph: 440-779-9913 ▪ Fx: 440-779-9151

Union of Needletrades, Industrial and Textile Employees www.uniteunion.org
275 7th Ave   New York NY 10001
Ph: 212-265-7000 ▪ Fx: 212-265-3415 ▪ TF: 800-238-6483

Union of Orthodox Rabbis of the US & Canada
235 E Broadway   New York NY 10002
Ph: 212-964-6337

Union of Poles in America www.unionofpoles.com
9999 Grainger Rd   Garfield Heights OH 44125
Ph: 216-478-0120 ▪ Fx: 216-478-0122

Union for Radical Political Economics www.urpe.org
37 Howe St   New Haven CT 06511
Ph: 203-777-4605

Union, Teamsters for a Democratic www.tdu.org
PO Box 10128   Detroit MI 48210
Ph: 313-842-2600 ▪ Fx: 313-842-0227

Union for Traditional Judaism   www.utj.org
811 Palisade Ave   Teaneck NJ 07666
Ph: 201-801-0707 ▪ Fx: 201-801-0449

Unionism, Concerned Educators Against Forced   www.nrtwc.org
8001 Braddock Rd Suite 500   Springfield VA 22160
Ph: 703-321-8519 ▪ Fx: 703-321-9319 ▪ TF: 800-326-3600

Unionists, Coalition of Black Trade   www.cbtu.org
PO Box 66268   Washington DC 20035
Ph: 202-429-1203 ▪ Fx: 202-429-1102

Unions, Congress of Independent
303 Ridge St   Alton IL 62002
Ph: 618-462-2447 ▪ Fx: 618-462-5579

Unions International, Association of College   www.acui.org
120 W 7th St 1 City Ctr Suite 200   Bloomington IN 47404
Ph: 812-855-8550 ▪ Fx: 812-855-0162

Unions, National Federation of Independent   www.nfiu.org
1166 S 11th St   Philadelphia PA 19147
Ph: 215-336-3300 ▪ Fx: 215-755-3542 ▪ TF: 888-595-6348

(Unitarian) Interweave Continental   www.qrd.org/qrd/www/orgs/uua/uu-interweave.html
Inc

Unitarian Universalist Association   www.uua.org
25 Beacon St   Boston MA 02108
Ph: 617-742-2100 ▪ Fx: 617-367-3237

Unitarian Universalist Christian Fellowship   www.uua.org/uucf
PO Box 629   Lancaster MA 01523
Ph: 978-365-2427 ▪ Fx: 978-368-0194

Unitarian Universalist Ministers Association   www.uuma.org
25 Beacon St   Boston MA 02108
Ph: 617-848-0498 ▪ Fx: 617-848-0973

Unitarian Universalist Musicians' Network   www.uua.org/uumn
2208 Henery Tuckers Ct   Charlotte NC 28270
Ph: 800-969-8866

Unitarian Universalist Poets Cooperative   www.puddinghouse.com/unitarian.htm
c/o Pudding House Publications 81 Shadymere Ln   Columbus
    OH 43213
Ph: 614-986-1881

Unitarian Universalist Service Committee   www.uusc.org
130 Prospect St   Cambridge MA 02139
Ph: 617-868-6600 ▪ Fx: 617-868-7102 ▪ TF: 800-388-3920

Unitarian Universalists, Young Religious   www.uua.org/YRUU
25 Beacon St   Boston MA 02108
Ph: 617-948-4350 ▪ Fx: 617-367-4798

UNITE   www.uniteunion.org
275 7th Ave   New York NY 10001
Ph: 212-265-7000 ▪ Fx: 212-265-3415 ▪ TF: 800-238-6483

United Agribusiness League   www.ual.org
54 Corporate Pk   Irvine CA 92606
Ph: 949-975-1424 ▪ Fx: 949-975-1671 ▪ TF: 800-223-4590

United Animal Nations   www.uan.org
PO Box 188890   Sacramento CA 95818
Ph: 916-429-2457 ▪ Fx: 916-429-2456

United Applications Standards Group   www.uasg.org
PO Box 1435   Des Moines IA 50305
Ph: 515-289-4467 ▪ Fx: 515-289-4468

United Association of Equipment Leasing   www.uael.org
78120 Calle Estado Suite 201   La Quinta CA 92253
Ph: 760-564-2227 ▪ Fx: 760-564-2206

United Association of Journeymen & Apprentices of the   www.ua.org
Plumbing Pipe Fitting Sprinkler Fitting Industry of the US &
Canada   901 Massachusetts Ave NW   Washington DC
    20001
Ph: 202-628-5823 ▪ Fx: 202-628-5024

United Association Manufacturers' Representatives   www.uamr.com
PO Box 986   Dana Point CA 92629
Ph: 949-240-4966 ▪ Fx: 949-240-7001

United Auto Workers   www.uaw.org
8000 E Jefferson Ave   Detroit MI 48214
Ph: 313-926-5000 ▪ Fx: 313-823-6016

United Black Fund of America Inc   www.ubfinc.org
2500 ML King Jr Ave SE PO Box 7051   Washington DC 20032
Ph: 202-783-9300 ▪ Fx: 202-347-2564

United Board for Christian Higher Education in Asia   www.unitedboard.org
475 Riverside Dr Suite 1221   New York NY 10115
Ph: 212-870-2610 ▪ Fx: 212-870-2322

United Braford Breeders   www.brafords.org
422 E Main St Suite 218   Nacogdoches TX 75961
Ph: 936-569-8200 ▪ Fx: 936-569-9556

United Brotherhood of Carpenters & Joiners of America   www.carpenters.org
101 Constitution Ave NW   Washington DC 20001
Ph: 202-546-6206 ▪ Fx: 202-543-5724

United Burmese Cat Fanciers
2395 NE 185th St   North Miami Beach FL 33180
Ph: 305-931-0104

United Catholic Music & Video Association   www.ucmva.com
PO Box 230   Donnellson IA 52625
Ph: 319-835-9340 ▪ Fx: 319-835-9071 ▪ TF: 877-668-2682

United Cerebral Palsy   www.ucp.org
1660 L St NW Suite 700   Washington DC 20036
Ph: 202-776-0406 ▪ Fx: 202-776-0414 ▪ TF: 800-872-5827

United Church of Christ   www.ucc.org
700 Prospect Ave   Cleveland OH 44115
Ph: 216-736-2100 ▪ Fx: 216-736-2103

United Church of Christ Justice & Witness Ministries   www.ucc.org/justice/index.html
700 Prospect Ave   Cleveland OH 44115
Ph: 216-736-3704 ▪ Fx: 216-736-3703

United Dance Merchants of America   www.udma.org
1609 Tabor Ct   Lafayette IN 47909
Ph: 765-471-0442 ▪ Fx: 765-477-5840 ▪ TF: 800-304-8362

United Daughters of the Confederacy   www.hqudc.org
328 North Blvd   Richmond VA 23220
Ph: 804-355-1636 ▪ Fx: 804-353-1396

United Drag Racers Association   www.udra.org
18823 High Point   Chagrin Falls OH 44023
Ph: 440-543-4272

United Egg Producers   www.unitedegg.com
1720 Windward Concourse Suite 230   Alpharetta GA 30005
Ph: 770-360-9220 ▪ Fx: 770-360-7058

United Electrical Radio & Machine Workers of America   www.ranknfile-ue.org
1 Gateway Ctr Suite 1400   Pittsburgh PA 15222
Ph: 412-471-8919 ▪ Fx: 412-471-8999

United Farm Workers   www.ufw.org
PO Box 62   Keene CA 93531
Ph: 661-822-5571 ▪ Fx: 661-823-6177

United Federation of Doll Clubs Inc   www.ufdc.org
10900 N Pomona Ave   Kansas City MO 64153
Ph: 816-891-7040 ▪ Fx: 816-891-8360

United Federation of Police Officers
540 N State Rd   Briarcliff Manor NY 10510
Ph: 914-941-4103 ▪ Fx: 914-941-4472

United Fire Equipment Service Association
500 Telser Rd   Lake Zurich IL 60047
Ph: 847-438-2343 ▪ Fx: 847-438-1869

United Food & Commercial Workers International Union   www.ufcw.org
1775 K St NW   Washington DC 20006
Ph: 202-223-3111 ▪ Fx: 202-466-1562 ▪ TF: 800-551-4010

United Fresh Fruit & Vegetable Association   www.uffva.org
1901 Pennsylvania Ave NW Suite 1100   Washington DC 20006
Ph: 202-303-3400 ▪ Fx: 202-303-3433

United Fund Inc, National Black   www.nbuf.org
40 Clinton St 5th Fl   Newark NJ 07102
Ph: 973-643-5122 ▪ Fx: 973-648-8350 ▪ TF: 800-223-0866

United in Group Harmony Association   www.ugha.org
PO Box 185   Clifton NJ 07011
Ph: 973-365-0049

United Hellenic Voters of America   www.smartbiz.net/uhva
525 W Lake St   Addison IL 60101
Ph: 630-628-0820 ▪ Fx: 630-543-7001

United Humanitarians   www.unitedhumanitarians.com
PO Box 14587   Philadelphia PA 19115
Ph: 215-750-0171

United Indian Missions International   www.uim.org
PO Box 336010   Greeley CO 80633
Ph: 970-330-7788 ▪ Fx: 970-330-2559

United Indians of All Tribes Foundation   www.unitedindians.com
PO Box 99100   Seattle WA 98199
Ph: 206-285-4425 ▪ Fx: 206-282-3640

United Inventors Association   www.uiausa.org
PO Box 23447   Rochester NY 14692
Ph: 585-359-9310 ▪ Fx: 585-359-1132

United Jewish Communities   www.ujc.org
111 8th Ave Suite 11E   New York NY 10011
Ph: 212-284-6500 ▪ Fx: 212-284-6835

United Kennel Club Inc   www.ukcdogs.com
100 E Kilgore Rd   Kalamazoo MI 49002
Ph: 269-343-9020 ▪ Fx: 269-343-7037

United Lithuanian Relief Fund of America
4545 W 63rd St   Chicago IL 60629
Ph: 773-767-3401 ▪ Fx: 773-767-3402

United Lutheran Society
PO Box 947   Ligonier PA 15658
Ph: 724-238-9505 ▪ Fx: 724-238-9506 ▪ TF: 800-235-0857

United Methodist Association of Health & Welfare Ministries   www.umassociation.org
601 W Riverview Ave   Dayton OH 45406
Ph: 937-227-9494 ▪ Fx: 937-222-7364 ▪ TF: 800-411-9901

United Methodist Church, General Commission on Archives &   www.gcah.org
History of the   36 Madison Ave PO Box 127   Madison NJ
    07940
Ph: 973-408-3189 ▪ Fx: 973-408-3909

United Methodist Church, National Association of Schools Colleges &
Universities of the   PO Box 340007   Nashville TN 37203
Ph: 615-340-7399 ▪ Fx: 615-340-7379

United Methodist Committee on Relief   gbgm-umc.org/umcor
475 Riverside Dr Suite 330   New York NY 10115
Ph: 212-870-3816 ▪ Fx: 212-870-3624 ▪ TF: 800-554-8583

United Methodist Youth Organization   umyouth.org
1001 19th Ave S PO Box 340003   Nashville TN 37203
Ph: 615-340-7184 ▪ Fx: 615-340-1764 ▪ TF: 877-899-2780

United Methodists of Color for a Fully Inclusive Church   www.umoc.org
3801 N Keeler Ave   Chicago IL 60641
Ph: 773-736-5526

United Mine Workers of America   www.umwa.org
8315 Lee Hwy   Fairfax VA 22031
Ph: 703-208-7200 ▪ Fx: 703-208-7227

United Ministries in Higher Education   www.umhe.org
7407 Steele Creek Rd   Charlotte NC 28217
Ph: 704-588-2182 ▪ Fx: 704-588-3652

United Mitochondrial Disease Foundation   www.umdf.org
8085 Saltsburg Rd Suite 201   Pittsburgh PA 15239
Ph: 412-793-8077 ▪ Fx: 412-793-6477

United Motorcoach Association   www.uma.org
113 S West St 4th Fl   Alexandria VA 22314
Ph: 703-838-2929 ▪ Fx: 703-838-2950 ▪ TF: 800-424-8262

United National Indian Tribal Youth   www.unityinc.org
PO Box 800   Oklahoma City OK 73101
Ph: 405-236-2800 ▪ Fx: 405-971-1071

United Nations Children's Fund   www.unicef.org
3 UN Plaza   New York NY 10017
Ph: 212-326-7000 ▪ Fx: 212-888-7465 ▪ TF: 800-553-1200

United Nations Foundation — www.unfoundation.org
1225 Connecticut Ave NW 4th Fl   Washington DC 20036
Ph: 202-887-9040 ▪ Fx: 202-887-9021

United Nations Women's Guild — www.iaea.or.at/unwg

United Negro College Fund Inc — www.uncf.org
8260 Willow Oaks Corporate Dr   Fairfax VA 22031
Ph: 703-205-3400 ▪ Fx: 703-205-3597 ▪ TF: 800-331-2244

United Neighborhood Centers of America Inc — www.unca.org
3631 Perkins Ave 4th Fl   Cleveland OH 44114
Ph: 216-391-3028 ▪ Fx: 216-391-6206

United Network for Organ Sharing — www.unos.org
700 N 4th St   Richmond VA 23219
Ph: 804-330-8500 ▪ Fx: 804-782-4817 ▪ TF: 888-894-6361

United Order True Sisters Inc — www.uots.org
100 State St Suite 1020   Albany NY 12207
Ph: 518-436-1670 ▪ Fx: 518-436-1573

United Ostomy Association — www.uoa.org
19772 MacArthur Blvd Suite 200   Irvine CA 92612
Ph: 949-660-8624 ▪ Fx: 949-660-9262 ▪ TF: 800-826-0826

United Paperworkers International Union
PO Box 1475   Nashville TN 37202
Ph: 615-834-8590 ▪ Fx: 615-831-6791

United Pentecostal Church International — www.upci.org
8855 Dunn Rd   Hazelwood MO 63042
Ph: 314-837-7300 ▪ Fx: 314-837-4503

United Poultry Concerns Inc — www.upc-online.org
12325 Seaside Rd PO Box 150   Machipongo VA 23405
Ph: 757-678-7875 ▪ Fx: 757-678-5070

United Producers Inc — www.uproducers.com
5909 Cleveland Ave   Columbus OH 43231
Ph: 614-890-6666 ▪ Fx: 614-890-4776 ▪ TF: 800-456-3276

United Producers Livestock Association — www.uproducers.com
210 Landmark Dr Suite D   Normal IL 61761
Ph: 309-888-9907

United Product Formulators & Distributors Association — www.pestworld.org/upfda
2034 Beaver Run Rd   Norcross GA 30071
Ph: 770-417-1418 ▪ Fx: 770-417-1419

United Professional Horsemen's Association — www.uphaonline.com
4059 Iron Works Pkwy Suite 2   Lexington KY 40511
Ph: 859-231-5070 ▪ Fx: 859-255-2774

United Scenic Artists — www.usa829.org
29 W 38th St 15th Fl   New York NY 10018
Ph: 212-581-0300 ▪ Fx: 212-977-2011 ▪ TF: 877-728-5635

United Schutzhund Clubs of America — www.germanshepherddog.com
3810 Paule Ave   Saint Louis MO 63125
Ph: 314-638-9686 ▪ Fx: 314-683-0609

United Seniors Association — www.unitedseniors.org
3900 Jermantown Rd Suite 450   Fairfax VA 22030
Ph: 703-359-6500 ▪ Fx: 703-359-6510 ▪ TF: 800-887-2872

United Service Organizations — www.uso.org
1008 Eberle Pl SE Suite 301   Washington Navy Yard DC 20374
Ph: 202-610-5700 ▪ Fx: 202-610-5699

United Sidecar Association — www.sidecar.com
130 S Michigan Ave   Villa Park IL 60181
Ph: 630-833-6732

United Silver Fanciers — www.unitedsilverfanciers.com

United South & Eastern Tribes Inc — usetinc.org
711 Stewarts Ferry Pike Suite 100   Nashville TN 37214
Ph: 615-872-7900 ▪ Fx: 615-872-7417

United Soybean Board — www.unitedsoybean.org
16640 Chesterfield Grove Rd Suite 130   Chesterfield MO 63005
Ph: 636-530-1777 ▪ Fx: 636-530-1560 ▪ TF: 800-989-8721

United Sportsmen's Association of North America — www.usanamtc.com
224 Sandbridge Rd   Pittsgrove NJ 08318
Ph: 856-358-4891

United Steelworkers of America — www.uswa.org
5 Gateway Ctr Rm 802   Pittsburgh PA 15222
Ph: 412-562-2400 ▪ Fx: 412-562-2445 ▪ TF: 800-248-8792

United Steelworkers of America PAC
5 Gateway Ctr   Pittsburgh PA 15222
Ph: 412-562-2400 ▪ Fx: 412-562-2445

United Steelworkers of America Rubber/Plastics Industry Conference
5 Gateway Ctr 7th Fl   Pittsburgh PA 15222
Ph: 412-562-6971 ▪ Fx: 412-562-6963

United Street Machine Association Inc — www.usmacarshows.com
430 N Batchewana St   Clawson MI 48017
Ph: 248-280-0342

United Suffolk Sheep Association — www.u-s-s-a.org
PO Box 256   Newton UT 84327
Ph: 435-563-6105 ▪ Fx: 435-563-9356

United Synagogue of Conservative Judaism — www.uscj.org
155 5th Ave   New York NY 10010
Ph: 212-533-7800 ▪ Fx: 212-353-9439

United Synagogue Youth — www.usy.org
155 5th Ave   New York NY 10010
Ph: 212-533-7800 ▪ Fx: 212-353-9439

United Telecom Council — www.utc.org
1901 Pennsylvania Ave NW 5th Fl   Washington DC 20006
Ph: 202-872-0030 ▪ Fx: 202-872-1331

United Thoroughbred Trainers of America
PO Box 7065   Louisville KY 40257
Ph: 502-893-0025 ▪ Fx: 502-893-0026 ▪ TF: 800-325-3487

United Transportation Union — www.utu.org
14600 Detroit Ave   Lakewood OH 44107
Ph: 216-228-9400 ▪ Fx: 216-228-5755

United Ukrainian American Relief Committee Inc — www.uuarc.org
1206 Cottman Ave   Philadelphia PA 19111
Ph: 215-728-1630 ▪ Fx: 215-728-1631

United Union of Roofers Waterproofers & Allied Workers — www.unionroofers.com
1660 L St NW Suite 800   Washington DC 20036
Ph: 202-463-7663 ▪ Fx: 202-463-6906

United Way of America — national.unitedway.org
701 N Fairfax St   Alexandria VA 22314
Ph: 703-836-7100 ▪ Fx: 703-683-7840 ▪ TF: 800-892-2757

United Way International — www.uwint.org
701 N Fairfax St   Alexandria VA 22314
Ph: 703-519-0092 ▪ Fx: 703-519-0097

United World Mission Inc — www.uwm.org
9401-B Southern Pines Blvd   Charlotte NC 28273
Ph: 704-357-3355 ▪ Fx: 704-357-6389 ▪ TF: 800-825-5896

United Worldwide Marriage Encounter USA — www.uwwme.org

Unity Churches, Association of — www.unity.org
401 SW Oldham Pkwy PO Box 610   Lee's Summit MO 64063
Ph: 816-524-7414 ▪ Fx: 816-525-4020

Unity Fellowship Church Movement
5148 W Jefferson Blvd   Los Angeles CA 90016
Ph: 323-938-8322 ▪ Fx: 323-965-8322

Universal Fellowship of Metropolitan Community Churches — www.mccchurch.org
8704 Santa Monica Blvd 2nd Fl   West Hollywood CA 90069
Ph: 310-360-8640 ▪ Fx: 310-360-8680

Universal Ship Cancellation Society — www.uscs.org

Universities, American Association of State Colleges & — www.aascu.org
1307 New York Ave NW 5th Fl   Washington DC 20005
Ph: 202-293-7070 ▪ Fx: 202-296-5819

Universities, Association of American — www.aau.edu
1200 New York Ave NW Suite 550   Washington DC 20005
Ph: 202-408-7500 ▪ Fx: 202-408-8184

Universities, Association of American Colleges & — www.aacu-edu.org
1818 R St NW   Washington DC 20009
Ph: 202-387-3760 ▪ Fx: 202-265-9532

Universities Club of New York, British Schools & — www.bsuc.org
24 E 39th St   New York NY 10016
Ph: 212-713-5713

Universities & Colleges, Association of Governing Boards of — www.agb.org
1 Dupont Cir NW Suite 400   Washington DC 20036
Ph: 202-296-8400 ▪ Fx: 202-223-7053 ▪ TF: 800-356-6317

Universities, Council for Christian Colleges & — www.cccu.org
321 8th St NE   Washington DC 20002
Ph: 202-546-8713 ▪ Fx: 202-546-8913

Universities Foundation, British Schools & — www.bsuf.org
575 Madison Ave Suite 1006   New York NY 10022
Ph: 212-662-5576

Universities, Hispanic Association of Colleges & — www.hacu.net
8415 Datapoint Dr Suite 400   San Antonio TX 78229
Ph: 210-692-3805 ▪ Fx: 210-692-0823 ▪ TF: 800-780-4228

Universities & Land Grant Colleges, National Association of State — www.nasulgc.org
1307 New York Ave NW Suite 400   Washington DC 20005
Ph: 202-478-6040 ▪ Fx: 202-478-6046

Universities, National Association of Independent Colleges & — www.naicu.edu
1025 Connecticut Ave NW Suite 700   Washington DC 20036
Ph: 202-785-8866 ▪ Fx: 202-835-0003

Universities Research Association Inc — www.ura-hq.org
1111 19th St NW Suite 400   Washington DC 20036
Ph: 202-293-1382 ▪ Fx: 202-293-5012

Universities for Research in Astronomy, Association of — www.aura-astronomy.org
1200 New York Ave NW Suite 350   Washington DC 20005
Ph: 202-483-2101 ▪ Fx: 202-483-2106

Universities Space Research Association — www.usra.edu
10227 Wincopin Cir American City Bldg Suite 212   Columbia MD 21044
Ph: 410-730-2656 ▪ Fx: 410-730-3496

University Anesthesiologists, Association of — www.auahq.org
520 Northwest Hwy   Park Ridge IL 60068
Ph: 847-825-5586

University Athletic Association — www.uaa.rochester.edu
575 Mt Hope Ave   Rochester NY 14620
Ph: 716-273-5881 ▪ Fx: 716-275-8322

University Attorneys, National Association of College & — www.nacua.org
1 Dupont Cir NW Suite 620   Washington DC 20036
Ph: 202-833-8390 ▪ Fx: 202-296-8379

University Aviation Association — uaa.auburn.edu
3410 Skyway Dr   Auburn AL 36830
Ph: 334-844-2434 ▪ Fx: 334-844-2432

University Business & Economic Research, Association for — www.auber.org
Univ of Colorado Leeds School of Business UCB 419   Boulder CO 80309
Ph: 303-492-3196 ▪ Fx: 303-492-3620

University Business Officers, National Association of College & — www.nacubo.org
2501 M St NW Suite 400   Washington DC 20037
Ph: 202-861-2500 ▪ Fx: 202-861-2583

University Centers on Disabilities, Association of — www.aucd.org
8630 Fenton St Suite 410   Silver Spring MD 20910
Ph: 301-588-8252 ▪ Fx: 301-588-2842

University & College Designers Association — www.ucda.com
153 Front St   Smyrna TN 37167
Ph: 615-459-4559 ▪ Fx: 615-459-5229

University Consortium for Advanced Internet Development — www.internet2.edu
3025 Boardwalk Suite 200   Ann Arbor MI 48108
Ph: 734-913-4250 ▪ Fx: 734-913-4255

University Continuing Education Association — www.ucea.edu
1 Dupont Cir NW Suite 615   Washington DC 20036
Ph: 202-659-3130 ▪ Fx: 202-785-0374

University Corporation for Atmospheric Research — www.ucar.edu
1850 Table Mesa Dr   Boulder CO 80305
Ph: 303-497-1000 ▪ Fx: 303-497-1654

University Council for Educational Administration — www.ucea.edu
Univ of Missouri-Columbia 205 Hill Hall   Columbia MO 65211
Ph: 573-884-8300 ▪ Fx: 573-884-8302

University Film & Video Foundation
www.ufva.org
Univ of Illinois Press 1325 S Oak St   Champaign IL 61820
Ph: 217-224-0626 ▪ Fx: 217-244-9910 ▪ TF: 866-244-0626

University Fisheries & Wildlife Programs,   www.ag.iastate.edu/departments/aecl/naufwp
National Association of   Univ of Montana 310 Lewis Hall Box
173460   Bozeman MT 59717
Ph: 406-994-2270 ▪ Fx: 406-994-3190

University Foundation, International
1301 S Noland Rd   Independence MO 64055
Ph: 816-461-3633 ▪ Fx: 816-461-4925 ▪ TF: 800-369-0009

University Housing Officers International, Association   www.acuho.ohio-state.edu
of College &   941 Chatham Ln Suite 318   Columbus OH
43221
Ph: 614-292-0099 ▪ Fx: 614-292-3205

University Interior Designers, Association of
www.auid.org

University Libraries, Canadian Association of   www.cla.ca/divisions/cacul/cacul.htm
College &   328 Frank St   Ottawa ON K2P0X8
Ph: 613-232-9625 ▪ Fx: 613-563-9895

University of the Negev, American Associates Ben-Gurion
www.aabgu.org
1430 Broadway 8th Fl   New York NY 10018
Ph: 212-687-7721 ▪ Fx: 212-302-6443 ▪ TF: 800-962-2248

University Planning, Society for College &
www.scup.org
339 E Liberty St Suite 300   Ann Arbor MI 48104
Ph: 734-998-7832 ▪ Fx: 734-998-6532

University Presses, Association of American
www.aaupnet.org
71 W 23rd St Suite 901   New York NY 10010
Ph: 212-989-1010 ▪ Fx: 212-989-0275

University Professional Association for Human Resources, College &   www.cupahr.org
1233 20th St NW Suite 301   Washington DC 20036
Ph: 202-429-0311 ▪ Fx: 202-429-0149

University Professors, American Association of
www.aaup.org
1012 14th St NW Suite 500   Washington DC 20005
Ph: 202-737-5900 ▪ Fx: 202-737-5526 ▪ TF: 800-424-2973

University Professors of Ophthalmology, Association of
PO Box 420369   San Francisco CA 94142
Ph: 415-561-8548 ▪ Fx: 415-561-8531

University Programs in Health Administration, Association of   www.aupha.org
730 11th St NW 4th Fl   Washington DC 20001
Ph: 202-638-1448 ▪ Fx: 202-638-3429

University Radiologists, Association of
www.aur.org
820 Jorie Blvd   Oak Brook IL 60523
Ph: 630-368-3730 ▪ Fx: 630-571-7837

University Research Administrators, National Council of
www.ncura.edu
1 Dupont Cir NW Suite 220   Washington DC 20036
Ph: 202-466-3894 ▪ Fx: 202-223-5573

University Research Parks, Association of
www.aurrp.org
12100 Sunset Hills Rd Suite 130   Reston VA 20190
Ph: 703-234-4088 ▪ Fx: 703-435-4390

University/Resident Theatre Association
www.urta.com
1560 Broadway Suite 712   New York NY 10036
Ph: 212-221-1130 ▪ Fx: 212-869-2752

University Risk Management & Insurance Association
www.urmia.org
342 N Main St   West Hartford CT 06117
Ph: 860-586-7565 ▪ Fx: 860-586-7550

University Surgeons, Society of
www.susweb.org
1133 W Morse Blvd Suite 201   Winter Park FL 32789
Ph: 407-647-7714 ▪ Fx: 407-629-2502

University Technology Managers, Association of
www.autm.net
60 Revere Dr Suite 500   Northbrook IL 60062
Ph: 847-559-0846 ▪ Fx: 847-480-9282

University Women, American Association of
www.aauw.org
1111 16th St NW   Washington DC 20036
Ph: 202-785-7700 ▪ Fx: 202-872-1425 ▪ TF: 800-326-2289

University Women, National Association of
www.nauw.org
1001 'E' St SE   Washington DC 20003
Ph: 202-547-3967 ▪ Fx: 202-547-5226

Unmanned Vehicle Systems International, Association for
www.auvsi.org
3401 Columbia Pike Suite 400   Arlington VA 22204
Ph: 703-920-2720 ▪ Fx: 703-920-2889

Unrepresented Nations & Peoples Organization
www.unpo.org
444 N Capitol St Suite 846   Washington DC 20001
Ph: 202-637-0475 ▪ Fx: 202-637-0585

Up With People
www.upwithpeople.org
1675 Broadway Suite 1460   Denver CO 80202
Ph: 303-460-7100 ▪ Fx: 303-225-4649 ▪ TF: 877-264-8856

Upholstered Furniture Action Council
www.ufac.org
PO Box 2436   High Point NC 27261
Ph: 336-885-5065 ▪ Fx: 336-885-5072

Upper Mississippi River Conservation Committee   www.mississippi-river.com/umrcc
4469 48th Ave Ct   Rock Island IL 61201
Ph: 309-793-5800 ▪ Fx: 309-793-5804

Upsilon Pi Epsilon Association
www.acm.org/upe
California State Univ Chico Dept of Computer Science   Chico
CA 95929
Ph: 530-898-6442 ▪ Fx: 530-898-5995

URAC
www.urac.org
1220 L St NW Suite 400   Washington DC 20005
Ph: 202-216-9010 ▪ Fx: 202-216-9006

Urasenke Tea Ceremony Society
153 E 69th St   New York NY 10021
Ph: 212-988-6161 ▪ Fx: 212-517-7594

Urban Affairs Association
www.udel.edu/uaa
Univ of Delaware 298 Graham Hall   Newark DE 19716
Ph: 302-831-1681 ▪ Fx: 302-831-4225

Urban Affairs, Higher Education Consortium for
www.hecua.org
2233 University Ave W Suite 210   Saint Paul MN 55114
Ph: 651-646-8831 ▪ Fx: 651-659-9421 ▪ TF: 800-554-1089

Urban Agriculture Council, National
www.nuac.org
1015 18th St NW Suite 600   Washington DC 20036
Ph: 202-429-4344 ▪ Fx: 202-429-4342

Urban Economics Association, American Real Estate &
www.areuea.org
PO Box 1148   Portage MI 49081
Ph: 866-273-8321 ▪ Fx: 313-731-0174

Urban Education Associations, National Council of
www.nea.org/ncuea
1201 16th St NW Suite 410   Washington DC 20036
Ph: 202-822-7376 ▪ Fx: 202-822-7624

Urban Ethnic Affairs, National Center for
PO Box 20 Cardinal Stn   Washington DC 20064
Ph: 202-319-5129 ▪ Fx: 202-319-6289

Urban Financial Services Coalition
www.ufscnet.org
1300 L St NW Suite 825   Washington DC 20005
Ph: 202-289-8335 ▪ Fx: 202-842-0567

Urban Habitat, Council on Tall Buildings &
www.ctbuh.org
Illinois Institute of Technology SR Crown Hall 3360 S State
St   Chicago IL 60616
Ph: 312-909-0253

Urban Hospitals, National Association of
www.nauh.org
10 Pidgeon Hill Dr Suite 150   Sterling VA 20165
Ph: 703-444-0989 ▪ Fx: 703-444-3029

Urban Institute
www.urban.org
2100 M St NW   Washington DC 20037
Ph: 202-833-7200 ▪ Fx: 202-223-3043

Urban Land Institute
www.uli.org
1025 Thomas Jefferson St NW Suite 500W   Washington DC
20007
Ph: 202-624-7000 ▪ Fx: 202-624-7140 ▪ TF: 800-321-5011

Urban League Inc, National
www.nul.org
120 Wall St 8th Fl   New York NY 10005
Ph: 212-558-5300 ▪ Fx: 212-344-5332

Urban Libraries Council
www.urbanlibraries.org
1603 Orrington Ave Suite 1080   Evanston IL 60201
Ph: 847-866-9999 ▪ Fx: 847-866-9989

(Urban Ministry) World Impact
www.worldimpact.org
2001 S Vermont Ave   Los Angeles CA 90007
Ph: 323-735-1137 ▪ Fx: 323-735-2576

Urban National & Transnational/Global Anthropology, Society for   www.sunta.org
c/o American Anthropological Assn 2200 Wilson Blvd Suite
600   Arlington VA 22201
Ph: 703-528-1902 ▪ Fx: 703-528-3546

(Urban Planning) Waterfront Center
www.waterfrontcenter.org
1622 Wisconsin Ave NW   Washington DC 20007
Ph: 202-337-0356 ▪ Fx: 202-625-1654

Urban & Regional Information Systems Association
www.urisa.org
1460 Renaissance Dr Suite 305   Park Ridge IL 60068
Ph: 847-824-6300 ▪ Fx: 847-824-6363

Urban Technology Center, National
www.urbantech.org
55 John St Suite 300   New York NY 10038
Ph: 212-528-7400 ▪ Fx: 212-528-7355 ▪ TF: 800-998-3212

Urogynecologic Society, American
www.augs.org
2025 M St NW Suite 800   Washington DC 20036
Ph: 202-367-1167 ▪ Fx: 202-367-2167

Urologic Cryosurgeons, Society of
1950 Old Tustin Ave   Santa Ana CA 92705
Ph: 714-550-9155 ▪ Fx: 714-550-9234

Urologic Disease, American Foundation for
www.afud.org
1000 Corporate Blvd Suite 110   Lithicum MD 21090
Ph: 410-689-3990 ▪ Fx: 410-689-3998 ▪ TF: 800-242-2383

Urologic Nurses & Associates, Society of
www.suna.org
PO Box 56   Pitman NJ 08071
Ph: 856-256-2335 ▪ Fx: 856-589-7463 ▪ TF: 888-827-7862

Urological Association, American
www.auanet.org
1000 Corporate Blvd   Linthicum MD 21090
Ph: 410-689-3700 ▪ Fx: 410-689-3800 ▪ TF: 866-746-4282

Urologists Inc, American Association of Clinical
www.aacuweb.org
1111 N Plaza Dr Suite 550   Schaumburg IL 60173
Ph: 847-517-1050 ▪ Fx: 847-517-7229

Urology, American Board of
www.abu.org
2216 Ivy Rd Suite 210   Charlottesville VA 22903
Ph: 434-979-0059 ▪ Fx: 434-979-2066

Urology Society of America
www.urologysocietyofamerica.org
305 Ave Second Ave Suite 200   Waltham MA 02451
Ph: 781-895-9078 ▪ Fx: 781-895-9088

Urology, Society of Women in
www.swiu.org
1111 N Plaza Dr Suite 550   Schaumburg IL 60173
Ph: 847-517-7225 ▪ Fx: 847-517-7229

Uroradiology, Society for
www.uroradiology.org
4550 Post Oak Pl Suite 342   Houston TX 77027
Ph: 713-965-0566 ▪ Fx: 713-960-0488

Ursuline Companions in Mission
www.ursulinecompanions.org
210 Glennon Heights Rd   Crystal City MO 63019
Ph: 636-937-6206 ▪ Fx: 636-937-7627

US Advanced Ceramics Association
www.advancedceramics.org
1800 M St NW Suite 300   Washington DC 20036
Ph: 202-293-6253 ▪ Fx: 202-223-5537

US Aikido Federation
www.usaikifed.com
98 State St   Northampton MA 01060
Ph: 413-586-7122

US Amateur Ballroom Dancers Association
www.usabda.org
PO Box 128   New Freedom PA 17349
Ph: 717-235-6656 ▪ Fx: 717-235-4183 ▪ TF: 800-447-9047

US Amateur Boxing Inc
www.usaboxing.org
1 Olympic Plaza   Colorado Springs CO 80909
Ph: 719-866-4506 ▪ Fx: 719-632-3426

US Amateur Jump Rope Federation
www.usajrf.org

US-Angola Chamber of Commerce
www.us-angola.org
1100 Connecticut Ave NW Suite 1000   Washington DC 20036
Ph: 202-223-0540 ▪ Fx: 202-223-0551

US Animal Health Association
www.usaha.org
PO Box K 227   Richmond VA 23229
Ph: 804-285-3210 ▪ Fx: 804-285-3367

US Apple Association   www.usapple.org
8233 Old Courthouse Rd Suite 200   Vienna VA 22182
Ph: 703-442-8850 ▪ Fx: 703-790-0845 ▪ TF: 800-781-4443

US Aquaculture Suppliers Association   www.aquaculturesuppliers.com
PO Box 901303   Homestead FL 33090
Ph: 305-248-4205 ▪ Fx: 305-248-1756

US Army Warrant Officers Association   www.penfed.org/usawoa
462 Herndon Pkwy Suite 207   Herndon VA 20170
Ph: 703-742-7727 ▪ Fx: 703-742-7728 ▪ TF: 800-587-2862

US-ASEAN Business Council   www.us-asean.org
1101 17th St NW Suite 411   Washington DC 20036
Ph: 202-289-1911 ▪ Fx: 202-289-0519

US-Asia Institute   www.usasiainstitute.org
232 E Capitol St NE   Washington DC 20003
Ph: 202-544-3181 ▪ Fx: 202-543-1748

US Association of Blind Athletes   www.usaba.org
33 N Institute St   Colorado Springs CO 80903
Ph: 719-630-0422 ▪ Fx: 719-630-0616

US Association for Computational Mechanics   www.usacm.org
Scientific Computation Research Ctr 7011 CIL Bldg   Troy NY
    12180
Ph: 518-276-3590 ▪ Fx: 518-276-4886

US Association for Energy Economics   www.usaee.org
28790 Chagrin Blvd Suite 350   Cleveland OH 44122
Ph: 216-464-2785 ▪ Fx: 216-464-2768

US Association of Former Members of Congress   www.usafmc.org
233 Pennsylvania Ave SE Suite 200   Washington DC 20003
Ph: 202-543-8676 ▪ Fx: 202-543-7145

US Association of Importers of Textiles & Apparel   www.usaita.com
13 E 16th St 6th Fl   New York NY 10003
Ph: 212-463-0089 ▪ Fx: 212-463-0583

US Association of Independent Gymnastic Clubs Inc   www.usaigc.com
22 River Terr Suite 20D   New York NY 10282
Ph: 212-227-9792 ▪ Fx: 212-227-9793 ▪ TF: 800-480-0201

US-Austrian Chamber of Commerce   www.usatchamber.com
165 W 46th St   New York NY 10036
Ph: 212-819-0117 ▪ Fx: 212-819-0345

US Auto Club   www.usacracing.com
4910 W 16th St   Speedway IN 46224
Ph: 317-247-5151 ▪ Fx: 317-247-0123

US Basketball Writers Association   www.sportswriters.net/usbwa
1818 Chouteau Ave   Saint Louis MO 63103
Ph: 314-421-0339 ▪ Fx: 314-421-3505

US Beet Sugar Association
1156 15th St NW Suite 1019   Washington DC 20005
Ph: 202-296-4820 ▪ Fx: 202-331-2065

US Biathlon Association   www.usbiathlon.org
29 Ethan Allen Ave   Colchester VT 05446
Ph: 802-654-7833 ▪ Fx: 802-654-7830 ▪ TF: 800-242-8456

US Billiard Association   www.uscarom.org
1800 Beach Dr Rm 1823   Gulfport MS 39507
Ph: 228-897-8290

US Blind Golfers' Association   www.blindgolf.com
3094 Shamrock St N   Tallahassee FL 32308
Ph: 850-893-4511

US Bobsled & Skeleton Federation   www.usbsf.com
421 Old Military Rd   Lake Placid NY 12946
Ph: 518-523-1842 ▪ Fx: 518-523-9491 ▪ TF: 800-262-7533

US Bocce Federation   www.bocce.com
44 Park Ln   Park Ridge IL 60068
Ph: 847-692-6223 ▪ Fx: 847-692-6221

US Book Exchange   www.usbe.com
2969 W 25th St   Cleveland OH 44113
Ph: 216-241-6960 ▪ Fx: 216-241-6966

US Boomerang Association   www.usba.org

US Bowling Instructors Association
PO Box 564   Palatine IL 60078
Ph: 847-359-0682 ▪ Fx: 847-550-0218

US Business Council for Southeastern Europe   www.usbizcouncil.org
PO Box 1521 Wall St Stn   New York NY 10268
Ph: 212-439-9025 ▪ Fx: 212-439-9105 ▪ TF: 800-203-8900

US Business & Industry Council   www.usbusiness.org
910 16th St NW Suite 300   Washington DC 20006
Ph: 202-728-1980 ▪ Fx: 202-728-1981

US Business & Industry Council Educational Foundation   www.usbusiness.org
910 16th St NW Suite 300   Washington DC 20006
Ph: 202-728-1990 ▪ Fx: 202-728-1981

(US-Canada Boundary) International Joint Commission   www.ijc.org
1250 23rd St NW Suite 100   Washington DC 20440
Ph: 202-736-9024 ▪ Fx: 202-736-9015

US & Canadian Academy of Pathology   www.uscap.org
3643 Walton Way Ext   Augusta GA 30909
Ph: 706-733-7550 ▪ Fx: 706-733-8033

US Canoe Association   www.uscanoe.com
606 Ross St   Middletown OH 45044
Ph: 513-422-3739

US Canola Association   www.uscanola.com
600 Penn Ave SE Suite 320   Washington DC 20003
Ph: 202-969-8113 ▪ Fx: 202-969-7036

US Capitol Historical Society   www.uschs.org
200 Maryland Ave NE   Washington DC 20002
Ph: 202-543-8919 ▪ Fx: 202-544-8244

US Catholic Mission Association   www.uscatholicmission.org
3029 4th St NE   Washington DC 20017
Ph: 202-832-3112 ▪ Fx: 202-832-3688

US Cavalry Association   www.uscavalry.org
PO Box 2325   Fort Riley KS 66442
Ph: 785-784-5797

US Chess Federation   www.uschess.org
3054 US Rt 9 W   New Windsor NY 12553
Ph: 845-562-8350 ▪ Fx: 845-561-2437 ▪ TF: 800-388-5464

US-China Arts Exchange, Center for   www.columbia.edu/cu/china
423 W 118th St Suite 1E   New York NY 10027
Ph: 212-280-4648 ▪ Fx: 212-662-6346

US-China Business Council   www.uschina.org
1818 N St NW Suite 200   Washington DC 20036
Ph: 202-429-0340 ▪ Fx: 202-775-2476

US China Peoples Friendship Association   www.uscpfa.org
1214 W Schwartz St   Carbondale IL 62901
Ph: 618-549-1555 ▪ Fx: 618-549-9766

US Coast Guard Chief Petty Officers Association   www.uscgcpoa.org
5520-G Hempstead Way   Springfield VA 22151
Ph: 703-941-0395 ▪ Fx: 703-941-0397

US Committee of the International Council on   www.icomos.org/usicomos
Monuments & Sites   National Building Museum 401 F St NW
    Rm 331   Washington DC 20001
Ph: 202-842-1866 ▪ Fx: 202-842-1861

US Committee on Irrigation & Drainage   www.uscid.org
1616 17th St Suite 483   Denver CO 80202
Ph: 303-628-5430 ▪ Fx: 303-628-5431

US Committee for Refugees   www.irsa-uscr.org
1717 Massachusetts Ave NW Suite 200   Washington DC 20036
Ph: 202-347-3507 ▪ Fx: 202-347-3418

US Competitive Aerobics Federation   www.sportaerobics-nac.com
Association of National Aerobic Championships Worldwide 8033
    Sunset Blvd Suite 920   Los Angeles CA 90046
Ph: 323-850-3777 ▪ Fx: 323-850-7795

US Conference of Catholic Bishops   www.usccb.org
3211 4th St NE   Washington DC 20017
Ph: 202-541-3000 ▪ Fx: 202-541-3322

US Conference of City Human Services Officials
1620 'I' St NW   Washington DC 20006
Ph: 202-293-7330 ▪ Fx: 202-293-2352

US Conference of Mayors   www.usmayors.org
1620 'I' St NW Suite 400   Washington DC 20006
Ph: 202-293-7330 ▪ Fx: 202-293-2352

US Council for International Business   www.uscib.org
1212 Ave of the Americas 18th Fl   New York NY 10036
Ph: 212-354-4480 ▪ Fx: 212-944-0012

US Council for International Friendship
745 Leader Bldg   Cleveland OH 44114
Ph: 216-861-5542 ▪ Fx: 216-861-5064

US Council of Society of Saint Vincent de Paul   www.svdpusa.org
58 Progress Pkwy   Maryland Heights MO 63043
Ph: 314-576-3993 ▪ Fx: 314-576-6755

US Court Reporters Association   www.uscra.org
PO Box 465   Chicago IL 60690
Ph: 800-628-2730

US Croquet Association   www.croquetamerica.com
700 Florida Mango Rd   West Palm Beach FL 33406
Ph: 561-478-0760 ▪ Fx: 561-686-5507

US Cross Country Coaches Association   www.usccca.org
Michigan State Univ Jenison Fieldhouse   East Lansing MI
    48824
Ph: 517-355-1640 ▪ Fx: 517-432-3339

US Curling Association   www.usacurl.org
PO Box 866   Stevens Point WI 54481
Ph: 715-344-1199 ▪ Fx: 715-344-2279 ▪ TF: 888-287-5377

US Cutting Tool Institute   www.uscti.com
1300 Sumner Ave   Cleveland OH 44115
Ph: 216-241-7333 ▪ Fx: 216-241-0105

US Dairy Export Council   www.usdec.org
2101 Wilson Blvd Suite 400   Arlington VA 22201
Ph: 703-528-3049 ▪ Fx: 703-528-3705

US Deaf Cycling Association   home.earthlink.net/~skedsmo/usdca.htm

US Dental Tennis Association   www.dentaltennis.org
2180 Briarcliff Dr   Idaho Falls ID 83404
Ph: 800-445-2524 ▪ Fx: 208-523-9004

US Distance Learning Association   www.usdla.org
8 Winter St   Boston MA 02108
Ph: 800-275-5162 ▪ Fx: 617-399-1771

US Diving Inc   www.usadiving.org
201 S Capitol Ave Suite 430   Indianapolis IN 46225
Ph: 317-237-5252 ▪ Fx: 317-237-5257

US Dressage Federation   www.usdf.org
PO Box 6669   Lincoln NE 68506
Ph: 402-434-8550 ▪ Fx: 402-434-8570

US Durum Growers Association   www.durumgrowers.com
4023 State St   Bismarck ND 58503
Ph: 701-222-2204 ▪ Fx: 701-223-0018 ▪ TF: 877-463-8786

US Energy Association   www.usea.org
1300 Pennsylvania Ave NW Suite 550   Washington DC 20004
Ph: 202-312-1230 ▪ Fx: 202-682-1826

US ENGLISH Inc   www.us-english.org
1747 Pennsylvania Ave NW Suite 1050   Washington DC 20006
Ph: 202-833-0100 ▪ Fx: 202-833-0108 ▪ TF: 800-873-4547

US Equestrian Federation Inc   www.usef.org
4047 Iron Works Pkwy   Lexington KY 40511
Ph: 859-225-6900 ▪ Fx: 859-231-6662

US Equestrian Team   www.uset.org
PO Box 355   Gladstone NJ 07934
Ph: 908-234-1251 ▪ Fx: 908-234-9417

US Eventing Association   www.eventingusa.com
525 Old Waterford Rd NW   Leesburg VA 20176
Ph: 703-779-0440 ▪ Fx: 703-779-0550

US Federation of Philippine American Chambers of Commerce Inc   www.fpacc.com
2887 College Ave Suite 1 Box 106   Berkeley CA 94705
Ph: 510-548-7952 ▪ Fx: 510-845-9901

US Fencing Association www.usfencing.org
1 Olympic Plaza   Colorado Springs CO 80909
Ph: 719-866-4511 ▪ Fx: 719-632-5737

US Fencing Coaches Association www.usfca.org
PO Box 1966   Hoboken NJ 07030
Ph: 888-927-6687

US Field Hockey Association www.usfieldhockey.com
1 Olympic Plaza   Colorado Springs CO 80909
Ph: 719-866-4567 ▪ Fx: 719-632-0979

US Figure Skating Association www.usfsa.org
20 1st St   Colorado Springs CO 80906
Ph: 719-635-5200 ▪ Fx: 719-635-9548

US Flag Foundation www.americanflags.org
Flag Plaza 1275 Bedford Ave   Pittsburgh PA 15219
Ph: 412-261-1776 ▪ Fx: 412-261-9132 ▪ TF: 800-615-1776

US Flag & Touch Football League www.usftl.com
7709 Ohio St   Mentor OH 44060
Ph: 440-974-8735 ▪ Fx: 440-974-8441

US Fund for UNICEF www.unicefusa.org
333 E 38th St 6th Fl   New York NY 10016
Ph: 212-922-2649 ▪ Fx: 212-779-1679 ▪ TF: 800-367-5437

US Golf Association www.usga.org
PO Box 708   Far Hills NJ 07931
Ph: 908-234-2300 ▪ Fx: 908-234-9687 ▪ TF: 800-336-4446

US Golf Teachers Federation www.usgtf.com
1295 SE Port St Lucie Blvd   Port Saint Lucie FL 34952
Ph: 772-335-3216 ▪ Fx: 772-335-3822 ▪ TF: 888-346-3290

US Grains Council www.grains.org
1400 K St NW Suite 1200   Washington DC 20005
Ph: 202-789-0789 ▪ Fx: 202-898-0522

US Green Building Council www.usgbc.org
1015 18th St NW Suite 805   Washington DC 20036
Ph: 202-828-7422 ▪ Fx: 202-828-5110

US Handball Association ushandball.org
2333 N Tucson Blvd   Tucson AZ 85716
Ph: 520-795-0434 ▪ Fx: 520-795-0465

US Hang Gliding Association Inc www.ushga.org
PO Box 1330   Colorado Springs CO 80901
Ph: 719-632-8300 ▪ Fx: 719-632-6417

US Hardware Industry Association www.associationhardware.com
PO Box 35189   Chicago IL 60607
Ph: 773-283-3880 ▪ Fx: 708-453-0083

US Hispanic Chamber of Commerce www.ushcc.com
2175 K St NW Suite 100   Washington DC 20037
Ph: 202-842-1212 ▪ Fx: 202-842-3221 ▪ TF: 800-874-2286

US Hispanic Publishers Federation Inc www.ushpf.org
c/o La Informacion 6065 Hillcroft St Suite 400-B   Houston TX 77081
Ph: 713-272-0100 ▪ Fx: 713-272-0011

US Historical Society www.ushs.org
1st & Main Sts   Richmond VA 23219
Ph: 804-648-4736 ▪ Fx: 804-648-0002 ▪ TF: 800-788-4478

US Icelandic Horse Congress www.icelandics.org
PO Box 1724   Santa Ynez CA 93460
Ph: 805-688-6355

US Indoor Soccer Association www.usindoor.com

US Industrial Fabrics Institute www.ifai.com/membership/divisions
1801 County Rd 'B' W   Roseville MN 55113
Ph: 651-222-2508 ▪ Fx: 651-631-9334

US Institute for Theatre Technology Inc www.usitt.org
6443 Ridings Rd   Syracuse NY 13206
Ph: 315-463-6463 ▪ Fx: 315-463-6525 ▪ TF: 800-938-7488

US Internet Council www.usinternetcouncil.org
503 N Roosevelt Blvd Unit A-220   Falls Church VA 22044
Ph: 703-536-5770

US Internet Industry Association www.usiia.org
5810 Kingstowne Center Dr Suite 120 PMB 212   Alexandria VA 22315
Ph: 703-924-0006 ▪ Fx: 703-924-4203

US Internet Service Providers Association www.usispa.org
1330 Connecticut Ave NW   Washington DC 20036
Ph: 202-862-3816 ▪ Fx: 202-261-0604

US-Japan Business Council www.usjbc.org
2000 L St NW Suite 515   Washington DC 20036
Ph: 202-728-0068 ▪ Fx: 202-728-0073

US Jaycees www.usjaycees.org
PO Box 7   Tulsa OK 74102
Ph: 918-584-2481 ▪ Fx: 918-584-4422 ▪ TF: 800-529-2337

US Jesuit Conference www.jesuit.org
1616 P St NW Suite 300   Washington DC 20036
Ph: 202-462-5200 ▪ Fx: 202-328-9212

US Judo Association www.usja-judo.org
21 N Union Blvd   Colorado Springs CO 80909
Ph: 719-633-7750 ▪ Fx: 719-633-4041

US Judo Federation www.usjf.com
PO Box 338   Ontario OR 97914
Ph: 541-889-8753

US Junior Chamber of Commerce www.usjaycees.org
PO Box 7   Tulsa OK 74102
Ph: 918-584-2481 ▪ Fx: 918-584-4422 ▪ TF: 800-529-2337

US Justice Foundation www.usjf.net
2091 E Valley Pkwy Suite 1-C   Escondido CA 92027
Ph: 760-741-8086 ▪ Fx: 760-741-9548 ▪ TF: 800-367-8753

US Kerry Blue Terrier Club www.uskbtc.com
2458 Eastridge Dr   Hamilton OH 45011
Ph: 513-863-5041

US Labor Education in the Americas Project www.usleap.org
PO Box 268-290   Chicago IL 60626
Ph: 773-262-6502 ▪ Fx: 773-262-6602

US Lacrosse Inc www.lacrosse.org
113 University Pkwy   Baltimore MD 21210
Ph: 410-235-6882 ▪ Fx: 410-366-6735

US Letter Carriers Mutual Benefit Association www.nalc.org/depart/mba
100 Indiana Ave NW Suite 510   Washington DC 20001
Ph: 202-638-4318 ▪ Fx: 202-783-6123 ▪ TF: 800-424-5184

US Lifesaving Association www.usla.org

US Lighthouse Society www.uslhs.org
244 Kearny St 5th Fl   San Francisco CA 94108
Ph: 415-362-7255 ▪ Fx: 415-362-7464

US Lipizzan Registry www.lipizzan-uslr.com
707 13th St SE Suite 275   Salem OR 97301
Ph: 503-589-3172 ▪ Fx: 503-362-6390

US Luge Association www.usaluge.org
35 Church St   Lake Placid NY 12946
Ph: 518-523-2071 ▪ Fx: 518-523-4106

US Marine Corps Combat Correspondents Association www.usmccca.org
238 Cornwall Cir   Chalfont PA 18914
Ph: 215-822-6898 ▪ Fx: 215-822-0163 ▪ TF: 888-999-7819

US Marine Safety Association www.usmsa.org
5050 Industrial Rd   Farmingdale NJ 07727
Ph: 732-751-0102 ▪ Fx: 732-751-0508

US Masters Swimming www.usms.org
PO Box 185   Londonderry NH 03053
Ph: 603-537-0203 ▪ Fx: 603-537-0204 ▪ TF: 800-550-7946

US Meat Export Federation Inc www.usmef.org
1050 17th St Suite 2200   Denver CO 80265
Ph: 303-623-6328 ▪ Fx: 303-623-0297

US Member Society of the International Society for Prosthetics & Orthotics www.usispo.org
1161 Francisco Rd   Columbus OH 43220
Ph: 614-457-4312 ▪ Fx: 614-538-1914

US Metric Association Inc lamar.colostate.edu/~hillger
10245 S Andasol Ave   Northridge CA 91325
Ph: 818-363-5606

US-Mexico Border Health Association www.usmbha.org
5400 Suncrest Dr Suite C-5   El Paso TX 79912
Ph: 915-833-6450 ▪ Fx: 915-833-7840

US-Mexico Chamber of Commerce www.usmcoc.org
1300 Pennsylvania Ave NW Suite 0003   Washington DC 20004
Ph: 202-312-1520 ▪ Fx: 202-312-1530

US Modern Pentathlon Association usmpa.home.texas.net
305 E Ramsey   San Antonio TX 78216
Ph: 210-229-2004 ▪ Fx: 210-340-4970

US National Committee to the International Dairy Federation www.usnac.org
PO Box 930398   Verona WI 53593
Ph: 608-848-6455 ▪ Fx: 608-848-7675

US National Committee for World Food Day
2175 K St NW   Washington DC 20437
Ph: 202-653-2404 ▪ Fx: 202-653-5760

US National Tennis Academy www.usnta.com
1014 Ferris Ave Suite 1042-E   Waxahachie TX 75165
Ph: 972-937-0311 ▪ Fx: 972-937-0450 ▪ TF: 800-452-8519

US Naval Institute www.usni.org
291 Wood Rd   Annapolis MD 21402
Ph: 410-268-6110 ▪ Fx: 410-269-7940 ▪ TF: 800-233-8764

(US Navy Destroyers) Tin Can Sailors www.destroyers.org
PO Box 100   Somerset MA 02726
Ph: 508-677-0515 ▪ Fx: 508-676-9740 ▪ TF: 800-223-5535

(US Navy) Tailhook Association www.tailhook.org
9696 Businesspark Ave   San Diego CA 92131
Ph: 858-689-9223 ▪ Fx: 858-578-8839 ▪ TF: 800-322-4665

US-New Zealand Council www.usnzcouncil.org
DACOR Bacon House 1801 F St NW   Washington DC 20006
Ph: 202-842-0772 ▪ Fx: 202-842-0749

US Oil & Gas Association
901 F St NW Suite 601   Washington DC 20004
Ph: 202-638-4400 ▪ Fx: 202-638-5967

US Olympic Committee www.olympic-usa.org
1 Olympic Plaza   Colorado Springs CO 80909
Ph: 719-632-5551 ▪ Fx: 719-866-4654 ▪ TF: 888-866-8687

US Optimist Dinghy Association www.usoda.org

US Orienteering Federation www.us.orienteering.org
PO Box 1444   Forest Park GA 30298
Ph: 404-363-2110

US Pacifist Party www.uspacifistparty.org
5729 S Dorchester Ave   Chicago IL 60637
Ph: 773-324-0654 ▪ Fx: 773-324-6426

US Pan Asian American Chamber of Commerce www.uspaacc.com
1329 18th St NW   Washington DC 20036
Ph: 202-296-5221 ▪ Fx: 202-296-5225

US Parachute Association www.uspa.org
1440 Duke St   Alexandria VA 22314
Ph: 703-836-3495 ▪ Fx: 703-836-2843 ▪ TF: 800-371-8772

US Personal Chef Association uspca.com
481 Rio Rancho Blvd NE   Rio Rancho NM 87124
Ph: 505-896-3522 ▪ Fx: 505-994-6399 ▪ TF: 800-995-2138

US Pharmacopeia www.usp.org
12601 Twinbrook Pkwy   Rockville MD 20852
Ph: 301-881-0666 ▪ Fx: 301-816-8525 ▪ TF: 800-877-6209

US Pilots Association www.uspilots.org
483 S Kirkwood Rd Suite 10   Saint Louis MO 63122
Ph: 314-849-8772

US Police Canine Association www.uspcak9.com
PO Box 80   Springboro OH 45066
Ph: 800-531-1614

US Polo Association www.us-polo.org
777 Corporate Dr Suite 505   Lexington KY 40503
Ph: 859-219-1000 ▪ Fx: 859-219-0520 ▪ TF: 800-232-8772

US Pony Clubs www.ponyclub.org
Kentucky Horse Park 4041 Iron Works Pkwy Lexington KY 40511
Ph: 859-254-7669 Fx: 859-233-4652

US Potato Board www.uspotatoes.com
7555 E Hampden Ave Suite 412 Denver CO 80231
Ph: 303-369-7783 Fx: 303-369-7718

US Poultry & Egg Association www.poultryegg.org
1530 Cooledge Rd Tucker GA 30084
Ph: 770-493-9401 Fx: 770-493-9257

US Power Squadrons www.usps.org
PO Box 30423 Raleigh NC 27622
Ph: 919-821-0281 Fx: 888-304-0813 TF: 888-367-8777

US Privacy Council
PO Box 302 Cabin John MD 20818
Ph: 301-229-7002 Fx: 301-229-8011

US Professional Tennis Association www.uspta.org
3535 Briarpark Dr Suite 1 Houston TX 77042
Ph: 713-978-7782 Fx: 713-978-7780 TF: 800-877-8248

US Psychotronics Association www.psychotronics.org
PO Box 45 Elkhorn WI 53121
Ph: 262-742-4790 Fx: 262-742-3670

US Racquet Stringers Association www.racquettech.com
330 Main St Vista CA 92084
Ph: 760-536-1177 Fx: 760-536-1171 TF: 888-900-3545

US Racquetball Association www.usra.org
1685 W Uintah St Colorado Springs CO 80904
Ph: 719-635-5396 Fx: 719-635-0685

US Rice Producers Association www.usriceproducers.com
2900 Wilcrest Dr Suite 180 Houston TX 77042
Ph: 713-974-7423 Fx: 713-974-7696

US Rowing Association www.usrowing.org
201 S Capitol Ave Suite 400 Indianapolis IN 46225
Ph: 317-237-5656 Fx: 317-237-5646 TF: 800-314-4769

US-Russia Business Council www.usrbc.org
1701 Pennsylvania Ave NW Suite 520 Washington DC 20006
Ph: 202-739-9180 Fx: 202-659-5920

US Sailing Association www.ussailing.org
15 Maritime Dr PO Box 1260 Portsmouth RI 02871
Ph: 401-683-0800 Fx: 401-683-0840 TF: 800-877-2451

US-Saudi Arabian Business Council www.us-saudi-business.org
1401 New York Ave NW Suite 720 Washington DC 20005
Ph: 202-638-1212 Fx: 202-638-2894

US Servas Inc www.usservas.org
11 John St Rm 505 New York NY 10038
Ph: 212-267-0252 Fx: 212-267-0292

US Ski & Snowboard Association www.usskiteam.com
PO Box 10045 Park City UT 84060
Ph: 435-649-9090 Fx: 435-649-3613

US Snowshoe Association www.snowshoeracing.com
678 County Rt 25 Corinth NY 12822
Ph: 518-654-7648 Fx: 518-643-8806

US Soccer Federation www.ussoccer.com
1801-1811 S Prairie Ave Chicago IL 60616
Ph: 312-808-1300 Fx: 312-808-1301 TF: 800-759-9636

US Society on Dams www.ussdams.org
1616 17th St Suite 483 Denver CO 80202
Ph: 303-628-5430 Fx: 303-628-5431

US Society for Education Through www.public.asu.edu/~ifmls/ussea/folder/ussea.html
Art Ohio State Univ 1739 N High St 4th Fl Columbus OH 43210
Ph: 614-247-7612

US Specialty Sports Association www.usssa.com
3935 S Crater Rd Petersburg VA 23805
Ph: 804-732-4099 Fx: 804-732-1704 TF: 800-635-0468

US Speedskating www.usspeedskating.org
PO Box 450639 Westlake OH 44145
Ph: 440-899-0128 Fx: 440-899-0109

US Sports Academy www.ussa.edu
1 Academy Dr Daphne AL 36526
Ph: 251-626-3303 Fx: 251-625-1035 TF: 800-223-2668

US Sports Massage Federation
2156 Newport Blvd Costa Mesa CA 92627
Ph: 949-642-0735 Fx: 949-642-1729

US Sportsmen's Alliance www.ussportsmen.org
801 Kingsmill Pkwy Columbus OH 43229
Ph: 614-888-4868 Fx: 614-888-0326

US Squash Racquets Association www.us-squash.org/squash
PO Box 1216 Bala Cynwyd PA 19004
Ph: 610-667-4006 Fx: 610-667-6539

US Student Association www.usstudents.org
1413 K St NW 9th Fl Washington DC 20005
Ph: 202-347-8772 Fx: 202-393-5886 TF: 877-877-2669

US Submarine Veterans of World War II www.ussubvetsofworldwarii.org

US Surveyors Association www.navsurvey.com
13430 McGregor Blvd Fort Myers FL 33919
Ph: 800-245-4425 Fx: 941-481-5150

US Synchronized Swimming www.usasynchro.org
201 S Capitol Ave Suite 901 Indianapolis IN 46225
Ph: 317-237-5700 Fx: 317-237-5705

US Taekwondo Union www.ustu.org
1 Olympic Plaza Suite 104C Colorado Springs CO 80909
Ph: 719-866-4632 Fx: 719-866-4642

US-Taiwan Business Council www.us-taiwan.org
1700 N Moore St Suite 703 Arlington VA 22209
Ph: 703-465-2930 Fx: 703-465-2937

US Telecom Association www.usta.org
1401 H St NW Suite 600 Washington DC 20005
Ph: 202-326-7300 Fx: 202-326-7333

US Tennis Association www.usta.com
70 W Red Oak Ln White Plains NY 10604
Ph: 914-696-7000 Fx: 914-696-7167 TF: 800-990-8782

US Tennis Court & Track Builders Association www.ustctba.com
3525 Ellicott Mills Dr Suite N Ellicott City MD 21043
Ph: 410-418-4875 Fx: 410-418-4805

US Term Limits Foundation www.termlimits.org
10 G St NE Suite 410 Washington DC 20002
Ph: 202-379-3000 Fx: 202-379-3010 TF: 800-733-6440

US-Thailand Business Council www.ustbc.org
3050 K St NW Suite 205 Washington DC 20007
Ph: 202-337-5973 Fx: 202-337-0039

US Tour Operators Association www.ustoa.com
275 Madison Ave Suite 2014 New York NY 10016
Ph: 212-599-6599 Fx: 212-599-6744

US Trade Association, Southern www.susta.org
2 Canal St World Trade Ctr Suite 2515 New Orleans LA 70130
Ph: 504-568-5986 Fx: 504-568-6010

US Trotting Association www.ustrotting.com
750 Michigan Ave Columbus OH 43215
Ph: 614-224-2291 Fx: 614-224-4575 TF: 800-887-8782

US Trout Farmers Association www.ustfa.org
111 W Washington St Suite 1 Charles Town WV 25414
Ph: 304-728-2189 Fx: 304-728-2196

US Tuna Foundation www.ustuna.org
1101 17th St NW Suite 609 Washington DC 20036
Ph: 202-857-0610 Fx: 202-331-9686

US Twirling Association www.ustwirling.org
44 Drexel Dr PO Box 390 Copiague NY 11726
Ph: 631-231-7434 Fx: 208-474-9067

US Ultralight Association www.usua.org
PO Box 667 Frederick MD 21705
Ph: 301-695-9100 Fx: 301-695-0763

US Water Fitness Association www.uswfa.org
PO Box 3279 Boynton Beach FL 33424
Ph: 561-732-9908 Fx: 561-732-0950

US Wheat Associates www.uswheat.org
1620 'I' St NW Suite 801 Washington DC 20006
Ph: 202-463-0999 Fx: 202-785-1052

US Windsurfing Association www.uswindsurfing.org
PO Box 99 Chelsea MI 48118
Ph: 877-386-8708

US Women's Curling Association www.uswca.org
916 9th St S Virginia MN 55792
Ph: 218-741-0253

US Women's Track Coaches Association
7263 Heartcrest Ln Centerville OH 45458
Ph: 937-434-0383

US Youth Soccer Association usysa.org
899 Presidential Dr Suite 117 Richardson TX 75081
Ph: 972-235-4499 Fx: 972-235-4480 TF: 800-476-2237

USA Archery www.usarchery.org
1 Olympic Plaza Colorado Springs CO 80909
Ph: 719-866-4576 Fx: 719-632-4733

USA Badminton www.usabadminton.org
1 Olympic Plaza Colorado Springs CO 80909
Ph: 719-578-4808 Fx: 719-578-4507

USA Baseball www.usabaseball.com
PO Box 1133 Durham NC 27702
Ph: 919-474-8721 Fx: 919-474-8822

USA Basketball www.usabasketball.com
5465 Mark Dabling Blvd Colorado Springs CO 80918
Ph: 719-590-4800 Fx: 719-590-4811

USA Bowling www.bowl.com/bowl/usa
5301 S 76th St Greendale WI 53129
Ph: 800-514-2695

USA Boxing Inc www.usaboxing.org
1 Olympic Plaza Colorado Springs CO 80909
Ph: 719-866-4506 Fx: 719-632-3426

USA Canoe/Kayak www.usacanoekayak.org
230 S Tryon St Suite 220 Charlotte NC 28202
Ph: 704-348-4330 Fx: 704-348-4418

USA-China Chamber of Commerce www.usccc.org
55 W Monroe St Suite 630 Chicago IL 60603
Ph: 312-368-9030 Fx: 312-368-9922

USA Cycling Inc www.usacycling.org
1 Olympic Plaza Colorado Springs CO 80909
Ph: 719-866-4581 Fx: 719-866-4628

USA Deaf Sports Federation www.usadsf.org
102 N Krohn Pl Sioux Falls SD 57103
Ph: 605-367-5760 Fx: 605-367-5958

USA Dry Pea & Lentil Council www.pea-lentil.com
2780 W Pullman Rd Moscow ID 83843
Ph: 208-882-3023 Fx: 208-882-6406

USA Film Festival www.usafilmfestival.com
6116 N Central Expy Suite 105 Dallas TX 75206
Ph: 214-821-6300 Fx: 214-821-6364

USA Gymnastics www.usa-gymnastics.org
201 S Capitol Ave Suite 300 Indianapolis IN 46225
Ph: 317-237-5050 Fx: 317-237-5069 TF: 800-345-4719

USA Hockey www.usahockey.com
1775 Bob Johnson Dr Colorado Springs CO 80906
Ph: 719-576-8724 Fx: 719-538-1160

USA Hockey InLine www.usahockey.com/inline
1775 Bob Johnson Dr Colorado Springs CO 80906
Ph: 719-576-8724 Fx: 719-538-1160

USA Judo Inc www.usjudo.org
1 Olympic Plaza Suite 202 Colorado Springs CO 80909
Ph: 719-866-4730 Fx: 719-866-4733

USA Jump Rope www.usajrf.org

USA Karate Federation www.usakarate.org
1300 Kenmore Blvd   Akron OH 44314
Ph: 330-753-3114 ※ Fx: 330-753-6888

USA Plowing Organization
7660 Burns Rd   Versailles OH 45380
Ph: 937-526-3525 ※ Fx: 937-526-3100

USA Poultry & Egg Export Council www.usapeec.org
2300 W Park Place Blvd Suite 100   Stone Mountain GA 30087
Ph: 770-413-0006 ※ Fx: 770-413-0007

USA Rice Council
9800 Richmond Ave Suite 235   Houston TX 77042
Ph: 713-270-6699 ※ Fx: 713-270-9021

USA Rice Federation www.usarice.com
9800 Richmond Ave Suite 235   Houston TX 77042
Ph: 713-270-6699 ※ Fx: 713-270-9021

USA Rice Millers' Association
4301 N Fairfax Dr Suite 305   Arlington VA 22203
Ph: 703-351-8161 ※ Fx: 703-236-2301

USA Roller Sports www.usarollersports.org
4730 South St   Lincoln NE 68506
Ph: 402-483-7551 ※ Fx: 402-483-1465

USA Rugby www.usarugby.org
3595 E Fountain Blvd   Colorado Springs CO 80910
Ph: 719-637-1022 ※ Fx: 719-637-1315 ※ TF: 800-280-6302

USA Shooting www.usashooting.com
1 Olympic Plaza   Colorado Springs CO 80909
Ph: 719-578-4670

USA Swimming www.usa-swimming.org
1 Olympic Plaza   Colorado Springs CO 80909
Ph: 719-866-4578 ※ Fx: 719-866-4669

USA Table Tennis www.usatt.org
1 Olympic Plaza   Colorado Springs CO 80909
Ph: 719-866-4583 ※ Fx: 719-632-6071

USA Team Handball www.usateamhandball.org
1 Olympic Plaza   Colorado Springs CO 80909
Ph: 719-866-4036 ※ Fx: 719-866-4055

USA Toy Library Association usatla.deltacollege.org
1326 Wilmette Ave   Wilmette IL 60091
Ph: 847-920-9030 ※ Fx: 847-920-9032

USA Track & Field www.usatf.org
1 RCA Dome Suite 140   Indianapolis IN 46225
Ph: 317-261-0500 ※ Fx: 317-261-0481

USA Triathlon www.usatriathlon.org
616 W Monument St   Colorado Springs CO 80904
Ph: 719-597-9090 ※ Fx: 719-597-2121

USA for UNHCR www.usaforunhcr.org
1775 K St NW Suite 290   Washington DC 20006
Ph: 202-296-1115 ※ Fx: 202-296-1081 ※ TF: 800-770-1100

USA Water Polo www.usawaterpolo.com
1685 W Uintah St   Colorado Springs CO 80904
Ph: 719-634-0699 ※ Fx: 719-634-0866

USA Water Ski www.usawaterski.org
1251 Holy Cow Rd   Polk City FL 33868
Ph: 863-324-4341 ※ Fx: 863-325-8259 ※ TF: 800-533-2972

USA Weightlifting www.usaweightlifting.org
1 Olympic Plaza   Colorado Springs CO 80909
Ph: 719-866-4508 ※ Fx: 719-866-4741

USA Wrestling www.usawrestling.org
6155 Lehman Dr   Colorado Springs CO 80918
Ph: 719-598-8181 ※ Fx: 719-598-9440 ※ TF: 800-999-8531

Usability Professionals' Association www.upassoc.org
140 N Bloomingdale Rd   Bloomingdale IL 60108
Ph: 630-980-1997 ※ Fx: 630-351-8490

USBIC Educational Foundation www.usbusiness.com
910 16th St NW Suite 300   Washington DC 20006
Ph: 202-728-1990 ※ Fx: 202-728-1981

Used Equipment Dealers, International Association of www.iaued.org
214 Edgewood Dr Suite 100   Wilmington DE 19809
Ph: 302-765-3571

Used Truck Association www.uta.org
7355 N Woodland Dr   Indianapolis IN 46278
Ph: 800-827-7468

USENIX Association www.usenix.org
2560 9th St Suite 215   Berkeley CA 94710
Ph: 510-528-8649 ※ Fx: 510-548-5738

(User Group) Encompass www.encompassus.org
401 N Michigan Ave 22nd Fl   Chicago IL 60611
Ph: 312-321-5151 ※ Fx: 312-673-4609 ※ TF: 877-354-9887

User Groups, Association of Personal Computer www.apcug.org
3150 Payne Ave Suite 12   Cleveland OH 44114
Ph: 301-423-1618

User Services Association, Reference & www.ala.org/rusa
50 E Huron St   Chicago IL 60611
Ph: 312-280-4398 ※ Fx: 312-944-8085 ※ TF: 800-545-2433

Users Group, International Function Point www.ifpug.org
191 Clarksville Rd   Princeton Junction NJ 08550
Ph: 609-799-4900 ※ Fx: 609-799-7032

Users Group, International Oracle www.ioug.org
401 N Michigan Ave   Chicago IL 60611
Ph: 312-245-1579 ※ Fx: 312-527-6785

Users Group, Regis System
11 Spring St   Hallowell ME 04347
Ph: 207-395-4837

USFN - America's Mortgage Banking Attorneys www.usfn.org
14471 Chambers Rd Suite 260   Tustin CA 92780
Ph: 714-838-7167 ※ Fx: 714-573-2650 ※ TF: 800-635-6128

USS Iowa, Veteran's Association of the www.ussiowa.org

USS Landing Craft Infantry National Association www.usslci.com

USS Liberty Veterans Association www.ussliberty.org/

USS North Carolina Battleship Association www.battleshipnc.com
PO Box 480   Wilmington NC 28402
Ph: 910-251-5797 ※ Fx: 910-251-5807

Utah Pioneers, International Society Daughters of www.dupinternational.org
300 N Main St   Salt Lake City UT 84103
Ph: 801-538-1050 ※ Fx: 801-538-1119

Utilities, Institute of Public www.ipu.msu.edu
Michigan State Univ 240 Nisbet Bldg   East Lansing MI 48823
Ph: 517-355-1876 ※ Fx: 517-355-1854

Utility Allocation Association, National Submetering & www.nsuaa.org
1866 Sheridan Rd Suite 201   Highland Park IL 60035
Ph: 847-681-8475 ※ Fx: 847-681-1869

Utility Commissioners, National Association of Regulatory www.naruc.org
1101 Vermont Ave NW Suite 200   Washington DC 20005
Ph: 202-898-2200 ※ Fx: 202-898-2213

Utility Communicators International www.uci-online.com
5525 E Grandview Dr   Scottsdale AZ 85254
Ph: 602-971-1989 ※ Fx: 602-971-2738

Utility Consumer Advocates, National Association of State www.nasuca.org
8300 Colesville Rd Suite 101   Silver Spring MD 20910
Ph: 301-589-6313 ※ Fx: 301-589-6380

Utility Contractors Association, National www.nuca.com
4301 N Fairfax Dr Suite 360   Arlington VA 22203
Ph: 703-358-9300 ※ Fx: 703-358-9307 ※ TF: 800-662-6822

Utility Professionals, Women's International Network of www.winup.org
PO Box 335   Whites Creek TN 37189
Ph: 615-876-5444

Utility Shareholders Association
52 Woods Rd   Little Falls NJ 07424
Ph: 973-785-1609

Utility Workers Union of America www.uwua.org
815 16th St NW   Washington DC 20006
Ph: 202-974-8200 ※ Fx: 202-974-8201

Utopian Studies, Society for www.utoronto.ca/utopia
Univ of Texas at Arlington English Dept   Arlington TX 76019
Ph: 817-272-2729

UWC - Strategic Services on Unemployment & www.uwcstrategy.org
Workers' Compensation   1331 Pennsylvania Ave NW Suite
600   Washington DC 20004
Ph: 202-637-3464 ※ Fx: 202-783-1616

Uzbekistan Chamber of Commerce, American- www.erols.com/aucc
1800 Massachusetts Ave NW Suite 600   Washington DC 20036
Ph: 202-828-4317 ※ Fx: 202-659-7010

V

VA Physicians & Dentists, National Association of www.navapd.org
11 Canal Ctr Plaza Suite 110   Alexandria VA 22314
Ph: 703-548-0280 ※ Fx: 703-683-7939

VAAD Harabonim of America, American Board of www.angelfire.com/ny2/abor
Rabbis   292 5th Ave 4th Fl   New York NY 10001
Ph: 212-714-3598

Vacation Rental Managers Association www.vrma.com
PO Box 1202   Santa Cruz CA 95061
Ph: 831-426-8762 ※ Fx: 831-458-3637 ※ TF: 800-871-8762

Vaccine Information Center, National www.909shot.com
421-E Church St   Vienna VA 22180
Ph: 703-938-3783 ※ Fx: 703-938-5768 ※ TF: 800-909-7468

Vacuum Coaters, Society of www.svc.org
71 Pinon Hill Pl NE   Albuquerque NM 87122
Ph: 505-856-7188 ※ Fx: 505-856-6716

Vacuum Dealers Trade Association www.vdta.com
2724 2nd Ave   Des Moines IA 50313
Ph: 515-282-9101 ※ Fx: 515-282-4483 ※ TF: 800-367-5651

Vacuum Equipment Manufacturers International, Association of www.avem.org
71 Pinon Hill Pl NE   Albuquerque NM 87122
Ph: 505-856-6924 ※ Fx: 505-856-6716

Vagabundos del Mar Boat & Travel Club www.vagabundos.com
190 Main St   Rio Vista CA 94571
Ph: 707-374-5511 ※ Fx: 707-374-6843 ※ TF: 800-474-2252

Valedictorian Society, National www.valedictorian.org
PO Box 250   Louviers CO 80131
Ph: 303-343-4000 ※ Fx: 303-343-4300

Valentine Collectors' Association, National
PO Box 1404   Santa Ana CA 92702
Ph: 714-547-1355

Valley Forge, Society of the Descendants of www.valleyforgesociety.org
Washington's Army at

Valley Wayne & Gladys Foundation
1939 Harrison St Suite 510   Oakland CA 94612
Ph: 510-466-6060 ※ Fx: 510-466-6067

Valor of the USA, Legion of www.legionofvalor.com
4706 Calle Reina   Santa Barbara CA 93110
Ph: 805-692-2244

Valuation Analysts, National Association of Certified www.nacva.com
1111 E Brickyard Rd Suite 200   Salt Lake City UT 84106
Ph: 801-486-0600 ※ Fx: 801-486-7500 ※ TF: 800-677-2009

Value Foundation, Lawrence Delos Miles www.valuefoundation.org
5505 Connecticut Ave NW Suite 149   Washington DC 20015
Ph: 703-237-2050 ※ Fx: 703-237-2113

Value Inquiry, American Society for
Bergen Community College Humanities Dept 400 Paramus
Rd   Paramus NJ 07652
Ph: 201-447-9282 ※ Fx: 201-612-8225

Values & Philosophy, Council for Research in　　www.crvp.org
PO Box 261 Cardinal Stn　Washington DC 20064
Ph: 202-319-6089

Valve & Fittings Industry Inc, Manufacturers Standardization　　www.mss-hq.com
Society of the　127 Park St NE　Vienna VA 22180
Ph: 703-281-6613 ▪ Fx: 703-281-6671

Valve Manufacturers Association of America　　www.vma.org
1050 17th St NW Suite 280　Washington DC 20036
Ph: 202-331-8105 ▪ Fx: 202-296-0378

Valve Repair Council　　www.vma.org/vrc_homepage.html
1050 17th St NW Suite 280　Washington DC 20036
Ph: 202-331-0104 ▪ Fx: 202-296-0378

Van Alen Institute: Projects in Public Architecture　　www.vanalen.org
30 W 22nd St　New York NY 10010
Ph: 212-924-7000 ▪ Fx: 212-366-5836

Van Andel Education Institute　　www.vai.org/vaei
333 Bostwick NE　Grand Rapids MI 49503
Ph: 616-234-5000 ▪ Fx: 616-234-5001

Van Andel Jay & Betty Foundation　　www.vai.org
333 Bostwick Ave NE　Grand Rapids MI 49503
Ph: 616-234-5000 ▪ Fx: 616-234-5001

Vanished Children's Alliance　　www.vca.org
991 W Hedding St Suite 101　San Jose CA 95126
Ph: 408-296-1113 ▪ Fx: 408-296-1117 ▪ TF: 800-826-4743

Variable Electronic Components Institute　　www.veci-vrci.com
PO Box 1070　Vista CA 92085
Ph: 760-631-0178 ▪ Fx: 760-631-7827

Variable Star Observers, American Association of　　www.aavso.org
25 Birch St　Cambridge MA 02138
Ph: 617-354-0484 ▪ Fx: 617-354-0665 ▪ TF: 800-223-0138

Variety Artists, American Guild of
363 7th Ave 17th Fl　New York NY 10001
Ph: 212-675-1003 ▪ Fx: 212-633-0097

Variety International - The Children's Charity　　www.varietychildrenscharity.com
350 5th Ave Suite 1119　New York NY 10118
Ph: 212-695-3818 ▪ Fx: 212-695-3857

Vasa Order of America　　www.vasaorder.com
　　www.navannet.org

Vascular Access Networks, National Association of
11441 S State St Suite A113　Draper UT 84020
Ph: 801-576-1824 ▪ Fx: 801-553-9137 ▪ TF: 888-576-2826

Vascular & Interventional Radiographers, Association of　　www.avir.org
10201 Lee Hwy Suite 500　Fairfax VA 22030
Ph: 703-691-2350 ▪ Fx: 703-691-8540

Vascular Laboratories, Intersocietal Commission for the　　www.icavl.org
Accreditation of　8840 Stanford Blvd Suite 4900　Columbia
MD 21045
Ph: 410-872-0100 ▪ Fx: 410-872-0030

Vascular Nursing, Society for　　www.svnnet.org
7794 Grow Dr　Pensacola FL 32514
Ph: 888-536-4786 ▪ Fx: 850-484-8762

Vascular Surgery, Society for　　svs.vascularweb.org
900 Cummings Ctr Suite 221-U　Beverly MA 01915
Ph: 978-526-8330 ▪ Fx: 978-526-4018

Vascular Surgery, Society for Clinical　　scvs.vascularweb.org
900 Cummings Ctr Suite 221-U　Beverly MA 01915
Ph: 978-927-8330 ▪ Fx: 978-927-4018

Vascular Ultrasound, Society for　　www.svunet.org
4601 Presidents Dr Suite 260　Lanham MD 20706
Ph: 301-459-7550 ▪ Fx: 301-459-5651 ▪ TF: 800-788-8346

Vatican Library, American Friends of the
581 E 14 Mile Rd　Clawson MI 48017
Ph: 248-588-1222

Vault Association, National Concrete Burial　　ncbva.org
900 Fox Valley Dr Suite 204　Longwood FL 32779
Ph: 407-788-1996 ▪ Fx: 407-774-6751 ▪ TF: 800-538-1423

Vault Technicians Association, Safe &　　www.savta.org
3003 Live Oak St　Dallas TX 75204
Ph: 214-827-7233 ▪ Fx: 214-827-1810

Vaulting Association, American　　www.americanvaulting.org
642 Alford Pl NW　Bainbridge Island WA 98110
Ph: 206-780-9353 ▪ Fx: 206-780-9355

VD Awareness, Citizens Alliance for
800 W Central Rd Suite 128　Mount Prospect IL 60056
Ph: 847-398-3378 ▪ Fx: 847-398-7309

Vector Ecology, Society for　　www.sove.org/
1966 Compton Ave　Corona CA 92881
Ph: 909-340-9792 ▪ Fx: 909-340-2515

Vedic Astrology, American Council of　　www.vedicastrology.org/
PO Box 2149　Sedona AZ 86339
Ph: 928-282-6595 ▪ Fx: 928-282-6097 ▪ TF: 800-900-6595

Vegan Action　　www.vegan.org
PO Box 4288　Richmond VA 23220
Ph: 804-502-8736

Vegan Society, American　　www.americanvegan.org
56 Dinshah Ln PO Box 369　Malaga NJ 08328
Ph: 856-694-2887 ▪ Fx: 856-694-2288

Vegetable Association, United Fresh Fruit &　　www.uffva.org
1901 Pennsylvania Ave NW Suite 1100　Washington DC 20006
Ph: 202-303-3400 ▪ Fx: 202-303-3433

Vegetarian Resource Group　　www.vrg.org
PO Box 1463　Baltimore MD 21203
Ph: 410-366-8343 ▪ Fx: 410-366-8804

Vegetarian Society, North American　　www.navs-online.org
PO Box 72　Dolgeville NY 13329
Ph: 518-568-7970 ▪ Fx: 518-568-7979

Vegetarians of North America, Jewish　　www.jewishveg.com

Vegetation Management Association, National Roadside　　www.nrvma.org
6402 Betty Cook Dr　Austin TX 78723
Ph: 512-933-9930 ▪ Fx: 512-933-9971

Vehicle Association, Human Powered　　www.ihpva.org/hpva
PO Box 1307　San Luis Obispo CA 93406
Ph: 805-772-5888 ▪ Fx: 805-545-9005

Vehicle Club, Holiday Rambler Recreational　　www.hrrvc.org
PO Box 587　Wakarusa IN 46573
Ph: 574-862-7330 ▪ Fx: 574-862-7390 ▪ TF: 877-702-5415

Vehicle Coalition, Natural Gas　　www.ngvc.org
400 N Capitol St NW　Washington DC 20001
Ph: 202-824-7360 ▪ Fx: 202-824-7367

Vehicle Conservation Council Inc, National Off-Highway　　www.nohvcc.org
4718 S Taylor Dr　Sheboygan WI 53081
Ph: 800-348-6487 ▪ Fx: 920-458-3446

Vehicle Institute of America, Specialty　　www.atvsafety.org
2 Jenner St Suite 150　Irvine CA 92618
Ph: 949-727-3727 ▪ Fx: 949-727-4216 ▪ TF: 800-887-2887

Vehicle Leasing Association, National　　www.nvla.org
1900 Arch St　Philadelphia PA 19103
Ph: 215-564-3484 ▪ Fx: 215-963-9785

Vehicle Network, Alternative Fuel
11621 San Antonio Dr NE　Albuquerque NM 87122
Ph: 505-856-8585 ▪ Fx: 505-856-5904

Vehicle Preservation Association, Military　　www.mvpa.org
PO Box 520378　Independence MO 64052
Ph: 816-833-6872 ▪ Fx: 816-833-5115

Vehicle Preservation, International Society for
PO Box 50046　Tucson AZ 85703
Ph: 520-622-2201 ▪ Fx: 520-792-8501

Vehicle Safety Alliance, Commercial　　www.cvsa.org
1101 17th St NW Suite 803　Washington DC 20036
Ph: 202-775-1623 ▪ Fx: 202-775-1624

Vehicle Safety Institute, All-Terrain　　www.atvsafety.org
2 Jenner St Suite 150　Irvine CA 92618
Ph: 949-727-3727 ▪ Fx: 949-786-3323 ▪ TF: 800-887-2887

Vehicle Systems International, Association for Unmanned　　www.auvsi.org
3401 Columbia Pike Suite 400　Arlington VA 22204
Ph: 703-920-2720 ▪ Fx: 703-920-2889

(Vehicles) COVA/CVAG Inc　　www.covacvag.org
PO Box 2136　West Paterson NJ 07424
Ph: 973-881-8838 ▪ Fx: 973-279-3779

Vehicular Technology Society, IEEE　　www.vtsociety.org
IEEE Operations Ctr 445 Hoes Ln　Piscataway NJ 08854
Ph: 732-981-0060 ▪ Fx: 732-981-1721

Velasquez Willie Institute　　www.wcvi.org
206 Lombard St 1st Fl　San Antonio TX 78226
Ph: 210-922-3118 ▪ Fx: 210-932-4055

Venceremos Brigade　　www.venceremosbrigade.org
PO Box 5202　Englewood NJ 07631
Ph: 212-560-4360

Veneer Association, Hardwood Plywood &　　www.hpva.org
PO Box 2789　Reston VA 20195
Ph: 703-435-2900 ▪ Fx: 703-435-2537

Venezuelan-American Association of the US
30 Vesey St Suite 506　New York NY 10007
Ph: 212-233-7776 ▪ Fx: 212-233-7779

Venezuelan-American Chamber of Commerce　　venezuelanchamber.org
2332 Galiano St　Coral Gables FL 33134
Ph: 305-728-7042 ▪ Fx: 305-728-7043

Venous Forum, American　　www.venous-info.com
900 Cummings Ctr Suite 221-U　Beverly MA 01915
Ph: 978-526-8330 ▪ Fx: 978-526-4018

Ventilating Institute, Home　　www.hvi.org
30 W University Dr　Arlington Heights IL 60004
Ph: 847-394-0150 ▪ Fx: 847-253-0088

Ventriloquists, North American Association of　　www.maherstudios.com
PO Box 420　Littleton CO 80160
Ph: 800-250-5125 ▪ Fx: 720-344-2907

Venture Capital Alliance, Community Development　　www.cdvca.org
330 7th Ave 19th Fl　New York NY 10001
Ph: 212-594-6747 ▪ Fx: 212-594-6717

Venture Capital Association, National　　www.nvca.org
1655 N Fort Myer Dr Suite 850　Arlington VA 22209
Ph: 703-524-2549 ▪ Fx: 703-524-3940

Venture PAC
1655 N Fort Myer Dr Suite 850　Arlington VA 22209
Ph: 703-524-2549 ▪ Fx: 703-524-3940

Vera Institute of Justice　　www.vera.org
233 Broadway 12th Fl　New York NY 10279
Ph: 212-334-1300 ▪ Fx: 212-941-9407

Verbatim Reporters Association, National　　www.nvra.org
207 3rd Ave　Hattiesburg MS 39401
Ph: 601-582-4345 ▪ Fx: 601-582-3354

Verdi Studies, American Institute for　　www.nyu.edu/projects/verdi
New York Univ Music Dept 24 Waverly Pl Rm 268　New York
NY 10003
Ph: 212-998-2587 ▪ Fx: 212-995-4147

Vermont Maple Industry Council
655 Spear St　Burlington VT 05405
Ph: 802-656-5433 ▪ Fx: 802-656-5422

Vertical Transportation Professionals, National Association of　　www.navtp.org
PO Box 636 Bowie　Bowie MD 20718
Ph: 301-262-3150 ▪ Fx: 301-262-3194

Vessel Operators Hazardous Materials Association, International　　www.vohma.com
1118 Bay Rd　Lake George NY 12845
Ph: 518-761-0263 ▪ Fx: 518-792-7781

Veteran Motor Car Club of America　　www.vmcca.org
4441 W Altadena Ave　Glendale AZ 85304
Ph: 800-428-7327

Veteran Railway Employees, National Association of Retired &　　www.narvre.com
300 Cedar Blvd Suite 201A　Pittsburgh PA 15228
Ph: 412-563-5611 ▪ Fx: 412-563-5612

Veterans of the Abraham Lincoln Brigade — www.alba-valb.org
799 Broadway Rm 227   New York NY 10003
Ph: 212-674-5552

Veterans Affairs, National Association of State Directors of — www.nasdva.com

Veterans Affairs, Nurses Organization of — www.vanurse.org
1726 M St NW Suite 1101   Washington DC 20036
Ph: 202-296-0888 ▪ Fx: 202-833-1577

Veterans of America Foundation, Vietnam — www.vvaf.org
1725 'I' St NW 4th Fl   Washington DC 20006
Ph: 202-483-9222 ▪ Fx: 202-483-9312

Veterans of America, Paralyzed — www.pva.org
801 18th St NW   Washington DC 20006
Ph: 202-872-1300 ▪ Fx: 202-416-7641 ▪ TF: 800-424-8200

Veterans of America, Vietnam — www.vva.org
8605 Cameron St Suite 400   Silver Spring MD 20910
Ph: 301-585-4000 ▪ Fx: 301-585-0519 ▪ TF: 800-882-1316

(Veterans) American Legion — www.legion.org
700 N Pennsylvania St   Indianapolis IN 46204
Ph: 317-630-1200 ▪ Fx: 317-630-1223 ▪ TF: 800-433-3318

(Veterans) AMVETS — www.amvets.org
4647 Forbes Blvd   Lanham MD 20706
Ph: 301-459-9600 ▪ Fx: 301-459-7924 ▪ TF: 877-726-8387

(Veterans) Army & Navy Union USA — www.armynavy.net
2002 Tallmadge Ave   Kent OH 44240
Ph: 330-343-9015

Veterans Association, Bay of Pigs
1821 SW 9th St   Miami FL 33135
Ph: 305-649-4719 ▪ Fx: 305-649-9769

Veterans Association, China-Burma-India
PO Box 780676   Orlando FL 32878
Ph: 407-282-0346

Veterans Association, Korean War — www.kwva.org
PO Box 10806   Arlington VA 22210
Ph: 703-522-9629

Veterans Association, SHAEF/ETOUSA — www.shaef.org
2301 Broadway   San Francisco CA 94115
Ph: 415-921-8322

Veteran's Association of the USS Iowa — www.ussiowa.org

Veterans Association, USS Liberty — www.ussliberty.org/

Veterans' Association, Women's Army Corps — www.armywomen.org

Veterans Auxiliary, Catholic War — www.cwv.org/laux/laux.htm
441 N Lee St   Alexandria VA 22314
Ph: 703-549-3622 ▪ Fx: 703-684-5196

Veterans Auxiliary, Disabled American — www.dav.org/dava
3725 Alexandria Pike   Cold Spring KY 41076
Ph: 859-441-7300 ▪ Fx: 859-442-2095

Veterans of the Battle of the Bulge — www.tfl.net/bulge.html
PO Box 11129   Arlington VA 22210
Ph: 703-528-4058

Veterans of the Civil War, Auxiliary to Sons of Union
2449 Center Ave   Alliance OH 44601
Ph: 330-823-6919

Veterans, Disabled American — www.dav.org
3725 Alexandria Pike   Cold Spring KY 41076
Ph: 859-441-7300 ▪ Fx: 859-441-1416 ▪ TF: 877-426-2838

Veterans that Enlisted Underage, American — www.avteu.org
100 Village Ln   Philadelphia PA 19154
Ph: 215-632-2332 ▪ Fx: 215-637-9566 ▪ TF: 800-595-1006

Veterans of Foreign Wars of the US — www.vfw.com
406 W 34th St   Kansas City MO 64111
Ph: 816-756-3390 ▪ Fx: 816-968-1149

(Veterans) Forty & Eight — fortyandeight.org
777 N Meridian St Rm 204   Indianapolis IN 46204
Ph: 317-634-1804 ▪ Fx: 317-632-9365

Veterans, Friends of Israel Disabled — fidv-bh.com
419 Park Ave S Suite 905   New York NY 10016
Ph: 212-689-3220 ▪ Fx: 212-689-3236 ▪ TF: 800-648-2125

Veterans of Israel, American
136 E 39th St   New York NY 10016
Ph: 631-499-4327

Veterans Link, Bowlers to — www.bowlforveterans.org
PO Box 2289   Rockville MD 20847
Ph: 301-881-8333 ▪ Fx: 301-881-4042

Veterans Medical Airlift Service, American
931 Flanders Rd PO Box 1065   La Canada Flintridge CA 91011
Ph: 818-952-6212

Veterans Memorial Foundation Inc, Rainbow Division — www.rainbowvets.org
16916 George Franklyn Dr   Independence MO 64055
Ph: 816-373-5041

Veterans Memorial Fund, Vietnam — www.vvmf.org
1023 15th St NW 2nd Fl   Washington DC 20005
Ph: 202-393-0090 ▪ Fx: 202-393-0029

Veterans, National Coalition for Homeless — www.nchv.org
333 1/2 Pennsylvania Ave SE   Washington DC 20003
Ph: 202-546-1969 ▪ Fx: 202-546-2063 ▪ TF: 800-838-4357

Veterans Organization of America, National — www.nvo.org/
7700 Alabama St PO Box 640064   El Paso TX 79904
Ph: 915-759-8387 ▪ Fx: 915-587-3028

Veterans for Peace Inc — www.veteransforpeace.org
438 N Skinker Blvd   Saint Louis MO 63130
Ph: 314-725-6005

Veterans Program Administrators, National Association of — www.navpa.org

Veterans' Research & Education Foundations, National Association of   5018 Sangamore Rd Suite 300   Bethesda MD 20816 — www.navref.org
Ph: 301-229-1048 ▪ Fx: 301-229-0442

Veterans of Safety — www.veteransofsafety.org
Central Missouri State Univ Safety Ctr Humphreys Bldg Rm 201   Warrensburg MO 64093
Ph: 660-543-4281 ▪ Fx: 660-543-4482

Veterans for Social Justice Inc, Black — www.bvsj.org
665 Willoughby Ave   Brooklyn NY 11221
Ph: 718-852-6004 ▪ Fx: 718-852-4805

Veterans, Sons of Confederate — www.scv.org
PO Box 59   Columbia TN 38402
Ph: 800-380-1896 ▪ Fx: 931-381-6712

Veterans, Sons of Spanish American War — www.spanamwar.com/SSAWV.htm
32028 Mt Vernon   Rockwood MI 48173
Ph: 734-379-4996

Veterans of the USA, Catholic War — www.cwv.org
441 N Lee St   Alexandria VA 22314
Ph: 703-549-3622 ▪ Fx: 703-684-5196

Veterans of the USA, Jewish War — www.jwv.org
1811 R St NW   Washington DC 20009
Ph: 202-265-6280 ▪ Fx: 202-234-5662

Veterans of the USA - National Ladies Auxiliary, Jewish War
1811 R St NW   Washington DC 20009
Ph: 202-667-9061 ▪ Fx: 202-667-6689

Veterans of the Vietnam War Inc — www.vvnw.org
805 S Township Blvd   Pittston PA 18640
Ph: 570-603-9740 ▪ Fx: 570-603-9741 ▪ TF: 800-843-8626

Veterans of World War II, US Submarine — www.ussubvetsofworldwarii.org

Veterinarians, American Association of Industrial
PO Box 488   Oskaloosa KS 66066
Ph: 785-863-2389 ▪ Fx: 785-863-3141

Veterinarians, American Association of Swine — www.aasv.org
902 1st Ave   Perry IA 50220
Ph: 515-465-5255 ▪ Fx: 515-465-3832

Veterinarians, American Association of Zoo — www.aazv.org
6 N Pennell Rd   Media PA 19063
Ph: 610-892-4812 ▪ Fx: 610-892-4813

Veterinarians for Animal Rights, Association of — avar.org
PO Box 208   Davis CA 95617
Ph: 530-759-8106 ▪ Fx: 530-759-8116

Veterinarians, Association of Avian — www.aav.org
PO Box 811720   Boca Raton FL 33481
Ph: 561-393-8901 ▪ Fx: 561-393-8902

Veterinarians Association, Flying
101 Bingham Rd   Columbia MO 65203
Ph: 573-449-4497

Veterinarians, National Association of Federal — users.erols.com/nafv
1101 Vermont Ave NW Suite 710   Washington DC 20005
Ph: 202-289-6334 ▪ Fx: 202-842-4360

Veterinary Acupuncture Society, International — www.ivas.org
PO Box 271395   Fort Collins CO 80527
Ph: 970-266-0666 ▪ Fx: 970-266-0777

Veterinary Allergy & Clinical Immunology, Academy of — www.avaci.org
330 Waukegan Rd   Glenview IL 60025
Ph: 847-729-5200 ▪ Fx: 847-729-5214

(Veterinary) American Association of Small Ruminant Practitioners — www.aasrp.org
1910 Lyda Ave Suite 200   Bowling Green KY 42104
Ph: 270-793-0781 ▪ Fx: 270-782-0188

Veterinary Cancer Society — www.vetcancersociety.org
PO Box 1763   Spring Valley CA 91979
Ph: 619-474-8929 ▪ Fx: 619-474-8947

Veterinary Clinicians, American Association of — www.craiggroup.com/aavc.htm
37 W Broad St Suite 480   Columbus OH 43215
Ph: 614-358-0417 ▪ Fx: 614-241-2215

Veterinary & Comparative Toxicology, American Academy of
Murray State Univ Breathitt Veterinary Ctr 715 North Dr PO Box 2000   Hopkinsville KY 42240
Ph: 270-886-3959 ▪ Fx: 270-886-4295

Veterinary Dental Society, American — www.avds-online.org
618 Church St Suite 220   Nashville TN 37219
Ph: 800-332-2837 ▪ Fx: 615-254-7047

Veterinary Dermatology, American College of — www.acvd.org
5610 Kearny Mesa Rd Suite B   San Diego CA 92111
Ph: 858-560-9393 ▪ Fx: 858-560-0206

Veterinary Distributors Association, American — www.avda.net
2105 Laurel Bush Rd Suite 200   Bel Air MD 21015
Ph: 443-640-1040 ▪ Fx: 443-640-1031

Veterinary Exhibitors Association, American
712 N Broadway   Menominee WI 54751
Ph: 715-231-6312 ▪ Fx: 715-232-9936

Veterinary Homeopathy, Academy of — www.theavh.org
PO Box 9280   Wilmington DE 19809
Ph: 866-652-1590

Veterinary Hospital Managers Association Inc — www.vhma.org
48 Howard St   Albany NY 12207
Ph: 518-433-8911 ▪ Fx: 518-463-8656

Veterinary Immunologists, American Association of — www.cvm.missouri.edu/aavi

Veterinary Internal Medicine, American College of — www.acvim.org
1997 Wadsworth Blvd Suite A   Lakewood CO 80214
Ph: 303-231-9933 ▪ Fx: 303-231-0880 ▪ TF: 800-245-9081

Veterinary Medical Association, American — www.avma.org
1931 N Meacham Rd Suite 100   Schaumburg IL 60173
Ph: 847-925-8070 ▪ Fx: 847-925-1329

Veterinary Medical Association, American Holistic — www.ahvma.org
2218 Old Emmorton Rd   Bel Air MD 21015
Ph: 410-569-0795 ▪ Fx: 410-569-2346

Veterinary Medical Association, Canadian — www.cvma-acmv.org
339 Booth St   Ottawa ON K1R7K1
Ph: 613-236-1162 ▪ Fx: 613-236-9681

Veterinary Medical Colleges, Association of American — www.aavmc.org
1101 Vermont Ave NW Suite 710   Washington DC 20005
Ph: 202-371-9195 ▪ Fx: 202-842-0773

(Veterinary) Omega Tau Sigma   www.cvm.uiuc.edu/ots
9947 E Bloomfield Hills Dr   Effingham IL 62401
Ph: 217-868-5095

Veterinary Ophthalmologists, American College of   www.acvo.com
PO Box 1311   Meridian ID 83680
Ph: 208-466-7624 ▪ Fx: 208-466-7693

Veterinary Orthopedic Society   www.vet.ohio-state.edu/docs/vos
PO Box 313   Newmarket NH 03857
Ph: 603-659-7989

Veterinary Parasitologists, American Association of   www.aavp.org
2001 W Main St MS GL52 PO Box 708   Greenfield IN 46140
Ph: 317-277-4439 ▪ Fx: 317-651-4532

Veterinary Pathologists, American College of   www.acvp.org
7600 Terrace Ave Suite 203   Middleton WI 53562
Ph: 608-833-8725 ▪ Fx: 608-831-5122

Veterinary Pharmacology & Therapeutics, American Academy of   www.aavpt.org
621 W Hill St   Champaign IL 61820
Ph: 217-359-0661 ▪ Fx: 217-244-1652

Veterinary Practitioners Inc, American Board of   www.abvp.com
618 Church St Suite 220   Nashville TN 37219
Ph: 615-254-3687 ▪ Fx: 615-254-7047

Veterinary Radiology, American College of   www.acvr.ucdavis.edu
777 E Park Dr PO Box 8820   Harrisburg PA 17105
Ph: 717-558-7865 ▪ Fx: 717-558-7841

Veterinary State Boards, American Association of   www.aavsb.org
4106 Central St   Kansas City MO 64111
Ph: 816-931-1504 ▪ Fx: 816-931-1604 ▪ TF: 877-698-8482

Veterinary Surgeons, American College of   www.acvs.org
4401 East-West Hwy Suite 205   Bethesda MD 20814
Ph: 301-913-9550 ▪ Fx: 301-913-2034

Vexillological Association, North American   www.nava.org

VFW, Ladies Auxiliary   www.ladiesauxvfw.com
406 W 34th St   Kansas City MO 64111
Ph: 816-561-8655 ▪ Fx: 816-931-4753

VHL Family Alliance   www.vhl.org
171 Clinton Rd   Brookline MA 02445
Ph: 617-277-5667 ▪ Fx: 617-734-8233 ▪ TF: 800-767-4845

VIA   www.viaprograms.org
PO Box 20266   Stanford CA 94309
Ph: 650-723-3228 ▪ Fx: 650-725-1805

Viatical & Life Settlement Association of America   www.viatical.org
800 Mayfair Cir   Orlando FL 32803
Ph: 407-894-3797 ▪ Fx: 407-897-1325 ▪ TF: 800-842-9811

Vibration Institute   www.vibinst.org/vabout.htm
6262 S Kingery Hwy Suite 212   Willowbrook IL 60527
Ph: 630-654-2254 ▪ Fx: 630-654-2271

Victim Assistance, National Organization for   www.try-nova.org
1730 Park Rd NW   Washington DC 20010
Ph: 202-232-6682 ▪ Fx: 202-462-2255 ▪ TF: 800-879-6682

Victim Compensation Boards, National Association of Crime   www.nacvcb.org
PO Box 16003   Alexandria VA 22302
Ph: 703-313-9500

Victims of Choice Inc   www.victimsofchoice.com
PO Box 815   Naperville IL 60566
Ph: 630-378-1680 ▪ Fx: 630-759-5030 ▪ TF: 888-267-3998

Victims of Crime, National Center for   www.ncvc.org
2000 M St NW Suite 480   Washington DC 20036
Ph: 202-467-8700 ▪ Fx: 202-467-8701 ▪ TF: 800-394-2255

Victims of Predatory Abduction, Jimmy Ryce Center for   www.jimmyryce.org
5050 Collins Ave Suite 1036   Miami Beach FL 33140
Ph: 305-864-1344 ▪ Fx: 305-864-4161 ▪ TF: 800-546-7923

Victorian Periodicals, Research Society for   www.aztecfreenet.org/rsvp/
Univ of South Florida FA 0209   Tampa FL 33620
Ph: 813-974-3365 ▪ Fx: 813-974-0810

Victorian Society in America   www.victoriansociety.org
205 S Camac St   Philadelphia PA 19107
Ph: 215-545-8340 ▪ Fx: 215-545-8379

Video Arts, Film/   www.fva.com
462 Broadway Suite 520   New York NY 10013
Ph: 212-941-8787 ▪ Fx: 212-219-8924

Video Association, United Catholic Music &   www.ucmva.com
PO Box 230   Donnellson IA 52625
Ph: 319-835-9340 ▪ Fx: 319-835-9071 ▪ TF: 877-668-2682

Video Electronics Standards Association   www.vesa.org
920 Hillview Ct Suite 140   Milpitas CA 95035
Ph: 408-957-9270

Video & Filmmakers, Association of Independent   www.aivf.org
304 Hudson St 6th Fl   New York NY 10013
Ph: 212-807-1400 ▪ Fx: 212-463-8519

Video Foundation, University Film &   www.ufva.org
Univ of Illinois Press 1325 S Oak St   Champaign IL 61820
Ph: 217-244-0626 ▪ Fx: 217-244-9910 ▪ TF: 866-244-0626

Video Laboratories, Association of Cinema &   www.acvl.org

Video Preservation, National Center for Film &
c/o American Film Institute 2021 N Western Ave   Los Angeles CA 90027
Ph: 323-856-7708 ▪ Fx: 323-586-7616

Video Software Dealers Association   www.vsda.org
16530 Ventura Blvd Suite 400   Encino CA 91436
Ph: 818-385-1500 ▪ Fx: 818-385-0567 ▪ TF: 800-955-8732

Video, Women in Film &   www.wifv.org
1919 M St NW Suite 225   Washington DC 20036
Ph: 202-429-9438 ▪ Fx: 202-429-9440

Videographers Association International, Wedding & Event   www.weva.com
8499 S Tamiami Trail PMB 208   Sarasota FL 34238
Ph: 941-923-5334 ▪ Fx: 941-921-3836

Vietnam Charities   www.vietnamcharities.org
2476 Bolsover St Suite 214   Houston TX 77005
Ph: 713-661-6506 ▪ Fx: 713-349-8366

(Vietnam) East Meets West Foundation   www.eastmeetswest.org
PO Box 29292   Oakland CA 94604
Ph: 510-763-7045 ▪ Fx: 510-763-6545

Vietnam Helicopter Pilots Association   www.vhpa.org
5530 Birdcage St Suite 200   Citrus Heights CA 95610
Ph: 916-966-7592 ▪ Fx: 916-966-8743 ▪ TF: 800-505-8472

Vietnam Human Rights Network   www.vnhrnet.org
4745 El Cajon Blvd Suite 104   San Diego CA 92115
Ph: 619-284-5111 ▪ Fx: 619-284-5115

Vietnam Veterans of America   www.vva.org
8605 Cameron St Suite 400   Silver Spring MD 20910
Ph: 301-585-4000 ▪ Fx: 301-585-0519 ▪ TF: 800-882-1316

Vietnam Veterans of America Foundation   www.vvaf.org
1725 'I' St NW 4th Fl   Washington DC 20006
Ph: 202-483-9222 ▪ Fx: 202-483-9312

Vietnam Veterans Memorial Fund   www.vvmf.org
1023 15th St NW 2nd Fl   Washington DC 20005
Ph: 202-393-0090 ▪ Fx: 202-393-0029

Vietnam War Inc, Veterans of the   www.vvnw.org
805 S Township Blvd   Pittston PA 18640
Ph: 570-603-9740 ▪ Fx: 570-603-9741 ▪ TF: 800-843-8626

Vietnamese-American Chamber of Commerce of Hawaii   www.vacch.org
PO Box 2011   Honolulu HI 96805
Ph: 808-545-1889 ▪ Fx: 808-734-2315

Vietnamese-American Professionals Alliance   www.vapaonline.org
PO Box 70804   Sunnyvale CA 94086
Ph: 877-705-6671

Vietnamese Music, International Association for Research in
2005 Willow Ridge Cir   Kent OH 44240
Ph: 330-673-3763 ▪ Fx: 330-673-4434

Vikings, Independent Order of   www.iovikings.org
5250 S 6th St PO Box 5147   Springfield IL 62705
Ph: 877-241-6006 ▪ Fx: 217-241-6578

Villa-Lobos Music Society   www.rdpl.red-deer.ab.ca/villa/society.html
153 E 92nd St Unit 4R   New York NY 10128
Ph: 212-427-5103

Village Earth - Consortium for Sustainable Village-Based Development   PO Box 797   Fort Collins CO 80522   www.villageearth.org
Ph: 970-491-5754 ▪ Fx: 970-491-2729 ▪ TF: 800-648-8043

Vine, Brotherhood of the Knights of the   www.kov.org
2210 Northpoint Pkwy   Santa Rosa CA 95407
Ph: 707-579-3781 ▪ Fx: 707-579-3996

Vineyard Foundation, American   www.avf.org
PO Box 5779   Napa CA 94581
Ph: 707-252-6911

Vinifera Wine Growers Association
PO Box 10045   Alexandria VA 22310
Ph: 703-922-7049 ▪ Fx: 703-922-0617

Vintage BMW Motorcycle Owners Ltd   www.vintagebmw.org
PO Box 67   Exeter NH 03833
Ph: 603-772-9799

Vintage Chevrolet Club of America   www.vcca.org
PO Box 5387   Orange CA 92863
Ph: 714-633-1310

Vintage Fashion & Costume Jewelry Club   www.lizjewel.com/vf
PO Box 265   Glen Oaks NY 11004
Ph: 718-939-3095 ▪ Fx: 718-939-7988

Vintage Racing Association, Sportscar   www.svra.com
257 Dekalb Industrial Way   Decatur GA 30030
Ph: 404-298-3323 ▪ Fx: 404-298-3325

Vintage Sailplane Association   www.vintagesailplane.org

Vintage Thunderbird Club International   www.vintagethunderbirdclub.org

Vintners Association, American   www.americanwineries.org
1200 G St NW Suite 360   Washington DC 20005
Ph: 202-783-2756 ▪ Fx: 202-347-6341 ▪ TF: 800-879-4537

Vintners Association, Napa Valley   www.napavintners.com
PO Box 141   Saint Helena CA 94574
Ph: 707-963-3388 ▪ Fx: 707-963-3488 ▪ TF: 800-982-1371

Vintners & Growers Association, Monterey County   www.montereywines.org
Box 1793   Monterey CA 93942
Ph: 831-375-9400 ▪ Fx: 831-375-1116

Vinyl Acetate Council   www.vinylacetate.org
1250 Connecticut Ave NW Suite 700   Washington DC 20036
Ph: 202-637-9040 ▪ Fx: 202-637-9178

Vinyl Institute   www.vinylinfo.org
1300 Wilson Blvd   Arlington VA 22209
Ph: 703-741-5670 ▪ Fx: 703-741-5672

Vinyl Siding Institute   www.vinylsiding.org
1801 K St NW Suite 600K   Washington DC 20006
Ph: 202-974-5200 ▪ Fx: 202-296-7005 ▪ TF: 888-367-8741

Viola da Gamba Society of America   www.vdgsa.org

Viola Society, American   www.americanviolasociety.org
13140 Coit Rd Suite 320 LB 120   Dallas TX 75240
Ph: 972-233-9107 ▪ Fx: 972-490-4219

Violence in Education, Parents & Teachers Against   www.nospank.net
PO Box 1033   Alamo CA 94507
Ph: 925-831-1661 ▪ Fx: 925-838-8914

Violence-Free Society, Physicians for a   www.pvs.org
160 14th St   San Francisco CA 94103
Ph: 415-621-3582 ▪ Fx: 415-621-3438

Violence Hotline, National Domestic   www.ndvh.org
PO Box 161810   Austin TX 78716
Ph: 800-799-7233

Violence, National Coalition Against Domestic   www.ncadv.org
1201 E Colfax Ave Suite 385   Denver CO 80218
Ph: 303-839-1852 ▪ Fx: 303-831-9251 ▪ TF: 800-799-7233

Violence, National Resource Center on Domestic   www.nrcdv.org
6400 Flank Dr Suite 1300   Harrisburg PA 17112
Ph: 717-545-6400 ▪ Fx: 717-545-9456 ▪ TF: 800-537-2238

Violence Prevention Fund, Family endabuse.org
383 Rhode Island St Suite 304   San Francisco CA 94103
Ph: 415-252-8900 ▪ Fx: 415-252-8991 ▪ TF: 888-792-2873

Violet Society of America, African www.avsa.org
2375 North St   Beaumont TX 77702
Ph: 409-839-4725 ▪ Fx: 409-839-4329 ▪ TF: 800-770-2872

Violin Society of America www.vsa.to
48 Academy St   Poughkeepsie NY 12601
Ph: 845-542-7557

VIP Mentoring www.vipmentoring.org
220 Bagley St 1020 Michigan Bldg   Detroit MI 48226
Ph: 313-964-1110 ▪ Fx: 313-964-1145

Vira I Heinz Endowment www.heinz.org
625 Liberty Ave 30 Dominion Tower   Pittsburgh PA 15222
Ph: 412-281-5777 ▪ Fx: 412-281-5788

Virginia, Memorial Foundation of Germanna Colonies in www.germanna.org
PO Box 279   Locust Grove VA 22508
Ph: 540-423-1700 ▪ Fx: 540-423-1747

Virginia Woolf Society, International www.utoronto.ca/IVWS
Southern Connecticut State Univ Dept of English 501 Crescent
St   New Haven CT 06515
Ph: 203-392-6717 ▪ Fx: 203-392-6731

Virology, American Society for www.mcw.edu/asv

(Virtual Activism) NetAction www.netaction.org
PO Box 6739   Santa Barbara CA 93160
Ph: 415-215-9392

Virtual Assistants Association, International www.ivaa.org/
11024 Balboa Blvd Suite 315   Los Angeles CA 91344
Ph: 877-440-2750

Virtual Education Foundation, Paul G Allen www.pgafoundations.com/edu.asp
505 5th Ave S Suite 900   Seattle WA 98104
Ph: 206-342-2000 ▪ Fx: 206-342-3000

Vision, 20/20 www.2020vision.org
1828 Jefferson Pl NW   Washington DC 20036
Ph: 202-833-2020 ▪ Fx: 202-833-5307 ▪ TF: 800-669-1782

(Vision) Achromatopsia Network www.achromat.org
PO Box 214   Berkeley CA 94701
Ph: 510-540-4700 ▪ Fx: 510-540-4767

Vision Council of America www.visionsite.org
1700 Diagonal Rd Suite 500   Alexandria VA 22314
Ph: 703-548-4560 ▪ Fx: 703-548-4580 ▪ TF: 800-424-8422

Vision, Council of Citizens With Low www.cclvi.org
1155 15th St NW Suite 1004   Washington DC 20005
Ph: 202-467-5081 ▪ Fx: 202-467-5085 ▪ TF: 800-424-8666

Vision Education, Parents Active for www.pavevision.org
4135 54th Pl   San Diego CA 92105
Ph: 619-287-0081 ▪ Fx: 619-287-0084 ▪ TF: 800-728-3988

Vision Institute, Better www.visionsite.org
Vision Council of America 1700 Diagonal Rd Suite
500   Alexandria VA 22314
Ph: 703-548-4560 ▪ Fx: 703-548-4580 ▪ TF: 800-424-8422

(Vision) Lighthouse International www.lighthouse.org
111 E 59th St   New York NY 10022
Ph: 212-821-9200 ▪ Fx: 212-821-9708 ▪ TF: 800-829-0500

Vision & Ophthalmology, Association for Research in www.arvo.org
12300 Twinbrook Pkwy Suite 250   Rockville MD 20852
Ph: 240-221-2900 ▪ Fx: 240-221-0370

(Vision) ORBIS International Inc www.orbis.org
520 8th Ave 11th Fl   New York NY 10018
Ph: 646-674-5500 ▪ Fx: 646-674-5599 ▪ TF: 800-672-4787

Visionary Resources, Coalition of www.covr.org
1667 N Magnolia Ave   Tucson AZ 85712
Ph: 520-320-9338

Visions in Action www.visionsinaction.org
2710 Ontario Rd NW   Washington DC 20009
Ph: 202-625-7402 ▪ Fx: 202-588-9344

Visiting Nurse Associations of America www.vnaa.org
99 Summer St Suite 1700   Boston MA 02110
Ph: 617-737-3200 ▪ Fx: 617-737-1144 ▪ TF: 800-426-2547

Visiting Teachers Association, National www.nvta4partents.org
650 Howe Ave Suite 1014   Sacramento CA 95825
Ph: 916-921-6882 ▪ Fx: 916-921-1460

Visitor Bureaus, International Association of Convention & www.iacvb.org
2025 M St NW Suite 500   Washington DC 20036
Ph: 202-296-7888 ▪ Fx: 202-296-7889

Visitor Studies Association www.visitorstudies.org
8175-A Sheridan Blvd Suite 362   Arvada CO 80003
Ph: 303-467-2200 ▪ Fx: 303-467-0064

Visitors, National Council for International www.nciv.org
1420 K St NW Suite 800   Washington DC 20005
Ph: 202-842-1414 ▪ Fx: 202-289-4625 ▪ TF: 800-523-8101

Visual Anthropology, Society for www.societyforvisualanthropology.org
c/o American Anthropological Assn 2200 Wilson Blvd Suite
600   Arlington VA 22201
Ph: 703-528-1902 ▪ Fx: 703-528-3546

Visual Artists & Galleries Association
350 5th Ave Suite 2820   New York NY 10118
Ph: 212-736-6666 ▪ Fx: 212-736-6767

Visual Arts, Christians in the www.civa.org
255 Grapevine Rd   Wenham MA 01984
Ph: 978-867-4124 ▪ Fx: 978-867-4125

Visual Communicators, International Association of Audio www.iaavc.org
57 W Palo Verde Ave PO Box 250   Ocotillo CA 92259
Ph: 760-358-7000 ▪ Fx: 760-358-7569

Visual Education Partnership, Planning & www.visualstore.com/pave
3368A Oxford Ave   Saint Louis MO 63143
Ph: 314-645-0701

Visual Impairment, Council of Families with
1155 15th St NW Suite 1004   Washington DC 20005
Ph: 202-467-5081 ▪ Fx: 202-467-5085 ▪ TF: 800-424-8666

Visual Impairments, National Association for Parents of Children with www.spedex.com/napvi
PO Box 317   Watertown MA 02471
Ph: 617-972-7441 ▪ Fx: 617-972-7444 ▪ TF: 800-562-6265

Visual Literacy Association, International www.ivla.org/
Navarro College 3200 W 7th Ave   Corsicana TX 75110
Ph: 903-875-7441 ▪ Fx: 903-875-4636

Visual Resources Association www.vraweb.org

Visually Handicapped, National Association for www.navh.org
22 W 21st St 6th Fl   New York NY 10010
Ph: 212-889-3141 ▪ Fx: 212-727-2931

Visually Impaired, Association for Education & Rehabilitation of the Blind & www.aerbvi.org
1703 N Beauregard St Suite 440   Alexandria
VA 22311
Ph: 703-671-4500 ▪ Fx: 703-671-6391

Viticulture, American Society for Enology & www.asev.org
PO Box 1855   Davis CA 95617
Ph: 530-753-3142 ▪ Fx: 530-753-3318

Vitiligo Foundation, National www.vitiligofoundation.org
611 S Fleishel Ave   Tyler TX 75701
Ph: 903-531-0074 ▪ Fx: 903-525-1234

Vivisection Investigation League
95 Belden St   Falls Village CT 06031
Ph: 860-824-0831 ▪ Fx: 860-824-5460

Vocation Directors, National Conference of Diocesan www.ncdvd.org
PO Box 1570   Little River SC 29566
Ph: 843-280-7191 ▪ Fx: 843-280-0681

Vocational Education Research Association, American tiger.coe.missouri.edu/~pavtat/AVERA

Vocational Evaluation & Career Assessment Professionals www.vecap.org
PO Box 26273   Colorado Springs CO 80936
Ph: 719-638-4787 ▪ Fx: 719-638-6153

Vocational Evaluation Specialists, Commission on Certification of Work Adjustment & www.ccwaves.org
1835 Rohlwing Rd Suite E   Rolling
Meadows IL 60008
Ph: 847-342-1796 ▪ Fx: 847-394-2108

Vocational Instructional Materials, American Association for www.aavim.com
220 Smithonia Rd   Winterville GA 30683
Ph: 706-742-5355 ▪ Fx: 706-742-7005 ▪ TF: 800-228-4689

Vocational Rehabilitation, Council of State Administrators of www.rehabnetwork.org
4733 Bethesda Ave Suite 330   Bethesda MD 20814
Ph: 301-654-8414 ▪ Fx: 301-654-5542

Vocational Services, International Association of Jewish www.iajvs.org/
1845 Walnut St Suite 640   Philadelphia PA 19103
Ph: 215-854-0233 ▪ Fx: 215-854-0212

Voice for Animals Society www.v4a.org
PO Box 68119 162 Bonnie Doon Mall   Edmonton AB T6C4N6
Ph: 780-490-0905 ▪ Fx: 780-922-5287

Voice of China & Asia Missionary Society www.vocamissionarysociety.org
183 E Glenarm St PO Box 150   Pasadena CA 91102
Ph: 626-441-0640 ▪ Fx: 626-441-8124

Voice Foundation www.voicefoundation.org
1721 Pine St   Philadelphia PA 19103
Ph: 215-735-7999 ▪ Fx: 215-735-9293

Voice Input/Output Society, Applied www.avios.com
PO Box 20817   San Jose CA 95160
Ph: 408-323-1783 ▪ Fx: 408-323-1782

Voice of the Martyrs www.persecution.com
PO Box 443   Bartlesville OK 74005
Ph: 918-337-8015 ▪ Fx: 918-338-0189 ▪ TF: 800-747-0085

Voice Phenomena, American Association of Electronic aaevp.com
PO Box 13111   Reno NV 89507
Ph: 775-329-5980

Voice of the Retarded www.vor.net
5005 Newport Dr Suite 108   Rolling Meadows IL 60008
Ph: 847-253-6020 ▪ Fx: 847-253-6054

VOICES in Action www.voices-action.org

Voices for America's Children www.voicesforamericaschildren.org
1522 K St NW Suite 600   Washington DC 20005
Ph: 202-289-0777 ▪ Fx: 202-289-0776

Volkssport Association, American www.ava.org
1001 Pat Booker Rd Suite 101   Universal City TX 78148
Ph: 210-659-2112 ▪ Fx: 210-659-1212 ▪ TF: 800-830-9255

Volleyball Coaches Association, American www.avca.org
1227 Lake Plaza Dr Suite B   Colorado Springs CO 80906
Ph: 719-576-7777 ▪ Fx: 719-576-7778

Volleyball Officials, Professional Association of www.pavo.org
PO Box 780   Oxford KS 67119
Ph: 888-791-2074 ▪ Fx: 620-455-3800

Volleyball Professionals, Association of www.avp.com
6080 Center Dr 6th Fl   Los Angeles CA 90045
Ph: 310-426-8000 ▪ Fx: 310-426-8010

Voluntary International Action, American Council for www.interaction.org
1717 Massachusetts Ave NW Suite 701   Washington DC 20036
Ph: 202-667-8227 ▪ Fx: 202-667-8236

Voluntary Organizations Active in Disaster, National www.nvoad.org
14253 Ballinger Terr   Burtonsville MD 20866
Ph: 301-890-2119

Voluntary Protection Programs Participants' Association www.vpppa.org
7600-E Leesburg Pike Suite 440   Falls Church VA 22043
Ph: 703-761-1146 ▪ Fx: 703-761-1148

Volunteer Administration, Association for www.avaintl.org
PO Box 32092   Richmond VA 23294
Ph: 804-672-3353 ▪ Fx: 804-672-3368

Volunteer Center National Network, Points of Light Foundation & www.pointsoflight.org
1400 'I' St NW Suite 800   Washington DC
20005
Ph: 202-729-8000 ▪ Fx: 202-729-8100 ▪ TF: 800-750-7653

Volunteer Corps, Financial Services www.fsvc.org
10 E 53rd St 24th Fl   New York NY 10022
Ph: 212-771-1400 ▪ Fx: 212-421-2162

Volunteer Corps, Lutheran www.lvchome.org
1226 Vermont Ave NW   Washington DC 20005
Ph: 202-387-3222 ▪ Fx: 202-667-0037

Volunteer Fire Council, National www.nvfc.org
1050 17th St NW Suite 490   Washington DC 20036
Ph: 202-887-5700 ▪ Fx: 202-887-5291 ▪ TF: 888-275-6832

Volunteer Missionary Movement www.vmmusa.org
5980 W Loomis   Greendale WI 53129
Ph: 414-423-8660 ▪ Fx: 414-423-8964

Volunteer Program Directors, National Association of Retired Senior
12388 Warwick Blvd   Newport News VA 23601
Ph: 757-595-9037 ▪ Fx: 757-595-9047

Volunteer Service, Catholic Network of www.cnvs.org
6930 Carroll Ave Suite 506   Takoma Park MD 20912
Ph: 301-270-0900 ▪ Fx: 301-270-0901 ▪ TF: 800-543-5046

Volunteer Services, American Society of Directors of www.asdvs.org
1 N Franklin St 27th Fl   Chicago IL 60606
Ph: 312-422-3939 ▪ Fx: 312-422-4575

(Volunteers) Altrusa International Inc www.altrusa.com
332 S Michigan Ave Suite 1123   Chicago IL 60604
Ph: 312-427-4410 ▪ Fx: 312-427-8521

Volunteers of America www.voa.org
1660 Duke St   Alexandria VA 22314
Ph: 703-341-5000 ▪ Fx: 703-341-7000 ▪ TF: 800-899-0089

(Volunteers) Box Project Inc www.boxproject.org
PO Box 435   Plainville CT 06062
Ph: 860-747-8182 ▪ Fx: 860-793-8857 ▪ TF: 800-268-9928

(Volunteers) Epsilon Sigma Alpha International www.esaintl.com
363 W Drake Rd   Fort Collins CO 80526
Ph: 970-223-2824 ▪ Fx: 970-223-4456

Volunteers International, Jesuit www.jesuitvolunteers.org
PO Box 3756   Washington DC 20027
Ph: 202-687-1132 ▪ Fx: 202-687-5082

Volunteers for Israel www.vfi-usa.org
330 W 42nd St Suite 1618   New York NY 10036
Ph: 212-643-4848 ▪ Fx: 212-643-4855

Volunteers, Lasallian www.cbconf.org/cbc.nsf/pages/volunteers
4351 Garden City Dr Suite 200   Landover MD 20785
Ph: 301-459-9410 ▪ Fx: 301-459-8056

Volunteers in Overseas Cooperative Assistance, Agricultural www.acdivoca.org
Cooperative Development International/   50 F St NW Suite
1075   Washington DC 20001
Ph: 202-638-4661 ▪ Fx: 202-626-8726 ▪ TF: 800-929-8622

Volunteers Overseas Inc, Health www.hvousa.org
PO Box 65157   Washington DC 20035
Ph: 202-296-0928 ▪ Fx: 202-296-8018

Volunteers Partners in Development, Global www.globalvolunteers.org
375 E Little Canada Rd   Saint Paul MN 55117
Ph: 651-407-6100 ▪ Fx: 651-482-0915 ▪ TF: 800-487-1074

Volunteers for Peace www.vfp.org
1034 Tiffany Rd   Belmont VT 05730
Ph: 802-259-2759 ▪ Fx: 802-259-2922

Volunteers in Prevention Probation Prisons www.vipmentoring.org
220 Bagley St 1020 Michigan Bldg   Detroit MI 48226
Ph: 313-964-1110 ▪ Fx: 313-964-1145

(Volunteers) Sabre Foundation Inc www.sabre.org
872 Massachusetts Ave Suite 2-1   Cambridge MA 02139
Ph: 617-868-3510 ▪ Fx: 617-868-7916

(Volunteers) Tech Corps www.techcorps.org
2 Clock Tower Pl Suite 340   Maynard MA 01754
Ph: 978-897-8282 ▪ Fx: 978-897-4204

Volunteers in Technical Assistance www.vita.org
1600 Wilson Blvd Suite 1030   Arlington VA 22209
Ph: 703-276-1800 ▪ Fx: 703-243-1865

Volunteers Unlimited, Business www.businessvolunteers.org
200 Public Sq   Cleveland OH 44113
Ph: 216-736-7711 ▪ Fx: 216-736-7710

(Volunteers) Visions in Action www.visionsinaction.org
2710 Ontario Rd NW   Washington DC 20009
Ph: 202-625-7402 ▪ Fx: 202-588-9344

Von Braun Astronomical Society www.vbas.org
PO Box 1142   Huntsville AL 35807
Ph: 256-539-0316

Vote Coalition, Youth www.youthvote.org
1010 Vermont Ave NW Suite 715   Washington DC 20005
Ph: 202-783-4751 ▪ Fx: 202-783-4750

Vote, Project www.projectvote.org
6805 Oak Creek Dr   Columbus OH 43229
Ph: 614-523-2560 ▪ Fx: 614-523-2720 ▪ TF: 800-546-8683

Vote, Rock the www.rockthevote.com
10635 Santa Monica Blvd Suite 150   Los Angeles CA 90025
Ph: 310-234-0665 ▪ Fx: 310-234-0666

Vote Smart, Project www.vote-smart.org
1 Common Ground   Philipsburg MT 59858
Ph: 406-859-8686 ▪ Fx: 406-859-8680 ▪ TF: 888-868-3762

Voter Registration Education Project, Southwest www.svrep.org
206 Lombard St 2nd Fl   San Antonio TX 78226
Ph: 210-922-0225 ▪ Fx: 210-932-4055 ▪ TF: 800-404-8683

Voter Registration, National Student Campaign for
1533 Market St 2nd Fl   Denver CO 80202
Ph: 303-573-5885 ▪ Fx: 303-573-5999

Voters of America, United Hellenic www.smartbiz.net/uhva
525 W Lake St   Addison IL 60101
Ph: 630-628-0820 ▪ Fx: 630-543-7001

Voters, League of Conservation www.lcv.org
1920 L St NW Suite 800   Washington DC 20036
Ph: 202-785-8683 ▪ Fx: 202-835-0491

Voters, League of Private Property www.landrights.org/_private/lppvhome.htm
PO Box 423   Battle Ground WA 98604
Ph: 360-687-2471 ▪ Fx: 360-687-2973

Voters, League of Women www.lwv.org
1730 M St NW Suite 1000   Washington DC 20036
Ph: 202-429-1965 ▪ Fx: 202-429-0854 ▪ TF: 800-249-8683

Voting & Democracy, Center for www.fairvote.org
6930 Carroll Ave Suite 610   Takoma Park MD 20912
Ph: 301-270-4616 ▪ Fx: 301-270-4133

Voyager Association, American www.csonline.net/cybersite/american.htm
PO Box 253   Cypress IL 62923
Ph: 618-657-2664

VSA Arts www.vsarts.org
1300 Connecticut Ave NW Suite 700   Washington DC 20036
Ph: 202-628-2800 ▪ Fx: 202-737-0725 ▪ TF: 800-933-8721

Vulvar Pain Foundation www.vulvarpainfoundation.org
PO Drawer 177   Graham NC 27253
Ph: 336-226-0704 ▪ Fx: 336-226-8518

Vulvodynia Association, National www.nva.org
PO Box 4491   Silver Spring MD 20914
Ph: 301-299-0775 ▪ Fx: 301-299-3999

W

Wages for Housework Campaign, International www.allwomencount.net
c/o Crossroad Women's Ctr PO Box 86681   Los Angeles CA 90086
Ph: 323-292-7405

Wagner Richard Society of New York www.wagnersocietyny.org
PO Box 230949 Ansonia Stn   New York NY 10023
Ph: 212-749-4561 ▪ Fx: 212-749-1542

Waksman Foundation for Microbiology www.waksmanfoundation.org
Univ of Michigan Medical School Dept of Microbiology &
Immunology Medical Sciences Bldg II   Box 620   Ann
Arbor MI 48109
Ph: 734-995-2951 ▪ Fx: 734-995-9071

Walden Woods Project www.walden.org
44 Baker Farm   Lincoln MA 01773
Ph: 781-259-4700 ▪ Fx: 781-259-4710

Waldensian Society, American www.waldensian.org
102 Vultee St   Allentown PA 18103
Ph: 866-825-3373 ▪ Fx: 610-797-9723

Waldorf Early Childhood Association of North America
285 Hungry Hollow Rd   Spring Valley NY 10977
Ph: 845-352-1690 ▪ Fx: 845-352-1695

Waldorf Schools of North America, Association of www.awsna.org
3911 Bannister Rd   Fair Oaks CA 95628
Ph: 916-961-0927 ▪ Fx: 916-961-0715

Walkaloosa Horse Association www.walkaloosaregistry.com
PO Box 3170   Carefree AZ 85377
Ph: 480-595-1699

Walking Horse Owners Association of America www.walkinghorseowners.com
304 W Thompson Ln   Murfreesboro TN 37129
Ph: 615-494-8822 ▪ Fx: 615-494-8825

Walking Horse Trainers Association www.walkinghorsetrainers.com
PO Box 61   Shelbyville TN 37162
Ph: 931-684-5866 ▪ Fx: 931-684-5895

Walking, National Center for Bicycling & www.bikewalk.org
1506 21st St NW Suite 200   Washington DC 20036
Ph: 202-463-6622 ▪ Fx: 202-463-6625

Walking Pony Association, American
PO Box 5282   Macon GA 31208
Ph: 478-743-2321 ▪ Fx: 478-742-6021

Wall & Ceiling Industries International, Association of the www.awci.org
803 W Broad St Suite 600   Falls Church VA 22046
Ph: 703-534-8300 ▪ Fx: 703-534-8307

Wallace Foundation www.wallacefoundation.org
2 Park Ave 23rd Fl   New York NY 10016
Ph: 212-251-9700 ▪ Fx: 212-679-6990 ▪ TF: 800-771-9701

Wallcoverings Association www.wallcoverings.org
401 N Michigan Ave Suite 2200   Chicago IL 60611
Ph: 312-644-6618

Wally Byam Caravan Club International www.wbcci.org
PO Box 612   Jackson Center OH 45334
Ph: 937-596-5211 ▪ Fx: 937-596-5542

Walnut Manufacturers Association, American www.walnutassociation.org
PO Box 5046   Zionsville IN 46077
Ph: 317-873-8780

Walter & Elise Haas Fund www.haassr.org
1 Market St Suite 400   San Francisco CA 94105
Ph: 415-856-1400 ▪ Fx: 415-856-1500

Walton Family Foundation Inc www.wffhome.com
PO Box 2030   Bentonville AR 72712
Ph: 479-464-1570 ▪ Fx: 479-464-1580

Walton Izaak League of America www.iwla.org
707 Conservation Ln   Gaithersburg MD 20878
Ph: 301-548-0150 ▪ Fx: 301-548-0146 ▪ TF: 800-453-5463

WAND Education Fund www.wand.org
691 Massachusetts Ave   Arlington MA 02476
Ph: 781-643-6740 ▪ Fx: 781-643-6744

Wanderer Forum Foundation www.wandererforum.org
PO Box 542   Hudson WI 54016
Ph: 651-276-1429

War of 1812, General Society of the www.societyofthewarof1812.org
1219 Charmuth Rd   Lutherville MD 21093
Ph: 410-825-3015

War, American Ex-Prisoners of www.axpow.org
3201 E Pioneer Pkwy Suite 40   Arlington TX 76010
Ph: 817-649-2979 ▪ Fx: 817-649-0109

War, Center on Conscience &   www.nisbco.org
1830 Connecticut Ave NW   Washington DC 20009
Ph: 202-483-2220 ■ Fx: 202-483-1246 ■ TF: 800-379-2679

War, Children of   www.thechildrenofwar.org
PO Box 11321   Burke VA 22009
Ph: 703-923-0455

War Council, World Without   www.wwwc.org/wwwc/wwwc.html
1730 ML King Jr Way   Berkeley CA 94709
Ph: 510-845-1992 ■ Fx: 510-845-5721

(War Gaming) Strategy   www.gametableonline.com/StrategyGamingSociety.htm
Gaming Society   87-6 Park Ave   Worcester MA 01605
Ph: 508-831-5334

War Memorial Project, National Medical   www.medicalwarmemorial.org
PO Box 14492   Kansas City MO 64152
Ph: 816-452-0606 ■ Fx: 816-454-0897

War & Peace Foundation   www.warpeace.org
777 United Nations Plaza   New York NY 10017
Ph: 212-557-2501 ■ Fx: 212-557-2515

War Peace & the News Media, Center for   www.nyu.edu/cwpnm
New York Univ 418 Lafayette Suite 554   New York NY 10003
Ph: 212-998-7960 ■ Fx: 212-995-4143

War/Peace Studies, Center for   www.cwps.org
180 W 80th St Suite 211   New York NY 10024
Ph: 212-579-4206 ■ Fx: 212-579-4362

War Project, Korean   www.koreanwar.org
PO Box 180190   Dallas TX 75218
Ph: 214-320-0342

War Resisters League   www.warresisters.org
339 Lafayette St   New York NY 10012
Ph: 212-228-0450 ■ Fx: 212-228-6193 ■ TF: 800-975-9688

War Revolution & Peace, Hoover Institution on   www-hoover.stanford.edu
434 Galvez Mall   Stanford CA 94305
Ph: 650-723-1754 ■ Fx: 650-723-1687 ■ TF: 877-466-8374

War Risk Reinsurance Exchange, American Cargo   www.amich.org/acwHome.htm
30 Broad St 7th Fl   New York NY 10004
Ph: 212-405-2835 ■ Fx: 212-240-0654

War Veterans Association, Korean   www.kwva.org
PO Box 10806   Arlington VA 22210
Ph: 703-522-9629

War Veterans Auxiliary, Catholic   www.cwv.org/laux/laux.htm
441 N Lee St   Alexandria VA 22314
Ph: 703-549-3622 ■ Fx: 703-684-5196

War Veterans of the USA, Catholic   www.cwv.org
441 N Lee St   Alexandria VA 22314
Ph: 703-549-3622 ■ Fx: 703-684-5196

War Veterans of the USA, Jewish   www.jwv.org
1811 R St NW   Washington DC 20009
Ph: 202-265-6280 ■ Fx: 202-234-5662

War Veterans of the USA - National Ladies Auxiliary, Jewish
1811 R St NW   Washington DC 20009
Ph: 202-667-9061 ■ Fx: 202-667-6689

Wardens & Superintendents, North American Association of   corrections.com/naaws
PO Box 11037   Albany NY 12211
Ph: 518-786-6801

Warehouse Association, Bright Belt
PO Box 12004   Raleigh NC 27605
Ph: 919-828-8988

Warehouse Association, Performance   www.pwa-par.org
41-701 Corporate Way Suite 1   Palm Desert CA 92260
Ph: 760-346-5647 ■ Fx: 760-346-5847

Warehouse Companies Inc, Affiliated   www.awco.com
54 Village Ct PO Box 295   Hazlet NJ 07730
Ph: 732-739-2323 ■ Fx: 732-739-4154

Warehouse Distributors Association, Automotive   www.awda.org
4050 Pennsylvania Ave Suite 225   Kansas City MO 64111
Ph: 816-523-8693 ■ Fx: 816-523-7293

Warehouse Logistics Association, International   www.iwla.com
2800 River Rd Suite 260   Des Plaines IL 60018
Ph: 847-813-4699 ■ Fx: 847-813-0115

Warehouse Union, International Longshore &   www.ilwu.org
1188 Franklin St 4th Fl   San Francisco CA 94109
Ph: 415-775-0533 ■ Fx: 415-775-1302

Warehouses, International Association of Refrigerated   www.iarw.org
1500 King St Suite 201   Alexandria VA 22314
Ph: 703-373-4300 ■ Fx: 703-373-4301

Warehousing Education & Research Council   www.werc.org
1100 Jorie Blvd Suite 170   Oak Brook IL 60523
Ph: 630-990-0001 ■ Fx: 630-990-0256

Warmblood Registry, American   www.americanwarmblood.com
PO Box 211735   Royal Palm Beach FL 33421
Ph: 561-333-5848

Warmblood Society, American   www.americanwarmblood.org
2 Buffalo Run   Center Ridge AR 72027
Ph: 501-893-2777 ■ Fx: 501-893-2779

Warmblood & Sport Horse Guild, American
PO Box 5512   Grants Pass OR 97527
Ph: 541-855-8942

Warrant Officers Association, Chief Warrant &   www.cwoauscg.org
200 V St SW   Washington DC 20024
Ph: 202-544-7753 ■ Fx: 202-484-0641

Warrant Officers Association, US Army   www.penfed.org/usawoa
462 Herndon Pkwy Suite 207   Herndon VA 20170
Ph: 703-742-7727 ■ Fx: 703-742-7728 ■ TF: 800-587-2862

Warren William K Foundation
6585 S Yale Ave Suite 900   Tulsa OK 74136
Ph: 918-492-8100 ■ Fx: 918-481-7935

Wars of the US, Veterans of Foreign   www.vfw.com
406 W 34th St   Kansas City MO 64111
Ph: 816-756-3390 ■ Fx: 816-968-1149

Warsaw Ghetto Resistance Organization
122 W 30th St Suite 205   New York NY 10001
Ph: 212-564-1065 ■ Fx: 212-279-2926

Washer Manufacturers Association, Pressure   www.pwma.org
1300 Sumner Ave   Cleveland OH 44115
Ph: 216-241-7333 ■ Fx: 216-241-0105

Washers of North America, Power   www.pwna.org
6418 Grovedale Dr Suite 101B   Alexandria VA 22310
Ph: 703-971-4011 ■ Fx: 703-971-7772 ■ TF: 800-393-7962

Washington Calligraphers Guild   www.calligraphersguild.org
PO Box 3688   Merrifield VA 22116
Ph: 301-897-8637

Washington DC, Historical Society of   www.hswdc.org
801 K St NW   Washington DC 20001
Ph: 202-383-1800 ■ Fx: 202-383-1870

Washington Legal Foundation   www.wlf.org
2009 Massachusetts Ave NW   Washington DC 20036
Ph: 202-588-0302 ■ Fx: 202-588-0386

Washington Office on Africa   www.woaafrica.org
212 E Capitol St NE   Washington DC 20003
Ph: 202-547-7503 ■ Fx: 202-547-7505

Washington Office on Latin America   www.wola.org
1630 Connecticut Ave NW Suite 200   Washington DC 20009
Ph: 202-797-2171 ■ Fx: 202-797-2172

Washington Trails Association   www.wta.org
1305 4th Ave Suite 512   Seattle WA 98101
Ph: 206-625-1367 ■ Fx: 206-625-9249

Washington Workshops Foundation   www.workshops.org
3222 'N' St NW Suite 340   Washington DC 20007
Ph: 202-965-3434 ■ Fx: 202-965-1018 ■ TF: 800-368-5688

Washington's Army at Valley Forge, Society of   www.valleyforgesociety.org
the Descendants of

Waste Association of North America, Solid   www.swana.org
PO Box 7219   Silver Spring MD 20907
Ph: 301-585-2898 ■ Fx: 301-589-7068 ■ TF: 800-467-9262

Waste, Citizens Against Government   www.cagw.org
1301 Connecticut Ave NW Suite 400   Washington DC 20036
Ph: 202-467-5300 ■ Fx: 202-467-4253 ■ TF: 800-232-6479

Waste Equipment Technology Association   www.wastec.org
4301 Connecticut Ave NW Suite 300   Washington DC 20008
Ph: 202-244-4700 ■ Fx: 202-966-4818 ■ TF: 800-424-2869

Waste Incineration, Coalition for Responsible   www.crwi.org
1752 'N' St NW Suite 800   Washington DC 20036
Ph: 202-452-1241 ■ Fx: 202-887-8044

Waste Management Association, Air &   www.awma.org
420 Fort Duquesne Blvd 1 Gateway Ctr 3rd Fl   Pittsburgh PA 15222
Ph: 412-232-3444 ■ Fx: 412-232-3450 ■ TF: 800-270-3444

Waste Management Association, Municipal   www.usmayors.org/uscm/mwma
1620 'I' St NW Suite 300   Washington DC 20006
Ph: 202-293-7330 ■ Fx: 202-293-2352

Waste Management Officials, Association of State &   www.astswmo.org
Territorial Solid   444 N Capitol St NW Suite 315   Washington DC 20001
Ph: 202-624-5828 ■ Fx: 202-624-7875

Waste Reduction Technologies, Center for   www.aiche.org/cwrt
3 Park Ave   New York NY 10016
Ph: 212-591-7462 ■ Fx: 212-591-8895

Waste Safety, National Campaign for Radioactive   www.sric.org
105 Stanford SE PO Box 4524   Albuquerque NM 87106
Ph: 505-262-1862 ■ Fx: 505-262-1864

Waste Services Association, Integrated   www.wte.org
1401 H St NW Suite 220   Washington DC 20005
Ph: 202-467-6240 ■ Fx: 202-467-6225

Waste Transporters, National Association of   www.nawt.org
PO Box 70   Edgewater MD 21037
Ph: 410-798-0842 ■ TF: 800-236-6298

Wastes Management Association, National Solid   www.nswma.org
4301 Connecticut Ave NW Suite 300   Washington DC 20008
Ph: 202-244-4700 ■ Fx: 202-966-4818 ■ TF: 800-424-2869

Wastewater Equipment Manufacturers Association, Water &   www.wwema.org
PO Box 17402   Washington DC 20041
Ph: 703-444-1777 ■ Fx: 703-444-1779

Wastewater Pump Association, Submersible   www.swpa.org
1866 Sheridan Rd Suite 201   Highland Park IL 60035
Ph: 847-681-1868 ■ Fx: 847-681-1869

Wastewater Recycling Association, National Onsite   www.nowra.org
PO Box 1270   Edgewater MD 21037
Ph: 410-798-1697 ■ Fx: 410-798-5741

Watch Association, American
1201 Pennsylvania Ave NW PO Box 464   Washington DC 20044
Ph: 703-759-3377

Watch & Clock Collectors, National Association of   www.nawcc.org
514 Poplar St   Columbia PA 17512
Ph: 717-684-8261 ■ Fx: 717-684-0878

Watch Fob Association, International   www.watchfob.com
601 Patriot Pl   Holmen WI 54636
Ph: 608-526-2328

Watchmakers-Clockmakers Institute, American   www.awi-net.org
701 Enterprise Dr   Harrison OH 45030
Ph: 513-367-9800 ■ Fx: 513-367-1414 ■ TF: 866-367-2924

Watchman Fellowship   www.watchman.org
3337 W Pioneer Pkwy PO Box 13340   Arlington TX 76094
Ph: 817-277-0023 ■ Fx: 817-227-8089

Watchtower Bible & Tract Society of New York Inc   www.watchtower.org
25 Columbia Heights   Brooklyn NY 11201
Ph: 718-560-5000

Water Agencies, Association of Metropolitan   www.amwa.net
1717 K St NW Suite 801   Washington DC 20036
Ph: 202-331-2820 ▪ Fx: 202-785-1845

Water Association, International Bottled   www.bottledwater.org
1700 Diagonal Rd Suite 650   Alexandria VA 22314
Ph: 703-683-5213 ▪ Fx: 703-683-4074 ▪ TF: 800-928-3711

Water Association, National Rural   www.nrwa.org
2915 S 13th St   Duncan OK 73533
Ph: 580-252-0629 ▪ Fx: 580-255-4476

Water Buffalo Association, American   www.americanwaterbuffalo.org
PO Box 13533   Gainesville FL 32604
Ph: 352-392-2643 ▪ Fx: 352-846-0816

Water Companies, National Association of   www.nawc.com
1725 K St NW Suite 1212   Washington DC 20006
Ph: 202-833-8383 ▪ Fx: 202-331-7442

Water Conservation Society, Soil &   www.swcs.org
945 SW Ankeny Rd   Ankeny IA 50021
Ph: 515-289-2331 ▪ Fx: 515-289-1227 ▪ TF: 800-843-7645

Water & Energy Education, Foundation for   www.fwee.org

Water Environment Federation   www.wef.org
601 Wythe St   Alexandria VA 22314
Ph: 703-684-2400 ▪ Fx: 703-684-2492 ▪ TF: 800-666-0206

Water Fitness Association, US   www.uswfa.com
PO Box 3279   Boynton Beach FL 33424
Ph: 561-732-9908 ▪ Fx: 561-732-0950

Water Fund, Clean   www.cleanwaterfund.org
4455 Connecticut Ave NW Suite A300-16   Washington DC 20008
Ph: 202-895-0432 ▪ Fx: 202-895-0438

Water Gardening Society, International Water Lily &   www.iwgs.org
6828 26th St W   Bradenton FL 34207
Ph: 941-756-0880

Water PAC
2915 S 13th St   Duncan OK 73533
Ph: 580-252-0629 ▪ Fx: 580-255-4476

Water for People   www.waterforpeople.org
6666 W Quincy Ave   Denver CO 80235
Ph: 303-734-3490 ▪ Fx: 303-734-3499

Water Policy, Interstate Council on   www.icwp.org
1299 Pennsylvania Ave NW 8th Fl W   Washington DC 20004
Ph: 202-218-4196 ▪ Fx: 202-478-1738

Water Pollution Control Administrators, Association of   www.asiwpca.org
State & Interstate   750 1st St NE Suite 1010   Washington DC 20002
Ph: 202-898-0905 ▪ Fx: 202-898-0929

Water Polo Association, Collegiate   www.collegiatewaterpolo.org
28 W Airy St   Norristown PA 19401
Ph: 610-277-6787 ▪ Fx: 610-277-7382

Water Polo, USA   www.usawaterpolo.com
1685 W Uintah St   Colorado Springs CO 80904
Ph: 719-634-0699 ▪ Fx: 719-634-0866

Water Quality Association   www.wqa.org
4151 Naperville Rd   Lisle IL 60532
Ph: 630-505-0160 ▪ Fx: 630-505-9637

Water Quality Insurance Syndicate   www.wqis.com
80 Broad St 21st Fl   New York NY 10004
Ph: 212-292-8700 ▪ Fx: 212-292-8716

Water Resources Association, American   www.awra.org
4 W Federal St PO Box 1626   Middleburg VA 20118
Ph: 540-687-8390 ▪ Fx: 540-687-9395

Water Resources Association, Canadian   www.cwra.org
400 Clyde Rd PO Box 1329   Cambridge ON N1R7G6
Ph: 519-622-4764 ▪ Fx: 519-621-4844

Water Resources Association, International   www.iwra.siu.edu
Southern Illinois Univ Carbondale 4535 Faner Hall   Carbondale IL 62901
Ph: 618-453-5138 ▪ Fx: 618-453-6465

Water Resources Association, National   www.nwra.org
3800 N Fairfax Dr Suite 4   Arlington VA 22203
Ph: 703-524-1544 ▪ Fx: 703-524-1548

Water Safety Congress, National   www.watersafetycongress.org
PO Box 1632   Mentor OH 44061
Ph: 440-209-9805

Water & Sewer Distributors of America   www.wasda.com
1900 Arch St   Philadelphia PA 19103
Ph: 215-564-3484 ▪ Fx: 215-564-2175

Water Ski Educational Foundation, American   www.waterskihalloffame.com
1251 Holy Cow Rd   Polk City FL 33868
Ph: 863-324-4341 ▪ Fx: 863-325-8259

Water Ski, USA   www.usawaterski.org
1251 Holy Cow Rd   Polk City FL 33868
Ph: 863-324-4341 ▪ Fx: 863-325-8259 ▪ TF: 800-533-2972

Water & Steam, International Association for the Properties of   www.iapws.org

Water Systems Council   www.watersystemscouncil.org
1101 30th St NW Suite 500   Washington DC 20007
Ph: 202-625-4387 ▪ Fx: 202-625-4363 ▪ TF: 888-395-1033

Water Technologies, Association of   www.awt.org
8201 Greensboro Dr Suite 300   McLean VA 22102
Ph: 703-610-9012 ▪ Fx: 703-610-9005 ▪ TF: 800-858-6683

Water & Wastewater Equipment Manufacturers Association   www.wwema.org
PO Box 17402   Washington DC 20041
Ph: 703-444-1777 ▪ Fx: 703-444-1779

Water Works Association, American   www.awwa.org
6666 W Quincy Ave   Denver CO 80235
Ph: 303-794-7711 ▪ Fx: 303-347-0804 ▪ TF: 800-926-7337

Waterbird Society   www.waterbirds.org
c/o Upper Mississippi Environmental Sciences Ctr 2630 Fanta Reed Rd   La Crosse WI 54603
Ph: 608-783-6451

Watercolor Society, National   www.nws-online.org
915 S Pacific Ave   San Pedro CA 90731
Ph: 800-486-8670

Watercraft Industry Association, Personal   www.pwia.org
1819 L St NW Suite 700   Washington DC 20036
Ph: 202-721-1621 ▪ Fx: 202-721-1626

WateReuse Association   www.watereuse.org
635 Slaters Ln 3rd Fl   Alexandria VA 22314
Ph: 703-548-2409 ▪ Fx: 703-548-3075

Waterfowl Association, International Wild   www.wildwaterfowl.org
PO Box 36   Scotland Neck NC 27874
Ph: 252-826-5038 ▪ Fx: 252-826-5284

Waterfowl Foundation, Delta   www.deltawaterfowl.org
1305 E Central Ave   Bismarck ND 58501
Ph: 701-222-8857 ▪ Fx: 701-223-4645 ▪ TF: 888-987-3695

Waterfowl Society, American Pheasant &   www3.upatsix.com/apws
W2270 US Hwy 10   Granton WI 54436
Ph: 715-238-7291 ▪ Fx: 715-238-7623

Waterfowl USA   www.waterfowlusa.com
Waterfowl Bldg Box 50   Edgefield SC 29824
Ph: 803-637-5767 ▪ Fx: 803-637-6983

Waterfront Center   www.waterfrontcenter.org
1622 Wisconsin Ave NW   Washington DC 20007
Ph: 202-337-0356 ▪ Fx: 202-625-1654

Waterfront Employers, National Association of
2011 Pennsylvania Ave NW Suite 301   Washington DC 20006
Ph: 202-296-2810 ▪ Fx: 202-331-7479

WaterJet Technology Association   www.wjta.org
917 Locust St Suite 1100   Saint Louis MO 63101
Ph: 314-241-1445 ▪ Fx: 314-241-1449

Watermark Association of Artisans   www.watermarkusa.net
150 Hwy 158 E   Camden NC 27921
Ph: 252-338-0853 ▪ Fx: 252-338-1444 ▪ TF: 800-982-8337

Waterpark Association, World   www.waterparks.org
8826 Santa Fe Dr Suite 310   Overland Park KS 66212
Ph: 913-599-0300 ▪ Fx: 913-599-0520

Waterproofers & Allied Workers, United Union of Roofers   www.unionroofers.com
1660 L St NW Suite 800   Washington DC 20036
Ph: 202-463-7663 ▪ Fx: 202-463-6906

Waterproofing Contractors Association   www.thewaterproofers.org
8608 Timberwind Dr   Raleigh NC 27615
Ph: 919-870-0315

Waterproofing & Restoration Institute, Sealant   www.swrionline.org
14 W 3rd St Suite 200   Kansas City MO 64105
Ph: 816-472-7974 ▪ Fx: 816-472-7765

Waterproofing & Structural Repair Contractors, National   www.nawsrc.com
Association of   8015 Corporate Dr Suite A   Baltimore MD 21236
Ph: 410-931-3332 ▪ Fx: 410-931-2060 ▪ TF: 800-245-6292

Waters Foundation   www.watersfoundation.org
5635 N Campbell Ave   Tucson AZ 85750
Ph: 520-577-1384

Waterways Conference Inc, National   www.waterways.org
1130 17th St NW Suite 200   Washington DC 20036
Ph: 202-296-4415 ▪ Fx: 202-835-3861

Waterways Operators, American   www.americanwaterways.com
801 N Quincy St Suite 200   Arlington VA 22203
Ph: 703-841-9300 ▪ Fx: 703-841-0389

Watusi Association, World   www.watusicattle.com
PO Box 14   Crawford NE 69339
Ph: 308-665-3919 ▪ Fx: 308-665-1931

WAVE Inc   www.waveinc.org
525 School St SW Suite 500   Washington DC 20024
Ph: 202-484-0103 ▪ Fx: 202-488-7595 ▪ TF: 800-274-2005

Way International The   www.theway.org
5555 Wierwille Rd PO Box 328   New Knoxville OH 45871
Ph: 419-753-2523 ▪ Fx: 419-753-2903

Wayne & Gladys Valley Foundation
1939 Harrison St Suite 510   Oakland CA 94612
Ph: 510-466-6060 ▪ Fx: 510-466-6067

We Believe   www.webelieve.cc
1899 Pinehurst Ave   Saint Paul MN 55116
Ph: 651-698-1857 ▪ Fx: 651-699-8390

We Care Program   www.wecareprogram.org
5825 Hwy 21   Atmore AL 36502
Ph: 334-368-8818 ▪ Fx: 334-368-0932

We The People   www.wtp.org
200 Harrison St   Oakland CA 94607
Ph: 510-836-3273 ▪ Fx: 510-836-3063

Wealth, International Association for Research in Income &   www.econ.nyu.edu/iariw
New York Univ Dept of Economics 269 Mercer St Rm 700   New York NY 10003
Ph: 212-924-4386 ▪ Fx: 212-366-5067

Weather Association, Air   www.airweaassn.org
1697 Capri Way   Charlottesville VA 22911
Ph: 434-296-2832 ▪ Fx: 434-296-9966

Weather Association, National   www.nwas.org
1697 Capri Way   Charlottesville VA 22911
Ph: 434-296-9966

Weather Modification Association   www.weathermodification.org
PO Box 26926   Fresno CA 93729
Ph: 559-434-3486

Weather Risk Management Association   www.wrma.org
1156 15th St NW Suite 900   Washington DC 20005
Ph: 202-289-3800 ▪ Fx: 202-393-0336

Weather Service Employees Organization, National   www.nwseo.org
601 Pennsylvania Ave Suite 900   Washington DC 20004
Ph: 703-293-9651 ▪ Fx: 703-293-9653

Weatherhead Center for International Affairs   www.wcfia.harvard.edu
Harvard Univ 1033 Massachusetts Ave   Cambridge MA 02138
Ph: 617-495-4420 ▪ Fx: 617-495-8292

Weavers, National Association of Wheat   www.geocities.com/nawwstrawart

Web Consortium, World Wide   www.w3.org
MIT Laboratory for Computer Science 200 Technology
Sq   Cambridge MA 02139
Ph: 617-253-2613 ▪ Fx: 617-258-5999

Web Offset Association   www.gain.net/PIA_GATF/WOA/main.html
100 Daingerfield Rd   Alexandria VA 22314
Ph: 703-519-8100 ▪ Fx: 703-548-3227 ▪ TF: 800-742-2666

Web Sling & Tie Down Association   www.wstda.com
2105 Laurel Bush Rd Suite 200   Bel Air MD 21015
Ph: 443-640-1070 ▪ Fx: 443-640-1031

Webby Awards   www.webbyawards.com
3515 24th St   San Francisco CA 94110
Ph: 415-824-2268 ▪ Fx: 415-707-2015

Webmasters Association, International   www.iwanet.org
119 E Union St Suite F   Pasadena CA 91103
Ph: 626-449-3709 ▪ Fx: 626-449-8308

Webmasters, World Organization of   www.joinwow.org
9580 Oak Pkwy Suite 7-177   Folsom CA 95630
Ph: 916-608-1597 ▪ Fx: 916-987-3022

Wedding Careers Worldwide Association   www.weddingcareers.com
18087 Holly Forest   Houston TX 77084
Ph: 281-382-9936 ▪ Fx: 281-997-4143

Wedding Consultants, Association of Certified   www.weddingconsulting.com
PO Box 261163   Plano TX 75026
Ph: 972-596-7450 ▪ Fx: 972-985-4442 ▪ TF: 800-520-2292

Wedding Consultants, Association of Certified Professional   www.acpwc.com
7791 Prestwick Cir   San Jose CA 95135
Ph: 408-528-9000 ▪ Fx: 408-528-9333

Wedding & Event Videographers Association International   www.weva.com
8499 S Tamiami Trail PMB 208   Sarasota FL 34238
Ph: 941-923-5334 ▪ Fx: 941-921-3836

Wedding & Portrait Photographers International   www.wppinow.com/index2.tml
1312 Lincoln Blvd   Santa Monica CA 90406
Ph: 310-451-0090 ▪ Fx: 310-395-9058

Wedding Professionals International, Association for   www.afwpi.com
2730 Arden Way Suite 218   Sacramento CA 95825
Ph: 916-482-3010 ▪ Fx: 916-482-2025 ▪ TF: 800-242-4461

Weed Science Society of America   www.wssa.net
PO Box 7050   Lawrence KS 66044
Ph: 785-843-1235 ▪ Fx: 785-843-1274 ▪ TF: 800-627-0629

Weed Science Society, International   www.olemiss.edu/orgs/iws/DEFAULT.HTM
PO Box 8048   University MS 38677
Ph: 662-915-1036 ▪ Fx: 662-915-1035

Weekly Newspaper Editors, International Society of   www.iswne.org
Missouri Southern State Univ 3950 E Newman Rd   Joplin MO
64801
Ph: 417-625-9736 ▪ Fx: 417-659-4445

Weighing & Measurement, International Society of   www.iswm.org
15245 Shady Grove Rd Suite 130   Rockville MD 20850
Ph: 301-258-1115 ▪ Fx: 301-990-9771

Weight Discrimination, Council on Size &   www.cswd.org
PO Box 305   Mount Marion NY 12456
Ph: 845-679-1209 ▪ Fx: 845-679-1206

Weight Engineers, Society of Allied   www.sawe.org
204 Hubbard St   Glastonbury CT 06033
Ph: 860-633-0850 ▪ Fx: 860-633-8971

(Weight Loss) TOPS Club Inc   www.tops.org
4575 S 5th St   Milwaukee WI 53207
Ph: 414-482-4620 ▪ TF: 800-932-8677

Weight Watchers International Inc   www.weightwatchers.com
175 Crossways Pk W   Woodbury NY 11797
Ph: 516-390-1400 ▪ Fx: 516-390-1632 ▪ TF: 800-651-6000

Weightlifting, USA   www.usaweightlifting.org
1 Olympic Plaza   Colorado Springs CO 80909
Ph: 719-866-4508 ▪ Fx: 719-866-4741

Weights & Measures, National Conference on   www.ncwm.net
15245 Shady Grove Rd Suite 130   Rockville MD 20850
Ph: 240-632-9454 ▪ Fx: 301-990-9771

Weill Kurt Foundation for Music   www.kwf.org
7 E 20th St   New York NY 10003
Ph: 212-505-5240 ▪ Fx: 212-353-9663

Weingart Foundation   www.weingartfnd.org
1055 W 7th St Suite 3050   Los Angeles CA 90017
Ph: 213-688-7799 ▪ Fx: 213-688-1515

Weizmann Institute of Science, American Committee for the   www.weizmann-usa.org
130 E 59th St   New York NY 10022
Ph: 212-895-7900 ▪ Fx: 212-895-7999

Welara Pony Society, American   www.WelaraRegistry.com/
PO Box 401   Yucca Valley CA 92286
Ph: 760-364-2048

Welch Robert A Foundation   www.welch1.org
5555 San Felipe St Suite 1900   Houston TX 77056
Ph: 713-961-9884 ▪ Fx: 713-961-5168

Welder Manufacturers' Association, Resistance   www.rwma.org
1900 Arch St   Philadelphia PA 19103
Ph: 215-564-3484 ▪ Fx: 215-564-2175

Welding Bureau, National Certified Pipe   www.mcaa.org/ncpwb
1385 Piccard Dr   Rockville MD 20850
Ph: 301-869-5800 ▪ Fx: 301-990-9690

Welding Distributors Association, Gases &   www.gawda.org
1900 Arch St   Philadelphia PA 19103
Ph: 215-564-3484 ▪ Fx: 215-963-7184

Welding Institute, Edison   www.ewi.org
1250 Arthur E Adams Dr   Columbus OH 43221
Ph: 614-688-5000 ▪ Fx: 614-688-5001

Welding Research Council   www.forengineers.org/wrc/
3 Park Ave 27th Fl   New York NY 10016
Ph: 212-591-7956 ▪ Fx: 212-591-7183

Welding Society, American   www.aws.org
550 NW Le Jeune Rd   Miami FL 33126
Ph: 305-443-9353 ▪ Fx: 305-443-7559 ▪ TF: 800-443-9353

Weldors Association Inc, National Blacksmiths &   blacksmithing.tripod.com
PO Box 123   Arnold NE 69120
Ph: 308-848-2913

Welfare Agencies, Federation of Protestant   www.fpwa.org
281 Park Ave S   New York NY 10010
Ph: 212-777-4800 ▪ Fx: 212-673-4085

Welfare Association, Catholic Near East   www.cnewa.org
1011 1st Ave   New York NY 10022
Ph: 212-826-1480 ▪ Fx: 212-838-1344 ▪ TF: 800-442-6392

Welfare Association, Presbyterian Health Education &   www.pcusa.org/phewa
100 Witherspoon St Rm 3041   Louisville KY 40202
Ph: 502-569-5794 ▪ Fx: 502-569-8034 ▪ TF: 888-728-7228

Welfare Foundation Inc, Public   www.publicwelfare.org
1200 U St NW   Washington DC 20009
Ph: 202-965-1800 ▪ Fx: 202-265-8852 ▪ TF: 800-275-7934

Welfare Institute, Animal   www.awionline.org
PO Box 3650 Georgetown Stn   Washington DC 20007
Ph: 202-337-2332 ▪ Fx: 202-338-9478

Welfare Institute, Child   www.gocwi.org
3950 Shackleford Rd Suite 175   Duluth GA 30096
Ph: 770-935-8484 ▪ Fx: 770-935-0344

Welfare Law Center   www.welfarelaw.org
275 7th Ave Suite 1205   New York NY 10001
Ph: 212-633-6967 ▪ Fx: 212-633-6371

Welfare Ministries, United Methodist Association   www.umassociation.org
of Health &   601 W Riverview Ave   Dayton OH 45406
Ph: 937-227-9494 ▪ Fx: 937-222-7364 ▪ TF: 800-411-9901

Welfare Research Inc   www.welfareresearch.org
112 State St Suite 1020   Albany NY 12207
Ph: 518-432-2563 ▪ Fx: 518-432-2564

Welfare Warriors   welfarewarriors.org
2711 W Michigan Ave   Milwaukee WI 53208
Ph: 414-342-6662 ▪ Fx: 414-342-6667

Well Association, National Stripper
302 N Independence St   Enid OK 73702
Ph: 580-233-8955

Well Log Analysts, Society of Petrophysicists &   www.spwla.org
8866 Gulf Fwy Suite 320   Houston TX 77017
Ph: 713-947-8727 ▪ Fx: 713-947-7181

Well Spouse Foundation   www.wellspouse.org
63 W Main St Suite H   Freehold NJ 07728
Ph: 732-577-8899 ▪ Fx: 732-577-8644 ▪ TF: 800-838-0879

Wellness Councils of America   www.welcoa.org
9802 Nicholas St Suite 315   Omaha NE 68114
Ph: 402-827-3590 ▪ Fx: 402-827-3594

Wellness Institute, National   www.nationalwellness.org
1300 College Ct PO Box 827   Stevens Point WI 54481
Ph: 715-342-2969 ▪ Fx: 715-342-2979 ▪ TF: 800-243-8694

Wellness Nutritionists, Sports Cardiovascular &   www.scandpg.org
PO Box 60820   Colorado Springs CO 80960
Ph: 719-635-6005 ▪ Fx: 719-635-3587

Wellstart International   www.wellstart.org
PO Box 8077   San Diego CA 92138
Ph: 619-295-5192

Welsh-American Foundation, National   www.wales-usa.org
301 Stone Ave   Clarks Summit PA 18411
Ph: 570-587-4131 ▪ Fx: 570-586-4901

Welsh Corgi Club of America, Cardigan   www.cardigancorgis.com
7446 Park Pl   Boulder CO 80301
Ph: 303-530-7107

Welsh Corgi Club of America, Pembroke   www.pembrokecorgi.com
PO Box 2141   Duxbury MA 02331
Ph: 781-934-0110 ▪ Fx: 781-934-6597

Welsh Pony & Cob Society of America   www.welshpony.org
PO Box 2977   Winchester VA 22604
Ph: 540-667-6195

Wendt Center for Loss & Healing   www.wendtcenter.org
730 11th St NW   Washington DC 20001
Ph: 202-624-0010 ▪ Fx: 202-624-0062

Wensleydale Sheep Association, North American   www.wensleydalesheep.org
4589 Fruitland Rd   Loma Rica CA 95901
Ph: 530-743-5262

Wesleyan/Holiness Women Clergy International   www.messiah.edu/whwc
Messiah College 1 College Ave   Grantham PA 17027
Ph: 717-691-6021

West, Native Daughters of the Golden   www.ndgw.org
543 Baker St   San Francisco CA 94117
Ph: 415-563-9091 ▪ Fx: 415-563-5230 ▪ TF: 800-944-6349

West, Native Sons of the Golden   www.nsgw.org
414 Mason St   San Francisco CA 94102
Ph: 415-392-1223 ▪ Fx: 415-392-1230 ▪ TF: 800-337-1875

Westar Institute   www.westarinstitute.org
PO Box 6144   Santa Rosa CA 95406
Ph: 707-523-1323 ▪ Fx: 707-523-1350

Westbeth Corp   www.westbeth.org
463 West St   New York NY 10014
Ph: 212-691-1500 ▪ Fx: 212-691-1502

Western Association of Schools & Colleges   www.wascweb.org
985 Atlantic Ave Suite 100   Alameda CA 94501
Ph: 510-748-9001 ▪ Fx: 510-748-9797

Western Athletic Conference   www.wacsports.com
9250 E Costilla Ave Suite300   Englewood CO 80112
Ph: 303-799-9221 ▪ Fx: 303-799-3888

Western Canada Wilderness Committee   www.wildernesscommittee.org
227 Abbott St   Vancouver BC V6B2K7
Ph: 604-683-8220 ▪ Fx: 604-683-8229 ▪ TF: 800-661-9453

Western Catholic Union   www.wculife.com
510 Maine St   Quincy IL 62301
Ph: 217-223-9721 ▪ Fx: 217-223-9726 ▪ TF: 800-223-4928

Western Center on Law & Poverty   www.wclp.org
3701 Wilshire Blvd Suite 208   Los Angeles CA 90010
Ph: 213-487-7211 ▪ Fx: 213-487-0242

Western Collegiate Hockey Association   wcha.ocsn.com
2190 S High St   Denver CO 80208
Ph: 303-871-4223 ▪ Fx: 303-871-2600

Western Cover Society   www.westerncoversociety.org

Western Economic Association International   www.weainternational.org
7400 Center Ave Suite 109   Huntington Beach CA 92647
Ph: 714-898-3222 ▪ Fx: 714-891-6715

Western-English Trade Association   www.wetaonline.org
451 E 58th Ave Suite 4323   Denver CO 80216
Ph: 303-295-2001 ▪ Fx: 303-295-6108

Western Forestry & Conservation Association   www.westernforestry.org
4033 SW Canyon Rd   Portland OR 97221
Ph: 503-226-4562 ▪ Fx: 503-226-2515

Western Front Association - US Branch   www.wfa-usa.org
96 College Ave   Poughkeepsie NY 12603
Ph: 845-486-6189

Western Golf Association   www.westerngolfassociation.com
1 Briar Rd   Golf IL 60029
Ph: 847-724-4600 ▪ Fx: 847-724-7133

Western Growers Association   www.wga.com
17620 Fitch St   Irvine CA 92614
Ph: 949-863-1000 ▪ Fx: 949-863-9028 ▪ TF: 800-949-4704

Western Hardwood Association   www.westernhardwood.com
PO Box 1095   Camas WA 98607
Ph: 360-838-1600 ▪ Fx: 360-835-1900

Western History Association   www.unm.edu/~wha
Univ of New Mexico MSC 06 3770   Albuquerque NM 87131
Ph: 505-277-5234 ▪ Fx: 505-277-5275

Western Literature Association   www.usu.edu/westlit
Utah State Univ English Dept 3200 Old Main Hill   Logan UT 84322
Ph: 435-797-1603 ▪ Fx: 435-797-4099

Western Manufactured Housing Communities Association   www.wma.org
455 Capitol Mall Suite 800   Sacramento CA 95814
Ph: 916-444-7002

Western Music Association   www.westernmusic.org
PO Box 35008   Tucson AZ 85740
Ph: 877-588-3747

Western National Parks Association   www.wnpa.org
12880 N Vistoso Village Dr   Tucson AZ 85737
Ph: 520-622-1999 ▪ Fx: 520-623-9519

Western Pulp & Paper Workers, Association of   www.awppw.org
PO Box 4566   Portland OR 97208
Ph: 503-228-7486 ▪ Fx: 503-228-1346

Western Railway Historical Society, Ontario &   www.nyow.org

Western Red Cedar Lumber Association   www.wrcla.org
1501-700 W Pender St   Vancouver BC V6C1G8
Ph: 604-684-0266 ▪ Fx: 604-687-4930

Western Red Cedar Pole Association   www.preservedwood.com/wrcpa/main.html
2405 61st Ave SE   Mercer Island WA 98040
Ph: 800-410-1917 ▪ Fx: 206-275-4755

Western US Agricultural Trade Association   www.wusata.org
2500 Main St Suite 110   Vancouver WA 98660
Ph: 360-693-3373 ▪ Fx: 360-693-3464

Western Wood Products Association   www.wwpa.org
522 SW 5th Ave Yeon Bldg Suite 500   Portland OR 97204
Ph: 503-224-3930 ▪ Fx: 503-224-3934

Western Writers of America   www.westernwriters.org

Westminster Kennel Club   www.westminsterkennelclub.org
149 Madison Ave Suite 803   New York NY 10016
Ph: 212-213-3165

WeTip Inc   www.wetip.com
PO Box 1296   Rancho Cucamonga CA 91729
Ph: 909-987-5005 ▪ Fx: 909-987-2477 ▪ TF: 800-782-7463

Wetland Managers, Association of State   www.aswm.org
1434 Helderberg Trail PO Box 269   Berne NY 12023
Ph: 518-872-1804 ▪ Fx: 518-872-2171

Wetland Scientists, Society of   www.sws.org
1313 Dolley Madison Blvd Suite 402   McLean VA 22101
Ph: 703-790-1745 ▪ Fx: 703-790-2672

Wetlands Coalition, National   www.thenwc.org
1050 Thomas Jefferson St NW Suite 700   Washington DC 20007
Ph: 202-298-1800

Wetterling Jacob Foundation   www.jwf.org
2314 University Ave W Suite 14   Saint Paul MN 55114
Ph: 651-714-4673 ▪ Fx: 651-714-9098

Whale Adoption Project USA   www.whaleadoption.org
International Wildlife Coalition 70 E Falmouth Hwy   East Falmouth MA 02536
Ph: 508-548-8328 ▪ Fx: 508-548-8542

Whale Foundation, Pacific   www.pacificwhale.org
300 Maalaea Rd Suite 211   Wailuku HI 96793
Ph: 808-879-8811 ▪ Fx: 808-243-9021 ▪ TF: 800-942-5311

Whale Research, Center for   www.whaleresearch.com
PO Box 1577   Friday Harbor WA 98250
Ph: 360-378-5835 ▪ Fx: 360-378-5954

Whales, Save the   www.savethewhales.org
PO Box 2397   Venice CA 90291
Ph: 831-899-9957 ▪ Fx: 831-394-5555

Whaling Museum Society   www.cshwhalingmuseum.org
301 Main St PO Box 25   Cold Spring Harbor NY 11724
Ph: 631-367-3418 ▪ Fx: 631-692-7037

Wheat Associates, US   www.uswheat.org
1620 'I' St NW Suite 801   Washington DC 20006
Ph: 202-463-0999 ▪ Fx: 202-785-1052

Wheat Foods Council   www.wheatfoods.org
10841 S Crossroads Dr Suite 105   Parker CO 80138
Ph: 303-840-8787 ▪ Fx: 303-840-6877

Wheat Gluten Association, International   www.iwga.net
9300 Metcalf Ave Suite 300   Overland Park KS 66212
Ph: 913-381-8180 ▪ Fx: 913-381-8836

Wheat Growers, National Association of   www.wheatworld.org
415 2nd St NE Suite 300   Washington DC 20002
Ph: 202-547-7800 ▪ Fx: 202-546-2638

Wheat PAC
415 2nd St NE Suite 300   Washington DC 20002
Ph: 202-547-7800 ▪ Fx: 202-546-2638

Wheat Quality Council   www.wheatqualitycouncil.org
PO Box 966   Pierre SD 57501
Ph: 605-224-5187 ▪ Fx: 605-224-0517

Wheat Ridge Ministries   www.wheatridge.org
1 Pierce Pl Suite 250E   Itasca IL 60143
Ph: 630-766-9066 ▪ Fx: 630-766-9622 ▪ TF: 800-762-6748

Wheat Weavers, National Association of   www.geocities.com/nawwstrawart

Wheatland, James Buchanan Foundation for the Preservation of   www.lanccounty.com/wheatland
1120 Marietta Ave   Lancaster PA 17603
Ph: 717-392-8721 ▪ Fx: 717-295-8825

Wheel Manufacturers, Institute of Caster &   www.mhia.org/psc
8720 Red Oak Blvd Suite 201   Charlotte NC 28217
Ph: 704-676-1190 ▪ Fx: 704-676-1199 ▪ TF: 800-345-1815

Wheel & Rim Association, National   nationalwheelandrim.org
5121 Bowden Rd Suite 303   Jacksonville FL 32216
Ph: 904-737-2900 ▪ Fx: 904-636-9881

Wheelchair Bowling Association, American   www.awba.org
2912 Country Woods Ln   Palm Harbor FL 34683
Ph: 727-734-0023

Wheelchair Motorcycle Association
101 Torrey St   Brockton MA 02301
Ph: 508-583-8614

Wheelchair Softball Association, National   www.wheelchairsoftball.com
1616 Todd Ct   Hastings MN 55033
Ph: 612-437-1792 ▪ Fx: 612-437-3889

Wheelchair Sports USA   www.wsusa.org
10 Lake Cir Suite G19   Colorado Springs CO 80906
Ph: 719-574-1150 ▪ Fx: 719-574-9840

Wheelmen   www.thewheelmen.org
14 Mulford Ln   Montclair NJ 07042
Ph: 973-509-2523 ▪ Fx: 973-509-2562

Whirling Disease Foundation   www.whirling-disease.org
PO Box 327   Bozeman MT 59771
Ph: 406-585-0860

Whistleblower Center, National   www.whistleblowers.org
3238 P St NW   Washington DC 20007
Ph: 202-342-1902 ▪ Fx: 202-342-1904

Whitaker Foundation   www.whitaker.org
1700 N Moore St Suite 2200   Arlington VA 22209
Ph: 703-528-2430 ▪ Fx: 703-528-2431

White Bison Inc   www.whitebison.org
6145 Lehman Dr Suite 200   Colorado Springs CO 80918
Ph: 719-548-1000 ▪ Fx: 719-548-9407

White Horse & American Creme Horse Registry, American   www.whitehorseranchnebraska.com/registry.htm
90000 Edwards Rd   Naper NE 68755
Ph: 402-832-5560

White House Correspondents' Association   www.whca.net
1920 'N' St NW Suite 300   Washington DC 20036
Ph: 202-833-8000 ▪ Fx: 202-783-0841

White House Historical Association   www.whitehousehistory.org
740 Jackson Pl NW   Washington DC 20503
Ph: 202-737-8292 ▪ Fx: 202-789-0440

White House News Photographers' Association   www.whnpa.org
PO Box 7119 Ben Franklin Stn   Washington DC 20044
Ph: 202-785-5230

White House Project   www.thewhitehouseproject.org
110 Wall St 2nd Fl   New York NY 10005
Ph: 212-785-6001

White Lung Association   www.whitelung.org
PO Box 5171   Baltimore MD 21224
Ph: 410-282-4300

Whitehall Foundation Inc   www.whitehall.org
380 South County Rd PO Box 3423   Palm Beach FL 33480
Ph: 561-655-4474 ▪ Fx: 561-659-4978

Whitetails Unlimited   www.whitetailsunlimited.com
PO Box 720   Sturgeon Bay WI 54235
Ph: 920-743-6777 ▪ Fx: 920-743-4658 ▪ TF: 800-274-5471

Whitewater, American   www.americanwhitewater.org
1424 Fenwick Ln   Silver Spring MD 20910
Ph: 301-589-9453 ▪ Fx: 301-565-6714 ▪ TF: 866-262-8429

Wholesale Booksellers Association, American   www.awba.com
702 S Michigan St   South Bend IN 46601
Ph: 574-288-4141

Wholesale & Department Store Union, Retail   www.rwdsu.org
30 E 29th St   New York NY 10016
Ph: 212-684-5300 ▪ Fx: 212-779-2809

Wholesale Florist & Florist Supplier Association   www.wffsa.org
147 Old Solomons Island Rd Suite 302   Annapolis MD 21401
Ph: 410-573-0400 ▪ Fx: 410-573-5001 ▪ TF: 888-289-3372

Wholesale Furniture Association, International   www.iwfa.net
164 S Main St Suite 310 PO Box 2482   High Point NC 27261
Ph: 336-884-1566 ▪ Fx: 336-884-1350

Wholesale Marketers Association Inc, American www.awmanet.org
2750 Prosperity Ave Suite 550 Fairfax VA 22031
Ph: 703-208-3358 ▪ Fx: 703-573-5738 ▪ TF: 800-482-2962

Wholesale Sales Representatives, Bureau of www.bwsr.com
1100 Spring St NW Suite 700 Atlanta GA 30309
Ph: 404-870-7600 ▪ Fx: 404-870-7601 ▪ TF: 800-877-1808

Wholesale Variety Bakers Association
215 Eva St Saint Paul MN 55107
Ph: 651-224-5761 ▪ Fx: 651-224-9047

Wholesaler-Distributors, National Association of www.naw.org
1725 K St NW Suite 300 Washington DC 20006
Ph: 202-872-0885 ▪ Fx: 202-785-0586

Wholesalers Association, Farm Equipment www.fewa.org
Box 1347 Iowa City IA 52244
Ph: 319-354-5156 ▪ Fx: 319-354-5157

Whooping Crane Conservation Association www.whoopingcrane.com
1393 Henderson Hwy Breaux Bridge LA 70517
Ph: 337-228-7563 ▪ Fx: 337-228-7424

WIC Association, National www.nwica.org
2001 'S' St NW Suite 580 Washington DC 20009
Ph: 202-232-5492 ▪ Fx: 202-387-5281

Wicca, Church & School of www.wicca.org
PO Box 297-IN Hinton WV 25951
Ph: 304-466-2613 ▪ Fx: 304-466-1353

Wider Church Ministries www.ucc.org/wcm
700 Prospect Ave NE 7th Fl Cleveland OH 44115
Ph: 216-736-3200 ▪ Fx: 216-736-3203

Wider Opportunities for Women www.w-o-w.org
1001 Connecticut Ave NW Suite 930 Washington DC 20036
Ph: 202-464-1596 ▪ Fx: 202-464-1660

Wider Quaker Fellowship quaker.org/fwcc/Americas/wqf.html
1506 Race St Philadelphia PA 19102
Ph: 215-241-7293 ▪ Fx: 215-241-7285

Widows, Society of Military www.nous.org
5535 Hempstead Way Springfield VA 22151
Ph: 703-750-1342 ▪ Fx: 703-354-4380 ▪ TF: 800-842-3451

Wiegand EL Foundation
165 W Liberty St Suite 200 Wiegand Ctr Reno NV 89501
Ph: 775-333-0310 ▪ Fx: 775-333-0314

Wiener Malcolm Center for Social Policy www.ksg.harvard.edu/socpol
John F Kennedy School of Government Harvard University 79
John F Kennedy St Cambridge MA 02138
Ph: 617-495-1461 ▪ Fx: 617-496-9053

Wiesenthal Simon Center www.wiesenthal.com
1399 S Roxbury Dr Los Angeles CA 90035
Ph: 310-553-9036 ▪ Fx: 310-772-7655

Wild Animal Orphanage www.wildanimalorphanage.org
9626 Leslie Rd PO Box 690422 San Antonio TX 78269
Ph: 210-688-9038 ▪ Fx: 210-688-9514

Wild Bird Feeding Industry www.wbfi.org
PO Box 763 Scottsbluff NE 69361
Ph: 888-839-1237 ▪ Fx: 308-632-1590

Wild Blueberry Association of North America www.wildblueberries.com
59 Cottage St Bar Harbor ME 04609
Ph: 207-288-2655 ▪ Fx: 207-288-2656 ▪ TF: 800-233-9453

Wild Canid Survival & Research Center www.wolfsanctuary.org
PO Box 760 Eureka MO 63025
Ph: 636-938-5900 ▪ Fx: 636-938-6490

Wild Flower Society, New England www.newfs.org
180 Hemenway Rd Framingham MA 01701
Ph: 617-877-7630 ▪ Fx: 617-877-3658

Wild Horse & Burro Program, National wildhorseandburro.blm.gov
PO Box 3270 Sparks NV 89432
Ph: 775-475-2222 ▪ Fx: 775-861-6711 ▪ TF: 800-417-9647

Wild Sheep, Foundation for North American www.fnaws.org
PO Box 146 Douglas WY 82633
Ph: 307-358-3693 ▪ Fx: 307-358-3262

Wild Turkey Federation, National www.nwtf.com
770 Augusta Rd PO Box 530 Edgefield SC 29824
Ph: 803-637-3106 ▪ Fx: 803-637-0034 ▪ TF: 800-843-6983

Wild Waterfowl Association, International www.wildwaterfowl.org
PO Box 36 Scotland Neck NC 27874
Ph: 252-826-5038 ▪ Fx: 252-826-5284

Wildcat Service Corp
2 Washington St 3rd Fl New York NY 10001
Ph: 212-635-3800 ▪ Fx: 212-635-3872

Wilder Laura Ingalls Memorial Society www.liwms.com
PO Box 426 DeSmet SD 57231
Ph: 800-880-3383 ▪ Fx: 605-854-3064

Wilderness Alliance, Southern Utah www.suwa.org
1471 S 1100 East Salt Lake City UT 84105
Ph: 801-486-3161 ▪ Fx: 801-486-4233

Wilderness Committee, Western Canada www.wildernesscommittee.org
227 Abbott St Vancouver BC V6B2K7
Ph: 604-683-8220 ▪ Fx: 604-683-8229 ▪ TF: 800-661-9453

Wilderness Education Association www.ebl.org/wea
900 E 7th St Bloomington IN 47405
Ph: 812-855-4095 ▪ Fx: 812-855-8697

Wilderness Inquiry www.wildernessinquiry.org
808 14th Ave SE Minneapolis MN 55414
Ph: 612-676-9400 ▪ Fx: 612-676-9401 ▪ TF: 800-728-0719

Wilderness Institute, National www.nwi.org
PO Box 25766 Washington DC 20007
Ph: 703-836-7404 ▪ Fx: 703-836-7405

Wilderness League, Alaska www.alaskawild.org
122 C St NW Suite 240 Washington DC 20002
Ph: 202-544-5205 ▪ Fx: 202-544-5197

Wilderness Medical Society www.wms.org
5390 N Academy Blvd Suite 310 Colorado Springs CO 80910
Ph: 719-572-9255 ▪ Fx: 719-572-1514

Wilderness Society www.wilderness.org
1615 M St NW Washington DC 20036
Ph: 202-833-2300 ▪ Fx: 202-429-3958 ▪ TF: 800-843-9453

Wilderness Society, Canadian Parks & www.cpaws.org
880 Wellington St Suite 506 Ottawa ON K1R6K7
Ph: 613-569-7226 ▪ Fx: 613-569-7098 ▪ TF: 800-333-9453

Wildfowl Carving Association, International iwfca.com

Wildfowl Trust of North America www.wildfowltrust.org/
PO Box 519 Grasonville MD 21638
Ph: 410-827-6694 ▪ Fx: 410-827-6713

Wildland Fire, International Association of www.iawfonline.org
4025 Fair Ridge Dr Fairfax VA 22033
Ph: 785-423-1818 ▪ Fx: 785-542-3511

Wildlands, American www.wildlands.org
40 E Main St Suite 2 Bozeman MT 59715
Ph: 406-586-8175 ▪ Fx: 406-586-8242

Wildlands Project www.wildlandsproject.org
PO Box 455 Richmond VT 05477
Ph: 802-434-4077 ▪ Fx: 802-434-5980

Wildlife Agencies, Association of Midwest Fish &
c/o Nebraska Game & Parks Commission 2200 N 33rd St PO
Box 30370 Lincoln NE 68503
Ph: 402-471-5539 ▪ Fx: 402-471-5528

Wildlife Agencies, International Association of Fish & www.iafwa.org
444 N Capitol St NW Suite 544 Washington DC 20001
Ph: 202-624-7890 ▪ Fx: 202-624-7891

Wildlife Agencies, Southeastern Association of Fish & www.seafwa.org
8500 Freshwater Farms Rd Tallahassee FL 32309
Ph: 850-893-1204 ▪ Fx: 850-893-6204

Wildlife Alliance, Alaska www.akwildlife.org
PO Box 202022 Anchorage AK 99520
Ph: 907-277-0897 ▪ Fx: 907-277-7423

Wildlife Association, Exotic www.exoticwildlifeassociation.com
HC 7 Box 24C Ingram TX 78025
Ph: 830-367-7761 ▪ Fx: 830-895-4998

Wildlife Association, National Military Fish & www.nmfwa.org
6300 Somerset Way Cambria CA 93428
Ph: 805-238-8265

Wildlife Coalition, International www.iwc.org
70 E Falmouth Hwy East Falmouth MA 02536
Ph: 508-548-8328 ▪ Fx: 508-548-8542 ▪ TF: 800-548-8704

Wildlife Commission, Great Lakes Indian Fish & www.glifwc.org
100 Maple St PO Box 9 Odanah WI 54861
Ph: 715-682-6619

(Wildlife Conservation) Ruffed Grouse Society www.ruffedgrousesociety.org
451 McCormick Rd Coraopolis PA 15108
Ph: 412-262-4044 ▪ Fx: 412-262-9207 ▪ TF: 888-564-6747

Wildlife Conservation Society www.wcs.org
2300 Southern Blvd Bronx NY 10460
Ph: 718-220-5100 ▪ Fx: 718-220-2685 ▪ TF: 800-234-5128

Wildlife, Defenders of www.defenders.org
1130 17th St NW Washington DC 20006
Ph: 202-682-9400 ▪ Fx: 202-682-1331 ▪ TF: 800-989-8981

Wildlife Disease Association www.wildlifedisease.org
PO Box 1897 Lawrence KS 66044
Ph: 785-843-1221 ▪ Fx: 785-843-1274

Wildlife Federation, Canadian www.cwf-fcf.org
350 Michael Cowpland Dr Kanata ON K2M2W1
Ph: 613-599-9594 ▪ Fx: 613-599-4428 ▪ TF: 800-563-9453

Wildlife Federation, National www.nwf.org
11100 Wildlife Center Dr Reston VA 20190
Ph: 703-438-6000 ▪ Fx: 703-438-3570 ▪ TF: 800-822-9919

Wildlife Forever www.wildlifeforever.org
2700 Freeway Blvd Brooklyn Center MN 55430
Ph: 763-253-0222

Wildlife Foundation, African www.awf.org
1400 16th St NW Suite 120 Washington DC 20036
Ph: 202-939-3333 ▪ Fx: 202-939-3332 ▪ TF: 888-494-5354

Wildlife Foundation, National Fish & www.nfwf.org
1120 Connecticut Ave NW Rm 900 Washington DC 20036
Ph: 202-857-0166 ▪ Fx: 202-857-0162

Wildlife Foundation, Norcross www.norcrossws.org
250 W 88th St Suite 806 New York NY 10024
Ph: 212-362-4831

Wildlife Fund Canada, World www.wwf.ca
245 Eglinton Ave E Suite 410 Toronto ON M4P3J1
Ph: 416-489-8800 ▪ Fx: 416-489-3611 ▪ TF: 800-267-2632

Wildlife Fund, World www.worldwildlife.org
1250 24th St NW Suite 500 Washington DC 20037
Ph: 202-293-4800 ▪ Fx: 202-293-9211 ▪ TF: 800-225-5993

Wildlife Habitat Council www.wildlifehc.org
8737 Colesville Rd Suite 800 Silver Spring MD 20910
Ph: 301-588-8994 ▪ Fx: 301-588-4629

Wildlife Information Center www.wildlifeinfo.org
PO Box 198 Slatington PA 18080
Ph: 610-760-8889

Wildlife Management Institute www.wildlifemanagementinstitute.org
1146 19th St NW Suite 700 Washington DC 20036
Ph: 202-371-1808 ▪ Fx: 202-408-5059

Wildlife Planners, Organization of www.owpweb.org
402 W Washington St Rm W273 Indianapolis IN 46204
Ph: 317-232-4080 ▪ Fx: 317-232-8150

Wildlife Programs, National Association www.ag.iastate.edu/departments/aecl/naufwp
of University Fisheries & Univ of Montana 310 Lewis Hall
Box 173460 Bozeman MT 59717
Ph: 406-994-2270 ▪ Fx: 406-994-3190

Wildlife Refuge Association, National www.refugenet.org
1010 Wisconsin Ave NW Suite 200 Washington DC 20007
Ph: 202-333-9075 ▪ Fx: 202-333-9077 ▪ TF: 877-396-6972

Wildlife Rehabilitation Council, International
829 Bancroft Way   Berkeley CA 94710
Ph: 707-864-1761 ■ Fx: 707-864-3106
www.iwrc-online.org

Wildlife Rehabilitators Association, National
14 N 7th Ave   Saint Cloud MN 56303
Ph: 320-259-4086
www.nwrawildlife.org

Wildlife Research Education & Conservation, Jane Goodall Institute for   8700 Georgia Ave Suite 500   Silver Spring MD 20910
Ph: 301-565-0086 ■ Fx: 301-565-3188 ■ TF: 800-592-5263
www.janegoodall.org

Wildlife Society
5410 Grosvenor Ln Suite 200   Bethesda MD 20814
Ph: 301-897-9770 ■ Fx: 301-530-2471
www.wildlife.org

Wildlife Society of North America, Abundant
PO Box 2   Beresford SD 57004
Ph: 605-751-0979
www.aws.vcn.com

(Wildlife) TRAFFIC North America
1250 24th St NW Suite 500   Washington DC 20037
Ph: 202-293-4800 ■ Fx: 202-775-8287
www.traffic.org

Wildlife Trust
61 Rt 9W   Palisades NY 10964
Ph: 845-365-8337 ■ Fx: 845-365-8177 ■ TF: 888-978-4275
www.wildlifetrust.org

Willa Cather Pioneer Memorial & Educational Foundation
413 N Webster   Red Cloud NE 68970
Ph: 402-746-2653 ■ Fx: 402-746-2652
www.willacather.org

William & Flora Hewlett Foundation
2121 Sand Hill Rd   Menlo Park CA 94025
Ph: 650-234-4500 ■ Fx: 650-234-4501
www.hewlett.org

William Glasser Institute
22024 Lassen St Suite 118   Chatsworth CA 91311
Ph: 818-700-8000 ■ Fx: 818-700-0555 ■ TF: 800-899-0688
www.wglasser.com

William K Warren Foundation
6585 S Yale Ave Suite 900   Tulsa OK 74136
Ph: 918-492-8100 ■ Fx: 918-481-7935

William Penn Association
709 Brighton Rd   Pittsburgh PA 15233
Ph: 412-231-2979 ■ Fx: 412-231-8535 ■ TF: 800-848-7366
www.williampennassociation.org

William Penn Foundation
100 N 18th St 2 Logan Sq 11th Fl   Philadelphia PA 19103
Ph: 215-988-1830 ■ Fx: 215-988-1823
www.wpennfdn.org

William Randolph Hearst Foundation
888 7th Ave 45th Fl   New York NY 10106
Ph: 212-586-5404 ■ Fx: 212-586-1917
hearstfdn.org

William Wendt Center for Loss & Healing
730 11th St NW   Washington DC 20001
Ph: 202-624-0010 ■ Fx: 202-624-0062
www.wendtcenter.org

Williams Syndrome Association
PO Box 297   Clawson MI 48017
Ph: 248-244-2229 ■ Fx: 248-244-2230
www.williams-syndrome.org

Williamsburg Foundation, Colonial
PO Box 1776   Williamsburg VA 23187
Ph: 757-229-1000 ■ Fx: 757-220-7259
www.history.org

Willie Velasquez Institute
206 Lombard St 1st Fl   San Antonio TX 78226
Ph: 210-922-3118 ■ Fx: 210-932-4055
www.wcvi.org

Willow Mixed Media Inc
25 11th Ave   Glenford NY 12433
Ph: 845-657-2914
www.hudsonvalley.com/willow

Wilson Woodrow Birthplace Foundation
18-24 N Coalter St PO Box 24   Staunton VA 24402
Ph: 540-885-0897 ■ Fx: 540-885-9874 ■ TF: 888-496-6376
www.woodrowwilson.org

Wilson Woodrow International Center for Scholars
1 Woodrow Wilson Plaza 1300 Pennsylvania Ave NW   Washington DC 20004
Ph: 202-691-4000 ■ Fx: 202-691-4001
wwics.si.edu

Wilson Woodrow National Fellowship Foundation
5 Vaughn Dr CN 5281   Princeton NJ 08540
Ph: 609-452-7007 ■ Fx: 609-452-0066
www.woodrow.org

Wind Energy Association, American
122 C St NW Suite 380   Washington DC 20001
Ph: 202-383-2500 ■ Fx: 202-383-2505
www.awea.org

Window Cleaning Association, International
6418 Grovedale Dr Suite 101B   Alexandria VA 22310
Ph: 703-971-7771 ■ Fx: 703-971-7772 ■ TF: 800-875-4922
www.iwca.org

Window Covering Safety Council
355 Lexington Ave Suite 1700   New York NY 10017
Ph: 800-506-4636
www.windowcoverings.org

Window Coverings Association of America
3550 McKelvey Rd Suite 202C   Bridgeton MO 63044
Ph: 314-770-0229 ■ Fx: 314-770-0263 ■ TF: 888-298-9222
www.wcaa.org

Window & Door Manufacturers Association
1400 E Touhy Ave Suite 470   Des Plaines IL 60018
Ph: 847-299-5200 ■ Fx: 847-299-1286 ■ TF: 800-223-2301
www.wdma.com

Window Film Association, International
PO Box 3871   Martinsville VA 24115
Ph: 276-666-4932
www.iwfa.com

Window Institute, Steel
1300 Sumner Ave   Cleveland OH 44115
Ph: 216-241-7333 ■ Fx: 216-241-0105
www.steelwindows.com

Windstar Foundation
PO Box 656   Snowmass CO 81654
Ph: 970-927-5435
www.wstar.org

Windsurfing Association, US
PO Box 99   Chelsea MI 48118
Ph: 877-386-8708
www.uswindsurfing.org

Windward Foundation
55 Windward Ln   Klickitat WA 98628
Ph: 509-369-2000
www.windward.org

Wine Alliance for Research & Education, American
PO Box 765   Washington DC 20004
Ph: 800-700-4050
www.alcohol-aware.com

Wine & Allied Workers Div, UFCW International Union Distillery
219 Paterson Ave   Little Falls NJ 07424
Ph: 973-237-1241 ■ Fx: 973-890-1956

Wine Appreciation Guild
360 Swift Ave Suite 34   South San Francisco CA 94080
Ph: 650-866-3020 ■ Fx: 650-866-3513 ■ TF: 800-231-9463
www.wineappreciation.com

Wine & Beer Trade Association, Home
PO Box 1373   Valrico FL 33595
Ph: 813-685-4261 ■ Fx: 813-681-5625
www.hwbta.org

Wine Educators, Society of
1200 G St NW Suite 360   Washington DC 20005
Ph: 202-347-5677 ■ Fx: 202-347-5667
www.wine.gurus.com

Wine & Food, American Institute of
304 W Liberty St Suite 201   Louisville KY 40202
Ph: 800-274-2493 ■ Fx: 502-589-3602
www.aiwf.com

Wine & Food Institute, Italian
60 E 42nd St Suite 1341 PO Box 789   New York NY 10150
Ph: 212-867-4111 ■ Fx: 212-867-4114
www.italianwineandfoodinstitute.com

Wine & Grape Foundation, New York
350 Elm St   Penn Yan NY 14527
Ph: 315-536-7442 ■ Fx: 315-536-0719
www.newyorkwines.org

Wine Growers Association, San Joaquin Valley
PO Box 2908   Fresno CA 93745
Ph: 559-834-2525 ■ Fx: 559-834-1348

Wine Growers Association, Vinifera
PO Box 10045   Alexandria VA 22310
Ph: 703-922-7049 ■ Fx: 703-922-0617

Wine Institute
425 Market St Suite 1000   San Francisco CA 94105
Ph: 415-512-0151 ■ Fx: 415-442-0742
www.wineinstitute.org

Wine Institute, Greek Food &
34-80 48th St   Long Island City NY 11101
Ph: 718-729-5277 ■ Fx: 718-361-9725

Wine Society, American
3006 Latta Rd   Rochester NY 14612
Ph: 585-225-7613
www.americanwinesociety.com

Wine, Society of Medical Friends of
511 Jones Pl   Walnut Creek CA 94597
Ph: 925-933-9691 ■ Fx: 925-939-5224
medicalfriendsofwine.org

(Wine) Sommelier Society of America
PO Box 20080 West Village Stn   New York NY 10014
Ph: 212-679-4190 ■ Fx: 212-255-8959
www.sommeliersocietyofamerica.org

Wine & Spirits Shippers Association Inc
11800 Sunrise Valley Dr Suite 332   Reston VA 22091
Ph: 703-860-2300 ■ Fx: 703-860-2422 ■ TF: 800-368-3167
www.wssa.com

Wine & Spirits Wholesalers of America Inc
805 15th St NW Suite 430   Washington DC 20005
Ph: 202-371-9792 ■ Fx: 202-789-2405
www.wswa.org

Wine & Spirits Wholesalers of America PAC
805 15th St NW Suite 430   Washington DC 20005
Ph: 202-371-9792 ■ Fx: 202-789-2405

Winegrape Growers, California Association of
555 University Ave Suite 250   Sacramento CA 95825
Ph: 916-924-5370
www.cawg.org

Wineries Association, Sonoma County
5000 Roberts Lake Rd Suite A   Rohnert Park CA 94928
Ph: 707-586-3795 ■ Fx: 707-586-1383 ■ TF: 800-939-7666
www.sonomawine.com

Winery Suppliers, Association of
21 Tamal Vista Blvd Suite 196   Corte Madera CA 94925
Ph: 415-924-2640 ■ Fx: 415-927-0608

Wings Foundation
8725 W 14th Ave Suite 150   Lakewood CO 80215
Ph: 303-238-8660 ■ TF: 800-373-8671
www.wingsfound.org

Wings of Hope Inc
Spirit of St Louis Airport 18590 Edison Ave   Chesterfield MO 63005
Ph: 636-537-1302 ■ Fx: 636-537-3139 ■ TF: 800-448-9487
www.wings-of-hope.org

Wings Inc, a Wish with
917 W Sanford St   Arlington TX 76012
Ph: 817-469-9474 ■ Fx: 817-275-6005
www.awishwithwings.org

Winnebago-Itasca Travelers Club
PO Box 152   Forest City IA 50436
Ph: 641-585-3535 ■ Fx: 641-585-6966 ■ TF: 800-643-4892
www.winnebagoind.com/html/lifestyle/wit/wit.html

Winrock International
38 Winrock Dr   Morrilton AR 72110
Ph: 501-727-5435 ■ Fx: 501-727-5242
www.winrock.org

Winslow House Association, Historic
644 Careswell St   Marshfield MA 02050
Ph: 781-837-5753
www.winslowhouse.org

Winston Churchill Foundation of the US
PO Box 1240   New York NY 10028
Ph: 212-879-3480
www.thechurchillscholarships.com

Wire Association International
PO Box 578   Guilford CT 06437
Ph: 203-453-2777 ■ Fx: 203-453-8384
www.wirenet.org

Wire Cloth Institute, American
25 N Broadway   Tarrytown NY 10591
Ph: 914-332-0040 ■ Fx: 914-332-1541
www.wireclothinstitute.org

Wire Fabricators Association
710 E Ogden Ave Suite 600   Naperville IL 60563
Ph: 630-579-3278 ■ Fx: 630-369-2488
www.wirefabricators.org

Wire Producers Association, American
801 N Fairfax St Suite 211   Alexandria VA 22314
Ph: 703-299-4434 ■ Fx: 703-299-9233
www.awpa.org

Wire Reinforcement Institute
942 Main St Suite 300   Hartford CT 06103
Ph: 800-552-4974 ■ Fx: 860-808-3009
www.wirereinforcementinstitute.org

Wire Rope Fabricators, Associated
PO Box 20126   Lehigh Valley PA 18002
Ph: 610-974-9974 ■ Fx: 610-691-6833
www.awrf.org

Wire Rope Technical Board
801 N Fairfax St Suite 211   Alexandria VA 22314
Ph: 703-299-8550 ▪ Fx: 703-299-9233

Wireless Association, Antique   www.antiquewireless.org
PO Box E   Breesport NY 14816
Ph: 607-739-5443 ▪ Fx: 607-796-6230

Wireless Association, Quarter Century   www.qcwa.org
159 E 16th Ave   Eugene OR 97401
Ph: 541-683-0987 ▪ Fx: 541-683-4181

Wireless Communications Association International   www.wcai.com
1333 H St NW Suite 700W   Washington DC 20005
Ph: 202-452-7823 ▪ Fx: 202-452-0041

Wireless Dealers Association   www.wirelessindustry.com
9746 Tappenbeck Dr   Houston TX 77055
Ph: 713-467-0077 ▪ Fx: 800-820-2284 ▪ TF: 800-624-6918

Wireless Foundation   www.wirelessfoundation.org
1400 16th St NW Suite 600   Washington DC 20036
Ph: 202-785-0081 ▪ Fx: 202-467-5532

Wireless Infrastructure Association, PCIA -   www.pcia.com
500 Montgomery St Suite 700   Alexandria VA 22314
Ph: 703-739-0300 ▪ Fx: 703-836-1608 ▪ TF: 800-759-0300

Wireless Location Industry Association   www.wliaonline.org
1225 19th St NW   Washington DC 20036
Ph: 202-955-6067

Wireless Pioneers, Society of   www.sowp.org
PO Box 86   Geyserville CA 95441
Ph: 707-545-0766

Wireless Telecommunications Association, International   www.iwta.org
200 N Glebe Rd Suite 1000   Arlington VA 22203
Ph: 202-331-7773 ▪ Fx: 202-331-9062

Wiring Harness Manufacturers Association   www.whma.org
7500 Flying Cloud Dr Suite 900   Eden Prairie MN 55344
Ph: 952-253-6225 ▪ Fx: 952-835-4774

Wisconsin Cheese Makers Association   www.wischeesemakersassn.org
8030 Excelsior Dr Suite 305   Madison WI 53717
Ph: 608-828-4550 ▪ Fx: 608-828-4551

Wisconsin Dairy Products Association
8383 Greenway Blvd   Middleton WI 53562
Ph: 608-836-3336 ▪ Fx: 608-836-3334

Wisconsin Evangelical Lutheran Synod   www.wels.net
2929 N Mayfair Rd   Milwaukee WI 53222
Ph: 414-256-3888 ▪ Fx: 414-256-3899

Wise Giving Alliance, Council of Better Business Bureaus Inc   www.give.org
4200 Wilson Blvd Suite 800   Arlington VA 22203
Ph: 703-276-0100 ▪ Fx: 703-525-8277

Wish Foundation Inc, Special   www.spwish.org
5340 E Main St Suite 208   Columbus OH 43213
Ph: 614-575-9474 ▪ Fx: 614-575-1866 ▪ TF: 800-486-9474

WISH List   www.thewishlist.org
499 S Capitol St SW Suite 408   Washington DC 20003
Ph: 202-479-1230 ▪ Fx: 202-479-1231 ▪ TF: 800-756-9474

Wish with Wings Inc, a   www.awishwithwings.org
917 W Sanford St   Arlington TX 76012
Ph: 817-469-9474 ▪ Fx: 817-275-6005

With Arms Wide Open Foundation   www.witharmswideopen.org
525 E College Ave   Tallahassee FL 32301
Ph: 850-222-3882 ▪ Fx: 850-222-1461

Witness Ministries, United Church of Christ Justice &   www.ucc.org/justice/index.html
700 Prospect Ave   Cleveland OH 44115
Ph: 216-736-3704 ▪ Fx: 216-736-3703

Witness for Peace   www.witnessforpeace.org
1229 15th St NW   Washington DC 20005
Ph: 202-588-1471 ▪ Fx: 202-588-1472

Wives of America Inc, Gold Star   www.goldstarwives.org
5510 Columbia Pike Suite 205   Arlington VA 22204
Ph: 888-479-9788

WK Kellogg Foundation   www.wkkf.org
1 Michigan Ave E   Battle Creek MI 49017
Ph: 269-968-1611 ▪ Fx: 269-968-0413

WM Keck Foundation   www.wmkeck.org
550 S Hope St Suite 2500   Los Angeles CA 90071
Ph: 213-680-3833 ▪ Fx: 213-614-0934

Wolf, Mission: www.missionwolf.com
PO Box 211   Silver Cliff CO 81252
Ph: 719-859-2157

Woman Geographers, Society of   www.iswg.org
415 E Capital St SE   Washington DC 20003
Ph: 202-546-9228 ▪ Fx: 202-546-5232

Woman's Economic Development Corp, American   www.awed.org
216 E 45th St 10th Fl   New York NY 10017
Ph: 917-368-6100

Woman's Exchanges, Federation of
19 Upper Price Rd   Saint Louis MO 63132
Ph: 314-997-4364 ▪ Fx: 314-872-3505

Woman's Missionary Union   www.wmu.com
100 Missionary Ridge   Birmingham AL 35242
Ph: 205-991-8100 ▪ Fx: 205-991-4990 ▪ TF: 800-968-7301

Woman's National Democratic Club   www.democraticwoman.org
1526 New Hampshire Ave NW   Washington DC 20036
Ph: 202-232-7363 ▪ Fx: 202-986-2791

Woman's Party, National   www.sewallbelmont.org
144 Constitution Ave NE   Washington DC 20002
Ph: 202-546-1210 ▪ Fx: 202-546-3997

Woman's Society of Certified Public Accountants, American   www.awscpa.org
136 S Keowee St   Dayton OH 45402
Ph: 937-222-1872 ▪ Fx: 937-222-5794 ▪ TF: 800-297-2721

Women, 9to5 National Association of Working   www.9to5.org
152 W Wisconsin Ave Suite 408   Milwaukee WI 53203
Ph: 414-274-0925 ▪ Fx: 414-272-2870 ▪ TF: 800-522-0925

(Women) About-Face   www.about-face.org
PO Box 77665   San Francisco CA 94107
Ph: 415-436-0212

Women Accountants, American Society of   www.aswa.org
8405 Greensboro Dr Suite 800   McLean VA 22102
Ph: 703-506-3265 ▪ Fx: 703-506-3266

Women in Accounting, Educational Foundation for   www.efwa.org
PO Box 1925   Southeastern PA 19399
Ph: 610-407-9229 ▪ Fx: 610-644-3713

Women Active in Letters & Social Change   malcs.chicanas.com

Women in Aerospace   www.womeninaerospace.org
PO Box 16721   Alexandria VA 22302
Ph: 202-547-9451

Women Affirming Life   www.affirmlife.com
PO Box 35532   Brighton MA 02135
Ph: 617-254-2277 ▪ Fx: 617-254-2299

Women Against Military Madness   www.worldwidewamm.org
310 E 38th St Suite 222   Minneapolis MN 55409
Ph: 612-827-5364 ▪ Fx: 612-827-6433

Women & Aging, National Center on   heller.brandeis.edu/national/ind.html
Brandeis University Heller Graduate School MS 035   Waltham
MA 02454
Ph: 781-736-3866 ▪ Fx: 781-736-3865 ▪ TF: 800-929-1995

(Women) Aglow International   www.aglow.org
152 3rd Ave S Suite 103 PO Box 1749   Edmonds WA 98020
Ph: 425-775-7282 ▪ Fx: 425-778-9615 ▪ TF: 800-755-2456

Women Alive   www.women-alive.org
1566 S Burnside Ave   Los Angeles CA 90019
Ph: 323-965-1564 ▪ Fx: 323-965-9886 ▪ TF: 800-554-4876

Women for America, Concerned   www.cwfa.org
1015 15th St NW Suite 1100   Washington DC 20005
Ph: 202-488-7000 ▪ Fx: 202-488-0806

Women, American Association of   www.amwomen.org
337 Washington Blvd Suite 1   Marina del Ray CA 90292
Ph: 310-822-4449 ▪ Fx: 310-822-4577 ▪ TF: 800-867-7777

Women, American Association of University   www.aauw.org
1111 16th St NW   Washington DC 20036
Ph: 202-785-7700 ▪ Fx: 202-872-1425 ▪ TF: 800-326-2289

Women in Animation   www.womeninanimation.org

Women Artists, National Association of   www.nawanet.org
80 5th Ave Suite 1405   New York NY 10011
Ph: 212-675-1616

Women Association, International Aviation   www.iawa.org
PO Box 4491   New York NY 10163
Ph: 212-921-5100 ▪ Fx: 212-774-7415

Women, Association of Professional Insurance   www.apiw.org
551 5th Ave Suite 1625   New York NY 10176
Ph: 212-867-0228 ▪ Fx: 212-867-2544

Women, Association of Real Estate   www.arew.org
551 5th Ave Suite 3025   New York NY 10176
Ph: 212-599-6181 ▪ Fx: 212-687-4016

Women Athletic Administrators, National Association of Collegiate   www.nacwaa.org
4701 Wrightsville Ave Oak Park D-1   Wilmington NC 28403
Ph: 910-793-8244 ▪ Fx: 910-793-8246

Women in Aviation International   www.wai.org
101 Corsair Dr Suite 101   Daytona Beach FL 32114
Ph: 386-226-7996 ▪ Fx: 386-226-7998

Women in Aviation Maintenance, Association for   www.awam.org
PO Box 1030   Edgewater FL 32132
Ph: 386-424-5780 ▪ Fx: 386-428-3534

Women Band Directors International   www.eskimo.com/~moorhous

(Women) Beta Sigma Phi   www.betasigmaphi.org
1800 W 91st Pl   Kansas City MO 64114
Ph: 816-444-6800 ▪ Fx: 816-333-6206 ▪ TF: 800-821-3989

Women Bowling Writers Association, National   www.nwbw.freeservers.com
3001 21st St   Lubbock TX 79410
Ph: 806-795-3830

Women in Business, Asian   www.awib.org
358 5th Ave Suite 504   New York NY 10001
Ph: 212-868-1368 ▪ Fx: 212-868-1373

Women in Business, Graduate   www.gwib.org

Women Business Owners, Association of African-American
3363 Alden Pl NE   Washington DC 20019
Ph: 202-399-3645

Women Business Owners, National Association of   www.nawbo.org
8405 Greensboro Dr Suite 800   McLean VA 22102
Ph: 703-506-3268 ▪ Fx: 703-506-3266 ▪ TF: 800-556-2926

Women in Cable & Telecommunications   www.wict.org
14555 Avion Pkwy Suite 250   Chantilly VA 20151
Ph: 703-234-9810 ▪ Fx: 703-817-1595

Women Center for Education & Research,   www.cluw.org/programs-edresearch.html
Coalition of Labor Union   1925 K St NW Suite
402   Washington DC 20006
Ph: 202-223-8360 ▪ Fx: 202-776-0537

Women Chefs & Restaurateurs   www.womenchefs.org
304 W Liberty St Suite 201   Louisville KY 40202
Ph: 502-581-0300 ▪ Fx: 502-589-3602 ▪ TF: 877-927-7787

Women Children & Family Service Charities of America   www.womenandchildren.org
21 Tamal Vista Blvd Suite 209   Corte Madera CA 94925
Ph: 800-626-6481 ▪ Fx: 415-924-1379

Women in Church & Society, Black   www.itc.edu/WSP/WSPBWCS.htm
700 ML King Jr Dr   Atlanta GA 30314
Ph: 404-527-5713 ▪ Fx: 404-527-5715

Women Clergy, Association of Full Gospel   afgwc.org
PO Box 2628   Landover MD 20784
Ph: 301-879-6958

Women Clergy International, Wesleyan/Holiness   www.messiah.edu/whwc
Messiah College 1 College Ave   Grantham PA 17027
Ph: 717-691-6021

Women, Coalition of Labor Union www.cluw.org
1925 K St NW Suite 402   Washington DC 20006
Ph: 202-223-8360 ▪ Fx: 202-776-0537

(Women of Color) Links Inc www.linksinc.org
1200 Massachusetts Ave NW   Washington DC 20005
Ph: 202-842-8686 ▪ Fx: 202-842-4020 ▪ TF: 800-574-3720

Women of Color Resource Center www.coloredgirls.org
1611 Telegraph Ave Suite 303   Oakland CA 94612
Ph: 510-444-2700 ▪ Fx: 510-444-2711

(Women) Committee of 200 www.c200.org
625 N Michigan Ave Suite 500   Chicago IL 60611
Ph: 312-751-3477 ▪ Fx: 312-943-9401

Women in Communications, Association for www.womcom.org
780 Ritchie Hwy River Reach Ctr Suite 280-S   Severna Park
MD 21146
Ph: 410-544-7442 ▪ Fx: 410-544-4640

Women in Community Colleges, American Association for www.pc.maricopa.edu/aawcc
1202 W Thomas Rd   Phoenix AZ 85013
Ph: 602-285-7449 ▪ Fx: 602-285-7832

Women in Community Service Inc www.charityadvantage.com/wics
1900 N Beauregard St Suite 103   Alexandria VA 22311
Ph: 703-671-0500 ▪ Fx: 703-671-4489 ▪ TF: 800-442-9427

Women in Computing, Association for www.awc-hq.org
41 Sutter St Suite 1006   San Francisco CA 94104
Ph: 415-905-4663

Women in Conscious Creative Action www.wiccawomen.com
PO Box 5296   Eugene OR 97405
Ph: 541-485-3654

Women in Construction, National Association of www.nawic.org
327 S Adams St   Fort Worth TX 76104
Ph: 817-877-5551 ▪ Fx: 817-877-0324 ▪ TF: 800-552-3506

Women Construction Owners & Executives USA www.wcoeusa.org
4410A Connecticut Ave NW   Washington DC 20008
Ph: 800-788-3548

Women in Construction, Professional www.pwcusa.org
315 E 56th St   New York NY 10022
Ph: 212-486-7745 ▪ Fx: 212-486-0228

Women Contractors Association www.womencontractors.org
PO Box 130441   Houston TX 77219
Ph: 713-807-9977 ▪ Fx: 713-807-9917

Women, Cosmetic Executive www.cew.org
21 E 40th St Suite 1700   New York NY 10016
Ph: 212-685-5955 ▪ Fx: 212-685-3334

Women Dentists, American Association of www.womendentists.org
330 S Wells Suite 1110   Chicago IL 60606
Ph: 312-913-9327 ▪ Fx: 312-461-0238 ▪ TF: 800-920-2293

Women in Development Inc, Refugee www.refwid.org
5501 Seminary Rd Suite 1606-S   Falls Church VA 22041
Ph: 703-931-6442 ▪ Fx: 703-931-5906

Women Employed www.womenemployed.org
111 N Wabash Ave Suite 1300   Chicago IL 60602
Ph: 312-782-3902 ▪ Fx: 312-782-5249

Women in Endocrinology www.women-in-endo.org
Brigham & Women's Hospital Endocrine Div 22 Longwood
Ave   Boston MA 02115
Ph: 617-732-5768 ▪ Fx: 617-732-5764

Women in Engineering Programs & Advocates Network www.wepan.org
Purdue Univ 1284 CIVL Bldg   Rm G167   West Lafayette IN
47907
Ph: 765-494-5387 ▪ Fx: 765-494-9152

Women Engineers, Society of www.societyofwomenengineers.org
230 E Ohio St Suite 400   Chicago IL 60611
Ph: 312-596-5223 ▪ Fx: 312-596-5252

Women Executives in Public Relations www.wepr.org
PO Box 7657   New York NY 10150
Ph: 212-859-7375

Women for Faith & Family www.wf-f.org
PO Box 3286   Saint Louis MO 63132
Ph: 314-863-8385 ▪ Fx: 314-863-5858

Women & Families, National Partnership for www.nationalpartnership.org
1875 Connecticut Ave NW Suite 650   Washington DC 20009
Ph: 202-986-2600 ▪ Fx: 202-986-2539

Women Inc, Federally Employed www.few.org
PO Box 27687   Washington DC 20038
Ph: 202-898-0994

Women in Film www.wif.org
8857 W Olympic Blvd Suite 201   Beverly Hills CA 90211
Ph: 310-657-5144 ▪ Fx: 310-657-5154

Women in Film & Video www.wifv.org
1919 M St NW Suite 225   Washington DC 20036
Ph: 202-429-9438 ▪ Fx: 202-429-9440

Women in the Fire Service www.wfsi.org
PO Box 5446   Madison WI 53705
Ph: 608-233-4768 ▪ Fx: 608-233-4879

Women in Flavor & Fragrance Commerce Inc www.wffc.org
3301 Rt 66 Bldg C Suite 205   Neptune NJ 07753
Ph: 732-922-0500 ▪ Fx: 732-922-0560

Women in Franchising www.womeninfranchising.com
53 W Jackson Blvd Suite 205   Chicago IL 60604
Ph: 312-431-1467 ▪ Fx: 312-431-1469 ▪ TF: 800-222-4943

Women Geoscientists, Association for www.awg.org
PO Box 30645   Lincoln NE 68505
Ph: 402-489-8122

Women & Girls in Education, National Coalition for www.ncwge.org
c/o National Women's Law Ctr 11 Dupont Cir NW Suite
800   Washington DC 20036
Ph: 202-785-7730 ▪ Fx: 202-588-5185

Women, Global Fund for www.globalfundforwomen.org
1375 Sutter St Suite 400   San Francisco CA 94109
Ph: 415-202-7640 ▪ Fx: 415-202-8604

Women in Government www.womeningovernment.org
2600 Virginia Ave NW Suite 709   Washington DC 20037
Ph: 202-333-0825 ▪ Fx: 202-333-0875

Women in Government, Executive www.execwomeningov.org
PO Box 1046   Laurel MD 20725
Ph: 301-725-3500 ▪ Fx: 301-725-5323

Women in Government Relations www.wgr.org
801 N Fairfax St Suite 211   Alexandria VA 22314
Ph: 703-299-8546 ▪ Fx: 703-299-9233

(Women) Grail in the US The www.grail-us.org
932 O'Bannonville Rd   Loveland OH 45140
Ph: 513-683-2340 ▪ Fx: 513-683-4752

Women Grocers of America www.nationalgrocers.org/WGA.html
1005 N Glebe Rd Suite 250   Arlington VA 22201
Ph: 703-516-0700 ▪ Fx: 703-516-0115

Women, Hard Hatted www.hardhattedwomen.org
4207 Lorain Ave   Cleveland OH 44113
Ph: 216-961-4449 ▪ Fx: 216-961-0927

Women Highway Safety Leaders Inc, National Association of www.nawhsl.org
145 Berry Rd   Clinton MS 39056
Ph: 601-924-7815

Women in Hospitality, Network of Executive www.newh.org
PO Box 322   Shawano WI 54166
Ph: 715-526-5267 ▪ Fx: 715-526-5979

Women in Housing & Finance Inc www.whfdc.org
717 Princess St   Alexandria VA 22314
Ph: 703-683-4742 ▪ Fx: 703-683-0018

Women in Insurance & Financial Services www.w-wifs.org
9101 LBJ Fwy Suite 450   Dallas TX 75243
Ph: 469-621-3525 ▪ TF: 800-753-3973

Women, Inter-American Commission of www.oas.org/CIM/
1889 F St NW Rm 880   Washington DC 20006
Ph: 202-458-6084 ▪ Fx: 202-458-6094

Women, International Alliance for www.tiaw.org
8405 Greensboro Dr Suite 800   McLean VA 22102
Ph: 703-506-3284 ▪ Fx: 703-506-3266

Women, International Center for Research on www.icrw.org
1717 Massachusetts Ave NW Suite 302   Washington DC 20036
Ph: 202-797-0007 ▪ Fx: 202-797-0020

Women International, Executive www.executivewomen.org
515 South 700 E Suite 2-A   Salt Lake City UT 84102
Ph: 801-355-2800 ▪ Fx: 801-355-2852

Women International, Financial www.fwi.org
200 N Glebe Rd Suite 820   Arlington VA 22203
Ph: 703-807-2007 ▪ Fx: 703-807-0111

Women International, Jewish www.jewishwomen.org
2000 M St NW Suite 720   Washington DC 20036
Ph: 202-847-1300 ▪ Fx: 202-857-1380 ▪ TF: 800-343-2823

Women (International), National Association of Insurance www.naiw.org
1847 E 15th St   Tulsa OK 74104
Ph: 918-744-5195 ▪ Fx: 918-743-1968 ▪ TF: 800-766-6249

Women in International Security wiis.georgetown.edu
Georgetown Univ Walsh School of Foreign Service Ctr for
Peace & Security Studies 3240 Prospect St
NW   Washington DC 20057
Ph: 202-687-3366 ▪ Fx: 202-687-3233

Women in International Trade, Organization of www.owit.org
1413 K St NW 1st Fl Suite 857   Washington DC 20005
Ph: 202-785-9842

Women Journalists, Association for www.awjdfw.org/
PO Box 2199   Fort Worth TX 76113
Ph: 817-685-3876

Women Judges, National Association of www.nawj.org
1112 16th St NW Suite 520   Washington DC 20036
Ph: 202-393-0222 ▪ Fx: 202-393-0125

Women Law Enforcement Executives, National Association of www.nawlee.com

Women Law Students Association, National www.nwlsa.com

Women Lawyers, National Association of www.abanet.org/nawl
750 N Lake Shore Dr   Chicago IL 60611
Ph: 312-988-6186 ▪ Fx: 312-988-6281

Women, Legal Action for www.legalactionforwomen.org

Women, Legion of Young Polish
Copernicus Ctr 5216 W Lawrence Ave   Chicago IL 60630
Ph: 773-777-9037 ▪ Fx: 773-763-4069

Women Legislators, National Foundation for www.womenlegislators.org
910 16th St NW Suite 100   Washington DC 20006
Ph: 202-293-3040 ▪ Fx: 202-293-5430

Women Legislators, National Order of www.womenlegislators.org/nowl
910 16th St NW Suite 100   Washington DC 20006
Ph: 202-337-3565

Women, Life & Liberty for www.lifeandlibertyforwomen.org
1015 S Taft Hill Rd PMB 213   Fort Collins CO 80521
Ph: 970-416-6872

Women Make Movies www.wmm.com
462 Broadway Rm 500   New York NY 10013
Ph: 212-925-0606 ▪ Fx: 212-925-2052

Women in Managed Care Inc www.wimc.org
4435 Waterfront Dr Suite 101 PO Box 6026   Glen Allen VA
23058
Ph: 804-527-1905 ▪ Fx: 804-747-5316

Women in Management Inc www.wimonline.org
PO Box 9560   Springfield IL 62791
Ph: 877-946-6285 ▪ Fx: 847-683-3751

Women in Management, Association for www.womens.org
927 15th St NW Suite 1000   Washington DC 20005
Ph: 202-659-6364 ▪ Fx: 202-371-1467

Women in Mathematics, Association for
Univ of Maryland 4114 Computer & Space Science
Bldg   College Park MD 20742
Ph: 301-405-7892 ▪ Fx: 301-314-9363
www.awm-math.org

Women in Medicine Program
Association of American Medical Colleges 2450 'N' St
NW   Washington DC 20037
Ph: 202-828-0521 ▪ Fx: 202-828-1125
www.aamc.org/members/wim

(Women) Melpomene Institute
1010 Universitiy Ave W   Saint Paul MN 55104
Ph: 651-642-1951 ▪ Fx: 651-642-1871
www.melpomene.org

Women in the Metal Industries, Association of
515 King St Suite 420   Alexandria VA 22314
Ph: 703-739-8335 ▪ Fx: 703-684-6048
www.awmi.com

**Women in Military Service for America Memorial
Foundation Inc**   Dept 560   Washington DC 20042
Ph: 703-533-1155 ▪ Fx: 703-931-4208 ▪ TF: 800-222-2294
www.womensmemorial.org

Women in Mining
PO Box 260246   Lakewood CO 80226
Ph: 303-298-1535
www.womeninmining.org

Women in Ministry, American Baptist
PO Box 851   Valley Forge PA 19482
Ph: 610-768-2000 ▪ Fx: 610-768-2275 ▪ TF: 800-222-3872
www.abwim.org

Women of the Motion Picture Industry International
c/o Twentieth Century Fox PO Box 900   Beverly Hills CA 90213
Ph: 310-369-4083 ▪ Fx: 310-369-8903
www.wompi.org

Women, Ms Foundation for
120 Wall St 33rd Fl   New York NY 10005
Ph: 212-742-2300 ▪ Fx: 212-742-1653
www.ms.foundation.org

Women in Municipal Government
c/o National League of Cities 1301 Pennsylvania Ave NW Suite
550   Washington DC 20004
Ph: 202-626-3000 ▪ Fx: 202-626-3043

Women in Music, International Alliance for
Indiana University of Pennsylvania Dept of Music Rm
209   Indiana PA 15705
Ph: 724-357-7918 ▪ Fx: 724-357-9570
music.acu.edu/www/iawm

Women in Music National Network
31121 Mission Blvd Suite 300   Hayward CA 94544
Ph: 510-232-3897 ▪ Fx: 510-215-2846
www.womeninmusic.com

Women, National Association of Commissions for
8630 Fenton St Suite 934   Silver Spring MD 20910
Ph: 301-585-8101 ▪ Fx: 301-585-3445 ▪ TF: 800-338-9267
www.nacw.org

Women, National Association of Professional Mortgage
PO Box 2016   Edmonds WA 98020
Ph: 425-778-6162 ▪ Fx: 425-771-9588 ▪ TF: 800-827-3034
www.napmw.org

Women, National Association of University
1001 'E' St SE   Washington DC 20003
Ph: 202-547-3967 ▪ Fx: 202-547-5226
www.nauw.org

Women, National Coalition of 100 Black
38 W 32nd St Suite 1610   New York NY 10001
Ph: 212-947-2196 ▪ Fx: 212-947-2477
www.ncbw.org

Women Inc, National Congress of Black
8484 Georgia Ave Suite 420   Silver Spring MD 20910
Ph: 301-562-8000 ▪ Fx: 301-562-8303 ▪ TF: 877-274-1198
www.npcbw.org

Women, National Congress of Neighborhood
249 Manhattan Ave   Brooklyn NY 11211
Ph: 718-388-8915 ▪ Fx: 718-388-0285

Women, National Council of Catholic
200 N Glebe Rd Suite 703   Arlington VA 22203
Ph: 703-224-0990 ▪ Fx: 703-224-0991 ▪ TF: 800-506-9407
www.nccw.org

Women, National Council of Jewish
53 W 23rd St 6th Fl   New York NY 10010
Ph: 212-645-4048 ▪ Fx: 212-645-7466 ▪ TF: 800-829-6259
www.ncjw.org

Women Inc, National Council of Negro
633 Pennsylvania Ave NW   Washington DC 20004
Ph: 202-737-0120 ▪ Fx: 202-737-0476
www.ncnw.org

Women, National Federation of Democratic
19432 Burlington Dr   Detroit MI 48203
Ph: 313-892-6199 ▪ Fx: 313-892-8424
www.nfdw.org

Women, National Federation of Press
PO Box 5556   Arlington VA 22205
Ph: 703-534-2500 ▪ Fx: 703-534-5751 ▪ TF: 800-780-2715
www.nfpw.org

Women, National Federation of Republican
124 N Alfred St   Alexandria VA 22314
Ph: 703-548-9688 ▪ Fx: 703-548-9836
www.nfrw.org

Women, National League of American Pen
1300 17th St NW   Washington DC 20036
Ph: 202-785-1997 ▪ Fx: 202-452-6868
www.americanpenwomen.org

Women, National Organization for
733 15th St NW 2nd Fl   Washington DC 20005
Ph: 202-628-8669 ▪ Fx: 202-785-8576
www.now.org

Women, National Organization of Italian-American
445 W 59th St Rm 1248   New York NY 10019
Ph: 212-237-8574 ▪ Fx: 212-489-6130
www.noiaw.com

Women Nationally Active for Christ
5233 Mt View Rd PO Box 5002   Antioch TN 37011
Ph: 615-731-6812 ▪ Fx: 615-731-0771
www.nafwb.org/wnac

Women in Numismatics
www.money.org/sum-baber.html

Women PAC, National Organization for
733 15th St NW 2nd Fl   Washington DC 20005
Ph: 202-331-0066 ▪ Fx: 202-785-8576
www.nowpacs.org

Women in Packaging
4290 Bells Ferry Rd Suite 106-17   Kennesaw GA 30144
Ph: 770-924-3563 ▪ Fx: 770-928-2338
womeninpackaging.org

Women in Petroleum, Society of Professional
13511 Queensbury Ln   Houston TX 77079
Ph: 713-461-2898
www.spwp.org

Women, Pi Beta Phi Fraternity for
1154 Town & Country Commons Dr   Town and Country MO
63017
Ph: 636-256-0680 ▪ Fx: 636-256-8124
www.pibetaphi.org

(Women Pilots) Ninety-Nines Inc
4300 Amelia Earhart Rd   Oklahoma City OK 73159
Ph: 405-685-7969 ▪ Fx: 405-685-7985 ▪ TF: 800-944-1929
www.ninety-nines.org

Women Podiatrists Inc, American Association for
PO Box 593   Pleasanton CA 94566
Ph: 925-785-8285 ▪ Fx: 925-426-5617
www.aawpinc.com

Women Police, International Association of
www.iawp.org

Women Policy Studies, Center for
1211 Connecticut Ave NW Suite 312   Washington DC 20036
Ph: 202-872-1770 ▪ Fx: 202-296-8962
www.centerwomenpolicy.org

(Women in Politics) White House Project
110 Wall St 2nd Fl   New York NY 10005
Ph: 212-785-6001
www.thewhitehouseproject.org

Women in Radio & Television, American
8405 Greensboro Dr Suite 800   McLean VA 22102
Ph: 703-506-3290 ▪ Fx: 703-506-3266
www.awrt.org

Women Radiologists, American Association for
4550 Post Oak Pl Suite 342   Houston TX 77027
Ph: 713-623-8335 ▪ Fx: 713-960-0488
www.aawr.org

Women of Reform Judaism - Federation of Temple Sisterhoods
633 3rd Ave   New York NY 10017
Ph: 212-650-4050 ▪ Fx: 212-650-4059
www.rj.org/wrj

Women Religious, Leadership Conference of
8808 Cameron St   Silver Spring MD 20910
Ph: 301-588-4955 ▪ Fx: 301-587-4575
www.lcwr.org

Women, Resourceful
340 Pine St Suite 302   San Francisco CA 94104
Ph: 415-956-3023 ▪ Fx: 415-837-1144
www.rw.org

Women, RVing
PO Box 1940   Apache Junction AZ 85217
Ph: 480-671-6226 ▪ Fx: 480-671-6230 ▪ TF: 888-557-8464
www.rvingwomen.org

Women in Science Inc, Association for
1200 New York Ave NW Suite 650   Washington DC 20005
Ph: 202-326-8940 ▪ Fx: 202-326-8960 ▪ TF: 800-886-2947
www.awis.org

Women Singers Association, Professional
PO Box 884   New York NY 10024
Ph: 212-969-0590
www.womensingers.org

Women in Sisterhood for Action, Black
PO Box 1592   Washington DC 20013
Ph: 202-543-6013 ▪ Fx: 202-543-5719
www.bisa-hq.org

Women for Sobriety Inc
PO Box 618   Quakertown PA 18951
Ph: 215-536-8026 ▪ Fx: 215-538-9026
www.womenforsobriety.org

Women in Sport, National Association for Girls &
1900 Association Dr   Reston VA 20191
Ph: 703-476-3400 ▪ Fx: 703-476-4566 ▪ TF: 800-213-7193
www.aahperd.org

Women in Sports Media, Association for
www.awsmonline.org

Women Strike for Peace
110 Maryland Ave NE Suite 102   Washington DC 20002
Ph: 202-543-2660

Women Surgeons, Association of
414 Plaza Dr Suite 209   Westmont IL 60559
Ph: 630-655-0392 ▪ Fx: 630-655-0391
www.womensurgeons.org

Women & Technology, Institute for
1501 Page Mill Rd MS 1105   Palo Alto CA 94304
Ph: 650-236-4756 ▪ Fx: 650-852-8172
www.iwt.org

Women in Technology International
13351 Riverside Dr Suite 441   Sherman Oaks CA 91423
Ph: 818-788-9484 ▪ Fx: 818-896-4746 ▪ TF: 800-334-9484
www.witi.com

Women in Trades Technology & Science, Institute for
1150 Ballena Blvd Suite 102   Alameda CA 94501
Ph: 510-749-0200 ▪ Fx: 510-749-0500
www.iwitts.org

Women United, Church
475 Riverside Dr Rm1626   New York NY 10115
Ph: 212-870-2347 ▪ Fx: 212-870-2338 ▪ TF: 800-298-5551
www.churchwomen.org

Women in Urology, Society of
1111 N Plaza Dr Suite 550   Schaumburg IL 60173
Ph: 847-517-7225 ▪ Fx: 847-517-7229
www.swiu.org

Women of the US Inc, National Council of
777 UN Plaza   New York NY 10017
Ph: 212-697-1278 ▪ Fx: 212-972-0164
www.ncw-usa.org

Women/USA, Business & Professional
1900 M St NW Suite 310   Washington DC 20036
Ph: 202-293-1100 ▪ Fx: 202-861-0298
www.bpwusa.org

Women of the USA, National Association of Cuban American
308 38th St   Union City NJ 07087
Ph: 201-864-4879

Women Voters, League of
1730 M St NW Suite 1000   Washington DC 20036
Ph: 202-429-1965 ▪ Fx: 202-429-0854 ▪ TF: 800-249-8683
www.lwv.org

Women on Wheels Motorcycle Association
PO Box 14180   Saint Paul MN 55114
Ph: 651-647-4344
www.womenonwheels.org

Women, Wider Opportunities for
1001 Connecticut Ave NW Suite 930   Washington DC 20036
Ph: 202-464-1596 ▪ Fx: 202-464-1660
www.w-o-w.org

Women in the Wind Inc
www.womeninthewind.org

Women for Women International
1850 M St NW Suite 1090   Washington DC 20036
Ph: 202-737-7705 ▪ Fx: 202-737-7709
www.womenforwomen.org

Women Work! National Network for Women's Employment
1625 K St NW Suite 300   Washington DC 20006
Ph: 202-467-6346 ▪ Fx: 202-467-5366 ▪ TF: 800-235-2732
www.womenwork.org

Women Writers, National Association of — www.naww.org
PO Box 183812   Arlington TX 76096
Ph: 866-821-5829

(Women) Zonta International — www.zonta.org
557 W Randolph St   Chicago IL 60661
Ph: 312-930-5848 ▪ Fx: 312-930-0951

Women's Action for New Directions — www.wand.org
691 Massachusetts Ave   Arlington MA 02476
Ph: 781-643-6740 ▪ Fx: 781-643-6744

Women's Alliance of America, Polish — www.pwaa.org
205 S Northwest Hwy   Park Ridge IL 60068
Ph: 847-384-1200 ▪ Fx: 847-384-1222 ▪ TF: 888-522-1898

Women's Alliance for Theology Ethics & Ritual — www.his.com/~mhunt
8035 13th St   Silver Spring MD 20910
Ph: 301-589-2509 ▪ Fx: 301-589-3150

Women's American ORT — www.waort.org
315 Park Ave S   New York NY 10010
Ph: 212-505-7700 ▪ Fx: 212-674-3057 ▪ TF: 800-519-2678

Women's Appraisal Association, Professional
1224 N Nokomis NE   Alexandria MN 56308
Ph: 320-763-7626 ▪ Fx: 320-763-9290

Women's Aquatic Network Inc — www.womensaquatic.net
PO Box 4993   Washington DC 20008
Ph: 202-208-4646 ▪ Fx: 202-667-6916

Women's Army Corps Veterans' Association — www.armywomen.org

Women's Association, American Business — www.abwahq.org
9100 Ward Pkwy   Kansas City MO 64114
Ph: 816-361-6621 ▪ Fx: 816-361-4991 ▪ TF: 800-228-0007

Women's Association, American Medical — www.amwa-doc.org
801 N Fairfax St Suite 400   Alexandria VA 22314
Ph: 703-838-0500 ▪ Fx: 703-549-3864

Women's Bar Associations, National Conference of — www.ncwba.org
PO Box 82366   Portland OR 97282
Ph: 503-775-4396 ▪ Fx: 503-657-3932

Women's Basketball Coaches Association — www.wbca.org
4646 Lawrenceville Hwy   Lilburn GA 30047
Ph: 770-279-8027 ▪ Fx: 770-279-8473

Women's Bowling Association, Professional — pwba.com
7171 Cherryvale Blvd   Rockford IL 61112
Ph: 815-332-5756 ▪ Fx: 815-332-9636

Women's Business Council, National — www.nwbc.gov
409 3rd St SW Suite 210   Washington DC 20024
Ph: 202-205-3800 ▪ Fx: 202-205-6825

Women's Business Research, Center for — www.nfwbo.org
1411 K St NW Suite 1350   Washington DC 20005
Ph: 202-638-3060 ▪ Fx: 202-638-3064

Women's Campaign Fund — www.wcfonline.org
734 15th St NW Suite 500   Washington DC 20005
Ph: 202-393-8164 ▪ Fx: 202-393-0649 ▪ TF: 800-446-8170

Women's Cancer Network — www.wcn.org
230 W Monroe St Suite 2528   Chicago IL 60606
Ph: 312-578-1439 ▪ Fx: 312-578-9769

Women's Caucus for Art — www.nationalwca.com
PO Box 1498   New York NY 10013
Ph: 212-634-0007

Women's Classical Caucus — home.gwu.edu/~camatteo/Womens_Classical_Caucus
Univ of Illinois at Urbana-Champaign   Dept of the Classics 4080
    Foreign Languages Bldg   707 S Mathews Ave   Urbana IL
    61801
Ph: 217-333-1008

Women's Clergy Association, African-American
214 P St NW   Washington DC 20001
Ph: 202-518-8488 ▪ Fx: 202-518-1273

Women's Club, American News — www.anwc.org
1607 22nd St NW   Washington DC 20008
Ph: 202-332-6770 ▪ Fx: 202-265-6092

Women's Clubs, General Federation of — www.gfwc.org
1734 'N' St NW   Washington DC 20036
Ph: 202-347-3168 ▪ Fx: 202-835-0246

Women's Clubs Inc, National Association of Colored
1601 R St NW   Washington DC 20009
Ph: 202-667-4080 ▪ Fx: 202-667-4113

Women's Clubs Inc, National Association of Negro — www.nanbpwc.org
Business & Professional   1806 New Hampshire Ave
    NW   Washington DC 20009
Ph: 202-483-4206 ▪ Fx: 202-462-7253

Women's College Coalition — www.womenscolleges.org
125 Michigan Ave NE Suite 340   Washington DC 20017
Ph: 202-234-0443 ▪ Fx: 202-234-0445

Women's Congress, International Black — www.ibwc.info
555 Fenchurch St Suite 102   Norfolk VA 23510
Ph: 757-625-0500 ▪ Fx: 757-625-1905

Women's Council on Energy & the Environment — www.wcee.org
PO Box 33211   Washington DC 20033
Ph: 703-351-7850

Women's Council of REALTORS — www.wcr.org
430 N Michigan Ave   Chicago IL 60611
Ph: 312-329-8483 ▪ Fx: 312-329-3290

Women's Curling Association, US — www.uswca.org
916 9th St S   Virginia MN 55792
Ph: 218-741-0253

Women's Economic Agenda Project — www.weap.org
449 15th St 2nd Fl   Oakland CA 94612
Ph: 510-451-7379 ▪ Fx: 510-986-8628

Women's Economic Round Table — www.wert.org
1633 Broadway 37th Fl   New York NY 10019
Ph: 212-492-4439 ▪ Fx: 212-492-4436

Women's Fisheries Network — www.fis.com/wfn
2442 NW Market St Suite 243   Seattle WA 98107
Ph: 206-789-1987

Women's Foodservice Forum — www.womensfoodserviceforum.com
1 General Mills Blvd MS W05D   Golden Valley MN 55426
Ph: 763-293-1150 ▪ Fx: 763-293-1114

Women's Forum, Independent — www.iwf.org
1726 M St NW Suite 1001   Washington DC 20036
Ph: 202-419-1820 ▪ TF: 800-224-6000

Women's Forum, International — www.iwforum.org
1621 Connecticut Ave NW Suite 300   Washington DC 20009
Ph: 202-775-8917 ▪ Fx: 202-429-0271

Women's Forum, National Asian Pacific American — www.napawf.org
1112 16th St NW Suite 110   Washington DC 20036
Ph: 202-293-2688 ▪ Fx: 202-463-2119

Women's Foundation, Business & Professional — www.bpwusa.org
1900 M St NW Suite 310   Washington DC 20036
Ph: 202-293-1100 ▪ Fx: 202-861-0298

Women's Fraternity, Alpha Xi Delta — www.alphaxidelta.org
8702 Founders Rd   Indianapolis IN 46268
Ph: 317-872-3500 ▪ Fx: 317-872-2947

Women's Funding Network — www.wfnet.org
1375 Sutter St Suite 406   San Francisco CA 94109
Ph: 415-441-0706 ▪ Fx: 415-441-0827

Women's Golf Association, Executive — www.ewga.com
300 Ave of the Champions Suite 140   Palm Beach Gardens FL
    33418
Ph: 561-691-0096 ▪ Fx: 561-691-0012 ▪ TF: 800-407-1477

Women's Guild, United Nations — www.iaea.or.at/unwg

Women's Health Coalition, International — www.iwhc.org
24 E 21st St   New York NY 10010
Ph: 212-979-8500 ▪ Fx: 212-979-9009

Women's Health, Global Alliance for — www.gawh.org
823 UN Plaza Suite 712   New York NY 10017
Ph: 212-286-0424 ▪ Fx: 212-286-9561

Women's Health Imperative, Black — www.blackwomenshealth.org
600 Pennsylvania Ave SE Suite 310   Washington DC 20003
Ph: 202-548-4000 ▪ Fx: 202-543-9743

Women's Health, Jacobs Institute of — www.jiwh.org
409 12th St SW   Washington DC 20024
Ph: 202-863-4990 ▪ Fx: 202-488-4229

Women's Health, National Association of Nurse Practitioners in — www.npwh.org
503 Capitol Ct NE Suite 300   Washington DC 20002
Ph: 202-543-9693 ▪ Fx: 202-543-9858

Women's Health Network, National — www.nwhn.org
514 10th St NW Suite 400   Washington DC 20004
Ph: 202-347-1140 ▪ Fx: 202-347-1168

Women's Health Organization, National Asian — www.nawho.org
250 Montgomery St Suite 900   San Francisco CA 94104
Ph: 415-989-9747 ▪ Fx: 415-989-9758

Women's Health Research, Society for — www.womens-health.org
1828 L St NW Suite 625   Washington DC 20036
Ph: 202-223-8224 ▪ Fx: 202-833-3472

Women's History Project, National — www.nwhp.org
3343 Industrial Dr Suite 4   Santa Rosa CA 95403
Ph: 707-636-2888 ▪ Fx: 707-636-2909 ▪ TF: 800-691-8888

Women's Interart Center
549 W 52nd St   New York NY 10019
Ph: 212-246-1050

Women's International Bowling Congress — www.bowl.com/bowl/wibc
5301 S 76th St   Greendale WI 53129
Ph: 414-421-9000 ▪ Fx: 414-421-3014 ▪ TF: 800-514-2695

Women's International Center — www.wic.org
PO Box 880736   San Diego CA 92168
Ph: 619-295-6446 ▪ Fx: 619-296-1633

Women's International League for Peace & Freedom-US Section — www.wilpf.org
1213 Race St   Philadelphia PA 19107
Ph: 215-563-7110 ▪ Fx: 215-563-5527

Women's International Network of Utility Professionals — www.winup.org
PO Box 335   Whites Creek TN 37189
Ph: 615-876-5444

Women's International Public Health Network
7100 Oak Forest Ln   Bethesda MD 20817
Ph: 301-469-9210 ▪ Fx: 301-469-8423

Women's Jewelry Association — www.womensjewelry.org
373 US Hwy 46 W Suite E-215   Fairfield NJ 07004
Ph: 973-575-7190 ▪ Fx: 973-575-1445

Women's Law Center, National — www.nwlc.org
11 Dupont Cir NW Suite 800   Washington DC 20036
Ph: 202-588-5180 ▪ Fx: 202-588-5185

Women's League of America, Ukrainian National — www.unwla.org
203 2nd Ave   New York NY 10003
Ph: 212-533-4646 ▪ Fx: 212-533-5237

Women's League for Conservative Judaism — www.wlcj.org
475 Riverside Dr   New York NY 10015
Ph: 212-870-1260 ▪ Fx: 212-870-1261 ▪ TF: 800-628-5083

Women's League for Israel
160 E 56th St   New York NY 10022
Ph: 212-838-1997 ▪ Fx: 212-888-5972

Women's League, Older — www.owl-national.org
1750 New York Ave NW Suite 350   Washington DC 20006
Ph: 202-783-6686 ▪ Fx: 202-628-0458 ▪ TF: 800-825-3695

Women's Media Foundation, International — www.iwmf.org
1726 M St NW Suite 1002   Washington DC 20036
Ph: 202-496-1992 ▪ Fx: 202-496-1977

Women's Ministries, American Baptist — www.abwministries.org
PO Box 851   Valley Forge PA 19482
Ph: 610-768-2000 ▪ Fx: 610-768-2275 ▪ TF: 800-222-3872

Women's Missionary League, Lutheran — www.lwml.org
PO Box 411993   Saint Louis MO 63141
Ph: 314-268-1531 ▪ Fx: 314-268-1532 ▪ TF: 800-252-5965

Women's Missionary Society - AME Church www.amecnet.org/wms/main_fr.htm
1134 11th St NW   Washington DC 20001
Ph: 202-371-8886 ▪ Fx: 202-371-8820

Women's Motorcyclist Foundation Inc www.ponyexpressrides.org
7 Lent Ave   Le Roy NY 14482
Ph: 800-442-3550

Women's Mountain Bike & Tea Society www.wombats.org
PO Box 757   Fairfax CA 94978
Ph: 415-459-0980

Women's National Republican Club www.wnrc.org
3 W 51st St   New York NY 10019
Ph: 212-582-5454 ▪ Fx: 212-265-5633

Women's Organizations, National Council of www.womensorganizations.org
733 15th St NW Suite 1011   Washington DC 20005
Ph: 202-393-7122 ▪ Fx: 202-387-7915

Women's Political Caucus, National www.nwpc.org
1634 'I' St NW Suite 310   Washington DC 20006
Ph: 202-785-1100 ▪ Fx: 202-785-3605

Women's Prison Association www.wpa.org
110 2nd Ave   New York NY 10003
Ph: 212-674-1163 ▪ Fx: 212-677-1981

Women's Professional Billiards Association www.wpba.com
6407 South Blvd   Charlotte NC 28217
Ph: 704-556-1128 ▪ Fx: 704-556-0699

Women's Professional Rodeo Association www.wpra.com
1235 Lake Plaza Dr Suite 127   Colorado Springs CO 80906
Ph: 719-576-0900 ▪ Fx: 719-576-1386

Women's Regional Publications of America www.womensyellowpages.org
729 Bates St   Saint Louis MO 63111
Ph: 314-997-6262 ▪ Fx: 314-567-7849

(Women's Religion) Re-Formed Congregation of the Goddess www.rcgi.org
International   PO Box 6677   Madison WI 53716
Ph: 608-226-9998

Women's Research & Education Institute www.wrei.org
1750 New York Ave NW Suite 350   Washington DC 20006
Ph: 202-628-0444 ▪ Fx: 202-628-0458

Women's Resources, Foundation for www.womensresources.org
1115 San Jacinto Blvd Suite 250   Austin TX 78701
Ph: 512-459-1167 ▪ Fx: 512-459-1408

Women's Rights in Development, Association for www.awid.org
96 Spadina Ave Suite 401   Toronto ON M5V2J6
Ph: 416-594-3773 ▪ Fx: 416-594-0330

Women's Roundtable on Civic Participation, Black www.bigvote.org/bwr.htm
1025 Vermont Ave NW Suite 1010   Washington DC 20005
Ph: 202-659-4929 ▪ Fx: 202-659-5025

Women's Sports Foundation www.womenssportsfoundation.org
Eisenhower Pk   East Meadow NY 11554
Ph: 516-542-4700 ▪ Fx: 516-542-4716 ▪ TF: 800-227-3988

Women's Studies Association, National www.nwsa.org
7100 Baltimore Ave Suite 500   College Park MD 20740
Ph: 301-403-0525 ▪ Fx: 301-403-4137

Women's Tennis Association, National Senior www.nswta.com
PO Box 142   Lake Oswego OR 97034
Ph: 503-636-9292 ▪ Fx: 503-636-9660

Women's Track Coaches Association, US
7263 Heartcrest Ln   Centerville OH 45458
Ph: 937-434-0383

Women's Travel Organizations, International Federation of www.ifwto.org

Women's Union of America, Slovenian www.swua.org
431 N Chicago St   Joliet IL 60432
Ph: 815-727-1926

Women's Welfare Association Inc, Armenian www.awwa-inc.org
PO Box 191   Belmont MA 02478
Ph: 617-522-2600 ▪ Fx: 617-524-7024

Women's World Banking www.swwb.org
8 W 40th St   New York NY 10018
Ph: 212-768-8513 ▪ Fx: 212-768-8519

Women's Writing Guild, International www.iwwg.com
PO Box 810 Gracie Stn   New York NY 10028
Ph: 212-737-7536 ▪ Fx: 212-737-9469

Women's Zionist Organization of America Inc, Hadassah www.hadassah.org
50 W 58th St   New York NY 10019
Ph: 212-355-7900 ▪ Fx: 212-303-8282 ▪ TF: 888-303-3640

Wood Association, APA - Engineered www.apawood.org
7011 S 19th   Tacoma WA 98466
Ph: 253-565-6600 ▪ Fx: 253-565-7265

Wood Carvers Association, National www.chipchats.org
7424 Miami Ave   Cincinnati OH 45243
Ph: 513-561-9051

Wood Component Manufacturers Association www.woodcomponents.org
1000 Johnston Ferry Rd Suite A-130   Marietta GA 30068
Ph: 770-565-6660 ▪ Fx: 770-565-6663

Wood Flooring Association, National www.woodfloors.org
111 Chesterfield Industrial Blvd   Chesterfield MO 63005
Ph: 636-519-9663 ▪ Fx: 636-519-9664 ▪ TF: 800-422-4556

Wood Flooring Manufacturers Association, NOFMA: www.nofma.org
PO Box 3009   Memphis TN 38173
Ph: 901-526-5016 ▪ Fx: 901-526-7022

Wood Machinery Manufacturers of America www.wmma.org
1900 Arch St   Philadelphia PA 19103
Ph: 215-564-3484 ▪ Fx: 215-963-9785

Wood Moulding & Millwork Producers Association wmmpa.com
507 First St   Woodland CA 95695
Ph: 530-661-9591 ▪ Fx: 530-661-9586 ▪ TF: 800-550-7889

Wood-Preservers' Association, American www.awpa.com
PO Box 388   Selma AL 36702
Ph: 334-874-9800 ▪ Fx: 334-874-9008

Wood Preservers Institute, American www.preservedwood.com
12100 Sunset Hills Rd Suite 130   Reston VA 20190
Ph: 703-204-0500 ▪ Fx: 703-204-4610 ▪ TF: 800-356-2974

Wood Products Association, International www.iwpawood.org
4214 King St W   Alexandria VA 22302
Ph: 703-820-6696 ▪ Fx: 703-820-8550

Wood Products Association, Western www.wwpa.org
522 SW 5th Ave Yeon Bldg Suite 500   Portland OR 97204
Ph: 503-224-3930 ▪ Fx: 503-224-3934

Wood Products Manufacturers Association www.wpma.org
175 State Rd E   Westminster MA 01473
Ph: 978-874-5445 ▪ Fx: 978-874-9946

Wood Research Foundation, Engineered www.engineeredwood.org
PO Box 11700   Tacoma WA 98411
Ph: 253-565-6600 ▪ Fx: 253-565-7265

Wood Science & Technology, Society of www.swst.org
1 Gifford Pinchot Dr   Madison WI 53726
Ph: 608-231-9347 ▪ Fx: 608-231-9592

Wood Tank Institute, National
PO Box 2755   Philadelphia PA 19120
Ph: 215-329-9022 ▪ Fx: 215-329-1177

Wood Truss Council of America www.woodtruss.com
6300 Enterprise Ln   Madison WI 53719
Ph: 608-274-4849 ▪ Fx: 608-274-3329

Wooden Canoe Heritage Association Ltd www.wcha.org

Wooden Money Collectors, Dedicated
2084 N Brook Cir   York PA 17403
Ph: 717-845-4295

Wooden Pallet & Container Association, National www.nwpca.com
329 S Patrick St   Alexandria VA 22314
Ph: 703-519-6104 ▪ Fx: 703-519-4720

Woodland Owners Association, National www.nationalwoodlands.org
374 Maple Ave E Suite 310   Vienna VA 22180
Ph: 703-255-2700 ▪ Fx: 703-281-9200 ▪ TF: 800-476-8733

Woodmen Rangers Youth Program www.woodmen.com/about/rangers.cfm
Woodmen of the World/Omaha Woodmen Life Insurance Society
1700 Farnam St   Omaha NE 68102
Ph: 402-271-7258 ▪ Fx: 402-449-7733

Woodrow Wilson Birthplace Foundation www.woodrowwilson.org
18-24 N Coalter St PO Box 24   Staunton VA 24402
Ph: 540-885-0897 ▪ Fx: 540-885-9874 ▪ TF: 888-496-6376

Woodrow Wilson International Center for Scholars wwics.si.edu
1 Woodrow Wilson Plaza 1300 Pennsylvania Ave
NW   Washington DC 20004
Ph: 202-691-4000 ▪ Fx: 202-691-4001

Woodrow Wilson National Fellowship Foundation www.woodrow.org
5 Vaughn Dr CN 5281   Princeton NJ 08540
Ph: 609-452-7007 ▪ Fx: 609-452-0066

Woodruff Robert W Foundation Inc www.woodruff.org
50 Hurt Plaza Suite 1200   Atlanta GA 30303
Ph: 404-522-6755 ▪ Fx: 404-522-7026

Woodturners, American Association of woodturner.org
3499 Lexington Ave N Suite 103   Shoreview MN 55126
Ph: 651-484-9094 ▪ Fx: 651-484-1724

Woodwork Institute, Architectural www.awinet.org
1952 Isaac Newton Sq W   Reston VA 20190
Ph: 703-733-0600 ▪ Fx: 703-733-0584

Woodworking & Furnishings Suppliers, Association of www.awfssupplierfinder.org
5800 S Eastern Ave Suite 330   Los Angeles CA 90040
Ph: 323-838-9440 ▪ Fx: 323-838-9443 ▪ TF: 800-946-2837

Woodworking Machinery Industry Association www.wmia.org/
5024-R Campbell Blvd   Baltimore MD 21236
Ph: 410-931-8100 ▪ Fx: 410-931-8111

Wool Growers Association, Natural Colored www.ncwga.org
429 W US 30   Valparaiso IN 46385
Ph: 219-759-9665

Worcester Noah Dermatological Society www.noahw.org
61 Donna Rd   Newton MA 02459
Ph: 617-641-9761 ▪ Fx: 617-527-4423

Word of God, National Institute for the www.wordofgodinstitute.org
487 Michigan Ave NE   Washington DC 20017
Ph: 202-529-0001 ▪ Fx: 202-636-4460

Word of Life Fellowship Inc www.wol.org
PO Box 600   Schroon Lake NY 12870
Ph: 518-494-6000 ▪ Fx: 518-494-6306 ▪ TF: 800-331-9673

Work Adjustment & Vocational Evaluation Specialists, Commission www.ccwaves.org
on Certification of   1835 Rohlwing Rd Suite E   Rolling
Meadows IL 60008
Ph: 847-342-1796 ▪ Fx: 847-394-2108

Work Center, American Youth www.youthtoday.org
1200 17th St NW 4th Fl   Washington DC 20036
Ph: 202-785-0764 ▪ Fx: 202-728-0657

Work Dog Association, North American Police www.napwda.com
4222 Manchester Ave   Perry OH 44081
Ph: 440-259-3169 ▪ Fx: 440-259-3170 ▪ TF: 888-422-6463

Work & Learning, National Institute for www.niwl.org
1825 Connecticut Ave NW 7th Fl   Washington DC 20009
Ph: 202-884-8186 ▪ Fx: 202-884-8422

Work-Life Progress, Alliance for www.awlp.org
14040 N Northsight Blvd   Scottsdale AZ 85260
Ph: 800-874-9383 ▪ Fx: 480-603-0791

Work Inc, New Ways to www.nww.org
103 Morris St Suite A   Sebastopol CA 95472
Ph: 707-824-4000 ▪ Fx: 707-824-4410

Work Process Improvement, Association for www.tawpi.org
185 Devonshire St Suite M102   Boston MA 02110
Ph: 617-426-1167 ▪ Fx: 617-521-8675 ▪ TF: 800-998-2974

Work, Society for the Anthropology of www.aaanet.org/saw
c/o American Anthropological Assn 2200 Wilson Blvd Suite
600   Arlington VA 22201
Ph: 703-528-1902 ▪ Fx: 703-528-3546

Worker Justice, National Interfaith Committee for   www.nicwj.org
1020 W Bryn Mawr Ave 4th Fl   Chicago IL 60660
Ph: 773-728-8400 ▪ Fx: 773-728-8409

Worker Movement, Catholic   www.catholicworker.org
36 E 1st St   New York NY 10003
Ph: 212-777-9617

Worker Partnership, National Older
c/o National Council on the Aging 300 D St SW Suite
801   Washington DC 20024
Ph: 202-479-1200 ▪ Fx: 202-479-0735

Workers' Compensation, UWC - Strategic Services on   www.uwcstrategy.org
Unemployment &   1331 Pennsylvania Ave NW Suite
600   Washington DC 20004
Ph: 202-637-3464 ▪ Fx: 202-783-1616

Workers Solidarity Alliance   www.workersolidarity.org
339 Lafayette St Rm 202   New York NY 10012
Ph: 212-979-8353

Workflow & Reengineering International Association   www.waria.com
2436 N Federal Hwy Suite 374   Lighthouse Point FL 33064
Ph: 954-782-3376 ▪ Fx: 954-782-6365 ▪ TF: 800-749-2742

Workforce Agencies, National Association of State   www.naswa.org
444 N Capitol St NW Suite 142   Washington DC 20001
Ph: 202-434-8020 ▪ Fx: 202-434-8033

Workforce Boards, National Association of   www.nawb.org
1701 K St NW Suite 1000   Washington DC 20006
Ph: 202-775-0960 ▪ Fx: 202-775-0330

(Workforce Development) Iota Lambda Sigma
607 Park Way W   Oregon OH 43616
Ph: 419-693-6860 ▪ Fx: 419-693-6859

Workforce Development Professionals, National Association of   www.nawdp.org
810 1st St NE Suite 525   Washington DC 20002
Ph: 202-589-1790 ▪ Fx: 202-589-1799

Workforce Education, National Council for   www.ncwe.org
PO Box 3188   Dublin OH 43016
Ph: 614-659-0196 ▪ Fx: 614-336-8596

Workgroup for Electronic Data Interchange   www.wedi.org
12020 Sunrise Valley Dr Suite 100   Reston VA 20191
Ph: 703-391-2716 ▪ Fx: 703-391-2759

Working for America Institute, AFL-CIO   www.workingforamerica.org
815 16th NW   Washington DC 20006
Ph: 202-974-8100 ▪ Fx: 202-974-8101 ▪ TF: 800-842-4734

Working Families, Campaign for   www.campaignforfamilies.org
2800 Shirlington Rd Suite 605   Arlington VA 22206
Ph: 703-671-8800 ▪ Fx: 703-671-8899

Working Families, Labor Project for   www.laborproject.org
2521 Channing Way Suite 5555   Berkeley CA 94720
Ph: 510-643-7088 ▪ Fx: 510-642-6432

Working Moms, Home-Based   www.hbwm.com
PO Box 500164   Austin TX 78750
Ph: 512-266-0900 ▪ TF: 800-281-8565

Working People, American Association of   www.aawp.org
4435 Waterfront Dr Suite 101   Glen Allen VA 23058
Ph: 804-527-1905 ▪ Fx: 804-747-5316 ▪ TF: 800-722-0376

Working Today   www.workingtoday.org
55 Washington St Suite 557   Brooklyn NY 11201
Ph: 718-222-1099 ▪ Fx: 718-222-4440

Working Women, 9to5 National Association of   www.9to5.org
152 W Wisconsin Ave Suite 408   Milwaukee WI 53203
Ph: 414-274-0925 ▪ Fx: 414-272-2870 ▪ TF: 800-522-0925

Workman, Catholic   www.catholicworkman.org
1201 1st St NE PO Box 47   New Prague MN 56071
Ph: 952-758-2229 ▪ Fx: 952-758-6221 ▪ TF: 800-346-6231

Workmen's Benefit Fund of the USA   www.wbfusa.com
99 N Broadway   Hicksville NY 11801
Ph: 516-938-6060 ▪ Fx: 516-938-6882

Workmen's Circle/Arbeter Ring   www.circle.org
45 E 33rd St   New York NY 10016
Ph: 212-889-6800 ▪ Fx: 212-532-7518 ▪ TF: 800-922-2558

Workshops Foundation, Washington   www.workshops.org
3222 'N' St NW Suite 340   Washington DC 20007
Ph: 202-965-3434 ▪ Fx: 202-965-1018 ▪ TF: 800-368-5688

WORLD   www.womenhiv.org
414 13th St 2nd Fl   Oakland CA 94612
Ph: 510-986-0340 ▪ Fx: 510-986-0341

World Academy of Art & Science   www.worldacademy.org/
301 19th Ave S   Minneapolis MN 55455
Ph: 612-624-5592 ▪ Fx: 612-625-3513

World Affairs Councils of America   www.worldaffairscouncils.org
1800 K St NW Suite 1014   Washington DC 20006
Ph: 202-833-4557 ▪ Fx: 202-833-4555

World Affairs, Institute of   www.iwa.org
1321 Pennsylvania Ave SE   Washington DC 20003
Ph: 202-544-4141 ▪ Fx: 202-544-5115

World Airline Entertainment Association   www.waea.org
8201 Greensboro Dr Suite 300   McLean VA 22102
Ph: 703-610-9021 ▪ Fx: 703-610-9005

World Allergy Organization   www.worldallergy.org
611 E Wells St   Milwaukee WI 53202
Ph: 414-276-1791 ▪ Fx: 414-276-3349

World Aquaculture Society   www.was.org
Louisiana State Univ 143 JM Parker Coliseum   Baton Rouge LA
70803
Ph: 225-578-3137 ▪ Fx: 225-578-3493

World Aquatic Babies Congress   www.waterbabies.org
776 21st Ave N   Saint Petersburg FL 33704
Ph: 727-896-7625 ▪ Fx: 727-896-0019

World Assembly of Muslim Youth   www.wamyusa.org
PO Box 8096   Falls Church VA 22041
Ph: 703-783-8410 ▪ Fx: 703-783-8409

World Association of Alcohol Beverage Industries   www.waabi.org

World Association for Case Method Research & Application   www.wacra.org
23 Mackintosh Ave   Needham MA 02492
Ph: 781-444-8982 ▪ Fx: 781-444-1548 ▪ TF: 800-523-6468

World Association for Children & Parents   www.wacap.org
315 S 2nd St   Renton WA 98055
Ph: 206-575-4550 ▪ Fx: 206-575-4148

World Association for Infant Mental Health   www.waimh.org
Michigan State Univ Institute for Children Youth & Families
Kellogg Ctr Rm 27   East Lansing MI 48824
Ph: 517-432-3793 ▪ Fx: 517-432-3694

World Association of International Studies   wais.stanford.edu
Hoover Institution   Stanford CA 94305
Ph: 650-322-2026 ▪ Fx: 650-723-1687

World Association of Law Professors
1000 Connecticut Ave NW Suite 202   Washington DC 20036
Ph: 202-466-5428 ▪ Fx: 202-452-8540

World Association of People with Disabilities   www.wapd.org
4503 Sunnyview Dr Suite 1121 PO Box 14111   Oklahoma City
OK 73135
Ph: 405-672-4440 ▪ Fx: 405-672-4441

World Association for Public Opinion Research   www.unl.edu/wapor
UNL Gallup Research Ctr Univ of Nebraska - Lincoln 200 N 11th
St   Lincoln NE 68588
Ph: 402-458-2030 ▪ Fx: 402-458-2038

World Beechcraft Society   www.worldbeechcraft.com
500 SE Everett Mall Way Suite A7   Everett WA 98208
Ph: 425-267-9235

World Bird Sanctuary   www.worldbirdsanctuary.org
125 Bald Eagle Ridge Rd   Valley Park MO 63088
Ph: 636-861-3225 ▪ Fx: 636-861-3240

World Bocce Association   www.worldbocce.org/USA
188 Industrial Dr Suite 17A   Elmhurst IL 60126
Ph: 630-834-8349 ▪ Fx: 630-832-2174 ▪ TF: 800-652-6623

World Bowling Writers
122 S Michigan Ave Suite 1506   Chicago IL 60603
Ph: 312-341-1110 ▪ Fx: 312-341-1480

World Business Associates
1000 Connecticut Ave NW Suite 202   Washington DC 20036
Ph: 202-466-5428 ▪ Fx: 202-452-8540

World Care   www.worldcare.org
PO Box 64001   Tucson AZ 85728
Ph: 520-514-1588 ▪ Fx: 520-514-1589

World Chapter of Disneyana Enthusiasts
PO Box 22647   Lake Buena Vista FL 32830
Ph: 407-275-2756

World Concern   www.worldconcern.org
19303 Fremont Ave N   Seattle WA 98133
Ph: 206-546-7201 ▪ Fx: 206-546-7269 ▪ TF: 800-755-5022

World Conference of Religions for Peace   www.wcrp.org
777 United Nations Plaza   New York NY 10017
Ph: 212-687-2163 ▪ Fx: 212-983-0566

World Congress of Poets
3146 Buckeye Ct   Placerville CA 95667
Ph: 530-626-4166 ▪ Fx: 530-344-9427

World Constitution & Parliament Association   www.wcpa.biz

World Convention (Christian - Churches of Christ -   worldconv.home.comcast.net
Disciples of Christ)   4800 B Franklin Rd   Nashville TN 37220
Ph: 615-331-1824 ▪ Fx: 615-331-1864

World Council of Churches - US Office   www.wcc-coe.org
475 Riverside Dr Rm 1371   New York NY 10115
Ph: 212-870-3260 ▪ TF: 888-212-2920

World Council of Credit Unions Inc   www.woccu.org
5710 Minerial Point Rd   Madison WI 53705
Ph: 608-231-7130 ▪ Fx: 608-238-8020 ▪ TF: 800-356-2644

World Council for Curriculum & Instruction   www.alliant.edu/gsoe/wcci
Alliant International Univ Cross Cultural Studies Institute School
of Education 10455 Pomerado Rd   San Diego CA 92131
Ph: 858-635-4719 ▪ Fx: 858-635-4714

World Council for Gifted & Talented Children   www.worldgifted.org
18401 Hiawatha St   Northridge CA 91326
Ph: 818-368-7501 ▪ Fx: 818-368-2163

World Day of Prayer International Committee   www.worlddayofprayer.net
475 Riverside Dr Rm 560   New York NY 10115
Ph: 212-870-3049 ▪ Fx: 212-864-8648

World Development Federation   www.wdf.org
35 Technology Park Suite 150   Norcross GA 30092
Ph: 770-446-6996 ▪ Fx: 770-263-8825

World Economic Processing Zones Association   www.wepza.org
PO Box 986   Flagstaff AZ 86002
Ph: 928-779-0052 ▪ Fx: 928-774-8589

World Education Inc   www.worlded.org
44 Farnsworth St   Boston MA 02210
Ph: 617-482-9485 ▪ Fx: 617-482-0617

World Emergency Relief   www.worldemergency.org
2270 Camino Vida Roble Suite D   Carlsbad CA 92009
Ph: 760-930-8001 ▪ Fx: 760-930-9085 ▪ TF: 888-484-2543

World Environment Center   www.wec.org
419 Park Ave S Suite 500   New York NY 10016
Ph: 212-683-4700 ▪ Fx: 212-683-5053

World Evangelical Alliance   www.worldevangelical.org
PO Box 1839   Edmonds WA 98020
Ph: 425-778-5513 ▪ Fx: 425-640-3671

World Evangelism, Association of Baptists for   www.abwe.org
PO Box 8585   Harrisburg PA 17105
Ph: 717-774-7000 ▪ Fx: 717-774-1919

World Federation of Building Service Contractors   www.wfbsc.org
10201 Lee Hwy Suite 225   Fairfax VA 22030
Ph: 703-359-7090 ▪ Fx: 703-352-0493

World Federation of Direct Selling Associations
1275 Pennsylvania Ave NW Suite 800   Washington DC 20004
Ph: 202-347-8866 ▪ Fx: 202-347-0055
www.wfdsa.org

World Federation of Free Latvians
400 Hurley Ave   Rockville MD 20850
Ph: 301-340-7646 ▪ Fx: 301-762-5438
www.pbla.lv

World Federation of Neuroradiological Societies
2210 Midwest Rd Suite 207   Oak Brook IL 60523
Ph: 630-574-0220 ▪ Fx: 630-574-0661
www.wfnrs.org

World Federation of Orthodontists
401 N Lindbergh Blvd   Saint Louis MO 63141
Ph: 314-993-1700 ▪ Fx: 314-993-5208
www.wfo.org

World Federation of Public Health Association
800 'I' St NW   Washington DC 20001
Ph: 202-777-2486 ▪ Fx: 202-777-2530
www.wfpha.org

World Floor Covering Association
2211 E Howell Ave   Anaheim CA 92806
Ph: 714-978-6440 ▪ Fx: 714-978-6066 ▪ TF: 800-624-6880
www.wfca.org

World Folk Music Association
PO Box 40553   Washington DC 20016
Ph: 202-362-2225 ▪ Fx: 202-244-1543 ▪ TF: 800-779-2226
www.wfma.net

World Food Day, US National Committee for
2175 K St NW   Washington DC 20437
Ph: 202-653-2404 ▪ Fx: 202-653-5760

World Food Logistics Organization
1500 King St Suite 201   Alexandria VA 22314
Ph: 703-373-4300 ▪ Fx: 703-373-4301
www.wflo.org

World Food Programme, Friends of the
1341 Connecticut Ave NW   Washington DC 20036
Ph: 202-530-1694
www.friendsofwfp.org

World Forest Institute
4033 SW Canyon Rd   Portland OR 97221
Ph: 503-228-1367 ▪ Fx: 503-228-4608
www.worldforestry.org/wfi

World Forestry Center
4033 SW Canyon Rd   Portland OR 97221
Ph: 503-228-1367 ▪ Fx: 503-228-4608
www.worldforestry.org

World Foundation for Medical Studies in Female Health
405 Main St Suite 8   Port Washington NY 11050
Ph: 516-944-8655 ▪ Fx: 516-944-8663
www.wffh.org

World Future Society
7910 Woodmont Ave Suite 450   Bethesda MD 20814
Ph: 301-656-8274 ▪ Fx: 301-951-0394 ▪ TF: 800-989-8274
www.wfs.org

World Gold Council
444 Madison Ave Suite 301   New York NY 10022
Ph: 212-317-3800 ▪ Fx: 212-688-0410
www.gold.org

World Gospel Mission
PO Box 948   Marion IN 46952
Ph: 765-664-7331 ▪ Fx: 765-671-7230
www.wgm.org

World Heritage
10725 Boston St   Henderson CO 80640
Ph: 303-252-8215 ▪ Fx: 303-252-0629 ▪ TF: 800-888-9040
www.world-heritage.org

World History Association
Univ of Hawaii at Manoa Sakamaki Hall A203   2530 Dole
   St   Honolulu HI 96822
Ph: 808-956-7688
www.thewha.org

World Hope International
8136 Old Keene Mill Rd Suite 209A   Springfield VA 22152
Ph: 703-923-9414 ▪ Fx: 703-923-9418 ▪ TF: 888-466-4673
www.worldhope.org

World Hunger Year Inc
505 8th Ave Suite 2100   New York NY 10018
Ph: 212-629-8850 ▪ Fx: 212-465-9274 ▪ TF: 800-548-6479
www.worldhungeryear.org

World Impact
2001 S Vermont Ave   Los Angeles CA 90007
Ph: 323-735-1137 ▪ Fx: 323-735-2576
www.worldimpact.org

World Institute on Disability
510 16th St Suite 100   Oakland CA 94612
Ph: 510-763-4100 ▪ Fx: 510-763-4109
www.wid.org

World International Nail & Beauty Association
1221 N Lake View Ave   Anaheim CA 92807
Ph: 714-779-9883 ▪ Fx: 714-779-9971 ▪ TF: 800-624-5777

World Investigators Network
7501 Sparrows Point Blvd   Baltimore MD 21219
Ph: 410-477-8879 ▪ Fx: 410-388-0846 ▪ TF: 888-946-6389
www.worldinvestigatorsnetwork.com

World Jewish Congress
501 Madison Ave 17th Fl   New York NY 10022
Ph: 212-755-5770 ▪ Fx: 212-755-5883 ▪ TF: 800-755-5883
www.wjc.org.il

World Jurist Association
1000 Connecticut Ave NW Suite 202   Washington DC 20036
Ph: 202-466-5428 ▪ Fx: 202-452-8540
www.worldjurist.org

World Learning for International Development
1015 15th St NW Suite 750   Washington DC 20005
Ph: 202-408-5420 ▪ Fx: 202-408-5397
www.worldlearning.org

World Media Association
3600 New York Ave NE 3rd Fl   Washington DC 20002
Ph: 202-636-3124 ▪ Fx: 202-635-9227
www.wmassociation.com

World Medical Relief Inc
11745 Rosa Parks Blvd   Detroit MI 48206
Ph: 313-866-5333 ▪ Fx: 313-866-5588
www.worldmedicalrelief.com

World Mercy Fund
PO Box 227   Waterford VA 20197
Ph: 540-882-4425 ▪ Fx: 540-882-3226
www.worldmercyfund.ie

World Methodist Council
PO Box 518   Lake Junaluska NC 28745
Ph: 828-456-9432 ▪ Fx: 828-456-9433
www.worldmethodistcouncil.org

World Methodist Historical Society
36 Madison Ave PO Box 127   Madison NJ 07940
Ph: 973-408-3789 ▪ Fx: 973-408-3909
www.gcah.org/WMHS.htm

World Mission Prayer League
232 Clifton Ave   Minneapolis MN 55403
Ph: 612-871-6843 ▪ Fx: 612-871-6844
www.wmpl.org

World Neighbors Inc
4127 NW 122nd St   Oklahoma City OK 73120
Ph: 405-752-9700 ▪ Fx: 405-752-9393 ▪ TF: 800-242-6387
www.wn.org

World Ocean & Cruise Liner Society
PO Box 4850   Stamford CT 06907
Ph: 203-329-2787
www.oceancruisenews.com

World Opportunities International/Help the Children
1415 Cahuenga Blvd   Hollywood CA 90028
Ph: 323-466-7187 ▪ Fx: 323-871-1546
www.helpthechildren.org

World Organization of China Painters
2641 NW 10th St   Oklahoma City OK 73107
Ph: 405-521-1234 ▪ Fx: 405-521-1265
www.theshop.net/wocporg

World Organization of Dredging Associations
PO Box 5797   Vancouver WA 98668
Ph: 360-750-0209 ▪ Fx: 360-750-1445
www.westerndredging.org

World Organization of Webmasters
9580 Oak Pkwy Suite 7-177   Folsom CA 95630
Ph: 916-608-1597 ▪ Fx: 916-987-3022
www.joinwow.org

World Peace Foundation
79 John F Kennedy St   Cambridge MA 02138
Ph: 617-491-5085 ▪ Fx: 617-491-8588
www.worldpeacefoundation.org

(World Peace & Justice) WorldViews
worldviews.igc.org

World Peace Prayer Society
26 Benton Rd   Wassaic NY 12592
Ph: 845-877-6093 ▪ Fx: 845-877-6862
www.worldpeace.org

World Peace Through Technology Organization
150 Folsom St   San Francisco CA 94105
Ph: 415-371-8706 ▪ Fx: 415-348-0762
www.peacetour.org

World Peacemakers
11427 Scottsbury Terr   Germantown MD 20876
Ph: 301-972-4041 ▪ Fx: 301-916-5335
www.worldpeacemakers.org

World Pen Pals
PO Box 337   Saugerties NY 12477
Ph: 845-246-7828
www.world-pen-pals.com

World Phenomenology Institute
1 Ivy Pointe Way   Hanover NH 03755
Ph: 802-295-3487 ▪ Fx: 802-295-5963
www.phenomenology.org

World Policy Institute
66 5th Ave 9th Fl   New York NY 10011
Ph: 212-229-5808 ▪ Fx: 212-229-5579
worldpolicy.org

World Presidents' Organization
110 S Union St Suite 200   Alexandria VA 22314
Ph: 703-684-4900 ▪ Fx: 703-684-4955
www.wpo.org

World Pumpkin Confederation
56 E Union St   Hamburg NY 14075
Ph: 716-648-7982
www.pandpseed.com/wpc.htm

World Relief
7 E Baltimore St   Baltimore MD 21202
Ph: 443-451-1900
www.wr.org

World Research Foundation
41 Bell Rock Plaza   Sedona AZ 86351
Ph: 928-284-3300 ▪ Fx: 928-284-3530
www.wrf.org

World Resources Institute
10 G St NE Suite 800   Washington DC 20002
Ph: 202-729-7600 ▪ Fx: 202-729-7610
www.wri.org

World Salt Foundation Inc
PO Box 851   Lake Wales FL 33859
Ph: 863-638-0557
www.angelfire.com/fl3/worldsalt

World Science Fiction Society
worldcon.org

World Service Authority
1012 14th St NW Suite 205   Washington DC 20005
Ph: 202-638-2662 ▪ Fx: 202-638-0638
www.worldservice.org

World Shoe Association
20281 SW Birch St Suite 100   Newport Beach CA 92660
Ph: 949-851-8451 ▪ Fx: 949-851-8523
www.wsashow.com

World Sidesaddle Federation
PO Box 1104   Bucyrus OH 44820
Ph: 419-284-3176
www.sidesaddle.org

World Sign Associates
8774 Yates Dr Suite 120   Westminster CO 80031
Ph: 303-427-7252 ▪ Fx: 303-427-7090

World Socialist Party of the US
PO Box 440247   Somerville MA 02144
Ph: 617-628-9096 ▪ Fx: 617-628-5239
www.worldsocialism.org

World Society for the Protection of Animals
34 Deloss St   Framingham MA 01702
Ph: 508-879-8350 ▪ Fx: 508-620-0786 ▪ TF: 800-883-9772
www.wspa.org.uk

World Team USA
1431 Stuckert Rd   Warrington PA 18976
Ph: 215-491-4900 ▪ Fx: 215-491-4910 ▪ TF: 800-967-7109
www.worldteam.org

World Teleport Association
55 Broad St 14th Fl   New York NY 10004
Ph: 212-825-0218 ▪ Fx: 212-825-0075
www.worldteleport.org

World Trade Centers Association
60 E 42nd St Suite 1901   New York NY 10165
Ph: 212-432-2626 ▪ Fx: 212-488-0064
iserve.wtca.org

World Trade, Consumers for
1001 Connecticut Ave NW Suite 1110   Washington DC 20006
Ph: 202-293-2944 ▪ Fx: 202-293-0495
www.cwt.org

World Travel Exchange, Association for
38 W 88th St   New York NY 10024
Ph: 212-787-7706 ▪ Fx: 212-580-9283
www.international-counselors.org

World Vision Inc
PO Box 9716   Federal Way WA 98063
Ph: 253-815-1000 ▪ Fx: 253-815-3240 ▪ TF: 800-777-5777
www.worldvision.org

World War I Aeroplanes Inc
15 Crescent Rd   Poughkeepsie NY 12601
Ph: 845-473-3679 ▪ Fx: 845-452-7332
www.aviation-history.com/ww1aero.htm

(World War II) SHAEF/ETOUSA Veterans Association www.shaef.org
2301 Broadway   San Francisco CA 94115
Ph: 415-921-8322

World War II, US Submarine Veterans of www.ussubvetsofworldwarii.org

World Waterpark Association www.waterparks.org
8826 Santa Fe Dr Suite 310   Overland Park KS 66212
Ph: 913-599-0300 ▪ Fx: 913-599-0520

World Watusi Association www.watusicattle.com
PO Box 14   Crawford NE 69339
Ph: 308-665-3919 ▪ Fx: 308-665-1931

World Wide Pet Supply Association Inc www.wwpsa.com
406 S 1st Ave   Arcadia CA 91006
Ph: 626-447-2222 ▪ Fx: 626-447-8350 ▪ TF: 800-999-7295

World Wide Web Consortium www.w3.org
MIT Laboratory for Computer Science 200 Technology
Sq   Cambridge MA 02139
Ph: 617-253-2613 ▪ Fx: 617-258-5999

World Wildlife Fund www.worldwildlife.org
1250 24th St NW Suite 500   Washington DC 20037
Ph: 202-293-4800 ▪ Fx: 202-293-9211 ▪ TF: 800-225-5993

World Wildlife Fund Canada www.wwf.ca
245 Eglinton Ave E Suite 410   Toronto ON M4P3J1
Ph: 416-489-8800 ▪ Fx: 416-489-3611 ▪ TF: 800-267-2632

World Without War Council www.wwwc.org/wwwc/wwwc.html
1730 ML King Jr Way   Berkeley CA 94709
Ph: 510-845-1992 ▪ Fx: 510-845-5721

WorldatWork www.worldatwork.org
14040 N Northsight Blvd   Scottsdale AZ 85260
Ph: 480-951-9191 ▪ Fx: 480-483-8352 ▪ TF: 877-951-9191

World's Christian Endeavor Union www.christianendeavorworldwide.org
3575 Valley Rd PO Box 326   Liberty Corner NJ 07938
Ph: 908-604-9440 ▪ Fx: 908-604-6190

World's Fair Collectors Society members.aol.com/Bbqprod/wfcs.html
PO Box 20806   Sarasota FL 34276
Ph: 941-923-2590

WorldTeach www.worldteach.org
Harvard Univ Center for International Development 79 John F
Kennedy St   Cambridge MA 02138
Ph: 617-495-5527 ▪ Fx: 617-495-1599 ▪ TF: 800-483-2240

WorldViews worldviews.igc.org

Worldwatch Institute www.worldwatch.org
1776 Massachusetts Ave NW   Washington DC 20036
Ph: 202-452-1999 ▪ Fx: 202-296-7365 ▪ TF: 800-555-2028

Worldwide Aquatics Bodywork Association aspen.forest.net/waba
PO Box 889   Middletown CA 95461
Ph: 707-987-3801 ▪ Fx: 707-987-9638

Worldwide Assurance for Employees of Public Agencies www.waepa.org
7651 Leesburg Pike   Falls Church VA 22043
Ph: 703-790-8010 ▪ Fx: 703-790-4606 ▪ TF: 800-368-3484

Worldwide Camaro Club www.worldwidecamaro.com
5140 S Washington Ave   Titusville FL 32780
Ph: 321-269-9680 ▪ Fx: 321-383-2059 ▪ TF: 800-456-1957

Worldwide Employee Benefits Network Inc www.webnetwork.org
21165 Whitfield Pl   Potomac Falls VA 20165
Ph: 703-433-9696 ▪ Fx: 703-433-0369

Worldwide Kennel Club Ltd www.worldwidekennel.qpg.com
530 5th Ave   Pelham NY 10803
Ph: 914-654-8574 ▪ Fx: 914-654-0364

Worldwide Printing Thermographers Association www.thermographers.org
1156 15th St NW Suite 900   Washington DC 20005
Ph: 202-393-2818 ▪ Fx: 202-223-9741

Worldwide Responsible Apparel Production www.wrapapparel.org
200 N Glebe Rd Suite 1016   Arlington VA 22203
Ph: 703-243-0970 ▪ Fx: 703-243-8247

Wound Care, Association for the Advancement of www.aawcone.com
83 General Warren Blvd Suite 100   Malvern PA 19355
Ph: 610-560-0500 ▪ Fx: 610-560-0502 ▪ TF: 866-229-2999

Wound Management, American Academy of www.aawm.org
1255 23rd St NW Suite 200   Washington DC 20037
Ph: 202-521-0368 ▪ Fx: 202-833-3636

Wound Ostomy & Continence Nurses Society www.wocn.org
4700 W Lake Ave   Glenview IL 60025
Ph: 888-224-9626 ▪ Fx: 866-615-8560

Wrestling Association, National Collegiate www.ncwa.net
11411 N Central Expy Suite 100W   Dallas TX 75243
Ph: 214-378-8700 ▪ Fx: 214-378-9900

Wrestling Association, New York Arm www.nycarms.com
PO Box 670952   Flushing NY 11367
Ph: 718-544-4592 ▪ Fx: 718-261-8111 ▪ TF: 877-692-2767

Wrestling Coaches Association, www.nwcaadmin.bluestep.net/my/shared/home.jsp
National   PO Box 254   Manheim PA 17545
Ph: 717-653-8009 ▪ Fx: 717-653-8270

Wrestling, USA www.usawrestling.org
6155 Lehman Dr   Colorado Springs CO 80918
Ph: 719-598-8181 ▪ Fx: 719-598-9440 ▪ TF: 800-999-8531

Wright Frank Lloyd Foundation www.franklloydwright.org
Taliesin West PO Box 4430   Scottsdale AZ 85261
Ph: 480-860-2700 ▪ Fx: 480-391-4009

Wright Frank Lloyd Foundation www.franklloydwright.org
Taliesin West PO Box 4430   Scottsdale AZ 85261
Ph: 480-860-2700 ▪ Fx: 480-391-4009

Wright Frank Lloyd Preservation Trust www.wrightplus.org
931 Chicago Ave   Oak Park IL 60302
Ph: 708-848-1976 ▪ Fx: 708-848-1248

Wright George Society www.georgewright.org
PO Box 65   Hancock MI 49930
Ph: 906-487-9722 ▪ Fx: 906-487-9405

Write Your Congressman Inc, National www.nwyc.com
9696 Skillman St Suite 170   Dallas TX 75243
Ph: 214-342-0299 ▪ Fx: 214-342-9186 ▪ TF: 800-872-8683

Writers of America Inc, Mystery www.mysterywriters.org
17 E 47th St 6th Fl   New York NY 10017
Ph: 212-888-8171 ▪ Fx: 212-888-8107

Writers of America, Romance www.rwanational.org
16000 Stuebner Airline Rd Suite 140   Spring TX 77379
Ph: 832-717-5200 ▪ Fx: 832-717-5210

Writers of America Inc, Science Fiction & Fantasy www.sfwa.org
PO Box 877   Chestertown MD 21620
Ph: 410-778-3052

Writers of America, Western www.westernwriters.org

Writers & Artists Inc, International Black members.tripod.com/~IBWA
PO Box 43576   Los Angeles CA 90043
Ph: 323-964-3721

Writers Association of America, Baseball
78 Olive St   Lake Grove NY 11755
Ph: 631-981-7938 ▪ Fx: 631-585-4669

Writers Association of America, Bowling www.bowlingwriters.com

Writers Association of America Inc, Dog www.dwaa.org
173 Union Rd   Coatesville PA 19320
Ph: 610-384-2436 ▪ Fx: 610-384-2471

Writers Association of America, Football www.sportswriters.net/fwaa
c/o Dallas Morning News 18652 Vista Del Sol   Dallas TX 75287
Ph: 972-713-6198

Writers Association of America, Golf www.gwaa.com
10210 Greentree Rd   Houston TX 77042
Ph: 713-782-6664 ▪ Fx: 713-781-2575

Writers Association of America, Outdoor www.owaa.org
121 Hickory St Suite 1   Missoula MT 59801
Ph: 406-728-7434 ▪ Fx: 406-728-7445

Writers Association, American Medical www.amwa.org
40 W Gude Dr Suite 101   Rockville MD 20850
Ph: 301-294-5303 ▪ Fx: 301-294-9006

Writers Association, American Podiatric Medical
104-20 Queens Blvd Suite 17B   Forest Hills NY 11375
Ph: 718-897-9700 ▪ Fx: 718-896-5747

Writers Association, Construction www.constructionwriters.org
PO Box 5586   Buffalo Grove IL 60089
Ph: 847-398-7756 ▪ Fx: 847-590-5241

Writers Association, Education www.ewa.org
2122 P St NW Suite 201   Washington DC 20037
Ph: 202-452-8830 ▪ Fx: 202-452-9837

Writers Association, Garden www.gwaa.org
10210 Leatherleaf Ct   Manassas VA 20111
Ph: 703-257-1032 ▪ Fx: 703-257-0213

Writers Association, Horror www.horror.org
PO Box 50577   Palo Alto CA 94303
Ph: 888-893-4008

Writers Association, International Food Wine & Travel www.ifwtwa.org
PO Box 8249   Calabasas CA 91372
Ph: 818-999-9959 ▪ Fx: 818-347-7545

Writers Association, National www.nationalwriters.com
3140 S Peoria St Suite 295   Aurora CO 80014
Ph: 303-841-0246 ▪ Fx: 303-841-2607

Writers Association, National Women Bowling www.nwbw.freeservers.com
3001 21st St   Lubbock TX 79410
Ph: 806-795-3830

Writers' Association, New York Financial www.nyfwa.org
PO Box 338   Ridgewood NJ 07451
Ph: 201-612-0100 ▪ Fx: 201-612-9915

Writers Association, Renaissance Artists & rawa.ru.org
c/o Ananda Marga New York Sectorial Office 97-38 42nd
Ave   Corona NY 11368
Ph: 718-898-1603

Writers Association, US Basketball www.sportswriters.net/usbwa
1818 Chouteau Ave   Saint Louis MO 63103
Ph: 314-421-0339 ▪ Fx: 314-421-3505

Writers & Broadcasters Association Inc, American Auto Racing www.aarwba.org
922 N Pass Ave   Burbank CA 91505
Ph: 818-842-7005 ▪ Fx: 818-842-7020

Writers' Circle of the Americas, Native www.ou.edu/cas/nas/writers.html
Univ of Oklahoma 216 Ellison Hall 633 Elm Ave   Norman OK
73019
Ph: 405-325-2312 ▪ Fx: 405-325-0842

Writers Collaborative, Teachers & www.twc.org
5 Union Sq W   New York NY 10003
Ph: 212-691-6590 ▪ Fx: 212-675-0171 ▪ TF: 888-266-5789

Writers - College & University Educators, Nature & Environmental www.new-cue.org
Saint Thomas Aquinas College   Sparkill NY 10976
Ph: 845-398-4247 ▪ Fx: 845-398-4224

Writers Guild of America East www.wgaeast.org
555 W 57th St   New York NY 10019
Ph: 212-767-7800 ▪ Fx: 212-582-1909

Writers Guild of America West www.wga.org
7000 W 3rd St   Los Angeles CA 90048
Ph: 323-951-4000 ▪ Fx: 323-782-4800 ▪ TF: 800-548-4532

Writers Guild, TallGrass www.outriderpress.com/guildinfo.html
c/o Outrider Press 937 Patricia Ln   Crete IL 60417
Ph: 708-672-6630 ▪ Fx: 708-672-5820 ▪ TF: 800-933-4680

Writers & Illustrators, Society of Children's Book www.scbwi.org
8271 Beverly Blvd   Los Angeles CA 90048
Ph: 323-782-1010 ▪ Fx: 323-782-1892

Writers International, Boating www.bwi.org
108 9th St   Wilmette IL 60091
Ph: 847-736-4147

Writers on Legal Subjects, SCRIBES - American Society of www.scribes.org
Barry Univ School of Law 6441 E Colonial Dr   Orlando FL
32807
Ph: 407-275-2000 ▪ Fx: 407-275-6142

Writers, National Association of Science www.nasw.org
PO Box 890   Hedgesville WV 25427
Ph: 304-754-5077 ■ Fx: 304-754-5076

Writers, National Association of Women www.naww.org
PO Box 183812   Arlington TX 76096
Ph: 866-821-5829

Writers, National Conference of Editorial www.ncew.org
3899 N Front St   Harrisburg PA 17110
Ph: 717-703-3015 ■ Fx: 717-703-3014

Writers Network, Small Publishers Artists & www.spawn.org
323 E Matilija St Suite 110   Ojai CA 93023
Ph: 818-886-4281 ■ Fx: 818-886-3120

Writers Organizations, Council of
12724 Sagamore Rd   Leawood KS 66209
Ph: 913-451-9023 ■ Fx: 913-451-4866

(Writers) PEN American Center www.pen.org
568 Broadway   New York NY 10012
Ph: 212-334-1660 ■ Fx: 212-334-2181

Writers Inc, Poets & www.pw.org
72 Spring St   New York NY 10012
Ph: 212-226-3586 ■ Fx: 212-226-3963

Writers, Society of American Business Editors & www.sabew.org
Missouri School of Journalism 134A Neff Annex   Columbia MO
65211
Ph: 573-882-7862 ■ Fx: 573-884-1372

Writers, TravelJourno - North American Association of www.traveljourno.com
Travel Food & Wine   866 Oneonta Dr   Los Angeles CA 90065
Ph: 323-257-6269

Writers Union, National www.nwu.org
113 University Pl 6th Fl   New York NY 10003
Ph: 212-254-0279 ■ Fx: 212-254-0673

Writers, World Bowling
122 S Michigan Ave Suite 1506   Chicago IL 60603
Ph: 312-341-1110 ■ Fx: 312-341-1480

Writers & Writing Programs, Association of awpwriter.org
George Mason Univ 4400 University Dr Tallwood House MS
1E3   Fairfax VA 22030
Ph: 703-993-4301 ■ Fx: 703-993-4302

Writing Academy www.wams.org
4010 Singleton Rd   Rockford IL 61114
Ph: 815-877-9675

Writing, Center for Sutton Movement www.dancewriting.org
PO Box 517   La Jolla CA 92038
Ph: 858-456-0098 ■ Fx: 858-456-0020

Writing Centers Association, National
Univ of Toledo 2801 W Bancroft   Toledo OH 43606
Ph: 419-530-4913 ■ Fx: 419-530-4752

Writing Guild, International Women's www.iwwg.com
PO Box 810 Gracie Stn   New York NY 10028
Ph: 212-737-7536 ■ Fx: 212-737-9469

Writing Instrument Manufacturers Association www.wima.org
17000 Commerce Pkwy Suite C   Mount Laurel NJ 08054
Ph: 856-638-0426 ■ Fx: 856-439-0525

Writing Program Administrators, Council of www.wpacouncil.org

Writing Programs, Association of Writers & awpwriter.org
George Mason Univ 4400 University Dr Tallwood House MS
1E3   Fairfax VA 22030
Ph: 703-993-4301 ■ Fx: 703-993-4302

WTA Tour Inc www.wtatour.com
1 Progress Pl Suite 1500   Saint Petersburg FL 33701
Ph: 727-895-5000 ■ Fx: 727-894-1982

WWII Glider Pilots Association Inc, National www.ww2gp.org
21 Phyllis Rd   Freehold NJ 07728
Ph: 732-462-1838

Wyckoff House & Association Inc www.wyckoffassociation.org
5816 Clarendon Rd   Brooklyn NY 11023
Ph: 718-629-5400 ■ Fx: 718-629-3125

Wycliffe Bible Translators www.wycliffe.org
PO Box 628200   Orlando FL 32862
Ph: 407-852-3600 ■ Fx: 407-852-3601 ■ TF: 800-992-5433

X

Xerces Society www.xerces.org
4828 SE Hawthorne Blvd   Portland OR 97215
Ph: 503-232-6639 ■ Fx: 503-233-6794

Xeroderma Pigmentosum Society Inc www.xps.org
437 Snydertown Rd   Craryville NY 12521
Ph: 518-851-2612 ■ TF: 877-977-2873

Xi Psi Phi Dental Fraternity www.xipsiphi.org
1623 Washington Ave Suite 300   Alton IL 62002
Ph: 618-463-1889

Xplor International www.xplor.org
24238 Hawthorne Blvd   Torrance CA 90505
Ph: 310-373-3633 ■ Fx: 310-375-4240 ■ TF: 800-669-7567

Y

Y-ME National Breast Cancer Organization www.y-me.org
212 W Van Buren St   Chicago IL 60607
Ph: 312-986-8338 ■ Fx: 312-294-8597 ■ TF: 800-221-2141

Yacht Brokers Association of America www.ybaa.com
105 Eastern Ave Suite 104   Annapolis MD 21403
Ph: 410-263-1014 ■ Fx: 410-263-1659

Yacht Council Inc, American Boat & www.abycinc.org
3069 Solomon's Island Rd   Edgewater MD 21037
Ph: 410-956-1050 ■ Fx: 410-956-2737

Yacht Racing Association, El Toro International www.eltoroyra.org
1014 Hopper Ave Suite 419   Santa Rosa CA 95403
Ph: 707-526-6621 ■ Fx: 707-526-3838

Yacht Racing Association, International Star Class www.starclass.org
1545 Waukegan Rd   Glenview IL 60025
Ph: 847-729-0630 ■ Fx: 847-729-0718

Yachting Association, Inland Lake www.ilya.org
W4680 Tory's Trail PO Box 311   Fontana WI 53125
Ph: 262-275-6921

Yachting Club of America www.ycaol.com
PO Box 1040   Marco Island FL 34146
Ph: 239-642-4448 ■ Fx: 239-642-5284

Yachting Professionals, Association of
PO Box 460248   Fort Lauderdale FL 33346
Ph: 954-522-0184 ■ Fx: 954-462-6084

YAI/National Institute for People with Disabilities Network www.yai.org
460 W 34th St   New York NY 10001
Ph: 212-273-6100 ■ Fx: 212-563-4836

Yale-China Association www.yalechina.org/
442 Temple St PO Box 208223   New Haven CT 06520
Ph: 203-432-0881 ■ Fx: 203-432-7246

Yamaha 650 Society www.yamaha650society.com

Yarn Association of America, Textured www.tyaa.org
PO Box 66   Gastonia NC 28053
Ph: 704-824-3522 ■ Fx: 704-824-0630

Yarn Council of America, Craft www.craftyarncouncil.com
PO Box 9   Gastonia NC 28053
Ph: 704-824-7838

Yarn Spinners Association, American www.aysa.org
PO Box 99   Gastonia NC 28053
Ph: 704-824-3522 ■ Fx: 704-824-0630

Year-Round Education, National Association for www.nayre.org
PO Box 711386   San Diego CA 92171
Ph: 619-276-5298 ■ Fx: 858-571-5754

Yellow Pages Integrated Media Association www.ypima.org
820 Kirts Blvd Suite 100   Troy MI 48084
Ph: 248-244-6200 ■ Fx: 248-244-0700 ■ TF: 800-841-0639

Yellow Ribbon Suicide Prevention Program www.yellowribbon.org
PO Box 644   Westminster CO 80036
Ph: 303-429-3530 ■ Fx: 303-426-4496

Yellowstone Coalition, Greater www.greateryellowstone.org
13 S Willson Ave Suite 2   Bozeman MT 59771
Ph: 406-586-1593 ■ Fx: 406-556-2839

Yes I Can Foundation for Exceptional Children yesican.cec.sped.org
1110 N Glebe Rd Suite 300   Arlington VA 22201
Ph: 703-264-3660 ■ Fx: 703-264-9494 ■ TF: 800-224-6830

Yeshiva Principals, National Conference of
160 Broadway   New York NY 10038
Ph: 212-227-1000 ■ Fx: 212-406-6934

Yiddish Book Center, National www.yiddishbookcenter.org
1021 West St   Amherst MA 01002
Ph: 413-256-4900 ■ Fx: 413-256-4700

Yiddish Culture Organization, Central
25 E 21st St 3rd Fl   New York NY 10010
Ph: 212-505-8305 ■ Fx: 212-505-8044

Yiddish Inc, League for www.ibiblio.org/yiddish/YidLeague
200 W 72nd St Suite 40   New York NY 10023
Ph: 212-787-6675

Yiddish, Yugntruf Youth for www.yugntruf.org
200 W 72nd St Suite 40   New York NY 10023
Ph: 212-787-6675

Yisrael, Congregation Shema www.shema.com
28600 Lahser Rd PO Box 804   Southfield MI 48037
Ph: 248-593-5150

YIVO Institute for Jewish Research www.yivoinstitute.org
15 W 16th St   New York NY 10011
Ph: 212-246-6080 ■ Fx: 212-292-1892

YLEM: Artists Using Science & Technology www.ylem.org
PO Box 2590   Alameda CA 94501
Ph: 650-856-9593

YMCA International Camp Counselor Program www.ymcaiccp.org
5 W 63rd St 2nd Fl   New York NY 10023
Ph: 212-727-8800 ■ Fx: 212-727-8814

YMCA of the USA www.ymca.net
101 N Wacker Dr 14th Fl   Chicago IL 60606
Ph: 312-977-0031 ■ Fx: 312-977-9063 ■ TF: 800-872-9622

YMCAs in the US, Association of Professional Directors of www.apdymca.org
12 Broad St Suite 2-1   Westerly RI 02891
Ph: 401-604-0034 ■ Fx: 401-604-0036

(Yoga) 3HO Foundation www.3ho.org
Rt 2 Box 4   Espanola NM 87532
Ph: 505-753-4988 ■ Fx: 505-753-1999 ■ TF: 888-346-2420

Yoga Association, American www.americanyogaassociation.org
PO Box 19986   Sarasota FL 34276
Ph: 941-927-4977 ■ Fx: 941-921-9844

Yoga Research Foundation www.yrf.org
6111 SW 74th Ave   Miami FL 33143
Ph: 305-661-9296 ■ Fx: 305-666-4443

Yoga Science & Philosophy, Himalayan International www.himalayaninstitute.org
Institute of   RR 1 Box 1127   Honesdale PA 18431
Ph: 570-253-5551 ■ Fx: 570-253-9078 ■ TF: 800-822-4547

Yoga Society Inc, Agni www.agniyoga.org
319 W 107th St   New York NY 10025
Ph: 212-864-7752 ■ Fx: 212-864-7704

Yogurt Association, National
2000 Corporate Ridge Suite 1000   McLean VA 22102
Ph: 703-821-0770 ■ Fx: 703-821-1350

Yogurt Retailers Association, National Ice Cream & www.nicyra.org
184 Hicks Rd Suite C   Rolling Meadows IL 60008
Ph: 847-934-0926 ■ Fx: 847-202-4791

Yosemite Association   www.yosemite.org
PO Box 230   El Portal CA 95318
Ph: 209-379-2646 ▪ Fx: 209-379-2486

Young Adult Library Services Association   www.ala.org/yalsa
50 E Huron St   Chicago IL 60611
Ph: 312-280-4390 ▪ Fx: 312-664-7459 ▪ TF: 800-545-2433

Young American Bowling Alliance   www.bowl.com/bowl/yaba
5301 S 76th St   Greendale WI 53129
Ph: 414-421-4700 ▪ Fx: 414-421-1301 ▪ TF: 800-514-2695

Young America's Foundation   www.yaf.org
110 Elden St   Herndon VA 20170
Ph: 703-318-9608 ▪ Fx: 703-318-9122 ▪ TF: 800-292-9231

Young Astronaut Council   www.youngastronauts.com
5200 27th St NW   Washington DC 20015
Ph: 301-617-0923 ▪ Fx: 301-776-0858

Young Audiences Inc   www.youngaudiences.org
115 E 92nd St   New York NY 10128
Ph: 212-831-8110 ▪ Fx: 212-289-1202

Young Concert Artists   www.yca.org/
250 W 57th St Suite 1222   New York NY 10019
Ph: 212-307-6655 ▪ Fx: 212-581-8894

Young Democrats of America   www.yda.org
PO Box 77496   Washington DC 20013
Ph: 202-639-8585 ▪ Fx: 202-318-3221 ▪ TF: 877-639-8585

Young Entomologists Society   www.members.aol.com/yesbugs/bugclub.html
6907 W Grand River Ave   Lansing MI 48906
Ph: 517-886-0630

Young Entrepreneurs Organization   www.yeo.org
1199 N Fairfax St Suite 200   Alexandria VA 22314
Ph: 703-519-6700 ▪ Fx: 703-519-1864

Young Farmer Educational Association, National   www.nyfea.org
PO Box 20326   Montgomery AL 36120
Ph: 334-288-0097

Young Israel, National Council of   www.youngisrael.org
3 W 16th St   New York NY 10011
Ph: 212-929-1525 ▪ Fx: 212-727-9526

Young Judaea   www.youngjudaea.org
50 W 58th St   New York NY 10019
Ph: 212-303-8014 ▪ Fx: 212-303-4572

Young Lawyers Div, ABA   www.abanet.org/yld
750 N Lake Shore Dr   Chicago IL 60611
Ph: 312-988-5000 ▪ Fx: 312-988-6231

Young Life   www.younglife.org
PO Box 520   Colorado Springs CO 80901
Ph: 651-381-1800 ▪ Fx: 719-381-1756

Young Men's Christian Association of the USA   www.ymca.net
101 N Wacker Dr 14th Fl   Chicago IL 60606
Ph: 312-977-0031 ▪ Fx: 312-977-9063 ▪ TF: 800-872-9622

Young Menswear Association
47 W 34th St   New York NY 10001
Ph: 616-241-6422 ▪ Fx: 212-594-9349

Young Polish Women, Legion of
Copernicus Ctr 5216 W Lawrence Ave   Chicago IL 60630
Ph: 773-777-9037 ▪ Fx: 773-763-4069

Young Political Leaders, American Council of   www.acypl.org
1612 K St NW Suite 300   Washington DC 20006
Ph: 202-857-0999 ▪ Fx: 202-857-0027

Young Presidents' Organization   www.ypo.org
451 S Decker Dr Suite 200   Irving TX 75062
Ph: 972-650-4600 ▪ Fx: 972-650-7976 ▪ TF: 800-773-7976

Young Religious Unitarian Universalists   www.uua.org/YRUU
25 Beacon St   Boston MA 02108
Ph: 617-948-4350 ▪ Fx: 617-367-4798

Young Republican National Federation
PO Box 65337   Washington DC 20035
Ph: 202-608-1417

Young Women's Christian Association   www.ywca.org
1015 18th St NW Suite 1100   Washington DC 20036
Ph: 202-467-0801 ▪ Fx: 202-467-0802 ▪ TF: 800-992-2871

Youth Action for Global Justice, Just Act: www.justact.org
333 Valencia St Suite 325   San Francisco CA 94103
Ph: 415-431-4204 ▪ Fx: 415-431-5953

Youth Advocacy Coalition, National   www.nyacyouth.org
1638 R St NW Suite 300   Washington DC 20009
Ph: 202-319-7596 ▪ Fx: 202-319-7365 ▪ TF: 800-541-6922

Youth, Advocates for   www.advocatesforyouth.org
1025 Vermont Ave NW Suite 200   Washington DC 20005
Ph: 202-347-5700 ▪ Fx: 202-347-2263

Youth, American Romanian Orthodox   www.aroy.org
Romanian Orthodox Episcopate of America 2535 Grey Tower
Rd   Jackson MI 49201
Ph: 517-522-4800

Youth, America's Promise - The Alliance for   www.americaspromise.org
909 N Washington St Suite 400   Alexandria VA 22314
Ph: 703-684-4500 ▪ Fx: 703-535-3900 ▪ TF: 800-365-0153

Youth for Christ/USA   community.gospelcom.net/Brix/yfcusa/public
PO Box 228822   Denver CO 80222
Ph: 303-843-9000 ▪ Fx: 303-843-9002 ▪ TF: 800-735-3252

Youth Clubs, National Association of
1601 R St NW   Washington DC 20009
Ph: 202-667-4080 ▪ Fx: 202-667-4113

Youth Council, National Indian
318 Elm St SW   Albuquerque NM 87102
Ph: 505-247-2251 ▪ Fx: 505-247-4251

Youth Crime Watch of America   www.ycwa.org
9200 S Dadeland Blvd Suite 417   Miami FL 33156
Ph: 305-670-2409 ▪ Fx: 305-670-3805

(Youth Development) Big Picture Alliance   www.bigpicturealliance.org
1315 Walnut St Suite 1616   Philadelphia PA 19107
Ph: 215-735-5750 ▪ Fx: 215-735-9291

(Youth Development) WAVE Inc   www.waveinc.org
525 School St SW Suite 500   Washington DC 20024
Ph: 202-484-0103 ▪ Fx: 202-488-7595 ▪ TF: 800-274-2005

Youth Employment Coalition, National   www.nyec.org
1836 Jefferson Pl NW   Washington DC 20036
Ph: 202-659-1064 ▪ Fx: 202-659-0339

Youth for Environmental Sanity   www.yesworld.org
420 Bronco Rd   Soquel CA 95073
Ph: 877-293-7226 ▪ Fx: 831-462-6970

Youth & Families, Grantmakers for Children   www.gcyf.org
1522 K St NW Suite 1100   Washington DC 20005
Ph: 202-962-3940 ▪ Fx: 202-393-4148

Youth Federation, Armenian   www.ayf.org
80 Bigleow Ave   Watertown MA 02472
Ph: 617-923-1933

Youth Foundation, American   www.ayf.com
2331 Hampton Ave   Saint Louis MO 63139
Ph: 314-646-6000 ▪ Fx: 314-772-7542

Youth Foundation, American Zionist
633 3rd Ave 21st Fl   New York NY 10017
Ph: 212-318-6123 ▪ TF: 800-274-7723

Youth Foundation, Harness Horse   www.hhyf.org
14950 Greyhound Ct Suite 210   Carmel IN 46032
Ph: 317-848-5132 ▪ Fx: 317-848-5136

Youth Foundation, International   www.iyfnet.org
32 South St Suite 500   Baltimore MD 21202
Ph: 410-347-1500 ▪ Fx: 410-347-1188 ▪ TF: 800-446-2700

Youth Foundation, Natural Science for
130 Azalea Dr   Roswell GA 30075
Ph: 770-594-9367 ▪ Fx: 770-594-7738

(Youth) Girls Inc   www.girlsinc.org
120 Wall St 3rd Fl   New York NY 10005
Ph: 212-509-2000 ▪ Fx: 212-509-8708 ▪ TF: 800-374-4475

Youth Horse Council, American   www.ayhc.com
577 N Boyero Ave   Pueblo West CO 81007
Ph: 719-547-7677 ▪ TF: 800-879-2942

Youth Hostels, Hostelling International - American   www.hiusa.org
8401 Colesville Rd Suite 600   Silver Spring MD 20910
Ph: 301-495-1240 ▪ Fx: 301-495-6697

Youth Law, National Center for   www.youthlaw.org
405 14th St Suite 1500   Oakland CA 94612
Ph: 510-835-8098 ▪ Fx: 510-835-8099

Youth Leadership Council, National   www.nylc.org
1667 Snelling Ave N   Saint Paul MN 55108
Ph: 651-631-3672 ▪ Fx: 651-631-2955

Youth Leadership, Hugh O'Brian   www.hoby.org
10880 Wilshire Blvd Suite 410   Los Angeles CA 90024
Ph: 310-474-4370 ▪ Fx: 310-475-5426

Youth Ministries, Dynamic   www.gospelcom.net/dym
1333 Alger SE PO Box 7259   Grand Rapids MI 49510
Ph: 616-241-5616 ▪ Fx: 616-241-5558

Youth Ministry, National Federation for Catholic   www.nfcym.org
415 Michigan Ave NE Suite 40   Washington DC 20017
Ph: 202-636-3825 ▪ Fx: 202-526-7544

Youth With A Mission   www.ywam.org
7085 Battlecreek Rd SE   Salem OR 97301
Ph: 503-364-3837 ▪ Fx: 503-378-7026

Youth, National Conference of Synagogue   www.ou.org/ncsy
11 Broadway   New York NY 10004
Ph: 212-613-8232 ▪ Fx: 212-613-0633

Youth, National Network for   www.nn4youth.org
1319 F St NW Suite 401   Washington DC 20004
Ph: 202-783-7949 ▪ Fx: 202-783-7955

(Youth) New Ways to Work Inc   www.nww.org
103 Morris St Suite A   Sebastopol CA 95472
Ph: 707-824-4000 ▪ Fx: 707-824-4410

Youth Organization, B'nai B'rith   www.bbyo.org
2020 K St NW   Washington DC 20006
Ph: 202-857-6633 ▪ Fx: 202-857-6568

Youth Organization, Byelorussian-American
PO Box 1123   New Brunswick NJ 08903
Ph: 732-560-8610

Youth Organization, Lubavitch   www.lubavitch.qpg.com
305 Kingston Ave   Brooklyn NY 11213
Ph: 718-953-1000 ▪ Fx: 718-493-1000

Youth Organization, United Methodist   umyouth.org
1001 19th Ave S PO Box 340003   Nashville TN 37203
Ph: 615-340-7184 ▪ Fx: 615-340-1764 ▪ TF: 877-899-2780

Youth Organizations USA
12 Tenafly Rd PO Box 526   Englewood NJ 07631
Ph: 201-836-1838 ▪ Fx: 201-894-5117

Youth Program, Woodmen Rangers   www.woodmen.com/about/rangers.cfm
Woodmen of the World/Omaha Woodmen Life Insurance Society
1700 Farnam St   Omaha NE 68102
Ph: 402-271-7258 ▪ Fx: 402-449-7733

Youth Service America   www.servenet.org
1101 15th St NW Suite 200   Washington DC 20005
Ph: 202-296-2992 ▪ Fx: 202-296-4030

Youth Services, National Resource Center for   www.nrcys.ou.edu
4502 E 41st St Bldg 4 W   Tulsa OK 74135
Ph: 918-660-3700 ▪ Fx: 918-660-3737

Youth, Soccer Association for   www.saysoccer.org
1 N Commerce Park Dr Suite 320   Cincinnati OH 45215
Ph: 513-769-3800 ▪ Fx: 513-769-0500 ▪ TF: 800-233-7291

Youth Soccer Association, US   usysa.org
899 Presidential Dr Suite 117   Richardson TX 75081
Ph: 972-235-4499 ▪ Fx: 972-235-4480 ▪ TF: 800-476-2237

Youth Soccer Organization, American   soccer.org
12501 S Isis Ave   Hawthorne CA 90250
Ph: 310-643-6455 ▪ Fx: 310-643-5310 ▪ TF: 800-872-2976

Youth Sport Institute, North American — www.naysi.com
4985 Oak Garden Dr   Kernersville NC 27284
Ph: 336-784-4926 ▪ Fx: 336-784-5546 ▪ TF: 800-767-4916

Youth Sports Coaches Association, National — www.nays.org
2050 Vista Pkwy   West Palm Beach FL 33411
Ph: 561-684-1141 ▪ Fx: 561-684-2546 ▪ TF: 800-729-2057

Youth Sports, National Alliance for — www.nays.org
2050 Vista Pkwy   West Palm Beach FL 33411
Ph: 561-684-1141 ▪ Fx: 561-684-2546 ▪ TF: 800-729-2057

Youth Sports, National Council of — www.ncys.org
7185 SE Seagate Ln   Stuart FL 34997
Ph: 772-781-1452 ▪ Fx: 772-781-7298

Youth Sports Safety Foundation, National — www.nyssf.org
1 Beacon St Suite 3333   Boston MA 02108
Ph: 617-367-6677 ▪ Fx: 617-722-9999

Youth for Understanding International Exchange — www.yfu.org
6400 Goldsboro Rd Suite 100   Bethesda MD 20817
Ph: 240-235-2100 ▪ Fx: 240-235-2104 ▪ TF: 800-424-3691

Youth, United National Indian Tribal — www.unityinc.org
PO Box 800   Oklahoma City OK 73101
Ph: 405-236-2800 ▪ Fx: 405-971-1071

Youth, United Synagogue — www.usy.org
155 5th Ave   New York NY 10010
Ph: 212-533-7800 ▪ Fx: 212-353-9439

(Youth Volunteers) Kids Korps USA — www.kidskorps.org
265 Santa Helena Suite 110A   Solana Beach CA 92075
Ph: 858-259-3602 ▪ Fx: 858-259-3603

Youth Vote Coalition — www.youthvote.org
1010 Vermont Ave NW Suite 715   Washington DC 20005
Ph: 202-783-4751 ▪ Fx: 202-783-4750

(Youth) Woodmen Rangers Youth Program — www.woodmen.com/about/rangers.cfm
Woodmen of the World/Omaha Woodmen Life Insurance Society
1700 Farnam St   Omaha NE 68102
Ph: 402-271-7258 ▪ Fx: 402-449-7733

Youth Work Center, American — www.youthtoday.org
1200 17th St NW 4th Fl   Washington DC 20036
Ph: 202-785-0764 ▪ Fx: 202-728-0657

Youth, World Assembly of Muslim — www.wamyusa.org
PO Box 8096   Falls Church VA 22041
Ph: 703-783-8410 ▪ Fx: 703-783-8409

Youth for Yiddish, Yugntruf — www.yugntruf.org
200 W 72nd St Suite 40   New York NY 10023
Ph: 212-787-6675

Youthbuild USA — www.youthbuild.org
58 Day St PO 440322   Somerville MA 02144
Ph: 617-623-9900 ▪ Fx: 617-623-4331

Yugntruf Youth for Yiddish — www.yugntruf.org
200 W 72nd St Suite 40   New York NY 10023
Ph: 212-787-6675

Yukon Pioneers, Alaska-
2725 E Fir St Unit 71   Mount Vernon WA 98273
Ph: 360-428-1912 ▪ Fx: 360-428-4200

YWCA of the USA — www.ywca.org
1015 18th St NW Suite 1100   Washington DC 20036
Ph: 202-467-0801 ▪ Fx: 202-467-0802 ▪ TF: 800-992-2871

Z

Zebu Association, International Miniature — www.miniature-zebu-cattle.com
PO Box 66   Crawford NE 68339
Ph: 308-665-3919 ▪ Fx: 308-665-1931

Zen-Do Kai Martial Arts International — www.superior.net/~zendokai
PO Box 186   Johnstown NY 12095
Ph: 518-762-4723

Zero Balancing Health Association — www.zerobalancing.com
801 W Main St Suite 202   Charlottesville VA 22903
Ph: 434-244-2458 ▪ Fx: 434-244-2645

Zeta Beta Tau Fraternity Inc — www.zbt.org
3905 Vincennes Rd Suite 300   Indianapolis IN 46268
Ph: 317-334-1898 ▪ Fx: 317-334-1899

Zeta Phi Beta Sorority Inc — www.zphib1920.org
1734 New Hampshire Ave NW   Washington DC 20009
Ph: 202-387-3103 ▪ Fx: 202-232-4593 ▪ TF: 800-368-5772

Zeta Psi Fraternity of North America — www.zetapsi.org
15 S Henry St   Pearl River NY 10965
Ph: 845-735-1847 ▪ Fx: 845-735-1989 ▪ TF: 800-477-1847

Zeta Tau Alpha Fraternity — www.zetataualpha.org
3450 Founders Rd   Indianapolis IN 46268
Ph: 317-872-0540 ▪ Fx: 317-876-3948

Ziegfeld Club
593 Park Ave 5th Fl   New York NY 10021
Ph: 212-751-6688

Zinc Association, American — www.zinc.org
2025 M St NW Suite 800   Washington DC 20036
Ph: 202-367-1151 ▪ Fx: 202-367-2232

Zinc Research Organization, International Lead — www.ilzro.org
PO Box 12036   Research Triangle Park NC 27709
Ph: 919-361-4647 ▪ Fx: 919-361-1957

Zion Foundation Inc, Bnai — www.bnaizion.org
136 E 39th St   New York NY 10016
Ph: 212-725-1211 ▪ Fx: 212-684-6327 ▪ TF: 800-564-6399

(Zionism) MERCAZ USA — www.mercazusa.org
155 5th Ave   New York NY 10010
Ph: 212-533-7800 ▪ Fx: 212-533-2601

Zionist Alliance, Labor — www.laborzionist.org
275 7th Ave 17th Fl   New York NY 10001
Ph: 212-366-1194 ▪ Fx: 212-675-7685

(Zionist) Hashomer Hatzair USA — www.hashomerhatzair.org
114 W 26th St Suite 1001   New York NY 10001
Ph: 212-627-2830 ▪ Fx: 212-989-9840

Zionist Movement, American — www.azm.org
633 3rd Ave 21st Fl   New York NY 10017
Ph: 212-318-6100 ▪ Fx: 212-935-3578

Zionist Organization of America — www.zoa.org
4 E 34th St   New York NY 10016
Ph: 212-481-1500 ▪ Fx: 212-481-1515

Zionist Organization of America Inc, Hadassah Women's — www.hadassah.org
50 W 58th St   New York NY 10019
Ph: 212-355-7900 ▪ Fx: 212-303-8282 ▪ TF: 888-303-3640

Zionist Youth Foundation, American —
633 3rd Ave 21st Fl   New York NY 10017
Ph: 212-318-6123 ▪ TF: 800-274-7723

(Zionist Youth) Young Judaea — www.youngjudaea.org
50 W 58th St   New York NY 10019
Ph: 212-303-8014 ▪ Fx: 212-303-4572

Zonta International — www.zonta.org
557 W Randolph St   Chicago IL 60661
Ph: 312-930-5848 ▪ Fx: 312-930-0951

Zoo & Aquarium Association, American — www.aza.org
8403 Colesville Rd Suite 710   Silver Spring MD 20910
Ph: 301-562-0777 ▪ Fx: 301-562-0888

Zoo, Friends of the National — www.fonz.org
National Zoological Pk   Washington DC 20008
Ph: 202-673-4973 ▪ Fx: 202-673-4890

Zoo Keepers, American Association of — www.aazk.org
3601 SW 29th St Suite 133   Topeka KS 66614
Ph: 785-273-9149 ▪ Fx: 785-273-1980 ▪ TF: 800-242-4519

Zoo Veterinarians, American Association of — www.aazv.org
6 N Pennell Rd   Media PA 19063
Ph: 610-892-4812 ▪ Fx: 610-892-4813

Zoocheck Canada — www.zoocheck.com
3266 Yonge St Suite 1417   Toronto ON M4N3P6
Ph: 416-285-1744 ▪ Fx: 416-285-4670

Zoological Nomenclature, American Association for — www.iczn.org/aazn.htm
c/o Smithsonian Institution Dept of Zoology MRC
159   Washington DC 20013
Ph: 202-633-9786 ▪ Fx: 202-357-2986

Appendix to Chambers of Commerce

Chambers of Commerce - Canadian

Listings are organized by provinces and then are alphabetized within each province grouping according to the name of the city in which each chamber is located.

ALBERTA

Brooks & District Chamber of Commerce www.brookschamber.ab.ca
Box 400   Brooks AB T1R1B4
Ph: 403-362-7641 ▪ Fx: 403-362-6893

Calgary Chamber of Commerce www.calgarychamber.com
100 6th Ave SW   Calgary AB T2P0P5
Ph: 403-750-0400 ▪ Fx: 403-266-3413

Alberta Chambers of Commerce www.abchamber.ab.ca
10025 - 102A Ave Suite 1808 Edmonton Ctr   Edmonton AB
T5J2Z2
Ph: 780-425-4180 ▪ Fx: 780-429-1061

Edmonton Chamber of Commerce www.edmontonchamber.com
10123 99th St Suite 600   Edmonton AB T5J3G9
Ph: 780-426-4620 ▪ Fx: 780-424-7946

Fort McMurray Chamber of Commerce www.fortmcmurraychamber.ca
9612 Franklin Ave Suite 304   Fort McMurray AB T9H2J9
Ph: 780-743-3100 ▪ Fx: 780-790-9757

Grande Prairie & District Chamber of Commerce www.gpchamber.com
11330 106th St Suite 217   Grande Prairie AB T8V7X9
Ph: 780-532-5340 ▪ Fx: 780-532-2926

Lethbridge Chamber of Commerce www.lethchamber.org
529 6th St S Suite 200   Lethbridge AB T1J2E1
Ph: 403-327-1586 ▪ Fx: 403-327-1001

Medicine Hat & District Chamber of Commerce www.medicinehatchamber.com
413 6th Ave SE   Medicine Hat AB T1A2S7
Ph: 403-527-5214 ▪ Fx: 403-527-5182

Peace River Chamber of Commerce
PO Box 6599   Peace River AB T8S1S4
Ph: 780-624-4166 ▪ Fx: 780-624-4663

Red Deer Chamber of Commerce www.reddeerchamber.com
3017 Gaetz Ave   Red Deer AB T4N5Y6
Ph: 403-347-4491 ▪ Fx: 403-343-6188

Saint Albert Chamber of Commerce www.stalbertchamber.com
71 St Albert Rd   Saint Albert AB T8N6L5
Ph: 780-458-2833 ▪ Fx: 780-458-6515

BRITISH COLUMBIA

Abbotsford Chamber of Commerce www.abbotsfordchamber.com
32900 S Fraser Way Unit 207   Abbotsford BC V2S5A1
Ph: 604-859-9651 ▪ Fx: 604-850-6880

Burnaby Board of Trade www.burnabyboardoftrade.com
4555 Kings Way Suite 201   Burnaby BC V5H4T8
Ph: 604-412-0100 ▪ Fx: 604-412-0102

Campbell River & District Chamber of Commerce www.campbellriverchamber.ca
900 Alder St PO Box 400   Campbell River BC V9W5B6
Ph: 250-287-4636 ▪ Fx: 250-286-6490

Chilliwack Chamber of Commerce www.chilliwackchamber.com
46093 Yale Rd Suite 201   Chilliwack BC V2P2L8
Ph: 604-793-4323 ▪ Fx: 604-793-4303

Tri-Cities Chamber of Commerce www.tricitieschamber.com
1209 Pinetree Way   Coquitlam BC V3B7Y3
Ph: 604-464-2716 ▪ Fx: 604-464-6796

Comox Valley Chamber of Commerce www.comoxvalleychamber.com
2040 Cliffe Ave   Courtenay BC V9N2L3
Ph: 250-334-3234 ▪ Fx: 250-334-4908 ▪ TF: 888-357-4471

Delta Chamber of Commerce www.deltachamber.com
6201 60th Ave   Delta BC V4K4E2
Ph: 604-946-4232 ▪ Fx: 604-946-5285

Duncan Cowichan Chamber of Commerce duncancc.bc.ca
381 Trans Canada Hwy   Duncan BC V9L3R5
Ph: 250-748-1111 ▪ Fx: 250-746-8222

Fort Saint John & District Chamber of Commerce www.fortstjohnchamber.com
9325 100th St Suite 201   Fort Saint John BC V1J4N4
Ph: 250-785-6037 ▪ Fx: 250-785-7181

Kamloops Chamber of Commerce www.kamloopschamber.bc.ca/
1290 W Trans-Canada Hwy   Kamloops BC V2C6R3
Ph: 250-372-7722 ▪ Fx: 250-828-9500

Kelowna Chamber of Commerce www.kelownachamber.org
544 Harvey Ave   Kelowna BC V1Y6C9
Ph: 250-861-1515 ▪ Fx: 250-861-3624 ▪ TF: 800-663-4345

Langley Chamber of Commerce www.langleychamber.com
5761 Glover Rd Unit 1   Langley BC V3A8M8
Ph: 604-530-6656 ▪ Fx: 604-530-7066

Maple Ridge Chamber of Commerce www.mapleridge-chamber.bc.ca
22238 Lougheed Hwy   Maple Ridge BC V2X2T2
Ph: 604-463-3366 ▪ Fx: 604-463-3201

Mission Regional Chamber of Commerce www.city.mission.bc.ca
34033 Lougheed Hwy   Mission BC V2V5X8
Ph: 604-826-6914 ▪ Fx: 604-826-5916

Greater Nanaimo Chamber of Commerce www.nanaimochamber.bc.ca
777 Poplar St Suite E   Nanaimo BC V9S2H7
Ph: 250-753-1191 ▪ Fx: 250-754-5186

New Westminster Chamber of Commerce www.newwestchamber.com
601 Queens Ave   New Westminster BC V3M1L1
Ph: 604-521-7781 ▪ Fx: 604-521-0057

North Vancouver Chamber of Commerce www.nvchamber.bc.ca
124 W 1st St Suite 102   North Vancouver BC V7M3N3
Ph: 604-987-4488 ▪ Fx: 604-987-8272 ▪ TF: 877-880-4699

Parksville Chamber of Commerce www.chamber.parksville.bc.ca
PO Box 99   Parksville BC V9P2G3
Ph: 250-248-3613 ▪ Fx: 250-248-5210

Penticton & Wine Country Chamber of Commerce www.penticton.org
888 Westminster Ave W   Penticton BC V2A8S2
Ph: 250-492-4103 ▪ Fx: 250-492-6119

Alberni Valley Chamber of Commerce www.avcoc.com
RR 2 Site 215 Suite C-10   Port Alberni BC V9Y7L6
Ph: 250-724-6535 ▪ Fx: 250-724-6560

Prince George Chamber of Commerce www.pgchamber.bc.ca
890 Vancouver St   Prince George BC V2O2P5
Ph: 250-562-2454 ▪ Fx: 250-562-6510

Richmond Chamber of Commerce www.chamber.richmond.bc.ca
5811 Cooney Rd Suite 101   Richmond BC V6X3Mi
Ph: 604-278-2822 ▪ Fx: 604-278-2972

Saanich Peninsula Chamber of Commerce www.spcoc.org
PO Box 2014   Sidney BC V8L3S3
Ph: 250-656-3616 ▪ Fx: 250-656-7111

Surrey Chamber of Commerce www.surreychamber.org
14439 104th Ave Suite 101   Surrey BC V3R1M1
Ph: 604-581-7130 ▪ Fx: 604-588-7549

British Columbia Chamber of Commerce www.bcchamber.org
750 W Pender St Suite 1201   Vancouver BC V6C2T8
Ph: 604-683-0700 ▪ Fx: 604-683-0416

Vancouver Board Of Trade www.vancouver.boardoftrade.com
999 Canada Pl Suite 400   Vancouver BC V6C3E1
Ph: 604-681-2111 ▪ Fx: 604-681-0437

Greater Vernon Chamber of Commerce
701 Hwy 97 S   Vernon BC V1B3W4
Ph: 250-545-0771 ▪ Fx: 250-545-3114

Greater Victoria Chamber of Commerce www.victoriachamber.ca
850 Courtney St   Victoria BC V8W1C4
Ph: 250-383-7191 ▪ Fx: 250-385-3552

West Shore Chamber of Commerce westshore.bc.ca
2830 Aldwynd Rd   Victoria BC V9B3S7
Ph: 250-478-1130 ▪ Fx: 250-478-1584

West Vancouver Chamber of Commerce www.westvanchamber.com
1310 Marine Dr   West Vancouver BC V7T1B5
Ph: 604-926-6614 ▪ Fx: 604-926-6436

Westbank & District Chamber of Commerce www.westbankchamber.com
2375 Pamela Rd Unit 4   Westbank BC V4T2H9
Ph: 250-768-3378 ▪ Fx: 250-768-3465 ▪ TF: 866-768-3378

MANITOBA

Brandon Chamber of Commerce www.brandonchamber.ca
1043 Rosser Ave   Brandon MB R7A0L5
Ph: 204-571-5340 ▪ Fx: 204-571-5347

Portage & District Chamber of Commerce www.portagechamber.com
11 2nd St NE   Portage la Prairie MB R1N1R8
Ph: 204-857-7778 ▪ Fx: 204-857-4095

Saint-Boniface Chamber of Commerce www.ccfsb.mb.ca
383 boul Provencher Bureau 212   Saint-Boniface MB R2H0G9
Ph: 204-235-1406 ▪ Fx: 204-233-1017

Appendix

Selkirk & District Chamber of Commerce
PO Box 89   Selkirk MB R1A2B1
Ph: 204-482-7176 ■ Fx: 204-785-2331
Manitoba Chamber of Commerce   www.mbchamber.mb.ca
227 Portage Ave   Winnipeg MB R3B2A6
Ph: 204-948-0100 ■ Fx: 204-948-0110 ■ TF: 877-444-5222
Winnipeg Chamber of Commerce   www.winnipeg-chamber.com
259 Portage Ave Suite 100   Winnipeg MB R3B2A9
Ph: 204-944-8484 ■ Fx: 204-944-8492

NEW BRUNSWICK

Enterprise Fredericton   www.gfedc.nb.ca
570 Queen St   Fredericton NB E3B6Z6
Ph: 506-444-4686 ■ Fx: 506-444-4649 ■ TF: 800-200-1180
Fredericton Chamber of Commerce   www.frederictonchamber.ca/
PO Box 275   Fredericton NB E3B4Y9
Ph: 506-458-8006 ■ Fx: 506-451-1119
Greater Miramichi Chamber of Commerce   www.greatermiramichi.com
PO Box 693   Miramichi NB E1V3V4
Ph: 506-622-5522 ■ Fx: 506-622-5529
Atlantic Provinces Chamber of Commerce   www.apcc.ca
236 Saint George St Suite 21   Moncton NB E1C1W1
Ph: 506-857-3980 ■ Fx: 506-859-6131
Greater Moncton Chamber of Commerce   www.gmcc.nb.ca
910 Main St Suite 100   Moncton NB E1C1G6
Ph: 506-857-2883 ■ Fx: 506-857-9209
Saint John Board of Trade   www.sjboardoftrade.com
40 King St PO Box 6037   Saint John NB E2L4R5
Ph: 506-634-8111 ■ Fx: 506-632-2008

NEWFOUNDLAND & LABRADOR

Greater Corner Brook Board of Trade
11 Confederation Dr PO Box 475   Corner Brook NL A2H6E6
Ph: 709-634-5831 ■ Fx: 709-639-9710
Gander & Area Chamber of Commerce   www.ganderchamber.nf.ca
109 Trans Canada Hwy   Gander NL A1V1P6
Ph: 709-256-7110 ■ Fx: 709-256-4080
Exploits Regional Chamber of Commerce
PO Box 272   Grand Falls-Windsor NL A2A2J7
Ph: 709-489-7512 ■ Fx: 709-489-7532
Saint John's Board of Trade   www.boardoftrade.nfld.net
PO Box 5127   Saint John's NL A1C5V5
Ph: 709-726-2961 ■ Fx: 709-726-2003

NORTHWEST TERRITORIES

Northwest Territories Chamber of Commerce   www.nwtchamber.com
4910 50th St Suite 302   Yellowknife NT X1A3S5
Ph: 867-920-9505 ■ Fx: 867-873-4174

NOVA SCOTIA

Bridgewater & Area Chamber of Commerce   www.bridgewaterchamber.com
PO Box 100   Bridgewater NS B4V2W8
Ph: 902-543-4263 ■ Fx: 902-543-5000
Metropolitan Halifax Chamber of Commerce   www.halifaxchamber.com
PO Box 8990   Halifax NS B3K5M6
Ph: 902-468-7111 ■ Fx: 902-468-7333
Pictou County Chamber of Commerce   www.pictouchamber.com
980 E River Rd   New Glasgow NS B2H3S8
Ph: 902-755-3463 ■ Fx: 902-755-2848
Sydney & Area Chamber of Commerce   www.sydneyareachamber.ca
PO Box 131   Sydney NS B1P6G9
Ph: 902-564-6453 ■ Fx: 902-539-7487
Truro & District Chamber of Commerce   www.trurochamber.com
574 Prince St   Truro NS B2N1G3
Ph: 902-895-6328 ■ Fx: 902-897-6641
Yarmouth Chamber of Commerce   www.yarmouthchamber.ca
PO Box 532   Yarmouth NS B5A4B4
Ph: 902-742-3074 ■ Fx: 902-749-1383

ONTARIO

Aurora Chamber of Commerce   www.aurorachamber.on.ca
6-14845 Yonge St Suite 321   Aurora ON L4G6H8
Ph: 905-727-7262 ■ Fx: 905-841-6217
Greater Barrie Chamber of Commerce   www.barriechamber.com
97 Toronto St   Barrie ON L4M1V1
Ph: 705-721-5000 ■ Fx: 705-726-0973
Belleville & District Chamber of Commerce   www.city.belleville.on.ca/chamber
5 Moira St E   Belleville ON K8N5B3
Ph: 613-962-4597 ■ Fx: 613-962-3911 ■ TF: 888-852-9992
Caledon Chamber of Commerce   www.caledonchamber.com
PO Box 626   Bolton ON L7E5T5
Ph: 905-857-7393 ■ Fx: 905-857-7405
Brampton Board of Trade   www.bramptonbot.com
33 Queen St W 2nd Fl   Brampton ON L6Y1L9
Ph: 905-451-1122 ■ Fx: 905-450-0295

Brantford Regional Chamber of Commerce   www.brcc.ca
77 Charlotte St PO Box 1294   Brantford ON N3T5T6
Ph: 519-753-2617 ■ Fx: 519-753-0921
Burlington Chamber of Commerce   www.burlingtonchamber.com
414 Locust St Suite 201   Burlington ON L7S1T7
Ph: 905-639-0174 ■ Fx: 905-333-3956
Cambridge Chamber of Commerce   www.cambridgechamber.com
750 Hespeler Rd   Cambridge ON N3H5L8
Ph: 519-622-2221 ■ Fx: 519-622-0177
Chatham & District Chamber of Commerce   www.chathamchamber.on.ca
235 King St W   Chatham ON N7M1E6
Ph: 519-352-7540 ■ Fx: 519-352-8741
Vaughan Chamber of Commerce   www.vaughanchamber.ca
160 Applewood Crescent Unit 32   Concord ON L4K4H2
Ph: 905-761-1366 ■ Fx: 905-761-1918
Cornwall Chamber of Commerce   www.chamber.cornwall.on.ca
113 2nd St E   Cornwall ON K6J1Y5
Ph: 613-933-4004 ■ Fx: 613-933-8466
Dryden District Chamber of Commerce   www.cityofdryden.on.ca
284 Government St   Dryden ON P8N2P3
Ph: 807-223-2622 ■ Fx: 807-223-2626 ■ TF: 800-667-0935
Halton Hills Chamber of Commerce   www.haltonhillschamber.on.ca
170 Guelph St   Georgetown ON L7G4A7
Ph: 905-877-5116 ■ Fx: 905-877-5117
Guelph Chamber of Commerce   www.guelphchamber.com
PO Box 1268   Guelph ON N1H6N6
Ph: 519-822-8081 ■ Fx: 519-822-8451
Hamilton Chamber of Commerce   www.hamilton-cofc.on.ca
555 Bay St N   Hamilton ON L8L1H1
Ph: 905-522-1151 ■ Fx: 905-522-1154
Greater Kingston Chamber of Commerce   www.kingstonchamber.on.ca
67 Brock St   Kingston ON K7L1R8
Ph: 613-548-4453 ■ Fx: 613-548-4743
Chamber of Commerce of Kitchener & Waterloo   www.greaterkwchamber.com
80 Queen St N PO Box 2367   Kitchener ON N2H6L4
Ph: 519-576-5000 ■ Fx: 519-742-4760
Leamington District Chamber of Commerce   www.leamingtonchamber.com
PO Box 321   Leamington ON N8H3W3
Ph: 519-326-2721 ■ Fx: 519-326-3204 ■ TF: 800-250-3336
London Chamber of Commerce   www.londonchamber.com
PO Box 3295   London ON N6A4K3
Ph: 519-432-7551 ■ Fx: 519-432-8063
Markham Board of Trade   www.markhamboard.com
80 F Centurian Dr Suite 206   Markham ON L3R8C1
Ph: 905-474-0730 ■ Fx: 905-474-0685
Southern Georgia Bay Chamber of Commerce   www.southerngeorgianbay.on.ca
208 King St   Midland ON L4R3L9
Ph: 705-526-7884 ■ Fx: 705-526-1744
Milton Chamber of Commerce   www.chamber.milton.on.ca
251 Main St E Suite 104   Milton ON L9T1P1
Ph: 905-878-0581 ■ Fx: 905-878-4972
Mississauga Board of Trade   www.mbot.com
1447 Burnham Thorpe Rd W   Mississauga ON L5C2S7
Ph: 905-273-6151 ■ Fx: 905-273-4937
Newmarket Chamber of Commerce   www.newmarketchamber.com
470 Davis Dr   Newmarket ON L3Y2P3
Ph: 905-898-5900 ■ Fx: 905-853-7271
Niagara Falls Canada Chamber of Commerce   www.niagarafallschamber.com
4056 Dorchester Rd   Niagara Falls ON L2E6M9
Ph: 905-374-3666 ■ Fx: 905-374-2972
North Bay & District Chamber of Commerce   www.northbaychamber.com
1375 Seymour St PO Box 747   North Bay ON P1B8J8
Ph: 705-472-8480 ■ Fx: 705-472-8027 ■ TF: 888-249-8998
Oakville Chamber of Commerce   www.oakvillechamber.com
2521 Wyecroft Rd   Oakville ON L6L6P8
Ph: 905-845-6613 ■ Fx: 905-845-6475
Orangeville & District Chamber of Commerce   www.orangeville.org
PO Box 101   Orangeville ON L9W2Z5
Ph: 519-941-0490 ■ Fx: 519-941-0492
Greater Oshawa Chamber of Commerce   www.oshawachamber.com
44 Richmond St W Suite 100   Oshawa ON L1G1C7
Ph: 905-728-1683 ■ Fx: 905-432-1259
Canadian Chamber of Commerce   www.chamber.ca
350 Sparks St Delta Office Tower Suite 501   Ottawa ON K1R7S8
Ph: 613-238-4000 ■ Fx: 613-238-7643
Ottawa (Greater) Chamber of Commerce   www.greaterottawachamber.com
1701 Woodward Dr Suite LL20   Ottawa ON K2C0R4
Ph: 613-236-3631 ■ Fx: 613-236-7498
Upper Ottawa Valley Chamber of Commerce   www.upperottawavalleychamber.com
2 International Dr   Pembroke ON K8A6W5
Ph: 613-732-1492 ■ Fx: 613-732-5793
Perth & District Chamber of Commerce   www.heritageperth.com
34 Herriott St   Perth ON K7H1T2
Ph: 613-267-3200 ■ Fx: 613-267-6797
Greater Peterborough Chamber of Commerce   www.peterboroughchamber.com
175 George St N   Peterborough ON K9J3G6
Ph: 705-748-9771 ■ Fx: 705-743-2331
Port Colborne-Wainfleet Chamber of Commerce   www.niagara.com/pcwchamb
76 Main St W   Port Colborne ON L3K3V2
Ph: 905-834-9765 ■ Fx: 905-834-1542
Richmond Hill Chamber of Commerce   www.rhcoc.com
376 Church St S   Richmond Hill ON L4C9V8
Ph: 905-884-1961 ■ Fx: 905-884-1962
Saint Catharines Chamber of Commerce   www.scchamberofcommerce.com
PO Box 940   Saint Catharines ON L2R6Z4
Ph: 905-684-2361 ■ Fx: 905-684-2100
Saint Thomas & District Chamber of Commerce   www.stthomaschamber.on.ca
555 Talbot St   Saint Thomas ON N5P1C5
Ph: 519-631-1981 ■ Fx: 519-631-0466

Sault Sainte Marie Chamber of Commerce   www.ssmcoc.com
334 Bay St   Sault Sainte Marie ON P6A1X1
Ph: 705-949-7152 ▪ Fx: 705-759-8166

Scarborough Chamber of Commerce   www.scarboroughchamber.com
940 Progress Ave   Scarborough ON M1G3T5
Ph: 416-439-4140 ▪ Fx: 416-439-4147

Timmins Chamber of Commerce   www.timminschamber.on.ca
PO Box 985   Schumacher ON P4N7H6
Ph: 705-360-1900 ▪ Fx: 705-360-1193

Simcoe & District Chamber of Commerce   www.kwic.com/~chamber
95 Queensway W   Simcoe ON N3Y2M8
Ph: 519-426-5867 ▪ Fx: 519-428-7718

Stratford & District Chamber of Commerce   www.stratfordchamber.com
55 Lorne Ave E   Stratford ON N5A6S4
Ph: 519-273-5250 ▪ Fx: 519-273-2229

Greater Sudbury Chamber of Commerce   www.sudburychamber.com
166 Douglas St   Sudbury ON P3E1G1
Ph: 705-673-7133 ▪ Fx: 705-673-2944

Thunder Bay Chamber of Commerce   www.tb-chamber.on.ca
857 N May St   Thunder Bay ON P7C3S2
Ph: 807-624-2626 ▪ Fx: 807-622-7752

Canadian Chamber of Commerce Toronto Office   www.chamber.ca
181 Bay St PO Box 818 BCE Place   Toronto ON M5J2T3
Ph: 416-868-6415 ▪ Fx: 416-868-0189

Ontario Chamber of Commerce   www.occ.on.ca
180 Dundas St W Suite 505   Toronto ON M5G1Z8
Ph: 416-482-5222 ▪ Fx: 416-482-5879

Toronto Board of Trade   www.bot.com
1 First Canadian Pl PO Box 60   Toronto ON M5X1C1
Ph: 416-366-6811 ▪ Fx: 416-366-6460

Flamborough Chamber of Commerce   www.chamber.flamborough.on.ca
PO Box 1030   Waterdown ON L0R2H0
Ph: 905-689-7650 ▪ Fx: 905-689-1313

Welland/Pelham Chamber of Commerce   www.chamber.iaw.com
32 E Main St   Welland ON L3B3W3
Ph: 905-732-7515 ▪ Fx: 905-732-7151

Whitby Chamber of Commerce   www.whitbychamber.org
128 Brock St S   Whitby ON L1N4J8
Ph: 905-668-4506 ▪ Fx: 905-668-1894

Windsor & District Chamber of Commerce   www.windsorchamber.org
2575 Ouellette Pl   Windsor ON N8X1L9
Ph: 519-966-3696 ▪ Fx: 519-966-0603

Woodstock District Chamber of Commerce   www.woodstockchamber.on.ca
19 Wellington St N   Woodstock ON N4S6P1
Ph: 519-539-9411 ▪ Fx: 519-539-5433

PRINCE EDWARD ISLAND

Greater Charlottetown Area Chamber of Commerce   www.charlottetownchamber.com
PO Box 67   Charlottetown PE C1A7K2
Ph: 902-628-2000 ▪ Fx: 902-368-3570

QUEBEC

Chicoutimi Chamber of Commerce
31 rue Price O   Chicoutimi QC G7J1H1
Ph: 418-543-5941 ▪ Fx: 418-543-5576

La Chambre de Commerce de Drummond   www.ccid.qc.ca
234 rue Saint Marcel CP 188   Drummondville QC J2B6V7
Ph: 819-477-7822 ▪ Fx: 819-477-2823

Chambre de Commerce et d'Industrie de l'Outaouais
166 rue de Varennes Bureau 300   Gatineau QC J8T8G4
Ph: 819-243-2246 ▪ Fx: 819-243-3346

Chambre de Commerce du District de Granby
328 rue Principale Bureau 200   Granby QC J2G2W4
Ph: 450-372-6100 ▪ Fx: 450-372-3161

Laval Chamber of Commerce   www.ccilaval.qc.ca
1555 boul Chomedey Bureau 200   Laval QC H7V3Z1
Ph: 450-682-5255 ▪ Fx: 450-682-5735

Mont-Laurier Chamber of Commerce
177 boul Albiny - Paquette   Mont-Laurier QC J9L1J2
Ph: 819-623-3642 ▪ Fx: 819-623-6102

Board of Trade of Metropolitan Montreal   www.btmm.qc.ca
380 Saint Antoine St W Suite 6000   Montreal QC H2Y3X7
Ph: 514-871-4000 ▪ Fx: 514-871-1255

Canadian Chamber of Commerce Montreal Office   www.chamber.ca
1255 University St Suite 1510   Montreal QC H3B3X2
Ph: 514-866-4334 ▪ Fx: 514-866-7296

Chambre de Commerce du Quebec   www.ccq.ca
500 Place D'Armes Bureau 3030   Montreal QC H2Y2W2
Ph: 514-844-9571 ▪ Fx: 514-844-0226 ▪ TF: 800-361-5019

Chambre de Commerce et d'Industrie du Quebec Metropolitain   www.cciqm.qc.ca
17 rue Saint-Louis   Quebec QC G1R3Y8
Ph: 418-692-3853 ▪ Fx: 418-694-2286

Haut-Richelieu Chamber of Commerce   www.cchr.netc.net
315 rue MacDonald Bureau 232   Saint-Jean-sur-Richelieu QC J3B2C3
Ph: 450-346-2544 ▪ Fx: 450-346-3812

Sainte-Foy Chamber of Commerce   www.ccrsf.ca
2700 boul Laurier Ed Champlain Bureau 3200   Sainte-Foy QC G1V2L8
Ph: 418-651-7181 ▪ Fx: 418-651-5248

Sept-Iles Chamber of Commerce
700 boul Laure Bureau 204   Sept-Iles QC G4R1Y1
Ph: 418-968-3488 ▪ Fx: 418-968-3432

Chambre de Commerce de la Region Sherbrookoise
386 King St W 2nd Fl   Sherbrooke QC J1H1R4
Ph: 819-822-6151 ▪ Fx: 819-822-6156

Trois-Rivieres & District Chamber of Commerce
168 rue Bonaventure   Trois-Rivieres QC G9A5K4
Ph: 819-375-9628 ▪ Fx: 819-375-9083

SASKATCHEWAN

Moose Jaw & District Chamber of Commerce   www.mjchamber.com
88 Saskatchewan St E   Moose Jaw SK S6H0V4
Ph: 306-692-6414 ▪ Fx: 306-694-6463

Battlefords Chamber of Commerce   www.battlefordschamber.com
PO Box 1000   North Battleford SK S9A3E6
Ph: 306-445-6226 ▪ Fx: 306-445-6633

Prince Albert & District Chamber of Commerce   www.thechamberofcom.com
1084 Central Ave Suite 347   Prince Albert SK S6V7P3
Ph: 306-764-6222 ▪ Fx: 306-922-4727 ▪ TF: 888-568-8869

Regina Chamber of Commerce   www.reginachamber.com
2145 Albert St   Regina SK S4P2V1
Ph: 306-757-4658 ▪ Fx: 306-757-4668

Saskatoon & District Chamber of Commerce   www.eboardoftrade.com
345 3rd Ave S   Saskatoon SK S7K1M6
Ph: 306-244-2151 ▪ Fx: 306-244-8366

YUKON TERRITORY

Whitehorse Chamber of Commerce   www.whitehorsechamber.com
302 Steele St Suite 101   Whitehorse YT Y1A2C5
Ph: 867-667-7545 ▪ Fx: 867-667-4507

Yukon Chamber of Commerce   www.yukonchamber.com
101-307 Jarvis St   Whitehorse YT Y1A2H3
Ph: 867-667-2000 ▪ Fx: 867-667-2001

Appendix

Chambers of Commerce - US - State

US Chamber of Commerce
1615 H St NW   Washington DC 20062
Ph: 202-659-6000 ▪ Fx: 202-463-5836 ▪ TF: 800-638-6582
www.uschamber.com

Alabama Business Council
PO Box 76   Montgomery AL 36101
Ph: 334-834-6000 ▪ Fx: 334-262-7371 ▪ TF: 800-665-9647
www.bcatoday.org

Alaska State Chamber of Commerce
217 2nd St Suite 201   Juneau AK 99801
Ph: 907-586-2323 ▪ Fx: 907-463-5515
www.alaskachamber.com

Arizona Chamber of Commerce
1221 E Osborne Rd Suite 100   Phoenix AZ 85014
Ph: 602-248-9172 ▪ Fx: 602-265-1262 ▪ TF: 800-498-6973
www.azchamber.com

Arkansas State Chamber of Commerce
PO Box 3645   Little Rock AR 72203
Ph: 501-374-9225 ▪ Fx: 501-372-2722
www.statechamber-aia.dina.org

California Chamber of Commerce
PO Box 1736   Sacramento CA 95812
Ph: 916-444-6670 ▪ Fx: 916-444-6685 ▪ TF: 800-772-2399
www.calchamber.com

Colorado Association of Commerce & Industry
1600 Broadway Suite 1000   Denver CO 80202
Ph: 303-831-7411 ▪ Fx: 303-860-1439
www.cochamber.com

Connecticut Business & Industry Association
350 Church St   Hartford CT 06103
Ph: 860-244-1900 ▪ Fx: 860-278-8562
www.cbia.com

Delaware State Chamber of Commerce
PO Box 671   Wilmington DE 19899
Ph: 302-655-7221 ▪ Fx: 302-654-0691
www.dscc.com

District of Columbia Chamber of Commerce
1213 K St NW   Washington DC 20005
Ph: 202-347-7201 ▪ Fx: 202-638-6764
www.dcchamber.org

Florida Chamber of Commerce
136 S Bruno St   Tallahassee FL 32301
Ph: 850-521-1200 ▪ Fx: 850-521-1219 ▪ TF: 877-521-1200
www.flchamber.com

Georgia Chamber of Commerce
235 Peachtree St NE Suite 900   Atlanta GA 30303
Ph: 404-223-2264 ▪ Fx: 404-223-2290
www.gachamber.com

Hawaii Chamber of Commerce
1132 Bishop St Suite 402   Honolulu HI 96813
Ph: 808-545-4300 ▪ Fx: 808-545-4369
www.cochawaii.com

Idaho Association of Commerce & Industry
PO Box 389   Boise ID 83701
Ph: 208-343-1849 ▪ Fx: 208-338-5623
www.iaci.org

Illinois State Chamber of Commerce
311 S Wacker Dr Suite 1500   Chicago IL 60606
Ph: 312-983-7100 ▪ Fx: 312-983-7101
www.ilchamber.org

Indiana State Chamber of Commerce
115 W Washington St Suite 850 S   Indianapolis IN 46204
Ph: 317-264-3110 ▪ Fx: 317-264-6855
www.indianachamber.com

Iowa Association of Business & Industry
904 Walnut St Suite 100   Des Moines IA 50309
Ph: 515-280-8000 ▪ Fx: 515-282-8085 ▪ TF: 800-383-4224
www.iowaabi.org

Kansas Chamber of Commerce & Industry
835 SW Topeka Blvd   Topeka KS 66612
Ph: 785-357-6321 ▪ Fx: 785-357-4732
www.kansaschamber.org

Kentucky Chamber of Commerce
464 Chenault Rd   Frankfort KY 40601
Ph: 502-695-4700 ▪ Fx: 502-695-6824
www.kychamber.com

Louisiana Association of Business & Industry
3113 Valley Creek Dr   Baton Rouge LA 70808
Ph: 225-928-5388 ▪ Fx: 225-929-6054
www.labi.org

Maine State Chamber of Commerce
7 University Dr   Augusta ME 04330
Ph: 207-623-4568 ▪ Fx: 207-622-7723
www.mainechamber.org

Maryland Chamber of Commerce
60 West St Suite 100   Annapolis MD 21401
Ph: 410-269-0642 ▪ Fx: 410-269-5247
www.mdchamber.org

Michigan Chamber of Commerce
600 S Walnut St   Lansing MI 48933
Ph: 517-371-2100 ▪ Fx: 517-371-7224 ▪ TF: 800-748-0266
www.michamber.com

Minnesota Chamber of Commerce
400 Robert St N Suite 1500   Saint Paul MN 55101
Ph: 651-292-4650 ▪ Fx: 651-292-4656 ▪ TF: 800-821-2230
www.mnchamber.com

Mississippi Economic Council
PO Box 23276   Jackson MS 39225
Ph: 601-969-0022 ▪ Fx: 601-353-0247 ▪ TF: 800-748-7626
www.msmec.com

Missouri Chamber of Commerce
PO Box 149   Jefferson City MO 65102
Ph: 573-634-3511 ▪ Fx: 573-634-8855
www.mochamber.org

Montana Chamber of Commerce
PO Box 1730   Helena MT 59624
Ph: 406-442-2405 ▪ Fx: 406-442-2409
www.montanachamber.com

Nebraska Chamber of Commerce & Industry
PO Box 95128   Lincoln NE 68509
Ph: 402-474-4422 ▪ Fx: 402-474-5681
www.nechamber.com

Nevada State Chamber of Commerce
1 E 1st St 16th Fl   Reno NV 89501
Ph: 775-686-3030
www.reno-sparkschamber.org

New England Council Inc
98 N Washington St Suite 201   Boston MA 02114
Ph: 617-723-4009 ▪ Fx: 617-723-3943
www.newenglandcouncil.com

New Hampshire Business & Industry Association
122 N Main St 3rd Fl   Concord NH 03301
Ph: 603-224-5388 ▪ Fx: 603-224-2872 ▪ TF: 800-540-5388
www.nhbia.org

New Jersey State Chamber of Commerce
216 W State St   Trenton NJ 08608
Ph: 609-989-7888 ▪ Fx: 609-989-9696
www.njchamber.com

New Mexico Association of Commerce & Industry
PO Box 9706   Albuquerque NM 87119
Ph: 505-842-0644 ▪ Fx: 505-842-0734
www.aci.nm.org

(New York) Business Council of New York State Inc
152 Washington Ave   Albany NY 12210
Ph: 518-465-7511 ▪ Fx: 518-465-4389 ▪ TF: 800-358-1202
www.bcnys.org

North Carolina Citizens for Business & Industry
225 Hillsborough St Suite 460   Raleigh NC 27603
Ph: 919-836-1400 ▪ Fx: 919-836-1425
www.nccbi.org

North Dakota (Greater) Assn
PO Box 2639   Bismarck ND 58502
Ph: 701-222-0929 ▪ Fx: 701-222-1611 ▪ TF: 800-382-1405
www.gnda.com

Ohio Chamber of Commerce
230 E Town St   Columbus OH 43215
Ph: 614-228-4201 ▪ Fx: 614-228-6403 ▪ TF: 800-622-1893
www.ohiochamber.com

Oklahoma State Chamber
330 NE 10th St   Oklahoma City OK 73104
Ph: 405-235-3669 ▪ Fx: 405-235-3670 ▪ TF: 800-364-6465
www.okstatechamber.com

Pennsylvania Chamber of Business & Industry
417 Walnut St   Harrisburg PA 17101
Ph: 717-255-3252 ▪ Fx: 717-255-3298 ▪ TF: 800-225-7224
www.pachamber.org

Puerto Rico Chamber of Commerce
PO Box 902-4033   San Juan PR 00902
Ph: 787-721-6060 ▪ Fx: 787-723-1891
camarapr.zonai.com

Rhode Island Economic Development Corp
1 W Exchange St   Providence RI 02903
Ph: 401-222-2601 ▪ Fx: 401-222-2102
www.riedc.com

South Carolina Chamber of Commerce
1201 Main St Suite 1810   Columbia SC 29201
Ph: 803-799-4601 ▪ Fx: 803-779-6043 ▪ TF: 800-799-4601
www.scchamber.net

South Dakota Chamber of Commerce & Industry
108 N Euclid Ave   Pierre SD 57501
Ph: 605-224-6161 ▪ Fx: 605-224-7198
www.sdchamber.biz

Tennessee Chamber of Commerce & Industry
611 Commerce St Suite 3030   Nashville TN 37203
Ph: 615-256-5141 ▪ Fx: 615-256-6726
www.tnchamber.org

Texas Association of Business & Chamber of Commerce
1209 Nueces St   Austin TX 78701
Ph: 512-477-6721 ▪ Fx: 512-477-0836 ▪ TF: 800-856-6721
www.tabcc.org

Vermont Chamber of Commerce
PO Box 37   Montpelier VT 05601
Ph: 802-223-3443 ▪ Fx: 802-223-4257
www.vtchamber.com

Virginia Chamber of Commerce
9 S 5th St   Richmond VA 23219
Ph: 804-644-1607 ▪ Fx: 804-783-6112 ▪ TF: 800-477-7682
www.vachamber.com

(Washington) Association of Washington Business
PO Box 658   Olympia WA 98507
Ph: 360-943-1600 ▪ Fx: 360-943-5811 ▪ TF: 800-521-9325
www.awb.org

West Virginia Chamber of Commerce
PO Box 2789   Charleston WV 25330
Ph: 304-342-1115 ▪ Fx: 304-342-1130
www.wvchamber.com

Wisconsin Manufacturers & Commerce
PO Box 352   Madison WI 53701
Ph: 608-258-3400 ▪ Fx: 608-258-3413
www.wmc.org

Chambers of Commerce - US - Local

Chambers listed here represent areas with a population of 25,000 or more. Listings are organized by states and then are alphabetized within each state grouping according to the name of the city in which each chamber is located.

ALABAMA

Alexander City-Lake Martin Area Chamber of Commerce www.alexandercity.org
PO Box 926   Alexander City AL 35011
Ph: 256-234-3461 ▪ Fx: 256-234-0094

Calhoun County Chamber of Commerce www.calhounchamber.com
1330 Quintard Ave   Anniston AL 36201
Ph: 256-237-3536 ▪ Fx: 256-237-4338 ▪ TF: 800-489-1087

Athens-Limestone County Chamber of Commerce www.tourathens.com
PO Box 150   Athens AL 35612
Ph: 256-232-2600 ▪ Fx: 256-232-2609

Auburn Chamber of Commerce www.auburnchamber.com
PO Box 1370   Auburn AL 36831
Ph: 334-887-7011 ▪ Fx: 334-821-5500

North Ballwin Area Chamber of Commerce
301 McMeans Ave   Bay Minette AL 36507
Ph: 251-937-5665 ▪ Fx: 251-937-5670

Bessemer Area Chamber of Commerce www.bessemerchamber.com
321 N 18th St   Bessemer AL 35020
Ph: 205-425-3253 ▪ Fx: 205-425-4979 ▪ TF: 888-423-7736

Birmingham Area Chamber of Commerce www.birminghamchamber.com
505 N 20th St Suite 200   Birmingham AL 35203
Ph: 205-324-2100 ▪ Fx: 205-324-2560

Chilton County Chamber of Commerce www.chiltoncountychamber.com
PO Box 66   Clanton AL 35046
Ph: 205-755-2400 ▪ Fx: 205-755-8444 ▪ TF: 800-553-0493

Cullman Area Chamber of Commerce www.cullmanchamber.org
301 2nd Ave SW   Cullman AL 35055
Ph: 256-734-0454 ▪ Fx: 256-737-7443

Eastern Shore Chamber of Commerce www.eschamber.com
PO Drawer 310   Daphne AL 36526
Ph: 251-621-8222 ▪ Fx: 251-621-8001

Decatur-Morgan County Chamber of Commerce www.dcc.org
515 6th Ave NE   Decatur AL 35602
Ph: 256-353-5312 ▪ Fx: 256-353-2384

Dothan Area Chamber of Commerce www.dothan.com
102 Jamestown Blvd   Dothan AL 36301
Ph: 334-792-5138 ▪ Fx: 334-794-4796 ▪ TF: 800-221-1027

Eufaula/Barbour County Chamber of Commerce www.eufaula-barbourchamber.com
333 E Broad St   Eufaula AL 36027
Ph: 334-687-6664 ▪ Fx: 334-687-5240 ▪ TF: 800-524-7529

Shoals Chamber of Commerce www.shoalschamber.com
612 S Court St   Florence AL 35630
Ph: 256-764-4661 ▪ Fx: 256-766-9017 ▪ TF: 877-764-4661

South Baldwin Chamber of Commerce www.southbaldwinchamber.com
104 N McKenzie St   Foley AL 36535
Ph: 251-943-3291 ▪ Fx: 251-943-6810

Gadsden Area Chamber of Commerce www.gadsdenchamber.com
PO Box 185   Gadsden AL 35902
Ph: 256-543-3472 ▪ Fx: 256-543-9887 ▪ TF: 800-238-6924

Greenville Area Chamber of Commerce
1 Depot Sq   Greenville AL 36037
Ph: 334-382-3251 ▪ Fx: 334-382-3181 ▪ TF: 800-959-0717

Hoover Chamber of Commerce www.hooverchamber.org
PO Box 36005   Hoover AL 35236
Ph: 205-988-5672 ▪ Fx: 205-988-8383

Chamber of Commerce of Huntsville/Madison County www.hsvchamber.org
PO Box 408   Huntsville AL 35804
Ph: 256-535-2000 ▪ Fx: 256-535-2015

Chamber of Commerce of Walker County www.walkerchamber.com
PO Box 972   Jasper AL 35502
Ph: 205-384-4571 ▪ Fx: 205-384-4901 ▪ TF: 888-384-4571

Greater Valley Area Chamber of Commerce www.greatervalleyarea.com
PO Box 205   Lanett AL 36863
Ph: 334-642-1411 ▪ Fx: 334-642-1410

Mobile Area Chamber of Commerce www.mobilechamber.com
451 Government St   Mobile AL 36602
Ph: 251-433-6951 ▪ Fx: 251-432-1143

Monroeville Area Chamber of Commerce www.monroecountyal.com
36 N Alabama Ave   Monroeville AL 36460
Ph: 251-743-2879 ▪ Fx: 251-575-7934

Montgomery Area Chamber of Commerce www.montgomerychamber.org
41 Commerce St   Montgomery AL 36101
Ph: 334-834-5200 ▪ Fx: 334-265-4745

Lawrence County Chamber of Commerce www.lawrencealabama.com
PO Box 325   Moulton AL 35650
Ph: 256-974-1658 ▪ Fx: 256-974-2400

Blount County-Oneonta Chamber of Commerce www.coveredbridge.org
227 2nd Ave E PO Box 1487   Oneonta AL 35121
Ph: 205-274-2153 ▪ Fx: 205-274-2099

Ozark Area Chamber of Commerce www.ozarkareacoc.com
294 Painter Ave   Ozark AL 36360
Ph: 334-774-9321 ▪ Fx: 334-774-8736 ▪ TF: 800-582-8497

Greater Shelby County Chamber of Commerce www.shelbychamber.org
PO Box 324   Pelham AL 35124
Ph: 205-663-4542 ▪ Fx: 205-663-4524

Phenix City-Russell County Chamber of Commerce pcrcchamber.com/pcrcchamber.htm
PO Box 1326   Phenix City AL 36868
Ph: 334-298-3639 ▪ Fx: 334-298-3846 ▪ TF: 800-892-2248

Franklin County Chamber of Commerce www.franklincountychamber.org
PO Box 44   Russellville AL 35653
Ph: 256-332-1760 ▪ Fx: 256-332-1740

Greater Jackson County Chamber of Commerce www.jacksoncountychamber.com
PO Box 973   Scottsboro AL 35768
Ph: 256-259-5500 ▪ Fx: 256-259-4447 ▪ TF: 800-259-5508

Selma-Dallas County Chamber of Commerce www.selmaalabama.com
912 Selma Ave   Selma AL 36701
Ph: 334-875-7241 ▪ Fx: 334-875-7142 ▪ TF: 800-457-3562

Greater Talladega Area Chamber of Commerce www.talladegachamber.com
210 East St S   Talladega AL 35160
Ph: 256-362-9075 ▪ Fx: 256-362-9093

Pike County Chamber of Commerce www.pikecountychamber.com
300 US Hwy 231 N   Troy AL 36079
Ph: 334-566-2294 ▪ Fx: 334-566-2298

Chamber of Commerce of West Alabama www.tuscaloosachamber.com
PO Box 020410   Tuscaloosa AL 35402
Ph: 205-758-7588 ▪ Fx: 205-391-0565

ALASKA

Anchorage Chamber of Commerce www.anchoragechamber.org
441 W 5th Ave Suite 300   Anchorage AK 99501
Ph: 907-272-2401 ▪ Fx: 907-272-4117

Chugiak-Eagle River Chamber of Commerce www.cer.org
11401 Old Glenn Hwy Suite 105   Eagle River AK 99577
Ph: 907-694-4702 ▪ Fx: 907-694-1205

Fairbanks Chamber of Commerce www.fairbankschamber.org
800 Cushman St Suite 114   Fairbanks AK 99701
Ph: 907-452-1105 ▪ Fx: 907-456-6968

Juneau Chamber of Commerce www.juneauchamber.org
3100 Channel Dr Suite 300   Juneau AK 99801
Ph: 907-463-3488 ▪ Fx: 907-463-3489

ARIZONA

Apache Junction Chamber of Commerce www.apachejunctioncoc.com
567 W Apache Trail   Apache Junction AZ 85220
Ph: 480-982-3141 ▪ Fx: 480-982-3234 ▪ TF: 800-252-3141

Bullhead Area Chamber of Commerce www.bullheadchamber.com
1251 Hwy 95   Bullhead City AZ 86429
Ph: 928-754-4121 ▪ Fx: 928-754-5514 ▪ TF: 800-987-7457

Chandler Chamber of Commerce www.chandlerchamber.com
25 S Arizona Pl Suite 201   Chandler AZ 85225
Ph: 480-963-4571 ▪ Fx: 480-963-0188 ▪ TF: 800-963-4571

Cottonwood Chamber of Commerce cottonwood.verdevalley.com
1010 S Main St   Cottonwood AZ 86326
Ph: 928-634-7593 ▪ Fx: 928-634-7594

Flagstaff Chamber of Commerce www.flagstaffchamber.com
101 W Rt 66   Flagstaff AZ 86001
Ph: 928-774-4505 ▪ Fx: 928-779-1209

Gilbert Chamber of Commerce www.gilbertaz.com
PO Box 527   Gilbert AZ 85299
Ph: 480-892-0056 ▪ Fx: 602-250-5735

Glendale Chamber of Commerce www.glendaleazchamber.org
7105 N 59th Ave   Glendale AZ 85301
Ph: 623-937-4754 ▪ Fx: 623-937-3333 ▪ TF: 800-437-8669

Southwest Valley Chamber of Commerce
289 N Litchfield Rd   Goodyear AZ 85338
Ph: 623-932-2260 ▪ Fx: 623-932-9057
www.southwestvalleychamber.org

Kingman Area Chamber of Commerce
120 W Andy Devine Ave   Kingman AZ 86401
Ph: 928-753-6253 ▪ Fx: 928-753-1049
www.kingmanchamber.org

Lake Havasu Area Chamber of Commerce
314 London Bridge Rd   Lake Havasu City AZ 86403
Ph: 928-855-4115 ▪ Fx: 928-680-0010
www.havasuchamber.com

Mesa Chamber of Commerce
120 N Center St   Mesa AZ 85201
Ph: 480-969-1307 ▪ Fx: 480-827-0727
www.mesachamber.org

Nogales-Santa Cruz County Chamber of Commerce
123 W Kino Park   Nogales AZ 85621
Ph: 520-287-3685 ▪ Fx: 520-287-3688
www.nogaleschamber.com

Rim County Regional Chamber of Commerce
PO Box 1380   Payson AZ 85547
Ph: 928-474-4515 ▪ Fx: 928-474-8812 ▪ TF: 800-672-9766
www.rimcountrychamber.org

Peoria Chamber of Commerce
PO Box 70   Peoria AZ 85380
Ph: 623-979-3601 ▪ Fx: 623-486-4729 ▪ TF: 800-580-2645
www.peoriachamber.com

Greater Phoenix Chamber of Commerce
201 N Central Ave Suite 2700   Phoenix AZ 85073
Ph: 602-254-5521 ▪ Fx: 602-495-8913
www.phoenixchamber.com

North Phoenix Chamber of Commerce
2737 E Greenway Rd Suite 10   Phoenix AZ 85032
Ph: 602-482-3344 ▪ Fx: 602-482-2261
www.northphoenixchamber.com

Prescott Chamber of Commerce
117 W Goodwin St   Prescott AZ 86303
Ph: 928-445-2000 ▪ Fx: 928-445-0068 ▪ TF: 800-266-7534
www.prescott.org

Prescott Valley Chamber of Commerce
3001 N Main St Suite 2A   Prescott Valley AZ 86314
Ph: 928-772-8857 ▪ Fx: 928-772-4267
www.pvchamber.org

Graham County Chamber of Commerce
1111 Thatcher Blvd   Safford AZ 85546
Ph: 928-428-2511 ▪ Fx: 928-428-0744 ▪ TF: 888-837-1841
www.graham-chamber.com

Scottsdale Area Chamber of Commerce
7343 Scottsdale Mall   Scottsdale AZ 85251
Ph: 480-945-8481 ▪ Fx: 480-947-4523
www.scottsdalechamber.com

Sierra Vista Area Chamber of Commerce
21 E Wilcox Dr   Sierra Vista AZ 85635
Ph: 520-458-6940 ▪ Fx: 520-452-0878
www.sierravistachamber.org

Northwest Valley Chamber of Commerce
12801 W Bell Rd Suite 14   Surprise AZ 85374
Ph: 623-583-0692 ▪ Fx: 623-583-0694
www.northwestvalley.com

Tempe Chamber of Commerce
PO Box 28500   Tempe AZ 85285
Ph: 480-967-7891 ▪ Fx: 480-966-5365
www.tempechamber.org

Tucson Metropolitan Chamber of Commerce
465 W St Mary's Rd   Tucson AZ 85701
Ph: 520-792-2250 ▪ Fx: 520-882-5704
www.tucsonchamber.org

Yuma County Chamber of Commerce
180 W 1st St Suite A   Yuma AZ 85364
Ph: 928-782-2567 ▪ Fx: 928-343-0038
www.yumachamber.org

ARKANSAS

Bentonville/Bella Vista Chamber of Commerce
412 S Main St   Bentonville AR 72712
Ph: 479-273-2841 ▪ Fx: 479-273-2180
www.bentonvillebellavistachamber.com

Berryville Chamber of Commerce
PO Box 402   Berryville AR 72616
Ph: 870-423-3704
www.berryvillear.com

Conway Area Chamber of Commerce
900 Oak St   Conway AR 72032
Ph: 501-327-7788 ▪ Fx: 501-327-7790
www.conwayarkcc.org

El Dorado Chamber of Commerce
201 N Jackson St   El Dorado AR 71730
Ph: 870-863-6113 ▪ Fx: 870-863-6115
www.boomtown.org/community/chamber

Fayetteville Chamber of Commerce
123 W Mountain St   Fayetteville AR 72701
Ph: 479-521-1710 ▪ Fx: 479-521-1791
www.fayettevillear.com

Fort Smith Chamber of Commerce
612 Garrison Ave   Fort Smith AR 72901
Ph: 479-783-6118 ▪ Fx: 479-783-6110
www.fschamber.com

Phillips County Chamber of Commerce
PO Box 447   Helena AR 72342
Ph: 870-338-8327 ▪ Fx: 870-338-6445

Greater Hot Springs Chamber of Commerce
659 Ouachita Ave   Hot Springs AR 71901
Ph: 501-321-1700 ▪ Fx: 501-321-3551 ▪ TF: 800-467-4636

Jacksonville Chamber of Commerce
200 Dupree Dr   Jacksonville AR 72076
Ph: 501-982-1511 ▪ Fx: 501-982-1464
www.jacksonville-arkansas.com

Jonesboro Regional Chamber of Commerce
1709 E Nettleton St   Jonesboro AR 72401
Ph: 870-932-6691 ▪ Fx: 870-933-5758
www.jonesborochamber.org

Jonesboro Regional Chamber of Commerce
1709 E Nettleton St   Jonesboro AR 72401
Ph: 870-932-6691 ▪ Fx: 870-933-5758
www.jonesborochamber.org

Greater Little Rock Chamber of Commerce
1 Chamber Plaza   Little Rock AR 72201
Ph: 501-374-2001 ▪ Fx: 501-374-6018
www.littlerockchamber.com

Magnolia-Columbia County Chamber of Commerce
202 N Pine St   Magnolia AR 71753
Ph: 870-234-4352 ▪ Fx: 870-234-7937 ▪ TF: 800-482-3330
www.magnoliachamber.com

Mountain Home Area Chamber of Commerce
1023 Hwy 62 E   Mountain Home AR 72653
Ph: 870-425-5111 ▪ Fx: 870-425-4446 ▪ TF: 800-822-3536
www.enjoymountainhome.com

North Little Rock Chamber of Commerce
116 Main St   North Little Rock AR 72114
Ph: 501-372-5959 ▪ Fx: 501-372-5955
www.nlrchamber.org

Paragould-Greene County Chamber of Commerce
PO Box 124   Paragould AR 72451
Ph: 870-236-7684 ▪ Fx: 870-236-1517
www.paragould.org

Greater Pine Bluff Chamber of Commerce
510 S Main St   Pine Bluff AR 71601
Ph: 870-535-0110 ▪ Fx: 870-535-1643
www.pinebluffchamber.com

Rogers-Lowell Area Chamber of Commerce
317 W Walnut St   Rogers AR 72756
Ph: 479-636-1240 ▪ Fx: 479-636-5485 ▪ TF: 800-364-1240
www.rogerslowell.com

Russellville Chamber of Commerce
708 W Main St   Russellville AR 72801
Ph: 479-968-2530 ▪ Fx: 479-968-5894
www.russellvillechamber.org

Springdale Chamber of Commerce
PO Box 166   Springdale AR 72765
Ph: 479-872-2222 ▪ Fx: 479-751-4699 ▪ TF: 800-972-7261
www.springdale.com

West Memphis Area Chamber of Commerce
108 W Broadway   West Memphis AR 72301
Ph: 870-735-1134 ▪ Fx: 870-735-6283
www.wmcoc.com

CALIFORNIA

Alameda Chamber of Commerce
1416 Park Ave   Alameda CA 94501
Ph: 510-522-0414 ▪ Fx: 510-522-7677
www.alamedachamber.com

Alhambra Chamber of Commerce
104 S 1st St   Alhambra CA 91801
Ph: 626-282-8481 ▪ Fx: 626-282-5596
www.alhambrachamber.org

Altadena Chamber of Commerce
730 E Altadena Dr   Altadena CA 91001
Ph: 626-794-3988 ▪ Fx: 626-794-6015
www.abacus-es.com/acoc

Anaheim Chamber of Commerce
201 E Center St   Anaheim CA 92805
Ph: 714-758-0222 ▪ Fx: 714-758-0468
anaheimchamber.org

Calaveras County Chamber of Commerce
PO Box 1145   Angels Camp CA 95222
Ph: 209-736-2580 ▪ Fx: 209-736-2576
www.chamber@calaveras.org

Antioch Chamber of Commerce
324 G St   Antioch CA 94509
Ph: 925-757-1800 ▪ Fx: 925-757-5286
www.antiochchamber.com

Apple Valley Chamber of Commerce
17852 Hwy 18   Apple Valley CA 92307
Ph: 760-242-2753 ▪ Fx: 760-242-0303
www.avchamber.org

Aptos Chamber of Commerce
7605-A Old Dominion Ct   Aptos CA 95003
Ph: 831-688-1467 ▪ Fx: 831-688-6961
www.aptoschamber.com

Arcadia Chamber of Commerce
388 W Huntington Dr   Arcadia CA 91007
Ph: 626-447-2159 ▪ Fx: 626-445-0273
www.arcadiachamber.com

Atascadero Chamber of Commerce
6550 El Camino Real   Atascadero CA 93422
Ph: 805-466-2044 ▪ Fx: 805-466-9218
www.atascaderochamber.org

Atwater Chamber of Commerce
1181 3rd St   Atwater CA 95301
Ph: 209-358-4251 ▪ Fx: 209-358-0934
www.atwater.org/chambemm.htm

Auburn Area Chamber of Commerce
601 Lincoln Way   Auburn CA 95603
Ph: 530-885-5616 ▪ Fx: 530-885-5854
www.auburnchamber.net

Azusa Chamber of Commerce
240 W Foothill Blvd   Azusa CA 91702
Ph: 626-334-1507 ▪ Fx: 626-334-5217
www.azusachamber.org

Greater Bakersfield Chamber of Commerce
1725 Eye St   Bakersfield CA 93301
Ph: 661-327-4421 ▪ Fx: 661-327-8751
www.bakersfieldchamber.org

Kern County Board of Trade
PO Bin 1312   Bakersfield CA 93302
Ph: 661-861-2367 ▪ Fx: 661-861-2017 ▪ TF: 800-500-5376
www.visitkern.com

Baldwin Park Chamber of Commerce
14327 Ramona Blvd   Baldwin Park CA 91706
Ph: 626-960-4848 ▪ Fx: 626-960-2990
www.baldwinparkchamber.com

Beaumont Chamber of Commerce
726 Beaumont Ave   Beaumont CA 92223
Ph: 909-845-9541 ▪ Fx: 909-769-9080

Bell Chamber of Commerce
PO Box 294   Bell CA 90201
Ph: 323-560-8755 ▪ Fx: 323-560-2060

Bell Gardens Chamber
6006 Shull St   Bell Gardens CA 90201
Ph: 562-806-2355 ▪ Fx: 562-806-1585
www.bellgardenschamber.org

Bellflower Chamber of Commerce
16730 Bellflower Blvd   Bellflower CA 90706
Ph: 562-867-1744 ▪ Fx: 562-866-7545

Belmont Chamber of Commerce
1070 6th Ave Suite 102   Belmont CA 94002
Ph: 650-595-8696 ▪ Fx: 650-595-8731
www.belmontchamber.org

Benicia Chamber of Commerce
601 1st St Suite 100   Benicia CA 94510
Ph: 707-745-2120 ▪ Fx: 707-745-2275
www.beniciachamber.com

Berkeley Chamber of Commerce
1834 University Ave   Berkeley CA 94703
Ph: 510-549-7000
www.berkeleychamber.com

Beverly Hills Chamber of Commerce
239 S Beverly Dr   Beverly Hills CA 90212
Ph: 310-248-1000 ▪ Fx: 310-248-1020 ▪ TF: 800-345-2210
www.beverlyhillscc.org

Blythe Chamber of Commerce
201 S Broadway   Blythe CA 92225
Ph: 760-922-8166 ▪ Fx: 760-922-4010
www.blytheareachamberofcommerce.com

Brea Chamber of Commerce   www.breachamber.com
1 Civic Ctr Cir   Brea CA 92821
Ph: 714-529-4938 ▪ Fx: 714-529-6103

Buena Park Chamber of Commerce   www.buenaparkchamber.org
6601 Beach Blvd   Buena Park CA 90621
Ph: 714-521-0261 ▪ Fx: 714-521-1851

Burbank Chamber of Commerce   www.burbankchamber.org
200 W Magnolia Blvd   Burbank CA 91502
Ph: 818-846-3111 ▪ Fx: 818-846-0109

Burlingame Chamber of Commerce   burlingamechamber.org
290 California Dr   Burlingame CA 94010
Ph: 650-344-1735 ▪ Fx: 650-344-1763

Camarillo Chamber of Commerce   www.camarillochamber.org
2400 E Ventura Blvd   Camarillo CA 93010
Ph: 805-484-4383 ▪ Fx: 805-484-1395

Campbell Chamber of Commerce   www.campbellchamber.com
1628 W Campbell Ave   Campbell CA 95008
Ph: 408-378-6252 ▪ Fx: 408-378-0192

Canoga Park/West Hills Chamber of Commerce www.cpwhchamber.com
7248 Owensmouth Ave   Canoga Park CA 91303
Ph: 818-884-4222 ▪ Fx: 818-884-4604

Carlsbad Chamber of Commerce   www.carlsbad.org
5934 Priestly Dr   Carlsbad CA 92008
Ph: 760-931-8400 ▪ Fx: 760-931-9153

Carmichael Chamber of Commerce   www.carmichaelchamber.com
6825 Fair Oaks Blvd Suite 100   Carmichael CA 95608
Ph: 916-481-1002 ▪ Fx: 916-481-1003

Carson Chamber of Commerce   www.carsonchamber.org
530 E Del Amo Blvd Suite 101B   Carson CA 90746
Ph: 310-217-4590 ▪ Fx: 310-217-4591

Castro Valley Chamber of Commerce   www.mycastrovalley.com/chamber_of_commerce
3467 Castro Valley Blvd   Castro Valley CA 94546
Ph: 510-537-5300 ▪ Fx: 510-537-5335

Cathedral City Chamber of Commerce   www.cathedralcitycc.com
68845 Perez Rd Suite 6   Cathedral City CA 92234
Ph: 760-328-1213 ▪ Fx: 760-321-0659

Ceres Chamber of Commerce   www.cereschamber.org
2904 4th St   Ceres CA 95307
Ph: 209-537-2601 ▪ Fx: 209-537-2699

Cerritos Chamber of Commerce   www.cerritos.org
13259 E South St Suite 200   Cerritos CA 90703
Ph: 562-467-0800 ▪ Fx: 562-467-0840

Chatsworth Chamber of Commerce   www.chatsworthchamber.com
10038 Old Depot Plaza Rd   Chatsworth CA 91311
Ph: 818-341-2428 ▪ Fx: 818-341-4930

Chico Chamber of Commerce   www.chicochamber.com
300 Salem St   Chico CA 95928
Ph: 530-891-5556 ▪ Fx: 530-891-3613 ▪ TF: 800-852-8570

Chino Valley Chamber of Commerce   www.chinovalleychamber.com
13150 7th St   Chino CA 91710
Ph: 909-627-6177 ▪ Fx: 909-627-4180

Chula Vista Chamber of Commerce   www.chulavistachamber.org
233 4th Ave   Chula Vista CA 91910
Ph: 619-420-6602 ▪ Fx: 619-420-1269

Citrus Heights Chamber of Commerce   www.chchamber.com
7115-A Greenback Ln PO Box 191   Citrus Heights CA 95611
Ph: 916-722-4545 ▪ Fx: 916-722-4543

Claremont Chamber of Commerce   www.claremontchamber.org
205 Yale Ave   Claremont CA 91711
Ph: 909-624-1681 ▪ Fx: 909-624-6629

Clovis District Chamber of Commerce   www.clovischamber.com
325 Pollasky Ave   Clovis CA 93612
Ph: 559-299-7273 ▪ Fx: 559-299-2969

Colton Chamber of Commerce   www.coltonchamber.com
655 N La Cadena Dr   Colton CA 92324
Ph: 909-825-2222 ▪ Fx: 909-824-1650

Compton Chamber of Commerce
310 N Willowbrook Ave Suite 4A   Compton CA 90220
Ph: 310-631-8611 ▪ Fx: 310-631-2066

Greater Concord Chamber of Commerce   www.concordchamber.com
2280 Diamond Blvd Suite 200   Concord CA 94520
Ph: 925-685-1181 ▪ Fx: 925-685-5623

Corona Chamber of Commerce   www.coronachamber.org
904 E 6th St   Corona CA 92879
Ph: 909-737-3350 ▪ Fx: 909-737-3531

Coronado Chamber of Commerce   www.coronadochamber.com
1313 Ynez Place   Coronado CA 92118
Ph: 619-435-9260 ▪ Fx: 619-522-6577

Costa Mesa Chamber of Commerce   www.costamesachamber.com
1700 Adams Ave Suite 101   Costa Mesa CA 92626
Ph: 714-885-9092 ▪ Fx: 714-885-9094

Covina Chamber of Commerce   www.covina.org
935 W Badillo St Suite 100   Covina CA 91722
Ph: 626-967-4191 ▪ Fx: 626-966-9660

Culver City Chamber of Commerce   www.culvercitychamber.com
4249 Overland Ave   Culver City CA 90230
Ph: 310-287-3850 ▪ Fx: 310-287-1350

Cupertino Chamber of Commerce   www.cupertino-chamber.org
20455 Silverado Ave   Cupertino CA 95014
Ph: 408-252-7054 ▪ Fx: 408-252-0638

Cypress Chamber of Commerce
4951 Lincoln Ave   Cypress CA 90630
Ph: 714-827-2430 ▪ Fx: 714-827-1229

Daly City-Colma Chamber of Commerce   www.dalycity-colmachamber.org
355 Gellert Blvd Suite 138   Daly City CA 94015
Ph: 650-755-3900 ▪ Fx: 650-755-5160

Dana Point Chamber of Commerce   www.danapoint-chamber.com
24681 La Plaza Suite 115   Dana Point CA 92629
Ph: 949-496-1555 ▪ Fx: 949-496-5321 ▪ TF: 800-290-4262

Davis Chamber of Commerce   www.davischamber.com
130 G St Suite B   Davis CA 95616
Ph: 530-756-5160 ▪ Fx: 530-756-5190

Del Mar Regional Chamber of Commerce   www.delmarchamber.org
1104 Camino Del Mar Suite 1   Del Mar CA 92014
Ph: 858-755-4844 ▪ Fx: 858-356-0595

Diamond Bar Chamber of Commerce   www.diamondbarchamber.com
21845 E Copley Dr Suite 1170   Diamond Bar CA 91765
Ph: 909-860-1904 ▪ Fx: 909-860-6064

Downey Chamber of Commerce   www.downeychamber.com
11131 Brookshire Ave   Downey CA 90241
Ph: 562-923-2191 ▪ Fx: 562-869-0461

Dublin Chamber of Commerce   www.dublinchamberofcommerce.org
7080 Donlon Way Suite 110   Dublin CA 94568
Ph: 925-828-6200 ▪ Fx: 925-828-4247

San Diego East County Chamber of Commerce   www.eastcountychamber.org
201 S Magnolia Ave   El Cajon CA 92020
Ph: 619-440-6161 ▪ Fx: 619-440-6164

El Centro Chamber of Commerce & Visitors Bureau www.elcentrochamber.org
1095 S 4th St   El Centro CA 92243
Ph: 760-352-3681 ▪ Fx: 760-352-3246

El Monte/South El Monte Chamber of Commerce www.emsem.com
PO Box 5866   El Monte CA 91734
Ph: 626-443-0180 ▪ Fx: 626-443-0463

Elk Grove Chamber of Commerce   www.elkgroveca.com
9280 W Stockton Blvd Suite 104   Elk Grove CA 95758
Ph: 916-691-3760 ▪ Fx: 916-691-3810

Encinitas Chamber of Commerce   www.encinitaschamber.com
138 Encinitas Blvd   Encinitas CA 92024
Ph: 760-753-6041 ▪ Fx: 760-753-6270 ▪ TF: 800-953-6041

Encino Chamber of Commerce   www.encinochamber.com
4933 Balboa Blvd   Encino CA 91316
Ph: 818-789-4711 ▪ Fx: 818-789-2485

Escondido Chamber of Commerce   www.escondidochamber.org
720 N Broadway   Escondido CA 92025
Ph: 760-745-2125 ▪ Fx: 760-745-1183

Greater Eureka Chamber of Commerce   www.eurekachamber.com
2112 Broadway   Eureka CA 95501
Ph: 707-442-3738 ▪ Fx: 707-442-0079 ▪ TF: 800-356-6381

Fair Oaks Chamber of Commerce   www.fairoakschamber.com
PO Box 352   Fair Oaks CA 95628
Ph: 916-967-2903 ▪ Fx: 916-967-8536

Fairfield-Suisun Chamber of Commerce   www.ffsc-chamber.com
1111 Webster St   Fairfield CA 94533
Ph: 707-425-4625 ▪ Fx: 707-425-0826

Fallbrook Chamber of Commerce   www.fallbrookca.org
233-A E Mission Rd   Fallbrook CA 92028
Ph: 760-728-5845 ▪ Fx: 760-728-4031

Folsom Chamber of Commerce   www.folsomchamber.com
200 Wool St   Folsom CA 95630
Ph: 916-985-2698 ▪ Fx: 916-985-4117

Fontana Chamber of Commerce   www.fontanaacc.org
8435 Sierra Ave   Fontana CA 92335
Ph: 909-822-4433 ▪ Fx: 909-822-6238

Fort Bragg-Mendocino Coast Chamber of Commerce www.mendocinocoast.com
PO Box 1141   Fort Bragg CA 95437
Ph: 707-961-6300 ▪ Fx: 707-964-2056 ▪ TF: 800-726-2780

Foster City Chamber of Commerce   www.fostercitychamber.com
989 E Hillsdale Blvd Suite 160   Foster City CA 94404
Ph: 650-573-7600 ▪ Fx: 650-573-5201

Fountain Valley Chamber of Commerce   www.fvchamber.com
11100 Warner Ave Suite 204   Fountain Valley CA 92708
Ph: 714-668-0542 ▪ Fx: 714-668-9164

Fremont Chamber of Commerce   www.fremontbusiness.com
39488 Stevenson Pl Suite 100   Fremont CA 94539
Ph: 510-795-2244 ▪ Fx: 510-795-2240

Fresno Chamber of Commerce   www.fresnochamber.com
2331 Fresno St   Fresno CA 93721
Ph: 559-495-4800 ▪ Fx: 559-495-4811

Fullerton Chamber of Commerce   www.fullertonchamber.com
219 E Commonwealth Ave   Fullerton CA 92832
Ph: 714-871-3100 ▪ Fx: 714-871-2871

Garden Grove Chamber of Commerce   www.gardengrovechamber.org
12866 Main St Suite 102   Garden Grove CA 92840
Ph: 714-638-7950 ▪ Fx: 714-636-6672 ▪ TF: 800-959-5560

Gardena Valley Chamber of Commerce   www.gardenachamber.com
1204 W Gardena Blvd Suite E   Gardena CA 90247
Ph: 310-532-9905 ▪ Fx: 310-329-7307

Gilroy Chamber of Commerce   www.gilroy.org
7471 Monterey St   Gilroy CA 95020
Ph: 408-842-6437 ▪ Fx: 408-842-6010

Glendale Chamber of Commerce   www.glendalechamber.com
200 S Louise St   Glendale CA 91205
Ph: 818-240-7870 ▪ Fx: 818-240-2872

Glendora Chamber of Commerce   www.glendora-chamber.org
131 E Foothill Blvd   Glendora CA 91741
Ph: 626-963-4128 ▪ Fx: 626-914-4822

Goleta Valley Chamber of Commerce   www.goletavalley.com
PO Box 781 5582 Calle Real Suite A   Goleta CA 93116
Ph: 805-967-4618 ▪ Fx: 805-967-4615 ▪ TF: 800-646-5382

Granada Hills Chamber of Commerce   www.granadachamber.com
17723 Chatsworth St   Granada Hills CA 91344
Ph: 818-368-3235 ▪ Fx: 818-366-7425

Hanford Chamber of Commerce   www.hanfordchamber.com
200 Santa Fe Ave Suite D   Hanford CA 93230
Ph: 559-582-0483 ▪ Fx: 559-582-0960

Hawthorne Chamber of Commerce   www.hawthorne-chamber.com
4444 S El Segundo Blvd   Hawthorne CA 90250
Ph: 310-676-1163 ▪ Fx: 310-676-7661

Hayward Chamber of Commerce — www.hayward.org
22561 Main St   Hayward CA 94541
Ph: 510-537-2424 ▪ Fx: 510-537-2730

Hemet Jacinto Valley Chamber of Commerce — hemetsanjacintochamber.com
615 N San Jacinto St   Hemet CA 92543
Ph: 909-658-3211 ▪ Fx: 909-766-5013 ▪ TF: 800-334-9344

Hesperia Chamber of Commerce — www.hesperiachamber.org
16816-D Main St   Hesperia CA 92345
Ph: 760-244-2135 ▪ Fx: 760-244-1333

Highland Chamber of Commerce — www.highlandchamber.org
7750 Palm Ave Suite N   Highland CA 92346
Ph: 909-864-4073 ▪ Fx: 909-864-4583

San Benito County Chamber of Commerce — www.sanbenitocountychamber.com
650 San Benito St Suite 130   Hollister CA 95023
Ph: 831-637-5315 ▪ Fx: 831-637-1008

Hollywood Chamber of Commerce — www.hollywoodchamber.net
7018 Hollywood Blvd   Hollywood CA 90028
Ph: 323-469-8311 ▪ Fx: 323-469-2805

Huntington Beach Chamber of Commerce — www.hbchamber.org
19891 Beach Blvd Suite 140   Huntington Beach CA 92648
Ph: 714-536-8888 ▪ Fx: 714-960-7654

Greater Huntington Park Area Chamber of Commerce — www.hpchamber1.com
6330 Pacific Blvd Suite 208   Huntington Park CA 90255
Ph: 323-585-1155 ▪ Fx: 323-585-2176

Imperial Beach Chamber of Commerce & Visitors Bureau — www.ib-chamber.org
170 Palm Ave   Imperial Beach CA 91932
Ph: 619-424-3151 ▪ Fx: 619-424-3008

Indio Chamber of Commerce — www.indiochamber.org
82-503 Hwy 111   Indio CA 92201
Ph: 760-347-0676 ▪ Fx: 760-347-6069 ▪ TF: 800-444-6346

Inglewood Chamber of Commerce — www.inglewoodchamber.com
330 E Queen St   Inglewood CA 90301
Ph: 310-677-1121 ▪ Fx: 310-677-1001

Irvine Chamber of Commerce — www.irvinechamber.com
17755 Sky Park E Suite 101   Irvine CA 92614
Ph: 949-660-9112 ▪ Fx: 949-660-0829 ▪ TF: 800-558-4262

Orange County Business Council — www.ocbc.org
2 Park Plaza Suite 100   Irvine CA 92614
Ph: 949-476-2242 ▪ Fx: 949-476-9240

Amador County Chamber of Commerce — www.amadorcountychamber.com
PO Box 596   Jackson CA 95642
Ph: 209-223-0350 ▪ Fx: 209-223-4425 ▪ TF: 800-649-4988

Crescenta Valley Chamber of Commerce — www.lacrescenta.org
3131 Foothill Blvd Suite D   La Crescenta CA 91214
Ph: 818-248-4957 ▪ Fx: 818-248-9625

La Habra Area Chamber of Commerce — www.lahabrabiz.com/chamber
321 E La Habra Blvd   La Habra CA 90631
Ph: 562-697-1704 ▪ Fx: 562-697-8359

La Jolla Town Council — www.lajollatc.org
PO Box 1101   La Jolla CA 92038
Ph: 858-454-1444 ▪ Fx: 858-454-1848

La Mirada Chamber of Commerce — lmchamber.org
13714 La Mirada Blvd   La Mirada CA 90638
Ph: 562-902-3130 ▪ Fx: 562-902-3135

Puente Hills Area Chamber of Commerce
15849 E Main St   La Puente CA 91744
Ph: 626-330-3216 ▪ Fx: 626-330-0447

La Verne Chamber of Commerce — www.lavernechamber.org
2078 Bonita Ave   La Verne CA 91750
Ph: 909-593-5265 ▪ Fx: 909-596-0579

Laguna Beach Chamber of Commerce & Visitors Bureau — www.lagunabeachchamber.org
357 Glenneyre Ave   Laguna Beach CA 92651
Ph: 949-494-1018 ▪ Fx: 949-376-8916

Laguna Niguel Chamber of Commerce — www.lagunaniguelchamber.net
30011 Ivy Glenn Dr Suite 125   Laguna Niguel CA 92677
Ph: 949-363-0136 ▪ Fx: 949-363-9026

Lake Elsinore Valley Chamber of Commerce — www.levcc.org
132 W Graham Ave   Lake Elsinore CA 92530
Ph: 909-245-8848 ▪ Fx: 909-245-9127

Greater Lakeport Chamber of Commerce — www.lakeportchamber.com
875 Lakeport Blvd   Lakeport CA 95453
Ph: 707-263-5092 ▪ Fx: 707-263-5104 ▪ TF: 866-525-3767

Lakeside Chamber of Commerce — www.lakesideca.com
9924 Vine St   Lakeside CA 92040
Ph: 619-561-1031 ▪ Fx: 619-561-7951

Lakewood Chamber of Commerce — www.lakewoodchamber.com
PO Box 160   Lakewood CA 90714
Ph: 562-920-2120 ▪ Fx: 562-920-9191

Antelope Valley Board of Trade — www.avbot.org
548 W Lancaster Blvd Suite 103   Lancaster CA 93534
Ph: 661-942-9581 ▪ Fx: 661-723-9279

Antelope Valley Chambers of Commerce — www.avchambers.com
554 W Lancaster Blvd   Lancaster CA 93534
Ph: 661-948-4518 ▪ Fx: 661-949-1212

South Orange County Regional Chambers of Commerce — www.socchambers.com
26111 Antonio Pkwy Suite 400   Las Flores CA 92688
Ph: 949-635-5800 ▪ Fx: 949-635-1635

Lemon Grove Chamber of Commerce — www.lemongrovechamber.com
3443 Main St   Lemon Grove CA 91945
Ph: 619-469-9621 ▪ Fx: 619-469-0035

Livermore Chamber of Commerce — www.livermorechamber.org
2157 1st St   Livermore CA 94550
Ph: 925-447-1606 ▪ Fx: 925-447-1641

Lodi District Chamber of Commerce — www.lodichamber.com
35 S School St   Lodi CA 95240
Ph: 209-367-7840 ▪ Fx: 209-334-0528

Lompoc Valley Chamber of Commerce & Visitors Bureau — www.lompoc.com
PO Box 626   Lompoc CA 93438
Ph: 805-736-4567 ▪ Fx: 805-737-0453 ▪ TF: 800-240-0999

Long Beach Area Chamber of Commerce — www.lbchamber.com
1 World Trade Ctr Suite 206   Long Beach CA 90831
Ph: 562-436-1251 ▪ Fx: 562-436-7099

Los Altos Chamber of Commerce — www.losaltoschamber.org
321 University Ave   Los Altos CA 94022
Ph: 650-948-1455 ▪ Fx: 650-948-6238

Century City Chamber of Commerce — www.centurycitycc.com
2029 Century Park E Suite B-17   Los Angeles CA 90067
Ph: 310-553-2222 ▪ Fx: 310-553-4623

Eagle Rock Chamber of Commerce — www.eaglerockchamberofcommerce.com
PO Box 41354   Los Angeles CA 90041
Ph: 323-257-2197

East Los Angeles Chamber of Commerce
PO Box 63220   Los Angeles CA 90063
Ph: 323-722-2005 ▪ Fx: 323-722-2405

Highland Park Chamber of Commerce — www.nelanet.org/highland.park.chamber
PO Box 42949   Los Angeles CA 90050
Ph: 323-256-0920

Lincoln Heights Chamber of Commerce
2716 N Broadway Suite 210   Los Angeles CA 90031
Ph: 323-221-6571 ▪ Fx: 323-221-1513

Los Angeles Area Chamber of Commerce — www.lachamber.org
350 S Bixel St   Los Angeles CA 90017
Ph: 213-580-7500 ▪ Fx: 213-580-7511

Westchester/LAX- Marina del Rey Chamber of Commerce — www.wlaxmdrchamber.com
6151 W Century Blvd Suite 514   Los Angeles CA 90045
Ph: 310-645-5151 ▪ Fx: 310-645-0130

Los Gatos Chamber of Commerce — www.losgatosweb.com
349 N Santa Cruz Ave   Los Gatos CA 95030
Ph: 408-354-9300 ▪ Fx: 408-399-1594

Lynwood Chamber of Commerce — www.lynwoodchamber.org
3651 E Imperial Hwy   Lynwood CA 90262
Ph: 310-537-6484 ▪ Fx: 310-537-8143

Madera District Chamber of Commerce — www.maderachamber.com
120 N 'E' St   Madera CA 93638
Ph: 559-673-3563 ▪ Fx: 559-673-5009

Malibu Chamber of Commerce — www.malibu.org
23805 Stuart Ranch Rd Suite 100   Malibu CA 90265
Ph: 310-456-9025 ▪ Fx: 310-456-0195

Manhattan Beach Chamber of Commerce — www.manhattanbeachchamber.net
PO Box 3007   Manhattan Beach CA 90266
Ph: 310-545-5313 ▪ Fx: 310-545-7203

Manteca Chamber of Commerce — www.manteca.org
107 N Lincoln Ave   Manteca CA 95336
Ph: 209-823-6121 ▪ Fx: 209-823-9959

Marina Chamber of Commerce — www.marinachamber.com
PO Box 425   Marina CA 93933
Ph: 831-384-9155 ▪ Fx: 831-384-9155

Martinez Area Chamber of Commerce — www.martinezchamber.com
603 Marina Vista   Martinez CA 94553
Ph: 925-228-2345 ▪ Fx: 925-228-2356

Yuba-Sutter Chamber of Commerce — www.yubasutterchamber.com
429 10th St   Marysville CA 95901
Ph: 530-743-6501 ▪ Fx: 530-741-8645

Maywood Chamber of Commerce
5720 Heliotrope Ave   Maywood CA 90270
Ph: 323-562-3373 ▪ Fx: 323-562-2905

Menlo Park Chamber of Commerce — www.menloparkchamber.com
1100 Merrill St   Menlo Park CA 94025
Ph: 650-325-2818 ▪ Fx: 650-325-0920

Greater Merced Chamber of Commerce — www.merced-chamber.com
690 W 16th St   Merced CA 95340
Ph: 209-384-7092 ▪ Fx: 209-384-8472

Merced County Chamber of Commerce — www.mercedcountychamber.com
PO Box 1112   Merced CA 95341
Ph: 209-722-3864 ▪ Fx: 209-722-2406

Milpitas Chamber of Commerce — www.milpitas-chamber.com
138 N Milpitas Blvd   Milpitas CA 95035
Ph: 408-262-2613 ▪ Fx: 408-262-2823

Modesto Chamber of Commerce — www.modchamber.org
PO Box 844   Modesto CA 95353
Ph: 209-577-5757 ▪ Fx: 209-577-2673

Monrovia Chamber of Commerce — www.monroviacc.com
620 S Myrtle Ave   Monrovia CA 91016
Ph: 626-358-1159 ▪ Fx: 626-357-6036

Montclair Chamber of Commerce
5220 Benito St   Montclair CA 91763
Ph: 909-624-4569 ▪ Fx: 909-625-2009

Montebello Chamber of Commerce — www.montebellochamber.org
817 W Whittier Blvd Suite 200   Montebello CA 90640
Ph: 323-721-1153 ▪ Fx: 323-721-7946

Monterey Peninsula Chamber of Commerce — www.mpcc.com
380 Alvarado St   Monterey CA 93940
Ph: 831-648-5360 ▪ Fx: 831-649-3502

Monterey Park Chamber of Commerce — www.montereypark.com
700 El Mercado Ave   Monterey Park CA 91754
Ph: 626-570-9429 ▪ Fx: 626-570-9491

Moorpark Chamber of Commerce — www.moorparkchamber.com
225 W Los Angeles Ave   Moorpark CA 93021
Ph: 805-529-0322 ▪ Fx: 805-529-5304

Moreno Valley Chamber of Commerce
22500 Town Cir Suite 2226   Moreno Valley CA 92553
Ph: 909-697-4404 ▪ Fx: 909-697-0995

Morgan Hill Chamber of Commerce — www.morganhill.org
17450 Monterey Rd   Morgan Hill CA 95037
Ph: 408-779-9444 ▪ Fx: 408-779-5405

Mountain View Chamber of Commerce — www.chambermv.org
580 Castro St   Mountain View CA 94041
Ph: 650-968-8378 ▪ Fx: 650-968-5668

Murrieta Chamber of Commerce   www.murrieta.org
26370 Beckman Ct Unit B   Murrieta CA 92562
Ph: 909-677-7916 ▪ Fx: 909-677-9976

Napa Chamber of Commerce   www.napachamber.org
1556 1st St   Napa CA 94559
Ph: 707-226-7455 ▪ Fx: 707-226-1171

National City Chamber of Commerce   www.nationalcitychamber.org
901 National City Blvd   National City CA 91950
Ph: 619-477-9339 ▪ Fx: 619-477-5018 ▪ TF: 800-292-4624

Newark Chamber of Commerce   www.newark-chamber.com
6066 Civic Terrace Ave Suite 8   Newark CA 94560
Ph: 510-744-1000 ▪ Fx: 510-744-1003

Newport Beach Chamber of Commerce   www.newportbeach.com
1470 Jamboree Rd   Newport Beach CA 92660
Ph: 949-729-4400 ▪ Fx: 949-729-4417

Universal City-North Hollywood Chamber of Commerce   www.noho.org
11335 Magnolia Blvd Suite 2-D   North Hollywood CA 91601
Ph: 818-508-5155 ▪ Fx: 818-508-5156

Northridge/Porter Ranch Chamber of Commerce   www.nchamber.org
9017 Reseda Blvd Suite 205   Northridge CA 91324
Ph: 818-349-5676 ▪ Fx: 818-349-4343

Norwalk Chamber of Commerce   www.norwalkchamber.com
12040 Foster Rd   Norwalk CA 90650
Ph: 562-864-7785 ▪ Fx: 562-864-8539

Novato Chamber of Commerce   www.novatochamber.com
807 DeLong Ave   Novato CA 94945
Ph: 415-897-1164 ▪ Fx: 415-898-9097 ▪ TF: 800-897-1164

Eastern Madera County Chamber of Commerce   www.oakhurstchamber.com
49074 Civic Cir   Oakhurst CA 93644
Ph: 559-683-7766 ▪ Fx: 559-658-2942

Oakland Metropolitan Chamber of Commerce   www.oaklandchamber.com
475 14th St   Oakland CA 94612
Ph: 510-874-4800 ▪ Fx: 510-839-8817

Oceanside Chamber of Commerce   www.oceansidechamber.com
928 N Coast Hwy   Oceanside CA 92054
Ph: 760-722-1534 ▪ Fx: 760-722-8336

Ojai Valley Chamber of Commerce   www.ojaichamber.org
PO Box 1134   Ojai CA 93024
Ph: 805-646-8126 ▪ Fx: 805-646-9762

Ontario Chamber of Commerce   www.ontario.org
421 N Euclid Ave Suite B   Ontario CA 91762
Ph: 909-984-2458 ▪ Fx: 909-984-6439

Orange Chamber of Commerce   www.orangechamber.com
439 E Chapman Ave   Orange CA 92866
Ph: 714-538-3581 ▪ Fx: 714-532-1675 ▪ TF: 800-938-0073

Orangevale Chamber of Commerce   www.orangevalechamber.com
9267 Greenback Ln Suite B-91   Orangevale CA 95662
Ph: 916-988-0175 ▪ Fx: 916-988-1049

Oroville Area Chamber of Commerce   www.orovillechamber.net
1789 Montgomery St   Oroville CA 95965
Ph: 530-538-2542 ▪ Fx: 530-538-2546 ▪ TF: 800-655-4653

Oxnard Chamber of Commerce   www.oxnardchamber.org
400 S 'A' St   Oxnard CA 93030
Ph: 805-385-8860 ▪ Fx: 805-487-1763

Pacifica Chamber of Commerce   www.pacificachamber.com
225 Rockaway Beach Ave Suite 1   Pacifica CA 94044
Ph: 650-355-4122 ▪ Fx: 650-355-6949

Palm Desert Chamber of Commerce   www.pdcc.org
73710 Fred Waring Dr Suite 114   Palm Desert CA 92260
Ph: 760-346-6111 ▪ Fx: 760-346-3263

Palm Springs Chamber of Commerce   www.pschamber.org
190 W Amado Rd   Palm Springs CA 92262
Ph: 760-325-1577 ▪ Fx: 760-325-3609

Palmdale Chamber of Commerce   www.palmdalechamber.org
817 East Ave Q-9   Palmdale CA 93550
Ph: 661-273-3232 ▪ Fx: 661-273-8508

Palo Alto Chamber of Commerce   www.paloaltochamber.com
122 Hamilton Ave   Palo Alto CA 94301
Ph: 650-324-3121 ▪ Fx: 650-324-1215

Paradise Chamber of Commerce   www.paradisechamber.com
5550 Sky Way Suite 1   Paradise CA 95969
Ph: 530-877-9356 ▪ Fx: 530-877-1865 ▪ TF: 888-845-2769

Paramount Chamber of Commerce   www.paramountchamber.org
15357 Paramount Blvd   Paramount CA 90723
Ph: 562-634-3980 ▪ Fx: 562-634-0891

Pasadena Chamber of Commerce & Civic Association   www.pasadena-chamber.org
865 E Del Mar Blvd   Pasadena CA 91101
Ph: 626-795-3355 ▪ Fx: 626-795-5603

Petaluma Area Chamber of Commerce   www.petalumachamber.com
800 Baywood Dr Suite B   Petaluma CA 94954
Ph: 707-762-2785 ▪ Fx: 707-762-4721

Pico Rivera Chamber of Commerce   www.picoriverachamber.org
6771 S Passon Blvd   Pico Rivera CA 90660
Ph: 562-949-2473 ▪ Fx: 562-949-8320

Pittsburg Chamber of Commerce   www.pittsburg.org
2020 Railroad Ave   Pittsburg CA 94565
Ph: 925-432-7301 ▪ Fx: 925-427-5555

Placentia Chamber of Commerce   www.placentiachamber.org
201 E Yorba Linda Blvd Suite C   Placentia CA 92870
Ph: 714-528-1873 ▪ Fx: 714-528-1879

El Dorado County Chamber of Commerce   www.eldoradocounty.org
542 Main St   Placerville CA 95667
Ph: 530-621-5885 ▪ Fx: 530-642-1624 ▪ TF: 800-457-6279

Pleasant Hill Chamber of Commerce   www.pleasanthillchamber.com
91 Gregory Ln Suite 11   Pleasant Hill CA 94523
Ph: 925-687-0700 ▪ Fx: 925-676-7422

Pleasanton Chamber of Commerce   www.pleasanton.org
777 Peters Ave   Pleasanton CA 94566
Ph: 925-846-5858 ▪ Fx: 925-846-9697

Pomona Chamber of Commerce   www.pomonachamber.org
101 W Mission Blvd Suite 223   Pomona CA 91766
Ph: 909-622-1256 ▪ Fx: 909-620-5986

Porterville Chamber of Commerce   www.chamber.porterville.com
93 N Main St Suite A   Porterville CA 93257
Ph: 559-784-7502 ▪ Fx: 559-784-0770

Poway Chamber of Commerce   www.poway.com
PO Box 868   Poway CA 92074
Ph: 858-748-0016 ▪ Fx: 858-748-1710

Ramona Chamber of Commerce   www.ramonachamber.com
960 Main St   Ramona CA 92065
Ph: 760-789-1311 ▪ Fx: 760-789-1317

Rancho Cordova Area Chamber of Commerce   www.ranchocordova.org
3328 Mather Field Rd   Rancho Cordova CA 95670
Ph: 916-361-8700 ▪ Fx: 916-361-3049

Rancho Cucamonga Chamber of Commerce   www.ranchochamber.org
7945 Vineyard Ave Suite D5   Rancho Cucamonga CA 91730
Ph: 909-987-1012 ▪ Fx: 909-987-5917

Greater Redding Chamber of Commerce   www.reddingchamber.com
747 Auditorium Dr   Redding CA 96001
Ph: 530-225-4433 ▪ Fx: 530-225-4398

Redlands Chamber of Commerce   www.redlandschamber.org
1 E Redlands Blvd   Redlands CA 92373
Ph: 909-793-2546 ▪ Fx: 909-335-6388

Redondo Beach Chamber of Commerce   www.redondochamber.org
200 N Pacific Coast Hwy   Redondo Beach CA 90277
Ph: 310-376-6911 ▪ Fx: 310-374-7373

Redwood City-San Mateo County Chamber of Commerce   www.redwoodcitychamber.com
1450 Veterans Blvd Suite 125   Redwood City CA 94063
Ph: 650-364-1722 ▪ Fx: 650-364-1729

Reseda Chamber of Commerce
7033 Reseda Blvd   Reseda CA 91335
Ph: 818-345-1920 ▪ Fx: 818-345-1925

Rialto Chamber of Commerce   www.rialtochamber.org
120 N Riverside Ave   Rialto CA 92376
Ph: 909-875-5364 ▪ Fx: 909-875-6790

Richmond Chamber of Commerce   www.rcoc.com
3925 Macdonald Ave   Richmond CA 94805
Ph: 510-234-3512 ▪ Fx: 510-234-3540

Ridgecrest Chamber of Commerce   www.ridgecrestchamber.com
128 E California Ave Suite B   Ridgecrest CA 93555
Ph: 760-375-8331 ▪ Fx: 760-375-0365

Greater Riverside Chambers of Commerce   www.riverside-chamber.com
3985 University Ave   Riverside CA 92501
Ph: 909-683-7100 ▪ Fx: 909-683-2670

Jurupa Chamber of Commerce
7920 Limonite Ave Suite C   Riverside CA 92509
Ph: 909-681-9242 ▪ Fx: 909-681-2720

Rocklin Area Chamber of Commerce   www.rocklinchamber.com
5055 Pacific St   Rocklin CA 95677
Ph: 916-624-2548 ▪ Fx: 916-624-5743

Rohnert Park Chamber of Commerce   www.rpchamber.org
5000 Roberts Lake Rd Suite B   Rohnert Park CA 94928
Ph: 707-584-1415 ▪ Fx: 707-584-2945

Palos Verdes Peninsula Chamber of Commerce   www.palosverdeschamber.com
707 Silver Spur Rd Suite 100   Rolling Hills Estates CA 90274
Ph: 310-377-8111 ▪ Fx: 310-377-0614

Rosemead Chamber of Commerce   www.rosemeadcc.org
PO Box 425   Rosemead CA 91770
Ph: 626-288-0811 ▪ Fx: 626-288-2514

Roseville Chamber of Commerce   www.rosevillechamber.com
650 Douglas Blvd   Roseville CA 95678
Ph: 916-783-8136 ▪ Fx: 916-783-5261

Sacramento Metro Chamber of Commerce   www.metrochamber.org
917 7th St   Sacramento CA 95814
Ph: 916-552-6800 ▪ Fx: 916-443-2672

Salinas Valley Chamber of Commerce   www.salinaschamber.com
PO Box 1170   Salinas CA 93902
Ph: 831-424-7611 ▪ Fx: 831-424-8639

San Bernardino Area Chamber of Commerce
PO Box 658   San Bernardino CA 92402
Ph: 909-885-7515 ▪ Fx: 909-384-9979

San Bruno Chamber of Commerce   www.sanbrunochamber.com
618 San Mateo Ave   San Bruno CA 94066
Ph: 650-588-0180 ▪ Fx: 650-588-6473

San Carlos Chamber of Commerce   www.sancarloschamber.com
1500 Laurel St Suite B   San Carlos CA 94070
Ph: 650-593-1068 ▪ Fx: 650-593-9108

San Clemente Chamber of Commerce   www.scchamber.com
1100 N El Camino Real   San Clemente CA 92672
Ph: 949-492-1131 ▪ Fx: 949-492-3764

I-15 Diamond Gateway Chamber of Commerce   www.dgchamber.com
12778 Rancho Penasquitos Blvd Suite B   San Diego CA 92129
Ph: 858-484-2800 ▪ Fx: 858-484-2155

Peninsula Chamber of Commerce   www.peninsulachamber.com
PO Box 7018   San Diego CA 92107
Ph: 619-223-9767 ▪ Fx: 619-225-8843

Rancho Bernardo Chamber of Commerce   www.rbchamber.com
11650 Iberia Pl Suite 220   San Diego CA 92128
Ph: 858-487-1767 ▪ Fx: 858-487-8051

San Diego Regional Chamber of Commerce   sdchamber.org
402 W Broadway Suite 1000   San Diego CA 92101
Ph: 619-544-1300

San Dimas Chamber of Commerce   www.sandimaschamber.com
PO Box 175   San Dimas CA 91773
Ph: 909-592-3818 ▪ Fx: 909-592-8178

Northeast San Fernando Valley Chamber of Commerce   www.nesfvcc.org
519 S Brand Blvd   San Fernando CA 91340
Ph: 818-361-1184 ▪ Fx: 818-898-1986

Appendix

San Francisco Chamber of Commerce   www.sfchamber.com
235 Montgomery St 12th Fl   San Francisco CA 94104
Ph: 415-392-4520 ▪ Fx: 415-392-0485

San Francisco Hispanic Chamber of Commerce   www.sfhcc.com
35 Gilbert St   San Francisco CA 94103
Ph: 415-731-8139

San Gabriel Chamber of Commerce   www.sangabrielchamber.com
620 W Santa Anita St   San Gabriel CA 91776
Ph: 626-576-2525 ▪ Fx: 626-289-2901

San Jose Silicon Valley Chamber of Commerce   www.sjchamber.com
310 S 1st St   San Jose CA 95113
Ph: 408-291-5250 ▪ Fx: 408-286-5019

San Juan Capistrano Chamber of Commerce   www.sanjuanchamber.com
31781 Camino Capistrano Suite 306   San Juan Capistrano CA 92675
Ph: 949-493-4700 ▪ Fx: 949-489-2695

San Leandro Chamber of Commerce   www.sanleandrochamber.com
262 Davis St   San Leandro CA 94577
Ph: 510-351-1481 ▪ Fx: 510-351-6740

San Luis Obispo Chamber of Commerce   www.slochamber.org
1039 Chorro St   San Luis Obispo CA 93401
Ph: 805-781-2777 ▪ Fx: 805-543-1255

San Marcos Chamber of Commerce
939 Grand Ave   San Marcos CA 92069
Ph: 760-744-1270 ▪ Fx: 760-744-5230

San Mateo Chamber of Commerce   www.sanmateoca.org
1021 S El Camino Real 2nd Fl   San Mateo CA 94402
Ph: 650-341-5679 ▪ Fx: 650-341-0679

San Pablo Chamber of Commerce
PO Box 6204   San Pablo CA 94806
Ph: 510-234-2067 ▪ Fx: 510-234-0604

San Pedro Peninsula Chamber of Commerce   www.sanpedrochamber.com
390 W 7th St   San Pedro CA 90731
Ph: 310-832-7272 ▪ Fx: 310-832-0685 ▪ TF: 888-447-3376

San Rafael Chamber of Commerce   sanrafaelchamber.com
817 Mission Ave   San Rafael CA 94901
Ph: 415-454-4163 ▪ Fx: 415-454-7039 ▪ TF: 800-454-4163

San Ramon Chamber of Commerce   www.sanramon.org
12667 Alcosta Blvd Suite 160   San Ramon CA 94583
Ph: 925-242-0600 ▪ Fx: 925-242-0603

San Ysidro Chamber of Commerce & Visitor Information Center www.sanysidrochamber.org
663 E San Ysidro Blvd   San Ysidro CA 92173
Ph: 619-428-1281 ▪ Fx: 619-428-1294

Santa Ana Chamber of Commerce   www.santaanacc.org
PO Box 205   Santa Ana CA 92702
Ph: 714-541-5353 ▪ Fx: 714-541-2238

Santa Barbara Region Chamber of Commerce   www.sbchamber.com
924 Anacapa St Suite 1   Santa Barbara CA 93101
Ph: 805-965-3023 ▪ Fx: 805-966-5954

Santa Clara Chamber of Commerce   www.santaclarachamber.com
1850 Warburton Ave   Santa Clara CA 95050
Ph: 408-244-8244 ▪ Fx: 408-244-7830 ▪ TF: 800-272-6822

Santa Clarita Valley Chamber of Commerce   www.scvchamber.com
23920 Valencia Blvd Suite 100   Santa Clarita CA 91355
Ph: 661-259-4787 ▪ Fx: 661-259-8628

Santa Cruz Area Chamber of Commerce   www.santacruzchamber.org
611 Ocean St Suite 1   Santa Cruz CA 95060
Ph: 831-457-3713 ▪ Fx: 831-423-1847

Santa Maria Valley Chamber of Commerce   www.santamaria.com
614 S Broadway   Santa Maria CA 93454
Ph: 805-925-2403 ▪ Fx: 805-928-7559 ▪ TF: 800-331-3779

Santa Monica Chamber of Commerce   www.smchamber.com
501 Colorado Ave Suite 150   Santa Monica CA 90401
Ph: 310-393-9825 ▪ Fx: 310-394-1868

Santa Paula Chamber of Commerce   www.santapaulachamber.com
PO Box 1   Santa Paula CA 93061
Ph: 805-525-5561 ▪ Fx: 805-525-8950

Santa Rosa Chamber of Commerce   www.santarosachamber.com
637 1st St   Santa Rosa CA 95404
Ph: 707-545-1414 ▪ Fx: 707-545-6914

Santee Chamber of Commerce   www.santee-chamber.org
10315 Mission Gorge Rd   Santee CA 92071
Ph: 619-449-6572 ▪ Fx: 619-562-7906

Saratoga Chamber of Commerce   www.saratogachamber.org
14485 Big Basin Way   Saratoga CA 95070
Ph: 408-867-0753 ▪ Fx: 408-867-5213

Seal Beach Chamber & Business Association   www.sealbeachchamber.com
201 8th St Suite 120   Seal Beach CA 90740
Ph: 562-799-0179 ▪ Fx: 562-795-5637

Seaside-Sand City Chamber of Commerce   www.seaside-sandcity.com
505 Broadway Ave   Seaside CA 93955
Ph: 831-394-6501 ▪ Fx: 831-394-1977

Sebastopol Area Chamber of Commerce   www.sebastopol.org
PO Box 178   Sebastopol CA 95473
Ph: 707-823-3032 ▪ Fx: 707-823-8439 ▪ TF: 877-828-4748

Greater Sherman Oaks Chamber of Commerce   www.shermanoakschamber.org
14827 Ventura Blvd Suite 207   Sherman Oaks CA 91403
Ph: 818-906-1951 ▪ Fx: 818-783-3100

Simi Valley Chamber of Commerce   simivalleychamber.com
40 W Cochran St Suite 100   Simi Valley CA 93065
Ph: 805-526-3900 ▪ Fx: 805-526-6234

Sonoma Valley Chamber of Commerce   www.sonomachamber.com
651A Broadway   Sonoma CA 95476
Ph: 707-996-1033 ▪ Fx: 707-996-9402

Tuolumne County Chamber of Commerce   www.tcchamber.com
222 S Shepherd St   Sonora CA 95370
Ph: 209-532-4212 ▪ Fx: 209-532-8068

South Gate Chamber of Commerce   www.southgatechamber.org
3350 Tweedy Blvd   South Gate CA 90280
Ph: 323-567-1203 ▪ Fx: 323-567-1204

South Lake Tahoe Chamber of Commerce   www.tahoeinfo.com
3066 Lake Tahoe Blvd   South Lake Tahoe CA 96150
Ph: 530-541-5255 ▪ Fx: 530-541-7121

South San Francisco Chamber of Commerce   www.ssfchamber.com
213 Linden Ave   South San Francisco CA 94080
Ph: 650-588-1911 ▪ Fx: 650-588-1529

Spring Valley Chamber of Commerce   www.springvalleychamber.org
3322 Sweetwater Springs Blvd Suite 202   Spring Valley CA 91977
Ph: 619-670-9902 ▪ Fx: 619-670-9924

Stanton Chamber of Commerce   www.stanton-chamber.org
8381 E Katella Ave Suite H   Stanton CA 90680
Ph: 714-995-1485 ▪ Fx: 714-995-1184

Greater Stockton Chamber of Commerce   www.stocktonchamber.org
445 W Weber Ave Suite 220   Stockton CA 95203
Ph: 209-547-2770 ▪ Fx: 209-466-5271

Studio City Chamber of Commerce   www.studiocitychamber.com
4024 Radford Ave   Studio City CA 91604
Ph: 818-769-3213 ▪ Fx: 818-655-8392

Greater Menifee Valley Chamber of Commerce   www.menifeevalleychamber.org
27070 Sun City Blvd Suite B   Sun City CA 92586
Ph: 909-672-1991 ▪ Fx: 909-672-4022

Sun Valley Area Chamber of Commerce   www.chambersunvalleyca.org
8133-A San Fernando Rd   Sun Valley CA 91352
Ph: 818-768-2014 ▪ Fx: 818-767-1947

Sunnyvale Chamber of Commerce   www.svcoc.org
101 W Olive Ave   Sunnyvale CA 94086
Ph: 408-736-4971 ▪ Fx: 408-736-1919

Lassen County Chamber of Commerce   www.lassencountychamber.org
84 N Lassen St   Susanville CA 96130
Ph: 530-257-4323 ▪ Fx: 530-251-2561

Sylmar Chamber of Commerce
13867 Foothill Blvd Suite 104   Sylmar CA 91342
Ph: 818-367-1177 ▪ Fx: 818-367-1633

Tarzana Chamber of Commerce   www.tarzana.org
PO Box 570414   Tarzana CA 91357
Ph: 818-881-4900 ▪ Fx: 818-881-1465

Greater Tehachapi Chamber of Commerce   www.tehachapi.com
PO Box 401   Tehachapi CA 93581
Ph: 661-822-4180 ▪ Fx: 661-822-9036 ▪ TF: 866-822-4180

Temecula Valley Chamber of Commerce   www.temecula.org
26790 Ynez Ct   Temecula CA 92591
Ph: 909-676-5090 ▪ Fx: 909-694-0201

Temple City Chamber of Commerce   www.templecitychamber.org
9050 Las Tunas Dr   Temple City CA 91780
Ph: 626-286-3101 ▪ Fx: 626-286-2590

Harbor City-Harbor Gateway Chamber of Commerce   www.hchgchamber.com
19401 S Vermont Ave Suite G104   Torrance CA 90502
Ph: 310-516-7933 ▪ Fx: 310-516-7734

Torrance Area Chamber of Commerce   www.torrancechamber.com
3400 Torrance Blvd Suite 100   Torrance CA 90503
Ph: 310-540-5858 ▪ Fx: 310-540-7662

Tracy Chamber of Commerce   www.tracychamber.org
223 E 10th St   Tracy CA 95376
Ph: 209-835-2131 ▪ Fx: 209-833-9526

Sunland-Tujunga Chamber of Commerce
PO Box 571   Tujunga CA 91043
Ph: 818-352-4433

Greater Tulare Chamber of Commerce   www.tularechamber.org
220 E Tulare Ave   Tulare CA 93274
Ph: 559-686-1547 ▪ Fx: 559-686-4915

Turlock Chamber of Commerce   www.turlockchamber.com
115 S Golden State Blvd   Turlock CA 95380
Ph: 209-632-2221 ▪ Fx: 209-632-5289

Tustin Chamber of Commerce   www.tustinchamber.org
399 El Camino Real   Tustin CA 92780
Ph: 714-544-5341 ▪ Fx: 714-544-2083

Twentynine Palms Chamber of Commerce   www.29chamber.com
6455A Mesquite Ave   Twentynine Palms CA 92277
Ph: 760-367-3445 ▪ Fx: 760-367-3366

Ukiah Chamber of Commerce   www.ukiahchamber.com
200 S School St   Ukiah CA 95482
Ph: 707-462-4705 ▪ Fx: 707-462-2088

Union City Chamber of Commerce   www.unioncitychamber.com
33412 Alvarado-Niles Rd   Union City CA 94587
Ph: 510-471-3115 ▪ Fx: 510-471-6011

Upland Chamber of Commerce   www.uplandchamber.org
433 N 2nd Ave   Upland CA 91786
Ph: 909-931-4108 ▪ Fx: 909-931-4184

Vacaville Chamber of Commerce   www.vacavillechamber.com
300 Main St   Vacaville CA 95688
Ph: 707-448-6424 ▪ Fx: 707-448-0424

Vallejo Chamber of Commerce   www.vallejochamber.com
2 Florida St   Vallejo CA 94590
Ph: 707-644-5551 ▪ Fx: 707-644-5590

Mid Valley Chamber of Commerce   www.midvalleychamber.com
14540 Victory Blvd Suite 100   Van Nuys CA 91411
Ph: 818-989-0300 ▪ Fx: 818-989-3836

Venice Area Chamber of Commerce   www.venicechamber.net
PO Box 202   Venice CA 90294
Ph: 310-822-5425 ▪ Fx: 310-248-3837

Ventura Chamber of Commerce   www.venturachamber.org
801 S Victoria Ave Suite 200   Ventura CA 93003
Ph: 805-676-7500 ▪ Fx: 805-650-1414

Victorville Chamber of Commerce   www.vvchamber.com
PO Box 997   Victorville CA 92393
Ph: 760-245-6506 ▪ Fx: 760-245-6505

Visalia Chamber of Commerce   www.visaliachamber.org
720 W Mineral King Ave   Visalia CA 93291
Ph: 559-734-5876 ▪ Fx: 559-734-7479 ▪ TF: 877-847-2542

Vista Chamber of Commerce www.vistachamber.org
201 Washington St   Vista CA 92084
Ph: 760-726-1122 ▪ Fx: 760-726-8654

Walnut Chamber of Commerce www.walnutchamber.com
18800 Amar Rd Unit C-14   Walnut CA 91789
Ph: 626-965-1707 ▪ Fx: 626-965-1709

Walnut Creek Chamber of Commerce www.walnut-creek.com
1501 N Broadway Suite 110   Walnut Creek CA 94596
Ph: 925-934-2007 ▪ Fx: 925-934-2404

Pajaro Valley Chamber of Commerce www.pajarovalleychamber.com
PO Box 1748   Watsonville CA 95077
Ph: 831-724-3900 ▪ Fx: 831-728-5300

West Covina Chamber of Commerce www.westcovinachamber.com
811 S Sunset Ave   West Covina CA 91790
Ph: 626-338-8496 ▪ Fx: 626-960-0511

West Hollywood Chamber of Commerce www.wehochamber.com
8278-1/2 Santa Monica Blvd   West Hollywood CA 90046
Ph: 323-650-2688 ▪ Fx: 323-650-2689

West Sacramento Chamber of Commerce www.westsacramentochamber.com
1414 Merkley Ave Suite 1   West Sacramento CA 95691
Ph: 916-371-7042 ▪ Fx: 916-371-7007

Thousand Oaks/Westlake Village Regional Chamber of Commerce www.towlvchamber.com
600 Hampshire Rd Suite 200   Westlake Village CA 91361
Ph: 805-370-0035 ▪ Fx: 805-370-1083

Westminster Chamber of Commerce www.westminsterchamber.com
14491 Beach Blvd   Westminster CA 92683
Ph: 714-898-9648 ▪ Fx: 714-373-1499

Whittier Area Chamber of Commerce www.whittierchamber.com
8158 Painter Ave   Whittier CA 90602
Ph: 562-698-9554 ▪ Fx: 562-693-2700

Willows Chamber of Commerce www.willowschamber.com
123 S Tehama St Suite C   Willows CA 95988
Ph: 530-934-8150 ▪ Fx: 530-934-8710 ▪ TF: 888-799-4254

Wilmington Chamber of Commerce www.wilmington-chamber.com
544 N Avalon Blvd   Wilmington CA 90744
Ph: 310-834-8586 ▪ Fx: 310-834-8887

Woodland Area Chamber of Commerce www.woodlandchamber.com
307 1st St   Woodland CA 95695
Ph: 530-662-7327 ▪ Fx: 530-662-4086 ▪ TF: 888-843-2636

Woodland Hills Chamber of Commerce www.woodlandhillscc.net
22025 Ventura Blvd Suite 202   Woodland Hills CA 91364
Ph: 818-347-4737 ▪ Fx: 818-347-3321

Yorba Linda Chamber of Commerce www.yorbalindachamber.com
17670 Yorba Linda Blvd   Yorba Linda CA 92886
Ph: 714-993-9537 ▪ Fx: 714-993-7764

Yucaipa Valley Chamber of Commerce www.yucaipachamber.com
35139 Yucaipa Blvd   Yucaipa CA 92399
Ph: 909-790-1841 ▪ Fx: 909-790-3484

Yucca Valley Chamber of Commerce www.yuccavalley.org
56711 29 Palms Hwy   Yucca Valley CA 92284
Ph: 760-365-6323 ▪ Fx: 760-365-0763

COLORADO

Arvada Chamber of Commerce www.arvadachamber.org
7305 Grandview Ave   Arvada CO 80002
Ph: 303-424-0313 ▪ Fx: 303-424-5370

Aurora Chamber of Commerce www.aurorachamber.org
562 Sable Blvd Suite 200   Aurora CO 80011
Ph: 303-344-1500 ▪ Fx: 303-344-1564

Boulder Chamber of Commerce www.boulderchamber.com
2440 Pearl St   Boulder CO 80302
Ph: 303-442-1044 ▪ Fx: 303-938-8837

Broomfield Chamber of Commerce www.broomfieldchamber.com
Garden Ctr 4 Suite 210   Broomfield CO 80020
Ph: 303-466-1775 ▪ Fx: 303-466-9874

Cañon City Chamber of Commerce www.canoncitychamber.com
403 Royal Gorge Blvd   Canon City CO 81212
Ph: 719-275-2331 ▪ Fx: 719-275-2332 ▪ TF: 800-876-7922

South Metro Denver Chamber of Commerce www.bestchamber.com
6840 S University Blvd   Centennial CO 80122
Ph: 303-795-0142 ▪ Fx: 303-795-7520

Colorado Springs Chamber of Commerce www.coloradospringschamber.org
2 N Cascade Ave Suite 110   Colorado Springs CO 80903
Ph: 719-635-1551 ▪ Fx: 719-635-1571

Delta Area Chamber of Commerce www.deltacolorado.org
301 Main St   Delta CO 81416
Ph: 970-874-8616 ▪ Fx: 970-874-8618

Denver Metro Chamber of Commerce www.denverchamber.org
1445 Market St   Denver CO 80202
Ph: 303-534-8500 ▪ Fx: 303-534-3200

Durango Area Chamber of Commerce www.durangobusiness.org
111 S Camino del Rio   Durango CO 81303
Ph: 970-247-0312 ▪ Fx: 970-385-7884 ▪ TF: 800-463-8726

Fort Collins Area Chamber of Commerce www.fcchamber.org
225 S Meldrum St   Fort Collins CO 80521
Ph: 970-482-3746 ▪ Fx: 970-482-3774

Fort Morgan Area Chamber of Commerce www.fortmorganchamber.org
100 Ensign St   Fort Morgan CO 80701
Ph: 970-867-6702 ▪ Fx: 970-867-6121 ▪ TF: 800-354-8660

Greater Golden Chamber of Commerce www.goldencochamber.org
1010 Washington Ave   Golden CO 80401
Ph: 303-279-3113 ▪ Fx: 303-279-0332

Grand Junction Area Chamber of Commerce www.gjchamber.org
360 Grand Ave   Grand Junction CO 81501
Ph: 970-242-3214 ▪ Fx: 970-242-3694 ▪ TF: 800-352-5286

Greeley-Weld Chamber of Commerce www.greeleychamber.com
902 7th Ave   Greeley CO 80631
Ph: 970-352-3566 ▪ Fx: 970-352-3572

La Veta/Cuchara Chamber of Commerce www.lavetacucharachamber.com
PO Box 32   La Veta CO 81055
Ph: 719-742-3676

West Chamber of Commerce www.westchamber.org
PO Box 280748   Lakewood CO 80228
Ph: 303-233-5555 ▪ Fx: 303-237-7633

Longmont Area Chamber of Commerce www.longmontchamber.org
528 N Main St   Longmont CO 80501
Ph: 303-776-5295 ▪ Fx: 303-776-5657

Loveland Chamber of Commerce www.loveland.org
5400 Stone Creek Cir Suite 200   Loveland CO 80538
Ph: 970-667-6311 ▪ Fx: 970-667-5211

Montrose Chamber of Commerce www.montrosechamber.com
1519 E Main St   Montrose CO 81401
Ph: 970-249-5000 ▪ Fx: 970-249-2907 ▪ TF: 800-923-5515

Parker Chamber of Commerce www.parkerchamber.com
20118 E Main St Suite A   Parker CO 80134
Ph: 303-841-4268 ▪ Fx: 303-841-8061

Greater Pueblo Chamber of Commerce www.pueblochamber.com
302 N Santa Fe Ave   Pueblo CO 81003
Ph: 719-542-1704 ▪ Fx: 719-542-1624 ▪ TF: 800-233-3446

MetroNorth Chamber of Commerce www.metronorthchamber.com
500 E 84th Ave Suite CM1   Thornton CO 80229
Ph: 303-288-1000 ▪ Fx: 303-227-1050

Vail Valley Chamber of Commerce www.visitvailvalley.com
100 E Meadow Dr Suite 34   Vail CO 81657
Ph: 970-476-1000 ▪ Fx: 970-476-6008 ▪ TF: 800-525-3875

CONNECTICUT

Branford Chamber of Commerce www.branfordct.com
239 N Main St   Branford CT 06405
Ph: 203-488-5500 ▪ Fx: 203-488-5046

Bridgeport Regional Business Council www.brbc.org
10 Middle St 14th Fl   Bridgeport CT 06604
Ph: 203-335-3800 ▪ Fx: 203-366-0105

Greater Bristol Chamber of Commerce www.bristol-chamber.org
10 Main St 1st Fl   Bristol CT 06010
Ph: 860-584-4718 ▪ Fx: 860-584-4722

Cheshire Chamber of Commerce www.cheshirechamber.com
195 S Main St   Cheshire CT 06410
Ph: 203-272-2345 ▪ Fx: 203-271-3044

Greater Danbury Chamber of Commerce www.danburychamber.com
39 West St   Danbury CT 06810
Ph: 203-743-5565 ▪ Fx: 203-794-1439

Northeastern Connecticut Chamber of Commerce www.newenglanditgroup.com/nectcc
3 Central St   Danielson CT 06239
Ph: 860-774-8001 ▪ Fx: 860-774-4299

East Hartford Chamber of Commerce www.ehcoc.com
1137 Main St   East Hartford CT 06108
Ph: 860-289-0239 ▪ Fx: 860-289-0230

East Haven Chamber of Commerce www.easthavenchamber.org
157 Main St   East Haven CT 06512
Ph: 203-467-4305 ▪ Fx: 203-469-2299

Fairfield Chamber of Commerce www.fairfieldctchamber.com
1597 Post Rd   Fairfield CT 06824
Ph: 203-255-1011 ▪ Fx: 203-256-9990

Chamber of Commerce of Eastern Connecticut Inc www.chamberect.com
39 King's Hwy PO Box 726   Gales Ferry CT 06335
Ph: 860-464-7373 ▪ Fx: 860-464-7374

Glastonbury Chamber of Commerce www.glastonburychamber.org
2400 Main St   Glastonbury CT 06033
Ph: 860-659-3587 ▪ Fx: 860-659-0102

Greenwich Chamber of Commerce www.greenwichchamber.com
45 E Putnam Ave Suite 121   Greenwich CT 06830
Ph: 203-869-3500 ▪ Fx: 203-869-3502

Hamden Chamber of Commerce www.hamdenchamber.com
2969 Whitney Ave   Hamden CT 06518
Ph: 203-288-6431 ▪ Fx: 203-288-4499

Metro Hartford Chamber of Commerce www.metrohartford.com
31 Pratt St Suite 5   Hartford CT 06103
Ph: 860-525-4451 ▪ Fx: 860-293-2592

Greater Manchester Chamber of Commerce www.manchesterchamber.com
20 Hartford Rd   Manchester CT 06040
Ph: 860-646-2223 ▪ Fx: 860-646-5871

Greater Meriden Chamber of Commerce www.meridenchamber.com
3 Colony St   Meriden CT 06451
Ph: 203-235-7901 ▪ Fx: 203-686-0172

Middlesex County Chamber of Commerce www.middlesexchamber.com
393 Main St   Middletown CT 06457
Ph: 860-347-6924 ▪ Fx: 860-346-1043

Milford Chamber of Commerce www.milfordct.com
5 Broad St   Milford CT 06460
Ph: 203-878-0681 ▪ Fx: 203-876-8517

Mystic Chamber of Commerce www.mysticchamber.org
14 Holmes St   Mystic CT 06355
Ph: 860-572-9578 ▪ Fx: 860-572-9273 ▪ TF: 866-572-9578

Naugatuck Chamber of Commerce
235 Meadow St   Naugatuck CT 06770
Ph: 203-729-4511 ▪ Fx: 203-729-4512

New Britain Chamber of Commerce www.newbritainchamber.com
1 Court St 4th Fl   New Britain CT 06051
Ph: 860-229-1665 ▪ Fx: 860-223-8341

Greater New Haven Chamber of Commerce www.newhavenchamber.com
900 Chapel St 10th Fl   New Haven CT 06510
Ph: 203-787-6735 ▪ Fx: 203-782-4329

Greater New Milford Chamber of Commerce www.newmilford-chamber.com
11 Railroad St   New Milford CT 06776
Ph: 860-354-6080 ▪ Fx: 860-354-8526

Greater Norwalk Chamber of Commerce   www.norwalkchamberofcommerce.com
101 East Ave   Norwalk CT 06851
Ph: 203-866-2521 ▪ Fx: 203-852-0583

Old Saybrook Chamber of Commerce   www.oldsaybrookct.com
PO Box 625   Old Saybrook CT 06475
Ph: 860-388-3266 ▪ Fx: 860-388-9433

Greater Valley Chamber of Commerce   www.greatervalleychamber.com
900 Bridgeport Ave 2nd Fl   Shelton CT 06484
Ph: 203-925-4981 ▪ Fx: 203-925-4984

Greater Southington Chamber of Commerce   www.southingtoncoc.com
37 W Center St   Southington CT 06489
Ph: 860-628-8036 ▪ Fx: 860-276-9696

SACIA Business Council   www.sacia.org
1 Landmark Sq Suite 230   Stamford CT 06901
Ph: 203-359-3220 ▪ Fx: 203-967-8294

Stamford Chamber of Commerce   www.stamfordchamber.com
733 Summer St Suite 104   Stamford CT 06901
Ph: 203-359-4761 ▪ Fx: 203-363-5069

Chamber of Commerce of Northwest Connecticut   www.northwestchamber.org
333 Kennedy Dr Suite R 101   Torrington CT 06790
Ph: 860-482-6586 ▪ Fx: 860-489-8851

Tolland County Chamber of Commerce   www.tollandcountychamber.org
30 Lafayette Sq   Vernon CT 06066
Ph: 860-872-0587 ▪ Fx: 860-872-0588

Quinnipiac Chamber of Commerce   www.quinncham.com
350 Center St   Wallingford CT 06492
Ph: 203-234-0332 ▪ Fx: 203-269-1358

Greater Waterbury Chamber of Commerce   www.waterburychamber.com
83 Bank St PO Box 1469   Waterbury CT 06721
Ph: 203-757-0701 ▪ Fx: 203-756-3507

West Hartford Chamber of Commerce   www.whchamber.com
948 Farmington Ave   West Hartford CT 06107
Ph: 860-521-2300 ▪ Fx: 860-521-1996

West Haven Chamber of Commerce   www.westhavenchamber.com
334 Main St   West Haven CT 06516
Ph: 203-933-1500 ▪ Fx: 203-931-1940

Windham Region Chamber of Commerce   www.windhamchamber.com
1010 Main St   Willimantic CT 06226
Ph: 860-423-6389 ▪ Fx: 860-423-8235

Windsor Chamber of Commerce   www.windsorcc.org
PO Box 9   Windsor CT 06095
Ph: 860-688-5165 ▪ Fx: 860-688-0809

DELAWARE

Central Delaware Economic Development Council   www.cdedc.org
Treadway Towers Suite 2-B   Dover DE 19903
Ph: 302-678-3028 ▪ Fx: 302-678-0189 ▪ TF: 800-624-2522

Rehoboth Beach-Dewey Beach Chamber of Commerce   www.beach-fun.com
PO Box 216   Rehoboth Beach DE 19971
Ph: 302-227-2233 ▪ Fx: 302-227-8351 ▪ TF: 800-441-1329

FLORIDA

Amelia Island-Fernandina Beach-Yulee Chamber of Commerce   www.islandchamber.com
961687 Gateway Blvd   Amelia Island FL 32034
Ph: 904-261-3248 ▪ Fx: 904-261-6997 ▪ TF: 800-226-3542

Apalachicola Bay Chamber of Commerce   www.apalachicolabay.org
122 Commerce St   Apalachicola FL 32320
Ph: 850-653-9419 ▪ Fx: 850-653-8219

DeSoto County Chamber of Commerce   www.desotochamber.net
16 S Volusia Ave   Arcadia FL 34266
Ph: 863-494-4033 ▪ Fx: 863-494-3312

Florida Gold Coast Chamber of Commerce   www.flgoldcc.org
1100 Kane Concourse Suite 210   Bay Harbor Islands FL 33154
Ph: 305-866-6020 ▪ Fx: 305-866-0635

Belleview-South Marion Chamber of Commerce   www.bsmcc.org
5301 SE Abshier Blvd   Belleview FL 34420
Ph: 352-245-2178 ▪ Fx: 352-245-7673

Lower Keys Chamber of Commerce   www.lowerkeyschamber.com
PO Box 430511   Big Pine Key FL 33043
Ph: 305-872-2411 ▪ Fx: 305-872-0752 ▪ TF: 800-872-3722

Greater Boca Raton Chamber of Commerce   www.bocaratonchamber.com
1800 N Dixie Hwy   Boca Raton FL 33432
Ph: 561-395-4433 ▪ Fx: 561-392-3780

Bonita Springs Area Chamber of Commerce   www.bonitaspringschamber.com
25071 Chamber of Commerce Dr   Bonita Springs FL 34135
Ph: 239-992-2943 ▪ Fx: 239-992-5011 ▪ TF: 800-226-2943

Greater Boynton Beach Chamber of Commerce   www.boyntonbeach.org
639 E Ocean Ave Suite 108   Boynton Beach FL 33435
Ph: 561-732-9501 ▪ Fx: 561-734-4304

Manatee Chamber of Commerce   www.manateechamber.com
PO Box 321   Bradenton FL 34206
Ph: 941-748-3411 ▪ Fx: 941-745-1877

Greater Brandon Chamber of Commerce   www.brandonchamber.com
808 Oakfield Dr   Brandon FL 33511
Ph: 813-689-1221 ▪ Fx: 813-689-9440

Greater Hernando County Chamber of Commerce   www.hernandochamber.com
101 E Fort Dade Ave   Brooksville FL 34601
Ph: 352-796-0697 ▪ Fx: 352-796-3704

Flagler County Palm Coast Chamber of Commerce   www.flaglerpcchamber.org
20 Airport Rd   Bunnell FL 32110
Ph: 386-437-0106 ▪ Fx: 386-437-5700 ▪ TF: 800-881-1022

Cape Coral Chamber of Commerce   capecoralchamber.com
2051 Cape Coral Pkwy E   Cape Coral FL 33904
Ph: 239-549-6900 ▪ Fx: 239-549-9609 ▪ TF: 800-226-9609

Clearwater Regional Chamber of Commerce   www.clearwaterflorida.org
1130 Cleveland St   Clearwater FL 33755
Ph: 727-461-0011 ▪ Fx: 727-449-2889

Coral Gables Chamber of Commerce   cg.wliinc2.com
PO Box 347555   Coral Gables FL 33234
Ph: 305-446-1657 ▪ Fx: 305-446-9900

Coral Springs Chamber of Commerce   www.cschamber.com
11805 Heron Bay Blvd   Coral Springs FL 33076
Ph: 954-752-4242 ▪ Fx: 954-827-0543

Crestview Area Chamber of Commerce   www.crestviewchamber.com
502 S Main St   Crestview FL 32536
Ph: 850-682-3212 ▪ Fx: 850-682-7413

Citrus County Chamber of Commerce   www.citruscountychamber.com
28 NW Hwy 19   Crystal River FL 34428
Ph: 352-795-3149 ▪ Fx: 352-795-4260

Davie-Cooper City Chamber of Commerce   www.davie-coopercity.org
4185 Davie Rd   Davie FL 33314
Ph: 954-581-0790 ▪ Fx: 954-581-9684

Daytona Beach-Halifax Area Chamber of Commerce   www.daytonachamber.com
126 E Orange Ave   Daytona Beach FL 32114
Ph: 386-255-0981 ▪ Fx: 386-258-5104

Greater Deerfield Beach Chamber of Commerce   www.deerfieldchamber.com
1601 E Hillsboro Blvd   Deerfield Beach FL 33441
Ph: 954-427-1050 ▪ Fx: 954-427-1056

DeLand Area Chamber of Commerce   www.delandchamber.com
336 N Woodland Blvd   DeLand FL 32720
Ph: 386-734-4331 ▪ Fx: 386-734-4333

Greater Delray Beach Chamber of Commerce   www.delraybeach.com
64-A SE 5th Ave   Delray Beach FL 33483
Ph: 561-278-0424 ▪ Fx: 561-278-0555

Destin Area Chamber of Commerce   www.destinchamber.com
4484 Legendary Dr   Destin FL 32541
Ph: 850-837-6241 ▪ Fx: 850-654-5612

Dunedin Chamber of Commerce   www.dunedin-fl.com
301 Main St   Dunedin FL 34698
Ph: 727-733-3197 ▪ Fx: 727-734-8942

Dunnellon Area Chamber of Commerce Inc   dunnellonchamber.org
PO Box 868   Dunnellon FL 34430
Ph: 352-489-2320 ▪ Fx: 352-489-6846 ▪ TF: 800-830-2087

Englewood/Cape Haze Chamber of Commerce   www.englewoodchamber.com
601 S Indiana Ave   Englewood FL 34223
Ph: 941-474-5511 ▪ Fx: 941-475-9257 ▪ TF: 800-603-7198

Broward County Chamber of Commerce   www.browardbiz.com
3045 N Federal Hwy Suite 60   Fort Lauderdale FL 33306
Ph: 954-565-5750 ▪ Fx: 954-566-3398

Greater Fort Lauderdale Chamber of Commerce   www.ftlchamber.com
512 NE 3rd Ave   Fort Lauderdale FL 33301
Ph: 954-462-6000 ▪ Fx: 954-527-8766

Chamber of Southwest Florida   www.chamber-swflorida.com
1520 Royal Palm Sq Blvd Suite 210   Fort Myers FL 33919
Ph: 239-278-4001 ▪ Fx: 239-278-3319

Greater Fort Myers Chamber of Commerce   www.fortmyers.org
PO Box 9289   Fort Myers FL 33902
Ph: 239-332-3624 ▪ Fx: 239-332-7276 ▪ TF: 800-366-3622

Fort Myers Beach Chamber of Commerce   www.fmbchamber.com
17200 San Carlos Blvd   Fort Myers Beach FL 33931
Ph: 239-454-7500 ▪ Fx: 239-454-7910 ▪ TF: 800-782-9283

Greater Fort Walton Beach Chamber of Commerce   www.fwbchamber.com
PO Box 640   Fort Walton Beach FL 32549
Ph: 850-244-8191 ▪ Fx: 850-244-1935

Gainesville Area Chamber of Commerce   www.gainesvillechamber.com
300 E University Ave Suite 100   Gainesville FL 32601
Ph: 352-334-7100 ▪ Fx: 352-334-7141

Goldenrod Area Chamber of Commerce   www.goldenrodchamber.com
PO Box 61   Goldenrod FL 32733
Ph: 407-677-5980 ▪ Fx: 407-677-4928

Hallandale Pembroke Park Chamber of Commerce
PO Box 249   Hallandale FL 33008
Ph: 954-454-0541 ▪ Fx: 954-454-0930

Camara de Comercio Hispana de Hialeah
4410 W 16th Ave Suite 62   Hialeah FL 33012
Ph: 305-557-5060 ▪ Fx: 305-556-7333

Hialeah Chamber of Commerce & Industries   www.hialeahchamber.com
1840 W 49th St Suite 700   Hialeah FL 33012
Ph: 305-828-9898 ▪ Fx: 305-828-9777

Greater Hollywood Chamber of Commerce   www.hollywoodchamber.org
330 N Federal Hwy   Hollywood FL 33020
Ph: 954-923-4000 ▪ Fx: 954-923-8737 ▪ TF: 800-231-5562

Greater Homestead/Florida City Chamber of Commerce   www.chamberinaction.com
43 N Krome Ave   Homestead FL 33030
Ph: 305-247-2332 ▪ Fx: 305-246-1100 ▪ TF: 888-352-4891

Citrus County Chamber of Commerce   www.citruscountychamber.com
3495 S Suncoast Blvd   Homosassa Springs FL 34447
Ph: 352-628-2666 ▪ Fx: 352-621-0920

Citrus County Chamber of Commerce   www.citruscountychamber.com
208 W Main St   Inverness FL 34450
Ph: 352-726-2801 ▪ Fx: 352-637-6498

Islamorada Chamber of Commerce   www.islamoradachamber.com
PO Box 915   Islamorada FL 33036
Ph: 305-664-4503 ▪ Fx: 305-664-4289 ▪ TF: 800-322-5397

Jacksonville Chamber of Commerce   www.myjaxchamber.com
3 Independent Dr   Jacksonville FL 32202
Ph: 904-366-6600 ▪ Fx: 904-632-0617

Jacksonville Chamber of Commerce Beaches Div   www.myjaxchamber.com
325 Jacksonville Dr   Jacksonville Beach FL 32250
Ph: 904-249-3868 ▪ Fx: 904-241-7556

Jupiter Tequesta Juno Beach Chamber of Commerce   www.jupiterfl.org
800 N US Hwy 1   Jupiter FL 33477
Ph: 561-746-7111 ▪ Fx: 561-746-7715 ▪ TF: 800-616-7402

Key Largo Chamber of Commerce   www.keylargo.org
106000 Overseas Hwy Mile Marker 106   Key Largo FL 33037
Ph: 305-451-1414 ▪ Fx: 305-451-4726

Key West Chamber of Commerce   www.keywestchamber.org
402 Wall St   Key West FL 33040
Ph: 305-294-2587 ▪ Fx: 305-294-7806 ▪ TF: 800-527-8539

Kissimmee/Osceola County Chamber of Commerce   www.kissimmeechamber.com
1425 E Vine St   Kissimmee FL 34744
Ph: 407-847-3174 ▪ Fx: 407-870-8607

Lake City/Columbia County Chamber of Commerce   www.lakecitychamber.com
162 S Marion St   Lake City FL 32025
Ph: 386-752-3690 ▪ Fx: 386-755-7744

Seminole County/Lake Mary Regional Chamber of Commerce   www.seminolebusiness.org
725 Primera Blvd Suite 100   Lake Mary FL 32746
Ph: 407-333-4748 ▪ Fx: 407-829-2100

Greater Lake Placid Chamber of Commerce   www.lpfla.com
18 N Oak St   Lake Placid FL 33852
Ph: 863-465-4331 ▪ Fx: 863-465-2588

Lake Wales Area Chamber of Commerce   www.lakewaleschamber.com
340 W Central Ave   Lake Wales FL 33853
Ph: 863-676-3445 ▪ Fx: 863-676-3446

Greater Lake Worth Chamber of Commerce   www.lwchamber.com
807 Lucerne Ave   Lake Worth FL 33460
Ph: 561-582-4401 ▪ Fx: 561-547-8300

Lakeland Area Chamber of Commerce   www.lakelandchamber.com
35 Lake Morton Dr   Lakeland FL 33801
Ph: 863-688-8551 ▪ Fx: 863-683-7454

Central Pasco Chamber of Commerce   www.centralpascochamber.com
PO Box 98   Land O'Lakes FL 34639
Ph: 813-909-2722 ▪ Fx: 813-909-0827

Greater Largo Chamber of Commerce   www.largochamber.com
151 3rd Ave NW   Largo FL 33770
Ph: 727-584-2321 ▪ Fx: 727-586-3112

Lehigh Acres Chamber of Commerce   www.lehighacreschamber.org
4109 Lee Blvd   Lehigh Acres FL 33971
Ph: 239-369-3322 ▪ Fx: 239-368-0500

Suwannee County Chamber of Commerce   www.suwanneechamber.com
PO Drawer C   Live Oak FL 32064
Ph: 386-362-3071 ▪ Fx: 386-362-4758

Palms West Chamber of Commerce   www.palmswest.com
PO Box 1062   Loxahatchee FL 33470
Ph: 561-790-6200 ▪ Fx: 561-791-2069 ▪ TF: 800-790-2364

Maitland Area Chamber of Commerce   www.maitlandchamber.com
110 N Maitland Ave   Maitland FL 32751
Ph: 407-644-0741 ▪ Fx: 407-539-2529

Greater Marathon Chamber of Commerce   www.floridakeysmarathon.com
12222 Overseas Hwy   Marathon FL 33050
Ph: 305-743-5417 ▪ Fx: 305-289-0183 ▪ TF: 800-262-7284

Marco Island Chamber of Commerce   www.marcoislandchamber.org
1102 N Collier Blvd   Marco Island FL 34145
Ph: 239-394-7549 ▪ Fx: 239-394-3061 ▪ TF: 800-788-6272

Jackson County Chamber of Commerce   www.jcflchamber.com
PO Box 130   Marianna FL 32447
Ph: 850-482-8061 ▪ Fx: 850-482-8002

Melbourne-Palm Bay Area Chamber of Commerce   www.melpb-chamber.org
1005 E Strawbridge Ave   Melbourne FL 32901
Ph: 321-724-5400 ▪ Fx: 321-725-2093 ▪ TF: 800-771-9922

Cocoa Beach Area Chamber of Commerce   www.cocoabeachchamber.com
400 Fortenberry Rd   Merritt Island FL 32952
Ph: 321-459-2200 ▪ Fx: 321-459-2232

Greater Miami Chamber of Commerce   www.greatermiami.com
1601 Biscayne Blvd   Miami FL 33132
Ph: 305-350-7700 ▪ Fx: 305-374-6902 ▪ TF: 888-660-5955

Miami-Dade Chamber of Commerce   www.m-dcc.org
9190 Biscayne Blvd Suite 201   Miami FL 33138
Ph: 305-751-8648 ▪ Fx: 305-758-3839

North Dade Regional Chamber of Commerce   www.thechamber.cc
1300 NW 167th St Suite 1   Miami FL 33169
Ph: 305-690-9123 ▪ Fx: 305-690-9124

Miami Beach Chamber of Commerce   www.miamibeachchamber.com
1920 Meridian Ave 3rd Fl   Miami Beach FL 33139
Ph: 305-672-1270 ▪ Fx: 305-538-4336

Santa Rosa County Chamber of Commerce   www.srcchamber.com
5247 Stewart St   Milton FL 32570
Ph: 850-623-2339 ▪ Fx: 850-623-4413

Naples Area Chamber of Commerce   www.napleschamber.org
895 5th Ave S   Naples FL 34102
Ph: 239-262-6141 ▪ Fx: 239-435-9910

West Pasco Chamber of Commerce   westpasco.com
5443 Main St   New Port Richey FL 34652
Ph: 727-842-7651 ▪ Fx: 727-848-0202

Southeast Volusia Chamber of Commerce   www.sevchamber.com
115 Canal St   New Smyrna Beach FL 32168
Ph: 386-428-2449 ▪ Fx: 386-423-3512 ▪ TF: 877-460-8410

Niceville-Valparaiso Bay Area Chamber of Commerce   www.nicevillechamber.com
1055 E John Sims Pkwy   Niceville FL 32578
Ph: 850-678-2323 ▪ Fx: 850-678-2602

North Fort Myers Chamber of Commerce   www.northfortmyerschamber.org
3323 N Key Dr Suite 1   North Fort Myers FL 33903
Ph: 239-997-9111 ▪ Fx: 239-997-4026

Greater North Miami Chamber of Commerce   www.northmiamichamber.com
13100 W Dixie Hwy   North Miami FL 33161
Ph: 305-891-7811 ▪ Fx: 305-893-8522

North Miami Beach Chamber of Commerce   www.nmbchamber.com
1870 NE 171st St   North Miami Beach FL 33162
Ph: 305-944-8500 ▪ Fx: 305-944-8191

Sunny Isles Beach Resort Association   www.sunnyislesfla.com
17070 Collins Ave Suite 266B   North Miami Beach FL 33160
Ph: 305-947-5826 ▪ Fx: 305-956-9527

Ocala-Marion County Chamber of Commerce   www.ocalacc.com
110 E Silver Springs Blvd   Ocala FL 34470
Ph: 352-629-8051 ▪ Fx: 352-629-7651

Okeechobee Chamber of Commerce
55 S Parrott Ave   Okeechobee FL 34972
Ph: 863-763-6464 ▪ Fx: 863-763-3531

Clay County Chamber of Commerce   www.claychamber.org
1734 Kingsley Ave   Orange Park FL 32073
Ph: 904-264-2651 ▪ Fx: 904-264-0070

East Orlando Chamber of Commerce   www.eocc.org
10111 E Colonial Dr   Orlando FL 32817
Ph: 407-277-5951 ▪ Fx: 407-381-1720

Orlando Regional Chamber of Commerce   www.orlando.org
PO Box 1234   Orlando FL 32802
Ph: 407-425-1234 ▪ Fx: 407-835-2500

Ormond Beach Chamber of Commerce   www.ormondchamber.com
165 W Granada Blvd   Ormond Beach FL 32174
Ph: 386-677-3454 ▪ Fx: 386-677-4363

Putnam County Chamber of Commerce   www.putnamcountychamber.org
1100 Reid St   Palatka FL 32177
Ph: 386-328-1503 ▪ Fx: 386-328-7076

Northern Palm Beaches Chamber of Commerce   www.npbchamber.com
1983 PGA Blvd Suite 104   Palm Beach Gardens FL 33408
Ph: 561-694-2300 ▪ Fx: 561-694-0126

Greater Palm Harbor Area Chamber of Commerce   www.palmharborcc.org
1151 Nebraska Ave   Palm Harbor FL 34683
Ph: 727-784-4287 ▪ Fx: 727-786-2336

Bay County Chamber of Commerce   www.panamacity.org
235 W 5th St   Panama City FL 32401
Ph: 850-785-5206 ▪ Fx: 850-763-6229

Panama City Beaches Chamber of Commerce   www.pcbeach.org
415 Beckrich Rd Suite 200   Panama City Beach FL 32407
Ph: 850-234-3193 ▪ Fx: 850-235-2301

Southwest Broward Regional Chamber of Commerce
10100 Pines Blvd 4th Fl   Pembroke Pines FL 33026
Ph: 954-432-9808 ▪ Fx: 954-432-9193

Pensacola Area Chamber of Commerce   www.pensacolachamber.com
PO Box 550   Pensacola FL 32591
Ph: 850-438-4081 ▪ Fx: 850-438-6369

Pinellas Park Mid-County Chamber of Commerce   www.pinellasparkchamber.com
Park Side Mall 7200 US 19 N Suite 326   Pinellas Park FL 33781
Ph: 727-544-4777 ▪ Fx: 727-521-0085

Greater Plant City Chamber of Commerce   www.plantcity.org
106 N Evers St   Plant City FL 33563
Ph: 813-754-3707 ▪ Fx: 813-752-8793 ▪ TF: 800-760-2315

Greater Plantation Chamber of Commerce   www.plantationchamber.org
7401 NW 4th St   Plantation FL 33317
Ph: 954-587-1410 ▪ Fx: 954-587-1886

Greater Pompano Beach Chamber of Commerce   www.pompanobeachchamber.com
2200 E Atlantic Blvd   Pompano Beach FL 33062
Ph: 954-941-2940 ▪ Fx: 954-785-8358

Charlotte County Chamber of Commerce   www.charlottecountychamber.org
2702 Tamiami Trail   Port Charlotte FL 33952
Ph: 941-627-2222 ▪ Fx: 941-627-9730

Port Orange-South Daytona Chamber of Commerce   www.pschamber.com
3431 Ridgewood Ave   Port Orange FL 32129
Ph: 386-761-1601 ▪ Fx: 386-788-9165

Charlotte County Chamber of Commerce   www.charlottecountychamber.org
326 W Marion Ave Suite 112   Punta Gorda FL 33950
Ph: 941-639-2222 ▪ Fx: 941-639-6330

Gadsden County Chamber of Commerce   www.gadsdencc.org
PO Box 389   Quincy FL 32353
Ph: 850-627-9231 ▪ Fx: 850-875-3299 ▪ TF: 800-627-9231

Greater Riverview Chamber of Commerce   www.riverviewchamber.com
PO Box 128   Riverview FL 33568
Ph: 813-643-8000 ▪ Fx: 813-643-8500

Ruskin Chamber of Commerce   www.ruskinchamber.com
315 S Tamiami Tr   Ruskin FL 33570
Ph: 813-645-3808 ▪ Fx: 813-645-2099

Saint Augustine & Saint Johns County Chamber of Commerce   www.staugustinechamber.com
1 Riberia St   Saint Augustine FL 32084
Ph: 904-829-5681 ▪ Fx: 904-829-6477

Saint Cloud/Greater Osceola Chamber of Commerce   stcloudflchamber.com
1200 New York Ave   Saint Cloud FL 34769
Ph: 407-892-3671 ▪ Fx: 407-892-5289

Tampa Bay Beaches Chamber of Commerce   www.tampabaybeaches.com
6990 Gulf Blvd   Saint Pete Beach FL 33706
Ph: 727-360-6957 ▪ Fx: 727-360-2233 ▪ TF: 800-944-1847

Saint Petersburg Area Chamber of Commerce   www.stpete.com
100 2nd Ave N Suite 150   Saint Petersburg FL 33701
Ph: 727-821-4069 ▪ Fx: 727-895-6326

Sanford Seminole County Chamber of Commerce   www.sanfordchamber.com
400 E 1st St   Sanford FL 32771
Ph: 407-322-2212 ▪ Fx: 407-322-8160

Sanibel & Captiva Islands Chamber of Commerce   www.sanibel-captiva.org
1159 Causeway Rd   Sanibel FL 33957
Ph: 239-472-1080 ▪ Fx: 239-472-1070

Walton County Chamber of Commerce   www.waltoncountychamber.com
63 S South Ctr Trail   Santa Rosa Beach FL 32459
Ph: 850-267-0683 ▪ Fx: 850-267-0603

Greater Sarasota Chamber of Commerce   www.sarasotachamber.org
1945 Fruitville Rd   Sarasota FL 34236
Ph: 941-955-8187 ▪ Fx: 941-366-5621

Sebastian River Area Chamber of Commerce   sebastian.fl.us/chamber
700 Main St   Sebastian FL 32958
Ph: 772-589-5969 ▪ Fx: 772-589-5993

Greater Sebring Chamber of Commerce   www.sebringflchamber.com
309 S Circle St   Sebring FL 33870
Ph: 863-385-8448 ▪ Fx: 863-385-8810 ▪ TF: 877-844-6007

Appendix

Greater Seffner Area Chamber of Commerce
PO Box 1920   Seffner FL 33583
Ph: 813-684-4075 ▪ Fx: 813-655-1754   www.seffnerchamber.com

Greater Seminole Area Chamber of Commerce
8400 113th St N   Seminole FL 33772
Ph: 727-392-3245 ▪ Fx: 727-397-7753   www.seminolechamber.net

Chamber South
6410 SW 80th St   South Miami FL 33143
Ph: 305-661-1621 ▪ Fx: 305-666-0508   www.chambersouth.com

Stuart-Martin County Chamber of Commerce
1650 S Kanner Hwy   Stuart FL 34994
Ph: 772-287-1088 ▪ Fx: 772-220-3437 ▪ TF: 800-524-9704   www.goodnature.org

Sumter County Chamber of Commerce
PO Box 100   Sumterville FL 33585
Ph: 352-793-3099 ▪ Fx: 352-793-2120   www.gosumter.com

Sunrise Chamber of Commerce
12801 W Sunrise Blvd Suite 101   Sunrise FL 33323
Ph: 954-835-2428 ▪ Fx: 954-835-2431   www.sunrisechamber.org

Tallahassee Chamber of Commerce
PO Box 1639   Tallahassee FL 32302
Ph: 850-224-8116 ▪ Fx: 850-561-3860   www.talchamber.com/

Tamarac Chamber of Commerce
8525 W McNab Rd   Tamarac FL 33321
Ph: 954-722-1520 ▪ Fx: 954-721-2725   www.tamaracchamber.org

Greater Tampa Chamber of Commerce
615 Channelside Dr Suite 108   Tampa FL 33602
Ph: 813-228-7777 ▪ Fx: 813-223-7899 ▪ TF: 800-298-2672   www.tampachamber.com

Greater Town & Country Area Chamber of Commerce
7512 Paula Dr Suite 105   Tampa FL 33615
Ph: 813-884-5344 ▪ Fx: 813-885-2093   www.tncchamber.org

North Tampa Chamber of Commerce
11778 N Dale Mabry Hwy   Tampa FL 33618
Ph: 813-961-2420 ▪ Fx: 813-961-2903   www.northtampachamber.com

Ybor City Chamber of Commerce
1514 1/2 E 8th Ave   Tampa FL 33605
Ph: 813-248-3712 ▪ Fx: 813-247-1764   www.ybor.org

Tarpon Springs Chamber of Commerce
11 E Orange St   Tarpon Springs FL 34689
Ph: 727-937-6109 ▪ Fx: 727-937-2879   www.tarponsprings.com

Titusville Area Chamber of Commerce
2000 S Washington Ave   Titusville FL 32780
Ph: 321-267-3036 ▪ Fx: 321-264-0127   www.titusville.org

Venice Area Chamber of Commerce
597 Tamiami Trail S   Venice FL 24285
Ph: 941-488-2236 ▪ Fx: 941-484-5903   www.venicechamber.com

Indian River County Chamber of Commerce
1216 21st St   Vero Beach FL 32960
Ph: 772-567-3491 ▪ Fx: 772-778-3181   www.indianriverchamber.com

Chamber of Commerce of the Palm Beaches
401 N Flagler Dr   West Palm Beach FL 33401
Ph: 561-833-3711 ▪ Fx: 561-833-5582   www.palmbeaches.org

Weston Area Chamber of Commerce
1290 Weston Rd Suite 200   Weston FL 33326
Ph: 954-389-0600 ▪ Fx: 954-384-6133   www.westonchamber.com

West Orange Chamber of Commerce
12184 W Colonial Dr   Winter Garden FL 34787
Ph: 407-656-1304 ▪ Fx: 407-656-0221   www.wochamber.com

Winter Haven Area Chamber of Commerce
PO Box 1420   Winter Haven FL 33882
Ph: 863-293-2138 ▪ Fx: 863-297-5818 ▪ TF: 800-871-7027   www.winterhavenfl.com

Winter Park Chamber of Commerce
150 N New York Ave   Winter Park FL 32789
Ph: 407-644-8281 ▪ Fx: 407-644-7826 ▪ TF: 877-972-4262   www.winterpark.org

Zephyrhills Chamber of Commerce
38550 5th Ave   Zephyrhills FL 33542
Ph: 813-782-1913 ▪ Fx: 813-783-6060   www.zephyrhills.net/chamber.html

GEORGIA

Albany Area Chamber of Commerce
225 W Broad Ave   Albany GA 31701
Ph: 229-434-8700 ▪ Fx: 229-434-8716 ▪ TF: 800-475-8700   www.albanyga.com

Americus-Sumter County Chamber of Commerce
400 W Lamar St PO Box 724   Americus GA 31709
Ph: 229-924-2646 ▪ Fx: 229-924-8784   www.americus-sumterchamber.com

Athens Area Chamber of Commerce
246 W Hancock Ave   Athens GA 30601
Ph: 706-549-6800 ▪ Fx: 706-549-5636   www.athenschamber.net

Metro Atlanta Chamber of Commerce
235 Andrew Young International Blvd NW   Atlanta GA 30303
Ph: 404-880-9000 ▪ Fx: 404-586-8464   www.metroatlantachamber.com

Women's Chamber of Commerce of Atlanta
PO Box 18765   Atlanta GA 31126
Ph: 404-892-0538

Augusta Metro Chamber of Commerce
PO Box 1837   Augusta GA 30903
Ph: 706-821-1300 ▪ Fx: 706-821-1330   www.augustagausa.com

Bainbridge-Decatur County Chamber of Commerce
PO Box 755   Bainbridge GA 39818
Ph: 229-246-4774 ▪ Fx: 229-243-7633 ▪ TF: 800-243-4774   www.bainbridgega.com/chamber/index.html

Brunswick-Golden Isles Chamber of Commerce
4 Glynn Ave   Brunswick GA 31520
Ph: 912-265-0620 ▪ Fx: 912-265-0629   brunswick-georgia.com/chamber

Gordon County Chamber of Commerce
300 S Wall St   Calhoun GA 30701
Ph: 706-625-3200 ▪ Fx: 706-625-5062 ▪ TF: 800-887-3811   www.gordonchamber.org

Cherokee County Chamber of Commerce
PO Box 4998   Canton GA 30114
Ph: 770-345-0400 ▪ Fx: 770-345-0030   www.cherokee-chamber.com

Carroll County Chamber of Commerce
200 Northside Dr   Carrollton GA 30117
Ph: 770-832-2446 ▪ Fx: 770-832-1300   www.carroll-ga.org

Cartersville-Bartow County Chamber of Commerce
PO Box 307   Cartersville GA 30120
Ph: 770-382-1466 ▪ Fx: 770-382-2704   www.cartersvillechamber.com

Chatsworth-Murray County Chamber of Commerce
126 N 3rd Ave   Chatsworth GA 30705
Ph: 706-695-6060 ▪ Fx: 706-517-0198 ▪ TF: 800-969-9490   www.murraycountychamber.com

White County Chamber of Commerce
122 N Main St   Cleveland GA 30528
Ph: 706-865-5356 ▪ Fx: 706-865-0758 ▪ TF: 800-392-8279   www.whitecountychamber.org

Columbus Chamber of Commerce
1200 6th Ave   Columbus GA 31902
Ph: 706-327-1566 ▪ Fx: 706-327-7512 ▪ TF: 800-360-8552   www.columbusgachamber.com

Jackson County Area Chamber of Commerce
PO Box 1444   Commerce GA 30529
Ph: 706-335-1896 ▪ Fx: 706-335-3312   www.jacksoncountyga.com

Conyers-Rockdale Chamber of Commerce
1186 Scott St   Conyers GA 30012
Ph: 770-483-7049 ▪ Fx: 770-922-8415   www.conyers-rockdale.com

Habersham County Chamber of Commerce
PO Box 366   Cornelia GA 30531
Ph: 706-778-4654 ▪ Fx: 706-776-1416 ▪ TF: 800-835-2559   www.seehabersham.com

Covington-Newton County Chamber of Commerce
2100 Washington St   Covington GA 30014
Ph: 770-786-7510 ▪ Fx: 770-786-1294   www.newtonchamber.com

Cumming-Forsyth County Chamber of Commerce
212 Kelly Mill Rd   Cumming GA 30040
Ph: 770-887-6461 ▪ Fx: 770-781-8800   www.forsythchamber.org

Paulding County Chamber of Commerce
455 Jimmy Campbell Pkwy   Dallas GA 30132
Ph: 770-445-6016 ▪ Fx: 770-445-3050   www.pauldingcountygeorgia.com

Dalton-Whitfield Chamber of Commerce
524 Holiday Ave   Dalton GA 30720
Ph: 706-278-7373 ▪ Fx: 706-226-8739   www.daltonchamber.org

DeKalb Chamber of Commerce
750 Commerce Dr Suite 201   Decatur GA 30030
Ph: 404-378-8000 ▪ Fx: 404-378-3397   www.dekalbchamber.org

Douglas-Coffee County Chamber of Commerce
211 S Gaskin Ave   Douglas GA 31533
Ph: 912-384-1873 ▪ Fx: 912-383-6304 ▪ TF: 888-426-3334   www.douglasga.org

Douglas County Chamber of Commerce
6658 Church St   Douglasville GA 30134
Ph: 770-942-5022 ▪ Fx: 770-942-5876   www.douglascountygeorgia.com

Dublin-Laurens County Chamber of Commerce
PO Box 818   Dublin GA 31040
Ph: 478-272-5546 ▪ Fx: 478-275-0811   www.dublin-georgia.com

Gwinnett Chamber of Commerce
6500 Sugarloaf Pkwy   Duluth GA 30097
Ph: 770-232-3000 ▪ Fx: 770-232-8807   www.gwinnettchamber.org

Columbia County Chamber of Commerce
4424 Evans to Locks Rd   Evans GA 30809
Ph: 706-651-0018 ▪ Fx: 706-651-0023

Fayette County Chamber of Commerce
200 Courthouse Sq   Fayetteville GA 30214
Ph: 770-461-9983 ▪ Fx: 770-461-9622   www.fayettechamber.org

Greater Hall Chamber of Commerce
230 EE Butler Pkwy   Gainesville GA 30501
Ph: 770-532-6206 ▪ Fx: 770-535-8419   www.ghcc.com

Griffin-Spalding Chamber of Commerce
143 N Hill St   Griffin GA 30223
Ph: 770-228-8200 ▪ Fx: 770-228-8031   www.griffinchamber.com

Liberty County Chamber of Commerce
500 E Oglethorpe Hwy   Hinesville GA 31313
Ph: 912-368-4445 ▪ Fx: 912-368-5585   www.libertycounty.org

Clayton County Chamber of Commerce
2270 Mt Zion Rd   Jonesboro GA 30236
Ph: 678-610-4021 ▪ Fx: 678-610-4025   www.claytoncham.org

Camden-Kings Bay Area Chamber of Commerce
2603 Osborne Rd Suite R   Kingsland GA 31558
Ph: 912-729-5840 ▪ Fx: 912-576-7924   www.camdenchamber.com

LaGrange-Troup County Chamber of Commerce
PO Box 636   LaGrange GA 30241
Ph: 706-884-8671 ▪ Fx: 706-882-8012   www.lagrangechamber.com

Greater Macon Chamber of Commerce
305 Coliseum Dr   Macon GA 31217
Ph: 478-621-2000 ▪ Fx: 478-621-2021   www.maconchamber.com

Cobb Chamber of Commerce
PO Box 671868   Marietta GA 30006
Ph: 770-980-2000 ▪ Fx: 770-980-9510   www.cobbchamber.com

Henry County Chamber of Commerce
1709 Hwy 20 W West Ridge Business Ctr   McDonough GA 30253
Ph: 770-957-5786 ▪ Fx: 770-957-8030 ▪ TF: 800-436-7926   www.henrycounty.com

Milledgeville-Baldwin County Chamber of Commerce
130 S Jefferson St   Milledgeville GA 31061
Ph: 478-453-9311 ▪ Fx: 478-453-0051   www.milledgevillega.com

Walton County Chamber of Commerce
PO Box 89   Monroe GA 30655
Ph: 770-267-6594 ▪ Fx: 770-267-0961   www.waltonchamber.org

Moultrie-Colquitt County Chamber of Commerce
116 1st Ave SE   Moultrie GA 31768
Ph: 229-985-2131 ▪ Fx: 229-890-2638 ▪ TF: 888-408-4748   www.moultriechamber.com

Newnan-Coweta Chamber of Commerce
23 Bullsboro Dr   Newnan GA 30263
Ph: 770-253-2270 ▪ Fx: 770-253-2271   www.ncchamber.org

Catoosa County Area Chamber of Commerce
PO Box 52   Ringgold GA 30736
Ph: 706-965-5201 ▪ Fx: 706-965-8224 ▪ TF: 877-965-5201   www.gatewaytogeorgia.com

Appendix

Walker County Chamber of Commerce
PO Box 430   Rock Spring GA 30739
Ph: 706-375-7702 ▪ Fx: 706-375-7797
www.walkercochamber.com

Polk County Chamber of Commerce
604 Goodyear St   Rockmart GA 30153
Ph: 770-684-8760 ▪ Fx: 770-684-9155 ▪ TF: 800-226-2517
polk.ofgeorgia.org

Greater Rome Chamber of Commerce
1 Riverside Pkwy   Rome GA 30161
Ph: 706-291-7663 ▪ Fx: 706-232-5755 ▪ TF: 800-234-3154
www.romega.com

Greater North Fulton Chamber of Commerce
1025 Old Roswell Rd Suite 101   Roswell GA 30076
Ph: 770-993-8806 ▪ Fx: 770-594-1059
www.gnfcc.com

Savannah Area Chamber of Commerce
101 E Bay St   Savannah GA 31401
Ph: 912-644-6400 ▪ Fx: 912-644-6499 ▪ TF: 877-728-2662
www.savannahchamber.com

Effingham County Chamber of Commerce
PO Box 1078   Springfield GA 31329
Ph: 912-754-3301 ▪ Fx: 912-754-1236
www.effinghamcounty.com

Statesboro-Bulloch County Chamber of Commerce
PO Box 303   Statesboro GA 30459
Ph: 912-764-6111 ▪ Fx: 912-489-3108
www.statesboro-chamber.org

Thomaston-Upson Chamber of Commerce
PO Box 827   Thomaston GA 30286
Ph: 706-647-9686 ▪ Fx: 706-647-1703
www.thomastonchamber.com

Thomasville-Thomas County Chamber of Commerce
PO Box 560   Thomasville GA 31799
Ph: 229-226-9600 ▪ Fx: 229-226-9603
www.thomasvillechamber.com

Tifton-Tift County Chamber of Commerce
PO Box 165   Tifton GA 31793
Ph: 229-382-6200 ▪ Fx: 229-386-2232 ▪ TF: 800-550-8438
www.tiftonchamber.com

Toccoa-Stephens County Chamber of Commerce
901 E Currahee St   Toccoa GA 30577
Ph: 706-886-2132 ▪ Fx: 706-886-2133
www.toccoagachamber.com

South Fulton Chamber of Commerce
6400 Shannon Pkwy   Union City GA 30291
Ph: 770-964-1984 ▪ Fx: 770-969-1969
www.sfcoc.org

Valdosta-Lowndes County Chamber of Commerce
416 N Ashley St   Valdosta GA 31602
Ph: 229-247-8100 ▪ Fx: 229-245-0071
www.valdostachamber.com

Warner Robins Area Chamber of Commerce
1420 Watson Blvd   Warner Robins GA 31093
Ph: 478-922-8585 ▪ Fx: 478-328-7745
www.warner-robins.com

Waycross-Ware County Chamber of Commerce
317 Plant Ave   Waycross GA 31501
Ph: 912-283-3742 ▪ Fx: 912-283-0121

Barrow County Chamber of Commerce
PO Box 456   Winder GA 30680
Ph: 770-867-9444 ▪ Fx: 770-867-6366
www.barrowchamber.com

HAWAII

Hawaii Island Chamber of Commerce
106 Kamehameha Ave   Hilo HI 96720
Ph: 808-935-7178 ▪ Fx: 808-961-4435
www.hawaiiislandchamber.org

Maui Chamber of Commerce
250 Alamaha St Unit N16A   Kahului HI 96732
Ph: 808-871-7711 ▪ Fx: 808-877-6646
www.mauichamber.com

Kailua Chamber of Commerce
600 Kailua Rd Suite 103   Kailua HI 96734
Ph: 808-261-2727 ▪ Fx: 808-262-0867
www.visitkailua.com

Kona-Kohala Chamber of Commerce
75-5737 Kuakini Hwy Suite 208   Kailua-Kona HI 96740
Ph: 808-329-1758 ▪ Fx: 808-329-8564
www.kona-kohala.com

Kaua'i Chamber of Commerce
PO Box 1969   Lihue HI 96766
Ph: 808-245-7363 ▪ Fx: 808-245-8815
www.kauaichamber.org

IDAHO

Boise Metro Chamber of Commerce
PO Box 2368   Boise ID 83701
Ph: 208-472-5205 ▪ Fx: 208-472-5201
www.boisechamber.org

Caldwell Chamber of Commerce
704 Blaine St   Caldwell ID 83605
Ph: 208-459-7493 ▪ Fx: 208-454-1284
www.caldwellidaho.org

Coeur d'Alene Area Chamber of Commerce
PO Box 850   Coeur d'Alene ID 83816
Ph: 208-664-3194 ▪ Fx: 208-667-9338
www.cdachamber.com

Mini-Cassia Chamber of Commerce
1177 7th St   Heyburn ID 83336
Ph: 208-679-4793 ▪ Fx: 208-679-4794
www.minicassiachamber.org

Greater Idaho Falls Chamber of Commerce
630 W Broadway   Idaho Falls ID 83402
Ph: 208-523-1010 ▪ Fx: 208-523-2255 ▪ TF: 866-365-6943
www.idahofallschamber.com

Lewiston Chamber of Commerce
111 Main St Suite 120   Lewiston ID 83501
Ph: 208-743-3531 ▪ Fx: 208-743-2176 ▪ TF: 800-473-3543
www.lewistonchamber.org

Meridian Chamber of Commerce
PO Box 7   Meridian ID 83680
Ph: 208-888-2817 ▪ Fx: 208-888-2682
www.meridianchamber.org

Moscow Chamber of Commerce
411 S Main St   Moscow ID 83843
Ph: 208-882-1800 ▪ Fx: 208-882-6186 ▪ TF: 800-380-1801
www.moscowchamber.com

Nampa Chamber of Commerce
1305 3rd St S   Nampa ID 83651
Ph: 208-466-4641 ▪ Fx: 208-466-4677
www.nampa.com

Greater Pocatello Chamber of Commerce
343 W Center St   Pocatello ID 83204
Ph: 208-233-1525 ▪ Fx: 208-233-1527
www.pocatelloidaho.com

Sun Valley/Ketchum Chamber of Commerce
PO Box 2420   Sun Valley ID 83353
Ph: 208-726-3423 ▪ Fx: 208-726-4533 ▪ TF: 800-634-3347
www.visitsunvalley.com

Twin Falls Area Chamber of Commerce
858 Blue Lakes Blvd N   Twin Falls ID 83301
Ph: 208-733-3974 ▪ Fx: 208-733-9216 ▪ TF: 866-894-6325
www.twinfallschamber.com

ILLINOIS

Addison Association of Industry & Commerce
777 W Army Trail Rd Suite D   Addison IL 60101
Ph: 630-543-4300 ▪ Fx: 630-543-4355
www.addisonaic.org

Algonquin/Lake in the Hills Chamber of Commerce
106 S Main St   Algonquin IL 60102
Ph: 847-658-5300 ▪ Fx: 847-658-6546
www.algonquin-lith-chamber.com

Arlington Heights Chamber of Commerce
311 S Arlington Heights Rd   Arlington Heights IL 60005
Ph: 847-253-1703 ▪ Fx: 847-253-9133
www.arlingtonhtschamber.com

Greater Aurora Chamber of Commerce
40 W Downer Pl   Aurora IL 60506
Ph: 630-897-9214 ▪ Fx: 630-897-7002
www.aurorachamber.com

Deerfield Bannockburn & Riverwoods Chamber of Commerce
2101 N Waukegan Rd Suite 102   Bannockburn IL 60015
Ph: 847-945-4660 ▪ Fx: 847-940-0381
www.dbrchamber.com

Barrington Area Chamber of Commerce
325 N Hough St   Barrington IL 60010
Ph: 847-381-2525 ▪ Fx: 847-381-2540
www.barringtonchamber.com

Bartlett Chamber of Commerce
138 S Oak Ave   Bartlett IL 60103
Ph: 630-830-0324 ▪ Fx: 630-830-9724
www.bartlettchamber.com

Belvidere Area Chamber of Commerce
200 S State St   Belvidere IL 61008
Ph: 815-544-4357 ▪ Fx: 815-547-7654
www.belvidere.net/chamber

Berwyn Development Corp
3322 S Oak Pk Ave 2nd Fl   Berwyn IL 60402
Ph: 708-788-8100 ▪ Fx: 708-788-0966
www.berwyn.net

McLean County Chamber of Commerce
210 S East St   Bloomington IL 61702
Ph: 309-829-6344 ▪ Fx: 309-827-3940
www.mcleancochamber.org

Bolingbrook Chamber of Commerce & Industry
375 W Briarcliff Rd   Bolingbrook IL 60440
Ph: 630-226-8420 ▪ Fx: 630-759-9937
www.bolingbrook.org

Bradley-Bourbonnais Chamber of Commerce
1690 Newtown Dr   Bourbonnais IL 60914
Ph: 815-932-2222 ▪ Fx: 815-932-3294
www.bbchamber.com

Buffalo Grove Area Chamber of Commerce
50 1/2 Raupp Blvd   Buffalo Grove IL 60089
Ph: 847-541-7799 ▪ Fx: 847-541-7819
www.bgacc.org

Calumet City Chamber of Commerce
1243 Hirsch Ave   Calumet City IL 60409
Ph: 708-891-5888 ▪ Fx: 708-891-9451

Carbondale Chamber of Commerce
121 S Illinois Ave   Carbondale IL 62901
Ph: 618-549-2146 ▪ Fx: 618-529-5063
www.carbondalechamber.com

Champaign County Chamber of Commerce
1817 S Neil St Suite 201   Champaign IL 61820
Ph: 217-359-1791 ▪ Fx: 217-359-1809
www.ccchamber.com

Charleston Area Chamber of Commerce
501 Jackson Ave   Charleston IL 61920
Ph: 217-345-7041 ▪ Fx: 217-345-7042
www.charlestonchamber.com

Albany Park Chamber of Commerce
4745 N Kedzie Ave   Chicago IL 60625
Ph: 773-478-0202 ▪ Fx: 773-478-0282
www.kacm.com/albanypchamber.html

Chicagoland Chamber of Commerce
330 N Wabash Ave 1 IBM Plaza Suite 2800   Chicago IL 60611
Ph: 312-494-6700 ▪ Fx: 312-494-0196
www.chicagolandchamber.org

Cosmopolitan Chamber of Commerce
1455 S Michigan Ave Suite 220   Chicago IL 60605
Ph: 312-786-0212 ▪ Fx: 312-786-9079
www.cchamber.org

East Side Chamber of Commerce
3658 E 106th St   Chicago IL 60617
Ph: 773-721-7948 ▪ Fx: 773-721-7446

Hyde Park Chamber of Commerce
5211-D S Harper Ave   Chicago IL 60615
Ph: 773-288-0124 ▪ Fx: 773-288-0464
www.hpchamber.com

Jefferson Park Chamber of Commerce
4849 N Milwaukee Ave Suite 305   Chicago IL 60630
Ph: 773-736-6697 ▪ Fx: 773-736-3508
www.jeffersonpark.net

Lincoln Park Chamber of Commerce
2534 N Lincoln Ave Suite 234   Chicago IL 60614
Ph: 773-880-5200 ▪ Fx: 773-880-0266
www.lincolnparkchamber.com

Portage Park Chamber of Commerce
4805 W Irving Park Rd 2nd Fl   Chicago IL 60641
Ph: 773-777-2020 ▪ Fx: 773-777-0202

Uptown Chamber of Commerce
4753 N Broadway Suite 822   Chicago IL 60640
Ph: 773-878-1184 ▪ Fx: 773-878-3678
www.uptownchamber.com

Cicero Chamber of Commerce & Industry
5801 Cermak Rd   Cicero IL 60804
Ph: 708-863-6000 ▪ Fx: 708-863-8981
www.cicerochamber.org

Crete Area Chamber of Commerce
1182 Main St PO Box 263   Crete IL 60417
Ph: 708-672-9216 ▪ Fx: 708-672-7640
www.cretechamber.com

Crystal Lake Chamber of Commerce
427 Virginia St   Crystal Lake IL 60014
Ph: 815-459-1300 ▪ Fx: 815-459-0243
www.clchamber.com

Danville Area Chamber of Commerce
28 W North St Danville IL 61832
Ph: 217-442-1887 ▪ Fx: 217-442-1897

Chamber of Commerce for Decatur & Macon County
243 S Water St Suite 100 Decatur IL 62523
Ph: 217-422-2200 ▪ Fx: 217-422-4576 ▪ TF: 888-954-2550
www.decaturchamber.com

DeKalb Chamber of Commerce
164 E Lincoln Hwy DeKalb IL 60115
Ph: 815-756-6306 ▪ Fx: 815-756-5164
www.dekalb.org

Des Plaines Chamber of Commerce & Industry
1401 Oakton St Des Plaines IL 60018
Ph: 847-824-4200 ▪ Fx: 847-824-7932
www.dpchamber.com

Dolton Chamber of Commerce
PO Box 823 Dolton IL 60419
Ph: 708-841-4810 ▪ Fx: 708-841-4833

Downers Grove Area Chamber of Commerce
1015 Curtiss St Downers Grove IL 60515
Ph: 630-968-4050 ▪ Fx: 630-968-8368
www.downersgrove.org

Northern King County Chamber of Commerce
319 N River St East Dundee IL 60118
Ph: 847-426-8565 ▪ Fx: 847-426-1098

Greater East Saint Louis Chamber of Commerce
327 Missouri Ave Suite 602 East Saint Louis IL 62201
Ph: 618-271-2855 ▪ Fx: 618-271-4622
www.eaststlouischamber.org

Elgin Area Chamber of Commerce
31 S Grove Ave Elgin IL 60120
Ph: 847-741-5660 ▪ Fx: 847-741-5677
www.elginchamber.com

Greater O'Hare Association of Industry & Commerce
PO Box 1516 Elk Grove Village IL 60009
Ph: 630-350-2944 ▪ Fx: 630-350-2979
www.greater-ohare.com

Elmhurst Chamber of Commerce & Industry
PO Box 752 Elmhurst IL 60126
Ph: 630-834-6060 ▪ Fx: 630-834-6002
www.elmhurstchamber.org

Mont Clare-Elmwood Park Chamber of Commerce
11 Conti Pkwy Elmwood Park IL 60707
Ph: 708-456-8000 ▪ Fx: 708-456-8680
www.mcepchamber.org

Evanston Chamber of Commerce
1560 Sherman Ave Suite 860 Evanston IL 60201
Ph: 847-328-1500 ▪ Fx: 847-328-1510
www.evchamber.com

Evergreen Park Chamber of Commerce
3960 W 95 St 3rd Fl Evergreen Park IL 60805
Ph: 708-423-1118 ▪ Fx: 708-423-1859
www.everythingep.com/chamber

Freeport Area Chamber of Commerce
26 S Galena Ave Freeport IL 61032
Ph: 815-233-1350 ▪ Fx: 815-235-4038
www.freeportilchamber.com

Galesburg Area Chamber of Commerce
471 E Main St Galesburg IL 61401
Ph: 309-343-1194 ▪ Fx: 309-343-1195
www.galesburg.org

Glen Ellyn Chamber of Commerce
490 Pennsylvania Ave Glen Ellyn IL 60137
Ph: 630-469-0907 ▪ Fx: 630-469-0426
www.glenellynchamber.com

Glenview Chamber of Commerce
2320 Glenview Rd Glenview IL 60025
Ph: 847-724-0900 ▪ Fx: 847-724-0202
www.glenviewchamber.com

River Bend Growth Association
5800 Godfrey Rd Alden Hall Godfrey IL 62035
Ph: 618-467-2280 ▪ Fx: 618-466-8289
www.growthassociation.com

Chamber of Commerce of Southwestern Madison County
PO Box 370 Granite City IL 62040
Ph: 618-876-6400 ▪ Fx: 618-876-6448

Lake County Chamber of Commerce
5221 W Grand Ave Gurnee IL 60031
Ph: 847-249-3800 ▪ Fx: 847-249-3892
www.lakecounty-il.org

Highland Park Chamber of Commerce
508 Central Ave Suite 206 Highland Park IL 60035
Ph: 847-432-0284 ▪ Fx: 847-432-2802
www.highland-park.com

Hoffman Estates Chamber of Commerce
2200 W Higgins Rd Suite 201 Hoffman Estates IL 60195
Ph: 847-781-9100 ▪ Fx: 847-781-9172
www.hechamber.com

Chicago Southland Chamber of Commerce
1154 Ridge Rd Homewood IL 60430
Ph: 708-957-6950 ▪ Fx: 708-957-6968
www.chicagosouthland.com

Jacksonville Area Chamber of Commerce
155 W Morton Ave Jacksonville IL 62650
Ph: 217-245-2174 ▪ Fx: 217-245-0661
www.jacksonvilleil.org

Joliet Region Chamber of Commerce & Industry
63 N Chicago St Joliet IL 60432
Ph: 815-727-5371 ▪ Fx: 815-727-5374
www.jolietchamber.com

Joliet/Will County Center for Economic Development
116 N Chicago St Suite 101 Joliet IL 60432
Ph: 815-723-1800 ▪ Fx: 815-723-6972
www.willcountyced.com

Kankakee Area Chamber of Commerce
PO Box 905 Kankakee IL 60901
Ph: 815-933-7721 ▪ Fx: 815-933-7675
www.kankakee.org

West Suburban Chamber of Commerce
47 S 6th Ave La Grange IL 60525
Ph: 708-352-0494 ▪ Fx: 708-352-0620
www.westsuburbanchamber.org

Illinois Valley Area Chamber of Commerce & Economic Development
300 Bucklin St La Salle IL 61301
Ph: 815-223-0227 ▪ Fx: 815-223-4827
www.ivaced.org

Lake Zurich Area Chamber of Commerce
1 1st Bank Plaza Suite 304 Lake Zurich IL 60047
Ph: 847-438-5572 ▪ Fx: 847-438-5574
www.lzacc.com

Lansing Chamber of Commerce
3404 Lake St Lansing IL 60438
Ph: 708-474-4170

Green Oaks/Libertyville/Mundelein/Vernon Hills Area Chamber of Commerce & Industry
1123 S Milwaukee Ave Libertyville IL 60048
Ph: 847-680-0750 ▪ Fx: 847-680-0760
www.gcvchamber.org

Lincoln/Logan County Chamber of Commerce
303 S Kickapoo St Lincoln IL 62656
Ph: 217-735-2385 ▪ Fx: 217-735-9205
www.lincolnillinois.com

Lombard Area Chamber of Commerce
225 W St Charles Rd Lombard IL 60148
Ph: 630-627-5040 ▪ Fx: 630-627-5519
www.lombardchamber.com

Parks Chamber of Commerce
100 Heart Blvd Loves Park IL 61111
Ph: 815-633-3999 ▪ Fx: 815-633-4057
www.parkschamber.com

Macomb Area Chamber of Commerce
804 W Jackson St Macomb IL 61455
Ph: 309-837-4855 ▪ Fx: 309-837-4857
www.macomb.com/chamber

Greater Marion Area Chamber of Commerce
2305 W Main St Marion IL 62959
Ph: 618-997-6311 ▪ Fx: 618-997-4665 ▪ TF: 800-699-1760
www.marionillinois.com

Matteson Area Chamber of Commerce
PO Box 106 Matteson IL 60443
Ph: 708-747-6000 ▪ Fx: 708-747-6054
www.macclink.com

McHenry Area Chamber of Commerce
1257 N Green St McHenry IL 60050
Ph: 815-385-4300 ▪ Fx: 815-385-9142
www.mchenrychamber.com

Illinois Quad City Chamber of Commerce
622 19th St Moline IL 61265
Ph: 309-757-5416 ▪ Fx: 309-757-5435
www.quadcitychamber.com

Grundy County Chamber of Commerce & Industry
909 N Liberty St Morris IL 60450
Ph: 815-942-0113 ▪ Fx: 815-942-0117
www.grundychamber.com

Mount Prospect Chamber of Commerce
111 E Busse Ave Suite 601 Mount Prospect IL 60056
Ph: 847-398-6616 ▪ Fx: 847-398-6780
www.mountprospectchamber.org

Jefferson County Chamber of Commerce
PO Box 1047 Mount Vernon IL 62864
Ph: 618-242-5725 ▪ Fx: 618-242-5130
www.southernillinois.com

Naperville Area Chamber of Commerce
131 W Jefferson Ave Naperville IL 60540
Ph: 630-355-4141 ▪ Fx: 630-355-8335
www.naperville.net

Niles Chamber of Commerce
7900 N Milwaukee Ave Suite 225 Niles IL 60714
Ph: 847-966-7606 ▪ Fx: 847-966-7617
www.nileschamber.org

Northbrook Chamber of Commerce & Industry
2002 Walters Ave Northbrook IL 60062
Ph: 847-498-5555 ▪ Fx: 847-498-5510
www.northbrookchamber.org

Oak Forest Chamber of Commerce
15440 S Central Ave Oak Forest IL 60452
Ph: 708-687-4600 ▪ Fx: 708-687-7878
www.oakforest.org

Oak Lawn Chamber of Commerce
5314 W 95th St Oak Lawn IL 60453
Ph: 708-424-8300 ▪ Fx: 708-229-2236
www.oaklawnchamber.com

Oak Park-River Forest Chamber of Commerce
1110 North Blvd Oak Park IL 60301
Ph: 708-848-8151 ▪ Fx: 708-848-8182
www.oprfchamber.org

Orland Park Area Chamber of Commerce
8799 W 151 St Orland Park IL 60462
Ph: 708-349-2972 ▪ Fx: 708-349-7454
www.orlandparkchamber.org

Palatine Area Chamber of Commerce
625 N North Ct Suite 320 Palatine IL 60067
Ph: 847-359-7200 ▪ Fx: 847-359-7246
www.palatinechamber.com

Palatine Area Chamber of Commerce
625 N North Ct Suite 320 Palatine IL 60067
Ph: 847-359-7200 ▪ Fx: 847-359-7246
www.palatinechamber.com

Paris Area Chamber of Commerce
105 N Central Ave Paris IL 61944
Ph: 217-465-4179 ▪ Fx: 217-465-4170
www.parisilchamber.com

Park Ridge Chamber of Commerce
32 Main St Park Ridge IL 60068
Ph: 847-825-3121 ▪ Fx: 847-825-3122
www.parkridgeilchamber.com

Pekin Chamber of Commerce
PO Box 636 Pekin IL 61555
Ph: 309-346-2106 ▪ Fx: 309-346-2104
www.pekin.net

Peoria Area Chamber of Commerce
124 SW Adams St Suite 300 Peoria IL 61602
Ph: 309-676-0755 ▪ Fx: 309-676-7534
www.peoriachamber.org

Quincy Area Chamber of Commerce
300 Civic Ctr Plaza Suite 245 Quincy IL 62301
Ph: 217-222-7980 ▪ Fx: 217-222-3033
www.quincychamber.org

Rockford Area Chamber of Commerce
515 N Court St Rockford IL 61103
Ph: 815-987-8100 ▪ Fx: 815-987-8122
www.rockfordchamber.com

Rolling Meadows Chamber of Commerce
2775 Algonquin Rd Suite 230 Rolling Meadows IL 60008
Ph: 847-398-3730 ▪ Fx: 847-398-3745
www.rmchamber.org

Round Lake Area Chamber of Commerce & Industry
1777 N Cedar Lake Rd Round Lake IL 60073
Ph: 847-546-2002 ▪ Fx: 847-546-2254
www.rlchamber.org

Northwest & Schaumburg Association of Commerce & Industry
1450 E American Ln Suite 140 Schaumburg IL 60173
Ph: 847-517-7110 ▪ Fx: 847-517-7116
www.nsaci.org

Skokie Chamber of Commerce
PO Box 106 Skokie IL 60077
Ph: 847-673-0240 ▪ Fx: 847-673-0249
www.skokiechamber.org

Greater Springfield Chamber of Commerce
3 S Old State Capitol Plaza Springfield IL 62701
Ph: 217-525-1173 ▪ Fx: 217-525-8768
www.gscc.org

Illinois Association of Chamber of Commerce Executives
215 E Adams St Springfield IL 62701
Ph: 217-522-5512 ▪ Fx: 217-522-5518
www.iacce.org

Streamwood Chamber of Commerce
PO Box 545 Streamwood IL 60107
Ph: 630-837-5200 ▪ Fx: 630-837-5251
www.streamwoodchamber.com

Streator Area Chamber of Commerce www.streatoril.com
PO Box 360   Streator IL 61364
Ph: 815-672-2921 ▪ Fx: 815-672-1768

Tinley Park Chamber of Commerce www.tinleychamber.org
17316 S Oak Park Ave   Tinley Park IL 60477
Ph: 708-532-5700 ▪ Fx: 708-532-1475

Wheaton Chamber of Commerce www.ewheaton.com
108 E Wesley St   Wheaton IL 60187
Ph: 630-668-6464 ▪ Fx: 630-668-2744

Wheeling/Prospect Heights Area Chamber of Commerce & Industry www.wphchamber.com
395 E Dundee Rd Suite 300   Wheeling IL 60090
Ph: 847-541-0170 ▪ Fx: 847-541-0296

Wilmette Chamber of Commerce www.wilmettechamber.org
1150 Wilmette Ave Suite A   Wilmette IL 60091
Ph: 847-251-3800 ▪ Fx: 847-251-6321

Woodridge Chamber of Commerce www.woodridgechamber.org
5 Plaza Dr Suite 212   Woodridge IL 60517
Ph: 630-852-9878 ▪ Fx: 630-719-4906

Woodstock Chamber of Commerce & Industry www.woodstockilchamber.com
136 Cass St   Woodstock IL 60098
Ph: 815-338-2436 ▪ Fx: 815-338-2927

Chicago Ridge-Worth Chamber of Commerce
PO Box 356   Worth IL 60482
Ph: 708-923-2050 ▪ Fx: 708-229-2115

INDIANA

Chamber of Commerce for Anderson & Madison County www.andersoninchamber.com
PO Box 469   Anderson IN 46015
Ph: 765-642-0264 ▪ Fx: 765-642-0266

Angola Area Chamber of Commerce www.angolachamber.org
211 E Maumee St Suite B   Angola IN 46703
Ph: 260-665-3512 ▪ Fx: 260-665-7418

Auburn Chamber of Commerce www.chamberinauburn.com
208 S Jackson St   Auburn IN 46706
Ph: 260-925-2100 ▪ Fx: 260-925-2199

Greater Bloomington Chamber of Commerce www.chamber.bloomington.in.us
400 W 7th St Suite 102   Bloomington IN 47404
Ph: 812-336-6381 ▪ Fx: 812-336-0651

Warrick County Chamber of Commerce
224 W Main St   Boonville IN 47601
Ph: 812-897-2340 ▪ Fx: 812-897-2360

Carmel-Clay Chamber of Commerce www.carmelchamber.com
41 E Main St   Carmel IN 46032
Ph: 317-846-1049 ▪ Fx: 317-844-6843

Columbia City Area Chamber of Commerce www.columbiacity.org
PO Box 166   Columbia City IN 46725
Ph: 260-248-8131 ▪ Fx: 260-248-8162

Columbus Area Chamber of Commerce www.columbusareachamber.com
500 Franklin St   Columbus IN 47201
Ph: 812-379-4457 ▪ Fx: 812-378-7308

Connersville/Fayette County Chamber of Commerce
504 Central Ave   Connersville IN 47331
Ph: 765-825-2561 ▪ Fx: 765-825-4613

Chamber of Commerce of Harrison County www.tourindiana.com
310 N Elm St   Corydon IN 47112
Ph: 812-738-2137 ▪ Fx: 812-738-6438

Crawfordsville-Montgomery County Chamber of Commerce www.crawfordsvillechamber.com
309 N Green St   Crawfordsville IN 47933
Ph: 765-362-6800 ▪ Fx: 765-362-6900

Greater Elkhart Chamber of Commerce www.elkhart.org
418 S Main St   Elkhart IN 46516
Ph: 574-293-1531 ▪ Fx: 574-294-1859

Metropolitan Evansville Chamber of Commerce www.evansvillechamber.com
100 NW 2nd St Suite 100   Evansville IN 47708
Ph: 812-425-8147 ▪ Fx: 812-421-5883

Greater Fort Wayne Chamber of Commerce www.fwchamber.org
826 Ewing St   Fort Wayne IN 46802
Ph: 260-424-1435 ▪ Fx: 260-426-7232

Clinton County Chamber of Commerce www.ccinchamber.org
259 E Walnut St   Frankfort IN 46041
Ph: 765-654-5507 ▪ Fx: 765-654-9592

Gary Chamber of Commerce www.garychamber.com
504 Broadway Suite 328   Gary IN 46402
Ph: 219-885-7407 ▪ Fx: 219-885-7408

Goshen Chamber of Commerce www.goshen.org
232 S Main St   Goshen IN 46526
Ph: 574-533-2102 ▪ Fx: 574-533-2103 ▪ TF: 800-307-4204

Greencastle Chamber of Commerce www.gogreencastle.com
2 S Jackson St   Greencastle IN 46135
Ph: 765-653-4517 ▪ Fx: 765-653-6385

Greater Greenwood Chamber of Commerce www.greenwood-chamber.com
550 US 31 S   Greenwood IN 46142
Ph: 317-888-4856 ▪ Fx: 317-865-2609

Lakeshore Chamber of Commerce www.lakeshorechamber.com
5246 Hohman Ave Suite 100   Hammond IN 46320
Ph: 219-931-1000 ▪ Fx: 219-937-8778

Indianapolis Chamber of Commerce www.indychamber.com
111 Monument Cir Suite 1950   Indianapolis IN 46204
Ph: 317-464-2200 ▪ Fx: 317-464-2217

Lawrence Township Chamber of Commerce
9120 Otis Ave Suite 100   Indianapolis IN 46216
Ph: 317-541-9876 ▪ Fx: 317-546-5106

Kokomo/Howard County Chamber of Commerce www.kokomochamber.com
325 N Main St   Kokomo IN 46901
Ph: 765-457-5301 ▪ Fx: 765-452-4564

Lafayette-West Lafayette Chamber of Commerce www.lafayettechamber.com
337 Columbia St   Lafayette IN 47901
Ph: 765-742-4041 ▪ Fx: 765-742-6276

Lafayette-West Lafayette Chamber of Commerce www.lafayettechamber.com
337 Columbia St   Lafayette IN 47901
Ph: 765-742-4041 ▪ Fx: 765-742-6276

LaGrange County Chamber of Commerce www.lagrangechamber.org
901 S Detroit St Suite A   LaGrange IN 46761
Ph: 260-463-2443 ▪ Fx: 260-463-2683

Dearborn County Chamber of Commerce www.dearborncountychamber.org
555 Eads Pkwy E Suite 1715   Lawrenceburg IN 47025
Ph: 812-537-0814 ▪ Fx: 812-537-0845 ▪ TF: 800-322-8198

Boone County Chamber of Commerce www.boonechamber.org
221 N Lebanon St   Lebanon IN 46052
Ph: 765-482-1320 ▪ Fx: 765-482-3114

Logansport/Cass County Chamber of Commerce www.logan-casschamber.com
300 E Broadway Suite 103   Logansport IN 46947
Ph: 574-753-6388 ▪ Fx: 574-735-0909 ▪ TF: 800-425-2071

Madison Area Chamber of Commerce www.madisonchamber.org
975 Industrial Dr   Madison IN 47250
Ph: 812-265-3135 ▪ Fx: 812-265-5544

Marion-Grant County Chamber of Commerce www.marionchamber.org
215 S Adams St   Marion IN 46952
Ph: 765-664-5107 ▪ Fx: 765-668-5443

Merrillville Chamber of Commerce www.merrillvillecoc.com
255 W 80th Pl   Merrillville IN 46410
Ph: 219-769-8180 ▪ Fx: 219-736-6223

Michigan City Area Chamber of Commerce www.michigancitychamber.com
200 E Michigan Blvd   Michigan City IN 46360
Ph: 219-874-6221 ▪ Fx: 219-873-1204

Greater Monticello Chamber of Commerce www.monticelloin.com
PO Box 657   Monticello IN 47960
Ph: 574-583-7220 ▪ Fx: 574-583-3399

Mount Vernon Area Chamber of Commerce www.mtvernonposeycochamber.com
915 E 4th St   Mount Vernon IN 47620
Ph: 812-838-3639 ▪ Fx: 812-838-6358

Muncie-Delaware County Chamber of Commerce www.muncie.com
401 S High St   Muncie IN 47305
Ph: 765-288-6681 ▪ Fx: 765-751-9151 ▪ TF: 800-336-1373

Southern Indiana Chamber of Commerce www.sicc.org
4100 Charlestown Rd   New Albany IN 47150
Ph: 812-945-0266 ▪ Fx: 812-948-4664

Noblesville Chamber of Commerce www.noblesvillechamber.com
54 N 9th St Suite 100   Noblesville IN 46060
Ph: 317-773-0086 ▪ Fx: 317-773-1966

Jennings County Chamber of Commerce
265 E Main St PO Box 340   North Vernon IN 47265
Ph: 812-346-2339 ▪ Fx: 812-346-2065

Peru/Miami County Chamber of Commerce www.miamicochamber.com
13 E Main St   Peru IN 46970
Ph: 765-472-1923 ▪ Fx: 765-472-7099

Greater Portage Chamber of Commerce www.portageindianachamber.com
2642 Eleanor St   Portage IN 46368
Ph: 219-762-3300 ▪ Fx: 219-763-2450

Richmond-Wayne County Chamber of Commerce www.rwchamber.org
33 S 7th St Suite 2   Richmond IN 47374
Ph: 765-962-1511 ▪ Fx: 765-966-0882

Schererville Chamber of Commerce www.scherervillechamber.com
105 E Joliet St   Schererville IN 46375
Ph: 219-322-5412 ▪ Fx: 219-322-0598

Shelby County Chamber of Commerce www.shelbychamber.net
33 E Washington St   Shelbyville IN 46176
Ph: 317-398-6647 ▪ Fx: 317-392-3901 ▪ TF: 800-223-2210

Chamber of Commerce of Saint Joseph County www.sjchamber.org
PO Box 1677   South Bend IN 46634
Ph: 574-234-0051 ▪ Fx: 574-289-0358

Winchester Area Chamber of Commerce www.winchesterchamber.org
112 W Washington St   Winchester IN 47394
Ph: 765-584-3731 ▪ Fx: 765-584-5544

IOWA

Ames Chamber of Commerce www.chamber.ames.ia.us
1601 Golden Aspen Dr Suite 110   Ames IA 50010
Ph: 515-232-2310 ▪ Fx: 515-232-6716

Bettendorf Chamber of Commerce www.bettendorfchamber.com
2117 State St   Bettendorf IA 52722
Ph: 563-355-4753 ▪ Fx: 563-355-7913

Burlington/West Burlington Area Chamber of Commerce www.growburlington.com
610 N 4th St Suite 200   Burlington IA 52601
Ph: 319-752-6365 ▪ Fx: 319-752-6454 ▪ TF: 800-827-4837

Cedar Falls Chamber of Commerce www.cedarfalls.org
10 Main St   Cedar Falls IA 50613
Ph: 319-266-3593 ▪ Fx: 319-277-4325

Cedar Rapids Area Chamber of Commerce www.cedarrapids.org
424 1st Ave NE   Cedar Rapids IA 52401
Ph: 319-398-5317 ▪ Fx: 319-398-5228

Clinton Area Chamber of Commerce www.clintonia.com
PO Box 1024   Clinton IA 52733
Ph: 563-242-5702 ▪ Fx: 563-242-5803

Council Bluffs Chamber of Commerce www.councilbluffsiowa.com
7 N 6th St   Council Bluffs IA 51503
Ph: 712-325-1000 ▪ Fx: 712-322-5698 ▪ TF: 800-228-6878

Davenport Chamber of Commerce www.davenportone.com
130 W 2nd St   Davenport IA 52801
Ph: 563-322-1706 ▪ Fx: 563-322-7804

Greater Des Moines Partnership www.desmoinesmetro.com
700 Locust St Suite 100   Des Moines IA 50309
Ph: 515-286-4950 ▪ Fx: 515-286-4974 ▪ TF: 800-376-9059

Dubuque Area Chamber of Commerce www.dubuquechamber.com
PO Box 705   Dubuque IA 52004
Ph: 563-557-9200 ▪ Fx: 563-557-1591 ▪ TF: 800-798-4748

Fort Dodge Chamber of Commerce   www.fortdodgechamber.com
1406 Central Ave   Fort Dodge IA 50501
Ph: 515-955-5500 ▪ Fx: 515-955-3245

Iowa City Area Chamber of Commerce   www.iowacityarea.com
325 E Washington St Suite 100   Iowa City IA 52244
Ph: 319-337-9637 ▪ Fx: 319-338-9958

Keokuk Area Chamber of Commerce
329 Main St   Keokuk IA 52632
Ph: 319-524-5055 ▪ Fx: 319-524-5016

Marion Chamber of Commerce   www.cedarrapids.org/region/marion.asp
790 11th St   Marion IA 52302
Ph: 319-377-6316 ▪ Fx: 319-377-1576

Marshalltown Area Chamber of Commerce   www.marshalltown.org
PO Box 1000   Marshalltown IA 50158
Ph: 641-753-6645 ▪ Fx: 641-752-8373

Mason City Area Chamber of Commerce   www.masoncityia.com
15 W State St   Mason City IA 50401
Ph: 641-423-5724 ▪ Fx: 641-423-5725

Ottumwa Area Chamber of Commerce   www.ottumwaiowa.com
PO Box 308   Ottumwa IA 52501
Ph: 641-682-3465 ▪ Fx: 641-682-3466 ▪ TF: 800-564-5274

Siouxland Chamber of Commerce   www.siouxlandchamber.com
101 Pierce St   Sioux City IA 51101
Ph: 712-255-7903 ▪ Fx: 712-258-7578

Urbandale Chamber of Commerce   www.urbandalechamber.com
3600 86th St   Urbandale IA 50322
Ph: 515-331-6855 ▪ Fx: 515-278-3927

Waterloo Chamber of Commerce   www.waterloochamber.org
315 E 5th St   Waterloo IA 50703
Ph: 319-233-8431 ▪ Fx: 319-233-4580

West Des Moines Chamber of Commerce   www.wdmchamber.org
4200 Mills Civic Pkwy Suite E100   West Des Moines IA 50266
Ph: 515-225-6009 ▪ Fx: 515-225-7129

KANSAS

Arkansas City Area Chamber of Commerce   www.arkcity.org
PO Box 795   Arkansas City KS 67005
Ph: 620-442-0230 ▪ Fx: 620-441-0048

Dodge City Area Chamber of Commerce   www.dodgechamber.com
311 W Spruce St   Dodge City KS 67801
Ph: 620-227-3119 ▪ Fx: 620-227-2957

Emporia Area Chamber of Commerce   www.emporia.com
PO Box 703   Emporia KS 66801
Ph: 620-342-1600 ▪ Fx: 620-342-3223

Garden City Area Chamber of Commerce   www.gardencity.net/chamber
1511 E Fulton Terr   Garden City KS 67846
Ph: 620-276-3264 ▪ Fx: 620-276-3290

Hutchinson/Reno County Chamber of Commerce   www.hutchchamber.com
117 N Walnut St   Hutchinson KS 67501
Ph: 620-662-3391 ▪ Fx: 620-662-2168 ▪ TF: 800-691-4262

Junction City Area Chamber of Commerce   www.junctioncity.org/chamber
814 N Washington St   Junction City KS 66441
Ph: 785-762-2632 ▪ Fx: 785-762-3353

Kansas City Kansas Area Chamber of Commerce   www.kckchamber.com
PO Box 171337   Kansas City KS 66117
Ph: 913-371-3070 ▪ Fx: 913-371-3732

Women's Chamber of Commerce
PO Box 171337   Kansas City KS 66117
Ph: 913-371-3165 ▪ Fx: 913-371-3732

Leavenworth-Lansing Area Chamber of Commerce   www.lvarea.com/LLCofC.htm
518 Shawnee St   Leavenworth KS 66048
Ph: 913-682-4112 ▪ Fx: 913-682-8170

Lenexa Chamber of Commerce   www.lenexa.org
11180 Lackman Rd   Lenexa KS 66219
Ph: 913-888-1414 ▪ Fx: 913-888-3770

Liberal Area Chamber of Commerce   www.liberalkschamber.com
PO Box 676   Liberal KS 67901
Ph: 620-624-3855 ▪ Fx: 620-624-8851

Manhattan Chamber of Commerce   www.manhattan.org
501 Poyntz Ave   Manhattan KS 66502
Ph: 785-776-8829 ▪ Fx: 785-776-0679 ▪ TF: 800-759-0134

Olathe Area Chamber of Commerce   www.olathe.com
PO Box 98   Olathe KS 66051
Ph: 913-764-1050 ▪ Fx: 913-782-4636 ▪ TF: 800-921-5678

Overland Park Chamber of Commerce   www.opks.org
9001 W 110th St Suite 150   Overland Park KS 66210
Ph: 913-491-3600 ▪ Fx: 913-491-0393

Pittsburg Area Chamber of Commerce   www.pittsburgkschamber.com
PO Box 1115   Pittsburg KS 66762
Ph: 620-231-1000 ▪ Fx: 620-231-3178 ▪ TF: 800-879-1112

Salina Area Chamber of Commerce   www.salinakansas.org
120 W Ash St   Salina KS 67401
Ph: 785-827-9301 ▪ Fx: 785-827-9758

Shawnee Area Chamber of Commerce   www.shawneekschamber.com
15100 W 67th St Suite 202   Shawnee KS 66217
Ph: 913-631-6545 ▪ Fx: 913-631-9628 ▪ TF: 888-550-7282

Greater Topeka Chamber of Commerce   www.topekachamber.org
120 SE 6th St Suite 110   Topeka KS 66603
Ph: 785-234-2644 ▪ Fx: 785-234-8656

Wichita Area Chamber of Commerce   www.wichitakansas.org
350 W Douglas Ave   Wichita KS 67202
Ph: 316-265-7771 ▪ Fx: 316-265-7502

KENTUCKY

Ashland Alliance Chamber of Commerce   www.ashlandalliance.com
PO Box 830   Ashland KY 41105
Ph: 606-324-5111 ▪ Fx: 606-325-4607 ▪ TF: 888-524-6860

Knox County Chamber of Commerce   www.knoxcochamber.com
196 Daniel Boone Dr Suite 205   Barbourville KY 40906
Ph: 606-546-4300

Bardstown-Nelson County Chamber of Commerce   www.bardstownchamber.com
201 E Stephen Foster Ave   Bardstown KY 40004
Ph: 502-348-9545 ▪ Fx: 502-348-6478 ▪ TF: 866-894-9545

Marshall County Chamber of Commerce   www.marshallcounty.net
17 US Hwy 68 W   Benton KY 42025
Ph: 270-527-7665 ▪ Fx: 270-527-9193

Bowling Green Area Chamber of Commerce   www.bgchamber.com
812 State St   Bowling Green KY 42101
Ph: 270-781-3200 ▪ Fx: 270-843-0458

Danville-Boyle County Chamber of Commerce   www.danville-ky.com
304 S 4th St   Danville KY 40422
Ph: 859-236-2361 ▪ Fx: 859-236-3197

Elizabethtown-Hardin County Chamber of Commerce   www.elizabethtownchamber.org
111 W Dixie Ave   Elizabethtown KY 42701
Ph: 270-765-4334 ▪ Fx: 270-737-0690

Northern Kentucky Chamber of Commerce   www.nkychamber.com
PO Box 17416   Fort Mitchell KY 41017
Ph: 859-578-8800 ▪ Fx: 859-578-8802

Frankfort Area Chamber of Commerce   www.frankfortky.org
100 Capitol Ave   Frankfort KY 40601
Ph: 502-223-8261 ▪ Fx: 502-223-5942

Georgetown-Scott County Chamber of Commerce   www.gtown.org
160 E Main St   Georgetown KY 40324
Ph: 502-863-5424 ▪ Fx: 502-863-5756

Glasgow-Barren County Chamber of Commerce   www.glasgowbarrenchamber.com
118 E Public Sq   Glasgow KY 42141
Ph: 270-651-3161 ▪ Fx: 270-651-3122 ▪ TF: 800-264-3161

Greenville-Muhlenberg County Chamber of Commerce
PO Box 313   Greenville KY 42345
Ph: 270-338-5422 ▪ Fx: 270-338-5440

Harlan County Chamber of Commerce
PO Box 268   Harlan KY 40831
Ph: 606-573-4717 ▪ Fx: 606-573-4717

Henderson-Henderson County Chamber of Commerce   www.hendersonky.com
201 N Main St   Henderson KY 42420
Ph: 270-826-9531 ▪ Fx: 270-827-4461

Hopkinsville-Christian County Chamber of Commerce   www.commercecenter.org/chamber.htm
PO Box 1382   Hopkinsville KY 42241
Ph: 270-885-9096 ▪ Fx: 270-886-2059 ▪ TF: 800-842-9959

Jeffersontown Chamber of Commerce   www.jtownchamber.com
10434 Watterson Tr   Jeffersontown KY 40299
Ph: 502-267-1674 ▪ Fx: 502-267-6874

Oldham County Chamber of Commerce   www.oldhamcountychamber.com
PO Box 366   LaGrange KY 40031
Ph: 502-222-1635 ▪ Fx: 502-222-3159 ▪ TF: 800-813-9953

Greater Lexington Chamber of Commerce   www.lexchamber.com
330 E Main St Suite 100   Lexington KY 40507
Ph: 859-254-4447 ▪ Fx: 859-233-3304

Greater Louisville Inc   www.greaterlouisville.com
614 W Main St   Louisville KY 40202
Ph: 502-625-0000 ▪ Fx: 502-625-0010 ▪ TF: 800-500-1066

Madisonville-Hopkins County Chamber of Commerce   www.hopkinschamber.com
15 E Center St   Madisonville KY 42431
Ph: 270-821-3435 ▪ Fx: 270-821-9190

Mayfield-Graves County Chamber of Commerce   www.mayfieldchamber.com
201 E College St   Mayfield KY 42066
Ph: 270-247-6101 ▪ Fx: 270-247-6110

Bell County Chamber of Commerce   www.bellcountyworks.com
N 20th St   Middlesboro KY 40965
Ph: 606-248-1075 ▪ Fx: 606-248-8851

Murray-Calloway County Chamber of Commerce   www.murraylink.com
805 N 12th St   Murray KY 42071
Ph: 270-753-5171 ▪ Fx: 270-753-0948 ▪ TF: 800-900-5171

Jessamine County Chamber of Commerce
508 N Main St Sutie 1   Nicholasville KY 40356
Ph: 859-887-4351 ▪ Fx: 859-887-1211

Owensboro-Daviess County Chamber of Commerce   www.owensboro.com
PO Box 825   Owensboro KY 42302
Ph: 270-926-1860 ▪ Fx: 270-926-3364

Paducah Area Chamber of Commerce   www.paducahchamber.org
PO Box 810   Paducah KY 42002
Ph: 270-443-1746 ▪ Fx: 270-442-9152

Pike County Chamber of Commerce   www.pikecountychamber.org
787 Hambley Blvd   Pikeville KY 41501
Ph: 606-432-5504 ▪ Fx: 606-432-7295

Radcliff Hardin Chamber of Commerce   www.radcliffchamber.org
306 N Wilson Rd   Radcliff KY 40160
Ph: 270-351-4450 ▪ Fx: 270-352-4449

Logan County Chamber of Commerce   www.loganchamber.com
116 S Main St   Russellville KY 42276
Ph: 270-726-2206 ▪ Fx: 270-726-2237

Shelby County Chamber of Commerce   www.shelbycountykychamber.com
316 Main St   Shelbyville KY 40065
Ph: 502-633-1636 ▪ Fx: 502-633-7501

Bullitt County Chamber of Commerce   www.bullittcounty.org
229A Lees Valley Rd   Shepherdsville KY 40165
Ph: 502-543-6727 ▪ Fx: 502-543-1765

Somerset-Pulaski County Chamber of Commerce   www.spcchamber.com
209 E Mt Vernon St   Somerset KY 42502
Ph: 606-679-7323 ▪ Fx: 606-678-4099

Letcher County Chamber of Commerce   www.letchercountychamber.com
317 Main St Suite C   Whitesburg KY 41858
Ph: 606-633-0310 ▪ Fx: 606-632-9965

Appendix

Winchester-Clark County Chamber of Commerce — www.winchesterky.com/chamber
2 S Maple St   Winchester KY 40391
Ph: 859-744-6420 ▪ Fx: 859-744-9229

LOUISIANA

Central Louisiana Chamber of Commerce — www.cenlachamber.org
1118 3rd St PO Box 992   Alexandria LA 71309
Ph: 318-442-6671 ▪ Fx: 318-442-6734

Bastrop-Morehouse Parish Chamber of Commerce — www.bastrop-morehouse.com
110 N Franklin St   Bastrop LA 71220
Ph: 318-281-3794 ▪ Fx: 318-281-3781

Greater Baton Rouge Chamber of Commerce — www.brchamber.org
564 Laurel St   Baton Rouge LA 70801
Ph: 225-381-7125 ▪ Fx: 225-336-4306

Bossier Chamber of Commerce — www.bossierchamber.com
710 Benton Rd   Bossier City LA 71111
Ph: 318-746-0252 ▪ Fx: 318-746-0357

Saint Tammany West Chamber of Commerce — www.sttammanychamber.com
201 Holiday Blvd Suite 108   Covington LA 70433
Ph: 985-892-3216 ▪ Fx: 985-893-4244 ▪ TF: 888-826-6269

Greater Denham Springs Chamber of Commerce — www.denhamspringschamber.com
PO Box 591   Denham Springs LA 70727
Ph: 225-665-8155 ▪ Fx: 225-665-2411

Greater Beauregard Chamber of Commerce — www.beauregardchamber.com
PO Box 309   DeRidder LA 70634
Ph: 337-463-5533 ▪ Fx: 337-463-2244

Ascension Chamber of Commerce — www.ascensionchamber.com
PO Box 1204   Gonzales LA 70707
Ph: 225-647-7487 ▪ Fx: 225-647-5124

Houma-Terrebonne Chamber of Commerce — www.houmachamber.com
6133 Hwy 311   Houma LA 70360
Ph: 985-876-5600 ▪ Fx: 985-876-5611

Greater Jennings Chamber of Commerce — www.jenningschamber.com
414 N Cary Ave   Jennings LA 70546
Ph: 337-824-0933 ▪ Fx: 337-824-0934

Greater Lafayette Chamber of Commerce — www.lafchamber.org
804 E St Mary Blvd   Lafayette LA 70505
Ph: 337-233-2705 ▪ Fx: 337-234-8671

Chamber/Southwest Louisiana — www.chamberswla.org
120 W Pujo St   Lake Charles LA 70601
Ph: 337-433-3632 ▪ Fx: 337-436-3727

Chamber of Commerce of Lafourche & the Bayou Region — www.lafourchechamber.com
PO Box 1462   Larose LA 70373
Ph: 985-693-6700 ▪ Fx: 985-693-6702

Greater Vernon Chamber of Commerce — www.leesville-vernon.org
PO Box 1228   Leesville LA 71496
Ph: 337-238-0349 ▪ Fx: 337-238-0340

DeSoto Parish Chamber of Commerce — desotoparishchamber.net
PO Box 928   Mansfield LA 71052
Ph: 318-872-1310 ▪ Fx: 318-871-1875

Monroe Chamber of Commerce — www.monroe.org
212 Walnut St Suite 10.   Monroe LA 71201
Ph: 318-323-3461 ▪ Fx: 318-322-7594 ▪ TF: 888-531-9535

East Parish Chamber of Commerce
PO Box 2606   Morgan City LA 70381
Ph: 985-384-3830 ▪ Fx: 985-384-0771

Natchitoches Area Chamber of Commerce — www.natchitocheschamber.com
PO Box 3   Natchitoches LA 71458
Ph: 318-352-6894 ▪ Fx: 318-352-5385

Greater Iberia Chamber of Commerce — www.iberia.org
111 W Main St   New Iberia LA 70560
Ph: 337-364-1836 ▪ Fx: 337-367-7405

New Orleans Regional Chamber of Commerce — www.norcc.org
601 Poydras St Suite 1700   New Orleans LA 70130
Ph: 504-527-6900 ▪ Fx: 504-527-6950

Iberville Parish Chamber of Commerce — www.ibervillechamber.com
23675 Church St   Plaquemine LA 70764
Ph: 225-687-3560 ▪ Fx: 225-687-3575 ▪ TF: 888-687-3560

Ruston/Lincoln Chamber of Commerce — www.rustonlincoln.org
PO Box 1383   Ruston LA 71273
Ph: 318-255-2031 ▪ Fx: 318-255-3481 ▪ TF: 800-392-9032

Greater Shreveport Chamber of Commerce — www.shreveportchamber.org
400 Edwards St   Shreveport LA 71101
Ph: 318-677-2500 ▪ Fx: 318-677-2541 ▪ TF: 800-448-5432

Greater Slidell Area Chamber of Commerce — www.slidellchamber.com
118 W Hall Ave   Slidell LA 70460
Ph: 985-643-5678 ▪ Fx: 985-649-2460 ▪ TF: 800-471-3758

Thibodaux Chamber of Commerce — www.thibodauxchamber.com
318 E Bayou Rd PO Box 467   Thibodaux LA 70302
Ph: 985-446-1187 ▪ Fx: 985-446-1191

MAINE

Kennebec Valley Chamber of Commerce — www.augustamaine.com
PO Box 676   Augusta ME 04332
Ph: 207-623-4559 ▪ Fx: 207-626-9342

Bangor Region Chamber of Commerce — www.bangorregion.com
PO Box 1443   Bangor ME 04402
Ph: 207-947-0307 ▪ Fx: 207-990-1427

Bar Harbor Chamber of Commerce — www.barharborinfo.com
93 Cottage St PO Box 158   Bar Harbor ME 04609
Ph: 207-288-5103 ▪ Fx: 207-288-2565 ▪ TF: 888-540-9990

Chamber of Commerce of the Bath-Brunswick Region — www.midcoastmaine.com
45 Front St   Bath ME 04530
Ph: 207-443-9751 ▪ Fx: 207-442-0808

Belfast Area Chamber of Commerce — www.belfastmaine.org
PO Box 58   Belfast ME 04915
Ph: 207-338-5900 ▪ Fx: 207-338-3511

Chamber of Commerce of the Bath-Brunswick Region — www.midcoastmaine.com
59 Pleasant St   Brunswick ME 04011
Ph: 207-725-8797 ▪ Fx: 207-725-9787 ▪ TF: 800-725-8797

Calais Regional Chamber of Commerce — www.visitcalais.com
PO Box 368   Calais ME 04619
Ph: 207-454-2308 ▪ Fx: 207-454-2308 ▪ TF: 888-422-3112

Ellsworth Area Chamber of Commerce — www.ellsworthchamber.org
PO Box 267   Ellsworth ME 04605
Ph: 207-667-5584 ▪ Fx: 207-667-2617

Androscoggin County Chamber of Commerce — www.androscoggincounty.com
PO Box 59   Lewiston ME 04243
Ph: 207-783-2249 ▪ Fx: 207-783-4481

Greater Lincoln Lakes Region Chamber of Commerce — www.lincolnmechamber.org
63 Main St   Lincoln ME 04457
Ph: 207-794-8065 ▪ Fx: 207-794-2606 ▪ TF: 888-794-8065

Greater Portland Chambers of Commerce — www.portlandregion.com
60 Pearl St   Portland ME 04101
Ph: 207-772-2811 ▪ Fx: 207-772-1179

Biddeford-Saco Chamber of Commerce & Industry — www.biddefordsacochamber.org
110 Main St Suite 1202   Saco ME 04072
Ph: 207-282-1567 ▪ Fx: 207-282-3149

Sanford-Springvale Chamber of Commerce — www.sanfordchamber.org
917 Main St Suite B   Sanford ME 04073
Ph: 207-324-4280 ▪ Fx: 207-324-8290

Oxford Hills Chamber of Commerce — www.oxfordhillsmaine.com
PO Box 167   South Paris ME 04281
Ph: 207-743-2281 ▪ Fx: 207-743-0687

Mid-Maine Chamber of Commerce — www.midmainechamber.com
1 Post Office Sq   Waterville ME 04901
Ph: 207-873-3315 ▪ Fx: 207-877-0087

MARYLAND

Annapolis & Anne Arundel County Chamber of Commerce — www.annapolischamber.com
151 West St Suite 101   Annapolis MD 21401
Ph: 410-268-7676 ▪ Fx: 410-268-2317

Baltimore City Chamber of Commerce — www.pe.net/~rksnow/mdcountybaltimorecha.htm
3 W Baltimore St   Baltimore MD 21201
Ph: 410-837-7101 ▪ Fx: 410-837-7104

Eastern Baltimore Area Chamber of Commerce — www.baltcountycc.com
7835 Eastern Ave Suite 302   Baltimore MD 21224
Ph: 410-282-9100 ▪ Fx: 410-284-9864

Harford County Chamber of Commerce — www.harfordchamber.com
108 S Bond St   Bel Air MD 21014
Ph: 410-838-2020 ▪ Fx: 410-893-4715 ▪ TF: 800-682-8536

Greater Bethesda-Chevy Chase Chamber of Commerce — www.bccchamber.org
7910 Woodmont Ave Suite 1204   Bethesda MD 20814
Ph: 301-652-4900 ▪ Fx: 301-657-1973

Greater Bowie Chamber of Commerce — www.bowiechamber.org
6770 Race Track Rd   Bowie MD 20715
Ph: 301-262-0920 ▪ Fx: 301-262-0921

Dorchester County Chamber of Commerce — www.dorchesterchamber.org
528 Poplar St   Cambridge MD 21613
Ph: 410-228-3575 ▪ Fx: 410-228-6848

Queen Anne's County Chamber of Commerce — www.qacchamber.com
PO Box 511   Chester MD 21619
Ph: 410-643-8530 ▪ Fx: 410-643-8477

Howard County Chamber of Commerce — www.howardchamber.com
5560 Sterrett Pl Suite 105   Columbia MD 21044
Ph: 410-730-4111 ▪ Fx: 410-730-4584

Crofton Chamber of Commerce — www.croftonchamber.com
PO Box 4146   Crofton MD 21114
Ph: 410-721-9131 ▪ Fx: 410-721-0785

Allegany County Chamber of Commerce — www.alleganycountychamber.com
24 Frederick St   Cumberland MD 21502
Ph: 301-722-2820 ▪ Fx: 301-722-5995

Caroline County Chamber of Commerce
PO Box 494   Denton MD 21629
Ph: 410-479-4638 ▪ Fx: 410-479-5551

Talbot County Chamber of Commerce — www.talbotchamber.org
PO Box 1366   Easton MD 21601
Ph: 410-822-4606 ▪ Fx: 410-822-7922

Cecil County Chamber of Commerce — www.cecilchamber.com
PO Box 96   Elkton MD 21922
Ph: 410-392-3833 ▪ Fx: 410-392-6225

Essex-Middle River-White Marsh Chamber of Commerce — www.emrchamber.org
435C Eastern Blvd   Essex MD 21221
Ph: 410-686-2233 ▪ Fx: 410-687-9081

Frederick County Chamber of Commerce — frederickchamber.org
43A S Market St   Frederick MD 21701
Ph: 301-662-4164 ▪ Fx: 301-846-4427

Gaithersburg-Germantown Chamber of Commerce — www.ggchamber.org
4 Professional Dr Suite 132   Gaithersburg MD 20879
Ph: 301-840-1400 ▪ Fx: 301-963-3918

Northern Anne Arundel County Chamber of Commerce — www.naaccc.com
7477 Baltimore-Annapolis Blvd Suite 203   Glen Burnie MD 21061
Ph: 410-766-8282 ▪ Fx: 410-766-5722

Hagerstown-Washington County Chamber of Commerce — www.hagerstown.org
111 W Washington St   Hagerstown MD 21740
Ph: 301-739-2015 ▪ Fx: 301-739-1278

Charles County Chamber of Commerce — www.cccc-md.org
6360 Crain Hwy   La Plata MD 20646
Ph: 301-932-6500 ▪ Fx: 301-932-3945

Prince George's Chamber of Commerce   www.pgcoc.org
4640 Forbes Blvd Suite 130   Lanham MD 20706
Ph: 301-731-5000 ▪ Fx: 301-731-5013

Baltimore/Washington Corridor Chamber of Commerce   www.baltwashchamber.org
312 Marshall Ave Suite 104   Laurel MD 20707
Ph: 301-725-4000 ▪ Fx: 301-725-0776

Garrett County Chamber of Commerce   www.garrettchamber.com
15 Visitors Ctr Dr   McHenry MD 21541
Ph: 301-387-4386 ▪ Fx: 301-387-2080

Saint Mary's County Chamber of Commerce   www.smcchamber.com
28290 Three Notch Rd   Mechanicsville MD 20659
Ph: 301-884-5555 ▪ Fx: 301-884-2149

Ocean City Chamber of Commerce   www.oceancity.org
12320 Ocean Gateway   Ocean City MD 21842
Ph: 410-213-0144 ▪ Fx: 410-213-7521 ▪ TF: 888-626-3386

West Anne Arundel County Chamber of Commerce   www.waaccc.org
8373 Piney Orchard Pkwy Suite 100   Odenton MD 21113
Ph: 410-672-3422 ▪ Fx: 410-672-3475

Olney Chamber of Commerce   www.olneymd.org
PO Box 550   Olney MD 20830
Ph: 301-924-3555 ▪ Fx: 301-774-4944

Reisterstown-Owings Mills-Glyndon Chamber of Commerce   www.romgchamber.com
66 Painters Mill Rd Suite 1   Owings Mills MD 21117
Ph: 410-356-2888 ▪ Fx: 410-356-5112

Pikesville Chamber of Commerce   www.pikesvillechamber.com
7 Church Ln Suite 14   Pikesville MD 21208
Ph: 410-484-2337 ▪ Fx: 410-484-4151

Calvert County Chamber of Commerce   www.calvertchamber.com
PO Box 9   Prince Frederick MD 20678
Ph: 410-535-2577 ▪ Fx: 410-257-3140

Montgomery County Chamber of Commerce   www.montgomery-chamber.com
51 Monroe St Suite 1609   Rockville MD 20850
Ph: 301-738-0015 ▪ Fx: 301-738-8792

Rockville Chamber of Commerce   www.rockvillechamber.com
255 Rockville Pike Suite L10   Rockville MD 20850
Ph: 301-424-9300 ▪ Fx: 301-762-7599

Salisbury Area Chamber of Commerce   www.salisburyarea.com
144 E Main St   Salisbury MD 21801
Ph: 410-749-0144 ▪ Fx: 410-860-9925

Greater Severna Park Chamber of Commerce   www.severnaparkchamber.com
1 Holly Ave   Severna Park MD 21146
Ph: 410-647-3900 ▪ Fx: 410-647-3999

Greater Silver Spring Chamber of Commerce   www.silverspringchamber.com
8601 Georgia Ave Suite 203   Silver Spring MD 20910
Ph: 301-565-3777 ▪ Fx: 301-565-3377

Snow Hill Chamber of Commerce   www.snowhillmd.com
PO Box 176   Snow Hill MD 21863
Ph: 410-632-0809 ▪ Fx: 410-632-3158

Baltimore County Chamber of Commerce   www.baltcountycc.com
102 W Pennsylvania Ave Suite 101   Towson MD 21204
Ph: 410-825-6200 ▪ Fx: 410-821-9901

Carroll County Chamber of Commerce   www.carrollcountychamber.org
PO Box 871   Westminster MD 21158
Ph: 410-876-7212 ▪ Fx: 410-876-1023

Wheaton-Kensington Chamber of Commerce   www.wkchamber.org
2401 Blueridge Ave Suite 101   Wheaton MD 20902
Ph: 301-949-0080 ▪ Fx: 301-949-0081

MASSACHUSETTS

Middlesex West Chamber of Commerce   www.mwcoc.com
77 Great Rd Suite 214   Acton MA 01720
Ph: 978-263-0010 ▪ Fx: 978-264-0303

Amherst Area Chamber of Commerce   www.amherstarea.com
409 Main St   Amherst MA 01002
Ph: 413-253-0700 ▪ Fx: 413-256-0771

Arlington Chamber of Commerce   www.arlingtonchamberofcommerce.org
1 Whittemore Pk   Arlington MA 02474
Ph: 781-643-4600 ▪ Fx: 781-646-5581

North Quabbin Chamber of Commerce   www.northquabbinchamber.com
523 Main St   Athol MA 01331
Ph: 978-249-3849 ▪ Fx: 978-249-7151

Chamber of Commerce of the Attleboro Area   www.attleborochamber.com
42 Union St   Attleboro MA 02703
Ph: 508-222-0801 ▪ Fx: 508-222-1498

Beverly Chamber of Commerce   www.beverlychamber.com
28 Cabot St   Beverly MA 01915
Ph: 978-232-9559 ▪ Fx: 978-232-9372

Billerica Chamber of Commerce   www.billericachamber.com
574 Boston Rd Unit 1   Billerica MA 01821
Ph: 978-663-0036 ▪ Fx: 978-670-1020

Greater Boston Chamber of Commerce   www.bostonchamber.com
75 State St 2nd Fl   Boston MA 02109
Ph: 617-227-4500 ▪ Fx: 617-227-7505

Metro South Chamber of Commerce   www.metrosouthchamber.com
60 School St   Brockton MA 02301
Ph: 508-586-0500 ▪ Fx: 508-587-1340

Brookline Chamber of Commerce   www.brooklinechamber.com
1101 Beacon St   Brookline MA 02446
Ph: 617-739-1330 ▪ Fx: 617-739-1200

Cape Cod Canal Regional Chamber of Commerce   www.capecodcanalchamber.org
70 Main St   Buzzards Bay MA 02532
Ph: 508-759-6000 ▪ Fx: 508-759-6965

Cambridge Chamber of Commerce   www.cambridgechamber.org
859 Massachusetts Ave   Cambridge MA 02139
Ph: 617-876-4100 ▪ Fx: 617-354-9874

Chicopee Chamber of Commerce   www.chicopeechamber.org
264 Exchange St   Chicopee MA 01013
Ph: 413-594-2101 ▪ Fx: 413-594-2103

Wachusett Chamber of Commerce   www.wachusettchamber.com
1 Green St   Clinton MA 01510
Ph: 978-368-7687 ▪ Fx: 978-368-7689

North Shore Chamber of Commerce   www.northshorechamber.org
5 Cherry Hill Dr Suite 100   Danvers MA 01923
Ph: 978-774-8565 ▪ Fx: 978-774-3418

Nashoba Valley Chamber of Commerce   www.nvcoc.com
43 Buena Vista St   Devens MA 01432
Ph: 978-772-6976 ▪ Fx: 978-772-3503

East Boston Chamber of Commerce   www.eastbostonchamber.com
296 Bennington St 2nd Fl   East Boston MA 02128
Ph: 617-569-5000 ▪ Fx: 617-569-1945

Everett Chamber of Commerce   www.everettmachamber.org
467 Broadway   Everett MA 02149
Ph: 617-387-9100 ▪ Fx: 617-389-6655

Fall River Area Chamber of Commerce & Industry   www.fallriverchamber.com
200 Pocasset St   Fall River MA 02721
Ph: 508-676-8226 ▪ Fx: 508-675-5932

Falmouth Chamber of Commerce   www.falmouth-capecod.com
PO Box 582   Falmouth MA 02541
Ph: 508-548-8500 ▪ Fx: 508-548-8521 ▪ TF: 800-526-8532

Metro West Chamber of Commerce   www.metrowest.org
1671 Worcester Rd Suite 201   Framingham MA 01701
Ph: 508-879-5600 ▪ Fx: 508-875-9325

United Chamber of Commerce   www.unitedchamber.org
40 Kenwood Cir   Franklin MA 02038
Ph: 508-528-2800 ▪ Fx: 508-520-7864

Greater Gardner Chamber of Commerce   www.gardnerma.com
210 Main St   Gardner MA 01440
Ph: 978-632-1780 ▪ Fx: 978-630-1767

Cape Ann Chamber of Commerce   www.capeannvacations.com
33 Commercial St   Gloucester MA 01930
Ph: 978-283-1601 ▪ Fx: 978-283-4740 ▪ TF: 800-321-0133

Franklin County Chamber of Commerce   www.co.franklin.ma.us
PO Box 898   Greenfield MA 01302
Ph: 413-773-5463 ▪ Fx: 413-773-7008

Greater Haverhill Chamber of Commerce   www.haverhillchamber.com
87 Winter St   Haverhill MA 01830
Ph: 978-373-5663 ▪ Fx: 978-373-8060

Greater Holyoke Chamber of Commerce   www.holycham.com
177 High St   Holyoke MA 01040
Ph: 413-534-3376 ▪ Fx: 413-534-3385

Assabet Valley Chamber of Commerce   www.assabetvalleychamber.org
18 Church St   Hudson MA 01749
Ph: 978-568-0360 ▪ Fx: 978-562-4118

Cape Cod Chamber of Commerce   www.capecodchamber.org
PO Box 790   Hyannis MA 02601
Ph: 508-362-3225 ▪ Fx: 508-362-5711 ▪ TF: 888-332-2732

Hyannis Area Chamber of Commerce   www.hyannis.com
1481 Rt 132 PO Box 100   Hyannis MA 02601
Ph: 508-362-5230 ▪ Fx: 508-362-9499 ▪ TF: 800-449-6647

Merrimack Valley Chamber of Commerce   www.merrimackvalleychamber.com
264 Essex St   Lawrence MA 01840
Ph: 978-686-0900 ▪ Fx: 978-794-9953

North Central Massachusetts Chamber of Commerce   www.northcentralmass.com
110 Erdman Way   Leominster MA 01453
Ph: 978-840-4300 ▪ Fx: 978-840-4896

Lexington Chamber of Commerce   www.lexingtonchamber.org
1875 Massachusetts Ave   Lexington MA 02420
Ph: 781-862-2480 ▪ Fx: 781-862-5995

Greater Lowell Chamber of Commerce   www.glcc.biz
144 Merrimack St Suite 403   Lowell MA 01852
Ph: 978-459-8154 ▪ Fx: 978-452-4145

Lynn Area Chamber of Commerce   www.lynnchamber.com
100 Oxford St   Lynn MA 01901
Ph: 781-592-2900 ▪ Fx: 781-592-2903

Malden Chamber of Commerce   www.maldenchamber.org
200 Pleasant St Suite 416   Malden MA 02148
Ph: 781-322-4500 ▪ Fx: 781-322-4866

Marlborough Regional Chamber of Commerce   www.marlboroughchamber.org
11 Florence St   Marlborough MA 01752
Ph: 508-485-7746 ▪ Fx: 508-481-1819

Medford Chamber of Commerce   www.medfordchamberma.com
1 Shipyard Way Suite G-01   Medford MA 02155
Ph: 781-396-1277 ▪ Fx: 781-396-1278

Melrose Chamber of Commerce   www.melrosechamber.org
1 W Foster St   Melrose MA 02176
Ph: 781-665-3033 ▪ Fx: 781-665-5595

Cranberry Country Chamber of Commerce   www.cranberrycountry.org
40 N Main St   Middleboro MA 02346
Ph: 508-947-1499 ▪ Fx: 508-947-1446

Milford Area Chamber of Commerce   www.milfordchamber.org
258 Main St   Milford MA 01757
Ph: 508-473-6700 ▪ Fx: 508-473-8467

New Bedford Area Chamber of Commerce   www.newbedfordchamber.com
PO Box 8827   New Bedford MA 02742
Ph: 508-999-5231 ▪ Fx: 508-999-5237

Newton-Needham Chamber of Commerce   www.nnchamber.com
PO Box 590268   Newton MA 02459
Ph: 617-244-5300 ▪ Fx: 617-244-5302

North Attleboro-Plainville Chamber of Commerce   www.napcc.org
PO Box 1071   North Attleboro MA 02761
Ph: 508-695-6011 ▪ Fx: 508-695-6096

Greater Northampton Chamber of Commerce   www.northamptonuncommon.com
99 Pleasant St   Northampton MA 01060
Ph: 413-584-1900 ▪ Fx: 413-584-1934

Neposet Valley Chamber of Commerce   www.nvcc.com
190 Vanderbilt Ave   Norwood MA 02062
Ph: 781-769-1126 ▪ Fx: 781-769-0808

Quaboag Valley Chamber of Commerce   www.quaboagvalley.org
3 Converse St Suite 103   Palmer MA 01069
Ph: 413-283-2418   Fx: 413-289-1355

Peabody Chamber of Commerce   www.peabody-chamber.com
24 Main St Suite 28   Peabody MA 01960
Ph: 978-531-0384   Fx: 978-532-7227

Berkshire Chamber of Commerce   www.berkshirechamber.com
75 North St Suite 360   Pittsfield MA 01201
Ph: 413-499-4000   Fx: 413-447-9641

Plymouth Area Chamber of Commerce   www.plymouthchamber.com
15 Caswell Ln Suite 3   Plymouth MA 02360
Ph: 508-830-1620   Fx: 508-830-1621

South Shore Chamber of Commerce   www.southshorechamber.org
PO Box 690625   Quincy MA 02269
Ph: 617-479-1111   Fx: 617-479-9274

Reading-North Reading Chamber of Commerce   www.readingnreadingchamber.org
PO Box 771   Reading MA 01867
Ph: 781-944-8824   Fx: 781-944-6125

Revere Chamber of Commerce   www.reverechamber.org
4 Squire Rd   Revere MA 02151
Ph: 781-289-8009   Fx: 781-289-2166

Salem Chamber of Commerce   salem-chamber.org
63 Wharf St   Salem MA 01970
Ph: 978-744-0004   Fx: 978-745-3855

Saugus Chamber of Commerce   www.sauguschamber.org
335 Central St   Saugus MA 01906
Ph: 781-233-8407   Fx: 781-231-1145

Somerville Chamber of Commerce   www.somervillechamber.org
PO Box 440343   Somerville MA 02144
Ph: 617-776-4100   Fx: 617-776-1157

Agawam Chamber of Commerce   www.myonlinechamber.com
1441 Main St   Springfield MA 01003
Ph: 413-787-1555   Fx: 413-731-8530

Greater Springfield Chamber of Commerce
1441 Main St Suite 136   Springfield MA 01103
Ph: 413-787-1555   Fx: 413-731-8530

West Springfield Chamber of Commerce   www.myonlinechamber.com
1441 Main St   Springfield MA 01103
Ph: 413-787-1555   Fx: 413-731-8530

Tri-Community Area Chamber of Commerce   www.sturbridge.org
380 Main St   Sturbridge MA 01566
Ph: 508-347-2761   Fx: 508-347-5218   TF: 888-788-7274

Taunton Area Chamber of Commerce   www.tauntonareachamber.org
12 Taunton Green Suite 201   Taunton MA 02780
Ph: 508-824-4068   Fx: 508-884-8222

Wakefield Chamber of Commerce   www.wakefieldma.org/chamber_page.html
PO Box 585   Wakefield MA 01880
Ph: 781-245-0741

Waltham/West Suburban Chamber of Commerce   www.walthamchamber.com
84 South St   Waltham MA 02453
Ph: 781-894-4700   Fx: 781-894-1708

Watertown Chamber of Commerce   www.wbcc.org
PO Box 45   Watertown MA 02471
Ph: 617-926-1017   Fx: 617-926-2322

Wellesley Chamber of Commerce   www.wellesleyweb.com/chamber.htm
1 Hollis St Suite 111   Wellesley MA 02482
Ph: 781-235-2446   Fx: 781-235-7326

Greater Westfield Chamber of Commerce   www.westfieldchamber.org
53 Court St   Westfield MA 01085
Ph: 413-568-1618   Fx: 413-572-1453

Blackstone Valley Chamber of Commerce   www.blackstonevalley.org
110 Church St   Whitinsville MA 01588
Ph: 508-234-9090   Fx: 508-234-5152   TF: 800-841-0919

North Suburban Chamber of Commerce   www.northsuburbanchamber.com
76-R Winn St Suite 3D   Woburn MA 01801
Ph: 781-933-3499   Fx: 781-933-1071

Worcester Regional Chamber of Commerce   www.worcesterchamber.org
339 Main St   Worcester MA 01608
Ph: 508-753-2924   Fx: 508-754-8560

MICHIGAN

Lenawee County Chamber of Commerce   www.lenaweechamber.com
202 N Main St Suite A   Adrian MI 49221
Ph: 517-265-5141   Fx: 517-263-6065

Allen Park Chamber of Commerce
6543 Allen Rd   Allen Park MI 48101
Ph: 313-382-7303   Fx: 313-382-4409

Gratiot Area Chamber of Commerce   www.gratiot.org/chamber
110 W Superior St   Alma MI 48801
Ph: 989-463-5525   Fx: 989-463-6588

Alpena Area Chamber of Commerce   www.alpenachamber.com
PO Box 65   Alpena MI 49707
Ph: 989-354-4181   Fx: 989-356-3999   TF: 800-425-7362

Ann Arbor Area Chamber of Commerce   www.annarborchamber.org
425 S Main St Suite 103   Ann Arbor MI 48104
Ph: 734-665-4433   Fx: 734-665-4191

Battle Creek Area Chamber of Commerce   www.battlecreek.org/chamber
77 E Michigan Ave Suite 80   Battle Creek MI 49017
Ph: 269-962-4076   Fx: 269-962-6309

Bay Area Chamber of Commerce   www.baycityarea.com
901 Saginaw St   Bay City MI 48708
Ph: 989-893-4567   Fx: 989-895-5594

Belleville Area Chamber of Commerce   www.bellevillech.org
248 Main St   Belleville MI 48111
Ph: 734-697-7151   Fx: 734-697-1415

Cornerstone Alliance Chamber Services   www.cstonealliance.org
38 W Wall St   Benton Harbor MI 49023
Ph: 269-925-6100   Fx: 269-925-4471

Mecosta County Area Chamber of Commerce   www.mecostacounty.com
246 N State St   Big Rapids MI 49307
Ph: 231-796-7649   Fx: 231-796-1625

Birmingham-Bloomfield Chamber of Commerce   www.bbcc.com
124 W Maple Rd   Birmingham MI 48009
Ph: 248-644-1700   Fx: 248-644-0286

Greater Brighton Area Chamber of Commerce   www.brightoncoc.com
131 Hyne St   Brighton MI 48116
Ph: 810-227-5086   Fx: 810-227-5940

Brooklyn-Irish Hills Chamber of Commerce   www.brooklynmi.com
221 N Main St PO Box 805   Brooklyn MI 49230
Ph: 517-592-8907

Cadillac Area Chamber of Commerce   www.cadillac.org
222 Lake St   Cadillac MI 49601
Ph: 231-775-9776   Fx: 231-775-1440

Canton Chamber of Commerce   www.cantonchamber.com
5820 N Canton Ctr Rd Suite 110   Canton MI 48187
Ph: 734-453-4040   Fx: 734-453-4503

Clarkston Area Chamber of Commerce   www.clarkston.org
5856 S Main St   Clarkston MI 48346
Ph: 248-625-8055   Fx: 248-625-8041

Coldwater Branch County Chamber of Commerce   www.branch-county.com
20 Division St   Coldwater MI 49036
Ph: 517-278-5985   Fx: 517-278-8369

Davison Area Chamber of Commerce
105 E 2nd St Suite 7   Davison MI 48423
Ph: 810-653-6266   Fx: 810-653-0669

Dearborn Chamber of Commerce   www.dearbornchamber.org
15544 Michigan Ave   Dearborn MI 48126
Ph: 313-584-6100   Fx: 313-584-9818

Dearborn Heights Chamber of Commerce   www.dhol.org/community/chamber.htm
24624 W Warren Ave   Dearborn Heights MI 48127
Ph: 313-274-7480   Fx: 313-565-0913

Detroit Regional Chamber   www.detroitchamber.com
PO Box 33840 1 Woodward Ave Suite 1900   Detroit MI 48232
Ph: 313-964-4000   Fx: 313-964-0531

Eastpointe Chamber of Commerce   www.epchamber.com
21238 Gratiot Ave   Eastpointe MI 48021
Ph: 586-776-5520   Fx: 586-776-7808

Delta County Area Chamber of Commerce   www.deltami.org
230 Ludington St   Escanaba MI 49829
Ph: 906-786-2192   Fx: 906-786-8830   TF: 888-335-8264

Farmington/Farmington Hills Chamber of Commerce   www.ffhchamber.com
30903-B W 10-Mile Rd   Farmington Hills MI 48336
Ph: 248-474-3440   Fx: 248-474-9235

Ferndale Chamber of Commerce   www.ferndalechamber.com
407 E 9-Mile Rd   Ferndale MI 48220
Ph: 248-542-2160   Fx: 248-542-8979

Flint Area Chamber of Commerce   www.flintchamber.org
519 S Saginaw St Suite 200   Flint MI 48502
Ph: 810-232-7101   Fx: 810-233-7437

Garden City Chamber of Commerce   www.gardencity.org
30120 Ford Rd Suite D   Garden City MI 48135
Ph: 734-422-4448   Fx: 734-422-1601

Grand Blanc Chamber of Commerce   www.grandblancchamber.org
512 E Grand Blanc Rd   Grand Blanc MI 48439
Ph: 810-695-4222   Fx: 810-695-0053

Chamber Grand Haven Ferrysburg   www.grandhavenchamber.org
1 S Harbor Dr   Grand Haven MI 49417
Ph: 616-842-4910   Fx: 616-842-0379   TF: 800-303-4096

Grand Rapids Area Chamber of Commerce   www.grandrapids.org
111 Pearl St NW   Grand Rapids MI 49503
Ph: 616-771-0300   Fx: 616-771-0318

Hillsdale County Chamber of Commerce   www.hillsdalecountychamber.com
116 N Broad St   Hillsdale MI 49242
Ph: 517-439-4341   Fx: 517-439-9263

Holland Area Chamber of Commerce   www.hollandchamber.org
272 E 8th St   Holland MI 49423
Ph: 616-392-2389   Fx: 616-392-7379

Keweenaw Peninsula Chamber of Commerce   www.keweenaw.org
326 Shelden Ave   Houghton MI 49931
Ph: 906-482-5240   Fx: 906-482-5241

Howell Area Chamber of Commerce   www.howell.org
123 E Washington St   Howell MI 48843
Ph: 517-546-3920   Fx: 517-546-4115

Dickinson County Area Chamber of Commerce   www.dickinsonchamber.com
600 S Stephenson Ave   Iron Mountain MI 49801
Ph: 906-774-2002   Fx: 906-774-2004   TF: 800-236-2447

Greater Jackson Chamber of Commerce   www.gjcc.org
1 Jackson Sq Suite 1100   Jackson MI 49201
Ph: 517-782-8221   Fx: 517-782-0061

Jenison Area Chamber of Commerce
PO Box 405   Jenison MI 49429
Ph: 616-457-8555   Fx: 616-457-3670

Kalamazoo Regional Chamber of Commerce   www.kazoochamber.com
346 W Michigan Ave   Kalamazoo MI 49007
Ph: 269-381-4000   Fx: 269-343-0430

Orion Area Chamber of Commerce   orion.lib.mi.us/orion
1520 S Lapeer Rd Suite 220   Lake Orion MI 48360
Ph: 248-693-6300   Fx: 248-693-9227

Lansing Regional Chamber of Commerce   www.lansingchamber.com
300 E Michigan Ave Suite 300   Lansing MI 48933
Ph: 517-487-6340   Fx: 517-484-6910

Lapeer Area Chamber of Commerce   www.lapeerareachamber.org
431 N Court St   Lapeer MI 48446
Ph: 810-664-6641   Fx: 810-664-4349

Lincoln Park Chamber of Commerce
1335 Southfield Rd PO Box 382   Lincoln Park MI 48146
Ph: 313-386-0140   Fx: 313-386-0140

Livonia Chamber of Commerce   www.livonia.org
33233 5 Mile Rd   Livonia MI 48154
Ph: 734-427-2122 ■ Fx: 734-427-6055

Madison Heights Chamber of Commerce
724 W 11-Mile Rd   Madison Heights MI 48071
Ph: 248-542-5010 ■ Fx: 248-542-6821

Midland Area Chamber of Commerce   www.macc.org
300 Rodd St Suite 101   Midland MI 48640
Ph: 989-839-9901 ■ Fx: 989-835-3701

Huron Valley Chamber of Commerce   huronvcc.com
317 Union St   Milford MI 48381
Ph: 248-685-7129 ■ Fx: 248-685-9047

Monroe County Chamber of Commerce   chamber.monroeinfo.com
106 W Front St   Monroe MI 48161
Ph: 734-242-3366 ■ Fx: 734-242-7253

Central Macomb County Chamber of Commerce   www.central-macomb.com
49 Macomb St   Mount Clemens MI 48043
Ph: 586-493-7600 ■ Fx: 586-493-7602

Mount Pleasant Area Chamber of Commerce   www.mt-pleasant.net
114 E Broadway   Mount Pleasant MI 48858
Ph: 989-772-2396 ■ Fx: 989-773-2656

Muskegon Area Chamber of Commerce   www.muskegon.org
900 3rd St Suite 200   Muskegon MI 49443
Ph: 231-722-3751 ■ Fx: 231-728-7251

Anchor Bay Chamber of Commerce   www.anchorbaychamber.com
35054 23-Mile Rd Suite 110   New Baltimore MI 48047
Ph: 586-725-5148 ■ Fx: 586-725-5369

Four Flags Area Chamber of Commerce   www.nilesmi.com
PO Box 10   Niles MI 49120
Ph: 269-683-3720 ■ Fx: 269-683-3722 ■ TF: 888-683-8361

Novi Chamber of Commerce   www.novichamber.com
43700 Expo Ctr Dr Suite 100   Novi MI 48375
Ph: 248-349-3743 ■ Fx: 248-349-4523

Petoskey Regional Chamber of Commerce   www.petoskey.com
401 E Mitchell St   Petoskey MI 49770
Ph: 231-347-4150 ■ Fx: 231-348-1810

Plymouth Community Chamber of Commerce   www.plymouthchamber.org
386 S Main St   Plymouth MI 48170
Ph: 734-453-1540 ■ Fx: 734-453-1724

Pontiac Chamber of Commerce   www.pontiacchamber.com
30 N Saginaw St Suite 404   Pontiac MI 48342
Ph: 248-335-9600 ■ Fx: 248-335-9601

Greater Port Huron Area Chamber of Commerce   www.porthuron-chamber.com
920 Pine Grove Ave   Port Huron MI 48060
Ph: 810-985-7101 ■ Fx: 810-985-7311 ■ TF: 800-361-0526

Redford Township Chamber of Commerce   www.redfordchamber.com
26050 5-Mile Rd   Redford MI 48239
Ph: 313-535-0960 ■ Fx: 313-535-6356

Greater Rochester Chamber of Commerce
71 Walnut Blvd Suite 110   Rochester MI 48307
Ph: 248-651-6700 ■ Fx: 248-651-5270

Rockford Area Chamber of Commerce   www.rockfordmichamber.com
PO Box 520   Rockford MI 49341
Ph: 616-866-2000 ■ Fx: 616-866-2141

Romeo-Washington Chamber of Commerce   www.rwchamber.com
228 N Main St PO Box 175   Romeo MI 48065
Ph: 586-752-4436 ■ Fx: 586-752-2835

Greater Royal Oak Chamber of Commerce   www.virtualroyaloak.com
200 S Washington Ave   Royal Oak MI 48067
Ph: 248-547-4000 ■ Fx: 248-547-0504

Saginaw County Chamber of Commerce   www.saginawchamber.org
901 S Washington Ave   Saginaw MI 48601
Ph: 989-752-7161 ■ Fx: 989-752-9055

Metro East Chamber of Commerce
27601 Jefferson Ave   Saint Clair Shores MI 48081
Ph: 586-777-2741 ■ Fx: 586-777-4811

Sault Area Chamber of Commerce   www.saultstemarie.org
2581 I-75 Business Spur   Sault Sainte Marie MI 49783
Ph: 906-632-3301 ■ Fx: 906-632-2331

South Lyon Area Chamber of Commerce   www.southlyonchamber.com
125 N Lafayette St   South Lyon MI 48178
Ph: 248-437-3257 ■ Fx: 248-437-4116

Southfield Chamber of Commerce   www.southfieldchamber.com
17515 W 9-Mile Rd Suite 750   Southfield MI 48075
Ph: 248-557-6661 ■ Fx: 248-557-3931

Sterling Heights Area Chamber of Commerce   www.suscc.com
12900 Hall Rd Suite 110   Sterling Heights MI 48313
Ph: 586-731-5400 ■ Fx: 586-731-3521

Southern Wayne County Regional Chamber   www.swccc.org
20600 Eureka Rd Suite 315   Taylor MI 48180
Ph: 734-284-6000 ■ Fx: 734-284-0198

Traverse City Area Chamber of Commerce   www.tcchamber.org
202 E Grandview Pkwy   Traverse City MI 49684
Ph: 231-947-5075 ■ Fx: 231-946-2565

Troy Chamber of Commerce   www.troychamber.com
4555 Investment Dr Suite 300   Troy MI 48098
Ph: 248-641-8151 ■ Fx: 248-641-0545

Lakes Area Chamber of Commerce   www.lakesareachamber.com
305 N Pontiac Tr Suite B   Walled Lake MI 48390
Ph: 248-624-2826 ■ Fx: 248-624-2892

Warren-Center Line-Sterling Heights Chamber of Commerce   www.wcschamber.com
30500 Van Dyke Ave Suite 118   Warren MI 48093
Ph: 586-751-3939 ■ Fx: 586-751-3995

West Bloomfield Chamber of Commerce   www.westbloomfieldchamber.com
6668 Orchard Lake Rd Suite 207   West Bloomfield MI 48322
Ph: 248-626-3636 ■ Fx: 248-626-4218

Westland Chamber of Commerce   www.westlandchamber.com
36900 Ford Rd   Westland MI 48185
Ph: 734-326-7222 ■ Fx: 734-326-6040

Wyoming Area Chamber of Commerce   www.southkent.org
590 32nd St SE   Wyoming MI 49548
Ph: 616-531-5990 ■ Fx: 616-531-0252

Ypsilanti Area Chamber of Commerce   www.ypsichamber.org
301 W Michigan Ave Suite 101   Ypsilanti MI 48197
Ph: 734-482-4920 ■ Fx: 734-482-2021

MINNESOTA

Albert Lea-Freeborn County Chamber of Commerce   www.albertlea.org/chamber.htm
143 W Clark St   Albert Lea MN 56007
Ph: 507-373-3938 ■ Fx: 507-373-0344

Alexandria Lakes Area Chamber of Commerce   www.alexandriamn.org
206 Broadway   Alexandria MN 56308
Ph: 320-763-3161 ■ Fx: 320-763-6857 ■ TF: 800-235-9441

Anoka Area Chamber of Commerce   www.anokaareachamber.com
12 Bridge Sq   Anoka MN 55303
Ph: 763-421-7130 ■ Fx: 763-421-0577

Apple Valley Chamber of Commerce   www.applevalleychamber.com
7300 W 147th St Suite 101   Apple Valley MN 55124
Ph: 952-432-8422 ■ Fx: 952-432-7964 ■ TF: 800-301-9435

Bemidji Area Chamber of Commerce   www.bemidji.org
300 Bemidji Ave   Bemidji MN 56601
Ph: 218-444-3541 ■ Fx: 218-444-4276 ■ TF: 800-458-2223

Brainerd Lakes Area Chamber of Commerce   www.explorebrainerdlakes.com
PO Box 356   Brainerd MN 56401
Ph: 218-829-2838 ■ Fx: 218-829-8199 ■ TF: 800-450-2838

Burnsville Chamber of Commerce   www.burnsvillechamber.com
101 W Burnsville Pkwy Suite 150   Burnsville MN 55337
Ph: 952-435-6000 ■ Fx: 952-435-6972

Cloquet Area Chamber of Commerce   www.cloquet.com
225 Sunnyside Dr   Cloquet MN 55720
Ph: 218-879-1551 ■ Fx: 218-878-0223 ■ TF: 800-554-4350

Detroit Lakes Regional Chamber of Commerce   www.visitdetroitlakes.com
700 Washington Ave   Detroit Lakes MN 56501
Ph: 218-847-9202 ■ Fx: 218-847-9082 ■ TF: 800-542-3992

Duluth Area Chamber of Commerce   www.duluthchamber.com
5 W 1st St Suite 101   Duluth MN 55802
Ph: 218-722-5501 ■ Fx: 218-722-3223

Northern Dakota County Chambers of Commerce   www.ndcchambers.com
1121 Town Center Dr Suite 102   Eagan MN 55123
Ph: 651-452-9872 ■ Fx: 651-452-8978

Eden Prairie Chamber of Commerce   www.epchamber.org
7901 Flying Cloud Dr Suite 270   Eden Prairie MN 55344
Ph: 952-944-2830 ■ Fx: 952-944-0229

Forest Lake Area Chamber of Commerce   www.flacc.org
PO Box 474   Forest Lake MN 55025
Ph: 651-464-3200 ■ Fx: 651-464-3201

Grand Rapids Area Chamber of Commerce   www.grandmn.com
1 NW 3rd St   Grand Rapids MN 55744
Ph: 218-326-6619 ■ Fx: 218-326-4825 ■ TF: 800-472-6366

Hastings Area Chamber of Commerce & Tourism Bureau   www.hastingsmn.org
111 E 3rd St   Hastings MN 55033
Ph: 651-437-6775 ■ Fx: 651-437-2697 ■ TF: 888-612-6122

River Heights Chamber of Commerce   www.riverheights.com
5782 Blackshire Path   Inver Grove Heights MN 55076
Ph: 651-451-2266 ■ Fx: 651-451-0846

Lakeville Area Chamber of Commerce & Convention & Visitors Bureau   www.lakevillechamber.org
PO Box 12   Lakeville MN 55044
Ph: 952-469-2020 ■ Fx: 952-469-2028 ■ TF: 888-525-3845

Suburban Area Chamber of Commerce
3262 Rice St   Little Canada MN 55126
Ph: 651-256-4770 ■ Fx: 651-256-4771

Minneapolis Regional Chamber of Commerce   www.minneapolischamber.org
81 S 9th St Suite 200   Minneapolis MN 55402
Ph: 612-370-9132 ■ Fx: 612-370-9195

TwinWest Chamber of Commerce   www.twinwest.com
10550 Wayzata Blvd   Minnetonka MN 55305
Ph: 952-540-0234 ■ Fx: 952-540-0237

Chamber of Commerce of Fargo Moorhead   www.fmchamber.com
202 1st Ave N   Moorhead MN 56560
Ph: 218-233-1100 ■ Fx: 218-233-1200

Twin Cities North Chamber of Commerce   www.twincitiesnorth.org
5394 Edgewood Dr Suite 100   Mounds View MN 55112
Ph: 763-571-9781 ■ Fx: 763-572-7950

Lake Minnetonka Chamber of Commerce   www.lakeminnetonkachamber.com
PO Box 115   Navarre MN 55392
Ph: 952-471-0768 ■ Fx: 952-471-0577

North Hennepin Chamber of Commerce   www.nhachamber.com
101 Broadway St W Suite 102   Osseo MN 55369
Ph: 763-424-6744 ■ Fx: 763-424-6927

Owatonna Area Chamber of Commerce & Tourism   www.owatonna.org
320 Hoffman Dr   Owatonna MN 55060
Ph: 507-451-7970 ■ Fx: 507-451-7972 ■ TF: 800-423-6466

Richfield Chamber of Commerce   www.richfieldchambercvb.org
6601 Lyndale Ave S Suite 106   Richfield MN 55423
Ph: 612-866-5100 ■ Fx: 612-861-8302

Rochester Area Chamber of Commerce   www.rochestermnchamber.com
220 S Broadway Suite 100   Rochester MN 55904
Ph: 507-288-1122 ■ Fx: 507-282-8960

Saint Cloud Area Chamber of Commerce   www.stcloudareachamber.com
110 6th Ave S   Saint Cloud MN 56301
Ph: 320-251-2940 ■ Fx: 320-251-0081

Minnesota State Chamber of Commerce   www.mnchamber.com
400 Robert St N Suite 1500   Saint Paul MN 55101
Ph: 651-292-4650 ■ Fx: 651-292-4656 ■ TF: 800-821-2230

Saint Paul Area Chamber of Commerce   www.saintpaulchamber.com
401 N Robert St Suite 150   Saint Paul MN 55101
Ph: 651-223-5000 ■ Fx: 651-223-5119

Stillwater Area Chamber of Commerce www.stillwaterchamber.com
106 S Main St   Stillwater MN 55082
Ph: 651-439-7700 ▪ Fx: 651-439-4035
Leech Lake Area Chamber of Commerce www.leech-lake.com
PO Box 1089   Walker MN 56484
Ph: 218-547-1313 ▪ Fx: 218-547-1338 ▪ TF: 800-833-1118
White Bear Lake Area Chamber of Commerce www.whitebearchamber.com
4801 Hwy 61 Suite 109   White Bear Lake MN 55110
Ph: 651-429-8593 ▪ Fx: 651-429-8592
Willmar Lakes Area Chamber of Commerce www.willmarareachamber.com
2104 E Hwy 12   Willmar MN 56201
Ph: 320-235-0300 ▪ Fx: 320-231-1948
Winona Area Chamber of Commerce
67 Main St PO Box 870   Winona MN 55987
Ph: 507-452-2272 ▪ Fx: 507-454-8814

MISSISSIPPI

Monroe County Chamber of Commerce www.gomonroe.org
124 W Commerce St   Aberdeen MS 39730
Ph: 662-369-6488 ▪ Fx: 662-369-6489
Panola Partnership Inc
150-A Public Sq   Batesville MS 38606
Ph: 662-563-3126 ▪ Fx: 662-563-0704 ▪ TF: 888-872-6652
Hancock County Chamber of Commerce www.hancockchamber.org
412 Hwy 90 Suite 6   Bay Saint Louis MS 39520
Ph: 228-467-9048 ▪ Fx: 228-467-1573
Biloxi Bay Chamber of Commerce www.biloxibaychamber.com
PO Box 889   Biloxi MS 39533
Ph: 228-435-6149 ▪ Fx: 228-435-6334
Biloxi Chamber of Commerce www.biloxi.org
1048 Beach Blvd   Biloxi MS 39530
Ph: 228-374-2717 ▪ Fx: 228-374-2764
Rankin County Chamber of Commerce www.rankinchamber.com
PO Box 428   Brandon MS 39043
Ph: 601-825-2268 ▪ Fx: 601-825-1977
Brookhaven-Lincoln County Chamber of Commerce www.brookhavenchamber.com
230 S Whitworth Ave   Brookhaven MS 39601
Ph: 601-833-1411 ▪ Fx: 601-833-1412 ▪ TF: 800-613-4667
Clarksdale-Coahoma County Chamber of Commerce & Industrial Foundation www.clarksdale.com
PO Box 160   Clarksdale MS 38614
Ph: 662-627-7337 ▪ Fx: 662-627-1313
Cleveland-Bolivar County Chamber of Commerce www.clevelandmschamber.com
PO Box 490   Cleveland MS 38732
Ph: 662-843-2712 ▪ Fx: 662-843-2718
Marion County Development Partnership www.marionpartnership.org
200 2nd St   Columbia MS 39429
Ph: 601-736-6385 ▪ Fx: 601-736-6392
Alliance The www.corinth.ms/alliance2.html
PO Box 1089   Corinth MS 38835
Ph: 662-287-5269 ▪ Fx: 662-287-5260 ▪ TF: 877-347-0545
Greenville Area Chamber of Commerce www.greenvilleareachamber.com
915 Washington Ave   Greenville MS 38702
Ph: 662-378-3141 ▪ Fx: 662-378-3143
Greenwood-Leflore County Chamber of Commerce www.greenwoodms.com
402 Hwy 82   Greenwood MS 38930
Ph: 662-453-4152 ▪ Fx: 662-453-8003
Gulfport Chamber of Commerce
1401 20th Ave   Gulfport MS 39501
Ph: 228-863-2933 ▪ Fx: 228-863-2934
Mississippi Gulf Coast Chamber of Commerce www.mscoastchamber.com
1401 20th Ave   Gulfport MS 39501
Ph: 228-863-2942 ▪ Fx: 228-863-3080
Area Development Partnership www.hattiesburg-adp.org
1 Convention Center Plaza   Hattiesburg MS 39401
Ph: 601-296-7500 ▪ Fx: 601-296-7505 ▪ TF: 800-238-4288
Horn Lake Chamber of Commerce www.hornlakechamber.com
3040 Goodman Rd W Suite 2-A   Horn Lake MS 38637
Ph: 662-393-9897 ▪ Fx: 662-393-2942
MetroJackson Chamber of Commerce www.metrochamber.com
PO Box 22548   Jackson MS 39225
Ph: 601-948-7575 ▪ Fx: 601-352-5539
Jones County Chamber of Commerce
PO Box 527   Laurel MS 39441
Ph: 601-428-0574 ▪ Fx: 601-428-2047 ▪ TF: 800-392-9629
Pike County Chamber of Commerce & Economic Development District www.pikeinfo.com
PO Box 83   McComb MS 39649
Ph: 601-684-2291 ▪ Fx: 601-684-4899 ▪ TF: 800-399-4404
East Mississippi Business Development Corp www.embdc.org
PO Box 790   Meridian MS 39302
Ph: 601-693-1306 ▪ Fx: 601-693-5638
Natchez-Adams County Chamber of Commerce www.natchezchamber.com
PO Box 1403   Natchez MS 39121
Ph: 601-445-4611 ▪ Fx: 601-445-9361
Olive Branch Chamber of Commerce www.olivebranchms.com
6820 Cockrum St   Olive Branch MS 38654
Ph: 662-895-2600 ▪ Fx: 662-895-2625
Oxford-Lafayette County Chamber of Commerce www.oxfordms.com
PO Box 147   Oxford MS 38655
Ph: 662-234-4651 ▪ Fx: 662-234-4655 ▪ TF: 800-880-6967
Jackson County Chamber of Commerce www.jcchamber.com
720 Krebs Ave   Pascagoula MS 39567
Ph: 228-762-3391 ▪ Fx: 228-769-1726
Philadelphia-Neshoba County Chamber of Commerce www.neshoba.org
410 Poplar Ave PO Box 330   Philadelphia MS 39350
Ph: 601-656-1000 ▪ Fx: 601-656-1066 ▪ TF: 877-752-2643
Madison County Chamber of Commerce www.madisoncountychamber.com
PO Box 1276   Ridgeland MS 39158
Ph: 601-605-2554 ▪ Fx: 601-605-2260

Sardis Chamber of Commerce
120 S Main St PO Box 377   Sardis MS 38666
Ph: 662-487-3451
Southaven Chamber of Commerce www.southavenchamber.com
8700 Northwest Dr Suite 100   Southaven MS 38671
Ph: 662-342-6114 ▪ Fx: 662-342-6365 ▪ TF: 800-272-6551
Starkville Area Chamber of Commerce www.starkville.org
1 Research Blvd Suite 204   Starkville MS 39759
Ph: 662-323-3322 ▪ Fx: 662-323-5815 ▪ TF: 800-959-9978
Vicksburg-Warren County Chamber of Commerce www.vicksburg.org
2020 Mission 66   Vicksburg MS 39180
Ph: 601-636-1012 ▪ Fx: 601-636-4422 ▪ TF: 888-842-5728
Yazoo County Chamber of Commerce
212 E Broadway   Yazoo City MS 39194
Ph: 662-746-1273 ▪ Fx: 662-746-7238

MISSOURI

Affton Chamber of Commerce www.afftonchamber.com
10203 Gravois Rd Suite D   Affton MO 63123
Ph: 314-849-6499
West Saint Louis County Chamber of Commerce www.westcountychamber.com
14811 Manchester Rd Suite 100   Ballwin MO 63011
Ph: 636-230-9900 ▪ Fx: 636-230-9912
Blue Springs Chamber of Commerce www.bluespringschamber.com
1000 SW Main St   Blue Springs MO 64015
Ph: 816-229-8558 ▪ Fx: 816-229-1244
Branson/Lakes Area Chamber of Commerce www.bransonchamber.com
PO Box 1897   Branson MO 65615
Ph: 417-334-4136 ▪ Fx: 417-334-4139 ▪ TF: 800-214-3661
Cape Girardeau Chamber of Commerce www.capechamber.com
1267 N Mt Auburn Rd   Cape Girardeau MO 63701
Ph: 573-335-3312 ▪ Fx: 573-335-4686
Cassville Area Chamber of Commerce www.cassville.com
504 Main St   Cassville MO 65625
Ph: 417-847-2814 ▪ Fx: 417-847-0804 ▪ TF: 866-847-2814
Chesterfield Chamber of Commerce www.chesterfieldmochamber.com
101 Chesterfield Business Pkwy   Chesterfield MO 63005
Ph: 636-532-3399 ▪ Fx: 636-532-7446 ▪ TF: 888-242-4262
Columbia Chamber of Commerce chamber.columbia.mo.us
300 S Providence Rd   Columbia MO 65203
Ph: 573-874-1132 ▪ Fx: 573-443-3986
North County Chamber of Commerce www.northcountycc.com
119 Church St Suite 135   Ferguson MO 63135
Ph: 314-521-6000 ▪ Fx: 314-521-2897
Twin City Area Chamber of Commerce www.twincity.org
114 Main St   Festus MO 63028
Ph: 636-931-7697 ▪ Fx: 636-937-0925
Florissant Valley Chamber of Commerce www.florissantvalleycc.com
420 W Washington St   Florissant MO 63031
Ph: 314-831-3500 ▪ Fx: 314-831-9682
Kingdom of Callaway Chamber of Commerce www.callawaychamber.com
409 Court St   Fulton MO 65251
Ph: 573-642-3055 ▪ Fx: 573-642-5182 ▪ TF: 800-257-3554
Gladstone Area Chamber of Commerce www.gladstonechamber.com
6504 N Oak Traffic Way   Gladstone MO 64118
Ph: 816-436-4523 ▪ Fx: 816-436-4352
Grandview Area Chamber of Commerce www.grandview.org
12500 S 71 Hwy   Grandview MO 64030
Ph: 816-761-6505 ▪ Fx: 816-763-8460
Independence Chamber of Commerce www.independencechamber.com
210 W Truman Rd   Independence MO 64051
Ph: 816-252-4745 ▪ Fx: 816-252-4917
Jefferson City Area Chamber of Commerce www.jcchamber.org
213 Adams St   Jefferson City MO 65101
Ph: 573-634-3616 ▪ Fx: 573-634-3805
Joplin Area Chamber of Commerce www.joplincc.com
320 E 4th St   Joplin MO 64801
Ph: 417-624-4150 ▪ Fx: 417-624-4303
Greater Kansas City Chamber of Commerce www.kcchamber.com
911 Main St Suite 2600   Kansas City MO 64105
Ph: 816-221-2424 ▪ Fx: 816-221-7440
Northland Regional Chamber of Commerce www.northlandchamber.com
634 NW Englewood Rd   Kansas City MO 64118
Ph: 816-455-9911 ▪ Fx: 816-455-9933
South Kansas City Chamber of Commerce www.southkcchamber.com
5908 E Bannister Rd   Kansas City MO 64134
Ph: 816-761-7660 ▪ Fx: 816-761-7340
Kirkwood Area Chamber of Commerce www.kirkwoodarea.com
138 W Madison Ave   Kirkwood MO 63122
Ph: 314-821-4161 ▪ Fx: 314-821-5229
Lebanon Area Chamber of Commerce www.lebanonmissouri.com
186 N Adams St   Lebanon MO 65536
Ph: 417-588-3256 ▪ Fx: 417-588-3251 ▪ TF: 888-588-5710
Lee's Summit Chamber of Commerce www.leessummit.org
220 SE Main St   Lee's Summit MO 64063
Ph: 816-524-2424 ▪ Fx: 816-524-5246 ▪ TF: 888-816-5757
Neosho Area Chamber of Commerce www.neoshocc.com
308 W Spring St   Neosho MO 64850
Ph: 417-451-1925 ▪ Fx: 417-451-8097
O'Fallon Chamber of Commerce www.ofallonmochamber.com
2897 Hwy K Suite 200   O'Fallon MO 63366
Ph: 636-240-1818 ▪ Fx: 636-281-8288
Park Hills Chamber of Commerce
5 Municipal Dr   Park Hills MO 63601
Ph: 573-431-1051 ▪ Fx: 573-431-2327
Raytown Area Chamber of Commerce www.raytownchamber.com
5909 Raytown Trafficway   Raytown MO 64133
Ph: 816-353-8500 ▪ Fx: 816-353-8525

Appendix

Rolla Area Chamber of Commerce   www.rollachamber.org
1301 Kingshighway St   Rolla MO 65401
Ph: 573-364-3577 ▪ Fx: 573-364-5222 ▪ TF: 888-809-3817

Saint Charles Chamber of Commerce   www.stcharleschamber.org
2201 First Capitol Dr   Saint Charles MO 63301
Ph: 636-946-0633 ▪ Fx: 636-946-0301

Saint Joseph Area Chamber of Commerce   www.saintjoseph.com
3003 Frederick Ave   Saint Joseph MO 64506
Ph: 816-232-4461 ▪ Fx: 816-364-4873 ▪ TF: 800-748-7856

Maryland Heights Chamber of Commerce   www.mhcc.com
545 W Port Plaza   Saint Louis MO 63146
Ph: 314-576-6603 ▪ Fx: 314-576-6855

Northwest Chamber of Commerce   www.nwcommchamber.com
11965 St Charles Rock Rd Suite 203   Saint Louis MO 63114
Ph: 314-291-2131 ▪ Fx: 314-291-2153

Saint Louis Regional Commerce & Growth Association   www.stlrcga.org
1 Metropolitan Sq Suite 1300   Saint Louis MO 63102
Ph: 314-231-5555 ▪ Fx: 314-444-1122 ▪ TF: 877-785-7242

South County Chamber of Commerce   www.southcountychamber.com
6921 S Lindburg Blvd   Saint Louis MO 63125
Ph: 314-894-6800 ▪ Fx: 314-894-6888

Saint Peters Chamber of Commerce   www.stpeterschamber.com
1236 Jungermann Rd Suite C   Saint Peters MO 63376
Ph: 636-447-3336 ▪ Fx: 636-447-9575

Waynesville-Saint Robert Area Chamber of Commerce www.waynesville-strobertchamber.com
137 St Robert Blvd   Saint Robert MO 65584
Ph: 573-336-5121 ▪ Fx: 573-336-5472

Sedalia Area Chamber of Commerce & Convention & Visitors Bureau www.sedaliachamber.com
600 E 3rd St   Sedalia MO 65301
Ph: 660-826-2222 ▪ Fx: 660-826-2223 ▪ TF: 800-827-5295

Springfield Area Chamber of Commerce   www.springfieldchamber.com
202 S John Q Hammons Pkwy   Springfield MO 65806
Ph: 417-862-5567 ▪ Fx: 417-862-1611 ▪ TF: 800-879-7504

Washington Area Chamber of Commerce   www.washmo.org
323 W Main St   Washington MO 63090
Ph: 636-239-2715 ▪ Fx: 636-239-1381

MONTANA

Billings Area Chamber of Commerce   www.billingschamber.com
815 S 27th St   Billings MT 59101
Ph: 406-245-4111 ▪ Fx: 406-245-7333 ▪ TF: 800-735-2635

Bozeman Area Chamber of Commerce   www.bozemanchamber.com
2000 Commerce Way   Bozeman MT 59715
Ph: 406-586-5421 ▪ Fx: 406-586-8286

Butte-Silver Bow Chamber of Commerce   www.butteinfo.org
1000 George St   Butte MT 59701
Ph: 406-723-3177 ▪ Fx: 406-723-1215 ▪ TF: 800-735-6814

Great Falls Area Chamber of Commerce   www.greatfallschamber.org
710 1st Ave N   Great Falls MT 59401
Ph: 406-761-4434 ▪ Fx: 406-761-6129 ▪ TF: 800-735-8535

Bitterroot Valley Chamber of Commerce   www.bvchamber.com
105 E Main St   Hamilton MT 59840
Ph: 406-363-2400 ▪ Fx: 406-363-2402

Helena Area Chamber of Commerce   www.helenachamber.com
225 Cruse Ave   Helena MT 59601
Ph: 406-442-4120 ▪ Fx: 406-447-1532 ▪ TF: 800-743-5362

Kalispell Area Chamber of Commerce   www.kalispellchamber.com
15 Depot Park   Kalispell MT 59901
Ph: 406-758-2800 ▪ Fx: 406-758-2805

Missoula Area Chamber of Commerce   www.missoulachamber.com
825 E Front St   Missoula MT 59802
Ph: 406-543-6623 ▪ Fx: 406-543-6625

NEBRASKA

Bellevue Chamber of Commerce   www.bellevuenebraska.com
204 W Mission Ave   Bellevue NE 68005
Ph: 402-898-3000 ▪ Fx: 402-291-8729

Grand Island Area Chamber of Commerce   www.gichamber.com
PO Box 1486   Grand Island NE 68802
Ph: 308-382-9210 ▪ Fx: 308-382-1154

Kearney Area Chamber of Commerce   www.kearneycoc.org
1007 2nd Ave   Kearney NE 68847
Ph: 308-237-3101 ▪ Fx: 308-237-3103 ▪ TF: 800-652-9435

Lincoln Chamber of Commerce   www.lcoc.com
PO Box 83006   Lincoln NE 68501
Ph: 402-436-2350 ▪ Fx: 402-436-2360

North Platte Area Chamber of Commerce   www.northplattechamber.com
502 S Dewey St   North Platte NE 69101
Ph: 308-532-4966 ▪ Fx: 308-532-4827

Greater Omaha Chamber of Commerce   www.omahachamber.net
1301 Harney St   Omaha NE 68102
Ph: 402-346-5000 ▪ Fx: 402-346-7050

Sarpy County Chamber of Commerce   www.sarpychamber.org
501 Olson Dr Suite 4   Papillion NE 68046
Ph: 402-339-3050 ▪ Fx: 402-339-9968

NEVADA

Carson City Area Chamber of Commerce   www.carsoncitychamber.com
1900 S Carson St Suite 100   Carson City NV 89701
Ph: 775-882-1565 ▪ Fx: 775-882-4179

Elko Chamber of Commerce   www.elkonevada.com
1405 Idaho St   Elko NV 89801
Ph: 775-738-7135 ▪ Fx: 775-738-7136 ▪ TF: 800-428-7143

Greater Fallon Area Chamber of Commerce   www.fallonchamber.com
85 N Taylor St   Fallon NV 89406
Ph: 775-423-2544 ▪ Fx: 775-423-0540

Carson Valley Chamber of Commerce & Visitors Authority   www.carsonvalleynv.org
1513 Hwy 395 N   Gardnerville NV 89410
Ph: 775-782-8144 ▪ Fx: 775-782-1025 ▪ TF: 800-727-7677

Henderson Chamber of Commerce   www.hendersonchamber.com
590 S Boulder Hwy   Henderson NV 89015
Ph: 702-565-8951 ▪ Fx: 702-565-3115

Tahoe-Douglas Chamber of Commerce   www.tahoechamber.com
PO Box 7139   Lake Tahoe NV 89449
Ph: 775-588-4591 ▪ Fx: 775-588-4598

Las Vegas Chamber of Commerce   www.lvchamber.com
3720 Howard Hughes Pkwy   Las Vegas NV 89109
Ph: 702-735-1616 ▪ Fx: 702-735-0320

Latin Chamber of Commerce   www.lasvegaslatincc.com
PO Box 7500   Las Vegas NV 89125
Ph: 702-385-7367 ▪ Fx: 702-385-2614

North Las Vegas Chamber of Commerce   www.nlvchamber.com
2290 McDaniel St Suite 1A   North Las Vegas NV 89030
Ph: 702-642-9595 ▪ Fx: 702-642-0439

Sparks Community Chamber of Commerce   www.sparkschamber.org
831 Victorian Ave   Sparks NV 89431
Ph: 775-358-1976 ▪ Fx: 775-358-1992

Tonopah Chamber of Commerce   www.tonopahnevada.com
PO Box 408   Tonopah NV 89049
Ph: 775-482-3859 ▪ Fx: 775-482-3932

NEW HAMPSHIRE

Souhegan Valley Chamber of Commerce   www.souhegan.net
89 SR 101A   Amherst NH 03031
Ph: 603-673-4360 ▪ Fx: 603-673-5018

Greater Concord Chamber of Commerce   www.concordnhchamber.com
40 Commercial St   Concord NH 03301
Ph: 603-224-2508 ▪ Fx: 603-224-8128

Greater Derry Chamber of Commerce   www.derry-chamber.org
29 W Broadway   Derry NH 03038
Ph: 603-432-8205 ▪ Fx: 603-432-7938

Greater Dover Chamber of Commerce   www.dovernh.org
299 Central Ave   Dover NH 03820
Ph: 603-742-2218 ▪ Fx: 603-749-6317

Exeter Area Chamber of Commerce   www.exeterarea.org
120 Water St   Exeter NH 03833
Ph: 603-772-2411 ▪ Fx: 603-772-9965

Hampton Area Chamber of Commerce   www.hamptonareachamberofcommerce.com
1 Park Ave Suite 3G   Hampton NH 03842
Ph: 603-926-8718 ▪ Fx: 603-926-9977

Hanover Area Chamber of Commerce   www.hanoverchamber.org
PO Box 5105   Hanover NH 03755
Ph: 603-643-3115 ▪ Fx: 603-643-5606

Greater Keene Chamber of Commerce   www.keenechamber.com
48 Central Sq   Keene NH 03431
Ph: 603-352-1303 ▪ Fx: 603-358-5341

Greater Laconia-Weirs Beach Chamber of Commerce   www.laconia-weirs.org
11 Veterans Sq   Laconia NH 03246
Ph: 603-524-5531 ▪ Fx: 603-524-5534

Greater Manchester Chamber of Commerce   www.manchester-chamber.org
889 Elm St   Manchester NH 03101
Ph: 603-666-6600 ▪ Fx: 603-626-0910

Greater Nashua Chamber of Commerce   www.nashuachamber.com
151 Main St   Nashua NH 03060
Ph: 603-881-8333 ▪ Fx: 603-881-7323

Greater Portsmouth Chamber of Commerce   www.portsmouthchamber.org
500 Market St PO Box 239   Portsmouth NH 03802
Ph: 603-436-1118 ▪ Fx: 603-436-5118

Greater Rochester Chamber of Commerce   www.rochesternh.org
18 S Main St   Rochester NH 03867
Ph: 603-332-5080 ▪ Fx: 603-332-5216

Greater Salem Chamber of Commerce   www.salemnhchamber.com
224 N Broadway 1st Fl   Salem NH 03079
Ph: 603-893-3177 ▪ Fx: 603-894-5158

NEW JERSEY

Asbury Park Chamber of Commerce   www.asburyparkchamber.com
PO Box 649   Asbury Park NJ 07712
Ph: 732-775-7676 ▪ Fx: 732-775-7675

Atlantic City Regional Chamber of Commerce   www.atlanticcitychamber.com
1125 Atlantic Ave Suite 105   Atlantic City NJ 08401
Ph: 609-345-5600 ▪ Fx: 609-345-1666

Bayonne Chamber of Commerce   www.bayonnenj.org/commerce.htm
621 Ave C   Bayonne NJ 07002
Ph: 201-436-4333 ▪ Fx: 201-436-8546

Bergenfield Chamber of Commerce   www.bergenfieldboro.com
35 S Washington Ave   Bergenfield NJ 07621
Ph: 201-387-8300 ▪ Fx: 201-387-8302

Brick Township Chamber of Commerce   www.brickchamber.org
270 Chambers Bridge Rd   Brick NJ 08723
Ph: 732-477-4949 ▪ Fx: 732-477-5788

Bridgeton Area Chamber of Commerce   www.baccnj.com
PO Box 1063   Bridgeton NJ 08302
Ph: 856-455-1312 ▪ Fx: 856-453-9795

Mount Olive Area Chamber of Commerce   www.mtolivechambernj.com
PO Box 192   Budd Lake NJ 07828
Ph: 973-691-0109 ▪ Fx: 973-691-0110

Cape May County Chamber of Commerce   www.capemaycountychamber.com
PO Box 74   Cape May Court House NJ 08210
Ph: 609-465-7181 ▪ Fx: 609-465-5017

Salem County Chamber of Commerce   www.salemnjchamber.homestead.com
91-A S Virginia Ave   Carneys Point NJ 08069
Ph: 856-299-6699 ▪ Fx: 856-299-0299

Cherry Hill Regional Chamber of Commerce   www.cherryhillregional.com
1060 Kings Hwy N Suite 200   Cherry Hill NJ 08034
Ph: 856-667-1600 ▪ Fx: 856-667-1464

North Jersey Regional Chamber of Commerce   www.njrcc.org
1033 Rt 46 E   Clifton NJ 07013
Ph: 973-470-9300 ▪ Fx: 973-470-9245

East Brunswick Regional Chamber of Commerce   www.ebnjchamber.org
21 Brunswick Woods Dr PO Box 56   East Brunswick NJ 08816
Ph: 732-257-3009 ▪ Fx: 732-257-0949

Edison Chamber of Commerce   www.edisonchamber.com
629 Amboy Ave 1st Fl   Edison NJ 08837
Ph: 732-738-9482 ▪ Fx: 732-738-9485

Union County Chamber of Commerce
135 Jefferson Ave PO Box 300   Elizabeth NJ 07207
Ph: 908-352-0900 ▪ Fx: 908-352-0865

Englewood Chamber of Commerce   www.englewood-chamber.com
2-10 N Van Brunt St   Englewood NJ 07631
Ph: 201-567-2381 ▪ Fx: 201-871-4549

Fair Lawn Chamber of Commerce   www.fairlawnchamber.org
0-100 27th St   Fair Lawn NJ 07410
Ph: 201-796-7050 ▪ Fx: 201-475-0619

Greater Fort Lee Chamber of Commerce   www.fortleechamber.us
210 Whiteman St   Fort Lee NJ 07024
Ph: 201-944-7575 ▪ Fx: 201-944-5168

Western Monmouth Chamber of Commerce   www.wmchamber.com
17 Broad St   Freehold NJ 07728
Ph: 732-462-3030 ▪ Fx: 732-462-2123

Greater Hackensack Regional Chamber of Commerce   www.hackensackchamber.org
5 University Plaza Dr   Hackensack NJ 07601
Ph: 201-489-3700 ▪ Fx: 201-489-1741

Warren County Regional Chamber of Commerce   www.warrencountychamber.org
PO Box 546   Hackettstown NJ 07840
Ph: 908-852-1253 ▪ Fx: 908-852-5622

Greater Hammonton Chamber of Commerce
10 S Egg Harbor Rd PO Box 554   Hammonton NJ 08037
Ph: 609-561-9080 ▪ Fx: 609-561-9411

Howell Chamber of Commerce   www.howellchamber.com
PO Box 196   Howell NJ 07731
Ph: 732-363-4114 ▪ Fx: 732-363-8747

Irvington Chamber of Commerce
PO Box 323   Irvington NJ 07111
Ph: 973-372-4100 ▪ Fx: 973-673-5828

Hudson County Chamber of Commerce   www.hudsonchamber.org
660 Newark Ave Suite 220   Jersey City NJ 07306
Ph: 201-386-0699 ▪ Fx: 201-386-8480

Parsippany Area Chamber of Commerce   www.njpacc.org
12-14 N Beverwyck Rd   Lake Hiawatha NJ 07034
Ph: 973-402-6400 ▪ Fx: 973-334-2242

Lakewood Chamber of Commerce   www.mylakewoodchamber.com
395 Hwy 70 W Suite 125   Lakewood NJ 08701
Ph: 732-363-0012 ▪ Fx: 732-367-4453

Hunterdon County Chamber of Commerce   www.hunterdon-chamber.org
2200 Rt 31 Suite 15   Lebanon NJ 08833
Ph: 908-735-5955 ▪ Fx: 908-730-6580

Greater Long Branch Chamber of Commerce
PO Box 628   Long Branch NJ 07740
Ph: 732-222-0400 ▪ Fx: 732-571-3385

Matawan-Aberdeen Chamber of Commerce
PO Box 522   Matawan NJ 07747
Ph: 732-290-1125 ▪ Fx: 732-290-1125

Millville Chamber of Commerce   www.millville-nj.com
PO Box 831   Millville NJ 08332
Ph: 856-825-2600 ▪ Fx: 856-825-5333

Middlesex County Regional Chamber of Commerce   www.mcrcc.org
1 Distribution Way Suite 101   Monmouth Junction NJ 08852
Ph: 732-821-1700 ▪ Fx: 732-821-5852

Morris County Chamber of Commerce   www.morrischamber.org
25 Lindsley Dr Suite 105   Morristown NJ 07960
Ph: 973-539-3882 ▪ Fx: 973-539-3960

Randolph Area Chamber of Commerce   www.randolphchamber.org
PO Box 391   Mount Freedom NJ 07970
Ph: 973-361-3462 ▪ Fx: 973-895-3297

Burlington County Chamber of Commerce   www.bccoc.com
900 Briggs Rd   Mount Laurel NJ 08054
Ph: 856-439-2520 ▪ Fx: 856-439-2523

Northern Monmouth Chamber of Commerce   www.northernmonmouth.org
PO Box 521   Navesink NJ 07752
Ph: 732-291-7870 ▪ Fx: 732-291-7871

Sussex County Chamber of Commerce   www.sussexcountychamber.org
120 Hampton House Rd   Newton NJ 07860
Ph: 973-579-1811 ▪ Fx: 973-579-3031

Atlantic County Chamber of Commerce   www.atlanticcountychamber.com
1337 Tilton Rd Suite 201   Northfield NJ 08225
Ph: 609-646-2214 ▪ Fx: 609-646-2433

Nutley Chamber of Commerce   www.nutleychamber.com
610 Franklin Ave   Nutley NJ 07110
Ph: 973-667-5300 ▪ Fx: 973-667-0854

Orange Chamber of Commerce   www.orangechamber.biz
PO Box 1178   Orange NJ 07050
Ph: 973-676-8725 ▪ Fx: 973-673-5828

Commerce & Industry Association of New Jersey   www.cianj.org
S 61 Paramus Rd   Paramus NJ 07652
Ph: 201-368-2100 ▪ Fx: 201-368-3438

Paramus Chamber of Commerce   www.paramuschamber.com
58 E Midland Ave   Paramus NJ 07652
Ph: 201-261-3344 ▪ Fx: 201-261-3346

Greater Paterson Chamber of Commerce   www.greaterpatersoncc.org
100 Hamilton Plaza Suite 1201   Paterson NJ 07505
Ph: 973-881-7300 ▪ Fx: 973-881-8233

Perth Amboy Chamber of Commerce   www.perthamboychamber.com
214 Smith St Suite 210   Perth Amboy NJ 08861
Ph: 732-442-7400 ▪ Fx: 732-442-7450

Piscataway/Middlesex/South Plainfield Area Chamber of Commerce   www.pmcoc.org
1315 Stelton Rd   Piscataway NJ 08854
Ph: 732-394-0220 ▪ Fx: 732-394-0223

Point Pleasant Beach Chamber of Commerce   www.pointpleasantbeachnj.com
517-A Arnold Ave   Point Pleasant Beach NJ 08742
Ph: 732-899-2424 ▪ Fx: 732-899-0103

Chamber of Commerce of the Princeton Area   www.princetonchamber.org
216 Rockingham Row   Princeton NJ 08540
Ph: 609-520-1776 ▪ Fx: 609-520-9107

Eastern Monmouth Area Chamber of Commerce   www.emacc.org
170 Broad St   Red Bank NJ 07701
Ph: 732-741-0055 ▪ Fx: 732-741-6778

Ridgewood Chamber of Commerce   www.webridgewood.com
199 Dayton St   Ridgewood NJ 07450
Ph: 201-445-2600 ▪ Fx: 201-251-1958

Meadowlands Regional Chamber of Commerce   www.meadowlands.org
201 Rt 17 N   Rutherford NJ 07070
Ph: 201-939-0707 ▪ Fx: 201-939-0522

Southern Ocean County Chamber of Commerce   www.discoversouthernocean.com
265 W 9th St   Ship Bottom NJ 08008
Ph: 609-494-7211 ▪ Fx: 609-494-5807 ▪ TF: 800-292-6372

Chamber of Commerce of Franklin Township   www.franklinchamber.com
675 Franklin Blvd   Somerset NJ 08873
Ph: 732-545-7044 ▪ Fx: 732-545-7043

Somerset County Business Partnership   www.somersetbusinesspartnership.com
PO Box 833   Somerville NJ 08876
Ph: 908-218-4300 ▪ Fx: 908-722-7823

Suburban Chambers of Commerce   www.suburbanchambers.org
71 Summit Ave   Summit NJ 07901
Ph: 908-522-1700 ▪ Fx: 908-522-9252

Toms River-Ocean County Chamber of Commerce   www.oc-chamber.com
1200 Hooper Ave   Toms River NJ 08753
Ph: 732-349-0220 ▪ Fx: 732-349-1252

Mercer County Chamber of Commerce   www.mercerchamber.org
214 W State St   Trenton NJ 08608
Ph: 609-393-4143 ▪ Fx: 609-393-1032

Union Township Chamber of Commerce   www.unionchamber.org
355 Chestnut St   Union NJ 07083
Ph: 908-688-2777 ▪ Fx: 908-688-0338

Greater Vineland Chamber of Commerce   chamber.vineland.org
2115 S Delsea Dr   Vineland NJ 08360
Ph: 856-691-7400 ▪ Fx: 856-691-2113 ▪ TF: 800-309-0019

Chamber of Commerce of Southern New Jersey   www.chambersnj.com
Piazza 6014 at Main St   Voorhees NJ 08043
Ph: 856-424-7776 ▪ Fx: 856-424-8180

Southern Monmouth Area Chamber of Commerce   www.smcconline.org
2510 Belmar Blvd Unit I-20   Wall NJ 07719
Ph: 732-280-8800 ▪ Fx: 732-280-8505

Tri-County Chamber of Commerce   www.tricounty.org
2055 Hamburg Tpke   Wayne NJ 07470
Ph: 973-831-7788 ▪ Fx: 973-831-9112

North Essex Chamber of Commerce   www.northessexchamber.com
3 Fairfield Ave   West Caldwell NJ 07006
Ph: 973-226-5500 ▪ Fx: 973-403-9335

West Milford Chamber of Commerce   www.westmilford.com
PO Box 234   West Milford NJ 07480
Ph: 973-728-3150 ▪ Fx: 973-697-5177

Westfield Area Chamber of Commerce   westfieldchamber.com
173 Elm St   Westfield NJ 07090
Ph: 908-233-3021 ▪ Fx: 908-654-8183

Woodbridge Metro Chamber of Commerce   www.woodbridgechamber.org
52 Main St   Woodbridge NJ 07095
Ph: 732-636-4040 ▪ Fx: 732-636-3492

NEW MEXICO

Alamogordo Chamber of Commerce   www.alamogordo.com
1301 N White Sands Blvd   Alamogordo NM 88310
Ph: 505-437-6120 ▪ Fx: 505-437-6334 ▪ TF: 800-826-0294

Greater Albuquerque Chamber of Commerce   www.gacc.org
PO Box 25100   Albuquerque NM 87125
Ph: 505-764-3700 ▪ Fx: 505-764-3714

Carlsbad Chamber of Commerce   www.chamber.caverns.com
302 S Canal St   Carlsbad NM 88220
Ph: 505-887-6516 ▪ Fx: 505-885-1455 ▪ TF: 800-221-1224

Clovis/Curry County Chamber of Commerce   www.clovisnm.org
215 N Main St   Clovis NM 88101
Ph: 505-763-3435 ▪ Fx: 505-763-7266 ▪ TF: 800-261-7656

Espanola Valley Chamber of Commerce   www.espanolanmchamber.com
PO Box 190   Espanola NM 87532
Ph: 505-753-2831 ▪ Fx: 505-753-1252

Farmington Chamber of Commerce   www.gofarmington.com
105 N Orchard Ave   Farmington NM 87401
Ph: 505-325-0279 ▪ Fx: 505-327-7556 ▪ TF: 888-325-0279

Grants/Cibola County Chamber of Commerce   www.grants.org
PO Box 297   Grants NM 87020
Ph: 505-287-4802 ▪ Fx: 505-287-8224 ▪ TF: 800-748-2142

Hobbs Chamber of Commerce   www.hobbschamber.org
400 N Marland Blvd   Hobbs NM 88240
Ph: 505-397-3202 ▪ Fx: 505-397-1689 ▪ TF: 800-658-6291

Greater Las Cruces Chamber of Commerce   lascruces.org
760 W Picacho Ave   Las Cruces NM 88005
Ph: 505-524-1968 ▪ Fax: 505-527-5546
Las Vegas-San Miguel Chamber of Commerce   www.lasvegasnm.org
PO Box 128   Las Vegas NM 87701
Ph: 505-425-8631 ▪ Fax: 505-425-3057 ▪ TF: 800-832-5947
Rio Rancho Chamber of Commerce   www.rrchamber.org
1781 Rio Rancho Dr   Rio Rancho NM 87124
Ph: 505-892-1533 ▪ Fax: 505-892-6157
Roswell Chamber of Commerce   www.roswellnm.org
PO Box 70   Roswell NM 88202
Ph: 505-623-5695 ▪ Fax: 505-624-6870 ▪ TF: 877-849-7679
Santa Fe Chamber of Commerce   www.santafechamber.com
PO Box 1928   Santa Fe NM 87504
Ph: 505-988-3279 ▪ Fax: 505-984-2205
Silver City-Grant County Chamber of Commerce   www.silvercity.org
201 N Hudson St   Silver City NM 88061
Ph: 505-538-3785 ▪ Fax: 505-538-3786 ▪ TF: 800-548-9378

NEW YORK

Albany-Colonie Regional Chamber of Commerce   www.ac-chamber.org
107 Washington Ave   Albany NY 12210
Ph: 518-434-1214 ▪ Fax: 518-434-1339
Guilderland Chamber of Commerce   www.guilderlandchamber.com
2021 Western Ave Suite 105   Albany NY 12203
Ph: 518-456-6611 ▪ Fax: 518-456-6690
Orleans County Chamber of Commerce   www.orleanschamber.com
121 N Main St Suite 110   Albion NY 14411
Ph: 585-589-7727 ▪ Fax: 585-589-7326
Montgomery County Chamber of Commerce   www.montgomerycountyny.com
366 W Main St PO Box 309   Amsterdam NY 12010
Ph: 518-842-8200 ▪ Fax: 518-843-8327 ▪ TF: 800-743-7337
Cayuga County Chamber of Commerce   www.cayugacountychamber.com
36 South St   Auburn NY 13021
Ph: 315-252-7291 ▪ Fax: 315-255-3077
Greater Baldwinsville Chamber of Commerce   www.baldwinsvillechamber.com
50 Oswego St   Baldwinsville NY 13027
Ph: 315-638-0550
Genesee County Chamber of Commerce   www.geneseeny.com/chamain.html
210 E Main St   Batavia NY 14020
Ph: 585-343-7440 ▪ Fax: 585-343-7487 ▪ TF: 800-622-2686
Greater Bath Area Chamber of Commerce   www.bathnychamber.com
10 Pulteney Sq W   Bath NY 14810
Ph: 607-776-7122 ▪ Fax: 607-776-7122
Bay Shore Chamber of Commerce   www.bayshorecommerce.com
77 E Main St PO Box 5110   Bay Shore NY 11706
Ph: 631-665-7003 ▪ Fax: 631-665-5204
Chamber of Commerce of the Bellmores   www.bellmorechamber.com
PO Box 861   Bellmore NY 11710
Ph: 516-679-1875 ▪ Fax: 516-409-0544
Broome County Chamber of Commerce   www.greaterbinghamtonchamber.com
49 Court St   Binghamton NY 13902
Ph: 607-772-8860 ▪ Fax: 607-722-4513 ▪ TF: 800-836-6740
New Bronx Chamber of Commerce Inc   www.bronxmall.com/com/chamber
1029 E 163rd St   Bronx NY 10459
Ph: 718-328-0100
Brooklyn Chamber of Commerce   www.ibrooklyn.com
25 Elm Pl Suite 200   Brooklyn NY 11201
Ph: 718-875-1000 ▪ Fax: 718-237-4274
Coney Island Chamber of Commerce
1015 Surf Ave   Brooklyn NY 11224
Ph: 718-266-1234 ▪ Fax: 718-714-0379
Buffalo Niagara Partnership   www.thepartnership.org
300 Main Pl Tower   Buffalo NY 14202
Ph: 716-852-7100 ▪ Fax: 716-852-2761 ▪ TF: 800-241-0474
Saint Lawrence County Chamber of Commerce   www.stlawrencechamber.org
101 Main St   Canton NY 13617
Ph: 315-386-4000 ▪ Fax: 315-379-0134 ▪ TF: 877-228-7810
Carmel-Kent Chamber of Commerce Inc   carmelkentchamber.com
PO Box 447   Carmel NY 10512
Ph: 914-441-9623
Greene County Chamber of Commerce   www.greene-ny.com
1 Bridge St 2nd Fl   Catskill NY 12414
Ph: 518-943-4222 ▪ Fax: 518-943-1700
Cheektowaga Chamber of Commerce   www.cheektowaga.org
2875 Union Rd Suite 50   Cheektowaga NY 14227
Ph: 716-684-5838 ▪ Fax: 716-684-5571
Southern Saratoga County Chamber of Commerce   www.ssccc.org
PO Box 399   Clifton Park NY 12065
Ph: 518-371-7748 ▪ Fax: 518-371-5025
Long Island Association   www.longislandassociation.org
80 Hauppauge Rd   Commack NY 11725
Ph: 631-499-4400 ▪ Fax: 631-499-2194
Corning Area Chamber of Commerce
1 W Market St Suite 302   Corning NY 14830
Ph: 607-936-4686 ▪ Fax: 607-936-4685 ▪ TF: 866-463-6264
Cortland County Chamber of Commerce   www.cortlandchamber.com
26 N Main St   Cortland NY 13045
Ph: 607-756-2814 ▪ Fax: 607-756-4698
Delaware County Chamber of Commerce   www.delawarecounty.org
114 Main St   Delhi NY 13753
Ph: 607-746-2281 ▪ Fax: 607-746-3571 ▪ TF: 800-642-4443
Bethlehem Chamber of Commerce   www.bethlehemchamber.com
318 Delaware Ave   Delmar NY 12054
Ph: 518-439-0512 ▪ Fax: 518-475-0910
Chautauqua County Chamber of Commerce   www.chautauquachamber.com
212 Lake Shore Dr W   Dunkirk NY 14048
Ph: 716-366-6200 ▪ Fax: 716-366-4276

Greater East Aurora Chamber of Commerce   www.eanycc.com
431 Main St   East Aurora NY 14052
Ph: 716-652-8444 ▪ Fax: 716-652-8384 ▪ TF: 800-441-2881
Chemung County Chamber of Commerce   www.chemungchamber.org
400 E Church St   Elmira NY 14901
Ph: 607-734-5137 ▪ Fax: 607-734-4490 ▪ TF: 800-627-5892
Livingston County Chamber of Commerce   www.fingerlakeswest.com
4560 Millennium Dr   Geneseo NY 14454
Ph: 585-243-2222 ▪ Fax: 585-243-4824 ▪ TF: 800-538-7365
Adirondack Regional Chambers of Commerce   www.adirondackchamber.org
5 Warren St   Glens Falls NY 12801
Ph: 518-798-1761 ▪ Fax: 518-792-4147 ▪ TF: 888-516-7247
Fulton County Regional Chamber of Commerce   www.fultoncountyny.org
2 N Main St   Gloversville NY 12078
Ph: 518-725-0641 ▪ Fax: 518-725-0643 ▪ TF: 800-676-3858
Hamburg Chamber of Commerce   www.hamburg-chamber.org
8 S Buffalo St   Hamburg NY 14075
Ph: 716-649-7917 ▪ Fax: 716-649-6362 ▪ TF: 877-322-6890
Hempstead Village Chamber of Commerce
1776 Denton Green   Hempstead NY 11550
Ph: 516-483-2000 ▪ Fax: 516-489-5997
Hicksville Chamber of Commerce   www.hicksvillechamber.com
10 W Marie St   Hicksville NY 11801
Ph: 516-931-7170 ▪ Fax: 516-931-8546
Southern Ulster County Chamber of Commerce   www.southernulsterchamber.org
33 Main St   Highland NY 12528
Ph: 845-691-6070 ▪ Fax: 845-691-9194
Columbia County Chamber of Commerce   www.columbiachamber-ny.com
507 Warren St   Hudson NY 12534
Ph: 518-828-4417 ▪ Fax: 518-822-9539
Huntington Township Chamber of Commerce   www.huntingtonchamber.com
164 Main St   Huntington NY 11743
Ph: 631-423-6100 ▪ Fax: 631-351-8276 ▪ TF: 888-361-5710
Hyde Park Chamber of Commerce   www.hydeparkchamber.org
PO Box 17   Hyde Park NY 12538
Ph: 845-229-8612 ▪ Fax: 845-229-8638
Tompkins County Chamber of Commerce   www.tompkinschamber.org
904 E Shore Dr   Ithaca NY 14850
Ph: 607-273-7080 ▪ Fax: 607-272-7617
Chamber of Commerce of Borough of Queens   www.queenschamber.org
75-20 Astoria Blvd Suite 140   Jackson Heights NY 11370
Ph: 718-898-8500 ▪ Fax: 718-898-8599
Jamaica Chamber of Commerce
90-25 161st St Suite 505   Jamaica NY 11432
Ph: 718-657-4800 ▪ Fax: 718-658-4642
Chautauqua County Chamber of Commerce   www.chautauquachamber.com
101 W 5th St   Jamestown NY 14701
Ph: 716-484-1101 ▪ Fax: 716-487-0785
Kenmore-Town of Tonawanda Chamber of Commerce   www.ken-ton.org
3411 Delaware Ave   Kenmore NY 14217
Ph: 716-874-1202 ▪ Fax: 716-874-3151
Chamber of Commerce of Ulster County   www.ulsterchamber.com
1 Albany Ave Suite G-3   Kingston NY 12401
Ph: 845-338-5100 ▪ Fax: 845-338-0968
Lake Placid/Essex County Visitors Bureau   www.lakeplacid.com
216 Main St Olympic Ctr   Lake Placid NY 12946
Ph: 518-523-2445 ▪ Fax: 518-523-2605 ▪ TF: 800-447-5224
Latham Area Chamber of Commerce   www.lathamchamber.org
849 New Loudon Rd   Latham NY 12110
Ph: 518-785-6995 ▪ Fax: 518-785-7173
Sullivan County Chamber of Commerce   www.catskills.com
59 N Main St   Liberty NY 12754
Ph: 845-292-8500 ▪ Fax: 845-292-5366
Greater Liverpool Chamber of Commerce   www.liverpoolchamber.com
314 2nd St   Liverpool NY 13088
Ph: 315-457-3895 ▪ Fax: 315-234-3226
Long Beach Chamber of Commerce
350 National Blvd   Long Beach NY 11561
Ph: 516-432-6000 ▪ Fax: 516-432-0273 ▪ TF: 866-563-3275
Lewis County Chamber of Commerce   www.lewiscountychamber.org
7383-C Utica Blvd   Lowville NY 13367
Ph: 315-376-2213 ▪ Fax: 315-376-0326 ▪ TF: 800-724-0242
Chamber of Commerce of the Mahopacs Inc   www.mahopacchamber.com
PO Box 160   Mahopac NY 10541
Ph: 845-628-5553 ▪ Fax: 845-628-5962
Chamber of Commerce of the Massapequas
PO Box 1912   Massapequa NY 11758
Ph: 516-541-1443 ▪ Fax: 516-541-8625
Herkimer County Chamber of Commerce   www.herkimercountychamber.com
28 W Main St   Mohawk NY 13407
Ph: 315-866-7820 ▪ Fax: 315-866-7833 ▪ TF: 877-984-4636
Mount Vernon Chamber of Commerce   www.mvnycoc.org
22 W 1st St Suite 210   Mount Vernon NY 10550
Ph: 914-667-7500 ▪ Fax: 914-699-0139
Greater New Hyde Park Chamber of Commerce   www.nhpchamber.com
PO Box 247   New Hyde Park NY 11040
Ph: 516-437-2021
Chamber of Commerce of New Rochelle   www.newrochellechamber.org
459 Main St   New Rochelle NY 10801
Ph: 914-632-5700 ▪ Fax: 914-632-0708
Greater New York Chamber of Commerce   nyc.chamber.com
172 Madison Ave 7th Fl   New York NY 10016
Ph: 212-244-0003 ▪ Fax: 212-686-7232
Manhattan Chamber of Commerce   www.manhattancc.org
1555 3rd Ave Rm 202   New York NY 10128
Ph: 212-479-7772 ▪ Fax: 212-831-4244
New York City Partnership & Chamber of Commerce Inc   www.nycp.org
1 Battery Park Plaza 5th Fl   New York NY 10004
Ph: 212-493-7500 ▪ Fax: 212-344-3344

West Side Chamber of Commerce www.westsidechamber.org
1841 Broadway Suite 701   New York NY 10023
Ph: 212-541-8880 ▪ Fx: 212-541-8883

Orange County Chamber of Commerce www.orangeny.com
11 Racquet Rd   Newburgh NY 12550
Ph: 845-567-6229 ▪ Fx: 845-567-6271

Niagara USA Chamber of Commerce www.niagarachamber.org
345 3rd St Suite 500   Niagara Falls NY 14303
Ph: 716-285-9141 ▪ Fx: 716-285-0941

Chamber of Commerce of the Tonawandas www.the-tonawandas.com
15 Webster St   North Tonawanda NY 14120
Ph: 716-692-5120 ▪ Fx: 716-692-1867

Chenango County Chamber of Commerce www.chenangony.org
19 Eaton Ave   Norwich NY 13815
Ph: 607-334-1400 ▪ Fx: 607-336-6963 ▪ TF: 800-556-8596

Oceanside Chamber of Commerce
PO Box 1   Oceanside NY 11572
Ph: 516-763-9177

Greater Olean Area Chamber of Commerce www.oleanny.com
120 N Union St   Olean NY 14760
Ph: 716-372-4433 ▪ Fx: 716-372-7912

Otsego County Chamber www.otsegocountychamber.com
12 Carbon St   Oneonta NY 13820
Ph: 607-432-4500 ▪ Fx: 607-432-4506 ▪ TF: 877-568-7346

Orchard Park Chamber of Commerce www.orchardparkchamber.com
4211 N Buffalo St Suite 14   Orchard Park NY 14127
Ph: 716-662-3366 ▪ Fx: 716-662-5946

Greater Oswego Chamber of Commerce www.oswegochamber.com
156 W 2nd St   Oswego NY 13126
Ph: 315-343-7681 ▪ Fx: 315-342-0831

Tioga County Chamber of Commerce www.tiogachamber.com
188 Front St   Owego NY 13827
Ph: 607-687-2020 ▪ Fx: 607-687-9028

Hudson Valley Gateway Chamber of Commerce www.hvgatewaychamber.com
1 S Division St   Peekskill NY 10566
Ph: 914-737-3600 ▪ Fx: 914-737-0541

Plattsburgh North Country Chamber of Commerce www.northcountrychamber.com
PO Box 310   Plattsburgh NY 12901
Ph: 518-563-1000 ▪ Fx: 518-563-1028

Port Chester-Rye Brook Chamber of Commerce www.portchesterryebrookchamber.com
110 Willett Ave   Port Chester NY 10573
Ph: 914-939-1900 ▪ Fx: 914-939-2733

Tri-State Chamber of Commerce www.tristatechamber.org
PO Box 121   Port Jervis NY 12771
Ph: 845-856-6694 ▪ Fx: 845-856-6695

Port Washington Chamber of Commerce www.portwashington.org
PO Box 121   Port Washington NY 11050
Ph: 516-883-6566 ▪ Fx: 516-883-6591

Poughkeepsie Area Chamber of Commerce www.pokchamb.org
1 Civic Ctr Plaza Suite 400   Poughkeepsie NY 12601
Ph: 845-454-1700 ▪ Fx: 845-454-1702

Rochester Business Alliance www.rnychamber.com
55 Saint Paul St   Rochester NY 14604
Ph: 585-454-2220 ▪ Fx: 585-263-3679

Chamber of Commerce of the Rockaways www.rockawaychamberofcommerce.com
253 Beach 116th St   Rockaway Park NY 11694
Ph: 718-634-1300 ▪ Fx: 718-634-9623

Rome Area Chamber of Commerce www.romechamber.com
139 W Dominick St   Rome NY 13440
Ph: 315-337-1700 ▪ Fx: 315-337-1715

Saratoga County Chamber of Commerce www.saratoga.org
28 Clinton St   Saratoga Springs NY 12866
Ph: 518-584-3255 ▪ Fx: 518-587-0318 ▪ TF: 800-526-8970

Schenectady County Chamber of Commerce www.schenectadychamber.org
306 State St   Schenectady NY 12305
Ph: 518-372-5656 ▪ Fx: 518-370-3217 ▪ TF: 800-962-8007

Schoharie County Chamber of Commerce www.schohariechamber.com
315 Main St PO Box 400   Schoharie NY 12157
Ph: 518-295-7033 ▪ Fx: 518-295-7453 ▪ TF: 800-418-4748

Seneca County Chamber of Commerce www.senecachamber.org
PO Box 70   Seneca Falls NY 13148
Ph: 315-568-2906 ▪ Fx: 315-568-1730

Smithtown Chamber of Commerce www.smithtownchamber.com
1 W Main St Suite 5   Smithtown NY 11787
Ph: 631-979-8069 ▪ Fx: 631-979-2206

Southampton Chamber of Commerce www.southamptonchamber.com
76 Main St   Southampton NY 11968
Ph: 631-283-0402 ▪ Fx: 631-283-8707

Staten Island Chamber of Commerce www.sichamber.com
130 Bay St   Staten Island NY 10301
Ph: 718-727-1900 ▪ Fx: 718-727-2295

Greater Syracuse Chamber of Commerce www.syracusechamber.com
572 S Salina St   Syracuse NY 13202
Ph: 315-470-1800 ▪ Fx: 315-471-8545

Rensselaer County Regional Chamber of Commerce www.renscochamber.com
31 2nd St   Troy NY 12180
Ph: 518-274-7020 ▪ Fx: 518-272-7729

Mohawk Valley Chamber of Commerce www.mvchamber.org
520 Seneca St   Utica NY 13502
Ph: 315-724-3151 ▪ Fx: 315-724-3177

Greater Southern Dutchess Chamber of Commerce gsdcc.org
2582 South Ave   Wappingers Falls NY 12590
Ph: 845-296-0001

Warwick Valley Chamber of Commerce www.warwickcc.org
PO Box 202   Warwick NY 10990
Ph: 845-986-2720 ▪ Fx: 845-986-6982

Greater Watertown-North Country Chamber of Commerce www.watertownny.com
1241 Coffeen St   Watertown NY 13601
Ph: 315-788-4400 ▪ Fx: 315-788-3369

Webster Chamber of Commerce www.websterchamber.com
26 E Main St   Webster NY 14580
Ph: 585-265-3960 ▪ Fx: 585-265-3702

West Seneca Chamber of Commerce www.westseneca.org
950-A Union Rd   West Seneca NY 14224
Ph: 716-674-4900 ▪ Fx: 716-674-5846

Westchester County Chamber of Commerce www.westchesterny.org
108 Corporate Pk Dr Suite 101   White Plains NY 10604
Ph: 914-948-2110 ▪ Fx: 914-948-0122

Amherst Chamber of Commerce www.amherst.org
325 Essjay Rd Suite 200   Williamsville NY 14221
Ph: 716-632-6905 ▪ Fx: 716-632-0548

Yonkers Chamber of Commerce www.yonkerschamber.com
20 S Broadway Suite 1207   Yonkers NY 10701
Ph: 914-963-0332 ▪ Fx: 914-963-0455

NORTH CAROLINA

Ahoskie Chamber of Commerce
PO Box 7   Ahoskie NC 27910
Ph: 252-332-2042 ▪ Fx: 252-332-8617

Stanly County Chamber of Commerce www.stanlychamber.org
PO Box 909   Albemarle NC 28002
Ph: 704-982-8116 ▪ Fx: 704-983-5000

Archdale-Trinity Chamber of Commerce www.archdaletrinitychamber.com
213 Balfour Dr   Archdale NC 27263
Ph: 336-434-2073 ▪ Fx: 336-431-5845

Asheboro/Randolph Chamber of Commerce chamber.asheboro
317 E Dixie Dr   Asheboro NC 27203
Ph: 336-626-2626 ▪ Fx: 336-626-7077

Asheville Area Chamber of Commerce www.ashevillechamber.org
151 Haywood St   Asheville NC 28801
Ph: 828-258-6101 ▪ Fx: 828-251-0926 ▪ TF: 800-257-1300

Black Mountain-Swannanoa Chamber of Commerce www.blackmountain.org
201 E State St   Black Mountain NC 28711
Ph: 828-669-2300 ▪ Fx: 828-669-1407 ▪ TF: 800-669-2301

Blowing Rock Chamber of Commerce www.blowingrock.com
PO Box 406   Blowing Rock NC 28605
Ph: 828-295-7851 ▪ Fx: 828-295-3198 ▪ TF: 800-295-7851

Brevard-Transylvania Chamber of Commerce www.brevardncchamber.com
35 W Main St   Brevard NC 28712
Ph: 828-883-3700 ▪ Fx: 828-883-8550 ▪ TF: 800-648-4523

Alamance County Area Chamber of Commerce www.alamancechamber.com
PO Box 450   Burlington NC 27216
Ph: 336-228-1338 ▪ Fx: 336-228-1330

Cary Chamber of Commerce www.carychamber.com
307 N Academy St   Cary NC 27513
Ph: 919-467-1016 ▪ Fx: 919-469-2375 ▪ TF: 800-919-2279

Chapel Hill-Carrboro Chamber of Commerce www.carolinachamber.com
104 S Estes Dr   Chapel Hill NC 27515
Ph: 919-967-7075 ▪ Fx: 919-968-6874

Charlotte Chamber of Commerce www.charlottechamber.com
PO Box 32785   Charlotte NC 28232
Ph: 704-378-1300 ▪ Fx: 704-374-1903

Lake Norman Chamber of Commerce www.lakenormanchamber.org
20916 Torrence Chapel Rd PO Box 760   Cornelius NC 28031
Ph: 704-892-1922 ▪ Fx: 704-892-5313 ▪ TF: 800-305-2508

Greater Durham Chamber of Commerce www.durhamchamber.org
300 W Morgan St Suite 1400   Durham NC 27701
Ph: 919-682-2133 ▪ Fx: 919-688-8351

Elizabeth City Area Chamber of Commerce www.elizcity.com
PO Box 426   Elizabeth City NC 27907
Ph: 252-335-4365 ▪ Fx: 252-335-5732 ▪ TF: 888-258-4832

Elkin Jonesville Chamber of Commerce www.ejachamber.com
116 E Market St   Elkin NC 28621
Ph: 336-526-1111 ▪ Fx: 336-526-1879

Elkin Jonesville Chamber of Commerce www.ejachamber.com
116 E Market St   Elkin NC 28621
Ph: 336-526-1111 ▪ Fx: 336-526-1879

Fayetteville Area Chamber of Commerce www.fayettevillencchamber.org
201 Hay St 4th Fl   Fayetteville NC 28301
Ph: 910-483-8133 ▪ Fx: 910-483-0263

Fuquay-Varina Area Chamber of Commerce www.fuquay-varina.com
121 N Main St   Fuquay-Varina NC 27526
Ph: 919-552-4947 ▪ Fx: 919-552-1029

Gaston County Chamber of Commerce www.gastonchamber.com
601 W Franklin Blvd   Gastonia NC 28054
Ph: 704-864-2621 ▪ Fx: 704-854-8723 ▪ TF: 800-348-8461

Chamber of Commerce of Wayne County www.waynecountychamber.com
PO Box 1107   Goldsboro NC 27533
Ph: 919-734-2241 ▪ Fx: 919-734-2247

Greensboro Area Chamber of Commerce www.greensborochamber.com
342 N Elm St   Greensboro NC 27401
Ph: 336-275-8675 ▪ Fx: 336-230-1867

Greenville-Pitt County Chamber of Commerce www.greenvillenc.org
302 S Greene St   Greenville NC 27834
Ph: 252-752-4101 ▪ Fx: 252-752-5934

Henderson-Vance County Chamber of Commerce www.hendersonvance.org
PO Box 1302   Henderson NC 27536
Ph: 252-438-8414 ▪ Fx: 252-492-8989

Greater Hendersonville Chamber of Commerce www.hendersonvillechamber.org
330 N King St   Hendersonville NC 28792
Ph: 828-692-1413 ▪ Fx: 828-693-8802

Catawba County Chamber of Commerce www.catawbachamber.org
PO Box 1828   Hickory NC 28603
Ph: 828-328-6111 ▪ Fx: 828-328-1175

High Point Chamber of Commerce www.highpointchamber.org
1101 N Main St   High Point NC 27262
Ph: 336-889-8151 ▪ Fx: 336-889-9499

Jacksonville/Onslow Chamber of Commerce   www.jacksonvilleonline.org
1099 Gum Branch Rd   Jacksonville NC 28541
Ph: 910-347-3141 ▪ Fx: 910-347-4705

Cabarrus Regional Chamber of Commerce   www.cabarruschamber.org
3003 Dale Earnhardt Blvd   Kannapolis NC 28083
Ph: 704-782-4000 ▪ Fx: 704-782-4050 ▪ TF: 800-848-3702

Outer Banks Chamber of Commerce   www.outerbankschamber.com
PO Box 1757   Kill Devil Hills NC 27948
Ph: 252-441-8144 ▪ Fx: 252-441-0338

Kinston-Lenoir County Chamber of Commerce   www.commercekinstonlc.com
301 N Queen St   Kinston NC 28501
Ph: 252-527-1131 ▪ Fx: 252-527-1914

Laurinburg/Scotland County Area Chamber of Commerce   www.laurinburgchamber.com
606 Atkinson St   Laurinburg NC 28353
Ph: 910-276-7420 ▪ Fx: 910-277-8785

Caldwell County Chamber of Commerce   www.caldwellcochamber.org
1909 Hickory Blvd SE   Lenoir NC 28645
Ph: 828-726-0616 ▪ Fx: 828-726-0385

Lincolnton-Lincoln County Chamber of Commerce   www.lincolnchambernc.org
PO Box 1617   Lincolnton NC 28093
Ph: 704-735-3096 ▪ Fx: 704-735-5449

Franklin County Chamber of Commerce   www.franklin-chamber.org
PO Box 62   Louisburg NC 27549
Ph: 919-496-3056 ▪ Fx: 919-496-0422

Lumberton Area Chamber of Commerce   www.lumbertonchamber.com
800 N Chestnut St   Lumberton NC 28358
Ph: 910-739-4750 ▪ Fx: 910-671-9722

Western Rockingham Chamber of Commerce   www.westernrockinghamchamber.com
112 W Murphy St   Madison NC 27025
Ph: 336-548-6248 ▪ Fx: 336-548-4466

McDowell Chamber of Commerce   www.mcdowellnc.org/chamber
1170 W Tate St   Marion NC 28752
Ph: 828-652-4240 ▪ Fx: 828-659-9620

Davie County Chamber of Commerce   www.daviecounty.com/commerce
135 S Salisbury St   Mocksville NC 27028
Ph: 336-751-3304 ▪ Fx: 336-751-5697

Union County Chamber of Commerce   www.unioncountycoc.com
PO Box 1789   Monroe NC 28111
Ph: 704-289-4567 ▪ Fx: 704-282-0122

Mooresville-South Iredell Chamber of Commerce   www.mooresvillenc.org
149 E Iredell Ave   Mooresville NC 28115
Ph: 704-664-3898 ▪ Fx: 704-664-2549

Carteret County Chamber of Commerce   www.nccoastchamber.com
PO Box 3605   Morehead City NC 28557
Ph: 252-726-6350 ▪ Fx: 252-726-3505 ▪ TF: 800-622-6278

Burke County Chamber of Commerce   www.burkecounty.org
110 E Meeting St   Morganton NC 28655
Ph: 828-437-3021 ▪ Fx: 828-437-1613

Greater Mount Airy Chamber of Commerce   www.mtairyncchamber.org
200 N Main St   Mount Airy NC 27030
Ph: 336-786-6116 ▪ Fx: 336-786-1488 ▪ TF: 800-948-0949

Mount Olive Area Chamber of Commerce   www.moachamber.com
123 N Center St   Mount Olive NC 28365
Ph: 919-658-3113 ▪ Fx: 919-658-3125

Cherokee County Chamber of Commerce   www.cherokeecountychamber.org
805 W US 64   Murphy NC 28906
Ph: 828-837-2242 ▪ Fx: 828-837-6012

New Bern Area Chamber of Commerce   www.newbernchamber.com
316 S Front St   New Bern NC 28560
Ph: 252-637-3111 ▪ Fx: 252-637-7541

Wilkes Chamber of Commerce   www.wilkesnc.org
PO Box 727   North Wilkesboro NC 28659
Ph: 336-838-8662 ▪ Fx: 336-838-3728

Granville County Chamber of Commerce   www.granvillecountyonline.com
107 Williamsboro St   Oxford NC 27565
Ph: 919-693-6125 ▪ Fx: 919-693-6126

Raeford/Hoke Chamber of Commerce   www.hoke-raeford.com/chamber.htm
101 N Main St   Raeford NC 28376
Ph: 910-875-5929 ▪ Fx: 910-875-1010

Greater Raleigh Chamber of Commerce   www.raleighchamber.org
PO Box 2978   Raleigh NC 27602
Ph: 919-664-7000 ▪ Fx: 919-664-7099

Roanoke Valley Chamber of Commerce   www.rvchamber.com
1640 Julian Allsbrook Hwy   Roanoke Rapids NC 27870
Ph: 252-537-3513 ▪ Fx: 252-535-5767

Richmond County Chamber of Commerce   www.richmondcountychamber.com
PO Box 86   Rockingham NC 28380
Ph: 910-895-9058 ▪ Fx: 910-895-9056 ▪ TF: 800-858-1688

Rocky Mount Area Chamber of Commerce   www.rockymountchamber.org
PO Box 392   Rocky Mount NC 27802
Ph: 252-446-0323 ▪ Fx: 252-446-5103

Roxboro Area Chamber of Commerce   www.roxboronc.com
PO Box 209   Roxboro NC 27573
Ph: 336-599-8333 ▪ Fx: 336-599-8335

Rutherford County Chamber of Commerce   www.rutherfordcoc.org
162 N Main St   Rutherfordton NC 28139
Ph: 828-287-3090 ▪ Fx: 828-287-0799

Rowan County Chamber of Commerce   www.rowanchamber.com
PO Box 559   Salisbury NC 28145
Ph: 704-633-4221 ▪ Fx: 704-639-1200

Sanford Area Chamber of Commerce   www.sanford-nc.com/sacc.html
143 Charlotte Ave Suite 101   Sanford NC 27330
Ph: 919-775-7341 ▪ Fx: 919-776-6244

Brunswick County Chamber of Commerce   www.brunswickcountychamber.org
PO Box 1185   Shallotte NC 28459
Ph: 910-754-6644 ▪ Fx: 910-754-6539 ▪ TF: 800-426-6644

Cleveland County Chamber of Commerce   www.clevelandchamber.org
PO Box 879   Shelby NC 28151
Ph: 704-487-8521 ▪ Fx: 704-487-7458

Chatham County United Chamber of Commerce   www.ccucc.net
1609 E 11th St   Siler City NC 27344
Ph: 919-742-3333 ▪ Fx: 919-742-1333

Greater Smithfield-Selma Area Chamber of Commerce   www.smithfieldselma.com
PO Box 467   Smithfield NC 27577
Ph: 919-934-9166 ▪ Fx: 919-934-1337

Sandhills Area Chamber of Commerce   www.sandhillschamber.com
PO Box 458   Southern Pines NC 28388
Ph: 910-692-3926 ▪ Fx: 910-692-0619

Jackson County Chamber of Commerce   www.mountainlovers.com
773 W Main St   Sylva NC 28779
Ph: 828-586-2155 ▪ Fx: 828-586-4887 ▪ TF: 800-962-1911

Tarboro Edgecombe Chamber of Commerce   www.edgecombe.cc.nc.us/chamber
PO Drawer F   Tarboro NC 27886
Ph: 252-823-7241 ▪ Fx: 252-823-1499

Alexander County Chamber of Commerce   www.alexandercountychamber.com
16 W Main Ave   Taylorsville NC 28681
Ph: 828-632-8141 ▪ Fx: 828-632-1096

Thomasville Area Chamber of Commerce
PO Box 1400   Thomasville NC 27361
Ph: 336-475-6134 ▪ Fx: 336-475-4802

Polk County Chamber of Commerce   www.polkchamber.org
2753 Lynn Rd Suite A   Tryon NC 28782
Ph: 828-859-6236 ▪ Fx: 828-859-2301

Washington-Beaufort County Chamber of Commerce   www.wbcchamber.com
102 Stewart Pkwy   Washington NC 27889
Ph: 252-946-9168 ▪ Fx: 252-946-9169

Haywood County Chamber of Commerce   www.haywood-nc.com
PO Box 600   Waynesville NC 28786
Ph: 828-456-3021 ▪ Fx: 828-452-7265 ▪ TF: 877-456-3073

Martin County Chamber of Commerce   www.martincountync.com
419 East Blvd   Williamston NC 27892
Ph: 252-792-4131 ▪ Fx: 252-792-1013

Greater Wilmington Chamber of Commerce   www.wilmingtonchamber.org
1 Estell Lee Pl   Wilmington NC 28401
Ph: 910-762-2611 ▪ Fx: 910-762-9765

Wilson Chamber of Commerce   www.wilsonncchamber.com
PO Box 1146   Wilson NC 27894
Ph: 252-237-0165 ▪ Fx: 252-243-7931

Windsor Area Chamber of Commerce   www.albemarle-nc.com/windsor/chamber
102 N York St   Windsor NC 27983
Ph: 252-794-4277 ▪ Fx: 252-794-5070

Greater Winston-Salem Chamber of Commerce   www.winstonsalem.com
PO Box 1408   Winston-Salem NC 27102
Ph: 336-725-2361 ▪ Fx: 336-721-2209

Yadkin County Chamber of Commerce   www.yadkinchamber.org
205 S Jackson St   Yadkinville NC 27055
Ph: 336-679-2200 ▪ Fx: 336-679-3034

NORTH DAKOTA

Bismarck Mandan Chamber of Commerce   www.chmbr.org
2000 Schafer St   Bismarck ND 58502
Ph: 701-223-5660 ▪ Fx: 701-255-6125

Grand Forks Chamber of Commerce   www.gfchamber.com
202 N 3rd St   Grand Forks ND 58203
Ph: 701-772-7271 ▪ Fx: 701-772-9238

Jamestown Area Chamber of Commerce   www.jamestownchamber.com
210 10th St SE   Jamestown ND 58401
Ph: 701-252-4830 ▪ Fx: 701-252-4837

Minot Area Chamber of Commerce   www.minotchamber.org
1020 20th Ave SW   Minot ND 58701
Ph: 701-852-6000 ▪ Fx: 701-838-2488

OHIO

Greater Akron Chamber   www.greaterakronchamber.org
1 Cascade Plaza 17th Fl   Akron OH 44308
Ph: 330-376-5550 ▪ Fx: 330-379-3164 ▪ TF: 800-621-8001

Alliance Area Chamber of Commerce   www.allianceohiochamber.org
210 E Main St   Alliance OH 44601
Ph: 330-823-6260 ▪ Fx: 330-823-4434

Ashtabula Area Chamber of Commerce   www.ashtabulachamber.net
4536 Main Ave   Ashtabula OH 44004
Ph: 440-998-6998 ▪ Fx: 440-992-8216

Athens Area Chamber of Commerce   www.athenschamber.com
5 N Court St   Athens OH 45701
Ph: 740-594-2251 ▪ Fx: 740-594-2252

Barberton Area Chamber of Commerce   www.southsummitchamber.org
503 W Park Ave   Barberton OH 44203
Ph: 330-745-3141 ▪ Fx: 330-745-4559

Beavercreek Chamber of Commerce   www.beavercreekchamber.org
3299 Kemp Rd   Beavercreek OH 45431
Ph: 937-426-2202 ▪ Fx: 937-426-2204

Logan County Chamber of Commerce   www.logancountyohio.com
100 S Main St   Bellefontaine OH 43311
Ph: 937-599-5121 ▪ Fx: 937-599-2411

Muskingum Valley Area Chamber of Commerce   www.tourohio.com/mvacc
PO Box 837   Beverly OH 45715
Ph: 740-984-8259

Bowling Green Chamber of Commerce   www.bowlinggreen-oh.com
163 N Main St   Bowling Green OH 43402
Ph: 419-353-7945 ▪ Fx: 419-353-3693

Brunswick Area Chamber of Commerce   www.brunswickareachamber.org
3511 Center Rd Suite A-B   Brunswick OH 44212
Ph: 330-225-8411 ▪ Fx: 330-273-8172

Cambridge Area Chamber of Commerce   www.cambridgeohiochamber.com
918 Wheeling Ave Cambridge OH 43725
Ph: 740-439-6688 Fx: 740-439-6689

Canton Regional Chamber of Commerce   www.cantonchamber.org
222 Market Ave N Canton OH 44702
Ph: 330-456-7253 Fx: 330-452-7786 TF: 800-533-4302

Carroll County Chamber of Commerce & Economic Development www.carrollohchamber.com
PO Box 277 Carrollton OH 44615
Ph: 330-627-4811 Fx: 330-627-3647 TF: 800-956-4684

Celina-Mercer County Chamber of Commerce   www.celinamercer.com
226 N Main St Celina OH 45822
Ph: 419-586-2219 Fx: 419-586-8645

Chagrin Valley Chamber of Commerce   www.cvcc.org
16 S Main St Chagrin Falls OH 44022
Ph: 440-247-6607 Fx: 440-247-6503

Chillicothe-Ross Chamber of Commerce   www.chillicotheohio.com
165 S Paint St Chillicothe OH 45601
Ph: 740-702-2722 Fx: 740-702-2727

Anderson Area Chamber of Commerce   www.andersonareachamber.com
8072-B Beechmont Ave Cincinnati OH 45255
Ph: 513-474-4802 Fx: 513-474-4857

Greater Cincinnati Chamber of Commerce   www.gccc.com
441 Vine St Carew Tower Suite 300 Cincinnati OH 45202
Ph: 513-579-3100 Fx: 513-579-3102

Hamilton County Chamber of Commerce
PO Box 42250 Cincinnati OH 45242
Ph: 513-984-6555 Fx: 513-793-1063

Pickaway County Chamber of Commerce
PO Box 462 Circleville OH 43113
Ph: 740-474-4923 Fx: 740-477-6800 TF: 800-897-9420

Greater Cleveland Growth Association   www.clevelandgrowth.com
50 Public Sq Suite 200 Cleveland OH 44113
Ph: 216-621-3300 Fx: 216-621-6013 TF: 800-562-7121

Greater Columbus Chamber of Commerce   www.columbus-chamber.org
37 N High St Columbus OH 43215
Ph: 614-221-1321 Fx: 614-221-9360 TF: 800-950-1321

Coshocton County Chamber of Commerce   www.coshoctonchamber.com
101 N Whitewoman St Coshocton OH 43812
Ph: 740-622-5411 Fx: 740-622-9902 TF: 800-589-2430

Cuyahoga Falls Chamber of Commerce   www.cuyahogafallschamberofcommerce.com
2020 Front St Suite 103 Cuyahoga Falls OH 44221
Ph: 330-929-6756 Fx: 330-929-4278

Dayton Area Chamber of Commerce   www.daytonchamber.org
1 Chamber Plaza Suite 200 Dayton OH 45402
Ph: 937-226-1444 Fx: 937-226-8254

South Metro Regional Chamber of Commerce   www.smrcoc.org
8087 Washington Village Dr Suite 100 Dayton OH 45458
Ph: 937-433-2032 Fx: 937-433-6881

Defiance Area Chamber of Commerce   www.defiancechamber.com
615 W 3rd St Defiance OH 43512
Ph: 419-782-7946 Fx: 419-782-0111

East Liverpool Area Chamber of Commerce   www.elchamber.com
529 Market St PO Box 94 East Liverpool OH 43920
Ph: 330-385-0845 Fx: 330-385-0581

Eaton-Preble County Chamber of Commerce   www.pcdl.lib.oh.us/chamber
PO Box 303 Eaton OH 45320
Ph: 937-456-4949 Fx: 937-456-4949

Englewood-Northmont Chamber of Commerce   www.englewood-northmontcoc.com
PO Box 62 Englewood OH 45322
Ph: 937-836-2550 Fx: 937-836-2485

Euclid Chamber of Commerce   www.euclidchamberofcommerce.com
21935 Lake Shore Blvd Euclid OH 44123
Ph: 216-731-9322 Fx: 216-731-8354

Fairborn Area Chamber of Commerce   www.fairborn.com
12 N Central Ave Fairborn OH 45324
Ph: 937-878-3191 Fx: 937-878-3197

Fairfield Chamber of Commerce   www.fairfieldchamber.com
670 Wessel Dr Fairfield OH 45014
Ph: 513-881-5500 Fx: 513-881-5503

Findlay-Hancock County Chamber of Commerce   www.findlayhancockchamber.com
123 E Main Cross St Findlay OH 45840
Ph: 419-422-3313 Fx: 419-422-9508

Fostoria Area Chamber of Commerce   www.fostoriaoh.org/chamber
121 N Main St Fostoria OH 44830
Ph: 419-435-0486 Fx: 419-435-0936

Chamber of Commerce of Sandusky County   www.scchamber.org
101 S Front St Fremont OH 43420
Ph: 419-332-1591 Fx: 419-332-8666

Gahanna Area Chamber of Commerce   www.gahannaareachamber.com
94 N High St Gahanna OH 43230
Ph: 614-471-0451 Fx: 614-471-5122

Gallia County Chamber of Commerce   www.galliachamber.org
PO Box 465 Gallipolis OH 45631
Ph: 740-446-0596 Fx: 740-446-7031 TF: 888-895-1700

Garfield Heights Chamber of Commerce   www.garfieldchamber.com
5284 Transportation Blvd Garfield Heights OH 44125
Ph: 216-475-7775 Fx: 216-475-2237

Geneva Area Chamber of Commerce   www.genevachamber.org
PO Box 84 Geneva OH 44041
Ph: 440-466-8694 Fx: 440-466-0823

Brown County Chamber of Commerce   www.browncountyohio.org
110 E State St Georgetown OH 45121
Ph: 937-378-4784 Fx: 937-378-1634 TF: 888-276-9664

Darke County Chamber of Commerce   www.darkecountyohio.com
622 S Broadway Greenville OH 45331
Ph: 937-548-2102 Fx: 937-548-5608

Greater Hamilton Chamber of Commerce   www.hamilton-ohio.com
201 Dayton St Hamilton OH 45011
Ph: 513-844-1500 Fx: 513-844-1999

Highland County Chamber of Commerce   www.highlandcountychamber.com
1575 N High St Suite 400 Hillsboro OH 45133
Ph: 937-393-1111 Fx: 937-393-2697

Huber Heights Chamber of Commerce   www.huberheightschamber.com
4756 Fishburg Rd Huber Heights OH 45424
Ph: 937-233-5700 Fx: 937-233-5769

Jackson Area Chamber of Commerce   www.jacksonohio.org
234 Broadway St Jackson OH 45640
Ph: 740-286-2722 Fx: 740-286-8443

Jackson-Beldon Chamber of Commerce   www.jbcc.org
5735 Wales Ave NW Jackson Township OH 44646
Ph: 330-833-4400 Fx: 330-833-4456

Kent Area Chamber of Commerce   www.kentbiz.com
155 E Main St Kent OH 44240
Ph: 330-673-9855 Fx: 330-673-9860

Hardin County Chamber of Commerce   www.hardinohio.org
225 S Detroit St Kenton OH 43326
Ph: 419-673-4131 Fx: 419-674-4876

Kettering-Moraine-Oakwood Area Chamber of Commerce   www.kmo-coc.org
2977 Far Hills Ave Kettering OH 45419
Ph: 937-299-3852 Fx: 937-299-3851

Lakewood Chamber of Commerce   www.lakewoodchamber.org
14701 Detroit Ave Suite 130 Lakewood OH 44107
Ph: 216-226-2900 Fx: 216-226-1340

Lancaster-Fairfield County Chamber of Commerce   www.lancoc.org
PO Box 2450 Lancaster OH 43130
Ph: 740-653-8251 Fx: 740-653-7074

Lima/Allen County Chamber of Commerce   www.limachamber.com
147 N Main St Lima OH 45801
Ph: 419-222-6045 Fx: 419-229-0266

Logan-Hocking Chamber of Commerce   www.logan-hockingchamber.com
PO Box 838 Logan OH 43138
Ph: 740-385-6836 Fx: 740-385-7259 TF: 800-414-6731

Lorain County Chamber of Commerce   www.loraincountychamber.com
6100 S Broadway Suite 201 Lorain OH 44053
Ph: 440-233-6500 Fx: 440-246-4050

Madison-Perry Area Chamber of Commerce   www.mpacc.org
PO Box 4 Madison OH 44057
Ph: 440-428-3760 Fx: 440-428-6668

Mansfield-Richland Area Chamber of Commerce   www.mrachamber.com
55 N Mulberry St Mansfield OH 44902
Ph: 419-522-3211 Fx: 419-526-6853

Marietta Area Chamber of Commerce   www.mariettachamber.com
316 3rd St Marietta OH 45750
Ph: 740-373-5176 Fx: 740-373-7808

Marion Area Chamber of Commerce   www.marion.net/chamber
205 W Center St Marion OH 43302
Ph: 740-382-2181 Fx: 740-387-7722

Union County Chamber of Commerce   www.unioncounty.org
227 E 5th St Marysville OH 43040
Ph: 937-642-6279 Fx: 937-644-0422 TF: 800-642-0087

Massillon Area Chamber of Commerce   www.massillonohchamber.com
137 Lincoln Way E Massillon OH 44646
Ph: 330-833-3146 Fx: 330-833-8944

Mentor Chamber of Commerce   www.mentorchamber.org
7547 Mentor Ave Suite 302 Mentor OH 44060
Ph: 440-946-2625 Fx: 440-946-2626

Mid-Miami Valley Chamber of Commerce   www.mmvchamber.org
1500 Central Ave Middletown OH 45044
Ph: 513-422-4551 Fx: 513-422-6831

Clermont County Chamber of Commerce   www.clermontchamber.com
553 Chamber Dr Milford OH 45150
Ph: 513-576-5000 Fx: 513-576-5001

Milford-Miami Township Chamber of Commerce   www.milfordmiamitownship.com
100 Cemetery Rd Milford OH 45150
Ph: 513-831-2411 Fx: 513-831-3547

Holmes County Chamber of Commerce   www.holmescountychamber.com
35 N Monroe St Millersburg OH 44654
Ph: 330-674-3975 Fx: 330-674-3976

Morrow County Chamber of Commerce   www.morrowcochamber.com
17 1/2 W High St Mount Gilead OH 43338
Ph: 419-946-2821 Fx: 419-946-3861

Mount Vernon-Knox County Chamber of Commerce   www.knoxchamber.com
7 E Ohio Ave Mount Vernon OH 43050
Ph: 740-393-1111 Fx: 740-393-1590

Napoleon/Henry County Chamber of Commerce   www.ohiohenrycounty.com
611 N Perry St Napoleon OH 43545
Ph: 419-592-1786 Fx: 419-592-4945

Perry County Chamber of Commerce   www.perrycountyohiocofc.com
103 W Brown St New Lexington OH 43764
Ph: 740-342-3547 Fx: 740-342-3547

Tuscarawas County Chamber of Commerce   www.tuschamber.com
1323 4th St NW New Philadelphia OH 44663
Ph: 330-343-4474 Fx: 330-343-6526

Newark & Licking County Chamber of Commerce   www.newarkchamber.com
PO Box 702 Newark OH 43058
Ph: 740-345-9757 Fx: 740-345-5141 TF: 800-589-8224

North Canton Area Chamber of Commerce   www.northcantonchamber.org
121 S Main St North Canton OH 44720
Ph: 330-499-5100 Fx: 330-499-7181

North Olmsted Chamber of Commerce   www.nolmstedchamber.org
25045 Lorain Rd North Olmsted OH 44070
Ph: 440-777-3368 Fx: 440-777-9361

North Royalton Chamber of Commerce
13737 State Rd North Royalton OH 44133
Ph: 440-237-6180 Fx: 440-237-6181

Eastern Maumee Bay Chamber of Commerce   www.embchamber.org
4209 Corduroy Rd Oregon OH 43616
Ph: 419-693-5580 Fx: 419-693-9990

Appendix

Painesville Area Chamber of Commerce   www.painesvilleohchamber.org
319 W Washington St   Painesville OH 44077
Ph: 440-357-7572 ■ Fx: 440-357-8752

Parma Area Chamber of Commerce   www.parmaareachamber.org
5255 Regency Dr Rm 201   Parma OH 44129
Ph: 440-886-1700 ■ Fx: 440-886-1770

Perrysburg Area Chamber of Commerce   www.perrysburgchamber.com
105 W Indiana Ave   Perrysburg OH 43551
Ph: 419-874-9147 ■ Fx: 419-872-9347

Portsmouth Area Chamber of Commerce   www.portsmouth.org
PO Box 509   Portsmouth OH 45662
Ph: 740-353-7647 ■ Fx: 740-353-5824 ■ TF: 800-648-2574

Reynoldsburg Area Chamber of Commerce   www.reynoldsburgchamber.com
1580 Brice Rd   Reynoldsburg OH 43068
Ph: 614-866-4753 ■ Fx: 614-866-7313

Salem Area Chamber of Commerce   www.salemohio.com/chamber
713 E State St   Salem OH 44460
Ph: 330-337-3473

Erie County Chamber of Commerce   www.eriecountyohiocofc.com
225 W Washington Row   Sandusky OH 44870
Ph: 419-625-6421 ■ Fx: 419-625-7914

Shelby Chamber of Commerce   www.shelbyoh.com
142 N Gamble St Suite A   Shelby OH 44875
Ph: 419-342-2426 ■ Fx: 419-342-2189 ■ TF: 888-245-2426

Sidney-Shelby County Chamber of Commerce   www.sidneyshelbychamber.com
101 S Ohio Ave 2nd Fl   Sidney OH 45365
Ph: 937-492-9122 ■ Fx: 937-498-2472

Greater Lawrence County Area Chamber of Commerce   www.lawrencecountyohio.org
PO Box 488   South Point OH 45680
Ph: 740-377-4550 ■ Fx: 740-377-2091 ■ TF: 800-408-1334

Springfield-Clark County Chamber of Commerce   www.springfieldnet.com
333 N Limestone St Suite 201   Springfield OH 45503
Ph: 937-325-7621 ■ Fx: 937-325-8765 ■ TF: 800-803-1553

Jefferson County Chamber of Commerce   www.jeffersoncountychamber.com
630 Market St PO Box 278   Steubenville OH 43952
Ph: 740-282-6226 ■ Fx: 740-282-6285

Stow-Munroe Falls Chamber of Commerce   www.smfcc.com
4381 Hudson Dr Suite K2   Stow OH 44224
Ph: 330-688-1579 ■ Fx: 330-688-6234

Strongsville Chamber of Commerce   www.strongsvillecofc.com
18829 Royalton Rd   Strongsville OH 44136
Ph: 440-238-3366 ■ Fx: 440-238-7010

Sylvania Area Chamber of Commerce   www.sylvaniachamber.org
6616 Monroe St Suite 8   Sylvania OH 43560
Ph: 419-882-2135 ■ Fx: 419-885-7740

Tiffin Area Chamber of Commerce   www.tiffinchamber.com
62 S Washington St   Tiffin OH 44883
Ph: 419-447-4141 ■ Fx: 419-447-5141 ■ TF: 800-253-3314

Toledo Area Chamber of Commerce   www.toledochamber.com
300 Madison Ave Suite 200   Toledo OH 43604
Ph: 419-243-8191 ■ Fx: 419-241-8302

Trotwood Chamber of Commerce   www.exopoint.com/Yutori/TrotwoodCC
4000 Lake Center Dr   Trotwood OH 45426
Ph: 937-837-1484 ■ Fx: 937-837-1508

Upper Arlington Area Chamber of Commerce   www.uachamber.org
2120 Tremont Ctr   Upper Arlington OH 43221
Ph: 614-481-5710 ■ Fx: 614-481-5711

Champaign County Chamber of Commerce   www.champaignohio.com/chamber
113 Miami St   Urbana OH 43078
Ph: 937-653-5764 ■ Fx: 937-652-1599 ■ TF: 877-873-5764

Van Wert Area Chamber of Commerce   www.vanwertchamber.com
118 W Main St   Van Wert OH 45891
Ph: 419-238-4390 ■ Fx: 419-238-4589

Vandalia-Butler Chamber of Commerce   www.vandaliabutlerchamber.com
76 Ford Way Dr   Vandalia OH 45377
Ph: 937-898-5351 ■ Fx: 937-898-5491

Fayette County Chamber of Commerce   www.fayettecountychamberoh.com
101 E East St   Washington Court House OH 43160
Ph: 740-335-0761 ■ Fx: 740-335-0762

Southeastern Butler County Chamber of Commerce   www.sebcchamber.com
8945 Brookside Ave Suite 101   West Chester OH 45069
Ph: 513-777-3600 ■ Fx: 513-777-0188

Adams County Chamber of Commerce   www.adamscountyohchamber.org
PO Box 398   West Union OH 45693
Ph: 937-544-5454 ■ Fx: 937-544-6957 ■ TF: 888-223-5454

Westerville Area Chamber of Commerce   www.westervillechamber.com
99-B Commerce Pk Dr   Westerville OH 43082
Ph: 614-882-8917 ■ Fx: 614-882-2085

West Shore Chamber of Commerce   www.westshorechamber.org
24600 Center Ridge Rd Suite 480   Westlake OH 44145
Ph: 440-835-8787 ■ Fx: 440-835-8798

Willougby Area Chamber of Commerce   www.wacoc.com
28 Public Sq   Willoughby OH 44094
Ph: 440-942-1632 ■ Fx: 440-942-0586

Wilmington Clinton County Chamber of Commerce   www.wccchamber.com
40 N South St   Wilmington OH 45177
Ph: 937-382-2737 ■ Fx: 937-383-2316

Wooster Area Chamber of Commerce   www.wooster-wayne.com
377 W Liberty St   Wooster OH 44691
Ph: 330-262-5735 ■ Fx: 330-262-5745

Worthington Area Chamber of Commerce   www.worthington.org/business/chamber.htm
25 W New England Ave   Worthington OH 43085
Ph: 614-888-3040 ■ Fx: 614-841-4842

Xenia Area Chamber of Commerce   www.xacc.com
334 W Market St   Xenia OH 45385
Ph: 937-372-3591 ■ Fx: 937-372-2192

Youngstown Warren Regional Chamber of Commerce   www.regionalchamber.com
1200 Stambaugh Bldg   Youngstown OH 44503
Ph: 330-744-2131 ■ Fx: 330-746-0330

Zanesville-Muskingum County Chamber of Commerce   www.zmchamber.com
205 N 5th St   Zanesville OH 43701
Ph: 740-455-8282 ■ Fx: 740-454-2963

OKLAHOMA

Ada Area Chamber of Commerce   www.adachamber.com
PO Box 248   Ada OK 74820
Ph: 580-332-2506 ■ Fx: 580-332-3265

Ardmore Chamber of Commerce   www.ardmore.org
410 W Main St   Ardmore OK 73401
Ph: 580-223-7765 ■ Fx: 580-223-7825

Bartlesville Area Chamber of Commerce   www.bartlesville.com/chamberindex.html
PO Box 2366   Bartlesville OK 74005
Ph: 918-336-8708 ■ Fx: 918-337-0216

Broken Arrow Chamber of Commerce   www.brokenarrow.org
123 N Main St   Broken Arrow OK 74012
Ph: 918-251-1518 ■ Fx: 918-251-1777

Del City Chamber of Commerce
4505 SE 15th St   Del City OK 73115
Ph: 405-677-1910 ■ Fx: 405-677-2275

Durant Area Chamber of Commerce   www.durantchamber.org
215 N 4th St   Durant OK 74701
Ph: 580-924-0848 ■ Fx: 580-924-0348

Edmond Area Chamber of Commerce   www.edmondchamber.com
825 E 2nd St   Edmond OK 73034
Ph: 405-341-2808 ■ Fx: 405-340-5512

Greater Enid Chamber of Commerce   www.enidchamber.com
PO Box 907   Enid OK 73702
Ph: 580-237-2494 ■ Fx: 580-237-2497 ■ TF: 888-229-2443

Lawton Chamber of Commerce & Industry   www.lcci.org
629 SW 'C' Ave Suite A   Lawton OK 73501
Ph: 580-355-3541 ■ Fx: 580-357-3642 ■ TF: 800-872-4540

Midwest City Chamber of Commerce   www.midwestcityok.com/chamber.html
PO Box 10980   Midwest City OK 73140
Ph: 405-733-3801 ■ Fx: 405-733-5633

Moore Chamber of Commerce   www.moorechamber.com
105 Industrial Blvd   Moore OK 73160
Ph: 405-794-3400 ■ Fx: 405-794-8555

Greater Muskogee Area Chamber of Commerce   www.muskogeechamber.org
PO Box 797   Muskogee OK 74402
Ph: 918-682-2401 ■ Fx: 918-682-2403

Norman Chamber of Commerce   www.normanok.org
PO Box 982   Norman OK 73070
Ph: 405-321-7260 ■ Fx: 405-360-4679

Greater Oklahoma City Chamber of Commerce   www.okcchamber.com
123 Park Ave   Oklahoma City OK 73102
Ph: 405-297-8900 ■ Fx: 405-297-8916 ■ TF: 800-616-1114

South Oklahoma City Chamber of Commerce   www.southokc.com
701 SW 74th St   Oklahoma City OK 73139
Ph: 405-634-1436 ■ Fx: 405-634-1462

Owasso Chamber of Commerce   www.owassochamber.com
315 S Cedar St   Owasso OK 74055
Ph: 918-272-2141 ■ Fx: 918-272-8564

Ponca City Area Chamber of Commerce   www.poncacitychamber.com
420 E Grand Ave   Ponca City OK 74601
Ph: 580-765-4400 ■ Fx: 580-765-2798

Poteau Chamber of Commerce   poteau.org
201 S Broadway   Poteau OK 74953
Ph: 918-647-9178 ■ Fx: 918-647-4099

Sallisaw Chamber of Commerce
PO Box 251   Sallisaw OK 74955
Ph: 918-775-2558 ■ Fx: 918-775-9550

Greater Shawnee Area Chamber of Commerce   www.shawneechamber.com
PO Box 1613   Shawnee OK 74802
Ph: 405-273-6092 ■ Fx: 405-275-9851

Stillwater Chamber of Commerce   www.stillwaterchamber.org
409 S Main St   Stillwater OK 74076
Ph: 405-372-5573 ■ Fx: 405-372-4316 ■ TF: 800-593-5573

Tulsa Metro Chamber   www.tulsachamber.com
2 W 2nd St Suite 150 Williams Ctr Tower II   Tulsa OK 74103
Ph: 918-585-1201 ■ Fx: 918-585-8016

Yukon Chamber of Commerce   www.yukoncc.com
510 Elm St   Yukon OK 73099
Ph: 405-354-3567 ■ Fx: 405-350-0724

OREGON

Albany Area Chamber of Commerce   www.albanychamber.com
435 W 1st Ave   Albany OR 97321
Ph: 541-926-1517 ■ Fx: 541-926-7064

Beaverton Area Chamber of Commerce   www.beaverton.org
4800 SW Griffith Dr Suite 100   Beaverton OR 97005
Ph: 503-644-0123 ■ Fx: 503-526-0349

Bend Chamber of Commerce   www.bendchamber.org
777 NW Wall St Suite 200   Bend OR 97701
Ph: 541-382-3221 ■ Fx: 541-385-9929 ■ TF: 800-905-2363

Bay Area Chamber of Commerce   www.oregonsbayareachamber.com
50 Central Ave   Coos Bay OR 97420
Ph: 541-269-0215 ■ Fx: 541-269-2861 ■ TF: 800-824-8486

Corvallis Area Chamber of Commerce   www.corvallischamber.com
420 NW 2nd St   Corvallis OR 97330
Ph: 541-757-1505 ■ Fx: 541-766-2996

Cottage Grove Area Chamber of Commerce   www.cgchamber.com
700 E Gibbs Ave Suite C   Cottage Grove OR 97424
Ph: 541-942-2411 ■ Fx: 541-767-0783

Eugene Chamber of Commerce
1401 Willamette St   Eugene OR 97401
Ph: 541-484-1314 ▪ Fx: 541-484-4942
www.eugenechamber.com

Florence Area Chamber of Commerce
270 Hwy 101   Florence OR 97439
Ph: 541-997-3128 ▪ Fx: 541-997-4101 ▪ TF: 800-524-4864
www.florencechamber.com

Grants Pass/Josephine County Chamber of Commerce
PO Box 970   Grants Pass OR 97528
Ph: 541-476-7717 ▪ Fx: 541-476-9574 ▪ TF: 800-547-5927
www.grantspasschamber.org

Gresham Area Chamber of Commerce
PO Box 1768   Gresham OR 97030
Ph: 503-665-1131 ▪ Fx: 503-666-1041
www.greshamchamber.org

Hermiston Chamber of Commerce
415 S Hwy 395   Hermiston OR 97838
Ph: 541-567-6151 ▪ Fx: 541-564-9109
www.hermistonchamber.com

Hillsboro Chamber of Commerce
334 SE 5th Ave   Hillsboro OR 97123
Ph: 503-648-1102 ▪ Fx: 503-681-0535
www.hillchamber.org

Keizer Chamber of Commerce
980 Chemawa Rd NE   Keizer OR 97303
Ph: 503-393-9111 ▪ Fx: 503-393-1003
www.keizerchamber.com

Klamath County Chamber of Commerce
507 Main St   Klamath Falls OR 97601
Ph: 541-884-5193 ▪ Fx: 541-884-5195 ▪ TF: 877-552-6284
www.klamath.org

La Grande-Union County Chamber of Commerce
102 Elm St   La Grande OR 97850
Ph: 541-963-8588 ▪ Fx: 541-963-3936
www.unioncountychamber.org

Lake Oswego Chamber of Commerce
242 B Ave   Lake Oswego OR 97034
Ph: 503-636-3634 ▪ Fx: 503-636-7427
www.lake-oswego.com

Chamber of Medford/Jackson County
101 E 8th St   Medford OR 97501
Ph: 541-779-4847 ▪ Fx: 541-776-4808
www.medfordchamber.com

North Clackamas County Chamber of Commerce
7740 SE Harmony Rd   Milwaukie OR 97222
Ph: 503-654-7777 ▪ Fx: 503-653-9515
www.yourchamber.com

Greater Newport Chamber of Commerce
555 SW Coast Hwy   Newport OR 97365
Ph: 541-265-8801 ▪ Fx: 541-265-5589 ▪ TF: 800-262-7844
www.newportchamber.org

Oregon City Chamber of Commerce
PO Box 226   Oregon City OR 97045
Ph: 503-656-1619 ▪ Fx: 503-656-2274
www.oregoncity.org

Portland Business Alliance
520 SW Yamhill St Suite 1000   Portland OR 97204
Ph: 503-224-8684 ▪ Fx: 503-323-9186
www.portlandalliance.com

Salem Area Chamber of Commerce
1110 Commercial St NE   Salem OR 97301
Ph: 503-581-1466 ▪ Fx: 503-581-0972
www.salemchamber.org

Springfield Chamber of Commerce
101 S 'A' St PO Box 155   Springfield OR 97477
Ph: 541-746-1651 ▪ Fx: 541-726-4727 ▪ TF: 866-346-1651
www.springfield-chamber.org

Tigard Area Chamber of Commerce
12345 SW Main St   Tigard OR 97223
Ph: 503-639-1656 ▪ Fx: 503-639-6302
www.tigardchamber.com

PENNSYLVANIA

Lehigh Valley Chamber of Commerce
462 Walnut St   Allentown PA 18102
Ph: 610-841-5800 ▪ Fx: 610-437-4907
www.lehighvalleychamber.org

Altoona-Blair County Chamber of Commerce
3900 Industrial Pk Dr Suite 12   Altoona PA 16602
Ph: 814-943-8151 ▪ Fx: 814-943-5239
www.blairchamber.com

Beaver County Chamber of Commerce
250 Insurance St Suite 300   Beaver PA 15009
Ph: 724-775-3944 ▪ Fx: 724-728-3666 ▪ TF: 888-832-7591
www.bcchamber.com

Bedford County Chamber of Commerce
137 E Pitt St   Bedford PA 15522
Ph: 814-623-2233 ▪ Fx: 814-623-6089
www.bedfordcountychamber.org

Bellefonte Intervalley Chamber of Commerce
320 W High St   Bellefonte PA 16823
Ph: 814-355-2917 ▪ Fx: 814-355-2761
bellefontechamber.org

Berwick Area Chamber of Commerce
206 Mulberry St   Berwick PA 18603
Ph: 570-752-3601 ▪ Fx: 570-752-3602
www.berwickpa.org

Bethlehem Area Chamber of Commerce
509 Main St   Bethlehem PA 18018
Ph: 610-867-3788 ▪ Fx: 610-758-9533
www.bethlehemchamber.org

Bloomsburg Area Chamber of Commerce
238 Market St   Bloomsburg PA 17815
Ph: 570-784-2522 ▪ Fx: 570-784-2661
www.bloomsburg.org

Allegheny Valley Chamber of Commerce
1030 Broadview Blvd   Brackenridge PA 15014
Ph: 724-224-3400 ▪ Fx: 724-224-3442
www.alleghenyvalleychamber.com

Butler County Chamber of Commerce
PO Box 1082   Butler PA 16033
Ph: 724-283-2222 ▪ Fx: 724-283-0224
www.butlercountychamber.com

West Shore Chamber of Commerce
4211 Trindle Rd   Camp Hill PA 17011
Ph: 717-761-0702 ▪ Fx: 717-761-4315
www.wschamber.org

Greater Chambersburg Chamber of Commerce
75 S 2nd St   Chambersburg PA 17201
Ph: 717-264-7101 ▪ Fx: 717-267-0399
www.chambersburg.org

Clarion Area Chamber of Commerce
41 S 5th Ave   Clarion PA 16214
Ph: 814-226-9161 ▪ Fx: 814-226-4903
www.clarionpa.com

Perkiomen Valley Chamber of Commerce
351 E Main St   Collegeville PA 19426
Ph: 610-489-6660 ▪ Fx: 610-454-1270
www.pvchamber.net

Greater Connellsville Chamber of Commerce
923 W Crawford Ave   Connellsville PA 15425
Ph: 724-628-5500 ▪ Fx: 724-628-5676
www.greaterconnellsville.org

Central Bucks Chamber of Commerce
115 W Court St   Doylestown PA 18901
Ph: 215-348-3913 ▪ Fx: 215-348-7154
www.centralbuckschamber.com

Two Rivers Area Chamber of Commerce
PO Box 637   Easton PA 18044
Ph: 610-253-4211 ▪ Fx: 610-253-6114
www.eastonareachamber.org

Erie Area Chamber of Commerce
109 Boston Store Pl   Erie PA 16501
Ph: 814-454-7191 ▪ Fx: 814-459-0241 ▪ TF: 800-524-3743
www.eriechamber.com

Exton Region Chamber of Commerce
PO Box 314   Exton PA 19341
Ph: 610-363-7746 ▪ Fx: 610-363-2374
www.ercc.net

Lower Bucks County Chamber of Commerce
409 Hood Blvd   Fairless Hills PA 19030
Ph: 215-943-7400 ▪ Fx: 215-943-7404
www.lbccc.org

Franklin Area Chamber of Commerce
1259 Liberty St   Franklin PA 16323
Ph: 814-432-5823 ▪ Fx: 814-437-2453 ▪ TF: 888-547-2377
www.franklin-pa.org

Gettysburg-Adams County Area Chamber of Commerce
18 Carlisle St Suite 203   Gettysburg PA 17325
Ph: 717-334-8151 ▪ Fx: 717-334-3368
www.gettysburg-chamber.org

Central Westmoreland Chamber of Commerce
RR1 Box 240   Greensburg PA 15601
Ph: 724-834-2900 ▪ Fx: 724-837-7635
www.westmorelandchamber.com

Hanover Area Chamber of Commerce
146 Carlisle St   Hanover PA 17331
Ph: 717-637-6130 ▪ Fx: 717-637-9127
www.hanoverchamber.com

Harrisburg Regional Chamber of Commerce
3211 N Front St Suite 201   Harrisburg PA 17110
Ph: 717-232-4099 ▪ Fx: 717-232-5184
www.harrisburgregionalchamber.org

Wayne County Chamber of Commerce
303 Commercial St   Honesdale PA 18431
Ph: 570-253-1960 ▪ Fx: 570-253-1517 ▪ TF: 800-433-9008
www.waynecountycc.com

Horsham Chamber of Commerce
PO Box 141   Horsham PA 19044
Ph: 215-443-7154 ▪ Fx: 215-443-7409
www.horshamchamber.com

Huntingdon County Business & Industry
241 Mifflin St   Huntingdon PA 16652
Ph: 814-643-4322 ▪ Fx: 814-643-4324
www.hcbi.com

Indiana County Chamber of Commerce
1019 Philadelphia St   Indiana PA 15701
Ph: 724-465-2511 ▪ Fx: 724-465-3706
www.indianapa.com/chamber

Norwin Chamber of Commerce
321 Main St   Irwin PA 15642
Ph: 724-863-0888 ▪ Fx: 724-863-5133
www.norwinchamber.com

Greater Johnstown/Cambria County Chamber of Commerce
111 Market St   Johnstown PA 15901
Ph: 814-536-5107 ▪ Fx: 814-539-5800 ▪ TF: 800-790-4522
www.johnstownchamber.com

Southern Chester County Chamber of Commerce
PO Box 395   Kennett Square PA 19348
Ph: 610-444-0774 ▪ Fx: 610-444-5105
www.scccc.com

King of Prussia Chamber of Commerce
101 Bill Smith Blvd   King of Prussia PA 19406
Ph: 610-265-1776 ▪ Fx: 610-265-0473
www.kopinn.com

Armstrong County Chamber of Commerce
124 Market St   Kittanning PA 16201
Ph: 724-543-1305 ▪ Fx: 724-548-2951 ▪ TF: 800-979-3348
www.armstrongchamber.org

Lancaster Chamber of Commerce & Industry
100 S Queen St   Lancaster PA 17603
Ph: 717-397-3531 ▪ Fx: 717-293-3159
www.lancasterchamber.com

North Penn Chamber of Commerce
229 S Broad St   Lansdale PA 19446
Ph: 215-362-9200 ▪ Fx: 215-362-0393
www.northpenn.org

Latrobe Area Chamber of Commerce
10 Lloyd Ave   Latrobe PA 15650
Ph: 724-537-2671 ▪ Fx: 724-537-2690
www.latrobearea.com

Lebanon Valley Chamber of Commerce
728 Walnut St PO Box 899   Lebanon PA 17042
Ph: 717-273-3727 ▪ Fx: 717-273-7940
www.lvchamber.org

Juniata Valley Area Chamber of Commerce
152 E Market St Suite 103   Lewistown PA 17044
Ph: 717-248-6713 ▪ Fx: 717-248-6714 ▪ TF: 877-568-9739
www.juniatavalley.org

Clinton County Economic Partnership
212 N Jay St   Lock Haven PA 17745
Ph: 570-748-5782 ▪ Fx: 570-893-0433 ▪ TF: 888-388-6991
www.clintoncountyinfo.com

Western Crawford County Chamber of Commerce
211 Chestnut St   Meadville PA 16335
Ph: 814-337-8030 ▪ Fx: 814-337-8022
www.meadvillechamber.com

Delaware County Chamber of Commerce
602 E Baltimore Pike   Media PA 19063
Ph: 610-565-3677 ▪ Fx: 610-565-1606
www.delcochamber.org

Pike County Chamber of Commerce
101 Rt 209 S   Milford PA 18337
Ph: 570-296-8700 ▪ Fx: 570-296-3921
www.pikechamber.com

Monroeville Area Chamber of Commerce
4268 Northern Pike   Monroeville PA 15146
Ph: 412-856-0622 ▪ Fx: 412-856-1030 ▪ TF: 888-753-5522
www.monroevillechamber.com

Pittsburgh Airport Area Chamber of Commerce
850 Beaver Grade Rd   Moon Township PA 15108
Ph: 412-264-6270 ▪ Fx: 412-264-1575
www.paacc.com

Laurel Highlands Chamber of Commerce
537 W Main St   Mount Pleasant PA 15666
Ph: 724-547-7521 ▪ Fx: 724-547-5530 ▪ TF: 888-547-7521
www.laurelhighlandschamber.com

Nazareth Area Chamber of Commerce
201 N Main St PO Box 173   Nazareth PA 18064
Ph: 610-759-9188 ▪ Fx: 610-759-5262
www.nazarethchamber.com

Lawrence County Chamber of Commerce   www.lawrencecountychamber.com
138 W Washington St   New Castle PA 16101
Ph: 724-654-5593 ▪ Fx: 724-654-3330

MONTCO Chamber of Commerce   www.montcocc.org
1341 Sandy Hill Rd   Norristown PA 19401
Ph: 610-277-9500 ▪ Fx: 610-277-2659

Pennridge Chamber of Commerce   www.pennridge.com
538 W Market St   Perkasie PA 18944
Ph: 215-257-5390 ▪ Fx: 215-257-6840

Greater Northeast Philadelphia Chamber of Commerce   www.gnpcc.org
8601 E Roosevelt Blvd   Philadelphia PA 19152
Ph: 215-332-3400 ▪ Fx: 215-332-6050

Greater Philadelphia Chamber of Commerce   www.gpcc.org
200 S Broad St Suite 700   Philadelphia PA 19102
Ph: 215-545-1234 ▪ Fx: 215-790-3600

Moshannon Valley Economic Development Partnership   www.mvedp.org
200 Shady Ln   Philipsburg PA 16866
Ph: 814-342-2260 ▪ Fx: 814-342-2878

Phoenixville Area Chamber of Commerce   www.phoenixvillechamber.org
171 E Bridge St   Phoenixville PA 19460
Ph: 610-933-3070 ▪ Fx: 610-917-0503

East Liberty Quarter Chamber of Commerce
5907 Penn Ave Suite 305   Pittsburgh PA 15206
Ph: 412-661-9660 ▪ Fx: 412-661-9661

Greater Pittsburgh Chamber of Commerce   www.pittsburghchamber.com
425 6th Ave 6th Fl   Pittsburgh PA 15219
Ph: 412-392-4500 ▪ Fx: 412-392-4520 ▪ TF: 800-843-8772

North Side Chamber of Commerce
809 Middle St   Pittsburgh PA 15212
Ph: 412-231-6500 ▪ Fx: 412-321-6760

Penn Hills Chamber of Commerce   www.pennhillschamber.org
13049 Frankstown Rd   Pittsburgh PA 15235
Ph: 412-795-8741 ▪ Fx: 412-795-7993

South Hills Chamber of Commerce   www.shchamber.org
1815 Washington Rd   Pittsburgh PA 15241
Ph: 412-833-1177 ▪ Fx: 412-833-1354

South Side Chamber of Commerce
PO Box 42380   Pittsburgh PA 15203
Ph: 412-431-3360

Greater Pittston Chamber of Commerce   www.pittstonchamber.org
Kennedy Blvd & William St   Pittston PA 18640
Ph: 570-655-1424 ▪ Fx: 570-655-0336

Tri County Area Chamber of Commerce   www.tricountyareachamber.com
135 High St   Pottstown PA 19464
Ph: 610-326-2900 ▪ Fx: 610-970-9705

Schuylkill Chamber of Commerce   www.schuylkillchamber.com
91 S Progress Ave   Pottsville PA 17901
Ph: 570-622-1942 ▪ Fx: 570-622-1638 ▪ TF: 800-755-1942

Upper Bucks Chamber of Commerce   www.ubcc.org
2170 Portzer Rd   Quakertown PA 18951
Ph: 215-536-3211 ▪ Fx: 215-536-7767

Berks County Chamber of Commerce   www.berkschamber.org
601 Penn St Suite 101   Reading PA 19601
Ph: 610-376-6766 ▪ Fx: 610-376-4135

Greater Scranton Chamber of Commerce   www.scrantonchamber.com
222 Mulberry St   Scranton PA 18503
Ph: 570-342-7711 ▪ Fx: 570-347-6262

Central Susquehanna Valley Chamber of Commerce   www.gsvcc.org
Rt 15 PO Box 10   Shamokin Dam PA 17876
Ph: 570-743-4100 ▪ Fx: 570-743-1221 ▪ TF: 800-410-2880

Shenango Valley Chamber of Commerce   www.svchamber.com
41 Chestnut St   Sharon PA 16146
Ph: 724-981-5880 ▪ Fx: 724-981-5480

Shippensburg Area Chamber of Commerce   www.shippensburg.org
75 W King St   Shippensburg PA 17257
Ph: 717-532-5509 ▪ Fx: 717-532-7501

Somerset County Chamber of Commerce   www.somersetcntypachamber.org
601 N Center Ave   Somerset PA 15501
Ph: 814-445-6431 ▪ Fx: 814-443-4313

Chamber of Business & Industry of Centre County   www.cbicc.org
200 Innovation Blvd Suite 150   State College PA 16803
Ph: 814-234-1829 ▪ Fx: 814-234-5869

Pocono Mountains Chamber of Commerce   www.poconochamber.net
556 Main St   Stroudsburg PA 18360
Ph: 570-421-4433 ▪ Fx: 570-424-7281

Indian Valley Chamber of Commerce   www.indianvalleychamber.com
100 Penn Ave   Telford PA 18969
Ph: 215-723-9472 ▪ Fx: 215-723-2490

Fayette Chamber of Commerce   www.faycham.org
65 W Main St   Uniontown PA 15401
Ph: 724-437-4571 ▪ Fx: 724-438-3304 ▪ TF: 800-916-9365

StrongLand Chamber of Commerce   www.strongland.org
1129 Industrial Pk Rd Box 10 Suite 108   Vandergrift PA 15690
Ph: 724-845-5426 ▪ Fx: 724-845-5428

Warren County Chamber of Commerce   www.warrenpachamber.com
308 Market St   Warren PA 16365
Ph: 814-723-3050 ▪ Fx: 814-723-6024

Washington County Chamber of Commerce   www.washcochamber.com
20 E Beau St   Washington PA 15301
Ph: 724-225-3010 ▪ Fx: 724-228-7337

Main Line Chamber of Commerce   www.mlcc.org
175 Strafford Ave Suite 130   Wayne PA 19087
Ph: 610-687-6232 ▪ Fx: 610-687-8085

Greater Waynesboro Chamber of Commerce   www.waynesboro.org
323 E Main St   Waynesboro PA 17268
Ph: 717-762-7123 ▪ Fx: 717-762-7124

Chamber of Commerce of Greater West Chester Inc   www.greaterwestchester.com
40 E Gay St   West Chester PA 19380
Ph: 610-696-4046 ▪ Fx: 610-696-9110

Mon-Yough Chamber of Commerce   www.regionalbusinessalliance.com
3001 Jacks Run Rd   White Oak PA 15131
Ph: 412-678-2450 ▪ Fx: 412-678-2451

Greater Wilkes-Barre Chamber of Business & Industry   www.wilkes-barre.org
2 Public Sq PO Box 5340   Wilkes-Barre PA 18710
Ph: 570-823-2101 ▪ Fx: 570-822-5951 ▪ TF: 800-331-0912

Williamsport/Lycoming Chamber of Commerce   www.williamsport.org
100 W 3rd St   Williamsport PA 17701
Ph: 570-326-1971 ▪ Fx: 570-321-1208

Greater Willow Grove Chamber of Commerce   www.willowgrovechamber.com
117 Park Ave Suite 100   Willow Grove PA 19090
Ph: 215-657-2227 ▪ Fx: 215-657-8564

York County Chamber of Commerce   www.yorkchamber.com
1 Market Way E   York PA 17401
Ph: 717-848-4000 ▪ Fx: 717-843-6737 ▪ TF: 888-878-9675

RHODE ISLAND

Greater Cranston Chamber of Commerce   www.cranstonchamber.com
48A Rolfe Sq   Cranston RI 02910
Ph: 401-785-3780 ▪ Fx: 401-785-3782

East Providence Chamber of Commerce   www.eastprovchamber.com
850 Waterman Ave   East Providence RI 02914
Ph: 401-438-1212 ▪ Fx: 401-435-4581

North Central Chamber of Commerce   www.ncrichamber.com
1126 Hartford Ave Suite 201A   Johnston RI 02919
Ph: 401-273-1310 ▪ Fx: 401-273-2570

Northern Rhode Island Chamber of Commerce   www.nrichamber.com
6 Blackstone Valley Pl Suite 301   Lincoln RI 02865
Ph: 401-334-1000 ▪ Fx: 401-334-1009

Newport County Chamber of Commerce   www.newportchamber.com
45 Valley Rd   Middletown RI 02842
Ph: 401-847-1600 ▪ Fx: 401-849-5848

North Kingstown Chamber of Commerce   www.northkingstown.com
8045 Post Rd   North Kingstown RI 02852
Ph: 401-295-5566 ▪ Fx: 401-295-5582

Greater Providence Chamber of Commerce   www.provchamber.com
30 Exchange Terr   Providence RI 02903
Ph: 401-521-5000 ▪ Fx: 401-751-2434

South Kingstown Chamber of Commerce   www.skchamber.com
322 Main St PO Box 289   Wakefield RI 02880
Ph: 401-783-2801 ▪ Fx: 401-789-3120

East Bay Chamber of Commerce   www.eastbaychamberri.org
654 Metacom Ave   Warren RI 02885
Ph: 401-245-0750 ▪ Fx: 401-245-0110 ▪ TF: 888-278-9948

Central Rhode Island Chamber of Commerce   www.centralrichamber.com
3288 Post Rd   Warwick RI 02886
Ph: 401-732-1100 ▪ Fx: 401-732-1107

Pawtuxet Valley Chamber of Commerce
1192 Main St   West Warwick RI 02893
Ph: 401-823-3349 ▪ Fx: 401-823-8162

SOUTH CAROLINA

Greater Abbeville Chamber of Commerce   www.abbevillecitysc.com/chamberdev/
107 Court Sq   Abbeville SC 29620
Ph: 864-459-4600 ▪ Fx: 864-459-4068

Greater Aiken Chamber of Commerce   www.aikenchamber.net
PO Box 892   Aiken SC 29802
Ph: 803-641-1111 ▪ Fx: 803-641-4174 ▪ TF: 800-542-4536

Anderson Area Chamber of Commerce   www.andersonscchamber.com
706 E Greenville St   Anderson SC 29621
Ph: 864-226-3454 ▪ Fx: 864-226-3300

Bennettsville Chamber of Commerce
PO Box 364   Bennettsville SC 29512
Ph: 843-479-3941 ▪ Fx: 843-479-4859

Kershaw County Chamber of Commerce   www.camden-sc.org
607 S Broad St   Camden SC 29020
Ph: 803-432-2525 ▪ Fx: 803-432-4181 ▪ TF: 800-968-4037

West Metro Chamber of Commerce   www.westmetrochamber.com
1006 12th St   Cayce SC 29033
Ph: 803-794-6504 ▪ Fx: 803-794-6505

Charleston Metro Chamber of Commerce   www.charlestonchamber.net
81 Mary St   Charleston SC 29403
Ph: 843-577-2510 ▪ Fx: 843-723-4853

Chester County Chamber of Commerce   www.chesterchamber.com
PO Box 489   Chester SC 29706
Ph: 803-581-4142 ▪ Fx: 803-581-2431

Laurens County Chamber of Commerce   www.laurenscounty.org
291 Professional Park Rd   Clinton SC 29325
Ph: 864-833-2716 ▪ Fx: 864-833-6935

Greater Columbia Chamber of Commerce   www.columbiachamber.com
930 Richland St   Columbia SC 29201
Ph: 803-733-1110 ▪ Fx: 803-733-1149

Conway Area Chamber of Commerce   www.conwayscchamber.com
203 Main St   Conway SC 29526
Ph: 843-248-2273 ▪ Fx: 843-248-0003

Greater Darlington Chamber of Commerce   www.darlingtonchamber.com
38 Public Sq   Darlington SC 29532
Ph: 843-393-2641 ▪ Fx: 843-393-8059

Dillon County Chamber of Commerce
100 N MacArthur Ave   Dillon SC 29536
Ph: 843-774-8551 ▪ Fx: 843-774-0114 ▪ TF: 800-444-6838

Greater Easley Chamber of Commerce   www.easleychamber.org
PO Box 241   Easley SC 29641
Ph: 864-859-2693 ▪ Fx: 864-859-1941

Greater Florence Chamber of Commerce   www.florencescchamber.com
610 W Palmetto St   Florence SC 29501
Ph: 843-665-0515   Fx: 843-662-2010

Cherokee County Chamber of Commerce   www.cherokeechamber.org
225 S Limestone St   Gaffney SC 29340
Ph: 864-489-5721   Fx: 864-487-3399

Georgetown County Chamber of Commerce   www.georgetownchamber.com
PO Box 1776   Georgetown SC 29442
Ph: 843-546-8436   Fx: 843-520-4876   TF: 800-777-7705

Greater Greenville Chamber of Commerce   www.greenvillechamber.org
24 Cleveland St   Greenville SC 29601
Ph: 864-242-1050   Fx: 864-282-8509

Greenwood Chamber of Commerce   www.greenwoodscchamber.org
PO Box 980   Greenwood SC 29648
Ph: 864-223-8431   Fx: 864-229-9785

Greater Hartsville Chamber of Commerce   www.hartsvillechamber.org
214 N 5th St   Hartsville SC 29550
Ph: 843-332-6401   Fx: 843-332-8017   TF: 888-427-8720

Hilton Head Island Chamber of Commerce   www.hiltonheadisland.org
1 Chamber Dr   Hilton Head Island SC 29928
Ph: 843-785-3673   Fx: 843-785-7110   TF: 800-523-3373

Williamsburg Hometown Chamber of Commerce   www.williamsburgsc.org
130 E Main St   Kingstree SC 29556
Ph: 843-355-6431   Fx: 843-354-3343

Lancaster County Chamber of Commerce   www.lancasterchambersc.org
PO Box 430   Lancaster SC 29721
Ph: 803-283-4105   Fx: 803-286-4360

Lexington Chamber of Commerce   www.lexingtonsc.org
PO Box 44   Lexington SC 29071
Ph: 803-359-6113   Fx: 803-359-0634

Clarendon County Chamber of Commerce   www.clarendoncounty.com
19 N Brooks St   Manning SC 29102
Ph: 803-435-4405   Fx: 803-435-4406   TF: 800-731-5253

Berkeley County Chamber of Commerce   www.bcoc.com
PO Box 968   Moncks Corner SC 29461
Ph: 843-761-8238   Fx: 843-899-6491   TF: 800-882-0337

Myrtle Beach Area Chamber of Commerce   www.myrtlebeachinfo.com/chamber/
1200 N Oak St   Myrtle Beach SC 29577
Ph: 843-626-7444   Fx: 843-626-0009   TF: 800-356-3016

Newberry County Chamber of Commerce   www.newberrycounty.org
1109 Main St PO Box 396   Newberry SC 29108
Ph: 803-276-4274   Fx: 803-276-4373

North Augusta Chamber of Commerce   www.northaugusta.net/chamber
PO Box 6246   North Augusta SC 29861
Ph: 803-279-2323   Fx: 803-279-0003

Orangeburg County Chamber of Commerce   www.orangeburgsc.net/chamber/chamber.html
PO Box 328   Orangeburg SC 29116
Ph: 803-534-6821   Fx: 803-531-9435   TF: 800-545-6153

York County Regional Chamber of Commerce   www.yorkcountychamber.com
PO Box 590   Rock Hill SC 29731
Ph: 803-324-7500   Fx: 803-324-1889

Spartanburg Area Chamber of Commerce   www.spartanburgchamber.com
PO Box 1636   Spartanburg SC 29304
Ph: 864-594-5000   Fx: 864-594-5055

Greater Summerville-Dorchester County Chamber of Commerce   www.gsdcchamber.org
402 N Main St   Summerville SC 29483
Ph: 843-873-2931   Fx: 843-875-4464

Greater Sumter Chamber of Commerce   www.sumterchamber.com
32 E Calhoun St   Sumter SC 29150
Ph: 803-775-1231   Fx: 803-775-0915

Union County Chamber of Commerce   www.unionsc.com
135 W Main St   Union SC 29379
Ph: 864-427-9039   Fx: 864-427-9030   TF: 877-202-8755

Walterboro-Colleton Chamber of Commerce   www.walterboro.org
PO Box 426   Walterboro SC 29488
Ph: 843-549-9595   Fx: 843-549-5775

SOUTH DAKOTA

Aberdeen Area Chamber of Commerce   www.aberdeen-chamber.com
516 S Main St   Aberdeen SD 57401
Ph: 605-225-2860   Fx: 605-225-2437   TF: 800-874-9038

Brookings Area Chamber of Commerce
2308 6th St E   Brookings SD 57006
Ph: 605-692-6125   Fx: 605-697-8109   TF: 800-699-6125

Pierre Area Chamber of Commerce   www.pierrechamber.com
PO Box 548   Pierre SD 57501
Ph: 605-224-7361   Fx: 605-224-6485   TF: 800-962-2034

Rapid City Area Chamber of Commerce   www.rapidcitychamber.com
PO Box 747   Rapid City SD 57709
Ph: 605-343-1744   Fx: 605-343-6550

Sioux Falls Area Chamber of Commerce   www.siouxfalls.com
200 N Phillips Ave Suite 102   Sioux Falls SD 57104
Ph: 605-336-1620   Fx: 605-336-6499

TENNESSEE

Cheatham County Chamber of Commerce   www.cheathamchamber.org
PO Box 354   Ashland City TN 37015
Ph: 615-792-6722   Fx: 615-792-5001

Bartlett Area Chamber of Commerce   www.bartlettchamber.org
2969 Elmore Pk Rd   Bartlett TN 38134
Ph: 901-372-9457   Fx: 901-372-9488

Bristol Chamber of Commerce   www.bristolchamber.org
20 Volunteer Pkwy   Bristol TN 37620
Ph: 423-989-4850   Fx: 423-989-4867

Chattanooga Area Chamber of Commerce   www.chattanoogachamber.com
811 Broad St   Chattanooga TN 37402
Ph: 423-756-2121   Fx: 423-267-7242

Clarksville Area Chamber of Commerce   www.clarksvillechamber.com
312 Madison St   Clarksville TN 37041
Ph: 931-647-2331   Fx: 931-645-1574

Cleveland/Bradley Chamber of Commerce   www.clevelandchamber.com
PO Box 2275   Cleveland TN 37320
Ph: 423-472-6587   Fx: 423-472-2019   TF: 800-472-6588

Anderson County Chamber of Commerce   www.andersoncountychamber.org
245 N Main St Suite 200   Clinton TN 37716
Ph: 865-457-2559   Fx: 865-463-7480

Collierville Chamber of Commerce   www.colliervillechamber.com
101 Walnut St   Collierville TN 38017
Ph: 901-853-1949   Fx: 901-853-2399

Maury Alliance   www.mauryalliance.com
PO Box 1076   Columbia TN 38402
Ph: 931-388-2155   Fx: 931-380-0335

Cookeville Area-Putnam County Chamber of Commerce   www.cookevillechamber.com
1 W 1st St   Cookeville TN 38501
Ph: 931-526-2211   Fx: 931-526-4023   TF: 800-264-5541

Covington-Tipton County Chamber of Commerce
106 W Liberty St   Covington TN 38019
Ph: 901-476-9727   Fx: 901-476-0056

Crossville Cumberland County Chamber of Commerce   www.crossville-chamber.com
34 S Main St   Crossville TN 38555
Ph: 931-484-8444   Fx: 931-484-7511   TF: 877-465-3861

Crossville Cumberland County Chamber of Commerce   www.crossville-chamber.com
34 S Main St   Crossville TN 38555
Ph: 931-484-8444   Fx: 931-484-7511   TF: 877-465-3861

Jefferson County Chamber of Commerce   www.jefferson-tn-chamber.org
PO Box 890   Dandridge TN 37725
Ph: 865-397-9642   Fx: 865-397-0164   TF: 877-237-3847

Dayton Chamber of Commerce
107 Main St   Dayton TN 37321
Ph: 423-775-0361   Fx: 423-570-0105

Dickson County Chamber of Commerce   www.dicksoncountychamber.com
119 Hwy 70 E   Dickson TN 37055
Ph: 615-446-2349   Fx: 615-441-3112   TF: 877-718-4967

Weakley County Chamber of Commerce   www.weakleycountychamber.com
PO Box 67   Dresden TN 38225
Ph: 731-364-3787   Fx: 731-364-2099

Dyersburg/Dyer County Chamber of Commerce   ddcc.dyercountychamber.com
PO Box 747   Dyersburg TN 38025
Ph: 731-285-3433   Fx: 731-286-4926

Elizabethton/Carter County Chamber of Commerce
PO Box 190   Elizabethton TN 37644
Ph: 423-547-3850   Fx: 423-547-3854

Fayetteville-Lincoln County Chamber of Commerce   www.vallnet.com/chamberofcommerce
PO Box 515   Fayetteville TN 37334
Ph: 931-433-1234   Fx: 931-433-9087   TF: 888-433-1238

Williamson County-Franklin Chamber of Commerce   www.williamson-franklinchamber.com
PO Box 156   Franklin TN 37065
Ph: 615-794-1225   Fx: 615-790-5337   TF: 800-356-3445

Germantown Area Chamber of Commerce   www.germantownchamber.com
2195 S Germantown Rd   Germantown TN 38138
Ph: 901-755-1200   Fx: 901-755-9168

Greene County Partnership & Chamber of Commerce   www.greenecountypartnership.com
115 Academy St   Greeneville TN 37743
Ph: 423-638-4111   Fx: 423-638-5345

Hendersonville Area Chamber of Commerce   www.hendersonvillechamber.com
101 Wessington Pl   Hendersonville TN 37075
Ph: 615-824-2818   Fx: 615-822-7498

Donelson-Hermitage Chamber of Commerce   www.dhchamber.com
5653 Frist Blvd Suite 740   Hermitage TN 37076
Ph: 615-883-7896   Fx: 615-391-4880

Carroll County Chamber of Commerce   www.carrollcounty-tn-chamber.com
PO Box 726   Huntingdon TN 38344
Ph: 731-986-4664   Fx: 731-986-2029

Jackson Area Chamber of Commerce   www.jacksontn.com
197 Auditorium St   Jackson TN 38301
Ph: 731-423-2200   Fx: 731-424-4860   TF: 800-858-5596

Johnson City/Jonesborough/Washington County Chamber of Commerce   www.johnsoncitytn.com
603 E Market St   Johnson City TN 37601
Ph: 423-461-8000   Fx: 423-461-8047   TF: 800-852-3392

Kingsport Area Chamber of Commerce   www.kingsportchamber.org
151 E Main St   Kingsport TN 37660
Ph: 423-392-8800   Fx: 423-246-7234

Roane County Chamber of Commerce   www.roanealliance.org
1209 N Kentucky St   Kingston TN 37763
Ph: 865-376-5572   Fx: 865-376-4978

Knoxville Area Chamber Partnership   www.knoxvillechamber.com
601 W Summit Hill Dr Suite 300   Knoxville TN 37902
Ph: 865-637-4550   Fx: 865-523-2071

Lawrence County Chamber of Commerce   www.chamberofcommerce.lawrence.tn.us
1609 N Locust Ave   Lawrenceburg TN 38464
Ph: 931-762-4911   Fx: 931-762-3153   TF: 877-388-4911

Lebanon-Wilson County Chamber of Commerce   www.wilsoncounty.com/lebanonchamber
149 Public Sq   Lebanon TN 37087
Ph: 615-444-5503   Fx: 615-443-0596

Loudon County Chamber of Commerce   www.loudoncountychamber.com
PO Box 129   Loudon TN 37774
Ph: 865-458-2067   Fx: 865-458-1206

Madison Rivergate Area Chamber of Commerce   www.madisonchamber.net
PO Box 97   Madison TN 37116
Ph: 615-865-5400   Fx: 615-865-0448

Monroe County Chamber of Commerce   www.monroecountychamber.org
4765 Hwy 68   Madisonville TN 37354
Ph: 423-442-4588   Fx: 423-442-9016

Blount County Chamber of Commerce   www.blountchamber.com
201 S Washington St   Maryville TN 37804
Ph: 865-983-2241   Fx: 865-984-1386

McMinnville-Warren County Chamber of Commerce   www.warrentn.com
PO Box 574   McMinnville TN 37111
Ph: 931-473-6611   Fx: 931-473-4741

Memphis Regional Chamber of Commerce   www.memphischamber.com
22 N Front St Suite 200   Memphis TN 38103
Ph: 901-543-3500   Fx: 901-543-3510

Morristown Area Chamber of Commerce   www.morristownchamber.com
825 W 1st North St   Morristown TN 37814
Ph: 423-586-6382   Fx: 423-586-6576

Mount Juliet/West Wilson County Chamber of Commerce
2592 N Mt Juliet Rd   Mount Juliet TN 37122   www.mtjulietchamber.com
Ph: 615-758-3478   Fx: 615-754-8595

Rutherford County Chamber of Commerce   www.rutherfordchamber.org
501 Memorial Blvd   Murfreesboro TN 37129
Ph: 615-893-6565   Fx: 615-890-7600   TF: 800-716-7560

Nashville Chamber of Commerce   www.nashvillechamber.com
211 Commerce St Suite 100   Nashville TN 37201
Ph: 615-743-3012   Fx: 615-256-3074   TF: 800-657-6910

Newport/Cocke County Chamber of Commerce   cockecounty.org
433-B Prospect Ave   Newport TN 37821
Ph: 423-623-7201   Fx: 423-623-7216

Oak Ridge Chamber of Commerce   www.orcc.org
1400 Oak Ridge Tpke   Oak Ridge TN 37830
Ph: 865-483-1321   Fx: 865-483-1678

Paris-Henry County Chamber of Commerce   www.paris.tn.org
2508 Eastwood St   Paris TN 38242
Ph: 731-642-3431   Fx: 731-642-3454   TF: 800-345-1103

Giles County Chamber of Commerce   www.gilescountychamber.com
110 N 2nd St   Pulaski TN 38478
Ph: 931-363-3789   Fx: 931-363-7279

Rogersville/Hawkins County Chamber of Commerce   www.welcome.to/hawkinscounty
107 E Main St Suite 100   Rogersville TN 37857
Ph: 423-272-2186   Fx: 423-272-2186

Shelbyville-Bedford County Chamber of Commerce   www.shelbyvilletn.com
100 N Cannon Blvd   Shelbyville TN 37160
Ph: 931-684-3482   Fx: 931-684-3483   TF: 888-662-2525

Fayette County Chamber of Commerce   fayettecountychamber.com
107 W Court Sq PO Box 411   Somerville TN 38068
Ph: 901-465-8690   Fx: 901-465-6497

Springfield-Robertson County Chamber of Commerce   members.aol.com/tngenweb/chamber.html
100 5th Ave W   Springfield TN 37172
Ph: 615-384-3800   Fx: 615-384-1260

Claiborne County Chamber of Commerce   www.claibornecounty.com
3222 Hwy 25 E Suite 1   Tazewell TN 37879
Ph: 423-626-4149   Fx: 423-626-1611   TF: 800-332-8164

Greater Gibson County Area Chamber of Commerce   www.gibsoncountytn.com
PO Box 464   Trenton TN 38382
Ph: 731-855-0973   Fx: 731-855-0979

Obion County Chamber of Commerce   www.obioncounty.com
214 E Church St   Union City TN 38261
Ph: 731-885-0211   Fx: 731-885-7155

Franklin County Chamber of Commerce   www.franklincountychamber.com
PO Box 280   Winchester TN 37398
Ph: 931-967-6788   Fx: 931-967-9418

TEXAS

Abilene Chamber of Commerce   www.abilene.com/chamber
PO Box 2281   Abilene TX 79604
Ph: 325-677-7241   Fx: 325-677-0622

Alice Chamber of Commerce   www.alicetx.org
612 E Main St   Alice TX 78332
Ph: 361-664-3454   Fx: 361-664-2291   TF: 877-992-5423

Allen Chamber of Commerce   www.allenchamber.com
210 W McDermott Dr   Allen TX 75013
Ph: 972-727-5585   Fx: 972-727-9000

Alvin-Manvel Area Chamber of Commerce   www.alvinmanvelchamber.org
105 W Willis St   Alvin TX 77511
Ph: 281-331-3944   Fx: 281-585-8662   TF: 800-331-4063

Amarillo Chamber of Commerce   www.amarillo-chamber.org
1000 S Polk St   Amarillo TX 79101
Ph: 806-373-7800   Fx: 806-373-3909

Arlington Chamber of Commerce   www.arlingtontx.com
505 E Border St   Arlington TX 76010
Ph: 817-275-2613   Fx: 817-261-7535   TF: 800-834-3928

Atlanta Area Chamber of Commerce   www.atlantatexas.org/Chamber/index.htm
PO Box 29   Atlanta TX 75551
Ph: 903-796-3296   Fx: 903-796-5711

Greater Austin Chamber of Commerce   www.austinchamber.org
210 Barton Springs Rd   Austin TX 78704
Ph: 512-478-9383   Fx: 512-478-6389   TF: 800-856-5602

Bastrop Chamber of Commerce   www.bastropchamber.com
927 Main St   Bastrop TX 78602
Ph: 512-321-2419   Fx: 512-303-0305

Baytown Chamber of Commerce   www.baytownchamber.com
4721 Garth Rd Suite C   Baytown TX 77521
Ph: 281-422-8359   Fx: 281-428-1758

Beaumont Chamber of Commerce   www.bmtcoc.org
1110 Park St   Beaumont TX 77701
Ph: 409-838-6581   Fx: 409-833-6718

Hurst-Euless-Bedford Chamber of Commerce   www.heb.org
PO Box 969   Bedford TX 76095
Ph: 817-283-1521   Fx: 817-267-5111

Bee County Chamber of Commerce   www.beeville.net/chamberofcommerce
1705 N Saint Mary's St   Beeville TX 78102
Ph: 361-358-3267   Fx: 361-358-3966

Greater Southwest Houston Chamber of Commerce   www.gswhcc.org
PO Box 788   Bellaire TX 77402
Ph: 713-666-1521   Fx: 713-666-1523

Bonham Area Chamber of Commerce   www.bonhamchamber.com
110 E 1st St   Bonham TX 75418
Ph: 903-583-4811   Fx: 903-583-7972

Washington County Chamber of Commerce   www.brenhamtexas.com
314 S Austin St   Brenham TX 77833
Ph: 979-836-3695   Fx: 979-836-2540   TF: 888-273-6426

Brownsville Chamber of Commerce   www.brownsvillechamber.com
1600 E Elizabeth St   Brownsville TX 78520
Ph: 956-542-4341   Fx: 956-504-3348

Brownwood Area Chamber of Commerce   www.brownwoodchamber.org
600 E Depot St   Brownwood TX 76801
Ph: 325-646-9535   Fx: 325-643-6686

Bryan-College Station Chamber of Commerce   www.bcschamber.org
4001 E 29th St Suite 175   Bryan TX 77802
Ph: 979-260-5200   Fx: 979-260-5208   TF: 800-777-8292

Burleson Area Chamber of Commerce   www.burleson.org
1044 SW Wilshire Blvd   Burleson TX 76028
Ph: 817-295-6121   Fx: 817-295-6192

Canyon Chamber of Commerce   www.canyonchamber.org
1518 5th Ave   Canyon TX 79015
Ph: 806-655-1183   Fx: 806-655-4608   TF: 800-999-9481

Metrocrest Chamber of Commerce   www.metrocrestchamber.com
1204 Metrocrest Dr   Carrollton TX 75006
Ph: 972-416-6600   Fx: 972-416-7874

Panola County Chamber of Commerce   www.carthagetexas.com/chamber.htm
300 W Panola St   Carthage TX 75633
Ph: 903-693-6634   Fx: 903-693-8578

Cleburne Chamber of Commerce   www.cleburnechamber.com
PO Box 701   Cleburne TX 76033
Ph: 817-645-2455   Fx: 817-641-3069

Brazosport Area Chamber of Commerce   www.brazosport.org
420 W Hwy 332   Clute TX 77531
Ph: 979-265-2505   Fx: 979-265-4246   TF: 888-477-2505

Conroe Chamber of Commerce   www.conroe.org
505 W Davis St   Conroe TX 77301
Ph: 936-756-6644   Fx: 936-756-6462   TF: 800-283-6645

Greater Conroe/Lake Conroe Area Chamber of Commerce www.conroe.org
505 W Davis St   Conroe TX 77301
Ph: 936-756-6644   Fx: 936-756-6462   TF: 800-283-6645

Coppell Chamber of Commerce   www.coppellchamber.org
200 E Belt Line Rd Suite 102   Coppell TX 75019
Ph: 972-393-2829   Fx: 972-393-7485

Copperas Cove Chamber of Commerce   www.copperascove.com
204 E Robertson Ave   Copperas Cove TX 76522
Ph: 254-547-7571   Fx: 254-547-5015

Corpus Christi Chamber of Commerce   www.corpuschristichamber.org
1201 N Shoreline Blvd   Corpus Christi TX 78401
Ph: 361-881-1800   Fx: 361-888-5627   TF: 877-385-3437

Corsicana Area Chamber of Commerce   www.corsicana.org
120 N 12th St   Corsicana TX 75110
Ph: 903-874-4731   Fx: 903-874-4187   TF: 877-376-7477

Dallas Northeast Chamber of Commerce   www.dallasnortheastchamber.net
6260 E Mockingbird Ln Suite 250   Dallas TX 75214
Ph: 214-828-1400   Fx: 214-828-9994

Greater Dallas Chamber of Commerce   www.dallaschamber.org
700 N Pearl St Suite 1200   Dallas TX 75201
Ph: 214-746-6600   Fx: 214-746-6799

North Dallas Chamber of Commerce   www.ndcc.org
10707 Preston Rd   Dallas TX 75230
Ph: 214-368-6485   Fx: 214-691-5584

Oak Cliff Chamber of Commerce   www.oakcliffchamber.org
660 S Zang Blvd   Dallas TX 75208
Ph: 214-943-4567   Fx: 214-943-4582

Southeast Dallas Chamber of Commerce   www.sedcc.org
PO Box 170132   Dallas TX 75217
Ph: 214-398-9590   Fx: 214-398-9591

Deer Park Chamber of Commerce   www.deerpark.org
110 Center St   Deer Park TX 77536
Ph: 281-479-1559   Fx: 281-476-4041

Del Rio Chamber of Commerce   www.drchamber.com
1915 Veterans Blvd   Del Rio TX 78840
Ph: 830-775-3551   Fx: 830-774-1813   TF: 800-889-8149

Denton Chamber of Commerce   www.denton-chamber.org
414 Parkway St   Denton TX 76202
Ph: 940-382-9693   Fx: 940-382-0040   TF: 888-381-1818

DeSoto Chamber of Commerce   www.desotochamber.org
PO Box 220   DeSoto TX 75123
Ph: 972-224-3565   Fx: 972-224-7228

North Galveston County Chamber of Commerce   www.northgalvestonchamber.com
2718 FM 517 E   Dickinson TX 77539
Ph: 281-337-3434   Fx: 281-337-0641

Duncanville Chamber of Commerce   www.duncanvillechamber.com
300 E Wheatland Rd   Duncanville TX 75116
Ph: 972-780-4990   Fx: 972-298-9370

Eagle Pass Chamber of Commerce   www.eaglepasstexas.com
PO Box 1188   Eagle Pass TX 78853
Ph: 830-773-3224   Fx: 830-773-8844   TF: 888-355-3224

Edinburg Chamber of Commerce   www.edinburg.com
PO Box 85   Edinburg TX 78540
Ph: 956-383-4974   Fx: 956-383-6942   TF: 800-800-7214

Greater El Paso Chamber of Commerce   www.elpaso.org
10 Civic Ctr Plaza   El Paso TX 79901
Ph: 915-534-0500   Fx: 915-534-0513   TF: 800-651-8065

Farmers Branch Chamber of Commerce   www.fbchamber.com
12875 Josey Ln Suite 150   Farmers Branch TX 75234
Ph: 972-243-8966   Fx: 972-243-8968

Flower Mound Chamber of Commerce   www.flowermoundchamber.com
700 Parker Sq Suite 100   Flower Mound TX 75028
Ph: 972-539-0500 ▪ Fx: 972-539-4307

Fort Worth Chamber of Commerce   www.fortworthcoc.org
777 Taylor St Suite 900   Fort Worth TX 76102
Ph: 817-336-2491 ▪ Fx: 817-877-4034

Friendswood Chamber of Commerce   www.friendswood-chamber.com
1100 S Friendswood Dr Suite A   Friendswood TX 77546
Ph: 281-482-3329 ▪ Fx: 281-482-3911

Gainesville Area Chamber of Commerce   www.gainesvilletexas.org
PO Box 518   Gainesville TX 76241
Ph: 940-665-2831 ▪ Fx: 940-665-2833 ▪ TF: 888-585-4468

Galveston Chamber of Commerce   www.galvestonchamber.com
519 25th St   Galveston TX 77550
Ph: 409-763-5326 ▪ Fx: 409-763-8271

Garland Chamber of Commerce   www.garlandchamber.com
914 S Garland Ave   Garland TX 75040
Ph: 972-272-7551 ▪ Fx: 972-276-9261

Georgetown Chamber of Commerce   www.georgetownchamber.org
100 Stadium Dr PO Box 346   Georgetown TX 78627
Ph: 512-930-3535 ▪ Fx: 512-930-3587

Gilmer Area Chamber of Commerce   www.gilmerareachamber.com
106 Buffalo St   Gilmer TX 75644
Ph: 903-843-2413 ▪ Fx: 903-843-3759

Lake Granbury Area Chamber of Commerce   www.granburychamber.com
3408 E Hwy 377   Granbury TX 76049
Ph: 817-573-1622 ▪ Fx: 817-573-0805

Grapevine Chamber of Commerce   www.grapevinechamber.org
PO Box 368   Grapevine TX 76099
Ph: 817-481-1522 ▪ Fx: 817-424-5208

Greater Cedar Creek Lake Area Chamber of Commerce   www.cclake.net
1907 W Main St   Gun Barrel City TX 75156
Ph: 903-887-3152 ▪ Fx: 903-887-3695 ▪ TF: 877-222-5253

Northeast Tarrant Chamber of Commerce   www.netarrant.org
5001 Denton Hwy   Haltom City TX 76117
Ph: 817-281-9376 ▪ Fx: 817-281-9379

Harlingen Area Chamber of Commerce   www.harlingen.com
311 E Tyler St   Harlingen TX 78550
Ph: 956-423-5440 ▪ Fx: 956-425-3870 ▪ TF: 800-531-7346

Henderson Area Chamber of Commerce   www.hendersontx.com
201 N Main St   Henderson TX 75652
Ph: 903-657-5528 ▪ Fx: 903-657-9454

Clear Lake Area Chamber of Commerce   www.clearlakearea.com/chamber.html
1201 NASA Pkwy   Houston TX 77058
Ph: 281-488-7676 ▪ Fx: 281-488-8981

Cy-Fair Houston Chamber of Commerce   www.cyfairchamber.com
11050 FM 1960 W Suite 100   Houston TX 77065
Ph: 281-955-1100 ▪ Fx: 281-955-0138

Galleria Area Chamber of Commerce   www.galleriachamber.com
5075 Westheimer Rd Suite 660   Houston TX 77056
Ph: 713-629-5555 ▪ Fx: 713-629-6403

Greater Heights Area Chamber of Commerce   www.heightschamber.com
545 W 19th St 2nd Fl   Houston TX 77008
Ph: 713-861-6735 ▪ Fx: 713-861-9310

Greater Houston Partnership   www.houston.org
1200 Smith St Suite 700   Houston TX 77002
Ph: 713-844-3600 ▪ Fx: 713-844-0200

Houston Northwest Chamber of Commerce   www.hnwcc.org
14511 Falling Creek Suite 205   Houston TX 77014
Ph: 281-440-4160 ▪ Fx: 281-440-5229

Houston West Chamber of Commerce   www.hwcoc.org
10777 Westheimer St Suite 916   Houston TX 77042
Ph: 713-785-4922 ▪ Fx: 713-785-4944

North Channel Area Chamber of Commerce   www.northchannelarea.com
PO Box 9759   Houston TX 77213
Ph: 713-450-3600 ▪ Fx: 713-450-0700

North Houston-Greenspoint Chamber of Commerce   www.nhgcc.org
16825 Northchase Dr Suite 140   Houston TX 77060
Ph: 281-872-8700 ▪ Fx: 281-872-8095

South Belt-Ellington Chamber of Commerce   www.southbeltchamber.com
10500 Scarsdale Blvd   Houston TX 77089
Ph: 281-481-5516 ▪ Fx: 281-922-7045

Humble Area Chamber of Commerce   www.humbleareachamber.org
110 W Main St   Humble TX 77338
Ph: 281-446-2128 ▪ Fx: 281-446-7483

Huntsville-Walker County Chamber of Commerce   chamber.itemonline.com
1327 11th St   Huntsville TX 77340
Ph: 936-295-8113 ▪ Fx: 936-295-0571 ▪ TF: 800-289-0389

Greater Irving & Las Colinas Chamber of Commerce   www.irvingchamber.com
3333 N MacArthur Blvd Suite 100   Irving TX 75062
Ph: 972-252-8484 ▪ Fx: 972-252-6710

Kerrville Area Chamber of Commerce   www.kerrvilletx.com
1700 Sidney Baker St Suite 100   Kerrville TX 78028
Ph: 830-896-1155 ▪ Fx: 830-896-1175

Greater Killeen Chamber of Commerce   www.gkcc.com
1 Santa Fe Plaza   Killeen TX 76541
Ph: 254-526-9551 ▪ Fx: 254-526-6090 ▪ TF: 800-869-8265

Kingsville Chamber of Commerce   www.kingsville.org
PO Box 1030   Kingsville TX 78364
Ph: 361-592-6438 ▪ Fx: 361-592-0866

La Porte-Bayshore Chamber of Commerce   www.laportechamber.org
PO Box 996   La Porte TX 77572
Ph: 281-471-1123 ▪ Fx: 281-471-1710

Laredo-Webb County Chamber of Commerce   www.laredochamber.com
2310 San Bernardo Ave   Laredo TX 78042
Ph: 956-722-9895 ▪ Fx: 956-791-4503

Lewisville Chamber of Commerce   www.lewisville-chamber.org
551 N Valley Pkwy   Lewisville TX 75067
Ph: 972-436-9571 ▪ Fx: 972-436-5949 ▪ TF: 800-657-9571

Liberty-Dayton Area Chamber of Commerce   www.libertydaytonchamber.com
PO Box 1270   Liberty TX 77575
Ph: 936-336-5736 ▪ Fx: 936-336-1159

Polk County Chamber of Commerce   www.livingston.net/chamber
PO Box 600   Livingston TX 77351
Ph: 936-327-4929 ▪ Fx: 936-327-2660

Longview Partnership   www.longviewchamber.com
410 N Center St   Longview TX 75601
Ph: 903-237-4000 ▪ Fx: 903-237-4049

Lubbock Chamber of Commerce   lubbock.org
1301 Broadway Suite 101   Lubbock TX 79401
Ph: 806-761-7000 ▪ Fx: 806-761-7010 ▪ TF: 800-321-5822

Lufkin/Angelina County Chamber of Commerce   www.lufkintexas.org
PO Box 1606   Lufkin TX 75901
Ph: 936-634-6644 ▪ Fx: 936-634-8726 ▪ TF: 800-409-5659

Greater Marshall Chamber of Commerce   www.marshall-chamber.com
213 W Austin St   Marshall TX 75670
Ph: 903-935-7868 ▪ Fx: 903-935-9982 ▪ TF: 800-953-7868

McAllen Chamber of Commerce   www.mcallenchamber.com
PO Box 790   McAllen TX 78505
Ph: 956-682-2871 ▪ Fx: 956-631-8571 ▪ TF: 877-622-5536

McKinney Chamber of Commerce   www.mckinneytx.org
1650 W Virginia St Suite 110   McKinney TX 75069
Ph: 972-542-0163 ▪ Fx: 972-548-0876

Mesquite Chamber of Commerce   www.mesquitechamber.com
617 N Ebrite St   Mesquite TX 75149
Ph: 972-285-0211 ▪ Fx: 972-285-3535 ▪ TF: 800-541-2355

Midland Chamber of Commerce   www.midlandtxchamber.com
109 N Main St   Midland TX 79701
Ph: 432-683-3381 ▪ Fx: 432-682-9205 ▪ TF: 800-624-6435

Mineral Wells Area Chamber of Commerce   www.mineralwellstx.com
511 E Hubbard St   Mineral Wells TX 76067
Ph: 940-325-2557 ▪ Fx: 940-328-0850 ▪ TF: 800-252-6989

Mission Chamber of Commerce   www.missionchamber.com
220 E 9th St   Mission TX 78572
Ph: 956-585-2727 ▪ Fx: 956-585-3044 ▪ TF: 800-580-2700

Mount Pleasant-Titus County Chamber of Commerce   www.mtpleasanttx.com
1604 N Jefferson Ave   Mount Pleasant TX 75455
Ph: 903-572-8567 ▪ Fx: 903-572-0613

Nacogdoches County Chamber of Commerce   www.nacogdoches.org
2516 North St   Nacogdoches TX 75965
Ph: 936-560-5533 ▪ Fx: 936-560-3920

New Braunfels Chamber of Commerce   www.nbcham.org
390 S Seguin St   New Braunfels TX 78130
Ph: 830-625-2385 ▪ Fx: 830-625-7918 ▪ TF: 800-572-2626

Odessa Chamber of Commerce   www.odessachamber.com
PO Box 3626   Odessa TX 79760
Ph: 432-332-9111 ▪ Fx: 432-333-7858 ▪ TF: 800-780-4678

Greater Orange Area Chamber of Commerce   www.goacc.org
1012 Green Ave   Orange TX 77630
Ph: 409-883-3536 ▪ Fx: 409-886-3247

Lamar County Chamber of Commerce   www.paristexas.com
1125 Bonham St   Paris TX 75460
Ph: 903-784-2501 ▪ Fx: 903-784-2503 ▪ TF: 800-727-4789

Pasadena Chamber of Commerce   www.pasadenachamber.org
4334 Fairmont Pkwy   Pasadena TX 77504
Ph: 281-487-7871 ▪ Fx: 281-487-5530

Pearland Area Chamber of Commerce   www.pearlandchamber.com
3501 Liberty Dr   Pearland TX 77581
Ph: 281-485-3634 ▪ Fx: 281-485-2420

Greater Pflugerville Chamber of Commerce   www.gpcc.pflugerville.tx.us
PO Box 483   Pflugerville TX 78691
Ph: 512-251-7799 ▪ Fx: 512-251-7802

Pharr Chamber of Commerce   www.visitpharr.com
PO Box 1715   Pharr TX 78577
Ph: 956-787-1481 ▪ Fx: 956-787-7972

Plainview Chamber of Commerce   www.plainviewtex.com
710 W 5th St   Plainview TX 79072
Ph: 806-296-7431 ▪ Fx: 806-296-0819 ▪ TF: 800-658-2685

Plano Chamber of Commerce   www.planocc.org
PO Drawer 940287   Plano TX 75094
Ph: 972-424-7547 ▪ Fx: 972-422-5182

Greater Port Arthur Chamber of Commerce   www.portarthurtexas.com
4749 Twin City Hwy Suite 300   Port Arthur TX 77642
Ph: 409-963-1107 ▪ Fx: 409-963-3322

Quinlan Area Chamber of Commerce   www.quinlanchamber.com
PO Box 1722   Quinlan TX 75474
Ph: 903-356-4703 ▪ Fx: 903-356-2130

Richardson Chamber of Commerce   www.telecomcorridor.com
411 Belle Grove Dr   Richardson TX 75080
Ph: 972-234-4141 ▪ Fx: 972-680-9103 ▪ TF: 800-777-8001

Rockwall Area Chamber of Commerce   www.rockwallchamber.org
PO Box 92   Rockwall TX 75087
Ph: 972-771-5733 ▪ Fx: 972-772-3642

Rosenberg-Richmond Area Chamber of Commerce   www.roserichchamber.com
4120 Ave H   Rosenberg TX 77471
Ph: 281-342-5464 ▪ Fx: 281-342-2990

Round Rock Chamber of Commerce   www.roundrockchamber.org
212 E Main St   Round Rock TX 78664
Ph: 512-255-5805 ▪ Fx: 512-255-3345 ▪ TF: 800-747-3479

Rowlett Chamber of Commerce   www.rowlettchamber.com
PO Box 610   Rowlett TX 75030
Ph: 972-475-3200 ▪ Fx: 972-463-1699 ▪ TF: 800-796-8644

San Angelo Chamber of Commerce   www.sanangelo.org/rchamindex.html
418 W Avenue B   San Angelo TX 76903
Ph: 325-655-4136 ▪ Fx: 325-658-1110 ▪ TF: 800-375-1206

Greater San Antonio Chamber of Commerce   www.sachamber.org
PO Box 1628   San Antonio TX 78296
Ph: 210-229-2100 ▪ Fx: 210-229-1600

Appendix

North San Antonio Chamber of Commerce　　www.northsachamber.com
12930 Country Pkwy　San Antonio TX 78216
Ph: 210-344-4848　▪　Fx: 210-525-8207

South San Antonio Chamber of Commerce　　www.southsachamber.org
908 McCreless Mall　San Antonio TX 78223
Ph: 210-533-5867　▪　Fx: 210-532-7788

San Benito Chamber of Commerce　　www.sanbenitochamber.org
210 E Heywood St　San Benito TX 78586
Ph: 956-399-5321　▪　Fx: 956-399-5421

San Marcos Area Chamber of Commerce　　www.sanmarcostexas.com
PO Box 2310　San Marcos TX 78667
Ph: 512-393-5900　▪　Fx: 512-393-5912　▪　TF: 888-200-5620

Seguin Area County Chamber of Commerce　www.chamber.seguinonline.com
427 N Austin St　Seguin TX 78155
Ph: 830-379-6382　▪　Fx: 830-379-6971

Randolph Metrocom Chamber of Commerce　　www.randolphchamber.net
9330 Corporate Dr Suite 707　Selma TX 78154
Ph: 210-658-8322　▪　Fx: 210-658-1817

Sherman Area Chamber of Commerce　　www.shermantexas.com
307 W Washington St Suite 100　Sherman TX 75090
Ph: 903-893-1184　▪　Fx: 903-893-4266　▪　TF: 888-893-1188

Springtown Chamber of Commerce　　www.springtowntexas.com
PO Box 296　Springtown TX 76082
Ph: 817-523-7828　▪　Fx: 817-523-3268

Fort Bend Chamber of Commerce　　www.visitfortbend.com
445 Commerce Green Blvd　Sugar Land TX 77478
Ph: 281-491-0800　▪　Fx: 281-491-0112

Hopkins County Chamber of Commerce　　www.sulphursprings-tx.com
1200 Houston St　Sulphur Springs TX 75482
Ph: 903-885-6515　▪　Fx: 903-885-6516　▪　TF: 888-300-6623

Temple Chamber of Commerce　　www.temple-tx.org
PO Box 158　Temple TX 76503
Ph: 254-773-2105　▪　Fx: 254-773-0661　▪　TF: 800-374-9123

Texarkana Chamber of Commerce　　www.texarkanachamber.com
PO Box 1468　Texarkana TX 75504
Ph: 903-792-7191　▪　Fx: 903-793-4304　▪　TF: 877-275-5289

Texas City-La Marque Chamber of Commerce　　www.texascitychamber.com
PO Box 1717　Texas City TX 77592
Ph: 409-935-1408　▪　Fx: 409-935-5186

The Colony Chamber of Commerce　　www.thecolonychamber.org
PO Box 560006　The Colony TX 75056
Ph: 972-625-4916　▪　Fx: 972-625-8027

South Montgomery County Woodlands Chamber of Commerce　　www.smcwcc.org
1400 Woodloch Forest Dr Suite 500　The Woodlands TX 77380
Ph: 281-367-5777　▪　Fx: 281-292-1655

Tyler Area Chamber of Commerce　　www.tylertexas.com
315 N Broadway Ave　Tyler TX 75702
Ph: 903-592-1661　▪　Fx: 903-593-2746　▪　TF: 800-235-5712

Victoria Chamber of Commerce　　www.victoriachamber.org
700 Main Ctr Suite 100　Victoria TX 77901
Ph: 361-573-5277　▪　Fx: 361-573-5911

Greater Waco Chamber of Commerce　　www.wacochamber.com
PO Box 1220　Waco TX 76703
Ph: 254-752-6551　▪　Fx: 254-752-6618

Weatherford Chamber of Commerce　　www.weatherford-chamber.com
PO Box 310　Weatherford TX 76086
Ph: 817-596-3801　▪　Fx: 817-613-9216　▪　TF: 888-594-3801

Rio Grande Valley Chamber of Commerce　　www.valleychamber.com
PO Box 1499　Weslaco TX 78599
Ph: 956-968-3141　▪　Fx: 956-968-0210

Weslaco Area Chamber of Commerce　　www.weslaco.com
1710 E Pike Blvd　Weslaco TX 78596
Ph: 956-968-2102　▪　Fx: 956-968-6451　▪　TF: 888-968-2102

Lake Tawakoni Area Chamber of Commerce　　www.tawakoni.org
605 E Hwy 276　West Tawakoni TX 75474
Ph: 903-447-3020　▪　Fx: 903-447-3820

Wichita Falls Board of Commerce & Industry　　www.wichitafallscommerce.com
PO Box 1860　Wichita Falls TX 76301
Ph: 940-723-2741　▪　Fx: 940-723-8773

UTAH

Davis Chamber of Commerce　　www.davischamberofcommerce.com
PO Box 457　Centerville UT 84014
Ph: 540-295-6944　▪　Fx: 801-298-1114

Cache Chamber of Commerce　　www.cachechamber.com
160 N Main St　Logan UT 84321
Ph: 435-752-2161　▪　Fx: 435-753-5825

Murray Area Chamber of Commerce　　www.murraychamber.net
5250 S Commerce Dr Suite 180　Murray UT 84107
Ph: 801-263-2632　▪　Fx: 801-263-8262

Chamber Ogden/Weber　　www.echamber.cc/
2484 Washington Blvd Suite 400　Ogden UT 84401
Ph: 801-621-8300　▪　Fx: 801-392-7609　▪　TF: 888-621-8306

Commission for Economic Development in Orem　　www.cedo.org
777 S State St　Orem UT 84058
Ph: 801-226-1538　▪　Fx: 801-226-2678

Provo/Orem Chamber of Commerce　　www.thechamber.org
51 S University Ave Suite 215　Provo UT 84601
Ph: 801-379-2555　▪　Fx: 801-379-2557

Saint George Area Chamber of Commerce　　www.stgeorgechamber.com
97 E Saint George Blvd　Saint George UT 84770
Ph: 435-628-1658　▪　Fx: 435-673-1587

East Valley Chamber of Commerce
2299 Highland Dr Suite 200　Salt Lake City UT 84106
Ph: 801-467-0844　▪　Fx: 801-467-6740

Salt Lake City Area Chamber of Commerce　　www.saltlakechamber.org
175 E 400 South Suite 600　Salt Lake City UT 84111
Ph: 801-364-3631　▪　Fx: 801-328-5098

Sandy Area Chamber of Commerce　　www.sandychamber.com
8807 S 700 E　Sandy UT 84070
Ph: 801-566-0344　▪　Fx: 801-566-0346

South Salt Lake Chamber of Commerce　　www.southsaltlakechamber.com
2880 S Main St Suite 208　South Salt Lake UT 84115
Ph: 801-466-3377　▪　Fx: 801-467-3322

Tooele County Chamber of Commerce　　www.tooelechamber.com
PO Box 460　Tooele UT 84074
Ph: 435-882-0690　▪　Fx: 435-833-0946　▪　TF: 800-378-0690

West Jordan Chamber of Commerce　　www.westjordanchamber.com
8000 S Redwood Rd　West Jordan UT 84088
Ph: 801-569-5151　▪　Fx: 801-569-5153

ChamberWest　　www.chamberwest.com
3540 S 4000 West Suite 400　West Valley City UT 84120
Ph: 801-969-8755　▪　Fx: 801-969-3518

VERMONT

Central Vermont Chamber of Commerce　　www.central-vt.com/chamber/index.html
33 Stewart Rd　Barre VT 05641
Ph: 802-229-5711　▪　Fx: 802-229-5713　▪　TF: 877-887-3678

Great Falls Region Chamber of Commerce　　www.gfrcc.org
PO Box 554　Bellows Falls VT 05101
Ph: 802-463-4280　▪　Fx: 802-463-9882

Bennington Area Chamber of Commerce　　www.bennington.com
100 Veterans Memorial Dr　Bennington VT 05201
Ph: 802-447-3311　▪　Fx: 802-447-1163　▪　TF: 800-229-0252

Brattleboro Area Chamber of Commerce　　www.brattleborochamber.org
180 Main St　Brattleboro VT 05301
Ph: 802-254-4565　▪　Fx: 802-254-5675　▪　TF: 877-254-4565

Lake Champlain Regional Chamber of Commerce　　www.vermont.org
60 Main St Suite 100　Burlington VT 05401
Ph: 802-863-3489　▪　Fx: 802-863-1538　▪　TF: 877-686-5253

Addison County Chamber of Commerce　　www.midvermont.com
2 Court St　Middlebury VT 05753
Ph: 802-388-7951　▪　Fx: 802-388-8066　▪　TF: 800-733-8376

Vermont's North Country Chamber of Commerce　　www.vtnorthcountry.com
The Causeway　Newport VT 05855
Ph: 802-334-7782　▪　TF: 800-635-4643

Franklin County Regional Chamber of Commerce　　www.stalbanschamber.com
2 N Main St Suite 101　Saint Albans VT 05478
Ph: 802-524-2444　▪　Fx: 802-527-2256

Northeast Kingdom Chamber of Commerce　　www.nekchamber.com
51 Depot Sq Suite 3　Saint Johnsbury VT 05819
Ph: 802-748-3678　▪　Fx: 802-748-0731　▪　TF: 800-639-6379

VIRGINIA

Washington County Chamber of Commerce　　www.washingtonvachamber.org/area.htm
179 E Main St　Abingdon VA 24210
Ph: 276-628-8141　▪　Fx: 276-628-3984

Alexandria Chamber of Commerce　　www.alexchamber.com
801 N Fairfax St Suite 402　Alexandria VA 22314
Ph: 703-549-1000　▪　Fx: 703-739-3805

Mount Vernon-Lee Chamber of Commerce　　www.mtvernon-leechamber.org
8804-D Pear Tree Village Ct　Alexandria VA 22309
Ph: 703-360-6925　▪　Fx: 703-360-6928

Amherst County Chamber of Commerce　　www.amherstvachamber.org
PO Box 560　Amherst VA 24521
Ph: 434-946-0990　▪　Fx: 434-946-0879

Annandale Chamber of Commerce　　www.annandalechamber.com
7263 Maple Pl Suite 207　Annandale VA 22003
Ph: 703-256-7232　▪　Fx: 703-256-7233

Arlington Chamber of Commerce　　www.arlingtonchamber.org
2009 N 14th St Suite 111　Arlington VA 22201
Ph: 703-525-2400　▪　Fx: 703-522-5273

Hanover Association of Businesses & Chamber of Commerce
PO Box 16　Ashland VA 23005
Ph: 804-798-8130　▪　Fx: 804-798-0014

Bedford Area Chamber of Commerce　　www.bedfordareachamber.com
305 E Main St　Bedford VA 24523
Ph: 540-586-9401　▪　Fx: 540-587-6650　▪　TF: 800-933-9535

Charlottesville Regional Chamber of Commerce　　www.cvillechamber.com
PO Box 1564　Charlottesville VA 22902
Ph: 434-295-3141　▪　Fx: 434-295-3144

Hampton Roads Chamber of Commerce-Chesapeake　　www.hamptonroadschamber.com
400 Volvo Pkwy　Chesapeake VA 23320
Ph: 757-622-2312　▪　Fx: 757-548-1835

Montgomery County Chamber of Commerce　　www.montgomeryccy.org
612 New River Rd　Christiansburg VA 24073
Ph: 540-382-4010　▪　Fx: 540-382-4390

Culpeper County Chamber of Commerce　　www.culpepervachamber.com
109 S Commerce St　Culpeper VA 22701
Ph: 540-825-8628　▪　Fx: 540-825-1449　▪　TF: 888-285-7373

Danville Pittsylvania County Chamber of Commerce　　www.dpchamber.org
635 Main St　Danville VA 24541
Ph: 434-793-5422　▪　Fx: 434-793-5424

Pulaski County Chamber of Commerce　　www.swva.net/pulaskichamber
4440 Cleburne Blvd Suite B　Dublin VA 24084
Ph: 540-674-1991　▪　Fx: 540-674-4163

Central Fairfax Chamber of Commerce　　www.cfcc.org
3975 University Dr Suite 350　Fairfax VA 22030
Ph: 703-591-2450　▪　Fx: 703-591-2820

Botetourt County Chamber of Commerce　　www.bot-co-chamber.com
PO Box 81　Fincastle VA 24090
Ph: 540-473-8280　▪　Fx: 540-473-8365

Greater Augusta Regional Chamber of Commerce www.augustachamber.org
732 Tinkling Spring Rd PO Box 1107   Fishersville VA 22939
Ph: 540-949-8203 ▪ Fx: 540-949-7740

Franklin-Southampton Area Chamber of Commerce
PO Box 531   Franklin VA 23851
Ph: 757-562-4900 ▪ Fx: 757-562-6138 www.fsachamber.com

Fredericksburg Regional Chamber of Commerce www.fredericksburgchamber.org
PO Box 7476   Fredericksburg VA 22404
Ph: 540-373-9400 ▪ Fx: 540-373-9570

Front Royal-Warren County Chamber of Commerce www.frontroyalchamber.com
305 E Main St   Front Royal VA 22630
Ph: 540-635-3185 ▪ Fx: 540-635-9758

Galax-Carroll-Grayson Chamber of Commerce www.gcgchamber.com
608 W Stuart Dr   Galax VA 24333
Ph: 276-236-2184 ▪ Fx: 276-236-1338

Gloucester County Chamber of Commerce www.gloucestervacc.com
PO Box 296   Gloucester VA 23061
Ph: 804-693-2425 ▪ Fx: 804-693-7193

Buchanan County Chamber of Commerce
Main St PO Box 2818   Grundy VA 24614
Ph: 276-935-4147 ▪ Fx: 276-935-5458

Virginia Peninsula Chamber of Commerce www.vpcc.org
1919 Commerce Dr Suite 320   Hampton VA 23666
Ph: 757-262-2000 ▪ Fx: 757-262-2009

Harrisonburg-Rockingham Chamber of Commerce www.hrchamber.org
800 Country Club Rd   Harrisonburg VA 22802
Ph: 540-434-3862 ▪ Fx: 540-434-4508

Carroll County Chamber of Commerce www.thecarrollchamber.com
PO Box 1184   Hillsville VA 24343
Ph: 276-728-5397 ▪ Fx: 276-728-7825

Hopewell-Prince George Chamber of Commerce www.hpgchamber.com
PO Drawer 1297   Hopewell VA 23860
Ph: 804-458-5536 ▪ Fx: 804-458-1342

Russell County Chamber of Commerce www.russellcountyva.org
PO Box 926   Lebanon VA 24266
Ph: 276-889-8041 ▪ Fx: 276-889-8002

Loudoun County Chamber of Commerce www.loudounchamber.org
PO Box 1298   Leesburg VA 20177
Ph: 703-777-2176 ▪ Fx: 703-777-1392 ▪ TF: 800-578-5222

Lexington-Rockbridge County Chamber of Commerce www.lexrockchamber.com
100 E Washington St   Lexington VA 24450
Ph: 540-463-5375 ▪ Fx: 540-463-3567

Lynchburg Regional Chamber of Commerce www.lynchburgchamber.com
2015 Memorial Ave   Lynchburg VA 24501
Ph: 434-845-5966 ▪ Fx: 434-522-9592

Prince William County-Greater Manassas Chamber of Commerce www.pwcgmcc.org
8963 Center St   Manassas VA 20110
Ph: 703-368-6600 ▪ Fx: 703-368-4733

Chamber of Commerce of Smyth County www.smythchamber.com
PO Box 924   Marion VA 24354
Ph: 276-783-3161 ▪ Fx: 276-783-8003

Martinsville-Henry County Chamber of Commerce www.mhcchamber.com
PO Box 709   Martinsville VA 24114
Ph: 276-632-6401 ▪ Fx: 276-632-5059

Eastern Shore of Virginia Chamber of Commerce www.esvachamber.org
PO Box 460   Melfa VA 23410
Ph: 757-787-2460 ▪ Fx: 757-787-8687

Hampton Roads Chamber of Commerce www.hrccva.com
420 Bank St   Norfolk VA 23510
Ph: 757-622-2312 ▪ Fx: 757-622-5563

Wise County Chamber of Commerce www.wisecountychamber.org
765 Park Ave   Norton VA 24273
Ph: 276-679-0961 ▪ Fx: 276-679-2655

Petersburg Chamber of Commerce www.petersburgcc.com
PO Box 928   Petersburg VA 23804
Ph: 804-733-8131 ▪ Fx: 804-733-9891

Hampton Roads Chamber of Commerce Portsmouth
200 High St Wachovia Bank Bldg Suite 201   Portsmouth VA 23704
Ph: 757-664-2561 ▪ Fx: 757-397-4483

Prince William Regional Chamber of Commerce www.regionalchamber.org
4320 Ridgewood Ctr Dr   Prince William VA 22192
Ph: 703-590-5000 ▪ Fx: 703-590-9815

Greater Reston Chamber of Commerce www.restonchamber.org
1763 Fountain Dr   Reston VA 20190
Ph: 703-707-9045 ▪ Fx: 703-707-9049

Greater Richmond Chamber of Commerce www.grcc.com
201 E Franklin St   Richmond VA 23219
Ph: 804-648-1234 ▪ Fx: 804-783-9366

Roanoke Regional Chamber of Commerce www.roanokechamber.org
212 S Jefferson St   Roanoke VA 24011
Ph: 540-983-0700 ▪ Fx: 540-983-0723

Franklin County Chamber of Commerce www.franklincounty.org
PO Box 158   Rocky Mount VA 24151
Ph: 540-483-9542 ▪ Fx: 540-483-0653

Salem/Roanoke County Chamber of Commerce www.s-rcchamber.org
PO Box 832   Salem VA 24153
Ph: 540-387-0267 ▪ Fx: 540-387-4110

Halifax County Chamber of Commerce www.halifaxchamber.net
515 Broad St   South Boston VA 24592
Ph: 434-572-3085 ▪ Fx: 434-572-1733

Greater Springfield Chamber of Commerce www.springfieldchamber.org
6434 Brandon Ave Suite 3A   Springfield VA 22150
Ph: 703-866-3500 ▪ Fx: 703-866-3501

Hampton Roads Chamber of Commerce-Suffolk
1001 W Washington St   Suffolk VA 23434
Ph: 757-622-2312 ▪ Fx: 757-925-1281

Tazewell Area Chamber of Commerce
Tazewell Mall Box 6   Tazewell VA 24651
Ph: 276-988-5091 ▪ Fx: 276-988-5093

Fairfax County Chamber of Commerce www.fccc.org
8230 Old Courthouse Rd Suite 350   Vienna VA 22182
Ph: 703-749-0400 ▪ Fx: 703-749-9075

Vienna-Tysons Regional Chamber of Commerce www.vtrcc.org
513 Maple Ave W 2nd Fl   Vienna VA 22180
Ph: 703-281-1333

Fauquier County Chamber of Commerce www.fauquierchamber.org
183-A Keith St   Warrenton VA 20186
Ph: 540-347-4414 ▪ Fx: 540-347-7510

Williamsburg Area Chamber of Commerce www.williamsburgcc.com
PO Box 3620   Williamsburg VA 23187
Ph: 757-229-6511 ▪ Fx: 757-229-2047

Winchester-Frederick County Chamber of Commerce www.winchesterva.org
2 N Cameron St Suite 200   Winchester VA 22601
Ph: 540-662-4118 ▪ Fx: 540-722-6365

Wytheville-Wythe-Bland Chamber of Commerce Inc chamber.wytheville.com
150 E Monroe St   Wytheville VA 24382
Ph: 276-223-3365 ▪ Fx: 276-223-3315

WASHINGTON

Grays Harbor Chamber of Commerce www.graysharbor.org
506 Duffy St   Aberdeen WA 98520
Ph: 360-532-1924 ▪ Fx: 360-533-7945 ▪ TF: 800-321-1924

Auburn Area Chamber of Commerce www.auburnareawa.org
108 S Division St Suite B   Auburn WA 98001
Ph: 253-833-0700 ▪ Fx: 253-735-4091

Bellevue Chamber of Commerce www.bellevuechamber.org
10500 NE 8th St Suite 212   Bellevue WA 98004
Ph: 425-454-2464 ▪ Fx: 425-462-4660

Bellingham/Whatcom Chamber of Commerce & Industry www.bellingham.com
1435 Railroad Ave   Bellingham WA 98225
Ph: 360-734-1330 ▪ Fx: 360-734-1332

Bremerton Area Chamber of Commerce www.bremertonchamber.org
301 Pacific Ave   Bremerton WA 98337
Ph: 360-479-3579 ▪ Fx: 360-479-1033

Camas-Washougal Chamber of Commerce www.cwchamber.com
PO Box 919   Camas WA 98607
Ph: 360-834-2472 ▪ Fx: 360-834-9171

Twin Cities Chamber of Commerce www.chamberway.com
500 NW Chamber Way   Chehalis WA 98532
Ph: 360-748-8885 ▪ Fx: 360-748-8763 ▪ TF: 800-525-3323

Greater Des Moines Chamber of Commerce
22030 7th Ave S Suite 104   Des Moines WA 98198
Ph: 206-878-7000 ▪ Fx: 206-824-8779

Greater Edmonds Chamber of Commerce www.edmondswa.com
PO Box 146   Edmonds WA 98020
Ph: 425-670-1496 ▪ Fx: 425-712-1808

Enumclaw Area Chamber of Commerce chamber.enumclaw.wa.us
1421 Cole St   Enumclaw WA 98022
Ph: 360-825-7666 ▪ Fx: 360-825-8369

Everett Area Chamber of Commerce www.everettchamber.com
2000 Hewitt Ave Suite 205   Everett WA 98201
Ph: 425-257-3222 ▪ Fx: 425-257-2074

Greater Federal Way Chamber of Commerce www.federalwaychamber.com
1230 S 336th St Suite F   Federal Way WA 98003
Ph: 253-838-2605 ▪ Fx: 253-661-9050

Gig Harbor/Peninsula Area Chamber of Commerce www.gigharborchamber.com
3302 Harborview Dr   Gig Harbor WA 98332
Ph: 253-851-6865 ▪ Fx: 253-851-6881

Greater Issaquah Chamber of Commerce www.issaquahchamber.com
155 NW Gilman Blvd   Issaquah WA 98027
Ph: 425-392-7024 ▪ Fx: 425-392-8101

Northshore Chamber of Commerce www.northshorecc.org
6524 NE 181st St Suite 4   Kenmore WA 98028
Ph: 425-486-1245 ▪ Fx: 425-485-0321

Tri-City Area Chamber of Commerce www.tcacc.com
3180 W Clearwater Ave Suite F   Kennewick WA 99336
Ph: 509-736-0510 ▪ Fx: 509-783-1733

Kent Chamber of Commerce www.kentchamber.com
524 W Meeker St Suite 1   Kent WA 98032
Ph: 253-854-1770 ▪ Fx: 253-854-8567

Greater Kirkland Chamber of Commerce www.kirklandchamber.org
401 Park Pl Suite 102   Kirkland WA 98033
Ph: 425-822-7066 ▪ Fx: 425-827-4878

Lacey-Thurston County Chamber of Commerce www.laceychamber.com
4705-B Lacey Blvd SE   Lacey WA 98503
Ph: 360-491-4141 ▪ Fx: 360-491-9403

Lakewood Chamber of Commerce www.lakewood-wa.com
6122 Motor Ave   Lakewood WA 98499
Ph: 253-582-9400 ▪ Fx: 253-581-5241

Kelso Longview Chamber of Commerce www.kelsolongviewchamber.org
1563 Olympia Way   Longview WA 98632
Ph: 360-423-8400 ▪ Fx: 360-423-0432

South Snohomish County Chamber of Commerce www.sscchamber.org
3500 188th St SW Suite 490   Lynnwood WA 98037
Ph: 425-774-0507 ▪ Fx: 425-774-4636

Greater Maple Valley-Black Diamond Chamber of Commerce www.maplevalley.com
PO Box 302   Maple Valley WA 98038
Ph: 425-432-0222 ▪ Fx: 425-413-8017

Moses Lake Area Chamber of Commerce www.moseslake.com
324 S Pioneer Way   Moses Lake WA 98837
Ph: 509-765-7888 ▪ Fx: 509-765-7891 ▪ TF: 800-992-6234

Greater Oak Harbor Chamber of Commerce www.oakharborchamber.org
32630 SR 20   Oak Harbor WA 98277
Ph: 360-675-3755 ▪ Fx: 360-679-1624

Olympia/Thurston County Chamber of Commerce www.thurstonchamber.com
PO Box 1427   Olympia WA 98507
Ph: 360-357-3362 ▪ Fx: 360-357-3376

Greater Pasco Area Chamber of Commerce   www.pascochamber.org
2705 St Andrews Loop Suite C   Pasco WA 99301
Ph: 509-547-9755 ▪ Fx: 509-547-9756

Port Orchard Chamber of Commerce   www.portorchard
1014 Bay St Suite 8   Port Orchard WA 98366
Ph: 360-876-3505 ▪ Fx: 360-895-1920 ▪ TF: 800-982-8139

Pullman Chamber of Commerce   www.pullmanchamber.com
415 N Grand Ave   Pullman WA 99163
Ph: 509-334-3565 ▪ Fx: 509-332-3232 ▪ TF: 800-365-6948

Eastern Pierce County Chamber of Commerce   www.puyallupchamber.com
PO Box 1298   Puyallup WA 98371
Ph: 253-845-6755 ▪ Fx: 253-848-6164

Redmond Chamber of Commerce   www.redmondchamber.org
PO Box 628   Redmond WA 98073
Ph: 425-885-4014 ▪ Fx: 425-882-0996

Greater Renton Chamber of Commerce   www.renton-chamber.com
300 Rainier Ave N   Renton WA 98055
Ph: 425-226-4560 ▪ Fx: 425-226-4287

Richland Chamber of Commerce   www.richlandchamberofcomm.com
710-A George Washington Way   Richland WA 99352
Ph: 509-946-1651 ▪ Fx: 509-943-6187 ▪ TF: 877-218-7729

Ballard Chamber of Commerce   www.ballardchamber.com
2208 NW Market St Suite 100   Seattle WA 98107
Ph: 206-784-9705 ▪ Fx: 206-783-8154

Greater Seattle Chamber of Commerce   www.seattlechamber.com
1301 5th Ave Suite 2400   Seattle WA 98101
Ph: 206-389-7200 ▪ Fx: 206-389-7288

Greater University Chamber of Commerce   www.udistrictchamber.org
4710 University Way NE Suite 212   Seattle WA 98105
Ph: 206-547-4417 ▪ Fx: 206-547-5266

Lake City Chamber of Commerce   www.lakecitychamber.org
12345 30th Ave NE Suite FG   Seattle WA 98125
Ph: 206-363-3287 ▪ Fx: 206-363-6456

Southwest King County Chamber of Commerce   www.swkcc.org
PO Box 58591   Seattle WA 98138
Ph: 206-575-1633 ▪ Fx: 206-575-2007 ▪ TF: 800-638-8613

White Center Chamber of Commerce
1327 SW 102nd St   Seattle WA 98146
Ph: 206-763-4196 ▪ Fx: 206-763-1042

Shelton-Mason County Chamber of Commerce   www.sheltonchamber.org
PO Box 2389   Shelton WA 98584
Ph: 360-426-2021 ▪ Fx: 360-426-8678 ▪ TF: 800-576-2021

Shoreline Chamber of Commerce   shorecham.org
18560 1st Ave NE   Shoreline WA 98155
Ph: 206-361-2260 ▪ Fx: 206-361-2268

Spokane Regional Chamber of Commerce   www.spokanechamber.org
801 W Riverside Ave Suite 100   Spokane WA 99201
Ph: 509-624-1393 ▪ Fx: 509-747-0077

Spokane Valley Chamber of Commerce   www.spokanevalleychamber.org
8817 E Mission Ave Suite B   Spokane Valley WA 99212
Ph: 509-924-4994 ▪ Fx: 509-924-4992

Tacoma-Pierce County Chamber of Commerce   www.tacomachamber.org
950 Pacific Ave Suite 300   Tacoma WA 98401
Ph: 253-627-2175 ▪ Fx: 253-597-7305

Greater Vancouver Chamber of Commerce   www.vancouverusa.com
1101 Broadway Suite 120   Vancouver WA 98660
Ph: 360-694-2588 ▪ Fx: 360-693-8279

Walla Walla Valley Chamber of Commerce   www.wwchamber.com
PO Box 644   Walla Walla WA 99362
Ph: 509-525-0850 ▪ Fx: 509-522-2038 ▪ TF: 877-998-4748

Wenatchee Valley Chamber of Commerce   www.wenatchee.org
300 S Columbia St 3rd Fl   Wenatchee WA 98801
Ph: 509-662-2116 ▪ Fx: 509-663-2022

Greater Yakima Chamber of Commerce   www.yakima.org
10 N 9th St   Yakima WA 98901
Ph: 509-248-2021 ▪ Fx: 509-248-0601

WEST VIRGINIA

Beckley-Raleigh County Chamber of Commerce   www.brccc.com
245 N Kanawha St   Beckley WV 25801
Ph: 304-252-7328 ▪ Fx: 304-252-7373 ▪ TF: 800-718-1474

Buckhannon-Upshur Chamber of Commerce   www.buchamber.com
16 S Kanawha St   Buckhannon WV 26201
Ph: 304-472-1722 ▪ Fx: 304-472-4938

Jefferson County Chamber of Commerce   www.jeffersoncounty.com
PO Box 426   Charles Town WV 25414
Ph: 304-725-2055 ▪ Fx: 304-728-8307 ▪ TF: 800-624-0577

Charleston Regional Chamber of Commerce   www.charlestonwvchamber.com
106 Capitol St Suite 100   Charleston WV 25301
Ph: 304-345-0770 ▪ Fx: 304-345-0776

Harrison County Chamber of Commerce   www.harrisoncountychamber.com
168 W Main St Suite 100   Clarksburg WV 26301
Ph: 304-624-6331 ▪ Fx: 304-624-5190

Elkins-Randolph County Chamber of Commerce   www.randolphcountywv.com
315 Railroad Ave Suite 1   Elkins WV 26241
Ph: 304-636-2717 ▪ Fx: 304-636-8046 ▪ TF: 800-422-3304

Marion County Chamber of Commerce   www.marionchamber.com
110 Adams St   Fairmont WV 26554
Ph: 304-363-0442 ▪ Fx: 304-363-0480 ▪ TF: 800-296-3379

Huntington Regional Chamber of Commerce   www.huntingtonchamber.com
720 4th Ave   Huntington WV 25701
Ph: 304-525-5131 ▪ Fx: 304-525-5158

Mineral County Chamber of Commerce   www.mineralcounty.org
Grand Central Business Ctr Suite 2011   Keyser WV 26726
Ph: 304-788-2513 ▪ Fx: 304-788-3887

Preston County Chamber of Commerce   www.prestonchamber.com
200 1/2 W Main St   Kingwood WV 26537
Ph: 304-329-0576 ▪ Fx: 304-329-1407

Greater Greenbrier Chamber of Commerce   www.greenbrierwv.com/greenbrier
111 N Jefferson St   Lewisburg WV 24901
Ph: 304-645-1000 ▪ Fx: 304-647-3001 ▪ TF: 800-833-2068

Logan County Chamber of Commerce   www.chamber.logan.wv.us
214 Stratton St   Logan WV 25601
Ph: 304-752-1324 ▪ Fx: 304-752-5988

Martinsburg-Berkeley County Chamber of Commerce   www.berkeleycounty.org
198 Viking Way   Martinsburg WV 25401
Ph: 304-267-4841 ▪ Fx: 304-263-4695 ▪ TF: 800-332-9007

Upper Kanawha Valley Chamber of Commerce
PO Box 831   Montgomery WV 25136
Ph: 304-442-5756 ▪ Fx: 304-442-3052

Morgantown Area Chamber of Commerce   www.mgnchamber.org
1009 University Ave   Morgantown WV 26507
Ph: 304-292-3311 ▪ Fx: 304-296-6619 ▪ TF: 800-618-2525

Marshall County Chamber of Commerce   www.marshallcountychamber.com
609 Jefferson Ave   Moundsville WV 26041
Ph: 304-845-2773 ▪ Fx: 304-845-2773

Greater New Martinsville Development Corp   www.gnmdc.com
201 Main St   New Martinsville WV 26155
Ph: 304-455-3825 ▪ Fx: 304-455-3637

Fayette County Chamber of Commerce   www.fayettecounty.com
310 Oyler Ave   Oak Hill WV 25901
Ph: 304-465-5617 ▪ Fx: 304-465-5618 ▪ TF: 800-927-0263

Chamber of Commerce of Mid-Ohio Valley   www.parkersburgchamber.com
214 8th St   Parkersburg WV 26101
Ph: 304-422-3588 ▪ Fx: 304-422-3580

Mason County Area Chamber of Commerce   www.masoncountychamber.org
305 Main St   Point Pleasant WV 25550
Ph: 304-675-1050 ▪ Fx: 304-675-2838

Princeton-Mercer County Chamber of Commerce   www.pmccc.org
910 Oakvale Rd   Princeton WV 24740
Ph: 304-487-1502 ▪ Fx: 304-425-0227

Putnam County Chamber of Commerce   www.putnamcounty.org
PO Box 553   Teays WV 25569
Ph: 304-757-6510 ▪ Fx: 304-757-6562

Wheeling Area Chamber of Commerce   www.wheelingchamber.com
1310 Market St   Wheeling WV 26003
Ph: 304-233-2575 ▪ Fx: 304-233-1320

Tug Valley Chamber of Commerce   www.tugvalleychamberofcommerce.com
PO Box 376   Williamson WV 25661
Ph: 304-235-5240 ▪ Fx: 304-235-4509

WISCONSIN

Fox Cities Chamber of Commerce & Industry   www.foxcitieschamber.com
227 S Walnut St   Appleton WI 54911
Ph: 920-734-7101 ▪ Fx: 920-734-7161 ▪ TF: 800-999-3224

Greater Beloit Chamber of Commerce   www.greaterbeloitchamber.com
520 E Grand Ave   Beloit WI 53511
Ph: 608-365-8835 ▪ Fx: 608-365-9345 ▪ TF: 800-683-2774

Greater Brookfield Chamber of Commerce   www.brookfieldchamber.com
1305 N Barker Rd Suite 5   Brookfield WI 53045
Ph: 262-786-1886 ▪ Fx: 262-786-1959

Chippewa Falls Area Chamber of Commerce   www.chippewachamber.org
10 S Bridge St   Chippewa Falls WI 54729
Ph: 715-723-0331 ▪ Fx: 715-723-0332

Eau Claire Area Chamber of Commerce   www.eauclairechamber.org
3625 Gateway Dr Suite B   Eau Claire WI 54701
Ph: 715-834-1204 ▪ Fx: 715-834-1956

Fond du Lac Area Association of Commerce   www.fdlac.com
207 N Main St   Fond du Lac WI 54935
Ph: 920-921-9500 ▪ Fx: 920-921-9559

Green Bay Area Chamber of Commerce   www.titletown.org
400 S Washington St   Green Bay WI 54301
Ph: 920-437-8704 ▪ Fx: 920-437-1024

Greenfield Chamber of Commerce   greenfieldchamber.org
4818 S 76th St   Greenfield WI 53220
Ph: 414-327-8500 ▪ Fx: 414-421-6797

Heart of the Valley Chamber of Commerce   www.heartofthevalleychamber.com
101 E Wisconsin Ave   Kaukauna WI 54130
Ph: 920-766-1616 ▪ Fx: 920-766-5504

Kenosha Area Chamber of Commerce   www.kenoshaareachamber.com
715 56th St   Kenosha WI 53140
Ph: 262-654-1234 ▪ Fx: 262-654-4655

Greater La Crosse Area Chamber of Commerce   www.lacrossechamber.com
712 Main St   La Crosse WI 54601
Ph: 608-784-4880 ▪ Fx: 608-784-4919 ▪ TF: 800-889-0539

Greater Madison Chamber of Commerce   www.greatermadisonchamber.com
615 E Washington Ave   Madison WI 53703
Ph: 608-256-8348 ▪ Fx: 608-256-0333

Manitowoc-Two Rivers Area Chamber of Commerce   www.manitowocchamber.com
1515 Memorial Dr PO Box 903   Manitowoc WI 54221
Ph: 920-684-5575 ▪ Fx: 920-684-1915 ▪ TF: 800-262-7892

Menomonee Falls Chamber of Commerce   www.menomoneefallschamber.com
N 88 W 16621 Appleton Ave   Menomonee Falls WI 53051
Ph: 262-251-2430 ▪ Fx: 262-251-0969

Greater Menomonie Area Chamber of Commerce   www.menomoniechamber.com
342 E Main St   Menomonie WI 54751
Ph: 715-235-9087 ▪ Fx: 715-235-2824

Merrill Area Chamber of Commerce   www.merrillchamber.com
120 S Mill St   Merrill WI 54452
Ph: 715-536-9474 ▪ Fx: 715-539-2043 ▪ TF: 877-907-2757

Metropolitan Milwaukee Association of Commerce   www.mmac.org
756 N Milwaukee St   Milwaukee WI 53202
Ph: 414-287-4100 ▪ Fx: 414-271-7753

Monroe Chamber of Commerce & Industry   www.monroechamber.org
1505 9th St   Monroe WI 53566
Ph: 608-325-7648 ▪ Fx: 608-325-7710

New Berlin Chamber of Commerce   www.nb-chamber.org
2140 S Calhoun Rd   New Berlin WI 53151
Ph: 262-786-5280 ▪ Fx: 262-786-9165

SECUB-Southeastern Chamber United in Business   www.secub.net
8580 S Howell Ave   Oak Creek WI 53154
Ph: 414-768-5845 ▪ Fx: 414-768-5848

Oconomowoc Area Chamber of Commerce   www.oconomowoc.org
152 E Wisconsin Ave   Oconomowoc WI 53066
Ph: 262-567-2666 ▪ Fx: 262-567-3477

Oshkosh Chamber of Commerce   www.oshkoshchamber.com
120 Jackson St   Oshkosh WI 54901
Ph: 920-303-2266 ▪ Fx: 920-303-2263

Racine Area Mfg & Commerce   www.racinechamber.com
300 5th St   Racine WI 53403
Ph: 262-634-1931 ▪ Fx: 262-634-7422

Ripon Area Chamber of Commerce   www.ripon-wi.com
PO Box 305   Ripon WI 54971
Ph: 920-748-6764 ▪ Fx: 920-748-6784

Shawano Area Chamber of Commerce   www.shawanocountry.com
213 E Green Bay St   Shawano WI 54166
Ph: 715-524-2139 ▪ Fx: 715-524-3127 ▪ TF: 800-235-8528

Sheboygan County Chamber of Commerce   www.sheboygan.org
712 Riverfront Dr Suite 101   Sheboygan WI 53081
Ph: 920-457-9491 ▪ Fx: 920-457-6269 ▪ TF: 800-457-9497

Portage County Business Council   www.portagecountybiz.com
5501 Vern Holmes Dr   Stevens Point WI 54481
Ph: 715-344-1940 ▪ Fx: 715-344-4473

Superior-Douglas County Chamber of Commerce   www.superiorwi.net
205 Belknap St   Superior WI 54880
Ph: 715-394-7716 ▪ Fx: 715-394-3810

Waukesha Area Chamber of Commerce   www.waukesha.org
223 Wisconsin Ave   Waukesha WI 53186
Ph: 262-542-4249 ▪ Fx: 262-542-8068

Wausau Area Chamber of Commerce   www.wausauchamber.com
PO Box 6190   Wausau WI 54402
Ph: 715-845-6231 ▪ Fx: 715-845-6235

West Suburban Chamber of Commerce
2421 N Mayfair Rd Suite 17   Wauwatosa WI 53226
Ph: 414-453-2330 ▪ Fx: 414-453-2336

West Allis Chamber of Commerce   www.westallis.org
7149 W Greenfield Ave   West Allis WI 53214
Ph: 414-302-9901 ▪ Fx: 414-302-9918

West Bend Area Chamber of Commerce   www.wbachamber.org
735 S Main St Suite 101   West Bend WI 53095
Ph: 262-338-2666 ▪ Fx: 262-338-1771 ▪ TF: 888-338-8666

Heart of Wisconsin Business & Economic Alliance   www.heartofwi.com
1120 Lincoln St   Wisconsin Rapids WI 54494
Ph: 715-423-1830 ▪ Fx: 715-423-1865

WYOMING

Casper Area Chamber of Commerce   www.casperwyoming.org
500 N Center St   Casper WY 82602
Ph: 307-234-5311 ▪ Fx: 307-265-2643 ▪ TF: 866-234-5311

Greater Cheyenne Chamber of Commerce   www.cheyennechamber.org
301 W 16th St   Cheyenne WY 82001
Ph: 307-638-3388 ▪ Fx: 307-778-1407

Campbell County Chamber of Commerce   www.gillettechamber.com
314 S Gillette Ave   Gillette WY 82716
Ph: 307-682-3673 ▪ Fx: 307-682-0538

Jackson Hole Chamber of Commerce   www.jacksonholechamber.com
990 W Broadway St   Jackson WY 83001
Ph: 307-733-3316 ▪ Fx: 307-733-5585

Laramie Area Chamber of Commerce   www.laramie.org
800 S 3rd St   Laramie WY 82070
Ph: 307-745-7339 ▪ Fx: 307-745-4624 ▪ TF: 866-876-1012

Rock Springs Chamber of Commerce   www.rockspringswyoming.net
PO Box 398   Rock Springs WY 82902
Ph: 307-362-3771 ▪ Fx: 307-362-3838 ▪ TF: 800-463-8637

Sheridan County Chamber of Commerce   www.sheridanwyomingchamber.org
PO Box 707   Sheridan WY 82801
Ph: 307-672-2485 ▪ Fx: 307-672-7321 ▪ TF: 800-453-3650

Appendix

Acronyms Index

Acronyms Index

Each acronym listed in this index is accompanied by the organization's full name and the page number on which contact data for that organization is located. If an organization has an acronym as its official name, then the acronym is presented both as the acronym and as the name. Example: AARP is now officially named AARP. Its index citation shows AARP as the acronym and as the name of the organization.

Acronyms Index

565

J

Acronyms Index

Acronyms Index

N

Acronyms Index

Acronyms Index

Acronyms Index

Acronyms Index

T

U

Acronyms Index

587

Acronyms Index